HART AND WECHSLER'S

THE FEDERAL COURTS
AND
THE FEDERAL SYSTEM

FOURTH EDITION

by

RICHARD H. FALLON, JR.
Professor of Law, Harvard Law School

DANIEL J. MELTZER
Professor of Law, Harvard Law School

DAVID L. SHAPIRO
William Nelson Cromwell Professor of Law,
Harvard Law School

WESTBURY, NEW YORK
THE FOUNDATION PRESS, INC.
1996

Library of Congress Cataloging-in-Publication Data

Hart, Henry Melvin.
    Hart and Wechsler's the federal courts and the federal system. —
4th ed. / by Richard H. Fallon, Jr., Daniel J. Meltzer, David L.
Shapiro.
      p.   cm. — (University casebook series)
    Includes index.
    ISBN 1–56662–335–9 (hardcover)
    1. Courts—United States—Cases. 2. Jurisdiction—United States—
Cases. 3. Judicial power—United States—Cases. I. Wechsler,
Herbert, 1909–   . II. Fallon, Richard H., 1952–   . III. Title.
IV. Series.
KF8718.H32 1996
347.73'2—dc20
[347.3071]   96–10876

 *TEXT IS PRINTED ON 10% POST CONSUMER RECYCLED PAPER* 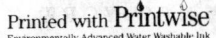 Printed with Printwise
Environmentally Advanced Water Washable Ink

The first edition of this book was dedicated to
FELIX FRANKFURTER
*who first opened our minds
to these problems*

The second edition was dedicated to the memory of
HENRY M. HART, JR.
*profound and passionate
student and teacher*

*The third edition was dedicated
to the memory of*
HENRY J. FRIENDLY
*man for all seasons in the law;
master of this subject*

The editors of the fourth edition add a dedication to
HERBERT WECHSLER
*a continuing source of inspiration and wisdom,
and our link to a grand tradition*

*

PREFACE
TO THE
FOURTH EDITION

I

As editors of the Fourth Edition of a book that helped create its field of study, we have tried both to carry on the tradition created by Professors Hart and Wechsler and to meet a range of important present-day teaching and scholarly objectives. Among the goals that we have attempted to fulfill are:

– To preserve the historical depth, breadth of inquiry, and level of sophistication that we believe have marked each earlier edition;

– To carry forward the book's objective of functioning not only as a vehicle for teaching an important and difficult subject but also as a reference tool and a source of ideas capable of contributing to the growth of the law;

– To make the book more compact and more accessible to students (the book is in fact some 160 pages shorter than the Third Edition), and to provide it with more of a contemporary flavor;

– To acquaint readers with and to participate in debates within the field and to link them to important general currents in legal scholarship.

The extraordinary work of the authors of the First Edition (whose preface is excerpted after this one), and of Paul Mishkin and Paul Bator on successor editions has contributed immeasurably to the structure, scope, and analysis of the present edition. And we note especially our sorrow at the passing of Paul Bator, whose death shortly after publication of the Third Edition has deprived us not only of a close friend but of a creative, rigorous, and challenging colleague.

II

The Third Edition made some major structural changes in the format of the book, and for the most part, those structural changes have been preserved in the present edition. But there are significant changes in this edition as well: for example, reorganization of materials in a number of chapters; the addition and substitution of important principal cases (both old and new) in Chapters II,[1] IV,[2] V,[3] VII,[4] IX,[5] X,[6] XI,[7] and XII;[8] the condensing and refocusing of the discussion

---

[1] In Section 2, Muskrat v. United States has been restored; Lujan v. Defenders of Wildlife has been added in Section 3, as has Abbott Laboratories v. Gardner in Section 5; in Section 6, Nixon v. United States has replaced Baker v. Carr.

[2] Tafflin v. Levitt has been added to Section 3, and Dice v. Akron C. & Y. R.R. has been moved to Section 3 (from Chapter V).

[3] In Section 2, State Tax Comm'n v. Van Cott has replaced Standard Oil v. Johnson; Staub v. Baxley and Cardinale v. Louisiana have replaced Herndon v. Georgia and Michel v. Louisiana.

[4] In Section 1, Boyle v. United Technologies Corp. has replaced Miree v. DeKalb Coun-

See footnotes 5–8 on page vi.

of the famous Steel Seizure litigation, so that it now appears at the end of Chapter IX as an embodiment of the related themes of sovereign immunity, official immunity, and equitable discretion; and the expansion and reworking of the materials in Chapter XI on habeas corpus for state prisoners, accompanied by a reduction in the materials on collateral relief for federal prisoners.

One change in the present edition deserves special comment. The notes in Chapter IV, involving congressional control of jurisdiction, attempt to present the historical and legal materials, and particularly the range of views expressed in the literature, in enriched detail. In the context of these revisions, we decided not to include in Chapter IV the full text of Professor Hart's famous article, *The Power of Congress to Limit the Jurisdiction of Federal Courts: An Exercise in Dialectic*, 66 Harv.L.Rev. 1362 (1953). This decision does not reflect the view that the Dialogue has diminished in importance, and indeed students are urged to read it in the full text. Rather, the omission results from our view that four decades of development have made it virtually impossible adequately to update Professor Hart's discussion in the footnotes and, of greater import, that more effective pedagogical use of the Dialogue can be made by liberal quotation from its text at appropriate places in the body of the Chapter. Indeed, we gathered from discussion with a number of our colleagues that very few were assigning the Dialogue in its entirety.

Finally, we have decided to include as a valuable indexing and research tool not only a Table of Cases but also a Table of Authorities.[9]

III

We readily acknowledge that no course currently given in any law school (or even to be imagined) could cover the entire book, and we therefore tender these brief suggestions for the selection of materials in three and four credit courses—those that are most commonly offered. Chapter I (at least in substantial part) is important background reading for any course. But the central materials in Chapter II are treated in many Constitutional Law courses, while much of Chapter VI is usually considered in the basic course in Civil Procedure. A teacher of a three-credit course might therefore try to cover at least Sections 1 and 3 of Chapter IV, Sections 1 and 2A–B of Chapter V (together with portions of Chapter XI), a few selections from Chapter VI, the bulk of Chapter VII, Chapter VIII (Sections 1–4), and much of Chapters IX and X. Some or all of Chapter XII might be added. A teacher of a four credit course could also include some or all of the remainder of Chapters IV, V, IX, X, and XII, and also assign some or all of Chapters II and XI (and perhaps the materials on supplemental jurisdiction in Chapters VIII and XIII).

IV

We have sought and are grateful to have received advice from many colleagues throughout the country. Their suggestions ranged from specific corrections,

ty. Ward v. Love County has been moved to Section 2 of this Chapter from Chapter V, and also in Section 2, Cannon v. University of Chicago has replaced J.I. Case v. Borak.

[5] In Section 2, Hans v. Louisiana has been added; Pennsylvania v. Union Gas Co. has replaced Atascadero State Hospital v. Scanlon; and Zinermon v. Burch has replaced Parratt v. Taylor. In Section 3, Harlow v. Fitzgerald has replaced Butz v. Economou.

[6] In Section 1, Kline v. Burke Constr. Co. has been added. In Section 2E, Ankenbrandt v. Richards has replaced Markham v. Allen.

[7] In Section 2, Teague v. Lane has been added.

[8] In Section 2, Heck v. Humphrey has replaced Preiser v. Rodriguez.

[9] We have attempted to make the book current in every respect as of January 1, 1996.

to advice on particular issues, to more general recommendations for new directions and approaches. Among those to whom we are especially indebted are Akhil Amar, William Casto, William Fletcher, Arthur Hellman, Vicki Jackson, Larry Kramer, Paul Mishkin, Henry Monaghan, Wendy Parmet, Judith Resnik, Anne-Marie Slaughter, Detlev Vagts, and Larry Yackle. We have benefited greatly from their thoughts, even though we found ourselves unable to adopt all their proposals while maintaining the essential structure and approach of the book. And we have made special efforts—both in response to a number of suggestions and in pursuing our own desire to explore issues of contemporary debate in greater depth—to expand the discussion of issues of "parity" between state and federal courts, to probe the significance of competing visions of the proper role of the federal courts, and to encourage discussion of issues of policy raised not only by court decisions but also by a wide range of proposals for legislative change.

V

Although every chapter is the product of extensive review and comment among the three authors, primary responsibility was divided among us as follows:

Fallon: Chapters I, II, IV, X (Sections 2A–C).

Meltzer: Chapters III, V, VII, X (Sections 1 and 2D–E), XI.

Shapiro: Chapters VI, VIII, IX, XII, XIII, XIV, XV.

VI

A few notes on form and related matters are in order. Although we recognize that the denial of certiorari by the Supreme Court may have some significance to persons besides the litigants, we have economized on space by omitting this reference, except in the few instances where it has special relevance. With respect to principal cases and quotations in text, no indication of footnotes or citations omitted is normally given; those footnotes that have been retained carry their original numbers. All other omissions, whether of a few words, a paragraph, or several pages, are indicated by spaced asterisks.

Several of the authors of this and prior editions participated in various ways as counsel in some of the cases discussed in this book. As in prior editions, we concluded that it would constitute an excess of caution to advert, in each case, to such participation. We are confident that our editorial process has fairly guarded us against partisan treatment (or undue leaning over backwards) with respect to the cases in question.

VII

We are grateful to a number of our present and former students for their research and for invaluable assistance in checking the manuscript and preparing the index: Ted Cruz, Allen Ferrell, Devri Glick, Melissa Hart, Sam Kaplan, Meredith Kotler, Ed McNicholas, Jennifer Peppet, Scott Peppet, Rachel Selinfreund, Chris Vergonis, and Jonathan Zittrain. Our thanks also to Lise Berg, Maura Kelley, and Nancy Thompson for their splendid secretarial assistance, and to the Library Reference and Word Processing staffs at Harvard Law School for their extraordinary willingness to help on a number of difficult problems.

VIII

We acknowledge with thanks permission to quote excerpts from the following copyrighted works: Fallon & Meltzer, *New Law, Non–Retroactivity, and Constitutional Remedies,* 104 Harv.L.Rev. 1731 (1991), © 1991 by The Harvard Law Review Association; Friendly, *In Praise of Erie—And of the New Federal Common Law,* 39 N.Y.U.L.Rev. 383 (1964), © 1964 by New York University; Friendly, *Is Innocence Irrelevant? Collateral Attack on Criminal Judgments,* 38 U.Chi.L.Rev. 142 (1970), © 1970 by the University of Chicago; Hart, *The Power of Congress to Limit the Jurisdiction of Federal Courts: An Exercise in Dialectic,* 66 Harv.L.Rev. 1362 (1953), © 1953 by The Harvard Law Review Association; and Shapiro, *Jurisdiction and Discretion,* 60 N.Y.U.L.Rev. 543 (1985), © 1985 by New York University.

R. H. F.
D. J. M.
D. L. S.

January 1996

EXCERPTS FROM PREFACE
TO THE
FIRST EDITION

I.

One of the consequences of our federalism is a legal system that derives from both the Nation and the states as separate sources of authority and is administered by state and federal judiciaries, functioning in far more subtle combination than is readily perceived. The resulting legal problems are the subject of this book. They are examined here mainly from the point of view of the federal courts and of Congress when it legislates respecting the judicial system. The frequently neglected problems posed in the administration of federal law by state courts have not, however, been ignored.

The jurisdiction of courts in a federal system is an aspect of the distribution of power between the states and the federal government. Federal jurisdiction, as our subject is usually called, would surely be a sterile topic were it not explored in this perspective. Questions of jurisdiction, however, bear commonly a subordinate or derivative relation to the distinct problem of determining the respective spheres of operation of federal and state law. It is in the effort to identify and to delineate these areas of federal and state authority that the nature of federalism and its crucial problems are, in our view, most significantly revealed. The book is concerned, therefore, with the relationship of federal and state law, both as guides to judicial decision and in everyday affairs, no less than with the jurisdiction of the federal courts and the relation of those courts to the tribunals of the states.

Problems of federal and state legislative competence are, of course, the main subject of elementary courses in constitutional law. Such courses tend, however, to deal with issues of this kind as they arise in clear-cut instances of conflict between federal and state assertions, calling for the adjudication of competing claims of power. These dramatic conflicts touch only the beginnings of the problems, as the materials in this volume should make clear. For every case in which a court is asked to invalidate a square assertion of state or federal legislative authority, there are many more in which the allocation of control does not involve questions of ultimate power; Congress has been silent with respect to the displacement of the normal state-created norms, leaving courts to face the problem as an issue of the choice of law. The book tries to suggest something of the variety of these questions and of their significance; it points to the importance of the postulates of federalism in the common run of litigation; it asks the question whether Congress cannot profitably give increased attention to these issues and attempts to show respects in which such conscious management of our federalism, on this mundane, working level, might produce important gains.

Without depreciating the importance of the problems facing courts, we are concerned throughout with the issues of legislative policy that the nature of our system puts to Congress. The legislative possibilities have received less attention than they merit, though they arise throughout the field.

The book deals mainly with these problems of federal-state relationships but it also has two secondary themes. In varying contexts we pose the issue of what courts are good for—and are not good for—seeking thus to open up the whole range of questions as to the appropriate relationship between the federal courts and other organs of federal and state government. We also pose throughout problems of the organization and management of the federal courts, wishing to promote understanding of the task of federal judicial administration and of the means available for its improvement.

The study of federal jurisdiction has commonly been coupled with that of federal procedure. What has been said will make clear why it is uncoupled here. Procedural problems remain in plenty, to be sure, as they must in any study of law administration, but they are raised and dealt with only as incidents of other problems posited by the main themes. In the editors' own schools, systematic instruction in federal practice takes place in procedure courses built around the Federal Rules of Civil Procedure or in which those Rules play a central part. Independently of this, however, we are convinced that studying procedure for its own sake, as of course it should be studied, is alien to the main inquiries projected by this book. The effort to combine them in law teaching serves, in our view, to produce a misalliance that accords to neither subject the attention it deserves.

* * *

III.

A word should be said about editorial method. The principal cases, less than a hundred and fifty in number, have been chosen with a view to their usefulness as the chief centers of classroom discussion. Related cases are abstracted, and related problems discussed, in the accompanying text notes. The text notes, it will be evident, raise many more questions than class discussion can hope to explore. We have proceeded here on the conviction that over-simplification is no service to advanced students and have tried to put before the reader something of the breadth of background and knowledge that an experienced teacher brings to a subject—or a teacher's manual seeks to give an inexperienced one. The general, if not invariable, rule, moreover, has been that references to variant decisions or important secondary discussions ought not to be blind. An effort has accordingly been made to tell enough about the decision or comment referred to so that the reader will not need to get the book from the shelf before he can begin to think about the problem. This relative fullness of discussion, it is hoped, will enhance the usefulness of the book to practitioners as well as to students.

* * *

H. M. H., Jr.
H. W.

August, 1953

SUMMARY OF CONTENTS

*

TABLE OF CONTENTS

TABLE OF CASES

Principal cases are in bold type. Cases cited or discussed
are in roman type. References are to Pages.

TABLE OF AUTHORITIES

THE CONSTITUTION OF THE UNITED STATES OF AMERICA

We the People of the United States, in Order to form a more perfect Union, establish Justice, insure domestic Tranquility, provide for the common defence, promote the general Welfare, and secure the Blessings of Liberty to ourselves and our Posterity, do ordain and establish this Constitution for the United States of America.

Article I

Section 1. All legislative Powers herein granted shall be vested in a Congress of the United States, which shall consist of a Senate and House of Representatives.

Section 2. The House of Representatives shall be composed of Members chosen every second Year by the People of the several States, and the Electors in each State shall have the Qualifications requisite for Electors of the most numerous Branch of the State Legislature.

No Person shall be a Representative who shall not have attained to the Age of twenty five Years, and been seven Years a Citizen of the United States, and who shall not, when elected, be an Inhabitant of that State in which he shall be chosen.

Representatives and direct Taxes shall be apportioned among the several States which may be included within this Union, according to their respective Numbers, which shall be determined by adding to the whole Number of free Persons, including those bound to Service for a Term of Years, and excluding Indians not taxed, three fifths of all other Persons. The actual Enumeration shall be made within three Years after the first Meeting of the Congress of the United States, and within every subsequent Term of ten Years, in such Manner as they shall by Law direct. The Number of Representatives shall not exceed one for every thirty Thousand, but each State shall have at Least one Representative; and until such enumeration shall be made, the State of New Hampshire shall be entitled to chuse three, Massachusetts eight, Rhode Island and Providence Plantations one, Connecticut five, New York six, New Jersey four, Pennsylvania eight, Delaware one, Maryland six, Virginia ten, North Carolina five, South Carolina five, and Georgia three.

When vacancies happen in the Representation from any State, the Executive Authority thereof shall issue Writs of Election to fill such Vacancies.

The House of Representatives shall chuse their Speaker and other Officers; and shall have the sole Power of Impeachment.

Section 3. The Senate of the United States shall be composed of two Senators from each State, chosen by the Legislature thereof, for six Years; and each Senator shall have one Vote.

Immediately after they shall be assembled in Consequence of the first Election, they shall be divided as equally as may be into three Classes. The Seats of the Senators of the first Class shall be vacated at the Expiration of the Second Year, of the second Class at the Expiration of the fourth Year, and of the third Class at the Expiration of the sixth Year, so that one third may be chosen every second Year; and if Vacancies happen by Resignation, or otherwise, during the Recess of the Legislature of any State, the Executive thereof may make temporary Appointments until the next Meeting of the Legislature, which shall then fill such Vacancies.

No Person shall be a Senator who shall not have attained to the Age of thirty Years, and been nine Years a Citizen of the United States, and who shall not, when elected, be an Inhabitant of that State for which he shall be chosen.

The Vice President of the United States shall be President of the Senate, but shall have no Vote, unless they be equally divided.

The Senate shall chuse their other Officers, and also a President pro tempore, in the Absence of the Vice President, or when he shall exercise the Office of President of the United States.

The Senate shall have the sole Power to try all Impeachments. When sitting for that Purpose, they shall be on Oath or Affirmation. When the President of the United States is tried, the Chief Justice shall preside: And no Person shall be convicted without the Concurrence of two thirds of the Members present.

Judgment in Cases of Impeachment shall not extend further than to removal from Office, and disqualification to hold and enjoy any Office of honor, Trust, or Profit under the United States: but the Party convicted shall nevertheless be liable and subject to Indictment, Trial, Judgment, and Punishment, according to Law.

Section 4. The Times, Places and Manner of holding Elections for Senators and Representatives, shall be prescribed in each State by the Legislature thereof; but the Congress may at any time by Law make or alter such Regulations, except as to the Places of chusing Senators.

The Congress shall assemble at least once in every Year, and such Meeting shall be on the first Monday in December, unless they shall by Law appoint a different Day.

Section 5. Each House shall be the Judge of the Elections, Returns, and Qualifications of its own Members, and a Majority of each shall constitute a Quorum to do Business; but a smaller Number may adjourn from day to day, and may be authorized to compel the Attendance of absent Members, in such Manner, and under such Penalties as each House may provide.

Each House may determine the Rules of its Proceedings, punish its Members for disorderly Behavior, and, with the Concurrence of two thirds, expel a Member.

Each House shall keep a Journal of its Proceedings, and from time to time publish the same, excepting such Parts as may in their Judgment require Secrecy; and the Yeas and Nays of the Members of either House on any question shall, at the Desire of one fifth of those Present, be entered on the Journal.

Neither House, during the Session of Congress, shall, without the Consent of the other, adjourn for more than three days, nor to any other Place than that in which the two Houses shall be sitting.

Section 6. The Senators and Representatives shall receive a Compensation for their Services, to be ascertained by Law, and paid out of the Treasury of the United States. They shall in all Cases, except Treason, Felony and Breach of the Peace, be privileged from Arrest during their Attendance at the Session of their respective Houses, and in going to and returning from the same; and for any Speech or Debate in either House, they shall not be questioned in any other Place.

No Senator or Representative shall, during the Time for which he was elected, be appointed to any civil Office under the Authority of the United States, which shall have been created, or the Emoluments whereof shall have been increased during such time; and no Person holding any Office under the United States, shall be a member of either House during his Continuance in Office.

Section 7. All Bills for raising Revenue shall originate in the House of Representatives; but the Senate may propose or concur with Amendments as on other Bills.

Every Bill which shall have passed the House of Representatives and the Senate, shall, before it become a Law, be presented to the President of the United States; If he approve he shall sign it, but if not he shall return it, with his Objections to the House in which it shall have originated, who shall enter the Objections at large on their Journal, and proceed to reconsider it. If after such Reconsideration two thirds of that House shall agree to pass the Bill, it shall be sent together with the Objections, to the other House, by which it shall likewise be reconsidered, and if approved by two thirds of that House, it shall become a Law. But in all such Cases the Votes of both Houses shall be determined by Yeas and Nays, and the Names of the Persons voting for and against the Bill shall be entered on the Journal of each House respectively. If any Bill shall not be returned by the President within ten Days (Sundays excepted) after it shall have been presented to him, the Same shall be a Law, in like Manner as if he had signed it, unless the Congress by their Adjournment prevent its Return in which Case it shall not be a Law.

Every Order, Resolution, or Vote, to Which the Concurrence of the Senate and House of Representatives may be necessary (except on a question of Adjournment) shall be presented to the President of the United States; and before the Same shall take Effect, shall be approved by him, or being disapproved by him, shall be repassed by two thirds of the Senate and House of Representatives, according to the Rules and Limitations prescribed in the Case of a Bill.

Section 8. The Congress shall have Power to lay and collect Taxes, Duties, Imposts and Excises, to pay the Debts and provide for the common Defence and general Welfare of the United States; but all Duties, Imposts and Excises shall be uniform throughout the United States;

To borrow money on the credit of the United States;

To regulate Commerce with foreign Nations, and among the several States, and with the Indian Tribes;

To establish an uniform Rule of Naturalization, and uniform Laws on the subject of Bankruptcies throughout the United States;

To coin Money, regulate the Value thereof, and of foreign Coin, and fix the Standard of Weights and Measures;

To provide for the Punishment of counterfeiting the Securities and current Coin of the United States;

To Establish Post Offices and Post Roads;

To promote the Progress of Science and useful Arts, by securing for limited Times to Authors and Inventors the exclusive Right to their respective Writings and Discoveries;

To constitute Tribunals inferior to the supreme Court;

To define and punish Piracies and Felonies committed on the high Seas, and Offenses against the Law of Nations;

To declare War, grant Letters of Marque and Reprisal, and make Rules concerning Captures on Land and Water;

To raise and support Armies, but no Appropriation of Money to that Use shall be for a longer Term than two Years;

To provide and maintain a Navy;

To make Rules for the Government and Regulation of the land and naval Forces;

To provide for calling forth the Militia to execute the Laws of the Union, suppress Insurrections and repel Invasions;

To provide for organizing, arming, and disciplining, the Militia, and for governing such Part of them as may be employed in the Service of the United States, reserving to the States respectively, the Appointment of the Officers, and the Authority of training the Militia according to the discipline prescribed by Congress;

To exercise exclusive Legislation in all Cases whatsoever, over such District (not exceeding ten Miles square) as may, by Cession of particular States and the Acceptance of Congress, become the Seat of the Government of the United States, and to exercise like Authority over all Places purchased by the Consent of the Legislature of the State in which the Same shall be, for the Erection of Forts, Magazines, Arsenals, dock-Yards, and other needful Buildings;—And

To make all Laws which shall be necessary and proper for carrying into Execution the foregoing Powers, and all other Powers vested by this Constitution in the Government of the United States, or in any Department or Officer thereof.

Section 9. The Migration or Importation of Such Persons as any of the States now existing shall think proper to admit, shall not be prohibited by the Congress prior to the Year one thousand eight hundred and eight, but a Tax or duty may be imposed on such Importation, not exceeding ten dollars for each Person.

The privilege of the Writ of Habeas Corpus shall not be suspended, unless when in Cases of Rebellion or Invasion the public Safety may require it.

No Bill of Attainder or ex post facto Law shall be passed.

No Capitation, or other direct, Tax shall be laid, unless in Proportion to the census or Enumeration herein before directed to be taken.

No Tax or Duty shall be laid on Articles exported from any State.

No Preference shall be given by any Regulation of Commerce or Revenue to the Ports of one State over those of another: nor shall Vessels bound to, or from, one State be obliged to enter, clear, or pay Duties in another.

No money shall be drawn from the Treasury, but in Consequence of Appropriations made by Law; and a regular Statement and Account of the Receipts and Expenditures of all public Money shall be published from time to time.

No Title of Nobility shall be granted by the United States: And no Person holding any Office of Profit or Trust under them, shall, without the Consent of the Congress, accept of any present, Emolument, Office, or Title, of any kind whatever, from any King, Prince, or foreign State.

Section 10. No State shall enter into any Treaty, Alliance, or Confederation; grant Letters of Marque and Reprisal; coin Money; emit Bills of Credit; make any Thing but gold and silver Coin a Tender in Payment of Debts; pass any Bill of Attainder, ex post facto Law, or Law impairing the Obligation of Contracts, or grant any Title of Nobility.

No State shall, without the Consent of the Congress, lay any Imposts or Duties on Imports or Exports, except what may be absolutely necessary for executing its inspection Laws: and the net Produce of all Duties and Imposts, laid by any State on Imports or Exports, shall be for the Use of the Treasury of the United States; and all such Laws shall be subject to the Revision and Controul of the Congress.

No State shall, without the Consent of Congress, lay any Duty of Tonnage, keep Troops, or Ships of War in time of Peace, enter into any Agreement or Compact with another State, or with a foreign Power or engage in War, unless actually invaded, or in such imminent Danger as will not admit of delay.

Article II

Section 1. The executive Power shall be vested in a President of the United States of America. He shall hold his Office during the Term of four Years, and, together with the Vice President, chosen for the same Term, be elected, as follows:

Each State shall appoint, in such Manner as the Legislature thereof may direct, a Number of Electors, equal to the whole Number of Senators and Representatives to which the State may be entitled in the Congress; but no Senator or Representative, or Person holding an Office of Trust or Profit under the United States, shall be appointed an Elector.

The Electors shall meet in their respective States, and vote by Ballot for two Persons, of whom one at least shall not be an Inhabitant of the same State with themselves. And they shall make a List of all the Persons voted for, and of the Number of Votes for each; which List they shall sign and certify, and transmit sealed to the Seat of the Government of the United States, directed to the President of the Senate. The President of the Senate shall, in the Presence of the Senate and House of Representatives, open all the Certificates, and the Votes shall then be counted. The Person having the greatest Number of Votes shall be the President, if such Number be a Majority of the whole Number of Electors appointed; and if there be more than one who have such Majority, and have an equal Number of Votes, then the House of Representatives shall immediately chuse by Ballot one of them for President; and if no Person have a Majority, then from the five highest on the List the said House shall in like

Manner chuse the President. But in chusing the President, the Votes shall be taken by States, the Representation from each State having one Vote; A quorum for this Purpose shall consist of a Member or Members from two thirds of the States, and a Majority of all the States shall be necessary to a Choice. In every Case, after the Choice of the President, the Person having the greater Number of Votes of the Electors shall be the Vice President. But if there should remain two or more who have equal Votes, the Senate shall chuse from them by Ballot the Vice President.

The Congress may determine the Time of chusing the Electors, and the Day on which they shall give their Votes; which Day shall be the same throughout the United States.

No person except a natural born Citizen, or a Citizen of the United States, at the time of the Adoption of this Constitution, shall be eligible to the Office of President; neither shall any Person be eligible to that Office who shall not have attained to the Age of thirty five Years, and been fourteen Years a Resident within the United States.

In case of the removal of the President from Office, or of his Death, Resignation or Inability to discharge the Powers and Duties of the said Office, the Same shall devolve on the Vice President and the Congress may by Law provide for the Case of Removal, Death, Resignation or Inability, both of the President and Vice President, declaring what Officer shall then act as President, and such Officer shall act accordingly, until the Disability be removed, or a President shall be elected.

The President shall, at stated Times, receive for his Services, a Compensation, which shall neither be increased nor diminished during the Period for which he shall have been elected, and he shall not receive within that Period any other Emolument from the United States, or any of them.

Before he enter on the Execution of his Office, he shall take the following Oath or Affirmation: "I do solemnly swear (or affirm) that I will faithfully execute the Office of President of the United States, and will to the best of my Ability, preserve, protect and defend the Constitution of the United States."

Section 2. The President shall be Commander in Chief of the Army and Navy of the United States, and of the militia of the several States, when called into the actual Services of the United States; he may require the Opinion, in writing, of the principal Officer in each of the Executive Departments, upon any Subject relating to the Duties of their respective Offices and he shall have Power to grant Reprieves and Pardons for Offenses against the United States, except in Cases of Impeachment.

He shall have Power, by and with the Advice and Consent of the Senate, to make Treaties, provided two thirds of the Senators present concur; and he shall nominate, and by and with the Advice and Consent of the Senate, shall appoint Ambassadors, other public Ministers and Consuls, Judges of the supreme Court, and all other Officers of the United States, whose Appointments are not herein otherwise provided for, and which shall be established by Law; but the Congress may by Law vest the Appointment of such inferior Officers, as they think proper, in the President alone, in the Courts of Law, or in the Heads of Departments.

The President shall have Power to fill up all Vacancies that may happen during the Recess of the Senate, by granting Commissions which shall expire at the End of their next Session.

Section 3. He shall from time to time give to the Congress Information of the State of the Union, and recommend to their Consideration such Measures as he shall judge necessary and expedient; he may, on extraordinary Occasions, convene both Houses, or either of them, and in Case of Disagreement between them, with Respect to the Time of Adjournment, he may adjourn them to such Time as he shall think proper; he shall receive Ambassadors and other public Ministers; he shall take Care that the Laws be faithfully executed, and shall Commission all the Officers of the United States.

Section 4. The President, Vice President and all civil Officers of the United States, shall be removed from Office on Impeachment for, and Conviction of, Treason, Bribery, or other high Crimes and Misdemeanors.

Article III

Section 1. The judicial Power of the United States, shall be vested in one supreme Court, and in such inferior Courts as the Congress may from time to time ordain and establish. The Judges, both of the supreme and inferior Courts, shall hold their Offices during good Behaviour, and shall, at stated Times, receive for their Services a Compensation, which shall not be diminished during their Continuance in Office.

Section 2. The judicial Power shall extend to all Cases, in Law and Equity, arising under this Constitution, the Laws of the United States, and Treaties made, or which shall be made, under their Authority;—to all Cases affecting Ambassadors, other public Ministers and Consuls;—to all Cases of admiralty and maritime Jurisdiction;—to Controversies to which the United States shall be a Party;—to Controversies between two or more States;—between a State and Citizens of another State;—between Citizens of different States;—between Citizens of the same State claiming Lands under the Grants of different States, and between a State, or the Citizens thereof, and foreign States, Citizens or Subjects.

In all Cases affecting Ambassadors, other public Ministers and Consuls, and those in which a State shall be a Party, the supreme Court shall have original Jurisdiction. In all the other Cases before mentioned, the supreme Court shall have appellate Jurisdiction, both as to Law and Fact, with such Exceptions, and under such Regulations as the Congress shall make.

The trial of all Crimes, except in Cases of Impeachment, shall be by Jury; and such Trial shall be held in the State where the said Crimes shall have been committed; but when not committed within any State, the Trial shall be at such Place or Places as the Congress may by Law have directed.

Section 3. Treason against the United States, shall consist only in levying War against them, or, in adhering to their Enemies, giving them Aid and Comfort. No Person shall be convicted of Treason unless on the Testimony of two Witnesses to the same overt Act, or on Confession in open Court.

The Congress shall have Power to declare the Punishment of Treason, but no Attainder of Treason shall work Corruption of Blood, or Forfeiture except during the Life of the Person attainted.

Article IV

Section 1. Full Faith and Credit shall be given in each State to the public Acts, Records, and judicial Proceedings of every other State. And the Congress may by general Laws prescribe the Manner in which such Acts, Records and Proceedings shall be proved, and the Effect thereof.

Section 2.   The Citizens of each State shall be entitled to all Privileges and Immunities of Citizens in the several States.

A Person charged in any State with Treason, Felony, or other Crime, who shall flee from Justice, and be found in another State, shall on demand of the executive Authority of the State from which he fled, be delivered up, to be removed to the State having Jurisdiction of the Crime.

No Person held to Service or Labour in one State, under the Laws thereof, escaping into another, shall, in Consequence of any Law or Regulation therein, be discharged from such Service or Labour, but shall be delivered up on Claim of the Party to whom such Service or Labour may be due.

Section 3.   New States may be admitted by the Congress into this Union; but no new State shall be formed or erected with the Jurisdiction of any other State; nor any State be formed by the Junction of two or more States, or Parts of States, without the Consent of the Legislatures of the States concerned as well as of the Congress.

The Congress shall have Power to dispose of and make all needful Rules and Regulations respecting the Territory or other Property belonging to the United States; and nothing in this Constitution shall be so construed as to Prejudice any Claims of the United States, or of any particular State.

Section 4.   The United States shall guarantee to every State in this Union a Republican Form of Government, and shall protect each of them against Invasion; and on Application of the Legislature, or of the Executive (when the Legislature cannot be convened) against domestic Violence.

Article V

The Congress, whenever two thirds of both Houses shall deem it necessary, shall propose Amendments to this Constitution, or, on the Application of the Legislatures of two thirds of the several States, shall call a Convention for proposing Amendments, which, in either Case, shall be valid to all Intents and Purposes, as part of this Constitution, when ratified by the Legislatures of three fourths of the several States, or by Conventions in three fourths thereof, as the one or the other Mode of Ratification may be proposed by the Congress; Provided that no Amendment which may be made prior to the Year One thousand eight hundred and eight shall in any Manner affect the first and fourth Clauses in the Ninth Section of the first Article; and that no State, without its consent, shall be deprived of its equal Suffrage in the Senate.

Article VI

All Debts contracted and Engagements entered into, before the Adoption of this Constitution, shall be as valid against the United States under this Constitution, as under the Confederation.

This Constitution, and the Laws of the United States which shall be made in Pursuance thereof; and all treaties made, or which shall be made, under the Authority of the United States, shall be the supreme Law of the Land; and the Judges in every State shall be bound thereby, any Thing in the Constitution or Laws of any State to the Contrary notwithstanding.

The Senators and Representatives before mentioned, and the Members of the several State Legislatures, and all executive and judicial Officers, both of the United States and of the several States, shall be bound by Oath or Affirmation, to support this Constitution; but no religious Test shall ever be required as a Qualification to any Office or public Trust under the United States.

Article VII

The Ratification of the Conventions of nine States shall be sufficient for the Establishment of this Constitution between the States so ratifying the Same.

ARTICLES IN ADDITION TO, AND AMENDMENT OF, THE CONSTITUTION OF THE UNITED STATES OF AMERICA, PROPOSED BY CONGRESS, AND RATIFIED BY THE LEGISLATURES OF THE SEVERAL STATES PURSUANT TO THE FIFTH ARTICLE OF THE ORIGINAL CONSTITUTION.

Amendment I [1791]

Congress shall make no law respecting an establishment of religion, or prohibiting the free exercise thereof; or abridging the freedom of speech, or of the press; or the right of the people peaceably to assemble, and to petition the Government for a redress of grievances.

Amendment II [1791]

A well regulated Militia, being necessary to the security of a free State, the right of the people to keep and bear Arms, shall not be infringed.

Amendment III [1791]

No Soldier shall, in time of peace be quartered in any house, without the consent of the Owner, nor in time of war, but in a manner to be prescribed by law.

Amendment IV [1791]

The right of the people to be secure in their persons, houses, papers, and effects, against unreasonable searches and seizures, shall not be violated, and no Warrants shall issue, but upon probable cause, supported by Oath or affirmation, and particularly describing the place to be searched, and the persons or things to be seized.

Amendment V [1791]

No person shall be held to answer for a capital, or otherwise infamous crime, unless on a presentment or indictment of a Grand Jury, except in cases arising in the land or naval forces, or in the Militia, when in actual service in time of War or public danger; nor shall any person be subject for the same offence to be twice put in jeopardy of life or limb; nor shall be compelled in any criminal case to be a witness against himself, nor be deprived of life, liberty, or property, without due process of law; nor shall private property be taken for public use, without just compensation.

Amendment VI [1791]

In all criminal prosecutions, the accused shall enjoy the right to a speedy and public trial, by an impartial jury of the State and district wherein the crime shall have been committed, which district shall have been previously ascertained by law, and to be informed of the nature and cause of the accusation; to be confronted with the witnesses against him; to have compulsory process for obtaining witnesses in his favor, and to have the Assistance of Counsel for his defence.

Amendment VII [1791]

In Suits at common law, where the value in controversy shall exceed twenty dollars, the right of trial by jury shall be preserved, and no fact tried by jury, shall be otherwise re-examined in any Court of the United States, than according to the rules of the common law.

Amendment VIII [1791]

Excessive bail shall not be required, nor excessive fines imposed, nor cruel and unusual punishments inflicted.

Amendment IX [1791]

The enumeration in the Constitution, of certain rights, shall not be construed to deny or disparage others retained by the people.

Amendment X [1791]

The powers not delegated to the United States by the Constitution, nor prohibited by it to the States, are reserved to the States respectively, or to the people.

Amendment XI [1798]

The Judicial power of the United States shall not be construed to extend to any suit in law or equity, commenced or prosecuted against one of the United States by Citizens of another State, or by Citizens or Subjects of any Foreign State.

Amendment XII [1804]

The Electors shall meet in their respective states and vote by ballot for President and Vice President, one of whom, at least, shall not be an inhabitant of the same state with themselves; they shall name in their ballots the person voted for as President, and in distinct ballots the person voted for as Vice President, and they shall make distinct lists of all persons voted for as President, and of all persons voted for as Vice President, and of the number of votes for each, which lists they shall sign and certify, and transmit sealed to the seat of the government of the United States, directed to the President of the Senate;—The President of the Senate shall, in the presence of the Senate and House of Representatives, open all the certificates and the votes shall then be counted;—The person having the greatest number of votes for President, shall be the President, if such number be a majority of the whole number of Electors appointed; and if no person have such majority, then from the persons having the highest numbers not exceeding three on the list of those voted for as President, the House of Representatives shall choose immediately, by ballot, the President. But in choosing the President, the votes shall be taken by states, the representation from each state having one vote; a quorum for this purpose shall consist of a member or members from two-thirds of the states, and a majority of all the states shall be necessary to a choice. And if the House of Representatives shall not choose a President whenever the right of choice shall devolve upon them before the fourth day of March next following, then the Vice President shall act as President, as in the case of the death or other constitutional disability of the President.—The person having the greatest number of votes as Vice President, shall be the Vice President, if such number be a majority of the whole number of Electors appointed, and if no person have a majority, then from the two highest numbers on the list, the Senate shall choose the Vice President; a quorum for the purpose shall consist of two-thirds of the whole number of Senators, and a majority of the whole number shall be necessary to a choice. But no person constitutionally ineligible to the office of President shall be eligible to that of Vice President of the United States.

Amendment XIII [1865]

Section 1. Neither slavery nor involuntary servitude, except as a punishment for crime whereof the party shall have been duly convicted, shall exist within the United States, or any place subject to their jurisdiction.

Section 2. Congress shall have power to enforce this article by appropriate legislation.

Amendment XIV [1868]

Section 1. All persons born or naturalized in the United States, and subject to the jurisdiction thereof, are citizens of the United States and of the State wherein they reside. No State shall make or enforce any law which shall abridge the privileges or immunities of citizens of the United States; nor shall any State deprive any person of life, liberty, or property, without due process of law; nor deny to any person within its jurisdiction the equal protection of the laws.

Section 2. Representatives shall be apportioned among the several States according to their respective numbers, counting the whole number of persons in each State, excluding Indians not taxed. But when the right to vote at any election for the choice of electors for President and Vice President of the United States, Representatives in Congress, the Executive and Judicial officers of a State, or the members of the Legislature thereof, is denied to any of the male inhabitants of such State, being twenty-one years of age, and citizens of the United States, or in any way abridged, except for participation in rebellion, or other crime, the basis of representation therein shall be reduced in the proportion which the number of such male citizens shall bear to the whole number of male citizens twenty-one years of age in such State.

Section 3. No person shall be a Senator or Representative in Congress, or elector of President and Vice President, or hold any office, civil or military, under the United States, or under any State, who having previously taken an oath, as a member of Congress, or as an officer of the United States, or as a member of any State legislature, or as an executive or judicial officer of any State, to support the Constitution of the United States, shall have engaged in insurrection or rebellion against the same, or given aid or comfort to the enemies thereof. But Congress may by a vote of two-thirds of each House, remove such disability.

Section 4. The validity of the public debt of the United States, authorized by law, including debts incurred for payment of pensions and bounties for services in suppressing insurrection or rebellion, shall not be questioned. But neither the United States nor any State shall assume or pay any debt or obligation incurred in aid of insurrection or rebellion against the United States, or any claim for the loss or emancipation of any slave; but all such debts, obligations and claims shall be held illegal and void.

Section 5. The Congress shall have power to enforce, by appropriate legislation, the provisions of this article.

Amendment XV [1870]

Section 1. The right of citizens of the United States to vote shall not be denied or abridged by the United States or by any State on account of race, color, or previous condition of servitude.

Section 2. The Congress shall have power to enforce this article by appropriate legislation.

Amendment XVI [1913]

The Congress shall have power to lay and collect taxes on incomes, from whatever source derived, without apportionment among the several States, and without regard to any census or enumeration.

Amendment XVII [1913]

[1] The Senate of the United States shall be composed of two Senators from each State, elected by the people thereof, for six years; and each Senator shall have one vote. The electors in each State shall have the qualifications requisite for electors of the most numerous branch of the State legislatures.

[2] When vacancies happen in the representation of any State in the Senate, the executive authority of such State shall issue writs of election to fill such vacancies: *Provided,* that the legislature of any State may empower the executive thereof to make temporary appointments until the people fill the vacancies by election as the legislature may direct.

[3] This amendment shall not be so construed as to affect the election or term of any Senator chosen before it becomes valid as part of the Constitution.

Amendment XVIII [1919]

Section 1. After one year from the ratification of this article the manufacture, sale, or transportation of intoxicating liquors within, the importation thereof into, or the exportation thereof from the United States and all territory subject to the jurisdiction thereof for beverage purposes is hereby prohibited.

Section 2. The Congress and the several States shall have concurrent power to enforce this article by appropriate legislation.

Section 3. This article shall be inoperative unless it shall have been ratified as an amendment to the Constitution by the legislatures of the several States, as provided in the Constitution, within seven years from the date of the submission hereof to the States by the Congress.

Amendment XIX [1920]

[1] The right of citizens of the United States to vote shall not be denied or abridged by the United States or by any State on account of sex.

[2] Congress shall have power to enforce this article by appropriate legislation.

Amendment XX [1933]

Section 1. The terms of the President and Vice President shall end at noon on the 20th day of January, and the terms of Senators and Representatives at noon on the 3d day of January, of the years in which such terms would have ended if this article had not been ratified; and the terms of their successors shall then begin.

Section 2. The Congress shall assemble at least once in every year, and such meeting shall begin at noon on the 3d day of January, unless they shall by law appoint a different day.

Section 3. If, at the time fixed for the beginning of the term of the President, the President elect shall have died, the Vice President elect shall become President. If the President shall not have been chosen before the time fixed for the beginning of his term, or if the President elect shall have failed to qualify, then the Vice President elect shall act as President until a President shall have qualified; and the Congress may by law provide for the case wherein neither a President elect nor a Vice President elect shall have qualified, declaring who shall then act as President, or the manner in which one who is to act shall be selected, and such person shall act accordingly until a President or Vice President shall have qualified.

Section 4. The Congress may by law provide for the case of the death of any of the persons from whom the House of Representatives may choose a President whenever the right of choice shall have devolved upon them, and for the case of the death of any of the persons from whom the Senate may choose a Vice President whenever the right of choice shall have devolved upon them.

Section 5. Sections 1 and 2 shall take effect on the 15th day of October following the ratification of this article.

Section 6. This article shall be inoperative unless it shall have been ratified as an amendment to the Constitution by the legislatures of three-fourths of the several States within seven years from the date of its submission.

Amendment XXI [1933]

Section 1. The eighteenth article of amendment to the Constitution of the United States is hereby repealed.

Section 2. The transportation or importation into any State, Territory, or possession of the United States for delivery or use therein of intoxicating liquors, in violation of the laws thereof, is hereby prohibited.

Section 3. This article shall be inoperative unless it shall have been ratified as an amendment to the Constitution by conventions in the several States, as provided in the Constitution, within seven years from the date of the submission hereof to the States by the Congress.

Amendment XXII [1951]

Section 1. No person shall be elected to the office of the President more than twice, and no person who has held the office of President, or acted as President, for more than two years of a term to which some other person was elected President shall be elected to the office of President more than once. But this

Article shall not apply to any person holding the office of President when this Article was proposed by the Congress, and shall not prevent any person who may be holding the office of President, or acting as President, during the term within which this Article becomes operative from holding the office of President or acting as President during the remainder of such term.

Section 2. This article shall be inoperative unless it shall have been ratified as an amendment to the Constitution by the legislatures of three-fourths of the several States within seven years from the date of its submission to the States by the Congress.

Amendment XXIII [1961]

Section 1. The District constituting the seat of Government of the United States shall appoint in such manner as the Congress may direct:

A number of electors of President and Vice President equal to the whole number of Senators and Representatives in Congress to which the District would be entitled if it were a State, but in no event more than the least populous state; they shall be in addition to those appointed by the states, but they shall be considered, for the purposes of the election of President and Vice President, to be electors appointed by a state; and they shall meet in the District and perform such duties as provided by the twelfth article of amendment.

Section 2. The Congress shall have power to enforce this article by appropriate legislation.

Amendment XXIV [1964]

Section 1. The right of citizens of the United States to vote in any primary or other election for President or Vice President, for electors for President or Vice President, or for Senator or Representative in Congress, shall not be denied or abridged by the United States or any State by reason of failure to pay any poll tax or other tax.

Section 2. The Congress shall have power to enforce this article by appropriate legislation.

Amendment XXV [1967]

Section 1. In the case of the removal of the President from office or of his death or resignation, the Vice President shall become President.

Section 2. Whenever there is a vacancy in the office of the Vice President, the President shall nominate a Vice President who shall take office upon confirmation by a majority vote of both Houses of Congress.

Section 3. Whenever the President transmits to the President pro tempore of the Senate and the Speaker of the House of Representatives his written declaration that he is unable to discharge the powers and duties of his office, and until he transmits to them a written declaration to the contrary, such powers and duties shall be discharged by the Vice President as Acting President.

Section 4. Whenever the Vice President and a majority of either the principal officers of the executive departments or of such other body as Congress may by law provide, transmit to the President pro tempore of the Senate and the Speaker of the House of Representatives, their written declaration that the President is unable to discharge the powers and duties of his office, the Vice

President shall immediately assume the powers and duties of the office as Acting President.

Thereafter, when the President transmits to the President pro tempore of the Senate and the Speaker of the House of Representatives his written declaration that no inability exists, he shall resume the powers and duties of his office unless the Vice President and a majority of either the principal officers of the executive department or of such other body as Congress may by law provide, transmit within four days to the President pro tempore of the Senate and the Speaker of the House of Representatives their written declaration that the President is unable to discharge the powers and duties of his office. Thereupon Congress shall decide the issue, assembling within forty-eight hours for that purpose if not in session. If the Congress, within twenty-one days after receipt of the latter written declaration, or, if Congress is not in session, within twenty-one days after Congress is required to assemble, determines by two-thirds vote of both Houses that the President is unable to discharge the powers and duties of his office, the Vice President shall continue to discharge the same as Acting President; otherwise, the President shall resume the powers and duties of his office.

Amendment XXVI [1971]

Section 1. The right of citizens of the United States, who are eighteen years of age or older, to vote shall not be denied or abridged by the United States or by any State on account of age.

Section 2. The Congress shall have power to enforce this article by appropriate legislation.

Amendment XXVII [1992]

No Law, varying the compensation for the services of the Senators and Representatives, shall take effect, until an election of Representatives shall have intervened.

*

THE FEDERAL COURTS
AND
THE FEDERAL SYSTEM

*

CHAPTER I

THE DEVELOPMENT AND STRUCTURE OF THE FEDERAL JUDICIAL SYSTEM

INTRODUCTORY NOTE: THE JUDICIARY ARTICLE
IN THE CONSTITUTIONAL CONVENTION AND
THE RATIFICATION DEBATES

Article III, the judiciary article of the Constitution, emerged from the Convention that met in Philadelphia during the summer of 1787.[1] In the words of a leading scholar, however, to "one who is especially interested in the judiciary, there is surprisingly little on the subject to be found in the records of the convention".[2] For most of the delegates, the judiciary was a secondary or even a tertiary concern. To understand the Convention's deliberations about Article III, attention to context is therefore vital.

A. Background of the Convention

On the whole, the period from the end of the Revolution to the ratification of the Constitution was one of economic growth.[3] Nonetheless, an economic downturn in the middle of the 1780s caused significant dislocations, especially for debtors. For this among other reasons, "the Critical Period", as it has been

---

1. Farrand, The Records of the Federal Convention 20–23 (1911)(hereinafter cited as Farrand), is the basic document for the study of the Convention. Three volumes were published in 1911; a fourth, published in 1937, has been revised and expanded. Hutson, Supplement to Max Farrand's Records of the Federal Convention of 1787 (1987).

Secondary sources include Farrand, The Framing of the Constitution of the United States (1913)(hereinafter cited as Farrand, Framing); Goebel, History of the Supreme Court of the United States: Antecedents and Beginnings to 1801, 196–250 (1971); McDonald, Novus Ordo Seclorum: The Intellectual Origins of the Constitution (1985); Rossiter, 1787: The Grand Convention (1966); Murphy, The Triumph of Nationalism: State Sovereignty, The Founding Fathers, and the Making of the Constitution (1967); Collier &

Collier, Decision in Philadelphia (1986); and Charles Warren, The Making of the Constitution 3–54 (1937 ed.).

Professors Kurland and Lerner have assembled a five volume anthology, The Founders' Constitution (1987), which presents views expressed on constitutional problems before, during, and after the Convention, through 1835. The volumes are keyed to the provisions of the Constitution and the first twelve amendments.

2. Farrand, Framing, note 1, *supra,* at 154.

3. See generally Wood, The Creation of the American Republic, 1776–1787, at 393–96 (1969)(hereinafter cited as Wood, Creation); Jensen, The New Nation: A History of the United States During the Articles of Confederation, 1781–1789, at 256, 339–40, 423–244 (1950).

1

called,[4] was a time of frustration, tension, and anxiety.[5]

By all accounts, the prevailing structure of "national" government, the Articles of Confederation, had proved inadequate to the challenges confronting the new nation. The Articles provided no executive branch and no system of courts. Each state had equal representation in Congress, and the concurrence of nine was needed for most important matters, including the appropriation of money. To levy a tariff required unanimous consent, which was never forthcoming. Perhaps the most basic problem, however, was that Congress lacked mechanisms to enforce its mandates. It could pass resolutions and make recommendations, but had to rely on the states to implement them. The states proved increasingly unwilling to do so.

Efforts to enforce the Treaty with Great Britain illustrated the difficulty. The treaty guaranteed the integrity of some of the private debts owed to British subjects, provided for post-war return of certain British property interests acquired before the war, and limited private causes of action against British subjects arising out of legitimate war activities. Yet nearly all the states enacted statutes that violated these and other provisions of the treaty. Even when states formally allowed suits by aliens, the cherished right to trial by jury often functioned as an instrument of nullification in such lawsuits, as it sometimes did in other debtor-creditor actions.[6]

Under the circumstances, the nation suffered a series of humiliations in foreign affairs. And the need for a national power to tax and to regulate commerce was increasingly obvious. "By 1787 almost every political leader in the country, including most of the later Antifederalists, wanted something done to strengthen the Articles of Confederation."[7]

Related to the problems issuing from national weakness, but also possessing a dynamic of their own, were anxieties about emerging political currents in the state legislatures and elsewhere. By the 1780s, a burgeoning commercialism had broadly expanded networks of credit and debt, and resentments accumulated around debtor-creditor relations, including those between the states—most of which had borrowed heavily during the Revolution—and their debt holders. At least six states responded by authorizing paper money, which was widely expected to yield inflation.[8] Some feared that it would spawn a broad-based financial instability. In the state legislatures, movements were afoot to pass debtor relief laws. In Massachusetts, Shay's Rebellion—a revolt of western debtors—broke out.

To many of those who came to be called Federalists, "the rage for paper money, for an abolition of debts",[9] and similar proposals under discussion reflected not only bad policy but a form of political immorality—a breach of

---

4. The label apparently originated with John Fiske, The Critical Period of American History, 1783–89 (1883).

5. See generally Wood, Creation, note 3, *supra*, at 393–467.

6. See Holt, *"To Establish Justice": Politics, The Judiciary Act of 1789, and the Invention of the Federal Courts*, 1989 Duke L.J. 1421, 1427–58.

7. Wood, *Interests and Disinterestedness in the Making of the Constitution*, in Beeman, Botein, & Carter (eds.), Beyond Confederation: Origins of the Constitution and American National Identity 69, 72 (1987).

8. See, *e.g.*, Reisman, *Money, Credit, and Federalist Political Economy*, in Beeman et al., Beyond Confederation, note 7, *supra*, at 128, 150–51; Jensen, note 3, *supra*, at 313–26.

9. The Federalist, No. 10 (Madison).

honor, if not of natural right, and one that threatened to spawn both financial and political turmoil.[10] From this perspective, a new, national constitution was necessary to restore a regime of virtuous government—or, failing that, a scheme that would protect individual rights and the public good by ensuring that faction would be checked by faction[11] and ambition set against ambition.[12]

When the Constitutional Convention met in Philadelphia with a charge to amend the Articles of Confederation, it agreed immediately to ignore the limits on its mandate and instead to draft an entirely new constitution.[13] With the agenda thus framed, the principal questions involved the extent to which a new Constitution should create and empower a truly national government to replace the existing confederation. At one pole stood the nationalists.[14] At the other were those who preferred more minor departures from the existing confederated structure, with authority concentrated in the sovereign states and delegated to a federal government by the states for limited purposes only.

As recent historical studies of "republican" ideology[15] have emphasized, this division tended to correlate with, and at least partly reflected, a more profound disagreement about the foundations of legitimate government. The

---

10. See Wood, note 7, *supra.*

11. See The Federalist, No. 10 (Madison).

12. See The Federalist, No. 51 (Madison).

13. On the relationships among formal legality and illegality, popular sovereignty, and the theory of political legitimacy reflected in the framing and ratification of the Constitution, and on the implications of the implicit constitutional theory of the founding for subsequent American constitutional history, see Ackerman, 1 We the People: Foundations (1991); Ackerman & Katyal, *Our Unconventional Founding,* 62 U.Chi.L.Rev. 475 (1995); Amar, *Philadelphia Revisited: Amending the Constitution Outside Article V,* 55 U.Chi. L.Rev. 1043 (1988); Amar, *The Consent of the Governed: Constitutional Amendment Outside Article V,* 94 Colum.L.Rev. 457 (1994). Professor Ackerman generally sees the founders as breaking sharply with existing legal forms, in the name of higher law or "We the People", whereas Professor Amar asserts the availability of legal justifications for the course of action followed at the Convention and after.

14. Crosskey, Politics and the Constitution in the History of the United States (1953), makes especially strong claims about the nationalism of the Constitution that emerged from the Convention. For sharp criticism, see, *e.g.,* the reviews by Professors Brown and Hart, 67 Harv.L.Rev. 1439, 1456 (1954), and Goebel, *Ex Parte Clio,* 54 Colum.L.Rev. 450 (1954). On the general dismissal of Crosskey's work by a later genera-

tion of historians, see Beeman, *Introduction,* in Beeman, Botein & Carter, note 7, *supra,* at 6–8.

15. The pathbreaking works are Bailyn, The Ideological Origins of the American Revolution (1967); Wood, Creation, note 3, *supra;* and Pocock, The Machiavellian Moment: Florentine Political Thought and the Atlantic Republican Tradition (1975). For valuable overviews, see Beeman, *Introduction,* in Beeman, Botein, & Carter, note 7, *supra,* at 3–19; Shalhope, *Toward a Republican Synthesis: The Emergence of an Understanding of Republicanism in Early American Historiography,* 29 Wm. & Mary Q. 49 (1972); and Shalhope, *Republicanism in Early American Historiography,* 39 Wm. & Mary Q. 334 (1982). For a more skeptical survey, see Rodgers, *Republicanism: the Career of a Concept,* 79 J.Am.Hist. 11 (1992).

Legal scholars have been interested in republicanism largely as a theory that might inform legal, and especially constitutional, interpretation. The leading works see a republican foundation for judicial contributions to reasoned governmental deliberation, see, *e.g.,* Sunstein, *Interest Groups in American Public Law,* 38 Stan.L.Rev. 29 (1985); Sunstein, *Beyond the Republican Revival,* 97 Yale L.J. 1539 (1988), or to political freedom, see, *e.g.,* Michelman, *The Supreme Court, 1985 Term—Foreword: Traces of Self–Government,* 100 Harv.L.Rev. 4 (1986); Michelman, *Law's Republic,* 97 Yale L.J. 1493 (1988). For a critical assessment, see Fallon, *What Is Republicanism, and Is It Worth Reviving?,* 102 Harv.L.Rev. 1695 (1989).

nationalists—or "Federalists", as they came to be called—generally favored representative institutions in which enlightened leaders would be at least partly insulated from, and reasonably asked to rise above, the play of passions and factional interests that often characterized state and local politics. By contrast, those wishing to retain the centrality of more local institutions tended to be suspicious of political elitism and supportive of democratic egalitarianism.[16]

Against this backdrop, perhaps the most crucial decision of the Constitutional Convention was that a federal government should be established with powers to act directly on individuals, not just on the member state. The most important implementing decisions were those dividing power between state and national government and devising representative institutions in which the influence of passion and faction would be filtered if not eliminated. Almost without exception, decisions regarding the judiciary were ancillary, and reflected settlements and divisions concerning more centrally controverted issues.

B. The Convention

The Convention's principal decisions concerning the federal courts may be grouped under five headings:

First, that there should be a federal judicial power operating, like the legislative and executive powers, upon both states and individuals;

Second, that the power should be vested in a Supreme Court and in such inferior federal courts as Congress might establish;

Third, that the federal judiciary should be as "independent as the lot of humanity will admit"[17] and that its power should be judicial only but should include the power to pass upon the constitutionality of both state and federal legislation;

Fourth, that the power should extend to nine specified classes of cases; and

Fifth, that in certain cases the Supreme Court should have original jurisdiction and in the remainder "appellate Jurisdiction, both as to Law and Fact, with such Exceptions, and under such Regulations as the Congress shall make."

As attested by The Federalist Papers and other contemporary defenses, these decisions reflected a general view of the role of the judiciary in an overarching scheme of shared national and state authority. But at least some of their particulars can only be explained by reference to the processes of debate, deliberation, and drafting at the Philadelphia Convention. To understand the judicial structure chosen at the Convention, it is therefore necessary to have a general picture of the way the Convention worked. Its deliberations divided into three main phases.

The settlement of general principles (May 30 to July 26). Although the Convention was scheduled to convene on May 14, no quorum was present until May 25, and the Convention did not begin its substantive business until four

---

16. See generally Wood, note 3, *supra,* at 393–615; Wood, note 7, *supra.* For modern echoes of the anti-elitist populism that characterized Antifederalist opposition to the Constitution's ratification, see Parker, "Here

the People Rule": A Constitutional Populist Manifesto (1994).

17. Article XXIX of the Declaration of Rights of the Massachusetts Constitution of 1780.

days later. On May 29, Governor Edmund Randolph of Virginia presented fifteen resolutions, variously referred to as the "Virginia Plan" or the "Randolph Plan", that as amended and expanded ultimately became the Constitution of the United States.[18]

Jointly drafted by the Virginia delegation but with Madison exerting a heavy influence,[19] the Randolph Plan called for a national government consisting of legislative, executive, and judicial branches. It provided national legislative authority "in all cases to which the separate States are incompetent, or in which the harmony of the United States may be interrupted by individual legislation"; and it conferred a legislative veto over state legislation. The national legislature was to consist of two houses, each apportioned according to the states' free population or their contributions to the national treasury. The Randolph Plan contemplated a national executive and a judiciary "to consist of one or more supreme tribunals, and of inferior tribunals to be chosen by the national legislature".

Randolph's resolutions became the order of business when, on May 30, the Convention resolved itself into a Committee of the Whole to begin serious deliberation. On the same day Charles Pinckney of South Carolina proposed a draft constitution that was also referred to the committee.[20] As discussed and amended through two weeks of debate, the Randolph Plan provided the substance of the first report of the Committee of the Whole to the Convention on June 13.

Randolph's plan had a distinctly nationalist thrust, and, unsurprisingly, it precipitated a counter-proposal by William Paterson of New Jersey,[21] which would have retained the existing unicameral Congress, with each state continuing to possess an equal vote. Even the Paterson Plan, however, would have created a national executive and a national judiciary. During this period, Alexander Hamilton of New York presented the fourth and last of the complete plans before the Convention.[22] As a final contribution to the mix, the Convention probably had before it a draft, of a judiciary article only, in the handwriting of John Blair of Virginia.[23]

But it was the Randolph Plan, and to a lesser extent the Paterson alternative, on which the delegates principally focused. Upon the introduction of the Paterson Plan, both it and the Randolph Plan were returned to the Committee of the Whole. Following four days of debate, the Committee voted on June 19, seven states to three with Maryland divided,[24] to adhere to its original report of the Randolph resolutions.

There followed the second major round of debate, in the Convention proper, on the report of the Committee of the Whole. At the outset, progress stalled for nearly a month, as—amid threats that delegates from the small states would pull out—the Convention wrestled with the divisive issue of proportional versus equal representation of the states. Finally, on July 16, a

---

18. 1 Farrand 20–23.

19. See Banning, *The Practical Sphere of a Republic: James Madison, the Constitutional Convention, and the Emergence of Revolutionary Federalism,* in Beeman, Botein, & Carter, note 7, *supra,* at 162–87.

20. 3 Farrand 595–609 (Appendix D).

21. 1 *id.* 242–45, 3 *id.* 611–16 (Appendix E).

22. 1 *id.* 291–93, 3 *id.* 617–30 (Appendix F).

23. Blair's draft was later found in the papers of George Mason. 2 *id.* 432–33.

24. 1 *id.* 313, 322.

compromise was voted, under which representation would be proportional in the House but equal in the Senate. Remaining disagreements were worked out, frequently by compromise, over the next ten days.

The elaboration of detail (July 27 to September 10).[25] The Convention adjourned from July 27 to August 6 while a Committee of Detail, chaired by John Rutledge, prepared the first definite draft of the Constitution.[26] The Committee built upon the votes of the Convention adopting or modifying Randolph's Virginia Plan, but it drew also on the other plans that had been submitted, on the provisions of various state constitutions, and on a report drafted in 1781 by a committee of the Old Congress that had sought to revise the Articles of Confederation. The report of the Committee of Detail introduced the third major round of debate, during which the Convention finally came to agreement on all remaining problems of general principle.

Final settlement and polishing (September 10 to 15).[27] A Committee on Style, which made more than stylistic changes, reported to the Convention on September 12.[28] There ensued a final review, which produced minor amendments and culminated in the signing of the engrossed Constitution on Monday, September 17.

C. The Judiciary Article

1. A Federal Judicial Power

In the first day of substantive debate (May 30), the Committee of the Whole accepted Randolph's resolution "that a national government ought to be established consisting of a supreme Legislative, Judiciary, and Executive".[29] Again on June 4, Madison records in his notes, the first clause of Randolph's ninth resolution—"Resolved that a national Judiciary be established"—passed unanimously.[30]

What was thus agreed to, without discussion or further question, was a substantial innovation in American experience. The new states had tried to settle border disputes by the device of *ad hoc* tribunals.[31] In addition, Con-

---

25. This phase is described in Farrand, Framing, note 1, *supra*, at 124–75, and Warren note 1, *supra*, at 368–685.

26. 2 Farrand 177–89.

27. For this final phase, see Farrand, Framing, note 1, *supra*, at 176–95, and Warren, note 1, *supra*, at 686–721.

28. 2 Farrand 590–603.

29. Connecticut alone opposed, with New York divided. 1 *id.* 30–32.

30. Madison's Journal 108 (Scott ed. 1895). (Madison's Notes of Debates in the Federal Convention of 1787 are also available in a paperback edition (Koch ed., Norton, 1969).) See also 1 Farrand 104.

31. The Articles of Confederation provided a cumbersome machinery for resolving disputes between states, under which the disputing states selected seven judges by joint consent, any five of whom could constitute a quorum. If judges could not be agreed upon, Congress was to select three candidates from each state, and the court would be arrived at by alternate striking of names. The judgment of the court so selected was to be final. Articles of Confederation, Art. IX.

The only case ever decided under this provision involved a territorial dispute between Connecticut and Pennsylvania over territory on the banks of the Susquehanna river known as Wyoming. In 1775, prior to the enactment of the provision, a special committee of Congress was appointed, which recommended the terms of an armistice that should govern until the dispute could be settled. When a court was appointed in 1782, by joint consent, it sat for forty-two days in Trenton, New Jersey, then rendered a unanimous judgment against Connecticut. Although Connecticut acquiesced, individual Connecticut settlers were unwilling to cede

gress had possessed the power to "appoint" state courts for the trial of "piracies and felonies on the high seas",[32] and it had even established a distinctively national court to handle appeals in cases of capture.[33] But what was now proposed was much more than a specialized tribunal. It was a national judicial power joined with executive and legislative powers as part of a national government.

The Convention's unhesitating initial agreement about the need for a national judiciary was only a prelude to serious disagreements about the kinds of tribunals that should exercise the judicial power and about the scope of the jurisdiction that these tribunals should possess. Nonetheless, the unanimity bespoke impressively the general understanding that a sound and efficacious government requires courts.

2. The Tribunals Exercising the Power

Having agreed to the establishment of a national judiciary, the Convention proceeded swiftly to vote that the judicial branch should "consist of one supreme tribunal, and of one or more inferior tribunals."[34] The vote of June 4, reiterated on June 5, reflected an uncontroversial agreement, never to be

their lands, and uncertainty persisted. Carson, The Supreme Court of the United States 67–74 (1891).

32. Articles of Confederation, Art. IX. Congress exercised the power by providing for trial of such offenses by designated state judges in 1781. As early as 1775, Congress had suggested that the several states set up courts to determine all cases of capture in the first instance, or confer such jurisdiction on their existing courts. See Carson, note 31, *supra,* at 42–43. In all such cases an appeal was to lie to Congress, or such person or persons as they should appoint. All the states but New York complied, and even New York ultimately appears to have come into partial compliance. See *id.* at 45.

33. The first appeal from a state tribunal came up in August of 1776, and Congress appointed a special committee to hear it. The practice of appointing special committees continued until January, 1777, when a five-member Standing Committee was appointed. At length, however, in January, 1780, Congress resolved "that a Court be established for trial of all appeals from the Courts of Admiralty in these United States, in cases of capture, to consist of 3 Judges appointed and commissioned by Congress * * *." The court was called "The Court of Appeals in Cases of Capture". See Carson, note 31, *supra,* at 41–64.

Although this was the first national court, several needed powers were stricken from its authorizing provisions, including those of fining and imprisoning for contempt and disobedience and directing that the state admiralty courts should execute its decrees. *Id.* at 56. Indeed, the court was never really independent of its creator. In the case of the brig "Susannah", involving a delicate question of national power arising out of conflict between a New Hampshire statute and the act of Congress creating the Court of Appeals, Congress ordered that all proceedings upon the sentence of the court be stayed, and attempted to determine the dispute itself. Congress never took any final action in the case, but it defeated a motion, made during the debate, stating that it was improper for Congress in any manner to reverse or control the court's decisions. In December, 1784, business had dwindled; the court had cleared its docket; and after a few more occasional sessions, the Court ceased to function on May 16, 1787. *Id.* at 58–60.

Nonetheless, "some 118 cases were disposed of by the congressional committees and the Court of Appeals, and the idea became well fixed that admiralty and maritime cases pertained to federal jurisdiction". Hockett, The Constitutional History of the United States 157 (1939). See also Jameson, *The Predecessor of the Supreme Court,* in Essays in the Constitutional History of the United States 1–45 (1889).

34. 1 Farrand 104–05 (June 4), 119 (June 5).

reconsidered, that there should be one Supreme Court.[35] The decision concerning inferior federal courts proved less stable.[36]

On June 5, after an inconclusive discussion about where the power to appoint inferior tribunals should lie, Rutledge moved to reconsider the provision for their establishment at all. He urged that "the State tribunals might and ought to be left in all cases to decide in the first instance, the right of appeal to the supreme national tribunal being sufficient to secure the national rights & uniformity of Judgmts: that it was making an unnecessary encroachment on the jurisdiction of the States, and creating unnecessary obstacles to their adoption of the new system".[37] Sherman, supporting him, dwelled on the expense of an additional set of courts.[38]

Madison strongly opposed the motion. He argued that "unless inferior federal tribunals were dispersed throughout the Republic with *final* jurisdiction in *many* cases, appeals would be multiplied to a most oppressive degree".[39] Besides, he maintained, "an appeal would not in many cases be a remedy." "What was to be done after improper Verdicts in State tribunals obtained under the biassed directions of a dependent Judge, or the local prejudices of an undirected jury? To remand the cause for a new trial would answer no purpose. To order a new trial at the supreme bar would oblige the parties to bring up witnesses, tho' ever so distant from the seat of the Court. An effective Judiciary establishment commensurate to the legislative authority, was essential".[40] Wilson and Dickinson spoke in the same vein, with the former emphasizing the special need for an admiralty jurisdiction.[41]

Despite these appeals, Rutledge's motion to strike out "inferior tribunals" carried, five states to four with two divided.[42] This, however, was not the end of the matter. Picking up on a suggestion by Dickinson, Wilson and Madison moved a compromise resolution, which provided that "the National Legislature [should] be empowered" to "institute"—the verb recorded in Madison's notes[43]—or "appoint"—the word in the Convention Journal[44] and another set of contemporary notes[45]—"inferior tribunals". According to Madison, he and Wilson "observed that there was a distinction between establishing such tribunals absolutely, and giving a discretion to the Legislature to establish or not establish them".

Pierce Butler objected even to this compromise proposal that "The people will not bear such innovations. The States will revolt at such encroachments." Despite this protest, "the Madisonian Compromise", as it has come to be called, was agreed to, eight states to two with one divided.[46]

35. All the plans submitted to the Convention provided for a Supreme Court. See *id.* 21, 244, 292; 2 *id.* 432; 3 *id.* 600.

36. Although the Randolph and Pinckney plans called for mandatory establishment of inferior federal courts, the Paterson plan did not provide for any such courts at all. Hamilton's plan empowered Congress to create them for the determination of all matters of general concern. John Blair's plan provided only for lower courts of admiralty.

37. 1 Farrand 124.

38. *Id.* 125.

39. *Id.* 124.

40. *Id.*

41. *Id.* 124 (Wilson), 125 (Dickinson).

42. *Id.* 125.

43. *Id.*

44. *Id.* 118.

45. *Id.* 127 (Yates).

46. *Id.* 124–25 (June 5). Professor Collins sees a puzzle in the sequence of the Convention's actions on June 4–5: Why, within so short a span, did the Convention swing from unanimous approval of constitutionally mandated lower federal courts, to preclusion of lower federal courts altogether,

Opposition to a system of inferior federal courts was renewed when the report of the Committee of the Whole came before the Convention on July 18. But it was milder, with Sherman saying that he "was willing to give the power to the Legislature but wished them to make use of the State Tribunals whenever it could be done with safety to the general interest". This time the vote accepting the compromise was unanimous,[47] and the decision stood without further question.[48] The Committee of Detail reported a draft prescribing that the judicial power "shall be vested in one Supreme Court and in such inferior Courts as shall, when necessary, from time to time, be constituted by the Legislature of the United States."[49] The Committee of Style further altered the language to its current form.

3. Separation and Independence of the Judicial Power

a. Appointment of Judges

The method of appointing federal judges was a source of significant controversy. The Randolph Plan called for appointment by the legislature, but Madison objected that many legislators would be incompetent to assess judicial qualifications and proposed appointment by the "less numerous & more select" Senate.[50] The Committee of the Whole agreed to Madison's suggested amendment on June 13. The Convention adhered to this decision on July 21, when it rejected another proposal by Madison, who now feared that senatorial appointment would confer too much power on the states, in favor of appointment by the national executive, with or without the approval of the Senate.[51] In the closing days the issue was reopened yet again and finally resolved, as part of a general settlement on appointments, in favor of appointment by the executive

to approval of a compromise apparently authorizing Congress to "appoint" or "establish" lower federal courts? See Collins, *Article III Cases, State Court Duties, and the Madisonian Compromise* 1995 Wisc.L.Rev. 35, 116–19. During the interval between the vote to approve mandatory federal courts and adoption of Rutledge's motion to reconsider, the Convention voted to delete the provision of the Randolph Plan that the national judiciary should be elected by the national legislature and to leave open for the time being the question of judicial selection. Emphasizing this background, Collins speculates that Rutledge's motion to reconsider may have been motivated by the intervening debate on the selection of the federal judiciary; if the power did not lie with the legislature, the Convention might have considered it too dangerous to be vested elsewhere. See *id.*

A related suggestion ascribes significance to the contested wording of Madison's and Wilson's compromise resolution: if the approved discretionary power was a congressional power to "appoint" inferior tribunals, this formulation may hark back to the practice under the Articles of Confederation by which Congress "appointed" existing state courts, rather than creating independent federal courts, to conduct certain forms of judicial business. See Goebel, note 1, *supra,* at 211–12. On the subsequent alteration of the language to its final form, see *infra.*

47. 2 Farrand 45–46 (July 18).

48. In the debate on the report of the Committee of Detail, a motion, recorded only in the Journal, was made and seconded to give the inferior federal courts only an appellate jurisdiction over decisions of state courts, but the motion was withdrawn. *Id.* 424 (August 27).

49. *Id.* 186.

50. 1 Farrand 233 (June 13).

51. The first proposal for appointment by the President with the concurrence of the Senate was made by Hamilton on June 5. Motions for executive appointment alone, or executive appointment subject to Senate approval, were defeated on several occasions thereafter. See 1 *id.* 128, 224, 232–33; 2 *id.* 80–83; Warren, note 1, *supra,* at 327–29.

with the advice and consent of the Senate.[52]

b. *Tenure and Salary*

The provisions protecting the tenure and salary of judges received almost complete assent.[53] There was minor controversy over whether to prevent the temptation of pay increases. The Committee of the Whole first accepted language barring increase as well as diminution in salary during tenure in office,[54] but the prohibition against increases was rejected in the subsequent debate in the Convention and again in the debate on the report of the Committee of Detail.[55] Rejection rested largely on the practical ground that the cost of living might rise.

The lone assault on the principle of tenure during good behavior occurred in the debate on the report of the Committee of Detail, when Dickinson of Delaware, seconded by Gerry and Sherman, moved that the judges "may be removed by the Executive on the application by the Senate and House of Representatives". The motion drew strong opposition, however, and only Connecticut ultimately supported it.[56]

c. *Extra–Judicial Functions*

Randolph's eighth resolution proposed to create a council of revision composed of "the Executive and a convenient number of the National Judiciary" with authority, first, "to examine every act of the National Legislature before it shall operate", and, second, to review every negative exercised by the National Legislature upon an act of a state legislature, pursuant to a power proposed in the sixth resolution, before it "shall be final". The dissent of the council was to "amount to a rejection, unless the Act of the National Legislature be again passed, or that of a particular Legislature be again negatived by [blank] of the members of each branch".[57]

In an early vote of 8–2, the Committee of the Whole rejected this plan to mingle executive and judicial functions, and substituted a purely executive veto of national legislation.[58] Madison and Wilson renewed the proposal for a council of revision on three subsequent occasions, but it was defeated each time.[59]

---

52. Appointment by the Senate was retained in the draft reported by the Committee of Detail. 2 Farrand 132, 155, 169, 183. The final compromise was worked out between August 25 and September 7. See *id.* 498, 538–40; Warren, note 1, *supra,* at 639–42. For Hamilton's comments on the matter, see The Federalist, Nos. 76, 77.

53. All four of the principal plans provided that the judges should hold office during good behavior, and the Randolph, Pinckney, and Paterson plans forbade either a decrease or an increase in salary during continuance in office.

54. 1 Farrand 121.

55. 2 *id.* 44–45, 429–30; Warren, note 1, *supra,* at 532–34. See also Rosenn, *The Constitutional Guaranty Against Diminution*

of Judicial Compensation, 24 U.C.L.A. L.Rev. 308, 311–18 (1976).

56. 2 Farrand 428–29; Warren, note 1, *supra,* at 532. For the conflict over judicial tenure in the colonial period, see Klein, *Prelude to Revolution in New York: Jury Trials and Judicial Tenure,* 17 Wm. & Mary Q. 439 (1960). For an extensive analysis of the problems of tenure and removal in the Constitution, see Berger, Impeachment: The Constitutional Problems (1973).

57. 1 Farrand 21.

58. *Id.* 97–104, 108–110 (June 4).

59. The Committee of the Whole adhered to the rejection, eight votes to three, on June 6. *Id.* 138–140 (June 6). The Convention did likewise in the later debate on the report of the Committee of the Whole, this

In the view of Madison and Wilson, judicial participation in a council of revision would have furnished a necessary check upon legislative aggrandizement and provided an assurance of wiser laws. The arguments that prevailed against it were concisely stated by Gerry and King:

"Mr. Gerry doubts whether the Judiciary ought to form a part of it [the council of revision], as they will have a sufficient check agst. encroachments on their own department by their exposition of the laws, which involved a power of deciding on their Constitutionality. In some States the Judges had actually set aside laws as being agst. the Constitution. This was done too with general approbation. It was quite foreign from the nature of ye. office to make them judges of the policy of public measures."

King added "that the Judges ought to be able to expound the law as it should come before them, free from the bias of having participated in its formation".[60]

The last important reference to extra-judicial functions occurred near the close of the Convention, when Dr. Johnson moved to extend the judicial power to cases arising under the Constitution of the United States, as well as under its laws and treaties.[61] Madison, responding, "doubted whether it was not going too far to extend the jurisdiction of the Court generally to cases arising under the Constitution, & whether it ought not to be limited to cases of a Judiciary Nature. The right of expounding the Constitution in cases not of this nature ought not to be given to that Department." Madison's concern notwithstanding, "The motion of Docr. Johnson was agreed to *nem. con.*: it being generally supposed that the jurisdiction given was constructively limited to cases of a Judiciary nature."[62]

4. The Power to Declare Statutes Unconstitutional

As Madison's comment on Dr. Johnson's motion indicates, the power of judicial review was taken for granted throughout the debates at the Constitutional Convention.[63] The point became perhaps most explicit in a debate over the proposed congressional negative of state laws, during which the existence of a

time by four votes to three with two states divided. 2 *id.* 73–80 (July 21). Madison and Wilson made their final attempt in the debate on the report of the Committee of Detail, but their proposal, which this time took a somewhat different form, again failed. *Id.* 298 (August 15).

60. 1 *id.* 97–98, 109 (June 4).

61. The Convention permitted two other plans for using judges non-judicially to die without coming to votes. The first was a suggestion advanced by Ellsworth and put in more elaborate form by Gouverneur Morris to make the Chief Justice a member of the projected Privy Council of the President. See Warren, note 1, *supra*, at 643–50. The second was a proposal by Charles Pinckney that "Each branch of the Legislature, as well as the Supreme Executive shall have authority to require the opinions of the supreme Judicial Court upon important questions of law,

and upon solemn occasions". 2 Farrand 340–41 (August 20). Pinckney's proposal went to the Committee of Detail, but was never reported out.

62. 2 Farrand 430 (August 27).

63. The historical case is perhaps most strongly made in Berger, Congress v. The Supreme Court (1969). Wood, Creation, note 3, *supra*, argues that developments in political theory in the 1780s, especially the substitution of popular sovereignty for the traditional Blackstonian notion of legislative sovereignty, made possible the institution of judicial review. Nelson, *Changing Conceptions of Judicial Review: The Evolution of Constitutional Theory in the States, 1790–1860,* 120 U.Pa.L.Rev. 1166 (1972), gives an interesting account of the evolution of judicial review into "an unchallenged dogma" in the period between Marbury v. Madison and the Civil War.

power in the federal courts to invalidate unconstitutional state laws was common ground. The crux of the controversy was whether this was a sufficient safeguard.[64] Resolution came through acceptance of Luther Martin's proposal of the Supremacy Clause, which strengthened the judicial check by express statement of the parallel power and responsibility of state judges.[65]

The existence of a judicial safeguard against unconstitutional federal laws was similarly recognized on both sides in the debates over the proposal for a council of revision of acts of the national legislature. Gerry's statement of the judicial power, already quoted, was substantially echoed at least eight times.[66]

The only note of challenge came in the fourth and last debate on the proposal when Mercer, a recently arrived delegate, speaking in support of the alternative plan of judicial participation in the veto, said that he "disapproved of the Doctrine that the Judges as expositors of the Constitution should have authority to declare a law void". Dickinson then observed that he was impressed with Mr. Mercer's remark and "thought no such power ought to exist" but "he was at the same time at a loss what expedient to substitute". Gouverneur Morris at once said that he could not agree that the judiciary "should be bound to say that a direct violation of the Constitution was law", and there the discussion ended.[67]

Meanwhile, the first version of the Supremacy Clause had been approved. At no time was there a suggestion that the responsibility of the judges under this clause was any less with respect to federal than state laws. On the contrary, the changes in the clause in the closing days of the Convention suggest that it was the same.[68] The Convention's matter-of-course approval of

---

64. Wilson thus summarized the proponents' case: "The power of self-defence had been urged as necessary for the State Governments—It was equally necessary for the General Government. The firmness of Judges is not of itself sufficient. Something further is requisite—It will be better to prevent the passage of an improper law, than to declare it void when passed." 2 Farrand 391 (August 23).

65. The proposal of a legislative negative, first advanced and vigorously supported throughout by Madison, was embodied in Randolph's sixth resolution, which authorized a negative only of state laws "contravening in the opinion of the National Legislature the articles of Union". 1 Farrand 21. In this form it was initially approved by the Committee of the Whole on May 31 without debate or dissent. *Id.* 54. The plan was first discussed on June 8, when the Committee rejected Charles Pinckney's motion to extend the negative to "all laws which they shd. judge to be improper". *Id.* 171. Rumblings of opposition then appeared and culminated in a debate in the Convention of July 17, when the plan was rejected. 2 *id.* 21–22.

Madison, in support, urged that states "can pass laws which will accomplish their injurious objects before they can be repealed

by the Genl Legislre, or be set aside by the National Tribunals". Sherman and Gouverneur Morris, in opposition, relied upon the courts to set aside unconstitutional laws, with Sherman saying that the proposal "involves a wrong principle, to wit, that a law of a State contrary to the articles of the Union, would if not negatived, be valid and operative". None doubted the judicial power. When the negative was defeated, Luther Martin at once proposed the first version of the Supremacy Clause, "which was agreed to *nem. con.*" *Id.* 27–29. See also *id.* 390–91.

66. See Rufus King, 1 Farrand 109 (June 4); Wilson, 2 *id.* 73 (July 21); Madison, *id.* 74 (July 21), and 92–93 (July 23); Martin, *id.* 76 (July 21); Mason, *id.* 78 (July 21); Pinckney, *id.* 298 (August 15); G. Morris, *id.* 299 (August 15). See also Williamson, *id.* 376 (August 22).

67. 2 Farrand 298–99 (August 15).

68. In its original form the clause referred only to "Legislative acts of the United States made by virtue and in pursuance of the Articles of Union" and to treaties, and it declared them to be the supreme law only "of the respective States". 2 Farrand 28–29 (July 17). On August 23 the Convention amended the clause without debate to declare

the express grant of jurisdiction in cases arising under the Constitution gives further indication of the scope of the intended power of judicial review.[69]

5. The Scope of Jurisdiction

As initially formulated, the Randolph Plan contemplated apparently mandatory federal jurisdiction of "all piracies & felonies on the high seas, captures from an enemy; cases in which foreigners or citizens of other States applying to such jurisdictions may be interested, or which respect the collection of the National revenue; impeachments of any National officers, and questions which may involve the national peace and harmony".[70] When the Committee of the Whole first discussed this subject on June 12 and 13, however, Randolph concluded that it was "the business of a subcommittee to detail" the jurisdiction. He "therefore moved to obliterate such parts of the resolve so as only to establish the principle, to wit, that the jurisdiction of the national judiciary shall extend to all cases of national revenue, impeachment of national officers, and questions which involve the national peace or harmony". The Committee agreed to this proposal by unanimous vote.[71]

In considering the report of the Committee of the Whole on July 18, the Convention again confined itself to general principle. But "several criticisms having been made on the definition [of jurisdiction]; it was proposed by Mr. Madison so to alter as to read thus—'that the jurisdiction shall extend to all cases arising under the Natl. laws: And to such other questions as may involve the Natl. peace & harmony.' which was agreed to *nem. con.*"[72]

With only this general direction, the Committee of Detail took the lead in defining the categories to which the federal judicial power would actually or potentially extend. The nine headings of federal jurisdiction that eventually emerged in Article III, § 2 can be grouped in various ways. Thematically, for example, the enumerated jurisdictional categories appear to contemplate federal judicial power to promote four central purposes: (i) to protect and enforce federal authority (jurisdiction of federal question cases and cases to which the United States is a party); (ii) to resolve disputes relating to foreign affairs (jurisdiction of suits affecting foreign envoys, admiralty cases, and suits involving foreign nations); (iii) to provide an interstate umpire (suits between states or involving their conflicting land grants); (iv) and to furnish an impartial tribunal where state court bias was feared (party-based cases involving citizens of different states, a state and a non-citizen, or an alien).

On the face of the text, however, a linguistically striking divide exists between the first three and the last six jurisdictional categories. With respect to the first three categories, which are defined mostly if not exclusively by subject matter,[73] Article III, § 2 provides that the judicial power of the United

---

expressly the supremacy of "This Constitution and the laws of the United States made in pursuance thereof". *Id.* 389. The final draft of the Committee on Style declared the Constitution, laws, and treaties to be "the supreme law of the land" and not merely "of the respective States". *Id.* 603.

69. See text at note 62, *supra*.

70. 1 Farrand 22. All of the plans respecting the judiciary that were put before

the Convention specified various definite heads of federal jurisdiction.

71. 1 Farrand 238 (June 13, Yates' notes). See also *id.* 220 (June 12), 223–24, 232 (June 13).

72. 2 *id.* 46 (July 18).

73. The jurisdiction for the first and third of these categories, involving "all Cases * * * arising under" the Constitution, laws, and treaties of the United States and "all

States shall extend to "all Cases". With respect to the last six, which are defined by reference to the status of the parties, the "all" disappears, and the judicial power is extended to "Controversies", not "Cases".

The shift in language seems sufficiently sharp and deliberate to require explanation. Yet there is no explicitly recorded discussion of its significance in the Committee of the Whole or on the floor of the Convention.[74] Partly as a result, whether the change of language marks a distinction of constitutional intent—especially with reference to Congress' power over the jurisdiction of the federal courts—is much controverted and will be explored more fully in later Chapters.[75]

Regardless of its intended significance, the linguistic division provides a useful framework for examining the scope of federal jurisdiction authorized, if not required, by Article III.

a. Jurisdiction Based Primarily on Subject Matter: The First Three Headings

(i) *Cases Arising Under the Constitution, Laws, and Treaties of the United States.* Faithful to the vote of July 18, the Committee of Detail placed at the head of its list of subjects of jurisdiction "all cases arising under laws passed by the Legislature of the United States".[76] Save only for the change in wording by the Committee of Style, this provision was accepted and incorporated into the Constitution without further question or discussion.[77]

But the provision for jurisdiction of cases "arising under [federal] laws" was not left standing alone. As already noted, in a general discussion of the judiciary article as crafted by the Committee of Style, Dr. Johnson moved to insert an express provision for jurisdiction of cases under "this Constitution", and the motion carried without opposition.[78] Immediately thereafter, accord-

Cases of admiralty and maritime Jurisdiction", is based unequivocally on subject matter. By contrast, the second category of "all Cases affecting Ambassadors, other public Ministers and Consuls" arguably straddles the distinction between subject-matter-based and party-based jurisdiction.

74. But *cf.* Amar, *A Neo–Federalist View of Article III: Separating the Two Tiers of Federal Jurisdiction,* 65 B.U.L.Rev. 205, 242–45 (1985)(arguing that documents used in drafting by the Committee of Detail, coupled with the Convention's specific reinsertion of the word "all" in the clause setting out the Supreme Court's appellate jurisdiction, after it had been omitted by the Committee of Style, reflects deliberate advertence to this point and an intention to make federal jurisdiction mandatory in the first three jurisdictional categories).

75. For further discussion of the possible significance of the distinction for Congress' power to define and limit federal jurisdiction in the various categories of cases, see Chap. IV, Sec. 1, *infra.* For exploration of the distinction's possible bearing on questions of state sovereign immunity and the meaning of the Eleventh Amendment, see Chap. IX, Sec. 2, *infra.*

76. 2 Farrand 186 (August 6). The clause had antecedents, partial or complete, in all of the judiciary plans: Randolph: cases "which respect the collection of the National revenue", 1 *id.* 22; Pinckney: "all cases arising under the laws of the United States", 3 *id.* 600; Paterson: all cases "which may arise on any of the Acts for regulation of trade, or the collection of the federal Revenue", 1 *id.* 244; Hamilton: "all causes in which the revenues of the general Government * * * are concerned", with power in the legislature "to institute Courts in each State for the determination of all matters of general concern", *id.* 292; Blair: "all cases in law and equity arising under * * * the laws of the United States", 2 *id.* 432.

77. 2 Farrand 600 (committee report), 628 (September 15, entire Article approved).

78. See note 62, *supra,* and accompanying text. Among the plans presented to the Convention, only the Blair plan had included such a provision. 2 Farrand 432.

ing to Madison's notes, Rutledge moved to extend the jurisdictional category to encompass cases involving "treaties made or which shall be made" under the authority of the United States. The vote to adopt the motion was again unanimous.[79]

(ii) *Affecting Ambassadors, Other Public Ministers, or Consuls.* Under the Articles of Confederation, the United States could give no assurance of legal protection to the representatives of foreign countries living in the United States. "The Convention was convinced that if foreign officials were either to seek justice at law or be subjected to its penalties, it should be at the hand of the national government."[80] The present clause was reported out of the Committee of Detail and passed without dispute, and, again without dispute, was included in the Supreme Court's original jurisdiction.[81]

(iii) *Admiralty and Maritime Cases.* The inclusion of admiralty and maritime jurisdiction in the report of the Committee of Detail went unchallenged.[82] The principal commerce of the period was, of course, maritime; and, as Wilson pointed out on the floor, it was in the admiralty jurisdiction that disputes with foreigners were most likely to arise.[83] In addition, maritime law had been administered by British vice-admiralty rather than colonial courts before the war,[84] and state courts had therefore not been accustomed to exercising general maritime jurisdiction. Following the break with England, some states established courts with admiralty jurisdiction, but others did not.[85] Moreover, experience during the Revolution with state court adjudication of prize cases had shown the need for a federal tribunal with adequate authority.[86]

79. 2 *id.* 431 (August 27). This amendment could easily be viewed as implementing the Convention's earlier determination that federal judicial power should extend to "questions which involve the national peace and harmony". In his early proposal to settle the scope of jurisdiction in terms of general principle, Randolph made clear that this language was intended to include questions of "the security of foreigners where treaties are in their favor". 1 Farrand 238 (June 13). Nevertheless, the Committee of Detail omitted any express reference to treaties, perhaps because of the provisions giving jurisdiction when foreigners were parties.

By all indications, the Convention regarded federal judicial power to enforce treaties as possessing vital importance. All the other plans except Pinckney's contemplated a similar jurisdiction. Paterson: appellate jurisdiction where construction of a treaty involved, 1 Farrand 244; Hamilton: where "citizens of foreign nations are concerned", *id.* 292; Blair: cases arising under a treaty, 2 *id.* 432. In addition, the Convention at one time had extended the proposed negative on state laws, upon motion by Benjamin Franklin, to include laws contravening "any treaties subsisting under the authority of the Union." 1 *id.* 54 (May 31).

80. Frank, *Historical Bases of the Federal Judicial System*, 13 Law & Contemp.Prob. 3, 14 (1948). All the plans contemplated such a jurisdiction. The Paterson plan gave the Supreme Court appellate jurisdiction in cases "touching the rights of ambassadors", as well as in cases "in which foreigners may be interested". 1 Farrand 244. The Pinckney plan gave the Court original jurisdiction in cases "affecting Ambassadors & other public Ministers". 3 *id.* 600. The Blair plan added consuls, in substantially the language of the present grant. 2 *id.* 432. The Randolph and Hamilton plans provided generally for jurisdiction where foreigners were concerned. 1 *id.* 22, 292.

81. 2 Farrand 186, 431.

82. *Id.* 186. See The Federalist No. 80 (Hamilton): "The most bigoted idolizers of state authority, have not thus far shown a disposition to deny the National Judiciary the cognizance of maritime causes".

83. 1 Farrand 124 (June 5).

84. See Benedict, Benedict on Admiralty § 713 (6th ed. 1941).

85. See *id.* at § 719, p. 438.

86. See note 33, *supra.*

b. *Jurisdiction Based on Party Status: The Remaining Categories*

(i) *United States a Party.*   Under the Articles of Confederation the United States had to go into state courts for enforcement of its laws and collection of its claims.[87]   Of the five plans before the Convention, however, only Blair's included a general grant of jurisdiction in cases to which the United States was a party.[88]   Possibly the clause was omitted in the others, and in the initial report of the Committee of Detail, because the problem was thought to be addressed through jurisdiction in cases arising under various federal laws.   But responding to a motion by Charles Pinckney, the committee later made a special recommendation, on August 22, that jurisdiction be given in controversies "between the United States and an individual State or the United States and an individual person".[89]   The provision as it stands was inserted on the floor on August 27, on a motion by Madison and G. Morris apparently intended to reflect this recommendation.   Soon after, on the same day, it was moved that "in cases in which the United States shall be a party the jurisdiction shall be original or appellate as the Legislature may direct", but the motion failed,[90] with the result that the jurisdiction of the Supreme Court was made appellate only.

(ii) *Controversies Between Two or More States.*   Border disputes had plagued the new states.[91]   In a speech introducing his resolutions, Governor Randolph said: "Are we not on the eve of war, which is only prevented by the hopes from the convention?"[92]   Though not specifically mentioned, a jurisdiction in controversies between states could be viewed as implicit in Randolph's "national peace and harmony" provision.

When the Committee of Detail reported, it qualified its proposed grant of jurisdiction to the Supreme Court in "controversies between two or more States" with an exception for "such as shall regard Territory or Jurisdiction".   For these disputes, an analogue to the cumbersome machinery of the Articles of Confederation was retained, and the Senate was charged with implementing

---

87.   Thus, even treason against the United States had to be left to trial in state courts by state law.   In 1781 Congress recommended to the state legislatures that they pass laws punishing infractions of the law of nations, and erect courts or clothe existing courts with authority to decide what constituted such an offense.   Where an official of the United States Post Office was guilty of misdemeanor in office, Congress could only prescribe penalties and let the Postmaster General bring an action in debt in a state court to recover them.   In settling accounts of the military and in recovering debts from individuals, Congress recommended that the state legislatures pass laws empowering Congress' agents to bring such actions in state courts.   Carson, note 31, *supra,* at 83–86.

88.   2 Farrand 432.   One version of the Paterson plan included a resolution that "provision ought to be made for hearing and deciding upon all disputes arising between the United States and an individual State respecting territory".   3 *id.* 611.

89.   2 *id.* 367 (August 22).   This report was distributed to the members, *id.* 376, but seems not to have been acted upon.   For Pinckney's earlier motion, see *id.* 342 (August 20).

90.   *Id.* 424–25, 430.

91.   See note 31, *supra.*

92.   1 Farrand 26 (May 29).   This view was by no means singular.   When the Convention was close to complete impasse, Gerry appealed to the members to keep trying.   Without a Union, "We should be without an Umpire to decide controversies and must be at the mercy of events".   *Id.* 515 (July 2).   Sherman listed a national power to prevent internal disputes and resorts to force as one of the four basic objects of a Union.   *Id.* 133 (June 6).

it.[93] On the floor, in the debate on the legislative articles, Rutledge moved to strike these provisions, saying that they were "necessary under the Confederation, but will be rendered unnecessary by the National Judiciary now to be established". Doubts were expressed whether the judiciary was appropriate, since "the Judges might be connected with the States being parties". But the motion to strike carried eight states to two, with only North Carolina and Georgia dissenting.[94]

(iii) *State and Citizens of Another State*. The grant of jurisdiction in controversies between a state and citizens of another state had no specific forerunner in any of the five plans before the Convention.[95] The clause first appears in a marginal note in Rutledge's handwriting on Randolph's draft for the Committee of Detail,[96] and was reported out by that committee in its present form.[97] There was no discussion of it, though concern about prejudice seems the only possible explanation.

(iv) *Citizens of Different States*. The grant of diversity jurisdiction aroused bitter controversy in the ratification debates, and the controversy has continued intermittently ever since.[98] Strangely, the clause passed without question in the Convention, and thus without clarification of its purposes.

Randolph's initial plan provided for jurisdiction in "cases in which foreigners or citizens of other States applying to such jurisdictions may be interested",[99] in contrast with Paterson's, Hamilton's, and Blair's, which protected only foreigners, and Pinckney's, which had no provision against bias. When the Committee of the Whole first considered Randolph's proposal on June 12, it voted to give jurisdiction in "cases in which foreigners or citizens of two distinct States of the Union" may be interested.[100] This specification was submerged in the more general votes of principle on June 13 and July 18. But in the report of the Committee of Detail it reappeared in its present form, and was accepted without challenge on August 27.[101]

(v) *Citizens of the Same State, Land Grants Under Different States*. The Committee of Detail proposed the same mode of settling these controversies as for controversies over territory or jurisdiction between the states themselves; and both proposals were stricken by the same vote.[102] Sherman moved the insertion of the present provision in the later debate on the judiciary article, however, and the motion passed unanimously.[103]

---

93. See the proposed Art. IX, Sec. 3, 2 Farrand 183–84. The provision seems to have originated in Randolph's draft in the Committee of Detail. *Id.* 144.

94. *Id.* 400–01 (August 24).

95. Randolph's original resolution would have given jurisdiction to inferior federal courts in "cases in which foreigners or citizens of other States applying to such jurisdictions may be interested". 1 Farrand 22. But this would not have guarded against the possibility of antagonism when a state was suing in the courts of another state. Moreover, if Hamilton was right in The Federalist, No. 81, that the Convention did not contemplate that a state could be sued by a citizen of another state without its consent, it would have been of no assistance to an out-of-state citizen as plaintiff.

96. 2 Farrand 147.

97. *Id.* 186.

98. The problem is more fully treated in the *Note on the Historical Background of the Diversity Jurisdiction*, Chap. XIII, p. 1522, *infra*.

99. See note 95, *supra*.

100. 2 Farrand 431–32.

101. 1 *id.* 22.

102. See note 94, *supra*.

103. 2 Farrand 431–32 (August 27).

(vi) *States, or Citizens Thereof, and Foreign States, Citizens or Subjects.*
All the plans except Pinckney's provided for jurisdiction where foreigners were
interested;[104] and the need for a grant going beyond cases involving treaties
and foreign representatives seems to have been undisputed. The clause came
out of the Committee of Detail in its present form.[105]

5. Jurisdiction of the Supreme Court

a. *Original Jurisdiction*

The Randolph plan, which required the establishment of lower federal courts,
made no provision for an original jurisdiction of the Supreme Court, but all the
other plans did.[106] In the Committee of Detail, one draft of the Constitution in
Randolph's handwriting gave the Supreme Court original jurisdiction in cases
of impeachment and such other cases as the legislature might prescribe.[107] In
a later draft in Wilson's handwriting, and in the draft submitted to the
Convention, original jurisdiction was given in cases of impeachment, in cases
affecting ambassadors and other public ministers and consuls, and in cases in
which a state was a party. This, however, was subject to a general power in
the legislature to assign this jurisdiction, except for a trial of the President, to
inferior federal courts.[108] The provision for impeachments and the legislative
power of assignment were stricken on the floor.[109]

b. *Appellate Jurisdiction*

The decisions as to the scope of the Supreme Court's original jurisdiction
settled that the balance of the jurisdiction should be appellate.[110]

The important provision that the appellate jurisdiction should be subject to
exceptions and regulations by Congress was contained in none of the plans.[111]
It is foreshadowed in Randolph's draft for the Committee of Detail and then
appears in a later draft in Wilson's handwriting in substantially the form in
which the committee reported it.[112] There was no discussion in the Convention.

Discussions on the floor of the Convention do speak, however, to another
question that would later occasion bitter political controversy. In debates
about whether lower federal courts should be constitutionally mandatory or

---

104. See note 79, *supra.*

105. 2 Farrand 186.

106. Paterson's plan, contemplating
primarily an appellate jurisdiction from state
courts, provided for original jurisdiction in
cases of impeachment. *Id.* 244. Pinckney's
gave original jurisdiction in impeachment
and in cases affecting ambassadors and other
public ministers, see 3 *id.* 600; Hamilton's,
in cases of captures, see 1 *id.* 292; and
Blair's, "in all cases affecting ambassadors,
other public ministers and consuls, and those
in which a State shall be a party, and suits
between persons claiming lands under grants
of different states", see 2 *id.* 432.

107. 2 Farrand 147.

108. *Id.* 173, 186–87.

109. See *id.* 423–24, 430–31 (August
27).

110. The expectation that this should
include jurisdiction to review the decisions of
state courts was shared even by those most
devoted to protecting states' rights. See text
following note 36, *supra.* Only Paterson's and
Blair's plans provided in terms for such a
jurisdiction. 1 Farrand 243–44; 2 *id.* 433.

111. All the plans appear to have made
the appellate jurisdiction a constitutional requirement and Blair's even went to the point
of prescribing a constitutional jurisdictional
amount.

112. 2 Farrand 147, 173, 186.

prohibited, it was universally assumed that the Supreme Court would have jurisdiction to review the decisions of state courts on matters of federal concern.[113] Indeed, it was the staunchest partisans of state authority themselves who most insistently urged the appropriateness of this method of protecting federal interests.

The provision that the jurisdiction should extend to both law and fact was added on the floor of the Convention.[114] G. Morris asked if the appellate jurisdiction extended to matters of fact as well as law, and Wilson said he thought that was the intention of the Committee of Detail. Dickinson then moved to add the words "both as to law and fact", and his motion was unanimously agreed to.[115]

The phrase "and fact" opened the Constitution to the charge that the Supreme Court was authorized to re-examine the verdicts of juries.[116] The charge was made even as to criminal cases, where the right of trial by jury was guaranteed, but more especially as to civil cases, where it was not.[117] It bore fruit, of course, in the Seventh Amendment, which not only established the right of trial by jury in civil cases but provided that "no fact tried by a jury, shall be otherwise re-examined in any Court of the United States, than according to the rules of the common law".

D. The Ratification Debates and Proposals for Amendment

The judiciary article, which had aroused only relatively minor disagreement in the Convention, became a center of controversy in the ratification debates. The conventions of six of the initially ratifying states suggested amendments,

113. See text accompanying notes 37–49, *supra*.

114. A similar provision had been in the Paterson plan. 1 Farrand 243. Blair's plan gave jurisdiction as to law only, except in cases of equity and admiralty. 2 *id.* 433. But the point was not touched on in the report of the Committee of Detail.

115. *Id.* 431 (August 27).

116. According to a recent study, for the framing generation "there was no clear distinction between the *functions* of an 'appellate' court and a 'trial' court", since appellate courts routinely retried entire cases. Ritz, Rewriting the History of the Judiciary Act of 1789, at 6 (Holt & LaRue eds. 1990). "Distinctness and hierarchy did not characterize the [then familiar] court structures, and 'superior' usually meant only that a reviewing court had more judges sitting on it." *Id.*

117. None of the five plans referred to trial by jury except Blair's. His plan, while contemplating the trial of crimes in state courts, required that the trial should be by jury. It said nothing of civil cases. 2 Farrand 433.

The provision in Article III for trial of crimes by jury first appears in a draft for the Committee of Detail in Wilson's handwriting, *id.* 173, and was included in the Committee's report. *Id.* 187. It was amended in the Convention to provide for the venue of trial for crimes not committed in any state and approved unanimously on August 28. *Id.* 438.

On September 12, while the report of the Committee of Style was being printed, Mr. Williamson "observed to the House that no provision was yet made for juries in Civil cases and suggested the necessity of it". Gorham said it was impossible "to discriminate equity cases from those in which juries are proper", and added that the "Representatives of the people may be safely trusted in this matter". Gerry supported Williamson. Mason said he saw the difficulty of specifying jury cases, but, broadening the discussion, said that a bill of rights "would give great quiet to the people"; and Gerry and Mason moved that a committee be appointed to prepare such a bill. Sherman thought the state bills of rights sufficient, and repeated Gorham's points about juries. The Convention voted down the motion unanimously. *Id.* 587–88.

and all of these but South Carolina wanted changes in Article III.[118]   Indeed, no fewer than 19 of the 103 amendments proposed by these six states related to the judiciary or judicial proceedings.[119]   According to Charles Warren, "The principal Amendments which were regarded as necessary, relative to the Judiciary, were (a) an express provision guaranteeing jury trials in civil as well as criminal cases; (b) the confinement of appellate power to questions of law, and not of fact; (c) the elimination of any Federal Courts of first instance, or, at all events, the restriction of such original Federal jurisdiction to a Supreme Court with very limited original jurisdiction; (d) the elimination of all jurisdiction based on diverse citizenship and status as a foreigner."[120]

Ames lists 173 amendments proposed in the first session of the first Congress, although this figure includes many repetitions. Of the total, 48 can be counted as primarily concerned with courts and court proceedings; most had to do with trial by jury and various rights of defendants in criminal proceedings.[121]   The Fourth, Fifth, Sixth, Seventh, and Eighth Amendments respond to the central concerns. The House approved a proposal to exclude appeals to the Supreme Court "where the value in controversy shall not amount to one thousand dollars", but it failed in the Senate.[122]

EXCERPTS FROM THE FEDERALIST PAPERS

Of the eighty-five Federalist papers, only five (Nos. 78 to 82) deal directly with the judiciary. But references to the courts and the judicial power are woven into the argument throughout. Of chief importance in showing the place of the courts in the frame of the analysis are the eight papers, five by Hamilton and three by Madison, concerning the defects of the confederacy (Nos. 15 to 22). These follow fourteen introductory papers about the need and utility of an effective union, and introduce the consideration of what is requisite to accomplish such a union.

118. Rhode Island's belated convention in 1790 also proposed amendments to Article III. Ames, Proposed Amendments to the Constitution, 1789–1889, at 310 (1897).

On the process of ratification generally, and on the character of anti-federalist opinion, see Main, The Anti–Federalists: Critics of the Constitution, 1781–1788 (1961); Mason, The States Rights Debate: Antifederalism and the Constitution (1964); Kenyon, The Anti–Federalists (1966); Rutland, The Ordeal of the Constitution: The Anti–Federalists and the Ratification Struggle of 1787– 1788 (1966); Goebel, note 1, *supra,* at 251– 91; Storing, The Complete Anti–Federalist (1981); and Wood, note 3, *supra.* On the debate over the judiciary during the ratification process, see Clinton, *A Mandatory View of Federal Court Jurisdiction: A Guided Quest for the Original Understanding of Article III,* 132 U.Pa.L.Rev. 741, 797–829 (1984).

119. Ames, note 118, *supra,* at 307–10.

120. Warren, *New Light on the History of the Federal Judiciary Act of 1789,* 37 Harv. L.Rev. 49, 56 (1923).

121. Ames, note 118, *supra,* at 310–21 (Nos. 135–38, 140, 142–43, 169–76, 183–86, 188–89, 213–14, 221–24, 226–27, 254–55, 258, 292–94, 297).

On the origins of the Bill of Rights, see generally Rutland, The Birth of the Bill of Rights, 1776–1791 (1955); Levy, Legacy of Suppression: Freedom of Speech and Press in Early American History (1960); Brant, The Bill of Rights: Its Origin and Meaning (1965); Goebel, note 1, *supra,* at 413–56; Schwartz, The Bill of Rights: A Documentary History (1971).

122. Ames, note 118, *supra,* at 316 (No. 225, drawn from Nos. 141, 181, 182); Senate Journal, p. 130.

In No. 15 Hamilton launches the argument with the proposition that:

"The great, and radical vice, in the construction of the existing confederation, is in the principle of *legislation* for *states* or *governments,* in their *corporate* or *collective capacities,* and as contradistinguished from the *individuals* of whom they consist."

The papers then develop, with many historical examples, the thesis that the absence of any effective peaceful process dooms a mere confederacy, having power only to act upon the member states, to disintegrating resort to violence. Hamilton says:

"Government implies the power of making laws. It is essential to the idea of a law, that it be attended with a sanction; or, in other words, a penalty or punishment for disobedience. If there be no penalty annexed to disobedience, the resolutions or commands which pretend to be laws, will in fact amount to nothing more than advice or recommendation. This penalty, whatever it may be, can only be inflicted in two ways; by the agency of the courts and ministers of justice, or by military force; by the COERCION of the magistracy, or by the COERCION of arms. The first kind can evidently apply only to men; the last kind must of necessity be employed against bodies politic, or communities or states. It is evident, that there is no process of a court by which their observance of the laws can, in the last resort, be enforced. Sentences may be denounced against them for violations of their duty; but these sentences can only be carried into execution by the sword. In an association, where the general authority is confined to the collective bodies of the communities that compose it, every breach of the laws must involve a state of war, and military execution must become the only instrument of civil obedience. Such a state of things can certainly not deserve the name of government, nor would any prudent man choose to commit his happiness to it."

In the final paper of the series (No. 22) he concludes:

"A circumstance, which crowns the defects of the confederation, remains yet to be mentioned—the want of a judiciary power. Laws are a dead letter, without courts to expound and define their true meaning and operation."

The next group of papers (Nos. 23 to 51) deals with a series of general problems concerning the new plan of government. Then come three series devoted more particularly to the three branches of government, of which the series on the judiciary, all by Hamilton, is the last.

The first of the judiciary papers (No. 78), which is addressed immediately to the question of tenure and independence of the judges, contains Hamilton's famous argument on judicial review. This paper strongly evidences a prevailing understanding that the Constitution contemplates judicial review. The next paper treats, more briefly, the protection of judicial independence by security of salary.

The first part of No. 80, excerpts from No. 81, and No. 82 are reproduced below. The final judiciary paper, which is not reproduced, discusses trial by jury.

No. 80, Hamilton

To judge with accuracy of the due extent of the federal judicature, it will be necessary to consider, in the first place, what are its proper objects.

It seems scarcely to admit of controversy, that the judiciary authority of the union ought to extend to these several descriptions of cases; 1st. To all those which arise out of the laws of the United States, passed in pursuance of their just and constitutional powers of legislation; 2nd. To all those which concern the execution of the provisions expressly contained in the articles of union; 3rd. To all those in which the United States are a party; 4th. To all those which involve the PEACE of the CONFEDERACY, whether they relate to the intercourse between the United States and foreign nations, or to that between the States themselves; 5th. To all those which originate on the high seas, and are of admiralty or maritime jurisdiction; and lastly, to all those in which the state tribunals cannot be supposed to be impartial and unbiassed.

The first point depends upon this obvious consideration, that there ought always to be a constitutional method of giving efficacy to constitutional provisions. What, for instance, would avail restrictions on the authority of the state legislatures, without some constitutional mode of enforcing the observance of them? The states, by the plan of the convention, are prohibited from doing a variety of things; some of which are incompatible with the interests of the union, others, with the principles of good government. The imposition of duties on imported articles, and the emission of paper money, are specimens of each kind. No man of sense will believe that such prohibitions would be scrupulously regarded, without some effectual power in the government to restrain or correct the infractions of them. * * *

As to the second point, it is impossible, by any argument or comment, to make it clearer than it is in itself. If there are such things as political axioms, the propriety of the judicial power of a government being co-extensive with its legislative, may be ranked among the number. The mere necessity of uniformity in the interpretation of the national laws, decides the question. Thirteen independent courts of final jurisdiction over the same causes, arising upon the same laws, is a hydra in government, from which nothing but contradiction and confusion can proceed.

Still less need be said in regard to the third point. Controversies between the nation and its members or citizens, can only be properly referred to the national tribunals. Any other plan would be contrary to reason, to precedent, and to decorum.

The fourth point rests on this plain proposition, that the peace of the WHOLE ought not to be left at the disposal of a PART. The union will undoubtedly be answerable to foreign powers for the conduct of its members. And the responsibility for an injury ought ever to be accompanied with the faculty of preventing it. As the denial or perversion of justice by the sentences of courts is with reason classed among the just causes of war, it will follow that the federal judiciary ought to have cognizance of all causes in which the citizens of other countries are concerned. * * * So great a proportion of the controversies in which foreigners are parties, involve national questions, that it is by far most safe, and most expedient, to refer all those in which they are concerned to the national tribunals.

The power of determining causes between two states, between one state and the citizens of another, and between the citizens of different states, is perhaps not less essential to the peace of the union, than that which has been just examined. * * *

            * * *

The fifth point will demand little animadversion. The most bigoted idolizers of state authority, have not thus far shown a disposition to deny the national judiciary the cognizance of maritime causes. These so generally depend on the laws of nations, and so commonly affect the rights of foreigners, that they fall within the considerations which are relative to the public peace. The most important part of them are, by the present confederation, submitted to federal jurisdiction.

The reasonableness of the agency of the national courts, in cases in which the state tribunals cannot be supposed to be impartial, speaks for itself. No man ought certainly to be a judge in his own cause, or in any cause, in respect to which he has the least interest or bias. This principle has no inconsiderable weight in designating the federal courts, as the proper tribunals for the determination of controversies between different states and their citizens. And it ought to have the same operation, in regard to some cases, between the citizens of the same state. Claims to land under grants of different states, founded upon adverse pretensions of boundary, are of this description. The courts of neither of the granting states could be expected to be unbiassed. The laws may have even prejudged the question, and tied the courts down to decisions in favour of the grants of the state to which they belonged. And where this had not been done, it would be natural that the judges, as men, should feel a strong predilection to the claims of their own government. * * *

PUBLIUS.

No. 81, Hamilton

Let us now return to the partition of the judiciary authority between different courts, and their relations to each other.

"The judicial power of the United States is to be vested in one supreme court, and in such inferior courts as the congress may from time to time ordain and establish." That there ought to be one court of supreme and final jurisdiction, is a proposition which is not likely to be contested. * * * [Hamilton here discusses the need for an independent judiciary and undertakes to refute claims that there is danger of encroachment by the judiciary department upon the legislative.]

Having now examined, and I trust removed, the objections to the distinct and independent organization of the supreme court; I proceed to consider the propriety of the power of constituting inferior courts,[1] and the relations which will subsist between these and the former.

The power of constituting inferior courts is evidently calculated to obviate the necessity of having recourse to the supreme court in every case of federal cognizance. It is intended to enable the national government to institute or *authorize* in each state or district of the United States, a tribunal competent to the determination of matters of national jurisdiction within its limits.

But why, it is asked, might not the same purpose have been accomplished by the instrumentality of the state courts? This admits of different answers. Though the fitness and competency of these courts should be allowed in the utmost latitude: yet the substance of the power in question may still be

---

1. This power has been absurdly represented as intended to abolish all the county courts in the several states, which are commonly called inferior courts. But the expressions of the constitution are to constitute "tribunals INFERIOR TO THE SUPREME COURT," and the evident design of the provision is, to enable the institution of local courts, subordinate to the supreme, either in states or larger districts. It is ridiculous to imagine, that county courts were in contemplation.—Publius.

regarded as a necessary part of the plan, if it were only to authorize the national legislature to commit to them the cognizance of causes arising out of the national constitution. To confer upon the existing courts of the several states the power of determining such causes, would perhaps be as much "to constitute tribunals," as to create new courts with the like power. But ought not a more direct and explicit provision to have been made in favour of the state courts? There are, in my opinion, substantial reasons against such a provision: The most discerning cannot foresee how far the prevalency of a local spirit may be found to disqualify the local tribunals for the jurisdiction of national causes; whilst every man may discover that courts constituted like those of some of the states would be improper channels of the judicial authority of the union. State judges, holding their offices during pleasure, or from year to year, will be too little independent to be relied upon for an inflexible execution of the national laws. And if there was a necessity for confiding to them the original cognizance of causes arising under those laws, there would be a correspondent necessity for leaving the door of appeal as wide as possible. In proportion to the grounds of confidence in, or distrust of the subordinate tribunals, ought to be the facility or difficulty of appeals. And well satisfied as I am of the propriety of the appellate jurisdiction, in the several classes of causes to which it is extended by the plan of the convention, I should consider everything calculated to give, in practice, an unrestrained course to appeals, as a source of public and private inconvenience.

I am not sure but that it will be found highly expedient and useful to divide the United States into four or five, or half a dozen districts; and to institute a federal court in each district, in lieu of one in every state. The judges of these courts may hold circuits for the trial of causes in the several parts of the respective districts. Justice through them may be administered with ease and dispatch; and appeals may be safely circumscribed within a narrow compass. This plan appears to me at present the most eligible of any that could be adopted, and in order to it, it is necessary that the power of constituting inferior courts should exist in the full extent in which it is seen in the proposed constitution.

These reasons seem sufficient to satisfy a candid mind, that the want of such a power would have been a great defect in the plan. Let us now examine in what manner the judicial authority is to be distributed between the supreme and the inferior courts of the union.

The supreme court is to be invested with original jurisdiction only "in cases affecting ambassadors, other public ministers and consuls, and those in which A STATE shall be a party." Public ministers of every class are the immediate representatives of their sovereigns. All questions in which they are concerned are so directly connected with the public peace, that as well for the preservation of this, as out of respect to the sovereignties they represent, it is both expedient and proper that such questions should be submitted in the first instance to the highest judicatory of the nation. Though consuls have not in strictness a diplomatic character, yet as they are the public agents of the nations to which they belong, the same observation is in a great measure applicable to them. In cases in which a state might happen to be a party, it would ill suit its dignity to be turned over to an inferior tribunal. * * *

[Hamilton here digresses to refute the objection that a state would be open to suit, without its consent, by a citizen of another state. See Monaco v. Mississippi, p. 307, *infra*.]

Let us resume the train of our observations; we have seen that the original jurisdiction of the supreme court would be confined to two classes of causes, and those of a nature rarely to occur. In all other cases of federal cognizance, the original jurisdiction would appertain to the inferior tribunals, and the supreme court would have nothing more than an appellate jurisdiction, "with such *exceptions,* and under such *regulations,* as the congress shall make."

The propriety of this appellate jurisdiction has been scarcely called in question in regard to matters of law; but the clamours have been loud against it as applied to matters of fact. * * *

The amount of the observations hitherto made on the authority of the judicial department is this: That it has been carefully restricted to those causes which are manifestly proper for the cognizance of the national judicature; that, in the partition of this authority, a very small portion of original jurisdiction had been reserved to the supreme court, and the rest consigned to the subordinate tribunals; that the supreme court will possess an appellate jurisdiction, both as to law and fact, in all the cases referred to them, but subject to any *exceptions* and *regulations* which may be thought advisable; that this appellate jurisdiction does, in no case, *abolish* the trial by jury; and that an ordinary degree of prudence and integrity in the national councils, will insure us solid advantages from the establishment of the proposed judiciary, without exposing us to any of the inconveniences which have been predicted from that source.

PUBLIUS.

No. 82, Hamilton

The erection of a new government, whatever care or wisdom may distinguish the work, cannot fail to originate questions of intricacy and nicety; and these may, in a particular manner, be expected to flow from the establishment of a constitution founded upon the total or partial incorporation of a number of distinct sovereignties. Time only can mature and perfect so compound a system, liquidate the meaning of all the parts, and adjust them to each other in a harmonious and consistent WHOLE.

Such questions accordingly have arisen upon the plan proposed by the convention, and particularly concerning the judiciary department. The principal of these respect the situation of the state courts, in regard to those causes which are to be submitted to federal jurisdiction. Is this to be exclusive, or are those courts to possess a concurrent jurisdiction? If the latter, in what relation will they stand to the national tribunals? These are inquiries which we meet with in the mouths of men of sense, and which are certainly entitled to attention.

The principles established in a former paper[1] teach us that the states will retain all *pre-existing* authorities, which may not be exclusively delegated to the federal head; and that this exclusive delegation can only exist in one of three cases; where an exclusive authority is, in express terms, granted to the union; or where a particular authority is granted to the union, and the exercise of a like authority is prohibited to the states; or, where an authority is granted to the union, with which a similar authority in the states would be utterly incompatible. Though these principles may not apply with the same force to the judiciary, as to the legislative power; yet I am inclined to think that they

1. No. XXXII.—Publius.

are in the main, just with respect to the former, as well as the latter. And under this impression I shall lay it down as a rule that the state courts will *retain* the jurisdiction they now have, unless it appears to be taken away in one of the enumerated modes.

The only thing in the proposed constitution, which wears the appearance of confining the causes of federal cognizance, to the federal courts, is contained in this passage: "The JUDICIAL POWER of the United States *shall be vested* in one supreme court, and in *such* inferior courts as the congress shall from time to time ordain and establish." This might either be construed to signify that the supreme and subordinate courts of the union should alone have the power of deciding those causes, to which their authority is to extend; or simply to denote that the organs of the national judiciary should be one supreme court, and as many subordinate courts, as congress should think proper to appoint; in other words, that the United States should exercise the judicial power with which they are to be invested, through one supreme tribunal, and a certain number of inferior ones, to be instituted by them. The first excludes, the last admits, the concurrent jurisdiction of the state tribunals: And as the first would amount to an alienation of state power by implication, the last appears to me the most defensible construction.

But this doctrine of concurrent jurisdiction is only clearly applicable to those descriptions of causes, of which the state courts have previous cognizance. It is not equally evident in relation to cases which may grow out of, and be *peculiar* to, the constitution to be established: For not to allow the state courts a right of jurisdiction in such cases can hardly be considered as the abridgement of a pre-existing authority. I mean not therefore to contend that the United States, in the course of legislation upon the objects entrusted to their direction, may not commit the decision of causes arising upon a particular regulation, to the federal courts solely, if such a measure should be deemed expedient; but I hold that the state courts will be divested of no part of their primitive jurisdiction, further than may relate to an appeal; and I am even of opinion, that in every case in which they were not expressly excluded by the future acts of the national legislature, they will, of course, take cognizance of the causes to which those acts may give birth. This I infer from the nature of judiciary power, and from the general genius of the system. The judiciary power of every government looks beyond its own local or municipal laws, and in civil cases, lays hold of all subjects of litigation between parties within its jurisdiction, though the causes of dispute are relative to the laws of the most distant part of the globe. Those of Japan, not less than of New York, may furnish the objects of legal discussion to our courts. When in addition to this we consider the state governments and the national governments, as they truly are, in the light of kindred systems, and as parts of ONE WHOLE, the inference seems to be conclusive, that the state courts would have a concurrent jurisdiction in all cases arising under the laws of the union, where it was not expressly prohibited.

Here another question occurs; what relation would subsist between the national and state courts in these instances of concurrent jurisdiction? I answer, that an appeal would certainly lie from the latter, to the supreme court of the United States. The constitution in direct terms, gives an appellate jurisdiction to the supreme court in all the enumerated cases of federal cognizance, in which it is not to have an original one; without a single expression to confine its operation to the inferior federal courts. The objects of appeal, not the tribunals from which it is to be made, are alone contemplated. From this circumstance, and from the reason of the thing, it ought to be construed to extend to the state tribunals. Either this must be the case, or the local courts must be excluded from a concurrent jurisdiction in matters of national concern, else the judiciary authority of the union may be eluded at the pleasure of every plaintiff or prosecutor. Neither of these consequences ought, without evident necessity, to be involved; the latter would be entirely inadmissible, as it would defeat some of the most important and avowed purposes of the proposed government, and would essentially embarrass its measures. Nor do I perceive any foundation for such a supposition. Agreeably to the remark already made, the national and state systems are to be regarded as ONE WHOLE. The courts of the latter will, of course, be natural auxiliaries to the execution of the laws of the union, and an appeal from them will as naturally lie to that tribunal, which is destined to unite and assimilate the principles of national justice and the rules of national decision. The evident aim of the plan of the convention is, that all the causes of the specified classes shall, for weighty public reasons, receive their original or final determination in the courts of the union. To confine, therefore, the general expressions which give appellate jurisdiction to the supreme court, to appeals from the subordinate federal courts, instead of allowing their extension to the state courts, would be to abridge the latitude of the terms, in subversion of the intent, contrary to every sound rule of interpretation.

But could an appeal be made to lie from the state courts, to the subordinate federal judicatories? This is another of the questions which have been raised, and of greater difficulty than the former. The following considerations countenance the affirmative. The plan of the convention, in the first place, authorizes the national legislature "to constitute tribunals inferior to the supreme court."[2] It declares in the next place, that "the JUDICIAL POWER of the United States *shall be vested in* one supreme court, and in such inferior courts as congress shall ordain and establish;" and it then proceeds to enumerate the cases, to which this judicial power shall extend. It afterwards divides the jurisdiction of the supreme court into original and appellate, but gives no definition of that of the subordinate courts. The only outlines described for them are, that they shall be "inferior to the supreme court," and that they shall not exceed the specified limits of the federal judiciary. Whether their authority shall be original or appellate, or both, is not declared. All this seems to be left to the discretion of the legislature. And this being the case, I perceive at present no impediment to the establishment of an appeal from the state courts, to the subordinate national tribunals; and many advantages attending the power of doing it may be imagined. It would diminish the motives to the multiplication of federal courts, and would admit of arrangements calculated to contract the appellate jurisdiction of the supreme court. The state tribunals may then be left with a more entire charge of federal causes; and appeals in most cases in which they may be deemed proper, instead of being carried to the supreme court, may be made to lie from the state courts, to district courts of the union.

PUBLIUS.

———

2. Section 8th, Article 1st.—Publius.

NOTE ON THE ORGANIZATION AND DEVELOPMENT OF THE FEDERAL JUDICIAL SYSTEM

A. The First Judiciary Act

The judiciary article of the Constitution was not self-executing, and the first Congress therefore faced the task of structuring a court system and, within limits established by the Constitution, of defining its jurisdiction. The job was daunting. Among other things, the controversies that had flared during the ratification debates made it clear that the definition of federal judicial jurisdiction was freighted with political ramifications.

The Judiciary Act of 1789,[1] the twentieth statute enacted by the first Congress, represented Congress' response to multiple pressures.[2] The Act is of interest today along at least two dimensions. First, the 1789 Act reflects the beginning of an organic development. It is impossible to understand the current judicial structure without a basic awareness of the foundations from which it evolved.[3] Second, the first Judiciary Act is widely viewed as an indicator of the original understanding of Article III and, in particular, of Congress' constitutional obligations concerning the vesting of federal jurisdiction.

1. Court Organization

The Supreme Court. The first section of the 1789 Act provided that "the supreme court of the United States shall consist of a chief justice and five associate justices". It called for two sessions annually at the seat of government, with one commencing the first Monday of February and the other the first Monday of August.

The circuit and district courts. The "transcendent achievement"[4] of the First Judiciary Act lay in the decision to take up the constitutional option to establish a system of federal trial courts.[5] Nonetheless, the system seems a curious one today. The Act provided for two tiers of trial courts: district courts, each with its own district judge, and circuit courts, without judges of their own. The circuit courts, which were to hold two sessions a year in each

---

1. Act of Sept. 24, 1789, 1 Stat. 73.

2. On the 1789 Act, see, *e.g.,* Goebel, History of the Supreme Court of the United States: Antecedents and Beginnings to 1801, at 457–508 (1971); Ritz, Rewriting the History of the Judiciary Act of 1789 (Holt & LaRue eds. 1990); Amar, *The Two–Tiered Structure of the Judiciary Act of 1789,* 138 U.Pa.L.Rev. 1499 (1990); Holt, *"To Establish Justice": Politics, the Judiciary Act of 1789, and the Invention of the Federal Courts,* 1989 Duke L.J. 1421; Clinton, *A Mandatory View of Federal Court Jurisdiction: Early Implementation of and Departures from the Constitutional Plan,* 86 Colum.L.Rev. 1515 (1986); Casto, *The First Congress's Understanding of its Authority over the Federal Courts' Jurisdiction,* 26 B.C.L.Rev. 1101 (1985); and Warren, *New Light on the History of the Federal Judiciary Act of 1789,* 37 Harv.L.Rev. 49 (1923).

3. Still perhaps the most valuable source on the sequence of federal judiciary acts is Frankfurter & Landis, The Business of the Supreme Court (1928). For a useful summary, see Bator, *Judicial System, Federal,* 3 Encyclopedia of The American Constitution 1068–75 (1986). For a brief but valuable description of the historical development of the jurisdiction of the lower federal courts, see Frankfurter, *Distribution of Judicial Power Between United States and State Courts,* 13 Corn.L.Q. 499, 507–15 (1928).

4. Frankfurter & Landis, note 3, *supra,* at 4.

5. See Frank, *Historical Bases of the Federal Judicial System,* 13 Law & Contemp.Prob. 3, 9–11 (1948).

district within the circuit, were to be constituted by one district judge and two Supreme Court justices sitting on circuit.

The Act divided the eleven states then in the union into thirteen districts with boundaries corresponding to state lines, except that the parts of Massachusetts and Virginia that later became Maine and Kentucky were made into separate districts. The Act thus established a precedent, still unbroken, against the crossing of state lines in setting the boundaries of federal judicial districts. Eleven of the thirteen districts were in turn divided into three circuits, with special provision made for the remote Maine and Kentucky districts.[6]

2. Jurisdiction of the District and Circuit Courts

The jurisdiction of the district courts was entirely original. Part of the jurisdiction was exclusive of the state courts, as it remains today, and part was concurrent.[7]

The circuit courts also had an important original jurisdiction, as well as authority to review on writ of error final decisions of the district courts in civil cases in which the matter in controversy exceeded $50, and, on appeal, final decrees in admiralty and maritime cases in which the matter in controversy exceeded $300.

The original jurisdiction of both sets of courts can usefully be considered together, as the jurisdiction of the Supreme Court will be below, under the nine jurisdictional headings of Article III.

a. Jurisdiction Based Primarily on Subject Matter

(i) *Cases Arising Under the Constitution, Laws, and Treaties of the United States.* In the sphere of private civil litigation, the 1789 Act, curiously, made no use of the grant of judicial power over cases arising under the Constitution or laws of the United States.[8] The district courts were, however, given "exclusive original cognizance of all seizures on land, or other waters than as aforesaid, made, and of all suits for penalties and forfeitures incurred, under the laws of the United States."[9]

With respect to criminal cases, the Act vested the circuit courts with "exclusive cognizance of all crimes and offences cognizable under the authority

---

6. The district courts in these two districts were authorized to sit also as circuit courts, a device afterward repeatedly used in outlying areas.

7. For a discussion of exclusive federal jurisdiction, see Chap. IV, Sec. 3, *infra*.

8. Engdahl, *Federal Question Jurisdiction Under the 1789 Judiciary Act*, 14 Okla. City U.L.Rev. 521, 522 (1989) argues that "all cases which could then have been contemplated as within" the "federal question" category of Article III were in fact provided for under the Act, although the jurisdiction had to be established under various grants of party-based and subject matter jurisdiction. But this position depends on a number of doubtful claims. Compare Casto, *An Orthodox View of the Two–Tier Analysis of Congressional Control over Federal Jurisdiction*, 7 Const. Commentary 89, 97 (1990)(stating that the 1789 Act "completely excluded a number of federal question cases from original and appellate federal jurisdiction"). For further discussion, see pp. 32-33, *infra*.

The development of later statutory grants of "arising under" jurisdiction is traced in Chap. VIII, pp. 878-83, *infra*.

9. § 9, 1 Stat. 73, 77.

of the United States", subject to a concurrent jurisdiction of the district courts to try certain minor criminal offenses.[10]

The only reference to suits arising under treaties came in a provision conferring district court jurisdiction, concurrent with the state courts or the circuit courts, of "all Causes where an Alien sues for a tort only in violation of * * * a Treaty of the United States".[11]

(ii) *Cases Affecting Ambassadors, Other Public Ministers, and Consuls.* Suits affecting ambassadors were provided for through the original jurisdiction of the Supreme Court.[12] But the Act conferred district court jurisdiction, exclusive of the state courts, of all suits against consuls and vice-consuls (except criminal cases triable in the circuit courts).[13]

(iii) *Admiralty jurisdiction.* The district courts were given, in terms that in substance survive today, "exclusive original cognizance of all civil causes of admiralty and maritime jurisdiction, * * * saving to suitors, in all cases, the right of a common law remedy, where the common law is competent to give it".[14] This grant included jurisdiction of "all seizures under laws of impost, navigation or trade of the United States, where the seizures are made, on waters which are navigable from the sea by vessels of ten or more tons burthen, within their respective districts as well as upon the high seas."

b. Jurisdiction Based on Party Status

(i) *United States a Party.* The Act did not in terms contemplate the possibility of suits against the United States.

In addition to the jurisdiction for civil and criminal enforcement actions by the United States arising under federal law, discussed above, the 1789 Act gave the circuit courts concurrent jurisdiction with the state courts of all civil suits at common law or in equity in which "the United States are plaintiffs, or petitioners" and the matter in dispute exceeded five hundred dollars.[15] The district courts were given jurisdiction, similarly concurrent, "of all suits at common law where the United States sue, and the matter in dispute amounts * * * to the sum or value of one hundred dollars."[16]

(ii) *Diversity jurisdiction.* The Act made prompt use of the constitutional grant of judicial power in cases of diverse citizenship. But the initial grant was carefully and significantly limited to controversies "between a citizen of the State where the suit is brought, and a citizen of another State";[17] and the Supreme Court, in Strawbridge v. Curtiss, 7 U.S. (3 Cranch)(1806), shortly construed this language to require "complete diversity" when there are multiple parties on one or more sides of a case. In addition, to prevent defendants from being summoned long distances to defend small claims, the jurisdiction was restricted to cases in which the matter in dispute exceeded five hundred dollars. The jurisdiction was concurrent with state courts.[18]

---

10. § 10, 1 Stat. 73, 78–79.

11. § 9, 1 Stat. 73, 77.

12. See p. 31, *infra;* Chap. III, Sec. 2, *infra.*

13. § 9, 1 Stat. 73, 77.

14. § 9, 1 Stat. 73, 77. For the current provision, see 28 U.S.C. § 1333; see also pp. 874-81, *infra.*

15. § 11, 1 Stat. 73, 78.

16. § 9, 1 Stat. 73, 77.

17. § 11, 1 Stat. 73, 78.

18. For the development of the diversity jurisdiction, see Chap. XIII, *infra.*

The circuit courts received a further jurisdiction dependent upon the character of the parties, also concurrent with the state courts, in all suits of a civil nature at common law or equity where an alien was a party, again when more than five hundred dollars was in dispute.[19] The circuit courts were also given concurrent jurisdiction "of all causes where an alien sues for a tort only in violation of the law of nations or a treaty of the United States."[20]

These various grants of jurisdiction dependent upon the character of the party were qualified by the famous "assignee clause", framed to avoid collusive assignments to create jurisdiction, which with various changes survived until 1948. Under its terms, no district or circuit court was to "have cognizance of any suit to recover the contents of any promissory note or other chose in action in favor of any assignee, unless a suit might have been prosecuted in such court * * * if no assignment had been made, except in cases of foreign bills of exchange."[21]

The First Judiciary Act also originated the device, since continuously in use, of authorizing the removal to a federal court, before trial, of certain types of proceedings begun in the state courts.[22] The removal was to a circuit court, and was subject to the jurisdictional amount requirement of five hundred dollars. The privilege of removing was given to three classes of parties:

(a) to a defendant who was an alien;

(b) to a defendant who was a citizen of another state, when sued by a plaintiff who was a citizen of the state where suit was brought; and

(c) to either party, where title to land was in dispute, if one party claimed under a grant from another state and the other party claimed under a grant of the state in which the suit was brought.

3. Jurisdiction of the Supreme Court

a. *Original Jurisdiction*[23]

Either not foreseeing the later-established doctrine that the original jurisdiction of the Supreme Court is derived directly from the Constitution, or not content to rely on forecast, the framers of the First Judiciary Act provided for the Court's original jurisdiction in terms that are nearly but not exactly coextensive with the constitutional grant. Under the 1789 Act, the original jurisdiction included:[24]

(1) "all controversies of a civil nature, where a state is a party, except between a state and its citizens;" and

(2)(a) "all such jurisdiction * * * as a court of law can have or exercise consistently with the law of nations" of suits "against ambassadors, or other public ministers, or their domestics, or domestic servants;" and

---

19. *Id.*

20. § 9, 1 Stat. 73, 77. The successor provision is 28 U.S.C. § 1350. See Chap. VII, Sec. 1, pp. 809-10, *infra.*

21. § 11, 1 Stat. 73, 79. The successor provision is 28 U.S.C. § 1359. See Chap. XIII, Sec. 5, *infra.*

22. § 12, 1 Stat. 73, 79. For the later history of the removal provisions, see Chap. VIII, Sec. 4, and Chap. XIV, Sec. 3, *infra.*

23. See generally Chap. III, *infra.*

24. § 13, 1 Stat. 73, 80–81.

(b) "all suits brought by ambassadors, or other public ministers, or in which a consul, or vice consul, shall be a party."[25]

The Act distinguished, as all later acts have also, between instances in which this original jurisdiction was exclusive of other courts and those in which it was not. The jurisdiction was exclusive in the cases in clause (1), above, except suits "between a state and citizens of other states, or aliens", and in all the cases in clause 2(a).

b. Appellate Jurisdiction[26]

The 1789 Act did not provide for Supreme Court review of all decisions of the lower federal courts. Final judgments or decrees of the circuit courts in civil cases were made reviewable on writ of error if but only if "the matter in dispute exceeds the sum or value of two thousand dollars, exclusive of costs".[27] Further, there was no provision for review of federal criminal cases. The Act did, however, confer a habeas corpus jurisdiction, which was later classified by the Court as appellate, to review federal detentions.[28]

With respect to state court decisions, the Act's famous Section 25 provided for Supreme Court review of final judgments or decrees "in the highest court of law or equity of a State in which a decision in the suit could be had," in three classes of cases:

(a) "* * * where is drawn in question the validity of a treaty or statute of, or an authority exercised under the United States, and the decision is against their validity;" or

(b) "* * * where is drawn in question the validity of a statute of, or an authority exercised under any State, on the ground of their being repugnant to the constitution, treaties or laws of the United States, and the decision is in favor of such their validity;" or

(c) "* * * where is drawn in question the construction of any clause of the constitution, or of a treaty, or statute of, or commission held under the United States, and the decision is against the title, right, privilege or exemption specially set up or claimed" thereunder.[29]

In all cases within the Court's appellate jurisdiction, review was to be by "writ of error". The effect of this limitation "was to eliminate all possibility of a second trial of the facts, by jury or otherwise", in Supreme Court review.[30]

4. The Overall Scope of Federal Jurisdiction Under the First Judiciary Act

When the respective jurisdictions of district and circuit courts and the Supreme Court are viewed together, the 1789 Act fell short of vesting federal jurisdiction in "all Cases" in which Article III would have permitted jurisdiction based primarily on subject matter.

---

25. The jurisdiction conferred by clause 2 was thus framed in terms of party status, rather than echoing the broader constitutional language authorizing jurisdiction in all cases "*affecting* Ambassadors, other public Ministers and Consuls".

26. See Chap. XV, Sec. 2, *infra.*

27. § 22, 1 Stat. 73, 84.

28. See Chap. III, Sec. 3, *infra.*

29. For the later development, see Chap. V, Sec. 1, *infra.*

30. Ritz, note 2, *supra,* at 88.

(i) In the category of cases arising under federal law, Congress provided no general federal question jurisdiction in the lower federal courts. Nor, under section 25, did the Supreme Court's appellate jurisdiction extend to cases originating in the state courts in which the federal claim was *upheld.* Further habeas corpus aside, the Supreme Court lacked appellate jurisdiction over federal criminal cases.

(ii) In the category of cases affecting ambassadors, other public ministers and consuls, section 13 of the 1789 Act conferred original Supreme Court jurisdiction over a broad category of suits to which denominated officials, and in some cases their servants, were *parties.* Nonetheless, section 13 fell short of the Constitution's more compendious authorization of jurisdiction in all suits by which ambassadors, other public ministers, and consuls might be "affect[ed]".

(iii) In the category of admiralty and maritime jurisdiction, section 9 gave the federal courts exclusive jurisdiction in admiralty, but saved "to suitors, in all cases, the right of a common law remedy". In practice, this provision has meant that every claim that can be enforced in a federal court in admiralty can also be enforced in a state court in personam action.

With respect to Article III's authorizations of jurisdiction based on party status, the 1789 Act did not provide in terms for suits against the United States. By contrast, the Act did authorize jurisdiction of a variety of civil suits to which states were parties, "except between a state and its citizens," without expressly limiting the grant to cases in which the states were plaintiffs or petitioners. The diversity jurisdiction included a significant amount-in-controversy limitation, and was construed by the Supreme Court as limited to cases of "complete diversity" in cases involving multiple parties.

The scope of these jurisdictional provisions and limitations continues to be much controverted, as does the question of the first Congress' understanding of the scope of its constitutional obligation, if any, to vest federal jurisdiction in various classes of cases.[31] For further discussion, see Chap. IV, Sec. 1, *infra.*

B. The Ante–Bellum Years

The ante-bellum years witnessed the emergence of two enduring patterns in the judicial history of the United States. The first involved the relative stability of the structure of courts established by the First Judiciary Act—at

---

31. Professor Amar argues that, when the meaning of various provisions of the 1789 Act is correctly understood, the congruence between the statutory and constitutional grants is almost complete and testifies to Congress' felt obligation to provide for federal jurisdiction in "all Cases" within the subject matter headings of Article III. See, *e.g.,* Amar, *A Neo–Federalist View of Article III: Separating the Two Tiers of Federal Jurisdiction,* 65 B.U.L.Rev. 205, 260–62 (1985); Amar, note 2, *supra.* See also Engdahl, note 8, *supra.* For a skeptical view, which portrays the shortfall of the 1789 Act as larger and more significant, see Meltzer, *The History and Structure of Article III,* 138 U.Pa. L.Rev. 1569 (1990); and Casto, note 2, *supra.*

See also Bourguignon, *The Federal Key to the Judiciary Act of 1789,* 46 S.Car.L.Rev. 647 (1995). For Amar's response to some of the skeptics, see Amar, *Reports of My Death Are Greatly Exaggerated: A Reply,* 138 U.Pa. L.Rev. 1651 (1990).

For a partly parallel exchange, focused on the broader claim that the 1789 Act came close to the full constitutional grant in all nine of Article III's jurisdictional categories, compare Clinton, *A Mandatory View of Federal Jurisdiction: A Guided Quest for the Original Understanding of Article III,* 132 U.Pa. L.Rev. 741, 749–50 (1984); and Clinton, note 2, *supra,* with Casto, note 2, *supra.*

least at its base in the district courts and its apex in the Supreme Court.[32] The circuit courts quickly emerged as a weak spot, due to their lack of any judges of their own and the inordinate burden that circuit riding cast upon the Supreme Court Justices. The burden was reduced in 1793 by requiring only one Justice on the circuit court;[33] but the reduction came at the cost of establishing a two-judge court, which created a problem of split decisions.[34]

A second emerging pattern concerned the incremental adjustment of federal jurisdiction to reflect shifting political currents and, in particular, preferences for greater or lesser national authority vis-a-vis the states. The famous Law of the Midnight Judges,[35] enacted by a lame duck Federalist Congress after the Federalist party had lost control of both Congress and the Presidency in the elections of 1800, furnishes an especially egregious example. The new Act, which aimed in part to protect the nationalist values of the outgoing administration, gave the district and circuit courts, taken together, a jurisdiction almost coextensive with the constitutional authorization and abolished circuit riding by Supreme Court Justices. It also provided five of the circuit courts with a bench of three circuit judges each and the sixth (the western circuit) with a single circuit judge. As part of the plan, all of the new circuit judges were Federalists.

The incoming Jeffersonians, their anger heightened by the behavior of some of the new judges, repealed the act and abolished the judgeships.[36] For the most part, the new Act of April 29, 1802,[37] prescribed a return to the *status quo ante*. Among its innovations, the Act made provision for the circuit courts, in cases where the judges were divided, to certify the question at issue to the Supreme Court.[38] In addition to its old jurisdiction in error, the Supreme Court was empowered to hear appeals from the circuit courts in equity, admiralty, and prize cases where the amount in dispute exceeded $2,000.

In the wake of the 1802 Act, the circuit courts became more and more rickety. Though Congress remained attached to circuit riding as a means of keeping Supreme Court Justices in touch with the people, the burgeoning number of judicial districts put increasing strains on the system. To allow for circuit court sessions in each, the Act had reduced the number of Supreme Court sessions to one a year and authorized the holding of the circuit court by a single district judge. As the country grew, however, the Justices increasingly

---

32. For a detailed account of the administration and business of the district and circuit courts under the First Judiciary Act from 1789 to 1801, see Henderson, Courts for a New Nation (1971); see also Goebel, note 2, *supra*, at 552–661.

33. Act of March 2, 1793, 1 Stat. 333. See Frankfurter & Landis, note 3, *supra*, at 14–30, and 1 Warren, The Supreme Court in United States History 85–90 (1926) for discussions of contemporary criticisms of the circuit riding obligation.

34. Professor White reports that in the early nineteenth century, the Justices sometimes deliberately created divisions when riding circuit, in order to permit Supreme Court review on certificate of decisions that otherwise were not reviewable. See White, III–IV History of the Supreme Court of the United States: The Marshall Court and Cultural Change, 1815–35, at 173–74 (1988).

35. Act of February 13, 1801, 2 Stat. 89. See generally Surrency, *The Judiciary Act of 1801*, 2 Am.J. Legal Hist. 53 (1958); Turner, *The Midnight Judges*, 109 U.Pa. L.Rev. 494 (1961); Turner, *Federalist Policy and the Judiciary Act of 1801*, 22 Wm. & Mary Q. 3 (1965).

36. Act of March 8, 1802, 2 Stat. 132. See Frankfurter & Landis, note 3, *supra*, at 24–30; 1 Warren, note 33, *supra*, at 184–230.

37. 2 Stat. 156, as amended by the Act of March 3, 1803, 2 Stat. 244.

38. Certification was optional in civil and mandatory in criminal cases.

invoked the privilege of non-attendance in remote districts. Correspondingly, circuit court review of district court decisions became increasingly futile.

In 1807 Congress created a seventh circuit to meet the needs of Kentucky, Tennessee, and Ohio.[39] This action automatically triggered the appointment of a sixth associate Justice for the new circuit. With the size of the Supreme Court tied to the circuit system, Congress proved unable to agree upon similar action for later-entering states for more than twenty years. As a result, these states remained outside the circuit system. At length, in 1837, the country was re-divided into nine circuits, and the membership of the Supreme Court increased to nine.[40] California (joined soon after by Oregon) became a tenth circuit in 1855;[41] and in 1863 Congress briefly added a tenth Justice to the Supreme Court,[42] before shortly reorganizing the districts into nine circuits[43] and reducing the size of the Supreme Court.[44]

Meanwhile, a series of collisions between federal and state authority had provoked Congress, characteristically, to extend federal jurisdiction to meet threats to federal interests. New England's resistance to the War of 1812 led Congress to provide for removal of suits against federal officers and others enforcing customs duties from state to federal court.[45] Similarly, the "Force Bill" of 1833[46] responded to South Carolina's threats of nullification by authorizing removal of suits and prosecutions based on acts done under federal customs laws[47] and conferring federal jurisdiction to grant writs of habeas corpus in cases of confinement "for any act done, or omitted to be done, in pursuance of a law of the United States".[48] The advent of the Civil War predictably occasioned further removal acts.[49]

C. Reconstruction

Reconstruction Congresses complemented the profound changes in constitutional structure wrought by the Civil War amendments with a compendious series of statutes extending the jurisdiction of the federal courts.[50] Congress authorized federal courts to issue writs of habeas corpus on behalf of prisoners held by state authorities in violation of the Constitution, laws, and treaties of the United States.[51] In addition, the various civil rights acts included jurisdictional grants. At least twelve pieces of removal legislation were enacted during

---

39. Act of Feb. 24, 1807, 2 Stat. 420, amended by the Act of March 22, 1808, 2 Stat. 477, and the Act of Feb. 4, 1809, 2 Stat. 516.

40. Act of March 3, 1837, 5 Stat. 176.

41. Act of March 2, 1855, 10 Stat. 631.

42. Act of March 3, 1863, 12 Stat. 794, amended by the Act of Feb. 19, 1864, 13 Stat. 4.

43. Act of July 23, 1866, § 2, 14 Stat. 209.

44. The number of Justices was reduced to seven, *id.*, § 1, to keep President Johnson from filling vacancies; but three years later the number was restored to nine, Act of April 10, 1869, 16 Stat. 44, where it has ever since remained.

45. See Act of Feb. 4, 1815, § 8, 3 Stat. 195, 198. For further discussion, see p. 951, *infra.*

46. Act of March 2, 1833, 4 Stat. 632.

47. For discussion of the removal provisions, see p. 951, *infra.*

48. For discussion of the habeas corpus provisions, see p. 1340, *infra.*

49. See p. 951, *infra.*

50. For useful overviews, see Kutler, Judicial Power and Reconstruction Politics (1968); Wiecek, *The Reconstruction of Federal Judicial Power, 1863–1875,* 13 Am.J.Legal Hist. 333 (1969).

51. See Act of Feb. 5, 1867, ch. 28, § 1, 14 Stat. 385. See generally Chapter XI, *infra.*

the Reconstruction era.[52] Most sweepingly, the Judiciary Act of 1875 conferred on the federal judiciary a general jurisdiction over all civil cases "arising under" federal law, subject only to an amount-in-controversy requirement.[53] With the enactment of this statute, the Supreme Court later observed, "the lower federal courts * * * 'became the primary and powerful reliances for vindicating every right given by the Constitution, the laws, and treaties of the United States' ".[54]

D. Structural Reforms

The surge in federal judicial business in the years following the Civil War and Reconstruction imposed intolerable burdens on the federal judicial structure. Congress enacted a minor but necessary reform in 1869, when it finally yielded to the old Federalist plan for the appointment of circuit judges, and authorized one circuit judge for each of the nine circuits.[55] At the same time, it reduced the circuit-riding duty of the Supreme Court Justices to attendance at one term every two years in each district of the circuit to which the Justice was assigned.

Nonetheless, docket pressures continued to mount. Growth in the Supreme Court's caseload resulted both from an increased population and from congressional additions to the Court's jurisdiction, including civil rights,[56] habeas corpus,[57] and patent and copyright[58] cases. When a restriction on appellate jurisdiction was finally enacted in 1875, it took the questionable form of an increase in the jurisdictional amount to $5,000.[59] Yet even this restriction was partially offset by further enlargements in the years immediately following.[60] By 1890, the number of cases on the Court's docket was nearly three times as large as in 1870, with no end of the growth in sight.[61]

In the lower federal courts, which were the principal feeders of the stream, the condition was the same. "In 1873 the number of cases pending in the circuit and district courts was twenty-nine thousand and thirteen, of which five thousand one hundred and eight were bankruptcy cases. In 1880, despite the fact that the repeal of the Bankruptcy Act had dried up that source of business, the number had increased to thirty-eight thousand and forty-five. The year 1890 brings the total to fifty-four thousand one hundred and ninety-four."[62]

---

52. See Kutler, note 50, *supra*, at 147.

53. See pp. 880-81, *infra*.

54. Steffel v. Thompson, 415 U.S. 452, 464 (1974)(quoting Frankfurter & Landis, note 3, *supra*, at 65).

55. Act of April 10, 1869, 16 Stat. 44.

56. Act of April 9, 1866, § 10, 14 Stat. 27, 29; Act of April 20, 1871, 17 Stat. 13.

57. Act of Feb. 5, 1867, § 1, 14 Stat. 385, 386. An intermediate appeal to the circuit court was also provided for. Congress abolished appeals to the Supreme Court under this law by the Act of March 27, 1868, § 2, 15 Stat. 44, see Ex parte McCardle, p. 356, *infra,* but restored them by the Act of March 3, 1885, 23 Stat. 437.

58. Act of Feb. 18, 1861, 12 Stat. 130.

59. Act of Feb. 16, 1875, § 3, 18 Stat. 315.

60. To the matters reviewable without regard to the amount in controversy, Congress added more civil rights cases by the Act of March 1, 1875, § 5, 18 Stat. 335, 337, and jurisdictional questions by the Act of Feb. 25, 1889, 25 Stat. 693. In 1889, writs of error were for the first time permitted in cases of capital crime. Act of Feb. 6, 1889, § 6, 25 Stat. 655, 656. On the further development of appeals in federal criminal cases, see Chap. XV, *infra*.

61. See Frankfurter & Landis, note 3, *supra*, at 60.

62. *Id.*

Congress finally responded to the crisis with the Judiciary Acts of 1887–88, which put a series of curbs on access to the lower federal courts,[63] and especially with the Evarts Act (the Circuit Court of Appeals Act of 1891[64]), which substantially fixed the framework of the contemporary system. The Act established circuit courts of appeals, consisting of three judges each, for each of the nine existing circuits. The legislation also created an additional circuit judgeship in each circuit, thus providing two circuit judges in all the circuits except the second, which, having received an additional judge in 1887,[65] now had three. The third place was ordinarily to be filled by a district judge, but Supreme Court Justices were also eligible to sit.[66]

With respect to the Supreme Court's appellate jurisdiction, the Evarts Act introduced the then revolutionary, but now familiar, principle of discretionary review of federal judgments on writ of certiorari.[67] Circuit court of appeals' decisions were declared to be "final" in diversity litigation, in suits under the revenue and patent laws, in criminal prosecutions, and in admiralty suits; but in all such cases the Supreme Court, "by certiorari or otherwise," was authorized, regardless of the amount in controversy, to order the judgment brought before it for review. Despite this innovation, the Act continued to permit Supreme Court review as of right in important classes of cases, subject in general to a jurisdictional amount requirement of $1,000. In addition, as remains true today, a circuit court of appeals was authorized to "certify to the Supreme Court * * * any questions or propositions of law concerning which it desires the instruction of that court for its proper decision."[68]

The principle of discretionary review, which was introduced by the Evarts Act, was also an important feature of the structurally important Act of

63. See Act of March 3, 1887, 24 Stat. 552, corrected by Act of Aug. 13, 1888, 25 Stat. 433. The specific restrictions of jurisdiction that the Act introduced were each relatively minor although considerable in the aggregate:

(1) The jurisdictional amount was raised to $2,000.

(2) The privilege of removal was withdrawn from plaintiffs and confined to defendants; in diversity cases it was confined to nonresident defendants.

(3) It was made clear that the general removal jurisdiction did not extend to any cases except those that might have been brought originally in a federal court.

(4) No longer was venue proper in any district in which the defendant "shall be found" but only in the district of which he was an "inhabitant", with an option in diverse citizenship cases of the district of either the plaintiff's or the defendant's residence.

(5) No longer were national banking associations to be allowed to sue in federal courts merely on the ground that they were incorporated under the laws of the United States.

(6) The assignee clause limiting diversity jurisdiction was broadened.

These restrictions of the 1887 act, however, were partly offset by the Tucker Act, 24 Stat. 505, which was signed on the same day. See Chap. IX, Sec. 1(C), *infra*.

64. Act of March 3, 1891, 26 Stat. 826. The Judiciary Acts of 1887–1888 had put a series of curbs on access to the lower federal courts, see Act of March 3, 1887, 24 Stat. 552, corrected by Act of Aug. 13, 1888, 25 Stat. 433, but their reforms had proved insufficient.

65. Act of March 3, 1887, 24 Stat. 492.

66. In deference to the traditionalists, the Act did not abolish the old circuit courts, although it took away their appellate jurisdiction over the district courts. For another twenty years there remained two sets of federal trial courts. The Circuit Courts were finally abolished by the Judicial Code of 1911. See Act of March 3, 1911, 36 Stat. 1087.

67. The Evarts Act did not alter the prevailing scheme of review of state court judgments by writ of error.

68. See Chap. XV, pp. 1636–37, 1674–76, *infra*, for further discussion of the Evarts Act and for consideration of certification.

December 23, 1914.[69] Animated at least partly by hostility to state court decisions invalidating legislation under the Due Process Clause,[70] Congress expanded the Supreme Court's appellate jurisdiction to encompass for the first time cases in which a state court rendered a decision favorable to a claim of federal right. To protect the Court from further docket overload, the statute provide for review of such cases by writ of certiorari. Congress further expanded the scope of discretionary Supreme Court review in the Act of February 13, 1925,[71] which was drafted by a committee of Supreme Court Justices (led by Justice Van Devanter). Since then, the principle of review at the Court's discretion has become ever more dominant.[72]

E. Political Responses to Federal Jurisdiction and Judicial Administration: The Lochner Era and Beyond

In the late nineteenth and early twentieth centuries, during the so-called Lochner era, the federal courts began to engage in broader and potentially more intrusive scrutiny of state and federal legislation than ever before. The substantive constitutional theory underlying judicial review of economic legislation occasioned controversy from the outset, and federal injunctions against the enforcement of state law by state officials were viewed as a special irritant to the structure of American federalism.

Congress responded with a number of jurisdictional enactments. In 1910, Congress provided that federal interlocutory injunctions against the enforcement of state statutes on constitutional grounds could only be issued by special, three-judge courts, with direct appeal as of right to the Supreme Court.[73]

The Johnson Act, passed in 1934, sharply circumscribed the district courts' jurisdiction to issue injunctions interfering with state regulation of public utilities whenever "[a] plain, speedy, and efficient remedy may be had at law or in equity in the courts of" the state.[74]

The Tax Injunction Act of 1937 similarly forbade federal injunctions against "the assessment, levy or collection of any tax imposed by or pursuant to the laws of any State" as long as "a plain, speedy, and efficient remedy may be had at law or in equity in the courts of such state."[75]

Another congressional enactment of the same era, the Norris–LaGuardia Act of 1932,[76] sought to protect unions and their right to strike by narrowly restricting the authority of the federal courts to issue injunctions in "a case involving or growing out of a labor dispute". The Act further provided that so-called "yellow-dog" contracts "shall not be enforceable in any court of the

---

69. Act of Dec. 23, 1914, 38 Stat. 790.

70. See Frankfurter & Landis, note 3, *supra,* at 187–98.

71. 43 Stat. 936. See generally Frankfurter & Landis, note 3, *supra,* 255–94; Mason, William Howard Taft: Chief Justice 88–120 (1964).

72. On review of state court decisions, see further Chap. V, *infra;* on review of federal decisions, Chap. XV, *infra.* On the certiorari policy, see Chap. XV, Sec. 3, *infra.*

73. 36 Stat. 557. For a discussion of this statute and its subsequent history, see Chap. X, Sec. 1, and Chap. XV, Sec. 1, *infra.*

74. The Johnson Act of 1934, 48 Stat. 775, now codified at 28 U.S.C. § 1342. For further discussion, see Chap. X, § 1, *infra.*

75. 50 Stat. 738, now 28 U.S.C. § 1341. For further discussion, see Chap. X, § 1, *infra.*

76. 47 Stat. 70, now codified at 29 U.S.C. §§ 101–115.

United States", despite Supreme Court precedent holding that state legislation similarly limiting employers' remedies violated the Due Process Clause.[77]

In 1937, after decisions of the Supreme Court in 1934–36 had invalidated important portions of the New Deal program[78] and raised apprehensions concerning the remainder, President Franklin Roosevelt determined to try to salvage the situation by "packing" the federal courts and especially the Supreme Court with New Deal sympathizers.[79] The Plan submitted to Congress[80] would have authorized the President to appoint one additional judge to the federal courts, including the Supreme Court, for any federal judge who had served 10 years and who, after reaching the age of 70, did not retire or resign.[81]

But the plan, which the President initially defended on the dubious ground that it was needed to keep the Supreme Court abreast of its work,[82] aroused wide-spread opposition as an attack on the independence of the federal judiciary and on the principle of judicial review.[83] The Senate Judiciary Committee reported the plan adversely in June, 1937,[84] and in late July the Senate allowed it to die.[85] In the meantime, the Supreme Court had upheld the constitutionality of a number of regulatory statutes,[86] Justice Van Devanter had retired, and the Lochner era had come to an end. Scholars continue to debate whether Justice Roberts' "switch in time", which provided the critical fifth vote to

77. For discussion, see Chap. IV, Sec. 1, pp. 363-65, *infra.*

78. See, *e.g.,* Panama Refining Co. v. Ryan, 293 U.S. 388 (1935); Railroad Retirement Board v. Alton R. Co., 295 U.S. 330 (1935); A.L.A. Schechter Poultry Corp. v. United States, 295 U.S. 495 (1935); United States v. Butler, 297 U.S. 1 (1936); Carter v. Carter Coal Co., 298 U.S. 238 (1936).

79. Before settling on this plan, the Administration canvassed a number of other possible measures, including restrictions on the courts' jurisdiction and substantive constitutional amendments. See Leuchtenburg, *The Origins of Franklin D. Roosevelt's "Court–Packing" Plan,* 1966 Sup.Ct.Rev. 347. See also Burns, Roosevelt: The Lion and the Fox ch. 15 (1956).

80. S. 1392, 75th Cong., 1st Sess. (1937), printed in Sen.Rep. No. 711, 75th Cong., 1st Sess. (1937)(Reorganization of the Federal Judiciary).

81. Not more than 50 additional judges were to be so appointed, and the membership of the Supreme Court was to be limited to 15. The proposal would have allowed President Roosevelt to add six Justices to the Supreme Court, if none of the sitting members over 70 had stepped down.

82. See the President's Message to Congress of February 5, 1937, printed in Sen. Rep. No. 711, note 80, *supra,* at 25–27. Subsequently the President became much more forthright in justifying his plan on the ground that the Court's decisions were an intolerable obstacle to his program. See generally Burns, note 79, *supra.* See also 6 The Public Papers and Addresses of Franklin D. Roosevelt lxv (1941): "I made one major mistake when I first presented the plan. I did not place enough emphasis upon the real mischief—the kind of decisions which, as a studied and continued policy, had been coming down from the Supreme Court. I soon corrected that mistake—in the speeches which I later made about the plan."

83. The suggestion that the plan was justified by the needs of judicial administration was strongly rebutted by Chief Justice Hughes, speaking also for Justices Brandeis and Van Devanter, in a celebrated letter to Senator Wheeler, which stated that the Court was abreast of its work and that the appointment of additional Justices would impair the effectiveness of the Court. See Sen.Rep. No. 711, note 80, *supra,* at 38–40 (quoting the letter). On the drafting of the letter and its impact, see 2 Pusey, Charles Evans Hughes 754–56, 766 (1951); Freund, *Charles Evans Hughes as Chief Justice,* 81 Harv.L.Rev. 4, 21–34 (1967). On reactions within the Court, see Mason, Harlan Fiske Stone ch. 28 (1956).

84. Sen.Rep. No. 711, note 80, *supra.*

85. See Burns, note 79, *supra,* at 306–09.

86. See, in particular, West Coast Hotel Co. v. Parrish, 300 U.S. 379 (1937); NLRB v. Jones & Laughlin Steel Corp., 301 U.S. 1 (1937).

uphold New Deal legislation, was influenced by President Roosevelt's court-packing scheme.[87]

After only a brief respite from the vortex of controversy, the substance of federal judicial action again began to occasion proposals to curb federal jurisdiction during the reign of the Warren Court.[88] None of the proposals was enacted, however.

F. Further Reforms: The Article III Courts Today

The defeat of the Court-packing plan left the basic organization of the federal court system in the form established by the Evarts Act and the Judges' Bill of 1925.[89] The Judicial Code of 1948 (the present codification of the organization and business of the federal courts) retained that structure while making many important changes in the statutory formulation governing the courts' jurisdiction. In 1958 came enactments restricting access to the federal courts by increasing the jurisdictional amount in federal question and diversity cases from $3,000 to $10,000, redefining corporate citizenship, and permitting certain interlocutory appeals to the courts of appeals from the district courts.

Since 1958, the major legislative changes in the federal judicial system have included:

1. The virtual elimination of the requirement that certain cases be heard before a district court of three judges, with a right of direct appeal to the Supreme Court.[90] The story of the rise and fall of this requirement is told in Chap. X, Sec. 1(B), *infra*.

2. Elimination of several other provisions for direct appeal to the Supreme Court of federal district court decisions.[91]

3. Elimination of the amount-in-controversy requirement in federal question cases brought under 28 U.S.C. § 1331.[92]

4. Division of the Fifth Circuit into a new Fifth Circuit (Louisiana, Mississippi, and Texas), and a new Eleventh Circuit (Alabama, Florida, and Georgia).[93]

5. Numerous changes in the character and scope of the specialized federal courts, including the creation of a new Court of Appeals for the Federal Circuit. These changes are described in Parts G and H of this Note.

6. Elimination of the Supreme Court's mandatory appellate jurisdiction in the general jurisdictional statutes governing review of state and lower federal

---

87. Justice Frankfurter later reported having received a memo from Justice Roberts that detailed the sequence of events and established that Roberts had cast his crucial votes in the West Coast Hotel and Jones & Laughlin cases, note 86, *supra*, before the President's announcement of his court-packing proposal. See Frankfurter, *Mr. Justice Roberts*, 104 U.Pa.L.Rev. 311 (1955); see also Freund, note 83, *supra* at 29–30. Frankfurter's claims are doubted in Ariens, *A Thrice-Told Tale, or Felix the Cat*, 107 Harv.L.Rev. 620 (1994). For a rebuttal, see Friedman, *A Reaffirmation: The Authenticity of the Roberts Memorandum, or Felix the Non–Forger*, 142 U.Pa.L.Rev. 1985 (1994).

88. For discussion, see Chap. IV, Sec. 1, p. 350, *infra*.

89. The present Tenth Circuit had been created in 1929. Act of Feb. 28, 1929, 45 Stat. 1346.

90. Act of Aug. 12, 1976, 90 Stat. 1119.

91. See, *e.g.*, Omnibus Crime Control Act of 1970, 18 U.S.C. § 3731, as amended by Act of Jan. 2, 1971, § 14(a), 84 Stat. 1890; Act of Dec. 21, 1974, 88 Stat. 1708–09 (amending the Expediting Act).

92. Act of Dec. 1, 1980, 94 Stat. 2369.

93. Act of Oct. 14, 1980, 94 Stat. 1994.

court judgments and substitution of discretionary review by writ of certiorari. The major amendments are described at pp. 493, 1640, *infra*.

7. An increase of the amount in controversy required in federal diversity actions brought under 28 U.S.C. § 1332 from $10,000 to $50,000. 102 Stat. 4642, 4646 (1988).[94]

G. Specialized Courts Under Article III

For the most part, the Article III courts have been courts of broad-based, if not "general", jurisdiction,[95] and the diversity of the federal docket has been viewed as a large asset in attracting able lawyers to the bench and achieving cross-pollination among different areas of the law.[96] There are important exceptions, however, as well as a continuing debate about whether the benefits of specialization (with respect to at least some subject matters) might outweigh the drawbacks.[97]

a. The Court of International Trade

In 1926 the old Board of General Appraisers, which had been established to hear appeals from decisions of customs collectors, was given formal status as a

94. The Judicial Improvements Act of 1990, 104 Stat. 5089, besides creating 85 new judgeships (11 at the appellate level and 74 at the district court level)(§§ 201–06, 104 Stat. 5098–5104), required that each district court formulate a plan to reduce the cost and delay of civil litigation (§ 103, 104 Stat. 5090, adding §§ 471–482 to Title 28). For discussion, see, *e.g.*, Johnston, *Civil Justice Reform: Juggling Between Politics and Perfection*, 62 Ford.L.Rev. 833 (1994); Haig & Stone, *Does All This Litigation "Reform" Really Benefit the Client?*, 67 St.John's L.Rev. 843 (1993); Mullenix, *The Counter–Reformation in Procedural Justice*, 77 Minn.L.Rev. 375 (1992); Peck, *"Users United": The Civil Justice Reform Act of 1990*, 54 L. & Contemp.Prob. 105 (Summer 1991).

95. Congress has from time to time constituted tribunals with specialized jurisdiction but staffed with Article III judges who, when sitting on other courts, exercise a broader jurisdiction. Examples include:

(a) An Emergency Court of Appeals with exclusive jurisdiction to entertain challenges to orders and regulations issued under the Emergency Price Control Act of 1942, 56 Stat. 23. For discussion, see pp. 380–84, *infra*.

(b) The Temporary Emergency Court of Appeals, created by the 1971 amendments to the Economic Stabilization Act of 1970 (Act of Dec. 22, 1971, 85 Stat. 743) to hear all appeals from district court decisions arising

under the Act or its implementing regulations. The duties of this court, staffed by appointment of regular federal judges from other courts, were later expanded to include appeals from the district courts in cases arising under the Emergency Petroleum Allocation Act of 1973, the Energy Policy and Conservation Act of 1975, and the Emergency Natural Gas Act of 1977. Congress abolished the Temporary Emergency Court of Appeals in 1992, and transferred its jurisdiction over appeals under the Economic Stabilization Act to the Court of Appeals for the Federal Circuit. P.L. 102–572, § 102, 106 Stat. 4506, 4507 (1992).

(c) The Rail Reorganization Court, established by the Regional Rail Reorganization Act of 1973, 45 U.S.C. § 701 *et seq.*, primarily to determine the value of properties transferred pursuant to the Act by seven bankrupt railroads. The court is staffed by three federal judges designated by the Panel on Multidistrict Litigation. The constitutionality of the statute creating the court was upheld in Regional Rail Reorganization Act Cases, 419 U.S. 102 (1974).

(d) The Judicial Panel on Multidistrict Litigation, also staffed by regular federal judges from other courts, authorized by 28 U.S.C. § 1407 to transfer certain actions pending in different districts to a single district "for coordinated or consolidated pretrial proceedings".

96. See, *e.g.*, Posner, The Federal Courts: Crisis and Reform 147–60 (1985).

97. For a brief discussion, see p. 65, *infra*.

specialized court with the name of the United States Customs Court.[98] The court was declared to be an Article III court in 1956,[99] and in 1980 was redesignated the United States Court of International Trade.[100] The provisions governing its organization are collected in Chapter 11 of the Judicial Code and the jurisdictional provisions in Chapter 95.[101]

b. The Court of Appeals for the Federal Circuit

In 1982, Congress created a new United States Court of Appeals for the Federal Circuit.[102] This court has exclusive jurisdiction to hear appeals from (1) the Court of Federal Claims,[103] (2) the Federal Merit System Protection Board, (3) agency boards of contract appeals under the Contract Disputes Act of 1978, (4) the Court of International Trade, (5) the Patent Office in patent and trademark cases,[104] (6) the district courts in certain actions in which district court jurisdiction was based in whole or in part on the "Little Tucker Act" (28 U.S.C. § 1346(a)(2)), and (7) the district courts in all patent cases in which district court jurisdiction was based in whole or in part on 28 U.S.C. § 1338.[105]

98. Act of May 28, 1926, § 1, 44 Stat. 669, 1948. See also Act of June 17, 1930, § 518, 46 Stat. 590, 737; Act of Oct. 10, 1940, 54 Stat. 1101; Act of June 2, 1970, 84 Stat. 278.

99. Act of July 14, 1956, 70 Stat. 532.

100. Act of Oct. 10, 1980, 94 Stat. 1727.

101. See generally Symposium, *Sixth Annual Judicial Conference of the U.S. Court of International Trade,* 14 Fordham Int.L.J. 7 (1990–91).

102. The Federal Courts Improvement Act of 1982, 96 Stat. 25, 37–38. The relevant provision appears in the Judicial Code at 28 U.S.C. § 1295.

103. The relation between the new court of appeals and the Court of Federal Claims is similar in important respects to the relation between the judges of the former Court of Claims and the commissioners of that court. For further discussion of the Court of Federal Claims and its history, see Chap. II, Sec. 2, pp. 110-15, and Chap. IX, Sec. 1, pp. 1028-29, *infra.*

104. Items (4) and (5) embrace the jurisdiction of the former Court of Customs and Patent Appeals. That court was established in 1909 as the second of the specialized federal courts with nationwide jurisdiction to hear appeals from the Board of General Appraisers—appeals that were then swamping some of the regular courts. Act of Aug. 5, 1909, 36 Stat. 11, 105. The court continued to hear these appeals after the board became the Customs Court in 1926, and in 1929 Congress gave the court the jurisdiction over appeals from the Patent Office that had been vested in the Court of Appeals of the District of Columbia. Act of March 2, 1929, 45 Stat. 1475. See also Act of June 17, 1930, § 646, 46 Stat. 590, 762; Act of Dec. 24, 1970, 84 Stat. 1558.

105. For one court's expression of concern over the jurisdictional "quagmire" created by some of the provisions of the 1982 Act, see Van Drasek v. Lehman, 762 F.2d 1065, 1072 (D.C.Cir.1985). See also Christianson v. Colt Industries Operating Corp., 486 U.S. 800 (1988) (deciding whether a federal action arises under the patent or antitrust laws, which in turn determines whether the Federal Circuit or the regional court of appeals has appellate jurisdiction); United States v. Hohri, 482 U.S. 64 (1987)(ambiguity in 1982 Act is resolved by holding that Federal Circuit has exclusive jurisdiction over "mixed cases" involving claims under both the Little Tucker Act and the Tort Claims Act). See generally Comment, 36 Am.Univ. L.Rev. 943 (1987).

For a generally favorable assessment of the Federal Circuit's exercise of its patent jurisdiction, see Dreyfuss, *The Federal Circuit: A Case Study in Specialized Courts,* 64 N.Y.U.L.Rev. 1 (1989). For a more mixed view, with criticism of the court's asserted failure to frame rules adequately cabining its "discretion" in an important category of cases, see Landry, *Certainty and Discretion in Patent Law: The On Sale Bar, The Doctrine of Equivalents, and Judicial Power in the Federal Circuit,* 67 S.Cal.L.Rev. 1151 (1994).

H. Non–Article III Courts and Adjudicators

Although this Note has so far focused on the Article III federal courts, Congress, from the very first, has asserted a power to organize tribunals under Article I.[106] Judges of these Article I tribunals lack the Article III guarantees of tenure during good behavior and non-reduction in salary, but the tribunals' functions are frequently indistinguishable from those of the Article III courts.

There is wide agreement to the highly general principle that Article III must impose at least some limits on Congress' power to vest judicial power in non-Article III federal tribunals, but much less consensus or certainty concerning precisely what those limits are. The relevant doctrine and its perplexities are explored in Chap. IV, Sec. 2, *infra*.

For present purposes, it will be useful to distinguish three broad categories: (i) legislative courts, (ii) administrative agencies, and (iii) adjuncts to the federal district courts.

1. Legislative Courts

Legislative courts—so-called because they are established not under Article III, but pursuant to Congress' legislative powers under Article I—typically are charged with adjudicating disputes involving specialized subject matters or with exercising jurisdiction in discrete geographical enclaves, such as the federal territories. They are characteristically constituted as "courts" and are seldom assigned significant executive or legislative functions.[107]

a. *Courts of the District of Columbia*

The organization of the District of Columbia compelled the establishment of tribunals to perform the functions of local courts as well as of ordinary federal courts. From the beginning the District has had inferior courts with distinctively local jurisdiction. From 1863 to 1893 this judicial system was headed by a Supreme Court of the District of Columbia, which was comparable both to a circuit court and to a state supreme court. In the latter year Congress established the Court of Appeals of the District of Columbia as a superior tribunal corresponding to the new circuit courts of appeals.[108] Both these courts had a local as well as a federal jurisdiction. But by successive steps the former District supreme court was given the title and status of a district court of the United States, and the former court of appeals became a United States Court of Appeals.[109]

In 1970 the District of Columbia Court Reorganization Act[110] ended the system of combining federal and local jurisdictions in the courts of the District. Under this Act, the United States District Court for the District of Columbia and the United States Court of Appeals for the District of Columbia Circuit exercise only the jurisdiction exercised by other federal district courts and

---

106. See Chap. IV, Sec. 2, *infra*.

107. For further generalizations about the characteristic nature of legislative courts, as well as some qualifications, see Chap. IV, Sec. 2, pp. 417-19, *infra*.

108. Act of Feb. 9, 1893, 27 Stat. 434. For the history of this court and of the old District supreme court, see O'Donoghue v. United States, 289 U.S. 516, 548 (1933).

109. For the present provisions, see 28 U.S.C. §§ 41, 43 (court of appeals), and §§ 88, 132 (district court).

110. Act of July 29, 1970, 84 Stat. 473. See generally Kern, *The District of Columbia Court Reorganization Act of 1970: A Dose of the Conventional Wisdom and a Dash of Innovation*, 20 Am.U.L.Rev. 237 (1971).

circuit courts of appeals. The remaining local jurisdiction of those courts was transferred to two local courts. The highest local court continues to be the District of Columbia Court of Appeals,[111] an appellate court whose judgments are in turn reviewable by the Supreme Court under 28 U.S.C. § 1257 as if they were rendered by the highest court of a state. The Superior Court of the District of Columbia is now the trial court of general jurisdiction,[112] and is divided into Civil, Criminal, Family, Probate, and Tax Divisions.[113] The judges of both these local courts serve for fifteen-year terms.[114] (For further discussion of the courts of the District of Columbia, and especially of their status under the Constitution, see Palmore v. United States, 411 U.S. 389 (1973)).

b. The Territorial and Related Courts

The statutes organizing each of the territories have likewise had to make provision for courts of local as well as federal jurisdiction. Today the Commonwealth of Puerto Rico has a system of local courts, headed by the Supreme Court of Puerto Rico;[115] decisions of the latter are reviewed by the United States Supreme Court much as state court judgments are.[116] In addition, a United States District Court for the District of Puerto Rico,[117] exercising federal jurisdiction, sits in the Commonwealth.

Guam, the Virgin Islands, and the Northern Mariana Islands all have courts, designated as "district courts" but organized under Article I, not Article III, that exercise both local and federal jurisdiction.[118] These territories also have local inferior courts.

c. The Tax Court

Until 1969 the Tax Court of the United States, which hears taxpayer petitions contesting deficiency determinations, was an independent agency in the Executive Branch. It was then declared to be a "court".[119] Its judgments are reviewed by the courts of appeals.

111. D.C. Code 1981 §§ 11–701 et seq.

112. D.C.Code 1981 §§ 11–901 et seq.

113. D.C.Code 1981 §§ 11–902, 11–1301.

114. D.C.Code 1981 § 11–1502.

115. See Puerto Rico Constitution Art. V, superseding 48 U.S.C. § 861.

116. 28 U.S.C. § 1258.

117. This district court is constituted among the regular district courts by Chapter 5 of the Judicial Code, 28 U.S.C. §§ 119, 132. Its judges have life tenure by virtue of the Act of September 12, 1966, 80 Stat. 764, amending 28 U.S.C. § 134(a). The district court is attached to the First Circuit, 28 U.S.C. § 41, and its judgments are reviewable in the normal manner under 28 U.S.C. §§ 1291 and 1292.

118. See 48 U.S.C. §§ 1611–14 (Virgin Islands), 1424 (Guam), 1694 (Northern Mariana Islands). Although these district courts are not among those constituted by Chapter 5 of the Judicial Code, many of the Code's provisions are expressly made applicable to them. See, e.g., 28 U.S.C. §§ 1291, 1294(2), 1294(3) and 1294(4)(review by the Courts of Appeals of the Third and Ninth Circuits of judgments of the district courts of the Virgin Islands and Guam).

On the status of the courts of Guam, see Territory of Guam v. Olsen, 431 U.S. 195 (1977).

119. Act of Dec. 30, 1969, 83 Stat. 730, amending 26 U.S.C. § 7441. Tax Court judges are appointed for 15–year terms. 26 U.S.C. § 7443(e).

For an exhaustive historical study of the Tax Court, see the series of articles appearing in the Albany Law Review from 1975 to 1978 by Dubroff, Cook, & Grossman. The articles appear in Volume 40 at pp. 7, 53, and 253; Volume 41 at pp. 1 and 639, and Volume 42 at pp. 161, 191, and 353. For critical comment on the court's assertedly pro-Treasury leanings, see Geier, *The Tax Court, Article III, and the Proposal Advanced By the Feder-*

d. The Court of Federal Claims

The story of the establishment of the Court of Claims by statutes of 1855, 1863, and 1866, and its replacement in 1982 by the United States Claims Court, which was itself retitled the Court of Federal Claims a decade later,[120] is summarized in Chap. II, Sec. 2.[121] Chapter 7 of the Judicial Code contains the provisions governing the organization of the Court of Federal Claims; Chapter 91 includes the provisions governing its jurisdiction.

e. Military Courts

Throughout American history, Congress has provided a separate set of military courts with jurisdiction over service-connected offenses.[122] Three tiers of tribunals currently exist. At the trial level, the least serious form of court-martial may be presided over by a commissioned officer, but trials of more serious offenses usually require a military judge—a position that has formally existed only since 1968—as presiding officer.[123] As of 1994, there were 99 judges, all attorneys and all commissioned officers, certified to preside at various types of courts-martial.[124] The trial-level judges do not serve for fixed terms and perform judicial duties only when assigned to do so by the Judge Advocate General of the service of which they are members.

At the first appellate tier are Courts of Military Review for each of the services. The appellate judges may be either military officers or civilians. They do not serve for fixed terms and are assigned by the appropriate Judge Advocate General.[125] As of 1994, there were 31 military appellate judges.

At the top of the system is a five-member, all-civilian Court of Appeals for the Armed Services, the judges of which are appointed by the President, with the advice and consent of the Senate, to 15–year terms.[126] The Court of Appeals' decisions are subject to review on certiorari by the Supreme Court of the United States.[127]

2. Administrative Agencies

Administrative agencies are often charged with significant responsibilities for adjudicating rights and obligations under their organic statutes. In perhaps the classic "agency model", ultimate adjudicative authority resides in "the agency" or its head. Agencies characteristically differ from legislative courts along several dimensions,[128] perhaps the most important of which is that agencies frequently perform a mix of functions, including rulemaking and

---

al Courts Study Committee: A Study in Applied Constitutional Theory, 76 Corn.L.Rev. 985 (1991).

120. See P.L. 102–572, § 902(a), 106 Stat. 4506, 4516 (1992).

121. See also Glidden Co. v. Zdanok, 370 U.S. 530 (1962); Chap. IX, Sec. 1(C), infra. Under the 1982 statute, Court of Federal Claims judges are appointed for 15–year terms. 28 U.S.C. § 172.

122. For a discussion of military justice and its relation to Article III, see Note, 103 Harv.L.Rev. 1909 (1990).

123. See Art. 26, Uniform Code of Military Justice ("UCMJ"), 10 U.S.C. § 826.

124. See Weiss v. United States, 114 S.Ct. 752, 756 (1994).

125. See Art. 66, UCMJ, 10 U.S.C. § 866.

126. Arts. 67, 142, UCMJ, 10 U.S.C. §§ 867, 942 (1988 ed., Supp. IV (1994)).

127. See 28 U.S.C. § 1259. There is also a limited opportunity to test the judgments of military courts in federal habeas corpus actions.

128. The differences are explored in Chap. IV, Sec. 2, pp. 417-19, infra.

enforcement as well as adjudication. In the modern agency, initial adjudication is typically performed by an "administrative judge" or "administrative law judge", who enjoys relative insulation from pressure by officials performing other functions, but nonetheless is an employee of the agency.

Though administrative adjudication is often overlooked in portrayals of the "judicial" system, by the early 1990s the federal government employed over 1,100 officials denominated as "administrative law judges" and an additional 2,700 "administrative judges". Strauss, Rakoff, Schotland, & Farina, Gellhorn & Byse's Administrative Law Cases and Comments 959 (9th ed. 1995). Each of these two categories of officials renders decisions in roughly 350,000 on-the-record adjudications per year. By itself, the Social Security Administration has a caseload larger than the civil docket of all Article III courts combined.

The adjudicative decisions of federal administrative agencies are most often, but not always, reviewable on appeal by the Article III federal courts. According to at least one commentator, this relationship between agencies and the Article III courts demonstrates that traditional thought about the federal judicial system has lagged behind the reality: Reconceptualization is needed to account for a fourth tier of federal adjudication (beneath the federal district courts, the courts of appeals, and the Supreme Court). See Resnik, *Rereading "The Federal Courts": Revising the Domain of Federal Courts Jurisprudence at the End of the Twentieth Century,* 47 Vand.L.Rev. 1021 (1994). For further materials bearing on this theme, administrative adjudication, and the Article III and other constitutional limits on administrative adjudication, see Chap. IV, Sec. 2, *infra.*

3. Adjuncts to the District Courts

a. *Bankruptcy Courts*

Until enactment of the Bankruptcy Act of 1978, the district courts acted as bankruptcy courts. Proceedings were generally conducted before court-appointed referees; the district court could at any time withdraw the case from the referee; and the referee's final order was appealable to the district court. In the 1978 Act, however, Congress created, as "an adjunct to the district court" for each district a "court of record known as the United States Bankruptcy Court." The judges of the new courts were appointed by the President and confirmed by the Senate to serve 14–year terms; they were removable by the judicial councils of the circuits; and their salaries were not protected against diminution.

The system of bankruptcy courts created by this statute failed to survive constitutional challenge. See Northern Pipeline Construction Co. v. Marathon Pipe Line Co., 458 U.S. 50 (1982), pp. 399–416, *infra.* After considerable delay and controversy, Congress in 1984 changed the system once again. Under the law as revised, bankruptcy judges are appointed as officers of the district courts for a term of fourteen years; appointments are made by the courts of appeals for the districts within their respective circuits, and the judges in each district "constitute a unit of the district court to be known as the bankruptcy court for that district." 28 U.S.C. §§ 151, 152. As of 1994, there were 314 bankruptcy judges, and 12 additional positions were vacant.[129] On the volume of bankrupt-

---

129. 1994 Annual Report of the Director of the Administrative Office of the United States Courts, Table 13.

cy cases filed each year and primarily handled by bankruptcy judges, see pp. 51-52 *infra*. For further discussion of the bankruptcy courts and constitutional issues surrounding their jurisdiction, see Chap. IV, Sec. 2, *infra*.

b. *Magistrate Judges*

The Federal Magistrates Act of 1968, 82 Stat. 1108, as amended, 28 U.S.C. §§ 631 *et seq.*, created the position of "magistrate", which was subsequently retitled as that of "magistrate judge".[130] Magistrate judges are appointed by the federal district judges, in such numbers as the Judicial Conference may determine. They may be appointed on a full-time basis for an eight-year term, or on a part-time basis for a four-year term. Magistrate judges were initially given (a) the powers previously exercised by United States commissioners (*e.g.*, issuing warrants, conducting probable cause and other preliminary hearings in criminal cases), (b) jurisdiction to try "minor offenses," and (c) "such additional duties as are not inconsistent with the Constitution and laws" and as might be established at the district court level, including service as special masters in civil cases, assistance in discovery or other pretrial proceedings, and preliminary review of applications for post-conviction relief.

Congress further expanded the role of magistrates in the Federal Magistrates Act of 1979,[131] which authorized magistrates to hear, determine, and enter final judgment in both jury and nonjury civil cases if all parties consent. Magistrate judges may also try criminal misdemeanor cases if the defendant consents. Appeal is provided for in all such cases (in some cases to the district court, in others to the court of appeals).

In 1994, there were 406 full-time and 88 part-time magistrate judges,[132] who conducted more than 500,000 judicial proceedings.[133] For a statistical breakdown of the kinds of matters handled by magistrate judges, see p. 52, *infra*. For further discussion of the precise nature of the role of magistrate judges and of the constitutional and statutory issues that it presents, see *Note on Magistrate Judges*, p. 437, *infra*.

I. The Business of the Article III Courts

1. The District Courts

Chapter 5 of the Judicial Code of 1948 (Title 28, U.S. Code) codified the statutes establishing the district courts. It now provides for 94 district courts: 92 for the fifty states, and one each for the District of Columbia and Puerto Rico.[134]

Each state has at least one district court. The more populous states are divided into two, three, or four districts. Many districts are in turn divided into divisions. On September 30, 1994, there were 649 authorized district

---

130. See the Judicial Improvements Act of 1990, section 321, 104 Stat. 5089, 5117.

131. 93 Stat. 643, amending 28 U.S.C. §§ 604, 631, 633–36, 1915(b), 18 U.S.C. § 3401.

132. 1994 Annual Report of the Director of the Administrative Office of the United States Courts, Table 14.

133. *Id.* at 19.

134. In addition, district courts are established for the Virgin Islands, Guam, and the Northern Mariana Islands. See p. 44 & note 118, *supra*.

judgeships. (The largest increase occurred in 1991, when 74 new judgeships were created.) In addition, there were 292 senior district judges.[135]

Chapter 85 of the Code (§§ 1331–62) collects the principal grants to the district courts of original jurisdiction in civil cases. Chapter 90 deals with bankruptcy cases. The principal removal provisions are collected in Chapter 89. The criminal jurisdiction of the district courts rests upon 18 U.S.C. § 3231, which gives them in sweeping terms "original jurisdiction, exclusive of the courts of the States, of all offenses against the laws of the United States."

In the preparation of these codes, as of earlier versions, an effort was made to bring together all the statutory provisions affecting the jurisdiction of the federal courts. But the effort was not completely successful. Drafters of substantive statutes have persisted in inserting jurisdictional provisions as sections of those statutes rather than as amendments of the Judicial Code; and the codifiers have never been able wholly to unravel their work. In determining the jurisdiction of a district court over a particular proceeding, it thus remains necessary to examine not only the applicable code but also the relevant substantive statutes.

The current business of the district courts (as well as of other federal courts) is described in extensive detail in the Annual Reports of the Director of the Administrative Office of the United States Courts.[136] Although nothing ages more quickly than statistics, and these are no exceptions, this and the following subsections of Part I attempt to give a summary picture of the work of the federal courts.

In fiscal 1994, 287,864 civil and criminal cases were commenced in the district courts. (By contrast, the Third Edition of this book noted that 296,318 civil and criminal cases were commenced in 1986, 127,280 in 1970, and 89,091 in 1960.) In addition a total of 837,797 bankruptcy petitions were filed (477,856 bankruptcy petitions were filed in 1986, 194,399 in 1970, and 110,034 in 1960.)

Civil and criminal suits commenced in fiscal 1994 broke down as follows (comparative figures noted in the Third Edition for 1986 and 1970 are also

135. These figures are drawn from the 1994 Annual Report of the Director of the Administrative Office of the United States Courts, Table 12.

136. These will be cited hereafter in this chapter as Ad.Off.Rep. with the appropriate date. Except where otherwise stated, the statistics concerning current litigation that follow are taken from these reports. Various tables, however, have been derived from materials scattered through the reports.

For writings by political scientists about the work of the federal courts, see, *e.g.,* Baum, American Courts: Process & Policy (2d ed.1990); Richardson & Vines, The Politics of Federal Courts (1970); The Federal Judicial System: Readings in Process and Behavior (Goldman & Jahnige eds.1968). For analysis of specific aspects of this work, see Dolbeare, *The Federal District Courts and*

Urban Public Policy, in Frontiers of Judicial Research 373 (Grossman & Tanenhaus eds. 1969); *The Effects of Gender in the Federal Courts: The Final Report of the Ninth Circuit Gender Bias Task Force,* 67 S.Calif.L.Rev. 745 (1994).

A detailed account of the history of the various district courts is Surrency, History of the Federal Courts (1987). See also Wheeler & Harrison, Creating the Federal Judicial System (2d ed.1994); Clark, *Adjudication to Administration: A Statistical Analysis of Federal District Courts in the Twentieth Century,* 55 S.Calif.L.Rev. 65 (1981). Thomas Baker has compiled an extensive bibliography that includes, *inter alia,* several works detailing the history of the federal courts. See Baker, *A Bibliography for the United States Courts of Appeals,* 25 Tex.Tech.L.Rev. 335 (1994).

given:)[137]

	1970	1986	1994
Private civil cases:			
Federal Question (including admiralty)	34,846	98,747	135,853
Diversity	22,854	63,672	54,886
United States civil cases:			
U.S. plaintiff	13,310	60,779	15,805
U.S. defendant	11,655	31,051	29,605
Criminal cases:	39,959	41,490	45,473
TOTAL	122,624	295,739	281,622

Private Civil Cases. The table in the footnote lists some of the significant categories of private litigation commenced in 1994.[138]

Most of the cases filed in federal district court never come to trial. Of the 180,501 private civil cases terminated in the district courts in 1994, trials were held in only 7,101 (of which 4,298 were before a jury). The percentage of cases reaching trial was 3.5 for federal question cases, 4.9 for diversity cases.[139] Of the cases terminated without trial, 31,987 were ended without court action by withdrawal or settlement; 122,814 were disposed of by court action before pretrial; and 18,599 were concluded by court action during or after pretrial.

Although the total volume of federal question litigation continues to increase, there is considerable variance among the subcategories. In some areas the growth is noteworthy—for example, in civil rights (29,636 cases (other than prisoner petitions) in 1994, compared with 20,128 such cases in

137. Cases involving local jurisdiction—of which there were 4,656 in 1970, 579 in 1986, and 242 in 1994—are not included in this table. Here and in the remainder of this Part, unless otherwise indicated, figures refer to fiscal, not calendar, years and are derived from Table C–2 (for civil cases) and from Table D–1 (for criminal cases) in the annual Ad.Off.Reps.

138. Federal Question:

Antitrust	658
Civil rights (other than prisoner cases)	29,636
Commerce (ICC rates, etc.)	841
Copyright	2,828
Fair Labor Standards Act	1,251
Labor Mgmt Relations Act	2,013
Marine contracts	2,478
Marine torts	2,372
Patent	1,603
Prisoners' (state) petitions	
—Habeas corpus	11,908
—Mandamus, etc.	395
—Civil rights	37,925
Securities laws	1,579
Trademark	2,441

Diversity of Citizenship:

Contract actions	
—Insurance	6,278
—Other	14,070
Tort actions	
—Motor vehicle	4,570
—Asbestos	2,038
—Other	24,315

139. The figures in this paragraph are derived from 1994 Ad.Off.Rep. Table C–4.

1986), and litigation under the Fair Labor Standards Act. Other categories, however, have seen a decrease in the number of annual filings between 1986 and 1994. For example, in 1994, 658 antitrust suits were filed, compared with 877 such suits in 1986. Other reductions include suits under the securities laws (in 1994, 1579; in 1986, 3059) and the Labor Management Relations Act (in 1994, 2013; in 1986, 3681).

A relatively large percentage of federal litigation is commenced by prisoners. After an explosive increase in habeas corpus petitions filed by state prisoners in the 1960s (872 in 1960; 8,963 in 1970), the number of these filings leveled off for a period (in 1986, 9040), but has increased slowly in recent years, with 11,908 habeas petitions filed in 1994.[140] The number of non-habeas prisoners' civil rights suits has swollen dramatically from 2,653 in 1970 to 20,071 in 1986 to 38,320 in 1994.[141] For further discussion of and statistics concerning prisoner litigation, see Chap. XI, *infra*.

Though the number of diversity cases filed has also grown substantially, the ratio of diversity filings to total civil filings has declined in recent decades—from 33.4% (17,048 diversity cases) in 1960, to 26.2% (22,854 diversity cases) in 1970, to 25.0% (63,672 diversity cases) in 1986, to 23.2% (54,886 diversity cases) in 1994. (This last period has also seen an absolute decline.)

United States Civil Cases. The table in the footnote lists some of the significant categories of litigation commenced in fiscal 1994 by and against the United States and its agencies and officers.[142] Cases involving the United States as defendant increased steadily from 5,854 in 1960, to 11,655 in 1970, to 31,051 in 1986. Since then, the pattern has been less consistent. The number of these cases first declined (24,740 in 1990), then rose again (31,242 in 1993), with another slight decline in 1994 (29,605 cases). Most of the suits in which the U.S. is a defendant are social security cases (despite a decline from 14,376 in 1986 to 10,863 in 1994) and federal prisoner petitions (which increased from 4,432 in 1986 to 7,700 in 1994).

---

140. These figures exclude a small number of local jurisdiction cases—100 in 1970, 5 in 1986, and 10 in 1994. The corresponding number of local jurisdiction cases for 1960 is not stated in the 1960 Ad.Off.Rep.

141. These figures also exclude local jurisdiction cases.

142.   United States plaintiff:

Antitrust	26
Civil rights	718
Forfeiture and penalty	3,067
Labor laws	569
Securities laws	222
Tax suits	893
Recovery of overpayments and enforcement of judgments	2,097
Other contract actions	1,933
Real property actions	4,554
United States defendant:	
Civil rights (excluding prisoner cases)	2,268
Prisoner petitions	
—Motions to vacate sentence	4,628
—Habeas corpus	1,441
—Mandamus and other	491
—Civil rights	1,140
Social security laws	10,863
Contract actions	785
Real property actions	514
Tort actions	3,074

Civil filings by the United States were relatively stable for many years, and actually declined from 1970 (13,310) to 1975 (12,742). But they rose sharply from 1975 to 1985, when they reached 79,371, and then declined to 60,779 in 1986. Since 1986, the number of these cases has been falling steadily, and in 1994 only 15,805 civil cases were filed by the United States. A particularly sharp drop has occurred in suits to recover overpayments and to enforce judgments, many of them in connection with defaulted student loans and overpayment of veterans' benefits. Student loans can now be collected through wage garnishment, and the Department of Veteran Affairs has increasingly used administrative processes to recover overpayments. As a result, the number of suits within these categories has diminished from 40,544 in 1986 to 2097 in 1994.

Of 46,947 United States cases terminated in 1994, only 799 went to trial, and only 146 were tried to a jury. The percentage of United States cases reaching trial (1.7%) was roughly half that for all civil filings (3.5%).[143]

Criminal Cases. The story on the criminal side is one of relative stability. Before World War I, filings ranged from 12,000 to 20,000 cases a year. During the Prohibition era, the number of annual filings climbed as high as 90,000, but well over half were prohibition cases. From 1934 to 1975, the number of filings ranged from about 30,000 to 50,000 with fluctuation due to such matters as price control and rationing cases during World War II, strenuous efforts to enforce the immigration laws in the fifties, and selective service cases in the early seventies. In the mid-seventies, the number of criminal prosecutions declined—partly as a result of efforts by the Justice Department to focus on organized and white collar crime and to transfer or divert other matters (*e.g.,* bank robberies, car thefts, cases involving juveniles) to the states. In the eighties, the number began to rise again because of increases in prosecutions involving drugs, weapons, and fraud. In 1986, total filings stood at 41,490. After a decade of steady increase, the number began to decline again in 1993. In 1994, the number of filings was 45,473.

Federal criminal cases terminated in 1994 involved 59,625 defendants.[144] Cases involving 8,669 defendants were dismissed, and 1,239 defendants were acquitted (546 by the court and 693 by a jury). Of the 49,717 who were convicted, 45,429 pleaded guilty or nolo contendere, 491 were convicted by the court, and 3,797 were convicted by a jury.

Bankruptcy Cases. The volume of bankruptcy cases is, of course, a function of both the size and the condition of the economy. Annual filings reached 70,000 in 1932, declined during World War II to a low of 10,000 in 1946, and with a few exceptions have been climbing ever since. After some decline from 254,484 cases in the recession year of 1975,[145] the figure began to increase once again, jumping 31% in 1986 alone to what was then an all-time high of 477,856 filings. The number of bankruptcy cases continued to increase to a peak of 977,478 in 1992, before decreasing in 1993 and again in 1994. Nonetheless, 837,797 cases were filed in 1994,[146] the vast majority of which (93.5%) were non-business bankruptcies; only 6.5% were business filings.

143. The figures in this paragraph are derived from 1994 Ad.Off.Rep. Table C–4.

144. Figures in this paragraph are derived from 1994 Ad.Off.Rep. Table D–4.

145. 1975 Ad.Off.Rep. 151.

146. The figures for 1994 appear in 1994 Ad.Off.Rep. 17.

The bulk of the work in bankruptcy cases is performed by the judges of the bankruptcy courts.[147]

Other Business.

(a) *The Probation System.* Various classes of offenders against federal laws who are not in confinement are supervised by probation officers, appointed by the district court and responsible to it. At the close of fiscal 1994, the Federal Probation System had a total of 89,103 persons under supervision.[148]

(b) *Naturalization.* Since the first naturalization law was enacted in 1790, the granting of American citizenship to aliens has been a function of the federal as well as of designated state courts.[149] For 116 years the courts performed this function unaided. Since 1906, however, all the steps in the process of naturalization prior to final hearing have been handled administratively, by what is now the Immigration and Naturalization Service; and a representative of the Service also participates in the final hearing, as an aid to the court with authority to oppose the application if in the judgment of the agency the public interest so requires. The volume of naturalizations reached a peak of 441,979 in fiscal 1944. In fiscal 1986, 252,679 persons were naturalized in the federal courts.[150] In fiscal 1994, the number of persons administered the oath of allegiance rose to 331,808.[151]

(c) *Federal Magistrate Judges.* The volume of judicial business handled by magistrate judges has increased steadily from 1972, soon after the new system began, to 1994. In 1994, magistrate judges disposed of 517,397 civil matters and received 47,780 references (involving motions, hearings, and conferences) in criminal felony cases. The number of civil cases disposed of by magistrate judges with the consent of the parties increased by 16 percent in 1994, and the number of civil trials conducted before magistrate judges grew by 36 percent.[152]

The following table reflects the expansion in matters handled by magistrates from 1972 to 1994:[153]

	1972	1986	1994
Trial Jurisdiction cases	72,082	91,570	87,519
—Petty offenses	62,915	79,272	75,381
—Misdemeanors	9,167	12,298	12,138
Preliminary Proceedings in Criminal Cases (warrants, arraignments, etc.)	131,522	129,526	196,990
Additional Duties	33,918	219,548	225,053
—Criminal (motions, pretrial conferences, etc.)	11,537	37,293	47,780
—Civil (motions, pretrial conferences, etc.)	15,595	158,451	146,814
—Prisoner litigation (habeas corpus, civil rights)	6,786	23,804	30,459
—Civil consent cases	—	4,931	7,835

147. See pp. 46–47, *supra*, pp. 421–22, *infra*.

148. 1994 Ad.Off.Rep. 19–20.

149. See 8 U.S.C. § 1421.

150. 1986 Ad.Off.Rep. 226. The district courts also processed 1,996 passport applications in 1986 and 737 in 1994. This function is now handled primarily by the U.S. Postal Service.

151. 1994 Ad.Off.Rep. A1–274 (Table P–1).

152. 1994 Ad.Off.Rep. 19.

153. The table is derived from 1986 Ad.Off.Rep. 40 (Table 13) and 1994 Ad.Off. Rep. 54 (Table S–19) and A1–251 to A1–261 (Tables M–1 and M–1A).

2. The Courts of Appeals

Chapter 3 of the Judicial Code of 1948 changed the name of the former circuit courts of appeals to the United States Courts of Appeals, and codified the provisions establishing them. It now provides for thirteen judicial circuits: eleven in the various states, one for the District of Columbia, and one for the Federal Circuit, located in the District of Columbia and other places as the court may direct by rule. The number of judges on each circuit ranges from six (First) to 28 (Ninth). 28 U.S.C. § 44. As of the end of fiscal 1994, 179 judgeships were authorized, and there were in addition 82 senior judges.[154]

The development of the statutory provisions governing the jurisdiction of the courts of appeals is described in Chap. XV. The courts' business can usefully be grouped in three categories: (1) review of decisions of district courts, including the district courts in the territories; (2) issuance of prerogative writs; and (3) review of decisions of certain administrative agencies and commissions.[155]

The statutory provisions conferring jurisdiction in the first category are codified in Chapter 83 of the Judicial Code. The jurisdiction of the courts of appeals to issue the prerogative writs rests on 28 U.S.C. § 1651.

The provisions for direct review by the courts of appeals of administrative decisions are dispersed among the various statutes establishing the agencies involved. This mode of review of administrative action was first adopted in 1914 in the Federal Trade Commission Act. The same pattern of review has since been followed for some or all of the decisions of many other agencies: *e.g.*, the SEC, the NLRB, and the FCC.

Cases in the courts of appeals are normally heard and determined by panels of three judges, but each court may, by vote of a majority of the judges in regular active service, order a hearing or rehearing by the court en banc. 28 U.S.C. § 46(c).[156] Rehearings en banc are rare; original hearings en banc are even rarer.[157] A number of circuits, however, have specified that panel decisions may be overruled only by the full bench sitting en banc.[158]

---

154. 1994 Ad.Off.Rep. 24–25. The most recent increase came from the Judicial Improvements Act of 1990, which authorized 11 additional judgeships.

155. In addition, the Court of Appeals for the Federal Circuit reviews decisions of the United States Court of Federal Claims and of the Court of International Trade.

156. A court en banc consists of all circuit judges in regular active service, except that (a) a senior circuit judge who sat on the decision being reviewed is also eligible to participate and (b) circuits with more than fifteen active judges—currently the fifth and ninth—may prescribe by rule the number of members required to perform en banc functions.

157. See United States v. American–Foreign S.S. Corp., 363 U.S. 685, 689 (1960)(en banc courts "are the exception, not the rule").

158. See. *e.g.*, Bonner v. City of Prichard, 661 F.2d 1206, 1209–11 (11th Cir.1981); United States v. Fatico, 603 F.2d 1053, 1058 (2d Cir.1979).

For examples of some of the difficulties that have arisen in the en banc process, see 16 Wright, Miller, Cooper, & Gressman, Federal Practice and Procedure § 3981 (1977 & 1995 Supp.). For discussion of efforts to reduce the costs and delays of en banc proceedings, see Note, 34 Cleve.St.L.Rev. 531 (1986). Stein, *Uniformity in the Federal Courts: A Proposal for Increasing the Use of En Banc Appellate Review*, 54 U.Pitt.L.Rev. 805, 808–819 (1993) provides interesting historical background and a breakdown of the frequency with which the different circuits use the en banc procedure and their reasons for authorizing rehearing. See generally Solimine, *Ideology and En Banc Review*, 67 N.C.L.Rev. 29 (1988); Note, 102 Harv.L.Rev. 864 (1989).

The number of appeals filed in the courts of appeals rose from 3,899 in 1960, to 11,662 in 1970, to 34,292 in 1986, and to 48,322 in 1994.[159] Nonetheless, the number of appeals filed actually decreased 3.8% from 1993 to 1994—the first decline since 1978.[160] In addition, for the first time since 1982, the number of cases terminated in the courts of appeals in 1994 (49,184) exceeded the number of filings. Of the cases terminated, 3,816 were disposed of by consolidation, and an additional 18,149 were disposed of without hearing or submission to the court.

The burden of the sharply increased caseload has led to dramatic changes in the procedures of the courts of appeals. Opportunity for oral argument has been sharply reduced in most circuits,[161] and the proportion of cases decided without any opinion, or by per curiam opinion, has increased.[162] In addition, at the urging of the Judicial Conference, most circuits have adopted rules with respect to their "unpublished" opinions and orders—rules that in various ways restrict the citation and use of these opinions and orders as precedent.[163] Serious questions have been raised about the meaning, validity, desirability, and enforceability of these rules.[164]

---

159. 1994 Ad.Off.Reps. Table B–1. The distribution of appeals filed in 1994 was as follows:

Criminal	10,674
U.S. prisoner petitions	2,951
Other U.S. civil	4,582
State prisoner petitions	10,110
Other private civil	14,666
Bankruptcy	1,382
Administrative appeals	3,369
Original proceedings	588

160. See 1994 Ad.Off.Rep., Table 2.

161. "Nationwide, between 40% and 50% of the appeals decided on the merits by the courts of appeals in recent years are being decided without oral argument. * * * Furthermore, when oral arguments are allowed, they are abbreviated; several courts routinely give some cases fifteen minutes of argument per side." Baker, *Intramural Reforms: How the U.S. Courts of Appeal Have Helped Themselves,* 22 Fla. St. U. L. Rev. 913, 916–17 (1995). For a bibliography of articles discussing oral argument reforms in the courts of appeals, see Baker, *A Bibliography for the United States Courts of Appeal,* 25 Tex.Tech.L.Rev. 335 (1994).

162. Judge Posner has reported that of all "contested terminations"—terminations after hearing or submission—the percentage disposed of by signed opinion declined from 74% in 1960 to 42% in 1983. Posner, note 96 *supra,* at 69–70. This trend has receded recently, but decisions rendered without an opinion remain common. See Baker, *Intramural Reforms,* note 161 *supra,* at 927–28.

For contrasting views of the values and problems inherent in the sorting out of cases for some form of summary treatment, compare Carrington, *Ceremony and Realism: Demise of Appellate Procedure,* 66 A.B.A.J. 860 (1980), with Godbold, *Improvements in Appellate Procedure: Better Use of Available Facilities,* 66 A.B.A.J. 863 (1980).

163. One of the most elaborate of these rules is Rule 35 of the Rules of the Seventh Circuit, which after defining "publication" and providing for limited distribution of unpublished orders, provides that an unpublished order may not be cited or used as precedent "in any federal court within the circuit in any written document or in oral argument or * * * by any such court for any purpose" except to support a claim of "res judicata, collateral estoppel or law of the case."

164. See, *e.g.,* Carrington, Meador, & Rosenberg, Justice on Appeal 37–41 (1976); Walther, *The Noncitation Rule and the Concept of Stare Decisis,* 61 Marq.L.Rev. 581 (1978). See also Posner, note 96, *supra,* at 120–27; Reynolds & Richman, *An Evaluation of Limited Publication in the United States Courts of Appeals: The Price of Reform,* 48 U.Chi.L.Rev. 573 (1981). But see Martineau, *Restrictions on Publication and Citation of Judicial Opinions: A Reassessment,* 28 U.Mich.J.L.Ref. 119 (1994)(summarizing and answering objections to rules restricting publication of judicial opinions and citation of unpublished opinions).

The problem of congestion in the courts of appeals has also led to increased reliance on "central" legal staffs,[165] and to proposals for such reforms as increased use of specialized courts, diversion of cases to alternative means of dispute resolution, an increase in the discretion of the appellate courts to deny review, statutory changes in the scope of review, and increased use of attorneys' fees awards to the prevailing party.[166]

3. The Supreme Court

The statutory provisions establishing the Supreme Court are now codified in Chapter 1 of the Judicial Code, and the major provisions governing its jurisdiction in Chapter 81. The development of the provisions for review of state and federal court decisions is described in Chap. V, Sec. 1, *infra* (state decisions), and Chap. XV, Secs. 1, 2, *infra* (federal decisions).

The business of the Court is summarized in statistical tables appearing every year in the Annual Report of the Administrative Office (though these tables are less detailed than they once were), in United States Law Week, and in the "Supreme Court Note"—a survey, both statistical and substantive, of the Court's work that is published annually in the November issue of the Harvard Law Review.[167]

At its 1994 Term, which ended in June 1995, the Supreme Court disposed of 7,170 cases (compared with 4,350 in 1986, 3,318 in 1970, 1,911 in 1960, and 1,202 in 1950).[168] An appreciation of the significance of this number and its relation to the Court's capacity to decide cases depends on an understanding of its various categories of business and of the ways in which it handles them.[169]

Original Cases. The Court disposed of two cases on its original docket in the 1994 Term. Original cases are few, but characteristically laborious and prolonged. Cases that are fully heard are usually referred to a master, and while they are pending call periodically for special consideration and interim orders.[170]

Appellate Cases. The remaining 7,168 cases disposed of in the 1994 Term fell within the Court's appellate jurisdiction, with the vast majority coming from the courts of appeals and the state courts.[171] Of these, 6,971 were cases

---

165. For a comprehensive account of this and related developments in one circuit, see Hellman, *Restructuring Justice: The Innovations of the Ninth Circuit and the Future of the Federal Courts* (1990); Oakley, *The Screening of Appeals: The Ninth Circuit's Experience in the Eighties and Innovations for the Nineties,* 1991 B.Y.U.L.Rev. 859.

166. Reform proposals of this kind are discussed in many of the authorities referred to in Part K, pp. 60-66, *infra.* See also 13 Wright, Miller, & Cooper, Federal Practice and Procedure § 3510 (1984 & 1995 Supp.).

167. Statistics for the pre–World War II Terms following the Judiciary Act of 1925 were reviewed in a series of articles in the Harvard Law Review by Professor Frankfurter and a number of collaborators. See 42 Harv.L.Rev. 1 (1928)(with Landis); 43 *id.* 33 (1929); 44 *id.* 1 (1930); 45 *id.* 271 (1931); 46 *id.* 726 (1932); 47 *id.* 245 (1933)(with Hart);

48 *id.* 238 (1934); 49 *id.* 68 (1935); 51 *id.* 577 (1938)(with Fisher); 53 *id.* 579 (1940)(with Hart).

168. Figures for the 1994 Term here and in the following discussion are derived from 64 U.S.L.W. 3094 (1995). Figures for the 1986 Term here and in the following discussion are taken from 56 U.S.L.W. 3102 (1987) unless otherwise indicated. Figures for 1970 are from 85 Harv.L.Rev. 346 (1971), for 1960 from 75 Harv.L.Rev. 85 (1961), and for 1950 from 65 Harv.L.Rev. 179 (1951).

169. See also Chap. XV, Sec. 3, *infra.* For a lively comparison, see *The Supreme Court in 1848 and 1948: A Review of Two Terms,* 23 S.Cal.L.Rev. 460 (1950).

170. See generally Chap. III, *infra.*

171. A few cases come from the district courts, either on application for an extraordinary writ or pursuant to one of the remain-

in which a petition for certiorari was denied or dismissed, an appeal was dismissed,[172] a petition for issuance of an extraordinary writ was denied or dismissed,[173] or the appeal or petition was withdrawn. The large majority of these dispositions were denials of petitions for certiorari. Such a denial is a decision only that the case will not be reviewed and imports no adjudication on the merits.[174]

Of the cases denied, dismissed, or withdrawn, 4,955—well over half—were cases in which the appellant or petitioner was proceeding *in forma pauperis*. Under 28 U.S.C. § 1915, any court of the United States may permit an action to be begun or an appeal taken without prepayment of fees and costs, or security for them, if the litigant submits a proper affidavit of inability to bear these expenses.[175] In such cases, an appellate court may also dispense with printing of the record and other papers, or direct that these expenses be borne by the United States.

In the Supreme Court, a party who seeks the benefit of § 1915 is permitted to file a single copy of a motion and of the certiorari petition or other papers (typewritten if possible), along with a copy of the record below. See Sup.Ct. Rule 39. The Court then, in a proper case, grants the motion and at the same time acts on the underlying petition or appeal.

Most of the *in forma pauperis* cases are filed by criminal defendants seeking relief from conviction or imprisonment. The percentage of such cases granted review, *i.e.*, not summarily denied, dismissed, or withdrawn, is far lower than the percentage of paid cases granted review.[176]

Of the relatively small number of cases surviving these various dispositions in the 1994 Term, 65 were decided by per curiam or memorandum decision and 95 were decided by written opinion, according to the statistical retrospective of the Harvard Law Review, contained in 109 Harv.L.Rev. 344, Table 1 (1995).

Trends in the Volume of Business. Comparisons over time are complicated by changes in the methods of keeping and reporting statistics. But one useful comparison is the number of cases reported by the Harvard Law Review as

ing provisions for direct appeal, *e.g.*, 28 U.S.C. §§ 1252, 1253. (See Chap. XV, Sec. 2, *infra*.) With the establishment of the Court of Appeals for the Federal Circuit, cases no longer go directly to the Supreme Court from the specialized courts that the new court has superseded.

172. Beginning in the 1971 Term of the Supreme Court, the statistics reported by the Clerk of the Supreme Court no longer distinguished between denials or dismissals of certiorari petitions on the one hand and dismissals of appeals on the other. See 86 Harv. L.Rev. 303 n.c (1972).

173. Like the other federal courts, the Supreme Court has authority under 28 U.S.C. § 1651 to issue extraordinary (or prerogative) writs—such as habeas corpus, mandamus, or prohibition—in aid of its jurisdiction. See Chap. III, Sec. 3, *infra*. Separate

statistics on applications received are no longer reported, but the number of such applications has always been relatively small. In the 1969 Term, for example, 124 motions for leave to file an application for an extraordinary writ were received; of these, 121 were summarily denied or dismissed. 1970 Ad.Off. Rep. 208 (Table A–4).

174. See Chap. XV, Sec. 3, *infra*.

175. Prepaid cases are assigned docket numbers beginning with 1. *In forma pauperis* cases are assigned docket numbers beginning with 5001. (In both categories, numbers are preceded by a designation of the Term in which the case was filed.)

176. In the 1994 Term, for example, review was granted in 3.9% of the paid cases and only .2% of the *in forma pauperis* cases docketed during the Term.

disposed of by written opinion, including per curiam opinions containing substantial discussion:[177]

Term of Court:	**1960**	**1970**	**1980**	**1990**	**1994**
Disposed of by Written opinion:	132	141	159	129	95

The increase in the number of cases docketed since 1960 has, of course, been more dramatic (although that number has itself leveled off in recent years):[178]

Term of Court:	**1960**	**1970**	**1980**	**1990**	**1994**
Cases docketed:	1,957	3,419	4,174	5,502	6,996

The two tables taken together indicate that although the Court has only limited control over the number of cases brought to it for review, it does have the capacity to keep within bounds the number of cases selected for intensive consideration. Thus in the period 1960–70, when the number of cases docketed rose 76.2%, the number of cases disposed of by written opinion rose only 6.4%, and in recent years the number of written opinions has actually declined. For further discussion, see Chap. XV, *infra*.

J. The Administration of the Federal Courts

From 1789 substantially to 1922, the federal courts were an aggregation of independent tribunals, tied together only by the authority of the superior courts to revise the judicial judgments of the inferior. There was little or no administrative direction or coordination. The defects of an uninformed and uncoordinated administration of justice appeared most acutely when questions of the need for new judges had to be decided.[179] Because no good statistics were kept, the play of political pressures was unchecked by any real knowledge.

In the Act of September 14, 1922,[180] following the leadership of Chief Justice Taft, Congress greatly liberalized the provisions for assignment of judges to areas with pressing needs. More important, the Act established an administrative structure for securing information about the needs of the federal judiciary, promoting better administration, and formulating recommendations to Congress. A central innovation was the creation of a conference of the senior circuit judges of each circuit to be summoned annually by the Chief Justice of the United States. On the basis of reports from the judges and the Attorney General, the conference was directed to "make a comprehensive

---

177. The sources of the figures in this table are: for 1960, 75 Harv.L.Rev. 85 (1961); for 1970, 85 Harv.L.Rev. 346 (1971); for 1980, 95 Harv.L.Rev. 342 (1981); for 1990, 105 Harv.L.Rev. 423 (1991); and for 1994, 109 Harv.L.Rev. 344 (1995).

Most of these opinions, but not all, were rendered after submission of briefs on the merits and oral argument. Some were dis-

posed of on the certiorari petition or jurisdictional statement, though the number of such dispositions has declined in recent years.

178. These figures are derived from the tables published each year in United States Law Week.

179. See Frankfurter & Landis, note 3, *supra*, at 220–21.

180. 42 Stat. 837.

survey of the condition of business in the courts of the United States and prepare plans for assignment and transfer of judges to or from circuits or districts where the state of the docket or condition of business indicates the need therefor," and to "submit such suggestions to the various courts as may seem in the interest of uniformity and expedition of business."

The Act of August 7, 1939[181] built on this foundation by strengthening the judicial conference as an instrument of coordination and direction of the judicial system. It also established the Administrative Office of the United States Courts, which provides staff assistance to the conference.

The 1939 Act was modified and altered in minor respects by the Judicial Code of 1948. The provisions with regard to Judicial Conferences and Councils are collected in Chapter 15; those with regard to the Administrative Office constitute Chapter 41. The Code also codified (and collected in Chapter 13, §§ 291–96) the provisions regarding temporary assignments of judges.

The former conference of senior circuit judges is now named the Judicial Conference of the United States, and the Chief Justice is expressly directed to "submit to Congress an annual report of the proceedings of the Judicial Conference and its recommendations for legislation."[182] The Judicial Conference operates in part through a large number of committees. Its reports are printed annually and bound with the reports of the Director of the Administrative Office.

By virtue of a provision added in 1958,[183] the Judicial Conference is charged with carrying on "a continuous study" of the rules of procedure prescribed by the Supreme Court and with making recommendations for changes and additions to the rules. Another 1958 amendment authorized the Judicial Conference to organize judicial "institutes and joint councils on sentencing" in order to achieve uniformity in sentencing procedures.[184] A further amendment in 1980 authorized the Conference, acting as such or through a standing committee, to exercise certain powers of investigation and judicial discipline provided in newly enacted subsection (c) of 28 U.S.C. § 372.[185]

---

181. 53 Stat. 1223. For a history of the Act, see Fish, *Crises, Politics, and Federal Judicial Reform: The Administrative Office Act of 1939*, 32 J. Politics 599 (1970). See also Chandler, *Some Major Advances in the Federal Judicial System 1922–1947*, 31 F.R.D. 307 (1963).

182. 28 U.S.C. § 331.

183. Act of July 11, 1958, 72 Stat. 356, added to 28 U.S.C. § 331. See further Chap. VI, Sec. 1, *infra*.

184. Act of Aug. 25, 1958, 72 Stat. 845, 28 U.S.C. § 334.

185. The Judicial Councils Reform and Judicial Conduct and Disability Act of October 15, 1980, § 4, 94 Stat. 2040. The Act permits the judicial council of each circuit to investigate complaints that a federal judge or magistrate judge has engaged in "behavior prejudicial to the effective and expeditious administration of the business of the courts." 28 U.S.C. § 372(c)(1988). For discussion of the remedial options available and examples of disciplinary and corrective actions actually taken under the Act, see Marcus, *Who Should Discipline Federal Judges, and How?*, 149 F.R.D. 375, 378–89 (1993); Barr & Willing, *Decentralized Self–Regulation, Accountability, and Judicial Independence Under the Federal Judicial Conduct and Disability Act of 1980*, 142 U.Pa.L.Rev. 25 (1993); Geyh, *Informal Methods of Judicial Discipline*, 142 U.Pa.L.Rev. 243 (1993). For diverse views on the constitutionality of the Act, and of non-impeachment discipline of federal judges generally, compare Shane, *Who May Discipline or Remove Federal Judges? A Constitutional Analysis*, 142 U.Pa.L.Rev. 209 (1993)(arguing that judicial disciplining of federal judges is constitutionally permissible), and Note, 62 S.Cal.L.Rev. 1263 (1989)(same) with Note, 94 Yale L.J 1117 (1985)(arguing that the Act is unconstitutional).

The Code also provides (1) for annual judicial conferences of the district judges in each circuit to be summoned by the chief judge "for the purpose of considering the business of the courts and advising means of improving the administration of justice within such circuit,"[186] and (2) for the calling of a semi-annual Judicial Council in each circuit, composed of the chief judge of the circuit and a number of circuit and district judges. Each Judicial Council has been given authority with respect to judicial discipline under 28 U.S.C. § 372, as well as broad authority to "make all necessary and appropriate orders for the expeditious administration of justice within its circuit."[187]

At the head of the Administrative Office of the United States Courts is a Director, who is appointed and subject to removal by the Supreme Court,[188] but whose duties are discharged "under the supervision and direction of the Judicial Conference of the United States."[189] The Administrative Office assists the Judicial Conference in a number of ways, most notably in preparation of the annual budget for the judicial system, in the collection and reporting of judicial statistics, and in the conduct of a wide variety of housekeeping tasks.

The tremendous growth in federal judicial business in recent decades has been accompanied by a corresponding expansion of administrative requirements. In 1960, the Administrative Office had a budget of $1.2 million. By 1986, the figure had soared to $28.4 million. Since then, the growth has continued unabated, with the budget reaching $44.9 million in 1994.[190] (The total budget for the federal judicial branch went from $48.3 million in 1960 to $1.044 billion in 1986 to $2.7 billion in 1994. These figures exclude the budget and personnel of the Supreme Court.)[191]

In 1967 the judicial branch acquired a research arm through the creation of the Federal Judicial Center.[192] The Center, which is run by a Board (chaired by the Chief Justice)[193] and a Director,[194] has four purposes: to conduct and stimulate "research and study of the operation of the [federal] courts"; to present to the Judicial Conference recommendations for improvements in the administration and management of the federal courts; to develop and conduct programs of continuing education for judges and other court personnel; and to provide research, staff, and planning assistance to the Judicial Conference and its committees.[195]

---

186. 28 U.S.C. § 333.

187. *Id.* § 332. See generally 16 Wright, Miller, Cooper & Gressman, Federal Practice and Procedure § 3939 (1977 and 1995 Supp.).

188. 28 U.S.C. § 601.

189. *Id.* § 604. For a discussion of the Administrative Office, see Chief Justice Rehnquist, *1994 Year–End Report on the Federal Judiciary,* 18 Am.J.Trial Advoc. 499, 505–06 (1995). On some of the Office's contemporary challenges, see Reske, *Growing Judiciary Worries Administrator,* 81 A.B.A.J. 28 (May 1995).

190. 1994 Ad.Off.Rep.: Activities of the Administrative Office of the United States Courts 5.

191. Figures for 1960 are taken from Meador, *The Federal Judiciary and its Future Administration,* 65 Va.L.Rev. 1031, 1038–39 (1979). Figures for 1994 are derived from 1994 Ad.Off.Rep.: Activities of the Administrative Office of the United States Courts 6.

192. Act of Dec. 20, 1967, 81 Stat. 664, adding Chapter 42 (§§ 620–29) to the Judicial Code. See Clark, *The New Federal Judicial Center,* 54 A.B.A.J. 743 (1968).

193. 28 U.S.C. §§ 621–24.

194. *Id.* § 625.

195. *Id.* § 620.

The proposal of a Judicial Conference in 1933 aroused the objection that it would give legislative and political functions to the courts. Today, for better or worse, the principle has been accepted that "judging is also administration."[196]

Among the issues of recent concern to administration is the matter of possible race, gender, and other bias in various aspects of the federal judicial system. Several circuit courts of appeals have provided for studies,[197] which indicate serious problems requiring urgent attention.[198]

K.   Proposals for Change

Since the 1960s, there has been renewed interest in fundamental changes in the jurisdiction of the federal courts and in the structure of the federal court system. The main proposals can be broken into five categories, involving: (i)

196. Justice Burton, *"Judging Is Also Administration": An Appreciation of Constructive Leadership,* 33 A.B.A.J. 1099 (1947). See also Chief Justice Warren, *Administrative Problems of the Federal Judiciary,* 23 Bus.Lawyer 7 (1967); Posner, note 96, *supra,* at 97–98.

For a comprehensive history of the administration of the federal court system over the fifty year period following the creation of the Judicial Conference in 1922, see Fish, The Politics of Federal Judicial Administration (1973). See also Fish, *William Howard Taft and Charles Evans Hughes: Conservative Politicians as Chief Judicial Reformers,* 1975 Sup.Ct.Rev. 123.

For warnings concerning the hazards of increasing the administrative and managerial tasks that judges are required to perform, see Glendon, A Nation Under Lawyers: How the Crisis in the Legal Profession is Transforming American Society 130–51 (1994); Hoffman, *The Bureaucratic Spectre: Newest Challenge to the Courts,* 66 Judicature 66 (1982); Resnik, *Managerial Judges,* 96 Harv.L.Rev. 374 (1982); Rubin, *The Bureaucratization of the Federal Courts: The Tension Between Justice and Efficiency,* 55 Notre Dame L.Rev. 648 (1980).

197. See *The Effects of Gender in the Federal Courts: The Final Report of the Ninth Circuit Gender Bias Task Force,* 67 S.Cal.L.Rev. 745 (1994); Draft Final Report of the Special Committee on Gender to the D.C. Circuit Task Force on Gender, Race & Ethnic Bias (Jan. 1995)(available from the Office of the Circuit Executive D.C. Circuit). Several state courts instituted task forces to investigate gender and race bias somewhat earlier—the Supreme Court of New Jersey in 1982 and the Michigan Supreme Court in 1989.

198. The Ninth Circuit task force—through public hearings, survey distribution, a review of court decisions, and the collection of other statistical data—found evidence of gender discrimination in virtually every area it studied, including judicial decision making and the interactions of judges, lawyers, court personnel, litigants, and witnesses. See *The Effects of Gender Bias in the Federal Courts,* note 197, *supra.* Women also reported demeaning forms of address, derogatory comments regarding their physical appearance, and verbal and physical sexual harassment. A similar study concerning the District of Columbia Circuit included comparable findings. See Draft Final Report of the Special Committee on Gender to the D.C. Circuit Task Force on Gender, Race & Ethnic Bias note 197, *supra.* See also Jackson, *Empiricism, Gender, and Legal Pedagogy: An Experiment in a Federal Courts Seminar at Georgetown University Law Center,* 83 Geo. L.J. 461 (1994).

Other studies have found indications of possible racial disparities, especially concerning sentencing. See, *e.g.,* Meierhoefer, Federal Judicial Center, The General Effect of Mandatory Minimum Prison Terms 20 (1992); Weatherspoon, *The Devastating Impact of the Justice System on the Status of African-American Males: An Overview Perspective,* 23 Cap.U.L.Rev. 23, 40 (1994). But *cf.* McDonald & Carlson, Bureau of Justice Statistics, U.S. Dept. of Justice, Sentencing in the Federal Courts: Does Race Matter? The Transition to Sentencing Guidelines, 1986–1990, at 1 (1993) (asserting that "[n]early all of the aggregate differences * * * can be attributed to characteristics of offenses and offenders that current law and sentencing guidelines establish as legitimate considerations"—and especially to higher sentences for trafficking in crack cocaine than for trafficking in powder cocaine).

the appellate jurisdiction of the Supreme Court, (ii) the original jurisdiction of the district courts, (iii) the jurisdiction of the courts of appeals, (iv) specialized tribunals, and (v) the size of the Article III judiciary.

1. Supreme Court Appellate Jurisdiction

Over the past two decades, various proposals have departed from the premise that the Supreme Court's workload has grown too large for it to fulfill effectively its role in clarifying and developing federal law.[199] In 1972, a committee under the chairmanship of Professor Paul Freund proposed elimination of the Court's obligatory review jurisdiction and creation of a new National Court of Appeals.[200] Under this recommendation, the new court would have "screened" all petitions for certiorari from state and federal courts, and would have had final authority (a) to resolve certain inter-circuit conflicts on the merits and (b) to deny certiorari and preclude further review in all other cases. Cases thought potentially worthy of Supreme Court review (estimated at some 400–500 annually) would have been certified to that Court, which would have selected among them for full review on the merits. The Freund Committee's proposal met a predominantly critical response, with most critics protesting that the Court's control of its docket should not be reduced.[201]

Since the Freund Committee, the idea of a "screening" court has generated little enthusiasm, but proposals to develop a national court of appeals— subordinate to the Supreme Court, but with jurisdiction to review decisions of the existing circuit courts of appeals—have recurred. The National Commission on Revision of the Federal Appellate System (the Hruska Commission) offered one such recommendation in 1975.[202] Chief Justice Warren Burger urged another in 1982.[203] In both cases, however, opponents argued, *inter alia,*

199. For data on the Supreme Court's workload, see pp. 55–57, *supra.*

200. Report of the Study Group on the Caseload of the Supreme Court (Federal Judicial Center 1972).

201. See, *e.g.,* Warren, *Let's Not Weaken The Supreme Court,* 60 A.B.A.J. 677 (1974); Brennan, *The National Court of Appeals: Another Dissent,* 40 U.Chi.L.Rev. 473 (1973); Black, *The National Court of Appeals: An Unwise Proposal,* 83 Yale L.J. 883 (1974). For defense of the Committee's proposals by two of its members, see Bickel, The Caseload of the Supreme Court (1973); Freund, *Why We Need the National Court of Appeals,* 59 A.B.A.J. 247 (1973).

202. Commission on Revision of the Federal Court Appellate System, Structure and Internal Procedures: Recommendations for Change (1975)(reprinted in 67 F.R.D. 195 (1975)). Designed primarily to increase the capacity of the federal judicial system for definitive adjudication of issues of national law, the seven-member court proposed by the Hruska Commission was to have (a) jurisdiction to decide cases referred to it by the Supreme Court and (b) "transfer" jurisdic-

tion to decide cases submitted to it (before decision) by any of the regional courts of appeals. All of its decisions were to be subject to review by the Supreme Court on certiorari.

203. See Burger, *Annual Report on the State of the Judiciary,* 69 A.B.A.J. 442, 447 (1983). Chief Justice Burger proposed the creation of a special appellate panel, consisting of designated judges from each circuit, to "hear and decide all intercircuit conflicts and possibly, in addition, a defined category of statutory interpretation cases". Following this proposal, bills were introduced in each House to establish an Intercircuit Tribunal consisting of 26 judges, two from each circuit, which was to sit in panels of five to hear cases referred to it by the Supreme Court on vote of five Justices. The Tribunal's judgments were to be reviewable on certiorari by the Supreme Court but until modified or overruled were to be binding on all federal courts and, with respect to federal questions, on state courts. S.645, 98th Cong., 1st Sess. §§ 601–607 (1983); H.R. 1970, 98th Cong., 1st Sess. (1983). A similar bill was introduced in the 99th Congress (S. 704); after hearings, it was reported out with amend-

that the Supreme Court's caseload was not in a state of crisis; that much could be accomplished by more modest steps (such as eliminating the Court's obligatory jurisdiction) and by more discriminating selection of cases for review; and that the creation of a new court might unduly narrow the scope of the Supreme Court's own work and create new and contentious issues of docket management.[204] Neither Senator Hruska's nor Chief Justice Burger's proposals were adopted.

The idea of a national court of appeals recently resurfaced, albeit in more modest form, as part of a comprehensive package of reform proposals by the Federal Courts Study Committee, a committee appointed by the Chief Justice at the direction of Congress.[205] The Committee proposed a five-year pilot

ments by the Judiciary Committee but never came to the floor.

204. See, *e.g., Intercircuit Panel of the United States Act: Hearings on S. 704 Before the Subcomm. on Courts of the Senate Comm. on the Judiciary,* 99th Cong., 1st Sess. (1985), at 94–121 (statements of Judges Patricia Wald, Harry Edwards, and Ruth Ginsburg). See also Hellman, *The Proposed Intercircuit Tribunal: Do We Need It? Will It Work?,* 11 Hastings Const.L.Q. 375 (1984); Ginsburg & Huber, *The Intercircuit Committee,* 100 Harv. L.Rev. 1417, 1432 (1987)(proposing, instead of a new national court, a "new standing committee" of Congress, whose function would be "to examine court decisions construing federal statutes and to draft bills to resolve actual or potential conflicts"); Estreicher & Sexton, Redefining the Supreme Court's Role 111–15 (1986).

The book by Professor Estreicher and Dean Sexton was based on an in-depth study of the Supreme Court's work during the 1982 Term. The study itself, entitled the New York University Supreme Court Project, is reported in three issues of the New York University Law Review beginning at 59 N.Y.U.L.Rev. 677 (1984). Its conclusions were summarized at the 1985 Hearings in a statement submitted by Professor Estreicher and Dean Sexton in opposition to the proposed legislation. See *Hearings, supra,* at 163.

The opposition and ultimate failure notwithstanding, the Burger proposal, in particular, drew strong support from a number of practitioners, judges, and members of the academic community. See, *e.g., Hearings, supra,* at 151 (Prof. Meador), 229 (Erwin N. Griswold), 256 (Robert L. Stern). See also Baker & McFarland, *The Need for a New National Court,* 100 Harv.L.Rev. 1400 (1987); McCree, *To Preserve an Endangered Species,* 52 U.Cin.L.Rev. 248 (1983); Rehnquist, *The*

Changing Role of the Supreme Court, 14 Fla. St.U.L.Rev. 1 (1986).

205. Report of the Federal Courts Study Committee (1990). Congress authorized the Committee and its report in the Federal Courts Study Act, 102 Stat. 4644 (1988). Parts I and II of the Report are reprinted in 22 Conn.L.Rev. 733 (1990). Part III consists of a set of papers underlying the analysis and recommendations in Parts I and II. A number of these papers also furnished the basis for a Federal Courts Symposium in 1990 Brigham Young L.Rev. No. 1.

The Report was submitted to Congress in 1990, and in that year, as part of the Judicial Improvements Act of 1990, 104 Stat. 5089, Congress enacted what the House Report described as "several of the more noncontroversial recommendations." H.R.Rep. No. 101–734, 101st Cong.2d Sess. 15 (1990). A number of those provisions are discussed elsewhere in this book. Some of the Committee's major proposals for changes in jurisdiction are still under consideration, and in § 302 of the 1990 Act, 104 Stat. 5104, the Federal Judicial Center was asked to conduct a study of intercircuit conflicts and to report back within two years. The report concluded that structural change would be unlikely to provide significant relief for the stresses posed by continuing expansion of federal jurisdiction without concomitant increases in judicial resources. See Federal Judicial Center, Structural and Other Alternatives For the Federal Courts of Appeals: Report to the United States Congress and the Judicial Conference of the United States (hereinafter cited as "Judicial Center Report")(1993).

Expressly not recommended by the Federal Courts Study Committee were the creation of either a national administrative appellate court or a new federal intermediate appellate court for resolving intercircuit conflicts (pp. 116–17).

project authorizing the Supreme Court to refer intercircuit conflicts to a court of appeals for an en banc, nationally binding decision. Report of the Federal Courts Study Committee 125–29 (1990). So far, Congress has not acted on this proposal.

2. Original Jurisdiction of the District Courts

A comprehensive American Law Institute Study, completed in 1969, made a number of proposals with respect to the jurisdiction of the district courts.[206] Included among these proposals was one substantially curtailing the diversity jurisdiction. The ALI proposal generated much discussion but no congressional action.[207]

Two more recent reports have offered reform proposals aimed predominantly at relieving mounting pressures on federal dockets.[208] The Report of the Federal Courts Study Committee called, *inter alia,* for (1) substantial reduction of the diversity jurisdiction (pp. 38–43), (2) vesting of nearly exclusive tax jurisdiction in the Article I Tax Court (coupled with the creation of an Article III appellate division of that court)(pp. 69–72), (3) creation of a new Article I Court of Disability Claims (pp. 55–59), and (4) reliance on non-judicial, or at least non-Article III, fora for resolving some disputes (pp. 55–66, 74–81). The Report also recommended (5) expansion of pendent and ancillary jurisdiction (pp. 47–48).

More recently, a committee of nine federal judges, commissioned by the Judicial Conference of the United States, has issued a report that also calls for sharp reductions in the diversity jurisdiction. See Committee on Long Range Planning of the Judicial Conference of the United States, Proposed Long Range Plan for the Federal Courts 29–32 (1995). In addition, the judges' committee suggests that not all federal civil statutes necessarily merit enforcement in a federal forum (pp. 27–29), and it proposes statutory changes to permit the filing of some federal criminal actions in state court (pp. 26–27). A more equivocal recommendation calls on Congress to "consider" authorizing federal judges to make discretionary judgments "in individual cases as to whether a particular case should be pursued in federal court or in state court" (p. 37). Responding to an earlier draft Long Range Planning Committee's report, one state judge protested that it would be unfair and ultimately dysfunctional to deal with overcrowded federal dockets by dumping cases into the equally overburdened state courts. See Kaye, *Federalism Gone Wild,* New York Times, Dec. 13, 1994,

For further comment on the Committee and its work, see, *e.g.,* Symposium, *The Federal Court Docket: Issues and Solutions,* 22 Conn.L.Rev. 615 (1990); Brown, *Nonideological Judicial Reform and Its Limits—The Report of the Federal Courts Study Committee,* 47 Wash. & Lee L. Rev. 973 (1990); Slate, *Report of the Federal Courts Study Committee: An Update,* 21 Seton Hall L.Rev. 336 (1991); Sporkin, *Reforming the Federal Judiciary,* 46 S.M.U.L.Rev. 751 (1992).

206. American Law Institute, Study of the Division of Jurisdiction Between State and Federal Courts (1969).

207. For appraisals, see Wright, *Restructuring Federal Jurisdiction: The Ameri-*can Law Institute Proposals, 26 Wash. & Lee L.Rev. 185 (1969); Currie, *The Federal Courts and The American Law Institute,* 36 U.Chi.L.Rev. I, 268 (1968–69).

208. For statistics on the district courts' caseload and its growth, see Part I(1), pp. 47-52, *supra.* For skeptical appraisals of the claims concerning the existence of a caseload crisis, see Galanter, *The Day After the Litigation Explosion,* 46 Md.L.Rev. 1 (1986); Mullenix, *Discovery and Disarray: The Pervasive Myth of Discovery Abuse and the Consequences for Unfounded Rulemaking,* 46 Stan.L.Rev. 1393 (1994).

p. A29. The final report proposes that "federal financial assistance should be provided to state justice systems to permit them to handle the increased workload that would result from the reduction or elimination of existing federal court jurisdiction" (p. 37).[209]

Factors that do and ought to bear on the allocation of original jurisdiction among state and federal courts are discussed repeatedly throughout this book. On the diversity jurisdiction, see especially Chapter XIII; on jurisdiction of cases arising under federal law, see especially Chap. IV, Sec. 3, and Chap. VIII.

3. Jurisdiction of the Courts of Appeals

Anxiety that a swelling caseload[210] threatens to overwhelm the courts of appeals has also spawned proposals to reform their jurisdiction or structure, though it is often assumed that reforms reducing the docket of the district courts would also alleviate pressures on the courts of appeals. The Federal Courts Study Committee termed abolition of appeal-as-of-right, and substitution of a certiorari-like jurisdiction, "a last resort".[211] By contrast, in 1993 the Federal Judicial Center prepared a report to the United States Congress and the Judicial Conference[212] including as alternative proposals creation of a writ system at the appeals court level (p. 123)[213] and what it described as a "two-track" appellate review structure. Under the latter proposal, parties would submit 15–page briefs at the Track One stage, and many cases would be disposed of on summary review at this point. Cases recommended for Track Two review would receive further briefing and oral argument (p. 128).

Other proposals, often but not invariably linked to problems of docket size, have included structural reforms that would, for example, (i) abandon or modify the present, geographically based definition of circuits, (ii) utilize intermediate appellate courts subordinate to the Supreme Court as a device for nationalizing precedential authority and thus promoting uniformity,[214] and/or

209. For discussion of the possibility that financial assistance might also be required under the Unfunded Mandate Reform Act of 1995, see Chap. IV, Sec. 3, pp. 478–79, *infra.*

210. On the caseload of the courts of appeals, see pp. 53–55, *supra.* See generally Gizzi, *Examining the Crisis of Volume in the Courts of Appeals,* 77 Judicature 96 (1993).

211. Study Committee Report, note 205, *supra,* at 116. See also Dalton, *Taking the Right to Appeal (More or Less) Seriously,* 95 Yale L.J. 62, 107 (1985)(advocating a "partial" certiorari system). The Federal Courts Study Committee called for further study of "[f]undamental structural alternatives" and listed, "[w]ithout endorsing", a diverse set of proposals (pp. 118–23).

212. Judicial Center Report, note 205, *supra.*

213. See also Clark, *Mules and Wagons—A Plea for Jurisdictional Reform,* 14 Miss.Coll.L.Rev. 263, 269 (1994)(noting that appeals as of right "are not a part of constitutional due process" and recommending

adoption of a discretionary system of appeals).

214. The Judicial Center Report, note 205, *supra,* advanced several, alternative proposals of these kinds as meriting consideration. These included creation of a single, consolidated court of appeals with judges assigned to move around the country to where they are needed (pp. 108–09); creation of 5 "mega" circuits within which judges would move around as needed (pp. 110–11); and adoption of a unified appeals court with one central division and many regional divisions of nine judges each, with appeal as of right to the regional divisions and possible discretionary review by the central divisions (p. 118). See also Weiss, *Disconnecting the Overloaded Circuits,* 39 St.L.U.L.Rev. 455 (1995)(proposing a unified court of appeals, divided into nine-judge divisions, with draft panel decisions subject to review by the other six judges within the division before they issue). On the more skeptical view of the Federal Courts Study Committee, and its much more limited

(iii) rely much more heavily on specialized appellate tribunals. For a critical survey and valuable bibliography, see Baker, *Imagining the Alternative Futures of the U.S. Courts of Appeals,* 28 Ga.L.Rev. 913 (1994).

4. Specialized Tribunals

Both the Federal Courts Study Committee and the Judicial Conference's recent long range planning report resisted what once had appeared to be gathering momentum in favor of specialized tribunals—though the Federal Courts Study Committee was willing to make exceptions for an Article I Court of Disability Claims, tax courts, and some alternative dispute resolution tribunals.[215] Specialized tribunals offer obvious advantages of expertise, efficiency, and enhanced likelihood of uniformity. On the other hand, specialization may reduce a court's prestige and deprive it of a valuable, generalist perspective. Judge Posner, a member of the Federal Courts Study Committee, is among those who have raised additional concerns: (i) even within legal specialties (including fields as diverse as patents and constitutional law), there is frequently division, which is rooted much more in ideology than in genuine expertise; (ii) these ideological cleavages would invite unhealthy efforts by the political branches to pack specialized courts with ideological judges; and (iii) specialized appeals courts could lack exposure to the range of issues conducive to a valuable cross-fertilization among different fields of law. See Posner, note 96, *supra,* at 147–60. For a direct rejoinder, see Bator, *The Judicial Universe of Judge Posner* (Book Review), 52 U.Chi.L.Rev. 1146, 1154–56 (1985)(advocating "increase[d] specialization at the court of appeals level" and arguing that specialization would "attract more real lawyers and fewer pseudo-politicians to the bench" and would subject them to the "kind of intellectual discipline that comes from having to demonstrate detailed substantive mastery over a field").[216]

5. The Size of the Article III Judiciary

One seemingly obvious solution to the problem of swelling federal caseloads—that of substantially increasing the number of federal judges—is viewed with distaste by the Committee on Long Range Planning of the Judicial Conference and was rejected in strong terms by the Federal Courts Study Committee. The Federal Courts Study Committee concluded (p. 7): "The independence secured to federal judges by Article III is compatible with responsible and efficient performance of judicial duties only if federal judges are carefully selected from a pool of competent and eager applicants and only if they are sufficiently few in number to feel a personal stake in the consequences of their actions." Were the judiciary greatly enlarged, "[t]he process of presidential nomination and senatorial confirmation would become pro forma * * *, [and] a sufficient

recommendations, see pp. 62–63 & n. 205, *supra.*

215. See p. 63, *supra.*

216. Other recent commentary on specialized courts and their advantages and drawbacks includes Bruff, *Specialized Courts in Administrative Law,* 43 Admin. L. Rev. 329 (1991); Dreyfuss, *Specialized Adjudication,* 1990 B.Y.U.L.Rev. 377; Dreyfuss, note 105, *supra*; Geier, note 119, *supra*; Revesz, *Specialized Courts and the Administrative Lawmaking System,* 138 U.Pa.L.Rev. 1111

(1990); and Stempel, *Two Cheers for Specialization,* 61 Brooklyn L.Rev. 67 (1995). To date, most specialized courts have been Article I courts. To what extent might the problems be alleviated if specialized courts were constituted under Article III? For discussion, see Meltzer, *Legislative Courts, Legislative Power, and the Constitution,* 65 Ind.L.J. 291, 294–95. On the experience with and prospects for specialized *state* courts, see Dreyfuss, *Forums of the Future: The Role of Specialized Courts in Resolving Business Disputes,* 61 Brooklyn L.Rev. 1 (1995).

number of highly qualified applicants could not be found unless the salaries of federal judges were greatly increased * * *." Moreover, in the Committee's view an expanded federal bench would increase the difficulties of coordination: more district judges generate more appeals; the more appeals, the more difficulty in maintaining uniformity both within and among the circuits. The Report posited that the total number of judgeships (then at 750) should not exceed 1000—a view shared by Judge Newman, among others. See Newman, *1,000 Judges—The Limit for an Effective Federal Judiciary,* 76 Judicature 187 (1993).

Contrasting perspectives are provided by Wells, *Against an Elite Federal Judiciary: Comments on the Report of the Federal Courts Study Committee,* 1991 B.Y.U.L.Rev. 923; Resnik, *The Mythic Meaning of Article III Courts,* 56 Colo.L.Rev. 581 (1985); Reinhardt, *Whose Federal Judiciary Is It Anyway?,* 27 Loy.L.A.L.Rev. 1 (1993); and Arnold, *The Future of the Federal Courts,* 60 Mo.L.Rev. 533 (1995). Directing his fire at the Report of the Federal Courts Study Committee, Professor Wells argues that the quality of judges would not necessarily be diluted if more were appointed and, in any event, that the Committee gave too little weight to the advantages of Article III courts, particularly their possibly greater receptivity to claims of federal right than other fora that might adjudicate such claims.

For further discussion of issues relating to the optimal size of the Article III judiciary, especially in light of the alternative of reliance on non-Article III federal tribunals and adjuncts, see Chap. IV, Sec. 2, *infra.*

CHAPTER II

The Nature of the Federal Judicial Function: Cases and Controversies

SECTION 1. GENERAL CONSIDERATIONS

Marbury v. Madison

5 U.S. (1 Cranch) 137, 2 L.Ed. 60 (1803).
On Petition for Mandamus.

■ * * * [T]he following opinion of the Court was delivered by the CHIEF JUSTICE:

Opinion of the Court. At the last term on the affidavits then read and filed with the clerk, a rule was granted in this case, requiring the secretary of state to show cause why a *mandamus* should not issue, directing him to deliver to William Marbury his commission as a justice of the peace for the county of Washington, in the district of Columbia.

No cause has been shown, and the present motion is for a *mandamus*. The peculiar delicacy of this case, the novelty of some of its circumstances, and the real difficulty attending the points which occur in it, require a complete exposition of the principles on which the opinion to be given by the court is founded.

* * *

In the order in which the court has viewed this subject, the following questions have been considered and decided.

1st. Has the applicant a right to the commission he demands?

2d. If he has a right, and that right has been violated, do the laws of his country afford him a remedy?

3d. If they do afford him a remedy, is it a *mandamus* issuing from this court?

* * * [The Court here addressed the first question and concluded that the withholding of the commission was "violative of a vested legal right."]

This brings us to the second enquiry; which is,

2dly. If he has a right, and the right has been violated, do the laws of the country afford him a remedy?

The very essence of civil liberty consists in the right of every individual to claim the protection of the laws, whenever he receives an injury. One of the first duties of government is to afford that protection. In Great Britain the king himself is sued in the respectful form of a petition, and he never fails to comply with the judgment of his court.

* * *

The government of the United States has been emphatically termed a government of laws and not of men. It will certainly cease to deserve this high appellation, if the laws furnish no remedy for the violation of a vested legal right.

[The Court next found that Marbury's case was not "one of *damnum absque injuria*; a loss without an injury."]

* * * Is the act of delivering or withholding a commission to be considered a mere political act, belonging to the executive department alone, for the performance of which, entire confidence is placed by our constitution in the supreme executive; and for any misconduct concerning which the injured individual has no remedy.

That there be such cases is not to be questioned; but that every act of duty, to be performed in any of the great departments of government, constitutes such a case, is not to be admitted.

* * *

* * * [T]he question, whether the legality of an act of the head of a department be examinable in a court of justice or not, must always depend on the nature of that act * * *.

By the Constitution of the United States, the President is invested with certain important political powers, in the exercise of which he is to use his own discretion, and is accountable only to his country in his political character, and to his conscience. To aid him in the performance of these duties, he is authorized to appoint certain officers, who act by his authority and in conformity with his orders.

In such cases, their acts are his acts; and whatever opinion may be entertained of the manner in which executive discretion may be used, still there exists, and can exist, no power to control that discretion. The subjects are political: they respect the nation, not individual rights, and being entrusted to the executive, the decision of the executive is conclusive. * * *

But when the legislature proceeds to impose on that officer other duties; when he is directed peremptorily to perform certain acts; when the rights of individuals are dependent on the performance of those acts; he is so far the officer of the law; is amenable to the laws for his conduct; and cannot at his discretion sport away the vested rights of others.

The conclusion from this reasoning is that, where the heads of departments are the political or confidential agents of the executive, merely to execute the will of the President, or rather to act in cases in which the executive possesses a constitutional or legal discretion, nothing can be more perfectly clear than that their acts are only politically examinable. But where a specific duty is assigned by law, and individual rights depend upon the performance of that duty, it seems equally clear that the individual who considers himself injured, has the right to resort to the laws of his country for a remedy.

* * *

[Mr. Marbury's right having been established,] it remains to be inquired whether,

 3d. He is entitled to the remedy for which he applies. This depends on,

 1st. The nature of the writ applied for; and,

 2d. The power of this court.

 1st. The nature of the writ.

  * * *

[T]o render the *mandamus* a proper remedy, the officer to whom it is to be directed, must be one to whom, on legal principles, such writ may be directed; and the person applying for it must be without any other specific and legal remedy.

 1st. With respect to the officer to whom it would be directed. The intimate political relation subsisting between the president of the United States and the heads of departments, necessarily renders any legal investigation of the acts of one of those high officers peculiarly irksome, as well as delicate; and excites some hesitation with respect to the propriety of entering into such investigation. Impressions are often received without much reflection or examination and it is not wonderful that in such a case as this the assertion, by an individual, of his legal claims in a court of justice, to which claims it is the duty of that court to attend, should at first view be considered by some, as an attempt to intrude into the cabinet, and to intermeddle with the prerogatives of the executive.

 It is scarcely necessary for the court to disclaim all pretensions to such a jurisdiction. An extravagance, so absurd and excessive, could not have been entertained for a moment. The province of the court is, solely, to decide on the rights of individuals, not to inquire how the executive, or executive officers, perform duties in which they have a discretion. Questions in their nature political, or which are, by the constitution and laws, submitted to the executive, can never be made in this court.

 But, if this be not such a question; if, so far from being an intrusion into the secrets of the cabinet, it respects a paper which, according to law, is upon record, and to a copy of which the law gives a right, on the payment of ten cents; if it be no intermeddling with a subject over which the executive can be considered as having exercised any control; what is there in the exalted station of the officer, which shall bar a citizen from asserting, in a court of justice, his legal rights, or shall forbid a court to listen to the claim, or to issue a *mandamus*, directing the performance of a duty, not depending on executive discretion, but on particular acts of congress, and the general principles of law?

 If one of the heads of departments commits any illegal act, under colour of his office, by which an individual sustains an injury, it cannot be pretended that his office alone exempts him from being sued in the ordinary mode of proceeding, and being compelled to obey the judgment of the law. How, then, can his office exempt him from this particular mode of deciding on the legality of his conduct, if the case be such a case as would, were any other individual the party complained of, authorize the process?

 It is not by the office of the person to whom the writ is directed, but the nature of the thing to be done, that the propriety or impropriety of issuing a *mandamus* is to be determined. Where the head of a department acts in a case, in which executive discretion is to be exercised; in which he is the mere organ of executive will; it is again repeated, that any application to a court to control, in any respect, his conduct would be rejected without hesitation.

But where he is directed by law to do a certain act affecting the absolute rights of individuals, in the performance of which he is not placed under the particular direction of the president, and the performance of which the president cannot lawfully forbid, and therefore is never presumed to have forbidden; as for example, to record a commission, or a patent for land, which has received all the legal solemnities; or to give a copy of such record; in such cases, it is not perceived on what ground the courts of the country are further excused from the duty of giving judgment that right be done to an injured individual, than if the same services were to be performed by a person not the head of a department. * * *

This, then, is a plain case for a *mandamus*, either to deliver the commission, or a copy of it from the record; and it only remains to be inquired,

Whether it can issue from this court.

The act to establish the judicial courts of the United States authorizes the supreme court, "to issue writs of *mandamus*, in cases warranted by the principles and usages of law, to any courts appointed or persons holding office, under the authority of the United States."

The secretary of state being a person holding an office under the authority of the United States, is precisely within the letter of the description; and if this court is not authorized to issue a writ of *mandamus* to such an officer, it must be because the law is unconstitutional, and therefore, absolutely incapable of conferring the authority, and assigning the duties which its words purport to confer and assign.

The constitution vests the whole judicial power of the United States in one supreme court, and such inferior courts as congress shall, from time to time, ordain and establish. This power is expressly extended to all cases arising under the laws of the United States; and, consequently, in some form, may be exercised over the present case; because the right claimed is given by a law of the United States.

In the distribution of this power it is declared, that "the supreme court shall have original jurisdiction in all cases affecting ambassadors, other public ministers and consuls, and those in which a state shall be a party. In all other cases, the supreme court shall have appellate jurisdiction."

It has been insisted, at the bar, that as the original grant of jurisdiction, to the supreme and inferior courts, is general, and the clause, assigning original jurisdiction to the supreme court, contains no negative or restrictive words, the power remains to the legislature, to assign original jurisdiction to that court in other cases than those specified in the article which has been recited; provided those cases belong to the judicial power of the United States.

If it had been intended to leave it in the discretion of the legislature to apportion the judicial power between the supreme and inferior courts according to the will of that body, it would certainly have been useless to have proceeded further than to have defined the judicial power, and the tribunals in which it should be vested. The subsequent part of the section is mere surplusage, is entirely without meaning, if such is to be the construction. If congress remains at liberty to give this court appellate jurisdiction where the constitution has declared their jurisdiction shall be original; and original jurisdiction where the constitution has declared it shall be appellate; the distribution of jurisdiction, made in the constitution, is form without substance.

Affirmative words are often, in their operation, negative of other objects than those affirmed; and in this case, a negative or exclusive sense must be given to them, or they have no operation at all.

It cannot be presumed that any clause in the constitution is intended to be without effect; and therefore, such a construction is inadmissible, unless the words require it.

If the solicitude of the convention, respecting our peace with foreign powers, induced a provision that the supreme court should take original jurisdiction in cases which might be supposed to affect them; yet the clause would have proceeded no further than to provide for such cases, if no further restriction on the powers of congress had been intended. That they should have appellate jurisdiction in all other cases, with such exceptions as congress might make, is no restriction; unless the words be deemed exclusive of original jurisdiction.

When an instrument organizing fundamentally a judicial system, divides it into one supreme, and so many inferior courts as the legislature may ordain and establish; then enumerates its powers, and proceeds so far to distribute them, as to define the jurisdiction of the supreme court, by declaring the cases in which it shall take original jurisdiction, and that in others it shall take appellate jurisdiction; the plain import of the words seems to be, that in one class of cases its jurisdiction is original, and not appellate; in the other it is appellate, and not original. If any other construction would render the clause inoperative, that is an additional reason for rejecting such other construction, and for adhering to their obvious meaning.

To enable this court, then, to issue a *mandamus*, it must be shown to be an exercise of appellate jurisdiction, or to be necessary to enable them to exercise appellate jurisdiction.

     * * *

It is the essential criterion of appellate jurisdiction, that it revises and corrects the proceedings in a cause already instituted, and does not create that cause. Although, therefore, a *mandamus* may be directed to courts, yet to issue such a writ to an officer for the delivery of a paper, is in effect the same as to sustain an original action for that paper, and, therefore, seems not to belong to appellate, but to original jurisdiction. Neither is it necessary in such a case as this, to enable the court to exercise its appellate jurisdiction.

The authority, therefore, given to the supreme court by the act establishing the judicial courts of the United States, to issue writs of *mandamus* to public officers, appears not to be warranted by the constitution; and it becomes necessary to inquire whether a jurisdiction so conferred can be exercised.

The question, whether an act, repugnant to the constitution, can become the law of the land, is a question deeply interesting to the United States; but, happily, not of an intricacy proportioned to its interest. It seems only necessary to recognize certain principles, supposed to have been long and well established, to decide it.

That the people have an original right to establish, for their future government, such principles, as in their opinion, shall most conduce to their own happiness is the basis on which the whole American fabric has been erected. The exercise of this original right is a very great exertion; nor can it, nor ought it, to be frequently repeated. The principles, therefore, so established, are deemed fundamental. And as the authority from which they proceed is supreme, and can seldom act, they are designed to be permanent.

This original and supreme will organizes the government, and assigns to different departments their respective powers. It may either stop here, or establish certain limits not to be transcended by those departments.

The government of the United States is of the latter description. The powers of the legislature are defined and limited; and that those limits may not be mistaken, or forgotten, the constitution is written. To what purpose are powers limited, and to what purpose is that limitation committed to writing, if these limits may, at any time, be passed by those intended to be restrained? The distinction between a government with limited and unlimited powers is abolished, if those limits do not confine the persons on whom they are imposed, and if acts prohibited and acts allowed, are of equal obligation. It is a proposition too plain to be contested, that the constitution controls any legislative act repugnant to it; or, that the legislature may alter the constitution by an ordinary act.

Between these alternatives, there is no middle ground. The constitution is either a superior paramount law, unchangeable by ordinary means, or it is on a level with ordinary legislative acts, and, like other acts, is alterable when the legislature shall please to alter it.

If the former part of the alternative be true, then a legislative act, contrary to the constitution, is not law: if the latter part be true, then written constitutions are absurd attempts, on the part of the people, to limit a power in its own nature, illimitable.

Certainly all those who have framed written constitutions contemplate them as forming the fundamental and paramount law of the nation, and, consequently, the theory of every such government must be, that an act of the legislature, repugnant to the constitution, is void.

This theory is essentially attached to a written constitution, and is consequently, to be considered, by this court, as one of the fundamental principles of our society. It is not therefore to be lost sight of, in the further consideration of this subject.

If an act of the legislature, repugnant to the constitution, is void, does it, notwithstanding its invalidity, bind the courts, and oblige them to give it effect? Or, in other words, though it be not law, does it constitute a rule as operative as if it was a law? This would be to overthrow in fact what was established in theory; and would seem, at first view, an absurdity too gross to be insisted on. It shall, however, receive a more attentive consideration.

It is emphatically the province and duty of the judicial department to say what the law is. Those who apply the rule to particular cases, must of necessity expound and interpret that rule. If two laws conflict with each other, the courts must decide on the operation of each.

So, if a law be in opposition to the constitution; if both the law and the constitution apply to a particular case, so that the court must either decide that case conformably to the law, disregarding the constitution; or conformably to the constitution, disregarding the law; the court must determine which of these conflicting rules governs the case. This is of the very essence of judicial duty.

If then, the courts are to regard the constitution, and the constitution is superior to any ordinary act of the legislature, the constitution, and not such ordinary act, must govern the case to which they both apply.

Those, then, who controvert the principle that the constitution is to be considered, in court, as a paramount law, are reduced to the necessity of maintaining that courts must close their eyes on the constitution, and see only the law. This doctrine would subvert the very foundation of all written constitutions. It would declare that an act which, according to the principles and theory of our government, is entirely void, is yet, in practice, completely obligatory. It would declare that if the legislature shall do what is expressly forbidden, such act, notwithstanding the express prohibition, is in reality effectual. It would be giving to the legislature a practical and real omnipotence, with the same breath which professes to restrict their powers within narrow limits. It is prescribing limits, and declaring that those limits may be passed at pleasure.

That it thus reduces to nothing, what we have deemed the greatest improvement on political institutions, a written constitution, would of itself be sufficient, in America, where written constitutions have been viewed with so much reverence, for rejecting the construction. But the peculiar expressions of the constitution of the United States furnish additional arguments in favour of its rejection.

The judicial power of the United States is extended to all cases arising under the constitution.

Could it be the intention of those who gave this power, to say that in using it the constitution should not be looked into? That a case arising under the constitution should be decided, without examining the instrument under which it arises?

This is too extravagant to be maintained.

In some cases, then, the constitution must be looked into by the judges. And if they can open it at all, what part of it are they forbidden to read or to obey?

There are many other parts of the constitution which serve to illustrate this subject.

It is declared, that "no tax or duty shall be laid on articles exported from any state." Suppose, a duty on the export of cotton, of tobacco, or of flour; and a suit instituted to recover it. Ought judgment to be rendered in such a case? ought the judges to close their eyes on the constitution, and only see the law?

The constitution declares "that no bill of attainder or *ex post facto* law shall be passed."

If, however, such a bill should be passed, and a person should be prosecuted under it; must the court condemn to death those victims whom the constitution endeavors to preserve?

"No person," says the constitution, "shall be convicted of treason unless on the testimony of two witnesses to the same overt act, or on confession in open court."

Here the language of the constitution is addressed especially to the courts. It prescribes, directly for them, a rule of evidence not to be departed from. If the legislature should change that rule, and declare *one* witness, or a confession *out* of court, sufficient for conviction, must the constitutional principle yield to the legislative act?

From these, and many other selections which might be made, it is apparent, that the framers of the constitution contemplated that instrument as a rule for the government of courts, as well as of the legislature.

Why otherwise does it direct the judges to take an oath to support it? This oath certainly applies in an especial manner, to their conduct in their official character. How immoral to impose it on them, if they were to be used as the instruments, and the knowing instruments, for violating what they swear to support!

The oath of office, too, imposed by the legislature, is completely demonstrative of the legislative opinion on this subject. It is in these words: "I do solemnly swear that I will administer justice without respect to persons, and do equal right to the poor and to the rich; and that I will faithfully and impartially discharge all the duties incumbent on me as _____, according to the best of my abilities and understanding, agreeably to the *constitution* and laws of the United States."

Why does a judge swear to discharge his duties agreeably to the constitution of the United States, if that constitution forms no rule for his government? if it is closed upon him, and cannot be inspected by him?

If such be the real state of things, this is worse than solemn mockery. To prescribe, or to take this oath, becomes equally a crime.

It is also not entirely unworthy of observation, that in declaring what shall be the *supreme* law of the land, the *constitution* itself is first mentioned; and not the laws of the United States, generally, but those only which shall be made in *pursuance* of the constitution, have that rank.

Thus, the particular phraseology of the constitution of the United States confirms and strengthens the principle, supposed to be essential to all written constitutions, that a law repugnant to the constitution is void; and that *courts*, as well as other departments, are bound by that instrument.

The rule must be discharged.

NOTE ON MARBURY v. MADISON

(1) *Historical Background.*[1] Control of the national government passed from Federalist to Republican hands for the first time in the national elections of 1800. The lines of political division were sharp. The Federalists generally favored a strong national government, a sound currency, and domestic and

1. For a comprehensive analysis of Marshall's opinion and a bibliography of major writings on the principles of the case, see Van Alstyne, *A Critical Guide to Marbury v. Madison*, 1969 Duke L.J. 1 (1969). A more sharply critical review is Haggard, *Marbury v. Madison: A Concurring/Dissenting Opinion*, 10 J. Law & Pol. 543 (1994). For more historical background, see Haskins & Johnson, 2 The Oliver Wendell Holmes Devise History of the Supreme Court of the United States: Foundations of Power: John Marshall, 1801–15 (1981); Robert McCloskey, The American Supreme Court 36–44 (1960).

foreign policies promoting mercantile interests. The Republicans, by contrast, were the party of states' rights and political and economic democracy.

Before the Republican Thomas Jefferson assumed office as President, the outgoing Federalists took a variety of measures to preserve their party's influence through the life-tenured federal judiciary. First, President John Adams appointed his Secretary of State, John Marshall, as Chief Justice of the United States, and the Senate quickly confirmed him. Marshall, while continuing to serve as Secretary of State, took office as Chief Justice on February 4, 1801. Second, a new Circuit Court Act of February 13, 1801, relieved Supreme Court Justices of their circuit-riding duties and created sixteen new circuit court judgeships. With only two weeks remaining in his term, Adams hurried to nominate Federalists to the newly created positions, and the Senate confirmed the "midnight judges" with equal alacrity. Finally, on February 27, Congress enacted legislation authorizing the President to appoint justices of the peace for the District of Columbia. Adams nominated forty-two justices on March 2, and the Senate confirmed them on March 3, the day before the conclusion of Adams' term. Adams signed the commissions, and John Marshall, as Secretary of State, affixed the great seal of the United States. Nonetheless, some of the commissions, including that of William Marbury, were not delivered before Adams' term expired, and the new President refused to honor those appointments.

While Marbury's suit was pending in the Supreme Court, the newly installed Republicans worked on a number of fronts to frustrate the outgoing Federalists' designs for the federal judiciary. Congress repealed the Circuit Court Act of 1801 and abolished the sixteen judgeships that it had created. By statute, Congress also abolished the Supreme Court's previously scheduled June and December Terms and provided that there be only one Term, in February. As a result, the Supreme Court did not meet at all in 1802. Having received Marbury's petition in December 1801, it could not hear his case until February 1803. Even more menacingly, the Jeffersonians embarked on a program of judicial impeachments. The House voted articles of impeachment against the Federalist district judge John Pickering of New Hampshire, an apparently insane drunkard, early in 1802. On the day after Pickering's conviction by the Senate in March 1804, the House impeached Supreme Court Justice Samuel Chase. The case against Chase failed in the Senate. Had it succeeded, the impeachment of John Marshall was widely expected to follow.

In this charged political climate, it seems doubtful, at least, that James Madison, Thomas Jefferson's Secretary of State, would have obeyed a judicial order to deliver Marbury's commission as a justice of the peace. Might this consideration have influenced Marshall's decision of the case?[2] Should it have?

---

2. O'Fallon, *Marbury,* 44 Stan.L.Rev. 219 (1992), asserts that conventional understandings of Marbury have not sufficiently emphasized the political context in which the case arose. He views Chief Justice Marshall as using the case to protect the Federalist judiciary, especially its capacity to resist the threats to property and other established rights that the Federalists believed were posed by the new Republican administration. For the contrary view that Marshall's opinion was essentially innocent of political motivation, see Clinton, Marbury v. Madison and Judicial Review 79–138 (1989). In a recent review of revisionist assessments of Marbury, Dean Alfange emphasizes that Marshall and the Supreme Court, in their decision the week after Marbury in Stuart v. Laird, 5 U.S. (1 Cranch) 299 (1803), declined to face the question of the constitutionality of the Repeal Act of 1802, which abolished the sixteen circuit court judgeships created by the Circuit

In light of his involvement in the events leading up to the case, should Marshall have recused himself?

(2) *A Political Masterstroke?* The Marbury opinion is widely regarded as a political masterstroke by John Marshall. Marshall seized the occasion to uphold the institution of judicial review, but he did so in the course of reaching a judgment that his political opponents could neither defy nor protest.

Is it ironic if Marbury, which authorizes the courts to hold some issues outside the bounds of permissible political decisionmaking, was itself a political decision?[3] Does the answer depend on sorting out various possible senses of "political" and determining in which sense, if any, Marbury should be so characterized?[4]

(3) *Marbury's Jurisdictional Holdings.* Marbury ultimately holds that the Supreme Court lacks jurisdiction to decide the case before it. Why didn't Marshall decide the jurisdictional question first?

The jurisdictional analysis proceeds in two steps. First, Marshall holds that section 13 of the 1789 Judiciary Act confers original Supreme Court jurisdiction in actions for mandamus. Is this holding necessary? Plausible? See Amar, *Marbury, Section 13, and the Original Jurisdiction of the Supreme Court*, 56 U.Chi.L.Rev. 443, 456 (1989)(arguing that "the mandamus clause is best read as simply giving the Court remedial authority—for both original and appellate cases after jurisdiction * * * has been independently established"). See also Van Alstyne, *supra* note 1, at 15. Should the Court have adopted Amar's construction under the principle favoring interpretations that render statutes constitutional?

Second, Marshall finds that the second paragraph of Article III, § 2 restricts the permissible scope of the Supreme Court's original jurisdiction to cases "affecting Ambassadors, other public Ministers and Consuls, and those in which a State shall be a Party." Is this the best interpretation? According to Van Alstyne, *supra* note 1, at 31, this clause "readily supports the interpretation that the Court's original jurisdiction may not be *reduced* by Congress, but that it may be supplemented". For further discussion of the Supreme Court's original jurisdiction, see Chap. III, Sec. 3, *infra*.

(4) *Marbury's Arguments for Judicial Review.* What arguments does Marshall offer to support the power of judicial review? Are those arguments persuasive?

Court Act of 1801—an omission that he regards as strongly probative of the Court's awareness of the political sensitivity of its situation and its willingness to shape its decisions accordingly. See Alfange, *Marbury v. Madison and Original Understandings of Judicial Review: In Defense of Traditional Wisdom*, 1993 Sup.Ct.Rev. 329.

3. See generally Nedelsky, *Confining Democratic Politics: Antifederalists, Federalists, and the Constitution*, 96 Harv. L. Rev 340 (1982).

4. See generally Dworkin, A Matter of Principle 162 (1985)(arguing that interpretation in law characteristically requires judges to choose among eligible interpretations on grounds of substantive preferability and that

legal interpretation is therefore "essentially political"). Do you agree?

Cf. Kahn, Legitimacy and History: Self–Government in American Constitutional Theory 24–29 (1992), arguing that "Marshall starts his discussion of judicial review with an inquiry into abstract political science", that he "speaks to the judicial function in any constitutional republic, not to any unique U.S. requirements", and that he says little or "nothing about the constitutional text—except that there is one—or the history of the text" (pp. 25–26). According to Professor Kahn, Marshall was characteristic of his generation in believing that "arguments from the abstract science of politics are essential to constitutional inquiry" (p. 28).

Consider the validity of the following criticism: Everyone accepted the proposition that the Constitution was binding on the national government. Dispute centered on the quite separate proposition that the courts were authorized to enforce their interpretations of the Constitution against the conflicting interpretations of Congress and the President. Marshall's arguments prove the first, undisputed proposition, but furnish no support for the second. In sum, Marshall's arguments beg the only question really in issue.[5]

In support of this criticism, note that there are matters concerning which courts accept as a basis of decision, without further inquiry, a formally correct determination of the legislative or executive branches—(*e.g.,* a statement that a certain statute has in fact been enacted in accordance with the prescribed procedure or an executive determination that a certain government is the established government of a country). See, further, Sec. 6, *infra.* Would it not be possible for courts, in all cases, similarly to accept the determination of Congress and the President (or in the case of a veto, of a special majority of Congress) that a statute is duly authorized by the Constitution?

On the other hand, does Congress in voting to enact a bill, or the President in approving it, typically make or purport to make such a determination? With respect to the validity of the statute as applied in particular situations, how could they?

Both Congress and the President can obviously contribute to the sound interpretation of the Constitution. But clearly neither branch is so organized as to be able, without aid from the courts, to build up a body of coherent and intelligible constitutional principle, and to carry public conviction that relevant principles are being observed. How important is it that such a body of constitutional principle should be developed? That people believe that constitutional principles guide or constrain governmental decisions? Are these considerations equally important with respect to all constitutional provisions? With respect to all kinds of official decisions? Are they especially important with respect to decisions authoritatively applying the law to specific individuals?

Do the considerations supporting judicial review help to indicate how much deference, if any, courts should accord to other branches' judgments concerning the constitutionality of their acts? Recent commentators have suggested that the theories of judicial review generally prevailing at the time of Marbury authorized judicial invalidation only in cases substantially free from doubt.[6] Is the reasoning of Marbury consistent with this "doubtful case rule"? Is Marbury's logic at least equally consistent with a more assertive judicial role?

(5) *Continuing Controversy.* Although the practice of judicial review is now firmly entrenched, debate persists over whether this judicial power was contemplated by the Constitution's framers and ratifiers.[7] Even more controverted, of

---

5. For a forceful statement of similar objections, see Bickel, The Least Dangerous Branch—The Supreme Court at the Bar of Politics 2–14 (1962).

6. See, *e.g.,* Alfange, note 2, *supra,* at 342–49; Casto, *James Iredell and the American Origins of Judicial Review,* 27 Conn. L.Rev. 329, 341–48 (1995).

7. On the understanding of the Conventions, see Chap. I, pp. 11–13, *supra.* See also Alfange, note 2, *supra,* at 366–67 (asserting that, at the time of Marbury's decision, the authority of the Supreme Court to declare acts of Congress unconstitutional "was all but universally conceded"); *cf.* Treanor, *The Case of the Prisoners and the Origins of Judicial Review,* 143 U.Pa.L.Rev. 491, 569–70 (1994)(suggesting that judicial review had

course, is the question of how, both substantively and methodologically, the power of judicial review should be exercised. Notable recent contributions to the vast literature include Ackerman, 1 We The People: Foundations (1991); Bork, The Tempting of America (1990); Dworkin, Law's Empire (1986); Ely, Democracy and Distrust (1980); Epstein, Takings (1985); Sunstein, The Partial Constitution (1993); and Michelman, *Law's Republic,* 97 Yale L.J. 1493 (1988).

NOTE ON MARBURY v. MADISON AND THE FUNCTION OF ADJUDICATION

(1) *The Derivation of Judicial Review.* In Marbury, an important strand of Marshall's reasoning derives the Court's power to declare acts of Congress unconstitutional, and hence its power to make authoritative determinations of constitutional law, solely from its function of deciding cases. Assume for the moment that this was the sole foundation for Marshall's arguments. Would there be any necessary implications for contemporary constitutional adjudication? If so, what would those implications be? Or would this aspect of Marshall's reasoning just be one relevant factor, among others, in defining the judicial role?

(2) *The "Dispute Resolution" or "Private Rights" Model.* In contemporary debate, insistence that the power of judicial review exists only as a necessary incident of the power to decide cases tends to cluster with a number of other views in what might be called a "dispute resolution" or "private rights" model of constitutional adjudication. Among the familiarly associated ideas are these. (a) The power of judicial review is anomalous under a substantially democratic Constitution and is tolerable only insofar as necessary to the resolution of cases. (b) The definition of justiciable "cases" should be restricted to the kinds of disputes historically viewed as appropriate for judicial resolution—paradigmatically, those in which a defendant's violation of a legal duty to the plaintiff has caused a distinct and palpable injury to an economic or other legally protected interest. (c) Courts should avoid any role as a general overseer of government conduct, and should especially avoid the award of remedies that invade traditional legislative and executive prerogatives.

The dispute resolution or private rights model draws support from a variety of sources. First, this model coheres well with a number of familiar axioms about constitutional adjudication, including the following: (i) Courts should avoid unnecessary decisions of constitutional law. (ii) Courts sit only to adjudicate claims of legal rights, not to pronounce on generalized grievances. (iii) One party may not assert the rights of another party. For further discussion of these asserted axioms and their validity, see Section 3 of this Chapter.

Second, the Framers plainly contemplated that the jurisdiction of the courts would be "limited to cases of a Judiciary nature." 2 Farrand, The Records of the Federal Convention 430 (1911). See Chap. I, pp. 10-11, *supra.* They also decisively rejected a proposal to establish a Council of Revision with

previously won uncontroversial acceptance in Marshall's home state of Virginia, perhaps   uniquely among the states, and that "Marshall's commitment to judicial review can be

the power to pronounce on the wisdom of proposed legislation. See 1 Farrand at 21, 94. According to Justice Harlan, "unrestricted public actions might well alter the [historic] allocation of authority among the three branches of the Federal Government" and thereby "go far toward" transforming the federal courts into "the Council of Revision which, despite Madison's support, was rejected by the Constitutional Convention." Flast v. Cohen, 392 U.S. 83, 130 (1968)(Harlan, J., dissenting).[1]

Third, the dispute resolution or private law model reflects a conception of the separation of powers, which many have found attractive, in which the courts should accord deference to the democratic legitimacy and practical competences of the legislative and executive branches. See, *e.g.,* Allen v. Wright, 468 U.S. 737 (1984), p. 123, *infra,* and the following Note.

Strictures by which courts limit the availability and scope of constitutional adjudication are supported from a somewhat different perspective by Brilmayer, *The Jurisprudence of Article III: Perspectives on the "Case or Controversy" Requirement,* 93 Harv.L.Rev. 297 (1979). Her theory rests on "three interrelated policies of Article III: the smooth allocation of power among courts over time; the unfairness of holding later litigants to an adverse judgment in which they may not have been properly represented; and the importance of placing control over political processes in the hands of the people most closely involved" (p. 302).[2]

(3) *The Public Rights Model.* In contrast with the dispute resolution or private rights model, a more diffused conception of the function of courts in public law matters has appeared in recent years (sometimes explicitly, sometimes assumed)—a conception that depicts constitutional (and sometimes statutory) interpretation by the courts as other than an incident of the power to resolve particular, ongoing disputes between identified litigants. This ap-

understood as having been shaped by [this] fact").

1. The historical pedigree of the private rights or dispute resolution model has not gone undisputed. See, *e.g.,* Berger, *Standing to Sue in Public Actions: Is it a Constitutional Requirement?,* 78 Yale L.L. 816 (1969)(arguing that the British legal traditions that informed the Framer's intentions in Article III included numerous provisions for parties without a personal interest in the outcome to bring judicial challenges to unlawful government actions); Winter, *The Metaphor of Standing and the Problem of Self–Governance,* 40 Stan.L.Rev. 1371 (1988)(arguing that, from colonial times through the twentieth century, courts did not view a personal stake as an element of the case or controversy requirement, but instead granted relief when authorized by the forms of action); Pushaw, *Article III's Case/Controversy Distinction and the Dual Functions of Federal Courts,* 69 Notre Dame L.Rev. 447 (1994)(arguing that the framers intended Article III "cases" and "controversies" to be distinct, and that in the former, which were not intended to require suit by an injured party in an adversary proceeding, the principal judicial function was to be norm articulation). See also Nichol, *Rethinking Standing,* 72 Cal. L.Rev. 68, 93–94 (1984)(arguing that the analogy between judicial power under a broad standing doctrine and the rejected judicial role in a Council of Revision is "inapt", since the proposed Council would have provided opinions on the wisdom of proposed laws as an aspect of the enactment process, not engaged in post-enactment review of constitutionality. Indeed, some have seen the foundation for an alternative conception of the judicial role in Marbury itself. See Paragraph (3), *infra.*

2. See also Eisenberg, *Participation, Responsiveness, and the Consultative Process: An Essay for Lon Fuller,* 92 Harv.L.Rev. 410, 430 (1978): "The underlying message of *Forms and Limits* [an article by Prof. Fuller] cannot be lightly disregarded: adjudication has a moral force, and this force is in major part a function of those elements that distinguish adjudication from all other forms of ordering. In the long run, the cost of departing from those elements may be a forfeiture of the moral force of the judicial role."

proach has at least three aspects. The first questions the importance of requiring that the plaintiff have a personal stake in the outcome of a lawsuit; in its purest form, it would permit any citizen to bring a "public action" to challenge allegedly unlawful government conduct. The second argues that the judiciary should not be viewed as a mere settler of disputes, but rather as an institution with a distinctive capacity to declare and explicate public values—norms that transcend individual controversies. The third defends the exercise by courts of broad remedial powers in cases challenging the operation of such public institutions as schools, prisons, and mental hospitals; it argues that relief cannot and should not be limited to undoing particular violations, but should involve judges (and their nominees) in the management and reshaping of those institutions.[3]

Support for the public rights approach, particularly in constitutional adjudication, is found by some commentators in Marbury itself. See, *e.g.*, Monaghan, *Constitutional Adjudication: The Who and When*, 82 Yale L.J. 1363 (1973); Fallon & Meltzer, *New Law, Non–Retroactivity, and Constitutional Remedies*, 104 Harv.L.Rev. 1731, 1800–01 (1991). According to Professor Monaghan, Marbury's "repeated emphasis that a written constitution imposes limits on every organ of the state * * * welded judicial review to the political axiom of limited government." (82 Yale L.J. at 1370). At least three other historical phenomena have contributed to the emergence of the public rights model.

The first involves the vast increase in governmental regulation, especially when administered by administrative agencies, that has created diffuse rights shared by large groups and new legal relationships that are hard to capture in traditional, private law terms. At the same time, a need has arisen for judicial control of the exercise of administrative power. See generally Jaffe, *Standing to Secure Judicial Review: Public Actions*, 74 Harv.L.Rev. 1265, 1282–84 (1961); Stewart, *The Reformation of American Administrative Law*, 88 Harv. L.Rev. 1667, 1674–81 (1975). Encouraged by statutes authorizing judicial review of administrative action, leading administrative law decisions gradually departed from the private rights model and permitted "standing" by representatives of interests not protected at common law to represent the "public interest" in statutory enforcement. See, *e.g.*, FCC v. Sanders Bros. Radio Station, 309 U.S. 470 (1940); Scripps–Howard Radio, Inc. v. FCC, 316 U.S. 4 (1942). For further discussion, see pp. 170–71, *infra.*

A second factor supporting the public rights model has been the substantive expansion of constitutional rights, especially under the Warren Court in the 1960s. For example, the broadly shared interests of voters in challenging a malapportioned legislative district, see Baker v. Carr, 369 U.S. 186 (1962), p. 284, *infra,* or of public school pupils in challenging school prayer, see School

---

3. For a range of commentary elaborating this approach in one or more of these three aspects, see, *e.g.*, Bandes, *The Idea of a Case*, 42 Stan.L.Rev. 227 (1990); Chayes, *The Role of the Judge in Public Law Litigation*, 89 Harv.L.Rev. 1281 (1976); Chayes, *Foreword: Public Law Litigation and the Burger Court*, 96 Harv.L.Rev. 4 (1982); Dworkin, Taking Rights Seriously 131–49 (1977); Fiss, *Foreword: The Forms of Justice*, 93 Harv. L.Rev. 1 (1979); Jaffe, *The Citizen as Litigant in Public Actions: The Non–Hohfeldian or Ideological Plaintiff*, 116 U.Pa.L.Rev. 1033 (1968); Pushaw, note 1, *supra*; Sunstein, *Standing and the Privatization of Public Law*, 88 Colum.L.Rev. 1432 (1988); Tushnet, *The New Law of Standing: A Plea for Abandonment*, 62 Cornell L.Rev. 633 (1977); Vining, Legal Identity: The Coming of Age of Public Administrative Law (1978).

Dist. v. Schempp, 374 U.S. 203 (1963), differ markedly from the liberty and economic interests recognized at common law.

Third, there has emerged an increasingly pervasive conception of constitutional rights not as shields against governmental coercion, but as swords authorizing the award of affirmative relief to redress injury to constitutionally protected interests. That development, the origins of which trace in part to the landmark decisions in Ex parte Young, 209 U.S. 123 (1908), p. 1058, *infra* (recognizing a judicially created equitable cause of action for violation of the Fourteenth Amendment's Due Process Clause), and Bivens v. Six Unknown Named Agents of Federal Bureau of Narcotics, 403 U.S. 388 (1971), p. 858, *infra* (recognizing a judicially created cause of action for damages for violation of the Fourth Amendment), also finds expression in the institutional reform litigation following Brown v. Board of Education, 347 U.S. 483 (1954). After the recognition of such rights as those to school desegregation, courts inevitably found themselves awarding remedies of a kind hard to square with at least some of the premises of the private rights or dispute resolution model.

(4) *Overlap of the Models.* The distinction between the somewhat simplistically depicted "dispute resolution" (or "private rights") and "public rights" models[4] is not watertight. School desegregation cases, for example, have their origin in individual grievances that may be assimilated to the dispute resolution or private rights model, but seemingly require the reshaping of institutions if the rights infringed are to be enforced. Conversely, an action seeking injunctive or declaratory relief against the future administration of a government policy (such as a police department's alleged policy of needlessly subjecting police detainees to life-threatening chokeholds) implicates the kind of publicly shared interests associated with the public rights model, but would not necessarily call for a broad or intrusive remedy. A prohibitory injunction or declaratory judgment would suffice. See Fallon, *Of Justiciability, Remedies, and Public Law Litigation: Notes on the Jurisprudence of Lyons,* 59 N.Y.U.L.Rev. 1, 3–9 (1984). The devices of the class action, as well as other techniques for broadening the scope of litigation, frequently reflect efforts to meld the private rights and public rights models, and many of the tensions about the proper role of the courts have been felt in the resulting cases and doctrines.[5]

---

4. For valuable discussion of similar models from a comparative perspective, see Damaska, The Faces of Justice and State Authority (1986). Professor Damaska develops the relationship between what he calls the "conflict solving" and "policy implementing" approaches to adjudication and visions of the state as "reactive" and "activist."

5. In his well-known essay, *The Forms and Limits of Adjudication,* 92 Harv.L.Rev. 353 (1978), Professor Fuller stresses the inappropriateness of adjudication for the resolution of "polycentric" disputes, which he claims have too many ramifications, too many interdependent aspects, to yield to rational, properly judicial solution; they are far more suited to disposition by processes of negotiation and managerial intuition.

In an essay on institutional reform litigation, Professor Horowitz notes the difficulties of casting the issues in such cases in terms of legal rights; the dangers of attempting to treat class plaintiffs and governmental defendants as if each side were always homogeneous and adverse to the other; the hazards of delegating authority to masters and of compromising judicial neutrality; and the inevitability of unintended consequences when judges necessarily "act on a piece, and neglect the rest." Horowitz, *Decreeing Organizational Change: Judicial Supervision of Public Institutions,* 1983 Duke L.J. 1265. See also Fletcher, *The Discretionary Constitution: Institutional Remedies and Judicial Legitimacy,* 91 Yale L.J. 635 (1982); Stewart, p. 80, *supra,* at 1802–05.

The distinction between the private and public rights models blurs, moreover, because the public rights model, sensibly construed, cannot be understood to license judicial review at the behest of any would-be litigant on the basis of any hypothesized set of facts or indeed no facts whatsoever. For there to be a constitutionally justiciable case under the public rights approach, "the functional requisites of effective adjudication" must be satisfied. See Fallon, *supra,* at 51. These functional requisites cannot be reduced to a short or determinate list, but involve such considerations as:

(a) The importance, in the judicial development of law, of a concrete set of facts as an aid to the accurate formulation of the legal issue to be decided;

(b) The importance of an adversary presentation of evidence as an aid to the accurate determination of the facts out of which the legal issue arises;

(c) The importance of an adversary presentation in the formulation and decision of the legal issue; and

(d) The importance of a concrete set of facts in limiting the scope and implications of the legal determination, and as an aid to its accurate interpretation.

Where the functional requisites of adjudication are not satisfied, adjudication would be inappropriate even under the public rights model. See generally Bandes, note 3, *supra;* Tushnet, *The Sociology of Article III: A Response to Professor Brilmayer,* 93 Harv.L.Rev. 1698 (1980). *Cf.* United States Parole Comm'n v. Geraghty, 445 U.S. 388 (1980), p. 227, *infra* (acknowledging that the plaintiff in a class action no longer had a "personal stake" in the litigation in the traditional sense, but holding the case not moot, partly because "[t]he imperatives of a dispute capable of judicial resolution"—"sharply presented issues in a concrete factual setting and self-interested parties vigorously advocating opposing positions"—were satisfied).

(5) *A Testing Case.* Suppose that a state employee, claiming that she is threatened with discharge in violation of her constitutional rights, brings a federal court action to enjoin her discharge and to require her state employer to institute certain procedures for dealing with cases like hers in the future. Two days after the complaint is filed, the plaintiff dies of unrelated causes, and her lawyer resists a motion to dismiss on the ground that the case raises important constitutional questions about the procedures and structure of the state employer. The lawyer seeks to substitute her client's husband, who is not a state employee, as plaintiff.

Of the functional requisites of adjudication cited above, some do not seem to be affected by the death of the original plaintiff, while others plainly are. But since only prospective relief was sought, the original plaintiff's death surely eliminates any ongoing dispute that the court's judgment and decree might resolve. Nor is there any indication in the character of the lawsuit that other employees of this agency confront similar problems, or, if they do, that they wish to press any claim they might have. Would a judicial decision passing on the constitutional question under these circumstances, and issuing an injunction requiring the agency to change its operations, be a legitimate exercise of judicial power? If you think so, would it matter if no evidence could be adduced that the original plaintiff had been threatened with discharge? If she had never been a public employee but had simply been seeking to determine whether the agency could discharge someone under certain conditions?

(6) *The Supreme Court and the Models.* The Supreme Court has never explicitly embraced the public rights model of the judicial role or disavowed the dispute resolution model. Indeed, its formal pronouncements have been consistently to the contrary.[6] Thus, for example, the Court has held that a federal district court exceeded its Article III jurisdiction when it considered a constitutional issue not raised by the parties, even though it did so at the express direction of the court of appeals. Williams v. Zbaraz, 448 U.S. 358, 367 (1980). Moreover, as will appear in the remainder of this chapter, the Court has recurrently rejected litigation avowedly aimed at generally policing official conduct rather than seeking relief for the complaining party; see, *e.g.,* Sierra Club v. Morton, p. 141, *infra;* O'Shea v. Littleton, p. 260, *infra*; City of Los Angeles v. Lyons, p. 266, *infra;* Rizzo v. Goode, p. 265 n. 1, *infra;* United States v. Richardson, p. 143, *infra.* There are, however, some holdings that may be seen as reflecting, though not in explicit terms, a shift in conception of the judicial role; see, *e.g.,* the developments discussed in the *Note on Mootness and Class Actions,* p. 236, *infra,* and in the *Note on the Scope of the Issue in First Amendment Cases,* p. 202, *infra.* See also Fallon & Meltzer, *supra,* at 1799–1800 (citing, *inter alia,* harmless error practice, the practice of providing alternative grounds for decision, and the exception to mootness doctrine for cases "capable of repetition, yet evading review" in support of the conclusion that "there exists a substantial body of case law, rising almost to the level of a general tradition, in which adjudication * * * functions more as a vehicle for the pronouncement of norms than for the resolution of particular disputes").

Note further that as the Supreme Court's appellate jurisdiction has become more and more discretionary, the Court has promulgated rules indicating that it will exercise its certiorari power based largely on the importance of the questions presented. See Sup.Ct.Rule 10; see generally Chap. XV, sec. 4, *infra.* However subtly, doesn't the Court's approach recognize the independent significance of norm-articulation as a judicial function?

Consider, as you work through these materials, whether a significant change in overall conception is occurring and, if so, whether such a change is warranted.

(7) *Discretion and the Judicial Function.* Does the power of judicial review upheld in Marbury carry with it a correlative duty to decide any claims of unconstitutionality in a properly presented case, or is there some measure of discretion to abstain from such decisions? In an important and controversial book, Professor Alexander Bickel argued that the Supreme Court must have flexibility to determine when it is appropriate to decide. This flexibility, he argued, is afforded not only by the discretion vested in the Court to grant or deny a writ of certiorari, but in the various doctrines of justiciability developed under such rubrics as standing, mootness, ripeness, and political question. Indeed, he suggested that these doctrines should be partly understood as

---

6. *But cf.* Chief Justice Rehnquist's dissenting opinion in Honig v. Doe, 484 U.S. 305, 329 (1988), a case in which the dispute had become moot only after the Supreme Court's grant of certiorari. The Chief Justice argued that the live controversy requirement is not an Article III command, but was originally a matter of judicial discretion, and that the Court should override the prohibition against deciding moot cases when there are good reasons to do so. Chief Justice Rehnquist based his argument in part on the "unique and valuable ability" of the Supreme Court to "decide a federal question in such a way as to bind all other courts" (p. 332).

techniques for avoiding the necessity of decision. See Bickel, *The Least Dangerous Branch–The Supreme Court at the Bar of Politics*, 111–98 (1962).

Does the virtual abolition of the Supreme Court's mandatory appellate jurisdiction deprive Bickel's theory of contemporary significance? What are its implications for lower courts?[7] Would a recognition that jurisdictional doctrines are "discretionary" imply judicial power to resolve questions beyond the framework of "cases" as that term is used in Article III?

Bickel's thesis has been vigorously challenged on the grounds that it tolerates, and even encourages, unprincipled judicial action and that it violates the basic tenets of Marbury itself. See, *e.g.*, Gunther, *The Subtle Vices of the "Passive Virtues"—A Comment on Principle and Expediency in Judicial Review*, 64 Colum.L.Rev. 1 (1964); Wechsler, *Book Review*, 75 Yale L.J. 672 (1966). See also Wechsler, *Toward Neutral Principles of Constitutional Law*, 73 Harv.L.Rev. 1, 6 (1959).

The debate about permissible judicial discretion is not limited to the context of justiciability, but also encompasses other circumstances in which courts have declined to reach the merits of federal claims, despite having jurisdiction to do so. Compare Shapiro, *Jurisdiction and Discretion*, 60 N.Y.U.L.Rev. 543 (1985)(arguing that jurisdictional doctrines frequently give courts some discretion in deciding whether to exercise jurisdiction), with Redish, The Federal Courts in the Political Order: Judicial Jurisdiction and American Political Theory 47–74 (1991)(arguing that federal judicial jurisdiction is mandatory and that failure to exercise jurisdiction conferred is an illegitimate usurpation of Congress' lawmaking power).

(8) *Retroactivity and Prospectivity of Judicial Decisions.* Other questions of judicial obligation and limits on judicial power have also been considered in terms of the functions of adjudication articulated in Marbury and implicit in Article III. Prominent among these are issues concerning the retroactivity, non-retroactivity, and prospectivity of judicial decisions. For example, when the Supreme Court overrules a past decision or departs significantly from settled understandings and establishes rights or obligations not previously recognized, to which cases should (or must) the newly announced rule of decision be applied?[8]

Traditionally, Supreme Court decisions have been fully "retroactive" in the sense of being applicable to all pending cases, including those awaiting appellate review and presenting applications for post-conviction remedies. Measured against this norm, a Supreme Court decision is "non-retroactive" insofar as it is not applied to cases pending at the time of its decision. Even further from the norm of full retroactivity are "purely prospective" decisions, which announce rules that are not applied even to the cases in which they are formulated.

---

7. Although Bickel prescribes his approach only for the Supreme Court, the justiciability doctrines that he invokes purport to govern the propriety of judicial intervention by all federal courts.

8. For general discussion of these questions, see Fallon & Meltzer, *supra*; Mishkin, *Foreword: The High Court, The Great Writ,* *and the Due Process of Time and Law,* 79 Harv.L.Rev. 56 (1965); Schwartz, *Retroactivity, Reliability, and Due Process: A Response to Professor Mishkin,* 33 U.Chi.L.Rev. 719 (1966); Beytagh, *Ten Years of Non-retroactivity: A Critique and a Proposal,* 61 Va.L.Rev. 1557 (1975); Note, 71 Yale L.J. 907 (1962).

Issues and debates concerning non-retroactivity (as defined above), which became current with the Warren Court, are the principal focus of this Paragraph. Although a dictum in Linkletter v. Walker, 381 U.S. 618, 621–22 & n. 3 (1965), denied any constitutional barrier to purely prospective decisions, the Court explained in Stovall v. Denno, 388 U.S. 293, 301 (1967), that "[s]ound practices of decision-making, rooted in the command of Article III of the Constitution that we resolve issues solely in cases or controversies, * * * militate against" pure prospectivity. Since then, pure prospectivity has seldom been treated as a live alternative. For a discussion of the issues that purely prospective decisionmaking would raise under the traditionally recognized Article III bar against "advisory opinions," see p. 95, *infra*.

(a) *Criminal Cases on Direct Review.* Initially, at least, there was broad agreement within the Warren Court that pathbreaking decisions need not be fully retroactive. In its landmark decision in Linkletter v. Walker, *supra*, the Supreme Court held that the rule of Mapp v. Ohio, 367 U.S. 643 (1961), though applied to the case in which it was announced, would not be applied retroactively to a state criminal conviction that had become final before Mapp was decided. A year later, in Johnson v. New Jersey, 384 U.S. 719 (1966), the Court asserted its power to make newly propounded rules of criminal procedure non-retroactive even to cases pending on direct review at the time the new rules were announced. The choice between retroactivity and non-retroactivity, the Court said, should depend on the purpose of the newly propounded rule, the reliance placed on prior decisions, and the effect of retroactive application on the administration of justice.

The Warren Court's non-retroactivity doctrine engendered fierce controversy. One criticism, rooted in Blackstone's "declaratory theory" of law, held that non-retroactivity doctrine smacks of judicial "law making" and is therefore impermissible. This line of argument obviously invites a jurisprudential debate, but is the question whether law is found or made really central to the issues of retroactivity and non-retroactivity? After a conviction has been obtained, aren't questions of entitlement to secure reversal, on the basis of newly propounded rules or otherwise, questions about the necessary or appropriate availability of constitutional remedies? If so, might they most usefully be addressed within the same kind of framework used to resolve other questions of entitlement to constitutional remedies? See generally Fallon & Meltzer, *supra*, at 1758–77; Chap. VII, Sec. 2, *infra*. But *cf.* Reynoldsville Casket Co. v. Hyde, 115 S.Ct. 1745 (1995)(suggesting, in a civil case, that a remedy-based analysis cannot be used to create exceptions to normally applicable retroactivity doctrine).

A second criticism of the Warren Court's non-retroactivity practice focused on its practical implications in facilitating the implementation of sweeping constitutional reform. It would have been virtually impossible for the Court to lay down the Miranda rules, for example, if the practical cost had involved the loss of criminal convictions in untold numbers of pending cases. Emphasizing considerations of this second kind, Justice Harlan, who had initially supported the Warren Court's retroactivity practices, became a forceful critic. The obligation to apply constitutional decisions to all cases pending on direct review, he concluded, was vital to enforce fidelity to precedent and to stop judicial decisionmaking from acquiring a starkly legislative aspect. See Desist v. United States, 394 U.S. 244, 256–69 (1969)(Harlan, J., dissenting); Mackey

v. United States, 401 U.S. 667, 675–702 (1971)(Harlan, J., concurring in part and dissenting in part).

After several decades of debate over the propriety of the Johnson approach and uncertainty over its application, the Court adopted Justice Harlan's view. In Griffith v. Kentucky, 479 U.S. 314 (1987), it decided that "failure to apply a newly declared constitutional rule to criminal cases pending on direct review violates basic norms of constitutional adjudication. * * * [A]fter we have decided a new rule in the case selected, the integrity of judicial review requires that we apply that rule to all similar cases pending on direct review" (pp. 322–23).

Which "basic norms of constitutional adjudication" did the Court believe that the prior practice violated? Do you agree with its assessment?

(b) *Habeas Corpus*. In Teague v. Lane, 489 U.S. 288 (1989), p. 1392, *infra*, the Supreme Court also adopted the basic outlines of Justice Harlan's preferred approach to habeas corpus, which he sharply differentiated from criminal cases on direct review. Emphasizing that habeas is an extraordinary and discretionary remedy and that the "finality" of criminal judgments should be upset only for weighty reasons, Teague held that petitions that either rely on or ask the court to establish "new" rules of law should, subject only to narrow exceptions, be dismissed at the threshold. For further discussion, see Chapter X, Section 2, *infra*.

Among its important implications, Teague sharply diminishes the role of federal habeas corpus courts in defining and protecting constitutional rights.

(c) *Civil Cases*. In Chevron Oil Co. v. Huson, 404 U.S. 97, 106–07 (1971), the Supreme Court laid down a relatively flexible test for determining whether new rules should be applied retroactively in civil cases. But following the Court's decision in Griffith v. Kentucky, *supra*, that new rules should be applied to all criminal cases on direct review, the Chevron test came under increasing attack from a number of Justices and eventually was discarded in favor of an approach that permits little if any non-retroactive adjudication. The new approach evolved in three cases in which state courts had refused to require the refund of tax payments exacted under measures held to be unconstitutional: American Trucking Ass'ns, Inc. v. Smith, 496 U.S. 167 (1990); James B. Beam Distilling Co. v. Georgia, 501 U.S. 529 (1991); and Harper v. Virginia Dep't of Taxation, 113 S.Ct. 2510 (1993).

In Harper, the only one of the cases featuring a majority opinion (per Thomas, J.), the Court reasoned that Griffith's concerns—that non-retroactive decisionmaking is the province of the legislature, and that such decisionmaking denies equal treatment to similarly situated litigants—were equally applicable in civil cases. Thus, the Court stated, "[w]hen this Court applies a rule of federal law to the parties before it, that rule * * * must be given full retroactive effect in all cases still open on direct review and as to all events, regardless of whether such events predate or postdate our announcement of the rule" (p. 2517).[9]

The Court's opinion does not clearly address the lawfulness of "pure prospectivity", in which a newly declared rule is not applied even in the case in

---

9. Compare Reynoldsville Casket Co. v. Hyde, 115 S.Ct. 1745 (1995), which includes dictum that is more equivocal on whether "special circumstances" might justify departure from Harper's non-retroactivity rule.

which it is announced. But much of the opinion's reasoning raises doubts that the Court would regard purely prospective adjudication as legitimate. Justice Scalia's concurring opinion included an attack on pure prospectivity, calling it "the handmaid of judicial activism" and "quite incompatible with the judicial power" (p. 2522).

Justice O'Connor's dissenting opinion (joined by the Chief Justice) expressed her preference for the "traditional equitable balancing test of Chevron Oil" (p. 2528). Non-retroactivity was more appropriate in civil than criminal cases, she argued, because in the former it did not systematically favor governmental over individual interests, and because civil litigants denied retroactive relief might still gain some benefit from a new ruling (for example, the prospective invalidation of an unconstitutional tax). Justice O'Connor also criticized the Court for intimating that purely prospective decisionmaking is unconstitutional. Justice Kennedy's opinion concurring in part and concurring in the judgment (which Justice White joined) expressed views generally consistent with those of Justice O'Connor, but concluded that because the 1989 decision had not established a new rule of law, there was no basis for making its application non-retroactive.[10]

Two cases decided during the 1994 Term cast further doubt on the permissibility of denying relief in civil cases, as a matter of remedial discretion, for violation of "novel" constitutional rules. Reynoldsville Casket Co. v. Hyde, 115 S.Ct. 1745 (1995), was an outgrowth of the Court's decision in Bendix Autolite Corp. v. Midwesco Enterprises, Inc., 486 U.S. 888 (1988), which invalidated an Ohio statute that tolled the state's two-year statute of limitations in suits against out-of-state defendants as an unconstitutional burden on interstate commerce. In Reynoldsville, the plaintiff filed a tort action against an out-of-state defendant more than two years after the underlying automobile accident, but before the decision in Bendix. The Ohio supreme court held that Bendix Autolite did not apply retroactively, but the Supreme Court reversed.

The Court, in an opinion by Breyer, J., began by noting plaintiff's concession that "as a result of Harper, [supra,] there is no question that Bendix retroactively invalidated" the tolling provision on which the timeliness of her suit depended. Eschewing a non-retroactivity theory, the plaintiff attempted to defend the Ohio supreme court's decision as a permissible denial of a *remedy* for the constitutional violation identified in Bendix, justified by the plaintiff's reliance on pre-Bendix law. Among other analogies, the plaintiff noted that official immunity doctrine frequently withholds damages remedies for violations of constitutional rights that were not "clearly established" at the time the violation occurred.

Rejecting the plaintiff's effort to characterize the case as involving constitutional remedies doctrine, the Court, per Breyer, J., relied heavily on Harper (p. 1749):

> "If Harper has anything more than symbolic significance, how could virtually identical reliance [by plaintiff], without more, prove sufficient to permit a virtually identical denial [of effect to Bendix] simply because it is characterized as a denial based on 'remedy' rather than 'non-retroactivity' "?

10. For a critique of Harper and an assessment of its implications, see Rakowski, *Harper and Its Aftermath*, 1 Fla.Tax.Rev. 445 (1993).

The Court acknowledged that constitutional remedies may be withheld under qualified immunity doctrine when the underlying constitutional violation depends on the establishment of a new rule of law, but it distinguished the cases: The "well-established general legal rule" of official immunity reflects not only reliance interests, but also "other significant policy justifications" missing in this case (*id.*).

Justice Scalia (joined by Justice Thomas), concurring, suggested that the case presented no proper question of remedial discretion; the result should rest entirely on the obligation of the Ohio courts to disregard an invalid statute. Justice Kennedy (joined by Justice O'Connor), also concurred in the judgment. He did "not read today's opinion to surrender in advance our authority to decide that in some exceptional cases, courts may shape relief in light of disruption of important reliance interests or the unfairness caused by unexpected judicial decisions" (p. 1752). In his view, however, the Bendix decision did not establish a new rule of law, and the plaintiff's claim of reliance therefore failed.

In Ryder v. United States, 115 S.Ct. 2031 (1995), the Court rejected the government's argument that a decision of the Court of Military Appeals finding invalid the appointment of judges to the Court of Military Review should, as a matter of remedial discretion pursuant to Chevron Oil Co. v. Huson, *supra*, be given prospective effect only. The Court found that, "whatever the continuing validity of Chevron Oil" after Harper, *supra*, and Reynoldsville Casket Co., *supra*, awarding retroactive relief to the petitioner would not entail "the sort of grave disruption or inequity * * * that would bring that doctrine into play" (115 S.Ct. at 2036–37).

For commentary on developments in non-retroactivity doctrine in a wide range of contexts, and for discussion of how the themes in those doctrines relate to the dispute resolution and public rights models of adjudication, see Fallon & Meltzer, *supra*.

(9) *Constitutional Interpretation by Non–Judicial Officials*. From Chief Justice Marshall's reasoning that courts must interpret the Constitution as a necessary incident of their function of deciding cases, does it follow that other public officials have a similar responsibility to interpret the Constitution in discharging their functions?[11] If so, won't serious conflicts inevitably result? These questions are far more complex and various than their grammatical form might suggest. In assessing the following expressions of views, try to identify the precise question of constitutional responsibility that triggered their utterance.

(a) President Franklin D. Roosevelt began a much-quoted letter of July 6, 1935, to Congressman Samuel B. Hill concerning constitutional questions surrounding a bill to regulate the bituminous coal mining industry with a brief argument that the measure was in fact constitutional. See 4 Public Papers and Addresses of Franklin D. Roosevelt 297–98 (1938). The letter concluded:

---

11. See Engdahl, *John Marshall's "Jeffersonian" Concept of Judicial Review,* 42 Duke L.J. 279 (1992)(discussing early debates about the appropriateness of constitutional interpretation by non-judicial public officials and arguing that Justice Marshall's opinion in Marbury was not intended to exclude oth-er branches from constitutional interpretation). For a broader argument that the President's interpretive responsibility encompasses determinations of whether to obey judicial decrees, see Paulsen, *The Most Dangerous Branch: Executive Power to Say What the Law Is,* 83 Geo.L.J. 217 (1994).

"Manifestly, no one is in a position to give assurance that the proposed act will withstand constitutional tests, for the simple fact that you can get not ten but a thousand differing legal opinions on the subject. But the situation is so urgent and the benefits of the legislation so evident that all doubts should be resolved in favor of the bill, leaving to the courts, in an orderly fashion, the ultimate question of constitutionality. A decision by the Supreme Court relative to this measure would be helpful as indicating, with increasing clarity, the constitutional limits within which this Government must operate. * * * I hope your committee will not permit doubts as to constitutionality, however reasonable, to block the suggested legislation."

For systematic discussion of how legislators should approach questions of constitutional interpretation, see Brest, *The Conscientious Legislator's Guide to Constitutional Interpretation*, 27 Stan.L.Rev. 586 (1975).

(b) In justifying his veto of a bill to continue the Bank of the United States, President Andrew Jackson maintained that the Bank was unconstitutional, despite Supreme Court decisions favorable to its constitutionality. 2 Richardson, Messages and Papers of the Presidents 576, 582 (1896). In his message of July 10, 1832, Jackson said:

"If the opinion of the Supreme Court covered the whole ground of this act, it ought not to control the coordinate authorities of this Government. * * * Each public officer who takes an oath to support the Constitution swears that he will support it as he understands it, and not as it is understood by others. It is as much the duty of the House of Representatives, of the Senate, and of the President to decide upon the constitutionality of any bill or resolution which may be presented to them for passage or approval as it is of the supreme judges when it may be brought before them for judicial decision. The opinion of the judges has no more authority over Congress than the opinion of Congress has over the judges, and on that point the President is independent of both. The authority of the Supreme Court must not, therefore, be permitted to control the Congress or the Executive when acting in their legislative capacities, but to have only such influence as the force of their reasoning may deserve."

(c) In his first inaugural address, Abraham Lincoln rejected the position that the Dred Scott decision conclusively deprived the federal government of power to prohibit expansion of slavery into federal territories (6 *id.*, at 5, 9):

"I do not forget the position assumed by some that constitutional questions are to be decided by the Supreme Court, nor do I deny that such decisions must be binding in any case upon the parties to a suit as to the object of that suit, while they are also entitled to very high respect and consideration in all parallel cases by all other departments of the Government. And while it is obviously possible that such decision may be erroneous in any given case, still the evil effect following it, being limited to that particular case, with the chance that it may be overruled and never become a precedent for other cases, can better be borne than could the evils of a different practice. At the same time, the candid citizen must confess that if the policy of the Government upon vital questions affecting the whole people is to be irrevocably fixed by decisions of the Supreme Court, the instant they are made in ordinary litigation between parties in personal actions the people will have ceased to be their own rulers, having to that extent practically resigned their Government into the hands of that eminent tribunal. Nor is there in this view any assault upon the court or the judges. It is a duty from which they may not shrink to decide cases properly brought before them, and it is no fault of theirs if others seek to turn their decision to political purposes."

Following the Supreme Court's decision in Roe v. Wade, 410 U.S. 113 (1973), a number of state legislatures enacted abortion-restricting measures, at least some of which seemed intended to provoke a reconsideration of Roe. Was it acceptable for legislators to act on the premise that Roe was constitutionally mistaken? See Wellington, Interpreting the Constitution 142–58 (1990). For public officials to resist school desegregation after Brown v. Board of Education, 347 U.S. 483 (1954)? For Lincoln to treat Dred Scott as binding on the parties but not as authoritatively resolving all of the constitutional issues that the decision addressed? What are the relevant differences, if any, among these cases?

See Wechsler, *The Court and the Constitution,* 65 Colum.L.Rev. 1001, 1008 (1965), building on the excerpt from Lincoln's First Inaugural quoted above: "[N]ote the purpose of the limitation [there] stated: to allow for the 'chance' that the decision 'may be overruled and never become a precedent for other cases.' When that chance has been exploited and has run its course, with reaffirmation rather than reversal of decision, has not the time arrived when its acceptance is demanded, without insisting on repeated litigation? The answer here, it seems to me, must be affirmative, both as the necessary implication of our constitutional tradition and to avoid the greater evils that will otherwise ensue." See also Bickel, *supra,* at 254–72, and especially at 261.

(d) In Cooper v. Aaron, 358 U.S. 1 (1958), the Supreme Court was asked to postpone the implementation of a court-approved desegregation program for Little Rock, Arkansas, because of extreme public hostility. Previously, the Governor had called out the National Guard to prevent black students from entering Little Rock Central High School and, though these troops were later withdrawn in response to a federal injunction against the Governor, black students were thereafter able to attend only under federal military protection. Though the School Board had been actively seeking to implement desegregation, it sought a two and one-half year postponement of the court-approved program. The District Court granted relief, but the Court of Appeals reversed. The Supreme Court affirmed, insisting that "[t]he constitutional rights of respondents are not to be sacrificed or yielded to the violence and disorder which have followed upon the actions of the Governor and Legislature" (p. 16).

The opinion of the Court, captioned in an extraordinary fashion with the names of all nine justices individually, continued (pp. 17–19):

"What has been said, in the light of the facts developed, is enough to dispose of the case. However, we should answer the premise of the actions of the Governor and Legislature that they are not bound by our holding in the Brown case. It is necessary only to recall some basic constitutional propositions which are settled doctrine.

"Article VI of the Constitution makes the Constitution the 'supreme Law of the Land.' In 1803, Chief Justice Marshall, speaking for a unanimous Court, referring to the Constitution as 'the fundamental and paramount law of the nation,' declared in the notable case of Marbury v. Madison,1 Cranch 137, 177, that 'It is emphatically the province and duty of the judicial department to say what the law is.' This decision declared the basic principle that the federal judiciary is supreme in the exposition of the law of the Constitution, and that principle has ever since been respected by this Court and the Country as a permanent and indispensable feature of our constitutional system. It follows that the interpretation of the Fourteenth Amendment enunciated by this Court in the Brown case is the supreme law of the land, and Art. VI of the Constitution makes it of binding effect on the States 'any Thing in the Constitution or Laws of any State to the Contrary notwithstanding.' Every state legislator and executive and judicial officer is solemnly committed by oath taken pursuant to Art. VI, cl. 3, 'to support this Constitution.' * * *

"* * * Chief Justice Marshall spoke for a unanimous Court in saying that: 'If the legislatures of the several states may, at will, annul the judgments of the courts of the United States, and destroy the rights acquired under those judgments, the constitution itself becomes a solemn mockery * * *.' United States v. Peters, 5 Cranch 115, 136. A Governor who asserts a power to nullify a federal court order is similarly restrained. If he had such power, said Chief Justice Hughes, in 1932, also for a unanimous Court, 'it is manifest that the fiat of a state Governor, and not the Constitution of the United States, would be the supreme law of the land; that the restrictions of the Federal Constitution upon the exercise of state power would be but impotent phrases * * *.' Sterling v. Constantin, 287 U.S. 378, 397–398."

Cooper v. Aaron involved the integrity of a court order, and the Court's language and result are therefore consistent with President Lincoln's position, Paragraph (c), *supra*. Does Marbury support any broader position concerning the pre-eminence of the Court's power of constitutional exposition? Are any broader assertions warranted?

(e) In United States v. Nixon, 418 U.S. 683 (1974)(the "Watergate" tapes case, in which a subpoena directed to the President was upheld), the Court dealt with the contention that the President's claim of privilege was not subject to judicial review by saying (p. 703): "In the performance of assigned constitutional duties each branch of the Government must initially interpret the Constitution, and the interpretation of its powers by any branch is due great respect from the others. The President's counsel * * * reads the Constitution as providing an absolute privilege of confidentiality for all Presidential communications. Many decisions of this Court, however, have unequivocally reaffirmed the holding of Marbury v. Madison * * * that '[i]t is emphatically the province and duty of the judicial department to say what the law is.' " The opinion then referred to a number of cases—admittedly none directly on point[12]—in which the power of judicial review had been exercised, and concluded this part of its discussion (p. 705): "We therefore reaffirm that it is the province and duty of this Court 'to say what the law is' with respect to the claim of privilege presented in this case. Marbury v. Madison * * *."

Was Marbury a sufficient response to the contention? Would it have been inconsistent with Marbury for the Court to hold that a President's determination that certain material was privileged had to be accepted as conclusive by the courts? Recall that sometimes the Court accepts determinations by other branches as to compliance with procedures for the enactment of a statute or as

---

12. The references included the steel seizure case, Youngstown Sheet & Tube Co. v. Sawyer, 343 U.S. 579 (1952); Powell v. McCormack, 395 U.S. 486 (1969); and a series of cases interpreting congressional mem-

to the identity of the "established" government of a foreign country.[13]

CORRESPONDENCE OF THE JUSTICES (1793)[1]

Letter from Thomas Jefferson, Secretary of State, to Chief Justice Jay and Associate Justices:

Philadelphia, July 18, 1793.

Gentlemen:

The war which has taken place among the powers of Europe produces frequent transactions within our ports and limits, on which questions arise of considerable difficulty, and of greater importance to the peace of the United States. These questions depend for their solution on the construction of our treaties, on the laws of nature and nations, and on the laws of the land, and are often presented under circumstances *which do not give a cognizance of them to the tribunals of the country.* Yet their decision is so little analogous to the ordinary functions of the executive, as to occasion much embarrassment and difficulty to them. The President therefore would be much relieved if he found himself free to refer questions of this description to the opinions of the judges of the Supreme Court of the United States, whose knowledge of the subject would secure us against errors dangerous to the peace of the United States, and their authority insure the respect of all parties. He has therefore asked the attendance of such of the judges as could be collected in time for the occasion, to know, in the first place, their opinion, whether the public may, with propriety, be availed of their *advice on these questions?* And if they may, to present, for their advice, the abstract questions which have already occurred, or may soon occur, from which they will themselves strike out such as any circumstances might, in their opinion, forbid them to pronounce on. I have the honour to be with sentiments of the most perfect respect, gentlemen,

Your most obedient and humble servant,

Thos. Jefferson.

The following are some of the questions submitted by the President to the Justices:

1. Do the treaties between the United States and France give to France or her citizens a *right,* when at war with a power with whom the United States are at peace, to fit out originally in and from the ports of the United States vessels armed for war, with or without commission?

2. If they give such a *right,* does it extend to all manner of armed vessels, or to particular kinds only? If the latter, to what kinds does it extend?

---

bers' immunity under the Speech or Debate Clause of Art. I, § 6.

13. See Gunther, *Judicial Hegemony and Legislative Autonomy: The Nixon Case and the Impeachment Process,* 22 U.C.L.A.L.Rev. 30, 33–35 (1974); Karst & Horowitz, *Presidential Prerogative and Judicial Review,* 22 U.C.L.A.L.Rev. 47, 55–61 (1974). See also Section 6 of this Chapter.

1. The letters are respectively taken from 3 Correspondence and Public Papers of John Jay 486–89 (Johnston ed. 1891) and 15 The Papers of Alexander Hamilton 111 n. 1 (H. Syrett ed. 1969), and the questions from 10 Sparks, Writings of Washington 542–45 (1836).

3. Do they give to France or her citizens, in the case supposed, a right to refit or arm anew vessels, which, before their coming within any port of the United States, were armed for war, with or without commission?

4. If they give such a right, does it extend to all manner of armed vessels, or to particular kinds only? If the latter, to what kinds does it extend? Does it include an *augmentation* of force, or does it only extend to replacing the vessel *in statu quo?*

17. Do the laws of neutrality, considered as aforesaid, authorize the United States to permit France, her subjects, or citizens, the sale within their ports of prizes made of the subjects or property of a power at war with France, before they have been carried into some port of France and there condemned, refusing the like privilege to her enemy?

18. Do those laws authorize the United States to permit to France the erection of courts within their territory and jurisdiction for the trial and condemnation of prizes, refusing that privilege to a power at war with France?

20. To what distance, by the laws and usages of nations, may the United States exercise the right of prohibiting the hostilities of foreign powers at war with each other within rivers, bays, and arms of the sea, and upon the sea along the coasts of the United States?

22. What are the articles, by name, to be prohibited to both or either party?

25. May we, within our own ports, sell ships to both parties, prepared merely for merchandise? May they be pierced for guns?

29. May an armed vessel belonging to any of the belligerent powers follow *immediately* merchant vessels, enemies, departing from our ports, for the purpose of making prizes of them? If not, how long ought the former to remain, after the latter have sailed? And what shall be considered as the place of departure from which the time is to be counted? And how are the facts to be ascertained?

On July 20, 1793, Chief Justice Jay and the Associate Justices wrote to President Washington expressing their wish to postpone the answer to Jefferson's letter until the sitting of the Court. On August 8, 1793, they wrote to the President as follows:

Sir:

We have considered the previous question stated in a letter written to us by your direction by the Secretary of State on the 18th of last month. The lines of separation drawn by the Constitution between the three departments of the government—their being in certain respects checks upon each other—and our being judges of a court in the last resort—are considerations which afford strong arguments against the propriety of our extrajudicially deciding the questions alluded to; especially as the power given by the Constitution to the President of calling on the heads of departments for opinions, seems to have been *purposely* as well as expressly limited to the *executive* departments.

NOTE ON ADVISORY OPINIONS

(1) *Consistent Practice.* The prohibition against advisory opinions has been termed "the oldest and most consistent thread in the federal law of justiciabili-

ty." Wright, Law of Federal Courts 65 (5th ed.1994). But what makes a judicial opinion "advisory" in the constitutional sense?[1] Would it be fair to describe the parts of Marbury v. Madison dealing with Marbury's right to the commission and the propriety of the remedy of mandamus as advisory?

(2) *Foundations.* To what extent was the Justices' decision controlled by the language and history of the Constitution?[2] According to Wright, *supra,* at 65, "the power of English judges to give advisory opinions was well recognized" by 1770.[3] Apparently for this reason, Felix Frankfurter concluded that the prohibition against advisory opinions must rest on policies implicit in Article III, rather than on historical pedigree. Frankfurter, *Advisory Opinions,* 1 Encyc. of the Social Sciences 475, 476 (1937). What are the policies to which Frankfurter referred? Are they the policies underlying the private rights or dispute resolution model of adjudication sketched on pp. 77–78, *supra?* Those associated with the "functional requisites" of effective adjudication acknowledged by the competing "public rights" model on pp. 79–81, *supra?*

To what extent would the objections to advisory opinions be lessened if the Court restricted itself to giving advisory rulings on definite states of fact, real or assumed? Consider the practices of administrative agencies in meeting demand for advance information of the agencies' policies and legal position. See generally Schwartz, Administrative Law 149–59 (3d ed. 1991).[4]

If the Justices had answered the questions presented to them, would their answers have been treated as authoritative in subsequent litigation?

If the Justices had answered the questions presented, how might the Supreme Court's role have been altered?[5] Would the Court's prestige, and the acceptability of its decisions, have been enhanced or diminished? Is there value in having courts function exclusively as organs of sober second thought, appraising action already taken, rather than as advisers at the stage of initial decision?

1. Note that Jefferson's questions to the Justices all sought clarification of existing law. Compare the proposal of Senator Schwellenbach in 1937 that the Supreme Court be requested to amend its rules so as to enable the Congress, on majority vote of both houses, to request and receive "advisory opinions as to the constitutionality of legislation pending before, and being considered by, the Congress of the United States." S.Res. 103, 75th Cong., 1st Sess., 81 Cong.Rec. 2804 (1937).

2. For an illuminating discussion of the incident, see Wheeler, *Extrajudicial Activities of the Early Supreme Court,* 1973 Sup.Ct.Rev. 123, 144–58.

3. The English history is exhaustively surveyed in Jay, *Servants of Monarch and Lords: The Advisory Role of Early English Judges,* 38 Am.J.Leg.Hist. 117 (1994).

4. Since Jefferson's efforts to obtain advice from the Supreme Court failed, the Attorney General has been the principal legal adviser to the President and the executive departments. See 28 U.S.C. §§ 511, 512, derived from § 35 of the First Judiciary Act; Cummings & McFarland, Federal Justice 40, 78–92, 511–20 (1937); Nealon, *The Opinion Function of the Federal Attorney General,* 25 N.Y.U.L.Rev. 825 (1950); Rhodes, *"Opinions of the Attorney General" Revived,* 64 A.B.A.J. 1374 (1978).

Formal opinions of the Attorney General have been published since 1841, but their number has declined consistently in recent years. Between 1977 and 1992, the Office of Legal Counsel, which is authorized to release certain opinions of the Attorney General, published only 22 of these opinions.

5. According to Wheeler, note 2, *supra,* "the 1793 incident was * * * part of a broader attempt by the early Supreme Court to deemphasize the obligatory extrajudicial service concept, so widely held in the early period" (p. 158).

(3) *Prospective Overruling, Harmless Error Doctrine, and Alternative Holdings.* Would a purely prospective overruling of a past decision by the Supreme Court, which did not apply the newly propounded rule of decision to the parties in the case in which the overruling was announced, constitute an advisory opinion forbidden by Article III?   For suggestions of an affirmative answer, see Teague v. Lane, 489 U.S. 288, 316 (1989); Note, 71 Yale L.J. 907, 930–33 (1961).   See also pp 86–87, *supra,* discussing the Justices' intimations concerning this issue in Harper v. Virginia Dep't of Taxation.

But is this view tenable?   When a court first identifies a constitutional violation, then denies relief under the harmless error or analogous doctrines, has it rendered a constitutionally impermissible advisory opinion?   See Teague, 489 U.S. at 318 (Stevens, J., concurring in part and concurring in the judgment); Fallon & Meltzer, *New Law, Non–Retroactivity, and Constitutional Remedies,* 104 Harv.L.Rev. 1731, 1798–1800 (1991).

When a Court renders alternative holdings, has it violated constitutional norms?   Settled practice surely suggests not, but why not?   Consider the relevance of the following factors: (i) a concretely framed dispute, (ii) adverse parties, (iii) adversarial presentation of competing arguments, (iv) res judicata and stare decisis effects of the judgment rendered in subsequent judicial actions; and (v) conclusiveness of the determination for other branches of government.

Is it possible to state necessary and/or sufficient conditions for the identification of advisory opinions lying beyond the judicial power under Article III? According to Lee, *Deconstitutionalizing Justiciability: The Example of Mootness,* 105 Harv.L.Rev. 603, 644–45 (1992), the Supreme Court has used the term "advisory opinion" to embrace "[a]ny judgment subject to review by a co-equal branch of government", "[a]dvice to a coequal branch of government prior to the other branch's contemplated action", "Supreme Court review of any state judgment for which there is or may be an adequate and independent state ground", "[a]ny opinion, or portion thereof, not truly necessary to the disposition of the case at bar (that is, dicta)", and "[a]ny decision on the merits of a case that is moot or unripe or in which one of the parties lacks standing". Lee concludes that "only the first two of these usages denote a constitutional bar.   The other three usages are a function of judicial discretion" (p. 645).

(4) *Extrajudicial Opinions of the Justices.*   Instances of extrajudicial expression of legal opinion by Justices of the Supreme Court have not been wanting. Three years before the *Correspondence,* President Washington wrote to the Justices, as they were about to set out on their first circuit riding, to invite them to feel free to communicate with him from time to time.   Chief Justice Jay and "a minority of the Members of that Court" wrote in response that the act requiring Supreme Court Justices to sit on circuit courts was unconstitutional.   See 4 Am.Jur. & Law Mag. 293 (1830).   (The letter may never have been sent, however.   See Wheeler, note 2, *supra,* at 148.)   The substantive point involved was later raised in Stuart v. Laird, 5 U.S. (1 Cranch) 299, 309 (1803), but resolved on the ground that the practice was too well established to be questioned at that late date.[6]

---

6.   Compare a personal letter of November 13, 1790, by Chief Justice Jay to President Washington in 3 Correspondence and   Public Papers of John Jay 405–08 (Johnston ed. 1891).

For later examples, see: Opinion given by Justice Johnson, with the approval of other members of the Court, to President Monroe, in 1 Warren, The Supreme Court in United States History 596–97 (1937 ed.); Letter of Chief Justice Hughes to Senator Wheeler, Chairman of the Senate Judiciary Committee, concerning President Roosevelt's proposals for reorganizing the Supreme Court, Sen.Rep. No. 711, 75th Cong., 1st Sess. (1937), at 38–40; Letter of Chief Justice Taney to Secretary of the Treasury Chase concerning the 1862 tax levied upon the salaries of federal judges, in Tyler, Memoir of Roger B. Taney 432–34 (1872).[7]

In recent years, sitting Justices have also published numerous books, articles, and lectures commenting on legal issues.[8] Does this practice compromise the values underlying the prohibition against advisory opinions? If not, why not?

(5) *Declaratory Judgments.* The Federal Declaratory Judgment Act of 1934, 48 Stat. 955, authorizes the federal courts to issue declaratory judgments establishing "the rights and legal relations of any interested party seeking such declaration" in "a case of actual controversy." For the present provision, see 28 U.S.C. §§ 2201–02. Why aren't declaratory judgments advisory opinions?

Language in Willing v. Chicago Auditorium Ass'n, 277 U.S. 274 (1928), raised apprehensions that the Supreme Court might regard declaratory judgment actions, which were permitted by statute in several states but had not been authorized by Congress, as outside the federal judicial power under Article III. But the Court gave res judicata effect to a state declaratory judgment in Fidelity Nat. Bank & Trust Co. v. Swope, 274 U.S. 123 (1927), observing (p. 132): "While ordinarily a case or judicial controversy results in a judgment requiring award of process of execution to carry it into effect, such relief is not an indispensable adjunct to the exercise of the judicial function." See also Old Colony Trust Co. v. Commissioner, 279 U.S. 716 (1929); Restatement (Second) of Judgments § 33 (1982).

In Nashville, C. & St.L.Ry. v. Wallace, 288 U.S. 249 (1933), the Court for the first time reviewed a state court declaratory judgment. The plaintiff had sued state tax officials and the state attorney general, asking for a declaratory

---

7. Taney protested that the tax was invalid. He gave as his reason for the form of the protest that all the judges would be disqualified if the question arose in litigation. When the same question arose under the Revenue Act of 1918, the Supreme Court held the tax invalid, referring to Taney's opinion. Evans v. Gore, 253 U.S. 245 (1920), substantially overruled in O'Malley v. Woodrough, 307 U.S. 277 (1939).

8. See, *e.g.,* Blackmun, *The First Amendment and its Religion Clauses: Where Are We? Where Are We Going?*, 14 Nova L.Rev. 29 (1989); Brennan, *The Bill of Rights and the States: The Revival of State Constitutions as Guardians of Individual Rights*, 61 N.Y.U.L.Rev. 535 (1986); Brennan, *Constitutional Adjudication and the Death Penalty: A View from the Court*, 100 Harv.L.Rev. 313 (1986); Marshall, *Remarks on the Death Penalty Made at the Judicial Conference of the Second Circuit*, 86 Colum.L.Rev. 1 (1986); O'Connor, *Foreword: The Establishment Clause and Endorsement of Religion*, 8 J.L. & Rel. 1 (1990); Rehnquist, *The Impeachment Clause: A Wild Card in the Constitution*, 85 Nw.U.L.Rev. 903 (1991); Rehnquist, *Presidential Appointments to the Supreme Court*, 2 Const.Commen. 319 (1985); Scalia, *The Rule of Law as a Law of Rules*, 56 U.Chi.L.Rev. 1175 (1989); Scalia, *Originalism: The Lesser Evil*, 57 U.Cinn.L.Rev. 849 (1989); Stevens, *The Freedom of Speech*, 102 Yale L.J. 1293 (1993); Stevens, *Is Justice Irrelevant?*, 87 Nw. U.L.Rev. 1121 (1993).

For a comprehensive review and compilation of informal comments through 1962, see Westin, *Out-of-Court Commentary by United States Supreme Court Justices, 1790–1962: Of Free Speech and Judicial Lockjaw*, 62 Colum.L.Rev. 633 (1962).

judgment that a state tax whose payment had been demanded violated the federal Constitution. Justice Stone, again speaking for a unanimous Court, said that the proceeding had all the elements of a traditional bill for an injunction, except that the plaintiffs sought no coercive decree and had not shown that they would suffer irreparable injury if preventive relief were not given. Neither of these elements, the Court held, was essential to a controversy in the constitutional sense.

Apparently encouraged by the Wallace decision, Congress passed the Federal Declaratory Judgment Act a year later, and the Court unanimously upheld the Act's constitutionality in Aetna Life Insurance Co. v. Haworth, 300 U.S. 227 (1937). The insurance company had brought the action to secure a declaration that four policies held by the defendant had lapsed for nonpayment of premiums, and that the company's only obligation was to pay $45 on the insured's death as extended insurance on one policy. The complaint asserted that the defendant claimed to be totally and permanently disabled, in which event two of the policies would oblige the company to pay disability benefits. The complaint added that the defendant, while making this claim repeatedly, had failed to institute any action in which the company could prove its falsity. The complaint pointed to the danger posed by the possible disappearance, illness, or death of witnesses, and to the necessity meanwhile of maintaining reserves against the policies in excess of $20,000.

Chief Justice Hughes, for the Court, said (pp. 239–40):

"* * * The Declaratory Judgment Act of 1934, in its limitation to 'cases of actual controversy,' manifestly has regard to the constitutional provision and is operative only in respect to controversies which are such in the constitutional sense. The word 'actual' is one of emphasis rather than of definition. Thus the operation of the Declaratory Judgment Act is procedural only. In providing remedies and defining procedure in relation to cases and controversies in the constitutional sense the Congress is acting within its delegated power over the jurisdiction of the federal courts which the Congress is authorized to establish. * * * Exercising this control of practice and procedure the Congress is not confined to traditional forms or traditional remedies."

After reviewing the earlier constitutional cases, the opinion continued (pp. 242–44):

"There is here a dispute between parties who face each other in an adversary proceeding. The dispute relates to legal rights and obligations arising from the contracts of insurance. The dispute is definite and concrete, not hypothetical or abstract. * * * It calls, not for an advisory opinion upon a hypothetical basis, but for an adjudication of present right upon established facts. * * *

"If the insured had brought suit to recover the disability benefits currently payable under two of the policies there would have been no question that the controversy was of a justiciable nature, whether or not the amount involved would have permitted its determination in a federal court. * * * [T]he character of the controversy and of the issue to be determined is essentially the same whether it is presented by the insured or by the insurer."

The Haworth case effectively disposed of a strict view, taken by some lower federal courts, that the statutory grant of jurisdiction to declare "rights and other legal relations" did not warrant a declaration of non-liability. Isn't this one of the areas in which the declaratory judgment is most useful?

Would it be safe to say that an actual controversy always exists if either party could maintain an action for coercive relief?

(6) *Advisory Opinions by State Courts.*   Article III's prohibition against advisory opinions by federal courts does not extend to state courts, and a number of state courts are authorized to render them.   For example, part 2, ch. 3, art. 2 of the constitution of Massachusetts (1780) provides: "Each branch of the legislature, as well as the governor or the council, shall have authority to require the opinions of the justices of the supreme judicial court, upon important questions of law, and upon solemn occasions."   There are variants of this provision in the constitutions of New Hampshire, Maine, Rhode Island, Florida, Colorado, and South Dakota.   In at least two states, Alabama and Delaware, advisory opinions are authorized, in certain circumstances, by statute.   Although there is no state statutory or constitutional authority for the practice, the justices of the North Carolina Supreme Court "acting in their individual capacities" have given advisory opinions to the governor and legislature on request.   These opinions do not "have the force of law", and the court has explicitly declined to provide advisory opinions "in its capacity as a court".   In re Advisory Opinion, 335 S.E.2d 890, 891 (N.C.1985).   Other states have had an advisory opinion procedure in the past, but have abandoned it through judicial decision, statutory repeal, or constitutional amendment.[9]

If a state court renders an advisory opinion on a question of federal law, that opinion may significantly affect the operations of state government.   How may federal interests be protected in such a case?   See pp. 154–57, *infra.*

(7) *Advisory Opinions in Other Legal Systems.*   The advisory opinion has been used in other legal systems.   See, *e.g.,* Davison, *The Constitutionality and Utility of Advisory Opinions,* 2 U.Toronto L.J. 254 (1938)(Canadian practice); Wade, *Consultation of the Judiciary by the Executive,* 46 L.Q.Rev. 169 (1939)(English practice).   Many European countries (including Germany, France, Italy, Spain, Portugal, and Belgium) employ courts established exclusively to review constitutional claims.   These tribunals characteristically require only "an *abstract* or *objective* question" to examine the constitutionality of a new law; "no concrete dispute involving individual situations" is necessary.   Louis Favoreu, *American and European Models of Constitutional Justice,* in Comparative and Private International Law: Essays in Honor of John Henry Merryman on His Seventieth Birthday 105, 113 (Clark, ed., 1990).   The European Court of Justice, the European Court of Human Rights, and the Inter–American Court of Human Rights all enjoy explicit grants of jurisdiction to render advisory opinions.[10]

9.   For critical commentary, favorable and adverse, on the advisory opinion practice, see Note, 29 Me.L.Rev. 305 (1978); Comment, 44 Fordham L.Rev. 81 (1975); Borchard, *Declaratory Judgments* 71–80 (2d ed. 1941); Frankfurter, p. 94, *supra;* Hudson, *Advisory Opinions of National and International Courts,* 37 Harv.L.Rev. 970 (1924). See also Brown, *Binding Advisory Opinions: A Federal Courts Perspective on the State School Finance Decisions,* 35 B.C.L.Rev. 543 (1994), observing that numerous state courts have held that school funding disparities violate state constitutional requirements, but

have typically declined to enter more than declaratory relief.   Although such opinions are not advisory in the technical sense, Brown sees close practical similarities.   Professor Brown generally approves the position taken by state courts as a potentially useful experiment, testing the utility of dialogues between state courts and state legislatures in finding remedies for legal wrongs.

10.   See Butterworth's Guide to the European Communities 29 (1992)(describing the jurisdiction granted to the European Court of Justice); Blaustein et al., eds., Human Rights

SECTION 2. ISSUES OF PARTIES, THE REQUIREMENT OF FINALITY, AND THE PROHIBITION AGAINST FEIGNED AND COLLUSIVE SUITS

Hayburn's Case

2 U.S. (2 Dall.) 408, 1 L.Ed. 436 (1792).
On Petition for Mandamus.

This was a motion for a *mandamus* to be directed to the *Circuit Court* for the district of *Pennsylvania,* commanding the said court to proceed in a certain petition of *Wm. Hayburn,* who had applied to be put on the pension list of the *United States,* as an invalid pensioner.

[The Invalid Pensions Act of 1792,[1] which provided financial assistance to injured veterans of the Revolutionary War, charged the federal circuit courts with entertaining petitions from would-be pensioners. The courts were to receive evidence of the petitioners' military service, their war injuries, their resulting disabilities, and the proportion of their monthly pay corresponding to those disabilities. If the court found that a petitioner qualified for a pension, it was directed to submit the petitioner's name, as well as a recommended sum, to the Secretary of War. The statute directed the Secretary to place any applicant certified by a circuit court on the pension list, except that, in cases of suspected "imposition or mistake", the Secretary was to withhold the suspected petitioner's name and so report to Congress.]

The Attorney General (Randolph) who made the motion for the *mandamus,* having premised that it was done *ex officio,* without an application from any particular person, but with a view to procure the execution of an act of Congress, particularly interesting to a meritorious and unfortunate class of citizens, THE COURT declared that they entertained great doubt upon his right, under such circumstances, and in a case of this kind, to proceed *ex officio;* and directed him to state the principles on which he attempted to support the right. The Attorney General, accordingly, entered into an elaborate description of the powers and duties of his office:—

But the COURT being divided in opinion on that question, the motion, made *ex officio,* was not allowed.

The Attorney General then changed the ground of his interposition, declaring it to be at the instance, and on behalf of Hayburn, a party interested; and he entered into the merits of the case, upon the act of Congress, and the refusal of the Judges to carry it into effect.

The COURT observed, that they would hold the motion under advisement, until the next term; but no decision was ever pronounced, as the Legislature, at an intermediate session, provided, in another way, for the relief of the pensioners.

Sourcebook 521, 606 (1987)(describing the jurisdiction of the courts of human rights).

1. [Ed.] Act of March 23, 1792, ch. 11, 1 Stat. 243 (1792)(repealed in part and amended by Act of Feb. 28, 1793, ch. 17, 1 Stat. 324 (1793).

[The following was added by the reporter as a footnote to the above report:]

As the reasons assigned by the Judges, for declining to execute the first act of Congress, involve a great Constitutional question, it will not be thought improper to subjoin them, in illustration of Hayburn's case.

■ The Circuit Court for the district of New York (consisting of JAY, CHIEF JUSTICE, CUSHING, JUSTICE, and DUANE, DISTRICT JUDGE) * * * were * * * unanimously, of opinion and agreed.

"That by the Constitution of the United States, the government thereof is divided into *three* distinct and independent branches, and that it is the duty of each to abstain from, and to oppose, encroachments on either.

"That neither the *Legislative* nor the *Executive* branches, can constitutionally assign to the *Judicial* any duties, but such as are properly judicial, and to be performed in a judicial manner.

"That the duties assigned to the Circuit courts, by this act, are not of that description, and that the act itself does not appear to contemplate them as such; in as much as it subjects the decisions of these courts, made pursuant to those duties, first to the consideration and suspension of the Secretary [of] War, and then to the revision of the Legislature; whereas by the Constitution, neither the Secretary [of] War, nor any other Executive officer, nor even the Legislature, are authorized to sit as a court of errors on the judicial acts or opinions of this court.

"As, therefore, the business assigned to this court, by the act, is not judicial, nor directed to be performed judicially, the act can only be considered as appointing commissioners for the purposes mentioned in it, by *official* instead of *personal* descriptions.

"That the Judges of this court regard themselves as being the commissioners designated by the act, and therefore as being at liberty to accept or decline that office.

"That as the objects of this act are exceedingly benevolent, and do real honor to the humanity and justice of Congress; and as the Judges desire to manifest, on all proper occasions, and in every proper manner, their high respect for the National Legislature, they will execute this act in the capacity of commissioners. * * *"[2]

The Circuit court for the district of Pennsylvania, (consisting of WILSON, and BLAIR, JUSTICES, and PETERS, DISTRICT JUDGE) made the following representation, in a joint letter to the President of the United States, on the 18th of April, 1792.

"* * * It is a principle important to freedom, that in government, the *judicial* should be distinct from, and independent of, the legislative department. To this important principle the people of the United States, in forming their Constitution, have manifested the highest regard. * * *

---

2. [Ed.] On the use of federal judges in other governmental roles, see generally *Note on Extra–Curricular Activities of Federal Judges* in the first edition of this book, at p. 102. See also the Code of Judicial Conduct approved by the American Bar Association, August 17, 1972; Canon 5(G) of the Code bars judges from accepting appointments to governmental commissions other than those concerned with the improvement of the law, the legal system, or the administration of justice.

"Upon due consideration, we have been unanimously of opinion, that, under this act, the Circuit court held for the Pennsylvania district could not proceed;

"1st. Because the business directed by this act is not of a judicial nature. It forms no part of the power vested by the Constitution in the courts of the United States; the Circuit court must, consequently, have proceeded *without* constitutional authority.

"2d. Because, if, upon that business, the court had proceeded, its *judgments* (for its *opinions* are its judgments) might, under the same act, have been revised and controuled by the legislature, and by an officer in the executive department. Such revision and controul we deemed radically inconsistent with the independence of that judicial power which is vested in the courts; and, consequently, with that important principle which is so strictly observed by the Constitution of the United States. * * *"

The Circuit court for the district of North Carolina, (consisting of IREDELL, JUSTICE, and SITGREAVES, DISTRICT JUDGE) made the following representation in a joint letter to the President of the United States, on the 8th of June, 1792. * * *

"1. That the Legislative, Executive, and Judicial departments, are each formed in a separate and independent manner; and that the ultimate basis of each is the Constitution only, within the limits of which each department can alone justify any act of authority.

"2. That the Legislature, among other important powers, unquestionably possess that of establishing courts in such a manner as to their wisdom shall appear best, limited by the terms of the constitution only; and to whatever extent that power may be exercised, or however severe the duty they may think proper to require, the Judges, when appointed in virtue of any such establishment, owe implicit and unreserved obedience to it.

"3. That at the same time such courts cannot be warranted, as we conceive, by virtue of that part of the Constitution delegating *Judicial power*, for the exercise of which any act of the legislature is provided, in exercising (even under the authority of another act) any power not in its nature *judicial*, or, if *judicial*, not provided for upon the terms the Constitution requires.

"4. That whatever doubt may be suggested, whether the power in question is properly of a judicial nature, yet inasmuch as the decision of the court is not made final, but may be at least suspended in its operation by the Secretary [of] War, if he shall have cause to suspect imposition or mistake; this subjects the decision of the court to a mode of revision which we consider to be unwarranted by the Constitution; for, though Congress may certainly establish, in instances not yet provided for, courts of appellate jurisdiction, yet such courts must consist of judges appointed in the manner the Constitution requires, and holding their offices by no other tenure than that of their good behaviour, by which tenure the office of Secretary [of] War is not held. And we beg leave to add, with all due deference, that no decision of any court of the United States can, under any circumstances, in our opinion, agreeable to the Constitution, be liable to a reversion [sic], or even suspension, by the Legislature itself, in whom no judicial power of any kind appears to be vested, but the important one relative to impeachments.

* * *

[The judges then indicated that they were of the opinion that they could not regard the Act as appointing them commissioners for the purpose of its execution, since the Act appeared to confer power on the circuit courts and not on the judges personally. Acknowledging their doubts as to the propriety of giving an advisory opinion (no application under the Act had as yet been made to them), they concluded that the present situation called for an exception, "upon every principle of humanity and justice", but stated that they would "most attentively hear" argument on the points on which an opinion had been expressed in the event that an actual application were made.]

NOTE ON HAYBURN'S CASE

(1) *Jurisdictional Basis.*   Jurisdiction in the mandamus proceeding in the Supreme Court was no doubt premised on the statute later held unconstitutional in Marbury v. Madison. Did the Court overlook the problem of the constitutionality of that statute? Or is this case distinguishable? See Ex parte Peru and materials in Chap. III, Sec. 3, *infra.*

(2) *The Ex Officio Action by the Attorney General.*   Why did three Justices conclude that the Attorney General could not proceed *ex officio*? In defense of his authority, Randolph argued that (i) the 1789 Judiciary Act authorized the Attorney General to "prosecute and conduct all suits in the Supreme Court in which the United States shall be concerned", (ii) the United States was "concerned" when a federal court failed to perform duties imposed on it by law, and (iii) the office of the English attorney general, on which its American counterpart was modeled, would be empowered to litigate to protect the public interest in a case such as this. See Bloch, *The Early Role of the Attorney General in Our Constitutional Scheme: In the Beginning There Was Pragmatism,* 1989 Duke L.J. 561, 601–04.

Was the problem that the Attorney General lacked a personal stake or interest in the outcome, as required by the private law model of adjudication, p. 78, *supra*?[1] Surely the Attorney General can enforce both the criminal law and federal regulatory statutes. What is the Attorney General's stake in those cases?

In Pasadena City Bd. of Educ. v. Spangler, 427 U.S. 424 (1976), high school students and their parents brought an action seeking injunctive relief from allegedly unconstitutional segregation in the Pasadena schools. The United States intervened as a party plaintiff pursuant to 42 U.S.C. § 2000h–2, which provides that upon such intervention, "the United States shall be entitled to the same relief as if it had instituted the action." By the time the case (involving issues as to remedy) reached the Supreme Court, all the student plaintiffs had graduated. The Court held that the continued presence of the United States was authorized by the statute, and that the case was therefore not moot.

With respect to the Attorney General's status as a party, what distinguishes Hayburn's Case from Spangler or other cases in which the Attorney

---

1. According to Marcus & Teir, *Hayburn's Case: A Misinterpretation of Precedent,* 1988 Wis.L.Rev. 527, 541–46, Hayburn's Case is frequently cited by the Supreme Court either for this proposition or for "some less well defined judicial restraint principle". For the authors' different interpretation, see *infra.*

General is authorized by statute to intervene or sue to enforce statutory prohibitions against private conduct?[2] For suggestions that the problem in Hayburn's Case did not arise from Article III's case or controversy requirement, but instead involved a possible lack of either presidential or congressional authorization for the Attorney General to proceed *ex officio*, see Bloch, *supra*, at 608–18; Marcus & Teir, note 1, *supra*, at 540–41.

Why might the Attorney General require congressional authorization to sue to enforce the law? Is it because public rights litigation, even by the Attorney General, has important implications for private rights and the separation of powers?[3] Why might the Attorney General require presidential authorization?[4]

(3) *The Reporter's Footnote.* The Supreme Court never pronounced a judgment on the motion for mandamus in Hayburn's Case; the opinions of the Justices on the merits emerge only through the reporter's footnote, which includes an opinion of the circuit court for the district of New York and letters from the circuit courts for the districts of Pennsylvania and North Carolina to President Washington. Were the latter two communications, at least, advisory opinions? Can the issuance of these letters be reconciled with the position taken in the Correspondence of the Justices, pp. 92–93, *supra?* There is at least one connecting theme between the Correspondence of the Justices and the opinions expressed in the reporter's footnote in Hayburn's Case: judicial independence requires that the Article III courts not be subject to enlistment by Congress or the Executive to act as subordinates to those two branches in the performance of their characteristic functions.

(4) *Adverse Parties.* Why did the Justices and district judges consider the functions assigned to the circuit courts by the Invalid Pensions Act of 1792 to be nonjudicial? Was it because a "case" or "controversy" requires at least two parties who are adverse to each other? Is there any intrinsic difficulty in making a "case" out of an application by a private person for a grant by the government of money or other tangible property or of an intangible permission? Note that Tutun v. United States, 270 U.S. 568 (1926), p. 107, *infra,* held that rulings on petitions for naturalization satisfy the case or controversy requirement. The Court recognized that many petitions are uncontested, but observed that the United States was "always a possible adverse party" (p. 577). Would it have made a difference if, under the Invalid Pensions Act, the government had been made a "possible" adverse party? Even if the government did not actually bother to contest any proceedings in the circuit courts?

(5) *Intergovernmental Litigation.* In Hayburn's Case, the original parties in the Supreme Court were the Attorney General and the Circuit Court for the District of Pennsylvania. Does the idea of a "case" entirely between the

2. See Bloch, *supra,* at 620–23. Bloch concludes that "echoes of the Hayburn Court's concern with the dangers of an uncontrolled Attorney General continue to reverberate today". *Id.* at 623.

3. Dissenting in Flast v. Cohen, p. 137, *infra,* Justice Harlan suggested that citizen standing to assert public rights should be permitted if *but only if* authorized by Con-gress. Should a comparable principle apply to the Attorney General?

4. For varying views of the extent to which the framers intended the executive branch to be subject to centralized presidential direction, see Bloch, *supra;* Lessig & Sunstein, *The President and the Administration,* 94 Colum.L.Rev. 1 (1994); Calabresi & Prakash, *The President's Power to Execute the Laws,* 104 Yale L.J. 541 (1994).

government and its own officials smack too much of the government litigating with itself? What if the adverse parties are both in the same branch?

In United States v. Nixon, 418 U.S. 683 (1974), enforcement of a subpoena against the President was sought by the Watergate Special Prosecutor, who was appointed—and also (under specified conditions) removable—by the Attorney General. The Court said (pp. 692–97):

"In the District Court, the President's counsel argued that the court lacked jurisdiction to issue the subpoena because the matter was an intra-branch dispute between a subordinate and superior officer of the Executive Branch and hence not subject to judicial resolution. That argument has been renewed in this Court with emphasis on the contention that the dispute does not present a 'case' or 'controversy' which can be adjudicated in the federal courts. * * *

"The mere assertion of a claim of an 'intra-branch dispute,' without more, has never operated to defeat federal jurisdiction; justiciability does not depend on such a surface inquiry.[5] * * * Our starting point is the nature of the proceeding for which the evidence is sought—here pending criminal prosecution [against John Mitchell, the former Attorney General, and others for a number of offenses]. * * * Under the authority of Art. II, § 2, Congress has vested in the Attorney General the power to conduct the criminal litigation of the United States Government. 28 U.S.C. § 516. It has also vested in him the power to appoint subordinate officers to assist him in the discharge of his duties. 28 U.S.C. §§ 509, 510, 515, 533. Acting pursuant to those statutes, the Attorney General has delegated the authority to represent the United States in these particular matters to a Special Prosecutor with unique authority and tenure. * * * [The opinion here referred to the regulation promulgated by the Attorney General giving the Special Prosecutor independent powers and preventing his removal except for "extraordinary improprieties." ']

"So long as this regulation is extant it has the force of law. * * * [I]t is theoretically possible for the Attorney General to amend or revoke the regulation defining the Special Prosecutor's authority. But he has not done so. So long as this regulation remains in force the Executive Branch is bound by it, and indeed the United States as the sovereign composed of the three branches is bound to respect and to enforce it. * * *

"In light of the uniqueness of the setting in which the conflict arises, the fact that both parties are officers of the Executive Branch cannot be viewed as a barrier to justiciability."

Whether or not the Court's stated ground was sufficient, wasn't the result correct on the issue of justiciability? As long as the Constitution permits the government to be structured so that some parts of the executive branch are not directly subordinate to others, can't a justiciable dispute exist between two factually independent units of government? See generally Herz, *United States v. United States: When Can the Federal Government Sue Itself?*, 32 Wm. & Mary L.Rev. 893 (1991).

(6) *The Problem of Executive Revision.* Why did the judges in the circuit courts think that the existence of an executive power of revision was fatal to

---

5. The Court here cited, *inter alia,* United States v. ICC, 337 U.S. 426 (1949)(action by the U.S., as shipper, to set aside reparations order of ICC), and United States ex rel. Chapman v. FPC, 345 U.S. 153 (1953)(action by Secretary of Interior challenging authority of FPC to grant license). Both the FPC and the ICC are "independent agencies". Does this matter?

the exercise of "judicial power"?[6] Note that the statutory scheme made short-run practical sense. The judges were in a better position than the Secretary of War to appraise the personal good faith of claimants and the extent of their disability, which was the job they were given to do, but the Secretary was in a better position to check the official military records. Did the objection to executive revision rest simply on judicial dignity and a desire to keep face? Or on more fundamental concerns about the integrity of the judicial process?

(a) Pursuant to the treaty of 1819 between the United States and Spain, Congress directed the judge of the territorial court, and later of the district court, in Florida to "receive, examine and adjudge" claims for losses suffered by certain Spanish citizens through operations of the American army in Florida. The judge was to report decisions in favor of the claimants, together with the supporting evidence, to the Secretary of the Treasury, who, if satisfied that the awards were just and within the provisions of the treaty, was to authorize payment. 3 Stat. 768, 6 *id.* 569, 9 *id.* 788. In United States v. Ferreira, 54 U.S. (13 How.) 40 (1852), the Supreme Court dismissed an appeal by the United States from an award by the district judge "for want of jurisdiction". The Court said that the judge was not acting judicially, but as a commissioner. It noted but did not decide the question whether the judge could be appointed in that capacity by statute rather than by the President with the advice and consent of the Senate.

(b) In Chicago & Southern Air Lines v. Waterman S.S. Corp., 333 U.S. 103 (1948), the question was whether an order of the Civil Aeronautics Board denying to one *citizen* air carrier and granting to another a certificate of convenience and necessity for an overseas air route was subject to judicial review. Section 801 of the Act provided that such an order must be submitted to the President before publication and was unconditionally subject to presidential approval. The judicial review section of the Act provided that "any order, affirmative or negative, issued by the Board under this Act, except any order in respect of any *foreign* air carrier subject to the approval of the President as provided in section 801 of this Act, shall be subject to review by the circuit courts of appeals * * *."

The Court held that final orders approved by the President could not be reviewed because such orders "embody Presidential discretion as to political matters beyond the competence of the courts to adjudicate" (p. 114). The court of appeals had avoided this difficulty by holding that after it had reviewed the final order the case should be resubmitted to the President so "that his power to disapprove would apply after as well as before the court acts". In rejecting this approach, the Court said (pp. 113–14):

"* * * But if the President may completely disregard the judgment of the court, it would be only because it is one the courts were not authorized to render. Judgments, within the powers vested in courts by the Judiciary Article of the Constitution, may not lawfully be revised, overturned or refused faith and credit by another Department of Government.

6. The Supreme Court has recently observed that "Hayburn's Case * * * stands for the principle that Congress cannot vest review of the decisions of Article III courts in officials of the Executive Branch." Plaut v. Spendthrift Farm, Inc., 115 S.Ct. 1447, 1453 (1995). How well does the Court's judicial action in Hayburn's Case support the principle for which the case is said to stand?

"To revise or review an administrative decision which has only the force of a recommendation to the President would be to render an advisory opinion in its most obnoxious form—advice that the President has not asked, tendered at the demand of a private litigant, on a subject concededly within the President's exclusive, ultimate control. This Court early and wisely determined that it would not give advisory opinions even when asked by the Chief Executive. It has also been the firm and unvarying practice of Constitutional Courts to render no judgments not binding and conclusive on the parties and none that are subject to later review or alteration by administrative action."

Four Justices, dissenting, thought that the order should be reviewed only after final action by the President, and that at that stage it would be feasible to separate those aspects of the order attributable to an exercise of Presidential discretion and review only those aspects relating to the validity of the Board's action.

Lower courts subsequently held Waterman inapplicable "where the action of the Board * * * is beyond the Board's power", on the theory that then, legally, the Board could have placed nothing before the President for action. American Airlines, Inc. v. CAB, 348 F.2d 349, 352 (D.C.Cir.1965); Pan American World Airways, Inc. v. CAB, 380 F.2d 770 (2d Cir.1967), *aff'd by an equally divided Court*, 391 U.S. 461 (1968).

(7) *Congressional Revision.* Was the power of Congress under the pension act to revise the decision of the judges open to the same objections as the power of the Secretary to do so? What if the Secretary had been directed to put all names certified by the courts on the pension roll, and Congress had simply retained power to refuse to pay any particular pension by virtue of its power over appropriations? See *Note on Claims Against the United States and the Problem of Legislative Revision*, p. 111, *infra*.

In Plaut v. Spendthrift Farm, Inc., 115 S.Ct. 1447 (1995), the Supreme Court ruled that a federal statute directing federal courts to reopen final judgments in private lawsuits violated Article III and the separation of powers. The original action between the parties, involving allegations of fraud and deceit in the sale of stock under § 10(b) of the Securities and Exchange Act and the SEC's Rule 10b–5, was dismissed with prejudice after the Supreme Court held in Lampf, Pleva, Lipkind, Prupis & Petigrow v. Gilbertson, 501 U.S. 350, 364 (1991), that litigation under § 10(b) and Rule 10b–5 "must be commenced within one year after the discovery of the facts constituting the violation and within three years of such violation." The decision in the Lampf case surprised many litigants by establishing a shorter limitations period than most courts had previously applied, and Congress responded by enacting legislation that authorized reinstatement of certain actions dismissed as time-barred under the Lampf decision. Relying on the congressional enactment, the petitioners moved to reopen their lawsuit. But the Supreme Court held that Congress had trenched on the judicial power. In an opinion for six Justices, Justice Scalia found that the Framers, having "lived among the ruins of a system of intermingled legislative and judicial powers" (p. 1453), wished to insulate *final* judicial judgments from legislative revision. The Court distinguished cases in which Congress had changed the applicable law while a case was pending but prior to entry of a final judgment, had waived the res judicata effect of a prior judgment in favor of the government, and had annulled judgments rendered by legislative (rather than Article III) courts. Justice

Breyer filed a concurring opinion. Justice Stevens, joined by Justice Ginsburg, dissented.

In the absence of a final judgment dismissing a lawsuit, the Court in Plaut did not question Congress' power to enact laws establishing the retroactive liability of one private party to another or to authorize suits that otherwise would be time-barred. What purposes are served by attaching so much significance to the form of a final judgment of an Article III court?

Tutun v. United States

270 U.S. 568, 46 S.Ct. 425, 70 L.Ed. 738 (1926).
Certificate from the Circuit Court of Appeals for the First Circuit.

■ MR. JUSTICE BRANDEIS delivered the opinion of the Court.

These cases present, by certificate, the question whether the Circuit Courts of Appeals have jurisdiction to review a decree or order of a federal District Court denying the petition of an alien to be admitted to citizenship in the United States. * * *

The "jurisdiction to naturalize aliens as citizens of the United States" is conferred by Act of June 29, 1906, c. 3592, § 3, upon the District Courts, among others. Jurisdiction to review the "final decision in the District Courts * * * in all cases," except as otherwise provided, was conferred by Act of March 3, 1891, c. 517, § 6, upon Circuit Courts of Appeals. * * * The substantial question is whether a petition for naturalization is a case within the meaning of the Circuit Court of Appeals Act.

The function of admitting to citizenship has been conferred exclusively upon courts continuously since the foundation of our government. See Act of March 26, 1790, c. 3. The federal District Courts, among others, have performed that function since the Act of January 29, 1795, c. 20. The constitutionality of this exercise of jurisdiction has never been questioned. If the proceeding were not a case or controversy within the meaning of article 3, § 2, this delegation of power upon the courts would have been invalid. Whether a proceeding which results in a grant is a judicial one does not depend upon the nature of the thing granted, but upon the nature of the proceeding which Congress has provided for securing the grant. The United States may create rights in individuals against itself and provide only an administrative remedy. It may provide a legal remedy, but make resort to the courts available only after all administrative remedies have been exhausted. It may give to the individual the option of either an administrative or a legal remedy. Or it may provide only a legal remedy. Whenever the law provides a remedy enforceable in the courts according to the regular course of legal procedure, and that remedy is pursued, there arises a case within the meaning of the Constitution, whether the subject of the litigation be property or status. A petition for naturalization is clearly a proceeding of that character.

The petitioner's claim is one arising under the Constitution and laws of the United States. The claim is presented to the court in such a form that the judicial power is capable of acting upon it. The proceeding is instituted and is conducted throughout according to the regular course of judicial procedure. The United States is always a possible adverse party. * * * Section 9 (Comp.

St. § 4368) provides that every final hearing must be held in open court, that upon such hearing the applicant and witnesses shall be examined under oath before the court and in its presence, and that every final order must be made under the hand of the court and shall be entered in full upon the record. The judgment entered, like other judgments of a court of record, is accepted as complete evidence of its own validity unless set aside. It may not be collaterally attacked. If a certificate is procured when the prescribed qualifications have no existence in fact, it may be canceled by suit. "It is in this respect," as stated in Johannessen v. United States, 225 U.S. 227, 238 "closely analogous to a public grant of land, or of the exclusive right to make, use and vend a new and useful invention."

The opportunity to become a citizen of the United States is said to be merely a privilege, and not a right. It is true that the Constitution does not confer upon aliens the right to naturalization. But it authorizes Congress to establish a uniform rule therefor. Article 1, § 8, cl. 4. The opportunity having been conferred by the Naturalization Act, there is a statutory right in the alien to submit his petition and evidence to a court, to have that tribunal pass upon them, and, if the requisite facts are established, to receive the certificate. There is, of course, no "right to naturalization unless all statutory requirements are complied with." United States v. Ginsberg, 243 U.S. 472, 475; Luria v. United States, 231 U.S. 9, 22. The applicant for citizenship, like other suitors who institute proceedings in a court of justice to secure the determination of an asserted right, must allege in his petition the fulfillment of all conditions upon the existence of which the alleged right is made dependent, and he must establish these allegations by competent evidence to the satisfaction of the court. In passing upon the application the court exercises judicial judgment. It does not confer or withhold a favor. * * *

Questions answered in the affirmative.

NOTE ON THE TUTUN CASE AND THE PROBLEM OF JUDICIAL REVISION

(1) *Res Judicata Effect and the Judicial Function.* Note the Court's statement that the district court's certificate could be cancelled on a subsequent judicial finding that "the prescribed qualifications have no existence in fact". Does the limited res judicata effect implied by the possibility of such reexamination raise any question concerning the consistency of the original naturalization proceeding with the judicial function?

(2) *Patent and Trademark Rulings.* For many years the U.S. Court of Appeals of the District of Columbia had jurisdiction of appeals from certain decisions of the Patent Office denying patent applications and disposing of claims of interference, and also from similar decisions of the Commissioner of Patents in trademark proceedings.[1] The statute provided that the decision on appeal "shall govern the further proceedings in the case. But no opinion or decision of the court in any such case shall preclude any person interested from

---

1. From 1929 to 1982 this jurisdiction was vested in the Court of Customs and Patent Appeals. Act of March 2, 1929, 45 Stat. 1476. In 1982, that court was abolished and its jurisdiction transferred to the new Court of Appeals for the Federal Circuit. See p. 42, *supra.*

the right to contest the validity of such patent in any court wherein the same may be called in question."   Rev.Stat. § 4914, 35 U.S.C. § 62 (1946).

In Postum Cereal Co. v. California Fig Nut Co., 272 U.S. 693 (1927), the Court held that it lacked jurisdiction under the Constitution to review a decision of the Court of Appeals of the District of Columbia in a trademark *inter partes* proceeding to which § 62 applied.   (Since that court was not viewed as limited in its jurisdiction by Article III, no question was raised as to its power under the Constitution to hear such appeals.)   Chief Justice Taft said (pp. 698–99):

"* * * The decision of the Court of Appeals * * * is not a judicial judgment.   It is a mere administrative decision.   It is merely an instruction to the Commissioner of Patents by a court which is made part of the machinery of the Patent Office for administrative purposes.   In the exercise of such function, it does not enter a judgment binding parties in a case as the term case is used in the third article of the Constitution * * *.   Neither the opinion nor decision of the Court of Appeals * * * precludes any person interested from having the right to contest the validity of such patent or trade-mark in any court where it may be called in question.   This result prevents an appeal to this Court, which can only review judicial judgments."

The unsuccessful party in the Patent Office, after an unsuccessful appeal, could resort to a bill in equity in a federal district court, under 35 U.S.C. § 63 (1946), to compel the granting of his application.[2]   The provisions of § 63 did not contain a provision like that of § 62 limiting the effect of the judgment.   In Hoover Co. v. Coe, 325 U.S. 79 (1945), the Court entertained an appeal by an applicant for a patent whose claims had been finally dismissed by the Patent Office, and who had been unsuccessful in a suit to review this decision brought under § 63 in the district court for the District of Columbia.   The court of appeals had held that the district court lacked jurisdiction.   Without adverting to the Postum case, the Supreme Court reversed, holding that the final denial of claims for a patent was a reviewable decision.

In 1952 Title 35 of the United States Code was revised, and § 62 was essentially carried over into new § 144.[3]   The provision of § 62 limiting the effect of the judgment was, however, omitted as "superfluous".   The Reviser's Note pointed out that, though § 63 had contained no equivalent provision, proceedings under that section had not precluded parties from subsequently raising questions of the patent's validity.

In Glidden Co. v. Zdanok, 370 U.S. 530, 576 (1962), Justice Harlan's plurality opinion pointed to that earlier provision of § 62 as "evidently instrumental in prompting" the Postum decision and concluded that the decision did not apply to the authority of the Court of Customs and Patent Appeals under the statutory scheme in effect in 1962.   (See note 1, *supra*.) He said:

"It may still be true that Congress has given to the equity proceeding a greater preclusive effect than that accorded to decisions of the Court of Customs and Patent Appeals.   Even so, that circumstance alone is insufficient to make those decisions nonjudicial.   Tutun v. United States, 270 U.S. 568,

---

2.   By the Act of March 2, 1927, 44 Stat. 1335, the applicant was required to elect between the appeal to the court of appeals and the bill in equity, but the Supreme Court nonetheless adhered to the rule of the Postum case.   See, *e.g.,* McBride v. Teeple, 311 U.S. 649 (1940).

3.   Section 63 was incorporated in new § 145.

decided by the same Court as Postum and not there questioned, is controlling authority. * * *

"Mr. Justice Brandeis, the author of the Tutun opinion, had also prepared the Court's opinion in United States v. Ness, 245 U.S. 319, which upheld the Government's right to seek denaturalization even upon grounds known to and asserted unsuccessfully by it in the naturalization court. Proceedings in that court, the opinion explained, were relatively summary, with no right of appeal, whereas the denaturalization suit was plenary enough to permit full presentation of all objections and was accompanied with appeal as of right. 245 U.S., at 326. These differences made it reasonable for Congress to allow the Government another chance to contest the applicant's eligibility.

"The decision in Tutun, coming after Ness, draws the patent and trademark jurisdiction now exercised by the Court of Customs and Patent Appeals fully within the category of cases or controversies. * * * Like naturalization proceedings in a District Court, appeals from Patent Office decisions under 35 U.S.C. § 144 are relatively summary—since the record is limited to the evidence allowed by that office—and are not themselves subject to direct review by appeal as of right. * * *

"We conclude that the Postum decision must be taken to be limited to the statutory scheme in existence before the transfer of patent and trademark litigation to that court" (pp. 577–79).

In Brenner v. Manson, 383 U.S. 519 (1966), the Court held that it could constitutionally review patent cases from the Court of Customs and Patent Appeals.

(3) *Further Developments.*   In the Ness case (cited by Justice Harlan, *supra*), Justice Brandeis pointed out that some, relatively minor, issues resolved in the naturalization proceeding might be foreclosed from subsequent re-examination. The Court has since made clear that while the burden of proof in the original naturalization proceeding is on the applicant, *e.g.,* Berenyi v. District Director, 385 U.S. 630 (1967), in seeking denaturalization the government must establish its case by "clear, unequivocal, and convincing evidence", *e.g.,* Chaunt v. United States, 364 U.S. 350 (1960). The present statute also provides for denaturalization only on the grounds that the naturalization was "illegally procured" or "procured by concealment of a material fact or by willful misrepresentation." 8 U.S.C. § 1451(a).

Does the validity of the Tutun holding depend on these or similar restrictions on the scope of re-examination? On the "relatively summary" nature of the original proceedings? What is the problem in having a judgment subject to later judicial revision? Is the prohibition against advisory opinions relevant, and if so, how?

United States v. Jones

119 U.S. 477, 7 S.Ct. 283, 30 L.Ed. 440 (1886).
Appeal from the Court of Claims.

■ Mr. Chief Justice Waite delivered the opinion of the Court.

The grounds of this motion [to dismiss the appeal] are:

1.   That under the law as it now stands no appeal lies from a judgment of the Court of Claims to this court; * * *.

The case of Gordon v. United States, 2 Wall. 561, holding that no appeal would lie from a judgment of the Court of Claims to this court, was announced March 10, 1865. The cause was originally submitted on the 18th of December, 1863, and on the 10th of April, 1864, it was ordered for argument on the second day of the next term. Chief Justice Taney died October 12, 1864, and the case was not reargued under the special order of the previous term until January 3, 1865. Consequently, the opinion published as an appendix to 117 U.S. 697 must have been prepared by him before the decision was actually made. * * * [I]n announcing the judgment Chief Justice Chase said: "We think that the authority given to the head of an Executive Department by necessary implication in the 14th section of the amended Court of Claims Act, to revise all the decisions of that court requiring payment of money, denies to it the judicial power, from the exercise of which alone appeals can be taken to this court. The reasons which necessitate this conclusion may be more fully announced hereafter. At present, we restrict ourselves to this general statement, and to the direction that the cause be dismissed for want of jurisdiction." This differs somewhat from the case as reported by Mr. Wallace, and shows precisely the ground of the opinion, to wit, the special provisions of § 14. That section was as follows:

"Sec. 14. That no money shall be paid out of the Treasury for any claim passed on by the Court of Claims till after an appropriation therefor shall have been estimated for by the Secretary of the Treasury."

At the next session of Congress after this decision the objectionable section was repealed by the Act of March 17, 1866, c. 19, and the Court of Claims was directed to transmit, at the end of every term, a copy of its decisions to the heads of departments and certain other officers specially mentioned. From that time until the presentation of this motion it has never been doubted that appeals would lie. Indeed, immediately after the repealing act went into effect, and before the adjournment of the term then being held, a set of rules regulating such appeals was promulgated by this court, and it is safe to say that there has never been a term since in which many cases of the kind have not been heard and decided without objection from any one. * * *

Reference is also made to an Act of March 3, 1875, c. 149, which provides for "deducting any debt due the United States from any judgment recovered against the United States by such debtor;" but this gives the accounting officers of the government no authority to reexamine the judgment. It only provides a way of payment and satisfaction if the creditor shall, at the time of the presentation of his judgment, be a debtor of the United States for anything except what is included in the judgment, which is conclusive as to everything it embraces.

We are entirely satisfied that, as the law now stands, appeals do lie to this court from the judgments of the Court of Claims in the exercise of its general jurisdiction. * * *

NOTE ON CLAIMS AGAINST THE UNITED STATES AND THE PROBLEM OF LEGISLATIVE REVISION

(1) *Origins of the Court of Federal Claims.*   Before 1855 no general statute gave the consent of the United States to suit on claims for money, and a

claimant's only recourse was to petition Congress for a private act.   The burden on Congress of private bills, the delays and inequities of the private bill procedure, and the resulting impairment of government credit prompted the Act of February 24, 1855, 10 Stat. 612, establishing the Court of Claims.   But while the 1855 act authorized the court to "hear and determine" most types of money claims not sounding in tort, and while the court made findings of fact and law, its decisions were to be embodied not in judgments but in reports to Congress when decisions were adverse, or in drafts of private bills when decisions were favorable.   Since the congressional committees were willing to re-examine claims *de novo* and to receive fresh evidence on either side, this procedure merely erected an additional hurdle for proper claims to surmount. The pressure of Civil War contracts led to the Act of March 3, 1863, which enlarged the court and authorized it to render judgment.[1]

For the present jurisdiction of the United States Court of Federal Claims, which (along with the Court of Appeals for the Federal Circuit) has succeeded to the jurisdiction of the Court of Claims, see 28 U.S.C. §§ 1491–1507; pp. 1028-29, *infra*.   The Court of Federal Claims is an Article I court, the Federal Circuit an Article III court.

(2) *Taney's Views.*   Chief Justice Taney's draft opinion in the Gordon case, referred to in United States v. Jones, took a much wider ground than the decision itself.   The opinion acknowledged that Congress could create the Court of Claims to help it pass upon claims against the United States, just as it could invoke the assistance of any executive or administrative officer.   But, it said (117 U.S. at 702–03):

"* * * Congress cannot extend the appellate power of this Court beyond the limits prescribed by the Constitution, * * * nor can Congress authorize or require this Court to express an opinion on a case where its judicial power could not be exercised, and where its judgment would not be final and conclusive upon the rights of the parties, and process of execution awarded to carry it into effect.

"The award of execution is a part, and an essential part of every judgment passed by a court exercising judicial power.   It is no judgment, in the legal sense of the term, without it.   Without such an award the judgment would be inoperative and nugatory, leaving the aggrieved party without a remedy.   * * *

"It is true the act speaks of the judgment or decree of this Court.   But all that the Court is authorized to do is to certify its opinion to the Secretary of the Treasury, and if he inserts it in his estimates, and Congress sanctions it by an appropriation, it is then to be paid, but not otherwise.   And when the Secretary asks for this appropriation, the propriety of the estimate for this claim, like all other estimates of the Secretary, will be opened to debate, and whether the appropriation will be made or not will depend upon the majority of each House. The real and ultimate judicial power will, therefore, be exercised by the Legislative Department, and not by that department to which the Constitution has confided it."

(3) *Advisory Functions.*   The 1855, 1863, and 1866 acts all gave the Court of Claims advisory functions on reference from either house of Congress or from the head of an executive department.   In Sanborn v. United States, 27 Ct.Cl.

---

1. See generally Richardson, History, Jurisdiction and Practice of the Court of Claims (2d ed. 1885).

485 (1892), Chief Justice Richardson, assuming his court to be one created under Article III, explained these functions as extra-judicial tasks voluntarily undertaken by the judges in the capacity of commissioners. The Supreme Court seems more often to have regarded these functions, as Chief Justice Taney did in the Gordon case, as those of a "legislative court" created under Article I and hence not subject to the restrictions of Article III. Action of the Court of Claims in the exercise of its advisory functions was of course not subject to Supreme Court review. In re Sanborn, 148 U.S. 222 (1893).

Note the assumption in United States v. Jones that review of a "judicial" decision by a "legislative court" (as the Court of Claims was then regarded) is an exercise of "appellate jurisdiction" within the meaning of Article III. The problem of legislative courts is considered further in Chap. IV, Sec. 2, *infra*.

In 1953, the Court of Claims was congressionally "declared to be a court established under article III," 28 U.S.C. § 171, and the departmental reference responsibility (28 U.S.C. § 1493) repealed. 67 Stat. 226. After the Supreme Court upheld the general Article III characterization in Glidden Co. v. Zdanok, 370 U.S. 530 (1962), and expressed doubt about the validity of the congressional reference advisory role, those functions were transferred from the Court of Claims itself to its chief commissioner. They are now vested in the chief judge of the Court of Federal Claims (which, as noted above, is an Article I court). See 28 U.S.C. § 1492.

(4) *The Justiciability of Claims Requiring Appropriations.* From 1956 to 1977, Congress provided that judgments of $100,000 or less were to be paid by the General Accounting Office; judgments in excess of that amount were to be certified by the Secretary of the Treasury to Congress for consideration. The effect of that provision on the justiciability of money claims against the United States was considered by the Supreme Court on two occasions.

(a) In Glidden Co. v. Zdanok, 370 U.S. 530 (1962), Justice Harlan's plurality opinion found such claims justiciable even when they exceeded $100,-000. He referred to a study (46 Harv.L.Rev. 677, 685–86 n. 63 (1933)) that discovered only 15 instances in 70 years when Congress had refused to pay a judgment. "This historical record," he said, "surely more favorable to prevailing parties than that obtaining in private litigation, may well make us doubt whether the capacity to enforce a judgment is always indispensable for the exercise of judicial power" (p. 570). He concluded: "If this Court may rely on the good faith of state governments or other public bodies to respond to its judgments, there seems to be no sound reason why the Court of Claims may not rely on the good faith of the United States" (p. 571).

(b) The Regional Rail Reorganization cases (Blanchette v. Connecticut General Ins. Corp., 419 U.S. 102 (1974)) involved a challenge to the constitutionality of amendments to the Bankruptcy Act enacted after eight northeastern railroads had filed for reorganization. The amendments required creditors and shareholders of the railroads to exchange their interests for stock and debt in Conrail (a government-created but private, for-profit corporation) and also required the railroads to continue operating until the exchange occurred. The Court held that the Tucker Act remedy in the Court of Claims remained available to compensate for any deficiency in the value of the Conrail securities and for losses incurred by reason of the mandatory continued operation. Justice Brennan, for the Court, relied on the above-quoted language in Glidden to answer the contention that this remedy was inadequate. Justice Douglas' dissent, joined on this issue by Justice Stewart, argued that while Congress ordinarily pays judgments over $100,000 as a matter of routine, "this is an exceptional case, involving the possibility of judgments in the billions of dollars" (p. 180).

In 1977, Congress eliminated the dollar amount limitation in the statute and provided generally for payment by the Comptroller General of final judgments, awards, and compromise settlements against the United States. See 31 U.S.C. § 1304.

(5) *Relevance of Congress' Power to Legislate.* As long as Congress makes lump sum appropriations, whether for judgments already entered or to be entered, particular judgments can be questioned only by means of an additional, separate legislative act. In the instances mentioned in the Harvard Note cited by Justice Harlan in Glidden, Paragraph (4)(a), *supra,* such a special act was the means actually used. Could Congress, consistently with its constitutional responsibility for appropriations, properly surrender the power to enact such legislation?

If a particular judgment against the United States may be defeated by the adoption of later legislation forbidding its payment, what conclusion follows? May not other judgments similarly be deprived of practical effect by subsequent legislation? Consider, for example, the effect upon an injunction of a statute validating the prohibited conduct.[2]

Many cases have upheld statutes waiving the benefit of judgments in favor of a public right. *E.g.,* Pennsylvania v. Wheeling & Belmont Bridge Co., 59 U.S. (18 How.) 421 (1855)(statute declaring bridge not to be an obstruction to navigation, after Supreme Court had enjoined its maintenance); Hodges v. Snyder, 261 U.S. 600 (1923)(statute validating district bonds after a judgment of invalidity); Cherokee Nation v. United States, 270 U.S. 476 (1926)(statute waiving the benefit of a judgment in favor of the United States); Pope v. United States, 323 U.S. 1 (1944)(upholding a statute, which the Court of Claims had declared unconstitutional, directing that court to rehear a claim and give judgment according to a different principle of proof under which the calculation of the amount due would be largely mechanical); United States v. Sioux Nation of Indians, 448 U.S. 371 (1980)(upholding a statute providing for de novo review, by the Court of Claims, of Indian Claims against United States without regard to defenses of res judicata or collateral estoppel based on a prior Court of Claims proceeding; Justice Rehnquist, dissenting, argued that "Congress may not constitutionally require the Court of Claims to reopen this proceeding" (p. 424)).[3]

(6) *Congressional Questioning of Judgments.* The validity of congressional action questioning judgments of the Court of Claims against the United States has come into issue in only a few cases.

---

2. Compare Watson v. Mercer, 33 U.S. (8 Pet.) 88 (1834)(upholding power of state legislature to cure formal defects in deeds, thereby causing title to revest in one previously ousted in a state court ejectment action); Paramino Lumber Co. v. Marshall, 309 U.S. 370 (1940)(upholding act of Congress directing review of a final administrative award of disability and the issuance of a new award taking account of subsequently discovered complications); 149 Madison Ave. Corp. v. Asselta, 331 U.S. 795 (1947)(modifying earlier judgment to give district court authority "to consider any matters presented to it under the Portal-to-Portal Act of 1947".

3. The Court in the Sioux Nation case also held that the statute did not constitute an impermissible attempt to prescribe the outcome of a judicial decision, distinguishing United States v. Klein, 80 U.S. (13 Wall.) 128 (1871). See p. 367, *infra.*

In District of Columbia v. Eslin, 183 U.S. 62 (1901), during the pendency of an appeal from the Court of Claims to the Supreme Court, Congress repealed the act under which the proceeding had been brought and directed that "no judgment heretofore rendered in pursuance of said act shall be paid". The Supreme Court, relying upon Chief Justice Taney's language in the Gordon case, declared: "As no judgment now rendered by this court would have the sanction that attends the exercise of judicial power, in its legal or constitutional sense, the present appeal must be dismissed for want of jurisdiction and without any determination of the rights of the parties."

In Pocono Pines Assembly Hotels Co. v. United States, 73 Ct.Cl. 447 (1932), the Court of Claims had rendered judgment against the United States for $227,239.53, and Congress, on a suggestion from the Comptroller General that the government had failed to present certain substantive defenses, passed a special act directing that the case be "remanded" to the Court of Claims "with complete authority, the statute of limitations or rule of procedure to the contrary notwithstanding, to hear testimony as to the actual facts involved in the litigation and with instructions to report its finding of facts to Congress at the earliest practicable moment." The Court of Claims rejected an argument that the statute was unconstitutional. It construed the act as leaving the prior judgment unimpaired and as constituting simply a reference to the court in its advisory capacity to secure information to guide Congress in determining whether the judgment should be paid. The Supreme Court denied without opinion a petition for a writ to prevent the Court of Claims from proceeding under the statute. 285 U.S. 526 (1932). See the discussion of the case in Note, 46 Harv.L.Rev. 677 (1933).

See also United States v. Klein, 80 U.S. (13 Wall.) 128 (1872), pp. 367-70, *infra*.

Muskrat v. United States

219 U.S. 346, 31 S.Ct. 250, 55 L.Ed. 246 (1911).
Appeal from the Court of Claims.

[In 1902, Congress provided for the transfer of Cherokee property from tribal to private ownership. Every citizen of the Cherokee Nation as of September 1, 1902, was entitled to be enrolled and, upon enrollment, to receive an allotment equal in value to 110 acres of the average allottable lands of the tribe (plus a proportionate share of any tribal funds on deposit in the U.S. Treasury and, presumably, of any land remaining after the allotments). In 1906, Congress extended the time for completion of the roll by permitting enrollment of minor children living on March 4, 1906. At the same time, it imposed new restraints on alienation by the original allottees. The Secretaries of the Interior and of the Treasury were charged with implementation of various aspects of these statutes.

[In 1907, Congress authorized certain named original allottees to bring suit against the United States in the Court of Claims, with a right of appeal by either party to the Supreme Court, "to determine the validity of any acts of Congress" passed after the 1902 act that purported to diminish their rights as allottees. Attorneys' fees for plaintiffs, if they prevailed, were to be paid by the Treasury out of tribal funds. Pursuant to this statute, Muskrat and other allottees brought suit in the Court of Claims, challenging the 1906 act on the ground that it deprived them of property without due process of law. The Court of Claims rejected this contention, and the case came to the Supreme Court on appeal.]

■ MR. JUSTICE DAY delivered the opinion of the Court.

     * * *

It is * * * evident that there is neither more nor less in this procedure than an attempt to provide for a judicial determination, final in this court, of the constitutional validity of an act of Congress. Is such a determination within the judicial power conferred by the Constitution, as the same has been interpreted and defined in the authoritative decisions to which we have referred? We think it is not. That judicial power is the right to determine actual controversies arising between adverse litigants, duly instituted in courts of proper jurisdiction. The right to declare a law unconstitutional arises because an act of Congress relied upon by one or the other of such parties in determining their rights is in conflict with the fundamental law. The exercise of this, the most important and delicate duty of this court, is not given to it as a body with revisory power over the action of Congress, but because the rights of the litigants in justiciable controversies require the court to choose between the fundamental law and a law purporting to be enacted within constitutional authority, but in fact beyond the power delegated to the legislative branch of the government. This attempt to obtain a judicial declaration of the validity of the act of Congress is not presented in a "case" or "controversy," to which, under the Constitution of the United States, the judicial power alone extends. It is true the United States is made a defendant to this action, but it has no interest adverse to the claimants. The object is not to assert a property right as against the government, or to demand compensation for alleged wrongs because of action upon its part. The whole purpose of the law is to determine the constitutional validity of this class of legislation, in a suit not arising between parties concerning a property right necessarily involved in the decision in question, but in a proceeding against the government in its sovereign capacity, and concerning which the only judgment required is to settle the doubtful character of the legislation in question. Such judgment will not conclude private parties, when actual litigation brings to the court the question of the constitutionality of such legislation. In a legal sense the judgment could not be executed, and amounts in fact to no more than an expression of opinion upon the validity of the acts in question. * * * [W]e think the Congress, in the act of March 1, 1907, exceeded the limitations of legislative authority, so far as it required of this court action not judicial in its nature within the meaning of the Constitution.

Nor can it make any difference that the petitioners had brought suits in the supreme court of the District of Columbia to enjoin the Secretary of the Interior from carrying into effect the legislation subsequent to the act of July 1, 1902, which suits were pending when the jurisdictional act here involved was passed. The latter act must depend upon its own terms and be judged by the authority which it undertakes to confer. If such actions as are here attempted, to determine the validity of legislation, are sustained, the result will be that this court, instead of keeping within the limits of judicial power, and deciding cases or controversies arising between opposing parties, as the Constitution intended it should, will be required to give opinions in the nature of advice concerning legislative action,—a function never conferred upon it by the

Constitution, and against the exercise of which this court has steadily set its face from the beginning.

The questions involved in this proceeding as to the validity of the legislation may arise in suits between individuals, and when they do and are properly brought before this court for consideration they, of course, must be determined in the exercise of its judicial functions. For the reasons we have stated, we are constrained to hold that these actions present no justiciable controversy within the authority of the court, acting within the limitations of the Constitution under which it was created. As Congress, in passing this act, as a part of the plan involved, evidently intended to provide a review of the judgment of the court of claims in this court, as the constitutionality of important legislation is concerned, we think the act cannot be held to intend to confer jurisdiction on that court separately considered. * * *

The judgments will be reversed and the cases remanded to the Court of Claims with directions to dismiss the petitions for want of jurisdiction.

 * * *

NOTE ON MUSKRAT AND ON TEST CASES FRAMED BY CONGRESS

(1) *The Holding.* Why did the Supreme Court find that the Muskrat case presented no justiciable controversy? Was the Court's concern influenced by doubts that a request for a declaratory judgment, without more, was a sufficient basis for the invocation of judicial power? See pp. 96-98, *supra.* If so, Muskrat would lack contemporary significance, wouldn't it? Yet the Supreme Court continues occasionally to cite the decision, with apparent acceptance of its authority, if not actual approval. See, *e.g.,* North Carolina v. Rice, 404 U.S. 244, 246 (1971); Sierra Club v. Morton, 405 U.S. 727, 732 n. 3 (1972); Williams v. Zbaraz, 448 U.S. 358, 368 (1980).

At the time of the Muskrat decision, the Supreme Court had pending before it another case, Gritts v. Fisher, 224 U.S. 640 (1912), in which three Cherokees enrolled under the 1902 act had sued under the general jurisdictional statutes for the District of Columbia courts to enjoin the Secretaries of Interior and Treasury from implementing the provision of the 1906 act for the inclusion of after-born children. Without mentioning Muskrat or adverting to any jurisdictional problem, the Court affirmed the dismissal of the bill on the merits.

(2) *Congressionally Framed Test Cases.* Is it constitutionally objectionable for Congress to frame a case for judicial resolution or to provide specifically for decision of a case by an Article III court?

In the Cherokee Intermarriage Cases, 203 U.S. 76 (1906), numerous protests had been filed with the Secretary of the Treasury by full-blooded Cherokees against the inclusion on the rolls (as Cherokee citizens) of white persons who had intermarried with Cherokees. The Secretary of the Treasury had referred the protests to the Court of Claims, in accordance with the Act of March 3, 1883, 22 Stat. 485. Thereafter Congress passed the Act of March 3, 1905, 33 Stat. 1048, 1071, authorizing the Court of Claims to render a final judgment, with the right in an aggrieved party to appeal to the Supreme Court. The Court of Claims entered an elaborate decree stating which classes of intermarried persons were and were not entitled to enrollment under the 1902 act. On appeal, the Supreme Court affirmed without referring to any jurisdictional problem.

On numerous other occasions, Congress has by special act empowered the Court of Claims or a federal district court, and the Supreme Court on review, to decide a particular case, and the Supreme Court has accepted jurisdiction. See, for example, La Abra Silver Mining Co. v. United States, 175 U.S. 423, 455–63 (1899); United States v. Alcea Band of Tillamooks, 329 U.S. 40 (1946); Northern Cheyenne Tribe v. Hollowbreast, 425 U.S. 649 (1976); McClure v. Carter, 513 F.Supp. 265 (D.Idaho 1981), *aff'd sub nom.* McClure v. Reagan, 454 U.S. 1025 (1981), p. 182, *infra.* What distinguishes the Muskrat statute?

(3) *Review Under the Voting Rights Act.* The Voting Rights Act of 1965 imposed certain requirements on states or political subdivisions that, as of November 1, 1964, maintained "any test or device" as a prerequisite to voting and had a voter turnout of less than 50% of all voting-age residents. Section 5 of the Act, 42 U.S.C. § 1973c, provided that whenever any such state or subdivision "shall enact or seek to administer any voting qualification or prerequisite to voting, or standard, practice, or procedure with respect to voting different from that in force or effect on November 1, 1964," it must either submit it to the Attorney General or "institute an action in the United States District Court for the District of Columbia for a declaratory judgment that" the newly introduced qualification or procedure "does not have the purpose and will not have the effect of denying or abridging the right to vote on account of race or color." If the Attorney General interposed an objection, the declaratory judgment might still be sought and would have to be obtained before the new law could be put into effect.

In South Carolina v. Katzenbach, 383 U.S. 301 (1966), the Supreme Court sustained the validity of § 5. The Court's opinion, by Chief Justice Warren, disposed of the justiciability question summarily (p. 335): "Nor has Congress authorized the District Court to issue advisory opinions, in violation of the principles of Article III * * *. The Act automatically suspends the operation of voting regulations enacted after November 1, 1964, and furnishes mechanisms for enforcing the suspension. A State or political subdivision wishing to make use of a recent amendment to its voting laws therefore has a concrete and immediate 'controversy' with the Federal Government. * * * An appropriate remedy is a judicial determination that continued suspension of the new rule is unnecessary to vindicate rights guaranteed by the Fifteenth Amendment."

Only Justice Black perceived a problem on this point (p. 357): "If it can be said that any case or controversy arises under this section, which gives the District Court for the District of Columbia jurisdiction to approve or reject state laws or constitutional amendments, then the case or controversy must be between a State and the United States Government. But it is hard for me to believe that a justiciable controversy can arise in the constitutional sense from a desire by the United States Government or some of its officials to determine in advance what legislative provisions a State may enact or what constitutional amendments it may adopt. If this dispute between the Federal Government and the States amounts to a case or controversy it is a far cry from the traditional constitutional notion of a case or controversy as a dispute over the meaning of enforceable laws or the manner in which they are applied."

Is there any significant difference, with regard to justiciability, between the procedures authorized by § 5 for testing the validity of a state law and an action brought by the Attorney General to enforce federal statutory or constitutional restrictions against state officials attempting to carry out that state law?

United States v. Johnson

319 U.S. 302, 63 S.Ct. 1075, 87 L.Ed. 1413 (1943).
Appeal from the District Court of the United States for the Northern District of Indiana.

■ PER CURIAM. One Roach, a tenant of residential property belonging to appellee, brought this suit in the district court alleging that the property was within a "defense rental area" established by the Price Administrator pursuant to §§ 2(b) and 302(d) of the Emergency Price Control Act of 1942; that the Administrator had promulgated Maximum Rent Regulation No. 8 for the area; and that the rent paid by Roach and collected by appellee was in excess of the maximum fixed by the regulation. The complaint demanded judgment for treble damages and reasonable attorney's fees, as prescribed by § 205(e) of the Act. The United States, intervening pursuant to 28 U.S.C. § 401, filed a brief in support of the constitutionality of the Act, which appellee had challenged by motion to dismiss. The district court dismissed the complaint on the ground—as appears from its opinion and judgment—that the Act and the promulgation of the regulation under it were unconstitutional because Congress by the Act had unconstitutionally delegated legislative power to the Administrator.

Before entry of the order dismissing the complaint, the Government moved to reopen the case on the ground that it was collusive and did not involve a real case or controversy. This motion was denied. The Government brings the case here on appeal, and assigns as error both the ruling of the district court on the constitutionality of the Act, and its refusal to reopen and dismiss the case as collusive. * * *

The affidavit of the plaintiff, submitted by the Government on its motion to dismiss the suit as collusive, shows without contradiction that he brought the present proceeding in a fictitious name; that it was instituted as a "friendly suit" at appellee's request; that the plaintiff did not employ, pay, or even meet, the attorney who appeared of record in his behalf; that he had no knowledge who paid the $15 filing fee in the district court, but was assured by appellee that as plaintiff he would incur no expense in bringing the suit; that he did not read the complaint which was filed in his name as plaintiff; that in his conferences with the appellee and appellee's attorney of record, nothing was said concerning treble damages and he had no knowledge of the amount of the judgment prayed until he read of it in a local newspaper.

Appellee's counter-affidavit did not deny these allegations. It admitted that appellee's attorney had undertaken to procure an attorney to represent the plaintiff and had assured the plaintiff that his presence in court during the trial of the cause would not be necessary. It appears from the district court's opinion that no brief was filed on the plaintiff's behalf in that court.

The Government does not contend that, as a result of this cooperation of the two original parties to the litigation, any false or fictitious state of facts was submitted to the court. But it does insist that the affidavits disclose the absence of a genuine adversary issue between the parties, without which a court may not safely proceed to judgment, especially when it assumes the grave responsibility of passing upon the constitutional validity of legislative action.

Even in a litigation where only private rights are involved, the judgment will not be allowed to stand where one of the parties has dominated the conduct of the suit by payment of the fees of both.

Here an important public interest is at stake—the validity of an Act of Congress having far-reaching effects on the public welfare in one of the most critical periods in the history of the country. That interest has been adjudicated in a proceeding in which the plaintiff has had no active participation, over which he has exercised no control, and the expense of which he has not borne. He has been only nominally represented by counsel who was selected by appellee's counsel and whom he has never seen. Such a suit is collusive because it is not in any real sense adversary. It does not assume the "honest and actual antagonistic assertion of rights" to be adjudicated—a safeguard essential to the integrity of the judicial process, and one which we have held to be indispensable to adjudication of constitutional questions by this Court. Chicago & G.T. Ry. Co. v. Wellman, 143 U.S. 339, 345. Whenever in the course of litigation such a defect in the proceedings is brought to the court's attention, it may set aside any adjudication thus procured and dismiss the cause without entering judgment on the merits. It is the court's duty to do so where, as here, the public interest has been placed at hazard by the amenities of parties to a suit conducted under the domination of only one of them. The district court should have granted the Government's motion to dismiss the suit as collusive. We accordingly vacate the judgment below with instructions to the district court to dismiss the cause on that ground alone. * * *

Judgment vacated with directions.

NOTE ON FEIGNED AND COLLUSIVE CASES

(1) *Collusive Litigation.* It is easy, in principle, to see why a constitutional issue of enormous public interest should not be determined in a proceeding in which one nominal party has dominated the conduct of the other. But why didn't the government's intervention in the Johnson case, pursuant to what is now 28 U.S.C. § 2403, cure the difficulty of lack of a party genuinely interested in supporting the constitutionality of the legislation?

(2) *Background to the Johnson Case.*

(a) In at least two early cases, Hylton v. United States, 3 U.S. (3 Dall.) 171 (1796)[1], and Fletcher v. Peck, 10 U.S. (6 Cranch) 87 (1810),[2] the Supreme Court reached the merits even though it appeared that the controversy was feigned or collusive. Indeed, according to Bloch, *The Early Role of the Attorney General in Our Constitutional Scheme: In the Beginning There Was Pragmatism,* 1989 Duke L.J. 561, 612, "Feigned and contrived suits were reasonably common in * * * [the 1790s], and appear to have raised no red flags". What, if any, is the relevance of this history? What accounts for the decisive change of attitude?

1. Hylton was an apparently contrived suit to settle the constitutionality of a federal tax, in which the Supreme Court overlooked a number of potential obstacles to justiciability, among them that the government had apparently paid Hylton's lawyers. See Currie, *The Constitution in the Supreme Court: 1789–1801,* 48 U.Chi.L.Rev. 819, 854 (1981).

2. Both cases are discussed in 1 Warren, The Supreme Court in United States History 147, 392–95 (rev.ed.1926).

(b) In Lord v. Veazie, 49 U.S. (8 How.) 251 (1850), Veazie had executed a deed to Lord warranting that he had certain rights claimed by third persons, and an action on the covenant by Lord against Veazie "was docketed by consent". The circuit court "gave judgment for the defendant *pro forma,* at the request of the parties, in order that the judgment and question might be brought before" the Supreme Court. On the third person's motion the Court dismissed the case, saying that the judgment below was a nullity upon which no writ of error would lie, and that "the whole proceeding was in contempt of the court, and highly reprehensible."

(c) Chicago & Grand Trunk Ry. Co. v. Wellman, 143 U.S. 339 (1892). A Michigan statute established a per mile passenger rate, graduated according to the earnings of the railroad per mile of road. On the day the law took effect, the plaintiff tried to buy a ticket at the reduced statutory rate and was refused. He brought an action for damages, and the case was quickly tried on an agreed statement of facts, together with testimony from two witnesses. The case came to the Supreme Court on writ of error from a decision of the state supreme court upholding the trial court's refusal to rule that the statute was unconstitutional. The Court affirmed the judgment, on the ground that unchallenged assertions about earnings and expenses afforded no adequate ground for declaring such a statute unconstitutional. Justice Brewer said (pp. 344–45):

"* * * The theory upon which, apparently, this suit was brought is that parties have an appeal from the legislature to the courts; and that the latter are given an immediate and general supervision of the constitutionality of the acts of the former. Such is not true. Whenever, in pursuance of an honest and actual antagonistic assertion of rights by one individual against another, there is presented a question involving the validity of any act of any legislature, State or Federal, and the decision necessarily rests on the competency of the legislature to so enact, the court must, in the exercise of its solemn duties, determine whether the act be constitutional or not; but such an exercise of power is the ultimate and supreme function of courts. It is legitimate only in the last resort, and as a necessity in the determination of real, earnest and vital controversy between individuals. It never was the thought that, by means of a friendly suit, a party beaten in the legislature could transfer to the courts an inquiry as to the constitutionality of the legislative act."

Was the trouble in this case that the suit was friendly, or that the defendant failed to make an adequate showing that the statute was unconstitutional? Are the two necessarily connected?

(3) *Test Cases.* Does the rule against feigned cases defeat the planning of a test case by the parties to a real controversy? See Evers v. Dwyer, 358 U.S. 202 (1958), in which the plaintiff (who was black) boarded a bus once, refused to obey an order to sit in the rear, got off, and brought a class action for a declaratory judgment against the enforced segregation. The Court held the action justiciable despite findings by the district court that the plaintiff had ridden a city bus on only that one occasion and then for the purpose of instituting the litigation. (Compare O'Shea v. Littleton, p. 260, *infra.*) See also Bankamerica Corp. v. United States, 462 U.S. 122, 124 (1983), in which the Court decided an issue of federal antitrust law after noting that the proceedings before it were "companion test cases" brought by the United States against ten corporations and five individuals. *Cf.* Buchanan v. Warley, 245 U.S. 60 (1917), a challenge to a segregated housing law that had every appearance of a

test case and in which the Court reached the merits without discussion of justiciability.

(4) *Parties in Agreement.* If one party agrees with the position of the other, does that necessarily preclude the presence of a case or controversy?

In Moore v. Charlotte–Mecklenburg Bd. of Educ., 402 U.S. 47 (1971), "confronted with the anomaly that both litigants desire precisely the same result, namely, a holding that the anti-busing statute is constitutional," the Court held, "There is, therefore, no case or controversy within the meaning of Art. III of the Constitution. Muskrat v. United States, 219 U.S. 346 (1911)." Did the Court cite Muskrat fairly?[3]

How does Moore square with the accepted judicial practice of entering consent decrees, resulting from a negotiated settlement among the parties, that are invested with the force of law? See, *e.g.,* New Hampshire v. Maine, 426 U.S. 363 (1976), p. 313 n. 3, *infra.* See generally Schwarzschild, *Public Law by Private Bargain: Title VII Decrees and the Fairness of Negotiated Institutional Reform,* 1984 Duke L.J. 887, 902–03. Of granting uncontested naturalization decrees? See Tutun v. United States, pp. 107-08, *supra.* Of expunging convictions? For an illuminating discussion of issues raised by practices such as these, see Resnik, *Whose Judgment? Vacating Judgments, Preferences for Settlement, and the Role of Adjudication at the Close of the Twentieth Century,* 41 U.C.L.A.L.Rev. 1471 (1994).

Issues arising from agreement among the parties have frequently drawn notice in cases involving the government. Government counsel who becomes convinced that the other side deserves to prevail can settle a case before judgment or, if the government is seeking review, withdraw the appeal or other petition. When the government has prevailed below, the problem becomes stickier; in a number of such instances the Solicitor General has confessed error in the judgment and asked to have it vacated or reversed. These confessions are generally accepted, but the Court not infrequently recites that it does so "upon an independent examination of the record." See, *e.g.,* Pope v. United States, 392 U.S. 651 (1968); Rosengart v. Laird, 405 U.S. 908 (1972). In Casey v. United States, 343 U.S. 808 (1952), the Court, without an independent examination, accepted a confession of error that there had been an unreasonable search and seizure, saying that to do so "in this case * * * would not involve the establishment of any precedent." Three justices dissented vigorously, arguing that "[w]hatever action we take is a precedent" and that "[o]nce we accept a confession of error at face value and make it the controlling and decisive factor in our decision, we no longer administer a system of justice under a government of laws" (pp. 811–12).[4]

---

3. With Moore, compare Immigration and Naturalization Service v. Chadha, 462 U.S. 919, 939–40 (1983)(in a challenge to the constitutionality of the legislative veto in an immigration case, a case or controversy exists, even though the Attorney General, representing the INS, agrees with Chadha and the decision of the court below that the legislative veto is unconstitutional; the INS had concluded that, if not for that decision, it would be required to comply with the order of the House of Representatives that Chadha be deported).

4. In Mariscal v. United States, 449 U.S. 405 (1981), the Court vacated and remanded per curiam "[i]n light of the Solicitor General's concession in this Court that the [petitioner's] mail fraud convictions were invalid." Justice Rehnquist, dissenting, suggested that the Court had been routinely vacating judgments on the basis of such concessions without independent examination. "[Congress] has not to my knowledge moved

In civil proceedings in which the government has found itself aligned with its adversary on one or more critical issues, the Court has sometimes appointed an *amicus curiae* to argue the other side. *E.g.,* Bob Jones University v. United States, 456 U.S. 922 (1982)(decided on the merits, 461 U.S. 574 (1983)); Cheng Fan Kwok v. Immigration and Naturalization Service, 392 U.S. 206 (1968). On occasion, the Court may suspect, or may be informed, that the Solicitor General's views are not shared by other agencies or branches of the government; in those instances the appointment of an *amicus* may be tantamount to allowing intervention by that other agency or branch.[5]

SECTION 3. SOME PROBLEMS OF STANDING TO SUE

SUBSECTION A: PLAINTIFFS' STANDING

Allen v. Wright

468 U.S. 737, 104 S.Ct. 3315, 82 L.Ed.2d 556 (1984).
Certiorari to the United States Court of Appeals for the District of Columbia Circuit.

■ JUSTICE O'CONNOR delivered the opinion of the Court.

Parents of black public school children allege in this nation-wide class action that the Internal Revenue Service (IRS) has not adopted sufficient standards and procedures to fulfill its obligation to deny tax-exempt status to racially discriminatory private schools. They assert that the IRS thereby harms them directly and interferes with the ability of their children to receive an education

the Office of the Solicitor General from the Executive Branch of the Federal Government to the Judicial Branch. Until it does, I think we are bound by our oaths either to examine independently the merits of a question presented for review on certiorari, or in the exercise of our discretion to deny certiorari" (p. 407).

In Watts v. United States, 422 U.S. 1032 (1975), the Solicitor General agreed with the judgment below rejecting petitioner's claim of double jeopardy but sought permission to dismiss the prosecution because it did not conform to a Department of Justice policy applicable in the event of a prior state court conviction involving the same acts. The Court vacated and remanded to allow dismissal, with three dissenters arguing that it was "not a judicial function" to aid the Department in implementation of its internal policies (p. 1036). See also Thompson v. United States, 444 U.S. 248 (1980).

Would the dissenters have thought it similarly inappropriate for the trial court to dismiss on such a representation prior to trial? If not, why was it inappropriate later? The dissenters implicitly answered this question by expressing displeasure at having to "sacrifice the careful work of the District Court and the Court of Appeals-to say nothing of the public funds which that work required-to the vagaries of administrative interpretation" (422 U.S. at 1036). For discussion of similar issues, see Chap. II, Sec. 4, pp. 225–26, *infra,* considering doctrines governing the vacating of judgments on appeal when cases are mooted by voluntary action or by agreement among the parties.

5. See, *e.g.,* United States v. Lovett, 328 U.S. 303 (1946), where counsel for Congress appeared and argued as *amicus* by authority of a joint resolution and by special leave of Court; *cf.* INS v. Chadha, note 3, *supra,* where formal intervention was allowed.

in desegregated public schools. The issue before us is whether plaintiffs have standing to bring this suit. We hold that they do not.

I

The IRS denies tax-exempt status under §§ 501(a) and (c)(3) of the Internal Revenue Code, 26 U.S.C. §§ 501(a) and (c)(3)—and hence eligibility to receive charitable contributions deductible from income taxes under §§ 170(a)(1) and (c)(2) of the Code, 26 U.S.C. §§ 170(a)(1) and (c)(2)—to racially discriminatory private schools.[1] The IRS policy requires that a school applying for tax-exempt status show that it [does not engage in discrimination. Moreover,] the IRS has established guidelines and procedures for determining whether a particular school is in fact racially nondiscriminatory. Failure to comply with the guidelines "will ordinarily result in the proposed revocation of" tax-exempt status.

* * * [T]he school must annually certify, under penalty of perjury, compliance with [the applicable] requirements. * * *

* * *

In 1976 respondents challenged these guidelines and procedures in a suit filed in Federal District Court against the Secretary of the Treasury and the Commissioner of Internal Revenue. The plaintiffs named in the complaint are parents of black children who, at the time the complaint was filed, were attending public schools in seven States in school districts undergoing desegregation. They brought this nation-wide class action "on behalf of themselves· and their children, and * * * on behalf of all other parents of black children attending public school systems undergoing, or which may in the future undergo, desegregation pursuant to court order [or] HEW regulations and guidelines, under state law, or voluntarily." They estimated that the class they seek to represent includes several million persons.

Respondents allege in their complaint that many racially segregated private schools were created or expanded in their communities at the time the public schools were undergoing desegregation. According to the complaint, many such private schools, including 17 schools or school systems identified by name in the complaint (perhaps some 30 schools in all), receive tax exemptions either directly or through the tax-exempt status of "umbrella" organizations that operate or support the schools. Respondents allege that, despite the IRS policy of denying tax-exempt status to racially discriminatory private schools and despite the IRS guidelines and procedures for implementing that policy, some of the tax-exempt racially segregated private schools created or expanded in desegregating districts in fact have racially discriminatory policies. [App.] 17–18 (IRS permits "schools to receive tax exemptions merely on the basis of adopting and certifying—but not implementing—a policy of nondiscrimination"); *id.*, at 25 (same).[11] Respondents allege that the IRS grant of tax

---

1. As the Court explained last Term in Bob Jones University v. United States, 461 U.S. 574, 579 (1983), the IRS announced this policy in 1970 and formally adopted it in 1971. This change in prior policy was prompted by litigation over tax exemptions for racially discriminatory private schools in the State of Mississippi, litigation that result-

ed in the entry of an injunction against the IRS largely if not entirely coextensive with the position the IRS had voluntarily adopted. * * *

11. * * * Contrary to Justice Brennan's statement, the complaint does not allege that each desegregating district in which they reside contains one or more racially

exemptions to such racially discriminatory schools is unlawful.[12]

Respondents allege that the challenged Government conduct harms them in two ways.   The challenged conduct

"(a) constitutes tangible federal financial aid and other support for racially segregated educational institutions, and

"(b) fosters and encourages the organization, operation and expansion of institutions providing racially segregated educational opportunities for white children avoiding attendance in desegregating public school districts and thereby interferes with the efforts of federal courts, HEW and local school authorities to desegregate public school districts which have been operating racially dual school systems." *Id.*, at 38–39.

Thus, respondents do not allege that their children have been the victims of discriminatory exclusion from the schools whose tax exemptions they challenge as unlawful.   Indeed, they have not alleged * * * that their children have ever applied or would ever apply to any private school.   Rather, respondents claim a direct injury from the mere fact of the challenged Government conduct and, as indicated by the restriction of the plaintiff class to parents of children in desegregating school districts, injury to their children's opportunity to receive a desegregated education.   The latter injury is traceable to the IRS grant of tax exemptions to racially discriminatory schools, respondents allege, chiefly because contributions to such schools are deductible from income taxes * * * and the "deductions facilitate the raising of funds to organize new schools and expand existing schools in order to accommodate white students avoiding attendance in desegregating public school districts."

Respondents * * * ask for a declaratory judgment that the challenged IRS tax-exemption practices are unlawful.   They also ask for an injunction requiring the IRS to deny tax exemptions to a considerably broader class of private schools than the class of racially discriminatory private schools, [including those with "insubstantial" minority populations that were "established or expanded at or about the same time" as local public schools were desegregating].   * * * Finally, respondents ask for an order directing the IRS to replace its 1975 guidelines with standards consistent with the requested injunction.

* * * [P]rogress in the lawsuit was stalled for several years.   During this period, the IRS reviewed its challenged policies and proposed new Revenue Procedures to tighten requirements for eligibility for tax-exempt status for private schools.   In 1979, however, Congress blocked any strengthening of the IRS guidelines at least until October 1980.[16]   The District Court thereupon

---

discriminatory private schools unlawfully receiving a tax exemption.

12.   The complaint alleges that the challenged IRS conduct violates several laws: § 501(c)(3) of the Internal Revenue Code, 26 U.S.C. § 501(c)(3); Title VI of the Civil Rights Act of 1964, 42 U.S.C. § 2000d *et seq.;* 42 U.S.C. § 1981; and the Fifth and Fourteenth Amendments to the United States Constitution.

Last Term, in Bob Jones University v. United States, 461 U.S. 574 (1983), the Court concluded that racially discriminatory private schools do not qualify for a tax exemption

under § 501(c)(3) of the Internal Revenue Code.

16.   [Provisions in appropriations acts] specifically forbade the use of funds to carry out the IRS's proposed Revenue Procedures * * * [and] more generally forbade the use of funds to make the requirements for tax-exempt status of private schools more stringent than those in effect prior to the IRS's proposal of its new Revenue Procedures.

These provisions expired on October 1, 1980, but * * * were reinstated for the period December 16, 1980, through September

considered and granted the defendants' motion to dismiss the complaint, concluding that respondents lack standing, that the judicial task proposed by respondents is inappropriately intrusive for a federal court, and that awarding the requested relief would be contrary to the will of Congress expressed in the 1979 ban on strengthening IRS guidelines.

The United States Court of Appeals for the District of Columbia Circuit reversed, concluding that respondents have standing to maintain this lawsuit. * * *

　　　* * *

We granted certiorari, and now reverse.

II

A

Article III of the Constitution confines the federal courts to adjudicating actual "cases" and "controversies." As the Court explained in Valley Forge Christian College v. Americans United for Separation of Church and State, Inc., 454 U.S. 464, 471–476 (1982), the "case or controversy" requirement defines with respect to the Judicial Branch the idea of separation of powers on which the Federal Government is founded. The several doctrines that have grown up to elaborate that requirement are "founded in concern about the proper—and properly limited—role of the courts in a democratic society." Warth v. Seldin, 422 U.S. 490, 498 (1975).

> "All of the doctrines that cluster about Article III—not only standing but mootness, ripeness, political question, and the like—relate in part, and in different though overlapping ways, to an idea, which is more than an intuition but less than a rigorous and explicit theory, about the constitutional and prudential limits to the powers of an unelected, unrepresentative judiciary in our kind of government." Vander Jagt v. O'Neill, 699 F.2d 1166, 1178–1179 ([D.C.Cir.] 1983)(Bork, J., concurring).

The case-or-controversy doctrines state fundamental limits on federal judicial power in our system of government.

The Art. III doctrine that requires a litigant to have "standing" to invoke the power of a federal court is perhaps the most important of these doctrines. "In essence the question of standing is whether the litigant is entitled to have the court decide the merits of the dispute or of particular issues." Warth v. Seldin, *supra*, at 498. Standing doctrine embraces several judicially self-imposed limits on the exercise of federal jurisdiction, such as the general prohibition on a litigant's raising another person's legal rights, the rule barring adjudication of generalized grievances more appropriately addressed in the representative branches, and the requirement that a plaintiff's complaint fall within the zone of interests protected by the law invoked. The requirement of standing, however, has a core component derived directly from the Constitution. A plaintiff must allege personal injury fairly traceable to the defendant's allegedly unlawful conduct and likely to be redressed by the requested relief.

30, 1981. For fiscal year 1982, Congress specifically denied funding for carrying out not only administrative actions but also court orders entered after the date of the IRS's proposal of its first revised Revenue Procedure. No such spending restrictions are currently in force.

Like the prudential component, the constitutional component of standing doctrine incorporates concepts concededly not susceptible of precise definition. The injury alleged must be, for example, "distinct and palpable," Gladstone, Realtors v. Village of Bellwood, 441 U.S. 91, 100 (1979)(quoting Warth v. Seldin, *supra*, at 501), and not "abstract" or "conjectural" or "hypothetical," Los Angeles v. Lyons, 461 U.S. 95, 101–102 (1983). The injury must be "fairly" traceable to the challenged action, and relief from the injury must be "likely" to follow from a favorable decision. See Simon v. Eastern Kentucky Welfare Rights Org., 426 U.S. [26,] 38, 41 [(1976)]. These terms cannot be defined so as to make application of the constitutional standing requirement a mechanical exercise.

The absence of precise definitions, however, * * * hardly leaves courts at sea in applying the law of standing. Like most legal notions, the standing concepts have gained considerable definition from developing case law. * * * More important, the law of Art. III standing is built on a single basic idea—the idea of separation of powers. It is this fact which makes possible the gradual clarification of the law through judicial application. * * *

Determining standing in a particular case may be facilitated by clarifying principles or even clear rules developed in prior cases. Typically, however, the standing inquiry requires careful judicial examination of a complaint's allegations to ascertain whether the particular plaintiff is entitled to an adjudication of the particular claims asserted. Is the injury too abstract, or otherwise not appropriate, to be considered judicially cognizable? Is the line of causation between the illegal conduct and injury too attenuated? Is the prospect of obtaining relief from the injury as a result of a favorable ruling too speculative? These questions and any others relevant to the standing inquiry must be answered by reference to the Art. III notion that federal courts may exercise power only "in the last resort, and as a necessity," Chicago & Grand Trunk R. Co. v. Wellman, 143 U.S. 339, 345 (1892), and only when adjudication is "consistent with a system of separated powers and [the dispute is one] traditionally thought to be capable of resolution through the judicial process," Flast v. Cohen, 392 U.S. 83, 97 (1968).

B

Respondents allege two injuries in their complaint to support their standing to bring this lawsuit. First, they say that they are harmed directly by the mere fact of Government financial aid to discriminatory private schools. Second, they say that the federal tax exemptions to racially discriminatory private schools in their communities impair their ability to have their public schools desegregated.

> * * *

* * * We conclude that neither suffices to support respondents' standing. The first fails under clear precedents of this Court because it does not constitute a judicially cognizable injury. The second fails because the alleged injury is not fairly traceable to the assertedly unlawful conduct of the IRS.[19]

---

19. The "fairly traceable" and "redressability" components of the constitutional standing inquiry were initially articulated by this Court as "two facets of a single causation requirement." C. Wright, Law of Feder-al Courts § 13, p. 68, n. 43 (4th ed. 1983). To the extent there is a difference, it is that the former examines the causal connection between the assertedly unlawful conduct and the alleged injury, whereas the latter exam-

1

Respondents' first claim of injury * * * might be a claim simply to have the Government avoid the violation of law alleged in respondents' complaint. Alternatively, it might be a claim of stigmatic injury, or denigration, suffered by all members of a racial group when the Government discriminates on the basis of race. Under neither interpretation is this claim of injury judicially cognizable.

This Court has repeatedly held that an asserted right to have the Government act in accordance with law is not sufficient, standing alone, to confer jurisdiction on a federal court. In Schlesinger v. Reservists Committee to Stop the War, 418 U.S. 208 (1974), for example, the Court rejected a claim of citizen standing to challenge Armed Forces Reserve commissions held by Members of Congress as violating the Incompatibility Clause of Art. I, § 6, of the Constitution. As citizens, the Court held, plaintiffs alleged nothing but "the abstract injury in nonobservance of the Constitution...." More recently, in Valley Forge, *supra,* we rejected a claim of standing to challenge a Government conveyance of property to a religious institution. Insofar as the plaintiffs relied simply on "their shared individuated right" to a Government that made no law respecting an establishment of religion, we held that plaintiffs had not alleged a judicially cognizable injury. * * *

Neither do they have standing to litigate their claims based on the stigmatizing injury often caused by racial discrimination. There can be no doubt that this sort of noneconomic injury is one of the most serious consequences of discriminatory government action and is sufficient in some circumstances to support standing. Our cases make clear, however, that such injury accords a basis for standing only to "those persons who are personally denied equal treatment" by the challenged discriminatory conduct.

* * *

If [an] abstract stigmatic injury were cognizable, standing would extend nationwide to all members of the particular racial groups against which the Government was alleged to be discriminating by its grant of a tax exemption to a racially discriminatory school, regardless of the location of that school. * * * A black person in Hawaii could challenge the grant of a tax exemption to a racially discriminatory school in Maine. Recognition of standing in such circumstances would transform the federal courts into "no more than a vehicle for the vindication of the value interests of concerned bystanders." United States v. SCRAP, 412 U.S. 669, 687 (1973). Constitutional limits on the role of the federal courts preclude such a transformation.

2

It is in their complaint's second claim of injury that respondents allege harm to a concrete, personal interest that can support standing in some circumstances.

ines the causal connection between the alleged injury and the judicial relief requested. Cases such as this, in which the relief requested goes well beyond the violation of law alleged, illustrate why it is important to keep the inquiries separate if the "redressability" component is to focus on the requested relief. Even if the relief respondents request might have a substantial effect on the desegregation of public schools, whatever deficiencies exist in the opportunities for desegregated education for respondents' children might not be traceable to IRS violations of law—grants of tax exemptions to racially discriminatory schools in respondents' communities.

The injury they identify—their children's diminished ability to receive an education in a racially integrated school—is, beyond any doubt, not only judicially cognizable but, as shown by cases from Brown v. Board of Education, 347 U.S. 483 (1954), to Bob Jones University v. United States, 461 U.S. 574 (1983), one of the most serious injuries recognized in our legal system. Despite the constitutional importance of curing the injury alleged by respondents, however, the federal judiciary may not redress it unless standing requirements are met. In this case, respondents' second claim of injury cannot support standing because the injury alleged is not fairly traceable to the Government conduct respondents challenge as unlawful.[22]

The illegal conduct challenged by respondents is the IRS's grant of tax exemptions to some racially discriminatory schools. The line of causation between that conduct and desegregation of respondents' schools is attenuated at best. From the perspective of the IRS, the injury to respondents is highly indirect and "results from the independent action of some third party not before the court." Simon v. Eastern Kentucky Welfare Rights Org., 426 U.S., at 42. * * *

The diminished ability of respondents' children to receive a desegregated education would be fairly traceable to unlawful IRS grants of tax exemptions only if there were enough racially discriminatory private schools receiving tax exemptions in respondents' communities for withdrawal of those exemptions to make an appreciable difference in public school integration. Respondents have made no such allegation. It is, first, uncertain how many racially discriminatory private schools are in fact receiving tax exemptions. Moreover, it is entirely speculative, as respondents themselves conceded in the Court of Appeals, whether withdrawal of a tax exemption from any particular school would lead the school to change its policies. It is just as speculative whether any given parent of a child attending such a private school would decide to transfer the child to public school as a result of any changes in educational or financial policy made by the private school once it was threatened with loss of tax-exempt status. It is also pure speculation whether, in a particular community, a large enough number of the numerous relevant school officials and parents would reach decisions that collectively would have a significant impact on the racial composition of the public schools.

The links in the chain of causation between the challenged Government conduct and the asserted injury are far too weak for the chain as a whole to sustain respondents' standing. * * *

---

22. Respondents' stigmatic injury, though not sufficient for standing in the abstract form in which their complaint asserts it, is judicially cognizable to the extent that respondents are personally subject to discriminatory treatment. See Heckler v. Mathews, 465 U.S. 728, 739–740 (1984) [involving the denial of monetary benefits on an allegedly discriminatory basis]. The stigmatic injury thus requires identification of some concrete interest with respect to which respondents are personally subject to discriminatory treatment. That interest must independently satisfy the causation requirement of standing doctrine.

* * *

In this litigation, respondents identify only one interest that they allege is being discriminatorily impaired—their interest in desegregated public school education. Respondents' asserted stigmatic injury, therefore, is sufficient to support their standing in this litigation only if their school-desegregation injury independently meets the causation requirement of standing doctrine.

The idea of separation of powers that underlies standing doctrine explains why our cases preclude the conclusion that respondents' alleged injury "fairly can be traced to the challenged action" of the IRS. That conclusion would pave the way generally for suits challenging, not specifically identifiable Government violations of law, but the particular programs agencies establish to carry out their legal obligations. Such suits, even when premised on allegations of several instances of violations of law, are rarely if ever appropriate for federal-court adjudication. * * *

The same concern for the proper role of the federal courts is reflected in cases like O'Shea v. Littleton, 414 U.S. 488 (1974), Rizzo v. Goode, 423 U.S. 362 (1976), and Los Angeles v. Lyons, 461 U.S. 95 (1983). In all three cases plaintiffs sought injunctive relief directed at certain systemwide law enforcement practices. The Court held in each case that, absent an allegation of a specific threat of being subject to the challenged practices, plaintiffs had no standing to ask for an injunction. Animating this Court's holdings was the principle that "[a] federal court * * * is not the proper forum to press" general complaints about the way in which government goes about its business.

Case-or-controversy considerations, the Court observed in O'Shea v. Littleton, *supra,* at 499, "obviously shade into those determining whether the complaint states a sound basis for equitable relief." The latter set of considerations should therefore inform our judgment about whether respondents have standing. Most relevant to this case is the principle articulated in Rizzo v. Goode, *supra,* at 378–379:

> "When a plaintiff seeks to enjoin the activity of a government agency, even within a unitary court system, his case must contend with 'the well-established rule that the Government has traditionally been granted the widest latitude in the' dispatch of its own internal affairs."

When transported into the Art. III context, that principle, grounded as it is in the idea of separation of powers, counsels against recognizing standing in a case brought, not to enforce specific legal obligations whose violation works a direct harm, but to seek a restructuring of the apparatus established by the Executive Branch to fulfill its legal duties. The Constitution, after all, assigns to the Executive Branch, and not to the Judicial Branch, the duty to "take Care that the Laws be faithfully executed." U.S. Const., Art. II, § 3. We could not recognize respondents' standing in this case without running afoul of that structural principle.[26]

C

The Court of Appeals relied for its contrary conclusion on Gilmore v. City of Montgomery, 417 U.S. 556 (1974), [and] Norwood v. Harrison, 413 U.S. 455 (1973) * * *. * * * [No case], however, requires that we find standing in this lawsuit.

In Gilmore v. City of Montgomery, *supra,* the plaintiffs * * * alleged that the city was violating [their] equal protection right by permitting racially

---

26. We disagree with Justice Stevens' suggestions that separation of powers principles merely underlie standing requirements, have no role to play in giving meaning to those requirements, and should be considered only under a distinct justiciability analysis. Moreover, our analysis of this case does not rest on the more general proposition that no consequence of the allocation of administrative enforcement resources is judicially cognizable. Rather, we rely on separation of powers principles to interpret the "fairly traceable" component of the standing requirement.

discriminatory private schools and other groups to use the public parks. The Court recognized plaintiffs' standing to challenge this city policy insofar as the policy permitted the exclusive use of the parks by racially discriminatory private schools * * *.

Standing in Gilmore thus rested on an allegation of direct deprivation of a right to equal use of the parks. * * *

In Norwood v. Harrison, *supra,* parents of public school children in Tunica County, Miss., filed a statewide class action challenging the State's provision of textbooks to students attending racially discriminatory private schools in the State. The Court held the State's practice unconstitutional because it breached "the State's acknowledged duty to establish a unitary school system." The Court did not expressly address the basis for the plaintiffs' standing.

In Gilmore, however, the Court identified the basis for standing in Norwood: "The plaintiffs in Norwood were parties to a school desegregation order and the relief they sought was directly related to the concrete injury they suffered." 417 U.S., at 571, n.10. Through the school-desegregation decree, the plaintiffs had acquired a right to have the State "steer clear" of any perpetuation of the racially dual school system that it had once sponsored. 413 U.S., at 467. The interest acquired was judicially cognizable because it was a personal interest, created by law, in having the State refrain from taking specific actions. * * *

* * *

III

"The necessity that the plaintiff who seeks to invoke judicial power stand to profit in some personal interest remains an Art. III requirement." Simon v. Eastern Kentucky Welfare Rights Org., 426 U.S., at 39. Respondents have not met this fundamental requirement. The judgment of the Court of Appeals is accordingly reversed, and the injunction issued by that court is vacated.

It is so ordered.

■ JUSTICE MARSHALL took no part in the decision of these cases.

■ JUSTICE BRENNAN, dissenting.

* * *

II

A

In these cases, the respondents have alleged at least one type of injury that satisfies the constitutional requirement of "distinct and palpable injury."[3] In

---

3. Because I conclude that the second injury alleged by the respondents is sufficient to satisfy constitutional requirements, I do not need to reach what the Court labels the "stigmatic injury." I note, however, that the Court has mischaracterized this claim of injury * * *. In particular, the respondents have not simply alleged that, as blacks, they have suffered the denigration injury "suffered by all members of a racial group when the Government discriminates on the basis of race." Rather, the complaint, fairly read, limits the claim of stigmatic injury from illegal governmental action to black children attending public schools in districts that are currently desegregating yet contain discriminatory private schools benefiting from illegal tax exemptions. Thus, the Court's "parade

particular, they claim that the IRS's grant of tax-exempt status to racially discriminatory private schools directly injures their children's opportunity and ability to receive a desegregated education. * * *

The Court acknowledges that this alleged injury is sufficient to satisfy constitutional standards. * * *

* * *

B

* * *

Viewed in light of the injuries they claim, the respondents have alleged a direct causal relationship between the Government action they challenge and the injury they suffer: their inability to receive an education in a racially integrated school is directly and adversely affected by the tax-exempt status granted by the IRS to racially discriminatory schools in their respective school districts. Common sense alone would recognize that the elimination of tax-exempt status for racially discriminatory private schools would serve to lessen the impact that those institutions have in defeating efforts to desegregate the public schools.

The Court admits that "[t]he diminished ability of respondents' children to receive a desegregated education would be fairly traceable to unlawful IRS grants of tax exemptions ... if there were enough racially discriminatory private schools receiving tax exemptions in respondents' communities for withdrawal of those exemptions to make an appreciable difference in public school integration," but concludes that "[r]espondents have made no such allegation." With all due respect, the Court has either misread the complaint or is improperly requiring the respondents to prove their case on the merits in order to defeat a motion to dismiss. For example, the respondents specifically refer by name to at least 32 private schools that discriminate on the basis of race and yet continue to benefit illegally from tax-exempt status. Eighteen of those schools * * * are located in the city of Memphis, Tenn., which has been the subject of several court orders to desegregate. * * * [T]here can be little doubt that the respondents have identified communities containing "enough racially discriminatory private schools receiving tax exemptions * * * to make an appreciable difference in public school integration."[6]

Moreover, the Court has previously recognized the existence, and constitutional significance, of such direct relationships between unlawfully segregated school districts and government support for racially discriminatory private schools in those districts. In Norwood v. Harrison, 413 U.S. 455 (1973), for example, we considered a Mississippi program that provided textbooks to students attending both public and private schools, without regard to whether any participating school had racially discriminatory policies. In declaring that program constitutionally invalid, we * * * [observed]:

of horribles" concerning black plaintiffs from Hawaii challenging tax exemptions granted to schools in Maine is completely irrelevant for purposes of Art. III standing in this action. Indeed, even if relevant, that criticism would go to the scope of the class certified or the relief granted in the lawsuit, issues that were not reached by the District Court or the Court of Appeals and are not now before this Court.

6. Even if the Court were correct in its conclusion that there is an insufficient factual basis alleged in the complaint, the proper disposition would be to remand in order to afford the respondents an opportunity to amend their complaint.

"The District Court laid great stress on the absence of a showing by appellants that 'any child enrolled in private school, if deprived of free textbooks, would withdraw from private school and subsequently enroll in the public schools.' * * * *We do not agree with the District Court in its analysis of the legal consequences of this uncertainty, for the Constitution does not permit the State to aid discrimination even when there is no precise causal relationship between state financial aid to a private school and the continued well-being of that school. A State may not grant the type of tangible financial aid here involved if that aid has a significant tendency to facilitate, reinforce, and support private discrimination.*" Id., at 465–466 (citations omitted)(emphasis added).

The Court purports to distinguish Norwood from the present litigation because "[t]he plaintiffs in Norwood were parties to a school desegregation order" and therefore "had acquired a right to have the State 'steer clear' of any perpetuation of the racially dual school system that it had once sponsored," whereas the "[r]espondents in this lawsuit * * * have no injunctive rights against the IRS that are allegedly being harmed." * * * Given that many of the school districts identified in the respondents' complaint have also been the subject of court-ordered integration, the standing inquiry in these cases should not differ. And, although the respondents do not specifically allege that they are named parties to any outstanding desegregation orders, that is undoubtedly due to the passage of time since the orders were issued, and not to any difference in the harm they suffer.

Even accepting the relevance of the Court's distinction, moreover, that distinction goes to the injury suffered by the respective plaintiffs, and not to the causal connection between the harm alleged and the governmental action challenged. The causal relationship existing in Norwood between the alleged harm (i.e., interference with the plaintiffs' injunctive rights to a desegregated school system) and the challenged governmental action (i.e., free textbooks provided to racially discriminatory schools) is indistinguishable from the causal relationship existing in the present cases, unless the Court intends to distinguish the lending of textbooks from the granting of tax-exempt status. * * *

* * *

III

More than one commentator has noted that the causation component of the Court's standing inquiry is no more than a poor disguise for the Court's view of the merits of the underlying claims. The Court today does nothing to avoid that criticism. * * *

■ JUSTICE STEVENS, with whom JUSTICE BLACKMUN joins, dissenting.

Three propositions are clear to me: (1) respondents have adequately alleged "injury in fact"; (2) their injury is fairly traceable to the conduct that they claim to be unlawful; and (3) the "separation of powers" principle does not create a jurisdictional obstacle to the consideration of the merits of their claim.

I

Respondents, the parents of black schoolchildren, have alleged that their children are unable to attend fully desegregated schools because large numbers of white children in the areas in which respondents reside attend private schools which do not admit minority children. The Court, JUSTICE BRENNAN and I all agree that this is an adequate allegation of "injury in fact." * * *

II

In final analysis, the wrong respondents allege that the Government has committed is to subsidize the exodus of white children from schools that would otherwise be racially integrated. The critical question in these cases, therefore, is whether respondents have alleged that the Government has created that kind of subsidy.

* * *

* * * Only last Term we explained the effect of * * * preferential [tax] treatment:

> "Both tax exemptions and tax deductibility are a form of subsidy that is administered through the tax system. A tax exemption has much the same effect as a cash grant to the organization of the amount of tax it would have to pay on its income. Deductible contributions are similar to cash grants of the amount of a portion of the individual's contributions." Regan v. Taxation With Representation of Washington, 461 U.S. 540, 544 (1983).

* * * If the granting of preferential tax treatment would "encourage" private segregated schools to conduct their "charitable" activities, it must follow that the withdrawal of the treatment would "discourage" them, and hence promote the process of desegregation.

* * *

This causation analysis is nothing more than a restatement of elementary economics: when something becomes more expensive, less of it will be purchased. * * * [W]ithout tax-exempt status, private schools will either not be competitive in terms of cost, or have to change their admissions policies, hence reducing their competitiveness for parents seeking "a racially segregated alternative" to public schools, which is what respondents have alleged many white parents in desegregating school districts seek. In either event the process of desegregation will be advanced in the same way that it was advanced in Gilmore and Norwood—the withdrawal of the subsidy for segregated schools means the incentive structure facing white parents who seek such schools for their children will be altered. * * *

III

Considerations of tax policy, economics, and pure logic all confirm the conclusion that respondents' injury in fact is fairly traceable to the Government's allegedly wrongful conduct. The Court therefore is forced to introduce the concept of "separation of powers" into its analysis. The Court writes that the separation of powers "explains why our cases preclude the conclusion" that respondents' injury is fairly traceable to the conduct they challenge.

The Court could mean one of three things by its invocation of the separation of powers. First, it could simply be expressing the idea that if the plaintiff lacks Art. III standing to bring a lawsuit, then there is no "case or controversy" within the meaning of Art. III and hence the matter is not within the area of responsibility assigned to the Judiciary by the Constitution. * * * While there can be no quarrel with this proposition, in itself it provides no guidance for determining if the injury respondents have alleged is fairly traceable to the conduct they have challenged.

Second, the Court could be saying that it will require a more direct causal connection when it is troubled by the separation of powers implications of the case before it. That approach confuses the standing doctrine with the justiciability of the issues that respondents seek to raise. The purpose of the standing inquiry is to measure the plaintiff's stake in the outcome, not whether a court has the authority to provide it with the outcome it seeks * * *.

Thus, the " 'fundamental aspect of standing' is that it focuses primarily on the *party* seeking to get his complaint before the federal court rather than 'on the issues he wishes to have adjudicated,' " United States v. Richardson, 418 U.S. 166, 174 (1974)(emphasis in original)(quoting Flast, 392 U.S., at 99). * * * If a plaintiff presents a nonjusticiable issue, or seeks relief that a court may not award, then its complaint should be dismissed for those reasons, and not because the plaintiff lacks a stake in obtaining that relief and hence has no standing. Imposing an undefined but clearly more rigorous standard for redressability for reasons unrelated to the causal nexus between the injury and the challenged conduct can only encourage undisciplined, ad hoc litigation * * *.

Third, the Court could be saying that it will not treat as legally cognizable injuries that stem from an administrative decision concerning how enforcement resources will be allocated. This surely is an important point. Respondents do seek to restructure the IRS's mechanisms for enforcing the legal requirement that discriminatory institutions not receive tax-exempt status. Such restructuring would dramatically affect the way in which the IRS exercises its prosecutorial discretion. The Executive requires latitude to decide how best to enforce the law, and in general the Court may well be correct that the exercise of that discretion, especially in the tax context, is unchallengeable.

However, as the Court also recognizes, this principle does not apply when suit is brought "to enforce specific legal obligations whose violation works a direct harm." For example, despite the fact that they were challenging the methods used by the Executive to enforce the law, citizens were accorded standing to challenge a pattern of police misconduct that violated the constitutional constraints on law enforcement activities in Allee v. Medrano, 416 U.S. 802 (1974). Here, respondents contend that the IRS is violating a specific constitutional limitation on its enforcement discretion. There is a solid basis for that contention. In Norwood, we wrote:

> "A State's constitutional obligation requires it to steer clear, not only of operating the old dual system of racially segregated schools, but also of giving significant aid to institutions that practice racial or other invidious discrimination." * * *

Respondents contend that these cases limit the enforcement discretion enjoyed by the IRS. They establish, respondents argue, that the IRS cannot provide "cash grants" to discriminatory schools through preferential tax treatment without running afoul of a constitutional duty to refrain from "giving significant aid" to these institutions. Similarly, respondents claim that the Internal Revenue Code itself, as construed in Bob Jones, constrains enforcement discretion. It has been clear since Marbury v. Madison that "[i]t is emphatically the province and duty of the judicial department to say what the law is." Deciding whether the Treasury has violated a specific legal limitation on its enforcement discretion does not intrude upon the prerogatives of the Executive, for in so deciding we are merely saying "what the law is." * * *

In short, I would deal with the question of the legal limitations on the IRS's enforcement discretion on its merits, rather than by making the untenable assumption that the granting of preferential tax treatment to segregated schools does not make those schools more attractive to white students and hence does not inhibit the process of desegregation. I respectfully dissent.

————

NOTE ON STANDING TO SUE

(1) *What Is Standing?* The Supreme Court has frequently stated that standing questions relate to parties—to the nature and sufficiency of the litigant's concern with the subject matter of the litigation—rather than to the fitness for adjudication of the legal issues tendered for decision. See, *e.g.,* Flast v. Cohen, 392 U.S. 83, 95 (1968), p. 137, *infra.* Consider whether Allen v. Wright, and the decisions discussed in this Note, are consistent with that statement.

However the standard is specified, the Supremacy Clause and the decision in Marbury v. Madison plainly imply that litigants always have standing to challenge judicial action (including the use of a rule of decision) claimed to violate their constitutional rights. Thus, in cases involving coercive action, there is little question that a defendant may challenge the judicial coercion as violating his or her rights; the only difficult question, discussed in Subsection B, is in what circumstances a litigant may invoke the rights of others. In the cases discussed in this Subsection, in which a plaintiff seeks a remedy other than relief from an adverse judicial action, the question of standing is more problematic.

(2) *The Origins of Standing Doctrine.* "The word *'standing'* * * * does not appear to have been commonly used until the middle of our own century." Vining, Legal Identity: The Coming of Age of Public Law 55 (1978).[1] Before then, most litigants asserted legal interests plainly recognized at common law. Even suits raising constitutional questions generally followed the private law model: the complaint would allege that official action invaded a legal interest protected at common law; to the defense of official authority, the plaintiff would respond that any purported authorization was unconstitutional, thereby leaving the official liable, like a private tortfeasor, for invasion of the protected interest. See *id.* at 20–27; Stewart, *The Reformation of American Administrative Law,* 88 Harv.L.Rev. 1667, 1717–18, 1723–24 (1975).[2]

During the twentieth century, courts became self-conscious about the concept of standing only after developments in the legal culture subjected the private law model to unfamiliar strains. Two sources of strain had special importance. One, which is further explored in the *Note on Lujan and Congressional Power to Confer Standing to Sue* and the *Note on Standing to Challenge*

---

1. Indeed, there appear to have been only eight Supreme Court references to "standing" before 1965, with the earliest coming in Stark v. Wickard, 321 U.S. 288 (1944). Sunstein, *What's Standing After Lujan? Of Citizen Suits, "Injuries," and Article III,* 91 Mich.L.Rev. 163, 169 (1992). On the history of standing as a concept, see Winter, *The Metaphor of Standing and the*

Problem of Self–Governance, 40 Stan.L.Rev. 1371, 1418–25 (1988).

2. At times, the prerogative writs or other forms of action permitted suit by litigants not asserting traditional common law interests. See Paragraph (3), *infra.* And particular forms of relief were sometimes authorized by state or federal legislation. See generally Chap. IX, Sec. 1(A), *infra.*

Federal Administrative Action, below, involved the advent of the administrative state and the enactment of statutes to protect interests, unprotected at common law, that were shared by large numbers of people.[3] The other was the increasing recognition of substantive constitutional rights, such as voting rights and rights to educational equality, that were broadly shared and that were not associated with the kind of liberty or property interests protected by the common law. Among the questions that arose was who, if anyone, should be able to sue to ensure governmental compliance with statutory and constitutional provisions intended to protect broadly shared interests of large numbers of citizens.

At the risk of some oversimplification, the private rights and public rights models introduced in Section 1, *supra,* exemplify perhaps the most prominent, rival approaches to questions such as this. The contrast between two decisions, Frothingham v. Mellon, 262 U.S. 447 (1923), and Flast v. Cohen, 392 U.S. 83 (1968), illustrates the rivalry and its stakes.

(a) *Frothingham and the Private Rights Model.* In Frothingham v. Mellon, 262 U.S. 447 (1923), a federal taxpayer challenged the Maternity Act of 1921, which provided federal financial support for state programs to reduce maternal and infant mortality, as beyond Congress' Article I powers and an invasion of state prerogatives under the Tenth Amendment. The plaintiff alleged that the Maternity Act would increase her tax liability and "thereby take her property without due process of law" (p. 486). The Supreme Court held unanimously that the action was nonjusticiable. Distinguishing cases that had allowed suits by municipal taxpayers, the Court found that the plaintiff's "interest in the moneys of the [federal] treasury" was "comparatively minute and indeterminable" and that "the effect upon future taxation of any payment out of" federal funds was "remote, fluctuating and uncertain" (p. 487).

"The administration of any statute, likely to produce additional taxation to be imposed upon a vast number of taxpayers, the extent of whose several liability is indefinite and constantly changing, is essentially a matter of public and not individual concern", the Court said (p. 487). "The party who invokes the [judicial] power must be able to show not only that the statute is invalid but that he has sustained or is immediately in danger of sustaining some direct injury as the result of its enforcement, and not merely that he suffers in some indefinite way in common with people generally" (p. 488). To accept jurisdiction, the Court concluded, "would be not to decide a judicial controversy, but to assume a position of authority over the governmental acts of another and co-equal department, an authority which plainly we do not possess" (p. 489).

(b) *Flast and the Public Rights Model.* The Supreme Court re-examined Frothingham in Flast v. Cohen, 392 U.S. 83 (1968), a suit by federal taxpayers alleging that a federal statute violated the Establishment Clause by providing financial support for educational programs in religious schools. Writing for the majority, Chief Justice Warren argued that standing doctrine contains a mix of "constitutional requirements and policy considerations" (p. 97) and suggested, though without holding, that Frothingham had rested on policy rather than constitutional grounds.

---

3. See generally Sunstein, *Standing and the Privatization of Public Law,* 88 Co- lum.L.Rev. 1432 (1988).

The government argued that the separation of powers presented an absolute bar to taxpayer suits challenging federal spending programs. According to the Court, however, any separation-of-powers barrier would involve "the substantive issues" that a plaintiff "seeks to have adjudicated" (p. 101). "The fundamental aspect of standing is that it focuses on the party seeking to get his complaint before a federal court and not on the issues he wishes to have adjudicated" (p. 99). "[I]n terms of Article III limitations on federal court jurisdiction, the question of standing is related only to whether the dispute sought to be adjudicated will be presented in an adversary context and in a form historically viewed as capable of judicial resolution" (p. 101).

With standing thus defined as distinct from the fitness of the issue presented for judicial resolution, Chief Justice Warren turned to "the problem of determining the circumstances under which a federal taxpayer will be deemed to have the personal stake and interest that impart the necessary concrete adverseness * * * so that standing can be conferred on the taxpayer *qua* taxpayer consistent with the constitutional limitations of Article III" (p. 101). Although it was "not relevant that the substantive issues in the litigation might be nonjusticiable," the Chief Justice found that "prior decisions establish that, in ruling on standing, it is both appropriate and necessary to look at the substantive issues for another purpose, namely, to determine whether there is a logical nexus between the status asserted and the claim sought to be adjudicated" (pp. 101–02). The Court continued: "The nexus demanded of federal taxpayers has two aspects to it. First, the taxpayer must establish a logical link between that status and the type of legislative enactment attacked. * * Secondly, the taxpayer must establish a nexus between that status and the precise nature of the constitutional infringement alleged" (p.102).

On the facts, the Court found both nexus requirements to be satisfied. It perceived a link between taxpayer status and the alleged "unconstitutionality only of exercises of congressional power under the taxing and spending clause of Art. I, § 8 of the Constitution" (p. 102). With respect to the second nexus, the Court found that the Establishment Clause at least partly resulted from concern that "the taxing and spending power would be used to favor one religion over another or to support religion in general" (p.103). The Court thus distinguished Frothingham as involving no allegation that Congress "had breached a specific limitation upon its taxing and spending power" (p. 105). Having held that the Establishment Clause specifically limited Congress' taxing and spending power, the Court reserved the question whether "the Constitution contains other specific limitations" that might be asserted in suits by federal taxpayers (*id.*).

Dissenting, Justice Harlan argued forcefully that "the Court's standard for the determination of standing", which focused on whether the plaintiff had the requisite personal stake in the outcome, was "entirely unrelated" to its double nexus test for whether this standard was satisfied (p. 122). "I am quite unable to understand how, if a taxpayer believes that a given public expenditure is unconstitutional, and if he seeks to vindicate that belief in a federal court, his interest in the suit can be said necessarily to vary according to [the nature of the spending program that he attacks or] the constitutional provision under which he states his claim" (p. 124).

To analyze the issues presented, Justice Harlan thought it necessary to distinguish between "Hohfeldian" plaintiffs, who possess "the personal and pecuniary interests of the traditional plaintiff", and "non-Hohfeldian plaintiffs", who assert rights "bereft of any personal or propriety considerations" (p. 119).[4] Justice Harlan found it clear that "non-Hohfeldian plaintiffs as such are not *constitutionally* excluded from the federal courts" (p. 120). The Court had "previously held that individual litigants have standing to represent the public interest, despite their lack of economic or other personal interests, if Congress has appropriately authorized such suits" (p. 131). Justice Harlan did think, however, that "'public actions' brought to vindicate public rights" presented "important hazards for the continued effectiveness of the federal judiciary" and threatened to "alter the allocation of authority among the three branches of the Federal government" (p. 130). In light of these concerns, Justice Harlan would have held that "individual litigants have standing to represent the public interest, despite their lack of economic or other personal interests, if [but only if] Congress has authorized such suits [as it had under various regulatory statutes]. * * * Any hazards to the proper allocation of authority among the three branches of the Government would be substantially diminished if public actions had been pertinently authorized by Congress" (pp. 131–32).

Justice Harlan was correct, wasn't he, about the transparent artificiality of Flast's double-nexus test for taxpayer standing? How is that artificiality to be explained? Was it a limited experiment with a public rights conception of standing in suits by taxpayers or in constitutional actions more generally?

Was Justice Harlan right in thinking that public actions should be allowed if but only if Congress authorizes them? Is this a sensible reflection of the separation-of-powers values that indisputably are at stake? Or is waiting for Congress to authorize suits challenging the constitutionality of federal legislation a violation of the principle that foxes should not be assigned to guard henhouses?

(c) *Standing and Rights*. Although sharply divergent in their apparent outlooks, Frothingham and Flast can be distinguished on a ground emphasized by Justice Stewart's concurring opinion in the latter case (392 U.S. at 114): Flast claimed a violation of her personal constitutional rights under the Establishment Clause, whereas Frothingham sought standing to enforce an essentially structural constitutional provision. Compare Warth v. Seldin, 422 U.S. 490 (1975), in which the Court said that the question of standing "is whether the constitutional or statutory provision on which the claim rests properly can be understood as granting persons in the plaintiff's position a right to judicial relief" (p. 500).[5]

According to Professor Fletcher, people should always have standing to seek redress for violations of their rights, and the standing question is essentially one of what rights particular individuals possess under particular constitutional and statutory provisions. See Fletcher, *The Structure of Standing*, 98 Yale L.J. 221 (1988). Fletcher stresses the link between decisions on standing (as he would formulate it) and implied rights of action cases, see Ch. VII, Sec. 2(B), *infra*: both involve the question of whether the plaintiff has asserted a

---

4. Justice Harlan adapted this terminology from Jaffe, *The Citizen as Litigant in Public Actions: The Non–Hohfeldian or Ideological Plaintiff*, 116 U.Pa.L.Rev. 1033 (1968).

5. Is that the same question as whether the plaintiff has stated a valid claim for re-

lief? See Albert, *Standing to Challenge Administrative Action: An Inadequate Surrogate for Claim for Relief*, 83 Yale L.J. 425 (1974); Currie, *Misunderstanding Standing*, 1981 Sup.Ct.Rev. 41 (1981).

valid claim to enforce the defendant's duty. He argues that the standing inquiry should be based not on a trans-substantive case or controversy doctrine, but rather on the meaning of the particular constitutional or statutory provision relied upon.

If this view were adopted, wouldn't many if not all of the same disputes about plaintiffs' standing recur, recast as arguments about which specific constitutional rights plaintiffs do and do not have? In Allen v. Wright, for example, mightn't the question whether the plaintiffs had an enforceable right under the Equal Protection Clause to enjoin Treasury officials depend on whether the defendants had caused them harm and whether relief would redress that harm? Even if many disputes did recur, however, might the adoption of Fletcher's position enhance the conceptual clarity of standing doctrine?

How does Fletcher's analysis relate to such concerns as (i) guaranteeing that controversies will be concrete and genuine; (ii) ensuring that litigants will be energetic adversaries; (iii) rationing a scarce and expensive resource; (iv) making sure that those most affected by a challenged practice are adequately represented; and (v) facilitating discretionary, prudential judgments whether the time is right for resolution of a particular controversy?

(d) *Cutbacks on Flast.* In the years following Flast v. Cohen, the Supreme Court grew increasingly wary of citizen and taxpayer standing to assert public rights. The Court's decision in Valley Forge Christian College v. Americans United for Separation of Church and State, Inc., 454 U.S. 464 (1982), cut especially close to Flast's core. Acting pursuant to a statute that authorized the lease or sale of surplus property to tax-exempt educational institutions, federal officials transferred a closed army hospital and 77 acres of land to a nonprofit Christian college, which, after a 100% public benefit allowance, received property valued at $577,500 for free.

When Americans United for Separation of Church and State, an organization with 90,000 taxpayer members, challenged the transfer under the Establishment Clause, the Supreme Court ruled that the members lacked standing, as did the organization as their representative. (On an organization's standing as the representative of its members, see Paragraph (7) of the *Note on The Standing of Taxpayers, Governments and Their Officials, and Organizations, and Other Capacity–Based Standing Issues*, pp. 178–87, *infra*.) The taxpayers failed the first prong of Flast's test—permitting challenges only to "exercises of congressional power under the taxing and spending clause"—for two reasons: first, "the source of their complaint is not a congressional action, but a decision by HEW to transfer a parcel of federal property"; second, the authorizing statute was "an * * * exercise of Congress' power under the Property Clause, Art. IV, § 3, cl. 2," rather than under the Taxing and Spending Clause (pp. 479–80).[6]

The Court also ruled (pp. 482–83) that standing could not be based on the claim of a "shared individuated right to a government that 'shall make no law respecting the establishment of religion.'" According to the Court, Schlesinger v. Reservists Comm. to Stop the War, 418 U.S. 208 (1974), and United States v.

---

6. In a footnote, the Court added the point—which it said was not necessary to its decision—that voiding the transfer would probably not increase government receipts, since the property would in all likelihood be transferred to "another nonprofit institution rather than a purchaser for cash" (pp. 480–81 n. 17).

Richardson, 418 U.S. 166 (1974), discussed in Paragraph (4), *infra,* had rejected similar attempts to establish individuated rights under other constitutional provisions, and "assertion of a right to a particular kind of Government conduct, which the Government has violated by acting differently, cannot alone satisfy the requirements of Art. III without draining those requirements of meaning."

Justice Brennan dissented, joined by Justices Blackmun and Marshall.[7] After reviewing the Establishment Clause's history, he concluded (p. 504) that "one of [its] primary purposes * * * was to prevent the use of tax moneys for religious purposes. *The taxpayer was the direct and intended beneficiary of the prohibition on financial aid to religion.*" This history explained, he suggested, why Flast treated a taxpayer challenge under the Establishment Clause differently from other taxpayer suits. Justice Brennan also rejected the Court's distinction of Flast as unconvincing.

Wasn't Justice Brennan right that the Court's distinction was unconvincing?

(3) *The Requirement of Injury in Fact.* The premise that injury-in-fact is a constitutional requirement for citizen challenges to governmental illegality has been disputed by commentators. Raoul Berger argues that when the Constitution was adopted, "the English practice in prohibition, certiorari, quo warranto, and informers' and relators' actions encouraged strangers to attack unauthorized action." Berger, *Standing to Sue in Public Actions: Is It a Constitutional Requirement?*, 78 Yale L.J. 816, 827 (1969). Winter, note 1, *supra,* similarly argues that, until the twentieth century, courts did not view standing either as part of the case or controversy requirement or as a prerequisite for seeking review of official action, but instead granted relief whenever a plaintiff asserted a right for which one of the forms of action afforded a remedy. Professor Winter adds that some of these forms, particularly the prerogative writs, permitted suit by persons lacking a distinctive personal stake in the dispute. See also Jaffe, Judicial Control of Administrative Action 329–36, 459–75 (1965)(describing the history, in England and in the state and federal courts, of the prerogative writs and of citizen and taxpayer standing).

Despite the historical pedigree of public actions, more recent cases have not questioned the principle that Article III requires the plaintiff to show injury by the conduct under challenge. Litigation has turned more often on disputes about what constitutes an "injury" for purposes of Article III.[8]

(a) In Sierra Club v. Morton, 405 U.S. 727 (1972), the Sierra Club sued the United States Forest Service, claiming that its approval of the development of a ski resort in the Sequoia National Forest violated federal statutes and regulations. Alleging that it had "a special interest in the conservation and sound maintenance of the national parks, game refuges, and forests of the country" and that the project would adversely affect the aesthetics and ecology of the area (p. 731), the Club claimed to be "adversely affected or aggrieved" under § 10 of the Administrative Procedure Act (APA), 5 U.S.C. § 702.[9]

---

7. Justice Stevens dissented separately.

8. On this question, see generally Nichol, *Injury and the Disintegration of Article III,* 74 Calif.L.Rev. 1915 (1986). For a discussion of Congress' power to create legal interests the violation of which might satisfy

the injury-in-fact requirement, see *Note on Lujan and Congressional Power to Confer Standing to Sue, infra.*

9. That section provides: "A person suffering legal wrong because of agency action, or adversely affected or aggrieved by

The Court ruled that the plaintiff lacked standing because it had not alleged that it would suffer "injury in fact" from the challenged action. Though non-economic harm of the kind alleged could satisfy that requirement, "the 'injury in fact' test requires more than an injury to a cognizable interest. It requires that the party seeking review be himself among the injured. * * * Nowhere * * * did the Club state that its members use [the area in question] for any purpose, much less that they use it in any way that would be significantly affected by the proposed actions of the [defendants]." The Court termed the requirement of injury a "rough attempt to put the decision as to whether review will be sought in the hands of those who have a direct stake in the outcome", and said that this goal would be "undermined" if organizations were permitted to sue under the APA merely to "vindicate their own value preferences through the judicial process" (pp. 734–35, 739–40).[10]

(b) In United States v. Students Challenging Regulatory Agency Procedures (SCRAP), 412 U.S. 669 (1973), a loose association of law students brought suit alleging that the ICC had failed to prepare an environmental impact statement, as required by federal law, before deciding not to suspend a temporary surcharge on railroad freight rates. The complaint averred that the surcharge, by raising the cost of recycled products, would increase consumption of natural resources, some of which might be taken from the Washington, D.C. area, which the association's members used for recreational purposes. The Supreme Court upheld the plaintiffs' standing. Unlike the Sierra Club, the complainant alleged injury to its *members*—that they "used the forests, streams, mountains, and other resources in the Washington metropolitan area * * * and that this use was disturbed by the adverse environmental impact caused by the nonuse of recyclable goods brought about by a rate increase on those commodities" (p. 685).

Was the dispute in SCRAP more genuine than the one in Sierra Club? Wasn't the Sierra Club likely to be at least as competent a litigant as the plaintiffs in SCRAP? Would it be proper for the Court to make ad hoc judgments about the litigating capacity of particular parties? Compare Scott, *Standing in the Supreme Court: A Functional Analysis*, 86 Harv.L.Rev. 645, 674 (1973)("If plaintiff did not have the minimal personal involvement and adverseness which Article III requires, he would not be engaging in the costly pursuit of litigation.").

(c) In Lujan v. National Wildlife Federation, 497 U.S. 871, 889 (1990), the Supreme Court first distinguished SCRAP, but then went on to suggest SCRAP may have been an aberration, whose "expansive expression of what would suffice for [APA] review * * * has never since been emulated by this Court." The National Wildlife Federation case involved a challenge to the administra-

agency action within the meaning of a relevant statute, is entitled to judicial review thereof." The Court had previously interpreted this provision to require that the plaintiff have suffered injury in fact. See pp. 174–76, *infra*. The decision that the club suffered no injury in *Sierra Club* itself had implications beyond cases brought under the APA.

10. Justice Blackmun (joined by Justice Brennan) dissented, calling for "an imagina-

tive expansion of our traditional concepts of standing in order to enable an organization such as the Sierra Club, possessed, as it is, of pertinent, bona fide and well-recognized attributes and purposes in the area of the environment, to litigate environmental issues" (p. 757). Justice Douglas also dissented; he would have upheld standing "in the name of the inanimate object about to be despoiled, defaced, or invaded by roads and bulldozers and where injury is the subject of public outrage" (p. 741).

tion of the Interior Department's "land withdrawal review program", which was alleged to have improperly permitted increased mining on certain public lands. The Supreme Court upheld the district court's grant of summary judgment to the defendants on the ground that the plaintiff lacked standing. Averments in two affidavits from the plaintiff's members that the government's policy would damage the environment and diminish the members' recreational opportunities were found to be too general, as the affidavits specified only that one of the members used "unspecified portions of an immense tract of territory, on some portions of which mining activity has occurred" (p. 889). SCRAP was "of no relevance here, since it involved not a Rule 56 motion for summary judgment but a Rule 12(b) motion to dismiss on the pleadings. The latter, unlike the former, presumes that general allegations embrace those specific facts that are necessary to support the claim" (*id.*).[11]

(4) *Injury and Generalized Grievances.* Closely related to cases about the adequacy of injury are those involving widely diffused harms, in which no single plaintiff suffers injury distinct from that suffered by many or all other citizens.

(a) Schlesinger v. Reservists Comm. to Stop the War, 418 U.S. 208 (1974), was a class action challenging the military reserve membership of certain Members of Congress as inconsistent with the "Incompatibility Clause" of Article I, § 6, cl. 2 ("no Person holding any Office under the United States, shall be a Member of either House during his Continuance in Office"). The plaintiffs—present and former members of the military reserves, and an association of members opposed to the Vietnam War—alleged as their injury that Members of Congress who belonged to the reserves would be subject to undue influence by the Executive, and that they had potentially conflicting obligations that would foster violations of their duties in each capacity to all citizens. The Court, per Burger, C.J., held that the plaintiffs had failed to assert sufficiently concrete, individualized injury, and merely sought to air " 'generalized grievances' about the conduct of Government" (p. 217). The Court continued (pp. 220–22): "Concrete injury * * * is that indispensable element of a dispute which serves in part to cast it in a form traditionally capable of judicial resolution."[12]

(b) In United States v. Richardson, 418 U.S. 166 (1974), decided the same day as Reservists, the Court ruled that the plaintiff lacked standing to litigate the question whether the CIA was violating Article I, § 9, cl. 7 (requiring "a regular Statement and Account of the Receipts and Expenditures of all public Money") by accounting for its expenditures, in accordance with a federal statute, "solely on the certificate of the Director." Chief Justice Burger's opinion actually addressed only the question whether the plaintiff had standing as a federal taxpayer (on that question, see pp. 178-80, *infra*); but it left no doubt that a complaint on behalf of a citizen-plaintiff would have fared no better (p. 179):

"It can be argued that if respondent is not permitted to litigate this issue, no one can do so. In a very real sense, the absence of any particular individual

---

11. See also Lujan v. Defenders of Wildlife, 504 U.S. 555, 559–61 (1992)(similarly distinguishing motions challenging standing filed under Rule 12 from those filed under Rule 56); Lucas v. South Carolina Coastal Council, 505 U.S. 1003 (1992)(same).

12. Dissenting, Justices Douglas and Marshall would have upheld plaintiffs' standing as citizens, while Justice Brennan would have upheld their standing as taxpayers.

or class to litigate these claims gives support to the argument that the subject matter is committed to the surveillance of Congress, and ultimately to the political process. * * * Slow, cumbersome, and unresponsive though the traditional electoral process may be thought at times, our system provides for changing members of the political branches when dissatisfied citizens convince a sufficient number of their fellow electors that elected representatives are delinquent in performing duties committed to them.''[13]

Justice Powell elaborated on this theme in his concurring opinion (pp. 188–92):

''* * * [R]epeated and essentially head-on confrontations between the life-tenured branch and the representative branches of government will not, in the long run, be beneficial to either. The public confidence essential to the former and the vitality critical to the latter may well erode if we do not exercise self-restraint in the utilization of our power to negative the actions of the other branches. * * * Indeed, taxpayer or citizen advocacy, given its potentially broad base, is precisely the type of leverage that in a democracy ought to be employed against the branches that were intended to be responsive to public attitudes about the appropriate operation of government. * * *

''* * * The irreplaceable value of the power [of judicial review] * * * lies in the protection it has afforded the constitutional rights and liberties of individual citizens and minority groups against oppressive or discriminatory government action. It is this role, not some amorphous general supervision of the operations of government, that has maintained public esteem for the federal courts and has permitted the peaceful coexistence of the countermajoritarian implications of judicial review and the democratic principles upon which our Federal Government in the final analysis rests.''

Reviewing the ''revolution in standing doctrine'' of recent years, he concluded (pp. 194–95): ''I recognize that the Court's allegiance to a requirement of particularized injury has on occasion required a reading of the concept that threatens to transform it beyond recognition. *E.g.,* Baker v. Carr, [p. 284, *infra*]; Flast v. Cohen, [p. 137, *supra*]. But despite such occasional digressions, the requirement remains, and I think it does so for the reasons outlined above. In recognition of those considerations, we should refuse to go the last mile towards abolition of standing requirements that is implicit in * * * allowing a citizen *qua* citizen to invoke the power of the federal courts to negative unconstitutional acts of the Federal Government.''

(c) Is there a difference between the kind of general judicial oversight feared by Chief Justice Burger and judicial interpretation of a constitutional provision as granting enforceable rights in all citizens? Compare SCRAP, Paragraph (3)(b), *supra,* at 687–88 (''standing is not to be denied simply because many people suffer the same injury''; otherwise, ''the most injurious and widespread Government actions could be questioned by nobody''); Public Citizen v. United States Dep't of Justice, 491 U.S. 440, 449–50 (1989)(upholding plaintiffs' standing to bring suit under the Federal Advisory Committee Act

---

13. The Court relied heavily on Ex parte Levitt, 302 U.S. 633 (1937), a challenge by a citizen and member of the Supreme Court bar to the appointment of Justice Black. The suit alleged a violation of Art. I, § 6, cl. 2, which prohibits the appointment of any Senator or Representative to any federal office whose emoluments were increased during the time in which he served in Congress. The Court ruled that Levitt lacked standing because he had suffered no ''direct injury'' and any interest he had was shared with ''all members of the public'' (p. 634).

to obtain information that had allegedly been wrongfully withheld, and rejecting the claim that because any citizen could seek the same information, plaintiffs asserted a mere generalized grievance: "The fact that other citizens * * * might make the same complaint * * * does not lessen appellant's asserted injury"). If there is a difference between general judicial oversight of government and the enforcement of the rights of all citizens, which side of the line do the claims presented in Schlesinger and Richardson fall on? The claim in Flast? The claim in Valley Forge? See generally Fletcher, Paragraph (2)(c), *supra.*

Consider Scalia, *The Doctrine of Standing as an Element of the Separation of Powers*, 17 Suffolk U.L.Rev. 891, 894 (1983): "[T]he law of standing roughly restricts courts to their traditional undemocratic role of protecting individuals and minorities against impositions of the majority, and excludes them from the even more undemocratic role of prescribing how the other two branches should function in order to serve the interest of the majority itself. * * * [U]nless the plaintiff can show some respect in which he is harmed *more* than the rest of us * * * he has not established any basis for concern that the majority is suppressing or ignoring the rights of a minority that wants protection, and thus has not established the prerequisite for judicial intervention."

Does the fact that a grievance is widely shared ensure that the political branches will respond to it—or that, if they do not, the grievance must not be very serious? Should the lack of any other or better plaintiff count in favor of upholding a litigant's standing? See, *e.g.,* Heckler v. Mathews and Orr v. Orr, Paragraph (5)(f), *infra.* See also Meltzer, *Deterring Constitutional Violations by Law Enforcement Officials: Plaintiffs and Defendants as Private Attorneys General,* 88 Colum.L.Rev. 247, 297–306 (1988). If there is reason to fear that adjudication of sensitive issues of governmental relations would result, isn't the political question doctrine the appropriate rubric under which to deal with that fear? See Sec. 6, *infra.*[14]

(d) Allen v. Wright formulates the rule barring adjudication of generalized grievances as an independent reason, apart from the injury requirement, for denying standing. Accord, *e.g.,* Valley Forge Christian College v. Americans United for Separation of Church and State, Inc., *supra,* 454 U.S. at 474–76; Warth v. Seldin, *supra,* 422 U.S. at 499–502. Wright adds that the rule is a judicially self-imposed, rather than a constitutionally mandated, requirement.[15] Is the Court justified in creating restrictions on standing not demanded by Article III?

(5) *Causation and Redressability Requirements.* Allen v. Wright holds that Article III requires not merely a cognizable injury, but also one that is "fairly traceable" to the challenged action and that will be redressed by a favorable decision. These requirements—often called "causation" and "redressability"—evolved in a series of important and controversial decisions.[16]

---

14. For commentary critical of notions of standing that stress the need for distinct injury to particular individuals, see, *e.g.,* Bandes, *The Idea of a Case,* 42 Stan.L.Rev. 227 (1990); Dow, *Standing and Rights,* 36 Emory L.J. 1195 (1987); Redish, *The Passive Virtues, The Counter–Majoritarian Principle, and the "Judicial–Political" Model of Consti-* *tutional Adjudication,* 22 Conn.L.Rev. 647 (1990).

15. Reservists, by contrast with Wright, appears to argue that a mere generalized grievance does not constitute injury under Article III.

16. For critical commentary, see Chayes, *Foreword: Public Law Litigation*

(a) Linda R.S. v. Richard D., 410 U.S. 614 (1973), was a class action, brought by the mother of an illegitimate child, against state officials whose policy was to bring non-support prosecutions against the fathers of legitimate children only. Asserting that the policy violated the Equal Protection Clause, the complaint sought an injunction requiring prosecution of the fathers of illegitimate children. Justice Marshall's opinion for the Court found no standing (pp. 617–18): "[I]n the unique context of a challenge to a criminal statute, appellant has failed to allege a sufficient nexus between her injury and the government action which she attacks to justify judicial intervention. * * * [T]he requested relief * * * would result only in the jailing of the child's father. The prospect that prosecution will, at least in the future, result in payment of support can, at best, be termed only speculative." The opinion also rested on the proposition that "in American jurisprudence at least, a private citizen lacks a judicially cognizable interest in the prosecution or nonprosecution of another" (p. 619).[17]

Since the suit was brought as a class action, is the result of prosecuting non-supporting fathers any more speculative than the general theory that the criminal law deters? Consider Professor Chambers' study, Making Fathers Pay: The Enforcement of Child Support (1979), which provides empirical evidence that aggressive prosecution of non-supporting fathers induces greater compliance. Should the decision in Linda R.S. be viewed instead as expressing doubts about the appropriateness of a judicial order requiring a prosecutor to bring an action?

(b) Warth v. Seldin, 422 U.S. 490 (1975), was an action alleging that the town zoning ordinance in Penfield, New York violated the Constitution and federal civil rights statutes, by preventing persons of low and moderate means (many of them minorities) from living in the town. The Court, per Powell, J., affirmed the dismissal of the complaint. The Court considered and rejected a number of theories of standing, of which two were central.

The first, asserted by several low-income individuals who wished to reside in Penfield, contended that enforcement of the ordinance had prevented construction of low-income housing in which they could afford to live. The Court found that even if the zoning law had increased housing costs, the complaint fell short of establishing standing because it did not "allege facts from which it reasonably could be inferred that, absent the [defendants'] restrictive zoning practices, there is a substantial probability that [plaintiffs] would have been able to purchase or lease in Penfield and that, if the court affords the relief requested, the asserted inability of [plaintiffs] will be removed." The record referred to only two efforts to develop low income housing, and the Court found no "indication that these projects, or other like projects, would have satisfied [the plaintiffs'] needs at prices they could afford, or that, were the court to

and the Burger Court, 96 Harv.L.Rev. 4, 17–19 (1982); Nichol, Causation as a Standing Requirement: The Unprincipled Use of Judicial Restraint, 69 Ky.L.Rev. 185 (1981); Tushnet, The New Law of Standing: A Plea for Abandonment, 62 Cornell L.Rev. 663, 680–88 (1977).

17. See also Leeke v. Timmerman, 454 U.S. 83 (1981)(per curiam)(relying on Linda R.S. in reversing a lower court damage award in a suit against officials who allegedly had conspired in bad faith to block a magistrate's issuance of arrest warrants, and noting that even had the warrants been issued, the prosecutor might have chosen not to press charges).

remove the obstructions attributable to [defendants], such relief would benefit" the plaintiffs (p. 506).[18]

The Court considered separately the standing of Metro–Act, a non-profit corporation interested in the housing needs of the poor. Metro–Act was permitted to serve as the representative of its members (see, on this point, pp. 87-187, *infra*), which led to consideration whether the members themselves had standing. The Court ruled that the allegation that some members, who lived in Penfield, were deprived by the zoning ordinance of the benefits of living in a racially and ethnically integrated community did not state a judicially cognizable injury. In doing so, the Court had to deal with Trafficante v. Metropolitan Life Ins. Co., 409 U.S. 205 (1972), which, in a suit specifically authorized by Congress for violations of the Civil Rights Act of 1968, had upheld the standing of tenants to sue their landlord for discrimination that deprived them of the benefits of an integrated community. Trafficante was different, the Court argued in Warth, because it involved a statutory right of action, and "Congress may create a statutory right or entitlement the alleged deprivation of which can confer standing to sue even where the plaintiff would have suffered no judicially cognizable injury in the absence of statute" (p. 514). For further discussion of Congress' power in this area, see *Note on Lujan and Congressional Power to Confer Standing to Sue*, p. 169, *infra*.

Can the diminished ability of residents of Penfield to live in an integrated community, found wanting in Warth, be distinguished from the diminished ability of the plaintiffs in Wright to obtain an education in a racially integrated school, which the Court held was judicially cognizable?

Consider too Warth's holding that the challenged ordinance did not cause (and relief from it would not redress) the absence of "affordable" housing in Penfield. Did the Court demand "intricacies of pleading that would have gladdened the heart of Baron Parke"? See Chayes, *The Role of the Judge in Public Law Litigation*, 89 Harv.L.Rev. 1281, 1305 (1976), so arguing.[19]

(c) The Court took an approach similar to that of Warth in Simon v. Eastern Kentucky Welfare Rights Org., 426 U.S. 26 (1976), a class action on behalf of all persons unable to afford hospital services. In another opinion by Justice Powell, Simon held that plaintiffs lacked standing to challenge an IRS Revenue Ruling eliminating a requirement that non-profit hospitals provide some care for indigents in order to qualify for favorable tax treatment. It was "purely speculative" that "the denial of access to hospital services [from which the plaintiffs suffered] in fact results from the petitioners' new Ruling, or that

18. Compare Village of Arlington Heights v. Metropolitan Housing Development Corp., 429 U.S. 252 (1977), in which a corporate housing developer, and a black would-be resident of the multiple-unit housing the developer planned to build, were each accorded standing to challenge the validity of an exclusionary single-family zoning ordinance. The developer had contracted to purchase the land for the project, engaged an architect, and begun design and other steps. The black plaintiff testified that he would qualify for the projected housing and would move there if it were built.

19. Compare Havens Realty Corp. v. Coleman, 455 U.S. 363, 377–78 (1982), discussed at p. 172, *infra*, holding that the allegations of injury were inadequate, but remanding to permit amendment of the complaint; "[u]nder the liberal federal pleading standards, * * * dismissal on the pleadings is inappropriate at this stage of the litigation."

a court-ordered return by petitioners to their previous policy would result in these respondents' receiving the hospital services they desire" (pp. 43–44).[20]

Do decisions like Allen, Linda R.S., and Simon—each involving allegations by plaintiffs that administrative officials violated the law by failing to take adverse action against third parties—systematically leave such violations unreviewable? Should standing be broadened to permit such actions, or more generally to permit review of regulatory action likely causing harms that are probabilistic in nature? Would allowing suits of this kind intrude excessively on the enforcement and prosecutorial discretion of executive officials? Or would other kinds of limits on judicial interference with executive enforcement decisions be available? See generally Sunstein, note 3, *supra,* at 1451–69; Comment, 76 Calif.L.Rev. 1061 (1988).[21]

(d) Could the plaintiffs in Warth v. Seldin, subparagraph (b), *supra,* have met the causation and redressability requirements by defining their injury differently—as the denial of the opportunity to participate in a housing market untainted by illegal conduct? Compare Regents of the University of California v. Bakke, 438 U.S. 265 (1978), involving a white plaintiff's challenge to the defendant's operation of a special admissions program for minority applicants to medical school. Some amici argued that Bakke lacked standing because he had not shown that his injury—exclusion from medical school—would be redressed by a favorable decision, since he might not have been admitted even absent any preference for minorities. In a portion of his opinion endorsed by four other Justices, Justice Powell affirmed Bakke's standing, arguing that relief would redress the injury Bakke had suffered by having been deprived, simply because of his race, of the chance to compete for every place in the entering class. The four Justices dissenting on the merits did not address the standing question.[22]

20. Justice Brennan, joined by Justice Marshall, concurred in the result on the ground that the plaintiffs had failed to establish either that the contested ruling altered the operation of all non-profit hospitals or that the tax-exempt status of the hospitals whose conduct affected the plaintiffs was in any way related to the ruling. He took sharp issue, however, with the Court's rationale. Justice Stewart concurred with the majority, but noted specially (p. 46): "I add only that I cannot now imagine a case, at least outside the First Amendment area, where a person whose own tax liability was not affected ever could have standing to litigate the federal tax liability of someone else."

21. For a recent and strict application of the causation and redressability requirements, see ASARCO Inc. v. Kadish, 490 U.S. 605 (1989), discussed at pp. 155–56, *infra.*

22. The Court took an approach similar to that of Bakke in Northeastern Florida Chapter of the Associated General Contractors of America v. City of Jacksonville, 113 S.Ct. 2297 (1993), which also involved a challenge to an affirmative action program. The court of appeals had ruled that plaintiff-contractors lacked standing to attack a municipal ordinance that set aside 10% of city contracts for "minority business enterprises" because they had not alleged that any particular contract would have been awarded to a non-minority bidder but for the set-aside provision. The Supreme Court reversed without dissent on this point. Under Bakke and other cases, the Court held, "[t]he 'injury in fact' in an equal protection case of this variety is the denial of equal treatment resulting from the imposition of [a barrier that makes it more difficult for members of a group to obtain a benefit], not the ultimate inability to obtain the benefit" (p. 2303).

The Court distinguished Warth v. Seldin, *supra,* on two grounds: (1) the plaintiffs in Warth complained not that they were excluded from competing for a benefit (in Warth, the benefit of zoning approval), but that they did not obtain the benefit; and (2) the plaintiffs in Warth did not allege that they had applied for zoning permits or variances with respect to any particular project, whereas here the contractors alleged that they had bid on city contracts affected by the ordinance.

Consider Sunstein, note 3, *supra*, at 1464–69: "The central problem [is] how to characterize the relevant injury. [In Simon,] for example, the plaintiffs might have characterized their injury as an impairment of the opportunity to obtain medical services under a regime undistorted by unlawful tax incentives. In Allen, the plaintiffs themselves argued that their injury should be characterized as the deprivation of an opportunity to undergo desegregation in school systems unaffected by unlawful tax deductions. Thus recharacterized, the injuries are not speculative at all."

Consider the suggestion of Professor Fletcher, Paragraph (2)(c), *supra*, that the causation and redressability questions should be asked at a broader level of generality—whether the plaintiff belongs to the class of people who are entitled to seek a particular form of relief for defendant's violation of a legal duty.

Would the constitutional requirements of standing doctrine be satisfied by a plaintiff who has been exposed to toxic chemicals, and has some statistical likelihood of contracting a serious illness as a result, but has not yet manifested any symptoms? What if the suit were a class action by all persons who have been or will be exposed, brought in a bankruptcy proceeding to protect the class's interests vis-a-vis other claimants to a debtor's assets? See Coffee, *Class Wars: The Dilemma of the Mass Tort Class Action*, 95 Colum.L.Rev. 1343, 1422–33 (1995). Suppose that a number of suits were brought against a defendant, some by plaintiffs who satisfied the standing requirement and others by plaintiffs who did not, and that the suits were consolidated under Fed.R.Civ.P. 42(a). Would it suffice that at least one plaintiff in the consolidated action had standing? See Steinman, *The Effects of Case Consolidation on the Procedural Rights of Litigants: What They Are, What They Might Be Part I: Justiciability and Jurisdiction (Original and Appellate)*, 42 U.C.L.A.L.Rev. 717, 726–50 (1995) (suggesting an affirmative answer).

(e) In Duke Power Co. v. Carolina Environmental Study Group, 438 U.S. 59 (1978), an environmental organization, a labor union, and forty individuals sued the Nuclear Regulatory Commission and a utility company that was constructing two nuclear power plants. The suit sought a declaration that the Price–Anderson Act, 42 U.S.C. § 2210, which limits liability in the event of a nuclear accident, effected an unconstitutional deprivation of property of potential accident victims. The Court, per Chief Justice Burger, affirmed standing and upheld the constitutionality of the Act. The Court found sufficient injury in the potential thermal pollution of several lakes in the vicinity of the plants under construction, and in the likelihood of low-level radiation from the plants. The requisite causal connection between this injury and the challenged conduct was found because of the "substantial likelihood" that, absent the Act, the utility would be unable to complete the two nuclear plants. The Court explicitly rejected any requirement, for Article III purposes, that the claimed injuries and the constitutional rights asserted have any connection. Restricting the "nexus" requirement of Flast v. Cohen, Paragraph 2(b) *supra*, to taxpayer suits, the Court refused to hold, in other kinds of lawsuits, that "a litigant must demonstrate anything more than injury in fact and a substantial likelihood that the judicial relief requested will prevent or redress the claimed injury" (p. 79).

For other decisions that interpret the causation and redressability requirements far less strictly than Warth, see, *e.g.*, Bryant v. Yellen, 447 U.S. 352, 366–68 (1980); Larson v. Valente, 456 U.S. 228, 238–43 (1982); Metropolitan Washington Airports Authority v. Citizens for the Abatement of Aircraft Noise, Inc., 501 U.S. 252 (1991).

Justice Stewart dissented on the standing issue, arguing that "[s]urely a plaintiff does not have standing simply because his challenge, if successful, will remove the injury relied on for standing purposes *only* because it will put the defendant out of existence. Surely there must be *some* direct relationship between the plaintiff's federal claim and the injury relied on for standing" (p. 95). Justice Stevens objected on similar grounds, and added (pp. 102–03): "The string of contingencies that supposedly holds this litigation together is too delicate for me. We are told that but for the Price–Anderson Act there would be no financing of nuclear power plants, no development of those plants by private parties, and hence no present injury to persons such as appellees; we are then asked to remedy an alleged due process violation that may possibly occur at some uncertain time in the future, and may possibly injure the appellees in a way that has no significant connection with any present injury. It is remarkable that such a series of speculations is considered sufficient * * * to establish appellees' standing."

Duke Power is virtually impossible to reconcile with prior authority, isn't it? It is perhaps most plausibly explained as responsive to ad hoc considerations—especially the desire to reverse on the merits the district court's ruling that an important federal statute was unconstitutional. See Stewart, *Review, Standing for Solidarity*, 88 Yale L.J. 1559, 1574 n. 62 (1979). See also Varat, *Variable Justiciability and the Duke Power Case*, 58 Tex.L.Rev. 273 (1980). If a result-oriented explanation is correct, to what extent and in what sense is Duke Power an anomaly?[23]

(f) A recurring question of standing has arisen in suits in which plaintiffs raise equal protection challenges to statutes or rules denying them the more favorable treatment enjoyed by others. If a violation can be established, the inequality might be eliminated either by treating the plaintiff more favorably or by denying the favorable treatment to others; in the latter case, the plaintiff would obtain no material benefit. The Supreme Court has nonetheless consistently upheld plaintiffs' standing. See, *e.g.*, Heckler v. Mathews, 465 U.S. 728 (1984); Orr v. Orr, 440 U.S. 268, 272 (1979); Stanton v. Stanton, 421 U.S. 7, 17–18 (1975); Iowa–Des Moines Nat. Bank v. Bennett, 284 U.S. 239, 247 (1931), p. 850, *infra*. See generally Kovacic, *Remedying Underinclusive Statutes*, 33 Wayne L.Rev. 39 (1986).

In the Mathews case, Congress had provided larger benefit awards under the Social Security Act to certain women than to similarly situated men. A severability clause provided that if the special provision were found to deny equal protection, men and women alike should receive the smaller amount. The Court upheld the standing of a male beneficiary to challenge the unequal treatment. Because he asserted "the right to receive 'benefits * * * distributed according to classifications which do not without sufficient justification differentiate * * * solely on the basis of sex,' and not a substantive right to any particular amount of benefits, [plaintiff's] standing does not depend on his ability to obtain increased Social Security payments. * * * Although the severability clause would prevent a court from redressing this inequality by increasing the benefits payable to [plaintiff], we have never suggested that the injuries caused by a constitutionally underinclusive scheme can be remedied

---

23. See also Franklin v. Massachusetts, 505 U.S. 788 (1992)(finding the redressability requirement satisfied where it was "substantially likely" that the President, although not subject to a judicial order, would alter his report concerning the states' respective representations in the House if a challenge to the calculation of the census were upheld).

only by extending the program's benefits to the excluded class. * * * [D]is-crimination itself, by perpetuating 'archaic and stereotypic notions' or by stigmatizing members of the disfavored group as 'innately inferior,' * * * can cause serious noneconomic injuries" (pp. 737–39).

Though, at least in a challenge to a *federal* statute, ordinarily "extension [of benefits] rather than nullification is the proper course, [Califano v. Westcott, 443 U.S. 76, 89 (1979)]", the Court explained that the question is one of legislative intent, and here Congress' clear expression of its preference for nullification should be honored (p. 739 n. 5). On the merits, the Court upheld the provision under attack.

Mathews is surely sound; to have denied standing would have effectively immunized the statute from judicial review. See Orr v. Orr, *supra,* 440 U.S. at 272. Can Mathews be squared, however, with the refusal in Allen v. Wright to find that the stigma suffered by plaintiffs was cognizable injury? Consider again the possible relevance of Professor Fletcher's theory, Paragraph (2)(c), *supra.* The plaintiff in Mathews asserted a claim of right under the Equal Protection Clause that, if valid, entailed a right to sue. But it is a much harder question, isn't it, whether the Equal Protection Clause should be construed to authorize the plaintiffs in Allen v. Wright to litigate the status and obligations of private schools under the Internal Revenue Code?

(6) *Standing and the Separation of Powers.* Article III's case or controversy requirement has often been said to implicate the separation of powers. See, *e.g.,* Valley Forge Christian College v. Americans United for Separation of Church and State, Inc., *supra,* 454 U.S. at 473–74; Flast v. Cohen, *supra,* 392 U.S. at 95; Scalia, Paragraph (4)(c), *supra.* But Allen v. Wright was distinctive in suggesting (see footnote 26) that the application of standing doctrine in a particular case should be guided by separation of powers considerations.[24] The Court was presumably concerned about the appropriate limits of relief against the Executive Branch. But even if the Court was right that case-or-controversy considerations "shade into" the question of the appropriateness of equitable relief, does it follow that "[t]he latter set of considerations should therefore inform our judgment about whether [plaintiffs] have standing"? Can the need for a particular kind of relief—and its impact on the Executive Branch—be adequately judged on the pleadings? See Fallon, *Of Justiciability, Remedies, and Public Law Litigation: Notes on the Jurisprudence of Lyons,* 59 N.Y.U.L.Rev. 1, 72 (1984). And aren't these equitable considerations, in any event, quite distinct from the question to which Wright deemed them relevant—namely, whether the IRS' conduct caused the harm in question? Compare Nichol, *Abusing Standing: A Comment on Allen v. Wright,* 133 U.Pa. L.Rev. 635 (1985), with Logan, *Standing to Sue: A Proposed Separation of Powers Analysis,* 1984 Wis.L.Rev. 37.

Would congressional authorization suffice to answer separation-of-powers concerns in cases such as Wright? Recall Justice Harlan's position in Flast v. Cohen, Paragraph (2)(b), *supra,* that standing by a "non-Hohfeldian" plaintiff should be deemed permissible under the separation of powers if but only if

---

24. For a more recent linkage, see Lujan v. Defenders of Wildlife, 504 U.S. 555 (1992), p. 157, *infra.* Compare Flast v. Cohen, Paragraph (2)(b) *supra,* which asserts that the question of standing "does not, by its own force, raise separation of powers problems related to improper judicial interference in areas committed to other branches of the Federal Government. Such problems arise, if at all, only from the substantive issues the individual seeks to have adjudicated" (392 U.S. at 100–01).

Congress authorizes the action. Does the distinction between "Hohfeldian" and "non-Hohfeldian" plaintiffs illuminate the separation-of-powers issues in Wright? In Heckler v. Mathews, Paragraph (5)(f), *supra*? For further discussion of Congress' power to authorize standing, see pp. 169–74, *infra*.

(7) *Asserting the Rights of Others.* Allen v. Wright notes that one of the Court's subconstitutional, "self-imposed limits on the exercise of federal jurisdiction * * * is a general prohibition on a litigant's raising another person's legal rights." A number of cases have forged exceptions to this rule. For example, in Pierce v. Society of Sisters, 268 U.S. 510 (1925), owners of a private school—whose enrollment had declined after enactment of a state law requiring parents to send their children to public schools—were permitted to enjoin enforcement of the statute on the ground that it violated the parents' rights to determine how their children should be educated. The Court relied on the "many * * * cases where injunctions have issued to protect business enterprises against interference with the freedom of patrons or customers" (p. 536).[25]

In City of Revere v. Massachusetts Gen. Hosp., 463 U.S. 239 (1983), municipal police officers wounded a suspect and then summoned an ambulance, which took the suspect to a private hospital. When the city refused to pay the bill, the hospital sued the city in state court. The state courts ruled for the hospital, concluding that the Cruel and Unusual Punishment Clause required that the city be held liable in order to ensure that persons in police custody receive adequate medical care. On review, the Supreme Court held that the hospital clearly had "standing in the Article III sense" to sue for recovery of payment for services rendered (p. 243), then concluded that the hospital should be able to assert its patient's rights. The hospital's assertion of third-party rights was not contested in the state courts, and a denial of standing in the Supreme Court, for merely "prudential reasons," would be a mistake, since it would "leav[e] intact the state court's judgment in favor of [the hospital], the purportedly improper representative of the third party's constitutional rights." In a footnote, the Court argued that standing and the merits were here " 'inextricably intertwined' "; both questions depended in part on "whether injured suspects will be deprived of their constitutional right to necessary medical care unless the government entity is required to pay hospitals for their services" (pp. 243–44 n. 5). On the merits, the Court reversed.

The Court again confronted the question of third-party standing in Caplin & Drysdale, Chartered v. United States, 491 U.S. 617 (1989). The dispute arose when the district court invoked a law permitting forfeiture of property derived from drug-law violations and forfeited virtually all the assets of a criminal defendant. The law firm representing him petitioned the court for an adjudication of its rights in the property, contending in part that the Sixth Amendment required that property used to pay legal fees be exempt from forfeiture. The Supreme Court upheld the firm's standing, although ruling against it on the merits. The firm's injury in fact was clear, as it stood to obtain legal fees if the forfeiture were voided. The prudential question whether the firm could assert the rights of others was more difficult, the Court said,

---

25. See also Singleton v. Wulff, 428 U.S. 106 (1976)(doctors permitted to challenge a state statute denying Medicaid benefits to patients who underwent abortions that were not medically indicated); Buchanan v. Warley, 245 U.S. 60 (1917)(white vendor of land sued black vendee for specific performance; vendor, in responding to defense of breach of a contractual condition, was permitted to challenge the constitutionality of a city ordinance purporting to forbid blacks from residing on the property in question).

and depended on three factors. One—the ability of the rightholder to bring suit asserting his own rights—argued against permitting the assertion of third-party rights, as the client faced no obstacle. But the other two factors weighed heavily the other way: first, the relationship (attorney-client) was of special consequence, and second, "it is credibly alleged that the statute at issue here may 'materially impair the ability of' third persons in [defendant's] position to exercise their constitutional rights" (p. 624 n. 3).

Can any of these cases be explained as involving the assertion of the plaintiff's own right to engage in a constitutionally protected relationship? See Warth v. Seldin, Paragraph (5)(b), *supra,* 422 U.S. at 501, citing Pierce as an example of the Court's having "found, in effect, that the constitutional or statutory provision in question implies a right of action in the plaintiff." For fuller discussion of assertion of the rights of others, see *Note on Asserting the Rights of Others,* Section 3(B) of this Chapter, pp. 187-95, *infra,* which discusses the more common situation of an actual or potential *defendant* who seeks to resist enforcement of a legal duty by asserting the rights of third persons.

(8) *Standing to Intervene, Appeal, and Challenge Removal.* In Diamond v. Charles, 476 U.S. 54 (1986), a pediatrician (Diamond) opposed to abortion was allowed to intervene as a defendant in a challenge to state legislation regulating abortions. After the court of appeals approved a permanent injunction against four sections of the statute, only Diamond appealed to the Supreme Court; the state merely filed a "letter of interest" noting that under the Court's rules it was an automatic appellee, and that its interest and Diamond's were identical. The Supreme Court dismissed the appeal on the ground that Diamond lacked standing. It first held that he could not ride "piggyback" on the state's undoubted ability to appeal; though the state was made a "party" by the Supreme Court's rules, it was not an appellant. The Court then rejected several theories under which Diamond claimed to have standing in his own right, one of which was based on his status as an intervenor. That status gave him a statutory right to seek review, but the Court ruled that he could continue the suit without the state's participation only "upon a showing * * * that he fulfills the requirements of Art. III" (p. 68). The Court added (pp. 68–69): "We need not decide today whether a party seeking to intervene before a District Court must satisfy not only the requirements of Rule 24(a)(2), but also the requirements of Art. III."[26]

Justice O'Connor, joined by Chief Justice Burger and Justice Rehnquist, concurred in part and concurred in the judgment. She agreed that Diamond in his own right had not alleged any injury cognizable under Article III, but thought the first part of the Court's opinion—holding that Diamond could not

---

26. See generally Shapiro, *Some Thoughts on Intervention Before Courts, Agencies, and Arbitrators,* 81 Harv.L.Rev. 721, 726–28 (1968): "[T]here is a difference between the question whether one is a proper plaintiff or defendant in an initial action and the question whether one is entitled to intervene. * * * A may not have a dispute with C that could qualify as a case or controversy [under Article III], but he may have a sufficient interest in B's dispute with C to warrant his participation in the case once it has begun, and the case or controversy limitation should impose no barrier to his admission" (p. 726). See also Tobias, *Standing to Intervene,* 1991 Wis.L.Rev. 415, 443 (arguing that, because "the judicial machinery has [already] been mobilized," intervenors should not be required to demonstrate standing under Article III, but that the policies underlying standing doctrine argue for permitting intervention when its contribution to the appropriate resolution of a dispute outweighs any disruptive impact it may have upon the parties or the court).

ride piggyback on the state's presence as a designated appellee—was inconsistent with an earlier precedent, Director, OWCP v. Perini North River Assoc., 459 U.S. 297 (1983). In Justice O'Connor's view, if Diamond was a proper party in the court of appeals, his statutorily authorized appeal brought a justiciable controversy (to which the state was a party) before the Supreme Court. She concluded, however, that Diamond was not a proper intervenor, at least in the court of appeals, and therefore she agreed that his appeal should be dismissed.[27]

In International Primate Protection League v. Administrators of Tulane Educational Fund, 500 U.S. 72 (1991), also discussed at p. 953, *infra,* a federal agency removed a state court action to a federal court under 28 U.S.C. § 1442(a)(1). The court of appeals held that (a) the action was removable and (b) the plaintiffs lacked Article III standing to sue on the merits. The Supreme Court, after granting certiorari on the question of removability, held that even if plaintiffs lacked Article III standing to prosecute the action in a federal court, their interest in litigating in state court gave them standing to object to the propriety of removal.[28]

(9) *The Bearing of State Law on Standing.* Article III's definition of judicial power applies only to the federal courts. The state courts are thus free to adjudicate federal questions even when there is no "case or controversy" within the meaning of Article III; some state courts, for example, issue advisory opinions. See p. 98, *supra.*

In Tileston v. Ullman, 318 U.S. 44 (1943)(per curiam), the Connecticut Supreme Court had rejected, on the merits, a physician's constitutional challenge to a state statute prohibiting the use or distribution of contraceptives. The Supreme Court dismissed his appeal on the ground that the only constitutional attack on the statute—that it worked a deprivation of life without due process—was based on the rights not of the physician but of his patients, which he had no standing to assert. See also Doremus v. Board of Educ., 342 U.S. 429, 434 (1952), p. 179 *infra* (dismissing, for want of standing, an appeal from a state judgment denying relief on the merits in a state taxpayer's challenge to a state statute).

(a) Suppose Dr. Ullman proceeded to distribute contraceptives and was prosecuted under the statute. Could the state supreme court's prior judgment

---

27. Compare Maine v. Taylor, 477 U.S. 131 (1986), a federal prosecution for transporting fish in interstate commerce in violation of state law. When the defendant contended that the state law unconstitutionally burdened interstate commerce, Maine intervened to defend the law. After the court of appeals reversed the defendant's conviction on the ground that the state law was indeed invalid, Maine (but not the United States) sought review. The Court ruled that Maine had standing to appeal in view of its interest in the continued enforceability of its statute and in the reinstatement of the defendant's conviction.

28. At this point, the Court dropped a footnote (p. 78 n. 4) in which it stated (a) that even if the plaintiffs lacked Article III standing, the case could properly be remanded to state court, where Article III requirements were not applicable, and (b) that the grant of certiorari did not extend to the question whether Article III standing requirements can be imposed on a plaintiff with respect to a state law claim removed under § 1442(a)(1), where the only basis for removal is a federal defense.

What is the answer to this question? Is removal analogous to an exercise of appellate jurisdiction? (Note the discussion in Justice Story's opinion for the Court in Martin v. Hunter's Lessee, 14 U.S. (1 Wheat.) 304 (1816), p. 495, *infra*). Consider also the relevance of the materials in Paragraph (9) of this Note.

preclude litigation of any constitutional challenge in the state courts? In the Supreme Court, on review of a judgment affirming his conviction? See Fidelity Nat. Bank & Trust Co. v. Swope, 274 U.S. 123 (1927), in which the Supreme Court assumed that if a state proceeding did not constitute a case or controversy within its appellate jurisdiction under Article III, a judgment rendered therein would not be res judicata in later proceedings in federal court.

(b) Suppose instead that the Connecticut Supreme Court had upheld Dr. Ullman's claim on the merits and enjoined enforcement of the statute. Does it follow from Tileston that the United States Supreme Court would have lacked power to review the state court's judgment? In ASARCO Inc. v. Kadish, 490 U.S. 605 (1989), the Supreme Court ruled that "[w]hen a state court has issued a judgment in a case where plaintiffs in the original action had no standing to sue under the principles governing the federal courts, we may exercise our jurisdiction on certiorari if the judgment of the state court causes direct, specific, and concrete injury to the parties who petition for our review, where the requisites of a case or controversy are also met" (pp. 623–24).

In ASARCO, state taxpayers and an association of public school teachers challenged a state statute governing mineral leases on state lands as void under federal law. The state supreme court found the statute invalid and remanded for entry of a declaratory judgment and consideration of injunctive relief. On certiorari, the Supreme Court held that it had power to review the judgment. Justice Kennedy's opinion (for four Justices) first concluded that in a federal court action, plaintiffs would lack standing.[29] Even accepting the plaintiffs' premise that the failure to comply with federal requirements had cost state school trust funds millions of dollars, the Court found it was "pure speculation" whether the relief sought would lead to tax reductions for the plaintiff-taxpayers (since any increased revenues might instead result in higher spending); therefore, the taxpayers had not demonstrated " 'direct injury,' pecuniary or otherwise" (pp. 613–614), quoting Doremus v. Board of Education, *supra*, 342 U.S. at 434. As for the plaintiff-teachers, it was equally speculative whether the relief sought would result in spending increases and better compensation (since the state might instead reduce education funds from other sources). Nor did it suffice that some plaintiffs—either the taxpayers or the teachers—would benefit whether taxes fell or educational spending increased. Rather, Justice Kennedy concluded, each plaintiff must independently satisfy the causation and redressability requirements of standing doctrine.[30]

---

29. The Chief Justice, Justice Stevens, and Justice Scalia joined this part of Justice Kennedy's opinion. Justices Brennan, White, Marshall, and Blackmun saw no reason to reach this issue, since they agreed with Justice Kennedy that the Court could review the judgment whether or not the suit could have been entertained in a federal district court. Justice O'Connor did not participate.

30. Compare Quinn v. Millsap, 491 U.S. 95 (1989), where the state courts rejected an equal protection challenge to a property ownership requirement for appointment to a local government body. The Court characterized

as "frivolous" the contention that the plaintiffs lacked standing because of the limits of federal district court power (noted in Supreme Court dicta) to require officials to make discretionary appointments in a particular way. "Whatever the limits of a federal court's power to *remedy* violations of the Equal Protection Clause, * * * those limits are plainly irrelevant when this Court is asked to review a state-court judgment [rejecting an Equal Protection claim]" (p. 104). Is this reasoning consistent with the "causation and redressability" requirements of Article III standing doctrine as applied in ASARCO?

Next, Justice Kennedy (here speaking for a majority of six) ruled that, even if a federal district court would have lacked power to hear the lawsuit, the Supreme Court could review the state court decision. Article III did not bar the state court from hearing the case, and the state adjudication adverse to the defendants "constitute[d] the kind of injury [to them] cognizable in this Court on review from the state courts. [Defendants] are faced with 'actual or threatened injury' that is sufficiently 'distinct and palpable' to support their standing to invoke the authority of a federal court" (p. 618, quoting Warth v. Seldin, 422 U.S. 490, 500–01 (1975)). The Court stressed that the record revealed a genuine case or controversy, that the parties were adverse, and that valuable legal rights would be affected by the decision.

The alternatives to reviewing the judgment were, in the Court's view, unsatisfactory. To vacate the state court judgment would in effect impose federal standing requirements on the state courts. To dismiss and leave the state judgment standing might have the same effect if, as the Court had intimated in earlier decisions such as Fidelity Nat. Bank & Trust, Paragraph (9)(a), *supra,* a state court judgment not reviewable by the Supreme Court would not be res judicata on an issue of federal law. The Solicitor General's suggestion that the defendants sue in a federal trial court to re-adjudicate the issues would "denigrate the authority of the state courts" by permitting a lower federal court to review the decision of the highest state court (p. 622), a course inconsistent with the Rooker–Feldman doctrine. (On that doctrine, see pp. 1501-04, *infra.*)

On the merits, the Court affirmed the state court's decision that the state statute regulating mineral leases was invalid.

In partial dissent, Chief Justice Rehnquist, joined by Justice Scalia, objected that the majority's recognition of standing created an unjustifiable disparity: "although the Doremus case is good law for plaintiffs who lack standing but lost in the state court on the merits of their federal claim, it is not good law for such plaintiffs who prevailed on the merits of the federal question * * *" (p. 634). That there was a genuine case or controversy and adverse parties did not suffice; that could be said in many cases where the Court had found no standing. The Chief Justice also found it unremarkable that some state court decisions about federal law might be unreviewable, for that was surely true when state courts rendered advisory opinions.

Do you agree with the ASARCO majority that there was no satisfactory alternative to reviewing the state court's judgment?[31] Wouldn't all of the difficulties discussed by the majority disappear if standing to raise federal questions (even in state court) were treated as matter of federal law? See the comments of Professor Freund, in Supreme Court and Supreme Law 35 (E. Cahn ed. 1954); Varat, Paragraph (6)(d), *supra,* at 311–13; Fletcher, *The "Case or Controversy" Requirement in State Court Adjudication of Federal Questions,* 78 Calif.L.Rev. 263 (1990). A strong objection might appear to arise from the traditionally accepted authority of state courts to give advisory opinions. See p. 98, *supra.* As Professor Fletcher has pointed out, however, treating standing to raise a federal question as a federal issue would not necessarily prohibit state courts from giving advisory opinions, as long as those opinions were given no res judicata or precedential effect.

---

31. The decision is defended as striking an appropriate balance between state and federal interests in Note, 69 N.Y.U.L.Rev. 77 (1994).

May a state court refuse, on standing grounds, to hear a federal cause of action in which a federal court would uphold standing? See generally Chap. IV, Sec. 3, *infra*; Chap. VII, Sec. 2, pp. 847-57, *infra*; Gordon & Gross, *Justiciability of Federal Claims in State Court,* 59 Notre Dame L.Rev. 1145 (1984).

Lujan v. Defenders of Wildlife

504 U.S. 555, 112 S.Ct. 2130, 119 L.Ed.2d 351 (1992).
Certiorari to the United States Court of Appeals for the Eighth Circuit.

■ JUSTICE SCALIA delivered the opinion of the Court with respect to Parts I, II, III–A, and IV, and an opinion with respect to Part III–B in which the CHIEF JUSTICE, JUSTICE WHITE, and JUSTICE THOMAS join.

I

The [Endangered Species Act of 1973 (ESA)] as amended, 16 U.S.C. § 1531 et seq., seeks to protect species of animals against threats to their continuing existence caused by man. * * * Section 7(a)(2) of the Act * * * provides, in pertinent part:

> "Each Federal agency shall, in consultation with and with the assistance of the Secretary [of the Interior], insure that any action authorized, funded, or carried out by such agency ... is not likely to jeopardize the continued existence of any endangered species or threatened species or result in the destruction or adverse modification of habitat of such species which is determined by the Secretary, after consultation as appropriate with affected States, to be critical."   16 U.S.C. § 1536(a)(2).

In 1978, the Fish and Wildlife Service (FWS) and the National Marine Fisheries Service (NMFS), on behalf of the Secretary of the Interior and the Secretary of Commerce respectively, promulgated a joint regulation stating that the obligations imposed by § 7(a)(2) extend to actions taken in foreign nations. [In 1986, however, these agencies promulgated a] revised joint regulation, reinterpreting § 7(a)(2) to require consultation only for actions taken in the United States or on the high seas * * *. 50 C.F.R. 402.01 (1991).

Shortly thereafter, respondents, organizations dedicated to wildlife conservation and other environmental causes, filed this action against the Secretary of the Interior, seeking a declaratory judgment that the new regulation is in error as to the geographic scope of § 7(a)(2), and an injunction requiring the Secretary to promulgate a new regulation restoring the initial interpretation. The District Court granted the Secretary's motion to dismiss for lack of standing. The Court of Appeals for the Eighth Circuit reversed by a divided vote. On remand, the Secretary moved for summary judgment on the standing issue, and respondents moved for summary judgment on the merits. The District Court denied the Secretary's motion, on the ground that the Eighth Circuit had already determined the standing question in this case; it granted respondents' merits motion, and ordered the Secretary to publish a revised regulation. The Eighth Circuit affirmed. We granted certiorari.

II

Over the years, our cases have established that the irreducible constitutional minimum of standing contains three elements: First, the plaintiff must have suffered an "injury in fact"—an invasion of a legally-protected interest which is (a) concrete and particularized, see [Allen v. Wright, 468 U.S. 737, 756 (1984)], and (b) "actual or imminent, not 'conjectural' or 'hypothetical,' " Whitmore [v. Arkansas, 495 U.S. 149, 155 (1990)], (quoting Los Angeles v. Lyons, 461 U.S. 95, 102 (1983)). Second, there must be a causal connection between the injury and the conduct complained of—the injury has to be "fairly ... trace[able] to the challenged action of the defendant, and not ... th[e] result [of] the independent action of some third party not before the court." Simon v. Eastern Kentucky Welfare Rights Org., 426 U.S. 26, 41–42 (1976). Third, it must be "likely," as opposed to merely "speculative," that the injury will be "redressed by a favorable decision." *Id.*, at 38, 43.

The party invoking federal jurisdiction bears the burden of establishing these elements. * * * [O]n a motion to dismiss we "presum[e] that general allegations embrace those specific facts that are necessary to support the claim," [Lujan v. National Wildlife Federation, 497 U.S. 871, 889 (1990).] In response to a summary judgment motion, however, the plaintiff can no longer rest on such "mere allegations," but must "set forth" by affidavit or other evidence "specific facts," Fed.Rule Civ.Proc. 56(e), which for purposes of the summary judgment motion will be taken to be true. * * *

When the suit is one challenging the legality of government action or inaction, the nature and extent of facts that must be averred (at the summary judgment stage) or proved (at the trial stage) in order to establish standing depends considerably upon whether the plaintiff is himself an object of the action (or forgone action) at issue. If he is, there is ordinarily little question that the action or inaction has caused him injury, and that a judgment preventing or requiring the action will redress it. When, however, as in this case, a plaintiff's asserted injury arises from the government's allegedly unlawful regulation (or lack of regulation) of *someone else,* much more is needed. In that circumstance, causation and redressability ordinarily hinge on the response of the regulated (or regulable) third party to the government action or inaction—and perhaps on the response of others as well. The existence of one or more of the essential elements of standing "depends on the unfettered choices made by independent actors not before the courts and whose exercise of broad and legitimate discretion the courts cannot presume either to control or to predict," ASARCO Inc. v. Kadish, 490 U.S. 605, 615 (1989)(opinion of KENNEDY, J.), and it becomes the burden of the plaintiff to adduce facts showing that those choices have been or will be made in such manner as to produce causation and permit redressability of injury. Thus, when the plaintiff is not himself the object of the government action or inaction he challenges, standing is not precluded, but it is ordinarily "substantially more difficult" to establish. Allen, *supra,* 468 U.S., at 758.

III

We think the Court of Appeals failed to apply the foregoing principles in denying the Secretary's motion for summary judgment. Respondents had not made the requisite demonstration of (at least) injury and redressability.

A

Respondents' claim to injury is that the lack of consultation with respect to certain funded activities abroad "increas[es] the rate of extinction of endangered and threatened species." Of course, the desire to use or observe an animal species, even for purely aesthetic purposes, is undeniably a cognizable interest for purpose of standing. See, *e.g.,* Sierra Club v. Morton, 405 U.S. [727, 734 (1972)]. "But the 'injury in fact' test requires more than an injury to a cognizable interest. It requires that the party seeking review be himself among the injured." *Id., at* 734–735. To survive the Secretary's summary judgment motion, respondents had to submit affidavits or other evidence showing, through specific facts, not only that listed species were in fact being threatened by funded activities abroad, but also that one or more of respondents' members would thereby be "directly" affected apart from their " 'special interest' in th[e] subject." *Id.,* at 735, 739.

With respect to this aspect of the case, the Court of Appeals focused on the affidavits of two Defenders' members—Joyce Kelly and Amy Skilbred. Ms. Kelly stated that she traveled to Egypt in 1986 and "observed the traditional habitat of the endangered nile crocodile there and intend[s] to do so again, and hope[s] to observe the crocodile directly," and that she "will suffer harm in fact as a result of [the] American . . . role . . . in overseeing the rehabilitation of the Aswan High Dam on the Nile . . . and [in] develop[ing] . . . Egypt's . . . Master Water Plan." Ms. Skilbred averred that she traveled to Sri Lanka in 1981 and "observed th[e] habitat" of "endangered species such as the Asian elephant and the leopard" at what is now the site of the Mahaweli Project funded by the Agency for International Development (AID), although she "was unable to see any of the endangered species;" "this development project," she continued, "will seriously reduce endangered, threatened, and endemic species habitat including areas that I visited . . . , [which] may severely shorten the future of these species;" that threat, she concluded, harmed her because she "intend[s] to return to Sri Lanka in the future and hope[s] to be more fortunate in spotting at least the endangered elephant and leopard." When Ms. Skilbred was asked at a subsequent deposition if and when she had any plans to return to Sri Lanka, she * * * confessed that she had no current plans * * *.

We shall assume for the sake of argument that these affidavits contain facts showing that certain agency-funded projects threaten listed species— though that is questionable. They plainly contain no facts, however, showing how damage to the species will produce "imminent" injury to Mss. Kelly and Skilbred. That the women "had visited" the areas of the projects before the projects commenced proves nothing. * * * And the affiants' profession of an "inten[t]" to return to the places they had visited before * * *—without any description of concrete plans, or indeed even any specification of *when* the some day will be—do not support a finding of the "actual or imminent" injury that our cases require.

Besides relying upon the Kelly and Skilbred affidavits, respondents propose a series of novel standing theories. The first, inelegantly styled "ecosystem nexus," proposes that any person who uses any part of a "contiguous ecosystem" adversely affected by a funded activity has standing even if the activity is located a great distance away. This approach, as the Court of Appeals correctly observed, is inconsistent with our opinion in National Wildlife Federation, which held that a plaintiff claiming injury from environmental damage must use the area affected by the challenged activity and not an area roughly "in the vicinity" of it. 497 U.S., at 887–889. It makes no difference that the general-purpose section of the ESA states that the Act was intended in part "to provide a means whereby the ecosystems upon which endangered species and threatened species depend may be conserved," 16 U.S.C. § 1531(b). To say that the

Act protects ecosystems is not to say that the Act creates (if it were possible) rights of action in persons who have not been injured in fact, that is, persons who use portions of an ecosystem not perceptibly affected by the unlawful action in question.

Respondents' other theories are called, alas, the "animal nexus" approach, whereby anyone who has an interest in studying or seeing the endangered animals anywhere on the globe has standing; and the "vocational nexus" approach, under which anyone with a professional interest in such animals can sue. Under these theories, anyone who goes to see Asian elephants in the Bronx Zoo, and anyone who is a keeper of Asian elephants in the Bronx Zoo, has standing to sue because the Director of AID did not consult with the Secretary regarding the AID-funded project in Sri Lanka. This is beyond all reason. * * * It is clear that the person who observes or works with a particular animal threatened by a federal decision is facing perceptible harm, since the very subject of his interest will no longer exist. It is even plausible—though it goes to the outermost limit of plausibility—to think that a person who observes or works with animals of a particular species in the very area of the world where that species is threatened by a federal decision is facing such harm, since some animals that might have been the subject of his interest will no longer exist, see Japan Whaling Assn. v. American Cetacean Soc., 478 U.S. 221, 231 n. 4 (1986). It goes beyond the limit, however, and into pure speculation and fantasy, to say that anyone who observes or works with an endangered species, anywhere in the world, is appreciably harmed by a single project affecting some portion of that species with which he has no more specific connection.

B

Besides failing to show injury, respondents failed to demonstrate redressability. * * *

* * * Since the agencies funding the projects were not parties to the case, the District Court could accord relief only against the Secretary: He could be ordered to revise his regulation to require consultation for foreign projects. But this would not remedy respondents' alleged injury unless the funding agencies were bound by the Secretary's regulation, which is very much an open question. * * * When the Secretary promulgated the regulation at issue here, he thought it was binding on the agencies. The Solicitor General, however, has repudiated that position here, and the agencies themselves apparently deny the Secretary's authority. * * *

Respondents assert that this legal uncertainty did not affect redressability (and hence standing) because the District Court itself could resolve the issue of the Secretary's authority as a necessary part of its standing inquiry. Assuming that it is appropriate to resolve an issue of law such as this in connection with a threshold standing inquiry, resolution by the District Court would not have remedied respondents' alleged injury anyway, because it would not have been binding upon the agencies. They were not parties to the suit, and there is no reason they should be obliged to honor an incidental legal determination the suit produced.[4] The Court of Appeals tried to finesse this problem by simply

---

4. We need not linger over the dissent's facially impracticable suggestion that one agency of the government can acquire the power to direct other agencies by simply claiming that power in its own regulations and in litigation to which the other agencies

proclaiming that "[w]e are satisfied that an injunction requiring the Secretary to publish [respondents' desired] regulatio[n] . . . would result in consultation." We do not know what would justify that confidence, particularly when the Justice Department (presumably after consultation with the agencies) has taken the position that the regulation is not binding.[5] * * *

A further impediment to redressability is the fact that the agencies generally supply only a fraction of the funding for a foreign project. AID, for example, has provided less than 10% of the funding for the Mahaweli Project. Respondents have produced nothing to indicate that the projects they have named will either be suspended, or do less harm to listed species, if that fraction is eliminated. As in Simon, 426 U.S., at 43–44, it is entirely conjectural whether the nonagency activity that affects respondents will be altered or affected by the agency activity they seek to achieve. There is no standing.

IV

The Court of Appeals found that respondents had standing for an additional reason: because they had suffered a "procedural injury." The so-called "citizen-suit" provision of the ESA provides, in pertinent part, that "any person may commence a civil suit on his own behalf (A) to enjoin any person, including the United States and any other governmental instrumentality or agency . . . who is alleged to be in violation of any provision of this chapter." 16 U.S.C. § 1540(g). The court held that, because § 7(a)(2) requires inter-agency consultation, the citizen-suit provision creates a "procedural righ[t]" to consultation in all "persons"—so that *anyone* can file suit in federal court to challenge the Secretary's (or presumably any other official's) failure to follow the assertedly correct consultative procedure, notwithstanding their inability to allege any discrete injury flowing from that failure. To understand the remarkable nature of this holding one must be clear about what it does *not* rest upon: This is not a case where plaintiffs are seeking to enforce a procedural requirement the disregard of which could impair a separate concrete interest of theirs (*e.g.*, the procedural requirement for a hearing prior to denial of their license application, or the procedural requirement for an environmental impact statement before a federal facility is constructed next door to them).[7] Nor is it

are not parties. As for the contention that the other agencies will be "collaterally estopped" to challenge our judgment that they are bound by the Secretary of Interior's views, because of their participation in this suit, [w]hether or not that is true now, it was assuredly not true when this suit was filed, naming the Secretary alone. "The existence of federal jurisdiction ordinarily depends on the facts as they exist when the complaint is filed." Newman–Green, Inc. v. Alfonzo–Larrain, 490 U.S., 826, 830 (1989) (emphasis added). It cannot be that, by later participating in the suit, the State Department and AID retroactively created a redressability (and hence a jurisdiction) that did not exist at the outset.

5. Seizing on the fortuity that the case has made its way to *this* Court, Justice Stevens protests that no agency would ignore

"an authoritative construction of the [ESA] by this Court." In that he is probably correct; in concluding from it that plaintiffs have demonstrated redressability, he is not. Since, as we have pointed out above, standing is to be determined as of the commencement of suit; since at that point it could certainly not be known that the suit would reach this Court; and since it is not likely that an agency would feel compelled to accede to the legal view of a district court expressed in a case to which it was not a party; redressability clearly did not exist.

7. There is this much truth to the assertion that "procedural rights" are special: The person who has been accorded a procedural right to protect his concrete interests can assert that right without meeting all the normal standards for redressability and immediacy. Thus, under our case-law, one liv-

simply a case where concrete injury has been suffered by many persons, as in mass fraud or mass tort situations. Nor, finally, is it the unusual case in which Congress has created a concrete private interest in the outcome of a suit against a private party for the government's benefit, by providing a cash bounty for the victorious plaintiff. Rather, the court held that the injury-in-fact requirement had been satisfied by congressional conferral upon all persons of an abstract, self-contained, non-instrumental "right" to have the Executive observe the procedures required by law. We reject this view.[8]

We have consistently held that a plaintiff raising only a generally available grievance about government—claiming only harm to his and every citizen's interest in proper application of the Constitution and laws, and seeking relief that no more directly and tangibly benefits him than it does the public at large—does not state an Article III case or controversy. * * *

    * * *

To be sure, our generalized-grievance cases have typically involved Government violation of procedures assertedly ordained by the Constitution rather than the Congress. But there is absolutely no basis for making the Article III inquiry turn on the source of the asserted right. Whether the courts were to act on their own, or at the invitation of Congress, in ignoring the concrete injury requirement described in our cases, they would be discarding a principle fundamental to the separate and distinct constitutional role of the Third Branch—one of the essential elements that identifies those "Cases" and "Controversies" that are the business of the courts rather than of the political branches. "The province of the court," as Chief Justice Marshall said in

---

ing adjacent to the site for proposed construction of a federally licensed dam has standing to challenge the licensing agency's failure to prepare an Environmental Impact Statement, even though he cannot establish with any certainty that the Statement will cause the license to be withheld or altered, and even though the dam will not be completed for many years. (That is why we do not rely, in the present case, upon the Government's argument that, even if the other agencies were obliged to consult with the Secretary, they might not have followed his advice.) What respondents' "procedural rights" argument seeks, however, is quite different from this: standing for persons who have no concrete interests affected—persons who live (and propose to live) at the other end of the country from the dam.

  8. The dissent's discussion of this aspect of the case distorts our opinion. We do not hold that an individual cannot enforce procedural rights; he assuredly can, so long as the procedures in question are designed to protect some threatened concrete interest of his that is the ultimate basis of his standing. The dissent, however, asserts that there exist "classes of procedural duties . . . so enmeshed with the prevention of a substantive, concrete harm that an individual plaintiff may be able

to demonstrate a sufficient likelihood of injury just through the breach of that procedural duty." If we understand this correctly, it means that the government's violation of a certain (undescribed) class of procedural duty satisfies the concrete-injury requirement by itself, without any showing that the procedural violation endangers a concrete interest of the plaintiff (apart from his interest in having the procedure observed). We cannot agree. The dissent is unable to cite a single case in which we actually found standing solely on the basis of a "procedural right" unconnected to the plaintiff's own concrete harm. Its suggestion that we did so in Japan Whaling Association, *supra*, and Robertson v. Methow Valley Citizens Council, 490 U.S. 332 (1989), is not supported by the facts. In the former case, we found that the environmental organizations had standing because the "whale watching and studying of their members w[ould] be adversely affected by continued whale harvesting," see 478 U.S., at 230–231, n. 4; and in the latter we did not so much as mention standing, for the very good reason that the plaintiff was a citizens' council for the area in which the challenged construction was to occur, so that its members would obviously be concretely affected.

Marbury v. Madison, 5 U.S. (1 Cranch) 137, 170 (1803) "is, solely, to decide on the rights of individuals." Vindicating the public interest (including the public interest in government observance of the Constitution and laws) is the function of Congress and the Chief Executive. The question presented here is whether the public interest in proper administration of the laws (specifically, in agencies' observance of a particular, statutorily prescribed procedure) can be converted into an individual right by a statute that denominates it as such, and that permits all citizens (or, for that matter, a subclass of citizens who suffer no distinctive concrete harm) to sue. If the concrete injury requirement has the separation-of-powers significance we have always said, the answer must be obvious: To permit Congress to convert the undifferentiated public interest in executive officers' compliance with the law into an "individual right" vindicable in the courts is to permit Congress to transfer from the President to the courts the Chief Executive's most important constitutional duty, to "take Care that the Laws be faithfully executed," Art. II, § 3. It would enable the courts, with the permission of Congress, "to assume a position of authority over the governmental acts of another and co-equal department," Frothingham v. Mellon, 262 U.S., at 489, and to become "virtually continuing monitors of the wisdom and soundness of Executive action." Allen, 468 U.S., at 760 (quoting Laird v. Tatum, 408 U.S. 1, 15 (1972)). We have always rejected that vision of our role * * *.

Nothing in this contradicts the principle that "[t]he ... injury required by Art. III may exist solely by virtue of 'statutes creating legal rights, the invasion of which creates standing.' " Warth, 422 U.S., at 500 (quoting Linda R.S. v. Richard D., 410 U.S. 614, 617, n. 3 (1973)). Both of the cases used by Linda R.S. as an illustration of that principle involved Congress's elevating to the status of legally cognizable injuries concrete, de facto injuries that were previously inadequate in law (namely, injury to an individual's personal interest in living in a racially integrated community, see Trafficante v. Metropolitan Life Ins. Co., 409 U.S. 205, 208–212 (1972), and injury to a company's interest in marketing its product free from competition, see Hardin v. Kentucky Utilities Co., 390 U.S. 1, 6 (1968)). As we said in Sierra Club, "[Statutory] broadening [of] the categories of injury that may be alleged in support of standing is a different matter from abandoning the requirement that the party seeking review must himself have suffered an injury." 405 U.S., at 738. Whether or not the principle set forth in Warth can be extended beyond that distinction, it is clear that in suits against the government, at least, the concrete injury requirement must remain.

      * * *

We hold that respondents lack standing to bring this action and that the Court of Appeals erred in denying the summary judgment motion filed by the United States. The opinion of the Court of Appeals is hereby reversed, and the cause remanded for proceedings consistent with this opinion.

It is so ordered.

■ JUSTICE KENNEDY, with whom JUSTICE SOUTER joins, concurring in part and concurring in the judgment.

Although I agree with the essential parts of the Court's analysis, I write separately to make several observations.

I agree with the Court's conclusion in Part III–A that, on the record before us, respondents have failed to demonstrate that they themselves are "among the injured." Sierra Club v. Morton, 405 U.S. 727, 735 (1972). * * *

While it may seem trivial to require that Mss. Kelly and Skilbred acquire airline tickets to the project sites or announce a date certain upon which they will return, this is not a case where it is reasonable to assume that the affiants will be using the sites on a regular basis, nor do the affiants claim to have visited the sites since the projects commenced. With respect to the Court's discussion of respondents' "ecosystem nexus," "animal nexus," and "vocational nexus" theories, I agree that on this record respondents' showing is insufficient to establish standing on any of these bases. I am not willing to foreclose the possibility, however, that in different circumstances a nexus theory similar to those proffered here might support a claim to standing.

In light of the conclusion that respondents have not demonstrated a concrete injury here sufficient to support standing under our precedents, I would not reach the issue of redressability that is discussed by the plurality in Part III–B.

I also join Part IV of the Court's opinion with the following observations. As government programs and policies become more complex and far-reaching, we must be sensitive to the articulation of new rights of action that do not have clear analogs in our common-law tradition. Modern litigation has progressed far from the paradigm of Marbury suing Madison to get his commission, Marbury v. Madison, 5 U.S. (1 Cranch) 137 (1803), or Ogden seeking an injunction to halt Gibbons' steamboat operations, Gibbons v. Ogden, 22 U.S. (9 Wheat.) 1 (1824). In my view, Congress has the power to define injuries and articulate chains of causation that will give rise to a case or controversy where none existed before, and I do not read the Court's opinion to suggest a contrary view. In exercising this power, however, Congress must at the very least identify the injury it seeks to vindicate and relate the injury to the class of persons entitled to bring suit. The citizen-suit provision of the Endangered Species Act does not meet these minimal requirements, because while the statute purports to confer a right on "any person . . . to enjoin . . . the United States and any other governmental instrumentality or agency . . . who is alleged to be in violation of any provision of this chapter," it does not of its own force establish that there is an injury in "any person" by virtue of any "violation." 16 U.S.C. § 1540(g)(1)(A).

The Court's holding that there is an outer limit to the power of Congress to confer rights of action is a direct and necessary consequence of the case and controversy limitations found in Article III. I agree that it would exceed those limitations if, at the behest of Congress and in the absence of any showing of concrete injury, we were to entertain citizen-suits to vindicate the public's nonconcrete interest in the proper administration of the laws. While it does not matter how many persons have been injured by the challenged action, the party bringing suit must show that the action injures him in a concrete and personal way. This requirement is not just an empty formality. It preserves the vitality of the adversarial process by assuring both that the parties before the court have an actual, as opposed to professed, stake in the outcome, and that "the legal questions presented . . . will be resolved, not in the rarefied atmosphere of a debating society, but in a concrete factual context conducive to a realistic appreciation of the consequences of judicial action." Valley Forge Christian College v. Americans United for Separation of Church and State, Inc.,

454 U.S. 464, 472 (1982). In addition, the requirement of concrete injury confines the Judicial Branch to its proper, limited role in the constitutional framework of government.

With these observations, I concur in Parts I, II, III–A, and IV of the Court's opinion and in the judgment of the Court.

■ JUSTICE STEVENS, concurring in the judgment.

Because I am not persuaded that Congress intended the consultation requirement in § 7(a)(2) * * * to apply to activities in foreign countries, I concur in the judgment of reversal. I do not, however, agree with the Court's conclusion that respondents lack standing because the threatened injury to their interest in protecting the environment and studying endangered species is not "imminent." Nor do I agree with the plurality's additional conclusion that respondents' injury is not "redressable" in this litigation.

I

In my opinion a person who has visited the critical habitat of an endangered species, has a professional interest in preserving the species and its habitat, and intends to revisit them in the future has standing to challenge agency action that threatens their destruction. * * *

The Court nevertheless concludes that respondents have not suffered "injury in fact" because they have not shown that the harm to the endangered species will produce "imminent" injury to them. I disagree. An injury to an individual's interest in studying or enjoying a species and its natural habitat occurs when someone (whether it be the government or a private party) takes action that harms that species and habitat. In my judgment, therefore, the "imminence" of such an injury should be measured by the timing and likelihood of the threatened environmental harm, rather than—as the Court seems to suggest—by the time that might elapse between the present and the time when the individuals would visit the area if no such injury should occur.

* * * [W]e have denied standing to plaintiffs whose likelihood of suffering any concrete adverse effect from the challenged action was speculative. In this case, however, the likelihood that respondents will be injured by the destruction of the endangered species is not speculative. If respondents are genuinely interested in the preservation of the endangered species and intend to study or observe these animals in the future, their injury will occur as soon as the animals are destroyed. Thus the only potential source of "speculation" in this case is whether respondents' intent to study or observe the animals is genuine. In my view, Joyce Kelly and Amy Skilbred have introduced sufficient evidence to negate petitioner's contention that their claims of injury are "speculative" or "conjectural." * * *

The plurality also concludes that respondents' injuries are not redressable in this litigation for two reasons. First, * * * even if * * * a new regulation is promulgated, there is no guarantee that federal agencies that are not parties to this case will actually consult with the Secretary. Furthermore, * * * even if the agencies consult with the Secretary and terminate funding for foreign projects, the foreign governments might nonetheless pursue the projects and jeopardize the endangered species. Neither of these reasons is persuasive.

We must presume that if this Court holds that § 7(a)(2) requires consultation, all affected agencies would abide by that interpretation and engage in the requisite consultations. Certainly the Executive Branch cannot be heard to argue that an authoritative construction of the governing statute by this Court may simply be ignored by any agency head. Moreover, if Congress has required consultation between agencies, we must presume that such consultation will have a serious purpose that is likely to produce tangible results. As Justice Blackmun explains, it is not mere speculation to think that foreign governments, when faced with the threatened withdrawal of United States assistance, will modify their projects to mitigate the harm to endangered species.

II

Although I believe that respondents have standing, I nevertheless concur in the judgment of reversal because I am persuaded that the Government is correct in its submission that § 7(a)(2) does not apply to activities in foreign countries. * * *

■ JUSTICE BLACKMUN, with whom JUSTICE O'CONNOR joins, dissenting.

I part company with the Court in this case in two respects. First, I believe that respondents have raised genuine issues of fact—sufficient to survive summary judgment—both as to injury and as to redressability. Second, I question the Court's breadth of language in rejecting standing for "procedural" injuries. I fear the Court seeks to impose fresh limitations on the constitutional authority of Congress to allow citizen-suits in the federal courts for injuries deemed "procedural" in nature. I dissent.

I

A

To survive petitioner's motion for summary judgment on standing, respondents * * * need show only a "genuine issue" of material fact as to standing. Fed.Rule Civ.Proc. 56(c). * * *

The Court never mentions the "genuine issue" standard. * * *

1

I think a reasonable finder of fact could conclude from the information in the affidavits and deposition testimony that either Kelly or Skilbred will soon return to the project sites, thereby satisfying the "actual or imminent" injury standard. * * *

By requiring a "description of concrete plans" or "specification of *when* the some day [for a return visit] will be," the Court, in my view, demands what is likely an empty formality. * * *

2

The Court also concludes that injury is lacking, because respondents' allegations of "ecosystem nexus" failed to demonstrate sufficient proximity to the site of the environmental harm. To support that conclusion, the Court mischaracterizes our decision in Lujan v. National Wildlife Federation as establishing a general rule that "a plaintiff claiming injury from environmental damage must use the area affected by the challenged activity." In National Wildlife Federation, the Court required specific geographical proximity because of the particular type of harm alleged in that case: harm to the plaintiff's visual enjoyment of nature from mining activities. One cannot suffer from the sight of a ruined landscape without being close enough to see the sites actually being mined. Many environmental injuries, however, cause harm distant from the area immediately affected by the challenged action. Environmental destruction may affect animals traveling over vast geographical ranges, see, *e.g.,* Japan Whaling Assn. v. American Cetacean Soc., 478 U.S. 221 (1986) * * *. It cannot seriously be contended that a litigant's failure to use the precise or exact site where animals are slaughtered * * * means he or she cannot show injury.

The Court also rejects respondents' claim of vocational or professional injury. The Court says that it is "beyond all reason" that a zoo "keeper" of Asian elephants would have standing to contest his government's participation in the eradication of all the Asian elephants in another part of the world. I am unable to see how the distant location of the destruction necessarily (for purposes of ruling at summary judgment) mitigates the harm to the elephant keeper. If there is no more access to a future supply of the animal that sustains a keeper's livelihood, surely there is harm.

B

A plurality of the Court suggests that respondents have not demonstrated redressability * * *. The plurality identifies two obstacles. The first is that the "action agencies" * * * are not directly bound as parties to the suit and are otherwise not indirectly bound by being subject to petitioner Secretary's regulation. Petitioner, however, officially and publicly has taken the position that his regulations regarding consultation under § 7 of the Act are binding on action agencies. 50 CFR § 402.14(a)(1991). And he has previously taken the same position in this very litigation * * *. I cannot agree with the plurality that the Secretary (or the Solicitor General) is now free, for the convenience of this appeal, to disavow his prior public and litigation positions. * * *

* * * Moreover, I wonder if the plurality has not overlooked the extensive involvement from the inception of this litigation by the Department of State and the Agency for International Development. Under principles of collateral estoppel, these agencies are precluded from subsequently relitigating the issues decided in this suit. * * *

The second redressability obstacle relied on by the plurality is that "the [action] agencies generally supply only a fraction of the funding for a foreign project." What this Court might "generally" take to be true does not eliminate the existence of a genuine issue of fact to withstand summary judgment. Even if the action agencies supply only a fraction of the funding for a particular foreign project, it remains at least a question for the finder of fact whether threatened withdrawal of that fraction would affect foreign government conduct sufficiently to avoid harm to listed species.

[Moreover], the relevant inquiry is not, as the plurality suggests, what will happen if AID or other agencies stop funding projects, but what will happen if AID or other agencies comply with the consultation requirement for projects abroad. Respondents filed suit to require consultation, not a termination of funding. Respondents have raised at least a genuine issue of fact that the projects harm endangered species and that the actions of AID and other U.S. agencies can mitigate that harm.

II

The Court concludes that any "procedural injury" suffered by respondents is insufficient to confer standing. It rejects the view that the "injury-in-fact requirement . . . [is] satisfied by congressional conferral upon *all* person of an abstract, self-contained, noninstrumental 'right' to have the Executive observe the procedures required by law." Whatever the Court might mean with that very broad language, it cannot be saying that "procedural injuries" *as a class* are necessarily insufficient for purposes of Article III standing.

Most governmental conduct can be classified as "procedural." * * * When the Government, for example, "procedurally" issues a pollution permit, those affected by the permittee's pollutants are not without standing to sue. Only later cases will tell just what the Court means by its intimation that "procedural" injuries are not constitutionally cognizable injuries. In the meantime, I have the greatest of sympathy for the courts across the country that will struggle to understand the Court's standardless exposition of this concept today.

The Court expresses concern that allowing judicial enforcement of "agencies' observance of a particular, statutorily prescribed procedure" would "transfer from the President to the courts the Chief Executive's most important constitutional duty, to 'take Care that the Laws be faithfully executed,' Art. II, sec. 3." In fact, the principal effect of foreclosing judicial enforcement of such procedures is to transfer power into the hands of the Executive at the expense—not of the courts—but of Congress, from which that power originates and emanates.

Under the Court's anachronistically formal view of the separation of powers, Congress legislates pure, substantive mandates and has no business structuring the procedural manner in which the Executive implements these mandates. To be sure, in the ordinary course, Congress does legislate in black-and-white terms of affirmative commands or negative prohibitions on the conduct of officers of the Executive Branch. In complex regulatory areas, however, Congress often legislates, as it were, in procedural shades of gray. That is, it sets forth substantive policy goals and provides for their attainment by requiring Executive Branch officials to follow certain procedures, for example, in the form of reporting, consultation, and certification requirements.

The Court recently has considered two such procedurally oriented statutes. In Japan Whaling Assn. v. American Cetacean Society, 478 U.S. 221 (1986), the Court examined a statute requiring the Secretary of Commerce to certify to the President that foreign nations were not conducting fishing operations or trading which "diminis[h] the effectiveness" of an international whaling convention. Id. at 226. The Court expressly found standing to sue. Id., at 230–231, n. 4. In Robertson v. Methow Valley Citizens Council, 490 U.S. 332, 348 (1989), this Court considered injury from violation of the "action-forcing" procedures of the National Environmental Policy Act (NEPA), in particular the requirements for issuance of environmental impact statements.

The consultation requirement of § 7 of the Endangered Species Act is a similar, action-forcing statute. Consultation is designed as an integral check on federal agency action, ensuring that such action does not go forward without full consideration of its effects on listed species. Once consultation is initiated, the Secretary is under a duty to provide to the action agency "a written statement setting forth the Secretary's opinion, and a summary of the information on which the opinion is based, detailing how the agency action affects the species or its critical habitat." 16 U.S.C. § 1536(b)(3)(A). The Secretary is also obligated to suggest "reasonable and prudent alternatives" to prevent jeopardy to listed species. Ibid. The action agency must undertake as well its own "biological assessment for the purpose of identifying any endangered species or threatened species" likely to be affected by agency action. § 1536(c)(1). After the initiation of consultation, the action agency "shall not make any irreversible or irretrievable commitment of resources" which would foreclose the "formulation or implementation of any reasonable and prudent alternative measures" to avoid jeopardizing listed species. § 1536(d). These action-forcing procedures are "designed to protect some threatened concrete interest," of persons who observe and work with endangered or threatened species. That is why I am mystified by the Court's unsupported conclusion that "[t]his is not a case where plaintiffs are seeking to enforce a procedural requirement the disregard of which could impair a separate concrete interest of theirs."

To prevent Congress from conferring standing for "procedural injuries" is another way of saying that Congress may not delegate to the courts authority deemed "executive" in nature. * * * Here Congress seeks not to delegate "executive" power but only to strengthen the procedures it has legislatively mandated. * * *

> * * *

It is to be hoped that over time the Court will acknowledge that some classes of procedural duties are so enmeshed with the prevention of a substantive, concrete harm that an individual plaintiff may be able to demonstrate a sufficient likelihood of injury just through the breach of that procedural duty. For example, in the context of the NEPA requirement of environmental-impact statements, this Court has acknowledged "it is now well settled that NEPA itself does not mandate particular results [and] simply prescribes the necessary process," but *"these procedures are almost certain to affect the agency's substantive decision."* Robertson v. Methow Valley Citizens Council, 490 U.S. 332, 350 (1989)(emphasis added). * * *

In short, determining "injury" for Article III standing purposes is a fact-specific inquiry. * * * There may be factual circumstances in which a congressionally imposed procedural requirement is so insubstantially connected to the prevention of a substantive harm that it cannot be said to work any conceivable injury to an individual litigant. But, as a general matter, the courts owe substantial deference to Congress' substantive purpose in imposing a certain procedural requirement. In all events, * * * [t]here is no room for a *per se* rule or presumption excluding injuries labeled "procedural" in nature.

III

In conclusion, I cannot join the Court on what amounts to a slash-and-burn expedition through the law of environmental standing. In my view, "[t]he very essence of civil liberty certainly consists in the right of every individual to claim the protection of the laws, whenever he receives an injury." Marbury v. Madison, 1 Cranch 137 (1803).

I dissent.

NOTE ON LUJAN AND CONGRESSIONAL POWER TO CONFER STANDING TO SUE

(1) *Precedents and Distinctions.* With the possible exceptions of the Court's old and cryptic opinion in Muskrat v. United States, 219 U.S. 346 (1911), p.

115, *supra,* and its unexplained summary affirmance in McClure v. Reagan, 454 U.S. 1025 (1981), discussed pp. 182–83, *infra,* Lujan v. Defenders of Wildlife is the first case in which the Supreme Court has found a congressional grant of standing to violate Article III. Justice Scalia, who often relies heavily on historic practice as a reason for rejecting constitutional challenges, did not discuss the English and American authorities permitting suits by persons who lack a distinctive personal stake. See p. 141, *supra.* The precedents on which he did rely—twentieth century decisions in which the Court refused to hear "generalized grievances"—did not involve congressional statutes authorizing the particular plaintiffs to bring suit. Is that a significant distinction?

(2) *Prior Congressional Grants of Standing.* As Justice Harlan recognized in Flast v. Cohen, p. 137, *supra,* Congress' power to confer standing where none otherwise would have existed was firmly established by administrative law decisions of the 1940s. In the absence of an authorizing statute, standing to challenge administrative action generally depended on the coercive infringement of a liberty or property interest recognized at common law. See Sunstein, *Standing and the Privatization of Public Law,* 88 Colum.L.Rev. 1432 (1988). In effect, this private law model of standing meant that the targets of regulatory action, but not the intended beneficiaries of regulatory statutes, possessed standing to sue. In a series of pathbreaking decisions, however, the Supreme Court held that Congress could authorize standing to protect the "public interest" in statutory enforcement.

(a) *Standing in Cases of Recognized Injury.* The evolution of competitors' standing provides a paradigmatic example of Congress' well-recognized power to create standing. The traditional rule was that the proprietor of a business lacks standing to object to the government's support of competing activities, because the common law does not recognize an interest in freedom from competition. See Tennessee Elec. Power Co. v. Tennessee Valley Auth., 306 U.S. 118, 137–38 (1939)(power companies that sell electricity lack standing to enjoin the TVA's competing operations, which are alleged to be unconstitutional). See also Alabama Power Co. v. Ickes, 302 U.S. 464 (1938). A major shift occurred in FCC v. Sanders Bros. Radio Station, 309 U.S. 470 (1940), where a radio station sought judicial review of the FCC's award of a broadcast license to a competitor. Section 402(b) of the Communications Act allowed an appeal "by any * * * person aggrieved or whose interests are adversely affected by a decision of the Commission granting or refusing any such application." The complainant argued that the Act created a legal interest in freedom from competition, which required consideration by the FCC of the economic impact of the award on existing licensees. The Court rejected this argument, but upheld the complainant's standing to protect the public interest (p. 477): "Congress * * * may have been of opinion that one likely to be financially injured by the issue of a license would be the only person having a sufficient interest to bring to the attention of the appellate court errors of law in the action of the Commission in granting the license. It is within the power of Congress to confer such standing to prosecute an appeal." See also Scripps–Howard Radio, Inc. v. FCC, 316 U.S. 4, 14 (1942)(under Sanders, "these private litigants have standing only as representatives of the public interest").

Defenders of Wildlife does not appear to threaten Congress' power to confer standing in cases such as Scripps–Howard and Sanders, since the plaintiffs in both suffered cognizable financial injury. Compare cases in which the Court has characterized the rule against asserting the rights of others as a "prudential" one that can be waived by Congress. See, *e.g.,* Warth v. Seldin, p. 146, *supra,* 422 U.S. at 500–01; Gladstone, Realtors v. Village of Bellwood, 441 U.S. 91, 103 n. 9 (1979).

(b) *Extending the Bounds of Actionable Injury?* As framed by modern doctrine, the issue of congressional power to confer standing becomes difficult only if Congress purports to confer standing in a case in which, absent legislation, the Court would have found no injury under Article III. Prior to Defenders of Wildlife, the Court's discussion of this issue had achieved little clarity.

In Trafficante v. Metropolitan Life Ins. Co., 409 U.S. 205 (1972), a white and a black tenant were held to have standing under § 810 of the Civil Rights Act of 1968, 42 U.S.C. § 3610, to seek injunctive relief and damages from their landlord for discriminating against non-white rental applicants. Section 810(d) of the Act provides that a "person aggrieved" may bring suit in federal court "to enforce rights granted or protected" by the Act. Section 810(a) defines "person aggrieved" to mean one "who claims to have been injured by a discriminatory housing practice * * *." The plaintiffs here claimed damages for (1) lost social benefits of living in an integrated community, (2) lost business and professional advantages, and (3) embarrassment and economic injury from being "stigmatized" as residents of a "white ghetto" (p. 208).

Justice Douglas, for a unanimous Court, held that the statute "showed 'a congressional intention to define standing as broadly as is permitted by Article III * * *'" insofar as tenants of the same housing unit * * * are concerned" (p. 209). The opinion further inferred from the Civil Rights Act's structure that, in achieving compliance, "the main generating force must be private suits in which * * * the complainants act not only on their own behalf but also 'as private attorneys general in vindicating a policy that Congress considered to be of the highest priority' " (pp. 210–11).[1]

Justice White, joined by Justices Blackmun and Powell, concurred in the opinion of the Court but wrote specially to note (p. 212): "Absent the Civil Rights Act of 1968, I would have great difficulty in concluding that petitioners' complaint in this case presented a case or controversy within the jurisdiction of the District Court under Article III of the Constitution. But with that statute purporting to give all those who are authorized to complain to the agency the right also to sue in court, I would sustain the statute insofar as it extends standing to those in the position of the petitioners in this case. * * *"

Justice White's approach was endorsed in Linda R.S. v. Richard D., p. 146, *supra,* 410 U.S. at 617 n. 3 (dictum)("Congress may enact statutes creating legal rights, the invasion of which creates standing, even though no injury would exist without the statute."), and in Warth v. Seldin, p. 146, *supra,* 422 U.S. at 500–01 (dictum)(emphasis added)("[t]he actual or threatened injury

---

1. In Gladstone, Paragraph (2)(a), *supra,* § 812 of the 1968 Civil Rights Act, which provides simply that specified rights granted by the Act "may be enforced by civil actions in appropriate United States district courts * * *", was given the same broad construction as § 810 had received in Trafficante. The Court held that a village and four white residents could sue realtors who allegedly

were "steering" non-white home-buyers into, and white buyers away from, a particular neighborhood. The residents were held to have standing under Trafficante. The village's Article III standing was upheld on the basis of the profound adverse consequences that could result from manipulation of the racial composition of its neighborhoods.

required by Art. III may exist *solely* by virtue of 'statutes creating legal rights, the invasion of which creates standing' ").

In Havens Realty Corp. v. Coleman, 455 U.S. 363, 372–74 (1982), the Court held that a black "tester"—who posed as a renter or purchaser of housing to collect evidence of racial steering practices—had standing to seek equitable and monetary relief against private parties under § 804 of the Fair Housing Act of 1968, 42 U.S.C. § 3604. The Court reasoned that the Act conferred on the tester an enforceable legal right not to be denied, because of racial steering, truthful information about the availability of housing. (A white tester, to whom the defendant had given truthful information, was held to lack standing under this theory.) But the Court also insisted that "the sole requirement for standing to sue under [the Act] is the Art. III minima of injury in fact: that the plaintiff allege that as a result of the defendant's actions he has suffered 'a distinct and palpable injury'" (p. 372); accord, *e.g.,* Gladstone, Paragraph (2)(a), *supra,* 441 U.S. at 100. Is it significant that the plaintiff in Havens sought damages as well as equitable relief?

(3) *Congressional Power and the Concept of "Injury."* In Part IV of its opinion, the Court in Lujan reaffirms the principle that "[t]he ... injury required by Art. III may exist solely in virtue of 'statutes creating legal rights, the invasion of which creates standing'" (p. 2145). But the sentences that follow suggest that Congress' power is solely one of "elevating to the status of legally cognizable injuries concrete, de facto injuries that were previously inadequate in law" (*id.*). How clear is the concept of a "concrete, de facto" injury? Suppose Congress amended the ESA to read: "Every citizen has a right to preservation of all species throughout the world against threats to which actions of the United States government contribute in any way. Any citizen may bring suit in federal court for all appropriate relief for violations of that right." Would Justice Scalia's opinion require a federal court to dismiss a suit, brought under such a statute, to enjoin an overseas project funded in part by the United States, where the plaintiff never has been and never will be in the project's vicinity? How would Justices Kennedy and Souter resolve this question?

Recall that in the Bakke case, p. 148, *supra,* the Court characterized the plaintiff's injury as deprivation of the chance to compete for every place in the medical school class, rather than deprivation of admission he would have gained but for the special admissions program. Why couldn't the injury in Defenders of Wildlife have been defined as deprivation of the opportunity to have the consultation process under the ESA result in greater protection of endangered species, without having to show that in fact such protection would have materialized? Does footnote 7 of the Court's opinion provide an adequate answer to this question—*i.e.,* that Congress, by statute, can establish that governmental failure to follow prescribed procedures can be presumed to be the *cause* of injuries to concrete interests (thus satisfying Article III's causation requirement), and that a judicial order directing government to follow such procedures can be presumed to *redress* an injury to a concrete interest (thus satisfying the redressability requirement), but that what Congress cannot do is to create a concrete interest where none previously existed? See Comment, 62 U.Chi.L.Rev. 275 (1994).

Congress has often given the Attorney General or other federal officials power to bring suit for the purpose of enforcing laws that do not benefit the agency or officials empowered to sue. See, *e.g.,* § 301 of the Voting Rights Act

Amendments of 1975, 42 U.S.C. § 1973bb; Title VII of the Civil Rights Act of 1964, §§ 706–07, as amended, 42 U.S.C. §§ 2000e–5 to 2000e–6. Does the Attorney General's standing depend on injury? In a regulatory scheme such as the Endangered Species Act, should Congress have equal power to use the device of suits by *private* attorneys general?[2] Compare Sunstein, *What's Standing After Lujan? Of Citizen Suits, "Injuries," and Article III*, 91 Mich. L.Rev. 163 (1992), and Fallon, *Of Justiciability, Remedies, and Public Law Litigation: Notes on the Jurisprudence of Lyons*, 59 N.Y.U.L.Rev. 1, 30–35, 54–56 (1984), with Kent & Shenkman, *Of Citizens Suits and Citizen Sunstein*, 91 Mich.L.Rev. 1793 (1993).

(4) *Possible Justifications.* If Allen v. Wright gave greater prominence than did prior decisions to separation of powers concerns in determining whether standing exists, see pp. 151–52, *supra*, Defenders of Wildlife takes matters a step further. Some have seen Justice Scalia's reliance on the "Take Care" Clause as linked to broader concerns he has expressed, often in dissenting opinions, about protecting the "unitary executive" from interference. See, *e.g.*, Morrison v. Olson, 487 U.S. 654, 727 (1988)(Scalia, J., dissenting). See also Kent & Shenkman, Paragraph (3), *supra;* Note, 106 Harv.L.Rev. 308, 316–18 (1992).

On what ground could it be said that recognition of standing in the plaintiffs (and, if they prevailed on the merits, issuance of an order requiring the Secretary of the Interior to comply with the ESA) would interfere improperly with executive independence? Isn't Professor Sunstein correct that the "Take Care" Clause confers a responsibility, not a license? See Sunstein, Paragraph (3), *supra*, at 212–13. Haven't courts recognized a power to enforce executive compliance with statutory duties since Marbury v. Madison? Kent & Shenkman, *supra*, at 1805–08, contend that considerations of political accountability, which are implicit in Article II, forbid congressional licensing of private attorneys general in cases in which no plaintiff or group of plaintiffs suffers "individuated" injury. But will the notion of "individuated injury" bear the weight that this argument requires? Moreover, if executive independence is the concern in Defenders of Wildlife, but "a court could set aside executive action at the behest of plaintiffs with a plane ticket, why does the Take Care Clause forbid it from doing so at the behest of plaintiffs without a ticket?" Sunstein, *supra*, at 213.

One of the themes of cases refusing to hear so-called "generalized grievances" is that the plaintiffs, not being a small minority, are well-positioned to seek change from the political process. But much political science literature about the organization of interest groups calls that contention into question. See, *e.g.*, Olson, The Logic of Collective Action: Public Goods and the Theory of Groups (1965). If Congress decides that there is a need for persons benefited by a statute (even if they constitute a majority) to be able to protect their

---

2. The federal Clean Air Act provides that "any person may commence a civil action on his own behalf" against a polluter who violates the Act, or against the Administrator of EPA for failing to perform a nondiscretionary duty. 42 U.S.C. § 7604(a). In Metropolitan Washington Coalition for Clean Air v. District of Columbia, 511 F.2d 809, 814 n. 26 (D.C.Cir.1975)(per curiam), the D.C. Circuit ruled that a plaintiff suing under this provision did not need to allege injury in order to establish standing. Even prior to Lujan, other courts disagreed. See, *e.g.*, NRDC, Inc. v. U.S. EPA, 507 F.2d 905, 908–11 (9th Cir.1974). See generally Currie, *Judicial Review Under Federal Pollution Laws*, 62 Iowa L.Rev. 1221, 1271–80 (1977).

Can the D.C. Circuit's view of congressional power be squared with the notion of "injury" as a constitutional limitation?

interests not only by voting but also by bringing citizen suits, should the Court be able to set aside that determination?

Can the approach of Defenders of Wildlife be justified on the view that "overenforcement" of regulatory statutes is a greater problem than "underenforcement"? See Pierce, *Lujan v. Defenders of Wildlife: Standing as a Judicially Imposed Limit on Legislative Power,* 42 Duke L.J. 1170, 1194–95 (1993)(noting that rights to participate in agency proceedings often track standing law, and expressing concern that such a pattern in response to Defenders of Wildlife could increase the extent of "agency capture" by regulatees). Shouldn't Congress have a role in determining what kinds of interference are unwarranted and whether judicial review is desirable to prevent agency capture and/or to monitor executive compliance with legislative mandates?

(5) *Future of the Citizen Suit.* Does Defenders of Wildlife preclude Congress from using the citizen suit? Consider again Justice Kennedy's suggestion that a different case might be presented if Congress purported to confer on every citizen a personal right to the preservation of endangered species and to recognize defined governmental actions that threatened endangered species as injuries to every citizen.

If Congress provided that any prevailing plaintiff in a suit to enforce the Endangered Species Act was entitled to a cash bounty from the government, would any citizen have standing to sue? Would it matter if the bounty were $10 or $10,000?

(6) *Literature.* For critical discussion of Defenders of Wildlife, see, in addition to the articles by Pierce and Sunstein, *supra,* Nichol, *Justice Scalia, Standing, and Public Law Litigation,* 42 Duke L.J. 1141 (1993). For more favorable commentary, see Breger, *Defending Defenders: Remarks on Nichol and Pierce,* 42 Duke L.J. 1202 (1993); Roberts, *Article III Limits on Statutory Standing,* 42 Duke L.J. 1219 (1993). An omnibus provision conferring citizen standing to enforce federal law is defended in Yackle, Reclaiming the Federal Courts 82–88 (1994).

NOTE ON STANDING TO CHALLENGE FEDERAL ADMINISTRATIVE ACTION: REQUIREMENTS BEYOND INJURY IN FACT

(1) *Traditional Doctrine.* Until 1970, the law of standing to challenge federal administrative action "was divided into three parts. In the absence of specific statutory provisions entitling designated persons or parties to judicial review, standing could be based upon present or threatened official infringement of an interest protected at common law; upon an interest substantively protected by a relevant organic statute (the statutorily protected-interest test); or upon an adverse economic impact when a relevant statute afforded standing to persons 'adversely affected' or 'aggrieved.'" Stewart, *Standing for Solidarity (Book Review),* 88 Yale L.J. 1559, 1569 (1979). See also pp. 78–81, 136–37, *supra.*

(2) *The Zone-of-Interests Test.* A major doctrinal shift was announced in Association of Data Processing Service Organizations, Inc. v. Camp, 397 U.S. 150 (1970). Sellers of data processing services sought review under the Administrative Procedure Act (APA), 5 U.S.C. § 702, of a ruling by the Comptroller of the Currency permitting national banks to provide data process-

ing services to other banks and to bank customers. (Section 702 provides: "A person suffering legal wrong because of agency action, or adversely affected or aggrieved by agency action within the meaning of a relevant statute, is entitled to judicial review thereof.") The district court dismissed for lack of standing, and the court of appeals affirmed, finding that the plaintiff must show either a "legal interest" or an explicit provision in the relevant statute permitting suit by any party "adversely affected or aggrieved." The Supreme Court reversed, with Justice Douglas writing for the Court. After finding that the plaintiffs had suffered the requisite injury in fact, Justice Douglas rejected any requirement formulated in terms such as a "legally protected interest." He referred to Tennessee Elec. Power Co. v. TVA, 306 U.S. 118 (1939), which denied a competitor standing on the basis that standing was unavailable "unless the right invaded is a legal right,—one of property, one arising out of contract, one protected against tortious invasion, or one founded on a statute which confers a privilege," and then continued:

"The 'legal interest' test goes to the merits. The question of standing is different. It concerns, apart from the 'case' or 'controversy' test, the question whether the interest sought to be protected by the complainant is arguably within the zone of interests to be protected or regulated by the statute or constitutional guarantee in question" (p. 153).

The opinion then referred to a statute that was not the principal ground of the plaintiffs' attack on the Comptroller's action, § 4 of the Bank Service Corporation Act of 1962, 12 U.S.C. § 1864: "No bank service corporation may engage in any activity other than the performance of bank services for banks." Although the Act itself had no provision authorizing review, the Court held that it established plaintiffs' standing because it "arguably brings a competitor within the zone of interests protected by it" (pp. 155–56).

In Barlow v. Collins, 397 U.S. 159 (1970), decided the same day as Data Processing, tenant farmers challenged a regulation of the Secretary of Agriculture as unauthorized by statute. The statute permitted farmers to assign certain government payments only "as security for cash or advances to finance making a crop." 16 U.S.C. § 590h(g). The challenged regulation defined this language to allow assignments to secure rent for a farm. Though this new definition increased the tenant farmers' freedom from governmental restraint, they objected because it allegedly permitted landlords to compel them to finance all their farm needs through the landlords at inflated cost. The court of appeals had denied the farmers standing on the ground that they had alleged no legally protected interest and also that they "have not shown us, nor have we found, any provision of the Food and Agriculture Act of 1965 which either expressly or impliedly gives [them] standing." Again speaking through Justice Douglas, the Court reversed. Relying on the legislative history of the specific substantive provision involved, which it viewed as indicating "a congressional intent to benefit the tenants," the Court held that "tenant farmers are clearly within the zone of interests protected by the Act" (p. 164).[1]

In Data Processing and Barlow, Justice Brennan, joined by Justice White, concurred in the judgment but disagreed with the Court's reasoning. In his view, the issue of standing presented a question only of injury in fact: "The

---

1. Davis, *The Liberalized Law of Standing,* 37 U.Chi.L.Rev. 450, 455–56 (1970), argues that the focus on the interests of tenant farmers in general, rather than on the *particular interest* asserted in the litigation, was inconsistent with Data Processing, may have been due to inadvertence, and was in any event wrong.

Constitution requires for standing only that the plaintiff allege that actual harm resulted to him from the agency action" (p. 178). To be sure, "[b]efore the plaintiff is allowed to argue the merits, it is true that a canvass of relevant statutory materials must be made in cases challenging agency action. But the canvass is made, not to determine *standing,* but to determine an aspect of *reviewability,* that is, whether Congress meant to deny or to allow judicial review of the agency action at the instance of the plaintiff" (p. 169).

(3) *Unanswered Questions.* Among the difficult questions raised by Data Processing and its immediate progeny were these: (i) Does the "zone-of-interests" test implicate the merits any less than the "legally protected interests" standard? (ii) May plaintiffs with standing nonetheless be defeated on the merits on the ground that the statute does not confer on them a legally protected interest?[2] (iii) Is the "zone-of-interests" test limited to cases under the APA? (iv) Do the grounds on which a litigant has been granted standing serve to limit the considerations that the litigant can raise on the merits?

For discussion of these and other questions, see Albert, *Standing to Challenge Administrative Action: An Inadequate Surrogate for Claim for Relief,* 83 Yale L.J. 425 (1974); Davis, note 1, *supra;* Jaffe, *Standing Again,* 84 Harv.L.Rev. 633 (1971); Scott, *Standing in the Supreme Court—A Functional Analysis,* 86 Harv.L.Rev. 645 (1973); Stewart, *The Reformation of American Administrative Law,* 88 Harv.L.Rev. 1667, 1723–47 (1975); Vining, Legal Identity: The Coming of Age of Public Law 34–35 (1978).

(4) *Reaffirmation.* In Control Data Corp. v. Baldrige, 655 F.2d 283, 291 (D.C.Cir.1981), the court of appeals observed that the Supreme Court had rarely invoked the zone-of-interests test in recent years, and that at least one commentator believed the test had been abandoned.[3] In Clarke v. Securities Industry Ass'n, 479 U.S. 388 (1987), however, the Supreme Court once again invoked the zone-of-interests test in a case involving review of agency action.[4] The suit was brought by a securities industry trade association, which challenged a decision of the Comptroller of the Currency permitting national banks to provide discount brokerage services in branch offices from which, under the federal banking laws, they would be forbidden to provide banking services. The plaintiff contended that the brokerage operations themselves constituted "branch banks" in violation of the federal law. In upholding the association's standing, the Court, per Justice White, stressed two implications of Data Processing (pp. 396–97): "*First.* The Court interpreted the phrase 'a relevant statute' in § 702 broadly; the data processors were alleging violations of [one statute], yet the Court relied on the legislative history of a much later statute * * * in holding that the data processors satisfied the zone of interest test. *Second.* The Court approved the 'trend * * * toward [the] enlargement of the class of people who may protest administrative action.'" He continued (pp. 399–400): "The test is not meant to be especially demanding; in particular,

---

2. Data Processing warned that an action might be dismissed if the plaintiff's interest was not legally protected. 397 U.S. at 158. But see Sierra Club v. Morton, 405 U.S. 727, 737 (1972), p. 141, *supra,* stating that a plaintiff with standing may argue "the public interest" in challenging agency action.

3. The commentator was Professor Davis, who later said that the Court "failed to mention the test in 27 opinions on standing since 1970, even when the test was relevant." 4 Davis, Administrative Law Treatise § 24:17, at 277 (2d ed. 1983).

4. The test had also been invoked, and found satisfied, in Japan Whaling Ass'n v. American Cetacean Soc'y, 478 U.S. 221, 230–31 n. 4 (1986).

there need be no indication of congressional purpose to benefit the would-be plaintiff."

The Court then held that the trade association had standing under the APA. The Court found in the federal banking laws a concern not only with limiting branch banking by national banks in states where state banks were barred from operating branches, but also with "keep[ing] national banks from gaining a monopoly control over credit and money through unlimited branching" (p. 403). The interest asserted by plaintiff has a "plausible relationship to [these] policies": the plaintiff's members compete with banks in providing discount brokerage services, and those services "give banks access to more money, in the form of credit balances, and enhanced opportunities to lend money." On the merits, the Court upheld the Comptroller's decision.[5]

(5) *Alteration of the Zone-of-Interests Test?* Since Clarke, the Supreme Court has twice confronted questions concerning the "zone of interests" in challenges to federal agency action.

In Air Courier Conference v. American Postal Workers Union, 498 U.S. 517 (1991), postal workers challenged a Postal Service ruling waiving its monopoly for certain international deliveries, claiming that the waiver harmed their employment opportunities. Conceding the existence of injury in fact, the majority held that (a) the relevant Act of Congress was the "Private Express Statutes (PES)," not the Postal Reorganization Act, in which the PES was included when it was codified in the new Postal Service Code, and (b) the postal workers were not within the zone of interests created by the PES, since the monopoly provisions of that Act were designed to protect revenues, not to provide employment opportunities. (Three Justices concurred on the ground that the APA's review provisions do not apply to the activities of the Postal Service.)

In Lujan v. National Wildlife Federation, p. 142, *supra,* the Court explained that to be "adversely affected or aggrieved * * * within the meaning of a relevant statute", a plaintiff must fall within the zone of interests sought to be protected by the statute "whose violation forms the legal basis for his complaint" (497 U.S. at 882).

Aren't these two decisions hard to square with Data Processing?

(6) *Reach of the Zone-of-Interests Test.* Why didn't the Data Processing test govern many of the subsequent decisions involving challenges to federal administrative action—*e.g.,* Allen v. Wright; Simon, p. 147, *supra*; Richardson, p. 143, *supra*; Valley Forge, p. 140, *supra*? When the Data Processing test does apply, does its "injury-in-fact" requirement include the questions of "causation" and "redressability" emphasized in cases such as Allen and Simon?

Consider Clarke v. Securities Industry Ass'n, Paragraph (4), *supra:* "The principal cases in which the 'zone of interest' test has been applied are those involving claims under the APA, and the test is most usefully understood as a gloss on the meaning of § 702. * * * Data Processing speaks of claims 'arguably within the zone of interests to be protected or regulated by the statute *or constitutional guarantee* in question.' We doubt, however, that it is possible to formulate a single inquiry that governs all statutory and constitu-

---

5. Justice Stevens, joined by Chief Justice Rehnquist and Justice O'Connor, concurred in part and concurred in the judgment. Finding that the case fell well within the rationale of prior decisions, he "decline[d] to join the Court's sweeping discussion of the zone of interest test" (p. 417). Justice Scalia did not participate.

tional claims. * * * We have occasionally listed the zone of interest inquiry among general prudential considerations bearing on standing, see, *e.g.,* Valley Forge Christian College v. Americans United for Separation of Church and State, Inc., 454 U.S. 464, 475 (1982), and have on one occasion conducted a 'zone of interest' inquiry in a case brought under the Commerce Clause, see Boston Stock Exch. v. State Tax Comm'n, 429 U.S. 318, 320–21 n. 3 (1977)'' (p. 400 n. 16). But the latter case "should not be taken to mean that the standing inquiry under whatever constitutional or statutory provision a plaintiff asserts is the same as it would be if the 'generous review provisions' of the APA apply" (*id.*).

(7) *Further References.* For a helpful discussion of standing under the APA, see Sunstein, *Standing and the Privatization of Public Law,* 88 Colum.L.Rev. 1432, 1440 n. 34 (1988). Professor Sunstein views § 702 of the APA as having created a cause of action in two situations: (i) when the plaintiff has suffered harm to an interest protected by common law, a federal statute, or the Constitution (the "legal wrong" test), and (ii) when an organic statute confers standing on a party to vindicate the interests of the public (the "adversely affected or aggrieved within the meaning of a relevant statute" test). For discussion of the parallels between the framework for review under the APA and that established for review of actions by state officials under 42 U.S.C. § 1983, see Monaghan, *Federal Statutory Review Under Section 1983 and the APA,* 91 Colum.L.Rev. 233 (1991).

————

NOTE ON THE STANDING OF TAXPAYERS, GOVERNMENTS AND THEIR OFFICIALS, AND ORGANIZATIONS, AND ON OTHER CAPACITY–BASED STANDING ISSUES

(1) *Federal Taxpayer Standing.* Three important decisions since Flast v. Cohen, p. 137, *supra,* have addressed the issue of taxpayer standing.

The first two, United States v. Richardson, 418 U.S. 166 (1974), and Schlesinger v. Reservists Comm. to Stop the War, 418 U.S. 208 (1974), were decided the same day, and in both the Court ruled against standing. (The facts of both cases are described at pp. 143–44, *supra.*)

In Richardson, the Court stressed the narrowness of Flast and the vitality of "the Frothingham holding left undisturbed" by Flast. "[Plaintiff] makes no claim that appropriated funds are being spent in violation of a 'specific constitutional limitation upon the * * * taxing and spending power * * *.' [Flast], 392 U.S., at 104," but only that the CIA's expenditures had not been reported in the manner required by the Constitution's Statement and Account Clause. "[T]here is no 'logical nexus' between the asserted status of taxpayer and the claimed failure of the Congress to require the Executive to supply a more detailed report of the expenditures of that agency" (pp. 174–75).

In Reservists, the Court found the complaint deficient under Flast because it "did not challenge an enactment under Art. I, § 8, but rather the action of the Executive Branch in permitting Members of Congress to maintain their Reserve status" (p. 228).[1]

---

1. Justice Stewart concurred in Reservists, but (joined by Justice Marshall) dissent-   ed in Richardson, where he argued (pp. 203–05) that the plaintiff was "in the position of a

The third major decision on taxpayer standing, Valley Forge Christian College v. Americans United for Separation of Church and State, Inc., 454 U.S. 464 (1982), which limited Flast nearly to its facts by denying taxpayer standing even under the Establishment Clause to challenge an executive decision to transfer property to a religious institution, is discussed on pp. 140–41, *supra*.[2]

After Valley Forge, does anything remain of federal taxpayer standing? Even from the perspective of the public rights model, is it possibly a mistake to focus on a taxpayer's stake in the expenditure of tax dollars rather than on what rights various constitutional provisions create and on who possesses those rights?

(2) *State and Municipal Taxpayers' Actions.*   Doremus v. Board of Educ., 342 U.S. 429 (1952), was a state court action to declare invalid under the federal Constitution a New Jersey statute requiring five verses of the Old Testament to be read without comment at the opening of every public school day.   The two plaintiffs stated that they were state and municipal taxpayers, but asserted no financial relation between their taxes and the statute complained of.   The state court expressed misgivings about the plaintiffs' standing but entertained the action and ruled against them on the merits.   The Supreme Court, 6–3, dismissed the appeal for want of a justiciable controversy.   Justice Jackson, speaking for the Court, said (pp. 434–35):

"We do not undertake to say that a state court may not render an opinion on a federal constitutional question even under such circumstances that it can be regarded only as advisory.   But, because our own jurisdiction is cast in terms of 'case or controversy,' we cannot accept as the basis for review, nor as the basis for conclusive disposition of an issue of federal law without review, any procedure which does not constitute such.

"The taxpayer's action can meet this test, but only when it is a good-faith pocketbook action.   It is apparent that the grievance which it is sought to litigate here is not a direct dollars-and-cents injury but is a religious difference. If appellants established the requisite special injury necessary to a taxpayer's case or controversy, it would not matter that their dominant inducement to action was more religious than mercenary.   It is not a question of motivation but of possession of the requisite financial interest that is, or is threatened to

---

traditional Hohfeldian plaintiff.   He contends that the Statement and Account Clause gives him a right to receive the information and burdens the Government with a correlative duty to supply it.   Courts of law exist for the resolution of such right-duty disputes." Justice Stewart drew an analogy to the standing of citizens under the Freedom of Information Act to bring suit contesting the government's failure to disclose information, and added (p. 204) that "it does not matter that those to whom the duty is owed may be many."   In his concurrence in Reservists, he said (pp. 228–29): "Here, unlike [Richardson], the [plaintiffs] do not allege that the [defendants] have refused to perform an affirmative duty imposed upon them by the Constitution."

For criticism of this distinction between constitutional duties and prohibitions, see Justice Powell's concurrence in Richardson, 418 U.S. at 185–88.

Justices Brennan, Douglas, and Marshall dissented in both cases.

2.   On Valley Forge, see Nichol, *Standing on the Constitution: The Supreme Court and Valley Forge*, 61 N.C.L.Rev. 798 (1983). For earlier commentary on taxpayer standing, see Bittker, *The Case of the Fictitious Taxpayer: The   Federal   Taxpayer's   Suit Twenty Years After Flast v. Cohen*, 36 U.Chi. L.Rev. 364 (1969); Davis, *The Case of the Real Taxpayer: A Reply to Professor Bittker*, 36 U.Chi.L.Rev. 375 (1969).

be, injured by the unconstitutional conduct.''[3]

It seems to go without saying that a state or municipal taxpayer's action will be entertained where a federal taxpayer would have standing. See, e.g., Grand Rapids School Dist. v. Ball, 473 U.S. 373, 380 n. 5 (1985)(upholding state taxpayer standing to challenge, under the Establishment Clause, aid to nonpublic schools, and citing nine similar decisions). If a state authorizes broader taxpayer standing (in its own courts) to police expenditures than would be permissible in federal court under Article III, should the state authorization establish standing for Supreme Court review? See ASARCO and the discussion at pp. 155-57, supra.

(3) *Actions by States and Municipalities.* On actions by states, consult the *Note on the Standing of a State as Parens Patriae to Sue the Federal Government,* p. 322, *infra.* See also the *Note on a State's Standing to Sue and Related Problems of Justiciability,* p. 316, *infra.*

Municipal corporations have generally been denied standing in the federal courts to attack state legislation as violative of the federal Constitution, on the ground that they have no rights against the state of which they are a creature. *E.g.,* Pawhuska v. Pawhuska Oil Co., 250 U.S. 394 (1919); Trenton v. New Jersey, 262 U.S. 182 (1923); Williams v. Mayor, 289 U.S. 36 (1933). This conclusion appears to rest largely if not exclusively on a proposition of *substantive* law. If so, might standing possibly depend on the particular constitutional or statutory provision on which a municipal corporation's suit against a state depends? See, *e.g.,* Rogers v. Brockette, 588 F.2d 1057 (5th Cir.1979)(upholding standing to challenge an obligation allegedly imposed in violation of the Supremacy Clause), *noted,* 93 Harv.L.Rev. 586 (1980); Collazo v. Acosta, 721 F.Supp. 385 (D.P.R.1989)(upholding standing of a municipality to sue the Commonwealth of Puerto Rico under the First Amendment). See also City of South Lake Tahoe v. California Tahoe Regional Planning Agency, 449 U.S. 1039, 1042 (1980)(White, J., joined by Marshall, J., dissenting from denial of certiorari)(asserting that "a per se" rule that "a municipal subdivision of a State may not raise constitutional objections to the validity of a state statute" is inconsistent with Supreme Court precedent and that the circuits are divided over the validity of such a rule).

(4) *Actions by Voters.* Many cases have recognized the standing of individual voters to sue to protect the integrity of their votes. See, *e.g.,* Smiley v. Holm, 285 U.S. 355 (1932); Leser v. Garnett, 258 U.S. 130 (1922).

In Baker v. Carr, 369 U.S. 186 (1962), p. 284, *infra,* registered state voters were held to have standing to challenge alleged malapportionment of the state legislature. The Court concluded that a sufficient "personal stake in the outcome of the adjudication" was alleged "to insure that concrete adverseness which sharpens the presentation of issues upon which the court so largely depends for illumination of difficult constitutional questions" (pp. 203–04). Why weren't these voters asserting a mere "generalized grievance"?

Since Baker, the standing of voters to challenge voting schemes on federal constitutional and statutory grounds has been recognized in suits involving alleged discrimination on racial, religious, and political grounds. See, *e.g.,* Rogers v. Lodge, 458 U.S. 613 (1982); Davis v. Bandemer, 478 U.S. 109 (1986).

---

3. See also ASARCO Inc. v. Kadish, 490 U.S. 605 (1989), discussed at pp. 157–59, *supra,* and its similarly restrictive approach.

What, precisely, is the nature of the injury in such cases? See Karlan, *The Rights to Vote: Some Pessimism About Formalism,* 71 Tex.L.Rev. 1705 (1993)(distinguishing among three kinds of interests that potentially might be at stake in voting rights cases: (i) an interest in being able to participate in elections, (ii) an interest in being able to aggregate one's vote with like-minded others to influence electoral outcomes, and (iii) an interest in achieving governance responsive to one's values and preferences).

In Shaw v. Reno, 113 S.Ct. 2816 (1993), the Supreme Court reversed a three-judge district court's decision dismissing a constitutional challenge to a congressional districting plan for the state of North Carolina. In objecting to a bizarrely shaped district that was drawn to create an additional district with an African–American majority, the plaintiffs did not allege any impediment to their capacity to participate in elections or dilution of the value of their votes (p. 2824); they asserted instead that the scheme violated their right under the Equal Protection Clause to participate in an electoral process whose structure was not unduly traceable to considerations of race. By allowing the suit to go forward, did the majority in Shaw v. Reno implicitly recognize an "expressive harm" to all citizens of the state, arising from the state's "impermissibl[e] endorse[ment of] too dominant a role for race"?[4]

The Court apparently gave a negative answer to that question in United States v. Hays, 115 S.Ct. 2431 (1995), holding that persons living outside a voting district lacked standing to challenge the legislation establishing the district as an unconstitutional racial gerrymander. Writing for eight Justices, Justice O'Connor concluded that the plaintiffs had failed to establish any constitutionally cognizable injury: they had not suffered the "representational harm[]" of having their representatives feel especially beholden to a racially defined constituency, nor been subjected personally to racially discriminatory treatment (pp. 2436–37). Justice Stevens concurred separately, in an opinion that closely linked his finding that the plaintiffs had suffered no cognizable injury with his conclusion that they had failed to allege a constitutional violation. Recall Professor Fletcher's thesis, discussed on pp. 139–40, *supra,* that inquiries into the nature and existence of constitutionally cognizable injuries distort standing analysis; in his view, standing determinations should be inseparable in principle from the judgment whether the Constitution, properly construed, gives the plaintiff a right to judicial relief on the facts alleged. Do the conceptual difficulties of determining standing in cases challenging voting schemes provide support for this approach?

(5) *Actions by Legislators.* In Coleman v. Miller, 307 U.S. 433 (1939), a bare majority of the Court held that Kansas state legislators who had voted against ratification of the Child Labor Amendment had standing to seek review of a

---

4. See Pildes & Niemi, *Expressive Harms, "Bizarre Districts," and Voting Rights: Evaluating Election–District Appearances After Shaw v. Reno,* 92 Mich.L.Rev. 483, 492–516 (1993). Is this the same *kind* of harm that underlies standing to challenge government practices under the Establishment Clause on the ground that they send a forbidden message of "endorsement" of religion? See *id.*

Without expressly adverting to standing doctrine, the Court in Shaw v. Reno respond-
ed to Justice Souter's objection that "racial gerrymandering is harmless unless it dilutes a racial group's voting strength" by observing that "reapportionment legislation that cannot be understood as anything other than an effort to classify * * * by race * * * reinforces racial stereotypes and threatens to undermine our system of representative democracy by signaling to elected officials that they represent a particular racial group rather than their constituency as a whole" (p. 2828).

state court's refusal to enjoin state officials from certifying that Kansas had ratified the amendment. One of the grounds of suit was that the amendment had been approved in the state senate only by virtue of the vote of the lieutenant-governor, as presiding officer, to break a tie, and that under the federal Constitution such a vote was ineffectual. The Court recognized not only the standing of state senators to raise this issue, in protection of their official vote, but also the standing of both state senators and representatives to urge that the ratification was invalid because a previous rejection by Kansas was final, and because the proposed amendment, having been outstanding for what was claimed to be more than a reasonable time, was no longer susceptible of ratification.

To what extent was the decision dependent on the fact that the Kansas court had accorded standing to the legislators, while denying them on the merits the relief they sought? See also Karcher v. May, note 8, *infra.*

In recent years, members of the House and Senate have often brought suit challenging official action alleged to impair their rights as legislators. The leading case upholding standing is Kennedy v. Sampson, 511 F.2d 430 (D.C.Cir. 1974), in which Senator Kennedy sought a declaratory judgment that a bill passed by the House and Senate, but neither signed nor vetoed by the President, had been enacted into law. The President took the position that because Congress had in the meantime adjourned, the bill had been subjected to a "pocket veto" and hence was invalid; the Senator contended that a pocket veto is unconstitutional. The court of appeals recognized Senator Kennedy's standing, on the ground that a pocket veto, if unconstitutional, improperly deprived him of an effective vote to enact legislation or to override a veto.[5] Standing has typically been denied, however, when members of Congress seek to challenge executive action as not in compliance with legislation for which they voted. See, *e.g.*, Harrington v. Bush, 553 F.2d 190 (D.C.Cir.1977).

With these cases, compare McClure v. Carter, 513 F.Supp. 265 (D.Idaho 1981), a challenge to the appointment of former Congressman Mikva to the United States Court of Appeals for the D.C. Circuit, on the ground that it violated Art. I, § 6, cl. 2, which prohibits the appointment of any Senator or Representative to any federal office whose emoluments were increased during the time for which the Senator or Representative was elected. A special statute passed by Congress several weeks after Mikva's confirmation authorized any Senator or Member of the House to bring suit before a three-judge district court to challenge under the Emoluments Clause any judicial appointment to the D.C. Circuit made during the 96th Congress. When Senator McClure, who

5. In Barnes v. Kline, 759 F.2d 21 (D.C.Cir.1984), *vacated as moot,* 479 U.S. 361 (1987), the court of appeals again held that plaintiffs—Members of Congress and the Senate itself (which filed suit pursuant to a Senate resolution)—could challenge a pocket veto, and on the merits found the veto unconstitutional. Judge Bork wrote a long dissent, in which he argued that recognition of Members of Congress as plaintiffs was "a major shift in basic constitutional arrangements", was "inconsistent with the judicial function", and would "subvert[] the constitutional roles of our political institutions" (pp. 41–42).

Recognition of standing could not be squared, he said, with the requirements set forth in cases such as Allen v. Wright and with the prohibition against adjudication of "generalized grievances."

See also Goldwater v. Carter, 617 F.2d 697 (D.C.Cir.1979)(en banc)(per curiam)(upholding the standing of Members of Congress to challenge President Carter's unilateral termination of a treaty with Taiwan), *vacated,* 444 U.S. 996 (1979)(per curiam), p. 289, *infra* (dispute held not justiciable; standing issue not reached).

had opposed the appointment, brought suit under this statute, the district court ruled that he had no standing. Ex parte Lévitt, p. 144 n. 13, *supra,* held that an ordinary citizen lacked standing to bring suit in just these circumstances. Unlike the legislators in Coleman v. Miller or Kennedy v. Sampson, Senator McClure could not assert that his vote had been impaired; he was simply on the losing side of the confirmation battle. Nor did the statutory authorization of suit change the outcome; "[i]t is difficult to see how this statute may, consistent with Article III, confer upon a senator or member of the House of Representatives a 'right' to seek a decision from a federal court that such a senator or member of the House would otherwise be powerless to procure" (p. 271). The Supreme Court summarily affirmed. McClure v. Reagan, 454 U.S. 1025 (1981).

Do the federal courts have a special role in settling questions of conformity to constitutional procedures defining the legitimacy of asserted governmental authority? Or, on the contrary, are there functional or prudential reasons to decline adjudication in cases like those just discussed? See, *e.g.,* the dissenting opinion of Judge Bork in Barnes v. Kline, discussed in note 5, *supra.* If so, should dismissal be based on lack of standing, lack of ripeness, the political question doctrine, or general equitable discretion?[6]

In Riegle v. Federal Open Market Comm., 656 F.2d 873 (D.C.Cir.1981), the D.C.Circuit, following a suggestion offered by one of its members (see McGowan, *Congressmen in Court: The New Plaintiffs,* 15 Ga.L.Rev. 241 (1981)), ruled that as a matter of equitable discretion a federal court should dismiss a suit brought by a Congressman who had standing, but who "could obtain substantial relief from his fellow legislators through the enactment, repeal, or amendment of a statute" (p. 881). The complaint in the Riegle case—that a statute providing for appointment of members of the Federal Open Market Committee without Senate approval was unconstitutional—was dismissed, since the plaintiff could seek to have the statute amended.[7] Citing Riegle and several subsequent cases, Professor Chemerinsky concludes that "under the current law articulated by the District of Columbia Circuit, a member of Congress has standing only if he or she alleges a complete nullification of a vote *and* convinces the court that it should use its equitable discretion to hear the case." Chemerinsky, Federal Jurisdiction § 2.3, p. 108 (2d ed. 1994). But see Barnes v. Kline, note 5, *supra,* following the different approach of Kennedy v. Sampson several years after the Riegle decision.

Should it matter whether suit is brought by an individual legislator, by one House of Congress pursuant to resolution, or by Congress itself under a joint resolution?[8]

6. For additional commentary, see Dessem, *Congressional Standing to Sue: Whose Vote Is This, Anyway?,* 62 Notre Dame L.Rev. 1 (1986); Note, 90 Harv.L.Rev. 1632 (1977)(urging reliance on the political question rubric); Note, 82 Colum.L.Rev. 526 (1982).

7. Under the approach of the Riegle case, should the suit in Kennedy v. Sampson have been dismissed, on the theory that Congress can hold up controversial bills passed just before a recess and send them to the White House after Congress reassembles? (Senator Mansfield, the former majority leader, was reported to have followed this practice. See N.Y. Times, Nov. 10, 1974, § 1, at 44, col. 1.)

8. In Barnes v. Kline, note 5, *supra,* the Senate was a plaintiff in a suit challenging the pocket veto. Compare, *e.g.,* United States v. American Tel. & Tel. Co., 551 F.2d 384 (D.C.Cir.1976)(subcommittee chairman allowed to intervene in suit by Executive to enjoin telephone company from complying

(6) *Actions Involving Executive Officials and Administrative Agencies.* Innumerable cases recognize the standing of administrative or executive officials to defend the constitutionality of the legislation that they are charged with administering or enforcing. See, *e.g.,* Coleman v. Miller, Paragraph (5), *supra,* 307 U.S. at 443–45 (citing cases).

On the other hand, the general rule at least until 1968 was that state officials lack standing to attack the validity under the federal Constitution of state statutes that they are charged with enforcing. Smith v. Indiana, 191 U.S. 138 (1903); Braxton County Court v. West Virginia, 208 U.S. 192 (1908); Columbus & Greenville Ry. v. Miller, 283 U.S. 96 (1931).

In Board of Educ. v. Allen, 392 U.S. 236 (1968), however, members of a school board were allowed to maintain an action against the New York commissioner of education challenging a state statute requiring them to lend textbooks to students in parochial schools. The Court disposed of the standing question in a footnote (p. 241 n. 5): "Appellees do not challenge the standing of appellants to press their claim in this Court. Appellants have taken an oath to support the United States Constitution. Believing § 701 to be unconstitutional, they are in the position of having to choose between violating their oath and taking a step—refusal to comply with § 701—that would be likely to bring their expulsion from office and also a reduction in state funds for their school districts. There can be no doubt that appellants thus have a 'personal stake in the outcome' of this litigation."

Are officials "better" litigants than taxpayers? Would routine litigation by officials to test the constitutionality of statutes they are charged with enforcing be desirable? If an official truly believes a statute to be invalid, should the official be required to refuse to enforce it, and to raise the question as a defense to whatever sanction—*e.g.,* dismissal—is imposed for refusal?[9]

with subcommittee's subpoena, where House retroactively passed resolution authorizing suit); Senate Select Comm. on Presidential Campaign Activities v. Nixon, 498 F.2d 725 (D.C.Cir.1974)(en banc)(congressional committee allowed to sue President to compel production of tape recordings of conversations between President and his former aide).

Cf. Karcher v. May, 484 U.S. 72 (1987), where, after New Jersey executive officials refused to defend the constitutionality of a "moment of silence" law challenged in federal court, the presiding officers of the New Jersey Senate and General Assembly intervened as defendants on behalf of the legislature. After the court of appeals affirmed the district court's judgment declaring the law unconstitutional, the two intervenor-defendants lost their leadership positions in the legislature. Though they appealed to the Supreme Court, their successors "withdrew" the appeal on behalf of the legislature. The intervenors nonetheless sought Supreme Court review as individual legislators and as representatives of the former legislature that had enacted the law, but the Court dismissed the appeal for want of jurisdiction. The

Court stressed that whether or not the appellants could have intervened in either of those capacities, they had not done so, and hence could not appeal on that basis; they had intervened only as representatives of the incumbent legislature, and no longer had authority to pursue an appeal on that basis. The intervenors argued, alternatively, that if the case could not be heard, the judgment must be vacated for want of a proper party-defendant below. The Court rejected this contention, finding that under state law the New Jersey legislature has authority to represent the state's interests in the courts. Concurring in the judgment, Justice White stressed the Court's acknowledgement that a state legislature (and its representative) may defend the constitutionality of a state statute challenged in federal court.

9. To have standing under Allen, must an official face some realistic threat of a sanction for failure to enforce the law? See City of South Lake Tahoe v. California Tahoe Regional Planning Agency, 625 F.2d 231 (9th Cir.1980), in which the court—reasoning that Allen had been undercut by subsequent Su-

Bender v. Williamsport Area School Dist., 475 U.S. 534 (1986), also raised a question of a local official's standing. There, high school students sued their school district, school officials, and nine school board members, challenging the refusal to permit a student religious club to meet on school premises. The district court granted summary judgment to the plaintiffs; no injunction was entered, however, and no relief was granted against any defendant individually. A majority of the school board decided to comply with the ruling, but a dissenting board member (Youngman) filed an appeal. When the case reached the Supreme Court, it ruled that Youngman lacked standing to appeal. He had been sued only in his official capacity, and therefore had no financial stake in the outcome of the litigation. And "[g]enerally speaking, members of collegial bodies do not have standing to perfect an appeal the body itself has declined to take" (p. 544). Allen was distinguished on the ground that "[u]nlike the members of the school board *majority* in Allen who were put 'in the position of having to choose between violating their oath and taking a step * * * that would be likely to bring their expulsion from office * * *,' Mr. Youngman has voted his conscience and, as a member of the Board, must abide by its decision not to appeal * * *" (p. 544 n. 7).[10]

If the responsibility for carrying out the board's decision was vested exclusively in the school superintendent and professional staff, would Youngman be in the same situation as a Member of Congress who lacks standing to contest the constitutionality of a law passed by the legislature? See, *e.g.*, Harrington v. Bush, Paragraph (5), *supra*. If, instead, Youngman had some responsibility for complying with the district court's ruling, wouldn't he be in the same bind, when deciding whether to comply with the order, as the officials in Allen? Can the sentiment of a majority eliminate the injury to an individual's conscience that was of concern in Allen?

The question of an administrative official's standing to appeal arose in a somewhat different posture in Director, Office of Workers' Compensation Programs v. Perini North River Associates, 459 U.S. 297 (1983). An administrative tribunal decided that an employee (Churchill) was not covered by the Longshore and Harbor Workers' Compensation Act. Churchill sought review in the court of appeals, and the Director of the OWCP participated as a respondent, filing a brief supporting the employee. After the court of appeals affirmed the decision, the Director alone sought review in the Supreme Court, which upheld his standing to appeal. Though the Director, as a party respondent below, clearly had statutory authority under 28 U.S.C. § 1254(1) to seek certiorari, the Court observed that "he *may* not have Art. III standing to argue the merits of Churchill's claim * * *" (p. 304). Having raised the question, however, the Court concluded that "the Director's petition makes Churchill an automatic respondent under our Rule 19.6, and in that capacity, Churchill 'may seek reversal of the judgment of the Court of Appeals on any ground urged in that court' "(p. 304).

preme Court decisions that tighten standing requirements and clearly reject citizen standing—refused to accord standing to plaintiff officials where the risk of civil liability for failing to enforce a law they believed to be unconstitutional was slight. The Supreme Court denied certiorari, over three dissents. 449 U.S. 1039 (1980).

10. The Court also ruled that the record did not support Youngman's standing as a parent of a pupil; Chief Justice Burger, and Justices White and Rehnquist, dissented on this point.

(7) *The Standing of Organizations.* Sierra Club v. Morton, p. 141, *supra,* held that organizations do not have standing to represent their particular conception of the public interest. The Court's position did not, however, restrict an organization's right to sue for injuries that it has itself suffered. For an expansive view of organizational injury, see Havens Realty Corp. v. Coleman, 455 U.S. 363, 378–79 (1982), p. 172, *supra* (nonprofit organization devoted to equal housing opportunity permitted to sue a landlord whose racial steering practices were alleged to impair the plaintiff's ability to provide services to low-income home seekers, with a consequent drain on the organization's resources).

Nor did Sierra Club cast doubt on the common practice of permitting associations to litigate as representatives of their members, as long as the members themselves would have standing to sue. The Court summed up prevailing doctrine in Hunt v. Washington State Apple Advertising Comm'n, 432 U.S. 333, 343 (1977): "Thus we have recognized that an association has standing to bring suit on behalf of its members when: (a) its members would otherwise have standing to sue in their own right; (b) the interests it seeks to protect are germane to the organization's purpose; and (c) neither the claim asserted nor the relief requested requires the participation of individual members in the lawsuit."

The Washington State Advertising Commission was not a membership organization but a statutory agency, consisting of 13 apple growers and dealers elected by growers and dealers. It sought declaratory and injunctive relief, on Commerce Clause grounds, against special grading and identification requirements imposed by North Carolina on apples sold in that state. The Court found that the commission performed the functions of a traditional trade association; that while there were no official "members" the relationship to the growers and dealers in fact carried all the indicia of membership; and, indeed, that the commission itself could be affected by the outcome of the litigation, because its annual assessments were tied to the volume of sales of Washington apples. The Court noted but did not specifically respond to the defendants' argument that the growers could easily have sued on their own, and upheld the Commission's standing without dissent.[11]

In International Union, UAW v. Brock, 477 U.S. 274 (1986), the UAW, suing on behalf of its members, challenged federal rules limiting eligibility for a federal program providing benefits to workers laid off because of foreign competition. The government urged the Court to reject the principles of associational standing recognized in Hunt. It argued that, "at least absent a showing of particularized need," members of an organization should be permitted to litigate common questions of law or fact against the same defendant only by filing a class action in accordance with Rule 23—which, unlike organizational standing doctrine, requires the plaintiff to be an adequate representative so as to protect the interests of class members (p. 288, quoting the government's

---

11. Compare Harris v. McRae, 448 U.S. 297, 320–21 (1980)(denying a church group standing to challenge, under the Free Exercise Clause, federal restrictions on Medicaid funding for abortions; because the claim required a showing of coercive effect on an individual's religious practice, and because there was a division of opinion within the plaintiff group on the abortion question, affected individuals must sue on their own

behalf); Warth v. Seldin, 422 U.S. 490, 515–16 (1975), p. 146, *supra* (association of developers lacks standing to challenge municipal zoning restrictions alleged to have harmed member firms; "the damages claims are not common to the entire membership, nor shared by all in equal degree," and thus "to obtain relief in damages, each member * * * who claims injury as a result of [the town's] practices must be a party to the suit").

brief).   The Court disagreed, concluding that this argument overlooked the distinctive value of organizational plaintiffs, whose ability to "draw upon a pre-existing reservoir of expertise and capital * * * can assist both courts and plaintiffs" (p. 289).   In addition, the Court observed that the primary reason that people join an organization—"to create an effective vehicle for vindicating interests that they share with others"—provides "some guarantee that the association will work to promote their interests" (p. 290).

The Court noted, however, that if an organization were in fact an ineffective representative, due process principles might prevent a judgment against it from precluding claims by its members.   The Court added (p. 290): "And were we presented with evidence that such a problem existed * * * we would have to consider how it might be alleviated."   But the Court found no reason to doubt the UAW's ability in the case at bar.[12]

Is it fair to say that the Court and the government differed on (i) whether the organization itself (rather than an affected member) can be the nominal plaintiff, and (ii) assuming the organization can be named as plaintiff, whether its adequacy as a representative should be presumed or must be proven?   Are these important differences?   See generally Note, 61 B.U.L.Rev. 174 (1981); Note, 1974 U.Ill.L.F. 663.

Should the UAW be required to identify particular members injured by the regulations, or does it suffice that the regulations will surely injure some members, even if it cannot now be shown which ones?   Compare *Note on "Ripeness" in Public Actions Challenging Patterns or Practices in the Administration of the Law*, pp. 265–70, *infra*, especially LaDuke v. Nelson, p. 270, *infra* (holding justiciable a class action challenging an official practice likely to harm some members of the class but unlikely to affect any particular member).

SUBSECTION B: DEFENDANTS' STANDING

NOTE ON ASSERTING THE RIGHTS OF OTHERS

(1) *Jus Tertii Doctrine.*   Defendants in enforcement proceedings, threatened with the imposition of state force, clearly face injury.   The standing question in such cases revolves around what issues defendants may raise.   Defendants may, of course, assert any claimed violation of their own rights, but may or may not be entitled to defend on the ground that the law being enforced violates the rights of others.

The question whether defendants should be able to assert the rights of others can be viewed from the perspective of either the private, dispute resolution or the public rights model of litigation.   From a private rights perspective, the judicial function is limited to vindicating the rights of the

---

12.   Justice Powell dissented from the standing decision.   He did not endorse the government's frontal attack on Hunt, focusing instead on the Court's traditional reluctance to permit parties to assert the rights of third persons "for fear of inadequate representation" (p. 296).   Absent a showing that more than a small number of UAW members had a stake in the lawsuit, he argued, the union's interest might be insufficient to assure the "concrete adverseness" that previous decisions had demanded (p. 297).

parties to the particular dispute before the court. From a public rights perspective, one party's litigation of the rights of others may provide an appropriate occasion for the declaration and enforcement of public norms.

Note, however, that third party standing (or *jus tertii*), the subject of this Note, is conceptually limited in a way that unrestricted defendants' standing to assert public rights would not be. The kind of third party standing considered in this Note is not only predicated on a concrete injury to the party who wishes to assert another's rights, but also requires that the application of the law against that party will harm those third parties whose rights the defendant seeks to litigate. Although the distinction is not always made clear in the cases, the doctrine governing *jus tertii* standing thus differs importantly from that governing overbreadth challenges, discussed at pp. 202-13, *infra*. "The overbreadth claimant seeks to assert the rights of hypothetical third persons to whom the challenged law conceivably might apply in a manner that would violate their constitutional rights. The most common example of such an attack arises under the first amendment, when a litigant whose speech may not itself be constitutionally protected claims that the relevant statute must be struck down because it could be applied to restrict speech that cannot constitutionally be burdened. Thus, overbreadth attacks involve both the application of the challenged law to the claimant and a different, hypothetical application of the law to third parties. Quite different from this sort of third party claim is an assertion of jus tertii—a litigant's claim that a single application of a law both injures him and impinges upon the constitutional rights of third persons." Note, *Standing to Assert Constitutional Jus Tertii*, 88 Harv.L.Rev. 423, 423–24 (1974).

(2) *The Traditional View*. The traditional rule was that parties to a lawsuit could only assert their own rights or immunities.

(a) In Tileston v. Ullman, 318 U.S. 44 (1943) (per curiam), the Connecticut Supreme Court had rejected, on the merits, a physician's constitutional challenge to the application to him of a state statute prohibiting the use or distribution of contraceptives. The Supreme Court dismissed his appeal on the ground that the only constitutional attack on the statute—that it worked a deprivation of liberty without due process—was based on the rights not of the physician but of his patients, which he had no standing to assert.[1]

Dr. Tileston was formally a plaintiff, but he was also a prospective defendant, bringing an anticipatory action (seeking a declaratory judgment or injunction) against a criminal statute directed at his own conduct. There is no reason, is there, to bar prospective defendants who bring anticipatory actions from making any legal arguments (including those based on the rights of others) that they would be entitled to raise in enforcement proceedings against them?

(b) McGowan v. Maryland, 366 U.S. 420 (1961), involved a prosecution of department store employees for Sunday sales in violation of the state's "Blue

---

1. Tileston is often cited as holding that a litigant may not assert the rights of third persons. Some have read the case more narrowly, as resting on the absence of any injury to the doctor himself: he failed to allege that the statute injured him economically, and the risk of a criminal prosecution was insufficiently ripe to constitute redressable injury. See Bickel, The Least Dangerous Branch 143–45 (1962); Scott, *Standing in the Supreme Court—A Functional Analysis*, 86 Harv.L.Rev. 645, 649 n. 14 (1973). On this view, the case stands merely for the proposition that a party not personally injured may not start a lawsuit solely to alleviate harm to others.

Laws". The Court denied the defendants' standing to assert their customers' First Amendment right to free exercise of religion (pp. 429–30):

"[A]ppellants * * * allege only economic injury to themselves; they do not allege any infringement of their own religious freedoms due to Sunday closing. * * * [Accordingly], we hold that appellants have no standing to raise [a challenge under the Free Exercise Clause]. Tileston v. Ullman, 318 U.S. 44, 46. * * * Those persons whose religious rights are allegedly impaired by the statutes are not without effective ways to assert these rights. Cf. N. A. A. C. P. v. Alabama, 357 U.S. 449, 459–460; Barrows v. Jackson, 346 U.S. 249, 257. Appellants present no weighty countervailing policies here to cause an exception to our general principles."[2]

(3) *Early Exceptions Allowing Third–Party Standing.* Consider how the following cases relate to the traditional rule forbidding one party to assert the rights of another.

(a) In Barrows v. Jackson, 346 U.S. 249 (1953), a state court damage action against a white woman for selling land in breach of a racially restrictive covenant, the vendor was permitted to defend on the ground that enforcement would amount to unconstitutional discrimination, even though she was not a member of the class discriminated against. Justice Minton wrote for the Court (pp. 255–57, 259):

"Ordinarily, one may not claim standing in this Court to vindicate the constitutional rights of some third party. * * * One reason for this rul[e] is that the state court, when actually faced with the question, might narrowly construe the statute to obliterate the objectionable feature, or it might declare the unconstitutional provisions separable. * * * It would indeed be undesirable for this Court to consider every conceivable situation which might possibly arise in the application of complex and comprehensive legislation. Nor are we so ready to frustrate the expressed will of Congress or that of the state legislatures. * * *

"* * * But in the instant case, we are faced with a unique situation in which it is the action of the state *court* which might result in a denial of constitutional rights and in which it would be difficult if not impossible for the persons whose rights are asserted to present their grievance before any court. Under the peculiar circumstances of this case, we believe the reasons which underlie our rule denying standing to raise another's rights, which is only a rule of practice, are outweighed by the need to protect the fundamental rights which would be denied by permitting the damages action to be maintained. * * *

"* * * The relation between the coercion exerted on respondent and her possible pecuniary loss thereby is so close to the purpose of the restrictive covenant, to violate the constitutional rights of those discriminated against, that respondent is the only effective adversary of the unworthy covenant in its last stand. She will be permitted to protect herself and, by so doing, close the gap to the use of this covenant, so universally condemned by the courts."

See also NAACP v. Alabama, 357 U.S. 449 (1958)(permitting the NAACP to assert the rights of its members in resisting an order to disclose its

---

2. In a companion case to McGowan involving Orthodox Jewish merchants, the Court rejected the free exercise challenge on the merits. See Braunfeld v. Brown, 366 U.S. 599 (1961).

membership list, and explaining that it was proper to permit an assertion of third party rights "where constitutional rights of persons who are not immediately before the Court could not be effectively vindicated except through an appropriate representative before the Court")(p. 459). Could the NAACP's members have intervened, as "John Does", to oppose the disclosure order? If so, couldn't they have asserted their right to anonymity without losing it?

(b) In Griswold v. Connecticut, 381 U.S. 479 (1965), a doctor and the Executive Director of the Planned Parenthood League were convicted as accessories to violation of the Connecticut birth control statute involved in Tileston v. Ullman, Paragraph (2)(a), *supra*. The Court went to the merits and held the underlying anti-use statute invalid as an invasion of "marital privacy". Justice Douglas wrote for the Court (p. 481):

"We think that appellants have standing to raise the constitutional rights of the married people with whom they had a professional relationship. Tileston v. Ullman is different, for there the plaintiff seeking to represent others asked for a declaratory judgment. In that situation we thought that the requirements of standing should be strict, lest the standards of 'case or controversy' in Article III of the Constitution become blurred. Here those doubts are removed by reason of a criminal conviction for serving married couples in violation of an aiding-and-abetting statute. Certainly the accessory should have standing to assert that the offense which he is charged with assisting is not, or cannot constitutionally be, a crime.

"This case is more akin to Truax v. Raich, 239 U.S. 33, where an employee was permitted to assert the rights of his employer; to Pierce v. Society of Sisters, 268 U.S. 510, where the owners of private schools were entitled to assert the rights of potential pupils and their parents; and to Barrows v. Jackson, 346 U.S. 249, where a white defendant, party to a racially restrictive covenant, who was being sued for damages by the covenantors because she had conveyed her property to Negroes, was allowed to raise the issue that enforcement of the covenant violated the rights of prospective Negro purchasers to equal protection, although no Negro was a party to the suit. The rights of husband and wife, pressed here, are likely to be diluted or adversely affected unless those rights are considered in a suit involving those who have this kind of confidential relation to them."

Was the second quoted paragraph necessary? Was not defendants' standing to challenge the validity of the birth control statute clearly established by the state law that made the accessory convictions dependent upon the substantive criminal prohibition?

(4) *Rationalizing Efforts.* Are the cases in Paragraph (3) that permit assertion of the rights of others better viewed as assertions by the litigants of their own rights?

Professor Sedler has argued that a litigant asserts his or her own rights in challenging a law as constitutionally invalid when (i) the litigant and third persons have some relationship, and (ii) it is in the context of that relationship that the challenged law works its allegedly unconstitutional deprivation. See Sedler, *The Assertion of Constitutional Jus Tertii: A Substantive Approach,* 70 Calif.L.Rev. 1308, 1329 (1982). Professor Monaghan similarly asserts that a litigant "asserts his own rights (not those of a third person) when he seeks to void restrictions that directly impair his freedom to interact with a third person who himself could not be legally prevented from engaging in the interaction."

Monaghan, *Third Party Standing,* 84 Colum.L.Rev. 277, 299 (1984).[3] Professor Monaghan suggests that this "first party" view is preferable because it eliminates "unanalyzed and ungrounded notions of judicial 'discretion.' " *Id.* at 278. Note, moreover, that under the "rights of others" view, Congress could presumably pass legislation barring the Court from exercising its discretion to hear *jus tertii* claims; by contrast, under the "first party" view, Congress would lack power to enact a law barring courts (at least in enforcement proceedings) from adjudicating the rights at issue.[4] A further asserted benefit of Sedler's and Monaghan's approach is that it supplies a straightforward answer to some troubling questions of judicial power, such as the source of a federal court's authority to disregard otherwise applicable law and provide relief to a party with no personal "right" to such relief.

Consider, however, whether the question of judicial power to provide remedies to parties with no personal right to relief, as a means of ensuring that the rights of others are not harmed, has not been implicitly resolved by well-established doctrine in other areas. The overbreadth doctrine arguably constitutes one relevant analogy. See pp. 202–13, *infra.* The exclusionary rule furnishes another. The Supreme Court has concluded that the Fourth Amendment's exclusionary rule does not prevent or redress any harm to the criminal defendant who invokes it, but instead simply helps to protect the citizenry at large by generally deterring constitutional violations. See, *e.g.,* United States v. Calandra, 414 U.S. 338, 353–54 (1974); United States v. Leon, 468 U.S. 897, 906 (1984). On this view, isn't the criminal defendant, in moving to suppress evidence, given standing to claim a remedy whose purpose is to safeguard the rights of others? See generally Meltzer, *Deterring Constitutional Violations by Law Enforcement Officials: Plaintiffs and Defendants as Private Attorneys General,* 88 Colum.L.Rev. 247 (1988); Monaghan, *supra,* at 279–82, 310–15.[5]

3. For earlier suggestions along similar lines, see Albert, *Standing to Challenge Administrative Action: An Inadequate Surrogate for Claim for Relief,* 83 Yale L.J. 425, 464–68 (1974); Jaffe, *Standing to Secure Judicial Review: Private Actions,* 75 Harv. L.Rev. 255, 270 (1961); Note, Paragraph (1), *supra.*

4. The "first party" view can also apply to suits by *plaintiffs* seeking to assert the rights of others. Recall Singleton v. Wulff, 428 U.S. 106 (1976), p. 152 n. 25, *supra,* in which physicians, who brought suit challenging the constitutionality of a Missouri statute that prohibited payment of Medicaid benefits for abortions that were not "medically indicated," were permitted to assert their patients' rights. Sedler, *supra,* at 1332, argues that the physicians should have been permitted to assert their own equal protection right to obtain payment for abortions as well as for other medical procedures; Monaghan, *supra,* at 306–07, disagrees, finding the interference with the doctor-patient relationship not sufficiently "direct" to violate the physicians' rights.

5. Private litigants are often permitted to raise questions of federalism or separation of powers in challenging a law or a government action that, if valid, affects their interests. See, *e.g.,* San Diego Bldg. Trades Council v. Garmon, 359 U.S. 236 (1959)(private litigant permitted to assert that state law under which he was sued is preempted by the National Labor Relations Act); INS v. Chadha, 462 U.S. 919 (1983)(permitting an alien to challenge a legislative veto of a decision suspending a deportation order against him, on the ground that the veto violated the separation of powers). Should these litigants be viewed as invoking the rights of a government or one of its branches? (Chadha rejected the argument that the alien lacked standing because he was advancing the interests of the Executive Branch in a dispute with Congress). See Choper, Judicial Review and the National Political Process: A Functional Reconsideration of the Role of the Supreme Court 209–10 (1980). Or do these litigants assert their own right to be regulated in accordance with a valid rule? Compare Dennis v. Higgins, 498 U.S. 439 (1991), discussed at p. 1137, *infra* (holding that one who challenges a state law under the "dormant" Commerce Clause asserts a right to engage in

(5) *Broader Exceptions.* Although the Supreme Court's pronouncements are less than perfectly consistent, decisions over the past several decades have created broad exceptions to the prohibition against defendants' assertions of third party rights. Consider what governing principles emerge from the following cases.

(a) Eisenstadt v. Baird, 405 U.S. 438 (1972), involved the validity of a Massachusetts conviction for giving away a contraceptive.[6] The challenged law prohibited the dispensing of any article for the prevention of conception, except by a registered physician or pharmacist administering to a married person. Baird, who was not a registered physician or pharmacist, challenged the statute on the ground that denial to unmarried persons of the same access to contraceptives as married persons violated the formers' right to equal protection. His claim was upheld.

On the question of Baird's standing to assert the rights of unmarried distributees, the Court first noted (p. 443) that he unquestionably "ha[d] sufficient interest in challenging the statute's validity to satisfy the 'case or controversy' requirement of Article III of the Constitution."[7] The Court continued (pp. 444–46):

"[A]ppellant contends that Baird's conviction rests on the restriction * * * on permissible distributors and that that restriction serves a valid health interest independent of the limitation on authorized distributees. * * * In any event, appellant concludes, since Baird was not himself a single person denied access to contraceptives, he should not be heard to assert their rights. We cannot agree.

"The Court of Appeals held that the statute under which Baird was convicted is not a health measure. If that view is correct, we do not see how Baird may be prevented, because he was neither a doctor nor a druggist, from attacking the statute in its alleged discriminatory application to potential distributees. * * * Appellant * * * argues that the absence of a professional or aiding-and-abetting relationship distinguishes this case from Griswold. Yet, as the Court's discussion of prior authority in Griswold indicates, the doctor-patient and accessory-principal relationships are not the only circumstances in which one person has been found to have standing to assert the rights of another. [The Court here cited and discussed Barrows v. Jackson, *supra.*] * * * And so here the relationship between Baird and those whose rights he seeks to assert is not simply that between a distributor and potential distributees, but that between an advocate of the rights of persons to obtain contraceptives and those desirous of doing so. * * *

"In any event, more important than the nature of the relationship between the litigant and those whose rights he seeks to assert is the impact of the litigation on the third-party interests. * * * Enforcement of the Massachusetts statute will materially impair the ability of single persons to obtain

commerce free from the challenged state regulation).

6. The case came to the Supreme Court on review of a federal habeas corpus proceeding. Is there any significant difference with regard to standing between a defendant in a criminal case and a petitioner in habeas?

7. A footnote appended at this point said (p. 443 n. 4): "This factor decisively distinguishes Tileston v. Ullman, 318 U.S. 44 (1943), where the Court held that a physician lacked standing to bring an action for declaratory relief to challenge, on behalf of his patients, the Connecticut law prohibiting the use of contraceptives. The patients were fully able to bring their own action * * *."

contraceptives. In fact, the case for according standing to assert third-party rights is stronger in this regard here than in Griswold because unmarried persons denied access to contraceptives in Massachusetts, unlike the users of contraceptives in Connecticut, are not themselves subject to prosecution and, to that extent, are denied a forum in which to assert their own rights. *Cf.* NAACP v. Alabama, 357 U.S. 449 (1958); Barrows v. Jackson, *supra*".

Justice White, joined by Justice Blackmun, pointed out that Baird had been convicted of giving away the contraceptive when he was not a physician or pharmacist, and not of giving it to an unmarried person; the state had not even offered proof as to the marital status of the recipient. He concurred in overturning the conviction on the limited ground that, since there was no indication that the foam involved danger to health, restriction of its distribution to medical channels was precluded by Griswold insofar as the recipients were married persons.

Chief Justice Burger dissented. On the standing question, he said that since Baird was not a physician or pharmacist and was on that basis prohibited by the statute from dispensing contraceptives to anyone, regardless of marital status, "the validity of this restriction on dispensing medicinal substances is the only issue before the Court, and appellee has no standing to challenge that part of the statute restricting the persons to whom contraceptives are available" (pp. 465–66).[8]

Wasn't Justice White correct that, if the restriction of distribution by nonprofessionals was invalid, Baird's conviction should have been reversed on that limited ground, whatever the marital status of the distributee?

Suppose, however, that the Court believed it to be constitutional to prohibit a nonprofessional from distributing contraceptives. Suppose, further, that the record indicated that Baird's distributee was unmarried, and the state argued that whether or not the ban on nonprofessional distribution was valid, the ban on *any* distribution to unmarried persons certainly was. Should Baird be permitted to argue that his conviction should be overturned because the statute also makes an unconstitutional distinction between married and unmarried persons? This question raises a conventional severability problem: is the ban on distribution by nonprofessionals severable from the ban on distribution (by anyone) to unmarried persons? On severability, see generally the materials immediately following this Note.

(b) Since Doe v. Bolton, 410 U.S. 179 (1973), a companion case to Roe v. Wade, 410 U.S. 113 (1973), the Supreme Court has frequently permitted doctors to assert their patients' rights in actions challenging abortion restrictions. See, *e.g.*, Planned Parenthood Ass'n v. Ashcroft, 462 U.S. 476 (1983)(permitting, without discussion, Planned Parenthood, two physicians, and an abortion clinic to challenge the constitutionality of state abortion restrictions).

(c) Craig v. Boren, 429 U.S. 190 (1976), involved Oklahoma laws that prohibited sales of 3.2% beer to males under 21, but permitted sale to females over 18. A licensed beer vendor who brought an anticipatory attack against the laws was permitted to assert the equal protection rights of 18–20 year-old men. The judicially created rule against *jus tertii* standing should not be followed in this case, the Court explained, because the vendor's standing had

---

8. Justices Powell and Rehnquist did   not participate.

not been challenged below and because the constitutional questions had been effectively presented.

The Court proceeded to hold (p. 194) that "[i]n any event", the vendor was "entitled to assert those concomitant rights of third parties that would be 'diluted or adversely affected' should her constitutional challenge fail and the statutes remain in force. Griswold v. Connecticut * * *. Otherwise, the threatened imposition of governmental sanctions might deter [the plaintiff] and other similarly situated vendors from selling 3.2% beer to young males, thereby ensuring that 'enforcement of the challenged restriction against the [vendor] would result indirectly in the violation of third parties' rights,' Warth v. Seldin, 422 U.S. 490, 510 (1975)" (p. 194). The Court found particular support for its result in Eisenstadt v. Baird, Paragraph (5)(a), *supra,* and concluded that since here, as there, the law prohibited distribution rather than use, the "obvious claimant" was the vendor (p. 197).[9] (On the merits, the Court held the statute unconstitutional.)

Chief Justice Burger alone dissented on the standing issue. He stressed (p. 216) that there was "no barrier whatever to Oklahoma males 18–20 years of age asserting, in an appropriate forum, any constitutional rights they may claim to purchase 3.2% beer." Nor did Griswold control: "It borders on the ludicrous to draw a parallel between a vendor of beer and the intimate professional physician-patient relationship which undergirded relaxation of standing rules in that case." Even Eisenstadt was distinguishable, involving as it did "the relationship between one who acted to protect the rights of a minority and the minority itself" (p. 216, quoting Eisenstadt).

After Craig, what is left of McGowan v. Maryland, Paragraph (2)(b), *supra?* As you read the remainder of this Paragraph, consider whether Craig was a watershed case, or whether a decisive turn occurred in Eisenstadt v. Baird.

(d) In United States Dept. of Labor v. Triplett, 494 U.S. 715 (1990), the Court held that an attorney who was resisting state court disciplinary proceedings for receiving contingent fees from claimants under the federal Black Lung Benefits Act had standing to assert the constitutional rights of his clients. (Such fees were prohibited by Department of Labor regulations issued under that Act.)[10]

(e) Powers v. Ohio, 499 U.S. 400 (1991), held that a criminal defendant had standing to assert that the prosecution had used peremptory challenges to exclude jurors of a race other than his own, even though the right being asserted was that of prospective jurors, not the defendant. The Court stated

---

9. The Court refused to distinguish Eisenstadt v. Baird on the ground that it involved an actual defendant prosecuted for a violation, while the vendor in Craig was only a prospective defendant: "The existence of Art. III 'injury in fact' and the structure of the claimant's relationship to the third parties are not altered by the litigative posture of the suit" (p. 196 n. 5).

10. See also Secretary of State of Maryland v. Joseph H. Munson Co., Inc., 467 U.S. 947, 954–58 (1984)(seller of fundraising services to charities has standing, in challenging statute making some of its fundraising activities unlawful, to assert the rights of chari-

ties); Carey v. Population Services, Intern., 431 U.S. 678 (1977)(mail-order vendor of contraceptives has standing, in challenge to state law forbidding it to advertise or distribute contraceptives, to assert the rights of its potential customers). But *cf.* Madsen v. Women's Health Center, 114 S.Ct. 2516, 2530 (1994)(in challenge to an injunction barring named protestors and those "in concert" with them from blocking access to an abortion clinic and from engaging in certain expressive activities tending to disrupt the clinic, named protestors may not assert the rights of non-parties).

that the defendant suffers injury in fact because such discrimination "places the fairness of a criminal proceeding in doubt" (p. 411); that as in Triplett and other cases, there was a "relation" with the third party—a relationship that "continues throughout the entire trial" (p. 413); and that there are significant practical barriers to the assertion by prospective jurors of their own rights.[11]

(6) *Current Doctrine.* How would you summarize the current doctrine dealing with a defendant's standing to assert a third party's rights? Two themes dominate the cases. One involves the requirement of a relationship between the parties, though it is less than clear what the nature of the relationship has to be. In Triplett, *supra,* the Supreme Court summarized its decisions as establishing that "[w]hen * * * enforcement of a restriction against the litigant prevents a third party from entering into a relationship with the litigant (typically a contractual relationship), to which relationship the third party has a legal entitlement (typically a constitutional entitlement), third-party standing has been held to exist" (494 U.S. at 720). This may well be a sufficient condition to justify *jus tertii* standing: Shouldn't litigants always be free to challenge the imposition on them of legal duties that prohibit them from acting in ways necessary for third parties to enjoy their constitutional rights—leaving to the merits the question whether, in fact, the third parties have such rights? See Note, p. 188, *supra,* at 431–33. But satisfaction of the Triplett formulation does not seem necessary to third party standing. See, *e.g.,* Powers, *supra,* in which no relationship of this kind existed between the criminal defendant and the prospective jurors' whose rights he was allowed to assert.

The other recurrent theme in the cases concerns obstacles to third parties' asserting their own rights in circumstances in which the would-be advocate would be an effective representative. Do the cases reflect a consistent view about how great the obstacle must be for third party standing to be justified wholly, or partly, on this basis?

Is the nature of the right possibly also a relevant factor? In Powers v. Ohio, for example, might it matter that the integrity of the judicial process itself was potentially at stake?

Is it significant that the Supreme Court, in recent years, appears seldom, if ever, to deny third-party standing to assert plausibly meritorious claims on the merits?

Yazoo & Mississippi Valley R. R. v. Jackson Vinegar Co.

226 U.S. 217, 33 S.Ct. 40, 57 L.Ed. 193 (1912).
Appeal from the Circuit Court of Hinds County, Mississippi.

■ Mr. Justice Van Devanter delivered the opinion of the Court.

This was an action to recover damages from a railway company for the partial loss of a shipment of vinegar carried over the company's line from one point to

---

11. The two dissenting Justices denied the existence of any first-party right (*i.e.,* of a prospective juror not to be excluded from a particular case through the use of a peremptory challenge), and also argued that the threshold requirement of injury in fact had not been met.

Powers was followed in Georgia v. McCollum, 505 U.S. 42 (1992), which held that prosecutors may challenge a criminal defendant's exercise of peremptory challenges on the basis of race: "The State's relation to potential jurors * * * is closer than the relationship[ ] approved in Powers", and the barriers to suit faced by excluded jurors in this case were "no less formidable" (p. 2357).

another in the state of Mississippi. This case originated in a justice's court and was taken on appeal to the circuit court of Hinds county, where the plaintiff recovered a judgment for actual damages and $25 as a statutory penalty. That being the highest court in the state to which the case could be carried, it was then brought here. The position of the railway company, unsuccessfully taken in the state court and now renewed, is that the Mississippi statute providing for the penalty is repugnant to the due process of law and equal protection clauses of the 14th Amendment to the Constitution of the United States. The statute reads:

"Railroads, corporations, and individuals engaged as common carriers in this state are required to settle all claims for lost or damaged freight which has been lost or damaged between two given points on the same line or system, within sixty days from the filing of written notice of the loss or damage with the agent at the point of destination; and where freight is handled by two or more roads or systems of roads, and is lost or damaged, claims therefor shall be settled within ninety days from the filing of written notice thereof, with the agent by consignee at the point of destination. A common carrier failing to settle such claims as herein required shall be liable to the consignee for $25 damages in each case, in addition to actual damages, all of which may be recovered in the same suit: Provided that this section shall only apply when the amount claimed is $200 or less."

The facts showing the application made of the statute are these: The plaintiff gave notice of its claim in the manner prescribed, placing its damages at $4.76, and, upon the railway company's failure to settle within sixty days, sued to recover that sum and the statutory penalty. Upon the trial the damages were assessed at the sum stated in the notice, and judgment was given therefor, with the penalty. Thus, the claim presented in advance of the suit, and which the railway company failed to settle within the time allotted, was fully sustained.

As applied to such a case, we think the statute is not repugnant to either the due process of law or the equal protection clause of the Constitution, but, on the contrary, merely provides a reasonable incentive for the prompt settlement, without suit, of just demands of a class admitting of special legislative treatment.

Although seemingly conceding this much, counsel for the railway company urge that the statute is not confined to cases like the present, but equally penalizes the failure to accede to an excessive or extravagant claim; in other words, that it contemplates the assessment of the penalty in every case where the claim presented is not settled within the time allotted, regardless of whether, or how much, the recovery falls short of the amount claimed. But it is not open to the railway company to complain on that score. It has not been penalized for failing to accede to an excessive or extravagant claim, but for failing to make reasonably prompt settlement of a claim which, upon due inquiry, has been pronounced just in every respect. Of course, the argument to sustain the contention is that, if the statute embraces cases such as are supposed, it is void as to them, and, if so void, is void *in toto*. But this court must deal with the case in hand, and not with imaginary ones. It suffices, therefore, to hold that, as applied to cases like the present, the statute is valid. How the state court may apply it to other cases, whether its general words may be treated as more or less restrained, and how far parts of it may be sustained if others fail, are matters upon which we need not speculate now.

The judgment is accordingly affirmed.

NOTE ON THE SCOPE OF THE ISSUE AND THE PROBLEM OF SEPARABILITY

(1) *Consistency of Application.* Except in cases involving the First Amendment and arguably a class of other fundamental rights, see pp. 202-13, *infra,* the Supreme Court has regularly followed Yazoo where a state's highest court has refused to deal with applications of a state statute not involved in the case before it.[1] The Court has similarly held that federal statues generally may be subject to constitutional challenge only as they are applied to the facts of particular cases. *See, e.g.,* United States v. Raines, 362 U.S. 17 (1960).

(2) *Underlying Policies.* Is the Yazoo approach, which generally precludes consideration of a statute's constitutionality as applied to the facts of other cases, a sound one? Consider Fallon, *Making Sense of Overbreadth,* 100 Yale L.J. 853, 860–61 (1991): "The Yazoo rule is harsh and in some ways counterintuitive. The challenged statute imposed pressure on railroads to settle even frivolous cases. The Court, in prescribing the approach that it did, bypassed a clear opportunity to consider the permissibility of the statutory policy and, it if found injustice, to end it." Does it matter that "preferred liberties", see Tribe, American Constitutional Law § 11–1, p. 770 (2d ed.1988), are not involved?

According to Fallon, *supra,* at 861, at least three policy reasons support the Yazoo approach: (i) if the defendant is guilty of prohibitable conduct that the state has attempted to forbid, the defendant has no personal right to escape punishment; (ii) to permit adjudication to turn on hypothetical disputes would give too abstract a flavor to constitutional litigation; (iii) it is a fundamental premise of constitutional federalism that state courts may play a lawmaking role, including one of narrowing statutes to bring them within constitutional bounds, and they should be given an opportunity to provide narrowing constructions on a case-by-case basis.

(3) *Separability and Reviewability.* Would it be open to the Mississippi courts to hold after Yazoo (a) that the statute involved in that case applied also to failure to settle groundless or excessive claims; (b) that as so applied the statute violated the federal Constitution; and (c) that the statute was inseparable, so that it could no longer be applied even to failure to settle meritorious claims? If so, does this suggest that the Supreme Court, in the Yazoo litigation, should have vacated the judgment and remanded the case to the state court, to permit the railroad to raise an argument based on this possible scenario? That it should have permitted the railroad to anticipate these questions in the Yazoo litigation? If the state court had anticipated them, should the Supreme Court then have treated question (b) as open to review?

---

1. The cases are collected in 13 Wright, Miller, & Cooper, Federal Practice and Procedure § 3531.9, at 589–90 & n. 87 (1984 & 1995 Supp.); Sedler, *Standing to Assert Con-* *stitutional Jus Tertii in the Supreme Court,* 71 Yale L.J. 599, 601–12 (1962); and Stern, *Separability and Separability Clauses in The Supreme Court,* 51 Harv.L.Rev. 76 (1937).

(4) *Deference to State Interpretations.*   In Dorchy v. Kansas, 264 U.S. 286 (1924), Dorchy sought review of his conviction under § 19 of the Court of Industrial Relations Act of Kansas, which he claimed was an unconstitutional restriction of the right to strike.   Pending the decision of this case, the Supreme Court held in another case that other provisions of the statute (providing for compulsory arbitration of labor disputes) violated the federal Constitution as there applied.   The Court pointed out that it would be unnecessary to consider Dorchy's objections to § 19 if that section were inseparable from the arbitration provisions.   It vacated the state court's judgment and remanded the case for a determination of that question.   The Court said (pp. 289–91):

"* * * Provisions within the legislative power may stand if separable from the bad.   * * * But a provision, inherently unobjectionable, cannot be deemed separable unless it appears both that, standing alone, legal effect can be given to it and that the legislature intended the provision to stand, in case others included in the act and held bad should fall.   * * * Whether § 19 is so interwoven with the system held invalid that the section cannot stand alone, is a question of interpretation and of legislative intent.   * * *

"The task of determining the intention of the state legislature in this respect, like the usual function of interpreting a state statute, rests primarily upon the state court.   Its decision as to the severability of a provision is conclusive upon this Court.   * * * In cases coming from the lower federal courts, such questions of severability, if there is no controlling state decision, must be determined by this Court.   * * * In cases coming from the state courts, this Court, in the absence of a controlling state decision, may, in passing upon the claim under the federal law, decide, also, the question of severability. But it is not obliged to do so.   The situation may be such as to make it appropriate to leave the determination of the question to the state court.   We think that course should be followed in this case."

(5) *Separability of Federal Statutes.*   Separability of a federal statute is, of course, an issue for the Supreme Court.   In applying the Yazoo approach to a *federal* statute and declining to consider the statute's constitutionality as applied to hypothetical facts, does the Supreme Court necessarily presume the statute's separability?

In United States v. Jackson, 390 U.S. 570 (1968), the district court had dismissed a federal kidnapping indictment after holding unconstitutional the statute's death penalty provision.   The Supreme Court agreed that the death penalty could not be imposed, but ruled that the kidnapping charge was nonetheless valid.   Quoting Champlin Refining Co. v. Corporation Comm'n, 286 U.S. 210, 234 (1932), the Court said (p. 585): "Unless it is evident that the legislature would not have enacted those provisions which are within its power, independently of that which is not, the invalid part may be dropped if what is left is fully operative as a law."   Though the statute at issue in Jackson (unlike that in Champlin) had no separability clause, the Court remarked that "the ultimate determination of severability will rarely turn on the presence or absence of such a clause" (p. 585 n. 27).   Accord, Buckley v. Valeo, 424 U.S. 1, 108 (1976) (also quoting Champlin); Regan v. Time, Inc., 468 U.S. 641, 653 (1984)(plurality opinion)(severability "is largely a question of legislative intent, but the presumption is in favor of severability").

Exactly what is the question of legislative intent that the Court asks in severability cases?   In Alaska Airlines, Inc. v. Brock, 480 U.S. 678 (1987), the

Court considered federal statutory provisions requiring airlines, when filling a vacancy, to give preference to certain former airline employees who lost their jobs after airline deregulation. The statute authorized the Secretary of Labor to issue regulations, subject to a legislative veto. Several airlines brought suit, contending that the first-hire provisions were void because inseparable from the legislative veto, which under INS v. Chadha, 462 U.S. 919 (1983), was unconstitutional. The court of appeals, in rejecting that argument, stated that the veto was severable unless "Congress would have preferred no airline employee protection provision at all to the existing provision *sans* the veto provision." 766 F.2d 1550, 1561. The Supreme Court offered a somewhat different formulation: "the unconstitutional provision must be severed unless the statute created in its absence is legislation that Congress would not have enacted" (p. 685). Was the Court right when it claimed (p. 685 n. 7) that its standard and that of the court of appeals are "completely consistent"?[2]

Coates v. City of Cincinnati

402 U.S. 611, 91 S.Ct. 1686, 29 L.Ed.2d 214 (1971).
Appeal from the Supreme Court of Ohio.

■ MR. JUSTICE STEWART delivered the opinion of the Court.

A Cincinnati, Ohio, ordinance makes it a criminal offense for "three or more persons to assemble * * * on any of the sidewalks * * * and there conduct themselves in a manner annoying to persons passing by * * *." The issue before us is whether this ordinance is unconstitutional on its face.

The appellants were convicted of violating the ordinance, and the convictions were ultimately affirmed by * * * the Supreme Court of Ohio * * *. An appeal from that judgment was brought here under 28 U.S.C. § 1257(2), and we noted probable jurisdiction. The record * * * tells us no more than that the appellant Coates was a student involved in a demonstration and the other appellants were pickets involved in a labor dispute. For throughout this litigation it has been the appellants' position that the ordinance on its face violates the First and Fourteenth Amendments of the Constitution.

---

2. In Alaska Airlines, the Supreme Court held that the veto provision was severable, stressing that the statute did not require the Secretary to issue regulations and "did not link specifically the operation of the first-hire provisions to the issuance of regulations" (p. 688). The Court also reviewed the first-hire provisions' legislative history, which, it said, paid far more attention to employee protection than to legislative oversight.

Chadha itself involved a provision of the Immigration and Nationality Act that authorized the Attorney General to suspend a deportation, subject to a legislative veto. The Court refused to invalidate the provision in its entirety: "we need not embark on [the] elusive inquiry" demanded by the Champlin case, since the Act included a severability clause, which "gives rise to a presumption" that the provision should not be declared invalid *in toto* (p. 932). The Court did examine the legislative history of the provision, finding that its purpose—to free Congress of the burdens of private immigration bills— would be undercut if the veto were found not to be severable.

See generally Smith, *From Unnecessary Surgery to Plastic Surgery: A New Approach to the Legislative Veto Severability Cases,* 24 Harv.J.Legis. 397 (1987).

In rejecting this claim and affirming the convictions the Ohio Supreme Court did not give the ordinance any construction at variance with the apparent plain import of its language. The court simply stated:

"The ordinance prohibits, *inter alia,* 'conduct * * * annoying to persons passing by.' The word 'annoying' is a widely used and well understood word; it is not necessary to guess its meaning. 'Annoying' is the present participle of the transitive verb 'annoy' which means to trouble, to vex, to impede, to incommode, to provoke, to harass or to irritate.

"We conclude, as did the Supreme Court of the United States in Cameron v. Johnson, 390 U.S. 611, 616, in which the issue of the vagueness of a statute was presented, that the ordinance 'clearly and precisely delineates its reach in words of common understanding. It is a "precise and narrowly drawn regulatory statute [ordinance] evincing a legislative judgment that certain specific conduct be * * * proscribed." ' "21 Ohio St.2d, at 69, 255 N.E.2d, at 249.

Beyond this, the only construction put upon the ordinance by the state court was its unexplained conclusion that "the standard of conduct which it specifies is not dependent upon each complainant's sensitivity." *Ibid.* But the court did not indicate upon whose sensitivity a violation does depend—the sensitivity of the judge or jury, the sensitivity of the arresting officer, or the sensitivity of a hypothetical reasonable man.

We are thus relegated, at best, to the words of the ordinance itself. If three or more people meet together on a sidewalk or street corner, they must conduct themselves so as not to annoy any police officer or other person who should happen to pass by. In our opinion this ordinance is unconstitutionally vague because it subjects the exercise of the right of assembly to an unascertainable standard, and unconstitutionally broad because it authorizes the punishment of constitutionally protected conduct.

Conduct that annoys some people does not annoy others. Thus, the ordinance is vague not in the sense that it requires a person to conform his conduct to an imprecise but comprehensible normative standard, but rather in the sense that no standard of conduct is specified at all. As a result, "men of common intelligence must necessarily guess at its meaning." Connally v. General Construction Co., 269 U.S. 385, 391.

It is said that the ordinance is broad enough to encompass many types of conduct clearly within the city's constitutional power to prohibit. And so, indeed, it is. The city is free to prevent people from blocking sidewalks, obstructing traffic, littering streets, committing assaults, or engaging in countless other forms of antisocial conduct. It can do so through the enactment and enforcement of ordinances directed with reasonable specificity toward the conduct to be prohibited. It cannot constitutionally do so through the enactment and enforcement of an ordinance whose violation may entirely depend upon whether or not a policeman is annoyed.

But the vice of the ordinance lies not alone in its violation of the due process standard of vagueness. The ordinance also violates the constitutional right of free assembly and association. Our decisions establish that mere public intolerance or animosity cannot be the basis for abridgment of these constitutional freedoms. * * * The First and Fourteenth Amendments do not permit a State to make criminal the exercise of the right of assembly simply because its exercise may be "annoying" to some people. If this were not the rule, the right of the people to gather in public places for social or political purposes would be continually subject to summary suspension through the good-faith enforcement of a prohibition against annoying conduct. And such a prohibition, in addition, contains an obvious invitation to discriminatory enforcement against those whose association together is "annoying" because their ideas, their lifestyle or their physical appearance is resented by the majority of their fellow citizens.

The ordinance before us makes a crime out of what under the Constitution cannot be a crime. It is aimed directly at activity protected by the Constitution. We need not lament that we do not have before us the details of the conduct found to be annoying. It is the ordinance on its face that sets the standard of conduct and warns against transgression. The details of the offense could no more serve to validate this ordinance than could the details of an offense charged under an ordinance suspending unconditionally the right of assembly and free speech.

The judgment is reversed.

■ MR. JUSTICE BLACK.

* * * As my Brother White states in his opinion (with which I substantially agree), this is one of those numerous cases where the law could be held unconstitutional because it prohibits both conduct which the Constitution safeguards and conduct which the State may constitutionally punish. Thus, the First Amendment which forbids the State to abridge freedom of speech, would invalidate this city ordinance if it were used to punish the making of a political speech, even if that speech were to annoy other persons. In contrast, however, the ordinance could properly be applied to prohibit the gathering of persons in the mouths of alleys to annoy passersby by throwing rocks or by some other conduct not at all connected with speech. It is a matter of no little difficulty to determine when a law can be held void on its face and when such summary action is inappropriate. This difficulty has been aggravated in this case, because the record fails to show in what conduct these defendants had engaged to annoy other people. In my view, a record showing the facts surrounding the conviction is essential to adjudicate the important constitutional issues in this case. I would therefore vacate the judgment and remand the case to the court below to give both parties an opportunity to supplement the record so that we may determine whether the conduct actually punished is the kind of conduct which it is within the power of the State to punish.

■ MR. JUSTICE WHITE, with whom THE CHIEF JUSTICE [BURGER] and MR. JUSTICE BLACKMUN join, dissenting.

* * * Any man of average comprehension should know that some kinds of conduct, such as assault or blocking passage on the street, will annoy others and are clearly covered by the "annoying conduct" standard of the ordinance. It would be frivolous to say that these and many other kinds of conduct are not within the foreseeable reach of the law.

It is possible that a whole range of other acts, defined with unconstitutional imprecision, is forbidden by the ordinance. But as a general rule, when a criminal charge is based on conduct constitutionally subject to proscription and clearly forbidden by a statute, it is no defense that the law would be unconstitutionally vague if applied to other behavior. Such a statute is not vague on its face. It may be vague as applied in some circumstances, but ruling on such a challenge obviously requires knowledge of the conduct with which a defendant is charged.

[Justice White then discussed several decisions rejecting vagueness challenges brought by litigants to whose conduct the statutes clearly applied]. This approach is consistent with the host of cases holding that "one to whom application of a statute is constitutional will not be heard to attack the statute on the ground that impliedly it might also be taken as applying to other persons or other situations in which its application might be unconstitutional." United States v. Raines, 362 U.S. 17, 21 (1960), and cases there cited.

Our cases, however, * * * recognize a different approach where the statute at issue purports to regulate or proscribe rights of speech or press protected by the First Amendment. Although a statute may be neither vague, overbroad, nor otherwise invalid as applied to the conduct charged against a particular defendant, he is permitted to raise its vagueness or unconstitutional overbreadth as applied to others. And if the law is found deficient in one of these respects, it may not be applied to him either, until and unless a satisfactory limiting construction is placed on the statute. The statute, in effect, is stricken down on its face. This result is deemed justified since the otherwise continued existence of the statute in unnarrowed form would tend to suppress constitutionally protected rights.

Even accepting the overbreadth doctrine with respect to statutes clearly reaching speech, the Cincinnati ordinance does not purport to bar or regulate speech as such. It prohibits persons from assembling and "conduct[ing]" themselves in a manner annoying to other persons. Even if the assembled defendants in this case were demonstrating and picketing, we have long recognized that picketing is not solely a communicative endeavor and has aspects which the State is entitled to regulate even though there is incidental impact on speech. In Cox v. Louisiana, 379 U.S. 559 (1965), the Court held valid on its face a statute forbidding picketing and parading near a courthouse. This was deemed a valid regulation of conduct rather than pure speech. The conduct reached by the statute was "subject to regulation even though [it was] intertwined with expression and association." *Id.*, at 563. The Court then went on to consider the statute as applied to the facts of record.

In the case before us, I would deal with the Cincinnati ordinance as we would with the ordinary criminal statute. The ordinance clearly reaches certain conduct but may be illegally vague with respect to other conduct. The statute is not infirm on its face and since we have no information from this record as to what conduct was charged against these defendants, we are in no position to judge the statute as applied. That the ordinance may confer wide discretion in a wide range of circumstances is irrelevant when we may be dealing with conduct at its core.

I would therefore affirm the judgment of the Ohio court.

NOTE ON THE SCOPE OF THE ISSUE IN FIRST AMENDMENT CASES

(1) *Distinguishing Overbreadth and Vagueness.* The overbreadth doctrine governs the permissibility of "facial" challenges to statutes brought on the ground that they reach constitutionally protected conduct by parties not before the court. Although Coates involved a challenge based on vagueness as well as an overbreadth issue, the doctrines are distinct. A statute may be overbroad without being vague. For example, a statute making it a crime to use the

words "kill" and "President" in the same sentence is not vague, but is clearly overbroad.   By contrast, a vague statute may or may not be overbroad; the vice of vagueness is that someone contemplating a course of conduct, expressive or otherwise, may be unable to tell what is forbidden.

(2) *Origins of First Amendment Overbreadth Doctrine.*   Conceived as an exception to the Yazoo rule that generally bars facial attacks even on overbroad statutes, the First Amendment overbreadth doctrine is usually traced to Thornhill v. Alabama, 310 U.S. 88 (1940).   An Alabama statute made it a crime for anyone "without a just cause" to "go near to or loiter about" any business for the purpose of influencing others not to deal with or be employed by that business, or to "picket the works or place of business" for the purpose of "hindering, delaying, or interfering with or injuring" the business.   Thornhill was convicted on a charge phrased substantially in the words of the statute.   In reversing the conviction under the First Amendment, the Court said (pp. 96–98):

"* * * The section in question must be judged upon its face. * * *

"* * * Proof of an abuse of power in the particular case has never been deemed a requisite for attack on the constitutionality of a statute purporting to license the dissemination of ideas.   * * * The power of the licensor * * * is pernicious not merely by reason of the censure of particular comments but by reason of the threat to censure comments on matters of public concern.   * * * One who might have had a license for the asking may therefore call into question the whole scheme of licensing when he is prosecuted for failure to procure it.   Lovell v. Griffin, 303 U.S. 444; Hague v. C.I.O., 307 U.S. 496.   A like threat is inherent in a penal statute, like that in question here, which does not aim specifically at evils within the allowable area of State control but, on the contrary, sweeps within its ambit other activities that in ordinary circumstances constitute an exercise of freedom of speech or of the press.   The existence of such a statute, which readily lends itself to harsh and discriminatory enforcement by local prosecuting officials, against particular groups deemed to merit their displeasure, results in a continuous and pervasive restraint on all freedom of discussion that might reasonably be regarded as within its purview. * * * An accused, after arrest and conviction under such a statute, does not have to sustain the burden of demonstrating that the State could not constitutionally have written a different and specific statute covering his activities as disclosed by the charge and the evidence introduced against him.   Schneider v. State, 308 U.S. 147, 155, 162, 163.   Where regulations of the liberty of free discussion are concerned, there are special reasons for observing the rule that it is the statute, and not the accusation or the evidence under it, which prescribes the limits of permissible conduct and warns against transgression."

(3) *The Rationale of the Doctrine.*   As developed and enforced in cases such as Thornhill and Coates, the First Amendment overbreadth doctrine rests on at least two assumptions.   First, as stated in Gooding v. Wilson, 405 U.S. 518, 521 (1972), constitutionally protected speech possesses "transcendent value to all society" and therefore merits special protection.   Second, if overbroad restrictions on speech could not be challenged on their face, "persons whose expression is constitutionally protected may well refrain from exercising their rights for fear of criminal sanctions."[1]   Are these assumptions well-founded?   For a

---

1. A third assumption—reflected with special force in cases subjecting to over- breadth attack statutes regulating the issu- ance of parade permits and similar licenses—

discussion of the importance of speech relative to other fundamental rights or preferred liberties, see Paragraph (10), *infra*. On the question whether constitutionally protected speech is likely to be "chilled" by overbroad statutes, compare Note, *The First Amendment Overbreadth Doctrine*, 83 Harv.L.Rev. 844 (1970), and Note, 69 Colum.L.Rev. 808 (1969), both supporting the premise, with Redish, *The Warren Court, The Burger Court, and the First Amendment Overbreadth Doctrine*, 78 Nw.U.L.Rev. 1031 (1983), questioning it. See also Fallon, *Making Sense of Overbreadth*, 100 Yale L.J. 853, 885–87 (1991), arguing that the degree of chill is likely to vary with the nature of the statute in question. For example, behavior targeted by a prohibition against "opprobrious language" is likely to be too spontaneous and emotional to be chilled, whereas a statute barring picketing affects conduct that is likely to be planned in advance by groups with access to legal advice concerning potentially applicable statutes.

Consider, too, how the likelihood of "chill" is affected by the prevailing doctrine concerning "narrowing constructions". The meaning of a state statute is a question of state law, of which state courts are authoritative expositors. As a result, the overbreadth doctrine applies to statutes as construed by state courts, not as written. See, *e.g.,* Osborne v. Ohio, 495 U.S. 103, 119–20 (1990). (Federal statutes may similarly be narrowed.) Indeed, the Supreme Court has held that a state court may provide a narrowing construction in the course of applying and enforcing a statute that, if read literally, would be unconstitutionally overbroad. See *id.* (upholding a state court's authority to provide a narrowing construction of a criminal statute in an appeal from a criminal conviction); Cox v. New Hampshire, 312 U.S. 569 (1941).[2]

is that statutes failing to establish clear standards are likely to be enforced in invidiously discriminatory ways. See, *e.g.,* City of Lakewood v. Plain Dealer Pub. Co., 486 U.S. 750, 757–69 (1988); Board of Airport Comm'rs v. Jews for Jesus, 482 U.S. 569, 576 (1987).

2. Does permitting a narrowing construction to occur for the first time in the course of a criminal prosecution deprive the defendant of fair warning? Or does the defendant have ample warning that the state wishes to forbid conduct within the terms of the statute as written if it is constitutionally entitled to do so? See Fallon, *supra*, at 878–79.

Cf. Shuttlesworth v. Birmingham, 394 U.S. 147 (1969), in which the Supreme Court invalidated a conviction for parading without a permit. Under applicable doctrine, a defendant who has failed to seek a permit may defend on the ground that a statute requiring parade permits fails to limit official discretion adequately and is therefore constitutionally overbroad. In Shuttlesworth, the Supreme Court of Alabama upheld a conviction by construing a parade ordinance that appeared overbroad on its face to allow the denial of permits only on narrow grounds. The Supreme Court reversed (pp. 155–58):

"* * * We may assume that * * * the ordinance as now authoritatively construed would pass constitutional muster. It does not follow, however, that the severely narrowing construction put upon the ordinance by the Alabama Supreme Court in November of 1967 necessarily serves to restore constitutional validity to a conviction that occurred in 1963 under the ordinance as it was written. * * *

"* * * In April of 1963 * * * [i]t would have taken extraordinary clairvoyance for anyone to perceive that [the ordinance] meant what the Supreme Court of Alabama was destined to find that it meant more than four years later; and, with First Amendment rights hanging in the balance, we would hesitate long before assuming that either the members of the Commission or the petitioner possessed any such clairvoyance at the time of the Good Friday march.

"But we need not deal in assumptions. * * * [The Court reviewed the events preceding the march, including two attempts to secure a permit, and concluded]:

"These 'surrounding relevant circumstances' make it indisputably clear, we think, that in April of 1963—at least with respect to this petitioner and his organization—the city

Does this approach accord with the *purposes* of the overbreadth doctrine? Isn't a statute that is overbroad on its face (prior to a narrowing judicial construction) likely to chill protected speech and conduct? One possible answer would be that (by the time an overbreadth challenge is presented as a defense against a criminal or civil action) any such chill necessarily occurred in the past; a narrowing construction should help to avert chill in the future; and a forward-looking remedy is sufficient. But if a forward-looking remedy will suffice, why shouldn't the Supreme Court, in cases such as Coates and Thornhill, remand to the state court (rather than reversing the conviction) to permit the state court to furnish a narrowing construction in light of a more accurate understanding of the First Amendment? *Cf.* Time, Inc. v. Hill, 385 U.S. 374 (1967)(vacating a state court judgment as founded on a rule of law that was invalid under the First Amendment, but remanding the case for further action in which a constitutionally valid rule might be applied).

Is it an aim of the overbreadth doctrine to create incentives for state legislatures to write narrow statutes and for state courts to be alert to develop narrowing constructions at the earliest opportunity? See Fallon, *supra,* at 885–89. Is this a legitimate aim if it pressures state legislatures to draft statutes that are less sweeping, and state courts to construe them more narrowly, than the Constitution requires?

The possibility that a state statute might be subject to a narrowing construction can raise formidable difficulties for lower federal courts in suits to enjoin enforcement of state statutes on grounds of overbreadth. An overbreadth attack should not succeed if the statute is "readily subject to a narrowing construction by the state courts." Erznoznik v. City of Jacksonville, 422 U.S. 205, 216 (1975). But how can a federal court know what construction a state court would adopt? In federal court actions seeking equitable relief from the enforcement of state laws alleged to be overbroad under the First Amendment, should the federal court abstain, or certify the question of state law to a state court, in order to obtain that court's authoritative construction of the statute? See Virginia v. American Booksellers Ass'n, Inc., 484 U.S. 383 (1988)(certifying state law questions in such an action). See generally Chap. X, Sec. 2(B), *infra*.

(4) *The Substantiality Requirement.* In Broadrick v. Oklahoma, 413 U.S. 601 (1973), the Supreme Court established that "where conduct and not merely speech is involved, * * * the overbreadth of a statute must be not only real, but substantial as well, judged in relation to the statute's plainly legitimate sweep", for a facial challenge to prevail (p. 615). Employing this standard, Justice White's opinion for the Court rejected a facial attack on Oklahoma's "Little Hatch Act," restricting political activities by state employees.

In a dissenting opinion joined by Justices Marshall and Stewart, Justice Brennan complained that the decision made no attempt to distinguish Coates, which had held a statute overbroad without reference to any substantiality requirement, and thus implicitly overruled it on this point (p. 632). Justice Brennan conceded that "[w]e have never held that a statute should be held invalid on its face merely because it is possible to conceive of a single impermissible application, and in that sense a requirement of substantial

authorities thought the ordinance meant exactly what it said. The petitioner was clearly given to understand that under no circumstances would he and his group be permitted to demonstrate in Birmingham, not that a demonstration would be approved if a time and place were selected that would minimize traffic problems. * * *"

overbreadth is already implicit in the doctrine'' (p. 630). He objected, however, to the apparent stringency of the Court's conception of substantiality.

In New York v. Ferber, 458 U.S. 747 (1982), the Court affirmed that the requirement of "substantial" overbreadth "is sound and should be applied in the present context involving the harmful employment of children to make sexually explicit materials for distribution" (p. 771). Accordingly, the Court rejected the overbreadth challenge of a defendant convicted under a statute barring the distribution of materials depicting sexual performances by children under 16, ruling that any overbreadth was not substantial. Brockett v. Spokane Arcades, Inc., 472 U.S. 491, 503 n. 12 (1985), expressly stated, in dictum, that Ferber had rejected the proposition that "the Broadrick substantial overbreadth requirement is inapplicable where pure speech rather than conduct is at issue."

Conceived in the abstract, the substantiality requirement is surely sound. As Justice Brennan conceded in Broadrick, statutes should not be invalidated based on a few aberrant, hypothetical applications. But does it make sense to measure substantial overbreadth, as the Court has sometimes suggested, as a kind of geometric proportion between constitutional and unconstitutional applications? Is this a manageable inquiry? Would it be preferable for courts frankly to weigh on a relatively ad hoc basis (i) the state's substantive interest in being able to employ a particular legal standard as opposed to some other, less restrictive substitute, against (ii) the First Amendment interest in encouraging narrow statutes and avoiding chill? See Alexander, *Is There an Overbreadth Doctrine*, 22 San Diego L.Rev. 541, 553–54 (1985). See also Redish, *supra* (advocating a balancing analysis). Compare Gunther, *Reflections on Robel,* 20 Stan.L.Rev. 1140, 1147–48 (1968), criticizing overbreadth decisions for suggesting, when striking down overbroad laws, that less sweeping enactments would be valid without providing any guidance concerning how to draft them.

(5) *Challenges by Protected Speakers.* Litigants always have standing to argue that a statute is unconstitutional as applied to their own speech or conduct. Should someone whose speech or conduct is constitutionally privileged be disabled from arguing that a statute is facially overbroad and therefore generally unenforceable?

In Brockett v. Spokane Arcades, Inc., 472 U.S. 491 (1985), only four days after the effective date of a Washington statute regulating obscenity, purveyors of sexually oriented books and movies brought a federal court challenge. The court of appeals ruled that the statute extended to protected as well as unprotected speech, and, finding that it "did not lend itself to a saving construction", declared it to be unconstitutional *in toto*. (In the court of appeals' view, the statute's vice was that it defined "prurient" to include "that which incites * * * lust" and thereby reached material that merely stimulated normal sexual responses.) The Supreme Court reversed. Though Justice O'Connor, joined by Chief Justice Burger and Justice Rehnquist, argued for abstention to permit the state courts to construe the new statute, the Court, per Justice White, rejected that course. Instead, the Court ruled that the court of appeals should have invalidated the statute only insofar as it reached protected expression. Acknowledging that the Court had invalidated statutes as facially overbroad in cases brought by "individual[s] whose own speech or expressive conduct may validly be prohibited" (p. 503), Justice White said that a different approach was called for "where the parties challenging the statute are those who desire to engage in protected speech that the overbroad statute purports to punish, or who seek to publish both protected and unprotected material. There is then no want of a proper party to challenge the statute, no concern that an attack on the statute will be unduly delayed or protected speech discouraged. The statute may forthwith be declared invalid to the extent it reaches too far, but otherwise left intact" (p. 504).

Total invalidation would be proper, the Court said, only if the state legislature had passed an inseverable statute or would not have passed the statute had its partial invalidity been recognized. Under Washington law, however, there was a presumption of severability, and the statute included a severability clause.

Should Brockett be taken to announce the apparently ironic conclusion that a litigant whose speech is constitutionally unprotected enjoys advantages over a litigant whose speech is constitutionally privileged in seeking to bar a statute from being enforced at all?[3] Would such a disparity be defensible on the ground that if a narrowing construction is the preferable result, courts should seize the opportunity in suits by protected challengers to hold statutes "invalid [only] to the extent that [they] reach[] too far"? Suppose that it is desirable to encourage narrowing constructions in at least some cases. Would that proposition require, in a case like Coates, that the Court determine whether the defendant's actual conduct was protected, so that it could in turn determine whether, in reversing his conviction, it should hold the ordinance unconstitutional on its face or only as applied?

Since the decision in the Brockett case, the Court has on a few occasions considered a facial overbreadth challenge without ruling on a challenge to the statute as applied. *E.g.*, Board of Airport Com'rs v. Jews for Jesus, Inc., 482 U.S. 569, 573–74 (1987). But in Board of Trustees, State Univ. of N.Y. v. Fox, 492 U.S. 469, 484–85 (1989), the Court said that its "usual" practice was to consider the as-applied challenge first, and noted that "the overbreadth question is ordinarily more difficult to resolve * * * since it * * * requires consideration of many more applications than those immediately before the Court." See also Renne v. Geary, 501 U.S. 312, 323–24 (1991)(dicta to the same effect).

(6) *Categorical Exceptions.* In Parker v. Levy, 417 U.S. 733 (1974), the Court rejected an overbreadth attack on general articles of the Uniform Code of Military Justice. In the Court's view, the reasons "dictating a different application of First Amendment principles in the military context" make less forceful the policies that support overbreadth attacks (p. 760).

---

3. Compare Secretary of State of Maryland v. Joseph H. Munson Co., Inc., 467 U.S. 947 (1984), a state court action by a fundraiser challenging the constitutionality of a state law that, subject to waiver provisions, prohibited charitable organizations from paying more than 25% of the proceeds of fundraising activities as expenses therefor. The Court of Appeals of Maryland struck down the statute on its face as overbroad, and the Supreme Court affirmed, 5–4. The majority cited 10 cases that it described as permitting facial rather than partial invalidation at the behest of litigants claiming that their own conduct was protected, which it explained on the ground that "any application of the legislation 'would create an unacceptable risk of the suppression of ideas' " (p. 965 n. 13, quoting City Council of Los Angeles v. Taxpayers for Vincent, 466 U.S. 789, 797 (1984)).

Justice Rehnquist and three other dissenters doubted "as a matter of original inquiry * * * whether an overbreadth challenge should ever be allowed" given the availability of declaratory and preliminary injunctive relief (p. 977). He viewed the statute under attack as constitutional in its "core" application to regulate the fees charged charities by outside fundraisers, and therefore not substantially overbroad.

In Bates v. State Bar of Arizona, 433 U.S. 350 (1977), in ruling that a state could not ban all advertising by attorneys and that the particular advertisement at issue was protected, the Court suggested that the overbreadth doctrine did not apply to commercial speech. "Since advertising is linked to commercial well-being, it seems unlikely that such speech is particularly susceptible to being crushed by overbroad regulation. * * * Moreover, concerns for uncertainty * * * are reduced; the advertiser seeks to disseminate information about a product or service that he provides, and presumably he can determine more readily than others whether his speech is truthful and protected" (p. 381). See also Waters v. Churchill, 114 S.Ct. 1878, 1885 (1994); Village of Hoffman Estates v. Flipside, Hoffman Estates, Inc., 455 U.S. 489, 496–97 (1982).

Do cases such as these suggest that application of the overbreadth doctrine necessarily requires a balancing of the value of the speech likely to be chilled against the state's interest in being able employ a broad regulatory standard? See the sources cited in Paragraph (3), *supra*.

(7) *Characterizations of Overbreadth Doctrine.* Overbreadth doctrine is almost uniformly portrayed as an exception to the rule against third party standing. This formulation, which assimilates overbreadth to the public rights model, raises an important issue of judicial power. By what authority does a court provide relief to a party whose own speech or expressive conduct is not constitutionally protected and falls within the terms of a state-enacted prohibition?

Consider the argument in Monaghan, *Overbreadth,* 1981 Sup.Ct.Rev. 1, that there is neither justification nor need for a special "standing" doctrine in First Amendment overbreadth cases. Professor Monaghan argues that litigants are always permitted to attack as constitutionally invalid the rule of law under which they are being sanctioned, whether or not the First Amendment is implicated, and whether or not their conduct is itself constitutionally protected. In his view, First Amendment overbreadth doctrine merely applies the requirement of a constitutionally valid rule in light of the substantive demands of the First Amendment. Under Yazoo, statutes are ordinarily assumed to be separable, and whatever remains of statutes after their invalid applications are severed will qualify as a constitutionally valid rule. According to Monaghan, the First Amendment mandates a substantive exception to the Yazoo doctrine. When parties claim First Amendment rights, a court must specifically articulate the constitutionally valid rule of law under which a defendant may be subject to sanctions; if an enforcement court fails to do so, it must be presumed that no constitutionally valid rule exists.

Compare Fallon, Paragraph (3), *supra,* at 867–77, asserting that First Amendment overbreadth doctrine has two elements: (i) a "rule-of-law" component, analogous to Monaghan's "valid rule" requirement, and (ii) a judge-made, prophylactic component aimed at averting chill and encouraging legislatures to draft statutes narrowly in the shadow of the First Amendment.[4] According to

---

4. Professor Fallon argues that Monaghan's theory cannot account for accepted judicial practice, especially in suits for declaratory and injunctive relief (pp. 871–75). In these cases, Fallon argues, the Supreme Court has deployed the overbreadth doctrine as a sword with which to protect the public against enforcement of overbroad statutes, rather than as a shield to protect individual defendants against the application of invalid rules in their particular cases. Fallon also argues that Professor Monaghan "has a far more forgiving view of what should count as an adequate narrowing construction than does the Supreme Court" and that his theory is unable "to explain why, if the overbreadth

Fallon, judicial discretion to create this "breathing space" for First Amendment freedoms is rooted in the First Amendment, but the Constitution does not directly dictate any particular set of rules for overbreadth cases.

In Massachusetts v. Oakes, 491 U.S. 576 (1989), the Massachusetts Supreme Court reversed a conviction under a statute making it a crime to photograph a minor "in a state of nudity" on the ground that the statute was unconstitutionally overbroad. Following this decision, the Massachusetts legislature amended the statute to include a "lascivious intent" requirement, but the state's attorney general continued to seek Supreme Court reversal of the Massachusetts court's overbreadth ruling. Writing for a plurality of four,[5] Justice O'Connor found that the overbreadth doctrine did not apply to statutes that have been amended or repealed. The purpose of the doctrine, according to the plurality, was to avert chill. Because chill was no longer a concern, the defendant was not entitled to an overbreadth defense. Did the Oakes plurality overlook the defendant's right, as framed by Professor Monaghan, not to be punished except pursuant to a constitutionally valid rule of law? What if the Massachusetts court had deemed the original statute constitutionally overbroad because it was not, as a matter of state law, susceptible of a narrowing construction?

(8) *The Strength of Overbreadth Medicine.* Both the Supreme Court and scholarly commentators have regularly characterized First Amendment overbreadth doctrine as "strong medicine" that ought to be applied sparingly. See, *e.g., Osborne v. Ohio,* 495 U.S. 103, 122 (1990); Redish, *supra,* at 1040 (both quoting *Broadrick v. Oklahoma,* 413 U.S. 601, 613 (1973)). Note, however, that a federal court has no authority to excise a law from a state's statute book. Moreover, because state courts and lower federal courts stand in a coordinate rather than a hierarchical relationship, a lower federal court's overbreadth determination generally will have binding effect only on the parties to the case. In an action against a non-party brought in state court, a lower federal court's overbreadth judgment generally would have only precedential effect. Even after the Supreme Court has held a statute unconstitutionally overbroad, state authorities remain free to seek narrowing constructions in state court actions for declaratory judgments. See, *e.g., Younger v. Harris,* 401 U.S. 37, 50–51 (1971); *Dombrowski v. Pfister,* 380 U.S. 479, 491–92 (1965). If an adequately narrow construction is obtained, the state can proceed with criminal prosecutions, possibly based on conduct occurring prior to the time that the narrowing construction was obtained. See *Dombrowski,* 380 U.S. at 491 n.7, quoted in *Osborne,* 495 U.S. at 115: "Our cases indicate that once an acceptable limiting construction is obtained, it may be applied to conduct occurring prior to the construction * * * provided such application affords fair warning to the defendants."

doctrine's sole concern is with individual rights and not with prophylactic protection of First Amendment values, a version of the 'Yazoo presumption' [of separability] should not apply even in First Amendment cases" (pp. 872–73).

5. Chief Justice Rehnquist, Justice White, and Justice Kennedy joined her opinion. Justice Scalia, writing on this point for four other Justices, concluded that the overbreadth doctrine remained applicable. According to him, if the statute was "overbroad and therefore invalid," the Court could not deny relief on grounds of policy. Joined on this point only by Justice Blackmun, however, Justice Scalia concluded that the statute was not "substantially" overbroad, and therefore concurred in the judgment vacating the state court's overbreadth ruling. Justices Brennan, Marshall, and Stevens argued in dissent that the statute was substantially overbroad and therefore unenforceable.

When all of these factors are taken into account, is it possible that the Supreme Court has substantially overestimated the strength of the overbreadth medicine? However this question is answered, it is clear that the protective effect of federal courts' overbreadth determinations may depend on principles of claim and issue preclusion. See Chap. XII, Sec. 1, *infra;* Shapiro, *State Courts and Federal Declaratory Judgments,* 74 Nw.L.Rev. 759 (1979). But should "ordinary" principles be applied in every case, or should preclusion law reflect the policies of First Amendment overbreadth doctrine, especially its aim of averting "chill" and encouraging legislatures not to trench carelessly on First Amendment interests? See Fallon, *supra,* arguing that the strength of the "medicinal" effects of federal overbreadth determinations should be viewed as largely a matter for federal judicial lawmaking under what he terms the "prophylactic" component of overbreadth doctrine.

(9) *Overbroad Federal Statutes.* If a litigant challenges a federal statute as overbroad, a federal court can of course give a narrowing construction, and indeed should presumably apply the canon of statutory construction that "where an otherwise acceptable construction of a statute will raise serious constitutional problems, * * * [the court should] construe the statute to avoid such problems unless such construction is plainly contrary to the intent of Congress." Edward J. DeBartolo Corp. v. Florida Gulf Coast Bldg. & Constr. Trades Council, 485 U.S. 568, 575 (1988). If a statute cannot be saved by construction, the question arises whether the invalid portions or applications can be severed. See Dorf, *Facial Challenges to State and Federal Statutes,* 46 Stan. L. Rev. 235, 288–93 (1994).[6]

In United States v. Thirty–Seven (37) Photographs, 402 U.S. 363 (1971), the Court considered the validity of a *federal* law prohibiting the importation of obscene material and providing for its seizure by customs officials. In a federal civil enforcement proceeding to forfeit allegedly obscene photographs, the owner counterclaimed for injunctive relief, alleging that the law was unconstitutional on its face and as applied. It was stipulated that some or all of the photographs were intended for use in a commercially distributed book. A three-judge district court held the statute unconstitutional, in part on the ground that it was overbroad as applied to the importation of materials for private use. A majority of the Court rejected this approach. Justice White's plurality opinion, joined by Chief Justice Burger and Justices Brennan and Blackmun, took the position that the statute was valid even as applied to private use, but specifically stated that had the district court's contrary view been correct, the proper approach would have been to "construe [the law] narrowly and hold it valid in its application to [the owner]" (p. 375 n. 3). Justice Harlan, concurring separately, stated (p. 378) that the commercial importer "lacked standing to raise the overbreadth claim." Justice Stewart concurred in the judgment, concluding that the statute was valid as applied to

---

6. Compare United States v. National Treasury Employees Union, 115 S.Ct. 1003 (1995), upholding an injunction granting relief to the plaintiff employees from a statutory ban on the collection of honoraria for speaking and writing, but limiting relief to the parties before the Court, since "the Government conceivably might advance a different justification for an honorarium ban limit-ed to more senior officials, thus presenting a different constitutional question" (p. 1019). The Court also declined to "redraft the statute to limit its coverage to cases involving an undesirable nexus between the speaker's official duties and either the subject matter of the speaker's expression or the identity of the payor" (*id.*).

the owner, while implying that it could not validly extend to importation for private use. Justices Black, Douglas, and Marshall dissented.[7]

The three-judge district court had also held that the statutory procedures for seizing obscene material were deficient because they did not contain time limits within which judicial review of any seizure must occur, as required by such cases as Freedman v. Maryland, 380 U.S. 51 (1965), and Teitel Film Corp. v. Cusack, 390 U.S. 139, 141 (1968). However, the Court found that "it is possible to construe the [law] to bring it in harmony with constitutional requirements," and distinguished its refusal to do so in Freedman and Teitel because the statutes there "were enacted pursuant to state rather than federal authority," and "we lack jurisdiction authoritatively to construe state legislation" (pp. 368–69). The Court held that its limiting construction applied in the present case.[8]

(10) *Overbreadth Beyond the First Amendment.* Are the considerations supporting First Amendment overbreadth doctrine any less forceful when applied to statutes whose overbreadth violates other fundamental rights? Several commentators have suggested not. See, *e.g.,* Monaghan, Paragraph (7), *supra,* at 37–38 (asserting that overbreadth analysis is appropriate "wherever the Supreme Court is serious about judicial review—wherever, that is, the minimum rationality standard does not prevail—* * * [and the doctrine is] concerned with the matter of least restrictive alternatives"); Dorf, Paragraph (9), *supra,* at 269 (arguing that overbreadth analysis should apply to all fundamental rights to engage in primary conduct that might be chilled by an overbroad statute).

In United States v. Salerno, 481 U.S. 739, 745 (1987), the Supreme Court stated that it had "not recognized an 'overbreadth' doctrine outside the limited context of the First Amendment." See also Schall v. Martin, 467 U.S. 253, 268 n.18 (1984). The pattern of decisions, however, may be more complex. "Virtually all of the abortion cases reaching the Supreme Court since Roe v. Wade * * * have involved facial attacks on state statutes, and the Court, whether accepting or rejecting the challenges on the merits, has typically accepted this framing of the question presented." Fallon, Paragraph (3), *supra,* at 859 n. 29. See, *e.g.,* Ohio v. Akron Ctr. for Reprod. Health, 497 U.S. 502 (1990); Hodgson v. Minnesota, 497 U.S. 417 (1990); Webster v. Reproductive Health Services., 492 U.S. 490 (1989). But see H.L. v. Matheson, 450 U.S. 398 (1981)(holding that the plaintiff, an unmarried 15–year old girl living with and dependent on her parents, could not present a facial challenge to a statute requiring parental notification).[9]

Compare Aptheker v. Secretary of State, 378 U.S. 500 (1964), involving a challenge to § 6 of the Subversive Activities Control Act of 1950. This section prohibited the use of a passport by any person who belonged to an organization that the person knew to be required to register under the Act. Two leaders of

---

7. In United States v. 12 200–Foot Reels, 413 U.S. 123 (1973), the Court later upheld that statute's constitutionality as applied to the importation of obscene material exclusively for private use.

8. For other decisions upholding federal statutes after narrowing constructions, see, *e.g.,* Hamling v. United States, 418 U.S. 87,

114–15 (1974); Buckley v. Valeo, 424 U.S. 1, 44, 76–80 (1976).

9. See also Bowers v. Hardwick, 478 U.S. 186 (1986), in which the Court upheld a state anti-sodomy statute as applied to homosexual sodomy, but refused to consider its constitutionality as applied, for example, to the conduct of a married couple.

the Communist Party brought suit to enjoin the State Department's efforts to revoke their passports. The Supreme Court held the statute "unconstitutional on its face" because it "too broadly and indiscriminately restricts the right to travel and thereby abridges the liberty guaranteed by the Fifth Amendment" (p. 505). Though it did not deny that a statutory ban on passport use by leaders of the Party might be valid, the Court refused to uphold the statute as applied to the plaintiffs. It suggested that an effort to supply a limiting construction would constitute "judicial[ ]rewriting" of the statute and would "inject an element of vagueness into the statute's scope and application. * * * [S]ince freedom of travel is a constitutional liberty closely related to rights of free speech and association, we believe that appellants in this case should not be required to assume the burden of demonstrating that Congress could not have written a statute constitutionally prohibiting their travel" (pp. 515–17). Should Aptheker be regarded as a First Amendment case?[10]

(11) *Vagueness.* "Vagueness doctrine, in its most familiar form, holds that criminal prohibitions, at least, may not be enforced when they are so unclear that people of ordinary intelligence would need to guess at whether their conduct was or was not forbidden. Although applicable in First Amendment cases, this minimal demand for fair notice does not stem from the First Amendment, and is not peculiar to free speech jurisprudence; the requirement of fair, individual warning stems from the Due Process Clause. There is, however, a separate, additional vagueness doctrine that applies in First Amendment cases and in other cases involving rights protected by strict scrutiny; as does overbreadth doctrine, First Amendment vagueness doctrine allows courts to declare statutes facially invalid, not merely unconstitutional as applied * * *. The purpose of this exception to 'ordinary' or non-First Amendment vagueness doctrine, as with the parallel 'ordinary' and 'First Amendment' overbreadth doctrines, is to avoid the chilling of constitutionally protected expression * * *." Fallon, Paragraph (3), *supra,* at 903–04 (footnotes omitted).

How should a court respond when First Amendment vagueness and overbreadth challenges are made against a single statute? Consider the view of Justice Marshall in Village of Hoffman Estates v. Flipside, Hoffman Estates, Inc., 455 U.S. 489, 494–95 (1982): "In a facial challenge to the overbreadth and vagueness of a law, a court's first task is to determine whether the enactment reaches a substantial amount of constitutionally protected conduct. If it does not, then the overbreadth challenge must fail. The court should then examine the facial vagueness challenge, and assuming the enactment implicates no constitutionally protected conduct, should uphold the challenge only if the enactment is impermissibly vague in all of its applications. A plaintiff who engages in some conduct that is clearly proscribed cannot complain of the vagueness of the law as applied to the conduct of others." See also Parker v. Levy, Paragraph (6), *supra,* 417 U.S. at 756.

This formulation implies that parties may not challenge a statute on vagueness grounds unless it is not only vague as to their conduct, but vague in all its applications. Is Coates consistent with this approach?

10. In any event, wouldn't a statute with an unconstitutional purpose be invalid in all its applications and therefore satisfy even the restrictive Salerno test for facial invalidation?

See also Dorf, *supra,* at 279–81 (asserting that "[i]in a variety of contexts, the Court has held that statutes with an unconstitutional purpose may be found facially invalid," but citing only cases under the First Amendment's Establishment Clause).

Compare Kolender v. Lawson, 461 U.S. 352 (1983), in which the majority characterized vagueness as "logically related and similar" to overbreadth and thus permitted a party to attack a statute, which clearly applied to his own conduct, on the ground that it would be impermissibly vague as applied to someone else (p. 359 n.8). The plaintiff in Kolender brought a facial attack against a California statute prohibiting loitering. The lower federal courts enjoined the law on the grounds that it was vague and that it violated the Fourth Amendment, and the Supreme Court affirmed on vagueness grounds. In dissent, Justice White, joined by Justice Rehnquist, argued that the statute did not implicate First Amendment concerns, and that because the statute was not vague in all of its possible applications, the Court's facial invalidation was inconsistent with the reasoning of cases like Hoffman Estates.[11] The majority, per O'Connor, J., responded (p. 359 n. 8) that Justice White's description of the precedents was inaccurate because (i) the Court permits facial challenges to laws that reach "a substantial amount of constitutionally protected conduct," quoting Hoffman Estates, and (ii) the standard of certainty is higher for criminal statutes. The Court further asserted that "[n]o authority cited by the dissent supports its argument about facial challenges in the arbitrary enforcement context."

Even in the First Amendment context, it seems indisputable that the Supreme Court has sent a mixed message about whether and when parties may challenge a statute that clearly applies to their conduct on the ground that the statute would be vague as applied to others. Compare Gooding v. Wilson, 405 U.S. 518, 521 (1972)(suggesting an affirmative answer), with Broadrick v. Oklahoma, 413 U.S. 601, 608 (1973)(suggesting a negative answer). If the Court was correct in Kolender that overbreadth and vagueness are indeed related doctrines, shouldn't the rules governing First Amendment overbreadth challenges, as discussed in Paragraphs (4)-(6), *supra*, apply equally to First Amendment vagueness cases?

On vagueness, see generally *Symposium: Void for Vagueness*, 82 Cal. L.Rev. 487 (1994); Note, *The Void–for–Vagueness Doctrine in the Supreme Court*, 109 U.Pa.L.Rev. 67 (1960).

SECTION 4. MOOTNESS

DeFunis v. Odegaard

416 U.S. 312, 94 S.Ct. 1704, 40 L.Ed.2d 164 (1974).
Certiorari to the Supreme Court of Washington.

■ PER CURIAM.

In 1971 the petitioner Marco DeFunis, Jr., applied for admission as a first-year student at the University of Washington Law School, a state-operated institution. The size of the incoming first-year class was to be limited to 150 persons, and the Law School received some 1,600 applications for these 150 places.

---

11. Justice White added that "if the statute on its face violates the Fourth or Fifth Amendment—and I express no views about that question—the Court would be justified in striking it down" (p. 374).

DeFunis was eventually notified that he had been denied admission. He thereupon commenced this suit in a Washington trial court, contending that the procedures and criteria employed by the Law School Admissions Committee invidiously discriminated against him on account of his race in violation of the Equal Protection Clause of the Fourteenth Amendment to the United States Constitution.

DeFunis brought the suit on behalf of himself alone, and not as the representative of any class, against the various respondents, who are officers, faculty members, and members of the Board of Regents of the University of Washington. He asked the trial court to issue a mandatory injunction commanding the respondents to admit him as a member of the first-year class entering in September 1971, on the ground that the Law School admissions policy had resulted in the unconstitutional denial of his application for admission. The trial court agreed with his claim and granted the requested relief. DeFunis was, accordingly, admitted to the Law School and began his legal studies there in the fall of 1971. On appeal, the Washington Supreme Court reversed the judgment of the trial court and held that the Law School admissions policy did not violate the Constitution. By this time DeFunis was in his second year at the Law School.

He then petitioned this Court for a writ of certiorari, and Mr. Justice Douglas, as Circuit Justice, stayed the judgment of the Washington Supreme Court pending the "final disposition of the case by this Court." By virtue of this stay, DeFunis has remained in law school, and was in the first term of his third and final year when this Court first considered his certiorari petition in the fall of 1973. Because of our concern that DeFunis' third-year standing in the Law School might have rendered this case moot, we requested the parties to brief the question of mootness before we acted on the petition. In response, both sides contended that the case was not moot. The respondents indicated that, if the decision of the Washington Supreme Court were permitted to stand, the petitioner could complete the term for which he was then enrolled but would have to apply to the faculty for permission to continue in the school before he could register for another term.[2]

We granted the petition for certiorari on November 19, 1973. The case was in due course orally argued on February 26, 1974.

In response to questions raised from the bench during the oral argument, counsel for the petitioner has informed the Court that DeFunis has now registered "for his final quarter in law school." Counsel for the respondents have made clear that the Law School will not in any way seek to abrogate this registration.[3] In light of DeFunis' recent registration for the last quarter of his final law school year, and the Law School's assurance that his registration is fully effective, the insistent question again arises whether this case is not moot, and to that question we now turn.

---

2. By contrast, in their response to the petition for certiorari, the respondents had stated that DeFunis "will complete his third year [of law school] and be awarded his J.D. degree at the end of the 1973–74 academic year regardless of the outcome of this appeal."

3. In their memorandum on the question of mootness, counsel for the respondents

unequivocally stated: "If Mr. DeFunis registers for the spring quarter under the existing order of this court during the registration period from February 20, 1974, to March 1, 1974, that registration would not be canceled unilaterally by the university regardless of the outcome of this litigation."

The starting point for analysis is the familiar proposition that "federal courts are without power to decide questions that cannot affect the rights of litigants in the case before them." North Carolina v. Rice, 404 U.S. 244, 246 (1971). The inability of the federal judiciary "to review moot cases derives from the requirement of Art. III of the Constitution under which the exercise of judicial power depends upon the existence of a case or controversy." Liner v. Jafco, Inc., 375 U.S. 301, 306 n. 3 (1964). Although as a matter of Washington state law it appears that this case would be saved from mootness by "the great public interest in the continuing issues raised by this appeal," the fact remains that under Art. III "[e]ven in cases arising in the state courts, the question of mootness is a federal one which a federal court must resolve before it assumes jurisdiction." North Carolina v. Rice, *supra,* at 246.

The respondents have represented that, without regard to the ultimate resolution of the issues in this case, DeFunis will remain a student in the Law School for the duration of any term in which he has already enrolled. Since he has now registered for his final term, it is evident that he will be given an opportunity to complete all academic and other requirements for graduation, and, if he does so, will receive his diploma regardless of any decision this Court might reach on the merits of this case. In short, all parties agree that DeFunis is now entitled to complete his legal studies at the University of Washington and to receive his degree from that institution. A determination by this Court of the legal issues tendered by the parties is no longer necessary to compel that result, and could not serve to prevent it. DeFunis did not cast his suit as a class action, and the only remedy he requested was an injunction commanding his admission to the Law School. He was not only accorded that remedy, but he now has also been irrevocably admitted to the final term of the final year of the Law School course. The controversy between the parties has thus clearly ceased to be "definite and concrete" and no longer "touch[es] the legal relations of parties having adverse legal interests." Aetna Life Ins. Co. v. Haworth, 300 U.S. 227, 240–241 (1937).

It matters not that these circumstances partially stem from a policy decision on the part of the respondent Law School authorities. The respondents, through their counsel, the Attorney General of the State, have professionally represented that in no event will the status of DeFunis now be affected by any view this Court might express on the merits of this controversy. And it has been the settled practice of the Court, in contexts no less significant, fully to accept representations such as these as parameters for decision. See Gerende v. Election Board, 341 U.S. 56 (1951) * * *.

There is a line of decisions in this Court standing for the proposition that the "voluntary cessation of allegedly illegal conduct does not deprive the tribunal of power to hear and determine the case, *i.e.,* does not make the case moot." United States v. W.T. Grant Co., 345 U.S. 629, 632 (1953); United States v. Trans–Missouri Freight Assn., 166 U.S. 290, 308–310 (1897) * * *. These decisions and the doctrine they reflect would be quite relevant if the question of mootness here had arisen by reason of a unilateral change in the *admissions procedures* of the Law School. For it was the admissions procedures that were the target of this litigation, and a voluntary cessation of the admissions practices complained of could make this case moot only if it could be said with assurance "that 'there is no reasonable expectation that the wrong will be repeated.'" United States v. W.T. Grant Co., *supra,* at 633. Otherwise, "[t]he defendant is free to return to his old ways," *id.,* at 632, and this fact would be enough to prevent mootness because of the "public interest in having the legality of the practices settled." *Ibid.* But mootness in the present case depends not at all upon a "voluntary cessation" of the admissions practices that were the subject of this litigation. It depends, instead, upon the simple fact that DeFunis is now in the final quarter of the final year of his course of study, and the settled and unchallenged policy of the Law School to permit him to complete the term for which he is now enrolled.

It might also be suggested that this case presents a question that is "capable of repetition, yet evading review," Southern Pacific Terminal Co. v. ICC, 219 U.S. 498, 515 (1911); Roe v. Wade, 410 U.S. 113, 125 (1973), and is thus amenable to federal adjudication even though it might otherwise be considered moot. But DeFunis will never again be required to run the gantlet of the Law School's admission process, and so the question is certainly not "capable of repetition" so far as he is concerned. Moreover, just because this particular case did not reach the Court until the eve of the petitioner's graduation from law school, it hardly follows that the issue he raises will in the future evade review. If the admissions procedures of the Law School remain unchanged,[4] there is no reason to suppose that a subsequent case attacking those procedures will not come with relative speed to this Court, now that the Supreme Court of Washington has spoken. This case, therefore, in no way presents the exceptional situation in which the Southern Pacific Terminal doctrine might permit a departure from "[t]he usual rule in federal cases * * * that an actual controversy must exist at stages of appellate or certiorari review, and not simply at the date the action is initiated." Roe v. Wade, *supra*, at 125; United States v. Munsingwear, Inc., 340 U.S. 36 (1950).

Because the petitioner will complete his law school studies at the end of the term for which he has now registered regardless of any decision this Court might reach on the merits of this litigation, we conclude that the Court cannot, consistently with the limitations of Art. III of the Constitution, consider the substantive constitutional issues tendered by the parties.[5] Accordingly, the judgment of the Supreme Court of Washington is vacated, and the cause is remanded for such proceedings as by that court may be deemed appropriate.

It is so ordered.

■ MR. JUSTICE DOUGLAS, dissenting.

I agree with MR. JUSTICE BRENNAN that this case is not moot, and because of the significance of the issues raised I think it is important to reach the merits.

* * *

---

4. In response to an inquiry from the Court, counsel for the respondents has advised that some changes have been made in the admissions procedures "for the applicants seeking admission to the University of Washington law school for the academic year commencing September, 1974." The respondents' counsel states, however, that "[these] changes do not affect the policy challenged by the petitioners * * * in that * * * special consideration still is given to applicants from 'certain ethnic groups.'"

5. It is suggested in dissent that "[a]ny number of unexpected events—illness, economic necessity, even academic failure—might prevent his graduation at the end of the term." "But such speculative contingencies afford no basis for our passing on the substantive issues [the petitioner] would have us decide," Hall v. Beals, 396 U.S. 45, 49 (1969), in the absence of "evidence that this is a prospect of 'immediacy and reality.'" Golden v. Zwickler, 394 U.S. 103, 109 (1969) * * *.

■ MR. JUSTICE BRENNAN, with whom MR. JUSTICE DOUGLAS, MR. JUSTICE WHITE, and MR. JUSTICE MARSHALL concur, dissenting.

I respectfully dissent. Many weeks of the school term remain, and petitioner may not receive his degree despite respondents' assurances that petitioner will be allowed to complete this term's schooling regardless of our decision. Any number of unexpected events—illness, economic necessity, even academic failure—might prevent his graduation at the end of the term. Were that misfortune to befall, and were petitioner required to register for yet another term, the prospect that he would again face the hurdle of the admissions policy is real, not fanciful; for respondents warn that "Mr. DeFunis would have to take some appropriate action to request continued admission for the remainder of his law school education, and *some discretionary action by the University on such request would have to be taken.*" (Emphasis supplied). Thus, respondents' assurances have not dissipated the possibility that petitioner might once again have to run the gantlet of the University's allegedly unlawful admissions policy. The Court therefore proceeds on an erroneous premise in resting its mootness holding on a supposed inability to render any judgment that may affect one way or the other petitioner's completion of his law studies. For surely if we were to reverse the Washington Supreme Court, we could insure that, if for some reason petitioner did not graduate this spring, he would be entitled to re-enrollment at a later time on the same basis as others who have not faced the hurdle of the University's allegedly unlawful admissions policy.

In these circumstances, and because the University's position implies no concession that its admissions policy is unlawful, this controversy falls squarely within the Court's long line of decisions holding that the "[m]ere voluntary cessation of allegedly illegal conduct does not moot a case." United States v. Phosphate Export Assn., 393 U.S. 199, 203 (1968) * * *. Since respondents' voluntary representation to this Court is only that they will permit petitioner to complete this term's studies, respondents have not borne the "heavy burden," United States v. Phosphate Export Assn., *supra,* at 203, of demonstrating that there was not even a "mere possibility" that petitioner would once again be subject to the challenged admissions policy. United States v. W.T. Grant Co., *supra,* at 633. On the contrary, respondents have positioned themselves so as to be "free to return to [their] old ways." *Id.,* at 632.

I can thus find no justification for the Court's straining to rid itself of this dispute. While we must be vigilant to require that litigants maintain a personal stake in the outcome of a controversy to assure that "the questions will be framed with the necessary specificity, that the issues will be contested with the necessary adverseness and that the litigation will be pursued with the necessary vigor to assure that the constitutional challenge will be made in a form traditionally thought to be capable of judicial resolution," Flast v. Cohen, 392 U.S. 83, 106 (1968), there is no want of an adversary contest in this case. Indeed, the Court concedes that, if petitioner has lost his stake in this controversy, he did so only when he registered for the spring term. But petitioner took that action only after the case had been fully litigated in the state courts, briefs had been filed in this Court, and oral argument had been heard. The case is thus ripe for decision on a fully developed factual record with sharply defined and fully canvassed legal issues. *Cf.* Sibron v. New York, 392 U.S. 40, 57 (1968).

Moreover, in endeavoring to dispose of this case as moot, the Court clearly disserves the public interest. The constitutional issues which are avoided today concern vast numbers of people, organizations, and colleges and universities, as evidenced by the filing of twenty-six *amicus curiae* briefs. Few constitutional questions in recent history have stirred as much debate, and they will not disappear. * * * Because avoidance of repetitious litigation serves the public interest, that inevitability counsels against mootness determinations, as here, not compelled by the record. Although the Court should, of course, avoid unnecessary decisions of constitutional questions, we should not transform principles of avoidance of constitutional decisions into devices for sidestepping resolution of difficult cases. *Cf.* Cohens v. Virginia, 6 Wheat. 264, 404–405 (1821)(Marshall, C.J.).

NOTE ON MOOTNESS: ITS RATIONALE AND APPLICATIONS

(1) *Standing Doctrine "in a time frame"?* In an influential formulation, Professor Henry Monaghan once characterized mootness as "the doctrine of standing in a time frame. The requisite personal interest that must exist at the commencement of the litigation (standing) must continue through its existence (mootness)." Monaghan, *Constitutional Adjudication: The Who and When,* 82 Yale L.J. 1363, 1384 (1973). As you read the rest of the materials in this Section, consider whether the doctrine does, and should, meet this description.

(2) *Foundations.* The Court in DeFunis viewed the mootness doctrine as a function of the Article III case or controversy requirement.[1] The Court apparently made this link explicit for the first time in 1964, in Liner v. Jafco, Inc., 375 U.S. 301 (1964), discussed in Paragraph (9), *infra.* Concurring in Honig v. Doe, 484 U.S. 305 (1988), Chief Justice Rehnquist conceded that "our recent cases have taken that position" (p. 330), but argued that the Court had erred; mootness doctrine, he contended, is rooted in policy judgments, not "forced upon us by the case or controversy requirement of Art. III itself" (*id.*). The Chief Justice rested his position partly on history; he thought it "very doubtful that the earliest case I have found discussing mootness, Mills v. Green, 159 U.S. 651 (1895), was premised on constitutional constraints; Justice Gray's opinion in that case nowhere mentions Art. III." 484 U.S. at 330. Chief Justice Rehnquist also maintained that the recognized exceptions to mootness doctrine for cases involving voluntary cessation of challenged conduct and for acts "capable of repetition, yet evading review", see Paragraphs (3) and (4), *infra,* could not be justified if Article III barred the adjudication of moot cases.

Justice Scalia, who thought the Honig case should be dismissed as moot, took issue with the Chief Justice's historical interpretation. Despite the failure to refer to Article III in Mills v. Green, Justice Scalia had "little doubt that the Court believed the [mootness] doctrine called into question the Court's power and not merely its prudence, for (in an opinion by the same Justice who wrote Mills) it had said two years earlier: '[T]he Court is not *empowered* to decide moot questions. * * * No stipulation of the parties or counsel * * * can enlarge the *power,* or affect the duty, of the court in this regard.' California v.

---

1. If DeFunis had brought his action as a class action, and all other facts had been the same, would the result have been different? See United States Parole Comm'n v. Geraghty and the following Note, p. 236, *infra.*

San Pable & Tulare R. Co., 149 U.S. 308, 314 (1893)(Gray, J.)" (emphasis added by Justice Scalia)(484 U.S. at 339).

Is Justice Gray's reference to what the Court is "empowered" to do necessarily a reference to the Article III case or controversy requirement? See Lee, *Deconstitutionalizing Justiciability: The Example of Mootness,* 105 Harv. L.Rev. 603 (1992)(suggesting that though there might be statutory, doctrinal, or prudential impediments to the adjudication of moot cases, they remain "cases" within the meaning of Article III). In any event, should historical practice be dispositive of the constitutional authority of Article III courts to decide moot cases? Of the bounds of mootness doctrine?

Is there any justification for treating mootness doctrine differently from standing?[2] If standing doctrine requires a live dispute at the outset of litigation, why should a continuing live dispute not be similarly required to avert mootness? Consider the following arguments: (i) an actual course of conduct, even if past, continues to frame litigation in a factual context and thereby focus judicial decisionmaking; (ii) the unlawful causation of a past injury deprives a defendant of any moral entitlement to freedom from judicial intervention;[3] (iii) sharp, adversarial presentation of issues may occur despite the mooting of a plaintiff's personal stake in the outcome; (iv) since a defendant who has caused wrongful conduct would otherwise remain free to repeat it, a judicial decision forbidding such conduct is not an advisory opinion in any objectionable sense; and (v) judicial investment in the resolution of an issue of public importance should not be squandered.

In light of considerations such as these, should the mootness doctrine be deemed inapplicable to cases on appeal to the Supreme Court? See Honig v. Doe, 484 U.S. 305, 331–32 (1988)(Rehnquist, C.J., concurring); Nichol, *Moot Cases, Chief Justice Rehnquist, and the Supreme Court,* 22 U.Conn.L.Rev. 703, 706 (1990). Treated as a prudential doctrine only? See Lee, *supra.* Should mootness bar adjudication only when the functional requisites of effective adjudication, such as effective adversarial presentation of sharply framed issues, are absent?[4]

(3) *Voluntary Cessation.* As noted in DeFunis, a long line of cases holds that an action for an injunction, or other judgment with continuing force, does not become moot merely because the conduct immediately complained of has

---

2. On the relation of standing and mootness doctrines, see Chemerinsky, *A Unified Approach to Justiciability,* 22 Conn. L.Rev. 677 (1990); Fallon, *Of Justiciability, Remedies, and Public Law Litigation: Notes on the Jurisprudence of Lyons,* 59 N.Y.U.L.Rev. 1, 24–30 (1984).

3. Note that claims for damages are seldom if ever mooted. Should it matter that a different form of relief is sought?

4. The policies underlying the mootness doctrine were at issue in Cardinal Chem. Co. v. Morton Int'l, Inc., 508 U.S. 83 (1993), in which the district court had rejected plaintiff's patent infringement claim and upheld the defendant's counterclaim of patent invalidity. The Court of Appeals for the Federal Circuit agreed that there was no infringement, but proceeded to vacate as moot the finding of patent invalidity without addressing its merits, reasoning that the only patent dispute between the parties—the infringement claim raised in the case—had been resolved by the finding of non-infringement. The Supreme Court reversed, stressing two points. First, in theory any decision of the Federal Circuit might be reviewed by the Supreme Court; and if the Court reversed the finding of non-infringement, it could surely reach the patent invalidity claim. Second, once it is established that a trial court has jurisdiction, courts may presume, absent a contrary showing, that the case has not become moot.

terminated, if there is a sufficient possibility of a recurrence that would be barred by a proper decree.[5] How likely does recurrence have to be for this exception to mootness doctrine to apply?

(a) In County of Los Angeles v. Davis, 440 U.S. 625 (1979), the Court held moot a challenge to certain proposed government hiring practices in light of the defendant's compliance with a district court decree over a period of five years, the resulting elimination of any discriminatory effects of the wrong complained of, and the asserted lack of any indication that defendant's hiring practices would change if the district court decree were dissolved.

(b) The Court, by a 5–4 vote, may have changed direction in Vitek v. Jones, 445 U.S. 480 (1980). Jones, a convicted felon, brought a federal court action challenging (on procedural grounds) his transfer from a prison to a mental hospital. While the case was pending, he was retransferred to prison, placed in the psychiatric ward, paroled on condition that he accept psychiatric treatment at a V.A. hospital, and subsequently returned to prison for violation of parole. The majority agreed with both parties that the case was not moot, stating that against the background of Jones' mental illness, it was not "absolutely clear" that the challenged wrong would not recur (p. 487).

Justice Stewart, for three dissenters, argued that the case was moot because there was "no demonstrated probability" of recurrence, and thus Jones was "simply one of thousands of [state] prisoners with no more standing than any other" (p. 501). Justice Blackmun, whose separate dissenting opinion also noted the absence of any indicated intention of transferring Jones to a mental hospital during his remaining prison term,[6] concluded that "the Court's analysis invites the criticism, increasingly voiced, that this Court's decisions on threshold issues 'are concealed decisions on the merits of the underlying constitutional claim.' Tushnet, *The New Law of Standing: A Plea for Abandonment*, 62 Cornell L.Rev. 663, 663 (1977)" (445 U.S. at 504 n. 3).[7]

---

5. See, *e.g.,* United States v. Concentrated Phosphate Export Ass'n, 393 U.S. 199, 202–04 (1968); United States v. W.T. Grant Co., 345 U.S. 629 (1953); United States v. Trans–Missouri Freight Ass'n, 166 U.S. 290, 307–09 (1897)(dissolution of allegedly unlawful combination did not moot the case, since a similar combination might be formed in the future). But *cf.* Preiser v. Newkirk, 422 U.S. 395, 402 (1975)(convict's retransfer from maximum to minimum security prison mooted his challenge to the original transfer).

6. Justice Blackmun also argued that the case presented less an issue of mootness than of ripeness. See Section 5, *infra.*

7. With Justice Blackmun's analysis, compare Justice Powell's observation that defendants' jurisdictional statement referred to "a very real expectation" of transfer if the lower court injunction were removed (p. 497 n. 1)(Powell, J., concurring in part).

For cases since Vitek, see Princeton University v. Schmid, 455 U.S. 100, 103 (1982)(change in University's regulations moots its appeal with respect to reversal of trespass conviction based on prior regulations); Iron Arrow Honor Society v. Heckler, 464 U.S. 67 (1983)(case mooted by voluntary act of non-party); City of Mesquite v. Aladdin's Castle, Inc., 455 U.S. 283, 288–89 (1982)(controversy not mooted by city's repeal of challenged provision after decision below; repeal would not preclude reenactment if the judgment were vacated, and the city had "announced just such an intention"). See also Northeastern Florida Chapter of the Associated General Contractors of America v. City of Jacksonville, 113 S.Ct. 2297, 2301 (1993), p. 148 n. 22, *supra* (case not moot when a municipal ordinance is replaced by one sufficiently similar that the challenged conduct in effect continues; two dissenting Justices viewed the modification of the ordinance as more significant and hence as mooting the dispute).

(4) *Capable of Repetition, Yet Evading Review.* Closely related to the "voluntary cessation" cases are a group, also discussed in DeFunis, in which the alleged wrong has ceased but the wrong is capable of repetition, yet evading review.[8] Does the Court's willingness to decide such cases suggest a kind of justiciability by necessity where there may otherwise be no way to obtain review of an important issue? Do you agree with Chief Justice Rehnquist that acceptance of jurisdiction in such cases is incompatible with viewing moot cases as outside of Article III? See Honig v. Doe, 484 U.S. at 331 (Rehnquist, C.J., concurring).

Recent decisions emphasize that, in the absence of a class action, the relevant question involves the possibility of recurrence with respect to the complaining party. See Weinstein v. Bradford, 423 U.S. 147, 149 (1975); Murphy v. Hunt, 455 U.S. 478, 482 (1982). Earlier cases seemed satisfied by the likelihood of recurrence between the defendant and another member of the public. See, *e.g.,* Southern Pac. Terminal Co. v. ICC, 219 U.S. 498, 515 (1911); Rosario v. Rockefeller, 410 U.S. 752, 756 n.5 (1973); Dunn v. Blumstein, 405 U.S. 330, 333 n.2 (1972).[9] The requisite likelihood is unclear. The Court has spoken of a "reasonable expectation" or "demonstrated probability" that the controversy would recur and insisted that a "mere physical or theoretical possibility" was insufficient. See, *e.g.,* Murphy v. Hunt, *supra,* at 482. Yet in Southern Pac. Term. Co. v. ICC, *supra,* there was no showing that the Commission proposed to issue similar short term orders in the future. And in Roe v. Wade, 410 U.S. 113, 124–25 (1973), a challenge to an abortion statute was held not moot even though the woman who had initiated the action was no longer pregnant. "Pregnancy," the Court said, "often comes more than once to the same woman * * * [and] truly could be 'capable of repetition, yet evading review.' "[10] *Cf.* Honig v. Doe, 484 U.S. at 318–19 n. 6 (finding, over two dissenting votes, that a "reasonable expectation" of recurrence may suffice to avoid mootness, even if there is no "demonstrated probability" of recurring, challengeable action).

(5) *Collateral Consequences.* Although it may become unnecessary or impossible to grant the primary relief requested, remaining or collateral consequences of judicial resolution of an issue on the merits may prevent a case from becoming moot. The cases, however, leave considerable uncertainty about

---

8. See, *e.g.,* Globe Newspaper Co. v. Superior Court, 457 U.S. 596 (1982)(order excluding press and public from certain portions of rape trial had expired with the completion of the trial); Nebraska Press Ass'n v. Stuart, 427 U.S. 539 (1976)(short-term judicial orders restricting press coverage of criminal proceedings had expired prior to Supreme Court review); Moore v. Ogilvie, 394 U.S. 814 (1969)(challenge to signature requirement on nominating petitions; election had occurred before Supreme Court review); Carroll v. President and Com'rs of Princess Anne, 393 U.S. 175 (1968)(ten-day injunction restraining white supremacist organization from holding public rallies had expired two years before); Southern Pac. Terminal Co. v. ICC, 219 U.S. 498 (1911)(short-term agency cease-and-desist order had expired).

9. In Dunn, the Court considered on the merits a challenge to a durational residency requirement for voting even though Blumstein had satisfied the requirement long before the case reached the Supreme Court. Neither party argued on appeal that the case was moot, and the Court said in a footnote that Blumstein had standing to challenge the requirement "as a member of the class of people affected by the presently written statute" (p. 333 n. 2). Although no class had actually been certified, the case may be seen as a harbinger of Sosna v. Iowa, 419 U.S. 393 (1975), p. 237, *infra.*

10. Since Roe was brought as a class action, the mootness question would presumably not be difficult today. See pp. 227-42, *infra.*

when such consequences will be determined to be present, or how likely they must be. Compare, *e.g.*, Bowen v. Roy, 476 U.S. 693 (1986)(holding, 7–2, but without a majority for any rationale, that a First Amendment challenge to a statute requiring plaintiffs to "supply" a Social Security number for their child as a precondition to AFDC aid was not moot even though the record showed that the child had received a number at birth), and Firefighters Local Union No. 1784 v. Stotts, 467 U.S. 561 (1984)(holding, 6–3, that challenge by a union to layoffs of white employees pursuant to a preliminary injunction was not moot even though all affected employees had been reinstated, since lower court's determination continued to affect relationships among the parties),[11] with, *e.g.*, Rhodes v. Stewart, 488 U.S. 1 (1988)(per curiam)(finding that the death of one prisoner and release of another prior to a § 1983 judgment in their favor prevented them from being "prevailing plaintiffs" under § 1988 and removed any basis for an award of attorney's fees), and University of Texas v. Camenisch, 451 U.S. 390 (1981)(question whether a preliminary injunction should have issued is moot because the terms of the injunction have been carried out, and any remaining question of liability on injunction bond should be resolved not on appeal but at trial on the merits).[12]

(6) *Mootness in Criminal Cases.* The doctrines discussed in this Note have been applied in criminal as well as civil cases. Indeed, some of the cases already cited (such as Murphy v. Hunt and Weinstein v. Bradford, Paragraph (4), *supra*) involved complaints by those in criminal custody. But two questions unique to criminal proceedings merit separate discussion: the ability of convicted defendants to attack their convictions or sentences after serving their sentences, and the effect of a defendant's death on the justiciability of such an attack.

(a) For many years, the general rule in the federal courts was that after criminal defendants had served their sentences, their cases were moot because "there was no longer a subject matter on which the judgment * * * could operate." St. Pierre v. United States, 319 U.S. 41, 42 (1943). But that rule was gradually eroded because of recognition, first, that issues characteristically involving only short sentences might forever escape review[13] and, second, that criminal convictions have collateral consequences that continue after a sentence is served (recidivism statutes, testimonial impeachment, etc.). The development is described in Sibron v. New York, 392 U.S. 40, 50–58 (1968), which

---

11. See also Jago v. Van Curen, 454 U.S. 14, 21–22 n. 3 (1981)(claim of right to hearing on withdrawal of parole recommendation was not moot, even though parole had been granted after petition filed; since parole might have been granted earlier, release from conditions of parole might now be an appropriate remedy); Super Tire Engineering Co. v. McCorkle, 416 U.S. 115 (1974)(holding, 5–4, that settlement of a strike did not moot employer's challenge to state regulations entitling striking workers to state welfare assistance); Church of Scientology of California v. United States, 506 U.S. 9 (1992) (holding that a challenge to an IRS summons requiring the production of records was not moot, even though the IRS had already obtained the records after the district court enforced

the summons, since a court could still "fashion *some* form of meaningful relief" by ordering the government to return the records and destroy all copies).

12. See also Local No. 8–6, Oil, Chem. & Atomic Workers Intern. Union v. Missouri, 361 U.S. 363 (1960)(injunctive relief mooted by termination of strike and government seizure; remaining penalty provisions severable and subject of separate action).

13. Note that unless the Court is predicting recidivism (which it has generally declined to do), this recognition is hard to square with the rule that the likelihood of repetition must exist with respect to the complaining party. See Paragraph (4), *supra.*

stated the rule (p. 57) that a criminal case is moot "only if it is shown that there is no possibility that any collateral consequences will be imposed on the basis of the challenged conviction". *Cf.* Carafas v. LaVallee, 391 U.S. 234 (1968), p. 1452, *infra.*

The defendant's interest in attacking a conviction surely guarantees the requisite adverseness in most instances.[14] But the Court has sustained claims of mootness in attacks on sentences. See Lane v. Williams, 455 U.S. 624 (1982); see also North Carolina v. Rice, 404 U.S. 244 (1971)(since the challenged sentence had been served, and the claim was directed not at the underlying conviction, the case would be moot unless it could be shown that collateral consequences flowed from the difference between the two sentences).

Should the stigma of a criminal conviction always be regarded as an answer to the argument that an attack on the conviction is moot, at least while the defendant is alive? *Cf.* Hart, *The Aims of the Criminal Law,* 23 Law & Contemp.Probs. 401, 404 (1958).

(b) The death of a criminal defendant moots the defendant's case on direct or collateral review. See, *e.g.,* Singer v. United States, 323 U.S. 338, 346 (1945).[15]

In Robinson v. California, 370 U.S. 660 (1962), a divided Court held in a novel decision that a law making drug addiction a crime constituted "cruel and unusual punishment" in violation of the Eighth and Fourteenth Amendments. Justice Stewart delivered the opinion of the Court; Justice Harlan concurred in the judgment; Justice Clark dissented, as did Justice White. Subsequently, the state informed the Court that the defendant in the case had died ten days before the appeal to the Supreme Court was taken, and petitioned for rehearing and abatement of the judgment. The petition was denied without opinion. 371 U.S. 905 (1962). Justice Clark, joined by Justices Harlan and Stewart, dissented, arguing that the judgment should be vacated as moot.

If the dissenters on the petition for rehearing in Robinson had prevailed, would the precedential force of the original Robinson decision have been affected? Should it be, if the case was handled by all concerned (including Robinson's counsel) on the assumption that Robinson was still alive?

(7) *Mootness and Discretion.* The result in DeFunis effectively postponed for several years a decision on the merits of a question that had stirred considerable public controversy. (The later decision on the merits was Regents of the University of California v. Bakke, 438 U.S. 265 (1978).) For a similar pair of decisions in another area of controversy over the scope of affirmative action, see Boston Firefighters Union, Local 718 v. Boston Chapter, NAACP, 461 U.S. 477 (1983)(finding mootness); Firefighters Local Union No. 1784 v. Stotts, 467 U.S. 561 (1984)(rejecting a suggestion of mootness). Consider whether these decisions reflect a "pattern" in cases "presenting hard issues of racial justice: a

---

14. In Pennsylvania v. Mimms, 434 U.S. 106, 108 n. 3 (1977), the Court rejected a claim of mootness by a defendant who had completed his sentence in view of the collateral consequences to the *state* of the judgment of reversal of which it sought review. Such consequences included the availability and amount of bail, length of sentence, and availability of probation in future proceedings against the defendant.

15. *Cf.* Wetzel v. Ohio, 371 U.S. 62 (1962)(per curiam decision granting motion on appeal in criminal case to substitute deceased appellant's wife as appellant; as administratrix and probable heir of appellant's estate, she had a substantial interest in protecting the estate from costs to be levied against it if conviction stood).

dubious decision not to decide one case * * * followed by an equally doubtful conclusion that a later case, presenting the same but now more 'percolated' issue, was fit for judicial resolution. The sequence does not seem coincidental. According to one celebrated argument,[16] justiciability doctrines perform an important function in allowing the Supreme Court to pick its time and its case for decision." Fallon and Weiler, *Firefighters v. Stotts: Conflicting Models of Racial Justice,* 1984 S.Ct.Rev. 1, 7–8.

If the result in DeFunis can be explained on this ground, do you think that this use of mootness doctrine as an avoidance device is warranted? Among other things, doesn't it sow confusion among the lower courts? Are there other devices—such as denial of the writ of certiorari—more appropriate to the task?

(8) *Disposition of Mooted Cases in the Federal System.* When a case in the federal system becomes moot on appeal, the disposition depends on the nature of the events that mooted the dispute.

(a) United States v. Munsingwear, Inc., 340 U.S. 36, 39 (1950), pronounced that "[t]he established practice of the Court in dealing with a civil case from a court in the federal system which has become moot while on its way here or pending our decision on the merits is to reverse or vacate the judgment below and remand with a direction to dismiss [citing many cases, together with four 'exceptions']."[17] The Munsingwear case had been mooted by a change in the applicable law, not any conduct of the parties intended to terminate the dispute, and the Court reasoned that vacatur was appropriate in such cases on the motion of a party to "clear[] the path for future relitigation of the issues between the parties and eliminate[] a judgment, review of which was prevented through happenstance" (p. 40).

Munsingwear quickly became the leading case on federal vacatur, and it remains the controlling authority for *civil* cases that, through happenstance, conduct not attributable to the parties, or the unilateral action of the prevailing party in the lower court, become moot on appeal, during the pendency of a

---

16. [Ed.] The "celebrated argument" is that of Professor Bickel, who catalogued a number of techniques for avoiding decision on the merits. See Bickel, The Least Dangerous Branch 111–98 (1962), pp. 83–84, *supra.*

17. The Court in Munsingwear nevertheless held res judicata a district court decision previously dismissed as moot on appeal, because the parties had failed to move in the court of appeals for vacation of the original judgment. Munsingwear originated when the United States filed a complaint in which, in separate counts, it sought injunctive and damages relief for violation of a price control regulation. The district court separated the two counts, holding the damages claim in abeyance "pending trial and final determination of the suit for an injunction" (p. 37). With the two counts in this posture, the court held that Munsingwear's prices complied with the regulation and dismissed the

complaint. The government sought appellate review, but while the appeal was pending, "the commodity involved was decontrolled", and the court of appeals granted a motion to dismiss the appeal as moot. Munsingwear then moved in the district court to dismiss the still pending damages action "on the ground that the unreversed judgment of the District Court in the injunctive suit was res judicata of" the damages claim (*id.*). The district court denied the motion, and the court of appeals and the Supreme Court both affirmed. The proper course for the government, the Court said, would have been to move to vacate the district court's judgment upon the mooting of the injunctive claim; the United States had "slept on its rights" and must suffer the consequences (p. 41).

Does it make sense to enforce a formal motion requirement after an appellate ruling of mootness?

petition for certiorari, or after the granting of such a petition but prior to decision by the Supreme Court.[18]

(b) In federal criminal cases, the Supreme Court held for a time that death abated "not only the appeal but also all proceedings had in the prosecution from its inception," thus requiring dismissal of the indictment. Durham v. United States, 401 U.S. 481, 483 (1971). But in Dove v. United States, 423 U.S. 325 (1976), the Court overruled this holding without discussion and dismissed a petition for certiorari on learning of petitioner's death.[19] Does any good reason support the disparity in the Court's practices concerning civil and criminal cases?

(c) In United States Bancorp Mortgage Co. v. Bonner Mall Partnership, 115 S.Ct. 386 (1994), the Supreme Court granted certiorari to resolve a question under the Bankruptcy Code, and the parties thereafter reached a settlement that mooted the case. Relying on Munsingwear, *supra*, Bancorp, the losing party in the court of appeals, asked the Supreme Court to vacate the judgment below as well as dismissing the writ. Bonner opposed the motion. Following briefing and argument, the Court, in an opinion by Justice Scalia, unanimously found Munsingwear distinguishable and ruled that "mootness by reason of settlement does not [ordinarily] justify vacatur of a judgment under review" (p. 393).

Justice Scalia began by rejecting an argument that, when a case becomes moot, a federal court loses jurisdiction to take any action, including entry of a vacatur order. Although mootness nullifies jurisdiction to pronounce on the merits, the court retains authority to take such ancillary action, including vacatur and the award of costs, as justice may require. The decision whether to vacate a judgment or simply to dismiss the case is thus governed by equitable principles. And while such principles generally support vacatur when one party has lost the opportunity to seek review of an adverse judgment as the result of happenstance, the "voluntary forfeiture of review" through settlement ordinarily shifts the balance of equities (p. 392). "Judicial precedents are presumptively correct and valuable to the legal community as a whole. They are not merely the property of private litigants and should stand unless a court concludes that the public interest would be served by vacatur." (*Id.*)(quoting Izumi Seimitsu Kogyo Kabushiki Kaisha v. U.S. Philips Corp.), 114 S.Ct. 425 (1993)(Stevens, J., dissenting).

The Court, in the United States Bancorp case, explicitly contemplated that its decision about vacatur standards in the Supreme Court would apply to "motions at the court of appeals level for vacatur of district court judgments" (p. 393). If vacatur depends on a balance of equities, however, is the decision best made at the appellate level? Might the district court be better able to weigh such arguably relevant factors as the strength of the authority support-

---

18. In Diffenderfer v. Central Baptist Church, 404 U.S. 412 (1972), involving a challenge to a state statute that had been superseded before the case reached the Supreme Court, the Court held the case moot and vacated the federal district court judgment. Yet because it found that the plaintiffs might wish to show that the superseded statute retained some continuing force, or might wish to attack its replacement, the Court did not direct dismissal of the action as

prescribed by the Munsingwear decision, but remanded the case to the district court with leave to the appellants to amend their complaint.

19. Dove was a case before the Supreme Court on direct review; the procedure was later followed on collateral review as well. Warden v. Palermo, 431 U.S. 911 (1977).

ing a decision and the public interest in preserving an authoritative resolution of a particular question?

The Bancorp decision is mostly of concern to litigants likely to be involved in a number of similar disputes, who have a keen interest not only in the outcome of any particular case, but also in the preclusive or precedential effects of any judicial resolution. Isn't there something unseemly about letting repeat players "buy up" judgments that they dislike by settling cases pending on appeal and seeking vacatur?[20]

(9) *Mootness and State Court Litigation.* In DeFunis, after concluding that the action was moot, the Supreme Court vacated the judgment and remanded "for such proceedings as by [the Washington Supreme Court] may be deemed appropriate."[21] If the state court on remand had reinstated a judgment on the merits, would it have had any binding effect in subsequent federal litigation, even between the same parties? See p. 155, *supra.* Could the Supreme Court have mandated dismissal of the action? (Recall that state courts are not bound by the Article III "case" or "controversy" limitation. See p. 154, *supra.*)

In ASARCO Inc. v. Kadish, 490 U.S. 605, 621 n. 1 (1989), discussed p. 155, *supra,* the Court noted its decision in DeFunis to vacate and remand for further proceedings in state court, but said that its more recent practice has been to dismiss cases that become moot on review from the state courts, leaving undisturbed the state court judgment (citing Kansas Gas & Elec. Co. v. State Corp. Comm'n of Kansas, 481 U.S. 1044 (1987); Times–Picayune Pub. Corp. v. Schulingkamp, 420 U.S. 985 (1975)).

If a state court holds moot a case involving a federal question, is Supreme Court review precluded? In Liner v. Jafco, Inc., 375 U.S. 301 (1964), a state court enjoined picketing in a labor dispute, despite a contention that its jurisdiction was federally preempted. Pending decision on appeal, construction at the site was completed, and the state appellate court held that the case had become moot (though it also expressed an opinion on the merits). The Supreme Court unanimously held, per Justice Brennan, that "in this case the question of mootness is itself a question of federal law upon which we must pronounce final judgment" (p. 304). In holding the case not moot, the Court cited an indemnity bond requiring payment if the injunction was "wrongfully" sued out, but also relied on the frustration of federal policy that might result if the state court's ruling on the preemption claim were immunized from review. See also, *e.g.,* Gannett Co., Inc. v. DePasquale, 443 U.S. 368 (1979).

---

20. For useful discussions, see Slavitt, *Selling the Integrity of the System of Precedent: Selective Publication, Depublication, and Vacatur,* 30 Harv.C.R.-C.L.L.Rev. 109 (1995); Fisch, *The Vanishing Precedent: Eduardo Meets Vacatur,* 70 Notre Dame L.Rev. 325(1994); Deyling, *Dangerous Precedent: Federal Government Attempts to Vacate Judicial Decisions Upon Settlement,* 27 J.Marshall L.Rev. 689 (1994). For an admirable exploration of the implications of the public and private rights models for vacatur and related issues, see Resnik, *Whose Judgment? Vacating Judgments, Preferences for Settlement, and the Role of Adjudication at* the Close of the Twentieth Century, 41 U.C.L.A.L.Rev. 1471 (1994).

21. On remand, DeFunis moved in the Washington Supreme Court to designate the case a class action and to reinstate the trial court judgment. The defendants countered with a motion to reinstate the prior judgment of the state supreme court.

Seven Justices joined in denying the motion to designate the suit as a class action, but no majority could be mustered on the other issues. DeFunis v. Odegaard, 84 Wash.2d 617, 529 P.2d 438 (1974).

United States Parole Commission v. Geraghty

445 U.S. 388, 100 S.Ct. 1202, 63 L.Ed.2d 479 (1980).
Certiorari to the United States Court of Appeals for the Third Circuit.

■ MR. JUSTICE BLACKMUN delivered the opinion of the Court.

This case raises the question whether a trial court's denial of a motion for certification of a class may be reviewed on appeal after the named plaintiff's personal claim has become "moot." * * * We granted certiorari to consider this issue of substantial significance, under Art. III of the Constitution, to class action litigation,[1] and to resolve the conflict in approach among the Courts of Appeals.

I

In 1973, the United States Parole Board adopted explicit Parole Release Guidelines for adult prisoners. * * *

Respondent John M. Geraghty was convicted in the United States District Court for the Northern District of Illinois of conspiracy to commit extortion, in violation of 18 U.S.C. § 1951, and of making false material declarations to a grand jury, in violation of 18 U.S.C. § 1623. On January 25, 1974, two months after initial promulgation of the release guidelines, respondent was sentenced to concurrent prison terms of four years on the conspiracy count and one year on the false declarations count. * * *

[Later, Geraghty's sentence was reduced by the District Court to 30 months]. Geraghty then applied for release on parole. His first application was denied in January 1976 * * * [with the explanation that under the Parole Release Guidelines, Geraghty should serve between 26 and 36 months]. If the customary release date applicable to respondent under the guidelines were adhered to, he would not be paroled before serving his entire sentence minus good-time credits. Geraghty applied for parole again in June 1976; that application was denied for the same reasons. He then instituted this civil suit as a class action in the United States District Court for the District of Columbia, challenging the guidelines as inconsistent with the PCRA [Parole Commission and Reorganization Act] and the Constitution, and questioning the procedures by which the guidelines were applied to his case.

Respondent sought certification of a class of "all federal prisoners who are or will become eligible for release on parole." Without ruling on Geraghty's

1. * * *

While the petition for a writ of certiorari was pending, respondent Geraghty filed a motion to substitute as respondents in this Court five prisoners, then incarcerated, who also were represented by Geraghty's attorneys. In the alternative, the prisoners sought to intervene. We deferred our ruling on the motion to the hearing of the case on the merits. These prisoners, or most of them, now also have been released from incarceration. [Another prisoner, whose petition to intervene had been denied by the District Court, had apparently also been released by the time the case reached the Su-

preme Court.] On September 25, 1979, a supplement to the motion to substitute or intervene was filed, proposing six new substitute respondents or intervenors; each of these is a presently incarcerated federal prisoner who, allegedly, has been adversely affected by the guidelines and who is represented by Geraghty's counsel.

Since we hold that respondent may continue to litigate the class certification issue, there is no need for us to consider whether the motion should be granted in order to prevent the case from being moot. We conclude that the District Court initially should rule on the motion.

motion, the court transferred the case to the Middle District of Pennsylvania, where respondent was incarcerated.   * * *

The District Court subsequently denied Geraghty's request for class certification and granted summary judgment for petitioners on all the claims Geraghty asserted.

Respondent, individually "and on behalf of a class," appealed to the United States Court of Appeals for the Third Circuit.   * * *

On June 30, 1977, before any brief had been filed in the Court of Appeals, Geraghty was mandatorily released from prison; he had served 22 months of his sentence, and had earned good-time credits for the rest.   Petitioners then moved to dismiss the appeals as moot.

The Court of Appeals, concluding that the litigation was not moot, reversed the judgment of the District Court and remanded the case for further proceedings.   * * *

II

Article III of the Constitution limits federal "Judicial Power," that is, federal court jurisdiction, to "Cases" and "Controversies."   This case or controversy limitation serves "two complementary" purposes.   Flast v. Cohen, 392 U.S. 83, 95 (1968).   It limits the business of federal courts to "questions presented in an adversary context and in a form historically viewed as capable of resolution through the judicial process," and it defines the "role assigned to the judiciary in a tripartite allocation of power to assure that the federal courts will not intrude into the areas committed to the other branches of government."   *Ibid.* Likewise, mootness has two aspects: "when the issues presented are no longer 'live' or the parties lack a legally cognizable interest in the outcome."   Powell v. McCormack, 395 U.S. 486, 496 (1969).

It is clear that the controversy over the validity of the Parole Release Guidelines is still a "live" one between petitioners and at least some members of the class respondent seeks to represent.   This is demonstrated by the fact that prisoners currently affected by the guidelines have moved to be substituted, or to intervene, as "named" respondents in this Court.   See n. 1, *supra.* We therefore are concerned here with the second aspect of mootness, that is, the parties' interest in the litigation.   The Court has referred to this concept as the "personal stake" requirement.   *E.g.,* Franks v. Bowman Transportation Co., 424 U.S. 747, 755 (1976).

* * *

III

On several occasions the Court has considered the application of the "personal stake" requirement in the class action context.   In Sosna v. Iowa, 419 U.S. 393 (1975), it held that mootness of the named plaintiff's individual claim *after* a class has been duly certified does not render the action moot.   It reasoned that "even though appellees * * * might not again enforce the Iowa durational residency requirement against [the class representative], it is clear that they will enforce it against those persons in the class that appellant sought to represent and that the District Court certified."   *Id.,* at 400.   The Court stated specifically that an Art. III case or controversy "may exist * * * between a named defendant and a member of the class represented by the named plaintiff, even though the claim of the named plaintiff has become moot." *Id.,* at 402.[6]

Although one might argue that Sosna contains at least an implication that the critical factor for Art. III purposes is the timing of class certification, other cases, applying a "relation back" approach, clearly demonstrate that timing is not crucial. When the claim on the merits is "capable of repetition, yet evading review," the named plaintiff may litigate the class certification issue despite loss of his personal stake in the outcome of the litigation. *E.g.,* Gerstein v. Pugh, 420 U.S. 103, 110, n. 11 (1975). The "capable of repetition, yet evading review" doctrine to be sure, was developed outside the class action context. But it has been applied where the named plaintiff does have a personal stake at the outset of the lawsuit, and where the claim may arise again with respect to that plaintiff; the litigation then may continue notwithstanding the named plaintiff's current lack of a personal stake. See, *e.g.,* Weinstein v. Bradford, 423 U.S. 147, 149 (1975); Roe v. Wade, 410 U.S. 113, 123–125 (1973). Since the litigant faces some likelihood of becoming involved in the same controversy in the future, vigorous advocacy can be expected to continue.

When, however, there is no chance that the named plaintiff's expired claim will reoccur, mootness still can be avoided through certification of a class prior to expiration of the named plaintiff's personal claim, *e.g.,* Franks v. Bowman Transportation Co., 424 U.S., at 752–757. See Kremens v. Bartley, 431 U.S. 119, 129–130 (1977). Some claims are so inherently transitory that the trial court will not have even enough time to rule on a motion for class certification before the proposed representative's individual interest expires. The Court considered this possibility in Gerstein v. Pugh, 420 U.S., at 110, n. 11. Gerstein was an action challenging pretrial detention conditions. The Court assumed that the named plaintiffs were no longer in custody awaiting trial at the time the trial court certified a class of pretrial detainees. There was no indication that the particular named plaintiffs might again be subject to pretrial detention. Nonetheless, the case was held not to be moot because:

> "The length of pretrial custody cannot be ascertained at the outset, and it may be ended at any time by release on recognizance, dismissal of the charges, or a guilty plea, as well as by acquittal or conviction after trial. It is by no means certain that any given individual, named as plaintiff, would be in pretrial custody long enough for a district judge to certify the class. Moreover, in this case the constant existence of a class of persons suffering the deprivation is certain. The attorney representing the named respondents is a public defender, and we can safely assume that he has other clients with a continuing live interest in the case." *Ibid.*

See also Sosna v. Iowa, 419 U.S., at 402, n. 11.

In two different contexts the Court has stated that the proposed class representative who proceeds to a judgment on the merits may appeal *denial* of class certification. First, this assumption was "an important ingredient," Deposit Guaranty Nat. Bank v. Roper, 445 U.S., at 338, in the rejection of

---

6. The claim in Sosna also fit the traditional category of actions that are deemed not moot despite the litigant's loss of personal stake, that is, those "capable of repetition, yet evading review." See Southern Pacific Terminal Co. v. ICC, 219 U.S. 498, 515 (1911). In Franks v. Bowman Transportation Co., 424 U.S., at 753–755, however, the Court held that the class action aspect of mootness doctrine does not depend on the class claim's being so inherently transitory that it meets the "capable of repetition, yet evading review" standard.

interlocutory appeals, "as of right," of class certification denials. Coopers & Lybrand v. Livesay, 437 U.S. 463, 469, 470, n. 15 (1978). The Court reasoned that denial of class status will not necessarily be the "death knell" of a small claimant action, since there still remains "the prospect of prevailing on the merits and reversing an order denying class certification." *Ibid.*

Second, in United Airlines, Inc. v. McDonald, 432 U.S. 385, 393–395 (1977), the Court held that a putative class member may intervene, for the purpose of appealing the denial of a class certification motion, after the named plaintiffs' claims have been satisfied and judgment entered in their favor. Underlying that decision was the view that "refusal to certify was subject to appellate review after final judgment at the behest of the named plaintiffs." *Id.,* at 393. And today, the Court holds that named plaintiffs whose claims are satisfied through entry of judgment over their objections may appeal the denial of a class certification ruling. Deposit Guaranty Nat. Bank v. Roper, 445 U.S. 326.

Gerstein, McDonald, and Roper are all examples of cases found not to be moot, despite the loss of a "personal stake" in the merits of the litigation by the proposed class representative. The interest of the named plaintiffs in Gerstein was precisely the same as that of Geraghty here. Similarly, after judgment had been entered in their favor, the named plaintiffs in McDonald had no continuing narrow personal stake in the outcome of the class claims. And in Roper the Court points out that an individual controversy is rendered moot, in the strict Art. III sense, by payment and satisfaction of a final judgment. 445 U.S., at 333.

These cases demonstrate the flexible character of the Art. III mootness doctrine.[7] As has been noted in the past, Art. III justiciability is "not a legal concept with a fixed content or susceptible of scientific verification." Poe v. Ullman, 367 U.S. 497, 508 (1961)(plurality opinion). * * *

IV

* * * [Petitioners] assert that a proposed class representative who individually prevails on the merits still has a "personal stake" in the outcome of the litigation, while the named plaintiff whose claim is truly moot does not. In the latter situation, where no class has been certified, there is no party before the court with a live claim, and it follows, it is said, that we have no jurisdiction to consider whether a class should have been certified.

We do not find this distinction persuasive. As has been noted earlier, Geraghty's "personal stake" in the outcome of the litigation is, in a practical sense, no different from that of the putative class representatives in Roper. * * *

---

7. Three of the Court's cases might be described as adopting a less flexible approach. In Indianapolis School Com'rs v. Jacobs, 420 U.S. 128 (1975), and in Weinstein v. Bradford, 423 U.S. 147 (1975), dismissal of putative class suits, as moot, was ordered after the named plaintiffs' claims became moot. And in Pasadena City Bd. of Education v. Spangler, 427 U.S. 424, 430 (1976), it was indicated that the action would have been moot, upon expiration of the named plaintiffs' claims, had not the United States intervened as a party plaintiff. Each of these, however, was a case in which there was an attempt to appeal the merits without first having obtained proper certification of a class. * * * Thus we do not find this line of cases dispositive of the question now before us.

Similarly, the fact that a named plaintiff's substantive claims are mooted due to an occurrence other than a judgment on the merits does not mean that all the other issues in the case are mooted. A plaintiff who brings a class action presents two separate issues for judicial resolution. One is the claim on the merits; the other is the claim that he is entitled to represent a class. * * *

Application of the personal stake requirement to a procedural claim, such as the right to represent a class, is not automatic or readily resolved. A "legally cognizable interest," as the Court described it in Powell v. McCormack, 395 U.S., at 496, in the traditional sense rarely ever exists with respect to the class certification claim. The justifications that led to the development of the class action include the protection of the defendant from inconsistent obligations, the protection of the interests of absentees, the provision of a convenient and economical means for disposing of similar lawsuits, and the facilitation of the spreading of litigation costs among numerous litigants with similar claims. * * * In order to achieve the primary benefits of class suits, the Federal Rules of Civil Procedure give the proposed class representative the right to have a class certified if the requirements of the rules are met. This "right" is more analogous to the private attorney general concept than to the type of interest traditionally thought to satisfy the "personal stake" requirement. See Roper, 445 U.S., at 338.

As noted above, the purpose of the "personal stake" requirement is to assure that the case is in a form capable of judicial resolution. The imperatives of a dispute capable of judicial resolution are sharply presented issues in a concrete factual setting and self-interested parties vigorously advocating opposing positions. We conclude that these elements can exist with respect to the class certification issue notwithstanding the fact that the named plaintiff's claim on the merits has expired. The question whether class certification is appropriate remains as a concrete, sharply presented issue. In Sosna v. Iowa it was recognized that a named plaintiff whose claim on the merits expires *after* class certification may still adequately represent the class. Implicit in that decision was the determination that vigorous advocacy can be assured through means other than the traditional requirement of a "personal stake in the outcome." Respondent here continues vigorously to advocate his right to have a class certified.

We therefore hold that an action brought on behalf of a class does not become moot upon expiration of the named plaintiff's substantive claim, even though class certification has been denied.[10] The proposed representative retains a "personal stake" in obtaining class certification sufficient to assure that Art. III values are not undermined. If the appeal results in reversal of the class certification denial, and a class subsequently is properly certified, the merits of the class claim then may be adjudicated pursuant to the holding in Sosna.

Our holding is limited to the appeal of the denial of the class certification motion. A named plaintiff whose claim expires may not continue to press the appeal on the merits until a class has been properly certified. See Roper, 445 U.S., at 336–337. If, on appeal, it is determined that class certification

---

10. We intimate no view as to whether a named plaintiff who settles the individual claim after denial of class certification may, consistent with Art. III, appeal from the adverse ruling on class certification. See Unit-

properly was denied, the claim on the merits must be dismissed as moot.[11]

Our conclusion that the controversy here is not moot does not automatically establish that the named plaintiff is entitled to continue litigating the interests of the class. "[I]t does shift the focus of examination from the elements of justiciability to the ability of the named representative to 'fairly and adequately protect the interests of the class.' Rule 23(a)." Sosna v. Iowa, 419 U.S., at 403. We hold only that a case or controversy still exists. The question of who is to represent the class is a separate issue.

We need not decide here whether Geraghty is a proper representative for the purpose of representing the class on the merits. No class as yet has been certified. Upon remand, the District Court can determine whether Geraghty may continue to press the class claims or whether another representative would be appropriate. We decide only that Geraghty was a proper representative for the purpose of appealing the ruling denying certification of the class that he initially defined. Thus, it was not improper for the Court of Appeals to consider whether the District Court should have granted class certification.

V

* * * Our holding that the case is not moot extends only to the appeal of the class certification denial. If the District Court again denies class certification, and that decision is affirmed, the controversy on the merits will be moot.

---

ed Airlines, Inc. v. McDonald, 432 U.S. 385, 393–394, and n. 14 (1977).

11. The erosion of the strict, formalistic perception of Art. III was begun well before today's decision.

* * *

* * * [T]he assumption thought to be "[p]ervading the Court's opinion" in [United Airlines, Inc. v. McDonald], and so vigorously attacked by [Justice Powell's] dissent there, is now relegated to "gratuitous" "dictum". Mr. Justice Powell, who [in his dissent in this case] finds the situation presented in the case at hand "fundamentally different" from that in Sosna and Franks, also found the facts of McDonald "sharply distinguishable" from those previous cases. 432 U.S., at 400.

We do not recite these cases for the purpose of showing that our result is mandated by the precedents. We concede that the prior cases may be said to be somewhat confusing, and that some, perhaps, are irreconcilable with others. Our point is that the strict, formalistic view of Art. III jurisprudence, while perhaps the starting point of all inquiry, is riddled with exceptions. And, in creating each exception, the Court has looked to practicalities and prudential considerations. The resulting doctrine can be characterized, aptly, as "flexible"; it has been developed, not irresponsibly, but "with some care," including the present case.

The dissent is correct that once exceptions are made to the formalistic interpretation of Art. III, principled distinctions and bright lines become more difficult to draw. We do not attempt to predict how far down the road the Court eventually will go toward premising jurisdiction "upon the bare existence of a sharply presented issue in a concrete and vigorously argued case." Each case must be decided on its own facts. We hasten to note, however, that this case does not even approach the extreme feared by the dissent. This respondent suffered actual, concrete injury as a result of the putatively illegal conduct, and this injury would satisfy the formalistic personal stake requirement if damages were sought. See, *e.g.,* Powell v. McCormack, 395 U.S., at 495–500. His injury continued up to and beyond the time the District Court denied class certification. We merely hold that when a District Court erroneously denies a procedural motion, which, if correctly decided, would have prevented the action from becoming moot, an appeal lies from the denial and the corrected ruling "relates back" to the date of the original denial. * * *

* * * The "relation back" principle, a traditional equitable doctrine applied to class certification claims in Gerstein v. Pugh, *supra,* serves logically to distinguish this case from the one brought a day after the prisoner is released. * * *

Furthermore, although the Court of Appeals commented upon the merits for the sole purpose of avoiding waste of judicial resources, it did not reach a final conclusion on the validity of the guidelines. Rather, it held only that summary judgment was improper and remanded for further factual development. Given the interlocutory posture of the case before us, we must defer decision on the merits of respondent's case until after it is determined affirmatively that a class properly can be certified.

The judgment of the Court of Appeals is vacated and the case is remanded for further proceedings consistent with this opinion.

It is so ordered.

■ MR. JUSTICE POWELL, with whom THE CHIEF JUSTICE, MR. JUSTICE STEWART and MR. JUSTICE REHNQUIST join, dissenting.

* * *

The Court's analysis proceeds in two steps. First, it says that mootness is a "flexible" doctrine which may be adapted as we see fit to "nontraditional" forms of litigation. Second, the Court holds that the named plaintiff has a right "analogous to the private attorney general concept" to appeal the denial of class certification even when his personal claim for relief is moot. Both steps are significant departures from settled law that rationally cannot be confined to the narrow issue presented in this case. Accordingly, I dissent.

I

As the Court observes, this case involves the "personal stake" aspect of the mootness doctrine. There is undoubtedly a "live" issue which an appropriate plaintiff could present for judicial resolution. The question is whether respondent, who has no further interest in this action, nevertheless may—through counsel—continue to litigate it.

Recent decisions of this Court have considered the personal stake requirement with some care. * * * The prudential aspect of standing aptly is described as a doctrine of uncertain contours. But the constitutional minimum has been given definite content: "In order to satisfy Art. III, the plaintiff must show that he personally has suffered some actual or threatened injury as a result of the putatively illegal conduct of the defendant." Gladstone, Realtors v. Village of Bellwood, 441 U.S. 91 (1979). * * *

As the Court notes today, the same threshold requirement must be satisfied throughout the action. * * *

* * *

[The] cases demonstrate, contrary to the Court's view today, that the core requirement of a personal stake in the outcome is not "flexible." * * *

II

* * * Art. III contains no exception for class actions. Thus, we have held that a putative class representative who alleges no individual injury "may not seek relief on behalf of himself or any other member of the class." O'Shea v. Littleton, 414 U.S. 488, 494 (1974). Only after a class has been certified in accordance with Rule 23 can it "acquir[e] a legal status separate from the interest asserted by [the named plaintiff]." Sosna v. Iowa, *supra,* 419 U.S. at 399 (1975). * * *

* * * [In this case, no] class has been certified, and the lone plaintiff no longer has any personal stake in the litigation. In the words of his own lawyer, respondent "can obtain absolutely no additional personal relief" in this case. Tr. of Oral Arg., at 25. Even the lawyer has evinced no interest in continuing to represent respondent as named plaintiff, as distinguished from other persons presently incarcerated. *Ibid.* In these circumstances, Art. III and the precedents of this Court require dismissal. But the Court * * * constructs new doctrine to breathe life into a lawsuit that has no plaintiff.

The Court announces today for the first time—and without attempting to reconcile the many cases to the contrary—that there are two categories of "the Art. III mootness doctrine": "flexible" and "less flexible." The Court then relies on cases said to demonstrate the application of "flexible" mootness to class action litigation. * * * In my view, the Court misreads the[] precedents.

A

In Sosna, the Court simply acknowledged that actual class certification gives legal recognition to additional adverse parties.[8] And in Gerstein the Court applied a rule long established, outside the class action context, by cases that never have been thought to erode the requirement of a personal stake in the outcome. Gerstein held that a class action challenging the constitutionality of pretrial detention procedures could continue after the named plaintiffs' convictions had brought their detentions to an end. The Court did not suggest that a personal stake in the outcome on the merits was unnecessary. The action continued only because of the transitory nature of pretrial detention, which placed the claim within "that narrow class of cases" that are "distinctly 'capable of repetition, yet evading review.'" 420 U.S., at 110, n. 11.[9]

McDonald and Roper sanction some appeals from the denial of class certification notwithstanding satisfaction of the class representative's claim on the merits. But neither case holds that Art. III may be satisfied in the absence of a personal stake in the outcome. * * *

There is dictum in McDonald that the "refusal to certify was subject to appellate review after final judgment at the behest of the named plaintiffs * * *." 432 U.S., at 393. That gratuitous sentence, repeated in Coopers & Lybrand v. Livesay, 437 U.S. 463, 469, 470, n. 15 (1978), apparently is elevated by the Court's opinion in this case to the status of new doctrine. There is

---

8. Certification is no mere formality. It represents a judicial finding that injured parties other than the named plaintiff exist. It also provides a definition by which they can be identified. Certification identifies and sharpens the interests of unnamed class members in the outcome; only thereafter will they be bound by the outcome. After certification, class members can be certain that the action will not be settled or dismissed without appropriate notice. * * * After certification, the case is no different in principle from more traditional representative actions involving, for example, a single party who cannot participate himself because of his incompetence but is permitted to litigate through an appointed fiduciary.

9. The Court's Gerstein analysis, which emphasized that "[p]retrial detention is by nature temporary" and that "[t]he individual could * * * suffer repeated deprivations" with no access to redress, falls squarely within the rule of Southern Pac. Terminal v. ICC, 219 U.S. 498, 515 (1911). In similar cases we have noted that the continuation of the action will depend "especially [upon] the reality of the claim that otherwise the issue would evade review." Swisher v. Brady, 438 U.S. 204, 213, n. 11 (1978), quoting Sosna v. Iowa, 419 U.S. 393, 402, n. 11 (1975). These limitations are inconsistent with the concept of "flexible" mootness and the redefinition of "personal stake" adopted today.

serious tension between this new doctrine and the much narrower reasoning adopted today in Roper. In Roper the Court holds that the named plaintiffs, who have refused to accept proffered individual settlements, retain a personal stake in sharing anticipated litigation costs with the class. 445 U.S., at 334, n. 6, 336. * * *

It is far from apparent how Roper can be thought to support the decision in this case. Indeed, the opinion by The Chief Justice in Roper reaffirms the obligation of a federal court to dismiss an appeal when the parties no longer retain the personal stake in the outcome required by Art. III. Here, there is not even a speculative interest in sharing costs, and respondent affirmatively denies that he retains any stake or personal interest in the outcome of his appeal. Thus, a fact that was critical to the analysis in Roper is absent in this case. One can disagree with that analysis yet conclude that Roper affords no support for the Court's ruling here.

B

The cases cited by the Court as "less flexible"—and therefore less authoritative—apply established Art. III doctrine in cases closely analogous to this one. Indianapolis School Com'rs v. Jacobs, 420 U.S. 128 (1975)(*per curiam*); Weinstein v. Bradford, 423 U.S. 147 (1975)(*per curiam*); Pasadena City Board of Education v. Spangler, 427 U.S. 424, 430 (1976). As they are about to become second class precedents, these cases are relegated to a footnote. But the cases are recent and carefully considered decisions of this Court. * * *

The Court suggests that Jacobs and Spangler may be distinguished because the plaintiffs there were not appealing the denial of class certification. The Court overlooks the fact that in each case the class representatives were defending a judgment on the merits from which the defendants had appealed. The plaintiff/respondents continued vigorously to assert the claims of the class. They did not take the procedural route of appealing a denial of certification only because the District Court had granted—albeit defectively—class status. We chose not to remand for correction of the oral certification order in Jacobs because we recognized that the putative class representative had suffered no injury that could be redressed by adequate certification. Underlying Jacobs, and Bradford as well, is the elementary principle that no one has a personal stake in obtaining relief for third parties, through the mechanism of class certification or otherwise.[13] The Court rejects that principle today.

III

While the Court's new concept of "flexible" mootness is unprecedented, the content given that concept is even more disturbing. The Court splits the class aspects of this action into two separate "claims": (i) that the action may be maintained by respondent on behalf of a class, and (ii) that the class is entitled to relief on the merits. Since no class has been certified, the Court concedes that the claim on the merits is moot. But respondent is said to have a personal stake in his "procedural claim" despite his lack of a stake in the merits.

13. In some circumstances, litigants are permitted to argue the rights of third parties in support of their claims. *E.g.,* Singleton v. Wulff, 428 U.S. 106, 113 (1976); Barrows v. Jackson, 346 U.S. 249, 255–256 (1953). In each such case, however, the Court has identified a concrete, individual injury suffered by the litigant himself.

The Court makes no effort to identify any injury to respondent that may be redressed by, or any benefit to respondent that may accrue from, a favorable ruling on the certification question.[14] Instead, respondent's "personal stake" is said to derive from two factors having nothing to do with concrete injury or stake in the outcome. First, the Court finds that the Federal Rules of Civil Procedure create a "right," "analogous to the private attorney general concept," to have a class certified. Second, the Court thinks that the case retains the "imperatives of a dispute capable of judicial resolution," which are identified as (i) a sharply presented issue, (ii) a concrete factual setting, and (iii) a self-interested party actually contesting the case.

The Court's reliance on some new "right" inherent in Rule 23 is misplaced. We have held that even Congress may not confer federal court jurisdiction when Art. III does not. Gladstone, Realtors v. Village of Bellwood, 441 U.S., at 100; O'Shea v. Littleton, 414 U.S., at 494, and n. 2; see Marbury v. Madison, 1 Cranch (5 U.S.) 137, 175–177 (1803). Far less so may a rule of procedure which "shall not be construed to extend * * * the jurisdiction of the United States district courts." Fed.Rule Civ.Proc. 82. Moreover, the "private attorney general concept" cannot supply the personal stake necessary to satisfy Art. III. It serves only to permit litigation by a party who has a stake of his own but otherwise might be barred by prudential standing rules. See Warth v. Seldin, 422 U.S., at 501; Sierra Club v. Morton, 405 U.S., at 737–738.

* * * Although we have refused steadfastly to countenance the "public action," the Court's redefinition of the personal stake requirement leaves no principled basis for that practice.[18] * * *

Class actions may advance significantly the administration of justice in appropriate cases. Indeed, the class action is scarcely a new idea. * * * The effect of mootness on the vitality of a device like the class action may be a relevant prudential consideration. But it cannot provide a plaintiff when none is before the Court, for we are powerless to assume jurisdiction in violation of Art. III.

* * *

NOTE ON MOOTNESS AND CLASS ACTIONS

(1) *Class Actions and Public Rights.* In 1973, Professor Monaghan wrote: "Marbury's analogy of constitutional litigation to 'ordinary' common law litiga-

---

14. In a footnote, the Court states:

"This respondent suffered actual, concrete injury as a result of the putatively illegal conduct, and this injury would satisfy the formalistic personal stake requirement if damages were sought. See, *e.g,* Powell v. McCormack, 395 U.S., at 495–500."

This appears to be a categorical claim of the actual, concrete injury our cases have required. Yet, again, the Court fails to identify the injury. The reference to damages is irrelevant here, as respondent sought no damages—only injunctive and declaratory relief. Moreover, counsel for respondent frankly conceded that his client "can obtain absolutely no additional personal relief" in this case. Tr. of Oral Arg. 25. * * *

18. The Court's view logically cannot be confined to moot cases. If a plaintiff who is released from prison the day after filing a class action challenging parole guidelines may seek certification of the class, why should a plaintiff who is released the day before filing the suit be barred? As an Art. III matter, there can be no difference.

tion strongly suggested that the occasions for judicial review were limited to the protection of identifiable and concrete personal rights, similar to those protected by the common law courts." Monaghan, *Constitutional Adjudication: The Who and When,* 82 Yale L.J. 1363, 1366 (1973). Later in the same piece, he concluded: "Perhaps more than any other single development, the mushrooming of class actions has rendered the private rights model [of Marbury] largely unintelligible" (p. 1383). *Cf.* Fiss, *Foreword: The Forms of Justice,* 92 Harv. L.Rev. 1, 19–21 (1974).

Does the majority opinion in Geraghty, written seven years later, bear out this thesis? Isn't Justice Powell correct that Geraghty had no personal stake in the outcome of the certification issue?[1] *Cf.* Lujan v. Defenders of Wildlife, 504 U.S. 555 (1992), p. 157, *supra.*

Is the dispute resolution model, pp. 78-79, *supra,* inconsistent with the recognition of group interests underlying the development of the class action? Or is the Geraghty majority at fault for not recognizing that the major goal of the class action—more vigorous and effective enforcement of group rights—can best be achieved by insistence that the litigation be prosecuted by a representative of the group who continues to share its concerns? Is it an answer that in any event the members of the group not themselves before the court have an ongoing dispute? See Deposit Guar. Nat'l Bank v. Roper, 445 U.S. 326, 342–44 (1980)(Stevens, J., concurring), Paragraph (4), *infra.* Does the court know whether they do, or what the true dimensions of that dispute are, without at least one of their number at the bar? Should it accept the assurances of their lawyer, on the theory that whether or not there is a "named plaintiff" with a live interest, it is really counsel who controls the litigation in such cases and determines its course?[2]

Geraghty itself was not written on a clean slate, and as the following Paragraphs suggest, was to a significant extent a consequence of earlier decisions.

(2) *Evolution of Mootness Doctrine in Class Actions.* The evolution of the mootness doctrine in class actions was extraordinarily rapid. Following a brief footnote alluding to the issue in Dunn v. Blumstein, 405 U.S. 330 (1972), the Court in Indiana Employment Sec. Div. v. Burney, 409 U.S. 540, 541–42 (1973), remanded a class action for consideration of mootness after the named plaintiff's claim had been fully settled. Then in Sosna v. Iowa, 419 U.S. 393 (1975), discussed in Geraghty, the Court announced that certification as a class action could save litigation from mootness even after the named plaintiff no longer had an individual claim. The Court, however, appeared to require that the controversy (over a state durational residency requirement for obtaining a divorce) be within the "capable of repetition, yet evading review" category (not

---

1. For forceful criticism of the Geraghty majority's reliance on a Rule 23 right to seek class certification (but a defense of the decision on other grounds), see Greenstein, *Bridging the Mootness Gap in Federal Court Class Actions,* 35 Stan.L.Rev. 897, 907– 08 (1983). Does such reliance raise a question under the Rules Enabling Act? (See Chap. VI, Sec. 1, *infra.*)

2. The court can, of course, seek to communicate with members of the class either before or after certification. But should that technique—which must to some degree operate through counsel—be regarded as a complete substitute for the requirement that the lawyer in such a case have a direct relationship with a live client? See Paragraph (5), *infra.*

for the named plaintiff but for the remaining members of the class) and that careful attention be given to the adequacy of representation.[3]

The first of these requirements crumbled in Franks v. Bowman Transp. Co., 424 U.S. 747 (1976), a class action in which the sole issue before the Supreme Court was a demand for retroactive seniority in employment and in which the plaintiff, the only named representative of the class, had been lawfully discharged by the employer after certification. In holding the case not moot, the Court, which was unanimous on this point, said (pp. 754–56): "[N]othing in our Sosna * * * [or other] opinions holds or even intimates that the fact the named plaintiff no longer has a personal stake in the outcome of a certified class action renders the class action moot unless there remains an issue 'capable of repetition, yet evading review.' * * *

"* * * Given a properly certified class action, Sosna contemplates that mootness turns on whether, in the specific circumstances of the given case at the time it is before this Court, an adversary relationship sufficient to fulfill this function [of 'concrete adverseness which sharpens the presentation of issues'] exists. In this case, that adversary relationship obviously obtained as to unnamed class members * * *."

How significant was it that other members of the class in the Franks case were "individually named in the record" and actively seeking relief? Wouldn't the mootness issue have been obviated if one or more had been added as a named plaintiff? If so, why wasn't that required? *Cf.* n. 1 of the majority opinion in Geraghty.

(3) *Uncertain Significance of Class Certification.* Even before Geraghty, the significance of class certification in the application of evolving mootness doctrine was in flux.

(a) In Board of School Comm'rs v. Jacobs, 420 U.S. 128 (1975), and Weinstein v. Bradford, 423 U.S. 147 (1975), discussed in both opinions in Geraghty, the Court held that the mootness of the named plaintiffs' claims mooted the entire case where class action status had been sought but formal certification had not been granted. Yet in Gerstein v. Pugh, 420 U.S. 103 (1975), relied on by the Geraghty majority, a putative class action challenging pretrial detention procedures was held by a unanimous Court to be not moot even though the named plaintiffs had evidently been tried before the district court certified the class. The Court said (pp. 110–11 n. 11): "Such a showing [that the case was not moot as to all named plaintiffs at the time of certification] ordinarily would be required to avoid mootness under Sosna. But this case is a suitable exception to that requirement. * * * It is by no means certain that any given individual, named as plaintiff, would be in pretrial custody long enough for a district judge to certify the class. Moreover, in this case the constant existence of a class of persons suffering deprivation is certain. The attorney representing the named respondents [plaintiffs] is a public defender, and we can safely assume that he has other clients with a continuing live interest in the case."

---

3. In Sosna itself, the Court said that "where it is unlikely that segments of the class appellant represents would have interests conflicting with those she has sought to advance, and where the interests of that class have been competently urged at each level of the proceeding, we believe that the [adequate representation] test of Rule 23(a) is met" (p. 403). For further discussion of this issue, see Paragraph (8) of this Note.

(b) Paralleling these decisions were several important cases dealing with appeals from district court denials of class certification motions. In United Airlines, Inc. v. McDonald, 432 U.S. 385 (1977), a class member was held entitled to intervene in order to appeal the denial of class certification, after the named plaintiffs' claims had been fully satisfied. And in Coopers & Lybrand v. Livesay, 437 U.S. 463 (1978), the Court held that a denial of a motion to certify was not an appealable final judgment under 28 U.S.C. § 1291. Both decisions explicitly assumed the appealability of a denial of class certification, at the behest of the named plaintiff, after final judgment, and both were invoked by the majority in support of the Geraghty result.

(4) *No Stopping Point?* If its prior decisions in this area were correct, could the Court responsibly have stopped short of the Geraghty result? Sosna and Franks established that neither constitutional nor prudential considerations invariably require the named plaintiff to have a continuing stake in the outcome. And Gerstein had eliminated formal certification prior to mootness of the named plaintiff's claim as an indispensable requirement. Indeed, is the act of formal certification as significant, either in constitutional or prudential terms, as Sosna suggested and Justice Powell, dissenting in Geraghty, insisted? (For a negative answer, see Greenstein, note 1, *supra.*) A class may be certified without any real contest between the parties, since certification may be to the advantage of both sides, and even after certification, other members of the class may be able to opt out (see Fed.R.Civ.P. 23(c)(2)), or to challenge the adequacy of representation and thus the binding effect of the judgment in a collateral proceeding (see Hansberry v. Lee, 311 U.S. 32 (1940)). Moreover, even if certification is critical, despite these considerations, why shouldn't an order of certification relate back, for purposes of determining mootness, when a request for class action status had been improperly denied before the case became moot? *Cf.* Fed.R.Civ.P. 15(c)(relation back of amended complaint for purposes of the statute of limitations). Wasn't the case for "relation back", and for appealability generally in a case like Geraghty, made even stronger by the Court's decision in Coopers & Lybrand to bar interlocutory appeals of certification denials as a matter of right?

The Court's momentum was also evident in Deposit Guar. Nat'l Bank v. Roper, 445 U.S. 326 (1980), decided the same day as Geraghty and discussed in both Geraghty opinions. Roper involved a damage suit for allegedly unlawful finance charges brought by credit card holders who sought to represent themselves as individuals and also to represent a class of similarly situated card holders. After the district court denied a motion to certify the class and an attempt to take an interlocutory appeal of that denial was rejected, the defendant tendered to each individual plaintiff the maximum amount each could have recovered. The plaintiffs refused to accept the tender, but the district court, on the basis of the tender, entered judgment over plaintiffs' objections and dismissed the action. Plaintiffs then sought review of the class certification ruling in the court of appeals and obtained a reversal of that ruling, with the appellate court rejecting the defendant's argument that the entry of judgment had mooted the case. The Supreme Court granted certiorari limited to the question of mootness and affirmed, 7–2. In an opinion for six Justices (with Justice Blackmun concurring on a broader ground), Chief Justice Burger emphasized that plaintiffs had rejected the offer of settlement and that, even after that offer, they retained "a continuing individual interest in the resolution of the class certification question in their desire to shift part of the costs of litigation [including attorney's fees] to those who will share in its benefits if the class is certified and ultimately prevails" (p. 336).

Dissenting for himself and Justice Stewart, Justice Powell argued that since no class had been certified, only the individual plaintiffs were involved at the time the tender of full relief to them was made, and such a tender "remedies a plaintiff's injuries and eliminates his stake in the outcome" (p. 347).

On the specific question of attorney's fees, Justice Powell noted that plaintiffs appeared to have entered a "customary type contingent fee" arrangement for payment to counsel of 25% of the final judgment. "[N]o one has explained", he continued, "how [plaintiffs'] obligation to pay 25% of their recovery to counsel could be reduced if a class is certified and its members become similarly obligated to pay 25% of their recovery" (pp. 350–51).

(5) *Possible Significance of a Plaintiff with a Personal Stake.* The constitutional argument for nonjusticiability in a case like Geraghty centers on the lack of an ongoing dispute involving the class member before the court. Whether or not that argument is accepted, does the absence of a named plaintiff with a stake in the outcome invoke prudential considerations favoring a refusal to adjudicate? Without a real, live client, is there sufficient insurance of counsel's competence, tenacity, and orientation? Does the simple fact that there is such a client impose significant limitations on the conduct of counsel?[4] As noted in Paragraph (2), *supra,* there were identified people who might well have come forward as representatives in Franks v. Bowman Transp. Co. (as there were in Geraghty), and they were apparently actively involved in the litigation. But didn't the Court's failure to insist that at least one actually be named as plaintiff make it less likely that in the future the Franks case would be limited to that situation? Why did the Court ignore that available alternative in Geraghty?[5]

(6) *Implications for Standing Doctrine?* What is the answer to the question posed in note 18 of Justice Powell's dissent? Given the relationship between

4. This question and its implications, and the general subject of possible divergence of interests between lawyers and clients, are of recurring importance in class action cases and other cases involving "public interest" lawyers. See, *e.g.,* Stewart, *The Reformation of American Administrative Law,* 88 Harv. L.Rev. 1667, 1762–69 (1975), and sources there cited; Bell, *Serving Two Masters: Integration Ideals and Client Interests in School Desegregation Litigation,* 85 Yale L.J. 470 (1976); Coffee, *Class Wars: The Dilemma of the Mass Tort Class Action,* 95 Colum.L.Rev. 1343 (1995). Compare Simon, *Homo Psychologicus: Notes on a New Legal Formalism,* 32 Stan.L.Rev. 487, 505 (1980): "Although it appears that the way the disadvantaged can most effectively use the legal system is through organization and through coordination and aggregation of claims, the bar continues to discourage and inhibit this kind of lawyering in the name of 'devotion to the interests of individual clients.' Issues con-

cerning the distribution of power in society are translated into issues of personal relations."

5. In some instances, insistence that the lawyer have an identifiable client with an ongoing interest may lead only to the naming of a class representative with little or no knowledge of the case who will play no role in the course of the litigation. Does it follow that such insistence is always and necessarily a sterile formalism? Or do Simon's concerns, note 4, *supra,* suggest that adherence to the requirement may in some instances temper the single-minded pursuit of some outsider's conception of the interests of the group?

For discussion of ways of increasing counsel's accountability to the class in "plaintiff class actions seeking structural reforms in public and private institutions", see Rhode, *Class Conflicts in Class Actions,* 34 Stan.L.Rev. 1183 (1982).

mootness and standing, can the courts turn away, on grounds of nonjusticiability, the plaintiff who is no longer a member of the class when the suit is filed, or who has never been in the class at all?

In Hall v. Beals, 396 U.S. 45 (1969), plaintiffs brought a federal court class action challenging a six-month residency requirement for voting. When the action was filed, they had resided in the state more than two but less than six months. While their appeal from dismissal of the complaint was pending, the election they had wanted to vote in was held, and the state legislature reduced the residency requirement to two months. The Court decided that the case had become moot, and emphasized that the class of voters disqualified by virtue of the new two-month requirement was "a class of which the appellants have *never* been members" (p. 49)(emphasis added).

Is Hall v. Beals still good law?[6] In terms of the interest in self-determination articulated by Professor Brilmayer as one of the policies underlying Article III, p. 79, *supra,* there may be a difference between a plaintiff who is no longer part of a class and one who has never been a member at all, but is this difference large enough to rationalize the conjunction of Geraghty with Hall v. Beals?

(7) *State Class Action Doctrine and Mootness on Appeal.* Richardson v. Ramirez, 418 U.S. 24 (1974), was a state court action against state election officials challenging a law disenfranchising convicted felons. The Supreme Court concluded that the state courts had treated the case as a class action and that, as such, it presented a justiciable controversy; even though the named plaintiffs had received all the relief that they sought, there was a continuing dispute involving "the unnamed members of the classes represented below by petitioners and respondents" (p. 40). Had the suit been brought in federal court, there "would be serious doubt as to whether it could have proceeded as a class action * * *. But California is at liberty to prescribe its own rules for class actions" (p. 39). The Court saw strong practical arguments militating against a holding of mootness, especially the fact that were the state judgment for the plaintiffs allowed to stand, the defendant officials would be "permanently bound by [the state court's] conclusion on a matter of federal constitutional law" (p. 35)—a conclusion that the U.S. Supreme Court went on to reverse. *Cf.* ASARCO Inc. v. Kadish, 490 U.S. 605 (1989), p. 155, *supra.*

(8) *Proper Class Representation.* Though the Court held in Geraghty that the question of class certification was justiciable, it emphasized that it was not deciding "whether Geraghty is a proper representative for the purpose of representing the class on the merits." That question calls for application of Rule 23 of the Federal Rules of Civil Procedure, and several Supreme Court decisions have applied the Rule 23 criteria to bar prosecution of a claim by the named plaintiff.[7]

---

6. See the last paragraph of footnote 11 of the Court's opinion in Geraghty. *Cf.* Blum v. Yaretsky, 457 U.S. 991, 999 (1982), in which the Court, without citing either Geraghty or Hall v. Beals, held part of a class action claim nonjusticiable, saying: "It is not enough that the conduct of which the plaintiff complains will injure *someone.* The complaining party must also show that he is within the class of persons who will be concretely affected."

7. *Cf.* Kremens v. Bartley, 431 U.S. 119 (1977), in which the Court held that changes in the law not only mooted the claims of the named plaintiffs but also served to fragment the original class and required reconsideration of the class definition as well as the substitution of representatives with live claims.

In General Tel. Co. v. Falcon, 457 U.S. 147 (1982), for example, an employee who claimed he had been denied a promotion because of his national origin brought a federal court class action against his employer on behalf of all Mexican–American employees *and* applicants for employment allegedly discriminated against with respect to promotion or hiring. The Supreme Court held, unanimously on this issue, that it was error, on these allegations alone, to certify the case as an "across-the-board" class action. Noting the overlap among the commonality, typicality, and adequacy-of-representation requirements of Rule 23(a), the Court said (pp. 158–59):

"Respondent's complaint provided an insufficient basis for concluding that the adjudication of his claim of discrimination in promotion would require the decision of any common question concerning the failure of petitioner to hire more Mexican–Americans. * * * If one allegation of specific discriminatory treatment were sufficient to support an across-the-board attack, every Title VII case would be a potential companywide class action."[8]

(9) *From Mootness to Rule 23.* The end result of Sosna and its progeny, on the one hand, and decisions like Falcon, on the other, is apparently to move consideration of issues bearing on the role of courts in certain class action cases from the context of the mootness doctrine to that of Rule 23. Can that move perhaps be justified in terms of Justice Stevens' argument in Roper that Article III is satisfied as long as there is a live dispute between the class and its adversary? Under this argument, the class itself is regarded as a legal entity, not simply as a device for the efficient litigation of many similar individual claims.

Even if such a view is adopted, isn't a question of standing raised with respect to the appropriateness of the named representative as litigator of that dispute? (See Sec. 3, *supra.*) Is that question of standing one of constitutional dimension, or may it be viewed as essentially prudential, to be determined in accordance with the criteria laid down in Rule 23?[9]

SECTION 5. RIPENESS

United Public Workers v. Mitchell

330 U.S. 75, 67 S.Ct. 556, 91 L.Ed. 754 (1947).
Appeal from the District Court for the District of Columbia.

■ MR. JUSTICE REED delivered the opinion of the Court. * * *

[The appellant federal employees and their union sought declaratory and injunctive relief from a provision of the Hatch Act and an implementing civil service rule that forbade executive officers and employees to "take any active part in political management or in political campaigns." This prohibition was

---

8. The Court also underscored "the potential unfairness to the class members bound by the judgment if the framing of the class is overbroad" (p. 161).

See also East Texas Motor Freight System Inc. v. Rodriguez, 431 U.S. 395 (1977);

Satterwhite v. City of Greenville, 578 F.2d 987 (5th Cir.1978) (en banc), *vacated and remanded,* 445 U.S. 940 (1980), *on remand,* 634 F.2d 231 (5th Cir.1981)(en banc).

9. For an able discussion of these issues, see Greenstein, note 1, *supra.*

claimed to violate the First, Fifth, Ninth, and Tenth Amendments to the Constitution.]

* * * It is alleged that the individuals desire to engage in acts of political management and in political campaigns. Their purposes are as stated in the excerpt from the complaint set out in the margin.[11] From the affidavits it is plain, and we so assume, that these activities will be carried on completely outside of the hours of employment. * * *

None of the appellants, except George P. Poole, has violated the provisions of the Hatch Act. They wish to act contrary to its provisions and those of * * * the Civil Service Rules and desire a declaration of the legally permissible limits of regulation. Defendants moved to dismiss the complaint for lack of a justiciable case or controversy. The [three-judge] District Court determined that each of these individual appellants had an interest in their claimed privilege of engaging in political activities, sufficient to give them a right to maintain this suit. The District Court further determined that the questioned provision of the Hatch Act was valid and * * * accordingly dismissed the complaint and granted summary judgment to defendants. * * *

Second. At the threshold of consideration, we are called upon to decide whether the complaint states a controversy cognizable in this Court. We defer consideration of the cause of action of Mr. Poole until section *Three* of this opinion. The other individual employees have elaborated the grounds of their objection in individual affidavits for use in the hearing on the summary judgment. We select as an example one that contains the essential averments of all the others and print below the portions with significance in this suit.[18]

11. "In discharge of their duties of citizenship, of their right to vote, and in exercise of their constitutional rights of freedom of speech, of the press, of assembly, and the right to engage in political activity, the individual plaintiffs desire to engage in the following acts: write for publication letters and articles in support of candidates for office; be connected editorially with publications which are identified with the legislative program of UFWA [former name of the present union appellant] and candidates who support it; solicit votes, aid in getting out voters, act as accredited checker, watcher, or challenger; transport voters to and from the polls without compensation therefor; participate in and help in organizing political parades; initiate petitions, and canvass for the signatures of others on such petitions; serve as party ward committeeman or other party official; and perform any and all acts not prohibited by any provision of law other than the second sentence of Section 9(a) and Section 15 of the Hatch Act, which constitute taking an active part in political management and political campaigns."

18. "At this time, when the fate of the entire world is in the balance, I believe it is not only proper but an obligation for all citizens to participate actively in the making of the vital political decisions on which the success of the war and the permanence of the peace to follow so largely depend. For the purpose of participating in the making of these decisions it is my earnest desire to engage actively in political management and political campaigns. I wish to engage in such activity upon my own time, as a private citizen.

"I wish to engage in such activities on behalf of those candidates for public office who I believe will best serve the needs of this country and with the object of persuading others of the correctness of my judgments and of electing the candidates of my choice. This objective I wish to pursue by all proper means such as engaging in discussion, by speeches to conventions, rallies and other assemblages, by publicizing my views in letters and articles for publication in newspapers and other periodicals, by aiding in the campaign of candidates for political office by posting banners and posters in public places, by distributing leaflets, by 'ringing doorbells', by addressing campaign literature, and by doing any and all acts of like character reasonably designed to assist in the election of candidates I favor.

"I desire to engage in these activities freely, openly, and without concealment.

Nothing similar to the fourth paragraph of the printed affidavit is contained in the other affidavits. The assumed controversy between affiant and the Civil Service Commission as to affiant's right to act as watcher at the polls on November 2, 1943, had long been moot when this complaint was filed. We do not therefore treat this allegation separately. The affidavits, it will be noticed, follow the generality of purpose expressed by the complaint. They declare a desire to act contrary to the rule against political activity but not that the rule has been violated. In this respect, we think they differ from the type of threat adjudicated in Railway Mail Association v. Corsi, 326 U.S. 88. In that case, the refusal to admit an applicant to membership in a labor union on account of race was involved. Admission had been refused. Definite action had also been taken in Hill v. Florida, 325 U.S. 538. In the Hill case an injunction had been sought and allowed against Hill and the union forbidding Hill from acting as the business agent of the union and the union from further functioning as a union until it complied with the state law. The threats which menaced the affiants of these affidavits in the case now being considered are closer to a general threat by officials to enforce those laws which they are charged to administer than they are to the direct threat of punishment against a named organization for a completed act that made the Mail Association and the Hill cases justiciable.

As is well known, the federal courts established pursuant to Article III of the Constitution do not render advisory opinions. For adjudication of constitutional issues, "concrete legal issues, presented in actual cases, not abstractions" are requisite. This is as true of declaratory judgments as any other field. These appellants seem clearly to seek advisory opinions upon broad claims of rights protected by the First, Fifth, Ninth and Tenth Amendments to the Constitution. As these appellants are classified employees, they have a right superior to the generality of citizens, compare Fairchild v. Hughes, 258 U.S. 126, but the facts of their personal interest in their civil rights, of the general threat of possible interference with those rights by the Civil Service Commission under its rules, if specified things are done by appellants, does not make a justiciable case or controversy. Appellants want to engage in "political management and political campaigns," to persuade others to follow appellants' views by discussion, speeches, articles and other acts reasonably designed to secure the selection of appellants' political choices. Such generality of objec-

However, I understand that the second sentence of Section 9(a) of the Hatch Act and the Rules of the C.S.C. provide that if I engage in this activity, the Civil Service Commission will order that I be dismissed from federal employment. Such deprivation of my job in the federal government would be a source of immediate and serious financial loss and other injury to me.

"At the last Congressional election I was very much interested in the outcome of the campaign and offered to help the party of my choice by being a watcher at the polls. I obtained a watcher's certificate but I was advised that there might be some question of my right to use the certificate and retain my federal employment. Therefore, on November 1, 1943, the day before the election, I called the regional office of the Civil Service Commission in Philadelphia and spoke to a person who gave his name as * * *. Mr. * * * stated that if I used my watcher's certificate, the Civil Service Commission would see that I was dismissed from my job at the * * * for violation of the Hatch Act. I, therefore, did not use the certificate as I had intended.

"I believe that Congress may not constitutionally abridge my right to engage in the political activities mentioned above. However, unless the courts prevent the Civil Service Commission from enforcing this unconstitutional law, I will be unable freely to exercise my rights as a citizen." [Identifying words omitted.]

tion is really an attack on the political expediency of the Hatch Act, not the presentation of legal issues. It is beyond the competence of courts to render such a decision.

The power of courts, and ultimately of this Court to pass upon the constitutionality of acts of Congress arises only when the interests of litigants require the use of this judicial authority for their protection against actual interference. A hypothetical threat is not enough. We can only speculate as to the kinds of political activity the appellants desire to engage in or as to the contents of their proposed public statements or the circumstances of their publication. It would not accord with judicial responsibility to adjudge, in a matter involving constitutionality, between the freedom of the individual and the requirements of public order except when definite rights appear upon the one side and definite prejudicial interferences upon the other.

The Constitution allots the nation's judicial power to the federal courts. Unless these courts respect the limits of that unique authority, they intrude upon powers vested in the legislative or executive branches. * * * Should the courts seek to expand their power so as to bring under their jurisdiction ill-defined controversies over constitutional issues, they would become the organ of political theories. Such abuse of judicial power would properly meet rebuke and restriction from other branches. * * * No threat of interference by the Commission with rights of these appellants appears beyond that implied by the existence of the law and the regulations. * * * These reasons lead us to conclude that the determination of the trial court, that the individual appellants, other than Poole, could maintain this action, was erroneous.

Third. The appellant Poole does present by the complaint and affidavit matters appropriate for judicial determination. The affidavits filed by appellees confirm that Poole has been charged by the Commission with political activity and a proposed order for his removal from his position adopted subject to his right under Commission procedure to reply to the charges and to present further evidence in refutation. We proceed to consider the controversy over constitutional power at issue between Poole and the Commission as defined by the charge and preliminary finding upon one side and the admissions of Poole's affidavit upon the other. Our determination is limited to those facts. This proceeding so limited meets the requirements of defined rights and a definite threat to interfere with a possessor of the menaced rights by a penalty for an act done in violation of the claimed restraint.

Because we conclude hereinafter that the prohibition of § 9 of the Hatch Act and Civil Service Rule 1, * * * are valid, it is unnecessary to consider, as this is a declaratory judgment action, whether or not this appellant sufficiently alleges that an irreparable injury to him would result from his removal from his position. Nor need we inquire whether or not a court of equity would enforce by injunction any judgment declaring rights. Since Poole admits that he violated the rule against political activity and that removal from office is therefore mandatory under the act, there is no question as to the exhaustion of administrative remedies. * * * Under such circumstances, we see no reason why a declaratory judgment action, even though constitutional issues are involved, does not lie. * * *

[The Court held that Poole had violated the Act, and that the Act as applied to him was valid.

[MR. JUSTICE FRANKFURTER delivered a concurring opinion dealing with a point of appellate procedure.

[MR. JUSTICE BLACK delivered a dissenting opinion, expressing the view that all the complaints stated a case or controversy, and that the Act as applied in all the cases was invalid.]

■ MR. JUSTICE DOUGLAS, dissenting in part.

I disagree with the Court on two of the four matters decided.

First. There are twelve individual appellants here asking for an adjudication of their rights. The Court passes on the claim of only one of them, Poole. It declines to pass on the claims of the other eleven on the ground that they do not present justiciable cases or controversies. With this conclusion I cannot agree.

* * *

The declaratory judgment procedure is designed "to declare rights and other legal relations of any interested party * * * whether or not further relief is or could be prayed." Judicial Code, § 274d, 28 U.S.C. § 400. The fact that equity would not restrain a wrongful removal of an office holder but would leave the complainant to his legal remedies is, therefore, immaterial. A judgment which, without more, adjudicates the status of a person is permissible under the Declaratory Judgment Act. Perkins v. Elg, 307 U.S. 325, 349, 350. * * * The right to hold an office or public position against such threats is a common example of its use. Borchard, Declaratory Judgments (2d ed.), pp. 858 *et seq.* Declaratory relief is the singular remedy available here to preserve the status quo while the constitutional rights of these appellants to make these utterances and to engage in these activities are determined. The threat against them is real not fanciful, immediate not remote. The case is therefore an actual not a hypothetical one. And the present case seems to me to be a good example of a situation where uncertainty, peril, and insecurity result from imminent and immediate threats to asserted rights.

Since the Court does not reach the constitutionality of the claims of these eleven individual appellants, a discussion of them would seem to be premature. * * *

Abbott Laboratories v. Gardner

387 U.S. 136, 87 S.Ct. 1507, 18 L.Ed.2d 681 (1967).
Certiorari to the United States Court of Appeals for the Third Circuit.

■ MR. JUSTICE HARLAN delivered the opinion of the Court.

In 1962 Congress amended the Federal Food, Drug, and Cosmetic Act * * * to require manufacturers of prescription drugs to print the "established name" of the drug "prominently and in type at least half as large as that used thereon for any proprietary [or brand] name * * *" on labels and other printed material * * *. The underlying purpose of the 1962 amendment was to bring to the attention of doctors and patients the fact that many of the drugs sold under familiar trade names are actually identical to drugs sold under their "established" or less familiar trade names at significantly lower prices. The

Commissioner of Food and Drugs, exercising authority delegated to him by the Secretary, * * * promulgated [a regulation providing that] * * *:

> "If the label or labeling of a prescription drug bears a proprietary name or designation for the drug or any ingredient thereof, the established name, if such there be, corresponding to such proprietary name or designation, shall accompany each appearance of such proprietary name or designation."

A similar rule was made applicable to advertisements for prescription drugs * * *.

The present action was brought by a group of 37 individual drug manufacturers and by the Pharmaceutical Manufacturers Association, of which all the petitioner companies are members, and which includes manufacturers of more than 90% of the Nation's supply of prescription drugs. They challenged the regulations on the ground that the Commissioner exceeded his authority under the statute by promulgating an order requiring labels, advertisements, and other printed matter relating to prescription drugs to designate the established name of the particular drug involved every time its trade name is used anywhere in such material.

The District Court, on cross motions for summary judgment, granted the declaratory and injunctive relief sought, finding that the statute did not sweep so broadly as to permit the Commissioner's "every time" interpretation. * * * The Court of Appeals for the Third Circuit reversed without reaching the merits of the case. * * * [T]he Court of Appeals held [inter alia] that no "actual case or controversy" existed * * *.

I.

[Congress did not] * * * intend to forbid pre-enforcement review of this sort of regulation promulgated by the Commissioner. * * * [Based on applicable precedents], only upon a showing of "clear and convincing evidence" of a contrary legislative intent should the courts restrict access to judicial review [quoting Rusk v. Cort, 369 U.S. 367, 379–80 (1962)]. * * *

Given this standard, we are wholly unpersuaded that the statutory scheme in the food and drug area excludes this type of action. * * *

* * *

II.

A further inquiry must, however, be made. The injunctive and declaratory judgment remedies are discretionary, and courts traditionally have been reluctant to apply them to administrative determinations unless these arise in the context of a controversy "ripe" for judicial resolution. Without undertaking to survey the intricacies of the ripeness doctrine it is fair to say that its basic rationale is to prevent the courts, through avoidance of premature adjudication, from entangling themselves in abstract disagreements over administrative policies, and also to protect the agencies from judicial interference until an administrative decision has been formalized and its effects felt in a concrete way by the challenging parties. The problem is best seen in a twofold aspect, requiring us to evaluate both the fitness of the issues for judicial decision and the hardship to the parties of withholding court consideration.

As to the former factor, we believe the issues presented are appropriate for judicial resolution at this time. First, all parties agree that the issue tendered is a purely legal one: whether the statute was properly construed by the Commissioner to require the established name of the drug to be used *every time* the proprietary name is employed. Both sides moved for summary judgment in the District Court, and no claim is made here that further administrative proceedings are contemplated. It is suggested that the justification for this rule might vary with different circumstances, and that the expertise of the Commissioner is relevant to passing upon the validity of the regulation. This of course is true, but the suggestion overlooks the fact that both sides have approached this case as one purely of congressional intent, and that the Government made no effort to justify the regulation in factual terms.

Second, the regulations in issue we find to be "final agency action" within the meaning of § 10 of the Administrative Procedure Act, 5 U.S.C. § 704, as construed in judicial decisions. * * *

* * *

This is also a case in which the impact of the regulations upon the petitioners is sufficiently direct and immediate as to render the issue appropriate for judicial review at this stage. These regulations purport to give an authoritative interpretation of a statutory provision that has a direct effect on the day-to-day business of all prescription drug companies; its promulgation puts petitioners in a dilemma that it was the very purpose of the Declaratory Judgment Act to ameliorate. As the District Court found on the basis of uncontested allegations, "Either they must comply with the every time requirement and incur the costs of changing over their promotional material and labeling or they must follow their present course and risk prosecution." 228 F.Supp. 855, 861. The regulations are clear-cut, and were made effective immediately upon publication; as noted earlier the agency's counsel represented to the District Court that immediate compliance with their terms was expected. If petitioners wish to comply they must change all their labels, advertisements, and promotional materials; they must destroy stocks of printed matter; and they must invest heavily in new printing type and new supplies. The alternative to compliance—continued use of material which they believe in good faith meets the statutory requirements, but which clearly does not meet the regulation of the Commissioner—may be even more costly. That course would risk serious criminal and civil penalties for the unlawful distribution of "misbranded" drugs.

It is relevant at this juncture to recognize that petitioners deal in a sensitive industry, in which public confidence in their drug products is especially important. To require them to challenge these regulations only as a defense to an action brought by the Government might harm them severely and unnecessarily. Where the legal issue presented is fit for judicial resolution, and where a regulation requires an immediate and significant change in the plaintiffs' conduct of their affairs with serious penalties attached to noncompliance, access to the courts under the Administrative Procedure Act and the Declaratory Judgment Act must be permitted, absent a statutory bar or some other unusual circumstance, neither of which appears here.

* * *

Reversed and remanded.

* * *

[The Court also upheld pre-enforcement review of an administrative regulation in the companion cases of Gardner v. Toilet Goods Ass'n, 387 U.S. 167 (1967), but reached a different conclusion as to ripeness in Toilet Goods Ass'n, Inc. v. Gardner, 387 U.S. 158 (1967), discussed p. 250, *infra*.*

[MR. JUSTICE FORTAS, joined by CHIEF JUSTICE WARREN and JUSTICE CLARK, concurred in the judgment in Toilet Goods Ass'n v. Gardner, but dissented from the decisions finding the controversies in Abbott Laboratories and Gardner v. Toilet Goods Ass'n ripe for review (p. 200):]

* * *

* * * Those challenging the regulations have a remedy and there are no special reasons to relieve them of the necessity of deferring their challenge to the regulations until enforcement is undertaken. In this way, and only in this way, will the administrative process have an opportunity to function—to iron out differences, to accommodate special problems, to grant exemptions, etc. The courts do not and should not pass on these complex problems in the abstract and the general—because these regulations peculiarly depend for their quality and substance upon the facts of particular situations. We should confine ourselves—as our jurisprudence dictates—to actual, specific, particularized cases and controversies, in substance as well as in technical analysis.

NOTE ON "RIPENESS" IN PUBLIC LITIGATION CHALLENGING THE VALIDITY OR APPLICATION OF STATUTES AND REGULATIONS

(1) *The Nature of Ripeness.* For what reason or reasons did the Supreme Court hold that the plaintiffs in UPW v. Mitchell (except for Poole) had failed to present a justiciable controversy? The Court refers to the impermissibility of advisory opinions, but would a decision on the merits have been "advisory"? The rights of the parties would have been determined, and the judgment would have had res judicata effect in any subsequent litigation between them.

Is the problem, then, that there was no threat of "actual interference" by the defendants with any constitutional rights of the plaintiffs? Inquiries into the presence or absence of actual threats are by no means unfamiliar in ripeness cases, but doesn't this focus substantially replicate the standing inquiry?

By contrast, there is a real issue in UPW v. Mitchell about whether the dispute was too "ill-defined" to be appropriate for judicial resolution until further developments had more sharply framed the issues for decision. If ripeness doctrine has a distinctive role or focus, mustn't this be it?

(2) *The Abbott Labs Test.* Abbott Laboratories is invariably cited as the leading case on the ripeness of challenges to federal administrative regulations, and its two-part test is often applied in cases involving constitutional attacks on state and federal statutes. How do the two parts of its test relate to each other? If a court first determines that "the issues tendered are appropriate for judicial resolution," may it still deem the case unripe because there would be no substantial "hardship to the parties if judicial relief is denied at that stage?"

---

* Justice Brennan did not take part in any of the three cases. Justice Douglas dissented in Toilet Goods Association v. Gardner.

Does the inquiry into hardship inform and influence the determination whether the issues presented are sufficiently defined for decision?

(a) A companion case to Abbott Laboratories, Toilet Goods Ass'n, Inc. v. Gardner, 387 U.S. 158 (1967), involved a pre-enforcement challenge to a regulation that required manufacturers of color additives to give "free access" to FDA inspectors; if access were denied, the regulation authorized the Commissioner to suspend the certification needed for manufacturers to market their products. With Justice Harlan again writing for the majority, the Court concluded that "the legal issue as presently framed" was "not appropriate for judicial resolution" (p. 162). The Court said:

"The regulation serves notice only that the Commissioner *may* under certain circumstances order inspection of certain facilities and data, and that further certification of additives *may* be refused to those who decline to permit a duly authorized inspection until they have complied in that regard. At this juncture we have no idea whether or when such an inspection will be ordered and what reasons the Commissioner will give to justify his order. * * * [Judicial review will] stand on a much surer footing in the context of a specific application of this regulation than could be the case in the framework of the generalized challenge made here" (pp. 162–63).

The Court went on to find that "the regulation challenged here" would not "be felt immediately by those subject to it in conducting their day-to-day affairs" (p. 164). "This is not a situation in which primary conduct is affected—when contracts must be negotiated, ingredients tested or substituted, or special records compiled. This regulation merely states that the Commissioner may authorize inspectors to examine certain processes or formulae; no advance action is required of cosmetics manufacturers, who since the enactment of the 1938 Act have been under a statutory duty to permit reasonable inspection[s] * * *" (*id.*). The Court added that "no irremediable adverse consequences flow from requiring a later challenge to this regulation by a manufacturer who refuses to allow this type of inspection. * * * [A] refusal to admit an inspector here would at most lead only to a suspension of certification services * * * [that] can then be promptly challenged through an administrative procedure" (pp. 164–65).

(b) In Lujan v. National Wildlife Federation, 497 U.S. 871 (1990), p. 142, *supra,* the Court, in addition to its ruling on standing, held that the agency's "land withdrawal review program" was not "agency action" or "final agency action" within the meaning of the APA, and was not "ripe" for review. A "wholesale" attack on an administrative program, wrote Justice Scalia for the majority, was inappropriate: "Under the terms of the APA, [plaintiff] must direct its attack against some particular 'agency action' that causes it harm. * * * [Absent a statutory provision permitting judicial review of broad regulations or policies], a regulation is not ordinarily considered the type of agency action 'ripe' for judicial review under the APA until the scope of the controversy has been reduced to more manageable proportions, and its factual components fleshed out, by some concrete action applying the regulation to the claimant's situation in a fashion that harms or threatens to harm him. (The major exception, of course [citing Abbott Laboratories, *supra*], is a substantive rule which as a practical matter requires the plaintiff to adjust his conduct immediately. Such agency action is 'ripe' for review at once, whether or not explicit statutory review apart from the APA is provided")(p. 891).

It is not clear why the Court went into the question of ripeness in Lujan, since the issue had not been presented by the parties, and in any event, the case was apparently disposed of by the ruling on standing. Under the Lujan standard for determining ripeness, what of a regulation that does not require anything of the party seeking review, or of anyone else, but that causes others to change their conduct toward that party?[1] What of a case in which nothing more will be learned by waiting for the regulation to be applied in a particular case?

(c) A narrow conception of ripeness was also at work in Reno v. Catholic Social Services, Inc., 509 U.S. 43 (1993), which involved disputes under the Immigration Reform and Control Act of 1986—legislation that permitted certain undocumented aliens to apply for and obtain authorization to reside permanently in the United States. In two class actions, undocumented aliens challenged INS regulations interpreting the Act as unduly restrictive. The Court (per Souter, J.) ruled, *sua sponte,* that the challenges were not ripe, stressing that the regulations imposed no penalty upon class members, but merely limited the availability of a benefit. Noting that class members might have their applications for adjustment of status denied because they failed to meet eligibility criteria unrelated to the challenged regulations, the Court ruled that plaintiffs would have a ripe claim only if their application were denied *because* of the challenged regulations. If and when that occurred, plaintiffs could obtain adequate judicial review on appeal of a deportation order, as provided by the Act.

The Court recognized that in some instances applications from aliens had been excluded from the formal review process altogether on grounds of facial ineligibility; in such cases no further judicial review was available under the Act; and some exclusions may have been based on the challenged regulations. The Court ruled that in such circumstances challenges to the regulations would be ripe, but it remanded the case because the record did not reveal whether any of the applications of any class members had been rejected on that basis. Four Justices dissented from the Court's ripeness analysis.

The Court did not suggest that the legal issues relating to the regulations' validity were not appropriate for judicial resolution. A forceful argument was made in dissent that in this case legal uncertainty alone caused considerable hardship to the plaintiffs—a continued need to live in a "shadow" status. Is the Court's differential treatment of regulatees (who, under Abbott Laboratories, will often be able to obtain immediate review of regulations) and regulatory beneficiaries (who, under this decision, will frequently be able to obtain review of regulations only after the benefit is denied) justifiable? Compare the approach to standing doctrine of Lujan v. Defenders of Wildlife, p. 157, *supra.* Do these decisions rest on a conception that is out of touch with a statutorily expressed policy of conferring protection on interests that were not protected at common law? Or are they justified on other grounds of prudence or administrative workability?

(d) In suits by regulatees, Abbott Labs has made pre-enforcement review of administrative regulations "the norm".[2] Mashaw, *Improving the Environ-*

---

1. In the following Term, in American Hospital Ass'n v. NLRB, 499 U.S. 606 (1991), the Court, without comment on the question of ripeness, reviewed such a regulation on the merits.

2. See, e.g., EPA v. National Crushed Stone Ass'n., 449 U.S. 64, 72–73 n. 12

ment of Agency Rulemaking: An Essay on Management, Games, and Accountability, 57 Law & Contemp. Prob. 185, 235–36 (1994). According to Professor Mashaw, this development has had significant adverse effects. Among other things, he argues, preenforcement review (i) creates incentives for the targets of regulation to litigate immediately rather than attempt to develop technologies needed to comply with regulations while maintaining economic viability (pp. 233–34); (ii) invites "the invocation of a laundry list of potential frailties in a rule's substantive content or procedural regularity," rather than a focused challenge to particular applications (p. 234); (iii) deprives agencies of an enforcement record on which to defend a rule as applied, confronts courts with increased uncertainties, and thereby increases the likelihood of judicial invalidation; and (iv) as a result, promotes "defensive" rulemaking (p. 234) or avoidance of rulemaking altogether. Mashaw traces these difficulties not only to Abbott Labs, but to a variety of statutes making specific agencies' rules immediately appealable. He sees the need for a context-sensitive legislative solution, rather than a blanket prohibition of or even a presumption against pre-enforcement review (pp. 237–38 & n.144).[3]

(e) Is the Abbott Labs approach to ripeness more or less appropriate in constitutional challenges to statutes than in challenges to administrative regulations? In his opinion in the Food, Drug, and Cosmetic Act cases, Justice Fortas suggested that at least some constitutional attacks might be entertained under a less restrictive standard than otherwise applied. He also said (p. 187): "Where personal status or liberties are involved, the courts may well insist upon a considerable ease of challenging administrative orders or regulations."[4]

(3) *Ripeness and the Merits.* What is the relationship between ripeness determinations and the merits of the underlying substantive claims?

(a) *First Amendment Overbreadth Challenges.* Adler v. Board of Education, 342 U.S. 485 (1952), was a state court action challenging New York statutes (including one known as the Feinberg Law) that required the dismissal of public school teachers who advocated the "doctrine that any government in the United States should be overthrown or overturned by force or violence" or who belonged to any organization so advocating. After the issuance of imple-

---

(1980)(mentioning conflict between the circuits as "yet another reason" in support of the conclusion of ripeness); FCC v. WNCN Listeners Guild, 450 U.S. 582 (1981)(without discussion of the issue). *Cf.* California Bankers Ass'n v. Shultz, 416 U.S. 21, 55–57, 72–75 (1974)(certain aspects of challenge to record-keeping requirements of Bank Secrecy Act held premature).

3. The Administrative Conference of the United States has recently adopted a similar view. See ACUS Recommendation #93–2, 58 Fed. Reg. 4510 (1993).

The costs and benefits of anticipatory adjudication are interestingly modeled in Landes & Posner, *The Economics of Anticipatory Adjudication,* 23 J.Leg.Stud. 683 (1994). For general discussions of the issue of ripeness in administrative law, see Jaffe, Judicial Control of Administrative Action 395–417 (1965); 3 Davis, Administrative Law Treatise, Chap. 15 (3d ed. 1994); Vining, *Direct Judicial Review and the Doctrine of Ripeness in Administrative Law,* 69 Mich.L.Rev. 1443 (1971). Note too the related concepts of exhaustion of administrative remedies and finality of administrative decision (both discussed in Davis, *supra,* and in Schwartz, *Timing of Judicial Review—A Survey of Recent Cases,* 8 Ad.L.J. 261 (1994)) as prerequisites to the availability of judicial review.

4. It has been argued that anticipatory actions asserting First Amendment claims should in particular be entertained at an early stage. See, *e.g.,* Note, 83 Harv.L.Rev. 1870 (1970). Indeed, the development of overbreadth doctrine as a means of facilitating such actions appears to have been responsive to these arguments. See *Note on the Scope of the Issue in First Amendment Cases,* p. 202, *supra.* See also Paragraph (3), *infra.*

menting rules, but before the publication of a list of organizations deemed subversive or any enforcement actions, the plaintiffs (including four teachers) sued to enjoin enforcement. They contended, *inter alia*, that the statute imposed invalid limitations on freedom of speech, press, and assembly and that the presumptive significance attached to membership in listed organizations denied due process of law. The New York Court of Appeals rejected these attacks, and the Supreme Court affirmed.

Justice Minton, for the Court, held that the statute and the rules did not deprive persons employed or seeking employment in the New York Schools of "any right to free speech or assembly" (p. 492); that the presumption of disqualification based on knowing membership in a listed organization did not offend due process; and that the term "subversive" as used in the statute was not unconstitutionally vague.

Justice Douglas, joined by Justice Black, dissented, saying (p. 511):

"* * * The Framers knew the danger of dogmatism; they also knew the strength that comes when the mind is free, when ideas may be pursued wherever they lead. We forget these teachings of the First Amendment when we sustain this law."

Justice Frankfurter alone perceived a ripeness problem (p. 504): "The allegations in the present action fall short of those found insufficient in the Mitchell case. These teachers do not allege that they have engaged in proscribed conduct or that they have any intention to do so. * * * They do not assert that they are threatened with action under the law, or that steps are imminent whereby they would incur the hazard of punishment for conduct innocent at the time, or under standards too vague to satisfy due process of law. * * * Since we rightly refused in the Mitchell case to hear government employees whose conduct was much more intimately affected by the law there attacked than are the claims of plaintiffs here, this suit is wanting in the necessary basis for our review."

In the Adler case, could the decision on the available record mean any more than that the challenged statutes were susceptible of valid applications or, insofar as the challenge rested on the First Amendment, that the statutes were not constitutionally overbroad?[5] If Adler is viewed as an overbreadth case, however, does it become obvious that the issue presented required little if any factual framing in order to be ripe?[6]

---

5. In Keyishian v. Board of Regents, 385 U.S. 589 (1967), the Court overturned Adler on the merits, holding invalid substantial portions of the Feinberg Law and some amendments to it. Adler was characterized as "a declaratory judgment suit in which the Court held, in effect, that there was no constitutional infirmity in [the New York Civil Service Law] or in the Feinberg Law on their faces and that they were capable of constitutional application" (p. 594).

6. See also Times Film Corp. v. Chicago, 365 U.S. 43 (1961). The plaintiff motion picture distributor refused to submit a film to the censorship board. After being denied a permit to show the movie, it sought injunctive relief from a federal court on the ground that the ordinance was void on its face as a prior restraint. Both lower courts dismissed the suit as unripe, but the Supreme Court found "that a justiciable controversy exists. * * * The claim is that this concrete and specific statutory requirement, the production of the film at the office of the Commissioner for examination, is invalid as a previous restraint on freedom of speech. * * * [T]he broad justiciable issue is therefore present as to whether the ambit of constitutional protection includes complete and absolute freedom to exhibit, at least once, any and every kind of motion picture. It is that question alone which we decide" (pp. 45–46).

If overbreadth cases require little factual illumination, does it follow that UPW v. Mitchell, which also presented an overbreadth challenge, implicitly held that the Hatch Act was *not* unconstitutionally overbroad (*i.e.*, that its validity could only be tested successfully "as applied", and that there were no "ripe" applications to test)?[7]

On this analysis, why did Justice Frankfurter, in Adler, refuse to join either the majority in rejecting or the dissenting Justices in upholding a facial attack on the New York statutes? Consider the suggestion in Scharpf, *Judicial Review and the Political Question: A Functional Analysis,* 75 Yale L.J. 517, 532 (1966): "For [Justice Minton, writing for the majority], the statute was clearly constitutional because it in no way deprived teachers of their freedoms of speech and association—it merely put before them the choice of either exercising these freedoms or continuing their employment in the public school system which, after all, was not a right but merely a privilege. Justices Black and Douglas, dissenting, also saw no reason to worry about standing or ripeness. For them the statute was clearly unconstitutional because it penalized teachers for the exercise of their 'absolute' freedoms of speech and association. The conclusion seems inevitable that Justice Frankfurter alone advocated avoidance because he alone defined the substantive issues in terms of a close balance between the equally legitimate interests of society in its self-preservation and of the teachers in their freedom of thought, inquiry and expression. Thus, in order to strike this balance in the particular case, Frankfurter would have had to know much more about the actual practices of enforcement and the degree of surveillance to which the teachers would be subjected than the bare text of an unenforced statute permitted him to know."

(b) *Takings Claims.* In Williamson County Regional Planning Comm'n v. Hamilton Bank, 473 U.S. 172 (1985), the Supreme Court held that a Fifth Amendment takings claim, challenging various zoning regulations, was not ripe because the plaintiff had failed to institute an inverse condemnation action under state law and had not applied for potentially available variances. Could

The ordinance was upheld, over sharp dissent on the merits.

7. In United States Civil Service Comm'n v. National Ass'n of Letter Carriers, 413 U.S. 548 (1973), the Court, without discussing ripeness, entertained and rejected on the merits anticipatory attacks on § 9(a) of the Hatch Act as facially vague and overbroad. The pleadings in Letter Carriers were somewhat more specific than in UPW v. Mitchell. In addition, there had been substantial experience in operation under the statute, as well as continual interpretation by the Civil Service Commission, in the interim between the two cases. The Court relied on these facts in deciding the merits. Are they also relevant to ripeness?

More recently, in Clements v. Fashing, 457 U.S. 957 (1982), the Court unanimously upheld the justiciability of a challenge by state judicial officers to state constitutional provisions (a) making them ineligible to run

for the state legislature during their term of office and (b) providing that an announcement of candidacy for any other office would result in automatic loss of their judicial post. The plaintiffs alleged that but for (b), they would announce their candidacy for higher judicial office and one said that but for (a), he would run for the legislature during his term. In a brief section of the opinion, the Court said that the challenge to (a) was not abstract or hypothetical and that as to (b): "Unlike the situation in Mitchell, [plaintiff] appellees have alleged in a precise manner that, but for the sanctions of the constitutional provision they seek to challenge, they would engage in the very acts that would trigger the enforcement of the provision" (p. 962).

Cf. Renne v. Geary, 501 U.S. 312 (1991), holding unripe a First Amendment challenge to a provision of the California constitution that prevents political parties from endorsing candidates for nonpartisan offices.

the Court's decision be viewed as a holding, on the merits, that no taking should be imputed to the defendant until these steps had been taken?[8]

Consider Nichol, *Ripeness and the Constitution*, 54 U.Chi.L.Rev. 153, 167 (1987): "[W]hile the first amendment allows citizens to attack regulations that may inhibit their speech even before such regulations have been enforced, the takings clause demands a showing by the challenger that the regulating authority has foreclosed all economically viable options. It is obviously more difficult, therefore, to present a ripe takings claim than a ripe first amendment challenge."

Pennell v. City of San Jose, 485 U.S. 1 (1988), involved a state court challenge to a local rent control ordinance under the Equal Protection, Due Process, and Takings Clauses. The pivotal provision authorized hearing officers to determine whether certain rent increases were "reasonable under the circumstances" by considering a range of specified factors, one of which was "hardship to tenant." The Court rejected plaintiffs' equal protection and due process challenges on the merits, but it held that the Takings Clause claim was premature. Plaintiffs had argued that the tenant hardship provision in the ordinance constituted a "forced subsidy", but the Court noted that no determination had been made that the rent charged by any plaintiff was unreasonable because of tenant hardship, and that hearing officers were authorized but not required to limit rent increases that would cause hardship. Dissenting, Justices Scalia and O'Connor found the takings claim not premature. They argued that if the ordinance allowed the hearing officer to consider the race of a tenant in fixing rents, the Court would not defer adjudication until the provision had been applied in a particular case.[9]

In Lucas v. South Carolina Coastal Council, 112 S.Ct. 2886 (1992), the plaintiff challenged a state law that prohibited construction of any habitable improvement on his recently acquired beachfront property. While the state's appeal from the state trial court's judgment for Lucas was pending before the South Carolina Supreme Court, the law was amended to give officials some discretion to authorize exceptions to the ban, so that Lucas *might* gain permission to develop his property. The South Carolina Supreme Court nonetheless reached the merits and rejected all of Lucas' claims.

8. *Cf.* Dames & Moore v. Regan, 453 U.S. 654, 688–90 (1981)(in Iranian assets case, question whether suspension of claims would constitute a taking is premature, but question whether petitioner would have a remedy in the Court of Claims in that event is ripe for review); Hodel v. Virginia Surface Mining & Reclamation Ass'n, Inc., 452 U.S. 264, 293–97 (1981)(holding unripe a claim that certain provisions of the Surface Mining Control and Reclamation Act constituted a taking and relying in part on failure of the appellees to seek relief pursuant to administrative procedures available under the Act.)

9. Similar issues were presented in Yee v. City of Escondido, 503 U.S. 519 (1992), a challenge to laws that restricted the rent charged by lessors of land parcels for mobile homes, and that also limited the lessors' ability to evict the tenants or to convert the property to other uses. The Court reached (and rejected on the merits) the claim that the laws constituted a "physical taking", but the claim of a "regulatory taking" was deemed unripe as applied to the lessors' property, since the lessors had not sought rent increases. In considered dictum, the Court stated that the "facial" attack on the law as a regulatory taking—a claim that the law failed substantially to advance a legitimate state interest—was ripe, for it did not depend on the particulars of the lessors' situations. The Court did not resolve that attack on the merits, however, because it was not embraced by the question as to which certiorari had been granted.

On review, the Supreme Court found that the possibility that Lucas might be allowed to develop the property rendered premature his claim of a permanent taking. But the Court held ripe his claim to have suffered a "temporary" taking in the period before the amendment took effect, as that claim, though not expressly addressed by the state supreme court, had effectively been denied on the merits. The possibility that Lucas might be permitted to develop the property went only to "prudential" aspects of ripeness, which the majority found insufficient to deny review (pp. 2891–92 & n. 3). On the merits, the Court reversed and remanded after considerable discussion of takings jurisprudence.

In dissent, Justice Blackmun objected that Lucas had never filed a plan for development or challenged the agency's initial inclusion of his property in the no-building zone—a right he had under the original, unamended statute. (The Court, in response, referred to the defendants' stipulation that such an application would have been denied.) He also objected to deciding the case on the basis of a trial court finding—that the property had lost all economic value—that he deemed to be "almost certainly erroneous" (p. 2908).[10]

(4) *Constitutional or Discretionary?* The Supreme Court has frequently associated the ripeness doctrine with Article III's case or controversy requirement. See, *e.g.*, Babbitt v. United Farm Workers Nat. Union, 442 U.S. 289, 297 (1979), Paragraph (6), *infra;* Duke Power Co. v. Carolina Environmental Study Group, Inc., 438 U.S. 59, 82 (1978), Paragraph (5), *infra*. In light of the constitutionalization of the "injury-in-fact" component of standing doctrine, see pp. 141–43, 170–74, *supra*, it may be understandable why any "injury" requirement in ripeness doctrine might also be regarded as constitutionally mandated. But should considerations of adequacy of factual framing, fitness of issues for review, and hardship to parties be elevated to constitutional stature?[11]

As a practical matter, does it make any difference whether ripeness is characterized in constitutional or discretionary terms? Consider the justiciability questions in Buckley v. Valeo, 424 U.S. 1 (1976). Buckley was an action for declaratory and injunctive relief attacking the constitutionality of all the major elements of the Federal Election Campaign Act of 1971, as amended in 1974: limitation of political contributions and expenditures, requirements of disclosure and recordkeeping of many such contributions and expenditures, public financing of national party conventions and presidential campaigns, and the constituting of a Federal Election Commission with responsibility for administering the Act. Plaintiffs included a presidential candidate and a committee organized on his behalf, a United States Senator running for re-election, a potential contributor, and a number of political organizations. The action, instituted shortly after enactment of the amending statute, was based in part on § 315(a) of the Act, 2 U.S.C. § 437h, which provides that: "The Commission, the national committee of any political party, or any individual eligible to vote in any election for the office of President of the United States may institute such actions in the appropriate district court of the United States, including actions for declaratory judgment, as may be appropriate to construe

---

10. Justice Souter echoed this point; he would have dismissed the writ of certiorari as improvidently granted. Justice Stevens' separate dissent objected to deciding the case when it was not clear that Lucas had suffered any injury, as the record did not disclose whether he had building plans whose implementation had been delayed by the development ban.

11. For a negative answer, see Nichol, *supra*.

the constitutionality of any provision of this Act [or related sections of the Criminal Code]." Because of the special expediting provisions of that section, the case was argued before the Supreme Court on November 10, 1975, and decided on January 30, 1976, near the beginning of the first national election campaign to be governed by the amended Act.

The Court passed on the merits of all the contentions with only the briefest treatment of the justiciability of the case as a whole, concluding (p. 12): "In our view, the complaint in this case demonstrates that at least some of the appellants have a sufficient 'personal stake' in a determination of the constitutional validity of each of the challenged provisions to present 'a real and substantial controversy admitting of specific relief through a decree of conclusive character, as distinguished from an opinion advising what the law would be upon a hypothetical state of facts.' "[12]

Should Congress' direction for speedy adjudication be relevant to the ripeness inquiry? Should it matter if the consequences of deferring adjudication—possibly until after the 1976 campaign—would have been unusually troublesome? If so, should the Court have been more explicit about these points?

(5) *Injury, Ripeness, and the Duke Power Case.* In Duke Power Co. v. Carolina Environmental Study Group, Inc., 438 U.S. 59 (1978), also discussed at pp. 149-50, *supra,* the Court first held that there was federal question jurisdiction over an action challenging the constitutionality of the Price–Anderson Act's limitation on liability for nuclear accidents at nuclear power plants, and that the plaintiffs had standing to sue. It then turned briefly to the ripeness of plaintiffs' challenge, indicating that any constitutional prerequisite was satisfied by the earlier conclusion as to standing "that appellees will sustain immediate [environmental] injury from the [routine] operation of the disputed power plants and that such injury would be redressed by the relief requested * * *" (p. 81). The Court went on to say (pp. 81–82) that "prudential considerations" also militated in favor of resolution of the issues presented, even though no nuclear accident had yet occurred; delayed resolution "would foreclose any relief from the present injury" and "would frustrate one of the key purposes of the Price–Anderson Act—the elimination of doubts concerning the scope of private liability in the event of major nuclear accident."

Of the three separate opinions concurring in the judgment of reversal but disagreeing with the decision to reach the merits, Justice Stevens' focused most

---

12. The attack on the validity of the Federal Election Commission's authority to issue regulations and perform other functions assigned by the Act—based upon the fact that its members were not appointed by the President (with or without the consent of the Senate) under Art. II, Sec. 2—gave the Court additional pause. Nonetheless, the Justices reversed the court of appeals' decision that the issue relating to the Commission's method of appointment was not "ripe". The Court noted that since the judgment of the lower court, the Commission had undertaken to issue regulations, and that as to yet unexercised powers, "the date of their all but certain exercise is now closer by several months than it was at the time the Court of Appeals ruled" (pp. 116–17). The opinion buttressed this conclusion by noting that Congress was "most concerned with obtaining a final adjudication of as many issues as possible litigated pursuant to the provisions of § 437h" (p. 117). On the merits, the Court held the Commission invalidly constituted to perform some of the major functions assigned to it, but delayed the effectiveness of that holding to give Congress time to establish a properly appointed body.

Why did the ripeness of the attack on the FEC's authority raise especially difficult questions?

squarely on ripeness: "The string of contingencies that supposedly holds this litigation together is too delicate for me. * * * [We are] asked to remedy an alleged due process violation [*i.e.,* the limitation of liability in the event of a nuclear accident] that may possibly occur at some uncertain time in the future and may possibly injure the appellees in a way that has no significant connection with any present injury. It is remarkable that such a series of speculations is considered sufficient either to make this litigation ripe for decision or to establish appellees' standing. * * * The Court's opinion will serve the national interest in removing doubts concerning the constitutionality of the [Act] * * *. But whenever we are persuaded by reasons of expediency to engage in the business of giving legal advice, we chip away a part of the foundation of our independence and our strength" (pp. 102–03).

In a perceptive discussion of Duke Power, Professor Varat concludes that for the first time, the Court "held the constitutional dimension of ripeness satisfied by the imminence of the injury that gave plaintiff standing [environmental injury from the plant's routine operation], instead of requiring the imminence of injury to the legal rights asserted in the suit [injury from a major nuclear accident]. The unacknowledged result was to collapse the article III ripeness inquiry into the article III standing inquiry and to alter the primary policy of ripeness from a concern with the issues to a concern with the plaintiff's cognizable injury in fact." Varat, *Variable Justiciability and the Duke Power Case,* 58 Tex.L.Rev. 273, 298 (1980).

Do you agree with Justice Stevens' claim, in dissent, that the Supreme Court's decision in Duke Power yielded illegitimately to "expediency"? Do you agree with Professor Varat's distinction between the injury relevant to standing and the injury relevant to ripeness?

(6) *Criminal Statutes.* The problems arising in challenges to criminal statutes substantially overlap those already discussed. Should it suffice, for example, that the plaintiff claims injury by virtue of the law's existence, or must the plaintiff also show a threat of enforcement by a particular official? Should such a requirement be viewed as only a dryly logical corollary of the principle of sovereign immunity—that the quarrel must be with the official and not with the statute book[13]—or should it be seen as serving a function also in assuring that the controversy is sufficiently concrete? Is this function significant only when the application of the statute to the conduct in question is a matter of some doubt?

Challenges to criminal statutes also confront the traditional doctrine—often honored in the breach—that equity will not enjoin a criminal prosecution. Should there be any special reluctance to entertain preventive attacks on criminal laws? On *state* criminal laws? See generally Chap. X, Sec. 2(C), *infra.*

In Pierce v. Society of Sisters, 268 U.S. 510 (1925), two private schools were allowed to sue to enjoin enforcement of a criminal statute requiring parents to send their children to public school, although the measure was not to be effective for several years. The complaints alleged that the defendant officials had announced their intention to proceed under the law, and that as a

---

13. See Chap. IX, Secs. 1(B), 2(A), *infra.* For a forceful statement of the close relationship between the "case or controversy" concept and the doctrine of sovereign immunity, with suggestions for rethinking both, see Monaghan, *Constitutional Adjudication: The Who and When,* 82 Yale L.J. 1363 (1973)(especially pp. 1386–89).

result parents were withdrawing children or refusing to enter them in complainants' schools, to their immediate and irreparable injury.

In Poe v. Ullman, 367 U.S. 497 (1961), married persons and their doctor brought a state court action for a declaratory judgment of the unconstitutionality of the state's law prohibiting the use of contraceptive devices or the giving of medical advice about them. An appeal from the state supreme court's decision upholding the statute was dismissed for nonjusticiability, with the plurality emphasizing the absence of any specific threat of enforcement, as well as the long history of non-enforcement.[14]

Yet only a few years later, in Epperson v. Arkansas, 393 U.S. 97 (1968), the Court held justiciable an attack on a 1928 state law prohibiting the teaching of evolution, even though there was no record of any prosecution under the statute. The law might be "more of a curiosity than a vital fact of life," but it was "properly here [on appeal from a state court], and it is our duty to decide the issues presented" (p. 102).

In Doe v. Bolton, 410 U.S. 179, 188 (1973), the Court allowed physicians consulted by pregnant women to challenge a state anti-abortion statute without any showing that they had been prosecuted or threatened with prosecution; but in the companion case of Roe v. Wade, 410 U.S. 113, 127–29 (1973), the Court refused to allow a similar challenge by a childless couple who alleged that they feared pregnancy for medical and personal reasons and that the inability to obtain a legal abortion in the state was forcing them to " 'the choice of refraining from normal sexual relations or of endangering [the plaintiff wife's] health through a possible pregnancy' " (p. 128). The Court said that the alleged injury was too speculative, resting as it did on possible contraceptive failure, possible pregnancy, and possible future impairment of health.

Six years later, in Babbitt v. United Farm Workers National Union, 442 U.S. 289 (1979), the Court allowed a pre-enforcement challenge to several provisions of a farm labor statute, though there had been no showing of probable prosecution. With respect to one of the provisions, the Court noted that the fear of prosecution was "not imaginary or wholly speculative", and with respect to another, that the state had "not disavowed any intention" of invoking it (p. 302).[15]

In Webster v. Reproductive Health Services, 492 U.S. 490 (1989), plaintiffs challenged, *inter alia*, the preamble to a state statute regulating abortions. The preamble set forth legislative "findings"—for example, that "[t]he life of each human being begins at conception"—and mandated that state laws be interpreted to provide unborn children with "all the rights, privileges, and immunities" afforded other persons, "subject only to the Constitution of the United States [and Supreme Court decisions interpreting it] * * *." The plaintiffs advanced what was in effect a facial challenge—that under Akron v. Akron Center for Reproductive Health, Inc., 462 U.S. 416, 444 (1983), "a State may not adopt one theory of when life begins to justify its regulation of abortions." The Court rejected that challenge on the merits, noting that the

14. Justice Brennan, concurring in the result, said that the "true controversy," not presented by the parties in the case, was "over the opening of birth-control clinics on a large scale" (p. 509). There were four dissents.

15. The Court held that challenges to several other provisions, governing access to employers' property and compulsory arbitration of certain disputes, were premature.

preamble did not itself regulate abortions. The Akron case, the Court reasoned, does not prohibit a state from expressing a value judgment, but only bars a state from justifying an otherwise invalid regulation of abortions on the basis of a theory of when life begins.

The Court refused, on ripeness grounds, to consider a second objection that the preamble might guide the interpretation of other provisions in the Act. The Court said that whether the preamble would have that effect "is something that only the courts of Missouri can definitively decide", and that "[i]t will be time enough for federal courts to address the meaning of the preamble should it be applied to restrict the activities of [plaintiffs] in some concrete way" (p. 506).

Justice Blackmun's dissent (joined by Justices Brennan and Marshall) objected that when statutory regulation of abortion is limited solely by the Court's constitutional decisions, the scheme is so uncertain as to chill the exercise of abortion rights. (Recall, as to this point, that the Court has often declined to view such "chilling effect" arguments as having merit outside the First Amendment area. See, *e.g.,* H.L. v. Matheson, 450 U.S. 398 (1981), p. 211, *supra,* and Bowers v. Hardwick, 478 U.S. 186 (1986)). He also noted that the preamble might unconstitutionally burden the use of contraceptive devices (such as the "morning after" pill) that prevent pregnancy only after conception. Justice Stevens dissented separately.

It is difficult to find a consistent pattern in these cases, isn't it? What factors ought to guide the application of ripeness doctrine to anticipatory challenges to criminal statutes?

Also relevant here is the line of cases allowing advance challenges to criminal statutes on the basis of a First Amendment claim of vagueness or overbreadth. See, *e.g.,* Erznoznik v. City of Jacksonville, 422 U.S. 205 (1975)(holding an ordinance invalid on its face); Brockett v. Spokane Arcades, Inc., 472 U.S. 491 (1985)(holding a statute invalid in part). See generally *Note on the Scope of the Issue in First Amendment Cases,* p. 202, *supra.* See also Paragraph (3)(a) of this Note, *supra.*

O'Shea v. Littleton

414 U.S. 488, 94 S.Ct. 669, 38 L.Ed.2d 674 (1974).
Certiorari to the United States Court of Appeals for the Seventh Circuit.

■ MR. JUSTICE WHITE delivered the opinion of the Court.

[Nineteen citizens of Cairo, Illinois, brought a civil rights action (alleging violations of various provisions of the Constitution and of 42 U.S.C. §§ 1981–83) against various government officials, including the city's police commissioner, the state's attorney for Alexander County, and a magistrate and judge of the county court. The complaint alleged a longstanding and continuing pattern of discriminatory law enforcement against blacks and, in particular, an effort to deter participation in an economic boycott of city merchants believed to engage in race discrimination. The magistrate and judge were alleged, *inter alia,* to set bond in criminal cases on a discriminatory basis and to impose higher sentences on blacks than on whites. The complaint cited examples of unlawful conduct committed against named plaintiffs by the state's attorney and his investigator, but contained only general allegations against the magistrate and judge. The plaintiffs sought to bring the case as a class action and requested injunctive (but no damages) relief.

[The district court dismissed the case, partly on grounds of lack of jurisdiction to award the relief requested. The court of appeals reversed, ruling that] in the event respondents proved their allegations, the District Court should proceed to fashion appropriate injunctive relief to prevent petitioners from depriving others of their constitutional rights in the course of carrying out their judicial duties in the future.[1] We granted certiorari.

I

We reverse the judgment of the Court of Appeals. The complaint failed to satisfy the threshold requirement imposed by Art. III of the Constitution that those who seek to invoke the power of federal courts must allege an actual case or controversy. * * * Plaintiffs * * * "must allege some threatened or actual injury resulting from the putatively illegal action before a federal court may assume jurisdiction." Linda R.S. v. Richard D., 410 U.S. 614, 617 (1973). The injury or threat of injury must be both "real and immediate," not "conjectural" or "hypothetical." Golden v. Zwickler, 394 U.S. 103 (1969); United Public Workers v. Mitchell, 330 U.S. 75, 89–91 (1947). Moreover, if none of the named plaintiffs purporting to represent a class establishes the requisite of a case or controversy with the defendants, none may seek relief on behalf of himself or any other member of the class.[2] * * *

In the complaint that began this action, the sole allegations of injury are that petitioners "have engaged in and continue to engage in, a pattern and practice of conduct * * * all of which has deprived and continues to deprive plaintiffs and members of their class of their" constitutional rights and, again, that petitioners "have denied and continue to deny to plaintiffs and members of their class their constitutional rights" by illegal bond-setting, sentencing, and jury-fee practices. None of the named plaintiffs is identified as himself having suffered any injury in the manner specified. In sharp contrast to the claim for relief against the State's Attorney where specific instances of misconduct with respect to particular individuals are alleged, the claim against petitioners alleges injury in only the most general terms. At oral argument, respondents' counsel stated that some of the named plaintiffs-respondents, who could be identified by name if necessary, had actually been defendants in proceedings

---

1. While the Court of Appeals did not attempt to specify exactly what type of injunctive relief might be justified, it at least suggested that it might include a requirement of "periodic reports of various types of aggregate data on actions on bail and sentencing." * * *

2. There was no class determination in this case as the complaint was dismissed on grounds which did not require that determination to be made. Petitioners assert that the lack of standing of the named respondents to raise the class claim is buttressed by the incongruous nature of the class respondents seek to represent. The class is variously and incompatibly defined in the complaint as those residents of Cairo, both Negro and white, who have boycotted certain businesses in that city and engaged in similar activities for the purpose of combatting racial discrimination, as a class of all Negro citizens suffering racial discrimination in the application of the criminal justice system in Alexander County (though two white persons are named respondents), and as all poor persons unable to afford bail, counsel, or jury trials in city ordinance cases. The absence of specific claims of injury as a result of any of the wrongful practices charged, in light of the ambiguous and contradictory class definition proffered, bolsters our conclusion that these respondents cannot invoke federal jurisdiction to hear the claims they present in support of their request for injunctive relief.

before petitioners and had suffered from the alleged unconstitutional practices. Past exposure to illegal conduct does not in itself show a present case or controversy regarding injunctive relief, however, if unaccompanied by any continuing, present adverse effects. Neither the complaint nor respondents' counsel suggested that any of the named plaintiffs at the time the complaint was filed were themselves serving an allegedly illegal sentence or were on trial or awaiting trial before petitioners. Indeed, if any of the respondents were then serving an assertedly unlawful sentence, the complaint would inappropriately be seeking relief from or modification of current, existing custody. See Preiser v. Rodriguez, 411 U.S. 475 (1973). Furthermore, if any were then on trial or awaiting trial in state proceedings, the complaint would be seeking injunctive relief that a federal court should not provide. Younger v. Harris, 401 U.S. 37 (1971). We thus do not strain to read inappropriate meaning into the conclusory allegations of this complaint.

Of course, past wrongs are evidence bearing on whether there is a real and immediate threat of repeated injury. But here the prospect of future injury rests on the likelihood that respondents will again be arrested for and charged with violations of the criminal law and will again be subjected to bond proceedings, trial, or sentencing before petitioners. Important to this assessment is the absence of allegations that any relevant criminal statute of the State of Illinois is unconstitutional on its face or as applied or that respondents have been or will be improperly charged with violating criminal law. If the statutes that might possibly be enforced against respondents are valid laws, and if charges under these statutes are not improvidently made or pressed, the question becomes whether any perceived threat to respondents is sufficiently real and immediate to show an existing controversy simply because they anticipate violating lawful criminal statutes and being tried for their offenses, in which event they may appear before petitioners and, if they do, will be affected by the allegedly illegal conduct charged. Apparently, the proposition is that *if* respondents proceed to violate an unchallenged law and *if* they are charged, held to answer, and tried in any proceedings before petitioners, they will be subjected to the discriminatory practices that petitioners are alleged to have followed. But it seems to us that attempting to anticipate whether and when these respondents will be charged with crime and will be made to appear before either petitioner takes us into the area of speculation and conjecture. See Younger v. Harris, *supra*, at 41–42. The nature of respondents' activities is not described in detail and no specific threats are alleged to have been made against them. Accepting that they are deeply involved in a program to eliminate racial discrimination in Cairo and that tensions are high, we are nonetheless unable to conclude that the case-or-controversy requirement is satisfied by general assertions or inferences that in the course of their activities respondents will be prosecuted for violating valid criminal laws. We assume that respondents will conduct their activities within the law and so avoid prosecution and conviction as well as exposure to the challenged course of conduct said to be followed by petitioners.

* * * We can only speculate whether respondents will be arrested, either again or for the first time, for violating a municipal ordinance or a state statute, particularly in the absence of any allegations that unconstitutional criminal statutes are being employed to deter constitutionally protected conduct. * * * Under these circumstances, where respondents do not claim any constitutional right to engage in conduct proscribed by therefore presumably permissible state laws, or indicate that it is otherwise their intention to so

conduct themselves, the threat of injury from the alleged course of conduct they attack is simply too remote to satisfy the case-or-controversy requirement and permit adjudication by a federal court.

* * *

II

The foregoing considerations obviously shade into those determining whether the complaint states a sound basis for equitable relief; and even if we were inclined to consider the complaint as presenting an existing case or controversy, we would firmly disagree with the Court of Appeals that an adequate basis for equitable relief against petitioners had been stated. The Court has recently reaffirmed the "basic doctrine of equity jurisprudence that courts of equity should not act, and particularly should not act to restrain a criminal prosecution, when the moving party has an adequate remedy at law and will not suffer irreparable injury if denied equitable relief." Younger v. Harris, [*supra,* at] 43–44. Additionally, recognition of the need for a proper balance in the concurrent operation of federal and state courts counsels restraint against the issuance of injunctions against state officers engaged in the administration of the State's criminal laws in the absence of a showing of irreparable injury which is "both great and immediate.'" *Id.,* at 46. * * *

Respondents do not seek to strike down a single state statute, either on its face or as applied; nor do they seek to enjoin any criminal prosecutions that might be brought under a challenged criminal law. In fact, respondents apparently contemplate that prosecutions will be brought under seemingly valid state laws. What they seek is an injunction aimed at controlling or preventing the occurrence of specific events that might take place in the course of future state criminal trials. The order the Court of Appeals thought should be available if respondents proved their allegations would be operative only where permissible state prosecutions are pending against one or more of the beneficiaries of the injunction. Apparently the order would contemplate interruption of state proceedings to adjudicate assertions of noncompliance by petitioners. This seems to us nothing less than an ongoing federal audit of state criminal proceedings which would indirectly accomplish the kind of interference that Younger v. Harris, *supra,* and related cases sought to prevent.

A federal court should not intervene to establish the basis for future intervention that would be so intrusive and unworkable. * * * [B]ecause an injunction against acts which might occur in the course of future criminal proceedings would necessarily impose continuing obligations of compliance, the question arises of how compliance might be enforced if the beneficiaries of the injunction were to charge that it had been disobeyed. Presumably, any member of respondents' class who appeared as an accused before petitioners could allege and have adjudicated a claim that petitioners were in contempt of the federal court's injunction order, with review of adverse decisions in the Court of Appeals and, perhaps, in this Court. Apart from the inherent difficulties in defining the proper standards against which such claims might be measured, and the significant problems of proving noncompliance in individual cases, such a major continuing intrusion of the equitable power of the federal courts into the daily conduct of state criminal proceedings is in sharp conflict with the principles of equitable restraint which this Court has recognized in the decisions previously noted.

Respondents have failed, moreover, to establish the basic requisites of the issuance of equitable relief in these circumstances—the likelihood of substantial and immediate irreparable injury, and the inadequacy of remedies at law. We have already canvassed the necessarily conjectural nature of the threatened injury to which respondents are allegedly subjected. And if any of the respondents are ever prosecuted and face trial, or if they are illegally sentenced, there are available state and federal procedures which could provide relief from the wrongful conduct alleged. * * *

* * *

Considering the availability of other avenues of relief open to respondents for the serious conduct they assert, and the abrasive and unmanageable intercession which the injunctive relief they seek would represent, we conclude that, apart from the absence of an existing case or controversy presented by respondents for adjudication, the Court of Appeals erred in deciding that the District Court should entertain respondents' claim.

Reversed.

■ MR. JUSTICE BLACKMUN, concurring in part.

I join the judgment of the Court and Part I of the Court's opinion which holds that the complaint "failed to satisfy the threshold requirement imposed by Art. III of the Constitution that those who seek to invoke the power of federal courts must allege an actual case or controversy."

When we arrive at that conclusion, it follows, it seems to me, that we are precluded from considering any other issue presented for review. Thus, the Court's additional discussion of the question whether a case for equitable relief was stated amounts to an advisory opinion that we are powerless to render. * * *

■ MR. JUSTICE DOUGLAS, with whom MR. JUSTICE BRENNAN and MR. JUSTICE MARSHALL concur, dissenting.

* * *

The allegations [in the complaint] support the likelihood that the named plaintiffs as well as members of their class will be arrested in the future and * * * subjected to the alleged discriminatory practices in the administration of justice.

These allegations of past and continuing wrongdoings clearly state a case or controversy in the Art. III sense. They are as specific as those alleged in Jenkins v. McKeithen, 395 U.S. 411, and in Doe v. Bolton, 410 U.S. 179, where we held that cases or controversies were presented.

Specificity of proof may not be forthcoming: but specificity of charges is clear.

What has been alleged here is not only wrongs done to named plaintiffs, but a recurring pattern of wrongs which establishes, if proved, that the legal regime under control of the whites in Cairo, Illinois, is used over and over again to keep the blacks from exercising First Amendment rights, to discriminate against them, to keep from the blacks the protection of the law in their lawful activities, to weight the scales of justice repeatedly on the side of white prejudices and against black protests, fears, and suffering. This is a more pervasive scheme for suppression of blacks and their civil rights than I have ever seen. It may not survive a trial. But if this case does not present a "case or controversy" involving the named plaintiffs, then that concept has been so watered down as to be no longer recognizable. This will please the white superstructure, but it does violence to the conception of evenhanded justice envisioned by the Constitution.

* * * It will be much more appropriate to pass on the nature of any equitable relief to be granted after the case has been tried. * * *

NOTE ON "RIPENESS" IN PUBLIC ACTIONS CHALLENGING PATTERNS OR PRACTICES IN THE ADMINISTRATION OF THE LAW

(1) *Scope of the Issue.* The line between the matters discussed in the preceding Note and those considered in this one is indistinct. But a case such as O'Shea is different from a case such as United Public Workers v. Mitchell or Roe v. Wade, p. 259, *supra,* in several respects. First, in O'Shea there is no challenged statute or regulation but rather a pattern of past events (and their implication for the future) that form the basis of the complaint and of the prayer for equitable relief. Second, in a case such as O'Shea, in which the matters complained of consist of official practices in law enforcement, it is especially difficult to identify the individuals who are likely to be harmed by those practices in the future. Such cases frequently involve requests for "structural relief"—for the shaping of a decree designed to modify significantly the way in which an arm of government (or, in some instances, a private institution) conducts its affairs. The Court's evident reluctance to become enmeshed in those affairs, especially when state institutions are at the bar, has been expressed, in part, in terms of justiciability doctrines—notably ripeness and standing.[1] Is the problem in these cases properly viewed as one of justiciability under Article III?

1. See also Rizzo v. Goode, 423 U.S. 362 (1976), in which the Supreme Court, partly on grounds of nonjusticiability, set aside a lower court order requiring Philadelphia police authorities to institute comprehensive civilian complaint procedures in accordance with specified guidelines. The order was based on some 19 instances in one year in which the police were found to have violated citizens' constitutional rights. The majority, per Justice Rehnquist, said that the considerations expressed in O'Shea "apply here with even more force, for the individual [plaintiffs'] claim to 'real and immediate' injury rests not upon what the named [defendants] might do to them in the future—such as set a bond on the basis of race—but upon what one of a small, unnamed minority of policemen might do to them in the future because of that unknown policeman's perception of departmental disciplinary procedures" (p. 372).

In Laird v. Tatum, 408 U.S. 1 (1972), plaintiffs sought to enjoin Army surveillance of civilian political activity, claiming they had been subjected to such surveillance and that the practice exerted a "chilling effect" on the exercise of First Amendment rights. The Court, 5–4, held the action not justiciable, stating that "[a]llegations of a subjective 'chill' are not an adequate substitute for a claim of specific present objective harm or a threat of specific future harm. * * *

"Stripped to its essentials, what respondents appear to be seeking is a broad-scale investigation, conducted by themselves * * * to probe into the Army's intelligence-gathering activities, with the district court determining at the conclusion of that investigation the extent to which those activities may or may not be appropriate to the Army's mission. * * *

"Carried to its logical end, this approach would have the federal courts as virtually continuous monitors of the wisdom and soundness of Executive action * * *" (pp. 13–15).

Consider O'Shea itself. Did the Court take adequate account of plaintiffs' allegation that the effect of defendants' continuing practices was "to deter them [plaintiffs] from engaging in their boycott and similar activities"? If this allegation was true, and the boycott and related activities had ceased as a result of the challenged practices, should the controversy have been deemed premature?

(2) *The Lyons Case.* In City of Los Angeles v. Lyons, 461 U.S. 95 (1983), Lyons, a black male, brought a civil rights action against the city and certain of its police officers in a federal district court, claiming that he had been unconstitutionally subjected to a "chokehold" after being stopped for a traffic violation. He alleged that pursuant to official authorization, chokeholds were routinely applied in situations where they were not warranted, and that many people had suffered injury as a consequence. (Since 1975, sixteen people, twelve of whom were black, had died as a result of police chokeholds.) Lyons sought both damages and declaratory and injunctive relief. The district court granted a preliminary injunction against the use of chokeholds "under circumstances which do not threaten death or serious bodily injury"—an injunction that was to continue in effect until an improved training and reporting program had been approved by the court—and the court of appeals affirmed.

The Supreme Court reversed on the ground that Lyons had "failed to demonstrate a case or controversy" that "would justify the equitable relief sought" (p. 105). Noting that only the question of an injunctive remedy was before it, and that the damages claim could be severed on remand, the Court relied on O'Shea and on Rizzo v. Goode, note 1, *supra,* in concluding that there was no jurisdiction to entertain the claim for equitable relief.[2]

First, the Court concluded that Lyons was not more immediately threatened than the plaintiffs in those cases: "[I]t is no more than conjecture to suggest that in every instance of a traffic stop, arrest, or other encounter between the police and a citizen, the police will act unconstitutionally and inflict injury without provocation or legal excuse. And it is surely no more than speculation to assert either that Lyons himself will again be involved in one of those unfortunate instances, or that he will be arrested in the future and provoke the use of a chokehold by resisting arrest, attempting to escape, or threatening deadly force or serious bodily injury" (p. 108).

Second, the Court decided that O'Shea and Rizzo could not be distinguished on the basis that in those proceedings, unlike the present one, "massive structural relief" had been sought (pp. 108–09).

Still relying on O'Shea, the Court went on to conclude that even if Lyons' pending damage suit "affords him Article III standing to seek an injunction as a remedy," the showing of irreparable injury prerequisite to that remedy had not been made: "We decline the invitation to slight the preconditions for equitable relief; for as we have held, recognition of the need for a proper balance between state and federal authority counsels restraint in the issuance of injunctions against state officers engaged in the administration of the States' criminal laws in the absence of irreparable injury which is both great

2. The Court summarily rejected a claim of mootness that was based on a six-month moratorium declared by the city on certain uses of the chokehold. The Court said (p. 101): "Intervening events have not 'irrevocably eradicated the effects of the alleged violation.' County of Los Angeles v. Davis, 440 U.S. 625, 631 (1979) [p. 220, *supra*]."

and immediate [citing O'Shea and Younger v. Harris, p. 1256, *infra*]" (pp. 111–12).

Justice Marshall, for four dissenters, focused on the majority's claim of lack of "standing" and argued that O'Shea and Rizzo were not controlling because the plaintiffs in those cases had not sought damages for past injury: "In addition to the risk that he will be subjected to a chokehold in the future, Lyons has suffered past injury. Because he has a live claim for damages, he need not rely solely on the threat of future injury to establish his personal stake in the outcome of the controversy.

* * *

"The Court provides no justification for departing from the traditional treatment of remedial issues and demanding a separate threshold inquiry into each form of relief a plaintiff seeks. It is anomalous to require a plaintiff to demonstrate 'standing' to seek each particular form of relief requested in the complaint when under Rule 54(c) the remedy to which a party may be entitled need not even be demanded in the complaint" (pp. 124, 130–31).

As to the majority's alternative ground—involving the failure to satisfy the traditional prerequisites for equitable relief—Justice Marshall urged that the question was not properly before the Court on the grant of certiorari. Moreover, he argued, Younger v. Harris was not in point because Lyons did not seek to enjoin state judicial proceedings; under general equitable principles the district court's findings that Lyons had been choked pursuant to city policy and that the policy posed grave risks of injury and death warranted preliminary relief. "The Court's decision," he concluded, "immunizes from prospective equitable relief any policy that authorizes persistent deprivations of constitutional rights as long as no individual can establish with substantial certainty that he will be injured, or injured again, in the future" (p. 137).[3]

(3) *Standing, Ripeness, Mootness.* The Court treated Lyons as a standing case. Since a forward-looking injunction would not be causally effective in remedying the injury that the plaintiff suffered when he was choked, a suit predicated on this past injury failed to satisfy the redressability requirement of standing doctrine. Is this a sound analysis?[4] No one disputed Lyons' standing to seek damages. Why shouldn't his past injury have established the existence of a

---

3. Compare Allee v. Medrano, 416 U.S. 802 (1974), in which the Court, in the same Term that it decided O'Shea, held that an injunction against continuing police harassment was "an appropriate exercise of the federal court's equitable powers" (p. 814). Plaintiffs were attempting to organize farmworkers in the state and complained of both police reliance on unconstitutional statutes and of police exercise of authority under valid laws in an unconstitutional manner. Without discussing any question of justiciability on this aspect of the case, the Court noted that the record showed not simply "isolated instances of police misconduct under valid statutes," but rather a "persistent pattern" of misconduct (p. 815). Hague v. CIO, 307 U.S. 496 (1939), was cited as a case involving "strikingly similar facts" (*id.*).

4. According to Little, *It's About Time: Unraveling Standing and Equitable Ripeness,* 41 Buff.L.Rev. 933, 944–45 (1993), the lower courts have almost unanimously held, in the wake of Lyons, that a plaintiff must establish standing for each type of relief sought, but the Ninth Circuit has determined otherwise. See Smith v. City of Fontana, 818 F.2d 1411, 1423 (9th Cir.), *cert. denied,* 484 U.S. 935 (1987)(modifying an even less restrictive standard "in light of Lyons" and holding no separate standing inquiry needed when claims for damages and injunction are predicated on same legal theory).

case or controversy focused largely on the appropriateness of equitable relief?[5]

Why wasn't Lyons a mootness case? At the time he was being choked, Lyons surely would have had a live controversy concerning the constitutionality of the city's alleged chokehold policy. Why, then, was he unable to benefit from the "flexible character of the Art. III mootness doctrine" (United States Parole Commission v. Geraghty, p. 227, supra)? Do all mootness cases also raise standing questions about whether declaratory or injunctive relief would redress past injuries that may or may not be repeated? Chemerinsky, A Unified Approach to Justiciability, 22 Conn.L.Rev. 677 (1990), suggests that the Lyons case would probably have been decided differently had the issue been viewed as one of mootness. Do you agree?

Or does it make more sense to conceive Lyons as a ripeness case, concerned with whether the threat of future injury to the plaintiff was sufficiently real and imminent to warrant immediate adjudication? See Little, note (4), supra, at 988–90.

Do the various justiciability doctrines fit together in a way that makes sense in light of underlying values and concerns?[6]

(4) *Justiciability and Institutional Remedies.* Although the injunction sought in Lyons was, as the Court conceded, less intrusive in scope and less "structural" in nature than the injunctions sought in O'Shea and in Rizzo, it was, like them, designed to effectuate a significant change in the law enforcement and administrative practices of a state government agency. The cases thus raise questions about the appropriate judicial role in reforming the operation of government in order to remedy constitutional violations.

Judicial efforts to reform or restructure governmental institutions seem inescapable in at least some instances, but undoubtedly place huge if not excessive demands on the practical competence of courts, and sometimes may even prove dysfunctional. For an analysis of substantive and remedial issues in "institutional" or structural reform litigation, with special emphasis on problems of remedial discretion, see Fletcher, *The Discretionary Constitution: Institutional Remedies and Judicial Legitimacy,* 91 Yale L.J. 635 (1982). For a range of views on the general subject, see, *e.g.,* Rosenberg, The Hollow Hope: Can Courts Bring About Social Change? (1991); Mishkin, *Federal Courts as*

---

5. See Fallon, *Of Justiciability, Remedies, and Public Law Litigation: Notes on the Jurisprudence of Lyons,* 59 N.Y.U.L.Rev. 1 (1984), arguing that in cases where past injury has occurred, the justiciability question in an action for equitable relief should be viewed, under the rubric of mootness, as a question of the likelihood of recurrence.

6. For suggestions concerning a further possible relation between ripeness and the "political question" doctrine, see the concurring opinion of Powell, J., in Goldwater v. Carter, 444 U.S. 996 (1979)(suggesting that a dispute over the President's authority to terminate a treaty without congressional approval should be regarded as political and unripe until Congress as an institution might "confront" the President and thereby present the Court with a justiciable controversy).

For discussion of Justice Powell's opinion and of the significance of discretion in determining questions of justiciability, see Shapiro, *Jurisdiction and Discretion,* 60 N.Y.U.L.Rev. 543, 552–55, 585–86 (1985).

See generally Chemerinsky, *supra.* Professor Chemerinsky criticizes the categories established under current justiciability doctrines and calls for a unified approach focused on four questions: "(1) Is the plaintiff legally entitled to relief * * * ? (2) Is there a sufficient likelihood that a federal court ruling for the claimant will have some effect? (3) Should the litigant be allowed to raise the claims of others not before the court? and (4) Is the claim based on a constitutional provision that the judiciary should not enforce * * * ?" (p. 697).

State Reformers, 35 Wash. & Lee L.Rev. 949 (1978); Nagel, *Separation of Powers and the Scope of Federal Equitable Remedies,* 30 Stan.L.Rev. 661 (1978); and authorities cited pp. 79–81, *supra.*

Is it appropriate for the Supreme Court to employ justiciability doctrines as a means of shielding the federal courts from the hazards of institutional reform litigation? Justiciability questions are generally resolved at the outset of litigation. By contrast, a framing of the central question as involving the law of remedies would allow a balancing of affected public and private interests upon a full record. Why has the Supreme Court rejected this approach? Is it significant that the doctrine of "remedial discretion" makes it difficult for appellate courts to set aside lower courts' remedial decrees and that a Supreme Court that is skeptical of institutional reform litigation can exercise more effective appellate control through the blunter instrument of justiciability doctrine? See Fallon, note (5), *supra,* at 39–43. Has the Court's insistence on examining these issues in Article III terms unduly restricted the power of Congress to deal with remedial questions in public law litigation?[7]

As a way of highlighting the remedial question, consider whether the Court in Lyons or in O'Shea might have taken a different view of the justiciability issue if the plaintiffs had sought only a declaration of the unlawfulness of the conduct engaged in.[8]

(5) *Justiciability and Class Actions.* What significance, if any, should attach to the fact that Lyons was not prosecuted as a class action? O'Shea had been brought as a class action, but no class determination had been made, and the Court (in footnote 3) expressed some doubt about the appropriateness of the class claim; at the same time, it indicated that a named plaintiff must individually satisfy the case or controversy requirement before being able to seek individual or class relief. In Rizzo, a class had been certified but the Court concluded that no showing had been made of a pattern of misbehavior toward the class as a whole that would warrant equitable relief. (It is noteworthy that in Rizzo the Court discussed the class claim only *after* the justiciability portion of the opinion, in a section addressed to the appropriateness of an injunctive remedy).

If Lyons could not establish a sufficient likelihood that he would be subjected to another chokehold, would there nevertheless have been a justiciable controversy if he had established his membership in an identifiable class at least some of whose members were virtually certain to be subjected to choke-

---

7. See generally Nichol, *Ripeness and the Constitution,* 54 U.Chi.L.Rev. 153 (1987); Fallon, note 5, *supra.*

8. *Cf.* Steffel v. Thompson, 415 U.S. 452 (1974), p. 1275, *infra.* But *cf.* Public Service Com'n v. Wycoff Co., 344 U.S. 237 (1952), in which the complainants had sought a declaratory judgment that their carriage of certain goods between points in Utah constituted interstate commerce and thus lay beyond the regulatory power of the state commission. (A prayer for an injunction had been abandoned, apparently because of lack of proof of irreparable injury.) A divided Court held that the discretionary remedy of declaratory relief should not be given in view of the inappropriateness of interfering with a state's administration of its law in the absence of a clear showing of need. But the Court also rested on a broader ground— based on its perception that the sole purpose of seeking the declaration was to hold it "in readiness for use should the Commission at any future time attempt to apply any part of a complicated regulatory statute to it. If there is any more definite or contemporaneous purpose to this case, neither this record nor the briefs make it clear to us. We think this for several reasons exceeds any permissible discretionary use of the Federal Declaratory Judgment Act" (p. 245).

holds in the near future?[9] Is the argument for justiciability—for treating the class itself as a legal entity—strengthened if the class has some characteristics (such as race or ethnicity) that distinguish it from the community at large? Do the cases relating to mootness of class claims, especially Geraghty (p. 227, *supra*) and Roper (p. 239, *supra*), support this argument? See LaDuke v. Nelson, 762 F.2d 1318, 1325–26 (9th Cir.1985), *amended*, 796 F.2d 309 (1986), in which the court (relying in part on Geraghty) held justiciable a class action for injunctive relief against Immigration and Naturalization Service checks of migrant housing units without sufficient cause. For discussion of these and other questions, see generally Meltzer, *Deterring Constitutional Violations By Law Enforcement Officials: Plaintiffs and Defendants as Private Attorneys General*, 88 Colum.L.Rev. 247 (1988).

SECTION 6. POLITICAL QUESTIONS

Nixon v. United States

506 U.S. 224, 113 S.Ct. 732, 122 L.Ed.2d 1 (1993).
Certiorari to the United States Court of Appeals for the District of Columbia Circuit.

■ CHIEF JUSTICE REHNQUIST delivered the opinion of the Court.

Petitioner Walter L. Nixon, Jr., asks this court to decide whether Senate Rule XI, which allows a committee of Senators to hear evidence against an individual who has been impeached and to report that evidence to the full Senate, violates the Impeachment Trial Clause, Art. I, § 3, cl. 6. That Clause provides that the "Senate shall have the sole Power to try all Impeachments." But before we reach the merits of such a claim, we must decide whether it is "justiciable," that is, whether it is a claim that may be resolved by the courts. We conclude that it is not.

Nixon, a former Chief Judge of the United States District Court for the Southern District of Mississippi, was convicted by a jury of two counts of making false statements before a federal grand jury and sentenced to prison. * * * The grand jury investigation stemmed from reports that Nixon had accepted a gratuity from a Mississippi businessman in exchange for asking a local district attorney to halt the prosecution of the businessman's son. Because Nixon refused to resign from his office as a United States District Judge, he continued to collect his judicial salary while serving out his prison sentence. * * *

On May 10, 1989, the House of Representatives adopted three articles of impeachment for high crimes and misdemeanors. The first two articles charged Nixon with giving false testimony before the grand jury and the third article charged him with bringing disrepute on the Federal Judiciary. * * *

After the House presented the articles to the Senate, the Senate voted to invoke its own Impeachment Rule XI, under which the presiding officer

9. Little, note (4), *supra*, at p. 943 n.53, reports that the lower courts are divided on this issue.

appoints a committee of Senators to "receive evidence and take testimony."[1] The Senate committee held four days of hearings, during which 10 witnesses, including Nixon, testified. * * * Pursuant to Rule XI, the committee presented the full Senate with a complete transcript of the proceeding and a report stating the uncontested facts and summarizing the evidence on the contested facts. * * * Nixon and the House impeachment managers submitted extensive final briefs to the full Senate and delivered arguments from the Senate floor during the three hours set aside for oral argument in front of that body. Nixon himself gave a personal appeal, and several Senators posed questions directly to both parties. * * * The Senate voted by more than the constitutionally required two-thirds majority to convict Nixon on the first two articles. * * * The presiding officer then entered judgment removing Nixon from his office as United States District Judge.

Nixon thereafter commenced the present suit, arguing that Senate Rule XI violates the constitutional grant of authority to the Senate to "try" all impeachments because it prohibits the whole Senate from taking part in the evidentiary hearings. See Art. I, § 3, cl. 6. Nixon sought a declaratory judgment that his impeachment conviction was void and that his judicial salary and privileges should be reinstated. The District Court held that his claim was nonjusticiable, and the Court of Appeals for the District of Columbia Circuit agreed.

A controversy is nonjusticiable—*i.e.*, involves a political question—where there is "a textually demonstrable constitutional commitment of the issue to a coordinate political department; or a lack of judicially discoverable and manageable standards for resolving it...." Baker v. Carr, 369 U.S. 186, 217 (1962). But the Courts must, in the first instance, interpret the text in question and determine whether and to what extent the issue is textually committed. See *ibid;* Powell v. McCormack, 395 U.S. 486 (1969). As the discussion that follows makes clear, the concept of a textual commitment to a coordinate political department is not completely separate from the concept of a lack of judicially discoverable and manageable standards for resolving it; the lack of judicially manageable standards may strengthen the conclusion that there is a textually demonstrable commitment to a coordinate branch.

---

1. Specifically, Rule XI provides:

"[I]n the trial of any impeachment the Presiding Officer of the Senate, if the Senate so orders, shall appoint a committee of Senators to receive evidence and take testimony at such times and places as the committee may determine, and for such purpose the committee so appointed and the chairman thereof, to be elected by the committee, shall (unless otherwise ordered by the Senate) exercise all the powers and functions conferred upon the Senate and the Presiding Officer of the Senate, respectively, under the rules of procedure and practice in the Senate when sitting on impeachment trials.

"Unless otherwise ordered by the Senate, the rules of procedure and practice in the Senate when sitting on impeachment trials shall govern the procedure and practice of the committee so appointed. The committee so appointed shall report to the Senate in writing a certified copy of the transcript of the proceedings and testimony had and given before such committee, and such report shall be received by the Senate and the evidence so received and the testimony so taken shall be considered to all intents and purposes, subject to the right of the Senate to determine competency, relevancy, and materiality, as having been received and taken before the Senate, but nothing herein shall prevent the Senate from sending for any witness and hearing his testimony in open Senate, or by order of the Senate having the entire trial in open Senate."

In this case, we must examine Art. I, § 3, cl. 6, to determine the scope of authority conferred upon the Senate by the Framers regarding impeachment. It provides:

> "The Senate shall have the sole Power to try all Impeachments. When sitting for the Purpose, they shall be on Oath or Affirmation. When the President of the United States is tried, the Chief Justice shall preside: And no Person shall be convicted without the Concurrence of two thirds of the Members present."

The language and structure of this Clause are revealing. The first sentence is a grant of authority to the Senate, and the word "sole" indicates that this authority is reposed in the Senate and nowhere else. The next two sentences specify requirements to which the Senate proceedings shall conform: the Senate shall be on oath or affirmation, a two-thirds vote is required to convict, and when the President is tried the Chief Justice shall preside.

Petitioner argues that the word "try" in the first sentence imposes by implication an additional requirement on the Senate in that the proceedings must be in the nature of a judicial trial. From there petitioner goes on to argue that this limitation precludes the Senate from delegating to a select committee the task of hearing the testimony of witnesses, as was done pursuant to Senate Rule XI. " '[T]ry' means more than simply 'vote on' or 'review' or 'judge.' In 1787 and today, trying a case means hearing the evidence, not scanning a cold record." * * * Petitioner concludes from this that courts may review whether or not the Senate "tried" him before convicting him.

There are several difficulties with this position which lead us ultimately to reject it. The word "try," both in 1787 and later, has considerably broader meanings than those to which petitioner would limit it. Older dictionaries define try as "[t]o examine" or "[t]o examine as a judge." See 2 S. Johnson, A Dictionary of the English Language (1785). In more modern usages the term has various meanings. For example, try can mean "to examine or investigate judicially," "to conduct the trial of," or "to put to the test by experiment, investigation, or trial." Webster's Third New International Dictionary 2457 (1971). Petitioner submits that "try," as contained in T. Sheridan, Dictionary of the English Language (1796), means "to examine as a judge; to bring before a judicial tribunal." Based on the variety of definitions, however, we cannot say that the Framers used the word "try" as an implied limitation on the method by which the Senate might proceed in trying impeachments. "As a rule the Constitution speaks in general terms, leaving Congress to deal with subsidiary matters of detail as the public interests and changing conditions may require * * *." Dillon v. Gloss, 256 U.S. 368, 376 (1921).

The conclusion that the use of the word "try" in the first sentence of the Impeachment Trial Clause lacks sufficient precision to afford any judicially manageable standard of review of the Senate's actions is fortified by the existence of the three very specific requirements that the Constitution does impose on the Senate when trying impeachments: the members must be under oath, a two-thirds vote is required to convict, and the Chief Justice presides when the President is tried. These limitations are quite precise, and their nature suggests that the Framers did not intend to impose additional limitations on the form of the Senate proceedings by the use of the word "try" in the first sentence.

Petitioner devotes only two pages in his brief to negating the significance of the word "sole" in the first sentence of Clause 6. As noted above, that sentence provides that "[t]he Senate shall have the sole Power to try all Impeachments." We think that the word "sole" is of considerable significance. Indeed, the word "sole" appears only one other time in the Constitution—with respect to the House of Representatives' "*sole* Power of Impeachment." Art. I, § 2, cl. 5 (emphasis added). The common sense meaning of the word "sole" is that the Senate alone shall have authority to determine whether an individual should be acquitted or convicted. The dictionary definition bears this out. "Sole" is defined as "having no companion," "solitary," "being the only one," and "functioning * * * independently and without assistance or interference." Webster's Third New International Dictionary 2168 (1971). If the courts may review the actions of the Senate in order to determine whether that body "tried" an impeached official, it is difficult to see how the Senate would be "functioning * * * independently and without assistance or interference."

* * *

The history and contemporary understanding of the impeachment provisions support our reading of the constitutional language. The parties do not offer evidence of a single word in the history of the Constitutional Convention or in contemporary commentary that even alludes to the possibility of judicial review in the context of the impeachment powers. * * * This silence is quite meaningful in light of the several explicit references to the availability of judicial review as a check on the Legislature's power with respect to bills of attainder, *ex post facto* laws, and statutes. See The Federalist No. 78, p. 524 (J. Cooke ed. 1961) ("Limitations ... can be preserved in practice no other way than through the medium of the courts of justice").

The Framers labored over the question of where the impeachment power should lie. Significantly, in at least two considered scenarios the power was placed with the Federal Judiciary. Indeed, Madison and the Committee of Detail proposed that the Supreme Court should have the power to determine impeachments. Despite these proposals, the Convention ultimately decided that the Senate would have "the sole Power to Try all Impeachments." Art. I § 3, cl. 6. According to Alexander Hamilton, the Senate was the "most fit depository of this important trust" because its members are representatives of the people. See The Federalist No. 65, p. 440 (J. Cooke ed. 1961). The Supreme Court was not the proper body because the Framers "doubted whether the members of that tribunal would, at all times, be endowed with so eminent a portion of fortitude as would be called for in the execution of so difficult a task" or whether the Court "would possess the degree of credit and authority" to carry out its judgment if it conflicted with the accusation brought by the Legislature—the people's representative. See *id.*, at 441. In addition, the Framers believed the Court was too small in number: "The awful discretion, which a court of impeachments must necessarily have, to doom to honor or to infamy the most confidential and the most distinguished characters of the community, forbids the commitment of the trust to a small number of persons." *Id.*, at 441–442.

There are two additional reasons why the Judiciary, and the Supreme Court in particular, were not chosen to have any role in impeachments. First, the Framers recognized that most likely there would be two sets of proceedings for individuals who commit impeachable offenses—the impeachment trial and a separate criminal trial. In fact, the Constitution explicitly provides for two separate proceedings. See Art. I, § 3, cl. 7. The Framers deliberately separated the two forums to avoid raising the specter of bias and to ensure independent judgments:

> "Would it be proper that the persons, who had disposed of his fame and his most valuable rights as a citizen in one trial, should in another trial, for the same offence, be also the disposers of his life and his fortune? Would there not be the greatest reason to apprehend, that error in the first sentence would be the parent of error in the second sentence? That the strong bias of one decision would be apt to overrule the influence of any new lights, which might be brought to vary the complexion of another decision?" The Federalist No. 65, p. 442 (J. Cooke ed. 1961).

Certainly judicial review of the Senate's "trial" would introduce the same risk of bias as would participation in the trial itself.

Second, judicial review would be inconsistent with the Framers' insistence that our system be one of checks and balances. In our constitutional system, impeachment was designed to be the *only* check on the Judicial Branch by the Legislature. * * *

* * * Judicial involvement in impeachment proceedings, even if only for purposes of judicial review, is counterintuitive because it would eviscerate the "important constitutional check" placed on the Judiciary by the Framers. See *id.*, No. 81, p. 545. Nixon's argument would place final reviewing authority with respect to impeachments in the hands of the same body that the impeachment process is meant to regulate.

Nevertheless, Nixon argues that judicial review is necessary in order to place a check on the Legislature. Nixon fears that if the Senate is given unreviewable authority to interpret the Impeachment Trial Clause, there is a grave risk that the Senate will usurp judicial power. The Framers anticipated this objection and created two constitutional safeguards to keep the Senate in check. The first safeguard is that the whole of the impeachment power is divided between the two legislative bodies, with the House given the right to accuse and the Senate given the right to judge. *Id.*, No. 66, p. 446. This split of authority "avoids the inconvenience of making the same persons both accusers and judges; and guards against the danger of persecution from the prevalency of a factious spirit in either of those branches." The second safeguard is the two-thirds supermajority vote requirement. Hamilton explained that "[a]s the concurrence of two-thirds of the senate will be requisite to a condemnation, the security to innocence, from this additional circumstance, will be as complete as itself can desire." *Ibid.*

In addition to the textual commitment argument, we are persuaded that the lack of finality and the difficulty of fashioning relief counsel against justiciability. See Baker v. Carr, 369 U.S., at 210. We agree with the Court of Appeals that opening the door of judicial review to the procedures used by the Senate in trying impeachments would "expose the political life of the country to months, or perhaps years, of chaos." * * * This lack of finality would manifest itself most dramatically if the President were impeached. The legitimacy of any successor, and hence his effectiveness, would be impaired severely, not merely while the judicial process was running its course, but during any retrial that a differently constituted Senate might conduct if its first judgment of conviction were invalidated. Equally uncertain is the question of what relief a court may give other than simply setting aside the judgment of conviction. Could it order the reinstatement of a convicted federal judge, or order Congress to create an additional judgeship if the seat had been filled in the interim?

Petitioner finally contends that a holding of nonjusticiability cannot be reconciled with our opinion in Powell v. McCormack, [*supra*]. The relevant issue in Powell was whether courts could review the House of Representatives' conclusion that Powell was "unqualified" to sit as a Member because he had been accused of misappropriating public funds and abusing the process of the New York courts. We stated that the question of justiciability turned on whether the Constitution committed authority to the House to judge its members' qualifications, and if so, the extent of that commitment. 395 U.S. at 519, 521. Article I, § 5 provides that "Each House shall be the Judge of the Elections, Returns and Qualifications of its own Members." In turn, Art. I, § 2 specifies three requirements for membership in the House: The candidate must be at least 25 years of age, a citizen of the United States for no less than seven years, and an inhabitant of the State he is chosen to represent. We held that, in light of the three requirements specified in the Constitution, the word "qualifications"—of which the House was to be the Judge—was of a precise, limited nature. *Id.*, at 522.

Our conclusion in Powell was based on the fixed meaning of "[q]ualifications" set forth in Art. I, § 2. The claim by the House that its power to "be the Judge of the Elections, Returns and Qualifications of its own Members" was a textual commitment of unreviewable authority was defeated by the existence of this separate provision specifying the only qualifications which might be imposed for House membership. The decision as to whether a member satisfied these qualifications *was* placed with the House, but the decision as to what these qualifications consisted of was not.

In the case before us, there is no separate provision of the Constitution which could be defeated by allowing the Senate final authority to determine the meaning of the word "try" in the Impeachment Trial Clause. We agree with Nixon that courts possess power to review either legislative or executive action that transgresses identifiable textual limits. As we have made clear, "whether the action of [either the Legislative or Executive Branch] exceeds whatever authority has been committed, is itself a delicate exercise in constitutional interpretation, and is a responsibility of this Court as ultimate interpreter of the Constitution." Baker v. Carr, *supra,* 369 U.S., at 211; accord, Powell, *supra,* 395 U.S., at 521. But we conclude, after exercising that delicate responsibility, that the word "try" in the Impeachment Clause does not provide an identifiable textual limit on the authority which is committed to the Senate.

For the foregoing reasons, the judgment of the Court of Appeals is

Affirmed.

■ Justice Stevens, concurring.

* * *

■ Justice White, with whom Justice Blackmun joins, concurring in the judgment.

Petitioner contends that the method by which the Senate convicted him on two articles of impeachment violates Art. I, § 3, cl. 6 of the Constitution, which mandates that the Senate "try" impeachments. The Court is of the view that the Constitution forbids us even to consider his contention. I find no such prohibition and would therefore reach the merits of the claim. I concur in the judgment because the Senate fulfilled its constitutional obligation to "try" petitioner.

I

It should be said at the outset that, as a practical matter, it will likely make little difference whether the Court's or my view controls this case. This is so because the Senate has very wide discretion in specifying impeachment trial procedures and because it is extremely unlikely that the Senate would abuse its discretion and insist on a procedure that could not be deemed a trial by reasonable judges. Even taking a wholly practical approach, I would prefer not to announce unreviewable discretion in the Senate to ignore completely the constitutional direction to "try" impeachment cases. When asked at oral argument whether that direction would be satisfied if, after a House vote to impeach, the Senate, without any procedure whatsoever, unanimously found the accused guilty of being "a bad guy," counsel for the United States answered that the Government's theory "leads me to answer that question yes." Especially in light of this advice from the Solicitor General, I would not issue an invitation to the Senate to find an excuse, in the name of other pressing business, to be dismissive of its critical role in the impeachment process.

Practicalities aside, however, since the meaning of a constitutional provision is at issue, my disagreement with the Court should be stated.

II

The majority states that the question raised in this case meets two of the criteria for political questions set out in Baker, [*supra*]. It concludes first that there is "a textually demonstrable constitutional commitment of the issue to a coordinate political department.'" It also finds that the question cannot be resolved for "a lack of judicially discoverable and manageable standards."
* * *

Of course the issue in the political question doctrine is *not* whether the Constitutional text commits exclusive responsibility for a particular governmental function to one of the political branches. There are numerous instances of this sort of textual commitment, *e.g.*, Art. I, § 8, and it is not thought that disputes implicating these provisions are nonjusticiable. Rather, the issue is whether the Constitution has given one of the political branches final responsibility for interpreting the scope and nature of such a power.

* * *

A

The majority finds a clear textual commitment in the Constitution's use of the word "sole" in the phrase "the Senate shall have the sole Power to try all impeachments." Art. I, § 3, cl. 6. It attributes "considerable significance" to the fact that this term appears in only one other passage in the Constitution.
* * *

In disagreeing with the Court, I note that the Solicitor General stated at oral argument that "[w]e don't rest our submission on sole power to try." The Government was well advised in this respect. The significance of the Constitution's use of the term "sole" lies not in the infrequency with which the term appears, but in the fact that it appears exactly twice, in parallel provisions concerning impeachment. That the word "sole" is found only in the House and Senate Impeachment Clauses demonstrates that its purpose is to emphasize the distinct role of each in the impeachment process. As the majority notes, the Framers, following English practice, were very much concerned to separate the prosecutorial from the adjudicative aspects of impeachment. * * * Giving each House "sole" power with respect to its role in impeachments effected this division of labor. While the majority is thus right to interpret the term "sole" to indicate that the Senate ought to "functio[n] independently and without assistance or interference," it wrongly identifies the judiciary, rather than the House, as the source of potential interference with which the Framers were concerned when they employed the term "sole."

Even if the Impeachment Trial Clause is read without regard to its companion clause, the Court's willingness to abandon its obligation to review the constitutionality of legislative acts merely on the strength of the word "sole" is perplexing. Consider, by comparison, the treatment of Art. I, § 1, which grants "All legislative powers" to the House and Senate. As used in that context "all" is nearly synonymous with "sole"—both connote entire and exclusive authority. Yet the Court has never thought it would unduly interfere with the operation of the Legislative Branch to entertain difficult and important questions as to the extent of the legislative power. * * *

> * * *

The historical evidence reveals above all else that the Framers were deeply concerned about placing in any branch the "awful discretion, which a court of impeachments must necessarily have." The Federalist No. 65, p. 441 (J. Cooke ed. 1961). Viewed against this history, the discord between the majority's position and the basic principles of checks and balances underlying the Constitution's separation of powers is clear. In essence, the majority suggests that the Framers conferred upon Congress a potential tool of legislative dominance yet at the same time rendered Congress' exercise of that power one of the very few areas of legislative authority immune from any judicial review. While the majority rejects petitioner's justiciability argument as espousing a view "inconsistent with the Framers' insistence that our system be one of checks and balances," it is the Court's finding of nonjusticiability that truly upsets the Framers' careful design. In a truly balanced system, impeachments tried by the Senate would serve as a means of controlling the largely unaccountable judiciary, even as judicial review would ensure that the Senate adhered to a minimal set of procedural standards in conducting impeachment trials.

B

The majority also contends that the term "try" does not present a judicially manageable standard. It notes that in 1787, as today, the word "try" may refer to an inquiry in the nature of a judicial proceeding, or, more generally, to experimentation or investigation. * * *

> * * *

Th[e] argument * * * that one simply cannot ascertain the sense of "try" which the Framers employed and hence cannot undertake judicial review, is clearly untenable. To begin with, one would intuitively expect that, in defining the power of a political body to conduct an inquiry into official wrongdoing, the Framers used "try" in its legal sense. That intuition is borne out by reflection on the alternatives. The third clause of Art. I, § 3 cannot seriously be read to mean that the Senate shall "attempt" or "experiment with" impeachments. It is equally implausible to say that the Senate is charged with "investigating" impeachments given that this description would substantially overlap with the House of Representatives' "sole" power to draw up articles of impeachment.

Art. I, § 2, cl. 5. That these alternatives are not realistic possibilities is finally evidenced by the use of "tried" in the third sentence of the Impeachment Trial Clause ("[w]hen the President of the United States is tried * * *"), and by Art. III, § 2, cl. 3 ("[t]he Trial of all Crimes, except in Cases of Impeachment * * *").

The other variant of the majority position focuses not on which sense of "try" is employed in the Impeachment Trial Clause, but on whether the legal sense of that term creates a judicially manageable standard. The majority concludes that the term provides no "identifiable textual limit." Yet, as the Government itself conceded at oral argument, the term "try" is hardly so elusive as the majority would have it. Were the Senate, for example, to adopt the practice of automatically entering a judgment of conviction whenever articles of impeachment were delivered from the House, it is quite clear that the Senate will have failed to "try" impeachments. Indeed in this respect, "try" presents no greater, and perhaps fewer, interpretive difficulties than some other constitutional standards that have been found amenable to familiar techniques of judicial construction, including, for example, "Commerce * * * among the several States," Art. I, § 8, cl. 3, and "due process of law." Amdt. 5.[3]

III

The majority's conclusion that "try" is incapable of meaningful judicial construction is not without irony. One might think that if any class of concepts would fall within the definitional abilities of the judiciary, it would be that class having to do with procedural justice. Examination of the remaining question—whether proceedings in accordance with Senate Rule XI are compatible with the Impeachment Trial Clause—confirms this intuition.

Petitioner bears the rather substantial burden of demonstrating that, simply by employing the word "try," the Constitution prohibits the Senate from relying on a factfinding committee. It is clear that the Framers were familiar with English impeachment practice and with that of the States employing a variant of the English model at the time of the Constitutional Convention. Hence there is little doubt that the term "try" as used in Art. I, § 3, cl. 6 meant that the Senate should conduct its proceedings in a manner somewhat resembling a judicial proceeding. Indeed, it is safe to assume that Senate trails were to follow the practice in England and the States, which contemplated a formal hearing on the charges, at which the accused would be represented by counsel, evidence would be presented, and the accused would have the opportunity to be heard.

---

3. The majority's *in terrorem* argument against justiciability—that judicial review of impeachments might cause national disruption and that the courts would be unable to fashion effective relief—merits only brief attention. In the typical instance, court review of impeachments would no more render the political system dysfunctional than has this litigation. Moreover, the same capacity for disruption was noted and rejected as a basis for not hearing Powell, [*supra*], at 549. The relief granted for unconstitutional impeachment trials would presumably be similar to the relief granted to other unfairly tried public employee-litigants. Finally, as applied to the special case of the President, the majority's argument merely points out that, were the Senate to convict the President without any kind of a trial, a constitutional crisis might well result. It hardly follows that the Court ought to refrain from upholding the Constitution in all impeachment cases. Nor does it follow that, in cases of Presidential impeachment, the Justices ought to abandon their Constitutional responsibilities because the Senate has precipitated a crisis.

Petitioner argues, however, that because committees were not used in state impeachment trials prior to the Convention, the word "try" cannot be interpreted to permit their use. It is, however, a substantial leap to infer from the absence of a particular device of parliamentary procedure that its use has been forever barred by the Constitution. And there is textual and historical evidence that undermines the inference sought to be drawn in this case.

* * *

[That] evidence reveals that the Impeachment Trial Clause was not meant to bind the hands of the Senate beyond establishing a set of minimal procedures. Without identifying the exact contours of these procedures, it is sufficient to say that the Senate's use of a factfinding committee under Rule XI is entirely compatible with the Constitution's command that the Senate "try all impeachments." Petitioner's challenge to his conviction must therefore fail.

IV

Petitioner has not asked the Court to conduct his impeachment trial; he has asked instead that it determine whether his impeachment was tried by the Senate. The majority refuses to reach this determination out of a laudable respect for the authority of the legislature. Regrettably, this concern is manifested in a manner that does needless violence to the Constitution.[4] The deference that is owed can be found in the Constitution itself, which provides the Senate ample discretion to determine how best to try impeachments.

■ JUSTICE SOUTER, concurring in the judgment.

I agree with the Court that this case presents a nonjusticiable political question. Because my analysis differs somewhat from the Court's, however, I concur in its judgment by this separate opinion.

As we cautioned in Baker v. Carr, [*supra*, at] 210–211, "the 'political question' label" tends "to obscure the need for case-by-case inquiry." The need for such close examination is nevertheless clear from our precedents, which demonstrate that the functional nature of the political question doctrine requires analysis of "the precise facts and posture of the particular case," and precludes "resolution by any semantic cataloguing," *id.*, at 217.

* * *

4. Although our views might well produce identical results in most cases, the same objection may be raised against the prudential version of the political question doctrine presented by Justice Souter. According to the prudential view, judicial determination of whether the Senate has conducted an impeachment trial would interfere unacceptably with the Senate's work and should be avoided except where necessitated by the threat of grave harm to the constitutional order. As articulated, this position is missing its premise: no explanation is offered as to why it would show disrespect or cause disruption or embarrassment to review the action of the Senate in this case as opposed to, say, the enactment of legislation under the Commerce Clause. * * *

In any event, the prudential view cannot achieve its stated purpose. The judgment it wishes to avoid—and the attendant disrespect and embarrassment—will inevitably be cast because the courts still will be required to distinguish cases on their merits. Justice Souter states that the Court ought not to entertain petitioner's constitutional claim because "[i]t seems fair to conclude," that the Senate tried him. In other words, on the basis of a preliminary determination that the Senate has acted within the "broad boundaries" of the Impeachment Trial Clause, it is concluded that we must refrain from making that determination. At best, this approach offers only the illusion of deference and respect by substituting impressionistic assessment for constitutional analysis.

Whatever considerations feature most prominently in a particular case, the political question doctrine is "essentially a function of the separation of powers," *ibid.*, existing to restrain courts "from inappropriate interference in the business of the other branches of Government," United States v. Munoz–Flores, 495 U.S. 385, 394 (1990), and deriving in large part from prudential concerns about the respect we owe the political departments. See Goldwater v. Carter, 444 U.S. 996, 1000 (1979)(Powell, J., concurring in the judgment); A. Bickel, The Least Dangerous Branch 125–126 (2d ed.1986); Finkelstein, Judicial Self–Limitation, 37 Harv.L.Rev. 338, 344–345 (1924). Not all interference is inappropriate or disrespectful, however, and application of the doctrine ultimately turns, as Learned Hand put it, on "how importunately the occasion demands an answer." L. Hand, The Bill of Rights 15 (1958).

This occasion does not demand an answer. The Impeachment Trial Clause commits to the Senate "the sole Power to try all Impeachments," subject to three procedural requirements: the Senate shall be on oath or affirmation; the Chief Justice shall preside when the President is tried; and conviction shall be upon the concurrence of two-thirds of the Members present. U.S. Const., Art. I, § 3, cl. 6. It seems fair to conclude that the Clause contemplates that the Senate may determine, within broad boundaries, such subsidiary issues as the procedures for receipt and consideration of evidence necessary to satisfy its duty to "try" impeachments. Other significant considerations confirm a conclusion that this case presents a nonjusticiable political question: the "unusual need for unquestioning adherence to a political decision already made," as well as "the potentiality of embarrassment from multifarious pronouncements by various departments on one question." Baker, *supra*, 369 U.S., at 217. As the Court observes, * * * judicial review of an impeachment trial would under the best of circumstances entail significant disruption of government.

One can, nevertheless, envision different and unusual circumstances that might justify a more searching review of impeachment proceedings. If the Senate were to act in a manner seriously threatening the integrity of its results, convicting, say, upon a coin-toss, or upon a summary determination that an officer of the United States was simply "a bad guy,'" (White, J., concurring in the judgment), judicial interference might well be appropriate. In such circumstances, the Senate's action might be so far beyond the scope of its constitutional authority, and the consequent impact on the Republic so great, as to merit a judicial response despite the prudential concerns that would ordinarily counsel silence. "The political question doctrine, a tool for maintenance of governmental order, will not be so applied as to promote only disorder." Baker, *supra*, at 215.

NOTE ON POLITICAL QUESTIONS

(1) *Political Questions and the Judicial Function.* What, exactly, did the Supreme Court mean by dismissing Nixon's lawsuit as raising a "political question"? Nixon's standing was not in question. He presented a live controversy, which was neither moot nor unripe, and there was no lack of adverse parties. How does the political question relate to Marbury v. Madison, p. 67, *supra,* and its assertions that it is "the province and duty of the judicial

department to say what the law is" and that, for every violation of a vested right, there should be a legal remedy?[1]

Note that, in Marbury itself, Chief Justice Marshall suggested that questions should be deemed "political", and therefore not subject to judicial review, if non-judicial officials possessed "discretion" to act as they did in the circumstances. Does the political question doctrine refer only to questions that are "political" in this sense? If so, a judicial holding that a suit was governed by the political question doctrine would amount to a decision that no "legal" rights of the plaintiff had been violated; the challenged action lay within the legal discretion of the officials who took it.

Consider Wechsler, Principles, Politics and Fundamental Law 11–14 (1961): "[A]ll the [political question] doctrine can defensibly imply is that the courts are called upon to judge whether the Constitution has committed to another agency of government the autonomous determination of the issue raised, a finding that itself requires an interpretation. * * * [T]he only proper judgment that may lead to an abstention from decision is that the Constitution has committed the determination of the issue to another agency of government than the courts. Difficult as it may be to make that judgment wisely, whatever factors may be rightly weighed in situations where the answer is not clear, what is involved is in itself an act of constitutional interpretation, to be made and judged by standards that should govern the interpretive process generally. That, I submit, is *toto caelo* different from a broad discretion to abstain or intervene."[2]

Is the Court's decision in Nixon v. United States consistent with Professor Wechsler's account?[3]

(2) *Textually Demonstrable Commitment to Another Branch.* The majority in the Nixon case appears to find a "textually demonstrable constitutional commitment of the issue" presented "to a coordinate political department".[4] Within the formulation of Marbury v. Madison, the decision how to "try" an

---

1. For an argument that the political question doctrine cannot be reconciled with the judicial function as it has descended from Marbury and should therefore be abandoned, see Redish, *Judicial Review and the "Political Question",* 79 Nw.U.L.Rev. 1031 (1985).

2. See also Henkin, *Is There a Political Question Doctrine?,* 85 Yale L.J. 597, 622–23 (1976)(arguing that the doctrine is "an unnecessary, deceptive packaging of several established doctrines" whose "proper content" relates to such matters as the obligation of the courts to "accept decisions by the political branches within their constitutional authority" and the ability of the courts to "refuse some (or all) remedies for want of equity").

3. Compare Brown, *When Political Questions Affect Individual Rights: The Other Nixon v. United States,* 1993 Sup.Ct.Rev. 125, 126 (criticizing the decision on the ground that separation of powers doctrine requires judicial review to protect individual rights).

4. Note that it does so only after conducting an inquiry into the "history and contemporary understanding of the impeachment provisions." Can or should the requirement of a "textually demonstrable commitment" be taken literally? Is there any reason why courts in political question cases should be denied access to ordinary sources of constitutional understanding such as history and precedent?

Would the evidence advanced by the Nixon majority to show a "textually demonstrable commitment", especially that involving the deliberate decision by the Constitutional Convention not to vest the Supreme Court with jurisdiction in impeachment cases, support the conclusion that such cases lie outside the judicial power under Article III? See Gerhardt, *Rediscovering Nonjusticiability: Judicial Review of Impeachments After* Nixon, 44 Duke L.J. 231, 271–73 (1994).

impeachment lay within the "discretion" of the Senate. But is it plausible to think that the Senate's discretion is constitutionally unbounded?

Powell v. McCormack, 395 U.S. 486 (1969), discussed in the Nixon case, presented the question whether an unbounded discretion was conferred on the House of Representatives by Art. I, § 5, which provides that "Each House shall be the Judge of the * * * Qualifications of its own Members." At issue was whether Adam Clayton Powell, Jr. was constitutionally entitled to take the seat in the House of Representatives to which he had been elected. It was conceded that he met the age, citizenship, and residence requirements of Art. I, § 2, but he had been denied his seat by a House resolution on the basis of findings by a Select Committee that he "had asserted an unwarranted privilege and immunity from the processes of the courts of New York; that he had wrongfully diverted House funds for the use of others and himself; and that he had made false reports on expenditures of foreign currency to the Committee on House Administration" (p. 492). Together with some voters in his district, Powell sued for a declaration that his exclusion was unconstitutional (and for back salary).

Chief Justice Warren, for the Court, held that the claim did not present a political question. After a lengthy historical examination, he concluded that the provision of Art. I, § 5, is "at most a 'textually demonstrable commitment' to Congress to judge only the qualifications expressly set forth in the Constitution" (p. 548).[5]

Does the approach of the majority in the Nixon case reflect a broader conception of the political question doctrine than the Court invoked in Powell v. McCormack? Note that Justice White's concurring opinion in Nixon v. United States took the majority to task for failing to inquire into constitutional bounds on the Senate's power.[6]

On the other hand, Justice White styled his approach a decision on the merits. If courts always had to inquire into whether other branches had acted within the bounds of their constitutionally permissible discretion, would there be any distinctive political question doctrine at all? Wouldn't every political question argument collapse into an argument on the merits about how the Constitution should be applied to particular, challenged action by a non-judicial official? In other words, wouldn't the question always be, *not* whether another branch of government was textually authorized to resolve a particular constitutional question, but whether that branch had resolved that question in a constitutionally acceptable way?

5. The Court also rejected several other arguments for concluding that the case presented a political question. Justice Stewart alone dissented on the ground that the case was moot.

6. For other cases involving claims of a textually demonstrable commitment to another branch, see, *e.g.,* INS v. Chadha, 462 U.S. 919, 940–43 (1983)(rejecting a claim that the constitutionality of a one-House veto of a suspension of deportation was a political question; the grant of power to Congress to "establish an uniform Rule of Naturaliza-tion" did not preclude the Court from considering whether Congress had chosen a permissible means of implementing that power); United States v. Nixon, 418 U.S. 683, 692–97 (1974)(rejecting the argument, in an action to enforce a subpoena against the President, that his claim of executive privilege raised a political question; the question was one arising in the regular course of a federal criminal prosecution and thus was "within the traditional scope of Art. III power"); Gilligan v. Morgan, 413 U.S. 1 (1973), note 17, *infra.*

(3) *Judicially Manageable Standards.* The Nixon majority was influenced in its conclusion by what it characterized as an absence of "judicially manageable standards". With respect to particular questions that might be put in dispute, it will often be plausible to think that other branches of government are better situated to provide an answer than the courts. But even in the absence of judicially manageable standards for making constitutionally optimal determinations, won't there frequently be manageable standards for determining that another branch has exceeded the bounds of its constitutional discretion? What if, to use Justice Souter's example, the Senate had "tried" Nixon by accepting the outcome of a coin-toss? Wouldn't there would be judicially manageable standards for finding that procedure constitutionally deficient?

Why might the majority wish to suggest otherwise? On the other hand, is the Senate much more likely than the Court to "try" a case by tossing a coin? Are there good reasons to think that entire subject areas ought to lie beyond the scope of judicial oversight?[7] To think that making no determination truly "final" until courts had completed judicial review would be constitutionally unwise?

The majority in the Nixon case specifically adverted to what it deemed the spectre of judicial review of a presidential impeachment. Consider Black, Impeachment: A Handbook 61–62 (1974): "If the Supreme Court [were] to order reinstatement of an impeached and convicted president, there would be, to say the least, a very grave and quite legitimate doubt whether that decree had any title to being obeyed, or whether it was [as] widely outside judicial jurisdiction as would be a judicial order to Congress to increase the penalty for counterfeiting. To cite the most frightening consequence, our military commanders would have to decide for themselves which president they were bound to obey, the reinstated one or his successor. * * * It would be most unfortunate if the notion got about that the Senate's verdict was somewhat tentative. * * * No senator should be encouraged to think he can shift to any court responsibility for an unpalatable or unpopular decision."[8]

(4) *Prudence.* In his concurring opinion in the Nixon case, Justice Souter argued that the political question doctrine requires case-by-case judgments that are sensitive to "prudential concerns". On the propriety of such an approach, Justice Souter cited the work of Alexander Bickel, the most celebrated proponent of a prudential theory of the political question doctrine. Bickel wrote: "[O]nly by means of a play on words can the broad discretion that the courts have in fact exercised be turned into an act of constitutional interpretation governed by the general standards of the interpretive process. The political-question doctrine simply resists being domesticated in this fashion. There is * * * something different about it, in kind not in degree; something greatly more flexible, something of prudence, not construction and not principle. And it is something that cannot exist within the four corners of Marbury v. Madison. * * *

7. For a further exploration of this issue in the context of the processes of constitutional amendment, see Paragraph (7), *infra.*

8. Compare Berger, Impeachment: The Constitutional Problems 103–21 (1973)(argu-

ing, primarily in the context of non-presidential impeachment proceedings, that the scope and content of the terms "other high Crimes and Misdemeanors" in Art. II, § 4, is a question of law subject to judicial review).

"* * * Such is the foundation, in both intellect and instinct, of the political-question doctrine: the Court's sense of lack of capacity, compounded in unequal parts of (a) the strangeness of the issue and its intractability to principled resolution; (b) the sheer momentousness of it, which tends to unbalance judicial judgment; (c) the anxiety, not so much that the judicial judgment will be ignored, as that perhaps it should but will not be; (d) finally ('in a mature democracy'), the inner vulnerability, the self-doubt of an institution which is electorally irresponsible and has no earth to draw strength from." Bickel, The Least Dangerous Branch 125–26, 184 (1962).

In Bickel's view, a fundamental problem of American constitutionalism lies in the necessity to reconcile adherence to principle, on which the legitimacy of judicial review depends, with the demands of sensible, prudent governance. He thought he found the key in a distinction between judicial judgments on the merits, which he argued must be unyieldingly principled, and determinations of justiciability, which he thought could and should turn largely on prudential concerns. Is this the approach that Justice Souter adopted in Nixon v. United States? Is it sound?[9] Is it reflected in at least some of the political question cases?

(5) *Baker v. Carr.* The leading modern political question case is undoubtedly Baker v. Carr, 369 U.S. 186 (1962), discussed in all of the opinions in Nixon v. United States.

(a) Baker presented the question whether an equal protection challenge to the apportionment of the Tennessee legislature raised a nonjusticiable political question. At the time the suit was brought, representation in both houses of the legislature was based on an apportionment scheme adopted in 1901. Since then, population shifts and uneven population growth had resulted in gross imbalances in the number of voters in various districts, and a situation had arisen in which even a substantial majority of the state's voters might fail to elect a majority in the legislature. At least partly as a result, every political effort to procure reapportionment had failed. As Justice Clark wrote in a concurring opinion: "The majority of voters have been caught up in a legislative strait jacket. * * * [The existing apportionment scheme] has riveted the present seats in the assembly to their respective constituencies, and by the votes of their incumbents a reapportionment of any kind is prevented" (p. 259).

In Colegrove v. Green, 328 U.S. 549 (1946), a narrowly divided Supreme Court had found that a challenge to congressional districting in Illinois, based on the Guarantee Clause, presented a nonjusticiable political question. Districting questions, the Court reasoned, were questions of political power and thus "not fit for judicial determination" (369 U.S. at 288 n.19).[10]

---

9. The question of judicial discretion to exercise jurisdiction conferred by the Constitution and by statute has come up before in these materials and will come up again. See generally Shapiro, *Jurisdiction and Discretion,* 60 N.Y.U.L.Rev. 543 (1985).

10. See also South v. Peters, 339 U.S. 276, 277 (1950)(noting that courts generally should not decide "cases posing political issues arising from a state's geographical distribution of electoral strength among its po-litical subdivisions"). In several cases, however, the Supreme Court had upheld judicial challenges to alleged racial discrimination in the drawing of election districts and in the organization of state political parties. See, *e.g.,* Gomillion v. Lightfoot, 364 U.S. 339 (1960) (drawing of political boundaries to disenfranchise blacks); Terry v. Adams, 345 U.S. 461 (1953)(discrimination by political party); Smith v. Allwright, 321 U.S. 649 (1944)(same).

In Baker, the Court distinguished Colegrove on the ground that it was a Guarantee Clause case, which had no relevance to a suit under the Equal Protection Clause. "Judicial standards under the Equal Protection Clause", Justice Brennan wrote, "are well developed and familiar" (p. 226).

In an angry dissenting opinion joined by Justice Harlan, Justice Frankfurter charged that Baker presented "a Guarantee Clause claim masquerading under a different label" (p. 297). In his view, the Equal Protection Clause provided no clearer standards for apportioning electoral power than did the Guarantee Clause. For a court to enter the dispute without such standards would embroil the judicial process in politics and threaten judicial legitimacy.[11]

(b) Baker v. Carr is notable, among other things, for its canvas of prior political question decisions. The Court began by identifying entire subject areas in which challenges to congressional or executive authority had sometimes been thought to raise non-justiciable political questions: foreign relations, questions involving dates of duration of hostilities, the formal validity of legislative enactments, the status of the Indian tribes, and questions about whether a republican form of government exists in the states (pp. 211–17). But the categorical divides were misleading, the Court concluded. "Much of the confusion results from the capacity of the 'political question' label to obscure the need for case-by-case inquiry" (pp. 210–11). From its survey, the Court distilled a list of governing criteria:

"Prominent on the surface of any case held to involve a political question is found a textually demonstrable constitutional commitment of the issue to a coordinate political department; or a lack of judicially discoverable and manageable standards for resolving it; or the impossibility of deciding without an initial policy determination of a kind clearly for nonjudicial discretion; or the impossibility of a court's undertaking independent resolution without expressing lack of the respect due coordinate branches of government; or an unusual need for unquestioning adherence to a political decision already made; or the potentiality of embarrassment from multifarious pronouncements by various departments on one question" (p. 217).

These criteria are regularly cited, as they were in Nixon v. United States, but the division over their applicability in that case was by no means unusual. As you read the rest of this Note, consider whether you would agree with Professor Chemerinsky's conclusions that "these criteria seem useless in identifying what constitutes a political question" and that it is therefore "hardly surprising that the doctrine is described as confusing and unsatisfactory". Chemerinsky, Federal Jurisdiction 144–45 (2d ed.1994).

(c) At the time Baker was decided, numerous commentators echoed Justice Frankfurter's themes that the Supreme Court had plunged into a political thicket and put its legitimacy at risk. Although these criticisms did not immediately abate with the pronouncement of the Warren Court's "one person, one vote" formula, see Reynolds v. Sims, 377 U.S. 533 (1964), that formula proved reasonably manageable in practice. Was this formula itself a result of

---

11. Justice Harlan, in a separate dissenting opinion also joined by Justice Frankfurter, argued that Tennessee's apportionment scheme offended no applicable constitutional standard and that the plaintiffs had therefore failed to state a valid claim on the merits. Were the dissenting opinions of Justices Frankfurter and Harlan, each joined by the other, mutually consistent?

the inability of the majority to discern or agree on any judicially manageable standard short of substantial arithmetical equality?

(d) Does the logic of Baker v. Carr imply that challenges to political gerrymanders are justiciable, notwithstanding the political question doctrine? In Davis v. Bandemer, 478 U.S. 109 (1986), the Court, while conceding that no similar arithmetical resolution could be applied in gerrymandering cases, relied heavily on the Baker line of decisions in rejecting the argument that judicially manageable standards were not available. (The Court also relied on several racial gerrymandering cases, *e.g.*, Rogers v. Lodge, 458 U.S. 613 (1982).)

In dissent, Justice O'Connor, for herself and two other Justices, argued that the question was a political one, due largely to the lack of manageable standards, since "the legislative business of apportionment is inherently a political affair" (p. 145). Any set of voting lines would inevitably advantage some groups relative to others, but the Equal Protection Clause did not require proportional political power for every group and sub-group. Thus the claim was qualitatively different from claims involving either numerical malapportionment or discrimination against racial groups. Justice O'Connor asserted that the claim of discrimination against a political group, if sustained, would inevitably lead to unwarranted judicial superintendence and to a requirement of "some loose form of proportionality" (p. 155).

(e) The influence of Baker v. Carr was also felt in United States Department of Commerce v. Montana, 503 U.S. 442 (1992), in which the state of Montana claimed that a statutorily-mandated method of apportioning members of the House of Representatives among the states violated the Constitution's Apportionment Clause. A unanimous Court (per Stevens, J.) rejected that challenge on the merits, but in doing so also rejected the government's contention that the choice among alternative methods of apportionment presented a nonjusticiable political question. The Court concluded, without substantial explanation, that the interpretation of the Apportionment Clause was "well within the competence of the judiciary", and that the factors enumerated in Baker v. Carr did not "place this kind of constitutional interpretation outside [the judiciary's] proper domain" (p. 1426).

The Court further observed that "[i]n invoking the political question doctrine, a court acknowledges the possibility that a constitutional provision may not be judicially enforceable. Such a decision is of course very different from determining that specific congressional action does not violate the Constitution" (p. 1425; footnote omitted). How sharp is this distinction? How consistently is it observed in political question cases?

(6) *The Guarantee Clause.* The leading early case on the political question doctrine, Luther v. Borden, 48 U.S. (7 How.) 1 (1849), involved Article IV, § 4, which provides that "[t]he United States shall guarantee to every State in the Union a Republican Form of Government". The case grew out "out of the unfortunate political differences which agitated the people of Rhode Island in 1841 and 1842" (p. 34). Despite popular unrest with a "charter" government elected under a state constitution that predated the American Revolution, incumbent officials thwarted reform, and the "Dorr Rebellion" broke out. As an aspect of that rebellion, Dorr was elected governor under the purported authority of a new constitution adopted outside established legal forms, but his effort to take power by force was repulsed, and the charter government implemented martial law. The charter government did, finally, call a constitu-

tional convention, and a new constitution was peaceably introduced in May of 1843.

Meantime, however, Borden and other state officers broke into the house of Luther, a Dorr supporter. When Luther sued for trespass, the forced entry was admitted; the claim turned on whether the defendants were lawfully authorized to enter; and this, the plaintiff maintained, depended on whether the charter government was indeed, as the defendants asserted and the plaintiff denied, the lawfully constituted, "republican" government of Rhode Island at the time of the entry. Rejecting the plaintiff's demand that it inquire into the charter government's lawful authority under the Guarantee Clause, the lower court entered judgment for the defendants, and the Supreme Court affirmed.

In an opinion by Chief Justice Taney, the Supreme Court offered several reasons for holding the issue nonjusticiable, including the practical difficulties that would ensue if judicial challenges to the lawful authority of state governments were invited. The Court's holding was that the question presented was one for congressional, not judicial, resolution: "Congress must necessarily decide what government is established in the state before it can determine whether it is republican or not. And when the senators and representatives of a state are admitted into the councils of the Union, the authority of the government under which they are appointed, as well as its republican character, is recognized by the proper constitutional authority. And its decision is binding on every other department of government, and could not be questioned in a judicial tribunal" (p. 42).

Since the Luther decision, the Supreme Court has never expressly found a Guarantee Clause claim to present a justiciable question, and indeed on several occasions has held such claims to be nonjusticiable. *E.g.,* Pacific States Tel. & Tel. Co. v. Oregon, 223 U.S. 118 (1912)(holding the question whether state laws enacted by initiative and referendum procedures were consistent with "republican" government to be nonjusticiable). Other decisions, however, are more ambiguous in their import. *E.g.,* Texas v. White, 74 U.S. (7 Wall.) 700 (1868)(a state engaged in rebellion against the Union in violation of the Constitution was depriving its citizens of a republican form of government)[12]; Coyle v. Smith, 221 U.S. 559 (1911)(holding that Congress could not rely on the Guarantee Clause—or any other provision—as a basis for conditioning the entry of a state into the Union on the state's agreement to locate its capital in a particular city for at least a decade). See generally Merritt, *The Guarantee Clause and State Autonomy: Federalism for a Third Century,* 88 Colum.L.Rev. 1 (1988); Bonfield, *The Guarantee Clause of Article IV, Section 4: A Study in Constitutional Desuetude,* 46 Minn.L.Rev. 513 (1962).

In New York v. United States, 505 U.S. 144 (1992), the state presented constitutional challenges to various provisions of the Low–Level Radioactive Waste Policy Amendments of 1985 under the Commerce Clause, the Tenth Amendment, and the Guaranty Clause. Per Justice O'Connor, the Court first ruled that a provision directing the states either to provide for the disposal of nuclear waste generated within their borders or to take title to such waste exceeded Congress' power under the Commerce Clause, thereby violating the

12. The Court in White went on to say that it did not need to determine whether every step taken by Congress to restore the state government after the rebellion complied with the Guarantee Clause, because the power to effectuate that clause was "primarily" a legislative power. 74 U.S. at 730.

Tenth Amendment. The Court therefore had no need to address the Guarantee Clause arguments against that provision. With respect to the argument that other provisions creating incentives for the states to provide for the disposal of nuclear waste violated the Guarantee Clause, Justice O'Connor noted that the Court had ruled on the merits of a number of Guarantee Clause cases in the late nineteenth and early twentieth centuries, "before the holding of Luther was elevated into a general rule of nonjusticiability" (p. 184). But Justice O'Connor found it unnecessary to resolve the circumstances, if any, under which Guarantee Clause claims might be justiciable, since the remaining provisions challenged by the state would "not pose any realistic threat of altering the form or the method of functioning of New York's government. Thus even indulging the assumption that the Guarantee Clause provides a basis upon which a State or its subdivisions may sue to enjoin the enforcement of a federal statute, petitioners have not made out such a claim in this case" (pp. 185–86).

Does this approach possibly signal a doctrinal change concerning the justiciability of Guarantee Clause claims in the wake of cases such as Baker v. Carr (which Justice Frankfurter, you will recall, characterized as "a Guarantee Clause claim masquerading under a different [equal protection] label")? Should it? Are judicially manageable standards any less available under the Guarantee Clause than under the Equal Protection Clause? Is there some other reason why all Guarantee Clause claims should be deemed political questions, or would a more contextualized approach be appropriate? See generally Symposium, *Guaranteeing a Republican Form of Government*, 65 Colo.L.Rev. 709 (1994).[13]

(7) *Constitutional Amendments*. In Coleman v. Miller, 307 U.S. 433 (1939), the Court "affirmed" a judgment of the Supreme Court of Kansas refusing to restrain the Kansas Secretary of State from certifying that Kansas had ratified the Child Labor Amendment. Chief Justice Hughes, in an opinion for three Justices, said (a) that the question whether Kansas, once having rejected the amendment, could later ratify it was a question that Congress had the ultimate authority to decide, and (b) that while ratification of a proposed amendment must occur within a "reasonable time" after promulgation of the proposal, decision of that question was "essentially political and not justiciable. * * * In determining whether a question falls within that category [of political questions], the appropriateness under our system of government of attributing finality to the action of the political departments and also the lack of satisfactory criteria for a judicial determination are dominant considerations" (pp. 454–55).

Justice Black, in an opinion for four Justices, said that "Congress has sole and complete control over the amending process, subject to no judicial review" (p. 459), and thus no opinion should be expressed even on the question whether ratification must take place within a reasonable time.[14]

---

13. In his contribution to the Symposium (p. 709), Judge Linde argues that, although Guarantee Clause claims are frequently nonjusticiable in *federal* court due to the deference owed by them to Congress' judgment, the relevant Supreme Court precedents impose no barrier to enforcement of Guarantee Clause claims by *state* courts. Do you agree?

14. Justice Butler, with whom Justice McReynolds joined, thought that mandamus should be granted on the ground that a reasonable time had expired.

Justice Black's view is supported by Scharpf, *Judicial Review and the Political Question: A Functional Analysis,* 75 Yale L.J. 517, 589 (1966): "It is one thing for the Court to strike down the Child Labor Law as incompatible with its choice of constitutional values * * * but it would seem to be quite a different matter if the Court could, by a narrow interpretation of the amendment procedures, prevent the ratification of the amendment which was intended to overrule [the Court's decision]. Of course, the amendment process is itself governed by the Constitution, and it is by no means inconceivable that an amendment might be unconstitutional. But this seems to be one instance in which the Court cannot assume responsibility for saying 'what the law is' without, at the same time, undermining the legitimacy of its power to say so."[15]

(8) *Foreign Relations.* In its survey of political question cases in Baker v. Carr, the Court observed that "[t]here are sweeping statements to the effect that all questions touching foreign relations are political questions" (p. 211), but rejected this conclusion. "Our cases in this field seem invariably to show a discriminating analysis of the particular question posed, in terms of the history of its management by the political branches, of its susceptibility to judicial handling in light of its nature and posture in the specific case, and of the possible consequences of judicial action" (pp. 211–12).[16]

(a) In Goldwater v. Carter, 444 U.S. 996 (1979), the Court, summarily and without opinion, vacated a lower court judgment holding, on the merits, that the President had authority to terminate a mutual defense treaty with Taiwan without the approval of either two-thirds of the Senate or a majority of both Houses of Congress. Justice Rehnquist, in an opinion for four Justices, concurred in the judgment. He argued that since the Constitution speaks only of the ratification of treaties, and not of their termination, the question of the President's power unilaterally to terminate a treaty is a political one. "[In] light of [the] fact that different termination procedures may be appropriate for different treaties, the [case] 'must surely be controlled by political standards' " (p. 1003)(quoting Dyer v. Blair, 390 F.Supp. 1291, 1302 (N.D.Ill.1975). Justice Rehnquist also emphasized that the question involved the politically sensitive area of foreign affairs and that, especially in this field, judicial intervention in "a dispute between coequal branches of our Government, each of which has resources available to protect and assert its interests" was inappropriate (p. 1004).[17]

15. Compare Professor Dellinger's argument for a substantially expanded judicial role in reviewing amending process issues, *The Legitimacy of Constitutional Change: Rethinking the Amendment Process,* 97 Harv. L.Rev. 386 (1983); Professor Tribe's reply, *A Constitution We Are Amending: In Defense of a Restricted Judicial Role,* 97 Harv.L.Rev. 433 (1983); and Professor Dellinger's response, *Constitutional Politics: A Rejoinder,* 97 Harv.L.Rev. 446 (1983).

16. On the justiciability of foreign affairs issues, see generally Ely, War and Responsibility: Constitutional Lessons of Vietnam and Its Aftermath 55–58 (1993); Franck, Political Questions/Judicial Answers: Does the Rule of Law Apply to Foreign Affairs (1992); Tigar, *Judicial Power, the "Po-litical Question Doctrine," and Foreign Relations,* 17 U.C.L.A.L.Rev. 1135 (1970); Champlin & Schwarz, *Political Question Doctrine and the Allocation of Foreign Affairs Power,* 13 Hofstra L.Rev. 215 (1985).

17. See also Gilligan v. Morgan, 413 U.S. 1 (1973), in which officers of the student government at Kent State University, acting in the aftermath of the shootings that occurred there in May 1970, sued for injunctive relief against the Ohio National Guard. The court of appeals had remanded for a determination whether the Guard employed a pattern of weaponry, training, and orders making inevitable the use of lethal force to quell civil disorders. The Supreme Court held that a combination of factors—possible mootness, doubts as to standing, and commitment of

Justice Powell, in a concurring opinion, disagreed with the view that the question was a political one; he argued that the case was not ripe—that prudential considerations militated against judicial involvement in a quarrel between the other two branches until and unless those branches were more at loggerheads than was indicated by the record before the Court.

Justice Brennan, who dissented, would have affirmed on the merits. Although the political question doctrine bars judicial review of some executive decisions in the field of foreign policy, he argued that "the doctrine does not pertain when a court is faced with the *antecedent* question whether a particular branch has been constitutionally designated as the repository of political decisionmaking power" (p. 1007). After addressing that antecedent question, he concluded that the Court should decide the question of presidential authority to terminate a treaty.[18]

(b) In Japan Whaling Ass'n v. American Cetacean Society, 478 U.S. 221 (1986), the Court (unanimously on this point) rejected the government's argument that it should not review a decision of the Secretary of Commerce refusing to certify that Japan's whaling practices diminished the effectiveness of an international conservation program. "[U]nder the Constitution," the Court said, "one of the judiciary's characteristic roles is to interpret statutes, and we cannot shirk this responsibility merely because our decision may have significant political overtones" bearing on American relations with Japan (p. 230).

When, if ever, could the political question doctrine be properly invoked in a statutory interpretation case? *Cf.* Chicago & S. Air Lines v. Waterman S.S. Corp., 333 U.S. 103, 111 (1948). Even if the political question doctrine does not strictly apply, note the analogy between that doctrine and the administrative law doctrine dealing with actions that are "committed to agency discretion by law" and thus not subject to judicial review. See generally Levin, *Understanding Unreviewability in Administrative Law,* 74 Minn.L.Rev. 689 (1990).

(c) During the late 1960s and early 1970s, a number of suits were brought attacking the legality of the Vietnam War. These cases included a variety of challenges (by individuals, groups, and even states) to executive actions taken in the absence of a formal declaration of war. The Supreme Court never gave plenary consideration to the justiciability of any of these challenges, though in

military functions to Congress and the Executive—rendered the issue nonjusticiable. In the course of its opinion, the Court agreed with the dissent below that the relief sought would offend every one of the Baker criteria, and noted: "[I]t is difficult to conceive of an area of governmental activity in which the courts have less competence. * * * The ultimate responsibility for these decisions [as to the composition, training, equipping, and control of a military force] is appropriately vested in branches of the government which are periodically subject to electoral accountability" (p. 10). But *cf.* Scheuer v. Rhodes, 416 U.S. 232, 249 (1974)(holding Gilligan v. Morgan not a bar to damages actions by the estates of students killed at the Kent State demonstration).

How do you explain the disparity between Gilligan and Scheuer with respect to the political question doctrine? Consider, *e.g.,* Nixon, *supra* (noting that "the difficulty of fashioning relief" may "counsel against justiciability"); Henkin, note 2, *supra,* at 622–23 (arguing that some cases resolved on political question grounds would be more aptly characterized as involving dismissal for lack of equity with respect to the remedy sought).

18. Justice Marshall concurred in the result. Justices White and Blackmun, dissenting from the summary disposition, would have "set the case for oral argument and give[n] it the plenary consideration it so obviously deserves" (p. 1006).

one case it summarily affirmed a three-judge court holding of nonjusticiability,[19] and in another summarily denied leave to file an original complaint.[20] But a number of lower courts did pass on this question, and invariably held all or a substantial part of the issues raised to be nonjusticiable.[21] Factors cited included the lack of manageable standards, commitment of final authority to other branches of the federal government, and the difficulty of gaining access to and determining the relevant facts. Several commentators urged, however, that at least some of the challenges did present justiciable issues of the scope of executive power. See, *e.g.,* Henkin, note 2, *supra,* at 623–24.[22]

More recently, Dellums v. Bush, 752 F.Supp. 1141 (D.D.C.1990), rejected the argument that the political question doctrine barred a suit challenging the constitutional authority of the Bush administration to launch the Gulf War without congressional authorization, but, because Congress as an institution had not acted with respect to the issue, the court dismissed the suit on ripeness grounds.

If American actions in Vietnam and Cambodia had been held to violate the Constitution, what consequences would have flowed from the decision? Was the Court right in Powell v. McCormack when it described as an "inadmissible suggestion" the risk that "action might be taken in disregard of a judicial determination" (p. 549, n. 86)? Do problems of enforcement and confrontation with other branches loom larger in a case challenging executive actions in Vietnam than in a case such as Powell? *Cf.* Youngstown Sheet & Tube Co. v. Sawyer, 343 U.S. 579 (1952), p. 1180, *infra.*

(9) *Respect for Coordinate Branches.* In United States v. Munoz–Flores, 495 U.S. 385 (1990), the Court considered on the merits a challenge to the validity of a provision of the Victims of Crime Act requiring those convicted of federal crimes to pay a special assessment to a Crime Victims Fund established by that Act. Munoz–Flores contended that the provision had originated in the Senate and therefore violated the requirement of the Origination Clause of the Constitution (Art. I, § 7, cl. 1) that "all Bills for raising Revenue shall originate in the House of Representatives." The Court rejected the position of the United States that the case presented a nonjusticiable political question. With respect to the suggestion that invalidation of a law on Origination Clause grounds would evidence a "lack of respect" for the House that passed the bill, the Court said: "[D]isrespect, in the sense the Government uses the term, cannot be sufficient to create a political question. If it were, *every* judicial

---

19. Atlee v. Richardson, 411 U.S. 911 (1973). Justices Douglas, Brennan, and Stewart would have noted probable jurisdiction.

20. Massachusetts v. Laird, 400 U.S. 886 (1970). Justices Harlan, Stewart, and Douglas dissented; Justice Douglas, in a separate opinion, considered the justiciability issue at some length. In several other cases involving similar challenges, there were dissents from decisions denying certiorari. *E.g.,* Mora v. McNamara, 389 U.S. 934 (1967); Da Costa v. Laird, 405 U.S. 979 (1972).

21. *E.g.,* Mitchell v. Laird, 488 F.2d 611 (D.C.Cir.1973); Orlando v. Laird, 443 F.2d 1039 (2d Cir.1971); Massachusetts v. Laird, 451 F.2d 26 (1st Cir.1971). In Orlando, the

court held that there was a manageable standard "imposing on the Congress a duty of mutual participation in the prosecution of war," but that the question of "[t]he form which congressional authorization should take is one of policy, committed to the discretion of Congress and outside the power and competency of the judiciary" (pp. 1042–43).

22. For echoes of the Vietnam decisions, see Crockett v. Reagan, 720 F.2d 1355 (D.C.Cir.1983), and Sanchez–Espinoza v. Reagan, 770 F.2d 202 (D.C.Cir.1985), holding nonjusticiable challenges to the Administration's activities in El Salvador and Nicaragua.

resolution of a constitutional challenge to a congressional enactment would be impermissible. * * * Nor do the House's incentives to safeguard its origination prerogative obviate the need for judicial review. * * * [T]he fact that one institution of government has mechanisms available to guard against incursions into its power by other governmental institutions does not require that the judiciary remove itself from the controversy by labeling the issue a political question" (pp. 390–93).

The Court then rejected the government's argument that judicial intervention was inappropriate since the case did not involve a question of individual rights. The argument, the Court said, is "simply irrelevant to the political question doctrine. * * * Furthermore, * * * [p]rovisions for separation of powers within the Legislative Branch are * * * *not* different in kind from provisions concerning relations between the branches: both sets of provisions safeguard liberty" (pp. 393–95).[23]

On the merits, the Court held that, even if the bill did not originate in the House, it did not violate the Origination Clause because a statute that does not raise revenue to support government generally, but rather creates and raises revenue to support a particular program, is not a "Bill for raising Revenue."

Justice Stevens, joined by Justice O'Connor, concurred on the ground that a bill that passes both Houses and is signed by the President becomes law even if it originated unconstitutionally. Justice Scalia, also concurring, argued that any enacted law that bears an attestation that it originated in the House (as this law did) should "establish[ ] that fact as officially and authoritatively as it establishes the fact that its recited text was adopted by both Houses" (p. 409). Although neither concurring opinion rested in terms on the political question doctrine, both interpret and apply the constitutional text in a manner that immunizes from judicial review certain actions of the legislature even when those actions violate the Constitution. Isn't that the core of the political question doctrine?

(10) *Political questions and political cases.* The mere fact that a case has political stakes or has generated political controversy clearly does not render it nonjusticiable under the political question doctrine. "The doctrine of which we treat is one of 'political questions,' not one of 'political cases.'" Baker v. Carr, 369 U.S. at 217.

Nagel, *Political Law, Legalistic Politics: A Recent History of the Political Question Doctrine,* 56 U.Chi.L.Rev. 643 (1989), argues that the political question doctrine is largely an anachronism. Today, he argues, we have come to expect a style of judicial reasoning that is not sharply distinguishable from characteristically political reasoning; it is therefore unsurprising that courts and commentators should have grown skeptical of a doctrine that views some questions as inappropriate for courts because they call for reasoning of a "political", not a "legal", kind (pp. 667–69).[24] Do you agree?

---

23. Compare Choper, Judicial Review and the National Political Process (1980), arguing that questions involving the proper relationship of Congress to the President (as well as questions involving the proper relationship between the states and the federal government) should be nonjusticiable. Professor Choper maintains that the political

process is capable of protecting the relevant interests, and that the courts should preserve their institutional capital for the protection of individual rights.

24. Compare Mulhern, *In Defense of the Political Question Doctrine,* 137 U.Pa.L.Rev. 97 (1988), arguing that the judiciary does not have a monopoly on constitutional interpretation and that the political question doctrine should be viewed as allocating responsibility for constitutional interpretation among the branches of government.

CHAPTER III

THE ORIGINAL JURISDICTION OF THE SUPREME COURT

INTRODUCTORY NOTE ON THE POWER OF CONGRESS
TO REGULATE THE JURISDICTION

(1) *The Constitutional Grant.* Article III, Sec. 2 specifically defines the original jurisdiction: "In all Cases affecting Ambassadors, other public Ministers and Consuls, and those in which a State shall be a Party, the supreme Court shall have original Jurisdiction." The Court has repeatedly said that the jurisdiction can be exercised without enabling action by Congress. See, *e.g.,* Arizona v. California, 373 U.S. 546, 564 (1963); Wisconsin v. Pelican Ins. Co., 127 U.S. 265, 300 (1888).

(2) *The Role of Congress.* Does Congress have power to contract or qualify the original jurisdiction? Beginning with § 13 of the Judiciary Act of 1789, Congress has specified the Court's original jurisdiction. The current provision, 28 U.S.C. § 1251, reads:

(a) The Supreme Court shall have original and exclusive jurisdiction of all controversies between two or more States.

(b) The Supreme Court shall have original but not exclusive jurisdiction of:

(1) All actions or proceedings to which ambassadors, other public ministers, consuls, or vice consuls of foreign states are parties;

(2) All controversies between the United States and a State;

(3) All actions or proceedings by a State against the citizens of another State or against aliens.

Like its predecessor in 1789, the current provision falls short of the constitutional grant—for example, by not including cases *affecting* foreign envoys but to which they are not parties,[1] disputes between a state and a foreign nation, and private suits against a state.[2] May the Supreme Court entertain such actions?

Doubts that Congress may limit the constitutional grant were expressed in California v. Arizona, 440 U.S. 59 (1979).[3] There, California brought an

---

1. But *cf.* United States v. Ortega, p. 336, *infra.*

2. Suits in the last two categories could ordinarily proceed only if sovereign immunity had been waived or abrogated. See pp. 307–08, *infra.*

3. Consider whether those doubts are supported by the proceedings at the Constitutional Convention. The draft of Article III reported by the Committee of Detail would have permitted the legislature to assign to the lower federal courts the cases in the Supreme Court's original jurisdiction—excepting trial of the President in an impeachment, which the draft allocated to the Supreme Court rather than to the Senate.

original action against Arizona and the United States, to quiet title to certain land. The Court found that the United States was an indispensable party and had consented, in 28 U.S.C. § 2409a(a), to such an action—notwithstanding 28 U.S.C. § 1346(f), which gives the *district* courts "exclusive original jurisdiction" of actions under § 2409a(a). Viewing the exclusivity provision as designed to bar state court jurisdiction rather than to divest the Supreme Court of its original jurisdiction, the Court said that any other construction would raise constitutional difficulties: "It is clear, of course, that Congress could refuse to waive the Nation's sovereign immunity in all cases or only in some cases but in all courts. Either action would bind this Court even in the exercise of its original jurisdiction. * * * But once Congress has waived the Nation's sovereign immunity, it is far from clear that it can withdraw the constitutional jurisdiction of this Court over such suits."

"The constitutional grant to this Court of original jurisdiction is limited to cases involving the States and the envoys of foreign nations. The Framers seem to have been concerned with matching the dignity of the parties to the status of the court. * * * Elimination of this Court's original jurisdiction would require those sovereign parties to go to another court, in derogation of this constitutional purpose. * * * [I]t is extremely doubtful that [Congress' powers] include the power to limit in this manner the original jurisdiction conferred upon this Court by the Constitution" (pp. 65–66).

Similar doubts are found in Justice O'Connor's separate opinion in South Carolina v. Regan, 465 U.S. 367 (1984). There the state sought to enjoin, as a violation of its Tenth Amendment rights, enforcement of federal tax provisions subjecting interest on state-issued bearer bonds (unlike interest on registered state bonds) to federal income tax. A possible barrier to suit was the Tax Code's Anti–Injunction Act, 26 U.S.C. § 7421(a), which provides that no suit to restrain the assessment or collection of any federal tax "shall be maintained in any court by any person, whether or not such person is the person against whom such tax was assessed." The Court found, however, that South Carolina had no effective way to raise its Tenth Amendment claim except by an injunctive or declaratory action, and held the Act inapplicable to aggrieved parties who lack an alternative forum for litigating a tax's validity. Justice O'Connor disagreed, finding the Act applicable even to plaintiffs who have no alternative remedy. She concluded, however, that the Act does not bar original actions brought by a state in the Supreme Court. To rule otherwise, she said, would raise the "grave" question "whether Congress constitutionally can impose remedial limitations so jurisdictional in nature that they effectively withdraw the original jurisdiction of this Court" (p. 395).[4]

Even assuming that Congress may not remove cases from the Supreme Court's original jurisdiction altogether, does it follow that original actions are

That assignment clause was eliminated on the floor. See p. 18, *supra*.

4. On the other hand, a Supplemental Memorandum filed in this case by the United States commented (p. 3 n. 4): "We do not fully understand how granting exclusive jurisdiction to a district court (or any other tribunal) over actions that previously were barred by sovereign immunity in *all* federal courts can be said to 'withdraw' (440 U.S. at 65) or 'limit' (*id.* at 66) this Court's original jurisdiction. * * * The Court may wish to reconsider the broad dictum of California v. Arizona * * * before States with claims under the Tucker Act or the Tort Claims Act, or the Internal Revenue Code, are emboldened to invoke this Court's original jurisdiction, notwithstanding provisions of the Judicial Code apparently restricting such suits to lower courts."

exempt from otherwise valid general legislation that regulates who may bring federal claims, what remedies they may seek, when claims may be brought, or what procedures apply? Assume that Congress may generally specify that the validity of a federal tax may be challenged only in a taxpayer's action for a refund. Should South Carolina's effort to obtain an injunction be exempt from that rule simply because it would fall within the original jurisdiction?[5] Does the purpose of the original jurisdiction—to afford states and foreign envoys access to a court having a status appropriate to their "sovereign" character—require such an exemption?

Justice O'Connor's analysis works only on the assumption that South Carolina has a *constitutional* right to an injunction to enforce its Tenth Amendment "rights". Does either the Tenth Amendment or Article III give a state such a right? *Cf.* General Oil v. Crain, p. 855, *infra.*

(3) *Cases vs. Controversies.* Professor Amar argues that Congress does have the power to limit the exercise of a portion of the original jurisdiction. His argument flows from his view, sketched in earlier writings, that the nine heads of jurisdiction defined in Article III, Sec. 1, fall into two tiers. The first tier comprises admiralty and federal question cases and cases affecting foreign envoys; Article III's definition of each is based on subject matter, and begins with the words "all cases". The second tier comprises the remaining six heads of jurisdiction, each of which is defined by party status, and begins with the word "controversies", unmodified by the word "all". He concludes that Article III requires Congress to vest original jurisdiction in the Supreme Court to hear "*all*" cases in the first tier, including those affecting foreign envoys. However, Congress has the power to eliminate from federal jurisdiction altogether all "controversies" (including those in which a state is a party) in the second tier; the grant of original jurisdiction simply requires that *if* Congress confers jurisdiction on the federal courts in such cases, it must allocate them to the Supreme Court—a kind of constitutional venue provision. See Amar, *Marbury, Section 13, and the Original Jurisdiction of the Supreme Court*, 56 U.Chi.L.Rev. 443, 478–88 (1989).

Amar's two-tier thesis is forcefully developed, though not without its difficulties. See generally pp. 371–72, *infra.* As to the original jurisdiction, the thesis leads to the surprising result that despite the mandatory language of Article III, Sec. 2, Congress has constitutional authority to leave the resolution of controversies involving the states—even controversies between two states—to the state courts. See Meltzer, *The History and Structure of Article III*, 138 U.Pa.L.Rev. 1569, 1608 (1990)(Hamilton's view in The Federalist No. 80—that Article III's grant of jurisdiction where a state is a party is grounded on the premise that "[n]o man ought certainly to be a judge in his own cause" —is "hard to square with Amar's view that the state courts, but not the lower federal courts, are free to entertain such actions"). For questions about the "venue" interpretation, see note 8, *infra.*[6]

---

5. Similarly, should it be unconstitutional, in actions falling within the original jurisdiction, to apply federal laws limiting the availability of injunctions in labor disputes, (see pp. 363–64, *infra*, discussing the Norris LaGuardia Act), or generally barring injunctions against state court proceedings (see pp. 1189–1215, *infra*, discussing the Anti–Injunc-

tion Act)—even if application of such a law would require dismissal of the action?

6. For further discussion of the reach of the original jurisdiction clauses, see p. 304, *infra*, discussing Pfander, *Rethinking the Supreme Court's Original Jurisdiction in State–Party Cases*, 82 Cal.L.Rev. 555 (1994).

(4) *Concurrent Jurisdiction.* Ever since 1789, Congress has assumed that the constitutional grant of original jurisdiction to the Supreme Court could be made concurrent with the jurisdiction of the lower federal courts or of state courts. Today, § 1251(a) prescribes exclusive jurisdiction over controversies between states; all other jurisdiction is made concurrent by § 1251(b). Subsection (b) does not itself grant jurisdiction to any other court, but simply permits the operation of any jurisdiction otherwise granted. See, *e.g.,* 28 U.S.C. § 1351, giving the district courts jurisdiction, exclusive of the state courts, "of all civil actions and proceedings against consuls or vice consuls of foreign states".

In United States v. Ravara, 2 U.S. (2 Dall.) 297 (C.C.Pa.1793), a divided circuit court of three judges, two of whom were Supreme Court Justices, upheld its authority to exercise such concurrent jurisdiction, as apparently did every other lower federal court before which the question came in the next 90 years. It was not until Börs v. Preston, 111 U.S. 252 (1884), and Ames v. Kansas, 111 U.S. 449 (1884), that the Supreme Court put to rest any doubts about the constitutionality of concurrent jurisdiction. The opinions in those cases lean heavily on the contemporaneous legislative construction and on the unbroken line of judicial authority. They also stress the inconvenience to the parties, and the burdens on the Supreme Court, that would arise if the Court had to hear every small claim involving a state or a foreign envoy.

The exercise of concurrent jurisdiction may appear to be less controversial when there remains the possibility of Supreme Court review. Thus, in Ames v. Kansas, the state chose to file in state rather than in federal court, but the case was removed (as one arising under federal law) to federal court and was subject to Supreme Court review.[7]

Is there more doubt about concurrent jurisdiction when its exercise will prevent the case ever from making its way to Supreme Court? That was the situation in Plaquemines Tropical Fruit Co. v. Henderson, 170 U.S. 511 (1898), where the Court refused to permit a collateral attack on a state court judgment rendered in an action by a state against citizens of another state—even though the defendants could not have removed the case to federal court and the state court's judgment was not reviewable by the Supreme Court. Does that result defeat the constitutional plan? Is it relevant that the state—the party whose presence gives rise to original jurisdiction—chose not to file in the Supreme Court? Should the "right" to file suit there be viewed as a waivable privilege belonging only to states and foreign envoys? (The possibility remains that an envoy, or a state, could be named as defendant in a state court action that, because no federal question was presented, could never reach the Supreme Court; but in most cases sovereign or diplomatic immunity, unless waived, would prevent the exercise of jurisdiction. See pp. 335–36, 1085–1105 *infra.* But see Nevada v. Hall, 440 U.S. 410 (1979), upholding California's power to render a state court judgment against Nevada as to an automobile accident, in California, involving a Nevada state employee who was driving a state-owned car.)

Note also the conclusion in Ohio v. Wyandotte Chem. Corp., p. 323, *infra,* that the Supreme Court may decline to hear a case of which it has original jurisdiction and remit the parties to a more appropriate forum—in that case, to a state trial court.

(5) *Additions to the Original Jurisdiction.* In Marbury v. Madison, 5 U.S. (1 Cranch) 137 (1803), the Court held unconstitutional § 13 of the Judiciary Act

---

7. On the Court's power to exercise *appellate* jurisdiction over state court decisions in cases that could have been brought in the *original* jurisdiction, see Paragraph (5), *infra.*

of 1789, because it purported to vest the Court with original jurisdiction in cases other than those set forth in Article III. Chief Justice Marshall declared (p. 174): "[I]f congress remains at liberty to give this court appellate jurisdiction, where the constitution has declared their jurisdiction shall be original; and original jurisdiction where the constitution has declared it shall be appellate; the distribution of jurisdiction, made in the constitution, is form without substance."

Do you agree? Surely the "dignity" rationale for original jurisdiction, see, *e.g.*, California v. Arizona, Paragraph (2), *supra*, can explain why Article III might bar Congress from depriving states or foreign envoys of an original hearing before the Supreme Court. Why should Article III preclude Congress from giving other litigants direct access to the Court? To protect those litigants from a possibly inconvenient forum?[8] To protect the Court from a crushing burden imposed by an irresponsible Congress?

Recall that Article III, after defining the original jurisdiction, provides that in all other cases, "the supreme Court shall have appellate Jurisdiction, both as to Law and Fact, with such Exceptions * * * as the Congress shall make." Does that language suggest that Congress may transfer cases from the appellate to the original jurisdiction? Or only that it may exclude them from the appellate jurisdiction in favor of other federal (or state) courts? Notwithstanding the dictum in Marbury and in Ex parte Bollman, 8 U.S. (4 Cranch) 75, 100–01 (1807), that the original and the appellate jurisdictions are mutually exclusive, Chief Justice Marshall later held in Cohens v. Virginia, 19 U.S. (6 Wheat.) 264, 392–403 (1821)(alternative holding), that Congress may grant appellate jurisdiction over cases falling within the original jurisdiction. Why can it not do the reverse?

For criticism of this aspect of Marbury, see Currie, The Constitution in the Supreme Court: The First Hundred Years, 1789–1888, at 68–69 (1985); Van Alstyne, *A Critical Guide to Marbury v. Madison*, 1969 Duke L.J. 1, 30–33.

---

8. Amar, Paragraph (3), *supra*, at 463–78, defends Marbury's holding that Congress may not add to the original jurisdiction. He contrasts the existence of eighteenth century sources stating (in his view) that the original jurisdiction extends *only* to the two categories in Article III with the lack of sources stating the contrary. He also argues that the original jurisdiction clause should be viewed as a constitutional venue provision. Trial before the Supreme Court in the nation's capital, he argues, would probably be convenient for foreign envoys likely to reside there, and for states, which are likely to have representatives there. In other cases, however, Article III prohibits Congress from conferring original jurisdiction on the Court because it is likely to be an inconvenient trial forum.

If geographic convenience had been the concern, why doesn't the Constitution read in those terms? After all, a lower federal court in the capital (which Amar would not bar from hearing Marbury's suit) is no more or less convenient than the Supreme Court. (Recall, moreover, that the Constitution does not guarantee that the Supreme Court would sit in the capital.) Furthermore, in many cases within the original jurisdiction—those involving consuls (many of whom resided outside the capital), or those between a state and a neighboring state or a citizen thereof—the Supreme Court is plainly less convenient than a lower federal court in or adjacent to the place of controversy. *Per contra*, the Supreme Court would seem to be a perfectly convenient forum for many cases that Marbury's holding precludes Congress from assigning to the Court (*e.g.*, suits where the United States is a party). See generally Meltzer, Paragraph (3), *supra*, at 1604–06 & nn. 126, 128, 130; Pfander, note 6, *supra*, at 568–72.

NOTE ON PROCEDURE IN ORIGINAL ACTIONS

Supreme Court Rule 17.2 provides that in an original action, the "form of pleadings and motions prescribed by the Federal Rules of Civil Procedure is followed.   In other respects, those Rules and the Federal Rules of Evidence may be taken as guides."   (Supreme Court Rule 20 governs procedure in applications for extraordinary writs.   See p. 344, *infra*.)

Rule 17.3 states that the "initial pleading shall be preceded by a motion for leave to file".   The adverse party has 60 days to file a brief in opposition to the motion (Rule 17.5).   The Court often disposes of major jurisdictional issues in its ruling on the motion for leave to file.   The Court apparently requires a majority to grant a motion for leave to file.   Oklahoma ex rel. Williamson v. Woodring, 309 U.S. 623 (1940)(motion denied by evenly divided Court);   see also p. 345, note 4, *infra*.   (Why should that be, given that four votes suffice to note probable jurisdiction of an appeal or to grant a writ of certiorari?   See pp. 1704–08, *infra*.)   During the period 1961–93, 50 of the 102 motions for leave to file were denied, generally without opinion.   See McKusick, *Discretionary Gatekeeping: The Supreme Court's Management of Its Original Jurisdiction Docket Since 1961*, 45 Me.L.Rev. 185, 188–90 (1993).

Although the Seventh Amendment applies to trials at common law in the Supreme Court (as 28 U.S.C. § 1872 recognizes), no jury trial seems to have been held since the eighteenth century,[1] as original cases have usually been equitable in character.   Invariably the Court has dealt with problems of taking evidence and preparing findings of fact by referring them to a special master; although the Court regularly accepts the master's findings, in theory they are advisory only.   See United States v. Raddatz, 447 U.S. 667, 683 n. 11 (1980); but *cf.* Maryland v. Louisiana, 451 U.S. 725, 765 (1981)(Rehnquist, J., dissenting)(referring to the "appellate-type review which this Court necessarily gives to [the special master's] findings and recommendations").   No statute or rule explicitly authorizes this procedure.[2]

See generally Stern, Gressman, Shapiro and Geller, Supreme Court Practice ch. 10 (7th ed.1993).

SECTION 1.   CASES IN WHICH A STATE IS A PARTY

United States v. Texas

143 U.S. 621, 12 S.Ct. 488, 36 L.Ed. 285 (1892).
Original.

■ MR. JUSTICE HARLAN delivered the opinion of the Court.

This suit was brought by original bill in this court pursuant to the act of May 2, 1890, providing a temporary government for the territory of Oklahoma.   The

---

1.   See Georgia v. Brailsford, 3 U.S. (3 Dall.) 1 (1794).   See also 1 Carson, History of the Supreme Court of the United States 169 n. 1 (1902), describing two unreported jury trials, in 1795 and 1797.   *Cf.* United States v. Louisiana, 339 U.S. 699, 706 (1950), denying Louisiana's motion for a jury trial.

2.   Compare Fed.R.Civ.Proc. 53, which empowers the *district* courts to appoint masters, states that such references "shall be the exception and not the rule", and requires judges in nonjury cases to accept the master's fact-findings unless clearly erroneous.

25th section recites the existence of a controversy between the United States and the state of Texas as to the ownership of what is designated on the map of Texas as "Greer County," and provides that the act shall not be construed to apply to that county until the title to the same has been adjudicated and determined to be in the United States. [In order to obtain a prompt judicial resolution of the disputed title, the Attorney General of the United States was authorized to institute an original action in the Supreme Court against the state of Texas, seeking a determination of the boundary between the United States and Texas.]

In support of the contention that the ascertainment of the boundary between a territory of the United States and one of the states of the Union is political in its nature and character, and not susceptible of judicial determination, the defendant cites Foster v. Neilson, 2 Pet. 253, 307, 309; Cherokee Nation v. Georgia, 5 Pet. 1, 21; U.S. v. Arredondo, 6 Pet. 691, 711; and Garcia v. Lee, 12 Pet. 511, 517. * * *

These authorities * * * relate to questions of boundary between independent nations, and have no application to a question of that character arising between the general government and one of the states composing the Union, or between two states of the Union. * * * At the time of the adoption of the constitution, there existed, as this court said in Rhode Island v. Massachusetts, 12 Pet. 657, 723, 724, controversies between 11 states, in respect to boundaries, which had continued from the first settlement of the colonies. The necessity for the creation of some tribunal for the settlement of these and like controversies that might arise, under the new government to be formed, must, therefore, have been perceived by the framers of the constitution; and consequently, among the controversies to which the judicial power of the United States was extended by the constitution, we find those between two or more states. And that a controversy between two or more states, in respect to boundary, is one to which, under the constitution, such judicial power extends, is no longer an open question in this court. [The Court here cited numerous decisions in original actions resolving boundary disputes between the states.] * * *

In view of these cases, it cannot with propriety be said that a question of boundary between a territory of the United States and one of the states of the Union is of a political nature, and not susceptible of judicial determination by a court having jurisdiction of such a controversy. The important question, therefore, is whether this court can, under the constitution, take cognizance of an original suit brought by the United States against a state to determine the boundary between one of the territories and such state. Texas insists that no such jurisdiction has been conferred upon this court, and that the only mode in which the present dispute can be peaceably settled is by agreement, in some form, between the United States and that state. Of course, if no such agreement can be reached,—and it seems that one is not probable,—and if neither party will surrender its claim of authority and jurisdiction over the disputed territory, the result, according to the defendant's theory of the constitution, must be that the United States, in order to effect a settlement of this vexed question of boundary, must bring its suit in one of the courts of Texas,—that state consenting that its courts may be opened for the assertion of claims against it by the United States,—or that in the end there must be a trial of physical strength between the government of the Union and Texas. The first alternative is unwarranted both by the letter and spirit of the constitution. Mr. Justice Story has well said: "It scarcely seems possible to raise a reasonable doubt as to the propriety of giving to the national courts jurisdiction of cases in which the United States are a party. It would be a perfect novelty in the history of national jurisprudence, as well as of public law, that a sovereign had no authority to sue in his own courts. * * *" Story, Const. § 1674. The second alternative above mentioned has no place in our constitutional system, and cannot be contemplated by any patriot except with feelings of deep concern.

The cases in this court show that the framers of the constitution did provide by that instrument for the judicial determination of all cases in law and equity between two or more states, including those involving questions of boundary. Did they omit to provide for the judicial determination of controversies arising between the United States and one or more of the states of the Union? This question is, in effect, answered by U.S. v. North Carolina, 136 U.S. 211. That was an action of debt brought in this court by the United States against the state of North Carolina upon certain bonds issued by that state. The state appeared, the case was determined here upon its merits, and judgment was rendered for the state. It is true that no question was made as to the jurisdiction of this court, and nothing was therefore said in the opinion upon that subject. But it did not escape the attention of the court, and the judgment would not have been rendered except upon the theory that this court has original jurisdiction of a suit by the United States against a state. As, however, the question of jurisdiction is vital in this case, and is distinctly raised, it is proper to consider it upon its merits. * * *

It is apparent upon the face of [Article III] that in one class of cases the jurisdiction of the courts of the Union depends "on the character of the cause, whoever may be the parties," and in the other, on the character of the parties, whatever may be the subject of controversy. Cohens v. Virginia, 6 Wheat. 264, 378, 393. The present suit falls in each class: for it is plainly, one arising under the constitution, laws, and treaties of the United States, and also one in which the United States is a party. It is therefore one to which, by the express words of the constitution, the judicial power of the United States extends. That a circuit court of the United States has not jurisdiction, under existing statutes, of a suit by the United States against a state, is clear; for by the Revised Statutes it is declared—as was done by the judiciary act of 1789—that "the supreme court shall have exclusive jurisdiction of all controversies of a civil nature where a state is a party, except between a state and its citizens, or between a state and citizens of other states, or aliens, in which latter cases it shall have original, but not exclusive, jurisdiction." Such exclusive jurisdiction was given to this court because it best comported with the dignity of a state that a case in which it was a party should be determined in the highest, rather than in a subordinate, judicial tribunal of the nation. Why, then, may not this court take original cognizance of the present suit, involving a question of boundary between a territory of the United States and a state?

The words in the constitution, "in all cases * * * in which a state shall be party, the supreme court shall have original jurisdiction," necessarily refer to all cases mentioned in the preceding clause in which a state may be made of right a party defendant, or in which a state may of right be a party plaintiff. It is admitted that these words do not refer to suits brought against a state by its own citizens or by citizens of other states, or by citizens or subjects of foreign states, even where such suits arise under the constitution, laws, and treaties of the United States, because the judicial power of the United States does not extend to suits of individuals against states. Hans v. Louisiana, 134 U.S. 1, and authorities there cited; North Carolina v. Temple, 134 U.S. 22. It is, however, said that the words last quoted refer only to suits in which a state is a party, and in which, also, the opposite party is another state of the Union or a foreign state. This cannot be correct, for it must be conceded that a state can bring an original suit in this court against a citizen of another state. Wisconsin v. Pelican Ins. Co., 127 U.S. 265, 287. Besides, unless a state is exempt altogether from suit by the United States, we do not perceive upon what sound rule of construction suits brought by the United States in this court—especially if they be suits, the correct decision of which depends upon the constitution, laws, or treaties of the United States—are to be excluded from its original jurisdiction as defined in the constitution. * * * We cannot assume that the framers of the constitution, while extending the judicial power of the United States to controversies between two or more states of the Union, and between a state of the Union and foreign states, intended to exempt a state altogether from suit by the general government. They could not have overlooked the possibility that controversies capable of judicial solution might arise between the United States and some of the states, and that the permanence of the Union might be endangered if to some tribunal was not entrusted the power to determine them according to the recognized principles of law. And to what tribunal could a trust so momentous be more appropriately committed than to that which the people of the United States, in order to form a more perfect Union, establish justice, and insure domestic tranquillity, have constituted with authority to speak for all the people and all the states upon questions before it to which the judicial power of the nation extends? * * *

The question as to the suability of one government by another government rests upon wholly different grounds. Texas is not called to the bar of this court at the suit of an individual, but at the suit of the government established for the common and equal benefit of the people of all the states. The submission to judicial solution of controversies arising between these two governments, "each sovereign, with respect to the objects committed to it, and neither sovereign with respect to the objects committed to the other," McCulloch v. State of Maryland, 4 Wheat. 316, 400, 410, but both subject to the supreme law of the land, does no violence to the inherent nature of sovereignty. The states of the Union have agreed, in the constitution, that the judicial power of the United States shall extend to all cases arising under the constitution, laws, and treaties of the United States, without regard to the character of the parties, (excluding, of course, suits against a state by its own citizens or by citizens of other states, or by citizens or subjects of foreign states,) and equally to controversies to which the United States shall be a party, without regard to the subject of such controversies, and that this court may exercise original jurisdiction in all such cases "in which a state shall be party," without excluding those in which the United States may be the opposite party. The exercise, therefore, by this court, of such original jurisdiction in a suit brought by one state against another to determine the boundary line between them, or in a suit brought by the United States against a state to determine the boundary between a territory of the United States and that state, so far from infringing in either case upon the sovereignty, is with the consent of the state sued. Such consent was given by Texas when admitted into the Union upon an equal footing in all respects with the other states.

We are of opinion that this court has jurisdiction to determine the disputed question of boundary between the United States and Texas. * * *

▉ MR. CHIEF JUSTICE FULLER, with whom concurred MR. JUSTICE LAMAR, dissenting.

Mr. Justice Lamar and myself are unable to concur in the decision just announced.

This court has original jurisdiction of two classes of cases only,—those affecting ambassadors, other public ministers, and consuls, and those in which a state shall be a party.

The judicial power extends to "controversies between two or more states," "between a state and citizens of another state," and "between a state, or the citizens thereof, and foreign states, citizens, or subjects." Our original jurisdiction, which depends wholly upon the character of the parties, is confined to the cases enumerated in which a state may be a party, and this is not one of them.

The judicial power also extends to controversies to which the United States shall be a party, but such controversies are not included in the grant of original jurisdiction. To the controversy here the United States is a party.

We are of opinion, therefore, that this case is not within the original jurisdiction of the court.

NOTE ON THE SCOPE OF THE JURISDICTION

(1) *The Structure of Article III.* Article III, Sec. 2's provision for original jurisdiction in "those [cases] in which a State shall be Party" might have been construed as an independent grant of jurisdiction to hear *all* such cases—including, for example, an action by a state against one of its own citizens to enforce a claim based on state law. However, this broadest of possible constructions has been uniformly rejected. "This second clause distributes the jurisdiction conferred upon the Supreme Court in the previous one into original and appellate jurisdiction; but does not profess to confer any." Pennsylvania v. Quicksilver Mining Co., 77 U.S. (10 Wall.) 553, 556 (1871).

(a) Recall that the first section of Article III contains three subject-matter heads of jurisdiction (admiralty, federal question, and cases affecting foreign envoys) and six party-based heads (including the United States as a party and three heads in which a state is a party). Decisions after United States v. Texas have rejected the view that the original jurisdiction extends to all of the nine classes of cases enumerated in the first section of Article III in which a state happens to be a party. Thus, in California v. Southern Pacific Co., 157 U.S. 229 (1895), a state sued a citizen of another state but joined also one of its own citizens. In denying jurisdiction, the Court said (pp. 257–58): "* * * The original jurisdiction depends solely on the character of the parties, and is confined to the cases in which are those enumerated parties and those only. Among those in which jurisdiction must be exercised in the appellate form are cases arising under the Constitution and laws of the United States. In one description of cases the character of the parties is everything, the nature of the case nothing. In the other description of cases the nature of the case is everything, the character of the parties nothing."

(b) No claim appears to have been made in the Southern Pacific litigation that the case arose under federal law. Nevertheless, in Texas v. ICC, 258 U.S.

158 (1922), where the suit filed by the state clearly did arise under federal law, the Court relied on Southern Pacific, without discussion, in holding that the presence as a defendant of a citizen of the plaintiff state was fatal to the jurisdiction. *Cf.* Minnesota v. Northern Securities Co., 184 U.S. 199, 245 (1902); New Mexico v. Lane, 243 U.S. 52 (1917).

Can Texas v. ICC be reconciled with United States v. Texas? Does the original jurisdiction in state-as-party cases that is distributed in section 2 of Article III extend only to those heads of jurisdiction in section 1 that are described in terms of parties rather than of subject matter? What would be the justification for such a limitation? (Compare the viewpoint of Professor Amar, p. 296, *supra*.) How could that limitation be reconciled with section 2's grant of original jurisdiction in cases *affecting* foreign envoys?

(c) A recent article by Professor Pfander (*Rethinking the Supreme Court's Original Jurisdiction in State–Party Cases*, 82 Cal.L.Rev. 555 (1994)) criticizes these decisions and contends more broadly that the state-as-party original jurisdiction was "at the center of the Framers' plan to secure the effective enforcement of federal law against the states" (p. 558). He reads Article III as leaving intact the traditional "common law" immunity of states from suits brought by individuals in the states' own courts, but views the original jurisdiction clause as abrogating the "law-of-nations" immunity of states to suit in the courts of the United States. The original jurisdiction was necessary to enforce individuals' federal rights against the states. After all, the Constitution did not require creation of lower federal courts. And the Supreme Court's appellate jurisdiction over state courts would not suffice because those courts might invoke common law immunity to defeat federal rights; rather than requiring state courts to hear federal claims, the "far simpler solution was to provide the only constitutionally mandated federal court—the Supreme Court— with original jurisdiction" over such claims (p. 560). That jurisdiction, however, need not be exclusive, and presumably Congress and the Court would remit most cases to the concurrent jurisdiction of the lower federal courts.

To buttress his argument, Professor Pfander musters an impressive range of sources and arguments. And he asserts that his account of the original jurisdiction is more persuasive than the traditional "dignified tribunal" theory in part because that theory is hard pressed to explain the exclusion from the original jurisdiction of cases in which the United States, or a foreign nation, is a party. Under his approach, the exclusion makes sense, for those sovereigns, unlike the states, were not subject (absent consent) to suit in federal court. But can't the traditional theory also explain those exclusions? There was no need for a "dignified tribunal" for foreign nations precisely because they (unlike the states) retained their immunity from unconsented actions; and the United States had no reason to fear suit in its own courts.

How does Pfander's understanding explain the grant of original jurisdiction in cases between states and non-citizens, without regard to the presence of a federal question? (He states that federal courts would not be justified in imposing liability on the states in individual claims based on non-federal law, in view of the surviving "common-law limits" on state suability.) How does his understanding fit with the foreign envoy branch of the original jurisdiction, whose principal purpose does not appear to have been enforcement of federal law?

In any event, Pfander's arguments raise important doubts about the correctness of the Court's decisions that the state-as-party jurisdiction does not include federal question (or admiralty) cases where state-citizen diversity is lacking. Could one question those decisions, however, without viewing the original jurisdiction as being primarily designed for, and central to the enforcement of, federal law against the states? Compare the discussion in Chap. IX, Sec. 2(A), pp. 1052–55, *infra*, of understandings of state sovereign immunity that would leave states suable in the lower federal courts in federal question cases, regardless of diversity. In practice, the results under those understandings would not differ significantly from those under Pfander's view, given his assumption that the Supreme Court would decline to hear most original federal question cases in favor of the concurrent jurisdiction of the federal district courts. (Pfander's view could burden the Supreme Court with additional motions for leave to file that would almost surely be denied.)

(2) *"Ancillary" Original Jurisdiction.* In the Southern Pacific case, although there would have been original jurisdiction in an action by California against the non-citizen defendant, the joinder as defendants of California citizens, who could not have been sued independently in the Supreme Court, was fatal to the jurisdiction. To the same effect, see the Northern Securities, Lane, and ICC cases, all cited in Paragraph (1)(c), *supra*.

In Louisiana v. Cummins, 314 U.S. 577 (1941), the state tried to distinguish the prior cases as involving ineligible parties who were indispensable, arguing that, by contrast, the Court in Cummins had jurisdiction to proceed without the in-state defendant. Still, the Court denied jurisdiction.

Was the Court wise to reject the argument that joinder should be permitted to permit resolution of the entire matter in controversy? See the views of Justices Harlan and Brewer, dissenting in California v. Southern Pac. Co., 157 U.S. at 262–71. Could Congress overrule this decision and authorize exercise of an "ancillary" original jurisdiction? Compare the district courts' supplemental jurisdiction, now governed by 28 U.S.C. § 1367. See Chap. VIII, Sec. 5, and Chap. XIII, Sec. 2, *infra*.

In actions by the United States against a state, the Court has repeatedly (and without discussion) permitted the joinder of individual defendants whom the United States could not have sued separately in the original jurisdiction. See, *e.g.*, United States v. Wyoming, 331 U.S. 440 (1947); United States v. West Virginia, 295 U.S. 463 (1935). Are these cases distinguishable?

(3) *"Penal" Actions.* A state's prosecution of a noncitizen seems to fall within the literal wording of the constitutional grant of original jurisdiction, and of § 1251.[1] But in Wisconsin v. Pelican Ins. Co., 127 U.S. 265, 297–98 (1888), the Court concluded that the constitutional grant of jurisdiction in state-as-party cases did not extend to original actions seeking to impose a penalty—there, an action on a judgment imposing statutory penalties on an insurer who had violated state regulations. The original jurisdiction in cases in which a state is a party, the Court said (p. 297), "is limited to controversies of a civil nature," and does not extend to "a suit or prosecution by the one State, of such a nature that it could not, on the settled principles of public and international law, be entertained by the judiciary of the other State at all" (p. 289).[2]

---

1. *But cf.* Meltzer, p. 296, *supra*, at 1575–76 & nn. 18, 22, and Fletcher, *Exchange on the Eleventh Amendment*, 57 U.Chi.L.Rev. 131, 133 (1990)(noting evidence that the word "controversy", used in Article III to define the state-as-party jurisdiction, was understood in the 18th century to encompass only civil cases); pp. 370–71, *infra*.

2. The Pelican case was disapproved in part in Milwaukee County v. M.E. White Co.,

The Pelican Court stressed the traditional reluctance of one jurisdiction to enforce the penal laws of another. Is that an adequate justification? (Note that (i) Cohens v. Virginia, p. 298, *supra*, p. 1048, *infra*, rejected the argument that Article III does not permit the exercise of the Supreme Court's *appellate* jurisdiction to review state criminal cases, and (ii) federal courts have removal jurisdiction over some state law prosecutions.) Is the Pelican decision justified by docket concerns? By the desire to provide convenient venues and local juries for criminal trials? By the limitation to "civil" cases in the jurisdiction granted over state-as-party cases by § 13 of the Judiciary Act of 1789? See generally Woolhandler & Collins, *State Standing*, 81 Va.L.Rev. 389, 422–46 (1995); Meltzer, p. 296, *supra*, at 1576.

(4) *The Docket*. State-as-party cases constitute virtually the entire original docket of the Supreme Court. Before the beginning of the 1961 Term, the Court had issued opinions in 121 original jurisdiction cases. From October 1, 1961 to April 1, 1993, the Court published 51 such opinions. See McKusick, p. 299, *supra*, at 186–88.[3] The Court's exercise of discretion to decline jurisdiction in favor of another forum has been an important factor limiting the docket. See pp. 323–34, *infra*.

NOTE ON ACTIONS BY THE UNITED STATES AGAINST A STATE

Under 28 U.S.C. § 1251(b)(2), the Supreme Court's original jurisdiction in "controversies between the United States and a State" is not exclusive.[1] See United States v. Nevada, 412 U.S. 534, 537 (1973). Section 1345's grant of district court jurisdiction over "all" civil actions commenced by the United States has been held to include actions against a state. See, *e.g.*, United States v. California, 328 F.2d 729 (9th Cir.1964). Other special jurisdictional provisions may also give the district courts concurrent jurisdiction in such cases.[2]

In cases between the United States and a state, the Court has exercised jurisdiction most readily in disputes over state-federal boundaries or title to tidelands or other property.

For discussion of the Court's discretion to deny leave to file in cases brought by the United States if a more convenient forum exists, see p. 331, *infra*.

---

296 U.S. 268 (1935), which held that a federal district court should take jurisdiction of an action on a judgment for taxes. The Court reserved opinion as to actions, outside the obligation-creating state, to enforce revenue laws or to enforce judgments "for an obligation created by a penal law, in the international sense" (p. 279).

3. McKusick's article is a thorough study of the original jurisdiction from the 1961 Term through April of 1993. For a study of original actions prior to July 1959, see Note, 11 Stan.L.Rev. 665 (1959).

1. Until 1948, jurisdiction in such actions was exclusive, see 28 U.S.C. § 341 (1940), except where § 341's exclusivity was overridden by special provisions conferring concurrent jurisdiction over particular matters on the district courts. See United States v. California, discussed above; Note, 38 N.Y.U.L.Rev. 405 (1963).

2. See, *e.g.*, United States v. Mississippi, 380 U.S. 128, 138–41 (1965), and United States v. Alabama, 362 U.S. 602 (1960)(both upholding district court suits by the United States against a state under the Civil Rights Act of 1957, 42 U.S.C. § 1971(c)).

NOTE ON THE BEARING OF SOVEREIGN IMMUNITY
AND THE ELEVENTH AMENDMENT

(1) *Suits by States Against the United States.* In Kansas v. United States, 204 U.S. 331 (1907), an alternative holding was that the United States is immune from suit by a state. The Court said only (p. 342): "It does not follow that because a State may be sued by the United States without its consent, therefore the United States may be sued by a State without its consent. Public policy forbids that conclusion." Accord Oregon v. Hitchcock, 202 U.S. 60 (1906); Minnesota v. United States, 305 U.S. 382 (1939).

(2) *Consent to Suit.* It is generally accepted that the doctrine of sovereign immunity does not qualify the constitutional grants of jurisdiction themselves, but simply erects a bar to the exercise of jurisdiction, which is removed when consent is given. See, *e.g.*, United States v. Louisiana, 123 U.S. 32, 35 (1887); Minnesota v. Hitchcock, 185 U.S. 373, 382–88 (1902).[1] However, California v. Arizona, pp. 294–95, *supra*, held that when the United States consents to suit, it may not avoid the Supreme Court's original jurisdiction by limiting its consent to another tribunal.

(3) *Suits by States Against Federal Officials.* Barred from suing the United States (absent its consent) by name, states have not infrequently sought to obtain similar relief by suing federal officials, as citizens of other states, in the original jurisdiction. Cases accepting jurisdiction include South Carolina v. Regan, p. 295, *supra;* Oregon v. Mitchell, 400 U.S. 112 (1970); South Carolina v. Katzenbach, 383 U.S. 301 (1966); and Ohio v. Helvering, 292 U.S. 360 (1934). But some suits of this form have been dismissed as in substance against the United States. See, *e.g.*, Hawaii v. Gordon, 373 U.S. 57 (1963); Oregon v. Hitchcock, 202 U.S. 60 (1906); New Mexico v. Lane, 243 U.S. 52 (1917). For discussion of when a suit nominally against an officer is barred as in substance against the United States, see pp. 1015–27, *infra*.

(4) *States as Defendants: The Bearing of the Eleventh Amendment.* The Eleventh Amendment has been interpreted as conferring on the states an immunity from suit in federal court, including the Supreme Court. For discussion of the historical, theoretical, and doctrinal complexities entailed, see Chap. IX, Sec. 2(A), *infra*.

In Monaco v. Mississippi, 292 U.S. 313 (1934), the Court denied Monaco's motion for leave to file, holding that a state possesses sovereign immunity from suit by a foreign government. Although the Eleventh Amendment applies in terms only to suits by private parties, the Court ruled that "[b]ehind the words of the constitutional provisions are postulates which limit and control"—in this case, that the states possess immunity from unconsented suit except "where there has been 'a surrender of this immunity in the plan of the convention'" (pp. 322–23, quoting The Federalist, No. 81). Although such a surrender was inherent in, and essential to, the Constitution when a state is sued by another state or by the United States, the Court found no such surrender when a foreign state, which lies "outside the structure of the Union", brings suit (p. 330).

Consider Article III's grant of jurisdiction in "Controversies * * * between a State * * * and foreign States * * *". If Mississippi had consented to suit,

---

1. The different view taken in Williams v. United States, 289 U.S. 553 (1933), as well as other aspects of Williams, seem to have been repudiated in Glidden Co. v. Zdanok, 370 U.S. 530 (1962). See generally Chap. IV, Sec. 2, pp. 420–21 note 9, *infra*.

would the Court have had jurisdiction? Would there be jurisdiction in the converse situation, if Mississippi were suing Monaco with Monaco's consent? Compare 28 U.S.C. § 1251(b).

(5) *Waiver of Eleventh Amendment Immunity.* The Eleventh Amendment states: "The Judicial power of the United States shall not be construed to extend to" the actions there listed. Yet the Supreme Court has consistently assumed that, like the sovereign immunity of the United States, "[t]he immunity from suit belonging to a State * * * is a personal privilege which it may waive at pleasure". Clark v. Barnard, 108 U.S. 436, 447 (1883). For further discussion of the issue of waiver, see pp. 1097–1100, *infra.*

(6) *Hybrid Cases.* In a suit against a state by another state or by the United States, would the intervention as plaintiff of someone other than a state violate the Eleventh Amendment? In Maryland v. Louisiana, 451 U.S. 725, 745 n. 21 (1981), the United States, one of its agencies, and private companies were allowed to intervene as plaintiffs in an original action between two states; Eleventh Amendment concerns were summarily waived aside. In Arizona v. California, 460 U.S. 605 (1983), a suit between two states in which the United States had intervened on behalf, *inter alia,* of Indian tribes, the Tribes themselves were subsequently allowed to intervene; citing Maryland v. Louisiana, the Court said that because the tribes did not seek to raise any new claims, "our judicial power * * * is not enlarged" and state "sovereign immunity * * * is not compromised" (p. 614). Compare p. 305, *supra* (refusing to exercise "ancillary" jurisdiction over co-defendants who could not have been sued independently before the Supreme Court).

Kentucky v. Indiana

281 U.S. 163, 50 S.Ct. 275, 74 L.Ed. 784 (1930).
Original.

■ MR. CHIEF JUSTICE HUGHES delivered the opinion of the Court.

In September, 1928, the Commonwealth of Kentucky and the State of Indiana, by their respective Highway Commissions, entered into a contract for the building of a bridge across the Ohio River between Evansville, Indiana, and Henderson, Kentucky. The contract was approved by the Governor, and as to legality and form, also by the Attorney General, of each State. The contract recited the acts of Congress and of the state legislatures which were deemed to authorize the enterprise. [Citations omitted.] The State of Indiana immediately began the performance of the covenants of the contract on its part, and thereupon nine citizens and taxpayers of Indiana brought suit in the Superior Court of Marion County in that State to enjoin the members of the Highway Commission and other officers of Indiana from carrying out the contract upon the ground that it was unauthorized and void.

The Commonwealth of Kentucky then asked leave to file the bill of complaint in this suit against the State of Indiana and the individuals who were plaintiffs in the suit in the state court, seeking to restrain the breach of the contract and the prosecution of that suit, and for specific performance. In its return to the order to show cause why this leave should not be granted the State of Indiana said that it had "no cause to show"; that the State intended ultimately to perform the contract, if performance were permitted or ordered by the courts in which the litigation over the contract was pending, but that it did not intend to do so until after that litigation had finally been disposed of favorably to its performance; that the State of Indiana had entered into the contract by virtue of authority of its own statutes and of the Act of Congress of March 2, 1927; that, as there was no court having complete jurisdiction over the parties and subject-matter, other than this Court, the State yielded to the jurisdiction of this Court, and that it was in the public interest that an early adjudication be had which would be final and binding upon all parties interested.

Leave being granted, the bill of complaint herein was filed. * * *

Separate answers were filed by the State of Indiana and by the individual defendants. The answer of the State of Indiana admitted that the allegations of the complaint were true. The answer then averred:

"The only excuse which the State of Indiana offers for failure to perform the contract set out in plaintiff's complaint is the litigation, mentioned in the complaint, instituted by her above-named co-defendants against the officers of the State of Indiana whose function it is to perform said contract. The resulting delay in performance of said contract is in breach of its terms, which contemplate immediate and continued performance."

* * *

"The State of Indiana believes said contract is valid. If this honorable court shall grant the relief prayed against Indiana by plaintiff Commonwealth of Kentucky * * *, the State of Indiana will thereupon immediately proceed with the performance of said contract * * *."

The individual defendants filed an answer and, at the same time, moved to dismiss the complaint * * *.

After hearing argument, the court overruled the motion to dismiss in so far as it questioned the jurisdiction of the court to entertain the bill of complaint and to proceed to a hearing and determination of the merits of the controversy, and directed that all other questions sought to be presented by that motion be reserved for further consideration at the hearing upon the merits. * * *

The question of the jurisdiction of this Court was determined on the hearing of the motion to dismiss. The State of Indiana, while desiring to perform its contract, is not going on with its performance because of a suit brought by its citizens in its own court. There is thus a controversy between the States, although a limited one.

[The Court proceeded to note that citizens, voters, and taxpayers, merely as such, have no separate right to contest the position taken by the state itself; the state stands as their representative. Individual defendants are not entitled to contest the merits of the making of the contract between two states or the obligations thereunder, as they have no separate and proper interest in the contract. Individual citizens sued by the complainant state, against whom that state could obtain some relief (which was merely incidental to the relief sought against the defendant state), have standing to contest the particular relief sought against them personally—the only question that concerns them individually rather than in common with their fellow citizens—but not to litigate the merits of a controversy between the states.]

In the present instance, * * * [t]he individual defendants were made parties solely for the purpose of obtaining an injunction against them restraining the prosecution of the suit in the state court. Such an injunction is not needed, as a decree in this suit would bind the State of Indiana, and, on being shown, would bar any inconsistent proceedings in the courts of that State. As no sufficient ground appears for maintaining the bill of complaint against the individual defendants, it should be dismissed as against them.

The question, then, is as to the case made by the Commonwealth of Kentucky against the State of Indiana. * * * [T]he State of Indiana admits the making of the contract and the authority of its officers to make it under the applicable legislation. * * * The only suggestion of a defense for its failure to perform the contract * * * is the pendency of this litigation in the state court. * * *

It is manifest that if, in accordance with the pleading of each State, the contract for the building of the bridge is deemed to be authorized and valid, the mere pendency of a suit brought by citizens to restrain performance does not constitute a defense. In that aspect, the question would be, not as to a defense on the merits, but whether this Court should withhold a final determination merely because of the fact that such a suit is pending. This question raises important considerations. It cannot be gainsaid that in a controversy with respect to a contract between States, as to which the original jurisdiction of this Court is invoked, this Court has the authority and duty to determine for itself all questions that pertain to the obligations of the contract alleged. The fact that the solution of these questions may involve the determination of the effect of the local legislation of either State, as well as of acts of Congress, which are said to authorize the contract, in no way affects the duty of this Court to act as the final, constitutional arbiter in deciding the questions properly presented. It has frequently been held that, when a question is suitably raised whether the law of a State has impaired the obligation of a contract, in violation of the constitutional provision, this Court must determine for itself whether a contract exists, what are its obligations, and whether they have been impaired by the legislation of the State. While this Court always examines with appropriate respect the decisions of state courts bearing upon such questions, such decisions do not detract from the responsibility of this Court in reaching its own conclusions as to the contract, its obligations and impairment, for otherwise the constitutional guaranty could not properly be enforced. Where the States themselves are before this Court for the determination of a controversy between them, neither can determine their rights *inter sese*, and this Court must pass upon every question essential to such a determination, although local legislation and questions of state authorization may be involved. A decision in the present instance by the state court would not determine the controversy here.

It is none the less true that this Court might await such a decision, in order that it might have the advantage of the views of the state court, if sufficient grounds appeared for delaying final action.* The question is as to the existence of such grounds in this case. The gravity of the situation cannot be ignored. The injury to the Commonwealth of Kentucky by the delay in the performance of the contract by the State of Indiana is definitely alleged and expressly admitted. That injury is concededly irreparable, without adequate

---

* [Ed.] For an instance where the Court, having acknowledged jurisdiction, continued an original case pending the resolution of state-law questions in state court litigation, see Arkansas v. Texas, 346 U.S. 368 (1953), dismissed as moot, 351 U.S. 977 (1956).

remedy at law.   * * *   In these circumstances there would appear to be no adequate ground for withholding the determination of this suit because of objections raised by individuals, merely in their capacity as citizens, voters, and taxpayers of Indiana, objections which the State itself declines to sponsor.

It would be a serious matter, where a State has entered into a contract with another State, the validity of the contract not being questioned by either State, if individual citizens could delay the prompt performance which was admittedly important, not only to the complainant State but to the people of both States, merely by bringing a suit.   It is not difficult to institute suits, and contracts between States, of increasing importance as interstate interests grow in complexity, would be at the mercy of individuals, if the action of the latter, without more, unsupported by any proper averments on the part of the State itself questioning its obligations, should lead this Court to stay its hand in giving the relief to which the complainant State would otherwise be entitled, and of which it stood seriously in need.

On such a record as we have in this case, it is unnecessary for the Court to search the legislation underlying the contract in order to discover grounds of defense which the defendant State does not attempt to assert.   The State of Indiana concludes its answer by saying that, if a decree goes against it as prayed for, the State will at once proceed with the performance of the contract and fully complete that performance according to its terms.

We conclude that the controversy between the States is within the original jurisdiction of this Court; that the defendant State has shown no adequate defense to this suit; that nothing appears which would justify delay in rendering a decree; and that the Commonwealth of Kentucky is entitled to the relief sought against the State of Indiana.

      * * *

Dismissed as to individual defendants.

Decree for complainant against the defendant State.

NOTE ON LITIGATION BETWEEN STATES

(1) *The State as Representative*.   Private interests may be bound not only, as in Kentucky v. Indiana, when a state serves as the representative of its citizens in litigation, see also Nebraska v. Wyoming, 115 S.Ct. 1933, 1944–45 (1995); Wyoming v. Colorado, 286 U.S. 494, 508–09 (1932) & cases cited, but also when disputes between states are settled by the alternative method of interstate compact, see, *e.g.*, Hinderlider v. La Plata River & Cherry Creek Ditch Co., 304 U.S. 92 (1938)(compact regulating apportionment of water in an interstate river governs right of private corporation to draw water from that river); see generally Frankfurter & Landis, *The Compact Clause of the Constitution—A Study in Interstate Adjustments*, 34 Yale L.J. 685 (1925).   Compare New Jersey v. New York, 345 U.S. 369 (1953), denying Philadelphia's motion to intervene in a dispute regarding the Delaware River on the ground that Pennsylvania (a party) adequately represented all its citizens, whereas the City represented only a special group.

(2) *The Subject Matter of Litigation.* Actions between states have been the most numerous class of cases in the Supreme Court's original jurisdiction.[1] "Evidencing the seriousness of some of these disputes is the fact that in at least four instances—New Jersey v. New York in the 1820's; Missouri v. Iowa in the 1840's; Louisiana v. Mississippi in the 1900's; and Oklahoma v. Texas in very recent years, armed conflicts between the militia or citizens of the contending States had been a prelude to the institution of the suits in the Court. And in several of the other suits, a state of facts was presented which, if arising between independent nations, might well have been a cause for war." Charles Warren, The Supreme Court and Sovereign States 38 (1924). See also Herbert A. Smith, The American Supreme Court as an International Tribunal (1920).

Boundary disputes were the first cases between states in which the Court exercised jurisdiction, and they have remained the most productive source of such litigation. See Rhode Island v. Massachusetts, 37 U.S. (12 Pet.) 657 (1838)(definitively establishing their justiciability). See also, *e.g.*, Georgia v. South Carolina, 497 U.S. 376 (1990); Nebraska v. Iowa, 406 U.S. 117 (1972).

Next in importance, ever since Kansas v. Colorado, 185 U.S. 125 (1902), have been conflicting claims to water from interstate streams, where the Court's task of apportioning water rights is enormously complex. See, *e.g.*, Arizona v. California, 373 U.S. 546 (1963). *Cf.* Idaho v. Oregon, 444 U.S. 380 (1980)(equitable apportionment between states of migrating fish).

Other interstate disputes have involved conflicting claims to escheat, see, *e.g.*, Texas v. New Jersey, 379 U.S. 674 (1965), suits to enforce interstate compacts, see, *e.g.*, Texas v. New Mexico, 462 U.S. 554 (1983), suits on contracts and debts (as in Kentucky v. Indiana), suits to prevent injuries to the citizens of the state, see, *e.g.*, Maryland v. Louisiana, 451 U.S. 725 (1981); Missouri v. Illinois, 180 U.S. 208 (1901), and challenges to state regulation, see, *e.g.*, Wyoming v. Oklahoma, 502 U.S. 437 (1992).[2]

---

1. See generally McKusick, p. 299, *supra*; Scott, Judicial Settlement of Controversies Between States of the American Union (1919); Barnes, *Suits Between States in the Supreme Court,* 7 Vand.L.Rev. 494 (1954).

2. The Court has experienced difficulty in determining whether to exercise original jurisdiction to resolve conflicting claims by two or more states that a decedent was a domiciliary at the time of death and therefore subject to its estate tax. In Texas v. Florida, 306 U.S. 398 (1939), the Court took jurisdiction of such an action, characterizing it as a "bill in the nature of interpleader" (p. 406), and noting the risk that the taxes levied by the four competing states would exceed the value of the peripatetic millionaire's estate.

But in California v. Texas, 437 U.S. 601 (1978), the Court without opinion denied California leave to file suit to determine which state had power to tax the estate of Howard Hughes. Three Justices concurred on the ground that Texas v. Florida, although indistinguishable, was "wrongly decided", and that no "case or controversy" exists until

different states have established enforceable claims to estate taxes that in the aggregate clearly exceed the decedent's assets. The concurring Justices also suggested that federal interpleader might be available (notwithstanding the Eleventh Amendment) to estates threatened with multiple taxation.

Four years later the Court reversed field again, granting California leave to file suit against Texas to secure a determination of Hughes' domicile at death. California v. Texas, 457 U.S. 164 (1982)(5–4). The Court concluded that California's allegation that the various state and federal tax claims would exceed the estate's value established an actual controversy between the states, and found the case indistinguishable from Texas v. Florida. The Court also noted that in view of its decision that very day, in Cory v. White, 457 U.S. 85 (1982), that the Eleventh Amendment barred the administrator of Hughes' estate from bringing an interpleader action in federal district court against the two states, exercise of the original jurisdiction was "appropriate" since there existed no

(3) *The Enforcement of Judgments.* There are evident political sensitivities and practical difficulties involved in enforcing a judgment against a state. See, *e.g.*, Virginia v. West Virginia, 222 U.S. 17, 19–20 (1911)("[A] State cannot be expected to move with the celerity of a private business man; it is enough if it proceeds, in the language of the English chancery, with all deliberate speed.")

The Supreme Court has been hesitant when asked to issue a writ of execution, a citation of contempt, or a writ of mandamus against state officials, preferring to wait, sometimes for considerable periods, to obtain voluntary compliance. For example, in Wyoming v. Colorado, 309 U.S. 572 (1940), Wyoming returned to the Court three times seeking to enforce a 1922 decree against Colorado that involved water rights. Wyoming's first two efforts resulted in clarification and broadening of the decree but no finding of violation by Colorado. The third time, in 1940, the Court found Colorado in violation but refused to adjudge it in contempt, stating: "In the light of all the circumstances [which included the consent of a Wyoming official to the illegal diversion of water], we think it sufficiently appears that there was a period of uncertainty and room for misunderstanding which may be considered in extenuation. In the future there will be no ground for any possible misapprehension * * *" (p. 582).

Concerns about enforcement were visible in the Court's decision in Vermont v. New York, 417 U.S. 270 (1974). There, Vermont sued New York and a paper company, alleging unlawful pollution of Vermont waters. The Special Master worked out a settlement and proposed consent decree. The decree included no findings of fact or conclusions of law, but contained elaborate provisions relating to steps to be taken with regard to the pollution problem, and provided for a Special Master to "police the execution of the settlement set forth in the Decree" and to "pass on to this Court his proposed resolution of contested issues that the future might bring forth" (p. 277). The Court declined to approve the proposed decree, noting that "continuing Court supervision over decrees of equitable apportionment of waters was undesirable" (p. 275) and that the Master's approach would have the Court acting in an "arbitral" manner, rather than in its accustomed role of "adjudicati[ng] * * * controversies between States according to principles of law, some drawn from the international field, some expressing a 'common law' formulated over the decades by this Court. * * * The proposals submitted by the * * * Master to this Court might be proposals having no relation to law. * * * Article III speaks of the 'judicial power' of this Court, which embraces application of principles of law or equity to facts, distilled by hearings or by stipulations. Nothing in the Proposed Decree nor in the mandate to be given the * * * Master speaks in terms of 'judicial power' "(p. 277).[3]

---

realistic alternative forum. The four dissenters would have adhered to the Court's view in 1978 that no ripe controversy existed until there were multiple judgments that the estate could not satisfy.

Cf. Massachusetts v. Missouri, p. 329, *infra.*

3. Compare New Hampshire v. Maine, 426 U.S. 363 (1976), accepting a proposed consent decree finally settling a boundary dispute in accordance with findings made on the basis of the evidence.

NOTE ON THE LAW APPLIED IN ACTIONS BETWEEN STATES

(1) *The Formulation of Federal Common Law.* The Court has fashioned a body of federal common law to apply in interstate disputes, as a necessary implication of the constitutional grant of jurisdiction and the obvious difficulty with application of the law of either disputant. See generally Hill, *The Law–Making Power of the Federal Courts: Constitutional Preemption*, 67 Colum.L.Rev. 1024, 1031–32 (1967); p. 790, *infra.* Thus, in Connecticut v. Massachusetts, 282 U.S. 660 (1931), a suit to enjoin Massachusetts from diverting waters from the watershed of the Connecticut River, Connecticut asked the Court to follow the common law of both states, which, it argued, gave riparian owners a vested right in the use of the flowing waters unimpaired by such a diversion. The Court replied (pp. 670–71):

"For the decision of suits between States, federal, state and international law are considered and applied by this Court as the exigencies of the particular case may require. The determination of the relative rights of contending States in respect of the use of streams flowing through them does not depend upon the same considerations and is not governed by the same rules of law that are applied in such States for the solution of similar questions of private right. Kansas v. Colorado, 185 U.S. 125, 146. And, while the municipal law relating to like questions between individuals is to be taken into account, it is not to be deemed to have controlling weight. As was shown in Kansas v. Colorado, 206 U.S. 46, 100, such disputes are to be settled on the basis of equality of right. But this is not to say that there must be an equal division of the waters of an interstate stream among the States through which it flows. It means that the principles of right and equity shall be applied having regard to the 'equal level or plane on which all the States stand, in point of power and right, under our constitutional system' and that, upon a consideration of the pertinent laws of the contending States and all other relevant facts, this Court will determine what is an equitable apportionment of the use of such waters. Wyoming v. Colorado, 259 U.S. 419, 465, 470."

See also Hinderlider v. La Plata River & Cherry Creek Ditch Co., 304 U.S. 92, 110 (1938), where, in reversing a decision that an interstate compact concerning water rights was invalid because it affected appropriation rights guaranteed by Colorado's constitution, Justice Brandeis said for the Court: "whether the water of an interstate stream must be apportioned between the two States is a question of 'federal common law' upon which neither the statutes nor the decisions of either State can be conclusive." This case was decided on the same day as Erie R. Co. v. Tompkins, p. 687, *infra.* For a recent example of the application of the federal common law of equitable apportionment of interstate waters, see Colorado v. New Mexico, 459 U.S. 176 (1982), and 467 U.S. 310 (1984).

(2) *The Possible Relevance of State Law.* Federal common law governs the question of the obligations created by contracts between states. And because Congress must approve interstate compacts, their interpretation in effect requires interpretation of an Act of Congress. Does that leave any role for state law in disputes arising under such compacts? See generally Engdahl, *Construction of Interstate Compacts: A Questionable Federal Question*, 51 Va.L.Rev. 987 (1965).

(a) In Kentucky v. Indiana, Chief Justice Hughes said that "this court has the authority and duty to determine for itself *all* questions that pertain to the obligations of the contract alleged" (emphasis added). He added that an injunction against the individual defendants "is not needed, as a decree in this suit would bind the state of Indiana, and, on being shown, would bar any inconsistent proceedings in the courts of that state."

Could the individual defendants in fact have been precluded in state court from questioning the state's authority, on the basis of a federal proceeding in which they were held not to have standing to raise the issue—and in which the issue (in view of the state's concession) was never litigated? Does the answer depend on whose law governs the question of the Indiana officials' authority to enter into the contract? If federal law were held to govern, would Indiana lose control of its governmental processes? If state law were held to govern, could the Supreme Court's decision of a state law issue have bound the state courts in the pending state court action?

On the other hand, if the Supreme Court's decision left the Indiana courts free in the pending suit to enjoin performance of the contract as unauthorized under state law, would Indiana be able to evade its federal obligations under the Compact Clause? *Cf.* Indiana ex rel. Anderson v. Brand and the *Note on Federal Protection of State–Created Rights,* Chap. V, Sec. 2(A), pp. 551–65, *infra.*

(b) Related questions were raised in West Virginia ex rel. Dyer v. Sims, 341 U.S. 22 (1951), where the Court reviewed a state court action involving the Ohio River Valley Sanitation Commission, a body formed by interstate compact. West Virginia members of the commission sued the West Virginia state auditor to compel him to take necessary action to pay West Virginia's contribution to the commission. The West Virginia court ruled that the state statute approving West Virginia's adherence to the compact was invalid under the state constitution because the compact purported (1) to delegate West Virginia's police power to other states and to the federal government, and (2) to bind future legislatures to make appropriations for the continued activities of the commission. The Supreme Court unanimously reversed, reaffirming its role in determining the nature and scope of obligations between states, whether they arise under compacts or under federal common law rules governing interstate disputes (as in Hinderlider, Paragraph (1), *supra*). While the Court will defer to the state courts' elaboration of state law, particularly as to "recondite or unique features of local law", the decisions in Kentucky v. Indiana and the Hinderlider case "make clear * * * that we are free to examine determinations of law by State courts in the limited field where a compact brings in issue the rights of other States and the United States" (p. 28). The Court concluded that the compact did not violate the West Virginia constitution.

Justice Reed, concurring, disputed the Court's power to override a state court's interpretation of its own constitution except where "the interpretation is a palpable evasion to avoid a federal rule." He added: "Under the Compact Clause, however, the federal questions are the execution, validity and meaning of federally approved state compacts. The interpretation of the meaning of the compact controls over a state's application of its own law through the Supremacy Clause and not by any implied federal power to construe state law" (p. 33). Justice Jackson concurred on the narrow ground that West Virginia was estopped to "raise an issue of *ultra vires,* decide it, and release herself from an interstate obligation", in the absence of "clear notice or fair warning to Congress or other States of any defect in her authority to enter into this Compact" (p. 35).

(c) The relevance of state law was also at issue in Petty v. Tennessee–Missouri Bridge Comm'n, 359 U.S. 275 (1959), where the Court held that federal law governs the question whether two states that had set up a bridge commission by an interstate compact approved by Congress thereby waived sovereign immunity in suits against the commission. (The Court went on to find a waiver in the case.) Justice Frankfurter, in dissent on the choice of law issue, distinguished Dyer v. Sims (which he wrote) on the ground that, although interpretation of an interstate compact is a federal question, that question "does not require a federal answer by way of a blanket, nationwide substantive doctrine where essentially local interests are at stake" (p. 285). (On this point, see generally pp. 767–68, *infra.*) He argued that the language of the compact, which Congress had not modified, should be given the legal significance that the two states placed upon it, just as the interpretation of ordinary contracts looks to the meaning that the parties attribute to the contract's language.

What would Justice Frankfurter have said if Missouri and Tennessee law differed on the question whether the bridge commission could be sued?

(3) *Choice of Law in Interstate Disputes About Escheat.* In Texas v. New Jersey, 379 U.S. 674 (1965), the question was which state may by escheat take abandoned intangible personal property (unclaimed small debts owed by Sun Oil Company to many unknown creditors). The Court held, as a matter of federal law, that jurisdiction to escheat lies in the "State of the creditor's last known address as shown by the debtor's books and records" (pp. 680–81), rejecting the claims of the state of the debtor's incorporation, the state housing the debtor's principal offices, and the state with the most significant "contacts" with the debt. For refinements of this rule, see Delaware v. New York, 507 U.S. 490 (1993); Pennsylvania v. New York, 407 U.S. 206 (1972)(whose rule of decision was thereafter modified by Congress, see 12 U.S.C. §§ 2501–03).

NOTE ON A STATE'S STANDING TO SUE AND RELATED PROBLEMS OF JUSTICIABILITY: HEREIN OF PARENS PATRIAE STANDING

(1) *Introduction.* States can bring suit in a number of different capacities— and sometimes in more than one capacity in a single litigation.

(a) In some cases, like Kentucky v. Indiana, states sue in their own proprietary capacity, much like private parties. Rules like those governing private parties—for example, the real party in interest rule—may apply in such cases, which are discussed in Paragraph (2).

(b) In boundary disputes, discussed in Paragraph (3), *supra,* the state's interest—preserving its sovereignty over property owned by others—is more intangible and less analogous to private interests.

(c) The most difficult standing cases, however, are those in which a state seeks to sue as *parens patriae.* Here, the state asserts interests that might be described as those of the citizenry in general, or, alternatively, as quasi-sovereign interests of a state—as, for example, when a state sues to prevent pollution to water or air that is enjoyed by large numbers of state citizens. The bulk of this Note—Paragraphs (4–8)—discusses the *parens patriae* decisions.

(2) *State as Real Party in Interest.* In New Hampshire v. Louisiana, 108 U.S. 76 (1883), the plaintiff states sued on defaulted bonds, as assignees for collection only, on behalf of certain of their citizens. The Court dismissed the bills as barred by the Eleventh Amendment, rejecting the argument that the

original jurisdiction should be available as a substitute for the traditional methods (war or diplomacy) by which sovereigns enforce their citizens' claims.

Since then it has become settled that a state, whatever the character of the defendant, has no standing to sue when it is merely sponsoring the claims of a small number of individual citizens. See, *e.g.,* Oklahoma v. Atchison, T. & S.F.Ry. Co., 220 U.S. 277 (1911)(state may not maintain bill to enjoin unlawful railroad rates where injury is to certain shippers); North Dakota v. Minnesota, 263 U.S. 365 (1923)(denying claim for damages made by state on behalf of individual farmers injured by flooding caused by neighboring state). *Cf.* New Jersey v. New York, p. 311, *supra.* However, as the discussion in Paragraphs (4–8), *infra,* reveals, this principle is somewhat in tension with later decisions that do permit states to sue, as parens patriae, to protect interests that are widely shared by citizens within the state.

South Dakota learned a lesson from the experience of New Hampshire and New York. She took absolute title (by gift from an individual) to defaulted North Carolina bonds and got judgment on them. South Dakota v. North Carolina, 192 U.S. 286 (1904).

(3) *States as Sovereign: Boundary and Water Cases.* When states sue neighboring states about water rights or boundaries questions, don't they seek to assert not an interest like that of a private citizen in property, but rather a distinct interest in sovereignty? (After all, the disputed property may be owned not by the state but by a private party.) That was the view of Chief Justice Taney, whose dissent in Rhode Island v. Massachusetts, 37 U.S. (12 Pet.) 657, 752 (1838) argued that such cases were therefore not justiciable. Can one accept his characterization without accepting his conclusion? Compare Justice Bradley's view of the boundary cases in Hans v. Louisiana, 134 U.S. 1, 15 (1890), as examples of suits made justiciable by the Constitution that were not so at common law.

(4) *States as Parens Patriae.* The recognition in boundary and water cases that states could sue to protect interests in sovereignty raises the question of the extent to which the state as *parens patriae* should be able to litigate in defense of quasi-sovereign interests, *i.e.,* public or governmental interests that concern the state as a whole. The rest of this Note, and the following *Note on the Standing of a State as Parens Patriae to Sue the Federal Government,* explore that issue. See generally Note, 11 Stan.L.Rev. 665, 671–80 (1959); Note, 125 U.Pa.L.Rev. 1069 (1977). Consider whether standards of justiciability should be more liberal in actions between states (where the original jurisdiction substitutes for war or diplomacy) than in actions by a state against individuals.

(5) *The Early Cases.*

(a) The Court was unreceptive to *parens patriae* standing in its first decision, Louisiana v. Texas, 176 U.S. 1 (1900). The case arose when a Texas official, enforcing drastic state quarantine regulations, embargoed all commerce between the state and New Orleans, where a case of yellow fever had been found. Louisiana sought to enjoin Texas and its officials from taking such action, alleging that the concern about yellow fever was a mere pretext for an effort to divert commerce from New Orleans to the port of Galveston, Texas. The Court dismissed the bill.

Later cases have explained the decision as based on (1) the absence of proof that the official's action was the act of the state, and (2) insufficient allegations of inescapable damage to justify intervention by a court of equity in a controversy between states. See, *e.g.*, Alabama v. Arizona, 291 U.S. 286, 291–92 (1934). But Chief Justice Fuller also placed the decision on broader grounds (176 U.S. at 19, 22):

"Inasmuch as the vindication of the freedom of interstate commerce is not committed to the State of Louisiana, and that State is not engaged in such commerce, the cause of action must be regarded not as involving any infringement of the powers of the State of Louisiana, or any special injury to her property, but as asserting that the State is entitled to seek relief in this way because the matters complained of affect her citizens at large. * * *

"But in order that a controversy between States, justiciable in this court, can be held to exist, something more must be put forward than that the citizens of one State are injured by the maladministration of the laws of another."

(b) The very next year, the Court broke new ground in Missouri v. Illinois, 180 U.S. 208 (1901), sustaining against demurrer a bill to enjoin the dumping of Chicago's sewage into a canal that drained into the Mississippi River, thereby poisoning the water supply in Missouri and injuring its land. The Court said (p. 241): "[A]n adequate remedy can only be found in this court at the suit of the State of Missouri. It is true that no question of boundary is involved, nor of direct property rights belonging to the complainant State. But it must surely be conceded that, if the health and comfort of the inhabitants of a State are threatened, the State is the proper party to represent and defend them. If Missouri were an independent and sovereign State all must admit that she could seek a remedy by negotiation, and, that failing, by force. Diplomatic powers and the right to make war having been surrendered to the general government, it was to be expected that upon the latter would be devolved the duty of providing a remedy and that remedy, we think, is found in the constitutional provisions we are considering."[1]

(c) The approach of Missouri v. Illinois was extended to a suit against a private party in Georgia v. Tennessee Copper Co., 206 U.S. 230 (1907), where the state sought to enjoin the company from discharging, at its works in Tennessee, noxious gas that passed over Georgia's territory. The state claimed an injury to both its own lands and the lands of its citizens generally. The Court referred to the proprietary claims as a "makeweight", but upheld the bill primarily on the ground that under the Constitution the states "did not renounce the possibility of making reasonable demands on the ground of their still remaining *quasi*-sovereign interests; and the alternative to force is a suit in this court" (p. 237). Justice Harlan's concurring opinion argued (p. 240) that the Court was not authorized to apply on behalf of a state "any principle or rule of equity that would not be applied, under the same facts, in suits wholly between private parties", but found that Georgia had met this test.[2]

---

1. For similar decisions, see New York v. New Jersey, 256 U.S. 296 (1921); North Dakota v. Minnesota, 263 U.S. 365 (1923); Wisconsin v. Illinois, 278 U.S. 367 (1929).

2. The Court relied on the Tennessee Copper decision in permitting Wyoming to file a cross-claim against the United States in Nebraska v. Wyoming, 115 S.Ct. 1933 (1995). The Court in 1945 had entered a decree, apportioning water among several states,

that was predicated on compliance by the United States (which had intervened in the action) with certain statutory and contractual obligations regarding its handling of storage water. When Wyoming later moved to enjoin the United States from violating those obligations, the Court rejected the United States' argument that the state was merely seeking to benefit individuals who were parties to storage contracts, ruling instead that Wyo-

(d) Four years later a unanimous Court in Oklahoma v. Atchison, T. & S.F. Ry. Co., 220 U.S. 277 (1911), held that the state could not maintain a bill seeking to enjoin railroad rates alleged to be "a hindrance to the growth of the State, as well as an injury to the property rights of its inhabitants" (p. 284). Both the rates' illegality and (in view of the state's power to regulate them) the need for equitable relief were in doubt.   But Justice Harlan, relying primarily on Louisiana v. Texas, Paragraph (5)(a), *supra*, placed the Court's decision on the broader ground that the alleged wrongs were to "be reached, without the intervention of the State, by suits instituted by the persons directly or immediately injured", and that the original jurisdiction did not reach "every cause in which the State * * * seeks not to protect its own property, but only to vindicate the wrongs of some of its people or to enforce its own laws or public policy against wrongdoers, generally" (p. 289).

Do these cases form a consistent pattern?   See Woolhandler & Collins, *State Standing*, 81 Va.L.Rev. 387, 450–55 (1995)(describing these cases as recognizing standing that derives from a state's police power to regulate for the public good).

(6) *The Extension of Parens Patriae Standing.*

(a) In Pennsylvania v. West Virginia and Ohio v. West Virginia, 262 U.S. 553 (1923), a divided Court enjoined enforcement of a West Virginia statute designed to limit the export of natural gas to the excess of output over the state's domestic needs.   The Court said (pp. 591–92):

"The attitude of the complainant States is not that of mere volunteers attempting to vindicate the freedom of interstate commerce or to redress purely private grievances.   Each sues to protect a two-fold interest—one as the proprietor of various public institutions and schools whose supply of gas will be largely curtailed or cut off by the threatened interference with the interstate current, and the other as the representative of the consuming public whose supply will be similarly affected.   * * *

"The private consumers in each State not only include most of the inhabitants of many urban communities but constitute a substantial portion of the State's population.   Their health, comfort and welfare are seriously jeopardized by the threatened withdrawal of the gas from the interstate stream.   This is a matter of grave public concern in which the State, as the representative of the public, has an interest apart from that of the individuals affected.   It is not merely a remote or ethical interest but one which is immediate and recognized by law."

The Court added (p. 592) that: "In principle these views have full support in prior decisions * * *."   Did they?   Or did this decision repudiate the statement in Louisiana v. Texas, Paragraph (5)(a), *supra*, that "the vindication of the freedom of interstate commerce is not committed to the [complaining state]?"   If so, was the change in course desirable?

(b) An expansive view of standing underlay the Court's 5–4 decision to permit Georgia to file a bill of complaint against twenty railroads to enjoin an alleged conspiracy to fix rates.   Georgia v. Pennsylvania R.R., 324 U.S. 439 (1945).   Georgia sued in two relevant capacities: (i) "as a quasi-sovereign or as

ming was properly suing under the 1945 de-   ests (p. 1944).
cree to vindicate its "quasi-sovereign" inter-

agent and protector of her people", and (ii) "as a proprietor to redress wrongs suffered by the State as the owner of a railroad and * * * of various institutions of the State" (p. 443). Standing as to the former capacity was supported by allegations that the high rates served "to frustrate and counteract the measures taken by the State to promote * * * the general progress and welfare of its people" and "to hold the Georgia economy in a state of arrested development" (p. 444).

In upholding *parens patriae* standing, the Court cited, among other cases, Georgia v. Tennessee Copper Co., Missouri v. Illinois, and Pennsylvania v. West Virginia, as holding that "Georgia may maintain this suit as *parens patriae* acting on behalf of her citizens though here, as in Georgia v. Tennessee Copper Co., * * * we treat the injury to the State as proprietor merely as a 'makeweight.' * * *

"Oklahoma v. Atchison, T. & S.F.R. Co., *supra*, is not opposed to this view. * * * This is not a suit in which a State is a mere nominal plaintiff, individual shippers being the real complainants. This is a suit in which Georgia asserts claims arising out of federal laws and the gravamen of which runs far beyond the claim of damage to individual shippers" (pp. 450–52).[3]

(7) *Modern Decisions.*

(a) The pendulum swung in a more restrictive direction in Pennsylvania v. New Jersey, 426 U.S. 660 (1976), which involved two different lawsuits by neighboring states premised on the unconstitutionality, under the Privileges and Immunities Clause, of commuter income taxes. The Court's earlier decision in Austin v. New Hampshire, 420 U.S. 656 (1975), had invalidated New Hampshire's 4% tax on the New Hampshire-derived income of nonresidents. In one case, Maine alleged that, because of the credit it afforded its residents for income taxes paid to other states, the invalid New Hampshire law had diverted some $3.5 million of taxes from Maine to New Hampshire. In the second case, Pennsylvania (which provided a similar tax credit) alleged that New Jersey's commuter income tax was invalid under Austin. Both states sought an accounting for "diverted" taxes.

The Court denied leave to file in both cases. It held, first, that "[t]he injuries to the plaintiffs' fiscs" were not caused by the defendant states, but were "self-inflicted, resulting from decisions by their respective state legislatures" to extend tax credits. Second, it held that no state has standing in its own right to complain of violations of the Privileges and Immunities Clause or the Equal Protection Clause: "both Clauses protect people, not States." Finally, the Court held that Pennsylvania could not sue *parens patriae*, as the action was "nothing more than a collectivity of private suits against New Jersey for taxes withheld from private parties" (pp. 664–66).

(b) In Maryland v. Louisiana, 451 U.S. 725 (1981), however, the Court permitted eight states to challenge the constitutionality of a Louisiana tax on the "first use" of previously untaxed natural gas coming into the state—a tax that fell heavily on gas from offshore wells passing through Louisiana for eventual sale to consumers in other states. Although imposed on private pipeline companies, the tax was passed through to their customers, among whom were the plaintiff states. Finding the suit "functionally indistinguish-

---

3. The Court also distinguished Massachusetts v. Mellon and Florida v. Mellon, pp. 322–23, *infra*, which refused to permit a state to sue to protect her citizens from the operation of federal statutes; unlike those cases, here the state sought not to invalidate federal laws but to asserts rights based on them.

able from Pennsylvania v. West Virginia", Paragraph (6)(a), *supra*, the Court upheld standing based on the states' direct proprietary interests, and found standing "also supported" by the states' interest in addressing the "substantial economic injury" visited by the tax to "a great many citizens in each of the plaintiff states" (pp. 738–39).

(c) The Court further expanded standing in Wyoming v. Oklahoma, 502 U.S. 437 (1992)(6–3). Wyoming challenged (as a violation of the dormant Commerce Clause) an Oklahoma statute requiring certain private utility plants in the state to burn a mixture of coal containing at least 10% Oklahoma-mined coal. Wyoming's claim of standing was based on the law's adverse effect on Wyoming's revenues from a severance tax on coal mined in Wyoming. In upholding standing, the Court distinguished a number of circuit court decisions holding states without standing to challenge federal actions that "injured the State's economy and thereby caused a decline in *general* tax revenues"; here, the Oklahoma statute deprived Wyoming of "*specific* tax revenues" (p. 797; emphases added). And the Court rejected Oklahoma's contention (endorsed by Justice Scalia in dissent) that because Wyoming was not engaged in commerce in coal that was affected by the Oklahoma law, Wyoming had not suffered the *kind* of injury cognizable under the Commerce Clause.

Cf. also the very broad language in Alfred L. Snapp & Son, Inc. v. Puerto Rico ex rel. Barez, note 5, *infra*.

(8) *Some Questions About The Parens Patriae Decisions.* The question of a state's standing has not generally been answered by reference to the doctrines governing the standing of private parties in the district courts. See Woolhandler & Collins, Paragraph (5)(d), *supra*, at 464–78 (suggesting, *inter alia*, that the decisions discussed in Paragraphs (6)-(7), *supra*, that upheld standing embraced a "public law" model of standing, see pp. 136–39, *supra*, long before it became available in actions by private individuals). Should a state have standing to assert "generalized grievances", compare p. 143, *supra*, or the rights of others, compare p. 152, *supra,* despite the Court's refusal to permit individuals to do so? See Maryland v. Louisiana, Paragraph (7)(b), *supra*, at 739, and Note, 125 U.Pa.L.Rev. 1069, 1099 (1977)(both suggesting the desirability of empowering states to sue in the Supreme Court's original jurisdiction when many citizens have suffered small claims for which individual redress is impractical). Compare the cases discussed in Chap. VII, Sec. 2(A), pp. 817–18, *infra*, dealing with efforts by the federal government to sue to protect private rights of its citizens.

Is the state a better or worse representative of others than, for example, a class representative under Fed.R.Civ.Proc. 23? Than an organizational plaintiff suing on behalf of its members? Compare p. 186, *supra*. Should the Court not merely presume that a state is a good representative but rather make a particularized inquiry whether that is so in each case—especially since a judgment in a *parens patriae* action ordinarily will preclude separate claims by the citizens whose interests were represented?[4] Does the possibility of preclusion bear on the appropriateness of recognizing standing in the first instance?

If *parens patriae* standing were rejected, how should the Court determine whether to accept a state's claim that it has standing to protect its own

---

4. See, *e.g*, Washington v. Washington State Commercial Passenger Fishing Vessel Ass'n, 443 U.S. 658, 692–93 n. 32 (1979) and City of Tacoma v. Taxpayers of Tacoma, 357 U.S. 320, 340–41 (1958), both involving former lower court judgments in suits by states as *parens patriae*; and Badgley v. City of New York, 606 F.2d 358, 364–66 (2d Cir.

interests? Should a state be limited to seeking redress for harm to interests that are among those sought to be protected by the statutory or constitutional provision under which it sues—as Justice Scalia suggested in his dissent in Wyoming v. Oklahoma, Paragraph (7)(c), *supra*. See also Woolhandler & Collins, *supra*, at 502–13. Does the fact that suits by states will often fall within the original jurisdiction—at once burdening the Court while depriving it of the chance to have issues first percolate in the lower courts—argue for a more limited conception of state standing? Should the recognition of state standing be broader if the state chooses, where jurisdiction is concurrent, to sue in district court?[5]

NOTE ON THE STANDING OF A STATE AS PARENS PATRIAE TO SUE THE FEDERAL GOVERNMENT

(1) *Massachusetts v. Mellon*. In Massachusetts v. Mellon, 262 U.S. 447 (1923), the state brought suit in the Supreme Court against the Secretary of the Treasury, arguing that a federal grant program was unconstitutional because it fell outside the scope of Congress' Article I powers and thus violated the Tenth Amendment. A unanimous Court held that Massachusetts lacked standing (pp. 484–86):

"* * * [I]n so far as the case depends upon the assertion of a right on the part of the State to sue in its own behalf, we are without jurisdiction. In that aspect of the case we are called upon to adjudicate, not rights of person or property, not rights of dominion over physical domain, not quasi-sovereign rights actually invaded or threatened, but abstract questions of political power, of sovereignty, of government. * * *

1979), involving a prior judgment in an original action in the Supreme Court. The Badgely decision precluded private parties from raising claims not only for injunctive relief but also for damages. But *cf.* Satsky v. Paramount Communications, Inc., 7 F.3d 1464, 1470 (10th Cir.1993)(prior judgment in *parens patriae* action does not preclude citizens from suing for damages not recoverable in the earlier action).

Compare Hawaii v. Standard Oil Co., 405 U.S. 251 (1972), a *district* court action brought by the state for treble damages for injuries to the state's "economy and prosperity" caused by violations of Section 4 of the Clayton Act. On review, the Supreme Court ruled that Hawaii could sue in its "proprietary capacity", but that permitting it to obtain damages as *parens patriae* for injury to the state's "general economy" would open the door to duplicate recoveries. See Comment, 48 N.C.L.Rev. 963 (1970). The Court did not discuss the possibility of preclusion.

5. Compare Alfred L. Snapp & Son, Inc. v. Puerto Rico ex rel. Barez, 458 U.S. 592 (1982), upholding a *district* court action by Puerto Rico, as *parens patriae*, against certain apple growers in the eastern states who allegedly had violated federal statutes creating a preference for domestic over temporary foreign workers. The Court discussed its original jurisdiction precedents, but noted (p. 603 n. 12) that the special considerations limiting *parens patriae* suits in the original jurisdiction may not apply to suits in the district courts—a point emphasized by four concurring Justices.

The Court also stated (p. 607) that although the determination whether a state may sue as *parens patriae* to redress injury to its citizens' health and welfare must be made case by case, "[o]ne helpful indication * * * is whether the injury is one that the State, if it could, would likely attempt to address through its sovereign lawmaking powers." The concurrence suggested that the state, "no ordinary litigant", should be able to determine which injuries to its citizens warranted protection via suit as *parens patriae* (p. 612). Does either of these notions place any serious limit on *parens patriae* standing?

"We come next to consider whether the suit may be maintained by the State as the representative of its citizens. To this the answer is not doubtful. We need not go so far as to say that a State may never intervene by suit to protect its citizens against any form of enforcement of unconstitutional acts of Congress; but we are clear that the right to do so does not arise here. * * * While the State, under some circumstances, may sue [as *parens patriae*] for the protection of its citizens (Missouri v. Illinois, 180 U.S. 208, 241), it is no part of its duty or power to enforce their rights in respect of their relations with the Federal Government. In that field it is the United States, and not the State, which represents them as *parens patriae,* when such representation becomes appropriate; and to the former, and not to the latter, they must look for such protective measures as flow from that status."

See also Florida v. Mellon, 273 U.S. 12, 18 (1927).[1]

(2) *South Carolina v. Katzenbach.* Some forty years later, the Court relied on Massachusetts v. Mellon in denying state standing to sue *parens patriae* on two of the state's claims against the federal government, while going ahead to reach the merits of a third claim. South Carolina v. Katzenbach, 383 U.S. 301 (1966), was a suit to enjoin the Attorney General from enforcing the Voting Rights Act of 1965—"the heart of [which] is a complex scheme of stringent remedies aimed at areas where voting discrimination has been most flagrant" (p. 315). The Court held that the state could not, as *parens patriae*, invoke the Due Process and Bill of Attainder Clauses against the federal government. But without discussing the issue of standing, the Court did pass on the merits of the state's contention, based on the Fifteenth Amendment, that the statute invaded the reserved power of the states to determine voter qualifications and regulate elections and exceeded the powers of Congress. Was the handling of the standing questions internally consistent? Consistent with prior cases? Correct? See Bickel, *The Voting Rights Cases,* 1966 Sup.Ct.Rev. 79, 80–93.[2]

Ohio v. Wyandotte Chemicals Corp.

401 U.S. 493, 91 S.Ct. 1005, 28 L.Ed.2d 256 (1971).
Original.

■ MR. JUSTICE HARLAN delivered the opinion of the Court.

By motion for leave to file a bill of complaint, Ohio seeks to invoke this Court's original jurisdiction. Because of the importance and unusual character of the

1. In Jones ex rel. Louisiana v. Bowles, 322 U.S. 707 (1944), the governor brought an original action on behalf of the state against the Price Administrator (in the hope of escaping the exclusive jurisdiction provisions of the Emergency Price Control Act of 1942, see p. 380, *infra*). The governor sought to enjoin enforcement of a regulation limiting prices for strawberries, which were alleged to be an important state crop. The motion for leave to file the complaint was denied "for want of jurisdiction of this Court to entertain it under Article III, Section 2, of the Constitution."

2. Compare Massachusetts v. Laird, 400 U.S. 886 (1970)(an unexplained refusal to allow Massachusetts to file an original bill

of complaint against the Secretary of Defense to challenge the legality of the Vietnam War; Justice Douglas dissented, while Justices Harlan and Stewart, also dissenting, would have set oral argument on "questions of standing and justiciability" (p. 900)).

See also Notes, 61 Minn.L.Rev. 691 (1977) and 125 U.Pa.L.Rev. 1069 (1977), both commenting on Pennsylvania v. Kleppe, 533 F.2d 668 (D.C.Cir.1976)(Pennsylvania lacks standing to challenge the Small Business Administration's designation of state as a Class B disaster area for purpose of distribution of federal disaster relief after 1972 hurricane).

But *cf.* Nebraska v. Wyoming, p. 318, note 2, *supra*.

issues tendered we set the matter for oral argument, inviting the Solicitor General to participate and to file a brief on behalf of the United States, as *amicus curiae*. For reasons that follow we deny the motion for leave to file.

The action, for abatement of a nuisance, is brought on behalf of the State and its citizens, and names as defendants Wyandotte Chemicals Corp. (Wyandotte), Dow Chemical Co. (Dow America), and Dow Chemical Company of Canada, Ltd. (Dow Canada). Wyandotte is incorporated in Michigan and maintains its principal office and place of business there. Dow America is incorporated in Delaware, has its principal office and place of business in Michigan, and owns all the stock of Dow Canada. Dow Canada is incorporated, and does business, in Ontario. * * *

The complaint alleges that Dow Canada and Wyandotte have each dumped mercury into streams whose courses ultimately reach Lake Erie, thus contaminating and polluting that lake's waters, vegetation, fish, and wildlife, and that Dow America is jointly responsible for the acts of its foreign subsidiary. [The state sought a decree requiring the defendants to cease introducing mercury into Lake Erie and its tributaries, to remove existing mercury from Lake Erie or to pay the costs of its removal, and to pay damages for harm done to the lake, to its fish, wildlife, and vegetation, and to the inhabitants of Ohio.]

     * * *

While we consider that Ohio's complaint does state a cause of action that falls within the compass of our original jurisdiction, we have concluded that this Court should nevertheless decline to exercise that jurisdiction.

I

* * * Beyond doubt, the complaint on its face reveals the existence of a genuine "case or controversy" between one State and citizens of another, as well as a foreign subject. Diversity of citizenship is absolute. Nor is the nature of the cause of action asserted a bar to the exercise of our jurisdiction. While we have refused to entertain, for example, original actions designed to exact compliance with a State's penal laws, Wisconsin v. Pelican Ins. Co., 127 U.S. 265 (1888), or that seek to embroil this tribunal in "political questions," Mississippi v. Johnson, 4 Wall. 475 (1867); Georgia v. Stanton, 6 Wall. 50 (1868), this Court has often adjudicated controversies between States and between a State and citizens of another State seeking to abate a nuisance that exists in one State yet produces noxious consequences in another. See Missouri v. Illinois and Sanitary Dist. of Chicago, 180 U.S. 208 (1901)(complaint filed), 200 U.S. 496 (1906)(final judgment); Georgia v. Tennessee Copper Co., [p. 318, *supra*; other citations omitted.] * * *

Ordinarily, the foregoing would suffice to settle the issue presently under consideration: whether Ohio should be granted leave to file its complaint. For it is a time-honored maxim of the Anglo–American common-law tradition that a court possessed of jurisdiction generally must exercise it. Cohens v. Virginia, 6 Wheat. 264, 404 (1821). Nevertheless, although it may initially have been contemplated that this Court would always exercise its original jurisdiction when properly called upon to do so, it seems evident to us that changes in the American legal system and the development of American society have rendered untenable, as a practical matter, the view that this Court must stand willing to adjudicate all or most legal disputes that may arise between one State and a citizen or citizens of another, even though the dispute may be one over which this Court does have original jurisdiction.

As our social system has grown more complex, the States have increasingly become enmeshed in a multitude of disputes with persons living outside their borders. Consider, for example, the frequency with which States and nonresidents clash over the application of state laws concerning taxes, motor vehicles, decedents' estates, business torts, government contracts, and so forth. It would, indeed, be anomalous were this Court to be held out as a potential principal forum for settling such controversies. The simultaneous development of "long-arm jurisdiction" means, in most instances, that no necessity impels us to perform such a role. And the evolution of this Court's responsibilities in the American legal system has brought matters to a point where much would be sacrificed, and little gained, by our exercising original jurisdiction over issues bottomed on local law. This Court's paramount responsibilities to the national system lie almost without exception in the domain of federal law. As the impact on the social structure of federal common, statutory, and constitutional law has expanded, our attention has necessarily been drawn more and more to such matters. We have no claim to special competence in dealing with the numerous conflicts between States and nonresident individuals that raise no serious issues of federal law.

This Court is, moreover, structured to perform as an appellate tribunal, ill-equipped for the task of factfinding and so forced, in original cases, awkwardly to play the role of factfinder without actually presiding over the introduction of evidence. Nor is the problem merely our lack of qualifications for many of these tasks potentially within the purview of our original jurisdiction; it is compounded by the fact that for every case in which we might be called upon to determine the facts and apply unfamiliar legal norms we would unavoidably be reducing the attention we could give to those matters of federal law and national import as to which we are the primary overseers.

Thus, we think it apparent that we must recognize "the need [for] the exercise of a sound discretion in order to protect this Court from an abuse of the opportunity to resort to its original jurisdiction in the enforcement by States of claims against citizens of other States." Massachusetts v. Missouri, 308 U.S. 1, 19 (1939), opinion of Chief Justice Hughes.[3] We believe, however, that the focus of concern embodied in the above-quoted statement of Chief Justice Hughes should be somewhat refined. In our opinion, we may properly exercise such discretion, not simply to shield this Court from noisome, vexatious, or unfamiliar tasks, but also, and we believe principally, as a technique for promoting and furthering the assumptions and value choices that underlie the current role of this Court in the federal system. Protecting this Court *per*

---

3. In our view * * * 28 U.S.C. § 1251(b)(3), providing that our original jurisdiction in cases such as these is merely concurrent with that of the federal district courts, reflects this same judgment. However, this particular case cannot be disposed of by transferring it to an appropriate federal district court since this statute by itself does not actually confer jurisdiction on those courts, and no other statutory jurisdictional basis exists. The fact that there is diversity of citizenship among the parties would not support district court jurisdiction under 28 U.S.C. § 1332 because that statute does not deal with cases in which a State is a party. Nor would federal question jurisdiction exist under 28 U.S.C. § 1331. So far as it appears from the present record, an action such as this, if otherwise cognizable in federal district court, would have to be adjudicated under state law.

se is at best a secondary consideration. What gives rise to the necessity for recognizing such discretion is pre-eminently the diminished societal concern in our function as a court of original jurisdiction and the enhanced importance of our role as the final federal appellate court. A broader view of the scope and purposes of our discretion would inadequately take account of the general duty of courts to exercise that jurisdiction they possess.

Thus, at this stage we go no further than to hold that, as a general matter, we may decline to entertain a complaint brought by a State against the citizens of another State or country only where we can say with assurance that (1) declination of jurisdiction would not disserve any of the principal policies underlying the Article III jurisdictional grant and (2) the reasons of practical wisdom that persuade us that this Court is an inappropriate forum are consistent with the proposition that our discretion is legitimated by its use to keep this aspect of the Court's functions attuned to its other responsibilities.

II

In applying this analysis to the facts here presented, we believe that the wiser course is to deny Ohio's motion for leave to file its complaint.

A

Two principles seem primarily to have underlain conferring upon this Court original jurisdiction over cases and controversies between a State and citizens of another State or country. The first was the belief that no State should be compelled to resort to the tribunals of other States for redress, since parochial factors might often lead to the appearance, if not the reality, of partiality to one's own. The second was that a State, needing an alternative forum, of necessity had to resort to this Court in order to obtain a tribunal competent to exercise jurisdiction over the acts of nonresidents of the aggrieved State.

Neither of these policies is, we think, implicated in this lawsuit. The courts of Ohio, under modern principles of the scope of subject matter and *in personam* jurisdiction, have a claim as compelling as any that can be made out for this Court to exercise jurisdiction to adjudicate the instant controversy, and they would decide it under the same common law of nuisance upon which our determination would have to rest.   * * *

B

Our reasons for thinking that, as a practical matter, it would be inappropriate for this Court to attempt to adjudicate the issues Ohio seeks to present are several. History reveals that the course of this Court's prior efforts to settle disputes regarding interstate air and water pollution has been anything but smooth. In Missouri v. Illinois, 200 U.S. 496, 520–522 (1906), Justice Holmes was at pains to underscore the great difficulty that the Court faced in attempting to pronounce a suitable general rule of law to govern such controversies. The solution finally grasped was to saddle the party seeking relief with an unusually high standard of proof and the Court with the duty of applying only legal principles "which [it] is prepared deliberately to maintain against all considerations on the other side," *id.*, at 521, an accommodation which, in cases of this kind, the Court has found necessary to maintain ever since. See, *e.g.*, New York v. New Jersey, 256 U.S. 296, 309 (1921). Justice Clarke's closing plea in New York v. New Jersey, *supra*, at 313, strikingly illustrates the sense of futility that has accompanied this Court's attempts to treat with the complex technical and political matters that inhere in all disputes of the kind at hand:

"We cannot withhold the suggestion * * * that the grave problem of sewage disposal presented by the large and growing populations living on the shores of New York Bay is one more likely to be wisely solved by cooperative study and by conference and mutual concession on the part of representatives of the States so vitally interested in it than by proceedings in any court however constituted."

The difficulties that ordinarily beset such cases are severely compounded by the particular setting in which this controversy has reached us. For example, the parties have informed us, without contradiction, that a number of official bodies are already actively involved in regulating the conduct complained of here. A Michigan circuit court has enjoined Wyandotte from operating its mercury cell process without judicial authorization. The company is, moreover, currently utilizing a recycling process specifically approved by the Michigan Water Resources Commission and remains subject to the continued scrutiny of that agency. Dow Canada reports monthly to the Ontario Water Resources Commission on its compliance with the commission's order prohibiting the company from passing any mercury into the environment.

Additionally, [Ohio and Michigan are participants in a federally-convened study of pollution (including mercury) in Lake Erie, whose purpose is to develop a plan for remedial action by the states or possibly for corrective action by the federal government. And a U.S.-Canadian Commission concerning the contamination of Lake Erie issued a 1971 report, one of whose recommendations would give the Commission authority to supervise such efforts.]

In view of all this, granting Ohio's motion for leave to file would, in effect, commit this Court's resources to the task of trying to settle a small piece of a much larger problem that many competent adjudicatory and conciliatory bodies are actively grappling with on a more practical basis.

The nature of the case Ohio brings here is equally disconcerting. It can fairly be said that what is in dispute is not so much the law as the facts. And the factfinding process we are asked to undertake is, to say the least, formidable. We already know, just from what has been placed before us on this motion, that Lake Erie suffers from several sources of pollution other than mercury; that the scientific conclusion that mercury is a serious water pollutant is a novel one; that whether and to what extent the existence of mercury in natural waters can safely or reasonably be tolerated is a question for which there is presently no firm answer; and that virtually no published research is available describing how one might extract mercury that is in fact contaminating water. * * * The notion that appellate judges, even with the assistance of a most competent Special Master, might appropriately undertake at this time to unravel these complexities is, to say the least, unrealistic. Nor would it suffice to impose on Ohio an unusually high standard of proof. That * * * would not lessen the complexity of the task of preparing responsibly to exercise our judgment, or the serious drain on the resources of this Court it would entail. Other factual complexities abound. For example, the Department of the Interior has stated that eight American companies are discharging, or have discharged, mercury into Lake Erie or its tributaries. We would, then, need to assess the business practices and relative culpability of each to frame appropriate relief as to the one now before us.

Finally, * * * we are not called upon by this lawsuit to resolve difficult or important problems of federal law and * * * nothing in Ohio's complaint distinguishes it from any one of a host of such actions that might, with equal justification, be commenced in this Court. * * *

To sum up, this Court has found even the simplest sort of interstate pollution case an extremely awkward vehicle to manage. And this case is an extraordinarily complex one both because of the novel scientific issues of fact inherent in it and the multiplicity of governmental agencies already involved. Its successful resolution would require primarily skills of factfinding, conciliation, detailed coordination with—and perhaps not infrequent deference to—other adjudicatory bodies, and close supervision of the technical performance of local industries. We have no claim to such expertise or reason to believe that, were we to adjudicate this case, and others like it, we would not have to reduce drastically our attention to those controversies for which this Court is a proper and necessary forum. Such a serious intrusion on society's interest in our most deliberate and considerate performance of our paramount role as the supreme federal appellate court could, in our view, be justified only by the strictest necessity, an element which is evidently totally lacking in this instance.

III

What has been said here cannot, of course, be taken as denigrating in the slightest the public importance of the underlying problem Ohio would have us tackle. * * * What is dealt with above are only considerations respecting the appropriate role this Court can assume in efforts to eradicate such environmental blights. * * *

Ohio's motion for leave to file its complaint is denied without prejudice to its right to commence other appropriate judicial proceedings.

It is so ordered.

■ MR. JUSTICE DOUGLAS, dissenting.

The complaint in this case presents basically a classic type of case congenial to our original jurisdiction. It is to abate a public nuisance. Such was the claim of Georgia against a Tennessee company which was discharging noxious gas across the border into Georgia. Georgia v. Tennessee Copper Co., 206 U.S. 230. * * *

Dumping of sewage in an interstate stream, Missouri v. Illinois, 200 U.S. 496, or towing garbage to sea only to have the tides carry it to a State's beaches, New Jersey v. New York City, 283 U.S. 473, have presented analogous situations which the Court has entertained in suits invoking our original jurisdiction. * * *

Much is made of the burdens and perplexities of these original actions. Some are complex, notably those involving water rights.

The drainage of Lake Michigan with the attendant lowering of water levels, affecting Canadian as well as United States interests, came to us in an original suit in which the Hon. Charles E. Hughes was Special Master. This Court entered a decree, Wisconsin v. Illinois, 278 U.S. 367, and has since that time entered supplementary decrees.

The apportionment of the waters of the Colorado between Arizona and California was a massive undertaking entailing a searching analysis by the

Special Master, the Hon. Simon H. Rifkind. Our decision was based on the record made by him and on exceptions to his Report. Arizona v. California, 373 U.S. 546.

The apportionment of the waters of the North Platte River among Colorado, Wyoming, and Nebraska came to us in an original action in which we named as Special Master, Hon. Michael J. Doherty. We entered a complicated decree, which dissenters viewed with alarm, Nebraska v. Wyoming, 325 U.S. 589, but which has not demanded even an hour of the Court's time during the 26 years since it was entered.

If in these original actions we sat with a jury, as the Court once did, there would be powerful arguments for abstention in many cases. But the practice has been to appoint a Special Master which we certainly would do in this case. We could also appoint—or authorize the Special Master to retain—a panel of scientific advisers. The problems in this case are simple compared with those in the water cases discussed above. * * *

* * *

The Department of Justice in a detailed brief tells us there are no barriers in federal law to our assumption of jurisdiction. I can think of no case of more transcending public importance than this one.

NOTE ON THE ORIGINAL JURISDICTION AS AN INAPPROPRIATE FORUM

(1) *The Origins of Discretion.* Massachusetts v. Missouri, 308 U.S. 1 (1939), a dispute involving potential multistate taxation of certain trusts, was the first case in which the Court declined to exercise its original jurisdiction squarely on the ground that it was inconvenient for the Court to adjudicate (and that a more convenient forum was available).[1] Having held that Massachusetts had no cause of action against Missouri (because there was no showing that the trusts would be depleted, and each state was free to press its claim), the Court then declined to adjudicate Massachusetts' tax claim against the Missouri trustees (pp. 18–19): "In the exercise of our original jurisdiction so as truly to fulfill the constitutional purpose we not only must look to the nature of the interest of the complaining State * * * but we must also inquire whether recourse to that jurisdiction in an action by a State merely to recover money alleged to be due from citizens of other States is necessary for the State's protection. * * * To open this Court to actions by States to recover taxes claimed to be payable by citizens of other States, in the absence of facts

---

1. Six years later, in Georgia v. Pennsylvania R.R., p. 319, *supra*, the entire Court asserted that it possessed such a power to decline (though the majority thought the power should not be exercised in that case). In support of the existence of the power both the majority and minority opinions cited (in addition to Massachusetts v. Missouri) North Dakota v. Chicago & N.W. R.R., 257 U.S. 485 (1922); Georgia v. Chattanooga, 264 U.S. 472, 483 (1924); and Oklahoma ex rel. Johnson v. Cook, 304 U.S. 387, 396 (1938). But in the first case the Court held that the United States was an indispensable party and that it had consented to suit only in the district court. In the second case the Court held that the bill lacked equity because Georgia had an adequate remedy at law in state court. And in the third case the Court's comments on the inconvenience of exercising original jurisdiction were made only to emphasize the importance of strict adherence to the doctrine that the complaining state must be the real party in interest.

showing the necessity for such intervention, would be to assume a burden which the grant of original jurisdiction cannot be regarded as compelling this Court to assume and which might seriously interfere with the discharge by this Court of its duty in deciding the cases and controversies appropriately brought before it. We have observed that the broad statement that a court having jurisdiction must exercise it (see Cohens v. Virginia, 6 Wheat. 264, 404) is not universally true but has been qualified in certain cases where the federal courts may, in their discretion, properly withhold the exercise of the jurisdiction conferred upon them where there is no want of another suitable forum."[2]

The Court quoted (p. 20) the Missouri Attorney General's statement that Massachusetts could sue in a Missouri state court "or in a federal district court in Missouri." The latter assertion seems plainly wrong. The former assertion would also have been wrong in the majority of states, which generally refuse, absent a reciprocity statute, to enforce each other's revenue laws.[3] Was it relevant whether Massachusetts could have sued the Missouri trustees in a Massachusetts court?

(2) *Declinations After Wyandotte.* Wyandotte was followed in Illinois v. Milwaukee, 406 U.S. 91 (1972), where Illinois moved for leave to file an original action against, *inter alia*, four Wisconsin cities to abate the alleged pollution of Lake Michigan.[4] The Court, after satisfying itself that the case could be filed under § 1331 in a federal district court, said that "while this original suit normally might be the appropriate vehicle for resolving this controversy, we exercise our discretion to remit the parties to an appropriate district court * * *" (p. 108).

2. The Court followed Massachusetts v. Missouri in Louisiana v. Cummins, 314 U.S. 580 (1941), an action to rescind a contract alleged to have been procured by fraud and to recover its proceeds. The state's attorney general pointed out that, since no federal district court would have jurisdiction, the Court's refusal to act would remit the controversy to the courts of whatever state the defendants could be served in. In the state's brief in support of its petition for rehearing (pp. 36–38), counsel said: "This completely defeats the purpose of the judiciary article of the Constitution, and places sovereign states in a worse position than private citizens and creatures of states—*i.e.* corporations—who can in similar circumstances invoke the diversity of citizenship jurisdiction. * * *

"* * * Truly the doctrine of a discretionary original jurisdiction in the Supreme Court has made a veritable *'Through the Looking-glass'* world out of the Judiciary Articles of the Constitution. Everything works backward! What was intended as a favor is turned into a burden. What was intended to give the parties a choice results in giving them no voice in the matter, and all the choice to the Court. The Act that was designed to give them recourse to the federal judiciary ends up in forcing them to accept the state judiciary. And the only practical method by which Congress can vest original jurisdiction in the Supreme Court, if indeed it can at all, is by withdrawing it from every other court. Such a system can not have been the intention either of the Founding Fathers, the Constitution, the Congress or the Court."

3. Coincidentally, Missouri held, seven years after Massachusetts v. Missouri, that it would accept such a suit. State ex rel. Oklahoma Tax Comm'n v. Rodgers, 238 Mo.App. 1115, 193 S.W.2d 919 (1946).

4. Illinois argued that the case was against the state within the meaning of the predecessor to § 1251(a), and that the Wyandotte doctrine was therefore inapplicable because the Supreme Court's jurisdiction was exclusive. But the Court held that political subdivisions of a state are not "States" within the meaning of § 1251(a), and that Wisconsin could but did not have to be joined as a defendant—thus leaving jurisdiction concurrent under § 1251(b). (The Court has since extended Wyandotte to cases within its exclusive original jurisdiction. See Paragraph (4), *infra.*)

On the same day, in Washington v. General Motors Corp., 406 U.S. 109 (1972), a unanimous Court applied the Wyandotte doctrine to deny a motion by eighteen states for leave to file a complaint against the four major automobile manufacturers and their trade associations. The complaint charged a conspiracy in violation of the antitrust laws to restrain the development of automobile air pollution control equipment. The Court stated that the federal district court was a more appropriate forum in view of the fact that "as a matter of law as well as practical necessity corrective remedies for air pollution * * * necessarily must be considered in the context of localized situations" (p. 116).

(3) *Suits by The United States.* The Court applied the Wyandotte doctrine to a suit by the United States in United States v. Nevada and California, 412 U.S. 534 (1973), a dispute over the waters of the Truckee River.[5] The Court stressed that original jurisdiction over the case was not exclusive, that "[w]e need not employ our original jurisdiction to settle competing claims to water within a single State," and that private users of the disputed waters could participate in a district court litigation but could not intervene in an original action in the Supreme Court (p. 538). The Court recognized that the United States could not join California in an action against Nevada in the Nevada district court, but it characterized the controversy between the United States and California as "remote" and one that could be settled in separate actions in the federal district courts in California (pp. 539–40).

(4) *Actions in Which the Supreme Court has Exclusive Jurisdiction.* The Court has dramatically extended the Wyandotte doctrine by applying it to cases falling within § 1251(a)'s grant of exclusive original jurisdiction. Can that extension be justified?

(a) The first case so holding was Arizona v. New Mexico, 425 U.S. 794 (1976). Arizona, suing both as a consumer of electricity and as *parens patriae* on behalf of its citizens, sought leave to file a complaint for a declaratory judgment that certain features of New Mexico's electrical energy tax were unconstitutional. The tax was already under attack in the courts of New Mexico by Arizona utility companies that generated electricity in New Mexico and were subject to the tax. In a brief per curiam, the Court denied leave to file because "we are persuaded that the pending state-court action provides an appropriate forum in which the *issues* tendered here may be litigated. If on appeal, the New Mexico Supreme Court should hold the electrical energy tax unconstitutional, Arizona will have been vindicated. If, on the other hand, the tax is held to be constitutional, the issues raised now may be brought to this Court by way of direct appeal under 28 U.S.C. § 1257(2).[6]

"In denying the State of Arizona leave to file, we are not unmindful that the legal incidence of the electrical energy tax is upon the utilities" (pp. 797–

---

5. Theretofore the United States had apparently been denied leave to file on only one occasion: United States v. Alabama, 282 U.S. 897 (1965). That declination, however, came on the same day that the Court granted leave in another original action, South Carolina v. Katzenbach, 382 U.S. 898 (1965), p. 323, *supra*, which raised identical questions as to the validity of the Voting Rights Act of 1965.

6. [Ed.] In 1988 Congress eliminated mandatory appeals under 28 U.S.C. § 1257; thus, there is no longer any guaranteed right of Supreme Court review of an unfavorable state court judgment in such a case. Does that amendment cast doubt on the continued appropriateness of the Wyandotte doctrine—either in general or specifically in cases between the states (where Congress has made the Court's jurisdiction exclusive)?

98).[7]

(b) The power to decline to hear a case within the exclusive original jurisdiction was reasserted, but not exercised, in Maryland v. Louisiana, 451 U.S. 725 (1981), discussed more fully at p. 320, *supra*. Justice White, for the Court, said (p. 739) that "we have construed the congressional grant of exclusive jurisdiction under § 1251(a) as requiring resort to our obligatory jurisdiction only in 'appropriate cases'". But he found this case to be "appropriate" and Arizona v. New Mexico to be distinguishable: (i) although the Louisiana tax was being challenged in various lower courts, in none of those cases were the plaintiff states adequately represented; (ii) the harm caused to other states by the Louisiana tax was far more severe than that involved in the Arizona case; and (iii) the Louisiana tax affected the interests of the United States (which had intervened as plaintiff) in the outer continental shelf. On the merits, the Court invalidated the tax. In dissent, Justice Rehnquist argued that the case was not "appropriate" for the exercise of original jurisdiction because the plaintiff states' claims did not involve any relation to their "sovereign" interests "qua States". He complained that the Court's opinion "articulates no limiting principles that would prevent this Court from being deluged by original actions brought by States simply in their role as consumers or on behalf of groups of their citizens as consumers" (p. 770).[8]

(c) In Louisiana v. Mississippi, 488 U.S. 990 (1988), the Court (in a one-sentence order) denied Louisiana's motion for leave to file a complaint against Mississippi over a boundary dispute. Justice White's dissent (joined by Justices Stevens and Scalia) objected that the dispute fell within the Court's exclusive jurisdiction under § 1251(a). The dissent argued that the denial was not justified by the pendency of a federal district court action concerning the ownership of land, which raised issues similar to those presented by Louisiana's complaint. That action was between private parties, but Louisiana had intervened. Justice White stated that even if the private suit were resolved in Louisiana's favor, the judgment would not bind Mississippi. For that reason, he supposed, Louisiana had filed a third-party complaint against Mississippi in

---

7. Justice Stevens concurred on the ground that Arizona lacked standing to sue. He added (pp. 798–99): "However, except to the extent that they apply to Arizona's attempt to litigate on behalf of an entity which has access to another forum, I do not believe the comments which the Court has previously made about its non-exclusive original jurisdiction adequately support an order denying a State leave to file a complaint against another State".

In Arizona Pub. Serv. Co. v. Snead, 441 U.S. 141 (1979), the Court in fact reviewed the New Mexico state court litigation described in Arizona v. New Mexico, and invalidated the tax as inconsistent with a federal statute.

8. Justice Stevens joined the Court's opinion, but a few months later—in a lone dissent to a summary denial of leave to file a suit by California against West Virginia alleging a breach of contract—stated that the Wyandotte "explanation" for discretionary refusals of original jurisdiction is "inapplicable to cases in which our jurisdiction is exclusive." California v. West Virginia, 454 U.S. 1027, 1028 (1981).

In Wyoming v. Oklahoma, 502 U.S. 437 (1992), discussed at p. 321, *supra*, the Court again held that the exercise of original jurisdiction was appropriate, as Wyoming's challenge raised important federalism concerns, there was no other appropriate forum in which Wyoming could obtain relief, and a significant amount of revenue was at stake. Justice Thomas, joined by the Chief Justice and Justice Scalia, dissented, arguing that the primary dispute was between private Wyoming mining companies and the state of Oklahoma, and that "an entirely derivative injury" of the type alleged by Wyoming did not justify the exercise of "discretionary original jurisdiction" (p. 476).

the district court, but that court, he argued, lacked jurisdiction in view of § 1251(a)'s exclusivity. And though the pending action might produce a judgment unfavorable to and binding on Louisiana, Justice White thought that denial of leave to file the complaint because of that possibility was "no way to treat a sovereign State that wants its dispute with another State settled in this Court" (p. 991).

After the Supreme Court denied the motion, the federal district court in Mississippi ruled that it did have jurisdiction over Louisiana's third-party complaint against Mississippi (and reached the merits). Ultimately, however, the Supreme Court disagreed and ordered the claim dismissed. The Court rejected the argument that its 1988 declination of original jurisdiction over that claim must be taken to indicate that the district court was a proper forum to hear it. While the Supreme Court may choose not to exercise jurisdiction under § 1251(a), the "uncompromising language" of exclusivity in that section "necessarily denies jurisdiction * * * to any other federal court." Mississippi v. Louisiana, 506 U.S. 73 (1992).[9]

Is § 1251(a)'s language less "uncompromising" in requiring the Supreme Court to hear such disputes than in forbidding lower federal courts from doing so? Was the Court's original decision in 1988 an abdication of duty? Was it unwise?

(d) Consider Justice White's statement in Maryland v. Louisiana, *supra*, that "the congressional grant of exclusive jurisdiction under § 1251(a) * * * requir[es] resort to our obligatory jurisdiction only in 'appropriate cases.'" Is it an oxymoron?

(5) *Questions About the Wyandotte Doctrine.*

(a) Reread the Court's words in California v. Arizona, quoted at the outset of this Chapter (pp. 294–95, *supra*), explaining why it would be in "derogation" of the purpose of the Framers—"matching the dignity of the parties to the status of the court"—for *Congress* to narrow the Court's original jurisdiction. Is it any less in derogation of that purpose for the *Court* to require "sovereign parties" to resort to another tribunal? See, for both a general discussion and criticism of the Court's approach when its jurisdiction is exclusive, Shapiro, *Jurisdiction and Discretion*, 60 N.Y.U.L.Rev. 543, 560–61, 576 (1985).

(b) If the exercise of discretion to decline jurisdiction is legitimate, what factors should inform that discretion? Clearly, although the Court handles few original cases each year, see p. 306, *supra*, they tend to be disproportionately lengthy and difficult, often involving elaborate factual rather than legal issues. But does the Wyandotte opinion demonstrate that the Supreme Court is a particularly inconvenient or inappropriate forum for that litigation, or merely that any court would find it extremely difficult to deal with the case? If the theory of the decision is that the Supreme Court has other, more significant, uses for its limited time, by what criteria does the Court justify the low priority assigned to such disputes?

Is the doctrine of forum non conveniens properly applied in a case where the convenience being served is that of the court rather than the litigants?

9. Thereafter, Louisiana commenced a new original action in the Supreme Court, which granted leave to file the bill of complaint. See Louisiana v. Mississippi, 114 S.Ct. 377 (1993), *decided on the merits,* 116 S.Ct. 290 (1995).

How carefully did the Wyandotte Court satisfy itself that the suit could be brought in another forum? An appropriate and convenient forum?

(c) In considering whether a more appropriate forum exists, is it enough that the *issues* that a state sought to litigate before the Supreme Court are under consideration in proceedings to which the state is not a party? Or should the Supreme Court have to satisfy itself that the state would have the right to participate as a party in an alternative forum?

(d) In suits between two states, is there any alternative forum? For example, in Arizona v. New Mexico, Paragraph (4)(a), *supra*, assuming that Arizona had a substantive right and standing to sue New Mexico (an issue the Court did not reach), where could it bring suit? Does § 1251(a)'s grant of exclusive jurisdiction preclude not only federal district court jurisdiction, see Paragraph (4)(c), *supra*, but also state court jurisdiction? If so, could Arizona avoid that barrier by suing only state officials? Will that tactic always work?

If not precluded by § 1251(a), could Arizona sue New Mexico in the *Arizona* state courts? (Compare Nevada v. Hall, 440 U.S. 410 (1979), upholding California's power to render a state court judgment against Nevada as to an automobile accident involving a Nevada state employee who was driving a state-owned car in California.) If Arizona sued instead in a New Mexico state court, would that court be obliged to hear the case? In any event, wasn't the Court right in Wyandotte when it said that "no State should be compelled to resort to the tribunals of other States for redress, since parochial factors might often lead to the appearance, if not the reality, of partiality to one's own"?

SECTION 2. CASES AFFECTING AMBASSADORS, OTHER PUBLIC MINISTERS, AND CONSULS

Ex Parte Gruber

269 U.S. 302, 46 S.Ct. 112, 70 L.Ed. 280 (1925).
Motion for Leave to File Petition for Mandamus.

■ MR. JUSTICE SUTHERLAND delivered the opinion of the Court.

This is an application for leave to file a petition and for a rule directing Albert Halstead, Consul General of the United States at Montreal, Canada, to show cause why a writ of mandamus should not issue commanding him to visa the passport or the certificate of origin and identity presented to him by one Rosa Porter, a citizen of Russia, who recently arrived in Montreal from Russia and from whom petitioner, a relative, desires a visit in the United States of several months' duration. We do not review the averments of the petition, since * * * it is clear that this court is without original jurisdiction.

Article III, § 2, cl. 2, of the Constitution provides that this court shall have original jurisdiction "in all cases affecting Ambassadors, other public Ministers and Consuls." Manifestly, this refers to diplomatic and consular representatives accredited to the United States by foreign powers, not to those representing this country abroad. The provision, no doubt, was inserted in view of the important and sometimes delicate nature of our relations and intercourse with foreign governments. It is a privilege, not of the official, but of the sovereign or government which he represents, accorded from high considerations of public policy, considerations which plainly do not apply to the United States in its own territory. [Citations omitted.]

The application is denied for want of original jurisdiction.

NOTE ON CASES AFFECTING FOREIGN DIPLOMATIC REPRESENTATIVES

(1) *The Paucity of Decisions.* Remarkably, Gruber and two other cases seem to be the only instances in which this head of the Supreme Court's original jurisdiction has been directly invoked.[1] Jones v. Le Tombe, 3 U.S. (3 Dall.) 384 (1798), a suit against the consul general of France, as the drawer of bills of exchange, was dismissed without opinion on the ground that the obligation was that of the government and not of the defendant as an individual. Casey v. Galli, 94 U.S. 673 (1877), was an original action in debt against a vice consul; judgment was rendered for the plaintiff without discussion of jurisdiction.

For whatever reasons of policy, representatives of foreign nations have not invoked the original jurisdiction as plaintiffs.

(2) *The Bearing of Diplomatic Immunity.* The dearth of suits against foreign diplomats is due to the wide immunity they enjoy. See generally Wilson, Diplomatic Privileges and Immunities (1967). That immunity has been in part codified ever since the Crimes Act of 1790, 1 Stat. 118, and is now found in the Diplomatic Relations Act of 1978, 22 U.S.C. §§ 254a *et seq.*[2]

(3) *Exclusive or Concurrent Jurisdiction?* Before 1978, the Court's jurisdiction of suits against ambassadors and other public ministers of foreign states was exclusive, but a 1978 amendment to § 1251 made the jurisdiction concurrent, see 92 Stat. 808. (Before 1978, the jurisdiction had been concurrent in suits brought *by* foreign envoys.) The lower federal courts have long had concurrent jurisdiction over actions against foreign *consuls* and *vice-consuls*—which, except for the period 1875–1911, has been exclusive of that of the state courts. See 28 U.S.C. § 1351. Litigation in the lower courts has been concerned largely with peripheral questions relating to the establishment of defenses, and only a handful of cases have reached the Court on review.[3]

---

1. Between 1961 and 1993, the Court summarily denied all five of the motions for leave to file under the foreign envoy jurisdiction; in two of the five the envoy was the plaintiff. For discussion of the apparent reason for each declination, see McKusick, p. 299, *supra*, at 206.

2. The 1978 Act implements the Vienna Convention on Diplomatic Relations, 28 U.S.T. 8227, April 18, 1961. See generally McClanahan, Diplomatic Immunity: Principles, Practices, Problems (1989); Shapiro, *Foreign Relations Law: Modern Developments in Diplomatic Immunity*, 1989 Ann. Surv.Am.L. 281.

Beginning with the Judiciary Act of 1789, there was further recognition of the immunity in the Supreme Court's jurisdictional statute. See, *e.g.* 28 U.S.C. § 1251(a)(2) (1948), which gave the Supreme Court only such jurisdiction as was "not inconsistent with the law of nations". See also Bergman v. De Sieyes, 170 F.2d 360 (2d Cir.1948)(holding that diplomatic immunity was broader than the then-existing statutory codification). However, the 1978 revision of § 1251 removed the language that had expressly limited the original jurisdiction in this respect.

3. As to who is a diplomat entitled to the immunity, see In re Baiz, 135 U.S. 403 (1890). As to the duration of the immunity, see Ex parte Hitz, 111 U.S. 766 (1884). As to waiver of the immunity, *cf.* Davis v. Packard (discussed in text).

State court actions against consuls raise problems with respect to the defense of exclusive jurisdiction similar to those raised by actions against higher diplomatic officials in the state or lower federal courts. See, *e.g.*, Davis v. Packard, 32 U.S. (7 Pet.) 276 (1833), holding that the failure to plead consular status at trial did not waive the defense on appeal, the privilege being that of the foreign government rather than of the official personally.

In Ohio ex rel. Popovici v. Agler, 280 U.S. 379 (1930), the Court held that the exclusion of state court jurisdiction did not extend to a suit for divorce by an American wife against a Rumanian vice-consul, in view of the traditional doctrine that domestic relations matters are reserved to the state courts. See Chap. X, Sec. 2(E), *infra*.

(4) *The Scope of the Jurisdiction "Affecting" Foreign Envoys.* Is the constitutional category of cases "affecting" foreign envoys exhausted by cases in which they are parties? Note the assumption of the draftsmen of § 1251 that it is.[4] (Compare Justice Frankfurter's comments in his dissent in Ex parte Peru, the next principal case.) The leading, if inconclusive, decision is United States v. Ortega, 24 U.S. (11 Wheat.) 467 (1826), holding that an indictment for offering violence to a foreign minister was not a case "affecting" the minister.

(5) *Representatives of International Organizations.* No decision of the Supreme Court casts direct light on the status of officials of the United Nations and other international organizations or of foreign delegates to them, for purposes either of the original jurisdiction or of the provisions of the Judicial Code excluding jurisdiction of state courts.[5]

SECTION 3. EXTRAORDINARY WRITS AND THE ORIGINAL JURISDICTION

Ex Parte Republic of Peru

318 U.S. 578, 63 S.Ct. 793, 87 L.Ed. 1014 (1943).
Motion for Leave to File Petition for a Writ of Prohibition and/or a Writ of Mandamus.

■ MR. CHIEF JUSTICE STONE delivered the opinion of the Court.

This is a motion for leave to file in this Court the petition of the Republic of Peru for a writ of prohibition or of mandamus. The petition asks this Court to prohibit respondent, a judge of the District Court for the Eastern District of Louisiana * * * from further exercise of jurisdiction over a proceeding in rem, pending in that court against petitioner's steamship Ucayali, and to direct the district judge to enter an order in the proceeding declaring the vessel immune from suit. * * *

---

4. Consider, however, the thesis of Professor Amar, p. 296, *supra*, which treats the foreign envoy jurisdiction as based on subject matter rather than on identity of the parties.

5. Relevant provisions are contained in the United Nations Charter, in the Headquarters Agreement between the United States and the United Nations, 61 Stat. 756, reprinted following 22 U.S.C.A. § 287, and in the International Organizations Immunities Act, 22 U.S.C. § 288 *et seq.*, and various executive orders of the President issued pursuant thereto. For discussion of the immunity of members of U.N. missions, see United States ex rel. Casanova v. Fitzpatrick, 214 F.Supp. 425 (S.D.N.Y.1963).

[The proceeding was commenced by a libel filed by a Cuban corporation against the ship for its failure to carry cargo from a Peruvian port to New York, as required by the terms of a charter party entered into by libelant with a Peruvian corporation acting as agent of the Peruvian Government. The petitioner procured the release of the vessel by filing a surety release bond in the sum of $60,000, and filed various claims and motions, each time asserting its sovereign immunity and disclaiming any waiver of this defense.]

In the meantime petitioner, following the accepted course of procedure, by appropriate representations, sought recognition by the State Department of petitioner's claim of immunity * * *. These negotiations resulted in formal recognition by the State Department of the claim of immunity. This was communicated to the Attorney General by the Under Secretary's letter of May 5, 1942. * * *

[In accordance with that letter's instructions,] the United States Attorney, on June 29th, filed in the district court a formal statement advising the court of the proceedings and communications mentioned, suggesting to the court and praying "that the claim of immunity made on behalf of the said Peruvian Steamship Ucayali and recognized and allowed by the State Department be given full force and effect by this court"; and "that the said vessel proceeded against herein be declared immune from the jurisdiction and process of this court". On July 1st petitioner moved for release of the vessel and that the suit be dismissed. The district court denied the motion on the ground that petitioner had waived its immunity by applying for extensions of time within which to answer, and by taking the deposition of the master—steps which the district court thought constituted a general appearance despite petitioner's attempted reservation of its right to assert its immunity as a defense in the suit.

The first question for our consideration is that of our jurisdiction. Section 13 of the Judiciary Act of 1789 conferred upon this Court "power to issue writs of prohibition to the district courts, when proceeding as courts of admiralty and maritime jurisdiction, and writs of mandamus, in cases warranted by the principles and usages of law, to any courts appointed, or persons holding office, under the authority of the United States". And § 14 provided that this Court and other federal courts "shall have power to issue writs of scire facias, habeas corpus, and all other writs not specially provided for by statute, which may be necessary for the exercise of their respective jurisdictions, and agreeable to the principles and usages of law." These provisions have in substance been carried over into * * * the Judicial Code * * *.

The jurisdiction of this Court as defined in Article III, § 2 of the Constitution is either "original" or "appellate". Suits brought in the district courts of the United States, not of such character as to be within the original jurisdiction of this Court under the Constitution, are cognizable by it only in the exercise of its appellate jurisdiction. Hence its statutory authority to issue writs of prohibition or mandamus to district courts can be constitutionally exercised only insofar as such writs are in aid of its appellate jurisdiction. Marbury v. Madison, 1 Cranch 137, 173, 180; Ex parte Siebold, 100 U.S. 371, 374, 375.

Under the statutory provisions, the jurisdiction of this Court to issue common law writs in aid of its appellate jurisdiction has been consistently sustained. The historic use of writs of prohibition and mandamus directed by an appellate to an inferior court has been to exert the revisory appellate power over the inferior court. The writs thus afford an expeditious and effective means of confining the inferior court to a lawful exercise of its prescribed jurisdiction, or of compelling it to exercise its authority when it is its duty to do so. Such has been the office of the writs when directed by this Court to district courts, both before the Judiciary Act of 1925,[1] and since.[2] In all these cases (cited in notes 1 and 2), the appellate, not the original, jurisdiction of this Court was invoked and exercised.[3]

The common law writs, like equitable remedies, may be granted or withheld in the sound discretion of the Court, and are usually denied where other adequate remedy is available. Ex parte Baldwin, 291 U.S. 610. And ever since the statute vested in the circuit courts of appeals appellate jurisdiction on direct appeal from the district courts, this Court, in the exercise of its discretion, has in appropriate circumstances declined to issue the writ to a district court, but without prejudice to an application to the circuit court of appeals, which likewise has power under § 262 of the Judicial Code to issue the writ.

After a full review of the traditional use of the common law writs by this Court, and in issuing a writ of mandamus, in aid of its appellate jurisdiction, to compel a district judge to issue a bench warrant in conformity to statutory requirements, this Court declared in Ex parte United States, 287 U.S. 241, 248, 249: "The rule deducible from the later decisions, and which we now affirm, is that this court has full power in its discretion to issue the writ of mandamus to a federal District Court, although the case be one in respect of which direct appellate jurisdiction is vested in the Circuit Court of Appeals—this court having ultimate discretionary jurisdiction by certiorari—but that such power will be exercised only where a question of public importance is involved, or where the question is of such a nature that it is peculiarly appropriate that such action by this court should be taken. In other words, application for the writ ordinarily must be made to the intermediate appellate court, and made to this court as the court of ultimate review only in such exceptional cases."[4]

1. [Citing numerous cases.]

2. Ex parte United States, 287 U.S. 241; State of Maryland v. Soper (No. 1), 270 U.S. 9, 27, 28; State of Maryland v. Soper (No. 2), 270 U.S. 36; State of Maryland v. Soper (No. 3), 270 U.S. 44; State of Colorado v. Symes, 286 U.S. 510; McCullough v. Cosgrave, 309 U.S. 634; Ex parte Kumezo Kawato, 317 U.S. 69; see Los Angeles Brush Mfg. Corp. v. James, 272 U.S. 701.

3. See particularly the discussion in State of Maryland v. Soper (No. 1), 270 U.S. 9, 28–30, and in Ex parte United States, 287 U.S. 241. Compare Ex parte Siebold, 100 U.S. 371.

Ex parte United States, supra, was not and could not have been a case of original jurisdiction. The Constitution confers original jurisdiction only in cases affecting ambassadors, other public ministers and consuls, and "those in which a State shall be Party" (Art. III, § 2, cl. 2). No state was made a party to Ex parte United States. The United States has never been held to be a "State"

within this provision—and it obviously is not—nor has it any standing to bring an original action in this Court which does not otherwise come within one of the provisions of Article III, § 2, cl. 2. United States v. Texas, 143 U.S. 621, relied upon to sustain a different view, was within the original jurisdiction because the state of Texas was the party defendant. And until now it has never been suggested that necessity, however great, warrants the exercise by this Court of original jurisdiction which the Constitution has not conferred upon it. Moreover, even if Congress had withdrawn this Court's appellate jurisdiction by the 1925 Act, there would have been no necessity in Ex parte United States for inventing an original jurisdiction which the Constitution had withheld, since a writ of mandamus could have been applied for in the circuit court of appeals.

4. The suggestion that the Judiciary Act of 1925 was intended to curtail the jurisdiction previously exercised by this Court in granting such writs to the district courts

We conclude that we have jurisdiction to issue the writ as prayed. And we think that—unless the sovereign immunity has been waived—the case is one of such public importance and exceptional character as to call for the exercise of our discretion to issue the writ rather than to relegate the Republic of Peru to the circuit court of appeals, from which it might be necessary to bring the case to this Court again by certiorari. The case involves the dignity and rights of a friendly sovereign state, claims against which are normally presented and settled in the course of the conduct of foreign affairs by the President and by the Department of State. When the Secretary elects, as he may and as he appears to have done in this case, to settle claims against the vessel by diplomatic negotiations between the two countries rather than by continued litigation in the courts, it is of public importance that the action of the political arm of the Government taken within its appropriate sphere be promptly recognized, and that the delay and inconvenience of a prolonged litigation be avoided by prompt termination of the proceedings in the district court. If the Republic of Peru has not waived its immunity, we think that there are persuasive grounds for exercising our jurisdiction to issue the writ in this case and at this time without requiring petitioner to apply to the circuit court of appeals * * *.

[The Court proceeded to find that Peru had not waived its immunity.]

The motion for leave to file is granted. We assume that, in view of this opinion, formal issuance of the writ will be unnecessary * * *.

■ MR. JUSTICE ROBERTS concurs in the result.

■ MR. JUSTICE FRANKFURTER, dissenting.

* * * [My brethren's and my] common starting point is that in taking hold of this case the Court is exercising its appellate jurisdiction.

We are also agreed that this Court "can exercise no appellate jurisdiction, except in the cases, and in the manner and form, defined and prescribed by congress". Amer. Const. Co. v. Jacksonville, T. & K.W. Railway Co., 148 U.S. 372, 378. Had this case arisen under the Evarts Act [of 1891, see p. 37, *supra*], appeal could have been taken from the district court, since its jurisdiction was in issue, directly to this Court without going to the Circuit Court of Appeals. And since the case would have been within the immediate appellate jurisdiction of this Court, §§ 13 and 14 of the first Judiciary Act, would have authorized this Court to issue an appropriate writ to prevent frustration of its appellate power, or have enabled it to accelerate its own undoubted reviewing authority where, under very exceptional circumstances, actual and not undefined interests of justice so required.

The power to issue these auxiliary writs is not a qualification or even a loose construction of the strict limits, defined by the Constitution and the Congress, within which this Court must move in reviewing decisions of lower courts. * * * The issuance of such a writ is, in effect, an anticipatory review of a case that can in due course come here directly. When the Act of 1891

finds no support in the history or language of the Act. * * * Ex parte United States, and most of the other cases cited in note 2, *supra*, were decided at a time when members of the Court's committee responsible for the 1925 Act were still members of the Court. The Court's unanimous concurrence in the existence of its jurisdiction in the cases subsequent to the 1925 Act establishes a practice which would be beyond explanation if there had been any thought that any provision of the Act had placed such a restriction on the Court's jurisdiction to issue the writs.

* * *

established the intermediate courts of appeals and gave to them a considerable part of the appellate jurisdiction formerly exercised by the Supreme Court, the philosophy and practice of federal appellate jurisdiction came under careful scrutiny. This Court uniformly and without dissent held that it was without power to issue a writ of mandamus in a case in which it did not otherwise have appellate jurisdiction. In re Commonwealth of Massachusetts, 197 U.S. 482, and In re Glaser, 198 U.S. 171. In these cases rules were discharged because, under the Circuit Court of Appeals Act, appeals could not be brought directly to the Supreme Court but would have to go to the Circuit Court of Appeals, and only thereafter could they come here, if at all, through certiorari. But review could be brought directly to this Court of cases in which the jurisdiction of the district court was in issue, and therefore writs of "prohibition or mandamus or certiorari as ancillary thereto", In re Commonwealth of Massachusetts, *supra*, 197 U.S. at 488, were available. Cases which came here directly, prior to the Judiciary Act of February 13, 1925, to review the jurisdiction of the district courts, whether on appeal or through the informal procedure of auxiliary writs, are therefore not relevant precedents for the present case. * * *

[The opinion then urges that the Judiciary Act of 1925 be read as removing the basis for issuance of an ancillary writ directly to a district court, save in the special situations in which direct review was authorized * * *. (Compare the present provision for direct review in 28 U.S.C. § 1253.) It cites the general purpose of the Act to remove "[t]he needless clog on the Court's proper business", in particular, by restricting appellate jurisdiction over the district courts.]

Finally, it is urged that practice since the Judicial Act of 1925 sanctions the present assumption of jurisdiction. Cases like Ex parte Northern Pac. R. Co., 280 U.S. 142, ordering a district judge to summon three judges to hear a suit under § 266 of the Judicial Code, must be put to one side. This is one of the excepted classes under the Act of 1925 in which direct review lies from a district court to the Supreme Court, and it is therefore an orthodox utilization of an ancillary writ within the rule of In re Commonwealth of Massachusetts, *supra*. Of all the other cases in which, since the Act of 1925, a writ was authorized to be issued, none is comparable to the circumstances of the present case. In one, Ex parte Kumezo Kawato, [317 U.S. 69 (1942)], the appellate jurisdiction of this court was invoked only after appellate jurisdiction was denied by a circuit court of appeals. Another, Ex parte United States, 287 U.S. 241, while in form a review of action by a district court, was in fact an independent suit by the United States because no appeal as such lay from the refusal of the district judge in that case to issue a bench warrant in denial of his duty. If the suit was a justiciable controversy through use of the ancillary writ, it was equally justiciable if regarded as an original suit by the United States. While, to be sure, it was not formally such, and while an ordinary suit by the United States to enforce an obligation against one of its citizens properly cannot be brought within the original jurisdiction of this Court, Ex parte United States, *supra,* was quite different. There the United States sought enforcement of a public duty for which no redress could be had in any other court. Therefore, the considerations which led this Court in United States v. Texas, 143 U.S. 621, to allow the United States to initiate an original suit in this Court, although the merely literal language of the Constitution precluded it (as the dissent in that case insisted), might have been equally potent to allow assumption of such jurisdiction in the circumstances of Ex parte United States. But, in any event, merely because there is no other available judicial relief is no reason for taking appellate jurisdiction. For some situations the only appropriate remedy is corrective legislation. Of the same nature were four other cases, three suits by Maryland and one by Colorado. State of Maryland v. Soper (1), 270 U.S. 9; State of Maryland v. Soper (2), 270 U.S. 36; State of Maryland v. Soper (3), 270 U.S. 44; State of Colorado v. Symes, 286 U.S. 510. These cases were not ordinary claims by a state against one of its citizens for which the state courts are the appropriate tribunals. They were in effect suits by states against federal functionaries in situations in which the citizenship of these functionaries was irrelevant to the controversy. And so the considerations that made the controversies by Maryland and Colorado justiciable through ancillary writs might have been equally relevant in establishing justiciability for original suits in this Court under Article III, Section 2. It is not without significance that the State of Maryland v. Soper cases and State of Colorado v. Symes, which the Court now regards as precedents for the ruling in Ex parte United States, were not even referred to in the opinion in the latter case.

If Ex parte United States, the State of Maryland v. Soper cases, and State of Colorado v. Symes, *supra,* are not to be supported on the basis of their peculiar circumstances which might have justified the Court in assuming jurisdiction, they should be candidly regarded as deviations from the narrow limits within which our appellate jurisdiction should move. They would then belong with the occasional lapses which occur when technical questions of jurisdiction are not properly presented to the Court and consciously met. * * *

     * * *

Had the Court jurisdiction, this case would furnish no occasion for its exercise. On whatever technical basis of jurisdiction the availability of these writs may have been founded, their use has been reserved for very special circumstances. * * *

No palpable exigency either of national or international import is made manifest for seeking this extraordinary relief here. * * *

To remit a controversy like this to the circuit court of appeals where it properly belongs is not to be indifferent to claims of importance but to be uncompromising in safeguarding the conditions which alone will enable this Court to discharge well the duties entrusted exclusively to us. * * *

Mr. Justice Reed is of the opinion that this Court has jurisdiction to grant the writ requested, Ex parte United States, 287 U.S. 241, but concurs in this dissent on the ground that application for the writ sought should have been made first to the Circuit Court of Appeals.

NOTE ON THE POWER TO ISSUE EXTRAORDINARY WRITS

(1) *Appellate versus Original Jurisdiction.* Article III gives the Supreme Court appellate jurisdiction "with such Exceptions, and under such Regulations as the Congress shall make". In Durousseau v. United States, 10 U.S. (6 Cranch) 307 (1810), the Court construed the Judiciary Act of 1789 as impliedly withdrawing appellate jurisdiction in every situation in which it was not expressly conferred. Hence power to issue an extraordinary writ (mandamus, prohibition, common-law certiorari, quo warranto, or habeas corpus) as an exercise of appellate

jurisdiction must be found in a statute that in turn is authorized by the Constitution.

The original jurisdiction, on the other hand, is conferred directly by the Constitution. Therefore, no statutory authorization is needed if issuance of an extraordinary writ would constitute a proper exercise of original jurisdiction;[1] and if it would not, under Marbury v. Madison no statute can authorize it, see pp. 297–98, *supra*.

Do Marbury v. Madison and Ex parte Peru, taken together, yield satisfactory criteria for deciding whether issuance of an extraordinary writ involves an exercise of appellate or of original jurisdiction?[2] Note that constitutional difficulties in this area could be met either by broadly construing the "appellate jurisdiction" in Article III, or by overruling Marbury v. Madison's holding that Article III's grant of original jurisdiction is not subject to enlargement by Congress.

(2) *The Limits of the Original Jurisdiction.* If the Republic of Peru had intervened in the litigation through its ambassador, would the Supreme Court have had original jurisdiction under the Constitution? Is it odd that the Court cannot hear, in its original jurisdiction, a case against a foreign country, but can hear a case against that country's envoy?

(3) *The Background to and Limits of Ex Parte Peru.* The Supreme Court at one time seems to have considered that its power, in the exercise of appellate jurisdiction, to issue mandamus or prohibition existed only when the writ was in aid of the proper disposition of a case then pending in the Supreme Court. Ex parte Warmouth, 84 U.S. (17 Wall.) 64 (1872). In re Massachusetts, 197 U.S. 482 (1905), recognized the propriety of issuing the writ in aid of the disposition of a case that was pending in a lower federal court and over which the Supreme Court had a power of direct review. Ex parte Peru moves one step further to bring in cases over which the power of direct review is vested in an intermediate court.

What of a case involving a federal question pending in a state court? (Section 13 of the Judiciary Act of 1789 permitted writs to be issued only to "courts appointed * * * under the authority of the United States", but the surviving authority in 28 U.S.C. § 1651(a) lacks that restriction.) The only decisions are two cases where the Court had already exercised appellate jurisdiction over the merits, and, without discussion of jurisdiction, subsequently granted leave to file a petition for a writ of mandamus ordering the state court to conform its decision to the Supreme Court's previous mandate. Deen v. Hickman, 358 U.S. 57 (1958); General Atomic Co. v. Felter, 436 U.S. 493 (1978); see p. 508, *infra*.[3]

---

1. For a discussion of some possible instances, see Oaks, *The "Original" Writ of Habeas Corpus in the Supreme Court*, 1962 Sup.Ct.Rev. 153, 156–59.

2. Consider Wolfson, *Extraordinary Writs in the Supreme Court Since Ex parte Peru*, 51 Colum.L.Rev. 977, 991 (1951): "In Ex parte Peru, doubtless as a result of Mr. Justice Frankfurter's scholarly dissent, the Supreme Court was compelled to articulate the criteria delimiting its power. When that was done, the Court found that, with respect to cases coming from the federal courts, its power was practically limitless. Thus, * * * the conflict moved into the area of discretion. It is true, of course, that the rules relating to power developed in the last hundred and fifty years have been influential in determining whether discretion should be exercised."

3. What of cases pending in a federal administrative agency, directly reviewable in a lower federal court? *Cf.* CAB v. American Air Transport, Inc., 344 U.S. 4 (1952), dis-

(4) *Habeas Corpus Practice.* Compare the practice in habeas corpus proceedings. In Ex parte Bollman, 8 U.S. (4 Cranch) 75 (1807), following United States v. Hamilton, 3 U.S. (3 Dall.) 17 (1795), and Ex parte Burford, 7 U.S. (3 Cranch) 448 (1806), the Court held that it was an exercise of its appellate jurisdiction for the Court to grant the writ to pass on the legality of a detention, based on a lower court's order (after a finding of probable cause) committing petitioners to stand trial—even though no appeal from a conviction had been authorized by Congress. The Court said (p. 101) that "the decision that the individual shall be imprisoned must always precede the application for a writ of *habeas corpus,* and this writ must always be for the purpose of revising that decision, and, therefore, appellate in its nature." See also Ex parte Watkins, 32 U.S. (7 Pet.) 568 (1833). Subsequently, in Ex parte Yerger, 75 U.S. (8 Wall.) 85 (1868), where a circuit court had granted and thereafter dismissed the writ sought by a military prisoner, the Supreme Court found that its jurisdiction was appellate—despite the congressional repeal of the statute authorizing an appeal from the denial of the writ by lower courts. See also Ex parte Siebold, 100 U.S. 371 (1880). But see Ex parte Barry, 43 U.S. (2 How.) 65 (1844)(no appellate jurisdiction to issue writ to test confinement by a private party in a child custody case). Stern, Gressman, Shapiro & Geller, p. 299, *supra,* at 502 report that "not since 1925 has any petitioner been successful in obtaining release on a habeas petition filed directly with the Court." See generally Oaks, note 1, *supra*; Chap XI, Sec. 1, pp. 1344–45, *infra.*

Does the power of a single Justice of the Supreme Court to issue a writ of habeas corpus (a power granted from 1789 to the present, see 28 U.S.C. § 2241(a)) involve original or appellate jurisdiction? The answer rests in obscurity. *Cf.* In re Kaine, 55 U.S. (14 How.) 103, 116, 130–31 (1852); Ex parte Clarke, 100 U.S. 399, 402–03 (1880); Locks v. Commanding General, Sixth Army, 89 S.Ct. 31 (1968)(Douglas, J., sitting as Circuit Justice).

(5) *Statutory Authority for the Issuance of Extraordinary Writs.* The 1948 revision of the Judicial Code repealed the successor provision to § 13 of the Judiciary Act of 1789; the revisers explained that it was "omitted as unnecessary". Thus, at present the only statutory authority for the issuance of the extraordinary writs other than habeas corpus (which is specially dealt with in 28 U.S.C. § 2241(a)) is the successor provision to § 14, the famous all-writs section—now 28 U.S.C. § 1651(a).

In LaBuy v. Howes Leather Co., 352 U.S. 249, 265–66 (1957), Justice Brennan's dissent, in discussing the powers of the courts of appeals (which were never covered by § 13), argued that the mandamus power granted by § 1651(a) is significantly narrower than that formerly granted by § 13. But he did not have to face the question whether the elimination of § 13 narrowed the *Supreme Court*'s power to issue mandamus. See also Chandler v. Judicial Council of the Tenth Circuit, 398 U.S. 74, 89, 117 n. 15 (1970)(Harlan, J., concurring).[4]

---

missing a certificate from a court of appeals in a case coming from an administrative agency; see also FTC v. Dean Foods Co., 384 U.S. 597 (1966).

4. The Chandler case raised, but did not answer, important questions about the Court's powers to issue extraordinary writs in connection with the disciplining of lower court judges. The Tenth Circuit Judicial Council found District Judge Chandler "unable or unwilling" to discharge his duties, and ordered that cases pending before him be reassigned and that no new cases be assigned to him. Judge Chandler filed a motion in the Supreme Court for leave to file a petition for writs of mandamus and/or prohibition,

(6) *Supreme Court Practice.* The 1980 revision of the Rules of the Supreme Court dispensed with the requirement that a petition for an extraordinary writ be preceded by a motion for leave to file.

The current Rules (as amended in 1995) provide in Rule 20.1 that issuance of extraordinary writs under § 1651(a) "is not a matter of right, but of discretion sparingly exercised. To justify the granting of any such writ, the petition must show that the writ will be in aid of the Court's appellate jurisdiction, that exceptional circumstances warrant the exercise of the Court's discretionary powers, and that adequate relief cannot be obtained in any other form or from any other court." A petition seeking issuance of a writ of prohibition or mandamus "shall set out with particularity why the relief sought is not available in any other court" (Rule 20.3(a)).

NOTE ON THE WAR CRIMES CASES

(1) *Introduction.* After World War II the Supreme Court was confronted with more than a hundred petitions for writs of habeas corpus, by or on behalf of persons convicted by or held for trial before various American or international

urging that the Council's order was unauthorized by statute, an attack on the independence guaranteed by Article III, and a usurpation of the impeachment power.

The Court did not decide whether it had jurisdiction. It would be "no mean feat", the Court said, to find that the action of the Judicial Council was reviewable as a "judicial act or decision by a judicial tribunal", "without doing violence to the constitutional requirement that [the Court's] review be appellate". Ruling that the question need not be resolved, since other, though unspecified, avenues of relief on the merits "may yet be open to Judge Chandler" (p. 86), the Court concluded (p. 89): "Whether the Council's action was administrative action not reviewable in this Court, or whether it is reviewable here, plainly petitioner has not made a case for the extraordinary relief of mandamus or prohibition."

In an elaborate concurring opinion, Justice Harlan would have granted the motion for leave to file, finding that Judge Chandler lacked other remedies, that the Judicial Council's orders were an exercise of judicial power, that the Supreme Court had appellate jurisdiction under Article III, and that § 1651(a) authorized issuance of the petition. On the last point, he wrote (p. 113): "Each of the prior cases in which this Court has invoked § 1651(a) to issue a writ 'in aid of [its jurisdiction]' has involved a particular lawsuit over which the Court would have statutory review jurisdiction at a later stage.

By contrast, petitioner's reliance on this statute is bottomed on the fact that the action of the Judicial Council 'touches, through Judge Chandler's fate, hundreds of cases over which this court has appellate or review jurisdiction.' Petition for Writ of Prohibition and/or Mandamus 13. He argues that the Council's orders, allocating to other judges in his district cases that would otherwise be decided by him, constitute a usurpation of power that cannot adequately be remedied on final review of those cases by certiorari or appeal in this Court. * * * Although this expansive use of § 1651(a) has no direct precedent in this Court, it seems to me wholly in line with the history of that statute and consistent with the manner in which it has been interpreted both here and in the lower courts."

On the merits, Justice Harlan found the Judicial Council's orders valid and thus would not have issued the writ. Justices Black and Douglas dissented, each arguing that the Court had jurisdiction and that the orders were invalid.

Should the Court's jurisdiction turn on whether the orders were "administrative" or "judicial"? *Cf.* Prentis v. Atlantic Coast Line Co. and District of Columbia Court of Appeals v. Feldman, pp. 1223–25, 1500–03, *infra.*

The Chandler case evoked copious comment. See, *e.g.*, Kurland, *The Constitution and the Tenure of Federal Judges: Some Notes From History*, 36 U.Chi.L.Rev. 665 (1969).

military tribunals abroad.[1] In almost none of these cases was relief first sought in a lower federal court.[2]

(2) *The Initial Denials.* Between 1946 and early 1948, the Court four times rebuffed German petitioners—at first "for want of original jurisdiction" (over three at least partial dissents);[3] then by order of an evenly divided Court (with Justice Jackson taking no part in view of his role at the Nuremberg trials);[4] and in the last two instances with a brief order simply stating that the petition was denied.[5]

(3) *Everett v. Truman.* Then in Everett v. Truman, 334 U.S. 824 (1948), a petition on behalf of 74 Germans convicted by the Military Government Court at Dachau, the per curiam decision stated:

"* * * The motion for leave to file a petition for an original writ of habeas corpus for relief from sentences upon the verdicts of a General Military Government Court at Dachau, Germany, is denied. The Chief Justice, Mr. Justice Reed, Mr. Justice Frankfurter, and Mr. Justice Burton are of the opinion that there is want of jurisdiction. U.S. Constitution, Article III, § 2, Clause 2; see Ex parte Betz and companion cases, all 329 U.S. 672 (1946); Milch v. United States, 332 U.S. 789 (1947); Brandt v. United States, 333 U.S. 836 (1948); In re Eichel, 333 U.S. 865 (1948). Mr. Justice Black, Mr. Justice Douglas, Mr. Justice Murphy, and Mr. Justice Rutledge are of the opinion that the motion for leave to file the petition should be granted and that the case should be set for argument forthwith. Mr. Justice Jackson took no part in the consideration or decision of the motion."

(4) *Hirota v. MacArthur.*

(a) After disposing by identical orders of more than two dozen petitions in the next six months, see Fairman, note 1, supra, at 599–600, the Court in December of 1948 set for oral argument motions for leave to file petitions on behalf of a group of Japanese, including former Premier Hirota, who had been

---

1. A comprehensive review of the war crime cases as of 1949 is found in Fairman, *Some New Problems of the Constitution Following the Flag*, 1 Stan.L.Rev. 587 (1949). See also Oaks, p. 342, note 1, *supra*, at 169–73.

2. An exception was Ex parte Quirin, 317 U.S. 1 (1942), involving the trial of German saboteurs by a military commission appointed by the President. During argument in the Supreme Court on the motion for leave to file petitions for habeas corpus, counsel perfected appeals from the district court's denial of the writ and petitioned for certiorari before judgment in the circuit court of appeals. The Supreme Court denied the applications for leave to file, but granted the petitions for certiorari and affirmed the district court's denial of the writ on the merits.

In re Yamashita, 327 U.S. 1 (1946), like Quirin, did not involve direct Supreme Court review of military tribunals. There a Japanese general, while on trial for war crimes before a military tribunal in the Philippines, sought leave to file petitions for writs of habeas corpus and prohibition in the Supreme Court. The Court stayed the case, 326 U.S. 693 (1945), pending receipt of a petition for certiorari from a decision of the Supreme Court of the Philippines that had denied similar relief. Subsequently the Court denied certiorari and leave to file, opining that Yamashita was not entitled to relief on the merits.

3. Ex parte Betz, 329 U.S. 672 (1946). Justices Black and Rutledge would have denied leave without prejudice to the filing of the petitions "in the appropriate District Court". Justice Murphy would have "heard and determined" the questions of jurisdiction and proper procedure.

4. Milch v. United States, 332 U.S. 789 (1947). See p. 299, *supra* (discussing whether four votes to grant a motion for leave to file should suffice).

5. Brandt v. United States, 333 U.S. 836 (1948); In re Eichel, 333 U.S. 865 (1948).

convicted by the International Military Tribunal of the Far East. Only two weeks later, following the argument, the Court rendered this opinion in Hirota v. MacArthur, 338 U.S. 197 (1948):

"PER CURIAM. The petitioners, all residents and citizens of Japan, are being held in custody pursuant to the judgment of a military tribunal in Japan. * * * They filed motions in this Court for leave to file petitions for *habeas corpus*. * * *

"We are satisfied that the tribunal sentencing these petitioners is not a tribunal of the United States. The United States and other allied countries conquered and now occupy and control Japan. General Douglas MacArthur has been selected and is acting as the Supreme Commander for the Allied Powers. The military tribunal sentencing these petitioners has been set up by General MacArthur as the agent of the Allied Powers.

"Under the foregoing circumstances the courts of the United States have no power or authority to review, to affirm, set aside or annul the judgments and sentences imposed on these petitioners and for this reason the motions for leave to file petitions for writs of *habeas corpus* are denied.

"Mr. Justice Murphy dissents.

"Mr. Justice Rutledge reserves decision and the announcement of his vote until a later time. [Justice Rutledge died September 10, 1949, without having announced his vote.]

"Mr. Justice Jackson took no part in the final decision on these motions.

"Mr. Justice Douglas concurs in the result for reasons to be stated in an opinion."

Justice Douglas delivered his concurring opinion on June 27, 1949. At the outset, he said (pp. 199–200):

"Respondents contend that the Court is without power to issue a writ of *habeas corpus* in these cases. It is argued that the Court has no original jurisdiction * * * since these are not cases affecting an ambassador, public minister, or consul; nor is a State a party. And it is urged that appellate jurisdiction is absent (1) because military commissions do not exercise judicial power within the meaning of Art. III, § 2 of the Constitution and hence are not agencies whose judgments are subject to review by the Court; and (2) no court of the United States to which the potential appellate jurisdiction of this Court extends has jurisdiction over this cause."

Justice Douglas found (p. 203) that the District Court of the District of Columbia had jurisdiction to hear the motions,[6] and that "[t]he appropriate course would be to remit the parties to it, reserving any further questions until the cases come here by certiorari. But the Court is unwilling to take that course, apparently because it deems the cases so pressing and the issues so unsubstantial that the motions should be summarily disposed of."

In the balance of his opinion, Justice Douglas objected to the sweep of the Court's decision that jurisdiction was barred merely because the committing tribunal was international. In his view, the appropriate course was to "ascertain whether, so far as American participation is concerned, there was authori-

---

6. For discussion of that court's jurisdiction in cases of aliens and citizens held under American authority abroad, see John- son v. Eisentrager, 339 U.S. 763 (1950), p. 365, *infra*.

ty to try the defendants for the precise crimes with which they are charged" (p. 205). Undertaking to do this, he concurred on the ground that "the capture and control of those who were responsible for the Pearl Harbor incident was a political question on which the President as Commander-in-Chief, and as spokesman for the nation in foreign affairs, had the final say" (p. 215).

(b) Is Justice Douglas assuming that the Supreme Court has "appellate jurisdiction", in the constitutional sense, in any case which is within the potential jurisdiction of a lower federal court? Is such an assumption sound? If it is, could the writ of mandamus have issued in Marbury v. Madison as an exercise of appellate jurisdiction? Does the majority opinion imply acceptance of the Douglas assumption? Did the Court actually exercise original jurisdiction in this case?

(5) *The Final Petitions.* Following the Hirota decision, a series of motions for leave to file petitions in war crimes cases were again denied. In one group of cases the Court was evenly divided: four Justices returned to their pre-Hirota ground of lack of original jurisdiction, while the other four stated that "argument should be heard on the motions for leave to file the petitions in order to settle what remedy, if any, the petitioners have". In re Dammann and companion cases, 336 U.S. 922 (1949); In re Muhlbauer and companion cases, 336 U.S. 964 (1949); In re Steimle, 337 U.S. 913 (1949); In re Felsch, 337 U.S. 953 (1949). In another case, however, the Court unanimously denied an application "without prejudice to the right to apply to any appropriate court that may have jurisdiction." In re Bush, 336 U.S. 971 (1949). (Three weeks earlier it had denied an application in "a somewhat comparable case" without comment. Bickford v. United States, 336 U.S. 950 (1949). See the reference to both cases in Hirota v. MacArthur, *supra*, 338 U.S. at 201–02 (Douglas, J., concurring).)

At the 1949 term, a reconstituted Court denied without explanation three more motions, with the notation that "Mr. Justice Black and Mr. Justice Douglas vote to deny without prejudice to making applications in a District Court." In re Hans, 339 U.S. 976 (1950).

(6) *Military Tribunals.* The question whether there is jurisdiction to entertain a petition for habeas corpus brought directly in the Supreme Court to challenge a criminal conviction rendered by a military tribunal is also raised by 28 U.S.C. § 1259. That provision authorizes direct Supreme Court review (on writ of certiorari) of decisions of the United States Court of Appeals for the Armed Services. That tribunal, like its predecessor, the Court of Military Appeals, is not an Article III court, and the cases it decides plainly do not fall within Article III's definition of the original jurisdiction. Yet the Supreme Court has reviewed decisions of the Court of Military Appeals without addressing this jurisdictional issue. See, *e.g.*, Solorio v. United States, 483 U.S. 435 (1987).

State courts, of course, are not Article III courts either, and yet Supreme Court review of state court decisions is not thought to be an exercise of original jurisdiction. But does it follow that Supreme Court review of *any* adjudicatory decision—even by a non-Article III federal tribunal—is an exercise of appellate jurisdiction? Could Congress provide for direct Supreme Court review of an NLRB decision in an unfair labor practice proceeding?

CHAPTER IV

CONGRESSIONAL CONTROL OF THE DISTRIBUTION OF JUDICIAL POWER AMONG FEDERAL AND STATE COURTS

SECTION 1. CONGRESSIONAL REGULATION OF FEDERAL JURISDICTION

INTRODUCTORY NOTE ON CONGRESSIONAL POWER OVER THE JURISDICTION OF THE ARTICLE III COURTS

(1) *Sources of Congressional Power.* Although Article III states that "the judicial Power of the United States *shall* be vested" (emphasis added), Congress possesses significant powers to apportion jurisdiction among state and federal courts and, in doing so, to define and limit the jurisdiction of particular courts. The precise limits of Congress' authority are controverted, but the existence of an important congressional power is not. Three sources of authority are particularly important.

(a) Article III, § 2. cl. 3 specifies that the appellate jurisdiction of the Supreme Court shall be subject to "such Exceptions * * * as the Congress shall make".

(b) Article III, § 1 provides for the vesting of federal judicial power in "one supreme Court, and in such inferior Courts as the Congress may from time to time ordain and establish". This language reflects a deliberate compromise reached at the Constitutional Convention between those who thought that the establishment of lower federal courts should be constitutionally mandatory and those who thought there should be no federal courts at all except for a Supreme Court with, *inter alia,* appellate jurisdiction to review state court judgments. See Chap. I, pp. 7-9, *supra.* Construed against the background of this "Madisonian Compromise", Congress' power to "ordain and establish" federal tribunals "inferior" to the Supreme Court has generally been understood to imply a power to create lower federal courts vested with less than the maximum jurisdiction that the Constitution would allow.

(c) Although state courts are bound by Article VI to respect and enforce federal law, "any Thing in the Constitution or Laws of any State to the Contrary notwithstanding", Congress can impose such limits on state court jurisdiction as may be "necessary and proper for carrying into Execution" the powers of the federal government.

(2) *Some Historical Limits on Federal Court Jurisdiction.* Beginning with the first Judiciary Act in 1789, Congress has never vested the federal courts with the entire "judicial Power" that would be permitted by Article III. A *partial* list of historical exclusions includes the following.

(a) *Jurisdiction of the Lower Federal Courts.* The first Judiciary Act did not provide for general federal question jurisdiction in civil cases "arising under" the Constitution, laws, or treaties of the United States. Federal question cases that did not fall into some more specialized grant of jurisdiction had to be litigated in state court, subject to Supreme Court review.[1] Only in 1875 did a Reconstruction Congress provide an enduring grant of general federal question jurisdiction.[2]

From 1875–1980, the general federal question statute limited federal jurisdiction in civil cases to disputes satisfying an amount-in-controversy requirement. The requisite amount was increased several times and stood at $10,000 when the requirement was repealed in 1980.[3] As a result, many "small" federal question claims could be filed only in state courts.

Even today, cases raising federal questions generally cannot be litigated under § 1331 unless the federal question appears on the face of the plaintiff's well-pleaded complaint.[4]

Congress has also imposed important exceptions on federal diversity jurisdiction. Although the first Judiciary Act authorized the lower federal courts to hear diversity cases,[5] it also established an amount-in-controversy requirement of $500.[6] This was a significant sum in 1789, and the amount has intermittently been increased to the current $50,000.[7] The rule of Strawbridge v. Curtiss, 7 U.S. (3 Cranch) 267 (1806), p. 1528, *infra,* requiring "complete diversity" when there are multiple parties on one or more sides of a case, also rests on an interpretation of the jurisdictional grant and restricts federal diversity jurisdiction more narrowly than the Constitution would allow.

(b) *Supreme Court Jurisdiction.* From 1789 to 1914, the Supreme Court had jurisdiction to review state court decisions of federal questions only if the state court had denied a claim of federal right.[8] Decisions favorable to federal claims were thus excluded from the Court's appellate jurisdiction. Nor, until 1891, did the Supreme Court possess statutory authority to review most decisions of lower federal courts in criminal cases. In addition, the Supreme Court has never had jurisdiction to review state court decisions on the basis that the parties are of diverse citizenship—even though such cases fall within the federal judicial power under Article III.

---

1. In a departure from this pattern, the Midnight Judges bill, the Act of February 13, 1801, § 2, 2 Stat. 89, did provide for federal jurisdiction in cases presenting federal questions, but this jurisdictional grant was repealed only a year later. Act of March 8, 1802, 2 Stat. 132.

2. Act of March 3, 1875, § 1, 18 Stat. 470.

3. Federal Question Jurisdictional Amendments Act of 1980, Pub. L. 96–486, § 1, 94 Stat. 2369 (amending 28 U.S.C. § 1331).

4. See generally see pp. 907-13, *infra.*

5. Act of Sept. 24, 1789, Sec. 11, 1 Stat. 73, 78.

6. Act of Sept. 24, 1789, Sec. 11, 1 Stat. 73, 78.

7. See Chap. XIII, Sec. 1, *infra.*

8. For reference to the relevant statutes, see Chap. V, § 1, pp. 492-93, *infra.*

(c) *State Court Jurisdiction.* By providing for exclusive federal jurisdiction in some cases[9] and for removal in others,[10] Congress has long exercised authority to limit the jurisdiction of the state courts.

(3) *Congressional Authority and Constitutional Controversy.* From the beginning of the Republic, perhaps the most controversial proposals to limit the jurisdiction of the federal courts have been those that reflect a substantive disagreement with the way the Supreme Court, the lower federal courts, or both have resolved particular issues. The subject matter of the proposed curbs has varied widely. "In the Marshall Court years, especially during the 1820's, those who perceived a tendency toward centralization in the Court's decisions proposed repealing section 25 of the 1789 Judiciary Act, which authorized Supreme Court review of certain state court judgments." Gunther, *Congressional Power to Curtail Federal Court Jurisdiction: An Opinionated Guide to the Ongoing Debate,* 36 Stan.L.Rev. 895, 896–97 (1984).[11] In the late 1950s and 1960s, controversy swarmed around legislative efforts to curb federal jurisdiction to review the admissibility of confessions in state criminal cases,[12] state legislative apportionments,[13] and legislation regulating or restricting subversive activities.[14]

Beginning in the early 1970s, a number of bills were introduced that were designed to use the power over jurisdiction to curb the authority of the federal courts to use busing as a remedy in school segregation cases.[15] More recently,

---

9. See pp. 452–55, *infra.*

10. See p. 453, *infra.*

11. See Chap. V, Sec. 1, pp. 506–07, *infra.*

12. S. 917, 90th Cong., 2d Sess. (1968), contained a provision withdrawing federal court jurisdiction to review a state court ruling "in any criminal prosecution admitting in evidence as voluntarily made an admission or confession of an accused if such ruling has been affirmed or otherwise upheld by the highest court of the State having appellate jurisdiction of the cause." Another provision of the bill was similarly designed to withdraw federal jurisdiction to apply the rule of United States v. Wade, 388 U.S. 218 (1967)(recognizing a right to counsel at post-indictment lineups). These provisions were eliminated when the bill reached the Senate floor. See 114 Cong.Rec. 14171–84 (1968).

13. H.R. 11926, 88th Cong., 2d Sess. (1964), which was introduced by Representative Tuck and passed the House before being defeated in the Senate, would have added the following provisions to Title 28:

§ 1259. "The Supreme Court shall not have the right to review the action of a Federal court or a State court of last resort concerning any action taken upon a petition or complaint seeking to apportion or reapportion any legislature of any State of the Union or any branch thereof. * * *"

§ 1331(c). "The district courts shall not have jurisdiction to entertain any petition or complaint seeking to apportion or reapportion the legislature of any State of the Union or any branch thereof."

This bill was one of more than fifty introduced in 1964 designed either to eliminate jurisdiction in or to "stay" reapportionment cases. None became law. See generally McKay, *Court, Congress, and Reapportionment,* 63 Mich.L.Rev. 255 (1964).

14. See, *e.g.,* the Jenner bill, S.2646, 85th Cong., 1st Sess. (1957), which would have deprived the Supreme Court of jurisdiction to review any case where there was drawn in question such matters as: the functions or practices of a congressional committee, any state law or regulation concerning subversive activities, or any state law or regulation relating to admission to the practice of law. The bill was voted down on the Senate floor, 49–41. See 104 Cong.Rec. 18687 (1958).

15. See, *e.g.,* Student Transportation Moratorium Act of 1972, S.3388, 92d Cong., 2d Sess.; H.R.13916, 92d Cong., 2d Sess.; Equal Educational Opportunities Act of 1972, S.3395, 92d Cong., 2d Sess.; H.R.13915, 92d Cong., 2d Sess.

two of the major efforts to limit jurisdiction have concerned abortion and school prayer.[16]

At least since the 1930s, no jurisdiction-stripping bill has become law.[17] But debates about the constitutionality of legislation withdrawing federal jurisdiction as a signal of substantive disagreement have spawned a body of literature that has been described as "choking on redundancy."[18] The issues generated by various forms of jurisdiction-limiting legislation are too diverse to be surveyed systematically in a summary introduction. In reading the materials that follow, however, consider whether curbs on jurisdiction aimed to stop the federal courts from enforcing the Constitution as they understand it are constitutionally different in kind from some or all of the historically familiar limitations on federal jurisdiction described in Paragraph (2), *supra*.

(4) *Residual Jurisdiction in the State Courts.* Although jurisdiction stripping proposals have been framed in widely varied ways, a common approach is reflected in several bills, introduced by Senator Jesse Helms, dealing with federal jurisdiction in cases involving prayer in the public schools and other public buildings. On various occasions he has introduced legislation providing that, notwithstanding any other provision of Title 28 of the United States Code, neither (a) the Supreme Court nor (b) any federal district court shall have jurisdiction of any case arising out of any state or local law or rule "which relates to voluntary prayer in public schools and buildings".[19]

Note that legislation worded in this way would not impair the jurisdiction of state courts to entertain challenges to the constitutionality of "voluntary prayer in public schools and buildings". There are various reasons why proponents of legislation that would strip federal jurisdiction might not seek to eliminate state court jurisdiction. Among them, legislation purporting to withhold *all* judicial review of allegedly unconstitutional action may present constitutional difficulties that legislation merely limiting *federal* jurisdiction does not. (For a discussion as to why, see pp. 373–79, *infra*).

Suppose that federal jurisdiction of school prayer cases were eliminated. Under the Supremacy Clause, state courts must enforce the Constitution as the supreme law of the land. Would they be obliged (i) to entertain challenges to school prayer? To accept Supreme Court precedent as establishing authoritatively what the Constitution means? Compare Wechsler, *The Courts and the Constitution,* 65 Colum.L.Rev. 1001, 1006–07 (1965)(maintaining the binding authority of Supreme Court precedent) with Caminker, *Why Must Inferior Courts Obey Superior Court Precedents?*, 46 Stan.L.Rev. 817, 837–38, 868–69 (1994)(arguing that inferior courts would have limited authority to reject Supreme Court precedents). Could all state courts realistically be expected to follow Supreme Court authority under such circumstances?

(5) *The "Parity" Debate.* Debates about congressional power to regulate federal jurisdiction are frequently bound up with disputes about the "parity" or "disparity" of state and federal courts. In thinking about the wisdom and constitutionality of restrictions on federal jurisdiction that would channel

16. See, *e.g.,* H.R. 326, 97th Cong., 1st Sess. (1981)(school prayer); H.R. 865, 97th Cong., 1st Sess. (1981)(school prayer); H.R. 867, 97th Cong., 1st Sess. (1981)(abortion).

17. For a discussion of legislation enacted during that era, see pp. 363–65, *infra.*

18. Gunther, *supra,* at 897 n. 9 (quoting Professor William Van Alstyne).

19. See, *e.g.,* S.481, 97th Cong., 1st Sess. (1981); S.1742, 97th Cong., 1st Sess. (1981).

litigation (especially of federal constitutional claims) exclusively to state courts, various forms of the "parity" question can be distinguished.

(a) *Parity as an Empirical or Sociological Concept.* For one set of debates, the relevant parity question is empirical or sociological, and asks whether state courts—in fact and on average—are as fair and as competent as federal courts.

(i) *Defining the Standard.* An immediate problem, however, involves the standard of comparison. Is the question whether federal or state courts are more likely to reach the *correct* resolution of constitutional issues, such as those involving prayer in public schools? If so, the parity question would seem inseparable from substantive issues about whether constitutional guarantees should be interpreted narrowly or broadly. In short, it would seem more normative than empirical or sociological.

Another way to frame the question is in terms of comparative sympathy or receptiveness to federal claims: are state courts as likely as federal courts to uphold claims of federal right? This question looks more capable of being given an empirical answer, and many commentators have explicitly adopted it— although others question the often implicit premise that giving a broader scope to federal rights is necessarily better. Compare Neuborne, *The Myth of Parity,* 90 Harv.L.Rev. 1105, 1105 (1977), with Bator *The State Courts and Federal Constitutional Litigation,* 22 Wm. & Mary L.Rev. 605 (1981).

(ii) *Time and Change.* In an influential contribution to the continuing debate, Professor Neuborne argued that three features of the federal courts tend to make them more sympathetic forums than state courts for the assertion of federal claims. See Neuborne, *supra.* (a) Federal judgeships are generally more prestigious and better paid than state judgeships and thus tend to be filled by more technically competent lawyers, who are more capable of grasping complex and novel arguments (p. 1121–22). (b) Federal judges, unlike the judges in all but a handful of states, enjoy life tenure and are therefore more insulated from majoritarian pressures to decide cases adversely to unpopular claims (p. 1127).[20] (c) Federal judges are participants in a proud tradition of protecting constitutional rights that may create a "psychological tilt" in favor of claims of constitutional rights (pp. 1124–27).

Are these arguments persuasive? Do they underestimate the influence of legal or political ideology and the extent to which the federal judiciary may be more or less liberal or conservative from time to time (largely as a result of whether liberal or conservative Presidents have appointed the most sitting judges)?[21] As will be discussed below, sound empirical studies are hard to come

---

20. For a broader argument that elective judiciaries are incompatible with the basis presupposition of constitutionalism that rights should be respected regardless of the views of democratic majorities, see Steven P. Croley, *The Majoritarian Difficulty: Elective Judiciaries and the Rule of Law,* 62 U.Chi. L.Rev. 689 (1995).

Compare the view of Judge Posner that Article III does not make federal judges *apolitical* so much as *autonomously political.* See Posner, The Federal Courts: Crisis and Reform 16 (1985).

21. When Jimmy Carter left the presidency in 1981, he had appointed approximately 40% of the federal bench, see Goldman, *Carter's Judicial Appointments: A Lasting Legacy,* 64 Judicature 344, 344 (1981), and an overall majority of federal judges had been appointed by Democratic presidents. By contrast, when George Bush left office in 1993, Republican Presidents had appointed more than 75% of the sitting federal judiciary. See Goldman, *Bush's Judicial Legacy: The Final Imprint,* 76 Judicature 282, 297 (1993).

by. By the early 1990s, however, when Republican Presidents had appointed a majority of sitting federal judges, the press began to report a large decline in the number of civil rights claims filed in federal courts and a corresponding increase in the number of such claims filed in state courts. See, *e.g.,* Cullen, *Scales Tip to State Courts,* The Boston Globe, p. 1, Dec. 28, 1991; Murphy, *Rights Cases Shift to State Courts,* The Boston Globe, p. 17, June 18, 1991. At about the same time, state supreme courts were increasingly reported to be upholding claims of rights, as a matter of state constitutional law, that had been rejected by the United States Supreme Court under the federal Constitution.[22]

(iii) *Empirical Studies.* Several reported studies have attempted to measure whether state courts, on average, are less likely than federal courts to uphold federal claims. (Note that this is not necessarily a measure of which courts are doing a better job of resolving federal claims *correctly.*) A prominent example is Solimine & Walker, *Constitutional Litigation in Federal and State Courts: An Empirical Analysis of Judicial Parity,* 10 Hastings Const.L.Q 213 (1983), which compared the decisions of federal district courts with those of state appellate courts concerning selected constitutional issues. The authors found that federal courts upheld the constitutional claim in 41% of the cases within their sample, while state courts did so in only 32% of the cases. Although this difference was "statistically significant"—*i.e.,* not random—the authors concluded that it was "unimportant", and interpreted the data as providing "support for the contention that there is no clear reluctance on the part of state courts to uphold a federal claim that would be upheld in federal district court" (pp. 240–41). In their view, the study established that " 'parity' does exist between federal and state courts" (p. 214–15). Among its weaknesses, however, the study by Solimine and Walker compared state appellate courts with federal trial courts and did not attempt to correct for possible differences in the content of the cases in state and federal court. For further criticisms, see Chemerinsky, *Parity Reconsidered: Defining a Role for the Federal Judiciary,* 36 U.C.L.A.L.Rev. 233, 261–69 (1988).

After examining the reported empirical studies, Professor Chemerinsky concludes that the methodological difficulties confronting inquiries of this kind—including those of controlling for differences in the types and difficulty of federal questions characteristically raised in state and federal court and of studying outcomes in state trial courts, which frequently fail to write opinions—are so daunting that, "[a]lthough parity is an empirical question, no empirical answer seems possible" (p. 273). Do you agree?

(b) *Parity as a Constitutional Concept.* A second question about "parity" is constitutional; it asks whether the Constitution (and Article III in particular) is indifferent whether adjudication occurs in a federal court or a state court. Anyone who believes that state courts are empirically less likely than federal courts to be hospitable to federal claims might feel a pull toward concluding, as a constitutional matter, that Article III requires a *federal* court to be available. Nonetheless, the constitutional and the empirical issue are conceptually distinct.

---

22. See, *e.g.,* Schuman, *The Right to "Equal Privileges and Immunities": A State's Version of "Equal Protection,"* 13 Vt. L.Rev. 221, 221 (1988); Wachtler, *Our Constitutions—Alive and Well,* 61 St. John's L.Rev. 381, 397 (1987); Doe v. Maher, 40 Conn.Sup. 394, 515 A.2d 134 (Conn.Super.Ct.1986)(regulation of funding for abortions violates rights of woman and physician under state constitution).

The pro-parity view regards the question of constitutional parity as resolved by the Madisonian Compromise, discussed at pp. 7-9, *supra,* and the structural logic of Article III: since Congress need not create any lower federal courts at all, Article III must be indifferent whether adjudication occurs in state or federal court; therefore state courts must be regarded as enjoying constitutional parity with federal courts.[23]

On the other side, some have advanced linguistic and structural arguments, often buttressed by the structural features stressed by Professor Neuborne, to support the position that Article III compels that the judicial power "shall be vested" in federal courts. Within the broad group embracing arguments of this kind, there are important differences, explored below, concerning both (a) whether Article III requires jurisdiction in the "inferior" federal courts or merely in *some* federal court (inferior or Supreme), and (b) whether this obligation extends to *all* of the nine categories of cases within the federal judicial power, or only to some (*e.g.,* constitutional cases, or in those defined by subject matter rather than party status, but not diversity cases).

The competing views about parity as a constitutional concept are much more fully explored on pp. 358-73, *infra.*

Sheldon v. Sill

49 U.S. (8 How.) 441, 12 L.Ed. 1147 (1850).
Appeal from the Circuit Court for the District of Michigan.

■ MR. JUSTICE GRIER delivered the opinion of the Court.

The only question which it will be necessary to notice in this case is, whether the Circuit Court had jurisdiction.

Sill, the complainant below, a citizen of New York, filed his bill in the Circuit Court of the United States for Michigan, against Sheldon, claiming to recover the amount of a bond and mortgage, which had been assigned to him by Hastings, the President of the Bank of Michigan.

Sheldon, in his answer, among other things, pleaded that "the bond and mortgage in controversy, having been originally given by a citizen of Michigan to another citizen of the same State, and the complainant being assignee of them, the Circuit Court had no jurisdiction."

The eleventh section of the Judiciary Act, which defines the jurisdiction of the Circuit Courts, restrains them from taking "cognizance of any suit to recover the contents of any promissory note or other chose in action, in favor of an assignee, unless a suit might have been prosecuted in such court to recover the contents, if no assignment had been made, except in cases of foreign bills of exchange."

The third article of the Constitution declares that "the judicial power of the United States shall be vested in one Supreme Court, and such inferior courts as the Congress may, from time to time, ordain and establish." The second section of the same article enumerates the cases and controversies of

---

23. See, *e.g.,* Bator, *supra;* Hart, *The Power of Congress to Limit the Jurisdiction of*   *Federal Courts: An Exercise in Dialectic,* 66 Harv.L.Rev. 1362 (1953).

which the judicial power shall have cognizance, and, among others, it specifies "controversies between citizens of different States."

It has been alleged, that this restriction of the Judiciary Act, with regard to assignees of choses in action, is in conflict with this provision of the Constitution, and therefore void.

It must be admitted, that if the Constitution had ordained and established the inferior courts, and distributed to them their respective powers, they could not be restricted or divested by Congress. But as it has made no such distribution, one of two consequences must result,—either that each inferior court created by Congress must exercise all the judicial powers not given to the Supreme Court, or that Congress, having the power to establish the courts, must define their respective jurisdictions. The first of these inferences has never been asserted, and could not be defended with any show of reason, and if not, the latter would seem to follow as a necessary consequence. And it would seem to follow, also, that, having a right to prescribe, Congress may withhold from any court of its creation jurisdiction of any of the enumerated controversies. Courts created by statute can have no jurisdiction but such as the statute confers. No one of them can assert a just claim to jurisdiction exclusively conferred on another, or withheld from all.

The Constitution has defined the limits of the judicial power of the United States, but has not prescribed how much of it shall be exercised by the Circuit Court; consequently, the statute which does prescribe the limits of their jurisdiction, cannot be in conflict with the Constitution, unless it confers powers not enumerated therein.

Such has been the doctrine held by this court since its first establishment. To enumerate all the cases in which it has been either directly advanced or tacitly assumed would be tedious and unnecessary.

In the case of Turner v. Bank of North America, 4 Dall. 10, it was contended, as in this case, that, as it was a controversy between citizens of different States, the Constitution gave the plaintiff a right to sue in the Circuit Court, notwithstanding he was an assignee within the restriction of the eleventh section of the Judiciary Act. But the court said,—"The political truth is, that the disposal of the judicial power (except in a few specified instances) belongs to Congress: and Congress is not bound to enlarge the jurisdiction of the Federal courts to every subject, in every form which the Constitution might warrant." This decision was made in 1799; since that time, the same doctrine has been frequently asserted by this court, as may be seen in McIntire v. Wood, 7 Cranch, 506; Kendall v. United States, 12 Peters, 616; Cary v. Curtis, 3 Howard, 245.

The only remaining inquiry is, whether the complainant in this case is the assignee of a "chose in action," within the meaning of the statute. * * *

The complainant in this case is the purchaser and assignee of a sum of money, a debt, a chose in action, not of a tract of land. He seeks to recover by this action a debt assigned to him. He is therefore the "assignee of a chose in action," within the letter and spirit of the act of Congress under consideration, and cannot support this action in the Circuit Court of the United States, where his assignor could not.

The judgment of the Circuit Court must therefore be reversed, for want of jurisdiction.

Ex Parte McCardle

74 U.S. (7 Wall.) 506, 19 L.Ed. 264 (1869).
Appeal from the Circuit Court for the Southern District of Mississippi.

[On February 5, 1867, Congress enacted legislation authorizing federal judges "to grant writs of habeas corpus in all cases where any person may be restrained of his or her liberty in violation of the constitution, or of any treaty or law of the United States". Act of Feb. 5, 1867, ch. 28, § 1, 14 Stat. 385. The main purpose of the Act was to establish federal habeas corpus jurisdiction to review detentions of prisoners by state and local authority; a jurisdiction to review federal detentions already existed. Among its provisions, the 1867 Act authorized a right of appeal from decisions of the circuit courts to the Supreme Court of the United States.

[McCardle, the editor of the Vicksburg Times, was arrested by federal military authorities acting pursuant to another piece of Reconstruction legislation, the Military Reconstruction Act. The charges against him, based solely on editorials published in his newspaper, included disturbing the peace, libel, incitement to insurrection, and impeding reconstruction. While he was awaiting trial, McCardle filed a habeas corpus petition with the federal Circuit Court for the Southern District of Mississippi, basing his application on the 1867 Act. The circuit court denied the petition, but nonetheless ordered McCardle released on bond pending decision of his appeal to the Supreme Court.

[McCardle's substantive arguments included a number of constitutional challenges to his threatened trial by court martial and, more generally, to the provisions of the Military Reconstruction Act placing ten states under military jurisdiction. The Court's decision in Ex parte Milligan, 71 U.S. (4 Wall.) 2 (1867), though not conclusive, suggested that these arguments might well be meritorious.[1]

[After the appeal had been argued but before conference or decision, Congress, over the President's veto, passed the Act of March 27, 1868, ch. 34, § 2, 15 Stat. 44, the second section of which provided: "* * * That so much of the act approved [February 5, 1867], entitled 'An act to amend "An act to establish the judicial courts of the United States," approved [September 24, 1789],' as authorizes an appeal from the judgment of the circuit court to the Supreme Court of the United States, or the exercise of any such jurisdiction by said Supreme Court on appeals which have been or may hereafter be taken, be, and the same is, hereby repealed."[2]]

---

1. Test cases also failed to produce a definitive adjudication on the merits in Mississippi v. Johnson, 71 U.S. (4 Wall.) 475, 501 (1867)(action to enjoin the President from executing the Reconstruction Acts dismissed for want of jurisdiction), and Georgia v. Stanton, 73 U.S. (6 Wall.) 50, 76–77 (1867)(action to enjoin executive branch officials from placing Georgia under military rule pursuant to Reconstruction Acts dismissed for want of jurisdiction).

2. For more historical background, see, e.g., Van Alstyne, *A Critical Guide to Ex Parte McCardle*, 15 Ariz.L.Rev. 229 (1973), and Fairman, Reconstruction and Reunion, 1864–88, Part One, ch. X (1971)(Volume VI of the Oliver Wendell Holmes Devise History of the Supreme Court of the United States).

The attention of the court was directed to this statute at the last term, but counsel having expressed a desire to be heard in argument upon its effect, and the Chief Justice being detained from his place here, by his duties in the Court of Impeachment, the cause was continued under advisement. Argument was now heard upon the effect of the repealing act. * * *

■ THE CHIEF JUSTICE delivered the opinion of the court.

The first question necessarily is that of jurisdiction; for, if the act of March, 1868, takes away the jurisdiction defined by the act of February, 1867, it is useless, if not improper, to enter into any discussion of other questions.

It is quite true, as was argued by the counsel for the petitioner, that the appellate jurisdiction of this court is not derived from acts of Congress. It is, strictly speaking, conferred by the Constitution. But it is conferred "with such exceptions and under such regulations as Congress shall make."

It is unnecessary to consider whether, if Congress had made no exceptions and no regulations, this court might not have exercised general appellate jurisdiction under rules prescribed by itself. For among the earliest acts of the first Congress, at its first session, was the act of September 24th, 1789, to establish the judicial courts of the United States. That act provided for the organization of this court, and prescribed regulations for the exercise of its jurisdiction.

The source of that jurisdiction, and the limitations of it by the Constitution and by statute, have been on several occasions subjects of consideration here. In the case of Durousseau v. The United States,* particularly, the whole matter was carefully examined, and the court held, that while "the appellate powers of this court are not given by the judicial act, but are given by the Constitution," they are, nevertheless, "limited and regulated by that act, and by such other acts as have been passed on the subject." The court said, further, that the judicial act was an exercise of the power given by the Constitution to Congress "of making exceptions to the appellate jurisdiction of the Supreme Court." "They have described affirmatively," said the court, "its jurisdiction, and this affirmative description has been understood to imply a negation of the exercise of such appellate power as is not comprehended within it."

The principle that the affirmation of appellate jurisdiction implies the negation of all such jurisdiction not affirmed having been thus established, it was an almost necessary consequence that acts of Congress, providing for the exercise of jurisdiction, should come to be spoken of as acts granting jurisdiction, and not as acts making exceptions to the constitutional grant of it.

The exception to appellate jurisdiction in the case before us, however, is not an inference from the affirmation of other appellate jurisdiction. It is made in terms. The provision of the act of 1867, affirming the appellate jurisdiction of this court in cases of *habeas corpus* is expressly repealed. It is hardly possible to imagine a plainer instance of positive exception.

We are not at liberty to inquire into the motives of the legislature. We can only examine into its power under the Constitution; and the power to make exceptions to the appellate jurisdiction of this court is given by express words.

What, then, is the effect of the repealing act upon the case before us? We cannot doubt as to this. Without jurisdiction the court cannot proceed at all in

---

* 6 Cranch, 312; Wiscart v. Dauchy, 3 Dallas, 321.

any cause. Jurisdiction is power to declare the law, and when it ceases to exist, the only function remaining to the court is that of announcing the fact and dismissing the cause. And this is not less clear upon authority than upon principle. * * *

It is quite clear, therefore, that this court cannot proceed to pronounce judgment in this case, for it has no longer jurisdiction of the appeal; and judicial duty is not less fitly performed by declining ungranted jurisdiction than in exercising firmly that which the Constitution and the laws confer.

Counsel seem to have supposed, if effect be given to the repealing act in question, that the whole appellate power of the court, in cases of *habeas corpus,* is denied. But this is an error. The act of 1868 does not except from that jurisdiction any cases but appeals from Circuit Courts under the act of 1867. It does not affect the jurisdiction which was previously exercised.**

The appeal of the petitioner in this case must be dismissed for want of jurisdiction.***

NOTE ON THE POWER OF CONGRESS TO LIMIT THE JURISDICTION OF FEDERAL COURTS

The question of Congress' power to limit federal court jurisdiction is not a unitary one. There are at least five separate issues, which this Note addresses in the following sequence: (i) the power of Congress to limit the jurisdiction of the lower federal courts on matters that continue to be within the jurisdiction of the Supreme Court; (ii) the power of Congress to limit the appellate jurisdiction of the Supreme Court over cases that continue to be within the jurisdiction of the lower federal courts; (iii) the power of Congress to withdraw certain matters from the jurisdiction of all *federal* courts (with state courts continuing to exercise jurisdiction over those matters); (iv) the power of Congress simultaneously to withdraw certain matters from the jurisdiction of both federal and state courts; and (v) the power of Congress to apportion jurisdiction among federal courts and, in particular, to divide responsibility for deciding issues presented by a single case.

A. Congressional Power to Exclude Cases from the Lower Federal Courts

(1) Assume, for the moment, that Congress excludes a class of cases—such as those involving school prayer—from the jurisdiction of the federal district courts but permits Supreme Court review of those cases following their decision by state courts. Congressional power to prescribe limits on the lower federal

---

** Ex parte McCardle, 6 Wallace, 324.

*** [Ed.] Following the suggestion in the penultimate paragraph of the McCardle opinion, the Court held in Ex parte Yerger, 75 U.S. (8 Wall.) 85 (1869), that the 1868 repealer act only affected the Court's appellate jurisdiction under the Habeas Corpus Act of 1867 and left intact its jurisdiction to entertain habeas corpus cases, which were not formally cast as "appeals", under Section 14 of the Judiciary Act of 1789, 1 Stat. 81–82. Terminology aside, the habeas corpus jurisdiction permitted the Supreme Court to exercise what was in effect review of lower federal court decisions. Adjudication of the challenges to military Reconstruction was again avoided, however, when the government released Yerger from the challenged military custody. See 2 Warren, The Supreme Court in United States History 496–97 (rev.ed. 1935).

courts' jurisdiction seems plainly contemplated by Article III and the Madisonian Compromise. Wouldn't it "make nonsense of" the compromise to hold that "the only power to be exercised is the all-or-nothing power to decide whether *none* or *all* of the cases to which the federal judicial power extends need the haven of a lower federal court"? Bator, *Congressional Power Over the Jurisdiction of the Federal Courts,* 27 Vill.L.Rev. 1030, 1031 (1982).[1]

If so, if there is any ground for objection under Article III, it would seemingly have to involve the *basis* for Congress' exercise of its acknowledged power. Do you agree with Professor Bator (p. 1031) that Article III and the Madisonian Compromise contemplate a general congressional power to make "political" judgments about the necessity or desirability of federal jurisdiction in particular classes of cases?

(2) *Mandatory Theories of Article III.* Notwithstanding the Madisonian Compromise and the historical practice reflected in cases such as Sheldon v. Sill, a variety of theories has been advanced to support a constitutional requirement of lower federal court jurisdiction in at least some cases. Nearly all of these theories build on views expressed by Justice Story.

(a) *The Views of Justice Story.* In his opinion for the Court in Martin v. Hunter's Lessee, 14 U.S. (1 Wheat.) 304 (1816), Justice Story wrote:

"* * * The language of [Article III] throughout is manifestly designed to be mandatory upon the legislature. Its obligatory force is so imperative, that congress could not, without a violation of its duty, have refused to carry it into operation. The judicial power of the United States *shall be vested* (not may be vested) in one supreme court, and in such inferior courts as congress may, from time to time, ordain and establish. Could congress have lawfully refused to create a supreme court, or to vest in it the constitutional jurisdiction? * * *

"If, then, it is a duty of congress to vest the judicial power of the United States, it is a duty to vest the *whole judicial power.* The language, if imperative as to one part, is imperative as to all. If it were otherwise, this anomaly would exist, that congress might successively refuse to vest the jurisdiction in any one class of cases enumerated in the constitution, and thereby defeat the jurisdiction as to all; for the constitution has not singled out any class on which congress are bound to act in preference to others.

"The next consideration is, as to the courts in which the judicial power shall be vested. It is manifest, that a supreme court must be established; but whether it is equally obligatory to establish inferior courts, is a question of some difficulty. If congress may lawfully omit to establish inferior courts, it might follow, that in some of the enumerated cases, the judicial power could

---

1. But see Goebel, History of the Supreme Court of the United States: Antecedents and Beginnings to 1801, at 246–47 (1971)(arguing the Congress must create lower federal courts and vest them with the full possible jurisdiction). Compare Eisenberg, *Congressional Authority to Restrict Lower Federal Court Jurisdiction,* 83 Yale L.J. 498 (1974). Professor Eisenberg asserts that the "national judiciary was intended * * * to be able to hear and do justice in all cases within

its jurisdiction" (p. 506). He then argues that since the Supreme Court can no longer perform this function alone, by reviewing every case that originates in state courts, it is "no longer reasonable to assert that Congress may simply abolish the lower federal courts" (p. 513). He concludes that "[t]he power to curtail [jurisdiction] is limited to prudent steps which help avoid case overloads" (p. 516). Do you find this argument persuasive?

nowhere exist. * * * Congress cannot vest any portion of the judicial power of the United States, except in courts ordained and established by itself; and if in any of the cases enumerated in the constitution, the state courts did not then possess jurisdiction, the appellate jurisdiction of the supreme court (admitting that it could act on state courts) could not reach those cases, and, consequently, the injunction of the constitution, that the judicial power *'shall be vested'*, would be disobeyed. It would seem, therefore, to follow, that congress are bound to create some inferior courts, in which to vest all that jurisdiction which, under the constitution, is *exclusively* vested in the United States, and of which the supreme court cannot take original cognizance. They might establish one or more inferior courts; they might parcel out the jurisdiction among such courts, from time to time, at their own pleasure. But the whole judicial power of the United States should be, at all times, vested either in an original or appellate form, in some courts created under its authority.

"This construction will be fortified by an attentive examination of the second section of the third article. The words are 'the judicial power *shall extend*,' & c. Much minute and elaborate criticism has been employed upon these words. It has been argued that they are equivalent to the words 'may extend,' and that 'extend' means to widen to new cases not before within the scope of the power. For the reasons which have been already stated, we are of opinion that the words are used in an imperative sense. They import an absolute grant of judicial power" (pp. 328–31).

A few pages later, Justice Story continued:

"[T]here are two classes of cases enumerated in the constitution, between which a distinction seems to be drawn. The first class includes cases arising under the constitution, laws, and treaties of the United States; cases affecting ambassadors, other public ministers and consuls, and cases of admiralty and maritime jurisdiction. In this class the expression is, and that the judicial power shall extend to *all cases*; but in the subsequent part of the clause which embraces all the other cases of national cognizance, and forms the second class, the word *'all'* is dropped seemingly *ex industria*. Here the judicial authority is to extend to controversies (not to *all* controversies) to which the United States shall be a party, & c. From this difference of phraseology, perhaps, a difference of constitutional intention may, with propriety, be inferred. It is hardly to be presumed that the variation in the language could have been accidental. It must have been the result of some determinate reason; and it is not very difficult to find a reason sufficient to support the apparent change of intention. In respect to the first class, it may well have been the intention of the framers of the constitution imperatively to extend the judicial power either in an original form or appellate form to *all cases;* and in the latter class to leave it to congress to qualify the jurisdiction, original or appellate, in such manner as public policy might dictate.

"The vital importance of all the cases enumerated in the first class to the national sovereignty, might warrant such a distinction. * * * All these cases, then, enter into the national policy, affect the national rights, and may compromit the national sovereignty. The original or appellate jurisdiction ought not, therefore, to be restrained, but should be commensurate with the mischiefs intended to be remedied, and, of course, should extend to all cases whatsoever.

"A different policy might well be adopted in reference to the second class of cases; for although it might be fit that the judicial power should extend to all controversies to which the United States should be a party, yet this power might not have been imperatively given, least it should imply a right to take cognizance of original suits brought against the United States as defendants in their own courts. It might not have been deemed proper to submit the sovereignty of the United States, against their own will, to judicial cognizance, either to enforce rights or to prevent wrongs; and as to the other cases of the second class, they might well be left to be exercised under the exceptions and regulations which congress might, in their wisdom, choose to apply. It is also worthy of remark, that congress seem, in a good degree, in * * * [the 1789 Judiciary Act] to have adopted this distinction. In the first class of cases, the jurisdiction is not limited except by the subject matter; in the second, it is made materially to depend upon the value in controversy" (pp. 333–36).

Note the three positions suggested in these excerpts. First, Justice Story argues that Congress is obligated to vest all of the judicial power "either in an original or appellate form" in some federal court. Second, he argues that if any cases described in Article III are beyond the jurisdiction of the state courts, and thus not capable of review on appeal from a state court to the Supreme Court, Congress would be obligated to create inferior federal courts in order that these cases might be entertained in some federal court. (The argument assumes that the cases do not fall within the Supreme Court's original jurisdiction.) Third, Justice Story appears to limit his argument of congressional obligation to the first three categories of cases described in Article III—to those in which the Framers used the adjective "all".[2]

How would these different positions bear on the question presented by Sheldon v. Sill? On the constitutionality of legislation removing federal district court (but not Supreme Court) jurisdiction over cases involving school prayer?

(b) *Contemporary Echoes of Justice Story's Arguments.*

Each of these three different positions developed by Justice Story in Martin v. Hunter's Lessee is echoed in contemporary debates.

(i) Based on a study of the historical materials, Professor Clinton has embraced a variant of the first position taken by Justice Story. He concludes that "Congress [must] allocate to the federal judiciary as a whole each and every type of case or controversy" within the scope of Article III "excluding, possibly, only those cases that Congress deemed to be so trivial that they would pose an unnecessary burden." Clinton, *A Mandatory View of Federal Court Jurisdiction: A Guided Quest for the Original Understanding of Article III*, 132 U.Pa.L.Rev. 741, 749–50 (1984); see also Clinton, *A Mandatory View of Federal Court Jurisdiction: Early Implementation of and Departures from the Constitutional Plan*, 86 Colum.L.Rev. 1515 (1986).[3] But the broad scope of the obligation that he infers runs into difficulties in interpreting the Exceptions Clause and in explaining the gaps left in federal jurisdiction by the Judiciary

---

2. A similar position with respect to the first of these categories—cases "arising under" federal law—was espoused by the Supreme Court reporter, Henry Wheaton, in a series of articles (signed "A Federalist of 1789") in *The New York American* in July and August 1821. (The identification of Wheaton as the author of these articles was made by Professor Gerald Gunther in the

course of his research on the Marshall Court.)

3. Clinton's view is challenged, based on a study of the first Judiciary Act, in Casto, *The First Congress's Understanding of Its Authority over the Federal Courts' Jurisdiction,* 26 B.C.L.Rev. 1101 (1985).

Act of 1789, see pp. 32-33, *supra,* notably with respect to diversity cases falling below the jurisdictional minimum.[4]

(ii) For a variant of Justice Story's second position, see Redish & Woods, *Congressional Power to Control the Jurisdiction of Lower Federal Courts: A Critical Review and a New Synthesis,* 124 U.Pa.L.Rev. 45 (1975). This argument builds on the assumption, which is hotly contested, that the Constitution precludes state courts from exercising jurisdiction in at least some cases in which the Constitution also requires that a court be available to rule on claims of legal right. See Tarble's Case, p. 459, *infra,* and the following *Note on Tarble's Case and State Court Proceedings Against Federal Officials.* As a preliminary matter, however, isn't this position in tension with the deliberate compromises of the Constitutional Convention and the resulting language of Article III, both of which reflected the understanding that the decision whether to create lower federal courts should be a matter for discretionary decision by Congress? See pp. 7-9, *supra.*[5]

(iii) Versions of Justice Story's third position have attained recent prominence as the result of influential articles by Professor Sager[6] and, especially, by Professor Amar.[7] The supporting arguments are explored more fully on pp. 370-73, *infra.* For now, note that this position is not incompatible with the result in Sheldon v. Sill, nor would it preclude the removal of federal district court jurisdiction in school prayer cases, as long as the Supreme Court retained jurisdiction to review state court decisions. For a discussion of the issues that would be raised if Congress attempted to preclude both federal original and appellate jurisdiction in cases presenting federal questions, see pp. 370-73, *infra.*

(3) *Internal and External Restraints.* Reserving the question whether Congress could simultaneously eliminate both original and appellate federal jurisdiction in cases covered by Justice Story's third argument for mandatory federal jurisdiction, consider the validity of the observation in Sheldon v. Sill that a statute prescribing limits on the jurisdiction of the lower federal courts "cannot be in conflict with the Constitution, unless it confers powers not enumerated therein". Is this a plausible claim? It is clear, isn't it, that Congress could not remove federal question jurisdiction over claims brought by plaintiffs who were black, or female, or Jewish?

The dictum in Sheldon presumably refers to conflict with Article III only. So understood, it asserts that there are no Article III (or what commentators

---

4. Sitting as a circuit judge in White v. Fenner, 1 Mason 520, 29 F.Cas. 1015 (C.C.D.R.I. 1818)(No. 17,547), Justice Story dismissed a diversity suit excluded from the statutory grant. Although pronouncing it "somewhat singular, that the jurisdiction actually conferred on the courts of the United States should have stopped so far short of the constitutional extent," he held the "court has no jurisdiction, which is not given by some statute" (pp. 1015–16). Were the dicta in Martin designed only to provide a basis for appeal to Congress?

5. Note, however, that state court availability may be limited by the reach of process when the relevant events occur overseas. *Cf.* Johnson v. Eisentrager, p. 365, *infra.*

6. Sager, *The Supreme Court, 1980 Term—Foreword: Constitutional Limitations on Congress' Authority to Regulate the Jurisdiction of the Federal Courts,* 95 Harv.L.Rev. 17 (1981).

7. See, *e.g.,* Amar, *A Neo–Federalist View of Article III: Separating the Two Tiers of Federal Jurisdiction,* 65 B.U.L.Rev. 205 (1985); Amar, *The Two–Tiered Structure of the Judiciary Act of 1789,* 138 U.Pa.L.Rev. 1499 (1990); Amar, *Reports of My Death Are Greatly Exaggerated: A Reply,* 138 U.Pa. L.Rev. 1651 (1990).

have sometimes called "internal") restrictions on Congress' power to limit lower federal court jurisdiction. But a statute barring the door to "suspect" classes of plaintiffs, even if it survived scrutiny under Article III, would surely run afoul of "external" restrictions imposed by other constitutional provisions, such as the equal protection component of the Fifth Amendment's Due Process Clause.

The statute at issue in Sheldon v. Sill did not plausibly violate any "external" limit on congressional power over jurisdiction, did it? Would any provision of the Constitution besides Article III bar Congress from withdrawing federal district court jurisdiction over challenges to prayer in public schools and buildings?

Professor Tribe has argued that to single out cases involving a particular category of constitutional claims for exclusion from the federal courts imposes an impermissible burden on the underlying constitutional right being asserted in those cases.[8] Note, however, that this argument rests heavily on the position that being required to litigate a federal question in a state court is a "burden". Given the Madisonian Compromise and the apparent underlying assumption that the allocation of original jurisdiction over federal claims is for Congress to decide, can it fairly be deemed a "burden", from a constitutional perspective, to send a case to a state court?

Is there a serious constitutional argument that the Reconstruction Amendments, and the fabric of judicial precedents construing them—although directed at the states, rather than at Congress—have relevantly altered the constitutional framework?[9]

(4) *The Norris–LaGuardia Act.* The Norris–LaGuardia Act of March 23, 1932, 29 U.S.C. §§ 101–115, narrowly restricted the authority of courts of the United States to issue a restraining order or a temporary or permanent injunction in "a case involving or growing out of a labor dispute", and provided that "yellow-dog"[10] contracts "shall not be enforceable in any court of the United States and shall not afford any basis for the granting of legal or equitable relief by any such court". The term "court of the United States" was defined to mean "any court of the United States whose jurisdiction has been or may be conferred or defined or limited by Act of Congress". The Act throughout was drawn as a limitation of the "jurisdiction" of those courts.

At the time of the Norris–LaGuardia Act's adoption, Truax v. Corrigan, 257 U.S. 312 (1921), had found state legislation similarly limiting employers' remedies to be unconstitutional. Somewhat more specifically, Truax found that the denial of *all* effective remedies for common law rights violations would offend due process (pp. 327–30). And, concerning injunctions, the Court held that state legislation depriving employers in labor disputes of injunctive reme-

---

8. See Tribe, *Jurisdictional Gerrymandering: Zoning Disfavored Rights Out of the Federal Courts,* 16 Harv.C.R.–C.L.L.Rev. 129, 142–43 (1981).

9. See generally Fallon, *Reflections on the Hart and Wechsler Paradigm,* 47 Vand. L.Rev. 953, 980–83 (1994), arguing that the Civil War Amendments reflected a conception of federalism different from that embodied in the original Constitution generally, and possibly Article III specifically, and claiming that

Federal Courts scholars should attend more self-consciously to resulting problems of "intertemporal synthesis". Compare Wells & Larson, *Original Intent and Article III,* 70 Tul.L.Rev. 75 (1995) (contending more broadly that reliance on the framers' intent to resolve federal courts issues is misguided).

10. A "yellow-dog" contract is one in which an employee agrees, as a condition of employment, not to join a labor union.

dies against the invasion of common law property rights, when injunctions were available to others who suffered similar invasions, violated the Equal Protection Clause (pp. 330–39). With respect to employers' substantive constitutional rights, Coppage v. Kansas, 236 U.S. 1 (1915), and Adair v. United States, 208 U.S. 161 (1908), had found a due process right to condition employment on an undertaking not to join a labor union or on non-membership.

In an employer's action for a federal court injunction against allegedly unlawful picketing and related activities, the Supreme Court, in Lauf v. E.G. Shinner & Co., 303 U.S. 323 (1938), cryptically rejected any suggestion that the Norris–LaGuardia Act's stringent restrictions on federal injunctions violated the Constitution. "There can be no question," the Court said, "of the power of Congress thus to define and limit the jurisdiction of the inferior courts of the United States" (p. 330).

Does Lauf v. Shinner establish that the Constitution does not "give people any right to proceed or be proceeded against, in the first instance, in a federal rather than a state court"? Hart, *The Power of Congress to Limit the Jurisdiction of Federal Courts: An Exercise in Dialectic,* 66 Harv.L.Rev. 1362, 1363 (1953)(hereinafter cited as "Hart, *Dialogue*").[11] Or should Lauf be read as resting on the narrow ground that withdrawal of the federal remedy sought on the specific facts of the case was constitutionally unexceptionable under Article III and the due process principles on which the plaintiff relied? See Young, *A Critical Reassessment of the Case Law Bearing on Congress's Power to Restrict the Jurisdiction of the Lower Federal Courts,* 54 Md.L.Rev. 132 (1995).[12]

Would it be fair to say that a purpose of the Norris–LaGuardia Act was to "burden" federal constitutional rights, as recognized by the Supreme Court, under the Due Process Clause? Consider also the pertinence of 28 U.S.C. §§ 1341, 1342, which preclude the district courts from entertaining certain constitutional challenges to state regulatory and taxing authority, and also reflect historic congressional disagreement with federal court decisions. (See Chap. X, Sec. 1(B), *infra.*)

Do these statutes, and the Supreme Court's acceptance of their constitutionality, establish that "the basic structure of article III affords" Congress the power to "redraw[] jurisdictional lines in part because it dislikes certain federal court decisions"? Gunther, *Congressional Power to Curtail Federal Court*

---

11. The Senate and House Judiciary Committees that drafted the Norris–LaGuardia Act believed that the availability of state remedies satisfied the Constitution. S.Rep. No. 163, 72d Cong., 1st Sess. 10 (1932); H.R.Rep. No. 669, 72d Cong., 1st Sess. 3 (1932). See also Frankfurter & Greene, The Labor Injunction 210–11 (1930).

Is it fair to say that the theory of the legislation was that the Constitution may impose more stringent limitations on state power to restrict state court jurisdiction than on federal power to restrict federal jurisdiction? Does this make sense?

12. Professor Young argues, *inter alia,* that (i) the Norris–LaGuardia Act did in fact allow labor injunctions in a narrow class of cases (p. 170); (ii) by 1938, when Lauf was decided, the Supreme Court no longer would have thought that the Due Process Clause required labor injunctions in any more than (at most) a narrow class of cases, of which Lauf on its facts was not a member (pp. 170–71, 176–78); (iii) the relevant holding of Truax v. Corrigan, which had found on its facts that a state could not withhold injunctions in cases arising from labor disputes, rested on the Equal Protection rather than the Due Process Clause (pp. 179–80); and (iv) the Supreme Court, in 1938, was not yet subjecting *federal* legislation to equal protection scrutiny (pp. 180–81).

Jurisdiction: An Opinionated Guide to the Ongoing Debate, 36 Stan.L.Rev. 895, 919–20 (1984).[13]

Would the analysis change if Congress' motive in withdrawing federal jurisdiction were to invite state court defiance of Supreme Court precedents interpreting the Constitution?[14]

(5) *Absence of State Court Jurisdiction.*   Are limits on federal jurisdiction permissible in a case beyond the reach of process of any state court?   See Eisentrager v. Forrestal, 174 F.2d 961 (D.C.Cir.1949).   Because the habeas corpus statute authorized federal courts to issue the writ only within their respective jurisdictions, the court of appeals found that no federal court had statutory jurisdiction to consider a petition by a person imprisoned by United States military authorities in Germany.   But the court held the statutory limitation unconstitutional, reasoning that Article III required "Congress to confer the whole of the federal judicial power upon some federal court" (pp. 965–66).   The Supreme Court reversed, saying only that the petitioners, who were German nationals confined upon conviction of war crimes, had failed to state a case.   Johnson v. Eisentrager, 339 U.S. 763 (1950).   The opinion does not make clear whether the detention was lawful or (whether lawful or not) simply beyond the reach of judicial inquiry.[15]

(6) *Affirmation of Congressional Power.*   For a broad restatement of congressional power over the jurisdiction of the lower federal courts, see Ankenbrandt v. Richards, 504 U.S. 689, 697 (1992), p. 1323, *infra* (affirming the power of Congress to create a "domestic relations" exception to federal diversity jurisdiction).

B.   Congressional Power over the Supreme Court's Appellate Jurisdiction

(1) *History.*   Article III's provision for congressional power to create "exceptions" to the Supreme Court's appellate jurisdiction was added to the Constitutional Convention's working draft by the Committee of Detail.   See p. 18,

---

13.   Compare Friedman, *A Different Dialogue: The Supreme Court, Congress and Federal Jurisdiction,* 85 Nw.U.L.Rev. 1 (1990), arguing that the bounds of authority established by the Constitution are "far less clear than commentary suggests" and that "the contours of federal jurisdiction are resolved as the result of an interactive process between Congress and the Court on the appropriate uses and bounds of the federal judicial power" (pp. 2–3).   A principal virtue of a "dialogic approach", Professor Friedman argues, is that "it is flexible enough to take into account changing conceptions of the roles of the lower federal courts and the Supreme Court in our constitutional system" (p. 3).   Replies to Professor Friedman's article, appearing in 85 Nw.U.L.Rev. 442–77 (1991), include: Amar, *Taking Article III Seriously: A Reply to Professor Friedman* (p. 442); Tushnet, *The Law, Politics, and Theory of Federal Courts: A Comment* (p. 454); and Wells, *Congress's Paramount Role in Set-*

ting the Scope of Federal Jurisdiction (p. 465).   See also Friedman, *Federal Jurisdiction and Legal Scholarship: A (Dialogic) Reply,* 85 Nw.U.L.Rev. 478 (1991).

14.   See Ely, *Legislative and Administrative Motivation in Constitutional Law,* 79 Yale L.J. 1205, 1306–08 (1970).   See also Gressman & Gressman, *Necessary and Proper Roots of Exceptions to Federal Jurisdiction,* 51 Geo.Wash.L.Rev. 495 (1983).

15.   In Burns v. Wilson, 346 U.S. 137 (1953), the Supreme Court, without discussing the issue, passed on a habeas corpus petition brought against the Secretary of Defense by a soldier held by the military in Japan; see the opinion of Frankfurter, J., commenting on the denial of rehearing, 346 U.S. at 844, 852 ("Petitioners have not discussed the question of jurisdiction, and the Government appears disinclined to argue it").   See also United States ex rel. Toth v. Quarles, 350 U.S. 11 (1955).

supra. Its intended purposes and possible limitations were not discussed on the floor of the Convention. Berger, Congress v. The Supreme Court 285–96 (1969), and Merry, *Scope of the Supreme Court's Appellate Jurisdiction: Historical Basis,* 47 Minn.L.Rev. 53 (1962), argue that the power to make exceptions to the appellate jurisdiction was intended to deal exclusively with the problem of appellate review of findings of fact by a jury. But this revisionist view has attracted little support.[16]

(2) *Can "Exceptions" Swallow the Rule?* Congress' power to limit the Supreme Court's appellate jurisdiction is presumably subject to the same "external" restraints from constitutional provisions other than Article III, such as the Due Process Clause, as is the power to define the lower courts' jurisdiction. See Paragraph (3), pp. 362–63, *supra.* But does Article III itself impose any limits on Congress' authority to create "exceptions"?

In his provocative and influential *Dialogue, supra,* Professor Hart offered the following exchange (66 Harv.L.Rev. at 1364–65):

"Q. * * * The *McCardle* case says that the appellate jurisdiction of the Supreme Court is entirely within Congressional control.

"A. You read the *McCardle* case for all it might be worth rather than the least it has to be worth, don't you?

"Q. No, I read it in terms of the language of the Constitution and the antecedent theory that the Court articulated in explaining its decision. This seems to me to lead inevitably to the same result, whatever jurisdiction is denied to the Court.

"A. You would treat the Constitution, then, as authorizing exceptions which engulf the rule, even to the point of eliminating the appellate jurisdiction altogether? How preposterous!

"Q. If you think an 'exception' implies some residuum of jurisdiction, Congress could meet that test by excluding everything but patent cases. This is so absurd, and it is so impossible to lay down any measure of a necessary reservation, that it seems to me the language of the Constitution must be taken as vesting plenary control in Congress.

"A. It's not impossible for me to lay down a measure. The measure is simply that the exceptions must not be such as will destroy the essential role of the Supreme Court in the constitutional plan. * * *

"Q. The measure seems pretty indeterminate to me.

"A. Ask yourself whether it is any more so than the tests which the Court has evolved to meet other hard situations. But whatever the difficulties of the test, they are less, are they not, than the difficulties of reading the Constitution as authorizing its own destruction?"

Is this argument persuasive?[17] In perhaps the most sustained effort to elaborate and apply the theory that Congress may not destroy the Supreme

---

16. Note the grammatical difficulties in limiting the exceptions power to questions of fact. Berger himself has substantially qualified his earlier position, especially with respect to matters arising under the Fourteenth Amendment. See Berger, Death Penalties: The Supreme Court's Obstacle Course 153–72 (1982); McAffee, *Berger v. The Supreme Court—The Implications of His Exceptions-Clause Odyssey,* 9 U.Dayton L.Rev. 219 (1984).

17. Hart's collaborator, Herbert Wechsler, appears not to think so:

Court's "essential role", Professor Ratner argues that, to be constitutionally valid, "exceptions" to the Court's appellate jurisdiction must not "negate" the Court's "essential constitutional functions of maintaining the uniformity and supremacy of federal law." Ratner, *Congressional Power Over the Appellate Jurisdiction of the Supreme Court,* 109 U.Pa.L.Rev. 157, 201–02 (1960). "[L]egislation that precludes Supreme Court review in every case involving a particular subject is an unconstitutional encroachment", he concludes (p. 201). See also Ratner, *Majoritarian Constraints on Judicial Review: Congressional Control of Supreme Court Jurisdiction,* 27 Vill.L.Rev. 929 (1981–82).[18]

How successful is Professor Ratner in giving content to the "essential functions" thesis? Is providing uniform application of federal law an irreducible aspect of the Supreme Court's role? If so, how does one explain the significant gaps in Supreme Court jurisdiction left by the provisions of the Judiciary Act of 1789—especially the lack of jurisdiction to review state court decisions upholding claims of federal right?[19] And if maintaining the supremacy of federal law is an essential function, is any scope left for the exceptions power in cases where there is an asserted conflict between federal law and state conduct? In light of difficulties such as these, Professor Gunther implies that essential functions arguments confuse "the familiar with the necessary, the desirable with the constitutionally mandated". Gunther, *supra,* at 905. Do you agree?

(3) *The Klein Case.* In United States v. Klein, 80 U.S. (13 Wall.) 128 (1871), plaintiff was the administrator of the deceased owner of property sold by agents of the government during the Civil War. He sued for the proceeds of the sale and recovered judgment in the Court of Claims, under legislation according this right of action to noncombatant rebel owners upon proof of loyalty. The Supreme Court had previously held that one who, like the decedent, had received a presidential pardon must be treated as loyal, and the Court of Claims awarded recovery on this basis. Pending appeal from the judgment by the United States, Congress passed an act providing in effect that no pardon should be admissible as proof of loyalty and, further, that acceptance without written protest or disclaimer of a pardon reciting that the claimant took part in or

"There is, to be sure, a school of thought that argues that 'exceptions' has a narrow meaning, not including cases that have constitutional dimension; or that the supremacy clause or the due process clause of the fifth amendment would be violated by an alteration of the jurisdiction motivated by hostility to the decisions of the Court. I see no basis for this view and think it antithetical to the plan of the Constitution for the courts— which was quite simply that the Congress would decide from time to time how far the federal judicial institution should be used within the limits of the federal judicial power; or, stated differently, how far judicial jurisdiction should be left to the state courts, bound as they are by the Constitution as 'the supreme Law of the Land * * * any Thing in the Constitution or Laws of any State to the Contrary notwithstanding.' Federal courts, including the Supreme Court, do not pass on constitutional questions because there is a special function vested in them to enforce the Constitution or police the other agencies of the government. They do so rather for the reason that they must decide a litigated issue that is otherwise within their jurisdiction and in doing so must give effect to the supreme law of the land. That is, at least, what Marbury v. Madison was all about. I have not heard that it has yet been superseded, though I confess I read opinions on occasion that do not exactly make its doctrine clear." Wechsler, *The Courts and the Constitution,* 65 Colum.L.Rev. 1001, 1005–06 (1965).

18. Attorney General William French Smith espoused this theory in a letter to Senator Strom Thurmond, May 6, 1982, printed in 128 Cong.Rec. S9093–97 (daily ed., May 6, 1982).

19. See pp. 32, 33 *supra.*

supported the rebellion should be conclusive evidence of the claimant's *disloyalty*. The statute directed the Court of Claims and the Supreme Court to dismiss for want of *jurisdiction* any pending claims based on a pardon.[20]

The Supreme Court held the supervening statute to be unconstitutional and affirmed the judgment of the Court of Claims. The brief opinion, which is hardly a model of clarity, includes at least three strands.

(a) The opinion emphasizes that the "denial of jurisdiction to this court, as well as to the Court of Claims, is founded solely on the application of a rule of decision, in causes pending, prescribed by Congress. The court has jurisdiction of the cause to a given point; but when it ascertains that a certain state of things exists, its jurisdiction is to cease and it is required to dismiss the cause for want of jurisdiction. * * * It seems to us that this is not an exercise of the acknowledged power of Congress to make exceptions and prescribe regulations to the appellate power" (p. 146).

Whatever else the Court may have had in mind, it is surely right, isn't it, that invocation of the language of "jurisdiction" is not a talisman, and that not every congressional attempt to influence the outcome of cases can be justified as the exercise of a power over jurisdiction?[21]

20. The statute provided that, with respect to any pending appeal in which a claimant had prevailed on proof of loyalty other "than such as is above required and provided, * * * the Supreme Court shall, on appeal, have no further jurisdiction of the cause, and shall dismiss the same for want of jurisdiction." Act of July 12, 1870, 16 Stat. 230, 235. Senator Edmunds, in response to a question whether this provision would simply require dismissal of the appeal (leaving the lower court judgment intact) said: "No; * * * we say they shall dismiss the case out of court for want of jurisdiction; not dismiss the appeal, but dismiss the case—everything." Cong.Globe, 41st Cong., 2d Sess. 3824 (1870).

21. In addition to the passage quoted in text, Klein contains other broad language questioning the power of Congress to "prescribe rules of decision to the Judicial Department of the government in cases pending before it" (p. 146). Given the context, such language should surely not be read as casting *general* doubt on the principle, clear since the decision in United States v. Schooner Peggy, 5 U.S. (1 Cranch) 103 (1801), that the courts are obligated to apply law (otherwise valid) as they find it at the time of their decision, including, when a case is on review, the time of the appellate judgment. See, *e.g.,* Carpenter v. Wabash Ry. Co., 309 U.S. 23 (1940); Vandenbark v. Owens–Illinois Glass Co., 311 U.S. 538 (1941); Cort v. Ash, 422 U.S. 66 (1975).

The general principle presupposes, however, that the law enacted by Congress must be otherwise valid, and thus anticipates the possibility of limits on Congress' power. The Court identified a constitutional limit on Congress' power to alter the applicable law in Plaut v. Spendthrift Farm, Inc., 115 S.Ct. 1447 (1995), p. 106, *supra.* Plaut held that Congress trenched on the judicial function under the separation of powers by enacting a statute that required Article III courts to reopen final judgments, entered before the statute's enactment, dismissing suits by one private party against another.

The scope of congressional power to influence the outcome in pending cases, and indirectly Klein's bearing on that issue, were also at stake in Robertson v. Seattle Audubon Soc'y, 503 U.S. 429 (1992). The case involved a challenge to a statutory provision that specifically noted two pending cases challenging the lawfulness of actions by the Bureau of Land Management and provided that "Congress hereby determines and directs that" certain actions by the Bureau satisfied "the statutory requirements that are the basis for [the two lawsuits]", 103 Stat. § 318(b)(6)(A), *quoted in* 503 U.S. at 432.

The Ninth Circuit, citing Klein, held the statute unconstitutional. Since the statute did not, "by its plain language, repeal or amend the environmental laws underlying this litigation", the court concluded that Congress had attempted to direct a result contrary to the law as judicially interpreted and thereby violated Article III (p. 1412).

The Supreme Court reversed. In the Court's view, Section 318 did not instruct a

(b) The Court found that the rule of decision in question impaired the effect of a presidential pardon and thus "infring[ed] the constitutional power of the Executive" (p. 147).[22]

(c) The Court suggested that jurisdiction-stripping legislation enacted "as a means to an end" that is itself constitutionally impermissible "is not an exercise of the acknowledged power of Congress to make exceptions and prescriptive regulations to the appellate power" (pp. 145–46).

Does this language support arguments that legislation precluding Supreme Court jurisdiction in cases challenging school prayer, for example, would be in service of a forbidden purpose and therefore beyond Congress' legitimate power to make exceptions to the Court's appellate jurisdiction?[23] Should Klein be read as holding no more than that an unconstitutional invasion of the judicial function occurs when Congress purports not to withdraw appellate jurisdiction

court in how to apply pre-existing legal standards to a pending case, but rather amended the statute. The Court thus found it unnecessary to consider whether (as the Ninth Circuit had concluded) Klein precludes Congress from directing a decision in a pending case without amending the governing law. (For an argument that Congress should not be able to dictate an outcome without changing the applicable law, because to do so would go beyond the legislative function of laying down general rules for which the legislature must accept political responsibility and intrude on the judicial function of deciding individual cases, see Redish, *Federal Judicial Independence: Constitutional and Political Perspectives*, 46 Mercer L.Rev. 697, 718–21 (1995).) The Court also declined to consider (because not properly presented) a broader argument that Klein restricts congressional power to enact amendments that sweep no more broadly than the range of applications at issue in pending cases.

22. Compare United States v. Sioux Nation of Indians, 448 U.S. 371 (1980), in which the Court upheld the constitutionality of a statute directing the Court of Claims to review the merits of a Fifth Amendment taking claim by the Sioux Nation, without reference to the res judicata effect of a previous Court of Claims decision favorable to the government. The Court distinguished Klein (over Justice Rehnquist's dissent) on the grounds that (1) in Klein, "Congress was attempting to decide the controversy at issue in the Government's own favor" and (2) "even more important, the proviso at issue in *Klein* had attempted to 'prescribe a rule for the decision of a cause in a particular way' * * * [while the amendment in the case at bar simply] waived the defense of res judicata so that a legal claim could be resolved on the

merits" (p. 405). Shouldn't the Court in Sioux Nation have added to the second distinction the point that the rule of decision prescribed in Klein was itself unconstitutional as an invasion of executive power?

23. Roughly contemporaneous cases decided on the authority of Klein include Armstrong v. United States, 80 U.S. (13 Wall.) 154 (1872), and Witkowski v. United States, 7 Ct.Cl. 393 (1872), in both of which the courts refused to be bound by the provision of the statute involved in Klein ordering courts to dismiss suits for want of jurisdiction upon the introduction of a pardon. According to Professor Young, these decisions take an important step beyond Klein, which in his terms involved a "puppeteering" provision of the statute ordering the Supreme Court to reverse a decision rendered by a lower court. See Young, *A Critical Reassessment of the Case Law Bearing on Congress's Power to Restrict the Jurisdiction of the Lower Federal Courts*, 54 Md.L.Rev. 132, 158–59 (1995). By contrast, Young argues, Armstrong and Witkowski involved a "court-stripping" portion of the statute purporting to deprive *trial* courts of jurisdiction over a defined class of cases. He concludes that "[i]t seems impossible to distinguish * * * the plaintiff in Armstrong from plaintiffs today who might seek federal court enforcement of modern constitutional rights, such as busing or abortion rights, despite a statute which purports to close off the federal courts" (p. 164). Do you agree? Under a statute that authorizes lower courts to entertain claims, but orders them to dismiss those claims for want of jurisdiction upon proof of a presidential pardon, is the line between "puppeteering" and "court stripping" as clear as Young suggests? If it is, on which side of the line do Armstrong and Witkowski belong?

completely, but to bind the Court to reach a result that is independently unconstitutional? *Cf.* Robertson v. Seattle Audubon Soc'y, note 21, *supra;* Public Citizen v. United States Dep't of Justice, 491 U.S. 440, 467 (1989)(Kennedy, J., concurring in the judgment).

For illuminating analysis of Klein and its significance for a variety of issues, see Young, *Congressional Regulation of Federal Courts' Jurisdiction and Processes:* United States v. Klein *Revisited,* 1981 Wis.L.Rev. 1189. See also Sager, note 6, *supra,* at 29, 70–77, 87–88.

(4) *Uncertainty and Its Consequences.* Is it perhaps politically healthy that the limits of congressional power over Supreme Court appellate jurisdiction have never been completely clarified? Does the existence of congressional power of unspecified scope contribute to the maintenance of a desirable tension between Court and Congress? In some circumstances, may not attempts to restrict jurisdiction be an important way for the political branches to register disagreement with the Court? And is it not enormously significant that, ever since McCardle, such "attempts" have, in the main, been just that—that Congress has not significantly cut back the Supreme Court's jurisdiction in a vindictive manner despite the great unpopularity of some of its rulings?

C. Congressional Power to Withdraw All Federal Jurisdiction

(1) *Framing the Issue.* Would *simultaneous* restrictions on lower federal court and Supreme Court appellate jurisdiction in the same class (or classes) of cases raise distinctive issues under Article III? Such limits have been historically accepted with respect to diversity cases, for example, but debate has swirled around the more central category of cases arising under federal law, and the Supreme Court appears never to have addressed directly the issues thus presented.

(2) *Constitutional Arguments.* As noted above, Justice Story developed the first, influential argument that denial of all federal jurisdiction of cases within Article III would offend the Constitution. The version of Justice Story's argument suggesting that all permissible jurisdiction must be vested in an Article III court in either original or appellate form, discussed on pp. 361–62, *supra,* is much embarrassed by the Judiciary Act of 1789—which is frequently viewed as a repository of insight into the original understanding of Article III—and by historical practice surrounding the diversity jurisdiction. See pp. 30, 33, *supra.* Recently, however, versions of another of Story's arguments—that Article III requires the vesting of federal jurisdiction in either original or federal appellate form in *some,* but not all, categories of cases—have achieved wide currency.

(a) Professor Sager has advanced an influential argument that the Constitution requires either original or appellate federal jurisdiction of *constitutional* claims. See Sager, *The Supreme Court, 1980 Term—Foreword: Constitutional Limitations on Congress' Authority to Regulate the Jurisdiction of the Federal Courts,* 95 Harv.L.Rev. 17 (1981). His thesis rests largely on the premise that these are the cases in which, in light of "the history and logic of the Constitution" (p. 45), there is the largest constitutional interest in adjudication by a judge with the safeguards from political influence established by Article III. How firmly is this appeal to "history and logic" anchored in the constitutional text? For criticism, see Redish, *Constitutional Limitations on Congressional Power to Control Federal Jurisdiction: A Reaction to Professor Sager,* 77 Nw.U.L.Rev. 143 (1982).

(b) Professor Amar has developed a somewhat more exhaustive argument that Article III requires the vesting of either original or appellate federal jurisdiction in three of the categories of cases listed in Article III, § 2. See, e.g., Amar, *A Neo–Federalist View of Article III: Separating the Two Tiers of Federal Jurisdiction*, 65 B.U.L.Rev. 205 (1985); Amar, *The Two–Tiered Structure of the Judiciary Act of 1789*, 138 U.Pa.L.Rev. 1499 (1990); Amar, *Reports of My Death Are Greatly Exaggerated: A Reply*, 138 U.Pa.L.Rev. 1651 (1990). In its textual dimension, Amar's argument (following Justice Story's) places considerable weight on the language of Article III, § 1 directing that the "judicial Power *shall* be vested" (emphasis added), but relies even more heavily on the selective use of the word "all" in Article III, § 2. With respect to the first three of the nine listed categories, Article III, § 2 says that the judicial power shall extend to "all cases". With respect to the remaining six, the word "all" is omitted, and Article III says simply that the judicial power shall extend to the denominated categories of "controversies". According to Amar, the text of Article III thus establishes two "tiers" of federal jurisdiction: a first tier, comprising the first three categories, in which federal jurisdiction (in either original or appellate form) is mandatory in "all cases"; and a second tier, consisting of the remaining six categories, in which the decision whether to vest federal jurisdiction is a matter for discretionary judgment by Congress.

This suggested interpretation leaves a role for congressional discretion, as contemplated by the Madisonian Compromise, about whether to create lower federal courts; federal appellate jurisdiction always suffices to satisfy Article III's mandate. The two-tier thesis also accords significance to Congress' power to create "exceptions" to the Supreme Court's appellate jurisdiction; even within the first tier of mandatory federal jurisdiction, exceptions are permissible wherever there is original federal jurisdiction. But what Congress may not do is to exercise its power to deny both Supreme Court and lower federal court jurisdiction with respect to the same class of cases within the mandatory tier.

Amar buttresses his proposed reading of Article III with a wide range of supporting arguments.

(i) Throughout the drafting process that eventually culminated in Article III, the central drafts approved by the Convention and the Committee of Detail all specified that the federal judicial power should extend to "all" cases arising under federal law, but omitted the "all" in listing other cases to which the judicial power would extend.

(ii) Despite some gaps, the 1789 Judiciary Act was reasonably consistent with the two-tier thesis.

(iii) Language supporting the two-tier thesis appears, not only in Martin v. Hunter's Lessee, but in other early Supreme Court opinions.[24]

(iv) The theory accords well with the structure of the Constitution, by ensuring adjudication in the cases of most profound national consequence by federal judges whose tenure and salary are constitutionally assured.

Amar's arguments on each of these points are skeptically probed in Meltzer, *The History and Structure of Article III*, 138 U.Pa.L.Rev. 1569 (1990).

---

24.   Amar cites American Ins. Co. v. 356 Bales of Cotton, 26 U.S. (1 Pet.) 511, 515 (1828); Osborn v. Bank of the United States, 22 U.S. (9 Wheat.) 738, 821–22 (1824); Cohens v. Virginia, 19 U.S. (6 Wheat.) 264, 378 (1821). See 138 U.Pa.L.Rev. at 1513 n.37. See also The Moses Taylor, 71 U.S. (4 Wall.) 411, 428–29 (1866); Stevenson v. Fain, 195 U.S. 165, 167 (1904).

(i) Meltzer notes that Amar's textual arguments are not self-evidently valid—that there are other possible explanations for the provision of jurisdiction of "all cases" in some categories and the reference to "controversies" in others.[25] Had the framers intended to establish the sharp distinction that Amar posits, other language could have made the point more clearly. What is more, Meltzer argues, there is virtually no support in either the Convention's records or the ratification debates for Amar's thesis. See 138 U.Pa.L.Rev. at 1578–82.

(ii) Meltzer argues that the fit between Amar's thesis and the 1789 Judiciary Act is less good than Amar suggests,[26] especially insofar as section 25 allowed review of federal questions decided in the state courts only when the decision was adverse to a claim of constitutional right.[27]

(iii) Meltzer views early Supreme Court dicta as much less probative than Amar suggests.

(iv) Meltzer challenges the claim that the two-tier thesis, with mandatory jurisdiction in the first tier, enjoys the "structural" superiority that Amar claims. Meltzer queries whether cases in which Amar views jurisdiction as mandatory—including cases of admiralty and maritime jurisdiction—are clearly more important than those in which the United States is a party and those between states, for example. See Meltzer, 138 U.Pa.L.Rev. at 1580–85. Meltzer also notes that "Charles Black, the dean of structural constitutional interpretation, has argued that congressional power to control federal court jurisdiction 'is the rock on which rests the legitimacy of the judicial work in a democracy.'" (p. 1621)(quoting Black, *The Presidency and Congress*, 32 Wash. & Lee L.Rev. 841, 846 (1975)).[28]

(3) *An Indian Law Perspective.* In Santa Clara Pueblo v. Martinez, 436 U.S. 49 (1978), the Supreme Court held that federal courts possess no jurisdiction over suits to enforce the federal Indian Civil Rights Act, 28 U.S.C. §§ 1301–03,[29] the express purpose of which is to "protect individual Indians

---

25. Perhaps most important, Meltzer argues, there is historical evidence that the framing generation understood the word "cases"—in contrast with the word "controversies"—to include both civil and criminal actions, and the word might have been used to indicate that both were encompassed. See Meltzer, 138 U.Pa.L.Rev. at 1574–76. (Amar replies that the historical evidence for the civil-criminal distinction is weak, and is in any event irrelevant because the explanation fails to make the word "all" anything but redundant. See Amar, 138 U.Pa.L.Rev. at 1656–57.)

26. On the 1789 Judiciary Act and the gaps in the jurisdiction that it conferred, see Chap. I, pp. 28–33, *supra*.

27. See, *e.g.*, Commonwealth Bank of Ky. v. Griffith, 39 U.S. (14 Pet.) 56 (1840)(denying jurisdiction to review a state court decision upholding a claim of federal right). Amar argues in response that a state court decision upholding a claim of federal right

would frequently trench on a federal right or interest of the opposing party and thus provide a basis for that party to seek Supreme Court review. For example, an overexpansive interpretation of the Article I, § 10 prohibition against bills of attainder "can be seen as a state court denial of the state's tenth amendment rights" that would have been reviewable, had the argument been framed properly, under section 25. See 138 U.Pa.L.Rev. at 1531. (Meltzer counters that this analytical claim corresponds poorly to historical understandings. See 138 U.Pa.L.Rev. at 1586–92.)

28. For other critical commentary, see Redish, *Text, Structure, and Common Sense in the Interpretation of Article III*, 138 U.Pa.L.Rev. 1633 (1990).

29. Although the Court found that there was no implied cause of action under the statute, the holding was limited to suits in federal court, and was explained partly by Congress' desire to respect tribal self-govern-

from arbitrary and unjust actions of tribal governments" by imposing "limitations on an Indian tribe in the exercise of its powers of self-government". S. Rep. No. 841, 90th Cong., 1st Sess. 6 (1967). Although the suits arise under federal law, enforcement actions can be filed only in tribal courts,[30] and there is no possibility of Supreme Court review.

Do the Indian Civil Rights Act and the Santa Clara Pueblo decision constitute a counterexample to the claim that Congress cannot preclude all federal jurisdiction over suits arising under federal law? An important counterexample? Does experience with the absence of any form of federal jurisdiction illustrate the normative attractiveness of theories such as Amar's, since tribal courts have often failed to enforce the Indian Civil Rights Act fully and fairly? See Worthen, note 29, *supra*, at 111–14. Or does it illustrate, at most, that Congress' decision may have been unwise?

D.   Congressional Preclusion of Both State and Federal Jurisdiction

(1) *Jurisdictional Limits and Judicial Review under the Portal-to-Portal Act.* The Fair Labor Standards Act of 1938, 29 U.S.C. §§ 201–219, guaranteed employees in industries covered by the Act compensation "at a rate not less than one and one-half times the regular rate" for a "work week longer than forty hours" and prescribed liability for unpaid overtime together with an additional, equal amount as liquidated damages.

In Tennessee Coal, Iron & R. Co. v. Muscoda Local No. 123, 321 U.S. 590 (1944); Jewell Ridge Coal Corp. v. Local No. 6167, 325 U.S. 161 (1945); and Anderson v. Mt. Clemens Pottery Co., 328 U.S. 680 (1946), the Supreme Court held that "work week", which the Act did not define, included underground travel in iron ore mines and similar preliminary and incidental activities of employees in connection with their work, which generally had not theretofore been regarded as compensable unless the parties so agreed.

Actions instituted in the federal district courts, based on these decisions, totaled 1,913 between July 1, 1946, and January 31, 1947, claiming in excess of $5,000,000,000. The potential liability of the United States on War Department cost-plus contracts was estimated at $1,400,000,000; and $128,500,000 was alleged to be owing by the Maritime Commission. See H.R.Rep. No. 71, 80th Cong., 1st Sess. 3, 4, 5 (1947).

Moved by these facts, Congress enacted the Portal-to-Portal Act of 1947, 29 U.S.C. §§ 251–62. The Act recited the finding of Congress that the recent decisions created immense, unexpected, and retroactive liabilities, which would result in financial ruin for many employers, unexpected windfall payments to employees, and serious financial consequences for the United States Treasury. Sections 2(a) and (b) of the Act then proceeded to wipe out the liabilities substantively by providing (with only limited exceptions) that "[n]o employer shall be subject to any liability or punishment" under the Fair Labor Standards

---

ment. See 436 U.S. at 70. Both federal and tribal courts have subsequently recognized that enforcement actions can be brought in tribal courts. See Worthen, *Shedding New Light on an Old Debate: A Federal Indian Law Perspective on Congressional Authority to Limit Federal Question Jurisdiction,* 75 Minn.L.Rev. 65, 90–91 (1990).

30. The one, partial exception involves federal habeas corpus actions, but many violations of the Act would not result in detention, and the custody requirement of habeas corpus jurisdiction would therefore not be satisfied.

Act for failure to compensate the preliminary and incidental work at issue. In addition, Section 2(d) provided:

"No court of the United States, of any State, Territory, or possession of the United States, or of the District of Columbia, shall have jurisdiction of any action or proceeding, whether instituted prior to or on or after May 14, 1947, to enforce liability or impose punishment for or on account of the failure of the employer to pay minimum wages or overtime compensation under the Fair Labor Standards Act of 1938, as amended, under the Walsh–Healey Act, or under the Bacon–Davis Act, to the extent that such action or proceeding seeks to enforce any liability or impose any punishment with respect to an activity which was not compensable under subsections (a) and (b) of this section."

The claim that the Act, in its retroactive operation, destroyed vested rights in violation of the Fifth Amendment was universally rejected on the merits. See, *e.g.*, Thomas v. Carnegie–Illinois Steel Corp., 174 F.2d 711 (3d Cir.1949). But the courts of appeals and most district courts treated it as open to decision, despite the jurisdictional provision and the separability clause. Judge Chase, writing for the Second Circuit in Battaglia v. General Motors Corp., 169 F.2d 254, 257 (2d Cir.1948), said:

"A few of the district court decisions sustaining section 2 of the Portal-to-Portal Act have done so on the ground that since jurisdiction of federal courts other than the Supreme Court is conferred by Congress, it may at the will of Congress be taken away in whole or in part. * * * [T]hese district court decisions would, in effect, sustain subdivision (d) of section 2 of the Act regardless of whether subdivisions (a) and (b) were valid. We think, however, that the exercise by Congress of its control over jurisdiction is subject to compliance with at least the requirements of the Fifth Amendment. That is to say, while Congress has the undoubted power to give, withhold, and restrict the jurisdiction of courts other than the Supreme Court,[a] it must not so exercise that power as to deprive any person of life, liberty, or property without due process of law or to take private property without just compensation. * * * Thus, regardless of whether subdivision (d) of section 2 had an independent end in itself, if one of its effects would be to deprive the appellants of property without due process or just compensation, it would be invalid." See also Seese v. Bethlehem Steel Co., 168 F.2d 58, 65 (4th Cir.1948), sustaining § 2(a) on the merits and then adding that "[w]hether the denial of jurisdiction would be valid if the provision striking down the claims were invalid is a question which does not arise".

(2) *The Reach of the Battaglia Principle.* Note that the court, in Battaglia, pointed to the Fifth Amendment, not Article III, in subjecting the Portal-to-Portal Act—including the provision purporting to preclude judicial review—to constitutional scrutiny. Under what circumstances might a withdrawal of jurisdiction from state and federal courts alike violate the Fifth Amendment?[31] In every case involving a claim to freedom from unconstitutional coercion? In

---

a. "It also has the power, of course, to make 'exceptions' to and 'regulations' regarding the Supreme Court's appellate jurisdiction. * * *"

31. It is hard to argue that due process requires the availability of jurisdiction in a *federal* court, isn't it? But see Redish, *Constitutional Limitations on Congressional Power to Control Federal Jurisdiction: A Reaction to Professor Sager*, 77 Nw.U.L.Rev. 143, 164–66 (1982).

every case presenting a constitutional claim, regardless of whether coercion is involved?

In Webster v. Doe, 486 U.S. 592 (1988), the Supreme Court held that, although Congress had precluded judicial review of non-constitutional claims based on an allegedly unlawful discharge by a former CIA employee against the CIA Director, Congress had not manifested its intent to preclude review of constitutional challenges with sufficient clarity for the statute to be construed as precluding such review. As part of its reason for demanding a "heightened showing" of intent to deny review of constitutional challenges, the Court cited an interest in avoiding the " 'serious constitutional question' that would arise if a federal statute were construed to deny any judicial forum for a colorable constitutional claim" (p. 603).

Other recent, important cases have similarly strained to construe statutes to permit judicial review of constitutional questions. See, *e.g.*, Bowen v. Michigan Academy of Family Physicians, 476 U.S. 667 (1986)(finding that Congress did not intend a statutory bar to judicial review of certain Medicare awards to encompass constitutional challenges and noting that the disposition avoided the "serious constitutional question" (p. 681 n.12) that would other-wise be presented); Johnson v. Robison, 415 U.S. 361, 366–67 (1974)(holding that a statute making benefits decisions of the Veterans Administration "final" and nonreviewable did not apply to constitutional challenges to the validity of legislative classifications, since preclusion would "raise serious questions con-cerning the constitutionality of" the provision generally barring judicial re-view). See also Bartlett v. Bowen, 816 F.2d 695, 699 (D.C.Cir.1987)(finding that Congress had not intended to preclude constitutional challenges to a provision of the Medicare Act, asserting that a preclusion of both state and federal judicial review would violate the Due Process Clause, and observing that "it has become something of a time-honored tradition for the Supreme Court and lower federal courts to find that Congress did not intend to preclude altogether judicial review of constitutional claims in light of the serious due process concerns that such preclusion would raise").

Note, however, that no Supreme Court case squarely holds that there is a constitutional right of access to a judicial forum in every case involving a constitutional claim. Does the political question doctrine refute the notion that courts must be available to rule on every claim of constitutional right? See Webster v. Doe, 486 U.S. at 612–13 (Scalia, J., dissenting)("we have found some constitutional claims to be beyond judicial review because they involve 'political questions' "). Does the doctrine of sovereign immunity? See Bartlett v. Bowen, 816 F.2d at 719–20 (Bork, J., dissenting)("the Supreme Court had never suggested * * * that there might be a constitutional difficulty in a statute that merely invoked sovereign immunity with respect to suits challeng-ing the constitutionality of a statutory denial of government benefits").

These are complex questions, but Justice Scalia and Judge Bork are surely right, aren't they, that (i) whether one has a constitutional right to judicial review is bound up with whether one has a constitutional right to a remedy, *and* (ii) as a result of sovereign and official immunity, among other doctrines, there may be circumstances in which the law provides no effective remedy for a particular violation of someone's constitutional rights? See Fallon, *Some Confusions About Due Process, Judicial Review, and Constitutional Remedies,* 93 Colum.L.Rev. 309, 329–39, 366–72 (1993). Questions involving rights to constitutional remedies and their relation to rights to judicial review are explored more fully in Chapter VII, pp. 847–77, *infra*. For now, consider the following, suggestive remarks from Professor Hart's *Dialogue*, 66 Harv.L.Rev. at 1366–71:

"Q. The power of Congress to regulate jurisdiction gives it a pretty complete power over remedies, doesn't it? To deny a remedy all Congress needs to do is to deny jurisdiction to any court to give the remedy.

"A. That question is highly multifarious. If what you are asking is whether the power to regulate jurisdiction isn't, in effect, a power to deny rights which otherwise couldn't be denied, why don't you come right out and ask it?

"Before you do, however, I'll take advantage of the question to make a point that may help in the later discussion. The denial of *any* remedy is one thing—that raises the question we're postponing. But the denial of one remedy while another is left open, or the substitution of one for another, is very different. It must be plain that Congress necessarily has a wide choice in the selection of remedies, and that a complaint about action of this kind can rarely be of constitutional dimension.

"Q. Why is that plain?

"A. History has a lot to do with it. Take, for example, the tradition of our law that preventive relief is the exception rather than the rule. That naturally makes it hard to hold that anybody has a constitutional right to an injunction or a declaratory judgment.

"But the basic reason, I suppose, is the great variety of possible remedies and the even greater variety of reasons why in different situations a legislature can fairly prefer one to another. That usually makes it hard to say, when one procedure has been provided, that it was unreasonable to make it exclusive. * * *

"Q. Please spell that out a little bit.

"A. Tax remedies furnish one of the best illustrations.

"More than a hundred years ago * * * the Supreme Court distressed Justice Story and many other people by holding that Congress had withdrawn the traditional right of action against a collector of customs for duties claimed to have been exacted illegally. [Cary v. Curtis, 44 U.S. (3 How.) 236 (1845).] Congress soon showed that it had never intended to do this, by restoring the right of action. But meanwhile the misunderstanding of the statute had produced a notable constitutional decision.

"Story thought it unconstitutional to abolish the right of action against the collector. The majority opinion by Justice Daniel poses very nicely the apparent dilemma which is the main problem of this discussion. It states the contention that the construction adopted would attribute to Congress purposes which 'would be repugnant to the Constitution, inasmuch as they would debar the citizen of his right to resort to the courts of justice'. In a bow to this position, it said: 'The supremacy of the Constitution over all officers and authorities, both of the federal and state governments, and the sanctity of the rights guarantied by it, none will question. These are *concessa* on all sides.'

"But then Justice Daniel stated the other horn of the dilemma as if it were an answer:

" 'The objection above referred to admits of the most satisfactory refutation. This may be found in the following positions, familiar in this and most other governments, viz: that the government, as a general rule, claims an exemption from being sued in its own courts. That although, as being charged with the administration of the laws, it will resort to those courts as means of securing this great end, it will not permit itself to be impleaded therein, save in instances forming conceded and express exceptions. Secondly, in the doctrine so often ruled in this court, that the judicial power of the United States, although it has its origin in the Constitution, is (except in enumerated instances, applicable exclusively to this court) dependent for its distribution and organization, and for the modes of its exercise, entirely upon the action of Congress, who possess the sole power of creating tribunals (inferior to the Supreme Court) for the exercise of the judicial power, and of investing them with jurisdiction either limited, concurrent, or exclusive, and of withholding jurisdiction from them in the exact degrees and character which to Congress may seem proper for the public good. To deny this position would be to elevate the judicial over the legislative branch of the government, and to give to the former powers limited by its own discretion merely.'

"Q. I can't see how to reconcile those two horns. How did Justice Daniel do it?

"A. He escaped by way of the power to select remedies. He said:

" 'The claimant had his option to refuse payment; the detention of the goods for the adjustment of duties, being an incident of probable occurrence, to avoid this it could not be permitted to effect the abrogation of a public law, or a system of public policy essentially connected with the general action of the government. The claimant, moreover, was not without other modes of redress, had he chosen to adopt them. He might have asserted his right to the possession of the goods, or his exemption from the duties demanded, either by replevin, or in an action of detinue, or perhaps by an action of trover, upon his tendering the amount of duties admitted by him to be legally due. The legitimate inquiry before this court is not whether all right of action has been taken away from the party, and the court responds to no such inquiry.'

"Q. Why bother with an old case that ducked the issue that way? What is today's law? Has a taxpayer got a constitutional right to litigate the legality of a tax or hasn't he?

"A. Personally, I think he has. But I can't cite any really square decision for the very reason I'm trying to tell you.[b] The multiplicity of remedies, and the fact that Congress has seldom if ever tried to take them all away, has prevented the issue from ever being squarely presented.

"For example, history and the necessities of revenue alike make it clear that the Government must have constitutional power to make people pay their taxes first and litigate afterward. Summary distraint to compel payment is proper. And injunctions against collection can be forbidden. But these decisions all proceeded on the express assumption that the taxpayer had other remedies.

---

b. [Ed.] Since the Dialogue was written, the Supreme Court has clearly recognized a due process right to litigate the constitutionality of a tax and, if the state provides no adequate opportunity before payment, to effective, post-payment remedies. See Reich v. Collins, 115 S.Ct. 547, 549 (1994). For further discussion, see Chap. VII, Sec. 2(C), *infra*.

"Correspondingly, a remedy after payment may be denied if the taxpayer had a remedy before, as Cary v. Curtis shows. Or the remedy may be conditioned upon following exactly a prescribed procedure. Rock Island, Ark. & La. Ry. v. United States, 254 U.S. 141 (1920).

"Q. The taxpayer has to watch out, then, or he'll lose his rights.

"A. He certainly does. As Justice Holmes said in the Rock Island case, 'Men must turn square corners when deal with the government.' That's true of constitutional rights generally. * * * There isn't often a constitutional right to a second bite at the apple.

* * *

"Q. * * * Granting [that there might be a constitutional right to litigate the constitutionality of taxes], you still have to reckon separately with the power of Congress to prevent its vindication by controlling jurisdiction. May I remind you of Sheldon and McCardle?

"A. There you go oversimplifying again.

"* * * The Bearing of Sovereign Immunity

"Q. Well, if it's too simple for you, let me complicate it a little bit. Justice Daniel mentioned sovereign immunity in Cary v. Curtis. That gives a double reason, doesn't it, why Congress has an absolute power over legal relations between the government and private persons? If it doesn't want to defeat private rights by regulating the jurisdiction of the federal courts, it can do it by withholding the Government's consent to suit.

"A. I can't deny that that does complicate things. But the power of withholding consent isn't as nearly absolute as it seems.

"Q. What mitigates it?

"A. You have to remember, in the first place, that the immunity is only to suits against the Government. This isn't the place to go into the question of what constitutes such a suit. My point now is that the possibility remains, as Cary v. Curtis indicates, of a personal action against an official who commits a wrong in the name of the Government.[c] Wherever the applicable substantive law allows such a remedy, the Government may be forced to protect its officers by providing a remedy against itself. The validity of any protection it tries to give may depend on its providing such a remedy and, indeed, the validity of other parts of its program. Consider, for example, the possibility that summary collection of taxes might be invalid if the Government did not waive its immunity to a suit for refund.

"Too, the Government may be under other kinds of practical pressure not to insist on its immunity. Take Government contracts, for example. * * * The business of the Government requires that people be willing to contract with it. * * * [T]his pressure made itself felt even before the Civil War and resulted in a blanket consent to suit [that has stood ever since] * * *.[d]

"Finally, no democratic government can be immune to the claims of justice and legal right. The force of those claims of course varies in different

c. [Ed.] On the personal responsibility of government officials in damages, see Chap. IX, *infra.*

d. [Ed.] See Chap. II, Sec. 2, pp. 111-15, *supra.* Some of the bracketed material in the

situations. If private property is taken, for example, the claim for just compensation has the moral sanction of an express constitutional guarantee; and it is not surprising that there is a standing consent to that kind of suit. 28 U.S.C. §§ 1346(a)(2), 1491(1). And where constitutional rights are at stake the courts are properly astute, in construing statutes, to avoid the conclusion that Congress intended to use the privilege of immunity, or of withdrawing jurisdiction, in order to defeat them."

In cases decided since Professor Hart wrote the *Dialogue*, the Supreme Court has held explicitly that the Constitution mandates the availability of effective remedies for "takings"[32] and for the coercive collection of taxes, and accordingly requires courts to provide those remedies, "the sovereign immunity States traditionally enjoy in their own courts notwithstanding". Reich v. Collins, 115 S.Ct. 547, 549 (1994). But it has not settled the question whether the Constitution mandates the availability of similar judicial protection for other rights.[33]

How does the possibility of constitutional violations for which the Constitution mandates no remedy relate to the right to judicial review contemplated by the Battaglia case? According to Hart, *Dialogue,* at 1372, it is "a necessary postulate of constitutional government" that "a court must always be available to pass on claims of constitutional right to judicial process, and to provide such process if the claim is sustained". Do you agree?[34]

Would a law precluding the use of forced busing as a remedy in school segregation cases offend the Constitution? Consider the argument of Fallon & Meltzer, *New Law, Non–Retroactivity, and Constitutional Remedies,* 104 Harv. L.Rev. 1731 (1991), that the constitutional tradition (which includes recognition of immunities for governments and their officials) reflects two remedial principles. The first, which prescribes that there should be individually effective redress for all violations of constitutional rights, is strong but not unyielding; it can sometimes be outweighed by the kinds of practical imperatives that underlie immunity doctrines, for example. The second, more structural principle, which "demands a system of constitutional remedies adequate to keep government generally within the bounds of law", is "more unyielding in its own terms, but can tolerate the denial of particular remedies, and sometimes of [any] individual redress' to the victim of a constitutional violation" (pp. 1778–79).

Would a serious constitutional question also be presented by preclusion of judicial review of suits alleging that official action has violated statutory, rather than constitutional, rights?[35]

---

text appeared in a footnote in the *Dialogue* as originally published.

32. See First English Evangelical Lutheran Church of Glendale v. Los Angeles County, 482 U.S. 304 (1987).

33. In a decision of uncertain but potentially large significance, Honda Motor Co., Ltd. v. Oberg, 114 S.Ct. 2331 (1994), held, 7–2, that an Oregon rule barring judicial review of the amount of jury punitive damages awards violates procedural due process. Justice Stevens' opinion for the Court rested heavily on nineteenth century common law practice, which he termed "a touchstone for constitutional analysis" (p. 2339).

34. See also Fallon, *supra,* 93 Colum.L.Rev. at 367–68: "[R]ights to review * * * define the judicial role as it has existed since Marbury v. Madison. Under Marbury, it is a judicial question whether there is a constitutional right to judicial review and, if review is granted and a violation of applicable norms is found, whether there is a right to a remedy."

35. For discussion, see Fallon, *Of Legislative Courts, Administrative Agencies, and Article III,* 101 Harv.L.Rev. 915, 976–86 (1988).

E. Congressional Apportionment of Jurisdiction Among Federal Courts and Limitations on the Authority of Enforcement Courts

(1) *The Price Control Act.* To combat wartime inflation, the Emergency Price Control Act of 1942, 56 Stat. 23, created the office of Price Administrator with the authority to issue regulations or orders fixing maximum prices and rents. To aid in enforcement, the Act created "a court of the United States to be known as the Emergency Court of Appeals" (ECA), to consist of three or more Federal District or Circuit Judges, and having "the powers of a district court with respect to the jurisdiction conferred on it", except that it had no power to issue any temporary restraining order or interlocutory decree staying the effectiveness of any order, regulation, or price schedule issued under the Act. Section 203(a) provided for attack on any order, regulation, or price schedule issued under the Act by filing a protest with the Administrator;[36] if the protest was denied, Section 204(a) gave the party aggrieved thirty days to file a complaint with the ECA. Section 204(d) provided that the judgments of that court could be reviewed by the Supreme Court. Section 204(d) also made the jurisdiction of the ECA (and of the Supreme Court on review of ECA's decisions) exclusive:

"Except as provided in this section, no court, Federal, State, or Territorial, shall have jurisdiction or power to consider the validity of any * * * regulation, order, or price schedule, or to stay, restrain, enjoin, or set aside, in whole or in part, any provision of this Act authorizing the issuance of such regulations or orders, or making effective any such price schedule, or any provision of any such regulation, order, or price schedule, or to restrain or enjoin the enforcement of any such provision."

Section 205 authorized the Administrator to bring suit to enjoin violations of the Act or secure an order directing compliance; declared willful violations criminal; and authorized treble damage suits in case of over-ceiling sales to be brought by a buyer or, in other cases, by the Administrator. Concurrent jurisdiction was conferred upon state courts, except in criminal prosecutions.[37]

(2) *The Lockerty Case.* Lockerty v. Phillips, 319 U.S. 182 (1943), involved a suit by wholesale meat dealers in a federal district court in New Jersey to restrain the United States Attorney from prosecuting violations of certain price regulations. The regulations and the Act were challenged on constitutional grounds.

The district court dismissed the suit for want of jurisdiction under § 204(d). The Supreme Court affirmed, with Chief Justice Stone writing (pp. 187–89):

36. As originally enacted, the statute required such a protest to be filed within 60 days after the issuance of the regulation or after the grounds of protest had arisen, but this time limit was removed in the Stabilization Extension Act of June 30, 1944, 58 Stat. 632.

37. As originally enacted, the statute made no provision for a stay of enforcement proceedings either to permit the filing of a protest or to await the disposition of a protest previously filed. The Stabilization Extension Act of June 30, 1944, 58 Stat. 632, however, added a new Section 204(e), which directed a stay of enforcement suits pending action on a protest already filed or review of its denial; it also gave a narrow scope for stays in certain cases to permit suits to be filed in the Emergency Court of Appeals where no protest had been filed.

"By this statute Congress has seen fit to confer on the Emergency Court (and on the Supreme Court upon review of decisions of the Emergency Court) equity jurisdiction to restrain the enforcement of price orders under the Emergency Price Control Act. At the same time it has withdrawn that jurisdiction from every other federal and state court. There is nothing in the Constitution which requires Congress to confer equity jurisdiction on any particular inferior federal court. All federal courts, other than the Supreme Court, derive their jurisdiction wholly from the exercise of the authority to 'ordain and establish' inferior courts, conferred on Congress by Article III, § 1 of the Constitution. Article III left Congress free to establish inferior federal courts or not as it thought appropriate. It could have declined to create any such courts, leaving suitors to the remedies afforded by state courts, with such appellate review by this Court as Congress might prescribe. * * * The Congressional power to ordain and establish inferior courts includes the power 'of investing them with jurisdiction either limited, concurrent, or exclusive, and of withholding jurisdiction from them in the exact degrees and character which to Congress may seem proper for the public good.' Cary v. Curtis, 3 How. 236, 245; Lauf v. E.G. Shinner & Co., 303 U.S. 323, 330. * * * In the light of the explicit language of the Constitution and our decisions, it is plain that Congress has power to provide that the equity jurisdiction to restrain enforcement of the Act, or of regulations promulgated under it, be restricted to the Emergency Court, and, upon review of its decisions, to this Court. Nor can we doubt the authority of Congress to require that a plaintiff seeking such equitable relief resort to the Emergency Court only after pursuing the prescribed administrative procedure. * * *

"Appellants also contend that the review in the Emergency Court is inadequate to protect their constitutional rights, and that § 204 is therefore unconstitutional, because § 204(c) prohibits all interlocutory relief by that court. We need not pass upon the constitutionality of this restriction. For, in any event, the separability clause of § 303 of the Act would require us to give effect to the other provisions of § 204, including that withholding from the district courts authority to enjoin enforcement of the Act—a provision which as we have seen is subject to no unconstitutional infirmity.

"Since appellants seek only an injunction which the district court is without authority to give, their bill of complaint was rightly dismissed. We have no occasion to determine now whether, or to what extent, appellants may challenge the constitutionality of the Act or the Regulation in courts other than the Emergency Court, either by way of defense to a criminal prosecution or in a civil suit brought for some other purpose than to restrain enforcement of the Act or regulations issued under it."[38]

38. Compare, with the provisions passed on in Lockerty, the Voting Rights Act of 1965, 42 U.S.C. § 1973, which provided that actions to exempt states from the coverage of the Act and actions to permit certain "suspended" state voting regulations to go into effect must be brought in the District Court for the District of Columbia. In South Carolina v. Katzenbach, 383 U.S. 301 (1966), the Court upheld this scheme, saying (pp. 331–32): "Congress might appropriately limit litigation under this provision to a single court in the District of Columbia, pursuant to its constitutional power under Art. III, § 1, to 'ordain and establish' inferior federal tribunals. See Bowles v. Willingham, 321 U.S. 503, 510–512; Yakus v. United States, 321 U.S. 414, 427–431; Lockerty v. Phillips, 319 U.S. 182. At the present time, contractual claims against the United States for more than $10,000 must be brought in the Court of Claims, and, until 1962, the District of Columbia was the sole venue of suits against federal officers officially residing in the Na-

(3) *Identifying the Proper Forum for a Constitutional Challenge.* In what court should the plaintiffs in Lockerty have attempted to test the constitutionality, under the Due Process Clause, of the Act's complete prohibition on interlocutory relief? Given that the jurisdiction of the Emergency Court was itself explicitly defined as not including the power to grant such relief, would their position have been stronger there than it was in the district court?

In a celebrated passage in his *Dialogue,* Professor Hart, who began with the assumption that Congress need not create any lower federal courts at all, pronounced the conclusion that state courts are "the primary guarantors of constitutional rights, and in many cases they may be the ultimate ones" (66 Harv.L.Rev. at 1401). Though Congress could withdraw all jurisdiction from the federal district courts, "[t]he state courts always have a general jurisdiction to fall back on", and in the exercise of that general jurisdiction they could strike down any unconstitutional limitation on their authority that Congress might attempt to impose.

If Professor Hart is correct that a state court would be obliged to pass on the validity of the remedial restriction in spite of the Act's provision completely withdrawing jurisdiction from state as well as federal courts, could Congress have meant the separability clause to deny a similar authority to the federal district courts?

Despite the force of Professor Hart's arguments concerning the ultimate power and responsibility of state courts, as a practical matter, the plaintiffs in Lockerty might have faced formidable obstacles to persuading a state court to rule on their challenge, due to the confusion surrounding state court power over suits against federal officers. See pp. 459-69, *infra.* But if it were assumed that a state court would not have been available to pass on the question, is it constitutionally tolerable for there to be *no* court in which the plaintiffs could raise their constitutional claim? In any event, doesn't the foundation for Lockerty's holding as to separability collapse?

(4) *Jurisdictional Limits on Enforcement Courts.*

(a) *The Yakus Case.* Yakus v. United States, 321 U.S. 414 (1944), presented one of the issues reserved in Lockerty: the status of a claim of invalidity of the Price Control Act or of a regulation as a defense to a criminal prosecution for a violation. Section 204(d) was interpreted to bar attack upon a regulation (at least one not invalid on its face) but not upon the Act itself. Thus construed, the provision was sustained against contentions that it effected a deprivation of due process, contravened the Sixth Amendment right to trial by jury of the state and district where a crime was committed, and worked an unconstitutional legislative interference with judicial power.

tion's Capital. We have discovered no suggestion that Congress exceeded constitutional bounds in imposing these limitations on litigation against the Federal Government, and the Act is no less reasonable in this respect."

South Carolina v. Katzenbach was an action to enjoin enforcement of various provisions of the Voting Rights Act, brought in the original jurisdiction of the Supreme Court. The parties do not seem to have referred to, and the Court decided the case without dis-cussing, section 14(b) of the Act, which provided that only the District Court for the District of Columbia "shall have jurisdiction to issue * * * any restraining order or temporary or permanent injunction" against enforcement of any provision of the Act. Did the Court, in deciding the case, sub silentio hold section 14(b) unconstitutional insofar as it restricted the Supreme Court's original jurisdiction? See Justice Black's dissent, 383 U.S. at 357 n.1; see generally Chap. III, pp. 294-96, *supra.*

On the due process issue, the opinion of the Court by Chief Justice Stone treats as the central question whether the procedure for review in the Emergency Court "affords to those affected a reasonable opportunity to be heard and present evidence" (p. 433). Concluding that it did, the opinion further holds that in "the circumstances of this case" there was "no denial of due process in the statutory prohibition of a temporary stay or injunction. * * * If the alternatives, as Congress could have concluded, were wartime inflation or the imposition on individuals of the burden of complying with a price regulation while its validity is being determined, Congress could constitutionally make the choice in favor of the protection of the public interest from the dangers of inflation" (pp. 437, 439). Upon the other issues, the opinion stated, *inter alia:*

"* * * [W]e are pointed to no principle of law or provision of the Constitution which precludes Congress from making criminal the violation of an administrative regulation, by one who has failed to avail himself of an adequate separate procedure for the adjudication of its validity, or which precludes the practice, in many ways desirable, of splitting the trial for violations of an administrative regulation by committing the determination of the issue of its validity to the agency which created it, and the issue of violation to a court which is given jurisdiction to punish violations. Such a requirement presents no novel constitutional issue * * *" (p. 444).

"Nor has there been any denial in the present criminal proceeding of the right, guaranteed by the Sixth Amendment, to a trial by a jury of the state and district where the crime was committed. Subject to the requirements of due process, which are here satisfied, Congress could make criminal the violation of a price regulation. The indictment charged a violation of the regulation in the district of trial, and the question whether petitioners had committed the crime thus charged in the indictment and defined by Congress, namely, whether they had violated the statute by willful disobedience of a price regulation promulgated by the Administrator, was properly submitted to the jury" (pp. 447–48).

Justice Rutledge, dissenting in an opinion in which Justice Murphy joined, found "the crux" of the case to lie in "the question whether Congress can confer jurisdiction upon federal and state courts in the enforcement proceedings, more particularly the criminal suit, and at the same time deny them 'jurisdiction or power to consider the validity' of the regulations for which enforcement is thus sought" (p. 467).

"It is one thing for Congress to withhold jurisdiction. It is entirely another to confer it and direct that it be exercised in a manner inconsistent with constitutional requirements or, what in some instances may be the same thing, without regard to them. * * * There are limits to the judicial power. Congress may impose others. And in some matters Congress or the President has final say under the Constitution. But whenever the judicial power is called into play, it is responsible directly to the fundamental law and no other authority can intervene to force or authorize the judicial body to disregard it. The problem therefore is not solely one of individual right or due process of law. It is equally one of the separation and independence of the powers of government and of the constitutional integrity of the judicial process, more especially in criminal trials" (p. 468).

After questioning the constitutional adequacy of the statutory procedure even in cases where it is pursued and the regulation under protest is declared invalid, Justice Rutledge found a "deeper fault" in a conviction "on a trial in two parts, one so summary and civil and the other criminal or, in the alternative, on a trial which shuts out what may be the most important of the issues material to * * * guilt" (pp. 478–79). Quoting the guarantee of jury trial in the Sixth Amendment and Article III, as well as the definition of the judicial power in Article III, he stated: "By these provisions the purpose hardly is to be supposed to authorize splitting up a criminal trial into separate segments, with some of the issues essential to guilt triable before one court in the state and district where the crime was committed and others, equally essential, triable in another court in a highly summary civil proceeding held elsewhere, or to dispense with trial on them because that proceeding has not been followed. * * * If Congress can remove these questions, it can remove also all questions of validity of the statute, or, it would seem, of law" (pp. 479–80).[39]

(b) *Falbo, Estep, and the Views of Professor Hart.* Consider the following excerpts from Professor Hart's *Dialogue*, 66 Harv.L.Rev. at 1380–83:

"Q. Does Yakus mark the maximum inroad on the rights of a criminal defendant to judicial process?

"A. No, unfortunately it doesn't. We have to take account of two World War II selective service cases, Falbo v. United States, 320 U.S. 549 (1944), and Estep v. United States, 327 U.S. 114 (1946). 'By the terms of' the selective service legislation, as Justice Douglas put it in Estep, 'Congress enlisted the aid of the federal courts only for enforcement purposes.' And so the question was sharply presented on what terms that could be done.

"The Court held in Falbo, with only Justice Murphy dissenting, that a registrant who was being prosecuted for failure to report for induction (or for work of national importance) could not defend on the ground that he had been wrongly classified and was entitled to a statutory exemption.

"Q. Doesn't that pretty well destroy your notion that there has to be some kind of reasonable means for getting a judicial determination of questions of law affecting liability for criminal punishment? All Congress has to do is to authorize an administrative agency to issue an individualized order, make the violation of the order a crime in itself, and at the same time immunize the order from judicial review. On the question of the violation of the order, all the defendant's rights are preserved in the criminal trial, except that they don't mean anything.

"A. Whoa! Falbo doesn't go that far. In Estep, after the fighting was over, the case was explained—and perhaps it had actually been decided—on the

---

39. Bowles v. Willingham, 321 U.S. 503 (1944), decided the same day, sustained the exclusion of the validity of the regulation from the scope of a civil action brought by the Administrator to enjoin a landlord from prosecuting in a state court a suit to restrain the issuance of an order reducing certain rentals to conform to the prescribed maximum. Concurring in the result, Justice Rutledge distinguished between such a civil proceeding and enforcement by criminal prosecution. He insisted, however, upon the following limitations, which he found to be satisfied: "(1) The order or regulation must not be invalid on its face; (2) the previous opportunity must be adequate for the pur-

pose prescribed, in the constitutional sense; and (3) * * * the circumstances and nature of the substantive problem dealt with by the legislature must be such that they justify both the creation of the special remedy and the requirement that it be followed to the exclusion of others normally available" (p. 526).

In Adamo Wrecking Co. v. United States, 434 U.S. 275 (1978), the Court dealt with issues similar to those in Yakus by construing the relevant statute to permit a particular defense to be raised in a criminal prosecution.

basis that the petitioner in failing to report for induction had failed to exhaust his administrative remedies. Considering the emergency, the requirement that claims be first presented at the induction center was pretty clearly a reasonable procedure.[a]

"Q. How about Estep?

"A. The petitioner there went to the end of the administrative road, and was indicted for refusing to submit to induction. The Court held that he was entitled to make the defense that the local board had 'acted beyond its jurisdiction'. Justice Douglas, speaking for himself and Justices Reed and Black, said (pp. 122–23):

" 'The provision making the decisions of the local boards "final" means to us that Congress chose not to give administrative action under this Act the customary scope of judicial review which obtains under other statutes. It means that the courts are not to weigh the evidence to determine whether the classification made by the local boards was justified. The decisions of the local boards made in conformity with the regulations are final even though they may be erroneous. The question of jurisdiction of the local board is reached only if there is no basis in fact for the classification which it gave the registrant.'

"Justices Murphy and Rutledge concurred specially on the ground that the Court's construction was required by the Constitution. Justice Frankfurter thought the construction wrong but concurred on the ground that there were other errors in the trial. Justice Burton and Chief Justice Stone dissented.

"Q. Well, the holding in the end wasn't such a departure after all, was it?

"A. Stop and think before you say that.

"Except for two Justices who are now dead, the whole Court dealt with the question as if it were merely one of statutory construction. Three Justices of the Supreme Court of the United States were willing to assume that Congress has power under Article I of the Constitution to direct courts created under Article III to employ the judicial power conferred by Article III to convict a man of a crime and send him to jail without his ever having had a chance to make his defenses.[b] No decision in 164 years of constitutional history, so far as I know, had ever before sanctioned such a thing. Certainly no such decision was cited. For these three didn't even see it as a problem. There is ground to doubt whether the first three in the majority did either.

"Bear in mind that the three dissenters from the Court's construction expressly recognized that the order of induction might have been erroneous in law. They said that the remedy for that was habeas corpus after induction. They seemed to say that the existence of the remedy of habeas corpus saved the constitutionality of the prior procedure. That turns an ultimate safeguard of

a. [Ed.] More recent cases indicate that even this "exhaustion" aspect of Falbo will be only selectively enforced, at least at a time when the nation is not fully engaged in war. Compare McKart v. United States, 395 U.S. 185 (1969) with McGee v. United States, 402 U.S. 479 (1971).

b. [Ed.] Would the objection to a refusal to permit a criminal defendant to show that an order of induction was erroneous in law lose its force if it were concluded that Congress might have made such an order a matter purely of the board's discretion? Is the power to do that material if the Congress has never exercised it?

Because Congress might have excluded the courts altogether from the process of raising an army in crisis, would it follow that it could also use them for the limited purpose of punishing as a civil crime a violation of a purely discretionary determination?

law into an excuse for its violation. And it strikes close to the heart of one of the main theses of this discussion—that so long at least as Congress feels impelled to invoke the assistance of courts, the supremacy of law in their decisions is assured."

(c) *The Mendoza–Lopez Case.* United States v. Mendoza–Lopez, 481 U.S. 828 (1987), presented the question whether an alien who had previously been deported, and was now being prosecuted for the crime of re-entry after having been deported, was entitled to challenge the validity of the underlying deportation order. The Court found that Congress had intended to preclude this form of collateral attack on deportation orders, but noted that the statutory determination "does not end our inquiry". Turning to constitutional issues, the Court first cited Yakus (along with other cases) for the proposition that "where a determination made in an administrative proceeding is to play a critical role in the subsequent imposition of a criminal sanction, there must be *some* meaningful review of the administrative proceeding" (pp. 837–38).[40] It then went on to hold that when defects in a prior deportation proceeding "effectively eliminate[d] the right of [an] alien to obtain judicial review", due process required that the alien be allowed to make a collateral challenge to the use of that proceeding as an element of a subsequent criminal offense (p. 839).

Chief Justice Rehnquist, joined by Justices White and O'Connor, dissented. Although agreeing that "there may be exceptional circumstances where the Due Process Clause prohibits the Government from using an alien's prior deportation as a basis for imposing criminal liability" (p. 842), the Chief Justice argued that the initial deportation proceedings had involved no due process violation and that there was no bar to relying on the prior deportation order on the facts of the case.

In a separate dissenting opinion, Justice Scalia contended that no prior decision of the Court "squarely holds that the Due Process Clause invariably forbids reliance upon the outcome of unreviewable administrative determinations in subsequent criminal proceedings" (p. 848). He continued:

"The Court's apparent adoption of that conclusion today seems to me wrong. To illustrate that point by one out of many possible examples, imagine that a State establishes an administrative agency that (after investigation and full judicial-type administrative hearings) periodically publishes a list of unethical businesses. Further imagine that the State, having discovered that a number of previously listed businesses are bribing the agency's investigators to avoid future listing, passes a law making it a felony for a business that has been listed to bribe agency investigators. It cannot be that the Due Process Clause

---

40. In a footnote appearing at this point, the Court said:

"Even with this safeguard, the use of the result of an administrative proceeding to establish an element of a criminal offense is troubling. While the Court has permitted criminal conviction for violation of an administrative regulation where the validity of the regulation could not be challenged in the criminal proceeding, *Yakus v. United States,* [*supra,*] the decision in that case was motivated by the exigencies of wartime, dealt with the propriety of regulations rather than the legitimacy of an adjudicative procedure, and, most significantly, turned on the fact that adequate judicial review of the validity of the regulation was available in another forum. Under different circumstances, the propriety of using an administrative ruling in such a way remains open to question. We do not reach this issue here, however, holding that, at a minimum, the result of an administrative proceeding may not be used as a conclusive element of a criminal offense where the judicial review that legitimated such a practice in the first instance has effectively been denied." 481 U.S. at 838 n.15.

forbids the State to punish violations of that law unless it either makes the agency's listing decisions judicially reviewable or permits those charged with violating the law to defend themselves on the ground that the original listing decisions were in some way unlawful."

Is Justice Scalia's argument by analogy persuasive?

Does the Mendoza–Lopez case cite Yakus correctly? Does it in any event effectively vindicate Professor Hart's position, including his criticisms of the opinions in Falbo and Estep?[41]

SECTION 2.   CONGRESSIONAL AUTHORITY TO ALLOCATE JUDICIAL POWER TO NON-ARTICLE III FEDERAL TRIBUNALS

Crowell v. Benson

285 U.S. 22, 52 S.Ct. 285, 76 L.Ed. 598 (1932).
Certiorari to the Circuit Court of Appeals for the Fifth Circuit.

■ MR. CHIEF JUSTICE HUGHES delivered the opinion of the Court.

This suit was brought in the District Court to enjoin the enforcement of an award made by petitioner Crowell, as Deputy Commissioner of the United States Employees' Compensation Commission, in favor of the petitioner Knudsen and against the respondent Benson. The award was made under the Longshoremen's and Harbor Workers' Compensation Act [33 U.S.C. §§ 901–950], and rested upon the finding of the deputy commissioner that Knudsen was injured while in the employ of Benson and performing service upon the navigable waters of the United States. The complainant alleged that the award was contrary to law for the reason that Knudsen was not at the time of his injury an employee of the complainant and his claim was not "within the jurisdiction" of the Deputy Commissioner. An amended complaint charged that the act was unconstitutional upon the grounds that it violated the due process clause of the Fifth Amendment, the provision of the Seventh Amendment as to trial by jury, that of the Fourth Amendment as to unreasonable search and seizure, and the provisions of article 3 with respect to the judicial

---

41. Compare Custis v. United States, 114 S.Ct. 1732 (1994), which ruled that a defendant in a federal sentencing proceeding generally has no constitutional right to mount a collateral attack on previous state convictions that are used for sentence enhancement. Writing for himself and five others, Chief Justice Rehnquist acknowledged Supreme Court precedent allowing defendants in sentence enhancement proceedings to attack prior convictions allegedly obtained without the assistance of counsel. The Chief Justice reasoned, however, that the failure to appoint counsel for an indigent defendant was a "unique" constitutional violation that rose to the level of "a jurisdictional defect." In support of limiting collateral attacks to cases involving the failure to appoint counsel for indigent defendants, the Court asserted that determination of constitutional claims such as the petitioner's claim of ineffective assistance of counsel "would require sentencing courts to rummage through frequently nonexistent or difficult to obtain state court transcripts or records" (pp. 1738–39).

Justice Souter, joined by Justices Blackmun and Stevens, dissented on statutory grounds.

Neither the majority nor the dissenting opinion cited Mendoza–Lopez. Was this an oversight? Is Custis consistent with Mendoza–Lopez?

power of the United States. The District Judge denied motions to dismiss and granted a hearing de novo upon the facts and the law, expressing the opinion that the act would be invalid if not construed to permit such a hearing. The case was transferred to the admiralty docket, answers were filed presenting the issue as to the fact of employment, and, the evidence of both parties having been heard, the District Court decided that Knudsen was not in the employ of the petitioner and restrained the enforcement of the award. The decree was affirmed by the Circuit Court of Appeals and this Court granted writs of certiorari. 283 U.S. 814.

The question of the validity of the act may be considered in relation to (1) its provisions defining substantive rights and (2) its procedural requirements. * * *

[The first part of the opinion sustains the substantive provisions of the Act as a proper exercise of "the general authority of the Congress to alter or revise the maritime law which shall prevail throughout the country".

[The second part of the opinion begins by describing the procedural provisions of the Act and the provisions for judicial review. Awards may be made by a deputy commissioner only after investigation, notice, and hearing. They may be enforced by a federal district court, on application of beneficiaries or of the deputy commissioner, if found to have been "made and served in accordance with law". Or they may be suspended or set aside, in whole or in part, on application of a respondent if "not in accordance with law".]

Second. The objections to the procedural requirements of the act relate to the extent of the administrative authority which it confers. * * *

1. The contention under the due process clause of the Fifth Amendment relates to the determination of questions of fact. Rulings of the deputy commissioner upon questions of law are without finality. * * *

Apart from cases involving constitutional rights to be appropriately enforced by proceedings in court, there can be no doubt that the act contemplates that as to questions of fact, arising with respect to injuries to employees within the purview of the act, the findings of the deputy commissioner, supported by evidence and within the scope of his authority, shall be final. To hold otherwise would be to defeat the obvious purpose of the legislation to furnish a prompt, continuous, expert, and inexpensive method for dealing with a class of questions of fact which are peculiarly suited to examination and determination by an administrative agency specially assigned to that task. The object is to secure within the prescribed limits of the employer's liability an immediate investigation and a sound practical judgment, and the efficacy of the plan depends upon the finality of the determinations of fact with respect to the circumstances, nature, extent, and consequences of the employee's injuries and the amount of compensation that should be awarded. And this finality may also be regarded as extending to the determination of the question of fact whether the injury "was occasioned solely by the intoxication of the employee or by the willful intention of the employee to injure or kill himself or another." While the exclusion of compensation in such cases is found in what are called "coverage" provisions of the act (section 3 [33 U.S.C.A. § 903]), the question of fact still belongs to the contemplated routine of administration, for the case is one of employment within the scope of the act, and the cause of the injury sustained by the employee as well as its character and effect must be ascertained in applying the provisions for compensation. The use of the administrative method for these purposes, assuming due notice, proper opportunity to be heard, and that findings are based upon evidence, falls easily within the principle of the decisions sustaining similar procedure against objections under the due process clauses of the Fifth and Fourteenth Amendments. * * *

2. The contention based upon the judicial power of the United States, as extended "to all cases of admiralty and maritime jurisdiction" (Const. Art. III), presents a distinct question. * * *

The question in the instant case, in this aspect, can be deemed to relate only to determinations of fact. The reservation of legal questions is to the same court that has jurisdiction in admiralty, and the mere fact that the court is not described as such is unimportant. * * * The Congress did not attempt to define questions of law, and the generality of the description leaves no doubt of the intention to reserve to the Federal court full authority to pass upon all matters which this Court had held to fall within that category. There is thus no attempt to interfere with, but rather provision is made to facilitate, the exercise by the court of its jurisdiction to deny effect to any administrative finding which is without evidence, or "contrary to the indisputable character of the evidence," or where the hearing is "inadequate," or "unfair," or arbitrary in any respect. * * *

As to determinations of fact, the distinction is at once apparent between cases of private right and those which arise between the government and persons subject to its authority in connection with the performance of the constitutional functions of the executive or legislative departments. The Court referred to this distinction in Murray's Lessee v. Hoboken Land & Improvement Company, 59 U.S. (18 How.) 272, 284 (1856), pointing out that "there are matters, involving public rights, which may be presented in such form that the judicial power is capable of acting on them, and which are susceptible of judicial determination, but which congress may or may not bring within the cognizance of the courts of the United States, as it may deem proper." Thus the Congress, in exercising the powers confided to it, may establish "legislative" courts (as distinguished from "constitutional courts in which the judicial power conferred by the Constitution can be deposited") which are to form part of the government of territories or of the District of Columbia, or to serve as special tribunals "to examine and determine various matters, arising between the government and others, which from their nature do not require judicial determination and yet are susceptible of it." But "the mode of determining matters of this class is completely within congressional control. Congress may reserve to itself the power to decide, may delegate that power to executive officers, or may commit it to judicial tribunals." Ex parte Bakelite Corporation, 279 U.S. 438, 451. Familiar illustrations of administrative agencies created for the determination of such matters are found in connection with the exercise of the congressional power as to interstate and foreign commerce, taxation, immigration, the public lands, public health, the facilities of the post office, pensions, and payments to veterans.

The present case does not fall within the categories just described, but is one of private right, that is, of the liability of one individual to another under the law as defined. But, in cases of that sort, there is no requirement that, in order to maintain the essential attributes of the judicial power, all determinations of fact in constitutional courts shall be made by judges. On the common-law side of the federal courts, the aid of juries is not only deemed appropriate but is required by the Constitution itself. In cases of equity and admiralty, it is historic practice to call to the assistance of the courts, without the consent of the parties, masters, and commissioners or assessors, to pass upon certain classes of questions, as, for example, to take and state an account or to find the amount of damages. * * *

* * * The statute has a limited application, being confined to the relation of master and servant, and the method of determining the questions of fact, which arise in the routine of making compensation awards to employees under the act, is necessary to its effective enforcement. The act itself, where it applies, establishes the measure of the employer's liability, thus leaving open for determination the questions of fact as to the circumstances, nature, extent and consequences of the injuries sustained by the employee for which compensation is to be made in accordance with the prescribed standards. Findings of fact by the deputy commissioner upon such questions are closely analogous to the findings of the amount of damages that are made according to familiar practice by commissioners or assessors, and the reservation of full authority to the court to deal with matters of law provides for the appropriate exercise of the judicial function in this class of cases. For the purposes stated, we are unable to find any constitutional obstacle to the action of the Congress in availing itself of a method shown by experience to be essential in order to apply its standards to the thousands of cases involved, thus relieving the courts of a most serious burden while preserving their complete authority to insure the proper application of the law.

3. What has been said thus far relates to the determination of claims of employees within the purview of the act. A different question is presented where the determinations of fact are fundamental or "jurisdictional,"[17] in the sense that their existence is a condition precedent to the operation of the statutory scheme. These fundamental requirements are that the injury occur upon the navigable waters of the United States and that the relation of master and servant exist. These conditions are indispensable to the application of the statute, not only because the Congress has so provided explicitly (section 3), but also because the power of the Congress to enact the legislation turns upon the existence of these conditions. * * *

In relation to these basic facts, the question is not the ordinary one as to the propriety of provision for administrative determinations. Nor have we simply the question of due process in relation to notice and hearing. It is rather a question of the appropriate maintenance of the federal judicial power in requiring the observance of constitutional restrictions. It is the question whether the Congress may substitute for constitutional courts, in which the judicial power of the United States is vested, an administrative agency—in this instance a single deputy commissioner—for the final determination of the existence of the facts upon which the enforcement of the constitutional rights of the citizen depend. The recognition of the utility and convenience of administrative agencies for the investigation and finding of facts within their proper province, and the support of their authorized action, does not require the conclusion that there is no limitation of their use, and that the Congress could completely oust the courts of all determinations of fact by vesting the authority to make them with finality in its own instrumentalities or in the

17. The term "jurisdictional," although frequently used, suggests analogies which are not complete when the reference is to administrative officials or bodies. In relation to administrative agencies, the question in a given case is whether it falls within the scope of the authority validly conferred.

executive department.   That would be to sap the judicial power as it exists under the federal Constitution, and to establish a government of a bureaucratic character alien to our system, wherever fundamental rights depend, as not infrequently they do depend, upon the facts, and finality as to facts becomes in effect finality in law.   * * *

* * *

In cases brought to enforce constitutional rights, the judicial power of the United States necessarily extends to the independent determination of all questions, both of fact and law, necessary to the performance of that supreme function.   The case of confiscation is illustrative, the ultimate conclusion almost invariably depending upon the decisions of questions of fact.   This court has held the owner to be entitled to "a fair opportunity for submitting that issue to a judicial tribunal for determination upon its own independent judgment as to both law and facts."   Ohio Valley Water Company v. Ben Avon Borough, 253 U.S. 287 (1920).   * * * Jurisdiction in the executive to order deportation exists only if the person arrested is an alien, and while, if there were jurisdiction, the findings of fact of the executive department would be conclusive, the claim of citizenship "is a denial of an essential jurisdictional fact" both in the statutory and the constitutional sense, and a writ of habeas corpus will issue "to determine the status."   Persons claiming to be citizens of the United States "are entitled to a judicial determination of their claims," said this Court in Ng Fung Ho v. White, 259 U.S. 276, 285 (1922), and in that case the cause was remanded to the federal District Court "for trial in that court of the question of citizenship."   * * *

[The Court then determined that, in order to avoid the serious constitutional question that would otherwise arise, the statute should be construed to permit the court "in determining whether a compensation order is in accordance with law" to "determine the fact of employment which underlies the operation of the statute".]

Assuming that the federal court may determine for itself the existence of these fundamental or jurisdictional facts, we come to the question, Upon what record is the determination to be made?   * * * We think that the essential independence of the exercise of the judicial power of the United States in the enforcement of constitutional rights requires that the federal court should determine such an issue upon its own record and the facts elicited before it. * * *

* * *

Decree affirmed.

■ Mr. Justice Brandeis (dissenting).

[The following excerpt from the long dissenting opinion indicates only one of the grounds of dissent.]

Sixth.   Even if the constitutional power of Congress to provide compensation is limited to cases in which the employer-employee relation exists, I see no basis for a contention that the denial of the right to a trial de novo upon the issue of employment is in any manner subversive of the independence of the federal judicial power.   Nothing in the Constitution, or in any prior decision of this Court to which attention has been called, lends support to the doctrine that a judicial finding of any fact involved in any civil proceeding to enforce a pecuniary liability may not be made upon evidence introduced before a properly constituted administrative tribunal, or that a determination so made may not be deemed an independent judicial determination. Congress has repeatedly exercised authority to confer upon the tribunals which it creates, be they administrative bodies or courts of limited jurisdiction, the power to receive evidence concerning the facts upon which the exercise of federal power must be predicated, and to determine whether those facts exist. The power of Congress to provide by legislation for liability under certain circumstances subsumes the power to provide for the determination of the existence of those circumstances. It does not depend upon the absolute existence in reality of any fact.

It is true that, so far as Knudsen is concerned, proof of the existence of the employer-employee relation is essential to recovery under the act. But under the definition laid down in Noble v. Union River Logging R. Co., 147 U.S. 165, 173, 174, that fact is not jurisdictional. It is quasi-jurisdictional. The existence of a relation of employment is a question going to the applicability of the substantive law, not to the jurisdiction of the tribunal. Jurisdiction is the power to adjudicate between the parties concerning the subject-matter. Obviously, the deputy commissioner had not only the power but the duty to determine whether the employer-employee relation existed. * * *

The "judicial power" of article 3 of the Constitution is the power of the federal government, and not of any inferior tribunal. There is in that article nothing which requires any controversy to be determined as of first instance in the federal District Courts. The jurisdiction of those courts is subject to the control of Congress. Matters which may be placed within their jurisdiction may instead be committed to the state courts. If there be any controversy to which the judicial power extends that may not be subjected to the conclusive determination of administrative bodies or federal legislative courts, it is not because of any prohibition against the diminution of the jurisdiction of the federal District Courts as such, but because, under certain circumstances, the constitutional requirement of due process is a requirement of judicial process. An accumulation of precedents, already referred to, has established that in civil proceedings involving property rights determination of facts may constitutionally be made otherwise than judicially; and necessarily that evidence as to such facts may be taken outside of a court. I do not conceive that article 3 has properly any bearing upon the question presented in this case. * * *

■ MR. JUSTICE STONE and MR. JUSTICE ROBERTS join in this opinion.

––––––––

NOTE ON CROWELL v. BENSON AND ADMINISTRATIVE ADJUDICATION

(1) *Historical Significance.* Henry Hart pointedly claimed that "[m]ost people * * * reading Crowell concentrate on what it said Congress could *not* do", but criticized this emphasis as a "simple mistake". Hart, *The Power of Congress to Limit the Jurisdiction of Federal Courts: An Exercise in Dialectic*, 66 Harv. L.Rev. 1362, 1374–75 (1953)(hereinafter cited as "Hart, *Dialogue*"). What did the Supreme Court say in Crowell that Congress *could* do in terms of investing federal administrative agencies with adjudicative authority?

In considering Professor Hart's assessment of the relative significance of Crowell's several holdings, note that by 1993, the federal government employed over 1,100 "administrative law judges"—executive branch officials, assigned to various federal agencies, who perform exclusively adjudicative functions and enjoy some statutory safeguards of decisional independence but lack life tenure and the Article III guarantee against reduction in salary. See Chap. I, p. ___, *supra*. Beyond those officials denominated as "administrative law judges", "studies undertaken for the Administrative Conference of the United States in the early 1990s identified 2700 federal administrative adjudicators (AJs) hearing on-the-record administrative adjudications * * *. Over 600 of these non-ALJ AJs have no other duties than hearing adjudications. * * * The ALJ and AJ groups each resolve roughly 350,000 on-the-record adjudications per year." Strauss, Rakoff, Schotland, & Farina, Gellhorn & Byse's Administrative Law Cases and Comments 959 (9th ed. 1995).

Because administrative adjudication is studied extensively in courses on Administrative Law, the discussion in this Note is necessarily brief and occasionally oversimplified. Nonetheless, any account of the contemporary role of the federal courts in the federal system would be seriously misleading if it did not reckon with (i) the vast scope of administrative adjudication, (ii) the relationship between administrative adjudicators and the Article III courts, and (iii) the strains that acceptance of administrative adjudication puts on efforts to develop a coherent theory of the necessary role of courts under Article III, the separation of powers, and the Due Process Clause.

(2) *Historical Foundations of Agency Adjudication.* How can Congress' vesting of any form of adjudicative power in federal administrative agencies be justified under Article III? Is it relevant that the first Congress assigned responsibilities to executive officials—including those of resolving disputes involving veterans' benefits and customs duties—that might instead have been vested in constitutional courts? See Fallon, *Of Legislative Courts, Administrative Agencies, and Article III,* 101 Harv.L.Rev. 915, 919 (1988).

Could Article III, the Due Process Clause, or the separation of powers reasonably be construed to exclude any role for adjudication by executive officials or administrative agencies? In Murray's Lessee v. Hoboken Land & Improvement Co., 59 U.S. (18 How.) 272 (1855), the Court upheld the power of an executive official to audit the accounts of a federal employee and, upon finding a deficit, to impose a summary attachment. In response to the argument that these were judicial acts that could be performed only by a court, the Supreme Court said: "[That the auditing of an official's accounts] may be, in an *enlarged* sense, a judicial act, must be admitted. So are all those administrative duties the performance of which involves an inquiry into the existence of facts and the application to them of rules of law. In this sense the act of the President in calling out the militia under [a federal statute] or of a commissioner who makes a certificate for the extradition of a criminal, under a treaty, is judicial" (p. 280).[1]

---

1. See also Bator, *The Constitution as Architecture: Legislative and Administrative Courts Under Article III,* 65 Ind.L.J. 233, 264–65 (1990): "Every time an official of the executive branch, in determining how faithfully to execute the laws, goes through the process of finding facts and determining the meaning and application of the relevant law, he is doing something which functionally is akin to the exercise of judicial power. Every time the Commissioner of Internal Revenue makes a determination that, on X facts, the Tax Code requires the collection of Y tax, and issues a tax assessment on that basis, or the Immigration Service determines that Z is a deportable alien and issues an order to deport, an implicit adjudicatory process is going on. Of course, many such executive determinations are informal. But it is only a step— and one quite consistent with the ideal of 'faithful' execution of the laws—from informal, implicit adjudication to the notion that

Since not every application of law to fact to determine legal rights can be deemed inherently judicial, isn't the question whether administrative adjudication is permissible under Article III a bit phony? Consider whether the real questions are not: (i) the extent to which the Constitution requires judicial *remedies* for injuries resulting from erroneous or unlawful actions by executive and administrative officials, and (ii) the extent to which an administrative official's or agency's findings of fact and law can be made *conclusive* on a court in subsequent litigation, including litigation to enforce an administrative judgment.

(3) *Constitutional Values at Stake.* What constitutional values need to be weighed in determining the outer bounds of Congress' power to vest authority that could instead by vested in Article III courts solely in administrative agencies or to give administrative findings conclusive effect in subsequent litigation?

Justice Brandeis, dissenting in Crowell, apparently regards the relevant constitutional norms as emanating entirely from the Due Process Clause. For the most part, he thinks, the Constitution is satisfied if the administrative process is sufficiently fair to satisfy due process, though occasionally "the constitutional requirement of due process is a requirement of judicial process" (p. 87). Is Justice Brandeis persuasive that "article 3 has properly [no] bearing upon the question presented"? Note the foundation of his argument. He assumes that Congress could confer jurisdiction of suits such as that in Crowell exclusively on the state courts, whose judges typically lack life tenure and guarantee against reduction in salary. If Article III is satisfied by adjudication in a state court, why shouldn't it also be satisfied by adjudication by a federal administrative agency?[2]

Writing for the majority, Chief Justice Hughes thinks that Article III concerns are implicated in one case but not the other. Why? Because federal agencies may be more susceptible than state courts to manipulation or control by Congress or the President? Because, even if state courts had exclusive original jurisdiction in cases involving federal claims, Article III might require federal *appellate* jurisdiction in at least some cases? What is the relationship of this question to the thesis discussed at pp. 370-73, *supra*, that Congress is

in making these determinations the official should hear the parties, make a record of the evidence, and give explicit formulations to his interpretation of the law. Determinations by the executive to apply law and judicial adjudication have a symbiotic relationship and flow naturally from and into each other. There is no *a priori* wall between them. * * * It is history and custom and expediency, rather than logic—or the text of the Constitution— that determine what needs to be the participation of the judges in the adjudicatory enterprise. * * * The judicial power is neither a platonic essence nor a pre-existing empirical classification. It is a purposive institutional concept, whose content is a product of history and custom distilled in the light of experience and expediency."

Professor Bator's article was the subject of a Symposium in the Indiana Law Journal.

Other articles in the Symposium include Easterbrook, *"Success" and the Judicial Power* (p. 277); Kramer, *The Constitution as Architecture: A Charette* (p. 283); Meltzer, *Legislative Courts, Legislative Power, and the Constitution* (p. 291); and Strauss, *Article III Courts and the Constitutional Structure* (p. 307).

2. Compare Meltzer, note 1, *supra*, arguing that review of federal administrative decisions is sometimes required by the Constitution, and, moreover, that if the constitutionally required review is by a federal tribunal, the judges must be Article III judges. Since due process does not generally require judges with life tenure (as, for example, in state court), Meltzer concludes that Article III must, at least in such cases, impose a requirement that the Due Process Clause does not impose (p. 299).

required to vest jurisdiction in *"all"* cases arising under federal law in some Article III court?

Consider the argument of Fallon, *supra,* that there are at least three Article III values at stake in cases such as Crowell: (i) ensuring fair adjudication to individual litigants, (ii) maintaining a system of judicial review and judicial remedies that suffices to keep government generally within the bounds of law, and (iii) preserving judicial integrity by not requiring a court to accept an agency's erroneous decision as conclusive of a legal issue and make that decision a predicate for the judicial imposition of civil or criminal penalties (pp. 937–43).

Are these values also embodied in the Due Process Clause? Ordinarily, of course, review of federal agency decisions is vested in Article III courts. But could Congress constitutionally provide that state courts have exclusive jurisdiction to review federal administrative adjudications denying claims for disability benefits under the Social Security Act? To review Federal Trade Commission cease-and-desist orders (which impose enforceable duties whose violation can lead to contempt citations)?[3]

(4) *Public Rights and Private Rights.* In fixing the bounds of constitutionally permissible adjudication by federal administrative agencies, Crowell v. Benson drew a categorical distinction between public rights and private rights.[4] The critical significance of the distinction was most influentially asserted in Murray's Lessee v. Hoboken Land & Improvement Co., *supra,* on which the Crowell decision specifically relied. The central passage from Murray's Lessee, which was only partly quoted in Crowell, is as follows (59 U.S. at 284):

"We do not consider Congress can either withdraw from judicial cognizance any matter which, from its nature, is the subject of a suit at the common law, or in equity, or admiralty; nor, on the other hand, can it bring under the judicial power a matter which, from its nature, is not a subject for judicial determination. At the same time, there are matters, involving public rights, which may be presented in such form that the judicial power is capable of acting on them, and which are susceptible of judicial determination, but which Congress may or may not bring within the cognizance of the courts of the United States, as it may deem proper."

(a) *Defining Public Rights.* Despite its historical lineage, the public rights category has never received a canonical formulation. Historically, however, three main classes of cases have formed the doctrine's core.

(i) Perhaps due to the influence of sovereign immunity, "claims against the United States" for "money, land or other things" have historically been regarded as involving public rather than private rights. Ex parte Bakelite Corp., 279 U.S. 438, 452 (1929).

(ii) Disputes arising from coercive governmental conduct outside the criminal law form a second component of the public rights category. Customs disputes are illustrative. The Supreme Court has established that government

---

3. Though stressing how unusual such arrangements would be, Meltzer, note 1, *supra,* argues that they would satisfy the requirements of Article III because the reviewing courts would be free from control by Congress or the federal executive. See pp. 299–300.

4. For a valuable history of the public rights doctrine, see Young, *Public Rights and the Federal Judicial Power: From Murray's Lessee Through Crowell to Schor,* 35 Buff. L.Rev. 765 (1986).

may coerce payment of duties at the border or seize disputed property and force the disputant to litigate later. See Bakelite, *supra,* 279 U.S. at 458. The Court has also settled that Congress can provide for subsequent litigation in federal tribunals other than Article III courts. *Id.*

(iii) "Apparently because of the longstanding assumption that the executive and legislative branches possess plenary power over immigration issues, the surrounding body of law falls within the public rights category." Fallon, *supra,* at 967.

(b) *Public Rights and Judicial Review.* Although the Supreme Court has sometimes suggested that public rights disputes can be removed from the purview of the courts altogether, the legal background has always included a range of common law and equitable remedies against government officers, who are often suable in their own names, even when the public rights and sovereign immunity doctrines bar unconsented suit against the government itself. Historically, this tradition of "officer suits" has diminished, but by no means eradicated, the tension between the public rights category on the one hand and, on the other, the ideal of the rule of law and the dictum of Marbury v. Madison promising a legal remedy for every deprivation of a legal right.

Did Crowell go unnecessarily far in suggesting that public rights cases could be committed exclusively to administrative adjudication? In this respect, how does Crowell fit with recent cases suggesting that there may be a right to judicial review of claims that administrative officials have violated constitutional rights? See pp. 374-75, *supra.*[5] With the weakening, if not the demise, of the right-privilege distinction?

(5) *The Judicial Power in Private Rights Cases.* Because Crowell was a private rights case, involving the liability of one private party to another, the Court, following the dictum in Murray's Lessee, assumed that Congress could not wholly preclude judicial consideration of the correctness of the administrative decision—at least in an action by a prospective defendant seeking to forestall an enforcement proceeding. The relevant question was thus the effect to be given to the administrative decision in the subsequent court action.

(a) *Questions of Fact.* As summarized by Professor Hart, "the apparently solid thing about Crowell is the holding that administrative findings of non-constitutional and jurisdictional facts may be made conclusive upon the courts, if not infected with any error of law, as a basis for judicial enforcement of a money liability of one private person to another". Hart, *Dialogue,* 66 Harv. L.Rev. at 1375. The Court apparently regarded this degree of agency conclusiveness as the minimum necessary to make the statutory scheme, including its contemplated reliance on administrative adjudication, workable. Should the Court have permitted this much transfer of adjudicative power from courts to agencies? How persuasive are the Court's analogies to the traditional judicial reliance on fact-finding by juries, masters, and commissioners?

In considering these questions, note that Congress' reasons for wanting to vest adjudicatory responsibility in administrative agencies have varied from time to time and from statute to statute. Recurrent themes include a desire to take advantage of specialized expertise, to adapt law and administration swiftly to changing priorities, and to avoid swelling the ranks of the Article III

---

5. For arguments that there is a constitutional right to judicial review of at least some questions in public rights cases, see Fallon, *supra,* at 950–91; Neuman, *The Constitutional Requirement of "Some Evidence",* 25 San Diego L.Rev. 631 (1988).

judiciary and thereby diminishing its prestige. In the case of statutes such as the Longshore and Harborworkers' Compensation Act, however, an additional impetus has involved the belief that regulatory statutes should be applied more purposively than neutrally, that adjudication furnished a fitting occasion for the elaboration of agency policy, and that fact-finding should be carried out in a way that promotes the remedial policies underlying particular statutes. Is this last rationale, in particular, in tension with constitutional values? See Strauss, note 1, *supra,* at 308–09.

Is it relevant that, in the years prior to Crowell, the Article III courts of the "Lochner era" were widely thought to have frustrated remedial schemes that departed from common law allocations of rights and responsibilities? In any case, was it naive or disingenuous for the Court to suggest that "the essential attributes of the judicial power" were all retained in Article III courts with agencies functioning as little more than fact-finding "adjuncts"?

(b) *Questions of "Jurisdictional Fact".* In striking a balance between the policies supporting expert implementation of remedial legislation on the one hand, and preservation of constitutional values on the other, the Court in Crowell insisted on de novo judicial review of questions of "jurisdictional fact"—that is, of those facts on which the jurisdiction of the agency depends. Earlier decisions had recognized a special need for de novo judicial review of agency determinations of "jurisdictional" facts, see Ng Fung Ho v. White, 259 U.S. 276 (1922), and also of "constitutional" facts—facts on which the adjudication of constitutional rights depends, see Ohio Valley Water Co. v. Ben Avon Borough, 253 U.S. 287 (1920). Which questions, in Crowell, did the Court regard as going to the jurisdiction of the agency?

What was Justice Brandeis' objection to the Court's identification of questions of jurisdictional fact? Does this category mark a sensible limitation on the bounds of an agency's power to adjudicate? Or is the line between jurisdictional and ordinary facts too uncertain to be administerable?

Although the distinction between constitutional and other facts was retained, an important shift of emphasis could be discerned in St. Joseph Stock Yards Co. v. United States, 298 U.S. 38, 54 (1936), which suggested that all relevant evidence should ordinarily be submitted to the agency and that review on the agency's record might therefore be sufficient in all but extraordinary cases. Today, the vitality of the constitutional and jurisdictional fact doctrines is disputed. It seems clear, however, that the requirement of independent judicial judgment on questions of jurisdictional fact is infrequently applied, and that independent judicial fact-finding—rather than redetermination of facts on the administrative record—virtually never occurs. See generally Monaghan, *Constitutional Fact Review,* 85 Colum.L.Rev. 229 (1985).

(c) *Questions of Law.* The Court in Crowell appeared to assume that Article III, the Due Process Clause, or both required independent judicial decision of questions of law in private rights cases. Has this assumption withstood more recent developments in administrative law?

Beginning as early as the 1940s, cases such as Gray v. Powell, 314 U.S. 402 (1941), and National Labor Relations Board v. Hearst Pub., Inc., 322 U.S. 111 (1944), suggested that courts should give deference to agency interpretations of their governing statutes. More recently, the important decision in Chevron v. Natural Resources Defense Council, 467 U.S. 837, 842–43 (1984), elaborates a two-step process to be followed by courts reviewing agency interpretations:

"When a court reviews an agency's construction of the statute which it administers, it is confronted with two questions. First, always, is the question whether Congress has directly spoken to the precise question at issue. If the intent of Congress is clear, that is the end of the matter * * * . If, however, the court determines Congress has not directly addressed the precise question at issue, the court does not simply impose its own construction on the statute, as would be necessary in the absence of an administrative interpretation. Rather, if the statute is silent or ambiguous with respect to the specific issue, the question for the court is whether the agency's answer is based on a permissible construction of the statute."

The Chevron case has given rise to many questions, including which interpretive tools courts may use in the search for congressional intent, and what should count as Congress' having spoken to "the precise question at issue".[6] Clearly, however, Chevron establishes that a reviewing court must often accept any reasonable agency construction, even if the court does not regard that construction as the best one.

Do cases such as Chevron vest the judicial power of the United States, or part of it, in administrative agencies? Do they, at the very least, authorize Congress to vest agencies, not courts, with the power to give conclusive determinations of questions of law in an important range of cases? Consider the following colloquy from Hart, *Dialogue*, 66 Harv.L.Rev. at 1377–78:

"Q. The Crowell case * * * has a dictum that questions of law * * * must be open to judicial consideration. And * * * Brandeis * * * [said] *that* was necessary to the supremacy of law. Have those statements stood up?

       * * *

"A. [Whether agencies are permitted 'to make final decisions of questions of law'] depends on how you define 'law'. * * *

"In recent years we've recognized increasingly a permissible range of administrative discretion in the shaping of judicially enforceable duties. How wide that discretion should be, and what are the appropriate ways to control it, are crucial questions in administrative law. But so long as the courts sit to answer the questions, the spirit of Brandeis' statement is maintained. And, since discretion by hypothesis is not law, the letter of it is not in question."

Compare Monaghan, *Marbury and the Administrative State*, 83 Colum.L.Rev. 1, 28–34 (1983), arguing that "[t]he opposition of 'discretion' to 'law' cannot dissolve Hart's problem," since "the result of the exercise of discretion is * * * an administrative formulation of a rule of law" (p. 29). Professor Monaghan concludes, however, that "there has never been a pervasive notion that limited government mandated an all-encompassing judicial duty to supply all of the relevant meaning of statutes. Rather, the judicial duty is to ensure that the administrative agency stays within the zone of discretion committed to it by its organic act" (p. 33).

(6) *What Is the Necessary Role of Constitutional Courts?* Consider the following argument. (i) Factfinding is as crucial to the fair resolution of individual cases as is the interpretation of relevant law. (ii) By allowing Congress to give conclusive effect to agency fact-finding, but not to agency determinations of law, Crowell suggests that Article III is more concerned with systemic or

---

6. For a fuller catalogue of questions, more than a few answers, and a valuable   bibliography, see Strauss et al., *supra*, at 620–36.

structural questions of agency compliance with law than with correct resolution of individual cases.   (iii) Chevron generally fits with this interpretation of Article III, but its very relaxed interpretation of what count as the "bounds of law" further diminishes the necessary role of constitutional courts in policing agency action.

If this argument is valid, would you agree that developments in administrative law are crucial to understanding the necessary role of constitutional courts in the contemporary constitutional order?

(7) *Appointments Issues.*   What are the constitutional constraints on the appointment of non-Article III federal adjudicators?   Freytag v. Commissioner, 501 U.S. 868 (1991), involved a challenge under the Appointments Clause (Art. II, § 2, cl. 2) to the statutory authority of the chief judge of the Tax Court to appoint and assign special trial judges to perform a variety of functions.   (The Appointments Clause provides, *inter alia,* that "Congress may by Law vest the Appointment of such inferior Officers, as they think proper, in the President alone, in the Courts of Law, or in the Heads of Departments.")

The Supreme Court rejected the challenge.   The Justices all agreed that special trial judges were not simply employees but rather were "inferior Officer[s]", but divided 5–4 on the reason why their appointment by the chief judge of the Tax Court satisfied the Appointments Clause.   Five Justices (in an opinion by Justice Blackmun) concluded that the Tax Court, though not an Article III court, was a "Court of Law" within the meaning of that clause. (Justice Blackmun never explained, however, how vesting the appointment power in the chief judge met the requirement of the clause that the power be vested in the court itself.)   Four Justices (in an opinion by Justice Scalia) concluded that the Tax Court is a "Department" in the executive branch and the chief judge is its head.[7]

Under the Administrative Procedure Act, 5 U.S.C. § 551 et. seq., administrative law judges are appointed, by the agency in which they work, from a short list of candidates certified on the basis of objective qualifications by the Office of Personnel Management.   Does this mode of appointment comport with the Constitution?

(8) *The Pertinence of the Seventh Amendment.*   In considering Congress' power to vest adjudicative power in administrative agencies, what is the pertinence of the Seventh Amendment's provision that "In suits at common law, where the value in controversy shall exceed twenty dollars, the right of trial by jury shall be preserved"?   See pp. 433–37, *infra.*

Northern Pipeline Construction Co.
v. Marathon Pipe Line Co.

458 U.S. 50, 102 S.Ct. 2858, 73 L.Ed.2d 598 (1982).
Appeal from the United States District Court for the District of Minnesota.

■ JUSTICE BRENNAN announced the judgment of the Court and delivered an opinion, in which JUSTICE MARSHALL, JUSTICE BLACKMUN, and JUSTICE STEVENS joined.

7.   See also Weiss v. United States, 114 S.Ct. 752 (1994)(because military officers have been appointed by the President, no further "appointment" is needed under the Appointments Clause for them to serve as military judges, and such assignments may therefore be made by the Judge Advocate General).

The question presented is whether the assignment by Congress to bankruptcy judges of the jurisdiction granted in 28 U.S.C. § 1471 by § 241(a) of the Bankruptcy Act of 1978 violates Art. III of the Constitution.

I

A

In 1978, after almost 10 years of study and investigation, Congress enacted a comprehensive revision of the bankruptcy laws. The Bankruptcy Act of 1978 (Act) made significant changes in both the substantive and procedural law of bankruptcy. It is the changes in the latter that are at issue in this case.

Before the Act, federal district courts served as bankruptcy courts and employed a "referee" system. Bankruptcy proceedings were generally conducted before referees,[2] except in those instances in which the district court elected to withdraw a case from a referee. The referee's final order was appealable to the district court. The bankruptcy courts were vested with "summary jurisdiction"—that is, with jurisdiction over controversies involving property in the actual or constructive possession of the court. And, with consent, the bankruptcy court also had jurisdiction over some "plenary" matters—such as disputes involving property in the possession of a third person.

The Act eliminates the referee system and establishes "in each judicial district, as an adjunct to the district court for such district, a bankruptcy court which shall be a court of record known as the United States Bankruptcy Court for the district." 28 U.S.C. § 151(a)(1976 ed., Supp. IV). The judges of these courts are appointed to office for 14–year terms by the President, with the advice and consent of the Senate. §§ 152, 153(a). They are subject to removal by the "judicial council of the circuit" on account of "incompetency, misconduct, neglect of duty or physical or mental disability." § 153(b). In addition, the salaries of the bankruptcy judges are set by statute and are subject to adjustment under the Federal Salary Act, 2 U.S.C. §§ 351–361. 28 U.S.C. § 154.

The jurisdiction of the bankruptcy courts created by the Act is much broader than that exercised under the former referee system. Eliminating the distinction between "summary" and "plenary" jurisdiction, the Act grants the new courts jurisdiction over all "civil proceedings arising under title 11 [the Bankruptcy title] or arising in or *related to* cases under title 11." 28 U.S.C. § 1471(b)(emphasis added). This jurisdictional grant empowers bankruptcy courts to entertain a wide variety of cases involving claims that may affect the property of the estate once a petition has been filed under Title 11. Included within the bankruptcy courts' jurisdiction are suits to recover accounts, controversies involving exempt property, actions to avoid transfers and payments as preferences or fraudulent conveyances, and causes of action owned by the debtor at the time of the petition for bankruptcy. The bankruptcy courts can hear claims based on state law as well as those based on federal law.

The judges of the bankruptcy courts are vested with all of the "powers of a court of equity, law, and admiralty," except that they "may not enjoin another court or punish a criminal contempt not committed in the presence of the judge of the court or warranting a punishment of imprisonment." 28 U.S.C. § 1481. In addition to this broad grant of power, Congress has allowed bankruptcy

---

2. Bankruptcy referees were redesignated as "judges" in 1973. For purposes of clarity, however, we refer to all judges under the old Act as "referees."

judges the power to hold jury trials, § 1480; to issue declaratory judgments, § 2201; to issue writs of habeas corpus under certain circumstances, § 2256; to issue all writs necessary in aid of the bankruptcy court's expanded jurisdiction, § 451; see 28 U.S.C. § 1651; and to issue any order, process or judgment that is necessary or appropriate to carry out the provisions of Title 11, 11 U.S.C. § 105(a).

The Act also establishes a special procedure for appeals from orders of bankruptcy courts. The circuit council is empowered to direct the chief judge of the circuit to designate panels of three bankruptcy judges to hear appeals. 28 U.S.C. § 160. These panels have jurisdiction of all appeals from final judgments, orders, and decrees of bankruptcy courts, and, with leave of the panel, of interlocutory appeals. § 1482. If no such appeals panel is designated, the district court is empowered to exercise appellate jurisdiction. § 1334. The court of appeals is given jurisdiction over appeals from the appellate panels or from the district court. § 1293. If the parties agree, a direct appeal to the court of appeals may be taken from a final judgment of a bankruptcy court. § 1293(b).[3]

* * *

B

This case arises out of proceedings initiated in the United States Bankruptcy Court for the District of Minnesota after appellant Northern Pipeline Construction Co. (Northern) filed a petition for reorganization in January 1980. In March 1980 Northern, pursuant to the Act, filed in that court a suit against appellee Marathon Pipe Line Co. (Marathon). Appellant sought damages for alleged breaches of contract and warranty, as well as for alleged misrepresentation, coercion, and duress. Marathon sought dismissal of the suit, on the ground that the Act unconstitutionally conferred Art. III judicial power upon judges who lacked life tenure and protection against salary diminution. The United States intervened to defend the validity of the statute.

The Bankruptcy Judge denied the motion to dismiss. But on appeal the District Court entered an order granting the motion, on the ground that "the delegation of authority in 28 U.S.C. § 1471 to the Bankruptcy Judges to try cases which are otherwise relegated under the Constitution to Article III judges" was unconstitutional. Both the United States and Northern filed notices of appeal in this Court. We noted probable jurisdiction.

II

A

Basic to the constitutional structure established by the Framers was their recognition that "[t]he accumulation of all powers, legislative, executive, and judiciary, in the same hands, whether of one, a few, or many, and whether hereditary, self-appointed, or elective, may justly be pronounced the very definition of tyranny." The Federalist No. 47, p. 300 (H. Lodge ed. 1888)(J. Madison). * * *

---

3. Although no particular standard of review is specified in the Act, the parties in the present cases seem to agree that the appropriate one is the clearly-erroneous standard, employed in old Bankruptcy Rule 810 for review of findings of fact made by a referee. * * *

The Federal Judiciary was therefore designed by the Framers to stand independent of the Executive and Legislature—to maintain the checks and balances of the constitutional structure, and also to guarantee that the process of adjudication itself remained impartial. Hamilton explained the importance of an independent Judiciary:

> "Periodical appointments, however regulated, or by whomsoever made, would, in some way or other, be fatal to [the courts'] necessary independence. If the power of making them was committed either to the Executive or legislature, there would be danger of an improper complaisance to the branch which possessed it; if to both, there would be an unwillingness to hazard the displeasure of either; if to the people, or to persons chosen by them for the special purpose, there would be too great a disposition to consult popularity, to justify a reliance that nothing would be consulted but the Constitution and the laws." The Federalist No. 78, p. 489 (H. Lodge ed. 1888).

* * *

As an inseparable element of the constitutional system of checks and balances, and as a guarantee of judicial impartiality, Art. III * * * [provides that the] judicial power of the United States must be exercised by courts having the attributes prescribed in Art. III. * * *

> "The Judges, both of the supreme and inferior Courts, shall hold their Offices during good Behaviour, and shall, at stated Times, receive for their Services, a Compensation, which shall not be diminished during their Continuance in Office." Art. III, § 1.

The "good Behaviour" Clause guarantees that Art. III judges shall enjoy life tenure, subject only to removal by impeachment. The Compensation Clause guarantees Art. III judges a fixed and irreducible compensation for their services. * * *[10]

B

It is undisputed that the bankruptcy judges whose offices were created by the Bankruptcy Act of 1978 do not enjoy the protections constitutionally afforded to Art. III judges. * * *

* * *

Appellants suggest two grounds for upholding the Act's conferral of broad adjudicative powers upon judges unprotected by Art. III. First, it is urged that "pursuant to its enumerated Article I powers, Congress may establish legislative courts that have jurisdiction to decide cases to which the Article III judicial power of the United States extends." Brief for United States 9. * * * Second, appellants contend that even if the Constitution does require that this bankruptcy-related action be adjudicated in an Art. III court, the Act in fact satisfies that requirement. * * * We consider these arguments in turn.

---

10. These provisions serve other institutional values as well. The independence from political forces that they guarantee helps to promote public confidence in judicial determinations. See The Federalist No. 78 (A. Hamilton). The security that they provide to members of the Judicial Branch helps to attract well-qualified persons to the federal bench. *Ibid.* The guarantee of life tenure insulates the individual judge from improper influences not only by other branches, but by colleagues as well, and thus promotes judicial individualism.

III

Congress did not constitute the bankruptcy courts as legislative courts.[13] Appellants contend, however, that the bankruptcy courts could have been so constituted, and that as a result the "adjunct" system in fact chosen by Congress does not impermissibly encroach upon the judicial power. In advancing this argument, appellants rely upon cases in which we have identified certain matters that "congress may or may not bring within the cognizance of [Art. III courts], as it may deem proper." Murray's Lessee v. Hoboken Land & Improvement Co., 18 How. 272, 284 (1856).[14] But when properly understood, these precedents represent no broad departure from the constitutional command that the judicial power of the United States must be vested in Art. III courts.[15] Rather, they reduce to three narrow situations not subject to that command, each recognizing a circumstance in which the grant of power to the Legislative and Executive Branches was historically and constitutionally so exceptional that the congressional assertion of a power to create legislative courts was consistent with, rather than threatening to, the constitutional mandate of separation of powers. * * *

Appellants first rely upon a series of cases in which this Court has upheld the creation by Congress of non-Art. III "territorial courts." This exception from the general prescription of Art. III dates from the earliest days of the Republic, when it was perceived that the Framers intended that as to certain geographical areas, in which no State operated as sovereign, Congress was to exercise the general powers of government. For example, in American Ins. Co. v. Canter, 1 Pet. 516 (1828), the Court observed that Art. IV bestowed upon Congress alone a complete power of government over territories not within the States that constituted the United States. The Court then acknowledged Congress' authority to create courts for those territories that were not in conformity with Art. III. Such courts were

> "created in virtue of the general right of sovereignty which exists in the government, or in virtue of that clause which enables Congress to make all needful rules and regulations, respecting the territory belonging to the

---

13. The Act designates the bankruptcy court in each district as an "adjunct" to the district court. 28 U.S.C. § 151(a). * * *

14. At one time, this Court suggested a rigid distinction between those subjects that could be considered only in Art. III courts and those that could be considered only in legislative courts. See Williams v. United States, 289 U.S. 553 (1933). But this suggested dichotomy has not withstood analysis. See C. Wright, Law of the Federal Courts 33–35 (3d ed. 1976). Our more recent cases clearly recognize that legislative courts may be granted jurisdiction over some cases and controversies to which the Art. III judicial power might also be extended. *E.g.,* Palmore v. United States, 411 U.S. 389 (1973). See Glidden Co. v. Zdanok, 370 U.S. 530, 549–551 (1962)(opinion of Harlan, J.).

15. Justice White's dissent finds particular significance in the fact that Congress could have assigned all bankruptcy matters to the state courts. But, of course, virtually all matters that might be heard in Art. III courts could also be left by Congress to state courts. This fact is simply irrelevant to the question before us. Congress has no control over state-court judges; accordingly the principle of separation of powers is not threatened by leaving the adjudication of federal disputes to such judges. See Krattenmaker, *Article III and Judicial Independence: Why the New Bankruptcy Courts are Unconstitutional,* 70 Geo.L.J. 297, 304–305 (1981). The Framers chose to leave to Congress the precise role to be played by the lower federal courts in the administration of justice. See Hart and Wechsler's The Federal Courts and the Federal System, at 11. But the Framers did not leave it to Congress to define the character of those courts—they were to be independent of the political branches and presided over by judges with guaranteed salary and life tenure.

United States. The jurisdiction with which they are invested * * * is conferred by Congress, in the execution of those general powers which that body possesses over the territories of the United States. Although admiralty jurisdiction can be exercised in the states in those Courts, only, which are established in pursuance of the third article of the Constitution; the same limitation does not extend to the territories. In legislating for them, Congress exercises the combined powers of the general, and of a state government." 1 Pet., at 546.

The Court followed the same reasoning when it reviewed Congress' creation of non-Art. III courts in the District of Columbia. * * *

Appellants next advert to a second class of cases—those in which this Court has sustained the exercise by Congress and the Executive of the power to establish and administer courts-martial. The situation in these cases strongly resembles the situation with respect to territorial courts: It too involves a constitutional grant of power that has been historically understood as giving the political Branches of Government extraordinary control over the precise subject matter at issue. Article I, § 8, cls. 13, 14 * * *

Finally, appellants rely on a third group of cases, in which this Court has upheld the constitutionality of legislative courts and administrative agencies created by Congress to adjudicate cases involving "public rights." [The Court here quoted the formulation of the "public rights" doctrine first set forth in Murray's Lessee v. Hoboken Land & Improvement Co., 59 U.S. 272, 285 (18 How. 1856), as quoted on p. 395, *supra.*]

This doctrine may be explained in part by reference to the traditional principle of sovereign immunity, which recognizes that the Government may attach conditions to its consent to be sued. See *id.*, at 283–285; see also Ex parte Bakelite Corp., 279 U.S. 438, 452 (1929). But the public-rights doctrine also draws upon the principle of separation of powers, and a historical understanding that certain prerogatives were reserved to the political Branches of Government. The doctrine extends only to matters arising "between the Government and persons subject to its authority in connection with the performance of the constitutional functions of the executive or legislative departments," Crowell v. Benson, 285 U.S. 22, 50 (1932), and only to matters that historically could have been determined exclusively by those departments, see Ex parte Bakelite Corp., *supra*, at 458. The understanding of these cases is that the Framers expected that Congress would be free to commit such matters completely to nonjudicial executive determination, and that as a result there can be no constitutional objection to Congress' employing the less drastic expedient of committing their determination to a legislative court or an administrative agency. Crowell v. Benson, *supra*, at 50.

* * * For example, the Court in Murray's Lessee looked to the law of England and the States at the time the Constitution was adopted, in order to determine whether the issue presented was customarily cognizable in the courts. Concluding that the matter had not traditionally been one for judicial determination, the Court perceived no bar to Congress' establishment of summary procedures, outside of Art. III courts, to collect a debt due to the Government from one of its customs agents.[20] On the same premise, the Court

---

20. Doubtless it could be argued that the need for independent judicial determination is greatest in cases arising between the Government and an individual. But the rationale for the public-rights line of cases lies not in political theory, but rather in Con-

in Ex parte Bakelite Corp., *supra,* held that the Court of Customs Appeals had been properly constituted by Congress as a legislative court:

> "The *full* province of the court under the act creating it is that of determining matters arising between the Government and others in the executive administration and application of the customs laws. * * * The appeals include nothing which inherently or necessarily requires judicial determination, but only matters the determination of *which may be, and at times has been, committed exclusively to executive officers.*" 279 U.S., at 458 (emphasis added).[21]

The distinction between public rights and private rights has not been definitively explained in our precedents. Nor is it necessary to do so in the present cases, for it suffices to observe that a matter of public rights must at a minimum arise "between the government and others." Ex parte Bakelite Corp., *supra,* at 451.[23] In contrast, "the liability of one individual to another under the law as defined," Crowell v. Benson, *supra,* at 51, is a matter of private rights. Our precedents clearly establish that *only* controversies in the former category may be removed from Art. III courts and delegated to legislative courts or administrative agencies for their determination. See Atlas Roofing Co. v. Occupational Safety and Health Review Comm'n, 430 U.S. 442, 450, n. 7 (1977); Crowell v. Benson, *supra,* at 50–51.[24] * * *

In sum, this Court has identified three situations in which Art. III does not bar the creation of legislative courts. * * * [25]

---

gress' and this Court's understanding of what power was reserved to the Judiciary by the Constitution as a matter of historical fact.

21. See also Williams v. United States, 289 U.S. 553 (1933)(holding that Court of Claims was a legislative court and that salary of a judge of that court could therefore be reduced by Congress).

23. Congress cannot "withdraw from [Art. III] judicial cognizance *any* matter which, *from its nature,* is the subject of a suit at the common law, or in equity, or admiralty." Murray's Lessee v. Hoboken Land & Improvement Co., 18 How. 272, 284 (1856)(emphasis added). It is thus clear that the presence of the United States as a proper party to the proceeding is a necessary but not sufficient means of distinguishing "private rights" from "public rights." And it is also clear that even with respect to matters that arguably fall within the scope of the "public rights" doctrine, the presumption is in favor of Art. III courts. See Glidden Co. v. Zdanok, 370 U.S., at 548–549, and n. 21 (opinion of Harlan, J.). See also Currie, *The Federal Courts and the American Law Institute,* Part 1, 36 U.Chi.L.Rev. 1, 13–14, n. 67 (1968). Moreover, when Congress assigns these matters to administrative agencies, or to legislative courts, it has generally provided, and we have suggested that it may be required to provide, for Art. III judicial review. See At-

las Roofing Co. v. Occupational Safety and Health Review Comm'n, 430 U.S., at 455, n. 13.

24. Of course, the public-rights doctrine does not extend to any criminal matters, although the Government is a proper party. See, *e.g.,* United States ex rel. Toth v. Quarles, 350 U.S. 11 (1955).

25. The "unifying principle" that Justice White's dissent finds lacking in all of these cases is to be found in the exceptional constitutional grants of power to Congress with respect to certain matters. Although the dissent is correct that these grants are not explicit in the language of the Constitution, they are nonetheless firmly established in our historical understanding of the constitutional structure. When these three exceptional grants are properly constrained, they do not threaten the Framers' vision of an independent Federal Judiciary. What clearly remains subject to Art. III are all private adjudications in federal courts within the States—matters from their nature subject to "a suit at common law or in equity or admiralty"—and all criminal matters, with the narrow exception of military crimes. There is no doubt that when the Framers assigned the "judicial Power" to an independent Art. III Branch, these matters lay at what they perceived to be the protected core of that power. * * *

We discern no * * * exceptional grant of power applicable in the cases before us. * * * Appellants argue that a discharge in bankruptcy is indeed a "public right," similar to such congressionally created benefits as "radio station licenses, pilot licenses, or certificates for common carriers" granted by administrative agencies. But the restructuring of debtor-creditor relations, which is at the core of the federal bankruptcy power, must be distinguished from the adjudication of state-created private rights, such as the right to recover contract damages that is at issue in this case. The former may well be a "public right," but the latter obviously is not. Appellant Northern's right to recover contract damages to augment its estate is "one of private right, that is, of the liability of one individual to another under the law as defined." Crowell v. Benson, 285 U.S., at 51.[26]

Recognizing that the present cases may not fall within the scope of any of our prior cases permitting the establishment of legislative courts, appellants argue that we should recognize an additional situation beyond the command of Art. III, sufficiently broad to sustain the Act. Appellants contend that Congress' constitutional authority to establish "uniform Laws on the subject of Bankruptcies throughout the United States," Art. I, § 8, cl. 4, carries with it an inherent power to establish legislative courts capable of adjudicating "bankruptcy-related controversies." * * * In support of this argument, appellants rely primarily upon a quotation from the opinion in Palmore v. United States, 411 U.S. 389 (1973), in which we stated that

> "both Congress and this Court have recognized that * * * the requirements of Art. III, which are applicable where laws of national applicability and affairs of national concern are at stake, must in proper circumstances give way to accommodate plenary grants of power to Congress to legislate with respect to specialized areas having particularized needs and warranting distinctive treatment." Id., 407–408.

Appellants cite this language to support their proposition that a bankruptcy court created by Congress under its Art. I powers is constitutional, because the law of bankruptcy is a "specialized area," and Congress has found a "particularized need" that warrants "distinctive treatment." Brief for United States 20–33.

Appellants' contention, in essence, is that pursuant to any of its Art. I powers, Congress may create courts free of Art. III's requirements whenever it finds that course expedient. * * *

The flaw in appellants' analysis is that it provides no limiting principle. It thus threatens to supplant completely our system of adjudication in independent Art. III tribunals and replace it with a system of "specialized" legislative courts. True, appellants argue that under their analysis Congress could create legislative courts pursuant only to some "specific" Art. I power, and "only when there is a particularized need for distinctive treatment." * * * But these "limitations" are wholly illusory. For example, Art. I, § 8, empowers Congress to enact laws, *inter alia*, regulating interstate commerce and punishing certain crimes. Art. I, § 8, cls. 3, 6. On appellants' reasoning Congress could provide

---

26. This claim may be adjudicated in federal court on the basis of its relationship to the petition for reorganization. See Williams v. Austrian, 331 U.S. 642 (1947); Schumacher v. Beeler, 293 U.S. 367 (1934). But this relationship does not transform the state-created right into a matter between the Government and the petitioner for reorganization. Even in the absence of the federal scheme, the plaintiff would be able to proceed against the defendant on the state-law contractual claims.

for the adjudication of these and "related" matters by judges and courts within Congress' exclusive control. * * * [28]

Appellants' reliance upon Palmore for such broad legislative discretion is misplaced. * * * Palmore was concerned with the courts of the District of Columbia, a unique federal enclave over which "Congress has * * * entire control * * * for every purpose of government." Kendall v. United States, 12 Pet., at 619. * * * [O]ur reference in Palmore to "specialized areas having particularized needs" referred only to *geographic* areas, such as the District of Columbia or territories outside the States of the Federal Union. In light of the clear commands of Art. III, nothing held or said in Palmore can be taken to mean that in every area in which Congress may legislate, it may also create non-Art. III courts with Art. III powers.

* * *

IV

Appellants advance a second argument for upholding the constitutionality of the Act: that "viewed within the entire judicial framework set up by Congress," the bankruptcy court is merely an "adjunct" to the district court, and that the delegation of certain adjudicative functions to the bankruptcy court is accordingly consistent with the principle that the judicial power of the United States must be vested in Art. III courts. * * * As support for their argument, appellants rely principally upon Crowell v. Benson, 285 U.S. 22 (1932), and United States v. Raddatz, 447 U.S. 667 (1980), cases in which we approved the

---

28. Justice White's suggested "limitations" on Congress' power to create Art. I courts are even more transparent. Justice White's dissent suggests that Art. III "should be read as expressing one value that must be balanced against competing constitutional values and legislative responsibilities," and that the Court retains the final word on how the balance is to be struck. The dissent would find the Art. III "value" accommodated where appellate review by Art. III courts is provided and where the Art. I courts are "designed to deal with issues likely to be of little interest to the political branches." But the dissent's view that appellate review is sufficient to satisfy either the command or the purpose of Art. III is incorrect. See n. 39, *infra*. And the suggestion that we should consider whether the Art. I courts are designed to deal with issues likely to be of interest to the political Branches would undermine the validity of the adjudications performed by most of the administrative agencies, on which validity the dissent so heavily relies. * * *

In applying its ad hoc balancing approach to the facts of this case, the dissent rests on the justification that these courts differ from standard Art. III courts because of their "extreme specialization." As noted above, "extreme specialization" is hardly an accurate description of bankruptcy courts designed to adjudicate the entire range of federal and state controversies. Moreover, the special nature of bankruptcy adjudications is in no sense incompatible with performance of such functions in a tribunal afforded the protection of Art. III. As one witness pointed out to Congress:

"Relevant to that question of need, it seems worth noting that Article III itself permits much flexibility; so long as tenure during good behavior is granted, much room exists as regards other conditions. Thus it would certainly be possible to create a special bankruptcy court under Article III and there is no reason why the judges of that court would have to be paid the same salary as district judges or any other existing judges. It would also be permissible to provide that when a judge of that court retired pursuant to statute, a vacancy for a new appointment would not automatically be created. And it would be entirely valid to specify that the judges of that court could not be assigned to sit, even temporarily, on the general district courts or courts of appeals." Hearings on H.R. 31 and H.R. 32 before the Subcommittee on Civil and Constitutional Rights of the House Committee on the Judiciary, 94th Cong., 2d Sess., 2697 (1976)(letter of Paul Mishkin).

use of administrative agencies and magistrates as adjuncts to Art. III courts. * * * The question to which we turn, therefore, is whether the Act has retained "the essential attributes of the judicial power," Crowell v. Benson, *supra,* at 51, in Art. III tribunals.

* * *

Crowell involved the adjudication of congressionally created rights. But this Court has sustained the use of adjunct factfinders even in the adjudication of constitutional rights—so long as those adjuncts were subject to sufficient control by an Art. III district court. In United States v. Raddatz, *supra,* the Court upheld the 1978 Federal Magistrates Act, which permitted district court judges to refer certain pretrial motions, including suppression motions based on alleged violations of constitutional rights, to a magistrate for initial determination. The Court observed that the magistrate's proposed findings and recommendations were subject to *de novo* review by the district court, which was free to rehear the evidence or to call for additional evidence. Moreover, it was noted that the magistrate considered motions only upon reference from the district court, and that the magistrates were appointed, and subject to removal, by the district court.[30] In short, the ultimate decisionmaking authority respecting all pretrial motions clearly remained with the district court. Under these circumstances, the Court held that the Act did not violate the constraints of Art. III.[31]

Together these cases establish two principles that aid us in determining the extent to which Congress may constitutionally vest traditionally judicial functions in non-Art. III officers. First, it is clear that when Congress creates a substantive federal right, it possesses substantial discretion to prescribe the manner in which that right may be adjudicated—including the assignment to an adjunct of some functions historically performed by judges.[32] * * * Second, the functions of the adjunct must be limited in such a way that "the essential attributes" of judicial power are retained in the Art. III court. * * *

These two principles assist us in evaluating the "adjunct" scheme presented in these cases. * * * [W]hile Crowell certainly endorsed the proposition that Congress possesses broad discretion to assign factfinding functions to an adjunct created to aid in the adjudication of congressionally created statutory rights, Crowell does not support the further proposition necessary to appellants' argument—that Congress possesses the same degree of discretion in assigning traditionally judicial power to adjuncts engaged in the adjudication of rights *not* created by Congress. Indeed, the validity of this proposition was

---

30. Thus in Raddatz there was no serious threat that the exercise of the judicial power would be subject to incursion by other branches. * * *

31. Appellants and Justice White's dissent also rely on the broad powers exercised by the bankruptcy referees immediately before the Bankruptcy Act of 1978. But those particular adjunct functions, which represent the culmination of years of gradual expansion of the power and authority of the bankruptcy referee, have never been explicitly endorsed by this Court. * * *

32. Contrary to Justice White's suggestion, we do not concede that "Congress may provide for initial adjudications by Art. I courts or administrative judges of all rights and duties arising under otherwise valid federal laws." Rather we simply reaffirm the holding of Crowell—that Congress may assign to non-Art. III bodies some adjudicatory functions. Crowell itself spoke of "specialized" functions. These cases do not require us to specify further any limitations that may exist with respect to Congress' power to create adjuncts to assist in the adjudication of federal statutory rights.

expressly denied in Crowell, when the Court rejected "the untenable assumption that the constitutional courts may be deprived in all cases of the determination of facts upon evidence even though a *constitutional* right may be involved," 285 U.S., at 60–61 (emphasis added)[33] * * *.

* * *

Although Crowell and Raddatz do not explicitly distinguish between rights created by Congress and other rights, * * * such a distinction seems to us to be necessary in light of the delicate accommodations required by the principle of separation of powers reflected in Art. III.   * * * [W]hen Congress creates a statutory right, it clearly has the discretion, in defining that right, to create presumptions, or assign burdens of proof, or prescribe remedies; it may also provide that persons seeking to vindicate that right must do so before particularized tribunals created to perform the specialized adjudicative tasks related to that right.   Such provisions do, in a sense, affect the exercise of judicial power, but they are also incidental to Congress' power to define the right that it has created.   No comparable justification exists, however, when the right being adjudicated is not of congressional creation.   In such a situation, substantial inroads into functions that have traditionally been performed by the Judiciary * * * suggest unwarranted encroachments upon the judicial power of the United States, which our Constitution reserves for Art. III courts.

We hold that the Bankruptcy Act of 1978 carries the possibility of such an unwarranted encroachment.   Many of the rights subject to adjudication by the Act's bankruptcy courts, like the rights implicated in Raddatz, are not of Congress' creation.   Indeed, the cases before us, which center upon appellant Northern's claim for damages for breach of contract and misrepresentation, involve a right created by *state* law, a right independent of and antecedent to the reorganization petition that conferred jurisdiction upon the Bankruptcy Court.[36]   Accordingly, Congress' authority to control the manner in which that right is adjudicated, through assignment of historically judicial functions to a non-Art. III "adjunct," plainly must be deemed at a minimum.   Yet it is equally plain that Congress has vested the "adjunct" bankruptcy judges with powers over Northern's state-created right that far exceed the powers that it has vested in administrative agencies that adjudicate only rights of Congress' own creation.

Unlike the administrative scheme that we reviewed in Crowell, the Act vests all "essential attributes" of the judicial power of the United States in the "adjunct" bankruptcy court.   First, the agency in Crowell made only specialized, narrowly confined factual determinations regarding a particularized area

---

33. The Court in Crowell found that the requirement of *de novo* review as to certain facts was not "simply the question of due process in relation to notice and hearing," but was "rather a question of the appropriate maintenance of the Federal judicial power." 285 U.S., at 56.   The dissent agreed that some factual findings cannot be made by adjuncts, on the ground that "under certain circumstances, the constitutional requirement of due process is a requirement of [Art. III] judicial process." *Id.*, at 87 (Brandeis, J., dissenting).

36. Of course, bankruptcy adjudications themselves, as well as the manner in which the rights of debtors and creditors are adjusted, are matters of federal law.   Appellant Northern's state-law contract claim is now in federal court because of its relationship to Northern's reorganization petition. See n. 26, *supra*.   But Congress has not purported to prescribe a rule of decision for the resolution of Northern's contractual claims.

of law. In contrast, the subject-matter jurisdiction of the bankruptcy courts encompasses not only traditional matters of bankruptcy, but also "all civil proceedings arising under title 11 or arising in or *related to* cases under title 11." 28 U.S.C. § 1471(b)(emphasis added). Second, while the agency in Crowell engaged in statutorily channeled factfinding functions, the bankruptcy courts exercise "*all* of the jurisdiction" conferred by the Act on the district courts, § 1471(c)(emphasis added). Third, the agency in Crowell possessed only a limited power to issue compensation orders pursuant to specialized procedures, and its orders could be enforced only by order of the district court. By contrast, the bankruptcy courts exercise all ordinary powers of district courts * * *. Fourth, while orders issued by the agency in Crowell were to be set aside if "not supported by the evidence," the judgments of the bankruptcy courts are apparently subject to review only under the more deferential "clearly erroneous" standard. Finally, the agency in Crowell was required by law to seek enforcement of its compensation orders in the district court. In contrast, the bankruptcy courts issue final judgments, which are binding and enforceable even in the absence of an appeal. In short, the "adjunct" bankruptcy courts created by the Act exercise jurisdiction behind the facade of a grant to the district courts, and are exercising powers far greater than those lodged in the adjuncts approved in either Crowell or Raddatz.[39]

We conclude that 28 U.S.C. § 1471, as added by § 241(a) of the Bankruptcy Act of 1978, has impermissibly removed most, if not all, of "the essential attributes of the judicial power" from the Art. III district court, and has vested those attributes in a non-Art. III adjunct. Such a grant of jurisdiction cannot be sustained as an exercise of Congress' power to create adjuncts to Art. III courts.

V

[The remainder of the opinion concluded that the grant of jurisdiction contained in 28 U.S.C. § 1471 could not be separated, by a court, into constitutionally valid as well as invalid parts and that the provision must therefore by ruled unconstitutional as a whole; held that its ruling of invalidity should apply only prospectively; and ordered that the judgment should be stayed until October 4, 1982, to "afford Congress an opportunity to reconstitute the bankruptcy courts

---

39. Appellants suggest that Crowell and Raddatz stand for the proposition that Art. III is satisfied so long as some degree of appellate review is provided. But that suggestion is directly contrary to the text of our Constitution: "The Judges, *both* of the supreme and inferior Courts, shall hold their Offices during good Behaviour, and shall * * * receive [undiminished] Compensation." Art. III, § 1 (emphasis added). Our precedents make it clear that the constitutional requirements for the exercise of the judicial power must be met at all stages of adjudication, and not only on appeal, where the court is restricted to considerations of law, as well as the nature of the case as it has been shaped at the trial level. * * *

Justice White's dissent views the function of the Third Branch as interpreting the Constitution in order to keep the other two Branches in check, and would accordingly find the purpose, if not the language, of Art. III satisfied where there is an appeal to an Art. III court. But in the Framers' view, Art. III courts would do a great deal more than, in an abstract way, announce guidelines for the other two Branches. While "expounding" the Constitution was surely one vital function of the Art. III courts in the Framers' view, the tasks of those courts, for which independence was an important safeguard, included the mundane as well as the glamorous, matters of common law and statute as well as constitutional law, issues of fact as well as issues of law. * * *

or to adopt other valid means of adjudication, without impairing the interim administration of the bankruptcy laws".]

■ JUSTICE REHNQUIST, with whom JUSTICE O'CONNOR joins, concurring in the judgment.

Were I to agree with the plurality that the question presented by these cases is "whether the assignment by Congress to bankruptcy judges of the jurisdiction granted in 28 U.S.C. § 1471 by § 241(a) of the Bankruptcy Act of 1978 violates Art. III of the Constitution," I would with considerable reluctance embark on the duty of deciding this broad question. But appellee Marathon Pipe Line Co. has * * * simply been named defendant in a lawsuit about a contract, a lawsuit initiated by appellant Northern after having previously filed a petition for reorganization under the Bankruptcy Act. Marathon may object to proceeding further with this lawsuit on the grounds that if it is to be resolved by an agency of the United States, it may be resolved only by an agency which exercises "[t]he judicial power of the United States" described by Art. III of the Constitution. But resolution of any objections it may make on this ground to the exercise of a different authority conferred on bankruptcy courts by the 1978 Act, should await the exercise of such authority. * * *

From the record before us, the lawsuit in which Marathon was named defendant seeks damages for breach of contract, misrepresentation, and other counts which are the stuff of the traditional actions at common law tried by the courts at Westminster in 1789. There is apparently no federal rule of decision provided for any of the issues in the lawsuit; the claims of Northern arise entirely under state law. No method of adjudication is hinted, other than the traditional common-law mode of judge and jury. The lawsuit is before the Bankruptcy Court only because the plaintiff has previously filed a petition for reorganization in that court.

The cases dealing with the authority of Congress to create courts other than by use of its power under Art. III do not admit of easy synthesis. * * * I need not decide whether these cases in fact support a general proposition and three tidy exceptions, as the plurality believes, or whether instead they are but landmarks on a judicial "darkling plain" where ignorant armies have clashed by night, as Justice White apparently believes them to be. None of the cases has gone so far as to sanction the type of adjudication to which Marathon will be subjected against its will under the provisions of the 1978 Act. To whatever extent different powers granted under that Act might be sustained under the "public rights" doctrine of Murray's Lessee v. Hoboken Land & Improvement Co., 18 How. 272 (1856), and succeeding cases, I am satisfied that the adjudication of Northern's lawsuit cannot be so sustained.

I am likewise of the opinion that the extent of review by Art. III courts provided on appeal from a decision of the bankruptcy court in a case such as Northern's does not save the grant of authority to the latter under the rule espoused in Crowell v. Benson, 285 U.S. 22 (1932). All matters of fact and law in whatever domains of the law to which the parties' dispute may lead are to be resolved by the bankruptcy court in the first instance, with only traditional appellate review by Art. III courts apparently contemplated. Acting in this manner the bankruptcy court is not an "adjunct" of either the district court or the court of appeals.

I would, therefore, hold so much of the Bankruptcy Act of 1978 as enables a Bankruptcy Court to entertain and decide Northern's lawsuit over Marathon's objection to be violative of Art. III of the United States Constitution. Because I agree with the plurality that this grant of authority is not readily severable from the remaining grant of authority to bankruptcy courts under § 1471, I concur in the judgment. I also agree with the discussion in Part V of the plurality opinion respecting retroactivity and the staying of the judgment of this Court.

■ CHIEF JUSTICE BURGER, dissenting.

* * *

It will not be necessary for Congress, in order to meet the requirements of the Court's holding, to undertake a radical restructuring of the present system of bankruptcy adjudication. The problems arising from today's judgment can be resolved simply by providing that ancillary common-law actions, such as the one involved in these cases, be routed to the United States district court of which the bankruptcy court is an adjunct.

■ JUSTICE WHITE, with whom THE CHIEF JUSTICE and JUSTICE POWELL join, dissenting.

* * *

* * * Any reader could easily take [Article III, § 1] * * * to mean that although Congress was free to establish such lower courts as it saw fit, any court that it did establish would be an "inferior" court exercising "judicial Power of the United States" and so must be manned by judges possessing both life tenure and a guaranteed minimal income. * * *

If this simple reading were correct and we were free to disregard 150 years of history, these would be easy cases and the plurality opinion could end with its observation that "[i]t is undisputed that the bankruptcy judges whose offices were created by the Bankruptcy Act of 1978 do not enjoy the protections constitutionally afforded to Art. III judges." The fact that the plurality must go on to deal with what has been characterized as one of the most confusing and controversial areas of constitutional law itself indicates the gross oversimplification implicit in the plurality's claim that "our Constitution unambiguously enunciates a fundamental principle—that the 'judicial Power of the United States' must be reposed in an independent Judiciary [and] provides clear institutional protections for that independence." While this is fine rhetoric, analytically it serves only to put a distracting and superficial gloss on a difficult question.

That question is what limits Art. III places on Congress' ability to create adjudicative institutions designed to carry out federal policy established pursuant to the substantive authority given Congress elsewhere in the Constitution. Whether fortunate or unfortunate, at this point in the history of constitutional law that question can no longer be answered by looking only to the constitutional text. This Court's cases construing that text must also be considered. In its attempt to pigeonhole these cases, the plurality does violence to their meaning and creates an artificial structure that itself lacks coherence.

I

* * *

The plurality concedes that Congress may provide for initial adjudications by Art. I courts or administrative judges of all rights and duties arising under otherwise valid federal laws. There is no apparent reason why this principle should not extend to matters arising in federal bankruptcy proceedings. The plurality attempts to escape the reach of prior decisions by contending that the bankrupt's claim against Marathon arose under state law. * * * For several reasons, the Court's judgment is unsupportable.

First, * * * [t]he plurality concedes that in adjudications and discharges in bankruptcy, "the restructuring of debtor-creditor relations, which is at the core of the federal bankruptcy power," and "the manner in which the rights of debtors and creditors are adjusted," are matters of federal law. Under the plurality's own interpretation of the cases, therefore, these matters could be heard and decided by Art. I judges. * * * Even if the Court is correct that * * * a state-law claim cannot be heard by a bankruptcy judge, there is no basis for doing more than declaring the section unconstitutional as applied to the claim against Marathon, leaving the section otherwise intact. * * *

Second, the distinction between claims based on state law and those based on federal law disregards the real character of bankruptcy proceedings. The routine in ordinary bankruptcy cases now, as it was before 1978, is to stay actions against the bankrupt, collect the bankrupt's assets, require creditors to file claims or be forever barred, allow or disallow claims that are filed, adjudicate preferences and fraudulent transfers, and make pro rata distributions to creditors, who will be barred by the discharge from taking further actions against the bankrupt. * * * [I]n the ordinary bankruptcy proceeding the great bulk of creditor claims are claims that have accrued under state law prior to bankruptcy—claims for goods sold, wages, rent, utilities, and the like. * * * Every such claim must be filed and its validity is subject to adjudication by the bankruptcy court. * * * Hence, the bankruptcy judge is constantly enmeshed in state-law issues.

The new aspect of the Bankruptcy Act of 1978, in this regard, therefore, is not the extension of federal jurisdiction to state-law claims, but its extension to particular kinds of state-law claims, such as contract cases against third parties or disputes involving property in the possession of a third person. Prior to 1978, a claim of a bankrupt against a third party, such as the claim against Marathon in this case, was not within the jurisdiction of the bankruptcy judge. The old limits were based, of course, on the restrictions implicit within the concept of *in rem* jurisdiction; the new extension is based on the concept of *in personam* jurisdiction. * * * The majority at no place explains why this distinction should have constitutional implications. * * *

* * *

In theory and fact, therefore, I can find no basis for that part of the majority's argument that rests on the state-law character of the claim involved here. * * * There is very little reason to strike down § 1471 on its face on the ground that it extends, in a comparatively minimal way, the referees' authority to deal with state-law questions. To do so is to lose all sense of proportion.

II

The plurality unpersuasively attempts to bolster its case for facial invalidity by asserting that the bankruptcy courts are now "exercising powers far greater than those lodged in the adjuncts approved in either Crowell or Raddatz." * * *

I * * * believe that the major premise of the plurality's argument is wholly unsupported: There is no explanation of why Crowell v. Benson, 285 U.S. 22 (1932), and United States v. Raddatz, 447 U.S. 667 (1980), define the outer limits of constitutional authority. Much more relevant to today's decision are, first, the practice in bankruptcy prior to 1978, which neither the majority nor any authoritative case has questioned, and, second, the practice of today's administrative agencies. Considered from this perspective, all of the plurality's arguments are unsupportable abstractions, divorced from the realities of modern practice. * * *

* * *

III

A

The plurality contends that the precedents upholding Art. I courts can be reduced to three categories. First, there are territorial courts * * *. Second, there are courts-martial * * *. Finally, there are those legislative courts and administrative agencies that adjudicate cases involving public rights * * *. Despite the plurality's attempt to cabin the domain of Art. I courts, it is quite unrealistic to consider these to be only three "narrow," limitations on or exceptions to the reach of Art. III. In fact, the plurality itself breaks the mold in its discussion of "adjuncts" in Part IV, when it announces that "when Congress creates a substantive federal right, it possesses substantial discretion to prescribe the manner in which that right may be adjudicated." Adjudications of federal rights may, according to the plurality, be committed to administrative agencies, as long as provision is made for judicial review.

The first principle introduced by the plurality is geographical: Art. I courts presumably are not permitted within the States.[8] The problem, of course, is that both of the other exceptions recognize that Art. I courts can indeed operate within the States. The second category relies upon a new principle: Art. I courts are permissible in areas in which the Constitution grants Congress "extraordinary control over the precise subject matter." Preliminarily, I do not know how we are to distinguish those areas in which Congress' control is "extraordinary" from those in which it is not. * * * But more importantly, in its third category, and in its treatment of "adjuncts," the plurality itself recognizes that Congress can create Art. I courts in virtually all the areas in which Congress is authorized to act, regardless of the quality of the constitutional grant of authority. At the same time, territorial courts or the courts of the District of Columbia, which are Art. I courts, adjudicate private, just as much as public or federal, rights.

Instead of telling us what it is Art. I courts can and cannot do, the plurality presents us with a list of Art. I courts. When we try to distinguish those courts from their Art. III counterparts, we find—apart from the obvious lack of Art. III judges—a series of nondistinctions. By the plurality's own admission, Art. I courts can operate throughout the country, they can adjudicate both private and public rights, and they can adjudicate matters arising from congressional

8. Had the plurality cited only the territorial courts, the principle relied on perhaps could have been the fact that power over the Territories is provided Congress in Art. IV. However, Congress' power over the District of Columbia is an Art. I power. As such, it does not seem to have any greater status than any of the other powers enumerated in Art. I, § 8.

actions in those areas in which congressional control is "extraordinary." I cannot distinguish this last category from the general "arising under" jurisdiction of Art. III courts.

The plurality opinion has the appearance of limiting Art. I courts only because it fails to add together the sum of its parts. Rather than limiting each other, the principles relied upon complement each other; together they cover virtually the whole domain of possible areas of adjudication. Without a unifying principle, the plurality's argument reduces to the proposition that because bankruptcy courts are not sufficiently like any of these three exceptions, they may not be either Art. I courts or adjuncts to Art. III courts. But we need to know why bankruptcy courts cannot qualify as Art. I courts in their own right.

* * *

IV

The complicated and contradictory history of the issue before us leads me to conclude that * * * [t]here is no difference in principle between the work that Congress may assign to an Art. I court and that which the Constitution assigns to Art. III courts. Unless we want to overrule a large number of our precedents upholding a variety of Art. I courts—not to speak of those Art. I courts that go by the contemporary name of "administrative agencies"—this conclusion is inevitable. It is too late to go back that far; too late to return to the simplicity of the principle pronounced in Art. III and defended so vigorously and persuasively by Hamilton in The Federalist Nos. 78–82.

To say that the Court has failed to articulate a principle by which we can test the constitutionality of a putative Art. I court, or that there is no such abstract principle, is not to say that this Court must always defer to the legislative decision to create Art. I, rather than Art. III, courts. Article III is not to be read out of the Constitution; rather, it should be read as expressing one value that must be balanced against competing constitutional values and legislative responsibilities. This Court retains the final word on how that balance is to be struck.

* * *

I do not suggest that the Court should simply look to the strength of the legislative interest and ask itself if that interest is more compelling than the values furthered by Art. III. The inquiry should, rather, focus equally on those Art. III values and ask whether and to what extent the legislative scheme accommodates them or, conversely, substantially undermines them. The burden on Art. III values should then be measured against the values Congress hopes to serve through the use of Art. I courts.

To be more concrete: Crowell, *supra,* suggests that the presence of appellate review by an Art. III court will go a long way toward insuring a proper separation of powers. Appellate review of the decisions of legislative courts, like appellate review of state-court decisions, provides a firm check on the ability of the political institutions of government to ignore or transgress constitutional limits on their own authority. Obviously, therefore, a scheme of Art. I courts that provides for appellate review by Art. III courts should be substantially less controversial than a legislative attempt entirely to avoid judicial review in a constitutional court.

Similarly, as long as the proposed Art. I courts are designed to deal with issues likely to be of little interest to the political branches, there is less reason to fear that such courts represent a dangerous accumulation of power in one of the political branches of government.   * * *

V

I believe that the new bankruptcy courts * * * satisfy this standard.

First, ample provision is made for appellate review by Art. III courts. * * *

Second, no one seriously argues that the Bankruptcy Act of 1978 represents an attempt by the political branches of government to aggrandize themselves at the expense of the third branch or an attempt to undermine the authority of constitutional courts in general. Indeed, the congressional perception of a lack of judicial interest in bankruptcy matters was one of the factors that led to the establishment of the bankruptcy courts: Congress feared that this lack of interest would lead to a failure by federal district courts to deal with bankruptcy matters in an expeditious manner. * * * Although some bankruptcies may indeed present politically controversial circumstances or issues, Congress has far more direct ways to involve itself in such matters than through some sort of subtle, or not so subtle, influence on bankruptcy judges. Furthermore, were such circumstances to arise, the Due Process Clause might very well require that the matter be considered by an Art. III judge * * *.

Finally, * * * I do not believe it is possible to challenge Congress' further determination that it was necessary to create a specialized court to deal with bankruptcy matters. * * *

The real question is not whether Congress was justified in establishing a specialized bankruptcy court, but rather whether it was justified in failing to create a specialized, Art. III bankruptcy court. My own view is that the very fact of extreme specialization may be enough, and certainly has been enough in the past,[18] to justify the creation of a legislative court. Congress may legitimately consider the effect on the federal judiciary of the addition of several hundred specialized judges: We are, on the whole, a body of generalists. The addition of several hundred specialists may substantially change, whether for good or bad, the character of the federal bench. Moreover, Congress may have desired to maintain some flexibility in its possible future responses to the general problem of bankruptcy. There is no question that the existence of several hundred bankruptcy judges with life tenure would have severely limited Congress' future options. Furthermore, the number of bankruptcies may fluctuate, producing a substantially reduced need for bankruptcy judges. Congress may have thought that, in that event, a bankruptcy specialist should not as a general matter serve as a judge in the countless nonspecialized matters that come before the federal courts. * * *

For all of these reasons, I would defer to the congressional judgment. Accordingly, I dissent.

---

18. Consider, for example, the Court of Customs Appeals involved in Ex parte Bakelite Corp., 279 U.S. 438 (1929), or the variety of specialized administrative agencies that engage in some form of adjudication.

NOTE ON THE NORTHERN PIPELINE CASE AND CONGRESSIONAL UTILIZATION OF LEGISLATIVE COURTS

(1) *Why Not Article III Status?* Why didn't Congress simply constitute the bankruptcy courts as Article III courts? In his dissenting opinion, Justice White notes the desirability of a specialized tribunal to deal with bankruptcy, but there is no constitutional barrier to creating Article III courts with specialized jurisdictions, is there?[1] Bankruptcy filings may ebb and flow, but isn't this also true of other kinds of cases?

In the background in Northern Pipeline was an aggressive lobbying effort by the Judicial Conference of the United States—the organization of Article III judges—and Chief Justice Warren Burger to prevent the conferral of Article III status on bankruptcy judges. See Countryman, *Scrambling to Define Bankruptcy Jurisdiction: The Chief Justice, the Judicial Conference, and the Legislative Process,* 22 Harv.J.Legis. 1, 7–12 (1985). At least two former judges, echoed by the chair of the Judicial Conference's ad hoc committee, testified before Congress that the Article III judiciary must remain relatively small to retain the elite status that has traditionally lured first-rate lawyers to the federal bench. See *id.* at 9. Do you agree?[2] If not, should all legislative courts—the nature and jurisdictions of which are described in Chap. I, pp. 43-45, *supra*—be reconstituted as Article III courts? Should the literally thousands of officials exercising adjudicative authority in administrative agencies (see pp. 45-46, *supra*) also receive Article III status?

Note that giving Article III status to all federal, administrative adjudicators would have vast consequences. (i) A large, new cost to phasing programs in and out would be introduced. (ii) It would be made much more difficult, if not impossible, for agencies to use adjudication as a policymaking vehicle. For example, if administrative law judges alone were turned into Article III judges, any appeal of their decisions to "the agency" would raise a problem of executive revision, wouldn't it? See generally Chap. II, Sec. 2, pp. 104-06, *supra*. (iii) The Senate would be subjected to the burden of confirming overwhelming numbers of judges and might cease to regard judicial confirmations as a significant act. (iv) Some diminution in the prestige of federal judgeships and the spirit of the Article III judiciary as an elite corps would likely result. (v) In some contexts, application of law to fact by Article III judges might prove more ad hoc and inconsistent than would decisionmaking by personnel subject to bureaucratically "rational" methods of discipline and hierarchical control. See Mashaw, Bureaucratic Justice (1983).

(2) *Distinguishing Legislative Courts from Administrative Agencies.* What is the difference between a legislative court and an administrative agency? Does adjudication by one raise more constitutional problems than adjudication by the other?

Consider the relevance of the following *generalizations* (which, of course, are subject to significant exceptions):

(a) *Enforceability of Judgments.* The decisions of administrative agencies often are not self-executing, but (as in Crowell v. Benson) instead require an

---

1. Existing Article III courts with specialized jurisdictions are discussed in Chap. I, pp. 41-42, *supra*. On the policy debate concerning the desirability of specialized tribunals, see Chap. I, p. 65, *supra*.

2. For a brief discussion and citations to some of the relevant literature, see Chap. I, pp. 65-66, *supra*.

enforcement action in a federal court. By contrast, the decisions of legislative courts are typically final and enforceable unless appealed. See Redish, *Legislative Courts, Administrative Agencies, and the Northern Pipeline Decision,* 1983 Duke L.J. 197, 216–17.

(b) *Policymaking Functions.* Administrative law doctrine generally permits agencies to use adjudication as an occasion for policymaking. (Administrative law judges, who characteristically make initial or recommended decisions, generally are not policymakers, but their decisions are typically subject to administrative review by officials who are.) Legislative courts, such as the bankruptcy courts in the Northern Pipeline case, are less likely to have any policymaking or enforcement responsibilities.

(c) *Traditions of Justification.* According to Fallon, *Of Legislative Courts, Administrative Agencies, and Article III,* 101 Harv.L.Rev. 915, 920–26, 946–47 (1988), legislative courts have usually been justified as permissible "exceptions" to Article III's requirement of tenure and salary protection. By contrast, at least since Crowell v. Benson, agency adjudication has frequently been justified *under* Article III on the theory that judicial review of the agency's decisionmaking retains "the essential elements" of the judicial power in an Article III court.

(3) *Identifying the Problem in Northern Pipeline.* Are you persuaded by the plurality's argument in Northern Pipeline that it is more problematic for Congress to commit state law claims than federal statutory claims to an Article I court? Don't federal territorial courts exercise supplemental jurisdiction of state law claims? Consider, too, Professor Redish's argument that it is "bizarre" to allow adjudication of federal claims by an Article I court while insisting that "suits between private individuals involving state-created common law rights" need to "be heard in article III courts", given that the latter cases may barely come within Article III at all. Redish, *supra,* at 208–09.[3]

Was the real problem, in the words of the Northern Pipeline plurality, that the government's argument concerning Congress' power to substitute legislative courts for constitutional courts contained "no limiting principle"?

3. It seems clear that Congress may not authorize a legislative court or agency to adjudicate a *diversity* case presenting no issues of federal law. (Do you see why?)

But suppose that, as in Northern Pipeline, the adjudication of the state law question by a federal tribunal is itself justified by a substantive grant of power to Congress to regulate matters of federal concern, so that the *case* in question can be deemed a case arising under federal law. Isn't it clear that the diversity-jurisdiction analysis does not *automatically* carry over to such a case—that additional considerations must be marshalled to compel the conclusion that here, too, Congress is limited to a choice between a state court and a full-blown Article III court?

As Justice White's dissent points out, long before the passage of the Bankruptcy Act of 1978, referees in bankruptcy were routinely adjudicating state-law issues in connection with the ordinary bankruptcy tasks of allowing and disallowing claims against the bankruptcy estate. These were conceptualized as proceedings "in rem", however, whereas the new act expanded the bankruptcy court's jurisdiction to actions in personam brought by the trustee against the bankrupt's debtors. Justice White asks why this should make a constitutional difference. Why should it? See, in this connection, Katchen v. Landy, 382 U.S. 323 (1966), ruling that a bankruptcy court had power to determine whether a payment to a creditor was a preference and to order the payment disgorged—even though these, normally, would be "in personam" claims that the trustee had to bring in state court. The holding that the bankruptcy court had jurisdiction was based on the fact that the creditor had himself filed a claim in bankruptcy, thus giving the bankruptcy court "constructive possession" of the preference.

Was this also a problem with the government's "adjuncts" argument? Was the degree of oversight by Article III courts really that much less in Northern Pipeline than in Crowell v. Benson? How significant is it that judgments of the bankruptcy court were self-executing unless appealed, whereas the orders of the agency in Crowell formally required judicial enforcement actions?

In the immediate aftermath of Northern Pipeline, commentators speculated that long established schemes of administrative adjudication had been put at risk. See, *e.g.,* Redish, *supra.* Do the opinions in the case support this assessment?

(4) *Possible Responses to "The Problem".* Assume (i) that the "deep" problem presented by Northern Pipeline was the possibility that the historic role of Article III courts in the constitutional scheme would be eroded by the piecemeal vesting of adjudicative responsibilities in non-Article III federal tribunals, and (ii) that the Government had indeed failed to furnish an adequate "limiting principle". How might the Court have responded?

(a) *Article III Literalism.* One relatively extreme possibility would have been to adopt a literal reading of Article III: if there are any federal adjudicative tribunals at all, they must be Article III courts. As the early development of "exceptions"[4] indicates, however, it is highly doubtful that this approach represented the original understanding of Congress' power. In any event, it was clearly too late, wasn't it, to upset the myriad schemes of federal, non-Article III adjudication—by both legislative courts and administrative agencies—that were in existence by 1982?

(b) *Historical Exceptions.* While recognizing the impossibility of "literalism", the plurality essentially accepted a literalist approach as reflecting the prevailing and constitutionally mandated norm: a short list of exceptions had been legitimated by some mix of textual analysis and historical acceptance, but departures from literalism could be justified only by reference to a historically accepted exception.[5] How workable was this approach? Justice White is surely correct, isn't he, that the plurality's categorical scheme would be difficult if not impossible to apply to future cases without the identification of some guiding principles?

Note, too, a possible irony arising from a historical exceptions approach. The Justices who joined the Northern Pipeline plurality opinion, in common with Justice Brennan who authored it, clearly were moved in large part by a desire to draw constitutional lines precluding Congress from diminishing the role of Article III courts as guardians of legal rights.[6] But in looking to history as its principal source of authority, the plurality accepted the controlling significance of a traditional line between public and private rights—a line frequently drawn for the express purpose of excluding from the courts altogeth-

---

4. See p. 393, *supra.*

5. A historical exception that the Northern Pipeline plurality did not list embraces military commissions established in areas captured from an enemy and empowered by the President to enforce discipline among civilian populations and to punish spies and saboteurs. See generally Bederman, *Article II Courts,* 44 Mercer L.Rev. 825 (1993).

6. See generally Brown, *Article III as a Fundamental Value—The Demise of Northern Pipeline and Its Implications for Congressional Power,* 49 Ohio St.L.J. 55 (1988).

er claims of right brought by citizens against the government.[7] Considered as a weapon with which to protect the role of Article III courts in enforcing citizens' rights, isn't the public rights tradition a two-edged sword at best?

(c) *Necessary and Proper Test.* At the opposite pole from Article III literalism would be an approach that views Article III as indifferent whether jurisdiction is vested in an Article III court, a legislative court, or an administrative agency. The only relevant questions would be whether use of a non-Article III federal tribunal was "necessary and proper" under Article I and whether it offended some other constitutional provision, such as the Due Process Clause or the Seventh Amendment.

(d) *Balancing.* Dissenting in the Northern Pipeline case, Justice White appeared to endorse a case-by-case balancing approach, in which Article III values are weighed against the interests supporting adjudication by a non-Article III federal tribunal. Is it possible to specify, with even moderate precision, what interests ought to count in the balance and how they ought to be weighed? Would a balancing approach give sufficient guidance to Congress and to lower federal courts?

(e) *Appellate Review.* A final position, built on the approach in Crowell v. Benson, would be to treat sufficiently searching appellate review by an Article III court as both necessary and sufficient to legitimate initial adjudication by a federal legislative court or administrative agency. See Fallon, *supra.* This approach claims the virtue of drawing only clear and enforceable lines.[8] As the price for doing so, it eschews efforts to inquire closely into the necessity or desirability of initial adjudication by a legislative court or administrative agency in a particular case. Compare Saphire & Solimine, *Shoring Up Article III: Legislative Court Doctrine in the Post CFTC v. Schor Era,* 68 B.U.L.Rev. 85, 135–51 (1988)(suggesting that review by an Article III court should be viewed as necessary, but not sufficient, to validate adjudication by a legislative court or administrative agency); Meltzer, *Legislative Courts, Legislative Power, and the Constitution,* 65 Ind.L.J. 291 (1990)(same).

(5) *Article III Cases and Controversies.* Note that all of the approaches identified in Paragraph (4), except for Article III literalism, and apparently all of the Justices in the Northern Pipeline case, accept that (i) at least some of the "cases" and "controversies" enumerated in Article III can be assigned by Congress to non-Article III federal tribunals, (ii) the decision to allocate judicial business of the kind referred to in Article III does not change the character of that business, and (iii) appellate review by an Article III court of the decisions of a federal legislative court or administrative agency is therefore permissible.

From these propositions, doesn't it follow that it is impossible to distinguish constitutional courts from legislative courts on the ground that the former exercise the exclusive power to adjudicate the judicial business enumerated in Article III, whereas the latter exercise judicial power in another class of cases? See Glidden v. Zdanok, 370 U.S. 530 (1962).[9]

---

7. See, *e.g.,* Strauss, *The Place of the Agencies in Government: Separation of Powers and the Fourth Branch,* 84 Colum.L.Rev. 573, 632 (1984); but *cf.* p. 396, *supra,* discussing the sometime availability of "officer suits" even in public rights cases.

8. Note, however, that hard questions would remain about the necessary scope of review. See Fallon, *supra,* at 974–92.

9. The most notorious instance of an attempt to act on the contrary view—that legislative courts may not adjudicate any of the cases and controversies enumerated in

(6) *Bankruptcy Jurisdiction after Northern Pipeline.*   After the Northern Pipeline decision (and after a short period during which an emergency rule, drafted by the Judicial Conference, was in effect in most districts), Congress in 1984 enacted a new Bankruptcy Act.   Act of July 10, 1984, 98 Stat. 333.[10]   The 1984 statute makes the bankruptcy judges (who are appointed by the courts of appeals for 14–year terms) "units" of the district court; it directs that each district court "may provide" that "any or all" cases or proceedings arising under Title 11, or arising in or related to a case under Title 11, shall be referred to the bankruptcy judges of the district.   If the matter is a "core" proceeding—corresponding, roughly, to the pre–1978 bankruptcy court's "summary" jurisdiction—the bankruptcy judge may "hear and determine" it.   But if the matter is a non-core proceeding, the bankruptcy judge makes only proposed findings and conclusions, and the final order is entered by the district judge after "reviewing de novo" all matters as to which an objection was made.[11] "Personal injury tort and wrongful death claims" must be adjudicated in the district court.

Article III—was Williams v. United States, 289 U.S. 553, referred to in the Northern Pipeline opinion, which held that the salaries of the judges of the Court of Claims were subject to reduction under the Economy Act of 1933.   Writing for the Court, Justice Sutherland set forth the holding in Ex parte Bakelite Corp., 279 U.S. 438 (1929), that the Court of Customs and Patent Appeals is an Article I court, and observed that the Court of Claims was in relevant respects similar to the Court of Customs and Patent Appeals. He then said (289 U.S. at 571):

"We might well rest the present case upon that determination; but must not do so without considering another view of the question, which seems to find support in some expressions of this court, namely, that when the United States consents to be sued, the judicial power of Article 3 at once attaches to the court upon which jurisdiction is conferred in virtue of the clause which in comprehensive terms extends the judicial power to 'controversies to which the United States shall be a party.' "

The opinion appeared to accept without question the premise of this argument— namely, that if cases in the Court of Claims are "controversies to which the United States shall be a party," in the constitutional sense, the court would have to be a constitutional court.   After elaborate consideration it rejected the argument on the sole ground that the constitutional provision must be treated "as though it read, 'controversies to which the United States shall be a party plaintiff or petitioner' "(*id.* at 577).

Among other things wrong with Justice Sutherland's reasoning, note (a) his failure to explain how the Supreme Court can have original jurisdiction of an action by a state against the United States when the United States consents, Minnesota v. Hitchcock, 185 U.S. 373 (1902), p. 307, *supra;* (b) the unexamined difficulties with the corollary of his conclusion that in other consented actions against the United States, the district courts, and the Supreme Court on appeal, must be exercising some other judicial power than "the judicial power defined by Article III"; and (c) his failure even to consider the question why cases in the Court of Claims, at least, are not "Cases * * * arising under * * * the Laws of the United States".

Can you explain how the intellectual disaster of the Williams case could have been perpetrated within a year of Crowell v. Benson?   Does the only possible explanation lie in the conceptual difficulty, if not intractability, of the subject matter?

10.   The intervening uncertainties and machinations are described vividly in Countryman, *supra*, at 19–33.

11.   In Celotex Corp. v. Edwards, 115 S.Ct. 1493 (1995), the Supreme Court held (7–2) that a bankruptcy court, pursuant to its jurisdiction over proceedings "related to" bankruptcies, may enjoin a judgment creditor from executing on a supersedeas bond following the entry of a final judgment by an Article III court.   Justice Stevens, joined in dissent by Justice Ginsburg, argued that a bankruptcy judge, lacking jurisdiction finally to "determine" a question only "related to" bankruptcy, also lacks jurisdiction to issue an

A number of constitutional issues have arisen under the 1984 Act. For a useful survey and analysis, see Ferriell, *The Constitutionality of the Bankruptcy Amendments and Federal Judgeship Act of 1984*, 63 Am.Bankr.L.J. 109 (1989). Some of the largest perplexities involve questions not considered in the Northern Pipeline case, including when the Seventh Amendment creates a right to trial by jury and whether the Article I bankruptcy courts are constitutionally and statutorily authorized to conduct such trials. For further discussion of these issues, see *Note on the Granfinanciera Case, the Relevance of the Distinction Between Public and Private Rights, and the Seventh Amendment*, p. 433, *infra*.

Commodity Futures Trading Comm'n v. Schor

478 U.S. 833, 106 S.Ct. 3245, 92 L.Ed.2d 675 (1986).
Certiorari to the United States Court of Appeals for the District of Columbia Circuit.

■ JUSTICE O'CONNOR delivered the opinion of the Court.

The question presented is whether the Commodity Exchange Act (CEA or Act), 7 U.S.C. § 1 *et seq.*, empowers the Commodity Futures Trading Commission (CFTC or Commission) to entertain state law counterclaims in reparation proceedings and, if so, whether that grant of authority violates Article III of the Constitution.

I

The CEA broadly prohibits fraudulent and manipulative conduct in connection with commodity futures transactions. In 1974, Congress "overhaul[ed]" the Act in order to institute a more "comprehensive regulatory structure to oversee the volatile and esoteric futures trading complex." H.R.Rep. No. 93–975, p. 1 (1974). Congress also determined that the broad regulatory powers of the CEA were most appropriately vested in an agency which would be relatively immune from the "political winds that sweep Washington." H.R.Rep. No. 93–975, pp. 44, 70. It therefore created an independent agency, the CFTC, and entrusted to it sweeping authority to implement the CEA.

Among the duties assigned to the CFTC was the administration of a reparations procedure through which disgruntled customers of professional commodity brokers could seek redress for the brokers' violations of the Act or CFTC regulations. Thus, § 14 of the CEA, 7 U.S.C.A. § 18, provides that any person injured by such violations may apply to the Commission for an order directing the offender to pay reparations to the complainant and may enforce that order in federal district court. Congress intended this administrative procedure to be an "inexpensive and expeditious" alternative to existing fora available to aggrieved customers, namely, the courts and arbitration. * * *

In conformance with the congressional goal of promoting efficient dispute resolution, the CFTC promulgated a regulation in 1976 which allows it to adjudicate counterclaims "aris[ing] out of the transaction or occurrence or series of transactions or occurrences set forth in the complaint." 17 CFR § 12.23(b)(2)(1983). This permissive counterclaim rule leaves the respondent

injunction preventing an Article III court
from determining such a question.

in a reparations proceeding free to seek relief against the reparations complainant in other fora.

The instant dispute arose in February 1980, when respondents Schor and Mortgage Services of America invoked the CFTC's reparations jurisdiction by filing complaints against petitioner ContiCommodity Services, Inc. (Conti), a commodity futures broker, and Richard L. Sandor, a Conti employee. Schor had an account with Conti which contained a debit balance because Schor's net futures trading losses and expenses, such as commissions, exceeded the funds deposited in the account. Schor alleged that this debit balance was the result of Conti's numerous violations of the CEA.

Before receiving notice that Schor had commenced the reparations proceeding, Conti had filed a diversity action in Federal District Court to recover the debit balance. Schor counterclaimed in this action, reiterating his charges that the debit balance was due to Conti's violations of the CEA. Schor also moved on two separate occasions to dismiss or stay the district court action, arguing that the continuation of the federal action would be a waste of judicial resources and an undue burden on the litigants in view of the fact that "[t]he reparations proceedings * * * will fully * * * resolve and adjudicate all the rights of the parties to this action with respect to the transactions which are the subject matter of this action."

Although the District Court declined to stay or dismiss the suit, Conti voluntarily dismissed the federal court action and presented its debit balance claim by way of a counterclaim in the CFTC reparations proceeding. * * *

After discovery, briefing and a hearing, the Administrative Law Judge (ALJ) in Schor's reparations proceeding ruled in Conti's favor on both Schor's claims and Conti's counterclaims. After this ruling, Schor for the first time challenged the CFTC's statutory authority to adjudicate Conti's counterclaim. The ALJ rejected Schor's challenge, stating himself "bound by agency regulations and published agency policies." The Commission declined to review the decision and allowed it to become final, at which point Schor filed a petition for review with the Court of Appeals for the District of Columbia Circuit.

After briefing and argument, the Court of Appeals upheld the CFTC's decision on Schor's claim in most respects, but ordered the dismissal of Conti's counterclaims on the ground that "the CFTC lacks authority (subject matter competence) to adjudicate" common law counterclaims. [Believing that] * * * the CFTC's exercise of jurisdiction over Conti's common law counterclaim gave rise to "[s]erious constitutional problems" under Northern Pipeline [Construction Co. v. Marathon Pipe Line Co., 458 U.S. 50 (1982),] * * * the Court of Appeals * * * concluded that, under well-established principles of statutory construction, the [CEA should not be construed to authorize CFTC jurisdiction over state law counterclaims]. * * *

* * *

We * * * granted certiorari, and now reverse.

II

* * *

* * * [T]he court below did not seriously contest that Congress intended to authorize the CFTC to adjudicate *some* counterclaims in reparations proceedings. Rather, the court read into the facially unqualified reference to counter-

claim jurisdiction a distinction between counterclaims arising under the Act or CFTC regulations and all other counterclaims. While the court's reading permitted it to avoid a potential Article III problem, it did so only by doing violence to the CEA, for its distinction cannot fairly be drawn from the language or history of the CEA, nor reconciled with the congressional purposes motivating the creation of the reparation proceeding.

* * *

Reference to the instant controversy illustrates the crippling effect that the Court of Appeals' restrictive reading of the CFTC's counterclaim jurisdiction would have on the efficacy of the reparations remedy. The dispute between Schor and Conti is typical of the disputes adjudicated in reparations proceedings: a customer and a professional commodities broker agree that there is a debit balance in the customer's account, but the customer attributes the deficit to the broker's alleged CEA violations and the broker attributes it to the customer's lack of success in the market. The customer brings a reparations claim; the broker counterclaims for the amount of the debit balance. In the usual case, then, the counterclaim "arises out of precisely the same course of events" as the principal claim and requires resolution of many of the same disputed factual issues.

Under the Court of Appeals' approach, the entire dispute may not be resolved in the administrative forum. Consequently, the entire dispute will typically end up in court, for when the broker files suit to recover the debit balance, the customer will normally be compelled either by compulsory counterclaim rules or by the expense and inconvenience of litigating the same issues in two fora to forgo his reparations remedy and to litigate his claim in court. * * * In sum, as Schor himself aptly summarized, to require a bifurcated examination of the single dispute "would be to emasculate if not destroy the purposes of the Commodity Exchange Act to provide an efficient and relatively inexpensive forum for the resolution of disputes in futures trading." * * *

As our discussion makes manifest, the CFTC's longheld position that it has the power to take jurisdiction over counterclaims such as Conti's is eminently reasonable and well within the scope of its delegated authority. * * *

III

* * *

Schor claims that [Article III] prohibit[s] Congress from authorizing the initial adjudication of common law counterclaims by the CFTC, an administrative agency whose adjudicatory officers do not enjoy the tenure and salary protections embodied in Article III.

Although our precedents in this area do not admit of easy synthesis, they do establish that the resolution of claims such as Schor's cannot turn on conclusory reference to the language of Article III. Rather, the constitutionality of a given congressional delegation of adjudicative functions to a non-Article III body must be assessed by reference to the purposes underlying the requirements of Article III. This inquiry, in turn, is guided by the principle that "practical attention to substance rather than doctrinaire reliance on formal categories should inform application of Article III." Thomas v. Union Carbide Agricultural Products Co., 473 U.S. 568, 584 (1985).

A

Article III, § 1 serves both to protect "the role of the independent judiciary within the constitutional scheme of tripartite government," Thomas, *supra*, at 582–83, and to safeguard litigants' "right to have claims decided before judges who are free from potential domination by other branches of government." United States v. Will, 449 U.S. 200, 218 (1980). * * *

Our precedents also demonstrate, however, that Article III does not confer on litigants an absolute right to the plenary consideration of every nature of claim by an Article III court. Moreover, as a personal right, Article III's guarantee of an impartial and independent federal adjudication is subject to waiver, just as are other personal constitutional rights that dictate the procedures by which civil and criminal matters must be tried. Indeed, the relevance of concepts of waiver to Article III challenges is demonstrated by our decision in Northern Pipeline, in which the absence of consent to an initial adjudication before a non-Article III tribunal was relied on as a significant factor in determining that Article III forbade such adjudication. * * *

In the instant case, Schor indisputably waived any right he may have possessed to the full trial of Conti's counterclaim before an Article III court. Schor expressly demanded that Conti proceed on its counterclaim in the reparations proceeding rather than before the District Court, and was content to have the entire dispute settled in the forum he had selected until the ALJ ruled against him on all counts * * *.

Even were there no evidence of an express waiver here, Schor's election to forgo his right to proceed in state or federal court on his claim and his decision to seek relief instead in a CFTC reparations proceeding constituted an effective waiver. * * *

B

As noted above, our precedents establish that Article III, § 1 not only preserves to litigants their interest in an impartial and independent federal adjudication of claims within the judicial power of the United States, but also serves as "an inseparable element of the constitutional system of checks and balances." Northern Pipeline, 458 U.S. at 58. * * * To the extent that this structural principle is implicated in a given case, the parties cannot by consent cure the constitutional difficulty for the same reason that the parties by consent cannot confer on federal courts subject matter jurisdiction beyond the limitations imposed by Article III, § 2. * * *

In determining the extent to which a given congressional decision to authorize the adjudication of Article III business in a non-Article III tribunal impermissibly threatens the institutional integrity of the Judicial Branch, the Court has declined to adopt formalistic and unbending rules. Thomas, 473 U.S., at 583. Although such rules might lend a greater degree of coherence to this area of the law, they might also unduly constrict Congress' ability to take needed and innovative action pursuant to its Article I powers. Thus, in reviewing Article III challenges, we have weighed a number of factors, none of which has been deemed determinative, with an eye to the practical effect that the congressional action will have on the constitutionally assigned role of the federal judiciary. Among the factors upon which we have focused are the extent to which the "essential attributes of judicial power" are reserved to Article III courts, and, conversely, the extent to which the non-Article III forum exercises the range of jurisdiction and powers normally vested only in Article

III courts, the origins and importance of the right to be adjudicated, and the concerns that drove Congress to depart from the requirements of Article III.
* * *

An examination of the relative allocation of powers between the CFTC and Article III courts in light of the considerations given prominence in our precedents demonstrates that the congressional scheme does not impermissibly intrude on the province of the judiciary. The CFTC's adjudicatory powers depart from the traditional agency model in just one respect: the CFTC's jurisdiction over common law counterclaims. While wholesale importation of concepts of pendent or ancillary jurisdiction into the agency context may create greater constitutional difficulties, we decline to endorse an absolute prohibition on such jurisdiction out of fear of where some hypothetical "slippery slope" may deposit us. Indeed, the CFTC's exercise of this type of jurisdiction is not without precedent. Thus, in Reconstruction Finance Corp. v. Bankers Trust Co., 318 U.S. 163, 168–171 (1943), we saw no constitutional difficulty in the initial adjudication of a state law claim by a federal agency, subject to judicial review, when that claim was ancillary to a federal law dispute. Similarly, in Katchen v. Landy, 382 U.S. 323 (1966), this Court upheld a bankruptcy referee's power to hear and decide state law counterclaims against a creditor who filed a claim in bankruptcy when those counterclaims arose out of the same transaction. We reasoned that, as a practical matter, requiring the trustee to commence a plenary action to recover on its counterclaim would be a "meaningless gesture." *Id.,* at 334.

In the instant case, we are likewise persuaded that there is little practical reason to find that this single deviation from the agency model is fatal to the congressional scheme. Aside from its authorization of counterclaim jurisdiction, the CEA leaves far more of the "essential attributes of judicial power" to Article III courts than did that portion of the Bankruptcy Act found unconstitutional in Northern Pipeline. The CEA scheme in fact hews closely to the agency model approved by the Court in Crowell v. Benson.

The CFTC, like the agency in Crowell, deals only with a "particularized area of law," Northern Pipeline, *supra,* 458 U.S., at 85, whereas the jurisdiction of the bankruptcy courts found unconstitutional in Northern Pipeline extended to broadly "all civil proceedings arising under title 11 or arising in or *related to* cases under title 11." 28 U.S.C. § 1471(b). CFTC orders, like those of the agency in Crowell, but unlike those of the bankruptcy courts under the 1978 Act, are enforceable only by order of the District Court. CFTC orders are also reviewed under the same "weight of the evidence" standard sustained in Crowell, rather than the more deferential standard found lacking in Northern Pipeline. The legal rulings of the CFTC, like the legal determinations of the agency in Crowell, are subject to *de novo* review. Finally, the CFTC, unlike the bankruptcy courts under the 1978 Act, does not exercise "all ordinary powers of district courts," and thus may not, for instance, preside over jury trials or issue writs of habeas corpus. 458 U.S., at 85.

Of course, the nature of the claim has significance in our Article III analysis quite apart from the method prescribed for its adjudication. The counterclaim asserted in this case is a "private" right for which state law provides the rule of decision. It is therefore a claim of the kind assumed to be at the "core" of matters normally reserved to Article III courts. * * * Yet this conclusion does not end our inquiry; just as this Court has rejected any attempt to make determinative for Article III purposes the distinction between public rights and private rights, Thomas, *supra,* at 585–86, there is no reason inherent in separation of powers principles to accord the state law character of a claim talismanic power in Article III inquiries. * * *

[W]here private, common law rights are at stake, our examination of the congressional attempt to control the manner in which those rights are adjudicated has been searching. In this case, however, "[l]ooking beyond form to the substance of what" Congress has done, we are persuaded that the congressional authorization of limited CFTC jurisdiction over a narrow class of common law claims as an incident to the CFTC's primary, and unchallenged, adjudicative function does not create a substantial threat to the separation of powers.

It is clear that Congress has not attempted to "withdraw from judicial cognizance" the determination of Conti's right to the sum represented by the debit balance in Schor's account. Congress gave the CFTC the authority to adjudicate such matters, but the decision to invoke this forum is left entirely to the parties and the power of the federal judiciary to take jurisdiction of these matters is unaffected. * * * This is not to say, of course, that if Congress created a phalanx of non-Article III tribunals equipped to handle the entire business of the Article III courts without any Article III supervision or control and without evidence of valid and specific legislative necessities, the fact that the parties had the election to proceed in their forum of choice would necessarily save the scheme from constitutional attack. But this case obviously bears no resemblance to such a scenario * * *.

When Congress authorized the CFTC to adjudicate counterclaims, its primary focus was on making effective a specific and limited federal regulatory scheme, not on allocating jurisdiction among federal tribunals. Congress intended to create an inexpensive and expeditious alternative forum through which customers could enforce the provisions of the CEA against professional brokers. Its decision to endow the CFTC with jurisdiction over such reparations claims is readily understandable given the perception that the CFTC was relatively immune from political pressures, see H.R.Rep. No. 93–975, pp. 44, 70, and the obvious expertise that the Commission possesses in applying the CEA and its own regulations. This reparations scheme itself is of unquestioned constitutional validity. See, *e.g.,* Thomas, *supra;* Northern Pipeline; Crowell v. Benson. It was only to ensure the effectiveness of this scheme that Congress authorized the CFTC to assert jurisdiction over common law counterclaims. Indeed, as was explained above, absent the CFTC's exercise of that authority, the purposes of the reparations procedure would have been confounded.

It also bears emphasis that the CFTC's assertion of counterclaim jurisdiction is limited to that which is necessary to make the reparations procedure workable. * * *

In such circumstances, the magnitude of any intrusion on the Judicial Branch can only be termed *de minimis.* Conversely, were we to hold that the Legislative Branch may not permit such limited cognizance of common law counterclaims at the election of the parties, it is clear that we would "defeat the obvious purpose of the legislation to furnish a prompt, continuous, expert and inexpensive method for dealing with a class of questions of fact which are peculiarly suited to examination and determination by an administrative agency specially assigned to that task." Crowell v. Benson, 285 U.S., at 46. We do not think Article III compels this degree of prophylaxis. * * *

C

Schor asserts that Article III, § 1, constrains Congress for reasons of federalism, as well as for reasons of separation of powers. He argues that the state law character of Conti's counterclaim transforms the central question in this case from whether Congress has trespassed upon the judicial powers of the Federal Government into whether Congress has invaded the prerogatives of state governments.

* * *

Even assuming that principles of federalism are relevant to Article III analysis, * * * we are unpersuaded that those principles require the invalidation of the CFTC's counterclaim jurisdiction. The sole fact that Conti's counterclaim is resolved by a *federal* rather than a *state* tribunal could not be said to unduly impair state interests, for it is established that a federal court could, without constitutional hazard, decide a counterclaim such as the one asserted here under its ancillary jurisdiction, even if an independent jurisdictional basis for it were lacking. * * *

The judgment of the Court of Appeals for the District of Columbia Circuit is reversed and the case remanded for further proceedings consistent with this opinion.

It is so ordered.

■ JUSTICE BRENNAN, with whom JUSTICE MARSHALL joins, dissenting.

* * *

* * * [The] important functions of Article III are too central to our constitutional scheme to risk their incremental erosion. The exceptions we have recognized for territorial courts, courts martial, and administrative courts were each based on "certain exceptional powers bestowed upon Congress by the Constitution or by historical consensus." Northern Pipeline, 458 U.S., at 70 (opinion of Brennan, J.). Here, however, there is no equally forceful reason to extend further these exceptions to situations that are distinguishable from existing precedents.

* * *

* * * Article III's prophylactic protections were intended to prevent just this sort of abdication to claims of legislative convenience. The Court requires that the legislative interest in convenience and efficiency be weighed against the competing interest in judicial independence. In doing so, the Court pits an interest the benefits of which are immediate, concrete, and easily understood against one, the benefits of which are almost entirely prophylactic, and thus often seem remote and not worth the cost in any single case. Thus, while this balancing creates the illusion of objectivity and ineluctability, in fact the result was foreordained, because the balance is weighted against judicial independence. See Redish, *Legislative Courts, Administrative Agencies, and the Northern Pipeline Decision*, 1983 Duke L.J. 197, 221–222. The danger of the Court's balancing approach is, of course, that as individual cases accumulate in which the Court finds that the short-term benefits of efficiency outweigh the long-term benefits of judicial independence, the protections of Article III will be eviscerated.

Perhaps the resolution of reparations claims such as respondent's may be accomplished more conveniently under the Court's decision than under my approach, but the Framers foreswore this sort of convenience in order to preserve freedom. As we explained in INS v. Chadha, 462 U.S. 919, 959 (1983):

> "The choices we discern as having been made in the Constitutional Convention impose burdens on governmental processes that often seem clumsy, inefficient, even unworkable, but those hard choices were consciously made by men who had lived under a form of government that permitted arbitrary governmental acts to go unchecked. * * *."

Moreover, in Bowsher v. Synar, 478 U.S. 714 (1986), we rejected the appellant's argument that legislative convenience saved the constitutionality of the assignment by Congress to the Comptroller General of essentially executive functions, stating that "the fact that a given law or procedure is efficient, convenient, and useful in facilitating functions of government, standing alone, will not save it if it is contrary to the Constitution. Convenience and efficiency are not the primary objectives—or the hallmarks—of democratic government * * *." Id., at 736 (quoting Chadha, supra, at 944).

It is impossible to reconcile the radically different approaches the Court takes to separation of powers in this case and in Bowsher. * * *

* * *

IV

The Court's reliance on Schor's "consent" to a non-Article III tribunal is also misplaced. The Court erroneously suggests that there is a clear division between the separation of powers and the impartial adjudication functions of Article III. The Court identifies Article III's structural, or separation of powers, function as preservation of the judiciary's domain from encroachment by another branch. The Court identifies the impartial adjudication function as the protection afforded by Article III to individual litigants against judges who may be dominated by other branches of government.

In my view, the structural and individual interests served by Article III are inseparable. The potential exists for individual litigants to be deprived of impartial decisionmakers only where federal officials who exercise judicial power are susceptible to congressional and executive pressure. That is, individual litigants may be harmed by the assignment of judicial power to non-Article III federal tribunals only where the Legislative or Executive Branches have encroached upon judicial authority and have thus threatened the separation of powers. The Court correctly recognizes that to the extent that Article III's structural concerns are implicated by a grant of judicial power to a non-Article III tribunal, "the parties cannot by consent cure the constitutional difficulty for the same reason that the parties by consent cannot confer on federal courts subject-matter jurisdiction beyond the limitations imposed by Article III, § 2." Because the individual and structural interests served by Article III are coextensive, I do not believe that a litigant may ever waive his right to an Article III tribunal where one is constitutionally required. In other words, consent is irrelevant to Article III analysis.

V

Our Constitution unambiguously enunciates a fundamental principle—that the "judicial power of the United States" be reposed in an independent judiciary. It is our obligation zealously to guard that independence so that our tripartite system of government remains strong and that individuals continue to be protected against decisionmakers subject to majoritarian pressures. Unfortunately, today the Court forsakes that obligation for expediency. I dissent.

———

FURTHER NOTE ON LEGISLATIVE COURTS

(1) *Developments Between the Northern Pipeline and Schor Cases.* As indicated in the Schor opinions, between Northern Pipeline and Schor the Supreme Court addressed the validity of an Article I tribunal in Thomas v. Union Carbide Agricultural Products Co., 473 U.S. 568 (1985). The Union Carbide case arose under the Federal Insecticide, Fungicide, and Rodenticide Act (FIFRA), 7 U.S.C. § 136 *et seq.*, which requires manufacturers of pesticides, as a precondition to obtaining the registration necessary to market a new product, to submit extensive research data to EPA concerning the product's health and environmental effects. In order to streamline the registration process and make it less costly, the statute permits the EPA in certain situations to use data previously submitted by another registrant in considering the registration application of a later ("me-too" or "follow-on") registrant. The Act authorizes the EPA to consider previously submitted data, however, only if the later registrant offers to compensate the original data submitter. If the original and follow-up registrants cannot agree on the terms of compensation, the issue must be submitted to binding arbitration before a private arbitrator, whose decision is subject to judicial review only for "fraud, misrepresentation, or other misconduct". See 7 U.S.C. § 136a(c)(1)(D)(ii).

In upholding the statute's arbitration provision against a challenge based on Article III,[1] Justice O'Connor's opinion for the Court stated that "an absolute construction of Article III is not possible", and that "the Court has long recognized that Congress is not barred from acting pursuant to its powers under Article I to vest decisionmaking authority in tribunals that lack the attributes of Article III courts" (p. 583). The lead opinion in Northern Pipeline spoke only for a plurality, Justice O'Connor emphasized. In addition, it adopted too categorical an approach in suggesting that the public rights/private rights dichotomy of Crowell and Murray's Lessee provides a bright-line test for determining the requirements of Article III and that, for a case to come within the public rights category, the government must be a party (pp. 584–86). "The enduring lesson of Crowell is that practical attention to substance rather than doctrinaire reliance on formal categories should inform application of Article III" (p. 587).

Turning to the dispute before it, the Court observed that although the liability of one private party to another was at stake, the case had "many of the characteristics" of a public rights dispute, apparently because it arose under a complex regulatory scheme (p. 589). The crucial point did not involve categorization, however. The administrative scheme represented "a pragmatic solution to the difficult problem of spreading the costs of generating adequate information regarding the safety, health, and environmental impact of a potentially dangerous product" (p. 590). The arbitration mechanism "incorporates

---

1. The Court said that it had no occasion to "identify the extent to which due process may require review of determinations by the arbitrator because the parties stipulated below to abandon any due process claims" (pp. 592–93). The Court also said, however, that because "review of constitutional error is preserved", FIFRA "does not obstruct whatever judicial review might be required by due process" (p. 592).

its own system of internal sanctions and relies only tangentially, if at all, on the Judicial Branch for enforcement. The danger of Congress or the Executive encroaching on the Article III judicial powers is at a minimum when no unwilling defendant is subjected to judicial enforcement * * * (p. 591)". Finally, "FIFRA limits but does not preclude review of the arbitration proceeding by an Article III court", since awards can be set aside for "fraud, misconduct or misrepresentation" and "review of constitutional error is preserved" (p. 592).

Justice Brennan, joined by Justices Blackmun and Marshall, concurred in the judgment in a separate opinion. He noted that the Northern Pipeline plurality had disclaimed any intent to create "a generally applicable definition of 'public rights' but concluded that at a minimum public rights disputes must arise 'between the government and others'" (p. 597). Then, however, Justice Brennan seemed to switch gears: "Though the issue before us in this case is not free of doubt, in my judgment the FIFRA compensation scheme challenged in this case should be viewed as involving a matter of public rights as that term is understood in the line of cases culminating in Northern Pipeline. In one sense the question of proper compensation for a follow-on registrant's use of test data is, under the FIFRA scheme, a dispute about 'the liability of one individual to another under the law as defined', Crowell v. Benson, at 51 (defining matters of private right). But the dispute arises in the context of a federal regulatory scheme that virtually occupies the field. Congress has decided that effectuation of the public policies of FIFRA demands not only a requirement of compensation from follow-on registrants in return for mandatory access to data but also an administrative process—mandatory negotiation followed by binding arbitration—to ensure that unresolved compensation disputes do not delay public distribution of needed products. This case, in other words, involves not only the congressional prescription of a federal rule of decision to govern a private dispute but also the active participation of a federal regulatory agency in resolving the dispute. Although a compensation dispute under FIFRA ultimately involves a determination of the duty owed one private party by another, at its heart the dispute involves the exercise of authority by a Federal Government arbitrator in the course of administration of FIFRA's comprehensive regulatory scheme" (pp. 600–01).

(2) *Balancing.* Does Schor adopt the balancing approach urged by Justice White's dissenting opinion in the Northern Pipeline case? Does it refine that approach by providing a list of factors to be taken into account?[2]

Does the majority respond adequately to the worry, expressed by Justice Brennan in his dissenting opinion, that the central role of the Article III judiciary might be eroded by a series of balancing decisions that, though individually innocuous, collectively deprived the courts of their fundamental role in the constitutional scheme?

Justice Brennan is right, isn't he, that the balancing approach of Schor is hard to square with the rigid view of the constitutionally mandated separation of powers adopted in INS v. Chadha, 462 U.S. 919 (1983)(holding legislative veto provisions constitutionally invalid), and Bowsher v. Synar, 478 U.S. 714 (1986)(invalidating a statute designed to trigger federal budgets cuts on the

---

2. Does Schor offer adequate guidance to Congress and the lower federal courts? See generally Whitten, *Consent, Caseload, and Other Justifications for Non–Article III* *Courts and Judges: A Comment on Commodities Futures Trading Comm'n v. Schor,* 20 Creighton L.Rev. 11 (1986).

ground that it vested executive functions in an employee potentially subject to congressional influence)? On the other hand, the "formalist" approach of the Chadha and Bowsher cases may be difficult to reconcile with Crowell v. Benson and, more generally, with the assignment of a mix of executive, rule-making, and adjudicative functions to administrative agencies. See generally Strauss, *Formal and Functional Approaches to Separation of Powers Questions—A Foolish Inconsistency?*, 72 Corn.L.Rev. 488 (1987).

Once a role for adjudication by administrative agencies and legislative courts is admitted, is some form of balancing possibly unavoidable, to determine the acceptable limits of a functionally or pragmatically justified role for non-Article III adjudicators? Consider Justice Brennan's own position in the Union Carbide case, where he held that a dispute about the liability of one private party to another "should be viewed as involving a matter of public rights" (p. 600) due to its connection with a congressionally established scheme, even though, historically, "public rights disputes must arise 'between the government and others' "(p. 597).

Note that not all balancing need be ad hoc. Another approach would be to hold, as the result of a more nearly categorical calculus, that Article III values *always* require—in "cases" (in that term's constitutional sense) initially assigned to non-Article III federal adjudicators—the availability of relatively broad powers of appellate review in an Article III court. Consider Fallon, *Of Legislative Courts, Administrative Agencies, and Article III*, 101 Harv.L.Rev. 915, 991 (1988):

"Northern Pipeline * * * was not only badly reasoned but wrongly decided. The availability of appellate review by Article III courts offered sufficient protection for Article III values. * * *

"Union Carbide should also have come out the other way. Decisions of federal law were committed to an arbitrator, whose rulings were subject to judicial review only for fraud and misconduct. In the absence of broader judicial review, investiture of authority to decide questions of law in a non-Article III decisionmaker encroaches too deeply on the fairness and separation-of-powers values that Article III embodies.

"Schor, by contrast, rightly upheld the CFTC's jurisdiction over state law counterclaims, because the statute provided for de novo review of questions of law by an Article III court."

(3) *The Significance of Consent.* The balancing analysis conducted in Schor was predicated on the waiver of any personal right to an Article III tribunal. Would it be fair to say that Schor gives no guidance whatever in the absence of waiver?[3] And what constitutes a valid waiver? In Schor, the Court held that merely invoking the CEA procedure constituted consent to a counterclaim. When federal programs provide for the compulsory arbitration of disputes, can every participant be deemed to have consented to arbitration simply by participating in the program? See generally Bruff, *Public Programs, Private Deciders: The Constitutionality of Arbitration in Federal Programs*, 67 Tex.L.Rev. 441 (1989).[4]

3. For a discussion of the importance of consent to the exercise of judicial power by magistrate judges, see *Note on Magistrate Judges*, p. 437, *infra*.

4. For a broad view of what constitutes valid consent, see Geldermann, Inc. v. CFTC, 836 F.2d 310, 316–21 (7th Cir.1987). The CFTC had adopted a rule obliging the Chica-

(4) *What Remains of the Northern Pipeline Approach?* Did the Supreme Court's decisions in the Union Carbide and Schor cases definitively reject the categorical approach of the Northern Pipeline plurality and, in particular, the central significance that it attached to the distinction between public and private rights? Many observers thought so—at least until the Supreme Court's confusing decision in Granfinanciera, S.A. v. Nordberg, 492 U.S. 33 (1989), discussed immediately below.

NOTE ON THE GRANFINANCIERA CASE, THE RELEVANCE OF THE DISTINCTION BETWEEN PUBLIC AND PRIVATE RIGHTS, AND THE SEVENTH AMENDMENT

(1) *The Granfinanciera Case.* Granfinanciera, S.A. v. Nordberg, 492 U.S. 33 (1989), arose when a trustee in bankruptcy filed suit in federal court to recover a sum of money alleged to have been fraudulently transferred to Granfinanciera. The district court referred the proceedings to the bankruptcy court for its district, which rejected Granfinanciera's claimed right to a jury trial on the ground that an action to recover a fraudulent conveyance is equitable, not legal. The court of appeals affirmed, but the Supreme Court reversed.

In a puzzling opinion by Justice Brennan, the Court first held the trustee's suit to be legal, not equitable, in nature. The Court concluded that the action would have had to be brought in law, not equity, in 18th century English courts prior to the merger of law and equity. It found further support for its determination in the nature of the relief—a payment of money—being sought (pp. 41–49).

The Court then turned to "whether the Seventh Amendment confers on petitioners a right to a jury trial in the face of Congress' decision to allow a non-Article III tribunal to adjudicate the claims against them" (p. 50). With the question framed in this way, Justice Brennan appeared to link the question of Congress' power to withhold trial by jury to the question of Congress' authority to provide for adjudication in a non-Article III federal tribunal: "if a statutory cause of action is legal in nature, the question whether the Seventh Amendment permits Congress to assign adjudication to a tribunal that does not employ juries as factfinders requires the same answer as the question whether Article III allows Congress to assign adjudication of that action to a non-Article III tribunal. * * * [I]f Congress may assign the adjudication of a statutory cause of action to a non-Article III tribunal, then the Seventh Amendment poses no independent bar to the adjudication of that action by a non-jury factfinder" (pp. 53–54).

Under both Article III and the Seventh Amendment, Justice Brennan held, the crucial inquiry was whether the right to recover a fraudulent conveyance

go Board of Trade (CBOT) to require its members (commodity brokers) to participate in arbitration proceedings initiated by their customers. One broker-member refused to arbitrate a customer's claim, then sued the CFTC and CBOT in federal court to enjoin enforcement of the arbitration requirement. Although the broker had to sign a membership agreement containing the arbitration clause in order to stay in business, the court held that under the Thomas decision the consent was valid, and under the Schor decision the use of arbitrators did not violate Article III.

should be viewed as "public" or "private".[1] To answer this question, Justice Brennan relied on the reformulation of the public rights doctrine offered in his concurring opinion in Thomas v. Union Carbide: "In our most recent discussion of the 'public rights' doctrine * * * we rejected the view that 'a matter of public right must at a minimum arise between the government and others'. * * * The crucial question, in cases not involving the Federal Government, is whether 'Congress * * * [has] create[d] a seemingly private right that is so closely integrated into a public regulatory scheme as to be a matter appropriate for agency resolution with limited involvement by the Article III judiciary' "(p. 54).

The right to recover a fraudulent conveyance, the Court held, did not qualify as a public right under this standard. It was a private right, legal in nature, which carried with it the Seventh Amendment guarantee of a trial by jury.[2]

Finally, having determined that Granfinanciera indeed had a Seventh Amendment right to trial by jury, Justice Brennan emphasized that important questions remained open to be decided upon remand: "We do not decide today whether the current jury trial provision—28 U.S.C. § 1411—permits bankruptcy courts to conduct jury trials in fraudulent conveyance actions like the one respondent initiated. Nor do we express any view as to whether the Seventh Amendment or Article III allows jury trials to be held before non-Article III bankruptcy judges subject to the oversight provided by the district courts" (p. 64).

Justice Scalia concurred in part and concurred in the judgment, but objected to the majority's suggestion that the public rights doctrine could encompass actions to which the government was not a party. He thought the traditional definition of the public rights category—and its enforcement to bar the transfer of private rights disputes to non-Article III federal tribunals— essential to the separation of powers. "This central feature of the Constitution must be anchored in rules, not set adrift in some multifactored 'balancing test' * * *" (p. 70).

Justice White's dissent (with which Justices Blackmun and O'Connor expressed general agreement) took a far broader view of public rights, and criticized the Court for "call[ing] into question the longstanding assumption * * * that the equitable proceedings of [bankruptcy] courts, adjudicating creditor-debtor disputes," involve public rights (p. 89).[3] Justice White also argued

1. Justice Brennan distinguished Schor, *supra,* which involved a private right, on the basis that there was consent to the exercise of jurisdiction by a non-Article III tribunal that did not employ a jury.

2. The Court distinguished Katchen v. Landy, 382 U.S. 323 (1966), which rejected a jury trial claim in a bankruptcy proceeding, essentially on the ground that it involved a claim *against* the bankrupt's estate. Langenkamp v. Culp, 498 U.S. 42 (1990)(per curiam), decided two Terms later, reinforced this distinction: The Court unanimously held that creditors who had submitted claims against a bankrupt's estate had no right to a jury when they were sued by the trustee to recover allegedly preferential transfers. The claim against the creditors, though in isolation a "legal" one under Granfinanciera, took on the "equitable" nature of the "claims-allowance process" when the creditors filed claims against the bankrupt's estate (p. 44).

3. Since Granfinanciera equated Article III and Seventh Amendment requirements, should Justice White now be less concerned in view of the holding in Langenkamp (note 2, *supra*) that there is no jury trial right in the bankruptcy court's restructuring of debtor-creditor relations?

that "[h]istory and our cases support the proposition that the right to a jury trial depends not solely on the nature of the issue to be resolved, but also on the forum in which it is to be resolved" (p. 79). He concluded that in a court of equity, where a jury trial would be anomalous, the Seventh Amendment does not apply.

(2) *Granfinanciera's Reasoning.* If the jury trial and Article III questions are coextensive, as the Court in an early part of the Granfinanciera opinion says they are, then how can the Court go on both (a) to determine that there is a jury trial right under the Seventh Amendment because the matter is one of private right, but (b) leave open the question whether the jury trial may be conducted in a bankruptcy court before a non-Article III bankruptcy judge? Given the premise of coextensiveness, isn't (b) inconsistent with (a)?[4]

In any event, doesn't Granfinanciera make it clear that the distinction between public and private rights retains significance in assessing Congress' power to assign cases to non-Article III federal tribunals?

Would trial by jury, even in a non-Article III federal court, alleviate many of the concerns about political pressure that underlie Article III?

(3) *Adjudication by Non–Article III Federal Tribunals and the Seventh Amendment.* What is Granfinanciera's holding with respect to the right to jury trial in private rights cases? Is Granfinanciera consistent with prevailing administrative practice and judicial precedent?

(a) NLRB v. Jones & Laughlin Steel Corp., 301 U.S. 1 (1937), held that Congress did not exceed its powers under the Commerce Clause in enacting the National Labor Relations Act and establishing the National Labor Relations Board. The Court then briefly addressed the argument that a decision by the NLRB awarding reinstatement and backpay to union members whom the company had unlawfully dismissed violated the Seventh Amendment (pp. 48–49):

"* * * [The Seventh Amendment] has no application to cases where recovery of money damages is an incident to equitable relief even though damages might have been recovered in an action at law. It does not apply where the proceeding is not in the nature of a suit at common law.

"The instant case is not a suit at common law or in the nature of such a suit. The proceeding is one unknown to the common law. Reinstatement of the employee and payment for time lost are requirements imposed for violation of the statute and are remedies appropriate to its enforcement."

(b) In Curtis v. Loether, 415 U.S. 189 (1974), the plaintiff sought actual and punitive damages for a violation of the fair housing provisions of the Civil Rights Act. The district court awarded the requested relief following trial without a jury, but the Supreme Court reversed. The Court ruled that "[t]he Seventh Amendment does apply to actions enforcing statutory rights, and

---

4. From 1989–94, the lower courts struggled inconclusively with both statutory and constitutional questions concerning the authority of bankruptcy courts to conduct jury trials. See Chemerinsky, Federal Jurisdiction 239 & n. 66 (2d ed.1994). Congress apparently resolved the question of the bankruptcy courts' statutory authority to conduct jury trials in the Bankruptcy Reform Act of 1994, P.L. 103–394, 108 Stat. 4106, § 112 of which amends 28 U.S.C. § 157 to provide: "(e) If the right to a jury trial applies in a proceeding that may be heard * * * by a bankruptcy judge, the bankruptcy judge may conduct the jury trial if specially designated to exercise such jurisdiction by the district court and with the express consent of the parties."

requires a jury trial upon demand, if the statute creates legal rights and remedies, enforceable in the ordinary courts of law". NLRB v. Jones & Laughlin Steel Corp., the Court said, "merely stands for the proposition that the Seventh Amendment is generally inapplicable in administrative proceedings, where jury trials would be incompatible with the whole concept of administrative adjudication and would substantially interfere with the NLRB's role in the statutory scheme" (pp. 194–95).

(c) Atlas Roofing Co. v. Occupational Safety & Health Review Commission, 430 U.S. 442 (1977), involved a Seventh Amendment challenge to an agency's assessment of a civil money penalty for noncompliance with a federal workplace safety statute and its accompanying regulations. In rejecting the challenge, the Court relied on the distinction between public and private rights: "At least in cases in which public rights are being litigated—e.g., cases in which the Government sues in its sovereign capacity to enforce public rights created by statutes within the power of Congress to enact—the Seventh Amendment does not prohibit Congress from assigning the factfinding function and initial adjudication to an administrative forum with which the jury would be incompatible" (p. 450).

(d) How much of this body of law, if any, does Granfinanciera change? Do you agree with Justice Scalia that the concept of a public right has been stripped of historical and analytic content? That it depends on "intuitive" judgments or the outcome of a balancing analysis?[5]

(e) Does Granfinanciera's Seventh Amendment analysis apply to suits in federal territorial courts?[6] Could an action at law involving an indisputably private right ever be litigated, without consent, in a non-Article III federal tribunal on the theory that it was "ancillary" to a public rights dispute? *Cf.* NLRB v. Jones & Laughlin Steel, *supra.*

(4) *Making Sense of Northern Pipeline, Schor, and Granfinanciera.* Can any coherent order be imposed on the dizzying succession of approaches reflected in Northern Pipeline, Schor, and Granfinanciera? Consider the following suggestion:

(i) To assess the constitutionality of any provision for adjudication by a non-Article III federal tribunal, ask first whether the provision falls within one of the "exceptional" categories identified by the Northern Pipeline plurality (involving territorial courts, military tribunals, and public rights) or within its "adjuncts" theory. If so, the provision passes muster under Article III.

(ii) If a provision cannot be justified under the test of the Northern Pipeline plurality, ask next whether it might nonetheless be justified under the kind of balancing test applied in Schor. In applying this test, note, first, that

---

5. For an argument that confusion will persist as long as the law is organized around this vague distinction, which unjustifiably portrays judicial review as least necessary in "public rights" suits against the government in which an independent judiciary is most crucially needed, see Chemerinsky, *Ending the Marathon: It Is Time to Overrule Northern Pipeline,* 65 Am.Bankr.L.J. 311, 314–16 (1991). See also Redish & La Fave, *Seventh Amendment Right to Jury Trial in Non-Article III Proceedings: A Study in Dysfunctional Constitutional Theory,* 4 Wm. & Mary Bill of Rts.J. 407 (1995) (arguing that the distinction between public and private rights is at best a "fig leaf", lacking historical foundations in Seventh Amendment doctrine, invoked to justify abdication of judicial responsibility to "preserve[]" the right to jury trial).

6. Note that, because the Seventh Amendment has not been incorporated into the Fourteenth Amendment, it creates no right to jury trial in state court.

consent will often be of crucial significance. Note, second, that in cases in which the functional justifications for utilizing a non-Article III tribunal are especially strong, one way to rationalize the result may be to classify the right in issue—even if involving the liability of one private party to another—as sufficiently bound up with an integrated regulatory scheme to come within the rationale, if not the historic scope, of the public rights doctrine. See Union Carbide.

(iii) In cases in which adjudication in a non-Article III federal tribunal is permissible under Article III, the question remains whether a jury trial is required under the Seventh Amendment. See Paragraph 3, *supra*. Ordinarily, the Article III and Seventh Amendment tests will be coextensive, but there may be exceptions, as possibly in cases such as Granfinanciera itself.

(iv) If a jury trial is required under the Seventh Amendment, and if a jury trial would be incompatible with the nature of the particular forum provided by Congress, this incompatibility may yield the conclusion that assignment of the dispute to that particular forum is constitutionally impermissible.

(v) Beyond the Seventh Amendment, proceedings that can permissibly occur in a non-Article III tribunal are of course subject to other constitutional restrictions, such as those arising from the Due Process Clause. But the Due Process Clause, of its own force, does not require adjudication by a judge with the tenure and salary guarantees of Article III in any case in which Article III does not apply of its own force.

Even if this summary is correct, would it be fair to say that the Supreme Court has brought little but confusion to this area since Crowell v. Benson?

NOTE ON MAGISTRATE JUDGES

(1) *Statutory History.*   In hopes of alleviating mounting administrative and docket pressures on the federal district courts, Congress enacted the Federal Magistrates Act of 1968, codified at 28 U.S.C. § 631 *et seq.*, which created the office of "magistrate"—a position retitled in 1990 as "magistrate judge". See Judicial Improvement Act of 1990, Pub. L. No. 101–650, § 321, 104 Stat. 5089, 5117 (1990); Smith, *From U.S. Magistrates to U.S. Magistrate Judges*, 75 Judicature 210 (1992). The position was not unprecedented.[1] The Judiciary Act of 1789 authorized magistrates to fix bail for those accused of federal crimes. In 1817, Congress redesignated magistrates as commissioners and modestly expanded their functions. Despite periodic revision and expansion of commissioners' functions, the system was widely regarded as ineffective by 1968, and the 1968 Act contemplated a major expansion in the functions that could be delegated by federal district judges. See Spaniol, *The Federal Magistrates Act: History and Development*, 1974 Ariz.L.Rev. 566. Under the 1968 Act, magistrates were authorized to serve as special masters, to provide "assistance to district judges in the conduct of pretrial or discovery proceedings in civil or criminal actions", and to conduct "preliminary review of motions for posttrial relief". See Pub. L. No. 90–578, 82 Stat. 1107, 1287 (1968). The

---

1. For historical background and analysis of issues involving the permissible role of federal magistrate judges, see Silberman, *Masters and Magistrates*, 50 N.Y.U.L.Rev. 1070 (*Part I: The English Model*), 1297 (*Part II: The American Analogue*)(1975).

1968 Act also contained an open-ended grant of authority to district judges to charge magistrates with additional duties.

Amendments enacted in 1976 and the Federal Magistrates Act of 1979 have greatly expanded the range of functions that magistrate judges are expressly authorized to perform. Overrruling the Supreme Court's decision in *Wingo v. Wedding*, 418 U.S. 461 (1974), the 1976 Amendments permit magistrate judges to conduct evidentiary hearings in habeas corpus cases and to "hear and determine" non-dispositive pre-trial motions, subject to review only to ensure that the decision is not "clearly erroneous or otherwise contrary to law", 28 U.S.C. § 636(b)(1)(A). The 1976 Amendments further specify that "dispositive" motions may be referred to a magistrate judge, but only for "proposed findings of fact and recommendations for the disposition", with the presiding judge still required to make a "de novo" determination of those findings to which objection is raised, 28 U.S.C. § 636(b)(1)(B). A catch-all provision, which is still in effect, provides that magistrate judges "may be assigned such additional duties as are not inconsistent with the Constitution and laws of the United States". 28 U.S.C. § 636(b)(3).

The Federal Magistrates Act of 1979 took yet a further step by establishing that magistrate judges, with the consent of the parties, "may conduct any or all proceedings in a jury or nonjury civil matter and order the entry of judgment in the case, when specifically designated to exercise such jurisdiction by the district court". 28 U.S.C. § 636(c)(1).[2] Aggrieved parties then have a right of appeal to the court of appeals or, with the consent of all parties, to a judge of the district court "in the same manner as on an appeal from a judgment of the district court to a court of appeals". 28 U.S.C. § 636(c)(3) & (c)(4).

Magistrate judges are appointed for a term of eight years by the judges of the federal judicial district in which they are employed. 28 U.S.C. § 631(e). During this term in office, a magistrate judge may be removed, by the judges of the judicial district, "only for incompetency, misconduct, neglect of duty, or physical or mental disability". 28 U.S.C. § 631(i). See generally, Administrative Office of the United States Courts, The Selection and Appointment of United States Magistrate Judges (1993).

As of 1994, there were 406 full-time and 88 part-time magistrate judges,[3] who disposed of over 500,000 judicial matters, including social security "appeals" and habeas petitions; dealt with over 47,000 references in criminal felony cases (involving motions, conferences, etc.); and conducted more than 1700 civil trials with the consent of the parties.[4] Some commentators have suggested that, without continued or even increasing reliance on magistrate judges, virtual paralysis would result in many judicial districts. See 1990 U.S.C.C.A.N. 6823; 1976 U.S.C.C.A.N. 6167–68.

Nearly all of the work done by magistrate judges, however, is judicial business that could be performed by Article III judges, and the assignment of that work to non-Article III officials cannot be justified on grounds that it requires specialized expertise. Would it be fair to say Congress has *no* reason for providing for the assignment of adjudicative functions to magistrate judges

---

2. "The court may, for good cause shown on its own motion, or under extraordinary circumstances shown by any party, vacate a reference of a civil matter to a magistrate". 28 U.S.C. § 636(c)(6).

3. 1994 Annual Report of the Director of the Administrative Office of the United States Courts, Table 14.

4. See *id.* at 54 (Table S–19). For further discussion, see p. 52, *supra.*

except that it prefers not to create more Article III judgeships? Is this a constitutionally adequate justification? Does reliance on magistrate judges create other problems under Article III or the Due Process Clause?

(2) *The Raddatz Case.* United States v. Raddatz, 447 U.S. 667 (1980), presented questions about the bounds of magistrates' (as they were then designated) permissible authority under both the Magistrates Act and the Constitution. The defendant, who was indicted for violation of a federal firearm statute, moved to suppress incriminating evidence, and the district judge referred the motion to a magistrate. After conducting a hearing that included the taking of evidence, the magistrate proposed findings of fact and recommended that the motion be denied.

The Supreme Court first interpreted the statute as not requiring an Article III judge to hear the evidence of witnesses on a suppression motion, even in a case where the "determination" of the motion turned on issues of demeanor and credibility. The statute required a de novo decision by such a judge, but not a de novo hearing of the evidence.

The Court then held that the statute, as so interpreted, survived challenge under the Due Process Clause. Writing for the majority, Chief Justice Burger noted that administrative agencies frequently follow an analogous procedure, with the agencies themselves making the ultimate findings based upon evidence presented to a hearing officer.

Finally, the Court rejected the suggestion that Crowell v. Benson, p. 387, *supra,* requires an Article III trial de novo on the "constitutional facts" at stake in a suppression motion. The district court had "plenary discretion" to decide to use a magistrate, to accept or reject the magistrate's recommendation, and to hear evidence de novo. It sufficed that "the entire process takes place under the district court's total control and jurisdiction" (pp. 681–84).

In an elaborate dissent, Justice Marshall, joined by Justice Brennan, argued that the due process principle that the "one who decides must hear" is violated when a judge is required to make a credibility determination, and does so without hearing the witnesses in a case where "the factual issues turned on issues of credibility that cannot be fairly resolved on the basis of the record" (p. 695). He argued further that under Crowell and Ng Fung Ho v. White, p. 397, *supra,* an Article III court must make an independent determination of "case-dispositive facts", including credibility issues, in cases where individual liberty is at stake (pp. 698–99).[5]

(3) *The Consent Jurisdiction.*

(a) The courts of appeals have been unanimous in upholding the validity of 28 U.S.C. § 636(c), which permits magistrate judges to adjudicate any civil case brought in a federal district court if both parties consent. See, *e.g.,* K.M.C. Co., Inc. v. Irving Trust Co., 757 F.2d 752, 755 (6th Cir.1985); Gairola v. Virginia Dept. of General Services, 753 F.2d 1281, 1284–85 (4th Cir.1985); Geras v. Lafayette Display Fixtures, Inc., 742 F.2d 1037, 1041–42 and cases cited (7th Cir.1984)(2–1).

---

5. In a separate dissent, Justice Stewart, joined by Justices Brennan and Marshall, concluded that the statute should be interpreted to require a de novo hearing where credibility issues are critical. In another opinion, Justice Powell dissented on the basis of the Due Process Clause.

(b) In Gomez v. United States, 490 U.S. 858 (1989), the Supreme Court considered "whether presiding at the selection of a jury in a felony trial without the defendant's consent is among those 'additional duties' " that (under 28 U.S.C. § 636) district courts may assign to magistrate judges (p. 860). After noting the doctrine of avoidance of constitutional issues, as well as its "serious doubts" whether it would be possible to conduct meaningful review of determinations made by a magistrate judge in the course of jury selection (p. 874–75), the Court unanimously concluded that no such authority existed.

(c) Two years later, in Peretz v. United States, 501 U.S. 923 (1991), the Court, seeing the question in a new light, held, 5–4, that under the "additional duties" clause of § 636, a magistrate judge may preside over jury selection in a felony trial when the parties consent.[6] Such delegation is constitutional because (i) any personal right of a defendant to an Article III judge may be waived (p. 936), and (ii) "[e]ven assuming that a litigant may not waive structural protections provided by Article III, we are convinced that such structural protections are not implicated by the procedure followed in this case. Magistrates are appointed and subject to removal by Article III judges. * * * Because 'the entire process takes place under the district court's total control and jurisdiction,' [quoting Raddatz, Paragraph (3), *supra*], there is no danger that use of the magistrate involves" an attempt to transfer jurisdiction for purposes of crippling the Article III courts (p. 937). As to review before an Article III judge, "nothing in the statute precludes a district judge from providing the review that the Constitution requires" (p. 939). (The Court did not explain what the content of such a requirement might be in this setting.)

Justice Marshall, joined by Justices White and Blackmun, dissented. His opinion protested that the Court had not explained how the "serious doubts" about meaningful review expressed in Gomez were now resolved and concluded that, in the absence of such review, the district court could not be said to have "total control and jurisdiction" (pp. 951–52).

For an argument that Peretz gives insufficient attention to the structural concerns embodied in Article III—concerns that might be analogized to the non-waivability of subject matter jurisdiction defects—see, *e.g.,* Note, 33 Wm. & Mary L.Rev. 253 (1991), and Note, 70 N.C.L.Rev. 1334 (1992).[7] Is that argument any stronger in this context than it was in the Schor case, p. 422, *supra?*

(4) *The Underlying Issues.* As courts and commentators have recognized, questions pertaining to the use of magistrate judges and other judicial auxiliaries within the Article III system are analytically distinct from the issue of the validity of legislative and administrative tribunals. Among other things, magistrate judges function within the Article III judicial structure, even though they are not Article III judges themselves, and there is an unusually broad array of levers for the supervision of magistrate judges and review of their judgments by Article III judges. Is it clear that these factors should alleviate, rather than heighten, constitutional concern?

---

6. Interestingly, although the government had relied on a *waiver* theory, the Court rested on the conceptually distinct basis of *consent.* Should the distinction make a difference under Article III?

7. Compare Meltzer, *Legislative Courts, Legislative Power, and the Constitution,* 65 Ind.L.J. 291, 304 (1990), concluding that "there is no inconsistency between an emphasis on Article III as the source of a right to judicial review * * * and a willingness to validate non-Article III adjudication to which litigants have consented".

A provocative student Note, 88 Yale L.J. 1023, 1052–58 (1979), argues that, given predictably increasing caseloads, there will be recurring pressure to appoint more magistrate judges, with the matters referred to them disproportionately involving "simple cases and needy litigants". The upshot, the author fears, will be a form of discrimination both among classes of litigants and areas of the law, with some receiving disproportionate inattention—a result that the author views as far from benign: "[T]he magistrate is not a judge. In addition to the familiar 'control' of appellate review that all higher federal tribunals exercise over the judges of lower courts, the magistrate is also subject to a qualitatively different form of bureaucratic control that may attend district court authority to determine his reappointment prospects and, more importantly, the day-to-day contents of his docket. Moreover, district judges must evaluate the magistrate's decisional record in the course of exercising their administrative functions, if only in order to maintain the standards of the court. The ongoing, informal oversight creates the risk of impermissible intrusion on the magistrate's substantive decisions. The danger is not that magistrates will come to function as judicial alter egos, but rather that they may be encouraged to adopt a risk-averse strategy of adjudication by the pressure of judicial scrutiny, a strategy eschewing unconventional decisions that might otherwise be prompted by novel legal claims or pressing factual idiosyncrasies. Such 'judicious' decisionmaking would be inconsistent with the * * * policy of autonomous adjudication within the federal courts that underlies the Article III judicial office".

A recent study by the Administrative Office Of the United States Courts—the organization of Article III judges themselves—found a "growing confidence in the magistrate system". *A Constitutional Analysis of Magistrate Judge Authority,* 150 F.R.D. 247, 271–72 (1993).

———

NOTE ON THE TIDEWATER PROBLEM

(1) *Introduction.* What are the limits on the scope of the jurisdiction that Congress may vest in an Article III court? This complex question will be explored more fully in Chapter VIII, *infra,* but the debate among the Justices in National Mutual Insurance Co. v. Tidewater Transfer Co., Inc., 337 U.S. 582 (1949), also sheds light on issues discussed in this Chapter.

(2) *The Tidewater Case and Its Bases for Decision.* The Tidewater case grew out of an action by a District of Columbia citizen against a citizen of Maryland on an insurance contract involving only issues of Maryland law. The suit was brought in the federal district court in Maryland, under a 1940 statute that gave the district courts jurisdiction in actions between citizens of the states and citizens of the District. The question was whether this statute was valid, and the Supreme Court held that it was. But the Justices whose votes were necessary to the judgment reached their conclusions by radically different paths of reasoning.

In the venerable case of Hepburn & Dundas v. Ellzey, 6 U.S. (2 Cranch) 445 (1805), Chief Justice Marshall had ruled that a citizen of the District was not a citizen of a "State" within the meaning of the Diversity Clause. In Tidewater, a seven-member majority of the Court declined to overrule this holding. But two Justices, Rutledge and Murphy, thought that Hepburn should be overruled; and on this basis they provided two of the votes necessary to uphold the challenged statute.

For the seven Justices who adhered to the holding of the Hepburn case, diversity of citizenship was absent, and the question became whether Congress' conferral of jurisdiction of suits between citizens of the states and citizens of the District of Columbia might be sustained on some other basis. Justice Jackson, joined by Justices Black and Burton, concluded that it could. And because the votes of these three Justices combined with those of Justices Rutledge and Murphy to make a majority for upholding the statute's validity, Justice Jackson announced the judgment of the Court and delivered a plurality opinion—even though, as discussed below, a majority of the Justices clearly rejected his central line of reasoning.

(3) *The Plurality Opinion.* According to Justice Jackson, Congress, pursuant to its Article I powers, may authorize Article III courts to adjudicate cases not falling within the Article III enumeration. In reaching this conclusion, the plurality relied partly on the proposition, most famously associated with the Supreme Court's opinion in Williams v. United States, 289 U.S. 553 (1933), discussed critically on pp. 420–21 n. 9 *supra,* that legislative courts are "incapable of receiving" Article III judicial power. He pointed out that, in many cases (*e.g.,* consented suits against the United States), the district courts have traditionally exercised a jurisdiction concurrent with that of legislative courts. For concurrent jurisdiction to be possible, he argued, both the legislative courts and the district courts must exercise an Article I judicial power entirely outside the scope of Article III.

Justice Jackson also cited Schumacher v. Beeler, 293 U.S. 367 (1934) and Williams v. Austrian, 331 U.S. 642 (1947), in which the Court had upheld provisions authorizing a district court to entertain non-diversity suits by bankruptcy trustees against debtors of the bankrupt based on state-law causes of action. Objecting to the view that these actions could be viewed as cases "arising under" federal law,[1] Justice Jackson said that "the fact that the congressional power over bankruptcy granted by Art. I could open the court to the trustee does not mean that such suits arise under the laws of the United States; but it does mean that Art. I can supply a source of judicial power for their adjudication" (p. 599).

Attempting to bound his argument, Justice Jackson stated that, although Congress is free to give the federal courts Article I judicial business that lies outside the enumeration of Article III, it must be *judicial* business: separation of powers postulates require that the jurisdiction conferred be "limited to controversies of a justiciable nature" (p. 591).

(4) *Other Views Expressed in Tidewater.* The remaining six Justices objected strongly to Justice Jackson's opinion. Justice Rutledge called it a "dangerous doctrine" (p. 626). Chief Justice Vinson, joined by Justice Douglas, also disagreed and dissented.

The remaining dissent was a passionate essay by Justice Frankfurter, joined by Justice Reed, reaffirming the classical proposition that the federal courts are courts of limited jurisdiction with no authority to adjudicate except in the instances specifically enumerated in Article III: "[I]f courts established

---

1. Here Justice Jackson cited cases such as Gully v. First National Bank, discussed in Chap. VIII, Sec. 3, *infra,* construing the statutory grant of "arising under" jurisdiction to the district courts.

under Article III can exercise wider jurisdiction than that defined and confined by Article III, * * * what justification is there for interpreting Article III as imposing one restriction in the exercise of those other powers of the Congress—the restriction to the exercise of 'judicial power'—yet not interpreting it as imposing the restrictions that are most explicit, namely, the particularization of the 'cases' to which 'the judicial Power shall extend' "? (p. 648).

Justice Frankfurter continued (pp. 650–55): "We are here concerned with the power of the federal courts to adjudicate merely because of the citizenship of the parties. Power to adjudicate between citizens of different states, merely because they are citizens of different states, has no relation to any substantive rights created by Congress. * * * The diversity jurisdiction of the federal courts was probably the most tenuously founded and most unwillingly granted of all the heads of federal jurisdiction which Congress was empowered by Article III to confer. * * * The process of reasoning by which this result is reached invites a use of the federal courts which breaks with the whole history of the federal judiciary and disregards the wise policy behind that history. It was because Article III defines and confines the limits of jurisdiction of the courts which are established under Article III that the first Court of Claims Act fell, Gordon v. United States, 69 U.S. (2 Wall.) 561.

"To find a source for 'the judicial Power,' therefore, which may be exercised by courts established under Article III of the Constitution outside that Article would be to disregard the distribution of powers made by the Constitution. * * *

"A substantial majority of the Court agrees that each of the two grounds urged in support of the attempt by Congress to extend diversity jurisdiction to cases involving citizens of the District of Columbia must be rejected—but not the same majority. And so, conflicting minorities in combination bring to pass a result—paradoxical as it may appear—which differing majorities of the Court find insupportable."

Justice Frankfurter is clearly correct about the last point, at least. Would it be fair to say that Tidewater stands for the proposition that Congress may *not* give an Article III court jurisdiction over a non-Article III case or function—with the case itself being a bizarre counterexample to the proposition for which it stands?

(5) *Comments and Questions.* Justice Jackson's first argument, that Article III courts must exercise an Article I power when they entertain suits that are also within the jurisdiction of Article I courts, rests on a discredited premise, doesn't it? See Paragraph (5) of the *Note on the Northern Pipeline Case and Congressional Utilization of Legislative Courts,* p. 420, *supra.*

Is his second argument, based on the exercise of federal jurisdiction in cases related to bankruptcies but involving only state law claims, so easily dismissed? See Cross, *Congressional Power to Extend Federal Jurisdiction to Disputes Outside Article III: A Critical Analysis from the Perspective of Bankruptcy,* 87 Nw.U.L.Rev. 1188 (1993); see also footnote 26 of the plurality opinion in Northern Pipeline, p. 406, *supra.* Or might federal jurisdiction of those cases be justified on some other basis? For further discussion, see pp. 894–96, 900–01, *infra* (discussing "protective jurisdiction" as a species of "arising under" jurisdiction).

Was Justice Frankfurter warranted in his apparent concern that the plurality's theory took a long and dangerous step down a slippery slope that might lead to congressionally conferred jurisdiction to issue advisory opinions or perform non-judicial functions?

May Congress confer jurisdiction on the federal courts in state-law actions between aliens? In Hodgson v. Bowerbank, 9 U.S. (5 Cranch) 303 (1809), the Court, in a short opinion by Chief Justice Marshall, held that jurisdiction may not be exercised in such a case notwithstanding the provision of the First Judiciary Act conferring jurisdiction in "all suits" in which an alien is a party. For an argument that this was a statutory, not a constitutional, holding, see Mahoney, *A Historical Note on Hodgson v. Bowerbank,* 49 U.Chi.L.Rev. 725 (1982). See also the Verlinden case, discussed at p. 903, *infra,* holding that such a case may, under certain circumstances, be deemed a case "arising under" federal law.

SECTION 3. FEDERAL AUTHORITY AND STATE COURT JURISDICTION

THE FEDERALIST, NO. 82

This paper is reprinted in Chap. I, pp. 25-27, *supra.*

Tafflin v. Levitt

493 U.S. 455, 110 S.Ct. 792, 107 L.Ed.2d 887 (1990).
Certiorari to the United States Court of Appeals for the Fourth Circuit

■ JUSTICE O'CONNOR delivered the opinion of the Court.

* * *

I

* * *

To resolve a conflict among the federal appellate courts and state supreme courts, we granted certiorari limited to the question whether state courts have concurrent jurisdiction over * * * [civil actions brought under the Racketeer Influenced and Corrupt Organizations Act (RICO)], Pub.L. 91–452, Title IX, 84 Stat. 941, as amended, 18 U.S.C. §§ 1961–1968.* We hold that they do * * *.

---

* [Ed.] RICO, which provides both criminal and civil liability for violations of the criminal law, authorizes victims to bring civil actions for treble damages plus attorney's fees.

On its facts, Tafflin involved a suit in federal court against the officers and directors of a failed, state-chartered savings and loan (among others) by holders of unpaid certificates of deposit. The question of a state court's jurisdiction over civil RICO actions arose in the federal action when the defendants argued, and the lower courts held,

that a federal court should "abstain" from resolving the RICO claims—and effectively require them to be litigated in state court— since (i) state courts had concurrent jurisdiction, (ii) the underlying causes of action had been raised in pending litigation in state court, and (iii) Maryland's "comprehensive scheme for the rehabilitation and liquidation of insolvent state-chartered savings and loan associations" made abstention appropriate under the doctrine of Burford v. Sun Oil Co., pp. 1247–51, *infra.* The Supreme Court's grant of certiorari limited its review to the first contention.

II

We begin with the axiom that, under our federal system, the States possess sovereignty concurrent with that of the Federal Government, subject only to limitations imposed by the Supremacy Clause.   Under this system of dual sovereignty, we have consistently held that state courts have inherent authority, and are thus presumptively competent, to adjudicate claims arising under the laws of the United States.   See, e.g., Claflin v. Houseman, 93 U.S. 130, 136–137 (1876);   Charles Dowd Box Co. v. Courtney, 368 U.S. 502, 507–508, 82 S.Ct. 519, 522–523 (1962);   Gulf Offshore Co. v. Mobil Oil Corp., 453 U.S. 473, 477–478 (1981).   As we noted in Claflin, "if exclusive jurisdiction be neither express nor implied, the State courts have concurrent jurisdiction whenever, by their own constitution, they are competent to take it."   93 U.S., at 136; see also Dowd Box, *supra*, 368 U.S. at 507–508 ("We start with the premise that nothing in the concept of our federal system prevents state courts from enforcing rights created by federal law.   Concurrent jurisdiction has been a common phenomenon in our judicial history, and exclusive federal court jurisdiction over cases arising under federal law has been the exception rather than the rule.").   See generally 1 J. Kent, Commentaries on American Law *400; The Federalist No. 82 (A. Hamilton);   F. Frankfurter & J. Landis, The Business of the Supreme Court 5–12 (1927);   H. Friendly, Federal Jurisdiction: A General View 8–11 (1973).

This deeply rooted presumption in favor of concurrent state court jurisdiction is, of course, rebutted if Congress affirmatively ousts the state courts of jurisdiction over a particular federal claim.   See, *e.g.,* Claflin, *supra*, 93 U.S. at 137 ("Congress may, if it see[s] fit, give to the Federal courts exclusive jurisdiction")(citations omitted).   As we stated in Gulf Offshore:

"In considering the propriety of state-court jurisdiction over any particular federal claim, the Court begins with the presumption that state courts enjoy concurrent jurisdiction.   Congress, however, may confine jurisdiction to the federal courts either explicitly or implicitly.   Thus, the presumption of concurrent jurisdiction can be rebutted by an explicit statutory directive, by unmistakable implication from legislative history, or by a clear incompatibility between state-court jurisdiction and federal interests."   453 U.S., at 478 (citations omitted).

* * * These principles, which have "remained unmodified through the years," Dowd Box, *supra*, 368 U.S. at 508, provide the analytical framework for resolving this case.

III

The precise question presented, therefore, is whether state courts have been divested of jurisdiction to hear civil RICO claims "by an explicit statutory directive, by unmistakable implication from legislative history, or by a clear incompatibility between state-court jurisdiction and federal interests."   Gulf Offshore, *supra,* 453 U.S. at 478.   * * *

At the outset, petitioners concede that there is nothing in the language of RICO—much less an "explicit statutory directive"—to suggest that Congress has, by affirmative enactment, divested the state courts of jurisdiction to hear civil RICO claims.   The statutory provision authorizing civil RICO claims provides in full:

"Any person injured in his business or property by reason of a violation of section 1962 of this chapter *may* sue therefor in any appropriate United States district court and shall recover threefold the damages he sustains and the cost of the suit, including a reasonable attorney's fee." 18 U.S.C. § 1964(c)(emphasis added).

This grant of federal jurisdiction is plainly permissive, not mandatory, for "[t]he statute does not state nor even suggest that such jurisdiction shall be exclusive.   It provides that suits of the kind described 'may' be brought in the federal district courts, not that they must be."   Dowd Box, *supra,* 368 U.S., at 506.   Indeed, "[i]t is black letter law . . . that the mere grant of jurisdiction to a federal court does not operate to oust a state court from concurrent jurisdiction over the cause of action."   Gulf Offshore, *supra,* 453 U.S., at 479 * * *.

Petitioners thus rely solely on the second and third factors suggested in Gulf Offshore, arguing that exclusive federal jurisdiction over civil RICO actions is established "by unmistakable implication from legislative history, or by a clear incompatibility between state-court jurisdiction and federal interests," 453 U.S., at 478.

Our review of the legislative history, however, reveals no evidence that Congress even considered the question of concurrent state court jurisdiction over RICO claims, much less any suggestion that Congress affirmatively intended to confer exclusive jurisdiction over such claims on the federal courts.   * * * Petitioners nonetheless insist that if Congress had considered the issue, it would have granted federal courts exclusive jurisdiction over civil RICO claims. This argument, however, is misplaced, for even if we could reliably discern what Congress' intent might have been had it considered the question, we are not at liberty to so speculate; the fact that Congress did not even *consider* the issue readily disposes of any argument that Congress unmistakably intended to divest state courts of concurrent jurisdiction.

Sensing this void in the legislative history, petitioners rely, in the alternative, on our decisions in Sedima, S.P.R.L. v. Imrex Co., 473 U.S. 479 (1985), and Agency Holding Corp. v. Malley–Duff & Assocs., 483 U.S. 143 (1987), in which we noted that Congress modeled § 1964(c) after § 4 of the Clayton Act, 15 U.S.C. § 15(a).   * * * Petitioners assert that, because we have interpreted § 4 of the Clayton Act to confer exclusive jurisdiction on the federal courts, see, *e.g.,* General Investment Co. v. Lake Shore & M.S.R. Co., 260 U.S. 261, 286–288 (1922), and because Congress may be presumed to have been aware of and incorporated those interpretations when it used similar language in RICO, Congress intended, by implication, to grant exclusive federal jurisdiction over claims arising under § 1964(c).

This argument is also flawed.   To rebut the presumption of concurrent jurisdiction, the question is not whether any intent at all may be divined from legislative silence on the issue, but whether Congress in its deliberations may be said to have affirmatively or unmistakably intended jurisdiction to be exclusively federal.   In the instant case, the lack of any indication in RICO's legislative history that Congress either considered or assumed that the importing of remedial language from the Clayton Act into RICO had any jurisdictional implications is dispositive.   The "mere borrowing of statutory language does not imply that Congress also intended to incorporate all of the baggage that may be attached to the borrowed language."   Lou, *supra,* at 737.   Indeed, to the extent we impute to Congress knowledge of our Clayton Act precedents, it makes no less sense to impute to Congress knowledge of Claflin and Dowd Box, under which Congress, had it sought to confer exclusive jurisdiction over civil RICO claims, would have had every incentive to do so expressly.

* * *

Petitioners finally urge that state court jurisdiction over civil RICO claims would be clearly incompatible with federal interests. We noted in Gulf Offshore that factors indicating clear incompatibility "include the desirability of uniform interpretation, the expertise of federal judges in federal law, and the assumed greater hospitality of federal courts to peculiarly federal claims." 453 U.S., at 483–484 (citation and footnote omitted). Petitioners' primary contention is that concurrent jurisdiction is clearly incompatible with the federal interest in uniform interpretation of federal criminal laws, see 18 U.S.C. § 3231, because state courts would be required to construe the federal crimes that constitute predicate acts defined as "racketeering activity," see 18 U.S.C. §§ 1961(1)(B), (C), and (D). Petitioners predict that if state courts are permitted to interpret federal criminal statutes, they will create a body of precedent relating to those statutes and that the federal courts will consequently lose control over the orderly and uniform development of federal criminal law.

We perceive no "clear incompatibility" between state court jurisdiction over civil RICO actions and federal interests. As a preliminary matter, concurrent jurisdiction over § 1964(c) suits is clearly not incompatible with § 3231 itself, for civil RICO claims are not "offenses against the laws of the United States," § 3231, and do not result in the imposition of criminal sanctions-uniform or otherwise. * * *

More to the point, however, our decision today creates no significant danger of inconsistent application of federal criminal law. Although petitioners' concern with the need for uniformity and consistency of federal criminal law is well-taken, see Ableman v. Booth, 62 U.S. 506, 517–518 (1859), federal courts, pursuant to § 3231, would retain full authority and responsibility for the interpretation and application of federal criminal laws, for they would not be bound by state court interpretations of the federal offenses constituting RICO's predicate acts. State courts adjudicating civil RICO claims will, in addition, be guided by federal court interpretations of the relevant federal criminal statutes, just as federal courts sitting in diversity are guided by state court interpretations of state law * * *. State court judgments misinterpreting federal criminal law would, of course, also be subject to direct review by this Court. * * *

Moreover, contrary to petitioners' fears, we have full faith in the ability of state courts to handle the complexities of civil RICO actions, particularly since many RICO cases involve asserted violations of state law, such as state fraud claims, over which state courts presumably have greater expertise. See 18 U.S.C. § 1961(1)(A)(listing state law offenses constituting predicate acts); Gulf Offshore, 453 U.S., at 484 ("State judges have greater expertise in applying" laws "whose governing rules are borrowed from state law"); * * * see also BNA, Civil RICO Report, Vol. 2, No. 44, p. 7 (Apr. 14, 1987)(54.9% of all RICO cases after Sedima involved "common law fraud" and another 18.0% involved either "nonsecurities fraud" or "theft or conversion"). * * *

* * *

Finally, we note that, far from disabling or frustrating federal interests, "[p]ermitting state courts to entertain federal causes of action facilitates the enforcement of federal rights." Gulf Offshore, 453 U.S., at 478, n. 4 * * *. Thus, to the extent that Congress intended RICO to serve broad remedial purposes, * * * concurrent state court jurisdiction over civil RICO claims will advance rather than jeopardize federal policies underlying the statute.

For all of the above reasons, we hold that state courts have concurrent jurisdiction to consider civil claims arising under RICO. * * * The judgment of the Court of Appeals is accordingly

Affirmed.

■ JUSTICE WHITE concurring.

        * * *

■ JUSTICE SCALIA, with whom JUSTICE KENNEDY joins, concurring.

I join the opinion of the Court, addressing the issues before us on the basis argued by the parties, which has included acceptance of the dictum in Gulf Offshore Co. v. Mobil Oil Corp., 453 U.S. 473, 478 (1981), that "the presumption of concurrent jurisdiction can be rebutted by an explicit statutory directive, by unmistakable implication from legislative history, or by a clear incompatibility between state-court jurisdiction and federal interests." * * * I write separately, before this * * * [dictum] has become too entrenched, to note my view that in one respect it is not a correct statement of the law, and in another respect it may not be.

State courts have jurisdiction over federal causes of action not because it is "conferred" upon them by the Congress; nor even because their inherent powers permit them to entertain transitory causes of action arising under the laws of foreign sovereigns, see, *e.g.,* McKenna v. Fisk, 1 How. 241, 247–249 (1843); but because "[t]he laws of the United States are laws in the several States, and just as much binding on the citizens and courts thereof as the State laws are.... The two together form one system of jurisprudence, which constitutes the law of the land for the State; and the courts of the two jurisdictions are not foreign to each other...." Claflin v. Houseman, 93 U.S. 130, 136–137 (1876).

It therefore takes an affirmative act of power under the Supremacy Clause to oust the States of jurisdiction—an exercise of what one of our earliest cases referred to as "the power of congress to *withdraw*" federal claims from state-court jurisdiction. Houston v. Moore, 5 Wheat. 1, 26 (1820)(emphasis added).

As an original proposition, it would be eminently arguable that depriving state courts of their sovereign authority to adjudicate the law of the land must be done, if not with the utmost clarity, cf. Atascadero State Hospital v. Scanlon, 473 U.S. 234, 243 (1985)(state sovereign immunity can be eliminated only by "clear statement"), at least *expressly.* That was the view of Alexander Hamilton:

> "When ... we consider the State governments and the national governments, as they truly are, in the light of kindred systems, and as parts of ONE WHOLE, the inference seems to be conclusive that the State courts would have a concurrent jurisdiction in all cases arising under the laws or the Union, where it was not expressly prohibited." The Federalist No. 82, p. 132 (E. Bourne ed. 1947).

* * * Although as early as Claflin, see 93 U.S., at 137, and as late as Gulf Offshore, we had *said* that the exclusion of concurrent state jurisdiction could be achieved by implication, the only cases in which to my knowledge we have

acted upon such a principle are those relating to the Sherman Act and the Clayton Act—where the full extent of our analysis was the less than compelling statement that provisions giving the right to sue in United States District Court "show that [the right] is to be exercised *only* in a 'court of the United States.'" General Investment Co. v. Lake Shore & Michigan Southern R. Co., 260 U.S. 261, 287 (1922)(emphasis added). * * * In the standard fields of exclusive federal jurisdiction, the governing statutes specifically recite that suit may be brought "only" in federal court, Investment Company Act of 1940, as amended, 15 U.S.C. § 80a–35(b)(5); that the jurisdiction of the federal courts shall be "exclusive," Securities Exchange Act of 1934, as amended, 15 U.S.C. § 78aa; Natural Gas Act of 1938, 15 U.S.C. § 717u; Employee Retirement Income Security Act of 1974, 29 U.S.C. § 1132(e)(1); or indeed even that the jurisdiction of the federal courts shall be "exclusive of the courts of the States," 18 U.S.C. § 3231 (criminal cases); 28 U.S.C. §§ 1333 (admiralty, maritime, and prize cases), 1334 (bankruptcy cases), 1338 (patent, plant variety protection, and copyright cases), 1351 (actions against consuls or vice consuls of foreign states), 1355 (actions for recovery or enforcement of fine, penalty, or forfeiture incurred under Act of Congress), 1356 (seizures on land or water not within admiralty and maritime jurisdiction).

Assuming, however, that exclusion by implication is possible, surely what is required is implication in the text of the statute, and not merely, as the second part of the Gulf Offshore dictum would permit, through "unmistakable implication from legislative history." 453 U.S., at 478. Although Charles Dowd Box Co. v. Courtney, 368 U.S. 502 (1962), after concluding that the statute "does not state nor even suggest that [federal] jurisdiction shall be exclusive," *id.*, at 506, proceeded quite unnecessarily to examine the legislative history, it did so to reinforce rather than contradict the conclusion it had already reached. We have never found state jurisdiction excluded by "unmistakable implication" from legislative history. * * * [I]t is simply wrong in principle to assert that Congress can effect this affirmative legislative act by simply talking about it with unmistakable clarity. What is needed to oust the States of jurisdiction is congressional *action* (*i.e.*, a provision of law), not merely congressional discussion.

It is perhaps also true that implied preclusion can be established by the fact that a statute expressly mentions only federal courts, plus the fact that state-court jurisdiction would plainly disrupt the statutory scheme. That is conceivably what was meant by the third part of the Gulf Offshore dictum, "clear incompatibility between state-court jurisdiction and federal interests." 453 U.S., at 478. If the phrase is interpreted more broadly than that, however-if it is taken to assert some power on the part of this Court to exclude state-court jurisdiction when systemic federal interests make it undesirable—it has absolutely no foundation in our precedent.

     * * *

In sum: As the Court holds, the RICO cause of action meets none of the three tests for exclusion of state-court jurisdiction recited in Gulf Offshore. Since that is so, the proposition that meeting any one of the tests would have sufficed is dictum here, as it was there. In my view meeting the second test is assuredly not enough, and meeting the third may not be.

NOTE ON TAFFLIN v. LEVITT AND CONGRESSIONAL
EXCLUSION OF STATE COURT JURISDICTION

(1) *Foundations of State Authority.* Do you see why states, more or less routinely, would authorize their courts to entertain federal claims? *Cf.* The Federalist, No. 82, p. 25, *supra.* For a discussion of situations in which states purport not to authorize jurisdiction of federal claims, and of the scope of their obligation to accept jurisdiction, see *Note on the Obligations of State Courts to Enforce Federal Law,* p. 472, *infra.*

Is state court authority to adjudicate federal claims an entailment of the Madisonian Compromise and Congress' discretion under Article III not to create lower federal courts? A presupposition thereof?

The proposition that the Constitution permits state court adjudication of federal claims, or at least of all classes of federal claims, has not always appeared self-evident. Justice Story, for example, believed that Article III makes federal jurisdiction "unavoidably * * * exclusive" in at least some classes of cases, including federal criminal cases, other cases arising under the Constitution and laws of the United States, and cases within the admiralty and maritime jurisdiction. See Martin v. Hunter's Lessee, 14 U.S. (1 Wheat.) 304, 337 (1816); *cf.* 3 Story, Commentaries on the Constitution 533, n. 3 (1833). See generally Collins, *Article III Cases, State Court Duties, and the Madisonian Compromise,* 1995 Wisc.L.Rev. 39 (arguing that it was commonly believed in the eighteenth and early nineteenth centuries that the constitutional plan required domains of exclusively federal jurisdiction).[2]

Do Tafflin v. Levitt and the authorities on which it relies decisively reject that view? Should they? For discussion of whether the Constitution might require exclusive federal jurisdiction in any other classes of cases, see pp. 463-69, *infra.*

(2) *Foundations of Congressional Authority.* The First Judiciary Act provided for exclusive federal jurisdiction of cases involving "crimes and offenses cognizable under the authority of the United States," "seizures" on land or water, "suits for penalties and forfeitures, incurred under the laws of the United States," "suits against consuls or vice-consuls", and "civil causes of admiralty and maritime jurisdiction * * * saving to suitors, in all cases, the right of a

---

2. Justice Story's view appears to have rested in part on a distinction between jurisdiction that existed in state courts "previous to the adoption of the constitution", which they retained, and jurisdiction of classes of disputes that could not previously have arisen, which "could not afterwards be directly conferred on them". Martin v. Hunter's Lessee, 14 U.S. (1 Wheat.) at 335. Whether intentionally or not, Justice Story's formulation echoes some of the language used by Hamilton (though not the conclusion that Hamilton reached) in The Federalist, No. 82, p. 25, *supra.* In discussing the relation of federal and state court jurisdiction, Hamilton emphasized that "the states will retain all *pre-existing* authorities, which may not be exclusively delegated to the federal head". For Hamilton, one principal point of the ar-

gument was that Congress could not divest the states of pre-existing jurisdiction; another was that Congress could, if it so chose, make federal jurisdiction exclusive in "cases which may grow out of, and be *peculiar* to, the constitution to be established: For not to allow the state courts a right of jurisdiction in such cases can hardly be considered as the abridgement of a pre-existing authority". With these two arguments in place, however, Hamilton—in sharp contrast with Justice Story—went on to "infer from the nature of judiciary power, and from the general genius of the system" that the state courts *would* enjoy concurrent jurisdiction of cases arising under the Constitution and laws of the United States unless expressly precluded by Congress.

common law remedy, where the common law is competent to give it". Act of Sept. 24, 1789, §§ 9, 11, 1 Stat. 76, 78. The Act also conferred exclusive Supreme Court jurisdiction in many civil actions to which states were parties. *Id.*, § 13. Pockets of exclusive jurisdiction have existed ever since; important surviving additions are rehearsed in Justice Scalia's concurring opinion in the Tafflin case, *supra.*[3]

Congress' power to create exclusive federal jurisdiction has seldom been challenged. As a result, the Supreme Court did not have occasion to pronounce on the question until The Moses Taylor, 71 U.S. (4 Wall.) 411 (1867), in which the Court reversed a state court judgment sustaining an *in rem* proceeding against a vessel, holding that such relief is not a "common law" remedy preserved by the saving clause in the exclusive grant of admiralty jurisdiction.[4] With respect to the constitutional question, Justice Field said (pp. 429, 430):

"* * * The Judiciary Act of 1789, in its distribution of jurisdiction to the several federal courts, recognizes and is framed upon the theory that in all cases to which the judicial power of the United States extends, Congress may rightfully vest exclusive jurisdiction in the Federal courts. It declares that in some cases, from their commencement, such jurisdiction shall be exclusive; in other cases it determines at what stage of procedure such jurisdiction shall attach, and how long and how far concurrent jurisdiction of the State courts shall be permitted. * * *

"The constitutionality of these provisions cannot be seriously questioned, and is of frequent recognition by both State and Federal courts."

For similar affirmations, see Houston v. Moore, 18 U.S. (5 Wheat.) 1, 25–26 (1820); Lockerty v. Phillips, p. 380, *supra;* Bowles v. Willingham, 321 U.S. 503 (1944); Brown v. Gerdes, 321 U.S. 178 (1944).

Under which grant(s) of authority might Congress exclude state court jurisdiction of federal claims? Would decisions such as The Moses Taylor support an act of Congress declaring the diversity jurisdiction exclusive? *Cf.* Hamilton in The Federalist, No. 82. Is Congress' power to exclude state court jurisdiction subject to the same sort of "external" limitations as Congress' power to limit federal jurisdiction? See pp. 362-63, *supra.*

(3) *Congressional Policy.* The conjunction of congressional powers to define the scope of federal jurisdiction (as discussed in Section 1 of this Chapter) and to make federal jurisdiction exclusive leaves Congress with an array of policy options. These include:

* exclusive state original jurisdiction, subject to appellate review by the Supreme Court;

* exclusive federal jurisdiction;

* concurrent federal and state jurisdiction, with state court decisions subject to Supreme Court review; and

* concurrent state and federal jurisdiction, but with a right of state court defendants to remove to federal court.

---

3. Section 256 of the former Judicial Code (28 U.S.C. § 371, 1940 ed.) purported to enumerate the areas from which state courts had been excluded, but the enumeration was incomplete and the section was repealed in the 1948 revision.

4. But *cf.* C.J. Hendry Co. v. Moore, 318 U.S. 133 (1943)(sustaining a state forfeiture proceeding, with an illuminating historical discussion).

Each of these options is employed with respect to at least some categories of cases involving federal claims.[5] The considerations that Congress might weigh in choosing among them are too complex and various to be pursued in detail here. It is important to bear in mind, however, that cases frequently involve a complex mix of state and federal issues. For example, a plaintiff may assert both state and federal causes of action, or a federal issue may come into a case only by way of defense or reply to a defense. In considering the forum in which cases involving a mixture of state and federal issues ought to be litigated, issues arise about how to identify and weigh the competing state and federal interests in adjudicating the entire case, see generally Chapter VIII, *infra,* and about the benefits and drawbacks of carving a case into parts so that the state elements can be adjudicated in state court and federal issues resolved in federal court, see generally Chapter X, *infra.* A few other issues should also be noted.[6]

(a) *Exclusive State Original Jurisdiction.* State jurisdiction is necessarily exclusive in cases not within the jurisdictional headings of Article III. With respect to cases within Article III, including those turning predominantly or even exclusively on federal law, a recurring issue is whether the bare interest in curbing the size of federal dockets constitutes a legitimate reason for withholding federal jurisdiction—and, as a frequent consequence, mandating the exercise of state jurisdiction, see pp. 478-79, *infra.*

(b) *Exclusive Federal Jurisdiction.* Arguments in favor of exclusive federal jurisdiction frequently invoke the desirability of uniform interpretation of federal law, the presumptive expertise of federal judges in dealing with federal issues, and "the probability that the federal courts will be more sympathetic to a new federal statute than will state courts". Note, 70 Harv.L.Rev. 509, 512 (1957). To a considerable extent, these arguments assume lack of parity between state and federal courts. See Fallon, *The Ideologies of Federal Courts Law,* 74 Va.L.Rev. 1202–07 (1988); see generally pp. 351-54, *supra* (discussing the concept of "parity"). Is that assumption warranted?[7] Even if it is, would the concern about the relative sympathy of state and federal forums to federal claims be adequately met by providing for concurrent state and federal jurisdiction and allowing a plaintiff to choose which to invoke?

How powerful are the other considerations supporting exclusive federal jurisdiction, notably the desire for uniformity?[8] Does their weight vary from

---

5. Other possibilities include exclusive state original jurisdiction, subject to appellate review in a federal court other than the Supreme Court, *cf.* The Federalist No. 82; exclusive state jurisdiction, but without provision for appellate review by a federal court, but *cf.* pp. 370-73, *supra* (canvassing arguments that this allocation would violate Article III); and concurrent state and federal jurisdiction, but with a right of federal court defendants to remove to state court, *cf.* Hicks v. Miranda, 419 U.S. 1018 (1974), p. 1291, *infra.* In contrast with the options discussed in text, these have not been employed.

6. For useful, recent discussions see Redish, *Reassessing the Allocation of Federal Judicial Business Between State and Federal Courts: Federal Jurisdiction and "The Martian Chronicles",* 78 Va.L.Rev. 1769 (1992);

Shapiro, *Reflections on Allocation of Business Between the State and Federal Courts,* 78 Va.L.Rev. 1839 (1992).

7. For a negative answer, see Solimine, *Rethinking Federal Jurisdiction,* 52 U.Pitt. L.Rev. 383, 411–19 (1991).

8. The interest in uniformity is at least partly compromised by the settled rule that when a federal issue arises defensively in a state court action, it must ordinarily be adjudicated in the state court even if it would otherwise lie within an area of exclusive federal jurisdiction. See, *e.g.,* Lear, Inc. v. Adkins, 395 U.S. 653 (1969)(state court may not award damages for breach of a patent license agreement if the patent is invalid and, accordingly, must rule on the issue of the patent's validity). It would of course be possible

statute to statute? Based on the catalogue of areas of exclusive federal jurisdiction provided by Justice Scalia's opinion in the Tafflin case, pp. 448–49, *supra,* do you think that Congress has made wise choices about when exclusive federal jurisdiction is appropriate?

(c) *Concurrent Jurisdiction.* Concurrent federal and state jurisdiction, with state court decisions subject to Supreme Court review, offers the benefit of convenience, when it is easier for litigants to appear in a state than a federal court. A regime of concurrent jurisdiction also "permits plaintiffs a relatively free choice of forum in the expectation that enlightened self-interest" will lead plaintiffs "into the forum most likely to enunciate an expansive vision of the rights of the individual". Neuborne, *Toward Procedural Parity in Constitutional Litigation,* 22 Wm. & Mary L.Rev. 725, 730 (1981). If a plaintiff believes that a state court is more likely than a federal court to give a broad construction of federal rights, should a defendant be able to remove to federal court, based on the premise that federal courts are more likely than state courts to decide federal issues *correctly*?

(d) *Concurrent Jurisdiction With Right of Removal.* In cases in which the plaintiff asserts a federal claim for relief, the jurisdictional arrangement most commonly employed by Congress is concurrent state and federal jurisdiction, subject to a right of the defendant to remove from state to federal court.[9] Typically, however, the right to remove depends on the contents of the plaintiff's well-pleaded complaint; with a few exceptions, removal is not allowed based on a federal defense or a federal reply to a defense. For extensive consideration of the intricacies of this scheme and of policy arguments for and against it, see Chapter VIII, *infra.*

If *both* litigants prefer state court, is there ever adequate justification for excluding state court jurisdiction and insisting on exclusive federal jurisdiction?[10] Further considerations that may bear on this question are discussed on pp. 478–79, *infra.*

(4) *Identifying Implied Exclusion.* Exclusive federal jurisdiction—a negation of state courts' authority to adjudicate federal claims—typically results from an express congressional policy choice. See, *e.g.,* 28 U.S.C. §§ 1333 (admiralty and maritime jurisdiction), 1338 (patents and copyrights), 1346(b)(U.S. as defendant in tort actions), 1351 (foreign consul or member of foreign mission as defendant), 1355 (action for recovery of fine, penalty, or forfeiture under federal legislation), 1356 (seizures under federal law but not within admiralty or maritime jurisdiction); 15 U.S.C. § 78aa (securities litigation); 18 U.S.C. § 3231 (federal crimes); 40 U.S.C. § 270b(b)(suits for payment on government building contracts). As reflected in the Tafflin case, however, the Supreme Court has also held that grants of federal jurisdiction should sometimes be read

---

to mandate removal from state to federal court at the point at which an issue within the exclusive federal jurisdiction arises, but it is at least conceivable that the federal issue might arise late in a case, without being presented in the original pleadings, and that removal would entail considerable costs and delay. See Note, *supra,* 70 Harv.L.Rev. at 514.

9. See 28 U.S.C. § 1441. In a few instances, however, Congress has precluded removal of a federal question case when it is brought in a state court. See 28 U.S.C. § 1445.

10. For an affirmative answer, see Redish, note 6, *supra,* at 1812.

as *impliedly* excluding state jurisdiction.[11] Impressive problems of interpretation and policy have grown up around the concept of implied exclusion.

(a) The leading case is Claflin v. Houseman, 93 U.S. 130 (1876), which upheld the right of an assignee in bankruptcy to sue in state court to recover assets of the bankrupt. Claflin held that a state court retains jurisdiction, notwithstanding a grant of federal jurisdiction, where state jurisdiction "is not excluded by express provision, or by incompatibility in its exercise arising from the nature of the particular case" (p. 136).

(b) In General Inv. Co. v. Lake Short & M.S. Ry., 260 U.S. 261, 287 (1922), and Freeman v. Bee Machine Co., 319 U.S. 448, 451 n. 6 (1943), without reference to the test framed in Claflin and with little discussion of any kind, the Court found that the federal antitrust laws impliedly exclude state court jurisdiction of federal antitrust claims.

(c) In Charles Dowd Box Co. v. Courtney, 368 U.S. 502 (1962), the Court specifically referred to and defended the Claflin presumption in favor of concurrent jurisdiction and concluded, after examination of the legislative history of § 301 of the Labor Management Relations Act, that Congress did not intend the grant of federal jurisdiction over certain contract actions for breach of a collective bargaining agreement to preclude the exercise of jurisdiction by state courts.

(d) Gulf Offshore Co. v. Mobil Oil Corp., 453 U.S. 473, 477–78 (1981), synthesized prior decisions to formulate the three-part test for implied exclusivity employed by the Court in the Tafflin case. Applying that test, it upheld state jurisdiction of a cause of action under the Outer Continental Shelf Lands Act.

(e) In Yellow Freight System, Inc. v. Donnelly, 494 U.S. 820 (1990), decided only a few months after Tafflin, a unanimous Court held that state courts have concurrent jurisdiction over private civil actions brought under Title VII of the 1964 Civil Rights Act. Justice Stevens, writing for the Court, said that the omission of any express provision making federal jurisdiction exclusive "is strong, and arguably sufficient, evidence that Congress had no such intent" (p. 823). The Court discussed the remaining two Gulf Offshore factors only briefly and attached little weight either to statements in the legislative history indicating an expectation that all Title VII cases would be tried in federal courts or to the frequent statutory references to procedures applicable in federal courts.

In light of these decisions, do you agree with the Court in Tafflin that the principles by which the Supreme Court identifies implied exclusion of state court jurisdiction "have 'remained unmodified through the years' "(p. 460, quoting Dowd Box, *supra,* 368 U.S. at 508)? With Judge Easterbrook that early decisions finding implied exclusion of state court jurisdiction to enforce the federal antitrust laws are "ripe for reexamination"? See Village of Bolingbrook v. Citizens Utilities Co., 864 F.2d 481, 485 (7th Cir.1988). With Professor Solimine that the Court's analysis in the Yellow Freight System case,

---

11. Statutes construed as impliedly excluding state jurisdiction include 28 U.S.C. §§ 1346(a)(U.S. as defendant in suits for recovery in tax and certain non-tax cases), 1491(a)(1)(Court of Federal Claims jurisdiction over express or implied contract actions where U.S. is the defendant), 2321–22 (enforcement of ICC orders), and 15 U.S.C. §§ 15 (antitrust damages), 26 (antitrust injunctions).

supra, implicitly abandons the three-part test employed in the Gulf Offshore and Tafflin cases and instead adopts Justice Scalia's view that only a clear statement by Congress can suffice to oust state court jurisdiction? See Solimine, note 7 *supra,* at 385.

(5) *Implied Preclusion and the Judicial Function.* What *should* be the courts' role in determining whether a grant of federal jurisdiction should be construed to exclude state jurisdiction? Is the decision to oust state court jurisdiction only for Congress to make? If so, in light of considerations of state sovereignty, should Congress have to make its intention evident in the legislative text? Or should courts eschew any such interpretive presumption and simply use ordinary methods of statutory interpretation? Or, moving beyond ordinary interpretation, should courts exercise a "creative lawmaking function" and determine whether federal jurisdiction is impliedly exclusive in light of "the potential impingement on important federal interests and programs that might result from [adjudication] by state judges who lack sufficient background, expertise or—on occasion—competence to deal with * * * uniquely federal concerns". Redish & Muench, *Adjudication of Federal Causes of Action in State Courts,* 75 Mich.L.Rev. 311, 329 (1976).

Which, if any, of these approaches are reflected in the leading cases? Is any mandated, or are some ruled out, by a sound understanding of the Constitution's structure?

Tennessee v. Davis

100 U.S. (10 Otto) 257, 25 L.Ed. 648 (1880).
Certificate from the Circuit Court for the Middle District of Tennessee.

[The defendant, James M. Davis, was indicted for murder in the Circuit Court of Grundy County, Tennessee. Before the trial of the indictment he presented to the Circuit Court of the United States for the proper district a petition for removal of the case from the state court. On the hearing of the motion, the judges were divided in opinion, and certified to the Supreme Court the following three questions:

[*First,* Whether an indictment of a revenue officer (of the United States) for murder, found in a State court, under the facts alleged in the petition for removal in this case, is removable to the Circuit Court of the United States, under § 643 of the Revised Statutes. * * *]

■ MR. JUSTICE STRONG delivered the opinion of the court.

The first of the questions certified is one of great importance, bringing as it does into consideration the relation of the general government to the government of the States, and bringing also into view not merely the construction of an act of Congress, but its constitutionality. That in this case the defendant's petition for removal of the cause was in the form prescribed by the act of Congress admits of no doubt. It represented that * * * he was acting by and under the authority of the internal-revenue laws of the United States; that what he did was done under and by right of his office, to wit, as deputy collector of internal revenue; that it was his duty to seize illicit distilleries and the apparatus that is used for the illicit and unlawful distillation of spirits; and that while so attempting to enforce the revenue laws of the United States, as deputy collector as aforesaid, he was assaulted and fired upon by a number of armed men, and that in defence of his life he returned the fire. * * * The language of the statute (so far as it is necessary at present to refer to it) is as follows: "When any civil suit or criminal prosecution is commenced in any court of a State against any officer appointed under, or acting by authority of, any revenue law of the United States, now or hereafter enacted, or against any person acting by or under authority of any such officer, on account of any act done under color of his office or of any such law, or on account of any right, title, or authority claimed by such officer or other person under any such law," the case may be removed into the Federal court. * * *

We come, then, to the inquiry, most discussed during the argument, whether sect. 643 is a constitutional exercise of the power vested in Congress. * * *

By the last clause of the eighth section of the first article of the Constitution, Congress is invested with power to make all laws necessary and proper for carrying into execution not only all the powers previously specified, but also all other powers vested by the Constitution in the government of the United States, or in any department or officer thereof. Among these is the judicial power of the government. That is declared by the second section of the third article to "extend to all cases in law and equity arising under the Constitution, the laws of the United States, and treaties made or which shall be made under their authority," & c. This provision embraces alike civil and criminal cases arising under the Constitution and laws. Cohens v. Virginia, 6 Wheat. 264. Both are equally within the domain of the judicial powers of the United States, and there is nothing in the grant to justify an assertion that whatever power may be exerted over a civil case may not be exerted as fully over a criminal one. And a case arising under the Constitution and laws of the United States may as well arise in a criminal prosecution as in a civil suit. What constitutes a case thus arising was early defined in the case cited from 6 Wheaton. It is not merely one where a party comes into court to demand something conferred upon him by the Constitution or by a law or treaty. A case consists of the right of one party as well as the other, and may truly be said to arise under the Constitution or a law or a treaty of the United States whenever its correct decision depends upon the construction of either. Cases arising under the laws of the United States are such as grow out of the legislation of Congress, whether they constitute the right or privilege, or claim or protection, or defence of the party, in whole or in part, by whom they are asserted. * * *

The constitutional right of Congress to authorize the removal before trial of civil cases arising under the laws of the United States has long since passed beyond doubt. It was exercised almost contemporaneously with the adoption of the Constitution, and the power has been in constant use ever since. The Judiciary Act of Sept. 24, 1789, was passed by the first Congress, many members of which had assisted in framing the Constitution; and though some doubts were soon after suggested whether cases could be removed from State courts before trial, those doubts soon disappeared. Whether removal from a State to a Federal court is an exercise of appellate jurisdiction, as laid down in Story's Commentaries on the Constitution, sect. 1745, or an indirect mode of exercising original jurisdiction, as intimated in Railway Company v. Whitton (13 Wall. 270), we need not now inquire. Be it one or the other, it was ruled in the case last cited to be constitutional. But if there is power in Congress to direct a removal before trial of a civil case arising under the Constitution or laws of the United States, and direct its removal because such a case has arisen, it is impossible to see why the same power may not order the removal of a criminal prosecution, when a similar case has arisen in it. * * *

The argument so much pressed upon us, that it is an invasion of the sovereignty of a State to withdraw from its courts into the courts of the general government the trial of prosecutions for alleged offences against the criminal laws of a State, even though the defence presents a case arising out of an act of Congress, ignores entirely the dual character of our government. It assumes that the States are completely and in all respects sovereign. But when the national government was formed, some of the attributes of State sovereignty were partially, and others wholly, surrendered and vested in the United States. Over the subjects thus surrendered the sovereignty of the States ceased to extend. Before the adoption of the Constitution, each State had complete and exclusive authority to administer by its courts all the law, civil and criminal, which existed within its borders. Its judicial power extended over every legal question that could arise. But when the Constitution was adopted, a portion of that judicial power became vested in the new government created, and so far as thus vested it was withdrawn from the sovereignty of the State. Now the execution and enforcement of the laws of the United States, and the judicial determination of questions arising under them, are confided to another sovereign, and to that extent the sovereignty of the State is restricted. The removal of cases arising under those laws, from State into Federal courts, is, therefore, no invasion of State domain. On the contrary, a denial of the right of the general government to remove them, to take charge of and try any case arising under the Constitution or laws of the United States, is a denial of the conceded sovereignty of that government over a subject expressly committed to it. * * *

It follows that the first question certified to us from the Circuit Court of Tennessee must be answered in the affirmative. * * *

■ MR. JUSTICE CLIFFORD, with whom concurred MR. JUSTICE FIELD, dissenting. * * *

NOTE ON THE POWER OF CONGRESS TO PROVIDE FOR REMOVAL FROM STATE TO FEDERAL COURTS

(1) *Historical and Constitutional Background.* In Martin v. Hunter's Lessee, 14 U.S. (1 Wheat.) 304 (1816), counsel conceded the authority of Congress to provide for a removal before final judgment of a case within the federal judicial power; they confined their attack to the review by the Supreme Court upon writ of error after judgment, as provided by Section 25 of the Judiciary Act of 1789. See Chap. V, Sec. 1, *infra.* Justice Story's theory of removal as a mode of exercising an "appellate jurisdiction" (14 U.S. at 347–51) thus used counsels' concession to refute their attack.

But the validity of a removal before judgment, though declared to be beyond doubt in The Moses Taylor, 71 U.S. (4 Wall.) 411, 429–30 (1867), was not directly determined in a civil action until The Mayor v. Cooper, 73 U.S. (6 Wall.) 247 (1868). This was a suit for trespass and conversion challenging a seizure under claim of federal authority during the Civil War, removed under the Act of March 3, 1863, 12 Stat. 756, p. 951, *infra.* Railway Co. v. Whitton, 80 U.S. (13 Wall.) 270 (1872), reaffirmed this decision in a case where the removal rested on diversity of citizenship. See also City of Greenwood v. Peacock, 384 U.S. 808, 833 (1966)("We may assume that Congress has constitutional power to provide that all federal issues be tried in the federal courts, that all be tried in the courts of the States, or that jurisdiction of such issues be shared. And in the exercise of that power, we may assume that Congress is constitutionally fully free to establish the conditions under which civil or criminal proceedings involving federal issues may be removed from one court to another.")

Unlike most removal statutes, the Act of 1863 applied after as well as before judgment in the state court, providing that the Circuit Court "shall thereupon proceed to try and determine the facts and law in such action in the same manner as if the same had been there originally commenced, the judgment in such case notwithstanding".[1] In The Justices v. Murray, 76 U.S. (9 Wall.) 274 (1870), an action for assault and battery and false imprisonment removed after a jury trial and verdict for the plaintiff, the Court held that the Seventh Amendment governed and that "so much of the Act of Congress * * * as provides for the removal of a judgment in a State court, and in which the cause was tried by a jury, to the Circuit Court of the United States for a retrial on the facts and law, is not in pursuance of the Constitution, and is void". See also McKee v. Rains, 77 U.S. (10 Wall.) 22 (1870).

(2) *Current Statutes and Issues.* Congress has provided since 1815 for the removal of state actions or prosecutions against federal officials likely to encounter sectional or state hostility. For an account of these statutes, see pp. 951-53, *infra.* The current statute, 28 U.S.C. § 1442, extending removal to any action or prosecution against any "officer" or "agency" or "person acting under him" for "any act under color of such office",[2] was broadly construed in Willingham v. Morgan, 395 U.S. 402 (1969)(allowing the warden and chief medical officer of a federal penitentiary to remove to federal court on a showing that their only contact with a prisoner who alleged a range of abuses had occurred inside the penitentiary).

The Supreme Court took a more cautious view in Mesa v. California, 489 U.S. 121 (1989), p. 905, *infra,* which interpreted 28 U.S.C. § 1442(a) as permitting federal officer removal only when the defendant avers a federal defense. In arguing for a broader interpretation, the United States contended that the defendant in Tennessee v. Davis had not asserted a federal defense to the killing, but only a state law self-defense claim. The Government argued, accordingly, that despite language in Tennessee v. Davis about the importance of federal adjudication of federal defenses, in fact the decision upheld removal in the absence of a federal defense. The Court rejected that interpretation of Davis, reasoning that whether Davis was acting in self-defense depended on whether he was lawfully trying to seize the still or was merely a thief; proof that he was not a simple thief depended on the federal revenue laws; hence, adjudication of the self-defense claim required application of federal law.

---

1. At present, removal of a civil action must ordinarily be effected within thirty days after receipt of the initial pleading (28 U.S.C. § 1446(b)), and removal of a criminal proceeding must be effected within thirty days after arraignment "or at any time before trial, whichever is earlier, except that for good cause shown the * * * [federal] court may enter an order granting the petitioner leave to file the [removal] petition at a later time" (28 U.S.C. § 1446(c)(1)).

2. See also 28 U.S.C. § 1442a, providing for removal of actions against members of the armed forces.

Clearly in the background in Mesa was a concern that, if § 1442 were construed to permit removal in the absence of a federal defense, the case might not "aris[e] under" federal law in the constitutional sense, and thus would not come within any of the authorized categories of federal jurisdiction under Article III.   Does Tennessee v. Davis establish that, as long as there is some issue of federal law in a case, there are no "external" limits (arising from the Tenth Amendment or the Constitution's structure) on Congress' authority to provide for federal jurisdiction of civil and criminal actions authorized by state law?

(3) *Additional Materials.*   For additional materials on removal, see pp. 948-62, 1615-31, *infra.*

Tarble's Case

80 U.S. (13 Wall.) 397, 20 L.Ed. 597 (1872).
Error to the Supreme Court of Wisconsin.

This was a proceeding on habeas corpus for the discharge of one Edward Tarble, held in the custody of a recruiting officer of the United States as an enlisted soldier, on the alleged ground that he was a minor, under the age of eighteen years at the time of his enlistment, and that he enlisted without the consent of his father.

The writ was issued on the 10th of August, 1869, by a court commissioner of Dane County, Wisconsin, an officer authorized by the laws of that State to issue the writ of habeas corpus upon the petition of parties imprisoned or restrained of their liberty, or of persons on their behalf.   It was issued in this case upon the petition of the father of Tarble, in which he alleged that his son, who had enlisted under the name of Frank Brown, was confined and restrained of his liberty by Lieutenant Stone, of the United States army, in the city of Madison, in that State and county * * *.

[The Supreme Court of Wisconsin affirmed] * * * the order of the commissioner discharging the prisoner.   This judgment was now before this court for examination on writ of error prosecuted by the United States.   * * *

■ MR. JUSTICE FIELD, after stating the case, delivered the opinion of the court, as follows:

The important question is presented by this case, whether a State court commissioner has jurisdiction, upon habeas corpus, to inquire into the validity of the enlistment of soldiers into the military service of the United States, and to discharge them from such service when, in his judgment, their enlistment has not been made in conformity with the laws of the United States.   The question presented may be more generally stated thus: Whether any judicial officer of a State has jurisdiction to issue a writ of habeas corpus, or to continue proceedings under the writ when issued, for the discharge of a person held under the authority, or claim and color of the authority, of the United States, by an officer of that government.   * * *

The decision of this court in the two cases which grew out of the arrest of Booth, that of Ableman v. Booth, and that of The United States v. Booth,*

---

* 21 Howard 506.

[Ed.] This decision, handed down in 1859, involved two habeas corpus petitions filed in Wisconsin state courts by Booth, a federal prisoner charged with aiding in the escape of a fugitive slave.   In the first peti-

disposes alike of the claim of jurisdiction by a State court, or by a State judge, to interfere with the authority of the United States, whether that authority be exercised by a Federal officer or be exercised by a Federal tribunal.   * * *

For a review in this court of the judgments in both of these cases, writs of error were prosecuted.   * * * The cases were afterwards heard and considered together, and the decision of both was announced in the same opinion.   In that opinion the Chief Justice details the facts of the two cases at length, and comments upon the character of the jurisdiction asserted by the State judge and the State court * * *.

And in answer to this assumption of judicial power by the judges and by the Supreme Court of Wisconsin thus made, the Chief Justice said as follows: If they "possess the jurisdiction they claim, they must derive it either from the United States or the State.   It certainly has not been conferred on them by the United States; and it is equally clear it was not in the power of the State to confer it, even if it had attempted to do so; for no State can authorize one of its judges or courts to exercise judicial power, by habeas corpus or otherwise, within the jurisdiction of another and independent government.   And although the State of Wisconsin is sovereign within its territorial limits to a certain extent, yet that sovereignty is limited and restricted by the Constitution of the United States.   And the powers of the General government and of the State, although both exist and are exercised within the same territorial limits, are yet separate and distinct sovereignties, acting separately and independently of each other, within their respective spheres.   And the sphere of action appropriated to the United States, is as far beyond the reach of the judicial process issued by a State judge or a State court, as if the line of division was traced by landmarks and monuments visible to the eye.   And the State of Wisconsin had no more power to authorize these proceedings of its judges and courts, than it would have had if the prisoner had been confined in Michigan, or in any other State of the Union, for an offence against the laws of the State in which he was imprisoned."

It is in the consideration of this distinct and independent character of the government of the United States, from that of the government of the several States, that the solution of the question presented in this case, and in similar cases, must be found.   There are within the territorial limits of each State two governments, restricted in their spheres of action, but independent of each other, and supreme within their respective spheres.   * * *

Such being the distinct and independent character of the two governments, within their respective spheres of action, it follows that neither can intrude with its judicial process into the domain of the other, except so far as such intrusion may be necessary on the part of the National government to preserve its rightful supremacy in cases of conflict of authority.   In their laws, and mode of enforcement, neither is responsible to the other.   How their respective laws shall be enacted; how they shall be carried into execution; and in what tribunals, or by what officers; and how much discretion, or whether any at all

tion, Booth challenged his arrest and detention on the ground, *inter alia,* of the unconstitutionality of the Fugitive Slave Act.   The state courts held in his favor and ordered his release.   Following that release, he was tried and convicted in a federal court for violation of the Act and was again imprisoned.   He then filed his second petition in state court attacking the act on the same grounds, and the state court again ordered his discharge.

shall be vested in their officers, are matters subject to their own control, and in the regulation of which neither can interfere with the other.

Now, among the powers assigned to the National government, is the power "to raise and support armies," and the power "to provide for the government and regulation of the land and naval forces." The execution of these powers falls within the line of its duties; and its control over the subject is plenary and exclusive. * * * Probably in every county and city in the several States there are one or more officers authorized by law to issue writs of habeas corpus on behalf of persons alleged to be illegally restrained of their liberty; and if soldiers could be taken from the army of the United States, and the validity of their enlistment inquired into by any one of these officers, such proceeding could be taken by all of them, and no movement could be made by the National troops without their commanders being subjected to constant annoyance and embarrassment from this source. The experience of the late rebellion has shown us that, in times of great popular excitement, there may be found in every State large numbers ready and anxious to embarrass the operations of the government, and easily persuaded to believe every step taken for the enforcement of its authority illegal and void. Power to issue writs of habeas corpus for the discharge of soldiers in the military service, in the hands of parties thus disposed, might be used, and often would be used, to the great detriment of the public service. In many exigencies the measures of the National government might in this way be entirely bereft of their efficacy and value. An appeal in such cases to this court, to correct the erroneous action of these officers, would afford no adequate remedy. Proceedings on habeas corpus are summary, and the delay incident to bringing the decision of a State officer, through the highest tribunal of the State, to this court for review, would necessarily occupy years, and in the meantime, where the soldier was discharged, the mischief would be accomplished. It is manifest that the powers of the National government could not be exercised with energy and efficiency at all times, if its acts could be interfered with and controlled for any period by officers or tribunals of another sovereignty.

It is true similar embarrassment might sometimes be occasioned, though in a less degree, by the exercise of the authority to issue the writ possessed by judicial officers of the United States, but the ability to provide a speedy remedy for any inconvenience following from this source would always exist with the National legislature. * * *

This limitation upon the power of State tribunals and State officers furnishes no just ground to apprehend that the liberty of the citizen will thereby be endangered. The United States are as much interested in protecting the citizen from illegal restraint under their authority, as the several States are to protect him from the like restraint under their authority, and are no more likely to tolerate any oppression. Their courts and judicial officers are clothed with the power to issue the writ of habeas corpus in all cases, where a party is illegally restrained of his liberty by an officer of the United States, whether such illegality consists in the character of the process, the authority of the officer, or the invalidity of the law under which he is held. And there is no just reason to believe that they will exhibit any hesitation to exert their power, when it is properly invoked. Certainly there can be no ground for supposing that their action will be less prompt and efficient in such cases than would be that of State tribunals and State officers.

It follows, from the views we have expressed, that the court commissioner of Dane County was without jurisdiction to issue the writ of habeas corpus for the discharge of the prisoner in this case * * *.

　　　* * *

Judgment reversed.

■ The Chief Justice [Chase], dissenting.

I cannot concur in the opinion just read. I have no doubt of the right of a State court to inquire into the jurisdiction of a Federal court upon habeas corpus, and to discharge when satisfied that the petitioner for the writ is restrained of liberty by the sentence of a court without jurisdiction. If it errs in deciding the question of jurisdiction, the error must be corrected in the mode prescribed by the 25th section of the Judiciary Act; not by denial of the right to make inquiry.

I have still less doubt, if possible, that a writ of habeas corpus may issue from a State court to inquire into the validity of imprisonment or detention, without the sentence of any court whatever, by an officer of the United States. The State court may err; and if it does, the error may be corrected here. The mode has been prescribed and should be followed.

To deny the right of State courts to issue the writ, or, what amounts to the same thing, to concede the right to issue and to deny the right to adjudicate, is to deny the right to protect the citizen by habeas corpus against arbitrary imprisonment in a large class of cases; and, I am thoroughly persuaded, was never within the contemplation of the Convention which framed, or the people who adopted, the Constitution. That instrument expressly declares that "the privilege of the writ of habeas corpus shall not be suspended, unless when, in case of rebellion or invasion, the public safety may require it."

NOTE ON TARBLE'S CASE AND STATE COURT PROCEEDINGS AGAINST FEDERAL OFFICIALS

(1) *Historical Practice.* Prior to the Booth case and Tarble's Case,[1] state courts "for a period of eighty years, continued to assert a right, through the issue of writs of *habeas corpus,* to take persons out of the custody of federal officials". Warren, *Federal and State Court Interference,* 43 Harv.L.Rev. 345, 353 (1930). (There were also prominent instances of refusal to interfere with federal enforcement activities, notably with respect to the Fugitive Slave Law, even in areas where its validity was most contested. See, *e.g.,* Passmore Williamson's Case, 26 Pa. 9 (1855); Warren, *supra,* at 355–56.)[2]

---

1. Note that Tarble's Case, unlike the Booth cases, did not involve state court interference with federal judicial processes, *cf.* Donovan v. City of Dallas, 377 U.S. 408 (1964), p. 1210, *infra,* but rather with executive action. This is a significant distinction, isn't it?

2. For an illuminating study of some Northern judges who were political opponents of slavery yet hesitated to press judicial

challenges to the Fugitive Slave Act and its enforcement, see Cover, Justice Accused: Antislavery and the Judicial Process (1975). Professor Cover's book explores the political, moral, psychological, and doctrinal contexts in which judicial decisions were rendered; he depicts those contexts as so highly impacted as to raise "the issue of whether the modern lawyer and scholar must forsake all the slavery cases as too infused with a substantive

Moreover, "such was the tenacity with which the state courts maintained their authority to issue writs of *habeas corpus,* that, for twelve years after the Booth decision, they continued to issue such writs against federal officials, on the ground that the Booth case only applied to instances where the prisoner was held under actual judicial federal process. Thus, during the Civil War, New York, Ohio, Iowa and Maine judges granted *habeas corpus* for persons serving in the United States Army. And as late as 1871, one Massachusetts court said that this power was so well settled by judicial opinion and long practice that it was not 'to be now disavowed, unless in obedience to an express act of congress, or to a direct adjudication of the supreme court of the United States'." Warren, *supra,* at 357, quoting Gray, J., in McConologue's Case, 107 Mass. 154, 160 (1871).

(2) *Constitutionally Mandated Exclusion?* To what extent does the decision in Tarble's Case rest on the proposition that the Constitution, of its own force, precludes the exercise of state habeas corpus jurisdiction against federal officials? Can the proposition that the Constitution precludes state habeas corpus jurisdiction over federal officers be squared with the Madisonian Compromise and the language of Article III making the establishment of "inferior" federal courts a matter of congressional discretion? Is this proposition consistent with Article I, section 9, which provides that "[t]he Privilege of the Writ of Habeas Corpus" shall not be suspended except in cases of rebellion or invasion?[3]

(a) In a recent article, Professor Collins offers a *historical* argument that among the generation that framed and ratified the Constitution, and its immediate successors, it was widely understood that some categories of federal jurisdiction—including federal criminal cases and suits against federal officers for specific relief—were inherently exclusive of state court jurisdiction. See Collins, *Article III Cases, State Court Duties, and the Madisonian Compromise,* 1995 Wisc.L.Rev. 39, 46–135 (1995).[4] Collins contends that Justice Story was only the most prominent of the jurists and treatise writers who thought the Constitution made some categories of jurisdiction exclusively federal (pp. 55–105); that the "Madisonian Compromise", discussed at pp. 7–9, 358–59, *supra,* was "secret" history that drew scant if any attention in public debates about the import of Article III (pp. 105–07, 114–16); and that it appeared plausible to many eighteenth and nineteenth century lawyers that if Congress wished to see the law enforced in cases in which the Constitution precluded state courts jurisdiction, it must exercise its constitutional option to create lower federal courts (pp. 129–35).

issue to be of any use in understanding our federal system" today (p. 166 n*).

Are the slavery cases *sui generis?* In the post-Civil War era, federal judicial concerns that racial prejudice may have corrupted state (and state court) decisionmaking has arguably had a large influence on doctrines of judicial federalism. See, for example, Glennon, *The Jurisdictional Legacy of the Civil Rights Movement,* 61 Tenn.L.Rev. 869 (1994); pp. 576–77 n. 2, *infra.*

3. According to Duker, A Constitutional History of Habeas Corpus 126–80 (1980), a principal purpose of the non-suspension clause was to protect state habeas corpus

jurisdiction from federal abrogation. See generally Chap. XI, Sec. 2, pp. 1368–69, *infra.*

4. According to Collins, the historical materials reflect a distinction between categories of cases in which the state courts had a "pre-existing" jurisdiction before the Constitution's ratification, and those in which they lacked a "pre-existing" jurisdiction. Where there was no pre-existing jurisdiction, the Constitution could not confer jurisdiction on a state court; and cases in which such conferral would have been necessary were widely thought to lie within the exclusive jurisdiction of the federal courts.

As Collins appears to acknowledge (pp. 84–105), important evidence against his thesis concerning the exclusivity of federal jurisdiction emerges from the practice of early Congresses, which authorized state courts to entertain actions seeking fines and other penalties, including criminal penalties, under a variety of federal laws. See Warren, *Federal Criminal Laws and the State Courts*, 38 Harv.L.Rev. 545 550–55, 570–73 (1925).[5] Perhaps for this reason, Collins appears to stop short of claiming that the intent of the framers or ratifiers of Article III was to exclude state court jurisdiction (and to insist only that it was thought by many to have this effect).[6]

Suppose it could be established that most of the framers or ratifiers of Article III understood it to preclude state court jurisdiction of certain classes of claims. Would that *specific* understanding necessarily be dispositive of the constitutional question? Would it be consistent with the structural logic of the constitutional plan for there to be no remedy available in any court for unconstitutional detentions or other coercive violations of national rights by federal officials?

(b) Redish & Woods, *Congressional Power to Control the Jurisdiction of Lower Federal Courts: A Critical Review and a New Synthesis*, 124 U.Pa.L.Rev. 45 (1975), give a negative answer to the latter question; they then go on to argue that because the rule of Tarble's Case bars a state court from providing constitutionally required review when a federal officer is the defendant, it would violate the Fifth Amendment to prevent the federal courts from hearing these cases. Thus, they conclude, Congress' power to control the jurisdiction of the lower federal courts must be limited by a Fifth Amendment obligation to provide a federal forum to protect constitutional rights where Tarble's Case prevents a state court from acting. In other words, the Madisonian Compromise and the language of Article III notwithstanding, Congress is constitutionally obliged to create lower federal courts.[7]

---

5. Collins quarrels with Warren's characterization of the scope of state *criminal*, rather than civil, jurisdiction contemplated by these federal statutes, but does not appear to deny that some state jurisdiction of federal criminal actions was authorized. See 1995 Wisc.L.Rev. at 86–89.

6. Collins argues that his implied-exclusivity thesis is consistent with the view of Hamilton in The Federalist No. 82, p. 25, *supra*. According to Collins, Hamilton is clear only that the Constitution did not divest the states of jurisdiction of "causes of which the states have *previous* cognizance". The Federalist No. 82, p. 26, *supra* (emphasis added). Professor Collins reads Hamilton as equivocal about cases, such as those under the Constitution and federal criminal statutes, of which the states could not be said to have "previous cognizance" or jurisdiction that antedated the Constitution (1995 Wisc. L.Rev. at 66–67). Will the language of The Federalist No. 82, especially that reproduced

on pp. 25-26, *supra*, support this interpretation?

7. In a subsequent passage Redish and Woods suggest a "potentially severe limitation on the reach of the new synthesis"— that "Congress can probably circumvent the difficulties created by Tarble's Case by *explicitly* authorizing state court jurisdiction over the acts of federal officials" (p. 106)(emphasis added). In a later piece, Redish dilutes his claim even further: "[A]ll my reading of Tarble's Case does is require that, before it excludes federal jurisdiction to review the alleged invasion of constitutional rights by federal officers, Congress be aware that (1) *some* judicial forum independent of congressional control will have to remain available to enforce constitutional rights, and that (2) with the federal courts removed from the picture, that forum will be the courts of the fifty states, with all the risks inherent in that avenue." Redish, *Constitutional Limitations on Congressional Power to Control Federal Jurisdiction: A Reaction to Professor Sager*, 77 Nw.U.L.Rev. 143, 159 (1982).

Is this argument persuasive? (Recall that Justice Story expressed similar views. See pp. 359–60, *supra*.) If not, where precisely does it break down? In its conclusions about the necessity of constitutional remedies for executive detentions? (For further exploration of issues involving constitutional remedies, see Chapter VII, pp. 847-77, *infra*.) In its assumption that the Supreme Court's reasoning in Tarble's Case, much of it unnecessary to the result, outweighs the seemingly plain contemplation of Article III that the decision whether to create "inferior" federal courts should be discretionary with Congress?

(3) *Alternative Foundations.* Suppose that the constitutional basis for the holding in Tarble's Case is adjudged untenable. Is the result possibly defensible on other grounds?

(a) Could the holding of Tarble's Case be justified on the ground that federal statutes (and not the Constitution of its own force) impliedly establish habeas corpus for persons in federal custody as a domain of exclusive federal jurisdiction? Is this attribution of congressional intent warranted by the acts of Congress with respect to federal habeas corpus? The acts of Congress with respect to the raising and government of the army? The conjunction of the two?

Could implied exclusion of state court jurisdiction be found under the test applied in Tafflin v. Levitt, *supra?*

(b) Could the result in Tarble's Case be justified by appeal to an inherent judicial power to develop a federal common law of state-federal relations, framed in the first instance by courts but subject to control by Congress? *Cf.* Meltzer, *State Court Forfeitures of Federal Rights,* 99 Harv.L.Rev. 1128, 1167– 85 (1986). On this interpretation, the decision might be defended as reflecting a synthesis of Reconstruction constitutionalism with Article III and the Madisonian Compromise: it would draw on premises of Reconstruction constitutionalism to presume state courts insufficiently trustworthy to issue mandatory orders to federal officials, but permit Congress to override that presumption by a sufficiently clear statement or, possibly, by failing to confer federal jurisdiction. But *cf.* McClung v. Silliman, Paragraph (4)(a), *infra*. Would judicial development of a common law of state-federal relations, subject to control by Congress, be any more problematic under the separation of powers than judicial development of presumptions and clear statement rules?[8]

(4) *State Jurisdiction in Other Proceedings Against Federal Officials.* How far does or should the rationale of Tarble's Case exclude other types of state proceedings challenging the legality of federal official action?

(a) *Mandamus.* In McClung v. Silliman, 19 U.S. (6 Wheat.) 598 (1821), the Supreme Court held that a state court lacked jurisdiction of a suit for mandamus to compel the register of a federal land office to make a conveyance. The Court rested its decision partly on the ground that the United States had denied its own courts authority to issue such a mandamus to an executive

---

8. See generally Sunstein, After the Rights Revolution: Reconstructing the Regulatory State 147–92 (1990)(discussing interpretive canons and their justifications, which sometimes involve considerations of constitutional structure and policy); *cf.* Eskridge & Frickey, *Quasi-Constitutional Law: Clear*

official,[9] but also reasoned that "no one will seriously contend, it is presumed, that it is among the reserved powers of the states, because not communicated by law to the courts of the United States" (p. 604).

According to the Court, "the one shadow of a ground on which" a state power to issue mandamus to federal officers "can be contended for" was "the general rights of legislation which the states possess over the soil within their respective territories" (*id.*). But that ground did not apply. "The question in this case is, as to the power of the state courts, over the officers of the general government, employed in disposing of" land under federal statutes "passed for that purpose" (*id.*). The conduct of a federal official implementing a federal statute "can only be controlled by the power that created him; since, whatever doubts have from time to time been suggested, as to the supremacy of the United States, in its legislative, judicial, or executive powers, no one has ever contested its supreme right to dispose of its property in its own way. And when we find it withholding from its own Courts, the exercise of this controlling power over its ministerial officers, * * * the inference clearly is, that all violations of private right, resulting from the acts of such officers, should be the subject of actions for damages, or to recover specific property, (according to the circumstances) in courts of competent jurisdiction. That is, the parties should be referred to the ordinary mode of obtaining justice, instead of resorting to the extraordinary and unprecedented mode of trying such questions on a motion for mandamus" (pp. 605).

Why did the Court presume that the power to issue mandamus to enforce the laws of the United States was not "among the reserved powers of the states" in cases involving the rights of their citizens? Recall the observation of Hamilton, in The Federalist, No. 82, that the "doctrine of concurrent jurisdiction is only clearly applicable to those descriptions of cases of which the state courts have previous cognizance". Mandamus suits against federal officials fall outside this category. See Collins, Paragraph (2)(a), p. 444, *supra*, at 98–105. Yet The Federalist, No. 82 went on to suggest that "in every case in which * * * [state courts are] not expressly excluded by future acts of the national legislature, they will, of course, take cognizance of the causes to which those acts may give birth".

The Court's opinion in the McClung case seemed to contemplate that state courts might exercise jurisdiction of suits against federal officials seeking damages or the recovery of specific property. See also Houston v. Moore, 18 U.S. (5 Wheat.) 1 (1820), holding that a state court had jurisdiction to try a militiaman for a violation of *federal* military law. Is there something *constitutionally* distinctive about the nature of mandamus?

Or was the crucial point that Congress, by failing to confer mandamus jurisdiction on the federal courts, signalled its intent to deny the power to state courts too?[10] Does the notion that Congress' *failure* to act somehow divested state courts of mandamus power make sense? Compare Justice Scalia's concurring opinion in Tafflin v. Levitt, p. 444, *supra*. Within a modern analytical

---

Statement Rules as Constitutional Lawmaking, 45 Vand.L.Rev. 593 (1992).

9. See McIntire v. Wood, 11 U.S. (7 Cranch) 504 (1813).

10. The Supreme Court held in Kendall v. Stokes, 37 U.S. (12 Pet.) 524 (1838), that

the territorial courts for the District of Columbia, apparently uniquely among the courts in the nation, possessed authority to issue writs of mandamus against federal officials.

framework, should McClung be viewed as a case in which federal jurisdiction, though nonexistent, is impliedly exclusive?

Or is McClung a case of judicial lawmaking, aimed at developing what the Court regarded as a sensible federal common law of state-federal relations? Appraised in that light, was the result indeed a sensible one? Note that McClung has been interpreted to exclude state mandamus against federal officials under any circumstances. See, *e.g.*, Armand Schmoll, Inc. v. Federal Reserve Bank, 286 N.Y. 503, 37 N.E.2d 225 (1941); Ex parte Shockley, 17 F.2d 133 (N.D.Ohio 1926).[11] See generally Arnold, *The Power of State Courts to Enjoin Federal Officers*, 73 Yale L.J. 1385, 1391–92 (1964).

Congress granted original jurisdiction to issue mandamus against federal officers to the *federal* district courts by the Act of October 5, 1962. See 28 U.S.C. § 1361. Does that statute, in conjunction with modern provisions for removal of actions filed in state court against federal officers, see 28 U.S.C. §§ 1442, 1442a, undercut McClung's rationale?

(b) *Damage Actions.* The Supreme Court has routinely sustained state court jurisdiction in damages actions against federal officials, averring tortious conduct unsupported by the claimed authority. See, *e.g.*, Teal v. Felton, 53 U.S. (12 How.) 284 (1852); Buck v. Colbath, 70 U.S. (3 Wall.) 334 (1866). But *cf.* Davis v. Passman, 442 U.S. 228, 245 n. 23 (1979)(p. 867, *infra*); Chap. IX, Sec. 3, *infra,* on the scope of substantive immunity.[12]

Why are suits for damages treated so differently from mandamus actions?

(c) *Actions at Law for Specific Relief.* Slocum v. Mayberry, 15 U.S. (2 Wheat.) 1 (1817), sustained a state court action for replevin of a cargo seized and held by customs officers, where the statutes gave no right to hold the cargo with the vessel. Chief Justice Marshall said that "the act of congress neither expressly, nor by implication, forbids the state courts to take cognizance of suits instituted for property in possession of an officer of the United States, not detained under some law of the United States; consequently their jurisdiction remains" (p. 12). The Court has also assumed that state courts may try ejectment actions against federal officers. See, *e.g.*, Scranton v. Wheeler, 179 U.S. 141 (1900). See generally Arnold, *supra,* at 1397 (asserting that state court "[j]urisdiction to award damages or possession of specific property, and to punish crime, is clear"). But *cf.* Malone v. Bowdoin, p. 1025, *infra.*

(d) *Injunctions.* The Supreme Court has not yet decided whether state courts have jurisdiction to entertain injunction actions against federal officers.[13] Other courts are divided on the question, though Redish & Woods,

---

11. In at least one case, however, the Supreme Court has decided on the merits a state-court mandamus action against a federal officer. Northern Pac. Ry. Co. v. North Dakota ex rel. Langer, 250 U.S. 135 (1919).

12. Professor Amar has suggested that states provide for "converse–1983" actions, in which state law furnishes a damages remedy for violations of the federal Constitution committed by federal officials, much as in 42 U.S.C. § 1983 the federal government has created a damages remedy for violations of federal law committed by state officials. See Amar, *Using State Law to Protect Federal*

Constitutional Rights: Some Questions and Answers about Converse–1983, 64 U.Colo. L.Rev. 159 (1993). Although recognizing that state court "converse–1983" suits would almost surely be removed to federal court, he contends that such actions would promote a healthy federalism, in which both state and federal governments would police the other's compliance with the federal Constitution.

13. A dictum in Keely v. Sanders, 99 U.S. 441, 443 (1878), stated that "no State court could, by injunction or otherwise, prevent federal officers from collecting Federal taxes." The government could have, but did

supra, at 89, conclude that "[t]he weight of reasoned opinion emanating from the state and lower federal courts supports the general denial of state court power" to enjoin federal officers.

Cf. Donovan v. City of Dallas, 377 U.S. 408 (1964), discussed at p. 1210, *infra,* in which the Court held that a state court lacked authority to enjoin a person from prosecuting an in personam action in a federal district court. Writing for a 6–3 majority, Justice Black reasoned (pp. 412–13): "While Congress has seen fit to authorize courts of the United States to restrain state-court proceedings in some special circumstances, it has in no way relaxed the old and well-established judicially declared rule that state courts are completely without power to restrain federal-court proceedings in personam actions like the one here. And it does not matter that the prohibition here was addressed to the parties rather than to the federal court itself * * * ".[14] See also General Atomic Co. v. Felter, 434 U.S. 12 (1977)(per curiam).

Can the uncertainty about the capacity of state courts to issue injunctions against federal officials be explained by viewing injunctions as occupying the middle of a spectrum, with mandamus and habeas corpus jurisdiction forbidden at one end and jurisdiction to award damages and specific relief just as clearly permitted at the other? See Arnold, *supra,* at 1397. If so, does any coherent set of principles underlie the grouping of cases along the spectrum? How should the uncertainty about injunctions be resolved?[15]

(5) *Consequences of Exclusion of State Jurisdiction.* A decision against state court jurisdiction, whether in an injunction or other type of suit, may mean that the plaintiff has no remedy at all against the defendant.[16] In Pennsylvania Turnpike Comm'n v. McGinnes, 179 F.Supp. 578 (E.D.Pa.1959), *aff'd per curiam,* 278 F.2d 330 (3d Cir.1960), plaintiff first sued in a federal district court, seeking to enjoin the Director of Internal Revenue from making a tax refund to a third party, who had allegedly obtained money from the plaintiff by fraud. The suit was dismissed for lack of jurisdiction on the ground that the plaintiff's case raised no federal question. When plaintiff subsequently sued in state court, defendant removed to federal court under 28 U.S.C. § 1442(a), and then obtained dismissal on the basis of the rule (then in force) that on removal a federal court cannot take jurisdiction over a case if the state court had none to begin with. Similarly, the holding in McClung v. Silliman, *supra,* came after the Supreme Court had already held that there was no original federal jurisdiction over the case. McIntire v. Wood, 11 U.S. (7 Cranch) 504 (1813).

---

not, raise the question in Tennessee Elec. Power Co. v. TVA, 306 U.S. 118 (1939). The issue was raised in Brooks v. Dewar, 313 U.S. 354, 360 (1941), but the Court was unwilling to resolve "asserted conflict touching issues of so grave consequence" where there was no case for injunction on the merits.

14. Justice Harlan, joined in dissent by Justices Stewart and Clark, argued that the power of a state court to enjoin a resident state court suitor from "conducting vexatious and harassing litigation in another forum" (p. 415) was well established by the Court's precedents.

15. For illuminating discussion and a powerful argument in favor of jurisdiction, see Arnold, *supra.* See also 1 Moore, Federal Practice ¶ 0.6[5] (2d ed. 1986); Warren, *Federal and State Court Interference,* 43 Harv. L.Rev. 345 (1930); Note, 53 Cornell L.Rev. 916, 926–29 (1968).

16. Until the amendments to 28 U.S.C. § 1331 in 1976 and 1980, there was a jurisdictional amount limitation on general federal question jurisdiction, and of course until 1875, there was no general federal question jurisdiction at all.

It is clear that in some cases, at least, the Constitution requires the availability of some court to provide a constitutionally adequate remedy for governmental lawlessness. See generally pp. 373-79, *supra,* and Chapter VII, Sec. 2(c), *infra.* If no federal court can provide a constitutionally required remedy, shouldn't—indeed, mustn't—the remedial imperative prevail over any competing principle restraining the exercise of state court jurisdiction?

———

Testa v. Katt

330 U.S. 386, 67 S.Ct. 810, 91 L.Ed. 967 (1947).
Certiorari to the Superior Court for Providence and Bristol Counties, Rhode Island.

■ MR. JUSTICE BLACK delivered the opinion of the Court.

Section 205(e) of the Emergency Price Control Act provides that a buyer of goods above the prescribed ceiling price may sue the seller "in any court of competent jurisdiction" for not more than three times the amount of the overcharge plus costs and a reasonable attorney's fee. Section 205(c) provides that federal district courts shall have jurisdiction of such suits "concurrently with State and Territorial courts." Such a suit under § 205(e) must be brought "in the district or county in which the defendant resides or has a place of business * * *."

The respondent was in the automobile business in Providence, Providence County, Rhode Island. In 1944 he sold an automobile to petitioner Testa, who also resides in Providence, for $1100, $210 above the ceiling price. The petitioner later filed this suit against respondent in the State District Court in Providence. Recovery was sought under § 205(e). The court awarded a judgment of treble damages and costs to petitioner. On appeal to the State Superior Court, where the trial was de novo, the petitioner was again awarded judgment, but only for the amount of the overcharge plus attorney's fees. Pending appeal from this judgment, the Price Administrator was allowed to intervene. On appeal, the State Supreme Court reversed. It interpreted § 205(e) to be "a penal statute in the international sense." It held that an action for violation of § 205(e) could not be maintained in the courts of that State. The State Supreme Court rested its holding on its earlier decision in Robinson v. Norato, 1945, 71 R.I. 256, 43 A.2d 467, 468 , in which it had reasoned that: A state need not enforce the penal laws of a government which is "foreign in the international sense"; § 205(e) is treated by Rhode Island as penal in that sense; the United States is "foreign" to the State in the "private international" as distinguished from the "public international" sense; hence Rhode Island courts, though their jurisdiction is adequate to enforce similar Rhode Island "penal" statutes, need not enforce § 205(e). Whether state courts may decline to enforce federal laws on these grounds is a question of great importance. For this reason, and because the Rhode Island Supreme Court's holding was alleged to conflict with this Court's previous holding in Mondou v. New York, N.H. & H.R. Co., 223 U.S. 1, we granted certiorari.

For the purposes of this case, we assume, without deciding, that § 205(e) is a penal statute in the "public international," "private international," or any other sense. So far as the question of whether the Rhode Island courts properly declined to try this action, it makes no difference into which of these categories the Rhode Island court chose to place the statute which Congress has passed. For we cannot accept the basic premise on which the Rhode Island Supreme Court held that it has no more obligation to enforce a valid penal law of the United States than it has to enforce a penal law of another state or a foreign country. Such a broad assumption flies in the face of the fact that the States of the Union constitute a nation. It disregards the purpose and effect of Article VI, § 2 of the Constitution which provides: "This Constitution, and the Laws of the United States which shall be made in Pursuance thereof; and all Treaties made, or which shall be made, under the Authority of the United States, shall be the supreme Law of the Land; and the Judges in every State shall be bound thereby, any Thing in the Constitution or Laws of any State to the Contrary notwithstanding."

It cannot be assumed, the supremacy clause considered, that the responsibilities of a state to enforce the laws of a sister state are identical with its responsibilities to enforce federal laws. Such an assumption represents an erroneous evaluation of the statutes of Congress and the prior decisions of this Court in their historic setting. Those decisions establish that state courts do not bear the same relation to the United States that they do to foreign countries. The first Congress that convened after the Constitution was adopted conferred jurisdiction upon the state courts to enforce important federal civil laws,[4] and succeeding Congress conferred on the states jurisdiction over federal crimes and actions for penalties and forfeitures.[5]

Enforcement of federal laws by state courts did not go unchallenged. Violent public controversies existed throughout the first part of the Nineteenth Century until the 1860's concerning the extent of the constitutional supremacy of the Federal Government. During that period there were instances in which this Court and state courts broadly questioned the power and duty of state courts to exercise their jurisdiction to enforce United States civil and penal statutes or the power of the Federal Government to require them to do so. But after the fundamental issues over the extent of federal supremacy had been resolved by war, this Court took occasion in 1876 to review the phase of the controversy concerning the relationship of state courts to the Federal Government. Claflin v. Houseman, 93 U.S. 130. The opinion of a unanimous court in that case was strongly buttressed by historic references and persuasive reasoning. It repudiated the assumption that federal laws can be considered by the states as though they were laws emanating from a foreign sovereign. Its teaching is that the Constitution and the laws passed pursuant to it are the supreme laws of the land, binding alike upon states, courts, and the people, "anything in the Constitution or Laws of any State to the contrary notwithstanding." It asserted that the obligation of states to enforce these federal laws is not lessened by reason of the form in which they are cast or the remedy which they provide. And the Court stated that "If an act of Congress gives a penalty to a party aggrieved, without specifying a remedy for its enforcement, there is no reason why it should not be enforced, if not provided otherwise by some act of Congress, by a proper action in a state court." Id. 93 U.S. at page 137.

4. Judiciary Act of 1789, 1 Stat. 73, 77 (suits by aliens for torts committed in violation of federal laws and treaties; suits by the United States).

5. 1 Stat. 376, 378 (1794)(fines, forfeitures and penalties for violation of the License Tax on Wines and Spirits); 1 Stat. 373, 375 (1794)(the Carriage Tax Act); 1 Stat. 452 (penalty for purchasing guns from Indians); 1 Stat. 733, 740 (1799)(criminal and civil actions for violation of the postal laws).

The Claflin opinion thus answered most of the arguments theretofore advanced against the power and duty of state courts to enforce federal penal laws. And since that decision, the remaining areas of doubt have been steadily narrowed. There have been statements in cases concerned with the obligation of states to give full faith and credit to the proceedings of sister states which suggested a theory contrary to that pronounced in the Claflin opinion. But when in Mondou v. New York, N.H. & H.R. Co., *supra,* this Court was presented with a case testing the power and duty of states to enforce federal laws, it found the solution in the broad principles announced in the Claflin opinion.

The precise question in the Mondou case was whether rights arising under the Federal Employers' Liability Act, 36 Stat. 291, could "be enforced, as of right, in the courts of the states when their jurisdiction, as prescribed by local laws, is adequate to the occasion. * * * "*Id.* 223 U.S. at page 46. The Supreme Court of Connecticut had decided that they could not. Except for the penalty feature, the factors it considered and its reasoning were strikingly similar to that on which the Rhode Island Supreme Court declined to enforce the federal law here involved. But this Court held that the Connecticut court could not decline to entertain the action. The contention that enforcement of the congressionally created right was contrary to Connecticut policy was answered as follows:

"The suggestion that the act of Congress is not in harmony with the policy of the State, and therefore that the courts of the state are free to decline jurisdiction, is quite inadmissible, because it presupposes what in legal contemplation does not exist. When Congress, in the exertion of the power confided to it by the Constitution, adopted that act, it spoke for all the people and all the states, and thereby established a policy for all. That policy is as much the policy of Connecticut as if the act had emanated from its own legislature, and should be respected accordingly in the courts of the state." Mondou v. New York, N.H. & H.R. Co., *supra,* 223 U.S. at page 57.

So here, the fact that Rhode Island has an established policy against enforcement by its courts of statutes of other states and the United States which it deems penal, cannot be accepted as a "valid excuse." Cf. Douglas v. New York, N.H. & H.R. Co., 279 U.S. 377, 388. For the policy of the federal Act is the prevailing policy in every state. Thus, in a case which chiefly relied upon the Claflin and Mondou precedents, this Court stated that a state court cannot "refuse to enforce the right arising from the law of the United States because of conceptions of impolicy or want of wisdom on the part of Congress in having called into play its lawful powers." Minneapolis & St. L.R. Co. v. Bombolis, 241 U.S. 211, 222.

The Rhode Island court in its Robinson decision on which it relies cites cases of this Court which have held that states are not required by the full faith and credit clause of the Constitution to enforce judgments of the courts of other states based on claims arising out of penal statutes. But those holdings have no relevance here, for this case raises no full faith and credit question. Nor need we consider in this case prior decisions to the effect that federal courts are not required to enforce state penal laws.

For whatever consideration they may be entitled to in the field in which they are relevant, those decisions did not bring before us our instant problem of the effect of the supremacy clause on the relation of federal laws to state courts. Our question concerns only the right of a state to deny enforcement to claims growing out of a valid federal law.

It is conceded that this same type of claim arising under Rhode Island law would be enforced by that State's courts. Its courts have enforced claims for double damages growing out of the Fair Labor Standards Act, 29 U.S.C.A. § 201 et seq. Thus the Rhode Island courts have jurisdiction adequate and appropriate under established local law to adjudicate this action. Under these circumstances the State courts are not free to refuse enforcement of petitioners' claim. See McKnett v. St. Louis & S.F.R. Co., 292 U.S. 230; and compare Herb v. Pitcairn, 324 U.S. 117; 325 U.S. 77. The case is reversed and the cause is remanded for proceedings not inconsistent with this opinion.

Reversed.

NOTE ON THE OBLIGATION OF STATE COURTS
TO ENFORCE FEDERAL LAW

(1) *From Power to Obligation.* How long is the leap from Claflin v. Houseman, discussed in Testa, which upheld state court *power* to exercise jurisdiction over a federal claim, to the holding of Testa itself that the state court was under an *obligation* to do so?[1]

(a) The question of congressional power to obligate the states to exercise jurisdiction was apparently first mooted by the Supreme Court in Prigg v. Pennsylvania, 41 U.S. (16 Pet.) 539 (1842), where the precise issue involved Congress' authority to impose a mandatory, concurrent jurisdiction to enforce the Fugitive Slave Act. Writing for himself and Justices Catron and McKinley, Justice Story—echoing a position he had taken in Martin v. Hunter's Lessee, 14 U.S. (1 Wheat.) 304, 337 (1816)—suggested that Congress lacked power to force the states to take jurisdiction. See Prigg, 41 U.S. at 608–626. But while Justice Story's opinion was styled as that of "the Court", "no five judges concurred in all of its reasoning", Cover, Justice Accused: Antislavery and the Judicial Process 166–67 (1975), and it is doubtful that a majority concurred in his analysis on this point. See *id.* at 166–68. The Court did not need to resolve this issue to reverse Prigg's conviction under a Pennsylvania kidnapping statute that forbade the forcible removal of a Negro from the state. The statute, Story reasoned, violated Article IV's Fugitive Slave Clause.

For a collection of nineteenth century cases expressing doubts about Congress' power to impose jurisdiction on the state courts, see Collins, *Article III, State Court Duties, and the Madisonian Compromise,* 1995 Wisc.L.Rev. 39, 145–94 (1995).[2]

---

1. For discussion of state court obligations, see Neuborne, *Toward Procedural Parity in Constitutional Litigation,* 22 Wm. & Mary L.Rev. 725, 753–66 (1981); Redish & Muench, *Adjudication of Federal Causes of Action in State Court,* 75 Mich.L.Rev. 311, 340–61 (1976); Sandalow, *Henry v. Mississippi and the Adequate State Ground: Proposals for a Revised Doctrine,* 1965 Sup.Ct.Rev. 187, 203–09. See also Warren, *New Light on the History of the Federal Judiciary Act of 1789,* 37 Harv.L.Rev. 49 (1923); Warren, *Federal Criminal Laws and the State Courts,* 38 Harv.L.Rev. 545 (1925); Note, 73 Harv. L.Rev. 1551 (1960).

2. To the objection that the lack of such a power would effectively force Congress to create lower federal courts and thus contravene the spirit of the Madisonian Compromise, Collins responds that, to eighteenth

Consider also the views expressed by Justice Frankfurter, concurring, in Brown v. Gerdes, 321 U.S. 178, 188 (1944):

"Since 1789, rights derived from federal law could be enforced in state courts unless Congress confined their enforcement to the federal courts. This has been so precisely for the same reason that rights created by the British Parliament or by the Legislature of Vermont could be enforced in New York courts. Neither Congress nor the British Parliament nor the Vermont Legislature has power to confer jurisdiction upon the New York courts. But the jurisdiction conferred upon them by the only authority that has power to create them and to confer jurisdiction upon them—namely the law-making power of the State of New York—enables them to enforce rights no matter what the legislative source of the right may be."

Is Testa v. Katt consistent with the views of Justice Frankfurter as to the basis of state jurisdiction to enforce federal rights of action?

(b) Is there greater compulsion on state courts to hear federal defenses than to take jurisdiction of causes of action that arise under federal law and, if so, why?

(c) In Mondou v. New York, N.H. & H.R.R., 223 U.S. 1 (1912), discussed in Testa v. Katt, the Court unanimously held that a Connecticut state court must accept jurisdiction of a claim under the Federal Employers' Liability Act. But the Court put its opinion, not on the ground that Congress had permissibly imposed an unconditional obligation to accept jurisdiction, but on the basis that a state court with acknowledged jurisdiction over analogous state law claims could not *discriminate* against federal claims based on an underlying policy disagreement with the federal statute.

(d) Under cases such as Mondou and Testa v. Katt, does a finding that (i) Congress has not *excluded* state jurisdiction imply that (ii) Congress has *bound* state courts to accept jurisdiction of federal claims whenever they would accept jurisdiction of analogous state claims? Does this result make sense? If (i) indeed implies (ii), should this consequence be a ground for hesitation in finding that Congress has created concurrent (rather than exclusively federal) jurisdiction?

(2) *The "Valid Excuse" Doctrine.* On what grounds may a state court refuse to accept jurisdiction of a federal cause of action? Does it make sense to suggest, as the Court has, that (i) state courts can be forbidden to discriminate against federal causes of action, but (ii) it is an open question whether they can be more straightforwardly required to hear federal claims?

Consider these questions in light of the Supreme Court's decisions in the following cases.

(a) In Douglas v. New York, N.H. & H.R.R., 279 U.S. 377 (1929), the New York courts had dismissed an action under the Federal Employers' Liability Act brought by a Connecticut resident against a Connecticut corporation based on an accident occurring in Connecticut. A New York statute permitted actions by a nonresident against a foreign corporation only in certain classes of cases,

and early nineteenth century lawyers, judges, and treatise writers (i) the Madisonian compromise was "secret" history that would not have been entitled to weight under prevailing interpretive understandings (pp. 105–07, 114–16), and (ii) the cost of allowing federal law to go unenforced in some cases was plausibly viewed as one to be weighed by Congress in determining whether to create lower federal courts (pp. 129–57).

of which this was not one. On appeal, plaintiff attacked the statute as a violation of the Article IV privileges and immunities clause. Justice Holmes, for the Court, rejected this attack on the ground that the statute applied equally to citizens of New York who were nonresidents of the state,[3] and then said (pp. 387–88):

"As to the grant of jurisdiction in the Employers' Liability Act, that statute does not purport to require State Courts to entertain suits arising under it, but only to empower them to do so, so far as the authority of the United States is concerned. It may very well be that if the Supreme Court of New York were given no discretion, being otherwise competent, it would be subject to a duty. But there is nothing in the Act of Congress that purports to force a duty upon such Courts as against an otherwise valid excuse. Second Employers' Liability Cases, 223 U.S. 1, 56, 57."

(b) In McKnett v. St. Louis & S.F. Ry., 292 U.S. 230 (1934), an Alabama statute had opened the doors of Alabama courts to suits against foreign corporations arising under the laws of other states. This statute superseded a previous rule of decision that no Alabama court had jurisdiction of any suit against a foreign corporation unless the cause of action arose in Alabama. The Alabama Supreme Court had dismissed an action under the Federal Employers' Liability Act that was based on an out-of-state accident on the ground that the statute lifted the prior bar only for causes of action arising under the laws of sister states. The Supreme Court reversed, Justice Brandeis saying (pp. 233–34):

"While Congress has not attempted to compel states to provide courts for the enforcement of the Federal Employers' Liability Act, Douglas v. New York, N.H. & H.R. Co., 279 U.S. 377, 387, the Federal Constitution prohibits state courts of general jurisdiction from refusing to do so solely because the suit is brought under a federal law. The denial of jurisdiction by the Alabama court is based solely upon the source of law sought to be enforced. The plaintiff is cast out because he is suing to enforce a federal act. A state may not discriminate against rights arising under federal laws."

(c) In Missouri ex rel. Southern Ry. v. Mayfield, 340 U.S. 1 (1950), the Missouri Supreme Court had quashed writs of mandamus to compel a state trial judge to exercise his discretion, on a plea of forum non conveniens, to dismiss actions brought by nonresidents under the Federal Employers' Liability Act. Justice Frankfurter, speaking for the Court, reiterated the statement of the Douglas case that there is nothing in the Act "which purported to 'force a duty' upon the State courts to entertain or retain Federal Employers' Liability litigation 'against an otherwise valid excuse' "(pp. 4–5). He made clear that the doctrine of forum non conveniens, if applied without discrimination to all nonresidents, constitutes a valid excuse. Because the state court might have acted under a misapprehension of a federal duty, its judgment was vacated and the cause remanded for further proceedings.[4]

---

3. But *cf.* Hicklin v. Orbeck, 437 U.S. 518, 524 n. 8 (1978). The Court in Hicklin, in invalidating a state law requiring preferential hiring of qualified state residents, said: "Although this Court has not always equated state residency with state citizenship * * * [citing Douglas and other cases], it is now established that the terms 'citizen' and 'resident' are 'essentially interchangeable' * * * for purposes of analysis of most cases under the Privileges and Immunities Clause of Art. IV, § 2."

4. The Court relied on Mayfield in American Dredging Co. v. Miller, 114 S.Ct. 981 (1994), which held, 7–2, that federal law

(d) In Howlett v. Rose, 496 U.S. 356 (1990), the Supreme Court unanimously ruled that Florida state courts were obliged to entertain a § 1983 action against a local school board. The Court began its analysis by citing Douglas, *supra,* for the proposition that "a state court may not deny a federal right, when the parties and controversy are properly before it, in the absence of a 'valid excuse' "(p. 369). Since a state statute had waived sovereign immunity in comparable actions under state law, the Court found the state's excuse—that the waiver did not extend to § 1983 actions—discriminatory and therefore invalid.[5]

(e) In Felder v. Casey, 487 U.S. 131 (1988), also discussed at pp. 487, 827, 1229, *infra,* the Court refused to permit application of a state notice-of-claim statute to a federal civil rights action filed in state court under 42 U.S.C. § 1983. (The statute made it a condition of a state court suit against a governmental body or one of its officers that the defendant be notified of the claim within 120 days of the alleged injury.) Though the statute treated state law and federal law claims against governmental defendants identically, the Court found that it discriminated against the precise type of civil rights action that Congress had created in § 1983.

The claim of discrimination is not very persuasive in Felder, is it?[6] The Court also argued that enforcement of the notice-of-claim requirement would interfere with federal civil rights policy. See p. 487, *infra.* If in fact such

does not preempt a state procedural rule rendering forum non conveniens doctrine inapplicable in Jones Act and maritime cases filed in state court under the "saving to suitors" clause. Although a federal district court would apply a different forum non conveniens rule, the Court, in an opinion by Justice Scalia, determined that forum non conveniens doctrine is procedural, not substantive, and that the policies of federal maritime law do not require complete procedural uniformity. Because the Jones Act adopts " 'the entire judicially developed doctrine of liability' under the [FELA]" (p. 989), Mayfield supported the Court's decision insofar as the Jones Act was involved. And, the Court concluded, to have a different rule for Jones Act than for general maritime law cases would disserve rather than promote the harmonization of general maritime law with federal statutes (p. 990).

Did the rule upheld by the Court discriminate against *defendants* in federal causes of action? Why shouldn't such discrimination be as suspect as discrimination against plaintiffs? Compare Norfolk & Western Ry. Co. v. Liepelt, 444 U.S. 490 (1980), p. 489, *infra,* and Monessen Southwestern Ry. Co. v. Morgan, 486 U.S. 330 (1988), p. 489, *infra.*

5. Compare National Private Truck Council, Inc. v. Oklahoma Tax Comm'n, 115 S.Ct. 2351 (1995), in which the Court held unanimously that § 1983 does not authorize suits for injunctions against state taxes when there is an adequate remedy under state law. Because the Tax Injunction Act, 28 U.S.C. § 1341, forbids federal courts to enjoin state taxes as long as state law furnishes a "plain, speedy and efficient remedy", see Chap. X(1)(B)(3), *infra,* plaintiffs sought an injunction (and attorneys' fees under 42 U.S.C. § 1988) in state (rather than federal) court. The Supreme Court "assume[d] * * * that state courts generally must hear § 1983 suits", though observed that it had never held explicitly that they must do so (p. 2355 & n. 4). But, "in light of the strong background principle against federal interference with state taxation", it found that § 1983 did not create an applicable cause of action.

6. Compare Herb v. Pitcairn, 324 U.S. 117 (1945). The plaintiff filed an FELA action in an Illinois city court that, under state law, lacked jurisdiction of causes of action, such as this one, arising outside the city. The plaintiff moved for a change of venue, but before a transfer occurred, the FELA's two-year statute of limitations had run. The state court dismissed on the ground that there was no timely filed action to transfer, and the Supreme Court affirmed. Acknowledging the state's authority to allocate jurisdiction among its courts, the Court found no violation of the "qualification that the cause of action must not be discriminated against because it is a federal one" (p. 123).

interference exists, wouldn't the opinion have been more persuasive had it rested on that ground alone, rather than also on a claim of state court discrimination? Doesn't the holding, if not the reasoning, of Felder make clear that not all non-discriminatory state rules may be enforced to close the doors of state courts against federal claims? See also General Oil v. Crain, 209 U.S. 211 (1908), discussed p. 855, *infra* (holding that a state law bar to jurisdiction of suits deemed to be against the state may not be enforced in a suit against a state official for an alleged violation of the federal Constitution).

(3) *The Tenth Amendment and Related Doctrines.* Do the Supreme Court's cases addressing Tenth Amendment and other structural limits on Congress' authority to regulate *nonjudicial* functions of state and local governments shed light on issues of congressional power to impose jurisdictional obligations on state courts?

(a) In National League of Cities v. Usery, 426 U.S. 833 (1976), a divided Court invalidated amendments to the Fair Labor Standards Act that extended the statute's minimum wage and maximum hours provisions to most state employees. The Court distinguished federal regulation of private activity from regulation "directed to the States as States" and held that regulation of traditional governmental functions involving matters "essential to [the] separate and independent existence" of the states lay beyond Congress' power under the Commerce Clause and the Tenth Amendment (p. 845).

Did Usery cast doubt on the validity of Testa? Did it constitutionalize the valid excuse doctrine?

(b) Federal Energy Regulatory Comm'n (FERC) v. Mississippi, 456 U.S. 742 (1982), involved a Tenth Amendment challenge to the Public Utilities Regulatory Policies Act of 1978 (PURPA), 16 U.S.C. §§ 2601 *et seq.*, which, *inter alia,* directed state utility regulatory authorities to implement certain federal rules, to "consider" the adoption of certain rate design and regulatory standards, and to follow certain procedures when considering these proposed standards. Distinguishing Usery, the Court relied heavily on Testa in upholding these requirements. The Court stressed that the area of public utility regulation was one that Congress could choose to preempt altogether and that the states could avoid the federal obligation by opting not to regulate.

Justice O'Connor, dissenting in part with two other Justices, argued that "[a]pplication of Testa to legislative power [such as that exercised by state utility regulatory commissions] * * * vastly expands the scope of that decision. Because trial courts of general jurisdiction do not choose the cases that they hear, the requirement that they evenhandedly adjudicate state and federal claims falling within their jurisdiction does not infringe any sovereign authority to set an agenda. * * * [But] the power to choose subjects for legislation is a fundamental attribute of legislative power, and interference with this power unavoidably undermines state sovereignty" (pp. 784–85).[7]

(c) After distinguishing Usery in FERC and several other cases,[8] the Court, noting that the Usery rationale had proved exceedingly difficult to apply,

---

7. Justice Powell, writing separately, expressed sympathy with Justice O'Connor's concerns, but limited his own dissent to that part of the majority opinion upholding the power of Congress to prescribe the "administrative and judicial *procedures* that States must follow" (p. 771)(emphasis added). On this issue, see pp. 479–91, *infra.*

8. Hodel v. Virginia Surface Mining & Reclamation Ass'n, Inc., 452 U.S. 264 (1981);

overruled Usery altogether (by a sharply divided 5–4 vote) in Garcia v. San Antonio Metropolitan Transit Auth., 469 U.S. 528 (1985). "[We] continue to recognize", the majority said, "that the States occupy a special and specific position in our constitutional system and that the scope of Congress' authority under the Commerce Clause must reflect that position. But the principal and basic limit on the federal commerce power is that inherent in all congressional action—the built-in restraints that our system provides through state participation in federal government action" (p. 556).

(d) In New York v. United States, 505 U.S. 144 (1992), the Supreme Court made clear that, despite Garcia, it had not wholly forsaken judicial enforcement of constitutional limits on Congress' power to regulate the states. Dividing 6–3, the Court invalidated a congressional act as outside the scope of the commerce power. The provision held unconstitutional required states that failed to provide for disposal of internally generated radioactive waste by a certain date to take title to the waste and thereby assume associated liabilities. In the Court's view, Congress lacked power either to "commandeer" the states into regulating waste disposal or to require states to take title to waste; accordingly, Congress lacked power to offer the states a choice between those two courses. Garcia was distinguished because it involved a statute that, unlike the "take title" provision, "subjected a State to the same legislation applicable to private parties" (p. 160).

The Court also distinguished FERC and Testa. The statute upheld in FERC differed from the take title provision by requiring only that the states give "consideration" to federal standards. Testa was distinguishable, the Court explained, because "[f]ederal statutes enforceable in state courts do, in a sense, direct state judges to enforce them, but this sort of federal 'direction' of state judges is mandated by the text of the Supremacy Clause. No comparable constitutional provision authorizes Congress to command state legislatures to legislate" (pp. 178–79).

Do the Court's dicta in New York v. United States clearly establish Congress' *power* to impose jurisdiction on otherwise competent state courts, even in the absence of "discrimination", where necessary and proper to implement federal policy?[9]

(e) In Gregory v. Ashcroft, 501 U.S. 452 (1991), the Supreme Court held that the federal Age Discrimination in Employment Act (ADEA), which forbids age-based mandatory retirement, did not apply to Missouri state judges, who are required by the state constitution to retire at age 70. Justice O'Connor's majority opinion reasoned that "[c]ongressional interference with this decision of the people of Missouri, defining their constitutional officers, would upset the

---

Hodel v. Indiana, 452 U.S. 314 (1981); United Transp. Union v. Long Island R.R.Co., 455 U.S. 678 (1982); EEOC v. Wyoming, 460 U.S. 226 (1983).

9. Compare the issues raised by Section 811 of the Fair Debt Collection Practices Act of 1977, 15 U.S.C. § 1692i. That section provides, *inter alia*, that "[a]ny debt collector who brings any legal action on a debt against any consumer" (other than an action to enforce an interest in real property) may bring the action "only in the judicial district or similar legal entity (A) in which such consumer signed the contract sued upon; or (B) in which such consumer resides * * *." The statute was specifically designed to encompass consumer debt actions arising under state law and brought in the state courts. Does Congress have the power to regulate the venue of state-law actions in the state courts? *Cf.* Mercantile National Bank v. Langdeau, 371 U.S. 555 (1963)(upholding federal limitations on venue in state court actions against national banks).

usual constitutional balance of federal and state powers" (p. 460). Without doubting Congress' power to do so, Justice O'Connor held that "[i]f Congress intends to alter 'the usual constitutional balance between the States and the Federal Government' it must make its intention to do so 'unmistakably clear in the language of the statute'" (*id.*)(citations omitted).[10]

After Gregory, should Congress be required to make any intent to bind the states to accept jurisdiction "unmistakably clear in the language of the statute"? Would a "plain statement rule" to this effect be desirable?

(4) *Federal Criminal Prosecutions in State Court.* If jurisdiction of federal criminal prosecutions were not made exclusive in the federal district courts, see 18 U.S.C. § 3231, could a United States Attorney prosecute criminal violations in a state court of general criminal jurisdiction? Compare the recent report of a panel of judges commissioned by the Judicial Conference of the United States, proposing statutory changes to permit some categories of federal criminal cases to be filed nearly exclusively in state court. Committee on Long Range Planning of the Judicial Conference of the United States, Proposed Long Range Plan for the Federal Courts 26–27 (1995). If a state court should hold its jurisdiction limited to crimes under state law, would its excuse be "valid" under Testa v. Katt?

(5) *State Jurisdictional Obligations and the Unfunded Mandate Reform Act.* The Unfunded Mandate Reform Act of 1995, P.L. 104–4, 109 Stat. 48 *et seq.*, generally provides that "[i]t shall not be in order in" either house of Congress to consider any proposed legislation that would impose aggregate annual compliance costs of $50 million or more (as estimated by the Congressional Budget Office) on state, local, or tribal governments, unless the proposed legislation also makes provision for federal funding of such costs. 109 Stat. 56–57. Any member may raise a point of order against a bill that would establish such unfunded mandates, though the point of order can be overridden by majority vote. The Act does not refer specifically to federal legislation that gives rise to state court obligations.

Do bills that seek to reduce the burden on federal courts by cutting back on federal jurisdiction, or by eliminating provisions that make federal jurisdiction exclusive (as in federal criminal cases, as discussed in Paragraph (4), *supra*), come within the Unfunded Mandate Reform Act? Legislation of this kind would presumably not state in terms that state courts must accept jurisdiction, but its clear purpose would be to channel more cases into state court, and the states' obligations (under the Supremacy Clause) to accept jurisdiction might be crucial to realizing this purpose. Under cases such as Testa v. Katt and the so-called "valid excuse" doctrine, is every statute creating a federal cause of action and contemplating *concurrent* state and federal jurisdiction potentially subject to the Unfunded Mandate Reform Act unless specifically exempted from the Act's coverage?[11] Or is the states' obligation to enforce federal law on a non-discriminatory basis imposed by the Constitution, rather than by the statutes

---

10. Justice White, joined by Justice Stevens, dissented from the Court's erection of a "plain statement" rule but concurred in the result on the ground that state judges are "policymaking" officials and therefore outside the statutory definition of covered "employee[s]". Justices Brennan and Marshall expressly agreed with Justice White's rejec-

tion of a plain statement rule and also dissented on the merits.

11. The Act does not apply to, *inter alia,* bills that provide for the enforcement of constitutional rights, antidiscrimination statutes, and "emergency" legislation. 48 Stat. 53.

that create federal causes of action (without saying expressly that jurisdiction must be exercised by state courts), so that the Unfunded Mandate Reform Act does not apply? If the Act does apply to all proposed federal legislation that contemplates concurrent federal and state court jurisdiction, does the Act reflect sound federal policy with respect to questions of judicial federalism?

Dice v. Akron, Canton & Youngstown R.R.

342 U.S. 359, 72 S.Ct. 312, 96 L.Ed. 398 (1952).
Certiorari to the Supreme Court of Ohio.

■ MR. JUSTICE BLACK delivered the opinion of the Court.

Petitioner, a railroad fireman, was seriously injured when an engine in which he was riding jumped the track. Alleging that his injuries were due to respondent's negligence, he brought this action for damages under the Federal Employers' Liability Act, in an Ohio court of common pleas. Respondent's defenses were (1) a denial of negligence and (2) a written document signed by petitioner purporting to release respondent in full for $924.63. Petitioner admitted that he had signed several receipts for payments made him in connection with his injuries but denied that he had made a full and complete settlement of all his claims. He alleged that the purported release was void because he had signed it relying on respondent's deliberately false statement that the document was nothing more than a mere receipt for back wages.

After both parties had introduced considerable evidence the jury found in favor of petitioner and awarded him a $25,000 verdict. The trial judge later entered judgment notwithstanding the verdict. In doing so he reappraised the evidence as to fraud, found that petitioner had been "guilty of supine negligence" in failing to read the release, and accordingly held that the facts did not "sustain either in law or in equity the allegations of fraud by clear, unequivocal and convincing evidence."[1] This judgment notwithstanding the verdict was reversed by the Court of Appeals of Summit County, Ohio, on the ground that under federal law, which controlled, the jury's verdict must stand because there was ample evidence to support its finding of fraud. The Ohio Supreme Court, one judge dissenting, reversed the Court of Appeals' judgment and sustained the trial court's action, holding that: (1) Ohio, not federal, law governed; (2) under that law petitioner, a man of ordinary intelligence who could read, was bound by the release even though he had been induced to sign it by the deliberately false statement that it was only a receipt for back wages; and (3) under controlling Ohio law factual issues as to fraud in the execution of this release were properly decided by the judge rather than by the jury. We granted certiorari because the decision of the Supreme Court of Ohio appeared to deviate from previous decisions of this Court that federal law governs cases arising under the Federal Employers' Liability Act.

First. We agree with the Court of Appeals of Summit County, Ohio, and the dissenting judge in the Ohio Supreme Court and hold that validity of releases under the Federal Employers' Liability Act raises a federal question to

---

1. The trial judge had charged the jury that petitioner's claim of fraud must be sustained "by clear and convincing evidence," but since the verdict was for petitioner, he does not here challenge this charge as imposing too heavy a burden under controlling federal law.

be determined by federal rather than state law. Congress in § 51 of the Act granted petitioner a right to recover against his employer for damages negligently inflicted. State laws are not controlling in determining what the incidents of this federal right shall be. * * * Manifestly the federal rights affording relief to injured railroad employees under a federally declared standard could be defeated if states were permitted to have the final say as to what defenses could and could not be properly interposed to suits under the Act. Moreover, only if federal law controls can the federal Act be given that uniform application throughout the country essential to effectuate its purposes. Releases and other devices designed to liquidate or defeat injured employees' claims play an important part in the federal Act's administration. Their validity is but one of the many interrelated questions that must constantly be determined in these cases according to a uniform federal law.

Second. In effect the Supreme Court of Ohio held that an employee trusts his employer at his peril, and that the negligence of an innocent worker is sufficient to enable his employer to benefit by its deliberate fraud. Application of so harsh a rule to defeat a railroad employee's claim is wholly incongruous with the general policy of the Act to give railroad employees a right to recover just compensation for injuries negligently inflicted by their employers. And this Ohio rule is out of harmony with modern judicial and legislative practice to relieve injured persons from the effect of releases fraudulently obtained. * * * We hold that the correct federal rule is that announced by the Court of Appeals of Summit County, Ohio, and the dissenting judge in the Ohio Supreme Court—a release of rights under the Act is void when the employee is induced to sign it by the deliberately false and material statements of the railroad's authorized representatives made to deceive the employee as to the contents of the release. The Trial Court's charge to the jury correctly stated this rule of law.

Third. Ohio provides and has here accorded petitioner the usual jury trial of factual issues relating to negligence. But Ohio treats factual questions of fraudulent releases differently. It permits the judge trying a negligence case to resolve all factual questions of fraud "other than fraud in the factum." The factual issue of fraud is thus split into fragments, some to be determined by the judge, others by the jury.

It is contended that since a state may consistently with the Federal Constitution provide for trial of cases under the Act by a nonunanimous verdict, Minneapolis & St. Louis R. Co. v. Bombolis, 241 U.S. 211, Ohio may lawfully eliminate trial by jury as to one phase of fraud while allowing jury trial as to all other issues raised. The Bombolis case might be more in point had Ohio abolished trial by jury in all negligence cases including those arising under the federal Act. But Ohio has not done this. It has provided jury trials for cases arising under the federal Act but seeks to single out one phase of the question of fraudulent releases for determination by a judge rather than by a jury. Compare Testa v. Katt, 330 U.S. 386.

We have previously held that "The right to trial by jury is 'a basic and fundamental feature of our system of federal jurisprudence' "and that it is "part and parcel of the remedy afforded railroad workers under the Employers' Liability Act." Bailey v. Central Vermont R. Co., 319 U.S. 350, 354. We also recognized in that case that to deprive railroad workers of the benefit of a jury trial where there is evidence to support negligence "is to take away a goodly portion of the relief which Congress has afforded them." It follows that the right to trial by jury is too substantial a part of the rights accorded by the Act to permit it to be classified as a mere "local rule of procedure" for denial in the manner that Ohio has here used. Brown v. Western R. Co., 338 U.S. 294.

The trial judge and the Ohio Supreme Court erred in holding that petitioner's rights were to be determined by Ohio law and in taking away petitioner's verdict when the issues of fraud had been submitted to the jury on conflicting evidence and determined in petitioner's favor. The judgment of the Court of Appeals of Summit County, Ohio, was correct and should not have been reversed by the Supreme Court of Ohio. The cause is reversed and remanded to the Supreme Court of Ohio for further action not inconsistent with this opinion.

Reversed and remanded with directions. It is so ordered.

■ MR. JUSTICE FRANKFURTER, whom MR. JUSTICE REED, MR. JUSTICE JACKSON and MR. JUSTICE BURTON join, concurring for reversal but dissenting from the Court's opinion.

Ohio, as do many other States, maintains the old division between law and equity even though the same judge administers both. The Ohio Supreme Court has told us what, on one issue, is the division of functions in all negligence actions brought in the Ohio courts: "Where it is claimed that a release was induced by fraud (other than fraud in the factum) or by mistake, it is * * * necessary, before seeking to enforce a cause of action which such release purports to bar, that equitable relief from the release be secured." 155 Ohio St. 185, 186, 98 N.E.2d 301, 304. Thus, in all cases in Ohio the judge is the trier of fact on this issue of fraud, rather than the jury. It is contended that the Federal Employers' Liability Act requires that Ohio courts send the fraud issue to a jury in the cases founded on that Act. To require Ohio to try a particular issue before a different fact-finder in negligence actions brought under the Employers' Liability Act from the fact-finder on the identical issue in every other negligence case disregards the settled distribution of judicial power between Federal and State courts where Congress authorizes concurrent enforcement of federally-created rights.

It has been settled ever since the Second Employers' Liability Cases (Mondou v. New York, N.H. & H.R. Co.) 223 U.S. 1, that no State which gives its courts jurisdiction over common law actions for negligence may deny access to its courts for a negligence action founded on the Federal Employers' Liability Act. Nor may a State discriminate disadvantageously against actions for negligence under the Federal Act as compared with local causes of actions in negligence. McKnett v. St. Louis & S.F. R. Co., 292 U.S. 230, 234; Missouri ex rel. Southern R. Co. v. Mayfield, 340 U.S. 1, 4. Conversely, however, simply because there is concurrent jurisdiction in Federal and State courts over actions under the Employers' Liability Act, a State is under no duty to treat actions arising under that Act differently from the way it adjudicates local actions for negligence, so far as the mechanics of litigation, the forms in which law is administered, are concerned. This surely covers the distribution of functions as between judge and jury in the determination of the issues in a negligence case.

In 1916 the Court decided without dissent that States in entertaining actions under the Federal Employers' Liability Act need not provide a jury system other than that established for local negligence actions. States are not compelled to provide the jury required of Federal courts by the Seventh

Amendment. Minneapolis & St. L. R. Co. v. Bombolis, 241 U.S. 211. In the thirty-six years since this early decision after the enactment of the Federal Employers' Liability Act, 35 Stat. 65 (1908), the Bombolis case has often been cited by this Court but never questioned. Until today its significance has been to leave to States the choice of the fact-finding tribunal in all negligence actions, including those arising under the Federal Act. * * *

Although a State must entertain negligence suits brought under the Federal Employers' Liability Act if it entertains ordinary actions for negligence, it need conduct them only in the way in which it conducts the run of negligence litigation. The Bombolis case directly establishes that the Employers' Liability Act does not impose the jury requirements of the Seventh Amendment on the States *pro tanto* for Employers' Liability litigation. If its reasoning means anything the Bombolis decision means that if a State chooses not to have a jury at all, but to leave questions of fact in all negligence actions to a court, certainly the Employers' Liability Act does not require a State to have juries for negligence actions brought under the Federal Act in its courts. Or, if a State chooses to retain the old double system of courts, common law and equity—as did a good many States until the other day, and as four States still do—surely there is nothing in the Employers' Liability Act that requires traditional distribution of authority for disposing of legal issues as between common law and chancery courts to go by the board. And if States are free to make a distribution of functions between equity and common law courts, it surely makes no rational difference whether a State chooses to provide that the same judge preside on both the common law and the chancery sides in a single litigation, instead of in separate rooms in the same building. So long as all negligence suits in a State are treated in the same way, by the same mode of disposing equitable, non-jury, and common law, jury issues, the State does not discriminate against Employers' Liability suits nor does it make any inroad upon substance.

Ohio and her sister States with a similar division of functions between law and equity are not trying to evade their duty under the Federal Employers' Liability Act; nor are they trying to make it more difficult for railroad workers to recover, than for those suing under local law. The States merely exercise a preference in adhering to historic ways of dealing with a claim of fraud; they prefer the traditional way of making unavailable through equity an otherwise valid defense. The State judges and local lawyers who must administer the Federal Employers' Liability Act in State courts are trained in the ways of local practice; it multiplies the difficulties and confuses the administration of justice to require, on purely theoretical grounds, a hybrid of State and Federal practice in the State courts as to a single class of cases. Nothing in the Employers' Liability Act or in the judicial enforcement of the Act for over forty years forces such judicial hybridization upon the States. The fact that Congress authorized actions under the Federal Employers' Liability Act to be brought in State as well as in Federal courts seems a strange basis for the inference that Congress overrode State procedural arrangements controlling all other negligence suits in a State, by imposing upon State courts to which plaintiffs choose to go the rules prevailing in the Federal courts regarding juries. Such an inference is admissible, so it seems to me, only on the theory that Congress included as part of the right created by the Employers' Liability Act an assumed likelihood that trying all issues to juries is more favorable to plaintiffs. At least, if a plaintiff's right to have all issues decided by a jury rather than the court is "part and parcel of the remedy afforded railroad workers under the Employers Liability

Act," the Bombolis case should be overruled explicitly instead of left as a derelict bound to occasion collisions on the waters of the law. We have put the questions squarely because they seem to be precisely what will be roused in the minds of lawyers properly pressing their clients' interests and in the minds of trial and appellate judges called upon to apply this Court's opinion. It is one thing not to borrow trouble from the morrow. It is another thing to create trouble for the morrow.

Even though the method of trying the equitable issue of fraud which the State applies in all other negligence cases governs Employers' Liability cases, two questions remain for decision: Should the validity of the release be tested by a Federal or a State standard? And if by a Federal one, did the Ohio courts in the present case correctly administer the standard? If the States afford courts for enforcing the Federal Act, they must enforce the substance of the right given by Congress. They cannot depreciate the legislative currency issued by Congress—either expressly or by local methods of enforcement that accomplish the same result. Davis v. Wechsler, 263 U.S. 22, 24. In order to prevent diminution of railroad workers' nationally-uniform right to recover, the standard for the validity of a release of contested liability must be federal.
* * *

NOTE ON "SUBSTANCE" AND "PROCEDURE" IN THE ENFORCEMENT OF FEDERAL RIGHTS OF ACTION IN STATE COURTS

(1) *Nature and Scope of the Issue in Dice.* What, exactly, were the nature and scope of the disagreement between the majority and dissenting opinions in the Dice case? Note the unanimity of the Court's holding that the standard governing the validity of the release is federal. What was the basis for this holding?[1]

Were the majority and dissenting Justices in Dice divided about a large issue of principle, or quibbling about how a shared principle ought to be applied?

(2) *Federal Rights and Federal "Procedures" under the FELA.* The scope of state court obligations to follow federal rules of proof, pleading, and procedure in adjudicating substantive federal rights has frequently arisen in suits under the FELA. Consider the following cases' relation to the holding in Dice. Do consistent principles run through the Court's decisions?

(a) Central Vermont Ry. Co. v. White, 238 U.S. 507 (1915), held inapplicable to an FELA action in a state court a state rule requiring the plaintiff to prove freedom from contributory negligence. The Court affirmed the "general principle that matters respecting the remedy—such as the form of action, sufficiency of the pleadings, rules of evidence, and the statute of limitations—depend upon the law of the place where the suit is brought". But Justice Lamar called it a "misnomer to say that the question as to the burden of proof as to contributory negligence is a mere matter of state procedure." Noting that "the United States courts have uniformly held that as a matter of general law the burden of proving contributory negligence is on the defendant" and

---

1. Does the release of federal rights of action necessarily raise a federal question? Garrett v. Moore–McCormack Co., 317 U.S. 239 (1942), cited by the Court, involved an admiralty claim.

that the "Federal courts have enforced that principle even in trials in States which hold that the burden is on the plaintiff", he concluded: "Congress in passing the Federal Employers' Liability Act evidently intended that the Federal statute should be construed in the light of these and other decisions of the Federal courts" (pp. 511–12).

(b) Minneapolis & St. Louis R.R. v. Bombolis, 241 U.S. 211 (1916), upheld a Minnesota provision for a civil verdict by five-sixths of the jury, after failure for twelve hours to achieve unanimity. Companion cases involved verdicts by three-fourths, St. Louis & San Francisco R.R. v. Brown, 241 U.S. 223 (1916); Louisville & Nashville R.R. v. Stewart, 241 U.S. 261 (1916), and trial to a jury of seven, Chesapeake & Ohio Ry. v. Carnahan, 241 U.S. 241 (1916). The cases decisively rejected the contention that state courts can enforce federal rights of action only if "such courts in enforcing the Federal right are to be treated as Federal courts and be subjected *pro hac vice* to the limitations of the Seventh Amendment". 241 U.S. at 221. See also Justice Holmes in Louisville & Nashville R.R. v. Stewart, *supra,* at 263.

Was there a stronger argument that Congress intended to displace state rules as to the burden of proof (the issue in the Central Vermont Railway case, *supra*) than state rules as to non-unanimous jury verdicts? Can the difference of outcome be explained by the state rules' differing consistency with the pro-plaintiff policies of the FELA[2]

Is the Bombolis decision still good law after Dice? Is there a valid distinction, as Justice Black suggests, between state failure to provide a jury trial as to "one phase of fraud" and failure to provide such trial on any issue? Can Congress have intended to displace the former practice but to leave the latter undisturbed?[3] If state procedure diminishes a federal right when it denies a jury trial on one issue, would it not do so *a fortiori* if it abolished jury trial on all issues? On the other hand, wouldn't it be more of an imposition on

2. The Bombolis decision does not prevent the Supreme Court from reversing a state court judgment directing a verdict for the railroad, where the Court deems the evidence sufficient to create an issue for the jury, although it would not overturn a jury verdict in defendant's favor. See, *e.g.,* Bailey v. Central Vermont Ry., 319 U.S. 350 (1943); Wilkerson v. McCarthy, 336 U.S. 53 (1949); Rogers v. Missouri Pac. R.R., 352 U.S. 500 (1957), p. 1699, *infra; cf.* Arnold v. Panhandle & S.F. Ry., 353 U.S. 360 (1957). The Court deals with this issue in such cases as it would if the case had been tried in a federal district court.

In Brady v. Southern Ry., 320 U.S. 476, 479 (1943), where the direction of a verdict was sustained, Justice Reed said: "Only by a uniform federal rule as to the necessary amount of evidence may litigants under the federal act receive similar treatment in all states. * * * It is true that this Court has held that a state need not provide in F.E.L.A. cases any trial by jury according to the requirements of the Seventh Amendment. * * * But when a state's jury system requires

the court to determine the sufficiency of the evidence to support a finding of a federal right to recover, the correctness of its ruling is a federal question."

Why? If the plaintiff has no federal right to have the facts determined by a jury, what federal right, as distinguished from rights under local practice, is denied if the facts are determined by the court, provided that the determination is supported by the evidence? *Cf.* Holmes, J., in Chicago, R.I. & Pac. Ry. v. Cole, 251 U.S. 54 (1919). Is there a general federal right to have the local practice properly applied in the adjudication of federal claims?

3. The Jones Act, 46 U.S.C. § 688, which extends the benefits of the FELA to seamen, expressly confers a right of "action for damages at law, with the right of trial by jury". Under the "saving clause" an action under the act may be maintained in a state court. See pp. 791–801, *infra.* What are the implications of the Bombolis case for a state court action under the Jones Act?

state courts to compel them to convene juries if they otherwise have none (or perhaps even to require juries larger than those otherwise employed in the state[4]) than to require submission of an additional issue to a jury already convened and functioning?

(c) In Brown v. Western Ry. of Alabama, 338 U.S. 294 (1949), the plaintiff alleged that he suffered injuries caused by "the negligence of the defendant", when he stepped on "a large clinker lying beside the tracks"; the railroad, he averred, had allowed clinkers and other debris to collect, "well knowing that * * * yards in such condition were dangerous for use by brakemen". The Georgia courts dismissed the complaint for failure to state a cause of action under the FELA; in doing so, they apparently interpreted a local rule requiring complaints to be construed "most strongly against the pleader" to require a specific pleading that the particular clinker inflicting the harm was not in plain view and therefore easily avoidable or that the railroad was negligent in allowing the particular clinker to be there.

The Supreme Court reversed. Justice Black, holding the allegations sufficient, said (pp. 296–98):

"* * * To what extent rules of practice and procedure may themselves dig into 'substantive rights' is a troublesome question at best as is shown in the very case on which respondent relies. Central Vermont R. Co. v. White, 238 U.S. 507. Other cases in this Court point up the impossibility of laying down a precise rule to distinguish 'substance' from 'procedure.' Fortunately, we need not attempt to do so. A long series of cases previously decided, from which we see no reason to depart, makes it our duty to construe the allegations of this complaint ourselves in order to determine whether petitioner has been denied a right of trial granted him by Congress. This federal right cannot be defeated by the forms of local practice. * * * And we cannot accept as final a state court's interpretation of allegations in a complaint asserting it. * * * This rule applies to FELA cases no less than to other types. * * *

"Strict local rules of pleading cannot be used to impose unnecessary burdens upon rights of recovery authorized by federal laws."

Justice Frankfurter, joined by Justice Jackson, dissented (pp. 300–03):

"* * * If a litigant chooses to enforce a Federal right in a State court, he cannot be heard to object if he is treated exactly as are plaintiffs who press like claims arising under State law with regard to the form in which the claim must be stated—the particularity, for instance, with which a cause of action must be described. Federal law, though invoked in a State court, delimits the Federal claim—defines what gives a right to recovery and what goes to prove it. But the form in which the claim must be stated need not be different from what the State exacts in the enforcement of like obligations created by it, so long as such a requirement does not add to, or diminish, the right as defined by Federal law, nor burden the realization of this right in the actualities of litigation. * * *

"These decisive differences are usually conveyed by the terms 'procedure' and 'substance.' The terms are not meaningless even though they do not have fixed undeviating meanings. They derive content from the functions they serve here in precisely the same way in which we have applied them in reverse

---

4. *Cf.* Ballew v. Georgia, 435 U.S. 223 (1978)(holding five-person juries constitution- ally impermissible in state criminal cases).

situations—when confronted with the problem whether the Federal courts respected the substance of State-created rights, as required by the rule in Erie R. Co. v. Tompkins, 304 U.S. 64, or impaired them by professing merely to enforce them by the mode in which the Federal courts do business. * * * Congress has authorized State courts to enforce Federal rights, and Federal courts State-created rights. Neither system of courts can impair these respective rights, but both may have their own requirements for stating claims (pleading) and conducting litigation (practice).

"In the light of these controlling considerations, I cannot find that the Court of Appeals of Georgia has either sought to evade the law of the United States or did so unwittingly. * * *"[5]

(3) *Basis of the Holding in Dice.* In what sense is jury trial "part and parcel of the remedy afforded railroad workers under the Employers' Liability Act"? The FELA makes no explicit grant of a right to trial by jury; it refers to jury trial only in the context of providing that contributory negligence shall not bar a recovery "but the damages shall be diminished by the jury in proportion to the amount of negligence" attributable to the employee. 45 U.S.C. § 53. (Indeed, as indicated by cases discussed in Paragraph (2), *supra,* this language has not been construed to mean that every FELA case must be submitted to the jury or even been cited by the Supreme Court in support of holdings regarding jury trials in state courts.)

Consider the statement in Bailey v. Central Vermont Ry., 319 U.S. 350, 354 (1943), referred to in the Dice opinion: "To deprive these workers of the benefit of a jury trial in close or doubtful cases is to take away a goodly portion of the relief which Congress has afforded them." Why is this true? On the premise that juries tend strongly to favor injured railroad workers? See Hill, note 5, *supra,* at 397.[6]

If the federal rule with respect to the jury's role in FELA cases is correctly seen as implementing congressional policy regarding risk-distribution, doesn't it follow that the Court was correct in imposing that rule on the state courts?

Cases such as Dice are often described as raising "reverse Erie" issues about the permissibility of state courts applying state procedural rules when

---

5. Consider the suggestion that "whatever the troubles [Brown] may have encountered in the state courts, they were not due to excessively burdensome pleading rules as such." Hill, *Substance and Procedure in State FELA Actions—The Converse of the Erie Problem?,* 17 Ohio St.L.J. 384, 407 & n. 143 (1956). Professor Hill notes: "Presumably it would have been easy for Brown to amend his complaint to set forth the more particularized allegations, but this would have been improvident if these allegations would have been difficult of proof *and* if as a matter of [federal] law he really did not have to adduce such proof to win. * * * This would suggest that the problem below was not the local pleading rules as such but rather a misconception concerning the minimum quantum of evidence needed in an FELA case". *Id.*

Compare Meltzer, *State Court Forfeitures of Federal Rights,* 99 Harv.L.Rev. 1128, 1142–43 n.65 (1986), arguing that on Hill's view, the proper disposition would have been a remand to permit the state courts to decide whether, on a proper understanding of federal law, the plaintiff had complied with state pleading rules, rather than a direction to the state courts to treat the plaintiff as having complied.

6. There is some historical evidence indicating that congressional policy favored jury trials in FELA cases, and possibly for plaintiff-favoring reasons, but it is far from conclusive. See Tiller v. Atlantic Coast Line R.R., 318 U.S. 54, 58–67 (1943); Rogers v. Missouri Pac.R.R., 352 U.S. 500, 508–09 (1957), and sources cited.

enforcing federal rights.[7] Is this terminology more misleading than helpful, since the respective obligations of state and federal courts are not, in view of the Supremacy Clause, symmetrical? Isn't the key point that a state court adjudicating a claim of federal right must also recognize any corollary rights, whether denominated substantive or procedural, that are necessary to implement the underlying federal policy? See generally Meltzer, note 5, *supra,* at 1176–85; Weinberg, *The Federal State Conflict of Laws: "Actual" Conflicts,* 70 Tex.L.Rev. 1743, 1773–96 (1992).

(4) *The Felder Case.* In Felder v. Casey, 487 U.S. 131 (1988), the state supreme court dismissed plaintiff's action under 42 U.S.C. § 1983 because of his noncompliance with the state's notice-of-claim statute. (That statute required written notice, within 120 days of the injury, of any claim against state or local governments (or their officials) as a condition of bringing suit.) In an opinion by Justice Brennan, the Supreme Court reversed, finding the statute preempted by federal law. The Court reasoned that the statute would burden civil rights plaintiffs in order to serve a purpose—minimizing governmental liability—that was impermissible under federal law; that the statute discriminated against federal rights (on this point, see p. 475, *supra*); and that enforcement of the statute was inconsistent with the decision in Patsy v. Board of Regents, p. 1225, *infra,* that exhaustion of administrative remedies is not required in § 1983 actions. Relying in part on Brown v. Western Ry. of Alabama, the Court argued that "[f]ederal law takes state courts as it finds them only insofar as those courts employ rules that do not 'impose unnecessary burdens upon rights of recovery authorized by federal laws.' * * * [E]nforcement of the notice-of-claim statute in § 1983 actions brought in state court so interferes with and frustrates the substantive right Congress created that, under the Supremacy Clause, it must yield to the federal interest" (pp. 150–51, quoting Brown).

The Court assumed that the notice-of-claim statute would have had no applicability had the suit been filed in federal court. Comparing the question before it to the application of the Erie doctrine, the Court said that the state could not "demand[] compliance with outcome-determinative rules that are inapplicable when such claims are brought in federal court. * * * The state notice-of-claim statute is more than a mere rule of procedure: [it] is a substantive condition on the right to sue governmental officials and entities, and the federal courts have therefore correctly recognized that the notice statute governs the adjudication of state-law claims in diversity actions. In Guaranty Trust [Co. v. York, 326 U.S. 99 (1945)], we held that, in order to give effect to a State's statute of limitations, a federal court could not hear a state-law action that a state court would deem time-barred. Conversely, a state court may not decline to hear an otherwise properly presented federal claim because that claim would be barred under a state law requiring timely filing of notice" (p. 152).[8]

Justice O'Connor, joined by the Chief Justice, dissented, finding that the state statute, unlike the rule in Brown, did not "diminish or alter any

---

7. The term apparently originated in Baxter, *Choice of Law and the Federal System,* 16 Stan.L.Rev. 1, 34 (1963).

8. Note that the Supreme Court retreated from Guaranty Trust v. York's "out-come-determinative" test for applying the Erie doctrine in Byrd v. Blue Ridge Rural Elec. Coop., Inc., p. 717, *infra,* and Hanna v. Plumer, p. 719, *infra.* Is reliance on York warranted in this context?

substantive right cognizable under § 1983" (p. 160).[9]

Is Justice Brennan's invocation of Erie helpful? See Paragraph (3), *supra.* If the state statute is preempted by federal law, it has no applicability whether a § 1983 action is filed in state or federal court. But if the statute were not preempted, is there any reason why it should not be applied even in a federal court—which would, for example, ordinarily apply a state statute of limitations? See pp. 820-29, *infra.*

(5) *Power, Policy, and Statutory Construction.* With Felder and other cases discussed in this Note, compare Hart, *The Relations Between State and Federal Law,* 54 Colum.L.Rev. 489, 508 (1954):

"The general rule, bottomed deeply in belief in the importance of state control of state judicial procedure, is that federal law takes the state courts as it finds them. * * * The Supreme Court in recent years has been disturbed by the recognition that differences between state and federal procedure may sometimes lead to different results in actions to enforce federally-created rights of which state and federal courts have concurrent jurisdiction. [Here citing Dice and other FELA cases.] * * * Some differences in remedy and procedure are inescapable if the different governments are to retain a measure of independence in deciding how justice should be administered. If the differences become so conspicuous as to affect advance calculations of outcome, and so to induce an undesirable shopping between forums, the remedy does not lie in the sacrifice of the independence of either government. It lies rather in provision by the federal government, confident of the justice of its own procedure, of a federal forum equally accessible to both litigants."

If intended to identify a constitutional limit on congressional power, Professor Hart's view has been clearly rejected by the Supreme Court, hasn't it? See in particular Felder v. Casey, *supra,* 487 U.S. at 150–51.

Would Hart's argument be more tenable or attractive if understood to address, not the *power* of Congress to impose obligations on state courts, but (i) the policies that Congress ought to follow in enacting substantive and jurisdictional legislation, (ii) the principles of statutory construction that courts should adopt in identifying the obligations that Congress has imposed, and (iii) the principles that should govern a judge-made federal common law of state-federal relations?

Note that the plaintiff in Dice chose the state forum. Having chosen the forum, why shouldn't the plaintiff have been stuck with that forum's allocation of responsibility between judge and jury? Or, to put a slightly different question, is it reasonable to attribute to Congress a policy of forcing state courts, not only to entertain FELA actions, but also to adopt federal allocations of responsibility between judges and juries in adjudicating such actions?

In considering these questions, note that Congress may wish to give litigants the convenience of state courts as forums for the enforcement of

---

9. In Howlett v. Rose, 496 U.S. 356 (1990), discussed at p. 475, *supra,* the Court, in requiring a state to entertain a federal claim under 42 U.S.C. § 1983, relied not only on the doctrine of Testa v. Katt but also on its decision in Felder v. Casey. "We conclude", the Court said, "that whether the question is framed in pre-emption terms, as petitioner would have it, or in the obligation to assume jurisdiction over a 'federal' cause of action, as respondents would have it, the Florida court's refusal to entertain one discrete category of § 1983 claims, when the court entertains similar state law claims against state defendants, violates the Supremacy Clause" (p. 375).

federal rights (this is a legitimate aim, isn't it?); that Congress may not always be able to anticipate all of the procedural issues likely to arise in the litigation of federal causes of action in state court; and that even plaintiffs who choose state courts may then be surprised by issues that arise in litigation. (In the Dice case, when the suit was filed in state court, neither the plaintiff nor his lawyer may have known that Dice had signed a paper that purported to be a release.)

(6) *Federal Limitations on the Enforceability of Federal Rights.*   In Dice and the other cases discussed so far, the issue has involved state law rules that directly or incidentally burden the enforcement of federal rights in state courts. Does federal law ever limit the permissible generosity of state procedural rules in suits to enforce federal rights?

(a) In Norfolk & Western Ry. Co. v. Liepelt, 444 U.S. 490 (1980), a wrongful death action under the FELA, the Supreme Court held that the Illinois trial court must (i) allow the defendant to introduce evidence to show the effect of income taxes on the decedent's projected future earnings, and (ii) on request, instruct the jury that their award will not be subject to federal income taxes. Justice Stevens, for the Court, held that both issues were governed by federal law. Saying simply, "It has long been settled that questions concerning the measure of damages in an FELA action are federal in character," (p. 493), he treated both issues on the merits without reference to what the state law might be.

Justice Blackmun, joined by Justice Marshall, dissented on both issues. On the issue of instructing the jury regarding the non-taxability of their award, he contended that the law of Illinois should govern. He argued that the necessity of giving such "purely cautionary" instructions should be governed by state law when an FELA action is brought in state court. Recognizing that "state rules that interfere with federal policy are to be rejected, even if they might be characterized as 'procedural' ", he said that he could not conclude "that a purely cautionary instruction to the jury not to misbehave implicates any federal interest" (pp. 502–04).[10]

(b) In Monessen Southwestern Ry. Co. v. Morgan, 486 U.S. 330 (1988), the Supreme Court ruled that in an FELA action, federal law barred prejudgment interest and required that damages for loss of future earnings be discounted to present value; conflicting state law was accordingly displaced. Justices Blackmun and Marshall, dissenting in part, urged a federal rule providing prejudgment interest. Justice O'Connor and Chief Justice Rehnquist also dissented in part; while generally agreeing with the Court, they would have given the states greater latitude in selecting a method for determining present value.

(c) What, precisely, is the question before the Court in cases such as these? Even if questions about the measure of damages are "federal in character", it does not follow that there must be a *uniform* federal rule; another possibility would be for federal law to "adopt" state law insofar as state law is not incompatible with federal policy. See generally Chap. VII, Sec. 1(B), *infra*. It is relatively easy to see why federal law would establish a floor of procedural

---

10.   See also St. Louis Southwestern Ry. Co. v. Dickerson, 470 U.S. 409 (1985)(federal law determines whether jury, in an FELA case, should be instructed that its award should reflect the present value of future losses).

safeguards to protect the integrity of federal rights. On what basis might the Court conclude that federal law also establishes a ceiling?[11]

(7) *Federal Procedures in State Administrative Processes.* In Federal Energy Regulatory Comm'n v. Mississippi, 456 U.S. 742 (1982), also discussed on p. 476, *supra,* the Court upheld provisions of the Public Utility Regulatory Policies Act of 1978 that imposed important federal procedural requirements on state commissions regulating energy. The Court acknowledged that the Act's procedural provisions were "more intrusive" than its "hortatory" substantive provisions, but said: "If Congress can require a state administrative body to consider proposed regulations as a condition to its continued involvement in a pre-emptible field—and we hold today that it can—there is nothing unconstitutional about Congress' requiring certain procedural minima as that body goes about undertaking its tasks" (p. 771). Justice Powell's dissent stated that "I know of no other attempt by the Federal Government to supplant state-prescribed procedures that in part define the nature of their administrative agencies" (p. 774). Justice O'Connor's dissent said that "[s]tate legislative and administrative bodies are not field offices of the national bureaucracy" (p. 777).[12]

Neither the Court nor the dissenters alluded to Dice or the other FELA cases. Does the rationale of those cases apply equally to the FERC case? Can you state, at this point, exactly what that rationale is?

(8) *Constitutional Cases.* With the issues discussed thus far, compare the debate between Justice Black, for the Court, and Justice Harlan, dissenting, about whether state or federal law should govern the question whether a state criminal conviction may stand, notwithstanding a federal constitutional error in the proceedings, because the error was "harmless." Chapman v. California, 386 U.S. 18 (1967). Justice Black said that "[w]hether a conviction for crime should stand when a State has failed to accord federal constitutionally guaranteed rights is every bit as much of a federal question as what particular federal constitutional provisions themselves mean, what they guarantee, and whether they have been denied" (p. 21). Justice Harlan said (pp. 46, 49): "I would hold that a state appellate court's reasonable application of a constitutionally proper state harmless-error rule to sustain a state conviction constitutes an independent and adequate state ground of judgment. * * * The challenged decision has no direct relation to federal constitutional provisions, rather it is an

---

11. Weinberg, *supra,* notes that the majority and dissenting opinions in Monessen Southwestern Ry. adopted very different approaches to statutory interpretation (pp. 1787–96). Justice White, for the majority, adopted an "historical" approach; he emphasized that at the time of the FELA's adoption, prejudgment interest was relatively uncommon and reasoned that Congress was unlikely to have intended to provide an unusual remedy when it did not say so expressly. By contrast, Justice Blackmun's partial dissent emphasizes the purpose of the F.E.L.A. to provide full compensation to injured plaintiffs. Which of these approaches is generally more appropriate? More appropriate under the F.E.L.A., a remedial statute first enacted in 1908? For discussion of

closely related issues, seen Chap. VII, Sec. 1(B), *infra.*

12. *Cf.* Caminker, *State Sovereignty and Subordinacy: May Congress Commandeer State Officers to Implement Federal Law?*, 95 Colum.L.Rev. 1001, 1043–87 (arguing that federal commandeering of state judicial, administrative, and legislative processes is consistent with the original understanding and otherwise constitutionally permissible); Prakash, *Field Office Federalism,* 79 Va. L.Rev. 1957 (1993)(arguing that the Framers did not intend to permit commandeering of states in their sovereign, legislative capacities, but were willing to have the federal government commandeer the state executives).

analysis of the question whether this admittedly improper comment had any significant impact on the outcome of the trial."[13]

In thinking about the respective roles of state and federal law in shaping harmless error doctrine, consider the pertinence of the following points.

First, harmless error doctrine is inherently *remedial*; it comes into play only on the hypothesis that a constitutional right has been violated and involves the circumstances under which the state must remedy the violation by reversing a conviction.

Second, the Supreme Court has said repeatedly that there is no constitutional right to appeal criminal convictions in the state judicial systems. *E.g.,* Goeke v. Branch, 115 S.Ct. 1275, 1277 (1995)(*per curiam*); Pennsylvania v. Finley, 481 U.S. 551, 555–56 (1987). If there is no federal right to appeal a criminal conviction at all, an obstacle arises to arguments that there is a federal right to relief (from a state's appellate courts) in cases in which a state deems any underlying violation of federal law to have been harmless.[14]

Third, there is a federal statutory right (and arguably a constitutional right, too) to seek Supreme Court review of state court decisions rejecting claims of constitutional right in criminal cases. The harmless error doctrine (if any) to be followed by the Supreme Court in exercising its appellate jurisdiction is surely bounded by federal law. Such a doctrine not only gauges the degree of risk that a particular error actually had an adverse effect; it also measures whether this risk is sufficiently small to permit exclusion of a case from the Court's constitutionally and statutorily prescribed functions in enforcing (by providing remedies for the violation of) federal rights.

In light of considerations such as these, should harmless error doctrine as applied by state appellate courts be regarded as reflecting at least in part a subconstitutional federal common law—crafted by judges to protect the integrity of federal rights and to facilitate Supreme Court review of state court judgments, but not strictly dictated by the Constitution, and therefore subject to modification and adjustment, if not total rejection, by Congress? See Meltzer, *Harmless Error and Constitutional Remedies,* 61 U.Chi.L.Rev. 1 (1994).

More generally, consider whether the notion of "federal common law" is helpful in illuminating the problems faced by the Supreme Court in determining the obligations of state courts to modify rules of pleading, proof, and procedure that are inhospitable to the vindication of federal rights. With only rare exceptions, neither congressional nor constitutional lawmakers are likely to have given the slightest attention to such ancillary considerations. When this is so, is it consistent or inconsistent with the separation of powers to recognize a role for creative judicial lawmaking to implement the policies reflected in federal statutory and constitutional provisions? For further discussion, see Chapter VII, *infra.*

---

13. For further development of this question, see Delaware v. Van Arsdall, 475 U.S. 673 (1986), p. 536, *infra.*

14. Even if there were a constitutional right to one appeal, questions would arise about why federal harmless error rules should prevail in further, discretionary appeals that the states frequently provide.

CHAPTER V

REVIEW OF STATE COURT DECISIONS BY THE SUPREME COURT

SECTION 1. THE ESTABLISHMENT OF THE JURISDICTION

DEVELOPMENT OF THE STATUTORY PROVISIONS

1. *The Judiciary Act of 1789 and the Amendments of 1867.* The following text, with accompanying footnotes, shows the original form of Section 25 of the Judiciary Act of 1789 (1 Stat. 73, 85), and the changes made by the Act of February 5, 1867 (14 Stat. 385, 386):[1]

"Sec. 25. And be it further enacted, That a final judgment or decree in any suit, in the highest court [of law or equity][2] of a State in which a decision in the suit could be had, where is drawn in question the validity of a treaty or statute of, or an authority exercised under the United States, and the decision is against their validity; or where is drawn in question the validity of a statute of, or an authority exercised under any State, on the ground of their being repugnant to the constitution, treaties or laws of the United States, and the decision is in favour of such their validity, [or where is drawn in question the construction of any clause of the constitution, or of a treaty, or statute of, or commission held under the United States,][3] and the decision is against the title, right, privilege or [exemption][4] specially set up or claimed by either party, under such [clause of the said][2] Constitution, treaty, statute [or] commission,[5] may be re-examined and reversed or affirmed in the Supreme Court of the United States upon a writ of error, the citation being signed by the chief justice, or judge or chancellor of the court rendering or passing the judgment or decree complained of, or by a justice of the Supreme Court of the United States, in the same manner and under the same regulations, and the writ shall have the same effect, as if the judgment or decree complained of had been rendered

---

1. The text is reproduced from Frankfurter & Shulman, Cases on Federal Jurisdiction and Procedure 627–28 (rev.ed.1937). For the text of the successive jurisdictional enactments, see Robertson & Kirkham, Jurisdiction of the Supreme Court of the United States, Appendix A, 931–41 (Wolfson & Kurland ed.1951).

2. The amendatory Act of Feb. 5, 1867, deleted these words.

3. The act of 1867 substituted the following: "or where any title, right, privilege, or immunity is claimed under the constitution, or any treaty or statute of or commission held, or authority exercised under the United States".

4. The Act of 1867 substituted "immunity".

5. The Act of 1867 added "or authority".

or passed in a [Circuit Court][6] and the proceeding upon the reversal shall also be the same, except that the Supreme Court, [instead of remanding the cause for a final decision as before provided,][2] may at their discretion, [if the cause shall have been once remanded before,][2] proceed to a final decision of the same, and award execution.[7] [But no other error shall be assigned or regarded as a ground of reversal in any such case as aforesaid, than such as appears on the face of the record, and immediately respects the before mentioned questions of validity or construction of the said constitution, treaties, statutes, commissions, or authorities in dispute.][2]"

The provisions of Section 25, as amended in 1867, were re-enacted in substantially the same form as § 709 of the Revised Statutes (1874) and § 237 of the Judicial Code (1911).

2. *The Judiciary Act of 1914.* The Act of December 23, 1914, c. 2, 38 Stat. 790, for the first time authorized the Supreme Court to review state court decisions that had upheld a claim of federal right.[8] The amendment was prompted largely by the decision in Ives v. South Buffalo Ry., 201 N.Y. 271, 94 N.E. 431 (1911), holding the first American workers' compensation act in conflict with the due process guaranties of both the federal and state constitutions. See Frankfurter & Landis, The Business of the Supreme Court 188–98 (1928).

The newly-authorized review, however, was not mandatory. While the writ of error was preserved for cases within the pre–1914 jurisdiction, the additional jurisdiction conferred in 1914 was to be exercised though a jurisdictional technique new to review of state court judgments: the discretionary writ of certiorari.[9]

3. *The Judiciary Act of 1916.* The Act of September 6, 1916, c. 448, § 2, 39 Stat. 726, expanded review on certiorari, by substituting it for the writ of error in cases where "any title, right, privilege or immunity is claimed under the Constitution, or any treaty or statute of, or commission held or authority exercised under the United States, and the decision is either in favor of or against the title, right, privilege, or immunity especially set up or claimed." Review on writ of error was retained from decisions against the validity of "an authority exercised under the United States", or from decisions refusing to invalidate "an authority exercised under any State" as "repugnant to the Constitution, treaties, or laws of the United States". Cases involving the validity of claims asserted under an "authority", as distinguished from the validity of the authority itself, were reviewable only on certiorari. See, *e.g.,*

---

6. The Act of 1867 substituted "court of the United States".

7. The Act of 1867 added "or remand the same to an inferior court".

8. For discussion of the decisions interpreting (and often denying review under) the pre–1914 jurisdictional statute, see Meltzer, *The History and Structure of Article III,* 138 U.Pa.L.Rev. 1569, 1585–92 (1990).

9. Thus, the Act authorized the Court to require to be certified for its review ("by certiorari or otherwise") any case within § 237 in which the decision of the state court "may have been in favor of the validity of the treaty or statute or authority exercised under the United States" or "against the validity of the State statute or authority claimed to be repugnant to the Constitution, treaties, or laws of the United States" or "in favor of the title, right, privilege, or immunity claimed under the Constitution, treaty, statute, commission, or authority of the United States."

The writ of certiorari had earlier been provided in the Evarts Act of 1891 for review of decisions of the federal circuit courts of appeals. See p. 37, *supra.*

Philadelphia & Reading Coal & Iron Co. v. Gilbert, 245 U.S. 162 (1917); Yazoo & Mississippi Valley R.R. v. Clarksdale, 257 U.S. 10, 15–16 (1921).

4. *The Judiciary Act of 1925.* Difficulty with the 1916 Act's subtle distinction between cases under an authority and those challenging the validity of an authority (see Frankfurter & Landis, *supra*, at 265) led to its abandonment in the Judges' Bill (Act of February 13, 1925, 43 Stat. 936). This Bill broadened review via certiorari still further; mandatory review of state judgments was preserved only for decisions against the validity of a treaty or Act of Congress, or in favor of the validity of a state statute attacked upon federal grounds. A new § 237(c) provided that when a writ of error was improperly sought or allowed in a certiorari case, the papers were to be treated by the Supreme Court as a petition for a writ of certiorari.

The Act of January 31, 1928, c. 14, 45 Stat. 54, as amended, substituted an appeal for writ of error in all cases reviewable as of right.

5. *The Revised Judicial Code of 1948.* This revision of the Judicial Code made no substantial change in § 237, but reformulated the basic provisions conferring jurisdiction to review state court decisions in 28 U.S.C. § 1257.[10] Three of the clauses of § 237 were made separate sections among Title 28's miscellaneous procedural provisions relating to Supreme Court review: § 2103 (formerly § 237(c)[11]); § 2104 (appeal from state court to be taken in same manner and with same effect as if judgment rendered by court of the United States); and § 2106 (power to affirm, modify, vacate, reverse, remand, direct entry of judgment or require further proceedings).

Under § 2101(c), the time in which to appeal or apply for certiorari in civil cases is ninety days; a Supreme Court Justice has power within this period to extend the time to apply for certiorari (but not the time to appeal) for not more than sixty days. Section 2101(d) defines the time in criminal cases as that "prescribed by rules of the Supreme Court." Supreme Court Rule 13.1 states that a petition for a writ of certiorari in a civil or criminal case is timely if filed within 90 days after the entry of the judgment of which review is sought. An application to extend the time to file may be made but "is not favored" (Rule 13.5).

6. *P.L. 100–352.* An Act of June 27, 1988, 102 Stat. 662, completed the gradual transition in this century from mandatory to discretionary review of state court decisions, amending § 1257 to eliminate appeals as of right and to make all state court judgments reviewable only by writ of certiorari. See generally Boskey & Gressman, *The Supreme Court Bids Farewell to Mandatory Appeals,* 109 S.Ct. No. 1, lxxxi (1988). As part of this change, § 2013, permitting the Court to treat an improvidently taken appeal as a petition for certiorari, was repealed as superfluous.

7. *Rules of the Supreme Court.* Supreme Court Rules 10–16 set out the

---

10. In 1970 a provision was added to § 1257 stating: "For the purposes of this section, the term 'highest court of a State' includes the District of Columbia Court of Appeals." Act of July 29, 1970, § 172(a)(1), 84 Stat. 590. In 1961, separate provisions parallel to § 1257 were adopted for review of the Supreme Court of the Commonwealth of Puerto Rico. See 28 U.S.C. § 1258.

11. Amended in 1962 to apply to appeals "improvidently taken" from federal courts of appeals as well. Act of Sept. 19, 1962, § 1, 76 Stat. 556.

procedure on petitions for certiorari.[12] The "character of the reasons the Court considers" in deciding whether to grant a petition include: "a state court of last resort has decided an important federal question in a way that conflicts with the decision of another state court of last resort or of a United States court of appeals", and "a state court * * * has decided an important question of federal law that has not been, but should be, settled by this Court, or has decided an important federal question in a way that conflicts with relevant decisions of this Court." Rule 10. See also Chap. XV, Sec. 3, *infra*.

Martin v. Hunter's Lessee

14 U.S. (1 Wheat.) 304, 4 L.Ed. 97 (1816).
Error to the Court of Appeals of Virginia.

[In 1791, Hunter filed an ejectment action, in the name of his lessee, against Denny Martin Fairfax in the Superior Court at Winchester, Virginia. At issue was a portion of the "waste and ungranted land" of a large tract known as the Northern Neck, owned by Lord Fairfax, a Virginia citizen, at his death in 1781. Hunter claimed under a grant from the commonwealth of Virginia made in 1789. The defendant, a British subject residing in England, was Lord Fairfax's nephew, and claimed as the devisee of the Fairfax estate. Originally known as Denny Martin, he succeeded to the Fairfax name.

[Because Hunter claimed as the grantee of Virginia, he had to establish how the commonwealth had acquired the land. In 1779 Virginia had enacted legislation purporting to declare the escheat or forfeiture of property then belonging to British subjects and prescribing a proceeding on inquest of office for escheat. A 1782 act provided that entries made with the surveyors of the Northern Neck after the death of Lord Fairfax should be as valid as those made previously, under his direction. An act of 1785 declared, among other things, that the commonwealth could grant unappropriated lands within the Northern Neck in the same manner as it could grant other unappropriated lands that it owned. Hunter's grant in 1789 was made under this last act. The land, however, had not been the subject of any inquest of office or other proceeding for escheat.

[A difficulty for Hunter's claim of title under the 1789 grant was posed by the Treaty of Peace with Great Britain of 1783, which provided that "no future confiscations shall be made". The Jay Treaty of 1794 further declared that "British subjects who now hold lands in the territories of the United States * * * shall continue to hold them * * * and may grant, sell or devise the same to whom they please, in like manner as if they were natives", and "neither they nor their heirs or assigns shall, so far as respects the said lands and the legal remedies incident thereto, be considered as aliens."

[On April 24, 1794, the Virginia Superior Court decided against Hunter.

[Events that transpired after the trial court's decision gave Hunter a second and distinct basis for his claim of title—the 1796 "Act of Compromise" of the Virginia legislature. That Act proposed that the commonwealth relin-

---

12. An authoritative work on Supreme Court practice is Stern, Gressman, Shapiro & Geller, Supreme Court Practice (7th ed.1993). A useful reference is Boskey, 1–1A West's Federal Forms (4th ed.1982).

quish "all claim to any lands specifically appropriated by * * * Lord Fairfax to his own use either by deed or actual survey * * * if the devises [sic] of Lord Fairfax, or those claiming under them, will relinquish all claims to lands * * * which were waste and unappropriated at the time of the death of Lord Fairfax." Prior to passage of the resolution, John Marshall—who with his brother James was part of a syndicate that two or three years earlier had contracted to purchase the main part of the Fairfax estate from Denny Martin Fairfax—wrote to the Speaker of the Virginia House of Delegates. Describing himself as "authorized to speak for all" of "the purchasers of the lands of Mr. Fairfax, Marshall wrote that he had" determined to accede to the proposition if the Act passed. 2 Beveridge, Life of John Marshall 208–09 (1911). John Marshall apparently had no personal interest in the land claimed by Hunter, but the purchase by the Marshall syndicate (finally consummated in 1806) of other land from the Fairfax estate did give him an interest in the general question of the validity of title claimed by the Fairfax interests and their devisees. See 4 Beveridge at 149–55.

[Hunter's appeal to the Court of Appeals of Virginia was argued in May 1796, but no decision appears to have been rendered by November 15, 1803, when the appeal abated by reason of the death of the appellee. It was revived by consent and was reargued in the Virginia Court of Appeals in October 1809.

[At that time, Hunter had alternative claims of title, resting on (i) the 1789 grant from Virginia (and the accompanying contentions that Denny Martin Fairfax as an alien had been incapable of holding land, and that in any case there had been an escheat of the land to the commonwealth despite the lack of any inquest of office) and (ii) the 1796 Act of Compromise. The Martin/Fairfax claim rested on the contention that the title obtained under the will of Lord Fairfax had not been divested by inquest of office or some equivalent act before the Treaty of Peace in 1783; and, further, that the Act of Compromise, passed after judgment in the Superior Court, did not affect the title and could not be introduced.

[In April, 1810, the Court of Appeals reversed the Superior Court's judgment, 2–0 (the third judge having disqualified himself). Separate opinions were rendered. Judge Roane, Marshall's political enemy, see 4 Beveridge at 146, held that Martin had acquired at best a defeasible title, that the Act of 1782 successfully vested the title in the commonwealth, and that the Treaty of Peace thus "had nothing left whereupon to operate". He also ruled that the Act of Compromise was binding, having been "intended to settle and determine *this*, among other suits". Hunter v. Fairfax's Devisee, 15 Va. (1 Munf.) 218, 231–32. Judge Fleming concurred solely on the basis of the Act of Compromise, disagreeing on the other points.

[On writ of error, the Supreme Court reversed. Fairfax's Devisee v. Hunter's Lessee, 11 U.S. (7 Cranch) 603 (1813). Justice Story's opinion held that an alien has the capacity to take title to land by devise, subject to divestiture by the sovereign; that none of the Virginia acts altered the common law requirement of inquest of office to vest title in the commonwealth; and, therefore, that the treaty of 1794 confirmed the undivested Fairfax title. Justice Johnson dissented on the ground that the "interest acquired under the devise was a mere *scintilla juris,* and that *scintilla* was extinguished by the grant of the state," the legislature being competent to dispense with inquest of office. He agreed, however, that under § 25 of the Judiciary Act an inquiry into "the title of the parties litigant" was necessary and "must, in the nature of things, precede the consideration how far the law, treaty and so forth, is applicable to it; otherwise an appeal to this court would be worse than nugatory" (p. 632).

[Neither Justice Story nor Justice Johnson mentioned the Act of Compromise relied upon by the Virginia court. Chief Justice Marshall did not participate.*

[The Supreme Court mandate, which was directed to "the Honorable the Judges of the Court of Appeals in and for the Commonwealth of Virginia," stated that the "Court is of opinion that there is error in the judgment of the Court of Appeals," and "adjudged and ordered, that the judgment of the Court of Appeals * * * in this case be, and the same is hereby reversed and annulled, and that the judgment of the District Court of Winchester be affirmed, with costs; and it is further ordered, that the said cause be remanded to the said Court of Appeals * * * with instructions to enter judgment for the appellant." It ended with the formal provision: "You therefore are hereby commanded that such proceedings be had in said cause, as according to right and justice, and the laws of the United States, and agreeably to said judgment and instructions of said Supreme Court ought to be had, the said writ of error notwithstanding". Hunter v. Martin, Devisee of Fairfax, 18 Va. (4 Munf.) 2–3.

["The question, whether this mandate should be obeyed, excited all that attention from the bench and bar, which its great importance truly merited" (*id.* at 3); and after oral argument, on December 16, 1815, the judges (Cabell, Brooke, Roane and Fleming) expressed their separate opinions *seriatim*, joining in the following conclusion (pp. 58–59):

["The court is unanimously of opinion that the appellate power of the Supreme Court of the United States, does not extend to this court, under a sound construction of the constitution of the United States;—that so much of the 25th section of the act of Congress * * * as extends the appellate jurisdiction of the Supreme Court to this court, is not in pursuance of the constitution of the United States; that the writ of error in this case was improvidently allowed under the authority of that act; that proceedings thereon in the Supreme Court were *coram non judice* in relation to this court; and that obedience to its mandate be declined by this court."

[The common grounds set forth for this conclusion are indicated by the following extracts from the opinion of Judge Cabell (pp. 8, 9, 12, 13):

["* * * The present government of the United States, grew out of the weakness and inefficacy of the confederation, and was intended to remedy its evils. Instead of a government of requisition, we have a government of power. But how does the power operate? On individuals in their individual capacity. No one presumes to contend, that the state governments can operate compulsively on the general government or any of its departments, even in cases of unquestionable encroachment on state authority. * * * Such encroachment of jurisdiction could neither be prevented nor redressed by the state government, or any of its departments, by any procedure acting on the Federal Courts. I can perceive nothing in the constitution which gives to the Federal Courts any stronger claim to prevent or redress, by any procedure acting on the state courts, an equally obvious encroachment on the Federal jurisdiction. The constitution of the United States contemplates the independence of both

---

* For the claim that John Marshall drafted the petition for a writ of error, see White, The Marshall Court and Cultural Change, 1815–35, at 167–68 (1988).

governments and regards the residuary sovereignty of the states, as not less inviolable, than the delegated sovereignty of the United States. It must have been foreseen that controversies would sometimes arise as to the boundaries of the two jurisdictions. Yet the constitution has provided no umpire, has erected no tribunal by which they shall be settled. The omission proceeded, probably, from the belief, that such a tribunal would produce evils greater than those of the occasional collisions which it would be designed to remedy. * * *

["If this Court should now proceed to enter a judgment in this case, according to instructions of the Supreme Court, the Judges of this Court, in doing so, must act either as Federal or as State Judges. But we cannot be made Federal Judges without our consent, and without commissions. * * * We must, then, in obeying this mandate, be considered still as State Judges. We are required, as State Judges to enter up a judgment, not our own, but dictated and prescribed to us by another Court. * * * But, before one Court can dictate to another, the judgment it shall pronounce, it must bear, to that other, the relation of an appellate Court. The term appellate, however, necessarily includes the idea of superiority. But one Court cannot be correctly said to be superior to another, unless both of them belong to the same sovereignty. It would be a misapplication of terms to say that a Court of Virginia is superior to a Court of Maryland, or vice versa. The Courts of the United States, therefore, belonging to one sovereignty, cannot be appellate Courts in relation to the State Courts, which belong to a different sovereignty— and, of course, their commands or instructions impose no obligation. * * *

["* * * If, therefore, I am correct in this position, the appellate jurisdiction of the Supreme Court of the United States [under the constitution], must have reference to the inferior Courts of the United States, and not to the State Courts. * * * It has been contended that the constitution contemplated only the objects of appeal, and not the tribunals from which the appeal is to be taken; and intended to give to the Supreme Court of the United States appellate jurisdiction in all the cases of federal cognizance. But this argument proves too much, and what is utterly inadmissible. It would give appellate jurisdiction, as well over the courts of England or France, as over the State courts; for, although I do not think the State Courts are foreign Courts in relation to the Federal Courts, yet I consider them not less independent than foreign Courts."

[To the argument that appellate jurisdiction over state courts was necessary to ensure uniformity of decision, Judge Cabell replied: "All the purposes of the constitution of the United States will be answered by the erection of Federal Courts, into which any party, plaintiff or defendant, concerned in a case of federal cognizance, may carry it for adjudication" (pp. 15–16). Judges Brooke and Fleming apparently shared this opinion (pp. 23, 58), on which Judge Roane expressed no view.

[Judges Roane and Fleming offered an additional ground for decision—that the case fell outside § 25 since the record did not show that the decision turned upon the federal treaty (see the last sentence of the text of section 25 on p. 493, *supra*) and that if the Supreme Court "had held itself at liberty, to go outside of the record", the report of the decision of the Virginia Court would have shown that it was based on the Act of Compromise (pp. 49, 50).

[The case returned to the Supreme Court on a writ of error from the judgment of the Court of Appeals of Virginia refusing to obey the Supreme Court's mandate. The plaintiff in error was Philip Martin, who had obtained the land by devise upon the death of his older brother, Denny Martin Fairfax. 4 Beveridge at 151, 160–61.]

■ STORY, J., delivered the opinion of the court * * *

Before proceeding to the principal questions, it may not be unfit to dispose of some preliminary considerations which have grown out of the arguments at the bar.

The constitution of the United states was ordained and established, not by the states in their sovereign capacities, but emphatically, as the preamble of the constitution declares, by "the People of the United States." There can be no doubt, that it was competent to the people to invest the general government with all the powers which they might deem proper and necessary; to extend or restrain these powers according to their own good pleasure, and to give them a paramount and supreme authority. As little doubt can there be, that the people had a right to prohibit to the states the exercise of any powers which were, in their judgment, incompatible with the objects of the general compact; to make the powers of the state governments, in given cases, subordinate to those of the nation, or to reserve to themselves those sovereign authorities which they might not choose to delegate to either. The constitution was not, therefore, necessarily carved out of existing state sovereignties, nor a surrender of powers already existing in state institutions, for the powers of the states depend upon their own constitutions; and the people of every state had the right to modify and restrain them, according to their own views of policy or principle. On the other hand, it is perfectly clear, that the sovereign powers vested in the state governments, by their respective constitutions, remained unaltered and unimpaired, except so far as they were granted to the government of the United States. These deductions do not rest upon general reasoning, plain and obvious as they seem to be. They have been positively recognized by one of the articles in amendment of the constitution, which declares, that "the powers not delegated to the United States by the constitution, nor prohibited by it to the states, are reserved to the states respectively, or to the people." * * *

The third article of the constitution is that which must principally attract our attention. * * *

      * * * 1

* * * We have already seen that appellate jurisdiction is given by the constitution to the supreme court in all cases where it has not original jurisdiction; subject, however, to such exceptions and regulations as congress may prescribe. It is, therefore, capable of embracing every case enumerated in the constitution, which is not exclusively to be decided by way of original jurisdiction. But the exercise of appellate jurisdiction is far from being limited by the terms of the constitution to the supreme court. There can be no doubt that congress may create a succession of inferior tribunals, in each of which it may vest appellate as well as original jurisdiction. The judicial power is delegated by the constitution in the most general terms, and may, therefore, be exercised by congress under every variety of form, of appellate or original jurisdiction. * * *

---

1. [Ed.] The omitted portion of the opinion develops the view that Article III's language is "designed to be mandatory" upon Congress. See p. 359, *supra*.

As, then, by the terms of the constitution, the appellate jurisdiction is not limited as to the supreme court, and as to this court it may be exercised in all other cases than those of which it has original cognizance, what is there to restrain its exercise over state tribunals in the enumerated cases?   The appellate power is not limited by the terms of the third article to any particular courts.   The words are, "the judicial power (which includes appellate power) shall extend *to all cases,*" & c., and "in all other cases before mentioned the supreme court shall have appellate jurisdiction."   It is the *case,* then, and not *the court,* that gives the jurisdiction.   * * *

If the constitution meant to limit the appellate jurisdiction to cases pending in the courts of the United States, it would necessarily follow that the jurisdiction of these courts would, in all cases enumerated in the constitution, be exclusive of state tribunals.   How otherwise could the jurisdiction extend to *all* cases arising under the constitution, laws, and treaties of the United States, or *to all cases* of admiralty and maritime jurisdiction?   If some of these cases might be entertained by state tribunals, and no appellate jurisdiction as to them should exist, then the appellate power would not extend to *all,* but to *some,* cases.   If state tribunals might exercise concurrent jurisdiction over all or some of the other classes of cases in the constitution without control, then the appellate jurisdiction of the United States might, as to such cases, have no real existence, contrary to the manifest intent of the constitution.   Under such circumstances, to give effect to the judicial power, it must be construed to be exclusive; and this not only when the *casus foederis* should arise directly, but when it should arise, incidentally, in cases pending in state courts.   This construction would abridge the jurisdiction of such court far more than has been ever contemplated in any act of congress.

On the other hand, if, as has been contended, a discretion be vested in congress to establish, or not to establish, inferior courts at their own pleasure, and congress should not establish such courts, the appellate jurisdiction of the supreme court would have nothing to act upon, unless it could act upon cases pending in the state courts.   Under such circumstances it must be held that the appellate power would extend to state courts; for the constitution is peremptory that it shall extend to certain enumerated cases, which cases could exist in no other courts.   Any other construction, upon this supposition, would involve this strange contradiction, that a discretionary power vested in congress, and which they might rightfully omit to exercise, would defeat the absolute injunctions of the constitution in relation to the whole appellate power.

But it is plain that the framers of the constitution did contemplate that cases within the judicial cognizance of the United States not only might but would arise in the state courts, in the exercise of their ordinary jurisdiction.   * * * [After quoting the Supremacy Clause of Article VI, the Court continued:] It is obvious that this obligation is imperative upon the state judges in their official, and not merely in their private, capacities.   * * *

A moment's consideration will show us the necessity and propriety of this provision in cases where the jurisdiction of the state courts is unquestionable.   * * * Suppose an indictment for a crime in a state court, and the defendant should allege in his defense that the crime was created by an *ex post facto* act of the state, must not the state court, in the exercise of a jurisdiction which has already rightfully attached, have a right to pronounce on the validity and sufficiency of the defense?   It would be extremely difficult, upon any legal principles, to give a negative answer * * *.   Innumerable instances of the same sort might be stated, in illustration of the position; and unless the state courts could sustain jurisdiction in such cases, this clause of the sixth article would be without meaning or effect, and public mischiefs, of a most enormous magnitude, would inevitably ensue.

It must, therefore, be conceded that the constitution not only contemplated, but meant to provide for cases within the scope of the judicial power of the United States, which might yet depend before state tribunals. It was foreseen that in the exercise of their ordinary jurisdiction, state courts would incidentally take cognizance of cases arising under the constitution, the laws, and treaties of the United States. Yet to all these cases the judicial power, by the very terms of the constitution, is to extend. It cannot extend by original jurisdiction if that was already rightfully and exclusively attached in the state courts * * *. It would seem to follow that the appellate power of the United States must, in such cases, extend to state tribunals * * *.

It is further argued, that no great public mischief can result from a construction which shall limit the appellate power of the United States to cases in their own courts: first, because state judges are bound by an oath to support the constitution of the United States, and must be presumed to be men of learning and integrity; and, secondly, because congress must have an unquestionable right to remove all cases within the scope of the judicial power from the state courts to the courts of the United States, at any time before final judgment, though not after final judgment. As to the first reason—admitting that the judges of the state courts are, and always will be, of as much learning, integrity, and wisdom, as those of the courts of the United States, (which we very cheerfully admit,) it does not aid the argument. It is manifest that the constitution has proceeded upon a theory of its own, and given or withheld powers according to the judgment of the American people, by whom it was adopted. We can only construe its powers, and cannot inquire into the policy or principles which induced the grant of them. The constitution has presumed (whether rightly or wrongly we do not inquire) that state attachments, state prejudices, state jealousies, and state interests, might sometimes obstruct, or control, or be supposed to obstruct or control, the regular administration of justice. Hence, in controversies between states; between citizens of different states; between citizens claiming grants under different states; between a state and its citizens, or foreigners, and between citizens and foreigners, it enables the parties, under the authority of congress, to have the controversies heard, tried, and determined before the national tribunals. No other reason than that which has been stated can be assigned, why some, at least, of those cases should not have been left to the cognizance of the state courts. In respect to the other enumerated cases—the cases arising under the constitution, laws, and treaties of the United States, cases affecting ambassadors and other public ministers, and cases of admiralty and maritime jurisdiction—reasons of a higher and more extensive nature, touching the safety, peace, and sovereignty of the nation, might well justify a grant of exclusive jurisdiction.

This is not all. A motive of another kind, perfectly compatible with the most sincere respect for state tribunals, might induce the grant of appellate power over their decisions. That motive is the importance, and even necessity of *uniformity* of decisions throughout the whole United States, upon all subjects within the purview of the constitution. Judges of equal learning and integrity, in different states, might differently interpret a statute, or a treaty of the United States, or even the constitution itself: If there were no revising authority to control these jarring and discordant judgments, and harmonize them into uniformity, the laws, the treaties, and the constitution of the United States would be different in different states, and might, perhaps, never have precisely the same construction, obligation, or efficacy, in any two states. The public mischiefs that would attend such a state of things would be truly deplorable; * * * and the appellate jurisdiction must continue to be the only adequate remedy for such evils.

There is an additional consideration, which is entitled to great weight. * * * The judicial power was * * * not to be exercised exclusively for the benefit of parties who might be plaintiffs, and would elect the national forum, but also for the protection of defendants who might be entitled to try their rights, or assert their privileges, before the same forum. Yet, if the construction contended for be correct, it will follow, that as the plaintiff may always elect the state court, the defendant may be deprived of all the security which the constitution intended in aid of his rights. Such a state of things can, in no respect, be considered as giving equal rights. To obviate this difficulty, we are referred to the power which it is admitted congress possess to remove suits from state courts to the national courts; and this forms the second ground upon which the argument we are considering has been attempted to be sustained.

This power of removal is not to be found in express terms in any part of the constitution; if it be given, it is only given by implication, as a power of removal is certainly not, in strictness of language, an exercise of original jurisdiction; it presupposes an exercise of original jurisdiction to have attached elsewhere. The existence of this power of removal is familiar * * *, and it is exercised before as well as after judgment. * * * If, then, the right of removal be included in the appellate jurisdiction, it is only because it is one mode of exercising that power, and as congress is not limited by the constitution to any particular mode, or time of exercising it, it may authorize a removal either before or after judgment. * * * A writ of error is, indeed, but a process which removes the record of one court to the possession of another court, and enables the latter to inspect the proceedings, and give such judgment as its own opinion of the law and justice of the case may warrant. * * *

The remedy, too, of removal of suits would be utterly inadequate to the purposes of the constitution, if it could act only on the parties, and not upon the state courts. * * * If state courts should deny the constitutionality of the authority to remove suits from their cognizance, in what manner could they be compelled to relinquish the jurisdiction? In respect to criminal cases, there would at once be an end of all control, and the state decisions would be paramount to the constitution; and though in civil suits the courts of the United States might act upon the parties, yet the state courts might act in the same way; and this conflict of jurisdictions would not only jeopardize private rights, but bring into imminent peril the public interests.

On the whole, the court are of opinion, that the appellate power of the United States does extend to cases pending in the state courts; and that the 25th section of the judiciary act, which authorizes the exercise of this jurisdiction in the specified cases, by a writ of error, is supported by the letter and spirit of the constitution. * * *

Strong as this conclusion stands upon the general language of the constitution, it may still derive support from other sources. It is an historical fact, that this exposition of the constitution, extending its appellate power to state courts, was, previous to its adoption, uniformly and publicly avowed by its friends, and admitted by its enemies, as the basis of their respective reasonings, both in and out of the state conventions. It is an historical fact, that at the time when the judiciary act was submitted to the deliberations of the first congress, composed, as it was, not only of men of great learning and ability, but of men who had acted a principal part in framing, supporting, or opposing that constitution, the same exposition was explicitly declared and admitted by the friends and by the opponents of that system. It is an historical fact, that the supreme court of the United States have, from time to time, sustained this appellate jurisdiction in a great variety of cases, brought from the tribunals of many of the most important states in the union, and that no state tribunal has ever breathed a judicial doubt on the subject, or declined to obey the mandate of the supreme court, until the present occasion. * * *

The next question which has been argued, is, whether the case at bar be within the purview of the 25th section of the judiciary act, so that this court may rightfully sustain the present writ of error. * * *

That the present writ of error is founded upon a judgment of the court below, which drew in question and denied the validity of a statute of the United States, is incontrovertible, for it is apparent upon the face of the record. That this judgment is final upon the rights of the parties is equally true * * *. The case, then, falls directly within the terms of the act. It is a final judgment in a suit in a state court, denying the validity of a statute of the United States; and unless a distinction can be made between proceedings under a mandate, and proceedings in an original suit, a writ of error is the proper remedy to revise that judgment. In our opinion no legal distinction exists between the cases. * * *

But it is contended, that the former judgment of this court was rendered upon a case not within the purview of this section of the judicial act, and that as it was pronounced by an incompetent jurisdiction, it was utterly void, and cannot be a sufficient foundation to sustain any subsequent proceedings. * * * [I]n ordinary cases a second writ of error has never been supposed to draw in question the propriety of the first judgment, and it is difficult to perceive how such a proceeding could be sustained upon principle. * * *

In this case, however, from motives of a public nature, we are entirely willing to waive all objections, and to go back and re-examine the question of jurisdiction as it stood upon the record formerly in judgment. * * *

The objection urged at the bar is, that this court cannot inquire into the title, but simply into the correctness of the construction put upon the treaty by the court of appeals; and that their judgment is not re-examinable here, unless it appear on the face of the record that some construction was put upon the treaty. If, therefore, that court might have decided the case upon the invalidity of the title, (and, *non constat*, that they did not,) independent of the treaty, there is an end of the appellate jurisdiction of this court. In support of this objection much stress is laid upon the last clause of the section, which declares, that no other cause shall be regarded as a ground of reversal than such as appears *on the face* of the record and *immediately* respects the construction of the treaty, & c., in dispute.

If this be the true construction of the section, it will be wholly inadequate for the purposes which it professes to have in view, and may be evaded at pleasure. But we see no reason for adopting this narrow construction; and there are the strongest reasons against it, founded upon the words as well as the intent of the legislature. What is the case for which the body of the section provides a remedy by writ of error? The answer must be in the words of the section, a suit where is drawn in question the construction of a treaty, and the decision is against *the title set up by the party.* It is, therefore, the decision against the title set up with reference to the treaty, and not the mere abstract construction of the treaty itself, upon which the statute intends to found the appellate jurisdiction. * * *

The restraining clause was manifestly intended for a very different purpose. It was foreseen that the parties might claim under various titles, and might assert various defenses, altogether independent of each other. The court might admit or reject evidence applicable to one particular title, and not to all, and in such cases it was the intention of congress to limit what would otherwise have unquestionably attached to the court, the right of revising all the points involved in the cause. It therefore restrains this right to such errors as respect the questions specified in the section; and in this view, it has an appropriate sense, consistent with the preceding clauses. We are, therefore, satisfied, that, upon principle, the case was rightfully before us, and if the point were perfectly new, we should not hesitate to assert the jurisdiction. * * *

It has been asserted at the bar that, in point of fact, the court of appeals did not decide either upon the treaty or the title apparent upon the record, but upon a compromise made under an act of the legislature of Virginia. If it be true (as we are informed) that this was a private act, to take effect only upon a certain condition, *viz.* the execution of a deed of release of certain lands, which was matter *in pais,* it is somewhat difficult to understand how the court could take judicial cognizance of the act, or of the performance of the condition, unless spread upon the record. At all events, we are bound to consider that the court did decide upon the facts actually before them. The treaty of peace was not necessary to have been stated, for it was the supreme law of the land, of which all courts must take notice. And at the time of the decision in the court of appeals and in this court, another treaty had intervened, which attached itself to the title in controversy, and, of course, must have been the supreme law to govern the decision, if it should be found applicable to the case. It was in this view that this court did not deem it necessary to rest its former decision upon the treaty of peace, believing that the title of the defendant was, at all events, perfect under the treaty of 1794. * * *

* * *

We have not thought it incumbent on us to give any opinion upon the question, whether this court have authority to issue a writ of mandamus to the court of appeals to enforce the former judgments, as we do not think it necessarily involved in the decision of this cause.

It is the opinion of the whole court, that the judgment of the court of appeals of Virginia, rendered on the mandate in this cause, be reversed, and the judgment of the district court, held at Winchester, be, and the same is hereby affirmed.

JOHNSON, J., * * * In this act I can see nothing which amounts to an assertion of the inferiority or dependence of the state tribunals. The presiding judge of the state court is himself authorized to issue the writ of error, if he will, and thus give jurisdiction to the supreme court: and if he thinks proper to decline it, no compulsory process is provided by law to oblige him. The party who imagines himself aggrieved is then at liberty to apply to a judge of the United States, who issues the writ of error, which (whatever the form) is, in substance, no more than a mode of compelling the opposite party to appear before this court, and maintain the legality of his judgment obtained before the state tribunal.   An exemplification of a record is the common property of every one who chooses to apply and pay for it, and thus the case and the parties are brought before us; and so far is the court itself from being brought under the revising power of this court, that nothing but the case, as presented by the record and pleadings of the parties, is considered, and the opinions of the court are never resorted to unless for the purpose of assisting this court in forming their own opinions.

The absolute necessity that there was for congress to exercise something of a revising power over cases and parties in the state courts, will appear from this consideration.

Suppose the whole extent of the judicial power of the United States vested in their own courts, yet such a provision would not answer all the ends of the constitution, for two reasons:

1st.   Although the plaintiff may, in such case, have the full benefit of the constitution extended to him, yet the defendant would not; as the plaintiff might force him into the court of the state at his election.

2dly.   Supposing it possible so to legislate as to give the courts of the United States original jurisdiction in all cases arising under the constitution, laws, & c., in the words of the 2d section of the 3d article, (a point on which I have some doubt, and which in time might, perhaps, under some *quo minus* fiction, or a willing construction, greatly accumulate the jurisdiction of those courts,) yet a very large class of cases would remain unprovided for.   Incidental questions would often arise, and as a court of competent jurisdiction in the principal case must decide all such questions, whatever laws they arise under, endless might be the diversity of decisions throughout the union upon the constitution, treaties, and laws, of the United States; a subject on which the tranquillity of the union, internally and externally, may materially depend.

I should feel the more hesitation in adopting the opinions which I express in this case, were I not firmly convinced that they are practical, and may be acted upon without compromising the harmony of the union, or bringing humility upon the state tribunals.   God forbid that the judicial power in these states should ever, for a moment, even in its humblest departments, feel a doubt of its own independence.   Whilst adjudicating on a subject which the laws of the country assign finally to the revising power of another tribunal, it can feel no such doubt.   An anxiety to do justice is ever relieved by the knowledge that what we do is not final between the parties.   And no sense of dependence can be felt from the knowledge that the parties, not the court, may be summoned before another tribunal.   With this view, by means of laws, avoiding judgments obtained in the state courts in cases over which congress has constitutionally assumed jurisdiction, and inflicting penalties on parties who shall contumaciously persist in infringing the constitutional rights of others—under a liberal extension of the writ of injunction and the *habeas corpus ad subjiciendum,* I flatter myself that the full extent of the constitutional revising power may be secured to the United States, and the benefits of it to the individual, without ever resorting to compulsory or restrictive process upon the state tribunals; a right which, I repeat again, congress has not asserted, nor has this court asserted, nor does there appear any necessity for asserting. * * *

NOTE ON THE ATTACKS UPON THE JURISDICTION

(1) *State Resistance to Section 25.* "Between 1789 and 1860 the courts of seven States denied the constitutional right of the United States Supreme Court to decide cases on writs of error to State courts—Virginia, Ohio, Georgia, Kentucky, South Carolina, California and Wisconsin. The Legislatures of all these states (except California), and also of Pennsylvania and Maryland, formally adopted resolutions or statutes against this power of the Supreme Court. Bills were introduced in Congress on at least ten occasions to deprive the Court of its jurisdiction—in 1821, 1822, 1824, 1831, 1846, 1867, 1868, 1871, 1872 and 1882." Warren, *Legislative and Judicial Attacks on the Supreme Court of the United States—A History of the Twenty–Fifth Section of the Judiciary Act, Part I*, 47 Am.L.Rev. 1, 3–4 (1913); see also Part II of Warren's article, 47 *id.* 161 (1913). The arguments advanced in these attacks ranged from the relatively narrow grounds adduced against the jurisdiction in the Hunter case to the extreme position, culminating in the doctrines of secession, that each state had an equal right to stand on its interpretation of the Constitution.[1]

The dissident remedies proposed included repeal of § 25, *e.g.,* H.R.Rep. No.43, 21st Cong., 2d Sess. (1831),[2] and constitutional amendment depriving the courts of authority to annul legislation, or vesting jurisdiction in the Senate, or establishing a new tribunal, differently composed, to mediate between the nation and the states. See Ames, The Proposed Amendments to the Constitution of the United States During the First Century of its History 158–63.

(2) *Cohens v. Virginia.* The Court's position, as defined by Justice Story, did not change throughout the period of controversy. It was strongly reaffirmed by Chief Justice Marshall in Cohens v. Virginia, 19 U.S. (6 Wheat.) 264 (1821), a writ of error to review a state court judgment affirming a criminal conviction. The Court, while affirming the judgment on the merits, reiterated its position in the Hunter case, and rejected two additional contentions urged against the jurisdiction: (1) that the Eleventh Amendment (or more generally, notions of state sovereign immunity) barred the writ of error as a suit against the state, see Chap. IX, Sec. 2(A), p. 1048, *infra;*[3] and (2) that review of the judgment under the Court's *appellate* jurisdiction was inconsistent with the constitutional

---

1. See generally Warren, *supra;* Haines, The Role of the Supreme Court in American Government and Politics 499–577 (1944); Corwin, *National Power and State Interposition,* 10 Mich.L.Rev. 535 (1912); Reference Note, *Interposition vs. Judicial Power—A Study of Ultimate Authority in Constitutional Questions,* 1 Race Rel.L.Rep. 465 (1956).

2. It is curious, in view of the issues raised by Southern states prior to the Civil War, that the "judicial power" of the Confederacy extended to "cases arising under" the Constitution, laws, and treaties of the Con-

federacy, and that the jurisdiction to review state decisions conferred on the Confederacy's Supreme Court by its Judiciary Act was even broader than that in § 25. Hostility to the Confederacy's judiciary article played a major part, however, in preventing the organization of a Confederate Supreme Court. See Robinson, Justice in Grey 48, 437–91 (1941).

3. For a recent re-affirmation of this aspect of Cohens, see McKesson Corp. v. Division of ABT, 496 U.S. 18, 26–28 (1990).

grant of *original* jurisdiction to the Supreme Court in cases where a state is a party, see Chap. III, Sec. 1, p. 298, *supra*.[4]

(3) *Supreme Court Review Today*. The constitutional validity of the Court's jurisdiction to review state court decisions has not been seriously challenged in the contemporary era. Brown v. Board of Education, 347 U.S. 483 (1954), did provoke attacks on the authoritativeness of Court decisions, including "interposition" resolutions by state legislatures reminiscent of the pre-Civil War pattern. See, *e.g.*, the "Southern Manifesto" signed by Congressmen and Senators, and the 1956 legislative resolutions of five Southern states, reprinted at 1 Race Rel.L.Rep. 435–47 (1956). For Supreme Court responses to such positions, see Cooper v. Aaron, 358 U.S. 1 (1958), p. 90, *supra;* Bush v. Orleans Parish Sch. Bd., 364 U.S. 803 (1960)(summarily rejecting the assertion that certain state statutes should be sustained on the ground that Louisiana "has interposed itself in the field of public education over which it has exclusive control").

There have been numerous attempts—none successful—to restrict the Court's jurisdiction over specific controversial subjects (*e.g.*, reapportionment, school prayer, abortion). See Chap. IV, Sec. 1, pp. 350–51, *supra*. A different proposal, advanced under the auspices of the Council of State Governments and echoing a similar scheme of the pre-Civil War era, would have created a "Court of the Union", composed of the chief justices of the fifty states, with power to review "any judgment of the Supreme Court relating to the rights reserved to the states or to the people by this Constitution." *Amending the Constitution to Strengthen the States in the Federal System*, 36 State Gov't 10, 13 (1963). See Kurland, *The Court of the Union or Julius Caesar Revised*, 39 Notre Dame Lawyer 636 (1964).

(4) *Review By Lower Federal Courts*. Note that Justice Story's opinion describes removal as an exercise of appellate jurisdiction. Does that suggest that Congress may authorize federal trial or circuit courts of appeals to review state court judgments? Would anything in Article III (*e.g.*, "The judicial Power * * * shall be vested in one supreme Court") prohibit such an arrangement? *Cf.* The Federalist No. 82, p. 25, *supra* (perceiving "no impediment" to such an arrangement).

A 1995 bill to create a uniform federal product liability law contained a provision that a decision by a federal circuit court of appeals interpreting a provision of that law shall (unless modified by the Supreme Court) be considered a "controlling precedent" by the court of any state falling within the geographical boundaries of that circuit. S.565, 104th Cong., 1st Sess., § 3(E), 104th Cong.Rec. S.3978–3980. (Under current law, a state court is not obliged to follow the decisions of any federal court of appeals on issues of federal law.) Is there any question about the provision's constitutionality?

NOTE ON ENFORCEMENT OF THE MANDATE

(1) *The Supreme Court's Mandate*. Normally the Supreme Court, when reversing a state court judgment, remands the cause for proceedings "not

---

4. The Court did not respond to Virginia's argument, see 19 U.S. (6 Wheat.) at 321–23, that Article III's grant of federal question jurisdiction did not extend to criminal cases. *Cf.* Wisconsin v. Pelican Ins. Co., Ch. III, Sec. 1, p. 305, *supra*.

inconsistent" with the Court's opinion. This mandate leaves the state court free to pass on any undetermined questions, or even to alter its determination of underlying state law. The reversal may not, therefore, be decisive of the final judgment. See, *e.g.*, Georgia Ry. & Elec. Co. v. Decatur, 297 U.S. 620 (1936); Schuylkill Trust Co. v. Pennsylvania, 302 U.S. 506 (1938).

Compare the mandate given upon the first review in the Hunter case, p. 497, *supra*. Would a more satisfactory result have been achieved if the mandate had been in usual form?

(2) *Mandamus to Enforce Compliance.* If a state court deviates from the Supreme Court's mandate, the proper remedy is to seek a new review of the judgment, as in Martin v. Hunter's Lessee. So long as such review is possible, mandamus has been considered inappropriate. In re Blake, 175 U.S. 114 (1899).

When immediate review is precluded by the absence of a final judgment in the state court, the Supreme Court has still generally denied, without explanation, leave to file a petition for mandamus. Lavender v. Clark, 329 U.S. 674 (1946); Ex parte Kedroff, 346 U.S. 893 (1953); International Ass'n of Machinists v. Duckworth, 368 U.S. 982 (1962). However, in Deen v. Hickman, 358 U.S. 57 (1958), after determining that the Texas courts were treating as open an issue it considered foreclosed by its prior decision, the Supreme Court granted leave to file a petition for mandamus; the writ itself was not issued, since the Court assumed that the Texas court "will of course conform to the disposition we now make". The opinion did not discuss the Court's power to issue mandamus to a state court.[1] The question of power was argued but undecided in Ex parte Texas, 315 U.S. 8 (1942). *Cf.* Chap. III, Sec. 3, *supra*. See also NAACP v. Alabama, 360 U.S. 240, 245 (1959)(granting certiorari and reversing state judgment inconsistent with prior mandate; leave to file petition for mandamus denied on the assumption state court will comply).

In General Atomic Co. v. Felter, 436 U.S. 493 (1978), the Supreme Court determined that a state trial court "has again done precisely what we held [in the Court's prior decision] that it lacked the power to do: interfere with attempts by [plaintiff] to assert in federal forums what it views as its entitlement to arbitration" (p. 496). Invoking the principle that "a lower court" that fails to "give full effect" to the Court's mandate may be controlled by writ of mandamus (without discussing the assumption that state courts fell within this principle), the Court granted the motion for leave to file a petition for mandamus. As in Deen, however, the Court did not issue the formal writ, assuming that the state court "will now conform to our previous judgment" (pp. 497–98).

(3) *Entry of Judgment.* The First Judiciary Act authorized the Supreme Court to enter judgment and award execution if the case had previously been remanded once; the requirement of one remand was eliminated in 1867, see pp. 492-93, *supra*. *Cf.* Judicial Code § 237(a), 28 U.S.C. § 344(a)(1940). In combination, 28 U.S.C. §§ 2106 and 1651(a) presumably confer no less authority than the Court had before the 1948 revision.

Thus state recalcitrance can be met by entry of judgment, as in Martin v. Hunter's Lessee, McCulloch v. Maryland, 17 U.S. (4 Wheat.) 316, 437 (1819),

---

1. On the same day, the Court summarily denied a petition for certiorari in the same case "in view of the order entered" in the mandamus proceeding. Deen v. Gulf, C. & S.F.Ry., 358 U.S. 874 (1958).

and Gibbons v. Ogden, 22 U.S. (9 Wheat.) 1, 239 (1824); by an award of execution, as in Tyler v. Magwire, 84 U.S. (17 Wall.) 253 (1873); or by remanding with directions to enter a specific judgment, as in Stanley v. Schwalby, 162 U.S. 255 (1896), and Poindexter v. Greenhow, 114 U.S. 270 (1885).

In NAACP v. Alabama ex rel. Flowers, 377 U.S. 288 (1964), after eight years of litigation (including four considerations by the Supreme Court) and obvious state court recalcitrance, the Court still refused the request to formulate its own decree for entry in the state courts. Accepting that it "undoubtedly" has the power to enter judgment, the Court "prefer[red] to follow our usual practice and remand the case to the Supreme Court of Alabama for further proceedings not inconsistent with this opinion." The opinion concluded (p. 310): "Should we unhappily be mistaken in our belief that the Supreme Court of Alabama will promptly implement this disposition, leave is given the Association to apply to this Court for further appropriate relief"—which proved to be unnecessary, see 277 Ala. 89, 167 So.2d 171 (1964).

(4) *Remedies for Violation of Mandates.* If a mandate to enter a specific judgment should be issued and defied, which of the following procedures, if any, might be pursued: (a) recall of mandate and entry of judgment with award of execution or other process (28 U.S.C. §§ 561–66, 672, 1651, 2241); (b) mandamus to the state court to enter the proper judgment; or (c) punishment for contempt for disobedience to "lawful * * * order * * * or command" under 18 U.S.C. § 401?

In United States v. Shipp, 203 U.S. 563 (1906), 214 U.S. 386 (1909), 215 U.S. 580 (1909), the Attorney General of the United States filed an information charging contempt of the Supreme Court. The information alleged that Shipp, a state sheriff with custody of a prisoner, and the other defendants had lynched the prisoner with knowledge that the Supreme Court had ordered a stay of the prisoner's execution pending an appeal, allowed by the Court, from a federal circuit court's denial of his habeas corpus petition. The Court appointed a commissioner to take testimony, rendered judgments of conviction, and sentenced the defendants to prison.

See also In re Herndon, 394 U.S. 399 (1969), where appellants in an election case moved the Supreme Court for a show-cause order to initiate contempt proceedings against a state official for disobedience of a temporary restraining order. The order had been entered originally by a three-judge district court (which later dissolved it) and reinstated by the Supreme Court pending appeal. The Court postponed decision on the motion until after completion of district court proceedings to determine whether the official's actions constituted contempt of that court's original order. Justice Douglas, joined by Justice Harlan, dissented on the ground that there was probable cause to find purposeful disobedience of the Supreme Court's order, and that the postponement of contempt prosecution might create difficulties under the Double Jeopardy Clause.

Should state judges, any more than executive officials, be shielded against a contempt sanction in a case of clear defiance? Does the story of Martin v. Hunter's Lessee have any bearing on the issue? See also the opinion of Justice Baldwin in Holmes v. Jennison, 39 U.S. (14 Pet.) 540, 586 (1840)(Appendix).

Murdock v. City of Memphis

87 U.S. (20 Wall.) 590, 22 L.Ed. 429 (1875).
Error to the Supreme Court of Tennessee.

* * *

Murdock filed a bill in one of the courts of chancery of Tennessee, against the city of Memphis, in that state. The bill and its exhibits made this case:

In July, 1844,—Congress having just previously authorized the establishment of a naval depot in that city, and appropriated a considerable sum of money for the purpose—the ancestors of Murdock—by ordinary deed of bargain and sale, without any covenants or declaration of trust on which the land was to be held by the city, but referring to the fact of "the location of the naval depot lately established by the United States at said town"—conveyed to the city certain land described in and near its limits "for the location of the naval depot aforesaid."

By the same instrument (a quadrupartite one) both the grantors and the city conveyed the same land to one Wheatley, in fee, in trust for the grantors and their heirs "in case the same shall not be appropriated by the United States for that purpose."

On the 14th of September, 1844, the city of Memphis, in consideration of the sum of $20,000 paid by the United States, conveyed the said land to the United States with covenant of general warranty; there being, however, in this deed to the United States no designation of any purpose to which the land was to be applied, nor any conditions precedent or subsequent, or of any kind whatsoever.

The United States took possession of the land for the purpose of the erection of a naval depot upon it, erected buildings, and made various expenditures and improvements for the said purpose; but in about ten years after, by an act of August 5th, 1854, transferred the land back to the city. The act was in these words:

"All the grounds and appurtenances thereunto belonging, known as the Memphis Navy Yard, in Shelby County, Tennessee, be, and the same is hereby, ceded to the mayor and aldermen of the city of Memphis, *for the use and benefit of said city.*"

* * *

The bill charged that by the failure of the United States to appropriate the land for a naval depot, and the final abandonment by the United States of any intention to do so, the land came within the clause of the deed of July 1844, conveying it to Wheatley in trust; or if not, that it was held by the city in trust for the original grantors, and the prayer sought to subject it to said trusts.

The answer, denying the construction put upon the deed of 1844, which established a trust, asserted that the land had been appropriated by the United States as a naval depot within the meaning and intent of the deed of July, 1844, and that the subsequent perpetual occupation of it was not a condition subsequent; and consequently that the abandonment of it as a naval depot was not a breach of a condition such as divested the title so conveyed by the deed.

It pleaded the statute of limitations. It also demurred to the bill as seeking to enforce a forfeiture for breach of condition subsequent.

The court sustained the demurrer, and also decreed that the city had a perfect title to the property against the complainants both under the act of Congress and the statute of limitations, and dismissed the bill. The Supreme Court of Tennessee affirmed this decree.

That court was also of opinion, and so declared itself to be, that the act of Congress "cedes the property in controversy in this cause to the mayor and aldermen of the city of Memphis, for the use of the city only, and not in trust for the complainant; and that the complainant takes no benefit under the said act."

The complainant thereupon sued out a writ of error to this court. * * *

■ MR. JUSTICE MILLER * * * delivered the opinion of the court.

In the year 1867 Congress passed an act * * * entitled an act to amend "An act to establish the judicial courts of the United States, approved September the 24th, 1789." This act consisted of two sections, the first of which conferred upon the Federal courts * * * additional power in regard to writs of habeas corpus, and regulated appeals and other proceedings in that class of cases. The second section was a reproduction, with some changes, of the twenty-fifth section of the act of 1789, to which, by its title, the act of 1867 was an amendment, and it related to the appellate jurisdiction of this court over judgments and decrees of State courts. * * *

The proposition is that by a fair construction of the act of 1867 this court must, when it obtains jurisdiction of a case decided in a State court, by reason of one of the questions stated in the act, proceed to decide every other question which the case presents which may be found necessary to a final judgment on the whole merits. To this has been added the further suggestion that in determining whether the question on which the jurisdiction of this court depends has been raised in any given case, we are not limited to the record which comes to us from the State court * * * but we may resort to any such method of ascertaining what was really done in the State court as this court may think proper, even to *ex parte* affidavits.

When the case standing at the head of this opinion came on to be argued, it was insisted by counsel for defendants in error that none of the questions were involved in the case necessary to give jurisdiction to this court, either under the act of 1789 or of 1867, and that if they were, there were other questions exclusively of State court cognizance which were sufficient to dispose of the case, and that, therefore, the writ of error should be dismissed.

Counsel for plaintiffs in error, on the other hand, argued that not only was there a question in the case decided against them which authorized the writ of error from this court under either act, but that this court having for this reason obtained jurisdiction of the case, should re-examine all the questions found in the record, though some of them might be questions of general common law or equity, or raised by State statutes, unaffected by any principle of Federal law, constitutional or otherwise.

When, after argument, the court came to consider the case in consultation, it was found that it could not be disposed of without ignoring or deciding some of these propositions, and it became apparent that the time had arrived when the court must decide upon the effect of the act of 1867 on the jurisdiction of this court as it had been supposed to be established by the twenty-fifth section of the act of 1789.

That we might have all the aid which could be had from discussion of counsel, the court ordered a reargument of the case on three distinct questions which it propounded, and invited argument, both oral and written, from any counsel interested in them.   This reargument was had, and the court was fortunate in obtaining the assistance of very eminent and very able jurists.[1]
* * *

With all the aid we have had from counsel, and with the fullest consideration we have been able to give the subject, we are free to confess that its difficulties are many and embarrassing, and in the results we are about to announce we have not been able to arrive at entire harmony of opinion.

The questions propounded by the court for discussion by counsel were these:

1.   Does the second section of the act of February 5th, 1867, repeal all or any part of the twenty-fifth section of the act of 1789, commonly called the Judiciary Act?[2]

2.   Is it the true intent and meaning of the act of 1867, above referred to, that when this court has jurisdiction of a case, by reason of any of the questions therein mentioned, it shall proceed to decide all the questions presented by the record which are necessary to a final judgment or decree?

3.   If this question be answered affirmatively, does the Constitution of the United States authorize Congress to confer such a jurisdiction on this court?
* * *

* * *

2.   The affirmative of the second question propounded above is founded upon the effect of the omission or repeal of the last sentence of the twenty-fifth section of the act of 1789.   That clause in express terms limited the power of the Supreme Court in reversing the judgment of a State court, to errors apparent on the face of the record and which respected questions, that for the sake of brevity, though not with strict verbal accuracy, we shall call Federal questions, namely, those in regard to the validity or construction of the Constitution, treaties, statutes, commissions, or authority of the Federal government.

The argument may be thus stated: 1. That the Constitution declares that the judicial power of the United States shall extend to *cases* of a character which includes the questions described in the section, and that by the word *case* is to be understood all of the cases in which such a question arises.   2. That by the fair construction of the act of 1789 in regard to removing those cases to this court, the power and the duty of re-examining the whole case would have been devolved on the court, but for the restriction of the clause omitted in the act of 1867; and that the same language is used in the latter act regulating the removal, but omitting the restrictive clause.   And, 3. That by re-enacting the statute in the same terms as to the removal of cases from the State courts,

---

1.   [Ed.] Among counsel who argued in support of the extended jurisdiction was former Justice Benjamin R. Curtis. His brief amicus curiae is summarized at 87 U.S. (20 Wall.) at 602–06 and printed in Curtis, Jurisdiction, Practice and Peculiar Jurisprudence of the Courts of the United States 54–58 (1880).

2.   [Ed.] The Court answered this first question in the affirmative.

without the restrictive clause, Congress is to be understood as conferring the power which that clause prohibited.[3]

We will consider the last proposition first.

What were the precise motives which induced the omission of this clause it is impossible to ascertain with any degree of satisfaction. In a legislative body like Congress, it is reasonable to suppose that among those who considered this matter at all, there were varying reasons for consenting to the change. No doubt there were those who, believing that the Constitution gave no right to the Federal judiciary to go beyond the line marked by the omitted clause, thought its presence or absence immaterial; and in a revision of the statute it was wise to leave it out, because its presence implied that such a power was within the competency of Congress to bestow. There were also, no doubt, those who believed that the section standing without that clause did not confer the power which it prohibited, and that it was, therefore, better omitted. It may also have been within the thought of a few that all that is now claimed would follow the repeal of the clause. But if Congress, or the framers of the bill, had a clear purpose to enact affirmatively that the court *should consider* the class of errors which that clause forbids, nothing hindered that they should say so in positive terms; and in reversing the policy of the government from its foundation in one of the most important subjects on which that body could act, it is reasonably to be expected that Congress would use plain, unmistakable language in giving expression to such intention.

There is, therefore, no sufficient reason for holding that Congress, by repealing or omitting this restrictive clause, intended to enact affirmatively the thing which that clause had prohibited. * * *

There is * * * nothing in the language of the act, as far as we have criticized it, which in express terms defines the extent of the re-examination which this court shall give to such cases.

But we have not yet considered the most important part of the statute, namely, that which declares that it is only upon the existence of certain questions in the case that this court can entertain jurisdiction at all. Nor is the mere existence of such a question in the case sufficient to give jurisdiction—the question must have been *decided* in the State court. Nor is it sufficient that such a question was raised and was decided. It must have been decided in a certain way, that is, against the right set up under the Constitution, laws, treaties, or authority of the United States. The Federal question may have been erroneously decided. It may be quite apparent to this court that a wrong construction has been given to the Federal law, but if the right claimed under it by plaintiff in error has been conceded to him, this court cannot entertain jurisdiction of the case, so very careful is the statute, both of 1789 and of 1867, to narrow, to limit, and define the jurisdiction which this court exercises over the judgments of the State courts. Is it consistent with this extreme caution to suppose that Congress intended, when those cases came here, that this court should not only examine those questions, but all others found in the record?—questions of common law, of State statutes, of controverted facts, and conflicting evidence. Or is it the more reasonable inference that Congress intended that the case should be brought here that *those questions* might be decided and *finally* decided by the court established by the Constitution of the Union, and the court which has always been supposed to be

---

3. [Ed.] For the text of this change, see pp. 492–93, *supra.*

not only the most appropriate but the only proper tribunal for their final decision? No such reason nor any necessity exists for the decision by this court of other questions in those cases. The jurisdiction has been exercised for nearly a century without serious inconvenience to the due administration of justice. The State courts are the appropriate tribunals, as this court has repeatedly held, for the decision of questions arising under their local law, whether statutory or otherwise. And it is not lightly to be presumed that Congress acted upon a principle which implies a distrust of their integrity or of their ability to construe those laws correctly.

Let us look for a moment into the effect of the proposition contended for upon the cases as they come up for consideration in the conference-room. If it is found that no such question is raised or decided in the court below, then all will concede that it must be dismissed for want of jurisdiction. But if it is found that the Federal question was raised and was decided against the plaintiff in error, then the first duty of the court obviously is to determine whether it was correctly decided by the State court. Let us suppose that we find that the court below was right in its decision on that question. What, then, are we to do? Was it the intention of Congress to say that while you can only bring the case here on account of this question, yet when it is here, though it may turn out that the plaintiff in error was wrong on that question, and the judgment of the court below was right, though he has wrongfully dragged the defendant into this court by the allegation of an error which did not exist, and without which the case could not rightfully be here, he can still insist on an inquiry into all the other matters which were litigated in the case? This is neither reasonable nor just.

In such case both the nature of the jurisdiction conferred and the nature and fitness of things demand that, no error being found in the matter which authorized the re-examination, the judgment of the State court should be affirmed, and the case remitted to that court for its further enforcement.

* * * We are of opinion that upon a fair construction of the whole language of the section the jurisdiction conferred is limited to the decision of the questions mentioned in the statute, and, as a necessary consequence of this, to the exercise of such powers as may be necessary to cause the judgment in that decision to be respected.

We will now advert to one or two considerations apart from the mere language of the statute, which seem to us to give additional force to this conclusion.

It has been many times decided by this court, on motions to dismiss this class of cases for want of jurisdiction, that if it appears from the record that the plaintiff in error raised and presented to the court * * * one of the questions specified in the statute, and the court ruled against him, the jurisdiction of this court attached, and we must hear the case on its merits. Heretofore these merits have been held to be to determine whether the propositions of law involved in the specific Federal question were rightly decided, and if not, did the *case* of plaintiff in error, on the pleadings and evidence, come within the principle ruled by this court. This has always been held to be the exercise of the jurisdiction and re-examination of the case provided by the statute. But if when we once get jurisdiction, everything in the case is open to re-examination, it follows that every case tried in any State court, from that of a justice of the peace to the highest court of the State, may be brought to this court for final decision on all the points involved in it. * * *

It is impossible to believe that Congress intended this result, and equally impossible that they did not see that it would follow if they intended to open the cases that are brought here under this section to re-examination on all the points involved in them and necessary to a final judgment on the merits.

The twenty-fifth section of the act of 1789 has been the subject of innumerable decisions * * *. These form a system of appellate jurisprudence relating to the exercise of the appellate power of this court over the courts of the States. That system has been based upon the fundamental principle that this jurisdiction was limited to the correction of errors relating solely to Federal law. And though it may be argued with some plausibility that the reason of this is to be found in the restrictive clause of the act of 1789, which is omitted in the act of 1867, yet an examination of the cases will show that it rested quite as much on the conviction of this court that without that clause and on general principles the jurisdiction extended no further. It requires a very bold reach of thought, and a readiness to impute to Congress a radical and hazardous change of a policy vital in its essential nature to the independence of the State courts, to believe that that body contemplated, or intended, what is claimed, by the mere omission of a clause in the substituted statute, which may well be held to have been superfluous, or nearly so, in the old one.

Another consideration, not without weight in seeking after the intention of Congress, is found in the fact that where that body has clearly shown an intention to bring the whole of a case which arises under the constitutional provision as to its subject-matter under the jurisdiction of a Federal court, it has conferred its cognizance on Federal courts of original jurisdiction and not on the Supreme Court.

* * * It was no doubt the purpose of Congress to secure to every litigant whose rights depended on any question of Federal law that that question should be decided for him by the highest Federal tribunal if he desired it, when the decisions of the State courts were against him on that question. That rights of this character, guaranteed to him by the Constitution and laws of the Union, should not be left to the exclusive and final control of the State courts.

There may be some plausibility in the argument that these rights cannot be protected in all cases unless the Supreme Court has final control of the whole case. But the experience of eighty-five years of the administration of the law under the opposite theory would seem to be a satisfactory answer to the argument. It is not to be presumed that the State courts, where the rule is clearly laid down to them on the Federal question, and its influence on the case fully seen, will disregard or overlook it, and this is all that the rights of the party claiming under it require. Besides, by the very terms of this statute, when the Supreme Court is of opinion that the question of Federal law is of such relative importance to the whole case that it should control the final judgment, that court is authorized to render such judgment and enforce it by its own process. It cannot, therefore, be maintained that it is in any case necessary for the security of the rights claimed under the Constitution, laws, or treaties of the United States that the Supreme Court should examine and decide other questions not of a Federal character.

And we are of opinion that the act of 1867 does not confer such a jurisdiction.

This renders unnecessary a decision of the question whether if Congress had conferred such authority, the act would have been constitutional. It will be time enough for this court to inquire into the existence of such a power when that body has attempted to exercise it in language which makes such an intention so clear as to require it. * * *

It is proper, in this first attempt to construe this important statute as amended, to say a few words on another point. What shall be done by this court when the question has been found to exist in the record, and to have been decided against the plaintiff in error, and *rightfully* decided, we have already seen, and it presents no difficulties.

But when it appears that the Federal question was decided erroneously against the plaintiff in error, we must then reverse the case undoubtedly, if there are no other issues decided in it than that. It often has occurred, however, and will occur again, that there are other points in the case than those of Federal cognizance, on which the judgment of the court below may stand; those points being of themselves sufficient to control the case.

Or it may be, that there are other issues in the case, but they are not of such controlling influence on the whole case that they are alone sufficient to support the judgment.

It may also be found that notwithstanding there are many other questions in the record of the case, the issue raised by the Federal question is such that its decision must dispose of the whole case.

In the two latter instances there can be no doubt that the judgment of the State court must be reversed, and under the new act this court can either render the final judgment or decree here, or remand the case to the State court for that purpose.

But in the other cases supposed, why should a judgment be reversed for an error in deciding the Federal question, if the same judgment must be rendered on the other points in the case? And why should this court reverse a judgment which is right on the whole record presented to us; or where the same judgment will be rendered by the court below, after they have corrected the error in the Federal question?

We have already laid down the rule that we are not authorized to examine these other questions for the purpose of deciding whether the State court ruled correctly on them or not. We are of opinion that on these subjects not embraced in the class of questions stated in the statute, we must receive the decision of the State courts as conclusive.

But when we find that the State court has decided the Federal question erroneously, then to prevent a useless and profitless reversal, which can do the plaintiff in error no good, and can only embarrass and delay the defendant, we must so far look into the remainder of the record as to see whether the decision of the Federal question alone is sufficient to dispose of the case, or to require its reversal; or on the other hand, whether there exist other matters in the record actually decided by the State court which are sufficient to maintain the judgment of that court, notwithstanding the error in deciding the Federal question. In the latter case the court would not be justified in reversing the judgment of the State court.

But this examination into the points in the record other than the Federal question is not for the purpose of determining whether they were correctly or erroneously decided, but to ascertain if any such have been decided, and their sufficiency to maintain the final judgment, as decided by the State court.

* * *

Finally, we hold the following propositions on this subject as flowing from the statute as it now stands:

1.   That it is essential to the jurisdiction of this court over the judgment of a State court, that it shall appear that one of the questions mentioned in the act must have been raised, and presented to the State court.

2.   That it must have been decided by the State court, or that its decision was necessary to the judgment or decree, rendered in the case.

3.   That the decision must have been against the right claimed or asserted by plaintiff in error under the Constitution, treaties, laws, or authority of the United States.

4.   These things appearing, this court has jurisdiction and must examine the judgment so far as to enable it to decide whether this claim of right was correctly adjudicated by the State court.

5.   If it finds that it was rightly decided, the judgment must be affirmed.

6.   If it was erroneously decided against plaintiff in error, then this court must further inquire, whether there is any other matter or issue adjudged by the State court, which is sufficiently broad to maintain the judgment of that court, notwithstanding the error in deciding the issue raised by the Federal question.   If this is found to be the case, the judgment must be affirmed without inquiring into the soundness of the decision on such other matter or issue.

7.   But if it be found that the issue raised by the question of Federal law is of such controlling character that its correct decision is necessary to any final judgment in the case, or that there has been no decision by the State court of any other matter or issue which is sufficient to maintain the judgment of that court without regard to the Federal question, then this court will reverse the judgment of the State court, and will either render such judgment here as the State court should have rendered, or remand the case to that court, as the circumstances of the case may require.[4]

Applying the principles here laid down to the case now before the court, we are of opinion that this court has jurisdiction, and that the judgment of the Supreme Court of Tennessee must be affirmed.   * * *

* * * The complainants, in their bill, and throughout the case, insisted that the effect of the act of 1854 was to vest the title in the mayor or aldermen of the city in trust for them.

It may be very true that it is not easy to see anything in the deed by which the United States received the title from the city, or the act by which they ceded it back, which raises such a trust, but the complainants claimed a right under this act of the United States, which was decided against them by the Supreme Court of Tennessee, and this claim gives jurisdiction of that question to this court.

---

4.   [Ed.] Do Justice Miller's seven propositions represent the Court's contemporary practice?   Return to this question after reading Sec. 2(A) of this Chapter.

But we need not consume many words to prove that neither by the deed of the city to the United States, which is an ordinary deed of bargain and sale for a valuable consideration, nor from anything found in the act of 1854, is there any such trust to be inferred.   The act, so far from recognizing or implying any such trust, cedes the property to the mayor and aldermen *for the use of the city*. We are, therefore, of opinion that this, the only Federal question in the case, was rightly decided by the Supreme Court of Tennessee.

But conceding this to be true, the plaintiffs in error have argued that the court having jurisdiction of the case must now examine it upon all the questions which affect its merits; and they insist that the conveyance by which the city of Memphis received the title previous to the deed from the city to the government, and the circumstances attending the making of the former deed are such, that when the title reverted to the city, a trust was raised for the benefit of plaintiffs.

After what has been said in the previous part of this opinion, we need discuss this matter no further.   The claim of right here set up is one to be determined by the general principles of equity jurisprudence, and is unaffected by anything found in the Constitution, laws, or treaties of the United States. Whether decided well or otherwise by the State court, we have no authority to inquire.   According to the principles we have laid down as applicable to this class of cases, the judgment of the Supreme Court of Tennessee must be Affirmed.

■ MR. JUSTICE CLIFFORD, with whom concurred MR. JUSTICE SWAYNE, dissenting:

I dissent from so much of the opinion of the court as denies the jurisdiction of this court to determine the whole case, where it appears that the record presents a Federal question and that the Federal question was erroneously decided to the prejudice of the plaintiff in error; as in that state of the record it is, in my judgment, the duty of this court, under the recent act of Congress, to decide the whole merits of the controversy, and to affirm or reverse the judgment of the State court. * * *

■ MR. JUSTICE BRADLEY, dissenting: * * *

* * * I deem it very doubtful whether the court has any jurisdiction at all over this particular case.   The complainants claim the property in question under the terms, and what they regard as the true construction, of the trust-deed of July, 1844 * * *.

* * * Proving that the government did not appropriate the land for a navy yard is a very different thing from setting up a claim to the land under an act of Congress.

I think, therefore, that in this case there was no title or right claimed by the appellants under any statute of, or authority exercised under, the United States; and consequently that there was no decision against any such title; and, therefore, that this court has no jurisdiction.

But supposing, as the majority of the court holds, that it has jurisdiction, I cannot concur in the conclusion that we can only decide the Federal question raised by the record.   If we have jurisdiction at all, in my judgment we have jurisdiction of the *case,* and not merely of a *question* in it. * * *

* * * The clause by its presence in the original act meant something, and effected something.   * * * The omission of the clause, according to a well-

settled rule of construction, must necessarily have the effect of removing the restriction which it effected in the old law.

In my judgment, therefore, if the court had jurisdiction of the case, it was bound to consider not only the Federal question raised by the record, but the whole case. As the court, however, has decided otherwise, it is not proper that I should express any opinion on the merits.

The case having been reargued, as well as argued originally, before the appointment of the Chief Justice, he took no part in the judgment.

———

NOTE ON MURDOCK v. MEMPHIS

(1) *Murdock and Reconstruction.* Is it possible that the Reconstruction Congress was so highly mistrustful of state courts that it did mean to authorize Supreme Court review of state court issues? See generally Matasar & Bruch, *Procedural Common Law, Federal Jurisdictional Policy, and Abandonment of the Adequate and Independent State Grounds Doctrine*, 86 Colum.L.Rev. 1291, 1319 (1986). Although Murdock concerned only the second section of the Act of 1867, is it relevant in construing that section to note that the first section of the Act gave the federal courts, for the first time, a general power to issue writs of habeas corpus to state prisoners? See Chap. XI, Sec. 1, p. 1341, *infra*; see generally Wiecek, *Murdock v. Memphis: Section 25 of the 1789 Judiciary Act and Judicial Federalism*, in Marcus (ed.), Origins of the Federal Judiciary 223 (1992).[1] Was the Court justified in requiring a clearer statement than the Act's deletion of the restrictive language of section 25? What could Congress have said that would have been clearer? Would a statute mandating the contrary result in Murdock have been constitutional?

(2) *Appellate vs. Original Federal Jurisdiction.* On the constitutional question, the Curtis brief (p. 512, note 1, *supra*) asserted: "Unless, therefore, some distinction can be made between the power of Congress to confer original and appellate jurisdiction, and neither the Constitution nor the decisions of this court permit this distinction, it is clear that Congress may confer appellate power over all cases to which the judicial power of the United States extends, and is not restricted by the Constitution to particular questions, by reason of which the cases are brought within the judicial power * * *."[2]

Note that where a federal court exercises original jurisdiction, it must decide the entire case, including state-law questions, in order to come to

---

1. Wiecek argues that the legislative history of the 1867 Act is unilluminating; concludes that Congress, in deleting the proviso to Section 25, may have approved a bill with far-reaching effects on American federalism without knowing what it was doing; observes that many commentators believe that Congress did intend the expansion of jurisdiction implicit in deletion of Section 25' proviso; views Murdock as one of a group of decisions in the 1870s that narrowed federal jurisdiction and retreated from federal protection of the newly freed slaves; and asserts that the Court, already feeling overworked,

was leery of taking on the added caseload that a contrary decision in Murdock would have generated. He concludes, however, that Murdock "was * * * a godsend for the American federal system" (p. 243).

2. *Cf.* 2 Crosskey, Politics and the Constitution in the History of the United States 711–817 (1953), arguing on a much broader basis for the Court's power to decide state law. But see Hart, *The Relations Between State and Federal Law*, 54 Colum.L.Rev. 489, 499–506 (1954).

judgment. When the Supreme Court exercises appellate jurisdiction, however, the state courts have, by hypothesis, already decided the state law question (or will on remand), and Supreme Court decision of the question is not necessary for complete adjudication. There is, therefore, a fundamental structural difference between original and appellate adjudication that the Curtis syllogism ignores.[3]

(3) *The Dissent's Position.* Suppose Murdock had been decided the other way, leaving the Supreme Court free (in a case otherwise within its appellate jurisdiction) to review a state's highest court on an issue of state law. What would be the future authority of such a Supreme Court determination, if the identical issue of state law arose:

(a) in the state's courts, in a case that did not involve any issue of federal law and was not otherwise within the federal judicial power?

(b) in the state's courts, in a case that, because there was a federal question presented, would potentially be subject to the Supreme Court's appellate jurisdiction?

(c) in the state's courts, in a case in which there was no federal question but there was diversity of citizenship?

(d) in a federal district court of that state, in a diversity action in which there was not (or, alternatively, there was) also a federal question?

(e) in a state court of a second state that, under applicable choice of law principles, would apply the law of the first state, and in which there was not (or, alternatively, there was) also a federal question?

Do these questions shed light on the correctness of Murdock as a matter of statutory interpretation? On whether the dissent's interpretation of the jurisdictional statute was constitutionally permissible?

Compare Field, *The Differing Federalisms of Canada and the United States*, 55 L. & Cont.Prob. 107 (1992)(noting that in Canada's federal system, the highest national court—the Canadian Supreme Court—has authority to review decisions of the provincial courts even on issues of provincial law).

(4) *Murdock and Erie.* The Court's clear recognition in Murdock that it lacks authority to review a state court on issues of state law should be contrasted with its conclusion in Swift v. Tyson, Ch. VI, Sec. 2, p. 676, *infra*, that the federal courts sitting in diversity need not follow state court decisions on issues of common law. What explains the two different developments?

(5) *"Antecedent" vs. "Independent" State Law Grounds.* In Murdock, the state trust law issue was logically (and functionally) quite independent of any issue of federal law; answering the state law question was not a necessary antecedent to any question of federal law. Put differently, if the Supreme Court had resolved the federal issue in favor of Murdock (the purported federal rightholder), he would have obtained all the relief he sought, regardless of the state court resolution of non-federal issues of trust law.

In Martin v. Hunter's Lessee, by contrast, the state law question (when did title vest in Virginia?) was an essential antecedent to the application of the

---

3. Consider, for example, whether the federal courts' undoubted constitutional power to entertain a diversity action based entirely on state law necessarily implies that the Supreme Court could exercise appellate jurisdiction over such an action that had been litigated in a state court. If so, what issues could the Court review?

federal treaty provisions giving protection to then-existing land titles. Put differently, to obtain the relief he sought, Martin had to prevail on both the state law issue (that his chain of title had not been divested at the time of the Treaty of Peace) and the federal law issue (that the Treaty protected that title against the Act of Compromise or other efforts to divest it).

The distinction between these two types of cases is critical to an understanding of this area of the law. Where the state issue is wholly independent, as in Murdock, is there any plausible argument that the Supreme Court needs power to review the correctness of the state ruling? On the other hand, where a state law ruling serves as an antecedent for determining whether a federal right has been violated, some review of the basis for the state court's determination of the state-law question is essential if the federal right is to be protected against evasion and discrimination—as Martin itself exemplifies. See Wechsler, *The Appellate Jurisdiction of the Supreme Court: Reflections on the Law and Logistics of Direct Review*, 34 Wash. & Lee L.Rev. 1043, 1050–56 (1977).

In evaluating revisionist proposals to abandon the "independent state ground" rule of Murdock, consider whether they overlook or slight this fundamental distinction and assume that *all* rulings on state law in cases where there is a federal question fall into the Martin category? See, *e.g.*, Matasar & Bruch, Paragraph (1), *supra*. Indeed, consider whether more systematic emphasis on this distinction would illuminate questions about the relation of state law (substantive and procedural) and federal law discussed in Section 2 of this Chapter.

SECTION 2. THE RELATION BETWEEN STATE AND FEDERAL LAW
SUBSECTION A: SUBSTANTIVE LAW

INTRODUCTORY NOTE: THE INTERSTITIAL
CHARACTER OF FEDERAL LAW

The First Edition of this book contained the following discussion:

"Federal law is generally interstitial in its nature. It rarely occupies a legal field completely, totally excluding all participation by the legal systems of the states. This was plainly true in the beginning when the federal legislative product (including the Constitution) was extremely small. It is significantly true today, despite the volume of Congressional enactments, and even within areas where Congress has been very active. Federal legislation, on the whole, has been conceived and drafted on an *ad hoc* basis to accomplish limited objectives. It builds upon legal relationships established by the states, altering or supplanting them only so far as necessary for the special purpose. Congress acts, in short, against the background of the total *corpus juris* of the states in much the way that a state legislature acts against the background of the common law, assumed to govern unless changed by legislation.

"That this is so was partially affirmed in § 34 of the First Judiciary Act, now 28 U.S.C. § 1652, but an attentive canvass of the total product of the Congress would establish its surprising generality and force. Indeed, the strength of the conception of the central government as one of delegated, limited authority is most significantly manifested on this mundane plane of working, legislative practice.

"The point involved is vital to appreciation of the legal issues posed by the materials in this and later chapters (especially [Chapters VI and VII]), concerned with the relationship between the law of the United States and of the states. It explains why frequently in litigation federal law bears only partially upon the case: the basis of a right asserted by the plaintiff which is open to defenses grounded in state law, the basis of a defense when a state-created right has been advanced, the foundation of a replication to a state defense or only of the rejoinder to a replication that would otherwise be good. It explains why federal law often embodies concepts that derive their content, or some portion of their content, from the states. It makes it less anomalous, at least, that substantive rights may be defined by Congress but the remedies for their enforcement left undefined or relegated wholly to the states; or that *per contra* national law may do no more than formulate remedies for vindicating rights that have their source and definition in state law.

"The diversity of these relationships is shown most plainly in cases that reach the Supreme Court from the authorized expositors of state law, the state courts."

In the 40 years since the First Edition was published, the process of expansion of federal legislation and administrative regulation noted in this discussion has continued if not accelerated. Today one finds many more instances in which federal enactments supply both right and remedy in, or wholly occupy, a particular field. This same period witnessed a broad extension of federal laws (constitutional and statutory) that protect individual rights and provide remedies for violations thereof. Thus, today federal law appears to be more primary than interstitial in numerous areas. Nonetheless, consider, in reading the material in this Section, whether the First Edition's thesis does not remain accurate over an extremely broad range of applications.[1]

Fox Film Corp. v. Muller

296 U.S. 207, 56 S.Ct. 183, 80 L.Ed. 158 (1935).
Certiorari to the Supreme Court of Minnesota.

■ MR. JUSTICE SUTHERLAND delivered the opinion of the Court.

This is an action brought in a Minnesota state court of first instance by the Film Corporation against Muller, to recover damages for an alleged breach of two contracts by which Muller was licensed to exhibit certain moving picture films belonging to the corporation. Muller answered, setting up the invalidity of the contracts under the Sherman Anti–Trust Act (15 U.S.C.A. §§ 1–7, 15 note). It was and is agreed that these contracts are substantially the same as

---

1. See generally, Hart, *The Relations Between State and Federal Law*, 54 Colum.L.Rev. 489 (1954). For analysis of relevant institutional factors, see, *e.g.*, Wechsler, *The Political Safeguards of Federalism: The Role of the States in the Composition and Selection of the National Government*, 54 Colum.L.Rev. 543 (1954); Choper, Judicial Review and the National Political Process (1980); Kaden, *Politics, Money, and State Sovereignty: The Judicial Role*, 79 Colum.L.Rev. 847 (1979); Kramer, *Understanding Federalism*, 47 Vand.L.Rev. 1485 (1994); Shapiro, Federalism: A Dialogue (1995).

the one involved in United States v. Paramount Famous Lasky Corporation et al., (D.C.) 34 F.2d 984, affirmed 282 U.S. 30; that petitioner was one of the defendants in that action; and that the "arbitration clause," paragraph 18 of each of the contracts sued upon, is the same as that held in that case to be invalid. * * *

The court of first instance held that each contract sued upon violated the Sherman Anti–Trust Act, and dismissed the action. In a supplemental opinion, that court put its decision upon the grounds, first, that the arbitration plan is so connected with the remainder of the contract that the entire contract is tainted; and, second, that the contract violates the Sherman Anti–Trust law. The state Supreme Court affirmed. * * *

In its opinion, the state Supreme Court, after a statement of the case, said: "The question presented on this appeal is whether the arbitration clause is severable from the contract, leaving the remainder of the contract enforceable or not severable, permeating and tainting the whole contract with illegality and making it void." That court then proceeded to refer to and discuss a number of decisions of state and federal courts, some of which took the view that the arbitration clause was severable, and others that it was not severable, from the remainder of the contract. After reviewing the opinion and decree of the federal District Court in the Paramount Case, the lower court reached the conclusion that the holding of the federal court was that the entire contract was illegal; and upon that view and upon what it conceived to be the weight of authority, held the arbitration plan was inseparable from the other provisions of the contract. Whether this conclusion was right or wrong we need not determine. It is enough that it is, at least, not without fair support.

Respondent contends that the question of severability was alone decided and that no federal question was determined by the lower court. This contention petitioner challenges, and asserts that a federal question was involved and decided. We do not attempt to settle the dispute; but, assuming for present purposes only that petitioner's view is the correct one, the case is controlled by the settled rule that where the judgment of a state court rests upon two grounds, one of which is federal and the other nonfederal in character, our jurisdiction fails if the nonfederal ground is independent of the federal ground and adequate to support the judgment. This rule had become firmly fixed at least as early as Klinger v. State of Missouri, 13 Wall. 257, 263, and has been reiterated in a long line of cases since that time. [Citing numerous decisions.]

Whether the provisions of a contract are nonseverable, so that if one be held invalid the others must fall with it, is clearly a question of general and not of federal law. The invalidity of the arbitration clause which the present contracts embody is conceded. It was held invalid by the federal District Court in the Paramount Case, and its judgment was affirmed here. * * * [T]he primary question to be determined by the court below was whether the concededly invalid clause was separable from the other provisions of the contract. The ruling of the state Supreme Court that it was not, is sufficient to conclude the case without regard to the determination, if, in fact, any was made, in respect of the federal question. It follows that the nonfederal ground is adequate to sustain the judgment.

The rule announced in *Enterprise Irr. Dist. v. Farmers' Mut. Canal Co.,* *supra,* and other cases, to the effect that our jurisdiction attaches where the nonfederal ground is so interwoven with the other as not to be an independent matter, does not apply. The construction put upon the contracts did not constitute a preliminary step which simply had the effect of bringing forward for determination the federal question, but was a decision which automatically took the federal question out of the case if otherwise it would be there. The nonfederal question in respect of the construction of the contracts and the federal question in respect of their validity under the Anti–Trust Act were clearly independent of one another. The case, in effect, was disposed of before the federal question said to be involved was reached. A decision of that question then became unnecessary; and whether it was decided or not, our want of jurisdiction is clear.

Writ dismissed for want of jurisdiction.

The Chief Justice took no part in the consideration or decision of this case.

PRELIMINARY NOTE ON THE INDEPENDENT AND ADEQUATE STATE GROUND

(1) *Early Development.* In the early decisions after Murdock, the rule that the Court would not review a judgment that rested on an adequate and independent state ground was apparently regarded merely as prudential (why should the Court engage in review that could not affect the judgment?). Later cases placed the rule squarely on lack of jurisdiction. See, *e.g.,* Enterprise Irrigation Dist. v. Farmers' Mut. Canal Co., 243 U.S. 157, 164 (1917)(where a nonfederal ground is sufficient to sustain the judgment, "we have no power to disturb it"). Indeed, in Herb v. Pitcairn, 324 U.S. 117, 126 (1945), the Court suggested that the jurisdictional barrier might be not merely statutory but constitutional: "our power is to correct wrong judgments, not to revise opinions. * * * [I]f the same judgment would be rendered by the state court after we corrected its view of federal laws, our review could amount to nothing more than an advisory opinion." For endorsements of this suggestion, see, *e.g.,* Coleman v. Thompson, 501 U.S. 722 (1991); Ake v. Oklahoma, 470 U.S. 68, 75 (1985).

Because a finding that a state-court judgment rests on an independent and adequate state-law ground implies that the Court lacks jurisdiction to review, the proper disposition is to dismiss for lack of jurisdiction, rather than to affirm (as Murdock itself suggested); and this has been the Court's practice since Eustis v. Bolles, 150 U.S. 361 (1893). Today, when a litigant petitions unsuccessfully for a writ of certiorari, the Court ordinarily will simply deny the petition without noting a reason, jurisdictional or otherwise.

(2) *Application of the Rule.* The rule that the Supreme Court will not review a federal question when, because of the state court's decision of issues of state law, federal review could not affect the outcome, has in principle been quite uncontroversial. But its administration engenders impressive difficulties and requires careful analysis of the relationship of state and federal law in the case at hand.[1]

---

1. See generally Hill, *The Inadequate State Ground*, 65 Colum.L.Rev. 943 (1965); Wechsler, *The Appellate Jurisdiction of the Supreme Court: Reflections on the Law and* *Logistics of Direct Review*, 4 Wash. & Lee L.Rev. 1043 (1977); Note, 74 Harv.L.Rev. 1375 (1961).

In performing that analysis, it is critical to keep in mind the key distinction (discussed at pp. 520–21, Paragraph (5), *supra*, and also noted in the last substantive paragraph of the Fox Film opinion) between (i) state law as antecedent to federal law and (ii) state law as independent of federal law.

(3) *State Law as Antecedent to Federal Law.* Cases like Martin v. Hunter's Lessee, in which state law is antecedent to the federal question, are relatively straightforward. If the state court denies relief to the federal rightholder by deciding the issue of state law adversely, and that ground is broad enough to support the judgment, then the Supreme Court has no jurisdiction. Review and reversal of the federal question in such a case would not change the judgment, since the rightholder must prevail on both state and federal grounds to obtain relief.[2] The hard question here, explored at pp. 551–65, 571–90, *infra*, is whether the state ground is adequate to support the judgment. And resolution of that question may require some review by the Supreme Court of the correctness of the state court's decision of state law issues (as in Martin) to ensure that federal rights are not being blocked by serious misapplications of state law.

Note, however, that if in cases like these the state court resolves the state law issue *in favor* of the federal rightholder, it must then reach the federal issue—and whichever way that issue is resolved, the Supreme Court has jurisdiction to review. Thus, federal reviewability often depends on who prevailed on the state law issue in state court.

(4) *State Law as Independent of Federal Law.* More complex possibilities are posed by cases like Fox Film and Murdock, in which state law is independent of federal law, so that the federal rightholder can obtain the relief sought by prevailing on *either* state or federal grounds. Suppose, for example, that a state tax statute is challenged, in a state-court refund action, as violative of both the federal and state constitutions.

(a) If the state supreme court holds the tax invalid solely under the state constitution, refusing to reach the federal question, there is clearly no jurisdiction to review. (This situation parallels that in Fox Film, on the defendant's view of the state court's decision in that case. Do you see why?)

(b) If the state supreme court holds the tax invalid under the federal constitution and also independently invalid under the state constitution, there is no jurisdiction to review. (This situation parallels that in Fox Film, on the plaintiff's view of the state court's decision in that case. Do you see why?)

Should one be concerned that in these cases state courts may put forth interpretations of federal law that are erroneous but unreviewable, and that might mislead litigants or other courts? Is correcting such errors reason enough to justify Supreme Court review, even though whatever the Court decides as to the federal issue, the taxpayer ultimately would get a refund?

---

2. This principle has been recognized in a variety of decisions refusing to review state court judgments resting on lack of remedial authority or similar quasi-procedural grounds. See, *e.g.,* Utley v. City of St. Petersburg, 292 U.S. 106 (1934)(laches is an adequate state ground); Enterprise Irrigation District v. Farmers' Mutual Canal Co., 243 U.S. 157 (1917)(estoppel is an adequate state ground); Wood v. Chesborough, 228 U.S. 672 (1913)(limitations is an adequate state ground); Coombes v. Getz, 217 Cal. 320, 18 P.2d 939 (1933), upon remand after reversal by the Supreme Court, 285 U.S. 434 (1932). The same principle operates when there is an antecedent state law *procedural* ground—ordinarily, that the party seeking Supreme Court review failed to raise the federal question in accordance with state procedural rules. See Sec. 2(B), *infra*.

Since the taxpayer would clearly prevail in the end, what incentive would there be for either party to litigate the federal question? *If* that same federal issue might again arise in future litigation in which both parties are interested, perhaps both sides would vigorously argue the point. But ordinarily wouldn't there be a serious risk that the federal question, if reviewed by the Supreme Court, would not be properly briefed and argued? But see Matasar & Bruch, p. 519, *supra* (discounting these risks and advocating review in just such a case).

(c) If the state court holds the tax statute *valid* under both constitutions, the state ground cannot independently support the judgment, and the federal-law ruling is plainly subject to review.

(d) If the state court invalidates the tax statute under the federal Constitution without considering the state-law issue, the settled rule is that the judgment is reviewable: the Supreme Court's jurisdiction depends on the state court's actual grounds of decision rather than on possible grounds. See, *e.g.*, Grayson v. Harris, 267 U.S. 352, 358 (1925); Regents of the Univ. of California v. Bakke, 438 U.S. 265, 279–80 (1978); Orr v. Orr, 440 U.S. 268, 274–77 (1979). If the Supreme Court reverses the state court with respect to the federal question, the proper disposition is to remand, to give the state court an opportunity to pass on the undetermined state-law issue. See, *e.g.*, California v. Ramos, 463 U.S. 992, 997–98 n. 7 (1983). The state court remains free to reinstate its prior judgment on that state-law ground. See, *e.g.*, Washington v. Chrisman, 455 U.S. 1 (1982), *reinstated on remand*, 100 Wash.2d 814, 676 P.2d 419 (1984); South Dakota v. Neville, 459 U.S. 553 (1983), *reinstated on remand*, 346 N.W.2d 425 (S.D.1984).

The Supreme Court's practice in cases like these has not, however, been uniform. On occasion the Court, rather than deciding the federal constitutional question, has instead vacated the state court judgment and remanded for consideration of possible state grounds whose decision might obviate the need to reach the constitutional question. See Kirkpatrick v. Christian Homes of Abilene, Inc., 460 U.S. 1074 (1983); Musser v. Utah, 333 U.S. 95 (1948).

In Paschall v. Christie-Stewart Inc., 414 U.S. 100 (1973), the Court declined to review a state court decision resting squarely on the Due Process Clause, instead remanding because the lawsuit might have been time-barred under state law. The case actually was one in which state law (the statute of limitations) was antecedent to the federal right (under the Due Process Clause), rather than a case like the tax refund illustration, in which state law is independent of federal law. But the Court's statement in Paschall—that if the suit was time-barred under state law, "any decision by this Court would be advisory and beyond our jurisdiction" (pp. 101–02)—has more general applicability.

Do you agree that Supreme Court review is advisory when the state court did not decide a state law issue that, had it been resolved in a particular way, would have established an independent and adequate state ground? Is an opinion always advisory if, at the end of the day, it turns out that it has not had a decisive effect on the final judgment? Even though, at the time it is rendered, it eliminates an erroneous ground on which the state court relied and that would otherwise have remained decisive? Would it be possible to administer a rule against advisory opinions that depended on advance knowledge of the final outcome of the case?

On the other hand, assuming the correctness of the Court's usual stance that it does have power to decide the federal constitutional question in such cases, might it sometimes be appropriate for the Court to seek to avoid doing so by vacating and remanding? What would justify use of this technique in some cases but not in others?[3]

(5) *The Responsibility of State Courts.* In a case like the hypothetical challenge to a state tax statute, involving a challenge on both state and federal constitutional grounds, if a state court views the tax as invalid under both the federal and state constitutions, should it rest its decision on state grounds alone, on federal grounds alone, or on both? This question has arisen more frequently in the last two decades, with the growth of state constitutional law.

Where state constitutional protections are defined independently of the content of parallel federal guarantees, does the state court have an obligation to avoid decision of the federal constitutional issue if possible?[4] May the Supreme Court impose such an obligation? May Congress? See Wechsler, note 1, *supra*, at 1056. How would such an obligation be enforced? (Presumably, the Court would vacate the state court judgment and remand with directions to decide the state law ground.[5] But note that the Court cannot, in such a case, itself enter judgment as a way of enforcing the mandate.)

(6) *Further Problems in Application.* Three further difficulties in the administration of the adequate and independent state ground rule are explored in the remaining materials in this section:

(a) Plainly, the Court's jurisdiction turns on whether a given issue in the case is properly regarded as one of federal or state law. Thus, in Fox Film itself, the finding of no jurisdiction was based on the prior determination that the issue of separability was governed by state law. Was this question as obvious as the Court seemed to think?[6]

3. In cases such as these, in which the state court did recognize a claim of federal right, Supreme Court review would serve the purpose of preventing the *overprotection* federal rights. On the question whether that should be a low priority for the Court, see Justice Stevens' opinion in Michigan v. Long (the next principal case) and the succeeding *Note on Review of State Decisions Upholding Claims of Federal Right.*

4. For analysis from the point of view of state courts' responsibilities, see Linde, *First Things First: Rediscovering the States' Bills of Rights*, 9 U.Balt.L.Rev. 379 (1980); Pollock, *State Constitutions as Separate Sources of Fundamental Rights*, 35 Rutgers L.Rev. 707 (1983). For an example of how failure to address state issues first may cause problems for the administration of the state courts, see State v. Kennedy, 295 Or. 260, 666 P.2d 1316, 1319 (1983). See also Kloppenberg, *Avoiding Constitutional Questions*, 35 B.C.L.Rev. 1003 (1994).

5. *Cf.* Massachusetts v. Upton, 466 U.S. 727 (1984), where Justice Stevens, concurring specially in a judgment reversing a state

court on the merits of a Fourth Amendment question, emphasized that the Massachusetts Supreme Judicial Court had committed "an error of a more fundamental character than the one this Court corrects today. It rested its decision on the Fourth Amendment to the United States Constitution without telling us whether the warrant was valid as a matter of Massachusetts law" (p. 735).

6. Even if the ruling of *inseparability* is correctly characterized as governed by state law, would a contrary ruling—that the rest of the contract was *severable* from the arbitration clause—be immune from review? Note that, on this hypothesis, the federal validity of the rest of the contract would in any event be reviewable. But suppose the Supreme Court agrees with a state court holding that the rest of the contract, independently viewed, is valid under the Sherman Act. Would it be foreclosed from determining whether, given the conceded invalidity of the arbitration clause, enforcing the rest of the contract violates the remedial policies of the Sherman Act?

(b) Once various issues are characterized as issues of federal or state law, the further question is whether the logical relationship between the two is such that the state law ground is "independent" of the federal for purposes of the Court's appellate jurisdiction. (Suppose, for example, that a state court rules that the state constitutional guarantee of free speech means exactly what the federal First Amendment provides—no more and no less—and then strikes down a state statute as invalid under the state's constitutional guarantee. Is the state ground truly independent of federal law? See pp. 544-51, *infra*.)

(c) Finally, a state court's opinion may not clearly indicate whether the judgment rested on an independent state-law ground, on federal law, or on both—a problem posed in the case that follows.

Michigan v. Long

463 U.S. 1032, 103 S.Ct. 3469, 77 L.Ed.2d 1201 (1983).
Certiorari to the Supreme Court of Michigan.

■ JUSTICE O'CONNOR delivered the opinion of the Court.

In Terry v. Ohio, 392 U.S. 1 (1968), we upheld the validity of a protective search for weapons in the absence of probable cause to arrest because it is unreasonable to deny a police officer the right "to neutralize the threat of physical harm," *id.*, at 24, when he possesses an articulable suspicion that an individual is armed and dangerous. We did not, however, expressly address whether such a protective search for weapons could extend to an area beyond the person in the absence of probable cause to arrest. In the present case, respondent David Long was convicted for possession of marihuana found by police in the passenger compartment and trunk of the automobile that he was driving. The police searched the passenger compartment because they had reason to believe that the vehicle contained weapons potentially dangerous to the officers. We hold that the protective search of the passenger compartment was reasonable under the principles articulated in Terry and other decisions of this Court. We also examine Long's argument that the decision below rests upon an adequate and independent state ground, and we decide in favor of our jurisdiction.

I

[The opinion here provides a detailed statement of the facts.]

The Barry County Circuit Court denied Long's motion to suppress the marihuana * * *. He was subsequently convicted of possession of marihuana. The Michigan Court of Appeals affirmed Long's conviction * * *. The Michigan Supreme Court reversed. The court held that "the sole justification of the Terry search, protection of the police officers and others nearby, cannot justify the search in this case." * * *

We granted certiorari * * *.

As you can see, in this area principles of reversibility do not always hold: a holding one way may be a "pure" state law holding, but a holding the other way may raise distinctive questions under federal law.

II

Before reaching the merits, we must consider Long's argument that we are without jurisdiction to decide this case because the decision below rests on an adequate and independent state ground. The court below referred twice to the State Constitution in its opinion, but otherwise relied exclusively on federal law.[3] Long argues that the Michigan courts have provided greater protection from searches and seizures under the State Constitution than is afforded under the Fourth Amendment, and the references to the State Constitution therefore establish an adequate and independent ground for the decision below.

It is, of course, "incumbent upon this Court * * * to ascertain for itself * * * whether the asserted non-federal ground independently and adequately supports the judgment." Abie State Bank v. Bryan, 282 U.S. 765, 773 (1931). Although we have announced a number of principles in order to help us determine whether various forms of references to state law constitute adequate and independent state grounds,[4] we openly admit that we have thus far not developed a satisfying and consistent approach for resolving this vexing issue. In some instances, we have taken the strict view that if the ground of decision was at all unclear, we would dismiss the case. See, *e.g.*, Lynch v. New York ex rel. Pierson, 293 U.S. 52 (1934). In other instances, we have vacated, see, *e.g.*, Minnesota v. National Tea Co., 309 U.S. 551 (1940), or continued a case, see, *e.g.*, Herb v. Pitcairn, 324 U.S. 117 (1945), in order to obtain clarification about the nature of a state court decision. See also California v. Krivda, 409 U.S. 33 (1972). In more recent cases, we have ourselves examined state law to determine whether state courts have used federal law to guide their application of state law or to provide the actual basis for the decision that was reached. See Texas v. Brown, 460 U.S. 730, 732–733, n. 1 (1983)(plurality opinion). *Cf.* South Dakota v. Neville, 459 U.S. 553, 569 (1983)(Stevens, J., dissenting). In Oregon v. Kennedy, 456 U.S. 667, 670–671 (1982), we rejected an invitation to remand to the state court for clarification even when the decision rested in part on a case from the state court, because we determined that the state case itself rested upon federal grounds. We added that "[e]ven if the case admitted of more doubt as to whether federal and state grounds for decision were inter-

---

3. On the first occasion, the court merely cited in a footnote both the State and Federal Constitutions. On the second occasion, at the conclusion of the opinion, the court stated: "We hold, therefore, that the deputies' search of the vehicle was proscribed by the Fourth Amendment to the United States Constitution and art. 1, § 11 of the Michigan Constitution."

4. For example, we have long recognized that "where the judgment of a state court rests upon two grounds, one of which is federal and the other non-federal in character, our jurisdiction fails if the non-federal ground is independent of the federal ground and adequate to support the judgment." Fox Film Corp. v. Muller, 296 U.S. 207, 210 (1935). We may review a state case decided on a federal ground even if it is clear that there was an available state ground for decision on which the state court could properly have relied. Beecher v. Alabama, 389 U.S. 35, 37, n. 3 (1967). Also, if, in our view, the state court "felt compelled by what it understood to be federal constitutional considerations to construe * * * its own law in the manner it did," then we will not treat a normally adequate state ground as independent, and there will be no question about our jurisdiction. Delaware v. Prouse, 440 U.S. 648, 653 (1979)(quoting Zacchini v. Scripps–Howard Broadcasting Co., 433 U.S. 562, 568 (1977)). Finally, "where the non-federal ground is so interwoven with the [federal ground] as not to be an independent matter, or is not of sufficient breadth to sustain the judgment without any decision of the other, our jurisdiction is plain." Enterprise Irrigation District v. Farmers' Mutual Canal Co., 243 U.S. 157, 164 (1917).

mixed, the fact that the state court relied to the extent it did on federal grounds requires us to reach the merits." *Id.*, at 671.

This ad hoc method of dealing with cases that involve possible adequate and independent state grounds is antithetical to the doctrinal consistency that is required when sensitive issues of federal-state relations are involved. Moreover, none of the various methods of disposition that we have employed thus far recommends itself as the preferred method that we should apply to the exclusion of others, and we therefore determine that it is appropriate to reexamine our treatment of this jurisdictional issue in order to achieve the consistency that is necessary.

The process of examining state law is unsatisfactory because it requires us to interpret state laws with which we are generally unfamiliar, and which often, as in this case, have not been discussed at length by the parties. Vacation and continuance for clarification have also been unsatisfactory both because of the delay and decrease in efficiency of judicial administration, see Dixon v. Duffy, 344 U.S. 143 (1952),[5] and, more important, because these methods of disposition place significant burdens on state courts to demonstrate the presence or absence of our jurisdiction. See Philadelphia Newspapers, Inc. v. Jerome, 434 U.S. 241, 244 (1978)(Rehnquist, J., dissenting); Department of Motor Vehicles v. Rios, 410 U.S. 425, 427 (1973)(Douglas, J., dissenting). Finally, outright dismissal of cases is clearly not a panacea because it cannot be doubted that there is an important need for uniformity in federal law, and that this need goes unsatisfied when we fail to review an opinion that rests primarily upon federal grounds and where the *independence* of an alleged state ground is not apparent from the four corners of the opinion. * * *

Respect for the independence of state courts, as well as avoidance of rendering advisory opinions, have been the cornerstones of this Court's refusal to decide cases where there is an adequate and independent state ground. It is precisely because of this respect for state courts, and this desire to avoid advisory opinions, that we do not wish to continue to decide issues of state law that go beyond the opinion that we review, or to require state courts to reconsider cases to clarify the grounds of their decisions. Accordingly, when, as in this case, a state court decision fairly appears to rest primarily on federal law, or to be interwoven with the federal law, and when the adequacy and independence of any possible state law ground is not clear from the face of the opinion, we will accept as the most reasonable explanation that the state court decided the case the way it did because it believed that federal law required it to do so. If a state court chooses merely to rely on federal precedents as it would on the precedents of all other jurisdictions, then it need only make clear by a plain statement in its judgment or opinion that the federal cases are being used only for the purpose of guidance, and do not themselves compel the result that the court has reached. * * * If the state court decision indicates clearly and expressly that it is alternatively based on bona fide separate, adequate, and independent grounds, we, of course, will not undertake to review the decision.

This approach obviates in most instances the need to examine state law in order to decide the nature of the state court decision, and will at the same time

---

5. Indeed, Dixon v. Duffy is also illustrative of another difficulty involved in our requiring state courts to reconsider their decisions for purposes of clarification. In Dixon, we continued the case on two occasions in order to obtain clarification, but none was forthcoming: "[T]he California court advised petitioner's counsel informally that it doubted its jurisdiction to render such a determination." 344 U.S., at 145. We then vacated the judgment of the state court, and remanded.

avoid the danger of our rendering advisory opinions.[6] It also avoids the unsatisfactory and intrusive practice of requiring state courts to clarify their decisions to the satisfaction of this Court. We believe that such an approach will provide state judges with a clearer opportunity to develop state jurisprudence unimpeded by federal interference, and yet will preserve the integrity of federal law. "It is fundamental that state courts be left free and unfettered by us in interpreting their state constitutions. But it is equally important that ambiguous or obscure adjudications by state courts do not stand as barriers to a determination by this Court of the validity under the federal constitution of state action." National Tea Co., *supra,* at 557.

The principle that we will not review judgments of state courts that rest on adequate and independent state grounds is based, in part, on "the limitations of our own jurisdiction." Herb v. Pitcairn, 324 U.S. 117, 125 (1945).[7] The jurisdictional concern is that we not "render an advisory opinion, and if the same judgment would be rendered by the state court after we corrected its views of federal laws, our review could amount to nothing more than an advisory opinion." *Id.,* at 126. Our requirement of a "plain statement" that a decision rests upon adequate and independent state grounds does not in any way authorize the rendering of advisory opinions. Rather, in determining, as we must, whether we have jurisdiction to review a case that is alleged to rest on adequate and independent state grounds, we merely assume that there are no such grounds when it is not clear from the opinion itself that the state court relied upon an adequate and independent state ground and when it fairly appears that the state court rested its decision primarily on federal law.[8]

Our review of the decision below under this framework leaves us unconvinced that it rests upon an independent state ground. Apart from its two

---

6. There may be certain circumstances in which clarification is necessary or desirable, and we will not be foreclosed from taking the appropriate action.

7. In Herb v. Pitcairn, 324 U.S., at 128, the Court also wrote that it was desirable that state courts "be asked rather than told what they have intended." It is clear that we have already departed from that view in those cases in which we have examined state law to determine whether a particular result was guided or compelled by federal law. Our decision today departs further from Herb insofar as we disfavor further requests to state courts for clarification, and we require a clear and express statement that a decision rests on adequate and independent state grounds. However, the "plain statement" rule protects the integrity of state courts for the reasons discussed above. The preference for clarification expressed in Herb has failed to be a completely satisfactory means of protecting the state and federal interests that are involved.

8. It is not unusual for us to employ certain presumptions in deciding jurisdictional issues. For instance, although the petitioner bears the burden of establishing our

jurisdiction, Durley v. Mayo, 351 U.S. 277, 285 (1956), we have held that the party who alleges that a controversy before us has become moot has the "heavy burden" of establishing that we lack jurisdiction. County of Los Angeles v. Davis, 440 U.S. 625, 631 (1979). That is, we presume in those circumstances that we have jurisdiction until some party establishes that we do not for reasons of mootness.

We also note that the rule that we announce today was foreshadowed by our opinions in Delaware v. Prouse, 440 U.S. 648 (1979), and Zacchini v. Scripps–Howard Broadcasting Co., 433 U.S. 562 (1977). In these cases, the state courts relied on both state and federal law. We determined that we had jurisdiction to decide the cases because our reading of the opinions led us to conclude that each court "felt compelled by what it understood to be federal constitutional considerations to construe and apply its own law in the manner it did." Zacchini, *supra,* at 568; Delaware, *supra,* at 653. In Delaware, we referred to prior state decisions that confirmed our understanding of the opinion in that case, but our primary focus was on the face of the opinion. In Zacchini,

citations to the State Constitution, the court below relied *exclusively* on its understanding of Terry and other federal cases. Not a single state case was cited to support the state court's holding that the search of the passenger compartment was unconstitutional. Indeed, the court declared that the search in this case was unconstitutional because "[t]he Court of Appeals erroneously applied the principles of Terry v. Ohio * * * to the search of the interior of the vehicle in this case." The references to the state constitution in no way indicate that the decision below rested on grounds in any way *independent* from the state court's interpretation of federal law. Even if we accept that the Michigan constitution has been interpreted to provide independent protection for certain rights also secured under the Fourth Amendment, it fairly appears in this case that the Michigan Supreme Court rested its decision primarily on federal law.

Rather than dismissing the case, or requiring that the state court reconsider its decision on our behalf solely because of a mere possibility that an adequate and independent ground supports the judgment, we find that we have jurisdiction in the absence of a plain statement that the decision below rested on an adequate and independent state ground. It appears to us that the state court "felt compelled by what it understood to be federal constitutional considerations to construe * * * its own law in the manner it did." Zacchini v. Scripps–Howard Broadcasting Co., 433 U.S. 562, 568 (1977).[10]

III

[The Court here ruled that the police action was valid under Terry v. Ohio.]

* * *

IV

[The Court concluded that a remand was necessary to permit the Michigan Supreme Court to address a different federal constitutional question that that court had not resolved in its earlier handling of Long's appeal.]

we relied entirely on the syllabus and opinion of the state court.

In dissent, Justice Stevens proposes the novel view that this Court should never review a state court decision unless the Court wishes to vindicate a federal right that has been endangered. The rationale of the dissent is not restricted to cases where the decision is arguably supported by adequate and independent state grounds. Rather, Justice Stevens appears to believe that even if the decision below rests exclusively on federal grounds, this Court should not review the decision as long as there is no federal right that is endangered.

The state courts handle the vast bulk of all criminal litigation in this country. * * * The state courts are required to apply federal constitutional standards, and they necessarily create a considerable body of "federal law" in the process. It is not surprising that this Court has become more interested in the application and development of federal law by state courts in the light of the recent signifi-

cant expansion of federally created standards that we have imposed on the States. * * *

10. There is nothing unfair about requiring a plain statement of an independent state ground in this case. Even if we were to rest our decision on an evaluation of the state law relevant to Long's claim, as we have sometimes done in the past, our understanding of Michigan law would also result in our finding that we have jurisdiction to decide this case. Under state search and seizure law, a "higher standard" is imposed under art. 1, § 11 of the 1963 Michigan Constitution. See People v. Secrest, 413 Mich. 521, 525, 321 N.W.2d 368, 369 (1982). If, however, the item seized is, *inter alia,* a "narcotic drug * * * seized by a peace officer outside the curtilage of any dwelling house in this state," art. 1, § 11 of the 1963 Michigan Constitution, then the seizure is governed by a standard identical to that imposed by the Fourth Amendment. See People v. Moore, 391 Mich. 426, 435, 216 N.W.2d 770, 775 (1974). * * *

V

The judgment of the Michigan Supreme Court is reversed, and the case is remanded for further proceedings not inconsistent with this opinion.

It is so ordered.

■ JUSTICE BLACKMUN, concurring in part and concurring in the judgment.

I join Parts I, III, IV, and V of the Court's opinion. While I am satisfied that the Court has jurisdiction in this particular case, I do not join the Court, in Part II of its opinion, in fashioning a new presumption of jurisdiction over cases coming here from state courts. Although I agree with the Court that uniformity in federal criminal law is desirable, I see little efficiency and an increased danger of advisory opinions in the Court's new approach.

[Justice Brennan, whom Justice Marshall joined, dissented on the merits of the Fourth Amendment issue. On the jurisdictional question, he said only: "I agree that the Court has jurisdiction to decide this case. See [footnote 10 of the Court's opinion]."]

* * *

■ JUSTICE STEVENS, dissenting.

The jurisprudential questions presented in this case are far more important than the question whether the Michigan police officer's search of respondent's car violated the Fourth Amendment. The case raises profoundly significant questions concerning the relationship between two sovereigns—the State of Michigan and the United States of America.

The Supreme Court of the State of Michigan expressly held "that the deputies' search of the vehicle was proscribed by the Fourth Amendment to the United States Constitution and *art 1, § 11 of the Michigan Constitution.*" (Emphasis added). The state law ground is clearly adequate to support the judgment, but the question whether it is independent of the Michigan Supreme Court's understanding of federal law is more difficult. Four possible ways of resolving that question present themselves: (1) asking the Michigan Supreme Court directly, (2) attempting to infer from all possible sources of state law what the Michigan Supreme Court meant, (3) presuming that adequate state grounds are independent unless it clearly appears otherwise, or (4) presuming that adequate state grounds are *not* independent unless it clearly appears otherwise. This Court has, on different occasions, employed each of the first three approaches; never until today has it even hinted at the fourth. In order to "achieve the consistency that is necessary," the Court today undertakes a reexamination of all the possibilities. It rejects the first approach as inefficient and unduly burdensome for state courts, and rejects the second approach as an inappropriate expenditure of our resources. Although I find both of those decisions defensible in themselves, I cannot accept the Court's decision to choose the fourth approach over the third * * *.

If we reject the intermediate approaches, we are left with a choice between two presumptions: one in favor of our taking jurisdiction, and one against it. Historically, the latter presumption has always prevailed. See, *e.g.,* Durley v. Mayo, 351 U.S. 277, 285 (1956); Lynch v. New York ex rel. Pierson, 293 U.S. 52 (1934). The rule, as succinctly stated in Lynch, was as follows:

"Where the judgment of the state court rests on two grounds, one involving a federal question and the other not, or if it does not appear upon

which of two grounds the judgment was based, and the ground independent of a federal question is sufficient in itself to sustain it, this Court will
not take jurisdiction. [Citing cases.]" *Id.*, at 54–55.

The Court today points out that in several cases we have weakened the
traditional presumption by using the other two intermediate approaches identified above. Since those two approaches are now to be rejected, however, I
would think that *stare decisis* would call for a return to historical principle.
Instead, the Court seems to conclude that because some precedents are to be
rejected, we must overrule them all.

Even if I agreed with the Court that we are free to consider as a fresh
proposition whether we may take presumptive jurisdiction over the decisions of
sovereign States, I could not agree that an expansive attitude makes good
sense. It appears to be common ground that any rule we adopt should show
"respect for state courts, and [a] desire to avoid advisory opinions." And I am
confident that all Members of this Court agree that there is a vital interest in
the sound management of scarce federal judicial resources. All of those policies
counsel against the exercise of federal jurisdiction. They are fortified by my
belief that a policy of judicial restraint—one that allows other decisional bodies
to have the last word in legal interpretation until it is truly necessary for this
Court to intervene—enables this Court to make its most effective contribution
to our federal system of government.

The nature of the case before us hardly compels a departure from tradition.
These are not cases in which an American citizen has been deprived of a right
secured by the United States Constitution or a federal statute. Rather, they
are cases in which a state court has upheld a citizen's assertion of a right,
finding the citizen to be protected under both federal and state law. The
attorney for the complaining party is an officer of the State itself, who asks us
to rule that the state court interpreted federal rights too broadly and "overpro-
tected" the citizen.

Such cases should not be of inherent concern to this Court. The reason
may be illuminated by assuming that the events underlying this case had arisen
in another country, perhaps the Republic of Finland. If the Finnish police had
arrested a Finnish citizen for possession of marihuana, and the Finnish courts
had turned him loose, no American would have standing to object. If instead
they had arrested an American citizen and acquitted him, we might have been
concerned about the arrest but we surely could not have complained about the
acquittal, even if the Finnish court had based its decision on its understanding
of the United States Constitution. That would be true even if we had a treaty
with Finland requiring it to respect the rights of American citizens under the
United States Constitution. We would only be motivated to intervene if an
American citizen were unfairly arrested, tried, and convicted by the foreign
tribunal.

In this case the State of Michigan * * * simply provided greater protection
to one of its citizens than some other State might provide or, indeed, than this
Court might require throughout the country.

I believe that in reviewing the decisions of state courts, the primary role of
this Court is to make sure that persons who seek to *vindicate* federal rights
have been fairly heard. That belief resonates with statements in many of our
prior cases. In Abie State Bank v. Bryan, 282 U.S. 765 (1931), the Supreme
Court of Nebraska had rejected a federal constitutional claim, relying in part on
the state law doctrine of laches. Writing for the Court in response to the

Nebraska Governor's argument that the Court should not accept jurisdiction because laches provided an independent ground for decision, Chief Justice Hughes concluded that this Court must ascertain for itself whether the asserted nonfederal ground independently and adequately supported the judgment "in order that constitutional guaranties may appropriately be enforced." * * *

Until recently we had virtually no interest in cases of this type. Thirty years ago, this Court reviewed only one. Nevada v. Stacher, 346 U.S. 906 (1953). Indeed, that appears to have been the only case during the entire 1953 Term in which a State even sought review of a decision by its own judiciary. Fifteen years ago, we did not review any such cases, although the total number of requests had mounted to three. Some time during the past decade, perhaps about the time of the 5–to–4 decision in Zacchini v. Scripps–Howard Broadcasting Co., 433 U.S. 562 (1977), our priorities shifted. The result is a docket swollen with requests by States to reverse judgments that their courts have rendered in favor of their citizens.[2] I am confident that a future Court will recognize the error of this allocation of resources. When that day comes, I think it likely that the Court will also reconsider the propriety of today's expansion of our jurisdiction.

The Court offers only one reason for asserting authority over cases such as the one presented today: "an important need for uniformity in federal law [that] goes unsatisfied when we fail to review an opinion that rests primarily upon federal grounds and where the independence of an alleged state ground is not apparent from the four corners of the opinion" (emphasis omitted). Of course, the supposed need to "review an opinion" clashes directly with our oft-repeated reminder that "our power is to correct wrong judgments, not to revise opinions." Herb v. Pitcairn, 324 U.S. 117, 126 (1945). The clash is not merely one of form: the "need for uniformity in federal law" is truly an ungovernable engine. That same need is no less present when it is perfectly clear that a state ground is both independent and adequate. In fact, it is equally present if a state prosecutor announces that he believes a certain policy of nonenforcement is commanded by federal law. Yet we have never claimed jurisdiction to correct such errors, no matter how egregious they may be, and no matter how much they may thwart the desires of the state electorate. We do not sit to expound our understanding of the Constitution to interested listeners in the legal community; we sit to resolve disputes. If it is not apparent that our views would affect the outcome of a particular case, we cannot presume to interfere.

Finally, I am thoroughly baffled by the Court's suggestion that it must stretch its jurisdiction and reverse the judgment of the Michigan Supreme Court in order to show "[r]espect for the independence of state courts."

Would we show respect for the Republic of Finland by convening a special sitting for the sole purpose of declaring that its decision to release an American citizen was based upon a misunderstanding of American law?

I respectfully dissent.

---

2. This Term, we devoted argument time to [twelve cases, here cited by Justice Stevens], as well as this case. And a cursory survey of the United States Law Week index reveals that so far this Term at least 80 petitions for certiorari to state courts were filed by the States themselves.

NOTE ON REVIEW OF STATE DECISIONS UPHOLDING
CLAIMS OF FEDERAL RIGHT

(1) *Justice Stevens' Argument.* Justice Stevens' dissent argues, quite apart from the problem of ambiguity (which is explored in the following Note), that the Court should not review state-court judgments that *uphold* claims of federal right.[1] He returned to this theme in his dissent in Delaware v. Van Arsdall, 475 U.S. 673 (1986), where the Court reviewed a Delaware decision that had found a violation of the Confrontation Clause of the Sixth Amendment. The Supreme Court agreed that the federal Constitution had been violated, but vacated the state court's judgment reversing the conviction. The Supreme Court concluded that (a) as a matter of federal law, the violation was not grounds for automatic reversal if the error was "harmless"; (b) the state court's reversal did not clearly rest on a state-law "automatic reversal" rule; and (c) the case should therefore be remanded to allow the state court to determine whether the error was "harmless" under federal standards.

Justice Stevens objected that this disposition "operates to expand this Court's review of state remedies that overcompensate for violations of federal constitutional rights" (p. 695). He added (p. 697): "the claim of these cases on our docket is secondary to the need to scrutinize judgments disparaging those rights." He also complained that reviewing such cases puts pressure on the state courts to confine *state* constitutional protections to the level required by the federal Constitution,[2] and noted that on remand the Delaware courts were free to impose an automatic reversal rule on the basis of state law.

Despite these arguments, the Court has adhered to the position that it has both the power and responsibility to review state court decisions that uphold individual claims of federal right. In addition to Michigan v. Long, see, *e.g.*, Fare v. Michael C., 442 U.S. 707, 716–17 (1979); Oregon v. Hass, 420 U.S. 714, 719–20 (1975).

(2) *The 1914 Expansion of Supreme Court Jurisdiction.* As Justice Stevens acknowledged in Van Arsdall (but not in Long), the Supreme Court's power to review state court determinations upholding claims of federal right was first conferred by the Judiciary Act of 1914, see p. 493, *supra*—which Justice Stevens described as having been enacted to allow the Court to review "Lochner-style" overenforcement of supposed federal limits on the states' power to enact social legislation. Does that history suggest that federal review in cases of "overenforcement" may be quite important? Is there a principled distinction between review in "Lochner-style" cases and in Long or Van Arsdall?

Or does the absence of review before 1914 support the view (advanced by Justice Stevens in Van Arsdall) that the Court should adopt a systematic policy (as against the normal case-by-case operation of the certiorari practice) disfavoring review in such cases? If Justice Stevens' "low priority" approach is justified, should the Court expressly state, in its Rules, that it follows that approach in determining whether to grant certiorari—much as the Rules state, for example, that there is a high priority for cases involving conflicts among the lower courts? If the answer is no, does this bear on the question whether a systematic "low priority" approach is justified?

---

1. In Minnesota v. Clover Leaf Creamery, 449 U.S. 456 (1981), and City of Revere v. Massachusetts Gen. Hosp., 463 U.S. 239 (1983), Justice Stevens voiced the same objection.

2. On this point, see p. 544, *infra*.

(3) *Supreme Court Review to Promote Uniformity and Protect States' Rights.* A significant purpose of Article III (now implemented by § 1257) is to permit the Supreme Court to unify federal law by review of state court decisions of federal questions—a point stressed, for example, by Hamilton in Federalist No. 82, see p. 25, *supra,* and by Justice Story in Martin, see p. 359, *supra.* How effectively could the Court play that role today if it never (or hardly ever) granted review of state court decisions upholding claims of federal right?

Beyond the uniformity problems lie other, deeper issues. Justice Stevens' arguments assume that the Constitution's guarantees of individual rights represent the only significant constitutional norms. Even if this were true of the Bill of Rights and the other amendments viewed in isolation, the Constitution as a whole "contains other sorts of values as well. It gives the federal government powers, but also enacts limitations on those powers. *The limitations, too, count as setting forth constitutional values.* * * * When a court upholds a state criminal statute against the claim that it violates the first amendment, it is rejecting one sort of constitutional claim, but it is also upholding principles of separation of powers and federalism which themselves have constitutional status." Bator, *The State Courts and Federal Constitutional Litigation,* 22 Wm. & Mary L.Rev. 605, 631–633 (1981). Does the reference to Lochner illustrate these points?

Consider, also, the distinct consideration that states, when they complain of "overenforcement" of federal constitutional norms, are often representing important individual or collective interests—as, for example, in Regents of the Univ. of California v. Bakke, 438 U.S. 265, 279–80 (1978), where the state challenged a state court's invalidation under the federal Constitution of an affirmative action plan. See Shapiro, Federalism: A Dialogue 99–104 (1995). But see Sager, *Fair Measure: The Legal Status of Underenforced Constitutional Norms,* 91 Harv.L.Rev. 1212, 1242–63 (1978)(*inter alia,* urging the Stevens position while discussing a number of objections thereto).

(4) *Supreme Court Review to "Unfreeze" State Political Processes.* If a state's highest court construes the state's own statutory or constitutional protections of individual rights more expansively than is required by federal constitutional norms, the state retains political power to disagree by amending the state statute or constitution. But a state court judgment that the federal Constitution bars the state government from action, if unreviewable by the Supreme Court, effectively freezes the law in that state (subject only to an amendment of the United States Constitution): no amendment of state law can overcome the decision. (The possibility that the state court might, in a subsequent case, reconsider and reverse its own judgment on the issue is remote, as is the possibility that the United States Supreme Court might review the same issue in a case from another state court that denied the same federal claim.) Is this a tolerable institutional situation?

If not, what of cases where the state court's judgment rests on both state and federal grounds? See p. 525, Paragraph 4(b), *supra.* Governor Deukmejian of California criticized his state's highest court for relying on both grounds as improperly insulating the court's decisions from any review: presence of the state ground bars Supreme Court review of the federal ground, while presence of the federal ground makes futile, or at least discourages, popular review of the state law ground. See Deukmejian & Thompson, *All Sail and No Anchor— Judicial Review Under the California Constitution,* 6 Hast.Const.L.Q. 975, 996– 97 (1979). But see Utter, *Swimming in the Jaws of the Crocodile: State Court*

Comment on Federal Constitutional Issues When Disposing of Cases on State Constitutional Grounds, 63 Texas L.Rev. 1025, 1029–41 (1985)(defending the practice of dual reliance as permitting state courts to contribute to the elaboration of the federal Constitution).

Should the Court review such cases, even though reversal of the federal ground could not change the judgment below, in order to avoid "freezing" the state's political processes?   Compare Bice, *Anderson and the Adequate State Ground*, 45 S.Calif.L.Rev. 750 (1972)(so arguing) with Falk, *The State Constitution: A More than "Adequate" Nonfederal Ground*, 61 Calif.L.Rev. 273 (1973)(criticizing the argument).   Is it likely that the presence of the federal ground will stop state politicians from trying to change state substantive law—especially since, if the state ground can be reversed, Supreme Court review of the federal ground would become available?   Even if the empirical claim is plausible, does it argue for the Supreme Court's rendering a wholly advisory opinion?   Or instead that the state should change its judicial practice—by state constitutional amendment if necessary—to require state courts not to rely on both federal and state constitutional grounds?

NOTE ON AMBIGUOUS STATE DECISIONS AND TECHNIQUES FOR CLARIFYING THEM

(1) *Possible Approaches to Ambiguous State Court Judgments.*   As Justice Stevens' dissent in Michigan v. Long points out, when it is uncertain whether a state decision rested on a federal ground, a state ground, or both, the Court can (a) seek clarification from the state court (either by obtaining from it a certificate[1] or by vacating and remanding with a request for clarification);[2] (b) try to resolve the ambiguity itself by examining the relevant state-law materials;[3] (c) dismiss on the ground that, in view of the ambiguity, the obligation affirmatively to establish the Court's jurisdiction has not been satisfied;[4] or (d) presume that the decision rested on a federal ground (the opposite stance from alternative "c".)   Over the years, the Court oscillated among the first three alternatives; Long was the first time that the fourth approach commended itself to the Court.

1.   See, *e.g.*, Lynum v. Illinois, 368 U.S. 908 (1961), 372 U.S. 528, 535–36 (1963)(consideration of certiorari petition deferred; certificate treated as conclusive to establish jurisdiction); Herb v. Pitcairn, Paragraph (2), *infra*.   Compare the difficulties in Dixon v. Duffy, discussed in footnote 5 of the Long opinion.

2.   See, *e.g.*, Philadelphia Newspapers, Inc. v. Jerome, 434 U.S. 241, 242 (1978); Minnesota v. National Tea Co., 309 U.S. 551 (1940).

3.   As early as Johnson v. Risk, 137 U.S. 300 (1890), the Court itself examined prior Tennessee decisions before concluding that a state court judgment (rendered without opinion) could plausibly have rested on the state statute of limitations; it added that if the

party seeking review "wished to claim that this cause was disposed of by the decision of a federal question, [he] should have obtained the certificate of the [state] Supreme Court to that effect * * *" (p. 307).   See also, *e.g.*, South Dakota v. Neville, 459 U.S. 553 (1983); Jankovich v. Indiana Toll Road Com'n, 379 U.S. 487 (1965).   Compare footnote 10 of the Court's opinion in Long.

4.   This was the approach of the earliest cases.   See, *e.g.*, Klinger v. Missouri, 80 U.S. (13 Wall.) 257 (1871); Eustis v. Bolles, 150 U.S. 361 (1893).   For more recent examples, see, *e.g.*, Lynch v. New York ex rel. Pierson, 293 U.S. 52, 54 (1934); Durley v. Mayo, 351 U.S. 277 (1956).

(2) *The Alternative of Vacation.* In Long, none of the Justices favored the alternative of vacation and remand. Yet might that alternative have best promoted what Justice O'Connor described as "the cornerstones of this Court's refusal to decide cases where there is an adequate and independent state ground"—"[r]espect for the independence of state courts [and] avoidance of rendering advisory opinions"?

As to avoiding advisory opinions, isn't vacation and remand plainly superior to the Court's position? Indeed, of the four alternatives, isn't the one selected by the Court *most* likely to generate unnecessary constitutional opinions (because on remand it becomes clear that the state court's original judgment did rest on state law) and to waste the Court's limited resources?

As for the Court's claim that asking state courts to clarify their opinions would be disrespectful, does it ring hollow? Long simply puts the burden of clarification on the state court in advance. And does imposition of that burden, at whatever stage it is imposed, truly reflect lack of respect? Compare the view of Justice Jackson in Herb v. Pitcairn, 324 U.S. 117, 128 (1945), mentioned in footnote 7 of the Long opinion, that where the state court opinion is unclear, "it seems consistent with the respect due the highest courts of states of the Union that they be asked rather than told what they have intended. If this imposes an unwelcome burden it should be mitigated by the knowledge that it is to protect their jurisdiction from unwitting interference as well as to protect our own from unwitting renunciation."

Finally, it is plain that the approach of seeking clarification is most likely to avoid errors—in the words of the Court in Minnesota v. National Tea Co., 309 U.S. 551, 557 (1940), "no other course assures that important federal issues, such as have been argued here, will reach this Court for adjudication; that state courts will not be the final arbiters of important issues under the federal constitution; and that we will not encroach on the constitutional jurisdiction of the states."

Isn't the principal problem with this approach that it causes delay? How serious is that problem in view of the fact that the Supreme Court is not a court of errors, and in view of the purposes for which it exercises its certiorari jurisdiction?

(3) *The Meaning of Long.* How significant a change in practice was the decision in Long? Note that the application of Long's presumption depends on a series of "soft" requirements: the state decision must "fairly appear" to rest "primarily" on federal law or be "interwoven" with federal law, and the independence of the state ground must be "not clear" from the face of the state opinion.[5] These are not self-applying concepts.[6]

5. Compare Ohio v. Johnson, 467 U.S. 493, 497 n. 7 (1984), where the Court stated Long's holding in the disjunctive: "we have jurisdiction * * * when the decision 'appears to rest primarily on federal law or to be interwoven with the federal law,' *or* if the 'adequacy and independence of any possible state law ground is not clear from the face of the opinion.'" Can you think of a case whose outcome might be affected by the difference in phrasing?

6. Presumably the Supreme Court may not review a state decision stating that "when this court cites federal or other State court opinions in construing provisions of the New Hampshire Constitution or statutes, we rely on those precedents merely for guidance and do not consider our results bound by those decisions. See Michigan v. Long * * *." State v. Ball, 124 N.H. 226, 471 A.2d 347, 352 (1983). But what if the state court routinely adds such a statement as boilerplate in every opinion (as is true of the New

Finally, in footnote 6 of Long the Court carefully reserved the right to seek clarification from the state court where this is "necessary or desirable". Does that safety valve suggest that the underlying policy tensions responsible for prior oscillations, with which the Court was clearly impatient, could still overcome the effort to work out a uniform approach?

(4) *Post-Long Decisions.* Since Long the Court has often relied on it to accept jurisdiction in the face of ambiguities in the state court opinion. See, *e.g.*, Arizona v. Evans, 115 S.Ct. 1185 & cases cited at 1189 n. 2 (1995).[7]

But in Capital Cities Media, Inc. v. Toole, 466 U.S. 378 (1984), the Court reverted to the practice of vacating and remanding. Here the trial judge had restricted media access to various aspects of a criminal trial. The Supreme Court of Pennsylvania, without opinion, denied a media petition (based on the First Amendment) for a writ of prohibition—a decision that might have rested on the ground that Pennsylvania law did not permit appellate review via writ of prohibition. The United States Supreme Court, per curiam, stated: "[T]he record does not disclose whether the Supreme Court of Pennsylvania passed on petitioners' federal claims or whether it denied their petition * * * on an adequate and independent state ground." The Court thus vacated the judgment and remanded for the state court to take further action to clarify the record (pp. 378–79).

What explains this shift in technique? Compare the relationship of state and federal law in Long and in Capital Cities. In Long, state and federal constitutional provisions provided independent grounds of relief, see p. 520, *supra*. In such cases, ambiguity about the presence of an adequate and independent state ground arises when the state court has upheld the position of the federal rightholder; the uncertainty is whether the grant of relief was premised on state and/or on federal grounds.

In Capital Cities, by contrast, the possible state ground (lack of jurisdiction to entertain a writ of prohibition) was antecedent to the federal right. In such a case, there is ambiguity about the presence of an adequate and independent state ground when the state court has denied the relief sought by the federal rightholder; the uncertainty is whether the denial was based on federal law or on the antecedent state ground.

The different approach followed in Capital Cities might have seemed to substantiate the many critics of Long who complained that the Burger Court, not generally known for its expansive view of federal jurisdiction,[8] was there

Hampshire Supreme Court, see Gardner, *The Failed Discourse of State Constitutionalism*, 90 Mich.L.Rev. 761, 801, 803–04 (1992)). What if, instead, such a statement is found not in the decision under review but only in a recent precedent that purports to establish the practice for the future?

7. In Evans, a search and seizure decision involving an arrest based on erroneous information in police computer records, Justice Ginsburg's dissent (joined by Justice Stevens) urged that Long be overruled. Arguing that Long "impedes the States' ability to serve as laboratories for testing solutions to novel legal problems" (p. 1198), she urged

that the Court presume that ambiguous state court opinions rested on state law. (Like the majority in Long, she would reserve power to vacate and remand in exceptional cases.)

8. As Justice Stevens noted, the Court's approach in Long cuts against the ordinary rule that a party invoking the jurisdiction of a federal court has the burden of establishing jurisdiction. See Philadelphia Newspapers, Inc. v. Jerome, 434 U.S. 241, 244 (1978)(Rehnquist, J., dissenting). But note that this rule usually applies where it is within the *party's* control (in filing a complaint or a petition for removal) to meet the burden. In the context of Supreme Court

extending Supreme Court jurisdiction in order to permit review of a state court decision challenged as going too far in protecting federal rights.[9] By contrast, the Court refused to apply Long's broad view of jurisdiction in Capital Cities at the behest of a petitioner complaining that the state court failed to protect federal rights.

In connection with this criticism, consider three post-Long decisions involving federal habeas corpus applications by state prisoners. All three cases involved operation of the principle that a federal district court ordinarily has habeas corpus jurisdiction to review a state prisoner's claim of a federal constitutional violation only if the claim was properly raised in state court. (See Chap. XI, Sec. 2, pp. 1413-40, *infra*.) Thus, in each case the question of state law (had the prisoner complied with state procedural rules when raising the federal claim in state court?) was antecedent to the federal questions presented. And in all three, there was uncertainty whether state court decisions refusing to overturn convictions rested on such state procedural grounds or instead on the merits.

(a) Harris v. Reed, 489 U.S. 255 (1989). A state prisoner was denied post-conviction relief in state court; the basis for the denial was ambiguous. The Supreme Court ruled that federal habeas corpus jurisdiction existed unless the state court "clearly and expressly states that its judgment rests on a state procedural bar" (p. 263; internal quotes omitted). A footnote stressed, however that had the state appellate court rendered alternative holdings, reaching the merits only after clearly finding a procedural default, federal habeas review would have been barred (p. 264 n. 10). Justice Stevens expressed approval of this application of Long in his concurrence, noting that federal habeas courts review only claims of state court *under*protection of federal rights, whereas in Long the Supreme Court reviewed state court *over*protection. Justice Kennedy dissented, suggesting that Long was right but this case was distinguishable: in Long, the Court stressed that the "most reasonable explanation" of the state court's decision was that it rested on federal law; here, he contended, the most reasonable explanation of the state court's opinion was that the prisoner failed to comply with state procedural rules.

(b) Coleman v. Thompson, 501 U.S. 722 (1991). After the state supreme court affirmed Coleman's conviction and death sentence, he filed a state postconviction proceeding raising a number of federal claims that he had not raised on direct appeal. The county court ruled against him, and the state

review, by contrast, if the state court's opinion is ambiguous, or the court writes no opinion, there is often nothing the losing party can do (or could have done) to meet the "burden" of establishing jurisdiction. Does that difference justify a departure from the ordinary approach?

9. Consider the statistics noted in Sager, p. 537, *supra*, at 1244: From 1960–69, the Supreme Court reviewed only eight cases in which state courts had upheld federal rights, and in four of those cases the Court affirmed the state court judgment; from 1970–78, the Court granted review in 25 such cases, and affirmed the state court in only one.

See also Hellman, *Case Selection in the Burger Court: A Preliminary Inquiry*, 60 No-

tre Dame Law. 947, 1044–46 (1985), noting that in the first four Terms of the 1980s, the Court granted roughly 24 of 2400 petitions for certiorari by state prisoners, while granting 26, vacating 40, and rejecting 125 petitions by state prosecutors. The disparity in ratios, he suggests, may be attributable in part to the greater sophistication of lawyers for the government (as repeat players), and to the availability of habeas corpus review to prisoners (but not to prosecutors) whose petitions are denied. In civil cases, he notes, the Court granted review in 71 cases where state courts denied federal rights, compared to only 9 where federal rights were upheld.

later moved to dismiss his appeal from that ruling on the sole ground that he had failed to file a notice of appeal within 30 days of the county court's denial of post-conviction relief, as required by state law. After briefs on that issue and on the merits, the state supreme court granted the motion to dismiss "upon consideration of" the filed papers. Coleman then filed a habeas petition in federal court raising the same federal claims. The Supreme Court held (6–3) that the claims were not subject to review in federal habeas, refusing to apply the presumption of Harris v. Reed even though the state supreme court's order of dismissal did not "expressly state" that it was based on a procedural ground. The majority found that the order "fairly appear[ed]" to rest primarily on state law because it did not mention federal law and because the motion to dismiss the appeal was based solely on the timing of the appeal notice (p. 740).

(c) Ylst v. Nunnemaker, 501 U.S. 797 (1991). In another capital case, the prisoner (Nunnemaker) raised a Miranda claim for the first time on appeal from his conviction, and the state court of appeals rejected the claim solely on state procedural grounds. After the summary denial of several *state* court habeas petitions raising that claim, Nunnemaker filed a federal habeas petition raising the Miranda claim. In a 6–3 decision, the Supreme Court held that the claim was barred by Nunnemaker's state procedural default. Justice Scalia, for the majority, acknowledged that the case was more difficult than Coleman, because neither the state court dispositions of the state habeas petitions nor the surrounding circumstances indicated that the basis of the state court actions was procedural default. But the opinion went on to conclude that where the last reasoned state court opinion on a federal claim rests on a finding of procedural default, there is a strong presumption, not rebutted in this case, that any subsequent state court decision on the claim did not disregard the default and consider the merits.

In the light of these three decisions, do you think the criticism of Long as result-oriented is warranted? [10] Does the Court's practice illustrate a general principle: jurisdictional rules tend to move in the direction of allowing more intensive supervision in areas of the law where the Supreme Court is in the process of changing the relevant substantive rules and wants to assure itself

---

10. Consider, also, two earlier decisions. In Colorado v. Nunez, 465 U.S. 324 (1984)(per curiam), the Court dismissed the writ of certiorari "as improvidently granted, it appearing that the judgment of the court below rested on independent and adequate state grounds." Justice White, joined by Chief Justice Burger and Justice O'Connor, concurred, but wrote separately simply to make clear his view that the federal Constitution did not grant the equivalent right. Justice Stevens in turn criticized his colleagues for issuing an advisory opinion.

Compare the more far-reaching discussion by Chief Justice Burger in Florida v. Casal, 462 U.S. 637 (1983)(per curiam). As in Nunez, the Court dismissed the writ of certiorari "as improvidently granted, it appearing that the judgment of the court below rested on independent and adequate state grounds." The Chief Justice's concurring opinion questioned the correctness of the state court's interpretation of the *state* constitution as requiring reversal of a criminal conviction, and called attention to the power of Florida's citizens to amend state constitutional or statutory provisions that provide more protection than the federal Constitution.

Was the Chief Justice any less justified in expressing that opinion than was Justice Brennan in putting forward a contrasting view in his influential article, *State Constitutions and the Protection of Individual Rights*, 90 Harv.L.Rev. 489 (1977)? Justice Brennan described a series of Supreme Court decisions that he viewed as reflecting unduly narrow constructions of federal constitutional provisions, and urged (p. 503) that "[w]ith federal scrutiny diminished, state courts must respond by increasing their own."

that the state courts are complying with the new dispensation? Is the different approach followed in Capital Cities a justifiable application of that principle, or an unprincipled discrimination against cases where federal rights may have been underprotected?

(5) *Other Justifications for Long.* Is any of the following arguments a convincing justification for the approach adopted in Long?

(a) By increasing the number of cases eligible for review, Long maximizes the Court's flexibility in managing its docket and in finding the right vehicle for resolving particular federal issues.

(b) Unlike most federal laws, the federal constitution has not had a merely interstitial role; in the domain of protection of individual rights, the federal constitution has been primary (and remains so despite the recent invigoration of state constitutional protections). Thus, as a matter of probability, an ambiguous state court opinion is more likely to have rested on federal than on state constitutional law.[11] Compare Coleman v. Thompson and Ylst v. Nunnemaker, *supra*, both making judgments about probabilities. Note, however, that Michigan v. Long appears to apply to all cases of ambiguity, not merely to those involving constitutional questions.

(c) State courts should be clear in the first instance whether their judgments rested on state or federal grounds (or both). Long makes it more likely that, in order to avoid the possibility of reversal, state court judges will clearly elaborate a state law ground when it exists.

(6) *The Reaction to Long.* The reaction of many commentators to Long has been hostile.[12] But some of the hostility is directed less to Long's treatment of ambiguous state court opinions and more to the Supreme Court's intensified review (and reversal) of state rulings *upholding* claims of federal right.

Putting aside that issue, is there any valid objection to the "presumption" approach of Long? That the Court is issuing opinions on delicate constitutional questions that are not necessary? That Long represents a result-oriented approach to jurisdictional decisionmaking? That Long increases the risk of friction with the state courts—by increasing the likelihood of reversal, and by

---

11. Note that a similar problem may arise when *federal court* actions are premised on both federal and state constitutional provisions. Although the Supreme Court has jurisdiction under 28 U.S.C. § 1254 to review a lower federal court decision, whether it rests on state or federal law (or both), in practice the Court is unlikely to grant review of a decision that rests at least in the alternative on state law grounds. See Sup.Ct.R. 10, p. 494, *supra*. But *cf.* Veronia School Dist. 47J v. Acton, 115 S.Ct. 2386 (1995), where the court of appeals had held that a school drug-testing policy violated the federal Fourth Amendment and the Oregon Constitution. The Supreme Court found no Fourth Amendment violation; argued that, as a result, the court of appeals' state law holding rested on a flawed premise; and therefore vacated and remanded for further proceedings.

12. See, *e.g.*, Welsh, *Reconsidering the Constitutional Relationship Between State and Federal Courts: A Critique of Michigan v. Long*, 59 Notre Dame L.Rev. 1118 (1984); Seid, *Schizoid Federalism, Supreme Court Power and Inadequate Adequate State Ground Theory: Michigan v. Long*, 18 Creighton L.Rev. 1 (1984); Matasar & Bruch, p. 519, *supra*, at 1367–82. For more favorable treatments, see Althouse, *How to Build a Separate Sphere: Federal Courts and State Power*, 100 Harv.L.Rev. 1485 (1987); Baker, *The Ambiguous Independent and Adequate State Ground in Criminal Cases: Federalism Along a Möbius Strip*, 19 Ga.L.Rev. 799 (1985); Redish, *Supreme Court Review of State Court "Federal" Decisions: A Study in Interactive Federalism*, 19 Ga.L.Rev. 861 (1985). For an earlier discussion of the problem, see Note, 62 Yale L.J. 822 (1962).

creating a significant risk that the Supreme Court's jurisdiction will be premised on a misunderstanding of the basis for the state court's decision?

How important is Long, in view of the fact that a state court that in fact relies on state law can, by simply so stating, avoid Supreme Court review? Compare Gardner, note 6, *supra*, at 785–88 (noting the frequent failure of state courts to indicate whether their decisions rest on state or federal constitutional grounds). Is Long's impact limited because, even if the Supreme Court does review an ambiguous decision and reverse on the federal issue, the state courts retain the power on remand to consider independent state-law issues, and to base ultimate judgment on them? Might the Supreme Court's decision (under the jurisdiction authorized by Long) on a question of federal constitutional law in some cases subtly influence the state court's resolution, on remand, of an uncertain question of state constitutional law? See See v. Commonwealth, 746 S.W.2d 401, 402 (Ky.1988), in which a criminal defendant claimed a violation of a constitutional right to confrontation that the Kentucky Supreme Court had recognized as a matter of federal law in a prior decision that in turn had been reversed by the Supreme Court. On remand, the state court recognized that it remained free under the Kentucky Constitution to uphold the claimed right, but in refusing to do so, stated that it was "not convinced that the [alleged error] is so violative of a basic right guaranteed by the Kentucky Constitution that we should place ourselves in direct opposition to an opinion of the United States Supreme Court".

State Tax Commission v. Van Cott

306 U.S. 511, 59 S.Ct. 605, 83 L Ed. 950 (1939).
Certiorari to the Supreme Court of Utah.

■ MR. JUSTICE BLACK delivered the opinion of the Court.

The State of Utah's income tax law * * * exempts all "Amounts received as compensation, salaries or wages from the United States ... for services rendered in connection with the exercise of *an essential governmental function*." (Italics supplied.) * * * [R]espondent claimed "as deduction" and "as exempt" salaries paid him as attorney for the Reconstruction Finance Corporation and the Regional Agricultural Credit Corporation, both federal agencies. The exemptions were denied by the Tax Commission of Utah, but the Utah Supreme Court reversed. Before the Commission and in the Supreme Court of Utah, respondent asserted, first, that his salaries were exempt by the terms of the state statute itself, and, second, that they could not be taxed by the State without violating an immunity granted by the Federal Constitution. In holding respondent's income not taxable, the Supreme Court of Utah said: "We shall have to be content to follow, as we think we must, the doctrine of the Graves Case [Rogers v. Graves, 299 U.S. 401 (1937)], until such time as a different rule is laid down by the courts, the Congress, or the people through amendment to the Constitution." The Graves case applied the doctrine that the Federal Constitution prohibits the application of state income taxes to salaries derived from federal instrumentalities. * * *

Respondent contends that the Utah Supreme Court's decision "was based squarely upon the construction of the Utah taxing statute which was held to omit respondent's salaries as a subject of taxation, and therefore that decision did not and could not reach the federal question and should not be reviewed." But that decision cannot be said to rest squarely upon a construction of the state statute. The Utah court stated that the question before it was whether respondent's salaries from the agencies in question were "taxable income for the purpose of the state income tax law," and that the answer depended upon whether these agencies exercised "essential governmental functions." But the opinion as a whole shows that the court felt constrained to conclude as it did because of the Federal Constitution and this Court's prior adjudications of Constitutional immunity. Otherwise, it is difficult to explain the court's declaration that respondent could not be taxed under the "doctrine of the Graves case *until such time as a different rule is laid down by the courts, the Congress or the people through amendment to the Constitution.*" (Italics supplied.) If the court were only incidentally referring to decisions of this Court in determining the meaning of the state law, and had concluded there-from that the statute was itself intended to grant exemption to respondent, this Court would have no jurisdiction to review that question. But, if the state court did in fact intend alternatively to base its decision upon the state statute and upon an immunity it thought granted by the Constitution as interpreted by this Court, these two grounds are so interwoven that we are unable to conclude that the judgment rests upon an independent interpretation of the state law. Whatever exemptions the Supreme Court of Utah may find in the terms of this statute, its opinion in the present case only indicates that "it thought the Federal Constitution [as construed by this Court] required" it to hold respondent not taxable.

* * *

We have now re-examined and overruled the doctrine of Rogers v. Graves in Graves v. O'Keefe, [306 U.S. 466 (1939)]. Salaries of employees or officials of the Federal Government or its instrumentalities are no longer immune, under the Federal Constitution, from taxation by the States. Whether the Utah income tax, by its terms, exempts respondent, can now be decided by the state's highest court apart from any question of Constitutional immunity, and without the necessity, so far as the Federal Constitution is concerned, of attempting to divide functions of government into those which are essential and those which are non-essential.

"We have frequently held that in the exercise of our appellate jurisdiction we have power not only to correct error in the judgment under review but to make such disposition of the case as justice requires. And in determining what justice does require, the Court is bound to consider any change, either in fact or in law, which has supervened since the judgment was entered. We may recognize such a change, which may affect the result, by setting aside the judgment and remanding the case so that the state court may be free to act. We have said that to do this is not to review, in any proper sense of the term, the decision of the state court upon a non-federal question, but only to deal appropriately with a matter arising since its judgment and having a bearing upon the right disposition of the case." [8]

Applying this principle, we vacate the judgment of the Supreme Court of Utah and remand the cause to that court for further proceedings.

Judgment vacated.

---

8. Patterson v. Alabama, 294 U.S. 600, 607.

■ THE CHIEF JUSTICE took no part in the consideration or decision of this case.

NOTE ON STATE INCORPORATION OF OR
REFERENCE TO FEDERAL LAW

(1) *Compelled Incorporation of Federal Law.* Suppose that the Supreme Court of Utah had clearly held that the federal Constitution required that Utah law be interpreted to exempt the taxpayer's salary from taxation. Wouldn't it be hard to find that there was an "independent" state law ground for a judgment in favor of the taxpayer? On this supposition, if the exemption in the state statute had been repealed, wouldn't the state court's understanding of federal law have required ruling for the taxpayer in any event? Note that in such a case, the federal doctrine of tax immunity would have been operative not merely because it had been incorporated by state law, but also because that doctrine was independently applicable to the facts in question, irrespective of state law. Where that is so, can't the state court's judgment be said to rest in substance on federal law, even if in form the state court rested its decision on an interpretation of state tax law?

(2) *The Remand in Van Cott.* On remand in the actual Van Cott proceeding, the Utah court reaffirmed that the salaries were not taxable, finding that its earlier judgment "correctly interpreted the intent of the Legislature in using the phrase 'essential governmental functions'" and that "such interpretation is still correct regardless of any change in decision of the United States Supreme Court." 98 Utah 264, 96 P.2d 740 (1939). Does that ruling suggest that the Supreme Court was wrong to accept review? Or merely that the state court's initial judgment was ambiguous about whether the interpretation of the state tax law (i) was based exclusively on perceived federal compulsion, or (ii) had an independent basis in state law? Compare Michigan v. Long, *supra*.

(3) *Other Examples of Compelled Incorporation of Federal Law.*

   (a) *United Air Lines v. Mahin.* An Illinois use tax applied to fuel stored in the state and then loaded onto United's airplanes for consumption in interstate flight. In 1963, the state Department of Revenue, rejecting its prior view that the tax covered only such fuel as was presumably "burned off" over Illinois, interpreted the tax to apply to all fuel loaded in Illinois for use by the receiving plane anywhere. Four of the seven Justices of the Illinois Supreme Court upheld this interpretation, but only two members of the majority rested on state law grounds alone; the other two rested in part on the ground that the older "burn off" rule was federally unconstitutional, because it exacted a tax on the privilege of using an instrumentality in interstate commerce. The three dissenters would have adhered to the "burn off" rule. (All of the Illinois Justices considered the new interpretation to be consistent with the federal Constitution.)

   On review, the Supreme Court examined the validity under the federal Constitution of both the new interpretation and the "burn off" rule. 410 U.S. 623 (1973). In reaching the latter issue, the Court noted that the two determining votes were premised on a construction of the federal Constitution, and held that "[t]his basis for construing a state statute creates a federal question" (p. 630)—even though the state court might have reached the same conclusion purely as a matter of state law. Holding that either state rule would be constitutional, the Court vacated the judgment and remanded for further proceedings.[1]

(b) *Parallel State Constitutions.* In Delaware v. Prouse, 440 U.S. 648 (1979), the state supreme court reversed a conviction on the ground that illegally seized evidence had been introduced, in violation of both the Fourth Amendment and the Delaware constitution. On certiorari, the Supreme Court upheld its jurisdiction: "As we understand the opinion below, Art I, § 6, of the Delaware Constitution will automatically be interpreted at least as broadly as the Fourth Amendment; that is, every police practice authoritatively determined to be contrary to the Fourth and Fourteenth Amendments will, without further analysis, be held to be contrary to Art. I, § 6. * * * The court * * * concluded that the Fourth Amendment foreclosed spot checks of automobiles, and summarily held that the State Constitution was therefore also infringed" (pp. 652–53).

If a state construes one of its constitutional guarantees to coincide fully with a parallel federal constitutional provision—to be no broader and no narrower, see, *e.g.*, People v. Luttenberger, 50 Cal.3d 1, 265 Cal.Rptr. 690, 696, 784 P.2d 633, 639 (1990)—isn't the Supreme Court justified in reviewing a judgment that rests, either exclusively or in the alternative, on the state constitution?[2]

To justify review in Prouse, however, was the Court required to find that the state court viewed the Delaware provision not only as prohibiting all searches forbidden by the Fourth Amendment, but also as prohibiting *only* those searches? Or was Supreme Court review justified in view of the possibility that the state court erroneously thought that federal law required exclusion of the evidence—in order to permit the state court, on remand, to determine (under a correct understanding of federal law) whether the state constitutional protections were broader than those afforded by federal law?

(c) *Long-Arm Statutes.* California, like a number of other states, provides by statute that its courts may exercise long-arm jurisdiction in any case permitted by the Federal Constitution. See Cal.Code Civ.Proc. § 410.10. Does every case where the California courts hold that jurisdiction cannot be obtained

---

1. On remand, the Illinois Supreme Court reaffirmed its prior judgment; the two concurring justices concluded that the current interpretation of the Act was "not improper". 298 N.E.2d 161 (Ill.1973).

See also Three Affiliated Tribes v. Wold Engineering, P.C., 467 U.S. 138 (1984)(correcting state court's misconceptions as to federal law that apparently caused it to decline jurisdiction over a case involving claims by an Indian Tribe; remand to enable state court to pass on state-law issues).

2. But see Roundhouse Constr'n Corp. v. Telesco Masons Supplies Co., 423 U.S. 809 (1975), where the Court had vacated and remanded to permit the state supreme court to explain whether its initial decision was based on state or federal constitutional grounds. On remand, the state court stated directly and without qualification that the federal and state constitutional provisions have the same meaning, and that its decision rested on both grounds; but the opinion included the comment, somewhat puzzling in light of that declaration, that decisions of the U.S. Supreme Court would be "at least very persuasive if not controlling authority". 170 Conn. 155, 365 A.2d 393, 394–95 (1976). Perhaps reading that language as qualifying the state court's declaration that state and federal provisions were congruent, the Supreme Court denied (over three dissents) a second petition for certiorari, "it appearing that the judgment below rests upon an adequate state ground." 429 U.S. 889 (1976). Was it only an oversight that the Court's final order did not say adequate *and independent* state ground?

under the state statute present a federal question subject to Supreme Court review? [3]

(4) *Gratuitous Incorporation of Federal Law.* Many states have enacted income tax laws that incorporate federal definitions of taxable income. Does every question of taxable income in such a state present a federal question? What about a state that adopts as its rules the Federal Rules of Civil Procedure and provides that the interpretation of state rules should track that of the federal rules?

Aren't these cases different from a state's incorporation of federal law in the cases in Paragraph (1), *supra*, because in these cases federal law applies *only* because the state chose to incorporate it? [4]

(5) *Gratuitous Incorporation of Federal Duties.* In some tort actions, a defendant's violation of a federal regulatory standard is treated by state law as negligence per se or at least as presumptive negligence. For example, a products liability action against a drug manufacturer may allege that the defendant violated FDA regulations, or a state law tort action against an intrastate railroad may allege violation of the duties set forth in the Federal Safety Appliance Act. In such a case, because it is not federal but state law

---

3. In California v. Byers, 402 U.S. 424 (1971), a driver was prosecuted for violation of the state "hit and run" statute. He contended that the statutory obligation to stop and identify himself following an accident violated his privilege against self-incrimination. The California Supreme Court agreed that there would be such a violation if disclosures compelled by the statute could be subsequently introduced into a criminal prosecution; it therefore read into the statute a prohibition on such use of the required disclosures; and it upheld the statute with that restriction. Nevertheless, the California Supreme Court restrained the prosecution on the ground that it would be "unfair" to punish someone who could not reasonably have anticipated the judicial promulgation of the use restriction.

Without discussing any jurisdictional issue, the Supreme Court vacated the state court judgment, holding that the statute would be valid even without a use restriction. Did the Court properly assume jurisdiction to decide the self-incrimination question? What if the state court had created the use restriction without actually deciding that its absence would make the statute invalid, but solely to avoid the *question* of constitutionality?

4. For a case in which state tax law incorporated a federal standard, but in which the issue was presented to the Supreme Court in a more complex posture, see Flournoy v. Wiener, 321 U.S. 253 (1944). The dispute involved a Louisiana inheritance tax whose definition of a taxable estate incorporated the standard of the federal estate tax laws—which, as applied to this case, included certain community property. The decedent's legatees claimed that the federal and state tax laws, by purporting to include the interest of the decedent's widow in the community property as part of the taxable estate, violated the Due Process Clauses of the 5th and 14th Amendments respectively. After the Supreme Court of Louisiana upheld these constitutional challenges, the state sought review only of the ruling that the federal definition of taxable estates violated the 5th Amendment. The U.S. Supreme Court found that any ruling on the constitutionality of the federal tax law would not affect the judgment below, resting as it did only on the constitutionality of the state tax law; that the constitutionality of the state tax had not been properly raised; and thus that the appeal must be dismissed for want of jurisdiction. Justice Frankfurter's dissent disagreed that the question was not properly raised, arguing that the invalidity of the state law was inseparable from the invalidity of the federal law. Relying on Smith v. Kansas City Title & Trust Co., 255 U.S. 180 (1921), Chap. VIII, Sec. 3, p. 928, *infra* (a case interpreting the "arising under" language of 28 U.S.C. § 1331) and Standard Oil Co. v. Johnson, Paragraph (6), *infra*, he concluded that "where a decision under state law necessarily involves the construction or validity of federal law the determination of such federal law in the application of state law gives rise to a federal question for review here" (p. 272).

that confers the private damages remedy, federal law is not independently operative in the tort suit itself. However, federal law could be said to be independently operative in the *circumstances* of the case (because federal law may lead to the imposition of other sanctions, like administrative sanctions, for the very conduct at issue).

There appears to be no doubt that a state court decision resting on an interpretation of the federal provision presents a federal question under § 1257. It was so held, for example, in St. Louis, I.M. & S. Ry. v. Taylor, 210 U.S. 281, 293 (1908), and considered dictum reaffirmed that position in Merrell Dow Pharmaceuticals, Inc. v. Thompson, 478 U.S. 804, 816 & n. 14 (1986), and Moore v. Chesapeake & O. Ry., 291 U.S. 205, 214 (1934). At the same time, the Merrell Dow case suggests that rarely if ever will such cases be viewed as "arising under" federal law for purposes of the original jurisdiction of the federal district courts under § 1331. See Chap. VIII, Sec. 3, *infra.*

What purposes are served by Supreme Court review in such cases? Clearly a defendant who contends that federal law preempts the state's power to impose liability for the particular conduct in question—whether liability rests on state law alone or on state law that incorporates a federal standard—could obtain Supreme Court review of the state court's denial of that preemption defense. But suppose that federal law is indifferent whether a state chooses to authorize damages for the particular conduct. If a state did so solely as a matter of state law, without incorporating a federal standard, there would be no Supreme Court review. If instead state law refers to a federal standard in imposing liability, why is Supreme Court review then needed? To ensure that federal law is given a correct and uniform interpretation?

(6) *Standard Oil Co. of California v. Johnson.* A leading decision, but one of uncertain import, on the question of state law incorporation of federal standards is Standard Oil Co. of California v. Johnson, 316 U.S. 481 (1942). A California tax on distribution of motor vehicle fuel exempted "any motor vehicle fuel sold to the government of the United States or any department thereof for official use of said government". A distributor to the United States Army Post Exchanges (PX) in California sued for a tax refund, arguing that the state tax (i) did not cover sales to the PX, and (ii) if construed to apply to such sales, was contrary to the federal Constitution. The state courts rejected these contentions, and the Supreme Court accepted jurisdiction of the taxpayer's appeal.

The Court unanimously reversed on the statutory issue. It found that the state court's construction of California tax was based not merely on local law but also on its examination "of the relationship between post exchanges and the government of the United States, a relationship which is controlled by federal law. For post exchanges operate under regulations of the Secretary of War pursuant to federal authority. These regulations and the practices under them establish the relationship between the post exchange and the United States government, and together with the relevant statutory and constitutional provisions from which they derive, afford the data upon which the legal status of the post exchange may be determined" (p. 483).

The Court proceeded to consider the "federal question" on which the state court's decision rested. It noted that in 1895 the War Department, acting pursuant to congressional authorization, had issued administrative regulations governing the PX; that facilities for the PX had been funded by congressional appropriations; that funds from disbanded posts in the 1930s had been paid to the U.S. Treasury; and that in 1936 Congress consented to state taxation of gasoline, sold by the PX, that was not for the exclusive use of the United States. The Court also noted that the purpose of the PX is to benefit soldiers and civilians working on military bases; that "[t]he commanding officer of an Army Post * * * has complete authority to establish and maintain an exchange"; that "government officers, under government regulations", are responsible for funds obtained by the exchange; and that profits go not to individuals but to improve life for the troops. "From all of this, we conclude that post exchanges as now operated are arms of the government deemed by it essential for the performance of governmental functions" (pp. 484–85).

The Court noted that the state might not have construed its law as it did had it "decided the issue of legal status of post exchanges in accordance with this opinion" (p. 485). Hence, the Court vacated and remanded without reaching the question whether the state could constitutionally tax sales to the PX.

Was federal review justified in this case? What purpose was served? Did the Court assume that there was a single concept of "federalness"—a kind of brooding omnipresence in the sky? Is that assumption justified? If not, what provision of federal law did the Supreme Court think that state law had incorporated and that the California courts had misinterpreted? Professor Shapiro notes that "federal money was at risk and the federal interest in immunity from taxation arguably did not stop at the border established by the Constitution itself; thus it was appropriate for the Supreme Court to correct a state court misunderstanding that inadvertently may have pushed the state too close to that border." *Jurisdiction and Discretion*, 60 N.Y.U.L.Rev. 543, 565 (1985). But what gives the Supreme Court authority to strike down state actions that come close to, but admittedly have not transgressed, constitutional borders?

(7) *Questions about State Incorporation of Federal Law.* Is there a principled basis for finding some but not all cases of gratuitous incorporation within the Supreme Court's jurisdiction under § 1257? Is the argument for review stronger in tort cases (incorporating federal regulatory standards) than in the cases incorporating federal procedural rules or definitions of taxable income?[5] See Shapiro, Paragraph (6), *supra*, at 565 (where "decision of a question of state law turns on a question of federal law", the Court has an "implicit power to choose" whether the case is reviewable in light of "the strength of the federal interest").[6]

5. See Greene, *Hybrid State Law in the Federal Courts*, 83 Harv.L.Rev. 289, 309 (1969)(in determining Supreme Court jurisdiction to review federal questions made relevant by state law, the "touchstone * * * is whether the federal law is itself operative in the circumstances of the case—whether Supreme Court jurisdiction could effect the coordination of two coextensive and possibly conflicting obligations.")

6. Thus, while Shapiro thinks there was a strong federal interest justifying review in the Standard Oil case, he finds little basis for federal concern in Miller v. Anderson, 150 U.S. 132 (1893)—where the state court held a

railroad's power to convey was limited by a state statute that simply incorporated the limits imposed by federal statute—and approves the Supreme Court's dismissal of the writ of error in that case for want of jurisdiction.

Compare St. Martin Evangelical Lutheran Church v. South Dakota, 451 U.S. 772 (1981). South Dakota, like all the other states, drafted its unemployment statute to meet the conditions of the Federal Unemployment Tax Act for allowing the states to recapture 90% of the tax that would otherwise be payable to the federal government. In this case, the Supreme Court reviewed a

Note that Standard Oil was an appeal falling within the Court's mandatory jurisdiction, as the state court had upheld against federal challenge the validity of a federal statute.   Since 1988, however, there is no longer mandatory jurisdiction in such a case.   Rather than engaging in a refined analysis of the federal interest to decide whether a case arises under § 1257, would it now be preferable simply to provide that jurisdiction under § 1257 extends to *every* case of state incorporation of federal law, compelled or gratuitous—leaving it to the Court's case-by-case discretion whether to grant certiorari?

Indiana ex rel. Anderson v. Brand

303 U.S. 95, 58 S.Ct. 443, 82 L.Ed. 685 (1938).
Certiorari to the Supreme Court of Indiana.

■ MR. JUSTICE ROBERTS delivered the opinion of the Court.

The petitioner sought a writ of mandate to compel the respondent to continue her in employment as a public school teacher.   Her complaint alleged that as a duly licensed teacher she entered into a contract in September, 1924, to teach in the township schools and, pursuant to successive contracts, taught continuously to and including the school year 1932–1933; that her contracts for the school years 1931–1932 and 1932–1933 contained this clause: "It is further agreed by the contracting parties that all of the provisions of the Teachers' Tenure Law, approved March 8, 1927, shall be in full force and effect in this contract"; and that by force of that act she had a contract, indefinite in duration, which could be canceled by the respondent only in the manner and for the causes specified in the act.   She charged that in July, 1933, the respondent notified her he proposed to cancel her contract for cause; that, after a hearing, he adhered to his decision and the county superintendent affirmed his action; that, despite what occurred in July, 1933, the petitioner was permitted to teach during the school year 1933–1934 and the respondent was presently threatening to terminate her employment at the end of that year.   The complaint alleged the termination of her employment would be a breach of her contract with the school corporation.   The respondent demurred on the grounds that (1) the complaint disclosed the matters pleaded had been submitted to the respondent and the county superintendent who were authorized to try the issues and had lawfully determined them in favor of the respondent; and (2) the Teachers' Tenure Law had been repealed in respect of teachers in township schools.   The demurrer was sustained and the petitioner appealed to the state Supreme Court which affirmed the judgment.   The court did not discuss the first ground of demurrer relating to the action taken in the school year 1932–1933, but rested its decision upon the second, that, by an act of 1933 the Teachers' Tenure Law had been repealed as respects teachers in township schools;   and held that the repeal did not deprive the petitioner of a vested

---

state court determination, based explicitly on interpretations of the federal statute and of the First Amendment, that church schools were not subject to the state statute.   The federal statute, unlike the First Amendment, was not independently operative in the case. But the Supreme Court found the federal statutory issue also to be reviewable, conclud-

ing that though the decision below "literally" concerned the coverage of the state tax statute, the South Dakota courts "deserve to be made aware of the proper and, here, significant interpretation of the intertwined federal law" (p. 780 n. 9).   Was there an important federal interest here?

property right and did not impair her contract within the meaning of the Constitution. * * *

The court below holds that in Indiana teachers' contracts are made for but 1 year; that there is no contractual right to be continued as a teacher from year to year; that the law grants a privilege to one who has taught 5 years and signed a new contract to continue in employment under given conditions; that the statute is directed merely to the exercise of their powers by the school authorities and the policy therein expressed may be altered at the will of the Legislature; that in enacting laws for the government of public schools, the Legislature exercises a function of sovereignty and the power to control public policy in respect of their management and operation cannot be contracted away by one Legislature so as to create a permanent public policy unchangeable by succeeding Legislatures. In the alternative the court declares that if the relationship be considered as controlled by the rules of private contract the provision for re-employment from year to year is unenforceable for want of mutuality.

As in most cases brought to this court under the contract clause of the Constitution, the question is as to the existence and nature of the contract and not as to the construction of the law which is supposed to impair it. The principal function of a legislative body is not to make contracts but to make laws which declare the policy of the state and are subject to repeal when a subsequent Legislature shall determine to alter that policy. Nevertheless, it is established that a legislative enactment may contain provisions which, when accepted as the basis of action by individuals, become contracts between them and the State or its subdivisions within the protection of article 1, § 10. If the people's representatives deem it in the public interest they may adopt a policy of contracting in respect of public business for a term longer than the life of the current session of the Legislature. This the petitioner claims has been done with respect to permanent teachers. The Supreme Court has decided, however, that it is the state's policy not to bind school corporations by contract for more than 1 year.

On such a question, one primarily of state law, we accord respectful consideration and great weight to the views of the state's highest court but, in order that the constitutional mandate may not become a dead letter, we are bound to decide for ourselves whether a contract was made, what are its terms and conditions, and whether the State has, by later legislation, impaired its obligation. This involves an appraisal of the statutes of the State and the decisions of its courts.

The courts of Indiana have long recognized that the employment of school teachers was contractual and have afforded relief in actions upon teachers' contracts. * * *

In 1927, the State adopted the Teachers' Tenure Act under which the present controversy arises. * * * By this act it was provided that a teacher who has served under contract for 5 or more successive years, and thereafter enters into a contract for further service with the school corporation, shall become a permanent teacher and the contract, upon the expiration of its stated term, shall be deemed to continue in effect for an indefinite period, shall be known as an indefinite contract, and shall remain in force unless succeeded by a new contract or canceled as provided in the Act. The corporation may cancel the contract, after notice and hearing, for incompetency, insubordination, neglect of duty, immorality, justifiable decrease in the number of teaching positions, or other good or just cause, but not for political or personal reasons. The teacher may not cancel the contract during the school term nor for a period 30 days previous to the beginning of any term (unless by mutual agreement) and may cancel only upon 5 days' notice.

By an amendatory act of 1933 township school corporations were omitted from the provisions of the Act of 1927. The court below construed this act as repealing the act of 1927 so far as township schools and teachers are concerned and as leaving the respondent free to terminate the petitioner's employment. But we are of opinion that the petitioner had a valid contract with the respondent, the obligation of which would be impaired by the termination of her employment.

Where the claim is that the state's policy embodied in a statute is to bind its instrumentalities by contract, the cardinal inquiry is as to the terms of the statute supposed to create such a contract. The State long prior to the adoption of the Act of 1927 required the execution of written contracts between teachers and school corporations * * *. These were annual contracts, covering a single school term. The Act of 1927 announced a new policy that a teacher who had served for 5 years under successive contracts, upon the execution of another was to become a permanent teacher and the last contract was to be indefinite as to duration and terminable by either party only upon compliance with the conditions set out in the statute. The policy which induced the legislation evidently was that the teacher should have protection against the exercise of the right, which would otherwise inhere in the employer, of terminating the employment at the end of any school term without assigned reasons and solely at the employer's pleasure. The state courts in earlier cases so declared.

The title of the Act is couched in terms of contract. It speaks of the making and canceling of indefinite contracts. In the body the word "contract" appears ten times in section 1, defining the relationship; eleven times in section 2, relating to the termination of the employment by the employer, and four times in section 4, stating the conditions of termination by the teacher.

The tenor of the act indicates that the word "contract" was not used inadvertently or in other than its usual legal meaning. By section 6 it is expressly provided that the act is a supplement to that of March 7, 1921, supra, requiring teachers' employment contracts to be in writing. By section 1 it is provided that the written contract of a permanent teacher "shall be deemed to continue in effect for an indefinite period and shall be known as an indefinite contract." Such an indefinite contract is to remain in force unless succeeded by a new contract signed by both parties or canceled as provided in section 2. No more apt language could be employed to define a contractual relationship. By section 2 it is enacted that such indefinite contracts may be canceled by the school corporation only in the manner specified. The admissible grounds of cancellation, and the method by which the existence of such grounds shall be ascertained and made a matter of record, are carefully set out. Section 4 permits cancellation by the teacher only at certain times consistent with the convenient administration of the school system and imposes a sanction for violation of its requirements. Examination of the entire act convinces us that the teacher was by it assured of the possession of a binding and enforceable contract against school districts.

Until its decision in the present case the Supreme Court of the State had uniformly held that the teacher's right to continued employment by virtue of the indefinite contract created pursuant to the act was contractual. * * *

[The opinion here reviews four decisions of the Indiana Supreme Court explicitly referring to teachers' contractual rights while also indicating that mandamus to compel reinstatement had been available.]

We think the decision in this case runs counter to the policy evinced by the Act of 1927, to its explicit mandate and to earlier decisions construing its provisions. * * *

The respondent urges that every contract is subject to the police power and that in repealing the Teachers' Tenure Act the Legislature validly exercised that reserved power of the State. The sufficient answer is found in the statute. By section 2 of the Act of 1927 power is given to the school corporation to cancel a teacher's indefinite contract for incompetency, insubordination (which is to be deemed to mean willful refusal to obey the school laws of the State or reasonable rules prescribed by the employer), neglect of duty, immorality, justifiable decrease in the number of teaching positions, or other good and just cause. The permissible reasons for cancellation cover every conceivable basis for such action growing out of a deficient performance of the obligations undertaken by the teacher, and diminution of the school requirements. Although the causes specified constitute in themselves just and reasonable grounds for the termination of any ordinary contract of employment, to preclude the assumption that any other valid ground was excluded by the enumeration, the Legislature added that the relation might be terminated for any other good and just cause. Thus in the declaration of the state's policy, ample reservations in aid of the efficient administration of the school system were made. * * * It is significant that the act of 1933 left the system of permanent teachers and indefinite contracts untouched as respects school corporations in cities and towns of the State. * * *

Our decisions recognize that every contract is made subject to the implied condition that its fulfillment may be frustrated by a proper exercise of the police power but we have repeatedly said that, in order to have this effect, the exercise of the power must be for an end which is in fact public and the means adopted must be reasonably adapted to that end, and the Supreme Court of Indiana has taken the same view in respect of legislation impairing the obligation of the contract of a state instrumentality. The causes of cancellation provided in the Act of 1927 and the retention of the system of indefinite contracts in all municipalities except townships by the act of 1933 are persuasive that the repeal of the earlier act by the later was not an exercise of the police power for the attainment of ends to which its exercise may properly be directed.

As the court below has not passed upon one of the grounds of demurrer which appears to involve no federal question, and may present a defense still open to the respondent, we reverse the judgment and remand the cause for further proceedings not inconsistent with this opinion.

So ordered.

■ MR. JUSTICE CARDOZO took no part in the consideration or decision of this case.

■ MR. JUSTICE BLACK, dissenting. * * *

The Indiana Supreme Court has consistently held, even before its decision in this case, that the right of teachers, under the 1927 Act, to serve until removed for cause, was *not given by contract, but by statute*. Such was the express holding in the two cases cited in the majority opinion * * *.

These cases demonstrate that the Supreme Court of Indiana has uniformly held that teachers did not hold their "indefinite" tenure under *contract*, but by grant of a repealable statute. In order to hold in this case that a contract was impaired, it is necessary to create a contract unauthorized by the Indiana Legislature and declared to be nonexistent by the Indiana Supreme Court. * * *

The clear purport of Indiana law is that its Legislature cannot surrender any part of its plenary constitutional right to repeal, alter or amend existing legislation relating to the school system whenever the conditions demand change for the public good. Under Indiana law the Legislature can neither barter nor give away its constitutional investiture of power. It can make no contract in conflict with this sovereign power. The construction of the constitution of Indiana by the Supreme Court of Indiana *must be accepted as correct.* That court holds that Indiana's Constitution invests Indiana's Legislature with *continuing* power to change Indiana's educational policies. It has here held that the Legislature did not attempt or intend to surrender its constitutional power by authorizing *definite* contracts which would prevent the future exercise of this continuing, constitutional power. If the Constitution and statutes of Indiana, as construed by its Supreme Court, prohibit the Legislature from making a contract which is inconsistent with a continuing power to legislate, there could have been no *definite* contracts to be impaired. * * *

Merits of a policy establishing a permanent teacher tenure law are not for consideration here. We are dealing with the constitutional right of the people of a sovereign state to control their own public school system as they deem best for the public welfare. This Court should neither make it impossible for states to experiment in the matter of security of tenure for their teachers, nor deprive them of the right to change a policy if it is found that it has not operated successfully. * * *

NOTE ON FEDERAL PROTECTION OF STATE–CREATED RIGHTS

Brand is illustrative of a range of cases, arising under different federal constitutional or statutory provisions, in which federal law protects interests that are created primarily, if not exclusively, by state law. This Note discusses some of the leading decisions, involving a variety of federal protections.

A.   The Contract Clause

(1) *Choice of Law.* The question whether an acknowledged contractual obligation is protected from impairment by the Contract Clause, or whether a particular impairment is forbidden, involves only interpretation of the Constitution. See, *e.g.*, El Paso v. Simmons, 379 U.S. 497, 506–08 (1965); Wright, The Contract Clause of the Constitution (1938); Hale, *The Supreme Court and the Contract Clause*, 57 Harv.L.Rev. 512, 621, 852 (1944).

But whose law governs the antecedent question whether there was a contract in the first place? The Brand opinion says that "the existence and nature of the contract" claimed to be impaired is a question "primarily of state law". And in General Motors Corp. v. Romein, 503 U.S. 181 (1992), the Court, in reviewing a state court determination that no contract existed, seemed to take a further step away from reliance on state law: "The question whether a contract was made is a federal question for purposes of Contract Clause analysis, * * * and 'whether it turns on issues of general or purely local law, we cannot surrender the duty to exercise our own judgment' " (p. 1110, quoting Appleby v. City of New York, 271 U.S. 364, 380 (1926)). At the same time, the Court in Romein acknowledged the "great weight" that it accords to—and in the end "saw no reason to disagree with"—the state court's views. See also Irving Trust Co. v. Day, 314 U.S. 556, 561 (1942).

Isn't it difficult to justify the view that the existence of a contract is governed by federal law? Is the Supreme Court in a position to formulate a complete body of federal contract law? Are the lower federal courts (in Contract Clause cases filed in federal district courts)? Even if such a body could be developed, should the question whether a particular contract creates an obligation be governed by one set of rules (state law) in a suit for breach, and by another (federal law) in litigation under the Contract Clause? *Cf.* the discussion of Murdock v. Memphis, p. 520, *supra.*

Isn't the existence of the contractual obligation in fact a question primarily, and usually exclusively, one of state law? See, *e.g.*, Ogden v. Saunders, 25 U.S. 213, 256–59, 326 (1827); Appleby v. City of New York, *supra*; Hale, *supra*. Would such a conclusion necessarily mean that Supreme Court review of the state court's determination is inappropriate?

(2) *Scope of Review*. While affirming the "independent judgment" rule, the Supreme Court usually has accorded respectful weight to the state court's determination—as the Court noted in Brand. Does independent review that accords great weight to the state court's views differ from limited review of the state court's decision for obvious error? Compare Hale v. Iowa State Bd., 302 U.S. 95, 101 (1937), where the Court said that it would accept the state court's judgment as to "the effect and meaning of the contract as well as its existence * * * unless manifestly wrong." See also, *e.g.*, Rapid Transit Corp. v. New York, 303 U.S. 573, 593 (1938); Atlantic Coast Line v. Phillips, 332 U.S. 168, 171 (1947). Can a state court be "manifestly wrong" on a matter of state law absent earlier decisions setting forth a different view? Was the state court "manifestly wrong" in Brand? Did Justice Black disagree with the majority on the scope of review, or on the meaning of Indiana law?

Note that the key question is not what state law *is* but rather what it *was* in the past.[1] Does that explain why in Brand the Supreme Court did not accept the Indiana court's determination? Is a state court less authoritative an expositor of what state law was than of what it now is?

(3) *Brand and Murdock*. Can the Supreme Court's willingness in the Brand case to review a state court's determination of an issue of state law be squared with Murdock v. Memphis? Note that in Brand, as in Martin v. Hunter's

---

1. The contract clause prohibits only impairment by legislation, not by judicial decision. Tidal Oil Co. v. Flanagan, 263 U.S. 444 (1924); Fleming v. Fleming, 264 U.S. 29 (1924); see Frankfurter & Landis, The Business of the Supreme Court 199–202 (1928). Although, in judging whether an obligation existed, the critical time would seem to be when the allegedly impairing legislation was enacted, the Court appears to have emphasized the date of the agreement. See, *e.g.*, El Paso v. Simmons and Appleby v. New York, *supra*; Ohio Life Ins. & Trust Co. v. Debolt, 57 U.S. (16 How.) 416, 431 (1854).

Lessee, state law is antecedent to federal law, whereas in Murdock state and federal law provided independent avenues of relief. See p. 520, *supra*. Isn't there a much stronger argument for some federal review of state law in the former situation? Does some tension remain between Brand and the reasoning in Murdock?

(4) *Review of Decisions Upholding Contractual Obligations.* In United States Mortgage Co. v. Matthews, 293 U.S. 232 (1934), the state court affirmed a contract obligation and invalidated the alleged impairment; there was no suggestion that the court viewed federal law as dictating the finding that an obligation existed. The Supreme Court, reversed, finding no obligation. *Cf.* Municipal Investors v. Birmingham, 316 U.S. 153 (1942), where the state court assumed, without deciding, that there was a contract right but found no unconstitutional impairment. The Supreme Court affirmed on the ground that no contract existed, saying it was obliged "to determine for itself the basic assumptions upon which interpretations of the Federal Constitution rest" (p. 157).

What justifies federal review of a state law determination that protects rather than potentially threatens federal rights? See Monaghan, *Of Liberty and Property*, 62 Corn.L.Rev. 405, 436 n. 201 (1977). Might review be justified if the state court had expressed the view that federal law compelled the finding that a contract existed?

B.   Due Process

A vast body of law considers the extent to which state law governs the question whether a challenged state deprivation constitutes an invasion of "property" or "liberty" interests within the meaning of the Due Process Clause.[2]

(1) *"Old Property."* The early cases involved traditional ("old") property interests. Thus, in Demorest v. City Bank Farmers Trust Co., 321 U.S. 36 (1944), a New York statute prescribed a default rule, when a will or trust was silent, for the apportionment of mortgage salvage operations between life tenancies and remainder interests. Those holding remainder interests contended that the statutory rule was less favorable to them than the decisional doctrines that it supplanted, and thus that the statute's retroactive application constituted a deprivation of property without due process. A divided New York Court of Appeals sustained the statute; the majority held that the earlier New York decisions concerning apportionment, rather than laying down fixed rules establishing property rights, merely set forth tentative guides to the discretion of trustees. In affirming, the Court (per Jackson, J.) said (pp. 42–43):

" 'Whether the state court has denied to rights asserted under local law the protection which the Constitution guarantees is a question upon which the petitioners are entitled to invoke the judgment of this Court. Even though the constitutional protection invoked be denied on non-federal grounds, it is the province of this Court to inquire whether the decision of the state court rests upon a fair or substantial basis. If unsubstantial, constitutional obligations may not be thus evaded.... But if there is no evasion of the constitutional

---

2. See generally Farina, *Conceiving Due Process*, 3 Yale J.L. & Fem. 189 (1991); Monaghan, Paragraph A(4), *supra*; Van Alstyne, *Cracks in "The New Property": Adjudicative Due Process in the Administrative State*, 62 Cornell L.Rev. 445 (1977); Herman, *The New Liberty*, 59 N.Y.U.L.Rev. 482 (1984). See also the perceptive surveys in Breyer & Stewart, Administrative Law and Regulatory Policy 729–66 (3d ed.1992), and Strauss *et al.*, Gellhorn and Byse's Administrative Law: Cases and Comments 739–835 (9th ed.1995).

issue, and the nonfederal ground of decision has fair support, . . . this Court will not inquire whether the rule applied by the state court is right or wrong, or substitute its own view of what should be deemed the better rule, for that of the state court.' [Quoting Broad River Power Co. v. South Carolina, 281 U.S. 537, 540 (1930).]

"Despite difference of opinion within the Court of Appeals as to the effect of its earlier cases, we think that the decision of the majority that they did not amount to a rule of property does rest on a fair and substantial basis." [3]

(2) *"New" Property and Liberty.* The recent cases are devoted almost exclusively to the question whether there has been a deprivation of liberty or property within the meaning of the Due Process Clause when, for example, the government fires an employee, denies an individual social welfare benefits, or disadvantages a prisoner (by, for example, a denial of parole or probation or a transfer to less desirable conditions of confinement). A key question in these cases is to what extent state law determines the existence of an entitlement.

This burgeoning body of case law started with Board of Regents v. Roth, 408 U.S. 564 (1972), where a state university teacher alleged that the failure to re-appoint him at the end of his one-year term, without statement of reasons or a hearing, deprived him of property without due process of law. The district court and the court of appeals so held, but the Supreme Court reversed (p. 577): "Property interests, of course, are not created by the Constitution. Rather they are created and their dimensions are defined by existing rules or understandings that stem from an independent source such as state law * * *. * * * [T]he terms of the respondent's appointment secured absolutely no interest in re-employment for the next year. * * * Nor, significantly, was there any state statute or University rule or policy that secured his interest in re-employment or that created any legitimate claim to it. In these circumstances, * * * he did not have a *property* interest sufficient to require the University authorities to give him a hearing * * *." Justice Marshall's dissent took the position that "every citizen who applies for a government job is entitled to it unless the government can establish some reason for denying the employment. This is the 'property' right that I believe is protected by the Fourteenth Amendment * * *. And it is also liberty—liberty to work—which is * * * secured by the Fourteenth Amendment" (pp. 588–89).

In the companion case of Perry v. Sindermann, 408 U.S. 593 (1972), the Court held that a similar claim by a state college teacher did "raise a genuine issue as to his interest in continued employment at [the particular] College. He alleged that this interest, though not secured by a formal contractual tenure provision, was secured by a no less binding understanding fostered by the college administration" (p. 599). The case was remanded for a hearing to allow the teacher to show a "legitimate claim of entitlement to continued employment absent 'sufficient cause' " (p. 602).

(3) *Choice of Law.* Detailed study of developments since Roth and Perry belongs primarily to courses in Administrative Law and Constitutional Law. Only a brief outline is presented here.

(a) The cases generally take the view that the question whether a "property" interest exists is governed by state law. See, *e.g.*, Cleveland Bd. of Educ. v.

---

3. See also the Broad River case, quoted by Justice Jackson; Muhlker v. Harlem R.R., 197 U.S. 544 (1905); Sauer v. New York, 206 U.S. 536 (1907); Fox River Paper Co. v. Railroad Comm., 274 U.S. 651 (1927).

Loudermill, 470 U.S. 532, 538–41 (1985)(state law created interest in school employment); Memphis Light, Gas & Water Division v. Craft, 436 U.S. 1, 9–12 (1978)(state-created interest in non-termination of utility service).[4]

(b) The relevance of state law to the existence of a constitutionally-protected "liberty" interest is more complicated. Clearly, state law can create "liberty" interests just as it can create property interests. See, *e.g.*, Board of Pardons v. Allen, 482 U.S. 369, 370–81 (1987)(state-law entitlement to parole). There is also significant authority recognizing a federal constitutional dimension to liberty, quite apart from entitlements based on positive law. Thus, without referring to state law, the Court has recognized, for example, liberty interests of a student in freedom from corporal punishment, see Ingraham v. Wright, 430 U.S. 651 (1977), a parent in not having parental rights terminated, see Santosky v. Kramer, 455 U.S. 745, 754 (1982), and a mentally retarded individual in the conditions of involuntary confinement, see Youngberg v. Romeo, 457 U.S. 307 (1982).[5] Plainly, federal law alone governs the question whether the Due Process Clause itself creates a liberty interest.

(c) Finally, if the case does involve a "property" or "liberty" interest (whether rooted in state or federal law), federal law governs the questions (i) whether there has been a deprivation,[6] and (ii) if so, whether due process was afforded.[7]

(4) *The Limits of State–Created Entitlements.* In deciding whether a state-created entitlement exists, the Court has not rested exclusively on an examination of state law and practice. Rather, the Supreme Court appears to have erected threshold federal standards that state laws and practices must satisfy in order to give rise to an entitlement for purposes of the Due Process Clause.

(a) First, despite suggestions in Perry, Paragraph B(2), *supra*, that "unwritten 'common law' " or "the existence of rules and *understandings*, promul-

---

4. Might there be a minimal conception of "property" in the Due Process Clause beneath which the states cannot (and almost never do) fall? Professor Monaghan asks whether federal law would permit a state to provide that "ownership" of an automobile is limited by the right of state officials to seize the car whenever they wish to—and answers his own question in the negative. See Monaghan, Paragraph A(4), *supra*, at 440; accord Fallon, *Some Confusions About Due Process, Judicial Review, and Constitutional Remedies*, 93 Colum.L.Rev. 309, 328–29 (1993). That the hypothetical is so extreme, however, indicates how rarely a state definition of property is likely to fall beneath any possible federal threshold. For discussion of a case that may be a rare example, see Webb's Fabulous Pharmacies, Inc. v. Beckwith, Paragraph B(5)(b), *infra*.

5. Occasionally the Court will find that state law and the Due Process Clause each independently gives rise to a liberty interest. See, *e.g.*, Vitek v. Jones, 445 U.S. 480, 487–94 (1980)(interest of prisoners in avoiding transfer to mental institutions); Washington v. Harper, 494 U.S. 210, 219–21 (1990)(mental-

ly ill inmate's interest in refusing anti-psychotic medications).

6. On the question of the meaning of deprivation, see Chap. IX, Sec. 2(C), p. 1150, *infra*.

7. In Arnett v. Kennedy, 416 U.S. 134 (1974), a case involving a federal employee, three Justices argued that since the government was free not to create a property interest at all, it should be free to create a property interest but to specify that only certain limited procedures must be followed before that interest could be impaired; according to this argument, the individual must "take the bitter with the sweet" (p. 154). Although there was no majority opinion in Arnett, the other six Justices rejected that position. And in Cleveland Bd. of Educ. v. Loudermill, 470 U.S. 532 (1985)(8–1), the Court squarely repudiated it, holding that although the existence of a "property" entitlement in state employment was governed by state law, the question of what procedures must be followed before depriving an individual of an entitlement is governed exclusively by federal law.

gated and *fostered* by state officials" can create an entitlement, 408 U.S. at 602 (emphasis added), more recent cases have qualified these suggestions. Not all interests recognized by state common law establish an entitlement under the Due Process Clause. See Paul v. Davis, 424 U.S. 693 (1976). And the Court has refused to recognize entitlements premised on institutional practice, see Connecticut Bd. of Pardons v. Dumschat, 452 U.S. 458, 465 (1981), insisting instead upon proof of "explicitly mandatory language" establishing "substantive predicates" governing official decisionmaking, whose satisfaction requires a particular outcome. Kentucky Dep't of Corrections v. Thompson, 490 U.S. 454, 462–63 (1989).

Why should the Supreme Court impose such a threshold requirement? Professor Fallon argues that "no constitutional value typically precludes a state from choosing as expansive a conception as it may wish; a state court that found a 'property' interest in a public employee's job, under circumstances in which the federal Constitution would not compel that characterization, should be deemed to commit no constitutional error." Fallon, note 4, *supra*, at 328. Compare United States Mortgage Co. v. Matthews, Paragraph A(4), *supra*.

If property is merely whatever "bundle of sticks" finds recognition in state law, doesn't Fallon's point have considerable force? On the other hand, could affording constitutional protection to whatever entitlement a state creates, no matter how unimportant, create a flood of due process claims asserting the deprivation of quite trivial interests?

(b) Concern about such a flood may have influenced the decision in Sandin v. Conner, 115 S.Ct. 2293 (1995), where the Court, in deciding whether a prisoner asserted a valid *liberty* interest, appears significantly to have shifted its approach to determining whether a state-created entitlement exists. The prisoner filed suit in *federal* court, objecting to his placement in disciplinary segregation for 30 days after having been found to have violated prison rules. Mandatory language in a state regulation (i) gave the prisoner a right to present evidence and (ii) permitted discipline only if the charge was supported by substantial evidence or admitted to by the prisoner. But with Chief Justice Rehnquist writing for a bare majority, the Court held that the prisoner lacked a liberty interest and thus could not challenge the discipline as a denial of due process. Acknowledging that it was departing from its precedents, the Court refused to treat mandatory language alone as sufficient to generate a state-created liberty interest. Doing so, the Court contended, "created disincentives for States to codify prison management procedures" and led "to the involvement of federal courts in the day-to-day management of prisons" (p. 2299). Instead, the Court held that a state-created liberty interest "will be generally limited to freedom from restraint which, while not exceeding the sentence in such an unexpected manner as to give rise to protection by the Due Process Clause of its own force [citing Vitek and Washington, note 5, *supra*], nonetheless imposes atypical and significant hardship on the inmate in relation to the ordinary incidents of prison life" (p. 2300). No such finding could be made here: the conditions of disciplinary segregation, when compared to ordinary prison life, did not "work a major disruption of [the prisoner's] environment" (p. 2301).[8]

---

8. Four Justices dissented. Justice Breyer (joined by Justice Souter) would have followed prior law, which he viewed as establishing three categories: deprivations so severe in kind or degree that they infringe liberty interests protected by the Due Process

It remains to be seen how major a shift in approach the Sandin decision heralds—whether, for example, it applies outside the prison context, or generally to property as well as liberty cases.

(5) *State-Created Entitlements: The Scope of Review.* Suppose that a state court finds that state law did not create a liberty or property interest. What standard of review should the Supreme Court apply in reviewing that decision?

(a) The question has not arisen often, since almost all the recent cases in this line have come to the Court from the lower federal courts, usually in actions under 42 U.S.C. § 1983.[9] The few cases that originated in the state courts shed little light on the scope of review. In Logan v. Zimmerman Brush Co., 455 U.S. 422 (1982), for example, the administrative agency dismissed an employment discrimination complaint because (through no fault of the employee) the agency had not convened a conference within 120 days, as required by state law. The Illinois Supreme Court affirmed, finding that the time-limit was mandatory and that the legislature could establish reasonable procedures for processing complaints. The Supreme Court reversed, citing federal decisions as having settled that "a cause of action is a species of property protected by the Fourteenth Amendment's Due Process Clause" (p. 428). The case is perhaps best read, however, as one where the state court did not deny that there was a property interest, but rather held that the state legislature, in creating that interest, could qualify it by specifying the procedures that would suffice to justify a deprivation—a position that the Supreme Court has specifically repudiated, see note 7, *supra.*[10]

(b) In one closely analogous decision under the Takings Clause, however, the Supreme Court did appear to disregard state property law. In Webb's Fabulous Pharmacies, Inc. v. Beckwith, 449 U.S. 155 (1980), the question was whether a Florida statute, which authorized a county to take the interest accruing on an interpleader fund deposited in state court, constituted a taking of property from the claimants to the fund. The state court said no, ruling that under the statute the interest was the property of the county, not of the claimants. The Supreme Court reversed. It acknowledged (quoting Roth) that

Clause directly; deprivations about minor matters (for example, the kind of lunch to be served) that are unprotected by the Due Process Clause, even if official conduct violated a clear-cut regulation; and an intermediate category of deprivations—like the one in this case—in which the existence of a liberty interest depends upon state law. He argued forcefully that the disciplinary segregation here was not a mere "minor matter" that should be deemed unprotected despite the state regulation. Justice Ginsburg, joined by Justice Stevens, agreed with Justice Breyer that the deprivation was serious, but took the view that the prisoner had a liberty interest rooted in the Due Process Clause itself—a result that avoided the concern (voiced by the majority) that states that formulate more rules subject themselves to stricter constitutional constraints.

9. In federal court actions, should the Supreme Court defer to the understanding of state law of the lower federal courts? In Bishop v. Wood, 426 U.S. 341 (1976)(5–4), the federal district court found that a discharged police officer had no state-created property right—a quite debatable reading, but one affirmed by the court of appeals and one that the Supreme Court thought was "tenable". Pointing to the district judge's familiarity with state law, the Supreme Court deferred to his ruling. Does that approach suggest that, had the case come up through the state courts, the Court would have accepted a state court finding of no property right, so long as it was "tenable"?

10. In Hicks v. Oklahoma, 447 U.S. 343 (1980), the Court also overturned a state court decision that had found no violation of due process in a sentencing decision, but because the liberty interest there involved was created directly by the Due Process Clause, federal review was de novo.

property interests are created not by the Constitution but by an independent source like state law. But it proceeded to cite numerous cases from jurisdictions other than Florida as supporting the proposition that, in the circumstances presented, the interest belonged to the claimants. Without examining Florida law further, the Court ruled that "a State, by ipse dixit, may not transform private property into public property without compensation" (p. 164). Does this suggest that the state's definition of property lacked fair support in Florida law? Or that the definition, however well-grounded, was impermissible under the Due Process Clause?

(c) Recall the standard set forth in Demorest, Paragraph B(1), *supra*—a case involving an "old" property interest (a remainder in proceeds paid to a trust). There the Court held that the decision of the state courts that there was no state-created property right will govern so long as there is fair support in state law for that decision.[11] Is that an appropriate approach for all due process cases—including those involving "new" liberty or property—insofar as the existence of an entitlement rests upon state law? Does that approach differ from the approach in Brand?

(d) Note, however, that the decisions discussed in Paragraph B(4), *supra*, indicate that under the Due Process Clause, as to "new" liberty or property interests, the existence of a "state-created" entitlement does not in fact always depend exclusively upon state law.

Imagine that a prison warden decides that a prisoner who violated certain rules must spend the next 12 months at hard labor; the state courts, in a lawsuit challenging that decision, rule that it implicates no state-created liberty interest.

(i) Suppose that the state court's ruling was based on the view that there was no consistent state law or practice limiting the warden's power to assign prisoners to hard labor. Shouldn't the Supreme Court exhibit deference—as under the Demorest standard—in reviewing that ruling?

(ii) Suppose, instead, that the state court took the view that the warden's decision, although arguably in violation of mandatory state rules limiting the circumstances in which prisoners may be given hard labor, did not "impose[] atypical and significant hardship" on the prisoner within the meaning of Sandin v. Connor, Paragraph B(4)(b), *supra*. Isn't that purely a question of federal law, as to which no deference is appropriate?

(iii) Suppose, finally, that the state courts' ruling that there is no liberty interest doesn't clearly articulate its basis. What should the Supreme Court do then? Does Michigan v. Long bear on that question?

C. Other Constitutional Protections of Liberty

Analogous claims involving constitutionally-protected liberties defined by state law may arise under provisions other than the Due Process Clause.

(1) *Expansion of Criminal Liability*. In Splawn v. California, 431 U.S. 595 (1977), the defendant was prosecuted for selling obscene films. He contended that (a) a state statute, enacted after the conduct for which he was being tried,

---

11. Even if that standard is generally the appropriate one, might there be rare cases in which a state's definition of the entitlement, though well-grounded in state law, is so aberrational that it subverts the purposes of the constitutional guarantee? See note 4, *supra*.

changed prior law to permit introduction of evidence of "pandering," and (b) application of the statute in his case violated the prohibition against ex post facto laws and the requirements of due process enunciated in Bouie v. City of Columbia, p. 624, *infra*.

The Supreme Court affirmed, ruling that the state court's decision—which found that the evidence would have been admissible under state law before the statute was passed—"is entitled to great weight in evaluating petitioner's constitutional contentions" (p. 600). The Court accepted the state court's conclusion, without explicit statement indicating independent verification of the state law question. The dissenters' position on the ex post facto issue was based on an independent assessment of state law.

(2) *Capital Punishment Statutes*. A problem analogous to that in Splawn arises in death penalty cases. Under prevailing doctrine, once a state has opted among a variety of constitutionally permissible schemes for imposition of capital punishment, the Eighth Amendment can be seen as protecting a state-created liberty interest: state law defines when a capital sentence is permitted, and the federal Constitution protects against capital punishment imposed other than in accordance with the state's statutes.

Although the Court has not described the problem in these terms, this approach may cast light on a number of difficult cases. For example, in Parker v. Dugger, 498 U.S. 308 (1991), the trial judge, in imposing a death sentence on Parker, had said that "[t]here are no mitigating circumstances that outweigh the aggravating circumstances". The state supreme court, in upholding the sentence, declared that the trial court had found no mitigating circumstances to balance against the aggravating circumstances. On federal habeas corpus, the Supreme Court, in a painstaking analysis of the record, concluded (1) that the trial court had in fact found non-statutory mitigating factors but concluded that they were outweighed by the aggravating circumstances, and (2) that as a result of the state supreme court's erroneous analysis of the trial court's decision, Parker had been deprived of the meaningful and individualized appellate review to which he was constitutionally entitled. Justice White, speaking for the four dissenters, argued that the trial judge's statements could plausibly be read as a finding of no mitigating circumstances, and that any error by the state supreme court was not "of federal constitutional dimensions. The Eighth Amendment 'does not, by its terms, regulate the procedures of sentencing as opposed to the substance of punishment' " (pp. 327–28)(quoting Walton v. Arizona, 497 U.S. 639, 670 (1990)(Scalia, J., concurring)).

Suppose that a state statute permits capital punishment only where at least one statutorily-specified aggravating factor is present; that a state trial judge—despite the clear language of the statute—imposes a death penalty, relying solely upon the presence of a different, unspecified aggravating factor; and that the death sentence is upheld on appeal. Suppose, further, that the Eighth Amendment does not independently preclude a state from relying solely on the unspecified aggravating factor in imposing the death penalty? Is the death sentence subject to reversal as a matter of federal law? [12]

---

12. In Ricketts v. Adamson, 483 U.S. 1 (1987), Adamson had been charged with first-degree murder but pled guilty to second-degree. The plea agreement provided that he would testify against two confederates, and that if he failed to do so, the agreement was void. Adamson testified as promised at the trial of the other two, who were convicted. Adamson's sentencing (which had been stayed) then took place. Thereafter, the con-

D. Full Faith and Credit

The Full Faith and Credit Clause (Article IV, Sec. 1) and implementing legislation (28 U.S.C. § 1738) require the forum state to determine the existence and nature of rights that a litigant claims to have acquired under a judgment of the state of the prior adjudication. The Supreme Court has jurisdiction to consider claims that the forum state failed to provide full faith and credit. See, *e.g.*, Clark v. Williard, 292 U.S. 112 (1934); Ford v. Ford, 371 U.S. 187 (1962).

In Adam v. Saenger, 303 U.S. 59 (1938), where the issue was whether a California judgment on which suit was brought in Texas had been rendered by a court with jurisdiction under California law, Justice Stone declared (p. 64): "While this Court reexamines such an issue with deference after its determination by a state court, it cannot, if the laws and Constitution of the United States are to be observed, accept as final the decision of the state tribunal as to matters alleged to give rise to the asserted federal right. This is especially the case where the decision is rested * * * upon the law of another state, as readily determined here as in a state court."

How much deference does the Supreme Court owe to Texas courts on a question of the law of California? [13]

E. Federal Statutes and Treaties

(1) *Martin v. Hunter's Lessee.* State-created rights may be protected not only by federal constitutional provisions, but also by federal statutes or treaties. Wasn't Martin v. Hunter's Lessee an example of a federal treaty that protected state-created rights? What was the scope of review on the question whether

victions of the other two were overturned on appeal. Adamson took the position that his obligation to testify under the agreement expired when he was sentenced, and thus he was not obliged to testify at the retrial. The state then declared him in breach of the agreement; as a result, his conviction was vacated and the first-degree murder charge was reinstated. Adamson's protests that he was not in breach and that the reinstated charge therefore constituted double jeopardy were rejected by the Arizona courts; the Arizona Supreme Court held that Adamson's interpretation of the agreement, although reasonable, was erroneous, and found that his breach left him unprotected by the Double Jeopardy Clause.

When the case reached the Supreme Court (on review of a federal habeas corpus proceeding), the Court found no double jeopardy violation. The majority said: "We will not second-guess the Arizona Supreme Court's construction of the language of the plea agreement. While we assess independently the plea agreement's effect on respondent's double jeopardy rights, the construction of the plea agreement and the concomitant obligations flowing therefrom are, within broad bounds of reasonableness,

matters of state law * * *" (p. 7 n. 3). Four dissenters argued that "even if one defers to the Arizona Supreme Court's construction of the plea agreement, one must conclude that Adamson never breached that agreement" (p. 12). The dissenters criticized the Court's acceptance of the state court's finding of breach, and relied on general principles of contract law (rather than on Arizona law specifically) in arguing that the state was not justified in treating Adamson's statements that he was not obliged to testify at the retrial as an anticipatory repudiation of the contractual promise.

13. The Supreme Court, rather than resolving questions of one state's law in the context of a full-faith-and-credit proceeding in the courts of another state, may be able to secure answers to those questions from the highest court of the original state. In Aldrich v. Aldrich, 378 U.S. 540 (1964), a case from West Virginia involving a question about the effect of a prior Florida decree, the Supreme Court delayed decision while certifying questions to the Florida Supreme Court under then established state procedures for such certification. See generally Chap. X, Sec. 2(B), p. 1245, *infra*.

the land had escheated to the Commonwealth of Virginia before the treaty took effect? What should it have been?

(2) *The Federal Arbitration Act.* In Volt Information Sciences, Inc. v. Board of Trustees of Leland Stanford Junior University, 489 U.S. 468 (1989), the defendant in a breach of contract suit sought to compel arbitration under the contract's arbitration clause. The California courts refused; they interpreted the contract's choice-of-law clause, which stated that any dispute would be governed by "the law of the place where the Project is located", as incorporating California's statutory rules, under which arbitration would not be compelled in the circumstances presented. The defendant appealed to the Supreme Court, claiming a denial of its rights under the Federal Arbitration Act (FAA), which, it argued, requires state courts to enforce arbitration clauses in contracts covered by the Act. The defendant argued, further, that the Court should review the state court's interpretation of the choice-of-law clause, as that interpretation was in effect a finding that defendant had "waived" its right under the FAA to compel arbitration.

In affirming, the Supreme Court refused to review the state court's contractual interpretation. Instead, the Court argued that the FAA gives no unqualified right to compel arbitration, but only a right to compel arbitration as provided for by the parties. The state court's decision "was not a finding that appellant had 'waived' an FAA-guaranteed right to compel arbitration of this dispute, but a finding that it had no such right in the first place, because the parties' agreement did not require arbitration to proceed in this situation" (p. 475).

Justice Brennan, joined by Justice Marshall, dissented. Relying, *inter alia*, on Brand, he said: "[T]he right of the instant parties to have their arbitration agreement enforced pursuant to the FAA could readily be circumvented by a state-court construction of their contract as having intended to exclude the applicability of federal law. It is therefore essential that, while according due deference to the decision of the state court, we independently determine whether we 'clearly would have judged the issue differently if [we] were the state's highest court'" (p. 484, quoting Wechsler, *The Appellate Jurisdiction of the Supreme Court: Reflections on the Law and Logistics of Direct Review*, 34 Wash. & Lee L.Rev. 1043, 1052 (1977)). Noting that past cases had employed a wide range of standards of review (from de novo review to determining merely whether the state court decision was "palpably erroneous"), he added: "I have no doubt that the proper standard of review is a narrow one" (p. 485 n. 6). He found no need to specify further, arguing that under any standard of review the state court had erred in reading the choice-of-law clause to speak to the interaction between state and federal law, rather than to the choice of California law over that of another state.

Can the majority's approach be squared with Brand? Wasn't it just as true in Brand that federal law (there the Contracts Clause) confers a right only when the parties' agreement is interpreted to create a contractual promise under the circumstances?

(3) *A General Standard?* Is there any reason why the scope of review, on the question of the existence of an antecedent state-created entitlement, should not be the same in all the various cases discussed in this Note? How do you explain the oscillation of the Justices in reviewing the state law issue— sometimes engaging in de novo review, sometimes in limited review, and sometimes deferring altogether?

SUBSECTION B: PROCEDURAL REQUIREMENTS

Cardinale v. Louisiana

394 U.S. 437, 89 S.Ct. 1161, 22 L.Ed. 398 (1969).
Certiorari to the Supreme Court of Louisiana.

■ MR. JUSTICE WHITE delivered the opinion of the Court.

Petitioner brutally murdered a woman near New Orleans, and then fled the State. * * * In the course of his flight petitioner came to Tucson, Arizona, where he decided to surrender. He flagged down a police car and, after an interruption by the police to warn him that he need not speak, that his speech might be used against him, and that he had a right to contact an attorney, was taken to the station house where he poured out a confession. His confession was introduced in its entirety in the subsequent trial for murder in which petitioner was convicted and sentenced to death. Petitioner does not now contend that his confession was involuntary or that his admission of guilt to the Tucson police was inadmissible in evidence. He objects solely to the admission of those parts of his confession which he argues were both irrelevant and prejudicial in his trial for murder. A Louisiana statute requires that confessions must be admitted in their entirety, La. Rev. Stat. § 15:450, and petitioner contends that this is unconstitutional.

Although certiorari was granted to consider this question, the fact emerged in oral argument that the sole federal question argued here had never been raised, preserved, or passed upon in the state courts below. It was very early established that the Court will not decide federal constitutional issues raised here for the first time on review of state court decisions. In Crowell v. Randell, 10 Pet. 368 (1836), Justice Story reviewed the earlier cases commencing with Owings v. Norwood's Lessee, 5 Cranch 344 (1809), and came to the conclusion that the Judiciary Act of 1789, c. 20, § 25, 1 Stat. 85, vested this Court with no jurisdiction unless a federal question was raised and decided in the state court below. "If both of these do not appear on the record, the appellate jurisdiction fails." 10 Pet. 368, 391. The Court has consistently refused to decide federal constitutional issues raised here for the first time on review of state court decisions both before the Crowell opinion, Miller v. Nicholls, 4 Wheat. 311, 315 (1819), and since, e.g., Safeway Stores, Inc. v. Oklahoma Retail Grocers Assn., Inc., 360 U.S. 334, 342, n. 7 (1959); State Farm Mutual Automobile Ins. Co. v. Duel, 324 U.S. 154, 160–163 (1945); [citing additional cases].

In addition to the question of jurisdiction arising under the statute controlling our power to review final judgments of state courts, 28 U.S.C. § 1257, there are sound reasons for this. Questions not raised below are those on which the record is very likely to be inadequate, since it certainly was not compiled with those questions in mind. And in a federal system it is important that state courts be given the first opportunity to consider the applicability of state statutes in light of constitutional challenge, since the statutes may be construed in a way which saves their constitutionality. Or the issue may be blocked by an adequate state ground. Even though States are not free to avoid constitutional issues on inadequate state grounds, O'Connor v. Ohio, 385 U.S. 92 (1966), they should be given the first opportunity to consider them.

In view of the petitioner's admitted failure to raise the issue he presents here in any way below, the failure of the state court to pass on this issue, the desirability of giving the State the first opportunity to apply its statute on an adequate record, and the fact that a federal habeas remedy may remain if no state procedure for raising the issue is available to petitioner, the writ is dismissed for want of jurisdiction.

It is so ordered.

■ MR. JUSTICE BLACK, MR. JUSTICE DOUGLAS, and MR. JUSTICE FORTAS concur in the dismissal of the writ, believing it to have been improvidently granted.

NOTE ON THE PRESENTATION AND PRESERVATION OF FEDERAL QUESTIONS

(1) *The Sources of the Rule.* As sources for the rule it follows, Cardinale invokes both 28 U.S.C. § 1257 (which requires that the federal question have been "drawn in question" or "specially set up and claimed") and a variety of policy concerns. See also Webb v. Webb, 451 U.S. 493, 499–501 (1981), elaborating on these sources.[1] Despite such references to § 1257, the Court in recent years has repeatedly acknowledged, in refusing to hear a federal issue not raised in state court, that it is unsettled whether the rule is merely prudential or is a strict jurisdictional requirement. See, *e.g.*, Yee v. City of Escondido, 503 U.S. 519, 533 (1992); Bankers Life & Cas. Co. v. Crenshaw, 486 U.S. 71, 79 (1988); Illinois v. Gates, 462 U.S. 213, 217–24 & cases cited (1983). Compare Wood v. Georgia, Paragraph (5), *infra*; Spann, *Functional Analysis of the Plain–Error Rule*, 71 Geo.L.J. 945 (1983)(arguing that the Court has jurisdiction to correct plain errors of federal law not raised in the state courts). See generally 16 Wright, Miller, Cooper & Gressman, Federal Practice and Procedure § 4022 (1977 & 1995 Supp.).

(2) *The Governing Standard.* The requirement of presenting the federal question to the state courts is often spoken of as if it were tested by federal-law

---

1. See also Supreme Court Rule 14.1(g)(i), which provides that a petition for certiorari to a state court shall contain "specification of the stage in the proceedings, both in the court of first instance and in the appellate courts, when the federal questions sought to be reviewed were raised; the method or manner of raising them and the way in which they were passed on by those courts; and pertinent quotations of specific portions of the record or summary thereof, with specific reference to the places in the record where the matter appears (*e.g.*, court opinion, ruling on exception, portion of court's charge and exception thereto, assignment of errors), so as to show that the federal question was timely and properly raised and that this Court has jurisdiction to review the judgment on a writ of certiorari."

When the Court gives a case plenary consideration after a grant of certiorari, there is a distinct requirement that the questions to be decided on the merits have been presented in the petition for certiorari. See Rule 14.1(a). On whether an issue argued on the merits was subsumed by a question presented in the petition, see, *e.g.*, Lebron v. National R.R. Passenger Corp., 115 S.Ct. 961, 964–66 (1995); Caspari v. Bohlen, 114 S.Ct. 948, 952–53 (1994); Yee v. City of Escondido, cited in text above. The Rules reserve to the Court, however, the power to "consider a plain error not among the questions presented but evident from the record *and otherwise within its jurisdiction to decide*" (Rule 24.1(a); emphasis added). The italicized language appears to authorize the Court to hear only an issue properly raised in state court but not presented in the petition for certiorari, rather than an issue not raised at all in state court. But *cf.* Vachon v. New Hampshire, Paragraph (4), *infra*.

standards: "There are various ways in which the validity of a state statute may be drawn in question on the ground that it is repugnant to the Constitution of the United States. No particular form of words or phrases is essential, but only that the claim of invalidity and the ground therefore be brought to the attention of the state court with fair precision and in due time." New York ex rel. Bryant v. Zimmerman, 278 U.S. 63, 67 (1928). See also Herndon v. Georgia, 295 U.S. 441, 443 (1935), p. 578, *infra*, which appears to recite a federal standard in stating "[t]he long-established general rule * * * that the attempt to raise a federal question after judgment, upon a petition for rehearing, comes too late * * *."

In Street v. New York, 394 U.S. 576 (1969), Justice Harlan, writing for the Court, said that the Court is not bound by the state court's determination as to whether the federal question was sufficiently raised, but he added: "[I]t is not entirely clear whether in such cases the scope of our review is limited to determining whether the state court has 'by-passed the federal right under forms of local procedure' or whether we should decide the matter '*de novo* for ourselves.' Ellis v. Dixon, 349 U.S. 458, 463 (1955)" (p. 582). When the highest state court fails to pass on a federal question, "it will be assumed that the omission was due to want of proper presentation" and that the burden is on appellant "affirmatively [to] show the contrary" (p. 582)—a burden that he found had been discharged in the case under review, both as a matter of federal law and under the New York authorities.[2]

(3) *Problems in Application.* There is considerable variation in the strictness with which the requirement of presentation to the state courts has been applied. A central difficulty in application is determining whether an issue raised before the Supreme Court was subsumed in questions put to and decided by the state courts, and how much variation and expansion of such questions is allowed.

(a) One set of cases has addressed the question whether a particular federal issue raised for the first time before the Supreme Court was subsumed in a slightly different federal issue that was raised in state court. For example, in Yee v. City of Escondido, 503 U.S. 519, 532 (1992), the Court reiterated the proposition that if a federal *claim* was properly raised in state court, a party can raise before the Supreme Court any *argument* in support of that claim, even if the *argument* was not raised in the state courts. The Court proceeded to hold that the argument that a rent control ordinance constituted a "regulatory taking" could be raised for the first time in the Supreme Court, as the litigant had raised, in state court, the claim that the ordinance was a "physical taking".[3] However, a substantive due process challenge to the ordinance was deemed to be a different claim not raised below and hence not reviewable.

The distinction between a new claim and a new argument is hardly clear-cut. For decisions in which the Justices divided on the question, see, *e.g.*, Eddings v. Oklahoma, 455 U.S. 104, 113–14 n. 9 (1982)(defendant's claim that imposition of the death penalty in his particular circumstances violated the Eighth Amendment sufficed to put in issue the legality of the trial judge's refusal to consider relevant mitigating evidence as required by Lockett v. Ohio,

---

2. But see p. 576, note 1, *infra*, for more recent decisions modifying that burden.

3. The Court nonetheless refused to decide the regulatory taking claim, on the distinct ground that it was not included within the question presented in the petition for certiorari (which was limited to the physical taking issue). See note 1, *supra*.

438 U.S. 586 (1978)—despite the failure to mention Lockett in state court;) Terminiello v. Chicago, 337 U.S. 1 (1949).[4]

(b) A second set of cases has focused on whether a litigant adequately indicated in state court that a claim was based on federal rather than on state law. For example, the Court has long required a litigant to show "that some provision of the Federal, as distinguished from the state, Constitution was relied upon," New York Central & H.R.Co. v. New York, 186 U.S. 269, 273 (1902). And claims that a state statute violates the Constitution, without more, will be viewed as referring to state and not federal provisions. See, *e.g.,* New York ex rel. Bryant v. Zimmerman, 278 U.S. 63, 67–68 (1928); Bowe v. Scott, 233 U.S. 658, 664–65 (1914)(reference to due process deemed to refer only to state constitution). What justifies that presumption? Compare Michigan v. Long, p. 528, *supra.*

The requirement that litigants show that their claims sounded in federal law is not limited to cases involving parallel federal and state constitutional provisions. Thus, for example, in Webb v. Webb, 451 U.S. 493 (1981), the Court, over Justice Marshall's lone dissent, held that a litigant who had complained in a custody suit about a failure to give "full faith and credit" to a prior judgment, but who had not mentioned the Full Faith and Credit Clause, had presented only a state law issue under the Uniform Child Custody Jurisdiction Act, and thus could not raise the federal constitutional issue in the Supreme Court.

(4) *Vachon v. New Hampshire.* The decision in Vachon v. New Hampshire, 414 U.S. 478 (1974), tested the outer limits of the requirement that the federal issue have been raised in state court. The defendant had been convicted of willfully contributing to the delinquency of a minor, for having sold a 14–year old girl a button containing a sexual slogan. On appeal to the state supreme court, he had unsuccessfully challenged the sufficiency of the evidence of willfulness. The Supreme Court, in a brief per curiam opinion, reversed, relying on the federal constitutional principle that due process is denied when there is no evidence of one element of a crime (here, willfulness).

In dissent, Justice Rehnquist protested (pp. 482–83): "A litigant seeking to preserve a constitutional claim for review in this Court must not only make clear to the lower courts the nature of his claim, but he must also make it clear that the claim is constitutionally grounded. The closest that appellant came in his brief on appeal to the Supreme Court of New Hampshire to discussing the issue on which this Court's opinion turns is in the sixth section, which is

---

4. In Terminiello, the petitioner, convicted of violating a disorderly conduct ordinance for making a speech, took no exception to a jury instruction that "misbehavior may constitute a breach of the peace if it stirs the public to anger, invites dispute, brings about a condition of unrest * * *". He did, however, move for a directed verdict on the ground that "what he said was protected by the first amendment" (Petition for Certiorari, pp. 4–5). His argument in the Supreme Court also focused wholly on the nature of his conduct.

The Supreme Court reversed, holding that the ordinance, as construed in the portion of the charge quoted above, was invalid,

and that the question had been adequately raised by the petitioner's contention that "inclusion of his speech within the ordinance was a violation of the Constitution" (337 U.S. at 6). Chief Justice Vinson, Justices Frankfurter, Jackson and Burton dissented. Justice Frankfurter objected (pp. 8–9): "For the first time in the course of the 130 years in which State prosecutions have come here for review, this Court is today reversing a sentence imposed by a State court on a ground that was urged neither here nor below and that was explicitly disclaimed on behalf of the petitioner at the bar of this Court."

headed: 'The State's failure to introduce any evidence of scienter should have resulted in dismissal of the charge following the presentation of the State's case.' Appellant in that section makes the customary appellate arguments of insufficiency of the evidence and does not so much as mention either the United States Constitution or a single case decided by this Court. The Supreme Court of New Hampshire treated these arguments as raising a classic state law claim of insufficient evidence of scienter; nothing in that court's opinion remotely suggests that it was treating the claim as having a basis other than in state law."[5]

The Vachon decision takes an unusually flexible view of the requirement that the federal issue be raised in state court. Compare, for example, Bailey v. Anderson, 326 U.S. 203 (1945), where the Court ruled that a state court challenge to the denial of interest in a condemnation action could not be converted, in the Supreme Court, into a federal constitutional question under the Just Compensation Clause.

Note, however, that Vachon fell within the Court's then-existing mandatory appellate jurisdiction. The Court's fact-specific decision enabled it to avoid the obligation it would otherwise have had to decide more difficult constitutional claims (under the void-for-vagueness doctrine and the First Amendment) that the appellant had properly raised. Today, because the Court no longer exercises a mandatory appellate jurisdiction over state court judgments, it would have the option of simply denying certiorari in a case like Vachon. But do the circumstances in Vachon suggest that the Court's jurisdictional determinations are likely to be influenced by whether the Court is eager (or reluctant) to reach a particular issue? Is that appropriate? Inevitable?

What other factors might influence the Court's administration of the rule? Whether the case is criminal rather than civil? Whether the petitioner is acting pro se? Whether the constitutional violation is flagrant? See generally Stern, Gressman, Shapiro & Geller, Supreme Court Practice 116–22 (7th ed.1993)(discussing such factors, and also suggesting that over time the Court may have become less strict in administering the rule).

(5) *Wood v. Georgia.* In Wood v. Georgia, 450 U.S. 261 (1981), the Court decided an issue that all the Justices acknowledged had not been raised in state court. There, three employees of "adult" establishments had been convicted of distributing obscene materials. Their sentence of probation was conditioned on their making installment payments of substantial fines. When those payments were not made, their probation was revoked. The Supreme Court granted review to decide whether it denies equal protection to imprison a probationer who is unable to make such payments.

But the Court (per Powell, J.) vacated the convictions on a different ground. Noting that the employees had been represented by a lawyer paid for by their employer, and that the employer had promised to pay any fines imposed, the Court found that there was a potential conflict of interest that might have denied the employees due process. The Court accordingly remand-

---

5. The Court relied on the predecessor provision to Rule 24.1(a), see note 1, *supra*. The dissent responded that that provision merely authorized the Court, when it had previously noted probable jurisdiction or granted certiorari, to decide issues other than those on which the earlier decision to afford plenary review had been made, rather than to hear issues never raised in state court.

ed the case so that the state courts could determine the nature and implications of any such conflict.

In dissent, Justice White objected that the Court lacked jurisdiction to resolve the due process issue. The Court argued, in response, that the lack of any presentation of the issue "merely emphasize[s] * * * why it *is* appropriate for us to consider the issue. The party who argued the appeal and prepared the petition for certiorari was the lawyer on whom the conflict-of-interest charge focused. It is unlikely that he would contend that he had continued improperly to act as counsel." And, Justice Powell continued, the state could not claim lack of notice, as it had pointed out the conflict at the revocation hearing. He concluded: "In this context, it is appropriate to treat the due process issue as one 'raised' below, and proceed to consider it here. Even if one considers that the conflict-of-interest question was not technically raised below, there is ample support for a remand required in the interests of justice. See 28 U.S.C. § 2106 (authorizing the Court to 'require such further proceedings to be had as may be just under the circumstances')" (p. 265 n. 5).

What is the holding of Wood? In Webb v. Webb, 451 U.S. 493, 502 (1981), Justice Powell, in a concurring opinion joined by Justice Brennan, characterized Wood as having "reaffirmed * * * that the Court has jurisdiction to review plain error unchallenged in the state court when necessary to prevent fundamental unfairness." Should Wood be limited to circumstances in which some defect in the state process prevented the litigant from raising the issue in the first instance?[6] If a litigant blames the failure to have raised the claim on counsel's inadvertence or incompetence, may the Supreme Court exercise jurisdiction? Might that not have been true in Cardinale itself?

Staub v. City of Baxley

355 U.S. 313, 78 S.Ct. 277, 2 L.Ed.2d 302 (1958).
Appeal from the Court of Appeals of Georgia.

■ MR. JUSTICE WHITTAKER delivered the opinion of the Court.

Appellant, Rose Staub, was convicted in the Mayor's Court of the City of Baxley, Georgia, of violation of a city ordinance and was sentenced to imprisonment for 30 days or to pay a fine of $300. The Superior Court of the county affirmed the judgment of conviction; the Court of Appeals of the State affirmed the judgment of the Superior Court; and the Supreme Court of the State denied an application for certiorari. The case comes here on appeal.

The ordinance in question is set forth in the margin.[1] Its violation, which is not denied, arose from the following undisputed facts * * *: Appellant was a

---

6. Compare the cases discussed on p. 577, Paragraph (4), *infra*.

1. [Section I of the ordinance required written application to the Mayor and City Council for a permit before anyone could "solicit membership for any organization, union or society of any sort which requires from its members the payments of membership fees" from citizens of Baxley.

[Section II required specific information about the organization and its representative (including places of residence for the past ten years and the names of three character references).

[Section III described the procedure for a hearing before the Mayor and Council of City of Baxley on the application.

salaried employee of the International Ladies' Garment Workers Union which was attempting to organize the employees of a manufacturing company located in the nearby town of Hazelhurst. A number of those employees lived in Baxley. On February 19, 1954, appellant * * * went to Baxley and, without applying for permits required under the ordinance, talked with several of the employees at their homes about joining the union. * * * Later that day a meeting was held at the home of one of the employees, attended by three other employees, at which, in the words of the hostess, appellant "just told us they wanted us to join the union, and said it would be a good thing for us to do ... and went on to tell us how this union would help us." * * * No money was asked or received from the persons at the meeting, but they were invited "to get other girls ... there to join the union" and blank membership cards were offered for that use. Appellant further explained that the immediate objective was to "have enough cards signed to petition for an election ... with the [National Labor Relations Board]."

On the same day a summons was issued and served by the Chief of Police commanding appellant to appear before the Mayor's Court three days later to answer "to the offense of Soliciting Members for an Organization without a Permit & License."

Before the trial, appellant moved to abate the action upon a number of grounds, among which were the contentions that the ordinance "shows on its face that it is repugnant to and violative of the 1st and 14th Amendments to the Constitution of the United States in that it places a condition precedent upon, and otherwise unlawfully restricts, the defendant's freedom of speech as well as freedom of the press and freedom of lawful assembly" by requiring, as conditions precedent to the exercise of those rights, the issuance of a "license" which the Mayor and city council are authorized by the ordinance to grant or refuse in their discretion, and the payment of a "license fee" which is discriminatory and unreasonable in amount * * *. [After conviction in the Mayor's Court, the appellant made the same contentions in the Superior Court, which affirmed the conviction.]

Those contentions were renewed in the Court of Appeals but that court declined to consider them. It stated that "[t]he attack should have been made against specific sections of the ordinance and not against the ordinance as a whole"; * * * and that since it "appears that * * * the defendant has made no effort to comply with any section of the ordinance ... it is not necessary to pass upon the sufficiency of the evidence, the constitutionality of the ordinance, or

[Section IV stated: "In passing upon such application the Mayor and Council shall consider the character of the applicant, the nature of the business of the organization for which members are desired to be solicited, and its effects upon the general welfare of citizens of the City of Baxley."

[Section V provided that the decision on granting a permit shall be determined "in the same manner as other matters are so granted or denied by the vote of the Mayor and Council."

[Section VI provided that an applicant who is salaried by the organization for which the applicant solicits members, or receives a fee from obtaining members, must pay $2,000 a year, and also $500.00 for each member obtained, in order to obtain a permit.

[Section VII stated that anyone soliciting citizens, or persons employed in, Baxley as members of an organization without having obtained a permit shall be punished "as provided by Section 85 of Criminal Code of City of Baxley."

[Section VIII repealed all city ordinances in conflict with this ordinance.

[Section IX contained a separability provision.]

any other phase of the case...." The court * * * affirmed the judgment of conviction.

* * * At the threshold, appellee urges that this appeal be dismissed because, it argues, * * * we are * * * without jurisdiction to entertain it. * * *

Appellee * * * contends that the holding of the Court of Appeals, that appellant's failure to attack "specific sections" of the ordinance rendered it unnecessary, under Georgia procedure, "to pass upon ... the constitutionality of the ordinance, or any other phase of the case ...," constitutes an adequate "non-federal ground" to preclude review in this Court. We think this contention is "without any fair or substantial support" (Ward v. Love County, [253 U.S. 17, 22]) and therefore does not present an *adequate* nonfederal ground of decision in the circumstances of this case. The several sections of the ordinance are interdependent in their application to one in appellant's position and constitute but one complete act for the licensing and taxing of her described activities. For that reason, no doubt, she challenged the constitutionality of the whole ordinance, and in her objections used language challenging the constitutional effect of all its sections. She did, thus, challenge all sections of the ordinance, though not by number. To require her, in these circumstances, to count off, one by one, the several sections of the ordinance would be to force resort to an arid ritual of meaningless form. Indeed, the Supreme Court of Georgia seems to have recognized the arbitrariness of such exaltation of form. Only four years ago that court recognized that an attack on such a statute was sufficient if "the [statute] so challenged was invalid in every part for some reason alleged." Flynn v. State, 209 Ga. 519, 522, 74 S.E.2d 461, 464 (1953). In enunciating that rule the court was following a long line of its own decisions. [Citing four decisions of the Georgia Supreme Court.]

We conclude that the decision of the Court of Appeals does not rest on an adequate nonfederal ground and that we have jurisdiction of this appeal.

[The Court proceeded to find that the ordinance violated the First Amendment, and therefore reversed the conviction.]

■ MR. JUSTICE FRANKFURTER, whom MR. JUSTICE CLARK joins, dissenting.

This is one of those small cases that carry large issues, for it concerns the essence of our federalism—due regard for the constitutional distribution of power as between the Nation and the States, and more particularly the distribution of judicial power as between this Court and the judiciaries of the States.

* * *

While the power to review the denial by a state court of a nonfrivolous claim under the United States Constitution has been centered in this Court, carrying with it the responsibility to see that the opportunity to assert such a claim be not thwarted by any local procedural device, equally important is observance by this Court of the wide discretion in the States to formulate their own procedures for bringing issues appropriately to the attention of their local courts, either in shaping litigation or by appeal. Such methods and procedures may, when judged by the best standards of judicial administration, appear crude, awkward and even finicky or unnecessarily formal when judged in the light of modern emphasis on informality. But so long as the local procedure does not discriminate against the raising of federal claims and, in the particular case, has not been used to stifle a federal claim to prevent its eventual consideration here, this Court is powerless to deny to a State the right to have the kind of judicial system it chooses and to administer that system in its own way. It is of course for this Court to pass on the substantive sufficiency of a claim of federal right, but if resort is had in the first instance to the state judiciary for the enforcement of a federal constitutional right, the State is not barred from subjecting the suit to the same procedures, *nisi prius* and appellate, that govern adjudication of all constitutional issues in that State. * * *

* * * The [United States Supreme] Court has long insisted, certainly in precept, on rigorous requirements that must be fulfilled before it will pass on the constitutionality of legislation, on avoidance of such determinations even by strained statutory construction, and on keeping constitutional adjudication, when unavoidable, as narrow as circumstances will permit. * * * [T]his Court will consider only those very limited aspects of a statute that alone may affect the rights of a particular litigant before the Court. * * * Surely a state court is not to be denied the like right to protect itself from the necessity—sometimes even the temptation—of adjudicating overly broad claims of unconstitutionality. Surely it can insist that such claims be formulated under precise (even if, in our view, needlessly particularized) requirements and restricted to the limited issues that concrete and immediately pressing circumstances may raise.

* * * The cases relied upon by the Georgia court in this case are part of a long line of decisions holding a comprehensive, all-inclusive challenge to the constitutionality of a statute inadequate and requiring explicit particularity in pleadings in order to raise constitutional questions. * * * Thus, allegations of unconstitutionality directed at a group of 16 sections of the Criminal Code, Rooks v. Tindall, 138 Ga. 863, 76 S.E. 378; a single named "lengthy section" of a statute, Crapp v. State, 148 Ga. 150, 95 S.E. 993; a single section of a city charter amendment, Glover v. City of Rome, 173 Ga. 239, 160 S.E. 249; a named Act of the General Assembly, Wright v. Cannon, 185 Ga. 363, 195 S.E. 168; and a 5–section chapter of the Code, Richmond Concrete Products Co. v. Ward, 212 Ga. 773, 95 S.E.2d 677, were held "too general" or "too indefinite" to raise constitutional questions because of their failure to define with particularity what portions offended claimed constitutional rights. * * *

There is nothing frivolous or futile (though it may appear "formal") about a rule insisting that parties specify with arithmetic particularity those provisions in a legislative enactment they would ask a court to strike down. This is so, because such exactitude helps to make concrete the plaintiffs' relation to challenged provisions. First, it calls for closer reflection and greater responsibility on the part of one who challenges legislation, for, in formulating specific attacks against each provision for which an infirmity is claimed, the pleader is more likely to test his claims critically and to reconsider them carefully than he would be if he adopted a "scatter-shot" approach. Secondly, the opposing party, in responding to a particularized attack, is more likely to plead in such a way as to narrow or even eliminate constitutional issues, as where he admits that a specific challenged provision is invalid.[6] Finally, where the parties identify particular language in a statute as allegedly violating a constitutional

---

6. One of the most vulnerable provisions of this ordinance, the drastically high license fee, was taken out of controversy in this suit by the respondent's admission of its invalidity. It is not out of question that more specific pleading might have drawn similar admissions as to other allegedly objectionable portions of the ordinance.

provision, the court will often be able to construe the words in such a way as to render them inoffensive.   * * *

* * * It may be—but it certainly is not clearly so—that with little expenditure of time and effort, and with little risk of misreading appellant's charges, a court could determine exactly what it is about the Baxley ordinance that allegedly infringes upon appellant's constitutional rights.   But rules are not made solely for the easiest cases they govern.   The fact that the reason for a rule does not clearly apply in a given situation does not eliminate the necessity for compliance with the rule.   So long as a reasonable rule of state procedure is consistently applied, so long as it is not used as a means for evading vindication of federal rights, see Davis v. Wechsler, 263 U.S. 22, 24–25, it should not be refused applicability.   * * *

The local procedural rule which controlled this case should not be disregarded by reason of a group of Georgia cases which, while recognizing and reaffirming the rule of pleading relied on by the Court of Appeals below, suggest a limited qualification.   It appears that under special circumstances, where a generalized attack is made against a statute without reference to specific provisions, the court will inquire into the validity of the entire body of legislation challenged.   The cases on which the Court relies as establishing this as the prevailing rule in Georgia strongly indicate that this approach will be used only where an allegation of unconstitutionality can be disposed of (one way or the other) relatively summarily and not where, as here, difficult issues are raised.   In the only case cited by the Court in which the Georgia Supreme Court overturned a statute on the basis of generalized allegations, Atlantic Loan Co. v. Peterson, 181 Ga. 266, 182 S.E. 15, the result was "plainly apparent."   181 Ga., at 274, 182 S.E., at 19.   In the other cases cited, the court gave varying degrees of recognition to this approach, refusing altogether to apply it in [Flynn v. State, 209 Ga. 519, 522, 74 S.E.2d 461, 464], where the court declined to accept "the burden of examining the act section by section and sentence by sentence."   Certainly it cannot be said that the Court of Appeals was out of constitutional bounds in failing to bring the instant case within the purview of whatever exception can be said to have been spelled out by these cases or that it is for this Court to formulate exceptions to the valid Georgia rule of procedure.

The record before us presents not the remotest basis for attributing to the Georgia court any desire to limit the appellant in the fullest opportunity to raise claims of federal right or to prevent an adverse decision on such claims in the Georgia court from review by this Court.   Consequently, this Court is left with no proper choice but to give effect to the rule of procedure on the basis of which this case was disposed of below.   "Without any doubt it rests with each State to prescribe the jurisdiction of its appellate courts, the mode and time of invoking that jurisdiction, and the rules of practice to be applied in its exercise; and the state law and practice in this regard are no less applicable when Federal rights are in controversy than when the case turns entirely upon questions of local or general law."   John v. Paullin, 231 U.S. 583, 585.

The appeal should be dismissed.

NOTE ON THE ADEQUACY OF STATE PROCEDURAL GROUNDS

(1) *Cardinale and Staub Compared.* There is a subtle difference between the jurisdictional questions in Cardinale and in Staub—a difference not always appreciated in the decisions. In Cardinale, the federal issue was never raised in any fashion in state court. The Supreme Court's refusal to hear the issue was based on the litigant's failure to have complied with a *federal* rule requiring that some presentation be made in the state court.

In Staub (and the other cases discussed in this Note), the federal issue was raised, but in a fashion that the state court found did not comply with state procedural law. The question for the Supreme Court was whether that *state law* ruling constituted an adequate state procedural ground barring Supreme Court review.

(2) *The Adequate State Procedural Ground and the Primacy of State Practice.* Justice Frankfurter is surely correct that, in general, state rules of practice presumptively determine the time when, and the mode by which, federal claims must be asserted in the state courts. See, *e.g.*, Edelman v. California, 344 U.S. 357 (1953); Beck v. Washington, 369 U.S. 541, 549–54 (1962); Exxon Corp. v. Eagerton, 462 U.S. 176 (1983). Thus, ordinarily when a state court litigant has committed a procedural default—that is, has failed to raise a federal question in accordance with state procedural rules—the state court will refuse to decide the federal question, and any effort to obtain Supreme Court review will be rejected on the basis that there is an independent and adequate state procedural ground precluding the exercise of jurisdiction. Decisions so holding are legion. See generally Stern, Gressman, Shapiro & Geller, Supreme Court Practice 122–30 (7th ed.1993). And in many other such instances, the Court simply denies certiorari, without noting specifically that jurisdiction was wanting.[1]

(3) *The Inadequate State Ground.* The decision in Staub is thus one of a small set of cases forming a limited exception to the general rule—cases in which the Supreme Court upholds its jurisdiction to review the federal issue in the case on the basis that the state procedural ground is "inadequate" to support the judgment below. The remainder of this Note examines this set of cases.

Many of the cases discussed in this Note, and in the succeeding Note, involved the refusal by Southern courts to adjudicate the rights of black criminal defendants; others involved similar refusals in cases (like Staub) involving members of unpopular social or political movements. Consider these questions: What are the limits of the Supreme Court's capacity to ensure, by reviewing state court judgments, that federal rights will not be undermined by recalcitrant state court judges? Did the Court bend the jurisdictional rules to be able adequately to deal with a pressing set of social, legal and political

---

1. Sometimes it is unclear whether a state court's denial of relief rests on a state procedural ground (which would ordinarily foreclose Supreme Court review) or on the merits of the federal issue (which would permit such review). In such cases, the earlier decisions declined jurisdiction, presuming that the state judgment rested on the procedural default. See, *e.g.*, Mutual Life Ins. Co. v. McGrew, 188 U.S. 291, 309–10 (1903); Bailey v. Anderson, 326 U.S. 203, 206–07 (1945). The recent decision in Harris v. Reed, p. 541, *supra*, suggests that the ordinary presumption may now be just the reverse; but compare the subsequent decisions in Coleman v. Thompson and Ylst v. Nunnemaker, pp. 541–42, *supra*, which qualify Harris' approach; and *cf.* the decision in Capital Cities Media, Inc. v. Toole, 466 U.S. 378 (1984), p. 540, *supra*, which resolved ambiguity as to the presence of an adequate state procedural ground not by presuming one way or the other but rather by remanding to the state court for clarification.

problems—and if so, was that appropriate? [2] Or is the problem that the Court failed to go far enough in trying to protect federal rights from being undermined in state court litigation? If there is concern about the quality of state court justice, is the proper solution for Congress to make available a federal trial forum rather than for the Court to displace state rules of practice? Would it in fact have been practical for Congress to confer federal jurisdiction over, for example, every state criminal prosecution in which federal constitutional issues are present? In the absence of congressional action, how should the Supreme Court respond to the underlying difficulties? Compare Hart, *The Relations Between State and Federal Law*, 54 Colum.L.Rev. 489, 508 (1954) with Meltzer, *State Court Forfeitures of Federal Rights*, 99 Harv.L.Rev. 1128, 1176–78 (1986).

(4) *Due Process Violations.* Supreme Court review plainly cannot be foreclosed by a litigant's noncompliance with a state procedural rule that, on its face or as applied, violates the Due Process Clause.

(a) *Unforeseeable Appellate Court Rulings.* In Brinkerhoff–Faris Trust & Savings Co. v. Hill, 281 U.S. 673 (1930), an equal protection challenge to a state tax was denied by the state appellate court because the taxpayer had failed first to seek administrative relief (which was no longer available)—even though earlier state decisions had held that the state administrative body lacked power to award relief. A petition for rehearing, objecting to this shift of course, was denied. The Supreme Court viewed the action of the state court as a denial of due process, and thus, brushing aside claims of procedural default, reversed the judgment and remanded so that the state court could consider the equal protection issue on the merits.[3]

2. *Cf.* the story related by Professors Eskridge & Frickey in their *Historical and Critical Introduction* to Hart & Sacks, The Legal Process: Basic Problems in the Making and Application of Law cxiii (Eskridge & Frickey eds.1994): "When Henry Hart taught 'Federal Courts' for the last time, during the Spring Term of 1965, he brought into class the Supreme Court's opinion in Hamm v. City of Rock Hill [379 U.S. 306 (1964)]. The Court applied the just-enacted Civil Rights Act of 1964 to abate Southern prosecutions of sit-in demonstrators. Hart stated the facts and relevant authorities, including a federal statute creating a presumption against finding abatement of prosecutions by new statutes. It was apparent from the professor's statement of the case and the authorities that the decision was about to be analytically dissected. But, rather than launching into the sort of devastating critique of which he was capable, Hart paused and reflected to himself, his eyes focused on his reprint of the Court's opinion. The class stopped for thirty breathless seconds. Finally, Hart looked up at the class and said: 'Sometimes, sometimes, you just have to do the right thing.' "

See also Glennon, *The Jurisdictional Legacy of the Civil Rights Movement*, 61 Tenn.L.Rev. 869 (1994)(arguing that in the mid–1950s and the 1960s, the Supreme Court modified doctrines, including that of the adequate state ground, that would otherwise have presented jurisdictional obstacles to the Court's support of the civil rights movement, and that subsequent changes in the South's legal and political systems have substantially diminished the need for expansive federal jurisdiction).

3. See also, *e.g.*, Saunders v. Shaw, 244 U.S. 317 (1917), where the highest state court had, on rehearing, rendered judgment on a finding as to a fact that the trial court, in accordance with appellant's contention, had held immaterial. After appellant's petition complaining of the shift was denied under a state rule precluding a second petition for rehearing, he filed in state court an assignment of errors raising a due process objection to the course of proceedings. On review, the Supreme Court reversed the state court judgment; although ordinarily a litigant would have had to raise the due process issue at an earlier stage, in this case "[w]e do not see what more he could have done" (p. 320).

Cf. also Missouri v. Gehner, 281 U.S. 313 (1930); Cole v. Arkansas, 333 U.S. 196 (1948), p. 624, *infra*.

But a similar attack on a state court's change of position was rejected in Herndon v. Georgia, 295 U.S. 441 (1935). Herndon, a black organizer for the Communist Party, was convicted of an attempt to incite insurrection, after the trial court instructed the jury that the defendant must have expected or advocated immediate serious violence against the state. On appeal, the defendant argued that there was insufficient evidence to convict him under the statute as interpreted by the trial court. The Supreme Court of Georgia affirmed his conviction, finding that the statute did not in fact require proof of the immediacy of the violence. Herndon challenged that court's construction of the statute as a violation of his First Amendment rights, first on motion for rehearing, which the state court denied, and then on appeal to the United States Supreme Court.

The Supreme Court held that Herndon had defaulted by not having challenged the statute until filing his motion for rehearing. The Court reasoned that while Herndon's motion for a new trial was pending in the trial court, the Supreme Court of Georgia had decided another case that had, in the Court's view, construed the statute in question as not requiring proof of the immediacy of violence; thus, the Georgia Supreme Court was justified in holding that Herndon should have anticipated the construction of which he complained and should have challenged it in his initial appeal in state court. In a powerful dissent, Justice Cardozo objected (p. 448) that "[i]t is novel doctrine that a defendant who has had the benefit of all he asks, and indeed of a good deal more, must place a statement on the record that if some other court at some other time shall read the statute differently, there will be a denial of liberties that at the moment of the protest are unchallenged and intact." He also argued persuasively that no decision of the Georgia courts had in fact put Herndon on notice of the construction of the statute later adopted on appeal in his case. Thus, he concluded (citing, *inter alia*, Brinkerhoff–Faris) that Herndon had given "seasonable notice" of his first amendment claim (p. 453).

(b) *Strict Time Limits for Pre–Trial Motions.* Reece v. Georgia, 350 U.S. 85 (1955) and Michel v. Louisiana, 350 U.S. 91 (1955), decided on the same day, both involved criminal defendants who failed to comply with state rules requiring prompt challenges to grand juries. In Reece, a black defendant was arrested for raping a white woman. Three days later he was indicted by a grand jury. Reece's lawyers were appointed the day after indictment, and six days later they challenged the exclusion of blacks from the grand jury. The Georgia courts treated the motion as untimely under a longstanding state rule requiring such challenges to be made prior to indictment.

Without holding the rule facially invalid, the Supreme Court unanimously ruled that its application to Reece's case denied due process (pp. 89–90): "Reece is a semi-illiterate Negro of low mentality. We need not decide whether, with the assistance of counsel, he would have had an opportunity to raise his objection during the two days he was in jail before indictment. But it is utterly unrealistic to say that he had such opportunity when counsel was not provided for him until the day after he was indicted. * * * The effective assistance of counsel in [a capital] case is a constitutional requirement of due process * * *. Georgia should have considered Reece's motion to quash on its merits."

The Michel case involved three defendants who, the Louisiana courts found, had failed to comply with a state rule requiring objections to the grand jury to be raised before the expiration of the third judicial day following the end of the grand jury's term, or before trial, whichever is earlier.

One defendant had a lawyer who, when the judge purported to appoint him (on the day the grand jury expired), told the judge of his reluctance and asked for a week to look the case over; the lawyer did not receive more definite notice of his appointment until three days after the grand jury had expired. Five days later, the lawyer filed a motion asserting racial discrimination in selecting the grand jury.

A second defendant had fled shortly after the crime with which he was charged, and was not returned to the state until 22 months after his indictment. His motion respecting the grand jury was filed more than a month after his return, and 11 days after his arraignment (where he was represented by counsel).

The third defendant was represented by an elderly lawyer whose first and only action in the case, coming 12 months after his appointment, was to move to withdraw.

In reviewing the state court's findings of procedural default, the Supreme Court declared (p. 93) that the state rule in question did not "raise[] an insuperable barrier to one making claim to federal rights. The test is whether the defendant has had 'a reasonable opportunity to have the issue as to the claimed right heard and determined by the state court.' Parker v. Illinois, 333 U.S. 571, 574"—a test that the Court appeared to equate with the meaning of due process (pp. 93–100). Over three dissents, the Court ruled that the application of the Louisiana rule was not "unreasonable" as to any of the three defendants.

(c) *The Relationship of Due Process and Inadequacy.* Plainly, the validity of a state procedural rule under the Due Process Clause raises an independent federal question that the Court has jurisdiction to review, apart from any other federal issue in the case. To the extent that such a rule may not constitutionally be enforced, presumably it could not more authorize a state court in refusing to hear a state law claim than in refusing to hear a federal claim. (Or is it possible that the Due Process Clause guarantees a more generous right to be heard with respect to a federal constitutional claim than to a claim based on state law?)

Nothing in the Reece opinion suggests that the defendant argued in the state trial or appellate courts that refusal to hear his grand jury discrimination claim would deny due process. Should he have been required to "present" the due process claim in state court?

(5) *Nonconstitutional Bases for Finding State Grounds Inadequate.* The opinion in the Michel case, Paragraph (4)(b), *supra*, appears to assume that a state procedural ground is inadequate only if it denies due process. In general, however, the decisions do not equate the two doctrines. For example, no language in Staub suggests that Georgia's application of its rule requiring the defendant to specify the sections of the ordinance she was challenging denied due process. See generally Fay v. Noia, 372 U.S. 391, 448, 465–66 (1963)(Harlan, J., dissenting); Meltzer, Paragraph (3), *supra*, at 1159–60; Note, 74 Harv.L.Rev. 1375 (1961); but *cf.* Hill, *The Inadequate State Ground*, 65 Colum.L.Rev. 943, 971–80 (1965).

The "nonconstitutional" bases for inadequacy can be broadly placed in two categories:

(a) *The state procedural ground is not fairly supported by state law because the requirement is novel or has been inconsistently applied.* Part of the reasoning in Staub is that the procedural ruling was inadequate because not supported by the Georgia precedents—a point vigorously disputed by Justice Frankfurter. Note the detailed examination of state law necessary to make such a determination.

Just five months after deciding Staub, the Court handed down a similar ruling in NAACP v. Alabama ex rel. Patterson, 357 U.S. 449 (1958). There, the NAACP had been held in contempt for failing to produce its membership lists, as required by a trial court order that the NAACP assailed as unconstitutional. The NAACP petitioned the Alabama Supreme Court for certiorari to review the contempt judgment. That court refused to consider the constitutional issues, holding that the Association should have sought appellate review prior to the contempt adjudication, by filing a petition for mandamus to quash the discovery order.

The Supreme Court unanimously held that the asserted state procedural ground was inadequate to bar consideration of the federal constitutional claims. That ruling, the Court said, could not be reconciled with the Alabama court's "past unambiguous holdings as to the scope of review available upon a writ of certiorari addressed to a contempt judgment" (p. 456). Though the Alabama authorities indicated that an order requiring production of evidence could be reviewed on petition for mandamus, the Court found (pp. 457–58) "nothing in the prior state cases which suggests that mandamus is the *exclusive* remedy for reviewing court orders after disobedience of them has led to contempt judgments. Nor, so far as we can find, do any of these prior decisions indicate that the validity of such orders can be drawn in question by way of certiorari only in instances where a defendant had no opportunity to apply for mandamus. * * * Even if that is indeed the rationale of the Alabama Supreme Court's present decision, such a local procedural rule, although it may now appear in retrospect to form a part of a consistent pattern of procedures to obtain appellate review, cannot avail the State here, because petitioner could not fairly be deemed to have been apprised of its existence. Novelty in procedural requirements cannot be permitted to thwart review in this Court applied for by those who, in justified reliance upon prior decisions, seek vindication in state courts of their federal constitutional rights. *Cf.* Brinkerhoff–Faris Co. v. Hill, 281 U.S. 673." [4]

See also, *e.g.*, James v. Kentucky, 466 U.S. 341, 345–48 (1984)(state rule requiring that a request for a jury charge be labeled as a request for a jury "instruction" rather than for an "admonition" had not been consistently applied in prior cases, and hence could not bar Supreme Court review of the refusal to grant the requested instruction); Hathorn v. Lovorn, 457 U.S. 255 (1982).[5]

4. The Court relied on the NAACP decision in Reich v. Collins, 115 S.Ct. 547, 551 (1994)(holding that where state courts had held out that taxpayers may challenge the validity of a tax by making payments and then seeking refunds, it may not subsequently refuse to provide such refunds on the ground that the exclusive remedy available to the taxpayers at bar—who had already paid their taxes—was to have withheld payment and to have challenged the tax's validity before payment).

5. In Ford v. Georgia, 498 U.S. 411 (1991), a capital defendant's challenge to the discriminatory exercise of peremptory challenges was turned aside by the state supreme court on the ground that the defendant had failed to comply with a rule requiring such an objection to be made after the jury was selected but before it was sworn. In a unani-

Inadequacy is also established by a demonstration that the state courts had not previously applied their stated rule "with the pointless severity" shown in the present case. See, *e.g.*, Rogers v. Alabama, 192 U.S. 226 (1904)(two-page motion to quash indictment stricken as prolix); NAACP v. Alabama ex rel. Flowers, 377 U.S. 288, 294–302 (1964)(formal arrangement of points in brief); Barr v. City of Columbia, 378 U.S. 146, 149–50 (1964)(generality of stated exceptions; same form accepted in other cases).[6]

For discussion of a closely related set of cases, involving state court refusals to exercise "discretion" to excuse procedural defaults, see pp. 587–90, *infra*.

(b) *The state procedural requirement is unacceptably burdensome.* In Davis v. Wechsler, 263 U.S. 22 (1923), a federal official defending a state court action entered a general denial and also pleaded a special federal jurisdictional objection. The official's successor, substituting as defendant, entered an appearance and adopted the previous pleadings; but the state court ruled that the appearance, coming just before the adoption of the pleadings, was a general one and waived the jurisdictional objection. The Supreme Court found the state ground unduly burdensome and therefore inadequate. In a much-quoted passage, Justice Holmes said: "Whatever springes the State may set for those who are endeavoring to assert rights that the State confers, the assertion of federal rights, when plainly and reasonably made, is not to be defeated under the name of local practice" (p. 24).

Cases finding state grounds inadequate because burdensome are especially rare. See Douglas v. Alabama, 380 U.S. 415, 422–23 (1965)(failure to repeat, after every question put to a witness, a constitutional objection that had been thrice made and whose repetition would have been futile and strategically harmful; state forfeiture ruling held inadequate); Shuttlesworth v. City of Birmingham, 376 U.S. 339 (1964)(failure to use proper paper for petition to review criminal conviction; state forfeiture ruling held inadequate); Brown v. Western Ry., 338 U.S. 294 (1949), Chap. IV, Sec. 3, p. 485, *supra* (in FELA action, dismissal of complaint for failure to satisfy extremely exacting state pleading rules deemed inadequate; quoting Davis v. Wechsler, Court held that strict local pleading rules cannot impose unnecessary burdens on rights of recovery authorized by federal law).[7]

mous opinion, the Supreme Court held this state procedural ground inadequate. Relying on James v. Kentucky, *supra*, the Court noted that the state decision establishing the procedural rule had not been handed down until after Ford's trial, and that that decision itself stated that the rule was to apply to claims that were made "hereafter". Although the rule itself was not an unreasonable one, the Court held that it could not be applied to bar Ford from asserting his federal claim.

Could the rule have been applied to bar Ford from raising a state constitutional challenge to discriminatory exercise of peremptory challenges? See Paragraph (4)(c), *supra*.

6. Note that a state ruling that is novel or inconsistent could be characterized either as a misapplication of state law or as an implicit revision of state law. Under either view, the state procedural ground will be deemed inadequate and thus will not block Supreme Court review; but the latter characterization would presumably permit the new ruling to be applied to future cases "once notice of the new interpretation is provided." Meltzer, *supra*, at 1139 n. 44.

7. Brown has been subject to varying interpretations. See p. 486, note 5, *supra*.

Cf. International Longshoremen's Ass'n v. Davis, 476 U.S. 380 (1986), in which a labor union, after it had been found liable in tort in state court, objected for the first time that the action was preempted under the federal labor laws. The state courts held the objection untimely and hence ruled that the union had waived the preemption defense. The Supreme Court disagreed, ruling 5–4

(c) *Relationship of the Varying Rubrics of Inadequacy.* Individual cases may fit within more than one rubric of inadequacy. In Staub, some of the majority's language—"To require her, in these circumstances, to count off, one by one, the several sections of the ordinance would be to force resort to an arid ritual of meaningless form"—suggests that the state court's ruling would have been deemed inadequate (because unduly burdensome) even if the Court had thought it was fairly supported by precedent. See also James v. Kentucky, *supra*, where the Court similarly regarded the state ruling (insisting that the word "instruction," rather than the word "admonition" be used when requesting a jury charge) as unjustifiably burdensome as well as inconsistent with prior state law.

(6) *The Source of Power to Find State Grounds Inadequate.* What is the basis for the Supreme Court's assertion of the power, in Staub and in other cases, to review a case where the state judgment rests on a procedural ruling that the Court finds "inadequate" to support the judgment—even though that ruling has not been found unconstitutional? Could Supreme Court review of federal questions be adequately effectuated if state procedural rulings with respect to the litigation of federal questions, once found constitutional, were wholly insulated from review? See Wechsler, *The Appellate Jurisdiction of the Supreme Court: Reflections on the Law and Logistics of Direct Review*, 34 Wash. & Lee L.Rev. 1043, 1053–56 (1977).

When the state court's application of a procedural rule is so novel or inconsistent as to lack fair support in state law, the case for treating it as inadequate seems relatively straightforward. Is this assertion of power more problematic than the Court's assertion of power to review the "adequacy" of state *substantive* rulings where the decision of the state law question is antecedent to a claim of federal right? See p. 520, *supra*. Are not all state procedural rulings that determine whether a federal question has been seasonably raised in the state courts "antecedent" in the relevant sense? Should the standard of review of the state law issue be the same for substantive and procedural grounds? See Wechsler, *supra*, at 1054 (so suggesting).

What is the justification, in the cases involving undue burden (see Paragraph (5)(b), *supra*), for treating as inadequate a ruling that has not been found either to lack fair support in state law or to deny due process? Does it make sense to read into § 1257, as informed by the Supremacy Clause, a requirement that state courts be reasonably hospitable to the litigation of federal claims? See Hart, *Foreword: The Time Chart of the Justices*, 73 Harv.L.Rev. 84, 117–18 (1959).

that the claim of "Garmon preemption" under the federal labor laws went to the state court's jurisdiction; as a matter of federal law that jurisdictional objection could not be waived, notwithstanding the state's procedural rules.

Does that conclusion follow ineluctably from the jurisdictional characterization? Does the fact that the federal courts treat the lack of federal subject matter jurisdiction as a non-waivable defect—an approach that has been sharply criticized, see Chap. XIV, Sec. 1, pp. 1580–83, *infra*—necessarily require state courts to do likewise? Although on the merits the Supreme Court affirmed the judgment against the union, rejecting its preemption defense, four Justices—who concurred in the judgment of affirmance but argued that the preemption issue had in fact been waived—objected that after the Davis decision, a defendant is free to wait until the verdict comes in before deciding whether to raise a preemption defense. For criticism of Davis, see Holzhauer, *Longshoremen v. Davis and the Nature of Labor Law Pre-Emption*, 1986 S.Ct. Rev. 135.

(7) *A Role for Federal Common Law?* The question of the source of the federal norms determining when state procedural grounds are inadequate is given a different answer in Meltzer, Paragraph (3), *supra*, at 1158–85. He suggests that the inadequate state ground cases should be viewed as applying a "federal common law" that places limits, in addition to those imposed by the Due Process Clause, on the freedom of states to hold that noncompliance with state procedural rules justifies forfeiture of the right to raise federal claims. He then uses the reformulation as the basis for advocating a somewhat more permissive standard for excusing state procedural defaults. *Id.* at 1208–26.

Consider the implications of this approach if, just after the decision in Staub v. Baxley, a case raising an indistinguishable procedural issue were to arise in Georgia. Professor Meltzer argues that the Supreme Court's decision in Staub—finding inadequate the Georgia rule that a litigant must object to each separate section of the statute—should not be regarded simply as regulating Supreme Court jurisdiction to review, but rather represents a federal common law rule that must be honored in the state courts. Compare Dice v. Akron, Canton & Youngstown RR., Chap. IV, Sec. 3, p. 479, *supra* (holding that in FELA actions, state courts must follow a federal procedural rule requiring jury trial on the issue whether a purported release of the claim was fraudulently obtained—even though the federal rule was not set forth in any federal constitutional or statutory enactment).[8]

(8) *State Court Excuse of Procedural Default.* In Staub and in the cases discussed in this Note, the state courts enforced their procedural rules by refusing to reach federal claims that were not properly presented. But in some cases in which a litigant has failed to comply with state procedural rules in raising a federal claim, the highest state court will excuse the procedural default and proceed to decide the federal question. Where the state court does reach the merits, the Supreme Court's jurisdiction to review the decision is secure. See, *e.g.*, Whitney v. California, 274 U.S. 357, 360–63 (1927); Orr v. Orr, 440 U.S. 268, 274–75 (1979); Payton v. New York, 445 U.S. 573, 582 n. 19 (1980). This rule creates an obvious risk that the record may not be adequately developed, but the elimination of mandatory appeals in 1988 permits the Court to deny certiorari whenever that appears to be the case.

NOTE ON (1) HENRY v. MISSISSIPPI, (2) THE RELATIONSHIP OF THE ADEQUATE STATE GROUND TO FEDERAL HABEAS CORPUS REVIEW OF STATE CONVICTIONS, AND (3) THE SIGNIFICANCE OF STATE COURT DISCRETION TO EXCUSE PROCEDURAL DEFAULTS

(1) *Henry v. Mississippi.* In Henry v. Mississippi, 379 U.S. 443 (1965), the defendant—a local NAACP leader—was convicted of disturbing the peace "by indecent proposals to and offensive contact with an 18–year-old hitchhiker". His motion, at the close of the state's case, for a directed verdict had objected in passing to the admission of evidence derived from an allegedly unconstitutional search. The Mississippi Supreme Court initially reversed the conviction on the Fourth Amendment ground; the court excused Henry's failure to have made a contemporaneous objection to the admission of the evidence, as required by

----

8. The question whether a finding of "inadequacy" should bind the state courts in future cases has divided the commentators. See Meltzer, *supra*, at 1150–52, 1202 n. 70.

state law, on the ground that he had been represented by out-of-state counsel unfamiliar with local procedure. When the state pointed out that Henry in fact had also been represented by local counsel, the Mississippi Supreme Court changed course and affirmed the conviction, refusing to reach the Fourth Amendment issue because of the lack of contemporaneous objection.

In a confusing opinion, the Supreme Court (per Brennan, J.) asserted that a state court may not forfeit a litigant's federal rights unless the procedural requirement that the litigant failed to satisfy serves a "legitimate state interest" (p. 447). Although Mississippi's contemporaneous objection rule satisfied this test, Justice Brennan added that the purpose served by the rule might have been substantially served by Henry's motion for a directed verdict, which adverted to the Fourth Amendment issue. If that were so, "giving effect to the contemporaneous-objection rule for its own sake 'would be to force resort to an arid ritual of meaningless form'" (p. 449, quoting Staub v. City of Baxley, 355 U.S. at 320).

But the Court refused in the end to decide whether application of the contemporaneous objection rule in these circumstances constituted an adequate state ground, in view of the possibility that Henry's lawyer had deliberately waived his federal claim. If that were so, Henry would have forfeited his right to have the claim heard. The Court thus vacated the judgment to permit a hearing on remand on the waiver question. Justice Brennan noted, however, that if no waiver were found, the defendant would be able, under the decision in Fay v. Noia, 372 U.S. 391 (1963), to challenge his conviction in a federal habeas corpus action, and suggested that the state might prefer litigating the Fourth Amendment issue on remand, rather than waiting until a habeas corpus petition was filed.[1]

The Henry decision appeared substantially to change the standard governing the adequacy of state procedural grounds on direct review (see Paragraphs (2–3), *infra*). Justice Brennan's opinion also highlighted the relationship between the standards governing procedural default on direct review in the Supreme Court and on collateral federal review via habeas corpus (see Paragraph (4), *infra*). A final issue raised by the case—how the Supreme Court should treat state court refusals to exercise discretion to excuse procedural defaults—is discussed in Paragraph (5), *infra*.

(2) *Henry's Standard of Inadequacy.* The Henry formulation—that a state procedural rule, to be accepted as a basis for forfeiting a federal claim, must be shown to serve a legitimate state interest—was somewhat novel, but "may be regarded as constructive." See Wechsler, p. 521, *supra*, at 1054. The more radical element in Henry was the suggestion that failure to comply with a rule that undoubtedly serves a legitimate interest should be overlooked because, in

---

1. For discussion of Justice Harlan's and Justice Black's dissents, see Paragraphs (2) and (5), *infra*. On Henry generally, see Hill, p. 579, *supra*; Sandalow, *Henry v. Mississippi and the Adequate State Ground: Proposals for a Revised Doctrine*, 1965 Sup.Ct. Rev. 187.

On remand, the Supreme Court of Mississippi found that Henry had knowingly waived his right to object to the evidence, and

the conviction was ultimately reinstated, 202 So.2d 40 (1967). The Supreme Court then denied certiorari, "without prejudice to the bringing of a proceeding for relief in federal habeas corpus." 392 U.S. 931 (1968). Such a proceeding was filed, and the federal district court (relying on evidence presented in addition to the state court records) found no waiver, upheld the Fourth Amendment claim, and granted the writ. Henry v. Williams, 299 F.Supp. 36 (N.D.Miss.1969).

the particular case, that interest could have been "substantially served" by some *other* procedure. Consider the following difficulties with that notion and with its application in Henry:

(a) As Justice Harlan's dissent in Henry (joined by Justices Clark and Stewart) convincingly showed, presentation of a Fourth Amendment claim as part of a motion for directed verdict did not in fact substantially serve the purposes of Mississippi's contemporaneous objection rule. Justice Harlan noted, *inter alia*, that (i) only one sentence in the lengthy motion referred to the search and seizure issue, making it was unrealistic to expect the judge to have been alerted to the claim; (ii) by focusing attention on the disputed evidence when it is introduced, a contemporaneous objection rule minimizes the risk of error; and (iii) assuming the evidence was in fact inadmissible, a contemporaneous objection would have permitted the trial to proceed (without the evidence), avoiding a mistrial.

(b) Many American jurisdictions, including the federal courts, have rules requiring contemporaneous objection to the admission of evidence. Why should a plainly constitutional rule of procedure that would be enforced in a federal court be deemed "inadequate" when enforced by a state court?[2]

(c) Isn't there a legitimate state interest in enforcing the rule as a *rule*? Is it feasible to require a judge, in the midst of trial, to determine before enforcing a general procedural rule whether noncompliance should be excused because some alternative procedure might be deemed adequate in the particular situation? Recall Justice Frankfurter's dissent in Staub: "[R]ules are not made solely for the easiest cases they govern. The fact that the reason for a rule does not clearly apply in a given situation does not eliminate the necessity for compliance with the rule" (355 U.S. at 333).

(3) *The Demise of Henry.* Despite its radical potential, the Henry decision has had little effect on the standards applied on direct review in judging the adequacy of state procedural grounds.[3] Some decisions finding state procedural grounds inadequate failed to cite Henry, even though it seemed pertinent;[4] when Henry was cited, the decision usually appeared to rest on more traditional formulations of inadequacy.[5]

---

2. See Meltzer, p. 577, *supra*, at 1202–08, for the argument that the rules for excusing procedural defaults in the state courts should not be more forgiving than the rules enforced in the federal courts. *Cf.* the discussion of Francis v. Henderson, 425 U.S. 536 (1976), Chap. XI, Sec. 2, p. 421, *infra*.

3. But *cf.* Camp v. Arkansas, 404 U.S. 69 (1971), where the defendant had raised, for the first time on appeal, a self-incrimination objection to the prosecutor's closing argument. The Arkansas court held that the failure to make a contemporaneous objection precluded appellate review. The Supreme Court summarily reversed in a brief per curiam: "Petitioner's alleged procedural default does not bar consideration of his constitutional claim in the circumstances of this case. See Henry v. Mississippi, 379 U.S. 443, 447–449 (1965)."

4. See Douglas v. Alabama, 380 U.S. 415 (1965); Parrot v. Tallahassee, 381 U.S. 129 (1965).

5. See, *e.g.*, James v. Kentucky, pp. 580, 582, *supra*, where the Court cited Henry for the proposition that a requirement that a request for a jury charge be labeled as one for an "instruction" rather than an "admonition" would further "no perceivable state interest".

A restrictive view of Henry is found in Michigan v. Tyler, 436 U.S. 499, 512 n. 7 (1978): "Failure to present a federal question in conformance with state procedure constitutes an adequate and independent ground of decision * * *, so long as the State has a legitimate interest in enforcing its procedural rule. [Citing Henry and two other cases.] The petitioner does not claim that

Other decisions (also not citing Henry) found state grounds adequate where Henry might have suggested the opposite.[6] But Monger v. Florida, 405 U.S. 958 (1972), is perhaps the clearest example of Henry's limited influence. There, the state supreme court dismissed a criminal appeal because the defendant filed his notice of appeal too *soon*: the notice was filed on the day the trial judge pronounced an oral judgment and imposed sentence (January 12), but the written judgment was entered on January 18, "*nunc pro tunc* January 12". The Supreme Court entered the following per curiam order: "Certiorari denied, it appearing that judgment [sic] of the Supreme Court of Florida rests upon an adequate state ground." Justice Douglas, joined by Justices Brennan and Stewart, dissented, citing Henry and arguing that there was "no state interest which would be served by rejecting a notice of appeal filed after an oral pronouncement of judgment but before a written order" (p. 962).

(4) *Procedural Default: The Relationship of Direct and Collateral Federal Review.* As the Henry opinion indicates, in Fay v. Noia, 372 U.S. 391 (1963), the Court held that a state criminal judgment resting on an adequate and independent state procedural ground could be collaterally attacked in a federal habeas corpus proceeding. Unless the defendant had "waived" a federal constitutional claim, a federal habeas court was free to reach the merits, even though the state court had refused to decide the claim because of noncompliance with state procedural rules. Noia also stated that only a "deliberate bypass" by the defendant personally (rather than by defense lawyer) would count as waiver.

The Henry decision appeared to many as the beginning of an effort to import the far more forgiving standards of Noia into direct review of state criminal convictions. Consider whether it is a stable institutional arrangement to maintain a wide disparity between the rules of forfeiture applicable on direct review and those applicable on collateral review—to hold, that is, that a litigant who is precluded from seeking direct federal review in the Supreme Court can then seek (perhaps the very next day) federal review of the same federal claim in a federal habeas corpus proceeding. What would justify broader availability of collateral than of direct review? See generally Chap. XI, Sec. 2, p. 1439, *infra.* Should the Court be more willing to enforce a forfeiture, especially one with potentially harsh consequences (as in a capital case), if habeas relief might be available? Would such an approach imply that there should be different standards of inadequacy on direct review, depending on whether the case is one for which habeas review would be available?

After it became clear that Henry did not herald a broadening of the notion of inadequacy on direct review, and after the Warren Court gave way to the Burger Court, the disparity in standards on direct and collateral review was in fact substantially eliminated—by narrowing access to collateral review. The regime of Fay v. Noia virtually ended with the decision in Wainwright v. Sykes, 433 U.S. 72 (1977), p. 1418, *infra*, a habeas corpus action where the Court refused to entertain a constitutional objection (under Miranda) to the admission of evidence on the ground that the defendant had not made a contempora-

Michigan's procedural rule serves no legitimate purpose."

6. See Johnson v. New Jersey, 384 U.S. 719 (1966)(state rule precluding reconsideration of issue adjudicated in prior litigation was adequate to bar that issue on Supreme Court review of state post-conviction proceedings); Parker v. North Carolina, 397 U.S. 790 (1970)(failure to object to grand jury composition prior to entry of guilty plea, as required by state rule, was adequate nonfederal ground).

neous objection at trial. The opinion strongly affirmed the *general* utility of contemporaneous objection rules, without discussing whether, in the circumstances of the case, alternatives would have adequately served the state's interest. Decisions since Sykes have further refined (and narrowed) the standard applied in federal habeas corpus proceedings for excusing state court procedural defaults. Today, that standard is only marginally broader than the traditional "inadequate state ground" doctrine applied on direct review. See generally Chap. XI, Sec. 2, pp. 1418–40, *infra*.

(5) *State Court "Discretionary" Refusals to Excuse A Procedural Default.* In Henry, Justice Black dissented from the Court's failure to decide the search and seizure question then and there, finding that the contemporaneous objection rule should not be "accept[ed] as an independent, adequate ground for the State Supreme Court's refusal to decide the [Fourth Amendment issue]." He argued (379 U.S. at 455) that nothing in Mississippi law denied the "*power* of the State Supreme Court * * * to consider and determine constitutional questions presented at the time this one was", and continued:

"I do not believe the cherished federal constitutional right of a defendant to object to unconstitutionally seized evidence * * * can be cut off irrevocably by state-court discretionary rulings which might be different in particular undefined circumstances in other cases. I think such a procedural device for shutting off our review of questions involving constitutional rights is too dangerous to be tolerated" (pp. 456–57).

Justice Black's opinion was not the first to suggest that the state court's failure to exercise available discretion might cast doubt on the adequacy of a state procedural ground.[7]

(a) In Patterson v. Alabama, 294 U.S. 600 (1935), an appeal arising out of the infamous Scottsboro trials, the defendant had been convicted of raping a white girl and sentenced to death for a third time after earlier convictions had been overturned. The Supreme Court of Alabama held that his challenge to the exclusion of blacks from the jury had not been made in timely fashion. In a companion case in which the same jury discrimination claim had been properly presented, the state court had affirmed the conviction on the merits. Granting review in both cases, the Supreme Court held in the companion case that discrimination was established. Norris v. Alabama, 294 U.S. 587 (1935), p. 590, *infra*. In Patterson's case, the Court found the state procedural ruling supported by earlier Alabama decisions, but nonetheless vacated the judgment. Chief Justice Hughes wrote (294 U.S. at 606–07):

"* * * We are not convinced that the [state] court, * * * confronting the anomalous and grave situation which would be created by a reversal of the judgment against Norris, and an affirmance of the judgment of death in the companion case of Patterson, * * * would have considered itself powerless to * * * [provide appropriate relief]. * * * At least the state court should have an opportunity to examine its powers in the light of the situation which has now developed."

Do you agree with the judgment of one of Chief Justice Hughes' biographers that in Patterson, "the technical requirements of law were subordinated

---

7. For discussion of some of the problems raised in this Paragraph, see the articles by Hill (at 985 n. 174) and Sandalow (at 225– 26) cited in note 1, *supra*; Meltzer, p. 577, *supra*, at 1139–42.

to the ends of justice"?   Hendel, Charles Evans Hughes and the Supreme Court 161 (1951).

A new trial was thereafter granted and a conviction sustained in Patterson v. State, 234 Ala. 342, 175 So. 371, *cert. denied*, 302 U.S. 733 (1937).

(b) In Williams v. Georgia, 349 U.S. 375 (1955)(6–3), Williams, a black man, was convicted of an inter-racial murder. The jury selection system used in his case facilitated discrimination against blacks, and in a decision handed down after Williams' conviction but a month before his lawyer filed an amended motion for new trial, the Supreme Court held that system unconstitutional. Avery v. Georgia, 345 U.S. 559 (1953). Williams' counsel first raised a jury discrimination claim six months later, in an extraordinary new trial motion filed after affirmance of the conviction. The state courts held the motion untimely: state practice required a challenge to the array before trial, and there had not been the due diligence necessary to justify an exception to that rule.

The Supreme Court, per Frankfurter, J., vacated and remanded. Although acknowledging the validity of the state rule, the Court said that "where a State allows questions of this sort to be raised at a later stage and be determined by its courts as a matter of discretion, we are not concluded from assuming jurisdiction and deciding whether the state court action in the particular circumstances is, in effect, an avoidance of the federal right" (p. 383). Noting numerous cases in which the Georgia courts had exercised discretion to entertain extraordinary motions challenging individual jurors, and finding no basis for distinguishing challenges to the array, the Court stated that "the discretionary decision to deny the motion does not deprive this Court of jurisdiction to find that the substantive issue is properly before us."

"But the fact that we have jurisdiction does not compel us to exercise it" (p. 389). Stressing that life was at stake and that the state had conceded the constitutional violation at oral argument, the Court concluded that "orderly procedure requires a remand * * *. Fair regard for the principles which the Georgia courts have enforced in numerous cases and for the constitutional commands binding on all courts compels us to reject the assumption that the courts of Georgia would allow this man to go to his death as the result of a conviction secured from a jury which the State admits was unconstitutionally impaneled" (p. 391).

Did the Williams majority hold the state ground inadequate? Or was it seeking "to cajole the Georgia court into reversing itself where the United States Supreme Court lacked grounds to do so"? Note, 69 Harv.L.Rev. 158, 160 (1955). On remand, the Georgia Supreme Court, without briefing or argument, "[a]dhered to" its earlier judgment, while protesting that the Supreme Court had lacked jurisdiction. 211 Ga. 763, 88 S.E.2d 376 (1954). Certiorari was denied. 350 U.S. 950 (1956).[8]

---

8. Dickson, *State Court Defiance and the Limits of Supreme Court Authority: Williams v. Georgia Revisited*, 103 Yale L.J. 1423 (1994), provides a rich account of the Williams case. He argues that the Justices failed to respond to the challenge offered on remand by the Georgia Supreme Court because they "feared that a showdown with the Southern states over this case would cost the Court too dearly in terms of image and authority, undermining the Court's efforts to secure Southern compliance with *Brown* [v. Board of Education]" (p. 1478). See also Burt, *Brown's Reflection*, 103 Yale L.J. 1483 (1994).

Cf. Wolfe v. North Carolina, 364 U.S. 177, 191–92 (1960)(finding Williams distin-

(c) In Sullivan v. Little Hunting Park, Inc., 396 U.S. 229 (1969), the trial court dismissed plaintiffs' complaints, which alleged violations of federal civil rights laws. The Supreme Court of Appeals of Virginia denied plaintiffs' appeals, holding that they had not been perfected in accordance with a Virginia rule requiring that opposing counsel be given reasonable notice of the tendering of the transcript and reasonable opportunity to examine it. The Supreme Court (per Douglas, J.) reversed, stating (pp. 233–34) that although the procedural ruling was not novel, the Virginia decisions "do not enable us to say that the Virginia court has so consistently applied its notice requirement as to amount to a self-denial of the power to entertain the federal claim here presented if the Supreme Court of Appeals desires to do so. * * * Such a rule, more properly deemed discretionary than jurisdictional, does not bar review here by certiorari." The Court proceeded to consider the merits and reverse.

Justice Harlan, joined by Chief Justice Burger and Justice White, dissented, arguing that certiorari should be dismissed because of the recent enactment of the Fair Housing Law. On the adequacy of the state ground, he said (pp. 243–45): "I agree with the majority's conclusion that there is no adequate state ground shown, but I find myself unable to subscribe to the majority's reasoning * * *.

"I am not certain what the majority means in its apparent distinction between rules that it deems 'discretionary' and those that it deems 'jurisdictional.' Perhaps the majority wishes to suggest that the dismissals of petitioners' writs of error by the Supreme Court of Appeals were simply *ad hoc* discretionary refusals to accept plenary review of the lower court's decisions, analogous to this Court's denial of certiorari. If this were all the Virginia Supreme Court of Appeals had done, review of a federal question properly raised below would of course not be barred here. * * *

"But this case clearly does not present this kind of discretionary refusal of a state appellate court to accept review. * * *

"The majority might have another meaning in mind * * *. It may be suggesting that 'reasonable written notice,' and 'reasonable opportunity to examine' are such flexible standards that the Virginia Supreme Court of Appeals has the 'discretion' to decide a close case either of two ways * * *. If this is what the majority means by 'discretionary rule,' then I must register my disagreement. This kind of 'discretion' is nothing more than 'the judicial formulation of law,' for a court has an obligation to be reasonably consistent and 'to explain the decision, including the reason for according different treatment to the instant case.' Surely a state ground is no less adequate simply because it involves a standard that requires a judgment of what is reasonable, and because the result may turn on a close analysis of the facts of a particular case in light of competing policy considerations."

Justice Harlan proceeded, however to find that "under the principle of NAACP v. Alabama, 357 U.S. 449 (1958)," p. 580, *supra*, the state ground was inadequate, because the state court had applied its rule here much more strictly than in prior cases.[9]

---

guishable because here the state court had without exception refused to excuse violations of the procedural rule in question).

9. In Sochor v. Florida, 504 U.S. 527 (1992), the state supreme court ruled that an Eighth Amendment objection to the vagueness of an "aggravating factor" in a capital punishment scheme was not preserved for appeal, because the defendant failed to renew an objection (previously advanced in a pre-

(d) If one accepts Justice Harlan's view of the significance of discretion, might there still be an argument in some cases for Supreme Court review of state court refusals to exercise that discretion? Suppose that the application of a state court's plain error standard depends on whether the issue that was not properly raised appears to have been meritorious, or obviously meritorious, or seriously prejudicial. If a state court refuses to exercise discretion to excuse a default, might not the Supreme Court be justified in reviewing the federal issue, on the theory that the decision might have differed had the state court realized that the federal claim had merit—and then remanding the case for the state to exercise its discretion in light of a correct understanding of federal law? Compare pp. 546–51, *supra*. Would such an approach justify the decision in Patterson? In Williams?

SUBSECTION C: APPLICATION OF LAW TO FACT

Norris v. Alabama

294 U.S. 587, 55 S.Ct. 579, 79 L.Ed. 1074 (1935).
Certiorari to the Supreme Court of Alabama.

■ MR. CHIEF JUSTICE HUGHES delivered the opinion of the Court.

Petitioner, Clarence Norris, is one of nine negro boys who were indicted in March, 1931, in Jackson county, Ala., for the crime of rape.* On being brought to trial in that county, eight were convicted. The Supreme Court of Alabama reversed the conviction of one of these and affirmed that of seven, including Norris. This Court reversed the judgments of conviction upon the ground that the defendants had been denied due process of law in that the trial court had failed in the light of the circumstances disclosed, and of the inability of the defendants at that time to obtain counsel, to make an effective appointment of counsel to aid them in preparing and presenting their defense. Powell v. Alabama, 287 U.S. 45.

After the remand, a motion for change of venue was granted and the cases were transferred to Morgan county. Norris was brought to trial in November, 1933. At the outset, a motion was made on his behalf to quash the indictment upon the ground of the exclusion of negroes from juries in Jackson county where the indictment was found. A motion was also made to quash the trial

trial motion) after the trial judge instructed the sentencing jury. The state supreme court added a sentence that the claim lacked merit in any event. The Supreme Court, per Souter, J., held that an adequate and independent state ground barred Supreme Court review. Dissenting from that conclusion, Justice Stevens stressed the defendant's pretrial objection, the state court's brief discussion (albeit in the alternative) of the merits, and "most important[ly]", the Florida Supreme Court's power to review "fundamental error" (p. 2127). In response, the majority disputed that the claim constituted "fundamental error" under Florida law.

* [Ed.] This was one of the infamous Scottsboro trials, in which the defendants, charged with raping two white girls on a train, were swiftly convicted by all-white juries and sentenced to death; with some understatement, the Supreme Court described the atmosphere surrounding the trials as one "of great hostility". Patterson v. Alabama, 287 U.S. 45, 51 (1932).

venire in Morgan county upon the ground of the exclusion of negroes from juries in that county. In relation to each county, the charge was of long-continued, systematic, and arbitrary exclusion of qualified negro citizens from service on juries, solely because of their race and color, in violation of the Constitution of the United States. The state joined issue on this charge and after hearing the evidence, which we shall presently review, the trial judge denied both motions, and exception was taken. The trial then proceeded and resulted in the conviction of Norris who was sentenced to death. On appeal the Supreme Court of the state considered and decided the federal question which Norris had raised and affirmed the judgment. We granted a writ of certiorari.

First. There is no controversy as to the constitutional principle involved. * * * [T]his Court thus stated the principle in Carter v. Texas, 177 U.S. 442, 447, in relation to exclusion from service on grand juries: "Whenever by any action of a state, whether through its Legislature, through its courts, or through its executive or administrative officers, all persons of the African race are excluded, solely because of their race or color, from serving as grand jurors in the criminal prosecution of a person of the African race, the equal protection of the laws is denied to him, contrary to the Fourteenth Amendment of the Constitution of the United States." * * * The principle is equally applicable to a similar exclusion of negroes from service on petit juries. And although the state statute defining the qualifications of jurors may be fair on its face, the constitutional provision affords protection against action of the state through its administrative officers in effecting the prohibited discrimination.

The question is of the application of this established principle to the facts disclosed by the record. That the question is one of fact does not relieve us of the duty to determine whether in truth a federal right has been denied. When a federal right has been specially set up and claimed in a state court, it is our province to inquire not merely whether it was denied in express terms but also whether it was denied in substance and effect. If this requires an examination of evidence, that examination must be made. Otherwise, review by this Court would fail of its purpose in safeguarding constitutional rights. Thus, whenever a conclusion of law of a state court as to a federal right and findings of fact are so intermingled that the latter control the former, it is incumbent upon us to analyze the facts in order that the appropriate enforcement of the federal right may be assured. [Citing, *inter alia*, Ward v. Board of County Com'rs. of Love County, 253 U.S. 17, 22; Davis, Director General, v. Wechsler, 263 U.S. 22, 24; Fiske v. Kansas, 274 U.S. 380, 385, 386.]

Second. *The evidence on the motion to quash the indictment.* In 1930, the total population of Jackson county, where the indictment was found, was 36,881, of whom 2,688 were negroes. The male population over twenty-one years of age numbered 8,801, and of these 666 were negroes.

The qualifications of jurors were thus prescribed by the state statute (Alabama Code 1923, § 8603): "The jury commission shall place on the jury roll and in the jury box the names of all male citizens of the county who are generally reputed to be honest and intelligent men, and are esteemed in the community for their integrity, good character and sound judgment, but no person must be selected who is under twenty-one or over sixty-five years of age, or, who is an habitual drunkard, or who, being afflicted with a permanent disease or physical weakness is unfit to discharge the duties of a juror, or who cannot read English, or who has ever been convicted of any offense involving moral turpitude. If a person cannot read English and has all the other qualifications prescribed herein and is a freeholder or householder, his name may be placed on the jury roll and in the jury box."

Defendant adduced evidence to support the charge of unconstitutional discrimination in the actual administration of the statute in Jackson county. The testimony, as the state court said, tended to show that "in a long number of years no negro had been called for jury service in that county." It appeared that no negro had served on any grand or petit jury in that county within the memory of witnesses who had lived there all their lives. Testimony to that effect was given by men whose ages ran from fifty to seventy-six years. Their testimony was uncontradicted. It was supported by the testimony of officials. The clerk of the jury commission and the clerk of the circuit court had never known of a negro serving on a grand jury in Jackson county. The court reporter, who had not missed a session in that county in twenty-four years, and two jury commissioners testified to the same effect. One of the latter, who was a member of the commission which made up the jury roll for the grand jury which found the indictment, testified that he had "never known of a single instance where any negro sat on any grand or petit jury in the entire history of that county."

That testimony in itself made out a prima facie case of the denial of the equal protection which the Constitution guarantees. The case thus made was supplemented by direct testimony that specified negroes, thirty or more in number, were qualified for jury service. Among these were negroes who were members of school boards, or trustees, of colored schools, and property owners and householders. It also appeared that negroes from that county had been called for jury service in the federal court. Several of those who were thus described as qualified were witnesses. While there was testimony which cast doubt upon the qualifications of some of the negroes who had been named, and there was also general testimony by the editor of a local newspaper who gave his opinion as to the lack of "sound judgment" of the "good negroes" in Jackson county, we think that the definite testimony as to the actual qualifications of individual negroes, which was not met by any testimony equally direct, showed that there were negroes in Jackson county qualified for jury service.

The question arose whether names of negroes were in fact on the jury roll. The books containing the jury roll for Jackson county for the year 1930–31 were produced. They were produced from the custody of a member of the jury commission which, in 1931, had succeeded the commission which had made up the jury roll from which the grand jury in question had been drawn. On the pages of this roll appeared the names of six negroes. They were entered, respectively, at the end of the precinct lists which were alphabetically arranged. The genuineness of these entries was disputed. It appeared that after the jury roll in question had been made up, and after the new jury commission had taken office, one of the new commissioners directed the new clerk to draw lines after the names which had been placed on the roll by the preceding commission. These lines, on the pages under consideration, were red lines, and the clerk of the old commission testified that they were not put in by him. The entries made by the new clerk, for the new jury roll, were below these lines.

The names of the six negroes were in each instance written immediately above the red lines. An expert of long experience testified that these names were superimposed upon the red lines, that is, that they were written after the lines had been drawn. The expert was not cross-examined and no testimony was introduced to contradict him.[1] In denying the motion to quash, the trial judge expressed the view that he would not "be authorized to presume that somebody had committed a crime" or to presume that the jury board "had been unfaithful to their duties and allowed the books to be tampered with." His conclusion was that names of negroes were on the jury roll.

We think that the evidence did not justify that conclusion. The Supreme Court of the state did not sustain it. That court observed that the charge that the names of negroes were fraudulently placed on the roll did not involve any member of the jury board, and that the charge "was, by implication at least, laid at the door of the clerk of the board." The court, reaching its decision irrespective of that question, treated that phase of the matter as "wholly immaterial" and hence passed it by "without any expression of opinion thereon."

The state court rested its decision upon the ground that even if it were assumed that there was no name of a negro on the jury roll, it was not established that race or color caused the omission. The court pointed out that the statute fixed a high standard of qualifications for jurors and that the jury commission was vested with a wide discretion. The court * * * regarded the testimony as being to the effect that "the matter of race, color, politics, religion or fraternal affiliations" had not been discussed by the commission and had not entered into their consideration, and that no one had been excluded because of race or color.

The testimony showed the practice of the jury commission. * * * It was shown that the clerk, under the direction of the commissioners, made up a preliminary list which was based on the registration list of voters, the polling list and the tax list, and apparently also upon the telephone directory. The clerk testified that he made up a list of all male citizens between the ages of twenty-one and sixty-five years without regard to their status or qualifications. The commissioner testified that the designation "col." was placed after the names of those who were colored. In preparing the final jury roll, the preliminary list was checked off as to qualified jurors with the aid of men whom the commissioners called in for that purpose from the different precincts. And the commissioner testified that in the selections for the jury roll no one was "automatically or systematically" excluded, or excluded on account of race or color; that he "did not inquire as to color," that was not discussed.

But, in appraising the action of the commissioners, these statements cannot be divorced from other testimony. As we have seen, there was testimony, not overborne or discredited, that there were in fact negroes in the county qualified for jury service. That testimony was direct and specific. After eliminating those persons as to whom there was some evidence of lack of qualifications, a considerable number of others remained. The fact that the testimony as to these persons, fully identified, was not challenged by evidence appropriately direct, cannot be brushed aside. There is no ground for an assumption that the names of these negroes were not on the preliminary list. The inference to be drawn from the testimony is that they were on that preliminary list, and were designated on that list as the names of negroes, and that they were not placed on the jury roll. There was thus presented a test of

1. The books containing the jury roll in question were produced on the argument at this bar and were examined by the Court. [Ed. See the dramatic account of this incident in Schmidt, *Juries, Jurisdiction, and Race Discrimination: The Lost Promise of Strauder v. West Virginia*, 61 Texas L.Rev. 1401, 1476–79 (1983).]

the practice of the commissioners. Something more than mere general asseverations was required. Why were these names excluded from the jury roll? Was it because of the lack of statutory qualifications? Were the qualifications of negroes actually and properly considered?

The testimony of the commissioner on this crucial question puts the case in a strong light. That testimony leads to the conclusion that these or other negroes were not excluded on account of age, or lack of esteem in the community for integrity and judgment, or because of disease or want of any other qualification. The commissioner's answer to specific inquiry upon this point was that negroes were "never discussed." We give in the margin quotations from his testimony.[3]

We are of the opinion that the evidence required a different result from that reached in the state court. We think that the evidence that for a generation or longer no negro had been called for service on any jury in Jackson county, that there were negroes qualified for jury service, that according to the practice of the jury commission their names would normally appear on the preliminary list of male citizens of the requisite age but that no names of negroes were placed on the jury roll, and the testimony with respect to the lack of appropriate consideration of the qualifications of negroes, established the discrimination which the Constitution forbids. The motion to quash the indictment upon that ground should have been granted.

Third. The evidence on the motion to quash the trial venire. The population of Morgan county, where the trial was had, * * * in 1930 was 46,176, and of this number 8,311 were negroes.

Within the memory of witnesses, long resident there, no negro had ever served on a jury in that county or had been called for such service. * * * Their testimony was not contradicted. A clerk of the circuit court, who had resided in the county for thirty years, and who had been in office for over four years, testified that during his official term approximately 2,500 persons had been called for jury service and that not one of them was a negro; that he did not recall "ever seeing any single person of the colored race serve on any jury in Morgan County."

---

3. "Q. Did you ever exclude from the jury rolls any negroes because you found first, he was a man under twenty-one years old or over sixty-five, and he was excluded by reason of his age; secondly because he was a person who wasn't esteemed in the community for being a decent and honorable citizen, for good sound common sense and judgment, did you ever see or hear of them not going to take that negro because he wasn't esteemed in the community for good sense and judgment? A. No, sir.

"Q. Did you ever have occasion to say, I can't take that negro because he is a fellow that has a disease which may affect or does affect, his mentality, did you ever say that to yourself, with reference to any particular negro? A. No, sir, negroes was never discussed.

"Q. Did you ever say to yourself as a jury commissioner in compiling those lists, I am

not going to take that negro because he has been convicted before of a crime involving moral turpitude, have you ever excluded a negro on that ground, did you ever find any negro that came within that category, under your personal knowledge in Jackson County? A. I couldn't recall any, no, sir, I don't know.

"Q. Have you ever known of any negro in Jackson County who was excluded by reason of the fact that he could not read English, and that negro at the same time wasn't a free holder or house holder, did you ever say I can't take that negro because he is prohibited under the rules from serving by reason of that provision? A. No, sir.

"Q. Or anybody in your presence? A. It never was discussed.

"* * *"

There was abundant evidence that there were a large number of negroes in the county who were qualified for jury service. Men of intelligence, some of whom were college graduates, testified to long lists (said to contain nearly 200 names) of such qualified negroes, including many business men, owners of real property and householders. When defendant's counsel proposed to call many additional witnesses in order to adduce further proof of qualifications of negroes for jury service, the trial judge limited the testimony, holding that the evidence was cumulative.

We find no warrant for a conclusion that the names of any of the negroes as to whom this testimony was given, or of any other negroes, were placed on the jury rolls. No such names were identified. The evidence that for many years no negro had been called for jury service itself tended to show the absence of the names of negroes from the jury rolls, and the state made no effort to prove their presence. * * *

For this long-continued, unvarying, and wholesale exclusion of negroes from jury service we find no justification consistent with the constitutional mandate. We have carefully examined the testimony of the jury commissioners upon which the state court based its decision. One of these commissioners testified in person and the other two submitted brief affidavits. By the state act in force at the time the jury roll in question was made up, the clerk of the jury board was required to obtain the names of all male citizens of the county over twenty-one and under sixty-five years of age, and their occupation, place of residence, and place of business. The qualifications of those who were to be placed on the jury roll were the same as those prescribed by the earlier statute which we have already quoted. The member of the jury board, who testified orally, said that a list was made up which included the names of all male citizens of suitable age; that black residents were not excluded from this general list; that in compiling the jury roll he did not consider race or color; that no one was excluded for that reason; and that he had placed on the jury roll the names of persons possessing the qualifications under the statute. The affidavits of the other members of the board contained general statements to the same effect.

We think that this evidence failed to rebut the strong prima facie case which defendant had made. * * * If, in the presence of such testimony as defendant adduced, the mere general assertions by officials of their performance of duty were to be accepted as an adequate justification for the complete exclusion of negroes from jury service, the constitutional provision-adopted with special reference to their protection-would be but a vain and illusory requirement. The general attitude of the jury commissioner is shown by the following extract from his testimony: "I do not know of any negro in Morgan County over twenty-one and under sixty-five who is generally reputed to be honest and intelligent and who is esteemed in the community for his integrity, good character and sound judgment, who is not an habitual drunkard, who isn't afflicted with a permanent disease or physical weakness which would render him unfit to discharge the duties of a juror, and who can read English, and who has never been convicted of a crime involving moral turpitude." In the light of the testimony given by defendant's witnesses, we find it impossible to accept such a sweeping characterization of the lack of qualifications of negroes in Morgan county. It is so sweeping, and so contrary to the evidence as to the many qualified negroes, that it destroys the intended effect of the commissioner's testimony.

In Neal v. Delaware, [103 U.S. 370], decided over fifty years ago, this Court observed that it was a "violent presumption," in which the state court had there indulged, that the uniform exclusion of negroes from juries, during a period of many years, was solely because, in the judgment of the officers, charged with the selection of grand and petit jurors, fairly exercised, "the black race in Delaware were utterly disqualified by want of intelligence, experience, or moral integrity, to sit on juries." Such a presumption at the present time would be no less violent with respect to the exclusion of the negroes of Morgan county. And, upon the proof contained in the record now before us, a conclusion that their continuous and total exclusion from juries was because there were none possessing the requisite qualifications, cannot be sustained.

We are concerned only with the federal question which we have discussed, and in view of the denial of the federal right suitably asserted, the judgment must be reversed and the cause remanded for further proceedings not inconsistent with this opinion.

It is so ordered.

■ MR. JUSTICE MCREYNOLDS did not hear the argument and took no part in the consideration and decision of this case.

NOTE ON CONTROL OF FACTFINDING AND OF APPLICATION OF LAW TO FACT

A. Introduction

(1) *Law, Historical Fact, and Application of Law to Fact.* Courts often divide the issues into cases in two categories, "fact" and "law", in allocating decision-making authority—in determining, for example, whether an issue is for jury or judge, or what standard of review governs on appeal. But adjudication typically involves not two functions, revolving around law and fact, but rather three. Consider a case involving an allegation of an unlawful arrest under the Fourth Amendment. One function consists of law declaration—of "formulating a proposition which affects not only the [present case] * * * but all others that fall within its terms", Hart & Sacks, The Legal Process: Basic Problems in the Making and Application of Law 350 (Eskridge & Frickey eds.1994); in the example, a court would declare (or follow) the proposition that an arrest is unlawful absent probable cause. The second function consists of finding the historical facts—that is, determining what happened in this particular case; in the example, a factfinder would determine what the police officer knew about the suspect at the time of arrest. The third function involves the application of legal propositions to the historical facts; in the example, a tribunal would determine whether what the officer knew about the suspect constituted probable cause to arrest. See generally *id.* at 350–51; Jaffe, Judicial Control of Administrative Action 546–623 (1967); Monaghan, *Constitutional Fact Review*, 85 Colum.L.Rev. 229, 236–38 (1985).

There has been no doubt that the Supreme Court may review a state court's declaration of federal law. This Note discusses review of the other two categories of issues: applications of law to fact (sometimes called "mixed questions" of law and fact) and findings of historical fact. As you will see, the lines among these three categories, although neither non-existent nor incoherent, are often blurred, and the categories may be more in the nature of points along a continuum, see Monaghan, *supra*, at 233.

Keep in mind, also, that even when a court purports to analyze the essence of the issue first, and then says that because an issue is one of fact (or law), it should be reviewed deferentially (or de novo), the actual chain of reasoning often runs in the other direction; the court may first determine who should decide, and then describe the issue as one of fact or law so as to implement that decision.

(2) *The Supreme Court's Role.*   The problems presented in this Note, though general ones faced in appellate review, are distinctive in the context of a federal Supreme Court that (i) reviews decisions of state courts that are legally bound to apply federal law, but whose fidelity may at times be in doubt; (ii) hears cases that nearly always have already received some appellate review; and (iii) has a limited docket governed by a discretionary jurisdiction reserved for cases of particular importance.   Consider whether the Supreme Court's role in reviewing questions of fact, or mixed questions, should differ from that of other appellate courts.   Consider, too, whether you agree that it "would pervert the concept of federalism for this Court to lay claim to a broader power of review over state-court judgments than it exercises in reviewing the judgments of intermediate federal courts."   Bose Corp. v. Consumers Union, 466 U.S. 485, 499 (1984); *cf.* Hill, *The Adequate State Ground*, 65 Colum.L.Rev. 943, 946–47 n. 18 (1965).

B.   Scope of Review Over Disputes About Historical Facts

(1) *Constitutional and Statutory Power.*   Article III specifies that the Supreme Court shall have appellate jurisdiction "both as to Law and Fact".   Doesn't a case like Norris, which arose from the infamous Scottsboro trials, highlight the wisdom of the Framers in authorizing the Court to assure itself that a federal claim is not undermined by state court misuse of the factfinding function?

Section 25 of the First Judiciary Act permitted review only via the writ of error, which, the Court ruled, gave no power to review state court findings of fact.   See, *e.g.*, Egan v. Hart, 165 U.S. 188 (1897); see generally Gibbons, *Federal Law and the State Courts, 1790–1860*, 36 Rutgers L.Rev. 399 (1984). But in this century that position eroded—and between 1914 and 1928 the writ of error was replaced by other forms of review not subject to the same limitation.   See pp. 493–94, *supra.*   It thus came to be accepted that where there is a dispute over a question of historical fact bearing on a federal claim, the Court is not powerless to review the state court factfinding.   The present § 1257, which simply provides that state court judgments may be reviewed, has been taken to confirm that power.

For discussion whether the Seventh Amendment limits the power of the Supreme Court to review of findings of fact made by state court juries, see Paragraph (B)(5), *infra.*

(2) *Scope of Review.*   When a state court fails to find the facts on a particular point, the Court will sometimes make findings on its own.   See, *e.g.*, Brooklyn Sav. Bank v. O'Neil, 324 U.S. 697, 703 (1945).   But the normal practice is to remand for the state courts to make the finding in the first instance.   See, *e.g.*, United Bldg. & Constr. Trades Council v. Mayor and Council of City of Camden, 465 U.S. 208, 223 (1984); Time, Inc. v. Firestone, 424 U.S. 448, 463–64 (1976).

When a finding of historical fact has been made and there is substantial evidence on *both* sides of the issue, the Court traditionally assesses the case on the basis of the facts found by the state court. Thus, in General Motors v. Washington, 377 U.S. 436, 444–42 (1964), the Court said: "[W]e have power to examine the whole record to arrive at an independent judgment as to whether constitutional rights have been invaded, but this does not mean that we will reexamine, as a court of first instance, findings of fact supported by substantial evidence." See also Taylor v. Mississippi, 319 U.S. 583, 585–86 (1943)("The evidence was contradictory and conflicting but the juries resolved the conflict against the appellants. We must, therefore, examine the questions presented on the basis of the proofs submitted by the State.").

Only in a rare case can one say that there is no conflict in the evidence, or (as in Norris) that even though there is *testimony* on one side of the case that has apparently been accepted by the factfinder, that testimony is not credible and does not constitute "substantial" evidence. Thus, despite the Court's authority to review state court findings of fact, in practice such findings are almost never disturbed.

(3) *Facts vs. Inferences.* In a dissenting opinion in Beck v. Ohio, 379 U.S. 89, 100–01 (1964), Justice Harlan suggested that while the Supreme Court should treat as authoritative state court factfindings resting on evaluations of credibility, "the Court is free to draw its own inferences from established facts, giving due weight to the conclusions of the state court, but not being conclusively bound by them".

In the analogous context of federal appellate review of factfindings based on "inferences" made at the trial level, the Court has rejected Justice Harlan's suggestion. In Anderson v. City of Bessemer City, 470 U.S. 564 (1985), the court of appeals had reversed the federal district judge's finding of intentional discrimination in employment. The Supreme Court reversed in turn. After holding that the question of intentional discrimination was one of fact (on this point, see Paragraph (B)(4)(a), *infra*), the Court said in dictum that the "clearly erroneous" standard of Fed.R.Civ.P. 52(a) applies to review even of factfindings that are based not on credibility determinations but on physical or documentary evidence or on inferences from other facts. Although Rule 52(a) "demands even greater deference to the trial court's findings" when credibility is at issue, the Rule does not except other findings from the clearly erroneous standard (p. 575). See also Resnik, *Tiers*, 57 So.Cal.L.Rev. 837, 998–1005 (1984).

The approach of Anderson was followed on review of a state court decision in Hernandez v. New York, 500 U.S. 352 (1991). There, a state prosecutor had exercised peremptory challenges against two prospective Latino jurors. When the defendant challenged that action as a denial of equal protection, the prosecutor explained that there would be Spanish-speaking witnesses, and that he was uncertain that the two Latinos would accept the interpreter's translation of the Spanish testimony. The trial judge found that the explanation was not pretextual.

The Supreme Court likewise rejected the defendant's claim. There was no majority opinion, but Justice Kennedy's plurality opinion (joined by three other Justices) relied, *inter alia*, on Anderson in finding that the issue whether the prosecutor had had a discriminatory purpose is one of "historical fact" (p. 367) that should be accepted because it was not clearly erroneous. The Court said (pp. 365–66):

"* * * Anderson was a federal civil case * * *. While no comparable rule exists for federal criminal cases, we have held that the same standard should apply to review of findings in criminal cases on issues other than guilt. * * *

"This case comes to us on direct review of the state court judgment. No statute or rule governs our review of facts found by state courts in cases with this posture. The reasons justifying a deferential standard of review in other contexts, however, apply with equal force to our review of a state trial court's findings of fact made in connection with a federal constitutional claim." The reversal in Norris was consistent with these principles, the Court said, because there "a finding of no discrimination was simply too incredible to be accepted by this Court" (p. 369).

Justice O'Connor (joined by Justice Scalia) concurred in the judgment. On this point she said only, "I agree with the plurality that we review for clear error the trial court's finding as to discriminatory intent" (p. 372).[1]

Although the plurality did not explicitly discuss the appropriate scope of review of state court factfindings based on inferences, it equated the standard for reviewing state court cases with the clearly erroneous standard under Rule 52(a). See also Bose Corp. v. Consumers Union, 466 U.S. 485, 498–99 (1984).

(4) *Historical Facts vs. Application of Law to Fact.* The Court's review of findings of historical fact differs sharply from its review of the application of law to fact; as to the latter, de novo review is common, though not invariable. See Paragraphs (C)(1–6), *infra*. Thus, an important, and often "vexing," question, Pullman–Standard v. Swint, 456 U.S. 273, 288 (1982), is whether a particular issue should be deemed to fall within one category or the other.

(a) *Discriminatory Purpose.* Consider the issue of intention to discriminate—whether in the selection of grand jurors in Norris, in the terms and conditions of employment in Anderson, or in the exercise of peremptory challenges in Hernandez. Couldn't one characterize the issues this way: the legal principle is that intentional discrimination violates the federal Constitution or federal civil rights statutes; the historical facts are what the jury commissioners or employer or prosecutor did and said; and the question whether those historical facts establish intentional discrimination requires an application of law to fact?

That characterization would not necessarily require less deferential review of findings of discrimination than was mandated in Anderson and Hernandez; as noted in Paragraph (C)(2), *infra*, the Court is free to defer to lower court applications of law to fact. And it may be that in many such cases, the determination whether there was a discriminatory motivation cannot effectively be separated from determinations as to credibility, which surely should be reviewed with deference. Would the reasoning in Hernandez have been more persuasive if the Court had urged deferential review not because the issue was one of historical fact, but instead because, even if the issue were deemed to be one of application of law to fact, de novo review would be impracticable or inappropriate?

---

1. The three dissenters did not discuss the standard of review, contending that whether or not the prosecutor's explanation was pretextual, it was insufficient to dispel the inference of racial animus created by his conduct.

(b) *Actual Malice.* Several defamation (and related) cases applying the "actual malice" standard of New York Times v. Sullivan, 376 U.S. 254 (1964), contain significant discussion of the appropriate standard of review on appeal.

(i) In the Sullivan decision itself, plaintiff, the Police and Fire Commissioner of Montgomery, Alabama, obtained a $500,000 jury verdict in a defamation suit predicated on the newspaper's publication of an advertisement charging the existence of "an unprecedented wave of terror" (p. 256) against blacks engaged in peaceful demonstration. The award rested on some inaccuracies in the ad, such as that Dr. Martin Luther King, Jr. had been arrested seven times (the correct number was four). The Supreme Court ruled that the First and Fourteenth Amendments "prohibit[] a public official from recovering damages for a defamatory falsehood unless he proves [with convincing clarity] that the statement was made with 'actual malice'—that is, with knowledge that it was false or with reckless disregard of whether it was false" (pp. 279–80). The state court had made no determination regarding actual malice. With no disagreement on this point, the Court treated the issue as one of application of law to fact that it should determine independently, and ruled that the record evidence did not furnish convincing proof of actual malice (pp. 284–86 & n. 26).

(ii) Disagreement surfaced, however, in Bose Corp. v. Consumers Union, 466 U.S. 485 (1984), a *federal* action for product disparagement that was governed by the actual malice standard. Justice Stevens' majority opinion conceded that it would "not stretch the language of [Fed.R.Civ.Proc. 52(a)] to characterize an inquiry into what a person knew at a given point in time as a question of 'fact' " (p. 498). Still, he followed Sullivan in treating the issue as one of application of law to fact that the Court should independently review— and found the evidence insufficient to support the trial judge's finding of actual malice. (The decision also stated that independent review was *required* by the First Amendment. See Paragraph (C)(3), *infra.*)

In dissent, Justice Rehnquist (joined by Justice O'Connor) argued that the finding of actual malice, like many other state-of-mind determinations, was "a question of pure historical fact" (p. 517 n. 1). Noting that such a finding would often be based on a determination of the defendant's credibility, he argued that it could be reversed under Rule 52(a) only if clearly erroneous. He acknowledged that the Sullivan decision looked the other way, but argued that independent review was justified there (i) because the factfinding was conducted by a jury whose general verdict, unlike the judge's written findings in Bose, did not resolve specific factual questions, and (ii) because of the narrow appellate review at common law of jury verdicts. Justice White's dissent contended that the "knowledge of falsity" component of actual malice is an historical fact but that "reckless disregard" is not.

(iii) In Bose, the trial judge's factfindings included an explicit statement that he did not believe a particular witness. How should the Bose requirement of independent review operate in the face of a *jury verdict* where there are credibility and demeanor issues? In Harte–Hanks Communications, Inc. v. Connaughton, 491 U.S. 657 (1989), a federal jury reached a special verdict finding a newspaper's story to be false and defamatory, and also finding, by clear and convincing evidence, that the story was published with actual malice. In affirming the judgment for plaintiff, the Supreme Court first indicated that "[t]he question whether the evidence in the record in a defamation case is sufficient to support a finding of actual malice is a question of law" (p. 685). The Court continued (p. 688, quoting Bose at 499–500): "credibility determinations are reviewed under the clearly erroneous standard because the trier of fact has had the 'opportunity to observe the demeanor of the witnesses' ". Reviewing the record in some detail, the Court reasoned that the jury must have rejected certain testimony of defense witnesses; based on those jury determinations and the undisputed evidence, "the conclusion that the newspaper acted with actual malice inextricably follows" (p. 691). Justice White's concurrence (joined by the Chief Justice) expressed his view that all historical facts (including but not limited to those dependent on credibility determinations) are reviewable under Rule 52's clearly erroneous standard. Justice Scalia, concurring in the judgment, noted that the circuits were split on whether an appellate court must make an independent assessment of the facts allegedly establishing actual malice, or instead should assume that the jury made all reasonable findings in favor of the plaintiff. He thought it odd for the Court to have judged the adequacy of the showing of actual malice on the basis of facts that the jury *did* find, rather than those that it could reasonably have found.

In many defamation cases, won't it be hard for a court, when reviewing a jury verdict in favor of the plaintiff, to determine by examining the record whether the jury (a) found the defendant's witnesses not credible (in which case deference would be called for), or (b) found those witnesses credible but still found actual malice (in which case independent review would be mandated)? Does this line of cases invite if not require state and federal courts to use detailed special verdicts in order to facilitate appellate review? Should those verdicts ask whether jurors believed particular witnesses?

(c) *The Lines of Decision Compared.* Why are findings regarding actual malice subject to independent review, while those regarding discriminatory purpose are not? Is there something different about the nature of the issues on the law/fact continuum? About the perceived need for appellate review? Is independent review more important under the First Amendment than under the Equal Protection Clause? See generally Paragraph (C)(3), *infra.*

For an excellent discussion of Bose, and of the problems canvassed in this Note, see Monaghan, Paragraph (A)(1), *supra.*

(5) *The Seventh Amendment.* The Seventh Amendment says that "no fact tried by jury, shall be otherwise reexamined in any Court of the United States, than according to the rules of the common law." In Chicago, B. & Q.R.R. v. Chicago, 166 U.S. 226, 242–43 (1897), the Court held that the Seventh Amendment applies to Supreme Court review of a state court jury verdict challenged as providing insufficient compensation for a taking of property.[2]

If a properly-instructed jury finds for the plaintiff in a defamation case, is the Supreme Court free to substitute its own determination? In the Sullivan case, the Court brushed the Seventh Amendment aside on the ground that the

---

2. The railroad claimed that the jury's award of one dollar deprived it of its federal constitutional right to due process. The Supreme Court upheld the jury verdict, noting that it was for the jury to ascertain the facts (a category that included the extent of interference with the railroad's property and the amount of the resulting loss in value), while the courts were to ascertain the legal principles. The Court said that the Seventh Amendment prohibited it from retrying what the jury had found; but it also noted that the scope of review on the writ of error did not extend to the facts, and included a discussion suggesting that the jury's decision was reasonable.

Cf. also p. 458, *supra* (discussing the applicability of the Seventh Amendment to cases removed to federal court after a state jury verdict).

issue was not one of historical fact but of application of law to fact. See 376 U.S. at 285 n. 26. See also Bose Corp., *supra*, at 508 n. 27 ("the limitation on appellate review of factual determinations under Rule 52(a) is no more stringent than the limitation on federal appellate review of a jury's factual determinations under the Seventh Amendment"). Many cases follow Sullivan in reviewing a jury's application of law to fact, see, *e.g.*, Fiske v. Kansas, Paragraph (C)(1), *infra*; Jenkins v. Georgia, Paragraph (C)(6)(d), *infra*, so that in practice, the Seventh Amendment has not proven to be an important limit on Supreme Court review.[3]

Is the question of a libel defendant's knowledge of falsity less "factual" than the question of how to value governmental interference with property rights? If an FELA case were tried in state court, could (should) the Supreme Court engage in de novo review of the jury's finding regarding negligence on the ground that it involves application of law to fact?

(6) *Cox v. Louisiana*. Cases like Norris, in which the Court overturns state court findings on issues that are undoubted historical facts, are rare.[4] (A 1995 addition to Sup.Ct.R. 10 expressly states that "[a] petition for writ of certiorari is rarely granted when the asserted error consists of erroneous factual findings".) Consider whether the Court overturned or made new findings of historical fact in Cox v. Louisiana, 379 U.S. 536 (1965), and if so, whether the Court was justified in doing so.

In the midst of an on-going civil rights protest in Baton Rouge in 1961, Cox led a large march of some 2000 students to protest the arrest and jailing the previous day of 23 students who had been picketing stores with segregated lunch counters. At one point during the march, when Cox told city officials that the group was going to pass by the courthouse, the officers requested that they disband; that request was refused, and the group began moving toward the courthouse. Cox then spoke with the Police Chief, who testified that he informed Cox that "he must confine" the demonstration "to the West side of the street"; in his testimony, the Chief added: "This, of course, was not—I didn't mean it in the import that I was giving him any permission to do it, but I was presented with a situation that was accomplished and I had to make a decision" (p. 541). The march proceeded on the sidewalk across the street from the courthouse. There followed some chanting and singing by the protesters; responses from the students in jail; a speech by Cox urging the

3. Are there countervailing constitutional considerations that favor judicial review of jury verdicts in some cases? Professor Monaghan argues that the evolution of the First Amendment from a guarantee of majority criticism of unrepresentative government to a guarantee protecting unpopular speech against majority standards requires a "reevaluation of the assumption that the jury is a reliable factfinder in free speech cases". Monaghan, *First Amendment "Due Process"*, 83 Harv.L.Rev. 518, 527–29 (1970). *Cf.* Honda Motor Co., Ltd. v. Oberg, 114 S.Ct. 2331 (1994), p. 607, note 9, *infra* (holding that due process requires some judicial review, for excessiveness, of the amount of jury punitive damage awards—though under a very forgiving standard).

4. For another example of such a case, see Moore v. Michigan, 355 U.S. 155 (1957). The Court found that the defendant had not waived his right to counsel (a mixed question of law and fact), but in making that determination rejected the trial judge's finding that the defendant's purported waiver was not based on his fear, while in pre-trial custody, of a threat of mob violence. The Court relied heavily on testimony by the sheriff (that he had told Moore that if he was guilty, he might be better owning up to it, because "tension is very high out there" and there could be trouble) that the trial judge had found "insignificant". The Court also appeared squarely to reject the trial judge's assessment of Moore's own credibility.

group to sit-in at segregated lunch counters; and finally the use by police of tear gas to disperse the group.

In a bench trial at which there were sharp disputes about the basic historical facts, Cox was convicted of disturbing the peace, obstructing public passages, and interfering with the administration of justice. Those convictions were affirmed by the Louisiana Supreme Court, but reversed by the U.S. Supreme Court. Justice Goldberg's majority opinion began with a factual recitation of what had occurred that was based not on state-court factfindings, but rather on his reading of the testimony in the record.

(a) As to the breach of the peace conviction, the Court reviewed in detail the testimony of defense and prosecution witnesses, found that the demonstration was "orderly" (p. 547), and stated that "our independent examination of the record, which we are required to make [because the case involves a claim of constitutional right], shows no conduct which the State had a right to prohibit as a breach of the peace" (p. 545).[5]   Compare the state supreme court's description of the events (156 So.2d at 452): "There were silent prayers and a display of signs"; "Cox then made a speech"; "[t]he crowd then sang songs, answered by the prisoners in the jailhouse, and this in turn evoked loud and frenzied outbursts and 'wild yells' from the demonstrators"; "[w]hereupon 'grumbling' was heard among the white people"; "[a]t this time, the prisoners in jail were 'hollering' ".

In making its findings, the Supreme Court relied heavily on a news film of the events, which the state had put in evidence at trial. Was this appropriate? Though a movie may convey a great sense of verisimilitude, its import and credibility inevitably depend upon the perspective and choices of the photographer and editor.

(b) The conviction for obstructing public passages was overturned on the ground that testimony at trial, and a statement by the counsel for the state in oral argument, indicated that some meetings or parades that obstruct traffic had been permitted with prior approval of officials, but no standards governed the officials' decision; "[t]he situation is thus the same as if the statute itself expressly provided that there could only be peaceful parades or demonstrations in the unbridled discretion of the local officials" (p. 557).

Justice White (joined by Justice Harlan) dissented as to this conviction: "The sole indication in the record from the state court that such has occurred was contained in the testimony of the Chief of Police who * * * said 'most organizations that want to hold a parade or a meeting of any kind, they have no reluctance to evidence their desires at the start.' There is no evidence in the record that other meetings of this magnitude had been allowed on the city streets, had been allowed in the vicinity of the courthouse or had been permitted completely to obstruct the sidewalk and to block access to abutting buildings. Indeed, the sheriff testified that 'we have never had such a demonstration since I have been in law enforcement in this parish.' * * *

"At the oral argument * * *, counsel said, 'arrangements are usually made depending on the size of the demonstration, of course, arrangements are made with the officials and their cooperation is not only required it is needed where you have such a large crowd.' In my view, however, all of this evidence

---

5. The Court ruled in the alternative that the breach of the peace statute was unconstitutionally overbroad.

together falls far short of justification for converting this prohibitory state statute into an open-ended licensing statute invalid under prior decisions of this Court as applied to this case. This is particularly true since the Court's approach is its own invention and has not been urged or litigated by the parties either in this Court or the courts below. Certainly the parties have had no opportunity to develop or to refute the factual basis underlying the Court's rationale * * *" (pp. 591–93).

(c) Cox's conviction of interfering with the administration of justice was overturned on the ground that the statute, in failing to define when a demonstration is near enough to the courthouse to constitute an interference, "foresees a degree of on-the-spot administrative interpretation by official charged with responsibility for administering and enforcing it. * * * The record here clearly shows that the officials present gave permission for the demonstration to take place across the street from the courthouse.[6] * * * In effect, [Cox] was advised that a demonstration at the place it was held would not be one 'near' the courthouse within the terms of the statute." To uphold a conviction under such circumstances "would be to sanction an indefensible sort of entrapment by the state" (pp. 568–71).

Justice Clark dissented as to this conviction. His description of the facts asserted that Cox, "in an effort to influence and intimidate the courts and legal officials of Baton Rouge and to procure the release of 23 prisoners being held for trial, agitated and led a mob of over 2,000 students in the staging of a modern Donnybrook Fair across from the courthouse and jail" (p. 585). This "mob of young Negroes * * * was not only within sight but in hearing distance of the courthouse. The record is replete with evidence that the demonstrators with their singing, cheering, clapping and waving of banners drew the attention of the whole courthouse square as well as the occupants and officials of the court building itself. Indeed, one judge was obliged to leave the building. * * * The law enforcement officials were confronted with a direct obstruction to the orderly administration of their duties as well as an interference with the courts. One hardly needed an on-the-spot administrative decision that the demonstration was 'near' the courthouse with the disturbance being conducted before the eyes and ringing in the ears of court officials, police officers and citizens throughout the courthouse" (p. 586).[7]

(d) Do the circumstances in Cox (a high visibility civil rights case) explain the Court's lack of deference to state court factfindings? If so, what is Cox's precedential significance?

(7) *The Limits of Supreme Court Review.* Suppose the Supreme Court believes that there is a significant danger of systemic erosion of certain federal claims, or of federal rights asserted by certain litigants, because of state court resistance? Suppose it believed that the problems in Norris and Cox were not episodic, but exemplified the treatment of racial issues during those periods in

---

6. In a footnote, the Court added: "It is true that the Police Chief testified that he did not subjectively intend to grant permission, but there is no evidence at all that this subjective state of mind was ever communicated to * * * [anyone present]" (p. 570 n. 4).

7. Justice Black (with whom Justices White and Harlan agreed in this respect) also dissented, arguing (p. 582): "But quite apart from the fact that a police chief cannot authorize violations of his State's criminal laws, there was strong, emphatic testimony that if any consent was given it was limited to telling Cox and his group to come no closer to the courthouse than they had already come without the consent of any official, city, state, or federal."

many Southern courts? Would a federal trial forum, provided by original or removal jurisdiction in federal question cases, be more satisfactory than an expanded scope of appellate review?

(8) *The Relevance of Federal Habeas Corpus.* A different mechanism of federal review is provided by federal habeas corpus jurisdiction, which authorizes the federal courts to entertain petitions from state prisoners alleging that their convictions or sentences were tainted by federal constitutional violations. The jurisdiction is limited to persons still in custody, and thus is not available in many criminal (and virtually all civil) cases. The remedy is available, moreover, only after state remedies have been exhausted, and is subject to numerous restrictions. See generally Chap. XI, Sec. 2, *infra.*

In considering habeas petitions, the federal courts are free to engage in de novo review of applications of law to fact, but since 1966 the habeas statute (28 U.S.C. § 2254(d)) has contained elaborate, though not unbending, rules of deference to state court factfindings.[8]

Unlike the Supreme Court, a habeas court has the capacity to hear evidence—although that power has been sharply narrowed by recent Supreme Court decisions, see pp. 1371–76, *infra,* and has been exercised exceedingly rarely. For the resolution of factual issues that are unclear on the record and that involve demeanor and credibility of witnesses or other elements that may depend on the "feel" of the trial, Justice Harlan suggested that "[f]ederal habeas corpus * * * provides a far more satisfactory vehicle [than Supreme Court review] * * *, for the judge can evaluate for himself the on-the-spot considerations which no appellate court can estimate with assurance on a cold record." Beck v. Ohio, 379 U.S. 89 (1964)(dissenting opinion).

Would habeas review have been preferable in Norris or Cox? Would that depend on the identity of the federal trial judge in Alabama or Louisiana who would have considered the habeas petition? On how long the defendant would realistically have had to wait (and, in Norris' case, whether a stay of execution would have been available) before obtaining review?

C. Techniques for Controlling the Law–Applying Functions

(1) *Jurisdiction to Review Application of Law to Fact.* The Court regularly reviews a state court's application of federal legal standards to the facts as found, usually without exhibiting any deference to the state court's determination.

A leading example is Fiske v. Kansas, 274 U.S. 380 (1927), where the defendant was convicted, after a jury trial, of criminal syndicalism for having distributed literature of, and solicited members for, a branch of the Industrial Workers of the World (IWW). The state supreme court, in rejecting his claim that the Kansas Syndicalism Act, insofar as it purported to criminalize the acts in question, violated the federal Constitution, concluded that the preamble to

---

8. Under 2254(d), the Supreme Court has rendered a number of decisions, not all of which are clear or convincing, differentiating between "fact" and "application of law to fact". See the *Note on Relitigating the Facts on Habeas Corpus,* p. 1371, *infra.* Those decisions in turn may have application on direct review. Thus, for example, Arizona v. Fulminante, 499 U.S. 279, 287 (1991), a case on direct review, followed the holding in Miller v. Fenton, 474 U.S. 104, 110 (1985), a habeas corpus case, that "the ultimate issue of 'voluntariness' [of a confession] is a legal question requiring independent federal determination." (On the confession cases, see Paragraph (C)(4), *infra.*)

the IWW constitution could have been found by the jury to advocate physical violence.

On writ of error, the Court reversed, stating (pp. 385–86): "[T]his Court will review the finding of facts by a State court where a Federal right has been denied as the result of a finding shown by the record to be without evidence to support it; or where a conclusion of law as to a Federal right and a finding of fact are so intermingled as to make it necessary, in order to pass upon the Federal question, to analyze the facts." The Court proceeded to find that "[n]o substantial inference can, in our judgment, be drawn from the language of this preamble, that the organization taught, advocated or suggested the duty, necessity, propriety, or expediency of crime, criminal syndicalism, sabotage, or other unlawful acts or methods" (p. 386).

Like Fiske, other cases state that the Court will exercise its own judgment when findings of fact are intermingled with conclusions of law. *E.g.*, Feiner v. New York, 340 U.S. 315, 323 (1951); Pollock v. Williams, 322 U.S. 4, 13 (1944). In a different verbal formulation, the Court often states that it has the power to engage in an independent examination of the record, see, *e.g.*, NAACP v. Claiborne Hardware Co., 458 U.S. 886, 915–16 n. 50 (1982); Edwards v. South Carolina, 372 U.S. 229, 235 (1963), but generally the actual review is only of the application of law to fact.

(2) *The Question of Policy.* How far the Supreme Court (or, more generally, appellate courts) should attempt to supervise individual instances of law application (which in constitutional cases are sometimes referred to as "constitutional facts") has been an important problem of judicial administration. See generally Louis, *Allocating Adjudicative Decision Making Authority Between the Trial and Appellate Levels: A Unified View of the Scope of Review, the Judge/Jury Question, and Procedural Discretion*, 64 N.C.L.Rev. 993 (1986). See also Lee, *Principled Decision Making and the Proper Role of Federal Appellate Courts: The Mixed Questions Conflict*, 64 S.Cal.L.Rev. 235 (1991)(noting that some *federal* appellate courts engage in de novo review of district court applications of law to fact, while others apply a clearly erroneous standard, and favoring the former approach only when appellate review would create meaningful precedent).

As the Court noted in Container Corp. of America v. Franchise Tax Board, 463 U.S. 159 (1983), its approach to this problem has not been uniform. The case turned on whether a corporation's activities constituted a "unitary business" under the federal constitutional doctrines pertaining to state taxing jurisdiction. The Court remarked (p. 176): "The factual records in such cases * * * tend to be long and complex, and the line between 'historical fact' and 'constitutional fact' is often fuzzy at best. * * * It will do the cause of legal certainty little good if this Court turns every colorable claim that a state court erred in a particular application of those principles into a de novo adjudication, whose unintended nuances would then spawn further litigation and an avalanche of critical comment. Rather, our task must be to determine whether the state court applied the correct standards to the case; and if it did, whether its judgment 'was within the realm of permissible judgment.'" But in a footnote the Court added: "This approach is, of course, quite different from the one we follow in certain other constitutional contexts" (p. 176 n. 13, citing New York Times v. Sullivan, Paragraph B(4)(b), *supra*, and Brooks v. Florida, 389 U.S. 413 (1967)(per curiam)(involving admissibility of an allegedly involuntary confession)).

What principle explains or justifies the different approaches followed in different substantive areas? Professor Monaghan, Paragraph A(1), *supra*, at 271, suggests two circumstances that call for de novo review: "first, the danger of systemic bias of other actors in the judicial system; second, the perceived need for a case-by-case development of the law in a given area." Does (should) the nature of the federal right at issue matter? Are constitutional errors pertaining to the limits of state taxing power more tolerable than those involving deprivations of free speech or of rights in the criminal process?

Must the Court be consistent on these questions? For example, in determining whether particular sets of circumstances constitute "probable cause" within the meaning of the Fourth Amendment, must the Court always display the same degree of deference? Or is it appropriate to rely on a "situation sense" to determine whether a specific case calls for more intensive review— even if the Court is unable or unwilling to articulate the reasons for its intuition?

(3) *Bose and The Obligation of Independent Review*. The Container Corp. decision appeared to suggest that the Court had the power, though not necessarily the obligation, to review state court applications of law to fact. But in the Bose decision, Paragraph B(4)(b), *supra*, which involved application by a federal district judge of the "actual malice" standard of New York Times v. Sullivan, the Court declared that "in cases raising First Amendment issues we have repeatedly held that an appellate court has an obligation to 'make an independent examination of the whole record' in order to make sure 'that the judgment does not constitute a forbidden intrusion on the field of free expression'" (p. 499, quoting Sullivan at 284–86). Justice Stevens said (p. 501): "[T]he rule of independent review assigns to judges a constitutional responsibility that cannot be delegated to the trier of fact, whether the factfinding function be performed in the particular case by a jury or by a trial judge." "When the standard governing the decision of a particular case is provided by the Constitution, this Court's role in marking out the limits of the standard through the process of case-by-case adjudication is of special importance. This process has been vitally important in cases involving restrictions on the freedom of speech protected by the First Amendment, particularly in those cases in which it is contended that the communication in issue is within one of the few classes of 'unprotected' speech" (p. 503). "Providing triers of fact with a general description of the type of communication whose content is unworthy of protection has not, in and of itself, served sufficiently to narrow the category, nor served to eliminate the danger that decisions by triers of fact may inhibit the expressed of protected ideas" (p. 505). "The requirement of independent appellate review * * * is a rule of federal constitutional law. * * * It reflects a deeply held conviction that judges—and particularly Members of this Court— must exercise such review in order to preserve the precious liberties established and ordained by the Constitution" (pp. 510–11).

Does the Bose decision imply that:

(a) There is a constitutional right to some judicial review of application of law to fact in defamation actions?[9] If so, should a trial court, in deciding a

---

9. *Cf.* Honda Motor Co., Ltd. v. Oberg, 114 S.Ct. 2331 (1994), which invalidated a provision of the Oregon Constitution that was understood to permit judicial review of a jury's punitive damages award only as to the question whether there was evidence to support any award of punitive damages, but to prohibit review of the amount of an award.

motion for a judgment as a matter of law, abandon the normal deferential standard and engage in independent review of the jury's application of law to fact (on the theory that if it doesn't, the appellate court will)? See Paragraph B(5), *supra* (discussing the applicability of the Seventh Amendment).

(b) There is a right to *appellate* review of a trial judge's fact-findings, even if the trial judge has denied motions for judgment as a matter of law and for a new trial? Compare Monaghan, Paragraph A(1), *supra*, and Meltzer, *Harmless Error and Constitutional Remedies*, 61 U.Chi.L.Rev. 1 (1993)(noting the lack of an established right to appellate review not only in civil but even in criminal cases). Or is the point in Bose that if there is a statutory right to appeal, the scope of appellate review cannot be limited? But why should that be? How would any claim of a right to appellate review apply before the Supreme Court, in view of its discretion to grant certiorari limited to a particular question presented or to deny certiorari altogether?

(c) There must be independent appellate review of the application of law to fact as to other issues (for example, the size of damage awards) in defamation actions (but *cf.* Chicago, B. & Q.R.R. v. Chicago, 166 U.S. 226, 242–43 (1897), Paragraph B(5), *supra*)? As to all First Amendment issues (compare the obscenity cases in Paragraph C(6), *infra*)? As to all constitutional questions (but compare the Container Corp. decision, Paragraph C(2), *supra*)?

(d) There must be independent review of a finding at trial that there was *not* actual malice?

For persuasive criticism of Bose's announcement of a constitutional obligation, see generally Monaghan, *supra*. See also Strong, *The Persistent Doctrine of "Constitutional Fact"*, 46 N.Cal.L.Rev. 223 (1968).

(4) *Involuntary Confessions.* In the period 1940–1965, the Court reviewed a large number of state court holdings admitting into evidence confessions alleged to be coerced. See, *e.g.*, Haley v. Ohio, 332 U.S. 596 (1948); Watts v. Indiana, 338 U.S. 49 (1949); Haynes v. Washington, 373 U.S. 503 (1963). The disputes usually centered not on the historical facts, but rather on the question whether the confession was "voluntary". But that question, resting as it did on the totality of the circumstances, was heavily dependent on factual variations. Each Supreme Court decision detailed the particular circumstances and held that the specific confession was (or less often, was not) coerced, without developing more clear cut constitutional standards for determining admissibility. Although the Court devoted a considerable portion of its docket to this aspect of criminal procedure, its efforts to supervise the state courts seemed unsuccessful.

Miranda v. Arizona, 384 U.S. 436 (1966)(5–4), which held that a statement made during custodial interrogation is inadmissible unless the suspect had been

The Court found that Oregon's prohibition departed from the Anglo–American tradition and from the practice of the other 49 states, and that "[p]unitive damages pose an acute danger of arbitrary deprivation of property" (p. 2340).

The Court's decision sounded in procedural due process. It was not entirely clear whether excessiveness is to be judged under a federal standard, see, *e.g.*, TXO Prod. Corp. v. Alliance Resources, Corp., 113 S.Ct. 2711, 2718–19, 2731 (1993)(five Justices, in separate opinions, agreeing that grossly excessive punitive damages would violate Due Process Clause), or under the state law standards on which the jury was instructed in the case; but the Court did clearly indicate that the standard was a deferential one (p. 2341 n. 10).

given the now-familiar "Miranda warnings" and had waived his right to silence, largely eliminated the need for the Court to review the "voluntariness" of confessions.[10] The few post-Miranda decisions under that standard have involved unusual factual situations to which Miranda may not apply. See, *e.g.*, Arizona v. Fulminante, 499 U.S. 279 (1991)(confession made to a prison informant who offered to protect the defendant from threats of violence in prison in exchange for the truth); Colorado v. Connelly, 479 U.S. 157 (1986)(psychotic individual approaches a police officer and voluntarily confesses).

(5) *Substantive Rules and Evidentiary Rules.* Miranda is an example of a change in substantive law designed to protect federal rights against erosion: adoption of per se rules minimized the need for case-by-case consideration of specific circumstances relevant to a more open-ended voluntariness standard.[11] Was the Court justified in adopting those rules if, in order to make them adequately clear in application, they result in prohibiting much conduct that would not have been illegal under even the most rights-protective application of the involuntariness test? Compare Grano, *Prophylactic Rules in Criminal Procedure: A Question of Article III Legitimacy*, 80 Nw.U.L.Rev. 100 (1985), with Strauss, *The Ubiquity of Prophylactic Rules*, 55 U.Chi.L.Rev. 190 (1988).

Can the Court accomplish some of the same results by declaring federal rules directed to the fact-finding process, governing matters such as scope of review or burden of proof? Recall the requirement of New York Times v. Sullivan, 376 U.S. 254, 285–86 (1964), that the evidence of "actual malice" be shown with "convincing clarity", and the requirement of independent review set forth in Bose.

Reconsider also Norris v. Alabama. Did the Court merely review a particular set of factual circumstances, or did it create a new legal rule, in the form of a rebuttable presumption of unconstitutional discrimination when the statistical evidence shows disparities? See Whitus v. Georgia, 385 U.S. 545, 551 (1967)("[w]hile the [jury] commissioners testified that no one was included or rejected on the jury list because of race or color, this has been held insufficient to overcome the prima facie case. Norris v. State of Alabama, * * *").

(6) *Obscenity.* What should the Court do when it has provided as much specification of the substantive federal standards, and related evidentiary or procedural rules, as it thinks possible, and yet lacks confidence that the state courts (or the lower federal courts) are applying these standards "correctly"?

---

10. But see Mincey v. Arizona, 437 U.S. 385 (1978)(confession that is involuntary, unlike one that merely violates Miranda, may not be introduced to impeach the defendant's testimony).

11. Compare the evolution of the constitutional right to counsel in state criminal cases from Powell v. Alabama, 287 U.S. 45 (1932) and Betts v. Brady, 316 U.S. 455 (1942)(counsel must be appointed when circumstances make such assistance fundamental to fair trial) to Gideon v. Wainwright, 372 U.S. 335 (1963) and Scott v. Illinois, 440 U.S. 367 (1979)(counsel required in any case resulting in imprisonment). See Wechsler, The Nationalization of Civil Liberties and Civil Rights 18–19 (1969): "[T]here can be no doubt but that the administration of a standard of due process calling for the closest scrutiny of records to appraise essential fairness has proved to be increasingly intractable and burdensome, and to exert too little impact on the grave abuse so frequently revealed by the cases in the Court. The pressure to decree more rigid rules more easily applied has grown accordingly apace."

The most vivid example of this problem of judicial administration comes from the intractable field of obscenity.

The general constitutional standards governing the materials that may be suppressed as "obscene" under the First Amendment have been defined in a small number of well-known cases, but beginning with Roth v. United States, 355 U.S. 852 (1957), all of the formulations developed have been notoriously open-ended. In these cases the historical facts (sale or possession of particular publication, or exhibition of a particular film) are rarely in doubt; the hard question has been whether the Court should (or must) review individual applications of the First Amendment standards.

(a) In Jacobellis v. Ohio, 378 U.S. 184 (1964), the Court reversed a conviction for possessing and exhibiting Louis Malle's film, *Les Amants*. There was no majority opinion. The Justices split sharply on the content of the constitutional standard for punishable "obscenity", and even more so on the issue of whether the Court should make its own determination of whether a particular film is "obscene".

Justice Brennan, joined by Justice Goldberg in the first plurality opinion, noted (pp. 188–96):

"* * * [T]he question whether a particular work is obscene necessarily implicates an issue of constitutional law. * * * [W]e reaffirm the principle that, in 'obscenity' cases as in all others involving rights derived from the First Amendment guarantees of free expression, this Court cannot avoid making an independent constitutional judgment on the facts of the case as to whether the material involved is constitutionally protected.

"The question of the proper standard for making this determination has been the subject of much discussion and controversy since our decision in Roth seven years ago. Recognizing that the test for obscenity enunciated there— 'whether to the average person, applying contemporary community standards, the dominant theme of the material taken as a whole appeals to prurient interest,' 354 U.S., at 489—is not perfect, we think any substitute would raise equally difficult problems, and we therefore adhere to that standard * * *.

"It has been suggested that the 'contemporary community standards' aspect of the Roth test implies a determination of the constitutional question of obscenity in each case by the standards of the particular local community from which the case arises. * * * We do not see how any 'local' definition of the 'community' could properly be employed in delineating the area of expression that is protected by the Federal Constitution. * * * It is, after all, a national Constitution we are expounding."

Justice Black, in a concurring opinion joined by Justice Douglas, maintained that the First Amendment permits all films to be shown. Justice Stewart concurred on the basis of a standard of obscenity limited to "hard-core pornography". Attempting no further definition, he nevertheless declared that "I know it when I see it, and the motion picture involved in this case is not that" (p. 197). Justice White concurred without opinion.

Chief Justice Warren, joined in dissent by Justice Clark, had a different view of the Supreme Court's role: "This Court hears cases such as the instant one not merely to rule upon the alleged obscenity of a specific film or book but to establish principles for the guidance of lower courts and legislatures. Yet most of our decisions since Roth have been given without opinion and have thus failed to furnish such guidance. Nor does the Court in the instant case—

which has now been twice argued before us—shed any greater light on the problem. * * *

"For all the sound and fury that the Roth test has generated, it has not been proved unsound, and I believe that we should try to live with it—at least until a more satisfactory definition is evolved. * * *

"* * * I would commit the enforcement of [the Roth] rule to the appropriate state and federal courts, and I would accept their judgments made pursuant to the Roth rule, limiting myself to a consideration only of whether there is sufficient evidence in the record upon which a finding of obscenity could be made * * *—requiring something more than merely any evidence but something less than 'substantial evidence on the record [including the allegedly obscene material] as a whole.' * * * This is the only reasonable way I can see to obviate the necessity of this Court's sitting as the Super Censor of all the obscenity purveyed throughout the Nation" (pp. 200–03).

Justice Harlan filed a separate dissent

(b) In Redrup v. New York, 386 U.S. 767 (1967), the Court again failed to achieve a consensus; after reviewing the Justices' differing approaches to review of obscenity cases, the opinion simply stated that "[w]hichever of these constitutional views is brought to bear upon the cases before us, it is clear that the judgments [of conviction on obscenity charges] cannot stand" (p. 771). Following Redrup, the Court summarily reviewed a substantial number of obscenity cases and disposed of them per curiam, most often simply reversing with a citation to Redrup without even describing the nature of the allegedly obscene matter. See, *e.g.*, the cases cited in Justice Harlan's concurrence in Ginsberg v. New York, 390 U.S. 676, 707 n. 11 (1968); Bloss v. Michigan, 402 U.S. 938 (1971).

(c) In Miller v. California, 413 U.S. 15 (1973), the Court reformulated the constitutional standard somewhat, defining obscenity as material that (i) " 'the average person, applying contemporary community standards,' would find * * *, taken as a whole, appeals to the prurient interest," (ii) depicts, "in a patently offensive way, sexual conduct specifically defined by * * * state law," and (iii) "taken as a whole, lacks serious literary, artistic, political, or scientific value" (p. 15). Chief Justice Burger added for the Court (p. 26): "In resolving the inevitably sensitive questions of fact and law, we must continue to rely on the jury system, accompanied by the safeguards that judges, rules of evidence, presumption of innocence, and other protective features provide * * *." A footnote appended to this sentence continued: "The mere fact juries may reach different conclusions as to the same material does not mean that constitutional rights are abridged" (p. 26 n. 9). In dissent, Justice Brennan (joined by Justices Stewart and Marshall) argued that statutes prohibiting distribution of obscene material to adults should be held unconstitutionally vague and overbroad, *inter alia*, because of the unpredictability, ineffectiveness, and inordinate burdens stemming from reliance upon case-by-case Supreme Court review for protection of First Amendment rights. He contended that independent review would continue to be necessary under the Court's new standard.

(d) Justice Brennan's prediction appeared to be borne out when, the year after Miller, the Court reversed a state conviction, after a jury trial, for showing Mike Nichols' film "Carnal Knowledge". Jenkins v. Georgia, 418 U.S. 153 (1974). Justice Rehnquist wrote for the majority: "Our own viewing of the film satisfies us that 'Carnal Knowledge' could not be found under the Miller standards to depict sexual conduct in a patently offensive way."[12] Concurring in the result, Justice Brennan (again joined by Justices Stewart and Marshall) said that the Court's need to view the film confirmed his prediction that the Miller formulation "does not extricate us from the mire of case-by-case determination of obscenity. * * * After the Court's decision today, there can be no doubt that Miller requires appellate courts—including this Court—to review independently the constitutional fact of obscenity" (pp. 162–63). Justice Douglas dissented separately.

Since Jenkins, although there have been some refinements in the constitutional standards governing obscenity,[13] the Court has tended to refuse to engage in *ad hoc* review of the application of those standards. See, *e.g.*, Pendleton v. California, 423 U.S. 1068 (1976)(appeal dismissed; dissent by Justice Brennan complains that Court is not discharging its responsibility to review facts independently).

(7) *Alternatives*. Is there a satisfactory solution to the dilemma presented to the Court in areas like obscenity? Is the answer to review a large number of cases and dispose of them per curiam? If summary dispositions do not help to delineate the constitutional standard, do they represent a wise use of the Court's limited time? Why in principle is the Court the "best" decider of these issues?

Are juries especially suspect in this area? See note 3, *supra*. If so, is the answer mandated appellate review, but not necessarily by the Supreme Court?

Or is the problem that *state* courts are particularly suspect? If so, is the answer to provide a federal trial forum, by way of original or removal jurisdiction—or to rely on federal habeas corpus?[14] In what cases? Is it more economical to have the Supreme Court review those obscenity decisions in which standards were misapplied than to permit defendants to remove all state court obscenity cases, including those in which tne state court would have gotten it right?

Jackson v. Virginia

443 U.S. 307, 99 S.Ct. 2781, 61 L.Ed.2d 560 (1979).
Certiorari to the United States Court of Appeals for the Fourth Circuit.

■ Mr. Justice Stewart delivered the opinion of the Court.

* * *

I

The petitioner was convicted after a bench trial * * * of the first-degree murder of a woman named Mary Houston Cole. Under Virginia law, murder is

12. Without mentioning the Seventh Amendment, see Paragraph B(5), *supra*, the Court's opinion said: "Even though questions of appeal to the 'prurient interest' or of patent offensiveness are 'essentially questions of fact,' it would be a serious misreading of Miller to conclude that juries have unbridled discretion in determining what is 'patently offensive' "(p. 160).

13. See, *e.g.*, Pinkus v. United States, 436 U.S. 293 (1978); Brockett v. Spokane Arcades, Inc., 472 U.S. 491 (1985); Pope v. Illinois, 481 U.S. 497 (1987); see also New York v. Ferber, 458 U.S. 747 (1982)(dealing with child pornography).

14. Recall that federal habeas corpus jurisdiction is subject to numerous restrictions. See Paragraph B(8), *supra*.

defined as "the unlawful killing of another with malice aforethought." Stapleton v. Commonwealth, 123 Va. 825, 96 S.E. 801. Premeditation, or specific intent to kill, distinguishes murder in the first from murder in the second degree; proof of this element is essential to conviction of the former offense, and the burden of proving it clearly rests with the prosecution.

That the petitioner had shot and killed Mrs. Cole was not in dispute at the trial. * * * [The opinion here reviews the evidence at some length, concluding with defendant's postarrest statement (introduced by the prosecution) that the shooting had been accidental and that he had been "pretty high" but not drunk at the time.] At the trial, his position was that he had acted in self-defense. Alternatively, he claimed that in any event the State's own evidence showed that he had been too intoxicated to form the specific intent necessary under Virginia law to sustain a conviction of murder in the first degree.[2]

The trial judge, declaring himself convinced beyond a reasonable doubt that the petitioner had committed first-degree murder, found him guilty of that offense. The petitioner's motion to set aside the judgment as contrary to the evidence was denied, * * * [as was a petition for writ of error to the Virginia Supreme Court.]

The petitioner then commenced this habeas corpus proceeding in the United States District Court for the Eastern District of Virginia, raising the same basic claim. Applying the "no evidence" criterion of Thompson v. Louisville, 362 U.S. 199, the District Court found the record devoid of evidence of premeditation and granted the writ. The Court of Appeals for the Fourth Circuit reversed the judgment. [That] court was of the view that some evidence that the petitioner had intended to kill the victim could be found in the facts that the petitioner had reloaded his gun after firing warning shots, that he had had time to do so, and that the victim was then shot not once but twice. The court also concluded that the state trial judge could have found that the petitioner was not so intoxicated as to be incapable of premeditation.

We granted certiorari * * *.

II

Our inquiry in this case is narrow. * * * As the record demonstrates, the judge sitting as factfinder in the petitioner's trial was aware that the State bore the burden of establishing the element of premeditation, and stated that he was applying the reasonable-doubt standard in his appraisal of the State's evidence. The petitioner, moreover, does not contest the conclusion of the Court of Appeals that under the "no evidence" rule of Thompson v. Louisville, *supra*, his conviction of first-degree murder is sustainable. And he has not attacked the sufficiency of the evidence to support a conviction of second-degree murder. His sole constitutional claim, based squarely upon [In re] Winship, [397 U.S. 358 (1970),] is that the District Court and the Court of Appeals were in error in not recognizing that the question to be decided in this case is whether any

---

2. Under Virginia law, voluntary intoxication—although not an affirmative defense to second-degree murder—is material to the element of premeditation and may be found to have negated it.

rational factfinder could have concluded beyond a reasonable doubt that the killing for which the petitioner was convicted was premeditated. * * *

III

A

This is the first of our cases to expressly consider the question whether the due process standard recognized in Winship constitutionally protects an accused against conviction except upon evidence that is sufficient fairly to support a conclusion that every element of the crime has been established beyond a reasonable doubt. Upon examination of the fundamental differences between the constitutional underpinnings of Thompson v. Louisville, *supra,* and of In re Winship, *supra,* the answer to that question, we think, is clear.

It is axiomatic that a conviction upon a charge not made or upon a charge not tried constitutes a denial of due process. * * * These standards no more than reflect a broader premise that has never been doubted in our constitutional system: that a person cannot incur the loss of liberty for an offense without notice and a meaningful opportunity to defend. * * * A meaningful opportunity to defend, if not the right to a trial itself, presumes as well that a total want of evidence to support a charge will conclude the case in favor of the accused. Accordingly, we held in the Thompson case that a conviction based upon a record wholly devoid of any relevant evidence of a crucial element of the offense charged is constitutionally infirm. * * * The "no evidence" doctrine of Thompson v. Louisville thus secures to an accused the most elemental of due process rights: freedom from a wholly arbitrary deprivation of liberty.

The Court in Thompson explicitly stated that the due process right at issue did not concern a question of evidentiary "sufficiency." 362 U.S., at 199. The right established in In re Winship, however, clearly stands on a different footing. Winship involved an adjudication of juvenile delinquency made by a judge under a state statute providing that the prosecution must prove the conduct charged as delinquent—which in Winship would have been a criminal offense if engaged in by an adult—by a preponderance of the evidence. Applying that standard, the judge was satisfied that the juvenile was "guilty," but he noted that the result might well have been different under a standard of proof beyond a reasonable doubt. In short, the record in Winship was not totally devoid of evidence of guilt.

The constitutional problem addressed in Winship was thus distinct from the stark problem of arbitrariness presented in Thompson v. Louisville. In Winship, the Court held for the first time that the Due Process Clause of the Fourteenth Amendment protects a defendant in a criminal case against conviction "except upon proof beyond a reasonable doubt of every fact necessary to constitute the crime with which he is charged." 397 U.S., at 364. * * * The standard of proof beyond a reasonable doubt, said the Court, "plays a vital role in the American scheme of criminal procedure," because it operates to give "concrete substance" to the presumption of innocence, to ensure against unjust convictions, and to reduce the risk of factual error in a criminal proceeding. 397 U.S., at 363. At the same time, by impressing upon the factfinder the need to reach a subjective state of near certitude of the guilt of the accused, the standard symbolizes the significance that our society attaches to the criminal sanction and thus to liberty itself. *Id.,* at 372 (Harlan, J., concurring).

* * * In short, Winship presupposes as an essential of the due process guaranteed by the Fourteenth Amendment that no person shall be made to suffer the onus of a criminal conviction except upon sufficient proof—defined as evidence necessary to convince a trier of fact beyond a reasonable doubt of the existence of every element of the offense.

B

* * * [T]he Federal Courts of Appeals have generally assumed that so long as the reasonable-doubt instruction has been given at trial, the no-evidence doctrine of Thompson v. Louisville remains the appropriate guide for a federal habeas corpus court to apply in assessing a state prisoner's challenge to his conviction as founded upon insufficient evidence.   * * *   We cannot agree.

The Winship doctrine requires more than simply a trial ritual. A doctrine establishing so fundamental a substantive constitutional standard must also require that the factfinder will rationally apply that standard to the facts in evidence. A "reasonable doubt," at a minimum, is one based upon "reason." Yet a properly instructed jury may occasionally convict even when it can be said that no rational trier of fact could find guilt beyond a reasonable doubt, and the same may be said of a trial judge sitting as jury. In a federal trial, such an occurrence has traditionally been deemed to require reversal of the conviction. * * * Under Winship, which established proof beyond a reasonable doubt as an essential of Fourteenth Amendment due process, it follows that when such a conviction occurs in a state trial, it cannot constitutionally stand.

A federal court has a duty to assess the historic facts when it is called upon to apply a constitutional standard to a conviction obtained in a state court. For example, on direct review of a state-court conviction, where the claim is made that an involuntary confession was used against the defendant, this Court reviews the facts to determine whether the confession was wrongly admitted in evidence. The same duty obtains in federal habeas corpus proceedings.

After Winship the critical inquiry on review of the sufficiency of the evidence to support a criminal conviction must be not simply to determine whether the jury was properly instructed, but to determine whether the record evidence could reasonably support a finding of guilt beyond a reasonable doubt. But this inquiry does not require a court to "ask itself whether *it* believes that the evidence at the trial established guilt beyond a reasonable doubt." Woodby v. INS, 385 U.S. [276], 282 [(1966)] (emphasis added). Instead, the relevant question is whether, after viewing the evidence in the light most favorable to the prosecution, *any* rational trier of fact could have found the essential elements of the crime beyond a reasonable doubt. This familiar standard gives full play to the responsibility of the trier of fact fairly to resolve conflicts in the testimony, to weigh the evidence, and to draw reasonable inferences from basic facts to ultimate facts. Once a defendant has been found guilty of the crime charged, the factfinder's role as weigher of the evidence is preserved through a legal conclusion that upon judicial review *all of the evidence* is to be considered in the light most favorable to the prosecution. The criterion thus impinges upon "jury" discretion only to the extent necessary to guarantee the fundamental protection of due process of law.

That the Thompson "no evidence" rule is simply inadequate to protect against misapplications of the constitutional standard of reasonable doubt is readily apparent. "[A] mere modicum of evidence may satisfy a 'no evidence' standard * * *." Jacobellis v. Ohio, 378 U.S. 184, 202 (Warren, C.J., dissenting). Any evidence that is relevant—that has any tendency to make the existence of an element of a crime slightly more probable than it would be without the evidence, *cf*. Fed.Rule Evid. 401—could be deemed a "mere modicum." But it could not seriously be argued that such a "modicum" of evidence could by itself rationally support a conviction beyond a reasonable doubt. The Thompson doctrine simply fails to supply a workable or even a predictable standard for determining whether the due process command of Winship has been honored.[14]

C

Under 28 U.S.C. § 2254 [the jurisdictional statute for federal habeas corpus for state prisoners], a federal court must entertain a claim by a state prisoner that he or she is being held in "custody in violation of the Constitution or laws or treaties of the United States." Under the Winship decision, it is clear that a state prisoner who alleges that the evidence in support of his state conviction cannot be fairly characterized as sufficient to have led a rational trier of fact to find guilt beyond a reasonable doubt has stated a federal constitutional claim. Thus, * * * such a claim is cognizable in a federal habeas corpus proceeding. The respondents have argued, nonetheless, that a challenge to the constitutional sufficiency of the evidence should not be entertained by a federal district court under 28 U.S.C. § 2254.

In addition to the argument that a Winship standard invites replication of state criminal trials in the guise of § 2254 proceedings—an argument that simply fails to recognize that courts can and regularly do gauge the sufficiency of the evidence without intruding into any legitimate domain of the trier of fact—the respondents have urged that any departure from the Thompson test in federal habeas corpus proceedings will expand the number of meritless claims brought to the federal courts, will duplicate the work of the state appellate courts, will disserve the societal interest in the finality of state criminal proceedings, and will increase friction between the federal and state judiciaries. * * * We disagree.

First, the burden that is likely to follow from acceptance of the Winship standard has, we think, been exaggerated. Federal-court challenges to the evidentiary support for state convictions have since Thompson been dealt with under § 2254. A more stringent standard will expand the contours of this type of claim, but will not create an entirely new class of cases cognizable on federal habeas corpus. Furthermore, most meritorious challenges to constitutional sufficiency of the evidence undoubtedly will be recognized in the state courts, and, if the state courts have fully considered the issue of sufficiency, the task of a federal habeas court should not be difficult. And this type of claim can almost always be judged on the written record without need for an evidentiary hearing in the federal court.

---

14. Application of the Thompson standard to assess the validity of a criminal conviction after Winship could lead to absurdly unjust results. Our cases have indicated that failure to instruct a jury on the necessity of proof of guilt beyond a reasonable doubt can never be harmless error. Thus, a defendant whose guilt was actually proved by overwhelming evidence would be denied due process if the jury was instructed that he could be found guilty on a mere preponderance of the evidence. Yet a defendant against whom there was but one slender bit of evidence would not be denied due process so long as the jury has been properly instructed on the prosecution's burden of proof beyond a reasonable doubt. Such results would be wholly faithless to the constitutional rationale of Winship.

Second, the problems of finality and federal-state comity arise whenever a state prisoner invokes the jurisdiction of a federal court to redress an alleged constitutional violation. * * * Although state appellate review undoubtedly will serve in the vast majority of cases to vindicate the due process protection that follows from Winship, the same could also be said of the vast majority of other federal constitutional rights that may be implicated in a state criminal trial. It is the occasional abuse that the federal writ of habeas corpus stands ready to correct. Brown v. Allen, [344 U.S. 443, 498–501 (1953)] (opinion of Frankfurter, J.).

* * *

* * * The question whether a defendant has been convicted upon inadequate evidence is central to the basic question of guilt or innocence. The constitutional necessity of proof beyond a reasonable doubt is not confined to those defendants who are morally blameless. Under our system of criminal justice even a thief is entitled to complain that he has been unconstitutionally convicted and imprisoned as a burglar.

We hold that in a challenge to a state criminal conviction brought under 28 U.S.C. § 2254—if the settled procedural prerequisites for such a claim have otherwise been satisfied—the applicant is entitled to habeas corpus relief if it is found that upon the record evidence adduced at the trial no rational trier of fact could have found proof of guilt beyond a reasonable doubt.[16]

IV

Turning finally to the specific facts of this case, we reject the petitioner's claim that under the constitutional standard dictated by Winship his conviction of first-degree murder cannot stand. A review of the record in the light most favorable to the prosecution convinces us that a rational factfinder could readily have found the petitioner guilty beyond a reasonable doubt of first-degree murder under Virginia law. * * *

For these reasons, the judgment of the Court of Appeals is affirmed.

■ MR. JUSTICE POWELL took no part in the consideration or decision of this case.

■ MR. JUSTICE STEVENS, with whom THE CHIEF JUSTICE and MR. JUSTICE REHNQUIST join, concurring in the judgment.

* * *

Today the Court creates a new rule of law—one that has never prevailed in our jurisprudence. According to the Court, the Constitution now prohibits the criminal conviction of any person—including, apparently, a person against whom the facts have already been found beyond a reasonable doubt by a jury, a trial judge, and one or more levels of state appellate judges—except upon proof sufficient to convince a *federal judge* that a "rational trier of fact could have found the essential elements of the crime beyond a reasonable doubt."

The adoption of this novel constitutional rule is not necessary to the decision of this case. Moreover, I believe it is an unwise act of lawmaking.

---

16. The respondents have suggested that this constitutional standard will invite intrusions upon the power of the States to define criminal offenses. Quite to the contrary, the standard must be applied with explicit reference to the substantive elements of the criminal offense as defined by state law. Whether the State could constitutionally make the conduct at issue criminal at all is, of course, a distinct question.

Despite its chimerical appeal as a new counterpart to the venerable principle recognized in Winship, I am persuaded that its precipitous adoption will adversely affect the quality of justice administered by federal judges. For that reason I shall analyze this new brainchild with some care.

* * *

I

* * * Most significantly, the Court has announced its new constitutional edict in a case in which it has absolutely no bearing on the outcome. The only factual issue at stake is whether petitioner intended to kill his victim. If the evidence is viewed "in the light most favorable to the prosecution," * * * there can be only one answer to that question no matter *what* standard of appellate review is applied. In Part IV of its opinion, the Court accepts this conclusion. There is, therefore, no need to fashion a broad new rule of constitutional law to dispose of this squalid but rather routine murder case. * * *

The Court's new rule is adopted simply to forestall some hypothetical evil that has not been demonstrated, and in my view is not fairly demonstrable. Although the Judiciary has received its share of criticism * * * I am aware of no general dissatisfaction with the accuracy of the factfinding process or the adequacy of the rules applied by state appellate courts when reviewing claims of insufficiency.

What little evidence the Court marshals in favor of a contrary conclusion is unconvincing. The Court is simply incorrect in implying that there are a significant number of occasions when federal convictions are overturned on appeal because no rational trier of fact could have found guilt beyond a reasonable doubt. * * *

Moreover, a study of the 127 federal criminal convictions that were reviewed by the various Courts of Appeals and reported in the most recent hardbound volume of the Federal Reporter, Second Series, Volume 589, reveals that only 3 were overturned on sufficiency grounds. And of those, one was overturned under a "no evidence" standard, while the other two, in which a total of only 3 out of 36 counts were actually reversed, arguably involved legal issues masquerading as sufficiency questions. It is difficult to believe that the federal courts will turn up more sufficiency problems than this on habeas review when, instead of acting as the first level of review, as in the cases studied, they will be acting as the second, third, or even fourth level of appellate review. In short, there is simply no reason to tinker with an elaborate mechanism that is now functioning well.

II

* * * [In Winship,] the Court merely extended to juveniles a protection that had traditionally been available to defendants in criminal *trials* in this Nation.

But nothing in the Winship opinion suggests that it also bore on appellate or habeas corpus procedures. Although it repeatedly emphasized the function of the reasonable-doubt standard as describing the requisite "subjective state of certitude" of the *"factfinder,"* it never mentioned the question of how appellate judges are to know whether the trier of fact really was convinced beyond a reasonable doubt, or, indeed, whether the factfinder was a "rational" person or group of persons.

Moreover, the mode of analysis employed in Winship finds no counterpart in the Court's opinion in this case. For example, in Winship, the Court pointed out the breadth of both the historical and the current acceptance of the reasonable-doubt *trial* standard. In this case, by contrast, the Court candidly recognizes that the Federal Courts of Appeals have "generally" *rejected* the habeas standard that it adopts today.

* * *

The primary reasoning of the Court in Winship is also inapplicable here. The Court noted in that case that the reasonable-doubt standard has the desirable effect of significantly reducing the risk of an inaccurate factfinding and thus of erroneous convictions, as well as of instilling confidence in the criminal justice system. In this case, however, it would be impossible (and the Court does not even try) to demonstrate that there is an appreciable risk that a factfinding made by a jury beyond a reasonable doubt, and twice reviewed by a trial judge in ruling on directed verdict and post-trial acquittal motions and by one or more levels of appellate courts on direct appeal, as well as by two federal habeas courts under the Thompson "no evidence" rule, is likely to be erroneous. * * *

* * * [T]he Court places all of its reliance on a dry, and in my view incorrect, syllogism: If Winship requires the factfinder to apply a reasonable-doubt standard, then logic requires a reviewing judge to apply a like standard. * * *

Time may prove that the rule the Court has adopted today is the wisest compromise between one extreme that maximizes the protection against the risk that innocent persons will be erroneously convicted and the other extreme that places the greatest faith in the ability of fair procedures to produce just verdicts. But the Court's opinion should not obscure the fact that its new rule is not logically compelled by the analysis or the holding in Winship or in any other precedent, or the fact that the rule reflects a new policy choice rather than the application of a pre-existing rule of law.

III

The Court cautions against exaggerating the significance of its new rule. It is true that in practice there may be little or no difference between a record that does not contain at least some evidence tending to prove every element of an offense and a record containing so little evidence that no rational factfinder could be persuaded of guilt beyond a reasonable doubt. Moreover, I think the Court is quite correct when it acknowledges that "most meritorious challenges to constitutional sufficiency of the evidence undoubtedly will be recognized in the state courts." But this only means that the new rule will seldom, if ever, provide a convicted state prisoner with any tangible benefits. It does not mean that the rule will have no impact on the administration of justice. On the contrary, I am persuaded that it will be seriously harmful both to the state and federal judiciaries.

The Court indicates that the new standard to be applied by federal judges in habeas corpus proceedings may be substantially the same as the standard most state reviewing courts are already applying. The federal district courts are therefore being directed simply to duplicate the reviewing function that is now being performed adequately by state appellate courts. * * * [T]o assign a single federal district judge the responsibility of directly reviewing, and inevitably supervising, the most routine work of the highest courts of a State can only undermine the morale and the esteem of the state judiciary—particularly when the stated purpose of the additional layer of review is to determine whether the State's factfinder is "rational."[9] Such consequences are intangible but none-theless significant.

The potential effect on federal judges is even more serious. Their burdens are already so heavy that they are delegating to staff assistants more and more work that we once expected judges to perform. The new standard will invite an unknown number of state prisoners to make sufficiency challenges that they would not have made under the old rule. Moreover, because the "rational trier of fact" must certainly base its decisions on *all* of the evidence, the Court's broader standard may well require that the entire transcript of the state trial be read whenever the factfinders' rationality is challenged under the Court's rule. Because this task will confront the courts of appeals as well as district courts, it will surely impose countless additional hours of unproductive labor on federal judges and their assistants. The increasing volume of work of this character has already led some of our most distinguished lawyers to discontinue or reject service on the federal bench. The addition of a significant volume of pointless labor can only impair the quality of justice administered by federal judges and thereby undermine "the respect and confidence of the community in applications of the * * * law." * * *

NOTE ON REVIEW OF THE SUFFICIENCY OF THE EVIDENCE IN ACTIONS BASED ON STATE LAW AND ON OTHER PROTECTIONS AGAINST ARBITRARINESS

(1) *Review of Factfinding as to Issues of State Law.*. Note how the problem in Jackson v. Virginia (and in Thompson v. Louisville) differs from that in Norris v. Alabama and the other decisions discussed in the preceding Note. In Norris and the cases discussed above, the Supreme Court reviews questions of evidentiary sufficiency that bear on issues of *federal* law; in Jackson and the cases discussed in this Note, the Court deals with the sufficiency of the evidence to establish violations of *state* law.

(2) *Thompson v. Louisville.* As the Jackson opinion notes, the Court's first foray into this area came in Thompson v. Louisville, 362 U.S. 199 (1960). Two police officers on a "routine check" saw Thompson, a black man, in a cafe at about 7:00 p.m. one Saturday evening "out there on the floor dancing by himself" (p. 200). According to one of the officers, the cafe's manager told them that Thompson had been there a little more than 30 minutes and had not bought anything. (At trial, Thompson testified that he had ordered food and drink; and the manager testified that he had told the officer only that he had

---

9. In the past, collateral review of state proceedings has been justified largely on the grounds (1) that federal judges have special expertise in the federal issues that regularly arise in habeas corpus proceeding, and (2) that they are less susceptible than state judges to political pressures against applying constitutional rules to overturn convictions. But neither of these justifications has any force in the present context. State judges are more familiar with the elements of state offenses than are federal judges and should be better able to evaluate sufficiency claims. Moreover, of all decisions overturning convictions, the least likely to be unpopular and thus to distort state decisionmaking processes are ones based on the inadequacy of the evidence. * * *

not *personally* sold Thompson anything.) The officers then asked Thompson "what was his reason for being in there" (*id.*); he said that he was waiting for a bus. He was then arrested for loitering, and a disorderly conduct charge was added when, outside the restaurant, Thompson was (in one officer's testimony) "argumentative".

At trial, the manager testified that Thompson was a regular patron and that he had never told Thompson that he was unwelcome. Thompson introduced in evidence a bus schedule showing that a bus to his home would have stopped within half a block of the cafe at about 7:30 p.m.

Thompson was convicted on both charges in the Police Court of Louisville. His motion for dismissal—on the grounds (1) that there was no evidence to support a finding of guilt, and (2) that the arrests and prosecutions constituted retaliation based on his having employed counsel to challenge prior, allegedly baseless charges by the police—was denied by that court. Thompson was fined $10 on each charge. Kentucky provided no appeal when a state police court imposes a fine of less than $20 on any single charge.

On review of the police court's judgment, the U.S. Supreme Court unanimously reversed. It noted that under the loitering ordinance, the city was required to establish that Thompson had been unable to give a satisfactory account of himself while loitering without the manager's consent, and found that "[t]he record is entirely lacking in evidence to support any of the charges" (p. 204). The manager's failing to object was "surely * * * implied consent, which the city admitted in oral argument satisfies the ordinance" (p. 205). As for the disorderly conduct charge, the Court noted that there was no evidence that Thompson had raised his voice, used vulgarity or resisted the officers; the Court added (p. 206): "We assume * * * that merely 'arguing' with a policeman is not, because it could not be, 'disorderly conduct' as a matter of the substantive law of Kentucky. Lanzetta v. New Jersey, 306 U.S. 451" [(invalidating, as void-for-vagueness, a statute that made it a crime to be a member of a "gang")]. The Court concluded that it is "a violation of due process to convict and punish a man without evidence of his guilt" (p. 206).

(3) *Applications of the "No Evidence Rule".*

(a) Garner v. Louisiana, 368 U.S. 157 (1961), dealt with three "sit-in" cases, in each of which a group of black students entered a segregated lunch counter and in an orderly manner awaited service; following a denial of service or a request to leave, the demonstrators were arrested. The students were convicted of disturbing the peace. On appeal, the Louisiana Supreme Court denied relief in an unreported oral opinion stating that it was without jurisdiction to review the facts and that "[t]he rulings of the district judge on matters of law are not erroneous."

Before the U.S. Supreme Court, petitioners claimed that the convictions violated their rights, *inter alia*, to freedom of speech and equal protection, but the Court reversed under the no-evidence doctrine. Recognizing that it was "bound by a State's interpretation of its own statute", the opinion analyzed the elements of the offense, relying heavily on a particular Louisiana Supreme Court case, and concluded that the statute was not intended to cover peaceful and orderly conduct, even if it might be offensive to others. Accepting that the Louisiana courts have authority to reinterpret that State's legislation, the Court saw "no indication that the Louisiana Supreme Court" had done so, and added that "we will not infer that an inferior Louisiana court intended to overrule a long-standing and reasonable interpretation of a state statute by that State's highest court. * * * However, because this case comes to us from a state court and necessitates a delicate involvement in federal-state relations, we are willing to assume with the respondent that the Louisiana courts might construe the statute more broadly to encompass the traditional common-law concept of disturbing the peace. Thus construed, it might permit the police to prevent an imminent public commotion even though caused by peaceful and orderly conduct on the part of the accused." In any event, the Court held that, "these records contain no evidence to support a finding that petitioners disturbed the peace, either by outwardly boisterous conduct or by passive conduct likely to cause a public disturbance," and reversed the convictions as denials of due process (pp. 165–66, 169, 173–74).

Justices Frankfurter, Douglas, and Harlan each concurred separately in the judgment.[1] But Justice Harlan, joined by Justice Douglas, specifically rejected the applicability of the Thompson "no-evidence" doctrine. In his view, "the State Supreme Court's refusal to review these convictions, taken in light of its assertion that the 'rulings of the district judge on matters of law are not erroneous,' must be accepted as an authoritative and binding state determination that the petitioners' activities, as revealed in these records, did violate the statute * * *" (p. 187).

(b) In Vachon v. New Hampshire, 414 U.S. 478 (1974), the Court, acting on the basis of the jurisdictional papers, summarily reversed a state court conviction on the ground that there was no evidence of one element of the crime. The Court described the case as follows:

"A 14–year-old girl bought a button inscribed 'Copulation Not Masturbation' at the Head Shop in Manchester, New Hampshire. In consequence, appellant, operator of the shop, was * * * [convicted] upon a charge of 'willfully' contributing to the delinquency of a minor * * *. In affirming the conviction, the New Hampshire Supreme Court held that the 'willfully' component of the offense required the State to prove that the accused acted 'voluntarily and intentionally and not because of mistake or accident or other innocent reason.' Thus, the State was required to produce evidence that appellant, knowing the girl to be a minor, personally sold her the button, or personally caused another to sell it to her. Appellant unsuccessfully sought dismissal of the charge at the close of the State's case on the ground that the State had produced no evidence to meet this requirement, and unsuccessfully urged the same ground as a reason for reversal in the State Supreme Court. * * *

"Our independent examination of the trial record discloses that evidence is completely lacking that appellant personally sold the girl the button or even that he was aware of the sale or present in the store at the time. * * * [Nor was there evidence that] 'he authorized such sales to minors * * *'" (pp. 479–80).

Justice Rehnquist's dissent, joined by Chief Justice Burger and Justice White, responded (pp. 484–86): "In Thompson [v. Louisville], the only state

---

1. Justice Frankfurter differed principally on the construction of state law. Justice Douglas concluded that the conviction constituted "state action" and denied petitioners equal protection of the laws. Justice Harlan thought that the statute was unconstitutionally vague and that (in two of the cases) its application violated petitioners' freedom of expression.

court proceedings reaching the merits of the case were in the Louisville Police Court from which there was no right of appeal to any higher state court, and there was therefore no state court opinion written which construed the statute under which Thompson was convicted.   * * *.

"Here, however, the Supreme Court of New Hampshire construed the state statute defining contributing to the delinquency of a minor, and held that the evidence adduced at the trial was sufficient to support a finding on each element of that offense.   While the Supreme Court of New Hampshire did say, as the Court indicates, that the State was required to prove that the accused acted 'voluntarily and intentionally and not because of mistake or accident or other innocent reason,' it said this in a context of several paragraphs of treatment of the elements of the offense.   * * *

"The Court simply casts aside this authoritative construction of New Hampshire law, seizes one phrase out of context, and concludes that there was no evidence to establish that the appellant '[knew] the girl to be a minor, personally sold her the button, or personally caused another to sell it to her.' The word 'personally' is the contribution of this Court to the New Hampshire statute; it is not contained in the statute, and is not once used by the Supreme Court of New Hampshire in its opinion dealing with the facts of this very case. Indeed, the entire thrust of the opinion of the Supreme Court of New Hampshire is that appellant need not *personally*, have sold the button to the minor nor *personally* have authorized its sale to a minor in order to be guilty of the statutory offense.   * * *"

Conceding that the state court's construction of the language "willfully" or "knowingly" may seem broad, Justice Rehnquist stressed that the Court must accept the state court's construction of state law.

(4) *Federal Limits on the Definition of State Law.*   Thompson, Garner, and Vachon illustrate that the determination whether there is "no evidence" requires a prior determination of the elements of the offense.   That is a question of state law, but subject to distinctive federal limitations, many of which help guard against arbitrary convictions.   See generally Comment, 79 Colum.L.Rev. 1577 (1979).

(a) *Constitutionally Protected Conduct.*   A state statute cannot be applied to penalize conduct that is protected under the Constitution.[2]   *Cf.* Gregory v. Chicago, 394 U.S. 111 (1969), where the Court overturned convictions for disorderly conduct arising out of an "orderly march" and the failure of the protesters to obey a police order to disperse when onlookers became unruly. The Court first cited First Amendment decisions establishing that a march like the one in question was constitutionally protected activity, and then added that because there was no evidence of disorderly conduct, the convictions violated due process.   Was the second point necessary?   Couldn't the Court just have rested on the ground that the conduct was constitutionally protected?

(b) *Void-for Vagueness.*   A state statute in which the prohibited conduct is so ill-defined as to deny fair warning and to invite arbitrary and discriminatory enforcement is void for vagueness.   See, *e.g.*, Papachristou v. Jacksonville, 405 U.S. 156, 162 (1972); Village of Hoffman Estates v. Flipside, Hoffman Estates,

---

2.   Alternatively, even if the defendant's conduct is unprotected, a statute may be unenforceable under the First Amendment overbreadth doctrine or because the statute's constitutional application in the case at bar is inseparable from unconstitutional ones.   See generally Chap. II, Sec. 3(B), *supra*.

Inc., 455 U.S. 489 (1982). See generally Amsterdam, *The Void-for-Vagueness Doctrine in the Supreme Court*, 109 U.Pa.L.Rev. 67 (1960); Jeffries, *Legality, Vagueness, and the Construction of Penal Statutes*, 71 Va.L.Rev. 189, 196 (1985); pp. 212–13, *supra*.

(c) *Retroactive Expansion of Criminal Liability.* Closely related to vagueness cases are those involving retroactive expansion of criminal liability. In Bouie v. City of Columbia, 378 U.S. 347 (1964), blacks were invited to patronize all departments in a large drug store in Columbia, South Carolina except its lunch counter. No signs announced this policy, though it seems to have been well understood. Shortly after the students sat down, a store employee put up a chain with a "no trespassing" sign hanging from it. The store owner then twice asked the students to leave. They refused, were arrested, and were subsequently convicted of criminal trespass under a state law that read: "Every entry upon the lands of another * * * after notice from the owner or tenant prohibiting such entry shall be a misdemeanor." Though the defendants entered the lunch counter area before any notice was given, the state supreme court affirmed the conviction, holding that the trespass statute also prohibited remaining on the premises after receiving notice to leave.

The Supreme Court reversed, finding that the state court's interpretation lacked support in South Carolina cases decided prior to the sit-in in question, and thus constituted an unforeseeable, retroactive judicial expansion of a criminal statute. Such an expansion operates like an ex post facto law in that it makes conduct, innocent when done, criminal, and thus denies due process.

Justice Black, joined by Justices Harlan and White, dissented; without quarreling directly with the majority's general thesis, he declared: "We cannot believe that either the petitioners or anyone else could have been misled by the language of this statute into believing that it would permit them to stay on the property of another over the owner's protest without being guilty of trespass" (pp. 366–67).[3]

(d) *Fair Notice of the Charge.* A failure to provide notice in the particular case of the nature of the charge may deny due process. In Cole v. Arkansas, 333 U.S. 196 (1948), defendants were convicted on a charge of violating § 2 of a statute declaring it "unlawful for any person acting in concert with one or more other persons, to assemble at or near any place where a 'labor dispute' exists and by force or violence prevent * * * any person from engaging in any lawful vocation, or for any person acting * * * in concert with one or more other persons, to promote, encourage or aid any such unlawful assemblage." On appeal, the state supreme court did not consider federal constitutional challenges to § 2, and instead affirmed the conviction under § 1 of the same statute, which made it a crime "for any person by the use of force or violence, or the threat of the use of force or violence, to prevent or attempt to prevent any person from engaging in any lawful vocation within this State." (Though similar to § 2, § 1 was broader, as it lacked a requirement of acting in concert and was not restricted to assemblies near labor disputes.) The Supreme Court

---

3. See also Marks v. United States, 430 U.S. 188 (1977), holding that, to the extent that the decision in Miller v. California, p. 611, *supra*, re-interpreted the First Amendment to expand the permissible scope of obscenity prosecutions, due process bars retro-active application of the new interpretation to conduct not punishable under preexisting authority.

For decisions rejecting attacks based on Bouie, see, *e.g.*, Ward v. Illinois, 431 U.S. 767 (1977); Rose v. Locke, 423 U.S. 48 (1975).

reversed, finding a denial of fair notice of the precise charge: "To conform to due process of law, petitioners were entitled to have the validity of their convictions appraised on consideration of the case as it was tried and as the issues were determined in the trial court" (p. 202). See also Cole v. Arkansas, 338 U.S. 345, 347–52 (1949).

Would a holding based on Cole allow re-trial of defendants on proper charges with new notice?

(5) *Insufficient Evidence vs. Redefinition of State Law.* An apparently unfounded state court decision can be viewed either as (1) applying established state law to convict where there is insufficient evidence as to some element of the offense, or (2) implicitly redefining the offense so as to comprehend the conduct in which the defendant engaged. The first interpretation raises questions under Jackson (or Thompson); the latter raises due process questions of notice and legality, see Paragraph (4), *supra.*

Reconsider the facts of Thompson, Garner and Vachon. In each case, might the Court, instead of finding no-evidence, have ruled that the state court had implicitly redefined the scope of the statute, and that such a determination denied due process on one or more of the grounds set forth in Paragraph (4)? (Vachon might also have been resolved on First Amendment grounds; the Court's actual disposition sidestepped that issue.) See Comment, Paragraph (4), *supra*, at 1588 (asserting that the convictions in all of the no-evidence cases could have been overturned on other constitutional grounds).

Which interpretation of a state court's decision should the Supreme Court accept?[4] Does it depend on the nature of the state court's opinion?[5] Compare Comment, Paragraph (4), *supra* (arguing that courts should consistently adopt the second interpretation).

Does the Thompson rule tempt the Court to avoid difficult and important constitutional questions by resting instead on the fact-specific "no-evidence" rubric? (Note that in Vachon, the federal claim of no-evidence had not been raised below, but the court raised it on its own motion, in arguable non-conformity with 28 U.S.C. § 1257. See p. 569, *supra.*) Is that rule a justified interpretation of procedural due process, which serves "norms of impartiality and conscientious attention to an individual's contributions"? Neuman, *The*

---

4. In the Thompson case, for example, the conviction might have been overturned either (i) because there was no evidence of loitering as traditionally defined under state law, or (ii) because if the definition of loitering was broadened to comprehend Thompson's dancing, that retroactive judicial expansion of criminal liability denied due process, see Paragraph (4)(b-d), *supra.* Though Thompson would prevail in either event, the latter interpretation would permit the state in the future to apply the redefined law to similar conduct, so long as that conduct was not itself constitutionally protected. See Comment, Paragraph (4), *supra*, at 1589 n. 5. *Cf.* p. 581, note 6, *supra.*

5. *Cf.* Douglas v. Buder, 412 U.S. 430 (1973)(in reversing a conviction on "no-evidence" grounds, stating that no state court had specifically construed state law to cover the facts of the case, and that, had they done so, retroactive application of such an interpretation would have denied due process under Bouie v. City of Columbia).

Reconsider the no-evidence cases: in Thompson, the state appellate courts provided no review at all; in Garner, there was no relevant state court opinion; and most of the scattered cases relying on the Thompson "no-evidence" rule have involved judgments without a state supreme court construction of the statute. See, *e.g.*, Barr v. Columbia, 378 U.S. 146 (1964); Shuttlesworth v. Birmingham, 382 U.S. 87 (1965). The danger of an arbitrary singling-out of a defendant is especially acute in such circumstances. By contrast, in Vachon there was an explicit state supreme court opinion on the issue.

Constitutional Requirement of "Some Evidence", 25 San Diego L.Rev. 631, 635 (1988).

(6) *The Meaning of "No Evidence."* Was there in fact *no* evidence in Thompson? That question was discussed in an opinion of Justice Stewart, dissenting from the denial of certiorari in Freeman v. Zahradnick, 429 U.S. 1111 (1977)—an opinion that presaged his opinion in Jackson. The petitioner had been sentenced to 10 years in prison for unlawful possession of a sawed-off shotgun. In a separate dissent from the denial of certiorari, Justice Marshall contended that there was no evidence to support the conviction. Justice Stewart disagreed on that point, making the argument he later made in Jackson (see the last paragraph of part III(B) of the Jackson opinion). He asked: "Indeed, in the Thompson case itself, could it fairly have been said that the mere fact that the defendant was found in a cafe, rather than home in bed, was *some* relevant evidence that he was guilty of loitering and disorderly conduct?" (p. 1114; emphasis added). He thus suggested that, at least in criminal cases, the Winship decision provided a sounder, and more intelligible, basis for review of evidentiary sufficiency than the no-evidence rule.

(7) *The Rule of Jackson: Direct and Collateral Review.* Did the Court in Jackson assume that federal review of a state court's application of a proposition of federal law (the Winship standard) to the facts was obligatory, rather than a matter of principled discretion? *Cf.* Bose Corp., p. 607, *supra*.

Jackson was a habeas corpus case. If direct review had been the only way to bring the issue before a federal court—as would be true, for example, if the convict were not "in custody"—would the Supreme Court have ruled as it did in Jackson?

In fact, the Supreme Court does not appear ever to have heard a case (whether on direct or collateral review) to consider application of the Jackson standard.[6] The Court's discretion to deny certiorari thus has prevented any serious docket burdens.[7] On the other hand, claims under Jackson are commonly presented to federal habeas courts, which are obliged (absent any procedural obstacle) to deal with them on the merits.

Insofar as the Court did have a choice about whether federal courts should review application of the Winship standard to the facts, didn't Justice Stevens have a point: the fact-specific nature of the inquiry means that federal review provides no guidance as to the meaning of federal law, and state courts lack neither expertise nor sympathy in reviewing claims of evidentiary sufficiency. On the other hand, is the Court's decision justified by the centrality of criminal guilt and the difficulty of tolerating error on that question?[8]

---

6. In Pilon v. Bordenkircher, 444 U.S. 1 (1979), a habeas corpus proceeding, a federal court of appeals, ruling prior to Jackson, had applied the no evidence rule to deny a petition founded on a claim of insufficient evidence. A few months after Jackson, the Court granted the prisoner's petition for certiorari, but the brief per curiam opinion merely vacated and remanded to give the court of appeals the opportunity to evaluate the claim of insufficient evidence under the new Jackson standard.

7. Before the elimination of mandatory appeals in 1988, a defendant might have tried to frame a Jackson claim as such an appeal under the former 28 U.S.C. § 1257(2). See Sec. 4, *infra*. The argument would have been that the state court had upheld the application to a defendant of the state criminal statute under which the prosecution was brought, in the face of a federal constitutional objection under Winship.

8. For more general discussion, in the context of federal habeas corpus jurisdiction, of the relevance of a prisoner's alleged inno-

(8) *The No–Evidence Rule: Life After Jackson?* Does Jackson swallow the doctrine of Thompson v. Louisville in the criminal area? Although the Court has never applied the "no-evidence" rule in a civil case, should the rule be retained for possible use in civil actions? (Recall that all that was at stake in Thompson itself was $20 in fines.)

Cf. Superintendent v. Hill, 472 U.S. 445, 455 (1985), where a prisoner challenged in state court the revocation of his good time credits. The Supreme Court held that in view of the liberty interest at stake, due process requires "some evidence" to support the decision to revoke.

If state court decisions that arbitrarily find sufficient evidence to support liability under state law raise due process questions, what about state court decisions that constitute arbitrary interpretations of the *meaning* of state law? Should there be a general due process protection against state court arbitrariness that applies even to cases raising no federal issue? See Note, 86 Mich. L.Rev. 2010 (1988), discussing the question but favoring a more limited interpretation of the no-evidence cases as designed to protect constitutional rights distinctive to the criminal process.

SECTION 3. FINAL JUDGMENTS AND THE HIGHEST STATE COURT

Cox Broadcasting Corp. v. Cohn

420 U.S. 469, 95 S.Ct. 1029, 43 L.Ed.2d 328 (1975).
Appeal from the Supreme Court of Georgia.

■ MR. JUSTICE WHITE delivered the opinion of the Court.

[During criminal proceedings against several youths charged with rape and murder, a television reporter broadcast a news story reporting the victim's name, which he had learned from records publicly available at the court. The victim's father brought a damage action against the reporter and the television station for invasion of his right to privacy. The father relied on Ga. Code Ann. § 26–9901, which made the publication or broadcast of the identity of a rape victim a misdemeanor. Despite the defendants' assertion that the imposition of civil liability would violate the First Amendment, the state trial court held that § 26–9901 implicitly created a civil remedy and granted summary judgment for the plaintiff.]

* * *

On appeal, the Georgia Supreme Court, in its initial opinion, held that the trial court had erred in construing § 26–9901 to extend a civil cause of action for invasion of privacy and thus found it unnecessary to consider the constitutionality of the statute. The court went on to rule, however, that the complaint stated a cause of action "for the invasion of the appellee's right of privacy, or for the tort of public disclosure"—a "common law tort exist[ing] in this jurisdiction without the help of the statute that the trial judge in this case relied on." * * * The court explained, however, that liability did not follow as a matter of law and that summary judgment was improper; whether the public

cence to the availability of federal review, see
Chap. XI, Sec. 2, pp. 1385–92, *infra*.

disclosure of the name actually invaded appellee's "zone of privacy," and if so, to what extent, were issues to be determined by the trier of fact. Also, "in formulating such an issue for determination by the fact-finder, it is reasonable to require the appellee to prove that the appellants invaded his privacy with willfull or negligent disregard for the fact that reasonable men would find the invasion highly offensive." The Georgia Supreme Court did agree with the trial court, however, that the First and Fourteenth Amendments did not, as a matter of law, require judgment for appellants. * * *

Upon motion for rehearing the Georgia court countered the argument that the victim's name was a matter of public interest and could be published with impunity by relying on § 26–9901 as an authoritative declaration of state policy that the name of a rape victim was not a matter of public concern. This time the court felt compelled to determine the constitutionality of the statute and sustained it as a "legitimate limitation on the right of freedom of expression contained in the First Amendment." * * *

We postponed decision as to our jurisdiction over this appeal to the hearing on the merits. We conclude that the Court has jurisdiction, and reverse the judgment of the Georgia Supreme Court.

II

* * *

B

Since 1789, Congress has granted this Court appellate jurisdiction with respect to state litigation only after the highest state court in which judgment could be had has rendered a "[f]inal judgment or decree." Title 28 U.S.C. § 1257 retains this limitation on our power to review cases coming from state courts. The Court has noted that "[c]onsiderations of English usage as well as those of judicial policy" would justify an interpretation of the final-judgment rule to preclude review "where anything further remains to be determined by a State court, no matter how dissociated from the only federal issue that has finally been adjudicated by the highest court of the State." Radio Station WOW, Inc. v. Johnson, 326 U.S. 120, 124 (1945). But the Court there observed that the rule had not been administered in such a mechanical fashion and that there were circumstances in which there has been "a departure from this requirement of finality for federal appellate jurisdiction." *Ibid.*

These circumstances were said to be "very few," *ibid.;* but as the cases have unfolded * * * [t]here are now at least four categories of * * * cases in which the Court has treated the decision on the federal issue as a final judgment for the purposes of 28 U.S.C. § 1257 and has taken jurisdiction without awaiting the completion of the additional proceedings anticipated in the lower state courts. In most, if not all, of the cases in these categories, these additional proceedings would not require the decision of other federal questions that might also require review by the Court at a later date,[6] and immediate rather than delayed review would be the best way to avoid "the mischief of

---

6. Eminent domain proceedings are of the type that may involve an interlocutory decision as to a federal question with another federal question to be decided later. "For in those cases the federal constitutional question embraces not only a taking, but a taking on payment of just compensation. A state judgment is not final unless it covers both aspects of that integral problem." North Dakota State Board of Pharmacy v. Snyder's Drug Stores, Inc., 414 U.S. 156, 163 (1973).

economic waste and of delayed justice," Radio Station WOW, Inc. v. Johnson, *supra*, at 124, as well as precipitate interference with state litigation.[7] In the cases in the first two categories considered below, the federal issue would not be mooted or otherwise affected by the proceedings yet to be had because those proceedings have little substance, their outcome is certain, or they are wholly unrelated to the federal question. In the other two categories, however, the federal issue would be mooted if the petitioner or appellant seeking to bring the action here prevailed on the merits in the later state-court proceedings, but there is nevertheless sufficient justification for immediate review of the federal question finally determined in the state courts.

In the first category are those cases in which there are further proceedings—even entire trials—yet to occur in the state courts but where for one reason or another the federal issue is conclusive or the outcome of further proceedings preordained. In these circumstances, because the case is for all practical purposes concluded, the judgment of the state court on the federal issue is deemed final. In Mills v. Alabama, 384 U.S. 214 (1966), for example, a demurrer to a criminal complaint was sustained on federal constitutional grounds by a state trial court. The State Supreme Court reversed, remanding for jury trial. This Court took jurisdiction on the reasoning that the appellant had no defense other than his federal claim and could not prevail at trial on the facts or any nonfederal ground. To dismiss the appeal "would not only be an inexcusable delay of the benefits Congress intended to grant by providing for appeal to this Court, but it would also result in a completely unnecessary waste of time and energy in judicial systems already troubled by delays due to congested dockets." *Id.*, at 217–218 (footnote omitted).[8]

Second, there are cases such as Radio Station WOW, *supra*, and Brady v. Maryland, 373 U.S. 83 (1963), in which the federal issue, finally decided by the highest court in the State, will survive and require decision regardless of the outcome of future state-court proceedings. In Radio Station WOW, the Nebraska Supreme Court directed the transfer of the properties of a federally licensed radio station and ordered an accounting, rejecting the claim that the transfer order would interfere with the federal license. The federal issue was held reviewable here despite the pending accounting on the "presupposition * * *

7. Gillespie v. United States Steel Corp., 379 U.S. 148 (1964), arose in the federal courts and involved the requirement of 28 U.S.C. § 1291 that judgments of district courts be final if they are to be appealed to the courts of appeals. In the course of deciding that the judgment of the District Court in the case had been final, the Court indicated its approach to finality requirements:

"And our cases long have recognized that whether a ruling is 'final' within the meaning of § 1291 is frequently so close a question that decision of that issue either way can be supported with equally forceful arguments, and that it is impossible to devise a formula to resolve all marginal cases coming within what might well be called the 'twilight zone' of finality. Because of this difficulty this Court has held that the requirement of finality is to be given a 'practical rather than a technical construction.' Cohen v. Beneficial Industrial Loan Corp., [337 U.S. 541, 546]. * * * Dickinson v. Petroleum Conversion Corp., 338 U.S. 507, 511, pointed out that in deciding the question of finality the most important competing considerations are 'the inconvenience and costs of piecemeal review on the one hand and the danger of denying justice by delay on the other.'" 379 U.S., at 152–153.

8. Other cases from state courts where this Court's jurisdiction was sustained for similar reasons include: Organization for a Better Austin v. Keefe, 402 U.S. 415, 418 n. (1971); Local No. 438 Construction and General Laborers' Union v. Curry, 371 U.S. 542, 550–551 (1963); Pope v. Atlantic C.L.R. Co., 345 U.S. 379, 382 (1953); Richfield Oil Corp. v. State Board, 329 U.S. 69, 73–74 (1946). * * *

that the federal questions that could come here have been adjudicated by the State court, and that the accounting which remains to be taken could not remotely give rise to a federal question * * * that may later come here * * *." 326 U.S., at 127.   * * * Nothing that could happen in the course of the accounting, short of settlement of the case, would foreclose or make unnecessary decision on the federal question.   Older cases in the Court had reached the same result on similar facts.   Carondelet Canal & Nav. Co. v. Louisiana, 233 U.S. 362 (1914);   Forgay v. Conrad, 6 How. 201 (1848).   * * *[9]

In the third category are those situations where the federal claim has been finally decided, with further proceedings on the merits in the state courts to come, but in which later review of the federal issue cannot be had, whatever the ultimate outcome of the case.   Thus, in these cases, if the party seeking interim review ultimately prevails on the merits, the federal issue will be mooted;   if he were to lose on the merits, however, the governing state law would not permit him again to present his federal claims for review.   The Court has taken jurisdiction in these circumstances prior to completion of the case in the state courts.   California v. Stewart, 384 U.S. 436 (1966)(decided with Miranda v. Arizona), epitomizes this category.   There the state court reversed a conviction on federal constitutional grounds and remanded for a new trial.   Although the State might have prevailed at trial, we granted its petition for certiorari and affirmed, explaining that the state judgment was "final" since an acquittal of the defendant at trial would preclude, under state law, an appeal by the State.

A recent decision in this category is North Dakota State Board of Pharmacy v. Snyder's Drug Stores, Inc., 414 U.S. 156 (1973), in which the Pharmacy Board rejected an application for a pharmacy operating permit relying on a state statute specifying ownership requirements which the applicant did not meet.   The State Supreme Court held the statute unconstitutional and remanded the matter to the Board for further consideration of the application, freed from the constraints of the ownership statute.   * * * [When the Board sought review, we exercised jurisdiction.]   The federal issue would not survive the remand, whatever the result of the state administrative proceedings.   The Board might deny the license on state-law grounds, thus foreclosing the federal issue, and the Court also ascertained that under state law the Board could not bring the federal issue here in the event the applicant satisfied the requirements of state law except for the invalidated ownership statute.   Under these circumstances, the issue was ripe for review.[10]

---

9. In Brady v. Maryland, 373 U.S. 83 (1963), the Maryland courts had ordered a new trial in a criminal case but on punishment only, and the petitioner asserted here that he was entitled to a new trial on guilt as well.   We entertained the case, saying that the federal issue was separable and would not be mooted by the new trial on punishment ordered in the state courts.

10. Cohen v. Beneficial Industrial Loan Corp., 337 U.S. 541 (1949), was a diversity action in the federal courts in the course of which there arose the question of the validity of a state statute requiring plaintiffs in stock-holder suits to post security for costs as a prerequisite to bringing the action.   The District Court held the state law inapplicable, the Court of Appeals reversed, and this Court, after granting certiorari, held that the issue of security for costs was separable from and independent of the merits and that if review were to be postponed until the termination of the litigation, "it will be too late effectively to review the present order, and the rights conferred by the statute, if it is applicable, will have been lost, probably irreparably."

Lastly, there are those situations where the federal issue has been finally decided in the state courts with further proceedings pending in which the party seeking review here might prevail on the merits on nonfederal grounds, thus rendering unnecessary review of the federal issue by this Court, and where reversal of the state court on the federal issue would be preclusive of any further litigation on the relevant cause of action rather than merely controlling the nature and character of, or determining the admissibility of evidence in, the state proceedings still to come. In these circumstances, if a refusal immediately to review the state-court decision might seriously erode federal policy, the Court has entertained and decided the federal issue, which itself has been finally determined by the state courts for purposes of the state litigation.

In Local No. 438 Construction and General Laborers' Union v. Curry, 371 U.S. 542 (1963), the state courts temporarily enjoined labor union picketing over claims that the National Labor Relations Board had exclusive jurisdiction of the controversy. The Court took jurisdiction for two independent reasons. First, the power of the state court to proceed in the face of the preemption claim was deemed an issue separable from the merits and ripe for review in this Court, particularly "when postponing review would seriously erode the national labor policy requiring the subject matter of respondents' cause to be heard by the * * * Board, not by the state courts." Second, the Court was convinced that in any event the union had no defense to the entry of a permanent injunction other than the preemption claim that had already been ruled on in the state courts. Hence the case was for all practical purposes concluded in the state tribunals.

In Mercantile National Bank v. Langdeau, 371 U.S. 555 (1963), two national banks [that had been sued in a particular county asserted that, under a federal venue statute,] they could properly be sued only in another county. Although trial was still to be had and the banks might well prevail on the merits, the Court, relying on Curry, entertained the issue as a "separate and independent matter, anterior to the merits and not enmeshed in the factual and legal issues comprising the plaintiff's cause of action." Moreover, it would serve the policy of the federal statute "to determine now in which state court appellants may be tried rather than to subject them * * * to long and complex litigation which may all be for naught if consideration of the preliminary question of venue is postponed until the conclusion of the proceedings."

Miami Herald Publishing Co. v. Tornillo, 418 U.S. 241 (1974), is the latest case in this category. There a candidate for public office sued a newspaper for refusing, allegedly contrary to a state statute, to carry his reply to the paper's editorial critical of his qualifications. The trial court held the act unconstitutional, denying both injunctive relief and damages. The State Supreme Court reversed, sustaining the statute against the challenge based upon the First and Fourteenth Amendments and remanding the case for a trial and appropriate relief, including damages. The newspaper brought the case here. We sustained our jurisdiction, relying on the principles elaborated in the North Dakota case and observing:

> "Whichever way we were to decide on the merits, it would be intolerable to leave unanswered, under these circumstances, an important question of freedom of the press under the First Amendment; an uneasy and unsettled constitutional posture of § 104.38 could only further harm the operation of a free press." 418 U.S., at 247 n. 6.

In light of the prior cases, we conclude that we have jurisdiction to review the judgment of the Georgia Supreme Court * * *, [which] is plainly final on the federal issue and is not subject to further review in the state courts. Appellants will be liable for damages if the elements of the state cause of action are proved. They may prevail at trial on nonfederal grounds, it is true, but if the Georgia court erroneously upheld the statute, there should be no trial at all. Moreover, even if appellants prevailed at trial and made unnecessary further consideration of the constitutional question, there would remain in effect the unreviewed decision of the State Supreme Court that a civil action for publishing the name of a rape victim disclosed in a public judicial proceeding may go forward despite the First and Fourteenth Amendments. Delaying final decision of the First Amendment claim until after trial will "leave unanswered * * * an important question of freedom of the press under the First Amendment," "an uneasy and unsettled constitutional posture [that] could only further harm the operation of a free press." Tornillo, *supra*, at 247 n. 6. On the other hand, if we now hold that the First and Fourteenth Amendments bar civil liability for broadcasting the victim's name, this litigation ends. Given these factors—that the litigation could be terminated by our decision on the merits[13] and that a failure to decide the question now will leave the press in Georgia operating in the shadow of the civil and criminal sanctions of a rule of law and a statute the constitutionality of which is in serious doubt—we find that reaching the merits is consistent with the pragmatic approach that we have followed in the past in determining finality. * * *

[The Court proceeded to invalidate § 26–9901 and the common-law privacy action on the merits, holding that the First and Fourteenth Amendments preclude states from basing liability on the publication of truthful information contained in official court records open to public inspection.]

Reversed.

■ [JUSTICE POWELL wrote a concurring opinion. CHIEF JUSTICE BURGER concurred in the judgment without opinion. JUSTICE DOUGLAS wrote an opinion concurring in the judgment.]

■ MR. JUSTICE REHNQUIST, dissenting.

    * * *

---

13. Mr. Justice Rehnquist is correct in saying that this factor involves consideration of the merits in determining jurisdiction. But it does so only to the extent of determining that the issue is substantial and only in the context that if the state court's final decision on the federal issue is incorrect, federal law forecloses further proceedings in the state court. That the petitioner who protests against the state court's decision on the federal question might prevail on the merits on nonfederal grounds in the course of further proceedings anticipated in the state court and hence obviate later review of the federal issue here is not preclusive of our jurisdiction. Curry, Langdeau, North Dakota State Board of Pharmacy, California v. Stewart, 384 U.S. 436 (1966)(decided with Miranda v. Arizona),

and Miami Herald Publishing Co. v. Tornillo, 418 U.S. 241 (1974), make this clear. In those cases, the federal issue having been decided, arguably wrongly, and being determinative of the litigation if decided the other way, the finality rule was satisfied.

The author of the dissent, a member of the majority in Tornillo, does not disavow that decision. He seeks only to distinguish it by indicating that the First Amendment issue at stake there was more important and pressing than the one here. This seems to embrace the thesis of that case and of this one as far as the approach to finality is concerned, even though the merits and the avoidance doctrine are to some extent involved.

Radio Station WOW, Inc. v. Johnson, 326 U.S. 120 (1945), established that in a "very few" circumstances review of state-court decisions could be had in this Court even though something "further remain[ed] to be determined by a State court." Over the years, however, * * * this Court has steadily discovered new exceptions to the finality requirement, such that they can hardly any longer be described as "very few." * * * Although the Court's opinion today does accord detailed consideration to this problem, I do not believe that the reasons it expresses can support its result.

I

The Court has taken what it terms a "pragmatic" approach to the finality problem presented in this case. In so doing, it has relied heavily on Gillespie v. United States Steel Corp., 379 U.S. 148 (1964). As the Court acknowledges, Gillespie involved 28 U.S.C. § 1291, which restricts the appellate jurisdiction of the federal courts of appeals to "final decisions of the district courts." Although acknowledging this distinction, the Court accords it no importance and adopts Gillespie's approach without any consideration of whether the finality requirement for this Court's jurisdiction over a "judgment or decree" of a state court is grounded on more serious concerns than is the limitation of court of appeals jurisdiction to final "decisions" of the district courts. * * *

According to Gillespie, the finality requirement is imposed as a matter of minimizing "the inconvenience and costs of piecemeal review." * * * Were judicial efficiency the only interest at stake there would be less inclination to challenge the Court's resolution in this case, although, as discussed below, I have serious reservations that the standards the Court has formulated are effective for achieving even this single goal. The case before us, however, is an appeal from a state court, and this fact introduces additional interests which must be accommodated in fashioning any exception to the literal application of the finality requirement. I consider § 1257 finality to be but one of a number of congressional provisions reflecting concern that uncontrolled federal judicial interference with state administrative and judicial functions would have untoward consequences for our federal system. This is by no means a novel view of the § 1257 finality requirement. In Radio Station WOW, Inc. v. Johnson, 326 U.S., at 124, Mr. Justice Frankfurter's opinion for the Court explained the finality requirement as follows:

"* * * *This prerequisite to review derives added force when the jurisdiction of this Court is invoked to upset the decision of a State court.* Here we are in the realm of potential conflict between the courts of two different governments. And so, ever since 1789, Congress has granted this Court the power to intervene in State litigation only after 'the highest court of a State in which a decision in the suit could be had' has rendered a 'final judgment or decree.' § 237 of the Judicial Code, 28 U.S.C. § 344(a). *This requirement is not one of those technicalities to be easily scorned. It is an important factor in the smooth working of our federal system.*" (Emphasis added.)

* * *

That comity and federalism are significant elements of § 1257 finality has been recognized by other members of the Court as well, perhaps most notably by Mr. Justice Harlan. See, *e.g.*, Hudson Distributors v. Eli Lilly, 377 U.S. [386, 397–98 (1964)] (dissenting). * * *

"Harmonious state-federal relations" are no less important today than when Mr. Justice Frankfurter penned Radio Station WOW * * *. Indeed, we have in recent years emphasized and re-emphasized the importance of comity and federalism in dealing with a related problem, that of district court interference with ongoing state judicial proceedings. See Younger v. Harris, 401 U.S. 37 (1971); Samuels v. Mackell, 401 U.S. 66 (1971). Because these concerns are important, and because they provide "added force" to § 1257's finality requirement, I believe that the Court has erred by simply importing the approach of cases in which the only concern is efficient judicial administration.

II

But quite apart from the considerations of federalism which counsel against an expansive reading of our jurisdiction under § 1257, the Court's holding today enunciates a virtually formless exception to the finality requirement, one which differs in kind from those previously carved out. * * *

* * * While the totality of [the exceptions previously recognized by the Court] certainly indicates that the Court has been willing to impart to the language "final judgment or decree" a great deal of flexibility, each of them is arguably consistent with the intent of Congress in enacting § 1257, if not with the language it used, and each of them is relatively workable in practice.

To those established exceptions is now added one so formless that it cannot be paraphrased, but instead must be quoted:

"Given these factors—that the litigation could be terminated by our decision on the merits and that a failure to decide the question now will leave the press in Georgia operating in the shadow of the civil and criminal sanctions of a rule of law and a statute the constitutionality of which is in serious doubt—we find that reaching the merits is consistent with the pragmatic approach that we have followed in the past in determining finality."

There are a number of difficulties with this test. One of them is the Court's willingness to look to the merits. It is not clear from the Court's opinion, however, exactly how great a look at the merits we are to take. On the one hand, the Court emphasizes that if we reverse the Supreme Court of Georgia the litigation will end, and it refers to cases in which the federal issue has been decided "arguably wrongly." On the other hand, it claims to look to the merits "only to the extent of determining that the issue is substantial." If the latter is all the Court means, then the inquiry is no more extensive than is involved when we determine whether a case is appropriate for plenary consideration; but if no more is meant, our decision is just as likely to be a costly intermediate step in the litigation as it is to be the concluding event. If, on the other hand, the Court really intends its doctrine to reach only so far as cases in which our decision in all probability will terminate the litigation, then * * * henceforth in determining our own jurisdiction we may be obliged to determine whether or not we agree with the merits of the decision of the highest court of a State.

Yet another difficulty with the Court's formulation is the problem of transposing to any other case the requirement that "failure to decide the question now will leave the press in Georgia operating in the shadow of the civil and criminal sanctions of a rule of law and a statute the constitutionality of which is in serious doubt." Assuming that we are to make this determination of "serious doubt" at the time we note probable jurisdiction of such an appeal, is it enough that the highest court of the State has ruled against any federal constitutional claim? If that is the case, then because § 1257 by other language imposes that requirement, we will have completely read out of the statute the limitation of our jurisdiction to a "final judgment or decree." Perhaps the Court's new standard for finality is limited to cases in which a First Amendment freedom is at issue. The language used by Congress, however, certainly provides no basis for preferring the First Amendment, as incorporated by the Fourteenth Amendment, to the various other Amendments which are likewise "incorporated," or indeed for preferring any of the "incorporated" Amendments over the due process and equal protection provisions which are embodied literally in the Fourteenth Amendment.

Another problem is that in applying the second prong of its test, the Court has not engaged in any independent inquiry as to the consequences of permitting the decision of the Supreme Court of Georgia to remain undisturbed pending final state-court resolution of the case. * * * In this case nothing more is at issue than the right to report the name of the victim of a rape. No hindrance of any sort has been imposed on reporting the fact of a rape or the circumstances surrounding it. Yet the Court unquestioningly places this issue on a par with the core First Amendment interest involved in Miami Herald Publishing Co. v. Tornillo, 418 U.S. 241 (1974), and Mills v. Alabama, *supra*, that of protecting the press in its role of providing uninhibited political discourse.

But the greatest difficulty with the test enunciated today is that it totally abandons the principle that constitutional issues are too important to be decided save when absolutely necessary, and are to be avoided if there are grounds for decision of lesser dimension * * *. [That principle is] primarily designed, not to benefit the lower courts, or state-federal relations, but rather to safeguard this Court's own process of constitutional adjudication. * * *

In this case there has yet to be an adjudication of liability against appellants, and unlike the appellant in Mills v. Alabama, they do not concede that they have no nonfederal defenses. Nonetheless, the Court rules on their constitutional defense. * * *

III

This Court is obliged to make preliminary determinations of its jurisdiction at the time it votes to note probable jurisdiction. At that stage of the proceedings, prior to briefing on the merits or oral argument, such determinations must of necessity be based on relatively cursory acquaintance with the record of the proceedings below. The need for an understandable and workable application of a jurisdictional provision such as § 1257 is therefore far greater than for a similar interpretation of statutes dealing with substantive law. * * * It is thus especially disturbing that the rule of this case, unlike the more workable and straightforward exceptions which the Court has previously formulated, will seriously compound the already difficult task of accurately determining, at a preliminary stage, whether an appeal from a state-court judgment is a "final judgment or decree."

* * *

* * * I would dismiss for want of jurisdiction.

NOTE ON THE FINAL JUDGMENT RULE AND THE HIGHEST STATE COURT REQUIREMENT

(1) *Evolution of the Finality Doctrine.* Section 25 of the Judiciary Act of 1789 limited Supreme Court review to "final judgment[s] or decree[s] in any suit, in the highest court of law or equity of a State in which a decision in the suit could be had." See p. 492, *supra.* Section 1257 today uses almost identical words. As Cox indicates, out of this deceptively simple language the Court has spun a complicated web.

For many years, the Court construed the requirement to permit review only when nothing was left to be done except entry or execution of judgment. See, *e.g.*, Houston v. Moore, 16 U.S. (3 Wheat.) 433 (1818). The first major inroad came with Carondelet Canal & Nav. Co. v. Louisiana, 233 U.S. 362 (1914), where the Court reviewed a state supreme court judgment ordering the transfer of the canal company's property despite its claim of federal protection; even though the case had been remanded by the state court for an accounting, the remaining dispute was narrow and the state judgment disposed of the federal right asserted.

As the doctrine further evolved, a "penumbral area" developed within which non-final judgments were nevertheless deemed final. Radio Station WOW, Inc. v. Johnson, 326 U.S. 120, 124 (1945). The holdings often involved state court judgments that in effect resolved a federal question in a manner threatening immediate and irreparable harm to a party.

In 1963, the Court decided Curry and Langdeau, both discussed in Cox. These cases substantially expanded the penumbra of finality; Curry's formulation included cases where "postponing review would seriously erode" national policy (371 U.S. at 550). The erosion standard now forms the central justification for the fourth Cox category and represents the loosest interpretation of the final judgment requirement.

(2) *The First Cox Category.* The first Cox category—cases where, despite a remand to the lower state court, the federal question finally decided by the state court is likely to be completely decisive—has not been very controversial.[1] A recent example is Duquesne Light Co. v. Barasch, 488 U.S. 299 (1989), where the state public utility commission had permitted a utility to raise its rates to recoup costs incurred from canceled nuclear plants. The state supreme court reversed and remanded for the commission to set lower rates not including those costs, rejecting the utility's argument that the lower rates constituted an unconstitutional "taking". In hearing the utility's appeal from that decision, the Supreme Court ruled that the state court had finally adjudicated the constitutional challenge to the state regulatory statute, and that all that remained was "straight-forward application of [the state supreme court's] clear directive to otherwise complete rate orders" (p. 307). Only Justice Blackmun dissented, arguing that because new rates would be set based on factors yet unknown, the Court was "strong-arming the finality concept" (p. 317).

Under this first category, finality may be affected by the parties' procedural steps and stipulations.[2] See Philadelphia v. New Jersey, 437 U.S. 617

---

1. See, *e.g.*, in addition to the Mills case discussed in Cox Broadcasting, Richfield Oil Corp. v. State Bd. of Equalization, 329 U.S. 69 (1946); Abood v. Detroit Bd. of Educ., 431 U.S. 209, 216 n. 8 (1977).

2. Is the state of the record also pertinent? See Minnick v. California Dep't of Corrections, 452 U.S. 105 (1981), where the Court first granted certiorari but then dis-

(1978)(appellants dismissed several counts with prejudice so that there would be a final judgment). Indeed, if a party represents that no further evidence will be offered below, that party may be precluded from adducing additional evidence on remand. See NAACP v. Alabama ex rel. Patterson, 360 U.S. 240 (1959). Should such a representation be required to establish finality in this kind of case?

(3) *The Second Cox Category.* The second Cox category allows review of federal claims that will eventually require decision no matter what happens during further state court proceedings. This category, based on the notion that the further state proceedings seem completely separate from the merits of the already adjudicated federal issues, represents the most traditional incursion into the finality requirement. See, *e.g.*, NAACP v. Claiborne Hardware Co., 458 U.S. 886, 907 n. 42 (1982)(holding "final" a state supreme court judgment determining that the First Amendment did not preclude tort liability but remanding for recomputation of damages; the judgment also left in effect an injunction, but that point was not stressed by the Court). Consider the suggestions (a) that each of the cases cited by the Court in support of this second category "arguably involved elements of hardship in addition to the simple burden of proceedings that might prove unnecessary, and this category of finality would be more convincing if it were restricted to such situations", 16 Wright, Miller, Cooper & Gressman, Federal Practice and Procedure § 4010, at 589 (1977), and (b) that in practice the prediction necessitated under this category is too difficult to make reliably, see Note, 91 Harv.L.Rev. 1004, 1017–20 (1978).

(4) *The Third Cox Category.* The third Cox exception allows immediate review where further proceedings may moot the federal question so that it becomes effectively unreviewable. Typical, and routinely reviewed, are criminal cases where the state court has decided a federal question in favor of the defendant— either in an interlocutory appeal or in reversing a conviction and remanding for retrial. See, *e.g.*, New York v. Quarles, 467 U.S. 649 (1984), California v. Trombetta, 467 U.S. 479 (1984), and Florida v. Meyers, 466 U.S. 380 (1984)(all three reviewing state court decisions suppressing evidence on federal constitutional grounds). *Cf.* 18 U.S.C. § 3731, expressly permitting interlocutory review in certain circumstances in federal criminal cases in order to protect the government from being bound by an acquittal that resulted from an otherwise unreviewable preliminary decision in the defendant's favor.

For a dispute over application of the third exception, see Pennsylvania v. Ritchie, 480 U.S. 39 (1987). Ritchie was charged with sexual offenses against his minor daughter. When he sought to subpoena the files of the state agency that had initially investigated the matter, the trial judge refused to require disclosure. On appeal from his conviction, the state supreme court ruled that the failure to require the agency to give defendant access to its files violated his Sixth Amendment rights under the Confrontation and Compulsory Process Clauses, and remanded for the trial court to determine whether the error was prejudicial.

missed the writ after argument, finding ambiguities in the record that clouded analysis of whether the constitutional questions under review might be affected by additional proceedings in state court. The Court's opinion never specified the precise basis for the dismissal, but Justice Rehnquist's concurrence explicitly described it as based on want of jurisdiction.

In a 5–4 decision, the Supreme Court (per Powell, J.) held that there was a final judgment, on the ground that the Sixth Amendment issue would not survive if review were not granted immediately. The Court argued that if, on the one hand, the error were found to be harmless, the state would prevail and would have no basis for seeking review—unless the defendant sought review of the adverse ruling on harmlessness, and the state filed a cross-petition raising the Sixth Amendment issues. (In dissent, Justice Stevens, joined by Justices Brennan, Marshall, and Scalia, responded that as the conviction would be affirmed, the prosecution would have suffered no harm from any non-reviewability.) On the other hand, if a new trial were granted, either the defendant would be convicted, "in which case the [state]'s ability to obtain review again will rest on Ritchie's willingness to appeal", or he would be acquitted, barring further appeal. (Justice Stevens responded that if the error were found prejudicial and a new trial ordered, Pennsylvania provided the prosecution with an interlocutory appeal of that order. In rejoinder, the majority contended that the law-of-the-case doctrine would govern any such interlocutory appeal in state court, so that the constitutional issue could be reviewed by the Supreme Court only after the Commonwealth's "fruitless" proceedings up the state court hierarchy.)

The Court also noted that unless it reviewed the case immediately, the harm that Pennsylvania sought to avoid—disclosure of the agency's confidential file—would occur and subsequent review would come too late. The dissent responded that here, as under § 1291, a witness (the agency) that seeks unsuccessfully to resist a subpoena should not be able to appeal until after having disobeyed and been found in contempt. See United States v. Ryan, 402 U.S. 530 (1971), p. 1653, *infra*. The Court rejoined that that rule applied to pre-trial proceedings; judicial economy had different implications when, as here, the trial was complete and the issue had already been decided by the state's highest court.

Clearly, in Ritchie, there were opportunities for future review. Does the case rest on the view that there might be irreparable harm (disclosure of the agency's file) that could not be remedied later? (On the merits, the Supreme Court ruled that the defendant was entitled to have the trial court review the file *in camera*, to determine (i) whether it contained relevant evidence and, (ii) if so, whether the failure to disclose was nonetheless harmless.) Do you think that some of the Justices' positions on finality might be linked to their view of the importance of reviewing state court decisions that "overprotect" federal constitutional rights? Compare pp. 536–38, *supra*.

(5) *The Fourth Cox Category*. The fourth Cox category embodies two requirements: reversal of the state court on the federal issue must end the litigation, and a refusal to review the federal issue immediately must threaten serious erosion of a significant federal policy. The range of policies encompassed has been broad. See, *e.g.*, Bullington v. Missouri, 451 U.S. 430 (1981) and Harris v. Washington, 404 U.S. 55 (1971)(constitutional policy against double jeopardy threatened if review postponed and defendant tried a second time); Goodyear Atomic Corp. v. Miller, 486 U.S. 174 (1988)(federal preemption of state safety rules for nuclear facilities threatened by workers' compensation award based on violation of those rules); Southland Corp. v. Keating, 465 U.S. 1 (1984)(Federal Arbitration Act's policy of preempting state-court jurisdiction eroded if state court decision ordering state proceedings not immediately reviewed); Belknap, Inc. v. Hale, 463 U.S. 491 (1983)(same with respect to NLRB's claim to

exclusive jurisdiction); Shaffer v. Heitner, 433 U.S. 186, 195–96 n. 12 (1977), and Calder v. Jones, 465 U.S. 783, (1984)(state court decisions upholding personal jurisdiction against due process objections reviewed even though state trials were to follow).[3] Is there a discernible limit to this category?

(6) *First Amendment Cases.* The Court has been especially willing to relax finality requirements in order to protect speech interests against the erosion that can attend delay. Such cases typically are accommodated by the fourth Cox category.

(a) A notable example, which built on earlier decisions,[4] is National Socialist Party v. Skokie, 432 U.S. 43 (1977). There, after Illinois appellate courts refused to stay a trial court order prohibiting petitioners from marching or parading, they applied for a stay from the United States Supreme Court. "Treating the application as a petition for certiorari from the order of the Illinois Supreme Court [denying a stay]," the Court granted certiorari and reversed: "The order is a final judgment for purposes of our jurisdiction * * *. It finally determined the merits of petitioners' claim that the outstanding injunction will deprive them of rights protected by the First Amendment during the period of appellate review which, in the normal course, may take a year or more to complete. If a State seeks to impose a restraint of this kind, it must provide strict procedural safeguards * * * including immediate appellate review * * *" (p. 44). Three Justices dissented, distinguishing Cox on the ground that there the state supreme court had finally decided the federal claim.[5]

3. With the last two cases, compare Gillette Co. v. Miner, 459 U.S. 86 (1982), a one sentence per curiam decision dismissing certiorari, after briefing and argument, for lack of a final judgment. The state supreme court had upheld the trial court's personal jurisdiction over *plaintiff* class-members, over the objection of the *defendant* that those class-members lacked substantial contacts with the forum state. The case was remanded for trial.

Can a defendant's interests be more fully protected after judgment on the merits in a case like this one than in the more typical case in which the defendant objects that it is not itself subject to the court's personal jurisdiction?

4. In Organization for a Better Austin v. Keefe, 402 U.S. 415 (1971), the Court held that a "temporary" injunction, prohibiting leafletting, that had been in effect for three years, with "marked impact on petitioners' First Amendment rights," was, in effect, final, with further proceedings "a formality" (p. 418 n. *).

In Nebraska Press Ass'n v. Stuart, 423 U.S. 1319 (1975), a trial court "gag" order prohibited media dissemination of certain materials relating to a pending criminal case. The Nebraska Supreme Court had taken the media's appeal but had yet to rule on the order's validity. Justice Blackmun, in chambers, stayed the order, finding that "[w]hen a reasonable time in which to review the restraint has passed, as here, we may properly regard the state court as having finally decided that the restraint should remain in effect during the period of delay" (p. 1330). After the Nebraska Supreme Court's affirmance of the trial court's order, which was clearly a final judgment, the Supreme Court granted reviewed and reversed—without expressing any judgment on Justice Blackmun's approach. Nebraska Press Ass'n v. Stuart, 427 U.S. 539 (1976).

5. For similar rulings, see, *e.g.*, M.I.C. Ltd. v. Bedford Township, 463 U.S. 1341 (1983)(Brennan, J., in chambers); Seattle Times Co. v. Rhinehart, 467 U.S. 20 (1984); Oklahoma Publishing Co. v. District Court for Oklahoma County, Oklahoma, 429 U.S. 967 (1976).

Note that the cases in this line assume that the power of the Court (or of a Justice) to grant a stay is limited to cases where the state decision is "final". This assumption is plainly correct where the stay is sought pursuant to 28 U.S.C. § 2101(f), which authorizes a stay in any case in which a final judgment is subject to Supreme Court review on writ of certiorari. But Sup.Ct.R. 23.1 says

Does the Court's reasoning suggest that interlocutory review may sometimes be a matter of constitutional right? Could such a right be limited to First Amendment cases? To cases involving constitutional rights? Would such a right, however broadly defined, extend to interlocutory review by the Supreme Court itself?

(b) In Fort Wayne Books, Inc. v. Indiana, 489 U.S. 46 (1989), the Supreme Court came close to holding reviewable any interlocutory order affecting the exercise of First Amendment rights. In a state RICO prosecution predicated on obscenity offenses, the trial court had dismissed the charges on the ground that the statute was unconstitutionally vague as applied to obscenity offenses. The Indiana Court of Appeals reversed, reinstating the charges. The Supreme Court (per White, J.) upheld its jurisdiction to review. Although acknowledging the general rule that in criminal cases finality is defined by judgment of conviction and imposition of sentence, the Court concluded that the case fell within Cox's fourth category: if the defendants prevailed at trial, that would preclude review of their First Amendment challenges to the RICO statute. Relying on the Skokie decision, the Court argued that leaving unresolved the question of possible First Amendment limits on federal and state efforts to apply RICO laws in obscenity cases would intolerably erode federal policy.

In dissent, Justice O'Connor (with whose views Justice Blackmun expressed agreement) disputed the judgment's finality. She relied heavily on Flynt v. Ohio, 451 U.S. 619 (1981)(per curiam)(5–4), where the state courts had denied defendants' motion to dismiss an obscenity prosecution on the ground that it constituted selective prosecution violating the First Amendment. The United States Supreme Court held the judgment not final (p. 622): Although it arguably fell within the fourth Cox category, "there is no identifiable federal policy that will suffer if the state criminal proceeding goes forward. * * * The resolution of this [Equal Protection] question can await final judgment without any adverse effect upon important federal interests. A contrary conclusion would permit the fourth exception [of Cox] to swallow the rule."[6]

In the Fort Wayne case, the majority distinguished Flynt as involving not a First Amendment claim, but rather a selective prosecution claim—albeit one in the context of a trial raising First Amendment issues. The majority added: "[N]o member of the Court concluded in Flynt—as Justice O'Connor does today—that where an important First Amendment claim *is* before us, the Court should refuse to invoke Cox's fourth exception and hold that we have no authority to address the issue" (p. 57).[7]

more generally that "A stay may be granted by a Justice as permitted by law." Would the All–Writs Act, 28 U.S.C. § 1651, provide an independent basis for the Court to stay a state court judgment that is concededly non-final? Would such a stay be "in aid of" the Court's jurisdiction within the meaning of § 1651? See the discussion in Stern, Gressman, Shapiro & Geller, Supreme Court Practice 671–704 (7th ed.1993); compare also the materials at Chap. III, Sec. 3, *supra*, and Chap. XV, Sec. 3, pp. 1666–70, *infra*.

6. The four dissenters in Flynt found in the First Amendment an identifiable federal policy of preventing this sort of prosecution.

7. In Fort Wayne, there was also a second proceeding before the Court, in which the State had brought a civil RICO action and then obtained an ex parte pretrial seizure order under which the defendants' stores were padlocked and their contents hauled away. On an interlocutory appeal, the Indiana Supreme Court upheld the constitutionality of the obscenity statute (the same constitutional issue presented in the criminal case) and of the pretrial seizure. On review of that judgment, the Supreme Court upheld its jurisdiction under § 1257, without dissent. Justice O'Connor's separate opinion expressed her agreement, noting that

(c) Note that neither the criminal prosecution in the Fort Wayne case nor the tort action in Cox involved an injunction against speech. Was Supreme Court review urgently needed in either case? Does the Court's approach in these cases echo First Amendment overbreadth doctrine in trying to prevent the "chilling effect" from statutes that purport to prohibit protected activity? Is the approach here more difficult to justify in the face of a congressional declaration of jurisdictional policy that non-final judgments are not reviewable?[8]

Recall Justice Rehnquist's invocation, in his dissent in Cox, of the policy of constitutional avoidance. Does the Court's approach, particularly in First Amendment cases, reflect a quite different conception of its role—one in which judicial articulation of constitutional values is to be encouraged rather than avoided? See generally pp. 78–83, *supra*.

(7) *Finality and Statutory Interpretation.* Does Cox—particularly in light of Flynt and Fort Wayne Books—provide a principled basis for determining when cases will be deemed final? (Note that even the four Cox categories may not exhaust the exceptions to the rule; Justice White speaks of "at least" four categories of exceptions.[9]) What is left of the final judgment requirement as a jurisdictional *rule*?

Does the Court's assertion of a power to create desirable exceptions to a strict conception of finality unjustifiably disregard a statutory limitation? Or does that approach properly try to accommodate a necessarily general legislative directive to multitudinous situations that Congress could not have anticipated?

Consider the relevance of the elimination in 1988 of mandatory appellate jurisdiction over state court judgments. Does the power simply to deny certiorari in any case argue for a less strict interpretation of finality as a matter of policy? As a matter of statutory interpretation? Or would additional flexibility encourage a flood of petitions for certiorari—seeking review of interlocutory judgments—that are particularly unlikely to be granted?

---

pretrial sanctions had already been imposed, and adding: "Where First Amendment interests are actually affected, we have held that such interlocutory orders are immediately reviewable by this Court" (p. 70). The availability of review in the civil case, however, was in her view another argument against the Court's decision that the judgment in the criminal proceeding was reviewable.

8. Professors Matasar and Bruch view the Court's willingness to depart from a strict interpretation of finality as serving the goal of Supreme Court protection of the supremacy and uniformity of federal law. They go on to argue that that same goal justifies abandonment of the independent and adequate state ground doctrine. In their view, for example, if a state supreme court held that a statute does not violate the First Amendment and, in the alternative, that the First Amendment objection had been forfeit-

ed by the failure to have raised it below, the Supreme Court should be free to review the federal issue. See Matasar & Bruch, p. 519, *supra*, at 1355.

Doesn't the analogy overlook important differences between the two jurisdictional doctrines—notably, the constitutional and practical difficulties presented when (as is *not* true under the approach of Cox) the Supreme Court's review is certain to have no effect on the state court's judgment?

9. For a particularly mysterious holding that a state judgment is final, even though it is hard to fit in any of the Cox categories, see American Export Lines, Inc. v. Alvez, 446 U.S. 274 (1980), discussed in 16 Wright, Miller, Cooper & Gressman, Federal Practice and Procedure § 4010, at 1026–29 (1995 Supp.).

(8) *Finality and Federalism.* In Cox, Justice Rehnquist's dissent argued that the finality rule of § 1257 should be more strictly construed than the analogous finality requirement in § 1291, governing review of district court decisions in the federal courts of appeals. (As to the latter, see Chap. XV, Sec. 2, *infra.*) The tradition has been to draw no distinction between the two statutes, and cases arising under them are apparently cited interchangeably. For example, in Cox, Justice White cited Forgay v. Conrad, 47 U.S. (6 How.) 201 (1848), a federal case, in the same breath with Carondelet Canal & Nav. Co. v. Louisiana, 233 U.S. 362 (1914), a case from a state court, for the proposition that the final judgment rule is to be given a liberal, non-technical construction; and he relied significantly (see footnote 7) on Gillespie v. United States Steel Corp., 379 U.S. 148 (1964), a federal case. Are there good reasons to distinguish between the finality rules of § 1257 and § 1291? If so, which way do they cut? See pp. 1653–54, *infra.*

(9) *Reviewability of Issues Not Previously Reviewable.* If a state court judgment is not final for purposes of Supreme Court review, the federal questions it determines will (if not mooted) be open in the Supreme Court on later review of the final judgment, whether or not under state law the initial adjudication is the law of the case on the second state review. See, *e.g.*, Great Western Tel. Co. v. Burnham, 162 U.S. 339 (1896). "[A] contrary rule would insulate interlocutory state court rulings on important federal questions from our consideration." Hathorn v. Lovorn, 457 U.S. 255, 262 (1982).

(10) *When to Seek Review: Prematurity and Preclusion.* Since the time within which to petition for certiorari runs from the date of final judgment, failure to seek review at an intermediate stage may result in forfeiture of the right to review if the judgment in question is deemed "final".

In Rio Grande Western R. Co. v. Stringham, 239 U.S. 44 (1915), the state supreme court reversed a judgment for defendants and ordered partial judgment for the plaintiff. After the trial court entered judgment as directed, plaintiff again appealed, challenging so much of the judgment as was entered for the defendants. The state supreme court denied relief, holding its prior opinion the law of the case. Plaintiff filed two writs of error in the Supreme Court, seeking to review both the first and second judgments. The Court held the first judgment reviewable (and affirmed on the merits); it dismissed the second writ of error, apparently because the state court's decision that the first judgment itself constituted the law of the case was, in view of the fact that the first judgment was reviewable, an adequate state ground precluding Supreme Court review. See also Department of Banking v. Pink, 317 U.S. 264 (1942); Cole v. Violette, 319 U.S. 581 (1943).

Though there was no substantive injustice in Rio Grande, to follow that decision today and dismiss a second writ of error would seem unfair and imprudent in light of the lack of definition of the final judgment rule. See Dyk, *Supreme Court Review of Interlocutory State–Court Decisions: "The Twilight Zone of Finality"*, 18 Stan.L.Rev. 907, 929–34 (1967); Frank, *Requiem For The Final Judgment Rule*, 45 Texas L.Rev. 292, 317–18 (1966). Suppose the writ of error as to the first judgment had been out of time, because the plaintiff mistakenly thought that judgment was not reviewable; would (should) the Court have been as quick to dismiss the writ as to the second judgment? If litigants act at their peril, they can be expected to seek review at every stage possible, which can only have an undesirable effect on the Supreme Court's docket. For this reason, as well as fairness to litigants, if the question of

finality is in doubt, shouldn't litigants be able to choose their time?   *Cf.* Corey
v. United States, 375 U.S. 169 (1963), p. 1654, *infra.*

(11) *Rehearing in State Court.*   Finality is unaffected by the reservation of
authority in the state court to grant a petition for rehearing, though if a timely
petition is filed, the date of final judgment is the date of its denial or of the
expiration of power to grant it, or, if rehearing is granted, of the new judgment.
See Sup.Ct.R. 13.3; Market Street Ry. Co. v. Railroad Comm'n, 324 U.S. 548,
551–52 (1945).   By the same token, the denial of a petition for habeas corpus is
a final judgment notwithstanding the authority of other courts to entertain a
new petition; and the existence of postconviction remedies does not preclude
direct review of a conviction.[10]

(12) *The Highest State Court Requirement.*   The "highest court of a State in
which a decision could be had" (28 U.S.C. § 1257) may be the lowest court in
the state system, *e.g.*, the city's Police Court in Thompson v. City of Louisville,
362 U.S. 199 (1960), p. 620, *supra*, or the order of a judge in chambers, as in
Betts v. Brady, 316 U.S. 455 (1942).   The sole criterion is whether further
appellate review is possible within the state.   If so, even though such review is
discretionary, it must have been sought to confer jurisdiction on the Supreme
Court.[11]

In Pacific Gas & Elec. Co. v. Public Util. Comm'n, 475 U.S. 1, 7 (1986), an
order of the state utility commission was reviewable only in the discretion of
state supreme court, which had refused to accept the appeal.   The Supreme
Court noted probable jurisdiction and decided the appellant's First Amendment
challenge.   Was this an exercise of the Supreme Court's original jurisdiction?[12]
(If so, it would appear to lack authorization under 28 U.S.C. § 1251 and to
violate the Eleventh Amendment.)

Suppose that in Cox no interlocutory review had been available within the
state court system, but that the relevant issue would have been open to state
review later after the trial court's final judgment.   Would the trial court
decision be subject to immediate review in the Supreme Court?   *Cf.* Organiza-

---

10.   In New York ex rel. Bryant v. Zimmerman, 278 U.S. 63 (1928), the relator, held
in custody to answer a criminal charge, successfully employed habeas corpus to test the
validity of the statute on which the charge
was based.   The state court judgment denying the writ was held final by the Supreme
Court, despite the fact that under that judgment the accused still had to stand trial.   Is
there a difference between such a judgment
in a collateral proceeding and a determination overruling a demurrer to the indictment
or information, based on the claim of invalidity?   See also Madruga v. Superior Court, 346
U.S. 556 (1954)(prohibition); Rescue Army v.
Municipal Court, 331 U.S. 549 (1947), p. 650,
infra (same).

11.   See, *e.g.*, Costarelli v. Massachusetts, 421 U.S. 193 (1975); Gotthilf v. Sills,
375 U.S. 79 (1963)(leave to appeal on certified questions must be sought); Gorman v.
Washington   University,   316   U.S.   98
(1942)(review of judgment of division of state

highest court by the court *en banc* is available and must be applied for); but *cf.* Teamsters Local 174 v. Lucas Flour Co., 369 U.S.
95 (1962)(petitioner need not apply for review *en banc* where such review is discretionary and treated as a rehearing, and state law
makes the division's actions the judgment of
whole court).

12.   If you are tempted to say yes, ask
yourself whether there is any federal criterion that distinguishes state "courts" (review of whose determinations would clearly
fall within the Supreme Court's appellate
jurisdiction) from other state tribunals that
engage in adjudication.   See Meltzer, *Legislative Courts, Legislative Power, and the
Constitution*, 65 Ind.L.J. 291, 297–301
(1990).

It is clear, however, that the Supreme
Court may not directly review a state tribunal's "legislative" action.   See Chap. X, Sec.
2(A), pp. 1223–25, *infra.*

tion for a Better Austin v. Keefe, 402 U.S. 415, 420 (1971)(Harlan, J., dissenting); Kentucky v. Powers, 201 U.S. 1, 37–39 (1906). For a discussion of the relationship between the highest state court requirement and finality, see the opinion of Brennan, J., dissenting from denial of certiorari, in Spradling v. Texas, 455 U.S. 971 (1982).

SECTION 4.   OBLIGATORY OR DISCRETIONARY REVIEW

NOTE ON THE HISTORICAL SCOPE OF THE APPELLATE JURISDICTION

(1) *The Evolution of Discretionary Jurisdiction.* The Court's jurisdiction to review state court judgments gradually shifted from being entirely mandatory (as it was prior to 1914) to being entirely discretionary (as it has been since 1988). The changes in the statutory formulation are set forth at pp. 493–94, *supra*. Thus, the *mandatory* jurisdiction is of merely historical interest.

(2) *The Dahnke–Walker Doctrine.* From 1916–25, the Court's obligatory jurisdiction (via writ of error) over state court decisions extended only to those decisions (a) ruling against the validity of "an authority exercised under the United States", or (b) refusing to invalidate "an authority exercised under any State" as in violation of federal law. Cases involving the validity of claims asserted under an "authority", as distinguished from the validity of the authority itself, were reviewable only on certiorari. (The Judges Bill of 1925 eliminated that elusive distinction, providing mandatory review only when the state court had upheld the validity of a state statute or had denied the validity of a federal statute or treaty.)

The leading decision on whether a state court judgment involved the validity of a statute (and thus was subject to obligatory review) was Dahnke–Walker Milling Co. v. Bondurant, 257 U.S. 282 (1921). There the defendant in a suit for breach of contract for the sale of wheat claimed the contract was unenforceable because the plaintiff corporation had failed to comply with a Kentucky statute prescribing the conditions on which out-of-state corporations could do business. The plaintiff replied that application of the statute to its business in Kentucky, which consisted only of purchasing wheat for shipment out-of-state, was invalid under the Commerce Clause. Viewing the commerce as not interstate in nature, the trial court upheld the statutory defense, and the judgment was affirmed on appeal.

The Supreme Court held that the plaintiff-corporation could seek review via writ of error: "[T]he plaintiff did not simply claim a right or immunity under the Constitution of the United States, but distinctly insisted that as to the transaction in question the Kentucky statute was void, and therefore unenforceable, because in conflict with the commerce clause of the Constitution" (pp. 298–99). By applying the statute, the state court affirmed its validity. "That the statute was not claimed to be invalid *in toto* and for every purpose does not matter" (p. 289).

Justice Brandeis' dissent argued that under the 1916 Act, review as of right extended only when "the question is a denial of the power of the legislature to enact the statute as construed", not when "the question concerns merely the propriety of * * * the manner of applying or administering" the statute (p. 294). He noted that the 1916 Act, in an effort to relieve the Court's caseload, had restricted mandatory review to cases that are usually of general interest. "But whether a valid state statute has in a particular case been so used as to violate a constitutional guaranty is ordinarily a matter of merely private interest" (*id*). Here, there was no doubt of the state's power to enact the statute, for it had been construed by the state's highest court as affecting only intrastate transactions of foreign corporations.[1]

(3) *The Impact of Dahnke–Walker*. Justice Brandeis' dissent also objected that if mandatory jurisdiction obtains whenever a litigant claims that a state statute is invalid when applied to particular facts, "the right to review will depend, in large classes of cases, not upon the nature of the constitutional question involved but upon the skill of counsel" (p. 298). That prediction was amply sustained by events.[2]

The approach of stating a claim of immunity to an abusive application of a statute as a claim of *pro tanto* statutory invalidity, though not subject to clear-cut limits, occasionally met defeat. Pennsylvania v. Board of Directors of City Trusts, 353 U.S. 230 (1957), involved a trust (with the City of Philadelphia named as trustee) to set up a "college" for "poor white male orphans". Some years later a state statute established a "Board of Directors of City Trusts of the City of Philadelphia" to administer the trust and the college. A state court action to compel the Board to admit blacks to the college was unsuccessful. Review in the Supreme Court was sought by appeal on the theory that the state judgment constituted an unconstitutional application of the statute creating the Board. The Supreme Court dismissed the appeal (although certiorari was granted under 28 U.S.C. § 2103, see p. 494, *supra*, and the judgment was reversed on the merits).

(4) *The Meaning of State "Statute"*. The Court took a broad view of what enactments counted as a state "statute" for purposes of the mandatory appellate jurisdiction. Included were: (a) municipal ordinances, see, *e.g.*, Metromedia, Inc. v. City of San Diego, 453 U.S. 490 (1981); (b) orders or regulations of a "legislative" character promulgated by state-wide bodies other than the legislature itself, see, *e.g.*, Sultan Ry. & Timber Co. v. Department of Labor, 277 U.S. 135 (1928); Zauderer v. Office of Disciplinary Counsel, 471 U.S. 626 (1985); and (c) state constitutional provisions, see, *e.g.*, PruneYard Shopping Center v. Robins, 447 U.S. 74 (1980).

(5) *Failure to Rule on A Statute's Validity*. A state court's failure to pass on the validity of a state statute that had been seasonably challenged was treated as equivalent to a determination of validity, and therefore (assuming that the decision did not rest on an adequate state ground) was reviewable. See, *e.g.*, Lawrence v. State Tax Comm'n, 286 U.S. 276, 282 (1932).

(6) *"Ancillary" Jurisdiction*. If a case presented a question that provided the basis for appeal, the normal order accepting an appeal for plenary consideration, "probable jurisdiction noted," brought before the Court all the federal

---

1. The Dahnke–Walker doctrine apparently also governed when a state court held an act of Congress invalid as applied. See Wissner v. Wissner, 338 U.S. 655 (1950).

2. Compare, *e.g.*, Gillespie v. Oklahoma, 257 U.S. 501 (1922) with Indian Territory Illuminating Oil Co. v. Board of Equalization, 287 U.S. 573, 288 U.S. 325 (1933); Citizens' National Bank v. Durr, 257 U.S. 99 (1921), with Senior v. Braden, 295 U.S. 422 (1935), and Dahnke–Walker, *supra;* Edwards v. South Carolina, 372 U.S. 229 (1963), and Gregory v. Chicago, 394 U.S. 111 (1969), with Cox v. Louisiana, p. 602, *supra*.

questions presented in the jurisdictional statement—even those that in themselves were reviewable only on certiorari. But the Court also held that it had power to restrict notations of probable jurisdiction to the appealable issues only. See, *e.g.*, Mishkin v. New York, 383 U.S. 502, 512–13 (1966).

NOTE ON THE PRELIMINARY DETERMINATION OF SUBSTANTIALITY AND ON THE PER CURIAM PRACTICE

(1) *The "Substantial" Question Requirement.* The Supreme Court developed the position that a federal question must be "substantial" to confer jurisdiction to entertain an appeal.[1] For example, in Zucht v. King, 260 U.S. 174 (1922), a student who had been excluded from public school because she lacked a certificate of vaccination challenged the governing ordinance. On writ of error from a state court judgment denying relief, the Supreme Court dismissed for want of jurisdiction, finding that, in light of the precedents, there was "no question as to the validity of the ordinance sufficiently substantial to support the writ of error" (p. 177).

The jurisdictional requirement of substantiality was of small consequence so long as all questions, including those of jurisdiction, were determined only on full argument; dismissal or affirmance hardly made a difference to the unsuccessful party. In 1872, the Court amended its rules to provide for the disposition of a motion to dismiss a writ of error on the printed brief, unless the Court expressed a wish for oral argument. 80 U.S. (13 Wall.) xi. This change was supplemented in 1876 by provision that a motion to dismiss might be accompanied by "a motion to affirm, on the ground, that * * * the writ was taken for delay only, or that the question on which jurisdiction depends is so frivolous as not to need further argument." 91 U.S. vii. Once these rules were established, treatment of the question of substantiality as jurisdictional laid the foundation for summary disposition on motion to dismiss or to dismiss or affirm. See generally Ulman & Spears, *"Dismissed for Want of a Substantial Federal Question"*, 20 B.U.L.Rev. 501 (1940).

There was, however, no procedure for eliminating frivolous invocations of jurisdiction without time-consuming oral argument unless the defendant in error made the motion. To surmount this difficulty, in 1928 a new rule required the appellant within 30 days of docketing the case to file a statement establishing jurisdiction, and indicated that the Court would note probable jurisdiction or dismiss upon the jurisdictional statement and the reply thereto. A 1936 amendment called expressly for a "statement of the grounds upon which it is contended the questions involved are *substantial*". 297 U.S. at 733 (emphasis added).

In 1954, the notion that, in order to dispose of a case without oral argument, the disposition must be "jurisdictional", was abandoned by Sup. Ct.R. 15(1)(e), which required that all appeals be docketed with a statement of "the reasons why the questions presented are so substantial as to require" plenary briefing and argument. Nevertheless, the dismissal for want of a substantial federal question remained the standard technique for dealing on the

---

1. That position developed late in the Court's history. Compare, *e.g.*, New Orleans v. New Orleans Water–Works Co., 142 U.S. 79 (1891) (following that view), with, *e.g.*, Murdock v. Memphis, 87 U.S. (20 Wall.) 590 (1875), p. 510, *supra*.

merits with a frivolous appeal from a state court judgment. (In cases from the lower federal courts, the tradition of such quasi-jurisdictional dismissals never developed, and cases not deserving oral argument were simply affirmed.)

(2) *The Determination of Substantiality.* The labeling of dismissals for want of a substantial federal question as "jurisdictional" engendered confusion about how to resolve the question of "substantiality". In theory the judgment to be made went only to whether the case should be decided without plenary briefing and oral argument; it did not relieve the Court of its statutory obligation to decide the appeal on the merits. The Court's discretion to deny certiorari is sharply different: it legitimately involves a judgment about whether the case should be decided at all.

The distinction, however, was subject to slippage for many years, and a number of informed commentators suggested that the Court's practice in appeals did not in fact differ sharply from that on certiorari. In 1975, retired Justice Tom Clark wrote that during the eighteen Terms in which he sat on the Supreme Court, "appeals from state court decisions received treatment similar to that accorded petitions for certiorari and were given about the same precedential weight." Hogge v. Johnson, 526 F.2d 833, 836 (4th Cir.1975)(concurring opinion; sitting by designation).[2] Note Professor Wechsler's response: "If that was so, and I well know, of course, that others have asserted that it was, the Court simply disregarded its statutory duty to decide appealed cases on the merits." Wechsler, *The Appellate Jurisdiction of the Supreme Court: Reflections on the Law and the Logistics of Direct Review*, 34 Wash. & Lee L.Rev. 1043, 1061 (1977). See also Griswold, *Equal Justice Under Law*, 33 Wash. & Lee L.Rev. 813, 818–21 (1976).

(3) *The Precedential Value of a Dismissal for Want of a Substantial Federal Question.* In Hicks v. Miranda, 422 U.S. 332 (1975), the Court ruled that dismissal of an appeal for want of a substantial federal question, unlike denial of certiorari, is an authoritative decision on the merits that binds the lower courts. In Miller v. California, 418 U.S. 915 (1974)(Miller II), the Court had dismissed, for want of a substantial federal question, an appeal from a state court judgment upholding a state statute against constitutional attack. The three-judge federal district court in Hicks nevertheless held itself not bound by the dismissal in Miller II and reaffirmed its earlier judgment that the very same state statute was invalid. The Supreme Court reversed. Justice White, for the Court, said (pp. 343–44) that because Miller II was an appeal, "we had no discretion to refuse adjudication of the case on the merits as would have been true had the case been brought here under our certiorari jurisdiction. We were not obligated to grant the case plenary consideration, and we did not; but we were required to deal with its merits." The three-judge court "was not free

2. See also, *e.g.*, Sidle v. Majors, 429 U.S. 945, 949 (1976)(Brennan, J., dissenting from the denial of certiorari)(referring to "the desirable latitude each of us formerly had [prior to Hicks v. Miranda, 422 U.S. 332 (1975), Paragraph (3), *infra*] to weigh, as in the case of petitions for certiorari, whether the issue presented is sufficiently important to merit plenary review, and whether in any event the question might better be addressed after we have had the benefit of the views of other courts"); Frankfurter & Landis, *The Business of the Supreme Court at October Term, 1929*, 44 Harv.L.Rev. 1, 12–14 (1930)(contending that the inevitable play of discretion in determining substantiality is bound to be influenced by the Court's docket, and where reasonable differences of opinion about substantiality arise, the Court's obligatory jurisdiction is subject to "discretionary considerations not unlike those governing certiorari").

to disregard" the Supreme Court's substantive pronouncement in Miller II that the constitutional challenge to the statute was not a substantial one.

(4) *Determining the "Precedent's" Meaning.* Hicks required lower courts to identify the principle or proposition that was deemed settled by a previous Supreme Court summary disposition. This was by no means always easy.

In Mandel v. Bradley, 432 U.S. 173 (1977)(per curiam), the Court vacated the decision of a three-judge federal district court that, the Court ruled, had incorrectly considered itself bound by a Supreme Court summary affirmance in a previous case materially distinguishable on its facts. The Court said (p. 176): "Because a summary affirmance is an affirmance of the judgment only, the rationale of the affirmance may not be gleaned solely from the opinion below. * * * Summary affirmances and dismissals for want of a substantial federal question without doubt reject the specific challenges presented in the statement of jurisdiction * * *. They do prevent lower courts from coming to opposite conclusions on the precise issues presented and necessarily decided by those actions. * * * Summary actions, however, * * * should not be understood as breaking new ground but as applying principles established by prior decisions to the particular facts involved."

Justice Brennan, concurring, said (p. 180): "After today, judges of the state and federal systems are on notice that, before deciding a case on the authority of a summary disposition by this Court in another case, they must (a) examine the jurisdictional statement in the earlier case to be certain that the constitutional questions presented were the same and, if they were, (b) determine that the judgment in fact rests upon decision of those questions and not even arguably upon some alternative non-constitutional ground."[3]

(5) *Summary Dispositions as Precedents for the Supreme Court.* The question at issue in Hicks v. Miranda and Mandel v. Bradley—the precedential value of summary dispositions in the lower courts—must be sharply distinguished from the question addressed in Edelman v. Jordan, 415 U.S. 651 (1974): the weight the Supreme Court itself should give to its summary dispositions. In Edelman the Court said (pp. 670–71): "This case * * * is the first opportunity the Court has taken to fully explore and treat the Eleventh Amendment aspects [of this case] in a written opinion. * * * [T]hree summary affirmances [of lower courts] obviously are of precedential value in support of the contention that the Eleventh Amendment does not bar the relief awarded by the District Court in this case. Equally obviously, they are not of the same precedential value as would be an opinion of this Court treating the question on the merits." See also, *e.g.*, Davis v. Bandemer, 478 U.S. 109 (1986); Caban v. Mohammed, 441 U.S. 380, 390 n. 9 (1979).

(6) *The Quality of Justice.* What does the Court's practice of treating its own summary decisions with reduced deference tell us about the quality of justice obtained by the litigants in the original case?

In Colorado Springs Amusements, Ltd. v. Rizzo, 428 U.S. 913, 916–19, 922 (1976), Justice Brennan, dissenting from a dismissal for want of a substantial federal question, said: "[T]he same reasons that lead us to deny conclusive precedential value in this Court to our summary dispositions require that we allow the same latitude to state and lower federal courts." He noted that such

---

3. On the precedential effect of summary dispositions, see also Illinois State Bd. of Elections v. Socialist Workers Party, 440 U.S. 173 (1979); Sporhase v. Nebraska ex rel. Douglas, 458 U.S. 941 (1982).

dispositions are made after consideration only of jurisdictional papers, whose purpose is to apprise the Court whether the issues warrant plenary review and "rarely contain more than brief discussions" of the merits.

He added that "summary dispositions are rarely supported even by a brief opinion identifying the federal questions presented or stating the reasons or authority upon which the disposition rests. * * * When presented with the contention that our unexplained dispositions are conclusively binding, puzzled state and lower court judges are left to guess as to the meaning and scope of our unexplained dispositions. * * *

"Even if the Court rejects my view that Hicks should be modified, at a minimum we have the duty to provide some explanation of the issues presented in the case and the reasons and authorities supporting our summary dispositions. This surely should be the practice in cases presenting novel issues or where there is a disagreement among us as to the grounds of the disposition, and I think it should be the practice in every case."

If one agrees that summary dispositions may be ambiguous and/or inadequately-considered precedents, does it follow that they should have no *authoritative* effect? Doesn't the Hicks rule impose some discipline on the Court's summary rulings; without it, wouldn't the problem of ill-considered summary dispositions be worse?[4]

(7) *Per Curiam Practice.* The Court's methods of protecting itself against having to give full consideration to frivolous appeals (dismissals of state-court appeals for want of a substantial federal question, and summary affirmance of federal-court appeals) comprised only two parts of a more general "summary per curiam practice"—cases that the Court decides on the merits without full briefing and oral argument. Even after mandatory appeals from state courts (and from nearly all lower federal courts) were eliminated in 1988, the Court has continued to use summary dispositions in reviewing cases on certiorari.[5]

4. For discussion of summary dispositions, see, *e.g.*, Linzer, *The Meaning of Certiorari Denials*, 79 Colum.L.Rev. 1227, 1291–99 (1979); Note, 64 Va.L.Rev. 117 (1978); Comment, 76 Colum.L.Rev. 508 (1976); Note, 52 B.U.L.Rev. 373 (1972).

5. The November issue of the Harvard Law Review reports the following statistics indicating, of all cases decided on the merits in the previous Term, the number disposed of by *per curiam* or memorandum decision:

Term	Total Dispositions On the Merits	Dispositions By Per Curiam Opinion
1980	274	115
1981	342	126
1982	301	119
1983	265	81
1984	266	91
1985	290	118
1986	277	102
1987	259	92
1988	256	86
1989	228	77
1990	241	112
1991	195	68
1992	226	107
1993	163	67
1994	160	65

Per curiam dispositions sometimes merely dispose of the case (*e.g.*, "affirmed"; "dismissed for want of jurisdiction"), sometimes include some citations of authority, and sometimes are accompanied by brief opinions. But both before and after 1988, summary dispositions have not been limited to instances of frivolous attacks on the judgment below. And at times the Court will summarily *reverse*.[6] Do you agree that the practice of summary *reversal* is "impossible to reconcile with the conventional conceptions of due process of law"? Hart, *Foreword: The Time Chart of the Justices*, 73 Harv.L.Rev. 84, 89 n. 13 (1959). Is the Supreme Court's practice in this regard different in principle from the practice in the courts of appeals? Does the acceptability of summary reversal (or summary dispositions more generally) depend on whether some explanation of the basis for decision is furnished?

NOTE ON DISMISSAL FOR WANT OF A "PROPERLY PRESENTED" QUESTION AND OTHER REFUSALS TO ADJUDICATE APPEALS

(1) *Discretion to Decline Jurisdiction?* Assuming that an appeal from a state court judgment raised a substantial federal issue, did the pre–1988 mandatory jurisdiction leave any room for the Supreme Court to refuse to entertain the merits? That question was the subject of sharp controversy for several decades. It implicated a broad set of concerns, reaching well beyond the specific problem of mandatory jurisdiction, relating to conceptions of judicial role and judicial discretion.

(2) *The Rescue Army Decision.* In Rescue Army v. Municipal Court of Los Angeles, 331 U.S. 549 (1947)(7–2), Murdock, a member of the Rescue Army, was prosecuted in Municipal Court for having violated city ordinances regulating charitable solicitations. The Rescue Army then sought a writ of prohibition against the Municipal Court's exercise of jurisdiction, on the ground that the ordinances violated the First and Fourteenth Amendments. The California Supreme Court denied the writ, on the authority of that court's decision several months earlier (in the Gospel Army case) rejecting a broad challenge to most of the provisions of the ordinances at issue in the Rescue Army proceeding.

In the U.S. Supreme Court, Justice Rutledge's majority opinion first noted that the Court had dismissed the appeal in Gospel Army because the state judgment there was not final. The Rescue Army suit, however, was free of that defect. "While therefore we are unable to conclude that there is no jurisdiction in this cause, nevertheless compelling reasons exist for not exercising it" (p. 568).

The *per curiam* decisions include cases where certiorari was granted and the case was summarily affirmed or reversed and cases on appeal summarily affirmed or reversed. It is unclear, however, whether these statistics include cases on appeal dismissed for want of a substantial federal question. Excluded from the per curiam figures are cases containing sufficient legal reasoning to be considered by the Harvard Law Review to be written opinions.

6. *E.g.*, Smith v. Ohio, 494 U.S. 541 (1990)(certiorari); Gelling v. Texas, 343 U.S. 960 (1952)(appeal). See also the detailed study and devastating criticism of summary reversal on certiorari in Brown, *Foreword: Process of Law*, 72 Harv.L.Rev. 77 (1958), and Sacks, *Foreword: The Supreme Court, 1953 Term*, 68 Harv.L.Rev. 96 (1954), further discussed in Chap. XV, Sec. 4, pp. 1712–13, *infra*.

The prime reason was the Court's policy of avoiding decision of constitutional issues except where "necessity compels it". He continued: "One aspect of the policy's application * * * has been by virtue of the presence of other grounds for decision. But when such alternatives are absent, as in this case, application must rest upon considerations relative to the manner in which the constitutional issue itself is shaped and presented" (p. 573).

Justice Rutledge found that, "for a variety of reasons the shape in which the underlying constitutional issues have reached this Court presents, we think, insuperable obstacles to any exercise of jurisdiction to determine them" (p. 574). The opinion pointed out the highly abstract form in which the constitutional issues appeared; the lack of clarity, on the record in this case, about the actual charges made; and the many unsettled questions of construction of the ordinance that would have to be resolved in the prosecution of Murdock, and whose resolution by the state courts could obviate or narrow the constitutional issues. Thus, Justice Rutledge concluded that the policy of constitutional avoidance obliged the Court to decline jurisdiction and dismiss the appeal "without prejudice to the determination in the future of any issues arising under the Federal Constitution from further proceedings in the Municipal Court" (p. 585).

(3) *Poe v. Ullman.* Poe v. Ullman, 367 U.S. 497 (1961), was a declaratory judgment action attacking the constitutionality of a Connecticut statute prohibiting the use of contraceptive devices or the giving of medical advice about them. The state courts upheld the statute, even as applied to married couples and despite allegations that conception would seriously threaten the health or lives of the plaintiff-wives. After plenary consideration in the Supreme Court, the appeal was dismissed.

There was no opinion of the Court. Justice Frankfurter, joined by Chief Justice Warren and Justices Clark and Whittaker, noted the absence of any specific threat of enforcement, the long history of non-enforcement of the statute, and the open and well-known sale of contraceptives in drug stores in the state. Accordingly, he found the controversy inappropriate for constitutional adjudication. Article III's case or controversy requirement is not, Justice Frankfurter argued, "the sole limitation on the exercise of our appellate powers, especially in cases raising constitutional questions" (pp. 502–03). He cited Justice Brandeis' celebrated discussion, in his concurrence in Ashwander v. Tennessee Valley Authority, 297 U.S. 288, 341, 346 (1936), of the rules of constitutional avoidance. "In part the rules summarized in the Ashwander opinion have derived from the historically defined, limited nature and function of courts and from the recognition that * * * the adjudicatory process is most securely founded when it is exercised under the impact of a lively conflict between antagonistic demands, actively pressed, which make resolution of the controverted issue a practical necessity. * * * In part they derive from the fundamental federal and tripartite character of our National Government and from the role—restricted by its very responsibility—of the federal courts, and particularly this Court, within that structure. * * *

"The Court has been on the alert against use of the declaratory judgment device for avoiding the rigorous insistence on exigent adversity as a condition for evoking Court adjudication. This is as true of state court suits for declaratory judgments as of federal. By exercising their jurisdiction, state courts cannot determine the jurisdiction to be exercised by this Court. * * * Indeed, * * * 'the discretionary element characteristic of declaratory jurisdiction, and imported perhaps from equity jurisdiction and practice without the remedial phase, offers a convenient instrument for making * * * effective * * *' the policy against premature constitutional decision. Rescue Army v. Municipal Court, 331 U.S. 549, 573, n. 41. * * *

"Justiciability is of course not a legal concept with a fixed content or susceptible of scientific verification. Its utilization is the resultant of many subtle pressures, including the appropriateness of the issues for decision by this Court and the actual hardship to the litigants of denying them the relief sought. Both these factors justify withholding adjudication of the constitutional issue raised under the circumstances and in the manner in which they are now before the Court."

Justice Brennan concurred in the result (p. 509): "The true controversy in this case is over the opening of birth-control clinics on a large scale; it is that which the State has prevented in the past, not the use of contraceptives by isolated and individual married couples. It will be time enough to decide the constitutional questions urged upon us when, if ever, that real controversy flares up again." Justices Black, Douglas, Harlan and Stewart each dissented separately.[1]

(4) *Possible Bases for Declination.* In both Rescue Army and Poe, the principal opinion clearly implies that dismissal was not compelled by the "case or controversy" requirement of Article III. If the problem was simply that the record was inadequate or ambiguous, couldn't the Court have remanded the case for further proceedings? If so, what justified the refusal to exercise mandatory appellate jurisdiction in these (and other) cases?[2]

(a) *Constitutional Avoidance.* The principal opinions in both cases rely heavily on Justice Brandeis' famous statement in Ashwander v. Tennessee Valley Authority, 297 U.S. 288, 346 (1936), of the policy of avoidance of constitutional questions and of seven rules that implement that policy. The Brandeisian conception of judicial role no longer has as strong a hold as it once did. See, *e.g.*, Chap. II, Sec. 1, pp. 78–83, *supra.* But even a disciple of constitutional avoidance would have difficulty premising the results in Rescue Army and Poe on that policy. As Professor Gunther notes, four of Brandeis' seven rules "involve * * * avoidance only of some or all of the *constitutional* questions argued, *not* avoidance of all decision on the merits of the case. * * * The remaining rules given by Brandeis deal with situations in which there is no

---

1. Compare Epperson v. Arkansas, 393 U.S. 97 (1968), where the Court (with only Justice Black dissenting on this point) decided the merits of a declaratory and injunction action challenging the validity of a 1928 law prohibiting the teaching of evolution, though there was no record of any prosecutions under it. "It is possible that the statute is presently more of a curiosity than a vital fact of life * * *. Nevertheless, the present case was brought, the appeal as of right is properly here, and it is our duty to decide the issues presented" (p. 102).

2. Applications of the Rescue Army approach were articulated in various forms. See, *e.g.*, International Bhd. of Teamsters v. Denver Milk Producers, Inc., 334 U.S. 809

(1948)(stressing "the inadequacy of the record"); DeBacker v. Brainard, 396 U.S. 28, 29–30 (1969)(stating that "resolution of the constitutional issues presented by appellant would not be appropriate in the circumstances of this case"); Simmons v. West Haven Housing Auth., 399 U.S. 510, 511 (1970)(noting "an ambiguity in the record"). Not uncommonly, cases were disposed of with nothing more than the notation, "Appeal dismissed for want of a properly presented federal question." See, *e.g.*, Cleveland Elec. Illuminating Co. v. Public Util. Com'n, 459 U.S. 1094 (1983); Doe v. Delaware, 450 U.S. 382 (1981). See generally 16 Wright, Miller, Cooper, & Gressman, Federal Practice and Procedure § 4015 (1977 & 1995 Supp.).

'case' or 'controversy' in terms of the jurisdictional content of Article III
* * *."

Gunther adds: "The Brandeis rules are a far cry from the neo-Brandeisian fallacy that there is a general 'Power To Decline the Exercise of Jurisdiction Which Is Given,' that there is a general discretion not to adjudicate though statute, Constitution, and remedial law present a 'case' for decision and confer no discretion. [The 'Power to Decline' quotation is from Bickel, The Least Dangerous Branch 127 (1962).]   Gunther, *The Subtle Vices of the 'Passive Virtues'—A Comment on Principle and Expediency in Judicial Review*, 64 Colum.L.Rev. 1, 16–17 (1964)".   See also Kloppenberg, *Avoiding Constitutional Questions*, 35 B.C.L.Rev. 1003 (1994).

(b) *Remedial Discretion.* Was the Court justified, in Rescue Army and Poe, in relying on concepts of judicial discretion in the awarding of equitable relief or declaratory judgments—even where the state court's denial of relief was based not on its remedial discretion but rather on the merits? Note that unlike a trial court's refusal to award such relief, the Court's refusal to hear these appeals left standing the state courts' judgments that there was no constitutional violation.

To be sure, it is significant that Rescue Army and Poe were actions seeking preventive relief against actual or potential criminal prosecution. The dismissal left the state free to prosecute; but (assuming the inapplicability of res judicata[3]) the federal questions presented in the anticipatory action could still be asserted as defenses to any prosecution, and, if conviction resulted, ultimately in an appeal to the U.S. Supreme Court.

But compare Mattiello v. Connecticut, 395 U.S. 209 (1969), where appellant, a 17–year-old girl, had been found to be "in manifest danger of falling into habits of vice," Conn.Gen.Stats. § 17–379, and was committed to the State Farm for Women until the age of 21. Her objection to the statute as unconstitutionally vague had been rejected by the state courts. On review, the Supreme Court dismissed the appeal after argument "for want of a properly presented federal question."

Should the Court have felt less freedom to decline to hear an appeal when the result was to permit a state to act coercively against a person who is asserting a federal constitutional defense?

(5) *Naim v. Naim.* Naim v. Naim, 350 U.S. 891 (1955), was a suit to annul a marriage on the ground that it violated Virginia's miscegenation statute. The marriage had been performed in North Carolina, but the Virginia statute specifically applied to couples leaving the state for the purpose of marriage and intending to return. The Virginia trial court, finding that the circumstances fell within the statute's proscription, decreed annulment, rejecting a challenge to the constitutionality of the statute. In the year following the initial decision in Brown v. Board of Education, the Supreme Court of Appeals of Virginia affirmed. On appeal to the United States Supreme Court, the judgment was vacated on the following opinion: "*Per Curiam*: The inadequacy of the record as to the relationship of the parties to the Commonwealth of Virginia at the time of the marriage in North Carolina and upon their return to Virginia, and

---

3. Even if the state court, applying issue preclusion, would refuse to reexamine any issues of federal law determined in the prior proceeding, that decision would probably not provide an adequate state ground barring direct review by the Supreme Court. See Fidelity Nat. Bank & Trust Co. v. Swope, 274 U.S. 123 (1927), p. 155, *supra*.

the failure of the parties to bring here all questions relevant to the disposition of the case, prevents the constitutional issue of the validity of the Virginia statute on miscegenation tendered here being [sic] considered 'in clean-cut and concrete form, unclouded' by such problems.   Rescue Army v. Municipal Court, 331 U.S. 549, 584.   The judgment is vacated and the case remanded to the Supreme Court of Appeals in order that the case may be returned to the Circuit Court of the City of Portsmouth for action not inconsistent with this opinion" (p. 891).

On remand, the Supreme Court of Appeals of Virginia reiterated the facts that had been established; declared that the record was fully adequate; said that state law provided no basis to return the case to the circuit court to reopen its previous adjudication; and reinstated the annulment.

A motion in the U.S. Supreme Court to recall the earlier mandate was denied, with a brief notation stating that "[t]he decision of the Supreme Court of Appeals of Virginia of January 18, 1956 in response to our order of November 14, 1955 leaves the case devoid of a properly presented federal question".   350 U.S. 985 (1956).

Note that the result of Naim was to permit the state, over constitutional objection, affirmatively to dissolve a marriage on the basis of the miscegenation statute.   Professor Wechsler has described this result as "wholly without basis in the law".   *Toward Neutral Principles of Constitutional Law*, in Principle, Politics, and Fundamental Law 47 (1961).   Compare the views of Professor Alexander Bickel: "[T]he Court, discounting the interest of the moving party, dismissed outright a case raising the constitutionality of state anti-miscegenation statutes.   Perhaps Virginia, whose statute was in question, had a 'right' to a decision, although the clamor from those quarters has been something short of deafening.   Actually a judgment legitimating such statutes would have been unthinkable, given the principle of the School Segregation Cases and of decisions made in their aftermath.   But would it have been wise, at a time when the Court had just pronounced its new integration principle, when it was subject to scurrilous attack by men who predicted that integration of the schools would lead directly to 'mongrelization of the race' and that this was the result the Court had really willed, would it have been wise, just then, in the first case of its sort on an issue that the Negro community as a whole can hardly be said to be pressing hard at the moment, to declare that the states may not prohibit racial intermarriage?"   The Least Dangerous Branch: The Supreme Court at the Bar of Politics 174 (1962).[4]

---

4.   See also the private memorandum of Mr. Justice Frankfurter on Naim v. Naim, read at the Court's conference on Nov. 4, 1955, reprinted as Appendix D to Hutchinson, *Unanimity and Desegregation: Decision-making in the Supreme Court, 1948–58*, 68 Geo.L.J. 1, 95–96 (1979), which said, in part: "So far as I recall, this is the first time since I've been here that I am confronted with the task of resolving a conflict between moral and technical legal considerations.   * * *

"Even if one regards the [constitutional challenge to the statute], as I do, of a seriousness that cannot be rejected as frivolous, I candidly face the fact that what I call moral considerations far outweigh the technical considerations in noting jurisdiction.   The moral considerations are, of course, those raised by the bearing of adjudicating this question to the Court's responsibility in not thwarting or seriously handicapping the enforcement of its decision in the segregation cases.   * * *   For I find it difficult to believe that there is a single member of this Court who does not think that to throw a decision of this Court other than validating this legislation into the vortex of the present disquietude would not seriously, I believe very seriously, embarrass the carrying-out of the Court's decree of last May."

Wasn't the real problem that the Court disregarded the right to appeal, not of Virginia, but of the person against whom Virginia was exercising coercion? Professor Bickel argues that even the obligatory appeal jurisdiction was subject to a general "power to decline the exercise of jurisdiction which is given" (p. 127). Compare Gunther, Paragraph (4)(a), *supra*, at 12, noting that there are "very few" instances (he viewed the miscegenation case as one) in which the Court engaged in "indefensible" dismissals, and criticizing Bickel for "exaggerat[ing] them to the level of the commonplace and * * * elevat[ing] them to the level of the desirable and the acceptable." If the Court believed that under the conditions of the time it had to avoid deciding Naim v. Naim without regard to legal obligation or cost, was it perhaps preferable to act as it did rather than to seek to rationalize and thus generalize the breach?

(6) *Discretion: Principled and Otherwise.* In a celebrated dictum, Chief Justice Marshall said: "It is most true that this Court will not take jurisdiction if it should not: but it is equally true, that it must take jurisdiction, if it should. * * * We have no more right to decline the exercise of jurisdiction which is given, than to usurp that which is not given. The one or the other would be treason to the constitution". Cohens v. Virginia, 19 U.S. (6 Wheat.) 264, 404 (1821).

Does Marshall's dictum correctly state the law? Professor Shapiro, in *Jurisdiction and Discretion*, 60 N.Y.U.L.Rev. 543 (1985), demonstrates (in discussing a wide range of traditional and contemporary doctrines) that it cannot be taken at face value: on many issues, courts have exercised a "principled discretion" (p. 578) in refusing to exercise jurisdiction seemingly granted by Congress. The discretion of which Shapiro approves is not ad hoc, but rather constitutes a fine-tuning of legislative enactments in accordance with criteria that are openly applied and that are "drawn from the relevant statutory * * * grant of jurisdiction or from the tradition within which the grant arose" (*ibid.*).

To what extent can the cases considered in this Note be brought within any notion of a principled discretion? Do some, or perhaps all, of them rest on a broad claim of discretion to determine, on the basis of judicial conceptions of prudence and statesmanship, whether to deny litigants a right to appeal to the Supreme Court? Is that claim consistent with Congress' creation of mandatory appellate jurisdiction? Is the answer to that question illuminated by asking the further question whether the Court would have been willing, in Naim v. Naim, for example, to articulate its true reason for declining jurisdiction? See *id.* at 553–54 & n. 65, 578–79 & nn. 215–16.

CHAPTER VI

THE LAW APPLIED IN CIVIL ACTIONS IN THE DISTRICT COURTS

SECTION 34, JUDICIARY ACT OF 1789

1 Stat. 92, Rev.Stat. § 721, 28 U.S.C. § 725 (1940 ed.)

That the laws of the several states, except where the constitution, treaties, or statutes of the United States shall otherwise require or provide, shall be regarded as rules of decision in trials at common law in the courts of the United States in cases where they apply.

---

28 U.S.C. § 1652

The laws of the several states, except where the Constitution or treaties of the United States or Acts of Congress otherwise require or provide, shall be regarded as rules of decision in civil actions in the courts of the United States, in cases where they apply.

SECTION 1. PROCEDURE

NOTE ON THE HISTORICAL DEVELOPMENT OF THE STATUTES AND RULES OF COURT

The same plan for the regulation of procedure is now in effect in each of the major fields of federal court jurisdiction: bankruptcy, other civil actions (including admiralty), and criminal actions. Some matters in each field are controlled directly by statute or constitutional provision. Primarily, however, procedure in each field is governed by a set of general rules that have been promulgated by the Supreme Court under authority of Congress and that remain continuously subject to revision by the Court. In addition, there are rules governing the procedure in all cases in the courts of appeals. The original goal of uniformity, however, has been significantly affected (some would say seriously undermined) by the proliferation of rules issued on the appellate level by individual circuits and on the district court level by each federal district.[1]

---

1. This tendency has been further encouraged by the passage in 1990 of the Civil Justice Reform Act, discussed at p. 668, *infra*. The authority of the district courts to pro-

The Supreme Court and all courts established by act of Congress are given general authority to prescribe rules for the conduct of their own business by 28 U.S.C. § 2071. The Supreme Court is given specific authority to prescribe rules of procedure for the lower federal courts in bankruptcy by 28 U.S.C. § 2075, and in other civil actions and in criminal actions by 28 U.S.C. § 2072. Section 2072 also delegates to the Supreme Court authority to prescribe rules of evidence.[2]

In equity, admiralty, and bankruptcy, the decision that federal procedure should be uniform (rather than conforming to the varied practices among the states) was readily arrived at. In criminal actions and, more notably, in civil actions at law, the approach made its way much more slowly, and indeed in the civil arena, is now under some strain. Here is another phase of a pervasive problem of federalism: the choice between uniformity and diversity.

A. Equity Before Merger

The story of equity is now merged in that of law. But for nearly a century and a half it had its own history as a distinctive branch of federal practice.

From the beginning, federal equity has had to administer the substantive law of the states as well as of the United States. Particularly where rights under state law were in issue, state procedure, in principle, had a claim for acceptance. But in 1789 equity was either non-existent or undeveloped in the courts of many of the states. Federal procedure was thus able to establish and maintain itself without serious challenge.

Even the Rules of Decision Act—the famous thirty-fourth section of the Judiciary Act of 1789—was not made to apply in terms to equity. Not until the 1948 revision, 28 U.S.C. § 1652, was the language broadened to cover all "civil actions".[3]

mulgate local rules is recognized in 28 U.S.C. § 2071 (discussed in text) and in the civil rules themselves, not only by the authorization of such rules in Rule 83 but by specific authorization allowing individual districts to opt out, in whole or in part, of important new disclosure requirements in the federal rules. See Rule 26(a)(1).

In addition to local rules and "plans" adopted pursuant to the Civil Justice Reform Act, many judges have adopted their own "standing orders", which establish special procedures applicable only in cases being litigated before them.

2. Section 2071 traces its origin to § 7 of The Act of March 2, 1793, 1 Stat. 333, 335 (giving authority to the several courts of the United States to "make rules and orders for their respective courts directing the returning of writs and processes, the filing of declarations and other pleadings, * * * and otherwise in a manner not repugnant to the laws of the United States, to regulate the practice of the said courts respectively, as shall be fit and necessary for the advancement of justice"). Section 2072, generally known as the Enabling Act, was originally enacted in 1934.

In addition to other rules discussed in this Note, the Supreme Court has prescribed the Copyright Rules, 17 U.S.C. following § 501.

Congress has also conferred certain rulemaking powers on the judicial councils of the circuits in connection with complaints of judicial misconduct and disability. See 28 U.S.C. § 372(c)(11); Burbank, *Procedural Reform Under the Judicial Conduct and Disability Act of 1980,* 131 U.Pa.L.Rev. 283 (1982).

3. The change was less significant than it might appear, in view of the often reiterated doctrine that the Rules of Decision Act "is merely declarative of the rule which would exist in the absence of the statute." See Guaranty Trust Co. v. York, p. 703, *infra.*

The first Congress dealt directly with civil procedure in the Process Act of September 29, 1789 (1 Stat. 93, 94), which provided that "the forms and modes of proceedings in causes of equity * * * shall be according to the course of the civil law". The second Congress replaced this avowedly stopgap measure with a formulation that lasted until law and equity were merged in 1938 (Act of May 8, 1792, § 2, 1 Stat. 275, 276). The forms of process in equity, except their style, and the forms and modes of proceedings were to be "according to the principles, rules and usages which belong to courts of equity * * *, as contra-distinguished from courts of common law".

This formulation's power of survival came from the qualification that provided needed flexibility:

"* * * subject however to such alterations and additions as the said courts respectively shall in their discretion deem expedient, or to such regulations as the supreme court of the United States shall think proper from time to time by rule to prescribe to any circuit or district court concerning the same".

The Supreme Court's rulemaking power was affirmed, in language that swept beyond the confines of equity (and admiralty) and extended to "suits at common law", in § 6 of the Act of August 23, 1842, 5 Stat. 516, 518. See also Rev.Stat. §§ 913, 917, 918 (1878).

The Supreme Court first exercised its power to prescribe rules for lower federal courts in 1822 when it promulgated thirty-three Equity Rules. 20 U.S. (7 Wheat.) xvii. Twenty years later these were replaced with ninety-two rules. 42 U.S. (1 How.) xli. Neither the 1822 nor the 1842 rules, however, were comprehensive codes. They assumed the existence of traditional chancery practice, and undertook only *ad hoc* modification or clarification of points of detail. The 1842 rules nevertheless lasted for seventy years, long after they had become archaic.

At length the Supreme Court undertook a comprehensive revision; the Equity Rules of 1912, effective February 1, 1913 (226 U.S. 627), worked a major reform. Three years later, Congress took a hand in the Law and Equity Act of 1915, 38 Stat. 956, making equitable defenses available in actions at law and providing for the transfer of cases brought on the wrong side of the court.

B. Admiralty

In many respects, the story in admiralty parallels that in equity.

Admiralty was thought of in 1789 as a distinct body of law, quasi-international in character. This traditional corpus comprised not only distinctive principles of liability and distinctive remedies but a distinctive practice. From the beginning the principle of federal uniformity both in substance and procedure was unquestioned.

Nonetheless, state law had played a significant role in relation to admiralty by virtue of the famous provision in § 9 of the First Judiciary Act (1 Stat. 73, 76) conferring on the district courts "exclusive original cognizance of all civil causes of admiralty and maritime jurisdiction", while "saving to suitors, in all cases, the right of a common law remedy, where the common law is competent to give it". The saving clause preserved remedies in the state courts and on the law side of the federal courts. But it did not affect the federal character of proceedings on the admiralty side of the federal courts.

The first Congress provided, 1 Stat. 93, 94, that in admiralty the forms and modes of proceedings "shall be according to the course of the civil law", and the second Congress provided that they should be "according to the principles, rules and usages which belong * * * to courts of admiralty * * *, as contradistinguished from courts of common law". Given content by exercise of the same rulemaking powers that applied in equity, this formulation survived until 1948, when it was swallowed entirely by the general rulemaking authorizations in 28 U.S.C. §§ 2071 and 2073.[4]

For more than half a century after the 1792 act, the Supreme Court left rulemaking in admiralty to the district courts, and divergent practices developed. Spurred apparently by the reaffirmation of its rulemaking authority in § 6 of the Act of August 23, 1842, *supra,* the Court in 1844 promulgated forty-seven "Rules of Practice of the Courts of the United States in Causes of Admiralty and Maritime Jurisdiction on the Instance Side of the Court" (44 U.S. (3 How.) ix). Like the first Equity Rules, the Admiralty Rules, while introducing certain simplifications, presupposed a traditional framework of practice.

The 1844 rules remained in effect, with rather frequent amendments, until they were superseded in 1921 (254 U.S. 671). The 1921 rules, in turn, were frequently amended until in 1966 admiralty procedure was merged with civil procedure, 383 U.S. 1029. The Federal Rules of Civil Procedure now apply in admiralty, but there are a number of special provisions and "supplemental rules for certain admiralty and maritime claims".[5] An Advisory Committee on Admiralty Rules, created in 1960, did not complete its work until 1971.

C. Bankruptcy

Congress has power under the Constitution to pass "uniform laws on the subject of Bankruptcies throughout the United States". In view of this constitutional requirement of uniformity and the absence of any applicable state court procedure, the need for a uniform federal procedure has been unquestioned. The need has been met, as in equity and admiralty, by authorizing the Supreme Court to promulgate general rules. 28 U.S.C. § 2075.

Within five months of the enactment of the Bankruptcy Act of July 1, 1898 (30 Stat. 544), the Court adopted the first "General Orders and Forms in Bankruptcy" (172 U.S. 653). These rules were completely revised in 1939 (305 U.S. 677) following enactment of the Chandler Act of 1938 (52 Stat. 840), and new rules were once again promulgated in the 1970s as a result of the work of the Advisory Committee on Bankruptcy Rules.

In 1978, Congress enacted a comprehensive statute (92 Stat. 2549), which codified bankruptcy law under Title 11 of the U.S. Code. At that time, Congress provided that existing bankruptcy rules, to the extent not inconsistent with the new law, were to remain effective until "repealed or superseded" by new rules. 11 U.S.C. § 405(d).

---

4. In 1966, the general Enabling Act provision, § 2072, was extended to admiralty, and § 2073 was repealed. (The present version of § 2073, discussed below, deals with other matters.)

5. See Fed.Rules 9(h), 14(a), 14(c), 38(e), 82, and Supplemental Rules A–F. Fed. Rule 81(a)(1) provides that the civil rules do not apply to prize proceedings governed by 10 U.S.C. §§ 7651–81.

The judges of the bankruptcy courts established by this act were to be appointed for fourteen year terms. They thus lacked life tenure, as well as other protections guaranteed to federal judges appointed under Article III. The act's broad grant of jurisdiction to these judges was held to violate Article III in Northern Pipeline Const. Co. v. Marathon Pipe Line Co., 458 U.S. 50 (1982), see p. 399, *supra*.

After a period of uncertainty in which the district courts (on recommendation of the Administrative Office) adopted stopgap rules, Congress made a number of substantive and procedural changes in the bankruptcy laws as part of the Bankruptcy Amendments and Federal Judgeship Act of 1984. See p. 421, *supra*. In 1985, an Advisory Committee proposed extensive amendments to the bankruptcy rules to conform to those statutory changes and for other purposes (107 F.R.D. 403 (1985)), and in March 1987, the Supreme Court ordered that amendments based on those proposals would become effective on August 1 (114 F.R.D. 193 (1987)). Since then, a number of further changes in the rules have taken effect.[6]

D. Criminal Prosecutions

Before adoption of the Rules of Criminal Procedure, federal criminal practice was a hodgepodge of judicial elaboration, common law rules, constitutional provisions, and *ad hoc* legislation. Though primarily uniform, the practice was interspersed with references to state law, called for by specific statutory direction or judicial interpretation.

Congress' first move to bring order out of this wilderness was restricted to proceedings after verdict. The Supreme Court was authorized to prescribe rules as to such proceedings by the Act of February 24, 1933, 47 Stat. 904, as amended by the Act of March 8, 1934, 48 Stat. 399. (See 18 U.S.C. § 3772.) The Court issued the first rules in 1934. 292 U.S. 661.

In the Act of June 29, 1940, 54 Stat. 688, Congress enlarged the Court's authority to include the prescription of rules of procedure for criminal proceedings prior to and including verdict. See 18 U.S.C. § 3771. The Court exercised this authority in 1944, Justices Black and Frankfurter withholding approval of the decision. 323 U.S. 821.[7]

The Rules of Criminal Procedure, which became effective on March 21, 1946, merged the 1934 post-verdict rules with the new rules. 327 U.S. 821 (1946). Since then, the rules have been amended on a number of occasions. As the pace of rulemaking has increased and the subjects of rulemaking have become more controversial, Congress has become more deeply enmeshed in the

---

6. The Bankruptcy Reform Act of 1994, Pub.L. No. 103–394, 108 Stat. 4106, made a number of changes in the powers of bankruptcy courts and in the options available to those seeking appellate review. (See p. 435, *supra*.) In addition, the Act amended the provision authorizing the promulgation of rules of evidence (discussed in Paragraph E(6), *infra*) to include rules applicable in bankruptcy proceedings.

7. Justice Black stated without explanation that he did not approve of the adoption of the rules. Justice Frankfurter objected not to the rules on their merits but to the remoteness of the Supreme Court from the day-to-day problems of the district courts, to the undesirability of appearing to prejudge questions that might come before the Court in litigation, and to the heavy burden that the Court was assuming in taking responsibility for the rules.

process, not infrequently modifying, postponing, or disapproving particular rules.[8]

The Supreme Court has also promulgated (in addition to the criminal rules) rules governing habeas corpus and other collateral proceedings under 28 U.S.C. §§ 2254 and 2255—which became effective, with changes by Congress, in 1977, see pp. 1348, 1442, 1467, *infra*—as well as rules for the trial of misdemeanors before United States magistrates. (The latter are authorized by 18 U.S.C. § 3402. See 445 U.S. 975 (1980)). The Federal Rules of Evidence, discussed in Part F, below, apply to criminal as well as civil cases.

E. Actions at Law Before Merger

(1) Section 34 of the Judiciary Act of 1789 (the Rules of Decision Act) blocked out a wide area for the application of state law in actions at law in federal courts but left uncertain whether this area included procedure. But the Process Act immediately following it (Act of Sept. 29, 1789) was unequivocal:

"That until further provision shall be made, and except where by this act or other statutes of the United States is otherwise provided, the forms of writs and executions, except their style, and modes of process and rates of fees, except fees to judges, in the circuit and district courts, in suits at common law, shall be the same in each state respectively as are now used or allowed in the supreme courts of the same."

The Act of May 8, 1792, reaffirmed this provision but made it subject to the same rulemaking power, both in the Supreme Court and the lower courts, that applied in equity and admiralty. See also the Act of March 2, 1793, § 7, 1 Stat. 333, 335, note 2, *supra*.

(2) The peculiarities of the conformity exacted by these provisions did not at once meet the eye. It was a static conformity. And, except for the rulemaking power, the provisions had no application to federal courts sitting in states that entered the union after 1789. As time passed, state procedure changed (notably, in many states, in favor of debtors). In Wayman v. Southard, 23 U.S. (10 Wheat.) 1 (1825), the Court was confronted with the question whether a federal court sitting in Kentucky should apply a Kentucky statute requiring a judgment plaintiff either to accept Kentucky bank notes in payment of the judgment or else to take a replevin bond from the defendant for the debt. The case evoked a notable, and notably difficult, constitutional opinion and projected the problem of the law governing federal procedure into the forefront of national politics.

The Court decided, in an opinion by Chief Justice Marshall, that the procedure on executions in the federal courts, as well as the procedure before judgment, was governed by the Process Act of 1792, which continued the Process Act of 1789. These acts adopted the state law "as it existed in September, 1789, * * * not as it might afterwards be made" (p. 32).

The Court recognized that the Rules of Decision Act, by contrast, called for a dynamic rather than a static conformity. But it rejected the claim that the section applied to executions. The Court also rejected the alternative suggestion that Congress lacked power to regulate executions on federal court judgments, and that state laws were independently operative (pp. 21–22):

8. See, *e.g.*, Pub.L. No. 93–361, 88 Stat. 397 (1974); Pub.L. No. 94–64, 89 Stat. 370 (1975); Pub.L. No. 94–349, 90 Stat. 822 (1976); Pub.L. No. 95–78, 91 Stat. 319 (1977); Pub.L. No. 96–42, 93 Stat. 326 (1979).

"'* * * The court cannot accede to this novel construction. The constitution concludes its enumeration of granted powers, with a clause authorizing congress to make all laws which shall be necessary and proper for carrying into execution the foregoing powers, and all other powers vested by this constitution in the government of the United States, or in any department or officer thereof. The judicial department is invested with jurisdiction in certain specified cases, in all which it has power to render judgment. That a power to make laws for carrying into execution all the judgments which the judicial department has power to pronounce, is expressly conferred by this clause, seems to be one of those plain propositions which reasoning cannot render plainer."

Had this been all, no question need have arisen as to the propriety of Congress' exercising this power by providing that the federal courts should follow current state procedure as it existed from time to time. But the Court recognized that its holding that the process acts were applicable involved the conclusion that the matters in issue could be regulated by rule of court. Then, in a pioneering discussion of delegation of legislative power, it went out of its way to consider and sustain the validity of this rulemaking authority (pp. 49–50):

"That the power claimed for the state is not given by the 34th section of the judiciary act, has been fully stated in the preceding part of this opinion. That it has not an independent existence in the state legislatures, is, we think, one of those political axioms, an attempt to demonstrate which, would be a waste of argument, not to be excused * * *. Its utter inadmissibility will at once present itself to the mind, if we imagine an act of a state legislature for the direct and sole purpose of regulating proceedings in the courts of the Union, or of their officers in executing their judgments. No gentleman, we believe, will be so extravagant as to maintain the efficacy of such an act. It seems not much less extravagant, to maintain, that the practice of the federal courts, and the conduct of their officers, can be indirectly regulated by the state legislatures, by an act professing to regulate the proceedings of the state courts, and the conduct of the officers who execute the process of those courts. It is a general rule, that what cannot be done directly, from defect of power, cannot be done indirectly. The right of congress to delegate to the courts the power of altering the modes (established by the process act) of proceedings in suits, has been already stated; but, were it otherwise, we are well satisfied that the state legislatures do not possess that power."

Marshall's result was politically unacceptable, and Congress overrode it. In apparent deference to his reasoning, however, it provided not for dynamic conformity but for static conformity brought, in part, up to date. The Process Act of May 19, 1828, 4 Stat. 278, required federal courts to follow, on writs of execution and other final process issued on judgments, the procedure of the state courts in force on the day the act became effective. State procedure in force on the same date was also made the rule for proceedings before judgment in federal courts sitting in states admitted after 1789. But for the original states the 1789 procedure remained the rule. Later legislation made parallel provision for states admitted after 1828. See, *e.g.*, the Act of Aug. 1, 1842, 5 Stat. 499.

Both the Supreme Court and the lower courts retained their rulemaking authority throughout the period of static conformity; the authority, indeed, was reiterated with fresh emphasis in the Act of Aug. 23, 1842, p. 658, *supra*. But the courts were reluctant to use the power. The adoption of the Field

Code by New York in 1848 and the spread of the code system to other states complicated the problem, and the situation became increasingly unsatisfactory.

(3) At length, in the Conformity Act of June 1, 1872, 17 Stat. 196, Congress withdrew the unused rulemaking authority, and adopted, with qualifications, the principle of dynamic conformity. Section 5 of the Act provided:

"That the practice, pleadings, and forms and modes of proceeding, in other than equity and admiralty causes in the circuit and district courts of the United States shall conform, as near as may be, to the practice, pleadings, and forms and modes of proceeding existing at the time in like causes in the courts of record of the State within which such circuit or district courts are held, any rule of court to the contrary notwithstanding: *Provided, however,* That nothing herein contained shall alter the rules of evidence under the laws of the United States, and as practiced in the courts thereof."

The Conformity Act eliminated the anachronism of federal adherence to no-longer-existent state practice. On more matters than not a lawyer in a federal court in a particular state could now follow the procedure currently prevailing in the courts of that state—an advantage particularly appreciated in the code states. But this conformity was confined to actions at law, and even as to such actions, exceptions and qualifications soon appeared.

The earlier process acts, in addition, had been held not to affect "jurisdiction", and the Conformity Act was similarly construed. See, *e.g.*, Davenport v. County of Dodge, 105 U.S. 237 (1881)(holding inapplicable a state statute permitting mandamus as an original proceeding). Finally, even when the Act plainly applied, its terms required the federal courts to conform to state procedure only "as near as may be", a phrase that opened a wide door for adherence to distinctive federal practices. See generally Clark & Moore, *A New Federal Civil Procedure,* 44 Yale L.J. 387, 401–11 (1935).

Partly in reliance on this latter phrase and partly by a restrictive interpretation of the three categories of "practice, pleadings, and forms and modes of proceedings", the Court withdrew from the operation of the Act a wide area of particularly important matters affecting the administration of federal justice. See, *e.g.*, McDonald v. Pless, 238 U.S. 264 (1915)(approving a ruling of the district court, on a motion to set aside a verdict as having been reached by compromise, refusing to permit one of the jurors to testify about proceedings in the jury room, and concluding that state practice on the question was not controlling). See also Herron v. Southern Pacific Co., 283 U.S. 91 (1931), p. 719, *infra*.

F. The Enabling Act, Merger, and Beyond

(1) The movement to reform federal procedure was prompted partly by the need to dispel the confusion created by the uneasy co-existence of several systems of procedure in the same forum. It was also motivated by the conviction that effective reform could be achieved only through the device of nationwide court rules, drafted with the assistance of bench and bar. Conformity, it was hoped, would not have to be sacrificed, if the states could be induced to copy the federal model. See generally Sunderland, *The Grant of Rule-Making Power to the Supreme Court of the United States,* 32 Mich.L.Rev. 1116 (1934).[9]

---

9. Virtually every state has been influenced by the federal model, and many have followed that model quite closely. See Wright, Federal Courts § 62, at 430 (5th ed. 1994).

The bill that became the Act of June 19, 1934 (now principally contained in 28 U.S.C. § 2072), had little legislative history of its own, but was preceded by several decades of debate and proposals for reform.[10] On March 1, 1934, Attorney General Cummings wrote identical letters to the chairmen of the House and Senate Judiciary Committees, as follows:

"I enclose herewith a draft of a bill to empower the Supreme Court of the United States to prescribe rules to govern the practice and procedure in civil actions at law in the District Courts of the United States and the courts of the District of Columbia. The enactment of the bill would bring about uniformity and simplicity in the practice in actions at law in Federal courts and thus relieve the courts and the bar of controversies and difficulties which are continually arising wholly apart from the merits of the litigation in which they are interested. It seems to me that there can be no substantial objection to the result, which, apart from its inherent merit, would also, it is believed, contribute to a reduction in the cost of litigation in the Federal courts.

"I request that you introduce the enclosed bill and hope that you may be able to give it your support."

In both House and Senate, the favorable committee reports were brief, see S.Rep. No. 1048, H.R.Rep. No. 1829, 73d Cong., 2d Sess. (1934), and the discussion in the two Houses consumed only a few minutes each. In each House, the floor manager paraphrased the Attorney General's letter and claimed the unanimous support of bar associations. In each, the objection that lawyers would have to learn two systems of practice was made by one member but was quickly withdrawn, and the bill was passed by unanimous consent. 78 Cong.Rec. 9362–63 (Senate); *id.* 10866 (House).[11]

(2) Under the leadership of Chief Justice Hughes, the Court made vigorous and effective use of the new power. On June 3, 1935, a distinguished Advisory Committee was appointed to draw up proposed rules. 295 U.S. 774. The Committee's proposals were subjected to considerable scrutiny and criticism, through the medium, among others, of special committees of the bench and bar established in the various circuits and districts. With minor changes, the final

---

10. For an exhaustive and informative study of the pre–1934 efforts at reform, with special emphasis on the period 1912–1930, see Burbank, *The Rules Enabling Act of 1934,* 130 U.Pa.L.Rev. 1015, 1035–98 (1982).

11. The Act provided as follows:

"That the Supreme Court of the United States shall have the power to prescribe, by general rules, for the district courts of the United States and for the courts of the District of Columbia, the forms of process, writs, pleadings, and motions, and the practice and procedure in civil actions at law. Said rules shall neither abridge, enlarge, nor modify the substantive rights of any litigant. They shall take effect six months after their promulgation, and thereafter all laws in conflict

therewith shall be of no further force or effect.

"SEC. 2. The court may at any time unite the general rules prescribed by it for cases in equity with those in actions at law so as to secure one form of civil action and procedure for both: *Provided, however,* That in such union of rules the right of trial by jury as at common law and declared by the seventh amendment to the Constitution shall be preserved to the parties inviolate. Such united rules shall not take effect until they shall have been reported to Congress by the Attorney General at the beginning of a regular session thereof and until after the close of such session." Act of June 19, 1934, 48 Stat. 1064.

proposals were approved by the Court, and the rules became effective September 16, 1938. See 308 U.S. 645–766.[12]

In 1958, in an amendment to 28 U.S.C. § 331, Congress instructed the Judicial Conference of the United States to "carry on a continuous study of the operation and effect of the general rules of practice and procedure now or hereafter in use as prescribed by the Supreme Court for the other courts of the United States pursuant to law. Such changes in and additions to those rules as the Conference may deem desirable * * * shall be recommended by the Conference from time to time to the Supreme Court for its consideration and adoption, modification or rejection, in accordance with law."

Pursuant to this provision, a Standing Committee of the Judicial Conference on Rules of Practice and Procedure was established in 1960, together with five Advisory Committees. The task of an Advisory Committee is to draft proposals, solicit public comment on them, and submit a report to the Standing Committee. The Standing Committee in turn reports to the Conference, which makes its recommendations to the Supreme Court.[13]

(3) In 1965, a sixth Advisory Committee, on Rules of Evidence, was appointed, and after several drafts were submitted for public comment, see 46 F.R.D. 161 (1969); 51 F.R.D. 315 (1971), the Supreme Court transmitted the Federal Rules of Evidence to Congress in November 1972. 56 F.R.D. 183 (1972). Justice Douglas, dissenting, argued that rules of evidence did not fall within the scope of authority delegated by Congress, that the Court had had little to do with drafting the rules, and that it was "so far removed from the trial arena that we have no special insight, no meaningful oversight to contribute" (p. 185).

Almost immediately, congressional opposition to the proposed rules surfaced, centering both on the content of certain rules and on the question whether the Court was empowered by the Rules Enabling Act to promulgate rules of evidence at all.[14] This opposition culminated in an enactment staying the effectiveness of the proposed rules until they should be affirmatively approved by Congress. Pub.L. No. 93–12, 87 Stat. 9 (1973). Following this resolution, Congress redrafted the rules, leaving much of the original Court text substantially unchanged, but making significant modifications, *inter alia*, in the rules relating to privileges and presumptions. Finally, the Federal Rules

---

12. For an extensive review of previously ignored materials relating to the work of the original Advisory Committee, see Burbank, note 10, *supra*, at 1131–84.

13. The results of the work of the Advisory Committees on the Admiralty, Bankruptcy, Criminal, and Appellate Rules have already been noted. (28 U.S.C. § 2072 was amended in 1966 to refer expressly to the power to make rules for all matters in the courts of appeals. At the same time, § 2073, dealing specifically with admiralty and maritime cases, and § 2074, relating to review of Tax Court decisions, were repealed.)

For discussion of the major changes in the Civil Rules adopted through 1980, see *Appendix A to the Report of the Standing Committee on Rules of Practice and Proce-*dure, 85 F.R.D. 538 (1980); *Advisory Committee's Explanatory Statement Concerning Amendments of the Discovery Rules,* 48 F.R.D. 487 (1970); Kaplan, *Continuing Work of the Civil Committee: 1966 Amendments of the Federal Rules of Civil Procedure,* 81 Harv.L.Rev. 356, 591 (1967, 1968); Kaplan, *Amendments of the Federal Rules of Civil Procedure, 1961–63,* 77 Harv.L.Rev. 601, 801 (1964).

14. Professor Burbank has concluded, on the basis of his study of pre–1934 materials, that rules relating to the admissibility of evidence—as distinguished from rules relating to the mode of taking and obtaining evidence—lie outside the scope of the 1934 Enabling Act. See Burbank, note 10, *supra*, at 1129–30, 1137–43.

of Evidence were enacted in statutory form, to become effective on July 1, 1975. Pub.L. No. 93–595, 88 Stat. 1926 (1975).[15]

The same statute contained a new "Enabling Act" to govern amendments to the rules of evidence. In 28 U.S.C. § 2076, the time allowed for congressional review of Supreme Court amendments to those rules was extended from the ninety days of § 2072 (the general Enabling Act) to one hundred eighty days, and a provision allowing *either* House of Congress to disapprove or defer a Supreme Court amendment was adopted. Moreover, amendments affecting privileges were not to be effective without approval by act of Congress.

For contemporary comment on, and criticism of, the balance struck by Congress in this area, see, *e.g.,* Moore & Bendix, *Congress, Evidence and Rulemaking,* 84 Yale L.J. 9 (1974). For a harsh appraisal of Congress' action in 1994 dealing with specific rules of evidence in sex abuse cases, see Duane, *The New Federal Rules of Evidence on Prior Acts of Accused Sex Offenders: A Poorly Drafted Version of a Very Bad Idea,* 157 F.R.D. 95 (1994).

(5) The concept of the "one-House veto" was successfully challenged In INS v. Chadha, 462 U.S. 919 (1983). In that case, the Supreme Court invalidated a section of the Immigration and Nationality Act, 8 U.S.C. § 244(c)(2), which provided that a decision by the Attorney General to suspend deportation of an alien could be nullified by a resolution of either House of Congress. Such nullification, the Court held, was legislative in character and thus under the Constitution could not take effect without the concurrence of both Houses and presentment to the President. (The Court further held that § 244(c)(2) was severable from the other provisions of the statute, and thus the Attorney General's statutory authority to suspend deportation remained intact.)

In the wake of Chadha, it seemed clear that the provision of the Rules of Evidence Enabling Act, 28 U.S.C. § 2076, which authorized either House to reject Supreme Court amendments to those rules, could not survive. Undoubtedly as a result of that decision, Congress, in amending the Enabling Acts in 1988, repealed § 2076, consolidated the rulemaking power with respect to civil procedure and evidence in § 2072, and in the process discarded the legislative veto provision formerly attached to § 2076.[16]

What of the provision (now appearing in § 2074(a)) that no changes in the rules shall go into effect until they have been reported to Congress and until the expiration of a specified period? Since this provision in terms requires only a report of any rule changes to Congress, and since Congress itself plainly cannot take action with respect to those changes without the concurrence of both Houses and presentment to the President, the Chadha decision would not appear to put the provision in jeopardy.

(6) The pace of rulemaking in all areas has increased dramatically in recent years. But at the same time, criticism of the process and the product has also increased, and Congress' responses to these criticisms have in turn generated their own critiques.

---

15. Several of the rules of evidence refer to state law in cases in which state law supplies the rule of decision. See Rule 302 (presumptions); Rule 501 (privileges); Rule 601 (competency of witnesses).

16. In § 2074(b), however, Congress preserved the provision (formerly in § 2076) that any revision of the rules governing evidentiary privilege shall have no force unless approved by an Act of Congress.

(a) From the beginning, a number of Supreme Court Justices have been skeptical, or disapproving, of their role in the process. The disagreements of Justices Black and Frankfurter with the promulgation of criminal rules, and of Justice Douglas with the rules of evidence, have already been mentioned. In 1938, Justice Brandeis stated without explanation that he did not approve of the adoption of the original civil rules. See 308 U.S. at 649. And Justices Black and Douglas together on several occasions voiced objection to the rule-making process, both in general and as applied. See, *e.g.*, 368 U.S. 1012 (1961); 374 U.S. 865 (1963); 383 U.S. 1032 (1966); 383 U.S. 1089 (1966); 398 U.S. 979 (1970); 401 U.S. 1019 (1971).

Similar objections were expressed by the Court itself in promulgating changes in the civil, criminal, appellate, and evidence rules in April 1993. (Some of these rules, especially as they related to lawyer discipline for filing or pursuing matters thought to be frivolous and to radical changes in the rules governing discovery, were significant and controversial.) Each of the transmittal letters to Congress, signed by the Chief Justice "[b]y direction of the Supreme Court", stated: "While the Court is satisfied that the required procedures [pursuant to 28 U.S.C. § 2072] have been observed, this transmittal does not necessarily indicate that the Court itself would have proposed these amendments in the form submitted." See, *e.g.*, 113 S.Ct. (Advance Sheet No. 15) CCII (1993). A separate statement of Justice White noted that "[s]ome of us * * * have silently shared Justice Black's and Justice Douglas' suggestion that the enabling statutes be amended". Justice White added that if the rulemaking process were not changed, he believed the Court's role was "to transmit the Judicial Conference's recommendations without change and without careful study, as long as there is no suggestion that the committee system has not operated with integrity"—even though on several occasions he had had "serious questions about the wisdom of particular proposals to amend certain rules." 113 S.Ct. (Advance Sheet No. 15) at CCCII, CCCIV (1993).

(b) Other criticisms of the process stressed the claimed inadequacy of public notice and participation and urged that the process be made more open. See, *e.g.*, Weinstein, Reform of Court Rule–Making Procedures (1977); Lesnick, *The Federal Rule–Making Process: A Time for Reexamination,* 61 A.B.A.J. 579 (1975); Hazard, *Undemocratic Legislation,* 87 Yale L.J. 1284 (1978)(reviewing Judge Weinstein's book).

(c) As a corollary to the lack of openness, some have faulted the predominance of judges in the rulemaking process, or have noted that those practitioners who are given a role tend to constitute a section of the bar more likely to represent the "haves" than the "have-nots." See, *e.g.*, Macey, *Judicial Preferences, Public Choice, and the Rules of Procedure,* 23 J.Leg.Stud. 627 (1994)(arguing that judges engaged in rulemaking will try to serve their own self-interest in a variety of ways).

(d) Still others have decried the lack of adequate empirical investigation, or cost-benefit analysis, as a basis for proposed rule changes, especially those of more than technical significance. One of the leaders of this group has been Laurens Walker who, in a series of articles, has proposed various techniques for avoiding changes that result in undue surprise or unintended consequences. See, *e.g.*, *Perfecting Federal Civil Rules: A Proposal for Restricted Field Experiments,* 51 L. & Cont.Probs. 67 (Summer 1988); *A Compromise Reform for Federal Civil Rulemaking,* 61 G.W.L.Rev. 455 (1993); *Avoiding Surprise*

From Civil Rulemaking: The Role of Economic Analysis, 23 J.Leg.Stud. 569 (1994).[17]

(e) Other criticisms of the federal rules as they were originally developed and have evolved include (1) a growing skepticism about "trans-substantive" rules that prescribe a uniform procedure for the entire range of cases (especially civil), even though that range covers an enormous variety of disputes, large and small, significant and trivial; (2) insistence on the need for open acknowledgment that the rulemaking process cannot be "neutral" and is necessarily political in its implications; and (3) a concern that many rules (such as those dealing with class actions and lawyer misconduct) have transgressed the limits imposed by the Enabling Acts. For discussion and appraisal, see the Symposium on Rulemaking in 59 B'klyn L.Rev. No. 3 (1993), especially (on the first two of the criticisms) articles by Marcus, *Of Babies and Bathwater* (p. 761), and Burbank, *Ignorance and Procedural Law Reform: A Call for a Moratorium* (p. 841).

(7) Some of these criticisms have led to proposals for legislative change, and Congress has responded to these proposals on several occasions.

(a) The 1988 amendments to the Enabling Acts (see 28 U.S.C. §§ 2071–2077) not only consolidated the rulemaking power with respect to civil procedure and evidence, see Paragraph (5), *supra,* but also specified procedures to be followed by the Judicial Conference and its committees (including the holding of open meetings by committees); provided mechanisms for the modification and abrogation of district and appellate court rules; and required notice and opportunity for comment as part of the rulemaking processes of the district and appellate courts. The new openness, while generally praised, has led some to question whether the broadening of participation may increase the politicization of the process. See, e.g., Mullenix, *Hope Over Experience: Mandatory Informal Discovery and the Politics of Rulemaking*, 69 N.C.L.Rev. 796 (1991).

(b) In 1990, Congress enacted the Civil Justice Reform Act (CJRA), codified as amended at 28 U.S.C. §§ 471–482. This Act requires every federal district to create an advisory group (which is to include attorneys and representatives of major categories of litigants) to assess the causes of "cost and delay" in civil litigation and to come up with recommendations based at least in part on assessment of certain specified factors. Each district must then adopt a plan, addressed to these problems, that will be reviewed by the Judicial Conference and evaluated annually. (Some districts were required to expedite adoption of their plans and to include certain principles in those plans.) The Judicial Conference is to report to Congress by the end of 1995, and the Act itself contains a 1997 sunset provision.[18]

The CJRA has resulted in the adoption and implementation of a variety of plans for reducing cost and delay, many of which focus on such matters as early

17. In a related criticism, Professor Mullenix has argued that the drafters of the Civil Justice Reform Act (discussed in Paragraph 7(b), *infra*) not only failed to undertake any empirical studies of their own but ignored existing and persuasive empirical evidence that cast serious doubt on many of the drafters' assumptions. See Mullenix, *Discovery in Disarray: The Pervasive Myth of Pervasive Discovery Abuse and the Consequences for Unfounded Rulemaking*, 46 Stan.L.Rev. 1393 (1994).

18. *Cf.* The Judicial Amendments Act of 1994, Pub.L.No. 103–420, 108 Stat. 4343, which, *inter alia,* extended the deadline for completion of certain congressionally authorized experiments and studies relating to judicial administration. The Act is discussed in Sanner & Tobias, *The Judicial Amendments Act of 1994,* 159 F.R.D. 649 (1995).

control and scheduling by judges and/or magistrate judges, mandatory or optional use of alternative dispute resolution techniques (such as mediation or non-binding arbitration), and other devices for encouraging settlement or expedition. See *Reformers Tout ADR Programs,* A.B.A.J. 28 (Aug. 1994).

At the same time, the Act has generated criticism on such grounds as the serious threat to uniformity (beyond that already inherent in the widespread adoption of local rules) that is posed by the almost inevitable "Balkanization" of procedures resulting from its provisions, at least on a temporary basis;[19] the appropriateness and even the constitutionality of such a high level of congressional involvement in procedural matters; the confusion surrounding the relationship between the CJRA and the Enabling Act; and the claim that the Act may constitute both a solution in search of a problem and an overemphasis of the evils of "delay" considered in isolation from other procedural values. For fuller discussion, see the Symposia in 46 Mercer L.Rev. No. 2 (1995), 67 St. Johns L.Rev. No. 4 (1993), and 46 Stan.L.Rev. No. 6 (1994); Tobias, *Civil Justice Reform and the Balkanization of Federal Civil Procedure,* 24 Ariz.St. L.J. 1393 (1992); Johnston, *Civil Justice Reform: Juggling Between Politics and Perfection,* 62 Ford.L.Rev. 833 (1994); Wesely, *The Civil Justice Reform Act; The Rules Enabling Act; The Amended Federal Rules of Civil Procedure; CJRA Plans; Rule 83–What Trumps What?,* 154 F.R.D. 563 (1994); and several articles by Mullenix, including: *The Counter–Reformation in Procedural Justice,* 77 Minn.L.Rev. 375 (1992), and *Unconstitutional Rulemaking: The Civil Justice Reform Act and Separation of Powers,* 77 Minn.L.Rev. 1283 (1993).[20]

Although many of these criticisms raise serious questions about the wisdom and soundness of the CJRA, the argument that Congress has overstepped constitutional bounds seems a good deal weaker. Professor Mullenix, in making this argument, relies heavily on the inconsistency between the CJRA and the Enabling Act, an inconsistency that is far from clear. In any event, it is difficult to see what constitutional obstacle precludes Congress from modifying the Enabling Act or repealing it altogether. The ability of Congress to legislate procedural change for the federal courts has never been seriously doubted, and whether or not each court must retain a certain modicum of ability to make decisions relevant to its internal affairs, the CJRA does not threaten that ability; indeed, if anything, it appears to vest in the district courts (at least temporarily) certain powers that the Enabling Act delegated in large part to a higher court.[21]

---

19. As noted at pp. 656–57, note 1, *supra,* the new discovery rules explicitly allow individual districts to opt out of some of their requirements—a grant of authority that was designed to reconcile the new rules with the provisions of the CJRA and that has been exercised by a very large number of districts. See 8 Wright, Miller & Marcus, Federal Practice and Procedure (1995 Supp.). Because the CJRA itself has a "sunset" provision, however, attention is already being given to efforts to restore a greater measure of uniformity after the period of district experimentation has run.

20. For the views of a former reporter for the Civil Rules Committee on the range of issues raised by the current rulemaking process, see Carrington, *Learning From the Rule 26 Brouhaha: Our Courts Need Real Friends,* 156 F.R.D. 295 (1994).

21. Professor Mullenix also relies on a New Jersey decision, Winberry v. Salisbury, a decision (discussed in the next section at p. 674, *infra*) that turns on a provision of the New Jersey constitution expressly granting

Sibbach v. Wilson & Co., Inc.

312 U.S. 1, 61 S.Ct. 422, 85 L.Ed. 479 (1940).
Certiorari to the Circuit Court of Appeals for the Seventh Circuit.

■ MR. JUSTICE ROBERTS delivered the opinion of the Court.

This case calls for decision as to the validity of Rules 35 and 37 of the Rules of Civil Procedure for District Courts of the United States.

In an action brought by the petitioner in the District Court for Northern Illinois to recover damages for bodily injuries, inflicted in Indiana, respondent answered denying the allegations of the complaint, and moved for an order requiring the petitioner to submit to a physical examination by one or more physicians appointed by the court to determine the nature and extent of her injuries. The court ordered that the petitioner submit to such an examination by a physician so appointed.

Compliance having been refused, the respondent obtained an order to show cause why the petitioner should not be punished for contempt. In response the petitioner challenged the authority of the court to order her to submit to the examination, asserting that the order was void. It appeared that the courts of Indiana, the state where the cause of action arose, hold such an order proper, whereas the courts of Illinois, the state in which the trial court sat, hold that such an order cannot be made. Neither state has any statute governing the matter.

The court adjudged the petitioner guilty of contempt, and directed that she be committed until she should obey the order for examination or otherwise should be legally discharged from custody. The petitioner appealed.

The Circuit Court of Appeals decided that Rule 35, which authorizes an order for a physical examination in such a case, is valid, and affirmed the judgment. The writ of certiorari was granted because of the importance of the question involved.   * * * [The opinion here quotes from the act authorizing the Rules of Civil Procedure, and from the then-existing versions of Rules 35(a) and 37(b).]

The contention of the petitioner, in final analysis, is that Rules 35 and 37 are not within the mandate of Congress to this court. This is the limit of permissible debate, since argument touching the broader questions of Congressional power and of the obligation of federal courts to apply the substantive law of a state is foreclosed.

rulemaking power to the courts. No such provision exists in the U.S. Constitution, and in any event, the Winberry decision has been severely criticized in its own right. See also Crocker v. First Hudson Associates, 569 F.Supp. 97, 102 (D.N.J.1983)(noting that in no reported case had the New Jersey court applied the Winberry "dictum" to a statute enacted following the promulgation of a court rule).

In Heckers v. Fowler, 69 U.S. (2 Wall.) 123 (1864)(the other case relied on by Profes-

sor Mullenix), the Supreme Court simply quoted the relevant statute conferring on the federal circuits the right to promulgate rules not inconsistent with federal law.

As this edition went to press, the debate over the constitutional issue intensified. Compare Redish, *Federal Judicial Independence: Constitutional and Political Perpectives,* 46 Mercer L.Rev. 697 (1995) with Mullenix, *Judicial Power and the Rules Enabling Act, id.* at 733.

Congress has undoubted power to regulate the practice and procedure of federal courts,[6] and may exercise that power by delegating to this or other federal courts authority to make rules not inconsistent with the statutes or Constitution of the United States; but it has never essayed to declare the substantive state law, or to abolish or nullify a right recognized by the substantive law of the state where the cause of action arose, save where a right or duty is imposed in a field committed to Congress by the Constitution. On the contrary it has enacted that the state law shall be the rule of decision in the federal courts.

Hence we conclude that the Act of June 19, 1934, was purposely restricted in its operation to matters of pleading and court practice and procedure. Its two provisos or caveats emphasize this restriction. The first is that the court shall not "abridge, enlarge, nor modify the substantive rights", in the guise of regulating procedure. The second is that if the rules are to prescribe a single form of action for cases at law and suits in equity, the constitutional right to jury trial inherent in the former must be preserved. There are other limitations upon the authority to prescribe rules which might have been, but were not mentioned in the Act; for instance, the inability of a court, by rule, to extend or restrict the jurisdiction conferred by a statute.

Whatever may be said as to the effect of the Conformity Act while it remained in force, the rules, if they are within the authority granted by Congress, repeal that statute, and the District Court was not bound to follow the Illinois practice respecting an order for physical examination. On the other hand if the right to be exempt from such an order is one of substantive law, the Rules of Decision Act required the District Court, though sitting in Illinois, to apply the law of Indiana, the state where the cause of action arose, and to order the examination. To avoid this dilemma the petitioner admits, and, we think, correctly, that Rules 35 and 37 are rules of procedure. She insists, nevertheless, that by the prohibition against abridging substantive rights, Congress has banned the rules here challenged. In order to reach this result she translates "substantive" into "important" or "substantial" rights. And she urges that if a rule affects such a right, albeit the rule is one of procedure merely, its prescription is not within the statutory grant of power embodied in the Act of June 19, 1934. She contends that our decisions and recognized principles require us so to hold.

* * * [Discussion of Union Pac. Ry. v. Botsford, 141 U.S. 250 (1891), and Camden & S.Ry. v. Stetson, 177 U.S. 172 (1900), omitted.]

We are thrown back, then, to the arguments drawn from the language of the Act of June 19, 1934. Is the phrase "substantive rights" confined to rights conferred by law to be protected and enforced in accordance with the adjective law of judicial procedure? It certainly embraces such rights. One of them is the right not to be injured in one's person by another's negligence, to redress infraction of which the present action was brought. The petitioner says the phrase connotes more; that by its use Congress intended that in regulating procedure this court should not deal with important and substantial rights theretofore recognized. Recognized where and by whom? The state courts are divided as to the power in the absence of statute to order a physical examina-

6. Wayman v. Southard, 10 Wheat. 1, 21; Bank of United States v. Halstead, 10 Wheat. 51, 53; Beers v. Haughton, 9 Pet. 329, 359, 361.

tion. In a number such an order is authorized by statute or rule. The rules in question accord with the procedure now in force in Canada and England.

The asserted right, moreover, is no more important than many others enjoyed by litigants in District Courts sitting in the several states, before the Federal Rules of Civil Procedure altered and abolished old rights or privileges and created new ones in connection with the conduct of litigation. The suggestion that the rule offends the important right to freedom from invasion of the person ignores the fact that as we hold, no invasion of freedom from personal restraint attaches to refusal so to comply with its provisions. If we were to adopt the suggested criterion of the importance of the alleged right we should invite endless litigation and confusion worse confounded. The test must be whether a rule really regulates procedure,—the judicial process for enforcing rights and duties recognized by substantive law and for justly administering remedy and redress for disregard or infraction of them. That the rules in question are such is admitted.

Finally, it is urged that Rules 35 and 37 work a major change of policy and that this was not intended by Congress. Apart from the fact already stated, that the policy of the states in this respect has not been uniform, it is to be noted that the authorization of a comprehensive system of court rules was a departure in policy, and that the new policy envisaged in the enabling act of 1934 was that the whole field of court procedure be regulated in the interest of speedy, fair and exact determination of the truth. The challenged rules comport with this policy. Moreover, in accordance with the Act, the rules were submitted to the Congress so that that body might examine them and veto their going into effect if contrary to the policy of the legislature.

The value of the reservation of the power to examine proposed rules, laws and regulations before they become effective is well understood by Congress. It is frequently, as here, employed to make sure that the action under the delegation squares with the Congressional purpose. Evidently the Congress felt the rule was within the ambit of the statute as no effort was made to eliminate it from the proposed body of rules, although this specific rule was attacked and defended before the committees of the two Houses. The Preliminary Draft of the rules called attention to the contrary practice indicated by the Botsford case, as did the Report of the Advisory Committee and the Notes prepared by the Committee to accompany the final version of the rules. That no adverse action was taken by Congress indicates, at least, that no transgression of legislative policy was found. We conclude that the rules under attack are within the authority granted.

The District Court treated the refusal to comply with its order as a contempt and committed the petitioner therefor. Neither in the Circuit Court of Appeals nor here was this action assigned as error. We think, however, that in the light of the provisions of Rule 37 it was plain error of such a fundamental nature that we should notice it. Section (b)(2)(iv) of Rule 37 exempts from punishment as for contempt the refusal to obey an order that a party submit to a physical or mental examination. The District Court was in error in going counter to this express exemption. The remedies available under the rule in such a case are those enumerated in Section (b)(2)(i)(ii) and (iii). For this error we reverse the judgment and remand the cause to the District Court for further proceedings in conformity to this opinion.

Reversed and remanded.

* * *

■ MR. JUSTICE FRANKFURTER (dissenting).

* * *

Speaking with diffidence in support of a view which has not commended itself to the Court, it does not seem to me that the answer to our question is to be found by an analytic determination whether the power of examination here claimed is a matter of procedure or a matter of substance, even assuming that the two are mutually exclusive categories with easily ascertainable contents. The problem seems to me to be controlled by the policy underlying the Botsford decision [refusing to order the plaintiff to submit to a physical examination on the grounds that no authority existed to issue such an order]. Its doctrine was not a survival of an outworn technicality. It rested on considerations akin to what is familiarly known in the English law as the liberties of the subject. To be sure, the immunity that was recognized in the Botsford case has no constitutional sanction. It is amenable to statutory change. But the "inviolability of a person" was deemed to have such historic roots in Anglo–American law that it was not to be curtailed "unless by clear and unquestionable authority of law". In this connection it is significant that a judge as responsive to procedural needs as was Mr. Justice Holmes, should, on behalf of the Supreme Judicial Court of Massachusetts, have supported the Botsford doctrine on the ground that "the common law was very slow to sanction any violation of or interference with the person of a free citizen". Stack v. New York, etc., R. Co., 177 Mass. 155, 157, 58 N.E. 686.

So far as national law is concerned, a drastic change in public policy in a matter deeply touching the sensibilities of people or even their prejudices as to privacy, ought not to be inferred from a general authorization to formulate rules for the more uniform and effective dispatch of business on the civil side of the federal courts. I deem a requirement as to the invasion of the person to stand on a very different footing from questions pertaining to the discovery of documents, pre-trial procedure and other devices for the expeditious, economic and fair conduct of litigation. That disobedience of an order under Rule 35 cannot be visited with punishment as for contempt does not mitigate its intrusion into an historic immunity of the privacy of the person. Of course the Rule is compulsive in that the doors of the federal courts otherwise open may be shut to litigants who do not submit to such a physical examination.

In this view little significance attaches to the fact that the Rules, in accordance with the statute, remained on the table of two Houses of Congress without evoking any objection to Rule 35 and thereby automatically came into force. Plainly the Rules are not acts of Congress and can not be treated as such. Having due regard to the mechanics of legislation and the practical conditions surrounding the business of Congress when the Rules were submitted, to draw any inference of tacit approval from non-action by Congress is to appeal to unreality. And so I conclude that to make the drastic change that Rule 35 sought to introduce would require explicit legislation.

Ordinarily, disagreement with the majority on so-called procedural matters is best held in silence. Even in the present situation I should be loath to register dissent did the issue pertain merely to diversity litigation. But Rule 35 applies to all civil litigation in the federal courts, and thus concerns the enforcement of federal rights and not merely of state law in the federal courts.

■ MR. JUSTICE BLACK, MR. JUSTICE DOUGLAS, and MR. JUSTICE MURPHY agree with these views.

NOTE ON CHALLENGES TO THE VALIDITY OF THE FEDERAL RULES

(1) *Decisions Rejecting Challenges Under the Enabling Act.* In Mississippi Publishing Corp. v. Murphree, 326 U.S. 438 (1946), a federal district court had held that a provision of Rule 4, permitting service of process anywhere within the state in which the district court sits, rather than within the district only, was invalid as in excess of the authority granted by the Enabling Act. The Supreme Court, while upholding the rule, was at pains to point out (p. 444) that "[t]he fact that this Court promulgated the rules as formulated and recommended by the Advisory Committee does not foreclose consideration of their validity, meaning or consistency".[1]

On several occasions the Court has had trouble interpreting the civil rules, and the results in some cases are difficult to square with the language of the rule involved. See, *e.g.*, Palmer v. Hoffman, 318 U.S. 109 (1943)(Fed.Rule 8(c)); Anderson v. Yungkau, 329 U.S. 482 (1947) (Fed.Rules 6(b) and 25(a)); Hickman v. Taylor, 329 U.S. 495 (1947) (former Fed.Rules 26, 30(b), 33, and 34); Ragan v. Merchants Transfer & Warehouse Co., 337 U.S. 530 (1949)(Fed.Rule 3); Walker v. Armco Steel Corp., 446 U.S. 740 (1980)(Fed.Rule 3). But to date, the Court has never squarely held a provision of the civil rules to be invalid on its face or as applied.[2]

(2) *Allocation of Authority Between the Legislative and Judicial Branches.* Observe the clear recognition both in the Enabling Act and in the Sibbach opinion of the power of Congress to override court-issued rules. Compare the elaborate dictum in Winberry v. Salisbury, 5 N.J. 240, 74 A.2d 406 (1950), that legislative power over practice and procedure was ousted by a provision of the state constitution that the state supreme court "shall make rules governing the administration of all courts in the State and, subject to law, the practice and procedure in all such courts * * *." Is the resulting disposition of power a

---

1. For criticism of the rationale in Murphree, and an argument that the Court's rulemaking authority in matters of personal jurisdiction and venue is quite limited, see Whitten, *Separation of Powers Restrictions on Rule Making: A Case Study of Federal Rule 4,* 40 Me.L.Rev. 41 (1988).

For discussion of the question whether (despite the dictum in the Sibbach opinion) Congress may delegate to the courts authority to define the scope of their subject-matter jurisdiction, see Chap. XV, Sec. 2, p. 1655, *infra.*

2. In Business Guides, Inc. v. Chromatic Communications Enterprises, Inc. 498 U.S. 533 (1991), the Court did take seriously, but ultimately rejected, an Enabling Act challenge to its interpretation of revised Rule 11 of the Federal Rules of Civil Procedure. (Under the Court's interpretation, and over a dissent joined by four Justices, the rule's provisions for sanctions were held applicable to a represented party who, in signing pleadings or other papers, failed to satisfy an objective standard of reasonableness.) The Court said that the rule as interpreted only incidentally affected substantive rights because it penalized conduct occurring during the litigation and was not directly tied to the outcome of the case.

See also Marek v. Chesny (and especially Justice Brennan's dissent), discussed in Paragraph (4), *infra.*

wise one? See Kaplan & Greene, *The Legislature's Relation to Judicial Rule–Making: An Appraisal of Winberry v. Salisbury,* 65 Harv.L.Rev. 234 (1951); Levin & Amsterdam, *Legislative Control Over Judicial Rulemaking: A Problem in Constitutional Revision,* 107 U.Pa.L.Rev. 1 (1958).

In view of the Enabling Act's language delegating authority to abrogate statutes, does the Supreme Court's rulemaking power allow it to supersede acts of Congress passed after the rules became effective? If Congress overrode a particular rule, could the Court thereafter reinstate the rule? Alter in any way the practice established by the overriding statute? (None of these questions has ever been squarely addressed by the Court, though the opinion in Sibbach surprisingly characterized the Enabling Act as giving the courts only the authority "to make rules not inconsistent with the statutes or Constitution of the United States".)[3]

(3) *Sibbach and the Substance/Procedure Distinction.* The substantive right asserted in the Sibbach case was state-created. What, if any, are the constitutional limits upon the power of Congress to regulate practice and procedure in actions for the enforcement of such rights? Does the Sibbach opinion yield a satisfactory test of what constitutes practice and procedure? Of when regulation of the former may transgress limits on the validity or appropriateness of federal regulation of the latter? Does the opinion cast any light on the difference, if any, between the constitutional power of Congress in this area and the power delegated by Congress to the Supreme Court?[4]

Compare Erie R.R. v. Tompkins and succeeding materials in Sections 2 and 3, *infra* (including materials on the significance of the Enabling Act and rules promulgated pursuant to it). Do you agree with the Sibbach Court's statement that if the right asserted were one of "substantive law", the Rules of Decision Act would require the application of Indiana law? Compare Klaxon Co. v. Stentor Elec. Mfg. Co., p. 695, *infra.*

(4) *Marek v. Chesny and the Limits of the Rulemaking Authority.* The tension between the rulemaking authority and the legislative powers of Congress was highlighted by the controversy in Marek v. Chesny, 473 U.S. 1 (1985). In that case the plaintiff, after prevailing in a civil rights action under 42 U.S.C. § 1983, moved for an award of attorney's fees as authorized by 42 U.S.C. § 1988. The district court denied the motion with respect to attorney's fees incurred after an offer of settlement had been made by the defendant, since the amount recovered after trial was less than the amount of the offer and since Rule 68 provides that in such circumstances, "the offeree must pay the costs

---

3. For arguments that the Enabling Act's delegation of authority to abrogate or alter statutes is unconstitutional, see Clinton, *Rule 9 of the Federal Habeas Corpus Rules: A Case Study on the Need for Reform of the Rules Enabling Acts,* 63 Iowa L.Rev. 15, 64–77 (1977); *Hearings on H.R. 3550 Before the Subcomm. on Courts, Civil Liberties, and the Administration of Justice of the House Comm. on the Judiciary,* 99th Cong., 2d Sess. 7–23 (1985)(testimony of Stephen Burbank, relying in substantial part on the Chadha case, see p. 666, *supra*).

In 1978, Congress, without explanation, repealed a similar delegation of authority in § 2075 as part of its revision of the bankruptcy laws. See p. 659, *supra.*

4. As noted in Paragraph (1), no federal rule has yet been held invalid by the Supreme Court. And although the Court has acknowledged that since the rules are not affirmatively enacted into law by Congress, they "are not entitled to that great deference as to constitutionality which we accord federal statutes * * * they at least come with the imprimatur of the rulemaking authority of this Court." Ticor Title Ins. Co. v. Brown, 114 S.Ct. 1359, 1361 (1994).

incurred after the making of the offer." The Supreme Court agreed with the district court, holding that (a) the term "costs" in Rule 68 includes attorney's fees whenever the underlying statute (here § 1988) defines costs to include those fees, and (b) as so construed Rule 68's policy of encouraging settlements is wholly consistent with § 1988's policy of encouraging meritorious civil rights suits.

Justice Brennan (joined by Justices Marshall and Blackmun) dissented on both grounds. He argued that the automatic provisions of Rule 68, if applied to attorney's fees, would put severe pressure on civil rights plaintiffs to settle even meritorious suits without adequate information and were thus wholly inconsistent with the broad discretion conferred by § 1988. He concluded that "[a]s construed by the Court * * * Rule 68 surely will operate to 'abridge' and to 'modify' [the] statutory right to reasonable attorney's fees. * * * [Thus] the Rules Enabling Act requires that the Court's interpretation give way." 473 U.S. at 36–37.[5]

SECTION 2. THE POWERS OF THE FEDERAL COURTS IN DEFINING PRIMARY LEGAL OBLIGATIONS THAT FALL WITHIN THE LEGISLATIVE COMPETENCE OF THE STATES

Swift v. Tyson

41 U.S. (16 Pet.) 1, 10 L.Ed. 865 (1842).
Certificate of Division from the Circuit Court for the Southern District of New York.

■ STORY, JUSTICE, delivered the opinion of the court.—This cause comes before us from the circuit court of the southern district of New York, upon a certificate of division of the judges of that court. The action was brought by the plaintiff, Swift, as indorsee, against the defendant, Tyson, as acceptor, upon a bill of exchange dated at Portland, Maine, on the first day of May 1836, for the sum of $1540.30, payable six months after date, and grace, drawn by one Nathaniel Norton and one Jairus S. Keith upon and accepted by Tyson, at the city of New York, in favor of the order of Nathaniel Norton, and by Norton indorsed to the plaintiff. The bill was dishonored at maturity.

At the trial, the acceptance and indorsement of the bill were admitted, and the plaintiff there rested his case. The defendant then introduced in evidence the answer of Swift to a bill of discovery, by which it appeared, that Swift took the bill, before it became due, in payment of a promissory note due to him by Norton & Keith; that he understood, that the bill was accepted in part payment of some lands sold by Norton to a company in New York; that Swift was a *bona fide* holder of the bill, not having any notice of anything in the sale

---

5. Justice Brennan's position finds support in Professor Burbank's study of the history of the 1934 Rules Enabling Act and earlier efforts at reform. See Burbank, *The Rules Enabling Act of 1934*, 130 U.Pa.L.Rev. 1015 (1982). In a later article applying that study in the context of sanctions for party or attorney misconduct or default, Professor Burbank concludes that while the rules may *authorize* the award of fees and other costs in such circumstances, they may not *require* their imposition without running afoul of the Enabling Act. Burbank, *Sanctions in the Proposed Amendments to the Federal Rules of Civil Procedure: Some Questions About Power,* 11 Hofstra L.Rev. 997 (1983).

or title to the lands, or otherwise impeaching the transaction, and with the full belief that the bill was justly due. The particular circumstances are fully set forth in the answer in the record; but it does not seem necessary further to state them. The defendant then offered to prove, that the bill was accepted by the defendant, as part consideration for the purchase of certain lands in the state of Maine, which Norton & Keith represented themselves to be the owners of, and also represented to be of great value, and contracted to convey a good title thereto; and that the representations were in every respect fraudulent and false, and Norton & Keith had no title to the lands, and that the same were of little or no value. The plaintiff objected to the admission of such testimony, or of any testimony, as against him, impeaching or showing a failure of the consideration, on which the bill was accepted, under the facts admitted by the defendant, and those proved by him, by reading the answer of plaintiff to the bill of discovery. The judges of the circuit court thereupon divided in opinion upon the following point or question of law—Whether, under the facts last mentioned, the defendant was entitled to the same defence to the action, as if the suit was between the original parties to the bill, that is to say, Norton, or Norton & Keith, and the defendant; and whether the evidence so offered was admissible as against the plaintiff in the action. And this is the question certified to us for our decision. * * *

In the present case, the plaintiff is a *bona fide* holder, without notice, for what the law deems a good and valid consideration, that is, for a pre-existing debt; and the only real question in the cause is, whether, under the circumstances of the present case, such a pre-existing debt constitutes a valuable consideration, in the sense of the general rule applicable to negotiable instruments. We say, under the circumstances of the present case, for the acceptance having been made in New York, the argument on behalf of the defendant is, that the contract is to be treated as a New York contract, and therefore, to be governed by the laws of New York, as expounded by its courts, as well upon general principles, as by the express provisions of the 34th section of the judiciary act of 1789, ch. 20. And then it is further contended, that by the law of New York, as thus expounded by its courts, a pre-existing debt does not constitute, in the sense of the general rule, a valuable consideration applicable to negotiable instruments.

In the first place, then, let us examine into the decisions of the courts of New York upon this subject. * * * [The opinion expresses doubt whether the doctrine asserted can "be treated as finally established" by the New York cases.]

But, admitting the doctrine to be fully settled in New York, it remains to be considered, whether it is obligatory upon this court, if it differs from the principles established in the general commercial law. It is observable, that the courts of New York do not found their decisions upon this point, upon any local statute, or positive, fixed or ancient local usage; but they deduce the doctrine from the general principles of commercial law. It is, however, contended, that the 34th section of the judiciary act of 1789, ch. 20, furnishes a rule obligatory upon this court to follow the decisions of the state tribunals in all cases to which they apply. That section provides "that the laws of the several states, except where the constitution, treaties or statutes of the United States shall otherwise require or provide, shall be regarded as rules of decision, in trials at common law, in the courts of the United States, in cases where they apply." In order to maintain the argument, it is essential, therefore, to hold, that the word "laws," in this section, includes within the scope of its meaning, the decisions of the local tribunals. In the ordinary use of language, it will hardly be contended, that the decisions of courts constitute laws. They are, at most, only evidence of what the laws are, and are not, of themselves, laws. They are often re-examined, reversed and qualified by the courts themselves, whenever they are found to be either defective, or ill-founded, or otherwise incorrect. The laws of a state are more usually understood to mean the rules and enactments promulgated by the legislative authority thereof, or long-established local customs having the force of laws. In all the various cases, which have hitherto come before us for decision, this court have uniformly supposed, that the true interpretation of the 34th section limited its application to state laws, strictly local, that is to say, to the positive statutes of the state, and the construction thereof adopted by the local tribunals, and to rights and titles to things having a permanent locality, such as the rights and titles to real estate, and other matters immovable and intraterritorial in their nature and character. It never has been supposed by us, that the section did apply, or was designed to apply, to questions of a more general nature, not at all dependent upon local statutes or local usages of a fixed and permanent operation, as, for example, to the construction of ordinary contracts or other written instruments, and especially to questions of general commercial law, where the state tribunals are called upon to perform the like functions as ourselves, that is, to ascertain, upon general reasoning and legal analogies, what is the true exposition of the contract or instrument, or what is the just rule furnished by the principles of commercial law to govern the case. And we have not now the slightest difficulty in holding, that this section, upon its true intendment and construction, is strictly limited to local statutes and local usages of the character before stated, and does not extend to contracts and other instruments of a commercial nature, the true interpretation and effect whereof are to be sought, not in the decisions of the local tribunals, but in the general principles and doctrines of commercial jurisprudence. Undoubtedly, the decisions of the local tribunals upon such subjects are entitled to, and will receive, the most deliberate attention and respect of this court; but they cannot furnish positive rules, or conclusive authority, by which our own judgments are to be bound up and governed. The law respecting negotiable instruments may be truly declared in the language of Cicero, adopted by Lord Mansfield in Luke v. Lyde, 2 Burr. 883, 887, to be in a great measure, not the law of a single country only, but of the commercial world. * * *

It becomes necessary for us, therefore, upon the present occasion, to express our own opinion of the true result of the commercial law upon the question now before us. And we have no hesitation in saying, that a pre-existing debt does constitute a valuable consideration, in the sense of the general rule already stated, as applicable to negotiable instruments. * * * And why, upon principle, should not a pre-existing debt be deemed such a valuable consideration? It is for the benefit and convenience of the commercial world, to give as wide an extent as practicable to the credit and circulation of negotiable paper, that it may pass not only as security for new purchases and advances, made upon the transfer thereof, but also in payment of, and as security for, pre-existing debts. The creditor is thereby enabled to realize or to secure his debt, and thus may safely give a prolonged credit, or forbear from taking any legal steps to enforce his rights. The debtor also has the advantage of making his negotiable securities of equivalent value to cash. But establish the opposite conclusion, that negotiable paper cannot be applied in payment of, or as security for, pre-existing debts, without letting in all the equities between the original and antecedent parties, and the value and circulation of such securities must be essentially diminished, and the debtor driven to the embarrassment of making a sale thereof, often at a ruinous discount, to some third person, and then, by circuity, to apply the proceeds to the payment of his debts. What, indeed, upon such a doctrine, would become of that large class of cases, where new notes are given by the same or by other parties, by way of renewal or security to banks, in lieu of old securities discounted by them, which have arrived at maturity? Probably, more than one-half of all bank transactions in our country, as well as those of other countries, are of this nature. The doctrine would strike a fatal blow at all discounts of negotiable securities for pre-existing debts.

This question has been several times before this court, and it has been uniformly held, that it makes no difference whatsoever, as to the rights of the holder, whether the debt, for which the negotiable instrument is transferred to him, is a pre-existing debt, or is contracted at the time of the transfer. * * * In England, the same doctrine has been uniformly acted upon. * * *

In the American courts, so far as we have been able to trace the decisions, the same doctrine seems generally, but not universally, to prevail. * * * We are all, therefore, of opinion, that the question on this point, propounded by the circuit court for our consideration, ought to be answered in the negative; and we shall, accordingly, direct it so to be certified to the circuit court.

CATRON, JUSTICE, said:—Upon the point of difference between the judges below, I concur, that the extinguishment of a debt, and the giving a past consideration, such as the record presents, will protect the purchaser and assignee of a negotiable note from the infirmity affecting the instrument before it was negotiated. But I am unwilling to sanction the introduction into the opinion of this court, a doctrine aside from the case made by the record, or argued by the counsel, assuming to maintain, that a negotiable note or bill, pledged as collateral security for a previous debt, is taken by the creditor in the due course of trade; and that he stands on the foot of him who purchases in the market for money, or takes the instrument in extinguishment of a previous debt. State courts of high authority on commercial questions have held otherwise; and that they will yield to a mere expression of opinion of this court, or change their course of decision in conformity to the recent English cases referred to in the principal opinion, is improbable; whereas, if the question was permitted to rest until it fairly arose, the decision of it either way by this court, probably, would, and I think ought to settle it. * * *

NOTE ON SWIFT v. TYSON, ITS ANTECEDENTS AND RISE, AND THE INTIMATIONS OF ITS FALL

(1) *The Question in Swift.* Was the problem of Swift v. Tyson one only of statutory interpretation? What guides to decision would there have been if the Rules of Decision Act had never been enacted? What were the relevant postulates to limit and control the Act's interpretation?

(2) *Decisions Prior to Swift.* The first volume of American law reports was Kirby's Connecticut reports, published in 1789. In view of the paucity of reported decisions and the difficulties of establishing the grounds of unreported

ones, the problem of the authority of state decisions arose infrequently in the early years. See the account of the antecedents of Swift v. Tyson in 2 Crosskey, Politics and the Constitution in the History of the United States 822–62 (1953).

In Brown v. Van Bramm, 3 U.S. (3 Dall.) 344 (1797), the plaintiff had brought an action on bills of exchange in the United States Circuit Court for Rhode Island. He obtained judgment—on the ground of default in the court proceedings—for the principal, plus interest, protest charges, and (pursuant to a 1743 Rhode Island statute) damages of 10 per cent of the principal. On appeal to the Supreme Court, the defendant argued that the default had been improperly entered, that there was no right to damages under the state statute because timely protest had not been made, and that the damages, if authorized, should have been assessed by a jury. The Court affirmed the judgment with a brief statement that the result was warranted "under the laws, and the practical construction of the courts, of Rhode Island", and with the following footnote (p. 356): "Chase, Justice, observed, that he concurred in the opinion of the court; but that it was on common law principles, and not in compliance with the laws and practice of the state." 2 Crosskey, *supra,* at 823–24, argues that two of the three points in the case were matters of procedure and thus governed by the Process Acts of 1789 and 1792, while the third, though substantive, dealt with a question traditionally delegated to local law and in this instance governed by a state statute enacted before 1789. But whatever the significance of the holding, the argument of the appellee, quoted in part in the margin, is of particular interest.[1]

In Jackson v. Chew, 25 U.S. (12 Wheat.) 153 (1827)(a dispute over a testamentary disposition), the Court for the first time squarely recognized an obligation to conform to post–1789 decisions of state courts on matters of unwritten law. Justice Thompson said (p. 167):

"After such a settled course of decisions, and two of them in the highest court of law in the state, upon the very clause in the will now under consideration, * * * a contrary decision by this court would present a conflict between the state courts and those of the United States, productive of incalculable mischief. * * * And it will be seen, by reference to the decisions of this court, that to establish a contrary doctrine here, would be repugnant to the principles which have always governed this court in like cases.

"It has been urged, however, at the bar, that this court applies this principle only to state constructions of their own statutes. * * * But the same rule has been extended to other cases; and there can be no good reason assigned, why it should not be, when it is applying settled rules of real property. This court adopts the state decisions, because they settle the law

---

1. In a general introduction to his argument, the appellee said (p. 352): "This adoption of the State laws [in the Rules of Decision Act], extends as well to the unwritten, as to the written law;—to the law arising from established usage and judicial determinations, as well as to the law created by positive acts of the Legislature. And the act for regulating process, in language equally general adopts 'in each State respectively, such forms and modes as are used or allowed in the Supreme Courts of the same.' The only question, therefore, to ascertain the legal correctness of the present record, is—what are the laws and modes adopted by the State of Rhode Island, in relation to the controverted points? It is immaterial, how far the answer shall be inconsistent with certain dogma of the English common law; it is enough to show that such are the laws and modes of Rhode Island, and that they are competent to all the purposes of justice."

applicable to the case; and the reasons assigned for this course, apply as well to rules of construction growing out of the common law, as the statute law of the state, when applied to the title of lands. And such a course is indispensable, in order to preserve uniformity; otherwise, the peculiar constitution of the judicial tribunals of the states and of the United States, would be productive of the greatest mischief and confusion."

In the early case of Huidekoper's Lessee v. Douglass, 7 U.S. (3 Cranch) 1 (1805), Chief Justice Marshall, speaking for a unanimous Court, had decided an important question of title to lands turning upon the construction of a 1792 Pennsylvania statute, without reference to two earlier decisions of the Supreme Court of Pennsylvania that were flatly to the contrary. Professor Crosskey, in an elaborate review of the context of this decision, concluded that it evidenced an original understanding not only that the Supreme Court was free to disregard state court decisions of any kind, but that Supreme Court decisions of any kind, once given, were to be binding thereafter upon the state courts. 2 Crosskey, *supra,* at 719–53. But as Crosskey himself recognizes, the Supreme Court of Pennsylvania was not the highest court of the state in 1805; and other scholars have persuasively argued that the state law at the time was unsettled.[2] Moreover, while the Pennsylvania judges continued to reach results consistent with the Huidekoper decision, they never followed its reasoning or acknowledged its authority.

Meanwhile, as noted by Justice Thompson in Jackson v. Chew, the Supreme Court of the United States began more and more clearly to acknowledge the authority of state court decisions construing state statutes. See, particularly, Marshall, C.J., in Elmendorf v. Taylor, 23 U.S. (10 Wheat.) 152, 159–60 (1825). The question came to a head in its most difficult form in Green v. Neal's Lessee, 31 U.S. (6 Pet.) 291 (1832), in which the Court held itself obliged to abandon two of its own former decisions construing a state statute affecting land titles in order to conform to intervening decisions to the contrary by the Tennessee state courts. After reviewing earlier cases, Justice McLean said (pp. 299–300):

"If the construction of the highest judicial tribunal of a state form a part of its statute law, as much as an enactment by the legislature, how can this court make a distinction between them? There could be no hesitation in so modifying our decisions as to conform to any legislative alteration in a statute; and why should not the same rule apply, where the judicial branch of the state government, in the exercise of its acknowledged functions, should, by construction, give a different effect to a statute from what had at first been given to it?
* * *

"* * * Here is a judicial conflict, arising from two rules of property in the same state, and the consequences are not only deeply injurious to the citizens of the state, but calculated to engender the most lasting discontents. It is, therefore, essential to the interests of the country, and to the harmony of the judicial action of the federal and state governments, that there should be but one rule of property in a state."

Finally, in Wheaton v. Peters, 33 U.S. (8 Pet.) 591 (1834), a federal court copyright action in which the plaintiff relied in part on a claim of right under the common law, the majority opinion said: "It is clear, there can be no common law of the United States. The federal government is composed of

---

2. Bridwell & Whitten, The Constitution and the Common Law 101–05 (1977).

twenty-four sovereign and independent states; each of which may have its local usages, customs and common law. There is no principle which pervades the Union and has the authority of law, that is not embodied in the constitution or laws of the Union. The common law could be made a part of our federal system, only by legislative adoption. When, therefore, a common law right is asserted, we must look to the state in which the controversy originated" (pp. 657–58).[3]

(3) *The Rationale of Swift.* Viewed against this background, was the meaning that Justice Story attributed to the term "laws" in the Rules of Decision Act a defensible one? Note that he drew a distinction between "local" law (statutes and usages) on the one hand, and "general commercial law" on the other. A conception of the common law as a single system, and especially of the law merchant as "a branch of the law of nations" that had been received into that system, did have a substantial foundation in the thinking of his time and an even more substantial foundation in eighteenth century thought. See, *e.g.,* Hoffman, Course of Legal Study (2 vols., 2d ed. 1836), particularly Vol. I, pp. 415–16; and the materials in Crosskey, *supra,* particularly Chap. XVIII. See also Fletcher, *The General Common Law and Section 34 of the Judiciary Act of 1789: The Example of Marine Insurance,* 97 Harv.L.Rev. 1513 (1984). In 1842, however, the problems of conflicting applications of common law principles, even on matters of commerce, were already fully apparent. Did Story take adequate account of them?

Consider the basic character of those rules of law that guide people in everyday affairs, advising them, in advance of any dispute, of their primary duties and powers and of their corresponding rights and vulnerabilities. Is it consistent with the presuppositions of law to leave people in uncertainty about such matters—to tell them that the rules by which they are to be judged, with respect even to basic obligations and powers, will depend upon the unpredictable circumstance of what court they can get into, or may be haled into? Does the problem in this aspect vary significantly as between questions of local property law, or commercial law, or other types of obligations?

If Swift v. Tyson had been brought in a state court, would Congress have had power to authorize the Supreme Court to review the state court's decision in the light of the principles of general jurisprudence? Should the actual decision have been regarded as authoritative, under the Constitution, in later

---

3. Compare DuPonceau, A Dissertation on the Nature and Extent of the Jurisdiction of the Courts of the United States (1824):

"I think, then, I can lay it down as a correct principle, that the common law of England, as it was at the time of the declaration of independence, still continues to be the national law of this country, so far as it is applicable to our present state, and subject to the modifications it has received here in the course of near half a century" (pp. 89–90).

"It appears to me also that by the words 'the laws of the United States,' the framers of the Constitution only meant the statutes which should be enacted by the national Legislature * * *

"On the whole, therefore, I think I may venture to assert * * * that when the federal Courts are sitting in or for the States, they can, it is true, derive no jurisdiction from the common law, because the people of the United States, in framing their Constitution, have thought proper to restrict them within certain limits; but that whenever by the Constitution or the laws made in pursuance of it, jurisdiction is given to them either over the person or subject matter, they are bound to take the common law as their rule of decision whenever other laws, national or local, are not applied" (pp. 99, 101).

cases in the state courts? Between persons of diverse citizenship? Between co-citizens?

Would Congress have had power to enact the holding of Swift v. Tyson as a rule of decision in the federal courts? As a rule of decision in diverse citizenship cases in the state courts? As a rule of conduct between diverse citizens? As a general rule of conduct?

Would a federal court sitting in New York have been free to disregard a New York statute enacting a rule contrary to Swift v. Tyson?

Professor Crosskey appears to answer all the questions in the last three paragraphs in the affirmative. See 1 Crosskey, *supra*, Part III, entitled "A Unitary View of the National Governing Powers". He reads the Constitution, in other words, as providing for a national legislature with plenary powers to pass laws for the general welfare and a national judiciary with plenary powers to establish justice. (In support of this reading he argues that the "laws of the United States" referred to in the jurisdictional provisions of Article III include the common law, and that Congress should have provided for the exercise of jurisdiction in all common law cases.)

(4) *Contemporary Controversy*. Recent decades have seen a revival of interest among legal historians in the rationale and significance of the Swift decision. And these issues are in turn part of a larger debate about the nature of law and the role played by judges in nineteenth century American society.

Professor Horwitz, in The Transformation of American Law, 1780–1860, at 245–52 (1977), argues that the Swift decision is a leading example of the instances in which Justice Story and other judges of the period employed judicial powers as an instrument to aid in the redistribution of wealth and to promote commercial and industrial growth. Justice Story, he suggests, was well aware that the common law was not a brooding omnipresence—an awareness demonstrated by the approach taken in his treatise on Conflict of Laws in 1834—but was anxious to provide the shelter of the federal courts against the application of state policies hostile to commercial interests.

In response, Professors Bridwell and Whitten, in The Constitution and the Common Law 90 (1977), argue that Professor Horwitz' thesis misconstrues both the Swift decision and the perceptions of its author. They suggest that in the first half of the nineteenth century, Story and his contemporaries viewed the law of commercial transactions and contracts not as the command of the sovereign, but rather as the embodiment of prevailing customs and practices and as a process for applying them to the case at hand. To allow local customs to prevail over general practice, in the absence of some strong reason for doing so, would frustrate the understandings on which the transaction was based. Swift v. Tyson, they conclude, is "a prime example of how the diversity jurisdiction operated to preserve the intentions and expectations of the parties intact when their dealings had taken place against the assumed background of general commercial practice".[4]

---

4. In two related articles, Professor Heckman has argued that, for Story, the nature of commercial and contract law was such that *both* state statutes and state common law would and should yield to federal court decisions in the field and that those decisions would be binding on state as well as federal courts. Nineteenth century case authority is cited in support of this position. See Heckman, *Uniform Commercial Law in the Nineteenth Century: The Decline and Abuse of the Swift Doctrine*, 45 Emory L.J. 45 (1978); Heckman, *The Relationship of Swift v. Tyson to the Status of Commercial Law in the Nine-*

Finally, Professor Freyer, in Harmony and Dissonance: The Swift and Erie Cases in American Federalism (1981), after considering the "antebellum credit system, the role of the federal courts in this system, the character of the legal profession during the period, and prevalent jurisprudential assumptions" concludes that "Swift was thoroughly consistent with antebellum notions of American constitutionalism and federalism" (p. xiii). The unanimity of the Swift Court on the critical issues, he suggests, shows that even its Jacksonian members did not regard Story's approach as a threat to the interests of the states or to the principles of federalism (p. 26).[5]

(5) *Developments Following Swift.* After Swift, the Court continued to adhere, in general, to the doctrine of Green v. Neal's Lessee in matters of construction of state statutes. See Note, 37 Harv.L.Rev. 1129 (1924). But there were some notable exceptions, *e.g.,* Watson v. Tarpley, 59 U.S. (18 How.) 517, 521 (1855), in which the Court said: "[A]ny state law or regulation, the effect of which would be to impair the rights [under and defined by the general commercial law] * * * or to devest the federal courts of cognizance thereof, * * * must be nugatory and unavailing."[6]

Controversy over the Swift decision and its ramifications did not become intense until the period during and after the Civil War. See Hazard, Tait & Fletcher, Pleading and Procedure 486–87 (7th ed. 1994). Among the most controversial of the Court's actions during this period was the rule developed with respect to federal court actions on defaulted municipal bonds.[7] In Gelpcke v. City of Dubuque, 68 U.S. (1 Wall.) 175 (1863), the Court declined to follow a state court construction of the state constitution that would have invalidated the bonds, in view of the fact that the construction overruled decisions outstanding at the time the bonds were issued. Justice Swayne said for the Court (pp. 206–07):

"We are not unmindful of the importance of uniformity in the decisions of this court, and those of the highest local courts, giving constructions to the laws and constitutions of their own States. It is the settled rule of this court in such cases, to follow the decisions of the State courts. But there have been heretofore, in the judicial history of this court, as doubtless there will be hereafter, many exceptional cases. We shall never immolate truth, justice, and the law, because a State tribunal has erected the altar and decreed the sacrifice."

Suppose the question had come to the Supreme Court on review of the state court's overruling decision? Would the decision have been vulnerable to

---

teenth Century and the Federal System, 17 Am.J. Legal Hist. 246 (1973).

5. See also Fletcher, Paragraph (3), *supra.* Professor Fletcher draws on diversity cases involving marine insurance during the period 1800–1820 to show that well before Swift, state and federal courts succeeded in developing a uniform system of common law in the adjudication of these commercial disputes under the law merchant. He argues that § 34, and the lex loci principle it was thought to embody, were never seen as precluding the application of general common law in such cases.

6. For fuller discussion of this case, *see* Bridwell & Whitton, Paragraph (4), *supra,* at 77–78; Freyer, Paragraph (4), *supra,* at 51–55.

7. See Freyer, Paragraph (4), *supra,* at 58–61. According to one report, "the total of defaulted bonds across the nation amounted to between $100,000,000 and $150,000,000." *Id.* at 60. Thus it was not surprising that some 300 bond cases came to the Supreme Court in the last third of the nineteenth century. *Id.*

challenge under the Fourteenth Amendment or any other constitutional provision?[8] If not, can the Gelpcke decision be defended?

Again, in Burgess v. Seligman, 107 U.S. 20 (1883), the Court declined to follow a state court's construction (rendered in connection with the same insolvency involved in the case before it) of the state's statutes as imposing stockholder liability. Justice Bradley's opinion noted that the conflicting state court construction was handed down after the decision of the court below, and concluded (p. 34):

"* * * [Since] the very object of giving to the national courts jurisdiction to administer the laws of the States in controversies between citizens of different States was to institute independent tribunals which it might be supposed would be unaffected by local prejudices and sectional views, it would be a dereliction of their duty not to exercise an independent judgment in cases not foreclosed by previous adjudication. * * * "

Note the important differences between the reasoning of the Gelpcke and Burgess decisions and that of Story in Swift v. Tyson. How persuasive are these later cases?[9]

(6) *The Attack on Swift Before 1938*. The principle of Swift v. Tyson held sway for nearly a century in a wide area of commercial law, marked off only with difficulty from property and other matters of "local" law. Consistently with the language of Swift, the Court also looked to general principles, rather than to state precedents, in "the construction of ordinary contracts or other written instruments" like deeds and wills. *E.g.*, Lane v. Vick, 44 U.S. (3 How.) 464 (1845). And in an extension of the rationale much criticized even by Swift's present-day defenders,[10] it was held applicable in a tort case as early as 1862. Chicago v. Robbins, 67 U.S. (2 Black) 418 (1862). Reliance on Swift in Baltimore & O.R.R. v. Baugh, 149 U.S. 368 (1893), to uphold the fellow-servant defense in a federal court action, evoked a strenuous dissent by Justice Field.[11]

In Kuhn v. Fairmont Coal Co., 215 U.S. 349 (1910), the Court applied in a common law case a doctrine akin to that applied in Gelpcke and Burgess in statutory fields. With Holmes, White, and McKenna dissenting, it held itself free to take its own view of the legal effect of a deed of land when the state decisions had been unsettled at the time of the conveyance.

Finally, in Black & White Taxicab & Transfer Co. v. Brown & Yellow Taxicab & Transfer Co., 276 U.S. 518 (1928), the Court declined to follow state decisions holding that a railroad's agreement to give exclusive taxicab privileges was contrary to public policy, declaring the question to be one of general law.

---

8. *Cf.* Ohio & M. Railroad Co. v. McClure, 77 U.S. (10 Wall.) 511 (1870)(state court decision holding similar state statute unconstitutional held not reviewable by the Supreme Court under the jurisdictional statute then in effect).

9. For an argument that in order to protect against discrimination, federal courts acting in diversity cases were empowered to disregard state rules, especially in commercial matters, see Borchers, *The Origins of Diversity Jurisdiction, The Rise of Legal Pos-*

itivism, and a Brave New World for Erie and Klaxon, 72 Tex.L.Rev. 79, 86–115 (1993).

10. *E.g.*, Bridwell & Whitten, Paragraph (4), *supra,* at 119–27.

11. Excerpts from the dissent, which was an eloquent challenge to the validity of the concept of "general law", appear in the Court's Erie opinion, pp. 689–90, *infra.* For a suggestion that this dissent was motivated more by dislike of the fellow-servant rule than by considerations of jurisprudential theory, see Freyer, Paragraph (4), *supra,* at 173 n. 41.

The outcry against the decision was enhanced by the circumstance that the successful company had reincorporated itself in another state in order to establish diversity of citizenship with its rival and thus to take advantage of the federal rule.   The argument of Justice Holmes, who was joined in dissent by Justices Brandeis and Stone, is summarized and excerpted in Justice Brandeis' opinion in Erie, p. 690, *infra*.

When reading the Erie opinion, consider whether it is necessary to accept Justice Holmes' characterization of the "fallacy" underlying the Swift decision in order to justify rejection of that decision.

(7) *Increasing Criticism*.   In the decade following the Black & White case there was a perceptible erosion of Swift v. Tyson.[12]

In Burns Mortgage Co. v. Fried, 292 U.S. 487 (1934), for example, the circuit court of appeals had held that the construction by a state court of last resort of a state statute that was merely declaratory of the common law or law merchant did not bind the federal courts, and hence refused to follow a decision interpreting the Uniform Negotiable Instruments Law.   The Supreme Court, granting certiorari because of a conflict among the circuits, said (p. 495):

"We think the better view is that there is no valid distinction * * * between an act which alters the common law and one which codifies or declares it.   Both are within the letter of § 34 of the Judiciary Act * * *.   And a declaratory act is no less an expression of the legislative will because the rule it prescribes is the same as that announced in prior decisions of the courts of the state.   Nor is there a difference in this respect between a statute prescribing rules of commercial law and one concerned with some other subject of narrower scope."

And in Mutual Life Ins. Co. v. Johnson, 293 U.S. 335 (1934), Justice Cardozo built some prior expressions of the Court into a principle of large if indeterminate potentiality.   The question was whether an insured's failure to give notice of disability before default in premium was excused by his physical and mental condition.   The opinion said (pp. 339–40):

"In this situation we are not under a duty to make a choice for ourselves between alternative constructions as if the courts of the place of the contract were silent or uncertain.   Without suggesting an independent preference either one way or the other, we yield to the judges of Virginia expounding a Virginia policy and adjudging its effect.   * * * No question is here as to any general principle of the law of contracts of insurance * * * with consequences broader than those involved in the construction of a highly specialized condition.   All that is here for our decision is the meaning, the tacit implications, of a particular set of words, which, as experience has shown, may yield a different answer to this reader and to that one.   With choice so 'balanced with doubt', we accept as our guide the law declared by the state where the contract had its being."

(8) *Prelude to Erie*.   On April 24, 1938, the day before the Erie decision, it is doubtful whether an intelligible and principled formulation could have been put

---

12. For a discussion of legislative efforts in 1928 and 1929 to overrule Swift, see Burbank, *The Rules Enabling Act of 1934*, 130 U.Pa.L.Rev. 1015, 1109–10 n. 433 (1982). Professor Burbank notes that one of the bills introduced was "drafted by * * * [then Professor Frankfurter] and sent to Senator Walsh at the suggestion of Justice Brandeis."

forward with respect to the power and duty of federal judges to disregard decisions of a state's highest court on questions of state law.

Erie Railroad Co. v. Tompkins

304 U.S. 64, 58 S.Ct. 817, 82 L.Ed. 1188 (1938).
Certiorari to the Circuit Court of Appeals for the Second Circuit.

■ MR. JUSTICE BRANDEIS delivered the opinion of the Court.

The question for decision is whether the oft-challenged doctrine of Swift v. Tyson shall now be disapproved.

Tompkins, a citizen of Pennsylvania, was injured on a dark night by a passing freight train of the Erie Railroad Company while walking along its right of way at Hughestown in that state. He claimed that the accident occurred through negligence in the operation, or maintenance, of the train; that he was rightfully on the premises as licensee because on a commonly used beaten footpath which ran for a short distance alongside the tracks; and that he was struck by something which looked like a door projecting from one of the moving cars. To enforce that claim he brought an action in the federal court for Southern New York, which had jurisdiction because the company is a corporation of that state. It denied liability; and the case was tried by a jury.

The Erie insisted that its duty to Tompkins was no greater than that owed to a trespasser. It contended, among other things, that its duty to Tompkins, and hence its liability, should be determined in accordance with the Pennsylvania law; that under the law of Pennsylvania, as declared by its highest court, persons who use pathways along the railroad right of way—that is, a longitudinal pathway as distinguished from a crossing—are to be deemed trespassers; and that the railroad is not liable for injuries to undiscovered trespassers resulting from its negligence, unless it be wanton or willful. Tompkins denied that any such rule had been established by the decisions of the Pennsylvania courts; and contended that, since there was no statute of the state on the subject, the railroad's duty and liability is to be determined in federal courts as a matter of general law.

The trial judge refused to rule that the applicable law precluded recovery. The jury brought in a verdict of $30,000; and the judgment entered thereon was affirmed by the Circuit Court of Appeals, which held (2 Cir., 90 F.2d 603, 604), that it was unnecessary to consider whether the law of Pennsylvania was as contended, because the question was one not of local, but of general, law, and that "upon questions of general law the federal courts are free, in absence of a local statute, to exercise their independent judgment as to what the law is; and it is well settled that the question of the responsibility of a railroad for injuries caused by its servants is one of general law. * * * Where the public has made open and notorious use of a railroad right of way for a long period of time and without objection, the company owes to persons on such permissive pathway a duty of care in the operation of its trains. * * * It is likewise generally recognized law that a jury may find that negligence exists toward a pedestrian using a permissive path on the railroad right of way if he is hit by some object projecting from the side of the train."

The Erie had contended that application of the Pennsylvania rule was required, among other things, by section 34 of the Federal Judiciary Act of September 24, 1789 * * *.

Because of the importance of the question whether the federal court was free to disregard the alleged rule of the Pennsylvania common law, we granted certiorari, 302 U.S. 671.

First. Swift v. Tyson, 16 Pet. 1, 18, held that federal courts exercising jurisdiction on the ground of diversity of citizenship need not, in matters of general jurisprudence, apply the unwritten law of the state as declared by its highest court; that they are free to exercise an independent judgment as to what the common law of the state is—or should be * * *.

The Court in applying the rule of section 34 to equity cases, in Mason v. United States, 260 U.S. 545, 559, said: "The statute, however, is merely declarative of the rule which would exist in the absence of the statute." The federal courts assumed, in the broad field of "general law," the power to declare rules of decision which Congress was confessedly without power to enact as statutes. Doubt was repeatedly expressed as to the correctness of the construction given section 34, and as to the soundness of the rule which it introduced. But it was the more recent research of a competent scholar, who examined the original document, which established that the construction given to it by the Court was erroneous; and that the purpose of the section was merely to make certain that, in all matters except those in which some federal law is controlling, the federal courts exercising jurisdiction in diversity of citizenship cases would apply as their rules of decision the law of the state unwritten as well as written.[5]

Criticism of the doctrine became widespread after the decision of Black & White Taxicab & Transfer Co. v. Brown & Yellow Taxicab & Transfer Co., 276 U.S. 518 [see p. 685, *supra*] * * *.

Second. Experience in applying the doctrine of Swift v. Tyson, had revealed its defects, political and social; and the benefits expected to flow from the rule did not accrue. Persistence of state courts in their own opinions on questions of common law prevented uniformity; and the impossibility of discovering a satisfactory line of demarcation between the province of general law and that of local law developed a new well of uncertainties.[8]

On the other hand, the mischievous results of the doctrine had become apparent. Diversity of citizenship jurisdiction was conferred in order to prevent apprehended discrimination in state courts against those not citizens of the state. Swift v. Tyson introduced grave discrimination by noncitizens against citizens. It made rights enjoyed under the unwritten "general law" vary according to whether enforcement was sought in the state or in the federal court; and the privilege of selecting the court in which the right should be

---

5. Charles Warren, New Light on the History of the Federal Judiciary Act of 1789 (1923) 37 Harv.L.Rev. 49, 51–52, 81–88, 108.

8. Compare 2 Warren, The Supreme Court in United States History, Rev.Ed.1935, 89: "Probably no decision of the Court has ever given rise to more uncertainty as to legal rights; and though doubtless intended to promote uniformity in the operation of business transactions, its chief effect has been to render it difficult for business men to know in advance to what particular topic the Court would apply the doctrine. * * * ". The Federal Digest through the 1937 volume, lists nearly 1,000 decisions involving the distinction between questions of general and of local law.

determined was conferred upon the noncitizen.[9] Thus, the doctrine rendered impossible equal protection of the law. In attempting to promote uniformity of law throughout the United States, the doctrine had prevented uniformity in the administration of the law of the state.

The discrimination resulting became in practice far-reaching. This resulted in part from the broad province accorded to the so-called "general law" as to which federal courts exercised an independent judgment. In addition to questions of purely commercial law, "general law" was held to include the obligations under contracts entered into and to be performed within the state, the extent to which a carrier operating within a state may stipulate for exemption from liability for his own negligence or that of his employee; the liability for torts committed within the state upon persons resident or property located there, even where the question of liability depended upon the scope of a property right conferred by the state; and the right to exemplary or punitive damages. Furthermore, state decisions, construing local deeds, mineral conveyances, and even devises of real estate, were disregarded.

In part the discrimination resulted from the wide range of persons held entitled to avail themselves of the federal rule by resort to the diversity of citizenship jurisdiction. Through this jurisdiction individual citizens willing to remove from their own state and become citizens of another might avail themselves of the federal rule. And, without even change of residence, a corporate citizen of the state could avail itself of the federal rule by reincorporating under the laws of another state, as was done in the Taxicab Case.

The injustice and confusion incident to the doctrine of Swift v. Tyson have been repeatedly urged as reasons for abolishing or limiting diversity of citizenship jurisdiction. Other legislative relief has been proposed. If only a question of statutory construction were involved, we should not be prepared to abandon a doctrine so widely applied throughout nearly a century. But the unconstitutionality of the course pursued has now been made clear, and compels us to do so.

Third. Except in matters governed by the Federal Constitution or by acts of Congress, the law to be applied in any case is the law of the state. And whether the law of the state shall be declared by its Legislature in a statute or by its highest court in a decision is not a matter of federal concern. There is no federal general common law. Congress has no power to declare substantive rules of common law applicable in a state whether they be local in their nature or "general," be they commercial law or a part of the law of torts. And no clause in the Constitution purports to confer such a power upon the federal courts. As stated by Mr. Justice Field when protesting in Baltimore & Ohio R.R. Co. v. Baugh, 149 U.S. 368, 401, against ignoring the Ohio common law of fellow-servant liability: "I am aware that what has been termed the general law of the country—which is often little less than what the judge advancing the doctrine thinks at the time should be the general law on a particular subject— has been often advanced in judicial opinions of this court to control a conflicting law of a state. I admit that learned judges have fallen into the habit of repeating this doctrine as a convenient mode of brushing aside the law of a

---

9. It was even possible for a nonresident plaintiff defeated on a point of law in the highest court of a State nevertheless to win out by taking a nonsuit and renewing the controversy in the federal court. Compare Gardner v. Michigan Cent. R.R. Co., 150 U.S. 349; * * *.

state in conflict with their views. And I confess that, moved and governed by the authority of the great names of those judges, I have, myself, in many instances, unhesitatingly and confidently, but I think now erroneously, repeated the same doctrine. But, notwithstanding the great names which may be cited in favor of the doctrine, and notwithstanding the frequency with which the doctrine has been reiterated, there stands, as a perpetual protest against its repetition, the constitution of the United States, which recognizes and preserves the autonomy and independence of the states,—independence in their legislative and independence in their judicial departments. Supervision over either the legislative or the judicial action of the states is in no case permissible except as to matters by the constitution specifically authorized or delegated to the United States. Any interference with either, except as thus permitted, is an invasion of the authority of the state, and, to that extent, a denial of its independence."

The fallacy underlying the rule declared in Swift v. Tyson is made clear by Mr. Justice Holmes. The doctrine rests upon the assumption that there is "a transcendental body of law outside of any particular State but obligatory within it unless and until changed by statute," that federal courts have the power to use their judgment as to what the rules of common law are; and that in the federal courts "the parties are entitled to an independent judgment on matters of general law":

"But law in the sense in which courts speak of it today does not exist without some definite authority behind it. The common law so far as it is enforced in a State, whether called common law or not, is not the common law generally but the law of that State existing by the authority of that State without regard to what it may have been in England or anywhere else. * * *

"The authority and only authority is the State, and if that be so, the voice adopted by the State as its own [whether it be of its Legislature or of its Supreme Court] should utter the last word."

Thus the doctrine of Swift v. Tyson is, as Mr. Justice Holmes said, "an unconstitutional assumption of powers by the Courts of the United States which no lapse of time or respectable array of opinion should make us hesitate to correct." In disapproving that doctrine we do not hold unconstitutional section 34 of the Federal Judiciary Act of 1789 or any other act of Congress. We merely declare that in applying the doctrine this Court and the lower courts have invaded rights which in our opinion are reserved by the Constitution to the several states.

Fourth. The defendant contended that by the common law of Pennsylvania as declared by its highest court in Falchetti v. Pennsylvania R. Co., 307 Pa. 203, 160 A. 859, the only duty owed to the plaintiff was to refrain from willful or wanton injury. The plaintiff denied that such is the Pennsylvania law. In support of their respective contentions the parties discussed and cited many decisions of the Supreme Court of the state. The Circuit Court of Appeals ruled that the question of liability is one of general law; and on that ground declined to decide the issue of state law. As we hold this was error, the judgment is reversed and the case remanded to it for further proceedings in conformity with our opinion.

Reversed.

■ [Justice Reed delivered a concurring opinion joining "in the conclusions reached in this case, in the disapproval of the doctrine of Swift v. Tyson, and in the reasoning of the majority opinion except in so far as it relies upon the unconstitutionality of the 'course pursued' by the federal courts." JUSTICE BUTLER dissented in an opinion in which JUSTICE McREYNOLDS joined. JUSTICE CARDOZO did not participate.]

NOTE ON THE RATIONALE OF THE ERIE DECISION

(1) *The "First" Ground of Decision.* Under its *"First"* heading, the Court refers to, and relies heavily on, Warren, *New Light on the History of The Federal Judiciary Act of 1789,* 37 Harv.L.Rev. 49, 51–52, 81–88, 108 (1923). In that article Warren notes that section 34 was "not contained in the Draft Bill, as introduced in the Senate, but was proposed, probably by [Senator, later Chief Justice] Ellsworth, as an amendment * * *." Warren's examination of the records of the Senate revealed a slip of paper, believed to be in Ellsworth's handwriting, on which an earlier version of the amendment (including the bracketed material in the following quotation) was written:

"And be it further enacted, That [the Statute law of the several states in force for the time being and their unwritten or common law now in use-,] whether by adoption from the common law of England, the ancient statutes of the same or otherwise, except where the Constitution, Treaties or Statutes of the United States shall otherwise require or provide, shall be regarded as rules of decision in the trials at common law in the courts of the United States in cases where they apply."

Warren's conclusion, endorsed by the Court in Erie, was that in light of the earlier draft, the phrase "laws of the several states" (which Ellsworth had written in as a substitute for the phrase in brackets), was plainly designed to cover unwritten law. Do you agree? Even if you accept Warren's conclusion, could you still defend the result of Swift v. Tyson? See Friendly, *In Praise of Erie—And of the New Federal Common Law,* 39 N.Y.U.L.Rev. 383, 389–91 (1964); *cf.* Hill, *The Erie Doctrine and the Constitution,* 53 Nw.U.L.Rev. 427, 442–45 (1958).[1]

(2) *The "Second" Ground.* In discussing the mischievous results of Swift v. Tyson, under its *"Second"* heading, the Court emphasized the "grave discrimination by noncitizens against citizens" introduced by the decision. The Court seems to be suggesting that only noncitizens of a state have access to a federal court in that state on diversity grounds. This is true of removal but not of

---

1. Warren's scholarship is sharply challenged, and his conclusions rejected, in Ritz, Rewriting the History of the Judiciary Act of 1789 (Holt & LaRue eds.) 8–12, 126–48 (1990). Ritz' research indicates, contrary to Warren's assumption, that during its deliberations, the Senate did not use the manuscript version of Section 34 that Warren had discovered. Ritz argues that choice-of-law questions were not a matter of concern to the framers of Section 34, and that the phrase "the laws of the several states" was meant to refer to American law as distinguished from British law. He notes that if the section had meant to refer to the laws of individual states, contemporary usage would have favored the phrase "laws of the respective states," and also points out that both the statute and decisional law of individual states was, by and large, inaccessible at that time. He then suggests that the true focus of Section 34 may have been to authorize development of a federal common law of crimes as an interim measure pending the development of statutory criminal provisions. (He recognizes, as a major obstacle to acceptance of this view, that Section 34 nowhere explicitly limits its application to criminal cases.)

original jurisdiction. And as to removal, the problem could be resolved by broadening the removal right. Should the Court's point about discrimination have been phrased differently?

Is the Erie holding and rationale limited to issues arising in litigation between citizens of different states? Plainly, it does not extend to all such issues, even of a wholly substantive character, since federal law may be controlling on particular questions in a diversity case. See, *e.g.*, Gertz v. Robert Welch, Inc., 418 U.S. 323 (1974). But what of questions of state law arising in a nondiversity case? See Maternally Yours v. Your Maternity Shop, 234 F.2d 538, 540–41 n. 1 (2d Cir.1956), where the court said, with respect to a pendent state law claim in a federal question case: "[I]t is the *source* of the right sued upon, and not the ground on which federal jurisdiction is founded, that determines the governing law. * * * Thus, the Erie doctrine applies, whatever the ground for federal jurisdiction, to any issue or claim which has its source in state law." (Emphasis in original.) See also Chap. VII, Sec. 1, p. ——, *infra.*

(3) *The "Third" Ground.* In a letter to Justice Reed written before the Erie decision was handed down, Justice Brandeis insisted that his opinion did not "pass upon or discuss the constitutionality of section 34 as construed in Swift v. Tyson"; rather the *"Third"* section of the opinion was "addressed to showing that the action of the Court in disregarding state law is unconstitutional." Quoted in Freyer, Harmony and Dissonance: The Swift and Erie Cases in American Federalism 136 (1981). What is the distinction?

From the time of its rendition to the present day, controversy has surrounded the scope and meaning of Erie as a constitutional holding.[1] Is the Court saying that Congress itself could not have enacted a rule of decision to govern a case like Erie? Would your answer turn on whether Congress was (a) laying down a rule of decision to govern the rights of trespassers on railroads whose activities affect interstate commerce, or (b) laying down a rule of decision applicable with respect to the rights of any trespasser in a case brought in a federal court under the diversity jurisdiction? If Congress (and/or the federal courts) have such power under the first theory, does the constitutional ruling in Erie do anything more than state a principle that can be readily circumvented in view of the breadth of the powers delegated to the federal government? If Congress has such power under either theory, should similar power be denied to the courts on constitutional grounds?

If your answer to the last question is yes, how would you state such a prohibition or presumption against judicial lawmaking? Wouldn't an absolute prohibition introduce an unworkable rigidity into the constitutional regime? (See Chap. VII, *infra.*) But might a less absolute presumption against judicial lawmaking be warranted in the absence of an adequate basis in federal constitutional or statutory values or policies?

(4) *The Remand.* Under its heading *"Fourth"*, why did the Court assume that Pennsylvania law controlled when the action had been brought in a New York federal court? See the Klaxon case, p. 695, *infra.*

---

1. See generally Wright, Federal Courts § 56 and authorities cited nn. 15, 16 (5th ed. 1994); Chemerinsky, Federal Jurisdiction § 5.3 and authorities cited n. 138 (2d ed. 1994).

NOTE ON THE WAYS OF ASCERTAINING STATE LAW

(1) *Unresolved Questions of State Law.* With what attitude should a federal district court approach a question of state law not plainly resolved by the state's highest court? With the same sense of responsibility for the creative development of law that a state court would have—or that the district court itself would have if the question were federal?

Should the federal court entertain an argument that a prior decision of the highest state court should be overruled? That it should be narrowly distinguished? Should it honor the state court's dicta?

What weight should be given to decisions of an intermediate state appellate court? Or a state trial court? The same weight that would be given by the court that rendered the decision? Or by a coordinate state court? Or by the highest state court?

Should a federal court of appeals, or the Supreme Court itself, exercise any greater freedom in these respects than a district court?

(2) *Lower State Court Decisions.* The lower federal courts did not at first read Erie as requiring them to adhere to decisions of lower state courts. But the Supreme Court brought them up sharply in a series of cases at the 1940 term, particularly Fidelity Union Trust Co. v. Field, 311 U.S. 169 (1940).

The Field case held that a federal court in New Jersey was bound to follow a decision of the New Jersey Court of Chancery, a trial court of state wide jurisdiction, "in the absence of more convincing evidence of what the state law is" (p. 178). The Court recognized that the decision might not be followed by the Court of Errors and Appeals or by the Court of Chancery itself.[1] But it called this "merely a matter of conjecture" (p. 179). Nor did it seem to regard arguments against the soundness of the decision, however persuasive, as "convincing evidence".

Eight years later, in King v. Order of United Commercial Travelers, 333 U.S. 153 (1948), the Court unanimously upheld the refusal of the court of appeals to follow an unreported decision of a South Carolina court of common pleas (a trial court of limited territorial jurisdiction). The pendulum swing continued, perhaps in an effort to get back to dead center, in Bernhardt v. Polygraphic Co., 350 U.S. 198 (1956). One of the issues in this diversity case was whether a 1910 Vermont Supreme Court decision represented the state law on the question in 1956. The United States Supreme Court held that it did, stating (p. 205):

"* * * Were the question in doubt or deserving further canvass, we would of course remand the case to the Court of Appeals to pass on this question of Vermont law. But, as we have indicated, there appears to be no confusion in the Vermont decisions, no developing line of authorities that casts a shadow over the established ones, no dicta, doubts or ambiguities in the opinions of Vermont judges on the question, no legislative development that promises to undermine the judicial rule." *Cf.* Commissioner v. Estate of Bosch, 387 U.S. 456, 465 (1967)(a federal estate tax case in which the Court noted that under Erie, "federal authority may not be bound by an intermediate state appellate court ruling").

---

1. Indeed, the decision was not followed. See Clark, *State Law in The Federal* *Courts: The Brooding Omnipresence of Erie v. Tompkins,* 55 Yale L.J. 267, 291–92 (1946).

Note one difference between a federal court and an intermediate state court: a decision of the latter can be directly reversed by the state's highest court while a decision of the former cannot. (Compare the process of certification, referred to in Paragraph (3), below). How does this difference affect your view of the issues raised in this Note?

Professor Wright, summarizing the state of the law since the King and Bosch decisions, says that a federal judge "need no longer be a ventriloquist's dummy. Instead he or she is free, just as state judges are, to consider all the data the highest court of the state would use in an effort to determine how the highest court of the state would decide." Wright, Federal Courts § 58, at 395 (5th ed. 1994).[2]

(3) *Abstention and Other Refusals to Decide State law Questions.* Under what circumstances may a federal district court refuse to determine a question of state law because of its uncertainty and difficulty? In the event of such a refusal, should the court dismiss the action? Or should it retain jurisdiction, and if so, for what purpose? Do the considerations change if a state has a "certification" statute or rule authorizing the state's highest court to answer questions referred to it by a federal court in the course of litigation?[3]

For materials throwing some light on these questions, see Chap. X, Sec. 2, *infra.*

(4) *Appellate Review of District Court Decisions.* In reviewing the judgment of a federal district court, should the court of appeals give deference to the district court's interpretation of state law, or should it review the question of state law de novo? In Salve Regina College v. Russell, 499 U.S. 225 (1991), the Supreme Court, in a 6–3 decision in a diversity case, held that de novo review was required. The Court reasoned that this result was supported not only by the traditional scope of review on questions of law and by the "reflective dialogue and collective judgment" (p. 232) that attends appellate consideration, but also by the purposes of the Erie doctrine—to discourage forum shopping and to avoid inequitable administration of the laws. "[D]eferential appellate review," the Court said, "invites divergent development of state law among the federal trial courts even within a single State" (p. 234). In answer to the argument, advanced in the dissent, that the Supreme Court itself had often deferred to the judgment of lower federal courts on questions of state law, the Court stated: "We are not persuaded that the manner in which this Court chooses to expend its limited resources in the exercise of its discretionary jurisdiction has any relevance to the obligation of courts of appeals to review de novo those legal issues properly before them" (p. 235 n. 3).

Is the rule of Salve Regina required by Erie? If not, is it preferable to a rule that in the absence of a conflict among district court decisions in a district,

---

2. In Factors Etc., Inc. v. Pro Arts, Inc., 652 F.2d 278 (2d Cir.1981), a divided court held that if the controlling law is that of a state in another circuit, and if the question of state law is a novel and difficult one, the prediction of the other circuit as to the course of state law is entitled to deference.

3. For discussion of certification procedures, see p. 1245, *infra.* For diversity cases in which the Supreme Court urged resort to certification, see Clay v. Sun Ins. Office Ltd., 363 U.S. 207 (1960) (substantial constitutional questions hinged on construction of relevant state statute); Lehman Bros. v. Schein, 416 U.S. 386 (1974)(question involved unsettled law of a state located in a different circuit from the one in which suit was brought).

the circuit court will ordinarily defer to the (local) district judge's understanding of the content of local law?

Klaxon Co. v. Stentor Electric Manufacturing Co., Inc.

313 U.S. 487, 61 S.Ct. 1020, 85 L.Ed. 1477 (1941).
Certiorari to the Circuit Court of Appeals for the Third Circuit.

■ Mr. Justice Reed delivered the opinion of the Court.

The principal question in this case is whether in diversity cases the federal courts must follow conflict of laws rules prevailing in the states in which they sit. * * *

In 1918 respondent, a New York corporation, transferred its entire business to petitioner, a Delaware corporation. Petitioner contracted to use its best efforts to further the manufacture and sale of certain patented devices covered by the agreement, and respondent was to have a share of petitioner's profits. The agreement was executed in New York, the assets were transferred there, and petitioner began performance there although later it moved its operations to other states. Respondent was voluntarily dissolved under New York law in 1919. Ten years later it instituted this action in the United States District Court for the District of Delaware, alleging that petitioner had failed to perform its agreement to use its best efforts. Jurisdiction rested on diversity of citizenship. In 1939 respondent recovered a jury verdict of $100,000, upon which judgment was entered. Respondent then moved to correct the judgment by adding interest at the rate of six percent from June 1, 1929, the date the action had been brought. The basis of the motion was the provision in section 480 of the New York Civil Practice Act directing that in contract actions interest be added to the principal sum "whether theretofore liquidated or unliquidated." The District Court granted the motion, taking the view that the rights of the parties were governed by New York law and that under New York law the addition of such interest was mandatory. 30 F.Supp. 425, 431. The Circuit Court of Appeals affirmed, 3 Cir., 115 F.2d 268, 275, and we granted certiorari, limited to the question whether section 480 of the New York Civil Practice Act is applicable to an action in the federal court in Delaware.

The Circuit Court of Appeals was of the view that under New York law the right to interest before verdict under section 480 went to the substance of the obligation, and that proper construction of the contract in suit fixed New York as the place of performance. It then concluded that section 480 was applicable to the case because "it is clear by what we think is undoubtedly the better view of the law that the rules for ascertaining the measure of damages are not a matter of procedure at all, but are matters of substance which should be settled by reference to the law of the appropriate state according to the type of case being tried in the forum. The measure of damages for breach of a contract is determined by the law of the place of performance; Restatement, Conflict of Laws § 413." The court referred also to section 418 of the Restatement, which makes interest part of the damages to be determined by the law of the place of performance. Application of the New York statute apparently followed from the court's independent determination of the "better view" without regard to Delaware law, for no Delaware decision or statute was cited or discussed.

We are of opinion that the prohibition declared in Erie Railroad v. Tompkins, 304 U.S. 64, against such independent determinations by the federal courts extends to the field of conflict of laws. The conflict of laws rules to be applied by the federal court in Delaware must conform to those prevailing in Delaware's state courts. Otherwise the accident of diversity of citizenship would constantly disturb equal administration of justice in coordinate state and federal courts sitting side by side. See Erie Railroad v. Tompkins, *supra*, 304 U.S. at 74–77. Any other ruling would do violence to the principle of uniformity within a state upon which the Tompkins decision is based. Whatever lack of uniformity this may produce between federal courts in different states is attributable to our federal system, which leaves to a state, within the limits permitted by the Constitution, the right to pursue local policies diverging from those of its neighbors. It is not for the federal courts to thwart such local policies by enforcing an independent "general law" of conflict of laws. Subject only to review by this Court on any federal question that may arise, Delaware is free to determine whether a given matter is to be governed by the law of the forum or some other law. This Court's views are not the decisive factor in determining the applicable conflicts rule. And the proper function of the Delaware federal court is to ascertain what the state law is, not what it ought to be.

* * *

Respondent makes the further argument that the judgment must be affirmed because, under the full faith and credit clause of the Constitution, Art. 4, § 1, the state courts of Delaware would be obliged to give effect to the New York statute. The argument rests mainly on the decision of this Court in John Hancock Mutual Life Insurance Company v. Yates, 299 U.S. 178, where a New York statute was held such an integral part of a contract of insurance that Georgia was compelled to sustain the contract under the full faith and credit clause. Here, however, section 480 of the New York Civil Practice Act is in no way related to the validity of the contract in suit, but merely to an incidental item of damages, interest, with respect to which courts at the forum have commonly been free to apply their own or some other law as they see fit. Nothing in the Constitution ensures unlimited extraterritorial recognition of all statutes or of any statute under all circumstances. The full faith and credit clause does not go so far as to compel Delaware to apply section 480 if such application would interfere with its local policy.

Accordingly, the judgment is reversed and the case remanded to the Circuit Court of Appeals for decision in conformity with the law of Delaware.

Reversed and remanded.

NOTE ON CHOICE OF LAW IN CASES INVOLVING
STATE–CREATED RIGHTS

(1) *Klaxon and Erie.* Judged by Klaxon, was the premise of the remand in Erie (in the "Fourth" section of the opinion) incorrect?

(2) *Unpacking the Issues.* Is it possible to think soundly about the question Justice Reed states in his opening sentence, and purports to decide, as a single question?

What did Justice Reed mean by speaking of "the right" of a state "to pursue local policies diverging from those of its neighbors"? In a federal system, does this "right" have the same claim to recognition with respect to all who find themselves within the state's borders? The same claim with respect to matters primarily connected with another state as with respect to matters primarily connected with the forum state? The same claim with respect to matters of plainly substantive law as with respect to matters procedural or quasi-procedural?

(3) *Klaxon and the Constitution.* If the Court in Klaxon proceeded on the assumption that, as in Erie, the result was constitutionally compelled, it was plainly mistaken.

The question in Klaxon was whether New York or Delaware law determined the date from which interest was to be awarded in connection with a judgment. Even assuming that the right to interest is substantive and thus to be governed by state law under Erie, the choice of *which* state's law applies in a federal court is clearly a matter of federal concern. The vesting of jurisdiction in the federal courts in a category of cases carries with it the inherent authority (within the limits set by the Tenth Amendment, the Due Process Clause, and any other relevant provisions of the Constitution) to choose the applicable law. Moreover, even if it could not have legislated the substantive decisional rule for all diversity cases encompassed by Erie, surely Congress, acting under its power to make laws "necessary and proper" to the exercise of jurisdiction under Article III, could authorize the formulation of federal choice-of-law rules for the federal courts, or indeed require a federal court to apply the New York statute on interest in a case like Klaxon.

The point is buttressed by the fact that at least in civil cases, the Constitution does not prohibit the territorial jurisdiction of the federal district courts from cutting across state boundaries. If Congress were to eliminate the district courts of New York and Delaware, and to create a single "Federal District Court for the Middle Atlantic States," the Klaxon rule could not operate on the facts of the case itself. See Hill, *The Erie Doctrine and the Constitution,* 53 Nw.U.L.Rev. 541, 558 (1958).

Indeed, Congress has authority under the Full Faith and Credit Clause to federalize choice of law by enacting conflicts rules binding on state as well as federal courts. See Friendly, *In Praise of Erie—And of the New Federal Common Law,* 39 N.Y.U.L.Rev. 383, 401–02 (1964); Jackson, *Full Faith and Credit—The Lawyer's Clause of the Constitution,* 45 Colum.L.Rev. 1 (1945).[1]

Is this authority relevant to the issue posed by Justice Reed in his opening sentence?

Note that these points go no further than to criticize the rather simplistic extension of Erie in the Klaxon opinion. They do not make an affirmative case for a contrary result, since it may be desirable, even though not constitutionally compelled, to apply the choice-of-law rules of the forum state.

---

1. Horowitz, *Toward a Federal Common Law of Choice of Law,* 14 U.C.L.A.L.Rev. 1191 (1967), points to the Full Faith and Credit Clause, the Rules of Decision Act, 28 U.S.C. § 1652 (especially the words "in cases where they apply"), and such decisions as Banco Nacional de Cuba v. Sabbatino, 376 U.S. 398 (1964), p. 806, *infra,* as providing authority for the development of federal common law in this field.

(4) *The First Edition's Arguments Against the Klaxon Result.* In the First Edition of this book (pp. 634–35), the authors marshaled the arguments against Klaxon as follows:

"Consider the application of Erie and of Klaxon to problems of the choice of plainly substantive rules of decision, such as those involved in Erie itself and in Swift v. Tyson.

"Notice again that these rules do much more than provide the underlying premises of a decision on the merits when litigation occurs. They help to organize and guide people's everyday lives. Notice that confusion and uncertainty about the rules of law which are relevant at this stage of primary private activity is far more serious than uncertainty about rules which become material only if litigation eventuates. This is so, if for no other reason, because the number of instances of the application of law at the primary stage bears to the number of instances of its application in litigation the ratio of thousands or hundreds of thousands to one.

"As applied in non-conflicts situations, Erie might have been regarded, might it not, as based at least in significant part on the proposition that it is intolerable to have two different systems of courts deciding questions of 'plainly substantive' law differently, where it is unpredictable which system will acquire jurisdiction, since that not only introduces an element of retroactivity into every judicial disposition of such disputes as develop but confuses basic legal relations throughout the area of primary activity affected by the overlap? Notice that it was in the context of questions of this kind that Justice Brandeis spoke of the 'unconstitutionality' of the course which the federal courts had pursued. See Hill, *The Erie Doctrine in Bankruptcy*, 66 Harv.L.Rev. 1013, 1031–35 (1953).

"If this view of Erie had been taken, the problem of marking out the scope of its application in non-conflicts situations would have reduced itself, would it not, to one of distinguishing between (a) those rules of law which characteristically and reasonably affect people's conduct at the stage of primary private activity and should therefore be classified as substantive or quasi-substantive, and (b) those rules which are not of significant importance at the primary stage and should therefore be regarded as quasi-procedural or procedural?

"Consider the bearing which such an analysis of Erie would have had in situations involving state-versus-state conflicts of plainly substantive law.

"Notice that Swift v. Tyson had solved the problem of uncertainty about the applicable substantive law for people who could anticipate access to a federal court. Erie destroyed this assurance, but mitigated the damage with an alternative assurance of the uniform enforcement in any federal court of whatever state law was applicable. Klaxon destroyed the mitigation, did it not?

"Erie must largely have proceeded upon the assumption, must it not, that the prime need was for an assurance of state-federal conformity in the interest of people who could not be sure of a federal forum? Klaxon cut down the value of this new assurance, did it not, largely to those situations in which it is possible to foresee the state in which litigation will take place? In what proportion of situations *is* this possible, when the people involved are of diverse citizenship?

"Would it be accurate to conclude that Klaxon, in effect, treats Erie as if it had been unconcerned with the problem of uncertainty about the applicable substantive law at the stage of primary private activity? Was it necessary to do this? Why should forum-shopping between different courts in the same state have been regarded as the *summum malum* of diversity litigation while forum-shopping among courts in different geographical areas was dismissed as an inescapable weakness of a federal system? Did the Rules of Decision Act have to be read as authorizing the plaintiff, and the courts of the state he selects, to decide which state's laws are the laws which 'apply', rather than the federal court?''

Are the foregoing assumptions about uniformity—that uniformity among federal courts is more important than uniformity between state and federal courts in a given state—warranted? How certain can one be, at the stage of primary private activity, of access to a federal forum when the plaintiff can prevent removal by suing in the defendant's home state? Is it more likely that forum shopping for a favorable choice-of-law rule would occur within a given state or among states? Even in controversies between diverse citizens, the defendant may well not be subject to suit in a number of states. Further, neither the plaintiff nor the plaintiff's lawyer is likely to be indifferent about the choice of the state in which to sue even if there is no choice-of-law question.

(5) *Further Arguments Bearing on the Klaxon Rule.* Consider the argument that the federal courts in diversity cases are in a special and strategic position, as a disinterested forum, to work out solutions to problems of interstate conflict of laws that are consistent with the presuppositions of a federal judicial system. See Hart, *The Relations Between State and Federal Law,* 54 Colum.L.Rev. 489, 513–15 (1954).

This argument rests on the premise that a state's choice-of-law rules are likely to discriminate (unfairly, even if not unconstitutionally) against out-of-staters and that this is precisely the kind of prejudice that the diversity jurisdiction was designed to prevent. To paraphrase one commentator, allowing the state in which the action happens to be brought to resolve a conflict with another state is like allowing the pitcher to call balls and strikes whenever he manages to beat the batter to the call.[2]

Such an argument suggests that all choice-of-law questions in actions between diverse citizens should be federal questions, whether they arise in state or federal courts.[3] But whether or not the argument must carry that far, it raises some problems about the supremacy of state policy in matters of essentially state concern. Consider a case in which a product made in State X is sold in State Y, where a consumer is injured in the course of using it.[4] State X holds manufacturers liable only on a showing of negligence, or privity of warranty, while State Y holds them strictly liable for personal injuries caused by a defective product. If litigation occurs in State Y, should Y's rule of liability apply? What is the relevance of state court decisions in Y holding that the rule should have "extra-territorial" application in such a case? Can a federal court in State Y disregard the state's choice of its own law without seriously undermining a substantive state policy? See Hill, Paragraph (3), *supra,* at 546–68. Bear in mind that an out-of-state defendant would undoubt-

---

2. See Baxter, *Choice of Law and the Federal System,* 16 Stan.L.Rev. 1, 23 (1963).

3. Indeed, if Erie was rightly decided, how else would you explain the fact that Article III appears in terms to authorize review by the Supreme Court of *state court* decisions in diversity cases? On the basis

that a special exception for diversity cases would have been too awkward to draft? That the question didn't occur to the drafters at all?

4. See Baxter, note 2, *supra,* at 7–11.

edly remove a state court action if there were any advantage in doing so. Suppose the legislature of Y had enacted a statute explicitly imposing strict liability on all manufacturers, wherever located, whose products cause personal injury within the state. If a federal court in Y were to choose X's law in such a case, would that not, in effect, be a holding that, as a matter of federal law, Y could not furnish this substantive protection to those injured within its borders?

Is it an answer to these arguments that if the Y federal court disregards X's law limiting the manufacturer's liability in such a case, it is also frustrating a significant state policy? Note that the suit in this hypothetical case is almost certain to take place in Y if the state has a long-arm statute permitting out-of-state service of process, and that the decisions upholding the constitutionality of the reach of state process in such a case are themselves a recognition of the substantiality of Y's interest. Do they also suggest the appropriateness of applying Y's laws? See International Shoe Co. v. Washington, 326 U.S. 310 (1945). See generally von Mehren & Trautman, *Jurisdiction to Adjudicate: A Suggested Analysis,* 79 Harv.L.Rev. 1121, 1128–34, 1176–77 (1966).

How different is the situation if the forum state in our hypothetical diversity action is Z, a state having no connection whatever with the events in suit? Would any impairment of Z's policies result from a federal court's refusal to follow Z's choice-of-law rule on the issue of absolute liability? And if Z chooses to follow its own law on burden of proof, for instance, on the ground that the matter is "procedural", should a federal court be free to disregard the choice? Indeed, should the federal court have that freedom whenever a state looks to its own law simply on the ground that the matter is procedural and thus lex fori applies? The cases hold otherwise. *E.g.,* Wells v. Simonds Abrasive Co., 345 U.S. 514 (1953); Sampson v. Channell, 110 F.2d 754 (1st Cir.1940). Are these cases perhaps justified because it is extremely rare that the forum state is totally disinterested (and sometimes hard to tell whether it is or not), because under a state's "procedural" label there may lurk a significant substantive policy, and because there is in any event an independent value in discouraging forum shopping within a state?

An effort by the Fifth Circuit to develop an exception to Klaxon was rejected by the Supreme Court in Day & Zimmermann, Inc. v. Challoner, 423 U.S. 3 (1975). It held that a Texas federal court must apply Texas choice-of-law rules in a diversity case even if, in the federal court's view, the rationale of those rules was "not operative" under the facts and the case was one in which those rules would lead to the application of the law of a jurisdiction with "no interest * * *, no policy at stake" (p. 4). See Currie, *The Supreme Court and Federal Jurisdiction: 1975 Term,* 1976 Sup.Ct.Rev. 183, 217 (raising a question of the constitutionality of the particular Texas choice-of-law rule involved in the case).[5]

---

5. For an extraordinary effort to remain within the Klaxon framework and at the same time to apply a "federal law or national consensus law" of liability in a diversity case, see Judge Weinstein's opinion in In re Agent Orange Product Liability Litigation, 580 F.Supp. 690, 706 (E.D.N.Y.1984), discussed in Schuck, Agent Orange on Trial 128–31 (Enlarged ed. 1987). The Second Circuit ultimately upheld Judge Weinstein's approval of the settlement in this case, 818 F.2d 145 (2d Cir.1987), on grounds that enabled it to avoid ruling on the propriety of Judge Weinstein's approach to choice of law. See Schuck, *supra,* at 307–11. The court did note, however, that since every jurisdiction was "free to render its own choice of law decision, * * * common experience suggests

(6) *Commentary*. Klaxon has its defenders, of course. See, *e.g.*, Cavers, *The Changing Choice-of-Law Process and the Federal Courts*, 28 Law & Contemp.Probs. 732 (1963)(emphasizing the emergence of a "policy-oriented, issue-by-issue process for choosing law" (p. 734 n. 8), noting the constructive contribution to this approach that can be made by the federal courts on an *ad hoc* basis within the Klaxon framework, and expressing concern about the inroads on state authority that a rejection of Klaxon would entail); Ely, *The Irrepressible Myth of Erie*, 87 Harv.L.Rev. 693, 714–15 n. 125 (arguing, *inter alia*, that the Klaxon result is required by the Rules of Decision Act).

But Klaxon has its contemporary critics too. See, *e.g.*, Bridwell & Whitten, The Constitution and the Common Law 135 (1977)("The Rules of Decision Act itself embodies a direction to the federal courts to determine when a particular state's law will 'apply' under international conflict of laws rules, which the early cases indicate would have controlled even if the Act itself had never been passed"); Trautman, *The Relation Between American Choice of Law and Federal Common Law*, 41 Law & Contemp.Probs. No. 2, at 105, 120 n. 58 (Spring 1977)(Klaxon reintroduced some of the uncertainty that Erie was designed to eliminate); Borchers, *The Origins of Diversity Jurisdiction, The Rise of Legal Positivism, and a Brave New World for Erie and Klaxon*, 72 Tex.L.Rev. 79 (1995).[6]

(7) *Existing Constitutional Limits on Horizontal Choice of Law*. The Due Process and Full Faith and Credit Clauses have been held to place some limits on the free choice of law by state courts, though recent decisions indicate that those limits are quite expansive. See Allstate Ins. Co. v. Hague, 449 U.S. 302 (1981), and cases cited therein. But see Phillips Petroleum Co. v. Shutts, 472 U.S. 797, 821–22 (1985)(since state lacks "significant contact or significant aggregation of contacts" with respect to claims of many members of plaintiff class, application of that state's law to those claims is "sufficiently arbitrary and unfair as to exceed constitutional limits").[7] Federal courts are controlled

---

that the intellectual power of Chief Judge Weinstein's analysis alone would not be enough to prevent widespread disagreement" (818 F.2d at 165).

6. For discussion of proposals to create a federal common law governing choice of the applicable state law in multistate tort cases, see p. 805, *infra*. See also Trautman, *Toward Federalizing Choice of Law*, 70 Tex. L.Rev. 1715 (1992).

The American Law Institute, in a recently completed study, has proposed a federal choice of law code for complex cases involving state-created causes of action. See ALI, Complex Litigation: Statutory Recommendations and Analysis §§ 6.01–6.07 (1994). For extensive discussion of this and other aspects of the study, see Symposium, 54 La.L.Rev. No. 4 (March 1994).

7. See also Leflar, *Constitutional Limits on Free Choice of Law*, 28 Law & Contemp.Probs. 706 (1963); Brilmayer, *Legitimate Interests in Multistate Problems: As*

Between State and Federal Law, 79 Mich. L.Rev. 1315 (1981); Laycock, *Equal Citizens of Equal and Territorial States: The Constitutional Foundations of Choice of Law,* 92 Colum.L.Rev. 249 (1992); Pielemeier, *Why We Should Worry About Full Faith and Credit to Laws,* 60 S.Cal.L.Rev. 1299 (1987). These articles contain, *inter alia,* arguments for significant limits on state choice of law.

The reach of the Shutts decision itself may have been limited by Sun Oil Co. v. Wortman, 486 U.S. 717 (1988), also a state court class action. In Sun Oil the Court, per Scalia, J., held that the forum state could constitutionally apply its own, relatively long, statute of limitations to claims as to which, under Shutts, it could not constitutionally apply its substantive law. Justice Brennan, joined by Justices Marshall and Blackmun, concurred in the judgment, arguing that the forum had sufficient procedural interests in the application of its own limitations period. He objected, however, to the majority's reasoning, which suggested broadly that the fo-

by the same limitations in administering the Klaxon doctrine—at least to the extent those limitations derive from the Due Process Clauses. Do these limitations give adequate protection to federal interests by assuring against excessive provincialism in state choice-of-law rules?

(8) *The Applicability of Klaxon in Special Circumstances.* Whatever the merits of the Klaxon doctrine on the facts there presented, should the rule be different when a federal court in a diversity case exercises jurisdiction over a defendant who is beyond the reach of process issuing from the forum state's own courts? (Examples of such cases include interpleader actions under 28 U.S.C. § 2361, and actions in which additional parties across state lines but within 100 miles of the federal courthouse are brought in under Fed.Rule 4(k)(1)(B)). Note that the reach of federal process in the vast bulk of diversity actions does not exceed that of the forum state,[8] and thus application of the forum state's choice-of-law rules does not alter the resolution of conflicting interests among states that would be arrived at if there were no federal diversity jurisdiction. But the balance may be significantly affected if the federal court applies the forum state's rules in a case that is beyond that state's power to adjudicate. See Hill, Paragraph (3), *supra,* at 557–58, 566–68.

In Griffin v. McCoach, 313 U.S. 498 (1941), decided the same day as Klaxon, the Court held that the forum state's choice of law rules must be applied in a statutory interpleader case. The Court did not mention the fact that at least one of the claimants to the fund was almost certainly beyond the reach of the forum state's process, nor did it refer to any of the arguments suggested here.

But if the Court in Griffin had taken account of these arguments, and had authorized a federal choice-of-law rule in such cases, another problem would have arisen. Whenever the question of choice of law arose in an interpleader case, for example, it might have been necessary to determine whether the forum state would have been able to exercise jurisdiction over all the claimants. Would the extra work have been worth the resulting benefits? Bear in mind that venue choices in interpleader are not unlimited, see 28 U.S.C. § 1397, and that the plaintiff stakeholder will frequently have little incentive to shop for a favorable choice-of-law rule.

(9) *Klaxon and Transfer of Venue.* Given Klaxon, what choice-of-law rule is to be applied in an action that is transferred to another federal court under 28 U.S.C. § 1404? Under 28 U.S.C. § 1406? § 1407?

rum could apply its own law to all matters (such as limitations periods, remedies, and evidentiary burdens) that have traditionally been viewed as procedural under the Full Faith and Credit Clause. Instead, Justice Brennan urged adherence to the standard set forth in Shutts, which permits a forum to apply its own law when it has an interest in doing so arising from significant contacts with the matter in question.

For an historical and analytical argument that the Full Faith and Credit Clause had a far more limited purpose than that accorded to it by the Supreme Court, see Whitten, *The Constitutional Limitations on* *State–Court Jurisdiction: A Historical–Interpretative Reexamination of the Full Faith and Credit and Due Process Clauses* (Part One), 14 Creighton L.Rev. 499 (1981). In a later article, Professor Whitten argues that the Due Process Clause places a restriction on state choice of law that is "far narrower than even the 'modest check on state power' currently enforced by the Court." Whitten, *The Constitutional Limitations on State Choice of Law: Due Process,* 9 Hastings Const.L.Q. 851, 853 (1982).

8. See Fed.Rule 4(k)(1)(A). *Cf.* Arrowsmith v. United Press Int'l, 320 F.2d 219 (2d Cir.1963), p. 1599, *infra.*

In Van Dusen v. Barrack, 376 U.S. 612 (1964), p. 1602, *infra,* the Court held (in a case involving transfer under § 1404) that the law to be applied was the law that the courts of the transferor state would apply. The defendants in that case were seeking the transfer, and the law of the transferee state would have been more favorable to them. "The legislative history of § 1404(a)," the Court said, "certainly does not justify the rather startling conclusion that one might 'get a change of law as a bonus for a change of venue'" (pp. 635–36).[9]

Does the very existence of the issue raised in Van Dusen, which is discussed more fully at pp. 1612–14, *infra,* cast doubt on the soundness of the Klaxon result? Given Klaxon, was the Van Dusen holding the best of the available alternatives?

(10) *Klaxon and the Federal Rules of Evidence.* The Federal Rules of Evidence raise a number of horizontal choice-of-law questions, especially when, as in Rules 302, 501, and 601, the rules refer to state law but give no guide governing a choice among the laws of different states. Is a federal court bound by the choice the forum state would make? "[T]he decisions to date have all but unanimously endorsed this method." 23 Wright & Graham, Federal Practice and Procedure § 5435, at 868, and cases cited n. 24 (1980 & 1995 Supp.). But see, *e.g.,* Berger, *Privileges, Presumptions and Competency of Witnesses in the Federal Court: A Federal Choice-of-Laws Rule,* 42 Brook. L.Rev. 417 (1976).

If Klaxon controls, what if the question of evidence arises in a deposition in a federal court in State A in connection with an action pending in a federal court in State B? When the question is one of privilege, Wright & Graham, *supra,* at 884–85, conclude that "the better rule would seem to be that the deposition state should not require disclosure if the matter is privileged either under local law or the law that will be applied at trial." Do you agree?

SECTION 3.   ENFORCING STATE-CREATED OBLIGATIONS— EQUITABLE REMEDIES AND PROCEDURE

Guaranty Trust Co. v. York

326 U.S. 99, 65 S.Ct. 1464, 89 L.Ed. 2079 (1945).
Certiorari to the Circuit Court of Appeals for the Second Circuit.

■ MR. JUSTICE FRANKFURTER delivered the opinion of the Court.

* * *

In May, 1930, Van Sweringen Corporation issued notes to the amount of $30,000,000. Under an indenture of the same date, petitioner, Guaranty Trust Co., was named trustee with power and obligations to enforce the rights of the noteholders in the assets of the Corporation and of the Van Sweringen brothers. In October, 1930, petitioner, with other banks, made large advances to companies affiliated with the Corporation and wholly controlled by the Van Sweringens. In October, 1931, when it was apparent that the Corporation

---

9. See also Ferens v. John Deere Co., 494 U.S. 516 (1990), p. 1612, *infra* (holding that the transferor state's law governs in *all* cases transferred under § 1404, whether the transfer is initiated by the plaintiff, the defendant, or the court).

could not meet its obligations, Guaranty co-operated in a plan for the purchase of the outstanding notes on the basis of cash for 50% of the face value of the notes and twenty shares of Van Sweringen Corporation's stock for each $1,000 note. This exchange offer remained open until December 15, 1931.

Respondent York received $6,000 of the notes as a gift in 1934, her donor not having accepted the offer of exchange. In April, 1940, three accepting noteholders began suit against petitioner, charging fraud and misrepresentation. Respondent's application to intervene in that suit was denied, Hackner v. Guaranty Trust Co., 2 Cir., 117 F.2d 95, and summary judgment in favor of Guaranty was affirmed. Hackner v. Morgan, 2 Cir., 130 F.2d 300. After her dismissal from the Hackner litigation, respondent, on January 22, 1942, began the present proceedings.

The suit, instituted as a class action on behalf of non-accepting noteholders and brought in a federal court solely because of diversity of citizenship, is based on an alleged breach of trust by Guaranty in that it failed to protect the interests of the noteholders in assenting to the exchange offer and failed to disclose its self-interest when sponsoring the offer. Petitioner moved for summary judgment, which was granted, upon the authority of the Hackner case. On appeal, the Circuit Court of Appeals, one Judge dissenting, * * * held that in a suit brought on the equity side of a federal district court that court is not required to apply the State statute of limitations that would govern like suits in the courts of a State where the federal court is sitting even though the exclusive basis of federal jurisdiction is diversity of citizenship. 143 F.2d 503. The importance of the question for the disposition of litigation in the federal courts led us to bring the case here.

In view of the basis of the decision below, it is not for us to consider whether the New York statute would actually bar this suit were it brought in a State court. Our only concern is with the holding that the federal courts in a suit like this are not bound by local law. * * *

In exercising their jurisdiction on the ground of diversity of citizenship, the federal courts, in the long course of their history, have not differentiated in their regard for State law between actions at law and suits in equity. Although § 34 of the Judiciary Act of 1789 directed that the "laws of the several States * * * shall be regarded as rules of decision in trials of common law * * *", this was deemed, consistently for over a hundred years, to be merely declaratory of what would in any event have governed the federal courts and therefore was equally applicable to equity suits. Indeed, it may fairly be said that the federal courts gave greater respect to State-created "substantive rights", Pusey & Jones Co. v. Hanssen, 261 U.S. 491, 498, in equity than they gave them on the law side, because rights at law were usually declared by State courts and as such increasingly flouted by extension of the doctrine of Swift v. Tyson, while rights in equity were frequently defined by legislative enactment and as such known and respected by the federal courts. See, *e.g.*, Pusey & Jones Co. v. Hanssen, *supra*, 261 U.S. at page 498.

Partly because the States in the early days varied greatly in the manner in which equitable relief was afforded and in the extent to which it was available, * * * Congress provided that "the forms and modes of proceeding in suits * * * of equity" would conform to the settled uses of courts of equity. Section 2, 1 Stat. 275, 276. But this enactment gave the federal courts no power that they would not have had in any event when courts were given "cognizance", by the first Judiciary Act, of suits "in equity". From the beginning there has been a good deal of talk in the cases that federal equity is a separate legal system. And so it is, properly understood. The suits in equity of which the federal courts have had "cognizance" ever since 1789 constituted the body of law which had been transplanted to this country from the English Court of Chancery. But this system of equity "derived its doctrines, as well as its powers, from its mode of giving relief". Langdell, Summary of Equity Pleading (1877) xxvii. In giving federal courts "cognizance" of equity suits in cases of diversity jurisdiction, Congress never gave, nor did the federal courts ever claim, the power to deny substantive rights created by State law or to create substantive rights denied by State law.

This does not mean that whatever equitable remedy is available in a State court must be available in a diversity suit in a federal court, or conversely, that a federal court may not afford an equitable remedy not available in a State court. Equitable relief in a federal court is of course subject to restrictions: the suit must be within the traditional scope of equity as historically evolved in the English Court of Chancery, Payne v. Hook, 7 Wall. 425, 430; a plain, adequate and complete remedy at law must be wanting, § 16, 1 Stat. 73, 82, 28 U.S.C. § 384; explicit Congressional curtailment of equity powers must be respected, see, e.g., Norris–LaGuardia Act, 47 Stat. 70, 29 U.S.C. § 101 et seq.; the constitutional right to trial by jury cannot be evaded, Whitehead v. Shattuck, 138 U.S. 146. That a State may authorize its courts to give equitable relief unhampered by any or all such restrictions cannot remove these fetters from the federal courts. See Clark v. Smith, 13 Pet. 195, 203; In re Broderick's Will, 21 Wall. 503, 519, 520; * * *. State law cannot define the remedies which a federal court must give simply because a federal court in diversity jurisdiction is available as an alternative tribunal to the State's courts.[3] Contrariwise, a federal court may afford an equitable remedy for a substantive right recognized by a State even though a State court cannot give it. Whatever contradiction or confusion may be produced by a medley of judicial phrases severed from their environment, the body of adjudications concerning equitable relief in diversity cases leaves no doubt that the federal courts enforced State-created substantive rights if the mode of proceeding and remedy were consonant with the traditional body of equitable remedies, practice and procedure, and in so doing they were enforcing rights created by the States and not arising under any inherent or statutory federal law.

Inevitably, therefore, the principle of Erie R. Co. v. Tompkins, an action at law, was promptly applied to a suit in equity. Ruhlin v. New York Life Ins. Co., 304 U.S. 202.

3. In Pusey & Jones Co. v. Hanssen, *supra,* the Court had to decide whether a Delaware statute had created a new right appropriate for enforcement in accordance with traditional equity practice or whether the statute had merely given the Delaware Chancery Court a new kind of remedy. * * * [T]he Court construed the Delaware statute merely to extend the power to an equity court to appoint a receiver on the application of an ordinary contract creditor. By conferring new discretionary authority upon its equity court, Delaware could not modify the traditional equity rule in the federal courts that only someone with a defined interest in the estate of an insolvent person, *e.g.,* a judgment creditor, can protect that interest through receivership. But the Court recognized that if the Delaware statute had been one not regulating the powers of the Chancery Court of Delaware but creating a new interest in a contract creditor, the federal court would have had power to grant a receivership at the behest of such a simple contract creditor, as much so as in the case of a secured creditor. * * *

And so this case reduces itself to the narrow question whether, when no recovery could be had in a State court because the action is barred by the statute of limitations, a federal court in equity can take cognizance of the suit because there is diversity of citizenship between the parties. Is the outlawry, according to State law, of a claim created by the States a matter of "substantive rights" to be respected by a federal court of equity when that court's jurisdiction is dependent on the fact that there is a State-created right, or is such statute of "a mere remedial character", Henrietta Mills v. Rutherford Co., supra, 281 U.S. at page 128, which a federal court may disregard?

Matters of "substance" and matters of "procedure" are much talked about in the books as though they defined a great divide cutting across the whole domain of law. But, of course, "substance" and "procedure" are the same key-words to very different problems. Neither "substance" nor "procedure" represents the same invariants. Each implies different variables depending upon the particular problem for which it is used. See Home Ins. Co. v. Dick, 281 U.S. 397, 409. And the different problems are only distantly related at best, for the terms are in common use in connection with situations turning on such different considerations as those that are relevant to questions pertaining to ex post facto legislation, the impairment of the obligations of contract, the enforcement of federal rights in the State courts and the multitudinous phases of the conflict of laws. * * *

Here we are dealing with a right to recover derived not from the United States but from one of the States. When, because the plaintiff happens to be a non-resident, such a right is enforceable in a federal as well as in a State court, the forms and mode of enforcing the right may at times, naturally enough, vary because the two judicial systems are not identic. But since a federal court adjudicating a state-created right solely because of the diversity of citizenship of the parties is for that purpose, in effect, only another court of the State, it cannot afford recovery if the right to recover is made unavailable by the State nor can it substantially affect the enforcement of the right as given by the State.

And so the question is not whether a statute of limitations is deemed a matter of "procedure" in some sense. The question is whether such a statute concerns merely the manner and the means by which a right to recover, as recognized by the State, is enforced, or whether such statutory limitation is a matter of substance in the aspect that alone is relevant to our problem, namely does it significantly affect the result of a litigation for a federal court to disregard a law of a State that would be controlling in an action upon the same claim by the same parties in a State court?

It is therefore immaterial whether statutes of limitation are characterized either as "substantive" or "procedural" in State court opinions in any use of those terms unrelated to the specific issue before us. Erie R. Co. v. Tompkins was not an endeavor to formulate scientific legal terminology. It expressed a policy that touches vitally the proper distribution of judicial power between State and federal courts. In essence, the intent of that decision was to insure that, in all cases where a federal court is exercising jurisdiction solely because of the diversity of citizenship of the parties, the outcome of the litigation in the federal court should be substantially the same, so far as legal rules determine the outcome of a litigation, as it would be if tried in a State court. The nub of the policy that underlies Erie R. Co. v. Tompkins is that for the same transaction the accident of a suit by a non-resident litigant in a federal court instead of in a State court a block away, should not lead to a substantially different result. And so, putting to one side abstractions regarding "substance" and "procedure", we have held that in diversity cases the federal courts must follow the law of the State as to burden of proof, Cities Service Oil Co. v. Dunlap, 308 U.S. 208, as to conflict of laws, Klaxon Co. v. Stentor Co., 313 U.S. 487, as to contributory negligence, Palmer v. Hoffman, 318 U.S. 109, 117. And see Sampson v. Channell, 1 Cir., 110 F.2d 754. Erie R. Co. v. Tompkins has been applied with an eye alert to essentials in avoiding disregard of State law in diversity cases in the federal courts. A policy so important to our federalism must be kept free from entanglements with analytical or terminological niceties.

Plainly enough, a statute that would completely bar recovery in a suit if brought in a State court bears on a State-created right vitally and not merely formally or negligibly. As to consequences that so intimately affect recovery or nonrecovery a federal court in a diversity case should follow State law. * * *

Prior to Erie R. Co. v. Tompkins it was not necessary, as we have indicated, to make the critical analysis required by the doctrine of that case of the nature of jurisdiction of the federal courts in diversity cases. But even before Erie R. Co. v. Tompkins, federal courts relied on statutes of limitations of the States in which they sat. In suits at law State limitations statutes were held to be "rules of decision" within § 34 of the Judiciary Act of 1789 and as such applied in "trials at common law". [E.g.,] McCluny v. Silliman, 3 Pet. 270, 277. While there was talk of freedom of equity from such State statutes of limitations, the cases generally refused recovery where suit was barred in a like situation in the State courts, even if only by way of analogy. See, e.g., Godden v. Kimmell, 99 U.S. 201. However in Kirby v. Lake Shore & M.S. Co., 120 U.S. 130, the Court disregarded a State statute of limitations where the Court deemed it inequitable to apply it.

To make an exception to Erie R. Co. v. Tompkins on the equity side of a federal court is to reject the considerations of policy which, after long travail, led to that decision. * * *

Diversity jurisdiction is founded on assurance to non-resident litigants of courts free from susceptibility to potential local bias. The Framers of the Constitution, according to Marshall, entertained "apprehensions" lest distant suitors be subjected to local bias in State courts, or, at least, viewed with "indulgence the possible fears and apprehensions" of such suitors. Bank of the United States v. Deveaux, 5 Cranch 61, 87. And so Congress afforded out-of-State litigants another tribunal, not another body of law. The operation of a double system of conflicting laws in the same State is plainly hostile to the reign of law. Certainly, the fortuitous circumstance of residence out of a State of one of the parties to a litigation ought not to give rise to a discrimination against others equally concerned but locally resident. The source of substantive rights enforced by a federal court under diversity jurisdiction, it cannot be said too often, is the law of the States. Whenever that law is authoritatively declared by a State, whether its voice be the legislature or its highest court, such law ought to govern in litigation founded on that law, whether the forum of application is a State or a federal court and whether the remedies be sought at law or may be had in equity.

Dicta may be cited characterizing equity as an independent body of law. To the extent that we have indicated, it is. But insofar as these general observations go beyond that, they merely reflect notions that have been replaced by a sharper analysis of what federal courts do when they enforce rights that have no federal origin. And so, before the true source of law that is applied by the federal courts under diversity jurisdiction was fully explored, some things were said that would not now be said. But nothing that was decided, unless it be the Kirby case, needs to be rejected. * * *

Reversed.

■ MR. JUSTICE ROBERTS and MR. JUSTICE DOUGLAS took no part in the consideration or decision of this case.

■ MR. JUSTICE RUTLEDGE.

I dissent.

* * *

If any characteristic of equity jurisprudence has descended unbrokenly from and within "the traditional scope of equity as historically evolved in the English Court of Chancery," it is that statutes of limitations, often in terms applying only to actions at law, have never been deemed to be rigidly applicable as absolute barriers to suits in equity as they are to actions at law. That tradition, it would seem, should be regarded as having been incorporated in the various Acts of Congress which have conferred equity jurisdiction upon the federal courts. So incorporated it has been reaffirmed repeatedly by the decisions of this and other courts. It is now excised from those Acts. If there is to be excision, Congress, not this Court, should make it. * * *

Applicable statutes of limitations in state tribunals are not always the ones which would apply if suit were instituted in the courts of the state which creates the substantive rights for which enforcement is sought. The state of the forum is free to apply its own period of limitations, regardless of whether the state originating the right has barred suit upon it. * * *

It is not clear whether today's decision puts it into the power of corporate trustees, by confining their jurisdictional "presence" to states which allow their courts to give equitable remedies only within short periods of time, to defeat the purpose and intent of the law of the state creating the substantive right. If so, the "right" remains alive, with full-fledged remedy, by the law of its origin, and because enforcement must be had in another state, which affords refuge against it, the remedy and with it the right are nullified. I doubt that the Constitution of the United States requires this or that the Judiciary Acts permit it. A good case can be made, indeed has been made, that the diversity jurisdiction was created to afford protection against exactly this sort of nullifying state legislation.[10]

In my judgment this furnishes added reason for leaving any change, if one is to be made, to the judgment of Congress. The next step may well be to say that in applying the doctrine of laches a federal court must surrender its own judgment and attempt to find out what a state court sitting a block away would do with that notoriously amorphous doctrine.

■ MR. JUSTICE MURPHY joins in this opinion.

------

10. Frankfurter, Distribution of Judicial Power Between United States and State   Courts (1928), 13 Corn.L.Q. 499, 520. * * *

NOTE ON STATE LAW AND FEDERAL EQUITY

(1) *Guaranty's Predecessors.*

(a) In Guffey v. Smith, 237 U.S. 101 (1915), lessees under an oil and gas lease brought a federal diversity action to enjoin operations under a later lease and to obtain discovery and an accounting. The complainants' lease gave them an option to surrender it at any time, and though this provision did not, under state law, render the lease "void as wanting in mutuality," the holder of such a lease would have been unable to bring an action of ejectment at law or a suit in equity for injunctive relief in the state's courts. Those courts would have regarded the lease as "so lacking in mutuality" that the lessee's only remedy would have been one at law for damages.

The Supreme Court, in a meticulous opinion by Justice Van Devanter, held that equitable relief was available in a federal court. After noting that the lease was not void as a matter of state substantive law, and that an action of ejectment at law would not be available in a federal court in light of the Conformity Act, he turned to the state decisions denying equitable relief in such a case:

"* * * These decisions, it is insisted, should have been accepted and applied by the Circuit Court. To this we cannot assent. By the legislation of Congress and repeated decisions of this court it has long been settled that the remedies afforded and modes of proceeding pursued in the Federal courts, sitting as courts of equity, are not determined by local laws or rules of decision, but by general principles, rules and usages of equity having uniform operation in those courts wherever sitting" (p. 114).

The Court then went on to consider whether, under "the general principles and rules of equity administered in the Federal courts" (*id.*), there were grounds for denying equitable relief, and concluded that there were not. Finally, after determining that the lessee's failure to make certain payments on time did not constitute a forfeiture of the lease under state law, the Court modified the decree for an accounting and, in doing so, relied on its own prior decisions in other equitable proceedings.

Can Guffey stand after Erie? Does York save it?

Note that the end of the sentence in the York opinion following footnote 3 would have been a good place to cite Guffey, if it had been thought to be alive. But neither Guffey nor any other case is cited. What kind of case might the Court have had in mind? What are the relevant considerations in deciding when "a federal court may afford an equitable remedy for a substantive right recognized by a State even though a State court cannot give it"?

(b) Does Justice Frankfurter account adequately for all of the "talk in the cases that federal equity is a separate legal system"?

In Payne v. Hook, 74 U.S. (7 Wall.) 425, 430 (1869), cited in Guffey, the Court said: "We have repeatedly held 'that the jurisdiction of the courts of the United States over controversies between citizens of different States, cannot be impaired by the laws of the States, which prescribe the modes of redress in their courts, or which regulate the distribution of their judicial power.' If legal remedies are sometimes modified to suit the changes in the laws of the States, and the practice of their courts, it is not so with equitable. The equity jurisdiction conferred on the Federal courts is the same that the High Court of

Chancery in England possesses; is subject to neither limitation or restraint by State legislation and is uniform throughout the different States of the Union."

As Justice Frankfurter mentions, many states had no separate systems of equity at all in 1789, and often only rudimentary equitable doctrines. Recall that the first Congress not only gave the circuit courts diversity jurisdiction in suits "in equity" (Act of Sept. 24, 1789, § 11, 1 Stat. 73, 78), but refrained from making the Rules of Decision Act (§ 34) applicable in such proceedings. Congress provided instead, in § 16, which later became § 267 of the Judicial Code of 1911 and which was repealed in 1948, only that "suits in equity shall not be sustained in either of the courts of the United States, in any case where plain, adequate and complete remedy may be had at law".

Yet traditional equity was not, as the quotation in York from Langdell's *Summary of Equity Pleading* might be thought to imply, a system merely of distinctive remedies without distinctive substantive consequences. In the paragraph before the one from which the opinion quotes, Dean Langdell pointed out (pp. xxv–xxvi) that "of course, * * * it must not be supposed that equity in modern times is simply a different system of remedies from those administered in courts of law; for there are many extensive doctrines in equity, and some whole branches of law, which are unknown to the common-law courts". And he went on to give familiar examples, such as trusts, the mortgagee's equity of redemption, and the doctrine of equitable election, in which equity, because of its distinctive remedies, was able to recognize and enforce an interest that the law entirely denied. Compare also the many equitable defenses, enforced by separate bill in equity, by which the chancellor, having as always the last word, destroyed interests that the law did recognize, so as to reach a wholly different substantive result.

In this context it is likely that federal courts sitting in states lacking courts of equity jurisdiction did claim, and were intended to claim, "the power to deny substantive rights created by State law or to create substantive rights denied by State law". See 2 Crosskey, Politics and the Constitution in the History of the United States 877–902 (1953), so contending. Nevertheless, the cases are inconclusive. Compare, *e.g.,* Neves v. Scott, 54 U.S. (13 How.) 268, 272 (1851)(dictum) with, *e.g.,* Meade v. Beale, 16 Fed.Cas.No. 9,371, at 1291 (C.C.Md.1850)(Taney, C.J., on circuit).

See Hill, *The Erie Doctrine in Bankruptcy,* 66 Harv.L.Rev. 1013, 1024–35 (1953), concluding that federal equitable jurisdiction was not regarded as a special source of authority to override state substantive law; that insofar as the federal courts overrode state substantive law in equity they did so on the basis of assumptions concerning the nature of law and the nature of federal judicial power common both to law and equity; and that for these reasons the implications of Erie have been essentially the same in both law and equity.

(c) The Court in Guffey took great pains to acknowledge the underlying substantive interests recognized by state law, both decisional and statutory, and then distinguished between substantive right and legal remedy, on the one hand, and equitable remedy on the other.

Guffey might be defended on the ground that the federal court was merely giving a fuller and fairer remedy in the enforcement of state-created rights—a kind of "juster justice." But in doing so, is the federal court undercutting the state's purpose to give a *lessor* an option to break a lease and pay damages if the lease itself gives the *lessee* an option to withdraw at any time? At least since the insights of Holmes (in his lectures on The Path of the Law), should we not hesitate to draw bright lines between right and remedy? Suppose a state decides that the market in land will function more efficiently if specific performance of land contracts is denied except in extraordinary cases. Should a federal court in that state grant specific performance in "ordinary" cases?[1]

(2) *The Bernhardt Case and Federal Equity.* In Bernhardt v. Polygraphic Co., 350 U.S. 198 (1956), the defendant removed a breach of contract action to a Vermont federal court on diversity grounds, and then moved to stay the proceedings pending arbitration, pursuant to an arbitration clause in the contract. The district court denied the motion on the ground that under Vermont law an agreement to arbitrate is revocable at any time prior to an award and is therefore not enforceable. The Second Circuit reversed, but the Supreme Court agreed with the district court, saying (p. 203):

"* * * If the federal court allows arbitration where the state court would disallow it, the outcome of litigation might depend on the courthouse where suit is brought. For the remedy by arbitration, whatever its merits or shortcomings, substantially affects the cause of action created by the State. The nature of the tribunal where suits are tried is an important part of the parcel of rights behind a cause of action."

The Court held, as a matter of statutory construction, that the provisions for judicial enforcement of certain agreements to arbitrate in the United States Arbitration Act, 9 U.S.C. §§ 1–14,[2] did not apply to the case at hand, noting (p. 202) that "[i]f respondent's contention [that the Act applied] is correct, a constitutional question might be presented. Erie R. Co. v. Tompkins indicated that Congress does not have the constitutional authority to make the law that is applicable to controversies in diversity of citizenship cases."

Was anything left of Guffey after Bernhardt?[3] What "constitutional question" was the Court referring to in Bernhardt? How should it be resolved? See Ely, *The Irrepressible Myth of Erie,* 87 Harv.L.Rev. 693, 705–06 (1974); Hirshman, *The Second Arbitration Trilogy: The Federalization of Arbitration Law,* 71 Va.L.Rev. 1305, 1309–20 (1985).

1. See generally Crump, *The Twilight Zone of the Erie Doctrine: Is There Really a Different Choice of Remedies in the "Court a Block Away"?,* 1991 Wis.L.Rev. 1233 (recognizing that state law ordinarily controls the "proof elements" relevant to the availability of equitable remedies in diversity cases, but suggesting that, in general, courts adopt a "modified interest-balancing" approach for setting and applying the standards for granting such remedies).

2. The Arbitration Act, originally enacted in 1925, provides in § 2 that a written arbitration provision "in any maritime transaction or a contract evidencing a transaction involving commerce * * * shall be valid, irrevocable, and enforceable, save upon such grounds as exist at law or in equity for the revocation of any contract"; in § 3 that when suit is brought "in any of the courts of the United States" on an issue referable to arbitration by an arbitration agreement, the court must stay its own proceedings pending arbitration once it has decided that the issue is arbitrable under the agreement; and in § 4 that a "United States district court" whose assistance is properly invoked by a party to an arbitration agreement shall order arbitration.

3. See Stern v. South Chester Tube Co., 390 U.S. 606, 609–10 (1968): "We need not decide whether this [diversity action] is a case where such a federal remedy can be provided even in the absence of a similar state remedy, Skelly Oil Co. v. Phillips Co., 339 U.S. 667, 674 (1950); *cf.* Guffey v. Smith, 237 U.S. 101 (1915), because it is clear that state law here also provides for enforcement of the shareholder's right [to inspect corporate records] by a compulsory judicial order."

(3) *The Effect of the Federal Arbitration Act.* The constitutional question raised in Bernhardt was answered, in part, in Prima Paint Corp. v. Flood & Conklin Mfg. Co., 388 U.S. 395 (1967). In this diversity action, Prima sought rescission of a consulting agreement on the basis of fraudulent inducement, and Flood & Conklin, relying on the Arbitration Act, filed a motion to stay the action pending arbitration of the issue of fraud under an arbitration clause in the contract. The Supreme Court held, 6–3, that the stay was properly granted under the Act, even though such a stay (for arbitration of the issue of fraud) might not have been obtainable had the action been brought in a state court. The Arbitration Act applied because, unlike the contract at issue in Bernhardt, the contract in Prima was one "evidencing a transaction involving commerce" within the meaning of § 2 of the Act. Application of the Act was constitutionally permissible because the question in the case was "not whether Congress may fashion federal substantive rules to govern questions arising in simple diversity cases"; rather it was "whether Congress may prescribe how federal courts are to conduct themselves with respect to subject matter [interstate commerce] over which Congress plainly has power to legislate". The answer, the Court concluded, "can only be in the affirmative" (p. 405). But the Court carefully avoided any explicit endorsement of the view that the Arbitration Act embodied substantive policies that were to be applied to all contracts within its scope, whether sued on in state or federal courts.

How stable was the result in the Prima Paint case if it contemplated different remedies in federal and state courts for breach of the same contract?[4] In Moses H. Cone Memorial Hospital v. Mercury Construction Corp., 460 U.S. 1, 26 (1983), the Court moved at least part way toward the imposition of the Arbitration Act's remedial provisions on the state courts when it said, in dicta, that "state courts, as much as federal courts, are obliged to grant stays of litigation under § 3 of the Arbitration Act."[5] Then in Southland Corp. v. Keating, 465 U.S. 1 (1984), the Court held that a state law rendering certain claims in franchise agreements not arbitrable was in direct conflict with § 2 of the Act and therefore could not be applied by a state court to a contract within the scope of that Act.[6] Although the Court in Southland disclaimed direct

---

4. Compare the demise of a similar, but converse, distinction between state and federal remedies in Boys Markets, Inc. v. Retail Clerks, 398 U.S. 235 (1970). Prior to this decision, the Court had held that as a result of the Norris–LaGuardia Act, a plaintiff in an action under § 301 of the Taft–Hartley Act could obtain certain injunctive relief in a state court but not in a federal court.

5. The Court went on to say, however, that it was "less clear * * * whether the same is true of an order to compel arbitration under § 4 of the Act" (p. 26). It noted the difference between the language of § 3 ("any of the courts of the United States") and that of § 4 ("United States District Court"). See note 2, *supra.* But it observed that at least one state court had held that it was required by § 4 to order arbitration in an appropriate case. *Id.* at n. 35.

6. The Court ruled, over Justice Stevens' dissent on this point, that the California statute did not come under the savings clause of § 2 as "grounds * * * for the revocation of any contract." (Justices O'Connor and Rehnquist dissented more broadly, arguing that the Arbitration Act was directed only to the federal courts.)

See also Volt Information Sciences, Inc. v. Board of Trustees of Leland Stanford Junior University, 489 U.S. 468 (1989), where the Court upheld the state court's decision to stay arbitration. A choice-of-law provision in the contract called for application of California law. The state courts interpreted that provision as incorporating California's statutory rules governing arbitration, which authorized a stay in the circumstances presented. In response to the argument that the federal Act preempted state law, the Court

reliance on § 4 of the Act, its reversal of the state court's judgment effectively required that court to compel arbitration.[7]

For discussion of these decisions, and their choice-of-law implications, see Hirshman, Paragraph (2), *supra*.

(4) *Federal Denial of Equitable Relief.* Are considerations different from those in Guffey and Bernhardt involved when state law, and particularly the availability of an equitable remedy in the state courts, is urged not as a reason for denying federal equitable relief but for granting it? To what extent do Erie–Klaxon–York require federal courts to mirror state courts in this respect also?

In Pusey & Jones Co. v. Hanssen, 261 U.S. 491 (1923), a Delaware statute authorizing the appointment of a receiver upon the application of a simple contract creditor was denied enforcement. In a much-cited opinion for the Court, Justice Brandeis said (pp. 497–99):

"That this suit could not be maintained in the absence of the statute is clear. * * *

"That a remedial right to proceed in a federal court sitting in equity cannot be enlarged by a state statute is likewise clear. Scott v. Neely, 140 U.S. 106; Cates v. Allen, 149 U.S. 451. Nor can it be so narrowed. Mississippi Mills v. Cohn, 150 U.S. 202; Guffey v. Smith, 237 U.S. 101, 114. The federal court may therefore be obliged to deny an equitable remedy which the plaintiff might have secured in a state court. * * * [I]t is not true that this statute confers upon the creditor a substantive right. * * * Insolvency is made a condition of the Chancellor's jurisdiction; but it does not give rise to any substantive right in the creditor. Jones v. Maxwell Motor Co. (Del.Ch.) 115 Atl. 312, 314, 315. It makes possible a new remedy because it confers upon the Chancellor a new power. Whether that power is visitorial (as the petitioner insists), or whether it is strictly judicial, need not be determined in this case. Whatever its exact nature, the power enables the Chancellor to afford a remedy which theretofore would not have been open to an unsecured simple contract creditor. But because that which the statute confers is merely a remedy, the statute cannot affect proceedings in the federal courts sitting in equity."[8]

For differing views of the impact of Erie on such decisions as Pusey & Jones, see the opinions in Mintzer v. Arthur L. Wright & Co., 263 F.2d 823 (3d Cir.1959). See also Note, 67 Harv.L.Rev. 836 (1954).

described as "not without some merit" (p. 477) the view that §§ 3–4 of the Act are inapplicable to state court proceedings. The Court did not reach that issue, however, reasoning instead that even if §§ 3–4 did apply, they would not displace state statutory rules where, as here, the parties agreed to arbitrate by those rules. Justice Brennan's dissent (joined by Justice Marshall) did not take issue with this last point; he argued, instead, that the state courts had misinterpreted the choice-of-law provision and that the Supreme Court should have reviewed their interpretation. See p. 565, *supra*.

7. In Allied–Bruce Terminix Companies, Inc. v. Dobson, 115 S.Ct. 834 (1995), the majority reaffirmed the Southland decision and, in applying it to override a state court refusal to compel arbitration, held that § 2 of the Arbitration Act should be read broadly to extend to the limit of Congress' commerce power. In dissent, Justice Thomas (joined by Justice Scalia) argued vigorously that Southland should be overruled and that the Arbitration Act should be held inapplicable in state courts.

8. Compare Guardian Sav. & Trust Co. v. Road Improvement Dist. No. 7, 267 U.S. 1 (1925), which held that the power to appoint a receiver to collect taxes, in order to pay the money due on certain bonds, could be exercised by a federal court in a diversity case.

(5) *Door-closing Provisions*.   Is there any objection that can be raised on the score of Erie policy if the federal courts, without passing on the merits, simply close their doors to the complainant seeking equitable relief?   Does it matter whether the federal door-closing policy is based on decisional law, a federal rule of civil procedure, or an act of Congress (like the anti-injunction provisions of the Norris–LaGuardia Act, p. 363, *supra*)?   Or whether the policy is stated in terms of a limitation on subject-matter jurisdiction, as in the case of the jurisdictional amount requirement?   See Cohen v. Beneficial Ind. Loan Corp., 337 U.S. 541, 556 (1949).

A door-closing rule creates special problems if the defendant is able to remove a state court action and then have the case dismissed.   In Cates v. Allen, 149 U.S. 451 (1893), the Court held that a federal court sitting in equity in a removed diversity case should not enforce a state statute permitting a simple contract creditor to set aside a fraudulent conveyance.[9]   The Court concluded that the proper disposition was not to dismiss but rather to remand, since the case had been improperly removed.   Compare Venner v. Great Northern Ry., 209 U.S. 24 (1908)(upholding the existence of federal jurisdiction but affirming dismissal of the bill for "want of equity").   *Cf.* Section 4, *infra*.

NOTE ON THE "OUTCOME" TEST AND ITS EVOLUTION TO HANNA v. PLUMER

(1) *Guaranty and Klaxon*.   Hadn't the point raised by Justice Rutledge in the closing paragraphs of his dissent in York been answered by the Court four years earlier, in Klaxon?

(2) *The "Outcome–Determinative" Test*.

(a) What did Justice Frankfurter mean in York by "outcome" when he said that it was the intent of Erie that in diversity cases "the outcome of the litigation in the federal court should be substantially the same, so far as legal rules determine the outcome of a litigation, as it would be if tried in a State court"?

(i) Did he mean only that a federal decision finally settling the rights of the parties ought not to take a view of their primary legal relations that is different from the view that the state court would take if it were similarly making a final decision?

(ii) Or did he mean that a federal court should not only avoid using different premises about primary legal relations but should also refrain from giving any form of relief that is different from the relief the state court would give?

(iii) Or did he mean, in addition, that the federal court should refrain from acting at all on the controversy if the state court would refuse to act, even though the state court's refusal would be without prejudice?

---

9.   To use state law to expand the remedies available on the equity side of the federal court, the Court noted in Cates, would curtail the right of jury trial under the Seventh Amendment.   Would this objection serve as a valid basis today—under a merged procedure—for refusal to enforce the state statute?

(iv) Did he mean also that the federal court ought not to refuse to act on the controversy, even though it does so without prejudice, if the state court would be willing to act?

(b) What did Justice Frankfurter mean by "legal rules" that "determine" the outcome of a litigation?

(i) Did he mean to include legal rules, such as that empowering the federal judge to comment on the evidence, that may determine the outcome of the litigation as a practical matter but do not purport to do so?

(ii) Did he mean to include all legal rules that purport to direct, in given circumstances, the final decision? *E.g.*, a rule of evidence calling for reversal if it is violated? Or a rule of procedure calling for dismissal if an indispensable party has not been joined? Or a rule of pleading permitting dismissal if an answer is not filed in time?

(iii) Or did he mean to exclude all rules that depend for their application upon what the parties or counsel do after litigation is begun and that might have been done differently under different rules of procedure?

(iv) Did he mean to include at least all rules purporting to control the final judgment upon due proof or failure of proof of given pre-litigation circumstances? Only those rules?

(c) Is the outcome test a material improvement upon the ancient dichotomy between substance and procedure?

(3) *The 1949 Trilogy.* The questions raised in the preceding paragraphs have perplexed the federal courts at all levels ever since the York decision. During the first 13 years after the decision, the Court disposed of a number of important cases without suggesting a stopping place for the outcome test or even hinting, in the majority opinions, at any limitation on the rationale. Of particular interest are three cases decided on the same day: Ragan v. Merchants Transfer & Warehouse Co., 337 U.S. 530 (1949); Woods v. Interstate Realty Co., 337 U.S. 535 (1949); and Cohen v. Beneficial Indus. Loan Corp., 337 U.S. 541 (1949). Only four members of the Court joined in all three decisions (and only Justice Rutledge dissented in all three).

(a) In Cohen, a stockholder in a Delaware corporation (who owned about .0125% of the stock, worth less than $10,000) had brought a derivative action in a New Jersey federal court against the corporation and various officers and directors, alleging mismanagement. Jurisdiction was based on diversity of citizenship. The question was whether the federal court should apply a New Jersey statute whose general effect was "to make a plaintiff having so small an interest liable for the reasonable expenses and attorney's fees of the defense if he fails to make good his complaint and to entitle the corporation to indemnity before the case can be prosecuted" (pp. 544–45).

The Court held, 6–3, that the statute should be applied. It rejected a contention that the statute conflicted with Fed. Rule 23 (now 23.1) and stated (pp. 555–56):

"Even if we were to agree that the New Jersey statute is procedural, it would not determine that it is not applicable. Rules which lawyers call procedural do not always exhaust their effect by regulating procedure. But this statute is not merely a regulation of procedure. With it or without it the main action takes the same course. However, it creates a new liability where none existed before, for it makes a stockholder who institutes a derivative action liable for the expense to which he puts the corporation and other defendants, if he does not make good his claims. Such liability is not usual and it goes beyond payment of what we know as 'costs.' If all the Act did was to create this liability, it would clearly be substantive. But this new liability would be without meaning and value in many cases if it resulted in nothing but a judgment for expenses at or after the end of the case. Therefore, a procedure is prescribed by which the liability is insured by entitling the corporate defendant to a bond of indemnity before the outlay is incurred. We do not think a statute which so conditions the stockholder's action can be disregarded by the federal court as a mere procedural device."

The dissent argued that the statute "merely prescribes the method by which stockholders may enforce [a cause of action] * * *. This New Jersey statute, like statutes governing security for costs * * * need not be applied in this diversity suit in the federal court. Rule 23 of the Federal Rules of Civil Procedure defines that procedure for the federal courts" (p. 557).

(b) In the Woods case, a Tennessee corporation had brought a diversity action in a Mississippi federal court against a Mississippi resident for a broker's commission allegedly due for the sale of real estate in Mississippi. The defense contended that since the plaintiff had not qualified to do business in the state, the action had to be dismissed under a state statute providing that any foreign corporation failing to qualify "shall not be permitted to bring or maintain any action or suit in any of the courts of this state." The Court held, 6–3, that the defense should be sustained, stating (p. 538):

"* * * The York case was premised on the theory that a right which local law creates but which it does not supply with a remedy is no right at all for purposes of enforcement in a federal court in a diversity case; that where in such cases one is barred from recovery in the state court, he should likewise be barred in the federal court."

No mention was made in the opinion of Fed. Rule 17(b). Was it relevant?[1]

(c) In Ragan, a diversity action for injuries suffered in a highway accident had been brought in a Kansas federal court. Kansas had a two-year statute of limitations; the action was filed within two years of the accident, but the summons and complaint were not served until after the two-year period had run. The Court held, 8–1, that summary judgment for the defendant should have been granted, despite the provisions of Fed. Rule 3,[2] because of a state statute providing: "An action shall be deemed commenced within the meaning of this article, as to each defendant, at the date of the summons which is served on him * * *." In a brief opinion that referred to but did not discuss the apparent conflict with Rule 3, the Court noted the holding of the court below

---

1. Rule 17(b) requires that a corporation's capacity to sue be determined by the law of the state of incorporation. This provision may be viewed as a pro tanto modification of Klaxon—as the statement, in other words, of a uniform federal choice-of-law rule on the question of capacity. Can it be squared with the result in Woods? One commentator has suggested that it can because the federal rule should be restricted to questions of capacity in a "narrower sense" than

the matters dealt with by the state law in Woods. See Note, 82 Harv.L.Rev. 708, 711 (1969). See also 6A Wright, Miller & Kane, Federal Practice and Procedure § 1569 (1990). But see Little, *Out of Woods and Into the Rules*, 72 Va.L.Rev. 767 (1986).

2. This rule provides: "A civil action is commenced by filing a complaint with the court."

that the Kansas statute was "an integral part" of its statute of limitations and said (pp. 533–34):

"We can draw no distinction [from York] in this case because local law brought the cause of action to an end after, rather than before, suit was started in the federal court. * * * We cannot give it longer life in the federal court than it would have had in the state court without adding something to the cause of action. We may not do that consistently with Erie R. Co. v. Tompkins."[3]

(4) *The Byrd Decision: A New Approach.*

(a) The first sign of a change of direction appeared in Byrd v. Blue Ridge Rural Elec. Cooperative, Inc., 356 U.S. 525 (1958). In a diversity action brought in a South Carolina federal court for injuries resulting from alleged negligence, the defendant asserted that it was the plaintiff's employer under South Carolina law, and that the plaintiff's exclusive remedy therefore lay before the state's Industrial Commission under the state's Workers' Compensation Law. Although the state supreme court had made it clear that such a defense was to be passed on by the judge alone, the United States Supreme Court held that issues of fact relevant to the defense were to be tried to the jury in the federal proceeding.

The Court first addressed the basis for the state supreme court's decision that the issue was one for the judge and noted that no reasons for that result had been given. It continued (pp. 535–38):

"* * * The decisions cited to support the holding [of the state supreme court] * * * are concerned solely with defining the scope and method of judicial review of the Industrial Commission. * * * The conclusion is inescapable that the * * * [state supreme court's] holding is grounded in the practical consideration that the question had theretofore come before the South Carolina courts from the Industrial Commission and the courts had become accustomed to deciding the factual issue of immunity without the aid of juries. We find nothing to suggest that this rule was announced as an integral part of the special relationship created by the statute. Thus the requirement appears to be merely a form and mode of enforcing the immunity, Guaranty Trust Co. v. York, 326 U.S. 99, 108, and not a rule intended to be bound up with the definitions of the rights and obligations of the parties. * * *

"* * * But cases following Erie have evinced a broader policy to the effect that the federal courts should conform as near as may be—in the absence of other considerations—to state rules even of form and mode where the state rules may bear substantially on the question whether the litigation would come out one way in the federal court and another way in the state court if the federal court failed to apply a particular local rule. *E.g.,* Guaranty Trust Co. v. York, *supra;* Bernhardt v. Polygraphic Co., 350 U.S. 198. Concededly the nature of the tribunal which tries issues may be important in the enforcement of the parcel of rights making up a cause of action or defense, and bear significantly upon achievement of uniform enforcement of the right. It may well be that in the instant personal-injury case the outcome would be substantially affected by whether the issue [in question] * * * is decided by a judge or a jury. Therefore, were 'outcome' the only consideration, a strong case might appear for saying that the federal court should follow the state practice.

---

3. The problem raised in Ragan was again considered by the Court in Walker v. Armco Steel Corp., 446 U.S. 740 (1980), p. 729, *infra.*

"But there are affirmative countervailing considerations at work here. The federal system is an independent system for administering justice to litigants who properly invoke its jurisdiction. An essential characteristic of that system is the manner in which, in civil common-law actions, it distributes trial functions between judge and jury and, under the influence—if not the command—of the Seventh Amendment, assigns the decisions of disputed questions of fact to the jury. The policy of uniform enforcement of state-created rights and obligations, see, *e.g.,* Guaranty Trust Co. v. York, *supra,* cannot in every case exact compliance with a state rule—not bound up with rights and obligations—which disrupts the federal system of allocating functions between judge and jury. Herron v. Southern Pacific Co., 283 U.S. 91. Thus the inquiry here is whether the federal policy favoring jury decisions of disputed fact questions should yield to the state rule in the interest of furthering the objective that the litigation should not come out one way in the federal court and another way in the state court.

"We think that in the circumstances of this case the federal court should not follow the state rule. It cannot be gainsaid that there is a strong federal policy against allowing state rules to disrupt the judge-jury relationship in the federal courts. * * *"

(b) Note that in Byrd, perhaps for the first time since Erie, the Court looked to the state rule in an effort to determine whether the policy behind that rule would be frustrated if the federal court were not to follow it. At the same time, the Court recognized that even a state rule relating only to "form and mode"—if it might bear substantially on the outcome—ought not to be disregarded in the absence of "affirmative countervailing considerations". Why not? Because there is no reason to adopt a rule that encourages forum shopping but serves no other purpose?

How successful was the Court in analyzing the state's reasons for assigning the issue in question to a judge rather than a jury? Should the state supreme court's failure to give any reasons mean that it has failed to satisfy its "burden of proof" with respect to the policies underlying the rule?[4] Or should the federal courts conduct a more sympathetic search for those policies? In Byrd itself, the state rule might be supported by arguments (a) that only a judge would be able to view the company's defense as an aspect of a comprehensive statutory scheme of liability without fault for industrial accidents, and (b) that a jury could not articulate the basis for its findings in a way that would help to assure predictability and consistency of decisions for litigants faced with many lawsuits raising the same issue. If such considerations might have led to the state's assignment of the issue to the judge, wouldn't the state's policy be undermined if it were disregarded in the federal courts?

With respect to the "affirmative countervailing considerations" referred to by the Supreme Court, would it not have been simpler, and correct, to rest the result squarely on the Seventh Amendment?[5] The only hint on this point in

---

4. In Magenau v. Aetna Freight Lines, Inc., 360 U.S. 273 (1959), a case similar to Byrd in many respects, the majority held that certain issues should be tried to the jury because "[w]e have been given no reason for the distinction in the Pennsylvania practice of trying such disputed factual issues to the court" (p. 278).

5. The Seventh Amendment plainly applies in diversity cases in the federal courts. See Simler v. Conner, 372 U.S. 221 (1963); Scott v. Neely, 140 U.S. 106 (1891). (In Simler, decided after Byrd, the Court held-without any discussion of the policy behind the contrary state rule-that a jury was consti-

the Byrd opinion is at p. 537 n. 10, where the Court states that it leaves open the question whether "the Seventh Amendment embraces the factual issue of statutory immunity when asserted, as here, as an affirmative defense in a common-law negligence action".

If the Seventh Amendment does not apply to the trial of a particular issue, is there nevertheless a federal policy favoring trial by jury on that issue? If so, what is the source of the policy?

(c) The Byrd Court's reliance on Herron v. Southern Pac. Co., 283 U.S. 91 (1931), surprised many observers. In Herron, a pre-Erie diversity action, the Court held that neither the Conformity Act nor the Rules of Decision Act precluded a directed verdict against the plaintiff on the issue of contributory negligence, despite a state constitutional provision that the defense of contributory negligence "shall, in all cases whatsoever, be a question of fact and shall, at all times, be left to the jury". "[S]tate laws," the Court said (p. 94), "cannot alter the essential character or function of a federal court."

If Herron were to arise today for the first time, how would you argue for application of the state constitutional provision? Do you think you should win?[6]

(5) *Commentary.* For discussions of the Erie doctrine during the period covered by this Note, see, *e.g.,* Smith, *Blue Ridge and Beyond: A Byrd's–Eye View of Federalism in Diversity Litigation,* 36 Tul.L.Rev. 443 (1962); Vestal, *Erie R.R. v. Tompkins: A Projection,* 48 Iowa L.Rev. 248 (1963).

Hanna v. Plumer

380 U.S. 460, 85 S.Ct. 1136, 14 L.Ed.2d 8 (1965).
Certiorari to the United States Court of Appeals for the First Circuit.

■ MR. CHIEF JUSTICE WARREN delivered the opinion of the Court.

The question to be decided is whether, in a civil action where the jurisdiction of the United States district court is based upon diversity of citizenship between the parties, service of process shall be made in the manner prescribed by state law or that set forth in Rule 4(d)(1) of the Federal Rules of Civil Procedure.

On February 6, 1963, petitioner, a citizen of Ohio, filed her complaint in the District Court for the District of Massachusetts, claiming damages in excess of $10,000 for personal injuries resulting from an automobile accident in South Carolina, allegedly caused by the negligence of one Louise Plumer Osgood, a Massachusetts citizen deceased at the time of the filing of the complaint.

------

tutionally required in a diversity action in a federal court.)

6. Is the question in Herron any different from the question whether there should be an independent federal standard generally applicable to rulings on the sufficiency of the evidence in diversity cases? On the latter question, see 9A Wright & Miller, Federal Practice and Procedure § 2525 (1995), and authorities there cited.

For a discussion and analysis of contemporary (and conflicting) authority in a number of contexts relating to this issue, see Childress, *Judicial Review and Diversity Jurisdiction: Solving an Irrepressible Erie Mystery?,* 47 S.M.U.L.Rev. 271 (1994)(arguing, *inter alia,* that, especially in view of the provisions of amended Rule 50 of the Federal Rules of Civil Procedure, federal law should govern the standard for review of jury verdicts in diversity cases).

Respondent, Mrs. Osgood's executor and also a Massachusetts citizen, was named as defendant. On February 8, service was made by leaving copies of the summons and the complaint with respondent's wife at his residence, concededly in compliance with Rule 4(d)(1) [now embodied in substantial part in Rule 4(e)(2)-Ed.], which provides:

"The summons and complaint shall be served together. The plaintiff shall furnish the person making service with such copies as are necessary. Service shall be made as follows:

"(1) Upon an individual other than an infant or an incompetent person, by delivering a copy of the summons and of the complaint to him personally or by leaving copies thereof at his dwelling house or usual place of abode with some person of suitable age and discretion then residing therein * * *."

Respondent filed his answer on February 26, alleging, inter alia, that the action could not be maintained because it had been brought "contrary to and in violation of the provisions of Massachusetts General Laws (Ter.Ed.) Chapter 197, Section 9." That section provides:

"Except as provided in this chapter, an executor or administrator shall not be held to answer to an action by a creditor of the deceased which is not commenced within one year from the time of his giving bond for the performance of his trust, or to such an action which is commenced within said year unless before the expiration thereof the writ in such action has been served by delivery in hand upon such executor or administrator or service thereof accepted by him or a notice stating the name of the estate, the name and address of the creditor, the amount of the claim and the court in which the action has been brought has been filed in the proper registry of probate. * * *." Mass.Gen.Laws Ann., c. 197, § 9 (1958).

On October 17, 1963, the District Court granted respondent's motion for summary judgment, citing Ragan v. Merchants Transfer & Warehouse Co., 337 U.S. 530, and Guaranty Trust Co. of New York v. York, 326 U.S. 99, in support of its conclusion that the adequacy of the service was to be measured by § 9, with which, the court held, petitioner had not complied. On appeal, petitioner admitted noncompliance with § 9, but argued that Rule 4(d)(1) defines the method by which service of process is to be effected in diversity actions. The Court of Appeals for the First Circuit, finding that "[r]elatively recent amendments [to § 9] evince a clear legislative purpose to require personal notification within the year,"[1] concluded that the conflict of state and federal rules was

---

1. Section 9 is in part a statute of limitations, providing that an executor need not "answer to an action * * * which is not commenced within one year from the time of his giving bond * * *." This part of the statute, the purpose of which is to speed the settlement of estates, * * * is not involved in this case, since the action clearly was timely commenced. * * *

Section 9 also provides for the manner of service. *Generally,* service of process must be made by "delivery in hand," although there are two alternatives: acceptance of service by the executor, or filing of a notice of claim, the components of which are set out in the statute, in the appropriate probate court. The purpose of this part of the statute, which *is* involved here, is, as the court below noted, to insure that executors will receive actual notice of claims. Actual notice is of course also the goal of Rule 4(d)(1); however, the Federal Rule reflects a determination that this goal can be achieved by a method less cumbersome than that prescribed in § 9. In this case the goal seems to have been achieved; although the affidavit filed by respondent in the District Court asserts that he had not been served in hand nor had he accepted service, it does not allege lack of actual notice.

over "a substantive rather than a procedural matter," and unanimously affirmed. 331 F.2d 157. * * *

We conclude that the adoption of Rule 4(d)(1), designed to control service of process in diversity actions, neither exceeded the congressional mandate embodied in the Rules Enabling Act nor transgressed constitutional bounds, and that the Rule is therefore the standard against which the District Court should have measured the adequacy of the service. Accordingly, we reverse the decision of the Court of Appeals.

* * * Under the cases construing the scope of the Enabling Act, Rule 4(d)(1) clearly passes muster. Prescribing the manner in which a defendant is to be notified that a suit has been instituted against him, it relates to the "practice and procedure of the district courts." * * *

"The test must be whether a rule really regulates procedure,—the judicial process for enforcing rights and duties recognized by substantive law and for justly administering remedy and redress for disregard or infraction of them." Sibbach v. Wilson & Co., 312 U.S. 1, 14.

In Mississippi Pub. Corp. v. Murphree, 326 U.S. 438, this Court upheld Rule 4(f), which permits service of a summons anywhere within the State (and not merely the district) in which a district court sits:

"We think that Rule 4(f) is in harmony with the Enabling Act * * *. Undoubtedly most alterations of the rules of practice and procedure may and often do affect the rights of litigants. Congress' prohibition of any alteration of substantive rights of litigants was obviously not addressed to such incidental effects as necessarily attend the adoption of the prescribed new rules of procedure upon the rights of litigants who, agreeably to rules of practice and procedure, have been brought before a court authorized to determine their rights. Sibbach v. Wilson & Co., 312 U.S. 1, 11–14. The fact that the application of Rule 4(f) will operate to subject petitioner's rights to adjudication by the district court for northern Mississippi will undoubtedly affect those rights. But it does not operate to abridge, enlarge or modify the rules of decision by which that court will adjudicate its rights." Id., at 445–446.

Thus were there no conflicting state procedure, Rule 4(d)(1) would clearly control. * * * However, respondent, focusing on the contrary Massachusetts rule, calls to the Court's attention another line of cases, a line which—like the Federal Rules—had its birth in 1938. Erie R. Co. v. Tompkins, 304 U.S. 64, * * * held that federal courts sitting in diversity cases, when deciding questions of "substantive" law, are bound by state court decisions as well as state statutes. The broad command of Erie was therefore identical to that of the Enabling Act: federal courts are to apply state substantive law and federal procedural law. However, as subsequent cases sharpened the distinction between substance and procedure, the line of cases following Erie diverged markedly from the line construing the Enabling Act. Guaranty Trust Co. of New York v. York, 326 U.S. 99, made it clear that Erie-type problems were not to be solved by reference to any traditional or common-sense substance-procedure distinction:

"And so the question is not whether a statute of limitations is deemed a matter of 'procedure' in some sense. The question is * * * does it significantly affect the result of a litigation for a federal court to disregard a law of a State that would be controlling in an action upon the same claim by the same parties in a State court?" 326 U.S., at 109.

Respondent, by placing primary reliance on York and Ragan, suggests that the Erie doctrine acts as a check on the Federal Rules of Civil Procedure, that despite the clear command of Rule 4(d)(1), Erie and its progeny demand the application of the Massachusetts rule. Reduced to essentials, the argument is: (1) Erie, as refined in York, demands that federal courts apply state law whenever application of federal law in its stead will alter the outcome of the case. (2) In this case, a determination that the Massachusetts service requirements obtain will result in immediate victory for respondent. If, on the other hand, it should be held that Rule 4(d)(1) is applicable, the litigation will continue, with possible victory for petitioner. (3) Therefore, Erie demands application of the Massachusetts rule. The syllogism possesses an appealing simplicity, but is for several reasons invalid.

In the first place, it is doubtful that, even if there were no Federal Rule making it clear that in-hand service is not required in diversity actions, the Erie rule would have obligated the District Court to follow the Massachusetts procedure. "Outcome-determination" analysis was never intended to serve as a talisman. Byrd v. Blue Ridge Rural Elec. Cooperative, 356 U.S. 525, 537. Indeed, the message of York itself is that choices between state and federal law are to be made not by application of any automatic, "litmus paper" criterion, but rather by reference to the policies underlying the Erie rule. * * *

The Erie rule is rooted in part in a realization that it would be unfair for the character or result of a litigation materially to differ because the suit had been brought in a federal court. * * *

The decision was also in part a reaction to the practice of "forum-shopping" which had grown up in response to the rule of Swift v. Tyson. 304 U.S., at 73–74. That the York test was an attempt to effectuate these policies is demonstrated by the fact that the opinion framed the inquiry in terms of "substantial" variations between state and federal litigation. 326 U.S., at 109. Not only are nonsubstantial, or trivial, variations not likely to raise the sort of equal protection problems which troubled the Court in Erie; they are also unlikely to influence the choice of a forum. The "outcome-determination" test therefore cannot be read without reference to the twin aims of the Erie rule: discouragement of forum-shopping and avoidance of inequitable administration of the laws.[9]

The difference between the conclusion that the Massachusetts rule is applicable, and the conclusion that it is not, is of course at this point "outcome-determinative" in the sense that if we hold the state rule to apply, respondent prevails, whereas if we hold that Rule 4(d)(1) governs, the litigation will continue. But in this sense *every* procedural variation is "outcome-determinative." For example, having brought suit in a federal court, a plaintiff cannot then insist on the right to file subsequent pleadings in accord with the time

---

9. The Court of Appeals seemed to frame the inquiry in terms of how "important" § 9 is to the State. * * * One cannot meaningfully ask how important something is without first asking "important for what purpose?" Erie and its progeny make clear that when a federal court sitting in a diversity case is faced with a question of whether or not to apply state law, the importance of a state rule is indeed relevant, but only in the context of asking whether application of the rule would make so important a difference to the character or result of the litigation that failure to enforce it would unfairly discriminate against citizens of the forum State, or whether application of the rule would have so important an effect upon the fortunes of one or both of the litigants that failure to enforce it would be likely to cause a plaintiff to choose the federal court.

limits applicable in state courts, even though enforcement of the federal timetable will, if he continues to insist that he must meet only the state time limit, result in determination of the controversy against him. So it is here. Though choice of the federal or state rule will at this point have a marked effect upon the outcome of the litigation, the difference between the two rules would be of scant, if any, relevance to the choice of a forum. Petitioner, in choosing her forum, was not presented with a situation where application of the state rule would wholly bar recovery; rather, adherence to the state rule would have resulted only in altering the way in which process was served. Moreover, it is difficult to argue that permitting service of defendant's wife to take the place of in-hand service of defendant himself alters the mode of enforcement of state-created rights in a fashion sufficiently "substantial" to raise the sort of equal protection problems to which the Erie opinion alluded.

There is, however, a more fundamental flaw in respondent's syllogism: the incorrect assumption that the rule of Erie R. Co. v. Tompkins constitutes the appropriate test of the validity and therefore the applicability of a Federal Rule of Civil Procedure. The Erie rule has never been invoked to void a Federal Rule. It is true that there have been cases where this Court has held applicable a state rule in the face of an argument that the situation was governed by one of the Federal Rules. But the holding of each such case was not that Erie commanded displacement of a Federal Rule by an inconsistent state rule, but rather that the scope of the Federal Rule was not as broad as the losing party urged, and therefore, there being no Federal Rule which covered the point in dispute, Erie commanded the enforcement of state law.

"Respondent contends in the first place that the charge was correct because of the fact that Rule 8(c) of the Rules of Civil Procedure makes contributory negligence an affirmative defense. We do not agree. Rule 8(c) covers only the manner of pleading. The question of the burden of establishing contributory negligence is a question of local law which federal courts in diversity of citizenship cases * * * must apply." Palmer v. Hoffman, 318 U.S. 109, 117.[12]

(Here, of course, the clash is unavoidable; Rule 4(d)(1) says—implicitly, but with unmistakable clarity—that in-hand service is not required in federal courts.) At the same time, in cases adjudicating the validity of Federal Rules, we have not applied the York rule or other refinements of Erie, but have to this day continued to decide questions concerning the scope of the Enabling Act and the constitutionality of specific Federal Rules in light of the distinction set forth in Sibbach. *E.g.,* Schlagenhauf v. Holder, 379 U.S. 104.

Nor has the development of two separate lines of cases been inadvertent. The line between "substance" and "procedure" shifts as the legal context changes. * * * When a situation is covered by one of the Federal Rules, the question facing the court is a far cry from the typical, relatively unguided Erie choice: the court has been instructed to apply the Federal Rule, and can refuse to do so only if the Advisory Committee, this Court, and Congress erred in their prima facie judgment that the Rule in question transgresses neither the terms of the Enabling Act nor constitutional restrictions.

We are reminded by the Erie opinion that neither Congress nor the federal courts can, under the guise of formulating rules of decision for federal courts,

12. To the same effect, see Ragan v. Merchants Transfer & Warehouse Co., *supra;* Cohen v. Beneficial Indus. Loan Corp., 337 U.S. at 556 (Douglas, J., dissenting) * * *.

fashion rules which are not supported by a grant of federal authority contained in Article I or some other section of the Constitution; in such areas state law must govern because there can be no other law. But the opinion in Erie, which involved no Federal Rule and dealt with a question which was "substantive" in every traditional sense (whether the railroad owed a duty of care to Tompkins as a trespasser or a licensee), surely neither said nor implied that measures like Rule 4(d)(1) are unconstitutional. For the constitutional provision for a federal court system (augmented by the Necessary and Proper Clause) carries with it congressional power to make rules governing the practice and pleading in those courts, which in turn includes a power to regulate matters which, though falling within the uncertain area between substance and procedure, are rationally capable of classification as either. Cf. M'Culloch v. State of Maryland, 4 Wheat. 316, 421. Neither York nor the cases following it ever suggested that the rule there laid down for coping with situations where no Federal Rule applies is coextensive with the limitation on Congress to which Erie had adverted. Although this Court has never before been confronted with a case where the applicable Federal Rule is in direct collision with the law of the relevant State,[15] courts of appeals faced with such clashes have rightly discerned the implications of our decisions. * * *

Erie and its offspring cast no doubt on the long-recognized power of Congress to prescribe housekeeping rules for federal courts even though some of those rules will inevitably differ from comparable state rules. Cf. Herron v. Southern Pacific Co., 283 U.S. 91. * * * Thus, though a court, in measuring a Federal Rule against the standards contained in the Enabling Act and the Constitution, need not wholly blind itself to the degree to which the Rule makes the character and result of the federal litigation stray from the course it would follow in state courts, Sibbach v. Wilson & Co., supra, 312 U.S. at 13–14, it cannot be forgotten that the Erie rule, and the guidelines suggested in York, were created to serve another purpose altogether. To hold that a Federal Rule of Civil Procedure must cease to function whenever it alters the mode of enforcing state-created rights would be to disembowel either the Constitution's grant of power over federal procedure or Congress' attempt to exercise that power in the Enabling Act. Rule 4(d)(1) is valid and controls the instant case.

Reversed.

■ MR. JUSTICE BLACK concurs in the result.

■ MR. JUSTICE HARLAN, concurring.

It is unquestionably true that up to now Erie and the cases following it have not succeeded in articulating a workable doctrine governing choice of law in diversity actions. I respect the Court's effort to clarify the situation in today's opinion. However, in doing so I think it has misconceived the constitutional premises of Erie and has failed to deal adequately with those past decisions upon which the courts below relied.

Erie was something more than an opinion which worried about "forum-shopping and avoidance of inequitable administration of the laws," although to

---

15. In Sibbach v. Wilson & Co., supra, the law of the forum State (Illinois) forbade the sort of order authorized by Rule 35. However, Sibbach was decided before Klaxon Co. v. Stentor Electric Mfg. Co., supra, and the Sibbach opinion makes clear that the Court was proceeding on the assumption that if the law of any State was relevant, it was the law of the State where the tort occurred (Indiana), which, like Rule 35, made provision for such orders. 312 U.S., at 6–7, 10–11.

be sure these were important elements of the decision. I have always regarded that decision as one of the modern cornerstones of our federalism, expressing policies that profoundly touch the allocation of judicial power between the state and federal systems. Erie recognized that there should not be two conflicting systems of law controlling the primary activity of citizens, for such alternative governing authority must necessarily give rise to a debilitating uncertainty in the planning of everyday affairs. And it recognized that the scheme of our Constitution envisions an allocation of law-making functions between state and federal legislative processes which is undercut if the federal judiciary can make substantive law affecting state affairs beyond the bounds of congressional legislative powers in this regard. Thus, in diversity cases Erie commands that it be the state law governing primary private activity which prevails.

The shorthand formulations which have appeared in some past decisions are prone to carry untoward results that frequently arise from oversimplification. The Court is quite right in stating that the "outcome-determinative" test of Guaranty Trust Co. of New York v. York, 326 U.S. 99, if taken literally, proves too much, for any rule, no matter how clearly "procedural," can affect the outcome of litigation if it is not obeyed. In turning from the "outcome" test of York back to the unadorned forum-shopping rationale of Erie, however, the Court falls prey to like oversimplification, for a simple forum-shopping rule also proves too much; litigants often choose a federal forum merely to obtain what they consider the advantages of the Federal Rules of Civil Procedure or to try their cases before a supposedly more favorable judge. To my mind the proper line of approach in determining whether to apply a state or a federal rule, whether "substantive" or "procedural," is to stay close to basic principles by inquiring if the choice of rule would substantially affect those primary decisions respecting human conduct which our constitutional system leaves to state regulation.[2] If so, Erie and the Constitution require that the state rule prevail, even in the face of a conflicting federal rule.

The Court weakens, if indeed it does not submerge, this basic principle by finding, in effect, a grant of substantive legislative power in the constitutional provision for a federal court system (compare Swift v. Tyson, 16 Pet. 1), and through it, setting up the Federal Rules as a body of law inviolate. * * * So long as a reasonable man could characterize any duly adopted federal rule as "procedural," the Court, unless I misapprehend what is said, would have it apply no matter how seriously it frustrated a State's substantive regulation of the primary conduct and affairs of its citizens. Since the members of the Advisory Committee, the Judicial Conference, and this Court who formulated the Federal Rules are presumably reasonable men, it follows that the integrity of the Federal Rules is absolute. Whereas the unadulterated outcome and forum-shopping tests may err too far toward honoring state rules, I submit that the Court's "arguably procedural, *ergo* constitutional" test moves too fast and far in the other direction.

The courts below relied upon this Court's decisions in Ragan v. Merchants Transfer & Warehouse Co., 337 U.S. 530, and Cohen v. Beneficial Indus. Loan Corp., 337 U.S. 541. Those cases deserve more attention than this Court has

2. See Hart and Wechsler, The Federal Courts and the Federal System 678. Byrd v. Blue Ridge Rural Elec. Co-op., Inc., 356 U.S. 525, 536–540, indicated that state procedures would apply if the State had manifested a particularly strong interest in their employment. Compare Dice v. Akron, C. & Y.R. Co., 342 U.S. 359. However, this approach may not be of constitutional proportions.

given them, particularly Ragan which, if still good law, would in my opinion call for affirmance of the result reached by the Court of Appeals. Further, a discussion of these two cases will serve to illuminate the "diversity" thesis I am advocating.

* * * I think that the [Ragan] decision was wrong. At most, application of the Federal Rule would have meant that potential Kansas tort defendants would have to defer for a few days the satisfaction of knowing that they had not been sued within the limitations period. The choice of the Federal Rule would have had no effect on the primary stages of private activity from which torts arise, and only the most minimal effect on behavior following the commission of the tort. In such circumstances the interest of the federal system in proceeding under its own rules should have prevailed.

* * * The proper view of Cohen is in my opinion, that the statute was meant to inhibit small stockholders from instituting "strike suits," and thus it was designed and could be expected to have a substantial impact on private primary activity. Anyone who was at the trial bar during the period when Cohen arose can appreciate the strong state policy reflected in the statute. I think it wholly legitimate to view Federal Rule 23 as not purporting to deal with the problem. But even had the Federal Rules purported to do so, and in so doing provided a substantially less effective deterrent to strike suits, I think the state rule should still have prevailed. That is where I believe the Court's view differs from mine; for the Court attributes such overriding force to the Federal Rules that it is hard to think of a case where a conflicting state rule would be allowed to operate, even though the state rule reflected policy considerations which, under Erie, would lie within the realm of state legislative authority.

It remains to apply what has been said to the present case. The Massachusetts rule provides that an executor need not answer suits unless in-hand service was made upon him or notice of the action was filed in the proper registry of probate within one year of his giving bond. The evident intent of this statute is to permit an executor to distribute the estate which he is administering without fear that further liabilities may be outstanding for which he could be held personally liable. If the Federal District Court in Massachusetts applies Rule 4(d)(1) of the Federal Rules of Civil Procedure instead of the Massachusetts service rule, what effect would that have on the speed and assurance with which estates are distributed? As I see it, the effect would not be substantial. It would mean simply that an executor would have to check at his own house or the federal courthouse as well as the registry of probate before he could distribute the estate with impunity. As this does not seem enough to give rise to any real impingement on the vitality of the state policy which the Massachusetts rule is intended to serve, I concur in the judgment of the Court.

NOTE ON "FORUM SHOPPING" AND ON THE FEDERAL RULES

(1) *Justice Harlan's Rationale in Hanna.* The passage in the First Edition of this book to which Justice Harlan was apparently referring in his concurrence read as follows:

"Is it too late to return to a test which would seek to distinguish between (a) those rules of law which characteristically and reasonably affect people's conduct at the stage of primary private activity and should therefore be classified as substantive or quasi-substantive, and (b) those rules which are not of significant importance at the primary stage and should therefore be regarded as procedural or quasi-procedural?"[1]

If such a distinction were to be adopted, how would you classify a rule of state law allowing rescission or reformation of a contract for a mutual mistake of fact? Shifting the burden of proof with respect to the issue of contributory negligence? Allowing the recovery of reliance damages for breach of a contract within the statute of frauds? Do any such rules characteristically affect people's conduct at the stage of primary private activity? If not, should they be regarded as "quasi-procedural"—as rules that need not be followed in federal diversity actions?

In view of the importance of Erie as a statement about the allocation of law-making power between states and nation, is it perhaps a mistake to ask simply whether a particular state rule in fact affects people's conduct at the planning stage? Is not the more critical question whether that state rule embodies a significant state policy with respect to primary conduct and its effects?

(2) *Matters Not Governed by a Federal Rule of Civil Procedure.* The Court in Hanna suggests that when the matter is not governed by a federal statute or Federal Rule of Civil Procedure, the question is whether failure to follow the state rule would make such an important difference as to "discriminate against citizens of the forum State" or as to lead the "plaintiff to choose the federal court." What if the discrimination is against a *non-citizen* of the forum state? If the failure to follow the state rule leads the *defendant* to choose the federal court?

In any event, doesn't the Court's emphasis on forum-shopping make too short shrift of the Byrd analysis of the impact of state and federal policies? Can't there be affirmative considerations that might justify a uniform federal rule even in the absence of a statute or a Federal Rule of Civil Procedure? Consider, for example, the standard for determining the sufficiency of the evidence to take a case to the jury, p. 719, note 6, *supra.*

Sharply contrasting views on these issues have been expressed by Ely, *The Irrepressible Myth of Erie,* 87 Harv.L.Rev. 693 (1974), and Redish & Phillips, *Erie and The Rules of Decision Act: In Search of the Appropriate Dilemma,* 91 Harv.L.Rev. 356 (1977). Arguing that the Rules of Decision Act was designed to mark out enclaves of exclusive state concern, Ely concludes that the Act requires state law to be followed whenever disregard of that law would be

---

1. In discussing this question, the First Edition referred to Levinson v. Deupree, 345 U.S. 648 (1953), a libel in admiralty to enforce a state-created right of action for wrongful death. The Court held in that case that an amendment to the complaint alleging the appointment of the plaintiff as administrator was authorized under the Admiralty Rules, although the state courts would have held the amendment barred by the statute of limitations (p. 652): "Whether, if this were a diversity case, we would consider that we are here dealing with 'forms and modes' or with matters more seriously affecting the enforcement of the right, it is clear that we are not dealing with an integral part of the right created by [the state] * * *."

Should there be one analysis for diversity cases and another for the other situations in which federal courts enforce rights created by state law? Does any such implication survive Byrd and Hanna?

"likely to generate an outcome different from that which would result were the case litigated in the state court system and the state rules followed" (87 Harv.L.Rev. at 714). "[I]n light of [the Act's] fairness rationale—or, for that matter in light of a desire either to minimize forum shopping or to avoid 'uncertainty in the planning of everyday affairs'—it becomes clear that there is no place in the analysis for the sort of balancing of federal and state interests contemplated by the Byrd opinion" (p. 717 n. 130).

Redish and Phillips disagree. They see Erie and the Rules of Decision Act as warranting consideration not only of the interests of litigants in uniformity of outcome but of the state's interest in enforcement of its substantive policies and of the federal interest in the fair and efficient administration of justice. Thus they urge a "refined balancing test" that considers, *inter alia,* the federal interest in "doing justice" and in the avoidance of unnecessary cost or inconvenience (91 Harv.L.Rev. at 384–94).[2]

(3) *Matters Governed by the Federal Rules of Civil Procedure.* Justice Harlan criticizes the majority for clothing the Federal Rules of Civil Procedure with virtually absolute immunity by adopting an "arguably procedural, ergo constitutional" test. That test is surely appropriate for measuring the constitutionality of a rule of procedure laid down for the federal courts by Congress. And Sibbach seems to require that essentially the same test be applied in determining the validity under the Enabling Act of a rule promulgated by the Supreme Court. Did Hanna continue to apply this test? If so, the fault (if fault is to be found) may well lie with the Sibbach opinion. Was that opinion sufficiently sensitive to state interests, and to the language and purpose of the Enabling Act?[3]

2. A question of the choice between state and federal law in the absence of a governing federal statute or rule arose in Chambers v. NASCO, Inc., 501 U.S. 32 (1991). In a diversity action for specific performance of a contract, the district court found that Chambers, the defendant corporation's sole shareholder, had engaged in sanctionable conduct both before and after formal institution of the litigation, and imposed a sanction against him in the form of attorney's fees and expenses totaling almost $1 million. (The conduct included attempts to deprive the court of jurisdiction by acts of fraud, the filing of false and frivolous pleadings, and other tactics of delay, oppression, and harassment.) The district court, concluding that neither Rule 11 of the Federal Rules of Civil Procedure nor any federal statute was sufficient to support the sanction, relied on its "inherent power," and the Supreme Court, in a 5–4 decision, upheld its authority to do so. On the relevance of state law to the question of sanctions, the Court concluded that, in the context of the determination of sanctions for bad faith conduct in the course of litigation, the question was "not a matter of substantive remedy, but of vindicating judicial authority" (p. 55, quoting

from the opinion below), and thus the imposition of sanctions (like a fine for civil contempt) could not conflict with state substantive law.

The majority stressed that in its view, the district court "did not attempt to sanction [Chambers] for breach of contract", but rather imposed sanctions for the "fraud he perpetrated on the court and the bad faith he displayed toward both his adversary and the court throughout the course of the litigation" (p. 54). Justice Kennedy's dissent, disagreeing with this characterization, argued that the district court had violated Erie principles to the extent that the sanctions were based not on litigation conduct but on a bad faith breach of contract.

3. Ely, Paragraph (2), *supra,* argues that the Court in Sibbach failed to give adequate scope to what was then the second sentence, and what is now subsection (b), of the Enabling Act. That provision, in his view, does not require evisceration of the Federal Rules of Civil Procedure; it does require, however, that a federal rule of civil procedure must yield in the face of a state rule that does not merely represent a procedural disagreement but embodies a substan-

The majority in Hanna recognized, however, that federal rules and federal statutes must be interpreted by the courts applying them, and that the process of interpretation can and should reflect an awareness of legitimate state interests. Indeed, the existence of that awareness may account for the fact that the Court did not squarely confront the issue posed in Hanna until 27 years after Erie and 25 years after Sibbach.[4]

(4) *Problems of Conflict After Hanna.* The Supreme Court has continued since Hanna to interpret the federal rules to avoid conflict with important state regulatory policies.[5] Thus in Walker v. Armco Steel Corp., 446 U.S. 740 (1980),

tive policy. Such a policy, he argues, may be found whenever the purpose of a rule, in whole or in part, relates to matters other than the fairness or efficiency of the litigation process. See 87 Harv.L.Rev. at 718–27.

Professor Burbank, in *The Rules Enabling Act of 1934,* 130 U.Pa.L.Rev. 1015 (1982), also objects to the interpretation of the Enabling Act in Sibbach and Hanna, but on quite different grounds. Relying on his study of the pre–1934 history of the Act, he concludes that the first two sentences of the original Act "were intended to allocate power between the Supreme Court as rulemaker and Congress and thus to circumscribe the delegation of legislative power, that they were thought to be equally relevant in all actions brought in a federal court, and that the protection of state law was deemed a probable effect, rather than the primary purpose, of the allocation scheme established by the Act" (pp. 1025–26). The second sentence of the Act (now subsection (b)), he suggests, has no independent meaning (pp. 1107–08) but serves to underscore the test for the validity of a rule: "[Matters classified as substantive] involve at their core, either potential effects on 'rights' recognized by the 'substantive law' that are *predictable and identifiable,* or the creation of remedial rights that *predictably and identifiably* affect personal liberty or the use and enjoyment of property" (p. 1128).

Even if this standard is supported by the pre–1934 history of the Act, is it workable?

4. After Hanna, in Bangor Punta Operations, Inc. v. Bangor & A.R.R. Co., 417 U.S. 703, 708 n. 4 (1974), the Court recognized that there was a question of the validity, in a diversity case in which state law differed, of the "contemporaneous ownership" requirement of Federal Rule 23.1 in shareholder derivative actions. See Harbrecht, *The Contemporaneous Ownership Rule in Shareholders' Derivative Suits,* 25 U.C.L.A.L.Rev. 1041 (1978); 7C Wright, Miller & Kane, Federal Practice and Procedure § 1829 (1986).

Can the contemporaneous ownership provision of Rule 23.1 be upheld on the ground that it relates only to the adequacy of pleading and not to the requirement of proof? The Court so interpreted the rule in a related context in Kamen v. Kemper Financial Services, Inc. 500 U.S. 90 (1991), a stockholder's derivative action founded on the federal Investment Company Act. Kamen presented the question whether a demand to bring suit had to be made on the board of directors as a prerequisite to the filing of such an action. The Court stated that the matter was not controlled by Rule 23.1, since the provisions of that rule—that the complaint must state the efforts, if any, made to obtain the desired action from the directors—simply *"contemplate* both the demand requirement and the possibility that demand may be excused, [and do] not *create* a demand requirement of any particular dimension" (p. 96). *Cf.* Palmer v. Hoffman, 318 U.S. 109 (1943)(construing Rule 8(c), p. 674, *supra*).

If the contemporaneous ownership provision would not survive an Enabling Act challenge in a diversity case, in the face of a conflicting state law, could it survive in a federal question case as a codification of a federal decisional rule? See Hawes v. Oakland, 104 U.S. 450 (1881). Is the question a trivial one because the Court could fall back on the Hawes precedent if the rule were invalid? See Burbank, note 3, *supra,* at 1149–53.

5. But *cf.* Burlington N.R.R. v. Woods, 480 U.S. 1 (1987). In this federal diversity case, the defendant had appealed from a judgment for the plaintiff; the question was whether the federal appellate court should follow a state rule imposing a fixed penalty on any appellant who obtains a stay of a money judgment pending appeal if the judgment is affirmed without substantial modification. The Supreme Court held that the state rule should not apply, since it conflicted with the discretion to award damages for

the Court unanimously decided that Ragan was still good law,[6] and that state law rather than Rule 3 determined when a diversity action was commenced for the purpose of tolling the statute of limitations. The Court noted at the outset (p. 749) that the doctrine of stare decisis "weighs heavily" in favor of adherence to Ragan; it then observed that significant state policy interests would be frustrated if Rule 3 operated to supersede the state rule requiring actual service on the defendant in order to stop the running of the statute. The Court did not reach the question of the validity of Rule 3 in this context because the lack of any reference in the rule to the tolling of state limitations statutes meant that there was no "direct conflict between the Federal Rule and the state law" (pp. 750, 752).[7]

Does the Walker decision cast some doubt on the Hanna result? If the state law at issue in Hanna was essentially a provision for determining when and how the statute of limitations was tolled, should it have prevailed even though it went beyond the requirements of Rule 4? See Burbank, note 3, *supra*, at 1173–76.

(5) *Resolving a Perceived Conflict Between Federal and State Law With Respect to a Motion to Transfer*. The question of the relevance of state policy to a motion to transfer under § 1404 (a question made more complicated by the presence in the case of a contractual forum-selection clause that was disfavored by the law of the transferor state) led to a decision by a sharply divided Court in Stewart Org., Inc. v. Ricoh Corp., 487 U.S. 22 (1988). The decision is discussed in Section 4 of this Chapter, p. 734, *infra*.

(6) *Hanna and the Rulemaking Process*. To a significant extent, the result of Hanna's permissive standards for measuring the validity of the Federal Rules has been to remit important issues of federalism from the Court as a decider of cases to the Court (and its advisers) as a promulgator of rules, and to Congress in its review of those rules. Doesn't this result increase the significance of the rulemaking process and of the effective allocation of power within that process? (See pp. 663–69, *supra*.)

A case in point is the evolution of the rules relating to privilege in the Federal Rules of Evidence. As proposed by the Advisers and promulgated by the Supreme Court, the rules set out a federally-defined set of privileges for all

---

frivolous appeals under Rule 38 of the Federal Rules of Appellate Procedure. For criticism of Burlington, see Whitten, *Erie and the Federal Rules: A Review and Reappraisal after Burlington Northern Railway v. Woods*, 21 Creighton L.Rev. 1 (1987).

6. After observing that Rule 3 contains no specific statement about tolling of the statute of limitations, the Court quoted from the Advisory Committee's Notes on the Rule as originally promulgated; it concluded from those notes that while the Committee "predicted the problem which arose in Ragan", it did not "*intend*[]" the Rule to serve as a tolling provision; it only "thought the Rule *might* have that effect" (p. 750, n. 10).

7. The Court also stated, in a footnote: "We do not here address the role of Rule 3 as a tolling provision for a statute of limitations, whether set by federal law or borrowed from state law, if the cause of action is based on federal law (p. 751 n. 11). That question was addressed in West v. Conrail, 481 U.S. 35 (1987); the Court held that 'when the underlying cause of action is based on federal law and the absence of an express federal statute of limitations makes it necessary to borrow a limitations period from another statute, the action is not barred if it has been 'commenced' in compliance with Rule 3 within the borrowed period" (p. 39).

After Walker, the Seventh Circuit found no conflict with Fed.R.Civ.P. 68 that would prevent a federal court sitting in diversity from following a state statute relating to the effects of rejecting a *plaintiff's* settlement offer. S.A. Healy Co. v. Milwaukee Metro. Sewerage Dist., 60 F.3d 305 (7th Cir.1995).

civil and criminal litigation in the federal courts. In answer to the argument that at least in cases governed by state substantive law these rules might run afoul of Erie and the Enabling Act, the Advisers argued that Hanna gave a large measure of choice to the rulemakers, that state privileges had at most a "tenuous" substantive aspect, that they would have to give way in federal question cases in any event, and that the practical dimensions of the problem were not great. See Revised Draft of Proposed Rules of Evidence, 51 F.R.D. 315, 358–60 (1971).[8]

Congress refused to accept this approach. Moved by concern for privacy interests and by a desire to safeguard substantive state policies, Congress provided in Federal Rule of Evidence 501 that federal "common law" was to control on matters of privilege only with respect to claims or defenses governed by federal substantive law. When the claim or defense was governed by state law, the state law of privilege was to be applied. For the relevant legislative history, see H.R.Rep. No. 93–650, 93d Cong., 1st Sess. (1973); S.Rep. No. 93–1277, 93d Cong., 2d Sess. (1974); Conf.Comm.Rep. No. 93–1597, 93d Cong., 2d Sess. 1974.[9]

SECTION 4. THE EFFECT OF STATE LAW (AND OF PRIVATE AGREEMENT) ON THE EXERCISE OF FEDERAL JURISDICTION

Railway Co. v. Whitton's Administrator

80 U.S. (13 Wall.) 270, 20 L.Ed. 571 (1871).
Writ of Error to the Circuit Court for the Eastern District of Wisconsin.

[Henry Whitton, as administrator of the estate of his wife in Wisconsin, brought suit in a Wisconsin state court to recover damages for the death of his

8. Ely, Paragraph (2), *supra,* concluded that the proposed privilege rules would have violated the Enabling Act, though he thought they would pass muster under the Constitution if enacted by Congress (87 Harv.L.Rev. at 738–40). He did not indicate any distinction, with respect to either prong of this conclusion, between federal question and diversity litigation. For a broader attack on the validity of the proposed evidence rules, see Burbank, note 3, *supra,* at 1137–43.

9. In a recent, extensive analysis of Rule 501, Professor Dudley is quite critical of the choice made by Congress. Dudley, *Federalism and Federal Rule of Evidence 501: Privilege and Vertical Choice of Law,* 82 Geo. L.J. 1781 (1994). Professor Dudley argues that since privilege rules serve goals "extrinsic to fact-finding accuracy * * * federalism principles suggest that the central issue should be * * * whether the extra-courtroom

behavior protected or promoted by the [privilege] rule is regulated by federal or state law, rather than whether federal or state law provides the legal source of the claim or defense at issue. * * * [But because of the supremacy of federal law, even when the behavior is regulated by state law,] a uniform federal rule may be in order when the application of the evidentiary rule implicates some federal interest * * * that is paramount in context to the state interest in regulating the underlying behavior" (p. 1785).

Under such an approach, how should a federal court, for example, deal with an assertion of marital privilege in a civil or criminal case arising under federal law? With a similar assertion in a civil case in which substantive claims are asserted under *both* state and federal law? (For discussion of the latter question in the context of current Rule 501, see 23 Wright & Graham, Federal Practice and Procedure § 5434 (1980 and 1995 Supp.).

wife which was alleged to have been caused by the carelessness and culpable mismanagement of the defendant railroad. The action was brought under a Wisconsin statute which, after creating a right of action in favor of the decedent's personal representative, subjected it to the proviso that "such action shall be brought for a death caused in this State, and, in some court established by the constitution and laws of the same".

[While the case was pending, Congress passed the Act of March 2, 1867, 14 Stat. 558, which provided that in any suit then pending or later brought in a state court "in which there is a controversy between a citizen of the State in which the suit is brought and a citizen of another State, and the matter in dispute exceeds the sum of $500, exclusive of costs, such citizen of another State, whether he be plaintiff or defendant, if he will make and file in such State court an affidavit stating that he has reason to, and does believe that, from prejudice or local influence, he will not be able to obtain justice in such State court, may, at any time before the final hearing or trial of the suit", remove the case to the federal circuit court.

[The plaintiff removed the case to the federal court under this act and ultimately got judgment for $5,000. The excerpt from the opinion which follows deals with one only of three grounds upon which the jurisdiction of the circuit court was challenged on writ of error.]

■ MR. JUSTICE FIELD, having stated the case, delivered the opinion of the court as follows:

    * * *

Second; as to the limitation to the State court of the remedy given by the statute of Wisconsin. That statute, after declaring a liability by a person or a corporation to an action for damages when death ensues from a wrongful act, neglect, or default of such person or corporation, contains a proviso "that such action shall be brought for a death caused in this State, and, in some court established by the constitution and the laws of the same." This proviso is considered by the counsel of the defendant as in the nature of a condition, upon a compliance with which the remedy given by the statute can only be enforced.

It is undoubtedly true that the right of action exists only in virtue of the statute, and only in cases where the death was caused within the State. The liability of the party, whether a natural or an artificial person, extends only to cases where, from certain causes, death ensues within the limits of the State. But when death does thus ensue from any of those causes, the relatives of the deceased named in the statute can maintain an action for damages. The liability within the conditions specified extends to all parties through whose wrongful acts, neglect, or default death ensues, and the right of action for damages occasioned thereby is possessed by all persons within the description designated. In all cases, where a general right is thus conferred, it can be enforced in any Federal court within the State having jurisdiction of the parties. It cannot be withdrawn from the cognizance of such Federal court by any provision of State legislation that it shall only be enforced in a State court. The statutes of nearly every State provide for the institution of numerous suits, such as for partition, foreclosure, and the recovery of real property in particular courts and in the counties where the land is situated, yet it never has been pretended that limitations of this character could affect, in any respect, the jurisdiction of the Federal court over such suits where the citizenship of one of the parties was otherwise sufficient. Whenever a general rule as to property or personal rights, or injuries to either, is established by State legislation, its enforcement by a Federal court in a case between proper parties is a matter of course, and the jurisdiction of the court, in such case, is not subject to State limitation.   * * *

NOTE ON AGREEMENTS NOT TO RESORT TO THE FEDERAL COURTS

(1) *Agreements Not To Remove as a Statutory Condition of Doing Business.* The Supreme Court early and consistently held that an agreement by a foreign corporation, exacted by a state statute, not to remove to a federal court any case brought against it in a state court was ineffectual in ousting jurisdiction when the corporation later removed a case in defiance of the agreement.   The agreement was condemned independently of the statute on the basis of the common law doctrine that agreements in advance to oust the courts of the jurisdiction conferred by law are illegal and void.   The Court also held that the statute gave the agreement no added force, since the state was without power to impose conditions repugnant to the Constitution and laws of the United States.   Insurance Co. v. Morse, 87 U.S. (20 Wall.) 445 (1874).   In Barron v. Burnside, 121 U.S. 186 (1887), the Court held that a statute attempting to exact such an agreement was void, so that the penalties it provided for employees of non-complying corporations could not be enforced.   Then in Terral v. Burke Const. Co., 257 U.S. 529 (1922), the Court, overruling several earlier decisions, held that a state lacked power to revoke a foreign corporation's license to engage in intrastate business on the grounds that it had violated a state statute by removing a case to federal court:

"The principle established by the more recent decisions of this court is that a state may not, in imposing conditions upon the privilege of a foreign corporation's doing business in the state, exact from it a waiver of the exercise of its constitutional right to resort to the federal courts, or thereafter withdraw the privilege of doing business because of its exercise of such right, whether waived in advance or not.   The principle does not depend for its application on the character of the business the corporation does, whether state or interstate, although that has been suggested as a distinction in some cases.   It rests on the ground that the Federal Constitution confers upon citizens of one state the right to resort to federal courts in another, that state action, whether legislative or executive, necessarily calculated to curtail the free exercise of the right thus secured is void because the sovereign power of a state in excluding foreign corporations, as in the exercise of all others of its sovereign powers, is subject to the limitations of the supreme fundamental law" (pp. 532–33).

(2) *Private Agreements Limiting Choice of Forum.* What is the status of a private agreement, not exacted by state law, that precludes suit from being brought in a federal court originally or on removal?[1]   The courts of appeals had adopted differing approaches to this question, and the matter ultimately came before the Supreme Court in The M/S Bremen v. Zapata Off–Shore Co., 407

---

1. The focus of discussion in text is on an agreement that suit may be brought only in the court of another forum (*i.e.*, a court of a state or of another country).   Agreements to submit disputes to arbitration, though once disfavored, are now generally enforced under a variety of state and federal statutes.   See pp, 711–13, *supra;* Hirshman, *The Second Arbitration Trilogy: The Federalization of Arbitration Law,* 71 Va.L.Rev. 1305, 1309–12 (1985).

U.S. 1 (1972). Zapata, an American corporation, had contracted with Unterweser, a German corporation, for towage of Zapata's ocean-going drilling rig from Louisiana to the Adriatic Sea. The contract contained a clause providing: "Any dispute arising must be treated before the London Court of Justice." The rig was severely damaged during a storm in the Gulf of Mexico, and Zapata commenced a suit in admiralty in a Florida federal court seeking damages against Unterweser in personam and against Unterweser's deep sea tug, The Bremen, in rem. Unterweser moved to dismiss on the basis of the contract's forum selection clause or on forum non conveniens grounds, or in the alternative to stay the action pending submission of the dispute to the London Court of Justice. (Unterweser had subsequently commenced an action against Zapata for breach of the towage contract in the London court.) The federal district court refused to dismiss or stay the action and instead enjoined Unterweser from prosecuting its action in the London court. A majority of the Fifth Circuit, sitting en banc, affirmed, concluding that a forum selection clause should not be upheld unless the forum selected would be more convenient than the one in which suit was brought, and in this case it was not.

The Supreme Court reversed, 8–1. The view that "such clauses are prima facie valid and should be enforced unless enforcement is shown by the resisting party to be 'unreasonable' under the circumstances * * * is the correct doctrine to be followed by federal district courts sitting in admiralty" (p. 10). The Court noted that much undesirable uncertainty in international transactions can be eliminated by an advance agreement as to forum and that the party seeking to avoid its impact on such grounds as fraud, undue influence, "overweening bargaining power", or, perhaps, serious inconvenience should have a heavy burden of proof.

Zapata argued further that enforcement of the forum selection clause would violate public policy because the contract also contained a clause, exculpating Unterweser from liability, that an English court would honor but a federal court sitting in admiralty presumably would not. See Bisso v. Inland Waterways Corp., 349 U.S. 85 (1955). This argument was rejected on the ground that, though it might be improper for an American tower contracting with an American towee to avoid the Bisso policy by providing for an exclusive foreign forum to resolve disputes, that policy did not reach "a freely negotiated international commercial transaction between a German and an American corporation for towage of a vessel from the Gulf of Mexico to the Adriatic Sea" (p. 17).

Finally, the decision in Insurance Co. v. Morse, Paragraph (1), *supra*, was explained by the Court as "one in which a state statutory requirement was viewed as imposing an unconstitutional condition on the exercise of the federal right of removal" (pp. 9–10, n. 10).

Should the rationale of The Bremen extend beyond contracts involving international transactions? Carnival Cruise Lines, Inc. v. Shute, 499 U.S. 585 (1991), was an admiralty action in which the Court applied The Bremen to enforce a forum-selection clause contained in a standard form passenger ticket. A woman and her husband, residents of Washington state, filed an admiralty action in federal court in that state against a cruise line, alleging personal injuries suffered off the coast of Mexico. The passengers' ticket contained three pages of fine print, including a clause selecting as the appropriate forum any court located in the state of Florida. The Supreme Court held the clause enforceable. That the clause was undoubtedly not negotiated between the parties did not make it "unreasonable," the Court argued, stressing the advantages of such clauses.[2] The Court did state, however, that such clauses "are subject to judicial scrutiny for fundamental fairness" (p. 595).[3]

(3) *The Status of Private Agreements in Diversity Cases.* In diversity of citizenship cases, what is the bearing of the law of the forum state? In Stewart Org., Inc. v. Ricoh Corp., 487 U.S. 22 (1988), an Alabama corporation signed a dealership agreement to market copier products of a nationwide manufacturer headquartered in New Jersey. The agreement's forum selection clause provided that any contractual dispute could be litigated only in a state or federal court located in Manhattan. The dealer nonetheless filed suit in federal district court in Alabama, alleging primarily breach of contract but also fraud and federal antitrust violations. The manufacturer sought to transfer the case to the Southern District of New York under 28 U.S.C. § 1404(a), which provides that "* * * in the interest of justice, a district court may transfer any civil action to any other district or division where it might have been brought." The district court denied the motion, applying Alabama law, which looks on forum selection clauses with disfavor. On interlocutory appeal, the en banc court of appeals reversed.

The Supreme Court agreed that the district court had erred. Justice Marshall stated that under Hanna v. Plumer the critical issue was whether § 1404(a) itself controlled the question of transfer. The Court answered that question in the affirmative, noting that § 1404(a) gives district courts discretion to decide transfer motions on a case-by-case basis, taking into account a range of factors, of which a forum selection clause is only one. To give such a clause either dispositive weight (as the defendant urged) or no weight at all (as Alabama law might have it) would interfere with the multi-factored balance set forth in § 1404(a). Accordingly, the case was remanded for the district court to determine the appropriate effect under federal law of the forum-selection clause on the defendant's motion to transfer.

Concurring, Justices Kennedy and O'Connor stated that in view of the great value of forum selection clauses, federal law under § 1404(a) should give them "controlling weight in all but the most exceptional cases" (p. 33).

In dissent, Justice Scalia offered two reasons why § 1404(a) should not govern the effect of the forum selection clause. First, the statute is concerned with the just and convenient litigation of the case after it has been filed, not with the content and enforceability of an agreement made before suit. Before considering how much weight to give to a clause under § 1404(a), a court must first determine whether the clause is valid; if not, it deserves no weight. The Court, he argued, had failed to address the question of whose law governs this

---

2. The Court also rejected an argument that a provision of the federal shipping laws, 46 U.S.C.App. § 183c, prohibited enforcement of forum-selection clauses in personal injury actions by ship passengers. For discussion of the Byzantine workings of Congress in first amending and then restoring this provision to its original form after the Carnival Cruise Lines decision, see Compagno v. Commodore Cruise Line, Ltd., 1994 WL 462997 (E.D.La.1994).

3. For discussion of Carnival Cruise Lines, see, *e.g.*, Goldman, *My Way and the Highway: The Law and Economics of Choice of Forum Clauses in Consumer Form Contracts*, 86 Nw.U.L.Rev. 700 (1992); Mullenix, *Another Easy Case, Some More Bad Law: Carnival Cruise Lines and Contractual Personal Jurisdiction*, 27 Tex.Int'l L.J. 323 (1992); Purcell, *Geography as a Litigation Weapon: Consumers, Forum–Selection Clauses, and the Rehnquist Court*, 40 U.C.L.A.L.Rev. 423 (1992).

prior question of validity; he found no reason to depart from the normal rule that state law governs the validity of a contract. Second, he suggested that in interpreting ambiguous federal statutes relating to the adjudication of state law claims in federal court, the Court should be guided by the general policy of the Erie line of cases of striving for "substantial uniformity of predictable outcome between federal and state courts in adjudicating claims" (p. 37). Thus, "a broad reading [of a federal statute or rule] that would create significant disuniformity between state and federal courts should be avoided if the text permits" (p. 38, citing, *inter alia,* Walker v. Armco Steel Corp., p. 729, *supra*). In his view, the text of § 1404(a) permitted such a reading.

Justice Scalia also argued that "[s]ince no federal statute or Rule of Procedure governs the validity of a forum-selection clause, the remaining issue is whether federal courts may fashion a judge-made rule to govern the question. If they may not, the Rules of Decision Act, 28 U.S.C. § 1652, mandates the use of state law" (p. 38). He concluded that a federal judge-made rule should not be fashioned, since giving such clauses different effect in state and federal court would lead to forum-shopping and to discrimination between citizens and non-citizens.

Is it clear that the motion to transfer was properly brought under § 1404, or should the motion be regarded as arising under § 1406 because the forum selection clause meant that venue had been laid in the "wrong district"? Would it make any difference in the analysis of the case? In the law applicable in the transferee forum if the motion is granted? See pp. 1612–13, *infra*.[4]

What if the forum selection clause had designated (as the only available forum) a state court, or a court in a foreign country, to which transfer could not be effected under either § 1404 or § 1406? Would the law of the forum state then control whether dismissal should be granted?

For differing views of the Stewart decision, see Freer, *Erie's Mid–Life Crisis,* 63 Tul.L.Rev. 1087 (1989); Stein, *Erie and Court Access,* 100 Yale L.J. 1935 (1991). Freer argues that in Stewart (and elsewhere), federal courts have been paying inadequate attention to state substantive interests in choosing between state and federal law. And he concludes that in any event, forum selection clauses "are simply ancillary tools of choice of law", and that there is "no relevant federal interest" in enforcing such clauses (63 Tul.L.Rev. at 1139–40).

Stein begins by arguing that neither "litigant equality" nor "the substance-procedure distinction" lies at the heart of the Erie doctrine; rather "[t]he appropriate inquiry * * * is * * * whether the policies driving the state law are undermined by federal nonconformity" (100 Yale L.J. at 1941). In the context of the Stewart case, Stein concludes from an examination of Alabama precedent that the state's policy against forum selection clauses "emphasizes that private parties should not be able to constrict the jurisdiction of the state's courts. * * * Thus, as in Byrd, the state rule would seem to be bound up in concerns about the administration of its own courts, rather than in conferring privileges upon the litigants or achieving some other regulatory objective

---

4. If a state court in the transferor state would *dismiss* the suit, may a federal court transfer the action or must it also dismiss? If it may transfer, should the transferee court apply the transferor state's substantive law (including choice of law)? See generally Maltz, *Choice of Forum and Choice of Law in the Federal Courts: A Reconsideration of Erie Principles,* 79 Ky.L.Rev. 231 (1990–91).

relevant to federal practice. In choice of law parlance, there is a 'false conflict.' No value of federalism would be sacrificed here by federal nonconformity with state practice" (p. 1966).[5]

For a broad-ranging discussion (by a number of scholars) of the relation between the Erie doctrine and choice of forum agreements, see *Case One: Choice of Forum Clauses,* 29 New Eng.L.Rev. 517 (1995).

NOTE ON THE VARIED EFFECTS OF STATE LAW ON FEDERAL JURISDICTION

(1) *The Problem.* The following statement in 32 Am.Jur.2d, Federal Practice and Procedure § 5, p. 606 (1982), is typical of innumerable others:

"Although federal laws can affect state court jurisdiction, state laws cannot affect federal court jurisdiction. State legislation may neither confer jurisdiction on federal courts nor abridge or impair federal court jurisdiction."

The material in this Note raises the question whether this statement is tenable. In considering this question, note also cases like Smith v. Reeves, 178 U.S. 436 (1900), which held that in view of the Eleventh Amendment, a state may "give its consent to be sued in its own courts by private persons or by corporations in respect of any cause of action against it and at the same time exclude the jurisdiction of the Federal courts" (p. 445).[1]

(2) *The Stude Case.* In Chicago, R.I. & P.R.R. v. Stude, 346 U.S. 574 (1954), the railroad sought to condemn certain lands owned by Stude, and a state commission awarded damages to Stude and others interested in the land on the basis of its appraisal of the value of the property. The railroad then filed a diversity action in federal court alleging that the assessment was excessive. Acting pursuant to state law, the railroad also filed an appeal in state court, which docketed the case (in accordance with state law) with Stude as the plaintiff and the railroad as defendant. The railroad then filed a petition to remove the state court action to federal district court. The district court granted Stude's motion to dismiss the original action and denied a motion to remand the removed action. The court of appeals upheld the dismissal but reversed the decision not to remand.

The Supreme Court, in an opinion by Justice Minton, affirmed. It held that federal law determines who is a "defendant" entitled to remove under 28 U.S.C. § 1441, and here the railroad was plainly a plaintiff in the state action. As to the dismissal of the action commenced by the railroad in federal court,

---

5. On the special problem of agreements, before and after injury, restricting the plaintiff's choice of venue under the Federal Employers' Liability Act, see Boyd v. Grand Trunk Western R.R., 338 U.S. 263 (1949), and cases cited, particularly the concurring opinion of Chief Judge Learned Hand in Krenger v. Pennsylvania R.R., 174 F.2d 556, 560 (2d Cir.1949).

1. The Court went on to state, however, that such exclusion was "subject always to the condition, arising out of the supremacy of the Constitution of the United States and the laws made in pursuance thereof, that the final judgment of the highest court of the State in any action brought against it with its consent may be reviewed or reexamined, as prescribed by the act of Congress, if it denies to the plaintiff any right, title, privilege or immunity secured to him and specially claimed under the Constitution or laws of the United States" (p. 445).

For fuller discussion of Smith and related decisions, see p. 1098, *infra.*

the Supreme Court held that it was not an original civil action but rather an action for review of the assessment by the state commission. The federal district court, Justice Minton said, "does not sit to review on appeal action taken administratively or judicially in a state proceeding" (p. 581). Noting the provisions in the federal rules governing procedure in condemnation proceedings, the Court said this was not such a proceeding since the railroad's effort to obtain the land by eminent domain had begun (in accordance with state law) with an application to a local official and the resultant appointment of a panel to assess the value of the property.

Justice Black, in a brief dissent, argued that the action was properly brought as a "civil action" under the diversity jurisdiction. Justice Frankfurter, in a separate dissent, indicated his agreement with Justice Black and argued that once the "judicial" phase of the proceedings had begun under state law, all the requirements of the diversity jurisdiction had been fulfilled.

(3) *The Madisonville Case.* In Madisonville Traction Co. v. Saint Bernard Mining Co., 196 U.S. 239 (1905), relied on by Justice Frankfurter in his dissent in Stude, the traction company had filed an application in a Kentucky county court to condemn certain lands belonging to the mining company. Pursuant to state law, commissioners were appointed, who awarded $100 as damages, and the county court issued an order to show cause why the commissioners' report should not be confirmed. State law gave either party a right of appeal to the state circuit court, and to a trial de novo, but the mining company sought instead to remove to the federal court, alleging diversity of citizenship and more than $2,000 in controversy.[2] Jurisdiction on removal was upheld by the Supreme Court. Justice Harlan, speaking for the majority, held that the proceeding in the county court was a "judicial" one that could have been brought originally in a federal court. The law to be applied in such a case was state law, but the state could not confine the determination of the questions involved to its own judicial tribunals. The opinion recognized that the state might have established a nonjudicial process for determining the issue of condemnation, thus excluding concurrent federal diversity jurisdiction, but suggested that the state could not constitutionally do so with respect to the issue of compensation. Compare Prentis v. Atlantic Coast Line Co., 211 U.S. 210 (1908), p. 1223, *infra;* District of Columbia Court of Appeals v. Feldman, 460 U.S. 462 (1983)(proceedings before D.C. Court of Appeals for waiver of bar admission rule were "judicial"; federal district court lacked jurisdiction of independent action challenging the result in those proceedings).

For Justice Holmes, dissenting in Madisonville, the question of condemnation (as distinguished from compensation) was one involving "a prerogative of the State, which on the one hand may be exercised in any way that the State thinks fit, and on the other may not be exercised except by an authority which the State confers" (p. 257). Since the state had provided that the issue be determined in its own courts, "the United States has no constitutional right to intervene and to substitute other machinery" (p. 258). Can this view be squared with Whitton, p. 731, *supra?*

(4) *The Significance and Implications of the Stude Rationale.* Given the result in the Madisonville case, the state court appeal in Stude would evidently have been removable by Stude and the other respondents, as the Stude opinion

---

2. Federal law at that time did not impose a thirty-day time limit on removal of a civil case (as it does now under 28 U.S.C. § 1446(b)).

assumes. But since removal jurisdiction depends on the existence of concurrent original jurisdiction, how could the Court in Stude have found jurisdiction to be lacking in the original federal court action? Was the railroad's failure in that action due only to a mistake of form in designating its complaint an "appeal"? How should the complaint have been designated? Why can't a federal court review action taken administratively in a state proceeding?

At the end of the Stude opinion, the Court left open the question whether the railroad could have initiated the condemnation proceeding in the federal court, bypassing state procedures altogether. How would you answer this question?

Does the Stude case suggest that, in the Supreme Court's view, federal courts should not be handling condemnation cases arising under state law?[3] Compare Louisiana Power & Light Co. v. City of Thibodaux, 360 U.S. 25 (1959)(upholding a district court decision to abstain in an eminent domain proceeding; majority quotes with approval the dissent in Madisonville), and Kaiser Steel Corp. v. W.S. Ranch Co., 391 U.S. 593 (1968)(endorsing federal abstention in case involving appropriation of water rights under state law), with County of Allegheny v. Frank Mashuda Co., 360 U.S. 185 (1959)(holding it erroneous to abstain in a federal diversity action challenging a taking under state law). These cases are discussed in greater detail at pp. 1252–56, *infra*.

(5) *What is a "Civil Action"?* Federal courts have had difficulty over the years distinguishing between a "civil action", which may properly be brought in, or removed to, a federal court, and an administrative proceeding, which may not. Often the outcome will turn on a careful analysis of the precise questions to be decided by the tribunal under the governing state law, as well as of the character of the tribunal contemplated by that law. See, *e.g.,* Upshur County v. Rich, 135 U.S. 467, 472 (1890)(appeal to "county court" from an assessment for taxation is "not a suit within the meaning of the removal act"); Commissioners of Road Improvement Dist. No. 2 v. St. Louis S.W. Ry. Co., 257 U.S. 547 (1922)(proceeding before "county court" to review assessment on railroad for benefits from projected improvements may be removed to a federal court); Range Oil Supply Co. v. Chicago, R.I. & P.R. Co., 248 F.2d 477 (8th Cir.1957)(proceeding for review of administrative denial of application became "civil action" when filed in state court and may be removed).

(6) *The Horton Case: Diversity and Workers' Compensation.* The Supreme Court found the Stude case easily distinguishable in Horton v. Liberty Mut. Ins. Co., 367 U.S. 348 (1961). In holding that an action to determine workers' compensation benefits under state law was properly brought in a federal court, the Court said (pp. 354–55):

"* * * Aside from many other relevant distinctions which need not be pointed out, the Stude case is without weight here because, as shown by the Texas Supreme Court's interpretation of its compensation act: 'The suit to set aside an award of the board is in fact a suit, not an appeal * * *.' [T]he trial in court is not an appellate proceeding. It is a trial *de novo* wholly without reference to what may have been done by the Board." Note that in Range Oil, Paragraph (4), *supra,* there was no trial de novo; review was on the record

---

3. Compare the policy of the federal courts with respect to traditional types of claims in the fields of decedents' estates and domestic relations—matters thought to be of such peculiar concern to the states as to be inappropriate for determination by any separate (even though coordinate) system of courts. See Chap. X, Sec. 2(E), *infra*.

before the state agency and the federal courts upheld the state agency's findings as not unlawful or unreasonable.

How would you react to a proposed statute excluding from the diversity jurisdiction all actions for review of state administrative determinations? *Cf.* 28 U.S.C. § 1445(c), prohibiting removal of state court actions arising under the workers' compensation laws of that state.

NOTE ON THE EFFECT OF STATE DOOR–CLOSING AND "SCREENING" RULES

(1) *Introduction.* In the Whitton and Stude cases discussed in the preceding Note, state laws authorized certain litigation in state tribunals. Different considerations arise when the doors of the state tribunal would themselves be closed, and the claim in federal court is that a federal doctrine, rule, or statute referring to state law (notably the Rules of Decision Act) requires that the doors of the federal court must also be closed. This problem has already been explored in cases like Guaranty Trust, Ragan, and Woods (pp. 703, 715–17, *supra*), and is pursued further in this Note. The Note concludes with a discussion of the impact on federal court jurisdiction of special tribunals established under state law—tribunals such as screening panels in medical malpractice cases. This latter issue, which touches on the relevance to federal diversity jurisdiction of state-mandated techniques of alternative dispute resolution, brings together a number of themes developed throughout this chapter.

(2) *A Point of Departure: The Szantay Case.* In Szantay, v. Beech Aircraft Corp., 349 F.2d 60 (4th Cir.1965), Szantay purchased a Beech airplane in Nebraska and flew it to Florida, and then to South Carolina, where it was serviced by Dixie Aircraft, a South Carolina corporation. On the next leg of the journey, the plane crashed in Tennessee, killing all the occupants.

Basing jurisdiction on diversity of citizenship, the plaintiffs (all citizens of Illinois) brought companion wrongful death actions in a South Carolina federal court against Dixie and Beech (a Delaware corporation with its principal place of business in Kansas). Beech moved to dismiss on the ground that a South Carolina "door-closing" statute deprived the state's courts of jurisdiction over a suit brought by a nonresident against a foreign corporation on a "foreign cause of action".

After an extensive analysis of Supreme Court precedent (including the Byrd and Hanna decisions, as well as Angel v. Bullington, discussed in Paragraph (3), below), the court of appeals upheld the district court's refusal to dismiss the action. The parties agreed that the South Carolina statute was "procedural" and was not "intimately bound up with" the substantive rights in the case, rights that allegedly arose (at least as against Beech) under the laws of another state. The court of appeals proceeded to consider whether important South Carolina policies would nevertheless be frustrated by disregard of the state statute and, after noting the lack of state legislative or judicial material shedding light on the problem, concluded that no such frustration would occur. On the other hand, significant federal considerations militated against dismissal, considerations that included the existence of the grant of diversity jurisdiction, the possibility that the state rule discriminated against out-of-state plaintiffs, and the virtues of joining Beech in the only court in which (the court assumed) Dixie was subject to personal jurisdiction.

At the end of its opinion, the court noted (p. 66) that "[t]he superficiality of the South Carolina policy is demonstrated in this case by the fact that the plaintiffs could have gained access to a South Carolina court by simply qualifying as administrators under South Carolina law."

Suppose that a South Carolina state court, in discussing the state statute, had said: "The clear purpose of this provision is to encourage foreign corporations to do business in this state without fear of being subjected to lawsuits brought by nonresidents on foreign causes of action." What effect, if any, should such a statement be given by a federal court on the Szantay facts?[1]

Having taken jurisdiction in the Szantay case, should the federal court interpret Klaxon as requiring it to apply South Carolina's choice-of-law rules in determining Beech's liability? If not, what rules should govern?

(3) *The Source of the Right Affected by the State Door-closing Rule.* Does it matter whether the state door-closing rule is operating on a right created under the laws of another jurisdiction, as in Szantay, or on a right created by the forum? In David Lupton's Sons Co. v. Automobile Club, 225 U.S. 489 (1912), a Pennsylvania corporation had brought an action in a New York federal court for breach of a contract entered into and to be partially performed in New York. A New York statute provided that a foreign corporation that had not qualified to do business in the state was disabled from bringing suit in the state. (The statute, as construed by the New York Court of Appeals, did not purport to render void the local contracts of such a corporation.) The Court held that the statute did not preclude the federal action, saying (p. 500): "The State could not prescribe the qualifications of suitors in the courts of the United States, and could not deprive of their privileges those who were entitled under the Constitution and laws of the United States to resort to the federal courts for the enforcement of a valid contract."

In Angel v. Bullington, 330 U.S. 183 (1947), a statute of North Carolina forbade deficiency judgments in favor of a mortgagee who had resorted to a foreclosure sale of the mortgaged property, and a North Carolina state court had refused to award such a judgment to a Virginia plaintiff in connection with a sale of Virginia land. (The state court had said: "The statute operates upon the adjective law of the State, which pertains to the practice and procedure, or legal machinery by which the substantive law is made effective, and not upon the substantive law itself. It is a limitation of the jurisdiction of the courts of this State." 220 N.C. 18, 20, 16 S.E.2d 411, 412 (1941).)[2] The plaintiff then tried to obtain a similar judgment in a diversity action in a North Carolina federal court. Although the matter was complicated by the question of the res judicata effect of the prior state action, the Supreme Court made it clear that by virtue of Erie, North Carolina's rule was applicable in a federal court sitting in that state.[3] "Cases like Lupton's Sons Co. v. Automobile Club, 225 U.S. 489,

---

1. On several occasions, notably in Piper Aircraft Co. v. Reyno, 454 U.S. 235, 248 n. 13 (1981), the Supreme Court has expressly left open the question whether "state or federal law of *forum non conveniens* applies in a diversity case."

2. The point was made in response to a challenge to the constitutionality of applying the statute to the case at hand. See note 3, *infra.*

3. The Court did not consider whether North Carolina could constitutionally apply

are obsolete insofar as they are based on a view of diversity jurisdiction which came to an end with Erie Railroad v. Tompkins, 304 U.S. 64. That decision drastically limited the power of federal district courts to entertain suits in diversity cases that could not be brought in the respective State courts or were barred by defenses controlling in the State courts" (p. 192).

Whatever was left of Lupton's appeared to have been buried in Woods v. Interstate Realty Co., pp. 715–16, *supra*. Can Szantay be reconciled with these cases, or is it an indication that some of Erie's progeny are not enduring?[4] Is Angel v. Bullington a case in which a significant state substantive policy may have been involved, though it was not articulated by the state court?

(4) *State "Screening" Statutes and Other State Laws Mandating Resort to Alternative Dispute Resolution Techniques.* A contentious question in recent years has been the applicability in federal diversity actions of state statutes mandating resort to "screening" or "arbitration" panels. These statutes, which are an aspect of a larger effort to develop alternative means of dispute resolution, vary considerably in their terms. Some require resort as a condition to suit, while others constitute the panel as an arm of the court itself— akin to a master in the federal courts. Though one purpose of these panels is to relieve court congestion, it is clear that another purpose—in medical malpractice cases, for example—is to cut back on large jury verdicts and resulting high insurance costs. It is also clear that some plaintiffs have invoked federal diversity jurisdiction in such cases in order to avoid the necessity of submission to a panel before trial.

An example of a screening statute is Mass.Gen.Laws ch. 231, § 60B, which provides for a panel consisting of a state judge, a physician, and an attorney. The panel is required to determine whether "the evidence presented if properly substantiated is sufficient to raise a legitimate question of liability appropriate for judicial inquiry * * *." A plaintiff wishing to sue for medical malpractice may do so even in the event of a negative determination, but the determination is admissible in evidence, and the plaintiff must post a bond (now $6000) for costs and attorney's fees, payable to defendant "if the plaintiff does not prevail in the final judgment."

In Feinstein v. Massachusetts General Hospital, 643 F.2d 880 (1st Cir. 1981), the court held that in a diversity action for malpractice filed in a

---

its rule to a case involving a contract with a Virginia citizen for the sale of Virginia land.

4. In Poitra v. Demarrias, 502 F.2d 23 (8th Cir.1974), the court upheld diversity jurisdiction in an action between Indians living on a reservation, although the state court could not have entertained the case because the Tribe had not given the consent required for the exercise of such jurisdiction by 25 U.S.C. § 1322(a). The court of appeals reasoned that assumption of federal jurisdiction would not undermine any state policy, and that § 1322(a) was intended not to deprive Indians of state-created rights but to prevent the states from interfering with Indian affairs.

Dissenting from the denial of certiorari in the Poitra case, 421 U.S. 934 (1975), Justice White argued that there was a conflict with certain decisions of the Ninth Circuit that, in denying jurisdiction, had relied in part on Woods v. Interstate Realty.

In several decisions after Szantay, the Fourth Circuit applied South Carolina's door-closing statute, noting in each instance that there was an alternative forum where the plaintiff could obtain full relief. *E.g.,* Proctor & Schwartz, Inc. v. Rollins, 634 F.2d 738 (4th Cir.1980). But *cf.* Atkins v. Schmutz Mfg. Co., 435 F.2d 527 (4th Cir.1970), where the court relied heavily on the Szantay analysis in refusing to be bound by state law.

Massachusetts federal court, this procedure must be followed.[5] After concluding that the state law was designed to serve substantive policy objectives that would be undermined if the law were not observed in a federal diversity action, the court rejected the argument that the Whitton case, p. 731, *supra,* precludes the application of Section 60B. Section 60B, the court said, does not attempt to confine medical malpractice actions to state courts: "Rather, [it] creates a screening mechanism through which every malpractice claim must proceed before being pursued in court. No ouster of federal jurisdiction results when, by reason of the policies expressed in Erie, a federal court requires that a state's rule barring an action from proceeding in its courts must be applied to bar the action from the federal court. This principle is exemplified by Woods v. Interstate Realty Co. * * *" (p. 888).

The court went on to hold (1) that the state procedures were not inherently unfair to out-of-staters, (2) that the bond requirement was not so oppressive for a non-indigent litigant[6] as to interfere with the Seventh Amendment right to a jury trial, and (3) that the question of the admissibility in evidence of the panel's determination, and its effect on the jury trial right, need not then be decided in light of the severability provision in the state law.

Under the principle of the Feinstein decision, is there a point at which mandatory resort to a state-created tribunal runs afoul of the Whitton principle? Does the availability of a de novo judicial proceeding resolve all doubts? What if the state law provided that the determination of the screening tribunal was not just admissible but was "prima facie evidence" of the conclusions reached? What if the tribunal had authority not only to make a determination of probable cause but to decide on liability and to award damages? To what extent should federal courts follow state screening or arbitration procedures when it appears that the sole purpose of those procedures is to relieve court congestion and to provide a speedier, more efficient alternative to litigants? To what extent are federal courts free to adopt such procedures in diversity cases without reference to state law?[7]

Such questions have grown in importance with the increasing efforts to channel disputes into alternative fora. Surely, these efforts have limits under the Erie doctrine, the Rules of Decision Act, and the boundaries of Congress' power under Article III. On the last of these points, could Congress, for example, establish an administrative agency for the final resolution of all diversity cases filed in federal court? For their preliminary resolution subject only to limited judicial review? For nonbinding recommendations that a party may reject only by assuming the risk of incurring substantial additional costs? See generally Chapter IV, Sec. 1(B), *supra.*

---

5. The particular procedure followed by the district court, and upheld on appeal, was to refer the action to the state Superior Court for a § 60B hearing. This was done after the state Supreme Court, in response to a question certified to it by a federal judge, had said that if a screening panel was to be used, "the Federal court should not fashion its own tribunal" but should refer the matter to the Superior Court for appointment of the tribunal, "after which its findings will be transmitted to the clerk of the Federal court." Austin v. Boston University Hospital, 372 Mass. 654, 660, 363 N.E.2d 515, 519 (1977).

6. The plaintiff in the Feinstein case did not claim to be indigent. Under the state law, if the plaintiff is found to be indigent, the court "may reduce the amount of the bond but may not eliminate the requirement thereof."

7. Compare the discussion, in the previous Note, of federal court review of state administrative decisions. Compare also the rules on exhaustion of state administrative remedies, especially in cases not arising under 42 U.S.C. § 1983, Chap. X, Sec. 2A, *infra.*

CHAPTER VII

FEDERAL COMMON LAW

INTRODUCTION: THE SCOPE OF THIS CHAPTER

There is no longer serious dispute that the body of federal law legitimately includes judge-made law—law that cannot fairly be described as simply the application of federal statutory or constitutional enactments. But there remain perplexing questions about the nature, source, and scope of such federal common law.

The broad topic of federal common law has a somewhat miscellaneous quality in view of the wide variety of subject matters in which power to formulate such law might be recognized. Rather than attempting an exhaustive survey, this Chapter focuses on some of the major areas of judicial law-making activity in actions in the federal district courts.[1]

The Chapter draws a rough organizational distinction between federal court exercise of substantive common law authority to define primary legal obligations (Section 1) and the exercise of remedial authority to enforce those obligations (Section 2). The boundary, however, is difficult to maintain, as the nature of the remedy may have much to do with determining the significance and, at least as a practical matter, the very existence of the right. Indeed, some questions—like capacity to sue or the availability of a right of contribution—are hard to place on either side of the divide. Further, some developments are noted in passing whenever they seem most relevant, even at the risk of straining the distinction.

SECTION 1. DEFINING PRIMARY OBLIGATIONS

SUBSECTIONS A: CRIMINAL PROSECUTIONS

---

1. Judge-made rules calling for abstention from the exercise of jurisdiction, although arguably federal common law, are discussed in Chapter X, Sec. 2.

The formulation of federal common law in suits originating in the state courts is considered at greatest length in Sec. 2, pp. 847–57, *infra*. See also, *e.g.*, Reconstruction Fin. Corp. v. Beaver County, p. 769, *infra*; Dice v. Akron, Canton & Youngstown R.R., p. 479, *supra*; Meltzer, *State Court Forfeitures of Federal Rights*, 99 Harv.L.Rev. 1128 (1986), discussed at p. 583, *supra*.

United States v. Hudson & Goodwin

11 U.S. (7 Cranch) 32, 3 L.Ed. 259 (1812).

This was a case certified from the Circuit Court for the district of Connecticut, in which, upon argument of a general demurrer to an indictment for a libel on the president and congress of the United States, contained in the Connecticut Currant, of the 7th of May 1806, charging them with having in secret voted $2,000,000 as a present to Bonaparte, for leave to make a treaty with Spain, the judges of that court were divided in opinion upon the question, whether the circuit court of the United States had a common-law jurisdiction in cases of libel?

Pinkney, Attorney–General, in behalf of the United States, and *Dana*, for the defendants, declined arguing the case.

■ * * * [T]he following opinion was delivered * * * by JOHNSON, J.

The only question which this case presents is, whether the Circuit Courts of the United States can exercise a common-law jurisdiction in criminal cases. * * *

Although this question is brought up now for the first time to be decided by this Court, we consider it as having been long since settled in public opinion. In no other case for many years has this jurisdiction been asserted; and the general acquiescence of legal men shows the prevalence of opinion in favor of the negative of the proposition.

The course of reasoning which leads to this conclusion is simple, obvious, and admits of but little illustration. The powers of the general Government are made up of concessions from the several states—whatever is not expressly given to the former, the latter expressly reserve. The judicial power of the United States is a constituent part of those concessions * * *. Of all the Courts which the United States may, under their general powers, constitute, one only, the Supreme Court, possesses jurisdiction derived immediately from the constitution, and of which the legislative power cannot deprive it. All other Courts created by the general Government possess no jurisdiction but what is given them by the power that creates them, and can be vested with none but what the power ceded to the general Government will authorize them to confer.

It is not necessary to inquire, whether the general Government, in any and what extent, possesses the power of conferring on its Courts a jurisdiction in cases similar to the present; it is enough that such jurisdiction has not been conferred by any legislative act, if it does not result to those Courts as a consequence of their creation.

And such is the opinion of the majority of this Court: For, the power which congress possess to create Courts of inferior jurisdiction, necessarily implies the power to limit the jurisdiction of those Courts to particular objects; and when a Court is created, and its operations confined to certain specific objects, with what propriety can it assume to itself a jurisdiction—much more extended—in its nature very indefinite—applicable to a great variety of subjects—varying in every state in the Union—and with regard to which there exists no definite criterion of distribution between the district and Circuit Courts of the same district?

The only ground on which it has ever been contended that this jurisdiction could be maintained is, that, upon the formation of any political body, an implied power to preserve its own existence and promote the end and object of its creation, necessarily results to it. But, without examining how far this consideration is applicable to the peculiar character of our constitution, it may be remarked that it is a principle by no means peculiar to the common law. It is coeval, probably, with the first formation of a limited Government; belongs to a system of universal law, and may as well support the assumption of many other powers as those more peculiarly acknowledged by the common law of England.

But if admitted as applicable to the state of things in this country, the consequence would not result from it, which is here contended for. If it may communicate certain implied powers to the general Government, it would not follow that the Courts of that Government are vested with jurisdiction over any particular act done by an individual, in supposed violation of the peace and dignity of the sovereign power. The legislative authority of the Union must first make an act a crime, affix a punishment to it, and declare the Court that shall have jurisdiction of the offense.

Certain implied powers must necessarily result to our Courts of justice from the nature of their institution. But jurisdiction of crimes against the state is not among those powers. To fine for contempt—imprison for contumacy—enforce the observance of order, & c., are powers which cannot be dispensed with in a Court, because they are necessary to the exercise of all others: and so far our Courts no doubt possess powers not immediately derived from statute; but all exercise of criminal jurisdiction in common-law cases, we are of opinion, is not within their implied powers.

United States v. Coolidge

14 U.S. (1 Wheat.) 415, 4 L.Ed. 124 (1816).

This was an indictment in the circuit court for the district of Massachusetts, against the defendants, for forcibly rescuing a prize, which had been captured and taken possession of by two American privateers. The captured vessel was on her way, under the direction of a prizemaster and crew, to the port of Salem for adjudication. The indictment laid the offense as committed upon the high seas. The question made was, whether the circuit court has jurisdiction over common law offenses against the United States? on which the judges of that court were divided in opinion.

The *Attorney-General* stated that he had given to this case an anxious attention; as much so, he hoped, as his public duty, under whatever view of it, rendered necessary. That he had also examined the opinion of the court, delivered at February term, 1813, in the case of the United States v. Hudson and Goodwin. That considering the point as decided in that case, whether with or without argument on the part of those who had preceded him as the representative of the government in this court, he desired respectfully to state, without saying more, that it was not his intention to argue it now.

Story, J. I do not take the question to be settled by that case.

Johnson, J. I consider it to be settled by the authority of that case.

Washington, J. Whenever counsel can be found ready to argue it, I shall divest myself of all prejudice arising from that case.

Livingston, J. I am disposed to hear an argument on the point. This case was brought up for that purpose, but until the question is re-argued, the case of the United States v. Hudson and Goodwin must be taken as law.

■ JOHNSON, J., delivered the opinion of the court.

Upon the question now before the court a difference of opinion has existed, and still exists, among the members of the court. We should, therefore, have been willing to have heard the question discussed upon solemn argument. But the attorney-general has declined to argue the cause; and no counsel appears for the defendant. Under these circumstances the court would not choose to review their former decision in the case of the United States v. Hudson and Goodwin, or draw it into doubt. They will, therefore, certify an opinion to the circuit court in conformity with that decision.

Certificate for the defendant.

NOTE ON THE HUDSON AND COOLIDGE CASES

(1) *Antecedents and Historical Context.* Although the outcome in Hudson and Coolidge put an end to federal common law crimes, it was hardly a foregone conclusion. There had been earlier prosecutions for common law crimes, yielding some unreviewed convictions. *E.g.*, United States v. Worrall, 2 U.S. (2 Dall.) 384 (C.C.Pa.1798)(attempt to bribe Commissioner of Revenue); see generally Goebel, History of the Supreme Court of the United States: Antecedents and Beginnings to 1801, at 623ff (1971). According to Jay, *Origins of Federal Common Law*, 133 U.Pa.L.Rev. 1231, 1323 (1985)(Part II), a "survey of jurisdictional theory from the Hudson period" shows a general awareness that "federal courts had what we would term significant common-law powers". Professor Jay also argues that "Hudson was decided in a peculiar setting of partisan disturbance, and grew out of a fear that we can scarcely appreciate today—the belief that there was a scheme afoot to install a consolidated national government through incorporation of the British common law". *Id*; see also *id*. at 1003 (1985)(Part I).[1]

In his opinion upholding the indictment for the circuit court in the Coolidge case, Justice Story said (1 Gall. 488, 491, 25 F.Cas. 619):

"I would ask then, what are crimes and offenses against the United States, under the construction of its limited sovereignty, by the rules of the common law? Without pretending to enumerate them in detail, I will venture to assert generally, that all offenses against the sovereignty, the public rights, the public justice, the public peace, the public trade and the public police of the United States, are crimes and offenses against the United States. From the nature of the sovereignty of the United States, which is limited and circumscribed, it is clear that many common law offenses, under each of these heads, will still remain cognizable by the states; but whenever the offense is directed against

---

1. See also Note, 101 Yale L.J. 919 (1992)(arguing that Hudson represented a change in practice influenced greatly by the Jeffersonians' political triumph in 1800 and their opposition to the Alien and Sedition laws). On the crucial importance of the Hudson and Coolidge cases in the development of the conception of the nature of federal law, and the part they played in the struggle between the Federalists and the Jeffersonians, see 2 Crosskey, Politics and the Constitution in the History of the United States 767–84 (1953).

the sovereignty or powers confided to the United States, it is cognizable under its authority. Upon these principles and independent of any statute, I presume that treasons, and conspiracies to commit treason, embezzlement of the public records, bribery and resistance of the judicial process, riots and misdemeanors on the high seas, frauds and obstructions of the public laws of trade, and robbery and embezzlement of the mail of the United States, would be offenses against the United States. At common law, these are clearly public offenses, and when directed *against the United States*, they must upon principle be deemed *offenses against the United States*."

In principle, was there a stronger case for upholding the indictment in Coolidge than in Hudson?

(2) *The Judiciary Act of 1789.* In defining the criminal jurisdiction of the district and circuit courts, the Judiciary Act of 1789, §§ 9, 11, 1 Stat. 73, 76, 79, used the phrase "all crimes and offenses cognizable under the authority of the United States". Charles Warren concluded that had the Supreme Court looked at a manuscript of the original draft bill, Hudson and Coolidge might have been decided differently. See *New Light on the History of the Federal Judiciary Act of 1789*, 37 Harv.L.Rev. 49, 73 (1923):

"'* * * The Draft Bill gave to the District Courts, 'cognizance of all crimes and offenses that shall be cognizable under the authority of the United States *and defined by the laws of the same.*' The italicized words make it clear that the framers of the Bill meant to confine criminal jurisdiction to crimes specifically defined by Congress, and to them only. * * * It now appears, on comparison of the Draft Bill with the Act as passed, that by an amendment introduced in and adopted by the Senate, the restrictive clause—'and defined by the laws of the same'—was deliberately stricken out, thus leaving the District Courts with jurisdiction over crimes 'cognizable under the authority of the United States,' without any limitation. The only rational meaning that can be given to this action striking out the restrictive words is, that Congress did not intend to limit criminal jurisdiction to crimes specifically defined by it." Do you agree?

(3) *Contemporary Common Lawmaking in Criminal Cases.* "Although * * * nonstatutory federal crimes disappeared after the Coolidge decision, federal courts continued [through use of the contempt power] to exercise common law power to enforce law and order within their own precincts and continued to employ a variety of common law techniques, forms, and writs in the enforcement of congressionally defined crimes. * * * By its 'supervisory powers' over lower federal courts and, through them, over federal law enforcement officers, the Supreme Court can still be said, loosely, to exercise an interstitial common law authority with respect to federal crimes." Levy, *Federal Common Law of Crimes*, 4 Encyclopedia of the American Constitution 693 (1986).[2]

Many aspects of "common law authority" referred to in this passage relate not to the definition of legal rights and duties, but to methods of enforcement and remediation. See, *e.g.*, Marshall v. United States, 360 U.S. 310 (1959)(set-

---

2. Note, however, that recent decisions have narrowed the exercise of supervisory power. For example, United States v. Williams, 504 U.S. 36 (1992), held (5–4) that the federal courts lack authority under the "supervisory power" to prescribe standards of prosecutorial conduct before a federal grand jury. The Court distinguished the power of federal courts to fashion rules that (i) enforce standards of conduct prescribed by the Constitution, statutes, or court rules, or (ii) prescribe standards governing the conduct of litigants before the courts themselves.

ting aside a jury verdict, in exercise of the "supervisory power", because the jurors had been exposed to potentially prejudicial publicity); *cf.* Mapp v. Ohio, 367 U.S. 643 (1961)(exclusionary rule).   Is the exercise of such lawmaking power easier to defend against a charge that it usurps the legislative prerogative?

Consider, also, the thesis of Kahan, *Lenity and Federal Common Law Crimes*, 1994 Sup.Ct.Rev. 345, 347–48 "that Congress may *delegate* criminal lawmaking power to the courts"; "that federal criminal law, no less than other statutory domains, is dominated by judge-made law crafted to fill the interstices of open-textured statutory provisions"; and that "a regime of delegated criminal lawmaking is much more * * * effective than one in which Congress is obliged to make criminal law without judicial assistance".[3]   As illustrations, Kahan points to the Crimes Act of 1790, 1 Stat. 112, whose text "merely identified" without defining various offenses on the high seas and in federal enclaves; the mail fraud statute, 18 U.S.C. § 1341; and the RICO statute, 18 U.S.C. §§ 1961–68.

Insofar as Congress has delegated authority to the courts to define liability, is the exercise of such authority unproblematic?   Can the statutes that Kahan lists fairly be viewed as containing implicit delegations?   Is the interpretation of statutes—even when their provisions are extremely open-textured—distinguishable from common lawmaking?

All of these questions are explored at greater length in the next Subsection, dealing with judicial lawmaking in civil actions.   See especially the *Introductory Note on the Existence, Sources, and Scope of a Federal Common Law*, p. 752, *infra*, and the *Note on Theories of Statutory Interpretation And Their Pertinence to Federal Common Lawmaking*, p. 758, *infra*.   In studying the material that follows, consider whether, notwithstanding Kahan's argument, the limits that Hudson and Coolidge impose on judicial definition of primary duties in criminal cases are stricter than the parallel limits on lawmaking in civil cases—and if so, whether the difference in approach is justified.

SUBSECTION B: CIVIL ACTIONS

Clearfield Trust Co. v. United States

318 U.S. 363, 63 S.Ct. 573, 87 L.Ed. 838 (1943).
Certiorari to the Circuit Court of Appeals for the Third Circuit.

■ MR. JUSTICE DOUGLAS delivered the opinion of the Court.

On April 28, 1936, a check was drawn on the Treasurer of the United States through the Federal Reserve Bank of Philadelphia to the order of Clair A. Barner in the amount of $24.20 * * *[,] for services rendered by Barner to the Works Progress Administration.   The check was placed in the mail addressed to Barner at his address in Mackeyville, Pa. Barner never received the check.

---

3.   Kahan views the rule of lenity as a kind of non-delegation doctrine in criminal cases.

Some unknown person obtained it in a mysterious manner and presented it to the J.C. Penney Co. store in Clearfield, Pa., representing that he was the payee and identifying himself to the satisfaction of the employees of J.C. Penney Co. He endorsed the check in the name of Barner and transferred it to J.C. Penney Co. in exchange for cash and merchandise. * * * J.C. Penney Co. endorsed the check over to the Clearfield Trust Co. which accepted it as agent for the purpose of collection and endorsed it as follows: "Pay to the order of Federal Reserve Bank of Philadelphia, Prior Endorsements Guaranteed."[1] Clearfield Trust Co. collected the check from the United States through the Federal Reserve Bank of Philadelphia and paid the full amount thereof to J.C. Penney Co. Neither the Clearfield Trust Co. nor J.C. Penney Co. had any knowledge or suspicion of the forgery. Each acted in good faith. On or before May 10, 1936, Barner advised the timekeeper and the foreman of the W.P.A. project on which he was employed that he had not received the check in question. This information was duly communicated to other agents of the United States and on November 30, 1936, Barner executed an affidavit alleging that the endorsement of his name on the check was a forgery. No notice was given the Clearfield Trust Co. or J.C. Penney Co. of the forgery until January 12, 1937, at which time the Clearfield Trust Co. was notified. The first notice received by Clearfield Trust Co. that the United States was asking reimbursement was on August 31, 1937.

This suit was instituted in 1939 by the United States against the Clearfield Trust Co. * * *. The cause of action was based on the express guaranty of prior endorsements made by the Clearfield Trust Co. J.C. Penney Co. intervened as a defendant. The case was heard on complaint, answer and stipulation of facts. The District Court held that the rights of the parties were to be determined by the law of Pennsylvania and that since the United States unreasonably delayed in giving notice of the forgery to the Clearfield Trust Co., it was barred from recovery under the rule of Market Street Title & Trust Co. v. Chelten T. Co., 296 Pa. 230, 145 A. 848. It accordingly dismissed the complaint. On appeal the Circuit Court of Appeals reversed. * * *

We agree with the Circuit Court of Appeals that the rule of Erie R. Co. v. Tompkins, 304 U.S. 64, does not apply to this action. The rights and duties of the United States on commercial paper which it issues are governed by federal rather than local law. When the United States disburses its funds or pays its debts, it is exercising a constitutional function or power. This check was issued for services performed under the Federal Emergency Relief Act of 1935. The authority to issue the check had its origin in the Constitution and the statutes of the United States and was in no way dependent on the laws of Pennsylvania or of any other state. The duties imposed upon the United States and the rights acquired by it as a result of the issuance find their roots in the same federal sources.[2] *Cf.* Deitrick v. Greaney, 309 U.S. 190; D'Oench, Duhme & Co. v. Federal Deposit Ins. Corp., 315 U.S. 447. In absence of an applicable Act

---

1. Guarantee of all prior endorsements on presentment for payment of such a check to Federal Reserve banks or member bank depositories is required by Treasury Regulations. 31 Code of Federal Regulations §§ 202.32, 202.33.

2. Various Treasury Regulations govern the payment and endorsement of government checks and warrants and the reimbursement of the Treasurer of the United States by Federal Reserve banks and member bank depositories on payment of checks or warrants bearing a forged endorsement. See 31 Code of Federal Regulations §§ 202.0, 202.32–202.34. Forgery of the check was an offense against the United States. Criminal Code § 148, 18 U.S.C. § 262.

of Congress it is for the federal courts to fashion the governing rule of law according to their own standards. United States v. Guaranty Trust Co., 293 U.S. 340, is not opposed to this result. That case was concerned with a conflict of laws rule as to the title acquired by a transferee in Yugoslavia under a forged endorsement. Since the payee's address was Yugoslavia, the check had "something of the quality of a foreign bill" and the law of Yugoslavia was applied to determine what title the transferee acquired.

In our choice of the applicable federal rule we have occasionally selected state law. But reasons which may make state law at times the appropriate federal rule are singularly inappropriate here. The issuance of commercial paper by the United States is on a vast scale and transactions in that paper from issuance to payment will commonly occur in several states. The application of state law, even without the conflict of laws rules of the forum, would subject the rights and duties of the United States to exceptional uncertainty. It would lead to great diversity in results by making identical transactions subject to the vagaries of the laws of the several states. The desirability of a uniform rule is plain. And while the federal law merchant developed for about a century under the regime of Swift v. Tyson, 16 Pet. 1, represented general commercial law rather than a choice of a federal rule designed to protect a federal right, it nevertheless stands as a convenient source of reference for fashioning federal rules applicable to these federal questions.

United States v. National Exchange Bank, 214 U.S. 302, falls in that category. The Court held that the United States could recover as drawee from one who presented for payment a pension check on which the name of the payee had been forged, in spite of a protracted delay on the part of the United States in giving notice of the forgery. * * *

The National Exchange Bank case went no further than to hold that prompt notice of the discovery of the forgery was not a condition precedent to suit. It did not reach the question whether lack of prompt notice might be a defense. We think it may. If it is shown that the drawee on learning of the forgery did not give prompt notice of it and that damage resulted, recovery by the drawee is barred. [Citing lower federal court decisions.] The fact that the drawee is the United States and the laches those of its employees are not material. The United States as drawee of commercial paper stands in no different light than any other drawee. As stated in United States v. National Exchange Bank, 270 U.S. 527, 534, "The United States does business on business terms." It is not excepted from the general rules governing the rights and duties of drawees "by the largeness of its dealings and its having to employ agents to do what if done by a principal in person would leave no room for doubt." *Id.*, 270 U.S. at page 535. But the damage occasioned by the delay must be established and not left to conjecture. Cases such as Market St. Title & Trust Co. v. Chelten Trust Co., *supra*, place the burden on the drawee of giving prompt notice of the forgery—injury to the defendant being presumed by the mere fact of delay. But we do not think that he who accepts a forged signature of a payee deserves that preferred treatment. It is his neglect or error in accepting the forger's signature which occasions the loss. He should be allowed to shift that loss to the drawee only on a clear showing that the drawee's delay in notifying him of the forgery caused him damage. No such damage has been shown by Clearfield Trust Co. who so far as appears can still recover from J.C. Penney Co. The only showing on the part of the latter is contained in the stipulation to the effect that if a check cashed for a customer is returned unpaid or for reclamation a short time after the date on which it is cashed, the employees can often locate the person who cashed it. It is further stipulated that when J.C. Penney Co. was notified of the forgery in the present case none of its employees was able to remember anything about the transaction or check in question. The inference is that the more prompt the notice the more likely the detection of the forger. But that falls short of a showing that the delay caused a manifest loss. It is but another way of saying that mere delay is enough.

Affirmed.

[Justices Murphy and Rutledge did not participate.]

————

INTRODUCTORY NOTE ON THE EXISTENCE, SOURCES, AND SCOPE OF A FEDERAL COMMON LAW

(1) *Erie and the "New" Federal Common Law.* Consider Friendly, *In Praise of Erie—And of the New Federal Common Law*, 39 N.Y.U.L.Rev. 383, 405, 421–22 (1964): "[B]y banishing the spurious uniformity of Swift v. Tyson—what Mr. Justice Frankfurter was to call 'the attractive vision of a uniform body of federal law' but a vision only—and by leaving to the states what ought to be left to them, Erie led to the emergence of a federal decisional law in areas of national concern that is truly uniform because, under the supremacy clause, it is binding in every forum, and therefore is predictable and useful as its predecessor, more general in subject matter but limited to the federal courts, was not. The clarion yet careful pronouncement of Erie, 'There is no federal general common law,' opened the way to what, for want of a better term, we may call specialized federal common law. * * *

"So, as it seems to me, the Supreme Court, in the years since Erie, has been forging a new centripetal tool incalculably useful to our federal system. It has employed a variety of techniques—spontaneous generation as in the cases of government contracts or interstate controversies, implication of a private federal cause of action from a statute providing other sanctions, construing a jurisdictional grant as a command to fashion federal law, and the normal judicial filling of statutory interstices. * * *

"The complementary concepts—that federal courts must follow state decisions on matters of substantive law appropriately cognizable by the states whereas state courts must follow federal decisions on subjects within national legislative power where Congress has so directed or the basic scheme of the Constitution demands—seem so beautifully simple, and so simply beautiful, that we must wonder why a century and a half was needed to discover them, and must wonder even more why anyone should want to shy away once the discovery was made."[1]

(2) *The Need for Federal Common Law.* In D'Oench, Duhme & Co. v. FDIC, 315 U.S. 447 (1942), respondent sued in a federal district court in Missouri to recover on a note payable to an Illinois bank. The petitioner initially had sold

---

1. The Erie doctrine, although sometimes discussed as applying only in diversity of citizenship actions, in fact applies, whatever the basis of federal jurisdiction, to any issue governed by state law operating of its own force. (Consider, for example, a state law claim that falls within the federal courts' supplemental jurisdiction.)

the bank some bonds that had become past due. Petitioner then gave the bank the note in 1933, "with the understanding it will not be called for payment", to replace the bonds—so that they would not appear as assets of the bank. The FDIC insured the bank in 1934, and acquired the note in 1938 as collateral for a loan made in connection with the assumption of the bank's deposit liabilities by another bank. The circuit court of appeals followed general conflicts rules in applying Illinois law, under which the FDIC was held to be the equivalent of a holder in due course and entitled to recover.

On review, the Supreme Court found it unnecessary to determine if Missouri or Illinois law governed, ruling that "the liability of petitioner on the note involves decision of a federal, not a state, question" (p. 456). The Court found in various federal statutes "a federal policy to protect respondent, and the public funds which it administers, against misrepresentations as to the securities or other assets in the portfolios of the banks which respondent insures or to which it makes loans" (p. 457).

In the course of an illuminating concurring opinion, Justice Jackson said (pp. 467–69, 470–73):

"This case is not entertained by the federal courts because of diversity of citizenship. It is here because a federal agency brings the action, and the law of its being provides, with exceptions not important here, that: 'All suits of a civil nature at common law or in equity to which the Corporation shall be a party shall be deemed to arise under the laws of the United States * * *.' That this provision is not merely jurisdictional is suggested by the presence in the same section of the Act of the separate provision that the Corporation may sue and be sued 'in any court of law or equity, State or Federal.' "

"Although by Congressional command this case is to be deemed one arising under the laws of the United States, no federal statute purports to define the Corporation's rights as a holder of the note in suit or the liability of the maker thereof. There arises, therefore, the question whether in deciding the case we are bound to apply the law of some particular state or whether, to put it bluntly, we may make our own law from materials found in common-law sources.

"This issue has a long historical background of legal and political controversy as to the place of the common law in federal jurisprudence. * * * The federal courts have no *general* common law, as in a sense they have no general or comprehensive jurisprudence of any kind, because many subjects of private law which bulk large in the traditional common law are ordinarily within the province of the states and not of the federal government. But this is not to say that wherever we have occasion to decide a federal question which cannot be answered from federal statutes alone we may not resort to all the source materials of the common law, or that when we have fashioned an answer it does not become a part of the federal non-statutory or common law. * * *

"Were we bereft of the common law, our federal system would be impotent. This follows from the recognized futility of attempting all-complete statutory codes, and is apparent from the terms of the Constitution itself. * * *

"A federal court sitting in a non-diversity case such as this does not sit as a local tribunal. In some cases it may see fit for special reasons to give the law of a particular state highly persuasive or even controlling effect, but in the last analysis its decision turns upon the law of the United States, not that of any state. Federal law is no juridical chameleon, changing complexion to match that of each state wherein lawsuits happen to be commenced because of the accidents of service of process and of the application of the venue statutes. It is found in the federal Constitution, statutes, or common law. Federal common law implements the federal Constitution and statutes, and is conditioned by them. Within these limits, federal courts are free to apply the traditional common-law technique of decision and to draw upon all the sources of the common law in cases such as the present.

"The law which we apply to this case consists of principles of established credit in jurisprudence, selected by us because they are appropriate to effectuate the policy of the governing Act. The Corporation was created and financed in part by the United States to bolster the entire banking and credit structure. * * * Under the Act, the Corporation has a dual relation of creditor or potential creditor and of supervising authority toward insured banks. The immunity of such a corporation from schemes concocted by the cooperative deceit of bank officers and customers is not a question to be answered from considerations of geography. * * *

"I concur in the Court's holding because I think that the defense asserted is nowhere admissible against the Corporation and that we need not go to the law of any particular state as our authority for so holding."

(3) *Congressional Regulation of Federal Common Lawmaking.* The question whether it is appropriate for a federal court to fashion a federal rule of decision for a particular matter may turn importantly on whether congressional legislation appears to authorize, or to forbid, such lawmaking.

(a) *Congressional Delegation.* In rare cases Congress expressly delegates lawmaking authority to the federal courts. Thus, the first sentence of Rule 501 of the Federal Rules of Evidence—which, unlike most procedural rules applicable in the federal courts, were enacted directly by Congress (88 Stat. 1933 (1975))—provides: "Except as otherwise required * * * [by federal law], the privilege of a witness, person, government, State, or political subdivision thereof shall be governed by the principles of the common law as they may be interpreted by the courts of the United States in the light of reason and experience."

Other cases may involve claims of implied delegation. The broad language of Section 1 of the Sherman Act, 15 U.S.C. § 1, is often viewed as inviting the courts to fashion a common law of anti-competitive practices. See National Soc'y of Professional Eng'rs v. United States, 435 U.S. 679, 688 (1978); Merrill, *The Common Law Powers of Federal Courts*, 52 U.Chi.L.Rev. 1, 43–46 (1985); but see Posner, The Problems of Jurisprudence 289 (1990)(questioning that view). In D'Oench Duhme or Clearfield, did Congress implicitly delegate lawmaking authority to the federal courts? Are there any limits on the scope of permissible delegation?[2]

(b) *Congressional Prohibition.* In other instances Congress may prohibit the federal courts from engaging in lawmaking. The second sentence of Fed.R.Evid. 501 contains such a prohibition: with respect to claims or defenses in which state law supplies the rule of decision, Rule 501 requires that evidentiary privileges be determined "in accordance with State law".

---

2. Compare the argument of Kahan, p. 749, *supra*, that Congress has validly delegated authority to the federal courts to define federal criminal offenses.

What is the significance of the general direction in the Rules of Decision Act, 28 U.S.C. § 1652: "The laws of the several states, except where the Constitution or treaties of the United States or Acts of Congress otherwise require or provide, shall be regarded as rules of decision in civil actions in the courts of the United States, in cases where they apply"? Some have viewed this language as a general restriction on federal court lawmaking in civil actions. See, *e.g.*, Kurland, Politics, The Constitution, and the Warren Court 62 (1970); Redish, *Federal Common Law, Political Legitimacy, and the Interpretive Process: An "Institutionalist" Perspective*, 83 Nw.U.L.Rev. 761 (1989); Merrill, *supra*, at 27–32. Would such a reading be workable? Wouldn't it require drawing a line between permissible statutory interpretation and prohibited common lawmaking? Can such a line be drawn with adequate precision?

Clearfield and numerous cases thereafter have fashioned federal common law while ignoring the Rules of Decision Act. A rare decision discussing the Act's pertinence to federal common lawmaking is DelCostello v. International Bhd. of Teamsters, 462 U.S. 151, 158–59 & n. 13 (1983), p. 824, *infra*, where the Court rejected the view that the Act barred the fashioning of a judge-made statute of limitations for a federal right of action. Noting that the Act "authorizes application of state law only when federal law does not 'otherwise require or provide,'" the Court found no barrier to formulation of a federal rule of decision when called for by "the policies and requirements of the underlying cause of action".[3]

Does that reading of the Act render it a nullity? Compare, *e.g.*, Guaranty Trust Co. v. York, 326 U.S. 99, 103–04 (1945), Chap. VI, Sec. 3, p. 703, *supra*, stating that the Act is "merely declaratory of what would in any event have governed the federal courts". Or does the Act restate basic premises about the scope of federal court lawmaking power?

(c) *Residual Areas*. There remain the vast domains in which Congress has legislative authority under the Constitution and has neither authorized nor precluded federal common lawmaking. In some areas there is a strong consensus that lawmaking is either forbidden (as, for example, with common law crimes or creation of general rules of tort liability) or permissible (as, for example, in admiralty suits or in fashioning limitations periods for federal rights of action, as in DelCostello). In many others, the power to fashion federal common law remains controversial.

(4) *Common Lawmaking vs. Interpretation of Enactments*. Determining the proper role of federal common law is all the more difficult because it cannot be sharply distinguished from statutory or constitutional interpretation. As specific evidence of legislative purpose with respect to the issue at hand attenuates, interpretation shades into judicial lawmaking on a spectrum.

3. One can also argue that the phrase "in cases where [state rules] apply" means "in cases in which there is no federal common law preempting state rules of decision." See Meltzer, *State Court Forfeitures of Federal Rights*, 99 Harv.L.Rev. 1128, 1168 n. 194 (1986) & sources cited; Weinberg, *The Curious Notion That the Rules of Decision Act Blocks Supreme Federal Common Law*, 83 Nw.U.L.Rev. 860 (1989).

Professor Weinberg also points to an oddity that a more restrictive reading of the Act would create. The modern understanding is that where federal common law exists, it governs not only in federal but also in state courts, which are equally obliged to fashion and apply it. See Friendly, Paragraph (1), *supra*. Since § 1652 applies only to the federal courts, a restrictive reading of that provision might leave only the state courts to fashion federal common law.

Commentators have offered a range of definitions of federal common law.[4] We will use the term loosely to refer generally to federal rules of decision whose content cannot be traced by traditional methods of interpretation to federal statutory or constitutional commands—without suggesting that the definition is "correct" in some ultimate sense or that it resolves any of the hard problems of judicial authority.

Whether a rule of decision is viewed as statutory interpretation or as a common law rule designed to help implement the statute does not matter in one important respect: in either case Congress has the power to override the decision. Rules of decision inspired by *constitutional* provisions present an additional complication. Congress clearly cannot override most constitutional decisions. However, Professor Monaghan, in a noteworthy article (*Foreword: Constitutional Common Law*, 89 Harv.L.Rev. 1 (1975)), pointed to a variety of areas in which, he argued, the Supreme Court has fashioned "constitutional common law"—judge-made rules designed to promote constitutional policies, but not themselves "required" by the Constitution, and hence subject to legislative override. For further discussion, see pp. 876-77, *infra*.

(5) *The Scope of Federal Common Lawmaking.* An outpouring of writing attempts to formulate a unified theory to explain when federal common lawmaking has been or should be permitted. Consider these viewpoints:

(a) Professor Weinberg argues that "there are no fundamental constraints on the fashioning of rules of decision" by federal courts, and criticizes suggestions that there is a presumption against such lawmaking, or that lawmaking is limited to particular enclaves of special federal concern. Weinberg, *Federal Common Law*, 83 Nw.U.L.Rev. 805, 805 (1989). For her, just as state courts have general lawmaking power in areas (like torts or contracts) of state concern, federal courts have similar power in areas in which the Constitution authorizes federal legislative or executive action.

Professor Weinberg's very broad view finds little support in the case law, see, *e.g.*, Wallis v. Pan Am. Petroleum Corp., 384 U.S. 63, 68 (1966), or among commentators, see, *e.g.*, Mishkin, *The Variousness of "Federal Law": Competence and Discretion in the Choice of National and State Rules for Decision*, 105 U.Pa.L.Rev. 797, 802–04 (1957). One objection to her thesis lies in the view that policy decisions generally should be made by politically accountable branches of government. See, *e.g.*, Redish, The Federal Courts in the Political Order 29–46 (1991); Merrill, *The Judicial Prerogative*, 12 Pace L.Rev. 327 (1992). How strong is this separation of powers objection? If common law judges traditionally exercised broad lawmaking authority before and after 1789, why shouldn't Article III's grant of judicial power be interpreted as giving

---

4. The definition offered in Field, *Sources of Law: The Scope of Federal Common Law*, 99 Harv.L.Rev. 881, 890 (1986)(italics omitted), which includes "any rule of federal law created by a court * * * when the substance of that rule is not clearly suggested by federal enactments—constitutional or congressional", encompasses much of what others might call statutory or constitutional interpretation. By contrast, Professor Hill, while recognizing that the idea of "construing" a text is strained when courts interpret general standards like "restraint of trade" in the Sherman Act or determine what remedies should be provided in implementing a statutory program, would include these and similar cases within the reach of interpretation, noting that "the text provides at least a sense of direction in which the courts should go". See Hill, *The Law-Making Power of the Federal Courts: Constitutional Preemption*, 67 Colum.L.Rev. 1024, 1026 (1967).

federal judges similar latitude?[5] Does common lawmaking necessarily disserve legislative purposes?

A second objection to Professor Weinberg's approach sounds in federalism. The national government is one of limited powers. Congressional exercise of those powers must overcome the inertia of a legislative process requiring bicameral enactment and either Presidential assent or a legislative supermajority. Congressional action is further restrained by the "political safeguards of federalism"—the responsiveness of national legislators to the interests of the states. Lawmaking by federal courts, by contrast, is not subject to these restraints. See, e.g., Mishkin, *Some Further Last Words on Erie—The Thread,* 87 Harv.L.Rev. 1682, 1685 (1974); Field, *The Legitimacy of Federal Common Law,* 12 Pace L.Rev. 303, 305–06 (1992); Merrill, *supra,* 12 Pace L.Rev. at 349–50.

(b) Most judges and commentators believe that the federal courts' power to fashion law is considerably more limited than that of Congress. There exist, however, a wide variety of formulations of those views. For example:

(i) Professor Field offers a relatively broad view of the power, permitting lawmaking so long as the court can "point to a federal enactment, constitutional or statutory, that it interprets as authorizing the federal common law rule." Field, note 4, *supra,* at 887.

(ii) Professor Merrill would require a stricter showing: "either that Congress has enacted law delegating lawmaking power to courts, or that it is necessary to replace state with federal law in order to preserve a provision of enacted law." Merrill, Paragraph 5(a), *supra,* at 330–31. In his view, lawmaking in admiralty and in interstate disputes is harder to justify but not overly troublesome if confined to circumstances where the purpose of granting exclusive jurisdiction to the federal courts would be undermined if state law governed.

(iii) A different approach would limit federal common lawmaking to particular federal enclaves. Professor Hill argues that the Constitution preempts state lawmaking, and thus authorizes federal common lawmaking, in four areas—interstate controversies, admiralty, proprietary transactions of the United States, and international relations. Hill, note 4, *supra;* see also Texas Indus., Inc. v. Radcliff Materials, Inc., 451 U.S. 630, 641 (1981)(following this approach). However, Hill approves of many decisions that are sometimes viewed as making federal common law outside of these enclaves; he treats them instead as falling within the scope of his broad view of statutory or constitutional interpretation, see note 4, *supra.*[6]

------

5. Much (though not all) of the post–1789 state common lawmaking was authorized by state "reception" statutes, for which there is no federal analogue. See Kramer, *The Lawmaking Power of the Federal Courts,* 12 Pace L.Rev. 263, 280–81 (1992).

6. Professor Kramer's views can be roughly characterized as a hybrid of the views of Professors Field and Hill: "federal courts can make common law * * * so long

as whatever rules the courts fashion are consistent with and further an underlying federal enactment", or fall within areas (such as admiralty, foreign relations, and interstate disputes) in which the Constitution makes federal sovereignty exclusive. Kramer, note 5, *supra,* at 289.

For other commentary, see, in addition to the articles cited elsewhere in this Note, Brown, *Federal Common Law and the Role of*

NOTE ON THEORIES OF STATUTORY INTERPRETATION AND THEIR PERTINENCE TO FEDERAL COMMON LAWMAKING

(1) *Introduction.* Recent discussions of statutory interpretation have raised important questions about the nature of the legislative process, the nature of textual interpretation, and the appropriate judicial role.[1] These questions are also highly relevant to the debate about federal common lawmaking. A necessarily simplified summary of these discussions may highlight a range of issues important to the topic of judge-made federal law.

For example, recall Justice Jackson's classic defense of federal common lawmaking in his opinion in the D'Oench Duhme case, p. 752, *supra*, which can be seen as resting upon three premises: (i) the governing Act was passed by Congress to serve a public purpose; (ii) that purpose can be identified by the courts; and (iii) it is desirable for the courts to exercise lawmaking authority to fashion a rule that implements the congressional purpose. Consider to what extent the material in this Note calls those premises into question.

This Note uses as an organizational tool a distinction between "agency" theories of interpretation—in which a judge looks to the enacting legislature in seeking a statute's meaning—and "non-agency" theories, in which a judge looks, at least in substantial part, to other sources (*e.g.*, background norms of interpretation, views of the current legislature, or a statute's relationship to currently-held social understandings). The distinction is not a clear-cut one, and some might even view it as misplaced. Without doubt, theories grouped within each of the two categories differ sharply from one another. Nonetheless, the distinction may prove useful in organizing the material that follows.

(2) *Agency Theories of Interpretation.* Traditional theories of statutory interpretation view the judge as an agent of the enacting legislature. One variant advocates a judicial focus on the "plain meaning" of the legislative text. Another calls for implementation of the legislature's "intentions". Professors Hart & Sacks urged the judge not to seek the legislature's specific intention concerning the legal question at issue, but rather to presume that "the legislature was made up of reasonable persons pursuing reasonable purposes reasonably", and to interpret the statute to serve those more general purposes. Hart & Sacks, The Legal Process: Basic Problems in the Making and Application of Law 1378 (Eskridge & Frickey eds.1994).

(3) *Contemporary Concerns.* Increasingly, approaches to statutory interpretation are viewed as necessarily implicating theories about the legislative process, the constitutional structure, and the legal system—theories about which sharp disagreement can be expected. See, *e.g.*, Posner, The Problems of Jurisprudence 291–92 (1990). Two sets of concerns have been prominent in posing challenges for "agency" theories of statutory interpretation.

(a) Modern public choice theory argues that legislative enactments, rather than furthering public goals, tend to reflect private deals that favor special interests and that are approved by lawmakers seeking to win re-election.

Federal Courts in Private Law Adjudication—A (New) Erie Problem?, 12 Pace L.Rev. 229, 240 (1992); Doernberg, *Juridical Chameleons in the "New Erie" Canal,* 1990 Utah L.Rev. 759.

1. For a broad-ranging study (and rich source of references) by one of the leading commentators, see Eskridge, Dynamic Statutory Interpretation (1994).

Considerable disagreement exists over both the theory's descriptive accuracy and its normative implications.[2]

A distinct body of political science, which studies problems of collective choice and voting rules, contends that legislation cannot coherently reflect majority preferences[3]—a conclusion reinforced, in the view of some, by a variety of defects in our political process.

(b) A second, partly overlapping set of concerns involves the difficulty of determining legislative meaning: Is it intelligible to speak of the intention or purpose of a bicameral, multi-member legislature? How can it be ascertained? Are not such intentions or purposes likely to be multiple, conflicting, and capable of being described at varying levels of generality?

To these difficulties modern hermeneutic theory adds the claim that interpretation of a statutory text cannot avoid being influenced by the understandings and commitments of the judge who interprets it. Some conclude that statutory meaning is therefore largely or wholly indeterminate, while others stress that meaning depends on linguistic and cultural assumptions—which may or may not be broadly shared. See generally Schanck, *The Only Game in Town: An Introduction to Interpretive Theory, Statutory Construction, and Legislative Histories*, 38 Kan.L.Rev. 815 (1990).[4]

(c) Despite these criticisms, agency theories of interpretation retain academic supporters, see, *e.g.*, Redish & Chung, *Democratic Theory and the Legislative Process: Mourning the Death of Originalism in Statutory Interpretation*, 68 Tul.L.Rev. 803 (1994), as well as judicial adherents. In many of the cases discussed in this Chapter, the Court attempts to identify a particular policy associated with a statutory enactment—and then treats the failure of Congress to have provided an explicit rule of decision to further that policy as an oversight that courts should remedy. In view of the questions about attribution of legislative purpose raised in this Paragraph, is that a justifiable approach?

(4) *The Reinvigoration of Textualism.* In recent years, the textual approach to interpretation has enjoyed a resurgence. See the discussion in Eskridge, *The New Textualism*, 37 U.C.L.A. L.Rev. 621 (1990). Its most prominent standard-bearer, Justice Scalia, argues, *inter alia*, that only the text was enacted by constitutional processes; that legislative history is an unreliable and illegitimate guide to statutory meaning; and that non-textual approaches give judges excessive interpretive latitude, while inviting Congress improperly to leave difficult questions to the courts. See, *e.g.*, Green v. Bock Laundry Mach. Co., 490 U.S. 504, 527 (1989)(Scalia, J., concurring in the judgment).[5]

---

2. See generally Farber & Frickey, Public Choice (1991); Symposium, 74 Va.L.Rev. 167–518 (1988).

3. See, *e.g.*, Arrow, Social Choice and Individual Values (2d ed.1963).

4. An additional set of concerns involves the relationship of courts and administrative agencies, given (i) the rise of "intransitive statutes" that do not operate directly on private actors but rather authorize and direct agencies to create rules governing those actors, see Rubin, *Law and Legislation in the Administrative State*, 89 Colum.L.Rev. 369 (1989), and (ii) claims that policymaking and/or democracy is enhanced by judicial deference to agency interpretation of statutes, see, *e.g.*, Chevron, U.S.A., Inc. v. NRDC, Inc., 467 U.S. 837 (1984); sources cited in Eskridge & Frickey, "An Historical and Critical Introduction to the Legal Process", in Hart & Sacks, Paragraph (2), *supra*, at cxxx n. 337.

5. Judge Easterbrook, another textualist, has argued that courts should broadly construe statutes (like the Sherman Act) that delegate to the courts a common lawmaking

Critics of textualism respond that the meaning of a text inherently depends upon context and culture; that textualism is of little help in filling statutory gaps or ambiguities; and that to burden Congress with providing greater legislative specification is neither realistic nor desirable. Eskridge, note 1, *supra*, ch. 1; Sunstein, *Interpreting Statutes in the Regulatory State*, 103 Harv.L.Rev. 405, 414–51 (1989); Eisenberg, *Strict Textualism*, 29 Loyola of L.A.L.Rev. 1 (1995).

(5) *Theories Premised on a Creative Judicial Role.* Many theories of statutory interpretation propounded in recent years assert that judges should be, or inevitably are, influenced by concerns other than recovering a meaning fixed by the drafters' intention or purpose or by the text itself.

(a) Some commentators have advocated "dynamic statutory interpretation", which calls upon judges, as least in hard cases, to adjust statutes to changed circumstances, to the views of the current legislature, or more generally to evolving social understandings. See generally Eskridge, note 1, *supra*.[6] Supporters often assert not only that interpretation necessarily is shaped by the interpreter's commitments, but also that (i) the difficulty of a legislature's responding to changed circumstances calls for judges to step in to update statutes, and (ii) judges are capable of divining current needs and attitudes and of contributing to a process of deliberation about the public good. Critics argue that this approach disrespects legislative supremacy, gives judges too much latitude to construct a prevailing consensus where none in fact exists, and rests upon a highly critical view of Congress while downplaying the limitations of the judiciary.

(b) Another, sometimes overlapping, view urges judges to be consciously guided, at least in hard cases, by substantive canons of interpretation, drawn from the Constitution or from understandings about government performance or regulatory failure.[7] Professor Sunstein, a prominent advocate, argues that

power, but should construe narrowly statutes in which such delegation is lacking. Easterbrook, *Statutes' Domains*, 50 U.Chi.L.Rev. 533, 544 (1983). Underlying this view is skepticism about statutory regulation as too often consisting only of private deals, and the belief that factors contributing to legislative opacity or incompleteness—such as inertia or lack of time or foresight—are inherent in the legislative process and cannot be treated as problems for courts to remedy. See *id.* at 547–51; Easterbrook, *Text, History, and Structure in Statutory Interpretation*, 17 Harv.J.L. & Pub.Pol'y 61 (1994).

Can one adequately distinguish "deals" from "delegation"? Should a theory of interpretation be based on a predisposition against statutory regulation?

6. For a long list of articles, see Eskridge & Frickey, note 4, *supra*, at cxxix n. 333.

Compare the views in Dworkin, Law's Empire 313, 338 (1986)(a judge should not be a mere agent of the legislature, but rather "a partner continuing to develop in what [the

judge] believes is the best way, the statutory scheme Congress began"; a judge interprets not just a text but the statute's life, in light of new understandings of policy or principle drawn from contemporary public opinion, circumstances, or political decisions); Strauss, *On Resegregating the Worlds of Statute and Common Law*, 1994 Sup.Ct.Rev. 429 (criticizing recent Supreme Court decisions for treating statutes as one-time pronouncements of Congress and segregating their interpretation from the common law, rather than viewing courts as partners of Congress and reading statutes in light of their political history and implementation by the courts and administrative agencies).

7. These commentators argue that such canons differ from traditional "interpretive canons", which are often dismissed as unhelpful rationalizations of decisions reached on other grounds. For a forceful defense of the utility of these much-criticized canons, which argues against a sharp distinction between "interpretive" and "substantive" canons and notes approvingly that the

this approach does not skew statutory meaning because meaning inevitably is drawn from such background understandings. Sunstein, Paragraph (4), *supra*; see also Eskridge, note 1, *supra*, ch. 9. His canons include (among a much longer list): (i) non-preemption of state law; (ii) promoting political accountability; (iii) avoidance of recognition of naked transfers of wealth, in part through narrow construction of interest-group deals; (iv) protection of disadvantaged groups; (v) promoting consistency among regulatory programs; and (vi) expressing respect for "nonmarket values".[8]

Critics contend that these canons are themselves highly controversial; that the values a judge would enforce in applying them may differ significantly from those that the legislature would favor; and that frequently multiple canons with conflicting implications will apply. See, *e.g.*, Moglen & Pierce, *Sunstein's New Canons: Choosing the Fictions of Statutory Interpretation*, 57 U.Chi.L.Rev. 1203 (1990).

(c) To what extent is federal common lawmaking supported by the arguments that favor these forms of judicial creativity in interpreting statutes? To what extent is it subject to the criticisms that have been levelled against those theories?

(6) *Judicial Practice*. It is not clear how this wide-ranging academic debate has affected Supreme Court interpretative practices. Without doubt the Court in recent years has increasingly emphasized a statute's "plain meaning" as the critical constituent of statutory interpretation. See, *e.g.*, Estate of Cowart v. Nicklos Drilling Co., 505 U.S. 469, 475–77 (1992); K Mart Corp. v. Cartier, Inc., 486 U.S. 281, 291–92 (1988). Majority opinions continue to rely on legislative history, although Justice Thomas and occasionally Justice Kennedy have joined Justice Scalia's attack on that practice.[9] One careful study of recent decisions found the Court's interpretive approach to be "eclectic, relying not only on text and originalist sources, but on practical considerations and other dynamic sources as well." Zeppos, *The Uses of Authority in Statutory Interpretation: An Empirical Analysis*, 70 Tex.L.Rev. 1073, 1120 (1992).[10]

---

most significant and widely used canons favor continuity over change, see Shapiro, *Continuity and Change in Statutory Interpretation*, 67 N.Y.U.L.Rev. 921 (1992).

8. Compare Macey, *Promoting Public–Regarding Legislation Through Statutory Interpretation: An Interest–Group Model*, 86 Colum.L.Rev. 223, 251 (1986)(advocating "traditional" interpretive approaches that look to what statutes say, rather than efforts to determine the "deal" that was struck, because private interest legislation is generally justified in public terms and therefore traditional interpretation will make statutes more public-regarding).

For general criticism of theories of statutory interpretation that employ interest group theory to justify greater latitude in statutory (and constitutional) interpretation, see Elhauge, *Does Interest Group Theory Justify More Intrusive Review?*, 101 Yale L.J. 31 (1991)(answering his question in the negative).

9. See, *e.g.*, Conroy v. Aniskoff, 507 U.S. 511 (1993)(seven Justices joined the Court's opinion, one footnote of which relied upon legislative history; Justice Thomas joined all but the offending footnote; and Justice Scalia wrote a separate opinion, concurring in the judgment, that denounced the reliance upon legislative history); United States v. Thompson/Center Arms, 504 U.S. 505, 516 n. 8 (1992)(plurality opinion of Souter, J., joined by Rehnquist, C.J. and O'Connor, J.)(defending the use of legislative history); *id.* at 521 (Scalia, J., joined by Thomas and Kennedy, JJ.)(criticizing reliance upon legislative history).

10. In addition, the Supreme Court has adopted its own canons—quite different from those discussed in Paragraph (5)(b)—requiring a very clear statement from Congress before a statute will be interpreted, for example, (i) to apply extraterritorially, *e.g.*, EEOC v. Arabian American Oil Co., 499 U.S. 244 (1991); (ii) to subject integral aspects of state

(7) *Implications.* Even this brief survey reveals a considerable range of views about such issues as the nature of the legislative process, the relationship of judicial decisionmaking to that process, and the attribution of meaning to legislative enactments. Those same issues arise, in slightly different form, in debates about federal common lawmaking, and you should therefore keep them in mind as you read the material in the remainder of this Chapter.

———

NOTE ON (1) CHOICE OF LAW IN CASES INVOLVING THE LEGAL RELATIONS OF THE UNITED STATES, AND (2) FEDERAL COMMON LAW INCORPORATION OF STATE RULES OF DECISION

(1) *Antecedents of Clearfield.* Early cases involving proprietary and other interests asserted by the United States focused on the question whether the federal government could institute civil suits absent explicit congressional authorization. See generally Sec. 2(A), *infra.* The question whether federal or state law governed was not carefully considered.

Thus, in Cotton v. United States, 52 U.S. (11 How.) 229, 231 (1850), where the United States sued in federal court for trespass, the Court simply stated that the United States has "the same right to have [its property] protected by the local laws that other persons have." The same approach was followed in Mason v. United States, 260 U.S. 545 (1923), a bill in equity by the United States to quiet title and regain possession of public lands. The Court rejected the argument that the Rules of Decision Act, which then provided that "the laws of the several States shall be regarded as rules of decision in trials *at common law* in the courts of the United States" (emphasis added), by implication excludes such laws as rules of decision in suits in *equity*.[1] No reference was made to the possibility (raised in the briefs)[2] that federal law applied.

As the Brief for the United States in the Clearfield case pointed out (pp. 11–12), few cases had squarely presented the choice of law issue: "Under the regime of Swift v. Tyson, since the law of commercial contracts and negotiable instruments was of course regarded as 'general law', the courts found it unnecessary to consider separately the applicability of state decisional law to contracts or negotiable instruments involving the United States. The law merchant as interpreted by the federal courts was as a rule applied without discussion. Prior to Erie R. Co. v. Tompkins, an issue in regard to governing law insofar as the United States was concerned could have arisen only where the state law took the form of a state statute or state decisions interpreting such statutes. Such an issue seems to have been rarely presented and cannot be said to have been clearly considered or determined."

(2) *Board of County Commissioners.* The first Supreme Court case after Erie to consider the applicability of federal common law to suits involving the United States was Board of County Commissioners v. United States, 308 U.S. 3.3 (1939). The question was whether a judgment for the United States, in an action to recover county tax payments illegally exacted from a Native American

———

government to regulation, Gregory v. Ashcroft, 501 U.S. 452 (1991); or (iii) to subject a state to suit in federal court, Dellmuth v. Muth, 491 U.S. 223 (1989). See generally Eskridge, note 1, *supra,* ch. 9 & App. 3.

1. The 1948 revision extended the Act to civil actions generally. See 28 U.S.C. § 1652.

2. See Brief for Appellants at 45; Brief for the United States at 14–15.

exempt under a federal treaty, should include interest. The Court (per Frankfurter, J.) said (pp. 349–52):

"The issue is uncontrolled by any formal expression of the will of Congress. The United States urges that we must be indifferent to the law of the state * * *. Jackson County, on the other hand, urges that the law of Kansas [under which no interest is recoverable] controls. * * *

" * * *

"Having left the matter at large for judicial determination within the framework of familiar remedies equitable in their nature, * * * Congress has left us free to take into account appropriate considerations of 'public convenience'. * * * Nothing seems to us more appropriate than due regard for local institutions and local interests. We are concerned with the interplay between the rights of Indians under federal guardianship and the local repercussion of those rights. * * * With reference to other federal rights, the state law has been absorbed, as it were, as the governing federal rule not because state law was the source of the right but because recognition of state interests was not deemed inconsistent with federal policy. * * * In the absence of explicit legislative policy cutting across state interests, we draw upon a general principle that the beneficiaries of federal rights are not to have a privileged position over other aggrieved taxpayers in their relation with the states or their political subdivisions. To respect the law of interest prevailing in Kansas in no wise impinges upon the exemption which the Treaty of 1861 has commanded Kansas to respect and the federal courts to vindicate."

See also D'Oench, Duhme & Co. v. FDIC, p. 752, *supra*; Deitrick v. Greaney, 309 U.S. 190 (1940).

(3) *Criticism of Clearfield.* Was Clearfield itself correctly decided? Judge Friendly, in his article on federal common law (39 N.Y.U.L.Rev. at 410) says: "Clearfield decided not one issue but two. The first, to which most of the opinion was devoted and on which it is undeniably sound, is that the right of the United States to recover for conversion of a government check is a federal right, so that the courts of the United States may formulate a rule of decision. The second, over which the Supreme Court jumped rather quickly and not altogether convincingly, is whether, having this opportunity, the federal courts should adopt a uniform nation-wide rule or should follow state law. * * * [T]he question persists why it is more important that federal fiscal officials rather than Pennsylvanians dealing in commercial paper should have the solace of uniformity."

A footnote (n. 130) continues: "Although the direct consequence of the Government's victory in Clearfield was to impose liability on the paying bank in accordance with the 'uniform' federal rule, this would necessarily lead to an action by the bank against the endorser. If that action were held to be governed by state law, which would excuse the endorser because of the delay, this would destroy the whole substantive basis of the Clearfield decision, namely, that the bank did not suffer from the delay since, under federal law, it could recover from the endorser, and, as has been noted, 'the burden of financial loss will merely be shifted from the Government to the particular endorser whom it chooses to sue.' Mishkin, [105 U.Pa.L.Rev. 797] at 831. On the other hand, if, as would seem more sensible, decision in the action by the bank against the endorser must reflect the result of applying the federal rule in the Government's action against the bank, a rather nice distinction of the Bank of America case is required.[3] See *id.* at 831–32."[4]

(4) *Competence and Discretion to Fashion Federal Common Law.* Modern decisions—influenced by Judge Friendly and Professor Mishkin—often distinguish two questions. The first is the question of "competence": Do the federal courts have authority to apply a federal common law rule in the particular context? The second is the question of "discretion": If such authority exists, is its exercise appropriate? It is on the latter point, of course, that Judge Friendly differed with the Court in Clearfield.[5]

(5) *Kimbell Foods.* That Clearfield did not require the application of uniform federal law to all questions in federal government litigation, even in cases involving government contracts, was made plain in United States v. Kimbell Foods, Inc., 440 U.S. 715 (1979). The decision involved two cases in which the United States had loaned money and obtained contractual security interests. The key question was whether the priority of the government's liens as against competing liens was governed by ordinary state commercial law rules or by a federal common law rule.

In a unanimous opinion by Justice Marshall, the Court first affirmed that "federal law governs questions involving the rights of the United States arising under nationwide federal programs" (p. 726), and that in the absence of a statutory rule of decision, "Clearfield directs federal courts to fill the interstices of federal legislation 'according to their own standards'" (p. 727, quoting Clearfield, 313 U.S. at 367). But the Court stated that "when there is little need for a nationally uniform body of law, state law may be incorporated as the federal rule of decision" (p. 728). The Court found that the Government had not established that uniformity was needed, emphasizing that it would "reject generalized pleas for uniformity as substitutes for concrete evidence that adopting state law would adversely affect administration of the federal pro-

---

3.   [Ed.] The reference is to Bank of America Nat. Trust & Savings Ass'n v. Parnell, 352 U.S. 29 (1956). There, the bank had brought a federal court diversity action against Parnell to recover funds obtained by cashing certain United States bearer bonds that had been stolen from the bank. Two issues in the case were whether the bonds were overdue and whether Parnell had taken them in good faith. The Supreme Court held that the first issue was controlled by federal law: "Federal law of course governs the interpretation of the nature of the rights and obligations created by the Government bonds themselves" (p. 34). But the second was not; distinguishing the Clearfield case, the Court emphasized that "[t]he present litigation is purely between private parties and does not touch the rights and duties of the United States. The only possible interest of the United States in a situation like the one here * * * is that the floating of securities of the United States might somehow or other be adversely affected by the local rule of a particular State regarding the liability of a converter. This is far too speculative * * * to

justify the application of federal law to transactions essentially of local concern" (pp. 33–34).

4.   For decisions coming on the heels of, and following the result in Clearfield, see National Metropolitan Bank v. United States, 323 U.S. 454 (1945)(commercial paper issued by United States); Priebe & Sons v. United States, 332 U.S. 407 (1947)(government contracts); United States v. Standard Rice Co., 323 U.S. 106 (1944)(government contracts).

5.   Courts virtually never claim that as a matter of discretion, federal common law should be formulated, but competence is lacking. Does this suggest that the two-step analysis collapses into a single question of whether federal law should apply? See Field, *Sources of Law: The Scope of Federal Common Law*, 99 Harv.L.Rev. 881, 950–53 (1986). Consider, though, the situation where federal competence is acknowledged: does the two-step approach usefully require a court to focus on whether there is a genuine need to formulate a federal rule of decision?

grams'' (p. 730). Nor was a federal rule of decision necessary to safeguard the government's fiscal interests, for they could be protected in the course of negotiating each individual loan. Moreover, the Court observed that "businessmen depend on state commercial law to provide the stability essential for reliable evaluation of the risks involved," and that that stability could be undermined by the formulation of a federal rule of decision granting special priority to federal contractual liens. "Creditors who justifiably rely on state law to obtain superior liens would have their expectations thwarted whenever a federal contractual security interest suddenly appeared and took precedence. * * * Thus, the prudent course is to adopt the readymade body of state law as the federal rule of decision until Congress strikes a different accommodation" (pp. 739–40). The Court therefore concluded that the relative priority of the liens was to be determined under nondiscriminatory state rules.

Kimbell Foods provides a textbook lesson in how the opinion in Clearfield might have been written. Like other post-Clearfield decisions concerning the proprietary interests of the United States, Kimbell Foods does not question— indeed it expressly reaffirms—the *competence* of the federal courts to fashion a federal rule of decision to govern such matters. At the same time, Kimbell's conclusion that, as a matter of *discretion*, the particular matter in question does not require formulation of a federal rule of decision is one that the Court has frequently reached in post-Clearfield cases.[6] And several features of the Kimbell opinion are characteristic of the Court's current approach to federal common lawmaking—careful analysis of the alleged need for uniformity, concern that federal rules of decision will generate intrastate disuniformity, and a preference for incorporation of state law absent a demonstrated need for a federal rule of decision.

(6) *Tort Suits Involving the Federal Government.* Choice between state and federal law must also be exercised in tort litigation involving the United States and its officers.

---

6. In United States v. Yazell, 382 U.S. 341 (1966), a decision relied upon in Kimbell Foods, the government sued on a Small Business Administration loan made to a married couple; the question was whether the wife's separate property was exempt from recovery under a Texas law limiting the contractual powers of married women. The Court held (6–3) that state law governed, stressing that (1) the loan was individually negotiated, so that the government was chargeable with knowledge of the Texas law; (2) there was no need for uniformity; (3) the financial consequences to the treasury were small, as the Texas law had been repealed; and (4) solicitude for state interests, particularly in the family-property area, was desirable.

The approach of Kimbell Foods was followed in O'Melveny & Myers v. FDIC, 114 S.Ct. 2048 (1994), which involved an action for malpractice and breach of fiduciary duty brought by the FDIC, as receiver of a federally-insured bank, against a law firm that formerly represented the bank. The Supreme Court unanimously held that state law gov-

erned the question of whether the firm could defend on the ground that the knowledge of bank officials who were acting against the bank's interest is be imputed to the bank, and in turn to the FDIC as receiver of the bank. The Court noted, *inter alia*, the absence of any significant conflict between federal interests and use of a state rule of decision.

With these decisions, compare United States v. 93.970 Acres of Land, 360 U.S. 328 (1959)(Illinois law on "election of remedies" is inapplicable to bar United States, as landlord, from simultaneously seeking to obtain immediate possession by condemning the lessee's interest and, by relying on its claimed right to revoke, to eject the lessee without liability); United States v. Little Lake Misere Land Co., Inc., 412 U.S. 580, 594–97 (1973)(rejecting state law in connection with mineral rights reserved in federal government contracts, partly on the ground that the specific state law was "hostile to the interests of the United States").

(a) The Federal Tort Claims Act, 28 U.S.C. § 1346(b), makes the United States liable for the negligent and wrongful acts and omissions of its employees "under circumstances where the United States, if a private person, would be liable to the claimant in accordance with the law of the place where the act or omission occurred"—subject, however, to important statutory exceptions. See generally Chap. IX, Sec. 1(C), *infra*.[7]

(b) In United States v. Standard Oil Co., 332 U.S. 301 (1947), a Standard Oil truck had injured a soldier, and the United States had lost his services during convalescence and had incurred expenses for his hospitalization. The government sued the oil company for damages, asserting a somewhat novel right of action, by analogy to "the master's rights of recovery for loss of the services of his servant or apprentice; the husband's similar action for interference with the marital relation, including loss of consortium as well as the wife's services; and the parent's right to indemnity for loss of a child's services, including his action for a daughter's seduction" (p. 312).

The court of appeals had ruled that California law governed, and precluded recovery by the United States. The Supreme Court affirmed the judgment against the United States, but on a different theory. Justice Rutledge's opinion for the Court began by declaring (p. 305) "that the creation or negation of such a liability is not a matter to be determined by state law," relying on Clearfield and similar cases. Then, recognizing that " 'in our choice of the applicable federal rule we have occasionally selected state law' ", it rejected any such reference (pp. 309–11, quoting Clearfield). Turning to the content of a federal rule, the Court, seemingly without evaluating the Government's analogies, concluded that the question was one of "fiscal policy" for determination by Congress rather than by a federal court, stating (pp. 313–16):

"We would not deny the Government's basic premise of the law's capacity for growth, or that it must include the creative work of judges. * * * But in the federal scheme our part in that work, and the part of the other federal courts, outside the constitutional area is more modest than that of state courts, particularly in the freedom to create new common-law liabilities, as Erie R. Co. v. Tompkins itself witnesses.

"Moreover, * * * we have not here simply a question of creating a new liability in the nature of a tort. For grounded though the argument is in analogies drawn from that field, the issue comes down in final consequence to a question of federal fiscal policy, coupled with considerations concerning the need for and the appropriateness of means to be used in executing the policy sought to be established. * * *

"Whatever the merits of the policy, its conversion into law is a proper subject for congressional action, not for any creative power of ours. Congress, not this Court or the other federal courts, is * * * the primary and most often the exclusive arbiter of federal fiscal affairs. And these comprehend * * * securing the treasury or the government against financial losses however inflicted, including requiring reimbursement for injuries creating them, as well as filling the treasury itself. * * *

---

7. In Richards v. United States, 369 U.S. 1 (1962), the Court held that the "law of the place where the act or omission occurred" includes not only that state's tort law but also its choice of law rules. See Shapiro, *Choice of Law under the Federal Tort Claims Act: Richards and Renvoi Revisited*, 70 N.C.L.Rev. 641 (1992).

"When Congress has thought it necessary to take steps to prevent interference with federal funds, property or relations, it has taken positive action to that end. We think it would have done so here, if that had been its desire. This it still may do, if or when it so wishes."

Justice Jackson's lone dissent argued (p. 318): "If there is one function which I should think we would feel free to exercise under a Constitution which vests in us judicial power, it would be to apply well-established common law principles to a case whose only novelty is in facts. The courts of England, whose scruples against legislating are at least as sensitive as ours normally are, have not hesitated to say that His Majesty's Treasury may recover outlay to cure a British soldier from injury by a negligent wrongdoer and the wages he was meanwhile paid. Attorney General v. Valle–Jones, [1935] 2 K.B. 209. I think we could hold as much without being suspected of trying to usurp legislative function."

Why didn't Clearfield Trust involve a question of federal fiscal policy just as much as did the Standard Oil case?

Despite all the talk of deference to Congress, didn't the Court in Standard Oil in fact render a decision—that federal law precludes recovery in these circumstances? Absent that decision, the United States might have been free to recover in a suit brought in a different state whose law did authorize recovery in these circumstances. But doesn't Standard Oil displace state law with a federal rule of no liability?

Note that a decision that a given problem is governed by federal law excludes both state courts and state legislatures from contributing to its solution. If the federal courts then woodenly shift the responsibility to Congress, creative development by the judicial process is wholly foreclosed. Is it wise and practicable to rely so completely on the legislative method of lawmaking? Is Congress equipped, with respect to matters of the order of magnitude involved in Standard Oil, to assume sole responsibility for the constructive elaboration and application of legal principles?[8] See generally Hart & Sacks, The Legal Process: Basic Problems in the Making and Application of Law 522–27 (Eskridge & Frickey eds.1994). See also Texas Indus., Inc. v. Radcliff Materials, Inc., p. 845, *infra*.

(7) *The Various Ways in Which State Law Applies*. The general proposition that state law "applies" as the rule of decision for a particular issue can have a variety of different meanings, including these:

(a) The federal government (Congress as well as the federal courts) lacks lawmaking authority.

(b) Congress has lawmaking authority, but in the absence of legislative action, state law governs. (Wasn't that so in Erie itself?)

(c) Federal legislation calls for the application of state law as part of a federal scheme. See, *e.g.*, the Federal Tort Claims Act, Paragraph (6)(a), *supra*.

---

8. For cases exhibiting similar diffidence in fashioning rules of decision, see United States v. Gilman, 347 U.S. 507 (1954)(United States as employer may not seek indemnity from an employee whose negligence resulted in a judgment against the United States under the Federal Tort Claims Act); Francis v. Southern Pac. Co., 333 U.S. 445 (1948)(federal law governs and precludes interstate railroad's liability for ordinary negligence in an action by a railroad employee who was killed while riding on a free pass).

(d) Although federal common law governs a given question, state law furnishes an appropriate and convenient measure of the content of this federal law.   See, *e.g.*, Kimbell Foods, Paragraph (5), *supra*, and Board of County Commissioners v. United States, Paragraph (2), *supra*.

Does the particular way in which state law applies make any difference with regard to (i) the nature or extent of the applicability of state law, (ii) the rules for ascertaining the content of state law,[9] or (iii) the choice of which state's law governs?[10]   See generally von Mehren & Trautman, The Law of Multistate Problems 1049–59 (1965); Mishkin, p. 756, *supra*, at 802–10.

(8) *The Meaning of Federal Statutory Terms.*   Closely related to the choice between state law and judge-made federal law is the question whether a general term used in a federal statute should be given a uniform federal definition or should instead incorporate state law.

(a) Many cases articulate the view that "in the absence of a plain indication to the contrary, * * * Congress when it enacts a statute is not making the application of the federal act dependent on state law."   Jerome v. United States, 318 U.S. 101, 104 (1943)(federal bank robbery statute prohibits entering a bank with intent to commit a "felony"; whether particular conduct is a felony is governed by federal rather than state law standards).

Of course, the application of a federal law definition may require analysis of state law in some respect.   For example, in Dickerson v. New Banner Inst., Inc., 460 U.S. 103 (1983), federal law made it unlawful, *inter alia*, for someone who had been "convicted" of a crime punishable by imprisonment for a term exceeding one year to be a dealer in firearms.   The case raised the question of how that prohibition applied to someone who had pleaded guilty to a state offense punishable by up to five years in prison, but whose conviction was later expunged in accordance with state law.   The Supreme Court ruled that whether the individual had been "convicted" within the meaning of the federal statute was a question of federal, not state, law.   The Court did have to look carefully at state law as it bore on what had happened in the state criminal proceedings, as a predicate for determining whether those proceedings had given rise to a "conviction" within the meaning of federal law.[11]

9.   On this point, consider Commissioner v. Bosch's Estate, 387 U.S. 456 (1967), which refused to accept a state trial court's determination of an issue of state trust law on which federal tax liability depended.   Is there any reason why the rules for "finding" state law developed under Erie, Chap. VI, Sec. 2, p. 687, *supra*, should not apply here— at least putting aside situations where a taxpayer obtained a favorable ruling in a nonadversary state court proceeding in order to minimize federal tax liability?   See generally Wolfman, *Bosch, Its Implications and Aftermath*, 3d Ann.Inst. on Estate Planning ch. 69–2 (Univ. Miami Law Center 1969); Caron, *The Role of State Court Decisions in Federal Tax Litigation: Bosch, Erie, and Beyond*, 71 Or.L.Rev. 781 (1992).

10.   In footnote 3 of Boyle v. United Technologies Corp., 487 U.S. 500 (1988), the next principal case, Justice Scalia expressed a preference for the phrase "displacement of state law" rather than "displacement of federal-law reference to state law"—while reserving judgment on whether the differing phraseologies would ever call for different results.   Accord O'Melveny & Myers v. FDIC, 114 S.Ct. 2048, 2053–54 (1994)(Scalia, J. for a unanimous Court).

11.   Similar problems arise under the federal tax laws, where the Court has looked to state law to ascertain what legal interests were created, but then has determined tax liability by asking how federal law characterizes those state-created interests.   See, *e.g.*, Morgan v. Commissioner, 309 U.S. 78, 80 (1940)(definition of "general power of appointment" under tax statute); Helvering v. Stuart, 317 U.S. 154 (1942)(whether there is

(b) When might a court be justified in interpreting a federal statutory term as embodying a state law definition—even when the statute does not expressly call for such incorporation of state law?

(i) In Reconstruction Fin. Corp. v. Beaver County, 328 U.S. 204 (1946), a case that arose in *state* court, a federal statute barred state or local taxation of the personal property of the RFC (a federal agency) but permitted non-discriminatory taxation of its real property. The county had taxed a subsidiary of the RFC on certain heavy machines: most were not attached to the building, but were held in place by their weight; others were attached by easily removable screws and bolts; and some could be moved within the manufacturing plant.

Challenging the county's taxation of the machines as real property, the RFC relied "on the generally accepted principle that Congress normally intends that its laws shall operate uniformly throughout the nation" (p. 209). But the Court found uniformity unattainable under the statute before it, since that statute permitted taxation of real property at the varying tax rates of different localities. Local taxation was geared to "[c]oncepts of real property [that] are deeply rooted in state traditions * * * and laws" (p. 210), and to require tax authorities to define real property differently for the RFC than for other taxpayers would hamper local tax machinery. Thus, real property should be defined under state law, "so long as it is plain, as it is here, that the state rules do not effect a discrimination against the government, or patently run counter to the terms of the Act" (*id.*).

Wasn't the choice between federal and state law definitions of "real property" made easier by Congress' apparent purpose of maintaining uniformity in the treatment of taxpayers *within* each taxing authority?

(ii) The Court relied on the Beaver County case in De Sylva v. Ballentine, 351 U.S. 570 (1956). The copyright statute then in effect allowed "children" of a deceased author to renew the copyright. In a private suit (to which the United States was not a party), the question was whether illegitimates were included within the definition. The Court held that the question should be answered by reference to state law (pp. 580–82): "The scope of a federal right is, of course, a federal question, but that does not mean that its content is not to be determined by state, rather than federal law. [Citing, *inter alia*, Beaver County.] This is especially true where a statute deals with a familial relationship; there is no federal law of domestic relations, which is primarily a matter of state concern.

"If we look at the other persons who * * * are entitled to renew the copyright after the author's death, it is apparent that this is the general scheme of the statute. To decide who is the widow or widower of a deceased author, or who are his executors or next of kin, requires a reference to the law of the State which created those legal relationships. The word 'children,' although it to some extent describes a purely physical relationship, also describes a legal status not unlike the others. To determine whether a child has been legally adopted, for example, requires a reference to state law. We think it proper, therefore, to draw on the ready-made body of state law to define the word 'children' in § 24. This does not mean that a State would be entitled to use the word 'children' in a way entirely strange to those familiar with its ordinary usage, but at least to the extent that there are permissible variations in the

"power to revest" title to trust corpus in grantor).

ordinary concept of 'children' we deem state law controlling. (The Court added that the relevant part of state law was that defining whether a child would take as an heir.)

(iii) De Sylva was distinguished in Mississippi Band of Choctaw Indians v. Holyfield, 490 U.S. 30 (1989), a case that did not involve a federally-created proprietary interest, but rather a provision of the Indian Child Welfare Act giving tribal courts exclusive jurisdiction over adoption proceedings concerning an Indian child who "is domiciled within the reservation of such tribe". 25 U.S.C. § 1911(a). In deciding whether a state court had jurisdiction over a particular adoption, the Court held that the meaning of "domiciled" under the Act is governed by federal law (p. 43): "Congress sometimes intends that a statutory term be given content by the application of state law. [Citing De Sylva v. Ballentine.] We start, however, with the general assumption that 'in the absence of a plain indication to the contrary, ... Congress when it enacts a statute is not making the application of the federal act dependent on state law.' Jerome v. United States, 318 U.S. 101, 104 (1943). One reason for this rule of construction is that federal statutes are generally intended to have uniform application."

What made it so clear that Congress' intention as to the application of state law differed in the De Sylva and the Choctaw Indian situations?

(c) Do you think that a court's decision whether to fashion a federal rule of decision may be subtly affected by whether it characterizes the problem as one of statutory interpretation (where the presumption is that uniform federal law applies) or as one of federal common lawmaking (where a number of recent cases tend to favor the view that state law should be incorporated)? If so, is there a clear enough distinction between the two categories to justify a difference in approach?

Boyle v. United Technologies Corp.

487 U.S. 500, 108 S.Ct. 2510, 101 L.Ed.2d 442 (1988).
Certiorari to the United States Court of Appeals for the Fourth Circuit.

■ JUSTICE SCALIA delivered the opinion of the Court.

This case requires us to decide when a contractor providing military equipment to the Federal Government can be held liable under state tort law for injury caused by a design defect.

I

On April 27, 1983, David A. Boyle, a United States Marine helicopter copilot, was killed when the CH–53D helicopter in which he was flying crashed * * * during a training exercise. Although Boyle survived the impact of the crash, he was unable to escape from the helicopter and drowned. Boyle's father, petitioner here, brought this diversity action in Federal District Court against the Sikorsky Division of United Technologies Corporation (Sikorsky), which built the helicopter for the United States.

At trial, petitioner presented two theories of liability under Virginia tort law * * *. First, petitioner alleged that Sikorsky had defectively repaired a device called the servo in the helicopter's automatic flight control system, which allegedly malfunctioned and caused the crash. Second, petitioner alleged that Sikorsky had defectively designed the copilot's emergency escape system: the escape hatch opened out instead of in (and was therefore ineffective in a submerged craft because of water pressure), and access to the escape hatch handle was obstructed by other equipment. The jury returned a general verdict [awarding petitioner] $725,000. * * *

The Court of Appeals reversed and remanded with directions that judgment be entered for Sikorsky. It found, as a matter of Virginia law, that Boyle had failed to meet his burden of demonstrating that the repair work performed by Sikorsky, as opposed to work that had been done by the Navy, was responsible for the alleged malfunction of the flight control system. It also found, as a matter of federal law, that Sikorsky could not be held liable for the allegedly defective design of the escape hatch because, on the evidence presented, it satisfied the requirements of the "military contractor defense," which the court had recognized the same day in Tozer v. LTV Corp., 792 F.2d 403 (C.A.4 1986).

* * *. We granted certiorari.

II

Petitioner's broadest contention is that, in the absence of legislation specifically immunizing Government contractors from liability for design defects, there is no basis for judicial recognition of such a defense. We disagree. In most fields of activity, to be sure, this Court has refused to find federal pre-emption of state law in the absence of either a clear statutory prescription or a direct conflict between federal and state law. But we have held that a few areas, involving "uniquely federal interests," Texas Industries, Inc. v. Radcliff Materials, Inc., 451 U.S. 630, 640 (1981), are so committed by the Constitution and laws of the United States to federal control that state law is pre-empted and replaced, where necessary, by federal law of a content prescribed (absent explicit statutory directive) by the courts—so-called "federal common law." See, e.g., United States v. Kimbell Foods, Inc., 440 U.S. 715, 726–729 (1979); Banco Nacional v. Sabbatino, 376 U.S. 398, 426–427 (1964); Howard v. Lyons, 360 U.S. 593, 597 (1959); Clearfield Trust Co. v. United States, 318 U.S. 363, 366–367 (1943); D'Oench, Duhme & Co. v. FDIC, 315 U.S. 447, 457–458 (1942).

The dispute in the present case borders upon two areas that we have found to involve such "uniquely federal interests." We have held that obligations to and rights of the United States under its contracts are governed exclusively by federal law. See, e.g., United States v. Little Lake Misere Land Co., 412 U.S. 580, 592–594 (1973); Clearfield Trust, supra. The present case does not involve an obligation to the United States under its contract, but rather liability to third persons. That liability may be styled one in tort, but it arises out of performance of the contract * * *.

Another area that we have found to be of peculiarly federal concern, warranting the displacement of state law, is the civil liability of federal officials for actions taken in the course of their duty. We have held in many contexts that the scope of that liability is controlled by federal law. See, e.g., Howard v. Lyons, supra, 360 U.S., at 597. The present case involves an independent contractor performing its obligation under a procurement contract, rather than an official performing his duty as a federal employee, but there is obviously implicated the same interest in getting the Government's work done.[1]

We think the reasons for considering these closely related areas to be of "uniquely federal" interest apply as well to the civil liabilities arising out of the performance of federal procurement contracts.   * * *

* * * [It] is plain that the Federal Government's interest in the procurement of equipment is implicated by suits such as the present one—even though the dispute is one between private parties.   It is true that where "litigation is purely between private parties and does not touch the rights and duties of the United States," Bank of America Nat. Trust & Sav. Assn. v. Parnell, 352 U.S. 29, 33 (1956), federal law does not govern.   Thus, for example, in Miree v. DeKalb County, 433 U.S. 25, 30 (1977), which involved the question whether certain private parties could sue as third-party beneficiaries to an agreement between a municipality and the Federal Aviation Administration, we found that state law was not displaced because "the operations of the United States in connection with FAA grants such as these . . . would [not] be burdened" by allowing state law to determine whether third-party beneficiaries could sue, id., at 30, and because "any federal interest in the outcome of the [dispute] before us '[was] far too speculative, far too remote a possibility to justify the application of federal law to transactions essentially of local concern.' " Id., at 32–33, quoting Parnell, supra, 352 U.S. at 33–34.   But the same is not true here.   The imposition of liability on Government contractors will directly affect the terms of Government contracts: either the contractor will decline to manufacture the design specified by the Government, or it will raise its price.   Either way, the interests of the United States will be directly affected.

That the procurement of equipment by the United States is an area of uniquely federal interest does not, however, end the inquiry.   That merely establishes a necessary, not a sufficient, condition for the displacement of state law.[2]   Displacement will occur only where, as we have variously described, a "significant conflict" exists between an identifiable "federal policy or interest and the [operation] of state law," [Wallis v. Pan American Petroleum Corp., 384 U.S. 63, 68 (1966)], or the application of state law would "frustrate specific objectives" of federal legislation, Kimbell Foods, supra, 440 U.S., at 728.   The conflict with federal policy need not be as sharp as that which must exist for ordinary pre-emption when Congress legislates "in a field which the States

1.   The dissent misreads our discussion here to "intimat[e] that the immunity [of federal officials] . . . might extend . . . to non-government employees" such as a government contractor.   But we do not address this issue, as it is not before us.   We cite these cases merely to demonstrate that the liability of independent contractors performing work for the Federal Government, like the liability of federal officials, is an area of uniquely federal interest.

2.   We refer here to the displacement of state law, although it is possible to analyze it as the displacement of federal-law reference to state law for the rule of decision.   Some of our cases appear to regard the area in which a uniquely federal interest exists as being entirely governed by federal law, with federal law deigning to "borro[w]," United States v. Little Lake Misere Land Co., 412 U.S. 580, 594 (1973), or "incorporat[e]" or "adopt" United States v. Kimbell Foods, Inc., 440 U.S. 715, 728, 729, 730 (1979), state law except where a significant conflict with federal policy exists.   We see nothing to be gained by expanding the theoretical scope of the federal pre-emption beyond its practical effect, and so adopt the more modest terminology.   If the distinction between displacement of state law and displacement of federal law's incorporation of state law ever makes a practical difference, it at least does not do so in the present case.

have traditionally occupied." Rice v. Santa Fe Elevator Corp., 331 U.S. [218, 230 (1947)]. Or to put the point differently, the fact that the area in question *is* one of unique federal concern changes what would otherwise be a conflict that cannot produce pre-emption into one that can. But conflict there must be. In some cases, for example where the federal interest requires a uniform rule, the entire body of state law applicable to the area conflicts and is replaced by federal rules. See, *e.g.,* Clearfield Trust, 318 U.S., at 366–367 (rights and obligations of United States with respect to commercial paper must be governed by uniform federal rule). In others, the conflict is more narrow, and only particular elements of state law are superseded. See, *e.g.,* Little Lake Misere Land Co., 412 U.S., at 595 (even assuming state law should generally govern federal land acquisitions, particular state law at issue may not).

In Miree, *supra,* the suit was not seeking to impose upon the person contracting with the Government a duty contrary to the duty imposed by the Government contract. Rather, it was the contractual duty *itself* that the private plaintiff (as third party beneficiary) sought to enforce. Between Miree and the present case, it is easy to conceive of an intermediate situation, in which the duty sought to be imposed on the contractor is not identical to one assumed under the contract, but is also not contrary to any assumed. If, for example, the United States contracts for the purchase and installation of an air conditioning unit, specifying the cooling capacity but not the precise manner of construction, a state law imposing upon the manufacturer of such units a duty of care to include a certain safety feature would not be a duty identical to anything promised the Government, but neither would it be contrary. The contractor could comply with both its contractual obligations and the state-prescribed duty of care. No one suggests that state law would generally be pre-empted in this context.

The present case, however, is at the opposite extreme from Miree. Here the state-imposed duty of care that is the asserted basis of the contractor's liability (specifically, the duty to equip helicopters with the sort of escape-hatch mechanism petitioner claims was necessary) is precisely contrary to the duty imposed by the Government contract (the duty to manufacture and deliver helicopters with the sort of escape-hatch mechanism shown by the specifications). Even in this sort of situation, it would be unreasonable to say that there is always a "significant conflict" between the state law and a federal policy or interest. If, for example, a federal procurement officer orders, by model number, a quantity of stock helicopters that happen to be equipped with escape hatches opening outward, it is impossible to say that the Government has a significant interest in that particular feature. That would be scarcely more reasonable than saying that a private individual who orders such a craft by model number cannot sue for the manufacturer's negligence because he got precisely what he ordered.

* * *

There is * * * a statutory provision that demonstrates the potential for, and suggests the outlines of, "significant conflict" between federal interests and state law in the context of government procurement. In the Federal Tort Claims Act (FTCA), Congress authorized damages to be recovered against the United States for harm caused by the negligent or wrongful conduct of Government employees, to the extent that a private person would be liable under the law of the place where the conduct occurred. 28 U.S.C. § 1346(b). It excepted from this consent to suit, however, "[a]ny claim ... based upon the exercise or performance or the failure to exercise or perform a discretionary function or duty on the part of a federal agency or an employee of the Government, whether or not the discretion involved be abused." 28 U.S.C. § 2680(a).

We think that the selection of the appropriate design for military equipment to be used by our Armed Forces is assuredly a discretionary function within the meaning of this provision. It often involves not merely engineering analysis but judgment as to the balancing of many technical, military, and even social considerations, including specifically the trade-off between greater safety and greater combat effectiveness. And we are further of the view that permitting "second-guessing" of these judgments through state tort suits against contractors would produce the same effect sought to be avoided by the FTCA exemption. The financial burden of judgments against the contractors would ultimately be passed through, substantially if not totally, to the United States itself, since defense contractors will predictably raise their prices to cover, or to insure against, contingent liability for the Government-ordered designs. * * * In sum, we are of the view that state law which holds Government contractors liable for design defects in military equipment does in some circumstances present a "significant conflict" with federal policy and must be displaced.

We agree with the scope of displacement adopted by the Fourth Circuit here * * *. Liability for design defects in military equipment cannot be imposed, pursuant to state law, when (1) the United States approved reasonably precise specifications; (2) the equipment conformed to those specifications; and (3) the supplier warned the United States about the dangers in the use of the equipment that were known to the supplier but not to the United States. The first two of these conditions assure that the suit is within the area where the policy of the "discretionary function" would be frustrated—i.e., they assure that the design feature in question was considered by a Government officer, and not merely by the contractor itself. The third condition is necessary because, in its absence, the displacement of state tort law would create some incentive for the manufacturer to withhold knowledge of risks, since conveying that knowledge might disrupt the contract but withholding it would produce no liability. We adopt this provision lest our effort to protect discretionary functions perversely impede them by cutting off information highly relevant to the discretionary decision.

We have considered the alternative formulation of the Government contractor defense, urged upon us by petitioner * * *. That would preclude suit only if (1) the contractor did not participate, or participated only minimally, in the design of the defective equipment; or (2) the contractor timely warned the Government of the risks of the design and notified it of alternative designs reasonably known by it, and the Government, although forewarned, clearly authorized the contractor to proceed with the dangerous design. While this formulation may represent a perfectly reasonable tort rule, it is not a rule designed to protect the federal interest embodied in the "discretionary function" exemption. The design ultimately selected may well reflect a significant policy judgment by Government officials whether or not the contractor rather than those officials developed the design. In addition, it does not seem to us sound policy to penalize, and thus deter, active contractor participation in the design process, placing the contractor at risk unless it identifies all design defects.

III

[Finding some ambiguity in the court of appeals' opinion, the Court remanded to permit that court to determine whether there was sufficient evidence to submit the case to the jury under a proper formulation of the contractor's defense.]

■ JUSTICE BRENNAN, with whom JUSTICE MARSHALL and JUSTICE BLACKMUN join, dissenting.

* * * We may assume, for purposes of this case, that Lt. Boyle was trapped under water and drowned because respondent * * * negligently designed the helicopter's escape hatch. * * * Had respondent designed such a death trap for a commercial firm, Lt. Boyle's family could sue under Virginia tort law * * *. But respondent designed the helicopter for the Federal Government, and that, the Court tells us today, makes all the difference: Respondent is immune from liability so long as it obtained approval of "reasonably precise specifications"—perhaps no more than a rubberstamp from a federal procurement officer who might or might not have noticed or cared about the defects, or even had the expertise to discover them.

If respondent's immunity "bore the legitimacy of having been prescribed by the people's elected representatives," we would be duty bound to implement their will, whether or not we approved. United States v. Johnson, 481 U.S. 681, 703 (1987)(dissenting opinion of Scalia, J.). Congress, however, has remained silent—and conspicuously so, having resisted a sustained campaign by Government contractors to legislate for them some defense.[1] The Court—unelected and unaccountable to the people—has unabashedly stepped into the breach to legislate a rule denying Lt. Boyle's family the compensation that state law assures them. This time the injustice is of this Court's own making.

Worse yet, the injustice will extend far beyond the facts of this case, for the Court's newly discovered Government contractor defense is breathtakingly sweeping. It applies not only to military equipment * * *, but (so far as I can tell) to any made-to-order gadget that the Federal Government might purchase after previewing plans—from NASA's Challenger space shuttle to the Postal Service's old mail cars. The contractor may invoke the defense in suits brought not only by military personnel like Lt. Boyle, or Government employees, but by anyone injured by a Government contractor's negligent design, including, for example, the children who might have died had respondent's helicopter crashed on the beach. It applies even if the Government has not intentionally sacrificed safety for other interests like speed or efficiency, and, indeed, even if the equipment is not of a type that is typically considered dangerous; thus, the contractor who designs a Government building can invoke the defense when the elevator cable snaps or the walls collapse. And the defense is invocable regardless of how blatant or easily remedied the defect, so long as the contractor missed it and the specifications approved by the Government, however unreasonably dangerous, were "reasonably precise."

In my view, this Court lacks both authority and expertise to fashion such a rule, whether to protect the Treasury of the United States or the coffers of industry. Because I would leave that exercise of legislative power to Congress, where our Constitution places it, I would reverse the Court of Appeals and reinstate petitioner's jury award.

1. [Citing numerous bills introduced in   Congress between 1979 and 1987.]

I

* * * [Erie R. Co. v. Tompkins, 304 U.S. 64 (1938), proclaimed]: "Except in matters governed by the Federal Constitution or by Acts of Congress, the law to be applied in any case is the law of the State." 304 U.S., at 78. The Court explained that the expansive power that federal courts had theretofore exercised was an unconstitutional "invasion of the authority of the State and, to that extent, a denial of its independence." *Id.*, at 79 (citation omitted). Thus, Erie was deeply rooted in notions of federalism, and is most seriously implicated when, as here, federal judges displace the state law that would ordinarily govern with their own rules of federal common law.[2]

* * *

Accordingly, we have emphasized that * * * "absent some congressional authorization to formulate substantive rules of decision, federal common law exists only in such narrow areas as those concerned with the rights and obligations of the United States, interstate and international disputes implicating conflicting rights of States or our relations with foreign nations, and admiralty cases." Texas Industries, Inc. v. Radcliff Materials, Inc., 451 U.S. 630, 641 (1981)(footnotes omitted). * * * State laws "should be overridden by the federal courts only where clear and substantial interests of the National Government, which cannot be served consistently with respect for such state interests, will suffer major damage if the state law is applied." United States v. Yazell, 382 U.S. 341, 352 (1966).

II

Congress has not decided to supersede state law here (if anything, it has decided not to, see n. 1, *supra*) and the Court does not pretend that its newly manufactured "Government contractor defense" fits within any of the handful of "narrow areas," Texas Industries, *supra*, 451 U.S., at 641, of "uniquely federal interests" in which we have heretofore done so, 451 U.S., at 640. Rather, the Court creates a new category of "uniquely federal interests" out of a synthesis of two whose origins predate Erie itself: the interest in administering the "obligations to and rights of the United States under its contracts," and the interest in regulating the "civil liability of federal officials for actions taken in the course of their duty." This case is, however, simply a suit between two private parties. We have steadfastly declined to impose federal contract law on relationships that are collateral to a federal contract, or to extend the federal employee's immunity beyond federal employees. * * *

A

The proposition that federal common law continues to govern the "obligations to and rights of the United States under its contracts" is nearly as old as Erie itself. * * * Any such transaction necessarily "radiate[s] interests in transactions between private parties." Bank of America Nat. Trust & Sav. Assn. v. Parnell, 352 U.S. 29, 33 (1956). But it is by now established that our power to

2. Not all exercises of our power to fashion federal common law displace state law in the same way. For example, our recognition of federal causes of action based upon either the Constitution, see, *e.g.*, Bivens v. Six Unknown Fed. Narcotics Agents, 403 U.S. 388 (1971), or a federal statute, see Cort v. Ash, 422 U.S. 66 (1975), supplements whatever rights state law might provide, and therefore does not implicate federalism concerns in the same way as does pre-emption of a state-law rule of decision or cause of action. Throughout this opinion I use the word "displace" in the latter sense.

create federal common law controlling the *Federal Government's* contractual rights and obligations does not translate into a power to prescribe rules that cover all transactions or contractual relationships collateral to Government contracts.

In Miree v. DeKalb County, *supra,* for example, the county was contractually obligated under a grant agreement with the Federal Aviation Administration (FAA) to "restrict the use of land adjacent to . . . the Airport to activities and purposes compatible with normal airport operations including landing and takeoff of aircraft." At issue was whether the county breached its contractual obligation by operating a garbage dump adjacent to the airport, which allegedly attracted the swarm of birds that caused a plane crash. Federal common law would undoubtedly have controlled in any suit by the Federal Government to enforce the provision against the county or to collect damages for its violation. The diversity suit, however, was brought not by the Government, but by assorted private parties injured in some way by the accident. We observed that * * * "the United States has a substantial interest in regulating aircraft travel and promoting air travel safety." Nevertheless, we held that state law should govern the claim because "only the rights of private litigants are at issue here," and the claim against the county "will have *no direct effect upon the United States or its Treasury*" (emphasis added).

Miree relied heavily on Parnell, *supra,* and Wallis, 384 U.S. 63 * * *. In the former case, Parnell cashed certain government bonds that had been stolen from their owner, a bank. It is beyond dispute that federal law would have governed the United States' duty to pay the value bonds [sic] upon presentation; we held as much in Clearfield Trust, *supra.* Cf. Parnell, *supra,* 352 U.S., at 34. But the central issue in Parnell, a diversity suit, was whether the victim of the theft could recover the money paid to Parnell. That issue, we held, was governed by state law, because the "litigation [was] purely between private parties and [did] *not touch the rights and duties of the United States.*" 352 U.S., at 33 (emphasis added).

The same was true in Wallis, which also involved a Government contract. * * *

Here, as in Miree, Parnell, and Wallis, a Government contract governed by federal common law looms in the background. But here, too, the United States is not a party to the suit and the suit neither "touch[es] the rights and duties of the United States," Parnell, *supra,* 352 U.S., at 33, nor has a "direct effect upon the United States or its Treasury," Miree, *supra,* 433 U.S., at 29. The relationship at issue is at best collateral to the Government contract. * * *

That the Government might have to pay higher prices for what it orders if delivery in accordance with the contract exposes the seller to potential liability does not distinguish this case. Each of the cases just discussed declined to extend the reach of federal common law despite the assertion of comparable interests that would have affected the terms of the Government contract—whether its price or its substance—just as "directly" (or indirectly). Third-party beneficiaries can sue under a county's contract with the FAA, for example, even though—as the Court's focus on the absence of "*direct* effect on the United States or its Treasury," 433 U.S., at 29 (emphasis added), suggests—counties will likely pass on the costs to the Government in future contract negotiations. Similarly, we held that state law may govern the circumstances under which stolen federal bonds can be recovered, notwithstanding Parnell's argument that "the value of bonds to the first purchaser and hence their salability by the Government would be materially affected." Brief for Respondent Parnell in Bank of America Nat'l Trust & Sav. Assn. v. Parnell, O.T. 1956, No. 21, pp. 10–11. As in each of the cases declining to extend the traditional reach of federal law of contracts beyond the rights and duties of the *Federal Government,* "any federal interest in the outcome of the question before us 'is far too speculative, far too remote a possibility to justify the application of federal law to transactions essentially of local concern.'" Miree, 433 U.S., at 32–33.

B

Our "uniquely federal interest" in the tort liability of affiliates of the Federal Government is equally narrow. * * * Never before have we so much as intimated that [official] immunity (or the "uniquely federal interest" that justifies it) might extend * * * to cover also nongovernment employees * * *.

The historical narrowness of the federal interest and the immunity is hardly accidental. A federal officer exercises statutory authority, which not only provides the necessary basis for the immunity in positive law, but also permits us confidently to presume that interference with the exercise of discretion undermines congressional will. In contrast, a Government contractor acts independently of any congressional enactment. Thus, immunity for a contractor lacks both the positive law basis and the presumption that it furthers congressional will.

* * * The extension of immunity to Government contractors skews the balance we have historically struck. On the one hand, whatever marginal effect contractor immunity might have on the "effective administration of policies of government," its "harm to individual citizens" is more severe than in the Government-employee context. Our observation that "there are ... other sanctions than civil tort suits available to deter the executive official who may be prone to exercise his functions in an unworthy and irresponsible manner," [Barr v. Matteo, 360 U.S. 564, 576 (1959)], offers little deterrence to the Government contractor. On the other hand, a grant of immunity to Government contractors could not advance "the fearless, vigorous, and effective administration of policies of government" nearly as much as does the current immunity for Government employees. *Id.,* at 571. In the first place, the threat of a tort suit is less likely to influence the conduct of an industrial giant than that of a lone civil servant, particularly since the work of a civil servant is significantly less profitable, and significantly more likely to be the subject of a vindictive lawsuit. In fact, were we to take seriously the Court's assertion that contractors pass their costs—including presumably litigation costs—through, "substantially if not totally, to the United States," the threat of a tort suit should have only marginal impact on the conduct of Government contractors. More importantly, inhibition of the Government official who actually sets Government policy presents a greater threat to the "administration of policies of government," than does inhibition of a private contractor, whose role is devoted largely to assessing the technological feasibility and cost of satisfying the Government's predetermined needs. Similarly, unlike tort suits against Government officials, tort suits against Government contractors would rarely "consume time and energies" that "would otherwise be devoted to governmental service." 360 U.S., at 571.

In short, because the essential justifications for official immunity do not support an extension to the Government contractor, it is no surprise that we have never extended it that far.

C

* * *

III

* * * [T]he Court invokes the discretionary function exception of the Federal Tort Claims Act (FTCA), 28 U.S.C. § 2680(a). The Court does not suggest that the exception has any direct bearing here, for petitioner has sued a private manufacturer (not the Federal Government) under Virginia law (not the FTCA). * * *

* * * [T]he Court * * * [reasons] that federal common law must immunize Government contractors from state tort law to prevent erosion of the discretionary function exception's *policy* of foreclosing judicial "second-guessing" of discretionary governmental decisions. The erosion the Court fears apparently is rooted not in a concern that suits against Government contractors will prevent them from designing, or the Government from commissioning the design of, precisely the product the Government wants, but in the concern that such suits might preclude the Government from purchasing the desired product at the price it wants: "The financial burden of judgments against the contractors," the Court fears, "would ultimately be passed through, substantially if not totally, to the United States itself."

Even granting the Court's factual premise, which is by no means self-evident, the Court cites no authority for the proposition that burdens imposed on Government contractors, but passed on to the Government, burden the Government in a way that justifies extension of its immunity. However substantial such indirect burdens may be, we have held in other contexts that they are legally irrelevant.

* * *

* * * [Moreover,] the Government's immunity for discretionary functions is not even "a product of" the FTCA. Before Congress enacted the FTCA (when sovereign immunity barred any tort suit against the Federal Government) we perceived no need for a rule of federal common law to reinforce the Government's immunity by shielding also parties who might contractually pass costs on to it. Nor did we (or any other court of which I am aware) identify a special category of "discretionary" functions for which sovereign immunity was so crucial that a government contractor who exercised discretion should share the Government's immunity from state tort law.

* * * There is no more reason for federal common law to shield contractors now that the Government is liable for some torts than there was when the Government was liable for none. * * *

* * *

IV

At bottom, the Court's analysis is premised on the proposition that any tort liability indirectly absorbed by the Government so burdens governmental functions as to compel us to act when Congress has not. That proposition is by no means uncontroversial. The tort system is premised on the assumption that the imposition of liability encourages actors to prevent any injury whose expected cost exceeds the cost of prevention. If the system is working as it should, Government contractors will design equipment to avoid certain injuries (like the deaths of soldiers or Government employees), which would be certain to burden the Government. The Court therefore has no basis for its assumption that tort liability will result in a net burden on the Government (let alone a clearly excessive net burden) rather than a net gain.

Perhaps tort liability is an inefficient means of ensuring the quality of design efforts, but "[w]hatever the merits of the policy" the Court wishes to implement, "its conversion into law is a proper subject for congressional action, not for any creative power of ours." Standard Oil, 332 U.S., at 314–315. It is, after all, "Congress, not this Court or the other federal courts, [that] is the custodian of the national purse. By the same token [Congress] is the primary and most often the exclusive arbiter of federal fiscal affairs. And these comprehend, as we have said, securing the treasury or the Government against financial losses *however inflicted . . . .*" *Ibid.* (emphasis added). * * *

Were I a legislator, I would probably vote against any law absolving multibillion dollar private enterprises from answering for their tragic mistakes, at least if that law were justified by no more than the unsupported speculation that their liability might ultimately burden the United States Treasury. Some of my colleagues here would evidently vote otherwise (as they have here), but that should not matter here. We are judges not legislators, and the vote is not ours to cast.

I respectfully dissent.

■ JUSTICE STEVENS, dissenting.

When judges are asked to embark on a lawmaking venture, I believe they should carefully consider whether they, or a legislative body, are better equipped to perform the task at hand. There are instances of so-called interstitial lawmaking that inevitably become part of the judicial process. But when we are asked to create an entirely new doctrine—to answer "questions of policy on which Congress has not spoken," United States v. Gilman, 347 U.S. 507, 511 (1954)—we have a special duty to identify the proper decisionmaker before trying to make the proper decision.

When the novel question of policy involves a balancing of the conflicting interests in the efficient operation of a massive governmental program and the protection of the rights of the individual—whether in the social welfare context, the civil service context, or the military procurement context—I feel very deeply that we should defer to the expertise of the Congress. * * *

I respectfully dissent.

———

NOTE ON CHOICE OF LAW IN PRIVATE LITIGATION INVOLVING INTERESTS CREATED BY FEDERAL LAW

(1) *The Presumption that State Law Governs.* Many cases hold that in private litigation involving land, federal law does not generally govern merely because the chain of title includes a patent or grant from the United States. See Chap.

VIII, Sec. 3, p. 927, *infra*.[1] Similarly, the fact that patent and copyright interests are created by federal law does not automatically mean that contractual arrangements concerning these interests are governed by federal law.

In line with this tradition is Wallis v. Pan American Petroleum Corp., 384 U.S. 63 (1966), distinguished in Boyle. Wallis raised the question "whether in general federal or state law should govern the dealings of private parties in an oil and gas lease validly issued [by the United States] under the Mineral Leasing Act of 1920" (p. 67). The specific issues were the validity of an oral contract and the interpretation of a written contract allegedly assigning a share in the lease. The Court held (pp. 69–70) that these questions were governed by state law—under which, the district court had ruled, the oral contract was not valid, and the written contract was interpreted as not having assigned the lease: "In deciding whether rules of federal common law should be fashioned, normally the guiding principle is that a significant conflict between some federal policy or interest and the use of state law * * * must first be specifically shown. * * * We find nothing in the Mineral Leasing Act of 1920 expressing policies inconsistent with state law in the area that concerns us here." Although the statutory provision that leases shall be assignable might require a federal rule of decision if the state "interpose[d] unreasonable conditions on assignability", Louisiana provided a quite feasible method (written instruments) for transferring leases.

(2) *Miree v. DeKalb County.* The majority and dissent in Boyle disagree about whether the Court's decision is consistent with Miree v. DeKalb County, 433 U.S. 25 (1977). Who has the better of the argument?

(3) *Boyle's Analogies.* The doctrine that federal officials are immune from damage liability for common law torts is discussed in detail in Chap. IX, Sec. 3, pp. 1165–66, *infra*. When Boyle was decided, federal common law conferred on federal officials acting within the scope of their employment an absolute immunity from damages liability under state tort law, so long as the conduct was discretionary in nature. (Congress has since codified that immunity and extended it to ministerial conduct.)

Boyle also relies on the government's exemption in the Federal Tort Claims Act (FTCA) from tort liability for so-called discretionary functions. See generally Chap. IX, Sec. 1(C), pp. 1030–36, *infra*. Would it have been less appropriate for the Court to have fashioned the immunity that it did in Boyle in a similar case filed *before* enactment in 1946 of the FTCA and its discretionary functions exception? Even under a very broad conception of statutory interpretation, can the result in Boyle be deemed a construction of the FTCA?

(4) *The Scope of the Immunity.* Are the United States' interests necessarily threatened by a private contractor's tort liability whenever there was a design defect in reasonably precise contractual specifications? Should the Court have required clearer proof that the design of the escape hatch in fact implicated "judgment as to the balancing of many technical, military, and even social considerations"? Compare Trevino v. General Dynamics Corp., 865 F.2d 1474 (5th Cir.1989), where the court ruled that the fact that government employees

---

1. But see Hughes v. Washington, 389 U.S. 290 (1967), holding that federal rather than state law governs the ownership of "rights in accretion" to ocean-front lands conveyed by the United States to a private owner prior to statehood. The case makes the important point that the scope of the original grant from the United States continues to be governed by federal law even in private litigation.

had signed each page of the contractor's working drawings for a submarine diving chamber did not necessarily constitute "approval" within the meaning of Boyle. A rubber stamp, the court said, is not a discretionary function. And the court ruled that the Government's retention of a right of final approval, after delegating discretion to the contractor, does not by itself suffice to establish the government contractor defense.

Consider, also, the holding in Boyle that in order to fall within the immunity, a contractor must have warned the United States about dangers known to it but not to the Government. Why shouldn't contractors be liable if they failed to warn about dangers of which they *should* have known?[2]

(5) *The WDAY Case.* Neither opinion in Boyle discussed Farmers Educ. & Co-op. Union v. WDAY, Inc., 360 U.S. 525 (1959). The case involved a federal law requiring radio and television stations that permitted broadcasts by a political candidate to give equal time to competing candidates. The regulation forbade a station from censoring such "equal time" broadcasts. WDAY was sued for defamation for having broadcast a reply by one Townley to earlier broadcasts by rival candidates. The Court held that the "no censorship" provision implied that the station was immune from defamation liability arising from equal time broadcasts. A contrary holding would "sanction the unconscionable result of permitting civil and perhaps criminal liability to be imposed for the very conduct the statute demands of the licensee"—liability that might lead broadcasters to refuse to broadcast any candidates' speeches in the first instance, thereby "hamper[ing] the congressional plan to develop broadcasting as a political outlet" (pp. 531, 534–35).[3]

Was the WDAY case—involving immunity from tort liability arising from the defendant's adherence to federal rules—closely on point in Boyle? Indeed, was the case for federal common law *a fortiori* in Boyle, since WDAY involved neither a federally-created proprietary interest nor the risk that, absent immunity, costs would be shifted to the United States? Or is WDAY distinguishable because conferral of the immunity still left a different private party (Townley) whom the plaintiff could sue? Because the relevant federal statute denied the station *any* control over the allegedly offending broadcast, whereas United Technologies might have had some capacity to influence the helicopter's design?

In both Boyle and WDAY, the Court might have framed the question as whether state tort law was preempted. Is that the same question as whether a federal rule of decision should be formulated? Note Justice Scalia's statement in Boyle that "the fact that the area in question *is* one of unique federal concern changes what would otherwise be a conflict that cannot produce preemption into one that can." Why should that be?

(6) *Claims of Family Members to Federally–Provided Financial Interests.* The Court has had difficulty choosing between state and federal law in matters

2. For critical analyses of Boyle, see Cass & Gillette, *The Government Contractor Defense: Contractual Allocation of Public Risk,* 77 Va.L.Rev. 257 (1991); Green & Matasar, *The Supreme Court and the Products Liability Crisis: Lessons from Boyle's Government Contractor Defense,* 63 S.Cal.L.Rev. 637 (1990).

3. Justice Frankfurter's lone dissent argued that the Court should not "stifle" state action unless it "would truly entail contradictory duties or make actual, not argumentative, inroads on what Congress has commanded or forbidden" (p. 542). In his view, "there exists here not an explicit conflict but, at the very most, an interference with policy" (p. 546).

involving claims of family members to pensions, retirement pay, insurance proceeds, or bonds that are provided by federal law.

(a) In Wissner v. Wissner, 338 U.S. 655 (1950), Major Wissner had bought a National Service Life Insurance Policy and designated his mother as beneficiary. Premiums were paid out of Wissner's army pay. Under California law, half of the policy proceeds were payable to the Major's widow as community property. The Court held, however, that the governing federal statute, which gave the insured "the right to designate the beneficiary * * * and * * * at all times * * * to change the beneficiary", prevented application of the state's community property law (pp. 658–59). The statute was meant to afford "a uniform and comprehensive system of life insurance for members and veterans of the armed forces of the United States", and the statutory plan displayed "[a] liberal policy toward the serviceman and his named beneficiary * * *. Congress has spoken with force and clarity in directing that the proceeds belong to the named beneficiary and no other" (p. 658). Justice Minton, joined by Justices Frankfurter and Jackson, dissented: "I am not persuaded that * * * the choice of beneficiary * * * provision should carry the implication of wiping out family property rights, which traditionally have been defined by state law. * * * I cannot believe that Congress intended to say to a serviceman, 'You may take your wife's property and purchase a policy of insurance payable to your mother, and we will see that your defrauded wife gets none of the money' "(pp. 663–64).

(b) Two later decisions involved claims to federal bonds. Free v. Bland, 369 U.S. 663 (1962), held that federal law governed survivorship rights to federal bonds bought with community property, on the ground that the state probate law conflicted with the federal interest in making the bonds attractive to investors.[4] State law fared better in Yiatchos v. Yiatchos, 376 U.S. 306 (1964), where the Court held that (i) although federal law governs whether a person who purchased federal bonds and designated a beneficiary had "defrauded" his wife of interests protected by state property law, (ii) "in applying the federal standard we shall be guided by state law insofar as the property interests of the widow created by state law are concerned" (p. 309).

(c) Wissner was followed and Yiatchos distinguished in Ridgway v. Ridgway, 454 U.S. 46 (1981). A state court divorce decree ordered Sergeant Ridgway to keep in force, for the benefit of his children, a life insurance policy issued pursuant to the Serviceman's Group Life Insurance Act (SGLIA). Ridgway subsequently remarried and designated his second wife as the policy's beneficiary. After his death, the state supreme court held that the second wife should receive the policy proceeds as constructive trustee for the benefit of Ridgway's children by his first marriage. The U.S. Supreme Court reversed, 7–2, concluding that the constructive trust conflicted with the provisions of the SGLIA and implementing regulations giving the policyholder the right to change the beneficiary at any time, and also conflicted with the provision exempting policy proceeds "from the claims of creditors" and from any "attachment, levy, or seizure by or under any legal or equitable process whatever" (p. 61). Yiatchos was not controlling because the fraud alleged in that case was committed by the husband "acting in his capacity as manager of the general

---

4. Compare the rejection, in Bank of America Nat. Trust & Savings Ass'n v. Parnell, 352 U.S. 29 (1956), p. 764, note 3, *supra*, of the argument that in order to make federal bonds marketable, state law (as to an issue other than survivorship) had to be displaced by a federal rule of decision.

community property'', whereas Sergeant Ridgway misdirected property over which he had exclusive control (p. 59 n. 8).[5]

Didn't the Ridgway decision neglect the essentially interstitial character of federal law by too readily discerning a federal interest in conflict with an agreed upon division of property under state law? If such insurance policies cannot serve as the subject of binding family settlements, isn't their value to servicemen reduced? If so, isn't that a result Congress would want to avoid?[6]

Textile Workers Union v. Lincoln Mills

353 U.S. 448, 77 S.Ct. 912, 1 L.Ed.2d 972 (1957).
Certiorari to the United States Court of Appeals for the Fifth Circuit.

■ MR. JUSTICE DOUGLAS delivered the opinion of the Court.

Petitioner-union entered into a collective bargaining agreement in 1953 with respondent-employer, the agreement to run one year and from year to year thereafter, unless terminated on specified notices. The agreement provided that there would be no strikes or work stoppages and that grievances would be handled pursuant to a specified procedure. The last step in the grievance procedure—a step that could be taken by either party—was arbitration.

This controversy involves several grievances that concern work loads and work assignments. The grievances were processed through the various steps in the grievance procedure and were finally denied by the employer. The union requested arbitration, and the employer refused. Thereupon the union brought this suit in the District Court to compel arbitration.

The District Court concluded that it had jurisdiction and ordered the employer to comply with the grievance arbitration provisions of the collective bargaining agreement. The Court of Appeals reversed by a divided vote. It held that, although the District Court had jurisdiction to entertain the suit, the court had no authority founded either in federal or state law to grant the relief. The case is here on a petition for a writ of certiorari * * *.

The starting point of our inquiry is § 301 of the Labor Management Relations Act of 1947, 29 U.S.C. § 185, which provides:

5. In addition to the cases discussed in text, see Hisquierdo v. Hisquierdo, 439 U.S. 572 (1979)(federal law prohibits a state from treating as community property a divorcing husband's expectancy interest in pension benefits under the Railroad Retirement Act); McCarty v. McCarty, 453 U.S. 210 (1981)(federal law precludes a state court from dividing military retirement pay pursuant to state community property laws), *substantially overridden by* Uniformed Services Former Spouses' Protection Act, Pub.L.No. 97–252, §§ 1001–1006, 96 Stat. 718, 730 (1982)(permitting division of retirement or retainer pay in accordance with state law).

6. In Rose v. Rose, 481 U.S. 619 (1987), the Court upheld a state court's order requiring a veteran to pay child support out of service-connected disability benefits. The relevant federal statute contained language similar to that in the SGLIA, exempting disability benefits from the claims of creditors, but Ridgway was distinguished on the ground that in the present case the disability benefits were intended to support not only veterans but also their families. In a concurring opinion, Justice O'Connor (joined by Justice Stevens) said (p. 636): "[W]hile *stare decisis* concerns may counsel against overruling Ridgway's interpretation of the [SGLIA], I see no reason whatever to extend Ridgway's equation of business debts with family-support obligations absent the clearest congressional direction to do so." Only Justice White dissented.

"(a) Suits for violation of contracts between an employer and a labor organization representing employees in an industry affecting commerce as defined in this chapter, or between any such labor organizations, may be brought in any district court of the United States having jurisdiction of the parties, without respect to the amount in controversy or without regard to the citizenship of the parties.

"(b) Any labor organization which represents employees in an industry affecting commerce as defined in this chapter and any employer whose activities affect commerce as defined in this chapter shall be bound by the acts of its agents. Any such labor organization may sue or be sued as an entity and in behalf of the employees whom it represents in the courts of the United States. Any money judgment against a labor organization in a district court of the United States shall be enforceable only against the organization as an entity and against its assets, and shall not be enforceable against any individual member or his assets."

There has been considerable litigation involving § 301 and courts have construed it differently. There is one view that § 301(a) merely gives federal district courts jurisdiction in controversies that involve labor organizations in industries affecting commerce, without regard to diversity of citizenship or the amount in controversy. Under that view § 301(a) would not be the source of substantive law; it would neither supply federal law to resolve these controversies nor turn the federal judges to state law for answers to the questions. Other courts—the overwhelming number of them—hold that § 301(a) is more than jurisdictional—that it authorizes federal courts to fashion a body of federal law for the enforcement of these collective bargaining agreements and includes within that federal law specific performance of promises to arbitrate grievances under collective bargaining agreements. * * * That is our construction of § 301(a), which means that the agreement to arbitrate grievance disputes, contained in this collective bargaining agreement, should be specifically enforced.

From the face of the Act it is apparent that § 301(a) and § 301(b) supplement one another. Section 301(b) makes it possible for a labor organization, representing employees in an industry affecting commerce, to sue and be sued as an entity in the federal courts. Section 301(b) in other words provides the procedural remedy lacking at common law. Section 301(a) certainly does something more than that. Plainly, it supplies the basis upon which the federal district courts may take jurisdiction and apply the procedural rule of § 301(b). The question is whether § 301(a) is more than jurisdictional.

The legislative history of § 301 is somewhat cloudy and confusing. But there are a few shafts of light that illuminate our problem.

The bills, as they passed the House and the Senate, contained provisions which would have made the failure to abide by an agreement to arbitrate an unfair labor practice. S.Rep. No. 105, 80th Cong., 1st Sess., pp. 20–21, 23; H.R.Rep. No. 245, 80th Cong., 1st Sess., p. 21. This feature of the law was dropped in Conference. As the Conference Report stated, "Once parties have made a collective bargaining contract, the enforcement of that contract should be left to the usual processes of the law and not to the National Labor Relations Board." H.R.Conf.Rep. No. 510, 80th Cong., 1st Sess., p. 42.

Both the Senate and the House took pains to provide for "the usual processes of the law" by provisions which were the substantial equivalent of

§ 301(a) in its present form. Both the Senate Report and the House Report indicate a primary concern that unions as well as employees should be bound to collective bargaining contracts. But there was also a broader concern—a concern with a procedure for making such agreements enforceable in the courts by either party. At one point the Senate Report, *supra*, p. 15, states, "We feel that the aggrieved party should also have a right of action in the Federal courts. Such a policy is completely in accord with the purpose of the Wagner Act which the Supreme Court declared was 'to compel employers to bargain collectively with their employees to the end that an employment contract, binding on both parties, should be made * * *.' "

Congress was also interested in promoting collective bargaining that ended with agreements not to strike. The Senate Report, *supra*, p. 16 states:

"If unions can break agreements with relative impunity, then such agreements do not tend to stabilize industrial relations. The execution of an agreement does not by itself promote industrial peace. The chief advantage which an employer can reasonably expect from a collective labor agreement is assurance of uninterrupted operation during the term of the agreement. Without some effective method of assuring freedom from economic warfare for the term of the agreement, there is little reason why an employer would desire to sign such a contract.

"Consequently, to encourage the making of agreements and to promote industrial peace through faithful performance by the parties, collective agreements affecting interstate commerce should be enforceable in the Federal courts. Our amendment would provide for suits by unions as legal entities and against unions as legal entities in the Federal courts in disputes affecting commerce."

Thus collective bargaining contracts were made "equally binding and enforceable on both parties." *Id.*, p. 15. As stated in the House Report, *supra*, p. 6, the new provision "makes labor organizations equally responsible with employers for contract violations and provides for suit by either against the other in the United States district courts." To repeat, the Senate Report, *supra*, p. 17, summed up the philosophy of § 301 as follows: "Statutory recognition of the collective agreement as a valid, binding, and enforceable contract is a logical and necessary step. It will promote a higher degree of responsibility upon the parties to such agreements, and will thereby promote industrial peace."

Plainly the agreement to arbitrate grievance disputes is the *quid pro quo* for an agreement not to strike. Viewed in this light, the legislation does more than confer jurisdiction in the federal courts over labor organizations. It expresses a federal policy that federal courts should enforce these agreements on behalf of or against labor organizations and that industrial peace can be best obtained only in that way.

To be sure, there is a great medley of ideas reflected in the hearings, reports, and debates on this Act. Yet, to repeat, the entire tenor of the history indicates that the agreement to arbitrate grievance disputes was considered as *quid pro quo* of a no-strike agreement. And when in the House the debate narrowed to the question whether § 301 was more than jurisdictional, it became abundantly clear that the purpose of the section was to provide the necessary legal remedies. * * *

It seems, therefore, clear to us that Congress adopted a policy which placed sanctions behind agreements to arbitrate grievance disputes, by implication rejecting the common-law rule * * * against enforcement of executory agreements to arbitrate. We would undercut the Act and defeat its policy if we read § 301 narrowly as only conferring jurisdiction over labor organizations.

The question then is, what is the substantive law to be applied in suits under § 301(a)? We conclude that the substantive law to apply in suits under § 301(a) is federal law, which the courts must fashion from the policy of our national labor laws. The Labor Management Relations Act expressly furnishes some substantive law. It points out what the parties may or may not do in certain situations. Other problems will lie in the penumbra of express statutory mandates. Some will lack express statutory sanction but will be solved by looking at the policy of the legislation and fashioning a remedy that will effectuate that policy. The range of judicial inventiveness will be determined by the nature of the problem. Federal interpretation of the federal law will govern, not state law. But state law, if compatible with the purpose of § 301, may be resorted to in order to find the rule that will best effectuate the federal policy. Any state law applied, however, will be absorbed as federal law and will not be an independent source of private rights.

It is not uncommon for federal courts to fashion federal law where federal rights are concerned. See Clearfield Trust Co. v. United States, 318 U.S. 363, 366–367. Congress has indicated by § 301(a) the purpose to follow that course here. There is no constitutional difficulty. Article III, § 2, extends the judicial power to cases "arising under * * * the Laws of the United States * * *." The power of Congress to regulate these labor-management controversies under the Commerce Clause is plain. * * * A case or controversy arising under § 301(a) is, therefore, one within the purview of judicial power as defined in Article III.

The question remains whether jurisdiction to compel arbitration of grievance disputes is withdrawn by the Norris–LaGuardia Act, 29 U.S.C. § 101. Section 7 of that Act prescribes stiff procedural requirements for issuing an injunction in a labor dispute. The kinds of acts which had given rise to abuse of the power to enjoin are listed in § 4. The failure to arbitrate was not a part and parcel of the abuses against which the Act was aimed. * * * The congressional policy in favor of the enforcement of agreements to arbitrate grievance disputes being clear, there is no reason to submit them to the requirements of § 7 of the Norris–LaGuardia Act.

    * * *

The judgment of the Court of Appeals is reversed and the cause is remanded to that court for proceedings in conformity with this opinion.

Reversed.

■ Mr. Justice Black took no part in the consideration or decision of this case.

■ Mr. Justice Burton, whom Mr. Justice Harlan joins, concurring in the result.

    * * *

■ Mr. Justice Frankfurter, dissenting.

The Court has avoided the difficult problems raised by § 301 of the Taft–Hartley Act, by attributing to the section an occult content. This plainly procedural section is transmuted into a mandate to the federal courts to fashion a whole body of substantive federal law appropriate for the complicated and touchy problems raised by collective bargaining. I have set forth in my opinion in Association of Westinghouse Salaried Employees v. Westinghouse Electric Corp. the detailed reasons why I believe that § 301 cannot be so construed, even if constitutional questions cannot be avoided. 348 U.S. 437, 441–449, 452–459. But the Court has a "clear" and contrary conclusion emerge from the "somewhat," to say the least, "cloudy and confusing legislative history." This is more than can be fairly asked even from the alchemy of construction. Since the Court relies on a few isolated statements in the legislative history which do not support its conclusion, however favoringly read, I have deemed it necessary to set forth in an appendix the entire relevant legislative history of the Taft–Hartley Act and its predecessor, the Case Bill. This legislative history reinforces the natural meaning of the statute as an exclusively procedural provision, affording, that is, an accessible federal forum for suits on agreements between labor organizations and employers, but not enacting federal law for such suits.

I have also set forth in my opinion in the Westinghouse case an outline of the vast problems that the Court's present decision creates by bringing into conflict state law and federal law, state courts and federal courts. These problems are not rendered non-existent by disregard of them. It should also be noted that whatever may be a union's *ad hoc* benefit in a particular case, the meaning of collective bargaining for labor does not remotely derive from reliance on the sanction of litigation in the courts. Restrictions made by legislation like the Clayton Act of 1914, and the Norris–LaGuardia Act of 1932, upon the use of familiar remedies theretofore available in the federal courts, reflected deep fears of the labor movement of the use of such remedies against labor. But a union, like any other combatant engaged in a particular fight, is ready to make an ally of an old enemy, and so we also find unions resorting to the otherwise much excoriated labor injunction. Such intermittent yielding to expediency does not change the fact that judicial intervention is ill-suited to the special characteristics of the arbitration process in labor disputes; nor are the conditions for its effective functioning thereby altered. * * *

* * * Arbitration agreements are for specific terms, generally much shorter than the time required for adjudication of a contested lawsuit through the available stages of trial and appeal. Renegotiation of agreements cannot await the outcome of such litigation; nor can the parties' continuing relation await it. Cases under § 301 will probably present unusual rather than representative situations. A "rule" derived from them is more likely to discombobulate than to compose. A "uniform corpus" cannot be expected to evolve, certainly not within a time to serve its assumed function.

The prickly and extensive problems that the supposed grant would create further counsel against a finding that the grant was made. They present hazardous opportunities for friction in the regulation of contracts between employers and unions. They involve the division of power between State and Nation, between state courts and federal courts, including the effective functioning of this Court. Wisdom suggests self-restraint in undertaking to solve these problems unless the Court is clearly directed to do so. Section 301 is not such a direction. The legislative history contains no suggestion that these problems were considered; the terms of the section do not present them.

* * *

The Court * * * sees no problem of "judicial power" in casting upon the federal courts, with no guides except "judicial inventiveness," the task of applying a whole industrial code that is as yet in the bosom of the judiciary. There are severe limits on "judicial inventiveness" even for the most imaginative judges. The law is not a "brooding omnipresence in the sky," (Mr. Justice Holmes, dissenting, in Southern Pacific Co. v. Jensen, 244 U.S. 205, 222), and it cannot be drawn from there like nitrogen from the air. These problems created by the Court's interpretation of § 301 cannot "be solved by resort to the established canons of construction that enable a court to look through awkward or clumsy expression, or language wanting in precision, to the intent of the legislature. For the vice of the statute here lies in the impossibility of ascertaining, by any reasonable test, that the legislature meant one thing rather than another * * *." Connally v. General Construction Co., 269 U.S. 385, 394. But the Court makes § 301 a mountain instead of a molehill and, by giving an example of "judicial inventiveness," it thereby solves all the constitutional problems that would otherwise have to be faced.

Even on the Court's attribution to § 301 of a direction to the federal courts to fashion, out of bits and pieces elsewhere to be gathered, a federal common law of labor contracts, it still does not follow that Congress has enacted that an agreement to arbitrate industrial differences be specifically enforceable in the federal courts. On the contrary, the body of relevant federal law precludes such enforcement of arbitration clauses in collective-bargaining agreements. * * *

* * *

The second ground of my dissent from the Court's action is more fundamental. * * * [For the remaining portion of the dissent, dealing with the constitutionality of § 301 (on the assumption that it is merely a jurisdictional grant), and for the concurring opinion of Justice Burton, see Chap. VIII, Sec. 2, p. 892, *infra*.]

NOTE ON FEDERAL COMMON LAW IMPLIED BY JURISDICTIONAL GRANTS

(1) *Jurisdiction as a Source of Lawmaking Authority*. In our legal system, a jurisdictional grant does not necessarily—or even ordinarily—imply that the law of the forum supplies the rule of decision. For example, a state court's jurisdiction over a case does not automatically carry with it application of the forum's substantive law.

After Erie R.R. Co. v. Tompkins, this principle took on special force as to federal court jurisdiction. Thus, in Texas Industries, Inc. v. Radcliff Materials, Inc., 451 U.S. 630, 640–41 (1981), the Court said: "The vesting of jurisdiction in the federal courts does not in and of itself give rise to authority to formulate federal common law". Nonetheless, Lincoln Mills stands as one of three celebrated instances in which the federal courts' law-making power is based at least substantially on a jurisdictional grant.[1]

---

1. For discussion of areas other than the three referred to in text, see p. 876, note 16, *infra* (implied private rights of action under § 1331); Brilmayer, *State Forfeiture* *Rules and Federal Review of State Criminal Convictions*, 49 U.Chi.L.Rev. 741, 765–70 (1982)(federal habeas corpus jurisdiction);

Unlike Lincoln Mills, which rested on a statutory grant of jurisdiction, the other two examples rest on jurisdictional grants in the Constitution. The first—the power to create federal admiralty law, implied by Article III's grant of admiralty jurisdiction—is particularly dramatic, because the implication is the source not only of power to create judge-made law but also of Congress' power to legislate on admiralty matters. See generally Moragne v. States Marine Lines, Inc., p. 791, *infra*, and the *Note on the Sources of Law in Admiralty* which follows Moragne. The second example is the power to fashion law governing litigation between states, which is implied by Article III's jurisdictional grant over interstate controversies. See *Note on the Law Applied in Actions Between States*, Chap. III, Sec. 1, p. 314, *supra*.[2]

In light of these two examples, why doesn't Article III's grant of diversity jurisdiction equally confer lawmaking authority? One explanation would point to additional reasons, beyond the jurisdictional grant, that support lawmaking in admiralty and in interstate disputes—in admiralty, a perceived need for uniformity, see, *e.g.*, Kossick v. United Fruit Co., 365 U.S. 731, 738–40 (1961), the connection of maritime commerce to the (inherently federal) area of international relations, and the lack of a well-developed colonial or state body of maritime law; in interstate controversies, the obvious inappropriateness of using the law of one of the disputants.

Indeed, is it a mistake to think of lawmaking in admiralty and in interstate disputes as resting (exclusively? primarily?) on jurisdictional grants, rather than on a structural inference that the area is inherently federal? *Cf.* Hill, p. 757, *supra* (viewing these areas as ones in which the Constitution preempts state lawmaking, leaving federal common law to govern).

(2) *Lincoln Mills and § 301.* In Lincoln Mills, too, other factors besides the grant of jurisdiction favored creation of federal common law. Quite apart from the uncertain claim that Congress had delegated lawmaking authority, there was a strong argument that federal law, which fosters the negotiation of collective bargaining agreements and the use of arbitration as an alternative to industrial strife, would be undermined if, as was true under the law of some states, agreements to arbitrate could not be enforced. (Arguments have also been made that a uniform federal law was needed to avoid difficult choice-of-law problems for interstate agreements, or to forestall a "race to the bottom" by states seeking to attract businesses with anti-labor provisions, see Posner, The Federal Courts 184 (1985).)[3]

(3) *The Scope of Lincoln Mills.* While Lincoln Mills itself raised only the question of the enforceability of an undertaking in a collective agreement, its reasoning has been followed in other decisions raising questions about the character and existence of those undertakings. For example, Local 174 v. Lucas Flour Co., 369 U.S. 95 (1962), held, as a matter of federal law, that a

Chap. VI, Sec. 3, pp. 709–14, *supra* (federal equity jurisdiction).

2. These controversies, and the terms of their settlement, may also affect private interests. See Hinderlider v. La Plata River & Cherry Creek Ditch Co., 304 U.S. 92 (1938).

3. For discussion of Lincoln Mills and its aftermath, see Bickel & Wellington, *Legis-* *lative Purpose and the Judicial Process: The Lincoln Mills Case,* 71 Harv.L.Rev. 1 (1957); Shapiro, *Of Institutions and Decisions,* 22 Stan.L.Rev. 657, 663–66 (1970); Pfander, *Judicial Purpose and the Scholarly Process: The Lincoln Mills Case,* 69 Wash.U.L.Q. 243 (1991); Note, 28 U.Chi.L.Rev. 707 (1961); Note, 82 Harv.L.Rev. 1512, 1531–35 (1969).

union that agreed to a compulsory arbitration provision was contractually obligated not to strike over an arbitrable dispute.

Lucas Flour also held that the federal common law governs in suits within the scope of § 301 that are brought in state court (pp. 103–04): "[T]he subject matter of § 301(a) 'is peculiarly one that calls for uniform law.' Pennsylvania R. Co. v. Public Service Comm'n, 250 U.S. 566, 569. The possibility that individual contract terms might have different meanings under state and federal law would inevitably exert a disruptive influence upon both the negotiation and administration of collective agreements."[4]

Doesn't Lucas Flour suggest that state courts have not only the power but also the obligation to formulate federal common law? Can federal common lawmaking by state courts be justified by reference to § 301, which grants jurisdiction only to the federal courts? Does that question further indicate the problematic nature of claims that lawmaking power derives from a jurisdictional grant alone?

Moragne v. States Marine Lines, Inc.

398 U.S. 375, 90 S.Ct. 1772, 26 L.Ed.2d 339 (1970).
Certiorari to the United States Court of Appeals for the Fifth Circuit.

■ MR. JUSTICE HARLAN delivered the opinion of the Court.

We brought this case here to consider whether The Harrisburg, 119 U.S. 199, in which this Court held in 1886 that maritime law does not afford a cause of action for wrongful death, should any longer be regarded as acceptable law.

The complaint sets forth that Edward Moragne, a longshoreman, was killed while working aboard the vessel Palmetto State on navigable waters within the State of Florida. Petitioner, as his widow and representative of his estate, brought this suit in a state court against respondent States Marine Lines, Inc., the owner of the vessel, to recover damages for wrongful death and for the pain and suffering experienced by the decedent prior to his death. The claims were predicated upon both negligence and the unseaworthiness of the vessel.

States Marine removed the case to [federal district court] on the basis of diversity of citizenship, and there filed a third-party complaint against respondent Gulf Florida Terminal Company, the decedent's employer, asserting that Gulf had contracted to perform stevedoring services on the vessel in a workmanlike manner and that any negligence or unseaworthiness causing the accident resulted from Gulf's operations.

Both States Marine and Gulf sought dismissal of the portion of petitioner's complaint that requested damages for wrongful death on the basis of unseaworthiness. They contended that maritime law provided no recovery for wrongful death within a State's territorial waters, and that the statutory right of action for death under Florida law did not encompass unseaworthiness as a basis of liability. The District Court dismissed the challenged portion of the complaint on this ground, citing this Court's decision in The Tungus v. Skovgaard, 358

---

4. Two weeks earlier, the Court had held that § 301 does not by implication divest state courts of concurrent jurisdiction. Charles Dowd Box Co. v. Courtney, 368 U.S. 502 (1962).

U.S. 588 (1959), and cases construing the state statute. * * * [The Court of Appeals, on interlocutory appeal under 28 U.S.C. § 1292(b), affirmed.]

* * *

In The Tungus this Court divided on the consequences that should flow from the rule of maritime law that "in the absence of a statute there is no action for wrongful death," first announced in The Harrisburg. All members of the Court agreed that where a death on state territorial waters is left remediless by the general maritime law and by federal statutes, a remedy may be provided under any applicable state law giving a right of action for death by wrongful act. However, four Justices dissented from the Court's further holding that "when admiralty adopts a State's right of action for wrongful death, it must enforce the right as an integrated whole, with whatever conditions and limitations the creating State has attached." 358 U.S., at 592. The dissenters would have held that federal maritime law could utilize the state law to "supply a remedy" for breaches of federally imposed duties, without regard to any substantive limitations contained in the state law. *Id.*, at 597, 599.

The extent of the role to be played by state law under The Tungus has been the subject of substantial debate and uncertainty in this Court * * *. On fresh consideration of the entire subject, we have concluded that the primary source of the confusion is not to be found in The Tungus, but in The Harrisburg, and that the latter decision, somewhat dubious even when rendered, is such an unjustifiable anomaly in the present maritime law that it should no longer be followed. We therefore reverse the judgment of the Court of Appeals.

I

The Court's opinion in The Harrisburg acknowledged that the result reached had little justification except in primitive English legal history—a history far removed from the American law of remedies for maritime deaths. * * * [The Court] relied primarily on its then recent decision in Insurance Co. v. Brame, 95 U.S. 754 (1878), in which it had held that in American common law, as in English, "no civil action lies for an injury which results in death." *Id.*, at 756.[2] In The Harrisburg, as in Brame, the Court did not examine the justifications for this common-law rule; rather, it simply noted that "we know of no country that has adopted a different rule on this subject for the sea from that which it maintains on the land," and concluded, despite contrary decisions of the lower federal courts both before and after Brame, that the rule of Brame should apply equally to maritime deaths. 119 U.S., at 213.

Our analysis of the history of the common-law rule indicates that it was based on a particular set of factors that had, when The Harrisburg was decided, long since been thrown into discard even in England, and that had never existed in this country at all. Further, regardless of the viability of the rule in 1886 as applied to American land-based affairs, it is difficult to discern an adequate reason for its extension to admiralty, a system of law then already differentiated in many respects from the common law. * * *

---

2. Brame was decided, of course, at a time when the federal courts under Swift v. Tyson, 41 U.S. 1 (1842), expounded a general federal common law.

II

We need not, however, pronounce a verdict on whether The Harrisburg, when decided, was a correct extrapolation of the principles of decisional law then in existence. A development of major significance has intervened, making clear that the rule against recovery for wrongful death is sharply out of keeping with the policies of modern American maritime law. This development is the wholesale abandonment of the rule in most of the areas where it once held sway, quite evidently prompted by the same sense of the rule's injustice that generated so much criticism of its original promulgation.

To some extent this rejection has been judicial. The English House of Lords in 1937 emasculated the rule without expressly overruling it. Rose v. Ford, [1937] A.C. 826. * * *

Much earlier, however, the legislatures both here and in England began to evidence unanimous disapproval of the rule against recovery for wrongful death. * * *

In the United States, every State today has enacted a wrongful-death statute. * * * The Congress has created actions for wrongful deaths of railroad employees, Federal Employers' Liability Act, 45 U.S.C. §§ 51–59; of merchant seamen, Jones Act, 46 U.S.C. § 688; and of persons on the high seas, Death on the High Seas Act, 46 U.S.C. §§ 761, 762. Congress has also, in the Federal Tort Claims Act, 28 U.S.C. § 1346(b), made the United States subject to liability in certain circumstances for negligently caused wrongful death to the same extent as a private person. See, *e.g.*, Richards v. United States, 369 U.S. 1 (1962).

These numerous and broadly applicable statutes, taken as a whole, make it clear that there is no present public policy against allowing recovery for wrongful death. The statutes evidence a wide rejection by the legislatures of whatever justifications may once have existed for a general refusal to allow such recovery. This legislative establishment of policy carries significance beyond the particular scope of each of the statutes involved. The policy thus established has become itself a part of our law, to be given its appropriate weight not only in matters of statutory construction but also in those of decisional law. See Landis, Statutes and the Sources of Law, in Harvard Legal Essays 213, 226–227 (1934). * * *

The legislature does not, of course, merely enact general policies. By the terms of a statute, it also indicates its conception of the sphere within which the policy is to have effect. In many cases the scope of a statute may reflect nothing more than the dimensions of the particular problem that came to the attention of the legislature, inviting the conclusion that the legislative policy is equally applicable to other situations in which the mischief is identical. This conclusion is reinforced where there exists not one enactment but a course of legislation dealing with a series of situations, and where the generality of the underlying principle is attested by the legislation of other jurisdictions. On the other hand the legislature may, in order to promote other, conflicting interests, prescribe with particularity the compass of the legislative aim, erecting a strong inference that territories beyond the boundaries so drawn are not to feel the impact of the new legislative dispensation. We must, therefore, analyze with care the congressional enactments that have abrogated the common-law rule in the maritime field, to determine the impact of the fact that none applies in terms to the situation of this case. See Part III, *infra*. However, it is sufficient at this point to conclude, as Mr. Justice Holmes did 45 years ago, that the work of the legislatures has made the allowance of recovery for wrongful death the general rule of American law, and its denial the exception. Where death is caused by the breach of a duty imposed by federal maritime law, Congress has established a policy favoring recovery in the absence of a legislative direction to except a particular class of cases.

III

Our undertaking, therefore, is to determine whether Congress has given such a direction in its legislation granting remedies for wrongful deaths in portions of the maritime domain. We find that Congress has given no affirmative indication of an intent to preclude the judicial allowance of a remedy for wrongful death to persons in the situation of this petitioner.

From the date of The Harrisburg until 1920, there was no remedy for death on the high seas caused by breach of one of the duties imposed by federal maritime law. For deaths within state territorial waters, the federal law accommodated the humane policies of state wrongful-death statutes by allowing recovery whenever an applicable state statute favored such recovery. Congress acted in 1920 to furnish the remedy denied by the courts for deaths beyond the jurisdiction of any State, by passing two landmark statutes. The first of these was the Death on the High Seas Act, 46 U.S.C. § 761 *et seq.* * * * The second statute was the Jones Act, 46 U.S.C. § 688, which, by extending to seamen the protections of the Federal Employers' Liability Act, provided a right of recovery against their employers for negligence resulting in injury or death. This right follows from the seamen's employment status and is not limited to injury or death occurring on the high seas.[11]

The United States, participating as *amicus curiae*, contended at oral argument that these statutes, if construed to forbid recognition of a general maritime remedy for wrongful death within territorial waters, would perpetuate three anomalies of present law. The first of these is simply the discrepancy produced whenever the rule of The Harrisburg holds sway: Within territorial waters, identical conduct violating federal law (here the furnishing of an unseaworthy vessel) produces liability if the victim is merely injured, but frequently not if he is killed. As we have concluded, such a distinction is not compatible with the general policies of federal maritime law.

The second incongruity is that identical breaches of the duty to provide a seaworthy ship, resulting in death, produce liability outside the three-mile limit—since a claim under the Death on the High Seas Act may be founded on unseaworthiness—but not within the territorial waters of a State whose local statute excludes unseaworthiness claims. The United States argues that since the substantive duty is federal, and federal maritime jurisdiction covers naviga-

---

11. In 1927 Congress passed the Longshoremen's and Harbor Workers' Compensation Act, 33 U.S.C. §§ 901–950, granting to longshoremen the right to receive workmen's compensation benefits from their employers for accidental injury or death arising out of their employment. These benefits are made exclusive of any other liability for employers who comply with the Act. The Act does not, however, affect the longshoreman's remedies against persons other than his employer, such as a shipowner, and therefore does not bear on the problem before us except perhaps to serve as yet another example of congressional action to allow recovery for death in circumstances where recovery is allowed for nonfatal injuries.

ble waters within and without the three-mile limit, no rational policy supports this distinction in the availability of a remedy.

The third, and assertedly the "strangest" anomaly is that a true seaman— that is, a member of a ship's company, covered by the Jones Act—is provided no remedy for death caused by unseaworthiness within territorial waters, while a longshoreman, to whom the duty of seaworthiness was extended only because he performs work traditionally done by seamen, does have such a remedy when allowed by a state statute.[12]

There is much force to the United States' argument that these distinctions are so lacking in any apparent justification that we should not, in the absence of compelling evidence, presume that Congress affirmatively intended to freeze them into maritime law. There should be no presumption that Congress has removed this Court's traditional responsibility to vindicate the policies of maritime law by ceding that function exclusively to the States. However, respondents argue that an intent to do just that is manifested by * * * portions of the Death on the High Seas Act * * *.

The legislative history of the Act suggests that respondents misconceive the thrust of the congressional concern. * * *

Read in light of the state of maritime law in 1920, we believe this legislative history indicates that Congress intended to ensure the continued availability of a remedy, historically provided by the States, for deaths in territorial waters; its failure to extend the Act to cover such deaths primarily reflected the lack of necessity for coverage by a federal statute, rather than an affirmative desire to insulate such deaths from the benefits of any federal remedy that might be available independently of the Act. The void that existed in maritime law up until 1920 was the absence of any remedy for wrongful death on the high seas. Congress, in acting to fill that void, legislated only to the three-mile limit because that was the extent of the problem. The express provision that state remedies in territorial waters were not disturbed by the Act ensured that Congress' solution of one problem would not create another by inviting the courts to find that the Act pre-empted the entire field, destroying the state remedies that had previously existed.

The beneficiaries of persons meeting death on territorial waters did not suffer at that time from being excluded from the coverage of the Act. To the contrary, the state remedies that were left undisturbed not only were familiar but also may actually have been more generous than the remedy provided by the new Act. * * * Congress in 1920 * * * legislated against a backdrop of

---

12. A joint contributor to this last situation, in conjunction with the rule of The Harrisburg, is the decision in Gillespie v. United States Steel Corp., 379 U.S. 148 (1964), where the Court held that the Jones Act, by providing a claim for wrongful death based on negligence, precludes any state remedy for wrongful death of a seaman in territorial waters—whether based on negligence or unseaworthiness. * * * [T]he remedy under general maritime law that will be made available by our overruling today of The Harris-

burg seems to be beyond the preclusive effect of the Jones Act as interpreted in Gillespie. The existence of a maritime remedy for deaths of seamen in territorial waters will further, rather than hinder, "uniformity in the exercise of admiralty jurisdiction"; and, of course, no question of preclusion of a *federal* remedy was before the Court in Gillespie or its predecessor, Lindgren v. United States, 281 U.S. 38 (1930), since no such remedy was thought to exist at the time those cases were decided. * * *

state laws that imposed a standard of behavior generally the same as—and in some respects perhaps more favorable than—that imposed by federal maritime law.

Since that time the equation has changed drastically, through this Court's transformation of the shipowner's duty to provide a seaworthy ship into an absolute duty not satisfied by due diligence. See, *e.g.*, Mahnich v. Southern S.S. Co., [321 U.S. 96 (1944)]. The unseaworthiness doctrine has become the principal vehicle for recovery by seamen for injury or death, overshadowing the negligence action made available by the Jones Act, and it has achieved equal importance for longshoremen and other harbor workers to whom the duty of seaworthiness was extended because they perform work on the vessel traditionally done by seamen. The resulting discrepancy between the remedies for deaths covered by the Death on the High Seas Act and for deaths that happen to fall within a state wrongful death statute not encompassing unseaworthiness could not have been foreseen by Congress. Congress merely declined to disturb state remedies at a time when they appeared adequate to effectuate the substantive duties imposed by general maritime law. That action cannot be read as an instruction to the federal courts that deaths in territorial waters, caused by breaches of the evolving duty of seaworthiness, must be *damnum absque injuria* unless the States expand their remedies to match the scope of the federal duty.

* * *

* * * Our recognition of a right to recover for wrongful death under general maritime law will assure uniform vindication of federal policies, removing the tensions and discrepancies that have resulted from the necessity to accommodate state remedial statutes to exclusively maritime substantive concepts.[15] Such uniformity not only will further the concerns of both of the 1920 Acts but also will give effect to the constitutionally based principle that federal admiralty law should be "a system of law coextensive with, and operating uniformly in, the whole country." The Lottawanna, 88 U.S. 558, 575 (1875).

We conclude that the Death on the High Seas Act was not intended to preclude the availability of a remedy for wrongful death under general maritime law in situations not covered by the Act. Because the refusal of maritime law to provide such a remedy appears to be jurisprudentially unsound and to have produced serious confusion and hardship, that refusal should cease * * *. * * *

* * *

15. The incongruity of forcing the States to provide the sole remedy to effectuate duties that have no basis in state policy is highlighted in this case. The Florida Supreme Court ruled [in response to a question certified to it by the Court of Appeals] that the state wrongful-death act was concerned only with "traditional common-law concepts," and not with "concepts peculiar to maritime law such as 'unseaworthiness' and the comparative negligence rule." It found no reason to believe that the Florida Legisla-ture intended to cover, or even considered, the "completely foreign" maritime duty of seaworthiness. 211 So.2d, at 164, 166. Federal law, rather than state, is the more appropriate source of a remedy for violation of the federally imposed duties of maritime law. *Cf.* Hill, The Law-Making Power of the Federal Courts: Constitutional Preemption, 67 Col.L.Rev. 1024 (1967); Note, The Federal Common Law, 82 Harv.L.Rev. 1512, 1523–1526 (1969).

* * *

We accordingly overrule The Harrisburg, and hold that an action does lie under general maritime law for death caused by violation of maritime duties. * * *

Reversed and remanded.

MR. JUSTICE BLACKMUN took no part in the consideration or decision of this case.*

———

NOTE ON THE SOURCES OF LAW IN ADMIRALTY

(1) *Introduction.* Moragne raised the question whether federal or state law was "the more appropriate source of a remedy for violation of the federally imposed duties of maritime law" (footnote 15). Thus it should perhaps have been included in Sec. 2 of this Chapter, dealing with issues of remedy. But the significance and scope of the question in the case, and of the Court's answer, are difficult to understand without some appreciation of the sources of substantive rights and obligations in admiralty and of the complex relationship between state and federal law in this field. This Note provides only a brief introduction to these topics.[1]

(2) *The Jensen and Chelentis Decisions.* The modern doctrine, which holds that admiralty is a uniform body of substantive federal law applicable not only in federal admiralty courts but also in the state courts and on the "law side" of the federal courts, stems from the decisions in Southern Pacific Co. v. Jensen, 244 U.S. 205 (1917), and Chelentis v. Luckenbach S.S. Co., 247 U.S. 372 (1918).[2]

The Jensen case involved a stevedore killed while loading a vessel in the port of New York. His next of kin obtained an award of compensation under the New York [Workers'] Compensation Law, and the award was sustained by

* [Ed.] For commentary on Moragne, Compare Posner, *Legal Formalism, Legal Realism, and the Interpretation of Statutes and the Constitution*, 37 Case W.Res.L.Rev. 179, 201–03 (1986)(criticizing both the Court's analysis, for effectively deleting the word "High" from the statute, and its conclusion), with Shapiro, *Continuity and Change in Statutory Interpretation*, 67 N.Y.U.L.Rev. 921, 952 (1992) and Note, 82 Yale L.J. 258 (1972)(both approving the Court's approach).

1. For extensive accounts of the development of the law, see Robertson, Admiralty and Federalism (1970); Currie, *Federalism and the Admiralty: "The Devil's Own Mess"*, 1960 Sup.Ct.Rev. 158. Other valuable sources include Benedict on Admiralty (7th rev.ed.1969–82); Gilmore & Black, The Law of Admiralty (2d ed.1975); Baer, Admiralty Law of the Supreme Court (3d ed.1979); Lucas, Admiralty: Cases and Materials (3d ed.1987); Schoenbaum, Admiralty and Maritime Law (2d ed.1994). For a theoretical overview, see von Mehren & Trautman, The Law of Multistate Problems 1049–73 (1965).

See also *Note on the Admiralty Jurisdiction*, Chap. VIII, Sec. 6(A), *infra*.

2. For a splendid account of the historical development, which treated the jurisdictional grant of the admiralty clause as a source of substantive federal law-making power—both judicial and legislative—see Note, 67 Harv.L.Rev. 1214 (1954). And see Robertson, note 1, *supra*, ch. 9, for a detailed analysis of the nineteenth century cases; he challenges as an oversimplification the conventional view that until the Jensen decision, the federal admiralty courts applied uniform maritime law, whereas state courts and federal courts (on the "law side") applied state law when acting under the "saving" clause, see note 3, *infra*.

For an argument that the modern doctrine should be abandoned and that "with the possible exception of cases on the high seas" the regime of federal common law should be "replaced by applicable state legal principles," see Redish, Federal Jurisdiction: Tensions in the Allocation of Judicial Power 138–47 (2d ed.1990).

the state courts.[3]

The Supreme Court reversed. Recognizing that "it would be difficult, if not impossible, to define with exactness just how far the general maritime law may be changed, modified, or affected by state legislation" but that "this may be done to some extent," Justice McReynolds declared that "no such legislation is valid if it * * * works material prejudice to the characteristic features of the general maritime law or interferes with the proper harmony and uniformity of that law in its international or interstate relations." 244 U.S. at 216. Without explaining why a workers' compensation law would be more destructive of "harmony and uniformity" than state wrongful death statutes (which could be relied on to remedy some maritime deaths, see The Hamilton, 207 U.S. 398 (1907)), he concluded that "freedom of navigation between the States and with foreign countries would be seriously hampered" if the statute could apply (p. 217). Justice Holmes, disagreeing, thought it "too late to say that the mere silence of Congress excludes the statute or common law of a state from supplementing the wholly inadequate maritime law of the time of the Constitution * * *" (p. 223). His strong dissent and that of Justice Pitney were approved by Justices Brandeis and Clarke.

Chelentis involved a sailor injured on board a vessel at sea. Instead of pursuing a maritime remedy (*i.e.*, maintenance and cure), he brought a negligence action against his employer in a state court. There being diversity of citizenship, the case was removed to federal court. On review, the Supreme Court held that the negligence action could not be maintained. Justice McReynolds said (247 U.S. at 382): "Under the doctrine approved in Southern Pacific Co. v. Jensen, no state has power to abolish the well recognized maritime rule concerning measure of recovery and substitute therefore [sic] the full indemnity rule of the common law. Such a substitution would distinctly and definitely change or add to the settled maritime law; and it would be destructive of the 'uniformity and consistency at which the Constitution aimed on all subjects of a commercial character affecting the intercourse of the States with each other or with foreign states' ".

To the extent that the "uniformity" of Jensen and Chelentis applies, it does so whether the case is litigated in admiralty or in a common law court. The momentary doubts on this score raised in Caldarola v. Eckert, 332 U.S. 155 (1947), were laid to rest in Pope & Talbot, Inc. v. Hawn, 346 U.S. 406, 411 (1953)("the substantial rights of an injured person are not to be determined differently whether his case is labelled 'law side' or 'admiralty side' ").

As the Jensen case illustrates, however, it is not always clear whether application of state law "works material prejudice to" or "interferes with the proper harmony and uniformity of" federal maritime law. Thus, Kossick v. United Fruit Co., 365 U.S. 731 (1961), held that maritime contracts are not subject to state statutes of frauds. Professor Currie asks: "But is it clear that the absence of a writing requirement in admiralty reflects a policy of contractual freedom rather than a felt judicial inability to formulate the details of a statute of frauds? Compare admiralty's willingness before the enactment of a federal statute of limitations for maritime torts * * * to refer to state law or to

---

3. State court jurisdiction was asserted under the "saving clause" of the federal grant of jurisdiction, which gave the federal courts exclusive jurisdiction over all civil cases in admiralty and maritime jurisdiction, "saving to suitors, in all cases, the right of a common law remedy, where the common law is competent to give it." For the current

related federal statutes for a time limitation to use as a yardstick for applying the maritime doctrine of laches". Currie, Federal Courts 364 (4th ed.1990).

(3) *Workers' Compensation Cases*. One of the most puzzling areas has been the one dealt with in the Jensen case itself—the availability of workers' compensation for longshore and harbor workers.[4] After Jensen, Congress twice sought to fill the gap created by that holding, by explicitly authorizing state law to furnish compensation; the Court responded both times that Congress had exceeded its powers because the Constitution prevents state law from operating. See Knickerbocker Ice Co. v. Stewart, 253 U.S. 149 (1920); Washington v. W.C. Dawson & Co., 264 U.S. 219 (1924).[5] Simultaneously, however, the Court limited the Jensen doctrine, holding that if the injury involved was "maritime but local", state compensation law could operate.[6]

In 1927 Congress passed a federal compensation statute (now known as the Longshore and Harbor Workers' Compensation Act, see 33 U.S.C. §§ 901 *et seq.*), but apparently preserved the "maritime but local" rule by providing in § 903(a) that federal compensation shall be payable only "if recovery for the disability or death through workmen's compensation proceedings may not validly be provided by State law." A tangled series of distinctions defined the line between federal and state compensability under this provision. See Gilmore & Black, note 1, *supra*, at 418–20. A further complexity was added in Davis v. Department of Labor, 317 U.S. 249 (1942), where the Court—though not denying that state and federal coverage are in theory mutually exclusive—said that there exists a "twilight zone" where either a federal or a state award could be upheld on the basis of a "presumption" of validity. See Lucas, note 1, *supra*, at 1002–03.

In 1962 the Court greatly simplified the law when it repealed by fiat the proviso limiting federal compensation to cases that could not "validly" be compensable under state law; it held that the federal remedy was available for all injuries on navigable waters, even those that state law could validly compensate under the "maritime but local" rubric. Calbeck v. Travelers Ins. Co., 370 U.S. 114 (1962)(7–2).[7]

In 1972, Congress approved Calbeck by deleting the limitation in § 903(a); it also extended the coverage of the Act by defining "navigable waters" to include piers and other areas where loading, unloading, repairing, or building of vessels is customarily performed. See 86 Stat. 1251.

Given this extension of federal coverage and the provision of § 905 that liability under the federal act is "exclusive * * * of all other liability * * * to the employee", may state compensation be awarded when the injury is "local" for purposes of the Jensen rule? See Sun Ship, Inc. v. Pennsylvania, 447 U.S.

---

wording and discussion, see generally p. 981, *infra*.

4. See generally Robertson, note 1, *supra*, ch. 12 & authorities cited at 213 n. 45.

5. It is doubtful that the doctrine of these cases would be accepted today as a measure of Congress' authority. *Cf.* Wilburn Boat Co. v. Fireman's Fund Ins. Co., 348 U.S. 310, 321 n. 29 (1955); Askew v. American Waterways Operators Inc., 411 U.S. 325, 344 (1973).

6. See Grant Smith–Porter Ship Co. v. Rohde, 257 U.S. 469 (1922)(injury to a car-

penter engaged in building a vessel lying in navigable water is compensable under state law); State Industrial Com'n v. Nordenholt Corp., 259 U.S. 263 (1922)(compensation statute may be applied to claim of mother of a longshore worker killed on the dock while unloading a vessel).

7. For discussion of the predominantly hostile commentary on the case (which viewed it as high-handed judicial legislation), and a valiant attempt at a defense, see Robertson, note 1, *supra*, at 212–19, 304–18.

715, 719–22 (1980), answering this question in the affirmative. (The Court held that the 1972 amendments were not intended to preempt state remedies, and that § 905 was not germane because it predated those amendments.)

(4) *Wrongful Death Cases.* The problem of wrongful death dealt with in Moragne has also had a troublesome and complex history. Western Fuel Co. v. Garcia, 257 U.S. 233 (1921), reaffirmed the proposition that notwithstanding Jensen, an admiralty action could be brought on the basis of a state wrongful death statute.[8] Just v. Chambers, 312 U.S. 383 (1941), confirmed that state survival statutes could also be applied in admiralty. But in the late '50s and early '60s a divided Court proved unable to create stable and intelligible law prescribing the exact scope that state law should have in these actions. The leading cases, all apparently—and happily—rendered obsolete by Moragne, are discussed in Gilmore & Black, note 1, *supra,* at 365–67.[9]

In Miles v. Apex Marine Corp., 498 U.S. 19 (1990), the Court followed through on the implications of its discussion in Moragne and held that there is a general maritime cause of action—based on the unseaworthiness of the vessel—for the wrongful death of a sailor who was killed while aboard a vessel on territorial waters. (Moragne itself involved a longshore worker who had been killed while aboard a vessel.) But noting that in a wrongful death action based on negligence under the Jones Act, recovery would be limited to losses suffered during decedent's lifetime and would not comprehend non-pecuniary losses, the Court imposed similar restrictions on general maritime wrongful death and survival actions for recovery on the basis of unseaworthiness.

(5) *Personal Injury Suits.* Beginning with Chelentis itself, a strong line of authority affirms that uniform maritime law, and not state law, governs liability in personal injury litigation not involving death. See, *e.g.,* Garrett v. Moore–McCormack Co., 317 U.S. 239 (1942)(applying admiralty rule that defendant has burden of proof on question of validity of a release); Pope & Talbot, Inc. v. Hawn, 346 U.S. 406 (1953)(applying admiralty rule that contributory negligence does not bar recovery).[10] The impact of this line of authority

8. The Court also held that the state statute of limitations applied and barred the action. See generally pp. 820–26, *infra.*

9. Footnote 12 of the Moragne opinion indicates that another happy effect of that decision is to render irrelevant the doctrine first announced in Lindgren v. United States, 281 U.S. 38 (1930), and reaffirmed in Gillespie v. United States Steel Corp., 379 U.S. 148 (1964), that the Jones Act, now 46 U.S.C. § 688, precludes recovery under state wrongful death statutes for the death of a sailor in territorial waters whether the claim is based on negligence or unseaworthiness.

For a decision after Moragne, in which the Court divided sharply on the nature of its role in the development of rules governing wrongful death actions, see Sea–Land Services, Inc. v. Gaudet, 414 U.S. 573 (1974)(recovery by decedent in his lifetime does not bar subsequent wrongful death action by his widow).

Following Gaudet, the Court held in Mobil Oil Corp. v. Higginbotham, 436 U.S. 618 (1978), that damages for loss of society, approved in Gaudet for a death in territorial waters under the general maritime law announced in Moragne, were precluded for a death on the high seas by the Death on the High Seas Act, which limits damages to pecuniary losses. In Offshore Logistics, Inc. v. Tallentire, 477 U.S. 207 (1986), it was further held that a recovery under the Death on the High Seas Act could not be supplemented by nonpecuniary damages under a state wrongful death statute.

10. The counter-indications in Justice Frankfurter's ambiguous opinion for the Court in Caldarola v. Eckert, 332 U.S. 155 (1947), were deprived of continuing effectiveness by the Court's opinion (and indeed to some extent by Justice Frankfurter's own concurrence) in the Pope & Talbot case.

However, Pope and Talbot and Garrett were held to be distinguishable in American

has been magnified by the Court's expansions of the maritime remedy of unseaworthiness. See, *e.g.*, Mahnich v. Southern S.S. Co., 321 U.S. 96 (1944); Mitchell v. Trawler Racer, Inc., 362 U.S. 539 (1960).[11]

FURTHER NOTE ON FEDERAL COMMON LAW GENERATED BY FEDERAL STATUTES

(1) *The Range of Issues.* A broad category of cases raises the general question whether, in "filling in" the gaps left open by federal statutory regulation, or in interpreting general statutory phrases, the federal courts should fashion federal common law or should resort to state law. This category overlaps with a good deal of the material already discussed. Recall, for example:

(a) Farmers Educ. & Co–op. Union v. WDAY, Inc., 360 U.S. 525 (1959), p. 782, *supra*, where the Court held that imposition of defamation liability for a broadcast that was mandated by federal law, and over whose content the broadcaster lacked control, would interfere with federal purposes and thus was precluded by federal common law.[1]

(b) Dice v. Akron, Canton & Youngstown R.R. Co., 342 U.S. 359 (1952), Chap. IV, Sec. 3, p. 479, *supra*, a state court FELA action, in which the Court held that state law rules governing the validity of a fraudulently obtained release, and also the division of authority between judge and jury in determining fraud, had to yield to federal common law rules.

(c) Mississippi Band of Choctaw Indians v. Holyfield, 490 U.S. 30 (1989), p. 770, *supra*, where the Court relied on a federal rule of decision in defining the meaning of "domiciled" in the jurisdictional provisions of the Indian Child Welfare Act.

There are innumerable examples of choice-of-law problems arising within the ambits of federal regulatory programs.[2] This Note will discuss only a few

Dredging Co. v. Miller, 114 S.Ct. 981 (1994), p. 474, note 4, *supra* (state court may apply its own forum non conveniens rules in action, pursuant to "savings to suitor clause", under the Jones Act and general maritime law).

11. The Court extended the unseaworthiness remedy to longshore workers in Seas Shipping Co. v. Sieracki, 328 U.S. 85 (1946). But Congress effectively overruled this decision in its 1972 amendments to the Longshore and Harbor Workers' Compensation Act. See 33 U.S.C. § 905(b); Friendly, Federal Jurisdiction: A General View 131–32 (1973).

Compare Wilburn Boat Co. v. Fireman's Fund Ins. Co., 348 U.S. 310 (1955), holding that state law governs the question whether breach by plaintiff of warranties in a marine insurance contract precludes recovery on the contract. The decision was widely criticized. See, *e.g.*, Gilmore & Black, note 1, *supra*, at 48–49, 68–71; von Mehren & Trautman, note 1, *supra*, at 1057 (arguing that the issue is

federal but that the old federal rule needs to be overhauled).

1. Consider also International Union, UAW v. Johnson Controls, 499 U.S. 187 (1991), where the Court held that Title VII prohibits an employer from barring fertile women from jobs involving exposure to lead levels that could be dangerous to fetal health. Although the opinion did not definitively resolve whether employers would be immune from suit were a fetus to suffer injury from such exposure, the Court said that "[i]f state tort law furthers discrimination in the workplace and prevents employers from hiring women * * *, then it will impede the accomplishment of Congress' goals in enacting Title VII," citing WDAY as presenting a "similar situation" (p. 209).

2. See, *e.g.*, Countryman, *The Use of State Law in Bankruptcy Cases*, 47 N.Y.U.L.Rev. 407, 631 (1972); Hill, *The Law–Making Power of the Federal Courts:*

additional situations raising distinctive questions. Consider whether different views of statutory interpretation, see *Note on Theories of Statutory Interpretation and Their Pertinence to Federal Common Lawmaking*, p. 758, *supra*, may affect a judge's approach to these problems.

(2) *Conflict with Federal Purposes*. The general proposition that state law cannot contradict or impede a federal regulatory program is easily stated, but its application in particular cases raises difficult and subtle problems. Determining whether a conflict exists shades into the pervasive question of the extent to which federal regulation preempts state law. For a recent preemption decision that discusses many of the leading precedents, see Freightliner Corp. v. Myrick, 115 S.Ct. 1483 (1995).

Recall Justice Scalia's statement, in the Boyle decision, that for federal common lawmaking to be justified, "[t]he conflict with federal policy need not be as sharp as that which must exist for ordinary pre-emption when Congress legislates 'in a field which the States have traditionally occupied.' Rice v. Santa Fe Elevator Corp., 331 U.S. [218, 230 (1947)]. Or to put the point differently, the fact that the area in question *is* one of unique federal concern changes what would otherwise be a conflict that cannot produce pre-emption into one that can."

Is the justification for judicial lawmaking to fill the interstices of federal statutes necessarily stronger when, for example, the case involves federal proprietary interests, or when lawmaking power is inferred from a jurisdictional grant, than when (as in the cases noted in Paragraph (1), *supra*) such factors are lacking?

(3) *Parallel State Law*. Federal regulation may displace not only contradictory but also parallel state law.[3] In Sears, Roebuck & Co. v. Stiffel Co., 376 U.S. 225 (1964), and Compco Corp. v. Day–Brite Lighting, Inc., 376 U.S. 234 (1964), the Court held that state unfair competition law could not make actionable the copying of products not entitled to patent protection under federal law (pp. 230–33): "[T]he patent system is one in which uniform federal standards are carefully used to promote invention while at the same time preserving free competition. Obviously a State could not, consistently with the Supremacy Clause of the Constitution, extend the life of a patent beyond its expiration date or give a patent on an article which lacked the level of invention required for federal patents. * * * Just as a State cannot encroach upon the federal patent laws directly, it cannot, under some other law, such as that forbidding unfair

---

Constitutional Preemption, 67 Colum.L.Rev. 1024 (1967); Note, 75 Harv.L.Rev. 1395 (1962).

3. See, *e.g.*, Garner v. Teamsters Union, 346 U.S. 485 (1953)(state courts may not grant injunctions against activities prohibited by the National Labor Relations Act); Local 926, IUOE v. Jones, 460 U.S. 669 (1983)(state law damage action by supervisory employee against union for tortious interference with his employment contract was preempted because conduct was arguably prohibited by NLRA). Garner was extended to the limit of its logic—or beyond—by Guss v. Utah Labor Bd., 353 U.S. 1 (1957), holding

that state courts could not redress acts technically violating the NLRA even when the NLRB has declined jurisdiction because the case has only minor impact on interstate commerce. The resulting "gap" was cured by legislation. See 29 U.S.C. § 164(c).

See also Pennsylvania v. Nelson, 350 U.S. 497 (1956)(federal Smith Act preempts substantially identical state law against subverting the national government); In re Second Employers' Liability Cases, 223 U.S. 1 (1912)(FELA preempts state law personal injury actions by covered employees).

competition, give protection of a kind that clashes with the objectives of the federal patent laws.

"* * * To allow a State by use of its law of unfair competition to prevent the copying of an article which represents too slight an advance to be patented would be to permit the State to block off from the public something which federal law has said belongs to the public. The result would be that while federal law grants only 14 or 17 years' protection to genuine inventions, see 35 U.S.C. §§ 154, 173, States could allow perpetual protection to articles too lacking in novelty to merit any patent at all under federal constitutional standards. This would be too great an encroachment on the federal patent system to be tolerated."[4]

See also Lear, Inc. v. Adkins, 395 U.S. 653 (1969)(a state may not award damages for breach of a contract licensing the use of a patented product if the patent is invalid).

Recent cases have limited the rationale of these decisions. See, *e.g.*, Kewanee Oil Co. v. Bicron Corp., 416 U.S. 470 (1974)(state's trade secret law is not preempted by federal patent law); Aronson v. Quick Point Pencil Co., 440 U.S. 257 (1979)(enforcement of royalty contract under state law is allowed, even though patent application for product covered by the contract had been rejected).[5]

(4) *Interstate Water Pollution.* The Court has traveled up the hill and down on the role of federal common law in the complex and heavily regulated area of pollution of interstate waters.

(a) A rather casual dictum in Ohio v. Wyandotte Chemicals Corp., 401 U.S. 493, 498–99 n. 3 (1971), Chap. III, Sec. 1, p. 323, *supra*, suggested that state law would govern an action by a state to abate, as a nuisance, the pollution of Lake Erie by the dumping of mercury. But a year later, the Court held that federal common law governed an action by Illinois against four Wisconsin cities and two sewerage commissions to enjoin alleged pollution of Lake Michigan— and that accordingly the federal district court had subject matter jurisdiction. Illinois v. Milwaukee, 406 U.S. 91 (1972). After noting a variety of federal statutes asserting an interest in the problem, Justice Douglas said (pp. 102–04):

"The Federal Water Pollution Control Act in § 1(b) declares that it is federal policy 'to recognize, preserve, and protect the primary responsibilities and rights of the States in preventing and controlling water pollution.' But the Act makes clear that it is federal, not state, law that in the end controls the pollution of interstate or navigable waters. * * *

---

4. See also Bonito Boats, Inc. v. Thunder Craft Boats, Inc., 489 U.S. 141 (1989), holding that the federal patent laws preempted a Florida law prohibiting the unlicensed commercial use of "the direct molding process" to duplicate a component of a vessel made by another person. Unlike unfair competition laws, which generally protect consumers from confusion as to source, this law created patent-like protection for an invention, and thus squarely conflicted with federal policy favoring free competition in ideas not meriting federal patent protection.

5. In the area of copyright, see Goldstein v. California, 412 U.S. 546 (1973)(California statute proscribing "record or tape piracy" is not preempted by federal copyright law). The statute (as amended in 1976) now deals explicitly with the scope of federal preemption. See 17 U.S.C. § 301. See generally Goldstein, Copyright, Patent, Trademark and Related State Doctrines 21–22, 101–12, 759–72, 910–19 (3d ed.1990); Brown & Denicola, Copyright 583–618 (6th ed.1995).

"The remedy sought by Illinois is not within the precise scope of remedies prescribed by Congress. Yet the remedies which Congress provides are not necessarily the only federal remedies available. * * * When we deal with air or water in their ambient or interstate aspects, there is a federal common law * * *.

"The application of federal common law to abate a public nuisance in interstate or navigable waters is not inconsistent with the Water Pollution Control Act. Congress provided in § 10(b) of that Act that, save as a court may decree otherwise in an enforcement action, '[s]tate and interstate action to abate pollution of interstate and navigable waters shall be encouraged and shall not * * * be displaced by federal enforcement action.' "[6]

Given the absence of any close relation to a statutory or constitutional provision, was the rule of decision formulated in Illinois v. Milwaukee an example of what Judge Friendly, p. 752, *supra*, called "spontaneous generation" of federal common law?

(b) After this decision, Congress enacted the extensive Water Pollution Control Amendments of 1972, 33 U.S.C. § 1311 *et seq.*, which, among other things, made it illegal to discharge pollutants into the nation's waters without a permit. Permits were issued to the defendants in the Illinois case, who by this time had been duly served in an action by Illinois in an Illinois federal district court. The district court held that a nuisance had been established under federal common law and issued an elaborate decree. The court of appeals affirmed in part. However, the Supreme Court (per Rehnquist, J.) reversed, 6–3. Milwaukee v. Illinois, 451 U.S. 304 (1981):

"* * * Congress has not left the formulation of appropriate federal standards to the courts through application of often vague and indeterminate nuisance concepts and maxims of equity jurisprudence, but rather has occupied the field through the establishment of a comprehensive regulatory program supervised by an expert administrative agency. The 1972 Amendments to the Federal Water Pollution Control Act were not merely another law 'touching interstate waters' of the sort surveyed in Illinois v. Milwaukee, and found inadequate to supplant federal common law. Rather, the Amendments were viewed by Congress as a 'total restructuring' and 'complete rewriting' of the existing water pollution legislation considered in that case" (p. 317).

The 1972 amendments had explicitly preserved more stringent remedies under state law. For the majority, however, "the appropriate analysis in determining if federal statutory law governs a question previously the subject of federal common law is not the same as that employed in deciding if federal law pre-empts state law. In considering the latter question 'we start with the assumption that the historic police powers of the States were not to be superseded by the Federal Act unless that was the clear and manifest purpose of Congress.' * * * (quoting Rice v. Santa Fe Elevator Corp., 331 U.S. 218, 230 (1947))." But the concerns underlying that reluctance to displace state authority "are not implicated in the same fashion when the question is whether

---

6. In reaching its result the Court relied on Georgia v. Tennessee Copper Co., 206 U.S. 230 (1907), Chap. III, Sec. 1, p. 318, *supra*, a pre-Erie case, as well as on cases holding that federal law governs questions relating to the apportionment among states of the waters of interstate streams. Are these authorities persuasive? The Court might also have cited cases such as Sanitary Dist. of Chicago v. United States, 266 U.S. 405 (1925), discussed in Sec. 2(A), p. 816, *infra*.

federal statutory or federal common law governs, and accordingly the same sort of evidence of a clear and manifest purpose is not required. Indeed, as noted, in cases such as the present 'we start with the assumption' that it is for Congress, not federal courts, to articulate the appropriate standards to be applied as a matter of federal law" (pp. 316–17).

Justice Blackmun, for the dissenters, analyzed the 1972 amendments at length and concluded (p. 339): "[T]he language and structure of the Clean Water Act leave no doubt that Congress intended to preserve the federal common law of nuisance." As a parting shot, he noted (p. 353) that "the Court in effect is encouraging recourse to state law wherever the federal statutory scheme is perceived to offer inadequate protection against pollution from outside the State * * *. * * * Instead of promoting a more uniform federal approach to the problem of alleviating interstate pollution, I fear that today's decision will lead States to turn to their own courts for statutory or common-law assistance in filling the interstices of the federal statute."

It is difficult to evaluate the disagreement between the majority and the dissent without a good deal more information than can be presented here about the statute and the scope of regulation. But consider carefully the majority's suggestion that a court should always be more reluctant to find that a federal statute preempts state law than to find that the statute preempts federal common law.

(5) *Complex Tort Litigation.* Just as the presence of a clearly declared federal legislative policy has often resulted in the displacement of state law, so the absence of such a declaration has led to a refusal to displace state law, even under circumstances where strong arguments of uniquely federal interests could be made. Of special note is Jackson v. Johns–Manville Sales Corp., 750 F.2d 1314 (5th Cir.1985), in which a sharply divided court, sitting en banc, rejected an appeal for the development of federal common law governing liability for asbestos-related injuries. In answer to arguments that federal common law was required because of the nationwide impact of "a sequence of massive tort claims that has unparalleled geographic and financial dimension" (dissent, p. 1330), the majority emphasized that "Congress itself has yet to make policy on this issue", that many "practical problems would attend the displacement of state law", and that there was not available "any governing principle of easy application for the imposition of federal common law in the asbestos context" (pp. 1325–27). See also, *e.g.*, In re "Agent Orange" Product Liability Litigation, 635 F.2d 987 (2d Cir.1980)(holding, 2–1, that veterans' personal injury action against herbicide suppliers for injuries incurred during Vietnam War was not governed by federal common law); *cf.* Silkwood v. Kerr–McGee Corp., 464 U.S. 238 (1984)(award of punitive damages under state law, in action for plutonium contamination injuries, not preempted by federal law).

A number of commentators have urged the creation of a federal common law of torts in the mass accident context. See Mullenix, *Class Resolution of the Mass–Tort Case: A Proposed Federal Procedure Act*, 64 Texas L.Rev. 1039, 1077–79 & authorities cited at n. 201 (1986). In addition, there have been numerous proposals for congressional action dealing with specific or general issues of product liability, but so far, none has been enacted into law.

An alternative approach would be to formulate a federal common law not of substantive tort liability but of the choice of law rules to be applied to multiple tort suits consolidated in a single forum. See, *e.g.*, Atwood, *The Choice-of-Law Dilemma in Mass Tort Litigation: Kicking Around Erie, Klaxon, and Van Dusen*, 19 Conn.L.Rev. 9 (1986).[7] Some have doubted whether federalizing only choice of law would resolve the procedural difficulties of mass tort litigation. See, *e.g.*, Mullenix, *Federalizing Choice of Law for Mass–Tort Litigation*, 70 Tex.L.Rev. 1623 (1992), which also contains numerous references to additional commentary.

NOTE ON SABBATINO AND THE FEDERAL LAW OF INTERNATIONAL RELATIONS

(1) *Sabbatino and the Act of State Doctrine.* Still another category of federal common law emerged in Banco Nacional de Cuba v. Sabbatino, 376 U.S. 398 (1964). Defendant, a New York corporation, had contracted with American citizens to buy sugar in Cuba. The Cuban government expropriated the sugar under a decree that passed title to petitioner, a Cuban governmental agency.[1] Defendant secured a Cuban export license for the sugar by promising to pay the proceeds to the petitioner; but after export it refused to honor this promise and proposed to pay the former owners. Petitioner then brought a diversity action for conversion of the proceeds in a federal district court.

Both the district court and the court of appeals held that the Cuban expropriation violated international law and therefore did not convey good title to the petitioner. The Supreme Court (per Harlan, J.) reversed, relying on the "act of state doctrine", which "in its traditional formulation precludes the courts of this country from inquiring into the validity of the public acts a recognized foreign sovereign power committed within its own territory" (pp. 400–01). Thus, absent "a treaty or other unambiguous agreement regarding controlling legal principles", the courts would not examine whether Cuba's action violated "customary international law" (p. 428).

Compliance with the act of state doctrine, the Court stated, is itself neither dictated nor limited by international law, but is, rather, governed by the internal law of each country. Nor does the Constitution "require the act of state doctrine; it does not irrevocably remove from the judiciary the capacity to review the validity of foreign acts of state." But the doctrine does "have 'constitutional' underpinnings. It arises out of the basic relationships between branches of government in a system of separation of powers. * * * The doctrine * * * expresses the strong sense of the Judicial Branch that its engagement in the task of passing on the validity of foreign acts of state may hinder rather than further this country's pursuit of goals both for itself and for the community of nations as a whole in the international sphere. Many

---

7. The American Law Institute's Complex Litigation Project, doubting that Congress would in fact enact comprehensive substantive federal tort law standards, has proposed enactment of a statute that would authorize federal courts to apply federal choice of law standards in multistate cases. The Project did not expressly consider whether federal courts could formulate such rules absent congressional action. See ALI, Complex Litigation: Statutory Recommendations and Analysis, Ch. 6 (1994). See generally *American Law Institute Complex Litiga-* *tion Project: A Symposium*, 54 La.L.Rev. 833ff (1994). See also Reavley & Wesevich, *An Old Rule for New Reasons: Place of Injury as a Federal Solution to Choice of Law in Single–Accident Mass–Tort Cases*, 71 Tex. L.Rev. 1 (1992).

1. Although the decree purported to provide a system of compensation, the prospect of adequate recovery was dim.

The statement of the case has been simplified in minor respects.

commentators disagree with this view; they have striven by means of distinguishing and limiting past decisions and by advancing various considerations of policy to stimulate a narrowing of the apparent scope of the rule. Whatever considerations are thought to predominate, it is plain that the problems involved are uniquely federal in nature. If federal authority, in this instance this Court, orders the field of judicial competence in this area for the federal courts, and the state courts are left free to formulate their own rules, the purposes behind the doctrine could be as effectively undermined as if there had been no federal pronouncement on the subject" (pp. 423–24).

The Court added (p. 425): "It seems fair to assume that the Court did not have rules like the act of state doctrine in mind when it decided Erie R. Co. v. Tompkins." And it pointed out (pp. 426–27) that there are precedents for creating "enclaves of federal judge-made law which bind the States", citing Lincoln Mills, D'Oench, Duhme & Co., and Clearfield. "Perhaps more directly in point are the bodies of law applied between States over boundaries and in regard to the apportionment of interstate waters. * * * The problems surrounding the act of state doctrine are, albeit for different reasons, as intrinsically federal as are those involved in water apportionment or boundary disputes. The considerations supporting exclusion of state authority here are much like those which led the Court in United States v. California, 332 U.S. 19, to hold that the Federal Government possessed paramount rights in submerged lands though within the three-mile limit of coastal States. We conclude that the scope of the act of state doctrine must be determined according to federal law."[2]

Justice White's long dissent did not dispute that federal law governed.[3]

(2) *The Basis for Federal Common Law.* What is the basis for judicial lawmaking in Sabbatino? Does it implement statutory or constitutional provisions? See note 2, *supra.* Does the Constitution impliedly preempt state lawmaking related to foreign affairs? See Professor Hill's views, p. 757, *supra.* Or is Sabbatino another example of "spontaneous generation"? See Friendly, p. 752, *supra.*

(3) *The Implications of Sabbatino.* Among the questions left largely unanswered by the post-Sabbatino case law are these: To what extent does Sabbatino make any question involving foreign relations a federal question?[4] What is

---

2. At this point Justice Harlan has a footnote: "Various constitutional and statutory provisions indirectly support this determination, see U.S. Const., Art. I, § 8, cls. 3, 10; Art. II, §§ 2, 3; Art. III, § 2; 28 U.S.C. §§ 1251(a)(2), (b)(1), (b)(3), 1332(a)(2), 1333, 1350–1351, by reflecting a concern for uniformity in this country's dealings with foreign nations and indicating a desire to give matters of international significance to the jurisdiction of federal institutions. * * *"

3. Shortly after Sabbatino, Congress enacted overriding legislation, see 22 U.S.C. § 2370(e), barring judicial invocation of the act of state doctrine except under specified circumstances. This amendment was held to be retroactive, and defeated Cuba's claim on

remand of the Sabbatino case. See Banco Nacional v. Farr, 383 F.2d 166 (2d Cir.1967).

For subsequent views on the act of state doctrine, see First Nat'l City Bank v. Banco Nacional de Cuba, 406 U.S. 759 (1972); Alfred Dunhill of London, Inc., v. Republic of Cuba, 425 U.S. 682 (1976).

4. In Zschernig v. Miller, 389 U.S. 429, 432 (1968), the Court invalidated, as "an intrusion by the State into the field of foreign affairs which the Constitution entrusts to the President and the Congress", an Oregon statute that, as interpreted and administered, barred foreigners from inheriting if their country does not grant U.S. citizens reciprocal rights. "The statute as construed seems to make unavoidable judicial criticism of na-

the relationship of the federal courts' law-making authority in this field to the power of the federal political branches?[5]

In an interesting passage, Henkin, Foreign Affairs and the Constitution 219–20 (1972), wrote that after Sabbatino:

"There ought to be little doubt * * * that in the established areas of judicial law-making, law that is substantially related to foreign affairs—the determination of customary international law and comity for judicial purposes; guidelines for the interpretation of treaties and the meaning of particular treaty provisions; the principles of (international) conflicts-of-laws; rules as to access of foreign governments to domestic courts and the treatment of foreign judgments—the federal courts can make law for their own guidance and can decide also whether federal interests require that the States conform to them. * * *

"Later cases will have to answer the more difficult question, whether and which new subjects are also within the legislative power of the federal courts. * * * [O]ne may expect that without limiting their power in principle, they will legislate sparingly.

"* * * Judge-made law, the courts must recognize, can only serve foreign policy grossly and spasmodically; their attempts to draw lines and make exceptions must be bound in doctrine and justified in reasoned opinions, and they cannot provide flexibility, completeness, and comprehensive coherence."

(4) *Sabbatino and Judicial Integrity.* In his dissent in Sabbatino, one of Justice White's objections was that, under the act of state doctrine, "not only are the courts powerless to question acts of state proscribed by international law but they are likewise powerless to refuse to adjudicate the claim founded

tions established on a more authoritarian basis than our own", and could "impair the effective exercise of the Nation's foreign policy" (p. 440). The Court purported to leave standing Clark v. Allen, 331 U.S. 503 (1947), upholding a similar California "reciprocity" statute, saying that such statutes were not unconstitutional "on their face" but only if their application required state courts to appraise the quality of justice in foreign countries.

See generally Restatement (Third) of the Foreign Relations Law of the United States §§ 111 (and Comment d), 112 (and Comment a) (1987); Brilmayer, *Federalism, State Authority, and the Preemptive Power of International Law*, 1994 Sup.Ct.Rev. 295; Edwards, *The Erie Doctrine in Foreign Affairs Cases*, 42 N.Y.U.L.Rev. 674 (1967); Hill, *The Law-Making Power of the Federal Courts: Constitutional Preemption*, 67 Colum.L.Rev. 1024 (1967); Moore, *Federalism and Foreign Relations*, 1965 Duke L.J. 248.

See also Weisburd, *State Courts, Federal Courts, and International Cases*, 29 Yale J.Int.L. 1, 59 (1995)(criticizing broad claims that federal law governs all matters of for-

eign relations, and arguing that federal common law displaces state law only in cases that (i) require a decision about what counts as a foreign state, (ii) require formal judicial evaluation of a foreign state's public policy, or (iii) involve immigration matters).

5. Compare Barclays Bank, PLC v. Franchise Tax Bd., 114 S.Ct. 2268 (1994), a constitutional challenge to California's method for apportioning taxes on multinational corporations. In rejecting arguments that the challenged method, which differed from that used by the federal government, impaired national uniformity in international trade and was likely to provoke international retaliation, the Court said (pp. 2284–85): "This Court has no constitutional authority to make the policy judgments essential to regulating foreign commerce and conducting foreign affairs. Matters relating 'to the conduct of foreign relations ... are so exclusively entrusted to the political branches of government as to be largely immune from judicial inquiry or interference.' Harisiades v. Shaughnessy, 342 U.S. 580, 589 (1952)."

upon a foreign law; they must render judgment and thereby validate the lawless act." 376 U.S. at 439.

Suppose that a state court were to dismiss a case exactly like Sabbatino on the ground that, as a matter of state law, it has no power to render an affirmative judgment for a claimant without considering the lawfulness of the claim, and that Sabbatino precludes it from such consideration. Ignoring the legislation enacted by Congress after Sabbatino (see note 3, *supra*), do you think the decision would be reviewable by the Supreme Court? If so, should it be reversed?

(5) *The Alien Tort Statute.* In support of its conclusion that federal law governed, the Sabbatino Court cited a number of constitutional and statutory provisions, see note 2, *supra*, including 28 U.S.C. § 1350. That provision, which confers jurisdiction in a "civil action by an alien for a tort only, committed in violation of the law of nations * * *", was described by Judge Friendly as "a kind of legal Lohengrin; although it has been with us since the First Judiciary Act, no one seems to know whence it came." IIT v. Vencap, Ltd, 519 F.2d 1001, 1015 (2d Cir.1975). Recent years have seen controversy about whether § 1350 merely confers jurisdiction in cases in which some other source of federal law creates a cause of action; whether it creates a right of action itself; and if so, whether that right of action is an aspect of federal common law.

(a) In Filartiga v. Pena–Irala, 630 F.2d 876 (2d Cir.1980), the court held that § 1350 afforded jurisdiction over a claim brought by Paraguayan citizens against a former Paraguayan official (served while in the United States on an expired visitor's visa) for acts of torture allegedly committed in Paraguay. The Court rejected the argument that § 1350 violated Article III as there was neither a federal question nor the requisites for party-based jurisdiction: "The constitutional basis for the Alien Tort Statute is the law of nations, which has always been part of the federal common law" (p. 885).

Does that language suggest that quite apart from the statute, the federal common law incorporates the law of nations, and § 1350 merely confers jurisdiction over certain actions based on this law? On this view, once Congress enacted a general federal question jurisdictional provision in 1875, would an action alleging a violation of the law of nations arise under § 1331— even if, because it does not involve a tort by an alien, the action falls outside § 1350? Or would § 1331 alone not suffice to entertain a claim based on the law of nations—either (i) because the jurisdictional statute should not be construed to extend that far absent a clearer statement by Congress, or (ii) because § 1350 not only confers jurisdiction but also supplies a private damages remedy—not otherwise supplied by the law of nations—for torts in violation of duties imposed by the law of nations? See the cases cited in Kadic v. Karadzic, 70 F.3d 232, 246 (2d Cir.1995).

See generally Burley, *The Alien Tort Statute and the Judiciary Act of 1789: A Badge of Honor*, 83 Am.J.Int'l.L. 461 & sources cited at 465 n. 16 (1989). See also Crockett, *The Role of Federal Common Law in Alien Tort Statute Cases*, 14 B.C.Int'l & Comp.L.Rev. 29 (1991).

(b) Note that while Sabbatino was meant to preclude federal (and state) courts from reviewing the conformity of acts of state with the law of nations, Filartiga authorized review of the conformity of the acts of individual officials, acting under color of state law, with the law of nations. Can the cases be distinguished on the basis that judicial review is more appropriate where the action complained of violates not only the law of nations but also the law of the foreign sovereign?

(c) Although Filartiga's approach has been broadly accepted by other courts, see, *e.g.*, Trajano v. Marcos, 978 F.2d 493 (9th Cir.1992), some judges have expressed their doubts about it.[6] In part to eliminate those doubts, Congress enacted the Torture Victim Protection Act of 1991, P.L. 102–256, 106 Stat. 73 (1992), which authorizes a damages action against "an individual who, under actual or apparent authority, or color of law, of any foreign nation, subjects an individual to torture" or "to extrajudicial killing"; the Act extends that right of action to American citizens as well as to aliens. See 28 U.S.C. § 1350 note.[7] The Act requires that the claimant have exhausted "adequate and available remedies" in the place of the conduct at issue. Although the Act itself does not confer federal jurisdiction, suits under it may ordinarily be brought in federal court under § 1350.[8]

---

6. In Tel–Oren v. Libyan Arab Republic, 726 F.2d 774 (D.C.Cir.1984), the panel of three judges agreed only that the action should be dismissed. Plaintiffs in that case, primarily Israeli citizens, sued the PLO and others for alleged acts of terrorism committed in Israel. Judge Edwards endorsed the general approach in Filartiga, but found no right of action under § 1350 because the law of nations did not extend to terrorist acts by individuals not acting under color of any recognized state's law. Judge Bork argued that § 1350 did not create a private cause of action, nor did the relevant principles of international law, which "typically does not authorize individuals to vindicate rights by bringing actions in either international or municipal tribunals" (p. 817). Moreover, he urged, the very separation of powers principles that animated Sabbatino counseled against recognition of a cause of action that "would raise substantial problems of judicial interference with * * * the conduct of foreign relations" (p. 804). For Judge Robb, the case was controlled by the political question doctrine, since it involved standards that defied application and touched on sensitive matters of diplomacy historically within the exclusive jurisdiction of the other branches.

For a critical analysis of Filartiga and of the premise that that customary international law is federal common law, see Weisburd, note 4, *supra*.

7. In focusing on individual defendants, the Act does not disturb the holding in Argentine Republic v. Amerada Hess Shipping Corp., 488 U.S. 428 (1989), that Argentina could not be sued under § 1350 for an alleged violation of international law in bombing a private ship on the high seas during the war over the Falkland Islands; the Foreign Sovereign Immunities Act, the Court ruled, is the exclusive basis for federal court jurisdiction over a foreign state. And suits nominally against foreign officials acting in their official capacity will often be deemed to be one against the state, and thus barred by foreign sovereign immunity. See, *e.g.*, Chuidian v. Philippine Nat'l Bank, 912 F.2d 1095, 1099–1103 (9th Cir.1990); see also Fitzpatrick, *The Future of the Alien Tort Claims Act of 1789: Lessons from In re Marcos Human Rights Litigation*, 67 St.John's L.Rev. 491, 503–17 (1993).

For discussion of the distinct common law doctrine that a head-of-state recognized by the executive branch is absolutely immune (absent waiver by statute or by the foreign government) from suit in American courts, see Lafontant v. Aristide, 844 F.Supp. 128 (E.D.N.Y.1994).

8. The Committee Reports state that "claims based on torture or summary executions do not exhaust the list of actions that may appropriately be covered by section 1350. Consequently, that statute should remain intact." See S.Rep.102–249 and H.Rep. 102–367, 102d Congress, 2d.Sess. (1992).

See also Kadic v. Karadzic, 70 F.3d 232 (2d Cir.1995)(interpreting § 1350 to impose liability for certain acts in violation of the law of nations, even when undertaken by private individuals not acting under the authority of a state, and rejecting the argument that the "state action" requirement of Torture Victim Act applies to actions under § 1350).

SECTION 2.   ENFORCING PRIMARY OBLIGATIONS

SUBSECTION A: CIVIL ACTIONS BY THE FEDERAL GOVERNMENT

United States v. San Jacinto Tin Co.

125 U.S. 273, 8 S.Ct. 850, 31 L.Ed. 747 (1888).
Appeal from the Circuit Court for the District of California.

■ MR. JUSTICE MILLER delivered the opinion of the Court.

* * * [This bill in chancery filed in federal circuit court] purports to be brought by the Attorney General on behalf of the United States against [several corporations] * * * alleged to be in possession of a large body of land * * * for which a patent was issued by the United States on the 26th day of October, 1867, to Maria del Rosario Estudillo de Aguirre, and her heirs and assigns. The object of the bill is to set aside this patent, and have it declared void, upon the ground that the land described in the survey, which description is a part of the patent, is not the land granted by the Mexican government to said Maria, nor that which was confirmed to her under the proceedings before the land commission, and by the judgment of the District Court of the United States, and by this court also on appeal. The essential feature of the grievance relied on by the complainant is, that this survey was thus located by fraud to include different and more valuable land than that granted by Mexico, and confirmed by the courts, and on account of this fraud it is prayed that the survey and patent be set aside and annulled. * * *

It is alleged that throughout the whole transaction * * * all the proceedings were dictated by fraud, and all the officers of the government below the Secretary of the Interior who had anything to do with it were parties to that fraud, and to be benefited by it. * * *

        * * *

Another question, however, is raised by counsel for the defendant, which is earnestly insisted upon by them, and which received the serious consideration of the judges in the Circuit Court; namely, the right of the Attorney General of the United States to institute this suit.

The question as presented is one surrounded by some embarrassment. But as it is in some form or other of frequent recurrence recently, and if decided in favor of the appellees will require the dismissal of the case * * *, we feel called upon to give the matter our attention. It is denied that the Attorney General has any general authority under the Constitution and laws of the United States to commence a suit in the name of the United States to set aside a patent, or other solemn instrument issued by proper authority.

It is quite true that the Revised Statutes, in the title which establishes and regulates the Department of Justice, simply declares, in section 346, that "there shall be at the seat of government an Executive Department to be known as the Department of Justice, and an Attorney General, who shall be the head thereof." There is no very specific statement of the general duties of the Attorney General, but it is seen from the whole chapter referred to that he has the authority * * * to supervise the conduct of all suits brought by or against the United States, and to give advice to the President and the heads of the other departments of the government. There is no express authority vested in him to authorize suits to be brought against the debtors of the government, or upon bonds, or to begin criminal prosecutions, or to institute proceedings in any of the numerous cases in which the United States is plaintiff; and yet he is invested with the general superintendence of all such suits, and all the district attorneys who do bring them in the various courts in the country are placed under his immediate direction and control. And notwithstanding the want of any specific authority to bring an action in the name of the United States to set aside and declare void an instrument issued under its apparent authority, we cannot believe that where a case exists in which this ought to be done it is not within the authority of that officer to cause such action to be instituted and prosecuted. * * *

If the United States in any particular case has a just cause for calling upon the judiciary of the country, in any of its courts, for relief by setting aside or annulling any of its contracts, its obligations, or its most solemn instruments, the question of the appeal to the judicial tribunals of the country must primarily be decided by the Attorney General of the United States. That such a power should exist somewhere, and that the United States should not be more helpless in relieving itself from frauds, impostures, and deceptions than the private individual, is hardly open to argument. The Constitution itself declares that the judicial power shall extend to all cases to which the United States shall be a party, and that this means mainly where it is a party plaintiff is a necessary result of the well-established proposition that it cannot be sued in any court without its consent. There must, then, be an officer or officers of the government to determine when the United States shall sue, to decide for what it shall sue, and to be responsible that such suits shall be brought in appropriate cases. The attorneys of the United States in every judicial district are officers of this character, and they are by statute under the immediate supervision and control of the Attorney General. How, then, can it be argued that if the United States has been deceived, entrapped, or defrauded into the making, under the forms of law, of an instrument which injuriously affects its rights of property, or other rights, it cannot bring a suit to avoid the effect of such instrument, thus fraudulently obtained, without a special act of Congress in each case, or without some special authority applicable to this class of cases, while all other just grounds of suing in a court of justice concededly belong to the Department of Justice, and are in use every day? The judiciary act of 1789, in its third section, which first created the office of Attorney General, without any very accurate definition of his powers, in using the words that "there shall also be appointed a meet person, learned in the law, to act as Attorney General for the United States," 1 Stat. 93, c. 21, § 35, must have had reference to the similar office with the same designation existing under the English law. And though it has been said that there is no common law of the United States, it is still quite true that when acts of Congress use words which are familiar in the law of England, they are supposed to be used with reference to their meaning in that law. In all this, however, the Attorney General acts as the head of one of the Executive departments, representing the authority of the President in the class of subjects within the domain of that department, and under his control. * * *

We are not insensible to the enormous power and its capacity for evil thus reposed in that department of the government. Since the title to all of the land in more than half of the States and Territories of the Union depends upon patents from the government of the United States, it is to be seen what a vast power is confided to the officer who may order the institution of suits to set aside every one of these patents; and if the doctrine that the United States in bringing such actions is not controlled by any statute of limitations, or governed by the rule concerning *laches* be sound, of which we express no opinion at present, then the evil which may result would seem to be endless as well as enormous. But it has often been said that the fact that the exercise of power may be abused is no sufficient reason for denying its existence, and if restrictions are to be placed upon the exercise of this authority by the Attorney General, it is for the legislative body which created the office to enact them.

We do not think, therefore, that it can be successfully denied that there exists in the Attorney General, as the head of the Department of Justice, the right to institute, in the name of the United States, a suit to abrogate, annul, or set aside a patent for land which has been issued by the government in a case where such an instrument if permitted to stand would work serious injury to the United States, and prejudice its interests, and where it has been obtained by fraud, imposture, or mistake.

* * *

But we are of opinion that since the right of the government of the United States to institute such a suit depends upon the same general principles which would authorize a private citizen to apply to a court of justice for relief * * *, the government must show that, like the private individual, it has such an interest in the relief sought as entitles it to move in the matter. If it be a question of property a case must be made in which the court can afford a remedy in regard to that property; if it be a question of fraud which would render the instrument void, the fraud must operate to the prejudice of the United States; and if it is apparent that the suit is brought for the benefit of some third party, and that * * * there does not appear any obligation on the part of the United States to the public, or to any individual, or any interest of its own, it can no more sustain such an action than any private person could under similar circumstances.

In all the decisions [supporting our holding] it is either expressed or implied that this interest or duty of the United States must exist as the foundation of the right of action. * * * In the case before us the bill itself leaves a fair implication that if this patent is set aside the title to the property will revert to the United States, together with the beneficial interest in it. It is argued in the brief that this is not true * * *. This view is supported by some pretty strong testimony * * *.

* * *

But we are not so entirely satisfied of the want of interest of the United States in the whole or a part of the land which is covered by this patent as to justify us in saying that the bill in the present case ought to be dismissed on that ground. * * *

[Upon consideration of the merits, the Court affirmed the decree dismissing the bill.]

■ MR. JUSTICE FIELD, concurring: I concur in affirming the decree of the court below dismissing the bill in this case.   * * *

But * * * I cannot assent to the position announced in the opinion of the court, that the Attorney General has unlimited authority by virtue of his office to institute suits to set aside patents issued by the government.   * * * Whenever Congress has felt it important that patents for lands should be revoked, either because of fraud in their issue, or of breach of conditions in them, it has not failed to authorize legal proceedings for that purpose. In a multitude of cases titles to lands, upon which whole communities live, rest upon patents of the United States.   * * * I cannot believe that it is within the power of the Attorney General, to be exercised at any time in the future, this generation or the next—as no statute of limitations runs against the government—to institute suits to unsettle the title founded upon such patents, even where there are allegations of fraud in obtaining them. There must be a time when such allegations will not be heeded.   * * * If, without the authority of Congress, such proceedings may be instituted by him upon the repetition, as in this case, of old charges, or upon the unsupported statements of interested parties, a cloud may at any moment be cast upon the titles of a whole people and there would be in his hands a tremendous weapon of vexation and oppression.   * * *

I do not recognize the doctrine that the Attorney General takes any power by virtue of his office except what the Constitution and the laws confer. The powers of the executive officers of England are not vested in the executive officers of the United States government, simply because they are called by similar names. It is the theory, and I may add, the glory of our institutions, that they are founded upon law, that no one can exercise any authority over the rights and interests of others except pursuant to and in the manner authorized by law.

* * *

* * * [Th]ere is much in the opinion [of the Court] which gives me great satisfaction. [The Court holds that] the government must show, like a private individual, that it has such an interest in the relief sought as entitles it to move in the matter.   * * *

From this ruling some degree of peace and security may come to holders of titles derived by patent from the government.   * * *

NOTE ON THE IMPLICATION OF RIGHTS OF ACTION BY THE UNITED STATES

(1) *Antecedents.* The right of the United States to sue for breach of contract without benefit of statutory authorization was asserted in Dugan v. United States, 16 U.S. (3 Wheat.) 172 (1818), recognized in United States v. Buford, 28 U.S. (3 Pet.) 12, 28 (1830), and reasserted in United States v. Tingey, 30 U.S. (5 Pet.) 115, 127–28 (1831). In Tingey, Justice Story said that the right of the United States "to enter into a contract, or to take a bond, in cases not

previously provided by some law * * * is, in our opinion, an incident to the general right of sovereignty."[1]

The Constitution expressly recognizes the capacity of the United States to own property, and the Court decided early on that the United State may sue to protect its property, despite the lack of special statutory authorization. See Benton v. Woolsey, 37 U.S. (12 Pet.) 27 (1838); United States v. Gear, 44 U.S. (3 How.) 120 (1845). The decision in Cotton v. United States, 52 U.S. (11 How.) 229 (1850), permitting an action in trespass without special statutory authorization, confirmed that the Constitution alone empowers the federal government, in its contractual and proprietary relations, to claim the same protection of general law that legal persons enjoy.[2]

(2) *The Reach of the San Jacinto Decision.* Did the San Jacinto case imply that the United States may bring only those non-statutory actions that are analogous to rights of action of private persons?

(a) In United States v. American Bell Tel. Co., 128 U.S. 315 (1888), the Court upheld the right of the United States to maintain a bill in equity to vacate a patent for an invention as fraudulently obtained. Rejecting the defendant's interpretation of the San Jacinto rationale as limited to cases where the government has a "direct pecuniary interest", the Court explained (pp. 367–68) that it had said in San Jacinto "that the cases in which the instrumentality of the court cannot * * * be used are those where the United States has no pecuniary interest in the remedy sought, and is also under no obligation to the party who will be benefited to sustain an action for his use, and also where it does not appear that any obligation existed on the part of the United States to the public or to any individual. The essence of the right of the United States to interfere in the present case is its obligation to protect the public from the monopoly of the patent which was procured by fraud, and it would be difficult to find language more aptly used to include this in the class of cases which are not excluded from the jurisdiction of the court by want of interest in the government of the United States."

(b) Compare the grounds upon which the Court upheld the interposition of the United States in the Pullman strike of 1894, In re Debs, 158 U.S. 564 (1895). The local United States Attorney, acting at the Attorney General's direction, had sued in federal circuit court to enjoin the strike, alleging a conspiracy forcibly to obstruct the mails and interstate transportation. Relying mainly on the Sherman Act, the circuit court issued an injunction, the subsequent violation of which led to conviction and sentences of imprisonment for contempt. A petition for a writ of habeas corpus in the Supreme Court in turn challenged the circuit court's authority to enter the original decree.

Justice Brewer, speaking for a unanimous Court, upheld the decree without deciding whether the Sherman Act supported the circuit court's jurisdiction. "We prefer to rest our judgment on a broader ground," he said (p. 600), which he summarized this way (p. 599):

---

1. See also United States v. Bradley, 35 U.S. (10 Pet.) 343, 359–60 (1836); United States v. Fitzgerald, 40 U.S. (15 Pet.) 407, 421 (1841); United States v. Hodson, 77 U.S. (10 Wall.) 395, 407–08 (1870).

2. Closely related to the proprietary cases are those in which the United States has established its status as guardian of the Indian tribes and its standing in litigation to vindicate Indian rights. See, *e.g.*, Heckman v. United States, 224 U.S. 413 (1912); United States v. Board of Com'rs of Osage County, 251 U.S. 128 (1919).

"* * * [T]he government of the United States is one having jurisdiction over every foot of soil within its territory, and acting directly upon each citizen; that while it is a government of enumerated powers, it has within the limits of those powers all the attributes of sovereignty; * * * that the powers thus conferred upon the national government are not dormant, but have been assumed and put into practical exercise by the legislation of Congress; that in the exercise of those powers it is competent for the nation to remove all obstructions upon highways, natural or artificial, to the passage of interstate commerce or the carrying of the mail; that while it may be competent for the government (through the executive branch and in the use of the entire executive power of the nation) to forcibly remove all such obstructions, it is equally within its competency to appeal to the civil courts for an inquiry and determination as to the existence and character of the alleged obstructions, and if such are found to exist, or threaten to occur, to invoke the powers of those courts to remove or restrain such obstructions; that the jurisdiction of courts to interfere in such matters by injunction is one recognized from ancient times and by indubitable authority * * *."[3]

(c) In Sanitary Dist. of Chicago v. United States, 266 U.S. 405 (1925), the United States obtained a federal court injunction barring the Sanitary District (an Illinois corporation) from diverting more water from Lake Michigan than the Secretary of War had authorized. The Supreme Court affirmed, with Justice Holmes writing. The opinion rested in part on the government's power to carry out obligations to Britain under a Treaty that "expressly provides against uses 'affecting the natural level or flow of boundary waters' without the authority of the United States or the Dominion of Canada within their respective jurisdictions and the approval of the International Joint Commission agreed upon therein" (p. 426). But the "main ground" for upholding the injunction was "the authority of the United States to remove obstructions to interstate and foreign commerce. There is no question that this power is superior to that of the States to provide for the welfare or necessities of their inhabitants. In matters where the States may act the action of Congress overrides what they have done. * * * But in matters where the national importance is imminent and direct even where Congress has been silent the States may not act at all. Evidence is sufficient, if evidence is necessary, to show that a withdrawal of water on the scale directed by the statute of Illinois threatens and will affect the level of the Lakes, and that is a matter which cannot be done without the consent of the United States, even were there no international covenant in the case" (p. 426).[4]

---

3. For approval of the Debs decision, despite the "unpleasant" political background, see Black, Structure and Relationship in Constitutional Law 24 (1969), contending that the Constitution's authorization of a functioning national government "ought in general to imply the unlawfulness of interference with its performance of those functions." He argues that similar structural reasoning underlay the fashioning, in McCulloch v. Maryland, 17 U.S. (4 Wheat.) 316 (1819), of an implied constitutional immunity from state taxation that threatened operation of the Bank of the United States, and that there is no basis for importing a "state ac-

tion" requirement into arguments of this kind.

Is there any reason to distinguish affirmative rights of action (as in Debs) from defenses (as in McCulloch)? *Cf.* Subsections 2(B–C), *infra*.

4. The Court has relied on the San Jacinto and Sanitary District cases in awarding remedies to the United States (in addition to those provided by statute) for violations of the Rivers and Harbors Act of 1899. United States v. Republic Steel Corp., 362 U.S. 482 (1960); Wyandotte Transp. Co. v. United States, 389 U.S. 191 (1967). Both

(3) *The "Pentagon Papers" Case.* In New York Times Co. v. United States, 403 U.S. 713 (1971), the Attorney General sued on behalf of the United States to enjoin the New York Times (and in a companion case, the Washington Post) from publishing classified material on Vietnam. Before the Supreme Court, the government did not contend (as it had below) that publication would violate the Espionage Act. It argued instead that the constitutional authority of the President in foreign affairs and as Commander-in-Chief entitled the government to enjoin a publication posing a grave and irreparable danger to national security—specifically the conduct of delicate diplomatic negotiations and the prosecution of the Vietnam War. The Times did not dispute the "standing" of the government "to come into a Federal Court to protect its functional interest in the integrity of an established rule of law, whether it is established by statute or by the Constitution" (Brief for Petitioner, p. 37). It contended that publication was not forbidden by an Act of Congress; that neither the President nor the Court was empowered to fashion a rule of law forbidding publication; and that the publication was protected by the First Amendment, since nothing in the documents presented the grave and immediate danger that alone might justify a prior restraint.

In a brief *per curiam* the Court held only that the government had failed to meet the "heavy burden" under the First Amendment "of showing justification for the imposition of" a prior restraint. Justice Black noted and Justice Stewart emphasized that the government did not rely on any Act of Congress. Justices Douglas and Marshall concluded that the relevant penal statutes did not forbid publication and attributed importance to the fact that Congress had not authorized injunctive relief and had, indeed, rejected proposals to authorize the President to prohibit publication of "information relating to the national defense which, in his judgment, * * * might be useful to the enemy." Justice White accorded significance to the latter fact, though he stated that the publication might violate the penal statutes. Chief Justice Burger and Justices Harlan and Blackmun dissented, favoring a remand for further hearing. Among the questions that Justice Harlan thought "should have been faced" was whether "the Attorney General is authorized to bring these suits in the name of the United States" (403 U.S. at 753–54).

Did the New York Times concede unnecessarily, or too broadly, that the United States had "standing"? If the government could have made a stronger showing of the dangers threatened by publication, might an injunction have been proper?

(4) *Protection of "Private" Rights.* Congress has in a number of instances authorized the Attorney General to institute civil actions by the United States to redress deprivations of the rights of private individuals.[5] But does the government have inherent authority to sue to protect the rights of citizens even when Congress has not specifically authorized such action? The Debs opinion declared that "it is not the province of the Government to interfere in any mere matter of private controversy between individuals," as distinguished from

---

cases presented unusual circumstances that were difficult to anticipate in framing statutory remedies.

5. See, *e.g.*, 42 U.S.C. §§ 1973(d)(voting rights), 1973bb (voting rights), 1997c (rights of institutionalized persons), 2000a–5 (segregation and discrimination in public schools,

facilities and places of public accommodation), 12188(b)(rights of individuals with disabilities). For decisions rejecting challenges to the power of Congress to confer such authority, see, *e.g.*, United States v. Raines, 362 U.S. 17, 27 (1960); United Steelworkers v. United States, 361 U.S. 39, 43, 60–61 (1959).

"wrongs * * * such as affect the public at large * * * and concerning which the Nation owes the duty to all the citizens of securing to them their common rights * * *" (158 U.S. at 586).

Suppose the government sues to challenge allegedly unconstitutional practices of a city police department on behalf of victimized citizens, as in United States v. City of Philadelphia, 644 F.2d 187 (3d Cir.1980). Are those "wrongs * * * such as affect the public at large"? Does the defendant have a good objection that the government lacks standing to assert the rights of third parties?

These questions have arisen in a number of cases. In the Philadelphia decision and several others, federal courts refused to permit such extra-statutory actions[6]—although some authority looks the other way.[7] See generally Note, 61 B.U.L.Rev. 1159 (1981); Note, 89 Yale L.J. 118 (1979).

Compare the material on a state's standing to sue as *parens patriae* on behalf of its citizens, Chap. III, Sec. 1, pp. 316–22, *supra.*

(5) *United States as Statutory Beneficiary.* Do the foregoing cases shed light on the extent to which the United States should be able to sue under regulatory statutes that confer rights of action generally in favor of "any person"?

In United States v. Cooper Corp., 312 U.S. 600 (1941), the Court held that the United States, as a purchaser of goods, could not maintain an action under § 7 of the Sherman Act, which authorizes suit for treble damages by "any person who shall be injured in his person or property" by a violation of the Act. Without referring to any preexisting legal policy or principle, the majority determined that the "natural and ordinary sense" of the text "makes against the extension of the term 'person' to include the United States" (p. 614). The opinion also pointed out that the term "person" in other parts of the statute could not include the United States; stressed the negative implied by the express establishment of a public right of action for an injunction and of criminal sanctions; found support in the legislative history and the provisions of other statutes; and put special weight on the failure of Attorneys General for fifty years to assert the right of action. Three dissenting Justices invoked the general rule that the government may seek all legal remedies that others

6. In addition to the Philadelphia decision, see, *e.g.*, United States v. Mattson, 600 F.2d 1295 (9th Cir.1979) and United States v. Solomon, 563 F.2d 1121, 1129 (4th Cir. 1977)(both holding, prior to enactment of 42 U.S.C. § 1997, note 5, *supra*, that the U.S. may not sue to protect the constitutional rights of the mentally retarded in state hospitals). See also United States v. Yonkers Bd. of Educ., 624 F.Supp. 1276, 1522–23 (S.D.N.Y.1985)(suggesting in dictum that the U.S. could not sue to protect 14th amendment rights to a desegregated education absent statutory authorization—which had, however, been provided), *aff'd on other grounds*, 837 F.2d 1181 (2d Cir.1987).

7. See, *e.g.*, United States v. Brand Jewelers, Inc., 318 F.Supp. 1293 (S.D.N.Y. 1970)(U.S. may seek to enjoin widespread use of "sewer process"—false returns and affida-

vits—because of the burden on interstate commerce and the government's authority to correct widespread deprivations of property without due process); United States v. Brittain, 319 F.Supp. 1058 (N.D.Ala.1970)(U.S. may seek to enjoin state miscegenation law that had been invoked against military personnel); United States v. Marchetti, 466 F.2d 1309 (4th Cir.1972)(U.S. may seek to enjoin publication that would allegedly endanger national security). *Cf.* Halderman v. Pennhurst State School & Hospital, 612 F.2d 84, 90–92 (3d Cir.1979)(en banc)(expressing disagreement with the Solomon decision, note 6, *supra*, but ruling only that the United States may intervene in an already pending action challenging the conditions in a state mental hospital), *rev'd on other grounds*, 451 U.S. 1 (1981).

may seek, "both at common law and under statutes, unless there is something in a statute or in its history to indicate an intent to deprive the United States of that right" (p. 620).

In the light of San Jacinto and the other cases discussed in this Note, does the "natural and ordinary sense" of the term "person", when used in relation to proprietary rights of action, exclude the United States? Is it significant that when Congress in 1955 amended the antitrust laws to authorize a damage action by the government (15 U.S.C. § 15(a)), it confined the remedy to actual rather than treble damages?

(6) *Special Rules Favoring the Government.* In some instances, the United States comes into court not simply on a par with private litigants but with a number of advantages, court-made as well as statutory. For example, the United States is not bound by statutes of limitations (or by laches) unless a statute expressly so provides. See United States v. Summerlin, 310 U.S. 414, 416 (1940). (In 1966, Congress enacted a general statute of limitations, 28 U.S.C. §§ 2415–16, applicable to most actions brought by the United States or by a federal officer or agency.) Another judge-made rule excepts the United States, in actions to rescind land grants alleged to have been obtained by fraud, from the usual principle that a suitor "who seeks equity must do equity"; the government in such cases need not offer to return the consideration it had received. Causey v. United States, 240 U.S. 399, 402 (1916). See Note, 55 Colum.L.Rev. 1177 (1955). Nor does the doctrine of equitable estoppel apply against the government as it does against private litigants. See Office of Personnel Mgmt. v. Richmond, 496 U.S. 414 (1990).

An even broader principle was suggested in Chief Justice Vinson's opinion in United States v. United Mine Workers, 330 U.S. 258, 272 (1947)—an "old and well-known rule that statutes which in general terms divest pre-existing rights or privileges will not be applied to the sovereign without express words to that effect." The five cases cited in support of this rule, however, did not lend it unqualified support.[8]

The Mine Workers case itself involved the question whether the general language of the Norris–LaGuardia Act, limiting the jurisdiction of the district courts to grant injunctions in labor disputes, applied to a suit to enjoin a strike, brought by the government in its capacity as an employer after it had seized the coal mines under the War Disputes Act. The entire Court agreed that the Norris–LaGuardia Act would have applied were the government suing only as sovereign, in view of the many indications that the Act was designed to prevent injunctions like that granted in In re Debs, Paragraph (2)(b), *supra.* But Chief Justice Vinson asserted (over the vigorous dissent of four Justices) that

---

8. Two, relying on part on the English rule that bankruptcy proceedings do not discharge debts due to the Crown, had held that the United States was not bound by the Bankruptcy Act of 1867. United States v. Herron, 87 U.S. (20 Wall.) 251, 263 (1873); Lewis v. United States, 92 U.S. 618, 622 (1875). These decisions had been overridden in result, if not in reasoning, by decisions under the Bankruptcy Act of 1898. See Guarantee Title & Trust Co. v. Title Guaranty & Surety Co., 224 U.S. 152, 155–60 (1912).

The other three decisions simply refused to find a repeal by implication of a remedy previously available to the United States. None involved general language that, if held to include the United States as a legal person, would have directly barred the old remedy. Dollar Savings Bank v. United States, 86 U.S. (19 Wall.) 227, 238–40 (1873); United States v. American Bell Tel. Co., 159 U.S. 548, 553–55 (1895); United States v. Stevenson, 215 U.S. 190, 197 (1909).

Congress "did not intend that the Act should apply to situations in which the United States appears as an employer" (p. 276).

———

SUBSECTION B: PRIVATE CIVIL ACTIONS

———

NOTE ON STATUTES OF LIMITATIONS AND OTHER QUASI–PROCEDURAL RULES IN LITIGATION INVOLVING FEDERAL RIGHTS

(1) *Introduction.*   Federal statutory causes of action are often incomplete. Congress may neglect to specify a limitations period, the remedies that should be available, whether the action survives the plaintiff's death, and a range of other issues.   This Note discusses how courts should resolve issues such as these in the face of congressional silence, and focuses heavily, though not exclusively, on the many decisions involving limitations periods.

(2) *The Problem of Limitations Periods.*   Until 1990, Congress never saw fit to enact a general statute of limitations applicable to federal civil actions not governed by a specific limitations period.   Moreover, it frequently neglected to provide a limitations period when creating a particular cause of action.

In response to a recommendation of the Federal Courts Study Committee, Congress in 1990 added a new § 1658 to Title 28, providing a general four-year statute of limitations (in the absence of a specific limitations period) for all civil actions "arising under an Act of Congress enacted after the date of enactment of this section."

Because section 1658 applies only to subsequently enacted statutes, it leaves unaddressed the question of what statute of limitation should govern civil actions brought under the manifold federal statutes previously on the books that do not themselves specify any limitations period.[1]   In dealing with such a situation, a court can (a) borrow a limitations period from state law; (b) borrow a limitations period from a different federal statute; (c) itself decide how long the limitations period should be; or (d) provide that there is no limitations period whatever.

The last two options have been almost universally rejected.[2]   Should they have been?

(3) *The Presumption that State Law is Borrowed.*   The great majority of cases have borrowed an analogous limitation period from state law.   A good example is Johnson v. Railway Express Agency, Inc., 421 U.S. 454 (1975), which followed that approach despite forceful arguments that doing so disserved federal policy.

---

1.   What if an amendment to an existing statute creates a new federal cause of action (or significantly expands an existing one) but contains no specific limitations period?   Will the new four-year period apply?

For general discussion of § 1658, see Nelson, *The 1990 Federal "Fallback" Statute of Limitations: Limitations by Default*, 72 Neb.L.Rev. 454, 502–13 (1993); Norwood, *28 U.S.C. § 1658: A Limitations Period with Real Limitations*, 69 Ind.L.J. 477, 508–13 (1994).

2.   But *cf.* Occidental Life Ins. Co. v. EEOC, 432 U.S. 355, 367 (1977), note 6, *infra.*

Johnson had filed an employment discrimination charge, under Title VII of the Civil Rights Act of 1964, with the federal Equal Employment Opportunity Commission. Title VII requires pursuit of such administrative remedies before suit can be filed in court. Several years later, the EEOC told him that there was reasonable cause to believe his charges, and that he had thirty days to bring a Title VII action in court. He did so, and joined with his Title VII claim a discrimination claim (based on the same factual allegations) under 42 U.S.C. § 1981, a Reconstruction-era civil rights statute.[3] The § 1981 claim was not superseded by Title VII, and can be filed immediately in court without first pursuing administrative remedies.

The Title VII claim was clearly timely under the provisions of that statute. The timeliness of the § 1981 claim, however, was in dispute, as that statute contains no limitations period. The Supreme Court (per Blackmun, J.) cited numerous decisions for the proposition that "[s]ince there is no specifically stated or otherwise relevant federal statute of limitations for a cause of action under § 1981, the controlling period would ordinarily be the most appropriate one provided by state law"—which in this case was one year (p. 462). Under state limitations law, that period would not be tolled by the filing of the Title VII charge with the EEOC, and the Court refused to depart from the state's tolling rules. "In virtually all statutes of limitations the chronological length of the limitation period is interrelated with provisions regarding tolling, revival, and questions of application" (p. 464). Hence, Johnson's § 1981 claim was time-barred.

The Court conceded that that result might press employees who valued their § 1981 claims to take them to court before the EEOC had completed its work under Title VII, but concluded that any such pressure resulted from Congress' decision to retain § 1981 as a remedy "separate from and independent of the more elaborate and time-consuming procedures of Title VII. * * * [In] a very real sense, petitioner has slept on his § 1981 rights" (p. 466).

In dissent Justice Marshall, joined by Justices Douglas and Brennan, argued that tolling the limitations period under these circumstances would not frustrate any of the state's purposes in enacting the statute of limitations, as the EEOC charge had placed the defendant on notice of the substance of the discrimination claim. The Court's refusal to toll, he objected, would require litigants like Johnson to bring § 1981 suits within one year, even if the EEOC's efforts to secure voluntary compliance were not yet complete. That result would undercut the federal policy, embodied in Title VII, of seeking to "avoid unnecessary and costly litigation by making the informal investigatory and conciliatory offices of EEOC readily available to victims of unlawful discrimination" (p. 473). The Court's decision, he concluded, imposed on a complainant "the draconian choice of losing the benefits of [EEOC] conciliation or giving up the right to sue" (p. 476).

(4) *The Scope of Borrowing of State Limitations Periods: Incidental Questions.* Johnson's holding—that state law ordinarily supplies not only the time period but also the rules on closely-related matters like tolling or revival—was

---

3. This section provides, *inter alia*, that all persons within the jurisdiction of the United States "shall have the same right * * * to make and enforce contracts * * * and to the full and equal benefits of all laws and proceedings for the security of persons and property as is enjoyed by white citizens * * *." Under § 1981 plaintiffs may recover compensatory and punitive damages; monetary relief under Title VII, as it then stood, was limited to back pay.

reaffirmed in Board of Regents v. Tomanio, 446 U.S. 478 (1980). There the Court, relying both on Johnson and on 42 U.S.C. § 1988,[4] held that in a federal court action under 42 U.S.C. § 1983 alleging violations of federal constitutional rights, the court must adopt not only the state's statute of limitations but also its tolling rules—which on the facts of Tomanio would not suspend the running of the statute during the pendency of a prior state court proceeding involving the same occurrences. The Court found no inconsistency between the state rule and federal policy.[5]

Sometimes application of state tolling rules can help plaintiffs who are asserting federal claims. See Hardin v. Straub, 490 U.S. 536 (1989), unanimously ruling that a federal court applying a state statute of limitations to an inmate's § 1983 action should also apply a state provision tolling the limitations period, in suits by a person under a legal disability, until one year after the disability has been removed.

(5) *Which State Statute of Limitations?* When federal courts decide to borrow a state limitations period, they frequently encounter difficulty in deciding *which* statute to select—or, as Judge Posner put it, "which round peg to stuff

---

4. Section 1988 provides, in part, that in certain civil rights actions where the laws of the United States are not "adapted to the object, or are deficient in the provisions necessary to furnish suitable remedies * * *, the common law, as modified and changed by the constitution and statutes of the [forum] state * * *, so far as the same is not inconsistent with [federal law] * * *, shall be extended to and govern the said [federal] courts in the trial and disposition of the cause * * *." The Court in Tomanio held that since § 1983 is "deficient" in not including a federal statute of limitations, § 1988 requires resort to the state law of limitations unless it is inconsistent with federal law. The Court's method of analysis under § 1988 did not diverge significantly, however, from its approach in Johnson, where the matter was deemed to be a problem for judge-made law.

Professor Eisenberg argues that § 1988 has been widely misunderstood and that, properly viewed, it applies only to state-created causes of action removed from state to federal court under the civil rights removal provision (28 U.S.C. § 1443). Eisenberg, *State Law in Federal Civil Rights Cases: The Proper Scope of Section 1988,* 128 U.Pa. L.Rev. 499 (1980). Compare Kreimer, *The Source of Law in Civil Rights Actions: Some Old Light on Section 1988,* 133 U.Pa.L.Rev. 601 (1985)(arguing *inter alia* that § 1988 expressly provides for development of *federal* common law except where modified by state enactments not inconsistent with federal legislation).

5. Consider the approach to state tolling rules in Holmberg v. Armbrecht, 327 U.S.

392 (1946). A bill in equity was filed in federal court in New York by the creditors of a failed bank, seeking to recover from the banks' shareholders the par value of their stock—a liability imposed under a federal statute. The court of appeals dismissed the suit as time-barred under New York's ten-year statute of limitations. The Supreme Court unanimously reversed. The Court noted that in actions at law "it is federal policy to adopt the local law of limitation" (p. 395). But the present case involved a federal right "for which the sole remedy is in equity", where laches rather than a statute of limitations traditionally controls (pp. 395–96). Moreover, while a plaintiff's lack of due diligence may ordinarily preclude equitable relief, traditionally "fraudulent conduct on the part of the defendant may have prevented the plaintiff from being diligent and may make it unfair to bar appeal to equity because of mere lapse of time" (p. 396). That equitable doctrine would have been read into a federal limitations period had Congress prescribed one; it would be incongruous not to read it also into the state limitations period being borrowed.

Although the dissent in the Johnson case relied upon Holmberg, the majority opinions in Johnson and Tomanio discussed neither the Holmberg decision nor whether the plaintiffs' claims were legal or equitable in character. Is Holmberg, then, still good law? See Marcus, *Fraudulent Concealment in Federal Court: Toward a More Disparate Standard?,* 71 Geo.L.J. 829 (1983).

in a square hole." Short v. Belleville Shoe Mfg. Co., 908 F.2d 1385, 1393 (7th Cir.1990)(concurring opinion). In International Union, UAW v. Hoosier Cardinal Corp., 383 U.S. 696 (1966)—a suit under § 301 of the Taft–Hartley Act for violation of a collective bargaining agreement—the Court decided that (a) Indiana would apply its six-year statute governing contracts not in writing, and (b) this choice was acceptable as a matter of federal law. "[T]here is no reason to reject the characterization that state law would impose unless that characterization is unreasonable or otherwise inconsistent with national labor policy" (p. 706). The Court added (p. 707 n. 9): "Other questions would be raised if this case presented a state law characterization of a § 301 suit that reasonably described the nature of the cause of action, but required application of an unusually short or long limitations period."

Later decisions concerning the choice among a state's various statutes of limitations have centered on claims under federal civil rights statutes, especially 42 U.S.C. §§ 1981 and 1983—the statutes involved in Johnson and Tomanio. Vexing problems were presented because § 1983, in particular, comprehends a wide variety of different claims—from discrimination in public employment to illegal arrests or searches to violations of freedom of speech or religion—many of which lack precise analogues in state law. If a plaintiff alleges that the police unconstitutionally arrested and beat him, should the court adopt the state statute governing actions for false arrest? For battery? For suits against public officials? For violation of state civil rights laws? For personal injuries generally?

Wilson v. Garcia, 471 U.S. 261 (1985), involved just such allegations. Noting a broad range of approaches followed in the lower courts, the Supreme Court held that (1) as a matter of federal law, "a simple, broad characterization of all § 1983 claims best fits the statute's remedial purpose", and (2) such claims are "best characterized as personal injury actions" for purposes of selecting the applicable statute of limitations (pp. 272, 280). Justice O'Connor, the sole dissenter, argued that the Court's effort to legislate uniformity was inconsistent with a century of precedent and was at odds with the longstanding obligation under § 1983 (and § 1988, see note 4, *supra*) to "identify and apply the statute of limitations of the state claim most closely analogous to the *particular* § 1983 claim" (p. 280)(emphasis added).

What happens when, as is often true, a state has different limitations periods for different kinds of personal injury actions? In Owens v. Okure, 488 U.S. 235 (1989), a § 1983 suit involving allegations against law enforcement officials similar to those in Wilson, the Supreme Court again opted for an approach stressing ease of application. Passing over the state's one-year statute of limitations applicable to actions alleging assault, battery, false imprisonment and several other intentional torts, the Court ruled broadly that in § 1983 actions the court should borrow the state's general or residual statute for personal injury actions.

(6) *Borrowing Federal Statutes.* Two arguments are commonly made (but not often found persuasive) for overcoming the presumption in favor of state law and instead fashioning a federal rule of decision.

The first is the assertion that state limitations law conflicts with federal policy. The Johnson decision, Paragraph (3), *supra*, turned aside an argument of this sort—that Tennessee law, in refusing to toll the limitations period, undercut Title VII's policy of voluntary compliance.

The second objection stresses the injustice and complexity of subjecting plaintiffs in different states to different rules governing limitations periods. In Hoosier Cardinal Corp., Paragraph (5), *supra*, the majority acknowledged the difficulty of applying state law but held that course preferable to "the drastic sort of judicial legislation that is urged upon us" (p. 703).

A handful of Supreme Court decisions, however, have applied a limitations period drawn from federal rather than state law sources.[6]

(a) McAllister v. Magnolia Petroleum Co., 357 U.S. 221 (1958), was a *state court* action for negligence under the Jones Act and for unseaworthiness (under judge-made federal admiralty doctrine). The state supreme court held the unseaworthiness claim barred by Texas' two-year statute for personal injury cases. The Supreme Court reversed, holding that "where an action of unseaworthiness is combined with an action under the Jones Act a [state or federal] court cannot apply to the former a shorter period of limitations than Congress has prescribed for the latter. * * * Since the seaman must sue for both unseaworthiness and Jones Act negligence in order to make full utilization of his remedies for personal injury, and since that can be accomplished only in a single proceeding, a time limitation on the unseaworthiness claim effects in substance a similar limitation on the right of action under the Jones Act" (pp. 224–25).

(b) In DelCostello v. International Bhd. of Teamsters, 462 U.S. 151 (1983), the Court held that the six-month limitations period in the National Labor Relations Act for filing unfair labor practice charges to the NLRB should be applied in an employee's "hybrid action"—against his employer for breach of the collective bargaining agreement and against his union for breach of the duty of fair representation. Such an action, the Court reasoned, had no close parallel in state law; the analogies that had been suggested raised problems of "legal substance" (because they were generally only 90 days) and "practical application" (p. 165). In dissent, Justice O'Connor said: "I do not think that federal law implicitly rejects the practice of borrowing state periods of limitation in this situation" (pp. 174–75 n. 1).[7]

(c) The rationale of DelCostello was extended in Agency Holding Corp. v. Malley–Duff & Associates, Inc., 483 U.S. 143 (1987). This case involved a civil

6. In addition to the cases discussed in text, see Occidental Life Ins. Co. v. EEOC, 432 U.S. 355 (1977)(EEOC enforcement actions under Title VII are not subject to state limitations periods; courts have discretion, however, to deny retrospective relief if there is inordinate delay in filing an action); Oscar Mayer & Co. v. Evans, 441 U.S. 750 (1979)(the Age Discrimination in Employment Act, though it requires resort to certain state proceedings before bringing federal court action, does not require the state proceeding to be timely under state law); County of Oneida v. Oneida Indian Nation, 470 U.S. 226 (1985)(borrowing of state limitations period would be inconsistent with federal policy in the context of Indian claims). But *cf.* South Carolina v. Catawba Indian Tribe, Inc., 476 U.S. 498 (1986)(applying state limitations period to action seeking possession of former tribal lands).

7. In a separate dissent, Justice Stevens relied heavily on the Rules of Decision Act, 28 U.S.C. § 1652, which, he argued, called for application of state law. For the majority's response, see p. 755, *supra*.

While the NLRA's limitation period requires that the charge be both filed *and* served within the six-month period, in West v. Conrail, 481 U.S. 35 (1987), Chap. VI, Sec. 3, p. 730 n. 7, *supra*, the Court held that hybrid actions in federal court are governed by Fed.R.Civ.Proc. 3 and 4, which require only that the complaint be filed to commence an action. "The governing principle," the Court explained, "is that we borrow only what is necessary to fill the gap left by Congress" (p. 40 n. 6).

suit under the Racketeer Influenced and Corrupt Organizations Act (RICO). Because RICO encompasses a broad range of conduct—racketeering activity includes nine state felonies and over 25 federal crimes—the Court found that a uniform statute was needed to avoid "intolerable 'uncertainty and time-consuming litigation'" (p. 150, quoting Wilson v. Garcia, Paragraph (5), *supra*). The Court also observed that a uniform federal limitations period would avoid the possibility that, as in DelCostello, the applicable state statute might be so short as to thwart federal purposes. The Court proceeded to select a uniform statute from elsewhere in federal law—specifically, the four-year limitations period of the Clayton Anti–Trust Act. RICO's civil enforcement provisions—with private attorneys general authorized to recover treble damages and attorney's fees—were patterned after those in the Clayton Act. Moreover, satisfactory state analogues were lacking, and because "RICO cases commonly involve interstate transactions", "the use of state statutes would present the danger of forum shopping" and guarantee complex litigation about which state's law applies (p. 154).

Justice Scalia, concurring in the judgment, argued that early decisions suggested that state limitations statutes applied of their own force unless preempted by federal law; the later treatment of congressional silence as an affirmative directive to "borrow" state law was an analytical error. This error, he urged, was now compounded by the Court's willingness to depart from the practice of borrowing state statutes and to "prowl[] hungrily through the Statutes at Large for an appetizing federal limitations period" (p. 166). He concluded that "if [as in the case at hand] we determine that the state limitations period that would apply under state law is pre-empted because it is inconsistent with the federal statute, that is the end of the matter, and there is no limitation on the federal cause of action" (pp. 163–64).

See also Lampf, Pleva, Lipkind, Prupis & Petigrow v. Gilbertson, 501 U.S. 350 (1991), where, in an action under one provision of the Securities Exchange Act of 1934, the Court borrowed a statute of limitations from another section of the same Act.[8]

(7) *The State of the Doctrine.* Decisions like DelCostello, Agency Holding, and Lampf Pleva appeared to represent a growing willingness to borrow a federal limitations period—even though the opinion in each case recited the proposition that borrowing state law remains the norm. In the Court's most recent decision, North Star Steel Co. v. Thomas, 115 S.Ct. 1927 (1995), that proposition was repeated more emphatically—and followed, without dissent.

---

8. The suit was a private civil action alleging a violation of § 10(b) of the Act and of SEC Rule 10b–5. Section 10(b) does not expressly confer a private civil remedy (and hence contains no limitations period), but the Supreme Court had previously recognized an implied right of action. See p. 841, *infra*. However, other provisions of the 1934 Act (and amendments thereto) that do expressly provide a private right of action contain limitations periods. The Court ruled that "where, as here, the claim asserted is one implied under a statute that also contains an express cause of action with its own time limitation, a court should look first to the statute of origin to ascertain the proper limitations period" (p. 359). Only two Justices dissented from the decision not to look to state law, but the remaining Justices divided 5–2 on the appropriate period under federal law. (And the two dissenters on that issue also disagreed with the majority's decision to apply the new limitations period to the case at bar. See generally Chap. II, Sec. 1, pp. 84–88, *supra*).

For discussion of the congressional response to this decision, and the Court's treat-

The suit was brought under the Worker Adjustment and Retraining Notification Act (WARN), 29 U.S.C. §§ 2101 *et seq.*, which requires covered employers to give employees 60 days notice of a plant closing or mass layoff; employees denied such notice may obtain back pay for each day of violation, up to a maximum of 60 days. WARN contains no limitations period, and the Court (per Souter, J.) ruled that state law should be followed. Borrowing from federal law, he said, "is the exception, and we decline to follow a state limitations period 'only when a rule from elsewhere in federal law clearly provides a closer analogy than available state statutes, and when the federal policies at stake and the practicalities of litigation make that rule a significantly more appropriate vehicle for interstitial lawmaking' " (p. 1931, quoting Reed v. United Transp. Union, 488 U.S. 319, 324 (1989)(internal quotation omitted)).[9] There was no need, he added, to decide which of four possibly analogous state limitations periods—ranging from two to six years—was most appropriate, as suit was timely under any of them, and none posed a conflict with federal purposes.

The Court rejected the argument that it should select the six-month limitations period of the National Labor Relations Act in order to avoid the risk of forum shopping. Acknowledging that in the Agency Holding decision, the "practicalities of litigation" had influenced the choice of a federal analogue for RICO actions, the Court noted that the reasons favoring that approach—that RICO violations are commonly interstate and can be based on a broad range of predicate acts—were not present in the instant case.[10]

(8) *Other Quasi–Procedural Rules.* Apart from statutes of limitations and their incidents, to what extent do other state "procedural" and "quasi-procedural" rules play a role in federal question litigation? The decisions on this question are concentrated in federal civil rights cases.[11]

ment of that response, see Chap. II, Sec. II, p. 106, *supra.*

9. In the Reed case—an employee's suit against his union alleging violation of free speech rights protected by the federal Labor–Management Reporting and Disclosure Act—the Court upheld, 8–1, the application of the state's three-year limitations period for personal injury suits. The Court ruled that DelCostello's adoption of the NLRA's six-month federal statute of limitations for filing an unfair labor practice claim was distinguishable: unlike this case, DelCostello directly implicated the concern with prompt resolution of disputes relating to collective bargaining. By contrast, a six-month period was inappropriate here, given the special national interest in the free speech claim at issue—a claim analogous to a federal civil rights action under 42 U.S.C. § 1983, which is governed by state limitations periods (see Paragraph (5), *supra*).

10. Justice Scalia, concurring in the judgment, reiterated the view he had expressed in his separate opinion in Agency Holding, *supra*, that the Court should apply state law unless doing so would frustrate federal purposes—in which case state law

was preempted, leaving no limitations period in place. He agreed with the Court's conclusion that in this case none of the potentially applicable state limitations periods would frustrate purposes.

11. Such issues have also arisen in stockholders' derivative actions brought to enforce a federal right. The Court has taken the view that federal common law governs when suit can be maintained, but that as to questions affecting the allocation of governing power within the corporation, state law will presumptively be borrowed, so as not to upset the balance that each state has struck. Only if there is a conflict with federal policy—which the Court has generally found not to exist—would a federal rule of decision be adopted. See Kamen v. Kemper Fin. Services, Inc., 500 U.S. 90 (1991)(in derivative action against financial adviser of a mutual fund for an alleged violation of the Investment Company Act, state law governs whether plaintiff must make a pre-complaint demand on the fund's Board of Directors to take action against the adviser); Burks v. Lasker, 441 U.S. 471 (1979)(state law governs whether independent directors may ter-

(a) *Survival of § 1983 Actions.* Robertson v. Wegmann, 436 U.S. 584 (1978), raised a difficult issue: what law governs whether an action under 42 U.S.C. § 1983 against state officials survives if the plaintiff dies during the action and the executor of the estate is substituted as plaintiff? The Court, per Justice Marshall, held that 42 U.S.C. § 1988 required application of Louisiana law, which permits survival of this type of action only if (as was not true here) the decedent is survived by spouse, children, parents, or siblings.[12] The Court found no inconsistency between § 1983's policies and Louisiana's limitation on survival: the compensatory goals of the federal statute are unaffected by the Louisiana rule (since the victim is deceased), and its deterrent policies are adequately safeguarded—at least where there is no allegation that the defendants' illegal acts caused the plaintiff's death—because most Louisiana actions do survive.

Justice Blackmun, joined by Justices Brennan and White, dissented, arguing for a uniform federal rule assuring survival: it would better serve the purposes of the federal act, and was supported by the many cases holding that federal law governs the question whether a state official in a § 1983 action is immune from damages liability, see generally Chap. IX, Sec. 3, *infra.* Is that analogy persuasive?

(b) *Survival of "Bivens" Actions.* The Court declined to follow Robertson in Carlson v. Green, 446 U.S. 14 (1980), p. 869, *infra,* a federal civil rights action alleging that defendant federal officials violated the Eighth Amendment by imposing cruel and unusual punishment on (and thereby causing the death of) a federal prisoner. Because § 1983 is limited to action "under color of *state* law", suit was based on the judge-made right of action against federal officials who violate one's constitutional rights, as recognized in Bivens v. Six Unknown Named Agents of Fed. Bur. of Narcotics, 403 U.S. 388 (1971). See generally Sec. 3, *infra.* In Carlson, the Court fashioned a federal common-law rule that a Bivens-type action survives. Robertson was distinguished on several grounds: (a) § 1988, with its reference to state law, does not apply to Bivens actions; (b) the liability of *federal* officials should be uniform; (c) here the death itself was allegedly caused by the defendants' violations, so effective deterrence requires survival; and (d) the power to transfer prisoners among federal facilities would invite manipulation of state survival laws.

(c) *Damages in § 1983 Actions.* In Carey v. Piphus, 435 U.S. 247 (1978), the Court fashioned a federal rule with respect to the measure of damages in a § 1983 action alleging that state officials deprived the plaintiffs of procedural rights in violation of the Due Process Clause. The Court did not examine analogous state law.[13] Is the case distinguishable from Robertson?

(d) *Notice of Claim Requirements in § 1983 Suits.* In Felder v. Casey, 487 U.S. 131 (1988), Chap. IV, Sec. 3, p. 487, *supra,* the Supreme Court held that a state notice-of-claim provision—which required written notice, within 120 days of the injury, of any claim against state or local governments or their officials

---

minate a non-frivolous derivative action brought under the same act and under the Investment Adviser Act of 1940).

12. For criticism of the Court's reliance on § 1988, see Eisenberg, note 4, *supra.*

13. See also Smith v. Wade, 461 U.S. 30 (1983), holding, as a matter of federal law,

that punitive damages are available in a § 1983 action when the defendant's conduct involves reckless or callous indifference to the plaintiff's federally protected rights. The dissenters did not question that federal law controlled.

as a condition of bringing suit—was preempted as applied to a *state court* § 1983 action. The absence of such a provision in § 1983, the Court ruled, is not a "deficiency" under § 1988 that should be remedied by borrowing state law; unlike statutes of limitations, notice-of-claim provisions are neither universally familiar nor indispensable.[14]

(e) *Release-Dismissal Agreements in § 1983 Suits.* In Town of Newton v. Rumery, 480 U.S. 386 (1987), plaintiff signed an agreement (while advised by counsel) releasing any claims he might have arising from his arrest in exchange for the town's promise not to prosecute. He later filed a § 1983 action challenging the arrest as unconstitutional, and argued that the agreement was unenforceable. The Court ruled, 5–4, that federal law controlled the question of enforceability. Emphasizing generally the value of such agreements in protecting public agencies and officials from insubstantial but potentially expensive litigation, the Court rejected a per se rule barring release-dismissal agreements, and found the particular agreement to be enforceable. Justice Stevens' dissent (joined by Justices Brennan, Marshall, and Blackmun) argued that federal policies demanded a strong presumption, not overcome in this case, against enforcement of such agreements.

Were the majority and dissent right to assume that state law has no bearing on the question of enforceability? See Solimine, *Enforcement and Interpretation of Settlements of Federal Civil Rights Actions*, 19 Rutgers L.J. 295 (1988); compare Dice v. Akron, Chap. IV, Sec. 3, p. 479, *supra*. Would application of a state law rule rendering release-dismissal agreements void— which would facilitate rather than restrict recovery under § 1983—interfere with any federal policy? If not, why shouldn't that rule be given effect? On the other hand, whether a state rule holding such agreements valid should be followed depends on the value and risks of those agreements, considerations that the majority and dissent assessed quite differently. For powerful criticism of the majority's position, see Kreimer, *Releases, Redress, and Police Misconduct: Reflections on Agreements to Waive Civil Rights Actions in Exchange for Dismissal of Criminal Charges*, 136 U.Pa.L.Rev. 851 (1988).

(9) *Which State's Law?* When state law is borrowed to fill a gap in a federal cause of action, or when state law rights are enforced by federal courts in the context of federal regulatory purposes (as in bankruptcy), does the Klaxon rule, Chap. VI, Sec. 2, p. 695, *supra*, determine how a federal court decides *which* state's law to apply? This question has been reserved a number of times. See, *e.g.*, UAW v. Hoosier Cardinal Corp., Paragraph (5), *supra*, at 705 n. 8; D'Oench, Duhme & Co. v. FDIC, p. 752, *supra*, at 456.[15] See also Richards v.

---

14. *Cf.* McCarthy v. Madigan, 503 U.S. 140 (1992), p. 1229, note 10, *infra*, where the Court refused, in the particular circumstances presented, to require a federal prisoner to exhaust administrative remedies before filing a Bivens action in federal court, and based its refusal on federal rather than state law doctrines governing exhaustion.

15. Statutes of limitations present a special problem in this regard. Traditionally, the federal courts followed the limitations statute of the forum, whether jurisdiction was based on diversity of citizenship, Bauser-

man v. Blunt, 147 U.S. 647 (1893), or on the presence of a federal question, Campbell v. Haverhill, 155 U.S. 610 (1895). But no case seems squarely to have faced the problem.

In Cope v. Anderson, 331 U.S. 461, 466 (1947), Justice Black mentioned that "limitations on federally created rights to sue have similarly been considered to be governed by the limitations law of the state where the crucial combination of events transpired." But he got to the obviously appropriate statute of Kentucky, where the insolvent national bank had been located, only by the hard

United States, p. 766, note 7, *supra*; Note, 68 Harv.L.Rev. 1212 (1955).[16]

(10) *Congressional Specification: Desirability and Alternatives.* Wasn't the enactment in 1990 of a general federal statute of limitations long overdue in view of the difficulties encountered in selecting limitations periods from other sources? Should § 1658 have been extended to *all* federal causes of action arising after the statute's effective date? See Norwood, note 1, *supra*, at 502–08. Is four years invariably the appropriate period? Should Congress instead delegate authority to some body (the Judicial Conference of the United States, or a new agency) to fashion the most appropriate limitations period for each new statute lacking any express provision? See Short v. Belleville Shoe Mfg. Co., 908 F.2d 1385, 1393 (7th Cir.1990)(Posner, J., concurring); Note, 44 Vand.L.Rev. 1355 (1991).

Congress often fails to address a range of other issues in statutory programs—including, *e.g.*, the existence *vel non* of private rights of action (a topic explored in the material that immediately follows); the type of relief authorized; survivorship; preemption of state law actions; and statutory retroactivity. The Federal Courts Study Committee recommended that Congress (i) establish a checklist for use by legislative staff in drafting, so that such issues are expressly addressed by statute; (ii) enact statutory default rules (like § 1658); and (iii) create a new body in the Judicial Branch to advise Congress, *inter alia*, on problems in existing legislation that have come to light in judicial opinions. See generally Maggs, *Reducing the Costs of Statutory Ambiguity: Alternative Approaches and the Federal Courts Study Committee*, 29 Harv.J.Legis. 123 (1992).

Is congressional resolution of such quasi-procedural questions always desirable? If so, can it realistically be expected?

INTRODUCTORY NOTE ON THE IMPLICATION OF PRIVATE REMEDIES FOR STATUTORY VIOLATIONS

Federal statutes sometimes makes clear that private parties may bring suit to redress harm suffered as the result of another's violation of duties imposed by the statute in question. For example, the federal patent laws expressly authorize patent-holders to sue, and to obtain damages and/or injunctive relief against, a person who has infringed the plaintiff's patent.

But many federal statutes do not expressly authorize suit by persons injured as the result of a violation of statutory duties. Sometimes the statute says nothing about remedies in the event of violation; in other cases, the statute provides criminal sanctions but is silent about the availability of civil remedies; in still other cases, the statute establishes certain remedies (for example, by authorizing a federal administrative agency to take specified measures to enforce the statute) but says nothing about others. In each of these instances, if a private person seeks legal redress against another who has violated the statute at issue, the federal courts may be asked to determine

route of construction of the forum state's "borrowing statute".

16. *Cf.* Oil, Chemical and Atomic Workers v. Mobil Oil Corp., 426 U.S. 407 (1976)(under § 14(b) of the NLRA, allowing states to prohibit the union shop as a "condition of employment in any State," a federal standard governs whether a state may apply its right-to-work laws to a particular employment relationship).

whether remedies not expressly authorized by the governing statute should be recognized. The next principal case, and the Note that follows it, are concerned with federal common lawmaking in this context—specifically, with the appropriate role of the federal courts in implying private remedies for violations of federal statutes.

Cannon v. University of Chicago

441 U.S. 677, 99 S.Ct. 1946, 60 L.Ed.2d 560 (1979).
Certiorari to the United States Court of Appeals for the Seventh Circuit.

■ MR. JUSTICE STEVENS delivered the opinion of the Court.

[Cannon alleged that the University of Chicago's medical school, which receives federal funds, denied her admission on account of her sex. She sued the university under § 901(a) of Title IX of the Education Amendments of 1972, as amended, 20 U.S.C. § 1681, which provides in relevant part: "No person * * * shall, on the basis of sex, be excluded from participation in, be denied the benefits of, or be subjected to discrimination under any education program or activity receiving Federal financial assistance * * *." Cannon sought declaratory, injunctive, and monetary relief.

[Section 901 does not expressly authorize a private right of action by an injured person. The district court refused to infer such a right of action and dismissed the action. The court of appeals affirmed.]

* * *

* * * As our recent cases—particularly demonstrate, the fact that a federal statute has been violated and some person harmed does not automatically give rise to a private cause of action in favor of that person. Instead, before concluding that Congress intended to make a remedy available to a special class of litigants, a court must carefully analyze the four factors that Cort identifies as indicative of such an intent.[9] Our review of those factors persuades us, however, that * * * petitioner does have a statutory right to pursue her claim that respondents rejected her application on the basis of her sex. * * *

---

9. "In determining whether a private remedy is implicit in a statute not expressly providing one, several factors are relevant. First, is the plaintiff 'one of the class for whose *especial* benefit the statute was enacted,' Texas & Pacific R. Co. v. Rigsby, 241 U.S. 33, 39 (1916) (emphasis supplied)—that is, does the statute create a federal right in favor of the plaintiff? Second, is there any indication of legislative intent, explicit or implicit, either to create such a remedy or to deny one? See, *e.g.*, National Railroad Passenger Corp. v. National Assn. of Railroad Passengers, 414 U.S. 453, 458, 460 (1974)(Amtrak). Third, is it consistent with the underlying purposes of the legislative scheme to imply such a remedy for the plaintiff? See, *e.g.*, Amtrak, *supra*. And finally, is the cause of action one traditionally relegated to state law, in an area basically the concern of the States, so that it would be inappropriate to infer a cause of action based solely on federal law? See Wheeldin v. Wheeler, 373 U.S. 647, 652 (1963); *cf.* J. I. Case Co. v. Borak, 377 U.S. 426, 434 (1964); Bivens v. Six Unknown Federal Narcotics Agents, 403 U.S. 388, 394–395 (1971); *id.*, at 400 (Harlan, J., concurring in judgment)." 422 U.S., at 78.

I

First, the threshold question under Cort is whether the statute was enacted for the benefit of a special class of which the plaintiff is a member. That question is answered by looking to the language of the statute itself. Thus, the statutory reference to "any employee of any such common carrier" in the 1893 legislation requiring railroads to equip their cars with secure "grab irons or handholds," see 27 Stat. 532, 531, made "irresistible" the Court's earliest "inference of a private right of action"—in that case in favor of a railway employee who was injured when a grab iron gave way. Texas & Pacific R. Co. v. Rigsby, 241 U.S. 33, 40.

Similarly, it was statutory language describing the special class to be benefited by § 5 of the Voting Rights Act of 1965 that persuaded the Court that private parties within that class were implicitly authorized to seek a declaratory judgment against a covered State. Allen v. State Board of Elections, 393 U.S. 544, 554–555. The dispositive language in that statute—"no person shall be denied the right to vote for failure to comply with [a new state enactment covered by, but not approved under, § 5]"—is remarkably similar to the language used by Congress in Title IX.

The language in these statutes—which expressly identifies the class Congress intended to benefit—contrasts sharply with statutory language customarily found in criminal statutes, such as that construed in Cort, *supra*, and other laws enacted for the protection of the general public. There would be far less reason to infer a private remedy in favor of individual persons if Congress, instead of drafting Title IX with an unmistakable focus on the benefited class, had written it simply as a ban on discriminatory conduct by recipients of federal funds or as a prohibition against the disbursement of public funds to educational institutions engaged in discriminatory practices.

Unquestionably, therefore, the first of the four factors identified in Cort favors the implication of a private cause of action. * * *

Second, the Cort analysis requires consideration of legislative history. We must recognize, however, that the legislative history of a statute that does not expressly create or deny a private remedy will typically be equally silent or ambiguous on the question. Therefore, in situations such as the present one "in which it is clear that federal law has granted a class of persons certain rights, it is not necessary to show an intention to *create* a private cause of action, although an explicit purpose to *deny* such cause of action would be controlling." Cort, 422 U.S., at 82 (emphasis in original). But this is not the typical case. Far from evidencing any purpose to *deny* a private cause of action, the history of Title IX rather plainly indicates that Congress intended to create such a remedy.

Title IX was patterned after Title VI of the Civil Rights Act of 1964. Except for the substitution of the word "sex" in Title IX to replace the words "race, color, or national origin" in Title VI, the two statutes use identical language to describe the benefited class.* Both statutes provide the same administrative mechanism for terminating federal financial support for institu-

---

* [Ed.] Section 601 of Title VI of the Civil Rights Act of 1964, 78 Stat. 252, 42 U.S.C. § 2000d, provides: "No person in the United States shall, on the ground of race, color, or national origin, be excluded from partic- ipation in, be denied the benefits of, or be subjected to discrimination under any pro- gram or activity receiving Federal financial assistance."

tions engaged in prohibited discrimination. * * * The drafters of Title IX explicitly assumed that it would be interpreted and applied as Title VI had been during the preceding eight years.[19]

In 1972 when Title IX was enacted, the critical language in Title VI had already been construed as creating a private remedy. * * * [I]n this case, * * * we are especially justified in presuming both that those representatives were aware of the prior interpretation of Title VI and that that interpretation reflects their intent with respect to Title IX.

Moreover, * * * during the period between the enactment of Title VI in 1964 and the enactment of Title IX in 1972, this Court had consistently found implied remedies [under other statutory schemes]—often in cases much less clear than this.[23] It was after 1972 that this Court decided Cort v. Ash * * *. We, of course, adhere to the strict approach followed in our recent cases, but our evaluation of congressional action in 1972 must take into account its contemporary legal context.   In sum, it is not only appropriate but also realistic to presume that Congress was thoroughly familiar with these unusually important precedents from this and other federal courts and that it expected its enactment to be interpreted in conformity with them.

It is not, however, necessary to rely on these presumptions. The package of statutes of which Title IX is one part also contains a provision whose language and history demonstrate that Congress itself understood Title VI, and thus its companion, Title IX, as creating a private remedy. Section 718 of the Education Amendments authorizes federal courts to award attorney's fees to the prevailing parties, other than the United States, in private actions brought against public educational agencies to enforce Title VI in the context of elementary and secondary education. The language of this provision explicitly presumes the availability of private suits to enforce Title VI in the education context. For many such suits, no express cause of action was then available; hence Congress must have assumed that one could be implied under Title VI itself. * * *

Finally, the very persistence—before 1972 and since, among judges and executive officials, as well as among litigants and their counsel, and even implicit in decisions of this Court[33]—of the assumption that both Title VI and Title IX created a private right of action for the victims of illegal discrimination and the absence of legislative action to change that assumption provide further evidence that Congress at least acquiesces in, and apparently affirms, that assumption. * * *

Third, under Cort, a private remedy should not be implied if it would frustrate the underlying purpose of the legislative scheme. On the other hand, when that remedy is necessary or at least helpful to the accomplishment of the

---

19. [Citing excerpts from the Senate debates.]

23. In the decade preceding the enactment of Title IX, the Court decided six implied-cause-of-action cases. In all of them a cause of action was found. Superintendent of Insurance v. Bankers Life & Cas. Co., 404 U.S. 6; Sullivan v. Little Hunting Park, [396 U.S. 229]; Allen [v. State Bd. of Educ., 393 U.S. 544]; Jones v. Alfred H. Mayer Co., [392 U.S. 409]; Wyandotte Transportation Co. v.

United States, 389 U.S. 191; J.I. Case Co. v. Borak, 377 U.S. 426.

33. [The Court here cited Lau v. Nichols, 414 U.S. 563, 566–569, and Hills v. Gautreaux, 425 U.S 284, 286, both private actions to enforce Title VI in which the Court, without discussing whether the statute confers a private right of action, reached the merits and granted some relief.] * * *

* * *

statutory purpose, the Court is decidedly receptive to its implication under the statute.

Title IX, like its model Title VI, sought to accomplish two related, but nevertheless somewhat different, objectives.   First, Congress wanted to avoid the use of federal resources to support discriminatory practices;   second, it wanted to provide individual citizens effective protection against those practices.   * * *

The first purpose is generally served by the statutory procedure for the termination of federal financial support for institutions engaged in discriminatory practices.   That remedy is, however, severe and often may not provide an appropriate means of accomplishing the second purpose if merely an isolated violation has occurred.   In that situation, the violation might be remedied more efficiently by an order requiring an institution to accept an applicant who had been improperly excluded.   Moreover, in that kind of situation it makes little sense to impose on an individual, whose only interest is in obtaining a benefit for herself, or on HEW, the burden of demonstrating that an institution's practices are so pervasively discriminatory that a complete cutoff of federal funding is appropriate.   * * *

The Department of Health, Education, and Welfare, which is charged with the responsibility for administering Title IX, * * * takes the unequivocal position that the individual remedy will provide effective assistance to achieving the statutory purposes.   The agency's position is unquestionably correct.[42]

Fourth, the final inquiry suggested by Cort is whether implying a federal remedy is inappropriate because the subject matter involves an area basically of concern to the States.   No such problem is raised by a prohibition against invidious discrimination of any sort, including that on the basis of sex.   * * * Moreover, it is the expenditure of federal funds that provides the justification for this particular statutory prohibition.   * * *

In sum, there is no need in this case to weigh the four Cort factors;   all of them support the same result.   * * *

II

Respondents' principal argument against implying a cause of action under Title IX is that it is unwise to subject admissions decisions of universities to judicial scrutiny at the behest of disappointed applicants on a case-by-case basis.   * * *

This argument * * * addresses a policy issue that Congress has already resolved.

History has borne out the judgment of Congress.   Although victims of discrimination on the basis of race, religion, or national origin have had private Title VI remedies available at least since 1965, respondents have not come forward with any demonstration that Title VI litigation has been so costly or voluminous that either the academic community or the courts have been unduly burdened.   * * *

---

42. * * * HEW has candidly admitted that it does not have the resources necessary to enforce Title IX in a substantial number of circumstances * * *.
* * *

III

[In this Part of its opinion, the Court discussed, *inter alia*, the university's argument that a comparison of Title VI with other Titles of the Civil Rights Act of 1964 demonstrated that Congress created express private remedies whenever it found them desirable. The Court responded that "[e]ven if these arguments were persuasive with respect to Congress' understanding in 1964 when it passed Title VI, they would not overcome the fact that in 1972 when it passed Title IX, Congress was under the impression that Title VI could be enforced by a private action and that Title IX would be similarly enforceable." It added that "[t]he fact that other provisions of a complex statutory scheme create express remedies has not been accepted as a sufficient reason for refusing to imply an otherwise appropriate remedy under a separate section. See, *e.g.*, J.I. Case Co. v. Borak, 377 U.S. 426. Rather, the Court has generally avoided this type of 'excursion into extrapolation of legislative intent,' Cort v. Ash, 422 U.S., at 83 n. 14, unless there is other, more convincing, evidence that Congress meant to exclude the remedy."]

IV

When Congress intends private litigants to have a cause of action to support their statutory rights, the far better course is for it to specify as much when it creates those rights. But * * * under certain limited circumstances the failure of Congress to do so is not inconsistent with an intent on its part to have such a remedy available to the persons benefited by its legislation. Title IX presents the atypical situation in which *all* of the circumstances that the Court has previously identified as supportive of an implied remedy are present. We therefore conclude that petitioner may maintain her lawsuit, despite the absence of any express authorization for it in the statute.

The judgment of the Court of Appeals is reversed, and the case is remanded for further proceedings consistent with this opinion.

It is so ordered.

■ MR. CHIEF JUSTICE BURGER concurs in the judgment.

■ MR. JUSTICE REHNQUIST, with whom MR. JUSTICE STEWART joins, concurring.

* * * The question of the existence of a private right of action is basically one of statutory construction. And while state courts of general jurisdiction still enforcing the common law as well as statutory law may be less constrained than are federal courts enforcing laws enacted by Congress, the latter must surely look to those laws to determine whether there was an intent to create a private right of action under them.

We do not write on an entirely clean slate, however, and the Court's opinion demonstrates that Congress, at least during the period of the enactment of the several Titles of the Civil Rights Act, tended to rely to a large extent on the courts to *decide* whether there should be a private right of action, rather than determining this question for itself. * * *

I fully agree with the Court's statement that "[when] Congress intends private litigants to have a cause of action to support their statutory rights, the far better course is for it to specify as much when it creates those rights." It seems to me that the factors to which I have here briefly adverted apprise the lawmaking branch of the Federal Government that the ball, so to speak, may well now be in its court. Not only is it "far better" for Congress to so specify when it intends private litigants to have a cause of action, but for this very reason this Court in the future should be extremely reluctant to imply a cause of action absent such specificity on the part of the Legislative Branch.

■ MR. JUSTICE WHITE, with whom MR. JUSTICE BLACKMUN joins, dissenting.

* * *

■ MR. JUSTICE POWELL, dissenting.

I agree with Mr. Justice White that even under the standards articulated in our prior decisions, it is clear that no private action should be implied here. * * * But as mounting evidence from the courts below suggests, and the decision of the Court today demonstrates, the mode of analysis we have applied in the recent past cannot be squared with the doctrine of the separation of powers. The time has come to reappraise our standards for the judicial implication of private causes of action.

* * * As the Legislative Branch, Congress * * * should determine when private parties are to be given causes of action under legislation it adopts. As countless statutes demonstrate, including Titles of the Civil Rights Act of 1964, Congress recognizes that the creation of private actions is a legislative function and frequently exercises it. When Congress chooses not to provide a private civil remedy, federal courts should not assume the legislative role of creating such a remedy and thereby enlarge their jurisdiction.

* * *

* * * The "four factor" analysis of [Cort v. Ash, 422 U.S. 66 (1975)] is an open invitation to federal courts to legislate causes of action not authorized by Congress. It is an analysis not faithful to constitutional principles and should be rejected. Absent the most compelling evidence of affirmative congressional intent, a federal court should not infer a private cause of action.

I

The implying of a private action from a federal regulatory statute has been an exceptional occurrence in the past history of this Court. A review of those few decisions where such a step has been taken reveals in almost every case special historical circumstances that explain the result, if not the Court's analysis. * * *

A

The origin of implied private causes of actions in the federal courts is said to date back to Texas & Pacific R. Co. v. Rigsby, 241 U.S. 33 (1916). * * * The narrow question presented for decision was whether the standards of care defined by the Federal Safety Appliance Act's penal provisions applied to a tort action brought against an interstate railroad by an employee not engaged in interstate commerce at the time of his injury. The jurisdiction of the federal courts was not in dispute, the action having been removed from state court on the ground that the defendant was a federal corporation. Under the regime of Swift v. Tyson, 16 Pet. 1 (1842), then in force, the Court was free to create the substantive standards of liability applicable to a common-law negligence claim brought in federal court. The practice of judicial reference to legislatively determined standards of care was a common expedient to establish the existence of negligence. Rigsby did nothing more than follow this practice * * *.

For almost 50 years after Rigsby, this Court recognized an implied private cause of action in only one other statutory context.[3] Four decisions held that various provisions of the Railway Labor Act of 1926 could be enforced in a federal court. * * * [Justice Powell found the case for implication of judicial remedies in these cases to be especially strong in view of (i) particular evidence of congressional intent, (ii) the absence of an express administrative or judicial enforcement mechanism, and/or (iii) a 1934 amendment to the Act indicating congressional approval of the initial decision in Texas & N.O.R. Co. v. Railway Clerks, 281 U.S. 548 (1930).] In each of these cases enforcement of the Act's various requirements could have been restricted to actions brought by the Board of Mediation (later the Mediation Board), rather than by private parties. But whatever the scope of the judicial remedy, the implication of some kind of remedial mechanism was necessary to provide the enforcement authority Congress clearly intended.

During this same period, the Court frequently turned back private plaintiffs seeking to imply causes of action from federal statutes. See, *e.g.*, Wheeldin v. Wheeler, 373 U.S. 647 (1963); T.I.M.E. Inc. v. United States, 359 U.S. 464 (1959); Switchmen v. National Mediation Board, 320 U.S. 297 (1943). Throughout these cases, the focus of the Court's inquiry generally was on the availability of means other than a private action to enforce the statutory duty at issue. * * *

A break in this pattern occurred in J.I. Case Co. v. Borak, 377 U.S. 426 (1964). There the Court held that a private party could maintain a cause of action under § 14(a) of the Securities Exchange Act of 1934, in spite of Congress' express creation of an administrative mechanism for enforcing that statute. I find this decision both unprecedented and incomprehensible as a matter of public policy. The decision's rationale, which lies ultimately in the judgment that "[p]rivate enforcement of the proxy rules provides a necessary supplement to Commission action," 377 U.S., at 432, ignores the fact that Congress, in determining the degree of regulation to be imposed on companies covered by the Securities Exchange Act, already had decided that private enforcement was unnecessary. More significant for present purposes, however, is the fact that Borak, rather than signaling the start of a trend in this Court, constitutes a singular and, I believe, aberrant interpretation of a federal regulatory statute.

Since Borak, this Court has upheld the implication of private causes of actions derived from federal statutes in only three extremely limited sets of

---

3. During this period, the Court did uphold the implication of civil remedies in favor of the Government, see Wyandotte Transportation Co. v. United States, 389 U.S. 191 (1967); United States v. Republic Steel Corp., 362 U.S. 482 (1960), and strongly suggested that private actions could be implied directly from particular provisions of the Constitution, Bell v. Hood, 327 U.S. 678, 684 (1946). Both of these issues are significantly different from the implication of a private remedy from a federal statute. In Wyandotte and Republic Steel, the Government already had a "cause of action" in the form of its power to bring criminal proceedings under the pertinent statutes. Thus, the Court was confronted only with the question whether the Government could exact less drastic civil penalties as an alternative means of enforcing the same obligations. And this Court's traditional responsibility to safeguard constitutionally protected rights, as well as the freer hand we necessarily have in the interpretation of the Constitution, permits greater judicial creativity with respect to implied constitutional causes of action. Moreover, the implication of remedies to enforce constitutional provisions does not interfere with the legislative process in the way that the implication of remedies from statutes can.

circumstances. First, the Court in Jones v. Alfred H. Mayer Co., 392 U.S. 409 (1968); Sullivan v. Little Hunting Park, Inc., 396 U.S. 229 (1969); and Johnson v. Railway Express Agency, Inc., 421 U.S. 454 (1975), recognized the right of private parties to seek relief for violations of 42 U.S.C. §§ 1981 and 1982. But to say these cases "implied" rights of action is somewhat misleading, as Congress at the time these statutes were enacted expressly referred to private enforcement actions. Furthermore, as in the Railway Labor Act cases, Congress had provided no alternative means of asserting these rights. Thus, the Court was presented with the choice between regarding these statutes as precatory or recognizing some kind of judicial proceeding.

Second, the Court in Allen v. State Board of Elections, 393 U.S. 544 (1969), permitted private litigants to sue to enforce the preclearance provisions of § 5 of the Voting Rights Act of 1965. As the Court seems to concede, this decision was reached without substantial analysis, and in my view can be explained only in terms of this Court's special and traditional concern for safeguarding the electoral process. In addition * * * the remedy implied was very limited, thereby reducing the chances that States would be exposed to frivolous or harassing suits.

Finally, the Court in Superintendent of Insurance v. Bankers Life & Cas. Co., 404 U.S. 6 (1971), ratified 25 years of lower-court precedent that had held a private cause of action available under the Securities and Exchange Commission's Rule 10b–5. As the Court concedes, this decision reflects the unique history of Rule 10b–5, and did not articulate any standards of general applicability.

These few cases applying Borak must be contrasted with the subsequent decisions where the Court refused to imply private actions. * * *

B

It was against this background of almost invariable refusal to imply private actions, absent a complete failure of alternative enforcement mechanisms and a clear expression of legislative intent to create such a remedy, that Cort v. Ash, 422 U.S. 66 (1975), was decided. In holding that no private action could be brought to enforce 18 U.S.C. § 610 (1970 ed. and Supp. III), a criminal statute, the Court referred to four factors said to be relevant to determining generally whether private actions could be implied. * * * But, as the opinion of the Court today demonstrates, the Cort analysis too easily may be used to deflect inquiry away from the intent of Congress, and to permit a court instead to substitute its own views as to the desirability of private enforcement.

Of the four factors mentioned in Cort, only one refers expressly to legislative intent. The other three invite independent judicial lawmaking. Asking whether a statute creates a right in favor of a private party, for example, begs the question at issue. What is involved is not the mere existence of a legal right, but a particular person's right to invoke the power of the courts to enforce that right. Determining whether a private action would be consistent with the "underlying purposes" of a legislative scheme permits a court to decide for itself what the goals of a scheme should be, and how those goals should be advanced. Finally, looking to state law for parallels to the federal right simply focuses inquiry on a particular policy consideration that Congress already may have weighed in deciding not to create a private action.

* * *

II

* * *

* * * Cort allows the Judicial Branch to assume policymaking authority vested by the Constitution in the Legislative Branch. It also invites Congress to avoid resolution of the often controversial question whether a new regulatory statute should be enforced through private litigation. * * * Because the courts are free to reach a result different from that which the normal play of political forces would have produced, the intended beneficiaries of the legislation are unable to ensure the full measure of protection their needs may warrant. For the same reason, those subject to the legislative constraints are denied the opportunity to forestall through the political process potentially unnecessary and disruptive litigation. Moreover, the public generally is denied the benefits that are derived from the making of important societal choices through the open debate of the democratic process.

The Court's implication doctrine encourages, as a corollary to the political default by Congress, an increase in the governmental power exercised by the federal judiciary. * * *

It is true that the federal judiciary necessarily exercises substantial powers to construe legislation, including, when appropriate, the power to prescribe substantive standards of conduct that supplement federal legislation. But this power normally is exercised with respect to disputes over which a court already has jurisdiction, and in which the existence of the asserted cause of action is established. Implication of a private cause of action, in contrast, involves a significant additional step. By creating a private action, a court of limited jurisdiction necessarily extends its authority to embrace a dispute Congress has not assigned it to resolve.[17] This runs contrary to the established principle that "[t]he jurisdiction of the federal courts is carefully guarded against expansion by judicial interpretation . . . [.]" American Fire & Cas. Co. v. Finn, 341 U.S. 6, 17 (1951) * * *.

The facts of this case illustrate how the implication of a right of action not authorized by Congress denigrates the democratic process. * * * Arming frustrated applicants with the power to challenge in court his or her rejection inevitably will have a constraining effect on admissions programs. The burden of expensive, vexatious litigation upon institutions whose resources often are severely limited may well compel an emphasis on objectively measured academic qualifications at the expense of more flexible admissions criteria that

---

17. Because a private action implied from a federal statute has as an element the violation of that statute, the action universally has been considered to present a federal question over which a federal court has jurisdiction under 28 U.S.C. § 1331. Thus, when a federal court implies a private action from a statute, it necessarily expands the scope of its federal-question jurisdiction.

It is instructive to compare decisions implying private causes of action to those cases that have found nonfederal causes of action cognizable by a federal court under § 1331. E.g., Smith v. Kansas City Title & Trust Co., 255 U.S. 180 (1921). Where a court decides both that federal-law elements are present in a state-law cause of action, and that these elements predominate to the point that the action can be said to present a "federal question" cognizable in federal court, the net effect is the same as implication of a private action directly from the constitutional or statutory source of the federal-law elements. To the extent an expansive interpretation of § 1331 permits federal courts to assume control over disputes which Congress did not consign to the federal judicial process, it is subject to the same criticisms of judicial implication of private actions discussed in the text.

bring richness and diversity to academic life. If such a significant incursion into the arena of academic polity is to be made, it is the constitutional function of the Legislative Branch, subject as it is to the checks of the political process, to make this judgment.

Congress already has created a mechanism for enforcing the mandate found in Title IX against gender-based discrimination. * * * The current position of the Government notwithstanding, overlapping judicial and administrative enforcement of these policies inevitably will lead to conflicts and confusion * * *. * * *

III

* * * I would start afresh. Henceforth, we should not condone the implication of any private action from a federal statute absent the most compelling evidence that Congress in fact intended such an action to exist. Where a statutory scheme expressly provides for an alternative mechanism for enforcing the rights and duties created, I would be especially reluctant ever to permit a federal court to volunteer its services for enforcement purposes. Because the Court today is enlisting the federal judiciary in just such an enterprise, I dissent.

NOTE ON IMPLIED RIGHTS OF ACTION FOR STATUTORY VIOLATIONS[1]

(1) *Antecedents.* As the Cannon opinions suggest, there have been important shifts in the Court's thinking about implied rights of action.[2]

(a) *The Borak Approach.* The high-water mark of judicial implication of remedies may have been J.I. Case Co. v. Borak, 377 U.S. 426 (1964), where a unanimous court upheld a private party's right to sue under § 14(a) of the Securities Exchange Act of 1934, which prohibits fraud in the solicitation of proxy material. The Court adopted a broad rationale—emphasizing the value of private enforcement as a "necessary supplement" to SEC action—that was followed, in cases in other statutory settings, by the Supreme Court (see footnote 23 of the Cannon opinion) and by lower federal courts.

1. There has been an outpouring of writing on this topic. In addition to sources cited elsewhere in this Note, see, *e.g.*, Brown, *Of Activism and Erie—Implication Doctrine's Implications for the Nature and Role of the Federal Courts,* 69 Iowa L.Rev. 617, 627–49 (1984); Foy, *Some Reflections on Legislation, Adjudication, and Implied Private Actions in the State and Federal Courts,* 71 Corn.L.Rev. 501 (1986); Frankel, *Implied Rights of Action,* 67 Va.L.Rev. 553 (1981); Steinberg, *Implied Private Rights of Action Under Federal Law,* 55 Notre Dame Law. 33 (1979); Ziegler, *Rights Require Remedies: A New Approach to the Enforcement of Rights in the Federal Courts,* 38 Hastings L.J. 665 (1987).

2. One of the earliest issues to arise was the availability of a private damage rem-edy for employees injured as a result of violations of the Federal Safety Appliance Act, where the activity was not so directly involved in interstate commerce as to be covered by the express private remedy in the Federal Employers Liability Act. The wavering course of decisions led to the apparent conclusion that no such remedy was created by federal law, although violations were in this instance redressable as a matter of state law. See Minneapolis, St.P., & S.St.M. Ry. Co. v. Popplar, 237 U.S. 369 (1915); Texas & P.Ry. Co. v. Rigsby, 241 U.S. 33 (1916); Moore v. Chesapeake & O. Ry. Co., 291 U.S. 205 (1934); Jacobson v. New York, N.H. & H.R. Co., 206 F.2d 153 (1st Cir.1953), *aff'd per curiam,* 347 U.S. 909 (1954).

(b) *Retrenchment and Cort v. Ash.* By the mid–1970s, however, the Court had rebuffed several attempts to extend the Borak principle. See National R.R. Passenger Corp. v. National Ass'n of R.R. Passengers (the Amtrak case), 414 U.S. 453 (1974)(Amtrak Act provides exclusive remedies for breaches of obligations created by Act, and no additional private actions to enforce compliance may be inferred); Securities Investor Protection Corp. v. Barbour, 421 U.S. 412 (1975)(customers of broker-dealers do not have implied right of action under Securities Investor Protection Act to compel SIPC to exercise its statutory authority for their benefit); Cort v. Ash, 422 U.S. 66 (1975)(no private cause of action for damages may be inferred from a criminal prohibition in the Federal Election Campaign Act).

The decision in Cort v. Ash was especially noteworthy for its effort, through its four-part test, to harmonize and rationalize the law. And in several post–1975 cases the Court, applying that test, held that no private rights of action were to be inferred from various federal statutes.[3]

(2) *Post-Cannon Developments.* Justice Powell lost the battle in Cannon, but he won the war. Since that decision, the Court has generally rejected claims of implied federal remedies. A good example of the current approach is found in Touche Ross & Co. v. Redington, 442 U.S. 560 (1979)(7–1). There the Court refused to imply a right of action under § 17(a) of the Securities Act of 1934, which imposes recordkeeping and reporting requirements on broker-dealers and some other persons. Suit was brought against an accounting firm that had audited and prepared the required reports for a securities firm that became insolvent. Justice Rehnquist wrote for the Court, and carried through on the warning he issued in Cannon: "Here, the statute by its terms grants no private rights to any identifiable class and proscribes no conduct as unlawful. And * * * the legislative history of the 1934 Act simply does not speak to the issue of private remedies under § 17(a). At least in such a case as this, the inquiry ends there * * *" (p. 576).

Although the Cort v. Ash test has occasionally reappeared in recent opinions,[4] many cases view the question of implied remedies in a narrower frame—as one exclusively of legislative intent demonstrated in text or legislative history—that ordinarily leads to a finding of no implication.[5]

---

3. See, *e.g.*, Piper v. Chris–Craft Indus., Inc., 430 U.S. 1 (1977)(Section 14(e) of the Securities Exchange Act); Santa Clara Pueblo v. Martinez, 436 U.S. 49 (1978)(Indian Civil Rights Act of 1968).

4. See, *e.g.*, Thompson v. Thompson, 484 U.S. 174, 179 (1988); compare *id.* at 188 (Scalia, J., concurring in the judgment)(objecting that Cort was effectively overruled by Touche Ross).

5. See, *e.g.*, California v. Sierra Club, 451 U.S. 287 (1981)(Section 10 of Rivers and Harbors Appropriation Act of 1899); Universities Research Ass'n, Inc. v. Coutu, 450 U.S. 754 (1981)(Davis–Bacon Act); Karahalios v. National Fed'n of Fed. Employees, 489 U.S. 527 (1989)(breach of union's duty of fair representation under the Civil Service Reform

Act of 1978); Suter v. Artist M., 503 U.S. 347 (1992), Chap. IX, Sec. 2(C), p. 1136, note 6, *infra* (Adoption Assistance and Child Welfare Act).

Justice Scalia would take matters one step further. In Part I of his concurrence in Thompson v. Thompson, 484 U.S. 174 (1988), which Justice O'Connor joined, he criticized the majority for examining "the 'context' of the [Parental Kidnaping Prevention Act] for indication of an intent to create a private right of action, after having found no such indication in either text or legislative history" (p. 189). In Part II, speaking for himself alone, he urged the adoption of "a flat rule that private rights of action will not be implied in statutes hereafter enacted" (p. 192).

Since Cannon, the Court has not taken the step of overturning its earlier decisions that had recognized a private right of action. Thus, in Herman & MacLean v. Huddleston, 459 U.S. 375 (1983), the Court was unanimous (with Justice Powell not participating) in re-affirming the private right of action under § 10(b) of the Securities Exchange Act of 1934 for violation of Rule 10b–5, the anti-fraud regulation promulgated by the SEC pursuant to § 10(b). The lower courts had long recognized that right of action, as had the Supreme Court itself in Superintendent of Ins. v. Bankers Life & Cas. Co., 404 U.S. 6, 13 n. 9 (1971).[6]

But post-Cannon decisions recognizing a new implied right of action are extremely rare. In Merrill Lynch, Pierce, Fenner & Smith, Inc. v. Curran, 456 U.S. 353, 381 (1982), the Court by a 5–4 vote inferred a private cause of action under the Commodity Exchange Act, primarily on the theory that such a remedy was part of the "contemporary legal context" that was preserved when Congress undertook a comprehensive revision of the Act in 1974. The decision, like Cannon itself, thus rested on the premise that certain statutes were enacted during a period when the legislature's expectations with respect to implied remedies were influenced by the Borak line of decisions.[7]

(3) *Arguments of Principle and Policy.* Allowing a private plaintiff to sue for a violation of a federal statute always adds force to the deterrent effect of a statutory prohibition. Since Congress must have meant the prohibition to be taken seriously, why shouldn't private remedies always be implied in order to promote the statutory purpose?

Note the following six objections to this argument—and the possible responses thereto.

6. However, in Central Bank of Denver v. First Interstate Bank of Denver, 114 S.Ct. 1439 (1994), the Court, rejecting the view of the SEC and of all 11 courts of appeals that had considered the question, held (5–4) that there is no implied right of action for *aiding and abetting* a violation of § 10(b). Justice Kennedy's majority opinion did not, however, appear to rely primarily on the proposition that private remedies for a violation of § 10(b) were inappropriate in the aiding and abetting context. Instead, it rested on the broader ground that § 10(b), whose text reaches persons who "directly or indirectly" engage in prohibited conduct, simply does not regulate aiding and abetting at all. Thus, Justice Stevens' dissent opined that "[t]he majority leaves little doubt that the [Securities] Exchange Act does not even permit the *Commission* to pursue aiders and abettors in civil enforcement actions under § 10(b) and Rule 10b–5" (p. 1460).

For criticism of Central Bank, see Strauss, *On Resegregating the Worlds of Statute and Common Law,* 1994 Sup.Ct.Rev. 429, 509–13 (citing the decision as one of many that take a static view of statutory law, rather than trying to create a consistent fabric in which the text gains meaning when elaborat-

ed by lower courts and by administrative agencies). Compare Eisenberg, *Strict Textualism,* 29 Loyola of L.A.L.Rev. 1 (1995) (criticizing the majority's strict-textualist analysis of § 10(b) as intellectually incoherent) with Grundfest, *We Must Never Forget That It Is An Inkblot We Are Expounding: Section 10(b) As Rorschach Test,* 29 id. 41 (urging courts to give cryptic provisions like § 10(b) the narrowest practical interpretation).

The Private Securities Litigation Act of 1995, 109 Stat. 737, § 104, partially restored enforcement authority against aiders and abettors, by giving the SEC (but not private parties) the right to sue those who knowingly provide substantial assistance to principal violators.

7. For other post-Cannon examples of implication of remedies, see the Transamerica Mortgage case, Paragraph (6), *infra,* recognizing a right of action to seek rescission but not damages; and see the unusual case of Key Tronic Corp. v. United States, 114 S.Ct. 1960 (1994)(6–3), in which the Justices disagreed about what distinguishes "implied" from "express" rights of action.

First, the argument assumes that a statutory prohibition is motivated by a one-dimensional purpose to deter or require certain kinds of conduct. In fact, a statute is often the product of a pitched battle between competing interest groups, one outcome of which may be a compromise (shaped by some mixture of policy concerns and the balance of political power) that the available remedies would be limited—that full compliance was neither desired nor desirable.[8]

Was Title IX (or Title VI) such a compromise, and if so what were the terms? Can a court reliably answer such questions?

Second, even when full compliance with the prohibition is the statutory goal, private enforcement in the courts leads to serious problems of overinclusion or excessive deterrence that discourage socially productive conduct outside the scope of the prohibition.

Did the right of action recognized in Cannon pose such a threat? Does the force of the objection depend on how meritorious most such actions are? The likely response of universities to the threat of lawsuits? The costs of litigation?

Third, Congress may have wished to give an administrative agency authority to flesh out statutory meaning and to determine appropriate levels of enforcement. Indeed, regulatory statutes frequently issue commands to administrative officials rather than directly to regulated parties. Recognition of a private remedy may thwart congressional efforts to centralize enforcement with an administrative body.[9]

Did Congress wish to give HEW a monopoly over enforcement of Title IX? If so, does it follow that if Illinois provided a state law remedy for violation of federal regulatory statutes like Title IX, that remedy should be held to be preempted? Even if the majority was correct that HEW's only remedy—a fund cut-off—is too draconian to be regularly enforced?[10]

Fourth, whether to provide a private remedy is an important question that the legislature should decide; treating it as left to judicial implication makes it too easy for Congress to dodge the question, and unduly taxes the ingenuity and capacity of the federal courts.

If this objection to lawmaking is valid here, is it equally valid as to a congressional failure to provide, for example, a statute of limitations for federal causes of action? Or is creation of a private right of action a far more significant matter that should be left to Congress? Does the objection depend

---

8. See Posner, The Federal Courts: Crisis and Reform 270–72 (1985); Easterbrook, *Foreword: The Court and the Economic System*, 98 Harv.L.Rev. 4, 45–51 (1984).

9. For a fuller development of this and related ideas, see Stewart & Sunstein, *Public Programs and Private Rights*, 95 Harv.L.Rev. 1193 (1982). The authors consider private rights of action as one of several available forms of private initiative in the operation of regulatory programs. They suggest that such a private remedy is of greatest worth in a program emphasizing "entitlement values"—for example, the value of being treated with respect and without invidious discrimination—and is considerably more problematic in programs designed primarily to increase

productive efficiency. In the latter instance, however, they note that a remedy limited to damages for injuries suffered is far less likely than broader remedies (sweeping injunctions or damages not tied to harm suffered) to generate overdeterrence.

10. It has recently been argued that the SEC has authority, by administrative rule, to "dis-imply" private rights of action, like the one to enforce Rule 10b–5. See Grundfest, *Disimplying Private Rights of Action under the Federal Securities Laws: The Commission's Authority*, 107 Harv.L.Rev. 961 (1994). If such authority exists, should it affect the willingness of courts to imply private rights of action in the first instance?

upon the assumption that Congress (or the Constitution) does not contemplate judges' acting as junior partners of the legislature, helping to implement its statutory purposes? That courts cannot reliably determine what the statutory purposes were and/or their implications with respect to private rights of action? That the proper role of courts vis-a-vis the legislature is one of disciplinarian, holding Congress' feet to the fire? See generally *Note on Theories of Statutory Interpretation and Their Pertinence to Federal Common Lawmaking*, p. 758, *supra*.

Fifth, even if private remedies are desirable, a federal remedy may not be necessary or appropriate if state remedies are adequate to the task.

Before deciding whether to formulate a federal remedy in Cannon, should the Justices have asked whether Illinois provided a private right of action against universities for sex discrimination? Whether the other 49 states did so?

Sixth, judges should not recognize a private right of action, for doing so carries in its wake the creation of federal subject matter jurisdiction, which only Congress can confer. Indeed, when state law independently provides a private remedy for violation of a federal statutory duty, implication of a federal remedy may have little substantive importance but will be significant primarily in opening the door to the federal courthouse.

Does acceptance of this argument give a pro-defendant tilt to federal common lawmaking: pro-plaintiff private remedies may not be fashioned, for doing so would give rise to federal jurisdiction; but federal common law defenses (*e.g.*, the government contractor defense of the Boyle case, p. 770, *supra*) may be crafted because their recognition does not give rise to federal question jurisdiction under the well-pleaded complaint rule of § 1331? (Compare Justice Brennan's argument, in footnote 2 of his dissent in Boyle, that federalism concerns counsel more strongly against recognizing federal *defenses*—which preempt state law—than federal *rights of action*, which often merely supplement state law.) Suppose, before the Boyle decision, Congress had amended the jurisdictional statutes to provide for federal defense removal; would it then have been inappropriate for the Court to have fashioned the defense it did, because doing so would give rise to removal jurisdiction? In any event, doesn't § 1331 exist precisely to permit federal causes of action— whether express or judicially-implied—to be heard in federal court? Doesn't Justice Powell overstate his objections (others of which are very forceful) by attempting to cast them in jurisdictional terms?

(4) *Common-Lawmaking vs. Statutory Interpretation.* Consider the Court's recent insistence that the question whether to imply a remedy should be regarded essentially as a pure (or conventional) question of statutory interpretation, viewed in terms of "legislative intent". Does that insistence—especially if it relies heavily on the absence of textual warrant for an implied remedy— create a danger that effectuation of congressional purpose, more broadly and sympathetically viewed, will be thwarted? Or does it beg the question to assume that such a purpose exists and can be reliably ascertained by the courts?

Note that an effort to inquire more broadly into legislative purpose might itself lead to a rejection of any private remedy, especially when Congress has established a comprehensive scheme for administration of a regulatory program. Thus while Stewart and Sunstein, note 9, *supra*, are quite critical of the

Court's tendency to engage in simplistic analysis of statutory text and legislative intent, they regard the Court's retrenchment since 1974 as, in the main, consistent with their view of the values and policies at stake.

Do courts have the capacity to make intelligent judgments about which statutory schemes do, and do not, call for implication of private remedies? If they do not, then when Congress has not addressed the question in a particular statute, should the default rule be (i) a refusal to recognize a right of action (more or less the Court's current position) or (ii) implication (as in Borak)? Can any effort to put Congress on notice about how the Court will deal with these situations—and to force Congress to face up to the problem—overcome the attributes of the legislative process (inertia, lack of time, lack of foresight, sloppiness, incapacity or unwillingness to reach agreement on various matters) that give rise to statutory gaps and ambiguities in the first place?

(5) *Express Remedies under 42 U.S.C. § 1983.* In 42 U.S.C. § 1983, Congress created an *express* private right of action for violations of federal law that are committed "under color of" state law. The Court has interpreted § 1983 as comprehending suits for violation of federal statutes as well as of constitutional provisions. See Maine v. Thiboutot, 448 U.S. 1 (1980), Chap. IX, Sec. 2(C), p. 1133, *infra.* Thus, in suits against state and local officials for violation of federal laws, § 1983's grant of an express private right of action makes it unnecessary to reach the implied right of action question.

The private remedy that § 1983 generally supplies may, however, be deemed to be precluded in particular statutory contexts. Thus, in Middlesex County Sewerage Auth. v. National Sea Clammers Ass'n, 453 U.S. 1 (1981), plaintiffs sought relief against state and federal officials under the Federal Water Pollution Control Act and related statutes. Those statutes established remedial mechanisms for statutory violations, but those remedies were unavailable to the plaintiffs because of their failure to have complied with the statutory notice provisions. The Court held that Congress, in providing these "quite comprehensive enforcement mechanisms", intended not only to foreclose implied private actions, but also "to supplant any remedy that otherwise would be available under § 1983" (pp. 20–21).

For discussion of the significance of § 1983 after Thiboutot and Sea Clammers, see generally pp. 1133–37, *infra.*

(6) *The Reach of Remedies.* Does the appropriateness of recognizing an implied right of action depend on just what remedy is sought? Note that Justice Powell, in Cannon, distinguished Allen v. State Board of Elections, 393 U.S. 544 (1969)—where the Court had permitted private litigants to seek a declaratory judgment that certain legislation had to be submitted for preclearance under § 5 of the Voting Rights Act of 1965—on the ground that "the remedy implied was very limited, thereby reducing the chances that States would be exposed to frivolous or harassing suits."

Are those chances greater when actions for compensatory (or punitive) damages are recognized?[11] More generally, might the Court's increased restric-

---

11. Compare the Court's apparent willingness to permit private parties to bring suit to enjoin state laws as preempted by federal law, even absent express statutory authorization. Although many if not most such actions could today be brought under 42 U.S.C. § 1983, see Paragraph (5), *supra*, earlier decisions authorizing such suits appeared to rest upon an implied right to relief. See Franchise Tax Board v. Construction Laborers Vacation Trust, 463 U.S. 1, 20 n. 20 (1983),

tiveness reflect, in part, changes in the Justices' view, for example, of whether securities class actions generally constitute an important enforcement tool or, instead, meritless strike suits instituted by unscrupulous plaintiffs' lawyers?[12]

Consider in this regard the decision in Transamerica Mortgage Advisors, Inc. (TAMA) v. Lewis, 444 U.S. 11 (1979), involving § 206 of the Investment Advisers Act of 1940, which makes it unlawful for an investment adviser to "employ any device, scheme, or artifice to defraud", as well as § 215, which renders "void" any contract made in violation of the Act. Treating the issue as one of legislative intent, the Court construed § 215 as fairly implying a private remedy for rescission of the void contract and restitution of moneys paid, but refused (over four dissents) to recognize a right of action for damages under § 206.

The TAMA decision appears, however, to be limited to the specifics of the Investment Advisers Act. For in Franklin v. Gwinnett County Pub. Schools, 503 U.S. 60 (1992), all nine Justices agreed that where a private right of action exists under a federal statute, "[t]he general rule * * * is that absent clear direction to the contrary by Congress, the federal courts have the power to award any appropriate relief" (pp. 70–71). Thus, the Court held that in a private action under the same statute involved in Cannon—Title IX of the Education Amendments of 1972—a damages remedy was available.

(7) *Implied Rights of Action for Contribution.*

(a) *The Texas Industries Decision.* A different kind of question regarding implied rights of action was raised in Texas Industries, Inc. v. Radcliff Materials, Inc., 451 U.S. 630 (1981). After having been sued for conspiring to raise prices in violation of the Sherman Act, Texas Industries filed a third-party complaint against other alleged participants in the scheme, seeking contribution in the event it should be held liable. The antitrust laws make no mention of contribution.

The Supreme Court unanimously affirmed the lower courts' dismissal of the third-party claim. Although it outlined the complex debate about whether affording a right to contribution would be good antitrust policy, the Court rested on a lack of judicial authority to create one.

The Court first applied the Cort v. Ash test and concluded that Congress had neither expressly nor implicitly intended to create such a right, stressing that alleged conspirators like Texas Industries were not "beneficiaries" of the antitrust laws. The opinion then treated as a distinct question whether the court should fashion a right of contribution as a matter of federal common law. The Court offered an especially restrictive description of the "uniquely federal interests" that alone justify federal common lawmaking, and found none present. (Some of the language is quoted in Justice Brennan's dissent in the Boyle case, p. 776, *supra.*) Finally, the Court ruled that although Congress had delegated broad authority to the courts to develop substantive rules specifying

---

Chap. VIII, Sec. 3, p. 937, *infra*, and the Note following that opinion.

12. Compare, *e.g.*, Seligman, *The Merits Do Matter*, 108 Harv.L.Rev. 438 (1994)(reviewing, but finding wanting, objections that securities litigation discourages capital formation, that courts cannot filter out frivolous suits, and that many companies settle meritless claims because of the high cost of defending, while affirming that private enforcement serves important compensatory and deterrent purposes) with Grundfest, *Why Disimply*, 108 Harv.L.Rev. 727 (1995)(taking a much less favorable view of the evidence about securities litigation).

what conduct violates the antitrust laws, that delegation did not extend to the development of remedial rules (like contribution).

Does Texas Industries imply that the question of contribution is governed by *state* law? Wouldn't application of differing contribution rules on identical facts, depending on the locus of the forum or of the place where the events occurred, interfere with effective enforcement of antitrust goals—and in multistate controversies, inevitably give rise to vexing questions about which state's rule should govern? *Cf.* the Agency Holding decision, p. 824, *supra.*

But if state law is displaced, should the federal courts regard themselves as less capable of filling the void than would a state court in similar circumstances? Or does it beg the question to assume that a void existed? The antitrust laws create remedies only for plaintiffs (or for the government as prosecutor in criminal cases). Should one infer that Congress meant there to be no remedies for one defendant as against another, or merely that Congress did not address the problem? The question is similar to that raised in connection with United States v. Standard Oil, p. 766, *supra.* Is the Court properly subject to criticism for refusing to accept responsibility for the development of a coherent system of rights and remedies in Texas Industries? In Standard Oil?

Of course, a responsible court might decide that contribution should not be permitted as a matter of policy, or even that the contribution thicket is too hazardous to enter without more legislative guidance.[13] While such institutional considerations were discussed by the Court in Texas Industries, its concentration on the question of power seemed to blind it to the fact that its decision was not neutral—that the result was effectively to *deny* the existence of a right of contribution.

(b) *Musick, Peeler and 10b–5 Actions.* The Court was willing, however, to fashion a right of contribution in Musick, Peeler & Garrett v. Employers Ins. of Wausau, 508 U.S. 286 (1993)(6–3). The plaintiff's action there was based on the implied private right of action, previously recognized by the Court, under § 10(b) of the Securities Exchange Act of 1934 and SEC Rule 10b–5. See Paragraph (2), *supra.* The Court found Texas Industries to be distinguishable, because its central inquiries—whether Congress " 'expressly or by clear implication' envisioned" a right to contribution, or "whether Congress 'intended courts to have the power to alter or supplement the remedies enacted' "—are not helpful in the context of a judicially-created private right of action like the one under Rule 10b–5 (p. 2088). Rather, the Court must ask "how the 1934 Congress would have addressed the issue had the 10b–5 action been included as an express provision in the 1934 Act" (pp. 2089–90). Because analogous provisions in the Act that do create express private rights of action also provide a right to contribution, the Court concluded that Congress would have wanted a similar contribution right in 10b–5 actions.

---

13. In Northwest Airlines, Inc. v. Transport Workers Union, 451 U.S. 77 (1981), such institutional considerations did lead the Court not to recognize a right of contribution in an employment discrimination case. In view of the comprehensive statutory scheme of remedies, the Court said, the "judiciary may not * * * fashion new remedies that might upset carefully considered legislative programs" (p. 97).

SUBSECTION C: REMEDIES FOR CONSTITUTIONAL VIOLATIONS

Ward v. Love County

253 U.S. 17, 40 S.Ct. 419, 64 L.Ed. 751 (1920).
Certiorari to the Supreme Court of Oklahoma.

■ MR. JUSTICE VAN DEVANTER delivered the opinion of the Court.

This is a proceeding by and on behalf of Coleman J. Ward and sixty-six other Indians to recover moneys alleged to have been coercively collected from them by Love county, Oklahoma, as taxes on their allotments, which under the laws and Constitution of the United States were nontaxable. The county commissioners disallowed the claim and the claimants appealed to the district court of the county. There the claimants' petition was challenged by a demurrer, which was overruled and the county elected not to plead further. A judgment for the claimants followed, and this was reversed by the Supreme Court [of Oklahoma]. The case is here on writ of certiorari.

The claimants, who were members of the Choctaw Tribe and wards of the United States, received their allotments out of the tribal domain under a congressional enactment of 1898, which subjected the right of alienation to certain restrictions and provided that "the lands allotted shall be nontaxable while the title remains in the original allottee, but not to exceed twenty-one years from date of patent." Chapter 517, 30 Stat. 507. In the act of 1906, enabling Oklahoma to become a state, Congress made it plain that no impairment of the rights of property pertaining to the Indians was intended; and the state included in its Constitution a provision exempting from taxation "such property as may be exempt by reason of treaty stipulations, existing between the Indians and the United States government, or by federal laws, during the force and effect of such treaties or federal laws." Article 10, § 6. Afterwards Congress, by an act of 1908, removed the restrictions on alienation as to certain classes of allottees, including the present claimants, and declared that all land from which the restrictions were removed "shall be subject to taxation, * * * as though it were the property of other persons than allottees." Chapter 199, §§ 1, 4.

Following the last enactment the officers of Love and other counties began to tax the allotted lands from which restrictions on alienation were removed, and this met with pronounced opposition on the part of the Indian allottees, who insisted * * * that the tax exemption was a vested property right which could not be abrogated or destroyed consistently with the Constitution of the United States. Suits were begun in the state courts to maintain the exemption and enjoin the threatened taxation, one of the suits being prosecuted by some 8,000 allottees against the officers of Love and other counties. * * * [T]he state courts * * * sustained the power to tax. * * * The cases were then brought here, and this court held that the exemption was a vested property right which Congress could not repeal consistently with the Fifth Amendment, that it was binding on the taxing authorities in Oklahoma, and that the state courts had erred in refusing to enjoin them from taxing the lands. Choate v. Trapp, 224 U.S. 665; Gleason v. Wood, 224 U.S. 679; English v. Richardson, 224 U.S. 680.

While those suits were pending the officers of Love county, with full knowledge of the suits, and being defendants in one, proceeded with the taxation of the allotments, demanded of these claimants that the taxes on their lands be paid to the county, threatened to advertise and sell the lands unless the taxes were paid, did advertise and sell other lands similarly situated, and caused these claimants to believe that their lands would be sold if the taxes were not paid. So, to prevent such a sale and to avoid the imposition of a penalty of eighteen per cent., for which the local statute provided, these claimants paid the taxes. They protested and objected at the time that the taxes were invalid, and the county officers knew that all the allottees were pressing the objection in the pending suits.

    * * *

In reversing the judgment which the district court had given for the claimants the Supreme Court [of Oklahoma] held, first, that the taxes were not collected by coercive means, but were paid voluntarily, and could not be recovered back as there was no statutory authority therefore; and, secondly, that there was no statute making the county liable for taxes collected and then paid over to the state and municipal bodies other than the county—which it was assumed was true of a portion of these taxes—and that the petition did not show how much of the taxes was retained by the county, or how much paid over to the state and other municipal bodies, and therefore it could not be the basis of any judgment against the county.

The county challenges our jurisdiction * * * [and] insists that the Supreme Court [of Oklahoma] put its judgment entirely on independent nonfederal grounds which were broad enough to sustain the judgment.

    * * * [I]t is certain that the lands were nontaxable. This was settled in Choate v. Trapp, *supra*, and the other cases decided with it; and it also was settled in those cases that the exemption was a vested property right arising out of a law of Congress and protected by the Constitution of the United States. * * *

We accept so much of the Supreme Court's decision as held that, if the payment was voluntary, the moneys could not be recovered back in the absence of a permissive statute, and that there was no such statute. But we are unable to accept its decision in other respects.

The right to the exemption was a federal right, and was specially set up and claimed as such in the petition. * * * It * * * is within our province to inquire not only whether the right was denied in express terms, but also whether it was denied in substance and effect, as by putting forward nonfederal grounds of decision that were without any fair or substantial support. [Citing numerous Supreme Court decisions.] * * *

The facts set forth in the petition, all of which were admitted by the demurrer, * * * make it plain, as we think, that the finding or decision that the taxes were paid voluntarily was without any fair or substantial support. The claimants were Indians just emerging from a state of dependency and wardship. Through the pending suits and otherwise they were objecting and protesting that the taxation of their lands was forbidden by a law of Congress. But * * * the county * * * made it appear to the claimants that they must choose between paying the taxes and losing their lands. To prevent a sale and to avoid the imposition of a penalty of eighteen per cent, they yielded to the county's demand * * *. The moneys thus collected were obtained by coercive means—by compulsion. The county and its officers reasonably could not have regarded it otherwise; much less the Indian claimants. Atchison, Topeka & Santa Fe Ry. Co. v. O'Connor, 223 U.S. 280; Gaar, Scott & Co. v. Shannon, supra, 223 U.S. 471.

As the payment was not voluntary, but made under compulsion, no statutory authority was essential to enable or require the county to refund the money. It is a well-settled rule that "money got through imposition" may be recovered back; and, as this court has said on several occasions, "the obligation to do justice rests upon all persons, natural and artificial, and if a county obtains the money or property of others without authority, the law, independent of any statute, will compel restitution or compensation." Marsh v. Fulton County, 10 Wall. 676, 684. To say that the county could collect these unlawful taxes by coercive means and not incur any obligation to pay them back is nothing short of saying that it could take or appropriate the property of these Indian allottees arbitrarily and without due process of law. Of course this would be in contravention of the Fourteenth Amendment, which binds the county as an agency of the state.

If it be true, as the Supreme Court assumed, that a portion of the taxes was paid over, after collection, to the state and other municipal bodies, we regard it as certain that this did not alter the county's liability to the claimants. The county had no right to collect the money, and it took the same with notice that the rights of all who were to share in the taxes were disputed by these claimants and were being contested in the pending suits. In these circumstances it could not lessen its liability by paying over a portion of the money to others whose rights it knew were disputed and were no better than its own. In legal contemplation it received the money for the use and benefit of the claimants and should respond to them accordingly.

* * *

Judgment reversed.

NOTE ON REMEDIES FOR FEDERAL CONSTITUTIONAL RIGHTS

(1) *The Sources of Constitutional Remedies.* The Constitution refers explicitly to remedies in only two instances. First, the remedy of habeas corpus is safeguarded against "Suspension" by Congress. See Chap. XI, Sec. 2, p. 1368, *infra.* Second, the Just Compensation Clause of the Fifth Amendment "dictates the remedy for interference with property rights amounting to a taking"—a compensatory remedy for the impairment of value. First English Evangelical Lutheran Church of Glendale v. County of Los Angeles, 482 U.S. 304, 316 n. 9 (1987).[1]

But what remedies are required for violations of other constitutional provisions? "To the framers, special provision for constitutional remedies probably appeared unnecessary, because the Constitution presupposed a going legal system, with ample remedial mechanisms, in which constitutional guaran-

---

1. Although First English involved a suit against a local government body—which is not shielded by sovereign immunity—the opinion rejected the United States' submission that, in view of sovereign immunity, the Just Compensation Clause should not be read as requiring a monetary remedy.

tees would be implemented." Fallon & Meltzer, *New Law, Non–Retroactivity, and Constitutional Remedies,* 104 Harv.L.Rev. 1731, 1779 (1991). Those mechanisms were the recognized forms of action at common law and in equity.

In thinking about claims of entitlement to a particular remedy for a constitutional violation, consider whether the following analysis provides a helpful framework:

"Few principles of the American constitutional tradition resonate more strongly than one stated in Marbury v. Madison: for every violation of a right, there must be a remedy. Yet Marbury's apparent promise of effective redress for all constitutional violations reflects a principle, not an ironclad rule, and its ideal is not always attained.

"* * * Within our constitutional tradition, * * * the Marbury dictum reflects just one of two principles supporting remedies for constitutional violations. Another principle, whose focus is more structural, demands a system of constitutional remedies adequate to keep government generally within the bounds of law. Both principles sometimes permit accommodation of competing interests, but in different ways. The Marbury principle that calls for individually effective remediation can sometimes be outweighed; the principle requiring an overall system of remedies that is effective in maintaining a regime of lawful government is more unyielding in its own terms, but can tolerate the denial of particular remedies, and sometimes of individual redress" (*id.* at 1778–79).

(2) *The Source of the Remedy in Ward.* What was the source of the refund remedy in Ward? State law apparently provided a refund remedy for taxes not voluntarily paid. Was the Supreme Court, when it ruled that there was no fair or substantial support for the state court's conclusion that the taxes had been paid voluntarily, merely ensuring that the state courts were applying *state* remedial rules on a non-discriminatory basis to a claim based on federal law? See generally Chap. V, Sec. 2(A), *supra.* How does that reading square with the Supreme Court's statement: "As the payment was not voluntary * * *, no statutory authority was essential to enable or require the county to refund the money"?

In any event, the Supreme Court did not assert that fair or substantial support was lacking for the state court's holding that state law afforded no remedy against the county with respect to monies already paid over to the state. What was the source of the obligation imposed on the state courts to require the county to provide a refund?

The act of Congress would have furnished a defense in a proceeding to collect the tax, but did not explicitly create a right of action to recover taxes paid under compulsion. Did it create such a right by implication? Did that right arise directly from the Due Process Clause? Was it a matter of the general common law, as then understood? Of federal common law?[2]

(3) *Remedies for Equal Protection Violations.* Iowa–Des Moines Nat'l Bank v. Bennett, 284 U.S. 239 (1931), was also a tax refund suit, but one in which the alleged constitutional violation was, *inter alia,* a denial of equal protection.

---

2. See generally Hart, *The Relations Between State and Federal Law,* 54 Colum.L.Rev. 489, 523–25 (1954); Collins, *"Economic Rights," Implied Constitutional Actions, and the Scope of Section 1983,* 77 Geo.L.J. 1493, 1507–33 (1989); Hill, *Consti-* *tutional Remedies,* 69 Colum.L.Rev. 1109 (1969); Katz, *The Jurisprudence of Remedies: Constitutional Legality and the Law of Torts in Bell v. Hood,* 117 U.Pa.L.Rev. 1 (1968).

The suit sought to compel county officers to refund taxes levied on the plaintiffs' stock at a higher rate than was applied to the shares of competing domestic corporations. The Supreme Court of Iowa found or assumed that there was systematic discrimination but nonetheless affirmed a judgment denying relief, holding that the auditor had violated state law in reducing taxes on the competitors, and that the plaintiffs' remedy was to await (or to initiate proceedings to compel) collection of the higher tax from their competitors.

The Supreme Court (per Brandeis, J.) reversed (p. 246): "When a state official, acting under color of state authority, invades, in the course of his duties, a private right secured by the federal Constitution, that right is violated, even if the state officer not only exceeded his authority but disregarded special commands of state law." With respect to the remedy, the Court said (p. 247):

"'* * * It may be assumed that all ground for a claim for refund would have fallen if the State, promptly upon discovery of the discrimination, had removed it by collecting the additional taxes from the favored competitors. * * * The right invoked is that to equal treatment; and such treatment will be attained if either their competitors' taxes are increased or their own reduced. But it is well settled that a taxpayer who has been subjected to discriminatory taxation * * * cannot be required himself to assume the burden of seeking an increase of the taxes which the others should have paid. Nor may he be remitted to the necessity of awaiting such action by the state officials upon their own initiative.

"The petitioners are entitled to obtain in these suits refund of the excess of taxes exacted from them."[3]

(4) *The McKesson and Reich Decisions.*

(a) The source of the remedial obligation in Ward and Bennett was clarified in McKesson Corp. v. Division of ABT, 496 U.S. 18 (1990), which involved a state court claim for a refund of state taxes paid under a discriminatory tax that was held to violate the dormant Commerce Clause. The state court had enjoined future enforcement of the tax but had refused, on the basis of "equitable considerations", to award a refund of taxes previously paid. The Supreme Court unanimously held that if (as in this case) a state requires taxpayers to pay first and obtain review of the tax's validity later, the Due Process Clause requires the state to afford a meaningful opportunity to secure postpayment relief. The Court held that the state must either refund to the complaining taxpayer the constitutionally excessive portion of the taxes paid, or

---

3. In Allied Stores v. Bowers, 358 U.S. 522 (1959), an Ohio resident challenged a tax on property as a denial of equal protection, because the statute exempted similar property of nonresidents. The Ohio Supreme Court held that it lacked power to extend the exemption to residents; that, consequently, if the taxpayer's contention was valid, equal protection could be achieved only by eliminating the nonresident's exemption; and that because the taxpayer would then remain liable for the tax assessed, it was in any event not entitled to any relief. The United States Supreme Court interpreted the Ohio court's ground as being that the taxpayer "lacked standing to raise the constitutional question presented" (p. 525). Treating that issue as governed by federal law, the Court ruled that the taxpayer did have standing to prosecute its constitutional claim (which it denied on the merits).

See also Orr v. Orr, 440 U.S. 268, 272 (1979). Compare Heckler v. Mathews, 465 U.S. 728 (1984), Chap. II, Sec., 3, p. 150, *supra* (upholding plaintiff's standing in federal court action challenging sex discrimination in the award of social security benefits—even though a congressional mandate limited relief to reduction in the amount received by other beneficiaries, rather than an increase in plaintiff's benefits).

(to the extent consistent with other constitutional restrictions[4]) assess and collect back taxes from the taxpayer's competitors so as to eliminate the discrimination.[5]

(b) Was it significant that the Court treated the remedial obligation as arising not from the constitutional provision that was violated (the dormant Commerce Clause) but from the Due Process Clause?

(c) In McKesson, the Court placed some emphasis on the fact that Florida had opened its courts to refund actions and did not claim that they were barred by sovereign immunity. But in Reich v. Collins, 115 S.Ct. 547 (1994), also a state court action for a state tax refund, the Supreme Court stated the constitutional obligation more unqualifiedly. Citing, *inter alia*, McKesson, Bennett, and Ward, the Court unanimously reaffirmed that due process requires that a state provide a "clear and certain" remedy for taxes collected in violation of federal law, and that while the state has authority to choose between predeprivation and postdeprivation remedies, it must provide one or the other. The Court added that the obligation exists notwithstanding "the sovereign immunity States traditionally enjoy in their own courts" (p. 549).

(5) *Retroactivity and Remedies.* A series of cases has addressed the question whether the remedial obligation recognized in McKesson extends to claims for tax refunds based upon "new" principles of federal law not clearly established at the time the tax was collected.

(a) In American Trucking Ass'ns, Inc. v. Smith, 496 U.S. 167 (1990), a companion case to McKesson, Justice O'Connor's plurality opinion for four Justices refused to give retroactive effect to the Court's earlier decision that had held certain highway use taxes unconstitutional under the Commerce Clause.[6] Thus, while future tax collections were enjoined, taxpayers were not afforded a refund of monies previously collected under the unconstitutional enactment.

(b) The approach of the Smith plurality was rejected in Harper v. Virginia Dept. of Taxation, 113 S.Ct. 2510 (1993)(5–4).[7] The case involved the question whether the Court's decision in Davis v. Michigan Dept. of Treasury, 489 U.S. 803 (1989)—which invalidated a state tax on federal pension income—should be applied retroactively. In a suit brought by federal pensioners in Virginia to recover taxes paid under a state tax scheme clearly invalid under Davis, the

---

4. On the permissible scope of retroactive taxation of the favored class as a remedy for discrimination, see Rakowski, *Harper and Its Aftermath*, 1 Fla.Tax.Rev. 445, 489–99 & authorities cited (1993); *cf.* United States v. Carlton, 114 S.Ct. 2018 (1994)(applying doctrine that retroactive tax legislation is constitutional so long as there is a rational basis for retroactive application).

5. The Court considered and rejected several arguments made by the state that such a requirement would cause serious economic dislocation and heavy administrative burdens. The Court concluded that the state's interest in financial stability did not justify a refusal to provide relief, and that there were procedural measures that states could take in the future to "protect [their]

fiscal security when weighed against their obligation to provide meaningful relief for their unconstitutional taxation" (p. 50).

6. The fifth vote was provided by Justice Scalia who, while generally favoring full retroactivity, concurred in the judgment denying a refund because he disagreed with the precedent establishing the unconstitutionality of the tax. He stated that *stare decisis* did not obligate him to adhere to that precedent when doing so would upset the state's legitimate expectations.

7. An intervening decision in James B. Beam Distilling Co. v. Georgia, 501 U.S. 529 (1991) had generated five opinions, none of which garnered more than three votes.

Virginia courts had held that they could as a matter of state law deny a refund. In reversing, the Supreme Court stressed that in the Davis case itself, where the state had conceded that a refund was appropriate, the rule announced in that case was applied retroactively; that being so, there was no basis for denying retroactive relief to similarly situated taxpayers in Virginia. Some language in Justice Thomas' majority opinion intimated, and Justice Scalia's concurring opinion clearly stated, that retroactive relief must be afforded even in situations in which the new constitutional rule had not already been applied retroactively in a prior case.

Rather than order a refund (or retroactive taxation of state pensioners), however, the Court remanded to give the state courts the chance to hear Virginia's argument that because the federal pensioners in fact had a valid pre-payment remedy, under McKesson they had no entitlement to post-payment relief.

In dissent, Justice O'Connor (joined by Chief Justice Rehnquist) took issue with the claim that Davis had applied its own rule retroactively. But more broadly, she maintained that when a constitutional decision established a new principle of law, it need not be applied retroactively if the failure to give retroactive effect would not retard the rule's operation and was necessary to avoid substantial hardship—criteria she found satisfied in this case. Concurring in the judgment, Justices Kennedy and White agreed with the dissenters that "it is sometimes appropriate in the civil context to give only prospective application to a judicial decision" (p. 2524), but concluded that this was not such a case because the Davis decision was not sufficiently novel to warrant withholding of retroactive relief.

(c) Both the Court in Harper and the plurality in Smith treated the question before the court as whether a new rule of law should be applied retroactively. However, following an argument made by Fallon & Meltzer, Paragraph (1), *supra*, at 1764–70, Justice O'Connor argued in her Harper dissent that even if the Davis decision must be applied retroactively, the question of what remedy must be provided is a separate issue, and might in appropriate circumstances be answered so as to deny a full refund even where no predeprivation process was provided.

Don't courts often consider factors like surprise, arguable injustice from retroactive application of unforeseeable rulings, and relative hardship to litigants, in framing remedies? If so, may they consider such factors in framing remedies for *constitutional* violations? See generally Fallon & Meltzer, *supra* (discussing the question generally, and stating that in other areas—notably official immunity doctrines in constitutional tort suits, and habeas corpus actions—the novelty of a constitutional rule is often made the basis for denying any relief); compare Brown, *The Demise of Constitutional Prospectivity: New Life for Owen?*, 79 Iowa L.Rev. 273 (1994)(objecting to giving weight to legal novelty in shaping constitutional remedies).

(d) The decision in Reynoldsville Casket Co. v. Hyde, 115 S.Ct. 1745 (1995), although it involved somewhat different facts, cast doubt on the permissibility of denying relief, as a matter of remedial discretion, for violation of a "novel" constitutional rule. At issue was the rule of Bendix Autolite Corp. v. Midwesco Enterprises, Inc., 486 U.S. 888 (1988), which struck down, as a burden on interstate commerce, an Ohio provision that in effect exempted tort suits against out-of-state defendants from the two-year limitations period applicable to suits against in-state defendants. In Reynoldsville—a suit against an out-of-state defendant filed before Bendix was decided, but more than two years after the car accident in question—the Ohio Supreme Court refused to apply Bendix retroactively, and thus held the action not to be time-barred.

The Supreme Court reversed, rejecting plaintiff's effort to justify the state court's decision as simply denying the defendant a remedy because of plaintiff's reliance on pre-Bendix law. Noting that the Ohio Supreme Court's decision had not rested on that ground, the Court (per Breyer, J.) added (p. 1749): "If Harper has anything more than symbolic significance, how could virtually identical reliance [by plaintiff], without more, prove sufficient to permit a virtually identical denial [of relief] simply because it is characterized as a denial based on 'remedy' rather than 'non-retroactivity'?"

The plaintiff had drawn an analogy to the law of qualified immunity in constitutional tort actions, under which damages will be denied if an official's conduct, though illegal, did not violate "clearly established" law. Conceding that that doctrine "does reflect certain remedial considerations", the Court distinguished it on the ground that "a set of special federal policy consider-ations have led to the creation of a well-established, independent rule of law"—whereas Ohio had tried to create "what amounts to an ad hoc exemption from retroactivity" (p. 1751). (Is that an adequate distinction?) A second analogy offered by the plaintiff—the general unavailability of habeas corpus relief when sought on the basis of "new" rulings of constitutional law—was also found wanting by the Court; that doctrine was not a "remedial" limitation on retroactivity but rather a limitation inherent in retroactivity itself—and one based on special concerns about the finality of criminal convictions. (But since the Court has authorized habeas relief based on new law in exceptional circumstances, see generally Teague v. Lane, Chap. IX, Sec. 2, p. 1392, *infra*, isn't there in fact a remedial calculus at work in such cases?)

The opinion recognized, however, that sometimes a new rule of law will not require a retroactive remedy, pointing to the "well-established general legal rule" of official immunity—which, the Court said, "reflects *both* reliance interests and other significant policy justifications", and which "trumps the new rule of [constitutional] law" (p. 1751). In light of that recognition, to what extent does the decision foreclose consideration of whether retroactive remedies may be denied for violations of "new" constitutional rulings?[8]

(6) *Claims for Injunctive Relief.*

---

8. Justice Scalia's concurring opinion (joined by Justice Thomas) suggested that the case involved no question of remedial discretion at all, but only the obligation of the Ohio courts to disregard an invalid stat-ute. Justice Kennedy (joined by Justice O'Connor), concurring in the judgment, did "not read today's opinion to surrender in advance our authority to decide that in some exceptional cases, courts may shape relief in light of disruption of important reliance in-terests or the unfairness caused by unexpect-ed judicial decisions" (p. 1752), but thought that the Bendix decision did not establish a new rule of law and hence that plaintiff's claim of reliance fell short.

Cf. Ryder v. United States, 115 S.Ct. 2031, 2036 (1995)(rejecting the government's argument that a decision finding invalid the appointment of judges to the Court of Mili-tary Review should, as a matter of remedial decision pursuant to Chevron Oil Co. v. Hu-son, 404 U.S. 97 (1971), p. 86, *supra*, be given prospective effect only; "whatever the con-tinuing validity of Chevron Oil after [Harper and Reynoldsville Casket], there is not the sort of grave disruption or inequity involved in awarding retrospective relief to this peti-tioner that would bring that doctrine into play").

(a) *The Crain Decision.* In General Oil Co. v. Crain, 209 U.S. 211 (1908), suit was brought in Tennessee state court to enjoin a state official from enforcing a tax alleged, *inter alia*, to burden interstate commerce. Anticipatory relief in equity was premised on the penalties for violation, coupled with doubts that payments under protest could be recovered and with concern that a multiplicity of suits would be necessary for recovery.

The Supreme Court of Tennessee held that the state courts lacked jurisdiction to grant an injunction on the ground that the suit was one against the state. On appeal to the U.S. Supreme Court, Tennessee urged that the judgment "involved no Federal question, but only the powers and jurisdiction of the courts of the State of Tennessee, in respect to which the Supreme Court of Tennessee is the final arbiter." But the Supreme Court affirmed its jurisdiction (although it sustained the tax upon the merits). Justice McKenna said (p. 226):

"* * * Necessarily to give adequate protection to constitutional rights a distinction must be made between valid and invalid state laws, as determining the character of the suit against state officers. And the suit at bar illustrates the necessity. If a suit against state officers is precluded in the national courts by the Eleventh Amendment to the Constitution, and may be forbidden by a state to its courts, * * * without power of review by this court, * * * an easy way is open to prevent the enforcement of many provisions of the Constitution, and the Fourteenth Amendment, which is directed at state action, could be nullified as to much of its operation. * * *

"It being then the right of a party to be protected against a law which violates a constitutional right, whether by its terms or the manner of its enforcement, it is manifest that a decision which denies such protection gives effect to the law, and the decision is reviewable by this court."

Justice Harlan, disagreeing as to jurisdiction, said (pp. 232–33):

"The oil company seeks a reversal of the decree of the state court, contending that it was denied a right arising under the commerce clause of the Constitution. But back of any question of that kind was the question before the Supreme Court of Tennessee whether the inferior state court, under the law of * * * Tennessee, could entertain jurisdiction of the suit. * * * That certainly is a state, not a Federal question. * * * When, therefore, its highest court has declared that the Tennessee statute referred to in argument did not allow the inferior state court to take cognizance of a suit like this, that decision must be accepted as the interpretation to be placed on the local statute. Otherwise, this court will adjudge that the Tennessee court *shall* take jurisdiction of a suit of which the highest court of the State adjudges that it cannot do consistently with the laws of the State which created it and which established its jurisdiction. It seems to me that this court * * * has no alternative but to affirm the judgment, on the ground simply that the ground upon which it is placed is broad enough to support the judgment without reference to any question raised or discussed by counsel."

(b) *The Implications of Crain.* The majority's suggestion that the Eleventh Amendment would have prevented the oil company from obtaining an injunction in federal court is puzzling, for on the very same day, the Court decided Ex parte Young, 209 U.S. 123, p. 1058, *infra*, holding that the Amendment did not bar a similar federal court action to enjoin state officials from enforcing a state law that was challenged on federal constitutional grounds. But whether or not a federal court would have been open, does Crain necessarily hold that, if the tax were unconstitutional, the oil company had a federal right to injunctive relief?[9]

Traditionally injunctions are available only when there is no adequate remedy at law. If Tennessee had clearly made a refund remedy available, would its refusal to provide an injunctive remedy then have been an adequate state ground? See McCoy v. Shaw, 277 U.S. 302 (1928)(affirming a state's denial of anticipatory equitable relief against a state tax on the ground that the state could properly require payment and a suit for refund). Re-read the excerpt from Professor Hart's Dialogue, quoted at pp. 376-79, *supra*, stressing the broad discretion that Congress has in choosing among alternative remedies for constitutional violations, and more particularly, that it is "hard to hold that anybody has a constitutional right to an injunction or a declaratory judgment". Did the Tennessee legislature have latitude in Crain to choose among alternative remedies?

Was the adequacy of the remedies Tennessee actually did provide judged under a standard drawn from state law? From judge-made federal law? From the Commerce Clause (the constitutional provision allegedly violated)?

(c) *A Right to Injunctive Relief?* The notion that injunctive relief is exceptional has considerably less force today than it did when Crain was decided, or when Professor Hart wrote in 1953. Indeed, at least since Brown v. Board of Education was decided in 1954, injunctive remedies for constitutional violations have become the rule and actions at law (at least for damages) the exception in many areas of public law litigation—*e.g.*, suits attacking school segregation, legislative malapportionment, or prison conditions. The question whether, or to what extent, particular injunctive remedies (for example, a busing order in a school desegregation case) might be constitutionally required has not been sharply presented in these cases, as it might be if the legislature purported to prohibit such a remedy.[10] Controversy has focused instead on whether the courts have appropriately exercised a general grant of equity jurisdiction.

---

9. In this connection, compare Crain with Georgia R.R. & Banking Co. v. Musgrove, 335 U.S. 900 (1949). The Georgia Supreme Court had dismissed an action for injunctive relief against certain state taxes on the ground that the suit was an unconsented action against the state; the opinion suggested that other (unspecified) state remedies might be available. The Supreme Court dismissed the appeal on the ground that there was an adequate nonfederal ground for decision. (A later Supreme Court decision held that in view of the inadequacy of state court remedies, an injunction *was* available in *federal* court. Georgia R.R. & Banking Co. v. Redwine, 342 U.S. 299 (1952).)

Does Musgrove mean that the Crain obligation will not be enforced unless it is first demonstrated that no federal court remedy exists? Should the state's obligation to grant a remedy be contingent on the hypothetical availability of a federal action?

10. An exception is tax refund cases, where the Tax Injunction Act, 28 U.S.C. § 1341, generally precludes federal court injunctions, and state law generally prohibits state court injunctions, thus often leaving taxpayers with the choice of refusing to pay (where that is permitted) or, more commonly, of seeking a refund after payment. *Cf.* National Private Truck Council, Inc. v. Oklahoma Tax Comm'n, 115 S.Ct. 2351 (1995), Chap. X, Sec. 1(B), *infra* (holding that the federal right of action in 42 U.S.C. § 1983, which generally affords relief at law or in equity for action taken under color of state law that violates federal rights, must be read, in light of the strong background presumption against federal interference in state taxation, as not authorizing injunctive relief in tax cases where state law furnishes an "adequate" remedy).

One important question is whether a person subject to civil or criminal sanctions has a constitutional right to anticipatory relief—*i.e.*, the right to bring a declaratory or injunctive action challenging the constitutionality of some statutory or other duty, before having to choose between (i) forgoing conduct believed to be constitutionally protected, or (ii) engaging in that conduct and suffering the specified penalties if the claim of constitutional protection is found to lack merit. In Ex parte Young, 209 U.S. 123 (1908), Chap. IX, Sec. 2(A), p. 1058, *infra*, an anticipatory action was brought to enjoin the state attorney general from instituting suits to impose sanctions for violation of a state statute regulating railroad rates alleged to be confiscatory in violation of the Fourteenth Amendment. The sale of each ticket above the specified rates constituted a separate violation; for each violation, employees would be criminally liable. The Court deemed those sanctions so enormous "as to intimidate the company and its officers from resorting to the courts to test the validity of the legislation", just "as if the law in terms prohibited the company from seeking judicial construction of laws which deeply affect its rights" (p. 147). The Court thus held that because of the harsh sanctions imposed, the acts "are unconstitutional on their face, without regard to the question of the insufficiency of those rates" (p. 148).

Despite some echoes in other rate cases decided not long after Young[11]— and the desirability of permitting litigants to determine in advance whether a statutory prohibition can validly be enforced against them[12]—there is little clear authority for a general right to obtain anticipatory relief. *Cf.* Thunder Basin Coal Co. v. Reich, 114 S.Ct. 771, 781–82 (1994), where the Court upheld congressional preclusion of anticipatory attack, on *statutory* grounds, on an administrative order. The Court stated that the case was not one in which the "practical effect of coercive penalties for non-compliance was to foreclose all access to the courts. Nor does this approach a situation in which compliance is sufficiently onerous and coercive penalties sufficiently potent that a constitutionally intolerable choice might be presented."[13]

---

11. See Missouri Pac. Ry. Co. v. Tucker, 230 U.S. 340 (1913); Oklahoma Operating Co. v. Love, 252 U.S. 331 (1920); Pacific Tel. & Tel. Co. v. Kuykendall, 265 U.S. 196 (1924).

12. See Note, 80 Harv. L. Rev. 1490 (1967).

13. Compare Oestereich v. Selective Service System Local Bd., 393 U.S. 233 (1968), where plaintiff, though entitled to an exemption from military service, turned in his registration certificate to protest the Vietnam war. The draft board, adjudging him delinquent for violating the regulation requiring possession of the certificate, re-classified him as eligible to be drafted. A statutory provision appeared rather plainly to preclude pre-induction judicial review of a draft board's classification decision, leaving review available only as a defense to a criminal prosecution for refusing induction (or apparently in a habeas corpus action after accepting induction). But the Court construed the statute as permitting a pre-induction injunction to restrain a blatantly lawless action by the board in disregarding the plaintiff's statutory right to an exemption. Justice Harlan's concurrence argued that to deprive a person of liberty without the prior opportunity to challenge the lawfulness of the induction in any competent forum would raise serious constitutional problems. Justice Stewart's dissent replied that persons arrested for crime are routinely deprived of their liberty without prior opportunity to adjudicate the legality of their detentions.

Cf. Monaghan, *First Amendment "Due Process"*, 83 Harv.L.Rev. 518, 543–51 (1970)(arguing for a right to prospective relief in cases arising under the First Amendment).

Bivens v. Six Unknown Named Agents
of Federal Bureau of Narcotics

403 U.S. 388, 91 S.Ct. 1999, 29 L.Ed.2d 619 (1971).
Certiorari to the United States Court of Appeals for the Second Circuit.

■ MR. JUSTICE BRENNAN delivered the opinion of the Court.

* * *

In Bell v. Hood, 327 U.S. 678 (1946), we reserved the question whether violation of [the Fourth Amendment] by a federal agent acting under color of his authority gives rise to a cause of action for damages consequent upon his unconstitutional conduct. Today we hold that it does.

* * * Petitioner's complaint alleged that * * * respondents, agents of the Federal Bureau of Narcotics acting under claim of federal authority, entered his apartment and arrested him for alleged narcotics violations. The agents manacled petitioner in front of his wife and children, and threatened to arrest the entire family. They searched the apartment from stem to stern. Thereafter petitioner was taken to the federal courthouse in Brooklyn, where he was interrogated, booked, and subjected to a visual strip search.

* * * [P]etitioner brought suit in Federal District Court. In addition to the allegations above, his complaint asserted that the arrest and search were effected without a warrant, and that unreasonable force was employed in making the arrest; fairly read, it alleges as well that the arrest was made without probable cause. Petitioner claimed to have suffered great humiliation, embarrassment, and mental suffering as a result of the agents' unlawful conduct, and sought $15,000 damages from each of them. The District Court * * * dismissed the complaint on the ground, *inter alia*, that it failed to state a cause of action. The Court of Appeals * * * affirmed on that basis. We granted certiorari. We reverse.

I

Respondents do not argue that petitioner should be entirely without remedy for an unconstitutional invasion of his rights by federal agents. In respondents' view, however, the rights which petitioner asserts—primarily rights of privacy—are creations of state and not of federal law. Accordingly, they argue, petitioner may obtain money damages to redress invasion of these rights only by an action in tort, under state law, in the state courts. In this scheme the Fourth Amendment would serve merely to limit the extent to which the agents could defend the state law tort suit by asserting that their actions were a valid exercise of federal power: if the agents were shown to have violated the Fourth Amendment, such a defense would be lost to them and they would stand before the state law merely as private individuals. Candidly admitting that it is the policy of the Department of Justice to remove all such suits from the state to the federal courts for decision,[4] respondents nevertheless urge that we uphold dismissal of petitioner's complaint in federal court, and remit him to filing an action in the state courts in order that the case may properly be removed to the federal court for decision on the basis of state law.

4. * * * In light of this, it is difficult to understand our Brother Blackmun's complaint that our holding today "opens the door for another avalanche of new federal cases." * * *

We think that respondents' thesis rests upon an unduly restrictive view of the Fourth Amendment's protection against unreasonable searches and seizures by federal agents, a view that has consistently been rejected by this Court. Respondents seek to treat the relationship between a citizen and a federal agent unconstitutionally exercising his authority as no different from the relationship between two private citizens. In so doing, they ignore the fact that power, once granted, does not disappear like a magic gift when it is wrongfully used. An agent acting—albeit unconstitutionally—in the name of the United States possesses a far greater capacity for harm than an individual trespasser exercising no authority other than his own. *Cf.* Amos v. United States, 255 U.S. 313, 317 (1921); United States v. Classic, 313 U.S. 299, 326 (1941). Accordingly, as our cases make clear, the Fourth Amendment operates as a limitation upon the exercise of federal power regardless of whether the State in whose jurisdiction that power is exercised would prohibit or penalize the identical act if engaged in by a private citizen. It guarantees to citizens of the United States the absolute right to be free from unreasonable searches and seizures carried out by virtue of federal authority. And "where federally protected rights have been invaded, it has been the rule from the beginning that courts will be alert to adjust their remedies so as to grant the necessary relief." Bell v. Hood, 327 U.S., at 684. * * *

First. Our cases have long since rejected the notion that the Fourth Amendment proscribes only such conduct as would, if engaged in by private persons, be condemned by state law. * * * In light of these cases, respondents' argument that the Fourth Amendment serves only as a limitation on federal defenses to a state law claim, and not as an independent limitation upon the exercise of federal power, must be rejected.

Second. The interests protected by state laws regulating trespass and the invasion of privacy, and those protected by the Fourth Amendment's guarantee against unreasonable searches and seizures, may be inconsistent or even hostile. Thus, we may bar the door against an unwelcome private intruder, or call the police if he persists in seeking entrance. The availability of such alternative means for the protection of privacy may lead the State to restrict imposition of liability for any consequent trespass. A private citizen, asserting no authority other than his own, will not normally be liable in trespass if he demands, and is granted, admission to another's house. But one who demands admission under a claim of federal authority stands in a far different position. The mere invocation of federal power by a federal law enforcement official will normally render futile any attempt to resist an unlawful entry or arrest by resort to the local police; and a claim of authority to enter is likely to unlock the door as well. * * *

Nor is it adequate to answer that state law may take into account the different status of one clothed with the authority of the Federal Government. For just as state law may not authorize federal agents to violate the Fourth Amendment, * * * neither may state law undertake to limit the extent to which federal authority can be exercised. The inevitable consequence of this dual limitation on state power is that the federal question becomes not merely a possible defense to the state law action, but an independent claim both necessary and sufficient to make out the plaintiff's cause of action. * * *

Third. That damages may be obtained for injuries consequent upon a violation of the Fourth Amendment by federal officials should hardly seem a surprising proposition. * * * See Nixon v. Condon, 286 U.S. 73 (1932); Nixon

v. Herndon, 273 U.S. 536, 540 (1927); Swafford v. Templeton, 185 U.S. 487 (1902); Wiley v. Sinkler, 179 U.S. 58 (1900). Of course the Fourth Amendment does not in so many words provide for its enforcement by an award of money damages for the consequences of its violation. But "it is also well settled that where legal rights have been invaded, and a federal statute provides for a general right to sue for such invasion, federal courts may use any available remedy to make good the wrong done." Bell v. Hood, 327 U.S., at 684 (1946)(footnote omitted). The present case involves no special factors counselling hesitation in the absence of affirmative action by Congress. We are not dealing with a question of "federal fiscal policy," as in United States v. Standard Oil Co., 332 U.S. 301, 311 (1947). * * * Nor are we asked in this case to impose liability upon a congressional employee for actions contrary to no constitutional prohibition, but merely said to be in excess of the authority delegated to him by the Congress. Wheeldin v. Wheeler, 373 U.S. 647 (1963). Finally, we cannot accept respondents' formulation of the question as whether the availability of money damages is necessary to enforce the Fourth Amendment. For we have here no explicit congressional declaration that persons injured by a federal officer's violation of the Fourth Amendment may not recover money damages from the agents, but must instead be remitted to another remedy, equally effective in the view of Congress. The question is merely whether petitioner, if he can demonstrate an injury consequent upon the violation by federal agents of his Fourth Amendment rights, is entitled to redress his injury through a particular remedial mechanism normally available in the federal courts. "The very essence of civil liberty certainly consists in the right of every individual to claim the protection of the laws whenever he receives an injury." Marbury v. Madison, 1 Cranch 137, 163 (1803). Having concluded that petitioner's complaint states a cause of action under the Fourth Amendment, we hold that petitioner is entitled to recover money damages for any injuries he has suffered as a result of the agents' violation of the Amendment.

II

In addition to holding that petitioner's complaint had failed to state facts making out a cause of action, the District Court ruled that in any event respondents were immune from liability by virtue of their official position. This question was not passed upon by the Court of Appeals, and accordingly we do not consider it here. The judgment of the Court of Appeals is reversed and the case is remanded for further proceedings consistent with this opinion.

So ordered.

Judgment reversed and case remanded.

■ MR. JUSTICE HARLAN, concurring in the judgment.

My initial view of this case was that the Court of Appeals was correct in dismissing the complaint, but for reasons stated in this opinion I am now persuaded to the contrary. Accordingly, I join in the judgment of reversal.

    * * *

For the reasons set forth below, I am of the opinion that federal courts do have the power to award damages for violation of "constitutionally protected interests" and I agree with the Court that a traditional judicial remedy such as damages is appropriate to the vindication of the personal interests protected by the Fourth Amendment.

I

I turn first to the contention that the constitutional power of federal courts to accord Bivens damages for his claim depends on the passage of a statute creating a "federal cause of action." Although the point is not entirely free of ambiguity, I do not understand either the Government or my dissenting Brothers to maintain that Bivens' contention that he is entitled to be free from the type of official conduct prohibited by the Fourth Amendment depends on a decision by the State in which he resides to accord him a remedy. Such a position would be incompatible with the presumed availability of federal equitable relief, if a proper showing can be made in terms of the ordinary principles governing equitable remedies. See Bell v. Hood, 327 U.S. 678, 684 (1946). However broad a federal court's discretion concerning equitable remedies, it is absolutely clear—at least after Erie R. Co. v. Tompkins, 304 U.S. 64 (1938)—that in a nondiversity suit a federal court's power to grant even equitable relief depends on the presence of a substantive right derived from federal law. Compare Guaranty Trust Co. v. York, 326 U.S. 99, 105–107 (1945), with Holmberg v. Armbrecht, 327 U.S. 392, 395 (1946). See also H. Hart and H. Wechsler, The Federal Courts and the Federal System 818–819 (1953).

Thus the interest which Bivens claims—to be free from official conduct in contravention of the Fourth Amendment—is a federally protected interest.[3] Therefore, the question of judicial *power* to grant Bivens damages is not a problem of the "source" of the "right"; instead, the question is whether the power to authorize damages as a judicial remedy for the vindication of a federal constitutional right is placed by the Constitution itself exclusively in Congress' hands.

II

The contention that the federal courts are powerless to accord a litigant damages for a claimed invasion of his federal constitutional rights until Congress explicitly authorizes the remedy cannot rest on the notion that the decision to grant compensatory relief involves a resolution of policy considerations not susceptible of judicial discernment. Thus, in suits for damages based on violations of federal statutes lacking any express authorization of a

---

3. The Government appears not quite ready to concede this point. Certain points in the Government's argument seem to suggest that the "state-created right—federal defense" model reaches not only the question of the power to accord a federal damages remedy, but also the claim to any judicial remedy in any court. * * *

* * *

In truth, the legislative record as a whole behind the Bill of Rights is silent on the rather refined doctrinal question whether the framers considered the rights therein enumerated as dependent in the first instance on the decision of a State to accord legal status to the personal interests at stake. That is understandable since the Government itself points out that general federal question jurisdiction was not extended to the federal dis-

trict courts until 1875. Act of March 3, 1875, § 1, 18 Stat. 470. The most that can be drawn from this historical fact is that the authors of the Bill of Rights assumed the adequacy of common law remedies to vindicate the federally protected interest. One must first combine this assumption with contemporary modes of jurisprudential thought which appeared to link "rights" and "remedies" in a 1:1 correlation, *cf.* Marbury v. Madison, 1 Cranch 137, 163, 2 L.Ed. 60 (1803), before reaching the conclusion that the framers are to be understood today as having created no federally protected interests. And, of course, that would simply require the conclusion that federal equitable relief would not lie to protect those interests guarded by the Fourth Amendment. * * *

damage remedy, this Court has authorized such relief where, in its view, damages are necessary to effectuate the congressional policy underpinning the substantive provisions of the statute. J.I. Case Co. v. Borak, 377 U.S. 426 (1964); [citing two other decisions.][4]

If it is not the nature of the remedy which is thought to render a judgment as to the appropriateness of damages inherently "legislative," then it must be the nature of the legal interest offered as an occasion for invoking otherwise appropriate judicial relief. But I do not think that the fact that the interest is protected by the Constitution rather than statute or common law justifies the assertion that federal courts are powerless to grant damages in the absence of explicit congressional action authorizing the remedy. Initially, I note that it would be at least anomalous to conclude that the federal judiciary—while competent to choose among the range of traditional judicial remedies to implement statutory and common-law policies, and even to generate substantive rules governing primary behavior in furtherance of broadly formulated policies articulated by statute or Constitution, see Textile Workers Union v. Lincoln Mills, 353 U.S. 448 (1957); United States v. Standard Oil Co., 332 U.S. 301, 304–311 (1947); Clearfield Trust Co. v. United States, 318 U.S. 363 (1943)—is powerless to accord a damage remedy to vindicate social policies which, by virtue of their inclusion in the Constitution, are aimed predominantly at restraining the Government as an instrument of the popular will.

More importantly, the presumed availability of federal equitable relief against threatened invasions of constitutional interests appears entirely to negate the contention that the status of an interest as constitutionally protected divests federal courts of the power to grant damages absent express congressional authorization. * * *

If explicit congressional authorization is an absolute prerequisite to the power of a federal court to accord compensatory relief regardless of the necessity or appropriateness of damages as a remedy simply because of the status of a legal interest as constitutionally protected, then it seems to me that explicit congressional authorization is similarly prerequisite to the exercise of equitable remedial discretion in favor of constitutionally protected interests. Conversely, if a general grant of jurisdiction to the federal courts by Congress is thought adequate to empower a federal court to grant equitable relief for all areas of subject-matter jurisdiction enumerated therein, see 28 U.S.C. § 1331(a), then it seems to me that statute is sufficient to empower a federal court to grant a traditional remedy at law. Of course, the special historical traditions governing the federal equity system, see Sprague v. Ticonic National

---

4. The Borak case is an especially clear example of the exercise of federal judicial power to accord damages as an appropriate remedy in the absence of any express statutory authorization of a federal cause of action. There we "implied"—from what can only be characterized as an "exclusively procedural provision" affording access to a federal forum—a private cause of action for damages for violation of § 14(a) of the Securities Act of 1934, 15 U.S.C. § 78n(a). We did so in an area where federal regulation has been singularly comprehensive and elaborate administrative enforcement machinery had been provided. The exercise of judicial power involved in Borak simply cannot be justified in terms of statutory construction, see Hill, Constitutional Remedies, 69 Columbia 1109, 1120–1121 (1969); nor did the Borak Court purport to do so. The notion of "implying" a remedy, therefore, as applied to cases like Borak, can only refer to a process whereby the federal judiciary exercises a choice among *traditionally available* judicial remedies according to reasons related to the substantive social policy embodied in an act of positive law. See *ibid.*, and Bell v. Hood, *supra*, 327 U.S., at 684.

Bank, 307 U.S. 161 (1939), might still bear on the comparative appropriateness of granting equitable relief as opposed to money damages. That possibility, however, relates not to whether the federal courts have the power to afford one type of remedy as opposed to the other, but rather to the criteria which should govern the exercise of our power. To that question, I now pass.

III

The major thrust of the Government's position is that, where Congress has not expressly authorized a particular remedy, a federal court should exercise its power to accord a traditional form of judicial relief at the behest of a litigant, who claims a constitutionally protected interest has been invaded, only where the remedy is "essential," or "indispensable for vindicating constitutional rights." Govt. Brief, 19, 24. * * *

These arguments for a more stringent test to govern the grant of damages in constitutional cases seem to be adequately answered by the point that the judiciary has a particular responsibility to assure the vindication of constitutional interests such as those embraced by the Fourth Amendment. To be sure, "it must be remembered that legislatures are ultimate guardians of the liberties and welfare of the people in quite as great a degree as the courts." Missouri, Kansas & Texas R. Co. of Texas v. May, 194 U.S. 267, 270 (1904). But it must also be recognized that the Bill of Rights is particularly intended to vindicate the interests of the individual in the face of the popular will as expressed in legislative majorities; at the very least, it strikes me as no more appropriate to await express congressional authorization of traditional judicial relief with regard to these legal interests than with respect to interests protected by federal statutes.

The question then, is, as I see it, whether compensatory relief is "necessary" or "appropriate" to the vindication of the interest asserted. * * * In resolving that question, it seems to me that the range of policy considerations we may take into account are at least as broad as those a legislature would consider with respect to an express statutory authorization of a traditional remedy. In this regard I agree with the Court that the appropriateness of according Bivens compensatory relief does not turn simply on the deterrent effect liability will have on federal official conduct.[8] * * *

* * * I think it is clear that Bivens advances a claim of the sort that, if proved, would be properly compensable in damages. The personal interests protected by the Fourth Amendment are those we attempt to capture by the notion of "privacy"; while the Court today properly points out that the type of

---

8. And I think it follows from this point that today's decision has little, if indeed any, bearing on the question whether a federal court may properly devise remedies—other than traditionally available forms of judicial relief—for the purpose of enforcing substantive social policies embodied in constitutional or statutory policies. Compare today's decision with Mapp v. Ohio, 367 U.S. 643 (1961), and Weeks v. United States, 232 U.S. 383 (1914). The Court today simply recognizes what has long been implicit in our decisions concerning equitable relief and remedies implied from statutory schemes; *i.e.*, that a court of law vested with jurisdiction over the subject matter of a suit has the power—and therefore the duty—to make principled choices among traditional judicial remedies. Whether special prophylactic measures—which at least arguably the exclusionary rule exemplifies, see Hill, The Bill of Rights and the Supervisory Power, 69 Col.L.Rev. 181, 182–185 (1969)—are supportable on grounds other than a court's competence to select among traditional judicial remedies to make good the wrong done, *cf.* Bell v. Hood, *supra*, 327 U.S. at 684, is a separate question.

harm which officials can inflict when they invade protected zones of an individual's life are different from the types of harm private citizens inflict on one another, the experience of judges in dealing with private trespass and false imprisonment claims supports the conclusion that courts of law are capable of making the types of judgment concerning causation and magnitude of injury necessary to accord meaningful compensation for invasion of Fourth Amendment rights.

On the other hand, the limitations on state remedies for violation of common law rights by private citizens argue in favor of a federal damage remedy. The injuries inflicted by officials acting under color of law, while no less compensable in damages than those inflicted by private parties, are substantially different in kind, as the Court's opinion today discusses in detail. See Monroe v. Pape, 365 U.S. 167, 195 (1961)(Harlan, J., concurring). It seems to me entirely proper that these injuries be compensable according to uniform rules of federal law, especially in light of the very large element of federal law which must in any event control the scope of official defenses to liability. See Monroe v. Pape, 365 U.S. 167, 194–195 (Harlan, J., concurring); Howard v. Lyons, 360 U.S. 593 (1959). Certainly, there is very little federalism interest in preserving different rules of liability for federal officers dependent on the State where the injury occurs. *Cf.*, United States v. Standard Oil Co., 332 U.S. 301, 305–311 (1947).

Putting aside the desirability of leaving the problem of federal official liability to the vagaries of common law actions, it is apparent that damages in some form is the only possible remedy for someone in Bivens' alleged position. It will be a rare case indeed in which an individual in Bivens' position will be able to obviate the harm by securing injunctive relief from any court. However desirable a direct remedy against the Government might be as a substitute for individual official liability, the Sovereign still remains immune to suit. Finally, assuming Bivens' innocence of the crime charged, the "exclusionary rule" is simply irrelevant. For people in Bivens' shoes, it is damages or nothing.

The only substantial policy consideration advanced against recognition of a federal cause of action for violation of Fourth Amendment rights by federal officials is the incremental expenditure of judicial resources that will be necessitated by this class of litigation. There is, however, something ultimately self-defeating about this argument. For if, as the Government contends, damages will rarely be realized by plaintiffs in these cases because of jury hostility, the limited resources of the official concerned, etc., then I am not ready to assume that there will be a significant increase in the expenditure of judicial resources on these claims. Few responsible lawyers and plaintiffs are likely to choose the course of litigation if the statistical chances of success are truly *de minimis*. And I simply cannot agree with my Brother Black that the possibility of "frivolous" claims—if defined simply as claims with no legal merit—warrants closing the courthouse doors to people in Bivens' situation. There are other ways, short of that, of coping with frivolous lawsuits.

On the other hand, if—as I believe is the case with respect, at least, to the most flagrant abuses of official power—damages to some degree will be available when the option of litigation is chosen, then the question appears to be how Fourth Amendment interests rank on a scale of social values compared with, for example, the interests of stockholders defrauded by misleading proxies. See J.I. Case Co. v. Borak, *supra*. Judicial resources, I am well aware, are increasingly scarce these days. Nonetheless, when we automatically close the courthouse door solely on this basis, we implicitly express a value judgment on the comparative importance of classes of legally protected interests. And current limitations upon the effective functioning of the courts arising from budgetary inadequacies should not be permitted to stand in the way of the recognition of otherwise sound constitutional principles.

Of course, for a variety of reasons, the remedy may not often be sought. See generally, Foote, Tort Remedies for Police Violations of Individual Rights, 39 Minn.L.Rev. 493 (1955). And the countervailing interests in efficient law enforcement of course argue for a protective zone with respect to many types of Fourth Amendment violations. *Cf.* Barr v. Matteo, 360 U.S. 564 (1959)(opinion of Harlan, J.). But, while I express no view on the immunity defense offered in the instant case, I deem it proper to venture the thought that at the very least such a remedy would be available for the most flagrant and patently unjustified sorts of police conduct. Although litigants may not often choose to seek relief, it is important, in a civilized society, that the judicial branch of the Nation's government stand ready to afford a remedy in these circumstances. It goes without saying that I intimate no view on the merits of petitioner's underlying claim.

For these reasons, I concur in the judgment of the Court.

■ Mr. Chief Justice Burger, dissenting.

I dissent from today's holding which judicially creates a damage remedy not provided for by the Constitution and not enacted by Congress. We would more surely preserve the important values of the doctrine of separation of powers—and perhaps get a better result—by recommending a solution to the Congress as the branch of government in which the Constitution has vested the legislative power. Legislation is the business of the Congress, and it has the facilities and competence for that task—as we do not. * * *

■ Mr. Justice Black, dissenting.

* * * There can be no doubt that Congress could create a federal cause of action for damages for an unreasonable search in violation of the Fourth Amendment. Although Congress has created such a federal cause of action against *state* officials acting under color of state law,* it has never created such a cause of action against federal officials. If it wanted to do so, Congress could, of course, create a remedy against federal officials who violate the Fourth Amendment in the performance of their duties. But the point of this case and the fatal weakness in the Court's judgment is that neither Congress nor the State of New York has enacted legislation creating such a right of action. For us to do so is, in my judgment, an exercise of power that the Constitution does not give us.

Even if we had the legislative power to create a remedy, there are many reasons why we should decline to create a cause of action where none has existed since the formation of our Government. The courts of the United States as well as those of the States are choked with lawsuits. * * *

We sit at the top of a judicial system accused by some of nearing the point of collapse. Many criminal defendants do not receive speedy trials and neither society nor the accused are assured of justice when inordinate delays occur.

* [Ed.] Justice Black's reference is to 42 U.S.C. § 1983. See generally Chap. IX, Sec. 2(C), *infra.*

Citizens must wait years to litigate their private civil suits. Substantial changes in correctional and parole systems demand the attention of the lawmakers and the judiciary. If I were a legislator I might well find these and other needs so pressing as to make me believe that the resources of lawyers and judges should be devoted to them rather than to civil damage actions against officers who generally strive to perform within constitutional bounds. There is also a real danger that such suits might deter officials from the *proper* and honest performance of their duties.

All of these considerations make imperative careful study and weighing of the arguments both for and against the creation of such a remedy under the Fourth Amendment. I would have great difficulty for myself in resolving the competing policies, goals, and priorities in the use of resources, if I thought it were my job to resolve those questions. But that is not my task. The task of evaluating the pros and cons of creating judicial remedies for particular wrongs is a matter for Congress and the legislatures of the States. * * *

■ MR. JUSTICE BLACKMUN, dissenting.

I, too, dissent. I do so largely for the reasons expressed in Chief Judge Lumbard's thoughtful and scholarly opinion for the Court of Appeals. But I also feel that the judicial legislation, which the Court by its opinion today concededly is effectuating, opens the door for another avalanche of new federal cases. * * *

NOTE ON THE BIVENS DECISION AND ON THE RELATIONSHIP OF CONGRESS AND THE COURTS IN FORMULATING REMEDIES FOR CONSTITUTIONAL VIOLATIONS

(1) *Introduction.* The Bivens case and the materials in this Note deal with damage actions against federal officials as an implied remedy for constitutional violations. Ward v. Love County, McKesson Corp. v. Division of ABT, p. 851, *supra*, and similar tax refund cases also were suits for a compensatory remedy for unconstitutional action, but in those cases the nominal defendant was typically a state or local government rather than a federal official, and any judgment would be paid by the government itself rather than by the official personally.

Should officer suits for monetary relief be seen as different from suits against the government itself—because the relief does not come from the treasury—or as a functionally necessary surrogate for governmental immunity, without which such immunity would not be tolerable? Should the Court's willingness to imply a remedy depend on whether the suit challenges action under color of *state law* or under color of *federal law*? On the latter point, what significance should the Bivens Court have attached to the absence of any broad statutory authorization of private remedies comparable to 42 U.S.C. § 1983 (for violations under color of *state* law)?

The absence of any such statutory provision highlights a range of questions about the respective roles of Congress and the courts in fashioning remedies for constitutional violations: Should the federal courts have more (or less) freedom in this area than when creating remedies for violation of statutory obligations? How relevant are (a) the availability of a state law remedy for the particular violation, (b) the effect on federal district court jurisdiction of recognition of a federal remedy, (c) the nature of the remedy sought (*e.g.*, damages versus an injunction), or (d) the availability of other federal remedies under applicable statutes and regulations? For early commentary, see the articles cited at p. 850, note 2, *supra*.

(2) *Antecedents*. The question of the availability of a damages remedy for violation of a constitutional right had been mooted ever since the Court held in Bell v. Hood, 327 U.S. 678 (1946), Chap. VIII, Sec. 3, p. 934, *infra*, that a federal district court had jurisdiction under § 1331 of a claim for damages against federal officers for allegedly unconstitutional arrests and searches—but reserved the question whether there was a good claim on the merits under federal (as opposed to state) law. Is it surprising that the question was not resolved until the Bivens decision in 1971?[1]

Does the explanation lie in part in the availability of state damages remedies for a substantial range of violations and of federal statutory remedies (under such statutes as the Tort Claims Act) for others? Note that state court authority to issue *injunctions* against federal officers is not clearly established—see Chap. IV, Sec. 3, *supra*. Does that uncertainty help to account for the much earlier development of federal equitable remedies for constitutional violations?[2]

(3) *Initial Extension of the Bivens Approach*. The Bivens decision suggested that implication of a damages remedy might be inappropriate in a case presenting (i) "special factors counselling hesitation in the absence of affirmative action by Congress" or (ii) "an explicit congressional declaration that * * * [plaintiff should be] remitted to another remedy, equally effective in the view of Congress." But the Court's next two decisions in the Bivens line—Davis v. Passman, 442 U.S. 228 (1979), and Carlson v. Green, 446 U.S. 14 (1980)— suggested that implication of the damages remedy would be close to automatic.

(a) *Davis v. Passman*. In Davis v. Passman, 442 U.S. 228 (1979), the Court held that a damages remedy "can also be implied directly under the Constitution when the Due Process Clause of the Fifth Amendment is violated" (p. 230). The case was a damages action brought against Congressman Otto Passman by Shirley Davis, who claimed that she had been fired as his administrative assistant because she was a woman—in violation of the "equal protection" component of the Due Process Clause. Justice Brennan, writing for the majority, stated (pp. 241–44): "Statutory rights and obligations are established by Congress, and it is entirely appropriate for Congress, in creating these rights and obligations, to determine in addition who may enforce them

1. Dellinger, *Of Rights and Remedies: The Constitution as a Sword*, 85 Harv.L.Rev. 1532, 1544–45 (1972), contends that the Court's assertion in Bivens that "[h]istorically, damages have been regarded as the ordinary remedy for an invasion of personal interests in liberty" was not supported by the four cases there cited. Compare Collins, *"Economic Rights," Implied Constitutional Actions, and the Scope of Section 1983*, 77 Geo.L.J. 1493, 1507–33 (1989), arguing that a number of 19th and early 20th century decisions, in suits against state and local officials for constitutional violations, provided some recognition of implied damages remedies.

2. Professor Hill also suggests that pleading conventions in equity, unlike those at common law, required anticipation of constitutional issues that substantively arose only by way of reply to an expected defense. Therefore, equity actions—even if not resting on modern conceptions of direct federal remedies for violations of the federal Constitution—were more likely to satisfy the "well-pleaded complaint rule" and thus to fall within federal court jurisdiction. See Hill, p. 850, note 2, *supra*, at 1128–31. See also Collins, note 1, *supra*, at 1513–17.

and in what manner. For example, statutory rights and obligations are often embedded in complex regulatory schemes * * *. * * *

"The Constitution, on the other hand, does not 'partake of the prolixity of a legal code.' M'Culloch v. Maryland, 17 U.S. 316, 407 (1819). * * * And in 'its great outlines,' *ibid.*, the judiciary is clearly discernible as the primary means through which these rights may be enforced. * * *

"At least in the absence of 'a textually demonstrable constitutional commitment of [an] issue to a coordinate political department,' Baker v. Carr, 369 U.S. at 217, we presume that justiciable constitutional rights are to be enforced through the courts. And, unless such rights are to become merely precatory, the class of those litigants who allege that their own constitutional rights have been violated, and who at the same time have no effective means other than the judiciary to enforce these rights, must be able to invoke the existing jurisdiction of the courts for the protection of their justiciable constitutional rights. * * *"

As to the availability of a damages remedy, the Court noted that since Passman was no longer a Congressman, "for Davis, as for Bivens, 'it is damages or nothing' "(p. 245).

The defendant had offered a forceful argument that congressional action counseled against recognition of an implied right of action. In 1972 Congress extended Title VII of the Civil Rights Act of 1964 to certain federal employees, but excluded personal staff of members of Congress from protection. And the legislative history clearly reflected the premise that apart from Title VII, *no* remedies were available for federal-employee victims of discrimination. The Court nevertheless rejected the contention that Congress meant to exclude any implied damages remedy.

Four Justices dissented in three separate opinions. Chief Justice Burger (joined by Justices Powell and Rehnquist) emphasized the "grave questions of separation of powers" presented when courts interfere with the decisions of Members of Congress on how to fill their staff positions (pp. 249–51). For Justice Stewart (joined by Justice Rehnquist), the Court had erred in failing to address at the outset the question of immunity under the Speech or Debate Clause (a question expressly reserved by the majority). And for Justice Powell (joined by Chief Justice Burger and Justice Rehnquist), the Court had failed to recognize the proper criteria to be applied (p. 252):

"The Court's analysis starts with the general proposition that 'the judiciary is clearly discernible as the primary means through which [constitutional] rights may be enforced.' It leaps from this generalization, unexceptionable itself, to the conclusion that individuals who have suffered an injury to a constitutionally protected interest, and who lack an 'effective' alternative, '*must* be able to invoke the existing jurisdiction of the courts for the protection of their justiciable constitutional rights.' (Emphasis supplied.) Apart from the dubious logic of this reasoning, I know of no precedent of this Court that supports such an absolute statement of the federal judiciary's obligation to entertain private suits that Congress has not authorized. On the contrary, I have thought it clear that federal courts must exercise a principled discretion when called upon to infer a private cause of action directly from the language of the Constitution. * * *"

Note the extraordinary divergence in approach between Justice Brennan and Justice Powell. Justice Powell's call for "principled discretion" echoes Justice Harlan's suggestion in Bivens that in framing an appropriate remedial scheme for constitutional interests, the Court should consider a range of policy considerations "at least as broad" as that which a legislature considers.

If there is any discretion in the matter at all, note the factors weighing against the recognition of a damages remedy in Davis: (a) the action was against a high official of a coordinate branch making personnel decisions concerning his personal staff; (b) Congress had decided (about as explicitly as it could) that such officials should retain plenary discretion in making such decisions, and therefore provided no legal remedies to such staff members; and (c) allowing the action to proceed would require resolution of difficult and sensitive constitutional issues under the Speech and Debate Clause. Are there many cases that would present *more* difficult obstacles to inferring a cause of action?[3]

(b) *Carlson v. Green.* The following year, in Carlson v. Green, 446 U.S. 14 (1980), the Court upheld the availability of a damages remedy in an action alleging that the failure of federal prison officials to provide medical attention to plaintiff's deceased son constituted cruel and unusual punishment in violation of the Eighth Amendment. The Court, again per Justice Brennan, stated flatly that "the victims of a constitutional violation by a federal agent have a right to recover damages against the official in federal court despite the absence of any statute conferring such a right," unless (1) the defendant demonstrates "special factors counselling hesitation," or (2) "Congress has provided an alternative remedy which it explicitly declared to be a *substitute* for recovery directly under the Constitution and viewed as equally effective" (pp. 18–19)(emphasis in original). It dismissed with a few words the question of "special factors", finding none.

The second qualification posed more difficulty in light of the passage by Congress in 1974 of an amendment to the Federal Tort Claims Act (FTCA) to allow recovery against the United States for intentional torts of the kind at issue in Bivens and in Carlson. See Chap. IX, Sec. 1(B), p. 1034, *infra*. But the Court found nothing in the legislative text or history to indicate that the amendment was to be a substitute rather than an alternative remedy. And the Court suggested four ways in which the Bivens remedy might be more effective than the FTCA remedy: (a) an action against the individual wrongdoer is a more effective deterrent than an action against the government;[4] (b) unlike the FTCA, the Bivens remedy permits punitive damages; (c) a Bivens plaintiff can

---

3. The ironic result of Davis was that it granted federal employees in non-competitive positions (whom Congress did not intend to protect) a more direct and forceful remedy than that available to employees in the competitive service (whom Congress did intend to protect). The latter, because they were bound by the ruling in Brown v. GSA, 425 U.S. 820 (1976), that Title VII was their exclusive remedy for employment discrimination, had to proceed through the administrative mechanism of Title VII, and their only monetary remedy was back pay. (Note, however, that the plaintiff's burden of proof is heavier in a case resting solely on the Constitution than in a case under Title VII. See Washington v. Davis, 426 U.S. 229 (1976).)

Sixteen years after Davis, the Congressional Accountability Act of 1995, P.L. 104–1, 109 Stat. 3, extended coverage of Title VII to employees of the House and the Senate. They are required to exhaust administrative remedies before bringing suit in court, and may recover general compensatory (but not punitive) damages. Should that Act be viewed as precluding resort to the implied right of action recognized in Davis?

4. How certain is this claim, considering that the United States is the ultimate deep pocket, and that unlike officers sued under Bivens, it cannot invoke official immunity from damages liability when sued under the FTCA?

opt for jury trial, unavailable under the FTCA; and (d) the FTCA remedy applies only to acts that would be actionable under state law if committed by a private person (see 28 U.S.C. § 1346(b)), whereas uniform federal rules govern the extent of Bivens liability. "Plainly FTCA is not a sufficient protector of the citizens' constitutional rights," concluded Justice Brennan (p. 23).

Justice Powell, concurring with Justice Stewart, reiterated the view that the question whether a Bivens remedy should be inferred was a question of "principled discretion," and criticized the Court for "dramatically" restricting that discretion. "The Court now volunteers the view that defendant cannot defeat a Bivens action simply by showing that there are adequate alternative avenues for relief. The defendant also must show that Congress 'explicitly declared [its remedy] to be a *substitute* for recovery directly under the Constitution and viewed [it] as equally effective.' These are unnecessarily rigid conditions" (pp. 26–27). Justice Powell agreed, however, that in fact the FTCA was not an adequate substitute remedy and that there was no reason to deny the Bivens remedy in this case.

(4) *Retrenchment in the Face of Congressional Provision of Alternative Remedies.* Not long after Davis and Carlson, the tide began to run the other way, and on four occasions the Supreme Court has refused to imply a Bivens remedy. In two of these decisions, the Court's refusal was based primarily on the existence of alternative remedies provided by Congress.

(a) *Bush v. Lucas.* In Bush v. Lucas, 462 U.S. 367 (1983), Bush, an aerospace engineer employed by the federal government, sued his superior for damages, alleging, *inter alia,* that he had been demoted in retaliation for an exercise of First Amendment rights. The Civil Service Commission's Appeals Review Board had previously restored him to his former position and awarded him back pay.

The Supreme Court assumed that a federal right had been violated and that the civil service remedy was "less than complete" (because it did not provide attorney's fees or compensation for alleged emotional and dignitary harms). Nonetheless, it held (per Stevens, J.) that in this matter of "federal personnel policy" the "elaborate remedial system" constructed by Congress should not be "augmented by the creation of a new judicial remedy" (pp. 373, 380–81, 388). Relying in part on the Standard Oil case, p. 766, *supra,* the Court said: "[W]e decline 'to create a new substantive legal liability without legislative aid and as at the common law' * * * because we are convinced that Congress is in a better position to decide whether or not the public interest would be served by creating it" (p. 390).

The Court also stated that the remedy afforded by Congress was "constitutionally adequate",[5] even though it was not an "equally effective substitute" for the judicial remedy sought (p. 378 & n. 14). Thus, the Court said, it "need not reach the question whether the Constitution itself requires a judicially-

---

5. Note, however, that the alternative remedy in Bush had nearly all of the shortcomings that the Court in Carlson v. Green had associated with the FTCA. Does Bush cast doubt on the continuing force of Carlson?

Cf. also Parratt v. Taylor, 451 U.S. 527 (1981), Chap. IX, Sec. 2(C), p. 1149, *infra* (holding, in a constitutional tort action against state officials under 42 U.S.C. 1983, that the state's provision of a tort remedy—that had all of the "defects" that Carlson had found in the FTCA—"could have fully compensated" the plaintiff and was adequate to satisfy due process).

fashioned damages remedy in the absence of any other remedy to vindicate the underlying right, unless there is an express textual command to the contrary" (*id.*). Justice Marshall, joined by Justice Blackmun, concurred in the opinion but wrote separately to emphasize that in his view "a different case would be presented if Congress had not created a comprehensive scheme that was specifically designed to provide full compensation * * * and that affords a remedy that is substantially as effective as a damage action" (p. 390).

(b) *Schweiker v. Chilicky*. The Court extended the approach of Bush v. Lucas in Schweiker v. Chilicky, 487 U.S. 412 (1988). The plaintiffs there were improperly denied disability benefits under the Social Security Act, but subsequently were awarded, or had pending administrative applications for, full retroactive benefits. They sued federal and state policy-making officials, alleging that the defendants had denied them due process by adopting policies that resulted in the improper denials. The complaint sought equitable relief and damages for "emotional distress and for loss of food, shelter and other necessities proximately caused by [defendants'] denial of benefits" (p. 419).

The Supreme Court refused to permit a Bivens action for the alleged due process violation. The Court noted that the Social Security Act's elaborate administrative and judicial review remedy is limited to full restoration of improperly denied benefits. "Here, exactly as in Bush, Congress has failed to provide for 'complete relief': [plaintiffs] have not been given a remedy in damages for emotional distress or for other hardships suffered because of delays in their receipt of Social Security benefits. The creation of a Bivens remedy would obviously offer the prospect of relief for injuries that must now go unredressed. Congress, however, has not failed to provide meaningful safeguards or remedies for the rights of persons situated as [plaintiffs] were. Indeed, the system for protecting their rights is, if anything, considerably more elaborate than the civil service system considered in Bush" (p. 425).

The Court added that its decision in Bush rested not on the view that Bivens actions were uniquely disruptive in the civil service setting, but instead on the belief that "Congress is in a better position to decide whether or not the public interest would be served by creating" a new liability (p. 427, quoting Bush). Nor was Bush distinguishable on the ground that there the statutory remedy provided compensation for the constitutional violation itself, while here it merely redressed a violation of the statute; rather, the Court in Bush seemed to assume that civil servants would get the same remedy "whether or not they were victims of constitutional deprivation" (p. 427, quoting Bush).

Justice Brennan's dissent (joined by Justices Marshall and Blackmun) urged that Bush did not control, primarily for three reasons. First, the civil service system, though not permitting compensation for emotional harm, did at least permit compensation for most economic consequential damages, and hence was a more adequate alternative to a Bivens action than the remedy available here. Second, Congress has special expertise over government employment but not over the social welfare system. And third, when undertaking its recent reforms of the disability system, Congress did not anticipate that federal officials might violate constitutional rights; it therefore did not purport to balance administrative needs and appropriate redress for constitutional violations, as it had in such areas as the the civil service system.

(c) *Congressional Preclusion: Implicit or Explicit*. Note that in Bush and Chilicky, Congress had not "explicitly" declared a statutory remedy to be a substitute for a judicially created one—as Bivens had suggested was necessary.

Was the Court on firm ground in both cases in concluding that provision of a Bivens remedy would have been inconsistent with the administrative scheme that Congress had established?

(5) *Retrenchment in the Absence of an Effective Remedy.* Two other decisions refused to imply Bivens remedies in suits brought by current or former servicemen—without finding (as the Court had in Bush or Chilicky) that the alternative remedies were "adequate" or "meaningful".

(a) *Chappell v. Wallace.* In Chappell v. Wallace, 462 U.S. 296 (1983), Navy enlisted men brought an action against their superior officers, alleging racial discrimination in violation of their rights under the Constitution and federal civil rights legislation. The Court unanimously held that the constitutional claim could not be maintained, and stated that "the unique disciplinary structure of the Military Establishment and Congress' activity in the field constitute 'special factors' which dictate that it would be inappropriate to provide enlisted military personnel a Bivens-type remedy against their superior officers" (p. 304). The activity of Congress that the Court referred to embraced "a comprehensive internal system of justice to regulate military life," which included procedures "for the review and remedy of complaints and grievances such as those presented by respondents" (p. 302). (Nothing was said about that system's effectiveness.)[6]

(b) *United States v. Stanley.* In United States v. Stanley, 483 U.S. 669 (1987), a former serviceman sued military officers and civilians for injuries resulting from the administration to him of the drug LSD, without his consent, as part of an army experiment. The Supreme Court held, 5–4, that a Bivens action could not be maintained. The Court said that the special factors found in Chappell "extend beyond the situation in which an officer-subordinate relationship exists, and require abstention in the inferring of Bivens actions as extensive as the exception to the [Federal Tort Claims Act] established by Feres [v. United States, 340 U.S. 135 (1950), p. 1035, *infra*] * * *. We hold that no Bivens remedy is available for injuries that 'arise out of or are in the course of activity incident to [military] service' " (pp. 683–84, quoting Feres, 340 U.S. at 146).

Justice O'Connor, dissenting in part, contended that "conduct of the type alleged in this case is so far beyond the bounds of human decency that as a matter of law it simply cannot be considered a part of the military mission" (p. 709). In a lengthy opinion dissenting in part, Justice Brennan (joined by Justice Marshall and in part by Justice Stevens) argued that: (1) a Bivens action should be unavailable if and only if the defendant was shielded by official immunity (see Chap. IX, Sec. 3, *infra*), and thus the case should be remanded to see whether the defendants can show "that absolute immunity was necessary to the effective performance of their functions" (p. 698); (2) the Chappell decision was not on point because "the defendants are not alleged to be Stanley's superior officers" (p. 701); and (3) in contrast to the situation in Chappell, no intramilitary system " 'provides for the . . . remedy' of Stanley's complaint" (p. 706, quoting Chappell).

(6) *Bivens Actions Against the United States.* Does the Bivens remedy extend to suits seeking damages from the United States itself rather than from its

---

6. The Court left it to the lower court on remand to consider whether an action could be maintained for damages resulting from an alleged conspiracy in violation of 42 U.S.C. § 1985(3), a federal civil rights statute.

officials? Ordinarily the sovereign immunity of the United States prevents this issue from being joined, but it did arise in FDIC v. Meyer, 114 S.Ct. 996 (1994). The suit was brought by a former employee of an insolvent S & L, who alleged that his termination by the Federal Savings and Loan Insurance Corporation (FSLIC), which was serving as the S & L's receiver,[7] deprived him of a property right without due process of law. Named as a defendant in addition to the FSLIC was the FSLIC official responsible for the termination. The jury returned a $130,000 verdict against the FSLIC, but found for the official-defendant on qualified immunity grounds (determining that although his conduct was unconstitutional, at the time it did not violate "clearly established" law). The Ninth Circuit affirmed.

The Supreme Court agreed with the courts below that Congress had waived the FSLIC's sovereign immunity,[8] but reversed the judgment against the FSLIC on the ground that the Bivens right of action extends only to suits against government officials, not against government agencies. Justice Thomas' unanimous opinion stressed three points. First, Bivens remedies were implied in part because a direct action against the government was assumed to be unavailable. Plaintiff's real complaint, he wrote, was that the official-defendant had a qualified immunity; but Bivens clearly contemplated such immunities. Second, and more important, "the purpose of Bivens is to deter the *officer*" (p. 1005); if litigants could bypass officers and sue federal agencies directly, "the deterrent effects of the *Bivens* remedy would be lost" (*id.*). Finally, he found "special factors counselling hesitation"—the potentially "enormous financial burden for the Federal Government" of recognition of a direct action for damages. (To Meyer's argument that the government already spends significant amounts indemnifying its employees who are sued under Bivens, the Court responded that decisions involving federal fiscal policy are for Congress, not the courts.)

How persuasive are Justice Thomas' arguments against governmental liability for damages in the relatively rare case where sovereign immunity has been waived? With respect to deterrence, doesn't governmental liability discourage violations—especially when immunity otherwise would preclude *any* recovery? And don't Bivens remedies also have an important compensatory purpose?

(7) *Bivens in Practice.* A 1989 article by a former Justice Department lawyer reported that since 1971, more than 12,000 Bivens actions had been filed; that only 30 had resulted in judgments for plaintiffs at the trial level (some of which had been reversed on appeal); that only four judgments had actually been paid; and that settlements are rare. Rosen, *The Bivens Constitutional Tort: An Unfulfilled Promise*, 67 N.C.L.Rev. 337, 343–44 (1989).

Do results like these indicate that Justice Blackmun's objections and fears in his Bivens dissent were well-founded? Or do they suggest instead, as Mr. Rosen argues, that there are too many obstacles to recovery—particularly (i) broad official immunity doctrines, (ii) the hesitance of juries to hold individuals,

---

7. A 1989 statute abolished the FSLIC, and the FDIC was substituted for the FSLIC in the lawsuit.

8. In the course of that analysis, the Court held that constitutional tort claims are not cognizable under the Federal Tort Claims

as distinguished from the government, liable,[9] and (iii) the federal government's provision of free representation to defendant officials, while Bivens plaintiffs (unlike many civil rights plaintiffs) cannot avail themselves of statutory fee-shifting provisions. Does any of this bear on the wisdom of the decision in FDIC v. Meyer?

(8) *Is the Bivens Remedy Constitutionally Required?* Recall Professor Hart's contention (Chap. IV, Sec. 2, p. 376, *supra*) that "Congress necessarily has a wide choice in the selection of remedies." That principle may explain the decision in Bush v. Lucas and perhaps even the decision in Chilicky.

(a) *Unqualified Congressional Preclusion.* But suppose Congress purported to eliminate the remedy recognized in Bivens. Given that, for Bivens, it was damages or nothing, could such action be justified as merely a choice among remedies? If not, would the preclusion necessarily be unconstitutional?

Does the Constitution require *some* remedy for violations of the Fourth Amendment—even if the remedy does not necessarily have to be a traditional damages remedy provided by the courts? If so, would the unconstitutionality of providing no remedy whatsoever for someone in Bivens' shoes rest on the absence of adequate mechanisms to deter constitutional violations?[10] The absence of adequate compensation for Bivens himself? How strong is the latter claim in light of the decisions in Chilicky, Chappell, and especially Stanley?[11] Can these decisions be viewed as consistent with a principle or presumption generally favoring remediation—because in Chilicky a remedy was available (albeit one that provided no compensation for any injury to *constitutional* interests), and because Chappell and Stanley involved the military?

(b) *The Pertinence of Immunity Doctrines.* A series of Supreme Court opinions recognizes that official liability in Bivens actions is subject to official immunity from damages—which is sometimes qualified and sometimes absolute. That immunity, which is designed primarily to avoid dampening the ardor of officials in the performance of their duties, broadly prevents recovery against federal officials even where they have in fact violated constitutional rights—as illustrated by the proceedings in FDIC v. Meyer, Paragraph (6), *supra*. See generally Chap. IX, Sec. 3, *infra*. Moreover, even had the Court been willing in the Meyer case to recognize an implied right of action against

Act, which is limited to actions based on state tort law.

9. Rosen suggests (pp. 347–48) that factfinders are unaware that many federal agencies indemnify defendants in Bivens actions.

10. Other remedies besides damages obviously have deterrent force—including the exclusion of illegally obtained evidence, and injunctions against unconstitutional practices by law enforcement officials. For an examination of the constitutional and practical considerations surrounding judicial provision of deterrent remedies in the absence of legislative direction, see Meltzer, *Deterring Constitutional Violations by Law Enforcement Officials: Plaintiffs and Defendants as Private Attorneys General*, 88 Colum.L.Rev. 247 (1988).

11. If one views Bivens remedies as justified because constitutionally required, does it follow that decisions about the incidents of a Bivens action (*e.g.*, damage measures; immunity doctrines; statutes of limitations; exhaustion requirements) also must be justified on the ground that particular incidents are (or are not) constitutionally required? *Cf.* Meltzer, *State Court Forfeitures of Federal Rights*, 99 Harv.L.Rev. 1128, 1172–73 n. 218 (1986)(noting the difficulty of any argument that the right of survivorship recognized by the Court in Carlson v. Green, pp. 827, 869, *supra*, is constitutionally required). Or, once it is determined that some judicially-fashioned remedy is required, are courts vested with a more flexible authority to shape the remedy as they deem appropriate?

the United States, sovereign immunity virtually always bars an unconsented suit against the government itself.[12] The net result may be (again, as in *Meyer*) that a plaintiff who alleges injury from a constitutional violation is left without any remedy.

Can a claim that the *Bivens* remedy is constitutionally required be reconciled with official immunity? By arguing that immunity rests upon an implicit determination that protection of the ardor of federal officials is a "compelling state interest" justifying limits on what is otherwise a constitutional entitlement to a damages remedy?

(c) *Other Monetary Remedies for Constitutional Violations.* Recall that the Court has squarely recognized a constitutional obligation to provide a monetary remedy in at least two settings. First, in the context of the Fifth Amendment's Just Compensation Clause, the Court has ruled that "it is the Constitution that dictates the remedy for interference with property rights amounting to a taking." First English Evangelical Lutheran Church of Glendale v. County of Los Angeles, California, 482 U.S. 304, 316 n. 9 (1987). Second, in cases seeking refunds of state taxes unconstitutionally exacted, the Court has made clear that where there was no adequate pre-payment remedy, a state is under a due process obligation to provide a refund remedy.[13] See McKesson Corp. v. Division of ABT and Reich v. Collins, pp. 851–52, *supra.*

Given those two lines of decision, on what basis can the Court justify a refusal to provide a monetary remedy in a *Bivens* suit (especially where no other relief is available)? Is there a greater need for compensation or deterrence in those lines of decision than in *Bivens*? In the tax cases, is the monetary remedy especially appropriate given the restitutionary quality of a tax refund and its nearly perfect fit as a remedy for an unlawful exaction of taxes? (But why should the Constitution protect property interests more fully than liberty interests safeguarded by the First, Fourth, or Fourteenth Amendments?) Does a suit against an officer have a weaker claim to constitutional status than a tax refund or takings claim against the government—even when recovery from the officer is the only possible remedy? See generally Fallon & Meltzer, p. 850, *supra*, at 1824–30.

(d) *The Repudiation of Sovereign Immunity?* Some commentators have attempted to resolve these tensions by arguing that the sovereign immunity of the United States—a venerable principle, but one nowhere enshrined in the constitutional text—must yield to what they see as "the Constitution's structural principle of full remedies for violations of legal rights against government." Amar, *Of Sovereignty and Federalism*, 96 Yale L.J. 1425, 1489 (1987); accord, Bandes, *Reinventing Bivens: The Self-Executing Constitution*, 68 S.Cal. L.Rev. 289 (1995). In *Bivens* actions against the government, there would be no need for official immunity doctrines that now stand in the way of recovery in many cases. For doubts that the asserted principle of full remedies for constitutional violations (despite its surface attractiveness) can be squared with important elements of our constitutional and legal tradition, see Fallon & Meltzer, *supra*, at 1777–91.

---

12. With only the possible exception of claims under the Just Compensation Clause. See Sub–Paragraph (c), *infra.*

13. With the possible qualification, not greatly significant in practice, that in cases of unconstitutional discrimination, retroactive tax increases on the favored class might substitute for refunds to the disfavored class.

(9) *Bivens as Constitutional Common Law.* If damages remedies are *not* constitutionally compelled in cases like Bivens, Davis v. Passman, and Carlson v. Green—even where other effective remedies are lacking—then by what authority do the federal courts recognize Bivens remedies in the absence of legislative authorization? Professor Monaghan, in an important article (*Foreword: Constitutional Common Law*, 89 Harv.L.Rev. 1 (1975)), treated Bivens as one example of what he termed "constitutional common law"—a body of judge-made law that implements constitutional guarantees rather than statutory provisions.[15]   But unlike simple interpretations of the Constitution, which cannot be overturned by Congress, constitutional common law is subject to legislative modification or repeal precisely because it is not constitutionally required.

What source of lawmaking power authorizes judicial development of a penumbra of supplemental, quasi-constitutional protection?[16]   If there is a valid source for constitutional common law, can that body of law adequately be distinguished from "real" constitutional law? (The problem arises sharply, of course, only when Congress attempts to modify a constitutional common law decision.) For a critical response to Monaghan, see Schrock & Welsh, *Reconsidering the Constitutional Common Law*, 91 Harv.L.Rev. 1117 (1978).

But recall Justice Harlan's comment in Bivens: "I * * * note that it would be at least anomalous to conclude that the federal judiciary—while competent to choose among the range of traditional judicial remedies to implement statutory and common-law policies, and even to generate substantive rules governing primary behavior in furtherance of broadly formulated policies articulated by statute or Constitution—is powerless to accord a damages remedy to vindicate social policies which, by virtue of their inclusion in the Constitution, are aimed predominantly at restraining the Government as an instrument of the popular will." Consider, too, whether the option of fashion-

---

15. Other examples noted by Monaghan include the Fourth Amendment's exclusionary rule; the invalidation of state statutes under the dormant Commerce Clause; and the decision in Miranda v. Arizona, 384 U.S. 436 (1966).

16. Justice Stevens' opinion in Bush v. Lucas, Paragraph (4)(a), *supra*, rested the Court's lawmaking authority on the grant of federal question jurisdiction in 28 U.S.C. § 1331, see 462 U.S. at 374, and Justice Harlan's concurrence in Bivens also looks in that direction. Accord Hill, p. 850, note 2, *supra*, at 1112–14; see also Dellinger, p. 867, note 2, *supra*, at 1541–47 (resting on Article III's jurisdictional grant). If jurisdictional grants are an uncertain source of authority to define rights and duties, see pp. 789-91, *supra*, are they a surer source of authority for formulation of remedies? If § 1331 were repealed or limited by an amount in controversy requirement, necessitating that some or all Bivens actions be filed in state court, would those courts lack authority to formulate a damages remedy? If not, would the

source of authority be a grant of state court jurisdiction? For doubts about the reliance on jurisdictional grants, see Meltzer, note 10, *supra*, at 295; Nichol, *Bivens, Chilicky, and Constitutional Damages Claims*, 75 Va.L.Rev. 1117, 1130–31 (1989).

With respect to Bivens actions in state courts, *cf.* Amar, *Using State Law to Protect Federal Constitutional Rights: Some Questions and Answers About Converse–1983*, 64 U.Colo.L.Rev. 159 (1993), and Amar, *Five Views of Federalism: "Converse–1983" In Context*, 47 Vand.L.Rev. 1229 (1994), proposing that state law should provide a private remedy, enforceable in state court, for violations by federal officials of federal constitutional rights. Amar urges that such a scheme, like the federal statutory remedy in 42 U.S.C. § 1983 for constitutional torts by state officials, represents a sound checking by one government of misconduct by the other. The 1993 article in particular attempts to address the formidable difficulties presented by his proposal.

ing constitutional common law may avoid improvident constitutionalization in areas where state rules appear to impede federal policy.

Would acceptance of Monaghan's view make it easier to reconcile the decided cases? Or would that view make it too easy to accommodate possibly erroneous refusals to recognize a remedy in cases like Chilicky and Stanley? See Nichol, note 15, *supra*, at 1128.

(10) *The Respective Roles of Congress and the Courts.* Bush, Chilicky, and Chappell rely heavily on the proposition that Congress' capacity to determine appropriate remedies for constitutional violations is superior to that of the courts. But given that Bivens actions are at a minimum constitutionally *inspired*, should the Court, before finding legislative preclusion of a Bivens action, require a clear statement to that effect by Congress? See Grey, *Preemption of Bivens Claims: How Clearly Must Congress Speak?*, 70 Wash. U.L.Q. 1087 (1992)(so arguing); see also Brown, *Letting Statutory Tails Wag Constitutional Dogs—Have the Bivens Dissenters Prevailed?*, 64 Ind.L.J. 263, 265 (1988–89) (contending that "the Court's emphasis on the statutory component of the remedial issues tends to obscure and downgrade their constitutional dimension").[16] Should the Court require that there be a substitute remedy that meets a constitutional test of adequacy? See generally Nichol, note 15, *supra*.

Is the relationship between Congress and the Courts in fashioning remedies for violations of constitutional provisions different from their relationship in fashioning remedies for violations of statutory obligations? Recall Justice Powell's dissent in the Cannon case, p. 830, *supra*, objecting on a wide variety of grounds to any implication of remedies for statutory violations. Yet several weeks later, in his dissent in Davis, he argued that courts should exercise a "principled discretion" in implying remedies for constitutional violations; and less than a year after Cannon, in Carlson v. Green, he joined in recognizing a Bivens remedy. Unless one begins with the assumption that the Bivens remedy is constitutionally required—and Justice Powell clearly does not—is there justification for a sharp difference in judicial approach as between constitutional and statutory cases? (Reconsider, in this regard, footnote 3 of Justice Powell's dissent in Cannon.)

---

16. Compare Friedman, *When Rights Encounter Reality: Enforcing Federal Remedies*, 65 S.Cal.L.Rev. 735, 738–39, 779–780 (1992), arguing that judges legitimately may restrict the reach of remedies in response to majoritarian resistance to either broader remedies or to the underlying rights themselves, and that Bivens provides a "brilliant solution" by putting remedies in the hands of Congress, thus initiating a dialogue on appropriate rights and remedies (p. 779).

CHAPTER VIII

THE FEDERAL QUESTION JURISDICTION OF THE DISTRICT COURTS

SECTION 1. INTRODUCTION

This chapter surveys the federal question ("arising under") jurisdiction of the federal district courts. Section 2 deals with the constitutional scope of the jurisdiction. Section 3 studies the development of the statutory grant of original jurisdiction to the federal district courts. (Since a defendant's right to remove a federal question case from state to federal court is generally conditioned on whether the federal court would have had original jurisdiction over the case, see 28 U.S.C. § 1441, some of the important cases dealing with the scope of the original jurisdiction are removal cases.)

Section 4 is devoted to the distinctive problems of removal jurisdiction in the context of federal question litigation; more general problems of removal are studied in Chap. XIV, Sec. 3, *infra*. Section 5 is concerned with supplemental jurisdiction, and particularly with the impact of the new statutory authorization for the exercise of that jurisdiction (28 U.S.C. § 1367).

Section 6 is a brief survey of jurisdictional categories that are functionally closely tied to and frequently overlap the "arising under" jurisdiction: admiralty, and litigation instituted by the United States.

NOTE ON THE STATUTORY DEVELOPMENT OF THE JURISDICTION

Although the protection of federal rights was a primary purpose of the establishment of a system of federal courts, the first Judiciary Act generally required private litigants to look to the state tribunals in the first instance for vindication of federal claims, subject to limited review by the United States Supreme Court.[1] In the course of time, exceptions were made in the case of matters of a peculiarly federal nature or where political exigencies demanded. But it was not until the consolidation of national sentiment after the Civil War that the national courts became the primary forums for the vindication of federal rights.[2]

---

1. Act of Sept. 24, 1789, § 25, 1 Stat. 73, 85. See Chap. I, pp. 28–33, *supra*.

2. See Frankfurter & Landis, The Business of the Supreme Court 64–65 (1928).

Early Congresses did not approach the limits of their authority to vest the federal courts with jurisdiction of cases "arising under" the Constitution, laws, and treaties of the United States.[3] The Judiciary Act of 1789, besides the grant of jurisdiction of suits for "penalties and forfeitures * * * incurred" under federal laws,[4] limited the jurisdiction of the national courts to cases "where an alien sues for a tort only in violation of the law of nations or a treaty of the United States."[5] The first patent law imposed only limited duties on the district courts in proceedings to revoke wrongfully secured patents,[6] though subsequently jurisdiction was extended to infringement suits.[7] Certain functions were likewise to be performed by the federal courts under the 1792 pension law.[8] In 1801, after the Federalist Party lost ground at the polls, it sought refuge in the national courts[9] by vesting them with broad jurisdiction in this area. The Act of Feb. 13, 1801, § 11, 2 Stat. 89, 92, conferred jurisdiction in virtually the same language as the "arising under" clause of the Constitution and provided for removal of such suits from state courts. *Id.* § 13. The Federalist statute, however, lasted barely more than a year before its repeal in 1802.[10]

The story of the early removal acts for the protection of federal interests from hostile state action, which began with the Non–Intercourse Act of 1815, is told below.[11] Primarily, these statutes were concerned with state court proceedings against federal officers, but they extended also to actions against private persons for acts done under federal authority.

Until the second half of the nineteenth century, no other important additions were made to federal jurisdiction over federal questions. Jurisdiction was continued in patent cases,[12] and in 1846 the federal courts were empowered to enforce awards made by consuls under a treaty with Prussia.[13] But the Civil War brought on a great surge of national feeling and national power,[14] which resulted in the vesting of a large part of the constitutionally authorized jurisdiction in the federal courts.

The process began during the war, when removal was authorized of all suits and prosecutions "for any arrest or imprisonment made, or other tres-

---

3. See Casto, *An Orthodox View of the Two–Tier Analysis of Congressional Control Over Federal Jurisdiction,* 7 Const. Commentary 89, 93 (1990)(The 1789 Act "completely excluded a number of federal question cases from original and appellate federal jurisdiction. For example, the Act did not allow federal jurisdiction over a tremendous number of significant cases arising under the Treaty of Paris * * * ."). But see Engdahl, *Federal Question Jurisdiction Under the 1789 Judiciary Act,* 14 Okla. City U.L.Rev. 521, 522 (1989), who argues that "all cases which then could have been contemplated as within" the "federal question" terms of Article III were in fact provided for in the 1789 Act.

4. For this and other grants of jurisdiction in actions by the United States or federal officials, see pp. 982–84, *infra.*

5. Act of Sept. 24, 1789, § 9, 1 Stat. 73, 77. This jurisdiction was exclusive in the district courts. It is now concurrent. 28 U.S.C. § 1350.

6. Act of April 10, 1790, § 5, 1 Stat. 109, 111.

7. Act of Feb. 21, 1793, § 6, 1 Stat. 318, 322; see also, Act of Feb. 15, 1819, 3 Stat. 481. The jurisdiction was concurrent. It is now exclusive. 28 U.S.C. § 1338(a).

8. Act of March 23, 1792, §§ 2, 3, 1 Stat. 243, 244. See Hayburn's Case, p. 99, *supra.*

9. See 3 Beveridge, Life of John Marshall, chs. 1, 2 (1919).

10. Act of March 8, 1802, 2 Stat. 132.

11. See pp. 951–53, *infra.*

12. Act of July 4, 1836, 5 Stat. 117.

13. Act of Aug. 8, 1846, 9 Stat. 78.

14. See Frankfurter & Landis, note 2, *supra,* at 56 *et seq.*

passes or wrongs done or committed * * * [during the rebellion], by virtue or under color of any authority derived from * * * the President of the United States, or any Act of Congress * * *."[15]   In the period that followed, Congress freely invoked the federal courts to secure blacks' newly granted civil rights, enacting a series of jurisdictional and remedial provisions most of which have lasted to this day.[16]   The first Civil Rights Act gave the federal courts cognizance, both original and on removal, of "all causes, civil and criminal, affecting persons who are denied or cannot enforce in the courts * * * of the state or locality where they may be any of the rights secured to them by the first section of this act * * *."[17] Removal was available to any defendant who was sued or prosecuted "for any arrest or imprisonment, trespasses, or wrongs done * * * under color of authority derived from this act * * * or for refusing to do any act upon the ground that it would be inconsistent with this act. * * *"[18]   The Act of 1870 provided for federal jurisdiction of "all causes, civil and criminal, arising under" it.[19]   The following year Congress went further by adding a remedy in damages[20] and giving the federal courts cognizance of suits for their recovery.[21]   Removal was as usual authorized by anyone brought into court for an act done under color of the statute.[22]   The last Civil Rights Act of that series, that of 1875, enlarged the available remedies and again provided federal jurisdiction.[23]

In 1864, jurisdiction was also conferred over suits against national banks,[24] and four years later Congress authorized removal of suits against "any corporation, organized under a law of the United States. * * *"[25]   The Act of 1874, which imposed certain obligations (such as non-discrimination in rates) on the Pacific railroads, gave the federal courts cognizance of treble damage suits for injuries resulting from violations of the statute.[26]

The culmination of the movement toward expansion of federal court jurisdiction came with the passage of the 1875 Judiciary Act.   Although this legislation in a very real sense revolutionized the nature of the federal judiciary, it passed almost unnoticed inside or outside Congress.[27]   It gave the circuit courts concurrent jurisdiction, subject to a $500 amount requirement, of "all suits of a civil nature, at common law or in equity, * * * arising under the Constitution or laws of the United States, or treaties made, or which shall be

---

15. Act of March 3, 1863, § 5, 12 Stat. 755, 756, amended by Act of May 11, 1866, 14 Stat. 46. See p. 951, *infra.*

16. See 28 U.S.C. §§ 1343, 1344, 1443. See also 42 U.S.C. § 1983, discussed at pp. 1111–37, *infra.*

17. Act of April 9, 1866, § 3, 14 Stat. 27.

18. *Id.*   These provisions are now found in 28 U.S.C. § 1443, except that original jurisdiction of such cases is omitted.

19. Act of May 31, 1870, § 8, 16 Stat. 140, 142.

20. Act of Feb. 28, 1871, § 15, 16 Stat. 433, 438.

21. Act of April 20, 1871, §§ 2, 6, 17 Stat. 13, 14, 15.

22. Act of Feb. 28, 1871, § 16, 16 Stat. 433, 439.

23. Act of March 1, 1875, §§ 2, 3, 18 Stat. 335, 336.

24. Act of June 3, 1864, § 57, 13 Stat. 99, 116.

25. Act of July 27, 1868, § 2, 15 Stat. 226, 227.

26. Act of June 20, 1874, 18 Stat. 111, 112.

27. The Act started as a bill to expand diversity jurisdiction. The main body of the law was added by amendment and the original provision was stricken before the bill passed. See Frankfurter & Landis, note 2, *supra,* at 64–68.

made, under their authority * * *."[28] Such cases were also made removable by either party.[29] In its one cautionary note, Section 5 of the Act directed the federal court to dismiss or remand if it appeared at any time "that such suit does not really and substantially involve a dispute or controversy properly within [its] jurisdiction. * * *"[30]

The flood of litigation to which the federal courts were now subjected, especially after the expansive jurisdiction upheld in the Pacific Railroad Removal Cases,[31] moved Congress to pare down the federal question jurisdiction. In 1887 the jurisdictional amount was raised to $2000, removal by plaintiffs was eliminated, and orders remanding removed cases to the state courts were made non-appealable.[32] Prior to that, Congress had begun the long process of reducing jurisdiction based solely on federal incorporation to cases in which the United States owns more than half the corporation's stock.[33]

The history of federal question jurisdiction between 1875 and 1980 revolves largely around the creation by Congress of myriad new federal rights and provision for their enforcement in the national courts without regard to jurisdictional amount. The Judicial Code of 1911 listed the types of cases where no jurisdictional amount was required and also codified existing removal provisions.[34]

This codification proved to be but a momentary convenience, for Congress persisted in embodying new jurisdictional provisions in the particular substantive statutes without amending the Judicial Code. In 1948 the Revisers found 158 such provisions in various parts of the United States Code.[35] Most of these concerned controversies between private parties and the government or its officers or agencies under various regulatory laws, but many of them authorized private suits without regard to amount in controversy.[36]

Special removal provisions—or rather, provisions prohibiting removal in certain cases—were also enacted. For example, the Federal Employers' Liability Act, in order to secure to employees the exclusive choice of forum, declared that damage suits under it were non-removable,[37] and the Jones Act followed suit in the maritime field.[38] Railroads sued under federal law for damages to

---

28. Act of March 3, 1875, § 1, 18 Stat. 470.

29. Act of March 3, 1875, § 2, 18 Stat. 470, 471.

30. *Id.* § 5, 18 Stat. at 472.

31. 115 U.S. 1 (1885), p. 910, *infra.*

32. Act of March 3, 1887, 24 Stat. 552, corrected by Act of Aug. 13, 1888, 25 Stat. 433. Section 24 of the first Judicial Code [Act of March 3, 1911, 36 Stat. 1087, 1091] raised the amount to $3000, and the Act of July 25, 1958, 72 Stat. 415, to $10,000, where it stood until removed in 1980. 28 U.S.C. §§ 1331, 1441(a). Removal is still limited to defendants. 28 U.S.C. § 1441(a). And remand orders are still generally non-reviewable. 28 U.S.C. § 1447(d).

33. See p. 910, *infra.*

34. Act of March 3, 1911, §§ 24, 28, 33, 36 Stat. 1087, 1091, 1094–97.

35. Reviser's Notes to 28 U.S.C. § 1332.

36. *E.g.,* provisions of the Clayton Act of 1914 (now in 15 U.S.C. § 15) and of the Federal Communications Act of 1934 (now in 47 U.S.C. § 207). In addition, there was a provision (now 28 U.S.C. § 1337) containing a general grant of jurisdiction, without regard to amount in controversy, of cases arising under any act regulating commerce.

37. Act of April 22, 1908, 35 Stat. 65, as amended by Act of April 5, 1910, 36 Stat. 291. Now 28 U.S.C. § 1445(a).

38. See 46 U.S.C. § 688. The Act made the Federal Employers' Liability Act applicable to seamen by generic reference, and it is generally held that (at least in the absence of "waiver" by the plaintiff or the presence of a separate and independent removable claim under 28 U.S.C. § 1441(c)), an

goods shipped were prevented from removing (although they might be sued originally in the district courts) unless the claim was at least $3000.[39] And all suits under the 1933 Securities Act were made non-removable.[40]

The Judicial Code of 1948 did not attempt a new codification of these numerous provisions, nor did it purport to make more than a few significant changes in the district courts' jurisdiction.[41] Although § 1338(b) seemed on its face to expand the pendent jurisdiction in patent, copyright, and trademark cases, the Reviser's note declared the purpose to be merely that of codifying the rule of Hurn v. Oursler.[42] The revised code also made two important changes in removal jurisdiction.[43] The privilege of removal was extended to all federal officers and agencies sued or prosecuted "for any act under color of * * * office."[44] And the revisers, while purporting to narrow the old "separable controversy" provision that had previously applied only in diversity cases, expanded it (confusingly) to include some cases in which a removable federal claim was joined with a non-removable claim.[45]

The creation of a large number of special jurisdictional grants outside the corners of the Judicial Code[46] continued in the '50s and accelerated in the period of intense federal legislative activity in the late '60s and '70s.[47]

The same period, however, saw a development that eventually deprived these specific jurisdictional grants of their principal significance. That development consisted of the erosion, and eventual elimination, of the jurisdictional amount requirement in the provision governing general federal-question jurisdiction. The forerunner statute was a 1962 provision conferring jurisdiction of actions "in the nature of mandamus" to compel federal officials to carry out their duties, together with special venue and process for such actions. See 28

action under the Jones Act is not removable. See 14 Wright, Miller & Cooper, Federal Practice and Procedure § 3674, at 467–68 (1985 & 1995 Supp.).

39. Act of Jan. 20, 1914, 38 Stat. 278. The amount has since been raised to $10,000. See 28 U.S.C. § 1445(b).

40. Act of May 27, 1933, § 22(a), 48 Stat. 74, 87, 15 U.S.C. § 77v.

41. The provisions relating to original jurisdiction in the district courts are found in 28 U.S.C. §§ 1331–1366.

42. 289 U.S. 238 (1933). See p. 966, *infra*.

43. The removal provisions are 28 U.S.C. §§ 1441–1445.

44. 28 U.S.C. § 1442(a)(1). Other parts of this section retain old provisions for removal of suits against particular officials. See p. 952, *infra*.

45. 28 U.S.C. § 1441(c). The problem is discussed in Chap. XIV, Sec. 3, pp. 1625–27, *infra*.

46. Within Title 28 itself, significant changes in the 1948 revision and since have included: the addition of a new subsection, of

uncertain import, providing for jurisdiction over civil actions "under any Act of Congress providing for the protection of civil rights, including the right to vote" (28 U.S.C. § 1343(4)); a provision for jurisdiction without a required amount in controversy for actions by certain Indian tribes (28 U.S.C. § 1362); a provision for actions to enforce Senate subpoenas (28 U.S.C. § 1365); a provision for actions for the "protection of jurors' employment" under 28 U.S.C. § 1875 (28 U.S.C. § 1363); a provision governing supplemental jurisdiction (28 U.S.C. § 1367)(discussed at pp. 971–73, 1564–67, *infra*); and provisions for jurisdiction over certain controversies involving foreign states and foreign diplomats (28 U.S.C. §§ 1330, 1332(a)(4), 1364).

47. For discussion of this development (and supporting references), see Friendly, Federal Jurisdiction: A General View, 22–26 & n. 53 (1973); Leventhal, Book Review, 75 Colum.L.Rev. 1009, 1018 and n. 41 (1975). For a general survey of the various substantive heads of federal question jurisdiction, see 13B Wright, Miller & Cooper, Federal Practice and Procedure §§ 3568–85 (1984 & 1995 Supp.).

U.S.C. §§ 1361, 1391(e). This provision was overtaken by the amendment in 1976 of § 1331—the general federal question statute—to eliminate the jurisdictional amount requirement in any civil action "brought against the United States, any agency thereof, or any officer or employee thereof in his official capacity." Act of October 21, 1976, 90 Stat. 2721.[48] Finally, on December 1, 1980, § 1331 was amended by eliminating—for the first time since the passage of the original act in 1875—any jurisdictional amount requirement in "all civil actions arising under the Constitution, laws, or treaties of the United States." (The requirement was expressly preserved for suits under the Consumer Product Safety Act, 15 U.S.C. § 2072(a); and it presumably continues in effect under other substantive statutes that explicitly require a minimum amount in controversy.[49])

Does the 1980 amendment make the numerous specific grants of federal question jurisdiction in the various substantive statutes irrelevant? Caution must be exercised. Some of those grants provide for exclusive jurisdiction in the federal courts, while § 1331 has always been read as a grant of concurrent jurisdiction.

Other questions of interpretation may arise because, as the materials in this chapter show, § 1331 is encrusted with a complex gloss of interpretive doctrines. Whether and how some or all of these glosses apply in the context of specific substantive jurisdictional grants is, itself, a question of interpretation that can raise (and has raised) substantial difficulties.

SECTION 2. THE SCOPE OF THE CONSTITUTIONAL GRANT OF FEDERAL QUESTION JURISDICTION

Osborn v. Bank of the United States

22 U.S. (9 Wheat.) 738, 6 L.Ed. 204 (1824).
Appeal from the Circuit Court of Ohio.

The bill filed in this cause, was exhibited in the Court below, at September term 1819, in the name of the respondents, * * * praying an injunction to restrain Ralph Osborn, auditor of the State of Ohio, from proceeding against the complainants, under an act of the legislature of that State, passed February the 8th, 1819, entitled, "an act to levy and collect a tax from all banks, and individuals, and companies and associations of individuals, that may transact business in this State, without being allowed to do so by the laws thereof."

This act, after reciting that the Bank of the United States pursued its operations contrary to a law of the State, enacted, that if, after the 1st day of

---

48. The Supreme Court relied in part on the passage of this statute in holding that the judicial review provisions of the Administrative Procedure Act did not provide a basis for original jurisdiction in the district courts independent of the general federal question provision. See Califano v. Sanders, 430 U.S. 99 (1977).

49. *E.g.,* the proviso added in 1978 to 28 U.S.C. § 1337. With respect to this and other, similar provisions, see 13B Wright, Miller & Cooper, Federal Practice and Procedure § 3561.1 and n. 24 (1984).

the following September, the said Bank, or any other, should continue to transact business in the State, it should be liable to an annual tax of $50,000 on each office of discount and deposit.   * * *

[Soon thereafter a writ of injunction was issued, as prayed, and was served upon Osborn and upon Harper, who was alleged to have been employed by Osborn to collect the tax.

[An amended bill charged that Harper, after service of the injunction and a subpoena, proceeded by violence to the office of the bank at Chillicothe and took therefrom $100,000 in specie and bank-notes belonging to or on deposit with the plaintiffs. It appeared that $98,000 of this money was being held separately, with notice of the circumstances, by Sullivan, the present State treasurer, who was also made a defendant. The location of the remaining $2,000 was unclear; it may have been retained as a "commission" by one of the State officers.

[After a hearing upon the defendants' answers and upon the decrees nisi against Osborn and Harper, the Circuit court pronounced a decree directing them to restore to the bank the sum of $100,000, with interest on $19,830, the amount of specie in the hands of Sullivan.]

■ Mr. Chief Justice Marshall delivered the opinion of the Court.

* * *

The appellants contest the jurisdiction of the Court on two grounds:

1st. That the act of Congress has not given it.

2d. That, under the constitution, Congress cannot give it.

1. The first part of the objection depends entirely on the language of the act. The words are, that the bank shall be "made able and capable in law,"— "to sue and be sued, plead and be impleaded, answer and be answered, defend and be defended, in all State Courts having competent jurisdiction, and in any Circuit Court of the United States."

These words seem to the Court to admit of but one interpretation; they cannot be made plainer by explanation. They give, expressly, the right "to sue and be sued," "in every Circuit Court of the United States," and it would be difficult to substitute other terms which would be more direct and appropriate for the purpose. The argument of the appellants is founded on the opinion of this Court, in the Bank of the United States v. Deveaux (5 Cranch 85). In that case, it was decided, that the former Bank of the United States was not enabled, by the act which incorporated it, to sue in the federal Courts. The words of the 3d section of that act are, that the Bank may "sue and be sued," & c., "in Courts of record, or any other place whatsoever." The Court was of opinion, that these general words, which are usual in all acts of incorporation, gave only a general capacity to sue, not a particular privilege to sue in the Courts of the United States; * * * Whether this decision be right or wrong, it amounts only to a declaration, that a general capacity in the Bank to sue, without mentioning the Courts of the Union, may not give a right to sue in those Courts. To infer from this, that words expressly conferring a right to sue in those Courts, do not give the right, is surely a conclusion which the premises do not warrant.

The act of incorporation, then, confers jurisdiction on the Circuit Courts of the United States, if Congress can confer it.

2. We will now consider the constitutionality of the clause in the act of incorporation, which authorizes the Bank to sue in the federal Courts.

In support of this clause, it is said, that the legislative, executive and judicial powers of every well-constructed government, are co-extensive with each other; that is, they are potentially co-extensive. The executive department may constitutionally execute every law which the Legislature may constitutionally make, and the judicial department may receive from the Legislature the power of construing every such law. All governments which are not extremely defective in their organization, must possess, within themselves, the means of expounding, as well as enforcing, their own laws. If we examine the constitution of the United States, we find that its framers kept this great political principle in view. The 2d article vests the whole executive power in the president; and the 3d article declares, "that the judicial power shall extend to all cases in law and equity, arising under this constitution, the laws of the United States, and treaties made, or which shall be made, under their authority." This clause enables the judicial department to receive jurisdiction to the full extent of the constitution, laws and treaties of the United States, when any question respecting them shall assume such a form that the judicial power is capable of acting on it. * * *

The suit of the Bank of the United States v. Osborn and others, is a case, and the question is, whether it arises under a law of the United States?

The appellants contend, that it does not, because several questions may arise in it, which depend on the general principles of the law, not on any act of Congress.

If this were sufficient to withdraw a case from the jurisdiction of the federal Courts, almost every case, although involving the construction of a law, would be withdrawn; and a clause in the constitution, relating to a subject of vital importance to the government, and expressed in the most comprehensive terms, would be construed to mean almost nothing. There is scarcely any case, every part of which depends on the constitution, laws or treaties of the United States. The questions, whether the fact alleged as the foundation of the action, be real or fictitious; whether the conduct of the plaintiff has been such as to entitle him to maintain his action; whether his right is barred; whether he has received satisfaction, or has in any manner released his claims, are questions, some or all of which may occur, in almost every case; and if their existence be sufficient to arrest the jurisdiction of the Court, words which seem intended to be as extensive as the constitution, laws and treaties of the Union—which seem designed to give the Courts of the government the construction of all its acts, so far as they affect the rights of individuals—would be reduced to almost nothing.

In those cases in which original jurisdiction is given to the Supreme Court, the judicial power of the United States cannot be exercised in its appellate form. In every other case, the power is to be exercised in its original or appellate form, or both, as the wisdom of Congress may direct. With the exception of these cases, in which original jurisdiction is given to this Court, there is none to which the judicial power extends, from which the original jurisdiction of the inferior Courts is excluded by the constitution. Original jurisdiction, so far as the constitution gives a rule, is co-extensive with the judicial power. * * *

The constitution establishes the Supreme Court, and defines its jurisdiction. It enumerates cases in which its jurisdiction is original and exclusive;

and then defines that which is appellate, but does not insinuate, that in any such case, the power cannot be exercised in its original form, by Courts of original jurisdiction. It is not insinuated, that the judicial power, in cases depending on the character of the cause, cannot be exercised, in the first instance, in the Courts of the Union, but must first be exercised in the tribunals of the State; tribunals over which the government of the Union has no adequate control, and which may be closed to any claim asserted under a law of the United States. We perceive, then, no ground on which the proposition can be maintained, that Congress is incapable of giving the Circuit Courts original jurisdiction, in any case to which the appellate jurisdiction extends.

We ask, then, if it can be sufficient to exclude this jurisdiction, that the case involves questions depending on general principles? A cause may depend on several questions of fact and law. Some of these may depend on the construction of a law of the United States; others on principles unconnected with that law. If it be a sufficient foundation for jurisdiction, that the title or right set up by the party, may be defeated by one construction of the constitution or law of the United States, and sustained by the opposite construction, provided the facts necessary to support the action be made out, then all the other questions must be decided as incidental to this, which gives that jurisdiction. * * * On the opposite construction, the judicial power never can be extended to a whole case, as expressed by the constitution, but to those parts of cases only which present the particular question involving the construction of the constitution or the law. We say, it never can be extended to the whole case, because, if the circumstance that other points are involved in it, shall disable Congress from authorizing the Courts of the Union to take jurisdiction of the original cause, it equally disables Congress from authorizing those Courts to take jurisdiction of the whole cause, on an appeal, and thus will be restricted to a single question in that cause; and words obviously intended to secure to those who claim rights under the constitution, laws or treaties of the United States, a trial in the federal Courts, will be restricted to the insecure remedy of an appeal, upon an insulated point, after it has received that shape which may be given to it by another tribunal, into which he is forced against his will.

We think, then, that when a question to which the judicial power of the Union is extended by the constitution, forms an ingredient of the original cause, it is in the power of Congress to give the Circuit Courts jurisdiction of that cause, although other questions of fact or of law may be involved in it.

The case of the Bank is, we think, a very strong case of this description. The charter of incorporation not only creates it, but gives it every faculty which it possesses. The power to acquire rights of any description, to transact business of any description, to make contracts of any description, to sue on those contracts, is given and measured by its charter, and that charter is a law of the United States. This being can acquire no right, make no contract, bring no suit, which is not authorized by a law of the United States. It is not only itself the mere creature of a law, but all its actions and all its rights are dependent on the same law. Can a being, thus constituted, have a case which does not arise literally, as well as substantially, under the law?

Take the case of a contract, which is put as the strongest against the Bank.

When a Bank sues, the first question which presents itself, and which lies at the foundation of the cause, is, has this legal entity a right to sue? Has it a right to come, not into this Court particularly, but into any Court? This depends on a law of the United States. The next question is, has this being a right to make this particular contract? If this question be decided in the negative, the cause is determined against the plaintiff; and this question, too, depends entirely on a law of the United States. These are important questions, and they exist in every possible case. The right to sue, if decided once, is decided forever; but the power of Congress was exercised antecedently to the first decision on that right, and if it was constitutional then, it cannot cease to be so, because the particular question is decided. It may be revived at the will of the party, and most probably would be renewed, were the tribunal to be changed. But the question respecting the right to make a particular contract, or to acquire a particular property, or to sue on account of a particular injury, belongs to every particular case, and may be renewed in every case. The question forms an original ingredient in every cause. Whether it be, in fact, relied on or not, in the defence, it is still a part of the cause, and may be relied on. The right of the plaintiff to sue cannot depend on the defence which the defendant may choose to set up. His right to sue is anterior to that defence, and must depend on the state of things when the action is brought. The question which the case involved, then, must determine its character, whether those questions be made in the cause or not.

The appellants say, that the case arises on the contract; but the validity of the contract depends on a law of the United States, and the plaintiff is compelled, in every case, to show its validity. The case arises emphatically under the law. The act of Congress is its foundation. The contract could never have been made, but under the authority of that act. The act itself is the first ingredient in the case—is its origin—is that from which every other part arises. That other questions may also arise, as the execution of the contract, or its performance, cannot change the case, or give it any other origin than the charter of incorporation. The action still originates in, and is sustained by, that charter. * * *.

It is said, that a clear distinction exists between the party and the cause; that the party may originate under a law with which the cause has no connection; and that Congress may with the same propriety, give a naturalized citizen, who is the mere creature of law, a right to sue in the Courts of the United States, as give that right to the Bank.

This distinction is not denied; and if the act of Congress was a simple act of incorporation, and contained nothing more, it might be entitled to great consideration. But the act does not stop with incorporating the Bank. It proceeds to bestow upon the being it has made, all the faculties and capacities which that being possesses. Every act of the Bank grows out of this law, and is tested by it. * * *

A naturalized citizen is, indeed, made a citizen under an act of Congress, but the act does not proceed to give, to regulate, or to prescribe his capacities. He becomes a member of the society, possessing all the rights of a native citizen, and standing, in the view of the constitution, on the footing of a native. The constitution does not authorize Congress to enlarge or abridge those rights. The simple power of the national legislature is, to prescribe a uniform rule of naturalization, and the exercise of this power exhausts it, so far as respects the individual. The constitution then takes him up, and, among other rights, extends to him the capacity of suing in the Courts of the United States, precisely under the same circumstances under which a native might sue. He is distinguishable in nothing from a native citizen, except so far as the constitution makes the distinction; the law makes none.

There is, then, no resemblance between the act incorporating the Bank, and the general naturalization law.

Upon the best consideration we have been able to bestow on this subject, we are of opinion, that the clause in the act of incorporation, enabling the Bank to sue in the Courts of the United States, is consistent with the constitution, and to be obeyed in all Courts.

We will now proceed to consider the merits of the cause. * * *.

We think, then, that there is no error in the decree of the Circuit Court for the district of Ohio, so far as it directs restitution of the specific sum of $98,000, which was taken out of the Bank unlawfully, and was in the possession of the defendant, Samuel Sullivan, when the injunction was awarded, in September 1820, to restrain him from paying it away, or in any manner using it; and so far as it directs the payment of the remaining sum of $2000 by the defendants, Ralph Osborn and John L. Harper; but that the same is erroneous, so far as respects the interest on the coin, part of the said $98,000, it being the opinion of this Court, that, while the parties were restrained by the authority of the Circuit Court from using it, they ought not to be charged with interest. The decree of the Circuit Court for the district of Ohio is affirmed, as to the said sums of $98,000 and $2000; and reversed as to the residue.

■ MR. JUSTICE JOHNSON. (Dissenting.)—The argument in this cause presents three questions: 1. Has Congress granted to the Bank of the United States, an unlimited right of suing in the Courts of the United States? 2. Could Congress constitutionally grant such a right? 3. Has the power of the Court been legally and constitutionally exercised in this suit?

I have very little doubt, that the public mind will be easily reconciled to the decision of the Court here rendered: for, whether necessary or unnecessary, originally, a State of things has now grown up, in some of the States, which renders all the protection necessary, that the general government can give to this Bank. The policy of the decision is obvious, that is, if the Bank is to be sustained; and few will bestow upon its legal correctness, the reflection that it is necessary to test it by the constitution and laws, under which it is rendered.

The Bank of the United States is now identified with the administration of the national government. It is an immense machine economically and beneficially applied to the fiscal transactions of the nation. Attempts have been made to dispense with it, and they have failed; serious and very weighty doubts have been entertained of its constitutionality, but they have been abandoned; and it is now become the functionary that collects, the depository that holds, the vehicle that transports, the guard that protects, and the agent that distributes and pays away, the millions that pass annually through the national treasury; and all this, not only without expense to the government, but after paying a large *bonus,* and sustaining actual annual losses to a large amount; furnishing the only possible means of embodying the most ample security for so immense a charge.

Had its effects, however, and the views of its framers, been confined exclusively to its fiscal uses, it is more than probable, that this suit, and the laws in which it originated, would never have had existence. But it is well known, that with that object was combined another, of a very general, and not less important character.

The expiration of the charter of the former Bank, led to State creations of Banks; each new Bank increased the facilities of creating others; and the necessities of the general government, both to make use of the State Banks for their deposits, and to borrow largely of all who would lend to them, produced that rage for multiplying Banks, which, aided by the emoluments derived to the States in their creation, and the many individual incentives which they developed, soon inundated the country with new description of bills of credit, against which, it was obvious, that the provisions of the constitution opposed no adequate inhibition.

A specie-paying Bank, with an overwhelming capital, and the whole aid of the government deposits, presented the only resource to which the government could resort, to restore that power over the currency of the country, which the framers of the constitution evidently intended to give to Congress alone. But this necessarily involved a restraint upon individual cupidity, and the exercise of State power; and in the nature of things, it was hardly possible, for the mighty effort necessary to put down an evil, spread so wide, and arrived to such maturity, to be made, without embodying against it an immense moneyed combination, which could not fail of making its influence to be felt, wherever its claimances could reach, or its industry and wealth be brought to operate.
* * *

In the present instance, I cannot persuade myself, that the constitution sanctions the vesting of the right of action in this Bank, in cases in which the privilege is exclusively personal, or in any case, merely on the ground that a question might *possibly* be raised in it, involving the constitution, or constitutionality of a law of the United States.

When laws were heretofore passed for raising a revenue by a duty on stamped paper, the tax was quietly acquiesced in, notwithstanding it entrenched so closely on the questionable power of the States over the law of contracts; but had the same law which declared void contracts not written upon stamped paper, declared, that every person holding such paper should be entitled to bring his action "in any Circuit Court" of the United States, it is confidently believed, that there could have been but one opinion on the constitutionality of such a provision. The whole jurisdiction over contracts, might thus have been taken from the State Courts, and conferred upon those of the United States. Nor would the evil have rested there; by a similar exercise of power, imposing a stamp on deeds, generally, jurisdiction over the territory of the State, whoever might be parties, even between citizens of the same State—jurisdiction of suits instituted for the recovery of legacies or distributive portions of intestates' estates—jurisdiction, in fact, over almost every possible case, might be transferred to the Courts of the United States. Wills might be required to be executed on stamped paper; taxes may be, and have been, imposed upon legacies and distributions, and in all such cases, there is not only a possibility, but a probability, that a question may arise, involving the constitutionality, construction, & c., of a law of the United States. If the circumstance, that the questions which the case involves, are to determine its character, whether those questions be made in the case or not, then, every case here alluded to, may as well be transferred to the jurisdiction of the United States, as those to which this Bank is a party. But still further, as was justly insisted in argument, there is not a tract of land of the United States, acquired under laws of the United States, whatever be the number of mesne transfers that it may have undergone, over which the jurisdiction of the Court of the

United States might not be extended by Congress, upon the very principle on which the right of suit in this Bank is here maintained. Nor is the case of the alien, put in argument, at all inapplicable. The one acquires its character of individual property, as the other does his political existence, under a law of the United States; and there is not a suit which may be instituted to recover the one, nor an action of ejectment to be brought by the other, in which a right acquired under a law of the United States, does not lie as essentially at the basis of the right of action, as in the suits brought by this Bank. It is no answer to the argument, to say, that the law of the United States is but ancillary to the constitution, as to the alien; for the constitution could do nothing for him, without the law: and whether the question be upon law or constitution, still, if the possibility of its arising, be a sufficient circumstance to bring it within the jurisdiction of the United States Courts, that possibility exists with regard to every suit affected by alien disabilities; to real actions, in time of peace—to all actions, in time of war.

I cannot persuade myself, then, that, with these palpable consequences in view, Congress ever could have intended to vest in the Bank of the United States the right of suit to the extent here claimed. * * *

* * * I next proceed to consider, more distinctly, the constitutional question, on the right to vest the jurisdiction to the extent here contended for. And here I must observe, that I altogether misunderstood the counsel, who argued the cause for the plaintiff in error, if any of them contended against the jurisdiction, on the ground, that the cause involved questions depending on general principles. No one can question, that the Court which has jurisdiction of the principal question, must exercise jurisdiction over every question. Neither did I understand them as denying, that if Congress could confer on the Circuit Courts appellate, they could confer original, jurisdiction. The argument went to deny the right to assume jurisdiction, on a mere hypothesis. It was one of description, identity, definition; they contended, that until a question involving the construction or administration of the laws of the United States did actually arise, the *casus foederis* was not presented, on which the constitution authorized the government to take to itself the jurisdiction of the cause. That until such a question actually arose, until such a case was actually presented, *non constat,* but the cause depended upon general principles, exclusively cognisable in the State Courts; that neither the letter nor the spirit of the constitution sanctioned the assumption of jurisdiction on the part of the United States, at any previous stage.

* * *

Efforts have been made to fix the precise sense of the constitution, when it vests jurisdiction in the general government, in "cases arising under the laws of the United States." To me, the question appears susceptible of a very simple solution; that all depends upon the identity of the case supposed; according to which idea, a case may be such, in its very existence, or may become such, in its progress. An action may "live, move and have its being," in a law of the United States; such is that given for the violation of a patent-right, and four or five different actions given by this act of incorporation; particularly that against the president and directors for over-issuing; in all of which cases, the plaintiff must count upon the law itself as the ground of his action. And of the other description, would have been an action of trespass, in this case, had remedy been sought for an actual levy of the tax imposed. Such was the case of the former Bank against Deveaux, and many others that have occurred in this

Court, in which the suit, in its form, was such as occur in ordinary cases, but in which the pleadings or evidence raised the question on the law or constitution of the United States. In this class of cases, the occurrence of a question makes the case, and transfers it, as provided for under the twenty-fifth section of the Judiciary Act, to the jurisdiction of the United States. And this appears to me to present the only sound and practical construction of the constitution on this subject; for no other cases does it regard as necessary to place under the control of the general government. It is only when the case exhibits one or the other of these characteristics, that it is acted upon by the constitution. Where no question is raised, there can be no contrariety of construction; and what else had the constitution to guard against? As to cases of the first description, *ex necessitate rei,* the Courts of the United States must be susceptible of original jurisdiction; and as to all other cases, I should hold them also susceptible of original jurisdiction, if it were practicable, in the nature of things, to make out the definition of the case, so as to bring it under the constitution judicially, upon an original suit. But until the plaintiff can control the defendant in his pleadings, I see no practical mode of determining when the case does occur, otherwise than by permitting the cause to advance, until the case for which the constitution provides shall actually arise. If it never occurs, there can be nothing to complain of; and such are the provisions of the twenty-fifth section. The cause might be transferred to the Circuit Court, before an adjudication takes place; but I can perceive no earlier stage at which it can possibly be predicated of such a case, that it is one within the constitution; nor any possible necessity for transferring it then, or until the Court has acted upon it to the prejudice of the claims of the United States. It is not, therefore, because Congress may not vest an *original* jurisdiction, where they can constitutionally vest in the Circuit Courts *appellate* jurisdiction, that I object to this general grant of the right to sue; but because that the peculiar nature of this jurisdiction is such, as to render it impossible to exercise it, in a strictly original form, and because the principle of a possible occurrence of a question, as a ground of jurisdiction, is transcending the bounds of the constitution, and placing it on a ground which will admit of an *enormous accession*, if not an *unlimited assumption*, of jurisdiction. * * *

Textile Workers Union v. Lincoln Mills

353 U.S. 448, 77 S.Ct. 912, 1 L.Ed.2d 972 (1957).
Certiorari to the United States Court of Appeals for the Fifth Circuit.

[This federal court action, commenced by a labor union to compel arbitration under a collective bargaining agreement, was brought under Section 301(a) of the Taft–Hartley Act, 29 U.S.C. § 185(a), which confers jurisdiction on the federal courts over suits for violation of labor-management contracts in industries affecting commerce. A majority of the Supreme Court, in an opinion by Justice Douglas, concluded that "the substantive law to apply in suits under § 301(a) is federal law, which the courts must fashion from the policy of our national labor laws." In doing so, the majority pretermitted the constitutional issues that it would have had to address if § 301(a) had been read solely as a grant of subject-matter jurisdiction and not also as a grant of authority to fashion substantive rules of decision.]

■ MR. JUSTICE BURTON, whom MR. JUSTICE HARLAN joins, concurring in the result.

* * *

* * * I do not subscribe to the conclusion of the Court that the substantive law to be applied in a suit under § 301 is federal law. At the same time, I agree with Judge Magruder in International Brotherhood v. W.L. Mead, Inc., 230 F.2d 576, that some federal rights may necessarily be involved in a § 301 case, and hence that the constitutionality of § 301 can be upheld as a congressional grant to Federal District Courts of what has been called "protective jurisdiction."

■ MR. JUSTICE FRANKFURTER, dissenting.

* * * [The first portion of this opinion dissented from the Court's conclusion that § 301(a) authorized the creation of a species of federal common law to govern collective bargaining agreements subject to federal court jurisdiction. Justice Frankfurter then turned to the rationale of Justice Burton's concurrence.]

The second ground of my dissent from the Court's action is more fundamental. Since I do not agree with the Court's conclusion that federal substantive law is to govern in actions under § 301, I am forced to consider the * * * constitutionality of a grant of jurisdiction to federal courts over contracts that came into being entirely by virtue of state substantive law, a jurisdiction not based on diversity of citizenship, yet one in which a federal court would, as in diversity cases, act in effect merely as another court of the State in which it sits. The scope of allowable federal judicial power that this grant must satisfy is constitutionally described as "Cases, in Law and Equity, arising under this Constitution, the Laws of the United States, and Treaties made, or which shall be made, under their Authority." Art. III, § 2. While interpretive decisions are legion under general statutory grants of jurisdiction strikingly similar to this constitutional wording, it is generally recognized that the full constitutional power has not been exhausted by these statutes. See, e.g., Mishkin, The Federal "Question" in the District Courts, 53 Col.L.Rev. 157, 160; Wechsler, Federal Jurisdiction and the Revision of the Judicial Code, 13 Law & Contemp.Prob., 216, 224–225.

Almost without exception, decisions under the general statutory grants have tested jurisdiction in terms of the presence, as an integral part of plaintiff's cause of action, of an issue calling for interpretation or application of federal law. * * * The litigation-provoking problem has been the degree to which federal law must be in the forefront of the case and not collateral, peripheral or remote.

In a few exceptional cases, arising under special jurisdictional grants, the criteria by which the prominence of the federal question is measured against constitutional requirements have been found satisfied under circumstances suggesting a variant theory of the nature of these requirements. The first, and the leading case in the field, is Osborn v. Bank of United States, 9 Wheat. 738.

There, Chief Justice Marshall sustained federal jurisdiction in a situation—hypothetical in the case before him but presented by the companion case of Bank of United States v. Planters' Bank, 9 Wheat. 904—involving suit by a federally incorporated Bank upon a contract. Despite the assumption that the cause of action and the interpretation of the contract would be governed by state law, the case was found to "arise under the laws of the United States" because the propriety and scope of a federally granted authority to enter into contracts and to litigate might well be challenged. This reasoning was subsequently applied to sustain jurisdiction in actions against federally chartered railroad corporations. Pacific Railroad Removal Cases, 115 U.S. 1. The traditional interpretation of this series of cases is that federal jurisdiction under the "arising" clause of the Constitution, though limited to cases involving potential federal questions, has such flexibility that Congress may confer it whenever there exists in the background some federal proposition that might be challenged, despite the remoteness of the likelihood of actual presentation of such a federal question.[4]

The views expressed in Osborn and the Pacific Railroad Removal Cases were severely restricted in construing general grants of jurisdiction. But the Court later sustained this jurisdictional section of the Bankruptcy Act of 1898:

"The United States district courts shall have jurisdiction of all controversies at law and in equity, as distinguished from proceedings in bankruptcy, between trustees as such and adverse claimants concerning the property acquired or claimed by the trustees, in the same manner and to the same extent only as though bankruptcy proceedings had not been instituted and such controversies had been between the bankrupts and such adverse claimants." § 23, sub. a, as amended, 44 Stat. 664, 11 U.S.C. § 46, sub. a.

Under this provision the trustee could pursue in a federal court a private cause of action arising under and wholly governed by state law. Schumacher v. Beeler, 293 U.S. 367; Williams v. Austrian, 331 U.S. 642 (Chandler Act of 1938, 52 Stat. 840, 11 U.S.C.A. § 1 et seq.). To be sure, the cases did not discuss the basis of jurisdiction. It has been suggested that they merely represent an extension of the approach of the Osborn case; the trustee's right to sue might be challenged on obviously federal grounds—absence of bankruptcy or irregularity of the trustee's appointment or of the bankruptcy proceedings. National Mutual Ins. Co. of Dist. of Col. v. Tidewater Transfer Co., 337 U.S. 582, 611–613 (Rutledge, J., concurring). So viewed, this type of litigation implicates a potential federal question.

Apparently relying on the extent to which the bankruptcy cases involve only remotely a federal question, Mr. Justice Jackson concluded in National Mutual Insurance Co. of Dist. of Col. v. Tidewater Transfer Co., 337 U.S. 582, that Congress may confer jurisdiction on the District Courts as incidental to its powers under Article I. No attempt was made to reconcile this view with the restrictions of Article III; a majority of the Court recognized that Article III defined the bounds of valid jurisdictional legislation and rejected the notion that jurisdictional grants can go outside these limits.

With this background, many theories have been proposed to sustain the constitutional validity of § 301. In Textile Workers Union of America v. American Thread Co., 113 F.Supp. 137, 140, Judge Wyzanski suggested, among other possibilities, that § 301 might be read as containing a direction that controversies affecting interstate commerce should be governed by federal law incorporating state law by reference, and that such controversies would then arise under a valid federal law as required by Article III. Whatever may be said of the assumption regarding the validity of federal jurisdiction under an

---

4. Osborn might possibly be limited on the ground that a federal instrumentality, the Bank of the United States, was involved, see note 5, *infra*, but such an explanation could not suffice to narrow the holding in the Pacific Railroad Removal Cases.

affirmative declaration by Congress that state law should be applied as federal law by federal courts to contract disputes affecting commerce, we cannot argumentatively legislate for Congress when Congress has failed to legislate. To do so disrespects legislative responsibility and disregards judicial limitations.

Another theory, relying on Osborn and the bankruptcy cases, has been proposed which would achieve results similar to those attainable under Mr. Justice Jackson's view, but which purports to respect the "arising" clause of Article III. See Hart and Wechsler, The Federal Courts and the Federal System, pp. 744–747 [1st ed. 1953]; Wechsler, *Federal Jurisdiction and the Revision of the Judicial Code,* 13 Law & Contemp. Prob. 216, 224–225. Called "protective jurisdiction," the suggestion is that in any case for which Congress has the constitutional power to prescribe federal rules of decision and thus confer "true" federal question jurisdiction, it may, without so doing, enact a jurisdictional statute, which will provide a federal forum for the application of state statute and decisional law. Analysis of the "protective jurisdiction" theory might also be attempted in terms of the language of Article III—construing "laws" to include jurisdictional statutes where Congress could have legislated substantively in a field. This is but another way of saying that because Congress could have legislated substantively and thereby could give rise to litigation under a statute of the United States, it can provide a federal forum for state-created rights although it chose not to adopt state law as federal law or to originate federal rights.

Surely the truly technical restrictions of Article III are not met or respected by a beguiling phrase that the greater power here must necessarily include the lesser. In the compromise of federal and state interests leading to distribution of jealously guarded judicial power in a federal system, it is obvious that very different considerations apply to cases involving questions of federal law and those turning solely on state law. It may be that the ambiguity of the phrase "arising under the laws of the United States" leaves room for more than traditional theory could accommodate. But, under the theory of "protective jurisdiction," the "arising under" jurisdiction of the federal courts would be vastly extended. For example, every contract or tort arising out of a contract affecting commerce might be a potential cause of action in the federal courts, even though only state law was involved in the decision of the case. At least in Osborn and the bankruptcy cases, a substantive federal law was present somewhere in the background. But this theory rests on the supposition that Congress could enact substantive federal law to govern the particular case. It was not held in those cases, nor is it clear, that federal law could be held to govern the transactions of all persons who subsequently become bankrupt, or of all suits of a Bank of the United States. See Mishkin, *The Federal "Question" in the District Courts,* 53 Col.L.Rev. 157, 189.

"Protective jurisdiction," once the label is discarded, cannot be justified under any view of the allowable scope to be given to Article III. "Protective jurisdiction" is a misused label for the statute we are here considering. That rubric is properly descriptive of safeguarding some of the indisputable, staple business of the federal courts. It is a radiation of an existing jurisdiction. See Adams v. United States ex rel. McCann, 317 U.S. 269; 28 U.S.C. § 2283. "Protective jurisdiction" cannot generate an independent source for adjudication outside of the Article III sanctions and what Congress has defined. The theory must have as its sole justification a belief in the inadequacy of state tribunals in determining state law. The Constitution reflects such a belief in the specific situation within which the Diversity Clause was confined. The intention to remedy such supposed defects was exhausted in this provision of Article III.[5] That this "protective" theory was not adopted by Chief Justice Marshall at a time when conditions might have presented more substantial justification strongly suggests its lack of constitutional merit. Moreover, Congress in its consideration of § 301 nowhere suggested dissatisfaction with the ability of state courts to administer state law properly. Its concern was to provide access to the federal courts for easier enforcement of state-created rights.

Another theory also relies on Osborn and the bankruptcy cases as an implicit recognition of the propriety of the exercise of some sort of "protective jurisdiction" by the federal courts. Mishkin, op. cit. *supra,* 53 Col.L.Rev. 157, 184 *et seq.* Professor Mishkin tends to view the assertion of such a jurisdiction, in the absence of any exercise of substantive powers, as irreconcilable with the "arising" clause since the case would then arise only under the jurisdictional statute itself, and he is reluctant to find a constitutional basis for the grant of power outside Article III. Professor Mishkin also notes that the only purpose of such a statute would be to insure impartiality to some litigant, an objection inconsistent with Article III's recognition of "protective jurisdiction" only in the specified situation of diverse citizenship. But where Congress has "an articulated and active federal policy regulating a field, the 'arising under' clause of Article III apparently permits the conferring of jurisdiction on the national courts of all cases in the area—including those substantively governed by state law." *Id.,* at 192. In such cases, the protection being offered is not to the suitor, as in diversity cases, but to the "congressional legislative program." Thus he supports § 301: "even though the rules governing collective bargaining agreements continue to be state-fashioned, nonetheless the mode of their application and enforcement may play a very substantial part in the labor-management relations of interstate industry and commerce—an area in which the national government has labored long and hard." *Id.,* at 196.

Insofar as state law governs the case, Professor Mishkin's theory is quite similar to that advanced by Professors Hart and Wechsler and followed by the Court of Appeals for the First Circuit: The substantive power of Congress, although not exercised to govern the particular "case," gives "arising under" jurisdiction to the federal courts despite governing state law. The second "protective jurisdiction" theory has the dubious advantage of limiting incursions on state judicial power to situations in which the State's feelings may have been tempered by early substantive federal invasions.

Professor Mishkin's theory of "protective jurisdiction" may find more constitutional justification if there is not merely an "articulated and active"

---

5. To be sure, the Court upheld the removal statute for suits or prosecutions commenced in a state court against federal revenue officers on account of any act committed under color of office. State of Tennessee v. Davis, 100 U.S. 257, 25 L.Ed. 648. The Court, however, construed the action of Congress in defining the powers of revenue agents as giving them a substantive defense against prosecution under state law for commission of acts "warranted by the Federal authority they possess." *Id.,* 100 U.S. at page 263. That put federal law in the forefront as a defense. In any event, the fact that officers of the Federal Government were parties may be considered sufficient to afford access to the federal forum. See In re Debs, 158 U.S. 564, 584–586; Mishkin, 53 Col. L.Rev., at 193: "Without doubt, a federal forum should be available for all suits involving the Government, its agents and instrumentalities, regardless of the source of the substantive rule."

congressional policy regulating the labor field but also federal rights existing in the interstices of actions under § 301. * * *

Legislation must, if possible, be given a meaning that will enable it to survive. This rule of constitutional adjudication is normally invoked to narrow what would otherwise be the natural but constitutionally dubious scope of the language. * * * Here the endeavor of some lower courts and of this Court has resulted in adding to the section substantive congressional regulation even though Congress saw fit not to exercise such power or to give the courts any concrete guidance for defining such regulation.

* * * The suggestion that the section permits the federal courts to work out, without more, a federal code governing collective-bargaining contracts must, for reasons that have already been stated, be rejected. Likewise the suggestion that § 301 may be viewed as a congressional authorization to the federal courts to work out a concept of the nature of the collective-bargaining contract, leaving detailed questions of interpretation to state law. * * *.

There is a point, however, at which the search may be ended with less misgiving regarding the propriety of judicial infusion of substantive provisions into § 301. The contribution of federal law might consist in postulating the right of a union, despite its amorphous status as an unincorporated association, to enter into binding collective-bargaining contracts with an employer. [Justice Frankfurter was here referring to § 301(b) of the Taft–Hartley Act, which provides, *inter alia*, that labor organizations and employers whose activities affect interstate commerce are bound by the acts of their agents, and that "any such labor organization may sue or be sued as an entity and in behalf of the employees whom it represents in the courts of the United States."] The federal courts might also give sanction to this right by refusing to comply with any state law that does not admit that collective bargaining may result in an enforceable contract. It is hard to see what serious federal-state conflicts could arise under this view. At most, a state court might dismiss the action, while a federal court would entertain it. Moreover, such a function of federal law is closely related to the removal of the procedural barriers to suit. * * *

Even if this limited federal "right" were read into § 301, a serious constitutional question would still be present. It does elevate the situation to one closely analogous to that presented in Osborn v. Bank of United States, 9 Wheat. 738. Section 301 would, under this view, imply that a union is to be viewed as a juristic entity for purposes of acquiring contract rights under a collective-bargaining agreement, and that it has the right to enter into such a contract and to sue upon it. This was all that was immediately and expressly involved in the Osborn case, although the historical setting was vastly different and the juristic entity in that case was completely the creature of federal law, one engaged in carrying out essential governmental functions. Most of these special considerations had disappeared, however, at the time and in the circumstances of the decision of the Pacific Railroad Removal Cases, 115 U.S. 1. There is force in the view that regards the latter as a "sport" and finds that the Court has so viewed it. See Mishkin, 53 Col.L.Rev., at 160, n. 24, citing Gully v. First National Bank, 299 U.S. 109, 113–114 ("Only recently we said after full consideration that the doctrine of the charter cases was to be treated as exceptional, though within their special field there was no thought to disturb them."), and People of Puerto Rico v. Russell & Co., 288 U.S. 476, 485; see also Mr. Justice Holmes, in Smith v. Kansas City Title & Trust Co., 255 U.S. 180,

214–215 (dissenting opinion). The question is whether we should now so consider it and refuse to apply its holding to the present situation.

I believe that we should not extend the precedents of Osborn and the Pacific Railroad Removal Cases to this case even though there be some elements of analytical similarity. Osborn, the foundation for the Removal Cases, appears to have been based on premises that today, viewed in the light of the jurisdictional philosophy of Gully v. First National Bank, *supra,* are subject to criticism. The basic premise was that every case in which a federal question might arise must be capable of being commenced in the federal courts, and when so commenced it might, because jurisdiction must be judged at the outset, be concluded there despite the fact that the federal question was never raised. Marshall's holding was undoubtedly influenced by his fear that the bank might suffer hostile treatment in the state courts that could not be remedied by an appeal on an isolated federal question. There is nothing in Article III that affirmatively supports the view that original jurisdiction over cases involving federal questions must extend to every case in which there is the potentiality of appellate jurisdiction. We also have become familiar with removal procedures that could be adapted to alleviate any remaining fears by providing for removal to a federal court whenever a federal question was raised. In view of these developments, we would not be justified in perpetuating a principle that permits assertion of original federal jurisdiction on the remote possibility of presentation of a federal question. Indeed, Congress, by largely withdrawing the jurisdiction that the Pacific Railroad Removal Cases recognized, and this Court, by refusing to perpetuate it under general grants of jurisdiction, see Gully v. First National Bank, *supra,* have already done much to recognize the changed atmosphere.

Analysis of the bankruptcy power also reveals a superficial analogy to § 301. The trustee enforces a cause of action acquired under state law by the bankrupt. Federal law merely provides for the appointment of the trustee, vests the cause of action in him, and confers jurisdiction on the federal courts. Section 301 similarly takes the rights and liabilities which under state law are vested distributively in the individual members of a union and vests them in the union for purposes of actions in federal courts, wherein the unions are authorized to sue and be sued as an entity. While the authority of the trustee depends on the existence of a bankrupt and on the propriety of the proceedings leading to the trustee's appointment, both of which depend on federal law, there are similar federal propositions that may be essential to an action under § 301. Thus, the validity of the contract may in any case be challenged on the ground that the labor organization negotiating it was not the representative of the employees concerned, a question that has been held to be federal, or on the ground that subsequent change in the representative status of the union has affected the continued validity of the agreement. Perhaps also the qualifications imposed on a union's right to utilize the facilities of the National Labor Relations Board, dependent on the filing of non-Communist affidavits required by § 9(h), and the information and reports required by § 9(f) and (g), might be read as restrictions on the right of the union to sue under § 301, again providing a federal basis for challenge to the union's authority. Consequently, were the bankruptcy cases to be viewed as dependent solely on the background existence of federal questions, there would be little analytical basis for distinguishing actions under § 301. But the bankruptcy decisions may be justified by the scope of the bankruptcy power, which may be deemed to sweep within its scope interests analytically outside the "federal question" category, but sufficiently related to the main purpose of bankruptcy to call for comprehensive treatment. See National Mutual Ins. Co. v. Tidewater Transfer Co., 337 U.S. 582, 652, Note 3 (concurring in part, dissenting in part). Also, although a particular suit may be brought by a trustee in a district other than the one in which the principal proceedings are pending, if all the suits by the trustee, even though in many federal courts, are regarded as one litigation for the collection and apportionment of the bankrupt's property, a particular suit by the trustee, under state law, to recover a specific piece of property might be analogized to the ancillary or pendent jurisdiction cases in which, in the disposition of a cause of action, federal courts may pass on state grounds for recovery that are joined to federal grounds. See Hurn v. Oursler, 289 U.S. 238; Siler v. Louisville & Nashville R. Co., 213 U.S. 175; but see Mishkin, 53 Col.L.Rev., at 194, n. 161.

If there is in the phrase "arising under the laws of the United States" leeway for expansion of our concepts of jurisdiction, the history of Article III suggests that the area is not great and that it will require the presence of some substantial federal interest, one of greater weight and dignity than questionable doubt concerning the effectiveness of state procedure. The bankruptcy cases might possibly be viewed as such an expansion. But even so, not merely convenient judicial administration but the whole purpose of the congressional legislative program—conservation and equitable distribution of the bankrupt's estate in carrying out the constitutional power over bankruptcy—required the availability of federal jurisdiction to avoid expense and delay. Nothing pertaining to § 301 suggests vesting the federal courts with sweeping power under the Commerce Clause comparable to that vested in the federal courts under the bankruptcy power.

In the wise distribution of governmental powers, this Court cannot do what a President sometimes does in returning a bill to Congress. We cannot return this provision to Congress and respectfully request that body to face the responsibility placed upon it by the Constitution to define the jurisdiction of the lower courts with some particularity and not to leave these courts at large. Confronted as I am, I regretfully have no choice. For all the reasons elaborated in this dissent, even reading into § 301 the limited federal rights consistent with the purposes of that section, I am impelled to the view that it is unconstitutional in cases such as the present ones where it provides the sole basis for exercise of jurisdiction by the federal courts.

NOTE ON THE SCOPE OF THE CONSTITUTIONAL GRANT AND THE VALIDITY OF A PROTECTIVE JURISDICTION

(1) *The Significance of a "Sue and Be Sued" Clause.* Similar questions to those in the bank cases-involving the interpretation of a "sue and be sued" clause-were raised in American Nat'l Red Cross v. S.G., 505 U.S. 247 (1992). There, plaintiffs brought a state court tort action against the Red Cross, alleging that one of the plaintiffs had contracted AIDS from a blood transfusion. Pointing to its congressional charter, which authorizes the Red Cross "to sue and be sued in courts of law and equity, State or Federal, within the jurisdiction of the United States," the Red Cross removed the case under 28 U.S.C. § 1441, which permits removal of federal question suits that could have been filed in federal court in the first instance.

On review, the Supreme Court ruled that the charter did confer on the federal courts jurisdiction to entertain actions against the Red Cross. The Court interpreted Deveaux, Osborn, and other precedents as supporting "the rule that a congressional charter's 'sue and be sued' provision may be read to confer federal court jurisdiction if, but only if, it specifically mentions the federal courts" (p. 2471). The decision in Deveaux was distinguished principally on the ground that the act of incorporation there at issue did not mention the federal courts, but simply referred to all "courts of record" (p. 2471). Finally, the Court stated that its "holding leaves the jurisdiction of the federal courts well within Article III's limits," noting that Osborn and many cases since had recognized congressional power to confer jurisdiction over actions involving federally chartered corporations (pp. 2475–76).

Four dissenting Justices interpreted the charter as merely conferring the capacity to sue and be sued. They distinguished Osborn on the ground that the Act incorporating the Bank provided that the Bank could be sued in state courts having competent jurisdiction and in the federal circuit courts but did not mention the federal district courts; that wording necessarily implied that the Act conferred jurisdiction on a particular set of federal trial courts. Because the Red Cross' charter (like the statute at issue in Deveaux) applies to suits in all courts, the dissent concluded that it merely established the Red Cross as a juridical entity. The dissenters found it unnecessary to express a view on any constitutional question under Article III.

Is it likely that over the years, members of Congress were aware that the jurisdictional consequences of a charter would depend on whether it referred to "all state and federal courts" rather than to "all courts of record", especially when no prior case had stressed that distinction? No doubt, the political exigencies of the time help account for the broad interpretation of the statute in Osborn. Is there a strong reason to interpret the Red Cross' charter to permit tort suits (or any other state law actions) by or against the Red Cross to be litigated in federal court without regard to diversity of citizenship—especially given the entirely plausible basis for distinguishing Osborn suggested by the dissent? The Court's opinion may also oblige federal courts to entertain state law actions by or against many other entities whose congressional charters mention the federal courts.

(2) *Federal Question Jurisdiction and the Planter's Bank Case.* In a companion case to the Osborn case, in which the jurisdiction also was sustained, the Bank of the United States had brought suit in a federal circuit court as the bearer of negotiable notes made by a state bank. Bank of the United States v. Planters' Bank of Georgia, 22 U.S. (9 Wheat.) 904 (1824). Was the Court right in treating the two cases as raising the same question?

The Bank's existence as a federal corporation was only a relatively minor premise of its claim for relief in both cases.[1] But in the Osborn case, unlike Planter's Bank, the major premise was also federal—namely, the right under the Constitution and laws of the United States to be free from state taxation. (On the other hand, it may well have been state tort law that furnished the

---

1. As the Court recently noted in Lebron v. National R.R. Passenger Corp., 115 S.Ct. 961, 974 (1995), neither the Bank's federal charter nor the ownership of shares by the national government served to make the United States a "party" to suits brought by or against the Bank in the sense of Article III of the Constitution. (The Lebron decision held that despite this long-standing view, Amtrak—a similar entity—was "part of the [national] Government for purposes of the First Amendment" (*id*. at 974–75)).

Bank in Osborn with a cause of action for an injunction to prevent the seizure of its property and for subsequent recovery of the funds seized.)

(3) *Original and Appellate Federal Question Jurisdiction.* Consider Marshall's proposition that original jurisdiction "is coextensive with judicial power" and that Congress is capable of "giving the Circuit Courts original jurisdiction, in any case to which the appellate jurisdiction extends." Can this be right? (For example, what of a state court action in which a federal issue is raised for the first time by the opinion of the state's highest court?)

Does Marshall's formulation also suggest that appellate jurisdiction may be exercised in any case over which there would have been original jurisdiction? Can that be right? Osborn apparently holds that Congress has the constitutional authority to endow the federal district courts with original "arising under" jurisdiction in any case where any proposition of federal law "forms an ingredient" of the cause, even though the proposition is unchallenged and unchallengeable. Even if this is correct, should it lead to the conclusion that if such a case is litigated in a state court, and no question of federal law is in any way raised or decided in fact, the Supreme Court could constitutionally be given appellate jurisdiction over the case? *Per contra,* assume that the Osborn proposition is too broad. Isn't it still clear that if a case is litigated in a state court, and, unexpectedly, a federal question does in fact arise, the Supreme Court would have appellate jurisdiction even though (by hypothesis) there could not have been original jurisdiction?

The important point is that appellate jurisdiction can be tailored to the case as it has actually developed: the presence (or absence) of a federal "ingredient" is known by the time the appeal is taken. The original jurisdiction, on the other hand, must often be based on conjecture: it cannot be known with certainty what issues will turn out to be decisive. Doesn't this difference have implications for the question whether the constitutional scope of the appellate jurisdiction is wholly congruent with that of the original jurisdiction? See also the *Note on Murdock v. Memphis,* p. 510, *supra.*

(4) *The Osborn Result in Light of a Theory of "Protective Jurisdiction".* Justice Frankfurter, noting that Osborn's premises have been "subject to criticism", asserts that "we would not be justified in perpetuating a principle that permits assertion of original federal jurisdiction on the remote possibility of presentation of a federal question." Is Justice Frankfurter's perception of the Osborn principle correct? If so, and if the principle is still accepted, is there any case not potentially within the scope of the "arising under" jurisdiction of Article III? On any theory of the purposes of the constitutional grant, should it be deemed to include cases where the only federal interest is the entirely theoretical possibility that some federal issue could conceivably arise in the litigation?

(a) What are those purposes? Justice Johnson's view was that federal tribunals must be available as expositors of federal law. If this is the sole purpose of the constitutional grant, it can be fully served by (a) authorizing federal appellate review of state court decisions upon determinative points of federal law and (b) giving federal trial courts (i) original jurisdiction only in cases necessarily involving federal law, and (ii) removal jurisdiction in such cases and in other cases when and if a determinative federal issue has been framed.

But surely, a further, constitutionally permissible function of federal courts is to enforce federal law—to establish the facts determinative of the application of federal law even if the law's content and applicability are undisputed, and to enter and enforce the appropriate judgment. What additions to the original and removal jurisdiction would be required for federal courts fully to perform this function?

(b) Do these two functions fulfill all of the purposes of the framers "to make the judicial power coextensive with the legislative"?

Take the case of the Bank. Should Congress be held to have power to provide a federal forum for litigation in which the Bank might become involved only to the extent that the outcome of the litigation depends upon exposition and application of substantive federal law? Is the only risk of the Bank's litigating in state courts that those courts might hold the Bank to lack capacity to sue or to contract? If Congress' concern extended beyond that, to the ways in which state courts might handle other issues in Bank cases, should it have to enact federal substantive law to govern all those other issues—or even be sure of its power to do so—in order to bring those cases before a federal forum?

Does a basis for a "protective jurisdiction" exist to prevent discrimination against federal instrumentalities or interests even though there is no need to enact an encompassing federal substantive law? Where an active and articulated congressional legislative program is at stake, even though the particular cases may involve state substantive law only, can federal court jurisdiction in such cases be thought to serve the purposes of the "arising under" Clause in Article III?

Might an analogous theory have buttressed the argument of Justice Jackson in the Tidewater case, p. 441, *supra* (an argument that he based entirely on the power of Congress under Article I and that was rejected by the majority as inconsistent with the limits set by Article III)?

(5) *Jurisdiction in Bankruptcy Proceedings.*

Do Article III and the bankruptcy power conferred in Article I permit Congress to give the federal courts jurisdiction (absent diversity) over state law claims between the bankrupt's estate or its trustee and third parties? If so (perhaps because of the relationship of the claim to the resolution of the bankruptcy proceeding itself), is this an example of a "federal ingredient", of protective jurisdiction, or of some other factor?

(a) The Bankruptcy Act of 1867, 14 Stat. 517, as construed in Lathrop v. Drake, 91 U.S. 516 (1875), gave the district courts two distinct classes of jurisdiction: "first, jurisdiction as a court of bankruptcy over the proceedings in bankruptcy initiated by the petition, and ending in the distribution of assets amongst the creditors, and the discharge or refusal of a discharge of the bankrupt; secondly, jurisdiction, as an ordinary court, of suits at law or in equity brought by or against the assignee in reference to alleged property of the bankrupt, or to claims alleged to be due from or to him". The latter jurisdiction, the Court held, could be exercised, without regard to the citizenship of the parties, and was not confined to the court in which the bankruptcy proceedings were initiated. The Court also construed the act as giving the circuit courts concurrent jurisdiction, similarly without regard to citizenship, of any action "brought by the assignee in bankruptcy against any person claiming an adverse interest".

Without directly adverting to the question of the validity of this jurisdiction, the Court said (p. 518):

"* * * The State courts may undoubtedly be resorted to in cases of ordinary suits for the possession of property or the collection of debts; and it is not to be presumed that embarrassments would be encountered in those courts in the way of a prompt and fair administration of justice. But a uniform system of bankruptcy, national in its character, ought to be capable of execution in the national tribunals, without dependence upon those of the States in which it is possible that embarrassments might arise."

The Bankruptcy Act of 1898 adopted a sharply different policy with respect to independent suits by the trustee in bankruptcy. Section 23 of the Act, as amended, 44 Stat. 664 (1926), laid down the general rule that the federal courts should have jurisdiction of "controversies at law and in equity, as distinguished from proceedings in bankruptcy, between trustees as such and adverse claimants concerning the property acquired or claimed by the trustees, in the same manner and to the same extent only as though bankruptcy proceedings had not been instituted and such controversies had been between the bankrupts and such adverse claimants".

Among other exceptions to this general rule in the case of suits by the trustee, however, was the clause "unless by consent of the proposed defendant". This provision was construed in Schumacher v. Beeler, 293 U.S. 367 (1934), as restoring (in cases of consent) the general jurisdiction of the district courts over plenary suits by the trustee that had existed under the 1867 act. On the issue of power, Chief Justice Hughes said simply (p. 374): "The Congress, by virtue of its constitutional authority over bankruptcies, could confer or withhold jurisdiction to entertain such suits and could prescribe the conditions upon which the federal courts should have jurisdiction".

In Williams v. Austrian, 331 U.S. 642 (1947), the Court again found that Congress had authorized a similar jurisdiction of actions by the trustee, in the case of reorganizations under the Chandler Act of 1938, 52 Stat. 840. The Justices divided sharply over the issue of construction, but none doubted the constitutional power.

(b) In the Northern Pipeline case (458 U.S. 50 (1982), printed at p. 399, *supra*), the Supreme Court invalidated certain provisions of the Bankruptcy Act of 1978 on the ground that Article III had been violated when Congress had granted certain authority over private state law claims to non-Article III bankruptcy judges. But in a cryptic footnote (458 U.S. at 72 n. 26), the Court said that even in the absence of diversity, the claim in question (a state law claim in tort and contract brought by the petitioner for reorganization against a private party) "could have been adjudicated in federal court on the basis of its relationship to the petition for reorganization." Partly on the basis of this footnote, Congress, in revising the Act in 1984, retained the authority delegated to the federal courts in the 1978 Act but vested greater control in Article III judges in non-"core" proceedings. The Supreme Court has yet to rule on the constitutional validity of this arrangement in any of the varied contexts in which the problem might arise.[2]

---

2. An argument for the validity of the new arrangement is made, on protective jurisdiction grounds, in Galligan, *Article III and The "Related To" Bankruptcy Jurisdiction: A Case Study in Protective Jurisdiction*, 11 U. Puget Sound L.Rev. 1 (1987). Galligan finds the "essential ingredient" and "ancillary jurisdiction" approaches inadequate, and argues that an exercise of protective jurisdiction is valid when "Congress acts pursuant to a valid Article I power and the means it chooses * * * are rationally related to the ends"

(6) *The Foreign Sovereign Immunities Act.* In 1976 Congress enacted the Foreign Sovereign Immunities Act (FSIA),[3] a comprehensive statute designed to establish the substantive standards and procedural rules governing suits brought against foreign nations in the federal and state courts. The Act provides broadly that the federal district courts "shall have original jurisdiction without regard to amount in controversy of any nonjury civil action against a foreign state * * * as to any claim * * * with respect to which the foreign state is not entitled to immunity" either under the terms of the FSIA itself or under any applicable international agreement. 28 U.S.C. § 1330(a). Any such claim brought in a state court may be removed by the foreign state to a federal court. Section 1441(d). The Act sets forth detailed standards for determining when foreign states are immune from suit in the United States, whether in state or federal Court; no such immunity exists, *inter alia,* when immunity has been waived, when the claim arises from specified commercial activities of the foreign state carried on or causing effects in the United States, when certain rights in property taken in violation of international law are at stake, when rights in specified property located in the United States are at issue, or when the claim involves certain tortious injuries to persons or property within the United States. Sections 1604, 1605. When immunity does not apply, "the foreign state shall be liable in the same manner and to the same extent as a private individual under like circumstances." Section 1606. The Act specifies rules as to punitive damages (§ 1606), attachment and execution (§§ 1609–11), venue (§ 1391(f)), process (§ 1607), counterclaims (§ 1607), and default judgments (§ 1608(e)).

Verlinden B.V. v. Central Bank of Nigeria, 461 U.S. 480 (1983), involved a suit by a Dutch corporation against an instrumentality of the Government of Nigeria for breach of a contract allegedly having effects within the United States within the meaning of one of the FSIA provisions abrogating foreign sovereign immunity. The court of appeals held that, although the FSIA applies to suits by foreign plaintiffs against foreign states, the Act was unconstitutional insofar as it permits the federal courts to entertain such actions when the substantive claim is not itself based on federal law. 647 F.2d 320 (2d Cir.1981).

The Supreme Court reversed in a unanimous opinion by Chief Justice Burger. Agreeing that the Act applies to foreign plaintiffs (and thus cannot be justified as an instance of diversity jurisdiction), the Court stated that the "controlling decision" is Osborn, which "reflects a broad conception of 'arising under' jurisdiction, according to which Congress may confer on the federal courts jurisdiction over any case or controversy that might call for the applica-

(p. 71). Adequate safeguards against overreaching, he suggests, are to be found in the limitations of Article I itself and "the political process" (p. 72).

For another approach to "related to "jurisdiction under the new law, see Cross, *Viewing Federal Jurisdiction Through the Looking Glass of Bankruptcy,* 23 Seton Hall L.Rev. 530 (1993); Cross, *Congressional Power to Extend Federal Jurisdiction to Disputes Outside Article III: A Critical Analysis From the Perspective of Bankruptcy,* 87 Nw. U.L.Rev. 1188 (1993)(both contending that such jurisdiction is best explained as a species

of "ancillary jurisdiction"). For an analysis of both approaches and of the impact on bankruptcy proceedings of the new supplemental jurisdiction statute (28 U.S.C. § 1367), see Block–Lieb, *The Case Against Supplemental Bankruptcy Jurisdiction: A Constitutional, Statutory, and Policy Analysis,* 62 Fordham L.Rev. 721 (1994), discussed in Section 5, at p. 973, *infra.*

3. Act of October 21, 1976, 90 Stat. 2891–98. The FSIA is codified at 28 U.S.C. §§ 1330, 1332(a)(2)-(4), 1391(f), 1441(d), and 1602–1611.

tion of federal law." The Court continued (pp. 492–97): "The breadth of that conclusion has been questioned. It has been observed that, taken at its broadest, Osborn might be read as permitting 'assertion of original federal jurisdiction on the remote possibility of presentation of a federal question.' Textile Workers Union v. Lincoln Mills, 353 U.S. 448, 482 (1957)(Frankfurter, J., dissenting). See, *e.g.,* P. Bator, P. Mishkin, D. Shapiro, & H. Wechsler, Hart & Wechsler's The Federal Courts and the Federal System 866–867 (2d ed. 1973). We need not now resolve that issue or decide the precise boundaries of Art. III jurisdiction, however, since the present case does not involve a mere speculative possibility that a federal question may arise at some point in the proceeding. Rather, a suit against a foreign state under this Act necessarily raises questions of substantive federal law at the very outset, and hence clearly 'arises under' federal law, as that term is used in Art. III.

"By reason of its authority over foreign commerce and foreign relations, Congress has the undisputed power to decide, as a matter of federal law, whether and under what circumstances foreign nations should be amenable to suit in the United States. Actions against foreign sovereigns in our courts raise sensitive issues concerning the foreign relations of the United States, and the primacy of federal concerns is evident.

"To promote these federal interests, Congress exercised its Art. I powers by enacting a statute comprehensively regulating the amenability of foreign nations to suit in the United States. The statute must be applied by the district courts in every action against a foreign sovereign, since subject-matter jurisdiction in any such action depends on the existence of one of the specified exceptions to foreign sovereign immunity, 28 U.S.C. § 1330(a). At the threshold of every action in a district court against a foreign state, therefore, the court must satisfy itself that one of the exceptions applies—and in doing so it must apply the detailed federal law standards set forth in the Act. Accordingly, an action against a foreign sovereign arises under federal law, for purposes of Art. III jurisdiction.

"In reaching a contrary conclusion, the Court of Appeals relied heavily upon decisions construing 28 U.S.C. § 1331, the statute which grants district courts general federal-question jurisdiction over any case that 'arises under' the laws of the United States. The court placed particular emphasis on the so-called 'well-pleaded complaint' rule, which provides, for purposes of *statutory* 'arising under' jurisdiction, that the federal question must appear on the face of a well-pleaded complaint and may not enter in anticipation of a defense. * * *

"* * * Art. III 'arising under' jurisdiction is broader than federal-question jurisdiction under § 1331, and the Court of Appeals' heavy reliance on decisions construing that statute was misplaced. * * *

"Congress, pursuant to its unquestioned Art. I powers, has enacted a broad statutory framework governing assertions of foreign sovereign immunity. In so doing, Congress deliberately sought to channel cases against foreign sovereigns away from the state courts and into federal courts, thereby reducing the potential for a multiplicity of conflicting results among the courts of the 50 States. The resulting jurisdictional grant is within the bounds of Art. III, since every action against a foreign sovereign necessarily involves application of a body of substantive federal law, and accordingly 'arises under' federal law, within the meaning of Art. III."[4]

---

4. Verlinden was relied on by a plurality of the Court in an unusual case, Gutierrez de Martinez v. Lamagno, 115 S.Ct. 2227 (1995), also discussed in Chap. IX, at p. 1030,

(7) *The Federal Officer Removal Statute.* The question of the constitutionality of one variety of protective jurisdiction was avoided by statutory construction in Mesa v. California, 489 U.S. 121 (1989). There, two Postal Service employees faced state criminal prosecutions arising out of traffic violations that were committed in connection with their jobs. The United States removed their cases to federal court under 28 U.S.C. § 1442(a)(1), which authorizes removal of any civil or criminal action against an officer of the United States for (*inter alia*) any act "under color of such office". The government, relying in part on its interpretation of Tennessee v. Davis, p. 455, *supra,* argued that removal was proper even though the defendants asserted no colorable federal defense or immunity to the state charges. The Supreme Court rejected that view, ruling instead that § 1442(a) permits federal officer removal only when the defendant avers a federal defense. (For further discussion of the statutory question, see pp. 951–52, *infra.*)

Though relying primarily on precedent, the Court also stated that the government's view would "unnecessarily present grave constitutional problems.

infra. This was a federal court diversity action against a federal agent for personal injuries, and pursuant to statute (the West-fall Act, 28 U.S.C. § 2679(d)(1)), the Attorney General certified that the agent had been acting within the scope of his employment at the time of the alleged wrong. The result of the certification was to substitute the United States as defendant under the Federal Tort Claims Act, but since the relevant events occurred abroad, that Act precluded U.S. government liability, and thus the plaintiff sought judicial review of the Attorney General's certification, hoping to have the United States dismissed as a defendant and the individual defendant reinstated.

A 5–4 majority of the Court held that the Attorney General's certification was subject to judicial review, and four members of the majority went on to conclude that even in a state court action against a federal employee in which diversity was lacking and that was removed to federal court after the Attorney General's certification, no "grave" Article III problem would be presented if the result of judicial review was to set aside the certification and to reinstate the original state law tort action against the individual defendant. Citing Verlinden as an analogous decision, the plurality said that the Westfall Act question—whether the employee was acting within the scope of his employment—is a significant federal question presented at the outset of any such case. Moreover, the question was one that Congress plainly wanted to be "aired" in a federal forum, and if it was resolved against the certification, it was ap-

propriate (citing United Mine Workers v. Gibbs, p. 962, *infra*) for the federal forum "to proceed beyond the federal question to final judgment once it has invested time and resources on the initial scope of employment contest" (pp. 2236–37).

Justice O'Connor, concurring in the judgment, was plainly more troubled by the Article III question, but concluded that the desirability of avoiding that question by construing the statute not to permit judicial review was countered by the fact that the case before the Court did not itself present the question (since there was diversity jurisdiction in the suit against the individual defendant), as well as by the presumption in favor of judicial review of executive action.

Justice Souter, writing for four Justices in dissent, urged that the statute be construed to preclude judicial review and thus to avoid the Article III problem—a problem he viewed as a serious one. The challenge to certification, he argued, was a challenge to jurisdiction itself, and thus the Court's reasoning was "tantamount to saying the authority to determine whether a court has jurisdiction over the cause of action supplies the very jurisdiction that is subject to challenge" (p. 2240). Since evidence bearing on the scope of employment question is bound to overlap evidence on the underlying question of liability, federal question jurisdiction would be "inevitable" even when the case ends up presenting no federal issues whatever (*id.*).

How different, if any, is the Court's rationale in Verlinden from the plurality's reasoning in Gutierrez de Martinez?

* * * At oral argument the Government urged upon us a theory of 'protective jurisdiction' to avoid these Art. III difficulties. * * * The Government insists that the full protection of federal officers from interference by hostile state courts cannot be achieved if the averment of a federal defense must be a predicate to removal, * * * [and] that this generalized congressional interest in protecting federal officers from state court interference suffices to support Art. III 'arising under' jurisdiction.

"We have, in the past, not found the need to adopt a theory of 'protective jurisdiction' to support Art. III 'arising under' jurisdiction, and we do not see any need for doing so here because we do not recognize any federal interests that are not protected by limiting removal to situations in which a federal defense is alleged. In these prosecutions, no state court hostility or interference has even been alleged by petitioners * * *" (pp. 137–38). At the end of its opinion, the Court quoted language from Maryland v. Soper (No. 2), 270 U.S. 36, 43–44 (1926), stating that if state prosecutions come to be used to obstruct enforcement of federal law, "it will be for Congress in its discretion to amend [the earlier version of the officer removal statute] so that * * * any prosecution of a federal officer * * * which can be shown by evidence to have had its motive in a wish to hinder him in the enforcement of federal law, may be removed for trial to the proper federal court. We are not now considering * * * whether such an enlargement would be valid; but * * * the present language * * * can not be broadened by fair construction to give it such a meaning"(p. 139).[5]

Was the Court in Mesa correct, in light of the decisions discussed in this Note, in observing that it had not "in the past, * * * found the need to adopt a theory of 'protective jurisdiction' to support Article III 'arising under' jurisdiction"? Even if the Court has never explicitly followed this course, can all of its decisions be rationally explained without reference to it?

(8) *The Diplomatic Relations Act of 1978.* Pub.L. No. 95–393, added the following provision to the Judicial Code (28 U.S.C. § 1364):

"(a) The district courts shall have original and exclusive jurisdiction, without regard to the amount in controversy, of any civil action commenced by any person against an insurer who by contract has insured an individual, who is a member of a mission (as defined in the Vienna Convention on Diplomatic Relations) or a member of the family of such a member of a mission * * * against liability for personal injury, death, or damage to property.

"(b) Any direct action brought against an insurer under subsection (a) shall be tried without a jury, but shall not be subject to the defense that the insured is immune from suit, that the insured is an indispensable party, or in the absence of fraud or collusion, that the insured has violated a term of the contract, unless the contract was cancelled before the claim arose."

This provision was designed to provide a means of recovering damages, particularly for automobile accident injuries, caused by foreign diplomats who are themselves immune from suit. The Senate Judiciary Committee Report

---

5. For further discussions of protective jurisdiction, see Goldberg–Ambrose, *The Protective Jurisdiction of the Federal Courts,* 30 U.C.L.A.L.Rev. 542 (1983); Note, 57 N.Y.U.L.Rev. 933 (1982).

accompanying the bill (S.Rep. No. 1108, 95th Cong., 2d Sess. 5 (1978)), made clear that state liability law would govern such suits.

If, as seems likely, many actions within this section could not be considered "Cases affecting Ambassadors, other public Ministers and Consuls" within Article III,[6] may jurisdiction in these direct actions properly be predicated on the "arising under" Clause?

See also the "alien tort" statute (28 U.S.C. § 1350), conferring jurisdiction over "any civil action by an alien for a tort only, committed in violation of the law of nations or a treaty of the United States," discussed in Casto, *The Federal Courts' Protective Jurisdiction Over Torts Committed in Violation of the Law of Nations*, 18 Conn.L.Rev. 467 (1986). For further discussion of this statute, see pp. 809–10, *supra.*

(9) *The Clean Air Act.* Issues of "protective jurisdiction" may also arise under 42 U.S.C. § 7604, which authorizes private civil actions against any person alleged to be in violation of any "emission standard or limitation" issued under the Act, and provides for district court jurisdiction over such actions without regard to citizenship. "Emission standards" presumably include standards contained in state-promulgated "Implementation Plans"; these plans must meet federal requirements and be approved by EPA, but otherwise constitute detailed programs of implementation, maintenance and enforcement of air quality standards as a matter of state law.[7]

SECTION 3. THE SCOPE OF THE STATUTORY GRANT OF FEDERAL QUESTION JURISDICTION

Louisville & Nashville R. Co. v. Mottley

211 U.S. 149, 29 S.Ct. 42, 53 L.Ed. 126 (1908).
Appeal From the Circuit Court of the United States for the Western District of Kentucky.

■ MR. JUSTICE MOODY delivered the opinion of the Court.

[Appellees, husband and wife and citizens of Kentucky, brought suit for specific performance of a contract against the railroad, a Kentucky corporation. The contract provided that the Mottleys would release the railroad from all claims for damages arising from a certain collision; in return the railroad agreed to issue free passes to the Mottleys during the rest of their lives. The bill alleged that, beginning in 1907, the railroad declined to renew the passes, relying on the Act of Congress of June 29, 1906, forbidding the giving of free passes. The

6. See S.Rep. 95–1108, pp. 6–7, indicating that many members of missions within the statutory definition would not be of the level of ambassadors, ministers or consuls, and would thus be outside the scope of the Article III provision regarding them. The discussion of the Report at that point refers to another provision of the statute, amending 28 U.S.C. § 1351 so as to give the district courts exclusive jurisdiction over all civil actions against members of a diplomatic mission or their families. Is this jurisdictional provision valid?

7. For a decision upholding jurisdiction in an analogous situation under the Truth in Lending Act, 15 U.S.C. § 1640, although without discussion of the issue, see Ives v. W.T. Grant Co., 522 F.2d 749 (2d Cir.1975), commented on in Note, 89 Harv.L.Rev. 998 (1976).

bill further alleged that the statute properly construed did not prohibit free passes pursuant to contracts entered into before its passage; but that if construed retroactively to invalidate the Mottleys' contract, it violated the Fifth Amendment. The federal circuit court overruled the railroad's demurrer and entered a decree of specific performance; the railroad appealed to the Supreme Court.]

Two questions of law * * * have been argued before us. They are, first, whether that part of the act of Congress of June 29, 1906, which forbids the giving of free passes or the collection of any different compensation for transportation of passengers than that specified in the tariff filed, makes it unlawful to perform a contract for transportation of persons, who in good faith, before the passage of the act, had accepted such contract in satisfaction of a valid cause of action against the railroad; and, second, whether the statute, if it should be construed to render such a contract unlawful, is in violation of the Fifth Amendment of the Constitution of the United States. We do not deem it necessary, however, to consider either of these questions, because, in our opinion, the court below was without jurisdiction of the cause. Neither party has questioned that jurisdiction, but it is the duty of this court to see to it that the jurisdiction of the Circuit Court, which is defined and limited by statute, is not exceeded. This duty we have frequently performed of our own motion. [*E.g.,*] Mansfield & C. Railway Company v. Swan, 111 U.S. 379, 382 [discussed in Chap. XIV, Sec. 1, *infra*].

There was no diversity of citizenship and it is not and cannot be suggested that there was any ground of jurisdiction, except that the case was a "suit * * * arising under the Constitution and laws of the United States." It is the settled interpretation of these words, as used in this statute, conferring jurisdiction, that a suit arises under the Constitution and laws of the United States only when the plaintiff's statement of his own cause of action shows that it is based upon those laws or that Constitution. It is not enough that the plaintiff alleges some anticipated defense to his cause of action and asserts that the defense is invalidated by some provision of the Constitution of the United States. Although such allegations show that very likely, in the course of the litigation, a question under the Constitution would arise, they do not show that the suit, that is, the plaintiff's original cause of action, arises under the Constitution. In Tennessee v. Union & Planters' Bank, 152 U.S. 454, the plaintiff, the State of Tennessee, brought suit in the Circuit Court of the United States to recover from the defendant certain taxes alleged to be due under the laws of the State. The plaintiff alleged that the defendant claimed an immunity from the taxation by virtue of its charter, and that therefore the tax was void, because in violation of the provision of the Constitution of the United States, which forbids any State from passing a law impairing the obligation of contracts. The cause was held to be beyond the jurisdiction of the Circuit Court, the court saying, by Mr. Justice Gray (p. 464), "a suggestion of one party, that the other will or may set up a claim under the Constitution or laws of the United States, does not make the suit one arising under that Constitution or those laws." * * *

The interpretation of the act which we have stated was first announced in Metcalf v. Watertown, 128 U.S. 586, and has since been repeated and applied in * * * [citing 17 cases]. The application of this rule to the case at bar is decisive against the jurisdiction of the Circuit Court.

It is ordered that the *judgment be reversed and the case remitted to the Circuit Court with instructions to dismiss the suit for want of jurisdiction.*

NOTE ON THE MOTTLEY CASE AND THE WELL–PLEADED COMPLAINT RULE

(1) *The Interpretation of the Jurisdictional Statute.*

(a) What is the significance of the fact that the 1875 Act (conferring general federal question jurisdiction) and its successors have always used the language of the Constitution to describe the statutory jurisdiction?[1]

The Act originated as a Senate amendment to a House bill relating only to the removal jurisdiction, and was hurriedly enacted at the close of a session without substantial debate. See Frankfurter & Landis, The Business of the Supreme Court 65–69 (1928); Chadbourn & Levin, *Original Jurisdiction of Federal Questions,* 90 U.Pa.L.Rev. 639, 642–45 (1942); Forrester, *The Nature of a "Federal Question",* 16 Tul.L.Rev. 362 (1942). The most significant bit in the legislative history was a statement of Senator Carpenter, who was in charge of the bill. Speaking of the bill as a whole rather than of the federal question section, he first discussed the views of Justice Story, see Chap. IV, Sec. 1, pp. 359–62, *supra,* and then said:

"* * * The act of 1789 did not confer the whole power which the Constitution conferred; it did not do what the Supreme Court has said Congress ought to do; it did not perform what the Supreme Court has declared to be the duty of Congress. This bill does. * * * This bill gives precisely the power which the Constitution confers—nothing more, nothing less."

Relying on this statement and on the identity of language, Dean Forrester argued that the statutory and constitutional provisions should be "considered synonymous".[2]

---

1. The only possibly significant departure from the language of the Constitution was the use of the word "suits" instead of "cases". Justice Miller, dissenting in New Orleans, M. & T. Railroad Co. v. Mississippi, 102 U.S. 135, 143 (1880), seized upon this difference as the basis for his argument that, under the statute, jurisdiction depended on the law under which the plaintiff claimed and could not rest on a federal defense. The conclusion, though not the argument, was adopted in Tennessee v. Union & Planters' Bank, 152 U.S. 454 (1894), and it has not been affected by the substitution of the phrase, "matter in controversy", in 1911. Act of March 3, 1911, § 24, 36 Stat. 1087, 1091.

The current statute (§ 1331) substitutes "civil actions" for the term "suits of a civil nature, at common law or in equity".

2. Professors Chadbourn and Levin agree with Dean Forrester that the 1875 Act should have been read as conferring, in the first instance, the whole of the federal question jurisdiction permissible under the Constitution, or at least the whole of it permissible under the Osborn opinion. But, they say, the draftsmen recognized that "if this radical legislation was to prove practicable * * *, provision had to be made to protect the lower federal courts from a flood of litigation technically within the broad limits staked out by Marshall, but actually unrelated to the purpose of the Act". Such a provision they find in § 5 of the Act, requiring dismissal or remand if "it shall appear * * * at any time after such suit has been brought or removed * * * that such suit does not really and substantially involve a dispute or controversy properly within the jurisdiction of said circuit court". See Chadbourn & Levin, *supra,* at 650.

In only one case does the Supreme Court seem to have applied the act in this fashion. Robinson v. Anderson, 121 U.S. 522, 524 (1887).

(b) As pointed out in Justice Frankfurter's opinion in Lincoln Mills, the Court, in the Pacific Railroad Removal Cases, 115 U.S. 1 (1885), held that federal incorporation of a party *ipso facto* made a case one "arising under" national law within the 1875 Act. At the time of the decision the requirements for removal jurisdiction were not tied to those for original jurisdiction; the 1875 Act permitted removal by either party of any suit, involving the requisite amount, "arising under the Constitution or laws of the United States".

The Pacific Railroad Removal Cases go farther than any case decided before[3] or since to suggest that the 1875 Act filled the whole of the constitutional space provided for "arising under" cases. In light of the other cases already considered and to be considered in this Chapter, it would seem clear that they can no longer be regarded as authoritative in this regard. In addition to the discussions in Lincoln Mills and Verlinden, *supra,* see Shoshone Mining Co. v. Rutter, 177 U.S. 505, 506 (1900)("the question, therefore, is not one of the power of Congress, but of its intent"); Romero v. International Terminal Operating Co., 358 U.S. 354, 379 n. 51 (1959)("the many limitations which have been placed on jurisdiction under § 1331 are not limitations on the constitutional power of Congress to confer jurisdiction on the federal courts").

Congress has overruled the Pacific Railroad Removal Cases, save as to corporations in which the United States is the owner of more than one-half the capital stock. 28 U.S.C. § 1349. See Frankfurter, *Distribution of Judicial Power Between United States and State Courts,* 13 Cornell L.Q. 499, 509–11 (1928).

(c) In light of the manifest differences between the functions of the constitutional grant and the statutory grant, would it be appropriate to treat the language in the two provisions as encompassing identical territory? Would the expansive approach of Osborn be tenable if it were to define the scope of the statutory jurisdiction? How does the statute's legislative history bear on this question? How do the policy considerations affect the interpretation of the language used or the weight that should be given to the legislative history?[4]

The Mottley case, subsequent to the Supreme Court's decision, was adjudicated in the state courts; the federal issues were the only decisive questions. It was then reviewed by the United States Supreme Court. 219 U.S. 467 (1911). What lesson does this teach?

(2) *The Impact of the Mottley Rule.*

(a) The rule of the Mottley decision—that a case does not "arise under" federal law for purposes of the federal question statute unless an assertion as to federal law is part of the plaintiff's well-pleaded complaint—might be regarded as a technical rule of convenience, designed to avoid making original jurisdic-

---

3. For cases antedating the Pacific Railroad Removal Cases that appeared to construe the 1875 removal provision more narrowly (and which the Court continued to treat as authoritative), see, *e.g.,* Little York Gold–Washing & Water Co. v. Keyes, 96 U.S. 199 (1878)(defense to injunction action grounded on claim that mining titles from the United States conferred a federal right to do the complained-of acts; removal denied); Albright v. Teas, 106 U.S. 613 (1883)(suit by patentee for royalties under an assignment;

held not removable). Compare also Provident Savings Life Assurance Society v. Ford, 114 U.S. 635 (1885)(decided on same day as Pacific Railroad Removal Cases; suit on a federal court judgment does not, for that reason alone, "arise under" federal law).

4. For recent criticism of the well-pleaded complaint rule, see Doernberg, *There's No Reason for It; It's Just Our Policy: Why the Well–Pleaded Complaint Rule Sabotages the Purposes of Federal Question Jurisdiction,* 38 Hastings L.J. 597 (1987).

tion turn on speculation as to what issues will be decisive in the litigation.[5] But the rule has had a broader impact because, ever since 1887, the general removal statute has been limited to cases falling within the original jurisdiction of the district court. Thus, a case like Mottley, if brought in a state court, could not be removed to federal court—even though the federal issues raised by the railroad (and by the Mottleys in reply to the railroad) were the decisive issues in the litigation.

(b) A few statutes, *e.g.,* 28 U.S.C. § 1442, allow removal from a state court on the basis of a federal defense, but as noted, federal defense removal is generally not available to either party.

The requirement of S 1441, tying removal to original jurisdiction, has had a profound effect on the jurisdictional structure, and even on our ways of thinking about that structure. Debates about the "need for a federal forum" are frequently carried on as if the only issue were whether plaintiffs with a claim of federal right should have access to a federal court; defendants with a claim of federal immunity are characteristically forgotten about. See Bator, *The State Courts and Federal Constitutional Litigation,* 22 Wm. & Mary L.Rev. 605, 608–11 (1981). But what justifies the distinction? Why should defendants with a claim of federal right or privilege be forced to litigate in a state court? Is the point that, where the federal ingredient is in the plaintiff's case, it is likely to be the predominant element in the case, whereas a federal defense is more likely to be only one element in a case dominated by state-law issues?[6] That federal defenses (in civil as well as criminal cases) are readily conjured up by knowledgeable and imaginative lawyers?[7] Or is the point that where the claimant seeks to enforce state law, and the contention based on federal law is that the state law may not be validly enforced, considerations of federalism make it appropriate to give the state court—the "enforcement" court—first crack?[8]

---

5. Even conceding the soundness of this purpose, did it make sense to apply the rule where, as in Mottley itself, the jurisdictional issue arose for the first time on appeal, at a time when both parties and the court below agreed that the case turned entirely on federal issues? (Note also that in Mottley the question of jurisdiction was not raised at the Supreme Court level by either party, but solely by the Court.) As to the basis for, and wisdom of, the rule that a defect in subject matter jurisdiction *must* be considered by a court on its own motion (even if the defect relates solely to the jurisdiction of a lower court), see Chap. XIV, Sec. 1, *infra.*

6. But what about cases like Mottley, where the only issues actually in contention are federal?

7. Consider the views of Judge Posner: "In many [cases] the federal defense would have little merit—would, indeed, have been concocted purely to confer federal jurisdiction—yet this fact might be impossible to determine, with any confidence, without having a trial before the trial. Of course, frivolous federal claims are also a problem when

only plaintiffs can use them to get into court, but a less serious problem. If the plaintiff gets thrown out of federal court because his claim is frivolous, and must start over in state court, he has lost time; and the loss may be fatal if meanwhile the statute of limitations has run. But the defendant may be delighted to see the plaintiff's case thrown out of federal court when the court discovers that the federal defense is frivolous. This is why it would not be a complete answer to the problem of the frivolous federal defense to allow removal on the basis of a federal question first raised by way of defense but give the district court discretion to remand the case back to the state court." Posner, The Federal Courts: Crisis and Reform 190–91 (1985).

8. *Cf.* Wechsler, *Federal Jurisdiction and the Revision of the Judicial Code,* 13 Law & Contemp.Prob. 216, 233–34 (1948). Commenting on 28 U.S.C. § 1441 before its enactment, Professor Wechsler advocated allowance of removal "by the party who puts forth the federal right". He argued that "the reason for providing the initial federal forum is

Note, however, that federal defenses can frequently be recast as affirmative claims of federal right. For example, the jurisdictional statutes have often been read to open the doors of the federal courthouse to cases in which plaintiffs are seeking to enjoin state law as in violation of federal statutory or constitutional provisions. See, *e.g.,* Shaw v. Delta Airlines, p. 947, *infra,* and the line of cases flowing from Ex parte Young, 209 U.S. 123 (1908), discussed in Chap. IX, Section 2, *infra.* It is thus not the case that the existing law generally excludes from federal court all litigants whose contention is that state-law claims are rendered *pro tanto* invalid by federal law: if the relevant federal remedial law (express or implied) gives the claimant a federal cause of action, and the claimant reaches the federal courthouse first, federal jurisdiction is usually upheld.[9] On the other hand, if the state claim is raised first, in state court, the defendant may not remove on the basis of a claim of *pro tanto* invalidity. (He is also normally precluded from thereafter transforming himself into a plaintiff and bringing a separate federal action to enjoin or otherwise abort the pending state proceeding (see Chap. X, *infra*).)

Isn't the underlying difficulty that litigants do not come labeled as "plaintiffs" and "defendants" as a matter of preexisting Platonic reality? Whether one is a plaintiff or a defendant (when is the law a sword? when a shield?) is itself contingent, a product of our remedial and substantive rules.

In light of these considerations, do the existing jurisdictional lines reflect a sensible accommodation of policies in tension? Or are they merely an *ad hoc* patchwork?

(c) Closely related to federal defense cases, and perhaps analytically identical, are actions maintainable only if they fall within the scope of a federal permission. In such cases the plaintiff may or may not assert compliance with the permission in his complaint, and the issue of compliance may or may not be drawn by the defendant.

The leading case is Gully v. First National Bank, 299 U.S. 109 (1936). There a state tax collector sued a national bank to recover state taxes assessed upon the shares of a predecessor national bank, counting upon a contract by the defendant to assume its predecessor's debts. The taxes were permissible only by virtue of Rev.Stat. § 5219. Speaking for a unanimous Court, Justice Cardozo said (p. 116):

the fear that state courts will view the federal right ungenerously. That reason is quite plainly absent in * * * the case where the *defendant* may remove because the *plaintiff's* case is federal. If in any case the reason can be present, it is only in the situations where [under proposed § 1441] removal is denied."

Do you agree with this analysis? Does the person resisting the assertion of a federal right have a basis for concern that a state court may, through lack of sufficient understanding, *over*-enforce the asserted right?

9. But *cf.* Southland Corp. v. Keating, 465 U.S. 1 (1984), which held (in a case coming from a state court) that the United States Arbitration Act preempts a California statute that rendered certain claims unarbitrable. In a puzzling footnote the Court said: "While the Federal Arbitration Act creates federal substantive law requiring the parties to honor arbitration agreements, it does not create any independent federal-question jurisdiction under 28 U.S.C. § 1331 or otherwise" (p. 15 n. 9).

The Court in Southland apparently read the Arbitration Act—which makes agreements to arbitrate "valid, irrevocable, and enforceable" (9 U.S.C. § 2)—as a substantive provision (negativing a defense of unenforceability) rather than as one that creates or authorizes the implication of a federal right of action.

"[T]he right to be established is one created by the state. If that is so, it is unimportant that federal consent is the source of state authority. To reach the underlying law we do not travel back so far. By unimpeachable authority, a suit brought under a state statute does not arise under an act of Congress or the Constitution of the United States because prohibited thereby. Louisville & Nashville R. Co. v. Mottley, *supra.* With no greater reason can it be said to arise thereunder because permitted thereby."

Elsewhere in the Gully opinion, Justice Cardozo repeats a much-quoted statement from Shulthis v. McDougal, 225 U.S. 561, 569 (1912), the equivalent of which may be found in many other cases:

"A suit to enforce a right which takes its origin in the laws of the United States is not necessarily, or for that reason alone, one arising under those laws, for a suit does not so arise unless it really and substantially involves a dispute or controversy respecting the validity, construction or effect of such a law, upon the determination of which the result depends."

This statement has been the source of much confusion. It seems impossible to reconcile with the principle of the well-pleaded complaint rule: the complaint by itself can hardly be expected to demonstrate whether an issue of federal law will turn out to be "really and substantially" in dispute. And the formulation is inconsistent with the settled proposition that if the plaintiff's action is brought to enforce a federally-created right, it "arises under" federal law even if the only issues "really and substantially" in dispute are issues of state law, or issues of fact. Mishkin, *The Federal "Question" in the District Courts,* 53 Colum.L.Rev. 157, 170 (1953), suggests that Justice Cardozo's formulation represents "an uncritical transference to the lower federal courts of a standard developed for the exercise of the Supreme Court's appellate jurisdiction."

(d) The well-pleaded complaint rule has led to many complex refinements turning on the niceties of pleading lore, much of it deservedly forgotten today. See, *e.g.,* Hopkins v. Walker, 244 U.S. 486, 490 (1917), p. 929, *infra* (bill to remove a cloud on title; jurisdiction upheld where the validity of the competing title depended on federal law, since "the facts showing the plaintiff's title and the existence and invalidity of the instrument or record sought to be eliminated as a cloud upon the title are essential parts of the plaintiff's cause of action" both as a matter of "general" and of Montana law); compare Shulthis v. McDougal, 225 U.S. 561 (1912)(jurisdiction denied; in action to quiet title, allegations with respect to competing claims are not properly part of plaintiff's complaint), and Joy v. St. Louis, 201 U.S. 332 (1906)(jurisdiction denied in an action for ejectment by a plaintiff not in possession, since in such an action, allegations with respect to plaintiff's title (allegedly based on a federal grant) are not properly part of the plaintiff's pleading).

American Well Works Co. v. Layne & Bowler Co.

241 U.S. 257, 36 S.Ct. 585, 60 L.Ed. 987 (1916).
Error to the District Court of the United States for the Eastern District of Arkansas.

■ MR. JUSTICE HOLMES delivered the opinion of the Court.

This is a suit begun in a state court, removed to the United States court, and then, on motion to remand by the plaintiff, dismissed by the latter court, on the ground that the cause of action arose under the patent laws of the United States, that the state court had no jurisdiction, and that therefore the one to which it was removed had none.* There is a proper certificate and the case comes here direct from the district court.

Of course the question depends upon the plaintiff's declaration. That may be summed up in a few words. The plaintiff alleges that it owns, manufactures, and sells a certain pump, has or has applied for a patent for it, and that the pump is known as the best in the market. It then alleges that the defendants have falsely and maliciously libeled and slandered the plaintiff's title to the pump by stating that the pump and certain parts thereof are infringements upon the defendants' pump and certain parts thereof, and that without probable cause they have brought suits against some parties who are using the plaintiff's pump, and that they are threatening suits against all who use it. The allegation of the defendants' libel or slander is repeated in slightly varying form, but it all comes to statements to various people that the plaintiff was infringing the defendants' patent, and that the defendant would sue both seller and buyer if the plaintiff's pump was used. Actual damage to the plaintiff in its business is alleged to the extent of $50,000, and punitive damages to the same amount are asked.

It is evident that the claim for damages is based upon conduct; or, more specifically, language, tending to persuade the public to withdraw its custom from the plaintiff, and having that effect to its damage. Such conduct, having such effect, is equally actionable whether it produces the result by persuasion, by threats, or by falsehood (Moran v. Dunphy, 177 Mass. 485, 487), and it is enough to allege and prove the conduct and effect, leaving the defendant to justify if he can. If the conduct complained of is persuasion, it may be justified by the fact that the defendant is a competitor, or by good faith and reasonable grounds. If it is a statement of fact, it may be justified, absolutely or with qualifications, by proof that the statement is true. But all such justifications are defenses, and raise issues that are no part of the plaintiff's case. In the present instance it is part of the plaintiff's case that it had a business to be damaged; whether built up by patents or without them does not matter. It is no part of it to prove anything concerning the defendants' patent, or that the plaintiff did not infringe the same—still less to prove anything concerning any patent of its own. The material statement complained of is that the plaintiff infringes,—which may be true notwithstanding the plaintiff's patent. That is merely a piece of evidence. Furthermore, the damage alleged presumably is rather the consequence of the threat to sue than of the statement that the plaintiff's pump infringed the defendants' rights.

* [Ed.] Although the district court had concluded that the case was one arising under the patent laws of the United States, that court nevertheless determined (as Justice Holmes notes) that the action had to be dismissed. Federal jurisdiction was (and still is) exclusive in patent cases, and the law at the time required dismissal because the "derivative" nature of removal authority was thought to preclude federal removal jurisdiction of a case over which the state court lacked subject-matter jurisdiction. (The law has since been changed to allow removal in such cases. See 28 U.S.C. § 1441(e)). The Supreme Court's holding that the case was *not* one arising under the patent laws required reversal of the judgment of dismissal below so that the case could be remanded to the state court.

A suit for damages to business caused by a threat to sue under the patent law is not itself a suit under the patent law. And the same is true when the damage is caused by a statement of fact,—that the defendant has a patent which is infringed. What makes the defendants' act a wrong is its manifest tendency to injure the plaintiff's business; and the wrong is the same whatever the means by which it is accomplished. But whether it is a wrong or not depends upon the law of the state where the act is done, not upon the patent law, and therefore the suit arises under the law of the state. A suit arises under the law that creates the cause of action. The fact that the justification may involve the validity and infringement of a patent is no more material to the question under what law the suit is brought than it would be in an action of contract. If the state adopted for civil proceedings the saying of the old criminal law: the greater the truth, the greater the libel, the validity of the patent would not come in question at all. In Massachusetts the truth would not be a defense if the statement was made from disinterested malevolence. Rev.Laws, chap. 173, § 91. The state is master of the whole matter, and if it saw fit to do away with actions of this type altogether, no one, we imagine, would suppose that they still could be maintained under the patent laws of the United States.

Judgment reversed.

■ Mr. Justice McKenna dissents, being of opinion that the case involves a direct and substantial controversy under the patent laws.

Merrell Dow Pharmaceuticals Inc. v. Thompson

478 U.S. 804, 106 S.Ct. 3229, 92 L.Ed.2d 650 (1986).
Certiorari to the United States Court of Appeals for the Sixth Circuit.

■ Justice Stevens delivered the opinion of the Court.

The question presented is whether the incorporation of a federal standard in a state-law private action, when Congress has intended that there not be a federal private action for violations of that federal standard, makes the action one "arising under the Constitution, laws, or treaties of the United States," 28 U.S.C. § 1331.

I

The Thompson respondents are residents of Canada and the MacTavishes reside in Scotland. They filed virtually identical complaints against petitioner, a corporation, that manufactures and distributes the drug Bendectin. The complaints were filed in the Court of Common Pleas in Hamilton County, Ohio. Each complaint alleged that a child was born with multiple deformities as a result of the mother's ingestion of Bendectin during pregnancy. In five of the six counts, the recovery of substantial damages was requested on common-law theories of negligence, breach of warranty, strict liability, fraud, and gross negligence. In Count IV, respondents alleged that the drug Bendectin was "misbranded" in violation of the Federal Food, Drug, and Cosmetic Act (FDCA), 21 U.S.C. § 301 *et seq.* (1982 ed., Supp. II), because its labeling did not provide adequate warning that its use was potentially dangerous. Paragraph 26 alleged that the violation of the FDCA "in the promotion" of Bendectin "constitutes a rebuttable presumption of negligence." Paragraph 27 alleged that the "violation of said federal statutes directly and proximately caused the injuries suffered" by the two infants.

Petitioner filed a timely petition for removal from the state court to the Federal District Court alleging that the action was "founded, in part, on an alleged claim arising under the laws of the United States." After removal, the two cases were consolidated. Respondents filed a motion to remand to the state forum on the ground that the federal court lacked subject-matter jurisdiction. Relying on our decision in Smith v. Kansas City Title & Trust Co., 255 U.S. 180 (1921), the District Court held that Count IV of the complaint alleged a cause of action arising under federal law and denied the motion to remand. It then granted petitioner's motion to dismiss on *forum non conveniens* grounds.

The Court of Appeals for the Sixth Circuit reversed. We granted certiorari, and we now affirm.

II

Article III of the Constitution gives the federal courts power to hear cases "arising under" federal statutes. * * * Although the constitutional meaning of "arising under" may extend to all cases in which a federal question is "an ingredient" of the action, Osborn v. Bank of the United States, 9 Wheat. 738, 823 (1824), we have long construed the statutory grant of federal-question jurisdiction as conferring a more limited power. Verlinden B.V. v. Central Bank of Nigeria, 461 U.S. 480, 494–495 (1983); Romero v. International Terminal Operating Co., 358 U.S. 354, 379 (1959).

Under our longstanding interpretation of the current statutory scheme, the question whether a claim "arises under" federal law must be determined by reference to the "well-pleaded complaint." Franchise Tax Board, 463 U.S., at 9–10.** A defense that raises a federal question is inadequate to confer federal jurisdiction. Louisville & Nashville R. Co. v. Mottley, 211 U.S. 149 (1908). Since a defendant may remove a case only if the claim could have been brought in federal court, 28 U.S.C. § 1441(b), moreover, the question for removal jurisdiction must also be determined by reference to the "well-pleaded complaint."

As was true in Franchise Tax Board, *supra,* the propriety of the removal in this case thus turns on whether the case falls within the original "federal question" jurisdiction of the federal courts. There is no "single, precise definition" of that concept; rather, "the phrase 'arising under' masks a welter of issues regarding the interrelation of federal and state authority and the proper management of the federal judicial system." *Id.,* 463 U.S., at 8.

This much, however, is clear. The "vast majority" of cases that come within this grant of jurisdiction are covered by Justice Holmes' statement that a "suit arises under the law that creates the cause of action." *Id.,* at 8–9, quoting American Well Works Co. v. Layne & Bowler Co., 241 U.S. 257, 260 (1916). Thus, the vast majority of cases brought under the general federal-

---

** [Ed.] The Franchise Tax Board opinion is printed at p. 937, *infra,* since its holding and analysis are most significant in connection with the problems of declaratory judgments and of federal defense removal, which are considered later in this Chapter. But its general account of "arising under" jurisdiction, is frequently discussed in the opinions in Merrell Dow; the reader may, therefore, wish to read Part II of the Franchise Tax Board opinion at this point.

question jurisdiction of the federal courts are those in which federal law creates the cause of action.

We have, however, also noted that a case may arise under federal law "where the vindication of a right under state law necessarily turned on some construction of federal law." Franchise Tax Board, 463 U.S., at 9.[5] Our actual holding in Franchise Tax Board demonstrates that this statement must be read with caution; the central issue presented in that case turned on the meaning of the Employment Retirement Income Security Act of 1974, 29 U.S.C. § 1001 *et seq.* (1982 ed. and Supp. II), but we nevertheless concluded that federal jurisdiction was lacking.

This case does not pose a federal question of the first kind; respondents do not allege that federal law creates any of the causes of action that they have asserted.[6] This case thus poses what Justice Frankfurter called the "litigation-provoking problem," Textile Workers v. Lincoln Mills, 353 U.S. 448, 470 (1957)(dissenting opinion)—the presence of a federal issue in a state-created cause of action.

* * * We have consistently emphasized that, in exploring the outer reaches of § 1331, determinations about federal jurisdiction require sensitive judgments about congressional intent, judicial power, and the federal system. "If the history of the interpretation of judiciary legislation teaches us anything, it teaches the duty to reject treating such statutes as a wooden set of self-sufficient words. * * * The Act of 1875 is broadly phrased, but it has been continuously construed and limited in the light of the history that produced it, the demands of reason and coherence, and the dictates of sound judicial policy which have emerged from the Act's function as a provision in the mosaic of federal judiciary legislation." Romero v. International Terminal Operating Co., 358 U.S., at 379. * * *

In this case, both parties agree with the Court of Appeals' conclusion that there is no federal cause of action for FDCA violations. For purposes of our decision, we assume that this is a correct interpretation of the FDCA. Thus, as the case comes to us, it is appropriate to assume that, under the settled framework for evaluating whether a federal cause of action lies, some combination of the following factors is present: (1) the plaintiffs are not part of the class for whose special benefit the statute was passed; (2) the indicia of legislative intent reveal no congressional purpose to provide a private cause of action; (3) a federal cause of action would not further the underlying purposes of the legislative scheme; and (4) the respondents' cause of action is a subject traditionally relegated to state law. In short, Congress did not intend a private federal remedy for violations of the statute that it enacted.

This is the first case in which we have reviewed this type of jurisdictional claim in light of these factors. That this is so is not surprising. The

---

5. The case most frequently cited for that proposition is Smith v. Kansas City Title & Trust Co., 255 U.S. 180 (1921). In that case the Court upheld federal jurisdiction of a shareholder's bill to enjoin the corporation from purchasing bonds issued by the federal land banks under the authority of the Federal Farm Loan Act on the ground that the federal statute that authorized the issuance of the bonds was unconstitutional. * * *

6. Jurisdiction may not be sustained on a theory that the plaintiff has not advanced. See Healy v. Sea Gull Specialty Co., 237 U.S. 479, 480 (1915)("[T]he plaintiff is absolute master of what jurisdiction he will appeal to"); The Fair v. Kohler Die and Specialty Co., 228 U.S. 22, 25 (1913)("[T]he party who brings a suit is master to decide what law he will rely upon"). * * *

development of our framework for determining whether a private cause of action exists has proceeded only in the last 11 years, and its inception represented a significant change in our approach to congressional silence on the provision of federal remedies.[8]

The recent character of that development does not, however, diminish its importance. Indeed, the very reasons for the development of the modern implied remedy doctrine—the "increased complexity of federal legislation and the increased volume of federal litigation," as well as "the desirability of a more careful scrutiny of legislative intent," Merrill Lynch, Pierce, Fenner & Smith v. Curran, 456 U.S. 353, 377 (1982) (footnote omitted)—are precisely the kind of considerations that should inform the concern for "practicality and necessity" that Franchise Tax Board advised for the construction of § 1331 when jurisdiction is asserted because of the presence of a federal issue in a state cause of action.

The significance of the necessary assumption that there is no federal private cause of action thus cannot be overstated. For the ultimate import of such a conclusion, as we have repeatedly emphasized, is that it would flout congressional intent to provide a private federal remedy for the violation of the federal statute. We think it would similarly flout, or at least undermine, congressional intent to conclude that the federal courts might nevertheless exercise federal-question jurisdiction and provide remedies for violations of that federal statute solely because the violation of the federal statute is said to be a "rebuttable presumption" or a "proximate cause" under state law, rather than a federal action under federal law.

III

Petitioner advances three arguments to support its position that, even in the face of this congressional preclusion of a federal cause of action for a violation of the federal statute, federal-question jurisdiction may lie for the violation of the federal statute as an element of a state cause of action.

First, petitioner contends that the case represents a straightforward application of the statement in Franchise Tax Board that federal-question jurisdiction is appropriate when "it appears that some substantial, disputed question of federal law is a necessary element of one of the well-pleaded state claims." 463 U.S., at 13. Franchise Tax Board, however, did not purport to disturb the long-settled understanding that the mere presence of a federal issue in a state cause of action does not automatically confer federal-question jurisdiction.[11] Indeed, in determining that federal-question jurisdiction was not appropriate in the case before us, we stressed Justice Cardozo's emphasis on principled, pragmatic distinctions: "What is needed is something of that common-sense

---

8. See Merrill Lynch, Pierce, Fenner & Smith v. Curran, 456 U.S. 353, 377 (1982)("In 1975 the Court unanimously decided to modify its approach to the question whether a federal statute includes a private right of action"). * * *

11. See, *e.g.,* Gully v. First National Bank, 299 U.S. 109, 115 (1936)("Not every question of federal law emerging in a suit is proof that a federal law is the basis of the suit"); *id.,* at 118 ("If we follow the ascent far enough, countless claims of right can be discovered to have their source or their operative limits in the provisions of a federal statute or in the Constitution itself with its circumambient restrictions upon legislative power. To set bounds to the pursuit, the courts have formulated the distinction between controversies that are basic and those that are collateral, between disputes that are necessary and those that are merely possible. We shall be lost in a maze if we put that compass by").

accommodation of judgment to kaleidoscopic situations which characterizes the law in its treatment of causation * * * a selective process which picks the substantial causes out of the web and lays the other ones aside." *Id.*, at 20–21 (quoting Gully v. First National Bank, 299 U.S. 109, 117–118 (1936)).

Far from creating some kind of automatic test, Franchise Tax Board thus candidly recognized the need for careful judgments about the exercise of federal judicial power in an area of uncertain jurisdiction. Given the significance of the assumed congressional determination to preclude federal private remedies, the presence of the federal issue as an element of the state tort is not the kind of adjudication for which jurisdiction would serve congressional purposes and the federal system. This conclusion is fully consistent with the very sentence relied on so heavily by petitioner. We simply conclude that the congressional determination that there should be no federal remedy for the violation of this federal statute is tantamount to a congressional conclusion that the presence of a claimed violation of the statute as an element of a state cause of action is insufficiently "substantial" to confer federal-question jurisdiction.[12]

12. Several commentators have suggested that our § 1331 decisions can best be understood as an evaluation of the *nature* of the federal interest at stake. See, *e.g.,* Shapiro, *Jurisdiction and Discretion,* 60 N.Y.U.L.Rev. 543, 568 (1985); Wright, Federal Courts § 16, at 96 (4th ed.1983); Cohen, *The Broken Compass: The Requirement That A Case Arise "Directly" Under Federal Law,* 115 U.Pa.L.Rev. 890, 916 (1967). * * *

Focusing on the nature of the federal interest, moreover, suggests that the widely perceived "irreconcilable" conflict between the finding of federal jurisdiction in Smith v. Kansas City Title & Trust Co., 255 U.S. 180 (1921) and the finding of no jurisdiction in Moore v. Chesapeake & Ohio R. Co., 291 U.S. 205 (1934), see, *e.g.,* M. Redish, Federal Jurisdiction: Tensions in the Allocation of Judicial Power 67 (1980), is far from clear. For the difference in results can be seen as manifestations of the differences in the nature of the federal issues at stake. In Smith, as the Court emphasized, the issue was the constitutionality of an important federal statute. See 255 U.S., at 201 ("It is * * * apparent that the controversy concerns the constitutional validity of an act of Congress which is directly drawn in question. The decision depends upon the determination of this issue"). In Moore, in contrast, the Court emphasized that the violation of the federal standard as an element of state tort recovery did not fundamentally change the state tort nature of the action. See 291 U.S., at 216–217 ("The action fell within the familiar category of cases involving the duty of a master to his servant. This duty is defined by the common law, except as it may be modified by legisla-

tion. The federal statute, in the present case, touched the duty of the master at a single point and, save as provided in the statute, the right of the plaintiff to recover was left to be determined by the law of the State")(quoting Minneapolis, St. P. & S.S.M.R. Co. v. Popplar, 237 U.S. 369, 372 (1915)).

The importance of the nature of the federal issue in federal question jurisdiction is highlighted by the fact that, despite the usual reliability of the Holmes test as an inclusionary principle, this Court has sometimes found that formally federal causes of action were not properly brought under federal-question jurisdiction because of the overwhelming predominance of state-law issues. See Shulthis v. McDougal, 225 U.S. 561, 569–570 (1912)("A suit to enforce a right which takes its origin in the laws of the United States is not necessarily, or for that reason alone, one arising under those laws, for a suit does not so arise unless it really and substantially involves a dispute or controversy respecting the validity, construction or effect of such a law, upon the determination of which the result depends. This is especially so of a suit involving rights to land acquired under a law of the United States. If it were not, every suit to establish title to land in the central and western States would so arise, as all titles in those States are traceable back to those laws"); Shoshone Mining Co. v. Rutter, 177 U.S. 505, 507 (1900)("We pointed out in the former opinion that it was well settled that a suit to enforce a right which takes its origin in the laws of the United States is not necessarily one arising under the Constitution or laws of the United States, within the

Second, petitioner contends that there is a powerful federal interest in seeing that the federal statute is given uniform interpretations, and that federal review is the best way of insuring such uniformity. In addition to the significance of the congressional decision to preclude a federal remedy, we do not agree with petitioner's characterization of the federal interest and its implications for federal-question jurisdiction. To the extent that petitioner is arguing that state use and interpretation of the FDCA pose a threat to the order and stability of the FDCA regime, petitioner should be arguing, not that federal courts should be able to review and enforce state FDCA–based causes of action as an aspect of federal-question jurisdiction, but that the FDCA pre-empts state-court jurisdiction over the issue in dispute. Petitioner's concern about the uniformity of interpretation, moreover, is considerably mitigated by the fact that, even if there is no original district court jurisdiction for these kinds of action, this Court retains power to review the decision of a federal issue in a state cause of action.[14]

Finally, petitioner argues that, whatever the general rule, there are special circumstances that justify federal-question jurisdiction in this case. Petitioner emphasizes that it is unclear whether the FDCA applies to sales in Canada and Scotland; there is, therefore, a special reason for having a federal court answer the novel federal question relating to the extraterritorial meaning of the Act. We reject this argument. We do not believe the question whether a particular claim arises under federal law depends on the novelty of the federal issue. Although it is true that federal jurisdiction cannot be based on a frivolous or insubstantial federal question, "the interrelation of federal and state authority and the proper management of the federal judicial system," Franchise Tax Board, 463 U.S., at 8 would be ill-served by a rule that made the existence of federal-question jurisdiction depend on the district court's case-by-case apprais-al of the novelty of the federal question asserted as an element of the state tort. The novelty of an FDCA issue is not sufficient to give it status as a federal cause of action; nor should it be sufficient to give a state-based FDCA claim status as a jurisdiction-triggering federal question.[15]

IV

We conclude that a complaint alleging a violation of a federal statute as an element of a state cause of action, when Congress has determined that there should be no private, federal cause of action for the violation, does not state a claim "arising under the Constitution, laws, or treaties of the United States." 28 U.S.C. § 1331.

---

meaning of the jurisdiction clauses, for if it did every action to establish title to real estate (at least in the newer States) would be such a one, as all titles in those States come from the United States or by virtue of its laws").

14. See Moore v. Chesapeake & Ohio R. Co., 291 U.S. 205, 214–215 (1934) * * *.

15. Petitioner also contends that the Court of Appeals opinion rests on a view that federal question jurisdiction was inappropri-ate because, whatever the role of the federal issue in the FDCA–related count, the plaintiff could recover on other, strictly state law claims. See 766 F.2d, at 1006 (noting that "the jury could find negligence on the part of Merrell Dow without finding a violation of the FDCA"). To the extent that the opinion can be read to express such a view, we agree that it was erroneous. If the FDCA–related count presented a sufficient federal question, its relationship to the other, state-law claims would be determined by the ordinary princi-ples of pendent jurisdiction [see Sec. 5, *infra*]. For the reasons that we have stated, howev-er, there is no federal-question jurisdiction even with that possible error corrected.

The judgment of the Court of Appeals is affirmed.

■ JUSTICE BRENNAN, with whom JUSTICE WHITE, JUSTICE MARSHALL, and JUSTICE BLACKMUN join, dissenting.

* * * [Although the language of § 1331 "parrots" the language of Article III,] § 1331 has been construed more narrowly than its constitutional counterpart. Nonetheless, given the language of the statute and its close relation to the constitutional grant of federal question jurisdiction, limitations on federal question jurisdiction under § 1331 must be justified by careful consideration of the reasons underlying the grant of jurisdiction and the need for federal review. *Ibid.* I believe that the limitation on federal jurisdiction recognized by the Court today is inconsistent with the purposes of § 1331. Therefore, I respectfully dissent.

I

While the majority of cases covered by § 1331 may well be described by Justice Holmes' adage that "a suit arises under the law that creates the cause of action," * * * it is firmly settled that there may be federal question jurisdiction even though both the right asserted and the remedy sought by the plaintiff are state created. See C. Wright, Federal Courts § 17, at 95–96 (4th ed. 1983)(hereinafter Wright); M. Redish, Federal Jurisdiction: Tensions in the Allocation of Judicial Power 64–71 (1980)(hereinafter Redish). The rule as to such cases was stated in what Judge Friendly described as "[t]he path-breaking opinion" in Smith v. Kansas City Title & Trust Co., 255 U.S. 180 (1921). T.B. Harms Co. v. Eliscu, 339 F.2d 823, 827 (C.A.2 1964). * * *

The continuing vitality of Smith is beyond challenge. We have cited it approvingly on numerous occasions, and reaffirmed its holding several times— most recently just three Terms ago by a unanimous Court in Franchise Tax Board v. Construction Laborers Vacation Trust, 463 U.S., at 9. * * * Moreover, in addition to Judge Friendly's authoritative opinion in T.B. Harms v. Eliscu, *supra,* at 827, Smith has been widely cited and followed in the lower federal courts. * * * Furthermore, the principle of the Smith case has been recognized and endorsed by most commentators as well. Redish 67, 69; American Law Institute, Study of the Division of Jurisdiction Between State and Federal Courts 178 (1969)(hereinafter ALI); Wright § 17, p. 96; P. Bator, P. Mishkin, D. Shapiro, & H. Wechsler, Hart & Wechsler's The Federal Courts and the Federal System 889 (2d ed. 1973); Mishkin, The Federal "Question" in the District Courts, 53 Colum.L.Rev. 157, 166 (1953); Wechsler, Federal Jurisdiction and the Revision of the Judicial Code, 13 Law & Contemp.Prob. 216, 225 (1948).[1]

---

1. Some commentators have argued that the result in Smith conflicts with our decision in Moore v. Chesapeake & Ohio Ry., 291 U.S. 205 (1934). See, *e.g.,* Greene, Hybrid State Law in the Federal Courts, 83 Harv.L.Rev. 289, 323 (1969). * * *

The Court suggests that Smith and Moore may be reconciled if one views the question whether there is jurisdiction under § 1331 as turning upon "an evaluation of the nature of the federal interest at stake." *Ante,* n. 12 (emphasis in original). Thus, the Court explains, while in Smith the issue was the constitutionality of "an important federal statute," in Moore the federal interest was less significant in that "the violation of the federal standard as an element of state tort recovery did not fundamentally change the state tort nature of the action." *Ibid.*

In one sense, the Court is correct in asserting that we can reconcile Smith and Moore on the ground that the "nature" of the federal interest was more significant in Smith than in Moore. Indeed, as the Court

There is, to my mind, no question that there is federal jurisdiction over the respondents' fourth cause of action under the rule set forth in Smith and reaffirmed in Franchise Tax Board. Respondents pleaded that petitioner's labeling of the drug Bendectin constituted "misbranding" in violation of §§ 201 and 502(f)(2), and (j) of the Federal Food, Drug, and Cosmetics Act (FDCA), 21 U.S.C. § 301 *et seq.* (1982 ed. Supp. II), and that this violation "directly and proximately caused" their injuries. Respondents asserted in the complaint that this violation established petitioner's negligence *per se* and entitled them to recover damages without more. No other basis for finding petitioner negligent was asserted in connection with this claim. As pleaded, then, respondents' "right to relief depend[ed] upon the construction or application of the Constitution or laws of the United States." Smith, 255 U.S., at 199 * * *. Furthermore, although petitioner disputes its liability under the FDCA, it concedes that respondents' claim that petitioner violated the FDCA is "colorable, and rests upon a reasonable foundation." Smith, *supra,* 255 U.S., at 199. Of course, since petitioner must make this concession to prevail in this Court, it need not be accepted at face value. However, independent examination of respondents' claim substantiates the conclusion that it is neither frivolous nor meritless. * * * Thus, the statutory question is one which "discloses a need for determining the meaning or application of [the FDCA]," T.B. Harms v. Eliscu, 339 F.2d, at 827, and the claim raised by the fourth cause of action is one "arising under" federal law within the meaning of § 1331.

II

The Court apparently does not disagree with any of this—except, of course, for the conclusion. According to the Court, if we assume that Congress did not

appears to believe, *ibid.,* we could reconcile many of the seemingly inconsistent results that have been reached under § 1331 with such a test. But this is so only because a test based upon an ad hoc evaluation of the importance of the federal issue is infinitely malleable: at what point does a federal interest become strong enough to create jurisdiction? What principles guide the determination whether a statute is "important" or not? Why, for instance, was the statute in Smith so "important" that direct review of a state court decision (under our mandatory appellate jurisdiction) would have been inadequate? Would the result in Moore have been different if the federal issue had been a more important element of the tort claim? The point is that if one makes the test sufficiently vague and general, virtually any set of results can be "reconciled." However, the inevitable—and undesirable—result of a test such as that suggested in the Court's footnote 12 is that federal jurisdiction turns in every case on an appraisal of the federal issue, its importance and its relation to state law issues. Yet it is precisely because the Court believes that federal jurisdiction would be "ill-served" by such a case-by-case appraisal that it rejects petitioners' claim that the difficulty and

importance of the statutory issue presented by their claim suffices to confer jurisdiction under § 1331. The Court cannot have it both ways.

My own view is in accord with those commentators who view the results in Smith and Moore as irreconcilable. See, *e.g.,* Redish 67; Currie, Federal Jurisdiction in a Nutshell 109 (2d ed. 1981). That fact does not trouble me greatly, however, for I view Moore as having been a "sport" at the time it was decided and having long been in a state of innocuous desuetude. Unlike the jurisdictional holding in Smith, the jurisdictional holding in Moore has never been relied upon or even cited by this Court. Moore has similarly borne little fruit in the lower courts, leading Professor Redish to conclude after comparing the vitality of Smith and Moore that "the principle enunciated in Smith is the one widely followed by modern lower federal courts." Redish 67. Finally, as noted in text, the commentators have also preferred Smith. Moore simply has not survived the test of time; it is presently moribund, and, to the extent that it is inconsistent with the well-established rule of the Smith case, it ought to be overruled.

intend for there to be a private federal cause of action under a particular federal law (and, presumably, *a fortiori* if Congress' decision not to create a private remedy is express), we must also assume that Congress did not intend for there to be federal jurisdiction over a state cause of action that is determined by that federal law. Therefore, assuming—only because the parties have made a similar assumption—that there is no private cause of action under the FDCA,[4] the Court holds that there is no federal jurisdiction over the plaintiff's claim * * *.

The Court nowhere explains the basis for this conclusion. Yet it is hardly self-evident. Why should the fact that Congress chose not to create a private federal *remedy* mean that Congress would not want there to be federal *jurisdiction* to adjudicate a state claim that imposes liability for violating the federal law? Clearly, the decision not to provide a private federal remedy should not affect federal jurisdiction unless the reasons Congress withholds a federal remedy are also reasons for withholding federal jurisdiction. Thus, it is necessary to examine the reasons for Congress' decisions to grant or withhold both federal jurisdiction and private remedies, something the Court has not done.

A

* * * [W]ith one shortlived exception, Congress did not grant the inferior federal courts original jurisdiction over cases arising under federal law until 1875. Judiciary Act of 1875, ch. 137, § 1, 18 Stat. 470. The reasons Congress found it necessary to add this jurisdiction to the district courts are well known. First, Congress recognized "the importance, and even necessity of *uniformity* of decisions throughout the whole United States, upon all subjects within the purview of the constitution." Martin v. Hunter's Lessee, 1 Wheat., at 347–348 (Story, J.)(emphasis in original). Concededly, because federal jurisdiction is not always exclusive and because federal courts may disagree with one another, absolute uniformity has not been obtained even under § 1331. However, while perfect uniformity may not have been achieved, experience indicates that the availability of a federal forum in federal question cases has done much to advance that goal. * * *

In addition, § 1331 has provided for adjudication in a forum that specializes in federal law and that is therefore more likely to apply that law correctly. Because federal question cases constitute the basic grist for federal tribunals, "the federal courts have acquired a considerable expertise in the interpretation and application of federal law." ALI 164–165. By contrast, "it is apparent that federal question cases must form a very small part of the business of [state] courts." ALI 165. As a result, the federal courts are comparatively more skilled at interpreting and applying federal law, and are much more likely correctly to divine Congress' intent in enacting legislation.[6] * * *

---

4. It bears emphasizing that the Court does *not* hold that there is no private cause of action under the FDCA. Rather, it expressly states that "[f]or purposes of our decision, we assume that this is a correct interpretation of the FDCA." The Court simply holds petitioner to its concession that the FDCA provides no private remedy, and decides petitioner's claim on the basis of this concession. I shall do the same.

6. Another reason Congress conferred original federal question jurisdiction on the district courts was its belief that state courts are hostile to assertions of federal rights. See Hornstein 564–565; Redish 71. Although this concern may be less compelling today than it once was, the American Law Institute reported as recently as 1969 that "it is difficult to avoid concluding that federal

These reasons for having original federal question jurisdiction explain why cases like this one and Smith—*i.e.,* cases where the cause of action is a creature of state law, but an essential element of the claim is federal—"arise under" federal law within the meaning of § 1331. Congress passes laws in order to shape behavior; a federal law expresses Congress' determination that there is a federal interest in having individuals or other entities conform their actions to a particular norm established by that law. Because all laws are imprecise to some degree, disputes inevitably arise over what specifically Congress intended to require or permit. It is the duty of courts to interpret these laws and apply them in such a way that the congressional purpose is realized. As noted above, Congress granted the district courts power to hear cases "arising under" federal law in order to enhance the likelihood that federal laws would be interpreted more correctly and applied more uniformly. * * *

By making federal law an essential element of a state law claim, the State places the federal law into a context where it will operate to shape behavior: the threat of liability will force individuals to conform their conduct to interpretations of the federal law made by courts adjudicating the state law claim. It will not matter to an individual found liable whether the officer who arrives at his door to execute judgment is wearing a state or a federal uniform; all he cares about is the fact that a sanction is being imposed—and may be imposed again in the future—because he failed to comply with the federal law. Consequently, the possibility that the federal law will be incorrectly interpreted in the context of adjudicating the state law claim implicates the concerns that led Congress to grant the district courts power to adjudicate cases involving federal questions in precisely the same way as if it was federal law that "created" the cause of action. It therefore follows that there is federal jurisdiction under § 1331.

B

The only remaining question is whether the assumption that Congress decided not to create a private cause of action alters this analysis in a way that makes it inappropriate to exercise original federal jurisdiction. According to the Court, "the very reasons for the development of the modern implied remedy doctrine" support the conclusion that, where the legislative history of a particular law shows (whether expressly or by inference) that Congress intended for there to be no private federal remedy, it must also mean that Congress would not want federal courts to exercise jurisdiction over a state law claim making violations of that federal law actionable. These reasons are "the increased complexity of federal legislation," "the increased volume of federal litigation," and "the desirability of a more careful scrutiny of legislative intent." * * *

courts are more likely to apply federal law sympathetically and understandingly than are state courts." ALI 166. In any event, this rationale is, like the rationale based on the expertise of the federal courts, simply an expression of Congress' belief that federal courts are more likely to interpret federal law correctly.

One might argue that this Court's appellate jurisdiction over state court judgments in cases arising under federal law can be depended upon to correct erroneous state court decisions and to insure that federal law is interpreted and applied uniformly. However, having served on this Court for 30 years, it is clear to me that, realistically, it cannot even come close to "doing the whole job" and that § 1331 is essential if federal rights are to be adequately protected.

These reasons simply do not justify the Court's holding. Given the relative expertise of the federal courts in interpreting federal law, the increased complexity of federal legislation argues rather strongly in *favor* of recognizing federal jurisdiction. And, while the increased volume of litigation may appropriately be considered in connection with reasoned arguments that justify limiting the reach of § 1331, I do not believe that the day has yet arrived when this Court may trim a statute solely because it thinks that Congress made it too broad.[7]

This leaves only the third reason: "the desirability of a more careful scrutiny of legislative intent." *Ibid.* I certainly subscribe to the proposition that the Court should consider legislative intent in determining whether or not there is jurisdiction under § 1331. But the Court has not examined the purposes underlying either the FDCA or § 1331 in reaching its conclusion that Congress' presumed decision not to provide a private federal remedy under the FDCA must be taken to withdraw federal jurisdiction over a private state remedy that imposes liability for violating the FDCA. Moreover, such an examination demonstrates not only that it is consistent with legislative intent to find that there is federal jurisdiction over such a claim, but, indeed, that it is the Court's contrary conclusion that is inconsistent with congressional intent.

The enforcement scheme established by the FDCA is typical of other, similarly broad regulatory schemes. Primary responsibility for overseeing implementation of the Act has been conferred upon a specialized administrative agency, here the Food and Drug Administration (FDA). Congress has provided the FDA with a wide-ranging arsenal of weapons to combat violations of the FDCA, including authority to obtain an ex parte court order for the seizure of goods subject to the Act, see 21 U.S.C. § 334, authority to initiate proceedings in a federal district court to enjoin continuing violations of the FDCA, see *id.* § 332, and authority to request a United States Attorney to bring criminal proceedings against violators, see *id.* § 333. See generally, 1 J. O'Reilly, Food and Drug Administration chs. 6–10 (1985). Significantly, the FDA has no independent enforcement authority; final enforcement must come from the federal courts, which have exclusive jurisdiction over actions under the FDCA. See §§ 332(a), 333, 334(a)(1). * * *

Given that Congress structured the FDCA so that all express remedies are provided by the federal courts, it seems rather strange to conclude that it either "flout[s]" or "undermine[s]" congressional intent for the federal courts to adjudicate a private state law remedy that is based upon violating the FDCA. That is, assuming that a state cause of action based on the FDCA is not preempted, it is entirely consistent with the FDCA to find that it "arises under" federal law within the meaning of § 1331. Indeed, it is the Court's conclusion that such a state cause of action must be kept *out* of the federal courts that appears contrary to the legislative intent inasmuch as the enforce-

---

7. *Cf.* Cohens v. Virginia, 6 Wheat. 264, 404 (1821)(Marshall, C.J.)("It is most true that this Court will not take jurisdiction if it should not but it is equally true that it must take jurisdiction if it should. * * * We have no more right to decline the exercise of jurisdiction which is given, than to usurp that which is not given. * * *"). The narrow exceptions we have recognized to Chief Justice Marshall's famous dictum have all been justified by compelling judicial concerns of comity and federalism. See, *e.g.,* Younger v. Harris, 401 U.S. 37 (1971). It would be wholly illegitimate, however, for this Court to determine that there was no jurisdiction over a class of cases simply because the Court thought that there were too many cases in the federal courts.

ment provisions of the FDCA quite clearly express a preference for having federal courts interpret the FDCA and provide remedies for its violation.

It may be that a decision by Congress not to create a private remedy is intended to preclude all private enforcement. If that is so, then a state cause of action that makes relief available to private individuals for violations of the FDCA is pre-empted. But if Congress' decision not to provide a private federal remedy does *not* pre-empt such a state remedy, then, in light of the FDCA's clear policy of relying on the federal courts for enforcement, it also should not foreclose federal jurisdiction over that state remedy. * * *

* * * Congress' decision to withhold a private right of action and to rely instead on public enforcement reflects congressional concern with obtaining more accurate implementation and more coordinated enforcement of a regulatory scheme. See * * * Stewart & Sunstein, *Public Programs and Private Rights,* 95 Harv.L.Rev. 1193, 1208–1209 (1982). These reasons are closely related to the Congress' reasons for giving federal courts original federal question jurisdiction. Thus, if anything, Congress' decision not to create a private remedy *strengthens* the argument in favor of finding federal jurisdiction over a state remedy that is not preempted.

NOTE ON THE HOLMES TEST AND ON OTHER APPROACHES TO "ARISING UNDER" JURISDICTION

(1) *The American Well Works Rule and its Applications.*

(a) *Introduction.* As a principle of inclusion, Holmes' proposition in American Well Works should be uncontroversial: at least as a general rule, an action arises under federal law if the plaintiff asserts a federally created cause of action. The problem of jurisdiction when such a case involves only disputes as to the facts has bemused some commentators, but few courts (notwithstanding the formulation of Justice Cardozo in Gully, p. 912, *supra,* requiring a "dispute" about federal law).

(b) *Patent and Copyright Cases.* The scope of the Holmes proposition is illustrated by many cases under the patent and copyright laws. The current statute governing jurisdiction in such cases is 28 U.S.C. § 1338; but the controlling concepts of what cases "arise under" these laws appear interchangeable with those developed under § 1331. Note, however, that the jurisdiction granted over cases arising under the patent and copyright laws by § 1338 is exclusive, so that a holding that a case is within that section is equally a holding that the case may not be brought in a state court—and vice versa.

(i) The federal right created by the patent and copyright statutes is the right to the monopoly, enforceable by an action for infringement. Many cases hold that there is federal jurisdiction over such an action even though plaintiff's suit could have been based on a breach of a contract to license the patent, and even though the only dispute is whether such a license covers defendant's contract. See, *e.g.,* The Fair v. Kohler Die & Specialty Co., 228 U.S. 22 (1913)(the "party who brings a suit is master to decide what law he will rely upon").

(ii) It is equally clear that if a patentee's action is based on rights created by a contract, or on the common law of torts, the case is not one "arising under" federal law (at least for purposes of inclusion within the Holmes proposition). See, *e.g.* (in addition to the American Well Works case), Becher v. Contoure Laboratories, Inc., 279 U.S. 388 (1929); Luckett v. Delpark, Inc., 270 U.S. 496, 510–11 (1926).

(iii) The result of these jurisdictional rules is that in some cases within exclusive federal court jurisdiction the dispute will be entirely about issues of state law (as where the question of liability for infringement turns entirely on the interpretation of a licensing contract); *per contra,* some cases within the exclusive jurisdiction of the state courts will turn out to depend entirely on federal questions involving the patent and copyright laws.[1]

(iv) Does the wide power of state courts to pass on "patent questions" undermine the justification for exclusive federal jurisdiction of "patent cases"? Suggested solutions include legislation providing for enlargement of original federal jurisdiction to include all cases involving the licensing or assignment of patent rights or for removal, at the option of either party, whenever an issue of patent validity or infringement appears at any pleading stage. Note, 72 Harv.L.Rev. 328, 330–31 (1958). See also Cooper, *State Law of Patent Exploitation,* 56 Minn.L.Rev. 313 (1972).[2]

(c) *Cases Involving Disputes Over Land Originally Owned by the United States.* Disputes about land in which the chain of title includes a grant or patent from the United States have generated some of the most confusing and difficult cases under the federal question statute. Many—but not all—of these cases are excluded from federal court by the well pleaded complaint rule. In most others, it is clear that since state law creates the plaintiff's right of action, federal jurisdiction cannot be justified under the Holmes test.

But a problematic (and perhaps anomalous) case is Shoshone Mining Co. v. Rutter, 177 U.S. 505 (1900). In Rev.Stat. §§ 2325–26, Congress laid down the conditions for issuance of patents for mining claims by the Commissioner of the General Land Office. The law provided that if, after notice of an application, an adverse claim were filed, "it shall be the duty of the adverse claimant, within thirty days after filing his claim, to commence proceedings in a court of competent jurisdiction, to determine the question of the right of possession, and prosecute the same with reasonable diligence to final judgment"; and directed that the patent should issue in accordance with the judgment. Rev.Stat. §§ 2319, 2324, and 2332 provided that this right of possession could be determined by "local customs or rules of miners in the several mining districts, so far as the same are applicable and not inconsistent with the laws of the

---

1. Lear, Inc. v. Adkins, 395 U.S. 653 (1969), for example, involved a patentee's state court action for royalties under a licensing agreement not involving a price-fixing term or alleged antitrust violation. The state supreme court held that the defendant was estopped to deny the validity of his licensor's patent. Reconsidering the general estoppel rule in light of "the strong federal policy favoring free competition in ideas which do not merit patent protection" (p. 656), the Supreme Court reversed and remanded, holding that the validity of the patent was open

to attack in this proceeding and that arguments concerning this issue should first be considered by the state courts.

2. For a masterly exposition of the jurisdictional rules governing copyright cases, see the opinion of Judge Friendly in T.B. Harms Co. v. Eliscu, 339 F.2d 823 (2d Cir. 1964).

As to declaratory judgments in patent and copyright matters, see the Franchise Tax Board case, p. 937, *infra,* and the *Note on the Jurisdictional Significance of the Declaratory Judgment Act,* p. 946, *infra.*

United States", or "by the statute of limitations for mining claims of the State or Territory where the same may be situated."

In the Shoshone case, the Court held that such an adverse suit was not within the general grant of federal question jurisdiction. It said (p. 509):

"Inasmuch, therefore, as the 'adverse suit' to determine the right of possession may not involve any question as to the construction or effect of the Constitution or laws of the United States, but may present simply a question of fact as to the time of the discovery of the mineral, the location of the claim on the ground, or a determination of the meaning and effect of certain local rules and customs prescribed by the miners of the district, or the effect of state statutes, it would seem to follow that it is not one which necessarily arises under the Constitution and laws of the United States."

Earlier in its opinion the Court had said (p. 507): "[It is] well settled that a suit to enforce a right which takes its origin in the laws of the United States is not necessarily one arising under the Constitution or laws of the United States, within the meaning of the jurisdiction clauses, for if it did every action to establish title to real estate (at least in the newer States) would be such a one, as all titles in those States come from the United States or by virtue of its laws."

Note the ambiguity of the phrase "a suit to enforce a right which takes its origin in the laws of the United States." The "for if it did" clause in the rest of that sentence shows that the Court was thinking here of a vast range of cases where the chain of title includes a federal grant but there is no federal question in the forefront of the case and the right of action is entirely state-created. But in Shoshone itself the right to sue was created by Congress itself. Why wasn't that decisive? Does the case stand as an exception to the inclusive aspect of the Holmes rule? If so, was the exception justified as a matter of statutory interpretation?[3] (For arguments that it was, see Shapiro, *Jurisdiction and Discretion,* 60 N.Y.U.L.Rev. 543, 569–70 (1985). See also the reference to Shoshone in Justice Stevens' opinion in Merrell Dow at n. 12).[4]

(2) *Cases in Which the Cause of Action is Not Federally Created: From Smith to Merrell Dow.*

(a) The decision in Smith v. Kansas City Title & Trust Co., 255 U.S. 180 (1921), is referred to at some length in the opinions in Merrell Dow. The Court in Smith upheld original federal question jurisdiction in a suit by shareholders of a Missouri bank to enjoin the bank from investing in certain federal bonds. The shareholders, who argued that the federal statute violated the federal Constitution, claimed a right to relief under state law on the basis that state

---

3. Compare the question of statutory interpretation raised in the discussion of the Mottley case, at pp. 909–10, *infra.*

4. With Shoshone, compare Oneida Indian Nation v. County of Oneida, 414 U.S. 661 (1974), in which the Court found that it was federal, not state, law that gave the Indian Nation "a current right to possession" of certain lands, so that its action of ejectment "arose under" federal law for purposes of Section 1331. The Court relied on the long, unique, and continuous federal concern for Indian lands. The assertion of jurisdiction "rests on the not insubstantial claim that federal law now protects, and has continuously protected from the time of the formation of the United States, possessory right to tribal lands, wholly apart from the application of state law principles which normally and separately protect a valid right of possession" (p. 677).

Note the support for the result in Oneida in the quotation from Shulthis v. McDougal appearing at p. 913, *supra.*

law prohibited the bank from investing in bonds not issued pursuant to a valid law. Thus state law supplied both the claimed right and the claimed remedy. Nevertheless, the Supreme Court upheld jurisdiction on the ground that "the controversy concerns the constitutional validity of an act of Congress, which is directly drawn in question" (p. 201).

Justice Holmes, dissenting, argued (relying in significant part on his own decision in American Well Works) that "a suit cannot be said to arise under any other law than that which creates the cause of action" (p. 214). Conceding that under Osborn (which he did not distinguish as arising under a special statute), "[i]t may be enough that the law relied upon creates a part of the cause of action" (*id.*), he insisted that not even that minimal standard had been met in the case at hand.

(b) Supreme Court cases applying the Smith rule prior to Merrell Dow are rare.[5] One interesting case decided prior to Smith is Hopkins v. Walker, 244 U.S. 486 (1917), p. 913, *supra,* a suit to remove a cloud on title where federal law governed many of the issues with respect to the validity of the competing claims. Without referring to the undoubted fact that the underlying right to have a title free from cloud and the right of action to enforce it both came from state law, the Supreme Court upheld jurisdiction after satisfying itself that, as a matter of proper pleading, the federal issues were part of the plaintiff's complaint.[6] (It is noteworthy, however, that the complaint in Hopkins left no doubt that the meaning of the federal land grant was in dispute, since the plaintiff was required to plead the defendant's competing claim in order to satisfy the well-pleaded complaint rule. Thus the case was not one in which the federal grant was an uncontested link in the plaintiff's title.)

(c) Justice Holmes also said, in his dissent in Smith, that "the law of the United States has no force proprio vigore". Was he suggesting that there was no "real" federal question in the case at all? In every situation where a state cause of action incorporates an element of federal law, an antecedent question is whether the incorporation is such that the so-called "federal" issue can properly be characterized as a real question of federal law. This question can be tested by asking whether (if other requirements of reviewability were met) a state court decision of the case would be subject to Supreme Court review because of this "federal" element. See *Note on State Incorporation of or Reference to Federal Law*, p. 546, *supra.* If the answer is yes, the further, distinct question is whether the role the federal question plays in the case is such that it supports original "arising under" jurisdiction in the district courts under § 1331.

Would Justice Holmes have doubted that a decision by the Missouri Supreme Court granting plaintiff the relief he sought in Smith would have been

5. For lower court authority during this period, see 13B Wright, Miller & Cooper, Federal Practice and Procedure § 3562 at 43–44 nn. 51, 52 (1984)(noting a good deal of dictum, and "some holdings", sustaining jurisdiction on the basis of the Smith decision).

6. See also De Sylva v. Ballentine, 351 U.S. 570 (1956), p. 769, *supra,* where the Supreme Court decided on the merits—with-out discussing any jurisdictional question—a federal court action involving a state law claim to partial ownership of copyright renewal terms. "Since there was no diversity of citizenship, and no infringement, the only, and a sufficient, explanation for the taking of jurisdiction was the existence of two major questions of construction of the Copyright Act." T.B. Harms Co. v. Eliscu, 339 F.2d 823, 827 (2d Cir.1964).

reviewable by the Supreme Court? What of a state court decision *denying* relief?

(d) In Moore v. Chesapeake & Ohio Ry., 291 U.S. 205 (1934), the specific issue was one of venue—namely, whether, for the purposes of the predecessor of 28 U.S.C. § 1391(a), jurisdiction in an action in a federal district court was "founded only on diversity of citizenship", or whether the action was also one arising under federal law, namely the Federal Safety Appliance Act. The plaintiff employee alleged injuries received while he was engaged in *intrastate* commerce and sought recovery under the Employers' Liability Act of Kentucky. But the claim also set forth asserted violations of the Federal Safety Appliance Act, which (as amended in 1903, 32 Stat. 943) prescribes certain equipment for all cars used on any railroad that is a highway of interstate commerce, and thus applies even while a particular car is in use in intrastate commerce.

The Kentucky Act provided that no employee should be held "to have been guilty of contributory negligence" or "to have assumed the risk of his employment" in any case "where the violation by such common carrier of any statute, state or federal, enacted for the safety of employees contributed to the injury or death of such employee". As the Supreme Court stated (p. 213), "the Federal Safety Appliance Acts were manifestly embraced in this description."

The Court held that jurisdiction rested solely on diversity of citizenship. It said (pp. 214–17):

"* * * Questions arising in actions in state courts to recover for injuries sustained by employees in intrastate commerce and relating to the scope or construction of the Federal Safety Appliance Acts are, of course, federal questions which may appropriately be reviewed in this Court. * * * But it does not follow that a suit brought under the state statute which defines liability to employees who are injured while engaged in intrastate commerce, and brings within the purview of the statute a breach of the duty imposed by the federal statute, should be regarded as a suit arising under the laws of the United States * * *.

"* * * [N]othing in the Safety Appliance Acts precluded the State from incorporating in its legislation applicable to local transportation the paramount duty which the Safety Appliance Acts imposed as to the equipment of cars used on interstate railroads. As this Court said in Minneapolis, St. Paul & Sault Ste. Marie R. Co. v. Popplar [237 U.S. 369], as to an action for injuries sustained in intrastate commerce: 'The action fell within the familiar category of cases involving the duty of a master to his servant. This duty is defined by the common law, except as it may be modified by legislation. The federal statute, in the present case, touched the duty of the master at a single point and, save as provided in the statute, the right of the plaintiff to recover was left to be determined by the law of the State.' "

Can Moore be reconciled with the Smith case? Despite the footnote war on this question in Merrell Dow, perhaps there is a simple route to reconciliation. In Moore, the state statute did not give the plaintiff a remedy for violation of the federal statute; it merely said that such a violation will negate the defenses of contributory negligence and assumption of risk. Moore thus fails the well-pleaded complaint rule: the federal issue, as in Mottley, comes in by way of reply to a defense. Assume this analysis is correct. If the state statute in Moore had provided that violation of the Federal Act was actionable or constituted negligence for purposes of a state negligence action, the result might well have been different under the Smith rationale. Does Merrell Dow render the distinction irrelevant?

(3) *Cases in Which the Cause of Action is Not Federally Created: The Meaning and Impact of Merrell Dow.*

(a) The Court carefully refrained from overruling Smith in Merrell Dow.[7] Rather, it purported to find, in Congress' (hypothesized) decision not to create a federal cause of action for violations of the Food, Drug, and Cosmetics Act, special reasons militating against jurisdiction.

But in virtually all cases where the Smith rule (rather than the Holmes test) is in play, no federal right of action will be available. Won't the Merrell Dow analysis—that federal court adjudication would undermine the policy that animated the decision not to have a substantive federal cause of action—be applicable in most such situations? What then is left of Smith—except the unusual case where a federal right of action exists but plaintiff chooses to sue only on a state cause of action with a federal ingredient?

(b) Justice Stevens' opinion is replete with hints that the Court wishes to reserve a wide discretion to tailor the "arising under" jurisdiction to the practical needs of the particular situation. In note 12, he cites Cohen, *The Broken Compass: The Requirement That a Case Arise "Directly" Under Federal Law*, 115 U.Pa.L.Rev. 890 (1967), which argued against the use of any analytic formula for determining when a case "arises under" federal law for purposes of § 1331, and in favor of "pragmatic standards for a pragmatic problem."[8] Justice Stevens also cites Shapiro, *Jurisdiction and Discretion*, 60 N.Y.U.L.Rev. 543, 568–70 (1985), where the author said:

7. For a statement after Merrell Dow that a case arises under § 1331 if "the plaintiff's right to relief necessarily depends on resolution of a substantial question of federal law," see Christianson v. Colt Industries Operating Corp., 486 U.S. 800, 808 (1988)(Brennan, J.). The case was an antitrust action alleging that the defendant had driven plaintiffs out of business. One of plaintiffs' several theories was that the defendant told plaintiffs' customers that plaintiffs were misappropriating defendant's trade secrets; the plaintiffs denied misappropriation on the ground that defendant's patents were invalid. No cause of action under the patent laws was asserted.

Plaintiffs prevailed in the district court. The defendant appealed to the Court of Appeals for the Federal Circuit, which, under 28 U.S.C. § 1295(a)(1), has exclusive jurisdiction over appeals from decisions of district courts whose jurisdiction is based in whole or in part on 28 U.S.C. § 1338 (cases arising under the patent or copyright laws). If the case arose under the patent laws, the appeal was properly filed. If instead it arose under the antitrust laws, the Seventh Circuit had appellate jurisdiction. When the case reached the Supreme Court, it unanimously ruled that

the case did not arise under the patent laws, and hence the Federal Circuit did not have appellate jurisdiction. The Court stressed that the multiplicity of antitrust theories pleaded in the complaint gave rise to many reasons, wholly unrelated to the question of patent validity, why the plaintiffs might or might not be entitled to relief under the antitrust laws: "a claim supported by alternative theories in the complaint may not form the basis for § 1338(a) jurisdiction unless patent law is essential to each of those theories" (p. 810).

Was it wise in interpreting § 1295(a)(1) to use as a test of *appellate* jurisdiction the question whether the claim arose under the patent laws when the case was filed in *district* court? *Cf.* p. 900, Paragraph (3) [discussion of Marshall's Osborn opinion], *supra*.

8. Cohen suggests (p. 916) that the relevant "pragmatic" considerations should include "the extent of the caseload increase" if jurisdiction is recognized; the extent to which cases "of this class" turn on federal versus state law; "the extent of the necessity for an expert federal tribunal"; and the "extent of the necessity for a sympathetic federal tribunal."

"My own view is that no formulation can possibly explain or even begin to account for the variety of outcomes unless it accords sufficient room for the federal courts to make a range of choices based on considerations of judicial administration and the degree of federal concern.   * * * [The] cases suggest that the Court's authority, but not its obligation, is very broad indeed.   In Smith, the presence of a federal ingredient made relevant by state law was sufficient to confer jurisdiction, but in Shoshone [p. 927, *supra*], a federally created claim that turned on issues of state law was not.   Both cases, however, may be better understood if viewed in terms of the federal interest at stake and the effect on the federal docket.   Cases like Smith arise infrequently, but the issue—the ability of a party to invest in federally authorized securities—was a matter of great federal moment.   Cases like Shoshone must have arisen with monotonous regularity at the turn of the century, but the degree of federal interest in an outcome dependent on local custom was marginal at best."

(c) What is the proper role of "discretion" in determining the appropriate scope of § 1331 jurisdiction?   Professor Cohen's position appears to be that the *district* courts should exercise an ad hoc case-by-case discretion, unguided by any "formulation", in determining whether jurisdiction is justified by "pragmatic" factors.   Would such a regime be tolerable?   (Note that its effect would be both to narrow and complicate Supreme Court supervision of this area.   See *Note on Control of Factfinding and of Application of Law to Fact*, p. 596, *supra*.)

Professor Shapiro's position is different.[9]   He acknowledges that the Supreme Court has developed general standards for applying § 1331; but, finding anomalous cases at the margin, he explains them by surmising that the Court was influenced by factors of "federal interest" and "effect on the federal docket."   Approving this approach, he argues that it is consistent with the statutory grant of jurisdiction for the Supreme Court to create exceptions to the general § 1331 standards to reflect these concerns.

Except in footnote 12 of Merrell Dow, the Court has not explicitly indicated approval of any notion of "discretion" in interpreting § 1331.   Rather, it has based decisions such as Franchise Tax Board and Merrell Dow on statutory interpretation, finding in a particular substantive statute a congressional intent to create a special exception to the usual § 1331 rules.   Is this approach likely to lead to results that differ significantly from that advocated by Professor Shapiro?

For a powerful argument that rules of subject matter jurisdiction should be subject to a "bright line" test, see Chafee, Some Problems of Equity (1950), especially at pp. 1–102, discussing the mischief created by the "unclean hands" doctrine in equity.   See also Hirshman, *Whose Law Is It Anyway?   A Reconsideration of Federal Question Jurisdiction Over Cases of Mixed State and Federal Law*, 60 Ind.L.J. 17 (1984) supporting a return to the Holmes test.   For analysis and criticism of Merrell Dow itself, see Alleva, *Prerogative Lost: The*

---

9.   Professor Shapiro carefully disassociated himself from the *ad hoc* approach of Professor Cohen, stressing that the range of discretion under § 1331, "though extremely broad at the outset, has been significantly narrowed by the course of decisions since the jurisdictional statute was enacted" (p. 568 n. 149).   He concluded: "The discretion I advocate relates primarily to the existence of a range of permissible choices under the relevant grants of jurisdiction.   It is entirely consistent with this view for judicial precedent to narrow the scope of discretion and even to generate predictable rules" (pp. 588–89).

Trouble with Statutory Federal Question Doctrine After Merrell Dow, 52 Ohio St.L.J. 1477 (1991).

(d) The jurisdictional question presented in the Smith and Merrell Dow cases does not arise that often, and it may therefore be fair to ask whether the game is worth the candle: whether the Holmes test should be not only sufficient but necessary for original federal question jurisdiction under § 1331. Under such an approach, the Supreme Court would, in general, be available to review significant errors of federal law that were committed or sustained by a state's highest court.[10]

(e) In general, in those cases that have arisen, the lower courts have interpreted Merrell Dow to preclude federal question jurisdiction in cases in which Congress has not created an express cause of action. See, *e.g.,* Clark v. Velsicol Chem. Corp., 944 F.2d 196 (4th Cir.1991); Utley v. Varian Associates, 811 F.2d 1279 (9th Cir.1987); Seinfeld v. Austen, 39 F.3d 761 (7th Cir.1994). But in one case involving a careful and sophisticated analysis, the Second Circuit refused to find the absence of an express cause of action determinative and sustained federal question jurisdiction. West 14th St. Commercial Corp. v. 5 West 14th Owners Corp., 815 F.2d 188 (2d Cir.1987).[11]

(f) Suppose plaintiff sues in a federal court for violations of constitutional rights under 42 U.S.C. § 1983, or for violations of rights conferred by a federal statute, and is unsuccessful in that action. Would a suit by the former defendant against the former plaintiff for malicious prosecution "arise under" federal law within the meaning of § 1331? (Consider the relevance to this question of the remaining Paragraphs in this Note.) Unless the answer is "yes", the former plaintiff could not, under § 1441, remove such a case from state to federal court. Would that be a sound result? Compare Sweeney v. Abramovitz, 449 F.Supp. 213 (D.Conn.1978)(upholding jurisdiction on removal) with Berg v. Leason, 32 F.3d 422 (9th Cir.1994)(holding such a claim not removable). Note that the Sweeney case predated, and the Berg case postdated, the Supreme Court's decision in Merrell Dow.

(4) *Causes of Action Created by Federal Common Law.*

(a) The holding in Merrell Dow rests on the antecedent premise—not disputed in the case—that no federal common-law cause of action may properly be "implied" from the federal Food, Drug and Cosmetics Act. The case does not cast doubt on the distinct proposition—now well settled—that causes of action that are properly "implied" from federal statutes or the federal Consti-

---

10. But see Yackle, Reclaiming the Federal Courts 114–16 (1994), urging that general federal question jurisdiction be defined so as to authorize the exercise of such jurisdiction whenever a substantial question of federal law is an essential element of the plaintiff's case. Professor Yackle also proposes, *inter alia,* that original jurisdiction should extend to a case in which the plaintiff "alleges that a substantial federal question that may resolve the dispute will appear in an answer or other allowable pre-trial proceeding or motion." *Id.*

11. See also Additive Controls & Measurement Systems, Inc. v. Flowdata, Inc., 986

F.2d 476 (Fed.Cir.1993), upholding federal jurisdiction over a state law claim whose resolution depended on a substantial question of federal patent law. American Well Works was distinguished on the ground that, under the governing state law in that case, the truth or falsity of the defendant's charges was not controlling on the plaintiff's right to recover, and hence no federal issue arose under a well-pleaded complaint. The Federal Circuit also relied both on Smith and on the Supreme Court's post-Merrell Dow decision in the Christianson case, note 7, *supra.*

tution, or that are otherwise a creation of federal common law, do "arise under" federal law within the meaning of § 1331 and its predecessors.

(b) The Court's approach to this proposition began with cases where the substantive question—whether a federal cause of action could be maintained—was itself in doubt when the lawsuit was commenced.

The foundation case was Bell v. Hood, 327 U.S. 678 (1946), a suit against FBI agents, brought in a federal district court under the predecessor of § 1331, seeking damages for violations of the Fourth and Fifth Amendments. The complaint alleged unconstitutional arrests, searches, and seizures. The district court dismissed the action for want of jurisdiction on the ground that it was not one "aris[ing] under the Constitution or laws of the United States"; the Circuit Court of Appeals affirmed. The Supreme Court reversed, deciding the jurisdictional issue only.

The Court, per Justice Black, held that the district court must assume jurisdiction to decide whether the allegations state a cause of action on which the court can grant relief as well as to determine issues of fact arising in the controversy (pp. 682–85):

"Jurisdiction, therefore, is not defeated as respondents seem to contend, by the possibility that the averments might fail to state a cause of action on which petitioners could actually recover. For it is well settled that the failure to state a proper cause of action calls for a judgment on the merits and not for a dismissal for want of jurisdiction. Whether the complaint states a cause of action on which relief could be granted is a question of law and just as issues of fact it must be decided after and not before the court has assumed jurisdiction over the controversy. If the court does later exercise its jurisdiction to determine that the allegations in the complaint do not state a ground for relief, then dismissal of the case would be on the merits, not for want of jurisdiction. * * * The previously carved out exceptions are that a suit may sometimes be dismissed for want of jurisdiction where the alleged claim under the Constitution or federal statutes clearly appears to be immaterial and made solely for the purpose of obtaining jurisdiction or where such a claim is wholly insubstantial and frivolous. * * *

"* * * [T]he complaint does in fact raise serious questions, both of law and fact, which the district court can decide only after it has assumed jurisdiction over the controversy. The issue of law is whether federal courts can grant money recovery for damages said to have been suffered as a result of federal officers violating the Fourth and Fifth Amendments. That question has never been specifically decided by this Court. * * * Whether the petitioners are entitled to recover depends upon an interpretation of [the predecessor to § 1331], and on a determination of the scope of the Fourth and Fifth Amendments' protection from unreasonable searches and deprivations of liberty without due process of law. Thus, the right of the petitioners to recover under their complaint will be sustained if the Constitution and laws of the United States are given one construction and will be defeated if they are given another. For this reason the district court has jurisdiction."[12]

---

12. Upon the remand in Bell v. Hood the district court took jurisdiction, and "being of the opinion that neither the Constitution nor the statutes of the United States give rise to any cause of action in favor of plaintiffs upon the facts alleged," granted the defendants' motion to dismiss the complaint for failure to state a claim upon which relief could be granted. Bell v. Hood, 71 F.Supp.

(c) Wheeldin v. Wheeler, 373 U.S. 647 (1963), was a federal court action alleging that defendant—an investigator for the House Un–American Activities Committee—had, without lawful authority, subpoenaed plaintiff to appear before the Committee for the sole purpose of subjecting him to public stigma as a disloyal person. The question was "whether a federal claim for damages is stated." The Supreme Court, in an opinion by Justice Douglas, held that, under Bell v. Hood, the federal court had jurisdiction to determine that question, but concluded that, on the merits, "no federal cause of action can be made out (p. 649)."

Justice Brennan's dissent suggested, *inter alia,* that the complaint might be upheld as a federal right of action implied from the federal statutes specifying the authority to issue subpoenas, or as a federal common law action. "[W]here, as here, it is alleged that a federal officer acting under color of federal law has so abused his federal powers as to cause unjustifiable injury to a private person, I see no warrant for concluding that state law must be looked to as the sole basis for liability" (p. 664). Justice Brennan added: "[O]nce the federal common-law cause of action is recognized, the much-mooted problem remains whether such a cause arises under federal law within the meaning of 28 U.S.C. § 1331(a). This Court has never decided that question" (pp. 664–65).

(d) The question that Justice Brennan in Wheeldin described as "much mooted"—whether a case arising under federal common law falls within the scope of § 1331—was in fact controversial principally in the special context of admiralty litigation, where much debate surrounded the issue whether, in the absence of diversity, certain admiralty cases could be brought on the "law" side of the federal court under § 1331. (As to this, see Romero v. International Terminal Operating Co., 358 U.S. 354 (1959), discussed in the *Note on the Admiralty Jurisdiction,* p. 974, *infra;* see also Kurland, *The Romero Case and Some Problems of Federal Jurisdiction,* 73 Harv.L.Rev. 817, 831–33 (1960)). Apart from admiralty, no plausible reason was ever advanced why—once a claim was determined to be a creation of federal, rather than state, law—the appropriateness and need for a federal forum should turn on whether the case arose under a federal statute or under federal common law.

The Court finally came to that unsurprising conclusion in Illinois v. Milwaukee, 406 U.S. 91 (1972). See p. 803, *supra.* The Court denied a motion for leave to file an original action in the Supreme Court seeking to enjoin pollution of Lake Michigan, on the ground that a district court would be a more appropriate forum. As a predicate for its action, the Court determined that pollution of interstate and navigable waters is governed by federal common law (as well as by statutes), that cases asserting such common law rights are actions arising under the "laws" of the United States within § 1331, and that the district courts thus had jurisdiction of such cases. See also National Farmers Union Ins. Cos. v. Crow Tribe of Indians, 471 U.S. 845 (1985)(holding that § 1331 supports jurisdiction over an action in federal court to enjoin the

813, 820–21 (S.D.Cal.1947). The case went no further.

Did the eventual judgment have any different effect from the judgment that the Supreme Court reversed? (As to the problem of supplemental jurisdiction over a joined claim under state law, see Section 5, *infra.*)

Twenty-five years after Bell v. Hood, the Supreme Court held that the Fourth Amendment gives rise to an action for damages against federal officers who violate it. Bivens v. Six Unknown Named Agents of the Federal Bureau of Narcotics, 403 U.S. 388 (1971), p. 858, *supra.*

execution of a default judgment rendered by an Indian tribal court, where the plaintiff alleged that federal law divested the tribal court of jurisdiction).

(5) *The Substantiality of the Claimed Federal Cause of Action.*

(a) The Court in Bell v. Hood cited as "exceptions" to the general rule applied in the case before it that suit may "sometimes" be dismissed on jurisdictional grounds when the alleged federal claim "clearly appears to be immaterial and made solely for the purpose of obtaining jurisdiction or where such a claim is wholly insubstantial and frivolous." Justice Black indicated some unhappiness with these exceptions. Are they sound? Or should these questions go only to the issue whether, on the merits, plaintiff has stated a claim for which relief can be granted?

In a number of cases the Court has exploited the Bell v. Hood distinction between rulings on "jurisdiction" and rulings on the "merits" to limit the reach of the principle that, even if neither party objects to federal jurisdiction, the courts must on their own dismiss a case if there is no subject matter jurisdiction. (See Chap. XIV, Sec. 1.) Thus, in Mt. Healthy City Sch. Dist. Bd. of Educ. v. Doyle, 429 U.S. 274, 277–79 (1977), the Court first held that the federal claim asserted in the complaint was not frivolous, and that under Bell the federal court therefore had subject matter jurisdiction. The Court then turned around and held that because of the defendant's failure to challenge the asserted right of action on the merits, it could proceed on the assumption that there was such a federal right of action, without in fact deciding that difficult point. See also, *e.g.*, Duke Power Co. v. Carolina Environmental Study Group, Inc., 438 U.S. 59, 69–72 (1978).

Consider also Jackson Transit Authority v. Local Div.1285, 457 U.S. 15 (1982). Section 13(c) of the Urban Mass Transportation Act of 1964, 49 U.S.C. § 1609(c), provides that, as a condition of federal financial aid for the acquisition of private transit companies, state and local governments must make "arrangements" to preserve existing collective bargaining rights. The city of Jackson bought a private bus company with federal aid, and, under § 13(c), entered into a contract with the union guaranteeing existing collective bargaining rights. It later repudiated that contract. The union brought an action for damages and an injunction in a federal court "under" § 13(c). The court of appeals held that there was § 1331 jurisdiction under Bell v. Hood, and that § 13(c) implicitly provides a federal right of action. The Supreme Court reversed. Agreeing that, "strictly speaking", the district court had jurisdiction under Bell "for the purpose of determining whether the union stated a cause of action" (p. 21 n. 6), the Court nevertheless concluded that § 13(c) was not intended to generate a federal right to enforce such contracts in a federal court.

Doesn't this case show that, notwithstanding Bell, there is often a complete functional congruence between the question whether the plaintiff states a valid claim of federal right and the question whether, for jurisdictional purposes, the case "arises under" federal law?

(b) Whatever the weaknesses of the exceptions described in Bell v. Hood,[13] those exceptions (as indicated above) are well established. Although the

---

13. In a dissent from a denial of certiorari, Justice Rehnquist called for reexamination of the "cryptic" decision in Bell v. Hood, which he said requires a "three tiered analysis" of motions to dismiss and contradicts Rule 12 of the Federal Rules of Civil Procedure. Yazoo County Industrial Development Corp. v. Suthoff, 454 U.S. 1157 (1982).

exceptions did not defeat district court jurisdiction in the Wheeldin case itself, would there be original federal question jurisdiction over another case on identical facts brought after the Supreme Court decision in Wheeldin?

Franchise Tax Board of California v. Construction Laborers Vacation Trust

463 U.S. 1, 103 S.Ct. 2841, 77 L.Ed.2d 420 (1983).
Appeal from the United States Court of Appeals for the Ninth Circuit.

■ JUSTICE BRENNAN delivered the opinion of the Court.

The principal question in dispute between the parties is whether the Employee Retirement Income Security Act of 1974 (ERISA), 29 U.S.C. § 1001 *et seq.*, permits state tax authorities to collect unpaid state income taxes by levying on funds held in trust for the taxpayers under an ERISA-covered vacation benefit plan.   The issue is an important one, which affects thousands of federally regulated trusts and all nonfederal tax collection systems, and it must eventually receive a definitive, uniform resolution.   Nevertheless, for reasons involving perhaps more history than logic, we hold that the lower federal courts had no jurisdiction to decide the question in the case before us, and we vacate the judgment and remand the case with instructions to remand it to the state court from which it was removed.

I

None of the relevant facts is in dispute.   Appellee Construction Laborers Vacation Trust for Southern California (CLVT) is a trust established by an agreement between four associations of employers active in the construction industry in southern California and the Southern California District Council of Laborers, an arm of the District Council and affiliated locals of the Laborers' International Union of North America.   The purpose of the agreement and trust was to establish a mechanism for administering the provisions of a collective-bargaining agreement that grants construction workers a yearly paid vacation.   The trust agreement expressly proscribes any assignment, pledge, or encumbrance of funds held in trust by CLVT.   The Plan that CLVT administers is unquestionably an "employee welfare benefit plan" within the meaning of § 3 of ERISA, 29 U.S.C. § 1002(1), and CLVT and its individual trustees are thereby subject to extensive regulation under Titles I and III of ERISA.

Appellant Franchise Tax Board is a California agency charged with enforcement of that State's personal income tax law.   California law authorizes appellant to require any person in possession of "credits or other personal property or other things of value, belonging to a taxpayer" "to withhold * * * the amount of any tax, interest, or penalties due from the taxpayer * * * and to transmit the amount withheld to the Franchise Tax Board."   Cal.Rev. & Tax.Code Ann. § 18817 (West Supp.1983).   Any person who, upon notice by

----

For further criticism of the "substantiality" requirement as a jurisdictional rule, on grounds of both history and policy, see Matasar, *Rediscovering "One Constitutional Case": Procedural Rules and the Rejection of the Gibbs Test for Supplemental Jurisdiction,* 71 Calif.L.Rev. 1401, 1417–46 (1983).   Matasar argues that, even if the requirement is accepted as a matter of construction of the jurisdictional statutes, it should not be seen as going to the constitutional power of Congress or the federal courts.

the Franchise Tax Board, fails to comply with its request to withhold and to transmit funds becomes personally liable for the amounts identified in the notice. § 18818.

In June 1980, the Franchise Tax Board filed a complaint in state court against CLVT and its trustees. Under the heading "First Cause of Action," appellant alleged that CLVT had failed to comply with three levies issued under § 18817, concluding with the allegation that it had been "damaged in a sum * * * not to exceed $380.56 plus interest from June 1, 1980." Under the heading "Second Cause of Action," appellant incorporated its previous allegations and added:

> "There was at the time of the levies alleged above and continues to be an actual controversy between the parties concerning their respective legal rights and duties. The Board [appellant] contends that defendants [CLVT] are obligated and required by law to pay over to the Board all amounts held * * * in favor of the Board's delinquent taxpayers. On the other hand, defendants contend that section 514 of ERISA preempts state law and that the trustees lack the power to honor the levies made upon them by the State of California.

> "[D]efendants will continue to refuse to honor the Board's levies in this regard. Accordingly, a declaration by this court of the parties' respective rights is required to fully and finally resolve this controversy."

In a prayer for relief, appellant requested damages for defendants' failure to honor the levies and a declaration that defendants are "legally obligated to honor all future levies by the Board."

CLVT removed the case to the United States District Court for the Central District of California, and the court denied the Franchise Tax Board's motion for remand to the state court. On the merits, the District Court ruled that ERISA did not pre-empt the State's power to levy on funds held in trust by CLVT. CLVT appealed, and the Court of Appeals reversed. 679 F.2d 1307 (C.A.9 1982). * * * [A]n appeal was taken to this Court. We postponed consideration of our jurisdiction pending argument on the merits. We now hold that this case was not within the removal jurisdiction conferred by 28 U.S.C. § 1441, and therefore we do not reach the merits of the preemption question.

II

The jurisdictional structure at issue in this case has remained basically unchanged for the past century. * * * For this case—as for many cases where there is no diversity of citizenship between the parties—the propriety of removal turns on whether the case falls within the original "federal question" jurisdiction of the United States district courts * * *.

The most familiar definition of the statutory "arising under" limitation is Justice Holmes' statement, "A suit arises under the law that creates the cause of action." American Well Works Co. v. Layne & Bowler Co., 241 U.S. 257, 260 (1916). However, it is well settled that Justice Holmes' test is more useful for describing the vast majority of cases that come within the district courts' original jurisdiction than it is for describing which cases are beyond district court jurisdiction. We have often held that a case "arose under" federal law where the vindication of a right under state law necessarily turned on some construction of federal law, see, *e.g.,* Smith v. Kansas City Title & Trust Co., 255 U.S. 180 (1921); Hopkins v. Walker, 244 U.S. 486 (1917), and even the most ardent proponent of the Holmes test has admitted that it has been rejected as an exclusionary principle, see Flournoy v. Wiener, 321 U.S. 253, 270–272 (1944)(Frankfurter, J., dissenting). See also T.B. Harms Co. v. Eliscu, 339 F.2d 823, 827 (C.A.2 1964)(Friendly, J.). Leading commentators have suggested that for purposes of § 1331 an action "arises under" federal law "if in order for the plaintiff to secure the relief sought he will be obliged to establish both the correctness and the applicability to his case of a proposition of federal law." P. Bator, P. Mishkin, D. Shapiro, & H. Wechsler, Hart and Wechsler's The Federal Courts and the Federal System 889 (2d ed. 1973)(hereinafter Hart & Wechsler); cf. T.B. Harms Co., supra, at 827 ("a case may 'arise under' a law of the United States if the complaint discloses a need for determining the meaning or application of such a law").

One powerful doctrine has emerged, however—the "well-pleaded complaint" rule—which as a practical matter severely limits the number of cases in which state law "creates the cause of action" that may be initiated in or removed to federal district court, thereby avoiding more-or-less automatically a number of potentially serious federal-state conflicts.

* * * For better or worse, under the present statutory scheme as it has existed since 1887, a defendant may not remove a case to federal court unless the *plaintiff's* complaint establishes that the case "arises under" federal law.[9] * * *

For many cases in which federal law becomes relevant only insofar as it sets bounds for the operation of state authority, the well-pleaded complaint rule makes sense as a quick rule of thumb. * * *

The rule, however, may produce awkward results, especially in cases in which neither the obligation created by state law nor the defendant's factual failure to comply are in dispute, and both parties admit that the only question for decision is raised by a federal pre-emption defense. Nevertheless, it has been correctly understood to apply in such situations. * * *[12]

III

Simply to state these principles is not to apply them to the case at hand. Appellant's complaint sets forth two "causes of action," one of which expressly refers to ERISA; if either comes within the original jurisdiction of the federal courts, removal was proper as to the whole case. See 28 U.S.C. § 1441(c). Although appellant's complaint does not specifically assert any particular

---

9. * * *

It is possible to conceive of a rational jurisdictional system in which the answer as well as the complaint would be consulted before a determination was made whether the case "arose under" federal law, or in which original and removal jurisdiction were not coextensive. Indeed, until the 1887 amendments to the 1875 Act, the well-pleaded complaint rule was not applied in full force to cases removed from state court; the defendant's petition for removal could furnish the necessary guarantee that the case necessarily presented a substantial question of federal law. See Railroad Co. v. Mississippi, 102 U.S. 135, 140 (1880); Gold–Washing & Water Co. v. Keyes, 96 U.S. 199, 203–204 (1878). Commentators have repeatedly proposed that some mechanism be established to permit removal of cases in which a federal defense may be dispositive. But those proposals have not been adopted.

12. Note, however, that a claim of federal pre-emption does not always arise as a defense to a coercive action. See note 20, *infra.* And, of course, the absence of original jurisdiction does not mean that there is no federal forum in which a pre-emption defense may be heard. If the state courts reject a claim of federal pre-emption, that decision may ultimately be reviewed on appeal by this Court.

statutory entitlement for the relief it seeks, the language of the complaint suggests (and the parties do not dispute) that appellant's "first cause of action" states a claim under Cal.Rev. & Tax.Code Ann. § 18818 (West Supp.1983), and its "second cause of action" states a claim under California's Declaratory Judgment Act, Cal.Civ.Proc.Code Ann. § 1060 (West 1980). As an initial proposition, then, the "law that creates the cause of action" is state law, and original federal jurisdiction is unavailable unless it appears that some substantial, disputed question of federal law is a necessary element of one of the well-pleaded state claims, or that one or the other claim is "really" one of federal law.

A

Even though state law creates appellant's causes of action, its case might still "arise under" the laws of the United States if a well-pleaded complaint established that its right to relief under state law requires resolution of a substantial question of federal law in dispute between the parties. For appellant's first cause of action—to enforce its levy, under § 18818—a straightforward application of the well-pleaded complaint rule precludes original federal-court jurisdiction. California law establishes a set of conditions, without reference to federal law, under which a tax levy may be enforced; federal law becomes relevant only by way of a defense to an obligation created entirely by state law, and then only if appellant has made out a valid claim for relief under state law. The well-pleaded complaint rule was framed to deal with precisely such a situation. * * *

Appellant's declaratory judgment action poses a more difficult problem. Whereas the question of federal pre-emption is relevant to appellant's first cause of action only as a potential defense, it is a necessary element of the declaratory judgment claim. Under Cal.Civ.Proc.Code Ann. § 1060 (West 1980), a party with an interest in property may bring an action for a declaration of another party's legal rights and duties with respect to that property upon showing that there is an "actual controversy relating to the legal rights and duties" of the parties. The only questions in dispute between the parties in this case concern the rights and duties of CLVT and its trustees under ERISA. Not only does appellant's request for a declaratory judgment under California law clearly encompass questions governed by ERISA, but appellant's complaint identifies no other questions as a subject of controversy between the parties. Such questions must be raised in a well-pleaded complaint for a declaratory judgment. Therefore, it is clear on the face of its well-pleaded complaint that appellant may not obtain the relief it seeks in its second cause of action ("[t]hat the court declare defendants legally obligated to honor all future levies by the Board upon [CLVT],") without a construction of ERISA and/or an adjudication of its pre-emptive effect and constitutionality—all questions of federal law.

Appellant argues that original federal-court jurisdiction over such a complaint is foreclosed by our decision in Skelly Oil Co. v. Phillips Petroleum Co., 339 U.S. 667 (1950). As we shall see, however, Skelly Oil is not directly controlling.

In Skelly Oil, Skelly Oil and Phillips had a contract, for the sale of natural gas, that entitled the seller—Skelly Oil—to terminate the contract at any time after December 1, 1946, if the Federal Power Commission had not yet issued a certificate of convenience and necessity to a third party, a pipeline company to whom Phillips intended to resell the gas purchased from Skelly Oil. Their dispute began when the Federal Power Commission informed the pipeline company on November 30 that it would issue a conditional certificate, but did not make its order public until December 2. By this time Skelly Oil had notified Phillips of its decision to terminate their contract. Phillips brought an action in United States District Court under the federal Declaratory Judgment Act, 28 U.S.C. § 2201, seeking a declaration that the contract was still in effect.

* * * [W]e held that Phillips' claim was not within the federal-question jurisdiction conferred by § 1331. We reasoned:

> " '[T]he operation of the Declaratory Judgment Act is procedural only.' Aetna Life Ins. Co. v. Haworth, 300 U.S. 227, 240. Congress enlarged the range of remedies available in the federal courts but did not extend their jurisdiction. * * * But the requirements of jurisdiction—the limited subject matters which alone Congress had authorized the District Courts to adjudicate—were not impliedly repealed or modified." 339 U.S., at 671–672.

We then observed that, under the well-pleaded complaint rule, an action by Phillips to enforce its contract would not present a federal question. Skelly Oil has come to stand for the proposition that "if, but for the availability of the declaratory judgment procedure, the federal claim would arise only as a defense to a state created action, jurisdiction is lacking." 10A C. Wright, A. Miller, & M. Kane, Federal Practice and Procedure § 2767, pp. 744–745 (2d ed. 1983). *Cf.* Public Service Comm'n of Utah v. Wycoff Co., 344 U.S. 237, 248 (1952)(dictum).[14]

1. As an initial matter, we must decide whether the doctrine of Skelly Oil limits original federal-court jurisdiction under § 1331—and by extension removal jurisdiction under § 1441—when a question of federal law appears on the face of a well-pleaded complaint for a state-law declaratory judgment. Apparently, it is a question of first impression. * * *

* * * [W]hile Skelly Oil itself is limited to the federal Declaratory Judgment Act, fidelity to its spirit leads us to extend it to state declaratory judgment actions as well. If federal district courts could take jurisdiction,

---

14. In Wycoff Co., a company that transported films between various points within the State of Utah sought a declaratory judgment that a state regulatory commission had no power to forbid it to transport over routes authorized by the Interstate Commerce Commission. However, "[i]t offered no evidence whatever of any past, pending or threatened action by the Utah Commission." 344 U.S., at 240. We held that there was no jurisdiction, essentially because the dispute had "not matured to a point where we can see what, if any, concrete controversy will develop." *Id.,* at 245. We also added:

"Where the complaint in an action for declaratory judgment seeks in essence to assert a defense to an impending or threatened state court action, it is the character of the threatened action, and not of the defense, which will determine whether there is federal-question jurisdiction in the District Court. If the cause of action, which the declaratory defendant threatens to assert, does not itself involve a claim under federal law, it is doubtful if a federal court may entertain an action for a declaratory judgment establishing a defense to that claim. This is dubious even though the declaratory complaint sets forth a claim of federal right, if that right is in reality in the nature of a defense to a threatened cause of action. Federal courts will not seize litigations from state courts merely because one, normally a defendant, goes to federal court to begin his federal-law defense before the state court begins the case under state law." *Id.,* at 248.

either originally or by removal, of state declaratory judgment claims raising questions of federal law, without regard to the doctrine of Skelly Oil, the federal Declaratory Judgment Act—with the limitations Skelly Oil read into it—would become a dead letter. For any case in which a state declaratory judgment action was available, litigants could get into federal court for a declaratory judgment despite our interpretation of § 2201, simply by pleading an adequate state claim for a declaration of federal law. Having interpreted the Declaratory Judgment Act of 1934 to include certain limitations on the jurisdiction of federal district courts to entertain declaratory judgment suits, we should be extremely hesitant to interpret the Judiciary Act of 1875 and its 1887 amendments in a way that renders the limitations in the later statute nugatory. Therefore, we hold that under the jurisdictional statutes as they now stand[17] federal courts do not have original jurisdiction, nor do they acquire jurisdiction on removal, when a federal question is presented by a complaint for a state declaratory judgment, but Skelly Oil would bar jurisdiction if the plaintiff had sought a federal declaratory judgment.

2. The question, then, is whether a federal district court could take jurisdiction of appellant's declaratory judgment claim had it been brought under 28 U.S.C. § 2201. The application of Skelly Oil to such a suit is somewhat unclear. Federal courts have regularly taken original jurisdiction over declaratory judgment suits in which, if the declaratory judgment defendant brought a coercive action to enforce its rights, that suit would necessarily present a federal question.[19] Section 502(a)(3) of ERISA specifically grants trustees of ERISA–covered plans like CLVT a cause of action for injunctive relief when their rights and duties under ERISA are at issue, and that action is exclusively governed by federal law.[20] If CLVT could have sought an injunction under ERISA against application to it of state regulations that require acts

17. It is not beyond the power of Congress to confer a right to a declaratory judgment in a case or controversy arising under federal law—within the meaning of the Constitution or of § 1331—without regard to Skelly Oil's particular application of the well-pleaded complaint rule. The 1969 ALI report strongly criticized the Skelly Oil doctrine. * * * ALI Study § 1311, at 170–171. Nevertheless, Congress has declined to make such a change. At this point, any adjustment in the system that has evolved under the Skelly Oil rule must come from Congress.

19. For instance, federal courts have consistently adjudicated suits by alleged patent infringers to declare a patent invalid, on the theory that an infringement suit by the declaratory judgment defendant would raise a federal question over which the federal courts have exclusive jurisdiction. See E. Edelmann & Co. v. Triple–A Specialty Co., 88 F.2d 852 (C.A.7 1937); Hart & Wechsler 896–897. * * * Taking jurisdiction over this type of suit is consistent with the dictum in Public Service Comm'n of Utah v. Wycoff Co., 344 U.S. 237, 248 (1952), see n. 14, *supra*, in

which we stated only that a declaratory judgment plaintiff could not get original federal jurisdiction if the anticipated lawsuit by the declaratory judgment defendant would *not* "arise under" federal law. It is also consistent with the nature of the declaratory remedy itself, which was designed to permit adjudication of either party's claims of right. See E. Borchard, Declaratory Judgments 15–18, 23–25 (1934).

20. * * *

Even if ERISA did not expressly provide jurisdiction, CLVT might have been able to obtain federal jurisdiction under the doctrine applied in some cases that a person subject to a scheme of federal regulation may sue in federal court to enjoin application to him of conflicting state regulations, and a declaratory judgment action by the same person does not necessarily run afoul of the Skelly Oil doctrine. See, *e.g.*, Lake Carriers' Assn. v. MacMullan, 406 U.S. 498, 506–508 (1972); Rath Packing Co. v. Becker, 530 F.2d 1295, 1303–1306 (C.A.9 1975), aff'd *sub nom.* Jones v. Rath Packing Co., 430 U.S. 519 (1977).

inconsistent with ERISA,[21] does a declaratory judgment suit by the State "arise under" federal law?

We think not. We have always interpreted what Skelly Oil called "the current of jurisdictional legislation since the Act of March 3, 1875," 339 U.S., at 673, with an eye to practicality and necessity. "What is needed is something of that common-sense accommodation of judgment to kaleidoscopic situations which characterizes the law in its treatment of problems of causation * * * a selective process which picks the substantial causes out of the web and lays the other ones aside." Gully v. First National Bank in Meridian, 299 U.S., at 117–118. There are good reasons why the federal courts should not entertain suits by the States to declare the validity of their regulations despite possibly conflicting federal law. States are not significantly prejudiced by an inability to come to federal court for a declaratory judgment in advance of a possible injunctive suit by a person subject to federal regulation. They have a variety of means by which they can enforce their own laws in their own courts, and they do not suffer if the pre-emption questions such enforcement may raise are tested there.[22] The express grant of federal jurisdiction in ERISA is limited to suits brought by certain parties, as to whom Congress presumably determined that a right to enter federal court was necessary to further the statute's purposes.[23] It did not go so far as to provide that any suit *against* such parties must also be brought in federal court when they themselves did not choose to sue. The situation presented by a State's suit for a declaration of the validity of state law is sufficiently removed from the spirit of necessity and careful limitation of district court jurisdiction that informed our statutory interpretation in Skelly Oil and Gully to convince us that, until Congress informs us otherwise, such a suit is not within the original jurisdiction of the United States district courts. Accordingly, the same suit brought originally in state court is not removable either.

B

CLVT also argues that appellant's "causes of action" are, in substance, federal claims. Although we have often repeated that "the party who brings a suit is master to decide what law he will rely upon," The Fair v. Kohler Die & Specialty Co., 228 U.S. 22, 25 (1913), it is an independent corollary of the well-pleaded complaint rule that a plaintiff may not defeat removal by omitting to

21. We express no opinion, however, whether a party in CLVT's position could sue under ERISA to enjoin or to declare invalid a state tax levy, despite the Tax Injunction Act, 28 U.S.C. § 1341.

22. Indeed, as appellant's strategy in this case shows, they may often be willing to go to great lengths to avoid federal-court resolution of a pre-emption question. Realistically, there is little prospect that States will flood the federal courts with declaratory judgment actions; most questions will arise, as in this case, because a State has sought a declaration in state court and the defendant has removed the case to federal court. Accordingly, it is perhaps appropriate to note that considerations of comity make us reluctant to snatch cases which a State has brought from

the courts of that State, unless some clear rule demands it.

23. *Cf.* nn. 19 and 20, *supra*. Alleged patent infringers, for example, have a clear interest in swift resolution of the federal issue of patent validity—they are liable for damages if it turns out they are infringing a patent, and they frequently have a delicate network of contractual arrangements with third parties that is dependent on their right to sell or license a product. Parties subject to conflicting state and federal regulatory schemes also have a clear interest in sorting out the scope of each government's authority, especially where they face a threat of liability if the application of federal law is not quickly made clear.

plead necessary federal questions in a complaint, see Avco Corp. v. Aero Lodge No. 735, Int'l Assn. of Machinists, 376 F.2d 337, 339–340 (C.A.6 1967), aff'd, 390 U.S. 557 (1968).

CLVT's best argument stems from our decision in Avco Corp. v. Aero Lodge No. 735. In that case, the petitioner filed suit in state court alleging simply that it had a valid contract with the respondent, a union, under which the respondent had agreed to submit all grievances to binding arbitration and not to cause or sanction any "work stoppages, strikes, or slowdowns." The petitioner further alleged that the respondent and its officials had violated the agreement by participating in and sanctioning work stoppages, and it sought temporary and permanent injunctions against further breaches. It was clear that, had petitioner invoked it, there would have been a federal cause of action under § 301 of the Labor Management Relations Act, 1947 (LMRA), 29 U.S.C. § 185, see Textile Workers v. Lincoln Mills, 353 U.S. 448 (1957), and that, even in state court, any action to enforce an agreement within the scope of § 301 would be controlled by federal law, see Teamsters v. Lucas Flour Co., 369 U.S. 95, 103–104 (1962). It was also clear, however, under the law in effect at the time, that independent limits on federal jurisdiction made it impossible for a federal court to grant the injunctive relief petitioner sought. See Sinclair Refining Co. v. Atkinson, 370 U.S. 195 (1962)(later overruled in Boys Markets, Inc. v. Retail Clerks, 398 U.S. 235 (1970)).

The Court of Appeals held, and we affirmed, that the petitioner's action "arose under" § 301, and thus could be removed to federal court, although the petitioner had undoubtedly pleaded an adequate claim for relief under the state law of contracts and had sought a remedy available *only* under state law. The necessary ground of decision was that the pre-emptive force of § 301 is so powerful as to displace entirely any state cause of action "for violation of contracts between an employer and a labor organization." Any such suit is purely a creature of federal law, notwithstanding the fact that state law would provide a cause of action in the absence of § 301. Avco stands for the proposition that if a federal cause of action completely pre-empts a state cause of action any complaint that comes within the scope of the federal cause of action necessarily "arises under" federal law.

CLVT argues by analogy that ERISA, like § 301, was meant to create a body of federal common law, and that "any state court action which would require the interpretation or application of ERISA to a plan document 'arises under' the laws of the United States." Brief for Appellees 20–21. ERISA contains provisions creating a series of express causes of action in favor of participants, beneficiaries, and fiduciaries of ERISA–covered plans, as well as the Secretary of Labor. § 502(a), 29 U.S.C. § 1132(a). It may be that, as with § 301 as interpreted in Avco, any state action coming within the scope of § 502(a) of ERISA would be removable to federal district court, even if an otherwise adequate state cause of action were pleaded without reference to federal law. It does not follow, however, that either of appellant's claims in this case comes within the scope of one of ERISA's causes of action.

The phrasing of § 502(a) is instructive. Section 502(a) specifies which persons—participants, beneficiaries, fiduciaries, or the Secretary of Labor—may bring actions for particular kinds of relief. It neither creates nor expressly denies any cause of action in favor of state governments, to enforce tax levies or for any other purpose. It does not purport to reach every question relating to plans covered by ERISA.[28] Furthermore, § 514(b)(2)(A) of ERISA, 29 U.S.C. § 1144(b)(2)(A), makes clear that Congress did not intend to pre-empt entirely every state cause of action relating to such plans. With important, but express limitations, it states that "nothing in this subchapter shall be construed to exempt or relieve any person from any law of any State which regulates insurance, banking, or securities."

Against this background, it is clear that a suit by state tax authorities under a statute like § 18818 does not "arise under" ERISA. Unlike the contract rights at issue in Avco, the State's right to enforce its tax levies is not of central concern to the federal statute. For that reason, * * * on the face of a well-pleaded complaint there are many reasons completely unrelated to the provisions and purposes of ERISA why the State may or may not be entitled to the relief it seeks. Furthermore, ERISA does not provide an alternative cause of action in favor of the State to enforce its rights, while § 301 expressly supplied the plaintiff in Avco with a federal cause of action to replace its pre-empted state contract claim. Therefore, even though the Court of Appeals may well be correct that ERISA precludes enforcement of the State's levy in the circumstances of this case, an action to enforce the levy is not itself pre-empted by ERISA.

Once again, appellant's declaratory judgment cause of action presents a somewhat more difficult issue. The question on which a declaration is sought—that of the CLVT trustees' "power to honor the levies made upon them by the State of California,"—is undoubtedly a matter of concern under ERISA. It involves the meaning and enforceability of provisions in CLVT's trust agreement forbidding the trustees to assign or otherwise to alienate funds held in trust, and thus comes within the class of questions for which Congress intended that federal courts create federal common law. Under § 502(a)(3)(B) of ERISA, a participant, beneficiary, or fiduciary of a plan covered by ERISA may bring a declaratory judgment action in federal court to determine whether the plan's trustees may comply with a state levy on funds held in trust. Nevertheless, CLVT's argument that appellant's second cause of action arises under ERISA fails for the second reason given above. ERISA carefully enumerates the parties entitled to seek relief under § 502; it does not provide anyone other than participants, beneficiaries, or fiduciaries with an express cause of action for a declaratory judgment on the issues in this case. A suit for similar relief by some other party does not "arise under" that provision.

IV

* * * We hold that a suit by state tax authorities both to enforce its levies against funds held in trust pursuant to an ERISA–covered employee benefit plan, and to declare the validity of the levies notwithstanding ERISA, is neither a creature of ERISA itself nor a suit of which the federal courts will take jurisdiction because it turns on a question of federal law. Accordingly, we vacate the judgment of the Court of Appeals and remand so that this case may be remanded to the Superior Court of the State of California for the County of Los Angeles.

28. * * * [E]ven under § 301 we have never intimated that any action merely relating to a contract within the coverage of § 301 arises exclusively under that section. For instance, a state battery suit growing out of a violent strike would not arise under § 301 simply because the strike may have been a violation of an employer-union contract.

It is so ordered.

NOTE ON THE JURISDICTIONAL SIGNIFICANCE OF THE DECLARATORY JUDGMENT ACT

(1) *The Rule of the Skelly Oil Case and its Extension in Franchise Tax.*

(a) Note, *Developments in the Law: Declaratory Judgments—1941–1949,* 62 Harv.L.Rev. 787, 802–03 (1949), suggests that there are three possible views of the jurisdictional effect of the Declaratory Judgment Act: (i) that jurisdiction exists if the federal question is properly set forth in the complaint, even though the question would have arisen only as a defense in a coercive action between the same parties; (ii) that jurisdiction exists only if it would exist in a coercive action by the plaintiff against the defendant; and (iii) that jurisdiction exists if it would exist in a coercive action by either party against the other. The Harvard Note urged adoption of the third view.

The legislative history of the Declaratory Judgment Act strongly suggests that the first alternative was the one most consistent with legislative purpose. See the informative discussions in Doernberg & Mushlin, *The Trojan Horse: How the Declaratory Judgment Act Created a Cause of Action and Expanded Federal Jurisdiction While the Supreme Court Wasn't Looking,* 36 UCLA L.Rev. 529 (1989); Mishkin, *The Federal "Question" in the District Courts,* 53 Colum.L.Rev. 157, 178 n. 99 (1953). Congress was concerned with issues of justiciability (explored in Chap. II, pp. 96–98, *supra*), but the drafters and advocates of the legislation clearly saw it as an innovation designed to provide a new right of action to one who was living under a sword of Damocles because an adversary could bring a traditional coercive suit but refused to do so. Thus they recognized that parties who previously would not have had access to any forum might now be able to seek relief in a federal court on the basis of this new cause of action.

Despite this history, the Skelly Oil case—discussed and quoted in Franchise Tax—cited the Harvard Note with apparent approval and rejected the first alternative. But Skelly's language was less than clear on the choice between the second and third.

Where does Franchise Tax Board leave this question? The Court's opinion says that "federal courts" have "regularly" assumed jurisdiction over declaratory judgment suits where the declaratory *defendant* could have brought a coercive federal action against the declaratory plaintiff; and footnote 19 seems to approve the large body of decisions holding that an alleged patent infringer may bring an action for a declaration of non-infringement or of the invalidity of the patent in a federal district court.[1] Yet in Franchise Tax itself, didn't the Court assume that the declaratory defendant in the state court action could have brought a federal court suit (under ERISA or the doctrine discussed in footnote 20 of the opinion) for declaratory *and* injunctive relief? Should it have

---

1. The leading case holding that such an action "arises under" the patent laws, cited in Franchise Tax Board n. 19, is the Edelmann case in the Seventh Circuit, 88 F.2d 852 (1937), which has been widely followed. The Supreme Court has passed on the merits of such actions for a declaratory judgment without raising any question of jurisdiction. See, *e.g.,* Calmar, Inc. v. Cook Chem. Co., decided *sub nom.* Graham v. John Deere Co., 383 U.S. 1 (1966).

mattered in determining removability that the plaintiff state agency was not prejudiced by being in a state court?

(b) In the Skelly case, Chief Justice Vinson expressed "real doubts whether there is a federal question here at all" (p. 679). Were these doubts well founded? Did the fact that federal law was "incorporated" into the case by private contract differentiate the case from Standard Oil v. Johnson, p. 549, *supra,* and Smith v. Kansas City Title & Trust, p. 928, *supra?*

(2) *Federal Complaints Asserting that State Laws Are Preempted.*

(a) Shaw v. Delta Air Lines, Inc., 463 U.S. 85 (1983), decided on the same day as Franchise Tax Board, was an action by employees and employers for an injunction and declaratory judgment that certain provisions of New York's Human Rights Law and Disability Benefits Law were preempted by ERISA (the statute also at issue in Franchise Tax Board). The Court decided the case on the merits. The opinion states (p. 96 n. 14) that Franchise Tax Board "does not call into question the lower courts' jurisdiction to decide these cases. Franchise Tax Board was an action seeking a declaration that state laws were *not* preempted by ERISA. Here, in contrast, companies subject to ERISA regulation seek injunctions against enforcement of state laws they claim *are* pre-empted by ERISA, as well as declarations that those laws are pre-empted.

"It is beyond dispute that federal courts have jurisdiction over suits to enjoin state officials from interfering with federal rights. See Ex parte Young, 209 U.S. 123, 160–162 (1908). A plaintiff who seeks injunctive relief from state regulation, on the ground that such regulation is pre-empted by a federal statute which, by virtue of the Supremacy Clause of the Constitution, must prevail, thus presents a federal question which the federal courts have jurisdiction under 28 U.S.C. § 1331 to resolve. This Court, of course, frequently has resolved preemption disputes in a similar jurisdictional posture * * *."[2]

By indicating that ordinarily a person claiming immunity from state regulation may bring a federal court action under § 1331 seeking injunctive relief, rather than being relegated to raising a federal defense to a state law enforcement action, Shaw is obviously in tension with the Wycoff decision, discussed at n. 19 of the Franchise Tax decision. But apart from its consistency with precedent, isn't Shaw's rationale persuasive?

For criticism of the result and rationale in the Shaw case, see Monaghan, *Federal Statutory Review Under Section 1983 and the APA,* 91 Colum.L.Rev. 233, 238–41 (1991). Monaghan argues that "Shaw seems wrong, if read to permit any federal immunity holder automatic access to federal courts for declaratory and injunctive relief" (pp. 239–40), since such plaintiffs could not point to any federal law giving them a right to sue but only to a federal immunity from state regulation.[3] If this objection is sound, does the fault perhaps lie with the interpretation of the Declaratory Judgment Act as not furnishing a federal remedy when a plaintiff presents a justiciable controversy and founds his claim of right or immunity on federal law? Is the Court in

---

2. Shaw involved a suit seeking injunctive as well as declaratory relief. But in dictum in Lawrence County v. Lead–Deadwood School Dist. No. 40–1, 469 U.S. 256, 259 n. 6 (1985), the Court cited Shaw as upholding the existence of jurisdiction over a suit seeking a declaratory judgment that a state statute was preempted by federal law. Accord, Schneidewind v. ANR Pipeline Co., 485 U.S. 293 (1988).

3. *Cf.* Southland Corp. v. Keating, 465 U.S. 1 (1984), discussed at p. 912, note 9, *supra.*

Shaw perhaps suggesting that whenever a claim of immunity is founded on the preemptive effect of federal law under the Supremacy Clause, there is an implied federal declaratory and injunctive remedy that does not depend on the existence or interpretation of the Declaratory Judgment Act? How does the result in Shaw differ from the holding of Ex parte Young that an injunction is available in federal court when the Constitution "preempts" state regulation?[4]

(b) Duke Power Co. v. Carolina Environmental Study Group, Inc., 438 U.S. 59 (1978), involved a declaratory judgment action against, *inter alia*, the Nuclear Regulatory Commission for a declaration of the invalidity of the Price Anderson Act, 42 U.S.C. § 2210, which limits the liability of nuclear plants for nuclear accidents. Reading the complaint as stating a claim against the Commission "directly under" the Due Process Clause of the Fifth Amendment, the Court upheld § 1331 jurisdiction. Justice Rehnquist, dissenting, argued that the complaint involved a claim of "taking" and was subject to the special jurisdiction statutes limiting district court jurisdiction in favor of the Court of Claims. He also argued that, under Mottley, there was no § 1331 jurisdiction over the action against co-defendant Duke Power Company—a point not addressed by the majority.

(3) *The Significance of Congressional "Purpose": Merrell Dow and Franchise Tax.* In Merrell Dow the Court concluded that what might otherwise be a general rule allowing § 1331 jurisdiction is trumped if, in a particular statutory context, the Court discerns a congressional purpose not to give access to the federal courts. Justice Brennan's dissent challenges the appropriateness of this approach. But isn't it the very same approach that he adopted in Franchise Tax?

SECTION 4.   FEDERAL QUESTION REMOVAL

NOTE ON THE GENERAL REMOVAL STATUTE AND THE PROBLEM OF FEDERAL DEFENSE REMOVAL

(1) *Statutory History.* As in the case of original jurisdiction, no general grant of removal jurisdiction in "arising under" cases was enacted until 1875: before then, Congress contented itself with a series of specific statutes (prompted by occasions of sharp conflict with state authority) allowing removal by federal officials and persons acting under them. (As to these statutes, see the immediately following Note.)

The Act of March 3, 1875, 18 Stat. 470, went to the opposite extreme: subject to a $500 jurisdictional amount requirement, virtually every case removable under Article III was made removable by either a plaintiff or a defendant.

The present statutory pattern for federal question removal was created by the Judiciary Act of March 3, 1887, 24 Stat. 552, corrected by the Act of August 13, 1888, 25 Stat. 433. The key element was (and is) to tie removal jurisdiction to original jurisdiction: removal was restricted to cases in which "the circuit

---

4. For discussion of the related topic of the removability of certain cases raising is-sues of federal preemption, see Sec. 4, pp. 949–51, *infra.*

courts of the United States are given original jurisdiction." (The statute also limited removal to defendants.) The present general removal statute, 28 U.S.C. § 1441(a), states the identical rule. On procedural and other aspects of removal under this statute, see further Chap. XIV, Sec. 3, *infra*. For a detailed discussion of the background of federal question removal, see Collins, *The Unhappy History of Federal Question Removal,* 71 Iowa L.Rev. 717 (1986).[1]

(2) *The Unavailability Under § 1441 of Removal on the Basis of a Federal Defense.*

As discussed in the following Note, several specific statutory provisions do allow removal on the basis of certain federal defenses, but no general authorization for such removal is contained in § 1441. The question whether removal on the basis of a federal defense should be more widely available, to the defendant or to both parties, is discussed in Paragraph (2)(b) of the Note (p. 911, *supra*), following the Mottley case,

(3) *The "Complete Preemption" Rationale for Removal.*

(a) A claim of federal preemption is usually a defense to a state-law coercive action, and thus typically does not furnish a basis for removal. See generally 14A Wright, Miller & Cooper, Federal Jurisdiction and Procedure § 3722, at 244–50 (1985); text at and notes 12 and 20 of Franchise Tax Board, p. 937, *supra*. But if the plaintiff's claim, albeit cast as a state-law claim, is itself "really" a federal claim, removal will be permitted on the ground that the plaintiff should not, by artful pleading, be allowed to negate the defendant's removal rights. The leading case for this proposition is Avco Corp. v. Aero Lodge No. 735, IAM, 390 U.S. 557 (1968) (discussed in Part III(B) of Franchise Tax Board), holding that a claim that defendant had violated a collective bargaining agreement, although labeled as a state contract claim, "necessarily" arose under § 301 of the Taft Hartley Act and was therefore removable by the defendant. In Caterpillar Inc. v. Williams, 482 U.S. 386 (1987), the Supreme Court described this doctrine as the "'complete preemption' doctrine," under which, "once an area of state law has been completely preempted, any claim purportedly based on that preempted state law is considered, from its inception, a federal claim, and therefore arises under federal law" (p. 2430). Caterpillar itself held the complete preemption doctrine inapplicable to a claim for breach of individual employment contracts, concluding that § 301 did not wholly absorb such claims; removal was consequently denied.

(b) In Franchise Tax Board, the Court rejected the application of the "complete preemption" theory to California's claims, but stated that "[i]t may be that, as with § 301 as interpreted in Avco, any state [court] action coming within the scope of § 502(a) of ERISA would be removable to federal district court, even if an otherwise adequate state cause of action were pleaded without reference to federal law" (p. 944, *supra*). The question thus prefigured in

---

1. An unresolved question under the new supplemental jurisdiction provision, 28 U.S.C. § 1367 (discussed in detail in Sec. 5, *infra*) is whether it applies to removed as well as to original actions. Despite some indications to the contrary in the text and the legislative history of § 1367, a forceful argument that the provision should apply to removed cases is made in Steinman, *Supple-* *mental Jurisdiction in § 1441 Removed Cases: An Unsurveyed Frontier of Congress' Handiwork,* 35 Ariz.L.Rev. 305, 308–10 (1993). (Steinman also argues that in federal question cases, and despite the language of § 1441(a), only the defendants on the federal question claims should be required to join in the request for removal. *Id.* at 314–16.)

Franchise Tax Board came before the Court in Metropolitan Life Ins. Co. v. Taylor, 481 U.S. 58 (1987), involving state law tort and contract claims brought in a state court by an employee complaining that his employer had illegally terminated disability benefits due under a plan regulated by ERISA. The defendants removed the case to federal court, and the Supreme Court upheld removal. Relying on Pilot Life Ins. Co. v. Dedeaux, 481 U.S. 41 (1987), decided on the same day as Taylor, the Court first concluded that the state law claims were preempted by ERISA's substantive preemption provision, 29 U.S.C. § 1144(a). Turning to the question whether the common-law claims were "not only preempted" but "also displaced by ERISA's civil enforcement provision, § 502(a)(1)(B)" (p. 60), the Court indicated that it "was reluctant to find that extraordinary preemptive power, such as has been found with respect to § 301 of the LMRA, that converts an ordinary state common law complaint into one stating a federal claim for purposes of the well-pleaded complaint rule." But the Court found strong indications in the legislative history of ERISA that Congress intended the preemptive sweep of the statute to replicate that of § 301, showing that Congress wished "to make § 502(a)(1)(B) suits brought by participants or beneficiaries federal questions for the purposes of federal court jurisdiction in like manner as § 301 of the LMRA" (p. 66).

(c) How do you distinguish cases like Avco and Taylor from Mottley? In Mottley, the federal defense was that Congress had completely superseded the plaintiffs' contract action by rendering the contract illegal. In Avco and Taylor, the defense was that Congress had completely superseded the plaintiffs' common law actions by creating an exclusive federal remedy.[2] Why should a state court have exclusive jurisdiction to adjudicate the first defense but not the second? Is the point that in the second situation, Congress intended not only to provide a shield but created an "exclusive" federal sword as well, thus signifying an incremental intention to give access to the federal courts?[3] Is this a sufficient distinction? Does it suggest that whenever Congress provides for federal jurisdiction over a new federal cause of action, the question whether state remedies can continue to coexist with the new federal cause of action may

---

2. One case that does not fit this pattern, and in which removal was upheld, is Federated Department Stores, Inc. v. Moitie, 452 U.S. 394, 397 n. 2 (1981). The decision involved primarily a problem of res judicata, and the removal issue received only passing attention in a footnote. The plaintiffs in the case had attempted to frame their state court complaint under state laws regulating competition (laws that plainly were not preempted), and yet the court of appeals stated that removal was proper because the true nature of the complaint was rooted in the federal antitrust laws. The Supreme Court, in a surprising departure from the traditional view that the plaintiff is the master of the complaint, said that it would not disturb the "factual finding" of the court below that plaintiffs had attempted by "artful pleading" to disguise the federal nature of their complaint.

3. In a cryptic footnote in the Caterpillar case (482 U.S. at 392 n. 4), the Supreme Court rejected the attempt of the court below to distinguish Avco on the ground that for "complete preemption" to be found and to afford a basis for removal, federal law must supply the plaintiff with a remedy. The Court said that in Avco, "we held that a § 301 claim was properly removed to federal court although, at the time, the relief sought by the plaintiff [an injunction that was unavailable in a federal court under the then-prevailing interpretation of the Norris–La-Guardia Act] could be obtained only in state court."

Does the footnote in the Caterpillar case undermine the distinction suggested in text? Or can it be explained on the ground that although § 301 affords a general (and exclusive) federal remedy, removal is not precluded by the fact that the *specific* remedy sought in a particular case is not available under federal law?

be litigated in a federal court?[4] Or should some other meaning be attached to the language in the Franchise Tax case, p. 937, *supra*, that removability in such a case depends on how "powerful" is the preemptive force of the relevant federal statute?

NOTE ON REMOVAL STATUTES FOR THE PROTECTION OF FEDERAL OFFICERS AND AGENCIES

(1) *Removal Under § 1442(a)*. The four specialized grants of removal jurisdiction in § 1442(a) are the residue of a long series of enactments.

The series begins in 1815. Prompted by New England's resistance to the War of 1812, Congress inserted in an act for the collection of customs duties a provision—of limited duration—for the removal to the federal circuit court of any state court suit or prosecution begun in a state court against federal officers or other persons as a result of enforcement of the act.[1]

The first permanent legislation in the series—and the antecedent of the last clause of § 1442(a)(1)—was the "Force Bill" of 1833, passed in response to South Carolina's threats of nullification. This law authorized the removal of all suits or prosecutions against officers of the United States or other persons on account of any acts done under the customs laws.[2]

Then, with the Civil War, came a wave of removal acts. In 1863, Congress authorized, for the period only of the rebellion, the removal of cases brought against United States officers or others for acts committed during the rebellion and justified under the authority of the President or Congress.[3]

Soon afterward, the removal provisions of the "Force Bill" were extended to cases involving the collection of internal revenue as well as import duties.[4] What is now the last clause of § 1442(a)(1) continued through successive codifications to be thus limited to cases growing out of the revenue laws[5] until 1948, when the revisers, with no explanation other than that above quoted, added the reference to acts "for the apprehension or punishment of criminals".

4. For further discussion of the issues raised in Paragraph (3) of the text, see Twitchell, *Characterizing Federal Claims: Preemption, Removal, and the Arising–Under Jurisdiction of the Federal Courts,* 54 Geo. Wash.L.Rev. 812 (1986); Segreti, *The Federal Preemption Question—A Federal Question? An Analysis of Federal Jurisdiction over Supremacy Clause Issues,* 33 Cleve.St.L.Rev. 653 (1984–85); Comment, 35 U.C.L.A.L.Rev. 315 (1987); Ragazzo, *Reconsidering the Artful Pleading Doctrine,* 44 Hastings L.J. 273 (1993).

1. Act of Feb. 4, 1815, § 8, 3 Stat. 195, 198. See also Act of March 3, 1815, § 6, 3 Stat. 231, 233, extended for one year by the Act of April 27, 1816, § 3, 3 Stat. 315, and for another four years by the Act of March 3, 1817, § 2, 3 Stat. 396.

2. Act of March 2, 1833, 4 Stat. 632, 633–34.

3. Act of March 3, 1863, § 5, 12 Stat. 756, amended by Act of May 11, 1866, §§ 3–4, 14 Stat. 46, and the Act of Feb. 5, 1867, 14 Stat. 385. See also the Act of July 28, 1866, § 8, 14 Stat. 328, 329; and the Act of July 27, 1868, § 1, 15 Stat. 243.

4. This result was the net of a confusing series of enactments from 1864 to 1866. See Act of March 7, 1864, § 9, 13 Stat. 14, 17; Act of June 30, 1864, § 50, 13 Stat. 241; Act of July 13, 1866, §§ 67–68, 14 Stat. 98, 171–72. See Frankfurter & Landis, The Business of the Supreme Court 61–62 (1928).

5. See Rev.Stat. § 643; Judicial Code of 1911, Act of March 3, 1911, § 33, 36 Stat. 1087, 1097; 28 U.S.C. (1940 ed.) § 76.

Paragraph (2) of § 1442(a), providing for the removal of cases brought against a property holder claiming under a federal officer, where the case affects the validity of an act of Congress, grew out of the same group of Civil War revenue acts. Before 1948 it was similarly limited to cases involving the validity of a revenue law. Again without explanation, the drafters of the 1948 revision of the Judicial Code struck out the limitation to revenue laws.

The provisions of paragraph (4) of § 1442(a) for the removal of cases brought against an officer of either House of Congress for an act done under an order of the House originated in an appropriation bill in 1875.[6]

The provisions of paragraph (3) of the subsection, authorizing the removal of proceedings against an officer of a United States court for acts done under color of office, were added in 1916.[7] A few days later, in an enactment that in substance is still in effect, Congress extended similar protection to any member of the armed forces when proceeded against "on account of any act done under color of his office or status, or in respect to which he claims any right, title, or authority under any law of the United States respecting the military forces thereof, or under the law of war".[8]

The Federal Employees Liability Reform and Tort Compensation Act of 1988, 102 Stat. 4563, amended 28 U.S.C. § 2679(b) to make the Federal Tort Claims Act (FTCA) the exclusive remedy for torts committed by federal officials in the course of their official duties. Under § 2679(d)(1), as amended, if the Attorney General certifies that an employee who has been sued was acting within the scope of his employment, the proceeding shall be re-designated as a suit against the United States; if pending in state court, the suit shall be removed to federal court, § 2679(d); and the plaintiff may recover only if the United States is liable under the FTCA. This regime—precluding suits against employees, substituting the United States as defendant, and authorizing removal—existed before 1988 in the limited area of suits resulting from a federal employee's operation of a motor vehicle. The 1988 provision extended the regime generally to tort actions against federal employees (other than those actions claiming constitutional violations).

(2) *Removal Under § 1442(b)*. The peculiar grant of removal jurisdiction of personal actions brought by an alien against a nonresident who is, or was at the time the action accrued, a civil officer of the United States, originated in a brief enactment of 1872.[9] The drafters of § 1442(b) accepted this provision substantially *in haec verba*.

What purpose, if any, did it serve, in view of 28 U.S.C. §§ 1332(a)(2), and 1441(b)? Escape from the requirement of a jurisdictional amount in this class of cases? The protection of former officers?

Were it not for the diversity aspect of such cases, would the provision be constitutional?

(3) *Removal Under § 1443*. Deriving also from the Civil War period are the civil rights removal provisions of 28 U.S.C. § 1443. While this section has a

---

6. Act of March 3, 1875, § 8, 18 Stat. 371, 401.

7. Act of Aug. 23, 1916, 39 Stat. 532.

8. Act of Aug. 29, 1916, § 3, Art. 117, 39 Stat. 619, 669; Act of June 4, 1920, Art. 117, 41 Stat. 759, 811; Act of June 24, 1948, § 242, 62 Stat. 642; Act of May 5, 1950, § 9, 64 Stat. 145, 146, 50 U.S.C. § 738, superseded by Act of Aug. 10, 1956, 70A Stat. 626, 28 U.S.C. § 1442a.

9. Act of March 30, 1872, 17 Stat. 44.

broader application than does § 1442, subsection (2) of § 1443 covers proceedings against federal officers or persons acting under them, and the original statutes referred expressly to such cases.[10] See *Note on Civil Rights Removal Under 28 U.S.C. § 1443*, p. 959, *infra.*

(4) *Removal by a Federal Agency.* May § 1442(a)(1) be read to authorize removal if the action is against an agency rather than an officer thereof?

A unanimous Court answered this question in the negative in International Primate Protection League v. Administrators of Tulane Educational Fund, 500 U.S. 72 (1991).[11] The Court reasoned that this result was supported by both the section's grammar and its language—including the failure to set off the phrase "or any agency thereof" by commas, and the use of the phrases "acting under him" and "under color of such office." The Court also expressly rejected the argument that its construction of the statute would lead to absurd results: when the present statute and its predecessors were enacted, the Court explained, Congress might well have believed that federal officers needed the protection removal would afford because of the "complicated" question of the scope of their immunity. The determination of an agency's immunity, on the other hand, "was sufficiently straightforward that a state court, even if hostile to the federal interest, would be unlikely to disregard the law" (p. 85).

Did the language and grammar of the statute compel the Court's result? If so, why did the Court think it necessary to explain that the result made at least some sense? If the language did not compel the result, don't the considerations underlying the removal statute weigh strongly in favor of removal? Does this case mean that whenever a complaint against the federal government is not sufficiently grounded in federal law to warrant removal under § 1441, a plaintiff can prevent removal by suing only the agency involved? Or is the problem unlikely to arise often because an agency (unlike an individual officer defendant) is almost sure to have a valid claim of immunity? Would a suit complaining of federal agency action necessarily be regarded in most instances as arising under the Administrative Procedure Act, even if the only law allegedly violated is state law? If so, would removal be appropriate under § 1441?[12]

---

10. Act of April 9, 1866, § 3, 14 Stat. 27; and Act of May 31, 1870, § 18, 16 Stat. 144. See also Rev.Stat. § 641 (1874).

11. Despite the name of the case, the only party to the state court action that had sought removal was the defendant National Institutes of Health, a federal agency.

12. In American Policyholders Ins. Co. v. Nyacol Prods., Inc., 989 F.2d 1256 (1st Cir.1993), a company had been threatened with suit by the EPA for environmental liabilities under the federal "Superfund" statute; the company's insurer then brought a state court action against the insured, seeking a declaration that the insurer had no obligation to defend or compensate the insured. The complaint also named an EPA official as a defendant, seeking to prevent EPA from reaching the insurance policy to satisfy potential judgments under the Superfund statute. The official removed the case under § 1442, but when the case reached the First Circuit, that court raised the question of jurisdiction under § 1442, and ruled (contrary to the position of both sides) that there was no removal jurisdiction. The court reasoned that (i) the Primate Protection decision would bar removal of a state court action against the EPA itself, and (ii) since a suit like this one, against an official in her official capacity, is, in essence, a suit against the entity, it too should be held unremovable.

Was the court of appeals justified in taking a "functional" approach to § 1442, when the Supreme Court's approach was just the

Georgia v. Rachel

384 U.S. 780, 86 S.Ct. 1783, 16 L.Ed.2d 925 (1966).
Certiorari to the United States Court of Appeals for the Fifth Circuit.

■ Mr. Justice Stewart delivered the opinion of the Court. * * *

[This] case arises from a removal petition filed by Thomas Rachel and 19 other defendants seeking to transfer to the United States District Court for the Northern District of Georgia criminal trespass prosecutions pending against them in the Superior Court of Fulton County, Georgia. The petition stated that the defendants had been arrested on various dates in the spring of 1963 when they sought to obtain service at privately owned restaurants open to the general public in Atlanta, Georgia. The defendants alleged: "their arrests were effected for the sole purpose of aiding, abetting, and perpetuating customs, and usages which have deep historical and psychological roots in the mores and attitudes which exist within the City of Atlanta with respect to serving and seating members of the Negro race in such places of public accommodation and convenience upon a racially discriminatory basis and upon terms and conditions not imposed upon members of the so-called white or Caucasian race. Members of the so-called white or Caucasian race are similarly treated and discriminated against when accompanied by members of the Negro race."

Each defendant, according to the petition, was then indicted under the Georgia statute making it a misdemeanor to refuse to leave the premises of another when requested to do so by the owner or the person in charge. On these allegations, the defendants maintained that removal was authorized under both subsections of 28 U.S.C. § 1443. the defendants maintained broadly that they were entitled to removal under the First Amendment and the Due Process Clause of the Fourteenth Amendment. Specifically invoking the language of subsection (1), the "denied or cannot enforce" clause, their petition stated: "petitioners are denied and/or cannot enforce in the Courts of the State of Georgia rights under the Constitution and Laws of the United States providing for the equal rights of citizens of the United States * * * in that, among other things, the State of Georgia by statute, custom, usage, and practice supports and maintains a policy of racial discrimination."

Invoking the language of subsection (2), the "color of authority" clause, the petition stated: "petitioners are being prosecuted for acts done under color of authority derived from the constitution and laws of the United States and for refusing to do an act which was, and is, inconsistent with the Constitution and Laws of the United States."

On its own motion and without a hearing, the Federal District Court remanded the cases to the Superior Court of Fulton County, Georgia, finding that the petition did not allege facts sufficient to sustain removal under the federal statute. The defendants appealed to the Court of Appeals for the Fifth

---

opposite? Note the unfortunate interaction of the disparate approaches: Primate Protection restricts removal in a case where there is a functional need but arguably no statutory authorization; American Policyholders further restricts removal in a case where there is both a functional need and apparent statutory authorization, because in substance rather than form the case is hard to distinguish from Primate Protection. The result is a large hole in the protection that § 1442 provides to federal officers, and derivatively, to the federal government. Does the problem lie with Primate Protection? With American Policyholders? With the inconsistency between the two?

Circuit. [See 28 U.S.C. § 1447(d), allowing appeal of a remand order in such a case.]

While the case was pending in that court, two events of critical significance took place. The first of these was the enactment into law by the United States Congress of the Civil Rights Act of 1964. The second was the decision of this Court in Hamm v. City of Rock Hill, 379 U.S. 306. That case held that the Act precludes state trespass prosecutions for peaceful attempts to be served upon an equal basis in establishments covered by the Act, even though the prosecutions were instituted prior to the Act's passage. In view of these intervening developments in the law, the Court of Appeals reversed the District Court. * * *

We granted certiorari to consider the applicability of the removal statute to the circumstances of this case. No issues touching the constitutional power of Congress are involved. We deal only with questions of statutory construction.

* * *[8] In the case before us, the Court of Appeals for the Fifth Circuit dealt only with issues arising under the first subsection of § 1443, and we confine our review to those issues.

Section 1443(1) entitles the defendants to remove these prosecutions to the federal court only if they meet both requirements of that subsection. They must show both that the right upon which they rely is a "right under any law providing for * * * equal civil rights," and that they are "denied or cannot enforce" that right in the courts of Georgia.

The statutory phrase "any law providing for * * * equal civil rights" did not appear in the original removal provision in the Civil Rights Act of 1866. That provision allowed removal only in cases involving the express statutory rights of racial equality guaranteed in the Act itself. The first section of the 1866 Act secured for all citizens the "same" rights as were "enjoyed by white citizens" in a variety of fundamental areas. Section 3, the removal section of the 1866 Act, provided for removal by "persons who are denied or cannot enforce * * * the rights secured to them by the first section of this act * * *."

The present language "any law providing for * * * equal civil rights" first appeared in § 641 of the Revised Statutes of 1874. * * *

There is no substantial indication, however, that the general language of § 641 of the Revised Statutes was intended to expand the kinds of "law" to which the removal section referred. In spite of the potential breadth of the phrase "any law providing for * * * equal civil rights," it seems clear that in enacting § 641, Congress intended in that phrase only to include laws comparable in nature to the Civil Rights Act of 1866. * * *

On the basis of the historical material that is available, we conclude that the phrase "any law providing for * * * equal civil rights" must be construed to mean any law providing for specific civil rights stated in terms of racial equality. Thus, the defendants' broad contentions under the First Amendment and the Due Process Clause of the Fourteenth Amendment cannot support a valid claim for removal under § 1443, because the guarantees of those clauses

---

8. * * * The statistics on the number of criminal cases of all kinds removed from state to federal courts in recent years are revealing. For the fiscal years 1962, 1963, 1964, and 1965, there were 18, 14, 43, and 1,192 such cases, respectively. Of the total removed criminal cases for 1965, 1,079 were in the Fifth Circuit. See Annual Report of the Director of the Administrative Office of the United States Courts 213–217 (1965).

are phrased in terms of general application available to all persons or citizens, rather than in the specific language of racial equality that § 1443 demands. * * *

But the defendants in the present case did not rely solely on these broad constitutional claims in their removal petition. They also made allegations calling into play the Civil Rights Act of 1964. That Act is clearly a law conferring a specific right of racial equality, for in § 201(a) it guarantees to all the "full and equal enjoyment" of the facilities of any place of public accommodation without discrimination on the ground of race. By that language the Act plainly qualifies as a "law providing for * * * equal civil rights" within the meaning of 28 U.S.C. § 1443(1).

Moreover, it is clear that the right relied upon as the basis for removal is a "right under" a law providing for equal civil rights. The removal petition may fairly be read to allege that the defendants will be brought to trial solely as the result of peaceful attempts to obtain service at places of public accommodation. The Civil Rights Act of 1964 endows the defendants with a right not to be prosecuted for such conduct. As noted, § 201(a) guarantees to the defendants the equal access they sought. Section 203 then provides that, "No person shall * * * (c) punish or *attempt to punish* any person for exercising or attempting to exercise any right or privilege secured by section 201 or 202." (Emphasis supplied.) 78 Stat. 244. In Hamm v. City of Rock Hill, 379 U.S. 306, 311, the Court held that this section of the Act "prohibits prosecution of any person for seeking service in a covered establishment, because of his race or color." Hence, if the facts alleged in the petition are true, the defendants not only are immune from conviction under the Georgia trespass statute, but they have a "right under" the Civil Rights Act of 1964 not even to be brought to trial on these charges in the Georgia courts.

The question remaining, then, is whether within the meaning of § 1443(1), the defendants are "denied or cannot enforce" that right "in the courts of" Georgia. That question can be answered only after consideration of the legislative and judicial history of this requirement.

When Congress adopted the first civil rights removal provisions in § 3 of the Civil Rights Act of 1866, it incorporated by reference the procedures for removal established in § 5 of the Habeas Corpus Suspension Act of 1863, 12 Stat. 756. The latter section, in turn, permitted removal either at the pre-trial stage of the proceedings in the state court or after final judgment in that court. There can be no doubt that post-judgment removal was a practical remedy for civil rights defendants invoking either the "denied or cannot enforce" clause or the "color of authority" clause of the 1866 removal provision, in order to vindicate rights that had actually been denied at the trial. The scope of pre-trial removal, however, was unclear.

Congress eliminated post-judgment removal when it enacted § 641 of the Revised Statutes of 1874. * * * Pre-trial removal was retained, but the scope of the provision had never been clarified. It was in this historic setting that the Court examined the scope of § 641. In a series of cases commencing with Strauder v. West Virginia [100 U.S. 303], and Virginia v. Rives [100 U.S. 313], decided on the same day in the 1879 Term, the Court established a relatively narrow, well-defined area in which pre-trial removal could be sustained under the "denied or cannot enforce" clause of that section.

In Strauder, the removal petition of a Negro indicted for murder pointed to a West Virginia statute that permitted only white male persons to serve on a grand or petit jury. Since Negroes were excluded from jury service pursuant to that statute, the defendant claimed that the "probabilities" were great that he would suffer a denial of his right to the "full and equal benefit of all laws and proceedings in the State of West Virginia. * * *" 100 U.S., at 304. The state court denied removal, however, and the defendant was convicted. This Court held that pre-trial removal should have been granted because, in the language of § 641, it appeared even before trial that the defendant would be denied or could not enforce a right secured to him by a "law providing for * * * equal civil rights." The law specifically invoked by the Court was § 1977 of the Revised Statutes, now 42 U.S.C. § 1981. That law, the Court held, conferred upon the defendant the right to have his jurors selected without discrimination on the ground of race. Because of the direct conflict between the West Virginia statute and § 1977, the Court in Strauder held that the defendant would be the victim of "a denial by the statute law of the State." 100 U.S., at 312.

In Com. of Virginia v. Rives, however, the defendants could point to no such state statute as the basis for removal. Their petition alleged that strong community racial prejudice existed against them, that the grand and petit jurors summoned to try them were all white, that Negroes had never been allowed to serve on county juries in cases in which a Negro was involved in any way, and that the judge, the prosecutor, and the assistant prosecutor had all rejected their request that Negroes be included in the petit jury. Hence, the defendants maintained, they could not obtain a fair trial in the state court. But the only relevant Virginia statute to which the petition referred imposed jury duty on *all* males within a certain age range. Thus, the law of Virginia did not, on its face, sanction the discrimination of which the defendants complained. This Court held that the petition stated no ground for removal. Critical to its holding was the Court's observation that § 641 of the Revised Statutes authorized only pre-trial removal. The Court concluded: "the denial or inability to enforce in the judicial tribunals of a State, rights secured to a defendant by any law providing for * * * equal civil rights * * * of which sect. 641 speaks, is primarily, if not exclusively, a denial of such rights, or an inability to enforce them, resulting from the Constitution or laws of the State, rather than a denial first made manifest at the trial of the case. In other words, the statute has reference to a legislative denial or an inability resulting from it. * * *"

The Court distinguished the situation in Strauder:

"It is to be observed that [§ 641] gives the right of removal only to a person 'who is denied, or cannot enforce, in *the judicial tribunals of the State* his equal civil rights.' And this is to appear before trial. When a statute of the State denies his right, or interposes a bar to his enforcing it, in the judicial tribunals, the presumption is fair that they will be controlled by it in their decisions; and in such a case a defendant may affirm on oath what is necessary for a removal. Such a case is clearly within the provisions of sect. 641." 100 U.S., at 321. (Emphasis in original.)

Strauder and Rives thus teach that removal is not warranted by an assertion that a denial of rights of equality may take place and go uncorrected at trial. Removal is warranted only if it can be predicted by reference to a law of general application that the defendant will be denied or cannot enforce the specified federal rights in the state courts. A state statute authorizing the denial affords an ample basis for such a prediction. * * * [Discussion of subsequent cases, in which, the Court states, the Strauder–Rives doctrine was "consistently applied", is omitted.]

In Rives itself, however, the Court noted that the denial of which the removal provision speaks "is primarily, *if not exclusively,* a denial * * * resulting from the Constitution or laws of the State * * *." 100 U.S., at 319. (Emphasis supplied.) * * * The Court thereby gave some indication that removal might be justified, even in the absence of a discriminatory state enactment, if an equivalent basis could be shown for an equally firm prediction that the defendant would be "denied or cannot enforce" the specified federal rights in the state court. Such a basis for prediction exists in the present case.

In the narrow circumstances of this case, *any* proceedings in the courts of the State will constitute a denial of the rights conferred by the Civil Rights Act of 1964, as construed in Hamm v. City of Rock Hill, if the allegations of the removal petition are true. * * * The Civil Rights Act of 1964, however, as Hamm v. City of Rock Hill, 379 U.S. 306, made clear, protects those who refuse to obey such an order not only from conviction in state courts, but from *prosecution* in those courts. Hamm emphasized the precise terms of § 203(c) that prohibit any "attempt to punish" persons for exercising rights of equality conferred upon them by the Act. The explicit terms of that section compelled the conclusion that "nonforcible attempts to gain admittance to or remain in establishments covered by the Act, are immunized from prosecution * * *." 379 U.S., at 311. The 1964 Act therefore "substitutes a right for a crime." 379 U.S., at 314. Hence, if as alleged in the present removal petition, the defendants were asked to leave solely for racial reasons, then the mere pendency of the prosecutions enables the federal court to make the clear prediction that the defendants will be "denied or cannot enforce in the courts of [the] State" the right to be free of any "attempt to punish" them for protected activity. It is no answer in these circumstances that the defendants might eventually prevail in the state court. The burden of having to defend the prosecutions is itself the denial of a right explicitly conferred by the Civil Rights Act of 1964 as construed in Hamm v. City of Rock Hill, *supra.*

Since the Federal District Court remanded the present case without a hearing, the defendants as yet have had no opportunity to establish that they were ordered to leave the restaurant facilities solely for racial reasons. If the Federal District Court finds that allegation true, the defendants' right to removal under § 1443(1) will be clear. The Strauder–Rives doctrine requires no more, for the denial in the courts of the State then clearly appears without any detailed analysis of the likely behavior of any particular state court. Upon such a finding it will be apparent that the conduct of the defendants is "immunized from prosecution" in any court, and the Federal District Court must then sustain the removal and dismiss the prosecutions.

For these reasons, the judgment is affirmed.

Affirmed.

■ MR. JUSTICE DOUGLAS, with whom THE CHIEF JUSTICE, MR. JUSTICE BRENNAN and MR. JUSTICE FORTAS join, concurring. * * *

It is the right to equal service in restaurants and the right to be free of prosecution for asserting that right—not the right to have a trespass conviction reversed—that the present prosecutions threaten. It is this right which must be vindicated by complete insulation from the State's criminal process if it is to be wholly vindicated. It is this right which the defendants are "denied" so long as the present prosecutions persist.

Georgia claims that Hamm v. City of Rock Hill, *supra,* does not cover cases of sit-ins prosecuted for disorderly conduct or other unlawful acts. Of course that is true. But one of the functions of the hearing on the allegations of the removal petition will be to determine whether the defendants were ejected on racial grounds or for some other, valid reason. * * *

If service was denied for other reasons, no case for removal has been made out. And if, as is intimated, any doubt remains as to whether the restaurants in question were covered by the 1964 Act, that too should be left open in the hearing to be held before the District Court—a procedure to which the defendants do not object.

NOTE ON CIVIL RIGHTS REMOVAL UNDER 28 U.S.C. § 1443

(1) *The Peacock Decision.* City of Greenwood v. Peacock, 384 U.S. 808 (1966), was decided on the same day as Rachel. Twenty-nine defendants in state criminal proceedings, alleging that they were civil rights workers engaged in a drive to encourage black voter registration in Mississippi, sought to remove those proceedings to a federal court under § 1443(1) and (2). Their removal petitions claimed that the courts and law enforcement officers of the state were prejudiced against them because of their race or their association with blacks; that their arrests and prosecutions were for the sole purpose of punishing them for, and deterring them from, the exercise of their constitutional rights to protest racial discrimination; that they would be tried in segregated court-rooms; that blacks would be excluded from the juries; that the judges and prosecutors had gained office at elections at which black voters had been excluded; and that the statutes and ordinances under which they were charged were unconstitutionally vague and were unconstitutional as applied to their conduct.

The Supreme Court, reversing the Fifth Circuit, held the cases nonremova-ble. As to § 1443(2), the Court stated, the first phrase allowed removal only by "federal officers or agents and those authorized to act with or for them in affirmatively executing duties under any federal law providing for equal civil rights";[1] the second phrase, plainly inapplicable in Peacock, "is available only to state officers" (p. 824).

Turning to subsection (1), the Court said (384 U.S. at 826–28):

"* * * The present case differs from Rachel in two significant respects. First, no federal law confers an absolute right on private citizens—on civil rights advocates, or Negroes, or on anybody else—to obstruct a public street, to contribute to the delinquency of a minor, to drive an automobile without a license, or to bite a policeman. [These were among the offenses charged.] Second, no federal law confers immunity from state prosecution on such charges. * * * It is *not* enough to support removal under § 1443(1) to allege or show that the defendant's federal equal civil rights have been illegally and

---

1. In light of this holding, is any case removable under the first phrase of § 1443(2) that is not also removable under § 1442?

corruptly denied by state administrative officials in advance of trial, that the charges against the defendants are false, or that the defendant is unable to obtain a fair trial in a particular state court. The motives of the officers bringing the charges may be corrupt, but that does not show that the state trial court will find the defendant guilty if he is innocent, or that in any other manner the defendant will be 'denied or cannot enforce in the courts' of the State any right under a federal law providing for equal civil rights. The civil rights removal statute does not require and does not permit the judges of the federal courts to put their brethren of the state judiciary on trial."

The Court noted that remedies other than removal—including, in appropriate cases, injunctions, actions for damages under 42 U.S.C. § 1983, and habeas corpus—were available to defendants for vindicating their constitutional rights, and expressed apprehension that a broad construction of § 1443 would lead to an explosion of state criminal litigation in the federal courts. (See footnote 8 of the opinion in Rachel.) Such a change raised fundamental issues of policy for Congress to consider: "Has the historic practice of holding state criminal trials in state courts * * * been such a failure that the relationship of the state and federal courts should now be revolutionized? Will increased responsibility of the state courts in the area of federal civil rights be promoted and encouraged by denying those courts any power at all to exercise that responsibility?" (p. 834).[1]

(2) *The Aftermath: Johnson v. Mississippi.* A decade after Rachel and Peacock, the Court returned to the "murky language" of § 1443(1) and again construed it narrowly. In Johnson v. Mississippi, 421 U.S. 213 (1975), after a detailed review of the Rachel and Peacock cases, the Court held that the provision of the 1968 Civil Rights Act (18 U.S.C. § 245) that prohibits interference with certain federal rights "by force or threat of force," did not confer upon petitioners a right under § 1443(1) to remove a state criminal prosecution for conspiracy and unlawful boycott. (The petitioners had been picketing and urging the boycott of certain Vicksburg, Mississippi, merchants for alleged racial discrimination in their hiring practices.) "Whether or not § 245 * * * provides for 'specific civil rights stated in terms of racial equality' [within the meaning of Rachel] * * * it evinces no intention to interfere in any manner with state criminal prosecutions."

Justices Marshall and Brennan, dissenting in Johnson, argued that "[t]he use of force or the threat of force to intimidate or interfere with persons engaged in protected activity fairly describes an 'attempt to punish' the same persons" by arrest and prosecution (p. 236). Commenting on the Court's observation that "varied avenues of relief" still lay open for vindication of any federal rights which might actually be violated in the state prosecution, the dissent, citing Younger v. Harris, p. 1256, *infra,* concluded: "I only hope that the recent instances in which this Court has emphasized the values of comity and federalism in restricting the issuance of federal injunctions against state criminal * * * proceedings will not mislead the district courts into forgetting that at times these values must give way to the need to protect federal rights from being irremediably trampled" (p. 239).

(3) *"Equal Civil Rights".* What is included in the Rachel Court's formulation that a law providing for "equal civil rights" is any law providing for "specific civil rights stated in terms of racial equality"? Is the Equal Protection Clause

---

1.   Three Justices dissented, in an opinion written by Justice Douglas.

itself excluded?   What of a law designed to protect a racial minority that is not stated in terms of equality?   Is the right to equal employment opportunity under Title VII of the Civil Rights Act of 1964 a "civil right" or some other kind of right?   The lower court authorities are collected in 14A Wright, Miller & Cooper, Federal Practice and Procedure § 3728 (1985 & 1995 Supp.).

(4) *The Question of Post-Judgment Removal*.   After Congress eliminated the possibility of post-judgment removal, was the language "is denied or cannot enforce in the courts of the State" meaningful at all?   Note that in a 1977 amendment to 28 U.S.C. § 1446(c), Congress authorized removal even after the commencement of trial in a criminal case (but not in civil cases, to which § 1443 is also applicable) "for good cause shown".   In so doing, did Congress, perhaps inadvertently, breathe new life into § 1443 by allowing for post-judgment removal in criminal cases when the results of the state judicial proceeding have established that the claimed right was in fact denied or could not be enforced?   In any event, must all state court remedies first be exhausted?   Even so, might removal be available in such a case as a substitute, or supplement, to a petition for certiorari in the Supreme Court or for habeas corpus in the district court?   Or is the "good cause" provision designed to serve a narrower purpose?   The legislative history does not address these questions (and they do not appear to have been considered by any court).   Does the silence of the legislative history suggest that a change of this dimension is beyond the scope of the revision?

Absent the possibility of post-judgment removal, if the task of the federal court is to find some basis for a "firm prediction" of denial of federal rights, what relevance does the existence of a state law invalid on its face have to the making of such a prediction?   Even if relevant, should it be either sufficient or necessary?

(5) *Can the Rachel and Peacock Decisions Be Reconciled?*

(a) Consider the meaning and significance of the first ground of distinction from Rachel drawn by the Court in Peacock, Paragraph (1) *supra*.   Does it mean that a case is not removable unless the conduct *charged to be a violation of state law* (rather than merely the conduct engaged in) is protected by a federal law providing for equal civil rights?   If so, does this leave any room for the removal statute to operate?

(b) Note that the second ground of distinction advanced in Peacock—that "no federal law confers immunity from prosecution"—was the one further elaborated in Johnson v. Mississippi, Paragraph (2), *supra*.   The Court in Johnson insisted that the federal "right" in question be a statutory right not to be proceeded against in the state courts at all.   Did Rachel itself meet this test?

(6) *Other Possible Recourses*.   Among the other possible remedies alluded to by the Court in Peacock were federal injunction against state proceedings, see Chap. X, *infra*, and federal habeas corpus, see Chap. XI, *infra*.   What are the relative advantages and disadvantages of these remedies as devices for reconciling the vindication of federal rights with the state's interest in administering justice in the state's own courts?   See Bator, *The State Courts and Federal Constitutional Litigation*, 22 Wm. & Mary L.Rev. 605, 611–21 (1981).   What obstacles are placed in the path of a state defendant seeking to obtain an injunction, or to obtain a writ of habeas corpus before or after trial?

(7) *Commentary on § 1443*.   Writing before the Rachel and Peacock decisions, Professor Amsterdam urged a broader construction of § 1443(1) and (2) than

the Court adopted in these cases, though not so broad as the language of the statute might arguably permit. Amsterdam, *Criminal Prosecutions Affecting Federally Guaranteed Civil Rights: Federal Removal and Habeas Corpus Jurisdiction to Abort State Court Trial,* 113 U.Pa.L.Rev. 793 (1965). Describing the section as "a text of exquisite obscurity" (p. 843), Amsterdam explored in depth the history and interpretation of the statute, and found support for his arguments in the deep distrust of state courts as protectors of civil rights on the part of "bad Tad Stevens and his rads" (p. 830)—the principal architects of the 1866 legislation. His article also emphasized the harm to the civil rights movement that could be caused by groundless and discriminatory prosecutions, even if all convictions were ultimately set aside. See also Redish, *Revitalizing Civil Rights Removal Jurisdiction,* 64 Minn.L.Rev. 523 (1980), also arguing for a broader (though different) reading of § 1443.

For discussion of the origins and development of § 1443 in the context of the original 1866 Act (which provided for both original and removal jurisdiction), and of the little known federal prosecution of John Blyew in 1868, see Goldstein, *Blyew: Variations on a Jurisdictional Theme,* 41 Stan.L.Rev. 469 (1989). Goldstein contends that, starting with the Supreme Court's decision in the Blyew case (80 U.S. (13 Wall.) 581 (1872)), Congress and the federal courts have virtually eliminated the jurisdictional protections Congress sought to afford in 1866.

SECTION 5.   SUPPLEMENTAL (PENDENT) JURISDICTION

United Mine Workers of America v. Gibbs

383 U.S. 715, 86 S.Ct. 1130, 16 L.Ed.2d 218 (1966).
Certiorari to the United States Court of Appeals for the Sixth Circuit.

■ MR. JUSTICE BRENNAN delivered the opinion of the Court.

Respondent Paul Gibbs was awarded compensatory and punitive damages in this action against petitioner United Mine Workers of America (UMW) for alleged violations of § 303 of the Labor Management Relations Act, 1947, 61 Stat. 158, as amended, and of the common law of Tennessee. The case grew out of the rivalry between the United Mine Workers and the Southern Labor Union over representation of workers in the southern Appalachian coal fields. Tennessee Consolidated Coal Company, not a party here, laid off 100 miners of the UMW's Local 5881 when it closed one of its mines in southern Tennessee during the spring of 1960. Late that summer, Grundy Company, a wholly owned subsidiary of Consolidated, hired respondent as mine superintendent to attempt to open a new mine on Consolidated's property at nearby Gray's Creek through use of members of the Southern Labor Union. As part of the arrangement, Grundy also gave respondent a contract to haul the mine's coal to the nearest railroad loading point.

On August 15 and 16, 1960, armed members of Local 5881 forcibly prevented the opening of the mine, threatening respondent and beating an organizer for the rival union. * * * [At that point the UMW international union intervened.] There was no further violence at the mine site; a picket line was maintained there for nine months; and no further attempts were made to open the mine during that period.

Respondent lost his job as superintendent, and never entered into performance of his haulage contract. He testified that he soon began to lose other trucking contracts and mine leases he held in nearby areas. Claiming these effects to be the result of a concerted union plan against him, he sought recovery * * * against petitioner, the international union. The suit was brought in the United States District Court for the Eastern District of Tennessee, and jurisdiction was premised on allegations of secondary boycotts under § 303. The state law claim, for which jurisdiction was based upon the doctrine of pendent jurisdiction, asserted "an unlawful conspiracy and an unlawful boycott aimed at him and [Grundy] to maliciously, wantonly and willfully interfere with his contract of employment and with his contract of haulage."

The trial judge refused to submit to the jury the claims of pressure intended to cause mining firms other than Grundy to cease doing business with Gibbs; he found those claims unsupported by the evidence. The jury's verdict was that the UMW had violated both § 303 and state law. Gibbs was awarded $60,000 as damages under the employment contract and $14,500 under the haulage contract; he was also awarded $100,000 punitive damages. On motion, the trial court set aside the award of damages with respect to the haulage contract on the ground that damage was unproved. It also held that union pressure on Grundy to discharge respondent as supervisor would constitute only a primary dispute with Grundy, as respondent's employer, and hence was not cognizable as a claim under § 303. Interference with the employment relationship was cognizable as a state claim, however, and a remitted award was sustained on the state law claim. The Court of Appeals for the Sixth Circuit affirmed. We granted certiorari. We reverse.

I.

A threshold question is whether the District Court properly entertained jurisdiction of the claim based on Tennessee law. * * *

The Court held in Hurn v. Oursler, 289 U.S. 238, that state law claims are appropriate for federal court determination if they form a separate but parallel ground for relief also sought in a substantial claim based on federal law. The Court distinguished permissible from nonpermissible exercises of federal judicial power over state law claims by contrasting "a case where two distinct grounds in support of a single cause of action are alleged, one only of which presents a federal question, and a case where two separate and distinct causes of action are alleged, one only of which is federal in character. In the former, where the federal question averred is not plainly wanting in substance, the federal court, even though the federal ground be not established, may nevertheless retain and dispose of the case upon the non-federal *ground;* in the latter it may not do so upon the non-federal *cause of action*." 289 U.S., at 246. The question is into which category the present action fell.

Hurn was decided in 1933, before the unification of law and equity by the Federal Rules of Civil Procedure. At the time, the meaning of "cause of action" was a subject of serious dispute; the phrase might "mean one thing for one purpose and something different for another." United States v. Memphis Cotton Oil Co., 288 U.S. 62, 67–68. The Court in Hurn identified what it meant by the term by citation of Baltimore S.S. Co. v. Phillips, 274 U.S. 316, a case in which "cause of action" had been used to identify the operative scope of the doctrine of *res judicata*. In that case the Court had noted that "the whole tendency of our decisions is to require a plaintiff to try his whole cause of action and his whole case at one time." 274 U.S., at 320. * * * Had the Court found a jurisdictional bar to reaching the state claim in Hurn, we assume that the doctrine of *res judicata* would not have been applicable in any subsequent state suit. But the citation of Baltimore S.S. Co. shows that the Court found that the weighty policies of judicial economy and fairness to parties reflected in *res judicata* doctrine were in themselves strong counsel for the adoption of a rule which would permit federal courts to dispose of the state as well as the federal claims.

With the adoption of the Federal Rules of Civil Procedure and the unified form of action, Fed.Rule Civ.Proc. 2, much of the controversy over "cause of action" abated. The phrase remained as the keystone of the Hurn test, however, and, as commentators have noted, has been the source of considerable confusion. Under the Rules, the impulse is toward entertaining the broadest possible scope of action consistent with fairness to the parties; joinder of claims, parties and remedies is strongly encouraged. Yet because the Hurn question involves issues of jurisdiction as well as convenience, there has been some tendency to limit its application to cases in which the state and federal claims are, as in Hurn, "little more than the equivalent of different epithets to characterize the same group of circumstances." 289 U.S., at 246.

This limited approach is unnecessarily grudging. Pendent jurisdiction, in the sense of judicial *power,* exists whenever there is a claim "arising under [the] Constitution, the Laws of the United States, and Treaties made, or which shall be made, under their Authority * * *," U.S. Const., Art. III, § 2, and the relationship between that claim and the state claim permits the conclusion that the entire action before the court comprises but one constitutional "case." The federal claim must have substance sufficient to confer subject matter jurisdiction on the court. Levering & Garrigues Co. v. Morrin, 289 U.S. 103. The state and federal claims must derive from a common nucleus of operative fact. But if, considered without regard to their federal or state character, a plaintiff's claims are such that he would ordinarily be expected to try them all in one judicial proceeding, then, assuming substantiality of the federal issues, there is *power* in federal courts to hear the whole.[13]

That power need not be exercised in every case in which it is found to exist. It has consistently been recognized that pendent jurisdiction is a doctrine of discretion, not of plaintiff's right. Its justification lies in considerations of judicial economy, convenience and fairness to litigants; if these are not present a federal court should hesitate to exercise jurisdiction over state claims, even though bound to apply state law to them, Erie R. Co. v. Tompkins, 304 U.S. 64. Needless decisions of state law should be avoided both as a matter of comity and to promote justice between the parties, by procuring for them a surer-footed reading of applicable law. Certainly, if the federal claims are dismissed before trial, even though not insubstantial in a jurisdictional sense, the state claims should be dismissed as well. Similarly, if it appears that the state issues substantially predominate, whether in terms of proof, of the scope of the issues raised, or of the comprehensiveness of the remedy sought, the state claims may

---

13. While it is commonplace that the Federal Rules of Civil Procedure do not expand the jurisdiction of federal courts, they do embody "the whole tendency of our decisions * * * to require a plaintiff to try his * * * whole case at one time," Baltimore S.S. Co. v. Phillips, *supra,* and to that extent emphasize the basis of pendent jurisdiction.

be dismissed without prejudice and left for resolution to state tribunals. There may, on the other hand, be situations in which the state claim is so closely tied to questions of federal policy that the argument for exercise of pendent jurisdiction is particularly strong. In the present case, for example, the allowable scope of the state claim implicates the federal doctrine of preemption; while this interrelationship does not create statutory federal question jurisdiction, Louisville & N.R. Co. v. Mottley, 211 U.S. 149, its existence is relevant to the exercise of discretion. Finally, there may be reasons independent of jurisdictional considerations, such as the likelihood of jury confusion in treating divergent legal theories of relief, that would justify separating state and federal claims for trial, Fed.Rule Civ.Proc. 42(b). If so, jurisdiction should ordinarily be refused.

The question of power will ordinarily be resolved on the pleadings. But the issue whether pendent jurisdiction has been properly assumed is one which remains open throughout the litigation. Pretrial procedures or even the trial itself may reveal a substantial hegemony of state law claims, or likelihood of jury confusion, which could not have been anticipated at the pleading stage. Although it will of course be appropriate to take account in this circumstance of the already completed course of the litigation, dismissal of the state claim might even then be merited. For example, it may appear that the plaintiff was well aware of the nature of his proofs and the relative importance of his claims; recognition of a federal court's wide latitude to decide ancillary questions of state law does not imply that it must tolerate a litigant's effort to impose upon it what is in effect only a state law case. Once it appears that a state claim constitutes the real body of a case, to which the federal claim is only an appendage, the state claim may fairly be dismissed.

We are not prepared to say that in the present case the District Court exceeded its discretion in proceeding to judgment on the state claim. We may assume for purposes of decision that the District Court was correct in its holding that the claim of pressure on Grundy to terminate the employment contract was outside the purview of § 303. Even so, the § 303 claims based on secondary pressures on Grundy relative to the haulage contract and on other coal operators generally were substantial. Although § 303 limited recovery to compensatory damages based on secondary pressures, Teamsters Union v. Morton, *supra,* and state law allowed both compensatory and punitive damages, and allowed such damages as to both secondary and primary activity, the state and federal claims arose from the same nucleus of operative fact and reflected alternative remedies. Indeed, the verdict sheet sent in to the jury authorized only one award of damages, so that recovery could not be given separately on the federal and state claims.

It is true that the § 303 claims ultimately failed and that the only recovery allowed respondent was on the state claim. We cannot confidently say, however, that the federal issues were so remote or played such a minor role at the trial that in effect the state claim only was tried. Although the District Court dismissed as unproved the § 303 claims that petitioner's secondary activities included attempts to induce coal operators other than Grundy to cease doing business with respondent, the court submitted the § 303 claims relating to Grundy to the jury. The jury returned verdicts against petitioner on those § 303 claims, and it was only on petitioner's motion for a directed verdict and a judgment *n.o.v.* that the verdicts on those claims were set aside. The District Judge considered the claim as to the haulage contract proved as to liability, and held it failed only for lack of proof of damages. Although there was some risk of confusing the jury in joining the state and federal claims— especially since, as will be developed, differing standards of proof of UMW involvement applied—the possibility of confusion could be lessened by employing a special verdict form, as the District Court did. Moreover, the question whether the permissible scope of the state claim was limited by the doctrine of pre-emption afforded a special reason for the exercise of pendent jurisdiction; the federal courts are particularly appropriate bodies for the application of pre-emption principles. We thus conclude that although it may be that the District Court might, in its sound discretion, have dismissed the state claim, the circumstances show no error in refusing to do so. * * *

[The judgment was reversed because, even if the state-law claim was not preempted by the Labor–Management Relations Act, the proof of defendant's responsibility had not met the requirements imposed by § 6 of the Norris–LaGuardia Act, 29 U.S.C. § 106.]

NOTE ON SUPPLEMENTAL (PENDENT) JURISDICTION IN FEDERAL QUESTION AND OTHER NON–DIVERSITY CASES

(1) *The Statutory and Constitutional Bases of the Gibbs Holding.* The Gibbs opinion focuses on the question whether pendent jurisdiction is within the scope of the judicial power conferred by Article III, and simply assumes that, within that boundary, the federal courts have "discretion" to entertain or refuse the case. But this elides the question of the scope of § 1331, a provision that is not even alluded to in the Court's opinion. Should § 1331 have been read to authorize the exercise of pendent jurisdiction over state-law claims? (Consider the relevance of the fact that § 1331 uses the phrase "civil actions," not "cases.")[1]

(2) *Antecedents: The Hurn and Siler Cases.* Hurn v. Oursler, referred to in Gibbs, was a suit to enjoin production of a play on the grounds of copyright infringement and unfair competition. The action originally involved only the plagiarizing of a copyrighted play. The bill was subsequently amended to allege also unfair competition with a revised, uncopyrighted version of the same play. The Court held that the state law claim of unfair competition with respect to the copyrighted play was "but [a] different ground[] asserted in support of the same cause of action [as that stated in the federal claim]", and thus both could be adjudicated in federal court. But the state law claim with regard to the uncopyrighted play asserted a "separate and distinct" cause of action "entirely outside the federal jurisdiction". Thus the Hurn rationale rested on a notion of the scope of a "cause of action" that was considerably narrower than Gibbs' formulation of a "common nucleus of operative fact".

---

1. For a dissent from Gibbs' view of the relationship of § 1331 and Article III, see Matasar, *Rediscovering "One Constitutional Case": Procedural Rules and the Rejection of the Gibbs Test for Supplemental Jurisdiction,* 71 Calif.L.Rev. 1401 (1983)(arguing that Gibbs' conflation of statutory and constitutional tests unduly restricted the latter; the only constitutional limit to supplemental jurisdiction is the existence of a case or controversy as defined under lawfully adopted procedural rules for the joinder of claims and parties).

The Hurn opinion supported jurisdiction to decide some state claims joined with federal claims on the basis, *inter alia,* of Osborn v. Bank of the United States, p. 883, *supra.* It also relied upon Siler v. Louisville & Nashville R. Co., 213 U.S. 175 (1909). Siler first held, in an action to enjoin the enforcement of an order made by the Kentucky Railroad Commission fixing intrastate rates, that a claim that the rate order violated state law could stand together with a parallel claim that the order violated the federal Constitution. See p. 1109, *infra.* But the Court in Siler went further and held that, even in the absence of diversity of citizenship, the case should be disposed of, if possible, on state grounds in order to avoid reaching the federal constitutional question.

(3) *The Rationale of the Gibbs Rule.* The original edition of this book raised the following issues:

"Notice that a federal trial court would often be unable to function as a court at all, in the absence of the jurisdiction over state questions which Marshall asserted in Osborn v. Bank of the United States. At stake there was the ability of such a court, ever, to be sure of being able to decide a whole case.

"No such justification, obviously, is available for the ancillary jurisdiction asserted in Siler. The justification there, is it not, is different and twofold: namely, the policy in favor of avoiding avoidable decisions of federal constitutional questions, plus the policy in favor of having one lawsuit, if possible, instead of two?

"Hurn, however, is supported only by the single policy against piecemeal litigation. How strong is this policy? How far does it warrant stretching the constitutional concept of a 'case'?"

The last questions apply equally well to Gibbs, which explicitly asserts the justification for its conclusion in terms of "judicial economy, convenience and fairness to litigants." But beyond their intrinsic value, are these considerations—and the policy against piecemeal litigation—relevant to jurisdictional issues, even when perceived in terms of distribution of power? Consider the effect of a rule contrary to Gibbs. If in order to invoke a federal forum for a federal claim, a party who also has related state claims will have to litigate those claims separately, might that party not be deterred from going to federal court? Where federal jurisdiction is exclusive, this may effectively attenuate the value of the federal claim. Where federal and state courts have concurrent jurisdiction, such a party could litigate federal and state claims together only in the state tribunals.

Should analysis of pendent jurisdiction focus on those factors that would be significant to a prospective litigant of a federal claim in deciding whether to choose a federal forum? Would this focus produce a rule different from that of Gibbs?

(4) *Res Judicata Problems.* Isn't Justice Brennan correct in assuming that if a state claim is held to be outside the scope of the "case" or "civil action" that is the subject of federal court jurisdiction, no state court would later bar consideration of the merits of the state claim as a result of the federal adjudication? Indeed, would any other outcome be consistent with the Due Process Clause? With Article III and the Supremacy Clause?

On the other hand, if the federal court does (or would, if asked) exercise pendent jurisdiction over a state law claim, doesn't that suggest that the litigant who fails to assert such a claim runs the risk of finding that the claim is barred in a later action in any court? At least if the relevant law regards the doctrine of res judicata as based not on the plaintiff's "theory" of recovery but on the scope of the transaction sued upon?   For further discussion of this and related issues, see Chapter XII, p. 1468, *infra.*

(5) *The Issue of Substantiality.*   The rule that an insubstantial federal question does not provide a basis for federal question jurisdiction (a rule referred to at p. 936, *supra,* and reiterated in Gibbs) may have been diluted in Hagans v. Lavine, 415 U.S. 528 (1974).   The Court there had first determined that there was pendent jurisdiction for a special three-judge federal district court to decide a federal statutory claim under 28 U.S.C. § 1343(3) if there existed a "substantial" constitutional claim as well.[2]   It then concluded that the constitutional claim actually presented (an attack on the validity of state regulations allowing the state to make certain deductions from AFDC payments) was not so frivolous as to be beyond the jurisdiction of the district court: "[It is not] immediately obvious to us from the face of the complaint that recouping emergency rent payments from future welfare disbursements, which petitioners argue deprived needy children because of parental default, was so patently rational as to require no meaningful consideration.   * * * Nor can we say that petitioners' claim is 'so insubstantial, implausible, foreclosed by prior decisions of this Court or otherwise completely devoid of merit as not to involve a federal controversy within the jurisdiction of the District Court, whatever may be the ultimate resolution of the federal issues on the merits.'   Oneida Indian Nation v. County of Oneida, 414 U.S. 661, 666–67 (1974)" (pp. 539–41, 543).   The dissent argued that pendent jurisdiction requires a constitutional claim that has more than a "glimmer of merit" (p. 552); "under today's rationale it appears sufficient for jurisdiction that a plaintiff is able to plead his claim with a straight face" (p. 564); "this seems to be a classic case of the statutory tail wagging the constitutional dog" (p. 564).

(6) *The 1948 Revision of the Judicial Code.*   In 1948, Congress, in revising the Judicial Code, conferred jurisdiction over "a claim of unfair competition when joined with a substantial and related claim under the copyright, patent or trade-mark laws".   28 U.S.C. § 1338(b).[3]

The Reviser's Notes on this provision stated: "Subsection (b) is added and is intended to avoid 'piecemeal' litigation to enforce common-law and statutory copyright, patent, and trade-mark rights by specifically permitting such enforcement in a single civil action in the district court.   While this is the rule under federal decisions, this section would enact it as statutory authority.   The problem is discussed at length in Hurn v. Oursler. * * * "

Did the revisers fairly represent what they were doing?   What was their warrant for singling out the unfair competition aspect of the Siler–Hurn doctrine for special statutory mention?   They apparently forgot that Hurn itself was based on Siler.   Note that while cases under the copyright and patent laws are exclusively in federal jurisdiction, trademark cases are not.

2. Under the jurisdictional provisions in effect at the time (see p. 1212, *infra*), certain challenges to the constitutionality of state laws required the convening of a three-judge district court (and also provided for direct appeal of its decisions to the Supreme Court).   Thus the particular question of pendent jurisdiction (whether the three-judge court could also entertain a federal statutory claim) was sufficiently unusual that it may diminish the significance of the Hagans case in other contexts.

3. In 1970, claims under plant variety protection laws were added to § 1338(b) as well as to the categories of exclusive jurisdiction in § 1338(a). 84 Stat. 1559.

The lower courts struggled with the relationship between § 1338(b) and the Hurn doctrine, generally moving toward a wider definition of the term "related" in the statute, though certainly not with ease or unanimity. After Gibbs, however, § 1338(b) was often ignored, and the doctrine of pendent jurisdiction treated as a general judge-made gloss on the federal question jurisdiction. See 13B Wright, Miller & Cooper, Federal Practice and Procedure § 3567 (1984).

(7) *The Effect of the Eleventh Amendment.* The scope of the Siler–Hurn–Gibbs doctrine was significantly affected by the Court's ruling in Pennhurst State School & Hospital v. Halderman, 465 U.S. 89 (1984), p. 1077, *infra.* Pennhurst held that the Eleventh Amendment prohibits the federal courts from ordering state officials to conform their conduct to state law, and thereby bars the exercise of pendent jurisdiction over claims against state officials arising under state law where the relief sought "has an impact directly on the State itself" (p. 117). The Court acknowledged that Siler, and the numerous cases in its line, had approved the exercise of pendent jurisdiction in such cases (and had even held that the state-law issue should be adjudicated first[4]); but it stated that none of those cases had discussed the Eleventh Amendment. Pendent jurisdiction is a "judge-made doctrine of expediency and efficiency"; it should not override Eleventh Amendment barriers to federal court adjudication of state-law injunction actions against state officials (pp. 120–21). The resulting problem of "bifurcation of claims" (p. 122) raises a policy consideration that cannot outweigh the ban of the Eleventh Amendment. Justice Stevens' strong dissent (joined by three other justices) complained that the Siler rule has "an impressive historical pedigree" and is also "strongly supported by the interest in avoiding duplicative litigation and the unnecessary decision of federal constitutional questions" (p. 162).

The Eleventh Amendment aspect of Pennhurst is discussed at pp. 1077–84, *infra.* The case presumably leaves open the adjudication of pendent state-law claims against state officials where state consent has eliminated an Eleventh Amendment objection; and the ruling of course has no effect when the Eleventh Amendment is inapplicable (*e.g.,* suits against local governments and their officials).

(8) *"Pendent Party" Jurisdiction Before the Enactment of 28 U.S.C. § 1367.* After Gibbs, could a plaintiff who made a federal claim against one defendant append a state law claim against another defendant who could not otherwise be sued in a federal court? The Gibbs rationale led a number of lower federal courts to accept the notion of such pendent party jurisdiction when they concluded that the requirement of a "common nucleus of operative fact" was satisfied. See Miller, *Ancillary and Pendent Jurisdiction*, 26 So.Texas L.Rev. 1, 11 (1985).

(a) This development in the lower courts was, at the least, slowed by the Supreme Court's decision in Aldinger v. Howard, 427 U.S. 1 (1976). Aldinger was an action under 42 U.S.C. § 1983 against county officials for violating the plaintiff's constitutional rights. Jurisdiction was founded on 28 U.S.C. § 1343(3), the jurisdictional companion to what is now 42 U.S.C. § 1983. The

---

4. This latter rule had been reaffirmed as recently as 1982, the Court holding per curiam that it was an abuse of discretion under Gibbs for the court of appeals not to resolve a pendent state-law question (wheth-

er an affirmative action plan was invalid under state law), resolution of which might moot a federal constitutional question. Schmidt v. Oakland Unified School District, 457 U.S. 594 (1982).

established rule at that time (since overruled, see p. _____, *infra*) was that cities and counties were not "persons" liable under § 1983, and thus could not be sued in a federal court under § 1343(3). In Aldinger, however, plaintiff also asserted a pendent state-law claim against the defendant officials, and named the county as a defendant in that state-law claim.

The Supreme Court held that the claim against the county must be dismissed. Congress' determination that local governmental entities should not be liable as a matter of federal law in a federal court under §§ 1343(3) and 1983, the Court concluded, would be undermined by allowing them to be sued in federal court under the judge-made doctrine of pendent jurisdiction. "In Osborn and Gibbs Congress was silent on the extent to which the defendant, already properly in federal court under a statute, might be called upon to answer nonfederal questions or claims; the way was thus left open for the Court to fashion its own rules under the general language of Article III. But the extension of Gibbs [here] * * * must be decided, not in the context of congressional silence or tacit encouragement, but in quite the opposite context" (pp. 15–16).

(b) The Supreme Court further limited pendent party jurisdiction in Finley v. United States, 490 U.S. 545 (1989), and its decision led to a significant legislative response. In Finley, the plaintiff sued the United States under the Federal Tort Claims Act (FTCA), alleging that the FAA's negligence caused a plane crash in which her husband and two of her children died. Under the FTCA, federal court jurisdiction is exclusive. The district court later granted plaintiff's motion to add a tort claim against the local electric company (whose transmission lines the plane had struck) and the City of San Diego, asserting pendent party jurisdiction. The Ninth Circuit reversed.

Before the Supreme Court, the Solicitor General argued narrowly, on the basis of the FTCA's language and legislative history, that plaintiffs suing the United States under the Act could not join private parties as co-defendants. But Justice Scalia's opinion for a divided Court rested on broader ground. It stressed the principle that "[t]he Constitution must have given to the court the capacity to take [jurisdiction], *and an act of Congress must have supplied it....* To the extent that such action is not taken, the power lies dormant" (p. 548, quoting The Mayor v. Cooper, 73 U.S. (6 Wall.) 247, 252 (1868)(emphasis added)). In the Court's view, Gibbs' assertion of jurisdiction over pendent claims to the full extent permitted by Article III, "without specific examination of jurisdictional statutes," was in tension with this principle (p. 548). The Court's opinion continued:

"We may assume, without deciding, that the constitutional criterion for pendent-party jurisdiction is analogous to the constitutional criterion for pendent-claim jurisdiction, and that [plaintiff's] state-law claims pass that test. Our cases show, however, that with respect to the addition of parties, as opposed to the addition of only claims, we will not assume that the full constitutional power has been congressionally authorized, and will not read jurisdictional statutes broadly. [Here he relied heavily on two diversity cases: Zahn v. International Paper Co., 414 U.S. 291, 301 (1973), p. 1556, *infra* (holding that in a federal court class action, the court lacks jurisdiction over any plaintiff whose claim falls short of the jurisdictional amount), and Owen Equipment & Erection Co. v. Kroger, 437 U.S. 365, 374 (1978), p. 1558, *infra* (holding that there is no ancillary jurisdiction over a plaintiff's claim against a non-diverse third-party defendant)]. * * * While in a narrow class of cases a federal court may assert authority over [a claim against an additional party] 'ancillary' to jurisdiction otherwise properly vested—for example, when an additional party has a claim upon contested assets within the court's exclusive control, or when necessary to give effect to the court's judgment—we have never reached such a result solely on the basis that the Gibbs test has been met" (pp. 549–51).

The Court found that the language of the FTCA's jurisdictional grant over "civil actions on claims against the United States" (28 U.S.C. § 1346(b)) means "against the United States and no one else" (p. 552). Justice Scalia acknowledged that because of the exclusivity of federal jurisdiction over FTCA actions, the Court's decision would require plaintiff to file two suits, one in state court and one in federal court, but concluded that the FTCA permitted no other result.

The Court's concluding paragraph, however, could be viewed as reaching well beyond suits under the FTCA: "[O]ur cases do not display an entirely consistent approach with respect to the necessity that jurisdiction be explicitly conferred. The Gibbs line of cases was a departure from prior practice, and a departure that we have no intent to limit or impair. But Aldinger indicated that the Gibbs approach would not be extended to the pendent-party field, and we decide today to retain that line. * * * All our cases * * * have held that a grant of jurisdiction over claims involving particular parties does not itself confer jurisdiction over additional claims by or against different parties" (p. 556).[4]

(9) *Legislative Response.* Following considerable scholarly criticism both of the Finley result and of its implications in other contexts, the Federal Courts Study Committee made a specific recommendation for congressional action, and Congress responded by adding § 1367 to Title 28 as part of the Judicial Improvements Act of 1990. See Mengler, Burbank & Rowe, *Congress Accepts Supreme Court's Invitation to Codify Supplemental Jurisdiction,* 74 Judicature 213 (1991). One result of this provision was to substitute the term "supplemental" jurisdiction for the prevailing (and often confusing) references to pendent, ancillary, and even "tag-along" jurisdiction.

Subsection (a) of this new section provides in sweeping terms that (except as stated in subsections (b) and (c) or in another federal law), a district court having original jurisdiction over a case "shall have supplemental jurisdiction over all other claims" that form part "of the same case or controversy" under Article III, including claims involving additional parties. Subsection (b) excepts from the scope of subsection (a) a variety of claims by plaintiffs against additional parties, or by persons proposed to be joined or seeking to intervene, "when exercising supplemental jurisdiction over such claims would be inconsistent with the jurisdictional requirements of [the diversity jurisdiction as provided in] section 1332." (See pp. 1564–67, *infra.*) Subsection (c) gives district courts limited discretion to decline to exercise supplemental jurisdiction,[5] and subsection (d) provides for tolling of the statute of limitations governing supplemental claims that are filed and then dismissed.

---

4. Justice Blackmun and Justice Stevens (who was joined by Justices Brennan and Marshall) dissented.

5. The House Report accompanying the bill states, cryptically, that when a district court dismisses a supplemental claim under subsection (c), and the party chooses to refile the claim in state court, the federal court "in deciding the party's claims over which the court has retained jurisdiction, should accord no claim preclusive effect to a state court judgment on the supplemental claim." H.R.Rep. No. 101–734, 101st Cong., 2d Sess. 29–30 (1990). This result could certainly have been provided in the statute itself, but can it be squared with the requirements of

At least with respect to the question of pendent party jurisdiction, may the Finley decision and the legislature's response to it be seen as a model of successful dialogue between the Court and Congress? Or should the statute be understood as a specific remonstrance to a Court that had been taking too crabbed a view of the scope of federal jurisdiction?

(10) *Problems in the Interpretation and Application of § 1367.*[6]

(a) The text of § 1367 leaves no doubt that it applies to all federal court litigation other than matters excepted by its provisions. Thus, in the area of non-diversity litigation, the section plainly applies in admiralty as well as in "arising under" cases (see p. 975, *infra,* as to the distinction). It is also clear that the section contemplates the availability of supplemental jurisdiction with respect to such devices as counterclaims, cross-claims, intervention, and permissive and "necessary" joinder, so long as the specified criteria are met. See generally McLaughlin, *The Federal Supplementary Jurisdiction Statute–A Constitutional and Statutory Analysis,* 24 Arizona St.L.J.849, 925–34 (1992).[7]

(b) The Ninth Circuit, alone among the courts of appeals, has indicated constitutional doubts about the permissibility of "pendent party" jurisdiction, but has never spelled out its reasons. See Moberly, Moberly & Moberly, *Penetrating the Thicket: Pendent–Party Removal Jurisdiction in the Ninth Circuit,* 30 Idaho L.Rev. 1, 35–36 (1993–94). Given the rationale and scope of the Gibbs decision, and its close relationship to the exercise of pendent party jurisdiction, is there any basis for a flat constitutional prohibition on that exercise?

Assuming no such basis exists, what is the permissible reach of jurisdiction over "all other claims that are so related to the claims in the action within * * * original jurisdiction that they form part of the same case or controversy under Article III"? Must there be a "common nucleus of operative fact", as required by Gibbs, or are the constitutional bounds broad enough to reach other kinds of relationships? See McLaughlin, *supra* at 907–25 (arguing that a "logical relationship" is sufficient, and that some instances of permissive joinder and permissive counterclaims may qualify).[8]

(c) Section 1367 is not made explicitly applicable to cases originating in a state court and removed to a federal court, and the Supreme Court has yet to

§ 1738, as interpreted in the Marrese case, p. 1496, *infra*? If not, is this statement in the committee report sufficient to warrant an exception? *Cf.* England v. Louisiana State Board of Medical Examiners, 384 U.S. 885 (1966), p. 1243, *infra.*

6. This Paragraph, in all of its subdivisions, deals primarily with questions raised by § 1367 in the context of federal question and other non-diversity litigation. Questions relating to diversity litigation are discussed in Chap. XIII, Sec. 4, *infra.*

For discussion of the question whether § 1367 occupies the field with respect to supplemental (including pendent or ancillary) jurisdiction, see *id.,* p. 1567, note 5, *infra.*

7. As part of a general study of the effects of case consolidation on a number of

jurisdictional and other procedural issues, Professor Steinman argues that when a federal question case is consolidated with a case over which there is no independent basis of federal jurisdiction, the consolidation should be treated as creating a single civil action for purposes of determining the availability of supplemental jurisdiction under § 1367. Steinman, *The Effects of Case Consolidation on the Procedural Rights of Litigants: What They Are, What They Might Be: Part I: Justiciability and Jurisdiction (Original and Appellate),* 42 UCLA L.Rev. 717, 750–71, 792–93 (1995).

8. See also Matasar, note 1, *supra.* But in a recent decision, the Third Circuit, in refusing to uphold supplemental jurisdiction under § 1367, decided that the plaintiff's claim for overtime wages under the FLSA

speak on the question. For discussion of this question, and a suggestion that the provision does apply to removed cases, see p. 1565, *infra*.

(d) Subsection (a) of § 1367 authorizes exceptions only as specified in subsections (b) and (c) "or as expressly provided otherwise by federal statute". Does the quoted phrase leave room for an exception based, for example, on the Federal Tort Claims Act (the subject of the Finley decision), since the Act confers jurisdiction only over "civil actions on claims against the United States" (28 U.S.C. § 1346(b))? If not (and any other conclusion would appear to fly in the face of congressional purpose), how express must the exception be? Compare the discussion and interpretation in Mitchum v. Foster, p. 1195, *infra*, of similar language in 28 U.S.C. § 2283.[9]

(e) Section 1367(c) sets forth four specific grounds for the exercise of judicial discretion not to uphold supplemental jurisdiction over a claim, and none of these grounds refers in terms to the "fairness" or "efficiency" considerations articulated in Gibbs. Are those grounds for declining supplemental jurisdiction no longer available? McLaughlin, *supra*, at 974–82, argues that such factors may still be taken into account. But it is clear, as McLaughlin recognizes, that the statute rejects the language in Gibbs appearing to *require* dismissal of the supplemental claim if the federal claim is disposed of before trial. And at least one appellate court, in an elaborate and somewhat opaque opinion (and over one dissent), appears to read § 1367 as narrowing the scope of judicial discretion available prior to its enactment. Executive Software North America, Inc. v. U.S. District Court, 24 F.3d 1545 (9th Cir.1994).

The tolling provision of § 1367 does obviate one ground for a discretionary refusal to dismiss a state claim: that the statute of limitations has run on the claim since the suit was filed. At least it does so if the tolling provision passes constitutional muster even in a case in which the provision would open the doors of a state court that would otherwise be closed. For a persuasive argument that the tolling provision is valid even in that context, see McLaughlin, *supra*, at 985–89; *cf.* ALI Study of the Division of Jurisdiction Between State and Federal Courts 453–57 (1968).

SECTION 6.   RELATED HEADS OF JURISDICTION

---

lacked a common nucleus of operative fact with her state law claim for the employer's failure to pay a promised bonus. Lyon v. Whisman, 45 F.3d 758 (3d Cir.1995).

9. A special question of the scope of exceptions to § 1367 may be presented in bankruptcy cases, where 28 U.S.C. § 1334 provides not only for jurisdiction in cases "arising under" Title 11 (the bankruptcy laws) but also of cases "arising in or related to" cases under Title 11. Assuming that this language is narrower than that in § 1367, does the latter embrace claims that are related to a "related to" or "arising in" proceeding under § 1334—for example, a third-party indemnification action brought by defendants in an action by a bankruptcy trustee to avoid a preferential transfer? One commentator, in a comprehensive and perceptive analysis of the range of issues that may arise in bankruptcy cases, argues (*inter alia*) that serious constitutional questions would be presented by such a reading of § 1367 and that, to avoid these questions, the statute should not be so interpreted. Rather, § 1334 should be viewed as covering the full range of federal court jurisdiction in bankruptcy matters. Block–Lieb, *The Case Against Supplemental Bankruptcy Jurisdiction: A Constitutional, Statutory, and Policy Analysis,* 62 Fordham L.Rev. 721 (1994).

SUBSECTION A: ADMIRALTY JURISDICTION

NOTE ON THE ADMIRALTY JURISDICTION

(1) *Introduction.* This Note provides only a brief survey of the admiralty jurisdiction. For comprehensive accounts, see Gilmore & Black, The Law of Admiralty (2d ed. 1975) and Lucas, Admiralty: Cases and Materials Part One (3d ed. 1986). For a recent historical study contending that the original vision of federal admiralty jurisdiction focused not on private claims but on such "public" matters as prize cases, revenue cases, and criminal prosecutions, see Casto, *The Origins of Federal Admiralty Jurisdiction in an Age of Privateers, Smugglers, and Pirates,* 37 Am.J.Leg.Hist. 117 (1993).

(2) *The Judiciary Act of 1789.* "Section 9 of the First Judiciary Act granted the District Courts maritime jurisdiction [exclusive of the courts of the states]. This jurisdiction has remained unchanged in substance to the present day. Indeed it was recognition of the need for federal tribunals to exercise admiralty jurisdiction that was one of the controlling considerations for the establishment of a system of lower federal courts. * * *

"Section 9 not only established federal courts for the administration of maritime law; it recognized that some remedies in matters maritime had been traditionally administered by common-law courts of the original States. This role of the States * * * was preserved in the famous 'savings clause'—'saving to suitors, in all cases, the right of a common-law remedy, where the common law is competent to give it.' Since the original Judiciary Act also endowed the federal courts with diversity jurisdiction, common-law remedies for maritime causes could be enforced by the then Circuit Courts when the proper diversity of parties afforded access." Romero v. International Terminal Operating Co., 358 U.S. 354, 361–62 (1959).

(3) *Present Law.* The current provision granting admiralty jurisdiction, 28 U.S.C. § 1333(1), maintains the traditional language: "The district courts shall have original jurisdiction, exclusive of the courts of the States, of * * * [a]ny civil case of admiralty or maritime jurisdiction, saving to suitors in all cases all other remedies to which they are otherwise entitled."

(4) *The Purposes of Admiralty Jurisdiction.* What interests are served by making admiralty an area of federal jurisdiction? The original decision to do so was undoubtedly influenced by concern about international relations; consider, *e.g.,* the possible implications of prize cases, involving adjudication of the rights and status of foreign claimants and nations, neutral and belligerent. See The Federalist, No. 80 (Hamilton). Indeed, Casto, Paragraph (1), *supra,* reads the historical materials as supporting federal jurisdiction largely in terms of such "public litigation" (see *id.*, pp. 153–55). But in view of the breadth of the Admiralty Clause in Article III, it is not surprising that a broader jurisdiction has been upheld. (See pp. 154–55.) And policy support for a broad reading of the grant has been found in the perceived value of uniformity in maritime law, a notion that reflects the traditional view of the law of the sea as an independent and international body of rules transcending the power of territorial jurisdictions. A related point of contemporary significance may be a general federal interest in furthering maritime commerce.

Are any of these or all in combination sufficient to support exclusive federal jurisdiction? Concurrent jurisdiction? Could the interests be adequately protected by Supreme Court review of state court decisions?

(5) *The Romero Case.*

(a) What is the relationship between the jurisdiction of the federal courts sitting in admiralty and their "law" jurisdiction to decide cases "arising under" federal law? This was the issue in the celebrated case of Romero v. International Terminal Operating Co., 358 U.S. 354 (1959). Romero, a Spanish seaman, was injured aboard the S.S. Guadalupe while it was docked in New Jersey. He filed an action for damages in district court against the ship's Spanish owners. The complaint asserted a statutory claim under the Jones Act, 46 U.S.C. § 688, and claims under general judge-made maritime law for unseaworthiness and maintenance and cure. But Romero did not invoke the admiralty jurisdiction; he claimed the district court had jurisdiction under the Jones Act and 28 U.S.C. §§ 1331.[1]

Justice Frankfurter, writing for a majority of the Supreme Court, concluded that § 1331 did not give the district courts federal question jurisdiction (as distinct from admiralty jurisdiction) over claims arising out of judge-made maritime law (pp. 362–72):

"Up to the passage of the Judiciary Act of 1875 [the grant of admiralty jurisdiction in § 9 of the Judiciary Act, and the grant of diversity jurisdiction to adjudicate common-law claims] * * * provided the only claim for jurisdiction in the federal courts in maritime matters. [On the admiralty side], [t]his jurisdiction was exercised according to the historic procedure in admiralty, by a judge without a jury. * * * Except in diversity cases, maritime litigation brought in state courts could not be removed to the federal courts. * * *

"* * * The Constitution declares, that 'the judicial power shall extend to all cases in law and equity, arising under this Constitution, the laws of the United States, and treaties made, or which shall be made, under their authority; to all cases affecting ambassadors, or other public ministers, and consuls; to all cases of admiralty and maritime jurisdiction.'

"The Constitution certainly contemplates these as three distinct classes of cases; and if they are distinct, the grant of jurisdiction over one of them does not confer jurisdiction over either of the other two. The discrimination made between them, in the Constitution, is, we think, conclusive against their identity. See also The Sarah, 8 Wheat. 391.

"This lucid principle of constitutional construction * * * was part of the realm of legal ideas in which the authors of the Act of 1875 moved. * * *

"* * * The provision of the Act of 1875 with which we are concerned was designed to give a new content of jurisdiction to the federal courts, not to reaffirm one long-established, smoothly functioning since 1789. We have uncovered no basis for finding the additional design of changing the method by which federal courts had administered admiralty law from the beginning. * * * To draw such an inference is to find that a revolutionary procedural change had undesignedly come to pass. If we are now to attribute such a result

---

1. The Jones Act explicitly confers jurisdiction on the district courts in the action "at law" that it provides for a seaman's death or injury. See Paragraph (5)(b), *infra,* for discussion of the possible reasons for Romero's decision not to invoke the admiralty jurisdiction.

to Congress the sole remaining justification for the federal admiralty courts which have played such a vital role in our federal judicial system for 169 years will be to provide a federal forum for the small number of maritime claims which derive from state law, and to afford the ancient remedy of a libel *in rem* in those limited instances when an *in personam* judgment would not suffice to satisfy a claim. * * *

"[Moreover,] the infusion of general maritime jurisdiction into the Act of 1875 * * * would have a disruptive effect on the traditional allocation of power over maritime affairs in our federal system.

"Thus the historic option of a maritime suitor pursuing a common-law remedy to select his forum, state or federal, would be taken away by an expanded view of § 1331, since saving-clause actions would then be freely removable under § 1441 of Title 28. * * * [Further,] [b]y making maritime cases removable to the federal courts it would make considerable inroads into the traditionally exercised concurrent jurisdiction of the state courts in admiralty matters—a jurisdiction which it was the unquestioned aim of the saving clause of 1789 to preserve. * * *

"Although the corpus of admiralty law is federal in the sense that it derives from the implications of Article III evolved by the courts, to claim that all enforced rights pertaining to matters maritime are rooted in federal law is a destructive oversimplification of the highly intricate interplay of the States and the National Government in their regulation of maritime commerce. It is true that state law must yield to the needs of a uniform federal maritime law when this Court finds inroads on a harmonious system. But this limitation still leaves the States a wide scope. State-created liens are enforced in admiralty. State remedies for wrongful death and state statutes providing for the survival of actions, both historically absent from the relief offered by the admiralty, have been upheld when applied to maritime causes of action. Federal courts have enforced these statutes. State rules for the partition and sale of ships, state laws governing the specific performance of arbitration agreements, state laws regulating the effect of a breach of warranty under contracts of maritime insurance—all these laws and others have been accepted as rules of decision in admiralty cases, even, at times, when they conflicted with a rule of maritime law which did not require uniformity. * * *

"* * * If jurisdiction of maritime claims were allowed to be invoked under § 1331, it would become necessary for courts to decide whether the action 'arises under federal law,' and this jurisdictional decision would largely depend on whether the governing law is state or federal. Determinations of this nature are among the most difficult and subtle that federal courts are called upon to make. * * *"

The Court held, on the other hand, that Romero's "assertion [of a substantial claim that the Jones Act affords him a right of recovery for the negligence of his employer] was sufficient to empower the District Court to assume jurisdiction over the case and determine whether, in fact, the Act does provide the claimed rights" (p. 359). Further, though the Court rejected the argument that § 1331 provided "law" jurisdiction over the unseaworthiness and maintenance and cure claims, it saw no barrier to the district court exercising jurisdiction over these claims *pendent* to its Jones Act jurisdiction. (It did not decide "whether the District Court may submit to the jury the 'pendent' claims under the general maritime law" (p. 381)). Turning then to the merits, the Court held the Jones Act and unseaworthiness and maintenance and cure doctrines inapplicable to a foreign seaman on the facts before it.

Justice Brennan, writing for four dissenters, argued that the district court had jurisdiction under § 1331 (pp. 391–403):

"In a long series of decisions tracing from Southern Pacific Co. v. Jensen, 244 U.S. 205, this Court has made it clear that, in a seaman's action to recover damages for a maritime tort from his employer, the substantive law to be applied is federal maritime law made applicable as part of the laws of the United States by the Constitution itself, and that the right of recovery, if any, is a federally created right. * * *

"Since petitioner's causes of action for unseaworthiness and for maintenance and cure are created by federal law, his case arises under 'the laws * * * of the United States' within the meaning of § 1331, for it is clear that 'a suit arises under the law that creates the cause of action.' Holmes, J., in American Well Works Co. v. Layne & Bowler Co., 241 U.S. 257, 260. * * *

"* * * The issue before us is not whether all cases 'of admiralty and maritime jurisdiction' are *per se* encompassed in the statutory 'arising under' jurisdiction. A suit seeking the sort of remedy that the common law is not competent to give could not be fairly contended to lie under § 1331; it would clearly be the sort of suit in which the jurisdictional grant of § 1333 was intended to be exclusive. The issue before us concerns only actions maintainable in some forum 'at law' under the Saving Clause. And again, the issue is not even the narrower one whether Saving Clause actions are *per se* cognizable under § 1331. The tests of jurisdiction under § 1331 must still be met, and there is no contention that they are met merely by a showing that an action is one maintainable under the Saving Clause and involving the requisite jurisdictional amount. The plaintiff's right to recovery must still be one rooted in federal substantive law, and it has quite recently been made clear that there are Saving Clause actions that do not meet that test. Wilburn Boat Co. v. Fireman's Fund Ins. Co., 348 U.S. 310. The issue before us is only whether the fact that an action is a Saving Clause action excludes it from § 1331 where it would otherwise be maintainable thereunder. * * *

"* * * The fact that the jurisdictional categories are separate and distinct * * * does not mean that a particular action could not come under the heading of more than one of them. Everyone recognizes that this is the case in a maritime matter in which the parties are of diverse citizenship. I see no reason why it should not be true here of Romero's general maritime law claims against his employer. * * *"

(b) Why didn't Romero invoke the admiralty jurisdiction? In the hope that by not doing so, he would be able to have a jury on his claims under general maritime law? What was the significance of the Court's finding of "pendent jurisdiction" over the maritime law claims if it did not mean that those claims would go to the jury? On pendent jurisdiction generally, see Sec. 5, *supra*.

In Fitzgerald v. United States Lines, 374 U.S. 16 (1963), the Court held that when (as is the usual case) a seaman's claims for unseaworthiness and for maintenance and cure are joined in an action under the Jones Act on the "law side" of the district court, the general maritime claims must be submitted to the jury with the Jones Act claim as a matter of trial convenience.

In view of this holding, what is the ultimate significance of the Romero decision? Is the elaborateness of treatment explained by the suggestion that its question "wakes echoes in the deepest metaphysics of admiralty"? Gilmore & Black, The Law of Admiralty, 33 n. 118 (1st ed. 1957).

For thorough analyses, see Currie, *The Silver Oar and All That: A Study of the Romero Case,* 27 U.Chi.L.Rev. 1 (1959); Kurland, *The Romero Case and Some Problems of Jurisdiction,* 73 Harv.L.Rev. 817 (1960).

(c) Romero held that claims resting on the general federal maritime law do not come within § 1331. Would the same be true of a claim founded on a federal maritime statute? See Wethering, *Jurisdictional Bases of Maritime Claims Founded on Acts of Congress,* 18 U.Miami L.Rev. 163 (1963)(arguing that Romero does not apply to statutory claims).

(6) *The Scope of the Jurisdiction.*

(a) Historically, admiralty's powers have been limited to the high seas and to certain other waters within the country. The limits of those waters were defined by the Supreme Court in The Daniel Ball, 77 U.S. (10 Wall.) 557, 563 (1871), a case involving federal inspection and licensing of steam vessels operating in the navigable waters of the United States. "The doctrine of the common law as to the navigability of waters has no application in this country. Here the ebb and flow of the tide [the English common law limitation] do not constitute the usual test * * *. Those rivers must be regarded as public navigable rivers in law which are navigable in fact. And, they are navigable in fact when they are used, or are susceptible of being used, in their ordinary condition, as highways for commerce * * *. And they constitute navigable waters of the United States * * * where they form in their ordinary condition by themselves, or by uniting with other waters, a continued highway over which commerce is or may be carried on with other States or foreign countries * * *."

(b) The traditional view of admiralty tort jurisdiction turned on the locality of the tort. Maritime law governed torts occurring on navigable waters. See The Plymouth, 70 U.S. (3 Wall.) 20 (1866). The distinction produced anomalous results: if a vessel collided with a bridge, the bridge owner could not proceed against the ship by a libel in admiralty since the damage to the bridge was considered to be on land. Similarly, docks and piers were viewed as extensions of the land and injuries occurring on them were outside the admiralty jurisdiction. See, *e.g.,* State Industrial Comm'n v. Nordenholt Corp., 259 U.S. 263, 275 (1922); T. Smith & Son, Inc. v. Taylor, 276 U.S. 179, 182 (1928). Dissatisfaction with these results led Congress to enact the Admiralty Extension Act of 1948, 46 U.S.C. § 740, providing that "[t]he admiralty and maritime jurisdiction of the United States shall extend to and include all cases of damage or injury, to person or property, caused by a vessel on navigable water, notwithstanding that such damage or injury be done or consummated on land."[2]

---

2. Constitutional attacks on the statute failed in lower federal courts, *e.g.,* United States v. Matson Navigation Co., 201 F.2d 610, 614–16 (9th Cir.1953). And in Gutierrez v. Waterman Steamship Corp., 373 U.S. 206 (1963), a longshoreman's suit for injuries sustained when he slipped on beans spilled from a defective shipboard container onto a pier, the Supreme Court took jurisdiction under the Extension Act without discussing its constitutionality.

The Extension Act did not entirely eliminate the question whether the injury must occur on waters within the jurisdiction. In Victory Carriers v. Law, 404 U.S. 202 (1971), a longshoreman was injured by a defective forklift truck, owned by his stevedore employer, as he transferred cargo from a dock to a place on the pier where it would be picked up and stowed by the ship's equipment. He brought an action invoking the admiralty jurisdiction of the district court on a claim of unseaworthiness against the vessel and Victory Carriers, its owner. The Supreme Court, Justices Brennan and Douglas dissenting, held that federal maritime law did not govern the suit because the injury did not occur on waters within the jurisdiction and was not cognizable under the Extension Act because the ship's equipment had not been involved. See also Rodrigue v. Aetna Casualty & Surety Co., 395 U.S. 352 (1969)(recovery for death on artificial island oil drilling platform not within Death on the High Seas Act, which permits an action for wrongful death occurring on the high seas).

(c) The traditional rule that the locality of a tort alone sufficed to sustain admiralty jurisdiction was modified in Executive Jet Aviation, Inc. v. City of Cleveland, 409 U.S. 249 (1972). In that case, the plaintiff's tort claim arose out of the crash into the navigable waters of Lake Erie of a jet on a domestic flight. Writing for a unanimous Court, Justice Stewart recognized that admiralty jurisdiction in tort cases "has traditionally depended upon the locality of the wrong" (p. 253). But noting that "there has existed over the years a judicial, legislative, and scholarly recognition that * * * reliance on the relationship of the wrong to a traditional maritime activity is often more sensible and more consonant with the purposes of maritime law than is a purely mechanical application of the locality test" (p. 261), he concluded that "claims arising from airplane accidents are not cognizable in admiralty" unless "the wrong bear[s] a significant relationship to traditional maritime activity" (p. 268). The mere fact that aircraft falling into navigable waters may pose problems similar to those arising out of the sinking of a ship did not constitute such a relationship.

The opinion specifically left open the question of jurisdiction with respect to a transoceanic airliner, and the question whether the fact that particular commerce by air would previously have been carried on by water borne vessels is a "significant relationship to traditional maritime activity." It also noted that the holding as to land-based aircraft on domestic flights would not extend to circumstances where there is federal legislation providing for jurisdiction—as a possible example, the Death on the High Seas Act.

In Foremost Insurance Co. v. Richardson, 457 U.S. 668 (1982), the issue was whether the collision of two pleasure boats on navigable United States waters fell within the admiralty jurisdiction. All members of the Court agreed that the Executive Jet requirement that the wrong have a significant connection with traditional maritime activity was controlling, thus ending doubts as to whether the requirement was limited to the aviation context. But the Court split upon the application of the test. With Justice Marshall writing for a majority of five, the Court held that because the wrong "involves the negligent operation of a vessel on navigable waters, * * * it has a sufficient nexus to traditional maritime activity" (p. 674). The majority rejected an argument that, "because commercial shipping is at the heart of * * * traditional maritime activity," a nexus with commerce was required for jurisdiction: "The federal interest in protecting maritime commerce cannot be adequately served if admiralty jurisdiction is restricted to those individuals actually *engaged* in commercial maritime activity. This interest can be fully vindicated only if *all* operators of vessels on navigable waters are subject to uniform rules of conduct" (pp. 674–75). The minority would have denied jurisdiction, stating that since neither craft was engaged in commercial activity, there was "no connection with any historic federal admiralty interest," pleasure boating being "basically a new phenomenon" (pp. 680–81).[3]

It is not yet settled whether the Executive Jet nexus requirement will be applied in cases where the tort occurred on the high seas. See East River S.S. Corp. v. Transamerica Delaval, Inc., 476 U.S. 858 (1986), involving a products liability claim relating to turbines that failed while ships were on the high seas. The Court noted that Executive Jet and Foremost involved torts that occurred on navigable waters within the United States, and stated that it did not need to reach the question "whether a maritime nexus also must be established when a tort occurs on the high seas" because "were there such a requirement, it was clearly met" in East River.

For a collection of lower court cases applying the Executive Jet test, see 14 Wright, Miller & Cooper, Federal Practice & Procedure § 3676 (1985 & 1995 Supp.).

(d) Admiralty jurisdiction over contract cases "depends upon * * * the nature and character of the contract * * * as to whether it have reference to maritime service or maritime transactions." North Pacific S.S. Co. v. Hall Bros. Co., 249 U.S. 119, 125 (1919). The application of this generalization has produced rather blurred jurisdictional lines. For example, a contract to build a ship is not within the admiralty jurisdiction, People's Ferry Co. v. Beers, 61 U.S. (20 How.) 393 (1858), while a contract to reconstruct or repair a ship may be litigated in admiralty, The Jack–O–Lantern, 258 U.S. 96 (1922). For examples of maritime contracts, see Gilmore & Black, Paragraph (1), *supra,* at 22. Professor Black has said of the pattern, "[T]here is about as much 'principle' as there is in a list of irregular verbs." Black, *Admiralty Jurisdiction: Critique and Suggestion,* 50 Colum.L.Rev. 259, 264 (1950). Gilmore & Black, *supra,* at 31, suggest that the correct line may be drawn to include "those things principally connected with maritime transportation," and that on this view the courts have been under-inclusive as to contracts. For an attempt to formulate a general rule from the cases, see Moore & Pelaez, *Admiralty Jurisdiction—The Sky's the Limit,* 33 J.Air Law 3, 5 (1967)(contracts enforced in admiralty all concerned a "vessel").[4]

---

3. In Sisson v. Ruby, 497 U.S. 358 (1990), a yacht owner, whose yacht had caught fire while docked at a marina on navigable waters, brought a limitation of liability suit in federal district court. The Supreme Court, relying on its analysis in the Foremost case, held that the action was within the admiralty jurisdiction: storage and maintenance of a vessel on navigable waters "is substantially related to 'traditional maritime activity' "(p. 367).

Applying the criteria developed in Foremost and in Sisson, the Court upheld admiralty jurisdiction in an action by a barge owner to limit its liability for damages resulting from the flooding of a freight tunnel running under a navigable river—flooding that caused damage to many buildings in downtown Chicago. Jerome B. Grubart, Inc. v. Great Lakes Dredge & Dock Co., 115 S.Ct. 1043 (1995). Concurring in the judgment, Justice Thomas (joined by Justice Scalia) advocated abandoning the Sisson approach and "restoring the jurisdictional inquiry to the simple question whether the tort occurred on a vessel in the navigable waters of the United States" (*id.* at 1056–57).

4. In Exxon Corp. v. Central Gulf Lines, Inc., 500 U.S. 603 (1991), the Court, overruling Minturn v. Maynard, 58 U.S. (17 How.) 477 (1855), held that agency contracts are not per se excluded from the scope of

(7) *The Saving Clause and the Role of State Law.*

(a) The grant of exclusive jurisdiction to the district courts in § 1333 is honeycombed with actions maintainable in state courts by virtue of the saving clause. The current interpretation allows a plaintiff to institute an action in personam in federal admiralty court, in state court, or, if federal jurisdiction is otherwise supported, on the "law side" of the federal court. See 14 Wright, Miller & Cooper, *supra,* at 430–33. Only a maritime action in rem must be brought in a federal admiralty court. See The Moses Taylor, 71 U.S. (4 Wall.) 411 (1867).[5]

The original saving clause ("saving to suitors, in all cases, the right of a common law remedy, where the common law is competent to give it") was interpreted to permit a state court to order specific performance of a maritime contract—an equitable remedy unknown to the common law courts of 1789. See Red Cross Line v. Atlantic Fruit Co., 264 U.S. 109 (1924). The 1948 revision ("saving to suitors * * * all other remedies to which they are otherwise entitled") has been taken as intended to conform to the Red Cross decision, and, other than this change, has been read as preserving the meaning of the original language. See Madruga v. Superior Court, 346 U.S. 556, 560 n. 12 (1954).[6]

(b) Certain maritime actions are committed by statute to exclusive federal jurisdiction. *E.g.,* suits against the United States arising from the operation of government vessels, 46 U.S.C. §§ 741–42, 781–82; proceedings under the Limitation of Liability Act, 46 U.S.C. §§ 183–89; actions under the Ship Mortgage Act, 46 U.S.C. § 951.[7] On the utility of state court jurisdiction under the saving clause, consider Justice Brennan's dissent in Romero (pp. 409–10): "[I]n the five-year period 1953 to 1957 inclusive only about 150 decisions in Saving Clause actions have been rendered in the state courts of the country. * * * Saving Clause suitors seem long ago to have deserted the state courts." Compare the reasons advanced in support of concurrent jurisdiction by the Romero majority (p. 372). See also the proposal of Professor Black, Paragraph (6)(d), *supra,* 50 Colum.L.Rev. at 276–80 (exclusive federal jurisdiction in maritime industry contract and commercial matters; exclusive state court jurisdiction of all personal injury claims).

(c) On the roles of federal and state law in maritime matters, see the *Note on the Sources of Law in Admiralty,* p. 797, *supra.*

---

admiralty jurisdiction. The Exxon Court determined that admiralty jurisdiction extended to a suit for breach of contract brought for failure to reimburse an agent for money spent to purchase fuel for a vessel in a foreign port.

5. The in rem/in personam distinction has been criticized as without historical support in Casto, Paragraph (1), *supra,* at 140–42.

6. In American Dredging Co. v. Miller, 114 S.Ct. 981 (1994), a divided Supreme Court held that federal law does not preempt state forum non conveniens doctrine (which in this case did not require dismissal) in a maritime case filed in a state court under the "saving to suitors" clause and the Jones Act.

7. Some lower courts had held the Death on the High Seas Act, 46 U.S.C. § 761, to confer exclusive federal jurisdiction, but in dicta in Offshore Logistics, Inc. v. Tallentire, 477 U.S. 207 (1986), the Court stated that DOHSA jurisdiction was concurrent.

SUBSECTION B: ACTIONS BROUGHT BY THE FEDERAL GOVERNMENT

NOTE ON CIVIL ACTIONS INSTITUTED
BY THE FEDERAL GOVERNMENT*

(1) *Statutory History.* The present general grant of jurisdiction to the federal courts for civil litigation instituted by the United States is 28 U.S.C. § 1345. This provision had its roots in the First Judiciary Act, which gave the district courts jurisdiction, concurrent with the state courts, "of all suits at common law where the United States shall sue", subject to a jurisdictional amount requirement of $100. (Act of Sept. 24, 1789, § 9, 1 Stat. 73, 77.) It gave the circuit courts jurisdiction, also concurrent, "of all suits at common law or in equity", subject to a jurisdictional amount requirement of $500. (*Id.* § 11, 1 Stat. 78.)

In 1815 both the district courts and the circuit courts were given jurisdiction of "all suits at common law" where either "the United States, or any officer thereof, under the authority of an act of Congress, shall sue"; and the requirement of a jurisdictional amount was dropped. (Act of March 3, 1815, § 4, 3 Stat. 244, 245.)

The Judiciary Act of 1875 restored the jurisdictional amount requirement of $500 in the circuit courts in suits at common law as well as in equity "in which the United States are plaintiffs or petitioners", and for the first time authorized removal in such cases. (Act of March 3, 1875, §§ 1, 2, 18 Stat. 470.) Twelve years later removal was limited to nonresident defendants, and the requirement of a jurisdictional amount was permanently eliminated. (Act of March 3, 1887, 24 Stat. 552, as corrected by Act of August 13, 1888, 25 Stat. 433.)

When the circuit courts were abolished in 1911, their jurisdiction in these cases was transferred to the district courts, and to it was added cognizance of all civil actions brought by federal officers "authorized by law to sue". (Act of March 3, 1911, § 24, 36 Stat. 1087, 1091.) The last obstacle to federal access to the national courts was thus removed. The general grant in § 1345, which includes actions by "any agency" as well as officers of the United States, remains a concurrent jurisdiction.[1]

The First Judiciary Act also gave the district courts cognizance "of all seizures on land, or [on non-navigable waters] * * *, and of all suits for penalties and forfeitures incurred, under the laws of the United States." (Act of Sept. 24, 1789, § 9, 1 Stat. 73, 77.) The jurisdiction survives today in 28 U.S.C. §§ 1355–1356 and, like its predecessor in 1789, is exclusive.

In addition to the general grants of jurisdiction, there are a number of specific grants in the Judicial Code. *E.g.,* §§ 1336 (ICC orders), 1339 (postal

---

* Problems of actions against the United States and its agencies and officers—including the statutory bases of jurisdiction in such actions, and doctrines of sovereign and official immunity—are dealt with in Chapter IX. Implied causes of action for constitutional violations against federal officials are discussed in Chap. VII, Sec. 2C, p. 847, *supra.* Implied causes of action on behalf of the United States are discussed in Chap. VII, Sec. 2A, p. 811, *supra.*

1. Note also the provision for counterclaims in suits against the United States, 28 U.S.C. § 1346(c).

matters), 1340 (internal revenue; customs duties), and 1358 (eminent domain). (With the elimination of any jurisdictional amount requirement in suits brought by the government and in all federal question suits under § 1331, do these provisions serve any function?) And the other titles of the Code abound in specific provisions, embedded in substantive statutes, authorizing particular officers or agencies to bring actions, and frequently including an express grant of federal jurisdiction.

For general discussion of the United States as plaintiff, see 14 Wright, Miller & Cooper, Federal Practice and Procedure §§ 3651–53 (1985 & 1995 Supp.).

(2) *Types of Statutory Provisions*.

(a) Most rights of action by the United States or federal agencies rest on a statutory basis, but the statutes vary greatly in how explicitly and comprehensively they delineate the rights and remedies involved. (For a selective catalogue of such statutes, see 14 Wright, Miller & Cooper, Paragraph (1), *supra*, § 3653.)

The simplest kind of statutory formulation is illustrated by § 4 of the Sherman Act and § 15 of the Clayton Act (15 U.S.C. §§ 4, 25). The district courts are "invested with" jurisdiction "to prevent and restrain" violations of the statutes, and it is declared to be the "duty" of the United States "under the direction of the Attorney General, to institute proceedings in equity to prevent and restrain such violations."

Simplicity yields to complexity, however, when restrictive practices challenged by the Antitrust Division occur in regulated industries. The regime of regulation may itself condemn, or authorize an administrative agency to condemn, the challenged practice; it may authorize the agency to approve or disapprove the practice, with or without consideration of antitrust norms; and administrative approval may or may not immunize the practice from antitrust condemnation. In such situations the doctrine of "primary jurisdiction" (see Texas & Pacific Ry. Co. v. Abilene Cotton Oil Co., 204 U.S. 426 (1907)) may require the United States to apply to the administrative agency for relief before instituting action to enjoin. For discussion of this complex and important doctrine, see Pierce, Shapiro & Verkuil, Administrative Law and Process 192–200 (2d ed. 1992).

(b) What is the significance of a statutory right of action like § 4 of the Sherman Act? Would a right of action exist anyway under the San Jacinto and Debs cases, pp. 811, 815, *supra* (both of which recognize, in the particular circumstances, an implied right of action on behalf of the United States)? Are there material differences between such a "common law" remedy and a statutory remedy?

The cases are replete with statements that a statutory jurisdiction to grant injunctions is to be administered in the light of general equitable principles. *E.g.,* Appalachian Coals, Inc. v. United States, 288 U.S. 344, 377 (1933); Hecht Co. v. Bowles, 321 U.S. 321 (1944); De Beers Consolidated Mines, Ltd. v. United States, 325 U.S. 212, 218–23 (1945). Some of these statements may have been motivated by Article III concerns over the integrity of judicial processes. See Shreve, *Federal Injunctions and the Public Interest,* 51 Geo. Wash.L.Rev. 382, 397–405 (1983).

But should not a statutory grant be read as dispensing in some degree with the usual prerequisites of equity jurisdiction? *Cf.* United Steelworkers v.

United States, 361 U.S. 39 (1959), holding an 80–day injunction mandatory under § 208 of the Labor–Management Relations Act, 29 U.S.C. § 178, when statutory findings of fact are made by the court. And see generally Shreve, *supra,* at 405: "[T]he essentials of equitable restraint are rarely sacrificed in the face of the so-called mandatory injunction [provided for by a specific statutory provision]. Judicial reservations concerning substantiality, adequacy, and irreparability give way, as they should, in the face of special law-enforcement authority and the needs of the governmental plaintiff. Judicial reservations concerning imminence [of threatened harm] and manageability, in contrast, do not. They must be addressed in each case."

(3) *Judicial Discretion.* To what extent do district courts have authority to decline to exercise jurisdiction in actions brought by the United States or federal officers on the ground that they assert rights more appropriately asserted in state courts? See United States v. Bank of New York & Trust Co., 296 U.S. 463, 479–81 (1936); Markham v. Allen, p. 1334, *infra; cf.* Colorado River Water Conserv. Dist. v. United States, p. 1308, *infra.*

(4) *Intervention.* When the United States or a federal agency seeks to intervene as of right in a private action, should it be required to satisfy the conditions ordinarily imposed by Rule 24(a) of the Federal Rules of Civil Procedure—a sufficient "interest relating to the property or transaction which is the subject of the action" and a lack of adequate representation by existing parties? And what of third-party intervention in a civil action brought by the United States; is it more restricted than intervention in private civil actions? See generally Shapiro, *Some Thoughts on Intervention Before Courts, Agencies, and Arbitrators,* 81 Harv.L.Rev. 721 (1968).

Rule 24(b) was amended in 1948 to give the district courts discretion to permit intervention by a governmental officer or agency when a party to an action relies on a statute, order, regulation, requirement, or agreement issued or administered by that officer or agency. See 7C Wright, Miller & Kane, Federal Practice and Procedure § 1912 (1986). And the government has an absolute right to intervene in any private action "wherein the constitutionality of any Act of Congress affecting the public interest is drawn in question." 28 U.S.C. § 2403.[2]

(5) *Special Provisions.* In addition to certain judge-made doctrines favoring the United States as a party in civil litigation, see p. 819, *supra,* there are a number of special statutory and rule provisions affecting the government as a litigant. Thus there is a general statute of limitations, 28 U.S.C. § 2415, that applies to most actions brought by the government or a federal officer or agency. See also 28 U.S.C. § 2404 (no abatement of damage action on death of defendant); § 2405 (garnishment); § 2407 (delinquents for public money); § 2408 (security not required); § 2413 (executions in favor of the United States).[3]

---

2. The right was acquired as salvage from the 1937 court-packing proposal. See the discussion of the predecessor to § 2403 (former § 401) in Note, 51 Harv.L.Rev. 148 (1937).

3. Some statutory provisions permit the award of attorney's fees to prevailing private parties in actions by or against the United States in situations in which the generally accepted common law rule in this country would not permit such an award. See Chap. IX, pp. 1006–07, *infra.*

(6) *Control of Government Civil Litigation.*   The question of the control of government litigation is more complex on the civil side than it is on the criminal side.   (As to the latter, see pp. 991–92, *infra.*)

(a) The Gray Jacket, 72 U.S. (5 Wall.) 370, 371 (1866), was a Civil War prize case in which, following an appearance by Assistant Attorney General Ashton in support of the captors, Caleb Cushing sought to appear in behalf of the Treasury Department to support the opposing position of the claimants. The Court heard Mr. Cushing, but Chief Justice Chase announced a different rule for the future:

"The court * * * has instructed me to say that in causes where the United States is a party, and is represented by the Attorney–General or the Assistant Attorney–General, or special counsel employed by the Attorney–General, no counsel can be heard in opposition on behalf of any other of the departments of the government."

This ruling has in effect been codified in 28 U.S.C. § 516, which states that, except as otherwise provided by law, the conduct of litigation involving the United States and its interests is "reserved to officers of the Department of Justice, under the direction of the Attorney General." Thus the Attorney General and the Department of Justice have been vested with large power and responsibility in resolving conflicts of opinion within the government concerning the positions to be presented to the courts.[4]

(b) In recent decades, many officers and agencies (in addition to the Attorney General) have been expressly authorized to sue (as well as to be sued) in their own names.   See, *e.g.,* 47 U.S.C. § 401(b)(authorizing suit by the FCC or by the Attorney General); 15 U.S.C. §§ 77t(b), 78u(e)(SEC); 29 U.S.C. §§ 160(e), 160(j), 160(*l*)(NLRB); 15 U.S.C. §§ 45(*l*), 45(m), 53, 56, 57b (giving the FTC exclusive authority to represent itself in certain actions and discretion to represent itself in others, as well as discretion to represent itself before the Supreme Court).[5]

This trend away from concentration of litigating authority in the Department of Justice led Attorney General Griffin Bell, in 1978, to urge the development of a more centralized system for the conduct of government litigation.   See Bell, *The Attorney General: The Government's Chief Lawyer and Chief Litigator, or One Among Many?*, 46 Fordham L.Rev. 1049 (1978).   As a result, on July 18, 1979, the President issued Exec.Order No. 12146, 44

---

4. *Cf.* United States v. San Francisco, 310 U.S. 16 (1940), an injunction action against the city (to enjoin the disposal of municipally generated power to a private utility) brought by the Attorney General at the request of the Secretary of the Interior. The granting statute provided that in certain circumstances, "upon written request of the Secretary of the Interior, it is made the duty of the Attorney General" to bring all necessary proceedings to carry out the provisions of the Act.

What are the respective duties of the Secretary and the Attorney General under this not uncommon type of statute? Is it proper to oblige the Attorney General to institute litigation, at the "request" of a non-lawyer, if the Attorney General's professional conscience and sense of obligation as a sworn officer of the court militate strongly against institution of the litigation? To prevent the Attorney General from bringing an action in the absence of such a request?

5. *Cf.* Federal Election Comm'n v. NRA Political Victory Fund, 115 S.Ct. 537 (1994)(declining to read broad statutory grant of litigating authority to Commission as conferring independent authority on Commission to seek certiorari and to represent itself before the Supreme Court in the particular action).

Fed.Reg. 42657, entitled "Management of Federal Legal Resources." This Order established a Federal Legal Council, chaired by the Attorney General, whose duties would include promoting coordination among federal legal offices; the Order also "encourages" executive branch agencies to submit legal disputes to the Attorney General for resolution.[6]

(c) In some instances, the diffusion of authority has meant that both the Department of Justice and a concerned agency may present their views in the same case, and those views may be opposed. See, *e.g.,* Mitchell v. United States, 313 U.S. 80 (1941); *cf.* St. Regis Paper Co. v. United States, 368 U.S. 208, 217 (1961); Note, 78 Yale L.J. 1443, 1465 (1969). In other instances, in which both the agency and the United States are formal parties, the Department of Justice may be actively espousing the conflicting views of another government agency. Do these cases raise problems of justiciability when the only contesting parties are both agencies or officers of the United States? See Chap. II, Sec. 2, pp. 103–04, *supra.* Is the judicial process an appropriate way of resolving differences of opinion between executive departments of the same government? Between an executive department and an "independent" agency? Between two independent agencies? To the extent that the dispute involves a conflict between major statutory schemes, may there not be special value in resorting to the courts to determine how the schemes should be adjusted? See ICC v. Jersey City, 322 U.S. 503 (1944).[7]

(d) Incident to the general power (subject to the noted exceptions) to conduct government litigation, the Attorney General has almost plenary authority to settle or compromise such litigation. See, *e.g.,* New York v. New Jersey, 256 U.S. 296 (1921). In some instances, however, Congress has prescribed the procedure for compromise or has limited the amount that may be paid in settlement. See, *e.g.,* 28 U.S.C. § 2672 (tort claims); 10 U.S.C. § 224(b)(claims against the FBI).

What standards ought to guide the Attorney General in approving or disapproving proposed settlements? How free should a government attorney be to accept a compromise based on a prudent estimate of the probability of

---

6. For an informative analysis of the early history of the Office of the Attorney General, and of the roles of the President and of Congress in controlling that officer, see Bloch, *The Early Role of the Attorney General in Our Constitutional Scheme: In the Beginning There Was Pragmatism,* 1989 Duke L.J. 561.

7. See generally Bell, Paragraph 6(b), *supra,* at 1058; Stern, *"Inconsistency" in Government Litigation,* 64 Harv.L.Rev. 759 (1951).

For a comprehensive discussion of problems of the justiciability of intragovernmental disputes, see Herz, *United States v. United States: When Can the Federal Government Sue Itself?,* 32 Wm. & Mary L.Rev. 893 (1991). Herz notes that interagency litigation falls into three categories: "First, one agency may challenge a decision of another that applies directly to it [as when an em-

ploying agency challenges an order by the Federal Labor Relations Authority to bargain with a union representing its employees]. Second, agencies may disagree over actions that affect private parties. Third, agencies may have disputes over regulatory authority, such as disagreements over jurisdiction" (p. 938). Rejecting the notion that such litigation is necessarily precluded because the United States is a single entity, or that the idea of a "unitary executive" necessarily precludes litigation between two entities within the executive branch, Herz concludes that suits in his first and third categories are justiciable and that those in the second category are not. Suits in that category, he argues, violate a principle of "unitary execution" of the laws: the *"constitutionally assigned* task [of enforcement officers in the executive branch] is to figure out enforcement policy on their own" (p. 973).

success? When another government department or agency is involved, how far should the Department of Justice defer to its opinion?

(e) Compare with the foregoing the ancient (and recently expanded) notion of the qui tam action, *i.e.,* an action by a private citizen to recover money for the government and to share in the proceeds of the recovery.[8]

In 1986, an amendment to the False Claims Act, 31 U.S.C. §§ 3729–3732, increased the availability of such actions by persons seeking to share in the recovery of damages and civil penalties for defrauding the federal treasury. As a result, a number of such actions have been brought, and in several instances, defendants have asserted that the qui tam mechanism is unconstitutional because Article II precludes Congress from vesting public law enforcement authority in private citizens and because private citizens do not have a sufficient personal interest in the underlying controversy. So far, these challenges have been consistently rejected. See, *e.g.,* United States ex rel. Kreindler & Kreindler v. United Technologies Corp., 985 F.2d 1148 (2d Cir.1993); United States ex rel. Truong v. Northrop Corp., 728 F.Supp. 615 (C.D.Cal. 1989); United States ex rel. Newsham v. Lockheed Missiles and Space Co., 722 F.Supp. 607 (N.D.Cal.1989). As these courts have noted, the Department of Justice retains considerable control and oversight of qui tam actions under the False Claims Act, including authority to intervene in, dismiss, or settle the action.

For a discussion of these problems and a defense of the constitutionality of the qui tam action, see Caminker, *The Constitutionality of Qui Tam Actions,* 99 Yale L.J. 341 (1989). Caminker concludes: "Authorizing private citizens to enforce the United States' legal interests through qui tam actions, no less than authorizing citizens to enforce their own legislatively created interests as an indirect means of implementing public policy objectives, is within Congress' power to 'judge *what* to do, and *how* to do it' " (p. 388)(quoting Lincoln's 1858 acceptance speech to the Republican convention). See also Comment, 57 U.Chi.L.Rev. 543 (1990)(suggesting that for purposes of determining standing to sue, a private qui tam plaintiff should be viewed as a partial assignee of the government's claim); *cf.* Note, 62 Geo.Wash.L.Rev. 609 (1994)(arguing that to permit individual employees and officers of the executive branch to prosecute qui tam suits under the 1986 Act would violate the Constitution).

(f) Title VII of the Ethics in Government Act of 1978 (codified at 2 U.S.C. §§ 288–288n; 28 U.S.C. § 1365) establishes the Office of Senate Legal Counsel. The Counsel is charged, *inter alia,* to represent the Senate, its committees, subcommittees, members, officers, or employees in a wide variety of civil actions. The Attorney General is relieved of responsibility for representation in certain actions but retains any existing right to intervene or appear as amicus.

The rationale for this legislation was fully set forth in S.Rep. No. 95–170, 95th Cong., 1st Sess. 8–16 (1977). The Report concluded that the result of reliance on the Department of Justice (and occasionally on private counsel) for

---

8. See United States ex rel. Marcus v. Hess, 317 U.S. 537, 545–47 (1943)(holding that Marcus (the qui tam plaintiff) could maintain such an action in spite of the previous conviction of the offenders and in spite of the fact that Marcus might have "received his information not by his own investigation, but from the previous indictment").

representation had been that congressional interests were "often inadequately represented or [were] not represented at all."

NOTE ON CRIMINAL PROSECUTIONS INSTITUTED BY THE FEDERAL GOVERNMENT

(1) *Statutory History.* The First Judiciary Act, §§ 9, 11, 1 Stat. 73, 76, 79, gave the district and circuit courts jurisdiction (exclusive of the state courts) over crimes and offenses "cognizable under the authority of the United States"; the district courts were restricted to prosecutions "where no other punishment than whipping, not exceeding thirty stripes, a fine not exceeding one hundred dollars, or a term of imprisonment not exceeding six months, is to be inflicted." (For discussion of United States v. Hudson & Goodwin, 11 U.S. (7 Cranch) 32 (1812), refusing to recognize a common-law jurisdiction in criminal cases, see pp. 747–49, *supra.*)

In 1794, however, Congress provided for concurrent jurisdiction in the state courts to award all "fines, penalties, and forfeitures" under the Carriage Tax Act.[1] Subsequent federal criminal legislation occasionally authorized state court enforcement, although federal court enforcement remained the rule. See generally Warren, *Federal Criminal Laws and the State Courts*, 38 Harv.L.Rev. 545 (1925), which also discusses the power of Congress to require state courts to enforce federal penal laws.

On the questions of whether, and to what extent, the states may be authorized, or required, to enforce federal criminal laws, see further Chap. IV, Secs. 1 and 3.

The present jurisdiction is codified at 18 U.S.C. § 3231, and gives the district courts exclusive jurisdiction "of all offenses against the laws of the United States."

(2) *The Purposes of Federal Criminal Prosecution.* Most federal prosecutions involve the enforcement of general statutes, enacted in the exercise of constitutionally defined powers of Congress, that criminalize conduct without regard to its specific location within the United States. In an important article in 1948, Professor Louis Schwartz suggested that "federal criminal jurisdiction is being employed in three different ways: (1) to punish anti-social conduct of distinctively, if not exclusively, federal concern; (2) to punish conduct of local concern, with which local enforcement authorities are unable or unwilling to cope; and (3) to secure compliance with federal administrative regulations." *Federal Criminal Jurisdiction and Prosecutor's Discretion*, 13 L. & Contemp.Prob. 64, 66–67 (1948). Yet as Professor Schwartz noted, many of the most important federal crimes employ criteria (such as use of the mails, use of means of interstate commerce, or conduct involving interstate transportation of some kind) that relate imperfectly to these categories. Consider Friendly, Federal Jurisdiction: A General View 58–59 (1973): "Why should it make a difference that a New York pimp chooses Newark, N.J., rather than Nyack, N.Y., as the place where his employees transact their business? * * * Why should the federal government be concerned with a $100 robbery from a federally insured savings bank although it is not if someone burned down Macy's?"

---

1. Act of June 5, 1794, ch. 45, § 10, 1 Stat. 373.

Within the constitutional limits of federal power (see note 2, *infra*), when should federal authority and resources be used to hunt out and punish conduct that has already been denounced as criminal by the states? In addition to the purposes suggested by Schwartz, should federal criminal jurisdiction be used in order to respond to the public's indignation against particular types of crime and its greater confidence in the efficiency of federal law enforcement?

For a fuller discussion of "non-territorial" federal criminal offenses, see Abrams, Federal Criminal Law And Its Enforcement, chs. 3, 5–12 (1986).

(3) *Parallel Prosecutions.* The Supreme Court has repeatedly held to the controversial position that parallel prosecutions by federal and state governments for the same conduct do not constitute double jeopardy. See, *e.g.,* Bartkus v. Illinois, 359 U.S. 121 (1959); Abbate v. United States, 359 U.S. 187 (1959).[2] Consequently, federal criminal liability usually poses the theoretical risk, at least, of double liability.[3] A memorandum issued by Attorney General Rogers to United States Attorneys after the Abbate case, however, declared a departmental policy against federal prosecution following state prosecution for "substantially the same act or acts," unless "the reasons are compelling." (The policy is known as the "Petite policy".[4]) For a collection of lower court decisions holding that this policy may not be invoked against the government to bar prosecution, see Abrams, Paragraph (2), *supra,* at 779–80.

(4) *Exclusive Federal Jurisdiction on the Basis of the Location of the Offense.* In some areas federal criminal law bears the whole burden of maintaining public order. These include, in addition to federal territories and possessions: (i) the admiralty and maritime jurisdiction that falls outside the territorial jurisdiction of any state; and (ii) federal enclaves—areas within the territorial jurisdiction of the states over which the federal government has acquired exclusive jurisdiction, such as military reservations or national parks.

The Criminal Code now deals with the latter two areas by defining a distinct group of acts that constitute federal crimes when committed within the "special maritime and territorial jurisdiction" of the United States.[5] That

2. For discussion, see, *e.g.,* Miller, Double Jeopardy and the Federal System (1968).

In United States v. Lopez, 115 S.Ct. 1624 (1995), the Court (in a 5–4 decision) struck down, for the first time in some 60 years, a congressional effort to rely on the commerce power as a basis for the regulation of private activity. The statute in question made it a federal offense for a person knowingly to possess a firearm in a place that the person knows or has reason to believe is a school zone. The case has stimulated considerable public and professional comment.

3. Note, also, the statement in Bartkus v. Illinois that "the state prosecution was [not] a sham and a cover for a federal prosecution, and thereby in essential fact another federal prosecution" (359 U.S. at 124).

A few federal statutes bar prosecution after a state acquittal or conviction. See, *e.g.,* 18 U.S.C. §§ 659–60, 1992, 2117. Some state statutes or constitutional provisions similarly prohibit a state prosecution following a federal prosecution for the same conduct. See generally Abrams, Paragraph (2), *supra,* at 748–49.

4. So named for Petite v. United States, 361 U.S. 529 (1960), in which the Supreme Court granted the government's motion to vacate a judgment of conviction below and to dismiss the indictment because the federal prosecution violated this policy.

5. Criminal offenses within the District of Columbia are governed by the D.C. Code, which includes a plenary set of criminal prohibitions enacted by (or pursuant to delegation of authority from) the Congress. Jurisdiction over such offenses is vested in the local D.C. Superior Court, see D.C. Code § 11–923, but the United States District Court for the District of Columbia has jurisdiction over D.C. offenses that are joined in the same information or indictment with a federal criminal offense, see *id.* § 11–502.

jurisdiction is defined in 18 U.S.C. § 7 to include the high seas and waters within the admiralty and maritime jurisdiction and outside any state's jurisdiction (including any American aircraft in flight over these areas), as well as lands reserved or acquired for the use of the United States, any U.S. space vehicle in flight, and any place outside the jurisdiction of any nation "with respect to an offense by or against a national of the United States."[6]

As long ago as 1790, Congress provided for the punishment of "wilful murder" and manslaughter "within any fort, arsenal, dock-yard, magazine, or in any other place or district of country, under the sole and exclusive jurisdiction of the United States." See Act of April 30, 1790, §§ 3, 7, 1 Stat. 112, 113. Even today, Title 18 includes a number of provisions making it a federal crime to engage in specified conduct "within the special maritime and territorial jurisdiction of the United States." *E.g.,* 18 U.S.C. §§ 113 (assault), 661 (larceny), 662 (receiving stolen property), 1111–13 (murder and manslaughter), 2241–45 (sexual abuse).

But the need soon arose for more complete specification of conduct occurring within these areas of federal jurisdiction that should be criminally punished. Recognition of this need led to the enactment of § 3 of the Federal Crimes Act of March 3, 1825, 4 Stat. 115, known as the Assimilative Crimes Act, and today codified at 18 U.S.C. § 13. The Act makes it a federal crime to engage, in any place falling within the scope of § 7, in conduct "not made punishable by any enactment of Congress" that would be a crime if committed within the jurisdiction of the state (or territory or the District of Columbia) in which that place is located.[7]

Presumably to avoid constitutional doubts, the Act was originally construed as adopting only the state criminal laws in force at the time of its enactment, United States v. Paul, 31 U.S. (6 Pet.) 141 (1832). This limitation necessitated a series of re-enactments to bring the Act up to date. See Note, 101 U.Pa.L.Rev. 124, 133–34 (1952). In the 1948 revision of the Criminal Code, Congress for the first time adopted the approach that the Act incorporates subsequent modifications in state criminal laws, and the constitutionality of this approach was upheld in United States v. Sharpnack, 355 U.S. 286 (1958).[8]

(5) *Proposals for Reform.* Though most federal crimes—territorial and nonterritorial alike—are codified in Title 18, that title is not an integrated criminal

---

On the constitutionality of these provisions, see Palmore v. United States, 411 U.S. 389 (1973).

6. In most of the vast lands belonging to the United States, the federal interest is limited to ownership. Only a small fraction of these lands is thought by the government agencies concerned to be within exclusive federal jurisdiction, or even within its concurrent or partial jurisdiction (presumably encompassing territorial criminal jurisdiction). The problem of determining when the United States possesses special governmental powers in such areas has raised intricate questions.

7. On the difficulties of determining when conduct is "not made punishable by any enactment of Congress," see Williams v.

United States, 327 U.S. 711 (1946); Abrams, Paragraph (2), *supra,* at 673–87; Note, 70 Harv.L.Rev. 685 (1957).

8. See generally, on the questions discussed in this Paragraph, Twitty, The Respective Powers of the Federal and Local Governments Within Lands Owned or Occupied by the United States (1944); Report of the Interdepartmental Committee for the Study of Jurisdiction over Federal Areas Within the States, pt. II (1956); Abrams, *Comment on Assimilated Offenses,* 1 National Commission on Reform of Federal Criminal Laws, Working Papers 77, 82 (1970).

On the special problems of federal criminal jurisdiction in the "Indian Country", see 18 U.S.C. §§ 1151–1153, 1162.

code but rather a collection of diverse offenses enacted over the years. In 1970, the National Commission on Reform of the Federal Criminal Laws published a Study Draft (as well as two volumes of Working Papers), and in 1971 a Final Report draft, proposing a comprehensive revision of Title 18. Though the Commission's work has been the basis of many bills to reform the federal criminal code,[9] none has been enacted. Nonetheless, that work, and the commentary it generated,[10] remains a valuable source of analysis of the problems discussed in this Note.

(6) *Control of Criminal Investigations and Prosecutions.*

(a) In general, the Attorney General is vested with control of the initiation of federal criminal prosecutions. See 28 U.S.C. §§ 509, 515–16; *cf.* 28 U.S.C. § 547 (United States Attorneys). Appointment of the Watergate Special Prosecutor—whose almost autonomous position was created by an order of the Attorney General—qualified this control, but as the Supreme Court emphasized in United States v. Nixon, 418 U.S. 683, 696 (1974), the Attorney General had not rescinded that departmental order.

In Title VI of the Ethics in Government Act of 1978, 92 Stat. 1875, Congress established a new procedure for temporary appointment of "special prosecutors" (since renamed "independent counsel") with limited jurisdiction. The Act has been codified at 28 U.S.C. §§ 591–99, and after its expiration in 1992, was reenacted, with some significant changes, in 1994.

Under the present independent counsel law, the Attorney General is charged with undertaking a preliminary investigation in a variety of circumstances.[11] The Attorney General is then required, unless there is a finding "that there are no reasonable grounds to believe that further investigation is warranted" (§ 592), to apply to a three-judge division of the U.S. Court of Appeals for the D.C. Circuit, specially designated by the Chief Justice pursuant to 28 U.S.C. § 49, for the appointment of an independent counsel.[12] That division in turn is empowered to name an individual to serve as independent counsel, and to define the counsel's "prosecutorial jurisdiction", subject to possible future expansion by the division upon the application of the Attorney General (§ 593(b)). While in office the independent counsel has, with minor exceptions, all the powers and authority of the Attorney General and the

9. For discussion of early bills, see Schwartz, *Reform of the Federal Criminal Laws: Issues, Tactics, and Prospects,* 41 L. & Contemp.Prob. 1 (1977).

10. See, *e.g.,* Brown & Schwartz, *New Federal Criminal Code Is Submitted,* 56 A.B.A.J. 844, *Sentencing Under the Draft Criminal Code, id.* at 935, *Offenses Redefined Under Proposed Federal Criminal Code, id.* at 1181 (1970); McClellan, *Codification, Reform and Revision: The Challenge of a Modern Federal Criminal Code,* 1971 Duke L.J. 663.

11. These include instances in which the Attorney General has a basis for believing that certain offenses may have been committed by the President or Vice President, a Member of Congress, or a wide range of other high level officials, as well as instances in which investigation or prosecution by the Department of Justice may result in a conflict of interest (§ 591).

The Act extends only to serious offenses, however; it excludes infractions and minor misdemeanors.

12. Upon determination that a conflict of interest might otherwise exist, the Attorney General may also apply for appointment of an independent counsel to investigate other federal officials.

Members of the Judiciary Committees may also request that the Attorney General apply for appointment of an independent counsel. The Attorney General must then report to the requesting committee, giving reasons for the decision whether or not to begin a preliminary investigation (§ 591(e)).

Department of Justice with respect to matters within the counsel's prosecutorial jurisdiction (§ 594).

An independent counsel may be removed, other than by impeachment and conviction, only by "personal action" of the Attorney General for "good cause" or substantial disabilities, subject to judicial review in a civil action in the district court for the District of Columbia for reinstatement or other "appropriate relief" (§ 596(a)). The office of a particular independent counsel terminates when either the independent counsel or the three-judge division determines that the independent counsel's investigations and prosecutions are "completed" or "substantially completed" (§ 596(b)).

In Morrison v. Olson, 487 U.S. 654 (1988), the independent counsel statute was challenged on constitutional grounds, relating to assertions that it (i) interferes with the President's appointment and removal power, (ii) confers upon federal judges duties that fall outside of Article III's judicial power, and (iii) otherwise violates the separation of powers. The Court, over a vigorous dissent by Justice Scalia, upheld the Act.[13]

(b) In two decisions, the Supreme Court has considered the question of control of the prosecution of federal criminal contempt cases. In Young v. United States ex rel. Vuitton et Fils S.A., 481 U.S. 787 (1987), the district court appointed plaintiff's lawyer to prosecute the defendant, who had violated an injunction, for criminal contempt. The Supreme Court reversed the resulting conviction. Invoking its supervisory power, the Court ruled that a district court should request the United States Attorney to prosecute a criminal contempt; if the request is declined, the court should appoint a private lawyer other than the attorney for an interested party. Concurring in the judgment, Justice Scalia argued that Article III's judicial power does not include the power to prosecute crimes, and that the district courts accordingly have no power, inherent or otherwise, to initiate the prosecution of criminal contemnors. Necessarily, he argued, they lack any derivative power to appoint a private lawyer to prosecute.

In United States v. Providence Journal Co., 485 U.S. 693 (1988), a disinterested private lawyer had successfully prosecuted a criminal contempt case. After the court of appeals reversed the conviction, the Supreme Court granted certiorari. Thereafter, however, the Court ruled that 28 U.S.C. § 518, which vests in the Attorney General authority to conduct Supreme Court litigation in which "the United States is interested", required dismissal of the writ, because the petition for certiorari had been filed by the private prosecutor alone.[14]

---

13. As a dramatic illustration of the problems that can confront independent counsel, Lawrence Walsh, in his report on the Iran/Contra investigation, noted that his office had been forced to dismiss one case "when the Administration declined to declassify information necessary for the trial", information that Walsh asserted was already publicly known. I Final Report of the Independent Counsel for Iran/Contra Matters 565 (1993).

14. Bloch, p. 986, note 6, *supra*, considers a number of recent cases, including Morrison v. Olson, *supra*, and Providence Journal in light of the early history of the role of the Attorney General. This history, she concludes, shows that "ambiguity and tension are built into the constitutional scheme" and that the Constitution "gives Congress and the President considerable latitude in filling in the details" of governmental structure (p. 652). She therefore criticizes what she views as the disregard of history in Providence Journal, and praises the "pragmatic, functional approach of the Morrison majority" (p. 647).

(7) *The Role of Federal Magistrate Judges.* Beginning with the passage of the Federal Magistrates Act of October 17, 1968, 82 Stat. 1107, federal magistrate judges have been authorized, upon the election of the defendant, to try prosecutions for minor offenses. The pertinent provisions, as amended and now codified in 18 U.S.C. § 3401, extend this authority to any misdemeanor offense.[15] Appeal from a conviction before a magistrate judge may be taken to the district court. *Id.* § 3402. Is there any constitutional objection to these provisions? See Chap. IV, p. 437, *supra.*

15. Section § 3401(f) permits removal of a prosecution from the magistrate judge to the district court on the court's own motion, or on the government's motion for "good cause shown" (defined as including "the novelty, importance or complexity of the case").

CHAPTER IX

SUITS CHALLENGING OFFICIAL ACTION

SECTION 1. SUITS CHALLENGING FEDERAL OFFICIAL ACTION

NOTE ON THE SCOPE OF THIS SECTION

A lawsuit challenging federal official action implicates a variety of related doctrines. Such a suit may be filed only in a court that possesses subject matter jurisdiction, a point of special importance given the limited jurisdiction of the federal courts. The litigant bringing the lawsuit must also surmount the barrier of sovereign immunity—a barrier that, unless waived by Congress, generally bars suit against the United States *eo nomine* or its agencies and departments, and also bars some actions nominally against federal officials. Finally, the litigant must establish an entitlement to the particular remedy sought.

Though distinct, these doctrines are closely related. For example, one may ordinarily assume that Congress, by vesting a federal court with subject matter jurisdiction over particular suits against the United States, meant to provide a concomitant waiver of the United States' immunity from suit. Similarly, the doctrine of sovereign immunity is closely related to the evolution of remedies in suits nominally against federal officers: in practice, both damages and specific relief have often been available in such lawsuits, thereby providing methods of reviewing official action thought to be consistent with any concept of sovereign immunity. Finally, the appropriateness of a particular remedy may depend heavily upon whether Congress has waived sovereign immunity and thus made available an alternative form of relief.

This Section is divided into three parts. Subsection A provides an introductory overview of the evolution of remedies available in suits against federal officials and agencies. Subsection B then deals in depth with the doctrine of sovereign immunity and related remedial questions. Finally, Subsection C reviews the most important congressional enactments waiving the sovereign immunity of the United States.

SUBSECTION A: REMEDIES

AN OVERVIEW OF THE DEVELOPMENT OF REMEDIES IN ACTIONS AGAINST FEDERAL OFFICIALS AND FEDERAL AGENCIES*

The development of remedies against federal officials and agencies follows two important paths. The first, nonstatutory review, involves the system of remedies generally available against any defendant in judicial proceedings. The remedies may be derived from the common law (as with damage actions, injunctions, or the prerogative writs) or from a statute (as with the declaratory judgment). The second path, statutory review, involves more specialized remedies created by Congress for the distinctive purpose of reviewing the actions of federal officers or agencies.

A valuable introduction to the subject as a whole (which embraces questions of remedies against state as well as federal officials) is the comprehensive analysis by Woolhandler, *Patterns of Official Immunity and Accountability,* 37 Case W.Res.L.Rev. 396 (1986–87). Woolhandler structures her study around two models for evaluating actions seeking such remedies: a "legality" model that focuses on whether harm to the citizen has been caused by an unlawful act, and a "discretion" model, which focuses on the harm posed by potential liability to "the decisionmaking processes of the official" (p. 398). She suggests that the former model was predominant during the era of the Marshall Court, and the latter during the era of the Taney Court, with respect not only to coercive or prohibitory relief but to damages as well. She contends that the two models have continued to weave in and out of Supreme Court jurisprudence, with the ultimate "ascendance of the legality model for injunctive relief" and of what she describes as a "colorable legality" model (the successor to the discretionary model) for damages (*id.*). In studying the materials that follow, consider the extent to which these two models are helpful in understanding the approach of the federal courts to questions ranging from the doctrine of sovereign immunity to the amenability of federal officers to actions for coercive or compensatory relief.

A. Nonstatutory Review of Federal Official Action[1]

(1) *The English Heritage.* Nonstatutory review of the action of federal officials draws upon the English heritage, which provided a variety of remedies against an officer or agency of the Crown. While the King enjoyed sovereign immunity, his officers did not. They could be required, for example, to pay damages to private persons injured by illegal acts, on the theory that officials, like other wrongdoers, were subject to the law.

In this country, until recently "the basic judicial remedy for the protection of the individual against illegal official action [was] a private action for damages against the official in which the court determine[d], in the usual common-law manner and with the aid of a jury, whether or not the officer was legally authorized to do what he did in the particular case. The plaintiff [could not] sue to redress merely any unauthorized action by an officer. To maintain the suit the plaintiff [had to] allege conduct by the officer which, if not justified by

---

* For further discussion of remedial issues in actions against federal officers and entities, see the Note following United States v. Lee, p. 1007, *infra,* and the material on official immunity in Sec. 3, *infra.*

1. See generally Byse, *Proposed Reforms in Federal "Nonstatutory" Judicial Re-* view: *Sovereign Immunity, Indispensable Parties, Mandamus,* 75 Harv.L.Rev. 1479 (1962); Jaffe, *Suits Against Governments and Officers: Sovereign Immunity,* 77 Harv. L.Rev. 1 (1963).

his official authority, [was] a private wrong to the plaintiff, entitling the latter to recover damages." Attorney General's Committee on Administrative Procedure, Administrative Procedure in Government Agencies, S.Doc. No. 8, 77th Cong, 1st Sess. 81 (1941). (On whether officials can today assert a qualified or absolute immunity from personal liability in damages, see Sec. 3, *infra*.)

(2) *Writs Available Against Federal Officers: An Introduction.*

(a) *A Survey.* A litigant seeking specific relief against federal officials could similarly avail himself of the usual common law remedies, like ejectment or replevin, in appropriate cases. See, *e.g.,* United States v. Lee, p. 1007, *infra.* Also available were the prerogative writs—quo warranto, habeas corpus, prohibition, certiorari, and mandamus—that were issued by the King's Bench in England. As a result of the highly creative development of the English law, these writs were available against royal officers notwithstanding the sovereign immunity of the King.[2] In this country, too, the prerogative writs provided an important means of controlling official action, though each was subject to distinctive limitations.

The writ of quo warranto is ordinarily limited to testing the right to an office, as when an official has been unlawfully appointed or attempts to continue in office beyond his term.

The writ of habeas corpus is available to test the legality of official detention or custody. Its contemporary uses include challenges to the detention of aliens, of individuals in military service, and of persons confined pursuant to arrest or criminal conviction. For detailed discussion, see Chap. XI, *infra.*

The writ of prohibition is usually directed to an inferior judicial or quasi-judicial body, to bar it from exceeding its jurisdiction. This writ generally does not permit review of actions (even if unlawful) of a tribunal that does have jurisdiction, or of actions that are deemed to be purely administrative or ministerial. Moreover, the writ is discretionary, and is not to be awarded if another remedy is available. For these reasons, prohibition has been of limited importance in reviewing action by federal officials.

The writ of certiorari directs a lower tribunal to certify its record to a superior court (in England, the King's Bench) for review. It is generally limited to review of judicial or quasi-judicial action, and it too is available as a matter of discretion rather than right. Congress has never authorized its use in the federal district courts, and even in the District of Columbia courts—long regarded as common law courts—certiorari fell into disuse as a means of reviewing administrative action. See Degge v. Hitchcock, 229 U.S. 162 (1913).

(b) *Mandamus.* A remedy of wider applicability in suits seeking specific relief against officials is the writ of mandamus, which, under the conventional formulation, is available to compel an official to perform a ministerial (but not a discretionary) duty. An aggrieved party, however, has to find a court with jurisdiction to award the writ. By 1838 it was established that, largely as the result of historical accident, neither the state courts nor the federal courts generally, but only the Circuit Court for the District of Columbia, possessed

---

2. See generally Jaffe, Judicial Control of Administrative Action 165–93 (1965); Smith, *The Prerogative Writs,* 11 Camb.L.J. 40 (1951).

that jurisdiction.   See Kendall v. United States ex rel. Stokes, 37 U.S. (12 Pet.) 524, 619–26 (1838).[3]

At least since the mid-nineteenth century, Supreme Court decisions adhered to the conventional formulation of the circumstances in which mandamus would issue.[4]   In Work v. United States ex rel. Rives, 267 U.S. 175 (1925), Chief Justice Taft reformulated the ministerial-discretionary distinction by transforming its general concern with the existence of executive discretion into a particularistic concern with the construction of the specific enactment alleged to have been violated (pp. 177–78):

"Mandamus issues to compel an officer to perform a purely ministerial duty.   It can not be used to compel or control a duty in the discharge of which by law he is given discretion.   The duty may be discretionary within limits.   He can not transgress those limits, and if he does so, he may be controlled by injunction or mandamus to keep within them.   The power of the court to intervene, if at all, thus depends upon what statutory discretion he has.   * * * [There] are decisions in which the discretion is greater than in the Kendall Case and less than in the Decatur Case,[5] and its extent and the scope of judicial action in limiting it depend upon a proper interpretation of the particular statute and congressional purpose.   * * *"

How useful is the distinction between the exercise of discretion and the performance of a ministerial duty in the modern administrative state—in which

---

3. Section 13 of the First Judiciary Act—purporting to vest in the Supreme Court an original jurisdiction to issue writs of mandamus to any persons holding office under the authority of the United States—was held unconstitutional in Marbury v. Madison, p. 67, *supra.*

Efforts to obtain mandamus in the inferior federal courts also failed.   In McIntire v. Wood, 11 U.S. (7 Cranch) 504 (1813), the Supreme Court held that § 11 of the Judiciary Act did not authorize a federal circuit court to issue mandamus to a local federal official, and, subsequently, in McClung v. Silliman, 19 U.S. (6 Wheat.) 598, 604–05 (1821), the Court held that the state courts did not possess power to issue writs of mandamus to federal officials because Congress had not given that power to the federal courts.   Compare Union Pacific R.R. v. Hall, 91 U.S. 343 (1875)(permitting suit by a member of the public under a statute specifically authorizing the circuit courts to hear mandamus actions against the Union Pacific Railroad), discussed in Winter, *The Metaphor of Standing and the Problem of Self–Governance,* 40 Stan.L.Rev. 1371, 1404–05 (1988).

4.   Thus, in Kendall v. United States, *supra,* the Court upheld issuance of a writ of mandamus to the Postmaster General, compelling him to allow certain credits (for carriage of the mails) that had been upheld by

the Solicitor of the Treasury.   Congress had authorized the Solicitor to decide such claims, and the defendant was said to have no discretion to deny them.   Though the President in the exercise of constitutionally derived powers was "beyond the reach of any other departments" except via impeachment, executive officers are not under the President's exclusive direction, and Congress may impose official duties that "are subject to the control of the law * * *.   * * * [T]his is emphatically the case, where the duty enjoined is of a mere ministerial character."   37 U.S. (12 Pet.) at 610, 612–13.

Two years later, in Decatur v. Paulding, 39 U.S. (14 Pet.) 497 (1840), the Court (per Taney, C.J.) affirmed the refusal to issue mandamus to the Secretary of the Navy (who was by law trustee of a navy pension fund) to compel him to pay a pension claim.   The Court accepted but distinguished Kendall, finding that the Secretary did not have a merely ministerial duty to pay the claim: the official duties of the head of an executive department are generally discretionary since they require the exercise of judgment in expounding the law.   (The claim in the Decatur case—a claim by Stephen Decatur's widow for two government pensions—was not a very appealing one, and this fact may have affected the outcome.)

5.   [Ed.] On Kendall and Decatur, see note 4, *supra.*

most official decisions involve an element of discretion without being wholly unbounded? See Jaffe, note 2, *supra*, at 181.

Though mandamus is a legal remedy, it is governed by equitable principles. In its "equitable" discretion, a court may decline to issue mandamus "to compel the doing of an idle act, * * * or to give a remedy which would work a public injury or embarrassment," United States ex rel. Greathouse v. Dern, 289 U.S. 352, 359–60 (1933), or when other avenues of relief have not been exhausted, see Heckler v. Ringer, 466 U.S. 602, 616–17 (1984); United States ex rel. Girard Trust Co. v. Helvering, 301 U.S. 540, 543–44 (1937).

(c) *Statutory Revision in 1962.* The Mandamus and Venue Act of 1962, 28 U.S.C. § 1361, gave jurisdiction, without regard to amount in controversy, to all federal district courts (rather than just that of the District of Columbia) over actions "in the nature of mandamus" to compel a federal officer to perform his or her duty.[6] See generally Byse, note 1, *supra*.[7] In response to this enactment and to a more general movement toward expanded review of administrative action, two differing views of mandamus came to be articulated in the case law: the "orthodox" view that the writ "is intended to provide a remedy for a plaintiff * * * only if the defendant owes him a clear nondiscretionary duty", Heckler v. Ringer, 466 U.S. 602, 616 (1984), and the "reformed" view that mandamus is a more flexible remedy available whenever an official acts beyond the scope of lawful authority. See 4 Davis, Administrative Law Treatise §§ 23:12–13 (2d ed. 1983). (Note the relation between these two views and the two models described by Woolhandler, p. 995, *supra*.)

(3) *Other Non-statutory Remedies.* The unavailability of mandamus relief outside the District of Columbia before 1962, and uncertainty about its scope even after 1962, made it an imperfect remedy for review of official action. Particularly after the advent of general federal question jurisdiction in 1875, equitable remedies like the injunction (and, later, the declaratory judgment) came to be the predominant nonstatutory remedies for obtaining specific relief against unlawful action by federal officials. The injunction "rests on the same theory [as a private action for damages, see Paragraph (1), *supra*], namely, the answerability of a Government officer as a private individual for conduct injurious to another, and depends upon the assumption that unless enjoined, the officer will commit acts which will entitle the plaintiff to maintain an action for damages." Attorney General's Committee on Administrative Procedure, Paragraph (1), *supra,* at 81.

The issuance of "negative injunctions" was relatively straightforward in cases meeting the requisites for equitable relief and in which such relief was not otherwise barred. Prior to 1962, however, it was uncertain whether federal courts outside the District of Columbia could issue "mandatory injunctions" that, in compelling an official to take action, resembled writs of mandamus, which those courts lacked jurisdiction to issue.[8] The Mandamus and Venue Act clearly permits all federal district courts to issue orders in the nature of mandamus. The question remained, however, whether a plaintiff could obtain

---

6. In 1938, Fed.R.Civ.P. 81(b) abolished the separate writ of mandamus in the district courts, providing that relief previously available by mandamus "may be obtained by appropriate action or by appropriate motion under the practice prescribed in these rules."

7. For discussion of the Act's impact on questions of process and venue, see pp. 1591–93, *infra.*

8. In Smith v. Bourbon County, 127 U.S. 105 (1888), the Supreme Court intimated that the power did not exist. Nonetheless, the Court never squarely resolved the issue.

broader relief in a suit for a mandatory injunction than would have been available in an action seeking an order in the nature of mandamus.

The Supreme Court suggested in Panama Canal Co. v. Grace Line, Inc., 356 U.S. 309, 318 (1958), that a suit for a mandatory injunction should be judged by the same principles as mandamus, and lower courts have generally followed that lead.[9] The significance of Panama Canal depends, of course, upon which view of mandamus is used as the measure of the scope of relief.[10]

Before 1976, a litigant whose claim was not worth more than $10,000 could not bring a simple action for an injunction under 28 U.S.C. § 1331, and if § 1361 was resorted to, the litigant would encounter all of the traditional limitations upon mandamus. But in 1976 Congress eliminated the minimum jurisdictional amount in suits under § 1331 against federal officials in their official capacity. Pub.L. No. 94–574.

Suits for specific relief against federal official action often raise sensitive questions of separation of powers and judicial role, particularly when the President or other high officials are involved. For exploration of these questions, see the discussion of Youngstown Sheet & Tube Co. v. Sawyer, Sec. 3, pp. 1180–83, *infra.*

B. Statutory Review of Federal Official Action

(1) *Introduction.* Statutory review, largely a development of the twentieth century, has become the predominant method of reviewing federal official action.[11] Although nonstatutory review remains important with regard to the older executive departments (*e.g.,* State, Defense, Treasury, Justice, Interior, and Agriculture), Congress usually makes action by new agencies or under new programs subject to statutory review, through a variety of mechanisms.

(2) *Judicial Enforcement Actions.* In many instances an administrative order becomes binding only when the agency brings an action to enforce its order. The statute may provide for enforcement in an action in a federal court of appeals (as is true, for example, of orders of the National Labor Relations Board, see 29 U.S.C. § 160(e)), or in a federal district court (as is often true of agency reparation orders, see, *e.g.,* 49 U.S.C. § 11705 (c), (d)(orders of the Interstate Commerce Commission); 7 U.S.C. §§ 210(f), 499g(b)(certain orders of the Secretary of Agriculture)). In such a proceeding, the court will ensure that the order is within the scope of the agency's delegated authority and is otherwise valid before ordering enforcement. See generally Attorney General's Committee on Administrative Procedure, Paragraph A(1), *supra,* at 82–83.

(3) *Specific Statutory Provisions Authorizing Judicial Review.* Regulatory statutes often authorize judicial review at the instance of a private person who

---

9. See, *e.g.,* National Wildlife Federation v. United States, 626 F.2d 917, 918 n. 1, 923 (D.C.Cir.1980); Fallini v. Hodel, 783 F.2d 1343, 1345 (9th Cir.1986).

10. For cases importing the narrow view of mandamus into decisions concerning mandatory injunctions, see Huntt v. Government of the Virgin Islands, 382 F.2d 38, 45 & n. 3 (3d Cir.1967); Vann v. Housing Auth., 87 F.R.D. 642, 668–69 (W.D.Mo.1980); Sodus Central School Dist. v. Kreps, 468 F.Supp. 884, 885 (W.D.N.Y.1978).

11. Indeed, mandamus may be unavailable as a substitute for a congressionally prescribed statutory review mechanism. See, *e.g.,* Pittston Coal Group v. Sebben, 488 U.S. 105, 121–23 (1988)(mandamus did not lie because agency officials had no "clear, nondiscretionary duty" to re-open administrative denials of "black lung" benefits that had become final under the governing review provisions).

wishes to take the initiative in challenging official action. Though these statutory review provisions vary widely, probably the most common authorize a petition in a federal court of appeals to set aside an administrative order. Thus, the National Labor Relations Act specifies that final orders of the NLRB may be reviewed in an appropriate court of appeals, see 29 U.S.C. § 160(f), and similar provisions govern other agencies. Other statutes authorize review in a federal district court. An important example is section 205(g) of the Social Security Act, 42 U.S.C. § 405(g), which provides for district court review of final and adverse administrative decisions on claims for social security benefits.

(4) *The Administrative Procedure Act.* In addition to specific statutory review provisions, Congress in 1946 enacted the Administrative Procedure Act (APA), which in section 10, 5 U.S.C. §§ 701–06, generally authorizes judicial review at the behest of a person who suffers legal wrong because of final agency action or who is adversely affected by such action.[12] Though review under the APA may be denied, *inter alia,* when (1) the action is committed to agency discretion, (2) the governing regulatory statute expressly or impliedly precludes judicial review, (3) the challenge is not ripe, (4) the petitioner lacks standing, or (5) the petitioner has failed to meet specific requirements for the exhaustion of administrative remedies, the decisions have established a strong presumption that federal agency action is reviewable.[13]

(5) *The Effect of Statutory Review Provisions.*

(a) The various statutory review provisions differ as to matters like the timing of review and the weight to be attached to administrative determinations. Some provisions prescribe a new form for the action seeking review, such as a "petition to modify or set aside" an order. Absent this kind of specification, any appropriate nonstatutory method of review may be used, unless Congress is found to have intended no further review. See Section 10(b) of the APA, 5 U.S.C. § 703.

(b) Without much discussion, courts generally have assumed that statutes creating review mechanisms also contain corresponding waivers of sovereign immunity. See, *e.g.,* Huie v. Bowen, 788 F.2d 698, 705 (11th Cir.1986)("42 U.S.C. § 405(g) operates as a waiver of sovereign immunity by giving the federal courts the right to review and modify or reverse the Secretary's decisions."). The assumption seems wholly justified, since it would be futile for Congress to authorize judicial review that is nonetheless barred by sovereign immunity.

The lower courts were long divided, however, on whether the APA constituted a waiver of sovereign immunity. See the cases compiled in S.Rep. No. 94–996, 94th Cong., 2d Sess. at 10 n. 33 (1976). In 1976, Congress amended § 702 to effect a broad waiver of immunity in federal court suits seeking relief other than money damages against federal agencies. See Sec. 1(C), *infra.*

---

12. Resolving a dispute among the lower courts, in 1977 the Supreme Court held that the Act does not give the federal courts subject matter jurisdiction. Califano v. Sanders, 430 U.S. 99 (1977). But since Congress had amended § 1331 the year before to eliminate the amount in controversy requirement in suits against federal agencies or federal officials in their official capacity, see Paragraph (A)(4), *supra,* there is now virtually always subject matter jurisdiction under § 1331 for a review proceeding under the APA.

13. See Bowen v. Massachusetts, 487 U.S. 879 (1988), p. 1038, *infra,* for an important holding on the meaning of § 704, which provides that "agency action for which there is no other adequate remedy in any court shall be subject to judicial review."

(c) The many provisions enacted by Congress that have waived sovereign immunity as to particular kinds of actions may themselves be viewed as constituting a form of statutory review, providing remedies that would have been unavailable absent specific congressional action. Of these provisions, three stand out: (1) the 1976 amendment to the APA described in this Paragraph; (2) the Tucker Act, generally permitting suit against the United States on non-tort monetary claims; and (3) the Federal Tort Claims Act, generally permitting suit against the United States for common law torts committed by its employees. There are important exceptions and limitations to each of these three statutory schemes, which are discussed in Sec. 1(C), *infra*.

SUBSECTION B: THE SOVEREIGN IMMUNITY OF THE UNITED STATES AND ASSOCIATED REMEDIAL PROBLEMS*

PRELIMINARY NOTE

(1) *The Foundations of Sovereign Immunity.*

(a) What is the basis of the well-established doctrine that bars suit against the United States in the absence of its consent?[1] The traditional immunity of the sovereign, which survives by implication the grant of judicial power in Article III? See The Federalist, No. 81 (Hamilton). The inability of the courts to enforce a judgment? See Jay, C.J., in Chisholm v. Georgia, 2 U.S. (2 Dall.) 419, 478 (1793), p. 1047, *infra*. The "logical and practical ground that there can be no legal right as against the authority that makes the law on which the right depends"? See Holmes, J., in Kawananakoa v. Polyblank, 205 U.S. 349, 353 (1907). The avoidance of interference with governmental functions and with the government's control over its instrumentalities, funds, and property?

In reading the materials that follow, and especially United States v. Lee, consider to what extent each of these purposes (a) is worthy, (b) squares with the decided cases, or (c) might not better be served through other doctrines.

---

* This Subsection deals with federal sovereign immunity and related issues, while Subsection A of Section 2 deals with state sovereign immunity and related issues (especially the Eleventh Amendment). A third type of sovereign immunity—not dealt with in this Chapter—is that possessed by Indian tribes. Tribal immunity, and its distinct characteristics, are dealt with in a number of cases and comments, notably Santa Clara Pueblo v. Martinez, 436 U.S. 49 (1978); Wright, *Sovereignty: Indian Sovereignty and Tribal Immunity from Suit*, 8 Am. Indian L.Rev. 401 (1980); Feldman, *The Supreme Court's New Sovereign Immunity Doctrine and the McCarran Amendment: Toward Ending State Adjudication of Indian Water Rights*, 18 Harv.Envtl.L.Rev. 433 (1994).

1. See generally Jaffe, *Suits Against Governments and Officers: Sovereign Immunity*, 77 Harv.L.Rev. 1 (1963); Cramton, *Nonstatutory Review of Federal Administrative Action: The Need for Statutory Reform of Sovereign Immunity, Subject Matter Jurisdiction, and Parties Defendant*, 68 Mich.L.Rev. 387 (1970); Engdahl, *Immunity and Accountability for Positive Government Wrongs*, 44 U.Colo.L.Rev. 1 (1972). See also Krent, *Reconceptualizing Sovereign Immunity*, 45 Vand.L.Rev. 1529 (1992)(defending the doctrine as promoting a proper relationship among the branches of government and the primacy of majoritarian policymaking, and arguing that Congress' decisions whether to waive immunity have generally drawn an appropriate balance).

Consider, also, whether the Supreme Court has misunderstood the historical foundations of sovereign immunity, and has given it too broad a scope, while professing at times to regard it with disfavor.

(b) Many scholars have argued that the doctrine of sovereign immunity, as it had evolved in England prior to 1789, was less about *whether* the Crown or its agents could be sued than about *how*. In some instances, officers could be sued for damages, enjoined from doing wrong, or compelled to perform their duty. In other cases, relief could be obtained through the petition of right, which permitted suits directly against the Crown; this remedy was cumbersome and required consent by the sovereign, but according to Professor Jaffe, "when it was necessary to sue the Crown *eo nomine* consent apparently was given as of course." Jaffe, note 1, *supra*, at 1; see also Borchard, *Governmental Responsibility in Tort, VI,* 36 Yale L.J. 1, 17–36 (1926). Professor Jaffe concluded that the "so-called doctrine of sovereign immunity was largely an abstract idea without determinative impact on the subject's right to relief against government illegality", and that "[t]he one serious deficiency [in English law] was the nonliability of the government for torts of its servants." Jaffe, *supra,* at 18–19.

Despite the Constitution's silence on immunity (and, indeed, Article III's grant of jurisdiction over "Controversies to which the United States shall be a Party"[2]), early Supreme Court decisions assumed that the United States could not be sued *eo nomine* absent congressional consent. Yet the doctrine developed largely in dicta,[3] without careful scrutiny of its underpinnings.

The earliest cases upholding a plea of immunity by the United States appear to be United States v. McLemore, 45 U.S. (4 How.) 286 (1846), and Hill v. United States, 50 U.S. (9 How.) 386 (1850). Both rejected bills in equity to enjoin the enforcement of judgments at law in favor of the United States, though the first pointed out that the relief sought could be obtained in the law action, and the second suggested that it might have been. Still, in 1882 Justice Miller could state in United States v. Lee, 106 U.S. 196, 207 (1882), that "the principle has never been discussed or the reasons for it given, but it has always been treated as an established doctrine."

Do the lack of a monarch, the existence of a written constitution, and the institution of judicial review suggest a different role for sovereign immunity in this country than in England? See Chisholm v. Georgia, 2 U.S. (2 Dall.) 419, 453–66 (1793)(Wilson, J.).

(2) *The Role of Sovereign Immunity With Respect to Particular Constitutional Claims.* Sovereign immunity appears to play a more limited role in "takings" cases. First English Evangelical Lutheran Church v. County of Los Angeles, 482 U.S. 304 (1987), was a suit against a *county* that had adopted an interim flood control measure prohibiting construction in an area that included land owned by the plaintiff church. The church sought damages in a state court inverse condemnation action. That suit was dismissed on the ground that a landowner may not obtain damages for a "regulatory taking" until the challenged regulation has been held invalid and the government has nevertheless

---

2. But *cf.* the discredited decision in Williams v. United States, 289 U.S. 553 (1933), p. 420, note 9, *supra,* which interpreted this language to apply only when the United States is a plaintiff.

3. See, *e.g.,* Chisholm v. Georgia, 2 U.S. (2 Dall.) 419, 478 (1793)(Jay, C.J.); Cohens v. Virginia, 19 U.S. (6 Wheat.) 264, 383, 392, 411–12 (1821).

decided that it should remain in effect. The Supreme Court reversed, 6–3, holding that the Fifth Amendment's Just Compensation Clause, as applied to the states through the Fourteenth Amendment, requires the provision of damages for harm suffered even before a challenged regulation has been judicially determined to constitute a "taking".

In an important footnote, the Court said (p. 316 n. 9): "The Solicitor General urges that the prohibitory nature of the Fifth Amendment, combined with principles of sovereign immunity, establishes that the Amendment itself is only a limitation on the power of the Government to act, not a remedial provision. The cases cited in the text, we think, refute the argument of the United States that 'the Constitution does not, of its own force, furnish a basis for a court to award money damages against the government.' Though arising in various factual and jurisdictional settings, these cases make clear that it is the Constitution that dictates the remedy for interference with property rights amounting to a taking."

In determining whether the United States is immune from damages liability, is there a basis in the constitutional text or in other considerations for treating an action under the Just Compensation Clause differently from actions claiming other constitutional violations? See Young, *Congressional Regulation of Federal Courts' Jurisdiction and Processes: United States v. Klein Revisited*, 1981 Wis.L.Rev. 1189, 1224–33.[4]

(3) *The Scope of Consent.* The English practice of allowing suit to be brought against the Crown when royal consent was given was transformed in this country into the notion that the government is immune from suit absent consent of the legislature. In the nineteenth century, congressional consent was, in general, limited to certain money claims against the United States cognizable in the Court of Claims. Today, the scope of various congressional consents is far broader, though the courts have generally insisted that a waiver by Congress be unmistakably expressed. For discussion of the reach of these statutes and their interpretation, see Sec. 1(C), *infra*.

(4) *The Effect of Suit Brought by the United States; Set-offs and Counterclaims.*

(a) In The Siren, 74 U.S. (7 Wall.) 152 (1868), a ship captured by the United States, sailing under a Navy crew, rammed another ship. The United States filed its libel in prize against the captured ship, which was condemned, and the sale proceeds were deposited with the assistant treasurer of the United States. The owners of the other ship then asserted a claim for a maritime tort

---

4. Compare the series of decisions culminating in Reich v. Collins, 115 S.Ct. 547 (1994)(discussed in detail in Chap. VII, pp. 847–57, *infra*), involving state court actions against state officials for refund of taxes allegedly exacted in violation of the federal Constitution. The Court in Reich, relying in part on its earlier decisions, stated that due process requires the state to afford a clear and certain remedy in such cases, and that this obligation exists notwithstanding "the sovereign immunity States traditionally enjoy in their own courts" (p. 549).

It is not clear from these decisions whether the federal government's reliance on a claim of sovereign immunity in a tax refund action against the United States (assuming the lack of an adequate statutory remedy) would similarly prove unavailing. For arguments that notions of national sovereign immunity must yield to these *and other* claims of violation of constitutional rights, see Amar, *Of Sovereignty and Federalism*, 96 Yale L.J. 1425 (1987); Bandes, *Reinventing Bivens: The Self–Executing Constitution*, 68 S.Cal.L.Rev. 289 (1995). (Consider the relation between these arguments and the doctrines of official immunity discussed in Sec. 3, *infra*.)

against the prize ship. The Supreme Court held that the captured vessel was guilty of a maritime tort and subject to a lien for damages extending also to its proceeds, but that the lien could not be enforced against the United States without its consent. By seeking a judicial decree of sale, however, the government had consented to an adjudication of the tort claim and to its payment out of the sale proceeds.

Note that the theory of The Siren—that the tort claim was valid, but unenforceable against the United States until its suit put the claimed property into issue—is inconsistent with Justice Holmes' conception, Paragraph (1)(a), *supra,* that sovereign immunity flows from the absence of any underlying obligation of the sovereign. Evidently recognizing this inconsistency, Justice Holmes later stated that the discussion in The Siren of unenforceable liens was just a means of stating that any claims against the sovereign were "ethical only", but that when the sovereign came into court it consented to see justice done with regard to the subject matter of the suit. The Western Maid, 257 U.S. 419, 433–34 (1922). In United States v. The Thekla, 266 U.S. 328, 339–40 (1924), also involving a collision of two ships, Holmes wrote: "The trial of such cases in the ordinary course is upon libel and cross libel, consolidated under authority of statute. * * * [T]he subject matter is the collision, rather than the vessel first libelled. * * * The libel in such a case is like a bill for an account, which imports an offer to pay the balance if it should turn out against the party bringing the bill."

Is it useful or realistic to view the substantive law applied in rendering a judgment against the United States as having been created retroactively by the waiver of sovereign immunity? Is this conception tenable when the waiver of immunity in The Siren arose from a government official's presentation of a claim in court?

(b) When the United States sues as plaintiff, does sovereign immunity bar a defensive credit in favor of the defendant? In 1797, Congress provided that, with certain exceptions, in actions by the United States "no claim for a credit shall be admitted, upon trial" unless previously presented for examination to the accounting officers of the government and by them disallowed. Act of March 3, 1797, § 4, 1 Stat. 512, 515, which survives in substance in 28 U.S.C. § 2406. A series of Supreme Court cases held that, this procedural requirement being satisfied, the defendant was entitled to at least a purely defensive credit against any judgment for the United States as plaintiff.[5]

Though some language in Supreme Court cases could be read to interpret § 2406 as itself a waiver of sovereign immunity, see, *e.g.,* United States v. Shaw, 309 U.S. 495, 501 (1940), the Court in United States v. United States Fidelity & Guaranty Co., 309 U.S. 506, 511 (1940), noted the government's concession of the validity of a claim "upon the theory that a defendant may, without statutory authority, recoup on a counterclaim an amount equal to the principal claim."

Yet not all counterclaims may qualify for a defensive credit. Despite some broad language in dictum in United States v. Shaw, *supra,* 309 U.S. at 501, that "cross-claims are allowed to the amount of the government's claim, where the government voluntarily sues", the courts have permitted a defensive claim in

---

5. See, *e.g.,* United States v. Wilkins, 19 U.S. (6 Wheat.) 135, 143–45 (1821); United States v. Ringgold, 33 U.S. (8 Pet.) 150, 163–64 (1834).

recoupment, which arises out of the same transaction,[6] while refusing to permit a counterclaim (including a set-off) that arises from a distinct transaction.[7]

What underlies the cases allowing a defensive credit? The need for economical resolution of an entire dispute? A sense of injustice that only one party may litigate a claim arising from the transaction? Are these justifications consistent with the courts' routine insistence that immunity can be waived only by Congress, not by an officer of the United States?

(c) A defensive credit requires no affirmative enforcement against the United States. But may a court enter judgment for the defendant if a balance is found due the defendant on his counterclaim? United States v. Eckford, 73 U.S. (6 Wall.) 484 (1867), held such a judgment improper and hence unenforceable, but that decision appeared to conflict with The Thekla, Paragraph (4)(a), *supra*. The conflict was resolved in United States v. Shaw, 309 U.S. 495 (1940), in which Michigan courts allowed a claim by the United States against an estate and a larger cross-claim by the estate against the United States, and entered a judgment (on which enforcement might later have been sought in the Court of Claims) against the United States for the difference. The Supreme Court reversed, rejecting the estate's argument that when the United States seeks judicial aid, it assumes the position of a private suitor subject to the full jurisdiction of the court (p. 502): "It is not our right to extend the waiver of sovereign immunity more broadly than has been directed by the Congress. * * * Against the background of complete immunity we find no Congressional action modifying the immunity rule in favor of cross-actions beyond the amount necessary as a set-off.

"The Thekla turns upon a relationship characteristic of claims for collision in admiralty but entirely absent in claims and cross-claims in settlement of estates. * * * Libels and cross-libels for collision are one litigation and give rise to one liability. * * *"

The Shaw decision, read together with Fed.R.Civ.P. 13(d), seems to require a defendant to split a compulsory counterclaim that exceeds the amount of the United States' primary claim, using part as a defensive credit and seeking the balance in (for example) the United States Court of Federal Claims pursuant to a congressional waiver of immunity. In the subsequent action, could the claimant be barred by the doctrine of claim preclusion? Shaw, *supra*, at 504–05, and United States v. United States Fidelity & Guaranty Co., 309 U.S. 506 (1940), imply not. Could the United States be precluded from relitigating

---

6. See, *e.g.,* Frederick v. United States, 386 F.2d 481, 488 (5th Cir.1967). But see, *e.g.,* United States v. Iron Mountain Mines, Inc., 881 F.Supp. 1432, 1456 (E.D.Cal.1995)(holding recoupment inappropriate in an action by the government to recover environmental cleanup costs under CERCLA; the court said that "recoupment doctrine, with its tenuous basis in the common law, cannot serve as a substitute for clearly expressed congressional intent" in the context of an action under CERCLA).

7. See, *e.g.,* United States v. Timmons, 672 F.2d 1373, 1379–80 (11th Cir.1982); EEOC v. First Nat. Bank, 614 F.2d 1004, 1008 (5th Cir.1980). But see United States v. Buchanan, 49 U.S. (8 How.) 83, 105 (1850), in which the Court held that the statute extends "to matters even distinct from the cause of action, if only such as the defendant is entitled to a credit on, whether equitable or legal. * * * But any wrongs or torts done, and any unliquidated damages claimed, have never been permitted as a set-off."

Also barred, no doubt because not truly defensive in nature, are counterclaims seeking relief different in kind from that sought by the United States. See, *e.g.,* United States v. 2,116 Boxes of Boned Beef, 726 F.2d 1481, 1490–91 (10th Cir.1984). See Paragraph (4)(c), *infra*.

issues on which it lost in the first action? See Hahn v. United States, p. 1037, note 24, *infra.*

(d) The American Law Institute Study of the Division of Jurisdiction Between State and Federal Courts 38–39, 255–59 (1969) proposed that courts be permitted by statute to enter affirmative relief against the United States on any claim arising from the same transaction or occurrence as a claim already in suit if the former is a claim "of which any court of the United States would have jurisdiction"—a step that the courts have been unwilling to take on their own without legislative authorization. Is the government's filing a lawsuit sufficient reason to transfer to the district courts jurisdiction that would otherwise be vested exclusively in the Court of Federal Claims, see Sec. 1(C), *infra?*

(5) *Interest on Claims Against the United States.* In United States v. Alcea Band of Tillamooks, 341 U.S. 48, 49 (1951), the Court said: "It is the 'traditional rule' that interest on claims against the United States cannot be recovered in the absence of an express provision to the contrary in the relevant statute or contract. This rule precludes an award of interest even though a statute should direct an award of 'just compensation' for a particular taking. The only exception arises when the taking entitles the claimant to just compensation under the Fifth Amendment."

Since a suit seeking to compel the payment of treasury funds will almost surely be considered to be against the United States, the question of liability for interest usually arises in construing a statute that waives immunity with respect to a particular claim. When Congress has provided that justice should be done in the main matter, but has not specified whether interest should be paid,[8] is there any persuasive reason for assuming an intention to deny the usual incidents of justice? A few cases have exhibited this liberal attitude, see, *e.g.,* Standard Oil Co. v. United States, 267 U.S. 76, 79 (1925)(rule against interest inapplicable where government assumed the status of a private commercial enterprise); United States v. The Thekla, Paragraph (4)(a), *supra* (award permitted with little explanation), but the contrary approach seems to have carried the day in more recent cases, see, *e.g.,* Library of Congress v. Shaw, 478 U.S. 310 (1986).

(6) *Attorney's Fees.* The Supreme Court has consistently held that in the absence of an authorizing statute, the United States is not liable for costs or attorney's fees.[9] But statutory waivers in this field have played an increasingly significant role.

---

8. In some instances, Congress has reinforced the traditional rule by expressly precluding interest awards. See 28 U.S.C. § 2516 (prohibiting the allowance of interest on a judgment of the Court of Federal Claims); *id.* § 2674 (governing actions under the Federal Tort Claims Act). In many others, Congress has expressly authorized the allowance of interest. See, *e.g.,* 28 U.S.C. §§ 2411 (tax refund suits), 2516(b)(post-judgment interest on Claims Court judgments); 41 U.S.C. § 611 (interest on claims under the Contract Disputes Act).

9. See, *e.g.,* United States v. Bodcaw Co., 440 U.S. 202, 203–04 n. 3 (1979)(per curiam).

As stated in Note, 60 U.Chi.L.Rev. 1043 (1993), the lower courts have generally been willing to impose monetary sanctions on the government for violating the requirements of Fed.R.Civ.P. 11, and in doing so have either ignored the waiver issue or found a waiver in the rule itself or in other sources. This result is criticized by the author of the Note, who argues that such monetary sanctions should be available only against a government attorney, not against the government itself, but that the government may be sub-

In 1966 an amendment to 28 U.S.C. § 2412 permitted costs (other than attorney's fees) to be awarded in any civil action "brought by or against the United States or any agency or any official * * * acting in his or her official capacity," except as "otherwise specifically provided by statute."

The rule as to attorney's fees has also been changed by statute. See the Equal Access to Justice Act of 1980, codified at 28 U.S.C. § 2412. Section 2412(b) authorizes the award of attorney's fees to a party who prevails against the United States in the same circumstances in which courts would award fees against private parties. In addition, § 2412(d) provides that courts *shall* award attorney's fees to certain persons who prevail against the United States in non-tort civil actions, unless the United States' position was "substantially justified" or "special circumstances make an award unjust." There are, moreover, many statutory provisions authorizing the award of attorney's fees in particular kinds of actions. See generally Bennett, Winning Attorneys' Fees From the U.S. Government (1986).

United States v. Lee

106 U.S. 196, 1 S.Ct. 240, 27 L.Ed. 171 (1882).
Appeal from the Circuit Court for the Eastern District of Virginia.

[The United States purchased the Arlington, Virginia estate of General Robert E. Lee's wife, after an alleged failure to pay a $92 assessment under a tax to support the Civil War. The tax commissioners had refused a proffer of payment on behalf of the owner, under a rule (later held invalid) that only the owner in person could pay overdue taxes. The United States proceeded to use part of the estate for the Arlington Cemetery and a fort.

[The Lees' son (who claimed title under his grandfather's will) filed an ejectment action in state court against the two federal officers who, under authority of the Secretary of War, had charge of the property. The defendants removed the action to the Circuit Court of the United States for the Eastern District of Virginia. Though the United States was not a party, the Attorney General filed a pleading in the Circuit Court seeking dismissal of the suit, stating that the United States possessed the property in the exercise of its sovereign and constitutional powers, and that "the court has no jurisdiction of the subject in controversy." Plaintiff's demurrer to this pleading was sustained, and after a jury trial, judgment for the plaintiff was entered.

[Both the individual defendants and the United States filed a writ of error in the Supreme Court. The Solicitor General argued the case for the individual defendants and for the United States.]

MR. JUSTICE MILLER delivered the opinion of the Court.

[The Court expressed doubt that the United States, a non-party, could file a writ of error, but noted that the defendants' writ raised all the issues pressed by the United States. After upholding the jury's determination that the United States did not acquire valid title under the tax sale proceeding because of the

jected to such non-monetary sanctions as an order that certain disputed facts must be taken as established adversely to the United States.

illegal refusal to accept payment on behalf of the owner, the Court turned to the question of sovereign immunity.]

* * *

The counsel for plaintiffs in error and in behalf of the United States assert the proposition, that though it has been ascertained by the verdict of the jury, in which no error is found, that the plaintiff has the title to the land in controversy, and that what is set up in behalf of the United States is no title at all, the court can render no judgment in favor of the plaintiff against the defendants in the action, because the latter hold the property as officers and agents of the United States, and it is appropriated to lawful public uses.

This proposition rests on the principle that the United States cannot be lawfully sued without its consent in any case, and that no action can be maintained against any individual without such consent, where the judgment must depend on the right of the United States to property held by such persons as officers or agents for the government.

The first branch of this proposition is conceded to be the established law of this country and of this court at the present day; the second, as a necessary or proper deduction from the first, is denied.

In order to decide whether the inference is justified from what is conceded, it is necessary to ascertain, if we can, on what principle the exemption of the United States from a suit by one of its citizens is founded, and what limitations surround this exemption. In this, as in most other cases of like character, it will be found that the doctrine is derived from the laws and practices of our English ancestors; and * * * it is beyond question that from the time of Edward the First until now the King of England was not suable in the courts of that country, except where his consent had been given on petition of right * * *.

* * *

There is in this country, however, no such thing as the petition of right, as there is no such thing as a kingly head to the nation, or to any of the States which compose it. There is vested in no officer or body the authority to consent that the State shall be sued except in the law-making power, which may give such consent on the terms it may choose to impose. Congress has created a court [the Court of Claims] in which it has authorized suits to be brought against the United States, but has limited such suits to those arising on contract, with a few unimportant exceptions.

What were the reasons which forbid that the King should be sued in his own court, and how do they apply to the political body corporate which we call the United States of America? As regards the King, one reason given by the old judges was the absurdity of the King's sending a writ to himself to command the King to appear in the King's court. No such reason exists in our government, as process runs in the name of the President, and may be served on the Attorney–General, as was done in Chisholm v. Georgia, 2 Dall. 419. Nor can it be said that the government is degraded by appearing as a defendant in the courts of its own creation, because it is constantly appearing as a party in such courts, and submitting its rights as against the citizen to their judgment.

* * *

That the doctrine met with a doubtful reception in the early history of this court may be seen from the opinions of two of its justices in the case of Chisholm v. Georgia, where Mr. Justice Wilson, a member of the convention which framed the Constitution, after a learned examination of the laws of England and other states and kingdoms, sums up the result by saying: "We see nothing against, but much in favor of, the jurisdiction of this court over the State of Georgia, a party to this cause." Mr. Chief Justice Jay also considered the question as affected by the difference between a republican State like ours and a personal sovereign, and held that there is no reason why a state should not be sued, though doubting whether the United States would be subject to the same rule.

The first recognition of the general doctrine by this court is to be found in the case of Cohens v. Virginia, 6 Wheat. 264.

The terms in which Mr. Chief Justice Marshall there gives assent to the principle does not add much to its force. "The counsel for the defendant," he says, "has laid down the general proposition that a sovereign independent State is not suable except by its own consent." This general proposition, he adds, will not be controverted.

* * *

* * * [W]hile acceding to the general proposition that in no court can the United States be sued directly by original process as a defendant, there is abundant evidence in the decisions of this court that the doctrine, if not absolutely limited to cases in which the United States are made defendants by name, is not permitted to interfere with the judicial enforcement of the established rights of plaintiffs when the United States is not a defendant or a necessary party to the suit.

But little weight can be given to the decisions of the English courts on this branch of the subject, for two reasons:—

1. In all cases where the title to property came into controversy between the crown and a subject, whether held in right of the person who was king or as representative of the nation, the petition of right presented a judicial remedy,— a remedy which this court, on full examination in a case which required it, held to be practical and efficient. There has been, therefore, no necessity for suing the officers or servants of the King who held possession of such property, when the issue could be made with the King himself as defendant.

2. Another reason of much greater weight is found in the vast difference in the essential character of the two governments as regards the source and the depositaries of power.

* * *

Under our system the *people,* who are there called *subjects,* are the sovereign. Their rights, whether collective or individual, are not bound to give way to a sentiment of loyalty to the person of a monarch. The citizen here knows no person, however near to those in power, or however powerful himself, to whom he need yield the rights which the law secures to him when it is well administered. When he, in one of the courts of competent jurisdiction, has established his right to property, there is no reason why deference to any person, natural or artificial, not even the United States, should prevent him from using the means which the law gives him for the protection and enforcement of that right.

* * *

The earliest case in this court in which the true rule is laid down, and which, bearing a close analogy to the one before us, seems decisive of it, is United States v. Peters, 5 Cranch, 115. In an admiralty proceeding, * * * the District Court of the United States for Pennsylvania * * * had decided that the libellants were entitled to the proceeds of the sale of a vessel condemned as prize of war, which had come to the possession of David Rittenhouse as treasurer of Pennsylvania. * * * [O]n an application therefor, a writ of *mandamus* to compel the judge of the District Court to proceed in the execution of his decree was granted. In delivering the opinion, Mr. Chief Justice Marshall says: "The State cannot be made a defendant to a suit brought by an individual, but it remains the duty of the courts of the United States to decide all cases brought before them by citizens of one State against citizens of a different State, when a State is not necessarily a defendant. In this case, the suit was not instituted against the State or its treasurer, but against the executrixes of David Rittenhouse, for the proceeds of a vessel condemned in the Court of Admiralty, which were admitted to be in their possession. If these proceeds had been the actual property of Pennsylvania, however wrongfully acquired, the disclosure of that fact would have presented a case on which it was unnecessary to give an opinion; *but it certainly can never be alleged that a mere suggestion of title in a State to property in possession of an individual must arrest the proceedings of the court, and prevent their looking into the suggestion and examining the validity of the title.*"

* * *

It may be said—in fact it is said—that the present case differs from the one in 5 Cranch, because the officers who are sued assert no personal possession, but are holding as the mere agents of the United States, while the executors of Rittenhouse held the money until a better right was established. But the very next case in this court of a similar character, Meigs v. McClung's Lessee, 9 Cranch, 11, shows that this distinction was not recognized as sound. [In Meigs, the plaintiff brought an action against military officers in possession of property and prevailed over the objection that the action could not be maintained against the officers because they were acting for the benefit of the United States and under their direction. The lower court held that since title was in the plaintiff, he was entitled to recover possession, and the Supreme Court upheld the judgment.]

* * *

Osborn v. Bank of United States, 9 Wheat. 738, is a leading case, remarkable in many respects, and in none more than in those resembling the one before us.

It was this: The State of Ohio having levied a tax upon the branch of the Bank of the United States located in that State, which the bank refused to pay, Osborn, auditor of the State, was about to proceed to collect said tax by a seizure of the money of the bank in its vaults, and an amended bill alleged that he had so seized $100,000, and while aware that an injunction had been issued by the Circuit Court of the United States on the prayer of the bank, the money so seized had been delivered to the treasurer of the State, Curry, and afterwards came to the possession of Sullivan, who had succeeded Curry as treasurer. Both Curry and Sullivan were made defendants as well as Osborn and his assistant, Harper.

One of the objections pressed with pertinacity all through the case to the jurisdiction of the court was the conceded fact that the State of Ohio, though not made a defendant to the bill, was the real party in interest. That all the parties sued were her officers,—her auditor, her treasurer, and their agents,— concerning acts done in their official character, and in obedience to her laws. It was conceded that the State could not be sued, and it was earnestly argued there, as here, that what could not be done directly could not be done by suing her officers. And it was insisted that while the State could not be brought before the court, it was a necessary party to the relief sought, namely, the return of the money and obedience to the injunction, and that the bill must be dismissed.

A few citations from the opinion of Mr. Chief Justice Marshall will show the views entertained by the court on the question thus raised. * * *

[Chief Justice Marshall stated]: "* * * In cases where a State is a party on the record, the question of jurisdiction is decided by inspection. If jurisdiction depend not on this plain fact, but on the interest of the State, what rule has the Constitution given by which this interest is to be measured? If no rule is given, is it to be settled by the court? If so, the curious anomaly is presented of a court examining the whole testimony of a cause, inquiring into and deciding on the extent of a State's interest, without having a right to exercise any jurisdiction in the case. Can this inquiry be made without the exercise of jurisdiction?"

The decree of the Circuit Court ordering a restitution of the money was affirmed.

* * *

* * * [A]s late as the case of Davis v. Gray, 16 Wall. 203, the case of Osborn v. Bank of United States is cited with approval as establishing these among other propositions: "Where the State is concerned, the State should be made a party, if it can be done. That it cannot be done, is a sufficient reason for the omission to do it, and the court may proceed to decree against the officers of the State in all respects as if the State were a party to the record. In deciding who are parties to the suit, the court will not look beyond the record. Making a State officer a party does not make the State a party, *although her law may have prompted his action, and the State may stand behind him as a real party in interest.* A State can be made a party only by shaping the bill expressly with that view, as where individuals or corporations are intended to be put in that relation to the case."

Though not prepared to say now that the court can proceed against the officer in "all respects" as if the State were a party, this may be taken as intimating in a general way the views of the court at that time.

* * *

The objection [of sovereign immunity] is also inconsistent with the principle involved in the last two clauses of article 5 of the amendments to the Constitution of the United States, whose language is: "That no person * * * shall be deprived of life, liberty, or property without due process of law, nor shall private property be taken for public use without just compensation."

Conceding that the property in controversy in this case is devoted to a proper public use, and that this has been done by those having authority to establish a cemetery and a fort, the verdict of the jury finds that it is and was the private property of the plaintiff, and was taken without any process of law and without any compensation. Undoubtedly those provisions of the Constitution are of that character which it is intended the courts shall enforce, when cases involving their operation and effect are brought before them. The instances in which the life and liberty of the citizen have been protected by the judicial writ of *habeas corpus* are too familiar to need citation, and many of these cases, indeed almost all of them, are those in which life or liberty was invaded by persons assuming to act under the authority of the government. Ex parte Milligan, 4 Wall. 2.

If this constitutional provision is a sufficient authority for the court to interfere to rescue a prisoner from the hands of those holding him under the asserted authority of the government, what reason is there that the same courts shall not give remedy to the citizen whose property has been seized without due process of law, and devoted to public use without just compensation?

* * *

No man in this country is so high that he is above the law. No officer of the law may set that law at defiance with impunity. All the officers of the government, from the highest to the lowest, are creatures of the law, and are bound to obey it.

* * *

Courts of justice are established, not only to decide upon the controverted rights of the citizens as against each other, but also upon rights in controversy between them and the government; and the docket of this court is crowded with controversies of the latter class.

Shall it be said, in the face of all this, and of the acknowledged right of the judiciary to decide in proper cases, statutes which have been passed by both branches of Congress and approved by the President to be unconstitutional, that the courts cannot give a remedy when the citizen has been deprived of his property by force, his estate seized and converted to the use of the government without lawful authority, without process of law, and without compensation, because the President has ordered it and his officers are in possession?

If such be the law of this country, it sanctions a tyranny which has no existence in the monarchies of Europe, nor in any other government which has a just claim to well-regulated liberty and the protection of personal rights.

* * *

The evils supposed to grow out of the possible interference of judicial action with the exercise of powers of the government essential to some of its most important operations, will be seen to be small indeed compared to this evil, and much diminished, if they do not wholly disappear, upon a recurrence to a few considerations.

* * *

* * * [One such] consideration is, that since the United States cannot be made a defendant to a suit concerning its property, and no judgment in any suit against an individual who has possession or control of such property can bind or conclude the government, * * * the government is always at liberty, notwithstanding any such judgment, to avail itself of all the remedies which the law allows to every person, natural or artificial, for the vindication and assertion of its rights. Hence, taking the present case as an illustration, the United States may proceed by a bill in chancery to quiet its title, in aid of which, if a proper case is made, a writ of injunction may be obtained. Or it may bring an action of ejectment, in which, on a direct issue between the United States as plaintiff, and the present plaintiff as defendant, the title of the United States could be judicially determined. Or, if satisfied that its title has been shown to be invalid, and it still desires to use the property, or any part of it, for the purposes to which it is now devoted, it may purchase such property by fair negotiation, or condemn it by a judicial proceeding, in which a just compensation shall be ascertained and paid according to the Constitution.

If it be said that the proposition here established may subject the property, the officers of the United States, and the performance of their indispensable functions to hostile proceedings in the State courts, the answer is, that no case can arise in a State court, where the interests, the property, the rights, or the authority of the Federal government may come in question, which cannot be removed into a court of the United States under existing laws. * * *

* * *

The Circuit Court was competent to decide the issues in this case between the parties that were before it; in the principles on which these issues were decided no error has been found; and its judgment is

Affirmed.

■ MR. JUSTICE GRAY, with whom concurred MR. CHIEF JUSTICE WAITE, MR. JUSTICE BRADLEY, and MR. JUSTICE WOODS, dissenting.

* * * The case so deeply affects the sovereignty of the United States, and its relations to the citizen, that it is fit to announce the grounds of our dissent. * * *

This [action] * * * is brought to recover possession of land which the United States have for years held, and still hold, for military and other public purposes, claiming title under a certificate of sale for direct taxes, which is declared by the act of Congress of June 7, 1862, to be *prima facie* evidence of the regularity and validity of the sale and of the title of the purchaser * * *.

The principles upon which we are of opinion that the court below had no authority to try the question of the validity of the title of the United States in this action, and that this court has therefore no authority to pass upon that question, may be briefly stated.

The sovereign is not liable to be sued in any judicial tribunal without its consent. The sovereign cannot hold property except by agents. To maintain an action for the recovery of possession of property held by the sovereign through its agents, not claiming any title or right in themselves, but only as the representatives of the sovereign and in its behalf, is to maintain an action to recover possession of the property against the sovereign; and to invade such possession of the agents, by execution or other judicial process, is to invade the possession of the sovereign, and to disregard the fundamental maxim that the sovereign cannot be sued.

That maxim is not limited to a monarchy, but is of equal force in a republic. In the one, as in the other, it is essential to the common defence and general welfare that the sovereign should not, without its consent, be dispossessed by judicial process of forts, arsenals, military posts, and ships of war, necessary to guard the national existence against insurrection and invasion; of custom-houses and revenue cutters, employed in the collection of the revenue; or of light-houses and light-ships, established for the security of commerce with foreign nations and among the different parts of the country.

These principles appear to us to be axioms of public law, which would need no reference to authorities in their support, were it not for the exceeding importance and interest of the case, the great ability with which it has been argued, and the difference of opinion that has been manifested as to the extent and application of the precedents.

The exemption of the United States from being impleaded without their consent is, as has often been affirmed by this court, as absolute as that of the Crown of England or any other sovereign. * * *

* * *

To maintain this action, independently of any legislation by Congress, is to declare that the exemption of the United States from being impleaded without their consent does not embrace lands held by a disputed title; to defeat the exemption from judicial process in the very cases in which it is of the utmost importance to the public that it should be upheld; and to compel the United States to submit to the determination of courts and juries the validity of their title to any land held and used for military, naval, commercial, revenue, or police purposes.

[Justice Gray then argued that several precedents relied upon by the plaintiff, including Chisholm, Osborn, and Meigs, were distinguishable—Chisholm because the case did not hold that the United States could be sued without its consent, Osborn because the money in issue was in the personal possession of the defendants and the suit was one to enjoin federal constitutional violations, and Meigs because "no objection to the exercise of jurisdiction was made by the defendants or by the United States, or noticed by the Court".]

* * *

In the case of The Siren, 7 Wall. 152, the court said: "It is a familiar doctrine of the common law, that the sovereign cannot be sued in his own courts without his consent. The doctrine rests upon reasons of public policy; the inconvenience and danger which would follow from any different rule. It is obvious that the public service would be hindered, and the public safety endangered, if the supreme authority could be subjected to suit at the instance of every citizen, and consequently controlled in the use and disposition of the means required for the proper administration of the government. The exemption from direct suit is therefore without exception. This doctrine of the common law is equally applicable to the supreme authority of the nation,—the United States. They cannot be subjected to legal proceedings at law or in equity without their consent; and whoever institutes such proceedings must bring his case within the authority of some act of Congress." * * *

* * *

The view on which this court appears to have constantly acted, which reconciles all its decisions, and is in accord with the English authorities, is this: The objection to the exercise of jurisdiction over the sovereign or his property, in an action in which he is not a party to the record, is in the nature of a personal objection, which, if not suggested by the sovereign, may be presumed not to be intended to be insisted upon. If ejectment is brought by one citizen against another, the court *prima facie* has jurisdiction of the subject-matter and of the parties, and, if no objection is interposed in behalf of the sovereign, proceeds to judgment between the parties before it. If the property is in the possession of the defendants and not of the sovereign, an informal suggestion that it belongs to the sovereign will not defeat the action. But if the sovereign, in proper form and by sufficient proof, makes known to the court that he insists upon his exemption from suit, and that the property sued for is held by the nominal defendants exclusively for him and on his behalf as public property, the right of the plaintiff to prosecute the suit and the authority of the court to exercise jurisdiction over it cease, and all further proceedings must be stayed.

* * *

    * * * [W]e are of opinion that the court had no authority to proceed to trial and judgment * * *.

NOTE ON SOVEREIGN IMMUNITY IN SUITS AGAINST FEDERAL OFFICERS

(1) *The Doctrine of Official Responsibility.* Despite the concept of sovereign immunity, the idea of official responsibility to law has received extensive judicial development. As had been true in England, many suits in the federal courts in which the nominal defendant was an officer, rather than the government or an executive agency, were deemed to be against the individual and not the sovereign—even though the suit challenged the legality of official action, and the relief granted required the officer to take action affecting the government.

    After surveying the evolution of suits against officers, Professor Jaffe concluded that "the sensitive areas—the areas where consent to suit [was] likely to be required—[were] those involving the enforcement of contracts, treasury liability for tort, and the adjudication of interests in property which [had] come unsullied by tort into the bosom of the government." Jaffe, *Suits Against Governments and Officers: Sovereign Immunity,* 77 Harv.L.Rev. 1, 29 (1963). The cases are by no means easy to square. For helpful discussions, see, in addition to Jaffe, *supra,* Cramton, *Nonstatutory Review of Federal Administrative Action: The Need for Statutory Reform of Sovereign Immunity, Subject Matter Jurisdiction, and Parties Defendant,* 68 Mich.L.Rev. 387, 402–04 (1970), and Engdahl, *Immunity and Accountability for Positive Government Wrongs,* 44 U.Colo.L.Rev. 1, 20–21, 32–34 (1972).

    Is it useful to ask whether a particular action against government officials is "really" against the government? Government interests are fully implicated in Lee and other actions not barred by sovereign immunity. Isn't it a fiction that such suits against officers are not against the state—in the sense of implicating important government interests? Or is the fiction that there ever existed a broad doctrine of sovereign immunity that, outside of a few specific areas, barred relief at the behest of individuals complaining of government illegality?

Many decisions, like Lee, referred interchangeably to decisions in suits against federal officials and suits against state officials brought in federal court. The history of these cases in the nineteenth century is not easily described, and there may be differences between suits against a state and against the United States. At a minimum, in the former context, one must consider the pertinence of the Eleventh Amendment, which has been interpreted as embodying a principle of state sovereign immunity in federal court actions. See generally Sec. 2(A), *infra*.

(2) *Precedent.* In Little v. Barreme, 6 U.S. (2 Cranch) 170, 179 (1804), the Supreme Court affirmed a damage judgment against an American naval captain who, in seizing a Danish vessel, had acted under presidential orders issued through the Secretary of Navy and purportedly pursuant to an act of Congress. The Court (per Marshall, C.J.) found that the orders had been based upon a misconstruction of the statute, and that the seizure was thus a trespass unauthorized by federal law. Despite the presidential direction, the need for military obedience, and the harshness of holding the officer personally liable, the Court ruled that the captain's claim of official authority could not shield an act that, absent lawful authorization, constituted a simple trespass.

The same principle of official accountability was applied by Chief Justice Marshall in Meigs v. McClung's Lessee, 13 U.S. (9 Cranch) 11 (1815), United States v. Peters, 9 U.S. (5 Cranch) 115 (1809), and Osborn v. Bank of the United States, 22 U.S. (9 Wheat.) 738 (1824), all referred to in Lee. In these cases, the claimant was permitted, in a suit against an officer, to recover property to which the government claimed title. (Peters and Osborn were suits against state officials.)

In Osborn, the Chief Justice admitted that the state was an interested party, but said that since the Eleventh Amendment deprived the Bank of power to name Ohio as a defendant, the case could proceed without the state as a party (pp. 846–47). Marshall ruled, however, that the Eleventh Amendment was not implicated (p. 856): "It may, we think, be laid down as a rule which admits of no exception, that, in all cases where jurisdiction depends upon the party, it is the party named in the record. Consequently, the 11th amendment * * * is, of necessity, limited to those suits in which a state is a party on the record." As late as Davis v. Gray, 83 U.S. 203, 220 (1872), the Court suggested adherence to the party-of-record rule.[1]

Lee, while finding no barrier to suit, suggests that immunity may not be "absolutely limited to cases in which the United States are made defendants by name." The Court clearly rejected the party-of-record test in In re Ayers, 123 U.S. 443, 487 (1887), p. 1064, *infra*, and in this respect has followed Ayers ever since.

Rejection of the party-of-record rule, however, left in place a broad scope for suits against officers, so long as it could be shown that the officer had personally committed an actionable wrong. The officials in Lee, Peters, Osborn, and Little v. Barreme committed acts that, absent valid authorizations, constituted trespasses at common law. That the acts were committed under

---

1. At the same time, Marshall had signaled a retreat from the broad party-of-record rule in the complicated proceedings in Governor of Georgia v. Madrazo, 26 U.S. (1 Pet.) 110 (1828), p. 1050, *infra*.

color of office was not an automatic defense. And the officer not only could be enjoined from causing harm (*e.g.*, Philadelphia Co. v. Stimson,223 U.S. 605 (1912)), but could even be compelled to perform affirmative acts if he was shown to be required by law to discharge some duty. See, *e.g.*, Wilbur v. United States ex rel. Krushnic, 280 U.S. 306 (1930).

In contrast to the liability of officers engaging in tortious conduct, officers agreeing to contracts on behalf of the government would not, under principles of the general law, be personally liable if the government committed a breach. Thus, suit for breach of contract could be brought only against the government—and such an action was barred by immunity. See, *e.g.*, Louisiana ex rel. Elliott v. Jumel, 107 U.S. 711, 721, 727 (1883), p. 1063, *infra.* The particular sensitivity of suits involving breach of government contracts was clear from the resistance to such suits brought by bondholders of state governments following both the Revolutionary and Civil Wars. The Eleventh Amendment was enacted, and later interpreted, to protect state governments from federal jurisdiction to impose just such liability.

(3) *The Impact of Ex Parte Young.* In Ex parte Young, 209 U.S. 123 (1908), p. 1058, *infra,* the Supreme Court upheld the authority of a federal circuit court to enjoin a state attorney general from instituting suits to impose sanctions for violation of a state statute that allegedly conflicted with the Fourteenth Amendment. Although the threatened conduct of the defendant would not have been an actionable wrong at common law, the court in effect upheld a federal right of action for equitable relief from violations of the Constitution. The Court also held such an action not barred by the Eleventh Amendment.

Young remains a pivotal decision in the interpretation of the Eleventh Amendment and *state* sovereign immunity. And its principle has been easily absorbed in suits challenging *federal* official action. See, *e.g.*, Shields v. Utah Idaho Central R.R., 305 U.S. 177, 183–84 (1938); Rickert Rice Mills, Inc. v. Fontenot, 297 U.S. 110 (1936).

(4) *The Role of Mandamus.* The Supreme Court has held that mandamus actions are not barred by sovereign immunity. See Houston v. Ormes, 252 U.S. 469, 472–74 (1920); Minnesota v. Hitchcock, 185 U.S. 373, 386 (1902). Why should this be?[2] In Vishnevsky v. United States, 581 F.2d 1249, 1255–56 (7th Cir.1978), the court, in approving a writ of mandamus to compel IRS officials to credit plaintiffs with an overpayment of taxes, noted a long line of Supreme Court and lower court cases issuing mandamus to compel payment of funds out of the federal treasury, even absent consent by Congress.

NOTE ON THE LARSON CASE AND SUBSEQUENT DECISIONS
CONCERNING SOVEREIGN IMMUNITY IN SUITS
CHALLENGING FEDERAL OFFICIAL ACTION

(1) *The Facts and Opinions in the Larson Case.* In Larson v. Domestic & Foreign Commerce Corp., 337 U.S. 682 (1949), the Supreme Court rendered an

---

2. Recall that in England, mandamus and the other prerogative writs were issued by the King's Bench, over which the King once presided. His presence eventually became only a fiction, but the writ was still regarded as an indirect command of the sovereign himself. See Note, *Developments in the Law—Remedies Against the United States and its Officials,* 70 Harv.L.Rev. 827, 846 (1957).

important decision, much-criticized ever since, on the sovereign immunity of the United States. The facts were described in Justice Frankfurter's dissenting opinion as follows (pp. 706–07):

"The Government had some surplus coal at an Army camp in Texas. On March 11, 1947, the War Assets Administration, through the Regional Office in Dallas, Texas, invited a bid from the plaintiff, respondent here, for purchase of the coal. The Dallas office expressed thus its approval of the bid submitted by the plaintiff. * * * Thereupon the plaintiff arranged for resale of the coal and its shipment abroad. On April 1, 1947, the Dallas office wired the plaintiff that unless the sum of $17,500 was deposited in the First National Bank in Dallas by noon April 4, 'the sale will be cancelled and other disposition made.' Though claiming that this demand was in the teeth of the contract, the plaintiff arranged for an irrevocable letter of credit payable through the First National Bank of Dallas to the War Assets Administration. The Dallas office now insisted that unless cash was deposited 'the sale of 10,000 tons of coal * * * will be cancelled ten days from this date.' That office disregarded further endeavors by the plaintiff to adjust the matter, and on April 16 it informed the plaintiff that the contract was cancelled. Having learned that the coal was to be sold to another concern, the plaintiff, asserting ownership in the coal and the threat of irreparable damage, brought this suit in the District Court of the United States for the District of Columbia to restrain the War Assets Administrator and those under his control from transferring the coal to any other person than the plaintiff."

The district court granted a motion to dismiss the complaint on the ground, among others, that the court did not have jurisdiction because the suit was one against the United States. The court of appeals reversed, holding that the jurisdiction of the court depended on whether or not title to the coal had passed. The Supreme Court, with Justice Rutledge concurring only in the result and Justices Frankfurter, Burton, and Jackson dissenting, reversed "with directions that the complaint be dismissed".

Chief Justice Vinson, speaking for the Court, said (p. 695):

"We hold that if the actions of an officer do not conflict with the terms of his valid statutory authority, then they are the actions of the sovereign, whether or not they are tortious under general law, if they would be regarded as the actions of a private principal under the normal rules of agency. A Government officer is not thereby necessarily immunized from liability, if his action is such that a liability would be imposed by the general law of torts. But the action itself cannot be enjoined or directed, since it is also the action of the sovereign."

"The relief sought in this case," the Court explained (pp. 688–89), "was not the payment of damages by the individual defendant. To the contrary, it was asked that the court order the War Assets Administrator, his agents, assistants, deputies and employees and all persons acting under their direction, not to sell the coal involved and not to deliver it to anyone other than the respondent. The district court held that this was relief against the sovereign and therefore dismissed the suit. We agree."

The plaintiff contended, in the Court's words, that "[i]f an officer of the Government wrongly takes or holds specific property to which the plaintiff has title, then his taking or holding is a tort, and illegal as a matter of general law, whether or not it be within his delegated powers. He may therefore be sued individually to prevent the illegal taking or to recover the property illegally held" (p. 692). The Court responded that this theory was "erroneous," and "confuse[d] the doctrine of sovereign immunity with the requirement that a plaintiff state a cause of action. It is a prerequisite to the maintenance of any action for specific relief that the plaintiff claim an invasion of his legal rights, either past or threatened. He must, therefore, allege conduct which is illegal in the sense that the respondent suggests. * * * But, in a suit against an agency of the sovereign, it is not sufficient that he make such a claim. Since the sovereign may not be sued, it must also appear that the action to be restrained or directed is not action of the sovereign. The mere allegation that the officer, acting officially, wrongfully holds property to which the plaintiff has title does not meet that requirement. * * *" (p. 693).

Chief Justice Vinson recognized that the plaintiff would be entitled to maintain its action if it were asserting either that the defendant were seeking to enforce an unconstitutional enactment or "acting in excess of his authority or under an authority not validly conferred[11]." Here, however, he said (p. 703):

"* * * The very basis of the respondent's action is that the Administrator was an officer of the Government, validly appointed to administer its sales program and therefore authorized to enter, through his subordinates, into a binding contract concerning the sale of the Government's coal. There is no allegation of any statutory limitation on his powers as a sales agent. In the absence of such a limitation he, like any other sales agent, had the power and the duty to construe such contracts and to refuse delivery in cases in which he believed that the contract terms had not been complied with. His action in so doing in this case was, therefore, within his authority even if, for purposes of decision here, we assume that his construction was wrong and that title to the coal had, in fact, passed to the respondent under the contract. There is no claim that his action constituted an unconstitutional taking. It was, therefore, inescapably the action of the United States and the effort to enjoin it must fail as an effort to enjoin the United States."

The Chief Justice explained United States v. Lee as resting on "the assumed lack of the defendants' constitutional authority to hold the land against the plaintiff" and the further assumption "that if title had been in the plaintiff the taking of the property by the defendants would be a taking without just compensation and, therefore, an unconstitutional action." And he added (pp. 697–702):

"* * * The cases which followed Lee's do not require a different result. * * * With only one possible exception, * * * specific relief in connection with property held or injured by officers of the sovereign acting in the name of the sovereign has been granted only where there was a claim that the taking of the property or the injury to it was not the action of the sovereign because unconstitutional or beyond the officer's statutory powers. Certainly, the Court has repeatedly stated these to be the cases in which such relief could be granted. A contrary doctrine was stated in Goltra v. Weeks, 271 U.S. 536 (1926). In that case the United States had leased barges to the plaintiff under

---

11. "Of course, a suit may fail, as one against the sovereign, even if it is claimed that the officer being sued has acted unconstitutionally or beyond his statutory powers, if the relief requested can not be granted by merely ordering the cessation of the conduct complained of but will require affirmative action by the sovereign or the disposition of unquestionably sovereign property. North Carolina v. Temple, 134 U.S. 22 (1890)."

a contract which gave it a right to repossess under certain conditions. Believing that those conditions existed, officers of the Government attempted to repossess the barges. The Court held that a suit to enjoin them from doing so was not a suit against the United States. The Court said that the taking of the barges was alleged to be a trespass and hence 'illegal.' Therefore, the actions of the officers were personal actions, not the actions of the United States, and injunction against them would not be injunction against the United States. 271 U.S. at 544. For this conclusion the Court relied entirely upon the opinion of Mr. Justice Hughes in Philadelphia Co. v. Stimson, 223 U.S. 605 (1912). The reliance was misplaced, since the opinion in that case clearly and specifically rested on the claim that there was a lack of statutory power to act, not simply on a claim of tortious injury to the plaintiff.

"Opposed to the rationale of the Goltra opinion is the decision, by Mr. Justice Holmes, in Goldberg v. Daniels, 231 U.S. 218 (1913). There, as here, the question concerned the effect of a claimed sale of Government surplus property. The plaintiff submitted a sealed bid for a surplus war vessel, accompanied in that case by a certified check as payment in advance. When the bids were opened his was the highest. The Secretary of the Navy, however, determined not to accept the bid and refused to deliver the vessel. The plaintiff brought mandamus. * * * On appeal here, it was * * * held that * * * [t]he suit must fail as one against the United States, * * * whether or not the sale was complete. In so holding the Court said, in effect, that the question of title was immaterial to the court's jurisdiction. Wrongful the Secretary's conduct might be, but a suit to relieve the wrong by obtaining the vessel would interfere with the sovereign behind its back and hence must fail.

"Both cases are pressed upon us. The petitioner argues, and correctly, that the result in the Goldberg case calls for a similar result in this case—a dismissal of the suit for want of jurisdiction. The respondent argues, with equal correctness, that the theory of the Goltra opinion—that an allegation that the actions of Government officers are wrongful under general law is sufficient to show that they are 'unauthorized'—calls for an affirmance of the decision below. Since we must therefore resolve the conflict in doctrine we adhere to the rule applied in the Goldberg case and to the principle which has been frequently repeated by this Court, both before and after the Goltra case: the action of an officer of the sovereign (be it holding, taking or otherwise legally affecting the plaintiff's property) can be regarded as so 'illegal' as to permit a suit for specific relief against the officer as an individual only if it is not within the officer's statutory powers or, if within those powers, only if the powers, or their exercise in the particular case, are constitutionally void.[26]

" * * *

---

26. "In addition to Goltra v. Weeks, *supra,* three other cases are argued to be inconsistent with this principle, [of which one was Land v. Dollar, 330 U.S. 731 (1947)].

"In Land v. Dollar, where the plaintiffs alleged that they were entitled to stock held by the Maritime Commission because the stock was received by the Commission only as a pledge, it was contended that any other kind of acquisition would constitute a violation of § 207 of the Merchant Marine Act, which allegedly gave the Commission author-

ity to acquire stock only as collateral. The complaint therefore alleged that the members of the Commission acted in excess of their authority as public officers. 330 U.S. at 738."

[Ed.] Consider whether this description of Land v. Dollar is accurate in light of the following statement of the Court in that case (pp. 735–36): "The allegations of the complaint, if proved, would establish that [defendant officials] are unlawfully withholding

"There are the strongest reasons of public policy for the rule that such [specific] relief cannot be had against the sovereign. The Government, as representative of the community as a whole, cannot be stopped in its tracks by any plaintiff who presents a disputed question of property or contract right. * * *

"There are limits, of course. Under our constitutional system, certain rights are protected against governmental action and, if such rights are infringed by the actions of officers of the Government, it is proper that the courts have the power to grant relief against those actions. But in the absence of a claim of constitutional limitation, the necessity of permitting the Government to carry out its functions unhampered by direct judicial intervention outweighs the possible disadvantage to the citizen in being relegated to the recovery of money damages after the event.

"* * * The differentiations as to remedy which the Congress has erected would be rendered nugatory if the basis on which they rest—the assumed immunity of the sovereign from suit in the absence of consent—were undermined by an unwarranted extension of the Lee doctrine."

Justice Douglas concurred in Larson (337 U.S. at p. 705) on the ground "that the principles announced by the Court are the ones which should govern the selling of government property. Less strict applications of those principles would cause intolerable interference with public administration. To make the right to sue the officer turn on whether by the law of sales title had passed to the buyer would clog this governmental function with intolerable burdens."

In a dissenting opinion more than matching in length the long opinion of the Chief Justice, Justice Frankfurter undertook a comprehensive analysis of the cases against governmental agents, both state and federal, in which the defense of sovereign immunity was raised. He put them in four groups, as follows (pp. 709–10):

"(1) Cases in which the plaintiff seeks an interest in property which concededly, even under the allegation of the complaint, belongs to the government, or calls for an assertion of what is unquestionably official authority.

"(2) Cases in which action to the legal detriment of a plaintiff is taken by an official justifying his action under an unconstitutional statute.

"(3) Cases in which a plaintiff suffers a legal detriment through action of an officer who has exceeded his statutory authority.

"(4) Cases in which an officer seeks shelter behind statutory authority or some other sovereign command for the commission of a common-law tort."

On the point directly in issue, Justice Frankfurter said, *inter alia* (pp. 716–18, 726–27):

"The fourth category of cases brings us to the controversy immediately before the Court and demands detailed analysis. These are the cases, it will be recalled, in which an official seeks to screen himself behind the sovereign in a suit against him based on the commission of a common-law tort. * * * A plaintiff's right 'under general law to recover possession of specific property

[plaintiffs'] property under the claim that it belongs to the United States. That conclusion would follow if either of [plaintiffs'] contentions were established: (1) that the Commission had no authority to purchase the shares or acquire them outright; or (2) that, even though such authority existed, the * * * contract resulted not in an outright transfer but in a pledge of the shares."

wrongfully withheld' may be enforced against an official and he cannot plead the sovereign's immunity against the court's power to afford a remedy. Land v. Dollar, 330 U.S. 731, 736; Belknap v. Schild, 161 U.S. 10, 18–20; Hopkins v. Clemson Agricultural College, 221 U.S. 636, 643.

"The starting point of this line of cases is United States v. Lee, 106 U.S. 196. * * *

"While there was some talk in the Lee opinion, as well as in some of the cases which followed that decision, about taking property without compensation, the basis of the action was that the defendants were ordinary tortfeasors, not immunized for their wrongful invasion of the plaintiff's property by the fact that they claimed to have acted on behalf of the Government. * * * In this class of cases the governmental agent had valid statutory authority but he determined erroneously the condition which had to exist before he could exercise it. The basis of action in this class of cases is the defendant's personal responsibility for the commission of a tort, which makes it irrelevant that by waiving the case against the governmental agent the plaintiff might choose to sue the Government as for a contract. * * *

"* * * When a pleading raises a substantial claim that the defendant is wrongfully withholding from the plaintiff property belonging to him, the defendant has not heretofore been permitted to shield himself behind the immunity of the sovereign. Only after the preliminary question of ownership is decided against the plaintiff does the claim of sovereign immunity come into play. Only then can it be said that the decree will affect property of the sovereign.

"The Court tries to explain away Land v. Dollar, [see footnote 26 of the Court's opinion] by suggesting that it was a case where the officers acted in excess of their authority, although the opinion in that case makes clear that, even if the officers had authority, there still remained the issue whether the shares of stock were sold or pledged to the United States. If the latter, to hold after satisfaction of the pledge would be tortious, and the stock could be recovered in the suit against the defendants. [Moreover, the] Goltra case is now thrown into the discard because it did not cite Goldberg v. Daniels, 231 U.S. 218. * * *

"* * * Goldberg was not cited in Goltra for the conclusive reason that Goldberg had nothing to do with Goltra. In the Goldberg case the Court, on the basis of the pleadings before it, was dealing with a suit where 'the United States is the owner in possession of the vessel.' 231 U.S. 218, 221–222. Accordingly, the suit was not for a tortious withholding of the plaintiff's property and the Government's immunity barred suit. In Goltra, on the contrary, the claim was for the delivery of property allegedly belonging to the plaintiff and tortiously in possession of the individual defendants, and the Court held that the plaintiff is entitled to establish such a claim as he can, 'even though the United States for whom they [the defendants] may profess to act is not a party and can not be made one.' 271 U.S. at 544. That is this case."

(2) *The Government Agent's Responsibility for Tortious Conduct.* Observe that historically the most plainly permissible of all types of actions against government officials, federal or state, are those in which (a) the plaintiff seeks to enjoin conduct or threatened conduct which, if not officially justified, would constitute a common law tort, and (b) the relief sought can be given by simply

directing the defendant to abstain from what he is doing or threatening to do. Is "the Government, as representative of the community as a whole," any the less "stopped in its tracks" in such cases than it would have been in Larson?

Should the question whether an action is, in substance, against the government be made to depend upon whether the law under which an official's conduct is wrongful is statutory or judge-made? Notice the Chief Justice's suggestion of an implied exception to the implied constitutional prohibition of suits against the government in cases in which other constitutional guarantees are at stake. But notice also that at this point the opinion fails to refer to cases involving only "excess of statutory authority".

(3) *Alternative Rationales for the Larson Result: The Relevance of Legal Title.* Apart from cases in which the United States is named as a party defendant, the clearest class of cases open to the defense of sovereign immunity under the pre-Larson law consisted of actions to establish an interest in, or satisfy a claim out of, property of the United States, where the United States admittedly had title and the property was in possession of its officers or agents.[1] Should the Larson situation have been assimilated to these property cases, as Justice Douglas suggested? Is there ground for saying that the action, in substance, was one to enforce a merely equitable claim for fulfillment of the contract of sale and hence in principle governed by these decisions, as well as by the cases holding that the United States' consent to be sued for damages in contract actions does not extend to specific relief?

Or might the case have been more successfully handled as presenting, not a question of immunity, but a question only of the propriety of the remedy sought as a matter of sound exercise of equitable discretion?

Notice that the Larson decision not only limits United States v. Lee but overrides a series of pre-Lee cases holding that a claim of legal title to property may be tried in an action against a United States officer holding the property under a claim of title of the United States. In many of these cases it would have been difficult to identify an issue either of constitutional power or statutory authority. Were these cases, and the post-Lee cases discussed in the Larson dissent, unsound in principle?[2]

What of footnote 11 in Larson? Is Professor Jaffe correct that it can be reconciled with prior cases only by reading "may" in that footnote "as *may* and not as *must*"? Jaffe, *Suits Against Governments and Officers: Sovereign Immunity,* 77 Harv.L.Rev. 1, 34 (1963). Is the footnote nonetheless misleading? Consider Hawaii v. Gordon, Paragraph (6)(b), *infra.*

(4) *The United States as an Indispensable Party.* Actions against federal officers were often dismissed on the ground, easily confused with sovereign immunity, that the United States was an indispensable party and could not be

---

1. See, *e.g.,* The Siren, 74 U.S. at 154, p. 1003, *supra*; United States v. Alabama, 313 U.S. 274, 282 (1941); Maricopa County v. Valley Nat. Bank, 318 U.S. 357, 362 (1943).

Compare, with these cases, Carr v. United States, 98 U.S. 433 (1878), much of the language of which was disapproved in United States v. Lee.

2. Justice Frankfurter, in the first category of his Larson dissent, commingles the property cases with "cases in which the plaintiff * * * calls for an assertion of what is unquestionably official authority." To what extent should an action be deemed to be in substance against the United States because the relief sought requires the affirmative exercise of official authority? Consider the history of mandamus against federal officials, see pp. 996–98, *supra.*

joined.[3] Whether anything of substance hinged on the difference in stated grounds for dismissal was a controverted point. But the debate was preempted by a 1976 congressional enactment broadly waiving sovereign immunity, and providing that the United States may but need not be named as a party defendant in suits seeking relief other than money damages. See Sec. 1(C), *infra*.[4]

(5) *Preclusion Against the United States*. Is it material, in determining if an action is in substance against the United States, to decide whether the United States will be bound by the judgment? As the Lee case notes, the traditional rule held that the United States is not bound by a judgment in an in personam suit against one of its officers. See, *e.g.*, Carr v. United States, 98 U.S. 433 (1878); Hussey v. United States, 222 U.S. 88 (1911).[5]

Under modern preclusion law, an interested person who is active in the conduct of litigation is ordinarily bound by the judgment, at least by way of issue preclusion, even though he is not a party. Applying this rule in a case in which the government had employed special counsel to prosecute an action concerning title to Indian lands, the Eighth Circuit held that "the United States is as effectually concluded as if it were a party to the judgment." United States v. Candelaria, 16 F.2d 559, 562–63 (8th Cir.1926), following United States v. Candelaria, 271 U.S. 432, 444 (1926). Accord Montana v. United States, 440 U.S. 147 (1979)(United States is bound, in its federal court challenge to a state tax, by a state court judgment in a suit filed by a private party but in which the United States had the "laboring oar"); see also Drummond v. United States, 324 U.S. 316, 318 (1945).

There appears to be no reason why sovereign immunity should bar the application of this rule to bind the United States to a judgment in a prior action against one of its officers, when (as is customary) the government employed counsel to defend or assist in the officer's defense. See 28 U.S.C. §§ 517–18 (authorizing the Attorney General to direct Justice Department lawyers to conduct any federal court case in which the United States is interested). In Duncan v. United States, 667 F.2d 36, 38 (Ct.Cl.1981), the court held that plaintiffs, having previously obtained a federal court injunction forbidding unlawful action of the Secretary of the Interior, could preclude the United States, in a separate suit for damages in the Court of Claims, from denying the illegality of the action. That result is especially appropriate in view of the 1976 statute mentioned in Paragraph (4), *supra,* which treats suits for specific relief nominally against officers as indistinguishable from suits against the United States.

---

3. See, *e.g.,* Mine Safety Appliances Co. v. Forrestal, 326 U.S. 371, 374–75 (1945); Louisiana v. Garfield, 211 U.S. 70, 77–78 (1908).

4. A different and nettlesome problem of parties defendant, involving the substitution of successors in office, appears to have been cured by a 1961 amendment to Rule 25(d) of the Federal Rules of Civil Procedure. See generally 7C Wright, Miller & Kane, Federal Practice and Procedure §§ 1959–61 (1986 & 1995 Supp.).

5. There appears to be little doubt that a subordinate federal official may be precluded by a prior judgment either against another federal official (with whom the defendant in the subsequent action is deemed to be in privity), see Tait v. Western Maryland Ry., 289 U.S. 620, 627 (1933), or against the United States or one of its agencies, see Sunshine Anthracite Coal Co. v. Adkins, 310 U.S. 381, 402–03 (1940).

(6) *Supreme Court Decisions Since Larson.*[6] The Supreme Court has revisited the question of sovereign immunity in several decisions since Larson.

(a) In Malone v. Bowdoin, 369 U.S. 643 (1962), the plaintiffs sought to eject a federal forest service officer from certain land to which both plaintiffs and the federal government claimed title. The Supreme Court held that sovereign immunity barred the action (pp. 646–48):

"In a number of later cases, arising over the years in a variety of factual situations, the principles of the Lee case were approved. But in several other cases which came to the Court during the same period, it was held that suits against government agents, specifically affecting property in which the United States claimed an interest, were barred by the doctrine of sovereign immunity. * * *

"While not expressly overruling United States v. Lee, *supra,* the Court in Larson * * * interpreted Lee as simply 'a specific application of the constitutional exception to the doctrine of sovereign immunity.' 337 U.S., at 696. So construed, the Lee case has continuing validity only 'where there is a claim that the holding constitutes an unconstitutional taking of property without just compensation.' *Id.,* at 697.

"No such claim has been advanced in the present case. Nor has it been asserted that the petitioner was exceeding his delegated powers as an officer of the United States in occupying the land in question, or that he was in possession of the land in anything other than his official capacity. This suit, therefore, is not within the class of cases in which, under Larson, specific relief can be obtained against a government officer. * * *"

Justice Douglas in dissent argued that Lee controlled (pp. 650–53):

"[T]he Larson case was a suit for specific performance of a contract to sell coal, a matter that courts had long left to damage suits. As I said in my separate concurrence in that case, any other rule would 'clog' government procurement 'with intolerable burdens.' 337 U.S., at 705.

"Ejectment, on the other hand, is the classic form of action to try title. It takes place in the locality where the land is located. No judges are better qualified to try it than the local judges. * * * If the [United States] is aggrieved by the state or federal court ruling on title, it can bring its arsenal of power into play. Eminent domain—with the power immediately to take possession—is available. * * *

"The balance between the convenience of the citizen and the management of public affairs is a recurring consideration in suits determining when and where a citizen can sue a government official. The balance is, in my view, on the side of the citizen where he claims realty in the Government's possession and where there are ready means of adjudicating the title. If legal title is actually in the claimant, if the action of the official in taking possession under authority of the United States is *ultra vires,* what objectionable interference with governmental functions can be said to exist?"

Since the government claimed no authority to condemn the property if it belonged to the plaintiffs, wasn't their assertion of title an "assertion that the officer was exceeding his delegated powers"? Is it conceivable that the case

---

6. For discussion of the lower courts' struggle to limit Larson and its progeny, see Webster, *Beyond Federal Sovereign Immuni-* *ty: 5 U.S.C. § 702 Spells Relief,* 49 Ohio St.L.J. 725, 729 & nn. 31–32 (1988).

turned merely on the plaintiffs' failure to make this allegation explicit? Is the result of the decision to force the government to pay compensation for property it has no wish to occupy unless its claim of title is well founded?

(b) Hawaii v. Gordon, 373 U.S. 57 (1963), concerned the Hawaii Statehood Act, which in § 5(e) required the President to determine whether certain federal properties were no longer needed by the United States, and, if not, to convey them to the State of Hawaii. The President's designee, the Director of the Bureau of the Budget, decided that § 5(e) did not apply to lands obtained by the United States through purchase, condemnation, or gift. He therefore did not determine whether any such land was "needed". Hawaii brought an original action in the Supreme Court seeking to obtain an order requiring the Director to withdraw his decision, to exercise his discretion in determining whether certain land acquired through condemnation was needed and, if not needed, to convey it to Hawaii. The Court in a brief per curiam opinion held that the complaint should be dismissed as a suit against the United States.

Does the judgment rest upon the premise that the nature of the decision called for by the statute precluded its interpretation to confer a legal right? Can the disposition on immunity grounds mean that that question never was considered? Are there other reasons why Hawaii should be made to seek its remedy from Congress rather than from the Court?

(c) Dugan v. Rank, 372 U.S. 609 (1963), was a suit to enjoin the United States and officers of the Bureau of Reclamation from impounding water behind Friant Dam, a part of the Central Valley Project in California, on the ground that this retention interfered with the plaintiffs' rights to the use of the water downstream.

The Supreme Court unanimously held that the suit against the officers was barred by sovereign immunity. In the Court's view, Congress had authorized physical seizure of the water and had limited the relief available to affected persons to a suit against the United States under the Tucker Act. If the relief sought were granted, the Court said (p. 621), "[t]he Government would, indeed, be 'stopped in its tracks' [citing Larson]."

Discussing an alternative form of relief requiring federal construction of additional dams to meet the plaintiffs' needs, the Court said (pp. 621–23): "The physical solution has no less direct effect. The Secretary of the Interior, the President and the Congress have authorized the Project as now constructed and operated. Its plans do not include the 10 additional dams required by the physical solution to be built at government expense. The judgment, therefore, would not only 'interfere with the public administration' but also 'expend itself on the public treasury....' [citing Land v. Dollar]. Moreover, the decree would require the United States—contrary to the mandate of the Congress—to dispose of valuable irrigation water and deprive it of the full use and control of its reclamation facilities. It is therefore readily apparent that the relief granted operates against the United States.

"* * * The power to seize which was granted here had no limitation placed upon it by the Congress. * * * It follows that if any part of respondents' claimed water rights were invaded it amounted to an interference therewith and a taking thereof—not a trespass."

What was the significance of the finding of immunity if its existence turned on the antecedent conclusions that Congress had authorized the seizure, subject to suit under the Tucker Act for just compensation, and that the seizure on these terms was constitutional?

In light of the other cases considered in this section (as well as the Steel Seizure Case, p. 1180, *infra*) consider Dugan's "general rule"—that a suit is against the sovereign if the judgment sought would interfere with the public administration. Far from explaining such decisions, does the formulation even describe them?[7]

(7) *Larson and Pennhurst.* The Supreme Court's decision in Pennhurst State School & Hospital v. Halderman, 465 U.S. 89 (1984), p. 1077, *infra,* involved a state's Eleventh Amendment immunity, but it relied heavily upon Larson. The opinion in Pennhurst characterized as a fiction the view that an injunction against an officer (even when he is acting outside his constitutional or statutory authority) does not run against the government, and said "it may well be wondered what principled basis there is to the ultra vires doctrine as it was set forth in Larson * * *. * * * For present purposes, we do no more than question the continued vitality of the ultra vires doctrine in the Eleventh Amendment context" (pp. 114–15 n. 25). The Court held that the doctrine was in any event a narrow one that did not permit the suit in question.

Should this language be read as calling into question even the limited scope for equitable relief against government officers that Larson and subsequent decisions seemed to permit?

––––––––

SUBSECTION C: CONGRESSIONAL ENACTMENTS WAIVING THE SOVEREIGN IMMUNITY OF THE FEDERAL GOVERNMENT

––––––––

NOTE ON FEDERAL LEGISLATION WAIVING THE SOVEREIGN IMMUNITY OF THE UNITED STATES

The importance of federal sovereign immunity has declined substantially over time as Congress has enacted a variety of measures authorizing federal courts to hear suits that would otherwise be barred. It has been taken for granted that specific statutory review mechanisms contained in particular regulatory statutes constitute pro tanto waivers of sovereign immunity. There are also more general enactments, not tied to review of a particular regulatory program, in which Congress has waived the United States' immunity. Discussed below are the three most important schemes: the Tucker Act, governing non-tort monetary claims against the United States; the Federal Tort Claims Act,

---

7. Consider the suggestion, in the Second Edition of this book, that it might be preferable "to return to Marshall's position in [Osborn] * * * that the only actions against the United States are actions in which the United States is named as a party defendant or in which the court is asked to enter a judgment affecting the title to property admitted or found to belong to the United States and in its possession, or compelling the expenditure of public funds, while recognizing that there may be other instances in which the interests of the United States are so intimately involved that the action cannot in justice proceed in its absence." Whatever its virtues, is this suggestion subject to criticism (for both vagueness and overbreadth) in its references to the "expenditure of public funds" and to the possibility of the government as an indispensable party?

governing tort suits against the United States; and a 1976 statute governing all claims against the United States for relief other than money damages.[1] In reviewing the system that has arisen, consider whether it lives up to reasonable standards of rationality and comprehensiveness.

A. The United States Court of Federal Claims and the Tucker Act[2]

(1) *Creation of the Court of Claims in 1855.* Before 1855, no statute gave consent to suit against the United States on claims for money damages; such claims were disposed of, if at all, by private act. Because reliance on private acts had proved burdensome and inequitable, the Court of Claims was created in that year. It was authorized to determine all claims against the government founded upon any statute, executive regulation, or express or implied contract with the United States.[3]

(2) *The Tucker Act.* In 1887, the Tucker Act broadened the Court of Claims' jurisdiction to include all "claims founded upon the Constitution of the United States or any law of Congress, except for pensions, or upon any regulation of an Executive Department, or upon any contract, expressed or implied, with the Government of the United States, or for damages, liquidated or unliquidated, in cases not sounding in tort, in respect of which claims the party would be entitled to redress against the United States either in a court of law, equity, or admiralty if the United States were suable." Act of March 3, 1887, 24 Stat. 505. Concurrent jurisdiction of claims not exceeding $1,000 was given to the district courts, and of claims of $1,000 to $10,000 to the circuit courts. The basic structure established by the Tucker Act, now codified at 28 U.S.C. §§ 1346(a)(2), 1491(a)(1), remains. (On the history of the court's constitutional status, and the problem of legislative revision of its judgments, see pp. 111–15, *supra*.)

(3) *Creation of the Claims Court in 1982.* The United States Claims Court, an Article I court, was established in 1982 (and renamed the United States Court of Federal Claims in 1992) to assume the trial jurisdiction formerly possessed by the Court of Claims. The Court of Federal Claims thus has jurisdiction over all claims governed by the Tucker Act; its jurisdiction over claims (other than for a tax refund) in excess of $10,000 is exclusive,[4] while the district courts

---

1. Other important measures consenting to suit against the United States include legislation authorizing district court jurisdiction over specified land disputes, see 28 U.S.C. §§ 2409–2410, Paragraph C(3)(a), *infra;* and provisions authorizing jurisdiction of the United States Court of Federal Claims over (i) patent and copyright infringement cases, 28 U.S.C. § 1498, (ii) disputes with government contractors arising under the Contract Disputes Act of 1978, see *id.* § 1491(a)(2), and (iii) specified claims of Indian tribes, see *id.* § 1505. See generally *id.* §§ 1491–1509; Steadman, Schwartz, Jacoby, Lester & Noone, Litigation With the Federal Government (3d ed. 1994)(hereafter Steadman et al.); 14 Wright, Miller & Cooper, Federal Practice and Procedure § 3656 (1985 & 1995 Supp.)

Recall, also, the general provisions discussed at pp. 1006–07, *supra,* providing for the award of costs and attorney's fees against the United States.

2. See generally Steadman et al., note 1, *supra,* at 215–48; 17 Wright, Miller & Cooper, Federal Practice and Procedure § 4101 (1988 & 1995 Supp.).

3. Act of Feb. 24, 1855, 10 Stat. 612, as amended by Act of March 3, 1863, 12 Stat. 765, Act of March 17, 1866, 14 Stat. 9, and Act of June 25, 1868, 15 Stat. 75.

4. This exclusivity has given rise to difficult questions about district court jurisdiction under provisions other than the Tucker Act. See Paragraphs C(3)-(5), *infra.*

have concurrent jurisdiction of claims not exceeding $10,000. There is no right in either forum to jury trial under the Tucker Act. 28 U.S.C. § 2402.

(4) *Scope and Limits of the Tucker Act.* The Tucker Act is merely a grant of jurisdiction and a concomitant waiver of sovereign immunity; it does not itself create any substantive rights. A suit under the Tucker Act must not only establish a violation of a federal enactment, but must also "demonstrate that the source of substantive law * * * [relied] upon 'can fairly be interpreted as mandating compensation by the Federal Government for the damage sustained.'" United States v. Mitchell, 463 U.S. 206, 216–17 (1983), quoting United States v. Testan, 424 U.S. 392, 400 (1976). (But the Mitchell decision also determined that the claimant need not demonstrate a separate waiver of immunity in the substantive provision relied upon.) Constitutional claims founded on the Just Compensation Clause have been held to satisfy this standard. See, *e.g.,* United States v. Causby, 328 U.S. 256 (1946); *cf.* First English Evangelical Lutheran Church v. County of Los Angeles, 482 U.S. 304 (1987)(Just Compensation Clause, as incorporated against a local government by the Fourteenth Amendment, by its own force authorizes award of money damages).[5] The lower courts have consistently rejected Tucker Act suits based on violations of other constitutional provisions, however, on the ground that these provisions do not "expressly grant a money remedy", Featheringill v. United States, 217 Ct.Cl. 24, 33 (1978) (First Amendment claim); accord, *e.g.,* Hohri v. United States, 782 F.2d 227, 244–45 (D.C.Cir.1986)(claims based, *inter alia,* on Fourth Amendment, Due Process Clause, Sixth Amendment's counsel and fair trial provisions, and Cruel and Unusual Punishments Clause), *vacated on other grounds,* 482 U.S. 64 (1987). The Act also does not extend to claims based on contracts implied-in-law (*i.e.,* quasi-contract or restitution claims). See generally Steadman et al., note 1, *supra,* §§ 9.120–9.121.

The Tucker Act is strictly limited to claims for money. It gives no jurisdiction to hear claims for specific performance, delivery of property in kind, or equitable relief,[6] although other provisions give the Court of Federal Claims a limited power to award equitable relief.[7]

Judgments in cases under the Tucker Act, both in the Court of Federal Claims and (except for cases based on the internal revenue laws) in the district courts, are appealable only to the Court of Appeals for the Federal Circuit, an Article III tribunal established in 1982. See 28 U.S.C. § 1295(a); United States v. Hohri, note 26, *infra.*

---

5. But in Preseault v. ICC, 494 U.S. 1 (1990), the Court noted that "taking claims against the Federal Government are premature until the property owner has availed itself of the process provided by the Tucker Act" (p. 11, quoting Williamson County Regional Planning Comm'n v. Hamilton Bank, 473 U.S. 172, 195 (1985)).

6. See Richardson v. Morris, 409 U.S. 464 (1973)(per curiam)(refusing injunctive relief). See generally United States v. Mitchell, 463 U.S. 206, 218 (1983).

7. To limit the need for claimants to bring two actions, one in district court seeking specific relief and one in the Court of Federal Claims seeking monetary relief, the latter has authority, in cases in which a judgment for damages is entered under the Tucker Act, to provide incidental and collateral relief "directing restoration to office or position, placement in appropriate duty or retirement status, and correction of applicable records." 28 U.S.C. § 1491(a)(2).

B. The Federal Tort Claims Act[8]

(1) *Enactment in 1946.* The exclusion of tort claims from coverage under the Tucker Act left tort victims without any general remedy against the government itself (rather than against individual officers) until 1946, when Congress enacted the Federal Tort Claims Act (FTCA).[9] The Act establishes district court jurisdiction and waives sovereign immunity in suits against the United States "for injury or loss of property, or personal injury or death caused by the negligent or wrongful act or omission of any employee of the Government while acting within the scope of his office or employment, under circumstances where the United States, if a private person, would be liable to the claimant in accordance with the law of the place where the act or omission occurred." 28 U.S.C. § 1346(b). Though it contains significant exceptions and limitations, the FTCA for the first time recognized the general principle of governmental liability in tort.[10]

(2) *Procedures and Remedies.* Procedure under the FTCA differs from ordinary tort suits in important respects.[11] No suit may be filed unless the claimant has made a timely application to the involved agency for administrative settlement, and the claim has been denied or not acted upon for six months. 28 U.S.C. § 2675. Trial is de novo, however, and is to the court.

---

8. See generally Jayson, Handling Federal Tort Claims (1995).

9. 60 Stat. 842 (1946). The FTCA's grant of jurisdiction is codified in 28 U.S.C. § 1346(b); procedures for tort claims are set forth in *id.* §§ 1402, 2401–02, 2412, 2671–79; exceptions to the rule of liability are contained in *id.* § 2680.

There are dozens of other statutes that provide remedies against the government in particular circumstances for the tortious conduct of its employees. See 1 Jayson, note 8, *supra*, § 2.05.

10. The Federal Employees Liability Reform and Tort Compensation Act of 1988, 102 Stat. 4563, amended 28 U.S.C. § 2679(b), (d), to make the FTCA the *exclusive* remedy for torts committed by federal officials in the course of their official duties. Under § 2679(d) as amended, if the Attorney General certifies that an employee who has been sued was acting within the scope of his employment, the proceeding shall be redesignated as a suit against the United States; if pending in state court, the suit shall be removed to federal court, *id.* § 2679(d)(2); and the plaintiff may recover only if the United States is liable under the FTCA, *id.* § 2679(d)(4). (The Supreme Court has held that although *removal* of the action pursuant to this provision is not judicially reviewable, the federal court in which the action is pending has authority to review the question whether the employee was acting within the scope of employment for purposes of deter-

mining whether the action is properly one against the United States under the FTCA. Gutierrez de Martinez v. Lamagno, 115 S.Ct. 2227 (1995). For further discussion of this case, particularly its implications for the scope of federal question jurisdiction under Article III, see p. 904, note 4, *supra*.)

This regime—precluding suits against employees and substituting the United States as defendant—existed before 1988 in the limited area of suits resulting from a federal employee's operation of a motor vehicle. The 1988 amendment extended the regime generally to tort actions against federal employees.

The 1988 Act also amended 28 U.S.C. § 2671 to extend the FTCA's coverage to injuries caused by employees of the judicial and legislative branches, but provided (in an amendment to 28 U.S.C. § 2674) that the United States may assert any defense of judicial or legislative immunity that would have been available to the employee. These amendments do not appear to disturb the rule, generally recognized in the lower courts—see Comment, 47 Geo. Wash.L.Rev. 651 (1979); Arnsberg v. United States, 549 F.Supp. 55, 57 (D.Or.1982), *rev'd on other grounds,* 757 F.2d 971 (9th Cir.1985)—that the United States may not assert in an FTCA action an immunity that would have been available to an *executive* official whose conduct gave rise to the lawsuit.

11. See generally 1 Jayson, note 8, *supra*, §§ 4.01–4.11.

Relief is limited to money damages,[12] and punitive damages are barred.[13]

(3) *The "Discretionary Function" Exception.* There are a number of express exceptions to the FTCA. The most important, which has caused difficulty from the outset, excludes any claim "based upon the exercise or performance or the failure to exercise or perform a discretionary function or duty on the part of a federal agency or an employee of the Government, whether or not the discretion involved be abused." 28 U.S.C. § 2680(a).

(a) *The Dalehite Case.* This exception was first interpreted by the Supreme Court in Dalehite v. United States, 346 U.S. 15 (1953). Pursuant to a high level government decision, a program was developed to manufacture and ship to occupied Germany, Japan, and Korea large quantities of an ammonium nitrate fertilizer as a means of increasing food production. The material was being loaded on ships at Texas City when spontaneous combustion led to an explosion that killed 560 people, injured some 3,000, and leveled a portion of the city.

The District Court awarded damages in a test case, finding negligence in the manufacture, coating, and packaging of the fertilizer as well as in the failure to give warning of the danger of fire and explosion. Sustaining a reversal of the judgment by the Court of Appeals, Justice Reed relied upon the fact that the entire program, including the aspects of the operation held to involve negligence, had been planned "at a high level under a direct delegation of plan-making authority from the apex of the Executive Department" (p. 40). The "discretionary function or duty" exception "includes more than the initiation of programs and activities. It also includes determinations made by executives or administrators in establishing plans, specifications or schedules of operations. Where there is room for policy judgment and decision there is discretion. It necessarily follows that acts of subordinates in carrying out the operations of government in accordance with official directions cannot be actionable. If this were not so, the protection of § 2680(a) would fail at the time it would be needed, that is, when a subordinate performs or fails to perform a causal step, each action or nonaction being directed by the superior, exercising, perhaps abusing, discretion" (pp. 35–36).

Justice Jackson, joined by Justices Black and Frankfurter, filed a powerful dissent. He dealt with the "discretionary function" defense as follows:

"We do not predicate liability on any decision taken at 'Cabinet level' or on any other high-altitude thinking. * * * However, if decisions are being made at Cabinet levels as to the temperature of bagging explosive fertilizer, whether paper is suitable for bagging hot fertilizer, and how the bags should be labeled, perhaps an increased sense of caution and responsibility even at that height would be wholesome. The common sense of this matter is that a policy adopted in the exercise of an immune discretion was carried out carelessly by those in charge of the detail. We cannot agree that all the way down the line

---

12. The courts have divided on whether a declaratory judgment of liability is permissible as one step toward a money judgment. See 2 Jayson, note 8, *supra*, § 9.02.

13. 28 U.S.C. § 2674. On the distinction between punitive and compensatory damages, see, *e.g.*, Molzof v. United States, 502 U.S. 301 (1992)(holding damages to be compensatory and not punitive even when they extend beyond ordinary notions of compensation, so long as the *purpose* of the award is not to punish intentional or egregious misconduct).

there is immunity for every balancing of care against cost, of safety against production, of warning against silence.

"* * * [M]any acts of government officials deal only with the housekeeping side of federal activities. The Government, as landowner, as manufacturer, as shipper, as warehouseman, as shipowner and operator, is carrying on activities indistinguishable from those performed by private persons. In this area, there is no good reason to stretch the legislative text to immunize the Government or its officers from responsibility for their acts, if done without appropriate care for the safety of others. Many official decisions even in this area may involve a nice balancing of various considerations, but this is the same kind of balancing which citizens do at their peril and we think it is not within the exception of the statute" (pp. 57–58, 59–60).[14]

(b) *The Indian Towing Case.* Two years later, the Court divided 5–4 in deciding Indian Towing Co. v. United States, 350 U.S. 61 (1955). The action was for damage to a barge caused by the Coast Guard's negligent failure to check and discover defects, make repairs or give warning that a light in a government operated lighthouse had gone out. The government contended that in imposing liability to the same extent that a private individual would be liable under similar circumstances, the statute excluded liability for the performance of activities that private persons do not perform. Rejecting this argument and the government's analogies to the "casuistries of municipal liability for torts", Justice Frankfurter's opinion for the Court said:

"* * * The Government reads the statute as if it imposed liability to the same extent as would be imposed on a private individual 'under the same circumstances.' But the statutory language is 'under like circumstances' and it is hornbook tort law that one who undertakes to warn the public of danger and thereby induces reliance must perform his 'good Samaritan' task in a careful manner" (pp. 64–65).

The government conceded that the "discretionary function" exception, which it described as relieving from liability for negligent "exercise of judgment", did not apply. The Court appeared to agree with that conclusion and added that although the government "need not undertake the lighthouse service," once having done so, the Coast Guard was obliged to use due care to keep the light in working order or give warning that it was not functioning (p. 69).

(c) *Subsequent Decisions.* The Court returned to the discretionary function exception in United States v. S.A. Empresa de Viacao Aerea Rio Grandense (Varig Airlines), 467 U.S. 797 (1984), in which victims of airplane accidents alleged that the planes did not meet federal safety standards, and that the Federal Aviation Administration (FAA) had been negligent in certificating the planes for commercial use. As authorized by statute, the FAA had delegated

---

14. On a different theory, the Court found no liability for the Coast Guard's negligence in fighting the fire. "The Act did not create new causes of action where none existed before", and "if anything is doctrinally sanctified in the law of torts it is the immunity of communities and other public bodies for injuries due to fighting fire" (pp. 43, 44). This part of Dalehite was overruled four years later in Rayonier Inc. v. United States, 352 U.S. 315 (1957), holding that the United States could be liable for the Forest Service's negligence in fighting a fire, and stating that "the very purpose of the Tort Claims Act [was] to establish novel and unprecedented governmental liability" (p. 319). See also United States v. Muniz, 374 U.S. 150 (1963).

certain inspection and certification responsibilities to employees of aircraft manufacturers, whose work was subject to spot checks by FAA employees. There was no record that an FAA inspector had checked the aircraft at issue in the suit.

The Supreme Court held the claims barred by the discretionary function exception. While admitting that its decisions "ha[d] not followed a straight line," the Court rejected the plaintiffs' contention that, after Indian Towing, Dalehite "no longer represents a valid interpretation of the discretionary function exception" (pp. 811–12). The Court then offered this explanation (pp. 813–14): "First, it is the nature of the conduct, rather than the status of the actor, that governs whether the discretionary function exception applies in a given case. * * * Thus, the basic inquiry concerning the application of the * * * exception is whether the challenged acts of a Government employee— whatever his or her rank—are of the nature and quality that Congress intended to shield from tort liability.

"Second, whatever else the discretionary function exception may include, it plainly was intended to encompass the discretionary acts of the Government acting in its role as a regulator of the conduct of private individuals. Time and again the legislative history refers to the acts of regulatory agencies as examples of those covered by the exception * * *. Congress wished to prevent judicial 'second-guessing' of legislative and administrative decisions grounded in social, economic, and political policy through the medium of an action in tort."

In light of this second observation, the Court had little difficulty holding that the FAA's decision to delegate inspection responsibility to the manufacturers was a discretionary function exempt from liability.

Doesn't the Court's first factor reduce to a perfect circularity? Does the second factor clarify the exception's scope outside the context of regulation of private enterprise?

In Berkovitz v. United States, 486 U.S. 531 (1988), the Court clarified the application of the exception in the context of federal regulatory programs, holding unanimously that the exception does not preclude liability for all acts arising out of such programs. The plaintiff alleged that federal health officials had violated specific federal regulatory directives when they licensed the sale of a vaccine that injured the plaintiff. The Court stressed that the discretionary function exception does not apply when "the employee has no rightful option but to adhere to the directive", and that even where the conduct involves the exercise of judgment, the exception shields "only governmental actions and decisions based on considerations of public policy" (pp. 536–37). Plaintiff's claim that the officials had wrongfully issued a product license, without receiving data required by statute as a precondition to licensing, was not barred because the officials had no discretion under federal law to act as they had. And the claim that the officials wrongfully authorized the distribution of a particular lot of vaccine without first testing it survived a motion to dismiss, since the plaintiff had alleged that the applicable regulations gave the responsible officials no policy discretion to release untested lots; whether that allegation could be substantiated was left for trial on the merits.[15]

---

15. In United States v. Gaubert, 499 U.S. 315 (1991), a shareholder of an insolvent savings and loan association sued the United States under the FTCA, alleging that federal regulators had been negligent in their supervision of the institution. The Supreme Court

Does this series of decisions create a clear pattern?[16] Is the exception's rationale similar to that underlying (i) the doctrine of sovereign immunity itself, (ii) traditional limitations on the scope of mandamus, (iii) the scope of review of administrative actions under the Administrative Procedure Act, (iv) the political question doctrine, see Chap. II, Sec. 6, *supra,* or (v) historic notions of officers' immunity in tort, see Sec. 3, *infra?* Does the United States require more or less protection from damage actions in tort than from suits for specific relief? Is the discretionary function exception more likely to be found applicable when (as in Dalehite but not in Indian Towing) the potential liability in tort is enormous?[17]

(4) *Other Exceptions.* Of the numerous other exceptions to the FTCA,[18] four should be highlighted.

(a) In addition to claims arising from discretionary functions, § 2680 excludes those based upon the action of a government employee "exercising due care, in the execution of a statute or regulation, whether or not * * * valid." Note the contrasting rule of Monell v. Department of Social Services, 436 U.S. 658 (1978), p. 1126, *infra,* under which local government bodies are liable under 42 U.S.C. § 1983 for constitutional torts of their employees only when the allegedly unconstitutional conduct "implements or executes a policy statement, ordinance, regulation, or decision officially adopted and promulgated by that body's officers" (p. 690).

(b) Section 2680(h) excludes liability for any claim arising out of assault, battery, false imprisonment, false arrest, malicious prosecution, abuse of process, libel, slander, misrepresentation, deceit, or interference with contract rights. The legislative history sheds little light on the reason for exclusion of these intentional torts, and in 1974 Congress modified the exclusion in a statute (88 Stat. 50) that, in effect, permits recovery for assault, battery, false imprisonment, false arrest, abuse of process, and malicious prosecution (but not libel, slander, misrepresentation, deceit, or interference with contract rights) when the suit is based upon acts or omissions of investigative or law enforcement officers. See Boger, Gitenstein & Verkuil, *The Federal Tort Claims Act Intentional Torts Amendment: An Interpretative Analysis,* 54 N.C.L.Rev. 497 (1976).

(c) In Laird v. Nelms, 406 U.S. 797 (1972), the plaintiff brought suit for property damage suffered as a result of a sonic boom caused by military

held unanimously that the discretionary function exception exempted the United States from liability. The Court stated that the exception applied to decisions made at the "operational" as well as at the policy planning level of activity; the critical question was whether the activity in question involved the exercise of choice and judgment in matters directly related to public policy considerations.

16. See also Boyle v. United Technologies Corp., 487 U.S. 500 (1988), p. 770, *supra,* relying on the discretionary function exception in fashioning a federal common law immunity for government contractors.

17. For critical analyses of the present scope of the discretionary function exception,

see Cass, *The Discretionary Function Exception to the Federal Tort Claims Act,* in 2 Administrative Conference of the United States: Recommendations and Reports 1503 (1987); Krent, *Preserving Discretion Without Sacrificing Deterrence: Federal Governmental Liability in Tort,* 38 U.C.L.A.L.Rev. 871, 915 (1991)(suggesting that agency action should be protected when (1) "courts in other contexts would decline to review agency acts for fear of skewing agency decisionmaking", or (2) the agency has made a "deliberate" social, economic, or political policy choice, whether negligent or not).

18. See generally 28 U.S.C. § 2680; 2 Jayson, note 8, *supra,* §§ 13.01–13.12.

aircraft. The Court held that a tort suit based on a theory of strict liability for ultrahazardous activity could not be brought under the FTCA. Does any provision in the Act justify that result?

(d) Numerous cases have considered the FTCA's application to injuries suffered by military personnel. In 1950, the Court unanimously held the Act inapplicable to injuries to servicemen that "arise out of or are in the course of activity incident to service", notwithstanding the absence of any statutory language supporting that result. Feres v. United States, 340 U.S. 135, 146 (1950).[19] The Court later explained this doctrine as based primarily upon three considerations: the distinctively federal character of military relationships, the existence of alternative compensation systems, and the deleterious effect that tort suits could have upon military discipline. Stencel Aero Engineering Corp. v. United States, 431 U.S. 666, 673 (1977). More recently, the Court stressed that the last of these considerations is the most important,[20] and that "[t]he Feres doctrine cannot be reduced to a few bright-line rules." United States v. Shearer, 473 U.S. 52, 57 (1985).

The Feres doctrine has continued to command majority support, even in close cases, but not without strong objection. In United States v. Johnson, 481 U.S. 681 (1987), for example, the Court held that a wrongful death claim filed by the widow of a Coast Guard pilot, alleging negligence by civilian FAA personnel under whose control the pilot had been flying, was barred by Feres. Justice Powell stated broadly that "the Feres doctrine has been applied consistently to bar all suits on behalf of service members against the Government based upon service-related injuries. We decline to modify the doctrine at this late date" (pp. 687–88). He reiterated the three concerns underlying the doctrine, and argued that any service-related suit "necessarily implicates the military judgments and decisions that are inextricably intertwined with the conduct of the military mission" (p. 691).

Justice Scalia, joined by Justices Brennan, Marshall, and Stevens, dissented. In his view, the Feres decision was simply unjustified; Congress had created numerous express exceptions to the FTCA's general rule of governmental liability, and there was no adequate basis for judicial implication of an additional exception. He argued that whether or not Feres should be overruled in a proper case, it should not be extended to injuries caused by civilian conduct.[21]

(5) *The Relation Between the FTCA and the Bivens Doctrine.* Carlson v. Green, 446 U.S. 14 (1980), p. 869, *supra,* held that the FTCA does not preclude a Bivens action against individual officers. The FTCA does not in terms create liability for conduct in violation of the Constitution;[22] such conduct may be the basis for an FTCA claim if suit is not barred by some limitation upon FTCA liability and if the conduct violates the applicable tort law. Liability and

---

19. But in United States v. Brown, 348 U.S. 110 (1954), the Court held that a *discharged* veteran may sue under the FTCA for negligent treatment in a Veterans' Administration hospital for a service-connected disability.

20. Note that the first rationale is in some tension with Rayonier v. United States

and United States v. Muniz, note 14, *supra,* while the second cannot explain the differing outcomes of Feres and of Brown (note 19, *supra*).

21. The Feres doctrine is criticized in Note, 77 Mich.L.Rev. 1099 (1979).

22. See, *e.g.,* FDIC v. Meyer, 114 S.Ct. 996 (1994).

damages are determined, however, under state law, not under constitutionally derived standards.[23]

The Feres doctrine, which was developed under the FTCA (see Paragraph (4)(d), *supra*), has also had an impact on the availability of Bivens remedies. In United States v. Stanley, 483 U.S. 669 (1987), the Court held that a former serviceman could not maintain a Bivens action against military officers and civilians who had administered the drug LSD to him, without his consent, as part of an army experiment. Justice Scalia, now speaking for the Court, applied the approach of Chappell v. Wallace, 462 U.S. 296 (1983), p. 872, *supra,* which was held to require "abstention in the inferring of Bivens actions as extensive as the exception to the FTCA established by Feres and United States v. Johnson"—*i.e.,* whenever the injury is "incident to [military] service" (483 U.S. at 709). (The court of appeals had ruled that Stanley's injury was incident to service, and the Supreme Court refused to reexamine that ruling.)

Justice Brennan (joined by Justices Marshall and Stevens) dissented, as did Justice O'Connor. In Justice O'Connor's view, "conduct of the type alleged in this case is so far beyond the bounds of human decency that as a matter of law it simply cannot be considered a part of the military mission" (p. 709).

C. Suits for Relief Other Than Money Damages

(1) *Waiver of Immunity in 1976.* In a statute enacted in 1976, 90 Stat. 2721, Congress eliminated three barriers to federal court actions seeking specific relief against federal official action. First, the statute amended 28 U.S.C. § 1331 to abolish any jurisdictional minimum in suits thereunder "brought against the United States, any agency thereof, or any officer or employee thereof in his official capacity." Second, the statute waived sovereign immunity in federal court suits seeking relief other than money damages against federal agencies or officials. And third, it provided that the United States may be named as a defendant and have judgment entered against it, providing that any mandatory or injunctive order specify the officer(s) responsible for compliance.

The language waiving sovereign immunity is codified as the last three sentences of section 10(b) of the Administrative Procedure Act, 5 U.S.C. § 702, and reads as follows:

"An action in a court of the United States seeking relief other than money damages and stating a claim that an agency or an officer or employee thereof acted or failed to act in an official capacity or under color of legal authority shall not be dismissed nor relief therein be denied on the ground that it is against the United States or that the United States is an indispensable party. The United States may be named as a defendant in any such action, and a judgment or decree may be entered against the United States: *Provided,* that any mandatory or injunctive decree shall specify the Federal officer or officers (by name or by title), and their successors in office, personally responsible for compliance. Nothing herein (1) affects other limitations on judicial review or the power or duty of the court to dismiss any action or deny relief on any other appropriate legal or equitable ground; or (2) confers authority to grant relief if any other statute that grants consent to suit expressly or impliedly forbids the relief which is sought."

---

23. A judgment against the United States under the FTCA bars further suit against individual tortfeasors. 28 U.S.C. § 2676.

The House Report accompanying that legislation remarks:

"* * * [T]he amendment to 5 U.S.C. section 702 is not intended to permit suit in circumstances where statutes forbid or limit the relief sought. * * * In the terms of the proviso, a statute granting consent to suit, *i.e.,* the Tucker Act, 'impliedly forbids' relief other than the remedy provided by the act. Thus, the partial abolition of sovereign immunity brought about by this bill does not change existing limitations on specific relief, if any, derived from statutes dealing with such matters as government contracts, as well as patent infringement, tort claims, and tax claims."

(2) *Scope of the Waiver.* How complete is this statute's waiver of sovereign immunity in suits for specific relief? Though codified in the APA, the waiver applies to any suit, whether under the APA, § 1331, § 1361, or any other statute. Note, however, that § 702 applies only to suits in federal court, and that it covers only actions of an "agency" of the United States as that term is defined in 5 U.S.C. § 701(b)(1), thereby excluding, for example, suits against Congress, the federal courts, the District of Columbia, and the territories.

(3) *The Effect of the Waiver on Pre-existing Supreme Court Authority.* Does § 702 overrule Malone v. Bowdoin, p. 1025, *supra?* Dugan v. Rank, p. 1026, *supra?* The Larson decision?

(a) A case like Malone v. Bowdoin would today be permitted under a 1972 statute—86 Stat. 1176, codified in 28 U.S.C. §§ 1346(f), 1402(d), 2409a—that (subject to some exceptions) authorizes suit against the United States in the district courts "to adjudicate a disputed title to real property in which the United States claims an interest." This statute has been held to be the exclusive remedy for real property actions to which it pertains, and thus, under the second proviso of § 702, it constitutes an implied preclusion of relief under that section. Block v. North Dakota ex rel. Bd. of Univ. & School Lands, 461 U.S. 273, 280–86 & n. 22 (1983).

(b) In South Delta Water Agency v. United States Dep't of Interior, 767 F.2d 531 (9th Cir.1985), users of water from the same federal reclamation project at issue in Dugan v. Rank sued state and federal agencies, alleging that the defendants were operating their respective water facilities in violation of plaintiffs' rights under state and federal law. The court of appeals upheld the district court's jurisdiction under § 702 to award equitable relief, and found that the Tucker Act did not impliedly preclude non-monetary relief under the second proviso of § 702.

(c) Would that proviso be pertinent, however, if a suit like Larson were brought today? See Spectrum Leasing Corp. v. United States, 764 F.2d 891 (D.C.Cir.1985)(holding (i) that in requesting an injunction to compel the Government to continue making payments under a contract on the ground that failure to pay violated the Debt Collection Act of 1982, Spectrum was seeking "the classic contractual remedy of specific performance," and (ii) that the Tucker Act impliedly precludes contractual remedies other than money damages (p. 894)). Does a case like Spectrum suggest that it may often be difficult to distinguish specific performance from review of the legality of administrative action?[24]

---

24. See also, *e.g.,* Hahn v. United States, 757 F.2d 581 (3d Cir.1985)(conceding that exclusive Tucker Act jurisdiction may not be evaded by disguising a monetary claim as a claim for an injunction, but refusing to order dismissal of district court suit to enjoin

(4) *The Significance of the Exception for "Money Damages" in § 702 of the APA.* Bowen v. Massachusetts, 487 U.S. 879 (1988), involved a dispute between Massachusetts and the Department of Health and Human Services (HHS) about whether certain state-provided services qualified for reimbursement under Medicaid. The Court sustained the prospective declaratory and injunctive relief permitted by the court of appeals, and also ruled that the court of appeals had erred in refusing to uphold the district court's order reversing HHS's disallowance of reimbursement for past services. The Court noted that this order did not require payment by the United States; to the extent that an order reversing the agency's disallowance of reimbursement leads to monetary relief, it is "a mere by-product of [the district court's] primary function of reviewing the Secretary's interpretation of federal law" (p. 910). The Court also endorsed the position that monetary relief for past disallowances was not "money damages", thus implying that § 702 would not have barred a money judgment against the United States.

The government argued in Bowen that in view of the availability of a monetary remedy in the Claims Court under the Tucker Act, APA review was unavailable in light of § 10(c), 5 U.S.C. § 704, which provides that agency action "for which there is no other adequate remedy in any court shall be subject to judicial review." The Supreme Court rejected that argument: even if the Claims Court could award monetary relief—a question about which the Court expressed some doubt—the Claims Court's lack of general equitable powers prevented it from providing the kind of "special and adequate review" that, under the APA, will foreclose district court jurisdiction (p. 904).

Justice Scalia, joined by the Chief Justice and Justice Kennedy, dissented. He criticized, as exalting form over substance, the Court's holdings that the district court's reversal of HHS' order was not a money judgment and that the monetary aspects of the relief were not money damages. Both of these propositions, he objected, would permit inventive lawyers to escape the Claims Court's exclusive jurisdiction simply by denominating damage claims as suits for specific relief against the government for its refusal to pay, or as suits for monetary relief not constituting damages. Justice Scalia also argued that in any event, the state could bring suit under the Medicaid Act for damages in the Claims Court, and that in all but the most unusual circumstances, such relief would constitute an "adequate remedy" under § 704, thereby precluding suit under § 702.[25]

the denial of certain "constructive service credits" in computing pay levels of Public Health Service officers); Matthews v. United States, 810 F.2d 109 (6th Cir.1987)(per curiam)(dismissing, as within the Claims Court's exclusive jurisdiction, a district court action for reinstatement by air traffic controllers; provision of injunctive relief would effectively dispose of all issues pertinent to a back pay action except the amount, and would thus effectively require payments by the United States in excess of $10,000 per plaintiff); Massachusetts v. Department Grant Appeals Bd., 815 F.2d 778 (1st Cir.1987)(after ordering state to fund abortions under Medicaid, court holds that state's suit against federal agency for reimburse-ment of costs may be brought only in Claims Court).

In North Side Lumber Co. v. Block, 474 U.S. 931 (1985), Justice White, dissenting from the denial of certiorari, questioned the court of appeals' decision that the Tucker Act impliedly precludes district court jurisdiction over a suit seeking a declaration that plaintiffs' contracts with the United States were void.

25. For general discussion of the Bowen decision, see Noone & Lester, *Defining Tucker Act Jurisdiction After Bowen v. Massachusetts,* 40 Cath.U.L.Rev. 571 (1991); Webster, *Beyond Federal Sovereign Immunity: 5 U.S.C. § 702 Spells Relief,* 49 Ohio

(5) *Problems Confronting Litigants*. Note, in connection with the previous two Paragraphs, that a key purpose of the Federal Rules of Civil Procedure was to replace the forms of action and separate systems of law and equity with a single civil action in the district courts. But litigants suing the government face a far more complex system. Will it always be clear whether a suit seeking specific relief should be filed in district court, or, because it is "really" a disguised suit for specific performance of a contract, in the Court of Federal Claims? Whether a suit for monetary relief is for money damages, and thus outside § 702 (though perhaps cognizable in the Court of Federal Claims), or for some other kind of monetary relief, and therefore within the district court's jurisdiction under § 702? Whether a damage claim in excess of $10,000 lies under a contract (and thus within the Court of Federal Claims' exclusive jurisdiction under the Tucker Act), in tort (and thus within the district courts' FTCA jurisdiction), or both? Whether an official's taking of property worth more than $10,000 was "authorized", so that damages are available under the Tucker Act, or was not, so that only equitable relief in the district courts is available (see Hooe v. United States, 218 U.S. 322, 335–36 (1910)).[26]

To eliminate such problems, should Congress abolish the Court of Federal Claims, and give the district courts jurisdiction to entertain all claims against the United States under the Tucker Act, the FTCA, and every other statute consenting to suit? Should it instead expand the Court of Federal Claims' jurisdiction? Compare 28 U.S.C. § 1631 (permitting, in the interest of justice, transfer of a civil action from a court without jurisdiction to one in which the case could have been filed). Is there any sound basis for determining that suits against the United States for money damages should be tried before a semi-specialized non-Article III tribunal?

D.   The Interpretation of Statutes Consenting to Suit

(1) *The Supreme Court's Construction of Statutory Waivers.*

St.L.J. 725 (1988). For an important application of Bowen, see Hubbard v. EPA, 982 F.2d 531 (D.C.Cir.1992)(en banc)(holding, despite contrary dicta in Bowen, that § 702 does not waive sovereign immunity in a suit for back pay by an individual claiming denial of federal employment in violation of his First Amendment rights). See also City of Houston v. HUD, 24 F.3d 1421 (D.C.Cir. 1994)(award of monetary relief from any source of funds other than particular appropriation would constitute money damages rather than specific relief, and is thus unauthorized by § 702).

For discussion of the implications of the Bowen decision with respect to the jurisdiction of the Court of Federal Claims, see Fallon, *Claims Court at the Crossroads*, 40 Cath. U.L.Rev. 517 (1991).

26. Similar jurisdictional uncertainties can arise on appeal. In United States v. Hohri, 482 U.S. 64 (1987), Japanese–American citizens placed in internment camps during World War II brought damage actions against the United States in district court, alleging both Tucker Act claims (apparently not exceeding $10,000) and FTCA claims. The D.C. Circuit found that it did have appellate jurisdiction under 28 U.S.C. § 1291 to review the district court's dismissal of the suit, but the Supreme Court reversed. Under 28 U.S.C. § 1295(a)(2), the United States Court of Appeals for the Federal Circuit has exclusive jurisdiction over an appeal from a decision of a district court whose jurisdiction "was based, in whole or in part, on [28 U.S.C. § 1346], except that jurisdiction of an appeal in a case brought in a district court under [28 U.S.C. § 1346(b)] * * * shall be governed by [28 U.S.C. § 1291] * * *", and the Supreme Court held that this ambiguous statutory language should be read to give the Federal Circuit exclusive jurisdiction over "mixed" cases. This view is supported by the desirability of enabling the Federal Circuit to promote uniformity by exercising jurisdiction over every Tucker Act appeal.

(a) The view that statutes waiving immunity should be strictly construed seems to have been established in the early cases under the Court of Claims Act. See, *e.g.,* Borchard, *Government Liability in Tort,* 34 Yale L.J. 1, 28–41 (1924). But in Keifer & Keifer v. Reconstruction Finance Corp., 306 U.S. 381 (1939), in which the defendant was a regional government corporation, the Court found that the corporation was not protected by sovereign immunity, even though its authorizing legislation contained no "sue-and-be-sued" clause. Justice Frankfurter, writing for the Court, reasoned that since the parent corporation and many similarly situated entities lacked immunity, Congress could not have intended a different result for the regional corporation. He went on to say (pp. 388–89): "[T]he government does not become the conduit of its immunity in suits against its agents or instrumentalities merely because they do its work", and the immunity is not readily implied. Accord Federal Housing Admin., Region No. 4 v. Burr, 309 U.S. 242 (1940)(no immunity from garnishment and execution from state court against funds in hands of agency; at least in cases involving federal instrumentalities, "waivers by Congress of governmental immunity * * * should be liberally construed"); Franchise Tax Bd. v. United States Postal Service, 467 U.S. 512, 520 (1984)(Postal Service subject to state administrative tax levies on employees' wages; "Congress has 'launched [the Postal Service] into the commercial world'" and hence the Court must "liberally construe the sue-and-be-sued clause" and "must presume that the Service's liability is the same as that of any other business.)"

(b) Cases like Keifer & Keifer and Burr reflected doubts about sovereign immunity even outside the context of specialized government agencies or corporations. Keifer & Keifer spoke of the "present climate of opinion which has brought governmental immunity from suit into disfavor", 306 U.S. at 391; accord Burr, 309 U.S. at 245. The Supreme Court has continued to voice such misgivings, albeit in a halting and irregular fashion. In United States v. Yellow Cab Co., 340 U.S. 543 (1951), for example, in holding that the United States could be impleaded under the FTCA as a third party defendant and required to answer the claim of a joint tortfeasor for contribution, the Court said (p. 550): "Recognizing such a clearly defined breadth of purpose for the bill as a whole, and the general trend toward increasing the scope of the waiver by the United States of its sovereign immunity from suit, it is inconsistent to whittle it down by refinements."[27]

Interspersed with such statements, however, have been regular reiterations in other cases of the conventional position, which has been dominant in most recent Supreme Court decisions. See, *e.g.,* McMahon v. United States, 342 U.S. 25, 27 (1951); Library of Congress v. Shaw, 478 U.S. 310, 318, 321 (1986)(the Court "must construe waivers strictly in favor of the sovereign"; "policy, no matter how compelling, is insufficient, standing alone, to waive this immunity"); United States v. Mottaz, 476 U.S. 834, 851 (1986), quoting United States v. Mitchell, 445 U.S. 535, 538 (1980)(notwithstanding traditional solicitude for Indian plaintiffs, "[a] waiver of sovereign immunity 'cannot be lightly implied, but must be unequivocally expressed'").[28] But in FDIC v. Meyer, 114 S.Ct. 996

---

27. See also, *e.g.,* Smith v. United States, 507 U.S. 197 (1993); National City Bank of New York v. Republic of China, 348 U.S. 356, 359 (1955); Canadian Aviator, Ltd. v. United States, 324 U.S. 215, 222 (1945).

28. See also United States v. Nordic Village, Inc., 503 U.S. 30, 33 (1992)(waiver must be "unequivocally expressed"); United States Dep't of Energy v. Ohio, 503 U.S. 607, 618–20 (1992)(waiver in Clean Water Act applied to "coercive" but not "punitive" fines);

(1994), the Court held that a sue-and-be-sued clause in the Corporation's organic statute constituted a waiver of immunity. The Court said its precedents required a liberal construction of such clauses "notwithstanding the general rule that waivers of sovereign immunity are to be read narrowly in favor of the sovereign" (p. 1003). It indicated that a clear showing of congressional purpose would be required to overcome the presumption of waiver.

One commentator, reviewing the cases, has concluded that the Court's two apparently conflicting approaches can be reconciled by considering whether the waiver in question deals with a "limited circumstance" or with an effort (as in the FTCA) to expose the government to broad liability. See Feldman, p. 1001, note *, *supra,* at 462–63. Another recent study, while supporting a "presumption" against statutory waiver of federal immunity, argues forcefully against the recent tendency to restrict the *scope* of statutory waivers by application of a "clear statement" rule. Nagle, *Waiving Sovereign Immunity in an Age of Clear Statement Rules,* 1995 Wis.L.Rev. 771.

(2) *The Appropriateness of a Narrow or Broad Construction.* Should not any waiver of immunity be construed, if not liberally, at least sensibly—with a sympathetic assumption of congressional intent to introduce a regime of law infused with a spirit of equity? Why shouldn't a court find an implied consent to suit when Congress has authorized the government to incur debts or to make contracts, or to engage in activity that might cause harm of the kind that normally is actionable when caused by private actors? Consider in this connection the numerous state judicial decisions attenuating or rejecting sovereign immunity in actions under state law. See, *e.g.,* the cases collected in S.Rep. 94–996, 94th Cong., 2d. Sess. 4 n. 11 (1976), and Keeton, *et al.,* Prosser & Keeton on The Law of Torts § 131 (5th ed. 1984).

SECTION 2. SUITS CHALLENGING STATE OFFICIAL ACTION

SUBSECTION A: THE ELEVENTH AMENDMENT AND STATE SOVEREIGN IMMUNITY

Hans v. Louisiana

134 U.S. 1, 10 S.Ct. 504, 33 L.Ed. 842 (1890).
Error to the Circuit Court of the United States for the Eastern District of Louisiana.

[This was an action brought in the Circuit Court of the United States against the State of Louisiana by Hans, a citizen of that State, to recover the amount of certain coupons annexed to bonds of the State, issued under the provisions of an act of the legislature approved January 24, 1874. The coupons sued on were for interest accrued as of January 1, 1880. Hans alleged that an amendment to the state constitution barring the state from paying the interest owing was an

Ardestani v. INS, 502 U.S. 129, 135–37 (1991).

impairment of the obligation of contract in violation of the U.S. Constitution. The lower court dismissed the action for lack of jurisdiction, and Hans appealed to the Supreme Court.]

■ MR. JUSTICE BRADLEY delivered the opinion of the court.

The question is presented, whether a State can be sued in a Circuit Court of the United States by one of its own citizens upon a suggestion that the case is one that arises under the Constitution or laws of the United States.

The ground taken is, that under the Constitution, as well as under the act of Congress passed to carry it into effect, a case is within the jurisdiction of the federal courts, without regard to the character of the parties, if it arises under the Constitution or laws of the United States * * *. It is conceded that where the jurisdiction depends alone upon the character of the parties, a controversy between a State and its own citizens is not embraced within it; but it is contended that though jurisdiction does not exist on that ground, it nevertheless does exist if the case itself is one which necessarily involves a federal question; and with regard to ordinary parties this is undoubtedly true. The question now to be decided is, whether it is true where one of the parties is a State, and is sued as a defendant by one of its own citizens.

That a State cannot be sued by a citizen of another State, or of a foreign state, on the mere ground that the case is one arising under the Constitution or laws of the United States, is clearly established by the decisions of this court in several recent cases. Louisiana v. Jumel, 107 U.S. 711; Hagood v. Southern, 117 U.S. 52; In re Ayers, 123 U.S. 443. Those were cases arising under the Constitution of the United States, upon laws complained of as impairing the obligation of contracts, one of which was the constitutional amendment of Louisiana complained of in the present case. Relief was sought against state officers who professed to act in obedience to those laws. This court held that the suits were virtually against the States themselves and were consequently violative of the Eleventh Amendment of the Constitution, and could not be maintained. It was not denied that they presented cases arising under the Constitution; but, notwithstanding that, they were held to be prohibited by the amendment referred to.

In the present case the plaintiff in error contends that he, being a citizen of Louisiana, is not embarrassed by the obstacle of the Eleventh Amendment, inasmuch as that amendment only prohibits suits against a State which are brought by the citizens of another State, or by citizens or subjects of a foreign State. It is true, the amendment does so read: and if there were no other reason or ground for abating his suit, it might be maintainable; and then we should have this anomalous result, that in cases arising under the Constitution or laws of the United States, a State may be sued in the federal courts by its own citizens, though it cannot be sued for a like cause of action by the citizens of other States, or of a foreign state; and may be thus sued in the federal courts, although not allowing itself to be sued in its own courts. If this is the necessary consequence of the language of the Constitution and the law, the result is no less startling and unexpected than was the original decision of this court, that under the language of the Constitution and of the judiciary act of 1789, a State was liable to be sued by a citizen of another State, or of a foreign country. That decision was made in the case of Chisholm v. Georgia, 2 Dall. 419, and created such a shock of surprise throughout the country that, at the first meeting of Congress thereafter, the Eleventh Amendment to the Constitution was almost unanimously proposed, and was in due course adopted by the legislatures of the States. This amendment, expressing the will of the ultimate sovereignty of the whole country, superior to all legislatures and all courts, actually reversed the decision of the Supreme Court. It did not in terms prohibit suits by individuals against the States, but declared that the Constitution should not be construed to import any power to authorize the bringing of such suits. The language of the amendment is that "the judicial power of the United States shall *not be construed to extend* to any suit in law or equity, commenced or prosecuted against one of the United States by citizens of another State or by citizens or subjects of any foreign state." The Supreme Court had construed the judicial power as extending to such a suit, and its decision was thus overruled. The court itself so understood the effect of the amendment * * * [as shown by its later decisions].

This view of the force and meaning of the amendment is important. It shows that, on this question of the suability of the States by individuals, the highest authority of this country was in accord rather with the minority than with the majority of the court in the decision of the case of Chisholm v. Georgia; and this fact lends additional interest to the able opinion of Mr. Justice Iredell on that occasion. The other justices were more swayed by a close observance of the letter of the Constitution, without regard to former experience and usage; and because the letter said that the judicial power shall extend to controversies "between a State and citizens of another State;" and "between a State and foreign states, citizens or subjects," they felt constrained to see in this language a power to enable the individual citizens of one State, or of a foreign state, to sue another State of the Union in the federal courts. Justice Iredell, on the contrary, contended that it was not the intention to create new and unheard of remedies, by subjecting sovereign States to actions at the suit of individuals, (which he conclusively showed was never done before,) but only, by proper legislation, to invest the federal courts with jurisdiction to hear and determine controversies and cases, between the parties designated, that were properly susceptible of litigation in courts.

Looking back from our present standpoint at the decision in Chisholm v. Georgia, we do not greatly wonder at the effect which it had upon the country. Any such power as that of authorizing the federal judiciary to entertain suits by individuals against the States, had been expressly disclaimed, and even resented, by the great defenders of the Constitution whilst it was on its trial before the American people. As some of their utterances are directly pertinent to the question now under consideration, we deem it proper to quote them.

The eighty-first number of the Federalist, written by Hamilton, has the following profound remarks:

"It has been suggested that an assignment of the public securities of one State to the citizens of another, would enable them to prosecute that State in the federal courts for the amount of those securities; a suggestion which the following considerations prove to be without foundation:

"It is inherent in the nature of sovereignty not to be amenable to the suit of an individual without its consent. This is the general sense and the general practice of mankind; and the exemption, as one of the attributes of sovereignty, is now enjoyed by the government of every State in the Union. Unless, therefore, there is a surrender of this immunity in the plan of the convention, it will remain with the States, and the danger intimated must be merely ideal. * * * [T]here is no color to pretend that the state governments would, by the adoption of that plan, be divested of the privilege of paying their own debts in their own way, free from every constraint but that which flows from the obligations of good faith. The contracts between a nation and individuals are only binding on the conscience of the sovereign, and have no pretension to a compulsive force. They confer no right of action independent of the sovereign will. To what purpose would it be to authorize suits against States for the debts they owe? How could recoveries be enforced? It is evident that it could not be done without waging war against the contracting State; and to ascribe to the federal courts by mere implication, and in destruction of a pre-existing right of the state governments, a power which would involve such a consequence, would be altogether forced and unwarrantable."

* * * [L]ooking at the subject as Hamilton did, and as Mr. Justice Iredell did [in Chisholm], in the light of history and experience and the established order of things, the[ir] views * * * were clearly right,—as the people of the United States in their sovereign capacity subsequently decided.

But Hamilton was not alone in protesting against the construction put upon the Constitution by its opponents. In the Virginia convention the same objections were raised by George Mason and Patrick Henry, and were met by Madison and Marshall as follows. Madison said: "Its jurisdiction [the federal jurisdiction] in controversies between a State and citizens of another State is much objected to, and perhaps without reason. It is not in the power of individuals to call any State into court. The only operation it can have is that, if a State should wish to bring a suit against a citizen, it must be brought before the federal court. This will give satisfaction to individuals, as it will prevent citizens on whom a State may have a claim being dissatisfied with the state courts.... It appears to me that this [clause] can have no operation but this—to give a citizen a right to be heard in the federal courts; and if a State should condescend to be a party, this court may take cognizance of it." 3 Elliott's Debates, 2d ed. 533. Marshall, in answer to the same objection, said: "With respect to disputes between a State and the citizens of another State, its jurisdiction has been decried with unusual vehemence. I hope that no gentleman will think that a State will be called at the bar of the federal court.... It is not rational to suppose that the sovereign power should be dragged before a court. The intent is to enable States to recover claims of individuals residing in other States.... But, say they, there will be partiality in it if a State cannot be defendant—if an individual cannot proceed to obtain judgment against a State, though he may be sued by a State. It is necessary to be so, and cannot be avoided. I see a difficulty in making a State defendant which does not prevent its being plaintiff." Ib. 555.

It seems to us that these views of those great advocates and defenders of the Constitution were most sensible and just; and they apply equally to the present case as to that then under discussion. The letter is appealed to now, as it was then, as a ground for sustaining a suit brought by an individual against a State. The reason against it is as strong in this case as it was in that. It is an attempt to strain the Constitution and the law to a construction never imagined or dreamed of. Can we suppose that, when the Eleventh Amendment was adopted, it was understood to be left open for citizens of a State to sue their own state in the federal courts, whilst the idea of suits by citizens of other states, or of foreign states, was indignantly repelled? Suppose that Congress, when proposing the Eleventh Amendment, had appended to it a proviso that nothing therein contained should prevent a State from being sued by its own citizens in cases arising under the Constitution or laws of the United States:

can we imagine that it would have been adopted by the States? The supposition that it would is almost an absurdity on its face.

* * *

The suability of a State without its consent was a thing unknown to the law. This has been so often laid down and acknowledged by courts and jurists that it is hardly necessary to be formally asserted. It was fully shown by an exhaustive examination of the old law by Mr. Justice Iredell in his opinion in Chisholm v. Georgia; and it has been conceded in every case since, where the question has, in any way been presented, even in the cases which have gone farthest in sustaining suits against the officers or agents of States. Osborn v. Bank of United States, 9 Wheat. 738; Davis v. Gray, 16 Wall. 203; Board of Liquidation v. McComb, 92 U.S. 531; United States v. Lee, 106 U.S. 196; Poindexter v. Greenhow, 109 U.S. 63; Virginia Coupon Cases, 114 U.S. 269. In all these cases the effort was to show, and the court held, that the suits were not against the State or the United States, but against the individuals; conceding that if they had been against either the State or the United States, they could not be maintained.

* * *

Undoubtedly a State may be sued by its own consent, as was the case in Curran v. Arkansas et al., 15 How. 304, 309, and in Clark v. Barnard, 108 U.S. 436, 447. * * *

* * * [B]esides the presumption that no anomalous and unheard-of proceedings or suits were intended to be raised up by the Constitution—anomalous and unheard of when the Constitution was adopted—an additional reason why the jurisdiction claimed for the Circuit Court does not exist, is the language of the act of Congress by which its jurisdiction is conferred. The words are these: "The circuit courts of the United States shall have original cognizance, concurrent with the courts of the several States, of all suits of a civil nature at common law or in equity, ... arising under the Constitution or laws of the United States, or treaties," etc.—"Concurrent with the courts of the several States." Does not this qualification show that Congress, in legislating to carry the Constitution into effect, did not intend to invest its courts with any new and strange jurisdictions? The state courts have no power to entertain suits by individuals against a State without its consent. Then how does the Circuit Court, having only concurrent jurisdiction, acquire any such power? It is true that the same qualification existed in the judiciary act of 1789, which was before the court in Chisholm v. Georgia, and the majority of the court did not think that it was sufficient to limit the jurisdiction of the Circuit Court. Justice Iredell thought differently. In view of the manner in which that decision was received by the country, the adoption of the Eleventh Amendment, the light of history and the reason of the thing, we think we are at liberty to prefer Justice Iredell's views in this regard.

Some reliance is placed by the plaintiff upon the observations of Chief Justice Marshall, in Cohens v. Virginia, 6 Wheat. 264, 410. The Chief Justice was there considering the power of review exercisable by this court over the judgments of a state court, wherein it might be necessary to make the State itself a defendant in error. He showed that this power was absolutely necessary in order to enable the judiciary of the United States to take cognizance of all cases arising under the Constitution and laws of the United States. He also showed that making a State a defendant in error was entirely different from suing a State in an original action in prosecution of a demand against it, and was not within the meaning of the Eleventh Amendment; that the prosecution of a writ of error against a State was not the prosecution of a suit in the sense of that amendment, which had reference to the prosecution, by suit, of claims against a State. * * *

After * * * showing by incontestable argument that a writ of error to a judgment recovered by a State, in which the State is necessarily the defendant in error, is not a suit commenced or prosecuted against a State in the sense of the amendment, he added, that if the court were mistaken in this, its error did not affect that case, because the writ of error therein was not prosecuted by "a citizen of another State" or "of any foreign state," and so was not affected by the amendment; but was governed by the general grant of judicial power, as extending "to all cases arising under the Constitution or laws of the United States, without respect to parties." p. 412.

It must be conceded that the last observation of the Chief Justice does favor the argument of the plaintiff. But the observation was unnecessary to the decision, and in that sense *extra judicial*, and though made by one who seldom used words without due reflection, ought not to outweigh the important considerations referred to which lead to a different conclusion. With regard to the question then before the court, it may be observed, that writs of error to judgments in favor of the crown, or of the State, had been known to the law from time immemorial; and had never been considered as exceptions to the rule, that an action does not lie against the sovereign.

To avoid misapprehension it may be proper to add that, although the obligations of a State rest for their performance upon its honor and good faith, and cannot be made the subjects of judicial cognizance unless the State consents to be sued, or comes itself into court; yet where property or rights are enjoyed under a grant or contract made by a State, they cannot wantonly be invaded. Whilst the State cannot be compelled by suit to perform its contracts, any attempt on its part to violate property or rights acquired under its contracts, may be judicially resisted; and any law impairing the obligation of contracts under which such property or rights are held is void and powerless to affect their enjoyment.

It is not necessary that we should enter upon an examination of the reason or expediency of the rule which exempts a sovereign State from prosecution in a court of justice at the suit of individuals. This is fully discussed by writers on public law. It is enough for us to declare its existence. The legislative department of a State represents its polity and its will; and is called upon by the highest demands of natural and political law to preserve justice and judgment, and to hold inviolate the public obligations. Any departure from this rule, except for reasons most cogent, (of which the legislature, and not the courts, is the judge,) never fails in the end to incur the odium of the world, and to bring lasting injury upon the State itself. But to deprive the legislature of the power of judging what the honor and safety of the State may require, even at the expense of a temporary failure to discharge the public debts, would be attended with greater evils than such failure can cause.

The judgment of the Circuit Court is

Affirmed.

■ Mr. Justice Harlan, concurring.

I concur with the court in holding that a suit directly against a State by one of its own citizens is not one to which the judicial power of the United States extends, unless the State itself consents to be sued. Upon this ground alone I assent to the judgment. But I cannot give my assent to many things said in the opinion. The comments made upon the decision in Chisholm v. Georgia do not meet my approval. They are not necessary to the determination of the present case. Besides, I am of opinion that the decision in that case was based upon a sound interpretation of the Constitution as that instrument then was.

NOTE ON THE ORIGIN, MEANING, AND SCOPE
OF THE ELEVENTH AMENDMENT

(1) *The Decision in Chisholm*. In Chisholm v. Georgia, 2 U.S. (2 Dall.) 419 (1793), a South Carolina citizen filed an assumpsit claim against the State of Georgia as an original action in the Supreme Court. Rejecting Georgia's protest that an unconsenting state was immune from suit, the Supreme Court upheld its jurisdiction as consistent with Article III's grant of judicial power over controversies "between a State and Citizens of another State." Each of the five Justices wrote separately. Justices Blair and Cushing both relied on the clear language of Article III, noting that its grant of jurisdiction over controversies between two states contemplated that an unconsenting state could be a defendant (pp. 450–53, 466–69). Chief Justice Jay likewise relied on Article III's language, but argued in addition that the "feudal" doctrine of sovereign immunity was incompatible with popular sovereignty. Troubled, though, that this argument implied that the United States itself could be sued, notwithstanding the difficulty of enforcing a judgment against it, he ultimately left that question open (pp. 472–79). Justice Wilson argued most fully that the doctrine of sovereign immunity was incompatible with principles of public law and with a republican form of government, reasoning that a state was no more sovereign, and no less subject to the law, than a free man (pp. 453–58).

Justice Iredell's lone dissent proceeded from the premise that the Supreme Court could exercise only that jurisdiction conferred by Congress. He contended that the first Judiciary Act's grant of original jurisdiction should be interpreted in light of common law principles. English law would have permitted an action like Chisholm's only by petition of right, with the sovereign's consent;[1] when the Constitution and First Judiciary Act took effect, no state permitted "a compulsory suit for the recovery of money against a State" (pp. 434–35). Though acknowledging (pp. 449–50) that he strongly opposed "any construction of [the Constitution] which will admit, under any circumstances, a compulsive suit against a State for the recovery of money", he rested his conclusion on statutory grounds.[2]

---

1. On a petition of right.

2. For an illuminating account of Chisholm in historical context, arguing that assertion of federal jurisdiction over suits against the states was necessary to enforce the Peace Treaty of 1783 with Britain, see Gibbons, *The Eleventh Amendment and State Sovereign Immunity: A Reinterpretation*, 83 Co-

lum.L.Rev. 1889, 1895–1941 (1983). For an informative analysis of each of the opinions in the case, see Casto, The Supreme Court in the Early Republic 188–97 (1995). For a discussion of Justice Iredell's dissent, see Orth, *The Truth About Justice Iredell's Dissent in Chisholm v. Georgia (1793)*, 73 N.C.L.Rev. 255 (1994).

(2) *The Adoption of the Eleventh Amendment.* As noted in Hans, Chisholm "created such a shock of surprise" that the Eleventh Amendment was soon enacted.[3] A constitutional amendment to overrule Chisholm was introduced in the Senate only two days after the decision.[4] As finally adopted and ratified, the Eleventh Amendment provides:

"The Judicial power of the United States shall not be construed to extend to any suit in law or equity, commenced or prosecuted against one of the United States by Citizens of another State, or by Citizens or Subjects of any Foreign State."

(3) *The Eleventh Amendment and the Marshall Court.* Before the Civil War, the Supreme Court faced relatively few cases involving the Eleventh Amendment. And until 1875 (except for a very brief period), there was, of course, no general federal question jurisdiction.

(a) In Cohens v. Virginia, 19 U.S. (6 Wheat.) 264 (1821), defendants convicted in state court in Virginia for selling District of Columbia lottery tickets, in violation of Virginia law, sought review in the Supreme Court, asserting that under the Supremacy Clause they were immune from prosecution for selling tickets because the lottery was authorized by Congress.[5] The Court affirmed the convictions on the merits, but only after rejecting the state's contention that it was being sued without its consent for a writ of error in the Supreme Court, in violation of the Eleventh Amendment.[6] In discussing the Constitution *as originally enacted*, Chief Justice Marshall observed (p. 383) that "a case arising under the constitution or laws of the United States, is cognizable in the Courts of the Union, whoever may be the parties to that case." Turning to the effect of the *Eleventh Amendment* in the case at hand, Marshall concluded that at least in the context of a writ of error that was entirely defensive and sought no affirmative relief, such a writ was not a "suit" within the meaning of the Amendment (p. 407).

Following this analysis, Marshall added a brief alternative holding: If "we in this be mistaken, the error does not affect the case now before the Court", as the defendants were citizens of Virginia (p. 412). (In Worcester v. Georgia, 31

---

3. But see Gibbons, note 2, *supra*, at 1926 (contending that "Congress's initial reaction to the Chisholm decision hardly demonstrates the sort of outrage so central to the profound shock thesis"). For other commentary on the history and drafting of the Amendment—commentary that presents a range of perspectives—see, Casto, note 2, *supra*, at 197–212; Jacobs, The Eleventh Amendment and Sovereign Immunity 67–74 (1972); Amar, *Of Sovereignty and Federalism*, 96 Yale L.J. 1425, 1481–84 (1987); Fletcher, *A Historical Interpretation of the Eleventh Amendment: A Narrow Construction of an Affirmative Grant of Jurisdiction Rather than a Prohibition Against Jurisdiction*, 35 Stan.L.Rev. 1033, 1058–59 (1983).

4. See Gibbons, note 2, *supra*, at 1926–27 & n. 186.

5. The following discussion has benefited from the careful analysis of the Cohens case in Jackson, *The Supreme Court, the Eleventh Amendment, and State Sovereign Immunity*, 98 Yale L.J. 1, 13–25 (1988).

6. In several prior decisions, the Court had reviewed suits between states and private citizens without discussion of the Amendment. See, *e.g.*, McCulloch v. Maryland, 17 U.S. (4 Wheat.) 316 (1819).

A recent analysis of the Court's decision in Cohens concludes that the Court's affirmance of the state decision on the merits was highly questionable in light of both existing precedent and the national interest, and reflected The Marshall Court's reluctance to engage in a direct confrontation with powerful state forces by declaring state action unconstitutional. Graber, *The Passive–Aggressive Virtues: Cohens v. Virginia and the Problematic Establishment of Political Power,* 12 Const.Comm. 67 (1995).

U.S. (6 Pet.) 515 (1832), the party seeking a writ of error was a noncitizen; the Supreme Court exercised jurisdiction without discussing the Eleventh Amendment issue.)

Does Cohens, as interpreted and applied by the Court itself, in effect recognize an "exception" to the Eleventh Amendment for appellate review of state court judgments—an exception demanded by the need to ensure the supremacy of federal law?[7] How significant is the fact that Cohens, unlike Chisholm, was a federal question case? (Note that in the portion of the Cohens opinion focusing on the Eleventh Amendment, Marshall does not rely on this fact.)

(b) In Osborn v. Bank of the United States, 22 U.S. (9 Wheat.) 738 (1824), after the federal circuit court enjoined state officials from collecting an unconstitutional tax from the plaintiff Bank, an official seized $100,000 from a Bank office. The Supreme Court upheld a second decree ordering one official to return the $98,000 held in his possession but credited to the state, and ordering two others to repay the remaining $2000 (the location of which was not discussed in the opinion[8]), all over defendants' objection that the order violated the Eleventh Amendment.[9] Chief Justice Marshall stated for the Court (pp. 846–47): "The direct interest of the State in the suit, as brought, is admitted; and, had it been in the power of the Bank to make it a party, perhaps no decree ought to have been pronounced in the cause, until the State was before the Court. But this was not in the power of the Bank. The eleventh amendment of the constitution has exempted a State from the suits of citizen of other States, or aliens * * *." That provision, however, did not bar suit against the officers (pp. 857–58): "It may, we think, be laid down as a rule which admits of no exception, that, in all cases where jurisdiction depends on the party, it is the party named in the record. Consequently, the 11th amendment * * * is, of necessity, limited to those suits in which a State is a party on the record. The amendment has its full effect, if the constitution be construed as it would have been construed, had the jurisdiction of the Court never been extended to suits brought against a State, by the citizens of another State, or by aliens."

Does the first quotation from Osborn concede, albeit in dictum, that the Eleventh Amendment bars suit against an unconsenting state even in a federal question case? Gibbons, note 2, *supra,* at 1958 n. 370, reads the quoted language as a paraphrase of defense counsel's position. Does the second quotation suggest that the Amendment bars the exercise of judicial power only in cases, like Chisholm, that do not involve federal questions and in which jurisdiction over a defendant state is based entirely on party status?

---

7. Cohens was read broadly in McKesson Corp. v. Division of ABT, 496 U.S. 18 (1990)(also discussed at p. 851, *supra*). In that case, wholesale liquor distributors had brought a state court action against a state agency challenging the constitutionality of a state excise tax and seeking postpayment relief. On Supreme Court review of the denial of relief in the state courts, the state agency argued that the Eleventh Amendment precluded Supreme Court appellate jurisdiction. Citing Cohens, the Court held unanimously that "[t]he Eleventh Amendment does not constrain the appellate jurisdiction of the Supreme Court over cases arising from state courts" (p. 31).

8. Garraty, Quarrels That Shaped the Constitution 48 (1987), reports that the $2000 in question had been retained by one of the state officers as a "fee".

9. While a state has no immunity from suit brought by the United States, see Paragraph (4)(a), *infra,* the Bank was treated as a private party rather than as an arm of the United States.

(c) The Marshall Court was able to dispose of several admiralty cases without deciding whether the Eleventh Amendment applied to that head of jurisdiction. In United States v. Peters, 9 U.S. (5 Cranch) 115 (1809), a Connecticut sailor and the State of Pennsylvania both claimed proceeds of an admiralty prize sale, which had been paid to the state treasurer, since deceased, and were held by his personal representatives. The Supreme Court ruled that an order requiring the representatives to pay the proceeds to the sailor did not violate the Amendment, because the suit was against the officer (or his representatives), not the state. Chief Justice Marshall noted (p. 139) that "if these proceeds had been the actual property of Pennsylvania, however wrongfully acquired, the disclosure of that fact would have presented a case on which it is unnecessary to give an opinion * * *."[10]

In Governor of Georgia v. Madrazo, 26 U.S. (1 Pet.) 110 (1828), the Court dismissed a libel in admiralty brought in federal district court by Madrazo against the governor for possession of certain slaves (and the proceeds of the sale of others) seized under a state statute after allegedly having been imported in violation of federal law. The Court reasoned that the suit could be justified neither as an in rem action (because the slaves—treated by the Court as "property"—were not in the possession of the court) nor as an in personam action against the governor (because he was sued "not by his name, but by his title" and "[t]he demand made upon him, is not made personally, but officially")(p. 123). Therefore, "the state itself may be considered as a party on the record" (pp. 123–24). Even if the governor were treated as if he had been sued personally, "no case is made which justifies a decree against him personally" since he "acted in obedience to a law of the state, made for the purpose of giving effect to an Act of Congress; and has done nothing in violation of any law of the United States" (p. 124). Because the suit was against the state, it fell within the Supreme Court's, rather than the district court's, original jurisdiction.[11]

Madrazo subsequently filed a libel in admiralty against the State of Georgia as an original action in the Supreme Court. In a one paragraph opinion, Chief Justice Marshall dismissed the suit: it was not within the admiralty jurisdiction, as the property was not in the custody of either the court or any private person. "It is a mere personal suit against a state to recover proceeds in its possession, and in such a case no private person has a right to commence an original suit in this court against a state." Ex parte Madrazzo, 32 U.S. (7 Pet.) 627, 632 (1833).

Note that Ex parte Madrazzo—the only case prior to the Civil War in which the Court's opinion based a dismissal on Eleventh Amendment grounds—involved no federal cause of action.

(4) *The Interpretation of Hans, Its Aftermath, and the Continuing Controversy over Its Meaning and Validity.*

---

10. In a later stage of the litigation in a circuit court, Justice Washington reiterated the basis for decision in Peters, but added that the Amendment did not extend to admiralty, pointing to the text's limitation to suits at law or in equity, and noting that in an admiralty in rem proceeding, the "delicate" issue of enforcement against a state does not arise. United States v. Bright, 24 F.Cas. 1232, 1236 (D.Pa.1809)(No. 14,647). Over a century later, the Supreme Court rejected his view. See Paragraph (4)(a), *infra.*

11. For a thorough discussion of Madrazo, see Gibbons, note 2, *supra,* at 1961–68; see also Jaffe, *Suits Against Governments and Officers: Sovereign Immunity,* 77 Harv. L.Rev. 1, 21–24 (1963).

(a) *Introduction.* Prior to Hans, the Supreme Court had never held that as a result of the Eleventh Amendment (or any other provision), the Constitution barred the exercise of federal jurisdiction in a suit against a state by a citizen of that state who asserted judicial power based on a claim arising under federal law. Though (as shown by the discussion that follows in this Paragraph) there is continuing debate about the precise holding in Hans, there is no doubt that the decision marked a critical turning point, and that ever since, the Court has not adhered to a "literal" reading of the Amendment in determining its effect on federal jurisdiction. Thus, the Court has held, despite earlier dicta to the contrary, see, *e.g.,* Cherokee Nation v. Georgia, 30 U.S. (5 Pet.) 1, 15–16 (1831), that the effect of the Amendment is to bar suit against a state by a foreign country, Monaco v. Mississippi, 292 U.S. 313, 322 (1934), p. 307, *supra,* asserting that "[b]ehind the words of the constitutional provisions are postulates which limit and control." And in Ex parte New York, 256 U.S. 490 (1921), the Court reached the same conclusion with respect to suits in admiralty, despite the textual limitation to suits "in law or equity".

However, the Court has declined to bar either suits against a state by another state, see, *e.g.,* Kansas v. Colorado, 206 U.S. 46, 83 (1907); p. 312, *supra,*[12] or suits against a state by the United States, see, *e.g.,* United States v. Mississippi, 380 U.S. 128, 140–41 (1965). In Monaco v. Mississippi, the Court explained that the former holding "was essential to the peace of the Union" and "a necessary feature of the formation of a more perfect Union," while the latter was "inherent in the constitutional plan" (292 U.S. at 328–29).

Finally, the Court has held that a state's immunity from federal court suit may be waived, and that, at least in certain circumstances, state immunity may be abrogated by Congress. See pp. 1085–1105, *infra.*

(b) *The Nature of the Immunity Recognized in Hans and Its Progeny.* Is the immunity recognized by cases like Hans, Monaco v. Mississippi, and Ex parte New York plainly a *constitutional* immunity? If so, is it derived *solely* from the Eleventh Amendment, notwithstanding its wording? (Many modern decisions seem to so hold. See, *e.g.,* Florida Dept. of State v. Treasure Salvors, Inc., 458 U.S. 670, 683 n. 17 (1982); Edelman v. Jordan, 415 U.S. 651, 662–63 (1974), p. 1066, *infra.*) Or does the Amendment simply undo a mistake made in Chisholm, and restore the (implicit) understanding that Article III's judicial power does not extend to a suit against an unconsenting state by any plaintiff other than the United States or another state? See, *e.g.,* Employees of Dep't of Pub. Health & Welfare v. Department of Pub. Health & Welfare, 411 U.S. 279, 291–92 (1973)(Marshall, J., concurring in the result); Poindexter v. Greenhow, 114 U.S. 270, 337–38 (1885)(Bradley, J., dissenting).

At one time, Justice Brennan advanced the view that the Eleventh Amendment did create a constitutional immunity, but only in suits by citizens of other states or by aliens; Hans, he argued, recognized only a nonconstitutional immunity from suit by a state's own citizens, which could be overcome by congressional enactments. See, *e.g.,* Employees of Dep't of Pub. Health & Welfare, *supra,* 411 U.S. at 309–22 (Brennan, J., dissenting); Edelman v. Jordan, *supra,* 415 U.S. at 687–88 (Brennan, J., dissenting). Professor Field takes that argument one step further: she contends that the original Constitu-

---

12. But *cf.* New Hampshire v. Louisiana, 108 U.S. 76 (1883), discussed at p. 316, *supra,* and p. 1064, note 1, *infra.*

tion neither imposed nor abrogated state sovereign immunity, but simply left a common law immunity in place; the Eleventh Amendment returned, after Chisholm, to that understanding; and Hans recognized only that common law immunity. Field, *The Eleventh Amendment and Other Sovereign Immunity Doctrines: Part I*, 126 U.Pa.L.Rev. 515 (1978)(Field I); Field, *The Eleventh Amendment and Other Sovereign Immunity Doctrines: Congressional Imposition of Suit Upon the States*, 126 U.Pa.L.Rev. 1203 (1978)(Field II).[13]

Consider whether Field's view rests upon a strained reading of Hans and of the constitutional text. Under her view, it appears that Congress could authorize the federal courts to entertain an action against an unconsenting state by a citizen of another state, even when the only basis of jurisdiction under Article III was the status of the parties.[14]

Field also suggests that "in an era of freewheeling federal common law, the federal judiciary might itself make desired modifications" in sovereign immunity. Field I, *supra*, at 545 n. 98. But *cf.* Field II, *supra*, at 1262–65 (federal courts may *modify* immunity but judicial *abrogation* is not to be expected). Was it then the purpose of the Eleventh Amendment merely to overturn Chisholm to whatever extent federal judges thought desirable?

(5) *The "Diversity" Interpretation of the Eleventh Amendment.*

(a) The Supreme Court still follows the understanding set forth in Hans that the Eleventh Amendment embodies (or reinstates) a general constitutional principle of state sovereign immunity in federal court actions. But in Atascadero State Hosp. v. Scanlon, 473 U.S. 234 (1985), Justice Brennan presented a powerful revisionist view of the meaning of the Amendment. Drawing on the work of several recent commentators,[15] his dissent (which Justices Marshall, Blackmun, and Stevens joined) rested on two central distinctions. First, he sharply distinguished "sovereign immunity"—a traditional concept barring uncontested suit against the sovereign in any court—from the jurisdictional bar to suit in *federal* court erected by the Eleventh Amendment. The Eleventh Amendment, he argued, had nothing to do with sovereign immunity (in suits in state court, for example); it was designed exclusively to regulate the scope of federal judicial power.

Second, Justice Brennan distinguished between two grounds of federal jurisdiction under Article III: jurisdiction based on subject matter (such as suits arising under federal law) and that dependent on party status (such as citizen/state diversity). The Eleventh Amendment, he contended, barred federal jurisdiction in suits based on party status, but not those based on subject matter. More specifically, it barred jurisdiction in suits against an unconsenting state brought under the state-citizen diversity clause, but did not restrict

---

13. In addition to the writings of Professor Field discussed in text, there are many other studies of the Hans decision, and some of these studies make similar arguments that the case involved only recognition of a common law immunity. *E.g.*, Burnham, *Taming the Eleventh Amendment Without Overruling Hans v. Louisiana*, 40 Case W.Res.L.Rev. 931 (1989–90).

14. Field reads the language "The Judicial power of the United States shall not be construed to extend to * * *" to mean that

the judicial power should not be deemed, of its own force, "affirmatively to allow" such cases to be heard. But note that elsewhere, Article III uses the words "extend to" to mean simply "reach".

15. See, *e.g.*, Fletcher, note 3, *supra*; Gibbons, note 2, *supra*; Orth, *The Interpretation of the Eleventh Amendment, 1798–1908: A Case Study of Judicial Power*, 1983 U.Ill. L.Rev. 423. See also the subsequent article by Amar, note 3, *supra*.

suits against an unconsenting state brought under admiralty or federal question jurisdiction.

According to Justice Brennan, "in most of the States in 1789, the doctrine of sovereign immunity formally forbade the maintenance of suits against States in state courts" (p. 261). To permit federal court jurisdiction based on party status "was a particularly troublesome prospect to the States that had incurred debts, some of which dated back to the Revolutionary War. The debts would naturally find their way into the hands of noncitizens and aliens, who at the first sign of default could be expected promptly to sue the State in federal court. The State's effort to retain its sovereign immunity in its own courts would turn out to be futile" (p. 262).[16]

After concluding that neither the records of the Constitutional Convention nor the language of Article III provides much guidance as to the Amendment's intended scope, Justice Brennan reviewed at length the ratification debates over Article III, including the comments of Hamilton, Madison, and Marshall (pp. 263–64):

"The various references to state sovereign immunity all appear in discussions of the state-citizen diversity clause. Virtually all of the comments were addressed to the problem created by state debts that predated the Constitution, when the State's creditors may often have had meager judicial remedies in the case of default. Yet, even in this sensitive context, a number of participants in the debates welcomed the abrogation of sovereign immunity that they thought followed from the state-citizen and state-alien clauses.[17] The debates do not directly address the question of suits against States in admiralty or federal question cases, where federal law and not state law would govern.[18] Nonetheless, the apparent willingness of many delegates to read the state-citizen clause as abrogating sovereign immunity in state-law causes of action suggests that they would have been even more willing to permit suits against States in federal question cases, where Congress had authorized such suits in the exercise of its Article I or other powers."

Justice Brennan then examined the drafting of the Eleventh Amendment by Congress. He concluded that the language chosen "would have been a particularly cryptic way to embody" in the Constitution a consensus that the doctrine of state sovereign immunity would apply in federal court. Had the

---

16. For contrasting views of the doctrine's status in the colonies, compare Jacobs, note 3, *supra,* at 12 (sovereign immunity and limitations on its scope were well-established), with Gibbons, note 2, *supra,* at 1895–99 (governmental immunity was not an accepted doctrine) and Orth, The Judicial Power of the United States: The Eleventh Amendment in American History 23–24 (1987)(same).

17. [Ed.] The view that the Constitution abrogated immunity was advanced as an argument against ratification by some opponents (such as George Mason and Patrick Henry in Virginia) and various anti-Federalist publicists, but the view was also held by proponents of ratification (like Edmund Pendleton and Edmund Randolph of Virginia and Timothy Pickering and James Wilson of Pennsylvania). See 473 U.S. at 263–80. See generally Gibbons, note 2, *supra,* at 1902–08.

18. [Ed.] Later in his opinion, Justice Brennan observed (p. 282 n. 33): "Most likely, Chisholm could not have been brought directly under the Contracts Clause of the Constitution. Prior to Fletcher v. Peck, 6 Cranch 87 (1810), it was not at all clear that the Contracts Clause applied to contracts to which a state was a party. Moreover, the case involved a simple breach of contract, not a law impairing the obligation of the contract to which the Clause would have applied. Finally, it was certainly not clear at the time of Chisholm that the Contracts Clause provided a plaintiff with a private right of action for damages."

drafters wished that result, they could have "merely omitted the last fourteen words" of the Amendment. The language chosen—"The Judicial power of the United States shall not be construed to extend * * *"—parallels the phrasing of Article III, and was meant merely to abandon the construction of Article III in Chisholm, which permitted federal court suit against a state based simply upon party status. The Amendment, accordingly, singles out suits against a state by aliens or citizens of another state, in order to track (and restrict) the party-based jurisdiction in Article III (pp. 286–87).

Finally, Justice Brennan considered the Marshall Court's decisions in Cohens, Osborn, Peters, and both Madrazo cases. He argued that they were consistent with his interpretation of the Amendment: in none of the decisions did the Court decline jurisdiction in a suit against a state based upon federal law.

Recall that Chisholm was an assumpsit action. In drafting a provision to overrule it, the Framers of the Eleventh Amendment gave little if any explicit consideration to the question of an unconsenting state's liability under federal law. Are the justifications for a state's claim of sovereign immunity as weighty in that context?

The Atascadero case involved a claim that a state was liable in damages under a federal statute, while Hans involved a claim for a judicially-implied remedy directly under the Constitution. Justice Brennan's dissent did not specifically address the question whether the federal courts' power to imply damage remedies for violations of federal constitutional provisions (as in the Bivens line of cases) or of federal statutes should extend to remedies against the states themselves. (He did suggest, however, that the *result* in Hans, denying relief, might be justified. See note 18, *supra*.) Should the Amendment be viewed as resting on the theory that federal judges (who are presumably less politically responsive to state interests than are federal legislators) should not on their own hold states liable in damages—a theory that necessarily would preclude holding states liable under modern judicially-fashioned damages remedies? Is it sometimes imperative that unconsenting states be held liable in federal court suits in order adequately to redress violations of constitutional rights? See Amar, note 3, *supra,* at 1484–92, so arguing; and recall the more limited holding in First English Evangelical Lutheran Church v. County of Los Angeles, 482 U.S. 304, 316 n. 9 (1987), that the Fifth Amendment's Just Compensation Clause, as applied to the states by the Fourteenth Amendment, "of its own force, furnish[es] a basis for a court to award money damages against the government."[19]

If Justice Brennan's view—that the *Amendment* merely restricts party-based jurisdiction—were adopted, might the states nonetheless enjoy some form of immunity (derived from the common law rather than the Constitution) in federal court actions?[20]

(b) The questions whether Hans correctly interpreted the Eleventh Amendment as giving rise to a general rule of state sovereign immunity, and

---

19. For an expansive reading of the First English case, suggesting that it allows the federal courts to provide compensation for a broad range of constitutional violations notwithstanding the Eleventh Amendment, see Beermann, *Government Official Torts* *and the Takings Clause: Federalism and State Sovereign Immunity,* 68 B.U.L.Rev. 277 (1988).

20. See Jackson, note 5, *supra,* at 72–104 (advocating this view).

whether that interpretation is in any event too well-established to warrant reconsideration, were further debated in Welch v. Texas Dep't of Highways and Pub. Transp., 483 U.S. 468 (1987), also discussed at p. 1100, *infra*. There the Court held that the Amendment barred a suit in admiralty (for damages under the Jones Act, 46 U.S.C. § 688), brought against the State of Texas by an employee of a state-owned ferry. Justice Powell, writing for a plurality of four, strongly defended the Court's adherence to the Hans rule. Justice Brennan's dissent, again joined by Justices Marshall, Blackmun, and Stevens, reiterated the views he expressed in his Atascadero dissent.

Justice Scalia, concurring in part and concurring in the judgment, cast the deciding vote in favor of dismissing the action. For him, "both the correctness of Hans as an original matter, and the feasibility, if it was wrong, of correcting it without distorting what we have done in tacit reliance upon it, [are] complex enough questions that I am unwilling to address them in a case whose presentation focused on other matters" (p. 496). He then concluded that the Jones Act, which applies to common carriers by water, did not by its terms impose liability upon the states.[21] (Two terms after the Welch decision, in Pennsylvania v. Union Gas Co., 491 U.S. 1 (1989), p. 1085, *infra*, the Chief Justice and Justices White, O'Connor, Scalia, and Kennedy declined to overrule Hans v. Louisiana.)

(6) *The Constitutional Status of a Federal Question Suit in a Federal Court Action Brought Against a State by a Citizen of Another State: A Textualist Answer to the Critics of Hans?* Recall that in the Hans opinion, the Court notes that the Eleventh Amendment had previously been held to bar a suit against a state by a citizen of another state, even when the claim was based on a question of federal law.[22] How then, the Court asked, could a federal court suit on such grounds be permitted by a citizen of the defendant state? The point has been picked up by several commentators who are not all defenders of the holding in Hans itself but who contend that the Amendment does in any event apply in any case in which a state is sued by a non-citizen of that state. See, *e.g.*, Marshall, *Fighting the Words of the Eleventh Amendment*, 102 Harv.L.Rev. 1342 (1989); Massey, *State Sovereignty and the Tenth and Eleventh Amendments*, 56 U.Chi.L.Rev. 61 (1989). In reply, Professor Amar argues that the language and structure of Article III, as well as the language of the Amendment's withdrawal of federal judicial power, support a limitation of the Amendment to cases in which Article III jurisdiction would otherwise exist only "*because* a state is a party". Amar, *Marbury, Section 13, and the Original Jurisdiction of the Supreme Court*, 56 U.Chi.L.Rev. 443, 496 (1989). For another forceful reply focusing on historical materials, see Fletcher, *The Diversity Explanation of the Eleventh Amendment: A Reply to Critics*, 56 U.Chi.L.Rev. 1261 (1989).[23]

---

21. Justice Scalia's conclusion on this point was rejected by the Court in Hilton v. South Carolina Pub. Ry. Comm'n, 502 U.S. 197 (1991), a state court FELA action against a state-owned railway. For further discussion of this decision, see p. 1100, note 6, *infra*.

22. In these cases, however, the Court may well have viewed the claims as "arising under" general contract law rather than under the constitutional Contracts Clause.

23. In addition to the authorities already cited, recent commentary on the Eleventh Amendment includes: Althouse, *When to Believe a Legal Fiction: Federal Interests and the Eleventh Amendment*, 40 Hastings L.J. 1123 (1989)(arguing that, rather than overruling Hans, courts should openly make doctrinal choices on the basis of their perception of the federal interests at stake; such an approach favors allowing greater access to federal courts for constitutional than for non-

(7) *The Constitutional Status of a Suit Against a State in the Courts of Another State*. The Eleventh Amendment applies by its terms only in the federal courts. The question whether a state is free to subject a sister state to damage liability in its own courts was faced in Nevada v. Hall, 440 U.S. 410 (1979). A California plaintiff, who had been involved in a California automobile accident with an employee of the state of Nevada driving a state-owned car, sued Nevada in a California court. Service of process was made on Nevada under the California long-arm statute permitting service on nonresidents whose agents use California highways and are involved in an accident there. The Supreme Court affirmed a $1.15 million verdict against Nevada, holding that nothing in the federal Constitution requires California to accord Nevada immunity, and that consequently California has the same discretion that a sovereign nation would have in deciding whether to provide immunity in its courts to other sovereigns. In dissent, Justice Rehnquist argued that, even though nothing in the text of the Constitution speaks directly to this issue, cases like Hans and Principality of Monaco "recognized that Art. III and the Eleventh Amendment are built on important concepts of sovereignty" that are "of constitutional dimension because their derogation would undermine the logic of the constitutional scheme" (p. 439).[24]

On what theory can one justify holding that Nevada can be sued in California state court but not in a federal district court in California, when the latter is presumably less likely to favor parochial interests? Does Justice Rehnquist's view require a greater stretch of the constitutional text than Hans or Monaco because he would draw inferences about *state court* jurisdiction from provisions regulating *federal* judicial power?

Suppose Hall files suit to enforce her California judgment in a Nevada state court? Would Nevada be obliged to give the California judgment full faith and credit, notwithstanding a plea of sovereign immunity by the state? See Brilmayer, An Introduction to Jurisdiction in the American Federal System 183–84 (1986).

(8) *Federal Court Suits Against State Agencies and Local Governments*. A suit against a statewide agency is considered a suit against the state under the Eleventh Amendment. See, *e.g.,* Edelman v. Jordan, 415 U.S. 651 (1974); Ford Motor Co. v. Department of Treasury, 323 U.S. 459 (1945). However, Lincoln County v. Luning, 133 U.S. 529 (1890), decided the same day as Hans, held that the Eleventh Amendment does not bar an individual's suit in federal court against a county for nonpayment of a debt. The unanimous Court noted its "general acquiescence" in such suits over the prior thirty years (p. 530). The Court has adhered to this position as to local government bodies ever since. See, *e.g.,* Mount Healthy City School Dist. Bd. of Educ. v. Doyle, 429 U.S. 274, 280–81 (1977)(school board); Workman v. New York, 179 U.S. 552, 563–66

---

constitutional violations of federal law); Brown, *Has the Supreme Court Confessed Error on the Eleventh Amendment? Revisionist Scholarship and State Immunity,* 68 N.C.L.Rev. 867 (1990)(discussing the delicate balance between national supremacy and state sovereignty); Sherry, *The Eleventh Amendment and Stare Decisis: Overruling*

Hans v. Louisiana, 57 U.Chi.L.Rev. 1260 (1990)(since the policies supporting the Hans decision are weak, and since the foundations of the decision have been undermined by the downfall of Swift v. Tyson, Hans is ripe for overruling).

24. The Chief Justice and Justice Blackmun also dissented.

(1900)(city).[25]

Since a local government body is a creature of the state, it is hard to see any functional basis for distinguishing the two. See Note, 1979 Duke L.J. 1042. Professor Fletcher explains the different treatment on the ground that in the nineteenth century, a municipal corporation was viewed as more closely analogous to a private corporation than to a state government. Fletcher, note 3, *supra,* at 1099–1107. Professor Orth explains the opposing outcomes in Hans and Lincoln County as resting on the limits of judicial power: in Hans and other cases against debt-ridden southern states, the Court chose not to issue orders that, in the post-Reconstruction political environment, could never have been enforced; by contrast, enforcement of court orders was far easier against counties, especially western counties (like Lincoln County, Nevada) that depended upon maintaining their credit to permit further borrowing. See Orth, note 15, *supra,* at 110–20; accord Gibbons, note 2, *supra,* at 1973–2002.[26]

Note that unlike states and state agencies, local government bodies are in some instances liable in damages under 42 U.S.C. § 1983. See Monell v. Department of Social Services, 436 U.S. 658 (1978), p. 1126, *infra.* By what criteria does one determine whether, for purposes of the Eleventh Amendment, a governmental unit such as a school board or county welfare department—which may administer state laws, be subject to some control by state authorities, and share fiscal responsibility for its operations with the state—should be deemed to be an arm of the state (and hence immune), or a separate political subdivision (and hence not immune)? See, *e.g.,* Martinez v. Board of Educ. of Taos Mun. School Dist., 748 F.2d 1393 (10th Cir.1984); Holley v. Lavine, 605 F.2d 638 (2d Cir.1979); Note, 55 Fordham L.Rev. 101 (1986). What is the pertinence of federal and state law in answering that question?[27]

(9) *Federal Court Suits Against Multi–State Agencies.* In Lake Country Estates, Inc. v. Tahoe Regional Planning Agency, 440 U.S. 391 (1979), the Court held that a bi-state regional agency created by a congressionally approved interstate compact between California and Nevada to coordinate development of the Lake Tahoe area was not immune from suit in federal court: "Unless there is good reason to believe that the States structured the new agency to enable it to enjoy the special constitutional protection of the States themselves, and that Congress concurred in that purpose, there would appear to be no justification for reading additional meaning into the limited language of the Amendment" (p. 401).

The Court expanded on its holding in Tahoe in Hess v. Port Authority Trans–Hudson Corp. [PATH], 115 S.Ct. 394 (1994), a case in which injured railroad workers brought an FELA action against PATH, a bi-state railway created by a congressionally approved interstate compact. In a 5–4 decision, the Court held that PATH was not entitled to Eleventh Amendment immunity.

---

25. But *cf.* Paragraph (4) of the Note on the Pennhurst Case, p. 1083, *infra.*

26. For a spirited defense of the Lincoln County decision on both historical and functional grounds, see Durschlag, *Should Political Subdivisions be Accorded Eleventh Amendment Immunity,* 43 DePaul L.Rev. 577 (1994).

27. For discussion of the case law, see Note, 92 Colum.L.Rev. 1243 (1992)(criticizing the balancing approach adopted by many lower courts, and arguing, by analogy to state immunity from federal antitrust liability, that Eleventh Amendment immunity should be recognized if and only if (1) the state has, with unmistakable clarity, designated the entity a state agency, or (2) the entity lacks authority to raise its own revenues).

Despite the formal elements of state control over PATH, there were significant elements pointing away from immunity for an entity that was not itself a state, notably the lack of state financial responsibility for the Authority's liabilities.

The dissenters in the PATH case criticized the majority for placing too much emphasis on the bi-state nature of the Authority and on the single factor of financial responsibility, and not enough on the elements of control retained by the two states or on the precept that when sovereign states act together to create a new entity, the resulting body should in most situations be "as deserving of immunity as either State acting apart" (p. 409).

Ex Parte Young

209 U.S. 123, 28 S.Ct. 441, 52 L.Ed. 714 (1908).
Petition for Writs of Habeas Corpus and Certiorari.

[Shareholders of various railroads brought derivative actions in federal circuit court in Minnesota, alleging that state legislation regulating railroad rates was confiscatory and violated the Fourteenth Amendment. The companies' managements, plaintiffs alleged, had refused their demands that the companies not comply with the legislation.

[The trial court entered a temporary restraining order prohibiting Edward Young, the state's Attorney General, from enforcing the legislation, and after denying Young's motion under the Eleventh Amendment to dismiss, entered a preliminary injunction to the same effect. Young then defied the injunction by filing a state court action seeking to enforce the legislation against the railroads.

[The circuit court held Young in contempt, again rejecting his Eleventh Amendment defense. He then filed an application in the Supreme Court for leave to file a petition for writs of habeas corpus and certiorari.]

■ MR. JUSTICE PECKHAM * * * delivered the opinion of the court.

[The Court first concluded that the circuit court had "arising under" jurisdiction, as the suit raised several federal questions: (i) whether enforcement of the rates would take property without due process of law, (ii) whether the penalties for violation were so enormous as to deny equal protection and due process, and (iii) whether the legislation interfered with interstate commerce.]

* * *

Coming to the inquiry regarding the alleged invalidity of these acts, we take up the contention that they are invalid on their face on account of the penalties. For disobedience to the freight act the officers, directors, agents and employés of the company are made guilty of a misdemeanor, and upon conviction each may be punished by imprisonment in the county jail for a period not exceeding ninety days. Each violation would be a separate offense, and, therefore, might result in imprisonment of the various agents of the company who would dare disobey for a term of ninety days each for each offense. Disobedience to the passenger rate act renders the party guilty of a felony and subject to a fine not exceeding five thousand dollars or imprisonment in the state prison for a period not exceeding five years, or both fine and imprisonment. The sale of each ticket above the price permitted by the act would be a violation thereof. * * *

The company, in order to test the validity of the acts, must find some agent or employé to disobey them at the risk stated. The necessary effect and result of such legislation must be to preclude a resort to the courts (either state or Federal) for the purpose of testing its validity. * * * It may therefore be said that when the penalties for disobedience are by fines so enormous and imprisonment so severe as to intimidate the company and its officers from resorting to the courts to test the validity of the legislation, the result is the same as if the law in terms prohibited the company from seeking judicial construction of laws which deeply affect its rights.

* * * Ordinarily a law creating offenses in the nature of misdemeanors or felonies relates to a subject over which the jurisdiction of the legislature is complete in any event. In the case, however, of the establishment of certain rates without any hearing, the validity of such rates necessarily depends upon whether they are high enough to permit at least some return upon the investment (how much it is not now necessary to state), and an inquiry as to that fact is a proper subject of judicial investigation. If it turns out that the rates are too low for that purpose, then they are illegal. Now, to impose upon a party interested the burden of obtaining a judicial decision of such a question (no prior hearing having ever been given) only upon the condition that if unsuccessful he must suffer imprisonment and pay fines as provided in these acts, is, in effect, to close up all approaches to the courts, and thus prevent any hearing upon the question whether the rates as provided by the acts are not too low, and therefore invalid. * * *

We hold, therefore, that the provisions of the acts relating to the enforcement of the rates, either for freight or passengers, by imposing such enormous fines and possible imprisonment as a result of an unsuccessful effort to test the validity of the laws themselves, are unconstitutional on their face, without regard to the question of the insufficiency of those rates. * * *

* * *

* * * The question that arises is whether there is a remedy that the parties interested may resort to, by going into a Federal court of equity, in a case involving a violation of the Federal Constitution, and obtaining a judicial investigation of the problem, and pending its solution obtain freedom from suits, civil or criminal, by a temporary injunction, and if the question be finally decided favorably to the contention of the company, a permanent injunction restraining all such actions or proceedings.

This inquiry necessitates an examination of the most material and important objection made to the jurisdiction of the Circuit Court, the objection being that the suit is, in effect, one against the State of Minnesota * * *. This objection is to be considered with reference to the Eleventh and Fourteenth Amendments to the Federal Constitution. * * *

* * * We may assume that each [Amendment] exists in full force, and that we must give to the Eleventh Amendment all the effect it naturally would have, without cutting it down or rendering its meaning any more narrow than the language, fairly interpreted, would warrant. It applies to a suit brought against a State by one of its own citizens as well as to a suit brought by a citizen of another State. Hans v. Louisiana, 134 U.S. 1. * * *

* * *

The cases * * * [following adoption of the Eleventh Amendment] were reviewed, and it was held, In re Ayers, 123 U.S. 443, that a bill in equity brought against officers of a State, who, as individuals, have no personal interest in the subject-matter of the suit, and defend only as representing the State, where the relief prayed for, if done, would constitute a performance by the State of the alleged contract of the State, was a suit against the State (page 504), following in this respect Hagood v. Southern, [117 U.S. 52, 67].

A suit of such a nature was simply an attempt to make the State itself, through its officers, perform its alleged contract, by directing those officers to do acts which constituted such performance. The State alone had any interest in the question, and a decree in favor of plaintiff would affect the treasury of the State.

[The Court then discussed a number of its recent decisions that it viewed as "ample justification" for determining that a state official who is about to commence civil or criminal proceedings to enforce unconstitutional state legislation may be enjoined from such action by a federal court of equity. Those cases included Reagan v. Farmers' Loan & Trust Co., 154 U.S. 362 (1894) and Smyth v. Ames, 169 U.S. 466, 518 (1898). The Court continued:]

* * * In those cases the only wrong or injury or trespass involved was the threatened commencement of suits to enforce the statute as to rates, and the threat of such commencement was in each case regarded as sufficient to authorize the issuing of an injunction to prevent the same. The threat to commence those suits under such circumstances was therefore necessarily held to be equivalent to any other threatened wrong or injury to the property of a plaintiff which had theretofore been held sufficient to authorize the suit against the officer.

* * * It is contended that the complainants do not complain and they care nothing about any action which Mr. Young might take or bring as an ordinary individual, but that he was complained of as an officer, to whose discretion is confided the use of the name of the State of Minnesota so far as litigation is concerned, and that when or how he shall use it is a matter resting in his discretion and cannot be controlled by any court.

The answer to all this is the same as made in every case where an official claims to be acting under the authority of the State. The act to be enforced is alleged to be unconstitutional, and if it be so, the use of the name of the State to enforce an unconstitutional act to the injury of complainants is a proceeding without the authority of and one which does not affect the State in its sovereign or governmental capacity. It is simply an illegal act upon the part of a state official in attempting by the use of the name of the State to enforce a legislative enactment which is void because unconstitutional. If the act which the state Attorney General seeks to enforce be a violation of the Federal Constitution, the officer in proceeding under such enactment comes into conflict with the superior authority of that Constitution, and he is in that case stripped of his official or representative character and is subjected in his person to the consequences of his individual conduct. The State has no power to impart to him any immunity from responsibility to the supreme authority of the United States. * * *

It is further objected (and the objection really forms part of the contention that the State cannot be sued) that a court of equity has no jurisdiction to enjoin criminal proceedings, by indictment or otherwise, under the state law.

This, as a general rule, is true. But there are exceptions. When such indictment or proceeding is brought to enforce an alleged unconstitutional statute, which is the subject matter of inquiry in a suit already pending in a Federal court, the latter court having first obtained jurisdiction over the subject matter, has the right, in both civil and criminal cases, to hold and maintain such jurisdiction, to the exclusion of all other courts, until its duty is fully performed. But the Federal court cannot, of course, interfere in a case where the proceedings were already pending in a state court.

* * *

It is proper to add that the right to enjoin an individual, even though a state official, from commencing suits under circumstances already stated, does not include the power to restrain a court from acting in any case brought before it, either of a civil or criminal nature, nor does it include power to prevent any investigation or action by a grand jury. The latter body is part of the machinery of a criminal court, and an injunction against a state court would be a violation of the whole scheme of our Government. * * *

* * *

It is further objected that there is a plain and adequate remedy at law open to the complainants and that a court of equity, therefore, has no jurisdiction in such case. It has been suggested that the proper way to test the constitutionality of the act is to disobey it, at least once, after which the company might obey the act pending subsequent proceedings to test its validity. But in the event of a single violation the prosecutor might not avail himself of the opportunity to make the test, as obedience to the law was thereafter continued, and he might think it unnecessary to start an inquiry. If, however, he should do so while the company was thereafter obeying the law, several years might elapse before there was a final determination of the question, and if it should be determined that the law was invalid the property of the company would have been taken during that time without due process of law, and there would be no possibility of its recovery.

Another obstacle to making the test on the part of the company might be to find an agent or employé who would disobey the law, with a possible fine and imprisonment staring him in the face if the act should be held valid. Take the passenger rate act, for instance: A sale of a single ticket above the price mentioned in that act might subject the ticket agent to a charge of felony, and upon conviction to a fine of five thousand dollars and imprisonment for five years. It is true the company might pay the fine, but the imprisonment the agent would have to suffer personally. It would not be wonderful if, under such circumstances, there would not be a crowd of agents offering to disobey the law. The wonder would be that a single agent should be found ready to take the risk.

* * *

* * * [I]t must be remembered that jurisdiction of this general character has, in fact, been exercised by Federal courts from the time of Osborn v. United States Bank up to the present; the only difference in regard to the case of Osborn and the case in hand being that in this case the injury complained of is the threatened commencement of suits, civil or criminal, to enforce the act, instead of, as in the Osborn case, an actual and direct trespass upon or interference with tangible property. A bill filed to prevent the commencement of suits to enforce an unconstitutional act, under the circumstances already mentioned, is no new invention, as we have already seen. The difference between an actual and direct interference with tangible property and the enjoining of state officers from enforcing an unconstitutional act, is not of a radical nature, and does not extend, in truth, the jurisdiction of the courts over the subject matter. * * * The sovereignty of the State is, in reality, no more involved in one case than in the other. The State cannot in either case impart to the official immunity from responsibility to the supreme authority of the United States. See In re Ayers, 123 U.S. 507.

This supreme authority, which arises from the specific provisions of the Constitution itself, is nowhere more fully illustrated than in the series of decisions under the Federal *habeas corpus* statute, in some of which cases persons in the custody of state officers for alleged crimes against the State have been taken from that custody and discharged by a Federal court or judge, because the imprisonment was adjudged to be in violation of the Federal Constitution. The right to so discharge has not been doubted by this court, and it has never been supposed there was any suit against the State by reason of serving the writ upon one of the officers of the State in whose custody the person was found. * * *

* * *

The rule to show cause is discharged and the petition for writs of *habeas corpus* and certiorari is dismissed.

So ordered.

■ Mr. Justice Harlan, dissenting.

* * *

Let it be observed that the suit * * * in the Circuit Court of the United States was, as to the defendant Young, one against him *as, and only because he was,* Attorney General of Minnesota. No relief was sought against him individually but only in his capacity *as* Attorney General. And the manifest, indeed the avowed and admitted, object of seeking such relief was *to tie the hands* of the *State* so that it could not in any manner or by any mode of proceeding, *in its own courts,* test the validity of the statutes and orders in question. It would therefore seem clear that within the true meaning of the Eleventh Amendment the suit brought in the Federal court was one, in legal effect, against the State—as much so as if the State had been formally named on the record as a party—and therefore it was a suit to which, under the Amendment, so far as the State or its Attorney General was concerned, the judicial power of the United States did not and could not extend.

* * * [T]he intangible thing, called a State, however extensive its powers, can never appear or be represented or known in any court in a litigated case, except by and through its officers. When, therefore, the Federal court forbade the defendant Young, as Attorney General of Minnesota, from taking any action, suit, step or proceeding whatever looking to the enforcement of the statutes in question, it said in effect to the State of Minnesota: "* * * the Federal court adjudges that you, the State, although a sovereign for many important governmental purposes, shall not appear in your own courts, by your law officer, with the view of enforcing, or even for determining the validity of the state enactments which the Federal court has, upon a preliminary hearing, declared to be in violation of the Constitution of the United States."

This principle, if firmly established, would work a radical change in our governmental system. It would inaugurate a new era in the American judicial system and in the relations of the National and state governments. It would enable the subordinate Federal courts to supervise and control the official action of the States as if they were "dependencies" or provinces. It would place the States of the Union in a condition of inferiority never dreamed of when the Constitution was adopted or when the Eleventh Amendment was made a part of the Supreme Law of the Land. * * * Too little consequence has been attached to the fact that the courts of the States are under an obligation equally strong with that resting upon the courts of the Union to respect and enforce the provisions of the Federal Constitution as the Supreme Law of the Land, and to guard rights secured or guaranteed by that instrument. We must assume—a decent respect for the States requires us to assume—that the state courts will enforce every right secured by the Constitution. If they fail to do so, the party complaining has a clear remedy for the protection of his rights; for, he can come by writ of error, in an orderly, judicial way, from the highest court of the State to this tribunal for redress in respect of every right granted or secured by that instrument and denied by the state court. * * *

NOTE ON THE ELEVENTH AMENDMENT AND
SUITS AGAINST STATE OFFICERS

(1) *The "Party-of-Record" Rule.* Osborn v. Bank of United States, 22 U.S. (9 Wheat.) 738 (1824), p. 883, *supra,* held the Eleventh Amendment inapplicable to suits in which the state was not a party of record. Although the decision in Governor of Georgia v. Madrazo, 26 U.S. (1 Pet.) 110 (1828), p. 1050, *supra,* cast some doubt on the party-of-record rule, the rule was reiterated in Davis v. Gray, 83 U.S. (16 Wall.) 203 (1872), in which the Governor of Texas was enjoined from disturbing the plaintiff's possession of certain land previously granted by the state, on the ground that the new state constitution, which deemed the land forfeited, violated the Contracts Clause.

How does the party-of-record rule relate to the historical development of damages actions and other suits against officers as a means of ensuring official accountability? See pp. 1015–17, *supra.* What of Professor Currie's observation that "[p]eople are not likely to amend constitutions just to change captions on complaints"? Currie, *State Sovereign Immunity and Suits Against Government Officers,* 1984 Sup.Ct.Rev. 149, 151 n. 11.

(2) *The Post–Reconstruction Bond Cases.*

(a) The scope of Eleventh Amendment immunity in suits against state officers was shaped largely in cases involving the repudiation of bond obligations by southern states after Reconstruction. Recent accounts have stressed the political context in which those cases arose, in particular the so-called Compromise of 1877, which made it unlikely that a federal judgment recognizing such obligations would have proved enforceable. See Orth, The Judicial Power of the United States: The Eleventh Amendment in American History 47–120 (1987); Gibbons, *The Eleventh Amendment and State Sovereign Immunity: A Reinterpretation,* 83 Colum.L.Rev. 1978–2002 (1983).

(b) Louisiana ex rel. Elliott v. Jumel, 107 U.S. 711 (1883), held that the Eleventh Amendment barred a suit by Louisiana bondholders seeking to require state officials to honor contractual obligations to collect a property tax and devote its proceeds to paying state bonds. The Court stressed that the officials were not personally liable on the contract, and expressed its unwillingness to assume "the control of the administration of the fiscal affairs of the State to the extent that may be necessary" (p. 722).[1]

(c) The Virginia Coupon Cases involved a Virginia statute that flatly repudiated prior legislation authorizing the payment of state taxes with the interest coupons on state bonds. The Supreme Court upheld an award of restitution, damages, and injunctive relief against state officials who had seized or threatened to seize taxpayers' property in satisfaction of taxes that had already been paid by such coupons. See Poindexter v. Greenhow, 114 U.S. 270 (1885)(discussing the bearing of the Eleventh Amendment even though the case had been prosecuted in *state* court); White v. Greenhow, 114 U.S. 307 (1885); Allen v. Baltimore & O.R.R., 114 U.S. 311 (1885). In Poindexter, the Court said (p. 288) that because any law purporting to authorize the conduct violated the Contracts Clause, the official "stands * * * stripped of his official character; and, confessing a personal violation of the plaintiff's rights for which he must personally answer, he is without defence." Justice Bradley, joined by Chief Justice Waite and Justices Gray and Miller, dissented in Poindexter and the companion cases, contending that the suits were "virtually" suits against the state to compel specific performance of its contractual obligations (p. 330).

The State of Virginia responded by passing legislation ordering state officials to bring suit to recover taxes from taxpayers who had used the coupons as payment. In such actions, the coupons were to be considered *prima facie* counterfeit; the taxpayer had the burden of establishing their genuineness, but was barred from introducing expert testimony on that issue, and to prevail was required to produce the bond from which the coupons were cut. Some British bondholders sued in federal court to enjoin officials from bringing such actions, alleging that the legislation violated the Contracts Clause. The Supreme Court, in In re Ayers, 123 U.S. 443 (1887), held that the Eleventh Amendment barred the lower court's award of injunctive relief. The Virginia Coupon Cases were distinguished on the ground that there, "the defendants, though professing to act as officers of the State, [were] threatening a violation of the personal or property rights of the complainant, for which they [were] personally and individually liable" (p. 500). But "a bill, the object of which is by injunction, indirectly, to compel the specific performance of the contract, by forbidding all those acts and doings which constitute breaches of the contract [instead of requiring the acts that would constitute performance] must also, necessarily, be a suit against the State. In such a case, though the State be not nominally a party on the record, if the defendants are its officers and agents, through whom alone it can act in doing and refusing to do the things which constitute a breach of its contract, the suit is still, in substance, though not in form, a suit against the State. * * *

"* * * The acts alleged in the bill as threatened by the defendants * * * are violations of the assumed contract between the State of Virginia and the complainants, only as they are considered to be the acts of the State of Virginia.

---

1. Louisiana bondholders also failed to obtain relief when the States of New York and New Hampshire, having agreed to take assignment from their citizens of unpaid bonds, tried to bring what was in effect a parens patriae action suit against Louisiana in the Supreme Court's original jurisdiction. New Hampshire v. Louisiana, 108 U.S. 76 (1883), p. 316, *supra*.

The defendants, as individuals, not being parties to that contract, are not capable in law of committing a breach of it. * * * In a certain sense and in certain ways the Constitution of the United States protects contracts against laws of a State subsequently passed impairing their obligation, and this provision is recognized as extending to contracts between an individual and a State; but this, as is apparent, is subject to the other constitutional principle, of equal authority, contained in the 11th Amendment, which secures to the State an immunity from suit. * * * [The protection of contracts] is not a positive and substantive right of an absolute character, secured by the Constitution of the United States against every possible infraction, or for which redress is given as against strangers to the contract itself, for the injurious consequences of acts done or omitted by them" (pp. 502–04).

(d) Note the significance of the tort-contract distinction suggested by the decision in Poindexter, on the one hand, and that in Ayers, on the other. This distinction has been defended by some as consistent with the then-prevailing idea that an official could be enjoined only from the commission (or threatened commission) of a wrong for which the official would be personally liable at common law, *e.g.*, Engdahl, *Immunity and Accountability for Positive Government Wrongs,* 44 U.Colo.L.Rev. 1, 15–16, 37–38 (1972). But it has recently come under attack by Woolhandler, p. 995, *supra,* at 436–45, on the basis that then-existing precedent did recognize "breach of legal duty apart from tort as a ground for [individual] liability" and that, in any event, given "the flexibility of the common law, the legal duty strand easily merges with the tort strand" (p. 444).[2]

(3) *The Significance of Ex Parte Young.*

(a) Attorney General Young's announced readiness to prosecute for conduct in violation of state law was probably not tortious under traditional common law concepts. See Jacobs, The Eleventh Amendment and Sovereign Immunity 138–42 (1972). At the very least, then, the Young decision, as Woolhandler notes, "strengthened the [breach of] legal duty" notion as a basis for equitable relief, and also resolved whatever doubt may have existed about whether a plaintiff could obtain a federal injunction against the bringing of proceedings under an unconstitutional law. Woolhandler, p. 995, *supra,* at 441. Moreover, isn't it clear that in Young, the Court recognized a judicially implied *federal* cause of action for injunctive relief under the Fourteenth Amendment? Indeed, since the parties in Young were not diverse, on what other basis could federal jurisdiction have been predicated? *Cf.* Louisville & N.R.R. v. Mottley, 211 U.S. 149 (1908), p. 907, *supra.*

(b) Did Ex parte Young overrule In re Ayers? Georgia R.R. & Banking Co. v. Redwine, 342 U.S. 299 (1952), held that the Eleventh Amendment did not bar a federal court action, based on the Contracts Clause, seeking to enjoin the state revenue commissioner from imposing taxes upon property claimed to be exempt pursuant to a state charter. The Court purported to distinguish Ayers on the ground that there the "complainant had not alleged that officers

---

2. Among the authorities Woolhandler cites in support of this proposition is Amy v. Des Moines County Supervisors, 78 U.S. (11 Wall.) 136 (1870)(supervisors held liable in damages for failing to obey federal court order to levy taxes to pay federal judgment). Note also that on the facts of In re Ayers itself, such torts as malicious prosecution or interference with advantageous contractual relations seem not inapt, though it is unclear whether a plaintiff in 1887 could have invoked the theory of those torts as a basis for relief.

threatened to tax its property in violation of its constitutional rights", while in Redwine the plaintiff sought "to enjoin [the commissioner] from a threatened and allegedly unconstitutional invasion of its property" (p. 305). Shouldn't the Redwine opinion have acknowledged that Ex parte Young had undermined the basis of In re Ayers?[3]

Edelman v. Jordan

415 U.S. 651, 94 S.Ct. 1347, 39 L.Ed.2d 662 (1974).
Certiorari to the United States Court of Appeals for the Seventh Circuit.

■ MR. JUSTICE REHNQUIST delivered the opinion of the Court.

Respondent John Jordan filed a complaint in the United States District Court for the Northern District of Illinois, individually and as a representative of a class, seeking declaratory and injunctive relief against two former directors of the Illinois Department of Public Aid, the director of the Cook County Department of Public Aid, and the comptroller of Cook County. Respondent alleged that these state officials were administering the federal-state programs of Aid to the Aged, Blind, or Disabled (AABD) in a manner inconsistent with various federal regulations and with the Fourteenth Amendment to the Constitution.

AABD is one of the categorical aid programs administered by the Illinois Department of Public Aid pursuant to the Illinois Public Aid Code. Under the Social Security Act, the program is funded by the State and the Federal Governments. The Department of Health, Education, and Welfare (HEW), which administers these payments for the Federal Government, issued regulations prescribing maximum permissible time standards within which States participating in the program had to process AABD applications. Those regulations, originally issued in 1968, required, at the time of the institution of this suit, that eligibility determinations must be made by the States within 30 days of receipt of applications for aid to the aged and blind, and within 45 days of receipt of applications for aid to the disabled. For those persons found eligible, the assistance check was required to be received by them within the applicable time period.

During the period in which the federal regulations went into effect, Illinois public aid officials were administering the benefits pursuant to their own regulations as provided in the Categorical Assistance Manual of the Illinois Department of Public Aid. Respondent's complaint charged that the Illinois defendants, operating under those regulations, were improperly authorizing

---

3. A question about the proper scope of Ex parte Young is raised by Seminole Tribe v. Florida, 115 S.Ct. 932, pending in the Supreme Court as this edition went to press. The case, discussed at p. 1102, note 11, *infra,* involves an injunction action brought by the Tribe against both the state of Florida and its Governor under the Indian Gaming Regulatory Act. The principal issue presented is whether Congress could, and did, abrogate state sovereign immunity from such a suit, but another significant issue is whether the suit can in any event stand as an action against a state official under the doctrine of Ex parte Young. The court of appeals (11 F.3d 1016 (11th Cir.1994)) held that it could not, in part because federal courts exercising jurisdiction under the Young doctrine "cannot compel discretionary acts" of the kind the Tribe was seeking (*i.e.,* negotiation by the state), and in part because the suit was, in substance, directed against the state itself. See *id.* at 1028–29.

Is either of these grounds consistent with the Young decision?

grants to commence only with the month in which an application was approved and not including prior eligibility months for which an applicant was entitled to aid under federal law. The complaint also alleged that the Illinois defendants were not processing the applications within the applicable time requirements of the federal regulations; specifically, respondent alleged that his own application for disability benefits was not acted on by the Illinois Department of Public Aid for almost four months. Such actions of the Illinois officials were alleged to violate federal law and deny the equal protection of the laws. Respondent's prayer requested declaratory and injunctive relief, and specifically requested "a permanent injunction enjoining the defendants to award to the entire class of plaintiffs all AABD benefits wrongfully withheld."

In its judgment of March 15, 1972, the District Court declared § 4004 of the Illinois Manual to be invalid insofar as it was inconsistent with the federal regulations found in 45 CFR § 206.10(a)(3), and granted a permanent injunction requiring compliance with the federal time limits for processing and paying AABD applicants. The District Court, in paragraph 5 of its judgment, also ordered the state officials to "release and remit AABD benefits wrongfully withheld to all applicants for AABD in the State of Illinois who applied between July 1, 1968 [the date of the federal regulations] and April 16, 197[1] [the date of the preliminary injunction issued by the District Court] and were determined eligible * * *."

* * * [The court of appeals rejected defendants' argument that the Eleventh Amendment barred the award of retroactive benefits, and affirmed the district court judgment.]

* * * Because we believe the Court of Appeals erred in its disposition of the Eleventh Amendment claim, we reverse that portion of the Court of Appeals decision which affirmed the District Court's order that retroactive benefits be paid by the Illinois state officials.

* * *

While the Amendment by its terms does not bar suits against a State by its own citizens, this Court has consistently held that an unconsenting State is immune from suits brought in federal courts by her own citizens as well as by citizens of another State. It is also well established that even though a State is not named a party to the action, the suit may nonetheless be barred by the Eleventh Amendment. In Ford Motor Co. v. Department of Treasury, 323 U.S. 459 (1945), the Court said:

"[W]hen the action is in essence one for the recovery of money from the state, the state is the real, substantial party in interest and is entitled to invoke its sovereign immunity from suit even though individual officials are nominal defendants." *Id.,* at 464.

Thus the rule has evolved that a suit by private parties seeking to impose a liability which must be paid from public funds in the state treasury is barred by the Eleventh Amendment. Kennecott Copper Corp. v. State Tax Comm'n, 327 U.S. 573 (1946).

* * *

Petitioner concedes that Ex parte Young is no bar to that part of the District Court's judgment that prospectively enjoined petitioner's predecessors from failing to process applications within the time limits established by the federal regulations. Petitioner argues, however, that Ex parte Young does not extend so far as to permit a suit which seeks the award of an accrued monetary liability which must be met from the general revenues of a State, absent consent or waiver by the State of its Eleventh Amendment immunity, and that therefore the award of retroactive benefits by the District Court was improper.

Ex parte Young was a watershed case in which this Court held that the Eleventh Amendment did not bar an action in the federal courts seeking to enjoin the Attorney General of Minnesota from enforcing a statute claimed to violate the Fourteenth Amendment of the United States Constitution. This holding has permitted the Civil War Amendments to the Constitution to serve as a sword, rather than merely as a shield, for those whom they were designed to protect. But the relief awarded in Ex parte Young was prospective only; the Attorney General of Minnesota was enjoined to conform his future conduct of that office to the requirement of the Fourteenth Amendment. Such relief is analogous to that awarded by the District Court in the prospective portion of its order under review in this case.

But the retroactive portion of the District Court's order here, which requires the payment of a very substantial amount of money which that court held should have been paid, but was not, stands on quite a different footing. These funds will obviously not be paid out of the pocket of petitioner Edelman. * * *

* * *

The Court of Appeals, in upholding the award in this case, held that it was permissible because it was in the form of "equitable restitution" instead of damages, and therefore capable of being tailored in such a way as to minimize disruptions of the state program of categorical assistance. But we must judge the award actually made in this case, and not one which might have been differently tailored in a different case, and we must judge it in the context of the important constitutional principle embodied in the Eleventh Amendment.[11]

We do not read Ex parte Young or subsequent holdings of this Court to indicate that any form of relief may be awarded against a state officer, no matter how closely it may in practice resemble a money judgment payable out of the state treasury, so long as the relief may be labeled "equitable" in nature. The Court's opinion in Ex parte Young hewed to no such line. Its citation of Hagood v. Southern, 117 U.S. 52 (1886), and In re Ayers, 123 U.S. 443 (1887), which were both actions against state officers for specific performance of a contract to which the State was a party, demonstrate that equitable relief may be barred by the Eleventh Amendment.

As in most areas of the law, the difference between the type of relief barred by the Eleventh Amendment and that permitted under Ex parte Young will not in many instances be that between day and night. The injunction issued in Ex

---

11. It may be true, as stated by our Brother Douglas in dissent, that "[m]ost welfare decisions by federal courts have a financial impact on the States." But we cannot agree that such a financial impact is the same where a federal court applies Ex parte Young to grant prospective declaratory and injunctive relief, as opposed to an order of retroactive payments as was made in the instant case. * * * [W]here the State has a defina-ble allocation to be used in the payment of public aid benefits, and pursues a certain course of action such as the processing of applications within certain time periods as did Illinois here, the subsequent ordering by a federal court of retroactive payments to correct delays in such processing will invariably mean there is less money available for payments for the continuing obligations of the public aid system. * * *

parte Young was not totally without effect on the State's revenues, since the state law which the Attorney General was enjoined from enforcing provided substantial monetary penalties against railroads which did not conform to its provisions. Later cases from this Court have authorized equitable relief which has probably had greater impact on state treasuries than did that awarded in Ex parte Young. * * * But the fiscal consequences to state treasuries in these cases were the necessary result of compliance with decrees which by their terms were prospective in nature. State officials, in order to shape their official conduct to the mandate of the Court's decrees, would more likely have to spend money from the state treasury than if they had been left free to pursue their previous course of conduct. Such an ancillary effect on the state treasury is a permissible and often an inevitable consequence of the principle announced in Ex parte Young, *supra*.

But that portion of the District Court's decree which petitioner challenges on Eleventh Amendment grounds goes much further than any of the cases cited. It requires payment of state funds, not as a necessary consequence of compliance in the future with a substantive federal-question determination, but as a form of compensation to those whose applications were processed on the slower time schedule at a time when petitioner was under no court-imposed obligation to conform to a different standard. While the Court of Appeals described this retroactive award of monetary relief as a form of "equitable restitution," it is in practical effect indistinguishable in many aspects from an award of damages against the State. It will to a virtual certainty be paid from state funds, and not from the pockets of the individual state officials who were the defendants in the action. It is measured in terms of a monetary loss resulting from a past breach of a legal duty on the part of the defendant state officials.

Were we to uphold this portion of the District Court's decree, we would be obligated to overrule the Court's holding in Ford Motor Co. v. Department of Treasury, *supra*. There a taxpayer, who had, under protest, paid taxes to the State of Indiana, sought a refund of those taxes from the Indiana state officials who were charged with their collection. The taxpayer claimed that the tax had been imposed in violation of the United States Constitution. The term "equitable restitution" would seem even more applicable to the relief sought in that case, since the taxpayer had at one time had the money, and paid it over to the State pursuant to an allegedly unconstitutional tax exaction. Yet this Court had no hesitation in holding that the taxpayer's action was a suit against the State, and barred by the Eleventh Amendment. We reach a similar conclusion with respect to the retroactive portion of the relief awarded by the District Court in this case.

The Court of Appeals held in the alternative that even if the Eleventh Amendment be deemed a bar to the retroactive relief awarded respondent in this case, the State of Illinois had waived its Eleventh Amendment immunity and consented to the bringing of such a suit by participating in the federal AABD program. The Court of Appeals relied upon our holdings in Parden v. Terminal R. Co., 377 U.S. 184 (1964), and Petty v. Tennessee–Missouri Bridge Comm'n, 359 U.S. 275 (1959) * * *. The question of waiver or consent under the Eleventh Amendment was found in those cases to turn on whether Congress had intended to abrogate the immunity in question, and whether the State by its participation in the program authorized by Congress had in effect consented to the abrogation of that immunity.

But in this case the threshold fact of congressional authorization to sue a class of defendants which literally includes States is wholly absent. Thus respondent is [precluded from relying on those decisions] * * *.

The Court of Appeals held that as a matter of federal law Illinois had "constructively consented" to this suit by participating in the federal AABD program and agreeing to administer federal and state funds in compliance with federal law. Constructive consent is not a doctrine commonly associated with the surrender of constitutional rights, and we see no place for it here. In deciding whether a State has waived its constitutional protection under the Eleventh Amendment, we will find waiver only where stated "by the most express language or by such overwhelming implications from the text as [will] leave no room for any other reasonable construction." Murray v. Wilson Distilling Co., 213 U.S. 151, 171 (1909).

The mere fact that a State participates in a program through which the Federal Government provides assistance for the operation by the State of a system of public aid is not sufficient to establish consent on the part of the State to be sued in the federal courts. And while this Court has, in cases such as J.I. Case Co. v. Borak, 377 U.S. 426 (1964), authorized suits by one private party against another in order to effectuate a statutory purpose, it has never done so in the context of the Eleventh Amendment and a state defendant. Since [Employees v. Department of Public Health and Welfare, 411 U.S. 279 (1973)], where Congress had expressly authorized suits against a general class of defendants and the only thing left to implication was whether the described class of defendants included States, was decided adversely to the putative plaintiffs on the waiver question, surely this respondent must also fail on that issue. The only language in the Social Security Act which purported to provide a federal sanction against a State which did not comply with federal requirements for the distribution of federal monies was found in former 42 U.S.C. § 1384 (now replaced by substantially similar provisions in 42 U.S.C. § 804), which provided for termination of future allocations of federal funds when a participating State failed to conform with federal law. This provision by its terms did not authorize suit against anyone, and standing alone, fell far short of a waiver by a participating State of its Eleventh Amendment immunity.

Our Brother Marshall argues in dissent, and the Court of Appeals held, that although the Social Security Act itself does not create a private cause of action, the cause of action created by 42 U.S.C. § 1983, coupled with the enactment of the AABD program, and the issuance by HEW of regulations which require the States to make corrective payments after successful "fair hearings" and provide for federal matching funds to satisfy federal court orders of retroactive payments, indicate that Congress intended a cause of action for public aid recipients such as respondent. It is, of course, true that Rosado v. Wyman, 397 U.S. 397 (1970), held that suits in federal court under § 1983 are proper to secure compliance with the provisions of the Social Security Act on the part of participating States. But it has not heretofore been suggested that § 1983 was intended to create a waiver of a State's Eleventh Amendment immunity merely because an action could be brought under that section against state officers, rather than against the State itself. * * *

Respondent urges that since the various Illinois officials sued in the District Court failed to raise the Eleventh Amendment as a defense to the relief sought by respondent, petitioner is therefore barred[19] from raising the Eleventh Amendment defense in the Court of Appeals or in this Court.   The Court of Appeals apparently felt the defense was properly presented, and dealt with it on the merits.   We approve of this resolution, since it has been well settled since the decision in Ford Motor Co. v. Department of Treasury, *supra,* that the Eleventh Amendment defense sufficiently partakes of the nature of a jurisdictional bar so that it need not be raised in the trial court.   * * *

For the foregoing reasons we decide that the Court of Appeals was wrong in holding that the Eleventh Amendment did not constitute a bar to that portion of the District Court decree which ordered retroactive payment of benefits found to have been wrongfully withheld.   The judgment of the Court of Appeals is therefore reversed and the cause remanded for further proceedings consistent with this opinion.

So ordered.

■ Mr. Justice Douglas, dissenting.

* * *

■ Mr. Justice Brennan, dissenting.

This suit is brought by Illinois citizens against Illinois officials.   In that circumstance, Illinois may not invoke the Eleventh Amendment, since that Amendment bars only federal court suits against States by citizens of other States.   Rather the question is whether Illinois may avail itself of the nonconstitutional but ancient doctrine of sovereign immunity as a bar to respondent's claim for retroactive AABD payments.   In my view Illinois may not assert sovereign immunity for the reason I expressed in dissent in Employees v. Department of Public Health and Welfare, 411 U.S. 279, 298 (1973): the States surrendered that immunity in Hamilton's words, "in the plan of the Convention," that formed the Union, at least insofar as the States granted Congress specifically enumerated powers.   See *id.,* at 319 n. 7.   Congressional authority to enact the Social Security Act, of which AABD is a part, is to be found in Art. I, § 8, cl. 1, one of the enumerated powers granted Congress by the States in the Constitution.   I remain of the opinion that "because of its surrender, no immunity exists that can be the subject of a congressional declaration or a voluntary waiver," 411 U.S., at 300, and thus have no occasion to inquire whether or not Congress authorized an action for AABD retroactive benefits, or whether or not Illinois voluntarily waived the immunity by its continued participation in the program against the background of precedents which sustained judgments ordering retroactive payments.

I would affirm the judgment of the Court of Appeals.

■ Mr. Justice Marshall, with whom Mr. Justice Blackmun joins, dissenting.

The Social Security Act's categorical assistance programs, including the Aid to the Aged, Blind, or Disabled (AABD) program involved here, are fundamentally different from most federal legislation.   * * * [This] Act seeks to induce state participation in the federal welfare programs by offering federal matching funds in exchange for the State's voluntary assumption of the Act's require-

---

19. Respondent urges that the State of Illinois has abolished its common-law sovereign immunity in its state courts * * *. Whether Illinois permits such a suit to be brought against the State in its own courts is not determinative of whether Illinois has relinquished its Eleventh Amendment immunity from suit in the federal courts.   Chandler v. Dix, 194 U.S. 590, 591–592 (1904).

ments. I find this basic distinction crucial: it leads me to conclude that by
participation in the programs, the States waive whatever immunity they might
otherwise have from federal court orders requiring retroactive payment of
welfare benefits.

* * *

In agreeing to comply with the requirements of the Social Security Act and
HEW regulations, I believe that Illinois has also agreed to subject itself to suit
in the federal courts to enforce these obligations. I recognize, of course, that
the Social Security Act does not itself provide for a cause of action to enforce its
obligations. As the Court points out, the only sanction expressly provided in
the Act for a participating State's failure to comply with federal requirements is
the cutoff of federal funding by the Secretary of HEW.

But a cause of action is clearly provided by 42 U.S.C. § 1983, which in
terms authorizes suits to redress deprivations of rights secured by the "laws"
of the United States. And we have already rejected the argument that
Congress intended the funding cutoff to be the sole remedy for noncompliance
with federal requirements. In Rosado v. Wyman, 397 U.S. 397, 420–423
(1970), we held that suits in federal court under § 1983 were proper to enforce
the provisions of the Social Security Act against participating States.

* * *

I believe that Congress also intended the full panoply of traditional judicial
remedies to be available to the federal courts in these § 1983 suits. There is
surely no indication of any congressional intent to restrict the courts' equitable
jurisdiction. Yet the Court has held that "[u]nless a statute in so many words,
or by a necessary and inescapable inference, restricts the court's jurisdiction in
equity, the full scope of that jurisdiction is to be recognized and applied."
Porter v. Warner Holding Co., 328 U.S. 395, 398 (1946).

* * *

In particular, I am firmly convinced that Congress intended the restitution of
wrongfully withheld assistance payments to be a remedy available to the
federal courts in these suits. * * * No other remedy can effectively deter
States from the strong temptation to cut welfare budgets by circumventing the
stringent requirements of federal law. The funding cutoff is a drastic sanction,
one which HEW has proved unwilling or unable to employ to compel strict
compliance with the Act and regulations. See Rosado v. Wyman, *supra,* 397
U.S., at 426. Moreover, the cutoff operates only prospectively; it in no way
deters the States from even a flagrant violation of the Act's requirements for as
long as HEW does not discover the violation and threaten to take such action.

* * *

I have no quarrel with the Court's view that waiver of constitutional rights
should not lightly be inferred. But I simply cannot believe that the State could
have entered into this essentially contractual agreement with the Federal
Government without recognizing that it was subjecting itself to the full scope of
the § 1983 remedy provided by Congress to enforce the terms of the agreement.

* * *

A finding of waiver here is also consistent with the reasoning of the majority in
Employees [v. Department of Public Health and Welfare], which relied on a

distinction between "governmental" and "proprietary" functions of state government. This distinction apparently recognizes that if sovereign immunity is to be at all meaningful, the Court must be reluctant to hold a State to have waived its immunity simply by acting in its sovereign capacity—*i.e.*, by merely performing its "governmental" functions. On the other hand, in launching a profitmaking enterprise, "a State leaves the sphere that is exclusively its own," Parden v. Terminal R. Co., 377 U.S., at 196, and a voluntary waiver of sovereign immunity can more easily be found. While conducting an assistance program for the needy is surely a "governmental" function, the State here has done far more than operate its own program in its sovereign capacity. It has voluntarily subordinated its sovereignty in this matter to that of the Federal Government, and agreed to comply with the conditions imposed by Congress upon the expenditure of federal funds. In entering this federal-state cooperative program, the State again "leaves the sphere that is exclusively its own," and similarly may more readily be found to have voluntarily waived its immunity. * * *

NOTE ON THE KINDS OF RELIEF PERMITTED
IN SUITS AGAINST STATE OFFICERS

(1) *Some Questions About the Edelman Decision.* Consider the Court's statement that officers have always been immune from suits "seeking to impose a liability which must be paid from public funds in the state treasury." Prior federal cases had issued writs ordering state officials to perform ministerial duties—the traditional office of the writ of mandamus[1]—and some writs of mandamus issued against *federal* officials had required payments from the federal treasury.[2] Should Edelman be read to bar mandamus requiring state officers to perform ministerial duties that involve the payment of public funds? Why should a state have an immunity that is broader in this respect than that of the United States?

Would Edelman permit a bondholder to obtain an order, under the Contracts Clause, requiring officials of a state that passed legislation unconstitutionally repudiating bonds to make payments due *in the future? Cf.* Georgia R.R. & Banking Co. v. Redwine, 342 U.S. 299 (1952), p. 1065, *supra.*

A suit nominally against an unconsenting state itself (rather than an officer) is barred regardless of the kind of relief sought. See, *e.g.,* Alabama v. Pugh, 438 U.S. 781 (1978)(per curiam). What justifies making federal court jurisdiction over the claim for prospective relief in Edelman depend on whether the named defendant is the Illinois Department of Public Aid or its director?

(2) *The Prospective–Retrospective Distinction.* In Milliken v. Bradley, 433 U.S. 267 (1977)(Milliken II), after the Supreme Court had disapproved an interdistrict busing remedy to desegregate the Detroit schools, the district court ordered the provision of remedial education for pupils and in-service training for teachers and administrators, as well as the hiring of more counselors. The

---

1. See, *e.g.,* Board of Liquidation v. McComb, 92 U.S. 531 (1875); Tindal v. Wesley, 167 U.S. 204 (1897); Rolston v. Missouri Fund Comm'rs, 120 U.S. 390 (1887).

2. See, *e.g.,* Kendall v. United States, 37 U.S. (12 Pet.) 524 (1838), p. 997, note 4, *supra;* Roberts v. United States ex rel. Valentine, 176 U.S. 221 (1900).

state, which shared responsibility for the segregation, was ordered to pay half the cost of these programs; though the order ran only against state officials, it contemplated payment from the state treasury. The Supreme Court unanimously held that the decree "fits squarely within the prospective-compliance exception reaffirmed by Edelman. * * * The educational components * * * are plainly designed to wipe out continuing conditions of inequality produced by the inherently unequal dual school system long maintained by Detroit.

"* * * That the programs are also 'compensatory' in nature does not change the fact that they are part of a plan that operates *prospectively* to bring about the delayed benefits of a unitary school system" (pp. 289–90).

Wasn't the decree in Milliken II just as much an effort to redress past violations as the retroactive benefits in Edelman? Is Milliken distinguishable because the order required the state to purchase services for (rather than to pay cash to) the plaintiffs? Because the payments in Milliken would be made over a long period, giving more time for budgetary planning? Because of the continuing effects of past violations?[3] (Might not indigent beneficiaries in Edelman have been suffering continuing effects of previous denials of benefits?)

Does it help, in understanding Milliken II, to recall the history of the Supreme Court's efforts to eradicate school desegregation? Is it pertinent that the order that was upheld took the place of an earlier multidistrict busing order? Would that earlier order have been "prospective"?

(3) *Attorney's Fees Awards.* In Hutto v. Finney, 437 U.S. 678 (1978), after finding that the Arkansas penal system constituted cruel and unusual punishment and issuing various injunctive orders over the course of seven years, the district court ruled that defendant officials had acted in bad faith and ordered them to pay $20,000 "out of Department of Correction funds" to plaintiffs' attorneys. In upholding that fee award, the Supreme Court stressed the importance of enforcing federal court orders, and held (p. 691) that "[t]he power to impose a fine is properly treated as ancillary to the federal court's power to impose injunctive relief. In this case, the award of attorney's fees for bad faith served the same purpose as a remedial fine imposed for civil contempt. It vindicated the District Court's authority over a recalcitrant litigant." The Court also observed that the compensatory effect of the award did not distinguish it from a fine for civil contempt, and the award was not so large "that it interfered with the State's budgeting process" (p. 691 & n. 17). In a footnote (p. 692 n. 19), the Court added: "We do not understand the Attorney General to urge that the fees should have been awarded against the officers personally; that would be a remarkable way to treat individuals who have relied on the Attorney General to represent their interests throughout this litigation."

In dissent, Justice Rehnquist (joined by Justice White) argued that the injunction could have been enforced by fining the defendant officials personally, and noted that state law provided for reimbursement at least in some cases.

Hutto also upheld a second award of attorneys' fees on the distinct theory that Congress, in authorizing fee awards to plaintiffs prevailing in actions

---

3. In Papasan v. Allain, 478 U.S. 265 (1986), Mississippi officials were sued for allegedly underfunding certain public schools. The Court held, 5–4, that a theory of recovery based on a long-standing and continuing breach of trust was barred by the Eleventh Amendment, but held unanimously that another theory—that the State's *current* school funding methods constituted an invalid denial of equal protection—was not barred.

under federal civil rights legislation, had abrogated any Eleventh Amendment immunity. See p. 1101, *infra*. But in so ruling, the Court noted that "[c]osts have traditionally been awarded without regard for the States' Eleventh Amendment immunity," and though the precedents predate Edelman, such awards "do not seriously strain" the retrospective/prospective distinction; "[w]hen a State defends a suit for prospective relief, it is not exempt from the ordinary discipline of the courtroom" (p. 695 & n. 24).[4]

Is Hutto consistent with Edelman? With the treatment (see pp. 1006–07, *supra*) of attorney's fees in suits against the United States?

(4) *The Aftermath of Edelman: The Quern and Green Decisions.*

(a) After the Edelman case was remanded, the defendant state officials were ordered "to send a mere explanatory notice to members of the plaintiff class advising them that there are state administrative procedures available by which they are entitled to past welfare benefits." In Quern v. Jordan, 440 U.S. 332 (1979), the Supreme Court unanimously held (pp. 347–49) that "this relief falls on the Ex Parte Young side of the Eleventh Amendment line rather than on the Edelman side. Petitioner makes no issue of the incidental administrative expense connected with preparing and mailing the notice. Instead, he argues that giving the proposed notice will lead inexorably to the payment of state funds for retroactive benefits and therefore it, in effect, amounts to a monetary award. But the chain of causation which petitioners seek to establish is by no means unbroken * * *. The notice * * * simply apprises plaintiff class members of the existence of whatever administrative procedures may already be available under state law * * *. * * * Whether a recipient of notice decides to take advantage of those available state procedures is left completely to [the recipient's] discretion * * *. And whether or not the class member will receive retroactive benefits rests entirely with the State, * * * not with the federal court.

"The notice * * * is more properly viewed as ancillary to the prospective relief already ordered by the court. See Milliken v. Bradley * * *. The notice in effect simply informs class members that their federal suit is at an end, that the federal court can provide them with no further relief, and that there are existing state administrative procedures which they may wish to pursue."

(b) Green v. Mansour, 474 U.S. 64 (1985), was an action similar to Edelman. The plaintiff class sued the state Director of Social Services, alleging underpayment of AFDC benefits in violation of federal law. While the suit was pending in the district court, Congress modified the program and the state came into compliance with federal law. In these circumstances, the Supreme Court, per Rehnquist, J., ruled that plaintiffs' request for a declaratory judgment that the defendant's past conduct violated federal law, and for notice relief (as in Quern), was barred by the Eleventh Amendment (p. 427): "[A] request for a limited notice order will escape the Eleventh Amendment bar if the notice is ancillary to the grant of some other appropriate relief that can be

---

4. See also Missouri v. Jenkins, 491 U.S. 274 (1989)(ruling that the Eleventh Amendment does not prohibit enhancement of a fee award assessed against a state under 42 U.S.C. § 1988 in order to compensate for delay in payment). Justice O'Connor, dissenting in Jenkins, relied on the post-Hutto decision in Library of Congress v. Shaw, 478 U.S. 310 (1986), construing a statute authorizing fee awards against the federal government as not permitting enhancement of fees to compensate for delay. The majority in Jenkins distinguished Shaw by brute force, asserting that it "has no application, even by analogy" (p. 281).

'noticed.'" Injunctive relief could no longer be issued, the Court observed, because the state had come into compliance with the statute as amended; consequently, notice relief could be granted only as ancillary to a declaratory judgment. But to issue a federal court declaratory judgment as a step toward a state court damage remedy would be an "'end run' around our decision in Edelman v. Jordan" (p. 428).

Justice Brennan, joined by Justices Marshall, Blackmun, and Stevens, dissented, arguing that in Green, as in Quern, any "use of the declaratory judgment in the State's courts is * * * left completely to the discretion of individual notice recipients and the award of retroactive benefits 'rests entirely with the State * * *'" (p. 430, quoting Quern, 440 U.S. at 348). Nor could Quern be distinguished as involving notice relief ancillary to an injunction, for (as the Court in Quern had recognized) that injunction had been mooted by Congress' abolition of the program at issue in Quern three years before the notice relief was issued.

In light of the decisions since Edelman, how stable or coherent is the line between permissible and impermissible relief in suits against state officers? See generally Currie, *Sovereign Immunity and Suits Against Government Officers,* 1984 Sup.Ct.Rev. 149.

(5) *State Court Actions.* The Eleventh Amendment does not apply to actions in state courts. See Maine v. Thiboutot, 448 U.S. 1, 9 n. 7 (1980); Nevada v. Hall, 440 U.S. 410 (1979), p. 1056, *supra.* Is it the implication of the Court's dicta in Hans, of its opinion in Quern, and of the dissenting opinions in Green, that the state courts are free to refuse, on the ground of state sovereign immunity, to award retroactive benefits even if a claimant could establish that their denial violated federal law?[5] Would such a refusal be consistent with the decisions in Ward, McKesson, Reich, and Crain (pp. 847, 851, 852, 855, *supra*)?

Is it possible to view the Eleventh Amendment as being, in effect, a forum choice provision, which merely permits the states to resist *federal court* jurisdiction over suits (even if nominally against officials) seeking retrospective relief— while leaving the state courts obliged, under the Supremacy Clause, to provide such relief in suits under federal law? See, *e.g.,* Employees of Dep't of Pub. Health & Welfare v. Department of Pub. Health & Welfare, 411 U.S. 279, 291– 94 (1973)(Marshall, J., concurring in the result); *cf.* Atascadero State Hosp. v. Scanlon, 473 U.S. 234, 238–40 n. 2 (1985). See generally Wolcher, *Sovereign Immunity and the Supremacy Clause: Damages Against States in Their Own Courts for Constitutional Violations,* 69 Calif.L.Rev. 189 (1981).

(6) *The Relevance of Indemnification Agreements in Suits Against State Officers.* Under Edelman, the Eleventh Amendment does not bar judgments for monetary relief to be paid by an official personally. (Distinct doctrines establishing official immunities, however, will make such relief difficult to obtain. See Sec. 3, *infra.*) Can the state, by providing for indemnification of officials for such judgments, transform such actions into suits against the state that are barred by the Eleventh Amendment? Most courts have held not. See, *e.g.,*

---

5. After the decision in Quern v. Jordan, class members who filed state court actions for past benefits obtained a judgment in their favor and were ultimately paid. See Lichtenstein, *Retroactive Relief in the Federal Courts Since Edelman v. Jordan: A Trip Through the Twilight Zone,* 32 Case W.Res. L.Rev. 364, 375 n. 73 (1982).

Demery v. Kupperman, 735 F.2d 1139, 1146–48 (9th Cir.1984), and cases cited; Jackson v. Georgia Dep't of Transp., 16 F.3d 1573 (11th Cir.1994).

NOTE ON THE PENNHURST CASE AND THE BEARING OF
THE ELEVENTH AMENDMENT ON FEDERAL COURT
RELIEF FOR VIOLATIONS OF STATE LAW

(1) *The Facts and Opinions in the Pennhurst Case.* In Pennhurst State School & Hosp. v. Halderman, 465 U.S. 89 (1984), the Supreme Court sharply restricted the reach of federal court jurisdiction in suits against state officials for violations of state law. In this case, a resident of a Pennsylvania state institution for the mentally retarded (Pennhurst) filed a federal class action against the institution and various state and county officials, alleging that conditions at Pennhurst violated federal statutory and constitutional requirements, as well as the state's Mental Health and Mental Retardation Act of 1966 (the "MH/MR Act").[1] The district judge held that conditions at Pennhurst contravened state law, federal statutory requirements, and the federal Constitution, and that the mentally retarded who were cared for by the state were constitutionally entitled to live in "the least restrictive setting" consistent with their rehabilitative needs. The defendants were ordered, among other things, to close Pennhurst as soon as practicable and to provide "suitable community living arrangements" for the residents. A special master was appointed to implement the decision.

The Third Circuit upheld the decision on the merits, but rested its conclusion (that treatment must be afforded in the least restrictive setting) exclusively on the federal Developmentally Disabled Assistance and Bill of Rights Act. It also affirmed the district court's remedial order except insofar as it decreed that Pennhurst itself be closed.

On its initial review in 1981, the Supreme Court held that the federal statutory provisions relied on by the courts below did not create any substantive rights. Pennhurst State School & Hosp. v. Halderman, 451 U.S. 1 (1981). The case was remanded for a determination whether the remedial order could be supported under other provisions of state or federal law. On remand, the Third Circuit en banc affirmed its prior judgment, ruling that the state's MH/MR Act required placement of residents in the least restrictive setting.

In 1984, the Supreme Court again reversed, holding (5–4) that the Eleventh Amendment barred relief based on state law. 465 U.S. 89. Justice Powell wrote for the Court (pp. 101–06; some paragraphing omitted):

"The Eleventh Amendment bars a suit against state officials when 'the state is the real substantial party in interest.' Thus, '[t]he general rule is that relief sought nominally against an officer is in fact against the sovereign if the decree would operate against the latter.' Hawaii v. Gordon, 373 U.S. 57, 58 (1963)(per curiam).[11] * * *

---

1. The statement of facts is derived from Shapiro, *Wrong Turns: The Eleventh Amendment and the Pennhurst Case,* 98 Harv.L.Rev. 61 (1984).

11. "Respondents * * * suggest * * * that the suit here should not be considered to be against the State * * * because * * * petitioners were acting ultra vires their authority. * * * Larson v. Domestic & Foreign

"The Court has recognized an important exception to this general rule: a suit challenging the constitutionality of a state official's action is not one against the State. This was the holding in Ex parte Young * * *. The theory of the case was that an unconstitutional enactment is 'void' and therefore does not 'impart to [the officer] any immunity from responsibility to the supreme authority of the United States.' Since the State could not authorize the action, the officer was 'stripped of his official or representative character and [was] subjected to the consequences of his individual conduct.' * * * [T]he Young doctrine has been accepted as necessary to permit the federal courts to vindicate federal rights and hold state officials responsible to 'the supreme authority of the United States.' Young, *supra,* at 160. * * *

"The Court also has recognized, however, that the need to promote the supremacy of federal law must be accommodated to the constitutional immunity of the States. This is the significance of Edelman v. Jordan * * *, [where] we declined to extend the fiction of Young to encompass retroactive relief, for to do so would effectively eliminate the constitutional immunity of the States. * * *

"This need to reconcile competing interests is wholly absent, however, when a plaintiff alleges that a state official has violated *state* law. * * * [Relief in such a case] does not vindicate the supreme authority of federal law. On the contrary, it is difficult to think of a greater intrusion on state sovereignty than when a federal court instructs state officials on how to conform their conduct to state law. Such a result conflicts directly with the principles of federalism that underlie the Eleventh Amendment. We conclude that Young and Edelman are inapplicable in a suit against state officials on the basis of state law."

According to Justice Powell, the view of the dissenters that in Pennhurst, as in Ex parte Young, the officer's wrong stripped him of his official character, making the suit one against him personally rather than against the state, "would make the law a pretense. * * * And the dissent's underlying view that the named defendants here were acting beyond and contrary to their authority cannot be reconciled with reality—or with the record. The District Court in this case held that the individual defendants 'acted in the utmost good faith * * * *within the sphere of their official responsibilities*' and therefore were entitled to immunity from damages" (p. 107).

Justice Powell then considered a wealth of nineteenth and early twentieth century precedents on which the dissenters relied. Most, he argued, were distinguishable. Two other cases alleged only common law torts, not violations of state statutes, and "were explicitly" overruled in Larson v. Domestic & Foreign Commerce Corp., 337 U.S. 682 (1949), p. 1017, *supra.* Only one decision, he concluded, clearly held injunctive relief against state officials for failing to carry out their duties under state statutes to be consistent with the Eleventh Amendment—Rolston v. Missouri Fund Comm'rs, 120 U.S. 390 (1887)—and that case ordered compliance with a plain ministerial duty. In

Commerce Corp., 337 U.S. 682 (1949) [p. 1017, *supra,*] * * * and other modern cases make clear that a state officer may be said to act ultra vires only when he acts 'without any authority whatever.' * * * 'A claim of error in the exercise of [delegated] power is * * * not sufficient.' Larson, *supra,* at 690. Petitioners' actions in operating this mental

health institution plainly were not beyond their delegated authority in this sense. The MH/MR Act gave them broad discretion to provide 'adequate' mental health services. * * * The essence of respondents' claim is that petitioners have not provided such services adequately. * * *"

Justice Powell's view, analogous cases involving the sovereign immunity of the United States, though far from uniform, "make clear that suit may not be predicated on violations of state statutes that command purely discretionary duties. Since it cannot be doubted that the statutes at issue here gave petitioners broad discretion in operating Pennhurst, * * * the conduct alleged in this case would not be ultra vires even under the standards of the dissent's cases" (pp. 109–11 & nn. 18–20). He continued (pp. 111–14):

"Thus, while there is language in the early cases that advances the authority-stripping theory advocated by the dissent, this theory had never been pressed as far as Justice Stevens would do in this case. And when the expansive approach of the dissent was advanced, this Court plainly and explicitly rejected it. In Larson, the Court was faced with the argument that an allegation that a government official committed a tort sufficed to distinguish the official from the sovereign. * * * The Court rejected the argument, noting that it would make the doctrine of sovereign immunity superfluous. A plaintiff would need only to 'claim an invasion of his legal rights' in order to override sovereign immunity. In the court's view the argument 'confuse[d] the doctrine of sovereign immunity with the requirement that a plaintiff state a cause of action.' *Id.*, at 692–93. * * *25"

The Court then discussed the impact of its ruling on the doctrine of pendent jurisdiction:

"As the Court of Appeals noted, in Siler [v. Louisville & N.R.R., 213 U.S. 175 (1909)] and subsequent cases concerning pendent jurisdiction, relief was granted against state officials on the basis of state-law claims that were pendent to federal constitutional claims. In none of these cases, however, did the Court so much as mention the Eleventh Amendment in connection with the state-law claim" (p. 118). As for plaintiffs' argument that the Court's ruling "may cause litigants to split causes of action between state and federal courts" and could undercut the policy of constitutional avoidance by denying federal courts the opportunity to premise relief on state law grounds, Justice Powell responded that pendent jurisdiction was a "judge-made doctrine of expediency and efficiency," and that "neither pendent jurisdiction nor any other basis of jurisdiction may override the Eleventh Amendment" (pp. 120–21).

Justice Stevens, joined by Justices Brennan, Marshall, and Blackmun, filed an unusually long and bitter dissent. He noted (p. 126) that the Court was reversing the Third Circuit for having done, on remand from Pennhurst I, "precisely what this Court ordered it to do"—*i.e.*, for premising its remedial order on state law. After asserting (p. 127) that the Court's decision repudiated "at least 28 cases, spanning well over a century of this Court's jurisprudence," he continued (pp. 130–32):

"The majority proceeds as if this Court has not had previous occasion to consider the Eleventh Amendment argument made by petitioners, and contends that Ex parte Young, 209 U.S. 123 (1908), has no application to a suit seeking injunctive relief on the basis of state law. That is simply not the case. The

---

25. "We have noted that the authority-stripping theory of Young is a fiction that has been narrowly construed. In this light, it may well be wondered what principled basis there is to the ultra vires doctrine as it was set forth in Larson * * *. * * * For present purposes, however, we do no more than question the continued vitality of the ultra vires doctrine in the Eleventh Amendment context. We hold only that to the extent the doctrine is consistent with the analysis of this opinion, it is a very narrow exception that will allow suit only under the standards set forth in n. 11, *supra*."

Court rejected the argument that the Eleventh Amendment precludes injunctive relief on the basis of state law twice only two Terms ago. In Florida Dept. of State v. Treasure Salvors, Inc., 458 U.S. 670 (1982), four Justices concluded that a suit for possession of property in the hands of state officials was not barred by the Eleventh Amendment inasmuch as the State did not have even a colorable claim to the property under state law. See id., at 696–697 (opinion of Stevens, J., joined by Burger, C.J., and Marshall and Blackmun, JJ.)[2] Four additional Justices accepted the proposition that if the state officers' conduct had been in violation of a state statute, the Eleventh Amendment would not bar the action. Id., at 714 (White, J., concurring in the judgment in part and dissenting in part, joined by Powell, Rehnquist, and O'Connor, JJ.). And in just one short paragraph in Cory v. White, 457 U.S. 85 (1982), the Court thrice restated the settled rule that the Eleventh Amendment does not bar suits against state officers when they are 'alleged to be acting against federal or state law.'[3] These are only the two most recent in an extraordinarily long line of cases.''

Justice Stevens then cited a number of prior decisions—two of which are discussed below—for the proposition that the Eleventh Amendment does not bar suits alleging that state officials have acted tortiously as a matter of state law, or in violation of state statutes (pp. 134–38, 145–50, 153–56):

''* * * [I]n Rolston v. Missouri Fund Commissioners, 120 U.S. 390 (1887), the Court rejected the argument that a suit to enjoin a state officer to comply with state law violated the Eleventh Amendment. The Court wrote: 'Here the suit is to get a state officer to do what a statute requires of him. The litigation is with the officer, not the state.' Id., at 411.

''* * * The appellants in Scully v. Bird, 209 U.S. 481 (1908), brought a diversity suit seeking injunctive relief against the dairy and food commissioner

---

2. [Ed.] In this case, after a salvor discovered a wrecked vessel, it entered into a contract with the State of Florida, predicated on the assumed validity of Florida's claim under state law to own the vessel, that permitted the salvor to undertake salvage operations and to retain 75% of the value of material recovered.

In unrelated proceedings between Florida and the United States, the Supreme Court ruled that Florida's boundary was landward of the site of the wreck. The salvor then filed an admiralty in rem action in federal court, naming the vessel as defendant and claiming title to all property recovered from the wreck. The district court issued, on plaintiff's motion, a ''warrant of arrest'' directing the United States Marshal to take custody of artifacts in the possession of state officials that had already been recovered from the wreck. The officials contended that execution of the warrant was barred by the Eleventh Amendment.

The Supreme Court rejected the claim of immunity. Four Justices held that the officials' continued possession of the artifacts was beyond their statutory authority; four Justices disagreed. The deciding vote was cast by Justice Brennan, who reasoned that the Eleventh Amendment is inapplicable to suits against a state by one of its own citizens.

3. [Ed.] In Cory, the administrator of Howard Hughes' estate filed a statutory interpleader action against officials of California and Texas, alleging that each state sought to tax the estate. The Court ruled that Edelman v. Jordan had not overruled Worcester County Trust Co. v. Riley, 302 U.S. 292 (1937), which, in holding a nearly identical action to be barred, stated that ''generally suits to restrain action of state officials can * * * be prosecuted only when the action sought to be restrained is without the authority of state law or contravenes the statutes or Constitution of the United States'' (p. 297). There being no violation of state or federal law alleged, Edelman provided no basis for injunctive relief. Justice Powell, joined by Justices Marshall and Stevens, dissented.

of the State of Michigan, on the ground that 'under cover of his office' he had maliciously engaged in a course of conduct designed to ruin plaintiff's business in the State. [Rejecting an Eleventh Amendment objection], * * * [t]his Court * * * noted that the complaint alleged action 'in dereliction of duties enjoined by the statutes of the State,' and concluded that it was 'manifest from this summary of the allegations of the bill that this is not a suit against the State.' *Id.*, at 490.[4] * * *

"* * * [A]ll of [these cases] explicitly consider and reject the claim that the Eleventh Amendment prohibits federal courts from issuing injunctive relief based on state law * * *. The Court tries to explain away these cases by arguing that the applicable state statutes gave petitioners such 'broad discretion' over Pennhurst that their actions were not *ultra vires* * * *. The Court, however, does not dispute the Court of Appeals' conclusion that these state statutes gave petitioners *no discretion whatsoever* to disregard their duties with respect to institutionalization of the retarded as they did. Petitioners acted outside of their lawful discretion every bit as much as did the government officials in the cases I have discussed, which hold that when an official commits an act prohibited by law, he acts beyond his authority and is not protected by sovereign immunity. * * *

"The majority states that the holding of Ex parte Young is limited to cases in which relief is provided on the basis of federal law, and that it rests entirely on the need to protect the supremacy of federal law. That position overlooks the foundation of the rule of Young * * *.

"The pivotal consideration in Young was that it was not conduct of the sovereign that was at issue. The rule that unlawful acts of an officer should not be attributed to the sovereign has deep roots in the history of sovereign immunity and makes Young reconcilable with the principles of sovereign immunity found in the Eleventh Amendment, rather than merely an unprincipled accommodation between federal and state interests that ignores the principles contained in the Eleventh Amendment.

"This rule plainly applies to conduct of state officers in violation of state law. Young states that the significance of the charge of unconstitutional conduct is that it renders the state official's conduct 'simply an illegal act,' and hence the officer is not entitled to the sovereign's immunity. Since a state officer's conduct in violation of state law is certainly no less illegal than his violation of federal law, in either case the official, by committing an illegal act, is 'stripped of his official or representative character.' * * *

"That the doctrine of sovereign immunity does not protect conduct which has been prohibited by the sovereign is clearly demonstrated by the [Larson] case on which petitioners chiefly rely. The Larson opinion teaches that the actions of state officials are not attributable to the state—are *ultra vires*—in two different types of situations: (1) when the official is engaged in conduct that the sovereign has not authorized, and (2) when he has engaged in conduct that the sovereign has forbidden. A sovereign, like any other principal, cannot authorize its agent to violate the law. * * *

"* * * Under the second track of the Larson analysis, petitioners were acting *ultra vires,* because they were acting in a way that the sovereign, by statute, had forbidden."

---

4. [Ed.] The majority characterized Scully as involving only a common law tort, and hence as having been overruled by Larson. 465 U.S. at 110 n. 19.

Finally, Justice Stevens objected to the overruling of cases exercising pendent jurisdiction over state law claims against state officials. Such jurisdiction, he argued, not only serves the policy of constitutional avoidance, but "enhances the decisionmaking autonomy of the States * * * [by directing] the federal court to turn first to state law, which the State is free to modify or repeal." By contrast, under the Court's opinion, "federal courts are required to resolve cases on federal grounds that no state authority can undo" (p. 163).

(2) *Pennhurst and Larson.* Pennhurst can be viewed as extending Larson to cases where an official's conduct is not merely tortious under the common law, but violates a state statute—an extension of which Justice Stevens was sharply critical. But however powerful his arguments against that extension, shouldn't Justice Stevens have admitted that the implications of Larson for a case like Pennhurst were far more ambiguous than he suggested? And rather than accepting Larson as a given, should he have stressed that Larson itself was poorly reasoned and was a major departure from precedent?

On the other hand, Justice Stevens clearly demonstrates the difficulties with the majority's argument that the outcome in Pennhurst was consistent with the Court's prior decisions and was compelled by Larson.

What accounts for the majority's strained reading and repudiation of so many precedents?

(3) *The Implications of Pennhurst.*

(a) The Pennhurst lawsuit implicated questions about the appropriate scope of federal equitable relief in cases seeking to restructure institutions of state government. There are perils in such actions, especially when relief is based upon an interpretation of unsettled state law. But aren't "the eleventh amendment and sovereign immunity * * * inappropriately blunt instruments for dealing with these delicate matters," especially when "[o]ther, more precise * * * nonconstitutional doctrines of restraint" are available? Shapiro, note 1, *supra*, at 79. (On those doctrines more generally, see Chap. X, Secs. 2(B)–2(D), *infra*; on the availability of declaratory relief, see subparagraph (d), *infra*.)

Consider the options open after Pennhurst to a litigant like Halderman who has plausible claims under both state and federal law for equitable relief against a course of ongoing state action.

She is free, of course, to file in state court under both state and federal law—but to do so she must forgo her right under § 1331 to a federal forum for her federal cause of action.

She may instead file the federal claim in federal court.[5] But to do so, she must either forgo her state law claim altogether, or file a second lawsuit in state court asserting the state law claim. Even if she can afford to file two separate lawsuits, the result is patently inefficient for the judicial system and the litigants, and it may deprive the federal court of the chance to avoid a constitutional decision. And it raises further complications:

(i) Should one court stay its hand while the other proceeds? See generally Chap. X, Sec. 2(D), *infra*. If so, what standards govern whether the federal court, or the state court, should abstain? See Werhan, *Pullman Abstention After Pennhurst: A Comment on Judicial Federalism*, 27 Wm. & Mary L.Rev. 449 (1986).

---

5. This is the only option available, of course, if the federal claim falls within the exclusive jurisdiction of the federal courts—for example, a patent or copyright claim.

(ii) Suppose the state court action comes to judgment first. At a minimum, the doctrine of issue preclusion may prevent the plaintiff from obtaining an independent federal court adjudication of issues in her federal lawsuit. It is also possible that the entire federal action might be barred by a plea of claim preclusion. See Chap. XII, pp. 1492–1500, *infra.*

Is any satisfactory option left open after Pennhurst?[6]

(b) Absent consent, does Pennhurst foreclose the exercise of diversity jurisdiction in suits against state officials seeking injunctive relief under state law?

(c) Will it always be clear whether a federal injunction should be characterized as resting on state law (and hence barred by Pennhurst) or federal law (and hence permissible under Young and Edelman)? Consider, for example, the Education of the Handicapped Act, 20 U.S.C. §§ 1400–61, which conditions federal assistance upon a state's adopting a plan (that must be federally approved) for ensuring handicapped children the right to a free public education. May a district court award prospective relief upon a finding that state officials have not complied with state law requirements in a federally-approved plan, even if that plan provides greater protection to handicapped pupils than is minimally required under federal law? See, *e.g.,* Geis v. Board of Educ., 774 F.2d 575 (3d Cir.1985)(permitting such relief).

(d) Does Pennhurst permit a suit under state law against a state official for damages to be paid by the officer personally rather than by the state? In a footnote, Justice Powell distinguished several cases in which relief had been awarded against federal officials on the ground that the actions sought damages in tort against the individual officer, and stated that because such relief does not run directly against the government, "nothing in our opinion touches these cases" (p. 111 n. 21). Could the judgment in such a case have preclusive effect in a subsequent state court action against a state official, or the state itself, seeking injunctive relief under state law? *Cf.* Duncan v. United States, 667 F.2d 36, 38 (Ct.Cl.1981), p. 1024, *supra.*

Does a suit seeking a declaratory judgment that official action violates state law "operate against the sovereign"? Dwyer, *Pendent Jurisdiction and the Eleventh Amendment,* 75 Calif.L.Rev. 129 (1987), argues that Pennhurst should be read as barring only intrusive relief, such as structural injunctions, but not declaratory relief or even negative injunctions. Is that an attractive reading? A well-supported one? What purpose would be served by such a declaration "if [the federal court] cannot back up its decision with an injunctive decree if the decision is disregarded."? Shapiro, note 1, *supra,* at 82.[7]

(4) *Suits Against Local Officers.* Though local governments and their officials have no Eleventh Amendment immunity, see p. 1056, *supra,* the Court in Pennhurst refused to leave standing a judgment against the defendant county officials: "[e]ven assuming" that they have no immunity, the relief ordered relates to an institution run and funded by the state; the state law under

---

6. A rare good word for Pennhurst is found in Althouse, *How to Build A Separate Sphere: Federal Courts and State Power,* 100 Harv.L.Rev. 1485 (1987). The author argues that Pennhurst forestalls the misinterpretation of state law and encourages the states to provide mechanisms for reform of their own institutions in order to obtain independence from federal supervision.

7. Declaratory relief was refused in Everett v. Schramm, 587 F.Supp. 228, 235 n. 11 (D.Del.1984), *aff'd,* 772 F.2d 1114 (3d Cir. 1985).

which relief had been ordered "contemplates that the state and county officials will cooperate in operating mental retardation programs"; and any relief against the county officials would be partial and incomplete (465 U.S. at 123–24).

The lower courts have not read Pennhurst as casting general doubt upon their authority to award relief under state law against county officials absent some significant effect on the state treasury. See, *e.g.*, Crane v. Texas, 759 F.2d 412 (5th Cir.1985); Lundgren v. McDaniel, 814 F.2d 600, 605 n. 4 (11th Cir.1987)(dictum).[8]

(5) *Pennhurst and Ex Parte Young.* Given Justice Powell's view that Ex parte Young was really a suit against the State—one justified by the need to enforce federal supremacy—what reason is there for following the rule (see p. 1073, *supra*) that a suit nominally against the State, but, like Young, seeking only prospective relief under federal law, is barred by the Eleventh Amendment?

(6) *The Relevance of Erie.* Pennhurst is not novel in assuming that the Eleventh Amendment may immunize the state from federal court suit on a state law cause of action, even if state law provides no immunity.[9] But wholly apart from the Eleventh Amendment, a decision by Pennsylvania to give state officials or agencies immunity from a state law cause of action would, under the Erie doctrine, be binding in a federal court. See, *e.g.,* Zeidner v. Wulforst, 197 F.Supp. 23 (E.D.N.Y.1961); *cf.* Martinez v. California, 444 U.S. 277, 280–83 (1980). Is there then any need in such cases for *additional* protection under the Eleventh Amendment—for protection that is broader than the state's Eleventh Amendment immunity from suit on a *federal* cause of action?[10]

(7) *Additional Bibliography.* For discussion of Pennhurst, in addition to the articles already cited, see Brown, *Beyond Pennhurst—Protective Jurisdiction, the Eleventh Amendment, and the Power of Congress to Enlarge Federal Jurisdiction in Response to the Burger Court,* 71 Va.L.Rev. 343 (1985); Rudenstine, *Pennhurst and the Scope of Federal Judicial Power to Reform Social Institutions,* 6 Cardozo L.Rev. 71 (1984).

---

8. Suppose that a local government defendant claims, in a case seeking prospective relief under federal law, that the state is an indispensable party, because of its authority or responsibility under *state law* over the subject matter in question. Would joinder of state officials in such a case violate the Eleventh Amendment?

9. Professor Field argues that since Erie was decided, state law does govern in such cases. Field, *The Eleventh Amendment and Other Sovereign Immunity Doctrines: Part I,* 126 U.Pa.L.Rev. 515, 520 n. 24 (1978); Field, *The Eleventh Amendment and Other Sovereign Immunity Doctrines: Congressional Imposition of Suit Upon the States,* 126 U.Pa.L.Rev. 1203, 1254 n. 240, 1264 n. 272 (1978). Compare Shapiro, note 1, *supra,* at 70 n. 55 ("Perhaps it should, but neither Pennhurst nor most of the cases [Field] cites * * * lend much support to that view.").

10. There is one "advantage" to the state of Eleventh Amendment immunity; under existing law, the state may waive immunity in its own courts without waiving its Eleventh Amendment immunity in federal court. See Smith v. Reeves, 178 U.S. 436 (1900), p. 1098, *infra.* If in the Pennhurst case the state could not claim Eleventh Amendment immunity, it might either have to create a substantive state law immunity, which would bar relief in state as well as federal court, or provide no immunity at all, which would leave it subject to suit in federal court.

Pennsylvania v. Union Gas Co.

491 U.S. 1, 109 S.Ct. 2273, 105 L.Ed.2d 1 (1989).
Certiorari to the United States Court of Appeals for the Third Circuit.

■ JUSTICE BRENNAN announced the judgment of the Court and delivered an opinion of the Court with respect to Parts I and II, and an opinion with respect to Part III, in which JUSTICE MARSHALL, JUSTICE BLACKMUN, and JUSTICE STEVENS join.

This case presents the questions whether the Comprehensive Environmental Response, Compensation, and Liability Act of 1980 (CERCLA), 42 U.S.C. § 9601 *et seq.*, as amended by the Superfund Amendments and Reauthorization Act of 1986 (SARA), Pub.L. No. 99–499, 100 Stat. 1613, permits a suit for monetary damages against a State in federal court and, if so, whether Congress has the authority to create such a cause of action when legislating pursuant to the Commerce Clause. The answer to both questions is "yes."

I

For about 50 years, the predecessors of respondent Union Gas operated a coal gasification plant near Brodhead Creek in Stroudsburg, Pennsylvania, which produced coal tar as a byproduct. The plant was dismantled around 1950. A few years later, Pennsylvania took part in major flood-control efforts along the creek. In 1980, * * * the Commonwealth struck a large deposit of coal tar while excavating the creek. The coal tar began to seep into the creek, and the Environmental Protection Agency determined that the tar was a hazardous substance and declared the site the Nation's first emergency Superfund site. Working together, Pennsylvania and the Federal Government cleaned up the area, and the Federal Government reimbursed the State for cleanup costs of $720,000.

To recoup these costs, the United States sued Union Gas under § 104 and § 106 of CERCLA, claiming that Union Gas was liable for such costs * * *. Union Gas filed a third-party complaint against Pennsylvania, asserting that the State was responsible for at least a portion of the costs because it was an "owner or operator" of the hazardous-waste site, and because its flood-control efforts had negligently caused or contributed to the release of the coal tar into the creek. The District Court dismissed the complaint, accepting Pennsylvania's claim that its Eleventh Amendment immunity barred the suit. * * *

* * * [The court of appeals reversed.] We granted certiorari, and now affirm.

II

In Hans v. Louisiana, 134 U.S. 1 (1890), this Court held that the principle of sovereign immunity reflected in the Eleventh Amendment rendered the States immune from suits for monetary damages in federal court even where jurisdiction was premised on the presence of a federal question. Congress may override this immunity when it acts pursuant to the power granted it under § 5 of the Fourteenth Amendment, but it must make its intent to do so "unmistakably clear." See Atascadero State Hospital v. Scanlon, 473 U.S. 234, 242 (1985). Before turning to the question whether Congress possesses the same power of abrogation under the Commerce Clause, we must first decide whether CERCLA, as amended by SARA, clearly expresses an intent to hold States liable in damages for conduct described in the statute. * * *

CERCLA both provides a mechanism for cleaning up hazardous waste sites, and imposes the costs of the cleanup on those responsible for the contamination. Two general terms, among others, describe those who may be liable under CERCLA for the costs of remedial action: "persons" and "owners or operators." [42 U.S.C.] § 9607(a). "States" are explicitly included within the statute's definition of "persons." § 9601(21). The term "owner or operator" is defined by reference to certain activities that a "person" may undertake. § 9601(20)(A).

Section 101(20)(D) of SARA excludes from the category of "owners or operators" States that "acquired ownership or control involuntarily through bankruptcy, tax delinquency, abandonment, or other circumstances in which the government involuntarily acquires title by virtue of its function as sovereign." § 9601(20)(D). However, § 101(20)(D) continues, "[t]he exclusion provided under this paragraph shall not apply to any State or local government which has caused or contributed to the release or threatened release of a hazardous substance from the facility, and such a State or local government shall be subject to the provisions of this chapter in the same manner and to the same extent, both procedurally and substantively, as any nongovernmental entity, including liability under section 9607 of this title." The express inclusion of States within the statute's definition of "persons," and the plain statement that States are to be considered "owners or operators" in all but very narrow circumstances, together convey a message of unmistakable clarity: Congress intended that States be liable along with everyone else for cleanup costs recoverable under CERCLA. Section 101(20)(D) is an express acknowledgment of Congress' background understanding—evidenced first in its inclusion of States as "persons"—that States would be liable in any circumstance described in § 107(a) from which they were not expressly excluded. The "exclusion" furnished to the States in § 101(20)(D) would be unnecessary unless such a background understanding were at work.[2]

The plain language of another section of the statute reinforces this conclusion. Section 107(d)(2) of CERCLA, as set forth in 42 U.S.C. § 9607(d)(2), headed "State and local governments," provides: "No State or local government shall be liable under this subchapter for costs or damages as a result of actions taken in response to an emergency created by the release or threatened release of a hazardous substance generated by or from a facility owned by another person. This paragraph shall not preclude liability for costs or damages as a result of gross negligence or intentional misconduct by the State or local government." This section is, needless to say, an explicit recognition of the potential liability of States under this statute; Congress need not exempt States from liability unless they would otherwise be liable. Similarly, unless suits against the States were elsewhere permitted, Congress would have had no reason to specify that citizen suits—as opposed to the kind of lawsuit involved here—could be brought "against any person (including the United States and any other governmental instrumentality or agency, to the extent permitted by the eleventh amendment to the Constitution)." 42 U.S.C. § 9659(a)(1). * * *

It is also highly significant that, in § 101(20)(D), Congress used language virtually identical to that it chose in waiving the Federal Government's

---

2. * * * We do not say that CERCLA's definition of "persons" alone overrides the States' immunity, but instead read CERCLA and SARA together, and argue that SARA's wording must inform our understanding of the other definitional sections of the statute. * * *

immunity from suits for damages under CERCLA [in Section 120(a)(1)]. * * * It can be no coincidence that in describing the potential liability of the States in § 101(20)(D), Congress chose language mirroring that of § 120(a)(1). * * * Congress must have intended to override the States' immunity from suit, just as it waived the Federal Government's immunity in § 120(a)(1).

* * * In the face of such clarity, [Pennsylvania] bravely insists that CERCLA merely makes clear that States may be liable to the *United States*, not that they may be liable to private entities such as Union Gas. * * *

Although it is true that the inclusion of States within CERCLA's definition of "persons" would not be rendered meaningless if we held that CERCLA did not subject the States to suits brought by private citizens, it is equally certain that such a holding *would* deprive the last portion of § 101(20)(D) of all meaning. Congress would have had no cause to stress that States would be liable "to the same extent . . . as any nongovernmental entity," § 101(20)(D), if it had meant only that they could be liable to the United States. * * * [T]he Constitution presents no barrier to lawsuits brought by the United States against a State. For purposes of such lawsuits, States are naturally just like "any nongovernmental entity" * * *. Indeed, this Court has gone so far as to hold that *no* explicit statutory authorization is necessary before the Federal Government may sue a State. See United States v. California, 332 U.S. 19, 26–28 (1947). Unless Congress intended to permit suits brought by private citizens against the States, therefore, the highly specific language of § 101(20)(D) was unnecessary.

The same can be said about the clause of § 101(20)(D) specifying that States would be subject to CERCLA's provisions, "including liability under section 9607 of this title." Section 9607 provides for liability in damages, and liability in damages is considered a special remedy, requiring special statutory language, only where the States' immunity from suits by private citizens is involved. In light of § 101(20)(D)'s very precise language, it would be exceedingly odd to interpret this provision as merely a signal that the United States—rather than private citizens—could sue the States for damages under CERCLA.

* * *

* * * Pennsylvania also argues that § 101(20)(D) demonstrates no intent to hold the States liable because this provision *limits* the States' liability. * * * The Commonwealth fails to grasp, however, that a limitation of liability is nonsensical unless liability existed in the first place.

We thus hold that the language of CERCLA as amended by SARA clearly evinces an intent to hold States liable in damages in federal court.[3]

III

Our conclusion that CERCLA clearly permits suits for money damages against States in federal court requires us to decide whether the Commerce Clause grants Congress the power to enact such a statute. * * *

---

3. The language of the Rehabilitation Act Amendments of 1986, 100 Stat. 1807, is indeed more pointed on the subject of abrogation than is CERCLA, since it mentions the Eleventh Amendment by name. It is surprising that Justice White's opinion lays so much stress on this difference in wording, however, because it expressly disclaims any intent to require that the words "Eleventh Amendment" appear in a statute in order to find abrogation. * * *

A

Though we have never squarely resolved this issue of congressional power, our decisions mark a trail unmistakably leading to the conclusion that Congress may permit suits against the States for money damages. The trail begins with Parden v. Terminal Railway of Alabama Docks Dept., 377 U.S. 184 (1964). There, in responding to a State-owned railway's argument that Congress had no authority to subject the railway to suit, we concluded that * * * "[b]y empowering Congress to regulate commerce, ... the States necessarily surrendered any portion of their sovereignty that would stand in the way of such regulation," id., at 192. Although it is true that we have referred to Parden as a case involving a waiver of immunity, Fitzpatrick v. Bitzer, 427 U.S. 445, 451 (1976), the statements quoted above lay a firm foundation for the argument that Congress' authority to regulate commerce includes the authority directly to abrogate States' immunity from suit.

* * *

[More recently,] we have twice assumed that Congress has the authority to abrogate States' immunity when acting pursuant to the Commerce Clause. See Welch v. Texas Dept. of Highways and Public Transportation, 483 U.S. 468, 475–476, and n. 5 (1987); County of Oneida v. Oneida Indian Nation of New York State, 470 U.S. 226, 252 (1985).

* * *

* * * In Fitzpatrick v. Bitzer, supra, we held that Congress may subject States to suits for money damages in federal court when legislating under § 5 of the Fourteenth Amendment * * *.

* * *

* * * Like the Fourteenth Amendment, the Commerce Clause with one hand gives power to Congress while, with the other, it takes power away from the States. It cannot be relevant that the Fourteenth Amendment accomplishes this exchange in two steps (§§ 1–4, plus § 5), while the Commerce Clause does it in one. The important point, rather, is that the provision both expands federal power and contracts state power; that is the meaning, in fact, of a "plenary" grant of authority, and the lower courts have rightly concluded that it makes no sense to conceive of § 5 as somehow being an "ultraplenary" grant of authority.

* * * Justice Scalia [in dissent] casually announces: "Nothing in [Fitzpatrick's] reasoning justifies limitation of the principle embodied in the Eleventh Amendment through appeal to antecedent provisions of the Constitution." The operative word here is, it would appear, "antecedent"; and it is important to emphasize that, according to Justice Scalia, the Commerce Clause is antecedent, not to the Eleventh Amendment, but to *the principle embodied in* the Eleventh Amendment." But, according to Part II of Justice Scalia's dissenting opinion, this "principle" has been with us since the days before the Constitution was ratified—since the days, in other words, before the Commerce Clause. * * * Justice Scalia, therefore, has things backwards: it is not the Commerce Clause that came first, but "the principle embodied in the Eleventh Amendment" that did so. Antecedence takes this case closer to, not further from, Fitzpatrick.

Even if "the principle embodied in the Eleventh Amendment" made its first appearance at the same moment as the Commerce Clause, and not before, Justice Scalia could no longer rely on chronology in distinguishing Fitzpatrick. * * * [If Congress had the power to abrogate sovereign immunity] prior to the enactment of this Amendment, we would require a showing far more powerful than Justice Scalia can muster that the Amendment was intended to obliterate that authority. The language of the Eleventh Amendment gives us no hint that it limits *congressional* authority; it refers only to "the *judicial* power" and forbids "*constru[ing]*" that power to extend to the enumerated suits—language plainly intended to rein in the judiciary, not Congress. * * *

Justice Scalia attempts to avoid the pull of our prior decisions by claiming that Hans answered this constitutional question over 100 years ago. Because Hans was brought into federal court via the Judiciary Act of 1875 * * *, Justice Scalia argues, that case disposed of the question whether Congress has the authority to abrogate States' immunity when legislating pursuant to the powers granted it by the Constitution. This argument depends on the notion that, in passing the Judiciary Act, "Congress . . . *sought* to eliminate [the] State sovereign immunity" that Article III had not eliminated (emphasis in original). As [the dissent] is well aware, however, the Judiciary Act merely gave effect to the grant of federal-question jurisdiction under Article III, which was not self-executing. Thus, if Article III did not "automatically eliminate" sovereign immunity, then neither did the Judiciary Act of 1875. That unsurprising conclusion does not begin to address the question whether other congressional enactments, not designed simply to implement Article III's grants of jurisdiction, may override States' immunity. * * *

Our prior cases thus indicate that Congress has the authority to override States' immunity when legislating pursuant to the Commerce Clause. This conclusion is confirmed by a consideration of the special nature of the power conferred by that Clause.

B

We have recognized that the States enjoy no immunity where there has been "a surrender of this immunity in the plan of the convention." Monaco v. Mississippi, 292 U.S. 313, 322–323 (1934), quoting The Federalist, No. 81 (Hamilton). Because the Commerce Clause withholds power from the States at the same time as it confers it on Congress, and because the congressional power thus conferred would be incomplete without the authority to render States liable in damages, it must be that, to the extent that the States gave Congress the authority to regulate commerce, they also relinquished their immunity where Congress found it necessary, in exercising this authority, to render them liable. The States held liable under such a congressional enactment are thus not "unconsenting"; they gave their consent all at once, in ratifying the Constitution containing the Commerce Clause, rather than on a case-by-case basis.

It would be difficult to overstate the breadth and depth of the commerce power. It is not the vastness of this power, however, that is so important here: it is its effect on the power of the States. The Commerce Clause, we long have held, displaces state authority even where Congress has chosen not to act, and it sometimes precludes state regulation even though existing federal law does not pre-empt it. Since the States may not legislate at all in these last two situations, a conclusion that Congress may not create a cause of action for money damages against the States would mean that no one could do so. And in many situations, it is only money damages that will carry out Congress' legitimate objectives under the Commerce Clause.

* * *

According to Pennsylvania, however, to decide that Congress may permit suits against States for money damages in federal court is equivalent to holding that Congress may expand the jurisdiction of the federal courts beyond the bounds of Article III.   * * * We never have held, however, that Article III does not permit [damage actions by private citizens] where the States have consented to them. Pennsylvania's argument * * * is answered by Fitzpatrick v. Bitzer, 427 U.S. 445 (1976). The Fourteenth Amendment does not purport to expand or even change the scope of Article III. If Pennsylvania were right about the limitations on Article III, then our holding in Fitzpatrick would mean that the Fourteenth Amendment, though silent on the subject, expanded the judicial power as originally conceived. We do not share that view of Fitzpatrick.

IV

We hold that CERCLA renders States liable in money damages in federal court, and that Congress has the authority to render them so liable when legislating pursuant to the Commerce Clause. Given our ruling in favor of Union Gas, we need not reach its argument that Hans v. Louisiana, 134 U.S. 1 (1890), should be overruled. We affirm the judgment of the Court of Appeals for the Third Circuit, and remand the case for further proceedings consistent with this opinion.

■ Justice Stevens, concurring.

It is important to emphasize the distinction between our two Eleventh Amendments. There is first the correct and literal interpretation of the plain language of the Eleventh Amendment that is fully explained in Justice Brennan's dissenting opinion in Atascadero State Hospital v. Scanlon, 473 U.S. 234, 247 (1985). In addition, there is the defense of sovereign immunity that the Court has added to the text of the Amendment in cases like Hans v. Louisiana, 134 U.S. 1 (1890). With respect to the former—the legitimate scope of the Eleventh Amendment limitation on federal judicial power—I do not believe Congress has the power under the Commerce Clause, or under any other provision of the Constitution, to abrogate the States' immunity. A statute cannot amend the Constitution. With respect to the latter—the judicially created doctrine of state immunity even from suits alleging violation of federally protected rights—I agree that Congress has plenary power to subject the States to suit in federal court.

Because Justice Brennan's opinion in Atascadero and the works of numerous scholars have exhaustively and conclusively refuted the contention that the Eleventh Amendment embodies a general grant of sovereign immunity to the States, further explication on this point is unnecessary. Suffice it to say that the Eleventh Amendment carefully mirrors the language of the citizen-state and alien-state diversity clauses of Article III and *only* provides that "[t]he Judicial power of the United States shall not be construed to extend" *to these cases.* * * *

* * *

Several of this Court's decisions make clear that much of our state immunity doctrine has absolutely nothing to do with the limit on judicial power contained in the Eleventh Amendment. For example, it is well established that a State may waive its immunity, subjecting itself to possible suit in federal court. Yet, the cases are legion holding that a party may not waive a defect in subject matter jurisdiction or invoke federal jurisdiction simply by consent. * * * [These holdings demonstrate] that this immunity is not a product of the limitation of judicial power contained in the Eleventh Amendment.

Another striking example of the application of prudential—rather than true jurisdictional—concerns is found in our decision in Edelman v. Jordan, 415 U.S. 651 (1974). * * * If Edelman simply involved an application of the limitation on judicial power contained in the Eleventh Amendment, once judicial power was found to exist to award prospective relief (even at some monetary cost to the State, see, *e.g.*, Milliken v. Bradley, 433 U.S. 267 (1977)), it is difficult to understand why that same judicial power would not extend to award other forms of relief. In Pennhurst State School and Hospital v. Halderman, 465 U.S. 89, 104–106 (1984), the Court made explicit what was implicit in Edelman: the Young fiction "rests on the need to promote the vindication of federal rights," while Edelman represents an attempt to "accommodate" this protection to the "competing interest" in "the constitutional immunity of the States." * * *

The theme that thus emerges from cases such as Edelman [and Pennhurst] is one of balancing of state and federal interests. This sort of balancing, however, like waiver, is antithetical to traditional understandings of Article III subject-matter jurisdiction—either the judicial power extends to a suit brought against a State or it does not. As a result, these cases are better understood as simply invoking the comity and federalism concerns discussed in our abstention cases, although admittedly in a slightly different voice.[4] * * * Congress is not superseding a constitutional provision [when it abrogates], but rather is setting aside the Court's assessment of the extent to which the use of constitutionally prescribed federal authority is prudent.

Because Congress has decided that the federal interest in protecting the environment outweighs any countervailing interest in not subjecting States to the possible award of monetary damages in a federal court, and because the "judicial power" of the United States plainly extends to such suits, I join Justice Brennan's opinion. * * *

■ JUSTICE WHITE, with whom THE CHIEF JUSTICE, JUSTICE O'CONNOR, and JUSTICE KENNEDY join as to Part I, concurring in the judgment in part and dissenting in part.

I find no "unmistakably clear language," Welch v. Texas Dept. of Highways and Public Transportation, 483 U.S. 468, 478 (1987), in either CERCLA or SARA that expresses Congress' intent to abrogate the States' Eleventh Amendment immunity. However, a majority of the Court concludes otherwise,

---

4. This understanding of our state immunity cases explains an additional anomaly. Over the years, this Court has repeatedly exercised Article III power to review state-court judgments in cases involving claims that, under our post-Hans decisions, could not have been brought in federal district court. [Citing numerous decisions, including Cohens v. Virginia, p. 1048, *supra*]. * * * [I]f our post-Hans state-immunity cases are * * * understood as premised on a prudential balancing of state and federal interests, these cases are easily explained: a state-court decision defining federal law tips the balance in favor of federal review.

and therefore I reach the constitutional issue presented here. On that question, I concur in Justice Brennan's conclusion, but not his reasoning.

I

Our cases make it plain that * * * "Congress must express its intention to abrogate the Eleventh Amendment in unmistakable language in the statute itself." Atascadero State Hospital v. Scanlon, 473 U.S. 234, 243 (1985).

     * * *

A

I begin by examining CERCLA, in the form in which Congress originally adopted it in 1980. * * * [The Court suggests] that because CERCLA includes "States" within its definition of "persons," and because the statute makes "persons" who are "owners or operators" liable under § 9607, Congress expressed in CERCLA an "unmistakably clear intent" to make the States liable to suit by private parties in Federal court. I reject this conclusion for several reasons.

     * * *

* * * [T]he significance that the Court draws from CERCLA's inclusion of States within its definition of persons is suspect for its impact on other portions of the statute. The definitional section the Court relies on also includes the "United States Government" within the term "person." 42 U.S.C. § 9601(21). Yet Congress also adopted, in CERCLA, an entirely separate statutory provision rendering the Federal Government suable under the statute's liability provision, see 42 U.S.C. § 9607(g). If the Court's views about the significance of including States within the definition of persons is [sic] correct, then § 9607(g) was wholly redundant, because—by including the United States Government within the definition of persons—Congress had already stripped the Federal Government of its sovereign immunity.[1]

Rather than assuming that Congress wrote a wholly redundant subsection of § 9607, however, it seems more likely to conclude that Congress did not think that including the United States Government or the States within § 9601(21)'s general definition of "persons" subject to CERCLA's regime was enough to abrogate the sovereign immunity of either for damage awards. With respect to the Federal Government, Congress went on to enact a separate provision executing the requisite waiver of immunity, § 9607(g). However, with respect to the States, Congress made no such additional provision: the conclusion to be drawn is obvious.

Finally, and most importantly, the Court's reading of CERCLA employs the precise analytical approach we rejected in Employees v. Missouri Dept. of

---

1. In an effort to avoid the force of this observation, the Court unleashes its oft-repeated statement that it relies on a *"combination"* of CERCLA and SARA to reach its conclusion. The Court says that it is my "failure to recognize" this quality in its analysis that leads to my "confusion" about this case.

I do not "fail to recognize" the Court's approach—I reject it outright. * * *

As I see it, the analysis must be this: either Congress abrogated the Eleventh Amendment when it enacted CERCLA—in which case, § 9607(g) was superfluous when adopted—or Congress did not do so until it adopted SARA—which is a peculiar view, for reasons I explain in Part IB below—or Congress did not have an intent to abrogate in either instance. * * *

Public Health and Welfare, 411 U.S. 279 (1973). There, as is true here, the relevant statutory term that described who was covered by the Act * * * expressly included the State-defendant * * *. Nonetheless, in Employees, we held that Congress had not thereby abrogated the States' Eleventh Amendment immunity; instead, we concluded, Congress had meant only to make the States subject to enforcement actions brought by the Federal Government.

    * * *

* * * If Congress believes that making the States liable to private parties is critical to the scheme it has created in CERCLA, it is up to Congress to say so in unmistakable language. Since it has not, I believe that our "clear statement" precedents bar us from implying such a policy choice—even if it is "latent" in the statutory scheme, or an advisable means of achieving the statute's ends.

B

The question then becomes whether * * * the 1986 amendments to CERCLA (known as SARA) added such an "unmistakable" statement of abrogation to the statute.

    [The relevant portion of SARA is § 101(20)(D), codified at 42 U.S.C. § 9601(20)(D).] * * *

    Although Congress entitled the amendment "State or Local Government Limitation," the Court disparages the idea that § 9601(20)(D) was enacted solely as a limitation on governmental unit liability. The Court asserts that such a view ignores that § [9601(20)(D)] "would be unnecessary unless" the States could be liable under § 9607. But everyone agrees that States may be liable under § 9607: the liability of the Commonwealth of Pennsylvania to the United States. Section 9601(20)(D) * * * limits the circumstances under which State and local governments will be forced to pay the U.S. Government for clean-ups at involuntarily-acquired sites. Given this fact, § 9601(20)(D) makes perfectly good sense without any contortion of it to imply an intent of Congress to abrogate the Eleventh Amendment.

    * * *

* * * [For this and other reasons], I do not think that SARA's liability-limiting amendment to CERCLA contains an "unmistakably clear" statement by Congress that it wanted to abrogate the States' solemn immunity to private suit under the Eleventh Amendment.[7]

    7. * * * [J]ust eight days after it adopted SARA, Congress enacted the Rehabilitation Act Amendments of 1986, Pub.L. 99–506, 100 Stat. 1807, which included a provision setting aside the force of our holding in Atascadero that Congress had failed to provide a clear statement of abrogation of the Eleventh Amendment. The words Congress chose in that Act are instructive: "A State shall not be immune under the Eleventh Amendment ... from suit in Federal court for a violation of [portions of the Act]."

    While I would not go so far as to hold that Congress must use these precise words (*i.e.*, make reference to the Eleventh Amendment) before it will be deemed to have abrogated States' immunity, the words used by Congress to set aside Atascadero are legions more "unmistakably clear" than the tangled mess in § 9601(20)(D) * * *.

    * * *

II

My view on the statutory issue has not prevailed, however; a majority of the Court has ruled that the statute, as amended, plainly intended to abrogate the immunity of the States from suit in the federal courts. I accept that judgment. This brings me to the question whether Congress has the constitutional power to abrogate the States' immunity.[8] In that respect, I agree with the conclusion reached by Justice Brennan in Part III of his opinion, that Congress has the authority under Article I to abrogate the Eleventh Amendment immunity of the States, although I do not agree with much of his reasoning.

Accordingly, I would affirm the judgment of the Court of Appeals.

■ Justice Scalia, with whom The Chief Justice, Justice O'Connor, and Justice Kennedy join as to Parts II, III, and IV, concurring in part and dissenting in part.

I

I join Part II of Justice Brennan's opinion holding that the text of [CERCLA], as amended by [SARA], clearly renders States liable for money damages in private suits. Justice White's contention that there is no clear statement is given plausibility only by his methodology of considering CERCLA and SARA separately, finding that first the one and then the other does not necessarily import monetary liability to private individuals * * *.

That methodology * * * is perhaps correct, if one assumes that the task of a court of law is to plumb the intent of the particular Congress that enacted a particular provision. That methodology is not mine nor, I think, the one that courts have traditionally followed. It is our task, as I see it, not to enter the minds of the Members of Congress—who need have nothing in mind in order for their votes to be both lawful and effective—but rather to give fair and reasonable meaning to the text of the United States Code, adopted by various Congresses at various times. CERCLA, as amended by SARA, clearly holds the States liable for damages in private suits. * * *

Finding that the statute renders the States liable in private suits for money damages, I must consider the continuing validity of Hans v. Louisiana, 134 U.S. 1 (1890) * * *.

II

Eight members of the Court addressed the question whether to overrule Hans only two Terms ago—but inconclusively, since they were evenly divided. See Welch v. Texas Dept. of Highways and Public Transportation, 483 U.S. 468 (1987). Since the substantive issue was addressed so extensively * * * [there], I will only sketch its outlines here.

* * * If [the text of the Eleventh Amendment] were intended as a comprehensive description of state sovereign immunity in federal courts—that is, if there were no state sovereign immunity beyond its precise terms—then it would unquestionably be most reasonable to interpret it as providing immunity only when the *sole basis* of federal jurisdiction is the diversity of citizenship that it describes (which of course tracks some of the diversity jurisdictional

---

8. As a preliminary matter, I reiterate my view that, for the reasons stated by the plurality in Welch v. Texas Dept. of High-   ways, 483 U.S., at 478–95, Hans v. Louisiana should not be overruled.

grants in U.S. Const., Art. III, § 2). For there is no plausible reason why one would wish to protect a State from being sued in federal court for violation of federal law (a suit falling within the jurisdictional grant over cases "arising under ... the Laws of the United States") when the plaintiff is a citizen of another State or country, but to permit a State to be sued there when the plaintiff is [a] citizen of the State itself. * * *

About a century ago, in the landmark case of Hans v. Louisiana, the Court unanimously rejected this "comprehensive" approach to the Amendment, finding sovereign immunity where not only a nondiversity basis of jurisdiction was present, but even where * * * [the plaintiff was an in-state citizen.] What we said in Hans was, essentially, that the Eleventh Amendment was important not merely for what it said but for what it reflected: a consensus that the doctrine of sovereign immunity, for States as well as for the Federal Government, was part of the understood background against which the Constitution was adopted * * * . * * *

* * * The foremost argument urged in favor of overruling Hans is that a waiver of immunity against suits presenting federal questions is also implicit in the constitutional scheme. On this single point I add a few words to what was so recently said in Welch.

The inherent necessity of a tribunal for peaceful resolution of disputes between the Union and the individual States, and between the individual States themselves, is incomparably greater, in my view, than the need for a tribunal to resolve disputes on federal questions between individuals and the States. Undoubtedly the Constitution envisions the necessary judicial means to assure compliance with the Constitution and laws. But since the Constitution does not deem this to require that private individuals be able to bring claims against the *Federal Government* for violation of the Constitution or laws, it is difficult to see why it must be interpreted to require that private individuals be able to bring such claims against the *States*. * * *

Even if I were wrong, however, about the original meaning of the Constitution, or the assumption adopted by the Eleventh Amendment, or the structural necessity for federal-question suits against the States, it cannot possibly be denied that the question is at least close. In that situation, the mere venerability of an answer consistently adhered to for almost a century, and the difficulty of changing, or even clearly identifying, the intervening law that has been based on that answer, strongly argue against a change. * * * Moreover, unlike the vast majority of judicial decisions, Hans has had a pervasive effect upon statutory law, automatically assuring that private damages actions created by federal law do not extend against the States. * * * It is impossible to say how many extant statutes would have included an explicit preclusion of suits against States if it had not been thought that such suits were automatically barred. * * *

I would therefore decline respondents' invitation to overrule Hans v. Louisiana.

III

Justice Brennan's plurality opinion purports to assume the validity of Hans, and yet reaches the result that CERCLA's imposition of monetary liability is constitutional because Congress has the power to abrogate state sovereign immunity in the exercise of its Commerce Clause power. Justice White, who not merely assumes the validity of Hans, but actually believes in it, agrees with that disposition. Better to overrule Hans, I should think, than to perpetuate the complexities that it creates, but eliminate all its benefits to the federal system. If Hans means only that federal-question suits for money damages against the States cannot be brought in federal court unless Congress clearly says so, it means nothing at all. We do not need Hans for the "clear statement" rule—just as we do not need to rely on any constitutional prohibition of suits against the Federal Government to require a similar rule for elimination of the sovereign immunity of the United States. As far as I can discern, the course the Court today pursues—preserving Hans but permitting Congress to overrule it—achieves the worst of both worlds. * * *

To begin with, Hans did not merely hold that Article III failed to eliminate state sovereign immunity of its own force, without any congressional action to that end. In Hans, as here, there was a congressional statute that could be pointed to as eliminating state sovereign immunity—namely, the Judiciary Act of 1875, which gave United States courts jurisdiction over cases involving federal questions. * * *

I think it plain that the position adopted by the Court contradicts the rationale of Hans, if not its narrow holding. Hans was not expressing some narrow objection to the particular federal power by which Louisiana had been haled into court, but was rather enunciating a fundamental principle of federalism, evidenced by the Eleventh Amendment, that the States retained their sovereign prerogative of immunity. * * *

Our later cases are similarly clear that state immunity from suit in federal courts is a structural component of federalism, and not merely a default disposition that can be altered by action of Congress pursuant to its Article I powers. * * * The only attempt by either the plurality or Justice White to reconcile today's holding with the "broad constitutional principle of sovereign immunity" established by these precedents is the plurality's facile assertion that "in approving the commerce power, the States consented to suits against them based on congressionally created causes of action." The suggestion that this is the kind of consent our cases had in mind when reciting the familiar phrase, "the States may not be sued without their consent," does not warrant response.

* * *

The Court's error is clear enough from the embarrassing frailty of the case support to which the plurality opinion appeals. * * * In fact the only dicta even suggesting the position the Court today adopts were contained in Parden v. Terminal Railway of Alabama Docks Dept., 377 U.S. 184, 191–192 (1964) * * *. As our later cases have made plain, see Fitzpatrick v. Bitzer, 427 U.S. 445, 451 (1976), Parden's holding was based upon the State's waiver of its sovereign immunity. One aspect of the case has already been overruled, and another cast in doubt, see infra * * *.

Finally, the plurality opinion errs in relying on Fitzpatrick v. Bitzer, supra, which upheld a money award against a State under Title VII of the Civil Rights Act of 1964. * * * [T]he Civil Rights Act was enacted pursuant to § 5 of the Fourteenth Amendment. We held that "the Eleventh Amendment, and the principle of state sovereignty which it embodies, see Hans v. Louisiana, ... are necessarily limited" by the later Amendment, 427 U.S., at 456, whose substantive provisions were "by express terms directed at the States," id., at 453, and "were intended to be, what they really are, limitations of the power of the

States and enlargements of the power of Congress,"*id.*, at 454, quoting Ex parte Virginia, 100 U.S. 339, 345 (1880). Nothing in this reasoning justifies limitation of the principle embodied in the Eleventh Amendment through appeal to antecedent provisions of the Constitution.

* * *

IV

[Justice Scalia here rejected the argument that, under the Parden case, Pennsylvania had constructively waived its immunity by operating a site containing hazardous substances in the face of CERCLA and SARA. He noted that in Welch v. Texas Dep't of Highways & Pub. Transp., 483 U.S. 468 (1987), the Court overruled Parden "insofar as [it] spoke to the clarity of language necessary to constitute * * * a demand" by the federal government that a state waive its immunity as a condition of undertaking activity regulated under the Commerce Clause. But the Welch decision did not address the continued validity of Parden's theory that "the Commerce Clause provided the constitutional power to make such a demand." "I would drop the other shoe", Justice Scalia continued, arguing that there was little difference between the position that Congress can abrogate immunity (which he had just rejected) and the position that Congress can condition a state's activity on waiver of its immunity.]

The Court's holding today can be applauded only by those who think state sovereign immunity so constitutionally insignificant that Hans itself might as well be abandoned. * * * It is a particularly unhappy victory, since instead of cleaning up the allegedly muddled Eleventh Amendment jurisprudence produced by Hans, the Court leaves that in place, and adds to the clutter the astounding principle that Article III limitations can be overcome by simply exercising Article I powers. It is an unstable victory as well, since that principle is too much at war with itself to endure. We shall either overrule Hans in form as well as in fact, or return to its genuine meaning.

I would reverse the judgment of the Court of Appeals on the ground that federal courts have no power to entertain the present suit against the Commonwealth of Pennsylvania.

■ JUSTICE O'CONNOR, dissenting.

* * *

NOTE ON WAIVER AND ON CONGRESSIONAL ABROGATION OF ELEVENTH AMENDMENT IMMUNITY[1]

A. The Doctrine of Waiver

(1) *Introduction*. There has never been any doubt (as Justice Stevens notes in his opinion in Union Gas) that Article III's judicial power extends to suits against *consenting* states. See, *e.g.,* Petty v. Tennessee–Missouri Bridge Comm'n, 359 U.S. 275 (1959); Clark v. Barnard, 108 U.S. 436, 447 (1883). Is

---

1. Although the Union Gas case focused primarily on the power of Congress to abrogate a state's Eleventh Amendment immunity, the doctrines of waiver and abrogation (as shown by the Parden case, Paragraph (3), *infra*) are closely related, and are thus dealt with in a single Note.

this an anomaly (however well-established) in light of the ordinary rule that the parties lack power to confer jurisdiction on the federal courts? Or does the justification for the waiver rule depend upon why jurisdiction is limited in the first instance?

Less clear is what constitutes a valid waiver on the part of a state. Enactment of a state statute (or constitutional provision) consenting to suit is the clearest example of a valid waiver. On the other hand, the failure of attorneys representing the state to assert the defense does not waive it; indeed, the defect is deemed to be jurisdictional, as Edelman v. Jordan, 415 U.S. 651 (1974), p. 1066, *supra,* made clear.[2] Note, however, that in Clark v. Barnard, 108 U.S. 436 (1883), *supra,* the state was held to have waived its immunity after its officials filed an appearance by the state as a claimant to a fund.[3] Compare the similar holdings in federal sovereign immunity cases, p. 1003, *supra.*

What justifies the Supreme Court's insistence, in a number of decisions, that a *state* legislature's waiver be unmistakable?[4] Is a policy of clear statement appropriate when a federal court is construing a state rather than a federal statute?

(2) *Waivers Confined to State Tribunals.* Smith v. Reeves, 178 U.S. 436, 441 (1900), held that a state may waive sovereign immunity as to suits for tax refunds in its own courts, while retaining its Eleventh Amendment immunity from such lawsuits in federal court. Earlier cases looked the other way, see, *e.g.,* Reagan v. Farmers' Loan & Trust Co., 154 U.S. 362, 391 (1894), but Smith reasoned that a limitation upon tax refund actions could not be seen as "hostile to the General Government, or as touching upon any right granted or secured by the Constitution of the United States" (p. 445). Subsequent cases have permitted selective waiver by the state without regard to Smith's qualifications. See, *e.g.,* Edelman v. Jordan, *supra.* Should they have, especially when other efforts by states to restrict lawsuits to the state courts have been held unlawful? See, *e.g.,* Chicago & N.W. Ry. v. Whitton's Adm'r, 80 U.S. (13 Wall.) 270 (1871), p. 731, *supra,* holding that a state statute purporting to permit enforcement of a state wrongful death action only in state court could not prevent the exercise of federal diversity jurisdiction. See also Shapiro, *Wrong*

---

2. But later, in Patsy v. Board of Regents, 457 U.S. 496 (1982), the Supreme Court, in holding that the district court had erred in dismissing a § 1983 action on the ground that plaintiff had not exhausted administrative remedies, refused to reach a colorable Eleventh Amendment issue. That issue was first raised (but not vigorously pressed) before the court of appeals, which had not addressed it. Before the Supreme Court, the defendant had not briefed or argued the immunity issue (though it was mentioned in opposing the petition for certiorari). The Court denied that the Eleventh Amendment "is jurisdictional in the sense that it must be raised and decided by this Court on its own motion", and left the issue to the district court on remand (p. 515–16 n. 19).

3. This waiver doctrine has not been extended to counterclaims against a state

that do not arise from the same transaction as the state's claim, or that seek not merely a setoff or recoupment but rather an affirmative judgment against the state. See, *e.g.,* Maryland Port Admin. v. SS American Legend, 453 F.Supp. 584, 590 (D.Md.1978); Burgess v. M/V Tamano, 382 F.Supp. 351, 355–56 (D.Me.1974), *aff'd,* 559 F.2d 1200 (1st Cir.1977).

4. But *cf.* Port Auth. Trans–Hudson Corp. v. Feeney, 495 U.S. 299 (1990)(holding that there was a valid waiver even though the "consent to suit" provision in the relevant state statutes creating a bi-state entity did not explicitly consent to suit in federal court; the Court relied both on the expansive language of the consent provision and on the language of the venue provision in those statutes).

Turns: The Eleventh Amendment and the Pennhurst Case, 98 Harv.L.Rev. 61, 76–78 (1984). Or is the whole point of the Eleventh Amendment not to exempt the state from suit altogether, but to give it a forum choice?

(3) *"Constructive" Waiver.*

(a) In Parden v. Terminal Ry., 377 U.S. 184 (1964), the Supreme Court (per Brennan, J.) held, 5–4, that Alabama had constructively consented to a federal court negligence action under the Federal Employers' Liability Act (FELA) brought by an employee of a state-owned railway. In the Court's view, the case presented two questions (p. 187): "(1) Did Congress in enacting the FELA intend to subject a State to suit in these circumstances? (2) Did it have power to do so, as against the State's claim of immunity?"

On the first question, the Court ruled that the FELA, which provides a damage action against "every" railroad in interstate commerce, "meant what it said", and refused to "read a 'sovereign immunity exception' " into the statute: "we should not presume to say, in the absence of express provision to the contrary, that [Congress] intended to exclude a particular group of such workers from the benefits conferred by the Act" (pp. 187–90).

On the second question, the Court said that "the States surrendered a portion of their sovereignty when they granted Congress the power to regulate commerce. * * * Since imposition of the FELA right of action upon interstate railroads is within the congressional regulatory power, it must follow that application of the Act to such a railroad cannot be precluded by sovereign immunity" (pp. 191–92). The Eleventh Amendment, the Court insisted, was not being overridden (p. 192): "Our conclusion is simply that Alabama, when it began operation of an interstate railroad approximately 20 years after enactment of the FELA, necessarily consented to such suit as was authorized by that Act." That the Alabama constitution barred any waiver of immunity was immaterial, as "the question whether the State's act constitutes the alleged consent is one of federal law" (p. 196).

Was Parden internally inconsistent in arguing both that the states had ceded part of their sovereignty in the constitutional plan and that Alabama could be subjected to suit only if it waived its immunity? Did the Court unconstitutionally condition Alabama's operation of a railroad on surrender of its Eleventh Amendment immunity?

(b) In Employees of Dep't of Pub. Health and Welfare v. Department of Pub. Health & Welfare, 411 U.S. 279 (1973), employees of Missouri state hospitals and schools brought suit under the Fair Labor Standards Act for overtime compensation. Though the Act initially excluded all state employees, a 1966 amendment extended coverage to employees of state schools and hospitals. The Supreme Court held Missouri immune from federal court suit, distinguishing Parden as involving a "for profit" operation of the kind normally run by private parties (p. 284). The Court contended that its ruling would not leave plaintiffs unprotected; the Act provided other remedies against state employers, including suits by the Secretary of Labor for unpaid compensation or injunctive relief.[5]

---

5. Is it clear that a suit by the Secretary as parens patriae would be deemed a suit by the United States, as to which the Amendment does not apply? *Cf.* New Hampshire v. Louisiana, 108 U.S. 76 (1883), p. 1064, note 1, *supra.*

Justice Marshall (joined by Justice Stewart) concurred in the result. In his view, the Act gave the plaintiffs all of § 16(b)'s remedies, but the Eleventh Amendment barred the federal courts from providing them. The Eleventh Amendment, however, was "nothing more than a regulation of the forum in which these petitioners may seek a remedy," and the state's courts "have an independent constitutional obligation to entertain employee actions to enforce [their] rights" (p. 298).

(c) The question whether Parden's approach survived Employees, Edelman, and Atascadero (discussed at p. 1103, note 13, *infra,* and in Union Gas) was resolved in Welch v. Texas Dep't of Highways & Pub. Transp., 483 U.S. 468 (1987). The plaintiff, an employee of a Texas agency that operated a ferry, sought damages under the Jones Act for injuries suffered on the ferry dock. (Section 33 of that Act, 46 U.S.C. § 688, provides that "[a]ny seaman who shall suffer personal injury in the course of his employment" may bring a personal injury action under the provisions of the FELA.) After finding that the question of express waiver by the state had not been presented for review, Justice Powell (speaking for a plurality of four in a 5–4 decision) said that the plaintiff's remaining argument for jurisdiction rested upon congressional abrogation. Assuming without deciding that Congress' power to subject unconsenting states to federal court suit was not confined to § 5 of the Fourteenth Amendment, the plurality concluded that "Congress has not expressed in unmistakable statutory language its intention to allow States to be sued in federal court under the Jones Act" (p. 475). The decision in Parden, Justice Powell said (p. 477), failed to recognize that "the constitutional role of the States sets them apart from other employers". He declared that to the extent that Parden is inconsistent with the requirement that Congress express its intent to abrogate "in unmistakably clear language, it is overruled" (p. 478).

Justice Scalia, concurring in part and concurring in the judgment, agreed that Parden should be overruled, but on the different ground that, in light of the general acceptance of Hans v. Louisiana when the FELA and the Jones Act were enacted, those statutes should not be interpreted as providing a cause of action against a state employer.[6]

B. Abrogation

Union Gas is the most recent of several decisions dealing not with waiver but with the power of Congress to abrogate Eleventh Amendment immunity.

(1) *The Fitzpatrick Decision.* Fitzpatrick v. Bitzer, 427 U.S. 445 (1976), discussed in Union Gas, was a Title VII action alleging that Connecticut's retirement plan discriminated against male employees. (Title VII regulates any "person" employing the requisite number of employees in interstate commerce; in 1972 Congress amended the definition of "person" to include state and local "governments, governmental agencies, [and] political subdivisions.") The Supreme Court, per Rehnquist, J., held that the Eleventh

---

6. Justice Scalia's approach was rejected in Hilton v. South Carolina Pub. Ry. Comm'n, 502 U.S. 197 (1991), in which the Court allowed an injured worker to bring a *state court* FELA action against a state-owned railway. The Court in Hilton noted that (1) stare decisis militated against overruling the aspect of the Parden holding interpreting the FELA to create substantive state liability, and (2) in a state court action, a claim of Eleventh Amendment immunity is not available. The Court's decision avoided a "remedial gap", since the state's worker's compensation law excluded railroad employees on the assumption that they were covered by the FELA.

Amendment did not bar an award of retroactive retirement benefits and attorney's fees as allowed by Title VII. Here, the Court said, "the 'threshold fact of congressional authorization' * * * is clearly present" (p. 452).

The 1972 amendment was enacted pursuant to Congress' power under § 5 of the Fourteenth Amendment. That Amendment as a whole represented a "shift in the federal-state balance [that] has been carried forward by more recent decisions of this Court," and past decisions had "sanctioned intrusions by Congress, acting under the Civil War Amendments, into the judicial, executive, and legislative spheres of autonomy previously preserved to the States" (p. 455). Justice Rehnquist continued (p. 456):

"It is true that none of these previous cases presented the question of the relationship between the Eleventh Amendment and the enforcement power granted to Congress under § 5 of the Fourteenth Amendment. But we think that the Eleventh Amendment, and the principle of state sovereignty which it embodies, are necessarily limited by the enforcement provisions of § 5 of the Fourteenth Amendment. In that section Congress is expressly granted authority to enforce 'by appropriate legislation' the substantive provisions of the Fourteenth Amendment, which themselves embody significant limitations on state authority. When Congress acts pursuant to § 5, not only is it exercising legislative authority that is plenary within the terms of the constitutional grant, it is exercising that authority under one section of a constitutional Amendment whose other sections by their own terms embody limitations on state authority. We think that Congress may, in determining what is 'appropriate legislation' for the purpose of enforcing the provisions of the Fourteenth Amendment, provide for private suits against States or state officials which are constitutionally impermissible in other contexts."

(2) *The Significance of § 1983.* In a lengthy dictum in Quern v. Jordan, 440 U.S. 332 (1979), p. 1075, *supra,* the Court rejected the view that § 1983 should be interpreted to make states suable in federal court: "[Section] 1983 does not explicitly and by clear language indicate on its face an intent to sweep away the immunity of the States; nor does it have a history which focuses directly on the question of state liability and which shows that Congress considered and firmly decided to abrogate the Eleventh Amendment immunity of the States" (p. 345).[7]

---

7. In contrast to the Court's holding in Quern, the Fitzpatrick rationale was applied in Hutto v. Finney, 437 U.S. 678 (1978), also discussed at p. 1074, *supra,* a lawsuit under 42 U.S.C. § 1983 in which injunctive relief against state officials had been awarded. Plaintiffs sought attorney's fees under the Civil Rights Attorney's Fees Awards Act of 1976, 42 U.S.C. § 1988, which provides that in actions to enforce certain federal civil rights statutes (including § 1983), a court may award prevailing parties reasonable attorney's fees "as part of the costs". The Act does not specify that fees may be awarded against a state, but the Senate and House reports did say that fees may be collected, *inter alia,* "from the State," and the House report cited Fitzpatrick. The Court concluded that Congress intended to make states vulnerable to liability for attorney's fees in § 1983 actions, and that because § 1983 enforces the Fourteenth Amendment, the case fell within the principle of Fitzpatrick.

Justice Powell's dissent in Hutto argued that a provision overriding immunity must be "in statutory language sufficiently clear to alert every voting Member of Congress" (p. 705). That argument in turn evoked a concurrence from Justice Brennan, who contended that Fitzpatrick and other decisions had "seriously undermined" The Court's earlier determination that Congress did not, in § 1983, intend to override the states' Eleventh Amendment immunity.

(3) *The Reasoning of the Justices in Union Gas.* Part III of Justice Brennan's opinion in Union Gas relies on two notions: first, that by ratifying the Constitution, the states consented to congressionally-authorized suits against them; and second, that the Commerce Clause is special because even when dormant, it preempts state regulatory power. The first rationale would permit abrogation under any of Congress' enumerated powers; the second might not.

Justice White says that he agrees with the conclusion of Part III of Justice Brennan's opinion—that Congress can abrogate under the commerce power—but disagrees with much of Justice Brennan's reasoning. Doesn't a Justice who casts the deciding vote have some obligation to provide an explanation that is intelligible to the legal community?[8]

Justice Scalia says, with considerable force, that the effect of the decision—to preserve Hans while permitting Congress to override it—achieves "the worst of both worlds". Couldn't he have avoided that result by joining the four Justices who would overrule Hans? Since he conceded the question was so close, why didn't he?

(4) *The Scope of Congress' Abrogation Power.* After Union Gas, how should a lower federal court decide a case in which Congress clearly intended to abrogate sovereign immunity when exercising its legislative authority over, for example, bankruptcy,[9] or copyright,[10] or commerce with "the Indian Tribes",[11] or the jurisdiction of the federal courts?[12] Isn't the answer complicated, and the very

8. Do you understand Justice White's vote to concur in the judgment even though he thinks Congress did not abrogate Pennsylvania's immunity? Because a majority disagrees on that point, he accepts their judgment. Of course, a different majority held that Congress could abrogate under the commerce power; should the four Justices who disagreed on that point also have concurred in the judgment, rather than dissenting?

9. In United States v. Nordic Village, Inc., 503 U.S. 30 (1992), the Court held that Congress had not expressed with sufficient clarity an intention to abrogate federal or state immunity in bankruptcy matters. Congress responded to Nordic Village in 1994 by a clear abrogation of governmental immunity in many such matters (see 108 Stat. 4117), and the validity of this abrogation with respect to a state agency has been sustained by the Seventh Circuit. In re Merchants Grain, Inc., 59 F.3d 630 (7th Cir.1995).

10. After one court of appeals held that the language of the Copyright Act was not sufficiently clear to abrogate a state's Eleventh Amendment immunity (see Richard Anderson Photography v. Brown, 852 F.2d 114 (4th Cir.1988)), Congress amended the Copyright Act to authorize copyright actions against states, their instrumentalities, officers, and employees, and specifically abrogated any immunity "under the Eleventh Amendment * * * or under any other doctrine of sovereign immunity". P.L. 101–553,

104 Stat. 2749 (1990). See Chavez v. Arte Publico Press, 59 F.3d 539 (5th Cir.1995).

11. The question whether Congress intended, and has the authority, to abrogate the states' Eleventh Amendment immunity in the exercise of its power over commerce with the Indian Tribes is one of the issues raised in Seminole Tribe v. Florida, 11 F.3d 1016 (11th Cir.1994), cert. granted, 115 S.Ct. 932 (1995), a case pending before the Supreme Court at the time this book went to press. In this case, which involves an effort by the Tribe to obtain injunctive relief against a state and its governor compelling compliance with the Indian Gaming Regulatory Act, the court of appeals (in disagreement with another circuit) held, *inter alia,* that Ex parte Young did not authorize the relief sought against the governor (see p. 1066, note 3, *supra*) and that Congress did not have the power to abrogate the immunity of the state itself. (This latter question arises because the Supreme Court had previously held, in Blatchford v. Native Village of Noatak, 501 U.S. 775 (1991), that the Eleventh Amendment applies to a suit against a state by an Indian Tribe.)

12. Suppose Congress viewed the Pennhurst decision, p. 1077, *supra,* as having unduly discouraged litigants with parallel federal and state law claims against state officials from seeking relief in federal court. Does it have power to abrogate the state's Eleventh

holding of Union Gas itself made unstable, by the absence of a majority rationale?

(5) *The Requirement of a "Clear" Legislative Statement.* The same day that Union Gas was decided, the Court ruled in Dellmuth v. Muth, 491 U.S. 223 (1989)(5–4) that the Education of the Handicapped Act—enacted under § 5 of the Fourteenth Amendment—did not abrogate the states' Eleventh Amendment immunity. The Act gives handicapped children the right to a free public education appropriate to their needs. The suit sought reimbursement from the state for private school tuition payments necessitated by violations of the Act by the state and a local school district. (The Supreme Court had previously ruled, in a case against a *local* school district, that reimbursement for the cost of private schooling necessitated by a violation of the Act was an appropriate remedy.)

The Court, per Justice Kennedy, found that congressional intent to abrogate immunity from federal court suit was not "unmistakably clear in the language of the statute" (p. 230, quoting from the Atascadero decision,[13] discussed in Union Gas). The plaintiff's argument that abrogation was necessary to achieve the Act's goals was "beside the point. * * * Lest Atascadero be thought to contain any ambiguity, we reaffirm today that * * * evidence of congressional intent must be both unequivocal and textual. * * * [W]e reject the approach of the Court of Appeals, according to which, '[w]hile the text of the federal legislation must bear evidence of such an intention, the legislative history may still be used as a resource in determining whether Congress' intention to lift the bar has been made sufficiently manifest.' Legislative history generally will be irrelevant 'in determining whether Congress intended to abrogate (p. 230).' Turning to the text, the Court found no reference to either the Eleventh Amendment or state sovereign immunity, and reaffirmed that '[a] general authorization for suit in federal court' 'falls short of the mark (p. 231, quoting Atascadero). Justice Scalia, who provided the fifth vote, joined the Court's opinion 'with the understanding that its reasoning does not preclude congressional elimination of sovereign immunity in statutory text that clearly subjects States to suit for monetary damages, though without explicit reference to state sovereign immunity or the Eleventh Amendment' " (p. 233).

Suppose the text of a federal statute clearly provides that a state that violates the statute is liable for damages, but in a context in which state courts have concurrent jurisdiction, says nothing about whether that liability should

Amendment immunity as to all state law claims that fall within the federal courts' pendent jurisdiction? For an affirmative answer, see Brown, *Beyond Pennhurst—Protective Jurisdiction, the Eleventh Amendment, and the Power of Congress to Enlarge Federal Jurisdiction in Response to the Burger Court,* 71 Va.L.Rev. 343 (1985).

13. Atascadero itself involved a federal court suit against a state under the federal Rehabilitation Act—a suit the Court held unauthorized because of the lack of a sufficiently clear congressional statement abrogating Eleventh Amendment immunity. The year after that decision, Congress enacted legisla-
tion providing: "A State shall not be immune under the Eleventh Amendment * * * from suit in Federal court for a violation [occurring after the date of the legislation] of section 504 of the Rehabilitation Act * * * or the provisions of any other Federal statute prohibiting discrimination by recipients of Federal financial assistance." Pub.L. 99–506, § 1003, 100 Stat. 1807, 1845 (1986). See Lee, *The Political Safeguards of Federalism? Congressional Response to Supreme Court Decisions on State and Local Liability,* 20 Urb.L. 301 (1988)(arguing that these "safeguards" were not visibly at work in this instance).

be enforced in state or federal court. Would Justice Scalia vote to uphold the power of a *federal* court to award damages against a state?

(6) *Is There a Justification for the "Clear Statement" Rule?* Is the Court's now established requirement of clear statement to overcome Eleventh Amendment immunity a justifiable one? Can it be explained as a corollary of the political safeguards of federalism? "If Congress is the only source of protection of the states' interests, it does not seem unfair for the Court to force Congress to do its job." Brown, *State Sovereignty Under the Burger Court—How the Eleventh Amendment Survived the Death of the Tenth: Some Broader Implications of Atascadero State Hospital v. Scanlon,* 74 Geo.L.J. 363, 390 (1985). If ordinary techniques of statutory interpretation lead to the conclusion that Congress intended to subject the states to suit, why should the Court reach an opposite result? Would it make more sense to require a policy of clear statement on the question whether Congress meant to subject the states to regulation—and especially to regulation of their internal governmental affairs—than on the question whether such regulation is fully enforceable in federal court? (Note that the Court took that very tack in a later decision, Gregory v. Ashcroft, 501 U.S. 452 (1991), refusing to hold, in the absence of a sufficiently clear statement, that a federal law prohibiting mandatory retirement applied to appointed state judges.)

Does it matter, in answering these questions, whether state sovereign immunity is viewed as having common law or constitutional status? Whether, if federal court relief is barred, the state courts would be obliged to provide all relief authorized by the federal statute?

Even assuming that some policy of clear statement represents an appropriate accommodation of the competing constitutional values at stake, do the more recent cases articulate that policy with undue severity? (Note that in neither Fitzpatrick nor Hutto v. Finney (note 7, *supra*) did the statute unequivocally express Congress' intention to subject the states to suit in *federal court*. And in Employees, Quern, and Hutto, the Court consulted legislative history to help determine whether abrogation was intended.)

(7) *The Significance of Exclusive Federal Jurisdiction.* In Union Gas, federal jurisdiction was exclusive, see 42 U.S.C. § 9613(b)—a point not mentioned by the Court. If it is held in such a case that state immunity has not been abrogated with sufficient clarity, in what tribunal may a claimant seek relief?[14]

(8) *Using the Exception for Suits Against a State by the United States.* Given the recognized inapplicability of the Eleventh Amendment to suits against a state by the United States (p. 1051, *supra*), could Congress circumvent the problem of its abrogation power by authorizing individuals or other entities to sue in the name of the United States (as in a *qui tam* action) to compel state compliance with a federal duty, or to seek compensation for a state's violation of such a duty. See Siegel, *The Hidden Source of Congress's Power to Abrogate State Sovereign Immunity,* 73 Tex.L.Rev. 539 (1995)(arguing that such authority does exist). If Siegel is right, is there any remaining justification for viewing the doctrine of state sovereign immunity as anything more than a federal common law rule?

---

14. See Cloherty, *Exclusive Jurisdiction and the Eleventh Amendment: Recognizing the Assumption of State Court Availability in the Clear Statement Compromise,* 82 Calif.L.Rev. 1287 (1994)(urging an exception to the clear statement rule in exclusive jurisdiction cases).

(9) *Additional References.* In addition to the sources already cited in this Note, two interesting commentaries on the question of the power to abrogate are Tribe, *Intergovernmental Immunities in Litigation, Taxation, and Regulation: Separation of Powers Issues in Controversies About Federalism,* 89 Harv. L.Rev. 682 (1976), and Nowak, *The Scope of Congressional Power to Create Causes of Action Against State Government and the History of the Eleventh and Fourteenth Amendments,* 75 Colum.L.Rev. 1413 (1975). Both authors argue that Congress may abrogate the states' Eleventh Amendment immunity in the exercise of *any* of its enumerated powers, since that immunity, in their view, is directed at appointed federal judges rather than at politically accountable legislators.

SUBSECTION B: FEDERAL CONSTITUTIONAL PROTECTION AGAINST STATE OFFICIAL ACTION

Home Telephone & Telegraph Co. v. City of Los Angeles

227 U.S. 278, 33 S.Ct. 312, 57 L.Ed. 510 (1913).
Appeal from the United States District Court for the Southern District of California.

■ MR. CHIEF JUSTICE WHITE delivered the opinion of the Court.

The appellant, a California corporation furnishing telephone service in the city of Los Angeles, sued the city and certain of its officials to prevent the putting into effect of a city ordinance establishing telephone rates for the year commencing July 1, 1911.

It was alleged that by the Constitution and laws of the state the city was given a right to fix telephone rates, and had passed the assailed ordinance in the exercise of the general authority thus conferred. It was charged that the rates fixed were so unreasonably low that their enforcement would bring about the confiscation of the property of the corporation, and hence the ordinance was repugnant to the due process clause of the 14th Amendment. * * *

Being of the opinion that no jurisdiction was disclosed by the bill, the court refused to grant a restraining order or allow a preliminary injunction, and thereafter, on the filing of a formal plea to the jurisdiction the bill was dismissed for want of power as a Federal court to consider it. This direct appeal was then taken.

* * *

The ground of challenge to the jurisdiction advanced by the plea may be thus stated: As the acts of the state officials (the city government) complained of were alleged to be wanting in due process of law, and therefore repugnant to the 14th Amendment,—a ground which, on the face of the bill, if well founded, also presumptively caused the action complained of to be repugnant to the due-process clause of the state Constitution,—there being no diversity of citizenship, there was no Federal jurisdiction. In other words, the plea asserted that where, in a given case, taking the facts averred to be true, the acts of state officials violated the Constitution of the United States, and likewise, because of the coincidence of a state constitutional prohibition, were presumptively repugnant to the state Constitution, such acts could not be treated as acts of the state within the 14th Amendment, and hence no power existed in a Federal court to consider the subject until, by final action of an appropriate state court, it was decided that such acts were authorized by the state, and were therefore not repugnant to the state Constitution. * * *

Coming to consider the real significance of this doctrine, we think it is so clearly in conflict with the decisions of this court as to leave no doubt that plain error was committed in announcing and applying it. In view, however, of the fact that the proposition was sanctioned by the court below, and was by it deemed to be supported by the persuasive authority of two opinions of the circuit court of appeals for the ninth circuit, before coming to consider the decided cases we analyze some of the conceptions upon which the proposition must rest, in order to show its inherent unsoundness, to make its destructive character manifest, and to indicate its departure from the substantially unanimous view which has prevailed from the beginning.

In the first place, the proposition addresses itself not to the mere distribution of the judicial power granted by the Constitution, but substantially denies the existence of power under the Constitution over the subject with which the proposition is concerned. It follows that the limitation which it imposes would be beyond possible correction by legislation. Its restriction would, moreover, attach to the exercise of Federal judicial power under all circumstances, whether the issue concerned original jurisdiction or arose in the course of a controversy to which otherwise jurisdiction would extend. Thus, being applicable equally to all Federal courts, under all circumstances, in every stage of a proceeding, the enforcement of the doctrine would hence render impossible the performance of the duty with which the Federal courts are charged under the Constitution. Such paralysis would inevitably ensue, since the consequence would be that, at least in every case where there was a coincidence between a national safeguard or prohibition and a state one, the power of the Federal court to afford protection to a claim of right under the Constitution of the United States, as against the action of a state or its officers, would depend on the ultimate determination of the state courts, and would therefore require a stay of all action to await such determination. * * * [Moreover,] it would come to pass that in every case where action of a state officer was complained of as violating the Constitution of the United States, the Federal courts, in any form of procedure, or in any stage of the controversy, would have to await the determination of a state court as to the operation of the Constitution of the United States. It is manifest that, in necessary operation, the doctrine which was sustained would, in substance, cause the state courts to become the primary source for applying and enforcing the constitution of the United States in all cases covered by the 14th Amendment.

* * * [I]f there be no right to exert [Federal judicial] power until, by the final action of a state court of last resort, the act of a state officer has been declared rightful and to be the lawful act of the state as a governmental entity, the inquiry naturally comes whether, under such circumstances, a suit against the officer would not be a suit against the state, within the purview of the 11th Amendment. The possibility of such a result, moreover, at once engenders a further inquiry; that is, whether the effect of the proposition would not be to cause the 14th Amendment to narrow Federal judicial power instead of enlarg-

ing it and making it more efficacious. It must be borne in mind, also, that the limitations which the proposition, if adopted, would impose upon Federal judicial power, would not be in reason solely applicable to an exertion of such power as to the persons and subjects covered by the 14th Amendment, but would equally govern controversies concerning the contract and possibly other clauses of the Constitution.

The vice which not only underlies but permeates the proposition is not far to seek. It consists, first, in causing by an artificial construction the provisions of the 14th Amendment not to reach those to whom they are addressed when reasonably construed; and, second, in wholly misconceiving the scope and operation of the 14th Amendment, thereby removing from the control of that Amendment the great body of rights which it was intended it should safeguard, and in taking out of reach of its prohibitions the wrongs which it was the purpose of the Amendment to condemn.

Before demonstrating the accuracy of the statement just made as to the essential result of the proposition relied upon by a reference to decided cases, in order that the appreciation of the cases may be made more salient, we contrast the meaning as above stated, which the 14th Amendment would have if the proposition was maintained, with the undoubted significance of that Amendment as established by many decisions of this court.

By the proposition the prohibitions and guaranties of the Amendment are addressed to and control the states only in their complete governmental capacity, and as a result give no authority to exert Federal judicial power until, by the decision of a court of last resort of a state, acts complained of under the 14th Amendment have been held valid, and therefore state acts in the fullest sense. To the contrary, the provisions of the Amendment as conclusively fixed by previous decisions are generic in their terms, are addressed, of course, to the states, but also to every person, whether natural or juridical, who is the repository of state power. By this construction the reach of the Amendment is shown to be coextensive with any exercise by a state of power, in whatever form exerted. * * *

To speak broadly, the difference between the proposition insisted upon and the true meaning of the Amendment is this: that the one assumes that the Amendment virtually contemplates alone wrongs authorized by a state, and gives only power accordingly, while in truth the Amendment contemplates the possibility of state officers abusing the powers lawfully conferred upon them by doing wrongs prohibited by the Amendment. In other words, the Amendment, * * * [conceiving] that state powers might be abused by those who possessed them, and as a result might be used as the instrument for doing wrongs, provided against all and every such possible contingency. * * * [A] state officer cannot, on the one hand, as a means of doing a wrong forbidden by the Amendment, proceed upon the assumption of the possession of state power, and at the same time, for the purpose of avoiding the application of the Amendment, deny the power, and thus accomplish the wrong. * * *

Let us consider the decided cases in order to demonstrate how plainly they refute the contention here made by the court below, and how clearly they establish the converse doctrine which we have formulated in the two propositions previously stated. * * *

Although every contention pressed and authority now relied upon in favor of affirmance is disposed of by the general principles which we have previously stated, before concluding we specially advert to some of the contentions urged to the contrary. * * * Much reliance is placed upon the decisions in Barney v. New York, [193 U.S. 430 (1904)], and Memphis v. Cumberland Teleph. & Teleg. Co., 218 U.S. 624. The latter we at once put out of view with the statement that, on its face, the question involved was one of pleading, and in no sense of substantive Federal power. As to the other,—the Barney Case,—it might suffice to say * * * [that] if it conflicted with the doctrine * * * of the subsequent and leading case of Ex parte Young, [it] is now so distinguished or qualified as not to be here authoritative or even persuasive. But on the face of the Barney Case it is to be observed that * * * [since] the decision there rendered proceeded upon the hypothesis that the facts presented took the case out of the established rule, there is no ground for saying that that case is authority for overruling the settled doctrine which, abstractly, at least, it recognized. If there were room for such conclusion, in view of what we have said, it would be our plain duty to qualify and restrict the Barney Case in so far as it might be found to conflict with the rule here applied. * * *

Reversed.

NOTE ON THE SCOPE OF FEDERAL CONSTITUTIONAL PROTECTION AGAINST UNAUTHORIZED STATE ACTION

(1) *The Relation Between the Eleventh and Fourteenth Amendments.* Despite the Court's reliance on Ex parte Young, is Home Telephone's construction of the Fourteenth Amendment inconsistent with the construction of the Eleventh Amendment in Young?

(2) *The Barney Case and its Aftermath.*

(a) Barney v. City of New York, 193 U.S. 430 (1904), discussed in Home Telephone, was a suit to enjoin the city from proceeding with construction of the Park Avenue subway tunnel, which was adjacent to plaintiff's premises. The bill alleged that the construction deprived plaintiff of his property without due process in violation of the Fourteenth Amendment. It also asserted that the construction was not in accordance with the plan approved by the local authorities, and hence was forbidden under state law. The federal circuit court dismissed the bill for want of jurisdiction, and the Supreme Court affirmed.

The bill of complaint seems to have been framed principally upon the theory that the acts of the defendants constituted a taking of the complainant's property without due process of law, in violation of the Fourteenth Amendment, not because of their intrinsic nature but simply because they were a violation of state law. If so, the Court's substantive interpretation of the Fourteenth Amendment would surely be unexceptionable.

However, the bill also alleged (p. 433) that "said rapid transit act, so far as it purports to authorize the construction of a tunnel and railway in said Park avenue without the consent of abutting owners or compensation therefor, is void, because it deprives your orator of his property without due process of law, in violation of the provisions of the said amendment." It is doubtful that this allegation raised a substantial federal question. The defendants pointed out that the subway affected neither light nor air nor access of abutters, and argued (p. 436) that "the alleged impairment of the comfort to be enjoyed in the plaintiff's premises through the acts of the city and its Rapid Transit Board underneath the surface of its own streets is not a taking of property within the meaning of the Fourteenth Amendment". The opinion does not discuss this question.

(b) A few years later, in Siler v. Louisville & N.R.Co., 213 U.S. 175 (1909), the railroad sought to enjoin enforcement of a state administrative order fixing maximum rates, on the grounds that it was unauthorized under state law and that it violated various provisions of the federal Constitution. Relying upon Barney, the defendants argued that if the order was unauthorized, it was "not the action of the State" and hence there could be no constitutional violation (p. 192). The Supreme Court responded that if the bill alleged *only* "that the order was invalid because it was not authorized by the State * * * the objection might be good, but the bill sets up several Federal questions. * * * The various questions are entirely separate from each other. Under these circumstances there can be no doubt that the Circuit Court obtained jurisdiction over the case by virtue of the Federal questions set up in the bill * * *" (pp. 192–93).[1]

(c) Justice Frankfurter attempted to resuscitate the Barney doctrine in his concurrence in Snowden v. Hughes, 321 U.S. 1 (1944). There, an Illinois citizen sued the members of the State Primary Canvassing Board for damages under 42 U.S.C. § 1983, alleging that defendants had maliciously and arbitrarily refused to file a certificate of plaintiff's selection as a Republican candidate for election to the state legislature. The certificate was necessary for plaintiff to be included on the ballot, and in the particular circumstances, certification would have been tantamount to final election. The complaint alleged that defendants had violated Illinois law and the Privileges or Immunities and Equal Protection Clauses of the Fourteenth Amendment.

The Court held that plaintiff had failed on the merits to state a cause of action. Chief Justice Stone's opinion, which focused on the equal protection claim, stated (pp. 11, 13):

"The unlawful administration by state officers of a state statute fair on its face, resulting in its unequal application to those who are entitled to be treated alike, is not a denial of equal protection unless there is shown to be present in it an element of intentional or purposeful discrimination. * * *

"As we conclude that the right asserted by petitioner is not one secured by the Fourteenth Amendment and affords no basis for a suit brought under the sections of the Civil Rights Acts relied upon, we find it unnecessary to consider whether the action by the State Board of which petitioner complains is state action within the meaning of the Fourteenth Amendment. The authority of Barney v. City of New York, *supra,* on which the court below relied, has been so restricted by our later decisions, see [*inter alia*] Home Tel. & Tel. Co. v. City of Los Angeles, 227 U.S. 278, 294, that our determination may be more properly and more certainly rested on petitioner's failure to assert a right of a nature such as the Fourteenth Amendment protects against state action."

Justices Douglas and Murphy dissented on the "narrow ground" that the complaint sufficiently charged "an invidious, purposeful discrimination", and that the plaintiff should be given a chance to prove the claim.

---

1. *Cf.* United States v. Raines, 362 U.S. 17, 25–26 (1960)(discriminatory voting practices that violated state law were unlawful under the Fifteenth Amendment and federal civil rights legislation; "Barney must be regarded as having 'been worn away by the erosion of time' * * * and of contrary authority").

Justice Frankfurter apparently agreed with the dissenters on this point but concurred with the majority on another ground. He said (pp. 15–17):

"* * * [To constitute] unjust discrimination the action must be that of the state. Since the state, for present purposes, can only act through functionaries, the question naturally arises what functionaries, acting under what circumstances, are to be deemed the state for purposes of bringing suit in the federal courts on the basis of illegal state action. The problem is beset with inherent difficulties and not unnaturally has had a fluctuating history in the decisions of the Court. Compare Barney v. City of New York, 193 U.S. 430, with [*e.g.*,] Home Tel. & Tel. Co. v. City of Los Angeles, 227 U.S. 278. It is not to be resolved by abstract considerations such as the fact that every official who purports to wield power conferred by a state is pro tanto the state. Otherwise every illegal discrimination by a policeman on the beat would be state action for purpose of suit in a federal court.

"Our question is not whether a remedy is available for such an illegality, but whether it is available in the first instance in a federal court. Such a problem of federal judicial control must be placed in the historic context of the relationship of the federal courts to the states, with due regard for the natural sensitiveness of the states and for the appropriate responsibility of state courts to correct the action of lower state courts and state officials. * * *

"I am clear * * * that the action of the Canvassing Board taken, as the plaintiff himself acknowledges, in defiance of the duty of that Board under Illinois law, cannot be deemed the action of the State, certainly not until the highest court of the State confirms such action and thereby makes it the law of the State. I agree, in a word, with the court below that Barney v. City of New York, 193 U.S. 430, is controlling. * * * A different problem is presented when a case comes here on review from a decision of a state court as the ultimate voice of state law. See for instance Iowa–Des Moines Nat. Bank v. Bennett, 284 U.S. 239. And the case is wholly unlike Lane v. Wilson, 307 U.S. 268, in which the election officials acted not in defiance of a statute of a state but under its authority."

(3) *The Implications of Justice Frankfurter's View.* Would the guarantees of the Fourteenth Amendment be adequately protected by a constitutional interpretation that treated the prohibitions of the Amendment as addressed only to the state as a whole after it has spoken with its final judicial voice? Could Justice Frankfurter's proposed jurisdictional doctrine have been accepted without rethinking the whole course of constitutional history since the Home Telephone case?

(4) *The Relation Between the Home Telephone Doctrine and the Materials That Follow.* The question whether federal law should be construed to regulate the conduct of state officials acting without authorization under or contrary to state law has proven to be a persistent one. In the next subsection, dealing with the scope of federal *statutory* protection against unauthorized state action, this question (or some variant of it) resurfaces in two contexts: (i) as a question of the proper interpretation of the Civil Rights Act of 1871, 42 U.S.C. § 1983, see Monroe v. Pape, which follows immediately; Monell v. Department of Social Services, p. 1126, *infra;* and (ii) in cases considering whether the existence of state-law remedies to redress a state official's deprivation of liberty or property provide "due process of law" so as to preclude any constitutional

claim under the Due Process Clause, see Zinermon v. Burch, p. 1138, *infra,* and the following Note.

SUBSECTION C: FEDERAL STATUTORY PROTECTION AGAINST STATE OFFICIAL ACTION: HEREIN OF 42 U.S.C. § 1983

Monroe v. Pape

365 U.S. 167, 81 S.Ct. 473, 5 L.Ed.2d 492 (1961).
Certiorari to the United States Court of Appeals for the Seventh Circuit.

■ MR. JUSTICE DOUGLAS delivered the opinion of the Court.

This case presents important questions concerning the construction of 42 U.S.C. § 1983, which reads as follows:

> "Every person who, under color of any statute, ordinance, regulation, custom, or usage, of any State or Territory, subjects, or causes to be subjected, any citizen of the United States or other person within the jurisdiction thereof to the deprivation of any rights, privileges, or immunities secured by the Constitution and laws, shall be liable to the party injured in an action at law, suit in equity, or other proper proceeding for redress."

The complaint alleges that 13 Chicago police officers broke into petitioners' home in the early morning, routed them from bed, made them stand naked in the living room, and ransacked every room, emptying drawers and ripping mattress covers. It further alleges that Mr. Monroe was then taken to the police station and detained on "open" charges for 10 hours, while he was interrogated about a two-day-old murder, that he was not taken before a magistrate, though one was accessible, that he was not permitted to call his family or attorney, that he was subsequently released without criminal charges being preferred against him. It is alleged that the officers had no search warrant and no arrest warrant and that they acted "under color of the statutes, ordinances, regulations, customs and usages" of Illinois and of the City of Chicago. Federal jurisdiction was asserted under [§ 1983], which we have set out above, and 28 U.S.C. § 1343 and 28 U.S.C. § 1331.

The City of Chicago moved to dismiss the complaint on the ground that it is not liable under the Civil Rights Acts nor for acts committed in performance of its governmental functions. All defendants moved to dismiss, alleging that the complaint alleged no cause of action under those Acts or under the Federal Constitution. The District Court dismissed the complaint. The Court of Appeals affirmed * * *.

I.

Petitioners claim that the invasion of their home and the subsequent search without a warrant and the arrest and detention of Mr. Monroe without a warrant and without arraignment constituted a deprivation of their "rights, privileges, or immunities secured by the Constitution" within the meaning of [§ 1983]. * * *

Section [1983] came onto the books as § 1 of the Ku Klux Act of April 20, 1871. 17 Stat. 13. * * *

Its purpose is plain from the title of the legislation, "An Act to enforce the Provisions of the Fourteenth Amendment to the Constitution of the United States, and for other Purposes." 17 Stat. 13. Allegation of facts constituting a deprivation under color of state authority of a right guaranteed by the Fourteenth Amendment satisfies to that extent the requirement of [§ 1983]. So far petitioners are on solid ground. For the guarantee against unreasonable searches and seizures contained in the Fourth Amendment has been made applicable to the States by reason of the Due Process Clause of the Fourteenth Amendment. Wolf v. Colorado, 338 U.S. 25 * * *.

II.

There can be no doubt at least since Ex parte Virginia, 100 U.S. 339, 346–347, that Congress has the power to enforce provisions of the Fourteenth Amendment against those who carry a badge of authority of a State and represent it in some capacity, whether they act in accordance with their authority or misuse it. See Home Tel. & Tel. Co. v. Los Angeles, 227 U.S. 278, 287–296. The question with which we now deal is the narrower one of whether Congress, in enacting § [1983], meant to give a remedy to parties deprived of constitutional rights, privileges and immunities by an official's abuse of his position. We conclude that it did so intend.

It is argued that "under color of" enumerated state authority excludes acts of an official or policeman who can show no authority under state law, state custom, or state usage to do what he did. In this case it is said that these policemen, in breaking into petitioners' apartment, violated the Constitution and laws of Illinois. It is pointed out that under Illinois law a simple remedy is offered for that violation and that, so far as it appears, the courts of Illinois are available to give petitioners that full redress which the common law affords for violence done to a person; and it is earnestly argued that no "statute, ordinance, regulation, custom or usage" of Illinois bars that redress.

* * *

The legislation—in particular the section with which we are now concerned—had several purposes. * * * One who reads [the debates] in their entirety sees that the present section had three main aims.

First, it might, of course, override certain kinds of state laws. * * *

Second, it provided a remedy where state law was inadequate. * * *

But the purposes were much broader. The *third* aim was to provide a federal remedy where the state remedy, though adequate in theory, was not available in practice. * * *

This Act of April 20, 1871, sometimes called "the third 'force bill,'" was passed by a Congress that had the Klan "particularly in mind." The debates are replete with references to the lawless conditions existing in the South in 1871. * * * It was not the unavailability of state remedies but the failure of certain States to enforce the laws with an equal hand that furnished the powerful momentum behind this "force bill." Mr. Lowe of Kansas said:

> "While murder is stalking abroad in disguise, while whippings and lynchings and banishment have been visited upon unoffending American citizens, the local administrations have been found inadequate or unwilling

to apply the proper corrective. * * * Immunity is given to crime, and the records of the public tribunals are searched in vain for any evidence of effective redress."

* * *

There was, it was said, no quarrel with the state laws on the books. It was their lack of enforcement that was the nub of the difficulty. * * *

* * *

Senator Pratt of Indiana spoke of the discrimination against Union sympathizers and Negroes in the actual enforcement of the laws:

"Plausibly and sophistically it is said the laws of North Carolina do not discriminate against them; that the provisions in favor of rights and liberties are general; that the courts are open to all; that juries, grand and petit, are commanded to hear and redress without distinction as to color, race, or political sentiment.

"But it is a fact, asserted in the report, that of the hundreds of outrages committed upon loyal people through the agency of this Ku Klux organization not one has been punished. This defect in the administration of the laws does not extend to other cases. Vigorously enough are the laws enforced against Union people. They only fail in efficiency when a man of known Union sentiments, white or black, invokes their aid. Then Justice closes the door of her temples."

It was precisely that breadth of the remedy which the opposition emphasized. Mr. Kerr of Indiana referring to the section involved in the present litigation said:

"This section gives to any person who may have been injured in any of his rights, privileges, or immunities of person or property, a civil action for damages against the wrongdoer in the Federal courts. The offenses committed against him may be the common violations of the municipal law of his State. * * * It is a covert attempt to transfer another large portion of jurisdiction from the State tribunals, to which it of right belongs, to those of the United States. * * *"

* * *

The debates were long and extensive. It is abundantly clear that one reason the legislation was passed was to afford a federal right in federal courts because, by reason of prejudice, passion, neglect, intolerance or otherwise, state laws might not be enforced and the claims of citizens to the enjoyment of rights, privileges, and immunities guaranteed by the Fourteenth Amendment might be denied by the state agencies.

* * *

Although the legislation was enacted because of the conditions that existed in the South at that time, it is cast in general language and is as applicable to Illinois as it is to the States whose names were mentioned over and again in the debates. It is no answer that the State has a law which if enforced would give relief. The federal remedy is supplementary to the state remedy, and the latter need not be first sought and refused before the federal one is invoked. Hence the fact that Illinois by its constitution and laws outlaws unreasonable searches and seizures is no barrier to the present suit in the federal court.

We had before us in United States v. Classic, *supra,* § 20 of the Criminal Code, 18 U.S.C. § 242, which provides a criminal punishment for anyone who "under color of any law, statute, ordinance, regulation, or custom" subjects any inhabitant of a State to the deprivation of "any rights, privileges, or immunities secured or protected by the Constitution or laws of the United States." Section 242 first came into the law as § 2 of the Civil Rights Act, Act of April 9, 1866, 14 Stat. 27. After passage of the Fourteenth Amendment, this provision was re-enacted and amended by §§ 17, 18, Act of May 31, 1870, 16 Stat. 140, 144. The right involved in the Classic case was the right of voters in a primary to have their votes counted. The laws of Louisiana required the defendants "to count the ballots, to record the result of the count, and to certify the result of the election." United States v. Classic, *supra,* 325–326. But according to the indictment they did not perform their duty. In an opinion written by Mr. Justice (later Chief Justice) Stone, in which Mr. Justice Roberts, Mr. Justice Reed, and Mr. Justice Frankfurter joined, the Court ruled, "Misuse of power, possessed by virtue of state law and made possible only because the wrongdoer is clothed with the authority of state law, is action taken 'under color of' state law." *Id.,* 326. There was a dissenting opinion; but the ruling as to the meaning of "under color of" state law was not questioned.

That view of the meaning of the words "under color of" state law, 18 U.S.C. § 242, was reaffirmed in Screws v. United States, *supra,* * * * [and] in Williams v. United States, *supra,* * * *.

Mr. Shellabarger, reporting out the bill which became the Ku Klux Act, said of the provision with which we now deal:

> "The model for it will be found in the second section of the act of April 9, 1866, known as the 'civil rights act.' * * * This section of this bill, on the same state of facts, not only provides a civil remedy for persons whose former condition may have been that of slaves, but also to all people where, under color of State law, they or any of them may be deprived of rights. * * *"

Thus, it is beyond doubt that this phrase should be accorded the same construction in both statutes—in § [1983] and in 18 U.S.C. § 242.

* * *

In the Screws case we dealt with a statute that imposed criminal penalties for acts "wilfully" done. We construed that word in its setting to mean the doing of an act with "a specific intent to deprive a person of a federal right." 325 U.S., at 103. We do not think that gloss should be placed on § [1983] which we have here. The word "wilfully" does not appear in § [1983]. Moreover, § [1983] provides a civil remedy, while in the Screws case we dealt with a criminal law challenged on the ground of vagueness. Section [1983] should be read against the background of tort liability that makes a man responsible for the natural consequences of his actions.

So far, then, the complaint states a cause of action. There remains to consider only a defense peculiar to the City of Chicago.

III.

The City of Chicago asserts that it is not liable under § [1983]. We do not stop to explore the whole range of questions tendered us on this issue at oral argument and in the briefs. For we are of the opinion that Congress did not undertake to bring municipal corporations within the ambit of § [1983].

When the bill that became the Act of April 20, 1871, was being debated in the Senate, Senator Sherman of Ohio proposed an amendment which would have made "the inhabitants of the county, city, or parish" in which certain acts of violence occurred liable "to pay full compensation" to the person damaged or his widow or legal representative. The amendment was adopted by the Senate. The House, however, rejected it. The Conference Committee reported another version. The House rejected the Conference report. In a second conference the Sherman amendment was dropped and in its place § 6 of the Act of April 20, 1871, was substituted. This new section, which is now 42 U.S.C. § 1986, dropped out all provision for municipal liability and extended liability in damages to "any person or persons, having knowledge that any" of the specified wrongs are being committed. * * * The objection to the Sherman amendment stated by Mr. Poland [speaking for the House Conferees] was that "the House had solemnly decided that in their judgment Congress had no constitutional power to impose any obligation upon county and town organizations, the mere instrumentality for the administration of state law." The question of constitutional power of Congress to impose civil liability on municipalities was vigorously debated with powerful arguments advanced in the affirmative.

* * * It is said that doubts should be resolved in favor of municipal liability because private remedies against officers for illegal searches and seizures are conspicuously ineffective, and because municipal liability will not only afford plaintiffs responsible defendants but cause those defendants to eradicate abuses that exist at the police level. We do not reach those policy considerations. Nor do we reach the constitutional question whether Congress has the power to make municipalities liable for acts of its officers that violate the civil rights of individuals.

The response of the Congress to the proposal to make municipalities liable for certain actions being brought within federal purview by the Act of April 20, 1871, was so antagonistic that we cannot believe that the word "person" was used in this particular Act to include them. Accordingly we hold that the motion to dismiss the complaint against the City of Chicago was properly granted. But since the complaint should not have been dismissed against the officials the judgment must be and is reversed.

■ MR. JUSTICE HARLAN, whom MR. JUSTICE STEWART joins, concurring.

Were this case here as one of first impression, I would find the "under color of any statute" issue very close indeed. However, in Classic and Screws this Court considered a substantially identical statutory phrase to have a meaning which, unless we now retreat from it, requires that issue to go for the petitioners here.

    * * *

Those aspects of Congress' purpose which are quite clear in the earlier congressional debates, as quoted by my Brothers Douglas and Frankfurter in turn, seem to me to be inherently ambiguous when applied to the case of an isolated abuse of state authority by an official. * * * If attention is directed at the rare specific references to isolated abuses of state authority, one finds them neither so clear nor so disproportionately divided between favoring the positions of the majority or the dissent as to make either position seem plainly correct.

    * * *

The dissent considers that the "under color of" provision of § 1983 distinguishes between unconstitutional actions taken without state authority, which only the State should remedy, and unconstitutional actions authorized by the State, which the Federal Act was to reach. If so, then the controlling difference for the enacting legislature must have been either that the state remedy was more adequate for unauthorized actions than for authorized ones or that there was, in some sense, greater harm from unconstitutional actions authorized by the full panoply of state power and approval than from unconstitutional actions not so authorized or acquiesced in by the State. I find less than compelling the evidence that either distinction was important to that Congress.

I.

If the state remedy was considered adequate when the official's unconstitutional act was unauthorized, why should it not be thought equally adequate when the unconstitutional act was authorized? * * *

Since the suggested narrow construction of § 1983 presupposes that state measures were adequate to remedy unauthorized deprivations of constitutional rights and since the identical state relief could be obtained for state-authorized acts with the aid of Supreme Court review, this narrow construction would reduce the statute to having merely a jurisdictional function, shifting the load of federal supervision from the Supreme Court to the lower courts and providing a federal tribunal for fact findings in cases involving authorized action. Such a function could be justified on various grounds. It could, for example, be argued that the state courts would be less willing to find a constitutional violation in cases involving "authorized action" and that therefore the victim of such action would bear a greater burden in that he would more likely have to carry his case to this Court, and once here, might be bound by unfavorable state court findings. But the legislative debates do not disclose congressional concern about the burdens of litigation placed upon the victims of "authorized" constitutional violations contrasted to the victims of unauthorized violations. Neither did Congress indicate an interest in relieving the burden placed on this Court in reviewing such cases.

The statute becomes more than a jurisdictional provision only if one attributes to the enacting legislature the view that a deprivation of a constitutional right is significantly different from and more serious than a violation of a state right and therefore deserves a different remedy even though the same act may constitute both a state tort and the deprivation of a constitutional right. This view, by no means unrealistic as a common-sense matter,[5] is, I believe, more consistent with the flavor of the legislative history than is a view that the primary purpose of the statute was to grant a lower court forum for fact findings. * * *

     * * *

---

5. There will be many cases in which the relief provided by the state to the victim of a use of state power which the state either did not or could not constitutionally authorize will be far less than what Congress may have thought would be fair reimbursement for deprivation of a constitutional right. * * * Even the remedy for such an unauthorized search and seizure as Monroe was allegedly subjected to may be only the nominal amount of damages to physical property allowable in an action for trespass to land. It would indeed be the purest coincidence if state remedies for violations of common-law rights by private citizens were fully appropriate to redress those injuries which only a state official can cause and against which the Constitution provides protection.

II.

I think [the] limited interpretation of § 1983 fares no better when viewed from the other possible premise for it, namely that state-approved constitutional deprivations were considered more offensive than those not so approved. For one thing, the enacting Congress was not unaware of the fact that there was a substantial overlap between the protections granted by state constitutional provisions and those granted by the Fourteenth Amendment. * * * I hesitate to assume that the proponents of the present statute, who regarded it as necessary even though they knew that the provisions of the Fourteenth Amendment were self-executing, would have thought the remedies unnecessary whenever there were self-executing provisions of state constitutions also forbidding what the Fourteenth Amendment forbids. * * *

These difficulties in explaining the basis of a distinction between authorized and unauthorized deprivations of constitutional rights fortify my view that the legislative history does not bear the burden which *stare decisis* casts upon it. For this reason and for those stated in the opinion of the Court, I agree that we should not now depart from the holdings of the Classic and Screws cases.

■ MR. JUSTICE FRANKFURTER, dissenting except insofar as the Court holds that this action cannot be maintained against the City of Chicago.

* * *

III.

* * * [A]lthough this Court has three times found that conduct of state officials which is forbidden by state law may be "under color" of state law for purposes of the Civil Rights Acts, it is accurate to say that that question has never received here the consideration which its importance merits. * * *

* * *

* * * The issue in the present case concerns directly a basic problem of American federalism: the relation of the Nation to the States in the critically important sphere of municipal law administration. In this aspect, it has significance approximating constitutional dimension. * * * This imposes on this Court a corresponding obligation to exercise its power within the fair limits of its judicial discretion. * * *

* * *

IV.

* * * [Plaintiffs] assert that they have been deprived of due process of law and of equal protection of the laws under color of state law, although from all that appears the courts of Illinois are available to give them the fullest redress which the common law affords for the violence done them, nor does any "statute, ordinance, regulation, custom, or usage" of the State of Illinois bar that redress. Did the enactment by Congress of § 1 of the Ku Klux Act of 1871 encompass such a situation?

* * * Senator Trumbull, then Chairman of the Senate Judiciary Committee, in his remarks urging its passage over [President Johnson's] veto, expressed the intendment of the second section as those who voted for it read it:

> "If an offense is committed against a colored person simply because he
> is colored, in a State where the law affords him the same protection as if he

were white, this act neither has nor was intended to have anything to do with his case, because he has adequate remedies in the State courts; but if he is discriminated against under color of State laws because he is colored, then it becomes necessary to interfere for his protection."

* * *

The original text of the present § [1983] contained words, left out in the Revised Statutes, which clarified the objective to which the provision was addressed:

"That any person who, under color of any law, statute, ordinance, regulation, custom, or usage of any State, shall subject, or cause to be subjected, any person within the jurisdiction of the United States to the deprivation of any rights, privileges, or immunities secured by the Constitution of the United States, shall, *any such law, statute, ordinance, regulation, custom, or usage of the State to the contrary notwithstanding,* be liable to the party injured. * * *"

* * *

The Court now says, however, that "It was not the unavailability of state remedies but the failure of certain States to enforce the laws with an equal hand that furnished the powerful momentum behind this 'force bill.'" Of course, if the notion of "unavailability" of remedy is limited to mean an absence of statutory, paper right, this is in large part true. Insofar as the Court undertakes to demonstrate—as the bulk of its opinion seems to do—that § [1983] was meant to reach some instances of action not specifically authorized by the avowed, apparent, written law inscribed in the statute books of the States, the argument knocks at an open door. No one would or could deny this, for by its express terms the statute comprehends deprivations of federal rights under color of any "statute, ordinance, regulation, *custom, or usage*" of a State. (Emphasis added.) The question is, *what* class of cases other than those involving state statute law were meant to be reached. And, with respect to this question, the Court's conclusion is undermined by the very portions of the legislative debates which it cites. For surely the misconduct of individual municipal police officers, subject to the effective oversight of appropriate state administrative and judicial authorities, presents a situation which differs *toto coelo* from one in which "Immunity is given to crime, and the records of the public tribunals are searched in vain for any evidence of effective redress," or in which murder rages while a State makes "no successful effort to bring the guilty to punishment or afford protection or redress," or in which the "State courts * * * [are] unable to enforce the criminal laws * * * or to suppress the disorders existing," or in which, in a State's "judicial tribunals one class is unable to secure that enforcement of their rights and punishment for their infraction which is accorded to another," * * *. These statements indicate that Congress—made keenly aware by the post-bellum conditions in the South that States through their authorities could sanction offenses against the individual by settled practice which established state law as truly as written codes—designed § [1983] to reach, as well, official conduct which, because engaged in "permanently and as a rule," or "systematically," came through acceptance by law-administering officers to constitute "custom, or usage" having the cast of law. They do not indicate an attempt to reach, nor does the statute by its terms include, instances of acts in defiance of state law and which no settled state practice, no systematic pattern of official action or inaction, no "custom, or usage, of any State," insulates from effective and adequate reparation by the State's authorities.

* * * [A]ll the evidence converges to the conclusion that Congress by § [1983] created a civil liability enforceable in the federal courts only in instances of injury for which redress was barred in the state courts because some "statute, ordinance, regulation, custom, or usage" sanctioned the grievance complained of. This purpose, manifested even by the so-called "Radical" Reconstruction Congress in 1871, accords with the presuppositions of our federal system. The jurisdiction which Article III of the Constitution conferred on the national judiciary reflected the assumption that the state courts, not the federal courts, would remain the primary guardians of that fundamental security of person and property which the long evolution of the common law had secured to one individual as against other individuals. The Fourteenth Amendment did not alter this basic aspect of our federalism.

Its commands were addressed to the States. Only when the States, through their responsible organs for the formulation and administration of local policy, sought to deny or impede access by the individual to the central government in connection with those enumerated functions assigned to it, or to deprive the individual of a certain minimal fairness in the exercise of the coercive forces of the State, or without reasonable justification to treat him differently than other persons subject to their jurisdiction, was an overriding federal sanction imposed. * * *

* * *

* * * Suppose that a state legislature or the highest court of a State should determine that within its territorial limits no damages should be recovered in tort for pain and suffering, or for mental anguish, or that no punitive damages should be recoverable. * * * Should an unlawful intrusion by a policeman in Chicago entail different consequences than an unlawful intrusion by a hoodlum? These are matters of policy in its strictly legislative sense, not for determination by this Court. And if it be, as it is, a matter for congressional choice, the legislative evidence is overwhelming that § [1983] is not expressive of that choice. * * *

[Justice Frankfurter concluded that the general allegation that the police intrusion was under color of Illinois law failed to state a claim under § 1983 in the face of Illinois decisions holding such intrusions unlawful. However, the averment that it was the "custom or usage" of the Chicago police department to detain individuals for long periods on "open charges" did state a valid claim of unlawful detention.]

————

NOTE ON 42 U.S.C. § 1983: AN OVERVIEW*

(1) *The Meaning of "Under Color of Law".*

* For further discussion of § 1983 in these materials, see, in addition to the remainder of this chapter, Chapters X and XII. For extensive treatment of § 1983 and related civil rights statutes in other sources, as well as additional references to secondary materials, see Low & Jeffries, Civil Rights Actions: Section 1983 and Related Statutes (2d ed. 1994); Gunther, Constitutional Law ch. 10 (12th ed. 1991); Nahmod, Wells & Eaton, Constitutional Torts (1995); Schwartz

(a) *The Relationship of Monroe to Home Telephone.*   Monroe establishes two overlapping but distinct propositions: (1) § 1983 creates a federal remedy, cognizable in federal court, against a state official for violation of federal rights; and (2) that remedy is available even if the official's conduct is wholly unauthorized under state law.   In the view of some, the primary significance of § 1983 is procedural—*i.e.*, even when it affords no substantive relief that could not also be obtained under state law, the *federal* remedy permits the exercise of federal court jurisdiction.   See Chevigny, *Section 1983 Jurisdiction: A Reply,* 83 Harv.L.Rev. 1352 (1970); Whitman, *Constitutional Torts,* 79 Mich.L.Rev. 5, 22–25 (1980).

Note that Justice Frankfurter's position in Monroe (which permits immediate resort to federal court when the defendant's acts have formal sanction in state law) gives a greater role to the federal courts than they would have had under the argument of the defendants in the Home Telephone case (under which there is no state action until the particular defendant's acts in the very case have been passed on by the highest state court).[1]   Consider the question raised by Justice Harlan: if state court remedies are deemed adequate to redress federal constitutional violations when the officer's acts violate state law, why should immediate resort to a federal court be allowed—as Justice Frankfurter concedes it is—when the officer's act is formally sanctioned by a state law or practice?   Recall that in the latter case, too, the state courts are obliged under the Supremacy Clause to disregard the state law if it conflicts with the federal, and that failure to do so is subject to review in the Supreme Court.

Note also the awkward inquiry that Justice Frankfurter's test would force on the federal courts in determining whether state "custom or usage" sanctions an individual defendant's unconstitutional acts.   Do the difficulties of such an inquiry argue for the reading of § 1983 in Monroe—a reading that makes the inquiry unnecessary in actions against state officials?[2]

(b) *State Action and Private Conduct.*   To recover under § 1983 for a constitutional tort in violation of the Fourteenth Amendment, the plaintiff must establish an injury resulting from unconstitutional "state action".   See, *e.g.,* Flagg Bros., Inc. v. Brooks, 436 U.S. 149 (1978).   In a suit against a government official, the state action requirement is identical to § 1983's requirement of conduct under color of state law; satisfying the former necessarily satisfies the latter.   Lugar v. Edmondson Oil Co., 457 U.S. 922, 928, 930

& Kirklin, Section 1983 Litigation: Claims, Defenses, and Fees (2d ed. 1991).

1.   *Cf.* City of Columbus v. Leonard, 443 U.S. 905, 910–11 (1979)(Rehnquist, J., dissenting)(suggesting reconsideration of Monroe's holding that the state remedy "need not be first sought and refused before the federal one is invoked").

2.   Note, however, that a similar inquiry must, in essence, be made today—under post-Monroe decisions that extended § 1983 liability to local government entities but limited the basis of such liability—in ruling whether the governmental entity itself is liable.   The

determination has not proved easy to make. See pp. 1129–31, *infra.*

For contrasting views of the soundness of the Monroe decision, see Zagrans, *"Under Color of" What Law: A Reconstructed Model of Section 1983 Liability,* 71 Va.L.Rev. 499 (1985)(arguing that the legislative history of the 1871 Civil Rights Act supports Justice Frankfurter's opinion); Winter, *The Meaning of "Under Color of" Law,* 91 Mich.L.Rev. 323 (1992)(suggesting, on the basis of consistent understanding from the thirteenth through the nineteenth century, that Monroe was correctly decided).

(1982).[3]

On the extent of state involvement needed—in a suit against a person who is concededly not a state officer—in order to establish both state action under the Constitution and conduct under color of law, custom, or usage for purposes of § 1983, see Lugar v. Edmondson Oil Co., *supra;* Pennzoil Co. v. Texaco, Inc., 481 U.S. 1 (1987), p. 1303, *infra.*

(2) *Jurisdiction Over Section 1983 Actions.* Section 1 of the Civil Rights Act of 1871 contained not only a remedial provision, now codified as § 1983, but also a grant of what appeared to be exclusive jurisdiction to the federal courts (without regard to amount in controversy). When the Act was revised in 1874, the jurisdictional portion was cut loose from the remedial provision and was itself divided into several provisions dealing with the circuit and district courts. When the original jurisdiction of the circuit and district courts was merged in 1911, the jurisdictional provisions of the Civil Rights Act were also merged, and eventually came to rest in what is now 28 U.S.C. § 1343(3).[4] That provision, which has been rendered superfluous by the elimination of the jurisdictional amount requirement in the general federal question statute (§ 1331), was not written in terms suggesting that federal jurisdiction was exclusive, and thus the Supreme Court has held that state courts have concurrent jurisdiction in actions under § 1983. See Martinez v. California, 444 U.S. 277, 283–84 n. 7 (1980); Maine v. Thiboutot, 448 U.S. 1, 3 n. 1 (1980). See generally Herman, *Beyond Parity: Section 1983 and the State Courts,* 54 Brook.L.Rev. 1057 (1989); Steinglass, *The Emerging State Court § 1983 Analysis: A Procedural Review,* 38 U.Miami L.Rev. 381 (1984).

On the question whether state courts are *obliged* to entertain such suits, see pp. 469–79, *supra.*

(3) *The Growth in § 1983 Litigation.* Prior to Monroe, litigation under § 1983 was infrequent; one commentator reports that there were only 19 cases in the U.S.C.A. annotations under § 1983 in its first 65 years. See Note, 82 Harv. L.Rev. 1486, 1486 n. 4 (1969). However, many suits that might have been brought under § 1983 as interpreted by Monroe were treated instead as actions for a remedy (usually an injunction) implied directly under the Constitution.[5]

Since Monroe, § 1983 litigation has grown rapidly. According to statistics gathered by the Administrative Office of the United States Courts, in 1961 there were 296 civil rights cases filed (the 1961 records do not indicate whether the plaintiff was a prisoner); in 1986 there were over 40,000: 20,842 filed by prisoners, and 20,128 filed by nonprisoners. These data, however, included many civil rights cases not filed under § 1983.[6] The most recent available

---

3. But the question of an individual's status is not always a simple one. Compare Polk County v. Dodson, 454 U.S. 312, 319 (1981)(state public defender was not acting under color of law because she undertook an "essentially * * * private function * * * for which state office and authority are not needed") with West v. Atkins, 487 U.S. 42 (1988)(physician who was under part-time contract with state and who treated inmates at a prison hospital was acting under color of state law).

4. This complicated story is told in fuller detail in Justice Powell's dissent in Maine v. Thiboutot, 448 U.S. 1, 15–16 (1980).

5. See, *e.g.,* General Oil v. Crain Co., 209 U.S. 211 (1908), p. 855, *supra;* Ex parte Young, 209 U.S. 123 (1908), p. 1058, *supra;* Ward v. Love County, 253 U.S. 17 (1920), p. 847, *supra.*

6. More refined analysis of data available during this period disclosed a less striking pattern of increase in § 1983 suits, particularly in non-prisoner cases. Eisenberg &

Administrative Office data, for the fiscal year ending June 30, 1995, shows a total of 35,566 non-prisoner "civil rights" actions filed, of which less than one half (16,259) did not relate to voting, employment, housing and accommodations, or welfare.[7] The number of prisoner civil rights actions had risen to 41,312.[8]

The view that constitutional tort actions are less likely to prove meritorious than civil litigation in general has been confirmed as to both prisoner and nonprisoner actions by Professors Eisenberg & Schwab, note 6, *supra*, at 136–48, although it is in the former class that the general lack of substance is most striking. Prisoners are also far less likely to have counsel, making the winnowing process especially difficult.

While the actual increase in § 1983 litigation since Monroe may have been somewhat exaggerated for reasons suggested above, there is no doubt that a significant increase has occurred. Is the concern of some observers over that increase (especially during the 1960s and 1970s) well-founded? Or did the increase simply reflect a natural response to the expansion of individual rights recognized by the federal courts during that period?[9] If the latter, is the real issue whether that expansion was itself desirable? Is there more basis for concern over suits for injunctive relief or suits for damages? See Whitman,

Schwab, *The Reality of Constitutional Tort Litigation,* 72 Cornell L.Rev. 641 (1987), conducted a detailed review of one federal judicial district, and concluded that (i) only 50% of the Administrative Office's "civil rights cases" were constitutional tort actions brought under § 1983 or the Bivens line of cases (p. 669); (ii) much of the increase reflected in the Administrative Office's data was attributable to the burgeoning of other kinds of actions, such as those under Title VII (pp. 662–65); (iii) from 1975–84, the number of nonprisoner civil rights cases outside the employment area increased by 94%, while the number of all other civil cases increased more rapidly, by 125% (p. 666); and (iv) though prisoner civil rights cases rose by nearly 200% between 1975 and 1984, from 6,606 to 18,856, when one adjusts for increases in prison population, the rate of increase was only 101%, compared to a 119% increase in all civil cases other than prisoner civil rights actions (p. 667).

For additional reports and analysis of empirical data gathered during this period, see Schwab & Eisenberg, *Explaining Constitutional Tort Litigation: The Influence of the Attorney Fees Statute and the Government as Defendant,* 73 Cornell L.Rev. 719 (1988); Doumar, *Prisoners' Civil Rights Suits: A Pompous Delusion,* 11 Geo. Mason U.L.Rev. 1, 15–17 (1988)(fewer than 0.5% of § 1983 prisoner suits filed in one federal district resulted in outcomes favorable to plaintiff); Eisenberg & Schwab, *What Shapes Percep-* *tions of the Federal Court System?,* 56 U.Chi. L.Rev. 501 (1989)(those who participate in, or observe, the federal appellate process see constitutional tort litigation as posing a serious problem for federal court administration; those who focus on federal district court litigation see much less of a problem); Eisenberg, *Section 1983: Doctrinal Foundations and an Empirical Study,* 67 Cornell L.Rev. 482 (1982); Turner, *When Prisoners Sue: A Study of Prisoner Section 1983 Suits in the Federal Courts,* 92 Harv.L.Rev. 610 (1979).

7. Letter from the Administrative Office of the United States Courts to David Shapiro, 8/31/95. Presumably, a large majority of the suits in these four categories were brought under federal statutes dealing specifically with such matters (like the Voting Rights Act and the various Titles of the 1964 Civil Rights Act).

8. *Id.* Once again, the increase in this category was in significant part a function of the large increase in the prison population. *Cf.* note 6, *supra.*

9. Professor Weinberg contends that the large increase in civil rights cases in the 1960s was caused not so much by Monroe's holding as by the Warren Court's expansion of protections afforded by the Bill of Rights— especially those relating to the criminal process. See Weinberg, *The Monroe Mystery Solved: Beyond the "Unhappy History" Theory of Civil Rights Litigation,* 1991 B.Y.U.L.Rev. 737.

Paragraph (1)(a), *supra*, at 10–11.[10]

(4) *Remedial and Procedural Doctrines in § 1983 Actions.* Section 1983 provides a barebones cause of action, without specifying such important matters as the measure of damages, the immunities of official defendants, and the statute of limitations. From what sources should the courts fashion rules of decision to govern issues like these?

One approach, which the Court has sometimes followed in developing doctrines governing official immunities and the measure of damages in § 1983 actions, is to establish a federal common law rule of decision that is designed to promote the statutory purposes.[11] A second approach—borrowing analogous rules of decisions of the applicable state (at least so long as those rules do not interfere with federal purposes)—has been followed in deciding whether a § 1983 action survives if the plaintiff dies during the lawsuit and an executor is substituted, and in selecting the appropriate statute of limitations for § 1983 actions, see pp. 820–29, *supra*.[12] A third possible approach, which the Court has not taken, is to borrow analogous doctrines from other federal civil rights statutes.

To the extent the Court has discretion to choose, is its election to follow different approaches as to different issues a sound one? For discussion of this question, see Chap. VII, Sec. 2(B), pp. 820–29, *supra*.

Another important issue in § 1983 actions that was much mooted for several years was the extent to which preclusion doctrines would apply in determining the res judicata effect of a prior state court proceeding. The Supreme Court's decisions in Allen v. McCurry, 449 U.S. 90 (1980)(applying 28 U.S.C. § 1738 and holding normal preclusion doctrine applicable), and in subsequent cases are discussed in detail in Chap. XII, Sec. 1, *infra*.

(5) *Attorney's Fees.* The Civil Rights Attorney's Fees Awards Act of 1976, codified in 42 U.S.C. § 1988, provided that a court "in its discretion, may allow the prevailing party, other than the United States, a reasonable attorney's fee as part of the costs." This provision is applicable to § 1983 actions in state as well as federal courts. Maine v. Thiboutot, 448 U.S. 1, 8–11 (1980). And

---

10. One response of many lower federal courts to the growth in § 1983 cases (and the corresponding growth in Bivens actions against federal officials) was to impose on plaintiffs a "heightened pleading standard" in order to survive a motion to dismiss for failure to state a claim. But in Leatherman v. Tarrant County Narcotics Intelligence and Coordination Unit, 507 U.S. 163, (1993), the Supreme Court held that such a demanding standard could not be squared with the liberal system of notice pleading established by the Federal Rules of Civil Procedure. The Leatherman case involved a complaint asserting municipal liability under § 1983 (see p. 1126, *infra*), and the Court noted that the case afforded no occasion to consider whether any comparable standard might be appropriate in suits against individual government

officers claiming official immunity. (On that question, see Sec. 3, p. 1175, *infra*.)

11. See, *e.g.,* Memphis Community School Dist. v. Stachura, 477 U.S. 299 (1986)(rules governing the measure of compensatory damages); Smith v. Wade, 461 U.S. 30 (1983)(punitive damages may be awarded on a showing of recklessness by an official defendant); Felder v. Casey, 487 U.S. 131 (1988), p. 827, *supra* (state notice-of-claim statute was preempted in a state court action under § 1983); Town of Newton v. Rumery, 480 U.S. 386 (1987), p. 828, *supra* (enforceability of agreement releasing § 1983 claims is governed by federal law); Sec. 3, *infra* (on official immunity doctrines).

12. For discussion of the Court's frequent reliance in these cases on § 1988 (which mandates reference to state law under certain conditions), see p. 822, *supra*.

despite the statutory language, it is established that (i) awards to plaintiffs who prevail (by settlement as well as by judgment, Maher v. Gagne, 448 U.S. 122 (1980)) are required absent special circumstances—a very narrow category; and (ii) defendants may not automatically recover whenever they prevail, but only when the plaintiff's action was frivolous or vexatious, see Hughes v. Rowe, 449 U.S. 5 (1980)(per curiam).

The essentially one-way shifting of fees may well have contributed to efforts to fit claims for relief under § 1983, and may also have increased the total number of civil rights actions filed. See Rowe, *Predicting the Effects of Attorney Fee Shifting,* 47 Law & Contemp.Prob. 139, 147 (1984). But see Schwab & Eisenberg, note 6, *supra,* at 780 ("attorney fees statutes may have less of an effect on filing rates than is commonly believed"). Is a one-way approach warranted by the importance of the rights asserted in § 1983 actions? By the presumed impecuniousness of many plaintiffs? By the fact that relief in § 1983 suits often provides benefits to non-parties? Does the approach exacerbate problems associated with the increase in § 1983 litigation?

Section 1988 has generated considerable litigation over circumstances in which fees should be awarded and the calculation of particular awards. For a survey and analysis of the case law, see Low & Jeffries, note *, *supra,* ch. IV.

(6) *Relationship Between the Remedy Under § 1983 and the Writ of Federal Habeas Corpus.* The Supreme Court, in Preiser v. Rodriguez, 411 U.S. 475 (1973), and Heck v. Humphrey, 114 S.Ct. 2364 (1994), has effectively subordinated the § 1983 remedy to the writ of habeas corpus where the remedies overlap (and to some extent, even where they don't), holding that § 1983 may not be resorted to if the direct or indirect effect of granting relief would be to invalidate an existing state court conviction of the § 1983 plaintiff. For analysis of these and related decisions, see Chap. XII, Sec. 2, *infra.*

NOTE ON INDIVIDUAL OFFICERS, LOCAL GOVERNMENTS, AND STATES AS DEFENDANTS IN ACTIONS UNDER § 1983

(1) *Individual Officers as Defendants: Personal Capacity Suits.* The great preponderance of § 1983 actions name individual officers as defendants. When damages are sought, the officer is ordinarily sued in a "personal" or "individual" capacity, which means that any judgment will be paid out of the officer's funds, rather than by the government employer. Similarly, in a personal capacity action, attorney's fees can be awarded only against the officer, not against the government. Kentucky v. Graham, 473 U.S. 159 (1985). The Eleventh Amendment is inapplicable, since the relief does not directly affect the state.

Ever since Tenney v. Brandhove, 341 U.S. 367 (1951), however, it has been clear that officials sued under § 1983 in their personal capacity may avail themselves of immunity doctrines shielding them in many cases from damages liability. The Court has given extensive attention to the immunity doctrines applicable in § 1983 damages actions. These doctrines are discussed in detail in Section 3, *infra,* and for present purposes a summary of their broadest outlines will suffice. Most executive officials have a qualified immunity from damages liability unless their conduct violated "clearly established statutory or constitutional rights of which a reasonable person would have knowledge."

Harlow v. Fitzgerald, 457 U.S. 800, 812 (1982). Legislators, judges, and prosecutors enjoy absolute immunity from damages liability for conduct undertaken within their official capacities.

(2) *Individual Officers as Defendants: Official Capacity Suits.* Some damages actions under § 1983 are filed against an officer in the officer's "official" capacity. The designation of the individual as a defendant is a bit of a misnomer, as in an official capacity suit the plaintiff "must look to the government entity itself" as the source of any award, and that entity is the "real party in interest." Kentucky v. Graham, 473 U.S. 159, 166 (1985). Even though the government is not nominally the defendant, it can be ordered to pay damages and attorney's fees, provided that it had adequate notice and opportunity to defend. Brandon v. Holt, 469 U.S. 464 (1985). But because it will in fact be paid from the government treasury, a damages award in an official capacity suit is appropriate only in accordance with the rules about liability, immunity, and damages described in Paragraphs (4)–(6), (8), *infra,* governing actions against the government as such; the same appears to be true of awards of attorney's fees that are to be paid with government funds. See Kentucky v. Graham, *supra,* at 167–68.

When *equitable relief* is sought, the defendant official is ordinarily named in an official capacity. See, *e.g.,* Hutto v. Finney, 437 U.S. 678, 693 (1978); ACLU of Mississippi v. Finch, 638 F.2d 1336, 1338–42 (5th Cir.1981). Even in a suit thus captioned, the Eleventh Amendment interposes no bar, at least if the relief is deemed prospective in character. See pp. 1073–74, *supra.* (Don't be confused by the fact that even in an official capacity suit, the authority-stripping rationale of Ex parte Young applies, so that for purposes of the Eleventh Amendment the defendant is treated as stripped of his official character and subject, like any private tortfeasor, to an injunction against continuing harm).[1]

(3) *The Distinction Between Personal and Official Capacity Suits.* In Kentucky v. Graham, Paragraph (2), *supra,* the Supreme Court observed that the distinction between personal and official capacity suits "continues to confuse lawyers and confound lower courts." 473 U.S. at 165.[2] Wouldn't it make sense,

---

1. Especially given the theory of Young, it is not clear that a suit seeking prospective relief against an officer in that officer's "personal capacity" is defective. Surely any defect is sufficiently technical as to be remediable by amendment.

The label "personal" or "official" may have some practical importance in actions seeking equitable relief in which the named official ceases to hold office. Rule 25(d) of the Federal Rules of Civil Procedure and Rule 43(c)(1) of the Federal Rules of Appellate Procedure provide, in suits filed against an officer in an official capacity, for automatic substitution of a successor in office. However, the plaintiff, in order to establish a right to equitable relief, must show continuation by the successor of the challenged policy or practice. See, *e.g.,* Spomer v. Littleton, 414 U.S. 514 (1974).

2. In the case of equitable relief, it should ordinarily make no difference whether the suit is labelled as one against the officer personally or against him in his official capacity.

Insofar as plaintiff seeks damages, on the other hand, it is of some importance to know whether recovery is sought from the officer, the government entity, or both. The same is true when plaintiff seeks attorney's fees; since "fee liability runs with merits liability", Kentucky v. Graham, *supra,* at 168, the government is not liable for attorney's fees in a damages action unless the plaintiff has prevailed against it, and presumably an individual is not liable for fees in an "official capacity" suit. See Bender v. Williamsport Area School Dist., 475 U.S. 534, 543 n. 6 (1986)(by implication); but see Pulliam v. Allen, 466 U.S. 522 (1984)(state judge against whom

instead of using the somewhat elusive labels of official and personal capacity, simply to require the plaintiff to set forth in the complaint, or soon thereafter, the particular person or entity from which monetary relief or fees is sought? Naming the government rather than the official as the nominal defendant affects the plaintiff's ability to recover only when the plaintiff is seeking prospective relief against conduct of a state government; here, to avoid dismissal under the Eleventh Amendment, the plaintiff must name the official. But when monetary relief is sought from the government treasury, the plaintiff will have to establish that the government is liable under § 1983, and that the Eleventh Amendment poses no barrier to obtaining such relief in federal court—whether the nominal defendant is the government or an officer sued in an official capacity. So long as all defendants have fair notice, why should the caption of the complaint have significance?

(4) *Local Governments as Defendants: The Monell Decision.* Between 1961 and 1978 the Court reaffirmed and extended the subsidiary holding of Monroe v. Pape that municipalities are not "persons" within the meaning of § 1983. But in Monell v. Department of Social Services, 436 U.S. 658 (1978), the Court shifted course, holding that Monroe v. Pape had misread the legislative history of § 1983, and that Congress did intend to include local governments among the "persons" it rendered liable. In Monell, a class of female employees sued municipal agencies for back pay and injunctive relief, challenging defendants' policy of requiring pregnant employees to take unpaid leaves of absence. Reversing the lower courts, the Supreme Court, with Justice Brennan writing, ruled that cities and counties may be sued directly under § 1983 for damages or for declaratory and injunctive relief "where * * * the action that is alleged to be unconstitutional implements or executes a policy statement, ordinance, regulation or decision officially adopted and promulgated by that body's officers. Moreover * * * local governments * * * may be sued for constitutional deprivations visited pursuant to governmental 'custom' even though such a custom has not received formal approval through the body's official decision-making channels" (pp. 690–91).

The opinion's lengthy reexamination of the legislative history of the Civil Rights Act of 1871 led the Court to conclude that Monroe v. Pape had misinterpreted the import of the 42d Congress' rejection of the so-called Sherman Amendment. That amendment would have made municipalities liable not simply for violations of federal rights by municipal officials, but also for certain wrongful acts of *private citizens* within the municipality. In the view of the Monell Court, rejection of the Sherman amendment could not justify an inference that Congress sought to exclude municipal liability for conduct of *officials.* The Court found support for municipal liability in the legislative debates, and in the general understanding in 1871 that the term "person" included municipal corporations.

The Court clearly stated, albeit in dictum, that "a municipality cannot be held liable *solely* because it employs a tortfeasor—or, in other words, a municipality cannot be held liable under § 1983 on a *respondeat superior* theory" (p. 691). The language of the statute (in particular, "[a]ny person who * * * shall subject, or causes to be subjected," a person to the deprivation of federal rights) "cannot be easily read to impose liability vicariously on govern-

declaratory and injunctive relief is awarded   attorney's fees).
under § 1983 is also personally liable for

ing bodies solely on the basis of the existence of an employer-employee relationship" (pp. 691–92). The Court viewed the primary rationales for *respondeat superior* liability—loss-spreading and reduction of harm—as too close to the justifications for the Sherman Amendment to be the predicate for municipal liability. Thus, "it is [only] when execution of a government's policy or custom, whether made by its lawmakers or by those whose edicts or acts may fairly be said to represent official policy, inflicts the injury that the government as an entity is responsible under § 1983" (p. 694).

Justice Stevens concurred in part, refusing to join the Court's dictum rejecting *respondeat superior* liability. He later expressed his views on this question in a lone dissent in Oklahoma City v. Tuttle, 471 U.S. 808 (1985). Section 1983 was enacted, he argued, against a recognized background of *respondeat superior* liability in tort suits in general and specifically in tort suits against municipal corporations. The debate over the Sherman Amendment showed that Congress contemplated making municipalities more broadly (rather than more narrowly) liable than were private parties in 1871. Because the Fourteenth Amendment regulates only state action, an individual official can be liable under § 1983 only by virtue of the official's relationship to the government employer; that same relationship, Justice Stevens argued, justifies the application of normal principles of *respondeat superior*. He suggested that the policy considerations supporting the application of *respondeat superior* in common law tort suits against municipal corporations—compensation of victims, deterrence of misconduct, and fairness to individual officers "performing difficult and dangerous work"—also apply in constitutional tort actions (p. 844). The fear that broadened liability would bankrupt municipalities, though legitimate, was in Justice Stevens' view a matter primarily for Congress to consider, and in any event related to the question of damages rather than to the question of which classes of defendants could be held liable.[3]

(5) *The Scope of Municipal Damages Liability After Monell.* Even prior to Monell, local government entities could be effectively bound in injunctive or declaratory proceedings through the technique of suing their officials. The important consequence of Monell is, therefore, to render city, county, and school board treasuries liable in damages actions for violations of constitutional and statutory rights by their officials—but only when the violation is pursuant to government policy or custom. Note that Monell thus adopts the same line that Justice Frankfurter argued should govern the whole of § 1983 liability—a view the Court rejected in Monroe v. Pape. Is that line more appropriately invoked in measuring local government liability than in measuring the liability of individual officers? If not, does it argue for adoption of Justice Frankfurter's position more generally, or for adoption of broad *respondeat superior* liability for local governments, as Justice Stevens advocated?

Note that the imposition of governmental liability in damages *always* creates vicarious liability, in the sense that in the end it is the taxpayers who

---

3. Kramer & Sykes, *Municipal Liability Under § 1983: A Legal and Economic Analysis,* 1987 Sup.Ct.Rev. 249, lend support to Justice Stevens' position. The authors argue (pp. 250–51) that the Court in Monell read the language and history of § 1983 incorrectly (in their view, Congress intended to create a full-fledged federal tort remedy for depriva- tions of federal rights under color of state law), that the Monell approach has proven "extremely difficult to apply coherently", and that either a negligence rule or conventional respondeat superior liability (perhaps exoner- ating the municipality when the individual who was at fault enjoys an immunity de- fense) would be economically efficient.

foot the bill. Does this fact call for hesitation in holding local governments liable? One aspect of this question was at issue in Owen v. City of Independence, 445 U.S. 622, 638 (1980). There, the Court held, 5–4, that a municipality sued under Monell for violations committed by its officials does not have a qualified immunity from damages liability under § 1983, even if it can show that the officials would themselves be entitled to such an immunity in a § 1983 action against them personally.[4] Justice Brennan's opinion for the Court argued that officers' immunity was already deeply embedded in the common law when § 1983 was passed, so that the 42d Congress should be deemed to have enacted § 1983 in contemplation of such a defense; by contrast, there existed at the time no common-law tradition of immunity in actions against municipalities. Moreover, allowing the municipality to avail itself of the immunity of its officials would interfere with both the compensatory and the deterrent purposes of § 1983. The Court concluded by asserting that its holding, together with its previous decisions, "properly allocates [the costs of federal violations] among the three principals in the scenario of the § 1983 cause of action: the victim of the constitutional deprivation; the officer whose conduct caused the injury; and the public, as represented by the municipal entity. The innocent individual who is harmed by an abuse of governmental authority is assured of compensation. The offending official who conducts himself in good faith may go about his business secure in the knowledge that a qualified immunity will preclude personal liability for damages that are more appropriately chargeable to the populace as a whole. And the public will be forced to bear only the costs of injury inflicted by the 'execution of a government's policy or custom, whether made by its lawmakers or by those whose edicts or acts may fairly be said to represent official policy' [citing Monell]" (p. 657).[5]

Justice Powell's dissent, which was joined by Chief Justice Burger and Justices Stewart and Rehnquist, objected to the imposition of municipal liability in damages in a case in which government officials had violated "a constitutional right that was unknown when the events in this case occurred. * * * The Court's ruling also ignores the vast weight of common-law precedent as well as the current state law of municipal immunity" (p. 658).[6] Justice Powell also disputed the Court's assertion that municipal liability will not unduly inhibit officials in their decisionmaking.

4. *Cf.* the analogous holdings under the Federal Tort Claims Act, p. 1030, note 10, *supra,* that the United States is liable in tort even when the misbehaving officer would have an immunity defense.

5. Owen did not squarely decide whether local governments may be liable for acts by officials who are themselves shielded by an absolute (rather than merely a qualified) immunity. The major thrust of the opinion, however, is that all individual immunity defenses are irrelevant to suits against governmental entities, and the cases distinguished include holdings that an official is absolutely immune. (For a recent appellate court decision holding that municipalities do not enjoy immunity from damages liability for unconstitutional legislative enactments, despite the absolute immunity accorded to individual legislators, see Berkley v. Common Council, 63 F.3d 295 (4th Cir.1995)(en banc)).

6. On this point, Justice Brennan had argued that the common law tort immunity of a municipality in connection with its "governmental" functions was irrelevant, on the ground that § 1983, by making municipalities liable at all, automatically abrogated doctrines that derive from or are allied to sovereign immunity. Justice Brennan dealt with the common law immunity of municipalities in connection with their "discretionary" functions by declaring that a "municipality has no 'discretion' to violate the Federal Constitution; its dictates are absolute and imperative" (p. 649).

Is Justice Brennan's reasoning in Owen consistent with his rejection of *respondeat superior* liability in Monell? Do you agree with the Court that there is nothing unfair about imposing liability on taxpayers for official conduct where there was insufficient reason at the time the conduct occurred to believe that the conduct violated constitutional norms? *Cf.* City of Newport v. Fact Concerts, Inc., 453 U.S. 247, 258–71 (1981), where the Court held that municipalities may not be held liable under § 1983 for punitive damages. The opinion stressed that the common law did not subject municipalities to punitive damages awards, but also expressed the view that such an award would be a windfall to the plaintiff, while unfairly punishing "blameless or unknowing taxpayers" (p. 267).

(6) *The Meaning of "Policy" or "Custom".* The Supreme Court has dealt with the meaning of Monell's "custom or policy" standard in four subsequent cases.

(a) Oklahoma City v. Tuttle, 471 U.S. 808 (1985), was a § 1983 action alleging unconstitutional use of excessive force by a police officer. The jury's $1.5 million verdict against the city was overturned by the Supreme Court. Seven Justices found fault with the jury charge, which stated that "a single, unusually excessive use of force may be sufficiently out of the ordinary to warrant an inference that it was attributable to inadequate training or supervision amounting to 'deliberate indifference' or 'gross negligence' on the part of the officials in charge" (p. 813). Justice Rehnquist, writing for a four-Justice plurality, expressed doubt that inadequate training could constitute a "policy" in the absence of proof that decisionmakers "deliberately chose a training program which would prove inadequate" (p. 823). He also doubted that a policy (unlike the one in Monell) that was not *itself* unconstitutional could be the basis for liability;[7] at a minimum, plaintiff would need to show an "affirmative link" between such a policy and the violation (p. 823). Justice Brennan (joined by Justices Marshall and Blackmun), concurring in part and concurring in the judgment, agreed that the "single incident" instruction was erroneous, but disagreed with the majority's doubts that inadequate training could provide a basis for municipal liability.[8]

(b) In Pembaur v. City of Cincinnati, 475 U.S. 469 (1986), a physician, alleging that the county prosecutor had instructed police to make an unconstitutional entry into his clinic, sued the county under § 1983. The Supreme Court ruled that a single decision of a high official like the county prosecutor, who had authority under state law to decide whether the officers should enter and whose decision "may fairly be said to represent official policy," was an adequate basis for imposing governmental liability under § 1983 (p. 480, quoting Monell). Justice Powell, joined by Chief Justice Burger and Justice Rehnquist, dissented. He accused the Court of imposing what Monell rejected—*respondeat superior* liability—at least with regard to employees having final authority to make policy (p. 499). Because the prosecutor's *ad hoc* decision did not establish a "rule of general applicability", and was made "without time for thoughtful consideration or consultation," it did not, in

---

7. In City of St. Louis v. Praprotnik, Paragraph 6(c), *infra*, the plurality of four suggested in dictum that municipal liability must rest on the existence of an unconstitutional municipal policy. The Court held oth-

erwise, however, in City of Canton v. Harris, Paragraph 6(d), *infra*.

8. Justice Stevens dissented, arguing that recovery was justified on a *respondeat superior* theory. See Paragraph (4), *supra*.

Justice Powell's view, establish a policy within the meaning of Monell (pp. 499–501).

(c) In City of St. Louis v. Praprotnik, 485 U.S. 112 (1988), the Court confronted the question of which officials' decisions can render a municipality liable under § 1983. There a municipal employee brought suit contending that the Director of Urban Design (UD)(to whom plaintiff reported) in the St. Louis Community Development Agency (CDA), and CDA's Director, had violated the First Amendment by discharging plaintiff in retaliation for earlier appeals to the city's Civil Service Commission. The Supreme Court ruled, 7–1, that the city could not be held liable for these acts. Justice O'Connor's plurality opinion—an opinion later endorsed by a majority in Jett v. Dallas Indep. School Dist., 491 U.S. 701 (1989)—affirmed that state law determines who is a policymaking official; found that under state and local regulations, only the mayor and aldermen of St. Louis, and the Civil Service Commission, had policymaking authority over personnel decisions; and then concluded that no policymaker had adopted an unconstitutional municipal policy authorizing retaliatory discharges. The mere fact that policymakers had delegated to the Directors of UD and of CDA discretion to act—even if these subordinates' decisions were not in turn given de novo review by the policymakers—did not give the subordinate officials policymaking authority so as to make the municipality liable for their conduct.

Justice Brennan (joined by Justices Marshall and Blackmun) concurred in the judgment, agreeing that the record showed that the two subordinate officials lacked final authority to establish city policy. He questioned, however, the plurality's exclusive reliance on state statutory law in determining who the policymakers were. Instead, he argued that a factfinder must determine where policymaking authority actually resides, and not merely in whom the law formally vests it. Justice Brennan disagreed in particular with the plurality's view that an official whose decisions are formally subject to review by others cannot be deemed a policymaker when, because that review is never exercised, the official effectively makes final policy.[9]

(d) In City of Canton v. Harris, 489 U.S. 378 (1989), the Court dealt with the much-mooted question of the existence and extent of municipal liability for constitutional violations resulting from "failure to train" employees. In the Canton case, which involved a complaint that the due process rights of a person under arrest had been violated because he had been given inadequate medical attention by the police, the Court held that municipal liability for inadequate training is permitted by the statute, but "only where the failure to train amounts to deliberate indifference to the rights of persons with whom the police [the officials involved in the particular case] come into contact" (p. 388). Thus, the Court said, "the focus must be on [the] adequacy of the training program in relation to the tasks the particular officers must perform" (p. 390). The question, in other words, is the adequacy of the training program itself and its relation to the injury caused, not simply the mistake or indifference of the individual officer.[10]

---

9. Justice Stevens dissented, arguing that the city should be held liable for decisions made by "high officials" such as an agency head. Justice Kennedy did not participate.

10. Because the district court (whose judgment had been affirmed by the court of appeals) had imposed a lesser standard of proof, the case was remanded for further proceedings. Justice Brennan, concurring,

Justice O'Connor (joined by Justices Scalia and Kennedy), concurred in part but would have reversed the judgment below instead of remanding for consideration of the question whether there should be a new trial. The plaintiff, she said, had had every opportunity to adduce the evidence needed to get to the jury under the standard adopted by the Court, and, in her view, "there is no evidence in the record indicating that the city of Canton has been deliberately indifferent to the constitutional rights of pretrial detainees" (p. 394).[11]

(7) *An Appraisal of Monell and its Progeny.* In all of the decisions following Monell, the Justices seem to be trying to limit local government liability to those situations in which fault can be attributed not simply to an individual officer but to the governmental entity itself. Doesn't the history of the sovereign immunity of the United States, and of the Eleventh Amendment, cast doubt on the desirability of such an effort? Do you find workable or useful the distinctions drawn between (i) formal and informal delegations of policymaking authority, and (ii) an unconstitutional act resulting from an officer's mistake or indifference and an unconstitutional act resulting from a woefully inadequate training program? To the extent § 1983 leaves the courts a choice (*cf.* Kramer & Sykes, note 2, *supra*), has the course chosen been the best available?

With the liability of local governments under § 1983, contrast the liability of the federal government under the Federal Tort Claims Act. The United States is generally liable on a simple *respondeat superior* theory for the common law torts of its employees, 28 U.S.C. § 1346(b); there is an exception, however, for acts undertaken with "due care, in the execution of a statute or regulation, whether or not * * * valid," *id.* § 2680(a). Is there some reason to believe that opposing views of governmental liability are appropriate at the local and federal levels?

(8) *Implied Remedies Against Local Governments..* Prior to Monell, a number of lower courts, relying on the authority of the Bivens case, had implied a damages remedy directly under the Constitution against municipalities or other local governments for violations of constitutional rights by individual officials. See Note, 89 Harv.L.Rev. 922 (1976). Were such decisions justifiable against the background of Monroe v. Pape's holding that Congress, in enacting § 1983, had not imposed any liability upon local governments?[12]

After Monell, a plaintiff would need to seek an implied damages remedy directly under the Fourteenth Amendment against a city or county only in a "pure" *respondeat superior* case. In Jett v. Dallas Indep. School Dist., 491 U.S. 701 (1989)(5–4), an employee alleging racial discrimination sued the school district for damages under 42 U.S.C. § 1981, an equal rights statute derived

---

made clear his understanding that on remand, the court of appeals could order a new trial.

11. For a critique of this line of decisions, see Cushman, *Municipal Liability Under § 1983: Toward a New Definition of Municipal Policymaker,* 34 B.C.L.Rev. 693, 697 (1993)(arguing that municipal policymakers should be defined as "elected officials, officials designated by state or local law as policymakers, *and officials who are de facto policymakers by virtue of the absence of*

any review of their actions.") (Emphasis added.)

12. *Cf.* Amar, *Of Sovereignty and Federalism,* 96 Yale L.J. 1425, 1484–92 (1987)(arguing that the Constitution demands full and adequate remedies for constitutional violations, and that imposition of governmental liability in damages, apparently through a judicially-implied remedy, will often be necessary to provide effective redress).

from the Civil Rights Act of 1866. Without questioning decisions holding private parties liable under § 1981 on a *respondeat superior* theory, the Court refused to hold the school district liable on that basis, reasoning that "the express cause of action for damages created by § 1983 constitutes the exclusive federal remedy for violation of the rights guaranteed in § 1981 by state governmental units" (p. 733). Accordingly, the Court remanded the case for application of the Monell "custom or policy" standard.

Doesn't it follow *a fortiori* from the Court's unwillingness to recognize a statutorily-based remedy in Jett that it would not recognize a judicially-implied damages remedy in a pure *respondeat superior* case?

(9) *States and State Agencies as Defendants: The Will Decision.* Quern v. Jordan, 440 U.S. 332 (1979), p. 1075, *supra,* held that Congress did not clearly manifest an intention in § 1983 to override the states' Eleventh Amendment immunity. Thus Quern held only that a *federal* court lacks power to impose such a remedy against an unconsenting state. It did not answer the question whether § 1983 itself creates a remedy against a state.

That question was resolved in Will v. Michigan Dep't of State Police, 491 U.S. 58 (1989), a state court § 1983 action seeking damages from a state agency. The Supreme Court ruled that neither a state nor a state official acting in an official capacity is a "person" within the meaning of § 1983, at least when sued for retrospective relief. Justice White's opinion for the Court stated that in common usage, the term "person" does not include the sovereign. Invoking the "clear statement" requirement developed in Eleventh Amendment cases (p. 1103, *supra*), he insisted on application of a similar approach to the question presented and concluded that the language of § 1983 did not satisfy such a requirement. The Court also noted its holding in Quern that § 1983 does not abrogate state sovereign immunity, and that therefore a federal court cannot award retrospective relief against a state under § 1983. Given that a principal reason for enacting § 1983 was to provide a federal forum, the Court found it implausible that Congress meant to create a liability under § 1983 that was enforceable only in a state court. In an important footnote, the Court noted that a state official sued in an official capacity for *prospective* relief is a "person" for purposes of § 1983, because under Ex parte Young, such suits are not treated as actions against the state (p. 71 n. 10).[13]

Justice Brennan's dissent (joined by Justices Marshall, Blackmun, and Stevens) objected particularly to the Court's reliance on Eleventh Amendment jurisprudence, when that Amendment was inapplicable to the case at hand. As further support for upholding the state's liability, he pointed to the "Dictionary Act"—a set of rules of construction enacted by Congress in 1871 two months before § 1983 was passed—which defined "person" to include "bodies politic and corporate"; he noted that in the Monell decision the Court had relied on that definition in upholding municipal liability. (The majority interpreted that phrase to mean private and municipal corporations, not states.)[14]

---

13. In Hafer v. Melo, 502 U.S. 21 (1991), the Court unanimously rejected the defendant's claim that Will bars damages actions against state officers sued in their personal capacities when the conduct in question was part of the defendant's official duties.

14. In Ngiraingas v. Sanchez, 495 U.S. 182 (1990), the Supreme Court held, 6–2, that neither the Territory of Guam, nor an officer of the Territory acting in an official capacity, is a "person" within the meaning of § 1983. The Court did not, and could not, rely on Eleventh Amendment jurisprudence,

Is it reasonable to interpret a statute by applying a rule of construction developed in a different context a century after the statute's enactment?

Taken together, the Jett and Will cases indicate that there is no express or implied damages remedy against a state for violation of constitutional rights. Can that result be squared with the holding of the McKesson and Reich cases (pp. 851–52, *supra*) that, in the absence of an available prepayment remedy, a state must afford a meaningful postpayment remedy to one complaining of an unconstitutional tax? Assuming that at least in some instances such a remedy must consist of a refund of taxes paid, does the distinction lie in the difference between a tax refund (*i.e.,* restitution) and damages? Is the obligation to make restitution closer to the obligation to pay just compensation for property taken? *Cf.* First English Evangelical Lutheran Church v. County of Los Angeles, p. 849, *supra.* See generally, Chap. VII, Sec. 2(C), *supra.*

NOTE ON § 1983 AS A REMEDY FOR THE VIOLATION OF A FEDERAL STATUTE

(1) *Historical Background.* As originally enacted in 1871, 17 Stat. 13, the provision that is now § 1983 created a cause of action only for the deprivation of *constitutional* rights. The phrase "and laws" was added without helpful explanation as part of a revision of the statutes in 1874, at the same time that the jurisdictional provisions of the 1871 Act were severed from its remedial provisions (see p. 1121, *supra*). The significance of this revision, and the scope of § 1983's application to federal statutory violations, was not fully explored by the Supreme Court until over a century later.

(2) *Maine v. Thiboutot.* Section 1343(a)(3) of Title 28—the jurisdictional counterpart of § 1983—is limited to rights secured by the Constitution or "by any Act of Congress *providing for equal rights*" (emphasis added). In Chapman v. Houston Welfare Rights Org., 441 U.S. 600 (1979), the Court interpreted that jurisdictional provision as not extending to a federal court suit challenging the deprivation of welfare benefits as unlawful under the federal Social Security Act.

The question whether § 1983 itself should also be interpreted as limited to actions claiming violations of "equal rights" statutes was resolved in Maine v. Thiboutot, 448 U.S. 1 (1980), a similar challenge to the denial of welfare benefits, but one filed in state court, to which § 1343(a)(3) had no application.[1] The Supreme Court, per Brennan J., held that the complaint (which asserted no denial of equal rights) stated a good claim under § 1983. The Court reasoned that prior decisions had upheld provision of relief in such cases, and

as it had in Will. But it did note that the original 1871 Act made no reference to the territories, and that in the same 1874 statute in which Congress extended the Act to persons acting under color of law of any territory, it also amended the Dictionary Act (cited by Justice Brennan in his dissent in Will) to define "person" to include "partnerships and corporations" rather than "bodies politic and corporate". And in the legislative history of that change (discussed by the Court at p. 191), the revisers indicated that the elimination of "body politic" from the definition of "person" effectively excluded "States, Territories, foreign governments, & c."

1. As noted at p. 1121, *supra,* since the elimination in 1980 of the amount in controversy requirement in 28 U.S.C. § 1331, § 1343(a)(3) has been superfluous even in federal court actions.

that there was no contrary legislative history sufficiently clear to warrant departure from the plain statutory language.

Justice Powell (joined by Chief Justice Burger and Justice Rehnquist) wrote a lengthy dissent, arguing that the legislative history showed an intention to encompass only rights secured by the Constitution and laws providing for equal rights. He argued further that the original limitation on the coverage of statutory rights was left out of the 1874 predecessor to § 1983 by accident in the process of recodifying the United States statutes (pp. 15–16). Justice Powell also criticized the Court for imposing upon state and local governments and officials "liability whenever a person believes he has been injured by the administration of *any* federal-state cooperative program * * *. * * * [L]iterally hundreds of cooperative regulatory and social welfare enactments may be affected" (p. 22).[2]

(3) *The Implications of the Thiboutot Decision.*

(a) *Statutory Supersession of the § 1983 Remedy.* Middlesex County Sewerage Auth. v. National Sea Clammers Ass'n, 453 U.S. 1 (1981), involved a § 1983 action for an injunction and damages brought by commercial fishermen against state and local governments and their officials. Plaintiffs alleged that defendants' discharge of sewage and pollutants violated the Federal Water Pollution Control Act (FWPCA) and the Marine Protection, Research, and Sanctuaries Act of 1972 (MPRSA). Both statutes provided what the Court termed "elaborate enforcement provisions" (p. 13), expressly authorizing suits by federal administrators to impose sanctions, suits by private persons to obtain judicial review of federal administrative decisions, and citizen suits against polluters for injunctive relief. (Injunctive relief under the two statutes' citizen suit provisions was unavailable in the actual case because the plaintiffs had not given the requisite 60–day notice to federal and state officials).

The Supreme Court ruled that the plaintiffs could not obtain remedies other than those expressly provided in the two regulatory statutes.[3] The Court first rejected plaintiffs' argument that they were entitled to implied remedies under the two Acts: "it cannot be assumed that Congress intended to authorize implication of" additional remedies in suits by private citizens (p. 14). The Court then ruled that Congress intended, in providing these "quite comprehensive enforcement mechanisms", not only to foreclose implied private actions, but also "to supplant any remedy that otherwise would be available under § 1983" (pp. 20–21).[4] However, the majority denied the charge made by the

---

2. For the view that the historical record, though not unambiguous, favors the majority's interpretation in Thiboutot, see Sunstein, *Section 1983 and the Private Enforcement of Federal Law,* 49 U.Chi.L.Rev. 394, 396–411 (1982); for criticism of the majority, see Brown, *Whither Thiboutot? Section 1983, Private Enforcement, and the Damages Dilemma,* 33 De Paul L.Rev. 31, 36–40 (1983).

3. A decision that preceded Middlesex, and that recognized a different limit on the reach of Thiboutot, was Pennhurst State School & Hosp. v. Halderman (Pennhurst I), 451 U.S. 1 (1981), in which the Court held

that a § 1983 class action complaining of conditions at a state hospital could not be maintained on the basis of alleged violations of a federal statute because the statute in question did not confer any private rights enforceable under § 1983. (The "bill of rights" provision in the statute, 42 U.S.C. § 6010, stated, *inter alia,* that persons with developmental disabilities "have a right to appropriate treatment, services and habilitation for such disabilities * * * in the setting that is least restrictive of * * * [their] personal liberty".)

4. The Court has applied this reasoning to find that congressional programs can im-

dissenters that the decision placed on plaintiffs, in § 1983 actions based on rights created by Congress, the burden of demonstrating congressional intent to preserve the § 1983 remedy (p. 20 n. 31).[5]

For an application of Middlesex, see Wright v. Roanoke Redevelopment & Hous. Auth., 479 U.S. 418 (1987), a damages action under § 1983 by tenants of a federally-funded public housing project against the municipal housing authority. The tenants alleged that the charges for utility service violated a rent ceiling governing the project that was set by a federal statute and implementing regulations. The Court ruled that the suit could go forward. Federal law created enforceable rights in the tenants, and HUD's powers to audit its contract with the public housing authority and to cut off funds were insufficient to indicate congressional intent to foreclose enforcement under § 1983: "§ 1983 provides a remedial cause of action unless the state actor demonstrates by express provision or other specific evidence from the statute itself that Congress intended to foreclose such private enforcement. 'We do not lightly conclude that Congress intended to preclude reliance on § 1983 as a remedy' for the deprivation of a federally secured right" (p. 771, quoting Smith v. Robinson, note 4, *supra*). The four dissenters expressed uncertainty about whether § 1983 permitted suit for violation of federal administrative regulations, but argued that in any event neither the statute nor the regulations conferred judicially enforceable rights.

In its decision in Thiboutot, the Court did not consider the relationship between its construction of § 1983 and case law on whether to imply a private right of action under a federal statute that does not expressly provide one. See generally Chap. VII, Sec. 2(B), *supra*. Suppose that, in the absence of § 1983, no private remedy would be implied under a particular federal statute—as is generally the case under the recent implied right of action precedents. Did Thiboutot indicate that § 1983 is available to supply the missing remedy whenever the offender is a state official?

Did Middlesex subsequently suggest that the express private right of action under § 1983 for violation of an Act of Congress is preempted whenever a right of action would not have been inferred under the Act? Or does Thiboutot (even after Middlesex) mean that there is a presumption that § 1983 provides a

pliedly preclude relief under § 1983 even for constitutional violations. See Smith v. Robinson, 468 U.S. 992 (1984), holding that a handicapped child could not bypass the detailed and comprehensive administrative system established under the Education of the Handicapped Act (EHA) by suing local school officials under § 1983 for an alleged denial of equal protection. (Congress modified the precise holding of Smith, however, by providing in 1986 that, subject to a requirement of exhaustion of remedies afforded by the EHA, nothing in the Act should be construed as restricting rights, procedures, and remedies available under the Constitution or other federal statutes. See 20 U.S.C. § 1415(f)).

5. Both statutes in Middlesex contained savings clauses stating that the remedies provided by statute shall not "restrict any right which any persons (or class of persons) may

have under any statute or common law to seek enforcement [of any standard or limitation] or to seek any other relief * * *." These provisions, the Court held, preserved only remedies for violations of other regulatory statutes or of state common law, not a remedy under § 1983 for a violation of the FWCPA or MPRSA itself. Alternatively, the Court ruled that the savings clauses related only to the effect of the citizen suit provisions, and therefore did not bar a finding that the overall remedial schemes precluded relief under § 1983.

Justice Stevens, joined by Justice Blackmun, dissented, arguing that the plaintiffs' "right to proceed under § 1983 * * * could have been made more plain only had Congress substituted the citation '42 U.S.C. § 1983' for the words 'any statute' in the savings clauses" (p. 29).

private remedy, in contrast to the implied right of action cases, in which the presumption appears to be quite the opposite?

Aren't the benefits and risks of private enforcement of federal law—difficult issues that are explored extensively in Chap. VII, Sec. 2(B), *supra*—the same whether the plaintiff claims an express remedy under § 1983 or a judicially implied right of action? Should the invocation of § 1983 provide a satisfactory answer to the complex questions of regulatory policy?

(b) *The Application of § 1983 to Preemption Claims*. In Golden State Transit Corp. v. City of Los Angeles, 493 U.S. 103 (1989), the question presented involved the application of § 1983 to a claim of federal statutory preemption of state law. The plaintiff, Golden State, had challenged Los Angeles' effort to condition renewal of its taxicab franchise on settlement of a labor dispute. The Court upheld Golden State's ability to sue under § 1983 for both injunctive and compensatory relief for interference with a federally protected bargaining relationship. The Court reasoned that (a) the National Labor Relations Act did not benefit private parties merely "as an incident" of federal regulation; rather the Act "creates rights in labor and management both against one another and against the State" (p. 109); and (b) those rights are secured against state interference by the Supremacy Clause. The availability of a § 1983 remedy in such cases, the Court said, "turns on whether the statute, by its terms or as interpreted, creates obligations 'sufficiently specific and definite' to be within 'the competence of the judiciary to enforce,' is intended to benefit the putative plaintiff, and is not foreclosed 'by express provision or other specific evidence from the statute itself'" (p. 108, quoting Wright v. Roanoke Redevelopment & Hous. Auth., Paragraph (3)(a), *supra*).

Dissenting for himself, the Chief Justice, and Justice O'Connor, Justice Kennedy argued that plaintiff's only remedy was for declaratory and injunctive relief in an action under 28 U.S.C. § 1331. Although he recognized that § 1983 extended to interests secured by various federal statutes, he observed that "[n]one of these secured statutory interests * * * has been the sole result of a statute's pre-emptive effect * * *. Pre-emption concerns the federal structure of the Nation rather than the securing of rights, privileges, and immunities to individuals" (p. 117).[6]

---

6. The Court has also rendered several closely divided (and hard to reconcile) decisions on the question when the conditions attached to federal programs reimbursing states for specified expenditures create private rights enforceable under § 1983. Compare Wilder v. Virginia Hospital Ass'n, 496 U.S. 498 (1990)(holding that a health care provider could bring an action under § 1983 alleging that the state had failed to provide "reasonable and adequate" payments as required by federal law) with Suter v. Artist M., 503 U.S. 347 (1992)(holding that a suit could not be brought under § 1983 alleging that a state had failed to make the "reasonable efforts" required by federal law as a condition for reimbursement for foster care and adoption services).

Note that permitting a § 1983 action for violation of conditions governing the award of federal funds via a grant or contract may divert funds from the program itself to damages awards, while the threat of liability may deter state participation. There may also be special problems with judicial enforcement of these conditions, which are likely to be vague or unduly complex—problems that can be alleviated if enforcement is left to the discretion of the federal administrators who dispense the funds. Finally, it is argued that private enforcement exacerbates the tendency of these federal programs to undercut the political accountability of state and local governments. See Stewart, *Federalism and Rights*, 19 Ga.L.Rev. 917, 959 (1985).

On the other hand, if the only remedy under the statute is that of cutting off funding—one so drastic as almost never to be used—private enforcement may be particularly important.

The following Term, in Dennis v. Higgins, 498 U.S. 439 (1991), the Court held that a violation of the "dormant" Commerce Clause is cognizable in an action under § 1983. (The complaint alleged that certain state taxes and fees constituted an unlawful burden on interstate commerce, and sought declaratory and injunctive relief, refund of taxes paid, and attorney's fees and costs.) Relying on the rationale of its decision in Golden State, the Court stated that its own "repeated references to 'rights' under the Commerce Clause constitute a recognition that the Clause *was* intended to benefit those who, like petitioner, are engaged in interstate commerce" (p. 449). Justice Kennedy, dissenting for himself and the Chief Justice, said that the decision "compounds the error of Golden State. * * * The [Commerce] Clause assigned prerogatives to the general government, not personal rights to those who engaged in commerce" (pp. 451–53).

In an analysis of these decisions, and especially Golden State, Professor Monaghan suggests that their principal effect is to focus on the question whether federal law creates a "primary" right. See Monaghan, *Federal Statutory Review Under Section 1983 and the APA*, 91 Colum.L.Rev. 233 (1991). If it does, § 1983 will afford a remedy even though "federal law does not otherwise establish a 'remedial' right (*i.e.,* a right of action). * * * Section 1983 is, of course, unavailable if Congress has 'specifically' foreclosed the remedy. But both Golden State and Wilder [note 6, *supra*] shore up the intimations in prior case law that this limitation is exceedingly narrow" (p. 247). Thus, he concludes, the role of § 1983 in affording review of the compliance of *state* officials with federal norms is comparable to the role of the Administrative Procedure Act in ensuring compliance of *federal* officials with federal norms. (One difference, of course, is that § 1983 specifically contemplates a damages remedy in appropriate cases.)

(c) *Thiboutot and Original Intent.* Note how far Thiboutot and related decisions have taken § 1983 from its historical origins, in the Civil Rights Act of 1871, as a remedy for abuses based on race that were widespread in the South during Reconstruction. Has the added breadth of § 1983 perhaps led to a loss of depth in its protection against invidious discrimination? For example, had the statute remained more closely limited to its historical context, consider whether the Supreme Court might have held that § 1983 *was* intended to make individuals fully liable without any defense of official immunity, and to make local and state governments fully liable on a respondeat superior theory without any possible defense of governmental immunity.[7]

Is any of this relevant to the interpretation of § 1983 as applied to these kinds of programs?

7. For critical analysis of the dramatic expansion of the reach of § 1983, see Collins, *"Economic Rights," Implied Constitutional Actions, and the Scope of Section 1983,* 77 Geo.L.J. 1493 (1989).

Zinermon v. Burch*

494 U.S. 113, 110 S.Ct. 975, 108 L.Ed.2d 100 (1990).
Certiorari to the United States Court of Appeals for the Eleventh Circuit.

■ JUSTICE BLACKMUN delivered the opinion of the Court:

I

Respondent Darrell Burch brought this suit under 42 U.S.C. § 1983 against the 11 petitioners, who are physicians, administrators, and staff members at Florida State Hospital (FSH) in Chattahoochee, and others. Respondent alleges that petitioners deprived him of his liberty, without due process of law, by admitting him to FSH as a "voluntary" mental patient when he was incompetent to give informed consent to his admission. Burch contends that in his case petitioners should have afforded him procedural safeguards required by the Constitution before involuntary commitment of a mentally ill person, and that petitioners' failure to do so violated his due process rights.

Petitioners argue that Burch's complaint failed to state a claim under § 1983 because, in their view, it alleged only a random, unauthorized violation of the Florida statutes governing admission of mental patients. Their argument rests on Parratt v. Taylor, 451 U.S. 527 (1981), and Hudson v. Palmer, 468 U.S. 517 (1984), where this Court held that a deprivation of a constitutionally protected property interest caused by a state employee's random, unauthorized conduct does not give rise to a § 1983 procedural due process claim, unless the State fails to provide an adequate postdeprivation remedy. The Court in those two cases reasoned that in a situation where the State cannot predict and guard in advance against a deprivation, a postdeprivation tort remedy is all the process the State can be expected to provide, and is constitutionally sufficient.

* * * [The district court dismissed the complaint, and the court of appeals, sitting en banc, reversed and remanded for further proceedings.]

This Court granted certiorari to resolve the conflict—so evident in the divided views of the judges of the Eleventh Circuit—that has arisen in the Courts of Appeals over the proper scope of the Parratt rule.

Because this case concerns the propriety of a Rule 12(b)(6) dismissal * * * [, we] decide only whether the Parratt rule necessarily means that Burch's complaint fails to allege any deprivation of due process, because he was constitutionally entitled to nothing more than what he received—an opportunity to sue petitioners in tort for his allegedly unlawful confinement. The broader questions of what procedural safeguards the Due Process Clause requires in the context of an admission to a mental hospital, and whether Florida's statutes meet these constitutional requirements, are not presented in this case. Burch did not frame his action as a challenge to the constitutional adequacy of Florida's mental health statutes. Both before the Eleventh Circuit and in his brief here, he disavowed any challenge to the statutes themselves

---

* Before studying this difficult case, you may wish to read Paragraph (1) of the following Note, p. 1149, *infra,* as an aid to under-standing the significance of the case in the context of this Section.

and restricted his claim to the contention that petitioners' failure to provide constitutionally adequate safeguards in his case violated his due process rights.[1]

II

A

For purposes of review of a Rule 12(b)(6) dismissal, the factual allegations of Burch's complaint are taken as true. * * *

On December 7, 1981, Burch was found wandering along a Florida highway, appearing to be hurt and disoriented. He was taken to Apalachee Community Mental Health Services (ACMHS) in Tallahassee. * * * On December 10, the staff found that Burch was "in need of longer-term stabilization," and referred him to FSH, a public hospital owned and operated by the State as a mental health treatment facility. Later that day, Burch signed forms requesting admission and authorizing treatment at FSH. He was then taken to FSH by a county sheriff.

Upon his arrival at FSH, Burch signed other forms for voluntary admission and treatment. One form, entitled "Request for Voluntary Admission," recited that the patient requests admission for "observation, diagnosis, care and treatment of [my] mental condition," and that the patient, if admitted, agrees "to accept such treatment as may be prescribed by members of the medical and psychiatric staff in accordance with the provisions of expressed and informed consent." * * *

On December 23, Burch signed a form entitled "Authorization for Treatment." This form stated that he authorized "the professional staff of [FSH] to administer treatment, except electroconvulsive treatment"; that he had been informed of "the purpose of treatment; common side effects thereof; alternative treatment modalities; approximate length of care"; and of his power to revoke consent to treatment; and that he had read and fully understood the Authorization. Petitioner Zinermon, a staff physician at FSH, signed the form as the witness.

On December 10, Doctor Zinermon wrote a "progress note" indicating that Burch was "refusing to cooperate," would not answer questions, "appears distressed and confused," and "related that medication has been helpful." A nursing assessment form dated December 11 stated that Burch was confused and unable to state the reason for his hospitalization and still believed that "[t]his is heaven." Petitioner Zinermon on December 29 made a further report on Burch's condition, stating that, on admission, Burch had been "disoriented, semi-mute, confused and bizarre in appearance and thought," "not cooperative to the initial interview," and "extremely psychotic, appeared to be paranoid

---

1. Inasmuch as Burch does not claim that he was deprived of due process by an established state procedure, our decision in Logan v. Zimmerman Brush Co., 455 U.S. 422 (1982), is not controlling. In that case, the plaintiff challenged not a state official's error in implementing state law, but "the 'established state procedure' that destroys his entitlement without according him proper procedural safeguards." Id., at 436.

Burch apparently concedes that, if Florida's statutes were strictly complied with, no deprivation of liberty without due process would occur. If only those patients who are competent to consent to admission are allowed to sign themselves in as "voluntary" patients, then they would not be deprived of any liberty interest at all. And if all other patients—those who are incompetent and those who are unwilling to consent to admission—are afforded the protections of Florida's involuntary placement procedures, they would be deprived of their liberty only after due process.

and hallucinating." The doctor's report also stated that Burch remained disoriented, delusional, and psychotic.

Burch remained at FSH until May 7, 1982, five months after his initial admission to ACMHS. During that time, no hearing was held regarding his hospitalization and treatment.

* * *

In February 1985, Burch filed a complaint in [federal district court]. He alleged, among other things, that ACMHS and the 11 individual petitioners, acting under color of Florida law, and "by and through the authority of their respective positions as employees at FSH ... as part of their regular and official employment at FSH, took part in admitting Plaintiff to FSH as a 'voluntary' patient." Specifically, he alleged:

"Defendants, and each of them, knew or should have known that Plaintiff was incapable of voluntary, knowing, understanding and informed consent to admission and treatment at FSH. * * * For said period of 149 days, Plaintiff was without the benefit of counsel and no hearing of any sort was held at which he could have challenged his involuntary admission and treatment at FSH.

"... Defendants, and each of them, deprived Plaintiff of his liberty without due process of law in contravention of the Fourteenth Amendment to the United States Constitution. Defendants acted with willful, wanton and reckless disregard of and indifference to Plaintiff's Constitutionally guaranteed right to due process of law."

B

Burch's complaint thus alleges that he was admitted to and detained at FSH for five months under Florida's statutory provisions for "voluntary" admission. These provisions are part of a comprehensive statutory scheme under which a person may be admitted to a mental hospital in several different ways. * * * [The first three involve (1) short-term emergency admission, (2) detention for up to five days pursuant to court order, and (3) involuntary detention after notice and hearing.]

Finally, a person may be admitted as a voluntary patient. Mental hospitals may admit for treatment any adult "making application by express and informed consent," if he is "found to show evidence of mental illness and to be suitable for treatment." § 394.465(1)(a). "Express and informed consent" is defined as "consent voluntarily given in writing after sufficient explanation and disclosure ... to enable the person ... to make a knowing and willful decision without any element of force, fraud, deceit, duress, or other form of constraint or coercion." § 394.455(22). A voluntary patient may request discharge at any time. If he does, the facility administrator must either release him within three days or initiate the involuntary placement process. § 394.465(2)(a). At the time of his admission and each six months thereafter, a voluntary patient and his legal guardian or representatives must be notified in writing of the right to apply for a discharge. § 394.465(3).

Burch, in apparent compliance with § 394.465(1), was admitted by signing forms applying for voluntary admission. He alleges, however, that petitioners violated this statute in admitting him as a voluntary patient, because they knew or should have known that he was incapable of making an informed decision as to his admission. He claims that he was entitled to receive the procedural safeguards provided by Florida's involuntary placement procedure, and that petitioners violated his due process rights by failing to initiate this procedure. The question presented is whether these allegations suffice to state a claim under § 1983, in light of Parratt and Hudson.

III

A

* * *

[The general rule of Monroe v. Pape that overlapping state remedies are irrelevant to the existence of a cause of action under § 1983] applies in a straightforward way to two of the three kinds of § 1983 claims that may be brought against the State under the Due Process Clause of the Fourteenth Amendment. First, the Clause incorporates many of the specific protections defined in the Bill of Rights. A plaintiff may bring suit under § 1983 for state officials' violation of his rights to, *e.g.,* freedom of speech or freedom from unreasonable searches and seizures. Second, the Due Process Clause contains a substantive component that bars certain arbitrary, wrongful government actions "regardless of the fairness of the procedures used to implement them." Daniels v. Williams, 474 U.S., at 331. As to these two types of claims, the constitutional violation actionable under § 1983 is complete when the wrongful action is taken. *Id.*, at 338 (Stevens, J., concurring in judgments). A plaintiff, under Monroe v. Pape, may invoke § 1983 regardless of any state-tort remedy that might be available to compensate him for the deprivation of these rights.

The Due Process Clause also encompasses a third type of protection, a guarantee of fair procedure. A § 1983 action may be brought for a violation of procedural due process, but here the existence of state remedies *is* relevant in a special sense. In procedural due process claims, the deprivation by state action of a constitutionally protected interest in "life, liberty, or property" is not in itself unconstitutional; what is unconstitutional is the deprivation of such an interest *without due process of law*. Parratt, 451 U.S., at 537. The constitutional violation actionable under § 1983 is not complete when the deprivation occurs; it is not complete unless and until the State fails to provide due process. Therefore, to determine whether a constitutional violation has occurred, it is necessary to ask what process the State provided, and whether it was constitutionally adequate. This inquiry would examine the procedural safeguards built into the statutory or administrative procedure of effecting the deprivation, and any remedies for erroneous deprivations provided by statute or tort law.

In this case, Burch does not claim that his confinement at FSH violated any of the specific guarantees of the Bill of Rights. Burch's complaint could be read to include a substantive due process claim, but that issue was not raised in the petition for certiorari, and we express no view on whether the facts Burch alleges could give rise to such a claim. The claim at issue falls within the third, or procedural, category of § 1983 claims based on the Due Process Clause.

B

Due process, as this Court often has said, is a flexible concept that varies with the particular situation. To determine what procedural protections the Constitution requires in a particular case, we weigh several factors:

"First, the private interest that will be affected by the official action; second, the risk of an erroneous deprivation of such interest through the procedures used, and the probable value, if any, of additional or substitute procedural safeguards; and finally, the Government's interest, including the function involved and the fiscal and administrative burdens that the additional or substitute procedural requirement would entail." Mathews v. Eldridge, 424 U.S. 319, 335 (1976).

Applying this test, the Court usually has held that the Constitution requires some kind of a hearing *before* the State deprives a person of liberty or property.

In some circumstances, however, the Court has held that a statutory provision for a postdeprivation hearing, or a common-law tort remedy for erroneous deprivation, satisfies due process.

This is where the Parratt rule comes into play. Parratt and Hudson represent a special case of the general Mathews v. Eldridge analysis, in which postdeprivation tort remedies are all the process that is due, simply because they are the only remedies the State could be expected to provide. In Parratt, a state prisoner brought a § 1983 action because prison employees negligently had lost materials he had ordered by mail.[14] The prisoner did not dispute that he had a postdeprivation remedy. Under state law, a tort-claim procedure was available by which he could have recovered the value of the materials. 451 U.S., at 543–544. This Court ruled that the tort remedy was all the process the prisoner was due, because any predeprivation procedural safeguards that the State did provide, or could have provided, would not address the risk of *this kind* of deprivation. The very nature of a negligent loss of property made it impossible for the State to predict such deprivations and provide predeprivation process. The Court explained:

"The justifications which we have found sufficient to uphold takings of property without any predeprivation process are applicable to a situation such as the present one involving a tortious loss of a prisoner's property as a result of a random and unauthorized act by a state employee. In such a case, the loss is not a result of some established state procedure and the State cannot predict precisely when the loss will occur. It is difficult to conceive of how the State could provide a meaningful hearing before the deprivation takes place." *Id.*, at 541.

Given these special circumstances, it was clear that the State, by making available a tort remedy that could adequately redress the loss, had given the prisoner the process he was due. Thus, Parratt is not an exception to the Mathews balancing test, but rather an application of that test to the unusual case in which one of the variables in the Mathews equation—the value of predeprivation safeguards—is negligible in preventing the kind of deprivation at issue. Therefore, no matter how significant the private interest at stake and the risk of its erroneous deprivation, the State cannot be required constitutionally to do the impossible by providing predeprivation process.

In Hudson, the Court extended this reasoning to an intentional deprivation of property. A prisoner alleged that, during a search of his prison cell, a guard deliberately and maliciousl, destroyed some of his property, including legal

---

14. Parratt was decided before this Court ruled, in Daniels v. Williams, 474 U.S. 327, 336 (1986), that a negligent act by a state official does not give rise to § 1983 liability.

papers. Again, there was a tort remedy by which the prisoner could have been compensated. In Hudson, as in Parratt, the state official was not acting pursuant to any established state procedure, but, instead, was apparently pursuing a random, unauthorized personal vendetta against the prisoner. * * * [T]he Court found that an individual state employee's ability to foresee the deprivation is "of no consequence," because the proper inquiry under Parratt is "whether the *state* is in a position to provide for predeprivation process." *Id.*, at 534 (emphasis added).

C

Petitioners argue that the dismissal under Rule 12(b)(6) was proper because, as in Parratt and Hudson, the State could not possibly have provided predeprivation process to prevent the kind of "random, unauthorized" wrongful deprivation of liberty Burch alleges, so the postdeprivation remedies provided by Florida's statutory and common law necessarily are all the process Burch was due.[15]

Before turning to that issue, however, we must address a threshold question raised by Burch. He argues that Parratt and Hudson cannot apply to his situation, because those cases are limited to deprivations of property, not liberty.

* * *

It is true that Parratt and Hudson concerned deprivations of property. It is also true that Burch's interest in avoiding five months' confinement is of an order different from inmate Parratt's interest in mail-order materials valued at $23.50. But the reasoning of Parratt and Hudson emphasizes the State's inability to provide predeprivation process because of the random and unpredictable nature of the deprivation, not the fact that only property losses were at stake. In situations where the State feasibly can provide a predeprivation hearing before taking property, it generally must do so regardless of the adequacy of a postdeprivation tort remedy to compensate for the taking. Conversely, in situations where a predeprivation hearing is unduly burdensome in proportion to the liberty interest at stake, see [Ingraham v. Wright, 430 U.S. 651, 682 (1977)], or where the State is truly unable to anticipate and prevent a random deprivation of a liberty interest, postdeprivation remedies might satisfy due process. Thus, the fact that a deprivation of liberty is involved in this case does not automatically preclude application of the Parratt rule.

To determine whether, as petitioners contend, the Parratt rule necessarily precludes § 1983 liability in this case, we must ask whether predeprivation procedural safeguards could address the risk of deprivations of the kind Burch alleges. * * *

Persons who are mentally ill and incapable of giving informed consent to admission would not necessarily meet the statutory standard for involuntary placement, which requires either that they are likely to injure themselves or others, or that their neglect or refusal to care for themselves threatens their well-being. See § 394.467(1)(b). The involuntary placement process serves to guard against the confinement of a person who, though mentally ill, is harmless

---

15. Burch does not dispute that he had remedies under Florida law for unlawful con-   finement. * * *

and can live safely outside an institution. Confinement of such a person not only violates Florida law, but also is unconstitutional. Thus, it is at least possible that if Burch had had an involuntary placement hearing, he would not have been found to meet the statutory standard for involuntary placement and would not have been confined at FSH. Moreover, even assuming that Burch would have met the statutory requirements for involuntary placement, he still could have been harmed by being deprived of other protections built into the involuntary placement procedure, such as the appointment of a guardian advocate to make treatment decisions and periodic judicial review of placement. §§ 394.467(3) and (4).

* * *

We now consider whether predeprivation safeguards would have any value in guarding against the kind of deprivation Burch allegedly suffered. Petitioners urge that here, as in Parratt and Hudson, such procedures could have no value at all, because the State cannot prevent its officials from making random and unauthorized errors in the admission process. We disagree.

The Florida statutes, of course, do not allow incompetent persons to be admitted as "voluntary" patients. But the statutes do not direct any member of the facility staff to determine whether a person is competent to give consent, nor to initiate the involuntary placement procedure for every incompetent patient. A patient who is willing to sign forms but incapable of informed consent certainly cannot be relied on to protest his "voluntary" admission and demand that the involuntary placement procedure be followed. The staff are the *only* persons in a position to take notice of any misuse of the voluntary admission process and to ensure that the proper procedure is followed.

Florida chose to delegate to petitioners a broad power to admit patients to FSH, *i.e.*, to effect what, in the absence of informed consent, is a substantial deprivation of liberty. Because petitioners had state authority to deprive persons of liberty, the Constitution imposed on them the State's concomitant duty to see that no deprivation occurs without adequate procedural protections.

It may be permissible constitutionally for a State to have a statutory scheme like Florida's, which gives state officials broad power and little guidance in admitting mental patients. But when those officials fail to provide constitutionally required procedural safeguards to a person whom they deprive of liberty, the state officials cannot then escape liability by invoking Parratt and Hudson. It is immaterial whether the due process violation Burch alleges is best described as arising from petitioner's failure to comply with state procedures for admitting involuntary patients, or from the absence of a specific requirement that petitioners determine whether a patient is competent to consent to voluntary admission. Burch's suit is neither an action challenging the facial adequacy of a State's statutory procedures, nor an action based only on state officials' random and unauthorized violation of state laws. Burch is not simply attempting to blame the State for misconduct by its employees. He seeks to hold state officials accountable for their abuse of their broadly delegated, uncircumscribed power to effect the deprivation at issue.

This case, therefore, is not controlled by Parratt and Hudson, for three basic reasons:

First, petitioners cannot claim that the deprivation of Burch's liberty was unpredictable. Under Florida's statutory scheme, only a person competent to give informed consent may be admitted as a voluntary patient. There is, however, no specified way of determining, before a patient is asked to sign admission forms, whether he is competent. It is hardly unforeseeable that a person requesting treatment for mental illness might be incapable of informed consent, and that state officials with the power to admit patients might take their apparent willingness to be admitted at face value and not initiate involuntary placement procedures. Any erroneous deprivation will occur, if at all, at a specific, predictable point in the admission process—when a patient is given admission forms to sign.

* * *

Second, we cannot say that predeprivation process was impossible here. Florida already has an established procedure for involuntary placement. The problem is only to ensure that this procedure is afforded to all patients who cannot be admitted voluntarily, both those who are unwilling and those who are unable to give consent.

In Parratt, the very nature of the deprivation made predeprivation process "impossible." 451 U.S., at 541. * * * In Hudson, the errant employee himself could anticipate the deprivation since he intended to effect it, but the State still was not in a position to provide predeprivation process, since it could not anticipate or control such random and unauthorized intentional conduct. * * *

Here, in contrast, there is nothing absurd in suggesting that, had the State limited and guided petitioners' power to admit patients, the deprivation might have been averted. * * *

Third, petitioners cannot characterize their conduct as "unauthorized" in the sense the term is used in Parratt and Hudson. The State delegated to them the power and authority to effect the very deprivation complained of here, Burch's confinement in a mental hospital, and also delegated to them the concomitant duty to initiate the procedural safeguards set up by state law to guard against unlawful confinement. In Parratt and Hudson, the state employees had no similar broad authority to deprive prisoners of their personal property, and no similar duty to initiate (for persons unable to protect their own interests) the procedural safeguards required before deprivations occur. The deprivation here is "unauthorized" only in the sense that it was not an act sanctioned by state law, but, instead, was a "depriv[ation] of constitutional rights ... by an official's abuse of his position." Monroe, 365 U.S., at 172.[20]

We conclude that petitioners cannot escape § 1983 liability by characterizing their conduct as a "random, unauthorized" violation of Florida law which the State was not in a position to predict or avert, so that all the process Burch could possibly be due is a postdeprivation damages remedy. Burch, according to the allegations of his complaint, was deprived of a substantial liberty interest without either valid consent or an involuntary placement hearing, by the very state officials charged with the power to deprive mental patients of their liberty and the duty to implement procedural safeguards. Such a deprivation is foreseeable, due to the nature of mental illness, and will occur, if at all, at a

---

20. Contrary to the dissent's view of Parratt and Hudson, those cases do not stand for the proposition that in every case where a deprivation is caused by an "unauthorized ... departure from established practices," state officials can escape § 1983 liability simply because the State provides tort remedies. This reading of Parratt and Hudson detaches those cases from their proper role as special applications of the settled principles expressed in Monroe and Mathews.

predictable point in the admission process. Unlike Parratt and Hudson, this case does not represent the special instance of the Mathews due process analysis where postdeprivation process is all that is due because no predeprivation safeguards would be of use in preventing the kind of deprivation alleged.

* * *

The judgment of the Court of Appeals is affirmed.

■ JUSTICE O'CONNOR, with whom THE CHIEF JUSTICE, JUSTICE SCALIA, and JUSTICE KENNEDY join, dissenting.

Without doubt, respondent Burch alleges a serious deprivation of liberty; yet equally clearly he alleges no violation of the Fourteenth Amendment. The Court concludes that an allegation of state actors' wanton, unauthorized departure from a State's established policies and procedures, working a deprivation of liberty, suffices to support a procedural due process claim even though the State provides adequate postdeprivation remedies for that deprivation. The Court's opinion unnecessarily transforms well-established procedural due process doctrine and departs from controlling precedent. I respectfully dissent.

* * *

Burch alleges a deprivation occasioned by petitioners' contravention of Florida's established procedures. * * * Consistent with his disavowal of any attack upon the adequacy of the State's established procedures, Burch alleges that petitioners flagrantly and at least recklessly contravened those requirements. In short, Burch has alleged that petitioners' unauthorized actions worked the deprivation of his liberty.

Parratt and Hudson should readily govern procedural due process claims such as respondent's. Taken together, the decisions indicate that for deprivations worked by such random and unauthorized departures from otherwise unimpugned and established state procedures the State provides the process due by making available adequate postdeprivation remedies. * * *

Application of Parratt and Hudson indicates that respondent has failed to state a claim allowing recovery under 42 U.S.C. § 1983. Petitioners' actions were unauthorized: they are alleged to have wrongly and without license departed from established state practices. * * * The wanton or reckless nature of the failure indicates it to be random. The State could not foresee the particular contravention and was hardly "in a position to provide for predeprivation process," Hudson, *supra,* at 534, to ensure that officials bent upon subverting the State's requirements would in fact follow those procedures. For this wrongful deprivation resulting from an unauthorized departure from established state practice, Florida provides adequate postdeprivation remedies, as two courts below concluded, and which the Court and respondent do not dispute. Parratt and Hudson thus should govern this case and indicate that respondent has failed to allege a violation of the Fourteenth Amendment.

* * *

The unauthorized and wrongful character of the departure from established state practice makes additional procedures an "impracticable" means of preventing the deprivation. "The underlying rationale of Parratt is that when deprivations of property are effected through random and unauthorized conduct of a state employee, predeprivation procedures are simply 'impracticable' since the state cannot know when such deprivations will occur." Hudson, 468

U.S., at 533. * * * The state actor so indifferent to guaranteed protections would be no more prevented from working the deprivation by additional procedural requirements than would the mail handler in Parratt or the prison guard in Hudson. * * * In all three cases, the unpredictable, wrongful departure is beyond the State's reasonable control. Additional safeguards designed to secure correct results in the usual case do not practicably forestall state actors who flout the State's command and established practice.

* * *

Every command to act imparts the duty to exercise discretion in accord with the command and affords the opportunity to abuse that discretion. The Mathews test measures whether the State has sufficiently constrained discretion in the usual case, while the Parratt doctrine requires the State to provide a remedy for any wrongful abuse. The Court suggests that this case differs from Parratt and Hudson because petitioners possessed a sort of delegated power. Yet petitioners no more had the delegated power to depart from the admission procedures and requirements than did the guard in Hudson to exceed the limits of his established search and seizure authority, or the prison official in Parratt wrongfully to withhold or misdeliver mail. * * *

The suggestion that the State delegated to petitioners insufficiently trammeled discretion conflicts with positions that the Court ostensibly embraces. The issue whether petitioners possessed undue discretion is bound with, and more properly analyzed as, an aspect of the adequacy of the State's procedural safeguards, yet the Court claims Burch did not present this issue and purports not to decide it. * * * Petitioners were not charged with formulating policy, and the complaint does not allege widespread and common departure from required procedures. Neither do the Court's passing reflections that a hearing is constitutionally required in the usual case of treatment of an incompetent patient advance the argument. That claim either states the conclusion that the State's combined admission procedures are generally inadequate, or repudiates Parratt and Hudson's focus upon random and unauthorized acts and upon the State's ability to formulate safeguards. To the extent that a liberty interest exists in the application of the involuntary admission procedures whenever appropriate, it is the random and authorized action of state actors that effected the deprivation, one for which Florida also provides adequate postdeprivation process.

* * *

The Court's reliance upon the State's inappropriate delegation of duty also creates enormous line-drawing problems. Today's decision applies to deprivations occasioned by state actors given "little guidance" and "broadly delegated, uncircumscribed power" to initiate required procedures. At some undefined point, the breadth of the delegation of power requires officials to channel the exercise of that power or become liable for its misapplications. When guidance is provided and the power to effect the deprivation circumscribed, no liability arises. And routine exercise of the power must be sufficiently fraught with the danger of "erroneous deprivation." In the absence of this broadly delegated power that carries with it pervasive risk of wrongful deprivation, Parratt and Hudson still govern. In essence, the Court's rationale applies when state officials are loosely charged with fashioning effective procedures or ensuring that required procedures are not routinely evaded. In a roundabout way, this rationale states the unexceptional conclusion that liability exists when officials' actions amount to the established state practice, a rationale unasserted in this case and, otherwise, appropriately analyzed under the Mathews test.

* * * Until today, the reasoning embodied in Mathews largely determined * * * the measures a State must establish to prevent a deprivation of a protected interest from amounting to a constitutional violation. Mathews employed the now familiar three-part test (considering the nature of the private interest, efficacy of additional procedures, and governmental interests) to determine what predeprivation procedural safeguards were required of the State. 424 U.S., at 335. That test reflects a carefully crafted accommodation of conflicting interests, weighed and evaluated in light of what fundamental fairness requires. Parratt drew upon concerns similar to those embodied in the Mathews test. For deprivations occasioned by wrongful departures from unchallenged and established state practices, Parratt concluded that adequate postdeprivation process meets the requirements of the Due Process Clause because additional predeprivation procedural safeguards would be "impracticable" to forestall these deprivations. 451 U.S., at 541. The Mathews and Parratt doctrines work in tandem. State officials able to formulate safeguards must discharge the duty to establish sufficient predeprivation procedures, as well as adequate postdeprivation remedies to provide process in the event of wrongful departures from established state practice. The doctrines together define the procedural measures that fundamental fairness and the Constitution demand of the State.

The Court today discovers an additional realm of required procedural safeguards. Now, all procedure is divided into three parts. In place of the border clearly dividing the duties required by Mathews from those required by Parratt, the Court marks out a vast terra incognita of unknowable duties and expansive liability of constitutional dimension. The Mathews test, we are told, does not determine the State's obligation to provide predeprivation procedural safeguards. Rather, to avoid the constitutional violation a State must have fully circumscribed and guided officials' exercise of power and provided additional safeguards, without regard to their efficacy or the nature of the governmental interests. Even if the validity of the State's procedures is not directly challenged, the burden is apparently on certain state actors to demonstrate that the State sufficiently constrained their powers. Despite the many cases of this Court applying and affirming Mathews, it is unclear what now remains of the test. And the Parratt doctrine no longer reflects a general interpretation of the Due Process Clause or the complement of the principles contained in Mathews. It is, instead, displaced when the State delegates certain types of duties in certain inappropriate ways. This resulting "no man's land" has no apparent boundaries. * * * We are left only with the implication that where doubt exists, liability of constitutional dimension will be found. Without so much as suggesting that our prior cases have warned against such a result, the Court has gone some measure to "make of the Fourteenth Amendment a font of tort law to be superimposed upon whatever systems may already be administered by the States." Parratt, *supra,* at 544 (quoting Paul v. Davis, 424 U.S. 693, 701 (1976)).

* * *

The Court believes that Florida's statutory scheme contains a particular flaw. That statutory omission involves the determination of competence in the course of the voluntary admission process, and the Court signals that it believes that these suggested additional safeguards would not be greatly burdensome. The

Court further believes that Burch's complaint and argument properly raise these issues and that adopting the additional safeguards would provide relevant benefit to one in Burch's position. * * * While this approach, if made explicit, would have required a strained reading of respondent's complaint and arguments, that course would have been far preferable to the strained reading of controlling procedural due process law that the Court today adopts. Ordinarily, a complaint must state a legal cause of action, but here it may be said that the Court has stated a novel cause of action to support a complaint.

I respectfully dissent.

NOTE ON THE PARRATT/ZINERMON DOCTRINE: ITS RATIONALE AND IMPLICATIONS

(1) *Introduction*. The issues raised by the Zinermon case and its predecessors deal less with the problem of remedies for constitutional wrongs, or with the allocation of business between state and federal courts, than with the substantive content of the prohibitions of the Fourteenth Amendment. The cases are included here, however, for several reasons. First, the line between the focus of these materials and those falling within the realm of substantive constitutional law is an indistinct one, not infrequently crossed by courses in both subjects. Second, there is far from a consensus among academics and judges on the true significance of these cases, and the disagreement goes to the heart of the subject matter of this book. And finally, whatever the meaning and rationale of these decisions, they profoundly affect the business of the federal courts in actions brought under § 1983.

(2) *The Background of the Zinermon Decision*. The decisions preceding Zinermon are canvassed in the various opinions in that case, and need be summarized only briefly here.

(a) *The Parratt Decision*. In Parratt v. Taylor, 451 U.S. 527 (1981), the plaintiff in a federal court action under § 1983 was a state prisoner who complained of the loss of a hobby kit (worth $23.50) that he had ordered by mail. He alleged that the loss of the kit constituted a negligent deprivation of his property without due process of law, and sought damages against the warden and another prison official. He obtained summary judgment in the courts below, but the Supreme Court reversed. Justice Rehnquist, for the Court, conceded that the plaintiff had been deprived of property by action under color of law but held that relief should be denied because the plaintiff had failed to show that the deprivation occurred without due process of law. The availability of an adequate state postdeprivation remedy for the deprivation, the Court ruled, satisfied the demands of the Due Process Clause. To conclude otherwise, the Court said, would suggest that "any party who is involved in nothing more than an automobile accident with a state official could allege a constitutional violation under § 1983. Such reasoning 'would make of the Fourteenth Amendment a font of tort law to be superimposed upon whatever systems may already be administered by the States' [quoting Paul v. Davis, 424 U.S. 693, 701 (1976)]. We do not think that the drafters of the Fourteenth Amendment intended the Amendment to play such a role in our society" (p. 544).

Among the several concurring opinions, Justice Powell, concurring only in the result, denied that "negligent acts by state officials constitute a deprivation of property within the meaning of the Fourteenth Amendment, regardless of whatever subsequent procedure a State may or may not provide" (p. 546).

(b) *Questions Raised by Parratt.* In a § 1983 action, three distinct issues of scienter may arise: (i) Does § 1983 itself require any distinctive scienter? (ii) Is scienter required to establish a violation (for which relief under § 1983 is sought) of the constitutional provision in question? (iii) Does an official sued have a qualified immunity from damages if the official's conduct did not violate clearly established legal norms? (On the last of these, see Sec. 3, *infra*.)

With respect to the second question, decisions after Parratt moved in two directions. First, in Hudson v. Palmer, 468 U.S. 517 (1984), the Court extended the Parratt doctrine to intentional wrongs. In this case, plaintiff, also a state prison inmate, brought a § 1983 action against a prison official for intentionally and unjustifiably destroying some of his personal property during a prison shakedown. Summary judgment for the defendant was unanimously affirmed by the Supreme Court. The Court declined to distinguish Parratt on the ground that the deprivation here was intentional. The underlying rationale of Parratt, it said, was that an adequate postdeprivation remedy satisfies the demands of due process whenever deprivation occurs "through random and unauthorized conduct of a state employee" (p. 533). In such a situation, "predeprivation procedures are simply 'impracticable' since the state cannot know when such deprivations will occur" (*id.*).

The second direction that the Court followed after Parratt was its adoption of Justice Powell's position in his concurrence in that case—that negligent acts do not constitute a deprivation within the meaning of the Fourteenth Amendment. In Daniels v. Williams, 474 U.S. 327 (1986), still another state prisoner brought a § 1983 action alleging a deprivation without due process after he tripped over a pillow negligently left on a staircase by a prison official. The Supreme Court held that, whether or not the prisoner had an adequate post-injury state remedy, there was no constitutional violation because (overruling Parratt on the point) mere lack of due care by a state officer cannot constitute a deprivation of liberty or property under the Fourteenth Amendment.[1]

---

1. The prisoner in Daniels, in support of the argument that negligent conduct can deny due process, posited a case in which the state negligently failed to provide an inmate with a hearing before revoking his good time credit, as required by Wolff v. McDonnell, 418 U.S. 539, 558 (1974). The Court responded that "the relevant action of the prison officials in that situation is their deliberate decision to deprive the inmate of good-time credit, not their hypothetically negligent failure to accord him the procedural protections of the Due Process Clause" (pp. 333–34). Compare Logan v. Zimmerman Brush Co., subparagraph (c), *infra*.

In a companion case, Davidson v. Cannon, 474 U.S. 344 (1986), the Court, relying on Daniels, held that a state prisoner could not bring a § 1983 action for the failure of prison officials to protect him from assault by another inmate. Justice Blackmun, joined by Justice Marshall, dissented, arguing that in some contexts—as when the state has taken on sole responsibility for a person's safety—negligence could rise to the level of a deprivation of liberty or property. (He also suggested that the record might support a finding of recklessness—a finding that he contended should suffice, even after Daniels, to make out a claim of deprivation.)

Justice Stevens, concurring in Daniels and Davidson, disagreed with the conclusion that a constitutional deprivation could not result from an officer's negligence, but found the state post-deprivation remedies adequate despite the availability of a sovereign immunity defense. (On this last point, see Paragraph (5), *infra*.)

(c) *Conduct Pursuant to Established State Procedures.* The Court's opinion in Hudson v. Palmer stated that "postdeprivation remedies do not satisfy due process where a deprivation of property is caused by conduct pursuant to established state procedure, rather than random and unauthorized action" (468 U.S. at 532). The Hudson Court cited Logan v. Zimmerman Brush Co., 455 U.S. 422 (1982), as supporting that proposition. In Logan, an individual claiming employment discrimination filed a charge with the state equal opportunity commission, as required by state law. By statute, the commission had 120 days to schedule a factfinding conference, but, apparently due to inadvertence, it failed to do so within that time. Ruling on a motion of the employer, the Illinois Supreme Court held that because the 120–day limit was jurisdictional, the commission must dismiss the charge. The Supreme Court unanimously reversed, holding that Logan's cause of action was a property interest of which he had been deprived without due process. The employer argued that, because Logan could sue the commission in state court for damages, under Parratt there was no deprivation without due process, but the Court was unconvinced (p. 436): "Here * * * it is the state system itself that destroys a complainant's property interest, by operation of law, whenever the Commission fails to convene a timely conference * * *. * * * Unlike the complainant in Parratt, Logan is challenging not the Commission's error, but the 'established state procedure' that destroys his entitlement without according him proper procedural safeguards."

The tension between the analysis in Hudson and that in Logan resurfaced in Zinermon. Was the tension adequately resolved in that case?[2]

(3) *The Significance of the Zinermon Decision.* The Zinermon case appeared to put some issues to rest, though the sharp division within the Court may contribute to the instability of its result and rationale. First, the Court ruled unanimously that the Parratt doctrine applies to a claimed deprivation of liberty as well as of property. Second, the Court ruled, again unanimously, that the Parratt doctrine does not apply to alleged violations of "substantive" (as opposed to procedural) due process or of specific guarantees of the Bill of Rights—violations that are complete when the conduct complained of occurs.

Under one view of the decision, the latter holding means that the lengthy debate about the significance of Parratt has, in essence, been mooted by reducing the question raised in such cases to the familiar one whether procedural due process requires a predeprivation hearing (a question to be determined by applying the "three prong" test of Mathews v. Eldridge). Even under this view, the problem of distinguishing between a case in which the action complained of was wholly "random" and one in which the action was sufficiently "predictable" in light of the authority granted by state law will undoubtedly prove daunting, and indeed, some have concluded that the distinction is unworkable. See, *e.g.*, Easter House v. Felder, 910 F.2d 1387, 1408–12 (7th Cir.1990)(Easterbrook, J., concurring).

Another view, however, starts from the premise that Parratt and its progeny cannot be understood simply as procedural due process cases. Rather, they should be read as cases in which a substantive due process claim was unavailable, *either* because the conduct in question did not constitute sufficient-

---

2. Recall the difficulties courts have had in an analogous area: determining, for purposes of local government liability under § 1983, when conduct is undertaken pursuant to local policy or custom. See p. 1129, *supra.*

ly unacceptable government behavior to make out a violation,[3] *or* because the Court has, *sub silentio,* relegated certain kinds of substantive due process claims to state fora and to state remedies in a form of "abstention" analogous to the more overt examples considered in Chap. X, *infra.*[4] Under either of these alternatives, the rationale of Zinermon—suggesting as it does that officials may be liable for failing to follow procedures that the state itself may have no constitutional obligation to provide—makes little sense, and the case should be reinterpreted to fall outside the scope of Parratt because Florida's procedural scheme for voluntary commitments was itself unconstitutional. See Fallon, note 4, *supra,* at 347 n. 219.

If the Parratt line of cases is understood as involving the reach of substantive due process, that line can perhaps be analogized to such decisions as Whitley v. Albers, 475 U.S. 312 (1986)(holding that shooting of prisoner during an effort to quell a riot did not violate substantive due process), DeShaney v. Winnebago County Dep't of Social Services, 489 U.S. 189 (1989)(rejecting substantive due process claim based on failure of state to protect child against parental violence), and Collins v. City of Harker Heights, 503 U.S. 115 (1992)(rejecting substantive due process claim based on city's alleged responsibility for employee's accidental death). One way of framing such an approach would be to conclude that on the ultimate question whether the state has deprived a person of liberty or property without the process that is due, state law remedies are *always* an aspect of the very question whether the state has committed a constitutional wrong.

If the cases are understood as a form of abstention, or as representing the view that no due process issue can be analyzed without taking account of available state remedies, can they be reconciled either with Home Telephone, p. 1105, *supra,* or Monroe v. Pape, p. 1111, *supra?* Or must Parratt and its progeny be recognized as carving out an exception to the holdings of those cases for certain claimed constitutional violations?

(4) *Albright v. Oliver.* These confusing and conflicting strands were visible in several opinions in Albright v. Oliver, 114 S.Ct. 807 (1994). In this case, the Court held (but without a majority opinion) that an arrest without probable cause did not violate substantive due process.[5] Justice Kennedy, concurring in the judgment in an opinion joined by Justice Thomas, argued that Parratt (a case not cited by the plurality) was controlling: since any deprivation suffered by the plaintiff was "random and unauthorized", the official's conduct "cannot be challenged under 42 U.S.C. § 1983 so long as the State provides an adequate postdeprivation remedy" (p. 818). In passing, Justice Kennedy lamented that the Court's ambivalence about Parratt had transformed the case "into a mere pleading exercise" in which a claimant either attached a substantive label to a

---

3. See, *e.g.,* Wells & Eaton, *Substantive Due Process and the Scope of Constitutional Torts,* 18 Ga.L.Rev. 201 (1984).

4. See Fallon, *Some Confusions About Due Process, Judicial Review, and Constitutional Remedies,* 93 Colum.L.Rev. 309, 339–55 (1993). *Cf.* Monaghan, *State Law Wrongs, State Law Remedies, and the Fourteenth Amendment,* 86 Colum.L.Rev. 979, 990–91 (1986)(suggesting that in such cases, the Court should not have sought to refine no-

tions of due process but should rather have refined the concept of state action in the context of § 1983).

5. For reasons that were not entirely clear, the petitioner in Albright relied in his Supreme Court argument not on a claim under the Fourth Amendment but rather on a claimed substantive due process right to be free from prosecution without probable cause.

due process claim or attempted to recast a due process claim in terms of some other constitutional provision (p. 819). Justice Stevens, joined by Justice Blackmun in dissent, took issue with all the other opinions, urging in response to Justice Kennedy that if plaintiff's constitutional claim is substantive, "Parratt is categorically inapplicable" under Zinermon, and that if it is procedural, Parratt is inapplicable because the deprivation was "officially authorized" (p. 833).

Does this interchange in Albright clarify the significance of the Parratt doctrine, or confuse it even further?

(5) *The Adequacy of State Postdeprivation Remedies.* When the constitutional issue turns on the adequacy of state postdeprivation process, what are the criteria by which adequacy is judged? Parratt indicated that a constitutionally "meaningful" remedy need not track § 1983's procedures and remedies even in important respects. Parratt did state, however, that the state remedies available in that case "could have fully compensated the [plaintiff] for the property loss he suffered." In Hudson v. Palmer, Paragraph (2)(b), *supra,* the Court articulated its reasoning somewhat differently: "that Palmer might not be able to recover under these [state] remedies the full amount which he might receive in a § 1983 action is not * * * determinative of the adequacy of the state remedies" (468 U.S. at 535).

In Davidson v. Cannon, note 1, *supra,* Justice Blackmun (joined by Justice Marshall) and Justice Stevens, each having found that a deprivation of liberty had occurred, proceeded to consider whether the state provided an adequate postdeprivation remedy. The question revolved around a state statute that immunized all public officials and entities from liability in an action by one prisoner claiming injury by another prisoner. For Justice Stevens, this statute did not render the state's postdeprivation procedure constitutionally invalid so as to permit a § 1983 action. Just as "defenses such as contributory negligence or statutes of limitations may defeat recovery in particular cases without raising any question about the constitutionality of a State's procedures for disposing of tort litigation", so the provision of an immunity defense "does not justify the conclusion that [the state's] remedial system is constitutionally inadequate" (474 U.S. at 342). Aren't contributory negligence and limitations defenses distinguishable? The former in effect denies that a wrong was committed, while the latter does not bar relief altogether but simply conditions its provision on compliance with reasonable procedural rules.

Justice Blackmun disagreed with Justice Stevens, arguing that the state remedy was obviously inadequate (p. 359): "Conduct that is wrongful under § 1983 surely cannot be immunized by state law." Does Justice Blackmun put the cart before the horse by assuming the conduct was wrongful under § 1983 without first establishing that it constituted a denial of due process?

How, then, should a court determine whether, when a deprivation of liberty or property has occurred, the existence of immunities in any state court action denies the process that is due? If the state's sovereign and official immunity rules permit damages liability whenever, in a § 1983 action, such liability could be imposed, is the state remedy plainly adequate? If, instead, the immunities in state court are broader than those applicable in § 1983 actions, does the state necessarily deny due process? Recall that under

Parratt, the question of adequacy is measured by comparison not with § 1983 actions, but with a constitutionally-based standard of adequacy.[6]

Immunity laws are only one of a seemingly endless number of provisions applicable in postdeprivation proceedings that plaintiffs have contended make such proceedings inadequate within the meaning of Parratt.[7] Is a state tort remedy inadequate if it applies a remedial or procedural rule that would not be "incorporated" in a § 1983 suit (presumably because it was deemed either "deficient" in promoting, or inconsistent with, federal policies, see pp. 827–28, *supra*)?

For general discussion of these problems, see Fallon, note 4, *supra,* at 355–59; Smolla, *The Displacement of Federal Due Process Claims by State Remedies: Parratt v. Taylor and Logan v. Zimmerman Brush,* 1982 U.Ill.L.Rev. 831, 871–81.

(6) *The Pertinence of Parratt and Hudson to Constitutional Tort Actions Against Federal Officials.* How should a federal court deal with a Bivens-type action seeking damages, under the Fifth Amendment, for a procedural due process violation arising from the random and unauthorized conduct of federal officials? In Weiss v. Lehman, 676 F.2d 1320 (9th Cir.1982), the Supreme Court had vacated and remanded, "for further consideration in light of Parratt v. Taylor", a prior judgment of the court of appeals that had upheld a damages award in such a case. On remand, the court of appeals ruled that because the plaintiff had an adequate remedy under the Federal Tort Claims Act, no due process violation had occurred. Recall that the FTCA (i) makes actionable wrongs as defined by state law rather than by the federal Constitution, (ii) affords no jury trial, (iii) establishes governmental but not individual liability, and (iv) forbids punitive damages. These were the very "defects" that the Court held in Carlson v. Green, 446 U.S. 14 (1980), p. 869, *supra,* made the FTCA less effective than a Bivens suit, and therefore made it inappropriate not to infer a Bivens remedy in an action directly under the Eighth Amendment. On the other hand, the state remedy that Parratt found adequate to redress a

---

6. Consider the bearing of Martinez v. California, 444 U.S. 277 (1980). There, a state court action against state parole officials, brought by the representatives of an individual murdered by a released convict, was dismissed under a state statute conferring absolute immunity on public officials and public entities. The Supreme Court affirmed. It found plaintiffs' § 1983 claim without merit because the officials had not proximately caused the harm. Plaintiffs' state law wrongful death claim could, the Court admitted, be viewed as a property interest, but the state's interest in fashioning immunity rules was held to be paramount to any federal interest involved, except perhaps the interest in protecting individuals from wholly arbitrary action (a problem not raised by the immunity provision).

Is Martinez' highly deferential standard of review applicable only to "pure" state law claims like the wrongful death action?

7. Consider, for example, such holdings as these: (i) a state remedy for recovery of excess taxes assessed is inadequate because it permits no compensation for mental anguish, Rutherford v. United States, 702 F.2d 580, 584 (5th Cir.1983); (ii) state *administrative* remedies are not necessarily inadequate, Dusanek v. Hannon, 677 F.2d 538 (7th Cir. 1982); (iii) state judicial review of an agency's decision arguably depriving a tow-truck operator of a property right provides an adequate remedy, even though the operator's § 1983 suit sought damages, Alfaro Motors, Inc. v. Ward, 814 F.2d 883 (2d Cir.1987); (iv) state provision of damages but not specific relief for wrongful seizure of personal property of sentimental value is inadequate, Bumgarner v. Bloodworth, 738 F.2d 966 (8th Cir. 1984)(per curiam).

deprivation of property under the Fourteenth Amendment's Due Process Clause had all four of these "defects".

Are Parratt's concerns about excessive federal interference with state officials and state courts less forceful in suits against federal officials? Is that enough reason, however, to give different interpretations to the Due Process Clauses of the Fifth and Fourteenth Amendments? See Smolla, Paragraph (5), *supra,* at 881–83.

(7) *Bibliography.* There is considerable scholarly commentary on the issues raised in this Note, though much of it antedates the Zinermon decision. In addition to the authorities already cited, see, *e.g.,* Bandes, *Monell, Parratt, Daniels, and Davidson: Distinguishing a Custom or Policy from a Random, Unauthorized Act,* 72 Iowa L.Rev. 101 (1986); Brown, *De-federalizing Common Law Torts: Empathy for Parratt, Hudson, and Daniels,* 28 B.C.L.Rev. 813 (1987); Burnham, *Separating Constitutional and Common–Law Torts: A Critique and a Proposed Constitutional Theory of Duty,* 73 Minn.L.Rev. 515 (1989); Zensky, *Parratt v. Taylor: Unauthorized Deprivations and the Content of an Adequate Remedy,* 16 N.Y.U.Rev.L. & Soc. Change 161 (1987–88).

SECTION 3. OFFICIAL IMMUNITY

Harlow v. Fitzgerald

457 U.S. 800, 102 S.Ct. 2727, 73 L.Ed.2d 396 (1982).
Certiorari to the United States Court of Appeals for the District of Columbia Circuit.

■ JUSTICE POWELL delivered the opinion of the Court.

The issue in this case is the scope of the immunity available to the aides and advisers of the President of the United States in a suit for damages based upon their official acts.

I

In this suit for civil damages, petitioners Bryce Harlow and Alexander Butterfield are alleged to have participated in a conspiracy to violate the constitutional and statutory rights of the respondent * * *. Respondent avers that petitioners entered the conspiracy in their capacities as senior White House aides to former President Richard M. Nixon. * * * [T]he alleged conspiracy is the same as that involved in Nixon v. Fitzgerald [decided the same day, see p. 1171, *infra*. In both cases, Fitzgerald, a well-known "whistleblower", sought damages for the elimination of his federal job, claiming that this action and his ensuing dismissal violated the First Amendment and several federal statutes.] * * *

Respondent claims that Harlow joined the conspiracy in his role as the Presidential aide principally responsible for congressional relations. At the conclusion of discovery the supporting evidence remained inferential. As evidence of Harlow's conspiratorial activity respondent relies heavily on a series of conversations in which Harlow discussed Fitzgerald's dismissal with Air Force Secretary Robert Seamans. The other evidence most supportive of Fitzgerald's claims consists of a recorded conversation in which the President later voiced a tentative recollection that Harlow was "all for canning" Fitzgerald.

Disputing Fitzgerald's contentions, Harlow argues that exhaustive discovery has adduced no direct evidence of his involvement in any wrongful activity. He avers that Secretary Seamans advised him that considerations of efficiency required Fitzgerald's removal by a reduction in force, despite anticipated adverse congressional reaction. Harlow asserts he had no reason to believe that a conspiracy existed. He contends that he took all his actions in good faith.

Petitioner Butterfield also is alleged to have entered the conspiracy not later than May 1969. Employed as Deputy Assistant to the President and Deputy Chief of Staff to H. R. Haldeman, Butterfield circulated a White House memorandum in that month in which he claimed to have learned that Fitzgerald planned to "blow the whistle" on some "shoddy purchasing practices" by exposing these practices to public view. Fitzgerald characterizes this memorandum as evidence that Butterfield had commenced efforts to secure Fitzgerald's retaliatory dismissal. As evidence that Butterfield participated in the conspiracy to conceal his unlawful discharge and prevent his reemployment, Fitzgerald cites communications between Butterfield and Haldeman in December 1969 and January 1970. After the President had promised at a press conference to inquire into Fitzgerald's dismissal, Haldeman solicited Butterfield's recommendations. In a subsequent memorandum emphasizing the importance of "loyalty," Butterfield counseled against offering Fitzgerald another job in the administration at that time.

For his part, Butterfield denies that he was involved in any decision concerning Fitzgerald's employment status until Haldeman sought his advice in December 1969—more than a month after Fitzgerald's termination had been scheduled and announced publicly by the Air Force. Butterfield states that he never communicated his views about Fitzgerald to any official of the Defense Department. He argues generally that nearly eight years of discovery have failed to turn up any evidence that he caused injury to Fitzgerald.

Together with their codefendant Richard Nixon, petitioners Harlow and Butterfield moved for summary judgment on February 12, 1980. In denying the motion the District Court upheld the legal sufficiency of Fitzgerald's Bivens (Bivens v. Six Unknown Fed. Narcotics Agents, 403 U.S. 388 (1971)) claim under the First Amendment and his "inferred" statutory causes of action * * * .[10]

* * *

Independently of former President Nixon, petitioners invoked the collateral order doctrine [see Chap. XV, Sec. 2, *infra*] and appealed the denial of their immunity defense to the Court of Appeals for the District of Columbia Circuit. The Court of Appeals dismissed the appeal without opinion. Never having determined the immunity available to the senior aides and advisers of the President of the United States, we granted certiorari.

10. * * * The legal sufficiency of respondent's asserted causes of action is not, however, a question that we view as properly presented for our decision in the present posture of this case.

II

As we reiterated today in Nixon v. Fitzgerald, our decisions consistently have held that government officials are entitled to some form of immunity from suits for damages. As recognized at common law, public officers require this protection to shield them from undue interference with their duties and from potentially disabling threats of liability.

Our decisions have recognized immunity defenses of two kinds. For officials whose special functions or constitutional status requires complete protection from suit, we have recognized the defense of "absolute immunity." The absolute immunity of legislators, in their legislative functions, see, *e.g.,* Eastland v. United States Servicemen's Fund, 421 U.S. 491 (1975), and of judges, in their judicial functions, see, *e.g.,* Stump v. Sparkman, 435 U.S. 349 (1978), now is well settled. Our decisions also have extended absolute immunity to certain officials of the Executive Branch. These include prosecutors and similar officials, see Butz v. Economou, 438 U.S. 478, 508–512 (1978), executive officers engaged in adjudicative functions, *id.,* at 513–517, and the President of the United States, see Nixon v. Fitzgerald.

For executive officials in general, however, our cases make plain that qualified immunity represents the norm. In Scheuer v. Rhodes, 416 U.S. 232 (1974), we acknowledged that high officials require greater protection than those with less complex discretionary responsibilities. Nonetheless, we held that a governor and his aides could receive the requisite protection from qualified or good-faith immunity. *Id.,* at 247–248. In Butz v. Economou, *supra,* we extended the approach of Scheuer to high federal officials of the Executive Branch. Discussing in detail the considerations that also had underlain our decision in Scheuer, we explained that the recognition of a qualified immunity defense for high executives reflected an attempt to balance competing values: not only the importance of a damages remedy to protect the rights of citizens, 438 U.S., at 504–505, but also "the need to protect officials who are required to exercise their discretion and the related public interest in encouraging the vigorous exercise of official authority." *Id.,* at 506. Without discounting the adverse consequences of denying high officials an absolute immunity from private lawsuits alleging constitutional violations—consequences found sufficient in Spalding v. Vilas, 161 U.S. 483 (1896), and Barr v. Matteo, 360 U.S. 564 (1959), to warrant extension to such officials of absolute immunity from suits at common law—we emphasized our expectation that insubstantial suits need not proceed to trial:

"Insubstantial lawsuits can be quickly terminated by federal courts alert to the possibilities of artful pleading. Unless the complaint states a compensable claim for relief ..., it should not survive a motion to dismiss. * * * In responding to such a motion, plaintiffs may not play dog in the manger; and firm application of the Federal Rules of Civil Procedure will ensure that federal officials are not harassed by frivolous lawsuits." 438 U.S., at 507–508 (citations omitted).

* * *

III

A

Petitioners argue that they are entitled to a blanket protection of absolute immunity as an incident of their offices as Presidential aides. In deciding this claim we do not write on an empty page. In Butz v. Economou, *supra,* the Secretary of Agriculture—a Cabinet official directly accountable to the President—asserted a defense of absolute official immunity from suit for civil damages. We rejected his claim. In so doing we did not question the power or the importance of the Secretary's office. Nor did we doubt the importance to the President of loyal and efficient subordinates in executing his duties of office. Yet we found these factors, alone, to be insufficient to justify absolute immunity. "[T]he greater power of [high] officials," we reasoned, "affords a greater potential for a regime of lawless conduct." 438 U.S., at 506. Damages actions against high officials were therefore "an important means of vindicating constitutional guarantees." *Ibid.* Moreover, we concluded that it would be "untenable to draw a distinction for purposes of immunity law between suits brought against state officials under § 1983 and suits brought directly under the Constitution against federal officials." *Id.,* at 504.

Having decided in Butz that Members of the Cabinet ordinarily enjoy only qualified immunity from suit, we conclude today that it would be equally untenable to hold absolute immunity an incident of the office of every Presidential subordinate based in the White House. Members of the Cabinet are direct subordinates of the President, frequently with greater responsibilities, both to the President and to the Nation, than White House staff. The considerations that supported our decision in Butz apply with equal force to this case. It is no disparagement of the offices held by petitioners to hold that Presidential aides, like Members of the Cabinet, generally are entitled only to a qualified immunity.

B

In disputing the controlling authority of Butz, petitioners rely on the principles developed in Gravel v. United States, 408 U.S. 606 (1972). In Gravel we endorsed the view that "it is literally impossible ... for Members of Congress to perform their legislative tasks without the help of aides and assistants" and that "the day-to-day work of such aides is so critical to the Members' performance that they must be treated as the latter's alter egos...." *Id.,* at 616–617. Having done so, we held the Speech and Debate Clause derivatively applicable to the "legislative acts" of a Senator's aide that would have been privileged if performed by the Senator himself. *Id.,* at 621–622.

* * *

Petitioners' [reliance on Gravel] is not without force. Ultimately, however, it sweeps too far. If the President's aides are derivatively immune because they are essential to the functioning of the Presidency, so should the Members of the Cabinet—Presidential subordinates some of whose essential roles are acknowledged by the Constitution itself—be absolutely immune. Yet we implicitly rejected such derivative immunity in Butz. Moreover, in general our cases have followed a "functional" approach to immunity law. We have recognized that the judicial, prosecutorial, and legislative functions require absolute immunity. But this protection has extended no further than its justification would warrant. In Gravel, for example, we emphasized that Senators and their aides were absolutely immune only when performing "acts legislative in nature," and not when taking other acts even "in their official capacity." 408 U.S., at 625. Our cases involving judges[15] and prosecutors[16] have followed a similar line.

---

15. See, *e.g.,* Supreme Court of Virginia v. Consumers Union of United States, 446 U.S. 719, 731–737 (1980); Stump v. Sparkman, 435 U.S. 349, 362 (1978).

16. In Imbler v. Pachtman, 424 U.S. 409, 430–431 (1976), this Court reserved the question whether absolute immunity would extend to "those aspects of the prosecutor's

The undifferentiated extension of absolute "derivative" immunity to the President's aides therefore could not be reconciled with the "functional" approach that has characterized the immunity decisions of this Court, indeed including Gravel itself.[17]

C

Petitioners also assert an entitlement to immunity based on the "special functions" of White House aides. This form of argument accords with the analytical approach of our cases. For aides entrusted with discretionary authority in such sensitive areas as national security or foreign policy, absolute immunity might well be justified to protect the unhesitating performance of functions vital to the national interest. But a "special functions" rationale does not warrant a blanket recognition of absolute immunity for all Presidential aides in the performance of all their duties. This conclusion too follows from our decision in Butz, which establishes that an executive official's claim to absolute immunity must be justified by reference to the public interest in the special functions of his office, not the mere fact of high station.

Butz also identifies the location of the burden of proof. The burden of justifying absolute immunity rests on the official asserting the claim. We have not of course had occasion to identify how a Presidential aide might carry this burden. But the general requisites are familiar in our cases. In order to establish entitlement to absolute immunity a Presidential aide first must show that the responsibilities of his office embraced a function so sensitive as to require a total shield from liability.[20] He then must demonstrate that he was discharging the protected function when performing the act for which liability is asserted.

Applying these standards to the claims advanced by petitioners Harlow and Butterfield, we cannot conclude on the record before us that either has shown that "public policy requires [for any of the functions of his office] an exemption of [absolute] scope." Butz, 438 U.S., at 506. Nor, assuming that petitioners did have functions for which absolute immunity would be warranted, could we now conclude that the acts charged in this lawsuit—if taken at all—would lie within the protected area. We do not, however, foreclose the possibility that petitioners, on remand, could satisfy the standards properly applicable to their claims.

IV

Even if they cannot establish that their official functions require absolute immunity, petitioners assert that public policy at least mandates an application

---

responsibility that cast him in the role of an administrator or investigative officer." * * * [For later Supreme Court decisions dealing with this question, see pp. 1169–70, *infra*.]

17. Our decision today in Nixon v. Fitzgerald in no way abrogates this general rule. As we explained in that opinion, the recognition of absolute immunity for all of a President's acts in office derives in principal part from factors unique to his constitutional re-

sponsibilities and station. Suits against other officials—including Presidential aides— generally do not invoke separation-of-powers considerations to the same extent as suits against the President himself.

20. Here as elsewhere the relevant judicial inquiries would encompass considerations of public policy, the importance of which should be confirmed either by reference to the common law or, more likely, our constitutional heritage and structure.

of the qualified immunity standard that would permit the defeat of insubstantial claims without resort to trial. We agree.

A

The resolution of immunity questions inherently requires a balance between the evils inevitable in any available alternative. In situations of abuse of office, an action for damages may offer the only realistic avenue for vindication of constitutional guarantees. It is this recognition that has required the denial of absolute immunity to most public officers. At the same time, however, it cannot be disputed seriously that claims frequently run against the innocent as well as the guilty—at a cost not only to the defendant officials, but to society as a whole. These social costs include the expenses of litigation, the diversion of official energy from pressing public issues, and the deterrence of able citizens from acceptance of public office. Finally, there is the danger that fear of being sued will "dampen the ardor of all but the most resolute, or the most irresponsible [public officials], in the unflinching discharge of their duties." Gregoire v. Biddle, 177 F.2d 579, 581 (C.A.2 1949), cert. denied, 339 U.S. 949 (1950).

In identifying qualified immunity as the best attainable accommodation of competing values, in Butz, *supra,* at 507–508, as in Scheuer, 416 U.S., at 245–248, we relied on the assumption that this standard would permit "[i]nsubstantial lawsuits [to] be quickly terminated." 438 U.S., at 507–508. Yet petitioners advance persuasive arguments that the dismissal of insubstantial lawsuits without trial—a factor presupposed in the balance of competing interests struck by our prior cases—requires an adjustment of the "good faith" standard established by our decisions.

B

Qualified or "good faith" immunity is an affirmative defense that must be pleaded by a defendant official. Gomez v. Toledo, 446 U.S. 635 (1980). Decisions of this Court have established that the "good faith" defense has both an "objective" and a "subjective" aspect. The objective element involves a presumptive knowledge of and respect for "basic, unquestioned constitutional rights." Wood v. Strickland, 420 U.S. 308, 322 (1975). The subjective component refers to "permissible intentions." *Ibid.* Characteristically the Court has defined these elements by identifying the circumstances in which qualified immunity would *not* be available. Referring both to the objective and subjective elements, we have held that qualified immunity would be defeated if an official *"knew or reasonably should have known* that the action he took within his sphere of official responsibility would violate the constitutional rights of the [plaintiff], *or* if he took the action *with the malicious intention* to cause a deprivation of constitutional rights or other injury...." *Ibid.* (emphasis added).

The subjective element of the good-faith defense frequently has proved incompatible with our admonition in Butz that insubstantial claims should not proceed to trial. Rule 56 of the Federal Rules of Civil Procedure provides that disputed questions of fact ordinarily may not be decided on motions for summary judgment. And an official's subjective good faith has been considered to be a question of fact that some courts have regarded as inherently requiring resolution by a jury.

In the context of Butz' attempted balancing of competing values, it now is clear that substantial costs attend the litigation of the subjective good faith of government officials. Not only are there the general costs of subjecting officials to the risks of trial—distraction of officials from their governmental duties, inhibition of discretionary action, and deterrence of able people from public service. There are special costs to "subjective" inquiries of this kind. Immunity generally is available only to officials performing discretionary functions. In contrast with the thought processes accompanying "ministerial" tasks, the judgments surrounding discretionary action almost inevitably are influenced by the decisionmaker's experiences, values, and emotions. These variables explain in part why questions of subjective intent so rarely can be decided by summary judgment. Yet they also frame a background in which there often is no clear end to the relevant evidence. Judicial inquiry into subjective motivation therefore may entail broad-ranging discovery and the deposing of numerous persons, including an official's professional colleagues. Inquiries of this kind can be peculiarly disruptive of effective government.

Consistently with the balance at which we aimed in Butz, we conclude today that bare allegations of malice should not suffice to subject government officials either to the costs of trial or to the burdens of broad-reaching discovery. We therefore hold that government officials performing discretionary functions, generally are shielded from liability for civil damages insofar as their conduct does not violate clearly established statutory or constitutional rights of which a reasonable person would have known. See Procunier v. Navarette, 434 U.S. 555, 565 (1978); Wood v. Strickland, 420 U.S., at 322.[30]

Reliance on the objective reasonableness of an official's conduct, as measured by reference to clearly established law, should avoid excessive disruption of government and permit the resolution of many insubstantial claims on summary judgment. On summary judgment, the judge appropriately may determine, not only the currently applicable law, but whether that law was clearly established at the time an action occurred.[32] If the law at that time was not clearly established, an official could not reasonably be expected to anticipate subsequent legal developments, nor could he fairly be said to "know" that the law forbade conduct not previously identified as unlawful. Until this threshold immunity question is resolved, discovery should not be allowed. If the law was clearly established, the immunity defense ordinarily should fail, since a reasonably competent public official should know the law governing his conduct. Nevertheless, if the official pleading the defense claims extraordinary circumstances and can prove that he neither knew nor should have known of the relevant legal standard, the defense should be sustained. But again, the defense would turn primarily on objective factors.

30. This case involves no issue concerning the elements of the immunity available to state officials sued for constitutional violations under § 1983. We have found previously, however, that it would be "untenable to draw a distinction for purposes of immunity law between suits brought against state officials under § 1983 and suits brought directly under the Constitution against federal officials." Butz v. Economou, 438 U.S., at 504.

Our decision in no way diminishes the absolute immunity currently available to officials whose functions have been held to require a protection of this scope.

32. As in Procunier v. Navarette, 434 U.S., at 565, we need not define here the circumstances under which "the state of the law" should be "evaluated by reference to the opinions of this Court, of the Courts of Appeals, or of the local District Court."

By defining the limits of qualified immunity essentially in objective terms, we provide no license to lawless conduct. The public interest in deterrence of unlawful conduct and in compensation of victims remains protected by a test that focuses on the objective legal reasonableness of an official's acts. Where an official could be expected to know that certain conduct would violate statutory or constitutional rights, he should be made to hesitate; and a person who suffers injury caused by such conduct may have a cause of action. But where an official's duties legitimately require action in which clearly established rights are not implicated, the public interest may be better served by action taken "with independence and without fear of consequences." Pierson v. Ray, 386 U.S. 547, 554 (1967).[34]

C

In this case petitioners have asked us to hold that the respondent's pretrial showings were insufficient to survive their motion for summary judgment.[35] We think it appropriate, however, to remand the case to the District Court for its reconsideration of this issue in light of this opinion.[36] The trial court is more familiar with the record so far developed and also is better situated to make any such further findings as may be necessary.

V

The judgment of the Court of Appeals is vacated, and the case is remanded for further action consistent with this opinion.

■ JUSTICE BRENNAN, with whom JUSTICE MARSHALL and JUSTICE BLACKMUN join, concurring.

I agree with the substantive standard announced by the Court today, imposing liability when a public-official defendant "knew or should have known" of the constitutionally violative effect of his actions. This standard would not allow the official who *actually knows* that he was violating the law to escape liability for his actions, even if he could not "reasonably have been expected" to know what he actually did know. Thus the clever and unusually well-informed violator of constitutional rights will not evade just punishment for his crimes. I also agree that this standard applies "across the board," to all "government

---

34. We emphasize that our decision applies only to suits for civil *damages* arising from actions within the scope of an official's duties and in "objective" good faith. We express no view as to the conditions in which injunctive or declaratory relief might be available.

35. In Butz, we admonished that "insubstantial" suits against high public officials should not be allowed to proceed to trial. 438 U.S., at 507. We reiterate this admonition. Insubstantial lawsuits undermine the effectiveness of government as contemplated by our constitutional structure, and "firm application of the Federal Rules of Civil Procedure" is fully warranted in such cases. 438 U.S., at 508.

36. Petitioners also have urged us, prior to the remand, to rule on the legal suffi-

ciency of respondent's "implied" causes of action under 5 U.S.C. § 7211 and 18 U.S.C. § 1505 and his Bivens claim under the First Amendment. We do not view petitioners' argument on the statutory question as insubstantial. Nor is the Bivens question. *Cf.* Bush v. Lucas, 647 F.2d 573, 576 (C.A.5 1981)(holding that the "unique relationship between the Federal Government and its civil service employees is a special consideration which counsels hesitation in inferring a Bivens remedy"). As in Nixon v. Fitzgerald, however, we took jurisdiction of the case only to resolve the immunity question under the collateral order doctrine. We therefore think it appropriate to leave these questions for fuller consideration by the District Court and, if necessary, by the Court of Appeals.

officials performing discretionary functions." I write separately only to note that given this standard, it seems inescapable to me that some measure of discovery may sometimes be required to determine exactly what a public-official defendant did "know" at the time of his actions. * * * Of course, as the Court has already noted, summary judgment will be readily available to public-official defendants whenever the state of the law was so ambiguous at the time of the alleged violation that it could not have been "known" then, and thus liability could not ensue. * * *

* * *

■ CHIEF JUSTICE BURGER, dissenting.

The Court today decides in Nixon v. Fitzgerald, what has been taken for granted for 190 years, that it is implicit in the Constitution that a President of the United States has absolute immunity from civil suits arising out of official acts as Chief Executive. I agree fully that absolute immunity for official acts of the President is, like executive privilege, "fundamental to the operation of Government and inextricably rooted in the separation of powers under the Constitution." United States v. Nixon, 418 U.S. 683, 708 (1974).

In this case the Court decides that senior aides of the President do not have derivative immunity from the President. I am at a loss, however, to reconcile this conclusion with our holding in Gravel v. United States, 408 U.S. 606 (1972). * * *

In Gravel we held that it is implicit in the Constitution that aides of Members of Congress have absolute immunity for acts performed for Members in relation to their legislative function. We viewed the aides' immunity as deriving from the Speech or Debate Clause * * *. * * * The Clause says nothing about "legislative acts" outside the Chambers, but we concluded that the Constitution grants absolute immunity for legislative acts not only "in either House" but in committees and conferences and in reports on legislative activities.

Nor does the Clause mention immunity for congressional aides. Yet, going far beyond any words found in the Constitution itself, we held that a Member's aides who implement policies and decisions of the Member are entitled to the same absolute immunity as a Member. It is hardly an overstatement to say that we thus avoided a "literalistic approach," Gravel, *supra,* at 617, and instead looked to the structure of the Constitution and the evolution of the function of the Legislative Branch. In short, we drew this immunity for legislative aides from a functional analysis of the legislative process in the context of the Constitution taken as a whole and in light of 20th-century realities. Neither Presidents nor Members of Congress can, as they once did, perform all their constitutional duties personally.

We very properly recognized in Gravel that the central purpose of a Member's absolute immunity would be "diminished and frustrated" if the legislative aides were not also protected by the same broad immunity. * * *

The Court has made this reality a matter of our constitutional jurisprudence. How can we conceivably hold that a President of the United States, who represents a vastly larger constituency than does any Member of Congress, should not have "alter egos" with comparable immunity? * * *

* * *

I challenge the Court * * * to say that the effectiveness of Presidential aides will not "inevitably be diminished and frustrated," Gravel, *supra,* at 617, if they must weigh every act and decision in relation to the risks of future lawsuits. The Gravel Court took note of the burdens on congressional aides: the stress of long hours, heavy responsibilities, constant exposure to harassment of the political arena. Is the Court suggesting the stresses are less for Presidential aides? By construing the Constitution to give only qualified immunity to senior Presidential aides we give those key "alter egos" only lawsuits, winnable lawsuits perhaps, but lawsuits nonetheless, with stress and effort that will disperse and drain their energies and their purses.

* * *

We—judges collectively—have held that the common law provides us with absolute immunity for ourselves with respect to judicial acts, however erroneous or ill-advised. See, *e.g.,* Stump v. Sparkman, 435 U.S. 349 (1978). Are the lowest ranking of 27,000 or more judges, thousands of prosecutors, and thousands of congressional aides—an aggregate of not less than 75,000 in all—entitled to greater protection than two senior aides of a President?

Butz v. Economou, 438 U.S. 478 (1978), does not dictate that senior Presidential aides be given only qualified immunity. Butz held only that a Cabinet officer exercising discretion was not entitled to absolute immunity; we need not abandon that holding. A senior Presidential aide works more intimately with the President on a daily basis than does a Cabinet officer, directly implementing Presidential decisions literally from hour to hour.

* * *

The Court's analysis in Gravel demonstrates that the question of derivative immunity does not and should not depend on a person's rank or position in the hierarchy, but on the *function* performed by the person and the relationship of that person to the superior. Cabinet officers clearly outrank United States Attorneys, yet qualified immunity is accorded the former and absolute immunity the latter; rank is important only to the extent that the rank determines the function to be performed. The function of senior Presidential aides, as the "alter egos" of the President, is an integral, inseparable part of the function of the President. * * *

By ignoring Gravel and engaging in a wooden application of Butz, the Court significantly undermines the functioning of the Office of the President. Under the Court's opinion in Nixon today it is clear that Presidential immunity derives from the Constitution as much as congressional immunity comes from that source. Can there rationally be one rule for congressional aides and another for Presidential aides simply because the initial absolute immunity of each derives from different aspects of the Constitution? I find it inexplicable why the Court makes no effort to demonstrate why the Chief Executive of the Nation should not be assured that senior staff aides will have the same protection as the aides of Members of the House and Senate.

NOTE ON OFFICERS' ACCOUNTABILITY IN DAMAGES FOR OFFICIAL MISCONDUCT

(1) *Introduction: The Basis for Official Immunity.* Questions of official immunity ordinarily arise in suits (like Harlow) seeking damages to be paid by

individual officers personally, rather than by the government. (For discussion of individual officers' immunity from actions for other relief, see *Note on the Immunity of Government Officers From Relief Other Than Damages*, which follows this Note.)

A classic statement of the rationale for official immunity is found in Gregoire v. Biddle, 177 F.2d 579 (2d Cir.1949)(L. Hand, J.), upholding the absolute immunity not only of the Attorney General, but also of mid-level Justice Department officials, in a suit claiming that the defendants had, with malice and without justification, falsely imprisoned the plaintiff. The court wrote (p. 581):

"It does indeed go without saying that an official, who is in fact guilty of using his powers to vent his spleen upon others, or for any other personal motive not connected with the public good, should not escape liability for the injuries he may so cause; and, if it were possible in practice to confine such complaints to the guilty, it would be monstrous to deny recovery. The justification for doing so is that it is impossible to know whether the claim is well founded until the case has been tried, and that to submit all officials, the innocent as well as the guilty, to the burden of a trial and to the inevitable danger of its outcome, would dampen the ardor of all but the most resolute, or the most irresponsible, in the unflinching discharge of their duties. Again and again the public interest calls for action which may turn out to be founded on a mistake, in the face of which an official may later find himself hard put to it to satisfy a jury of his good faith. There must indeed be means of punishing public officers who have been truant to their duties; but that is quite another matter from exposing such as have been honestly mistaken to suit by anyone who has suffered from their errors. As is so often the case, the answer must be found in a balance between the evils inevitable in either alternative. In this instance it has been thought in the end better to leave unredressed the wrongs done by dishonest officers than to subject those who try to do their duty to the constant dread of retaliation. Judged as res nova, we should not hesitate to follow the path laid down in the books."

The view that executive actions were entitled to some form of "discretionary immunity" from actions for damages—a view expressed by the Supreme Court at the turn of the century in Spalding v. Vilas, 161 U.S. 483 (1896)—represented a major shift from earlier nineteenth century practice. See Woolhandler, *Patterns of Official Immunity and Accountability*, 37 Case W.Res.L.Rev 396, 453–57 (1986–87). See also Engdahl, *Immunity and Accountability for Positive Governmental Wrongs*, 44 U.Colo.L.Rev. 1, 41–56 (1972). Under the earlier view, officials sued in tort generally were treated like private tortfeasors and not shielded by any distinctive immunity—although pockets of immunity did evolve, as for judges and high federal officials.

The purpose of this Note is to explore this shift, to examine the present scope of immunity doctrine, and to consider whether the broadening of notions of immunity that has taken place in this century strikes a proper balance between the interest in compensating individuals for wrongs done to them and the interest in protecting government officers from undue harassment in the performance of their jobs.

(2) *The Relationship of State and Federal Immunity Rules.* Whether state or federal law governs the immunity issue in a damages action depends on whether the conduct is alleged to violate state or federal law, and whether the defendant is a state or a federal official.

(a) *State Law Actions.* Prior to 1988, when a state law tort action was brought against a federal officer, federal common law had established a shield of absolute immunity from damages liability for actions within the "outer perimeter of [the official's] line of duty", Barr v. Matteo, 360 U.S. 564, 575 (1959)(plurality opinion). In 1988, the Federal Employees Liability Reform and Tort Compensation Act, 102 Stat. 4563, amended 28 U.S.C. § 2679(b), (d) to make the FTCA the *exclusive* remedy for torts committed by federal officials in the course of their official duties. Under § 2679(d) as amended, if the Attorney General or his designate certifies that an employee who has been sued was acting within the scope of employment, the proceeding shall be re-designated as a suit against the United States; if pending in state court, the suit shall be removed to federal court, and the plaintiff may recover only if the United States is liable under the FTCA.

The immunity of *state* officials in actions based on state law is itself governed by state law, for absent wholly arbitrary action by the state, there is no distinctive federal interest. See Martinez v. California, 444 U.S. 277 (1980). This rule applies even in actions that fall within the federal courts' jurisdiction. See, *e.g.,* Oyler v. National Guard Ass'n, 743 F.2d 545 (7th Cir.1984).

(b) *Federal Law Actions.* The remainder of this Note focuses primarily upon the immunity rules in actions based on federal law, especially constitutional tort actions. Federal law governs the immunity in such actions, even when brought against state officials. Consider these closely related questions:

First, has the Court been correct in assuming that the immunities of state officials in § 1983 actions and of federal officials in Bivens actions should be co-extensive?[1] Since § 1983, as enacted by Congress, said nothing about official immunity (absolute or qualified), should the statute be interpreted as providing a remedy not restricted by the immunities recognized in other contexts? See Matasar, *Personal Immunities Under Section 1983: The Limits of the Court's Historical Analysis,* 40 Ark.L.Rev. 741 (1987). Had that understanding been accepted, could the state have protected its interest in not having officials' conduct influenced by the fear of litigation and liability by agreeing to provide counsel for and to indemnify officials sued under § 1983? See Eisenberg, *Section 1983: Doctrinal Foundations and an Empirical Study,* 67 Cornell L.Rev. 482, 491–504 (1982). Or is the Court right in assuming (as it consistently has) that if the 42d Congress had intended § 1983 to abrogate any and all immunities recognized at common law, that intent would have been more clearly signalled in the statute?

Second, on what sources should the Court rely in determining the scope of official immunity? In Tower v. Glover, 467 U.S. 914, 920 (1984), a § 1983 action, the Court described the appropriate inquiry this way: "If an official was accorded immunity from tort actions at common law when the Civil Rights Act was enacted in 1871, the Court next considers whether § 1983's history or purposes nonetheless counsel against recognizing the same immunity in § 1983 actions." Both of these inquiries may be quite open-ended. The common law history may be inapposite to the distinctive functions and organization of modern governments, or may simply be unclear. See generally Matasar, *supra.* Analysis of policy considerations may be quite indeterminate in view of the

---

1. A limited exception to this parity is the absolute immunity of the President, see Paragraph (6), *infra;* state governors have only a qualified immunity, Scheuer v. Rhodes, 416 U.S. 232 (1974).

complexity of the competing goals, the paucity of pertinent empirical data, and the need to consider damages suits as just one of many remedies for official misconduct.

A third question derives from the first two: what are the respective roles of the courts, the Congress, and the Constitution in shaping immunities? In Bivens actions, the immunities are fashioned from federal common law. The Court has sometimes described the immunities in § 1983 actions also as federal common law, see, *e.g.,* United States v. Gillock, 445 U.S. 360, 372 n. 10 (1980), but has asserted on other occasions that the statutory basis of immunities in § 1983 suits imposes distinctive constraints on judicial lawmaking—as, for example, in the Court's insistence, in Tower v. Glover, *supra,* at 922–23, that if no analogous immunity was recognized at common law when the Civil Rights Act of 1871 was enacted, "[w]e do not have a license to establish immunities from § 1983 actions in the interests of what we judge to be sound public policy." Yet in Harlow, a Bivens action in which the Court formulated a new standard for qualified immunity broader than that recognized at common law, the Court expressly said (in footnote 30) that the new standard was meant to govern § 1983 actions as well.

Could Congress narrow or abolish immunities in § 1983 actions? In Bivens actions? Conversely, could Congress constitutionally provide all officials with absolute immunity in all constitutional tort actions? Does the answer to the latter question depend on whether Congress has made available other remedies—for example, a remedy directly against the government, as under the FTCA? (Note that the Department of Justice has issued a policy statement providing that the Department may indemnify its employees for any monetary judgment against them resulting from conduct taken within the scope of their employment. 28 C.F.R. § 50.15(c).)

Fourth, is the Court correct, in § 1983 actions, to ignore the immunity law of the affected state? Suppose that a state prosecutor has only a qualified immunity from state tort actions. Is there any reason why the federal law applied in a § 1983 action should not incorporate state rules that would broaden, rather than narrow, the opportunities for recovery? *Cf.* Davis v. Scherer, Paragraph (9), *infra*.

(3) *Absolute vs. Qualified Immunity.* Absolute and qualified immunities differ both substantively and procedurally. Substantively, an absolute immunity cannot be defeated by proof that an official knew or should have known that the conduct in issue was unlawful.[2] Procedurally, precisely because an official with absolute immunity has no obligation to justify action taken, the suit can ordinarily be dismissed on a simple Rule 12(b)(6) motion; consequently, unlike qualified immunity, absolute immunity eliminates nearly all of the possible burden, expense, and anxiety of litigation.

(4) *Absolute Immunities Associated With the Judicial Process.*

(a) *Judicial Immunity.* The considerations offered by the Court as justifications for absolute judicial immunity have been summarized as follows: "(1) the need for a judge to 'be free to act upon his own conviction, without apprehension of personal consequences to himself'; (2) the controversiality and importance of the competing interests adjudicated by judges and the likelihood

---

2. But it does not matter, for purposes of either absolute or qualified immunity, whether the defendant sought to injure the plaintiff, or otherwise acted without justification or with improper motivation.

that the loser, feeling aggrieved, would wish to retaliate; (3) the record-keeping to which self-protective judges would be driven in the absence of immunity; (4) the availability of alternative remedies, such as appeal and impeachment, for judicial wrongdoing; and (5) the ease with which bad faith can be alleged and made the basis for 'vexatious litigation.'" Schuck, Suing Government: Citizen Remedies for Official Wrongs 90 (1983).

The only way to circumvent judicial immunity is to show that a judge was acting "in the clear absence of all jurisdiction" or was not performing a "judicial act". These tests, dating back at least to Bradley v. Fisher, 80 U.S. (13 Wall.) 335, 351 (1871), were applied in Stump v. Sparkman, 435 U.S. 349 (1978), in which an Indiana judge had approved *ex parte* a petition filed by parents of a fifteen year-old girl to have her sterilized without her knowledge. When she later sued the judge for damages under § 1983, the Supreme Court ruled that he was absolutely immune: since he presided over a court of general jurisdiction, he had not acted wholly outside his jurisdiction, and he did not lose his immunity simply because no state statute specifically authorized his conduct.

The Court also rejected the argument that because the petition was never docketed or filed with the clerk, no hearing was held, and no guardian *ad litem* was appointed, the judge's approval of the petition was not a "judicial act". In the Court's view, whether a judge's action is a "judicial act" depends on whether (i) it is a function normally performed by a judge, and (ii) the parties' expectations revealed that they were dealing with the judge in his judicial capacity. The Court found both criteria to be met, noting as to the former that Indiana judges are often called upon to approve petitions about minors' affairs (p. 362).

Justice Stewart, joined by Justices Marshall and Powell, wrote an angry dissent, arguing that *ex parte* approval of a parent's petition was not an act normally performed by Indiana judges. He continued by insisting (p. 367) that "false illusions as to a judge's power can hardly convert a judge's response to those illusions into a judicial act", and that "[a] judge is not free, like a loose cannon, to inflict indiscriminate damage whenever he announces that he is acting in his judicial capacity." Justice Powell's separate dissent emphasized (p. 370) that "[t]he complete absence of normal judicial process" made inoperative the assumption underlying judicial immunity that "there exist alternative forums and methods for vindicating [private] rights."[3]

After Stump, when will a judge (or quasi-judicial officer) be found to have acted outside the official's judicial capacity?[4] Many of the cases so finding deal

---

3. Compare Cleavinger v. Saxner, 474 U.S. 193 (1985), holding (6–3) that federal prison officials who are members of a prison's Institution Discipline Committee, on which they hear cases charging inmates with rules infractions, are not entitled to absolute immunity: though they perform an adjudicatory function, these officials are not professional hearing officers insulated from executive pressure.

4. In Mireles v. Waco, 502 U.S. 9 (1991)(per curiam), the Court recognized absolute immunity for a state judge who alleg- edly ordered police officers to seize "with excessive force", and bring to the judge's chambers, a public defender who had missed a calendar call (p. 10). Following Stump, the Court held (pp. 12–13) that whether an act is "judicial", and thus shielded by absolute immunity, depends on the general nature of the act (here, the proper judicial function of directing officers to bring a person in the courthouse before the judge), not on the particulars of the alleged conduct (the direction to use excessive force). Justice Stevens' dissent argued that the judge issued two distinct

with offbeat situations.[5] But Forrester v. White, 484 U.S. 219 (1988), raised a more important issue. There, a state judge was sued by a probation officer who alleged that the judge had dismissed her on account of her sex, in violation of the Fourteenth Amendment. The Supreme Court unanimously ruled that the judge was acting in an administrative rather than a judicial capacity, and hence was not entitled to absolute immunity; the question of his entitlement to qualified immunity was not resolved.

(b) *Prosecutorial Immunity.* The purposes and scope of prosecutorial immunity are similar to those of judicial immunity. Imbler v. Pachtman, 424 U.S. 409 (1976), was a § 1983 damages action alleging that a state prosecutor had knowingly introduced perjured testimony at plaintiff's trial, resulting in an erroneous conviction. The Court found that prosecutorial immunity was well-established at common law, and necessary to protect the prosecutor; if only a qualified immunity attached, a criminal defendant could "transform his resentment * * * into the ascription of improper and malicious actions to the State's advocate", and suits "could be expected with some frequency" (p. 425). These suits would require a retrial of the criminal case, could discourage the prosecutor from presenting relevant evidence, and might skew postconviction procedures because of a judge's subconscious knowledge that a decision favorable to the accused could lead to a prosecutor's civil liability. Accordingly, the Court held that a prosecutor is absolutely immune from damages suits arising from activities "intimately associated with the judicial phase of the criminal process." There was "no occasion", the Court added, "to consider whether like or similar reasons require immunity for those aspects of the prosecutor's responsibility that cast him in the role of an administrator or investigative officer rather than that of advocate" (pp. 430–31).[6]

In Mitchell v. Forsyth, 472 U.S. 511 (1985), the Court held with little discussion that former Attorney General Mitchell, in authorizing a warrantless wiretap for reasons of national security, was not acting in a prosecutorial capacity and hence was not shielded by absolute immunity.

In two later decisions, the Court further limited the reach of a prosecutor's absolute immunity. In the first, Burns v. Reed, 500 U.S. 478 (1991), the plaintiff alleged, *inter alia,* that the defendant had violated her constitutional rights (i) by improperly advising the police that they could question her under hypnosis and that they "probably had probable cause" to arrest her, and (ii) by presenting false and misleading evidence at a court appearance in support of an application for a search warrant. The Supreme Court held that the defen-

orders—one to bring plaintiff to the courtroom (a judicial act), and the second to commit a battery (not a judicial act).

5. See, *e.g.,* Zarcone v. Perry, 572 F.2d 52 (2d Cir.1978)(judge who ordered court officials to bring "in front of me in cuffs" the vendor of coffee that the judge thought tasted "putrid", and who then interrogated the vendor and threatened his "livelihood", acted outside his judicial capacity).

6. Public defenders do not ordinarily act under color of law, see Polk County v. Dodson, 454 U.S. 312 (1981), so that they are likely to be liable under § 1983 only if they

conspire with state officials. Tower v. Glover, 467 U.S. 914 (1984), held that in such a § 1983 action a defender has no immunity, noting the absence of any common law immunity for a defense lawyer's intentional misconduct.

Jurors and witnesses in judicial proceedings also enjoy an absolute immunity. See Briscoe v. LaHue, 460 U.S. 325 (1983); Schwartz & Kirklin, Section 1983 Litigation: Claims, Defenses, and Fees § 7.9 (1986). But court reporters enjoy only qualified immunity. Antoine v. Byers & Anderson, Inc., 508 U.S. 429 (1993).

dant's appearance and the presentation of evidence at the hearing on the search warrant were protected by absolute immunity, but that his acts of providing advice to the police were subject only to a qualified immunity defense. The Court noted the lack of any historical or common law support for extending absolute immunity to the provision of advice and stressed the rationale behind absolute prosecutorial immunity—"to free the *judicial process* from the harassment and intimidation associated with litigation" (p. 494). Moreover, one significant check on constitutional violations in the course of the judicial process—the availability of appellate review—"will not necessarily restrain out-of-court activities by a prosecutor that occur prior to the initiation of a prosecution," particularly "if a suspect is not eventually prosecuted" (p. 496).

In the second case, Buckley v. Fitzsimmons, 113 S.Ct. 2606 (1993), plaintiff alleged that prosecutors had fabricated evidence during the preliminary investigation of a crime, by obtaining testimony about a bootprint from an expert known to be unreliable. The suit also alleged that prosecutors had made false statements at a press conference announcing the return of an indictment. The Court ruled that the prosecutors were entitled only to qualified immunity with respect to both the press conference (on this point, the Court was unanimous) and the alleged fabrication (here, the Court divided 5–4). On the latter question, the Court reasoned that because the prosecutors lacked probable cause to arrest or charge the suspect at the time of the alleged fabrication, their mission in seeking the evidence was "entirely investigative in character. A prosecutor neither is, nor should consider himself to be, an advocate before he has probable cause to have anyone arrested" (p. 2616). It would be anomalous, after Burns, to hold prosecutors absolutely immune when conducting investigative work themselves but only qualifiedly immune when advising the police about investigations.

(5) *The Absolute Immunity of Legislators.* The only explicit source in the Constitution for official immunity of any kind is Article I, Section 6, which states that Senators and Representatives "shall in all Cases, except Treason, Felony, and Breach of Peace, be privileged from Arrest during their Attendance at the Session of their respective Houses, and in going to and returning from the same; and for any Speech or Debate in either House, they shall not be questioned in any other Place." Unlike judges and prosecutors, federal legislators are immune not merely from damages actions, but also from any form of judicial process that requires inquiry into so-called legislative acts. See *Note on the Immunity of Government Officers From Relief Other Than Damages,* which follows this Note.

The Supreme Court first considered the Speech or Debate Clause in Kilbourn v. Thompson, 103 U.S. 168, 200–05 (1880). Relying on the English tradition of parliamentary privilege, the Court held that federal legislators who had voted for a resolution ordering the plaintiff to be imprisoned for contempt of Congress were immune from damages liability in a suit for false imprisonment. Subsequent cases have interpreted the Speech or Debate Clause to shield all "legislative acts"—matters that are "an integral part of the deliberative and communicative processes by which Members participate in committee and House proceedings with respect to the consideration and passage or rejection of proposed legislation or with respect to other matters which the Constitution places within the jurisdiction of either House." Gravel v. United States, 408 U.S. 606, 625 (1972).[7]

---

7. Compare Doe v. McMillan, 412 U.S. 306 (1973)(House Members responsible for preparing a committee report were absolutely immune in a suit for invasion of privacy filed

The Gravel case—discussed at length in the Harlow opinions—also held, contrary to prior authority,[8] that the immunity extends not only to members of Congress but to their aides as well. By its terms, the Speech or Debate Clause extends only to federal legislators. But in Tenney v. Brandhove, 341 U.S. 367 (1951), the Court held a state legislator absolutely immune from damages liability in a § 1983 action that alleged that the defendant had called a hearing not for a legitimate legislative purpose, but instead to deprive plaintiff of his constitutional rights.

Like judicial immunity, legislative immunity attaches to functions, not offices. Thus, it extends to nonlegislative officials exercising legislative powers, such as judges who promulgate disciplinary rules for the bar. See Supreme Court of Virginia v. Consumers Union of the United States, Inc., 446 U.S. 719 (1980), p. 1177, *infra*.[9]

(6) *Absolute Immunity of the President.* In Nixon v. Fitzgerald, 457 U.S. 731 (1982), Fitzgerald (the plaintiff in the Harlow case) sought damages from President Nixon, who allegedly shared responsibility for the loss of his federal job. Justice Powell's opinion for the Court ruled that the President enjoyed an absolute immunity from damages liability for all acts within the "outer perimeter" of his official responsibilities (p. 756). This immunity, he argued, was a "functionally mandated incident of the President's unique office, rooted in the constitutional tradition of the separation of powers" (p. 749).[10] The Court stressed that the President's prominence made him an easy target for damages actions, and that if he had only a qualified immunity, the resulting diversion of his energies in defending himself would jeopardize the effective functioning of government. Justice White wrote a vigorous dissent, in which Justices Brennan, Marshall, and Blackmun joined, accusing the Court of mistakenly conferring immunity on an office rather than a function, and finding nothing in the nature of executive personnel decisions to warrant absolute rather than qualified immunity.[11]

by schoolchildren identified in the report, though the Superintendent of Documents and the Public Printer, who publicly disseminated the report, were not immune), with Hutchinson v. Proxmire, 443 U.S. 111 (1979)(Senator was not immune from a defamation action arising out of his publicizing his "Golden Fleece" award—for wasteful federal spending—in a press release, newsletter, and television program).

8. See, *e.g.,* Powell v. McCormack, 395 U.S. 486 (1969)(action challenging Congressman's exclusion from the House dismissed as to Members of Congress but not as to congressional employees).

9. On legislative immunity, see generally Reinstein & Silverglate, *Legislative Privilege and the Separation of Powers,* 86 Harv. L.Rev. 1113 (1973); Note, 88 Yale L.J. 1280 (1979); Comment, 56 U.Chi.L.Rev. 1121 (1989).

10. The Court left open the question whether the President could be subjected to

damages liability by explicit and affirmative congressional action (p. 748 n. 27).

11. A different question (and one not resolved by the Supreme Court) is that of the ability of a litigant to bring a civil suit against a sitting President for conduct occurring prior to the President's taking office. See Jones v. Clinton, 869 F.Supp. 690 (E.D.Ark.1994), *affirmed in part, reversed in part,* 72 F.3d 1354 (8th Cir.1996) (holding that trial of sexual harassment claim against President Clinton—relating to conduct occurring prior to his Presidency—may not go forward during his term of office, but that discovery may proceed). See also Amar & Katyal, *Executive Privileges and Immunities: The Nixon and Clinton Cases,* 108 Harv. L.Rev. 701 (1995)(suggesting various forms of temporary immunity for a sitting President).

Also unresolved is the question of the precise extent to which a President may be subject to a judicial order other than a judgment for damages. See pp. 1180–84, *infra*.

(7) *The Immunity of Presidential Aides.* While the Court in Harlow held that in the circumstances presented, presidential aides could claim only qualified immunity, the Court did suggest that absolute immunity might be appropriate for presidential aides with discretionary authority in national security matters or foreign affairs.

That suggestion was taken up in Mitchell v. Forsyth, 472 U.S. 511 (1985), a Bivens action against former Attorney General Mitchell for having authorized a warrantless wiretap for the purpose of protecting national security. Four of the seven participating Justices rejected Mitchell's claim of absolute immunity, finding no historical analog for it, and arguing that the secrecy of national security matters reduced both the likelihood of unfounded and burdensome lawsuits and the effectiveness of other possible mechanisms of restraining misconduct.

(8) *The Contrast Between Qualified and Absolute Immunity.* Consider Justice Rehnquist's criticism, dissenting in Butz v. Economou, 438 U.S. 478 (1978), of the Court's refusal to extend absolute immunity generally to executive officials sued for constitutional torts (438 U.S. at 528 n. *):

"If one were to hazard an informed guess as to why such a distinction in treatment between judges and prosecutors, on the one hand, and other public officials on the other, obtains, mine would be that those who decide the common law know through personal experience the sort of pressures that might exist for such decisionmakers in the absence of absolute immunity, but may not know or may have forgotten that similar pressures exist in the case of nonjudicial public officials to whom difficult decisions are committed. But the cynical among us might not unreasonably feel that this is simply another unfortunate example of judges treating those who are not part of the judicial machinery as 'lesser breeds without the law.' "

If Justice Rehnquist is correct, does this analysis argue for conferring absolute immunity on executive officials, or only a qualified immunity on judges and prosecutors? See, *e.g.,* Maher, *Federally–Defined Judicial Immunity: Some Quixotic Reflections on an Unwarranted Imposition,* 88 Dick.L.Rev. 326 (1984). Or should executive officials have less complete protection, because, as compared to judges, their incentives for misconduct are greater, because they are subject to fewer alternative checks on possible misbehavior, and because they face smaller risks of harassment? See Cass, *Damages Suits Against Public Officers,* 129 U.Pa.L.Rev. 1110, 1146–47 (1981).

(9) *The Reshaping of Qualified Immunity in Harlow.* The Court in Harlow deliberately moved toward an objective test for determining the availability of a claim of qualified immunity. But Justice Brennan suggested in his concurrence that the test might still contain a subjective element when he said that he "agree[d]" with the standard announced in the Court's opinion in Harlow—a standard he described as imposing liability on an official who "knew or should have known" of "the constitutionally violative effect of his actions."

Plainly, after Harlow bad motives will not in themselves defeat a qualified immunity claim if the action complained of is not itself in violation of constitutional rights. Moreover, given the structure of the Harlow opinion and the formulation of the immunity standard, it appears that "bad motives" will not defeat an immunity claim if the action in question was not *clearly* in violation of constitutional rights. But might there be a case in which the defendant's conduct violated the plaintiff's "clearly established" constitutional rights and the defendant in fact *knew* that it did, but could not reasonably be expected to have known it?   Or, in view of the requirement that the right be clearly established, does this category of cases constitute a virtually empty set?

Cases like Mitchell v. Forsyth, Paragraph (7), *supra*, and Davis v. Scherer, 468 U.S. 183, 191 (1984),[12] suggest that an inquiry into the defendant's state of mind is not ordinarily appropriate (except, as indicated in Harlow, when the official is claiming that special circumstances *afford* immunity even though the ordinary criteria for defeating such a claim have been shown).   But an argument that the defendant's actual knowledge remains relevant, and that Justice Brennan's approach is the preferable one, is made in Kinports, *Qualified Immunity in Section 1983 Cases: The Unanswered Questions*, 23 Ga.L.Rev. 597, 607–18 (1989).

Harlow's emphasis on facilitating dismissal of insubstantial suits against officials was visible in another aspect of Mitchell v. Forsyth, *supra, i.e.,* its holding that a trial court's denial of a defendant's motion for judgment on the ground of qualified immunity is immediately appealable as a "collateral order" under 28 U.S.C. § 1291.   (For further discussion of this aspect of the Mitchell case, and of the Court's recent narrowing of its holding on this point, see Chapter XV, pp. 1648–49, *infra*.)[13]

(10) *Further Questions on the Meaning of Harlow.*

(a) *The Meaning of Clearly Established Law.*[14] In Procunier v. Navarette, 434 U.S. 555 (1978), the Court (without dissent on this point) found no violation of clearly established law when, at the time prison officials interfered

---

12. The Davis case was a § 1983 suit brought by a state employee who challenged his discharge as a violation of due process. He argued that the defendants lost their qualified immunity because their conduct, even if not violative of clearly established law under the Fourteenth Amendment, violated clearly established state law.   The Court, in a 5–4 opinion, acknowledged that the argument had some force, but declined to "disrupt the balance" established by Harlow, and held that the plaintiff could overcome qualified immunity only by showing that the very law whose violation forms the basis of his federal action was clearly established (p. 195).   The Court contended that a federal judge might have difficulty resolving issues of state law on summary judgment, and that state officials may be subject to a plethora of vague and contradictory state law rules.

Justices Brennan, Marshall, Blackmun, and Stevens, in dissent, argued that the discharge did violate clearly established federal constitutional law.

13. In Wyatt v. Cole, 504 U.S. 158 (1992)(6–3), the Court rejected a claim of immunity by a private party.   Cole, after filing a state court replevin action against Wyatt, obtained (in accordance with state law) an ex parte order authorizing the sei-

zure of Wyatt's property.   Wyatt later sued Cole under § 1983, alleging that Cole had acted "under color of law" (see pp. 1119–21, *supra*), and that the seizure denied due process.   Reversing the lower courts, the Supreme Court held that the qualified immunity recognized in Harlow was not applicable. Conceding that at common law defendants sued for abuse of process or malicious prosecution had a good-faith defense, the Court stressed that Harlow departed from common law principles and established an immunity from suit rather than a defense to liability. Moreover, Harlow's concerns with permitting public officials to act forcefully when making discretionary decisions and with encouraging qualified persons to enter public service were inapplicable.   However, the Court left open the question whether Cole possessed a common law *defense,* based upon "good faith and/or probable cause" (p. 1834).

For discussion of the Wyatt case, and of the disagreement among the circuits as to its scope, see Note, 69 Notre Dame L.Rev. 735 (1994).

14. Compare the holding of Teague v. Lane, Chap. XI, p. 1392, *infra,* that federal habeas corpus will not lie to attack a state criminal conviction on the basis of a "new rule".

with a prisoner's outgoing mail, there was no decision of the Supreme Court, or of the pertinent federal circuit or district court, establishing the First Amendment right on which the suit was based, and other federal courts had divided on the First Amendment question. Davis v. Scherer, 468 U.S. 183 (1984), proved more difficult. There, the Court held, 5–4, that under the precedents as of 1977 (when the challenged conduct occurred), it was not clearly established that a permanent state employee who was terminated after various oral and written communications with his superiors had a right to a more formal hearing either before or promptly after his termination.

In many situations, the Supreme Court will not have addressed the legality of the conduct at issue. Can a single state court or lower federal court decision clearly establish the illegality of a practice if no other court has spoken? Even if all the circuits agree that a practice is illegal, isn't it possible that the Supreme Court would disagree?

Suppose instead that the lower courts have divided. Is an official immune if the legality of his conduct had previously been upheld by one court somewhere? What if that court is in Maine, the official works for the state of California, and both the California Supreme Court and the 9th Circuit had declared the practice unlawful before the conduct occurred?[15]

In the absence of a generally accepted and clearcut theory of the role of precedent in adjudication—an especially complex problem in a federal system— how stable would you expect application of the "clearly established law" standard to be?

Many of the cases applying the Harlow standard involved a question about a general proposition of law. See, *e.g.,* Mitchell v. Forsyth, Paragraph (7), *supra* (Attorney General reasonably could have believed in 1970 that he had authority to conduct warrantless electronic surveillance for national security purposes). Anderson v. Creighton, 483 U.S. 635 (1987), by contrast, was a case in which the governing principles of law were clear, but their application to the facts was in dispute. There, the court of appeals ruled that if a warrantless search of a home was unlawful, the officer could not obtain summary judgment on immunity grounds, because clearly established law prohibited entry of a dwelling absent probable cause and exigent circumstances. The Supreme Court reversed (6–3), holding that the court of appeals misapplied Harlow by identifying the legal rule that was violated at too high a level of generality: "The contours of the right must be sufficiently clear that a reasonable official would understand that *what he is doing* violates that right" (p. 640)(emphasis added). The Court also rejected the plaintiff's argument that since the Fourth Amendment prohibits "unreasonable searches and seizures", it is logically impossible to find an officer immune under Harlow, for to do so would imply that an officer "reasonably" acted unreasonably.

(b) *Advice of Counsel.* When would a "reasonable" official seek more specific advice from a government lawyer? If the lawyer advises an official that

---

15. One issue was resolved by the Court in Elder v. Holloway, 114 S.Ct. 1019 (1994). In that case, the Court held (unanimously) that an appellate court should resolve the issue of qualified immunity in light of *all* relevant precedents, including in Elder itself a Ninth Circuit decision not cited to or relied on by the district court.

For an argument that state decisional law should be given a greater role in "the qualified immunity calculus", see Saphire, *Qualified Immunity in Section 1983 Cases and the Role of State Decisional Law,* 35 Ariz.L.Rev. 621 (1993).

contemplated action would be lawful though under the precedents it clearly would not be, is the officer immune? Is this last situation covered by Harlow's statement that even an official whose conduct violates clearly established law is still immune if the official "claims extraordinary circumstances and can prove that he neither knew nor should have known of the relevant legal standard"?

Cf. Malley v. Briggs, 475 U.S. 335 (1986), in which a police officer presented arrest warrants to a state judge, who approved and signed them. The officer was later sued under § 1983 for having caused the arrest of individuals without probable cause. The Supreme Court refused to hold that the officer was absolutely immune because he had relied "on the judgment of a judicial officer in finding that probable cause exists and hence issuing the warrant" (p. 345). Though in an ideal system no judge would approve a defective application, it was not unreasonable to minimize the risk of error by holding an officer liable if "the warrant application is so lacking in indicia of probable cause as to render official belief in its existence unreasonable" (pp. 344–45). The Court remanded for application of the Harlow standard.

(c) *Procedural issues.* A number of procedural questions relating to claims of official immunity—and especially of qualified immunity—have yet to be resolved. It is clear that unless a claim of official immunity is made by the defendant, the issue is not in the case. See, *e.g.,* Graham v. Connor, 490 U.S. 386, 399 n. 12 (1989). But once such a claim has been asserted, it is not clear what burden, if any, is placed on the plaintiff in order to continue the litigation, *i.e.,* to engage in limited or general discovery or to survive a motion to dismiss or a motion for summary judgment, or in order to prevail if the case goes to trial.[16] For further discussion of these procedural questions, see Kinports, Paragraph (9), *supra.*

Another issue raised by a number of lower court decisions is whether the need to dispose of a qualified immunity defense without undue burden on the defendant justifies imposing on the plaintiff any special obligation to plead the facts with particularity. The Supreme Court has yet to rule on the issue, although a number of petitioners have sought to raise the question.[17] See, *e.g.,* Kimberlin v. Quinlan, 6 F.3d 789 (D.C.Cir.1993), *rev'd and remanded,* 115 S.Ct. 2552 (1995)(remanding, after grant of certiorari, for consideration of question of appealability). One difficulty with imposing such an obligation resides in the general rejection of detailed pleading requirements in the rules of civil procedure, particularly Fed.R.Civ.P. 8. (See the discussion in Siegert v. Gilley, 500 U.S. 226, 236 (1991)(Kennedy, J., concurring in the judgment)). In one recent effort to circumvent this difficulty, the Fifth Circuit invoked the discretionary authority of a trial court (under Fed.R.Civ.P. 7(a)) to require a reply by the plaintiff to the defendant's answer, and held it proper to order such a reply

---

16. The allocation of factfinding responsibility was at issue in Hunter v. Bryant, 502 U.S. 224 (1991)(per curiam), where the Court, in reversing a district court's denial of summary judgment on qualified immunity grounds, stressed that the question whether law enforcement officials could reasonably have believed there was probable cause to arrest is a question not for the jury but for the judge deciding the immunity question. Justice Stevens' dissent argued that any disputed factual questions must be resolved against the party moving for summary judgment, and that the lower courts properly found factual uncertainty that precluded them from concluding that the defendants' belief in the lawfulness of their conduct was reasonable.

17. For discussion of the Supreme Court's related holding that no special pleading obligation may be imposed on a plaintiff for purposes of determining whether or not the complaint has stated a claim under § 1983, see Sec. 2(C), p. 1123, note 10, *supra.*

when the defendant's answer contained a plea of immunity. Schultea v. Wood, 47 F.3d 1427 (5th Cir.1995).

(11) *Official Immunity and Systems of Liability for Official Misconduct.* Should an individual officer's liability in damages be limited, in general, to violations of "clearly established law"? The question cannot be answered in a vacuum, since it depends in part on whether governmental entities themselves are accountable for the same wrongs, on the extent to which government is willing to reimburse its officers for their liability and litigation costs, and on the utility of other forms of judicial relief (*i.e.,* injunctive remedies) and of nonjudicial mechanisms of control.

See generally Fallon & Meltzer, *New Law, Non–Retroactivity, and Constitutional Remedies,* 104 Harv.L.Rev. 1731, 1820–24 (1991). In dealing with the question of individual officer liability, they argue that "[t]he threshold issue [with respect to official immunity] is whether to frame the problem as one about the appropriate scope of remedies against individual officials or about government's liability for the costs of government" (p. 1824). Under the first of these approaches, "[i]f excessive caution [by enforcement officers] is a substantial worry, formulation of an immunity standard in terms of new law [*i.e.,* precluding liability for conduct that was not a violation of clearly established law] seems a sensible response. * * * [And if] officials are easily deterred from conscientious action by the threat of personal liability, an unusually broad conception of new law may be appropriate" (p. 1821). But if the second approach is followed and doctrines of official liability are seen as evolving because they were "functionally necessary surrogates for governmental liability", then there would be greater concern for the cost to the victims of unlawful conduct (p. 1822). The second approach would therefore suggest a narrowing of the scope of official immunity, perhaps preserving immunity only for "exceptional circumstances" in which, for example, later case law "establish[ed] the unconstitutionality of previously accepted and widespread employment practices". Such a course "would pressure government to provide indemnification and thereby internalize the costs of government, which in turn would permit victims to obtain relief even if the official tortfeasors themselves were judgment-proof" (pp. 1823–24).

(12) *Bibliography.* There has been a great deal of valuable scholarship in this area in recent decades. In addition to the authorities already cited in this Note, see, *e.g.,* Achtenberg, *Immunity Under 42 U.S.C. § 1983: Interpretive Approach and the Search for the Legislative Will,* 86 Nw.U.L.Rev. 497 (1992)(arguing, *inter alia,* that judges should give "hierarchical primacy" to the 42d Congress' goal of protecting individual rights); Bermann, *Integrating Governmental and Officer Tort Liability,* 77 Colum.L.Rev. 1175 (1977); Lewis & Blumoff, *Reshaping Section 1983's Asymmetry,* 140 U.Pa.L.Rev. 755 (1992); Madden & Allard, *Advice on Official Liability and Immunity,* in 2 Administrative Conference of the United States: Reports and Recommendations 201–442 (1982); Nahmod, *Constitutional Wrongs Without Remedies: Executive Official Immunity,* 62 Wash.U.L.Q. 221 (1984); Rudovsky, *The Qualified Immunity Doctrine in the Supreme Court: Judicial Activism and the Restriction of Constitutional Rights,* 138 U.Pa.L.Rev. 23 (1989); Whitman, *Government Responsibility for Constitutional Torts,* 85 Mich.L.Rev. 225 (1986); Wise, *Liability of Federal Officials: An Analysis of Alternatives,* 45 Pub.Ad.Rev. 746 (1985).

NOTE ON THE IMMUNITY OF GOVERNMENT OFFICERS
FROM RELIEF OTHER THAN DAMAGES

A. Civil Actions Against Officers Exercising Legislative Functions

(1) *The Eastland and Consumers Union Cases.* In Eastland v. United States Servicemen's Fund, 421 U.S. 491 (1975), a Senate Committee subpoenaed the bank records of an organization that was critical of the Vietnam War. The organization sued to enjoin enforcement of the subpoenas as a violation of the First Amendment. The Supreme Court, without extended consideration, held that the suit was barred by the Speech or Debate Clause: "Just as a criminal prosecution infringes upon the independence which the Clause is designed to preserve, a private civil action, whether for an injunction or damages, creates a distraction and forces Members to divert their time, energy, and attention from their legislative tasks to defend the litigation" (p. 503).

Immunity from injunctive relief was extended to state officials acting in a legislative capacity in Supreme Court of Virginia v. Consumers Union of the United States, Inc., 446 U.S. 719 (1980). There a consumer group sued, *inter alia,* the Supreme Court of Virginia and its Chief Justice under § 1983, seeking to enjoin (as inconsistent with the First Amendment) state bar rules restricting plaintiffs' ability to gather information about lawyers' fees. A three-judge federal court ultimately awarded the injunctive relief sought, as well as attorney's fees under 42 U.S.C. § 1988, against the Supreme Court of Virginia and the Chief Justice in his official capacity. On appeal, the Supreme Court ruled that officials acting in a legislative capacity could not be enjoined.

The Court first reasoned that "in promulgating the disciplinary rules the Virginia Supreme Court acted in a legislative capacity" (p. 731). Given the decision in Eastland, and the Court's general practice of "equat[ing] the legislative immunity to which state legislators are entitled under § 1983 to that accorded Congressmen under the Constitution" (p. 733), there was little doubt that a state legislator would be immune from suit seeking an injunction.[1] Even conceding that not all officials exercising delegated rulemaking power are necessarily immune from suit, the Court rejected the contention that "in *no* circumstances do those who exercise delegated legislative power enjoy legislative immunity" (p. 734). The Supreme Court of Virginia was "exercising the State's entire legislative power" and its members were the state's legislators with respect to regulation of the Bar; they could not be enjoined in that capacity (p. 734).

The injunction was upheld, however, under a different theory. The Supreme Court noted that the Virginia court performed non-legislative functions in connection with attorney discipline—it both adjudicated (on appeal) violations of bar disciplinary rules and had independent enforcement authority. "We need not decide whether judicial immunity would bar prospective relief, for we believe that the Virginia Court and its chief justice properly were held liable in their enforcement capacities", much as prosecutors—who enjoy abso-

---

1. The Court did not mention Bond v. Floyd, 385 U.S. 116 (1966). There, Julian Bond, who had been elected to the Georgia House of Representatives, sought declaratory and injunctive relief after the House had excluded him because of his statements op- posing the Vietnam War. A three-judge federal court found no constitutional violation, but the Supreme Court unanimously reversed, ruling that the exclusion violated Bond's First Amendment rights.

lute immunity from damages liability—may be enjoined from enforcing laws that violate the Constitution (p. 736).

Was the Court in Eastland justified in extending Speech or Debate Clause immunity to actions seeking prospective relief? To what extent do such lawsuits threaten to inhibit the fearless discharge by legislators of their duties, or to create injustice for individual legislators, given that Congress employs a legal staff to defend these actions? Does the answer to this question depend upon whether legislators may be held personally liable for attorney's fees? See Pulliam v. Allen, Paragraph (2), *infra*. In any event, don't suits for injunctive relief against prosecutors or other enforcement officials pose the same threats?

As Consumers Union itself shows, the extension of legislative immunity is relatively unimportant in suits seeking relief from unconstitutional legislation, precisely because enforcement officials are amenable to suit. But in legislative investigations, there may be no potential defendants other than legislators and their aides. Does Eastland mean that the only way to obtain judicial review of the constitutionality of committee process is to risk contempt?[2] Contrast the Court's argument in Consumers Union that prosecutors must be amenable to prospective relief, for otherwise "putative plaintiffs would have to await the institution of state-court proceedings against them in order to assert their federal constitutional claims" (p. 737). If an individual is held in contempt of Congress and detained, would legislators be immune from an action seeking a writ of habeas corpus? If so, is there no remedy whatever? If not, can habeas relief after contempt and injunctive relief before contempt really be distinguished with respect to their impact on legislative independence?

(2) *The Yonkers Litigation.* Some of the issues discussed in Paragraph (1) were presented, but not resolved, in Spallone v. United States, 493 U.S. 265 (1990). In this case, arising out of a civil rights action brought against the city of Yonkers, both the city and four members of the city council were held in civil contempt (and fines were imposed) as a result of the failure to enact a public housing ordinance required by a consent decree. After affirmance by the court of appeals, the Supreme Court denied the city's petition for certiorari but granted the petitions of the individual members. The members argued, *inter alia*, that under the doctrine of legislative immunity, they could not be held in contempt for voting against the ordinance. Without ruling on that argument, the Court held, 5–4, that "in view of the 'extraordinary' nature of" a civil contempt sanction against local legislative officers for refusing to vote as ordered, the district court "should have proceeded with such contempt sanctions first against the city alone in order to secure compliance with the remedial order. Only if that approach failed to produce compliance within a reasonable time should the question of imposing contempt sanctions against petitioners even have been considered" (p. 280).

The four dissenters argued that the district court had not abused its remedial discretion by imposing civil contempt fines on the individual members. With respect to the claim of legislative immunity, the dissenters distinguished the question presented from the question of the immunity of legislators from suit by a private plaintiff. Once the district court found, in an action brought against the city, "that the city (through acts of its council) had

---

2. Indeed, in Eastland itself, because the subpoenas were directed at the bank, the   plaintiff lacked even that option.

engaged in a pattern and practice of racial discrimination in housing and had issued a valid remedial order, the city councilmembers became obliged to respect the limits thereby placed on their legislative independence" (p. 302).

B. Civil Actions Against Officers Exercising Judicial Functions

The question left open in Consumers Union—whether judicial immunity bars suits for prospective relief—was answered in Pulliam v. Allen, 466 U.S. 522 (1984). Pulliam, a state magistrate, had a practice in criminal cases involving nonjailable offenses of setting bail and incarcerating persons who could not post it. Two arrestees subjected to this policy brought suit under § 1983, seeking injunctive and declaratory relief. The district court ruled that the practice was unconstitutional, and enjoined Pulliam from continuing it. The court also awarded the plaintiffs $7691 in costs, of which $7038 was attorney's fees awarded under 42 U.S.C. § 1988.

Dividing 5–4, the Supreme Court upheld the injunction and the fee award. Justice Blackmun's opinion for the Court began by noting that the propriety of the award depended on whether judicial immunity barred the injunction. The Court conceded that at common law there were no injunctions against judges. But a lengthy review of English history showed, in the Court's view, that judicial immunity from injunctive orders developed merely to protect the common law courts from overreaching by the courts of equity. That immunity coexisted with the exercise of significant control by the King's Bench "over inferior and rival courts through the use of prerogative writs", particularly prohibition and mandamus (p. 532). Though in theory these writs were used only to control the proper exercise of lower courts' jurisdiction, in practice "the King's Bench used and continues to use the writs to prevent a judge from committing all manner of errors, including departing from the rules of natural justice, proceeding with a suit in which he has an interest, misconstruing substantive law, and rejecting legal evidence" (p. 533). That practice, though "not precisely paralleled in our system by the relationship between state and federal courts[,] * * * indicates that, at least in the view of the common law, there was no inconsistency between a principle of immunity that protected judicial authority from 'a wide, wasting, and harassing persecution,' * * * and the availability of collateral injunctive relief in exceptional cases" (pp. 535–36).

Justice Blackmun also contended that immunity from injunctive relief was far less necessary than immunity from damages awards. The need to show the lack of an adequate remedy at law and a serious risk of irreparable harm "severely curtail[s] the risk that judges will be harassed and their independence compromised by the threat of having to defend themselves against suits by disgruntled litigants", as does the need to satisfy Article III's requirements (pp. 537–38 & n. 18).

Turning to the award of costs and fees, Justice Blackmun conceded that "[t]here is, perhaps, some logic to [the defendant's] reasoning" that "the chilling effect of a damages award is no less chilling when the award is denominated attorney's fees" (p. 543). However, he found that Congress had made unmistakable its intent that attorney's fees should be available "in any action to enforce a provision of § 1983[,] * * * even when damages would be barred or limited by 'immunity doctrines and special defenses available only to public officials' " (p. 543).

Justice Powell, joined by Chief Justice Burger and Justices Rehnquist and O'Connor, dissented. He found far more significance in the common law immunity of judges from injunctive relief, and less in the history of the writs of prohibition and mandamus, which "were intended only to control the proper exercise of jurisdiction" and therefore "posed no threat to judicial independence and implicated none of the policies of judicial immunity" (p. 550). Justice Powell also argued (p. 554) that "the burdens of harassing litigation, rather than the threat of pecuniary loss," constitute the key threat to judicial independence, and suits for prospective relief pose that threat as much as damages actions. The threat is magnified if an injunction is issued, and a judge may risk contempt if a subsequent decision is deemed to run afoul of the order. Finally, the dissenters emphasized the impact of § 1988 in stimulating litigation, opining that "[t]he Court * * * ignores reality when it suggests that the availability of injunctive relief under § 1983, combined with the prospect of attorney's fees under § 1988, poses no serious threat of harassing litigation with its potentially adverse consequences for judicial independence" (p. 557).

Consider whether the Pulliam majority might be correct that immunity does not bar injunctive relief, but mistaken in permitting the award of attorney's fees. On the latter point, the Court relied in part on the understanding of § 1988 in Hutto v. Finney, p. 1074, *supra*. But while the judgment in Hutto enjoined state officials, the fee award was to be paid by the state itself.

Could § 1988 be interpreted to impose fee liability upon only those officials who could be held liable for damages? Would it pose a problem for this view if government liability for fees requires the same showing needed to establish government liability for damages—that the violation was pursuant to government policy or custom? Isn't it likely that such a showing can be made, however, if the requisites for injunctive relief have been satisfied? And, at least where that showing is made, cannot judicial independence and Congress' policy in § 1988 both be honored by permitting fee awards only against the government?

C. Civil Actions Against Officers Exercising Executive Functions

(1) *Introduction.* Consumers Union indicates that executive officials in general have no immunity from suit for prospective relief—a conclusion supported by the entire history of suits against officers as a means of ensuring governmental accountability.

But the President's amenability to an injunction or writ of mandamus has never been authoritatively established. The following paragraphs, which discuss the famous Steel Seizure Case of 1952 and its doctrinal aftermath, may shed some light on this question, and also serve as a useful recapitulation of many of the themes of this Chapter.

(2) *The Steel Seizure Case of 1952.*

(a) *Facts and Holding.* In 1951, following unsuccessful negotiations to resolve a dispute between labor and management in the steel industry, the union gave notice of an intent to strike. After mediation efforts broke down, President Truman, claiming that a strike would jeopardize national defense, issued an Executive Order directing the Secretary of Commerce to take possession of most of the nation's steel mills and keep them running.

Following the seizure, the steel companies sued the Secretary of Commerce in a federal district court. Alleging that the seizure was not authorized by Act of Congress or by any constitutional provision, the companies' complaint sought injunctive relief. The district court issued a preliminary injunction, and on writ of certiorari granted before judgment in the court of appeals, the Supreme Court affirmed. Youngstown Sheet & Tube Co. v. Sawyer, 343 U.S. 579 (1952).

Justice Black, writing for the Court, concluded first that there was sufficient doubt about the adequacy and availability of a damages remedy in the Court of Claims to warrant consideration of the constitutional claim. He then noted that the President had not met the conditions of any statute authorizing him to take possession of property, and rejected the argument that the power asserted should be implied from the aggregate of executive power under the Constitution. In particular, he rejected the contention that the seizure could be sustained as an exercise of the President's power as Commander-in-Chief, and stressed that the executive power was limited to faithful execution of the laws enacted by Congress.

(b) *Concurring and Dissenting Opinions.* Justices Frankfurter, Douglas, Jackson, Burton, and Clark each delivered separate concurring opinions.

All of the concurring Justices went directly to the merits except Justice Frankfurter, who observed (pp. 595–96):

"[H]ere our first inquiry must be not into the powers of the President, but into the powers of a District Judge to issue a temporary injunction in the circumstances of this case. Familiar as that remedy is, it remains an extraordinary remedy. * * * [But to] deny inquiry into the President's power in a case like this, because of the damage to the public interest to be feared from upsetting its exercise by him, would in effect always preclude inquiry into challenged power, which presumably only avowed great public interest brings into action. And so, with the utmost unwillingness, with every desire to avoid judicial inquiry into the powers and duties of the other two branches of the government, I cannot escape consideration of the legality of [the] Executive Order."

On the merits Justice Douglas agreed with Justice Black that the President had exercised legislative power. The other concurring Justices all pinned their agreement on the merits to congressional enactments that in their view impliedly forbade the President to take the course he had chosen.

Chief Justice Vinson, joined by Justices Reed and Minton, dissented. Initially (pp. 677–78), the dissenters noted their assumption "that defendant Charles Sawyer is not immune from judicial restraint and that plaintiffs are entitled to equitable relief if we find the Executive Order under which defendant acts is unconstitutional." In urging the legality of the seizure, the dissenters stressed, *inter alia,* the legislative programs for increased production of military equipment and for economic stabilization that the President had the duty to execute; the gravity of the threat to those programs; the need for recognition of executive power to act in the face of emergency; the absence of any statute prohibiting seizure; and the temporary character of the taking and the right to just compensation for it.

(c) *The Issue of Judicial Power to Restrain Presidential Action.* The award of equitable relief in the Youngstown case, while not directly implicating the sovereign immunity of the United States, contrasts sharply with the ruling in the Larson case (Sec. 1, p. 1017, *supra*) that an injunction of far smaller dimension was not merely inappropriate but wholly beyond the judicial power. Youngstown therefore illustrates the relationship among the principal themes in this chapter—the questions raised by the doctrines of sovereign and official immunity—and does so in a context in which decisionmaking at the highest executive level lay at the heart of the controversy. Does the case illustrate the utility of the notion that a suit against an officer is not a suit against the sovereign? Or does it highlight its character as legal fiction?

In the district court proceedings, Judge Holtzoff raised the question whether an injunction would not "in essence and in spirit * * * be an injunction against the President". 1 The Steel Seizure Case 247 (82d Cong., 2d Sess., H.Doc. No. 534, Pt. I). In denying a temporary injunction, Judge Holtzoff cited Mississippi v. Johnson, 71 U.S. (4 Wall.) 475 (1866), in which the state sought unsuccessfully, in an original action in the Supreme Court, to restrain the President from executing the provisions of the Reconstruction Acts.[3] Judge Holtzoff concluded that the consideration that a court "should not do by indirection what it could not do directly, irrespective of whether the Court has the power to do so * * * is a consideration that should affect the exercise of the Court's discretion". 1 The Steel Seizure Case, *supra,* at 265.

In the hearing fifteen days later before a different judge (Judge Pine), Assistant Attorney General Baldridge, appearing for Secretary Sawyer, enlarged on Judge Holtzoff's suggestion, and on his reliance on Mississippi v. Johnson (*id.* at 362):

"Our position is that there is no power in the Courts to restrain the President and, as I say, Secretary Sawyer is the alter ego of the President and not subject to injunctive order of the Court."

The next morning Mr. Baldridge drew a somewhat different argument from Mississippi v. Johnson (*id.* at 379):

"* * * We do not say that it is an unconsented suit against the United States, but we do say that the President is an indispensable party and, because the President cannot be enjoined as a defendant, he is immune from judicial process."

The brief for the Secretary in the Supreme Court reduced the government's reliance on Mississippi v. Johnson to a suggestion in a footnote "that the courts should consider the inappropriateness of issuing what is in effect a

---

3. In Johnson, after referring to cases on mandamus against executive officers, and expressly reserving the question whether the President may be ordered to perform a purely ministerial act, Chief Justice Chase said (pp. 499–501):

"It is true that in the instance before us the interposition of the court is not sought to enforce action by the Executive under constitutional legislation, but to restrain such action under legislation alleged to be unconstitutional. But we are unable to perceive that this circumstance takes the case out of the general principles which forbid judicial interference with the exercise of Executive discretion. * * *

"* * *

"The impropriety of such interference will be clearly seen upon consideration of its possible consequences.

"Suppose the bill filed and the injunction prayed for allowed. If the President refuse obedience, it is needless to observe that the court is without power to enforce its process. If, on the other hand, the President complies with the order of the court and refuses to execute the acts of Congress, is it not clear that a collision may occur between the executive and legislative departments of the government?"

As is evident from these quotes, the Johnson decision contains strong elements not simply of immunity from suit but of the unreviewability of executive discretion and of the hazards of creating a direct conflict between Congress and the President (*i.e.,* of deciding a "political question"). See Woolhandler, p. 995, *supra,* at 433–35.

mandatory injunction to the President", and "the difficulties implicit" therein, as "a sound reason for denying the injunction sought on other grounds, if it is possible to do so." 2 The Steel Seizure Case, *supra*, at 760. Was the Johnson case worth more than this?

Would Mississippi v. Johnson have prevented an injunction directed against the President (as opposed to the Secretary of Commerce) in the steel situation? Is the problem different when the President is off in a corner by himself, and the Court is not confronted with the possibility of precipitating a conflict between him and Congress that it could not resolve?

Were government counsel in Youngstown wise in failing to press the objection that the suit was in substance against the United States? Is the Larson case (which was decided three years before Youngstown) plainly distinguishable? In terms of the rationale of sovereign immunity set forth in Larson?[4]

(3) *Post-Youngstown Decisions on Remedies Against the President.* In United States v. Nixon, 418 U.S. 683 (1974), the Supreme Court unanimously affirmed an order requiring President Nixon to respond to a grand jury subpoena seeking, *inter alia*, tape recordings of presidential conversations. The Court stressed the special importance of the government's demonstrated need for evidence in a criminal trial. It did not cite Mississippi v. Johnson, and the question of presidential immunity from process was submerged in a discussion of the merits of the President's claim of executive privilege.[5]

After the Nixon decisions, what is the nature and extent of the President's immunity from process in a civil suit seeking specific relief against allegedly unlawful executive conduct? Could it now be fairly argued that President (Andrew) Johnson had discretion to enforce the Reconstruction Acts if, as Mississippi alleged, the legislation was unconstitutional?

Franklin v. Massachusetts, 505 U.S. 788 (1992), may cast some light on this question. That case involved a suit naming President Bush and various federal officials as defendants, and challenging the government's reapportionment of congressional seats following the 1990 census. In an opinion for a plurality of four Justices, Justice O'Connor stated: "We have left open the question whether the President might be subject to a judicial injunction requiring the performance of a purely 'ministerial' duty, Mississippi v. Johnson, *supra*, at 498–99 (1867), and we have held that the President may be subject to a subpoena to provide information relevant to an ongoing criminal prosecution, United States v. Nixon, *supra*, but in general 'this court has no jurisdiction of a

---

4. For fuller treatment of the famous Youngstown case, see Marcus, Truman and the Steel Seizure Case: The Limits of Presidential Power (1977); Corwin, *The Steel Seizure Case: A Judicial Brick Without Straw,* 53 Colum.L.Rev. 53 (1953); Freund, *Foreword: The Year of the Steel Case,* 66 Harv. L.Rev. 89 (1952); Lea, *The Steel Case: Presidential Seizure of Private Industry,* 47 Nw. L.Rev. 289 (1952); Kauper, *The Steel Seizure Case: Congress, the President and the Supreme Court,* 51 Mich.L.Rev. 141 (1952).

5. See also Nixon v. Fitzgerald, 457 U.S. 731, 748 n. 27, 754 (1982), p. 1171,

supra, which held that the President is absolutely immune from damages liability for all acts "within the outer perimeter" of his official responsibilities—at least absent "explicit affirmative action by Congress". The Court recognized that such decisions as United States v. Nixon and Youngstown (cited with a *cf.*) required a balancing of the interests involved, but concluded that in the case of a "merely private suit for damages based on a President's official acts," the exercise of jurisdiction was not warranted.

bill to enjoin the President in the performance of his official duties.' " (pp. 2776–77, quoting Mississippi v. Johnson). Justice Scalia concurred in the judgment. He noted that Mississippi v. Johnson "left open the question whether the President might be subject to a judicial injunction requiring the performance of a purely 'ministerial' duty," but argued that "no court has authority to direct the President to take an official act" or to enter a declaratory judgment with respect to the concededly nonministerial function presented in the case at bar (pp. 2788–89 & n. 2).

See also Ray, *From Prerogative to Accountability: The Amenability of the President to Suit,* 80 Ky.L.J. 739 (1991–92).

D.   Criminal Prosecutions

Government officials possess no general immunity from criminal process, though of course in particular instances their governmental status may permit a defense of privilege that could not be asserted by a private person. Thus, in Imbler v. Pachtman, 424 U.S. 409, 429 (1976), p. 1169, *supra,* the Court stressed that it had "never suggested that the policy considerations which compel civil immunity for certain governmental officials [in that case, for prosecutors] also place them beyond the reach of the criminal law. Even judges, who have long been cloaked with absolute immunity from damages, could be punished criminally for willful deprivations of constitutional rights on the strength of 18 U.S.C. § 242, the criminal analog of § 1983. O'Shea v. Littleton, 414 U.S. 488, 503 (1974) * * *. The prosecutor would fare no better for his willful acts."

The Speech or Debate Clause, however, does limit the reach of criminal process against federal legislators. Thus, in a federal bribery prosecution of a Member of Congress, the prosecution may not introduce evidence about the defendant's "legislative acts". United States v. Helstoski, 442 U.S. 477, 488–89 (1979). See also United States v. Johnson, 383 U.S. 169 (1966). Other kinds of evidence, however—that a Congressman accepted a bribe to perform a legislative act, Helstoski, *supra,* or that he attempted to influence the Justice Department, Johnson, *supra*—may be introduced in a bribery trial, as such activities are not "related to the due functioning of the legislative process", *id.* at 172. See also Gravel v. United States, 408 U.S. 606 (1972)(senatorial aide is immune from grand jury questioning about a Senator's reading the Pentagon Papers in a subcommittee hearing, but not about the Senator's arrangements for their private publication).

United States v. Gillock, 445 U.S. 360 (1980), held that state legislators, unlike their federal counterparts, possess no immunity from the introduction, in a federal criminal prosecution, of evidence concerning their legislative acts. The defendant argued that here, as in constitutional tort actions, his immunity should be co-extensive with that enjoyed by federal legislators under the Speech or Debate Clause. But the Court responded that decisions affording state prosecutors and judges absolute immunity in § 1983 actions have been premised on the availability of federal criminal liability as a restraining influence on behavior, and argued that principles of comity to the state legislative process must yield to the needs of federal criminal prosecutions.

CHAPTER X

JUDICIAL FEDERALISM: LIMITATIONS ON DISTRICT COURT JURISDICTION OR ITS EXERCISE

INTRODUCTION: THE COORDINATION OF CONCURRENT JURISDICTION IN A FEDERAL SYSTEM

Kline v. Burke Construction Company

260 U.S. 226, 43 S.Ct. 79, 67 L.Ed. 226 (1922).
Certiorari to the Circuit Court of Appeals for the Eighth Circuit.

■ MR. JUSTICE SUTHERLAND delivered the opinion of the Court.

[On February 16, 1920, Burke Construction Company, a Missouri corporation, brought an action in law in federal district court in Arkansas against petitioners (citizens of Arkansas), invoking diversity jurisdiction. The suit alleged breach of a contract under which Burke was to pave certain streets in the town of Texarkana.]

[On March 19, 1920, petitioners brought a suit in equity in an Arkansas Chancery Court against Burke and the sureties on the bond given for the faithful performance of the contract. The bill alleged that Burke had abandoned the contract; it sought an accounting for the work that had been done and that remained, and prayed for judgment in the sum of $88,000. Burke removed the equity suit to federal district court, which remanded the case to the Arkansas Chancery Court.]

[Both actions were in personam and sought money judgments; they presented substantially the same issues; and the defendant's answer and cross-complaint in each alleged, in substance, the matters set forth as complainant in the other. The principal difference between the suits was the addition of the sureties as defendants in the equitable action.]

[In the federal action, following a mistrial, Burke sought to enjoin petitioners from further prosecuting the state court action. The federal district court denied the injunction, but the court of appeals reversed and remanded with instructions to issue the injunction.] From that decree the case comes here upon writ of certiorari.

Section 265 of the Judicial Code [the Anti–Injunction Act, now codified, as amended, as 28 U.S.C. § 2283] provides: "The writ of injunction shall not be granted by any court of the United States to stay proceedings in any court of a State, except in cases where such injunction may be authorized by any law relating to proceedings in bankruptcy." But this section is to be construed in connection with § 262 [the All Writs Act, now codified, as amended, as 28 U.S.C. § 1651], which authorizes the United States courts "to issue all writs not specifically provided for by statute, which may be necessary for the exercise of their respective jurisdictions, and agreeable to the usages and principles of law." It is settled that where a federal court has first acquired jurisdiction of the subject-matter of a cause, it may enjoin the parties from proceeding in a state court of concurrent jurisdiction where the effect of the action would be to defeat or impair the jurisdiction of the federal court. Where the action is *in rem* the effect is to draw to the federal court the possession or control, actual or potential, of the *res*, and the exercise by the state court of jurisdiction over the same *res* necessarily impairs, and may defeat, the jurisdiction of the federal court already attached. The converse of the rule is equally true, that where the jurisdiction of the state court has first attached, the federal court is precluded from exercising its jurisdiction over the same *res* to defeat or impair the state court's jurisdiction.

      * * *

But a controversy * * * over a mere question of personal liability does not involve the possession or control of a thing, and an action brought to enforce such a liability does not tend to impair or defeat the jurisdiction of the court in which a prior action for the same cause is pending. Each court is free to proceed in its own way and in its own time, without reference to the proceedings in the other court. Whenever a judgment is rendered in one of the courts and pleaded in the other, the effect of that judgment is to be determined by the application of the principles of *res adjudicata* by the court in which the action is still pending * * *. The rule, therefore, has become generally established that where the action first brought is *in personam* and seeks only a personal judgment, another action for the same cause in another jurisdiction is not precluded. [Citing numerous cases.]

      * * *

      * * * In the case now under consideration, however, the court below held otherwise, upon the ground that: "By the Constitution of the United States (article 3, § 2, and the acts of Congress) the constitutional right was granted to the Burke Company to ask and to have a trial and adjudication ... by the federal court."

      * * *

The force of the cases above cited is sought to be broken by the suggestion that in none of them was this question of constitutional right presented or considered.

    The right of a litigant to maintain an action in a federal court on the ground that there is a controversy between citizens of different States is not one derived from the Constitution of the United States, unless in a very indirect sense. * * * Only the jurisdiction of the Supreme Court is derived directly from the Constitution. Every other court created by the general government derives its jurisdiction wholly from the authority of Congress. * * * A right which thus comes into existence only by virtue of an act of Congress * * * cannot well be described as a constitutional right. The Construction Company, however, had the undoubted right under the statute to invoke the jurisdiction of the federal court and that court was bound to take the case and proceed to judgment. It could not abdicate its authority or duty in favor of the state jurisdiction. But, while this is true, it is likewise true that the state court had jurisdiction of the suit instituted by petitioners. Indeed, since the case presented by that suit was such as to preclude its removal to the federal jurisdiction, the state jurisdiction in that particular suit was exclusive. It was, therefore, equally the duty of the state court to take the case and proceed to judgment. There can be no question of judicial supremacy, or of superiority of individual right. * * * The rank and authority of the courts are equal but both courts cannot possess or control the same thing at the same time, and any attempt to do so would result in unseemly conflict. The rule, therefore, that the court first acquiring jurisdiction shall proceed without interference from a court of the other jurisdiction is a rule of right and of law based upon necessity, and where the necessity, actual or potential, does not exist, the rule does not apply. Since that necessity does exist in actions *in rem* and does not exist in actions *in personam*, involving a question of personal liability only, the rule applies in the former but does not apply in the latter.

The decree of the Circuit Court of Appeals is therefore reversed and the case remanded to the District Court for further proceedings in conformity with this opinion.

————

NOTE ON THE COORDINATION OF OVERLAPPING STATE COURT AND FEDERAL COURT JURISDICTION

(1) *The Prevalence of Overlapping Jurisdiction.* State and federal jurisdiction overlap pervasively. This is seen most clearly in 28 U.S.C. §§ 1331–32, which give the federal courts jurisdiction, *concurrently* with the state courts, over federal question and diversity cases.

But the overlap extends even to matters that at first glance appear to fall within the exclusive jurisdiction of the state or the federal courts. Consider, for example, a contractual dispute in which the defaulting party contends that the contract violates the federal antitrust or patent or copyright laws. If framed as a suit by the promisee for breach of contract, then (assuming no diversity of citizenship) the state courts have exclusive jurisdiction. But if framed as a suit by the promisor, under the federal statute in question, for declaratory or injunctive relief against contractual liability, then the federal courts have exclusive jurisdiction. Similarly, a claim that a state criminal statute is unconstitutional might be a defense to a state criminal prosecution (over which the state courts have exclusive jurisdiction) or the basis for a federal § 1983 action seeking declaratory or injunctive relief against the statute's enforcement (which would fall within the concurrent jurisdiction of the federal courts).

More generally, whether an asserted federal right is a "defense" or provides an "affirmative claim for relief" cannot be determined *a priori*; it is a product of a variety of remedial and substantive rules.

The possibility that suits relating to the same subject might be brought in both state and federal courts can thus be seen to be widespread. In some situations (as in the examples just discussed and in Kline) the defendant in one action may file a different action involving essentially the same dispute; in others, a plaintiff might sue the same defendant, on the same claim, in both state and federal court.

(2) *Accommodation of Jurisdictional Overlap.* The question of how to accommodate overlapping proceedings (pending or potential) in state and federal courts is a complex one, to which no general federal statute gives a clear answer.

(a) Kline suggests one solution: apart from actions *in rem*, there is no barrier to overlapping litigations, but the law of preclusion will apply once one of the actions has come to judgment.

(b) A different solution would give priority (absolute or presumptive) to the suit first filed. See, *e.g.*, James Rehnquist, *Taking Comity Seriously: How to Neutralize the Abstention Doctrine*, 46 Stan.L.Rev. 1049, 1068 (1994)(advocating replacement of all of the various abstention doctrines—under which a federal court may dismiss or stay proceedings within its statutory jurisdiction—with the rule that "[a] federal court should abstain if, and only if, the federal plaintiff has an adequate opportunity to litigate his federal claim in a duplicative suit already pending in state court").

(c) Still another approach might attempt to determine, either in particular cases or in general categories, which forum should be preferred, and to require the other to desist (perhaps even via an anti-suit injunction, if necessary).

(3) *Deference Where No State Proceeding is Pending.* The question of "preferred" tribunals extends beyond situations, like that in Kline, where there are duplicative proceedings underway in state and federal courts. A distinct question is whether federal courts should in some circumstances not exercise jurisdiction in order to permit state court adjudication, even when no state proceeding is yet pending. See Sections 2(A–C), 2(E), *infra*.

(4) *The Subjects of Federal Deference.* Some of the foregoing questions have arisen in areas that, for reasons of history or policy, have been thought (not always uncontroversially) to be outside of federal jurisdictional concern. Domestic relations and probate matters are notable examples. See Section 2(E), *infra*.

But the central arena in which these matters have been at issue has not been private suits like Kline, but rather suits against state and local officials. Exercise of the jurisdiction that was sanctioned in Ex parte Young and the Home Telephone case brought about a major shift in the distribution of power between state and nation. Because of its association with decisions enjoining state laws as unconstitutional under the jurisprudence of the Lochner era, the power sanctioned by Ex parte Young was, in Judge Friendly's words, "the *bête noire* of liberals in [my] law school days". Friendly, Federal Jurisdiction: A General View 3 n. 7 (1973). That power became more salient, but also more attractive to liberals, with the expansion of individual rights recognized by the Constitution and federal statutes, and the accompanying emergence of 42 U.S.C. § 1983 as a broad federal remedy to enforce those rights.

(5) *Statutory and Judicial Limitations on the Exercise of Federal Jurisdiction.* The change that Ex parte Young brought about in the working "small-letter" constitution of the country was not overlooked by Congress, by the spokesmen for the interests adversely affected, or by the federal courts.

(a) The early congressional response was embodied in three provisions of the Judicial Code:

— a requirement (all but a fragment of which was repealed in 1976) that a district court of three judges be convened to hear actions seeking injunctive relief against state statutes or administrative orders alleged to be unconstitutional;

— the Johnson Act of 1934, now 28 U.S.C. § 1342, limiting federal district court jurisdiction to enjoin state public utility rate orders; and

— the Tax Injunction Act of 1937, now 28 U.S.C. § 1341, limiting federal district court jurisdiction to enjoin the collection of state taxes.[1]

These provisions are considered in Section 1 of this Chapter, which begins with consideration of the Anti–Injunction Act, first enacted in 1793.

(b) The federal courts themselves have formulated additional doctrines under which they will abstain from adjudicating cases that fall within the literal terms of congressional grants of jurisdiction, so as to permit adjudication in state tribunals. Section 2 of this Chapter considers these doctrines.

(c) Both the statutory and judge-made doctrines raise important questions along numerous dimensions, including: (i) How can courts promote effective judicial administration in light of the pervasiveness of overlap and potential duplication? (ii) What are the distinctive qualities of federal and of state courts, see, *e.g*, Chap. IV, Sec. 1, pp. 351–53, *supra* (discussing whether state and federal courts should be viewed as in parity), and in what cases are those respective qualities (in)dispensable?[2] and (iii) What is the appropriate role of the federal courts in interpreting statutes, and in formulating judge-made doctrines, limiting the exercise of broad congressional grants of jurisdiction?

SECTION 1. STATUTORY LIMITATIONS ON FEDERAL COURT JURISDICTION

SUBSECTION A: THE ANTI–INJUNCTION ACT

Atlantic Coast Line R.R. v. Brotherhood of Locomotive Engineers

398 U.S. 281, 90 S.Ct. 1739, 26 L.Ed.2d 234 (1970).
Certiorari to the United States Court of Appeals for the Fifth Circuit.

■ MR. JUSTICE BLACK delivered the opinion of the Court.

Congress in 1793 * * * provided that in federal courts "a writ of injunction [shall not] be granted to stay proceedings in any court of a state." Act of

---

1. A 1913 provision directed a three-judge federal district court to suspend its proceedings whenever a state court stayed proceedings under the challenged enactment, pending state court determination of an action to enforce the same. It was largely ineffectual, see Hutcheson, *A Case for Three Judges*, 47 Harv.L.Rev. 795, 822–25 (1934), and was repealed in 1976.

2. When the limitations on federal district court jurisdiction described in this Chapter were created, state court decisions strik-

ing down a treaty or Act of Congress, or holding valid a state or local statute challenged on federal grounds, were reviewable as of right in the Supreme Court. In 1988, Congress eliminated mandatory appeals from state court decisions. See Chap. V, Sec. 1, p. 494, *supra*. Does the disappearance of one form of guaranteed federal review (Supreme Court review of state court decisions) affect the appropriateness of statutory or judicially-fashioned limits on another form of guaranteed federal review (original jurisdiction in the district courts)?

March 2, 1793, § 5, 1 Stat. 335. Although certain exceptions to this general prohibition have been added, that statute, directing that state courts shall remain free from interference by federal courts, has remained in effect until this time. Today that amended statute provides:

> "A court of the United States may not grant an injunction to stay proceedings in a State court except as expressly authorized by Act of Congress, or where necessary in aid of its jurisdiction, or to protect or effectuate its judgments." 28 U.S.C. § 2283.

Despite the existence of this longstanding prohibition, in this case a federal court did enjoin the petitioner, Atlantic Coast Line Railroad Co. (ACL), from invoking an injunction issued by a Florida state court which prohibited certain picketing by respondent Brotherhood of Locomotive Engineers (BLE). The case arose in the following way.

In 1967 BLE began picketing the Moncrief Yard, a switching yard located near Jacksonville, Florida, and wholly owned and operated by ACL.[2] As soon as this picketing began ACL went into federal court seeking an injunction. When the federal judge denied the request, ACL immediately went into state court and there succeeded in obtaining an injunction. No further legal action was taken in this dispute until two years later in 1969, after this Court's decision in Brotherhood of Railroad Trainmen v. Jacksonville Terminal Co., 394 U.S. 369. In that case the Court considered the validity of a state injunction against picketing by the BLE and other unions at the Jacksonville Terminal, located immediately next to Moncrief Yard. The Court * * * concluded that the unions had a federally protected right to picket under the Railway Labor Act, 45 U.S.C. § 151 et seq., and that that right could not be interfered with by state court injunctions. Immediately after a petition for rehearing was denied in that case, 394 U.S. 1024 (1969), the respondent BLE filed a motion in state court to dissolve the Moncrief Yard injunction, arguing that under the Jacksonville Terminal decision the injunction was improper. The state judge refused to dissolve the injunction, holding that this Court's Jacksonville Terminal decision was not controlling. The union did not elect to appeal that decision directly, but instead went back into the federal court and requested an injunction against the enforcement of the state court injunction. The District Judge granted the injunction * * *. The Court of Appeals summarily affirmed on the parties' stipulation * * *.

* * *

I

* * * While all the reasons that led Congress to adopt [the anti-injunction statute in 1793] are not wholly clear, it is certainly likely that one reason stemmed from the essentially federal nature of our national government. When this Nation was established by the Constitution each State surrendered only a part of its sovereign power to the national government. But those

---

2. There is no present labor dispute between the ACL and the BLE or any other ACL employees. ACL became involved in this case as a result of a labor dispute between the Florida East Coast Railway Co. (FEC) and its employees. FEC cars are hauled into and out of Moncrief Yard and switched around to make up trains in that yard. The BLE picketed the yard, encouraging ACL employees not to handle any FEC cars. * * *

powers that were not surrendered were retained by the States and unless a State was restrained by "the supreme Law of the Land" as expressed in the Constitution, laws or treaties of the United States, it was free to exercise those retained powers as it saw fit. One of the reserved powers was the maintenance of state judicial systems for the decision of legal controversies. * * *

While the lower federal courts were given certain powers in the [Judiciary Act of 1789], they were not given any power to review directly cases from state courts, and they have not been given such powers since that time. Only the Supreme Court was authorized to review on direct appeal the decisions of state courts. Thus from the beginning we have had in this country two essentially separate legal systems. Each system proceeds independently from the other with ultimate review in this Court of the federal questions raised in either system. Understandably this dual court system was bound to lead to conflicts and frictions. Litigants who foresaw the possibility of more favorable treatment in one or the other system would predictably hasten to invoke the powers of whichever court it was believed would present the best chance of success. Obviously this dual system could not function if state and federal courts were free to fight each other for control of a particular case. Thus, in order to make the dual system work and "to prevent needless friction between state and federal courts," Oklahoma Packing Co. v. Oklahoma Gas & Electric Co., 309 U.S. 4, 9 (1940), it was necessary to work out lines of demarcation between the two systems. Some of these limits were spelled out in the 1789 Act. Others have been added by later statutes as well as judicial decisions. The 1793 anti-injunction Act was at least in part a response to these pressures.

On its face the present Act is an absolute prohibition against enjoining state court proceedings, unless the injunction falls within one of three specifically defined exceptions. The respondent here has intimated that the Act only establishes a "principle of comity," not a binding rule on the power of the federal courts. The argument implies that in certain circumstances a federal court may enjoin state court proceedings even if that action cannot be justified by any of the three exceptions. We cannot accept any such contention. In 1954 when this Court interpreted this statute, it stated: "This is not a statute conveying a broad general policy for appropriate *ad hoc* application. Legislative policy is here expressed in a clear-cut prohibition qualified only by specifically defined exceptions." Amalgamated Clothing Workers v. Richman Brothers, 348 U.S. 511, 515–516 (1955). * * * [W]e * * * adhere to that position and hold that any injunction against state court proceedings otherwise proper under general equitable principles must be based on one of the specific statutory exceptions to § 2283 if it is to be upheld. Moreover since the statutory prohibition against such injunctions in part rests on the fundamental constitutional independence of the States and their courts, the exceptions should not be enlarged by loose statutory construction. Proceedings in state courts should normally be allowed to continue unimpaired by intervention of the lower federal courts, with relief from error, if any, through the state appellate courts and ultimately this Court.

II

In this case the Florida Circuit Court enjoined the union's intended picketing, and the United States District Court enjoined the railroad "from giving effect to or availing themselves of the benefits of" that state court order. Both sides agree that although this federal injunction is in terms directed only at the railroad it is an injunction "to stay proceedings in a state court." It is settled that the prohibition of § 2283 cannot be evaded by addressing the order to the parties or prohibiting utilization of the results of a completed state proceeding. * * * Thus if the injunction against the Florida court proceedings is to be upheld, it must be "expressly authorized by Act of Congress," "necessary in aid of [the District Court's] jurisdiction," or "to protect or effectuate [that court's] judgments."

Neither party argues that there is any express Congressional authorization for injunctions in this situation and we agree with that conclusion. The respondent union does contend that the injunction was proper either as a means to protect or effectuate the District Court's 1967 order, or in aid of that court's jurisdiction. We do not think that either alleged basis can be supported.

A

The argument based on protecting the 1967 order is not clearly expressed, but in essence it appears to run as follows: In 1967 the railroad sought a temporary restraining order which the union opposed. In the course of deciding that request, the United States District Court determined that the union had a federally protected right to picket Moncrief Yard and that this right could not be interfered with by state courts. When the Florida Circuit Court enjoined the picketing, the United States District Court could, in order to protect and effectuate its prior determination, enjoin enforcement of the state court injunction. Although the record on this point is not unambiguously clear, we conclude that no such interpretation of the 1967 order can be supported.

When the railroad initiated the federal suit it filed a complaint with three counts, each based entirely on alleged violations of federal law. The first two counts alleged violations of the Railway Labor Act, and the third alleged a violation of that Act and the Interstate Commerce Act as well. Each of the counts concluded with a prayer for an injunction against the picketing. * * * [T]he union * * * appeared at a hearing on a motion for a temporary restraining order and argued against the issuance of such an order. The union argued that it was a party to a labor dispute with the FEC,* that it had exhausted the administrative remedies required by the Railway Labor Act, and that it was thus free to engage in "self-help," or concerted economic activity. Then the union argued that such activity could not be enjoined by the federal court. In an attempt to clarify the basis of this argument the District Judge asked: "You are basing your case solely on the Norris–LaGuardia Act?" The union's lawyer replied: "Right. I think at this point of the argument, since Norris–LaGuardia is clearly in point here." At no point during the entire argument did either side refer to state law, the effects of that law on the picketing, or the possible preclusion of state remedies as a result of overriding federal law. The next day the District Court entered an order denying the requested restraining order. In relevant part that order included these conclusions of law:

"3. The parties of the BLE–FEC 'major dispute,' having exhausted the procedures of the Railway Labor Act, are now free to engage in self-help. * * *

"4. The conduct of the FEC pickets and that of the responding ACL employees are a part of the FEC–BLE major dispute. * * *

"* * *

* [Ed.]   See footnote 2.

"7. The Norris–LaGuardia Act, 29 U.S.C. § 101, and the Clayton Act, 29 U.S.C. § 52, are applicable to the conduct of the defendants here involved."

In this Court the union asserts that the determination that it was "free to engage in self-help" was a determination that it had a federally protected right to picket and that state law could not be invoked to negate that right. The railroad, on the other hand, argues that the order merely determined that the *federal* court could not enjoin the picketing, in large part because of the general prohibition in the Norris–LaGuardia Act, against issuance by federal courts of injunctions in labor disputes. * * *

* * *

* * * [After reviewing the record, the Court stated that it] conclusively shows that neither the parties themselves nor the District Court construed the 1967 order as the union now contends it should be construed. Rather we are convinced that the union in effect tried to get the Federal District Court to decide that the state court judge was wrong in distinguishing the Jacksonville Terminal decision. Such an attempt to seek appellate review of a state decision in the Federal District Court cannot be justified as necessary "to protect or effectuate" the 1967 order. * * *

B

This brings us to the second prong of the union's argument in which it is suggested that * * * once the decision in Jacksonville Terminal was announced, the District Court was then free to enjoin the state court on the theory that such action was "necessary to aid [the District Court's] jurisdiction." Again the argument is somewhat unclear, but it appears to go in this way: The District Court had acquired jurisdiction over the labor controversy in 1967 when the railroad filed its complaint, and it determined at that time that it did have jurisdiction. The dispute involved the legality of picketing by the union and the Jacksonville Terminal decision clearly indicated that such activity was not only legal, but was protected from state court interference. The state court had interfered with that right, and thus a federal injunction was "necessary in aid of its jurisdiction." For several reasons we cannot accept the contention.

First, a federal court does not have inherent power to ignore the limitations of § 2283 and to enjoin state court proceedings merely because those proceedings interfere with a protected federal right or invade an area preempted by federal law, even when the interference is unmistakably clear. * * * This conclusion is required because Congress itself set forth the only exceptions to the statute, and those exceptions do not include this situation. Second, if the District Court does have jurisdiction, it is not enough that the requested injunction is related to that jurisdiction, but it must be *"necessary in aid of"* that jurisdiction. While this language is admittedly broad, we conclude that it implies something similar to the concept of injunctions to "protect or effectuate" judgments. Both exceptions to the general prohibition of § 2283 imply that some federal injunctive relief may be necessary to prevent a state court from so interfering with a federal court's consideration or disposition of a case as to seriously impair the federal court's flexibility and authority to decide that case. Third, no such situation is presented here. * * * [T]he state and federal courts had concurrent jurisdiction in this case, and neither court was free to prevent either party from simultaneously pursuing claims in both courts. Kline v. Burke Constr. Co., 260 U.S. 226 (1922); *cf.* Donovan v. City of Dallas,

377 U.S. 408 (1964). Therefore the state court's assumption of jurisdiction over the state law claims and the federal preclusion issue did not hinder the federal court's jurisdiction so as to make an injunction *necessary* to aid that jurisdiction. An injunction was no more necessary because the state court may have taken action which the federal court was certain was improper under the Jacksonville Terminal decision. * * * If the union was adversely affected by the state court's decision, it was free to seek vindication of its federal right in the Florida appellate courts and ultimately, if necessary, in this Court. Similarly if, because of the Florida Circuit Court's action, the union faced the threat of immediate irreparable injury sufficient to justify an injunction under usual equitable principles, it was undoubtedly free to seek such relief from the Florida appellate courts, and might possibly in certain emergency circumstances seek such relief from this Court as well. * * *

III

This case is by no means an easy one. The arguments in support of the union's contentions are not insubstantial. But * * * [a]ny doubts as to the propriety of a federal injunction against state court proceedings should be resolved in favor of permitting the state courts to proceed in an orderly fashion to finally determine the controversy. The explicit wording of § 2283 itself implies as much, and the fundamental principle of a dual system of courts leads inevitably to that conclusion.

The injunction issued by the District Court must be vacated. * * *

■ [JUSTICE MARSHALL did not participate. JUSTICE HARLAN wrote a concurring opinion.]

■ MR. JUSTICE BRENNAN, with whom MR. JUSTICE WHITE joins, dissenting.

My disagreement with the Court in this case is a relatively narrow one. I do not disagree with much that is said concerning the history and policies underlying 28 U.S.C. § 2283. * * * Nevertheless, in my view the District Court had discretion to enjoin the state proceedings in the present case because it acted pursuant to an explicit exception to the prohibition of § 2283, that is, "to protect or effectuate [the District Court's] judgments." * * *

In my view, what the District Court decided in 1967 was that BLE had a federally protected right to picket at the Moncrief Yard and, by necessary implication, that this right could not be subverted by resort to state proceedings. I find it difficult indeed to ascribe to the District Judge the views which the Court now says he held, namely, that ACL, merely by marching across the street to the state court, could render wholly nugatory the District Judge's declaration that BLE had a federally protected right to strike at the Moncrief Yard. * * *

* * *

Accordingly, I would affirm the judgment of the Court of Appeals sustaining the District Court's grant of injunctive relief against petitioner's giving effect to, or availing itself of, the benefit of the state injunction.

———

Mitchum v. Foster

407 U.S. 225, 92 S.Ct. 2151, 32 L.Ed.2d 705 (1972).
Appeal from the United States District Court for the Northern District of Florida.

■ Mr. Justice Stewart delivered the opinion of the Court.

The federal anti-injunction statute provides that a federal court "may not grant an injunction to stay proceedings in a State court except as expressly authorized by Act of Congress, or where necessary in aid of its jurisdiction, or to protect or effectuate its judgments." An Act of Congress, 42 U.S.C. § 1983, expressly authorizes a "suit in equity" to redress "the deprivation," under color of state law, "of any rights, privileges, or immunities secured by the Constitution...." The question before us is whether this "Act of Congress" comes within the "expressly authorized" exception of the anti-injunction statute so as to permit a federal court in a § 1983 suit to grant an injunction to stay a proceeding pending in a state court. * * *

I

The prosecuting attorney of Bay County, Florida, brought a proceeding in a Florida court to close down the appellant's bookstore as a public nuisance under the claimed authority of Florida law. The state court entered a preliminary order prohibiting continued operation of the bookstore. After further inconclusive proceedings in the state courts, the appellant filed a complaint in the United States District Court for the Northern District of Florida, alleging that the actions of the state judicial and law enforcement officials were depriving him of rights protected by the First and Fourteenth Amendments. Relying upon 42 U.S.C. § 1983, he asked for injunctive and declaratory relief against the state court proceedings, on the ground that Florida laws were being unconstitutionally applied by the state court * * *. * * *

II

In denying injunctive relief, the District Court relied on this Court's decision in Atlantic Coast Line R. Co. v. Brotherhood of Locomotive Engineers, 398 U.S. 281. The * * * Court's opinion in that case * * * made clear that the statute imposes an absolute ban upon the issuance of a federal injunction against a pending state court proceeding, in the absence of one of the recognized exceptions * * *.

It follows, in the present context, that if 42 U.S.C. § 1983 is not within the "expressly authorized" exception of the anti-injunction statute, then a federal equity court is wholly without power to grant any relief in a § 1983 suit seeking to stay a state court proceeding.

Last Term, in Younger v. Harris, 401 U.S. 37, and its companion cases, the Court dealt at length with the subject of federal judicial intervention in pending state criminal prosecutions. In Younger a three-judge federal district court in a § 1983 action had enjoined a criminal prosecution pending in a California court. In asking us to reverse that judgment, the appellant argued that the injunction was in violation of the federal anti-injunction statute. But the Court carefully eschewed any reliance on the statute in reversing the judgment, basing its decision instead upon what the Court called "Our Federalism"— upon "the national policy forbidding federal courts to stay or enjoin pending state court proceedings except under special circumstances."

* * * At the same time, however, the Court clearly left room for federal injunctive intervention in a pending state court prosecution in certain exceptional circumstances—where irreparable injury is "both great and immediate," where the state law is "flagrantly and patently violative of express constitutional prohibitions," or where there is a showing of "bad faith, harassment, or * * * other unusual circumstances that would call for equitable relief." * * *

While the Court in Younger and its companion cases expressly disavowed deciding the question now before us—whether § 1983 comes within the "expressly authorized" exception of the anti-injunction statute—it is evident that our decisions in those cases cannot be disregarded in deciding this question. In the first place, if § 1983 is not within the statutory exception, then the anti-injunction statute would have absolutely barred the injunction issued in Younger, as the appellant in that case argued, and there would have been no occasion whatever for the Court to decide that case upon the "policy" ground of "Our Federalism." Secondly, if § 1983 is not within the "expressly authorized" exception of the anti-injunction statute, then we must overrule Younger and its companion cases insofar as they recognized the permissibility of injunctive relief against pending criminal prosecutions in certain limited and exceptional circumstances. * * *

The Atlantic Coast Line and Younger cases thus serve to delineate both the importance and the finality of the question now before us. And it is in the shadow of those cases that the question must be decided.

III

* * * In 1793, Congress enacted a law providing that no "writ of injunction be granted [by any federal court] to stay proceedings in any court of a state. . . ." Act of March 2, 1793; 1 Stat. 335. The precise origins of the legislation are shrouded in obscurity,[10] but the consistent understanding has been that its basic purpose is to prevent "needless friction between state and federal courts." Oklahoma Packing Co. v. Gas Co., 309 U.S. 4, 9. The law remained unchanged until 1874, when it was amended to permit a federal court to stay state court proceedings that interfered with the administration of a federal bankruptcy proceeding. The present wording of the legislation was adopted with the enactment of Title 28 of the United States Code in 1948.

---

10. "The history of this provision in the Judiciary Act of 1793 is not fully known. We know that on December 31, 1790, Attorney General Edmund Randolph reported to the House of Representatives on desirable changes in the Judiciary Act of 1789. * * * A section of the proposed bill submitted by him provided that 'no injunction in equity shall be granted by a district court to a judgment at law of a State court.' Randolph explained * * * *[:] 'it is enough to split the same suit into one at law, and another in equity, without adding a further separation, by throwing the common law side of the question into the State courts, and the equity side into the federal courts.' * * * * No action was taken until after Chief Justice Jay and his associates wrote the President that their circuit-riding duties were too burdensome. In response to this complaint, which was transmitted to Congress, the Act of March 2, 1793, was passed, containing in § 5, *inter alia*, the prohibition against staying state court proceedings.

"There is no record of any debates over the statute. It has been suggested that the provision reflected the then strong feeling against the unwarranted intrusion of federal courts upon state sovereignty. * * * Much more probable is the suggestion that the provision reflected the prevailing prejudices against equity jurisdiction. * * * *" Toucey v. New York Life Ins. Co., 314 U.S. 118, 130–132.

Despite the seemingly uncompromising language of the anti-injunction statute prior to 1948, the Court soon recognized that exceptions must be made to its blanket prohibition if the import and purpose of other Acts of Congress were to be given their intended scope. So it was that, in addition to the bankruptcy law exception that Congress explicitly recognized in 1874, the Court through the years found that federal courts were empowered to enjoin state court proceedings, despite the anti-injunction statute, in carrying out the will of Congress under at least six other federal laws. These covered a broad spectrum of congressional action: (1) legislation providing for removal of litigation from state to federal courts,[12] (2) legislation limiting the liability of shipowners,[13] (3) legislation providing for federal interpleader actions,[14] (4) legislation conferring federal jurisdiction over farm mortgages,[15] (5) legislation governing federal habeas corpus proceedings,[16] and (6) legislation providing for control of prices.[17]

In addition to the exceptions to the anti-injunction statute found to be embodied in these various Acts of Congress, the Court recognized other "implied" exceptions to the blanket prohibition of the anti-injunction statute. One was an *"in rem"* exception, allowing a federal court to enjoin a state court proceeding in order to protect its jurisdiction of a res over which it had first acquired jurisdiction. Another was a "relitigation" exception, permitting a federal court to enjoin relitigation in a state court of issues already decided in federal litigation. Still a third exception, more recently developed, permits a federal injunction of state court proceedings when the plaintiff in the federal court is the United States itself, or a federal agency asserting "superior federal interests."

In Toucey v. New York Life Ins. Co., 314 U.S. 118, the Court in 1941 issued an opinion casting considerable doubt upon the approach to the anti-

---

12. See French v. Hay, 22 Wall. 250; Kline v. Burke Construction Co., 260 U.S. 226. The federal removal provisions, both civil and criminal, 28 U.S.C. §§ 1441–1450, provide that once a copy of the removal petition is filed with the clerk of the state court, the "State court shall proceed no further unless and until the case is remanded." 28 U.S.C. § 1446(e).

13. See Providence & N.Y.S.S. Co. v. Hill Mfg. Co., 109 U.S. 578. The Act of 1851, as amended, provides that once a shipowner has deposited with the court an amount equal to the value of his interest in the ship, "all claims and proceedings against the owner with respect to the matter in question shall cease." 46 U.S.C. § 185.

14. See Treinies v. Sunshine Mining Co., 308 U.S. 66. The Interpleader Act of 1926 as currently written provides that in "any civil action of interpleader * * * a district court may * * * enter its order restraining [all claimants] * * * from instituting or prosecuting any proceeding in any State or United States court affecting the property, instrument or obligation involved in the interpleader action." 28 U.S.C. § 2361.

15. See Kalb v. Feuerstein, 308 U.S. 433. The Frazier–Lemke Farm–Mortgage Act, as amended in 1935, provides that in situations to which it is applicable a federal court shall "stay all judicial or official proceedings in any court." 11 U.S.C. § 203(s)(2)(1940 ed.).

16. See Ex parte Royall, 117 U.S. 241, 248–249. The Federal Habeas Corpus Act provides that a federal court before which a habeas corpus proceeding is pending may "stay any proceeding against the person detained in any State Court * * * for any matter involved in the habeas corpus proceeding." 28 U.S.C. § 2251.

17. Section 205(a) of the Emergency Price Control Act of 1942 provided that the Price Administrator could request a federal district court to enjoin acts that violated or threatened to violate the Act. In Porter v. Dicken, 328 U.S. 252, we held that this authority was broad enough to justify an injunction to restrain state court proceedings. * * *

injunction statute reflected in its previous decisions. The Court's opinion expressly disavowed the "relitigation" exception to the statute, and emphasized generally the importance of recognizing the statute's basic directive "of 'hands off' by the federal courts in the use of the injunction to stay litigation in a state court." The congressional response to Toucey was the enactment in 1948 of the anti-injunction statute in its present form in 28 U.S.C. § 2283, which, as the Reviser's Note makes evident, served not only to overrule the specific holding of Toucey, but to restore "the basic law as generally understood and interpreted prior to the Toucey decision."

We proceed, then, upon the understanding that in determining whether § 1983 comes within the "expressly authorized" exception of the anti-injunction statute, the criteria to be applied are those reflected in the Court's decisions prior to Toucey. A review of those decisions makes reasonably clear what the relevant criteria are. In the first place, it is evident that, in order to qualify under the "expressly authorized" exception of the anti-injunction statute, a federal law need not contain an express reference to that statute. * * * Indeed, none of the previously recognized statutory exceptions contains any such reference.[24] Secondly, a federal law need not expressly authorize an injunction of a state court proceeding in order to qualify as an exception. Three of the six previously recognized statutory exceptions contain no such authorization.[25] Thirdly, it is clear that, in order to qualify as an "expressly authorized" exception to the anti-injunction statute, an Act of Congress must have created a specific and uniquely federal right or remedy, enforceable in a federal court of equity, that could be frustrated if the federal court were not empowered to enjoin a state court proceeding. This is not to say that in order to come within the exception an Act of Congress must, on its face and in every one of its provisions, be totally incompatible with the prohibition of the anti-injunction statute. The test, rather, is whether an Act of Congress, clearly creating a federal right or remedy enforceable in a federal court of equity, could be given its intended scope only by the stay of a state court proceeding. * * *

With these criteria in view, we turn to consideration of 42 U.S.C. § 1983.

IV

Section 1983 was originally § 1 of the Civil Rights Act of 1871. * * * The predecessor of § 1983 was thus an important part of the basic alteration in our federal system wrought in the Reconstruction era through federal legislation and constitutional amendment. As a result of the new structure of law that emerged in the post-Civil War era—and especially of the Fourteenth Amendment, which was its centerpiece—the role of the Federal Government as a guarantor of basic federal rights against state power was clearly established. * * *

It is clear from the legislative debates surrounding passage of § 1983's predecessor that the Act was intended to enforce the provisions of the Fourteenth Amendment "against State action, * * * whether that action be executive, legislative, or *judicial*." Ex parte Virginia, 100 U.S. 339, 346 (emphasis supplied). Proponents of the legislation noted that state courts were being used to harass and injure individuals, either because the state courts were

24. See nn. 12, 13, 14, 15, 16, and 17, *supra*.

25. See nn. 12, 13, and 17, *supra*.
* * *

powerless to stop deprivations or were in league with those who were bent upon abrogation of federally protected rights.

As Representative Lowe stated, the "records of the [state] tribunals are searched in vain for evidence of effective redress [of federally secured rights]. * * * What less than this [the Civil Rights Act of 1871] will afford an adequate remedy? The Federal Government cannot serve a writ of mandamus upon State Executives or upon State courts to compel them to protect the rights, privileges and immunities of citizens. * * * The case has arisen * * * when the Federal Government must resort to its own agencies to carry its own authority into execution. Hence this bill throws open the doors of the United States courts to those whose rights under the Constitution are denied or impaired." Cong. Globe, 42d Cong., 1st Sess., 374–376 (1871). This view was echoed by [other legislators]. * * *

     * * *

This legislative history makes evident that Congress clearly conceived that it was altering the relationship between the States and the Nation with respect to the protection of federally created rights; it was concerned that state instrumentalities could not protect those rights; it realized that state officers might, in fact, be antipathetic to the vindication of those rights; and it believed that these failings extended to the state courts.

V

Section 1983 was thus a product of a vast transformation from the concepts of federalism that had prevailed in the late 18th century when the anti-injunction statute was enacted. The very purpose of § 1983 was to interpose the federal courts between the States and the people, as guardians of the people's federal rights—to protect the people from unconstitutional action under color of state law, "whether that action be executive, legislative, or judicial." Ex parte Virginia, 100 U.S., at 346. In carrying out that purpose, Congress plainly authorized the federal courts to issue injunctions in § 1983 actions, by expressly authorizing a "suit in equity" as one of the means of redress. And this Court long ago recognized that federal injunctive relief against a state court proceeding can in some circumstances be essential to prevent great, immediate, and irreparable loss of a person's constitutional rights. Ex parte Young, 209 U.S. 123 * * *. For these reasons we conclude that, under the criteria established in our previous decisions construing the anti-injunction statute, § 1983 is an Act of Congress that falls within the "expressly authorized" exception of that law.

In so concluding, we do not question or qualify in any way the principles of equity, comity, and federalism that must restrain a federal court when asked to enjoin a state court proceeding. These principles, in the context of state criminal prosecutions, were canvassed at length last Term in Younger v. Harris, 401 U.S. 37, and its companion cases. * * * Today we decide only that the District Court in this case was in error in holding that, because of the anti-injunction statute, it was absolutely without power in this § 1983 action to enjoin a proceeding pending in a state court under any circumstances whatsoever.

The judgment is reversed and the case is remanded to the District Court for further proceedings consistent with this opinion.

■ [JUSTICES POWELL and REHNQUIST did not participate. CHIEF JUSTICE BURGER, joined by JUSTICES WHITE and BLACKMUN, filed a concurring opinion stressing that the Court had not yet decided whether the principles of equity, comity, and federalism set forth in Younger v. Harris restricted federal injunctive relief against pending state *civil* proceedings. He urged the district court on remand to consider that question before proceeding to the merits.]

NOTE ON THE ANTI–INJUNCTION ACT (28 U.S.C. § 2283)

A.   Background, Purpose, and Interpretation of the Act

(1) *History and Purpose.*   Why should federal injunctions against state proceedings be disfavored, when a federal court may enjoin proceedings in a different federal court, see Chap. XIV, Sec. 4, *infra*, and a state court may enjoin proceedings in the court of a different state?[1]   Note the contrasting rhetoric of Atlantic Coast Line (stressing the independence of state legal systems) and Mitchum (arguing that Reconstruction worked a "vast transformation" in the concepts of federalism, and that federal jurisdiction is needed to protect federal rights that state courts are unable or unwilling to protect).   As you read the remainder of this Note, consider whether "the goal of a bright-line anti-injunction standard may be doomed never to succeed, because it attempts to incorporate two mutually inconsistent imperatives".   Wood, *Fine-Tuning Judicial Federalism: A Proposal for Reform of the Anti–Injunction Act*, 1990 B.Y.U.L.Rev. 289, 290.   See generally Fallon, *The Ideologies of Federal Courts Law*, 74 Va.L.Rev. 1141 (1988) (systematically elaborating two conflicting models of the relation of state and federal courts: the "Federalist" model exemplified by Atlantic Coast Line, and the "Nationalist" model exemplified by Mitchum).

1. The view set forth in Atlantic Coast Line and Mitchum of the Anti–Injunction Act's purpose has not gone unchallenged. Professor Mayton marshals considerable support for the view that the original Act of 1793 was designed merely to prohibit a *single Justice* of the Supreme Court from enjoining such proceedings while riding circuit. Mayton, *Ersatz Federalism under the Anti–Injunction Statute*, 78 Colum.L.Rev. 330 (1978). He relies in part on the fact that the bar on injunctions was included in the middle of section 5 of the 1793 Act, which governed the powers of a single Justice—though he does have some difficulty explaining the statute's syntax and its use at one point of the phrase "court or judge" (p. 335). He also observes that for over fifty years, the federal courts did not rely on the statute in considering requests for injunctions against state court proceedings, disposing of such cases instead on "equitable principles, * * * standards of comity * * *, and on general principles of federalism" (p. 338). The original meaning,

Mayton argues, was lost when, in Peck v. Jenness, 48 U.S. (7 How.) 612 (1849), the Supreme Court asserted without discussion that the 1793 Act barred federal injunctions against state court proceedings. That view was followed when the anti-injunction language was separated from the rest of section 5 in the 1874 statutory revision, which was not supposed to effect substantive changes. He concedes that the 1948 revision had a broader purpose, but argues that its true intent was to authorize the exercise of a sound discretion to protect the exercise of federal court jurisdiction.

See also Reaves & Golden, *The Federal Anti–Injunction Statute in the Aftermath of Atlantic Coast Line Railroad*, 5 Ga.L.Rev. 294, 297–99 (1971); Comment, 38 U.Chi. L.Rev. 612, 613 (1971)(arguing "that Congress in 1793 did not intend to prevent stays effected by writs other than injunction, and that Congress specifically approved the use of the [common-law] writ of certiorari to stay state proceedings").

(2) *Pre–1948 Exceptions*. A number of pre–1948 decisions recognized limitations to the anti-injunction statute.

(a) *Congressional Authorization*. Some of these limitations were founded on congressional enactments; they are summarized in Mitchum.

(b) *The Res Exception*. As Mitchum notes, a line of cases beginning with Hagan v. Lucas, 35 U.S. (10 Pet.) 400 (1836), announced an implied exception to the statute by declaring that the court (state or federal) that first assumes jurisdiction over property may exercise that jurisdiction, to the exclusion of any other court—if necessary by enjoining another court's proceedings. *Cf.* Freeman v. Howe, 65 U.S. (24 How.) 450 (1860). See also Kline v. Burke Construction, *supra*. No Supreme Court case actually has upheld an injunction against state proceedings on this basis.[2] But *cf.* Colorado River Water Conservation Dist. v. United States, p. 1308, *infra* (holding that district court should have declined to exercise jurisdiction in favor of pending state action that was analogized to an in rem proceeding). And keep in mind that the traditional distinction between *in rem* and *in personam* jurisdiction has for some decades been criticized as standing in the way of useful analysis, see, *e.g.*, Mullane v. Central Hanover Bank & Trust Co., 339 U.S. 306 (1950); von Mehren & Trautman, *Jurisdiction to Adjudicate: A Suggested Analysis*, 79 Harv.L.Rev. 1121 (1966), and more recently has suffered significant erosion, see, *e.g.*, Shaffer v. Heitner, 433 U.S. 186 (1977).

(c) *Fraudulent State Court Judgments*. Several Supreme Court decisions sustained the power of federal courts to enjoin litigants from enforcing judgments fraudulently obtained in state courts. See Paragraph C(2)(b), *infra*.

(3) *The Toucey Decision*. In Toucey v. New York Life Ins. Co., 314 U.S. 118 (1941), the Court (per Frankfurter, J.) broke with the tradition of implying exceptions to the statute, holding that the federal courts lacked authority to enjoin state relitigation of issues settled in a prior federal action. The opinion found the precedents upholding such injunctions to be at most "a tenuous basis for the exception which we are now asked explicitly to sanction"; "[w]e must be scrupulous in our regard for the limits within which Congress has confined the authority of the courts of its own creation" (pp. 140–41). While acknowledging the existence of the "res" exception, the Court argued that "[t]he fact that one exception has found its way into [the statute] is no justification for making another" (p. 139).

(4) *The 1948 Revision*. The only legislative history to § 2283, enacted in 1948, is found in the Revisers' Notes:

"An exception as to acts of Congress relating to bankruptcy was omitted and the general exception substituted to cover all exceptions.

"The phrase 'in aid of its jurisdiction' was added to conform to section 1651 of this title and to make clear the recognized power of the Federal courts to stay proceedings in State cases removed to the district courts.

---

2. Princess Lida of Thurn and Taxis v. Thompson, 305 U.S. 456 (1939), held that the filing of trust accounts gave a state court *quasi in rem* jurisdiction and empowered it to enjoin a later federal action against the trustees for an accounting and other relief. Compare Mandeville v. Canterbury, 318 U.S. 47 (1943)(holding that because federal court action concerning a trust was in personam, related state court action could not be enjoined). See also Markham v. Allen, 326 U.S. 490 (1946), p. 1334, *infra*.

"The exceptions specifically include the words 'to protect or effectuate its judgments,' for lack of which the Supreme Court held that the Federal courts are without power to enjoin relitigation of cases and controversies fully adjudicated by such courts. (See Toucey v. New York Life Ins. Co., * * *. A vigorous dissenting opinion * * * notes that at the time of the 1911 revision of the Judicial Code, the power of the courts of the United States to protect their judgments was unquestioned and that the revisers of that code noted no change and Congress intended no change).

"Therefore the revised section restores the basic law as generally understood and interpreted prior to the Toucey decision.

"Changes were made in phraseology."

(5) *Interpretative Approaches to § 2283*. The 1948 revision, though hardly a model of clarity, was designed both to overrule Toucey, which had departed from the tradition of judicial implication of exceptions, and to expand the scope of permissible injunctions. Given that background, how convincing are the statements in Atlantic Coast Line and Mitchum that § 2283's ban should be viewed as absolute unless the case falls within one of the three stated exceptions?[3]

In fact, the Court has not been quite as strict as those statements would suggest. In Leiter Minerals, Inc. v. United States, 352 U.S. 220 (1957), the Court recognized an additional exception for injunctions sought by the United States. Leiter sued lessees of the United States in state court, seeking a declaration that it owned certain mineral rights and an accounting. The United States subsequently brought a federal action against Leiter and others to quiet title to the mineral rights, and sought to enjoin the state proceedings. In upholding the injunction, Justice Frankfurter's opinion for the Court declared that the policy of preventing conflict between federal and state courts "is much more compelling" in litigation between private parties than "when * * * the United States * * * seeks a stay to prevent a threatened irreparable injury to a national interest. The frustration of superior federal interests * * * from precluding the Federal Government from obtaining a stay of state court proceedings except under the severe restrictions of 28 U.S.C. § 2283 would be so great that we cannot reasonably impute such a purpose to Congress from the general language of § 2283 alone" (pp. 225–26).

In NLRB v. Nash–Finch Co., 404 U.S. 138 (1971), the Court extended the Leiter rationale to an application for an injunction by the National Labor Relations Board.

Although the expansive view expressed in Leiter appeared as a harbinger of further judicial creativity, subsequent decisions, including Atlantic Coast Line and Mitchum, have closed the door on efforts to create additional exceptions to § 2283.

B. The Three Statutory Exceptions

(1) *Expressly Authorized by Congress.*

---

3. The courts have said that the statute is not strictly jurisdictional, but have nonetheless permitted its application to be raised on appeal sua sponte. *E.g.*, Gloucester Ma- rine Ry. Corp. v. Charles Parisi, Inc., 848 F.2d 12, 15 (1st Cir.1988); Hickey v. Duffy, 827 F.2d 234, 243 (7th Cir.1987).

(a) *The Scope of Mitchum.* The significance for anti-suit injunctions of the Mitchum decision, which holds § 1983 to be an expressly authorized exception to § 2283, plainly depends on the reach of the underlying § 1983 cause of action. One question about § 1983's scope relates to the requirement under § 1983 that the challenged action be taken "under color of law", and asks in what circumstances that requirement is satisfied by state court litigation between private parties. In the leading decision on this point, Lugar v. Edmondson Oil Co., Inc., 457 U.S. 922 (1982), a creditor sued on a debt, and, pursuant to a state statute, obtained ex parte a prejudgment attachment of the defendant's property. The Court held (5–4) that though "a private party's mere invocation of state legal procedures" was not action under color of law, the attachment was and hence could be challenged under § 1983.[4] And the issuance of a state court injunction surely constitutes action "under color of law." See, *e.g.*, Henry v. First Nat. Bank, 595 F.2d 291, 299–300 (5th Cir.1979); Machesky v. Bizzell, 414 F.2d 283, 286 (5th Cir.1969); *cf.* Shelley v. Kraemer, 334 U.S. 1 (1948).

A different question as to the scope of § 1983 was resolved in Maine v. Thiboutot, 448 U.S. 1 (1980), Chap. IX, Sec. 2(C), p. 1134, *supra*, which held that § 1983 provides a remedy for violations of federal rights conferred not only by the Constitution or by legislation relating to equal rights, but also by federal statutes generally. That holding, in combination with Mitchum, creates a large terrain in which anti-suit injunctions may be issued.

Indeed, reconsider the facts of Atlantic Coast Line. Could the union have sued under § 1983, arguing (i) that the state court injunction constituted action under color of law, and (ii) that the Railway Labor Act conferred a federal right to be free from that injunction? On the latter point, see Golden State Transit Corp. v. City of Los Angeles, 493 U.S. 103 (1989), p. 1136, *supra* (holding that federal statutes may create rights that operate through the Supremacy Clause to preempt regulation under state law and that are cognizable under § 1983).

How applicable is the legislative history of the Reconstruction era, on which Mitchum placed great weight, to a claim that the Railway Labor Act bars a state court injunction, or that an ex parte attachment denied due process?[5]

(b) *Mitchum's Interpretation of the Act.* A careful look at footnotes 12–17 of the Mitchum opinion shows that in five of the six statutes that had previously been found expressly to authorize injunctive relief against state proceedings, Congress clearly indicated that state proceedings should cease. (The exception is the Emergency Price Control Act of 1942.) Whether or not such an indication necessarily authorizes such federal intervention—the Su-

---

4. See also Pennzoil Co. v. Texaco, Inc., 481 U.S. 1 (1987), pp. 1303, 1503, *infra*, in which four Justices, concurring in the judgment, stated that a judgment creditor's invocation of state post-judgment collection procedures constitutes action under color of state law. The majority did not reach the issue.

5. In Hickey v. Duffy, 827 F.2d 234, 240–43 (7th Cir.1987), Judge Easterbrook held that the "rationale of Mitchum is limited to violations of the Constitution for which § 1983 supplies a remedy, and then only

when the state litigation is itself the violation of the Constitution." He admitted the logic of the broader view of Mitchum, but argued it would be odd to provide that when a federal statute provides detailed remedies (and thus preempts § 1983, see p. 1134, *supra*), no injunction can issue, but when Congress provides fewer remedies (so that § 1983 is not displaced), an injunction is available. He also rested on the fact that the jurisdictional counterpart to § 1983, 28 U.S.C. § 1343(3), does not extend to federal statutory claims generally. See p. 1121, *supra*.

premacy Clause, after all, obliges a state court to stay its own proceedings if federal law so dictates—isn't Mitchum still a further step, given the lack of any such indication in § 1983? Didn't Mitchum read "expressly authorized" to mean "impliedly authorized"?

(c) *The Vendo Decision.* The possibility that Mitchum's broad construction of the "expressly authorized" exception would be extended to other federal statutes may have been dimmed by the result in Vendo Co. v. Lektro–Vend Corp., 433 U.S. 623 (1977). Vendo sued Lektro–Vend (and others) in state court for breach of an agreement not to compete. Lektro–Vend countered with a federal court action against Vendo alleging that the agreement violated the federal antitrust laws and that the state court suit was designed to stifle competition and to harass. After a state court judgment against Lektro–Vend for over $7 million was affirmed, the federal district court enjoined enforcement of the judgment, holding that § 16 of the Clayton Act, 15 U.S.C. § 26 (which authorizes private suits for injunctive relief against antitrust violations) was an "expressly authorized" exception to § 2283. The Seventh Circuit affirmed.

A splintered Supreme Court reversed. Justice Rehnquist, for himself and Justices Stewart and Powell, argued that, unlike § 1983, § 16 of the Clayton Act could be given "its intended scope" without a stay of state court proceedings; there was no indication that Congress "was concerned with the possibility that state-court proceedings would be used to violate the Sherman or Clayton Acts" (p. 634). To rule otherwise would "eviscerate" § 2283 "since the ultimate logic of this position can mean no less than that virtually *all* federal statutes authorizing injunctive relief are exceptions to § 2283" (p. 636).

Justice Blackmun, joined by the Chief Justice, concurred, but on the very different theory that § 16 was an "expressly authorized" exception only in the "narrowly limited circumstances", not found in the present case, where state court proceedings "are themselves part of a 'pattern of baseless, repetitive claims' that are being used as an anticompetitive device" (p. 644). Justice Stevens, for the four dissenters, contended that prosecution of even a single state-court proceeding could (and in this case did) violate the antitrust laws; that to deny an injunction would deprive § 16 of its intended scope; and thus that § 16 was an "expressly authorized" exception.

The key disagreement between the four dissenting and the two concurring Justices concerned merely the circumstances when state court litigation violates the federal antitrust laws. Does it follow that after Vendo, any federal statute providing for injunctive relief against unlawful action is an "expressly authorized" exception to § 2283 whenever the prosecution of a state court suit is at least a significant part of such unlawful action?

Unsurprisingly, the lower court decisions since Vendo do not form a coherent pattern. See generally 17 Wright, Miller & Cooper, Federal Practice & Procedure § 4224 (1988 & 1995 Supp.). See generally Redish, *The Anti–Injunction Statute Reconsidered*, 44 U.Chi.L.Rev. 717 (1977), arguing, *inter alia*, that the three opinions in Vendo demonstrate the unworkability of the Mitchum test.

(2) *"In Aid of Its Jurisdiction".* The exception for injunctions "in aid of [the federal court's] jurisdiction" has been taken to have two primary concerns. First, most courts have viewed the language as confirming the "res" exception, see Paragraph A(2)(b), *supra*—despite the failure of the Reviser's Notes to so

indicate.[6] The Reviser's Notes do mention the second purpose—to confirm the power of the federal courts to stay proceedings in state cases that have been removed.[7]

(a) *Richman Brothers*. The principal Supreme Court decision discussing this exception is Amalgamated Clothing Workers v. Richman Brothers, 348 U.S. 511 (1955). There, a union sought to enjoin a state-court suit as preempted by the NLRB's exclusive jurisdiction. The Supreme Court affirmed the district court's refusal to issue an injunction: because no statute authorized the union to file the federal court suit, the federal injunction was not ancillary to an independently-based, ongoing proceeding; and the Court refused to permit an injunction merely when state court jurisdiction has allegedly been preempted.[8]

(b) *Exclusive Jurisdiction*. If the "in aid of jurisdiction" exception permits an injunction to protect federal court jurisdiction after removal, does it authorize an injunction against a state proceeding that falls within the federal courts' exclusive jurisdiction? There is some force to the analogy, but most lower courts have viewed Richman Brothers' refusal to authorize an injunction to protect the NLRB's exclusive jurisdiction as applying equally to protection of the federal courts' exclusive jurisdiction. See, *e.g.*, Piambino v. Bailey, 610 F.2d 1306, 1333–34 (5th Cir.1980). The existence of exclusive jurisdiction may be one relevant factor, however, in determining whether a statute constitutes an "express" exception within the meaning of Mitchum.

(c) *Complex Litigation*. May a federal court enjoin state court actions that threaten to interfere with administration of a pending federal class action? The question is not a unitary one, and may depend on such factors as: (i) the kind of federal class action (Rule 23(b)(1), (b)(2), or (b)(3)); (ii) whether the state court action was brought by members of the federal class; and (iii) whether the injunction is sought before certification, after certification but before the time for opting-out in (b)(3) actions, after formulation of a proposed settlement, or after entry of judgment.

In general, the lower courts have read the "in aid of jurisdiction" exception broadly in class actions so as to permit anti-suit injunctions. Many decisions rely on the statement in Atlantic Coast Line that some injunctive relief may be necessary "to prevent a state court from so interfering with a federal court's consideration or disposition of a case as to seriously impair the federal court's flexibility and authority to decide that case." See, *e.g.*, Carlough v. Amchem

---

6. For a collection of cases, see 17 Wright, Miller & Cooper, *supra*, § 4225 (1988 & Supp.1995).

7. Compare footnote 12 of Mitchum, which viewed the power to enjoin in removed cases as "expressly authorized by act of Congress" rather than "in aid of jurisdiction".

8. In Richman Brothers, the Court had to distinguish Capital Service, Inc. v. NLRB, 347 U.S. 501 (1954). There an employer, having obtained a state court injunction against a union's secondary boycott, filed an unfair labor practice charge with the NLRB. After issuing a complaint, the NLRB obtained a federal court injunction against enforcement of the state court injunction, on the ground that federal law preempts state

court jurisdiction over unfair labor practices. The Supreme Court affirmed the order as "necessary in aid of jurisdiction": to make effective its statutory power to seek injunctions, the NLRB "must have authority to take all steps necessary to preserve its case" (p. 505).

Richman Brothers distinguished Capital Service on the ground that the NLRB had a statutory right to file the federal action in which injunctive relief was sought. But perhaps Capital Service is best understood in light of the decisions, rendered only later, permitting anti-suit injunctions in actions by the United States or its agencies. See Paragraph A(5), *supra*.

Prods., Inc., 10 F.3d 189, 202 (3d Cir.1993). Can the subject matter of a class suit be analogized to a "res"?[9]

See generally Larimore, *Exploring the Interface Between Rule 23 Class Actions and the Anti–Injunction Act*, 18 Ga.L.Rev. 259 (1984); Sherman, *Class Actions and Duplicative Litigation*, 62 Ind.L.J. 507, 528–36 (1987). For discussion of the ALI's Study of Complex Litigation (1993), which proposes statutory reforms to permit consolidation of multi-party, multi-forum litigation in a single tribunal, and to broaden that tribunal's authority to enjoin state court proceedings relating to such matters, see p. 1322, *infra*.

(3) *The Relitigation Exception.*

(a) *Purpose.* The relitigation exception permits a federal court to enjoin a state court to respect the preclusive effect of a federal judgment. But why shouldn't the litigant relying on that judgment be relegated to a plea of res judicata in state court? Is it because the federal court is better able to determine the effect of a prior federal judgment?

(b) *The Chick Kam Choo Decision.* The relitigation exception was at issue in Chick Kam Choo v. Exxon Corp., 486 U.S. 140 (1988). There, a federal district court in Texas had dismissed plaintiff's wrongful death action, finding that (i) choice of law doctrine called for application of the law of Singapore rather than of Texas, and (ii) forum non conveniens called for dismissal of the suit so long as the defendants submitted to jurisdiction in Singapore. The plaintiff then filed suit in Texas state court, asserting claims under Texas law and under Singapore law. The defendants returned to federal court and obtained an injunction against the state court action. The Supreme Court ruled that § 2283 did not preclude the injunction insofar as it barred relitigation of the Texas law claim, which the federal court had previously held to lack merit when it held that Singapore law applied. But the Court overturned the injunction insofar as it barred state court litigation of the claim based on the law of Singapore: because federal and state forum non conveniens law might differ, the state court would not necessarily be asked to relitigate the federal court's forum non conveniens ruling; and (per Atlantic Coast Line) even if federal maritime law preempted Texas' application of its own forum non conveniens law, no injunction could issue on that basis because that preemption issue had not been decided by the federal district court.[10]

---

9. That analogy would seem especially strong in an action under Rule 23(b)(1)(B), which authorizes class suit (without a right to opt-out) when separate actions would effectively dispose of the interests of nonparties or substantially impair their ability to protect their interests. But in In re Federal Skywalk Cases, 680 F.2d 1175 (8th Cir.1982), the court held impermissible an order enjoining class members, including those with pending actions in state court, from settling their punitive damage claims until the federal court had resolved the issue.

Could that injunction have been upheld by analogy to the federal interpleader statute, see footnote 14 in Mitchum, which has been held to be an expressly authorized exception? Does Rule 23 count as an "Act of Congress"

for purposes of § 2283? Would an effort to read Rule 23 as creating an exception to § 2283 "abridge, enlarge, or modify" a substantive right in violation of the Rules Enabling Act? See In re Temple, 851 F.2d 1269, 1272 n. 3 (11th Cir.1988); 7B Wright, Miller & Kane, Federal Practice & Procedure § 1798.1 (1986 & 1995 Supp.).

10. Some language in the Chick Kam Choo opinion ("an essential prerequisite for applying the relitigation exception is that the claims or issues which the federal injunction insulates from litigation in state proceedings actually have been decided by the federal court" (p. 148)) has led some federal circuits to conclude that that exception permits enforcement of issue preclusion but not of claim preclusion. See generally Martinez, *The*

Should an injunction issue whenever the matter to be litigated in state court has already been litigated between the parties in federal court? Or should the moving party have to establish something more: that the state action is vexatious or highly inconvenient, or that there is need for speedier relief than can be afforded by a plea of res judicata in the state court? In Chick Kam Choo, the Court noted that merely because § 2883 *permitted* an injunction against relitigation of the Texas claim did not mean that an injunction was *required*.

(c) *The Parsons Steel Decision*. In Parsons Steel, Inc. v. First Alabama Bank, 474 U.S. 518 (1986), plaintiffs sued the bank in separate actions in federal and state court. The federal action came to judgment first, with the bank prevailing. The bank's assertion in state court of res judicata defenses, based on the federal judgment, was rejected, leading to a $4 million state court verdict against the bank.

The bank returned to federal court and obtained an injunction against the state court proceeding on the ground that the state court claims could have been raised as pendent claims in the prior federal action and thus should have been held by the state court to have been precluded by the federal judgment. The Supreme Court unanimously overturned the injunction. The Court noted that 28 U.S.C. § 1738 (the full faith and credit statute) generally requires a federal court to give a state court judgment the same effect that it would have under state law, see Chap. XII, Sec. 1, pp. 1484–1500, *infra*; that § 2283 was not an exception to § 1738; and that the relitigation exception was limited "to those situations in which the state court has not yet ruled on the merits of the res judicata issue. Once the state court has finally rejected a claim of res judicata, * * * federal courts must turn to state law to determine the preclusive effect of the state court's decision" (p. 772).

Doesn't Parsons Steel encourage a litigant who has obtained a favorable federal judgment to seek an immediate federal injunction against state court relitigation if there is any doubt that the state court will recognize the judgment's effect? Will the likely response produce more or less federal-state friction?

C. Questions of Coverage

(1) *Introduction*. Even where there is no exception to § 2283's prohibition, the question remains whether the particular "interference" by the federal court with state court proceedings is one that the Act forbids.

(2) *The Meaning of "Proceedings"*.

(a) *Commencement of Proceedings*. When do the state court "proceedings" referred to in § 2283 begin? Ex parte Young, 209 U.S. 123 (1908), p. 1058, *supra*, held the Act inapplicable to an injunction against criminal proceedings not yet instituted.[11] Consider how critical that holding has been to the vindication of federal rights.

Anti–Injunction Act: Fending Off the New Attack on the Relitigation Exception, 72 Neb. L.Rev. 643 (1993). Should one sentence in an opinion that involved only the question of issue preclusion be read as having such significance? Is there any reason to treat claim preclusion differently? Compare the Parsons Steel case, immediately following.

11. A related question: At what stage in the federal lawsuit must the state proceedings begin in order to constitute pending proceedings under § 2283? Dombrowski v. Pfister, 380 U.S. 479, 484 n. 2 (1965), ap-

In Lynch v. Household Finance Corp., 405 U.S. 538 (1972), the Court held (6–3) that a prejudgment garnishment was not a "proceeding" in state court within the scope of § 2283, and hence could be enjoined by a federal court, even though the garnishment might be necessary to obtain satisfaction of any subsequent judgment obtained by the creditor. The opinion emphasized that the garnishment could be instituted by the creditor's attorney, without judicial order, before filing suit (pp. 553–55).

(b) *Termination of Proceedings*. As to the termination of state proceedings, the problem is tied in with the authority of a federal court to enjoin enforcement of a fraudulently obtained state judgment. Cases upholding such injunctions—on the ground that there was an exception to the anti-injunction statute, see Hill v. Martin, 296 U.S. 393, 403 (1935), or that the statute did not apply to completed state proceedings, see Simon v. Southern Ry., 236 U.S. 115 (1915)—were questioned in Toucey v. New York Life Ins. Co., 314 U.S. 118, 136 (1941). After the Court's statement in Atlantic Coast Line that § 2283 "cannot be evaded by * * * prohibiting utilization of the results of a completed state proceeding", the lower courts, although divided, have tended to find such injunctions to be unauthorized. See Wright, Miller, & Cooper, *supra*, § 4223, at 518–19.

(c) *State Court Proceedings Against Different Parties*. In County of Imperial v. Munoz, 449 U.S. 54 (1980), the county obtained a state court injunction against a landowner barring him from selling water from a well on his property for use outside the county. Three persons who had agreements to buy water for use in Mexico then sued the county in federal court, alleging that the state court injunction violated the Commerce Clause. The Supreme Court reversed a grant of preliminary injunctive relief, relying on Atlantic Coast Line in rejecting the view that the state court proceedings had terminated.

The federal plaintiffs sought to avoid § 2283 by relying on Hale v. Bimco Trading, Inc., 306 U.S. 375 (1939). There, after one party obtained a state court order requiring a state agency to enforce a state statute, a different person obtained a federal court injunction barring the agency's enforcement of the statute. The Hale opinion upheld that injunction, rejecting the view that the Anti–Injunction Act in effect bars federal suit by strangers to a state court proceeding who seek to enjoin a statute that was the subject of that proceeding (pp. 377–78). In Munoz, the Court ruled that unless the federal plaintiffs were "strangers," the injunction they sought was barred by § 2283; the case was remanded for an appropriate determination (p. 60). Justice Blackmun, concur-

pears to hold (in the alternative) that when state grand jury indictments are returned after the filing of a federal complaint but before injunctive relief is issued, "no state 'proceedings' are pending within the intendment of § 2283." See Fiss, *Dombrowski*, 86 Yale L.J. 1103, 1108–09 (1977)(criticizing this holding). In Barancik v. Investors Funding Corp., 489 F.2d 933 (7th Cir.1973)(Stevens, J.), the court nonetheless indicated that the mere fact that the federal complaint was filed before the state proceeding was commenced did not preclude application of the Anti–Injunction Act, but went on to hold § 2283

inapplicable on the ground that the state proceeding was not filed until after the motion for federal injunctive relief had been made. *Contra*, Roth v. Bank of the Commonwealth, 583 F.2d 527 (6th Cir.1978), *cert. dismissed*, 442 U.S. 925 (1979).

Cf. Hicks v. Miranda, 422 U.S. 332 (1975), p. 1291, *infra*, holding that the equitable restraint doctrine of Younger v. Harris applies "in full force" when a state prosecution is filed after the federal action but "before any proceedings of substance on the merits" in federal court.

ring in result, was disturbed by the Court's implication that § 2283 does not apply when the state litigation involves different parties.[12]

Wouldn't acceptance of Justice Blackmun's view effectively transform a state court proceeding like that in Munoz into a defendant class action, without any due process safeguards?   See Vestal, *Protecting A Federal Court Judgment*, 42 Tenn.L.Rev. 635, 661–63 (1975).[13]

(3) *Declaratory Judgments.*   When § 2283 bars an injunction, may a federal plaintiff obtain declaratory relief?   This question was once of particular importance in suits challenging state or local official action as unlawful under federal law.   But because those suits fall under § 1983, under Mitchum even injunctions are no longer barred by the Anti-Injunction Act.[14]

An example of a case in which the availability of a declaratory judgment may still be in issue under § 2283 is Thiokol Chem. Corp. v. Burlington Indus., Inc., 448 F.2d 1328 (3d Cir.1971), where the court said it would be proper to award a declaratory judgment as to the validity of a patent even though a parallel state proceeding involving the same patent could not be enjoined. "Normally, the policy that precludes federal injunctions * * * is also applied to prohibit declaratory judgments * * *.   But if the state suit is likely to turn on a question of federal law with which a federal court is likely to be more familiar and experienced than the state court, and if the state court * * * manifests willingness to hold its hand pending federal decision on that question, we think it is neither necessary nor desirable to construe section 2283 as precluding the federal court from issuing a declaratory judgment on the common federal question" (p. 1332).

Assuming that a federal declaratory judgment has res judicata effect,[15] could the federal plaintiff turn a declaratory judgment into an injunction— either in every case, or at least whenever the state court refused to honor it?[16] In Munoz, Paragraph C(2)(c), *supra*, the Court rejected the plaintiffs' argument that (i) § 2283 does bar declaratory relief, (ii) such relief without an injunction would be a nullity, and (iii) therefore an injunction was necessary "in aid of" the federal court's jurisdiction.   While expressing no opinion about the first premise, the Court said that the argument "proves too much, since by its reasoning the exception, and not the rule, would always apply."   449 U.S. at 60 n. 4.   See generally 17 Wright, Miller & Cooper, *supra*, § 4222.

D.   Proposed Revisions of § 2283

(1) *The ALI Study.*   In 1969, the ALI's Study of the Division of Jurisdiction Between State and Federal Courts proposed a revision of § 2283 that specified seven exceptions to the general prohibition.[17]

---

12.   Justices Brennan and Stevens dissented, finding no reason to believe that two of the three plaintiffs were strangers.   Justice Marshall would have dismissed the writ of certiorari as improvidently granted.

13.   Similar questions arise in the application to nonparties of the equitable restraint doctrine of Younger v. Harris.   See pp. 1299–1300, *infra*.

14.   A year before Mitchum, Justice Brennan (joined by Justices White and Marshall) opined that § 2283 does not extend to

declarations.   See Perez v. Ledesma, 401 U.S. 82, 128–29 n. 18 (1971)(separate opinion).

15.   For discussion of this question, see p. 1287, *infra*.

16.   Analogous questions whether restrictions on federal injunctions should also govern federal declaratory judgments have arisen under several other congressional statutes limiting federal court interference with state court proceedings, see Sec. 1(B), *infra*, and in connection with Younger v. Harris and the judge-made doctrine of equitable restraint, see Sec. 2(C), pp. 1256-88, *infra*.

(2) *Professor Currie's Proposal.* Commenting on the ALI Study, Professor Currie argued instead for a statute providing not specific rules but a general standard: "The federal courts shall not enjoin pending or threatened proceedings in state courts unless there is no other effective means of avoiding grave and irreparable harm." See Currie, The Federal Courts and the American Law Institute, Part II, 36 U.Chi.L.Rev. 268, 329 (1969). Under such a standard, how should a court deal, for example, with Atlantic Coast Line? Bear in mind that, in labor disputes, the timing of economic pressure by either side may be critical, and a state court's preliminary injunction may effectively moot the controversy.

Would it be preferable in a case like Atlantic Coast Line to retain a bar on injunctions but to authorize removal to federal court based on a federal defense, at least if the defense is one of federal preemption?

(3) *The Federal Courts Study Committee.* In 1990, a Working Paper prepared for the Federal Courts Study Committee recommended a hybrid approach, under which injunctions could be issued if the case either (i) fell within one of seven specified circumstances,[18] or (ii) satisfied a general standard similar to that proposed Professor Currie.

(4) *Concluding Questions.* Which of the foregoing approaches is most sound? With regard to general jurisdictional provisions like § 2283, what do you conclude about the desirability of courts' exercising considerable interpretive latitude? Of congressional efforts to write detailed and comprehensive statutes?

NOTE ON THE POWER OF STATE COURTS TO ENJOIN FEDERAL COURT ACTIONS

(1) *The Donovan Decision.* No federal statute forbids state courts from enjoining overlapping federal actions.[1] And Donovan v. City of Dallas, 377 U.S. 408 (1964), provided about as strong a case as can be imagined for a state court injunction against federal *in personam* proceedings. There, 46 citizens brought

---

17. See proposed § 1372. The exceptions were largely a restatement of the pre-Mitchum law, except that injunctions could be issued (i) if an Act of Congress authorized (rather than "expressly" authorized) the relief, and (ii) against criminal prosecutions when the governing statute was plainly unconstitutional or its application was plainly discriminatory. The proposal denied authority (whose continued existence the ALI viewed as uncertain) to enjoin allegedly fraudulent state court judgments.

18. The Committee would have extended existing power by generally authorizing an injunction (i) when necessary to ensure the effectiveness of a judgment or consent decree entered by the federal court, but only if relief has first been sought in state court, (ii) when

necessary to ensure the effectiveness of a class action, of multidistrict litigation, or of court-ordered arbitration; or (iii) to prevent duplicative state court proceedings when federal proceedings are far advanced and no special circumstances favor state court litigation. See I Federal Court Study Committee, Working Papers 600–01 (1990).

1. Compare 2 Story, Equity Jurisprudence 186 (1st ed.1836)(asserting that "the State Courts cannot injoin proceedings in the Courts of the United States") with Arnold, *State Court Power to Enjoin Federal Court Proceedings,* 51 Va.L.Rev. 59, 65 (1965)(contending that in 1836 no reported case had so held). On the early precedents, see also Comment, 32 U.Chi.L.Rev. 471 (1965).

a state court class action to enjoin expansion of an airport and issuance of municipal bonds for that purpose. After losing in state court, 27 of the named plaintiffs joined with nearly 100 other persons in bringing a federal court action seeking similar relief. Under Texas law, no bonds could be issued while litigation challenging their validity was pending.

The city not only moved to dismiss the federal action, but also obtained a state court writ of prohibition, based upon a finding that plaintiffs had filed "vexatious and harassing litigation", that barred the federal plaintiffs from prosecuting their federal action and enjoined them from filing further actions contesting the validity of the bonds. On review of the state court decision, the Supreme Court reversed, 6–3, stating (pp. 412–13):

"It may be that a full hearing in an appropriate court would justify a finding that the state-court judgment in favor of Dallas in the first suit barred the issues raised in the second suit * * *. But plaintiffs in the second suit chose to file that case in the federal court. They had a right to do this * * * by reason of congressional enactments passed pursuant to congressional policy. And whether or not a plea of *res judicata* in the second suit would be good is a question for the federal court to decide. While Congress has seen fit to authorize courts of the United States to restrain state-court proceedings in some special circumstances, it has in no way relaxed the old and well-established judicially declared rule that state courts are completely without power to restrain federal-court proceedings in *in personam* actions like the one here."

Justice Harlan's dissent doubted that any of the precedents did or should negate the power of a state court to enjoin vexatious, duplicative federal litigation whose effect was to thwart an unfavorable state court judgment.[2]

(2) *General Atomic v. Felter*. That Donovan's reasoning also bars a state court injunction prohibiting the institution of future litigation was made clear in General Atomic Co. v. Felter, 434 U.S. 12, 18 (1977)(per curiam), which stressed the existence of a federal statutory right to federal court access. Given that § 2283 does not bar injunctions against future litigation, was this extension of Donovan inevitable? Desirable?

(3) *The Decisions Considered*. Why should state power to restrain federal court proceedings be more limited than federal power to restrain state court proceedings? Justice Rehnquist, the lone dissenter in the General Atomic case, suggested that a state court should have injunctive authority against vexatious federal court proceedings of the same scope as a federal court's authority under the Anti–Injunction Act. Compare the ALI Study's proposal to authorize a state court injunction when "necessary to protect against vexatious and harassing relitigation of matters determined by an existing judgment of the State court in a civil action" (proposed § 1373).[3]

---

2. Arnold, note 1, *supra*, argues that although state court injunctions may sometimes be necessary, in Donovan there was no need, as the federal court could have stayed the action before it and also enjoined the filing of any further lawsuits, thus clearing the way for issuance of the bonds. If this is true in Donovan, won't it always be true? See also Comment, note 1, *supra*; Note, 75 Yale L.J. 150 (1965).

3. A later ALI Study of Complex Litigation (1993) proposed statutory reforms that would authorize, in some circumstances, consolidation of related state and federal lawsuits in a single state court, which in turn would possess authority to enjoin state or federal proceedings whose continuation would impair the consolidated action. See p. 1322, *infra*.

How persuasive is the Donovan Court's reliance upon protecting access to federal court, when, as Section 2 of this Chapter shows, the Court, in furtherance of its conceptions of judicial federalism, has fashioned a wide variety of judge-made limitations on the exercise of federal jurisdiction?

(4) *The "Res" Exception.* Donovan and General Atomic are both expressly limited to *in personam* actions; Donovan clearly affirms (377 U.S. at 412) that a state court that has custody of property in *quasi in rem* or *in rem* proceedings may enjoin a federal proceeding when necessary to protect that custody. See p. 1201, note 2, *supra;* Colorado River Water Conservation Dist. v. United States, 424 U.S. 800, 817 (1976), p. 1308, *infra.* Would such an injunction be consistent with Donovan's theory that state courts may not curtail federal jurisdiction? Or should the state courts' *in rem* jurisdiction be deemed to be exclusive, so that there was no federal jurisdiction that could be curtailed? See Hornstein & Nagle, *State Court Power to Enjoin Federal Judicial Proceedings: Donovan v. City of Dallas Revisited*, 60 Wash.U.L.Q. 1 (1982).

SUBSECTION B: OTHER STATUTORY RESTRICTIONS ON FEDERAL COURT JURISDICTION

NOTE ON THREE–JUDGE DISTRICT COURTS, THE JOHNSON ACT OF 1934, AND THE TAX INJUNCTION ACT OF 1937

Introduction

This Note considers three congressional responses to the recognition, in Ex parte Young and Home Telephone, of the federal courts' jurisdiction to enjoin state officials: the three-judge court requirement; the Johnson Act of 1934; and the Tax Injunction Act of 1937.

A. The Rise and Decline of Three–Judge District Courts

(1) *The Reaction to Ex parte Young.* The storm of controversy that followed Ex parte Young centered on the power of a single federal judge to stop the implementation of state legislation in its tracks.[1] Responding to the particular abuses of *ex parte* restraining orders and interlocutory injunctions, Congress in 1910 required that applications for interlocutory injunctions against enforcement of state statutes on constitutional grounds be heard by a district court of three judges (at least one of whom had to be a judge of the court of appeals), with appeal as of right directly to the Supreme Court. 36 Stat. 557.[2] The statute was extended in 1913 to cover interlocutory injunctions against state administrative orders, and in 1925 and 1948 to encompass permanent injunctions.

----

1. See generally Frankfurter, *Distribution of Judicial Power Between United States and State Courts,* 13 Cornell L.Q. 499, 519 (1928); Lilienthal, *The Federal Courts and State Regulation of Public Utilities,* 43 Harv.L.Rev. 379 (1930); Lockwood, Maw, & Rosenberry, *The Use of the Federal Injunction* in Constitutional Litigation, 43 Harv.L.Rev. 426 (1930); Hutcheson, *A Case for Three Judges,* 47 Harv.L.Rev. 795 (1934).

2. This device had previously been used in certain antitrust cases, see 32 Stat. 823 (1903), and in suits challenging ICC orders, see 34 Stat. 584, 592 (1906).

From 1948–76, the provision was codified as 28 U.S.C. § 2281. A parallel provision, enacted in 1937 and codified from 1948–76 as 28 U.S.C. § 2282, required a three-judge court in suits seeking to enjoin federal statutes as unconstitutional.

(2) *Experience With Three–Judge Courts.* The burdens of conducting three-judge court hearings proved to be substantial. Moreover, the mandatory appeals from three-judge courts burdened the Supreme Court; in some years they constituted more than 20% of the argued cases.[3]

Responding to these problems, Congress in 1976 abolished nearly all three-judge courts. It repealed 28 U.S.C. §§ 2281–82, while enacting a new provision (codified as 28 U.S.C. § 2284) that calls for three-judge courts only in suits "challenging the constitutionality of the apportionment of congressional districts or the apportionment of any statewide legislative body," or "when otherwise required by Act of Congress." 90 Stat. 1119 (1976).[4] The latter phrase refers primarily to provisions of the Civil Rights Act of 1964, 42 U.S.C. §§ 1971(g), 2000a–5(b), 2000e–6(b), and the Voting Rights Act of 1965, as amended, *id.* §§ 1973b(a), 1973c, 1973h(c), 1973aa–2, 1973bb(a)(2)—although other statutes occasionally employ the device. See generally Williams, *The New Three–Judge Courts of Reapportionment and Continuing Problems of Three–Judge–Court Procedure*, 65 Geo.L.J. 971 (1977).

The pre–1976 law generated complex and confusing doctrines governing just when three judges were required, and how to obtain appellate review of an order by or relating to a three-judge court. Some of these doctrines remain of interest today in the limited areas in which the requirement survives, and hence are briefly discussed below.

(3) *Actions Subject to the Requirement.* The Supreme Court treated § 2281 "not as a measure of broad social policy to be construed with great liberality, but as an enactment technical in the strict sense of the term and to be applied as such." Phillips v. United States, 312 U.S. 246, 251 (1941).

(a) *Suits Against State Officers Challenging State Statutes.* Because of its limitation to suits against *state* officers seeking to restrain *state* statutes, § 2281 did not apply in suits challenging local ordinances or against local officials (unless they were functioning pursuant to a policy of statewide concern). See, *e.g.*, Moody v. Flowers, 387 U.S. 97, 101–02 (1967).

(b) *The Meaning of "Constitutional" Challenge.* Section 2281 was limited to federal constitutional challenges, and did not extend to a suit alleging that a state statute conflicts with a federal statute and hence is invalid under the Supremacy Clause. See, *e.g.*, Swift & Co. v. Wickham, 382 U.S. 111 (1965); but *cf.* Kesler v. Department of Public Safety, 369 U.S. 153 (1962).

(c) *Pendent Nonconstitutional Claims.* Florida Lime and Avocado Growers, Inc. v. Jacobsen, 362 U.S. 73 (1960), held that a properly convened three-judge court had jurisdiction over related nonconstitutional challenges to a state statute. Despite contrary intimations in the Florida Lime case, the Court later

---

3. S.Rep.No. 201, 94th Cong., 2d Sess. 4 (1976).

4. In 1974, the requirement of three-judge courts in certain antitrust actions, see note 2, *supra,* had been abolished, 88 Stat. 1706, and the following year, the require-

ment in suits to enjoin ICC orders was also repealed, 88 Stat. 1918. Still earlier, a provision for three-judge courts in condemnation suits involving the TVA, see 16 U.S.C. § 831x (1964), had been repealed. 82 Stat. 885 (1968).

held that a single judge could grant injunctive relief on a pendent nonconstitutional challenge. Hagans v. Lavine, 415 U.S. 528, 543–45 (1974).

(d) *Declaratory Judgment Actions.* In Kennedy v. Mendoza–Martinez, 372 U.S. 144 (1963), the Court held that an action for a declaration that a federal statute was unconstitutional was properly heard by a single judge rather than by three judges (under former § 2282). At present, § 2284 refers generally to suits challenging statutes without distinguishing injunctive from declaratory relief.

(e) *Mandatory or Permissive.* Section 2281 required a three-judge court in a proper case whether or not the parties so requested. The present statute says that a three-judge court "shall be convened" in a case meeting the specifications, 28 U.S.C. § 2284(a), but § 2284(b)(1) states that the special court shall be convened "[u]pon the filing of a request for three judges." The legislative history does not explain this apparent discrepancy.

(4) *The Powers of a Single Judge.* The Supreme Court rejected the view that the original three-judge court statute left undisturbed a single judge's power to *deny* injunctive relief, Ex parte Metropolitan Water Co., 220 U.S. 539 (1911), even if the denial was based not on the constitutional merits but rather on the failure to show the need for equitable relief. See Idlewild Bon Voyage Liquor Corp. v. Epstein, 370 U.S. 713 (1962).

In Ex parte Poresky, 290 U.S. 30 (1933), however, the Court held that a single judge may pass on the existence of jurisdiction, and may dismiss a bill on the "jurisdictional" ground, see p. 934, *supra,* that it presents no substantial federal question. Subsequent cases have said such dismissals will be "rare indeed." See, *e.g.,* Hagans v. Lavine, 415 U.S. 528, 537–43 (1974). See also Gonzalez v. Automatic Employees Credit Union, 419 U.S. 90, 100 (1974)(single judge may dismiss for lack of standing). The lower courts have followed these holdings in decisions under the 1976 law. See, *e.g.,* Simkins v. Gressette, 631 F.2d 287 (4th Cir.1980); Ryan v. State Bd. of Elections, 661 F.2d 1130 (7th Cir.1981).[5]

(5) *Review in Three–Judge Cases.* The sole route of appeal of a decision on the merits of a properly convened three-judge court is to the Supreme Court under 28 U.S.C. § 1253, a provision not modified in 1976. Aside from that easy case, the decisions on appellate review under former §§ 2281–82 presented a shifting and complex picture.

In a reversal of prior decisions, the Court held that dispositions by three-judge courts on issues "short of the merits" are appealable to the court of appeals, not directly to the Supreme Court. See, *e.g.,* Gonzalez v. Automatic Employees Credit Union, 419 U.S. 90 (1974)(lack of standing); MTM, Inc. v. Baxley, 420 U.S. 799 (1975)(Younger abstention). However, an injunction based on pendent nonconstitutional grounds is appealable directly to the Supreme Court. Philbrook v. Glodgett, 421 U.S. 707, 712 n. 8 (1975).

The precedents on the proper route of appeal where a single judge erroneously decided an issue that should have been assigned to a three-judge

---

5. In Bailey v. Patterson, 369 U.S. 31, 33 (1962)(per curiam), the Court reached the surprising conclusion that a single judge had power under former § 2281 to award injunctive relief in situations at the other end of the spectrum, where "prior decisions make frivo-lous any claim that a state statute on its face is not unconstitutional." Is that holding valid under the present law, which bars a single district judge from "enter[ing] judgment on the merits" (§ 2284(b)(3))?

court took an uneven course. See generally Currie, *Appellate Review of the Decision Whether or Not to Empanel a Three–Judge Federal Court*, 37 U.Chi. L.Rev. 159 (1969). In the end, the Court ruled that appeal should be taken to the court of appeals, Mengelkoch v. Industrial Welfare Com'n, 393 U.S. 83 (1968), which was empowered to review only whether a three-judge court should have been convened, see Schackman v. Arnebergh, 387 U.S. 427 (1967).

B.   The Johnson Act of 1934

(1) *Origins.* The Johnson Act of 1934, 48 Stat. 775, now 28 U.S.C. § 1342, was the culmination of a quarter century of effort by advocates of state utility regulation. The Act deprives the district courts of jurisdiction to enjoin the operation of, or compliance with, any order of a state administrative agency or local rate-making body fixing rates for a public utility, whenever four conditions are met:

"(1) Jurisdiction is based solely on diversity of citizenship or repugnance of the order to the Federal Constitution; and,

"(2) The order does not interfere with interstate commerce; and,

"(3) The order has been made after reasonable notice and hearing; and,

"(4) A plain, speedy and efficient remedy may be had in the courts of such State."

Notice how this statute overrides traditional doctrines of federal equity. Federal injunctive relief is barred not only, as before, when an adequate remedy is available on the law side of the federal court (which seldom happens in rate cases), but also when there is a sufficient remedy in the state courts (whether in equity, in an action at law, or via statutory review of the order).[6] This approach was followed by Congress three years later in the Tax Injunction Act of 1937, as discussed below, and is also reflected in the judicially-created equitable restraint doctrine, see Younger v. Harris, Subsection 2(C), *infra*.

(2) *The Statutory Criteria.* The Johnson Act comes into play only if all four statutory criteria are satisfied.

(a) *The Basis of Federal Jurisdiction.* The Act does not govern a challenge to a utility rate order as preempted by a federal statute. See, *e.g.*, IBEW v. Public Serv. Com'n, 614 F.2d 206, 211 (9th Cir.1980). Why should federal courts be allowed to hear preemption claims but not, for example, claims that a rate order is unconstitutional because confiscatory? Is it because, as the court suggested (p. 211) in the IBEW case, the former "involves more confining legal analysis and can hardly be thought to raise the worrisome possibilities that economic or political predilections will find their way into a judgment"?

(b) *Interference With Interstate Commerce.* Is the second criterion anything other than the question whether the rate order is constitutional under

---

6. It does not appear to be entirely settled whether the Act is "jurisdictional", applying even if neither party raises it. Compare, *e.g.*, Kentucky West Virginia Gas Co. v. Pennsylvania PUC, 791 F.2d 1111, 1112 n.1 (3d Cir.1986)(in reversing the district court's abstention order and remanding for decision on the merits, court of appeals noted in passing that although defendant had argued below that the Johnson Act barred the exercise of jurisdiction, it had not pursued the objection on appeal) with Kansas–Nebraska Natural Gas Co. v. City of St. Edward, 234 F.2d 436 (8th Cir.1956)(treating Johnson Act as non-waivable question of subject matter jurisdiction).

the dormant Commerce Clause? Why should Commerce Clause challenges, unlike other constitutional challenges, be cognizable in federal court?

(c) *Reasonable Notice and Hearing.* The third criterion—the adequacy of notice and hearing—is governed by federal law, see City of Meridian v. Mississippi Valley Gas Co., 214 F.2d 525 (5th Cir.1954), and is ordinarily quite straightforward. Two courts of appeals have held, however, that no injunction can issue, even absent notice and hearing, if there was no issue of fact and the only disputed question involved the government's power to issue the rate order in question. See General Inv. & Serv. Corp. v. Wichita Water Co., 236 F.2d 464 (10th Cir.1956); City of Monroe v. United Gas Corp., 253 F.2d 377 (5th Cir.1958).

(d) *Plain, Speedy, and Efficient Remedy.* The fourth criterion is the most important, and litigation has centered on the availability of an interlocutory stay in state court. In both Mountain States Power Co. v. Public Serv. Com'n of Montana, 299 U.S. 167 (1936), and Driscoll v. Edison Light & Power Co., 307 U.S. 104 (1939), the Supreme Court assumed that there was no plain, speedy, and efficient remedy absent an opportunity at least to appeal to the discretion of the state court for a stay *pendente lite.* The Court in Mountain States argued (p. 170) that the existence of a remedy "cannot be predicated upon the problematical outcome of future consideration"—thereby suggesting that substantial doubts would be resolved against the ouster of jurisdiction.[7]

(3) *Non-Injunctive Relief.* The lower courts have interpreted the Act as applicable to suits for declaratory relief, as well as those for damages. See Brooks v. Sulphur Springs Valley Elec. Coop., 951 F.2d 1050, 1053–54 & cases cited (9th Cir.1988).

(4) *Exceptions.* The Act has been held not to apply to suits brought by the United States. See, *e.g.,* United States v. PUC of Cal., 141 F.Supp. 168 (N.D.Cal.1956), *aff'd,* 355 U.S. 534 (1958).

C. The Tax Injunction Act of 1937

(1) *Origins.* The Tax Injunction Act of 1937, 50 Stat. 738, now 28 U.S.C. § 1341, states: "The district courts shall not enjoin, suspend or restrain the assessment, levy or collection of any tax under State law where a plain, speedy and efficient remedy may be had in the courts of such State." For purposes of the Act, local taxes have uniformly been held to be collected "under State law." See 17 Wright, Miller & Cooper, Federal Practice & Procedure § 4237 (1988).

Like the Johnson Act, this statute responded to what was viewed as an unwarranted expansion of federal jurisdiction in the wake of Ex parte Young. In addition, the Act was designed to eliminate disparities between those taxpayers who could obtain injunctive relief in federal court—usually out-of-state corporations asserting diversity jurisdiction—and those left to the state courts, which generally required taxpayers to pay first and litigate later. Congress was also concerned that taxpayers, with the aid of a federal injunction, could withhold large sums, thereby disrupting governmental finances.

---

7. If a state court empowered to issue a stay refuses to do so, may a federal district court review the state court's exercise of discretion and assume jurisdiction if it thinks the stay was wrongly denied? See generally Note, 50 Harv.L.Rev. 813 (1937); Comment, 44 Yale L.J. 119 (1934). If so, should the federal court simply grant interim relief pending further state court review, or proceed to hear the entire case? *Cf.* ALI Study, proposed § 1371(d).

S.Rep.No. 1035, 75th Cong., 1st Sess. 1–2 (1937); Rosewell v. LaSalle Nat. Bank, 450 U.S. 503, 522–23 & nn. 28–29, 527 (1981).

The Act, like the Johnson Act, displaces federal equity power when there is an adequate remedy in the state courts. Although the Act's language restricting the district courts' "jurisdiction" was removed in the 1948 statutory revision, the Act continues to be interpreted as "jurisdictional" and hence nonwaivable. See, *e.g.*, Hardwick v. Cuomo, 891 F.2d 1097, 1103–04 (3d Cir.1989).

(2) *"Plain, Speedy and Efficient Remedy"*.

(a) *The Relationship to Equity Practice*. Is "a plain, speedy, and efficient remedy" synonymous with an "adequate" remedy in pre–1937 equity practice? In early decisions under the Act, the Supreme Court often seemed to use the terms interchangeably.[8] But the argument that Congress meant to establish a more stringent standard for federal intervention in tax cases was found persuasive in Rosewell v. LaSalle Nat. Bank, 450 U.S. 503, 524–27 (1981).[9] But *cf.* Fair Assessment in Real Estate Ass'n v. McNary, 454 U.S. 100, 117 n. 8 (1981), Paragraph (4), *infra* (discerning no significant difference between remedies that are "plain, speedy and efficient" under § 1341, and those that are "plain, adequate, and complete" under the equitable restraint doctrine, Sec. 2(C), *infra*).

(b) *The Adequacy of State Remedies*. A taxpayer who has no offensive remedy in state court, but only a defensive one in an action to collect the tax, does have an adequate remedy. Kohn v. Central Distributing Co., Inc., 306 U.S. 531 (1939)(alternative holding). Also adequate, as the Act's purposes make clear, is a refund remedy conditioned upon payment under protest. See, *e.g.*, California v. Grace Brethren Church, 457 U.S. 393, 412 & n. 28 (1982).[10] That a taxpayer has forfeited a remedy that was formerly available does not make state remedies inadequate. See, *e.g.*, Randall v. Franchise Tax Bd., 453 F.2d 381 (9th Cir.1971).

The litigation burdens imposed by state remedies are pertinent to its "efficiency". A state remedy that "would require the filing of over three hundred separate claims in fourteen different counties to protect the single federal claim asserted by [the taxpayer]" was found wanting in Georgia R.R. & Banking Co. v. Redwine, 342 U.S. 299, 303 (1952). In Tully v. Griffin, Inc., 429 U.S. 68, 73 (1976), however, the Court said that a remedy is not inefficient merely because a taxpayer must travel across a state line to obtain it.

The Court first considered whether a remedy was "speedy" in Rosewell v. LaSalle Nat. Bank, *supra*. There, after reviewing statistics showing the serious delays in state and federal urban trial courts, the Court held that a customary delay of two years from payment under protest until receipt of a refund after state court litigation, though regrettable, was not so unusual as to make the remedy not "speedy."

---

8. See, *e.g.,* Great Lakes Dredge & Dock Co. v. Huffman, 319 U.S. 293 (1943), Paragraph (3), *infra;* Township of Hillsborough v. Cromwell, 326 U.S. 620 (1946), Paragraph (2)(b), *infra*.

9. Accord Comment, 93 Harv.L.Rev. 1016, 1021–22 (1980); Note, 59 Harv.L.Rev.

780, 784 (1946); Note, 70 Yale L.J. 636, 643 (1961).

10. What if a taxpayer lacks the funds to pay before litigating? See Wood v. Sargeant, 694 F.2d 1159 (9th Cir.1982)(federal relief barred), & cases cited.

Certainty that the remedy exists is also important. In Township of Hillsborough v. Cromwell, 326 U.S. 620, 625–26 (1946), the Court held that where it was at best "speculative" whether New Jersey followed the federal constitutional rule that a state may not "impos[e] on him against whom the discrimination has been directed the burden of seeking an upward revision of the taxes of other members of the class," federal jurisdiction would lie. In Tully, *supra*, at 76, the Court reiterated that "uncertainty concerning a State's remedy may make it less than 'plain' ", but was convinced after a detailed inquiry into state law that an adequate remedy existed.

More recently, the Court has stated that the "exception" to § 1341 permitting federal injunctions when state remedies are not plain, speedy, and efficient should be narrowly construed. California v. Grace Brethren Church, 457 U.S. 393, 413 (1982).

(c) *The LaSalle National Bank Decision*. In Rosewell v. LaSalle Nat. Bank, *supra*, the Court considered whether a refund remedy without interest was "plain, speedy, and efficient". The taxpayer, alleging a 300% over-assessment, sued in federal court under 42 U.S.C. § 1983 to enjoin collection of the tax as a violation of the Fourteenth Amendment. The Supreme Court, per Brennan, J., held that the suit should have been dismissed, advancing (450 U.S. at 512) a purely "procedural interpretation" of "plain, speedy and efficient". The legislative history of the Act emphasized the need for a taxpayer to have a "full hearing and judicial determination" (pp. 513–14). The state clearly provided that much, and so long as the taxpayer could raise in state court all substantive constitutional objections to the tax (including her claim of a federal right to interest), the federal court was stripped of jurisdiction to enjoin.[11]

Justice Stevens, joined by Justices Stewart, Marshall, and Powell, filed a vigorous dissent. He emphasized the roots of the Act in equity practice, under which the substance of available state remedies was considered. Conceding that the Act was designed to impose new limits on federal equity jurisdiction, he argued that it did so by reversing the prior rule that an adequate state equitable remedy would not defeat federal equity jurisdiction (p. 534 & n. 7). The Court had considered the substance of state remedies in the past, he argued,[12] and "there would be little purpose in denying a federal remedy to a litigant and sending him to state court to pursue a state remedy—albeit a quick and certain one—that provided no relief" (p. 537). On the specific question of interest, he suggested that its provision had been deemed necessary to make state remedies adequate under both early equity cases and post-Act cases (p. 541). Without concluding that a state remedy without interest is always inadequate, he argued that it was in this case, where the assessment was so excessive, and thus federal intervention was proper.

Assume that the Constitution does require payment of interest on the facts of the LaSalle National Bank case. Wasn't the Court right to hold that the state remedies were not inadequate when the taxpayer was free to raise that constitutional claim in state court?

11. The Court left open the question whether the state's failure to reassess the property in question after plaintiff's successful challenges (under state procedures) to prior years' assessments rendered the remedy deficient as to more recent tax years.

12. In the Township of Hillsborough case, Paragraph (2)(b), *supra*, the Court indicated that even had the state's rule been clear, the remedy would have been inadequate.

Suppose, however, that the Illinois Supreme Court had previously made clear its view that the Constitution never requires payment of interest on tax refunds. In that case, should the taxpayer be barred from federal court? The taxpayer could ultimately seek Supreme Court review of an unfavorable state court decision, but only after a futile exercise before state tribunals.[13] On the other hand, permitting the taxpayer to file in federal court would require that court, as part of its jurisdictional inquiry, to determine whether the precedents in the state courts make it futile to seek relief there. Does the existence of unfavorable or even clearly erroneous precedent constitute a denial of a "full and fair opportunity" to litigate under, for example, the doctrine of res judicata?

(3) *Declaratory Judgments.* The Tax Injunction Act was passed three years after the federal declaratory judgment act, now 28 U.S.C. § 2201. In Great Lakes Dredge & Dock Co. v. Huffman, 319 U.S. 293 (1943), the Court avoided the question whether § 1341 itself bars federal declaratory relief concerning state taxes, ruling instead that such relief ought not to be given in a situation in which, under traditional equity practice, the federal court would have stayed its hand because state remedies were adequate.

Nearly 40 years later, in California v. Grace Brethren Church, 457 U.S. 393 (1982), the Court squarely ruled (7–2) that § 1341 bars the issuance of declaratory judgments. The case was brought by religious institutions, seeking (i) to enjoin the Secretary of Labor from conditioning his approval of a state unemployment insurance program on its coverage of the plaintiffs' employees,[14] and (ii) to enjoin the state from collecting both tax information and the tax itself. As support for its holding, the Court relied upon language from the Great Lakes decision that equated the practical effect of a declaration and an injunction, and on the Act's prohibition of actions that not only "enjoin" but also "suspend or restrain" collection of state taxes. To be sure, the Act focuses on injunctions, but only because they were "the principal weapon used by business to delay or avoid state taxes"; Congress was concerned not with the form of relief, but rather with federal court interference with state tax administration (p. 409 n. 22).

(4) *Damage Actions.* A still more expansive limitation on federal court remedies for illegal state taxation was set forth in Fair Assessment in Real Estate Ass'n, Inc. v. McNary, 454 U.S. 100 (1981), decided one year before Grace Brethren Church. The plaintiffs sued under 42 U.S.C. § 1983, alleging that local officials had violated the Fourteenth Amendment by their unequal taxation of real property, and by targeting for reassessment taxpayers who had successfully appealed their assessments the previous year. Plaintiffs sought actual and punitive damages for past overassessments and for expenses incurred in combating them. The Court (per Rehnquist, J.) deemed it unnecessary to decide whether § 1341 barred plaintiffs' action, as "the principle of

---

13. Compare the rules governing exhaustion of remedies in federal habeas corpus, Chap. XI, Sec. 2, pp. 1443-50, *infra*, which do not require a prisoner to resort to state remedies where it would be futile to do so. *Cf.* Fuchs, *Prerequisites to Judicial Review of Administrative Agency Action*, 51 Ind. L.J. 817, 909 (1976)(citing numerous cases for the proposition that administrative reme-

dies need not be exhausted "if the agency, although legally empowered to consider the challenger's contention, has become rigidly precommitted against it").

14. Employers are entitled to a credit of up to 90% on their federal unemployment tax liability for payments to a federally-approved state unemployment compensation plan.

comity bars federal courts from granting damages relief" (p. 107), much as comity had been held to bar declaratory relief in Great Lakes. That principle barred any federal intervention whose practical effect was to suspend collection of state taxes, regardless of the form of federal relief sought (p. 111).[15]

The Court rejected the taxpayers' argument that their § 1983 suit did not disrupt the collection of taxes, as the suit sought damages from individual officers rather than from the county, and those officers would be shielded by a qualified immunity. Rather, the Court stated that in a damages action, the district court must "in effect * * * first enter a declaratory judgment like that barred in Great Lakes," a prospect as disruptive as an equitable remedy (p. 113). Moreover, the Court feared the disruptive effect of the litigation itself: plaintiffs' suit, hauling virtually every county tax official into federal court, with the risk of punitive damages and attorney's fees liability, could have a chilling effect upon the officials' conduct of their duties (pp. 115–16).

Justice Brennan, joined by Justices Marshall, Stevens, and O'Connor, concurred in the judgment. In his view, the principle of comity was associated with the discretion of a court of equity in exercising its extraordinarily intrusive powers, a view that he believed Great Lakes had followed. "There is little room for the 'principle of comity' in actions at law where, apart from matters of administration, judicial discretion is at a minimum" (pp. 121–22). In enacting § 1983, Congress clearly intended federal adjudication of damage actions for constitutional violations by state officials; the precedents prior to passage of the Tax Injunction Act supported federal court power to award damages in actions for wrongful collection of state taxes; and the Act's legislative history expressly suggested that refund actions would be permitted.

Justice Brennan noted, however, that in First Nat. Bank of Greeley v. Board of County Com'rs., 264 U.S. 450, 456 (1924), the Court held that a federal refund action based on an alleged violation of the Fourteenth Amendment was barred by the taxpayers' failure to exhaust state administrative remedies. He acknowledged that in general exhaustion should not be required in § 1983 actions. (On this point, see generally Sec. 2(A), *infra*.) But he argued that whether or not the Tax Injunction Act itself created an exception to the no exhaustion rule under § 1983, congressional policy called for an exhaustion requirement in suits challenging state taxes (p. 137). Thus, "[w]here administrative remedies are a precondition to suit for monetary relief in state court, absent some substantial consideration compelling a contrary result in a particular case, those remedies should be deemed a precondition to suit in federal court as well" (*id.*).

Can McNary be squared with the view of § 1983 articulated in Monroe v. Pape and Mitchum v. Foster? Are the majority's concerns truly implicated in a suit in which the taxpayer has already paid? To the extent they are, are they not also implicated in every § 1983 action? See Bravemen, *Fair Assessment And Federal Jurisdiction in Civil Rights Cases,* 45 U.Pitt.L.Rev. 351 (1984); Note, 46 U.Chi.L.Rev. 736 (1979).[16]

---

15. A footnote stated that "[w]e need not decide in this case whether * * * comity * * * would also bar a claim under § 1983 which requires no scrutiny whatever of state tax assessment practices, such as a facial attack on tax laws colorably claimed to be discriminatory as to race" (p. 107 n. 4).

16. May a federal court entertain a diversity action by a state or local government to collect a tax from an out-of-state taxpayer? If so, suppose the court upholds the taxpayer's defense that the tax violates federal law. Would entry of judgment to that effect "re-

(5) *Suits Between States or Suits Filed by the United States.* In Department of Employment v. United States, 385 U.S. 355 (1966), the Court held that the Act does not bar suits by the United States, or by a federal instrumentality, to enjoin state taxation of the instrumentality's employees, who asserted a federal immunity from the taxation.[17] In Maryland v. Louisiana, 451 U.S. 725, 745 n. 21 (1981), p. 320, *supra,* the Court held the Act (whose text mentions only the district courts) inapplicable to suits between two states in the original jurisdiction of the Supreme Court.

(6) *Claims of Exclusive Federal Jurisdiction.* In E–Systems, Inc. v. Pogue, 929 F.2d 1100 (5th Cir.1991), the sponsors of benefit plans sought federal declaratory and injunctive relief against a state tax alleged to be preempted by ERISA— which confers exclusive federal jurisdiction over suits claiming that state laws are preempted. The Fifth Circuit reasoned that the state courts therefore lack jurisdiction to decide the dispositive preemption issue, and hence ERISA must be viewed as an exception to the Tax Injunction Act. *Contra,* Ashton v. Cory, 780 F.2d 816 (9th Cir.1986).

Whether or not ERISA should be interpreted as creating an exception to the Tax Injunction Act—a question reserved in Franchise Tax Board v. Construction Laborers Vacation Trust, 463 U.S. 1, 20 n. 21 (1983), Chap. VIII, Sec. 3, p. 943, *supra*—wasn't the Fifth Circuit wrong to assume that ERISA necessarily precludes state courts from considering defenses, based on ERISA preemption, to enforcement actions under state law? Indeed, state courts routinely decide antitrust or patent defenses to contract actions, to take just two examples, even though there is exclusive federal jurisdiction for claims arising under the antitrust and patent laws.

(7) *Section 1983 Actions in State Courts.* By its terms, the Tax Injunction Act governs only the federal district courts. Is a state court obliged to entertain a suit under 42 U.S.C. § 1983 that asserts that a state tax violates federal law— and, if the tax is found invalid, to provide injunctive or declaratory relief of the sort ordinarily available in § 1983 actions?[18] The issue has practical importance no matter how complete the state law remedies, for relief under § 1983 carries with it the right to attorney's fees under 42 U.S.C. § 1988.

In National Private Truck Council, Inc. v. Oklahoma Tax Comm'n, 115 S.Ct. 2351 (1995), the state court had ordered tax refunds as authorized by state law, but had refused to award an injunction or attorney's fees under § 1983. A unanimous Supreme Court (per Thomas, J.) affirmed, declaring that the Tax Injunction Act was but "one manifestation of" a longstanding "aversion to federal interference with state tax administration" that dated back to

---

strain or suspend" collection of the tax in violation of § 1341? Does the answer depend on whether non-parties could avail themselves of the judgment? Does the government's initiation of suit constructively waive any objection under § 1341? *Cf.* Chap. IX, Sec. 1(B), pp. 1003–06, *supra.* See generally Diginet, Inc. v. Western Union ATS, Inc., 845 F.Supp. 1237, 1241–42 & cases cited (N.D.Ill. 1994).

17. See also Moe v. Confederated Salish and Kootenai Tribes, 425 U.S. 463 (1976), holding that § 1341 does not bar a suit by an Indian tribe that could have been brought by the United States on behalf of the tribe.

18. The issue had arisen in Spencer v. South Carolina Tax Com'n, 281 S.C. 492, 316 S.E.2d 386 (1984), where the state court's decision had been affirmed by an equally divided court (471 U.S. 82 (1985)); had been noted but not resolved in Arkansas Writers' Project, Inc. v. Ragland, 481 U.S. 221, 234 n. 7 (1987); and thereafter had given rise to a conflict among state courts. See generally Note, 95 Yale L.J. 414 (1985); Note, 103 Harv.L.Rev. 1888, 1908 (1990).

the time of § 1983's enactment during Reconstruction (p. 2354). Among other examples of that aversion, the Court noted the "particular relevance" of the McNary decision, Paragraph (4), *supra*, which it read as holding "that because of principles of comity and federalism, Congress never authorized federal courts to entertain damages actions under § 1983 against state taxes when state law furnishes an adequate remedy" (pp. 2354–55). Assuming without deciding that state courts generally must hear § 1983 suits, the Court ruled that "the background presumption that federal law generally will not interfere with administration of state taxes leads us to conclude that Congress did not authorize injunctive or declaratory relief under § 1983 in state tax cases when there is an adequate [state] remedy at law" (p. 2355).[12] Because no relief was available under § 1983, there was no basis for an award of attorney's fees under § 1988.[13]

If the background presumption that federal substantive law should not be interpreted as authorizing interference with state taxes is as clear and long-standing as Justice Thomas asserts, why was enactment of the Tax Injunction Act necessary? Solely to deal with diversity actions?

SECTION 2. JUDICIALLY-DEVELOPED LIMITATIONS ON FEDERAL COURT JURISDICTION: DOCTRINES OF EQUITY, COMITY, AND FEDERALISM

INTRODUCTORY NOTE

The central issue of this Section is whether, and in what circumstances, it is appropriate for federal courts to abstain from entertaining actions that appear to fall within the literal terms of congressional grants of jurisdiction. (That question has previously been raised by the decisions in McNary and in Great Lakes Dredge & Dock, pp. 1219–20, *supra,* notably in Justice Brennan's separate opinion in the former case). These materials consider the courts' response to continuing and conflicting pressures, including, on the one hand, the desire to avoid premature constitutional determinations, to defer to state tribunals on questions of state law, to avoid duplicative proceedings, and to

---

12. The Court added (p. 2357 n. 6): "there may be extraordinary circumstances under which injunctive or declaratory relief is available even when a legal remedy exists. For example, if the 'enforcement of the tax would lead to a multiplicity of suits, or produce irreparable injury, [or] throw a cloud upon the title,' equity might be invoked. Dows v. City of Chicago, 78 U.S. 108, 11 Wall. 108, 110 (1871)."

13. The Court did not discuss whether, notwithstanding the adequacy of state remedies, relief other than an injunction or declaratory relief against state taxation was ever available under § 1983, simply noting that

§ 1983 would not extend to any claim for a tax refund against the state (p. 2355 n. 5, citing Will v. Michigan Dep't of State Police, 491 U.S. 58 (1989)(holding that neither a state nor a state official may be sued under § 1983 for retrospective relief)). By contrast, local governments may be sued for retrospective relief with respect to conduct that represents official policy or custom. See Chap. IX, Sec. 2(C), pp. 1126–31, *supra.* Although the McNary decision would ordinarily bar a *federal court* from awarding a tax refund against a local government, would a state court be obliged to entertain a § 1983 action seeking such relief—and, if so, to award attorney's fees to a prevailing plaintiff?

interfere as little as possible with state processes; and, on the other hand, the desire to uphold a litigant's choice of a federal forum, to respect the policies of the jurisdictional grants, and to vindicate federal rights without undue delay.

This Section divides the judicially developed doctrines limiting district court jurisdiction into five groupings: (1) the requirement of exhaustion of state administrative and other nonjudicial remedies; (2) the doctrine derived from the Pullman case, often referred to as "Pullman abstention", and related abstention doctrines; (3) the doctrine, derived from equity practice and frequently labeled "Younger abstention", restricting the availability of federal equitable relief from pending state enforcement actions and particularly from pending criminal prosecutions; (4) the doctrine calling for a federal court to stay its hand in exceptional circumstances because of the pendency of a parallel proceeding in state court; and (5) the rules restricting the exercise of federal jurisdiction in probate and domestic relations matters.

The primary though not exclusive focus of the materials that follow is on federal actions against state officials.

SUBSECTION A: EXHAUSTION OF STATE NONJUDICIAL REMEDIES

NOTE ON EXHAUSTION OF STATE NONJUDICIAL REMEDIES

(1) *The Prentis Case.* In the same year that Ex parte Young was decided, the Supreme Court reviewed the decree of a federal circuit court enjoining enforcement of a rate order of the Virginia State Corporation Commission. In Prentis v. Atlantic Coast Line Co., 211 U.S. 210 (1908), the appellants argued that under state law the commission had the characteristics and powers of a court and that the Anti–Injunction Act, now 28 U.S.C. § 2283, forbade a federal injunction. The Court, speaking through Justice Holmes, held that, whatever the status of the commission in other types of proceedings, "[t]he establishment of a rate is the making of a rule for the future, and therefore is an act legislative not judicial in kind" (p. 226), to which the Anti–Injunction Act did not apply.

The Court noted, however, that the statute provided an appeal as of right to the Supreme Court of Appeals of Virginia, upon the record made in the commission, and that "that court, if it reverses what has been done, is to substitute such order as in its opinion the commission should have made" (p. 224). *Cf.* Federal Radio Comm'n v. General Elec. Co., 281 U.S. 464 (1930). In ruling that the railroads should have taken such an appeal before resorting to the federal court, Justice Holmes said (pp. 229–30):

"* * * Considerations of comity and convenience have led this court ordinarily to decline to interfere by habeas corpus where the petitioner had open to him a writ of error to a higher court of a State, in cases where there was no merely logical reason for refusing the writ. The question is whether somewhat similar considerations ought not to have some weight here.

"We admit at once that they have not the same weight in this case. The question to be decided, we repeat, is legislative, whether a certain rule shall be made. * * * We should hesitate to say, as a general rule, that a right to resort to the courts could be made always to depend upon keeping a previous watch upon the bodies that make laws, and using every effort and all the machinery available to prevent unconstitutional laws from being passed. * * *

"But this case hardly can be disposed of on purely general principles. The question that we are considering may be termed a question of equitable fitness or propriety, and must be answered on the particular facts. * * * The railroads went into evidence before the commission. They very well might have taken the matter before the Supreme Court of Appeals. No new evidence and no great additional expense would have been involved.

"The State of Virginia has endeavored to impose the highest safeguards possible upon the exercise of the great power given to the State Corporation Commission, not only by the character of the members of that commission, but by making its decisions dependent upon the assent of the same historic body that is entrusted with the preservation of the most valued constitutional rights, if the railroads see fit to appeal. It seems to us only a just recognition of the solicitude with which their rights have been guarded, that they should make sure that the State in its final legislative action would not respect what they think their rights to be, before resorting to the courts of the United States.

"If the rate should be affirmed by the Supreme Court of Appeals and the railroads still should regard it as confiscatory, it will be understood from what we have said that they will be at liberty then to renew their application to the Circuit Court, without fear of being met by a plea of res judicata. It will not be necessary to wait for a prosecution by the commission."[1]

(2) *The Legislative/Judicial Distinction.* The limits of the Prentis doctrine were marked, and its rationale made unmistakable, in Bacon v. Rutland R.R., 232 U.S. 134 (1914). There, in a suit to enjoin the Public Service Commission of Vermont from enforcing an order concerning a passenger station, the defendants invoked the Prentis case in objecting that the railroad had failed to utilize its statutory right of appeal to the state supreme court. But the Court, speaking again through Justice Holmes, held that at the judicial stage the railroads had a right to resort to the courts of the United States at once. Finding that no legislative powers had been conferred upon the Supreme Court of Vermont, it sustained the jurisdiction.

Following Prentis, whether a state court's role is characterized as legislative or judicial determines not only whether a litigant must take an appeal in the state courts before mounting a federal challenge, but also the proper forum in which to seek federal review. If the state court acts in a legislative capacity, a federal district court will have jurisdiction of a timely challenge, and the "administrative" findings will lack res judicata effect. Does it also follow from Prentis that the losing party in a case in which the highest state court acts legislatively cannot go directly to the Supreme Court of the United States?

1. Accord, Porter v. Investors' Syndicate, 286 U.S. 461 (1932), 287 U.S. 346 (1932), holding that a legislative remedy in a state district court against an administrative order under a state blue sky law must be exhausted before resort to a federal court.

But *cf.* Pacific Tel. & Tel. Co. v. Kuykendall, 265 U.S. 196, 204–05 (1924), where the utility alleged that existing rates were confiscatory and that no stay was available: "Under such circumstances comity yields to constitutional right, and the fact that the procedure on appeal in the legislative fixing of rates has not been concluded will not prevent a federal court of equity from suspending the daily confiscation, if it finds the case to justify it."

Would the Supreme Court in such a case be exercising appellate jurisdiction?[2] If, on the other hand, the state court's decision is "judicial", the Supreme Court has jurisdiction and the district courts do not, see pp. 1500–04, *infra,* discussing the "Rooker–Feldman" doctrine.

Is the characterization of state proceedings as legislative or judicial governed by state or federal law? In Oklahoma Packing Co. v. Oklahoma Gas & Elec. Co., 309 U.S. 4 (1940), the Supreme Court, after first upholding a plea of res judicata, withdrew its former opinion and overruled the plea in light of an intervening state court opinion characterizing the review as legislative.

(3) *The Traditional Requirement to Exhaust Administrative Remedies.* Analogous to the Prentis doctrine is the traditional, judicially developed principle that a federal court will not entertain an action against a state officer if the plaintiff has failed to exhaust remedies before a state administrative agency. As explained by courts and commentators, the exhaustion requirement is calculated to avoid premature interruption of agency procedures, to permit proper factual development, to take advantage of the agency's expertise, to give the agency the chance to correct its own errors, and to promote efficiency in both the judicial and administrative processes. See generally Fuchs, *Prerequisites to Judicial Review of Administrative Agency Action,* 51 Ind.L.J. 817, 859–911 (1976). At least until the developments discussed in Paragraphs (4) and (7), *infra,* it had become the norm that prospective plaintiffs must exhaust (non-judicial) administrative remedies as a precondition to raising federal challenges.[3] *See, e.g.,* Pacific Live Stock Co. v. Lewis, 241 U.S. 440 (1916); First Nat. Bank of Greeley v. Board of County Com'rs., 264 U.S. 450 (1924); Illinois Commerce Com'n v. Thomson, 318 U.S. 675, 686 (1943).

Regardless of the strength of the policy arguments supporting an exhaustion requirement, is it legitimate for courts to decline to exercise jurisdiction of cases within their jurisdictional grants? Should federal courts be viewed as possessing an inherent discretion to develop principled constraints on their exercise of jurisdiction? On the timing of their exercise of jurisdiction? For discussion of these and related issues, see pp. 1234–35 *infra.*

(4) *Inapplicability of Exhaustion Requirements to § 1983 Actions.* In Patsy v. Board of Regents of the State of Florida, 457 U.S. 496 (1982), the Supreme Court ruled that exhaustion of state administrative remedies is not required in actions under 42 U.S.C. § 1983.

2. See generally Chap. V, Sec. 3, *supra.* In Corporation Comm'n of Oklahoma v. Cary, 296 U.S. 452 (1935), a public utility, after having taken an unsuccessful appeal to the state supreme court (which, it was agreed on all sides, had power to act legislatively), obtained a federal court injunction against the commission's order. On appeal to the Supreme Court, the commission argued that the utility could have obtained Supreme Court review of the state court's decision, and its failure to do so barred the action for an injunction. But the Court ignored that contention, instead treating the case as if the

only issue was whether there was jurisdiction in equity in any state court to review judicially the decision of the state's highest court. Finding the remedy uncertain, the Court held that the Johnson Act, discussed p. 1215, *supra,* did not bar the federal injunction.

3. The exhaustion doctrine has always been subject to important limits. For example, exhaustion has not generally been required when undue delay would result, when the state remedy is inadequate, or when exhaustion would be futile. See generally 17 Wright, Miller & Cooper, Federal Practice & Procedure § 4233 (1988 & Supp.1995).

(a) *The Patsy Case.* Alleging that her employer, a state university, had discriminated against her on the basis of race and gender, Patsy filed a civil rights action in federal district court. The district court dismissed, based on Patsy's failure to exhaust administrative remedies. The en banc court of appeals reversed, ruling that a § 1983 plaintiff was required to exhaust administrative remedies when (but only when): (1) an orderly system of review is provided by statute or agency rule; (2) the agency can grant relief more or less commensurate with the claim; (3) relief is available without undue delay; (4) the procedures are fair, not burdensome, and are not used to harass those with legitimate claims; and (5) interim relief is available in appropriate cases. It remanded for the district court to determine whether exhaustion was appropriate under those standards.

The Supreme Court, per Justice Marshall, reversed. The Court noted that it had ruled in McNeese v. Board of Education, 373 U.S. 668 (1963), that exhaustion should not be required in § 1983 actions, and had adhered to that view in seven subsequent cases. That position was also supported by the legislative history of § 1 of the Civil Rights of 1871, the precursor to § 1983, whose "very purpose * * * was to interpose the federal courts between the States and the people, as guardians of the people's federal rights * * *" (p. 503, quoting Mitchum v. Foster, Sec. 1(A), *supra*). Though Congress in 1871 did not consider the question of exhaustion, the Court believed that the "tenor of the debates" did not support an exhaustion requirement (p. 502). The Court based this conclusion on three recurring themes in the legislative history: Congress' assignment "to the federal courts [of] a paramount role in protecting constitutional rights" (p. 503); Congress' belief "that the state authorities had been unable or unwilling to protect the constitutional rights of individuals or to punish those who violated those rights" (p. 505); and "the fact that many legislators interpreted the bill to provide dual or concurrent forums in the state and federal system, enabling the plaintiff to choose the forum in which to seek relief" (p. 506).

Justice Marshall also found support for the Court's holding in a 1980 amendment to the Civil Rights of Institutionalized Persons Act, 42 U.S.C. § 1997 *et seq.* That amendment requires adult prisoners, before seeking relief under § 1983, to exhaust administrative remedies that satisfy statutorily specified conditions. See Paragraph (5)(b), *infra*. In the Court's view, "[t]his detailed scheme is inconsistent with discretion to impose, on an ad hoc basis, a judicially developed exhaustion rule in other cases" (p. 511).

Justice Powell, joined by Chief Justice Burger, dissented. The court of appeals' exhaustion requirement was based, he said, on "sound considerations. It does not defeat federal-court jurisdiction, it merely defers it. It permits the States to correct violations through their own procedures, and it encourages the establishment of such procedures. It is consistent with the principles of comity that apply whenever federal courts are asked to review state action or supersede state proceedings" (pp. 532–33). A rule requiring exhaustion also conserves federal court resources, Justice Powell argued, a matter particularly important given the rapid growth of § 1983 litigation.

In Justice Powell's view, many of the Court's past decisions suggesting that exhaustion was not required in a § 1983 action "can be explained as applications of traditional exceptions to the exhaustion requirement. Other decisions speak to the question in an offhand and conclusory fashion without full briefing and argument" (p. 533). Nor did § 1997e support the Court's decision: that provision focused on the particular question of prisoners' suits, and simply did not bear on the general question of exhaustion in § 1983 actions.[4]

(b) *The Soundness of the Decision.*   Did the Court in Patsy confuse the question of exhaustion of state remedies in general (which Monroe v. Pape, 365 U.S. 167 (1961), p. 1111, *supra,* held is not required) with the question of exhaustion of distinctively administrative remedies?   In light of the considerable benefits associated with exhaustion, did the Court's opinion sweep too broadly?   Some state administrative regimes were created in response to federal court decisions holding that the failure to provide such administrative procedures denied due process.   Is it ironic that Patsy authorizes litigants to bypass these regimes altogether?

On the other hand, wouldn't an exhaustion requirement have been difficult to square with the rationale of Monroe v. Pape, as well as the results in a number of prior cases?   Consider, too, Justice Powell's assertion that exhaustion does not heavily burden the federal plaintiff; "[i]t does not defeat federal-court jurisdiction, it merely defers it."   Compare University of Tennessee v. Elliott, 478 U.S. 788 (1986), p. 1498, *infra,* holding that when a state administrative agency acting in a judicial capacity makes factual findings after the parties have had a fair opportunity to litigate, a federal court in a § 1983 action must give those findings the same preclusive effect that they would have in the state's courts.   On the facts of Patsy, a rule requiring exhaustion might not have resulted in preclusion, but that would not be true under many other administrative regimes governed by the rule of Patsy.   In cases in which administrative decisions would have preclusive effect in federal litigation, wouldn't a contrary decision have been in the teeth of Monroe v. Pape?

Was there a workable middle course?   For example, should the federal district courts have been required to determine on a case-by-case basis whether exhaustion should be required, using criteria such as those set forth by the court of appeals in Patsy?   See Comment, 41 U.Chi.L.Rev. 537 (1974).   Suppose that Patsy and the university had differed about the adequacy of available administrative remedies.   Would it be unreasonably burdensome to require litigation of issues such as these as a threshold matter?

(5) *Exceptions to the Patsy Rule.*   Patsy's general rule that exhaustion of administrative remedies is not required in § 1983 actions is subject to important limitations.

(a) *Plain, Adequate, and Complete Tax Remedies.*   The ruling in Fair Assessment in Real Estate Ass'n v. McNary, 454 U.S. 100 (1981), p. 1219, *supra,* interprets principles of comity to require federal courts to decline jurisdiction in suits seeking a damages remedy for state taxation whenever the state provides a plain, adequate, and complete remedy.   Though the four concurring Justices would not have required the federal court to decline jurisdiction where state *judicial* remedies were available, they agreed that when the state courts would require exhaustion of *administrative* remedies

---

4.   Justice O'Connor wrote a concurring opinion, in which Justice Rehnquist joined, endorsing an exhaustion requirement as sound policy, but noting that, "for the reasons set forth in the Court's opinion," that view had already been rejected by prior decisions.   Justice White concurred in part, expressing his disagreement with the Court's view that Congress' enactment of § 1997e supported the Court's decision.

before entertaining a challenge to state taxes in which monetary relief was sought, a federal court entertaining a § 1983 action should ordinarily do likewise.[5]

(b) *Actions by Prisoners.* In § 1983 actions filed by prisoners, 42 U.S.C. § 1997e authorizes a court to continue a case for a period not to exceed 180 days if: (i) it believes exhaustion of administrative remedies would be "appropriate and in the interests of justice," *id.* § 1997e(a)(1), and (ii) either the Attorney General or the court has determined that there exist prison grievance procedures that are "in substantial compliance" with federal standards established by regulation by the Attorney General,[6] or, following an amendment enacted in 1995, "are otherwise fair and effective".[7]

Suppose that, when a case is continued to permit exhaustion, the prisoner fails to file a grievance within the time or in the manner specified by the administrative scheme. May the prisoner then be barred from filing a § 1983 action? See Lewis v. Meyer, 815 F.2d 43, 45 (7th Cir.1987), and Rocky v. Vittorie, 813 F.2d 734, 736 (5th Cir.1987), arguing that the sanction of dismissal is necessary to ensure that prisoners actually resort to the scheme.[8]

(c) *Administrative Remedies, the Merits, and Ripeness.* Although not "exceptions" to Patsy in the technical sense, substantive doctrines and the "finality" requirement may sometimes compel plaintiffs to complete administrative processes prior to bringing a § 1983 action.

Under Parratt v. Taylor, p. 1149, *supra,* adequate postdeprivation *judicial* remedies can sometimes provide all the process that is constitutionally due and thus eliminate the basis for a suit under the Due Process Clause. Taking a further step, the lower courts have held that postdeprivation *administrative* remedies may have the same effect. See p. 1154, note 7.

The demand for "finality" in takings cases may also compel a resort to administrative remedies. See, *e.g.,* Williamson County Regional Planning Com'n v. Hamilton Bank of Johnson City, 473 U.S. 172 (1985)(finding a Takings Clause challenge to the action of a zoning board premature because the plaintiff had not sought a variance from the agency). The Court distinguished the finality and exhaustion doctrines, as follows: "[T]he finality requirement is concerned with whether the initial decision-maker has arrived at a definitive position on the issue that inflicts an actual, concrete injury; the exhaustion requirement generally refers to administrative * * * procedures by which an

---

5. National Private Truck Council, Inc. v. Oklahoma Tax Comm'n, 115 S.Ct. 2351 (1995), builds on Fair Assessment by holding that § 1983 does not authorize equitable or injunctive relief against state taxes, either in federal or state court, when state law provides an adequate legal remedy.

6. Detailed regulations have been issued and are codified at 28 C.F.R. §§ 40.1–40.22.

7. The amendment followed the recommendation of the Report of the Federal Courts Study Committee (1990), which, noting that "few states have sought and obtained certification under this statute," perhaps because of delays by the Justice Department or the onerousness of the min-

imum standards, urged that § 1997 be revised to eliminate specific federal standards for state institutional remedies and to require exhaustion if either the court or the Attorney General found the state's remedies to be "fair and effective" (pp. 48–51).

8. In the Rocky case, the court ruled that dismissal would be inappropriate where the prisoner had tried in good faith to comply with the administrative requirements. In the absence of similar good-faith efforts, subsequent Fifth Circuit decisions have followed the course outlined in Rocky and ordered dismissal to ensure utilization of state administrative procedures. See, *e.g.,* Gartrell v. Gaylor, 981 F.2d 254, 258 (5th Cir.1993).

injured party may seek review of an adverse decision and obtain a remedy if the decision is found to be unlawful or otherwise inappropriate. Patsy concerned the latter, not the former" (p. 193).[9]

(6) *Section 1983 Actions in State Court.* Does Patsy's rule of non-exhaustion apply to § 1983 suits filed in the state courts? Although the state courts were initially divided, the issue appears to have been resolved in Felder v. Casey, 487 U.S. 131 (1988), also discussed at pp. 475, 487, *supra.* There, the Wisconsin Supreme Court had dismissed a state court § 1983 suit because of plaintiff's noncompliance with the state's notice-of-claim statute, which required, as a condition of bringing suit in state court, provision of written notice, within 120 days of the injury, of any claim against state or local governments (or their officials). The Supreme Court reversed, reasoning that "[g]iven the evil at which the federal civil rights legislation was aimed, there is simply no reason to suppose that Congress meant 'to provide these individuals immediate access to the federal courts notwithstanding any provision of state law to the contrary,' yet contemplated that those who sought to vindicate their federal rights in state courts could be required to seek redress in the first instance from the very state officials whose hostility to those rights precipitated their injuries" (p. 147, quoting Patsy, 457 U.S. at 504). The "dominant characteristic" of a § 1983 action—that it is "judicially enforceable *in the first instance*"—holds as true in state court as in federal court suits (p. 148). Dissenting, Justice O'Connor (joined by Chief Justice Rehnquist) distinguished Patsy as resting on legislative history indicating that § 1983 was meant to provide access to a *federal* forum.

(7) *Exhaustion Requirements in Challenges to Federal Administrative Action.* The requirement that plaintiffs exhaust administrative remedies traditionally applied to challenges to federal as well as state administrative action. But in Darby v. Cisneros, 113 S.Ct. 2539 (1993), the Supreme Court held unanimously that when judicial review is authorized by the Administrative Procedure Act, a litigant who has exhausted all administrative remedies expressly prescribed by the governing regulatory statute or by agency rules has a right, under § 10(c) of the APA, to judicial review. In the Court's view, § 10(c) modified the judge-made exhaustion doctrine in cases governed by the APA and precludes the federal courts from requiring a litigant to exhaust *optional* federal administrative appeals before seeking judicial review. The Court noted that "the exhaustion doctrine continues to apply as a matter of judicial discretion in cases not governed by the APA" (p. 2548).[10] For sharply critical comment on Darby, see

---

9. In an alternate holding, the Court ruled that the claim was not ripe because plaintiff had not availed itself of state procedures for obtaining compensation (p. 194).

10. For a recent case illustrating the application of traditional exceptions to the exhaustion doctrine, see McCarthy v. Madigan, 503 U.S. 140 (1992), a case decided prior to Darby but not governed by the APA, in which the Court held that a prisoner bringing a Bivens action against federal prison officials need not exhaust available administrative remedies. The Court stated that its precedents recognized three broad sets of circumstance that weigh heavily against exhaustion: (i) when exhaustion may occasion undue prejudice to subsequent court action; (ii) when

the agency cannot provide effective relief; and (iii) when the agency is biased. The Court found the first two of these factors implicated because the Federal Bureau of Prisons' grievance procedure provided short deadlines, which created a trap for unwary inmates, and because the agency lacked the authority to award monetary relief.

Even in a suit not governed by the APA, might the availability of adequate state administrative remedies constitute a barrier to federal *equitable* relief? See Farmer v. Brennan, 114 S.Ct. 1970, 1984 (1994) (suggesting that a federal court of equity in a constitutional tort action may require a prisoner plaintiff to have pursued "adequate prison procedures").

Schwartz, *Timing of Judicial Review—A Survey of Recent Cases,* 8 Ad.L.J. 261, 285–88 (1994).

Note the partial symmetry of Darby with the Supreme Court's earlier decision in Patsy v. Board of Regents, Paragraph (4), *supra,* holding judge-made exhaustion rules displaced in cases brought under § 1983. Is the case that exhaustion requirements are statutorily precluded stronger or weaker in Darby than it was in Patsy? Is the Court growing more skeptical of the benefits of requiring exhaustion of administrative remedies? More reluctant to craft or apply jurisdiction-limiting doctrines not explicitly authorized by Congress?

———

SUBSECTION B: ABSTENTION: PULLMAN AND RELATED DOCTRINES

———

Railroad Commission of Texas v. Pullman Co.

312 U.S. 496, 61 S.Ct. 643, 85 L.Ed. 971 (1941).
Appeal from the United States District Court for the Western District of Texas.

■ MR. JUSTICE FRANKFURTER delivered the opinion of the Court.

In those sections of Texas where the local passenger traffic is slight, trains carry but one sleeping car. These trains, unlike trains having two or more sleepers, are without a Pullman conductor; the sleeper is in charge of a porter who is subject to the train conductor's control. As is well known, porters on Pullmans are colored and conductors are white. Addressing itself to this situation, the Texas Railroad Commission after due hearing ordered that "no sleeping car shall be operated on any line of railroad in the State of Texas * * * unless such cars are continuously in the charge of an employee * * * having the rank and position of Pullman conductor". Thereupon, the Pullman Company and the railroads affected brought this action in a federal district court to enjoin the Commission's order. Pullman porters were permitted to intervene as complainants, and Pullman conductors entered the litigation in support of the order. Three judges having been convened, the court enjoined enforcement of the order. From this decree, the case came here directly.

The Pullman Company and the railroads assailed the order as unauthorized by Texas law as well as violative of the Equal Protection, the Due Process and the Commerce Clauses of the Constitution. The intervening porters adopted these objections but mainly objected to the order as a discrimination against Negroes in violation of the Fourteenth Amendment.

The complaint of the Pullman porters undoubtedly tendered a substantial constitutional issue. It is more than substantial. It touches a sensitive area of social policy upon which the federal courts ought not to enter unless no alternative to its adjudication is open. Such constitutional adjudication plainly can be avoided if a definitive ruling on the state issue would terminate the controversy. It is therefore our duty to turn to a consideration of questions under Texas law.

The Commission found justification for its order in a Texas statute * * *.[1] It is common ground that if the order is within the Commission's authority its

———

1. Vernon's Anno. Texas Civil Statutes, Article 6445:

subject matter must be included in the Commission's power to prevent "unjust discrimination * * * and to prevent any and all other abuses" in the conduct of railroads. Whether arrangements pertaining to the staffs of Pullman cars are covered by the Texas concept of "discrimination" is far from clear. What practices of the railroads may be deemed to be "abuses" subject to the Commission's correction is equally doubtful. Reading the Texas statutes and the Texas decisions as outsiders without special competence in Texas law, we would have little confidence in our independent judgment regarding the application of that law to the present situation. The lower court did deny that the Texas statutes sustained the Commission's assertion of power. And this represents the view of an able and experienced circuit judge of the circuit which includes Texas and of two capable district judges trained in Texas law. Had we or they no choice in the matter but to decide what is the law of the state, we should hesitate long before rejecting their forecast of Texas law. But no matter how seasoned the judgment of the district court may be, it cannot escape being a forecast rather than a determination. The last word on the meaning of Article 6445 of the Texas Civil Statutes, and therefore the last word on the statutory authority of the Railroad Commission in this case, belongs neither to us nor to the district court but to the supreme court of Texas. In this situation a federal court of equity is asked to decide an issue by making a tentative answer which may be displaced tomorrow by a state adjudication. The reign of law is hardly promoted if an unnecessary ruling of a federal court is thus supplanted by a controlling decision of a state court. The resources of equity are equal to an adjustment that will avoid the waste of a tentative decision as well as the friction of a premature constitutional adjudication.

An appeal to the chancellor, as we had occasion to recall only the other day, is an appeal to the "exercise of the sound discretion, which guides the determination of courts of equity". Beal v. Missouri Pacific R.R., 312 U.S. 45, decided January 20, 1941. The history of equity jurisdiction is the history of regard for public consequences in employing the extraordinary remedy of the injunction. There have been as many and as variegated applications of this simple principle as the situations that have brought it into play. Few public interests have a higher claim upon the discretion of a federal chancellor than the avoidance of needless friction with state policies, whether the policy relates to the enforcement of the criminal law, Fenner v. Boykin, 271 U.S. 240; Spielman Motor Co. v. Dodge, 295 U.S. 89; or the administration of a specialized scheme for liquidating embarrassed business enterprises, Pennsylvania v. Williams, 294 U.S. 176; or the final authority of a state court to interpret doubtful regulatory laws of the state, Gilchrist v. Interborough Co.,

"Power and authority are hereby conferred upon the Railroad Commission of Texas over all railroads, and suburban, belt and terminal railroads, and over all public wharves, docks, piers, elevators, warehouses, sheds, tracks and other property used in connection therewith in this State, and over all persons, associations and corporations, private or municipal, owning or operating such railroad, wharf, dock, pier, elevator, warehouse, shed, track or other property to fix, and it is hereby made the duty of the said Commission to adopt all necessary rates, charges and regulations, to govern and regulate such railroads, persons, associations and corporations, and to correct abuses and prevent unjust discrimination in the rates, charges and tolls of such railroads, persons, associations and corporations, and to fix division of rates, charges and regulations between railroads and other utilities and common carriers where a division is proper and correct, and to prevent any and all other abuses in the conduct of their business and to do and perform such other duties and details in connection therewith as may be provided by law."

279 U.S. 159; cf. Hawks v. Hamill, 288 U.S. 52, 61. These cases reflect a doctrine of abstention appropriate to our federal system whereby the federal courts, "exercising a wise discretion", restrain their authority because of "scrupulous regard for the rightful independence of the state governments" and for the smooth working of the federal judiciary. See Cavanaugh v. Looney, 248 U.S. 453, 457; Di Giovanni v. Camden Ins. Ass'n., 296 U.S. 64, 73. This use of equitable powers is a contribution of the courts in furthering the harmonious relation between state and federal authority without the need of rigorous congressional restriction of those powers.   * * *

Regard for these important considerations of policy in the administration of federal equity jurisdiction is decisive here. If there was no warrant in state law for the Commission's assumption of authority there is an end of the litigation; the constitutional issue does not arise. The law of Texas appears to furnish easy and ample means for determining the Commission's authority. Article 6453 of the Texas Civil Statutes gives a review of such an order in the state courts. Or, if there are difficulties in the way of this procedure of which we have not been apprised, the issue of state law may be settled by appropriate action on the part of the State to enforce obedience to the order. Beal v. Missouri Pacific R.R., *supra;* Article 6476, Texas Civil Statutes. In the absence of any showing that these obvious methods for securing a definitive ruling in the state courts cannot be pursued with full protection of the constitutional claim, the district court should exercise its wise discretion by staying its hands. Compare Thompson v. Magnolia Co., 309 U.S. 478.

We therefore remand the cause to the district court, with directions to retain the bill pending a determination of proceedings, to be brought with reasonable promptness, in the state court in conformity with this opinion.

Reversed and remanded.

■ MR. JUSTICE ROBERTS took no part in the consideration or decision of this case.

NOTE ON ABSTENTION IN CASES INVOLVING A FEDERAL QUESTION

(1) *The Basis of the Pullman Doctrine.* In explaining its decision to order abstention in the Pullman case, the Supreme Court cited a number of considerations, including the following: (i) resolution of a state law question in a particular way would avoid the necessity to decide a federal constitutional question; (ii) the relevant state law was unclear; (iii) resolution of the federal constitutional question adversely to the defendants might generate "needless friction" with state policies; and (iv) "the federal constitutional question 'touche[d] a sensitive area of social policy upon which the federal courts ought not to enter unless no alternative to adjudication is open'". Do these factors, individually or jointly, justify the decision to abstain?[1]

1. Even before Pullman, the Supreme Court had endorsed federal court abstention on difficult, unsettled questions of state law. See, *e.g.*, Gilchrist v. Interborough Rapid Transit Co., 279 U.S. 159 (1929)(federal court action to prevent state commission from interfering with fare increase; action was filed only a few hours before commission sued in state court to compel compliance with existing fare); Railroad Com'n v. Rowan & Nichols Oil Co., 310 U.S. 573 (1940), rehear. denied, 311 U.S. 614 (1940)(rejecting on the merits a federal due process challenge to a regulatory order, and refusing to decide whether under state law there was a "reasonable basis" for the commission's order, so as

Recall that, in Siler v. Louisville & N. R.R., 213 U.S. 175 (1909), p. 1079, *supra,* the Court held that if a controverted question of state law was presented in an action that presented a federal constitutional issue, the federal district court should decide the state question first (even though the court had only pendent jurisdiction with respect to that question) in order to avoid, if possible, a constitutional decision. (This background to the Pullman case was importantly modified by Pennhurst State School & Hosp. v. Halderman, 465 U.S. 89 (1984), p. 1077, *supra,* the consequences of which are discussed in Paragraph (4), *infra.)* Is Pullman inconsistent with Siler? Or does Pullman simply implement Siler's injunction to avoid unnecessary constitutional decisions by a mechanism that also satisfies other legitimate concerns?

How significant is the worry that a federal court's decision of a difficult state law issue, in a case such as Pullman, might be "supplanted by a controlling decision of a state court"? Aren't federal courts frequently called upon to resolve hard questions of state law?[2]

In what sense is the friction generated by a federal remedy for unconstitutional state action "needless"? Is it somehow preferable for a state court, rather than a federal court, to invalidate a state law or state policy? If state policies are unlawful, isn't it the business of the federal courts to stop them, when asked to do so in the context of a properly presented case?

What did Justice Frankfurter mean in suggesting that the constitutional question "touche[d] a sensitive area of state policy"? Consider Resnik, *Rereading "The Federal Courts:" Revising the Domain of Federal Courts Jurisprudence at the End of the Twentieth Century,* 47 Vand.L.Rev. 1021, 1039 (1994)(footnotes omitted): "The testimony [in the record] in Pullman is filled with discussion of how white women feel 'a little bit safer . . . with a white man conductor in charge of that car.' * * * Further, in an effort to prop up the porters' claims, the record also includes testimony aimed at distinguishing 'the Pullman porter[s],' as 'pretty high-classed colored men,' from those other kinds of 'colored men.'

"* * * In 1941 it was, I take it, not obvious how federal constitutional law would decide [the equal protection] question [that Pullman presented]. It was not easy because national norms did not readily trump local customs and prejudices, indeed because national norms may well have shared such prejudices. [As Professor Resnik observes in a footnote, 'the United States Army remained segregated in 1941.'] Thus the case was 'sensitive,' the engagement

to avoid supplanting the commission's expert judgment). See also Thompson v. Magnolia Petroleum Co., 309 U.S. 478 (1940)(although federal bankruptcy court had jurisdiction to determine the title to property in trustee's possession, trustee should be directed to bring state court proceeding to settle the issue).

2. A nest of difficult issues lies behind the suggestion that erroneous federal determinations might be supplanted. For example, if a federal court does not abstain from deciding a question of state law and if it decides the state law question incorrectly, might the judgment nonetheless be res judicata in subsequent, state court litigation be-

tween the parties? If the judgment is adverse to the state or a state actor, will it have issue preclusive effect in subsequent actions by the relevant official seeking to enforce state law against other parties? See generally Shapiro, *State Courts and Federal Declaratory Judgments,* 74 Nw.U.L.Rev. 759 (1979). For specific discussion of the effect of federal judgments that state statutes are overbroad and therefore unenforceable—judgments that necessarily rest on a possibly erroneous determination of the meaning of those statutes as a matter of state law—see Fallon, *Making Sense of Overbreadth,* 100 Yale L.J. 853, 877–83, 898–903 (1991).

between federal and state law fraught with anxiety, and if some other point of law could determine the outcome without having to consider announcing federal constitutional rules about discrimination based on race, more the better."

On its facts, was Pullman a wise avoidance of a question better faced after prevailing social understandings had undergone further evolution? Was it an abdication of judicial responsibility?

(2) *Abstention and the Separation of Powers.* The federal district court possessed undoubted statutory jurisdiction over the Pullman case. By what legitimate authority, if any, could a federal court decline to exercise that jurisdiction in a properly presented case? In his much-quoted opinion in Cohens v. Virginia, 19 U.S. (6 Wheat.) 264, 404 (1821), Chief Justice Marshall wrote: "We have no more right to decline the exercise of a jurisdiction which is given, than to usurp that which is not given. The one or the other would be treason to the constitution." Did the Court in Pullman commit "treason to the constitution"?[3]

In considering this question, recall Justice Frankfurter's invocation of the traditions of equity, which license the exercise of judicial discretion in the award of equitable remedies. But the traditions of equity developed in England, and considerations of federalism therefore had no role in early equitable practice. Is it appropriate for federal courts to shape equitable doctrine to further federalism-based interests? To advance an interest in avoiding the possibly unnecessary decision of constitutional issues? In any event, does reference to equity simply beg the question whether the federal courts possess authority under the separation of powers to craft equitable doctrines to reflect their own notions of sound policy? Professor Redish so argues. See Redish, The Federal Courts in the Political Order: Judicial Jurisdiction and American Political Theory 59–60 (1991). In Redish's view, there is no demonstrated justification for assuming that Congress would have intended courts to retain discretionary authority to decline jurisdiction on account of federalism concerns, and in the absence of such demonstrated intent, a judicial claim of power to abstain reflects a power grab—a usurpation of congressional power to define the jurisdiction of the federal courts—that is incompatible with basic premises of constitutional democracy.[4]

Is this argument persuasive? Aren't the lines that divide judicial lawmaking, statutory interpretation, and the development and application of interpretive and evidentiary presumptions frequently vague and occasionally vanishing? Shouldn't the *precise* jurisdictional questions raised by cases such as Pullman be thoughtfully considered at least once by a responsible organ of government before they are held to be authoritatively resolved? Is democratic theory necessarily so rigid as to preclude the courts from playing this role?

3. Marshall's utterance came in a case involving the appellate jurisdiction of the Supreme Court. Does it provide persuasive authority for cases in which an alternative forum is available? On the historical and doctrinal context of Marshall's utterance, see James Rehnquist, *Taking Comity Seriously: How to Neutralize the Abstention Doctrine,* 46 Stan.L.Rev. 1049, 1102–05 (1994). Rehnquist concludes that the dictum is not incompatible with a judicial discretion to decline to exercise jurisdiction in some contexts.

4. To the suggestion that Pullman abstention merely delays rather than declines the exercise of federal jurisdiction, Professor Redish responds that "even a delay * * * may be considered a violation of the separation of powers if it has not been contemplated by Congress" (p. 60).

Compare Shapiro, *Jurisdiction and Discretion,* 60 N.Y.U.L.Rev. 543, 543–45, 574–75 (1985)(some paragraphing omitted):

"Judges and lawyers have often said that the federal courts are obligated to exercise the jurisdiction conferred on them by the Constitution and by Congress. * * * [For example,] Justice Brennan warned that the federal courts have a 'virtually unflagging obligation * * * to exercise the jurisdiction given them.'[5] * * *

"[S]uggestions of an overriding obligation, subject only and at most to a few narrowly drawn exceptions, are far too grudging in their recognition of judicial discretion in matters of jurisdiction. * * * [T]he existence of this discretion is much more pervasive than is generally realized, and * * * it has ancient and honorable roots at common law as well as in equity. * * *

"My point is not that the Constitution expressly 'provides' that a grant of jurisdiction carries with it certain discretion not to proceed, or that Congress necessarily 'intends' to confer such discretion when it authorizes the exercise of jurisdiction. Rather, I submit that, as experience and tradition teach, the question whether a court must exercise jurisdiction and resolve a controversy on its merits is difficult, if not impossible, to answer in gross. And the courts are functionally better adapted to engage in the necessary fine tuning than is the legislature. * * *

"A grant of jurisdiction obligates the court to receive and consider the plaintiff's complaint and, on appropriate occasions, to determine whether the ends of justice will be served best by declining to proceed. At the same time, nothing in our history or traditions permits a court to interpret a normal grant of jurisdiction as conferring unbridled authority to hear cases simply at its pleasure. * * * [W]hen jurisdiction is conferred, I believe that there is at least a 'principle of preference' that a court should entertain and resolve on its merits an action within the scope of the jurisdictional grant. For this preference to yield in a particular case, the court must provide an explanation based on the language of the grant, the historical context in which the grant was made, or the common law tradition behind it."

In Shapiro's view, experience suggests that the criteria for channeling discretion in matters of jurisdiction may be grouped under four headings—"equitable discretion, federalism and comity, separation of powers, and judicial administration"—that "in general, are to be weighed against the presumption favoring the assertion and exercise of jurisdiction" (p. 579). Compare Friedman, *A Different Dialogue: The Supreme Court, Congress, and Federal Jurisdiction,* 85 Nw.L.Rev. 1 (1990)(arguing that the Constitution authorizes a dialogic interaction between Congress and the courts in fixing the bounds of federal jurisdiction).[6]

---

5. Moses H. Cone Memorial Hosp. v. Mercury Constr. Co., 460 U.S. 1, 15 (1983) [p. 1317, *infra*].

6. The question whether judicially crafted abstention doctrines are permissible under the jurisdictional statutes and the separation of powers is a general one, by no means limited to Pullman abstention, and it has stimulated a broad debate. Professor Redish remains the leading proponent of the view that, in the absence of clear statutory authorization, abstention violates separation-of-powers principles. *E.g.,* Redish, *supra,* at 47–74; Redish, *Abstention, Separation of Powers, and the Limits of the Judicial Function,* 94 Yale L.J. 71 (1984). See also Dennis, *The Illegitimate Foundations of the Younger Abstention Doctrine,* 10 Bridgeport L.Rev. 311 (1990); Doernberg, *"You Can Lead a Horse to Water ..." The Supreme Court's Refusal to Allow the Exercise of Original Jurisdiction Conferred by Congress,* 40 Case W.Res.L.Rev.

(3) *The Evolution of Pullman Abstention.*

(a) *Early Years.* In the early years after Pullman, the Supreme Court frequently required abstention on unsettled state law issues when resolution of those issues was preliminary to consideration of a federal constitutional question. See, *e.g.,* Spector Motor Serv., Inc. v. McLaughlin, 323 U.S. 101 (1944); Albertson v. Millard, 345 U.S. 242 (1953); City of Meridian v. Southern Bell Tel. & Tel. Co., 358 U.S. 639 (1959).[7]

(b) *Extension to Actions at Law.* Despite Pullman's equitable foundations, the Court, without further discussion, has applied the doctrine to actions at law involving uncertain state law and potentially avoidable federal constitutional questions. See Clay v. Sun Ins. Office, Ltd., 363 U.S. 207 (1960); United Gas Pipe Line Co. v. Ideal Cement Co., 369 U.S. 134 (1962); Fornaris v. Ridge Tool Co., 400 U.S. 41 (1970). Can this extension be justified? Note that while Justice Frankfurter's defense of abstention in the Pullman case rested on the traditional discretion of courts of equity, Professor Shapiro's defense of judicial discretion in jurisdictional matters, *supra,* sweeps more broadly.

(c) *Diversity Cases.* The cases extending Pullman from equitable to legal actions also crossed a second divide, again without discussion from the Court. Whereas jurisdiction in the Pullman case rested on the general federal jurisdiction statute, 28 U.S.C. § 1331, Clay, United Gas Pipe Line, and Fornaris were all diversity cases. A major purpose of the diversity jurisdiction—to provide a neutral forum for the determination of state law issues, both hard and easy—is at least attenuated by abstention, whether or not the state law issue is preliminary to a federal question. *Cf. Note on the Abstention Doctrine In Cases Not Involving a Federal Question,* which follows this Note. Does this extension of Pullman flout the congressional policy expressed in the grant of diversity jurisdiction? See generally Redish, *supra.* Or should it be doubted that congressional intent with respect to the precise question raised by these cases is sufficiently clear to be flouted? In any event, shouldn't the Court have at least addressed the issue openly?

(d) *Section 1983 Actions.* Over the dissent of Justice Douglas, joined by Chief Justice Warren and Justice Brennan, the Supreme Court, in Harrison v.

---

999 (1989–90). For critical analyses of this view, in addition to Shapiro, *supra,* see Wells, *Why Professor Redish is Wrong About Abstention,* 19 Ga.L.Rev. 1097 (1985); Althouse, *The Humble and the Treasonous: Judge-Made Jurisdiction Law,* 40 Case W.Res. L.Rev. 1035 (1989–90); Beerman, *"Bad" Judicial Activism and Liberal Federal–Courts Doctrine: A Comment on Professor Doernberg and Professor Redish,* 40 Case W.Res.L.Rev. 1053 (1989–90); and Brown, *When Federalism and Separation of Powers Collide—Rethinking Younger Abstention,* 59 Geo.Wash. L.Rev. 114 (1990). For an intermediate position, approving abstention when based on concerns about judicial administration, but not when based on matters requiring "political choices", see Shreve, *Pragmatism without Politics–A Half Measure of Authority for Jurisdictional Common Law,* 1991 B.Y.U.L.Rev.

767. For an argument that abstention doctrines do not merely involve questions of policy, but are rooted in the Constitution, see Massey, *Abstention and the Constitutional Limits of the Judicial Power of the United States,* 1991 B.Y.U.L.Rev. 811.

7. In Propper v. Clark, 337 U.S. 472, 490 (1949), the Court made clear that abstention was inappropriate to avoid decision of *nonconstitutional* federal issues. (Justice Frankfurter dissented.) Most lower courts have resisted efforts to circumvent Propper by characterizing federal statutory challenges to state action as constitutional challenges under the Supremacy Clause. See, *e.g.,* United Services Automobile Ass'n v. Muir, 792 F.2d 356 (3d Cir.1986); 17 Wright, Miller, & Cooper, Federal Practice and Procedure § 4242 (1988 & Supp.1995).

NAACP, 360 U.S. 167 (1959), found Pullman abstention doctrine applicable to cases under § 1983. The dissenters emphasized the suspicion of state courts evinced in the legislative history of the Civil Rights Act of 1871 and asserted the special importance of a federal forum in civil rights cases (pp. 180–81). For other decisions abstaining in suits brought under § 1983, see, *e.g.*, Bellotti v. Baird, 428 U.S. 132 (1976); Carey v. Sugar, 425 U.S. 73 (1976); Boehning v. Indiana State Employees Ass'n, Inc., 423 U.S. 6 (1975)(per curiam). There is some tension between these decisions and the holdings of (i) Monroe v. Pape, refusing to limit the scope of § 1983 to suits challenging conduct authorized by state law or custom, and (ii) Patsy v. Board of Regents, refusing to require exhaustion of state administrative remedies in § 1983 actions. But an "exception" for § 1983 cases would swallow the rule, as that section extends to all constitutional violations by those acting under color of state law.[8]

(e) *Decline and Resurgence.* The Supreme Court's enthusiasm for Pullman abstention appeared to wane during the 1960s, as the Court expressed concern about the delays that abstention entails. (For discussion of this concern, see Paragraph (7), *infra.*) One commentator, writing in 1967, noted that in all seven cases raising a Pullman question after Justice Frankfurter's retirement in 1962, the Court had managed to find reasons not to require abstention, and called the doctrine a "judicial orphan". Note, 80 Harv.L.Rev. 604, 608 & n. 3 (1967).[9] The doctrine staged something of a comeback in the Burger Court, see, *e.g.*, Babbitt v. United Farm Workers Nat. Union, 442 U.S. 289 (1979); Harris County Com'rs Court v. Moore, 420 U.S. 77 (1975); Lake Carriers' Ass'n v. MacMullan, 406 U.S. 498 (1972), although since 1979 the Court has found it applicable in only one instance. See Virginia v. American Booksellers Ass'n, Inc., 484 U.S. 383 (1988). Despite the relative dearth of recent, supportive cases in the Supreme Court, the doctrine continues to be applied by the lower federal courts, although with some uncertainty and confusion. See generally Chemerinsky, Federal Jurisdiction 695–98 (2d ed.1994).

(4) *The Impact of Pennhurst.* In Pennhurst State School & Hosp. v. Halderman, 465 U.S. 89 (1984), p. 1079, *supra*, the Supreme Court held that the Eleventh Amendment denies federal courts jurisdiction to award injunctive relief against state officials based upon state law. Pennhurst does not bar federal court suits challenging state action under both state and federal law if the relief is not of the kind barred by the Eleventh Amendment—as is true of relief against a local government or its officials and of damages to be paid out of the public official's pocket. Nor is Pennhurst relevant to cases in which a plaintiff attempts to attack a state statute on its face, and the validity of the attack depends on how the statute would be construed by the state's courts.[10]

---

8. For a suggestion that particular classes of civil rights cases—for example, those raising equal protection or voting rights claims—should be exempt from Pullman abstention, see Wechsler, *Federal Jurisdiction and the Revision of the Judicial Code,* 13 Law & Contemp.Prob. 216, 230 (1948).

9. The cases were McNeese v. Board of Educ., 373 U.S. 668 (1963); Griffin v. County School Bd., 377 U.S. 218 (1964); Hostetter v. Idlewild Bon Voyage Liquor Corp., 377 U.S. 324 (1964); Davis v. Mann, 377 U.S. 678

(1964); Baggett v. Bullitt, 377 U.S. 360 (1964); Dombrowski v. Pfister, 380 U.S. 479 (1965); and Harman v. Forssenius, 380 U.S. 528 (1965).

10. In cases presenting First Amendment overbreadth and vagueness challenges, the question frequently arises whether abstention is appropriate pending a state court determination of a statute's actual reach. In City of Houston v. Hill, 482 U.S. 451 (1987), in which the plaintiff challenged a municipal

But if the Pullman case were filed today in federal court, under Pennhurst the court would lack power altogether to entertain a claim to enjoin the order as unauthorized by Texas law.

In such a case, should the federal court stay its hand pending state court resolution of the state law issue? In Askew v. Hargrave, 401 U.S. 476 (1971), Florida citizens filed a federal class action challenging a state school financing program under the Equal Protection Clause. A pending state action by a school board challenged the same law under the Florida constitution. The Court remanded for consideration whether to abstain, noting (p. 478) that the "claims under the Florida Constitution * * *, if sustained, will obviate the necessity of determining the [equal protection] question." Note that in Askew, unlike Pullman itself, abstention could be justified only to avoid a federal constitutional question, and not to prevent misconstruction of state law or possibly unjustified interference with a state program. Werhan, *Pullman Abstention After Pennhurst: A Comment on Judicial Federalism*, 27 Wm. & Mary L.Rev. 449, 490–99 (1986).[11] This is a significant extension of Pullman, isn't it? Should abstention be allowed on this basis?

What if a federal plaintiff raises only federal claims in a federal court action, and neither the federal plaintiff nor anyone else raises parallel state law claims in a state court action? Should a federal court abstain on the ground that the plaintiff *must* go to state court with claims that, if resolved favorably, might moot or modify the federal issue?[12] See Muskegon Theatres, Inc. v. City of Muskegon, 507 F.2d 199, 204 (6th Cir.1974)(refusing to permit the "simple expedient" of not raising the state law claim at all to "frustrate the policies underlying the doctrine of abstention"); International Brotherhood of Electrical Workers v. Public Serv. Com'm of Nevada, 614 F.2d 206, 212 (6th Cir.1980)(noting that union's decision not to raise state law claims "does not

ordinance making it a misdemeanor "to assault, strike, or in any manner oppose, molest, abuse or interrupt any policeman in the execution of his duty * * *", the Supreme Court stated that "abstention * * * is inappropriate for cases [where] * * * statutes are justifiably attacked on their face as abridging free expression" (p. 467, quoting Dombrowski v. Pfister, 380 U.S. 479, 489–90 (1965)), and that "the delay of state-court proceedings might itself effect the impermissible chilling of the very constitutional right [plaintiff] seeks to protect," (p. 468, quoting Zwickler v. Koota, 389 U.S. 241, 252 (1967)). (Justice Powell, joined by Chief Justice Rehnquist and Justices Scalia and O'Connor, concurred in the judgment, but did not agree that abstention is generally inappropriate in facial challenges under the First Amendment.) In contrast with Hill, the Court declined to consider First Amendment challenges to state statutes before the state courts had the chance to construe them in Babbitt v. United Farm Workers Nat. Union, 442 U.S. 289 (1979), and Virginia v. American Booksellers Ass'n, Inc., 484 U.S. 383 (1988). See also Harrison v. NAACP, 360

U.S. 167 (1959) (ordering abstention). For general discussion of the relationship between the Pullman abstention and First Amendment overbreadth doctrine, see Fallon, note 2 *supra,* at 901–02.

11. Werhan also notes that a different abstention doctrine, dealing specifically with the problem of a parallel pending proceeding in state court, might apply. See generally Sec. 2(D), *infra.*

12. As the Pullman case itself shows, the Court may clearly decide on its own motion to abstain. See, *e.g.,* Ohio Bureau of Employment Services v. Hodory, 431 U.S. 471, 480 n. 11 (1977)(though appeal from three-judge district court's award of injunctive relief did not contest the failure to abstain, "Pullman abstention, where deference to the state process may result in elimination or material alteration of the constitutional issue, surely does not require that this Court defer to the wishes of the parties concerning adjudication"); Bellotti v. Baird, 428 U.S. 132, 143 n. 10 (1976); Wisconsin v. Constantineau, Paragraph (6), *infra.*

affect our determination of the abstention issue"); *cf.* Allendale Leasing, Inc. v. Stone, 614 F.Supp. 1440 (D.R.I.1985)(first dismissing, under Pennhurst, pendent state law challenges to the validity of certain state regulations, and then refusing to adjudicate the federal constitutional challenges to the regulations until the state courts could hear the state law challenges). Is it reasonable to compel plaintiffs, at their own expense, to make state law claims they do not wish to make in a forum in which they do not wish to litigate, when resolution of the state claim is not *necessary* to consideration of the federal claim?

(5) *The Meaning of Unsettled State Law.* When is an issue of state law sufficiently "unsettled" or "unclear" to warrant abstention under the Pullman doctrine? The answer does not emerge easily from the decisions, since the Court frequently announces only its conclusion with little elaboration of its reasons.

Harrison v. NAACP, 360 U.S. 167 (1959), which involved a First Amendment challenge to Virginia statutes dealing with litigation and lobbying, especially with respect to racial matters, found abstention appropriate where the Court was "unable to agree that [there was] * * * no reasonable room" for a limiting construction (p. 177). Similar language appears in Fornaris v. Ridge Tool Co., 400 U.S. 41, 44 (1970), and Reetz v. Bozanich, 397 U.S. 82, 86–87 (1970). Other cases have articulated a narrower standard. See, *e.g.,* Hawaii Housing Auth. v. Midkiff, 467 U.S. 229 (1984), in which the Court stated without dissent that although "[i]n the abstract" the possibility of a limiting construction always exists, "the relevant inquiry is not whether there is a bare, though unlikely possibility that state courts *might* render adjudication of the federal question unnecessary. Rather, '[w]e have frequently emphasized that abstention is not to be ordered unless the statute is of an uncertain nature, and is obviously susceptible of a limiting construction' " (p. 237, quoting Zwickler v. Koota, 389 U.S. 241, 251 & n. 14 (1967)).

The newness of a state statute and the total absence of judicial precedent are clearly significant considerations. See, *e.g.,* the Pullman case itself; Lake Carriers' Ass'n v. MacMullan, Paragraph (3)(e), *supra;* Harrison, *supra.* On the other hand, the mere presence of judicially unconstrued state law does not automatically require abstention. See, *e.g.,* Brockett v. Spokane Arcades, Inc., 472 U.S. 491 (1985); Wisconsin v. Constantineau, 400 U.S. 433, 439 (1971); Toomer v. Witsell, 334 U.S. 385 (1948).

Most important, the uncertainty in state law must be such that construction by the state court might obviate the need for decision (or at least help to limit the scope) of the federal constitutional question. See, *e.g.,* Baggett v. Bullitt, 377 U.S. 360, 378 (1964)(rejecting an argument for abstention in a case challenging a statute as unconstitutionally vague where it was "fictional to believe that anything less than extensive adjudications, under the impact of a variety of factual situations," would cure the vagueness).

(6) *Unsettled State Constitutional Provisions.* Do different considerations govern the appropriateness of abstention due to the unclarity of state *constitutional* provisions—when, for example, a statute or official action is (or might be) attacked under both the state and federal constitutions? In Reetz v. Bozanich, 397 U.S. 82 (1970), the plaintiff sought a declaration that Alaska fishing laws and regulations, which limited eligibility to receive certain commercial fishing licenses, violated (i) the Fourteenth Amendment of the federal Constitution, and (ii) two provisions of the Alaska constitution—one reserving fishing rights to the people, and the other proscribing exclusive fishing rights. A three-judge

court upheld both contentions, but the Supreme Court vacated and remanded with directions to abstain, emphasizing that the Alaska constitutional provisions "have never been interpreted by an Alaska court" and that management of fish resources was "a matter of great state concern" (p. 86). See also Askew v. Hargrave, Paragraph (4), *supra.* By contrast, in Wisconsin v. Constantineau, 400 U.S. 433 (1971), the Court upheld the decision of a three-judge district court invalidating a Wisconsin statute providing for the public posting, without notice or hearing to the person affected, of the name of any person whose excessive drinking produced specified social problems. (The statute prohibited the provision of intoxicating beverages to any such person.) The Court declined to abstain, notwithstanding the dissenting protest of Chief Justice Burger and Justices Black and Blackmun that "[f]or all we know, the state courts would find this statute invalid under the State Constitution" (p.440).[13]

The Court sought to reconcile these decisions in Harris County Com'rs Court v. Moore, 420 U.S. 77 (1975), which ordered abstention to obtain a state court construction of the state constitution. The Court said (pp. 84–85 n. 8) that in Constantineau "we declined to order abstention where the federal due process claim was not complicated by an unresolved state-law question, even though the plaintiffs might have sought relief under a similar provision of the state constitution. But where the challenged statute is part of an integrated scheme of related constitutional provisions, statutes, and regulations, and where the scheme as a whole calls for clarifying interpretation by the state courts, we have regularly required the district courts to abstain [citing Reetz]."

The theme of Harris was repeated in Examining Board of Engineers v. Flores de Otero, 426 U.S. 572, 597–98 (1976), in which the Court refused to abstain simply because a challenged Puerto Rico statute might violate Puerto Rico's constitutional guarantees of equal protection and nondiscrimination. To require abstention because of the "broad and sweeping" provisions of the Puerto Rico constitution "would convert abstention from an exception into a general rule" (p. 598). See also Hawaii Housing Auth. v. Midkiff, 467 U.S. 229, 237 n. 4 (1984). Since most state constitutions contain guarantees analogous to those in the Bill of Rights, this is a powerful and general point, isn't it?[14]

(7) *The Problem of Delay.* During the early years of the Pullman doctrine, pursuit of the prescribed procedure sometimes occasioned delays of six or eight years before the final resolution of litigation,[15] and critics cited the problem of

---

13. A footnote to the Chief Justice's opinion at this point stated: "Although Wisconsin has no due process clause as such, Art. I, § 1, of the Wisconsin Constitution has been held by the Wisconsin Supreme Court to be substantially equivalent to the limitation on state action contained in the Due Process and Equal Protection Clauses of the Fourteenth Amendment" (p. 440 n. 1).

If Chief Justice Burger was correct in his analysis of Wisconsin constitutional law, would a state decision invalidating the state law under the state constitution necessarily have been reviewable by the Supreme Court? See Chap. V, Sec. 2(A), *supra.* Is the answer to that question relevant to the decision whether to abstain?

14. Consider Professor Currie's response: "If the doctrine itself is sound, it should be applied to all cases within its purpose. Perhaps the Court's unprincipled limitation of abstention indicates a healthy dissatisfaction with the doctrine itself. If so, it would be more consistent to abolish abstention altogether." Currie, *The Supreme Court and Federal Jurisdiction: 1975 Term,* 1976 Sup.Ct.Rev. 183, 212.

15. See, *e.g.,* Spector Motor Serv., Inc. v. O'Connor, 340 U.S. 602 (1951)(eight years); United States v. Leiter Minerals, Inc., 381 U.S. 413 (1965)(dismissed as moot eight years after abstention was ordered).

delay in urging that the doctrine be abolished.[16]   Today, however, nearly two-thirds of the states have procedures that allow a federal court to certify an unsettled question of state law directly to the state's highest court; one study found a median time of six months from certification to provision of an answer. Seron, *Certifying Questions of State Law: Experience of Federal Judges* 16 (Federal Judicial Center 1983).   For a further discussion of certification of questions of state law, see *Note on Procedural Aspects of Pullman Abstention*, immediately following this Note.[17]

(8) *Discretionary or Mandatory?*   The Supreme Court has occasionally cited protracted delay as an equitable factor supporting a refusal to abstain in particular cases.   See, *e.g.,* Harman v. Forssenius, 380 U.S. 528, 537 (1965); Hostetter v. Idlewild Bon Voyage Liquor Corp., 377 U.S. 324, 329 (1964); Griffin v. School Bd. of Prince Edward County, 377 U.S. 218, 228–29 (1964). Cases such as these imply that Pullman abstention is a discretionary doctrine that should be applied only after a balancing of competing considerations in the particular case.   So, arguably, does the Court's reference to the Pullman dispute as touching a "sensitive area of social policy".   Compare Davies, *Pullman and Burford Abstention: Clarifying the Roles of State and Federal Courts in Constitutional Cases,* 20 U.C. Davis L.Rev. 1, 19 (1986)(noting "interpretive confusion" among the lower courts in determining "when sensitive policy issues exist").   Yet the Supreme Court's recent decisions have not devoted much attention to the sensitivity of the state program, see, *e.g.,* Hawaii Housing Auth. v. Midkiff, Paragraph (6), *supra,* and it is not obvious that the issue in Clay v. Sun Ins. Office, Paragraph (3)(b), *supra,* for example, which involved contract damages in a diversity action between private parties, was particularly sensitive or affected an important state program.   Do these decisions suggest that Pullman should be applied automatically, whenever resolution of an uncertain state issue in a particular way might moot or modify a federal constitutional issue?   Compare City of Meridian v. Southern Bell Tel. & Tel. Co., 358 U.S. 639, 640 (1959).

Would some of the objections to Pullman be mooted if the doctrine were framed in explicitly prudential terms and the costs exacted only where they could be justified on a fact-specific basis?   Or would open-ended balancing only generate more confusion and strengthen contentions that abstention represents a troubling form of judicial lawlessness?   See Paragraph (2), *supra.*   Is there a

---

16.   See, *e.g.,* Kurland, *Toward a Cooperative Judicial Federalism: The Federal Court Abstention Doctrine,* 24 F.R.D. 481 (1959); Field, *The Abstention Doctrine Today,* 125 U.Pa.L.Rev. 590, 605 (1977); Currie, *The Federal Courts and the American Law Institute, Part II,* 36 U.Chi.L.Rev. 268, 317 (1969).   See also England v. Louisiana State Bd. of Medical Exam'rs, 375 U.S. 411, 423 (1964)(Douglas, J., concurring)(urging that the doctrine be reconsidered).

17.   With cases under the Pullman doctrine, in which the Supreme Court tolerates delay and sometimes the burden imposed on state courts by certification procedures, compare Michigan v. Long, 463 U.S. 1032 (1983), Chap. V, Sec. 2(A), *supra,* which involved the Supreme Court's jurisdiction to review a state court decision that might, but does not clearly, rest on an adequate and independent state constitutional ground.   The Court in Long rejected the option of vacating and remanding the case for clarification because of the resulting "delay and decrease in efficiency of judicial administration" and because of the "significant burdens" this approach would place on state courts (pp. 1040–41). Can the disparity of approaches be reconciled?

middle ground? Under what criteria, if any, would an appropriately principled form of discretion to abstain in Pullman-type cases be exercised?

NOTE ON PROCEDURAL ASPECTS OF PULLMAN ABSTENTION

(1) *Stay of Federal Proceedings.* When invoking the Pullman abstention doctrine, a federal court typically retains jurisdiction to permit it to resolve the federal question if a decision is ultimately necessary.[1] Retaining jurisdiction also enables the federal court to guard against the possibility of unreasonable delay or an unforeseen bar to relief in the state courts, and, where appropriate, to provide interim relief pending the outcome of the state court litigation.[2]

(2) *Commencing a State Proceeding.* If a federal court decides to abstain on an issue of state law and to remit the plaintiff to state court to seek a resolution of that issue, a variety of issues and obstacles may immediately present themselves.

(a) A state proceeding raising the issue may already be pending, as in Askew v. Hargrave, p. 1238, *supra,* but if (again as in Askew) the state proceeding involves different parties, the plaintiff may be unhappy with the adequacy of presentation of the issue and may be denied intervention. If so, the plaintiff may have to start the same lawsuit all over again in a state court.

(b) In some cases, the plaintiff may be able to take advantage of declaratory judgment legislation, adopted in virtually every state, and seek a declaration limited to the precise issue on which abstention was ordered. But the existence of such legislation is no assurance that the state courts will entertain an action in the abstention context. In United Serv. Life Ins. Co. v. Delaney, 328 F.2d 483 (5th Cir.1964), after the Fifth Circuit abstained (reserving jurisdiction to enter final judgment), the Texas Supreme Court held that declaratory relief was unavailable because the decision of the issue of state law would be only an "advisory opinion." 396 S.W.2d 855 (Tex.1965). Do you agree that in a state court that is constitutionally limited to cases and controversies, as federal courts are, such a request for declaratory relief is nonjusticiable?

What options remain available if a state court adopts the position of the Texas Supreme Court in Delaney? Harris County Com'rs Court v. Moore, 420 U.S. 77 (1975), ordered abstention in a case arising in Texas, and in view of the Delaney case, ruled that the district court should dismiss instead of retaining jurisdiction. "The dismissal", the Court specified, "should be without prejudice so that any remaining federal claim may be raised in a federal forum after the Texas courts have been given the opportunity to address the state law questions in this case" (pp. 88–89). This approach has since been followed by

---

1. For a discussion of the limited exceptions, see Paragraph (2), *infra.*

2. On the latter point, consider Babbitt v. United Farm Workers Nat. Union, 442 U.S. 289, 312 n. 18 (1979). There the Court found abstention appropriate in a First Amendment challenge to state law. In responding to plaintiff's request for an injunc- tion against enforcement of the statute at issue pending the state court proceeding, the Court said simply that "this is a matter that is best addressed by the District Court in the first instance." See generally Wells, *Preliminary Injunctions and Abstention: Some Problems in Federalism,* 63 Cornell L.Rev. 65 (1977).

the federal courts in Texas cases.[3]

(c) As an alternative to requiring the parties to commence a declaratory judgment action at the bottom of the state judicial ladder and to go up as far as they can, nearly two-thirds of the states allow a federal court to certify an unsettled question directly to the state's highest court. Certification and procedure in certified cases are discussed in Paragraph (6), *infra.* The discussion in all other Paragraphs of this Note involves cases in which, following a federal court's decision to abstain under the Pullman doctrine, the parties themselves had to commence litigation in state court.

(3) *Resolution of the Federal Questions.* Whether or not the federal court retains jurisdiction, the parties may present their federal as well as their state contentions to the state court for decision, and the loser may seek Supreme Court review. This was the course followed after Harrison v. NAACP, p. 1239, *supra,* and in NAACP v. Button, 371 U.S. 415 (1963), the Supreme Court ultimately passed on the constitutionality of the state statutes on certiorari to the Virginia Supreme Court of Appeals, saying (p. 427): "Where * * * the party remitted to the state courts elects to seek a complete and final adjudication of his rights in the state courts, the District Court's reservation of jurisdiction is purely formal, and does not impair our jurisdiction to review directly an otherwise final judgment."

But may a party elect not to submit the federal questions for state court decision? At least where those questions involve a constitutional challenge to the state statute being construed, the state court must be made aware of the nature of that challenge. In Government & Civic Employees Organizing Committee, CIO v. Windsor, 353 U.S. 364 (1957), the district court first abstained, and then, following a state court's construction of a state statute, ruled that the statute was constitutional. The Supreme Court vacated that ruling (p. 366–67): "The bare adjudication by the Alabama Supreme Court * * * does not suffice, since that court was not asked to interpret the statute in light of the constitutional objections presented to the District Court. If appellants' freedom-of-expression and equal protection arguments had been presented to the state court, it might have construed the statute in a different manner. Accordingly, the judgment of the District Court is vacated, and this cause is remanded to it with directions to retain jurisdiction until efforts to obtain an appropriate adjudication in the state courts have been exhausted."

(4) *The England Case.* Suppose the state supreme court, presented with the federal questions, chooses to decide them, and the litigant prefers not to seek Supreme Court review (or review is denied). May the litigant return to the federal court, or is the state decision res judicata? The Court answered this question in England v. Louisiana State Bd. of Medical Examiners, 375 U.S. 411 (1964), holding that a party is bound by the state court determination *only* if the party did in fact elect, in the words of Button, *supra,* "to seek a complete and final adjudication of his rights in a state court". The Court said (pp. 415–16):

---

3. A similar problem is presented when a state court is unwilling to hear an action substantially similar to one previously filed in a federal district court in that state, even if the federal court has chosen to abstain. See, *e.g.,* Eways v. Governor's Island, 326 N.C. 552, 391 S.E.2d 182 (1990), noted in 69 N.C.L.Rev. 1414 (1991). Should the state court's unwillingness lead the federal court to dismiss (even if dismissal might prejudice the federal plaintiff)? To refuse to abstain in the first instance?

"There are fundamental objections to any conclusion that a litigant who has properly invoked the jurisdiction of a Federal District Court to consider federal constitutional claims can be compelled, without his consent and through no fault of his own, to accept instead a state court's determination of those claims. * * * [Abstention's] recognition of the role of state courts as the final expositors of state law implies no disregard for the primacy of the federal judiciary in deciding questions of federal law. * * *

"It is true that, after a post-abstention determination and rejection of his federal claims by the state courts, a litigant could seek direct review in this Court. But such review, even when available by appeal rather than only by a discretionary writ of certiorari, is an inadequate substitute for the initial District Court determination * * *. This is true as to issues of law; it is especially true as to issues of fact. Limiting the litigant to review here would deny him the benefit of a federal trial court's role in constructing a record and making fact findings. How the facts are found will often dictate the decision of federal claims. * * *"

As to the hazards involved in the presentation required by Windsor, the Court said (pp. 421–22):

"* * * [A] party may readily forestall any conclusion that he has elected not to return to the District Court. He may accomplish this by making on the state record the 'reservation to the disposition of the entire case by the state courts' that we referred to in Button. That is, he may inform the state courts that he is exposing his federal claims there only for the purpose of complying with Windsor, and that he intends, should the state courts hold against him on the question of state law, to return to the District Court for disposition of his federal contentions. Such an explicit reservation is not indispensable; the litigant is in no event to be denied his right to return to the District Court unless it clearly appears that he voluntarily did more than Windsor required and fully litigated his federal claims in the state courts. When the reservation has been made, however, his right to return will in all events be preserved."[4]

After England, may litigants obtain Supreme Court review of a state court decision of the federal question despite their own efforts to reserve the question for the district court? If review is denied, may they then return to the district court?

After England, may a party submit some federal questions for binding state court decision and reserve others?[5] If a state court determination of fact is

---

4. In the specific case before it, the Court found that the litigants had submitted the federal question to the state court, but only in the belief that the Windsor case required them to do so; the Court therefore declined to apply its new rule to them, and held that the district court should pass on the merits of their federal contention.

Is the judicial pronouncement of a rule with purely prospective effect consistent with Article III? See Chap. II, Sec. 1, pp. 84–88, *supra.*

5. May *defendants,* as well as plaintiffs, reserve the right to litigate a federal question in federal court? In England, the Court (p. 422 n. 13) said: "The reservation [of the right to litigate the federal question in a federal court] may be made by any party to the litigation. Usually the plaintiff will have made the original choice to litigate in the federal court, but the defendant also, by virtue of the removal jurisdiction, 28 U.S.C. § 1441(b), has a right to litigate the federal question there. * * * The latter may protect his right by either declining to oppose the plaintiff's federal claim in the state court or opposing it with the appropriate reservation." Did the Court mean that a defendant may *always* make such a reservation, or may

relevant to both the state and federal questions, is the state court determination binding in the federal court after England? (Note that a principal, intended effect of the England procedure is to create at least a limited exception to the rules of claim and issue preclusion ordinarily prevailing under 28 U.S.C. § 1738. See generally Chap. XII, Sec. 1, *infra*.)

(5) *Appealability of Decisions Whether to Abstain.* For discussion of the appealability of orders granting or denying abstention, see Chapter XV, Sec. 1, *infra*.

(6) *The Option of Certification.* Although the standard Pullman procedure probably remains one in which plaintiffs are remitted to state court and whatever procedural hazards may lurk there, state certification procedures frequently furnish a more expeditious method of obtaining state court resolution of unsettled state law issues. As of 1994, it was reported that 37 jurisdictions (including Puerto Rico and the District of Columbia) have enacted laws or rules providing for certification, with many states basing their provisions on the Uniform Certification of Questions of Law Act, 12 U.L.A. 52 (1967), adopted by the Commissioners on Uniform State Laws. See 17 Wright, Miller & Cooper, Federal Practice & Procedure § 4248 (1988 & 1994 Supp.).

(a) *Doctrinal History.* The Supreme Court first ordered a lower federal court to avail itself of state certification procedures in Clay v. Sun Ins. Office, Ltd., 363 U.S. 207 (1960), p. 1236, *supra*. (The Clay case arose in Florida, which from 1945–65 was the only state with a statute authorizing its courts to answer certified questions.) More recently, the Court embraced the certification option in Lehman Brothers v. Schein, 416 U.S. 386 (1974), a case involving a difficult question of state law but no federal question. (On the doctrines governing abstention in cases not presenting a federal question, see *Note on Burford and Thibodaux Abstention,* immediately following this Note.) In Lehman Brothers, the Court said "We do not suggest that where there is doubt as to local law and where the certification procedure is available, resort to it is obligatory" (pp. 390–91). But, the Court continued, "It does, of course, in the long run save time, energy, and resources and helps build a cooperative judicial federalism" (p. 391).

(b) *Policy Issues.* Is there any reason why the Supreme Court's enthusiasm for certification in Lehman Brothers should not carry over from diversity cases to federal question cases? When Pullman abstention is warranted in any event, should federal courts use certification if it is available? See Field, *The Abstention Doctrine Today,* 125 U.Pa.L.Rev. 590, 605–09 (1977).

The majority of commentators have been enthusiastic about certification, especially as a substitute for a state declaratory judgment action. But there is always risk that the certified question will be badly drafted, too abstract,[6] or misunderstood by the state court, or that the federal court will be unsure of the significance of the answer.

(c) *Mechanics.* All states with certification procedures will respond to a question certified from the Supreme Court or a federal court of appeals; most

do so only when the original action was removable?

6. In re Richards, 223 A.2d 827 (Me. 1966), the Maine Supreme Judicial Court refused to answer a certified question on the ground that, because appropriate findings had not been made by the federal court, the question was not ripe for determination. Most states require, however, that the certified question be accompanied by a statement of facts, which is often drafted by the parties. See Note, 59 Notre Dame L.Rev. 1339, 1354–55 (1984).

but not all will also accept certified questions from a federal district court. See Seron, Certifying Questions of State Law: Experience of Federal Judges 2 (Federal Judicial Center 1983).[7] A federal court certifying a question of state law retains jurisdiction while awaiting a response.

Is the state court's response as much entitled to full faith and credit under 28 U.S.C. § 1738 as an ordinary state court judgment? Does Congress have the power to require states to entertain certified questions—and if so, should that power be exercised? Compare Kurland, *Mr. Justice Frankfurter, The Supreme Court and the Erie Doctrine in Diversity Cases,* 67 Yale L.J. 187, 214 (1957), with ALI Study at 295.

In general, certification tends to involve less time, money, and procedural complexity than other methods of shuttling back and forth between federal and state courts. A study of 48 cases in which certification was used found a median time of six months from certification to obtaining the state's answer, though the range extended from less than one month to two and a half years. Seron, *supra,* at 16. Some federal courts have nonetheless been reluctant to certify questions in view of the anticipated delay. See, *e.g.,* State ex rel. Shevin v. Exxon Corp., 526 F.2d 266, 275–76 (5th Cir.1976); Roth, *Certified Questions from the Federal Courts: Review and Re-proposal,* 34 U.Miami L.Rev. 1 (1979).

Should certification be denied to a party who chose the federal forum in the first place? For an argument that it should, see Yonover, *A Kinder, Gentler Erie: Reining In the Use of Certification,* 47 Ark.L.Rev. 305 (1994).[8]

(d) *Bearing on the Abstention Decision.* Should the availability of certification make a federal court more willing to abstain in Pullman-type cases? In Bellotti v. Baird, 428 U.S. 132, 151 (1976), the Court said: "The importance of speed in resolution of the instant litigation is manifest. * * * Although we do not mean to intimate that abstention would be improper in this case were certification not possible, the availability of certification greatly simplifies the analysis." See also Planned Parenthood Ass'n of Kansas City, Mo., Inc. v. Ashcroft, 462 U.S. 476, 493 n. 21 (1983)(noting as one reason for refusing to abstain that Missouri had no certification procedure, and that "[s]uch a procedure 'greatly simplifie[d]' our analysis in Bellotti"). But *cf.* Houston v. Hill, 482 U.S. 451, 470–71 (1987)(the availability of certification, though important in deciding whether to abstain, "is not in itself sufficient to render abstention appropriate"). Is there a risk that the availability of certification procedures will invite improvident abstention in Pullman-type cases?[9]

---

7. Most states require that the certified question be potentially determinative of the case. Thus, in Abrams v. West Virginia Racing Com'n, 164 W.Va. 315, 263 S.E.2d 103 (1980), the Court refused to decide a certified question because it believed that federal law would control regardless of the answer. Some states, however, impose the stricter requirement that the answer will certainly determine the case. See Note, note (7), *supra,* at 1349. How often will an answer *either way* determine the outcome? Wouldn't this stricter requirement make certification virtually unavailable in Pullman-type cases?

8. See also Seaboard Sur. Co. v. Garrison, Webb & Stanaland, P.A., 823 F.2d 434,

438 (11th Cir.1987)("[h]aving sought a Federal forum, [plaintiff in a diversity case] must abide by federal determination" of state law); American Law Institute, Study of the Division of Jurisdiction Between State and Federal Courts 296 (1969)(it is usually undesirable to allow a removing defendant a federal court determination of facts and a state court determination of state law).

9. There is apparently some reluctance on the part of federal judges to certify questions in constitutional or civil rights cases; nearly two-thirds of all certified questions arose in diversity actions like Lehman Brothers. Seron, *supra,* at 7–10.

(e) *Frequency of Utilization.* Judge Butzner reported in 1985 that the Fourth Circuit had certified fewer than a half-dozen of the approximately 23,000 cases filed since 1972. Butzner & Kelly, *Certification: Assuring the Primacy of State Law in the Fourth Circuit,* 42 Wash. & Lee L.Rev. 449, 455 (1985). Several years earlier, Chief Judge Brown stated that the Fifth Circuit has "reserved certification only for use in cases where important, probably recurrent state issues are involved." Brown, *Certification—Federalism in Action,* 7 Cumb.L.Rev. 455, 457 (1977). But some decisions suggest an enthusiasm for the device more likely to lead to its routine use than to its reservation for unusually important issues. See, *e.g.,* Walters v. Inexco Oil Co., 670 F.2d 476 (5th Cir.1982), a diversity case in which Judge Brown, in certifying a "narrow" question of Mississippi law to the state supreme court, without any finding that the issue was recurrent or of special significance, "seize[d] the opportunity to praise, extol, laud and proclaim the virtues of this wonderful device" (pp. 477–78). See generally 17A Wright, Miller & Cooper, Federal Practice and Procedure § 4248 (1988).

(f) *Literature on Certification.* For further discussion of certification procedures, see, in addition to the sources cited above, Lillich & Mundy, *Federal Court Certification of Doubtful State Law Questions,* 18 U.C.L.A.L.Rev. 888 (1971); McKusick, *Certification: A Procedure for Cooperation between State and Federal Courts,* 16 Me.L.Rev. 33 (1964). See also Corr & Robbins, *Interjurisdictional Certification and Choice of Law,* 41 Vand.L.Rev. 411 (1988); Robbins, *The Uniform Certification of Questions of Law Act: A Proposal for Reform,* 18 J.Legis. 127 (1992).

NOTE ON BURFORD AND THIBODAUX ABSTENTION

(1) *Departures from the Pullman Paradigm.* In its paradigmatic applications, the Pullman doctrine involves challenges to state action in which resolution of an unsettled state law issue could eliminate the need to decide (or at least narrow) a difficult federal question. Is abstention ever justified in the absence of a federal interest in avoiding a possibly unnecessary constitutional holding or at least narrowing a constitutional issue?

The cases discussed in this Note respond to this question. One, Burford v. Sun Oil Co., 319 U.S. 315 (1943), is conventionally viewed as the leading case establishing a form of so-called "Burford" or "administrative" abstention. Another, Louisiana Power & Light Co. v. City of Thibodaux, 360 U.S. 25 (1959), is thought to have launched another abstention doctrine applicable to at least some cases otherwise within the federal courts' diversity jurisdiction and not presenting any federal question at all.

Although often cited, the Burford and Thibodaux cases have produced few if any progeny in the Supreme Court, and attempts to apply them in the lower courts have frequently spawned confusion. As you read through the remainder of this Note, consider (i) whether the Burford and Thibodaux decisions can be justified, (ii) whether they truly have given rise to sufficiently clear principles and bodies of law to constitute "doctrines", and, if so, (iii) how those doctrines ought to be defined.

(2) *Burford Abstention.*

(a) *The Burford Case.*   Burford v. Sun Oil Co., 319 U.S. 315 (1943), was an action to enjoin the execution of an order of the Railroad Commission of Texas granting a neighboring leaseholder a permit to drill new wells. The order was attacked on federal constitutional and state grounds, and jurisdiction rested both on the federal question and diversity of citizenship. The Court held, 5–4, that the federal district court "as a matter of sound equitable discretion" should have declined to exercise jurisdiction and dismissed the case.

Justice Black's opinion emphasized the complexity of the problems of oil and gas regulation (pp. 318–20):

"* * * The East Texas field, in which the Burford tract is located, * * * is forty miles long and between five and nine miles wide, and over 26,000 wells have been drilled in it. * * * The chief forces causing oil to move are gas and water, and it is essential that the pressures be maintained at a level which will force the oil through wells to the surface. As the gas pressure is dissipated, it becomes necessary to put the well 'on the pump' at great expense, and the sooner the gas from a field is exhausted, the more oil is irretrievably lost. Since the oil moves through the entire field, one operator can not only draw oil from under his own surface area, but can also, if he is advantageously located, drain oil from the most distant parts of the reservoir. * * *

"For these and many other reasons based on geologic realities, each oil and gas field must be regulated as a unit for conservation purposes.   * * *

"Texas' interests in this matter are more than that very large one of conserving gas and oil, two of our most important natural resources. It must also weigh the impact of the industry on the whole economy of the State and must consider its revenue, much of which is drawn from taxes on industry and from mineral lands preserved for the benefit of its educational and eleemosynary institutions. * * * The primary task of attempting adjustment of these diverse interests is delegated to the Railroad Commission, which Texas has vested with 'broad discretion' in administering the law."

Justice Black condemned the results of previous federal court injunctions, particularly those that had proved to be based on "misunderstanding of local law". He continued (pp. 325–26, 332–34):

"In describing the relation of the Texas court to the Commission, no useful purpose will be served by attempting to label the court's position as legislative, Prentis v. Atlantic Coast Line Co., [p. 1223, *supra*] * * *, or judicial, Bacon v. Rutland Railroad Co., [p. 1224, *supra*] * * *—suffice it to say that the Texas courts are working partners with the Railroad Commission in the business of creating a regulatory system for the oil industry. * * *

"To prevent the confusion of multiple review of the same general issues, the legislature provided for concentration of all direct review of the Commission's orders in the state district courts of Travis County. * * *
          * * *

"These questions of regulation of the industry by the state administrative agency, whether involving gas or oil prorationing programs or [well spacing] cases, so clearly involve basic problems of Texas policy that equitable discretion should be exercised to give the Texas courts the first opportunity to consider them. * * *

"The State provides a unified method for the formation of policy and determination of cases by the Commission and by the state courts. The judicial review of the Commission's decisions in the state courts is expeditious and adequate. Conflicts in the interpretation of state law, dangerous to the success of state policies, are almost certain to result from the intervention of the lower federal courts. On the other hand, if the state procedure is followed from the Commission to the State Supreme Court, ultimate review of the federal questions is fully preserved here. * * * Under such circumstances, a sound respect for the independence of state action requires the federal equity court to stay its hand.''[1]

Justice Frankfurter, speaking for three other Justices, dissented vigorously. He found no uncertainty in state law akin to that in the Pullman case. Rather, he said, the case depended upon "narrowly defined standards of law established by Texas for review of the orders of its Railroad Commission", which federal judges "are certainly not incompetent to apply" (p. 342). Apparently regarding the federal issues as minor, he distinguished Pullman as "merely illustrative of one phase of the basic constitutional doctrine that substantial constitutional issues should be adjudicated only when no alternatives are open" (p. 338).

(b) *The Burford Doctrine in the Supreme Court.* The Supreme Court relied on Burford, not Pullman, in ordering abstention in Alabama Pub. Serv. Comm'n v. Southern Ry., 341 U.S. 341 (1951). After the Commission denied the railroad's request to discontinue two intrastate trains, the railroad bypassed available review in the state's courts and sued instead in federal court. Jurisdiction was based on diversity of citizenship and on a federal question, since the railroad alleged that the Commission's order constituted confiscation of property in violation of the Fourteenth Amendment. A three-judge court granted the requested injunction, but the Supreme Court reversed, ordering dismissal of the complaint. Chief Justice Vinson, writing for the Court, apparently conceded that there were no issues of unsettled state law in the case and no challenge to the constitutionality of the state statute on its face. But, he said (pp. 346–50):

"* * * This Court has held that regulation of intrastate railroad service is 'primarily the concern of the state.' North Carolina v. United States, 325 U.S. 507, 511 (1945). Statutory appeal from an order of the Commission is an integral part of the regulatory process under the Alabama Code. Appeals, concentrated in one circuit court, are 'supervisory in character.' * * * As adequate state court review of an administrative order based upon predominantly local factors is available to appellee, intervention of a federal court is not necessary for the protection of federal rights. * * * 'Few public interests have a higher claim upon the discretion of a federal chancellor than the avoidance of needless friction with state policies' [citing Pullman] * * *.''

Justice Frankfurter, joined by Justice Jackson, concurred in the result on the basis that the complaint failed to state a substantial claim, but again dissented from the abstention rationale (pp. 360–62).

The Supreme Court has not invoked Burford abstention since the Southern Railway decision. In McNeese v. Board of Education, 373 U.S. 668 (1963), the Court refused, over Justice Harlan's lone dissent, to abstain in a school desegregation case where the state claimed to have administrative procedures

---

1. Justices Douglas and Murphy concurred specially on the ground that "this decision is but an application of the principle expressed in" Pennsylvania v. Williams, p. 1254, *infra.*

for handling the dispute; Burford was distinguishable, because here the federal right was not "entangled in a skein of state law" and the legality under state law of the conduct was not at issue (p. 674). The Court also stressed the importance of federal court jurisdiction in civil rights cases. In Colorado River Water Conservation Dist. v. United States, 424 U.S. 800 (1976), Sec. 2(D), *infra,* a suit by the United States to adjudicate complex claims to water rights, the Court again found Burford abstention inappropriate, emphasizing that the state law was settled, and that although a federal decision might conflict with that of a state tribunal, it would not "impermissibly" impair state water policy.[2] The Supreme Court also distinguished Burford in its more recent decisions in Ankenbrandt v. Richards, 504 U.S. 689 (1992), p. 1323, *infra,* and New Orleans Public Service, Inc. ("NOPSI") v. Council of New Orleans, 491 U.S. 350 (1989), p. 1301, *infra.*

Nonetheless, the Court's references to Burford imply its continuing vitality. In Ankenbrandt, 504 U.S. 689, the Court suggested that Burford abstention might be appropriate in domestic relations cases that present "difficult questions of state law bearing on policy problems of substantial import whose importance transcends the result in the case then at bar"—as, for example, "if a federal suit were filed prior to effectuation of a divorce, alimony, or child custody decree, and the suit depended on a determination of the status of the parties". (The Court, however, found such factors absent in Ankenbrandt itself—a tort suit on behalf of two children alleging child abuse by their father and his companion.) In the NOPSI case, *supra,* the Court summarized the Burford doctrine as follows (489 U.S. at 361):

"Where timely and adequate state court review is available, a federal court sitting in equity must decline to interfere with the proceedings or orders of state administrative agencies: (1) when there are 'difficult questions of state law bearing on policy problems of substantial public import whose importance transcends the result in the case then at bar'; or (2) where the 'exercise of federal review * * * would be disruptive of state efforts to establish a coherent policy with respect to a matter of substantial public concern'" (quoting Colorado River Conservation Dist., *supra,* 424 U.S. at 814).[3]

(c) *The Rationale.* Can you clearly identify Burford's rationale? Are the criteria that govern its application sufficiently clear to permit reasonable predictability? How difficult must a question be for the doctrine to be triggered? Which state policies are and are not sufficiently important to justify abstention?

Would Burford abstention make most sense if restricted to cases in which a particular state court, through its exclusive appellate jurisdiction, works as a de

---

2. In a footnote, the Court noted (p. 815 n. 21) that Burford and Southern Railway both involved federal constitutional questions, and stated that "the presence of a federal basis for jurisdiction may raise the level of justification needed for abstention." The Court did order the federal court to stay its proceedings in deference to a parallel state proceeding under Colorado's elaborate procedures for handling disputes about water rights, but viewed that as a rationale distinct from Burford abstention.

3. Although the Court's summary seems to imply that Burford-type abstention is limited to cases involving state administrative agencies, the first two cases cited as exemplifying "difficult questions of state law" in the Colorado River case, from which the Court quoted its formulation, upheld abstention in cases not involving administrative proceedings. Those cases, Louisiana Power & Light Co. v. City of Thibodaux, 360 U.S. 25 (1959), and Kaiser Steel Corp. v. W.S. Ranch Co., 391 U.S. 593 (1968), are discussed in Paragraph (3), *infra.*

facto partner of a state administrative agency in developing state regulatory policy, and review of the agency's decision by a federal district court would disrupt the partnership relationship? See James Rehnquist, *Taking Comity Seriously: How to Neutralize the Abstention Doctrine,* 46 Stan.L.Rev. 1049, 1077–78 (1994). See also Young, *Federal Court Abstention and State Administrative Law From Burford to Ankenbrandt: Fifty Years of Judicial Federalism Under Burford v. Sun Oil Co. and Kindred Doctrines,* 42 DePaul L.Rev. 859, 886–99 (1993)(arguing that the decision in Burford reflected concerns such as these). On the other hand, if Burford abstention is based on the notion that a specialized state court has some attributes of an administrative agency, wouldn't it be rather difficult to square with the decision in Patsy v. Board of Regents, Sec. 2(A), *supra,* which held that plaintiffs need not exhaust available administrative remedies before bringing suit under 42 U.S.C. § 1983?

(d) *Burford and the Judicial Power.* In both Burford and Southern Railway, Justice Frankfurter protested that abstention was incompatible with the expressed policy of the jurisdictional statutes.[4] But was abstention in those cases any more at odds with the policy of the jurisdictional statutes than abstention in the Pullman decision (in which Justice Frankfurter wrote the majority opinion)?[5]

Note that there are at least two differences between the cases. (i) Jurisdiction in Burford and Southern Ry. rested on *both* federal question and diversity grounds, whereas in Pullman there was federal question jurisdiction only. Is abstention more problematic under the diversity than under the federal question grant? (ii) In Burford abstention, the federal court defers to the state court on federal as well as state issues, and unless the Supreme Court reviews the case, res judicata would preclude federal litigation of the federal issues.[6] In Pullman abstention, by contrast, the plaintiff retains the right, following an excursion to state court, to litigate federal claims in federal court.

(e) *Burford in the Lower Courts.* The lower courts have, not surprisingly, found the Supreme Court's pronouncements less than pellucid, and the decisions are contradictory. See Young, *supra,* at 900–06; Davies, *Pullman and Burford Abstention: Clarifying the Roles of State and Federal Courts in Constitutional Cases,* 20 U.C. Davis L.Rev. 1, 16–21 (1986).[7]

4. In Southern Railway, Justice Frankfurter also said that to recognize judicial discretion to abstain "based solely on the availability of a remedy in the State courts would for all practical purposes repeal the Act of 1875 [conferring federal jurisdiction of cases 'arising under' the Constitution and laws of the United States]" (341 U.S. at 355–57). And he noted in his dissent in Burford (p. 338 n.1) that the Johnson Act limits federal court jurisdiction over one class of public utility orders, those dealing with rates. See Sec. 1(B), *supra.* Does that limitation suggest that Congress had made a considered decision about when comity did and did not call for federal judicial abstention?

5. *Cf.* McManamon, *Felix Frankfurter: The Architect of "Our Federalism",* 27 Ga. L.Rev. 697 (1993)(arguing generally that

much of modern abstention law and its underlying notions of comity and federalism reflect Frankfurter's influence).

6. If Burford abstention is premised on the notion that a state reviewing court acts in a policymaking partnership with the state administrative agency, see Paragraph (2)(c), *supra,* would it follow that the state court's decision should be deemed legislative rather than judicial, and that ordinary res judicata principles should not apply? Compare Young, *supra,* at 977–78.

7. Among the issues on which the lower courts are divided is whether Burford abstention should be available in suits for damages. See, *e.g.,* Garamendi v. Allstate Ins. Co., 47 F.3d 350 (9th Cir.1995), *cert. granted sub nom.* Quackenbush v. Allstate Ins. Co., 116 S.Ct. 334 (1995).

(3) *Thibodaux Abstention.*

(a) *The Thibodaux Case.* Louisiana Power & Light Co. v. City of Thibodaux, 360 U.S. 25 (1959), was a proceeding by the City to take by eminent domain property owned by Louisiana Power & Light. The company removed the proceeding to federal court on the basis of diversity of citizenship. The issue in the case—aside from the amount of compensation—was whether as a matter of Louisiana law municipalities had the authority to condemn public utility properties. The district court stayed the action pending the institution of a state declaratory judgment action and decision of this issue by the state supreme court. The court of appeals reversed, but was in turn reversed by the Supreme Court. Justice Frankfurter stressed that eminent domain proceedings are "special and peculiar" and "intimately involved with sovereign prerogative", particularly where the issue "concerns the apportionment of governmental powers between City and State" (p. 28). He continued (pp. 29–30):

"The special nature of eminent domain justifies a district judge, when his familiarity with the problems of local law so counsels him, to ascertain the meaning of a disputed state statute from the only tribunal empowered to speak definitively—the courts of the State under whose statute eminent domain is sought to be exercised—rather than himself make a dubious and tentative forecast. This course does not constitute abnegation of judicial duty. On the contrary, it is a wise and productive discharge of it. There is only postponement of decision for its best fruition. Eventually the District Court will award compensation if the taking is sustained. If for some reason a declaratory judgment is not promptly sought from the state courts and obtained within a reasonable time, the District Court, having retained complete control of the litigation, will doubtless assert it to decide also the question of the meaning of the state statute. The justification for this power, to be exercised within the indicated limits, lies in regard for the respective competence of the state and federal court systems and for the maintenance of harmonious federal-state relations in a matter close to the political interests of a State. * * *

"* * * In providing on his own motion for a stay in this case, an experienced district judge was responding in a sensible way to a quandary about the power of the City of Thibodaux into which he was placed by an opinion of the Attorney General of Louisiana in which it was concluded that in a strikingly similar case a Louisiana city did not have the power here claimed by the City. A Louisiana statute apparently seems to grant such a power. But that statute has never been interpreted, in respect to a situation like that before the judge, by the Louisiana courts and it would not be the first time that the authoritative tribunal has found in a statute less than meets the outsider's eye. Informed local courts may find meaning not discernible to the outsider. The consequence of allowing this to come to pass would be that this case would be the only case in which the Louisiana statute is construed as we would construe it, whereas the rights of all other litigants would be thereafter governed by a decision of the Supreme Court of Louisiana quite different from ours."

Justice Brennan, joined by Chief Justice Warren and Justice Douglas, filed a long and vigorous dissent (pp. 31–33, 39):

"Until today, the standards for testing this order of the District Court sending the parties to this diversity action to a state court for decision of a state law question might have been said to have been reasonably consistent with the imperative duty of a District Court, imposed by Congress under 28

U.S.C. §§ 1332 and 1441, to render prompt justice in cases between citizens of different States. To order these suitors out of the federal court and into a state court in the circumstances of this case passes beyond disrespect for the diversity jurisdiction to plain disregard of this imperative duty. The doctrine of abstention, in proper perspective, is an extraordinary and narrow exception to this duty, and abdication of the obligation to decide cases can be justified under this doctrine only in the exceptional circumstances where the order to the parties to repair to the state court would clearly serve one of two important countervailing interests: either the avoidance of a premature and perhaps unnecessary decision of a serious federal constitutional question, or the avoidance of the hazard of unsettling some delicate balance in the area of federal-state relationships.

> * * *

"But neither of the two recognized situations justifying abstention is present in the case before us. * * *

"'* * * [M]ere difficulty of construing the state statute is not justification for running away from the task. * * *'"

Note that Justice Brennan appears to concede that, in principle, the avoidance of friction with significant state policies is an independent justification for abstention. Doesn't this concession seriously weaken his argument that abstention reflects a "plain disregard of [an] imperative duty"? Was Justice Brennan correct that federal adjudication of the state law issue in Thibodaux created no significant risk of federal/state friction?

Justice Frankfurter, who in the Burford and Southern Railway cases, *supra,* had offered anti-abstention arguments similar to those of Justice Brennan's dissent, once again supported abstention in the Thibodaux case (as he had in Pullman). Is there any thread of consistency among his positions?

(b) *Background to Thibodaux.* Justice Brennan's dissenting opinion in Thibodaux relied heavily on Meredith v. City of Winter Haven, 320 U.S. 228 (1943). Meredith was a municipal bondholders' action to enjoin the retirement of bonds on terms that were allegedly unlawful as a matter of state law. Jurisdiction rested solely on diversity of citizenship. The court of appeals directed dismissal without prejudice to the plaintiffs' right to proceed in the state courts, but the Supreme Court, per Chief Justice Stone, reversed. After a careful review of the cases, the Chief Justice held that a federal court could not refuse to exercise diversity jurisdiction merely because a case "involve[s] state law or because the law is uncertain or difficult to determine. * * * Decision here does not require the federal court to determine or shape state policy governing administrative agencies. It entails no interference with such agencies or with the state courts. No litigation is pending in the state courts in which the questions here presented could be decided. We are pointed to no public policy or interest which would be served by withholding from petitioners the benefit of the jurisdiction which Congress has created with the purpose that it should be availed of and exercised subject only to such limitations as traditionally justify courts in declining to exercise the jurisdiction which they possess. * * *"[8]

---

8. In a footnote in his opinion for the Court in Thibodaux (p. 27 n. 2), Justice Frankfurter distinguished Meredith largely on the basis that the court of appeals in that case had ordered the suit dismissed, whereas the district court in Thibodaux would retain

In a few cases prior to Meredith, however, the Supreme Court had indicated that under certain circumstances a federal court should refrain from deciding a case governed entirely by state law. See Hawks v. Hamill, 288 U.S. 52, 60 (1933)(concluding that a federal court should not enjoin legal actions by a state attorney general and county attorneys where jurisdiction rested on "no other basis than the accidents of residence"); Pennsylvania v. Williams, 294 U.S. 176 (1935)(federal diversity court should defer to impending state statutory proceeding for liquidating insolvent building and loan association); *cf.* Thompson v. Magnolia Petroleum Co., 309 U.S. 478 (1940).

(c) *The Thibodaux Rationale.* A reading of the Court's opinion in Thibodaux would surely justify the conclusion that some distinctive feature of eminent domain tips the scales heavily in favor of abstention. But in a case decided the same day, County of Allegheny v. Frank Mashuda Co., 360 U.S. 185 (1959), the Court declined (5–4) to abstain from deciding whether land taken by the county and then leased to a private party was validly condemned under state law. Like Thibodaux, the Allegheny County case was brought under the diversity jurisdiction, and Justice Brennan's majority opinion was an almost verbatim gloss of parts of his dissent in Thibodaux, which rejects any notion that federal adjudication of cases involving the eminent domain power of the states presents any special risks of friction with state authority. Justice Brennan added (p. 196): "Aside from the complete absence of any possibility that a District Court adjudication would * * * conflict with state policy, the state law that the District Court was asked to apply is clear and certain. All that was necessary * * * was to determine whether, as a matter of fact, the respondents' property was taken for private use * * *."

Justice Clark's dissent was joined by Justices Black, Frankfurter, and Harlan, all of whom were in the Thibodaux majority. Thus, of the nine Justices, seven evidently felt that Thibodaux and Mashuda were indistinguishable and dissented in either one or the other of the cases. Justices Stewart and Whittaker alone were in the majority in both cases, and only Justice Stewart attempted an explanation. In a concurrence in Thibodaux (p. 31), he said: "In a conscientious effort to do justice the District Court deferred immediate adjudication of this controversy pending authoritative clarification of a controlling state statute of highly doubtful meaning. Under the circumstances presented, I think the course pursued was clearly within the District Court's allowable discretion. * * *

"The case is totally unlike County of Allegheny v. Mashuda Co., decided today, except for the coincidence that both cases involve eminent domain proceedings. In Mashuda the Court holds * * * that, since the controlling state law is clear and only factual issues need be resolved, there is no occasion in the interest of justice to refrain from prompt adjudication."

The taking in Mashuda involved the enlargement of the Pittsburgh Airport; the property in controversy was leased by the county to a contractor for storing necessary materials. The issue was whether this was a private or a public use under Pennsylvania law. Were Justices Brennan and Stewart correct in characterizing this as an issue of fact and therefore distinguishable from the issue in Thibodaux?

Even if the answer to this question is "no", is there a basis for distinction? Do the two cases raise issues of equal breadth and import? In which case

jurisdiction while awaiting "controlling light
from the state court."

would a "wrong" decision of the question by a federal court create graver consequences for state policy? Was there an equal need in the two cases for affording the kind of protection for which the diversity jurisdiction was designed?

When enough factors are taken into account, it seems clear that Thibodaux and Mashuda can be distinguished, but it also remains doubtful that any ground of distinction could have commanded a majority of the Supreme Court. For further discussion of these cases, see, *e.g.*, Gowen & Izlar, *Federal Court Abstention in Diversity of Citizenship Cases,* 43 Tex.L.Rev. 194 (1964).

(d) *Current Status.* How much contemporary vitality does Thibodaux possess? Consider Rehnquist, note (2)(c), *supra,* at 1082: "Thibodaux's difficult and controversial birth perhaps left it too weak to generate much force. Not a single Supreme Court case has subsequently upheld abstention based solely on Thibodaux. Overloaded district courts have, for the most part, resisted the allure of Thibodaux's abstract principle: that unsettled state law permits abstention."

The Supreme Court, however, has continued to cite Thibodaux approvingly. In Colorado River Water Conservation District v. United States, 424 U.S. 800, 814 (1976), p. 1308, *infra,* the Court characterized Thibodaux as supporting abstention "where there have been presented difficult questions of state law bearing on policy problems of substantial public import whose importance transcends the result in the case at bar." In New Orleans Public Service, Inc. v. New Orleans, 491 U.S. 350, 361 (1989), this formulation reappeared, but as a description of one of two prongs of Burford abstention doctrine. See Paragraph (2)(b), *supra* (quoting NOPSI's formulation). Has Thibodaux abstention now been subsumed by Burford abstention? Is there sufficient difference between the two doctrines and their rationales to warrant a difference in label? Or do both reflect an amorphous notion that when state issues are sufficiently difficult, sufficiently important, and sufficiently bound up with other state law issues and state administration, federal courts should sometimes abstain?

Although the Supreme Court did not cite Thibodaux expressly, Kaiser Steel Corp. v. W.S. Ranch Co., 391 U.S. 593 (1968), might be regarded as a Thibodaux abstention case. In Kaiser Steel, a diversity action involving a dispute over rights to water on private land, the question was whether a New Mexico statute had authorized the defendant to take water, and, if so, whether the statute was valid under the state constitution, which permits takings only for "public use". In a per curiam decision reversing the court of appeals, the Supreme Court held that the suit should be stayed pending adjudication of the central issues in a state declaratory judgment action. The Court explained: "The state law issue which is crucial in this case is one of vital concern in the arid State of New Mexico, where water is one of the most valuable natural resources. The issue, moreover, is a truly novel one. The question will eventually have to be resolved by the New Mexico courts, and since a declaratory judgment action is actually pending there, in all likelihood that resolution will be forthcoming soon. Sound judicial administration requires that the parties in this case be given the benefit of the same rule of law which will apply to all other businesses and landowners concerned with the use of this vital state resource" (p. 594).[9]

---

9. Justice Brennan's brief concurrence, joined by Justices Douglas and Marshall, stressed that the importance of the issue of water use for New Mexico was a "special

What, finally, is the relevance of Lehman Brothers v. Schein, 416 U.S. 386 (1974), p. 1245, *supra,* a diversity case presenting no federal question, in which a unanimous Supreme Court vacated the court of appeals' decision of a difficult question of state law and directed the lower court to certify the question to the state's highest court? In cases subject to the Pullman doctrine, both courts and commentators have frequently treated federal courts' decisions to certify questions to state courts as decisions to abstain. See generally Paragraph (6) of the *Note on Procedural Aspects of Pullman Abstention,* p. 1242, *supra.* Is that characterization apt? If so, isn't Lehman Brothers a Thibodaux abstention case? If it is, is the Supreme Court's endorsement of certification procedures in Lehman Brothers at least partly an endorsement of a form of Thibodaux abstention?

(4) *The Rationales Re-examined.* Consider the validity of each of the following propositions:

(i) A necessary and desirable function of state courts, as of state administrative agencies, is to make law.

(ii) Burford counsels abstention in order not to disrupt coordinated policy-making by state agencies and state courts; Thibodaux takes the logical, parallel step of authorizing abstention, even in the absence of action by an administrative agency, when a federal court believes that adjudication of a state law issue would require "sensitive and uncertain decisions of policy better made by the state judiciary." Young, Paragraph (2)(c), *supra,* at 945.

(iii) The rationales of the Burford and Thibodaux doctrines are therefore closely linked, with Thibodaux being broader in that it omits the apparent Burford requirement of decisionmaking by a state administrative agency and unified review in the state court. It would thus be as true to say that Thibodaux subsumes, as that Thibodaux is an extension of, Burford.

(iv) A major difficulty with both Burford and Thibodaux lies in developing a metric to compare state interests favoring abstention with federal interests counseling against abstention and to weigh those interests in a reasonably predictable way.

SUBSECTION C: EQUITABLE RESTRAINT

Younger v. Harris

401 U.S. 37, 91 S.Ct. 746, 27 L.Ed.2d 669 (1971).
Appeal from the United States District Court for the Central District of California.

■ MR. JUSTICE BLACK delivered the opinion of the Court.

Appellee, John Harris, Jr., was indicted in a California state court, charged with violation of the California Penal Code §§ 11400 and 11401, known as the California Criminal Syndicalism Act * * *. He then filed a complaint in the Federal District Court, asking that court to enjoin the appellant, Younger, the

circumstance" justifying abstention, and included "*cf.*" cites to Burford and Southern Railway (pp. 594–95), which the majority did not cite.

District Attorney of Los Angeles County, from prosecuting him, and alleging that the prosecution and even the presence of the Act inhibited him in the exercise of his rights of free speech and press, rights guaranteed him by the First and Fourteenth Amendments. Appellees Jim Dan and Diane Hirsch intervened as plaintiffs in the suit, claiming that the prosecution of Harris would inhibit them as members of the Progressive Labor Party from peacefully advocating the program of their party, which was to replace capitalism with socialism and to abolish the profit system of production in this country. Appellee Farrell Broslawsky, an instructor in history at Los Angeles Valley College, also intervened claiming that the prosecution of Harris made him uncertain as to whether he could teach about the doctrines of Karl Marx or read from the Communist Manifesto as part of his classwork. All claimed that unless the United States court restrained the state prosecution of Harris each would suffer immediate and irreparable injury. A three-judge Federal District Court, convened pursuant to 28 U.S.C. § 2284, held that it had jurisdiction and power to restrain the District Attorney from prosecuting, held that the State's Criminal Syndicalism Act was void for vagueness and overbreadth in violation of the First and Fourteenth Amendments, and accordingly restrained the District Attorney from "further prosecution of the currently pending action against plaintiff Harris for alleged violation of the Act."

The case is before us on appeal by the State's District Attorney Younger, pursuant to 28 U.S.C. § 1253. In his notice of appeal and his jurisdictional statement appellant presented two questions: (1) whether the decision of this Court in Whitney v. California, 274 U.S. 357, holding California's law constitutional in 1927 was binding on the District Court and (2) whether the State's law is constitutional on its face. In this Court the brief for the State of California, filed at our request, also argues that only Harris, who was indicted, has standing to challenge the State's law, and that issuance of the injunction was a violation of a longstanding judicial policy and of 28 U.S.C. § 2283 * * *. Without regard to the questions raised about Whitney v. California, *supra*, since overruled by Brandenburg v. Ohio, 395 U.S. 444 (1969), or the constitutionality of the state law, we have concluded that the judgment of the District Court, enjoining appellant Younger from prosecuting under these California statutes, must be reversed as a violation of the national policy forbidding federal courts to stay or enjoin pending state court proceedings except under special circumstances.[2] We express no view about the circumstances under which federal courts may act when there is no prosecution pending in state courts at the time the federal proceeding is begun.

I

Appellee Harris has been indicted, and was actually being prosecuted by California for a violation of its Criminal Syndicalism Act at the time this suit was filed. He thus has an acute, live controversy with the State and its prosecutor. But none of the other parties plaintiff in the District Court, Dan, Hirsch, or Broslawsky, has such a controversy. None has been indicted, arrested, or even threatened by the prosecutor. * * *

---

2. Appellees did not explicitly ask for a declaratory judgment in their complaint. They did, however, ask the District Court to grant "such other and further relief as to the Court may seem just and proper," and the District Court in fact granted a declaratory judgment. For the reasons stated in our opinion today in Samuels v. Mackell, 401 U.S. 66, we hold that declaratory relief is also improper when a prosecution involving the challenged statute is pending in state court at the time the federal suit is initiated.

Whatever right Harris, who is being prosecuted under the state syndicalism law may have, Dan, Hirsch, and Broslawsky cannot share it with him. If these three had alleged that they would be prosecuted for the conduct they planned to engage in, and if the District Court had found this allegation to be true—either on the admission of the State's district attorney or on any other evidence—then a genuine controversy might be said to exist. But here appellees, Dan, Hirsch, and Broslawsky do not claim that they have ever been threatened with prosecution, that a prosecution is likely, or even that a prosecution is remotely possible. They claim the right to bring this suit solely because, in the language of their complaint, they "feel inhibited." We do not think this allegation even if true, is sufficient to bring the equitable jurisdiction of the federal courts into play to enjoin a pending state prosecution. A federal lawsuit to stop a prosecution in a state court is a serious matter. And persons having no fears of state prosecution except those that are imaginary or speculative, are not to be accepted as appropriate plaintiffs in such cases. See Golden v. Zwickler, 394 U.S. 103 (1969). Since Harris is actually being prosecuted under the challenged laws, however, we proceed with him as a proper party.

II

Since the beginning of this country's history Congress has, subject to few exceptions, manifested a desire to permit state courts to try state cases free from interference by federal courts. In 1793 an Act unconditionally provided: "[N]or shall a writ of injunction be granted to stay proceedings in any court of a state * * *." A comparison of the 1793 Act with 28 U.S.C. § 2283, its present-day successor, graphically illustrates how few and minor have been the exceptions granted from the flat, prohibitory language of the old Act. During all this lapse of years from 1793 to 1970 the statutory exceptions to the 1793 congressional enactment have been only three: (1) "except as expressly authorized by Act of Congress"; (2) "where necessary in aid of its jurisdiction"; and (3) "to protect or effectuate its judgments." In addition, a judicial exception to the longstanding policy evidenced by the statute has been made where a person about to be prosecuted in a state court can show that he will, if the proceeding in the state court is not enjoined, suffer irreparable damages. See Ex parte Young, 209 U.S. 123 (1908).

The precise reasons for this longstanding public policy against federal court interference with state court proceedings have never been specifically identified but the primary sources of the policy are plain. One is the basic doctrine of equity jurisprudence that courts of equity should not act, and particularly should not act to restrain a criminal prosecution, when the moving party has an adequate remedy at law and will not suffer irreparable injury if denied equitable relief. The doctrine may originally have grown out of circumstances peculiar to the English judicial system and not applicable in this country, but its fundamental purpose of restraining equity jurisdiction within narrow limits is equally important under our Constitution, in order to prevent erosion of the role of the jury and avoid a duplication of legal proceedings and legal sanctions where a single suit would be adequate to protect the rights asserted. This underlying reason for restraining courts of equity from interfering with criminal prosecutions is reinforced by an even more vital consideration, the notion of "comity," that is, a proper respect for state functions, a recognition of the fact that the entire country is made up of a Union of separate state governments, and a continuance of the belief that the National Government will fare best if the States and their institutions are left free to perform their separate functions in their separate ways. This, perhaps for lack of a better and clearer way to describe it, is referred to by many as "Our Federalism," and one familiar with the profound debates that ushered our Federal Constitution into existence is bound to respect those who remain loyal to the ideals and dreams of "Our Federalism." The concept does not mean blind deference to "States' Rights" any more than it means centralization of control over every important issue in our National Government and its courts. The Framers rejected both these courses. What the concept does represent is a system in which there is sensitivity to the legitimate interests of both State and National Governments, and in which the National Government, anxious though it may be to vindicate and protect federal rights and federal interests, always endeavors to do so in ways that will not unduly interfere with the legitimate activities of the States. It should never be forgotten that this slogan, "Our Federalism," born in the early struggling days of our Union of States, occupies a highly important place in our Nation's history and its future.

This brief discussion should be enough to suggest some of the reasons why it has been perfectly natural for our cases to repeat time and time again that the normal thing to do when federal courts are asked to enjoin pending proceedings in state courts is not to issue such injunctions. In Fenner v. Boykin, 271 U.S. 240 (1926), suit had been brought in the Federal District Court seeking to enjoin state prosecutions under a recently enacted state law that allegedly interfered with the free flow of interstate commerce. The Court, in a unanimous opinion made clear that such a suit, even with respect to state criminal proceedings not yet formally instituted, could be proper only under very special circumstances:

> "Ex parte Young, 209 U.S. 123, and following cases have established the doctrine that, when absolutely necessary for protection of constitutional rights, courts of the United States have power to enjoin state officers from instituting criminal actions. But this may not be done, except under extraordinary circumstances, where the danger of irreparable loss is both great and immediate. Ordinarily, there should be no interference with such officers; primarily, they are charged with the duty of prosecuting offenders against the laws of the state, and must decide when and how this is to be done. The accused should first set up and rely upon his defense in the state courts, even though this involves a challenge of the validity of some statute, unless it plainly appears that this course would not afford adequate protection." *Id.*, at 243–244.

These principles, made clear in the Fenner case, have been repeatedly followed and reaffirmed in other cases involving threatened prosecutions. See, *e.g.,* Spielman Motor Sales Co. v. Dodge, 295 U.S. 89 (1935); Beal v. Missouri Pac. R. Co., 312 U.S. 45 (1941); Watson v. Buck, 313 U.S. 387 (1941); Williams v. Miller, 317 U.S. 599 (1942); Douglas v. City of Jeannette, 319 U.S. 157 (1943).

In all of these cases the Court stressed the importance of showing irreparable injury, the traditional prerequisite to obtaining an injunction. In addition, however, the Court also made clear that in view of the fundamental policy against federal interference with state criminal prosecutions, even irreparable injury is insufficient unless it is "both great and immediate." Fenner, *supra.* Certain types of injury, in particular, the cost, anxiety, and inconvenience of having to defend against a single criminal prosecution, could not by themselves be considered "irreparable" in the special legal sense of that term. Instead, the threat to the plaintiff's federally protected rights must be one that cannot be eliminated by his defense against a single criminal prosecution.   * * *

This is where the law stood when the Court decided Dombrowski v. Pfister, 380 U.S. 479 (1965), and held that an injunction against the enforcement of certain state criminal statutes could properly issue under the circumstances presented in that case.[4] In Dombrowski, unlike many of the earlier cases denying injunctions, the complaint made substantial allegations that: "the threats to enforce the statutes against appellants are not made with any expectation of securing valid convictions, but rather are part of a plan to employ arrests, seizures, and threats of prosecution under color of the statutes to harass appellants and discourage them and their supporters from asserting and attempting to vindicate the constitutional rights of Negro citizens of Louisiana."

The appellants in Dombrowski had offered to prove that their offices had been raided and all their files and records seized pursuant to search and arrest warrants that were later summarily vacated by a state judge for lack of probable cause. They also offered to prove that despite the state court order quashing the warrants and suppressing the evidence seized, the prosecutor was continuing to threaten to initiate new prosecutions of appellants under the same statutes, was holding public hearings at which photostatic copies of the illegally seized documents were being used, and was threatening to use other copies of the illegally seized documents to obtain grand jury indictments against the appellants on charges of violating the same statutes. These circumstances, as viewed by the Court sufficiently establish the kind of irreparable injury, above and beyond that associated with the defense of a single prosecution brought in good faith, that had always been considered sufficient to justify federal intervention. See, *e.g.,* Beal, *supra,* 312 U.S., at 50. Indeed, after quoting the Court's statement in Douglas [v. City of Jeannette, *supra*] concerning the very restricted circumstances under which an injunction could be justified, the Court in Dombrowski went on to say:

"But the allegations in this complaint depict a situation in which defense of the State's criminal prosecution will not assure adequate vindication of constitutional rights. They suggest that a substantial loss of or impairment of

---

4. Neither the cases dealing with standing to raise claims of vagueness or overbreadth, *e.g.,* Thornhill v. Alabama, 310 U.S. 88 (1940), nor the loyalty oath cases, *e.g.,* Baggett v. Bullitt, 377 U.S. 360 (1964), changed the basic principles governing the propriety of injunctions against state criminal prosecutions. In the standing cases we allowed attacks on overly broad or vague statutes in the absence of any showing that the defendant's conduct could not be regulated by some properly drawn statute. But in each of these cases the statute was not merely vague or overly broad "on its face"; the statute was held to be vague or overly broad as construed and *applied* to a particular defendant in a particular case. If the statute had been too vague as written but sufficiently narrow as applied, prosecutions and convictions under it would ordinarily have been permissible. See Dombrowski, *supra,* 380 U.S., at 491 n. 7.

In Baggett and similar cases we enjoined state officials from discharging employees who failed to take certain loyalty oaths. We held that the States were without power to exact the promises involved, with their vague and uncertain content concerning advocacy and political association, as a condition of employment. Apart from the fact that any plaintiff discharged for exercising his constitutional right to refuse to take the oath would have had no adequate remedy at law, the relief sought was of course the kind that raises no special problem—an injunction against allegedly unconstitutional state action (discharging the employees) that is not part of a criminal prosecution.

freedoms of expression will occur if appellants must await the state court's disposition and ultimate review in this Court of any adverse determination. These allegations, if true, clearly show irreparable injury." 380 U.S., at 485–486.

And the Court made clear that even under these circumstances the District Court issuing the injunction would have continuing power to lift it at any time and remit the plaintiffs to the state courts if circumstances warranted. 380 U.S., at 491, 492. * * *

It is against the background of these principles that we must judge the propriety of an injunction under the circumstances of the present case. Here a proceeding was already pending in the state court, affording Harris an opportunity to raise his constitutional claims. There is no suggestion that this single prosecution against Harris is brought in bad faith or is only one of a series of repeated prosecutions to which he will be subjected. In other words, the injury that Harris faces is solely "that incidental to every criminal proceeding brought lawfully and in good faith," Douglas, *supra,* and therefore under the settled doctrine we have already described he is not entitled to equitable relief "even if such statutes are unconstitutional," Buck, *supra.*

The District Court, however, thought that the Dombrowski decision substantially broadened the availability of injunctions against state criminal prosecutions and that under that decision the federal courts may give equitable relief, without regard to any showing of bad faith or harassment, whenever a state statute is found "on its face" to be vague or overly broad, in violation of the First Amendment. We recognize that there are some statements in the Dombrowski opinion that would seem to support this argument. But, as we have already seen, such statements were unnecessary to the decision of that case, because the Court found that the plaintiffs had alleged a basis for equitable relief under the long-established standards. In addition, we do not regard the reasons adduced to support this position as sufficient to justify such a substantial departure from the established doctrines regarding the availability of injunctive relief. It is undoubtedly true, as the Court stated in Dombrowski, that "[a] criminal prosecution under a statute regulating expression usually involves imponderables and contingencies that themselves may inhibit the full exercise of First Amendment freedoms." 380 U.S., at 486. But this sort of "chilling effect," as the Court called it, should not by itself justify federal intervention. In the first place, the chilling effect cannot be satisfactorily eliminated by federal injunctive relief. In Dombrowski itself the Court stated that the injunction to be issued there could be lifted if the State obtained an "acceptable limiting construction" from the state courts. The Court then made clear that once this was done, prosecutions could then be brought for conduct occurring before the narrowing construction was made, and proper convictions could stand so long as the defendants were not deprived of fair warning. 380 U.S., at 491 n. 7. The kind of relief granted in Dombrowski thus does not effectively eliminate uncertainty as to the coverage of the state statute and leaves most citizens with virtually the same doubts as before regarding the danger that their conduct might eventually be subjected to criminal sanctions. The chilling effect can, of course, be eliminated by an injunction that would prohibit any prosecution whatever for conduct occurring prior to a satisfactory rewriting of the statute. But the States would then be stripped of all power to prosecute even the socially dangerous and constitutionally unprotected conduct that had been covered by the statute, until a new statute could be passed by the state legislature and approved by the federal courts in potentially lengthy trial and appellate proceedings. Thus, in Dombrowski itself the Court carefully reaffirmed the principle that even in the direct prosecution in the State's own courts, a valid narrowing construction can be applied to conduct occurring prior to the date when the narrowing construction was made, in the absence of fair warning problems.

Moreover, the existence of a "chilling effect," even in the area of First Amendment rights, has never been considered a sufficient basis, in and of itself, for prohibiting state action. Where a statute does not directly abridge free speech, but—while regulating a subject within the State's power—tends to have the incidental effect of inhibiting First Amendment rights, it is well settled that the statute can be upheld if the effect on speech is minor in relation to the need for control of the conduct and the lack of alternative means for doing so. Just as the incidental "chilling effect" of such statutes does not automatically render them unconstitutional, so the chilling effect that admittedly can result from the very existence of certain laws on the statute books does not in itself justify prohibiting the State from carrying out the important and necessary task of enforcing these laws against socially harmful conduct that the State believes in good faith to be punishable under its laws and the Constitution.

Beyond all this is another, more basic consideration. Procedures for testing the constitutionality of a statute "on its face" in the manner apparently contemplated by Dombrowski, and for then enjoining all action to enforce the statute until the State can obtain court approval for a modified version, are fundamentally at odds with the function of the federal courts in our constitutional plan. The power and duty of the judiciary to declare laws unconstitutional is in the final analysis derived from its responsibility for resolving concrete disputes brought before the courts for decision; a statute apparently governing a dispute cannot be applied by judges, consistently with their obligations under the Supremacy Clause, when such an application of the statute would conflict with the Constitution. Marbury v. Madison, 5 U.S. (1 Cranch) 137 (1803). But this vital responsibility, broad as it is, does not amount to an unlimited power to survey the statute books and pass judgment on laws before the courts are called upon to enforce them. Ever since the Constitutional Convention rejected a proposal for having members of the Supreme Court render advice concerning pending legislation it has been clear that, even when suits of this kind involve a "case or controversy" sufficient to satisfy the requirements of Article III of the Constitution, the task of analyzing a proposed statute, pinpointing its deficiencies, and requiring correction of these deficiencies before the statute is put into effect, is rarely if ever an appropriate task for the judiciary. The combination of the relative remoteness of the controversy, the impact on the legislative process of the relief sought, and above all the speculative and amorphous nature of the required line-by-line analysis of detailed statutes ordinarily results in a kind of case that is wholly unsatisfactory for deciding constitutional questions, whichever way they might be decided. In light of this fundamental conception of the Framers as to the proper place of the federal courts in the governmental processes of passing and enforcing laws, it can seldom be appropriate for these courts to exercise any such power of prior approval or veto over the legislative process.

For these reasons, fundamental not only to our federal system but also to the basic functions of the Judicial Branch of the National Government under our Constitution, we hold that the Dombrowski decision should not be regarded as having upset the settled doctrines that have always confined very narrowly the availability of injunctive relief against state criminal prosecutions. We do not think that opinion stands for the proposition that a federal court can properly enjoin enforcement of a statute solely on the basis of a showing that the statute "on its face" abridges First Amendment rights. There may, of course, be extraordinary circumstances in which the necessary irreparable injury can be shown even in the absence of the usual prerequisites of bad faith and harassment. For example, as long ago as the Buck case, *supra,* we indicated:

"It is of course conceivable that a statute might be flagrantly and patently violative of express constitutional prohibitions in every clause, sentence and paragraph, and in whatever manner and against whomever an effort might be made to apply it." 313 U.S., at 402.

Other unusual situations calling for federal intervention might also arise, but there is no point in our attempting now to specify what they might be. It is sufficient for purposes of the present case to hold, as we do, that the possible unconstitutionality of a statute "on its face" does not in itself justify an injunction against good-faith attempts to enforce it, and that appellee Harris has failed to make any showing of bad faith, harassment, or any other unusual circumstance that would call for equitable relief. Because our holding rests on the absence of the factors necessary under equitable principles to justify federal intervention, we have no occasion to consider whether 28 U.S.C. § 2283, which prohibits an injunction against state court proceedings "except as expressly authorized by Act of Congress" would in and of itself be controlling under the circumstances of this case.

The judgment of the District Court is reversed, and the case is remanded for further proceedings not inconsistent with this opinion.

■ MR. JUSTICE BRENNAN with whom MR. JUSTICE WHITE and MR. JUSTICE MARSHALL join, concurring in the result.

I agree that the judgment of the District Court should be reversed. Appellee Harris had been indicted for violations of the California Criminal Syndicalism Act before he sued in federal court. He has not alleged that the prosecution was brought in bad faith to harass him. His constitutional contentions may be adequately adjudicated in the state criminal proceeding, and federal intervention at his instance was therefore improper. * * *

■ MR. JUSTICE STEWART, with whom MR. JUSTICE HARLAN joins, concurring.

The questions the Court decides today are important ones. Perhaps as important, however, is a recognition of the areas into which today's holdings do not necessarily extend. In all of these cases, the Court deals only with the proper policy to be followed by a federal court when asked to intervene by injunction or declaratory judgment in a criminal prosecution which is contemporaneously pending in a state court.

In basing its decisions on policy grounds, the Court does not reach any questions concerning the independent force of the federal anti-injunction statute, 28 U.S.C. § 2283. Thus we do not decide whether the word "injunction" in § 2283 should be interpreted to include a declaratory judgment, or whether an injunction to stay proceedings in a state court is "expressly authorized" by § 1 of the Civil Rights Act of 1871, now 42 U.S.C. § 1983. And since all these cases involve state criminal prosecutions, we do not deal with the considerations that should govern a federal court when it is asked to intervene in state civil proceedings, where, for various reasons, the balance might be struck differently.[2]   Finally, the Court today does not resolve the problems involved when a federal court is asked to give injunctive or declaratory relief from *future* state criminal prosecutions.

The Court confines itself to deciding the policy considerations that in our federal system must prevail when federal courts are asked to interfere with pending state prosecutions.   Within this area, we hold that a federal court must not, save in exceptional and extremely limited circumstances, intervene by way of either injunction or declaration in an existing state criminal prosecution.[3] Such circumstances exist only when there is a threat of irreparable injury "both great and immediate."   A threat of this nature might be shown if the state criminal statute in question were patently and flagrantly unconstitutional on its face * * * or if there has been bad faith and harassment—official lawlessness—in a statute's enforcement * * *. * * *

■ Mr. Justice Douglas, dissenting.

* * *

Dombrowski represents an exception to the general rule that federal courts should not interfere with state criminal prosecutions.   The exception does not arise merely because prosecutions are threatened to which the First Amendment will be the proffered defense.   Dombrowski governs statutes which are a blunderbuss by themselves or when used *en masse*—those that have an "overbroad" sweep. * * *

* * *

Harris' "crime" was distributing leaflets advocating change in industrial ownership through political action.   The statute under which he was indicted was the one involved in Whitney v. California, 274 U.S. 357, a decision we overruled in Brandenburg v. Ohio, 395 U.S. 444, 449.

If the "advocacy" which Harris used was an attempt at persuasion through the use of bullets, bombs, and arson, we would have a different case.   But Harris is charged only with distributing leaflets advocating political action toward his objective.   He tried unsuccessfully to have the state court dismiss the indictment on constitutional grounds.   He resorted to the state appellate court for writs of prohibition to prevent the trial, but to no avail.   He went to the federal court as a matter of last resort in an effort to keep this unconstitutional trial from being saddled on him. * * *

---

2. Courts of equity have traditionally shown greater reluctance to intervene in criminal prosecutions than in civil cases. See Younger v. Harris, 401 U.S., at 43–44; Douglas v. City of Jeannette, 319 U.S. 157, 163–164. The offense to state interests is likely to be less in a civil proceeding. A State's decision to classify conduct as criminal provides some indication of the importance it has ascribed to prompt and unencumbered enforcement of its law. By contrast, the State might not even be a party in a proceeding under a civil statute.

These considerations would not, to be sure, support any distinction between civil and criminal proceedings should the ban of 28 U.S.C. § 2283, which makes no such distinction, be held unaffected by 42 U.S.C. § 1983.

3. The negative pregnant in this sentence—that a federal court may, as a matter of policy, intervene when such "exceptional and extremely limited circumstances" are found—is subject to any further limitations that may be placed on such intervention by 28 U.S.C. § 2283.

NOTE ON YOUNGER v. HARRIS AND THE DOCTRINE
OF EQUITABLE RESTRAINT

(1) *The History of Equitable Restraint Doctrine.* The pre-Younger history of equitable restraint doctrine is complex and multi-faceted. Consider its bearing on the specific problem presented in Younger.

(a) *English Origins.* A venerable maxim, which apparently originated in the English Court of Chancery, holds that equity will not enjoin a criminal prosecution. See Shapiro, *Jurisdiction and Discretion,* 60 N.Y.U.L.Rev. 543, 550 n. 37 (1985); Whitten, *Federal Declaratory and Injunctive Interference with State Court Proceedings: The Supreme Court and the Limits of Judicial Discretion,* 53 N.C.L.Rev. 591, 597–600 (1975). Also of English origin are the complementary maxims that equity will not provide relief unless (i) there is no adequate remedy at law and (ii) the plaintiff is threatened with irreparable injury. Because the legal remedy of defending a criminal proceeding was ordinarily considered adequate, the irreparable injury requirement also established a barrier to injunctions against criminal proceedings. Whitten, *supra,* at 600–04. From the beginning, however, the bar against injunction of criminal prosecutions admitted exceptions. For example, a court of equity would enjoin a party from litigating the same matter in a later-commenced criminal action, *id.* at 598, and some American cases permitted an injunction against a criminal prosecution that would infringe property rights, see Davis & Farnum Mfg. Co. v. Los Angeles, 189 U.S. 207, 217 (1903); Fitts v. McGhee, 172 U.S. 516, 531–32 (1899).

(b) *Early Reception in the United States.* Section 16 of the First Judiciary Act stated that "suits in equity shall not be sustained in * * * the courts of United States, in any case where plain, adequate, and complete remedy may be had at law," 1 Stat. 82—a limitation repealed in 1948, see p. 710, *supra.* That provision defeated the plaintiff's case for equitable relief, however, only if the remedy was available on the law side of a *federal* court; it was not intended to affect the plaintiff's right to a federal—as against a state—forum. See Atlas Life Ins. Co. v. W.I. Southern, Inc., 306 U.S. 563, 569 (1939).

(c) *Background to Modern Doctrine: Ex Parte Young.* In Ex parte Young, p. 1058, *supra,* a case best known for its Eleventh Amendment holding,[1] the Supreme Court sustained a federal injunction forbidding the Minnesota Attorney General to enforce railroad rate regulations alleged to deny due process. The Court noted that the "general rule" that "equity has no jurisdiction to enjoin [state] criminal proceedings * * * [was subject to] exceptions. When such * * * [a] proceeding is brought to enforce an alleged unconstitutional statute, which is the subject matter of inquiry in a suit already pending in a Federal court, the latter court having first obtained jurisdiction over the subject matter, has the right, in both civil and criminal cases, to hold and maintain such jurisdiction, to the exclusion of all other courts, until its duty is fully performed. But the Federal court cannot, of course, interfere in a case where the proceedings were already pending in a state court" (pp. 161–62).

---

1. For discussion of the precedents prior to Young, see Isseks, *Jurisdiction of the Lower Federal Courts to Enjoin Unauthorized Action of State Officials,* 40 Harv.L.Rev. 969 (1927); Taylor & Willis, *The Power of Federal Courts to Enjoin Proceedings in State Courts,* 42 Yale L.J. 1169, 1190–92 (1942); Warren, *Federal and State Court Interference,* 43 Harv.L.Rev. 345, 372–74 (1930); B. Wechsler, *Federal Courts, State Criminal Law and the First Amendment,* 49 N.Y.U.L.Rev. 740, 753–62 (1974); Whitten, *supra,* at 629–30.

The Court in Young also rejected the Attorney General's argument that the railroads had an adequate remedy at law—namely, to disobey the statute and then challenge its constitutionality in a subsequent prosecution. In part, this conclusion was based on the difficulty for the railroad of finding an employee willing to risk imprisonment in order to set up a test case. But the Court also advanced a broader argument: To force the railroad "[t]o await proceedings against the company in a state court, grounded upon a disobedience of the act, [and then if necessary seek Supreme Court review] would place the company in peril of large loss and its agents in great risk of fines and imprisonment if it should be finally determined that the act was valid. This risk the company ought not to be required to take" (p. 165).

(d) *Restriction, Exceptions, and the Decision in Douglas v. City of Jeannette.* In the years following Ex parte Young, federal courts seldom if ever enjoined pending criminal prosecutions, but while "a few prominent cases said that injunctions against *future* prosecutions [as in Ex parte Young] should be hard to get, in practice they become routine." Laycock, *Federal Interference with State Prosecutions: The Need for Prospective Relief,* 1977 Sup.Ct.Rev. 193, 193; see Soifer & MacGill, *The Younger Doctrine: Reconstructing Reconstruction,* 55 Tex.L.Rev. 1141, 1158 (1977).

Whatever the normal pattern in the years following Ex parte Young, there is no doubt about the generative significance of cases such as Douglas v. City of Jeannette, 319 U.S. 157 (1943), which not only denied equitable relief, but also forged the link between equitable concepts and a vision of American federalism in which federal courts should frequently defer to state institutions and especially state courts.[2] In the Douglas case, the Supreme Court, per Stone, C.J., ordered dismissal, for want of equity, of a class action by Jehovah's Witnesses (whose religious practice was to distribute books door-to-door) seeking to restrain, as a violation of the First Amendment, their prosecution under a city ordinance forbidding solicitation of orders for merchandise without a license. The Chief Justice noted first that Congress had adopted a deliberate policy of "leaving generally to the state courts the trial of criminal cases arising under state laws, subject to review by this Court of any federal questions involved" (p. 163). He then deployed equitable concepts to implement that policy, reasoning that a criminal prosecution, "even though alleged to be in violation of constitutional guarantees, is not a ground for equity relief since the lawfulness or constitutionality of the statute or ordinance on which the prosecution is based may be determined as readily in the criminal case as in the suit for an injunction" (p. 163).[3]

---

2. *But cf.* Laycock, *Federal Interference with State Prosecutions: The Cases Dombrowski Forgot,* 46 U.Chi.L.Rev. 636, 666 & n. 201 (1979). Professor Laycock notes that both before and after the Douglas case, the Supreme Court approved federal injunctions against threatened prosecution for future conduct, even when the federal plaintiff wishing to engage in a continuous course of conduct was already the subject of a pending state prosecution for past conduct. For example, in Cline v. Frink Dairy Co., 274 U.S. 445, 452–53, 466 (1927), a three-judge court had permanently enjoined state officials from

bringing criminal prosecutions under an unconstitutional state statute. The Supreme Court reversed the grant of relief as to a prosecution already pending when the federal suit was filed, but affirmed the grant as to the institution of future prosecutions.

3. Although Douglas is often read as barring any injunctions against state criminal enforcement actions, the previous cases had distinguished between pending and threatened prosecutions, see the articles by Laycock, *supra,* and the facts of Douglas were themselves somewhat exceptional. On the same day Douglas was decided, the Court, in

Is it appropriate to use "doctrines of equity—doctrines forged in the battles of English Chancery—to further views of federalism, a political principle central to American Government"? See Fiss, *Dombrowski*, 86 Yale L.J. 1103, 1107 (1977), for a negative view. Compare the line of equity cases declining, both prior and subsequent to enactment of the Tax Injunction Act, to restrain collection of state taxes in the face of an adequate *state* remedy at law. See pp. 1216-19, *supra*.

(e) *The Warren Era and the Dombrowski Case.* The Warren Court's expansion of constitutional rights in the sphere of criminal procedure and the events surrounding the civil rights movement conjoined to put new strains on doctrines demanding federal judicial deference to state court proceedings. The case most clearly exhibiting the emerging tension was Dombrowski v. Pfister, 380 U.S. 479 (1965), discussed at length in Younger. Suit was brought by a civil rights group and affiliated individuals to enjoin state officials from prosecuting or threatening to prosecute the plaintiffs for alleged violations of two Louisiana statutes criminalizing subversive activities. A divided Supreme Court, per Justice Brennan, purported to accept the position of the Douglas case that "the mere possibility of erroneous initial application of constitutional standards will usually not amount to the irreparable injury necessary to justify a disruption of orderly state proceedings" (pp. 484–85). But in the Court's view, the plaintiffs' allegations that the statutes were overbroad, if true, would establish the threat of "irreparable injury" warranting relief. The majority argued that when statutes are overbroad, "[t]he assumption that defense of a criminal prosecution will generally assure ample vindication of constitutional rights is unfounded * * *. * * * The chilling effect upon the exercise of First Amendment rights may derive from the fact of the prosecution, unaffected by the prospects of its success or failure" (pp. 486–87). The Court noted that the repeated invocation (and threatened invocation) of state criminal prosecutions, and concomitant searches and seizures, had frightened off potential members of the organization and "paralyzed operations", making the need for "immediate resolution" of the First Amendment claims especially pressing (p. 489).

The Court also concluded that the district court "erred in holding that it should abstain pending authoritative interpretation of the statutes in state court * * *. We hold the abstention doctrine is inappropriate for cases such as the present one where, unlike Douglas v. City of Jeannette, statutes are justifiably attacked on their face as abridging free expression, or as applied for the purpose of discouraging protected activities" (pp. 489–90). A state court's limiting construction would not eliminate the threat of bad faith harassment; moreover, citing Baggett v. Bullitt, 377 U.S. 360, 378 (1964), the Court stressed that "no readily apparent limiting construction suggests itself", and that plaintiffs were entitled to be free from the burdens of defending the multiple prosecutions necessary to hammer out the statute's meaning (p. 491).

The Court held that plaintiffs were entitled to an injunction against enforcement of the overbroad sections of one of the statutes. It then remanded, ordering the district court to frame a specific decree, to adjudicate the

---

reviewing the criminal convictions of some Jehovah's Witnesses who had already violated the ordinance, held it unconstitutional. Murdock v. Pennsylvania, 319 U.S. 105 (1943). In view of that authoritative ruling, the plaintiffs in Douglas did not face the same dilemma as to their continuing conduct faced by the plaintiffs in Ex parte Young. The Douglas opinion recognizes this point, see 319 U.S. at 165, though much of its language sweeps far more broadly.

merits of attacks on the other challenged provisions, and to hear plaintiffs' allegations that the defendants "threaten to enforce both statutes solely to discourage [plaintiffs] from continuing their civil rights activities" (p. 497).

Justice Harlan, joined by Justice Clark, dissented: "[U]nderlying the Court's major premise that enforcement of an overly broad statute affecting speech and association is itself a deterrent to the free exercise thereof seems to be the unarticulated assumption that state courts will not be as prone as federal courts to vindicate constitutional rights promptly and effectively" (p. 499). The Court, he thought, had departed from healthy traditions of federalism by creating a situation in which "[i]n practical effect * * * a State may no longer carry on prosecutions under statutes challengeable * * * on 'First Amendment' grounds without the prior approval of the federal courts" (p. 498).[4]

According to Professor Fiss, by the time of the Dombrowski decision, Justice Brennan had already concluded that the traditional vision of federalism championed by Justice Harlan in dissent "was wholly inconsistent with the revisions of federal jurisdiction that had occurred after the Civil War and that had given the citizen the right to choose which forum—state or federal—would best adjudicate his grievance against the state." Fiss, *supra*, at 1107. It later emerged as a weakness of the Dombrowski opinion, Fiss concludes, that Justice Brennan had not made his alternative vision explicit and had not more fully articulated its implications for cases in which plaintiffs sought federal equitable relief against state institutions and especially state judicial processes.

(f) Did the Supreme Court's prior decisions fairly determine the outcome in Younger, or might the Court reasonably have decided the case either way? If the latter, what factors led the Court to decide as it did? Was the decision well-advised?

(2) *Criticisms of Younger.* Although decided more than twenty-five years ago, Younger continues to be a subject of controversy. Three criticisms are especially common.

First, numerous commentators have objected that Younger fails to respect congressional policy by requiring abstention in suits under 42 U.S.C. § 1983—a statute whose purpose (according to Mitchum v. Foster, p. 1195, *supra*) "was to interpose the federal courts between the States and the people, as guardians of the people's federal rights".[5]

A second complaint is that Younger relegates plaintiffs claiming constitutional rights violations to state forums that they, at least, expect to be less sympathetic to their claims than the federal court in which they preferred to litigate. For discussion of the "parity" or "disparity" of state and federal courts, see Chap. IV, Sec. 1, pp. 351-54, *supra*.

A third objection is that Younger erects a frequently insuperable barrier to prospective and class relief—remedies typically unavailable from a criminal court. See, *e.g.*, Laycock, 1977 Sup.Ct.Rev., *supra*.

(3) *Younger's Near Unanimity.* Given Younger's controversiality, it is striking that eight of the nine Justices—including Justice Brennan, who had authored

4. Justices Black and Stewart did not participate.

5. For further discussion of the relation of Younger and Mitchum, see Paragraph (5), *infra*.

the opinion in Dombrowski, *supra*—concurred in the judgment. How do you account for the virtual unanimity? Consider the following suggestions:

(a) Younger involved a claim for an injunction against a *pending* criminal prosecution. Especially in light of the revolution worked by the Warren Court, it is hard to imagine a criminal prosecution in which a constitutional claim could not be raised; and it would be unworkable if every prosecution could be interrupted by suit for a federal injunction at any stage in the proceedings.[6] Nor need § 1983 be read to establish so dysfunctional a rule. Like any other statute, it should be interpreted in light of the general body of background law—including the traditional maxim that equity will not enjoin a criminal prosecution—and a traditionally recognized judicial discretion, often but not uniquely associated with equity, to decline to exercise jurisdiction granted. See generally Shapiro, *Jurisdiction and Discretion,* 60 N.Y.U.L.Rev. 543 (1985), quoted p. 1235, *supra.*[7]

(b) Whatever may have been the case in other eras, by 1971 there was no reason to think state courts generally untrustworthy in cases involving claimed federal rights, especially given the availability of federal habeas corpus as well as Supreme Court review. See, *e.g.,* Friedman, *A Revisionist Theory of Absten-tion,* 88 Mich.L.Rev. 530, 561–63 (1989). Nor did the facts of Younger exhibit any special factors that might tend to justify federal interference with a pending judicial action, such as a pattern of bad faith or harassment in which state courts were arguably complicit.

(c) Given the Court's holding that plaintiffs other than Harris lacked standing,[8] Younger did not involve a claim to class relief and did not implicate the federal interest in avoiding the chill of *future,* constitutionally protected conduct, which might deserve to be weighed in the scale against the state

6. *Cf.* Stefanelli v. Minard, 342 U.S. 117 (1951), in which a district court was asked to enjoin the use, in a state criminal proceeding, of evidence seized by state police officers in violation of the Federal Constitution. The Supreme Court held that the injunction should not issue, saying that the equity rule of Douglas v. City of Jeannette applies *a fortiori* where the request is "to intervene piecemeal to try collateral issues" in a criminal proceeding. For the subsequent, often complex, development of the Stefanelli principle, see Rea v. United States, 350 U.S. 214 (1956)(federal officers enjoined from testifying in state criminal proceeding as to evidence obtained by them in violation of Fed. R.Crim.P. 41); Wilson v. Schnettler, 365 U.S. 381 (1961)(upholding refusal to enjoin federal officers from testifying where allegation that the evidence was illegally obtained was insufficient); Pugach v. Dollinger, 365 U.S. 458 (1961)(refusing to enjoin state officer from testifying as to illegal wiretap); Cleary v. Bolger, 371 U.S. 392 (1963)(reversing grant of injunction prohibiting state officer from testifying as to evidence illegally gathered by federal officers).

7. Compare Bator, *The State Courts and Federal Constitutional Litigation,* 22 Wm. & Mary L.Rev. 605, 622 n. 49 (1981): "Statutes such as § 1983 and the Habeas Corpus Act use language which, if woodenly and anachronistically read, can be interpreted to provide an 'absolute' right of access to the federal courts. But these statutes were themselves passed against the background of a large body of standing law on matters of substance, remedy, and jurisdiction. As is true of all legislation, it is a major problem of *interpretation* how to fit the new enactment into this preexisting texture. No statute recreates the entire legal universe. The fact that a given remedial doctrine is not explicitly mentioned therefore does not automatically mean that the new statute was intended wholly to supersede it."

8. Did Younger heighten the standing requirement for plaintiffs who fear criminal prosecution for activities that they believe to be constitutionally protected but who have not been arrested or specifically threatened with arrest?

interest in avoiding disruption of a pending criminal prosecution.[9] (Even in such a case, the actual or prospective defendants might seek injunctive and class remedies in a state court of equity, but if a separate suit for such relief is to proceed, why shouldn't the plaintiff have a forum choice?)

In light of these considerations, might Younger itself reasonably be viewed as a relatively easy case. Even if so, it would not necessarily follow that Younger established an appropriate framework or rhetorical tone for resolving other cases.

(4) *Companion Cases.* On the day that Younger was decided, the Supreme Court handed down important decisions in two companion cases.

(a) In Samuels v. Mackell, 401 U.S. 66 (1971), the Court held that the Younger doctrine applies not only to injunctive but also to declaratory relief against a pending state criminal prosecution. The Court relied heavily on Great Lakes Dredge & Dock Co. v. Huffman, 319 U.S. 293 (1943), p. 1219, *supra,* which, though not literally extending the Tax Injunction Act to restrict declaratory judgments, had as an exercise of equitable discretion refused federal declaratory relief against the imposition of state taxes.[10] Justice Black, writing for the Court, said (p. 72):

"[O]rdinarily a declaratory judgment will result in precisely the same interference with and disruption of state proceedings that the long-standing policy limiting injunctions was designed to avoid. This is true for at least two reasons. In the first place, the Declaratory Judgment Act provides that after a declaratory judgment is issued the district court may enforce it by granting '[f]urther necessary or proper relief,' 28 U.S.C. § 2202, and therefore a declaratory judgment issued while state proceedings are pending might serve as the basis for a subsequent injunction against those proceedings to 'protect or effectuate' the declaratory judgment, 28 U.S.C. § 2283, and thus result in a clearly improper interference with the state proceedings. Secondly, even if the declaratory judgment is not used as a basis for actually issuing an injunction, the declaratory relief alone has virtually the same practical impact as a formal injunction would. As we said in [Public Service Comm'n of Utah v. Wycoff Co., 344 U.S. 237, 247 (1952)]:

> "Is the declaration contemplated here to be res judicata, so that the [state court] cannot hear evidence and decide any matter for itself? If so, the federal court has virtually lifted the case out of the State [court] before it could be heard. If not, the federal judgment serves no useful purpose as a final determination of rights."

Justice Black conceded that there might be "unusual circumstances" in which, despite a plaintiff's "strong claim for relief," an injunction would be withheld because it would have been "particularly intrusive or offensive," but in which "a declaratory judgment might be appropriate" (p. 73). He "ex-

---

9. For further discussion of distinctions among suits that seek relief from prosecution based on (i) past, (ii) future, and (iii) continuing conduct, see pp. 1285-87, *infra.*

10. The Court subsequently held that the Tax Injunction Act itself bars federal declaratory relief. See California v. Grace Brethren Church, 457 U.S. 393 (1982), p. 1219, *supra.*

Samuels did not refer to Kennedy v. Mendoza–Martinez, 372 U.S. 144 (1963), p. 1214, *supra,* in which the Court refused to equate declaratory and injunctive relief for purposes of the three-judge court requirement.

press[ed] no views on the propriety of declaratory relief when no state proceeding is pending at the time the federal suit is begun" (pp. 73–74).[11]

(b) In Perez v. Ledesma, 401 U.S. 82 (1971), the federal plaintiffs were being prosecuted in state court under state and local obscenity laws. A three-judge district court had upheld the constitutionality of the state obscenity law, but, finding that the arrest of plaintiffs and the seizure from them of allegedly obscene materials were unlawful, issued an injunction ordering that the materials be returned to plaintiffs and not used in evidence by state prosecutors. While recognizing that a three-judge court lacked jurisdiction over the question of the validity of a local ordinance without statewide applicability, the court expressed its view that the local ordinance was unconstitutional. Thereafter, the single district judge who initially referred the case to a court of three judges issued a declaratory judgment that the *local* ordinance was unconstitutional.

On direct review, the Supreme Court applied Younger to vacate the decision upholding the *state* statute's constitutionality on the merits, holding that the three-judge court should have dismissed the action. The Court reversed the injunction against use of the seized materials, noting that that order would "effectively stifle the then-pending state criminal prosecution" (p. 84), and that "[t]he propriety of arrests and the admissibility of evidence in state criminal prosecutions are ordinarily matters to be resolved by state tribunals, see Stefanelli v. Minard, 342 U.S. 117 (1951), subject, of course, to review by certiorari or appeal in this Court or, in a proper case, on federal habeas corpus" (pp. 84–85).[12] Finally, the Court ruled that it lacked jurisdiction to review directly the single judge's decision that the *local* ordinance was unconstitutional; appeal from that decision should have been taken to the court of appeals.

Justice Brennan, joined by Justices White and Marshall, dissented on this last point, concluding that the Court did have jurisdiction to review the declaratory judgment as to the local ordinance. He then argued that because criminal charges under the local ordinance had been dismissed before the three-judge court was convened, the declaratory judgment did not interfere with pending prosecutions. In a preview of the position he took for the Court in Steffel v. Thompson, p. 1275, *infra,* he argued that in such a situation, a declaratory judgment—which he called a "milder alternative" to an injunction—should be available.[13]

11. Justice Douglas wrote a separate concurring opinion stressing that the prosecutions were not "palpably unconstitutional" (p. 75). Justice Brennan, joined by Justices White and Marshall, concurred in the judgment on the ground that the state indictment preceded the federal suit, and there were no allegations amounting to bad faith harassment.

12. Justice Douglas alone dissented from this part of the ruling.

For a refusal to issue similar relief, see O'Shea v. Littleton, 414 U.S. 488, 499–504 (1974).

13. A somewhat different issue was presented in another companion case, Boyle v. Landry, 401 U.S. 77 (1971). Boyle was an action by a group of black residents of Chicago, who alleged that a number of state statutes and city ordinances—for example, laws prohibiting mob action, resisting arrest, aggravated assault, and intimidation—were being used to harass them. The only part of the case before the Court was the district court's decree enjoining the defendants from enforcing one section of the statute prohibiting certain kinds of "intimidation". The Supreme Court reversed. Stressing that none of the plaintiffs had ever been arrested, charged, prosecuted, or even threatened with prosecution under the statute, it held that the complaint did not allege the requisite irreparable injury to justify injunctive relief.

(5) *The Relationship of Younger to Mitchum v. Foster.* The question reserved in Younger—whether 28 U.S.C. § 2283 would bar an injunction in that case— was decided a year later in Mitchum v. Foster, 407 U.S. 225 (1972)(p. 1195, *supra*). Was it appropriate for the Court in Younger to decide the case on the basis of a judge-made doctrine of equitable restraint without first determining the reach of § 2283?

There is an obvious tension between Younger's trust in state enforcement of federal rights and the parallel distrust, coupled with a demand for federal court jurisdiction in § 1983 actions, expressed in cases such as Mitchum and Patsy v. Board of Regents of the State of Florida, p. 1225, *supra*. How do you account for the disparity? Would the Court clearly have decided Mitchum the same way if, as a consequence of that decision, cases such as Younger necessarily could have been litigated in federal court?

Even if the results in Younger and Mitchum could be reconciled, the Court's rhetoric in the two cases is starkly dissonant. Younger is written as if "Our Federalism" had remained stable since the founding, Mitchum as if Reconstruction had dramatically altered the relation of state and nation and especially of state and federal courts. Isn't it the Supreme Court's function to achieve a workable synthesis of Reconstruction legislation with preexisting doctrine?

(6) *The Relationship of Younger to Pullman Abstention.* Note the differences between the Pullman "abstention" doctrine and the equitable restraint doctrine of Younger. In conventional Pullman-type cases, the issue is whether federal plaintiffs—as a necessary condition of having the federal court adjudicate their federal claims—should be forced to commence separate state proceedings that might not otherwise occur at all. In the normal Younger-type case, on the other hand, the whole point is that a state proceeding either has been or is about to be commenced by the state authorities, and that the entire case should be litigated in that proceeding. The two doctrines thus have sharply different impacts on federal plaintiffs' ability to obtain federal court resolution of their federal claims. The Pullman doctrine ordinarily entails postponement, not relinquishment, of federal jurisdiction to pass on claims of federal right. In Younger cases, by contrast, the federal court dismisses the suit, and the underlying federal claims must typically be adjudicated in the context of a state criminal case, subject only to Supreme Court review. (As the Court later held in Allen v. McCurry, 449 U.S. 90 (1980), p. 1484, *infra,* the state court adjudication will have full res judicata effect in subsequent federal court proceedings, including those brought under 42 U.S.C. § 1983.)

Notwithstanding Younger, a state criminal defendant may ultimately reach federal court by filing a federal habeas corpus petition, but important limits apply to this remedy: (i) it comes only after state remedies have been exhausted; (ii) it is available only to defendants who are still "in custody" after exhaustion of state remedies; (iii) it ordinarily does not permit plenary federal litigation of the facts; (iv) it generally does not extend to Fourth Amendment claims; and (v) with only narrow exceptions, it will not provide relief based on "new" law. See generally Chapter XI, *infra.*

(7) *Exceptions to the Younger Doctrine.* Younger suggested that there might be exceptional cases warranting federal equitable relief against pending state criminal prosecutions. Subsequent decisions have stressed the narrowness of the possible openings. See generally Comment, 67 Calif.L.Rev. 1318 (1979). (As is discussed in detail in the *Note on Further Extension of Equitable*

Restraint Doctrine: Pending Civil Actions in State Court, State Administrative Proceedings, and Executive Action, pp. 1300-08, *infra,* the Younger doctrine has been extended to bar federal interference in some kinds of state court *civil* proceedings, and many of the cases discussed in this Paragraph involve intervention in civil matters.)

(a) *Bad Faith Prosecution or Harassment.*   The Supreme Court has never authorized intervention under this exception.   Among the cases in which the Court has refused to find bad faith are Cameron v. Johnson, 390 U.S. 611, 621 (1968)(rejecting the notion that bad faith could be inferred from the innocence of the accused and framing the question as whether enforcement was undertaken "with no expectation of convictions but only to discourage exercise of protected rights"), and Hicks v. Miranda, 422 U.S. 332, 350–51 (1975), p. 1291, *infra* (finding that the districts court's "vague and conclusory" findings concerning the "pattern of seizure" of the movie "Deep Throat" did not make out bad faith and harassment since each step in the pattern was authorized by judicial order, and even a showing "that the state courts were in error on some one or more issues of state or federal law" would not necessarily establish bad faith or harassment).

For a collection of a small number of lower court cases upholding federal interference under this exception, see 17A Wright, Miller & Cooper, Federal Practice and Procedure § 4255 (1988 & Supp.1995).

If Younger itself is sound, why should there be such an exception?   Is a state court unable to determine whether a prosecutor is acting in bad faith?   Or is the real problem one of harassment—of repeated, unfounded prosecutions that are dismissed before the defendant can obtain a favorable ruling?

(b) *Patent and Flagrant Unconstitutionality.*   Younger also suggested that federal courts might be justified in restraining prosecutions under statutes that are "flagrantly and patently violative of express constitutional prohibitions in every clause, sentence, and paragraph, and in whatever manner and against whomever an effort might be made to apply it."   The language is from Watson v. Buck, 313 U.S. 387, 402 (1941), which refused to enjoin an entire statute when parts could be severed or the legislation could be given a narrowing construction.   Not much is left of this "exception" after Trainor v. Hernandez, 431 U.S. 434, 446–47 (1977).[14]   There, the defendants in a state court action filed a federal suit challenging the constitutionality of a state court attachment against their property that had been obtained without any prior hearing, as authorized by state law.   The lower court, in enjoining the attachment, stated that the state's attachment procedure was "on its face patently violative of the due process clause."   405 F.Supp. at 762.   Dividing 5–4, the Supreme Court reversed.   Without clearly stating whether there was an exception to Younger for statutes found to be flagrantly unconstitutional, the majority simply said that if the lower court's statement constituted such a finding, it "would have not been warranted in light of our cases.   Compare North Georgia Finishing, Inc. v. Di–Chem, Inc., 419 U.S. 601 (1975), with Mitchell v. W.T. Grant Co., 416 U.S. 600 (1974)."

Justices Brennan, Stewart, Marshall, and Stevens dissented.   Justice Brennan's dissent argued that "a requirement that the * * * formulation [defining

---

14.   Indeed, what was left of this exception after Younger itself?   Two years earlier, Brandenburg v. Ohio, 395 U.S. 444 (1969), had invalidated a statute almost identical to the one under which Harris was being prosecuted.

this exception] must be literally satisfied renders the exception meaningless" (p. 457). Analyzing the statute in some detail, Justice Brennan found it clearly unconstitutional under North Georgia Finishing and clearly distinguishable from the statute upheld in W.T. Grant. Justice Stevens' dissent objected that the majority's view made the exception inapplicable whenever the statute had a separability clause, and argued that there was no reason "why all sections of any statute must be considered invalid in order to justify an injunction against a portion that is itself flagrantly unconstitutional" (p. 463).

See also New Orleans Public Serv., Inc. v. Council of New Orleans, 491 U.S. 350, 367 (1989)(concluding that an allegation that "requires further factual inquiry can hardly be deemed" to have satisfied the test for flagrant unlawfulness "for purposes of a threshold abstention determination").

Why might an exception for patently and flagrantly unconstitutional statutes be warranted at all? Isn't it a particular insult to the state courts to suggest that they will be unable to detect patent unconstitutionality in state statutes? Indeed, isn't it arguable that a defendant faces no risk of irreparable injury in the state court prosecution if a Supreme Court decision is clearly (and favorably) on point?

(c) *Other Extraordinary Circumstances.* What else might constitute "extraordinary circumstances" meriting an exception to Younger's policy of non-interference? In Gibson v. Berryhill, 411 U.S. 564 (1973), the Court refused to apply Younger to require deference to administrative proceedings before a state agency that the lower court had found to be "incompetent by reason of bias to adjudicate the issues pending before it. If the District Court's conclusion was correct in this regard, it was also correct that it need not defer to the Board. Nor, in these circumstances, would a different result be required simply because judicial review, de novo or otherwise, would be forthcoming at the conclusion of the administrative proceedings" (p. 577).[15]

Should the applicability of Younger, like the applicability of the Tax Injunction Act's bar on federal interference, depend on the existence of a "plain, speedy, and effective" remedy in state court? See Rosenfeld, *The Place of State Courts in the Era of Younger v. Harris,* 59 B.U.L.Rev. 597, 655–58 (1979). Is there, or should there be, a parallel here to doctrines that permit federal intervention if—but only if—there was not a full and fair opportunity to litigate the constitutional question in state court? See Bator, note 7, *supra,* at 626; Collins, *The Right to Avoid Trial: Justifying Federal Court Intervention into Ongoing State Court Proceedings,* 66 N.C.L.Rev. 49 (1987).

(8) *Younger and Pending Court–Martial Proceedings.* In Schlesinger v. Councilman, 420 U.S. 738 (1975), the Supreme Court held that the policies of Younger barred injunctive relief against pending court martial proceedings. The district court had granted an injunction on the ground that the offense was not service-connected and that the military courts therefore could not constitutionally exercise jurisdiction.[16] Reversing, the Court reasoned that "[w]hile the peculiar demands of federalism are not implicated, the deficiency is supplied by

15. In Kugler v. Helfant, 421 U.S. 117, 125 n. 4 (1975), the Court described Gibson as an example of an "extraordinary circumstance", other than bad faith/harassment or patent unconstitutionality, but concluded that the case was distinguishable because the plaintiff's claim (in Kugler) that he could not obtain a fair hearing in the state courts was without merit.

16. See O'Callahan v. Parker, 395 U.S. 258 (1969), *overruled,* Solorio v. United States, 483 U.S. 435 (1987).

factors equally compelling", especially the need for deference to the military (pp. 757–58). The Court distinguished prior cases permitting anticipatory federal court relief against courts-martial acting in excess of their constitutional jurisdiction as involving civilians; their federal court actions contested "the right of the military to try them at all", and "the expertise of military courts [did not extend] to the consideration of constitutional claims of the type presented" in those cases (p. 759). Justices Douglas, Brennan, and Marshall dissented, believing that these considerations applied equally to the lawsuit at bar.

What does this case suggest about whether Younger bars a federal suit seeking relief from a pending state court proceeding on the ground that the state court lacks jurisdiction? *Cf.* Ohio Civil Rights Com'n v. Dayton Christian Schools, Inc., 477 U.S. 619 (1986), p. 1306, *infra.*

(9) *Equitable Restraint—Mandatory or Permissive?* In Ohio Bureau of Employment Services v. Hodory, 431 U.S. 471 (1977), the state, in appealing a three-judge court's injunction against the enforcement of a state statute, argued for reversal on the merits but not for dismissal under Younger. The Supreme Court reached the merits and reversed, over the suggestion of an amicus that Younger called for dismissal. On this point, the Court said (p. 480): "If the State voluntarily chooses to submit to a federal forum, principles of comity do not demand that the federal court force the case back into the State's own system." Accord, Brown v. Hotel & Rest. Employees & Bartenders Local 54, 468 U.S. 491, 500 n. 9 (1984).[17]

By contrast, in Hodory the Court stated that it was not required to defer to the parties' wishes regarding Pullman abstention, which may result in avoidance of a constitutional question (p. 480 n. 11), though on the facts it found Pullman abstention inappropriate. Is the distinction valid? (Note that the Supreme Court has occasionally upheld the desirability of Younger abstention as a means of allowing state courts to provide narrowing constructions that might avoid constitutional questions. See, *e.g.,* Pennzoil Co. v. Texaco, Inc., 481 U.S. 1, 11–12 (1987); Moore v. Sims, 442 U.S. 415, 429–30 (1979).)

(10) *Appealability.* Decisions dismissing a federal action on Younger grounds are plainly appealable. On the appealability of the refusal to dismiss an action, see Chap. XV, pp. 1650-51, *infra.*

Steffel v. Thompson

415 U.S. 452, 94 S.Ct. 1209, 39 L.Ed.2d 505 (1974).
Certiorari to the United States Court of Appeals for the Fifth Circuit.

■ MR. JUSTICE BRENNAN delivered the opinion of the Court.

* * * This case presents the important question reserved in Samuels v. Mackell, 401 U.S. 66, 73–74 (1971), whether declaratory relief is precluded

---

17. In Ohio Civil Rights Comm'n v. Dayton Christian Schools, 477 U.S. 619 (1986), the federal plaintiff contended that the defendant had waived any claim for equitable restraint under Younger, because though the claim was raised in the federal district court and in oral argument before the Supreme Court, the defendant conceded in the district court that that court had jurisdiction. The Supreme Court ruled that this waiver argument "misconceive[d] the nature of Younger abstention," which is founded not on lack of jurisdiction but on "strong policies" of noninterference (p. 626). Hodory and Brown showed, the Court said, that a state may voluntarily submit to federal jurisdiction even though it could have invoked Younger, but in those two cases the state had expressly urged federal court adjudication of the merits; "there was no similar consent or waiver here, and we therefore address the [Younger issue]" (p. 626).

when a state prosecution has been threatened, but is not pending, and a showing of bad-faith enforcement or other special circumstances has not been made.

Petitioner, and others, filed a complaint in the District Court for the Northern District of Georgia, invoking the Civil Rights Act of 1871, 42 U.S.C. § 1983, and its jurisdictional implementation, 28 U.S.C. § 1343. The complaint requested a declaratory judgment pursuant to 28 U.S.C. §§ 2201–2202, that Ga.Code Ann. § 26–1503 (1972) was being applied in violation of petitioner's First and Fourteenth Amendment rights, and an injunction restraining respondents—the Solicitor of the Civil and Criminal Court of DeKalb County, the chief of the DeKalb County Police, the owner of the North DeKalb Shopping Center, and the manager of that shopping center—from enforcing the statute so as to interfere with petitioner's constitutionally protected activities.

The parties stipulated to the relevant facts: On October 8, 1970, while petitioner and other individuals were distributing handbills protesting American involvement in Vietnam on an exterior sidewalk of the North DeKalb Shopping Center, shopping center employees asked them to stop handbilling and leave. They declined to do so, and police officers were summoned. The officers told them that they would be arrested if they did not stop handbilling. The group then left to avoid arrest. Two days later petitioner and a companion returned to the shopping center and again began handbilling. The manager of the center called the police, and petitioner and his companion were once again told that failure to stop their handbilling would result in their arrests. Petitioner left to avoid arrest. His companion stayed, however, continued handbilling, and was arrested and subsequently arraigned on a charge of criminal trespass in violation of § 26–1503. Petitioner alleged in his complaint that, although he desired to return to the shopping center to distribute handbills, he had not done so because of his concern that he, too, would be arrested for violation of § 26–1503; the parties stipulated that, if petitioner returned and refused upon request to stop handbilling, a warrant would be sworn out and he might be arrested and charged with a violation of the Georgia statute.

After hearing, the District Court denied all relief and dismissed the action, finding that "no meaningful contention can be made that the state has [acted] or will in the future act in bad faith," and therefore "the rudiments of an active controversy between the parties * * * [are] lacking." Petitioner appealed only from the denial of declaratory relief. The Court of Appeals for the Fifth Circuit, one judge concurring in the result, affirmed the District Court's judgment refusing declaratory relief. * * *

We granted certiorari, and now reverse.

I

At the threshold we must consider whether petitioner presents an "actual controversy," a requirement imposed by Art. III of the Constitution and the express terms of the Federal Declaratory Judgment Act, 28 U.S.C. § 2201.

Unlike three of the appellees in Younger v. Harris, 401 U.S. [37, 41 (1971)], petitioner has alleged threats of prosecution that cannot be characterized as "imaginary or speculative," *id.*, at 42. He has been twice warned to stop handbilling that he claims is constitutionally protected and has been told by the police that if he again handbills at the shopping center and disobeys a warning to stop he will likely be prosecuted. The prosecution of petitioner's handbilling companion is ample demonstration that petitioner's concern with arrest has not been "chimerical," Poe v. Ullman, 367 U.S. 497, 508 (1961). In these circumstances, it is not necessary that petitioner first expose himself to actual arrest or prosecution to be entitled to challenge a statute that he claims deters the exercise of his constitutional rights. See, *e.g.,* Epperson v. Arkansas, 393 U.S. 97 (1968). Moreover, petitioner's challenge is to those specific provisions of state law which have provided the basis for threats of criminal prosecution against him. *Cf.* Boyle v. Landry, 401 U.S. 77, 81 (1971); Watson v. Buck, 313 U.S. 387, 399–400 (1941).

* * *

II

We now turn to the question of whether the District Court and the Court of Appeals correctly found petitioner's request for declaratory relief inappropriate.

Sensitive to principles of equity, comity, and federalism, we recognized in Younger v. Harris, *supra,* that federal courts should ordinarily refrain from enjoining ongoing state criminal prosecutions. We were cognizant that a pending state proceeding, in all but unusual cases, would provide the federal plaintiff with the necessary vehicle for vindicating his constitutional rights, and, in that circumstance, the restraining of an ongoing prosecution would entail an unseemly failure to give effect to the principle that state courts have the solemn responsibility, equally with the federal courts "to guard, enforce, and protect every right granted or secured by the constitution of the United States. * * *" Robb v. Connolly, 111 U.S. 624, 637 (1884). In Samuels v. Mackell, *supra,* the Court also found that the same principles ordinarily would be flouted by issuance of a federal declaratory judgment when a state proceeding was pending, since the intrusive effect of declaratory relief "will result in precisely the same interference with and disruption of state proceedings that the long-standing policy limiting injunctions was designed to avoid." 401 U.S., at 72.[11] We therefore held in Samuels that, "in cases where the state criminal prosecution was begun prior to the federal suit, the same equitable principles relevant to the propriety of an injunction must be taken into consideration by federal district courts in determining whether to issue a declaratory judgment. * * *" *Id.,* at 73.

Neither Younger nor Samuels, however, decided the question whether federal intervention might be permissible in the absence of a pending state prosecution. * * *

These reservations anticipated the Court's recognition that the relevant principles of equity, comity, and federalism "have little force in the absence of a pending state proceeding." Lake Carriers' Assn. v. MacMullan, 406 U.S. 498, 509 (1972). When no state criminal proceeding is pending at the time the federal complaint is filed, federal intervention does not result in duplicative legal proceedings or disruption of the state criminal justice system; nor can federal intervention, in that circumstance, be interpreted as reflecting negatively upon the state court's ability to enforce constitutional principles. In

---

11. The Court noted that under 28 U.S.C. § 2202 a declaratory judgment might serve as the basis for issuance of a later injunction to give effect to the declaratory judgment, and that a declaratory judgment might have a res judicata effect on the pending state proceeding. 401 U.S., at 72.

addition, while a pending state prosecution provides the federal plaintiff with a concrete opportunity to vindicate his constitutional rights, a refusal on the part of the federal courts to intervene when no state proceeding is pending may place the hapless plaintiff between the Scylla of intentionally flouting state law and the Charybdis of foregoing what he believes to be constitutionally protected activity in order to avoid becoming enmeshed in a criminal proceeding. *Cf.* Dombrowski v. Pfister, 380 U.S. 479, 490 (1965).

When no state proceeding is pending and thus considerations of equity, comity, and federalism have little vitality, the propriety of granting federal declaratory relief may properly be considered independently of a request for injunctive relief. Here, the Court of Appeals held that, because injunctive relief would not be appropriate since petitioner failed to demonstrate irreparable injury—a traditional prerequisite to injunctive relief, *e.g.*, Dombrowski v. Pfister, *supra*—it followed that declaratory relief was also inappropriate. Even if the Court of Appeals correctly viewed injunctive relief as inappropriate—a question we need not reach today since petitioner has abandoned his request for that remedy,[12] the court erred in treating the requests for injunctive and declaratory relief as a single issue. "[W]hen no state prosecution is pending and the only question is whether declaratory relief is appropriate[,] * * * the congressional scheme that makes the federal courts the primary guardians of constitutional rights, and the express congressional authorization of declaratory relief, afforded because it is a less harsh and abrasive remedy than the injunction, become the factors of primary significance." Perez v. Ledesma, 401 U.S. 82, 104 (1971)(separate opinion of Brennan, J.).

The subject matter jurisdiction of the lower federal courts was greatly expanded in the wake of the Civil War. A pervasive sense of nationalism led to enactment of the Civil Rights Act of 1871, empowering the lower federal courts to determine the constitutionality of actions, taken by persons under color of state law, allegedly depriving other individuals of rights guaranteed by the Constitution and federal law, see 42 U.S.C. § 1983, 28 U.S.C. § 1343(3). Four years later, in the Judiciary Act of March 3, 1875, Congress conferred upon the lower federal courts, for but the second time in their nearly century-old history, general federal-question jurisdiction subject only to a jurisdictional-amount requirement, see 28 U.S.C. § 1331. With this latter enactment, the lower federal courts "ceased to be restricted tribunals of fair dealing between citizens of different states and became the *primary* and powerful reliances for vindicating every right given by the Constitution, the laws, and treaties of the United States." F. Frankfurter & J. Landis, The Business of the Supreme Court 65 (1928)(emphasis added). These two statutes, together with the Court's decision in Ex parte Young, 209 U.S. 123 (1908)—holding that state officials who threaten to enforce an unconstitutional state statute may be enjoined by a federal court of equity and that a federal court may, in appropriate circumstances, enjoin future state criminal prosecutions under the unconstitutional Act—have "established the modern framework for federal protection of consti-

---

12. We note that, in those cases where injunctive relief has been sought to restrain an imminent, but not yet pending, prosecution *for past conduct,* sufficient injury has not been found to warrant injunctive relief, see Beal v. Missouri Pacific R. Co., 312 U.S. 45 (1941); Spielman Motor Sales Co. v. Dodge, 295 U.S. 89 (1935); Fenner v. Boykin, 271 U.S. 240 (1926). There is some question, however, whether a showing of irreparable injury might be made in a case where, although no prosecution is pending or impending, an individual demonstrates that he will be required to *forego* constitutionally protected activity in order to avoid arrest. Compare Dombrowski v. Pfister, 380 U.S. 479 (1965).

tutional rights from state interference." Perez v. Ledesma, *supra,* 401 U.S., at 107 (separate opinion of Brennan, J.).

A "storm of controversy" raged in the wake of Ex parte Young, focusing principally on the power of a single federal judge to grant *ex parte* interlocutory injunctions against the enforcement of state statutes, H. Hart & H. Wechsler, The Federal Courts and the Federal System 967 (2d ed. 1973). This uproar was only partially quelled by Congress' passage of legislation requiring the convening of a three-judge district court before a preliminary injunction against enforcement of a state statute could issue, and providing for direct appeal to this Court from a decision granting or denying such relief. See 28 U.S.C. §§ 2281, 1253. From a State's viewpoint the granting of injunctive relief— even by these courts of special dignity—"rather clumsily" crippled state enforcement of its statutes pending further review. Furthermore, plaintiffs were dissatisfied with this method of testing the constitutionality of state statutes, since it placed upon them the burden of demonstrating the traditional prerequisites to equitable relief—most importantly, irreparable injury. See, e.g., Fenner v. Boykin, 271 U.S. 240, 243 (1926).

To dispel these difficulties, Congress in 1934 enacted the Declaratory Judgment Act, 28 U.S.C. §§ 2201–2202. That Congress plainly intended declaratory relief to act as an alternative to the strong medicine of the injunction and to be utilized to test the constitutionality of state criminal statutes in cases where injunctive relief would be unavailable is amply evidenced by the legislative history of the Act, traced in full detail in Perez v. Ledesma, *supra,* at 111– 115 (separate opinion of Brennan, J.). The highlights of that history, particularly pertinent to our inquiry today, emphasize that:

> "* * *

> "The express purpose of the Federal Declaratory Judgment Act was to provide a milder alternative to the injunction remedy. * * * Of particular significance on the question before us, the Senate report makes it even clearer that the declaratory judgment was designed to be available to test state criminal statutes in circumstances where an injunction would not be appropriate. * * *

> "* * * Moreover, the Senate report's clear implication that declaratory relief would have been appropriate in Pierce v. Society of Sisters, 268 U.S. 510 (1925), and Village of Euclid v. Ambler Realty Co., 272 U.S. 365 (1926), both cases involving federal adjudication of the constitutionality of a state statute carrying criminal penalties, and the report's quotation from Terrace v. Thompson, 263 U.S. 197 (1923), which also involved anticipatory federal adjudication of the constitutionality of a state criminal statute, make it plain that Congress anticipated that the declaratory judgment procedure would be used by the federal courts to test the constitutionality of state criminal statutes."

It was this history that formed the backdrop to our decision in Zwickler v. Koota, 389 U.S. 241 (1967), where a state criminal statute was attacked on grounds of unconstitutional overbreadth and no state prosecution was pending against the federal plaintiff. There, we found error in a three-judge district court's considering, as a single question, the propriety of granting injunctive and declaratory relief. Although we noted that injunctive relief might well be unavailable under principles of equity jurisprudence canvassed in Douglas v. City of Jeannette, 319 U.S. 157 (1943), we held that "a federal district court has the duty to decide the appropriateness and the merits of the declaratory request irrespective of its conclusion as to the propriety of the issuance of the injunction." 389 U.S., at 254. Only one year ago, we reaffirmed the Zwickler v. Koota holding in Roe v. Wade, 410 U.S. 113 (1973), and Doe v. Bolton, 410 U.S. 179 (1973). In those two cases, we declined to decide whether the District Courts had properly denied to the federal plaintiffs, against whom no prosecutions were pending, injunctive relief restraining enforcement of the Texas and Georgia criminal abortion statutes; instead, we affirmed the issuance of declaratory judgments of unconstitutionality, anticipating that these would be given effect by state authorities. * * *

The "different considerations" entering into a decision whether to grant declaratory relief have their origins in the preceding historical summary. First, as Congress recognized in 1934, a declaratory judgment will have a less intrusive effect on the administration of state criminal laws. As was observed in Perez v. Ledesma, 401 U.S., at 124–126 (separate opinion of Brennan, J.):

> "* * * [W]here the highest court of a State has had an opportunity to give a statute regulating expression a narrowing or clarifying construction but has failed to do so, and later a federal court declares the statute unconstitutionally vague or overbroad, it may well be open to a state prosecutor, after the federal court decision, to bring a prosecution under the statute if he reasonably believes that the defendant's conduct is not constitutionally protected and that the state courts may give the statute a construction so as to yield a constitutionally valid conviction. * * * [E]ven though a declaratory judgment has 'the force and effect of a final judgment,' 28 U.S.C. § 2201, it is a much milder form of relief than an injunction. Though it may be persuasive, it is not ultimately coercive; noncompliance with it may be inappropriate, but is not contempt."[18]

Second, engrafting upon the Declaratory Judgment Act a requirement that all of the traditional equitable prerequisites to the issuance of an injunction be satisfied before the issuance of a declaratory judgment is considered would defy Congress' intent to make declaratory relief available in cases where an injunction would be inappropriate. * * *

Thus, the Court of Appeals was in error when it ruled that a failure to demonstrate irreparable injury * * * precluded the granting of declaratory relief.

The only occasions where this Court has disregarded these "different considerations" and found that a preclusion of injunctive relief inevitably led to a denial of declaratory relief have been cases in which principles of federalism militated altogether against federal intervention in a class of adjudications. See Great Lakes Dredge & Dock Co. v. Huffman, 319 U.S. 293 (1943)(federal policy against interfering with the enforcement of state tax laws); Samuels v. Mackell, 401 U.S. 66 (1971). In the instant case, principles of federalism not only do not preclude federal intervention, they compel it. Requiring the federal courts totally to step aside when no state criminal prosecution is pending against the federal plaintiff would turn federalism on its head. When federal claims are premised on 42 U.S.C. § 1983 and 28 U.S.C. § 1343(3)—as they are

---

18. The pending prosecution of petitioner's handbilling companion does not affect petitioner's action for declaratory relief. In Roe v. Wade, 410 U.S. 113 (1973), while the pending prosecution of Dr. Hallford under the Texas Abortion law was found to render his action for declaratory and injunctive relief impermissible, this did not prevent our granting plaintiff Roe, against whom no action was pending, a declaratory judgment that the statute was unconstitutional.

here—we have not required exhaustion of state judicial or administrative remedies, recognizing the paramount role Congress has assigned to the federal courts to protect constitutional rights. See, *e.g.,* McNeese v. Board of Education, 373 U.S. 668 (1963); Monroe v. Pape, 365 U.S. 167 (1961). But exhaustion of state remedies is precisely what would be required if both federal injunctive and declaratory relief were unavailable in a case where no state prosecution had been commenced.

III

Respondents, however, relying principally upon our decision in Cameron v. Johnson, 390 U.S. 611 (1968), argue that, although it may be appropriate to issue a declaratory judgment when no state criminal proceeding is pending and the attack is upon the *facial validity* of a state criminal statute, such a step would be improper where, as here, the attack is merely upon the constitutionality of the statute as applied, since the State's interest in unencumbered enforcement of its laws outweighs the minimal federal interest in protecting the constitutional rights of only a single individual. We reject the argument.
* * *

* * *

Indeed, the State's concern with potential interference in the administration of its criminal laws is of lesser dimension when an attack is made upon the constitutionality of a state statute as applied. A declaratory judgment of a lower federal court that a state statute is invalid *in toto*—and therefore incapable of any valid application—or is overbroad or vague—and therefore no person can properly be convicted under the statute until it is given a narrowing or clarifying construction—will likely have a more significant potential for disruption of state enforcement policies than a declaration specifying a limited number of impermissible applications of the statute. While the federal interest may be greater when a state statute is attacked on its face, since there exists the potential for eliminating any broad-ranging deterrent effect on would-be actors, see Dombrowski v. Pfister, 380 U.S. 479 (1965), we do not find this consideration controlling. The solitary individual who suffers a deprivation of his constitutional rights is no less deserving of redress than one who suffers together with others.[21]

We therefore hold that, regardless of whether injunctive relief may be appropriate, federal declaratory relief is not precluded when no state prosecution is pending and a federal plaintiff demonstrates a genuine threat of enforcement of a disputed state criminal statute, whether an attack is made on the constitutionality of the statute on its face or as applied. The judgment of the Court of Appeals is reversed, and the case is remanded for further proceedings consistent with this opinion.

It is so ordered.

■ MR. JUSTICE STEWART, with whom THE CHIEF JUSTICE joins, concurring.

21. Abstention, a question "entirely separate from the question of granting declaratory or injunctive relief," Lake Carriers' Assn. v. MacMullan, 406 U.S. 498, 509 n. 13 (1972), might be more appropriate when a challenge is made to the state statute as applied, rather than upon its face, since the reach of an uncertain state statute might, in that circumstance, be more susceptible of a limiting or clarifying construction that would avoid the federal constitutional question. *Cf.* Zwickler v. Koota, 389 U.S., at 249–252, 254; Baggett v. Bullitt, 377 U.S. 360, 375–378 (1964).

While joining the opinion of the Court, I add a word by way of emphasis.

Our decision today must not be understood as authorizing the invocation of federal declaratory judgment jurisdiction by a person who thinks a state criminal law is unconstitutional, even if he genuinely feels "chilled" in his freedom of action by the law's existence, and even if he honestly entertains the subjective belief that he may now or in the future be prosecuted under it. * * *

The petitioner in this case has succeeded in objectively showing that the threat of imminent arrest, corroborated by the actual arrest of his companion, has created an actual concrete controversy between himself and the agents of the State. He has, therefore, demonstrated "a genuine threat of enforcement of a disputed state criminal statute * * *." Cases where such a "genuine threat" can be demonstrated will, I think be exceedingly rare.

■ MR. JUSTICE WHITE, concurring.

I offer the following few words in light of Mr. Justice Rehnquist's concurrence in which he discusses the impact on a pending federal action of a later filed criminal prosecution against the federal plaintiff, whether a federal court may enjoin a state criminal prosecution under a statute the federal court has earlier declared unconstitutional at the suit of the defendant now being prosecuted, and the question whether that declaratory judgment is res judicata in such a later filed state criminal action.

It should be noted, first, that his views on these issues are neither expressly nor impliedly embraced by the Court's opinion filed today. Second, my own tentative views on these questions are somewhat contrary to my Brother's.

At this writing at least, I would anticipate that a final declaratory judgment entered by a federal court holding particular conduct of the federal plaintiff to be immune on federal constitutional grounds from prosecution under state law should be accorded res judicata effect in any later prosecution of that very conduct. There would also, I think, be additional circumstances in which the federal judgment should be considered as more than a mere precedent bearing on the issue before the state court.

Neither can I at this stage agree that the federal court, having rendered a declaratory judgment in favor of the plaintiff, could not enjoin a later state prosecution for conduct that the federal court has declared immune. The Declaratory Judgment Act itself provides that a "declaration shall have the force and effect of a final judgment or decree," 28 U.S.C. § 2201; eminent authority anticipated that declaratory judgments would be res judicata, E. Borchard, Declaratory Judgments 10–11 (2d ed. 1941); and there is every reason for not reducing declaratory judgments to mere advisory opinions. Toucey v. New York Life Insurance Co., 314 U.S. 118 (1941), once expressed the view that 28 U.S.C. § 2283 forbade injunctions against relitigation in state courts of federally decided issues, but the section was then amended to overrule that case, the consequence being that "[i]t is clear that the Toucey rule is gone, and that to protect or effectuate its judgment a federal court may enjoin relitigation in the state court." C. Wright, Federal Courts 180 (2d ed. 1970). I see no more reason here to hold that the federal plaintiff must always rely solely on his plea of res judicata in the state courts. The statute provides for "[f]urther necessary or proper relief * * * against any adverse party whose rights have been determined by such judgment," 28 U.S.C. § 2202, and it would not seem improper to enjoin local prosecutors who refuse to observe adverse federal judgments.

Finally, I would think that a federal suit challenging a state criminal statute on federal constitutional grounds could be sufficiently far along so that ordinary consideration of economy would warrant refusal to dismiss the federal case solely because a state prosecution has subsequently been filed and the federal question may be litigated there.

■ MR. JUSTICE REHNQUIST, with whom THE CHIEF JUSTICE joins, concurring.

I concur in the opinion of the Court. Although my reading of the legislative history of the Declaratory Judgment Act of 1934 suggests that its primary purpose was to enable persons to obtain a definition of their rights before an actual injury had occurred, rather than to palliate any controversy arising from Ex parte Young, 209 U.S. 123 (1908), Congress apparently was aware at the time it passed the Act that persons threatened with state criminal prosecutions might choose to forego the offending conduct and instead seek a federal declaration of their rights. Use of the declaratory judgment procedure in the circumstances presented by this case seems consistent with that congressional expectation. * * *

* * * The Court quite properly leaves for another day whether the granting of a declaratory judgment by a federal court will have any subsequent res judicata effect or will perhaps support the issuance of a later federal injunction. But since possible resolutions of those issues would substantially undercut the principles of federalism reaffirmed in Younger v. Harris, 401 U.S. 37 (1971), and preserved by the decision today, I feel it appropriate to add a few remarks.

First, the legislative history of the Declaratory Judgment Act and the Court's opinion in this case both recognize that the declaratory judgment procedure is an alternative to pursuit of the arguably illegal activity. There is nothing in the Act's history to suggest that Congress intended to provide persons wishing to violate state laws with a federal shield behind which they could carry on their contemplated conduct. Thus I do not believe that a federal plaintiff in a declaratory judgment action can avoid, by the mere filing of a complaint, the principles so firmly expressed in Samuels, *supra*. The plaintiff who continues to violate a state statute after the filing of his federal complaint does so both at the risk of state prosecution and at the risk of dismissal of his federal lawsuit. For any arrest prior to resolution of the federal action would constitute a pending prosecution and bar declaratory relief under the principles of Samuels.

Second, I do not believe that today's decision can properly be raised to support the issuance of a federal injunction based upon a favorable declaratory judgment. The Court's description of declaratory relief as "a milder alternative to the injunction remedy," having a "less intrusive effect on the administration of state criminal laws" than an injunction, indicates to me critical distinctions which make declaratory relief appropriate where injunctive relief would not be. It would all but totally obscure these important distinctions if a successful application for declaratory relief came to be regarded, not as the conclusion of a lawsuit, but as a giant step toward obtaining an injunction against a subsequent criminal prosecution. * * *

A declaratory judgment is simply a statement of rights, not a binding order supplemented by continuing sanctions. State authorities may choose to be guided by the judgment of a lower federal court, but they are not compelled to follow the decision by threat of contempt or other penalties. If the federal plaintiff pursues the conduct for which he was previously threatened with arrest and is in fact arrested, he may not return the controversy to federal court, although he may, of course, raise the federal declaratory judgment in the state court for whatever value it may prove to have.[3] In any event, the defendant at that point is able to present his case for full consideration by a state court charged, as are the federal courts, to preserve the defendant's constitutional rights. Federal interference with this process would involve precisely the same concerns discussed in Younger and recited in the Court's opinion in this case.

Third, attempts to circumvent Younger by claiming that enforcement of a statute declared unconstitutional by a federal court is *per se* evidence of bad faith should not find support in the Court's decision in this case.   * * *

If the declaratory judgment remains, as I think the Declaratory Judgment Act intended, a simple declaration of rights without more, it will not be used merely as a dramatic tactical maneuver on the part of any state defendant seeking extended delays. Nor will it force state officials to try cases time after time first in the federal courts and then in the state courts.   * * *   If the federal court finds that the threatened prosecution would depend upon a statute it judges unconstitutional, the State may decide to forgo prosecution of similar conduct in the future, believing the judgment persuasive. Should the state prosecutors not find the decision persuasive enough to justify forbearance, the successful federal plaintiff will at least be able to bolster his allegations of unconstitutionality in the state trial with a decision of the federal district court in the immediate locality. The state courts may find the reasoning convincing even though the prosecutors did not. Finally, of course, the state legislature may decide, on the basis of the federal decision, that the statute would be better amended or repealed. All these possible avenues of relief would be reached voluntarily by the States and would be completely consistent with the concepts of federalism discussed above. Other more intrusive forms of relief should not be routinely available.   * * *

NOTE ON STEFFEL v. THOMPSON AND ANTICIPATORY RELIEF

(1) *The Pending/Non–Pending Distinction.*   Do you agree with the Court's conclusion in Steffel that the "principles of equity, comity, and federalism" that underlay Younger v. Harris "have little or no force in the absence of a pending state proceeding"? Consider Redish, Federal Jurisdiction: Tensions in the Allocation of Judicial Power 356 (2d ed.1990): "[Steffel] appears to contradict two * * * recognized bases of Younger deference—the desire to avoid interference with state substantive legislative policies and with state prosecutorial discretion. For whether or not a prosecution has been filed, federal relief tells the prosecutor 'when and how'—and indeed if—he or she is to bring a prosecution."[1]

---

3. The Court's opinion notes that the possible res judicata effect of a federal declaratory judgment in a subsequent state court prosecution is a question "not free from diffi- culty." * * * I express no opinion on that issue here. * * *

1. Do you agree with Professor Redish that Steffel "seems committed to the theory that the *sole* purpose of 'Our Federalism' was

If there is a disparity of outlooks between Younger and Steffel,[2] how do you account for the Supreme Court's nearly total unanimity in *both* cases? (The decision in Steffel was unanimous, while eight of the nine Justices concurred in the result in Younger.) Is the distinction between pending and non-pending actions, on which Justice Brennan's opinion relied so heavily, a stable one? See generally Hicks v. Miranda, 422 U.S. 332 (1975), p. 1291, *infra;* Paragraph (6) of this Note (discussing the applicability of abstention doctrine to grand jury proceedings). Are there other grounds of principled distinction?

(2) *Interests in Anticipatory Relief.* Apart from any desire to litigate their federal rights in federal rather than state court, plaintiffs such as Steffel may have powerful interests in obtaining anticipatory relief from what they believe to be unconstitutional applications of state laws. To clarify the interests at stake, and to evaluate the extent to which they are in tension with the values underlying Younger v. Harris, it is useful to distinguish claims to federal relief against state prosecution for future, past, and continuing conduct.

(a) *Future Conduct.* Suppose that Steffel had never violated the Georgia anti-trespassing statute, but that he had definite plans to do so, and was deterred from carrying out those plans only by the threat of a criminal prosecution. As Justice Brennan points out in Steffel, to allow plaintiffs to obtain a declaration of their rights in such cases would appear to be a central purpose of the Declaratory Judgment Act. Exposing oneself to criminal prosecution is a perilous business; anticipatory federal relief is important to relieve parties acting in good faith from having to choose between forgoing conduct they believe to be constitutionally protected and risking criminal liability. In these circumstances, a declaratory judgment is plainly available under Steffel, provided that the "ripeness" barrier can be surmounted.[3]

(b) *Past Conduct.* Consider now the case of someone who has engaged in conduct in the past, but has no plan or wish to continue that conduct in the future, and who seeks a federal declaration that the past conduct was constitutionally protected. Declaratory relief designed to immunize past, noncontinuing conduct from state prosecution cannot spare a litigant the choice between violating the statute and forgoing possibly lawful activity; that choice has already been made. And if the state prevails in the federal action, a subse-

---

to avoid insult to state judges"? If so, Steffel would appear to be contradicted by subsequent decisions applying Younger-based abstention principles to suits seeking to enjoin state administrative proceedings, see, *e.g.,* Ohio Civil Rights Comm'n v. Dayton Christian Schools, Inc., 477 U.S. 619 (1986), p. 1306, *infra.*

2. Compare Fallon, *The Ideologies of Federal Courts Law,* 74 Va.L.Rev. 1141, 1164–72 (1988)(suggesting that Steffel's acceptance of the "Nationalist" premise that Congress intended the federal courts to be "the primary and powerful reliances for vindicating every right given by the Constitution" is dissonant with Younger's "Federalist presumption that Congress would wish to show deference to state courts or that rules

of equitable restraint should be crafted to do so").

3. The Supreme Court's ripeness decisions clearly have not taken a straight path. Nonetheless, despite Justice Stewart's suggestion in Steffel that cases where a genuine threat of prosecution can be demonstrated will be "exceedingly rare" and his emphasis on Steffel's having engaged in similar conduct in the past and on the prosecution of his companion, one commentator concludes that the Court "routinely entertain[s] suits to declare statutes unconstitutional, invoking the ripeness requirement only occasionally." Laycock, Modern American Remedies 498 (2d ed.1994). See also Ohio Civil Rights Com'n v. Dayton Christian Schools, Inc., 477 U.S. 619 (1986), p. 1306, *infra.* See generally Chap. II, Sec. 5, *supra.*

quent prosecution is likely to be highly duplicative, since the federal litigation will have at best very limited res judicata effect against the state criminal defendant.[4]

Doesn't Younger suggest that federal equitable intervention is unjustified if its only advantage over a state defense is the immediate provision of a *federal* forum? Is the point equally valid whether or not the state has chosen to file charges for the past violation?[5] The pertinent precedents on this issue prior to Younger and Steffel include Fenner v. Boykin, 271 U.S. 240 (1926), and Spielman Motor Sales Co. v. Dodge, 295 U.S. 89 (1935), both of which denied relief even though there was no pending prosecution when the federal action was instituted.

Does Steffel hold that federal declaratory relief might be appropriate in a case of past conduct only? Would such a result be sound?

(c) *Continuing Conduct.* Consider now the case of a plaintiff, like Steffel, engaged in a continuing course of conduct—someone who has already violated a criminal statute, but who seeks federal equitable relief from prosecution for similar actions not yet undertaken. In such a case, anticipatory federal intervention offers the federal plaintiff distinctive advantages over defending against a state prosecution. First, in appropriate cases interlocutory relief may be available, thereby largely eliminating the need for the federal plaintiff to choose, *pendente lite,* between desisting from conduct that the plaintiff believes to be constitutionally protected and risking additional criminal penalties. Second, if the federal court awards equitable relief based upon the protected nature of the plaintiff's conduct, the plaintiff has protection against a second prosecution for similar conduct undertaken in the future.[6] By contrast, a defendant's victory in the pending state criminal case will not necessarily preclude prosecution for engaging thereafter in the same conduct: an acquittal, or even a trial judge's dismissal of the charges, may not have preclusive effect, especially where the state could not appeal. See generally Laycock, *Federal Interference With State Prosecutions: The Need for Prospective Relief,* 1977 Sup.Ct.Rev. 193.[7]

On the other hand, in cases of continuing conduct as in cases of past conduct only, the availability of a federal suit for equitable relief may force the state prosecutor's hand about when and where to litigate. In addition, if the federal claim fails, duplicative litigation may ensue.

4. Although preclusion might apply to a pure issue of law—such as the facial validity of a statute—differences in the burden of proof in civil and criminal cases would ordinarily require relitigation of the application of law to fact. See generally Restatement (Second) of Judgments §§ 27, 28 (1982).

Does this suggest that there may be a stronger argument for federal intervention in cases involving past conduct if the federal plaintiff is challenging the state statute on its face rather than as applied?

5. On the applicability of Younger when grand jury proceedings are underway, see Paragraph (6), *infra.*

6. This assumes a federal declaratory judgment would be accorded res judicata effect in a subsequent state prosecution. For an examination of this assumption, see Paragraph (3), *infra.*

7. Professor Laycock also notes that the state criminal case may be disposed of without reaching the federal constitutional question. As a third advantage to federal intervention, Laycock notes the availability of class relief.

Even so, aren't the arguments for allowing federal equitable intervention much stronger in a case involving continuing conduct than in a case involving past conduct only?

(3) *Declaratory v. Injunctive Relief.* Justice Brennan's opinion in Steffel places considerable weight on the distinction between declaratory and injunctive relief. How well does that distinction bear up?

(a) *Intended Effect.* Isn't the intended effect of a declaratory judgment the same as that of an injunction? Of course, if a state prosecutor subsequently brings an action that "violates" a declaration, the prosecutor would not be in contempt, as would be the case had an injunction issued. But wouldn't the plaintiff surely seek and be entitled to a supplementary injunction under 28 U.S.C. §§ 2201–2202? If so, is there any virtue in leaving the threat of a federal contempt sanction an extra step away? *Cf.* General Atomic Co. v. Felter and Deen v. Hickman, Chap. V, Sec. 1, p. 508, *supra.*

Does a declaration leave the state with more freedom than it would have under an injunction to prosecute other persons under the statute and thereby to salvage its constitutional applications? If such flexibility is desired, couldn't an injunction be drawn to permit it?

(b) *The Res Judicata Effect of a Federal Declaratory Judgment on an Issue of Federal Law.* Is a declaratory judgment possibly less intrusive on state interests than an injunction because it lacks the same res judicata effect? Suppose that, on remand in Steffel, the district court entered a declaratory judgment that the plaintiff's leafletting was constitutionally protected, and thereafter the state indicted him for criminal trespass. In the state prosecution, could he invoke issue preclusion on the federal constitutional question, based on the federal judgment? Concurring in Steffel, Justice Rehnquist expressed doubts. See also Green v. Mansour, p. 1075, *supra.* But "[t]he very purpose of the declaratory judgment proceeding would appear to be thwarted were this determination to be regarded, in a subsequent proceeding between the same parties, as no more than the view of a coordinate court." Shapiro, *State Courts and Federal Declaratory Judgments,* 74 Nw.U.L.Rev. 759, 764 (1979); accord, Restatement (Second) of Judgments § 33.[8] Indeed, if a federal declaratory judgment lacked any significant preclusive effect, mightn't it constitute a constitutionally forbidden advisory opinion? See Chapter II, Sec. 1, *supra.*[9]

Suppose instead that the federal district court declared that the statute was *constitutional* as applied to Steffel's conduct. Should Steffel be precluded in the criminal case from relitigating the constitutional question?

For a related discussion, see Paragraph (4) of the *Further Note on Enjoining State Criminal Proceedings,* p. 1297, *infra.*

---

8. There should be no problem, should there, with binding the state in the criminal case on the basis of a federal action that, because of Eleventh Amendment constraints, named an official rather than the state as a defendant? See Shapiro, *supra,* at 764; *cf.* Duncan v. United States, p. 1024, *supra.*

9. Even if Steffel could invoke the preclusive effect of a favorable federal judgment, does it follow that a fellow protester who was not a party to the federal proceeding should be able to do so? See Shapiro, *supra,* at 770–76, arguing that to permit nonmutual preclusion could prevent the full ventilation of issues of law regarding matters of public importance. See also Chap. XII, Sec. 1, *infra.* (If, however, the federal suit can be and is filed as a class action, there may be no one outside the class against whom the state could bring an enforcement action.)

(c) *Federal Judgments Involving Issues of State Law.* Suppose that in the Steffel case, the federal district court on remand determined that (i) Steffel's conduct was not constitutionally protected, but (ii) the criminal trespass statute was nonetheless invalid because it reached other constitutionally protected conduct, and as a matter of state law no narrowing construction was possible. Might a federal *injunction* against prosecutions under the statute risk depriving the state of the opportunity, through further litigation, to obtain the state courts' authoritative resolution of the state law issue?

The answer is almost surely not: the state could in any event bring a state court declaratory action against Steffel to determine whether a narrowing construction could be given. Professor Shapiro argues that in such an action, the federal judgment on the state law issue should have no preclusive effect. See Shapiro, *supra,* at 769. In any event, the preclusive effect should not depend on whether the federal court issued an injunction or a declaration.

If the state court were to supply a valid narrowing construction that would make application of the statute to Steffel's conduct constitutional, could Steffel then be prosecuted for conduct he undertook prior to the narrowing construction, but after the initial federal declaration that the state statute was invalid? A dictum in Dombrowski v. Pfister, 380 U.S. 479, 491 n. 7 (1965), rather clearly suggested yes, but Shapiro, *supra,* at 769–70, finds it unpersuasive due to a problem of inadequate notice.[10]

(d) *Prohibitory Intent and Preclusive Effect Conjoined.* If the intended effect of a declaratory judgment is the same as that of an injunction, and if a federal declaratory judgment would enjoy the same preclusive effect as an injunction in subsequent state litigation, isn't the distinction between the two types of remedy less significant than Justice Brennan suggested in Steffel?[11] May a sharp line between declaratory and injunctive relief be based on other considerations, such as a possible symbolic difference between the messages that the two remedies communicate? Does the distinction help to effect a workable, if somewhat arbitrary, accommodation of the interests that underlay Younger on the one hand and those supporting Steffel on the other? Or, like most arbitrary lines, is the distinction between injunctive and declaratory relief inherently vulnerable to erosion?

(4) *After Steffel: Injunctions Against Non–Pending Actions.* In Wooley v. Maynard, 430 U.S. 705 (1977), the Court upheld a permanent injunction barring New Hampshire officials from enforcing against the plaintiffs a state law making it a misdemeanor to "obscure" the phrase "Live Free or Die" on state license plates. Maynard had previously been convicted three times for violating the statute. The Court held that "[t]he threat of repeated prosecutions in the future against both [Maynard] and his wife, and the effect of such a continuing threat on their ability to perform the ordinary tasks of daily life

10. But *cf.* Fallon, *Making Sense of Overbreadth,* 100 Yale L.J. 853, 878 (1991), asserting that the argument based on inadequate notice "is circular. If the legal rule clearly provided that states could subsequently punish conduct occurring prior to a saving construction, everyone would have notice of the state's intent and capacity (provided that it could get an adequate limiting construction) to bring subsequent prosecutions." Fallon argues that the preclusive effect of a federal determination of unconstitutional overbreadth is largely a question of federal common law that should be determined based on a range of policy considerations (pp. 884–903).

11. Compare California v. Grace Brethren Church, p. 1219, *supra* (Tax Injunction Act bars a federal action for declaratory judgment as to state taxes).

which require an automobile, is sufficient to justify injunctive relief" (p. 712). Justice White, joined by Justices Blackmun and Rehnquist, dissented on the Younger issue, arguing that there was no reason to believe that the state officials—who had simply been performing their jobs in obtaining the three prior convictions—would not comply with a declaration, and hence there was no special need for injunctive relief.

In more recent cases involving threatened prosecution for future conduct, the Court has sometimes approved final injunctions (rather than declaratory judgments) without comment or dissent. See, *e.g.,* Bellotti v. Baird, 443 U.S. 622, 651 (1979); Ray v. Atlantic Richfield Co., 435 U.S. 151, 156–57 (1978); Zablocki v. Redhail, 434 U.S. 374, 377 (1978).

The Justices took a slightly more cautious position in Morales v. TWA, Inc., 504 U.S. 374 (1992). The district court had enjoined the Texas Attorney General from bringing enforcement proceedings against various airlines under certain state advertising regulations held to be preempted by the federal Airline Deregulation Act. No enforcement actions were pending, but the Attorney General's office had sent several putative violators a letter that served "as formal notice of intent to sue." In affirming part of the injunction, the Court found that the requirements of irreparable injury and of no adequate remedy at law were satisfied "[w]hen enforcement actions are imminent[,] * * * at least when repetitive penalties attach to continuing or repeated violations and the moving party lacks the realistic option of violating the law once and raising its federal defenses" (p. 381). The Court nevertheless overturned the injunction insofar as it barred the Attorney General from enforcing *any* regulation regarding airline advertising, rates, routes, or services, finding this "blunderbuss" injunction invalid in the absence of any imminent enforcement action (p. 2036).

In the wake of Wooley and its successor cases, how disparate are the standards for declaratory and injunctive relief against non-pending enforcement actions? Are too many variables in play—including, for example, the distinction between past and future or continuing conduct—to permit a simple, confident answer?

(5) *Exhaustion of State Remedies and Res Judicata.* Once the doctrine of equitable restraint closes the door to the federal courthouse because a state proceeding is pending, does there ever come a time—for example, after the state trial court has rendered judgment—when access to a federal court is no longer barred? The answer to this question may depend on whether further state-court remedies are available at the time the federal suit is filed.

(a) *State Remedies Still Available.* In Huffman v. Pursue, Ltd., 420 U.S. 592 (1975), the state had brought a civil action under its obscenity laws to "abate" the showing of obscene movies by Pursue. After the state trial court had issued a final order of abatement, Pursue filed a § 1983 action in federal court challenging the validity of the state obscenity statute. The Supreme Court first ruled that Younger applied when this form of *civil* proceeding was pending in state court—a question discussed at pp. 1300-04, *infra.* The Court then ruled that a party in Pursue's position "must exhaust his state appellate remedies before seeking relief in the District Court, unless he can bring himself within one of the exceptions specified in Younger" (p. 608), and noted that at the time the federal action was commenced Pursue still had the right to appeal the state trial court's order. Refusing to "assum[e] that state judges will not be faithful to their constitutional responsibilities" (p. 611), the Court held that the exhaustion requirement is not excused merely because the prospects for success in the state courts are poor.

Is there any reason for saying that a state proceeding still open to review by the state appellate courts is not "pending" for Younger purposes? Is it possible nonetheless to find that an appeal is futile, given the state's precedents, without accusing the state courts of constitutional infidelity? Compare the exhaustion requirement in federal habeas corpus, pp. 1443–50, *infra*. Even if Younger were held not to apply when state remedies are futile, however, wouldn't res judicata doctrine foreclose any federal action based upon a federal issue that was fully and fairly litigated in state court?

(b) *State Remedies No Longer Available.* Suppose that at the time a federal action is filed, the federal plaintiff has forfeited state court appellate remedies that would have been available at an earlier point. This may have been the case in Huffman: the Court was not sure whether at the time the federal district court issued its injunction Pursue could still have appealed the state court's order, but said that it "may not avoid the standards of Younger by simply failing to comply with the procedures of perfecting its appeal within the Ohio judicial system" (p. 611 n. 22).

A similar question was presented in Ellis v. Dyson, 421 U.S. 426 (1975), decided two months after Huffman. On the basis of their pleas of *nolo contendere,* several individuals were convicted in a Texas municipal court of loitering, and fined $10 each. Under Texas law, they were entitled to trial de novo in a county court and thereafter to appellate review. But, fearing higher fines on reconviction, they allowed the municipal court convictions to become final. They then brought suit in federal district court, seeking (a) a declaratory judgment that the loitering ordinance was unconstitutional and could not be applied to them in the future, and (b) an order "expunging" the records of the municipal court convictions. The court of appeals affirmed the district court's holding that the federal plaintiffs were not entitled to relief absent a showing of bad faith. The Supreme Court, in a confusing and opaque opinion, reversed and remanded for reconsideration in light of the intervening decision in Steffel. Justice Powell, dissenting, argued that the collateral attack on the convictions raised an issue not of equitable restraint, but of res judicata. Justice Powell then concluded that plaintiffs' challenge was in any event barred by the doctrine that a defendant who enters a constitutionally valid guilty plea cannot litigate in a federal habeas corpus proceeding alleged violations of constitutional rights, see Tollett v. Henderson, 411 U.S. 258 (1973); as a result, there was no need to decide whether § 1983 could be used as a basis for collateral attack on state court judgments—a question subsequently resolved by Allen v. McCurry, 449 U.S. 90 (1980), p. 1484, *infra,* holding that § 1983 does not create an exception to ordinary preclusion doctrines.

Justice Powell was right, wasn't he, that if a federal § 1983 suit challenges the validity of a state statute under which a conviction has already become final, the real issue is res judicata rather than Younger and exhaustion? Is there any reason why the federal plaintiff's forfeiture of state remedies should preclude the § 1983 suit when res judicata doctrine would not?

On this point, consider Wooley v. Maynard, 430 U.S. 705 (1977), Paragraph (4), *supra.* There, Maynard, who had not appealed any of his three state convictions for obscuring his license plate, later joined with his wife in bringing a § 1983 action to enjoin enforcement of the state law under which he had been convicted. In finding no bar to the action, the Court distinguished Huffman:

there, the plaintiff was trying to "annul the results of a state trial"; by contrast, Maynard sought relief that was "wholly prospective, to preclude further prosecution," and did not seek expungement of his prior convictions or relief from their consequences (p. 711). Federal intervention was appropriate to avoid the dilemma of either risking punishment under state law or foregoing conduct that might be constitutionally protected.

The Court proceeded to award the Maynards federal injunctive relief without discussing whether the prior state judgment deserved issue preclusive effect in the federal action. The three-judge district court in Wooley had addressed this question, ruling that the Maynards were not precluded from challenging the statute's constitutionality because that issue was not actually litigated in the criminal prosecutions. 406 F.Supp. at 1385 n. 6. Moreover, although the district court did not say so, claim preclusion could not be invoked, since Maynard could not have counterclaimed in a misdemeanor prosecution for an injunction against enforcement of a state statute. But see Currie, *Res Judicata: The Neglected Defense,* 45 U.Chi.L.Rev. 317, 336–47, 349–50 (1978), questioning the lower court's reasoning, though not necessarily its result.

(6) *Grand Jury Proceedings.* When does a state criminal action become "pending" or otherwise move beyond the ambit of Steffel and into the category governed by Younger and Samuels v. Mackell? In Monaghan v. Deakins, 798 F.2d 632 (3d Cir.1986), the court of appeals found that Younger's non-interference policy did not apply to grand jury proceedings, but the issue was mooted in that case before it could be decided by the Supreme Court. See Deakins v. Monaghan, 484 U.S. 193 (1988). *Cf.* United States v. Williams, 504 U.S. 36 (1992), p. 748 n. 2, *supra,* holding that a federal grand jury is functionally independent of the judicial branch.

In Morales v. TWA, Inc., 504 U.S. 374 (1992), p. 1289, *supra,* the Court, although not relying on the Younger doctrine (because it had not been invoked), described it as "impos[ing] heightened requirements for an injunction to restrain an already-pending *or an about-to-be-pending* state criminal action" (pp. 381–82 n. 1; emphasis added). Does the italicized language suggest that Younger might apply even when no state enforcement action has been filed? Compare Ankenbrandt v. Richards, 504 U.S. 689, 705 (1992), p. 1323, *infra* ("we have never applied the notions of comity so critical to Younger's 'Our Federalism' when no state proceeding was pending").

Hicks v. Miranda

422 U.S. 332, 95 S.Ct. 2281, 45 L.Ed.2d 223 (1975).
Appeal from the United States District Court for the Central District of California.

■ MR. JUSTICE WHITE delivered the opinion of the Court.

* * *

I

On November 23 and 24, 1973 * * * the police seized four copies of the film "Deep Throat," each of which had been shown at the Pussycat Theatre in Buena Park, Orange County, California. On November 26 an eight-count criminal misdemeanor charge was filed in the Orange County Municipal Court against two employees of the theater, each film seized being the subject matter of two counts in the complaint. Also on November 26, the Superior Court of Orange County ordered [the owners of the theaters] to show cause why "Deep Throat" should not be declared obscene, an immediate hearing being available to appellees, who appeared that day, objected on state law grounds to the court's jurisdiction to conduct such a proceeding, purported to "reserve" all federal questions and refused further to participate. Thereupon, on November 27 the Superior Court held a hearing, viewed the film, took evidence and then declared the movie to be obscene and ordered seized all copies of it that might be found at the theater. This judgment and order were not appealed by appellees.

Instead, on November 29, they filed this suit in the District Court against appellants—four police officers of Buena Park and the District Attorney and Assistant District Attorney of Orange County. The complaint recited the seizures and the proceedings in the Superior Court, stated in the body of the complaint that the action was for an injunction against the enforcement of the California obscenity statute, prayed for judgment declaring the obscenity statute unconstitutional and for an injunction ordering the return of all copies of the film, but permitting one of the films to be duplicated before its return.

A temporary restraining order was requested and denied, the District Judge finding the proof of irreparable injury to be lacking and an insufficient likelihood of prevailing on the merits to warrant an injunction. He requested the convening of a three-judge court, however, to consider the constitutionality of the statute. Such a court was then designated on January 8, 1974.

Service of the complaint was completed on January 14, 1974, and answers and motions to dismiss, as well as a motion for summary judgment, were filed by appellants. Appellees moved for a preliminary injunction. None of the motions was granted and no hearings held, all of the issues being ordered submitted on briefs and affidavits. * * *

Meanwhile, on January 15, the criminal complaint pending in the Municipal Court had been amended by naming appellees as additional parties defendant and by adding four conspiracy counts, one relating to each of the seized films. * * *

On June 4, 1974, the three-judge court issued its judgment and opinion declaring the California obscenity statute to be unconstitutional * * * and ordering appellants to return to appellees all copies of "Deep Throat" which had been seized as well as to refrain from making any additional seizures. Appellants' claim that Younger v. Harris, *supra,* and Samuels v. Mackell, *supra,* required dismissal of the case was rejected, the court holding that no criminal charges were pending in the state court against appellees and that in any event the pattern of search warrants and seizures demonstrated bad faith and harassment on the part of the authorities, all of which relieved the court from the strictures of Younger v. Harris, *supra,* and its related cases.

* * *

III

The District Court committed error in reaching the merits of this case despite the State's insistence that it be dismissed under Younger v. Harris, *supra,* and Samuels v. Mackell, *supra.* When they filed their federal complaint, no state criminal proceedings were pending against appellees by name; but two employees of the theater had been charged and four copies of "Deep Throat" belonging to appellees had been seized, were being held and had been declared to be obscene and seizable by the Superior Court. Appellees had a substantial stake in the state proceedings, so much so that they sought federal relief, demanding that the state statute be declared void and their films be returned to them. Obviously, their interest and those of their employees were intertwined; and as we have pointed out, the federal action sought to interfere with the pending state prosecution. Absent a clear showing that appellees, whose lawyers also represented their employees, could not seek the return of their property in the state proceedings and see to it that their federal claims were presented there, the requirements of Younger v. Harris could not be avoided on the ground that no criminal prosecution was pending against appellees on the date the federal complaint was filed. The rule in Younger v. Harris is designed to "permit state courts to try state cases free from interference by federal courts," 401 U.S., at 43, particularly where the party to the federal case may fully litigate his claim before the state court. Plainly, "the same comity considerations apply," Allee v. Medrano, 416 U.S. 802, 831 (Burger, C.J., concurring), where the interference is sought by some, such as appellees, not parties to the state case.

What is more, on the day following the completion of service of the complaint, appellees were charged along with their employees in Municipal Court. Neither Steffel v. Thompson, 415 U.S. 452, nor any other case in this Court has held that for Younger v. Harris to apply, the state-criminal proceedings must be pending on the day the federal case is filed. Indeed, the issue has been left open;[17] and we now hold that where state criminal proceedings are begun against the federal plaintiffs after the federal complaint is filed but before any proceedings of substance on the merits have taken place in the federal court, the principles of Younger v. Harris should apply in full force. Here, appellees were charged on January 15, prior to answering the federal case and prior to any proceedings whatsoever before the three-judge court. Unless we are to trivialize the principles of Younger v. Harris, the federal complaint should have been dismissed on the State's motion absent satisfactory proof of those extraordinary circumstances calling into play one of the limited exceptions to the rule of Younger v. Harris and related cases.

[The Court then rejected the district court's finding of official harassment and bad faith. See p. 1273, *supra.*][20] * * *

* * * The District Court should have dismissed the complaint before it and we accordingly reverse its judgment.

---

17. At least some Justices have thought so. Perez v. Ledesma, 401 U.S. 82, at 117 n. 9 (opinion of Mr. Justice Brennan, joined by Justices White and Marshall). Also, Steffel v. Thompson, *supra,* did not decide whether an injunction, as well as a declaratory judgment, can be issued when no state prosecution is pending.

20. It has been noted that appellees did not appeal the Superior Court's order of November 27, 1973, declaring "Deep Throat" obscene and ordering all copies of it seized.

It may be that under Huffman v. Pursue, 420 U.S. 592, decided March 18, 1975, the failure of appellees to appeal the Superior Court order of November 27, 1973, would itself foreclose resort to federal court, absent extraordinary circumstances bringing the case within some exception to Younger v. Harris. Appellees now assert, seemingly contrary to their prior statement before Judge Ferguson, that the November 27 order was not appealable. In view of our disposition of the case, we need not pursue the matter further.

■ Mr. Chief Justice Burger, concurring.

* * *

■ Mr. Justice Stewart, with whom Mr. Justice Douglas, Mr. Justice Brennan, and Mr. Justice Marshall join, dissenting.

* * *

In Steffel v. Thompson, 415 U.S. 452, the Court unanimously held that the principles of equity, comity, and federalism embodied in Younger v. Harris, 401 U.S. 37, and Samuels v. Mackell, 401 U.S. 66, do not preclude a federal district court from entertaining an action to declare unconstitutional a state criminal statute when a state criminal prosecution is threatened but not pending at the time the federal complaint is filed. Today the Court holds that the Steffel decision is inoperative if a state criminal charge is filed at any point after the commencement of the federal action "before any proceedings of substance on the merits have taken place in the federal court." Any other rule, says the Court, would "trivialize" the principles of Younger v. Harris. I think this ruling "trivializes" Steffel, decided just last Term, and is inconsistent with those same principles of equity, comity, and federalism.[1]

There is, to be sure, something unseemly about having the applicability of the Younger doctrine turn solely on the outcome of a race to the courthouse. The rule the Court adopts today, however, does not eliminate that race; it merely permits the State to leave the mark later, run a shorter course, and arrive first at the finish line. This rule seems to me to result from a failure to evaluate the state and federal interests as of the time the state prosecution was commenced.

* * *

The duty of the federal courts to adjudicate and vindicate federal constitutional rights is, of course, shared with state courts, but there can be no doubt that the federal courts are "the primary and powerful reliances for vindicating every right given by the Constitution, the laws, and treaties of the United States." Frankfurter & Landis, The Business of the Supreme Court: A Study of the Federal Judicial System 65. The statute under which this action was brought, 42 U.S.C. § 1983, established in our law "the role of the Federal Government as a guarantor of basic federal rights against state power." Mitchum v. Foster, 407 U.S. 225, 239. Indeed, "[t]he very purpose of § 1983 was to interpose the

---

1. There is the additional difficulty that the precise meaning of the rule the Court today adopts is a good deal less than apparent. What are "proceedings of substance on the merits"? Presumably, the proceedings must be both "on the merits" and "of substance." Does this mean, then, that months of discovery activity would be insufficient, if no question on the merits is presented to the court during that time? What proceedings "on the merits" are sufficient is also unclear. An application for a temporary restraining order or a preliminary injunction requires the court to make an assessment about the likelihood of success on the merits. Indeed, in this case, appellees filed an application for a temporary restraining order along with six supporting affidavits on November 29, 1973. Appellants responded on December 3, 1973, with six affidavits of their own as well as additional documents. On December 28, 1973, Judge Lydick denied the request for a temporary restraining order, in part because appellees "have failed totally to make that showing of * * * likelihood of prevailing on the merits needed to justify the issuance of a temporary restraining order." These proceedings, the Court says implicitly, were not sufficient to satisfy the test it announces. Why that should be, even in terms of the Court's holding, is a mystery.

federal courts between the States and the people." *Id.*, at 242. And this central interest of a federal court as guarantor of constitutional rights is fully implicated from the moment its jurisdiction is invoked. How, then, does the subsequent filing of a state criminal charge change the situation from one in which the federal court's dismissal of the action under Younger principles "would turn federalism on its head" to one in which *failure* to dismiss would "trivialize" those same principles?

A State has a vital interest in the enforcement of its criminal law, and this Court has said time and again that it will sanction little federal interference with that important state function. But there is nothing in our decision in Steffel that requires a State to stay its hand during the pendency of the federal litigation. If, in the interest of efficiency, the State wishes to refrain from actively prosecuting the criminal charge pending the outcome of the federal declaratory judgment suit, it may, of course, do so. But no decision of this Court requires it to make that choice.

The Court today, however, goes much further than simply recognizing the right of the State to proceed with the orderly administration of its criminal law; it ousts the federal courts from their historic role as the "primary reliances" for vindicating constitutional freedoms. This is no less offensive to "Our Federalism" than the federal injunction restraining pending state criminal proceedings condemned in Younger v. Harris. The concept of federalism requires "sensitivity to the legitimate interests of *both* State and National Governments." *Id.*, 401 U.S., at 44 (emphasis added). Younger v. Harris and its companion cases reflect the principles that the federal judiciary must refrain from interfering with the legitimate functioning of state courts. But surely the converse is a principle no less valid.

The Court's new rule creates a reality which few state prosecutors can be expected to ignore. It is an open invitation to state officials to institute state proceedings in order to defeat federal jurisdiction. One need not impugn the motives of state officials to suppose that they would rather prosecute a criminal suit in state court than defend a civil case in a federal forum. Today's opinion virtually instructs state officials to answer federal complaints with state indictments. Today, the State must file a criminal charge to secure dismissal of the federal litigation; perhaps tomorrow an action "akin to a criminal proceeding" will serve the purpose, *see* Huffman v. Pursue, Ltd., 420 U.S. 592; and the day may not be far off when any state civil action will do.

The doctrine of Younger v. Harris reflects an accommodation of competing interests. The rule announced today distorts that balance beyond recognition.

FURTHER NOTE ON ENJOINING STATE CRIMINAL PROCEEDINGS

(1) *Hicks and Traditional Equity Practice.* Hicks is contrary to the settled rule that equity jurisdiction is not destroyed because an adequate legal remedy has become available after the equitable action was filed. See, *e.g.,* American Life Ins. Co. v. Stewart, 300 U.S. 203, 215 (1937)(Cardozo, J.); Dawson v. Kentucky Distilleries & Warehouse Co., 255 U.S. 288, 296 (1921)(Brandeis, J.).[1]

---

1. Neither the majority nor dissent in Hicks paid attention to the alternate holding in Dombrowski v. Pfister, 380 U.S. 479, 484 n. 2 (1965), that when grand jury indictments

Do you agree with Justice White that Hicks was needed to avoid trivializing Younger? With Justice Stewart that Hicks trivializes Steffel?

(2) *The Meaning of "Proceedings of Substance on the Merits".* What suffices to constitute "proceedings of substance on the merits" in the federal action? The not insignificant proceedings on the motion for a temporary restraining order in Hicks obviously did not suffice, a result that Justice Stewart deemed a "mystery".

Ordinarily, if a plaintiff obtains a temporary restraining order or preliminary injunction, the State will be barred from instituting suit. But suppose any injunctive order is later vacated, or is limited in scope, or indeed is defied; are the federal proceedings leading to the issuance of that order substantial enough to permit the federal court to retain jurisdiction notwithstanding a subsequently filed state proceeding? In Hawaii Housing Auth. v. Midkiff, 467 U.S. 229 (1984), the Supreme Court found that Younger did not bar consideration of a federal action seeking injunctive relief against a state land reform scheme, stating (p. 238): "Whether issuance of the February temporary restraining order was a substantial federal court action or not, issuance of the June preliminary injunction certainly was"; the court had by then "proceeded well beyond the 'embryonic stage,'" and no state judicial proceedings had yet been filed.

(3) *The Pertinence of Doran v. Salem Inn.* A week after the decision in Hicks v. Miranda, the Court decided Doran v. Salem Inn, Inc., 422 U.S. 922 (1975). Consider the pertinence of Doran to the issues raised by Hicks.

(a) *Doran's Facts and Holding.* The Doran case arose from a dispute about the constitutionality of an ordinance passed by the Town of North Hempstead, New York, that prohibited topless dancing in bars. Three local bars that had previously featured topless dancing initially complied with the ordinance, but three corporate bar owners (M & L, Salem, and Tim–Robb) brought suit in federal court seeking a declaration that the ordinance was unconstitutional as well as a temporary restraining order and a preliminary injunction against its enforcement. The day after the complaint was filed, M & L (but not the other two plaintiffs) resumed topless dancing; a criminal prosecution against it was commenced immediately. The district court granted plaintiffs' prayer for a preliminary injunction, and the Court of Appeals for the Second Circuit affirmed.

The Supreme Court first concluded that the three plaintiffs should not "be thrown into the same hopper for Younger" purposes; while there "may be some circumstances in which legally distinct parties are so closely related that they should all be subjected to the Younger considerations which govern any one of them, this is not such a case" (p. 928).[2] The court then held that M & L was barred from securing an injunction by Younger and a declaratory judgment by Samuels v. Mackell. "When the criminal summonses issued against M & L on the days immediately following the filing of the federal complaint, the federal litigation was in an embryonic stage" (p. 929). With regard to Salem

---

are returned after the filing of a federal complaint seeking interlocutory and permanent injunctive relief but before such relief is issued, "no state 'proceedings' were pending within the intendment of [the Anti–Injunction Act, 28 U.S.C. § 2283]."

2. The Court noted that, although the plaintiffs were represented by common counsel, they were unrelated in terms of ownership or management.

and Tim–Robb, the Court held their prayers for declaratory relief squarely governed by Steffel, since they were not subject to state criminal prosecution at any time. Further, the Court held that under the circumstances the issuance of a preliminary injunction barring enforcement of the ordinance was not subject to the restrictions of Younger. The Court reasoned that, at the end of trial on the merits, the plaintiffs' interests can generally be protected by a declaratory judgment; but "prior to final judgment there is no established declaratory remedy comparable to a preliminary injunction; unless preliminary relief is available upon a proper showing, plaintiffs in some situations may suffer unnecessary and substantial irreparable harm" (p. 931).

Turning to the merits, and stressing the narrow scope of appellate review, the Court held that it was not an abuse of discretion to grant the preliminary injunction, since a sufficient showing of both irreparable harm *pendente lite* and likelihood of ultimate success on the merits had been made.

(b) *The Relationship of Hicks and Doran.* In a situation involving continuing conduct, is there an underlying inconsistency between Hicks and Doran? Steffel permits federal intervention so long as no state prosecution is pending. Under Hicks, however, the state can preempt the federal action by commencing a prosecution before substantial proceedings occur in the federal case, and thereby bar federal relief even as to conduct not yet undertaken; that, indeed, is what happened to M & L in Doran.[3] But under Doran, the district court may issue a preliminary injunction against enforcement of the statute if the requisites for such relief have been satisfied. Does Doran, therefore, shut the door opened by Hicks v. Miranda in any case where a district court, at the outset of the federal litigation, concludes that, *pendente lite,* injunctive relief is appropriate?

Of course merely filing a motion for a preliminary injunction does not constitute "proceedings of substance on the merits", and a prosecutor can often file charges before much has happened in connection with such a motion. A plaintiff might seek still earlier federal intervention by way of a temporary restraining order, but even then would have to give prior notice to the defendant, unless it were clear that irreparable injury would result before notice could be provided, see Fed.R.Civ.Proc. 65(b). Isn't Hicks likely to give an alert prosecutor a "reverse removal power"? See Fiss, *Dombrowski*, 86 Yale L.J. 1103, 1136 (1977).

(4) *Doran and Issues Involving Federal Relief Pendente Lite.* Doran raises a number of questions about the availability and effect of federal injunctive relief *pendente lite.*

(a) *The Availability of Interim Relief.* In Doran, didn't M & L, during the pendency of the state prosecution against it, have just as much need as the other plaintiffs to avoid having either to suffer economic injury from suspending topless dancing or to run the risk of multiple prosecutions if the dancing continued? Given a proper showing of likely success on the merits and irreparable injury, why wasn't the district judge in Doran right, then, to grant M & L a preliminary injunction restraining the enforcement of the ordinance with respect to violations by M & L occurring *after* the injunction was granted

---

3. See also Roe v. Wade, 410 U.S. 113, 125–27 (1973), where a doctor who had already been indicted for performing abortions sought an injunction against further prosecution for performing additional abortions. The Supreme Court held that under Younger, this request for prospective relief was barred in view of the pending prosecution.

and before the constitutional issues were settled on the merits? (For suggestions along this line, see Laycock, *Federal Interference with State Prosecutions:
The Need for Prospective Relief,* 1977 Sup.Ct.Rev. 193, 238; *The Supreme
Court, 1974 Term,* 89 Harv.L.Rev. 151–69 (1975).) This would have allowed
the state to prosecute the single *past violation* and thus to preempt a full
federal trial on the merits under Hicks; on the other hand, the preliminary
injunction would have permitted M & L to continue the disputed activity while
the issue of constitutionality was being settled (either in the state prosecution
or, if none were brought, in federal court).[4]

(b) *The Effect of Preliminary Relief.* When preliminary relief is awarded—
as it was in fact in Doran to Salem and Tri–Robb—does it immunize the
plaintiff from criminal prosecution for acts taken after the injunction issued,
even if the statute is ultimately held constitutional in further proceedings in
state or federal court? The claim that it does was urged in Edgar v. MITE
Corp., 457 U.S. 624 (1982), as part of an argument that a federal action seeking
to restrain enforcement of a state statute was moot because (i) the only past
violation occurred during the pendency of a preliminary injunction forbidding
the statute's enforcement, and (ii) the plaintiff did not plan any future
violations of the challenged statute. The Court brushed aside the mootness
argument, concluding that the effect of the preliminary injunction "is an issue
to be decided when and if the [state official charged with enforcing the statute]
initiates an action" (p. 630).

Of the five Justices in the majority, only Justice Stevens reached the
question. In his concurring opinion he contended that whether or not such
immunity would be wise, federal judges were not empowered to confer it. He
suggested that even a final judgment declaring a state law unconstitutional
would not confer immunity from prosecution for post-judgment conduct if the
judgment were later reversed on appeal.

Justice Marshall's dissent on the mootness point—which Justice Brennan
joined and with which Justice Powell expressed general agreement—argued
that federal courts have the power to confer such immunity; that "whether a
particular injunction provides temporary or permanent protection becomes a
question of interpretation"; and that "in the ordinary case * * * it should be
presumed that an injunction secures permanent protection from penalties for
violations that occurred during the period it was in effect" (p. 657). He
insisted that people will be "reluctant to challenge [the validity of state
statutes] unless they can obtain permanent immunity from penalties", and that
"short-term protection is often only marginally better than no protection at
all" (pp. 657 n. 1, 658).[5] See also Paragraph (3)(b)-(c) of the *Note on Steffel v.
Thompson and Anticipatory Relief,* pp. 1287–88, *supra.*

---

4. Does the need for interim relief disappear if the state officials promise not to
seek additional sanctions for further violations pending resolution of the issue in the
pending prosecution? Is such a promise enforceable? See Laycock, *Modern American
Remedies* 245 (2d ed.1994).

5. Justice Rehnquist found the case
moot on other grounds without reaching the
immunity issue.

None of the opinions cited Oklahoma
Operating Co. v. Love, 252 U.S. 331
(1920)(Brandeis, J.), where in unanimously
affirming the award of a preliminary injunction against allegedly confiscatory rate regulation, the Court said (p. 338): "If upon final
hearing the maximum rates fixed should be
found not to be confiscatory, a permanent
injunction should, nevertheless, issue to restrain enforcement of penalties accrued *pendente lite,* provided that it also be found that

(c) *The Relationship Between Ongoing State and Federal Proceedings.* Suppose that M & L had been permitted to obtain a preliminary injunction *pendente lite*, notwithstanding the filing of a state prosecution against it. Note that the ultimate question of constitutionality would be resolved by the state court; at that point, the preliminary injunction would presumably be dissolved as unnecessary.

Should the federal court's role be so limited? While the state prosecution is pending (but before it has come to judgment), should the federal court be denied the power to enter a *final* judgment declaring the ordinance invalid, and *permanently* enjoining the institution of prosecutions against M & L for any conduct that occurs in the future? Courts sometimes proceed to enter final judgment after hearing a motion for preliminary relief when the legal issues are so well-developed that further proceedings are unnecessary. Moreover, note that a final injunction could presumably be entered, in an appropriate case, as to Salem and Tri–Robb, who had not yet violated the statute. Would M & L obtain any advantage from a final federal judgment in its favor, as compared with a federal preliminary injunction followed by a victory in the pending state prosecution? *See* Paragraph (4)(a), *supra.* Could the award of permanent federal relief be reconciled with Younger itself? Does the answer to the latter question depend on whether a final judgment favorable to M & L would preclude relitigation of the constitutional question in the pending state prosecution against M & L?[6] Recall that in Cline v. Frink Dairy Co., 274 U.S. 445, 452–53, 466 (1927), p. 1266 n. 2, *supra,* the Supreme Court, per Brandeis, J., affirmed the issuance of final injunctive relief against the institution of *future* prosecutions even though a state prosecution was pending when the federal action was filed.

(5) *The Pertinence of Pending Actions Against Nonparties.* Notice the contrary indications in Hicks and Doran with respect to whether Younger ever bars one party (X) from obtaining federal relief because of the pendency of state proceedings against another party (Y).[7] Did the Court in Hicks really mean to hold so casually (albeit in the alternative) that for Younger purposes a criminal prosecution against Y can oust X's right to litigate a constitutional claim in federal court because X and Y's interests are "intertwined", X and Y share the same lawyer, and X has not made a "clear showing" that his or her rights cannot be protected in state court? Compare the Court's refusal in Doran to

---

the plaintiff had reasonable ground to contest them as being confiscatory." See generally Laycock, note 4, *supra,* at 502–05.

6. It is unlikely, but not impossible, that a similar question might arise as to the res judicata effect of a federal judgment merely awarding preliminary relief. The Restatement (Second) of Judgments, § 13, Illustration 1 (1982), suggests that a decision on a motion for preliminary injunction can (but does not necessarily) have preclusive effect, and that suggestion has been endorsed in some cases. See, *e.g.,* Commodity Futures Trading Comm'n v. Board of Trade, 701 F.2d 653, 657–58 (7th Cir.1983); Miller Brewing Co. v. Jos. Schlitz Brewing Co., 605 F.2d 990, 995–96 (7th Cir.1979); *cf.* Lummus Co. v. Commonwealth Oil Refining Co., 297 F.2d

80, 89 (2d Cir.1961). But see United Books, Inc. v. Conte, 739 F.2d 30, 33 (1st Cir.1984)(asserting in passing and without qualification that a preliminary injunction against future prosecution would not have preclusive effect in a pending state prosecution).

7. In Steffel the Court dismissed the argument that the pendency of a prosecution against Steffel's handbilling companion barred Steffel's federal action. 415 U.S. at 471 n. 19. See also Roe v. Wade, 410 U.S. 113, 126–27 (1973)(pending prosecution against a physician who was a plaintiff-intervenor does not bar challenge to same statute by a different plaintiff).

withhold federal relief in favor of two bar owners because of the pending prosecution of the third: "while [the three owners] are represented by common counsel, * * * they are apparently unrelated in terms of ownership, control, and management" (pp. 928–29). Hicks, decided one week earlier, was not cited.

Aren't the interests of employees and owners potentially quite divergent in Hicks? Suppose, for example, the prosecutor were to offer a favorable plea to the employees if they would agree to implicate the owners. See Wood v. Georgia, 450 U.S. 261 (1981), discussed in Chap. V, p. 570, *supra.* Shouldn't parties X be barred from seeking federal relief only if they would be deemed to be in privity with Y (and hence to have their day in court) in the state court proceeding against Y?[8]

———

NOTE ON FURTHER EXTENSIONS OF EQUITABLE RESTRAINT DOCTRINE: PENDING CIVIL ACTIONS IN STATE COURT, STATE ADMINISTRATIVE PROCEEDINGS, AND EXECUTIVE ACTION

(1) *Civil Actions to Which the State Is a Party.* In Huffman v. Pursue, Ltd., 420 U.S. 592 (1975)(also discussed at p. 1289, *supra*), the state brought a civil action under its obscenity laws to "abate" the showing of obscene movies by Pursue. Dividing 6–3, the Supreme Court held that Younger applies to bar federal relief when "[t]he State is a party to the * * * proceeding, and the proceeding is both in aid of and closely related to criminal statutes" (p. 604).

(a) *The Huffman Opinions and Rationale.* In the view of the Huffman majority, the federalism strain of Younger—its policies of avoiding interference with state officials, duplicative proceedings, and negative reflection upon the state courts—all counseled restraint. The Court conceded that Younger's equitable component—the traditional reluctance to enjoin criminal proceedings—was not "strictly" on point. "But whatever may be the weight attached to this factor in civil litigation involving private parties, we deal here with a state proceeding which in important respects is more akin to a criminal prosecution than are most civil cases" (p. 604).

Justice Brennan's dissent, joined by Justices Douglas and Marshall, complained that the Court was taking a "first step toward extending to state *civil* proceedings generally the holding of Younger v. Harris" (p. 613). He argued that such a course would undermine Mitchum v. Foster, which, on virtually identical facts, held a federal court § 1983 action not barred by the Anti–Injunction Act, 28 U.S.C. § 2283.[1] Justice Brennan also cited functional differences between civil and criminal proceedings: while many safeguards are provided against the initiation of unwarranted criminal proceedings, state civil proceedings may be initiated "merely upon the filing of a complaint, whether or

———

8. Compare County of Imperial v. Munoz, 449 U.S. 54 (1980), p. 1208, *supra,* holding that the plaintiffs' federal action challenging on federal grounds a state court injunction against a different person was barred under the Anti–Injunction Act, 28 U.S.C. § 2283, unless the federal plaintiffs were "strangers" to the state court litigation.

1. Can one argue that § 2283 in fact supports the Court's holding? After all, (i) Younger relied heavily upon that Act as a source of the federal policy of noninterference, and (ii) the Act does not distinguish between criminal and civil proceedings.

not well founded" (p. 615). (The ease of filing a civil complaint may also facilitate a state official's exercise of the "reverse removal power" established by Hicks v. Miranda.)

To what extent does Younger's "bad faith" exception address Justice Brennan's concern about the ease of filing state civil proceedings? See p. 1273, *supra*.

One other difference between pending civil and criminal cases deserves mention. Unlike a criminal defendant, a civil defendant in state court will often be able to counterclaim for relief against enforcement of the challenged enactment—including declaratory relief, class relief, and relief *pendente lite*. But if a civil defendant fails to counterclaim, compulsory counterclaim and claim preclusion rules may bar later federal court consideration of the federal constitutional claim, even if the constitutional issue was not raised or decided in state court. Compare Wooley v. Maynard, p. 1288, *supra*.

(b) *Extension of Huffman.* The Court appeared to extend Younger more broadly to encompass all civil enforcement actions brought by the state in Trainor v. Hernandez, 431 U.S. 434 (1977). The Trainor case involved a state court civil action by the State of Illinois to recover welfare payments that the defendants had allegedly obtained by fraud. After the state attached some of the defendants' funds, they brought a federal challenge to the constitutional validity of Illinois' attachment procedures. The Supreme Court held, 5–4, that "the principles of Younger and Huffman are broad enough to apply to interference by a federal court with an ongoing civil enforcement action such as this, brought by the State in its sovereign capacity" (p. 444). The Court acknowledged that federal interference would be warranted if it would not be possible to challenge the validity of the attachment procedures in the Illinois litigation, and remanded the case for a determination of that question. In dissent, Justice Brennan (joined by Justice Marshall) continued to criticize the application of Younger to pending civil proceedings. In addition, he and Justice Stevens (who also wrote an opinion) argued that the case fell within exceptions to Younger, including that for challenges to "patently and flagrantly unconstitutional" statutes. (For discussion of this issue, see pp. 1273-74, *supra*.) Justice Stewart stated that he agreed "substantially" with both dissents.

In Moore v. Sims, 442 U.S. 415 (1979), the Court found that Younger foreclosed interference with a pending state proceeding in which the state sought custody of children who had allegedly suffered abuse by their parents. The Court divided 5–4 on the question whether the state proceedings afforded the federal plaintiffs a meaningful opportunity to raise their federal constitutional claims.

(c) *The NOPSI Case.* In New Orleans Public Service, Inc. v. Council of City of New Orleans ("NOPSI"), 491 U.S. 350 (1989), the Supreme Court limited the extension of Younger abstention principles in actions to which the state is a party. NOPSI, a utility company, sought a rate increase to cover its share of the costs of a nuclear reactor, as fixed by the Federal Energy Regulatory Commission. After the New Orleans City Council denied the requested rate increase, the utility sought federal injunctive and declaratory relief, alleging that the rate order violated federal law. But, fearful that the district court might abstain (as it had in two prior suits filed by NOPSI during the city council's consideration of the proposed rate increase), NOPSI also filed a petition for review of the city council's order in state court. The city council also filed its own state court action seeking a declaratory judgment of the lawfulness of its order, which was consolidated with NOPSI's state court action. Relying partly on the pendency of the state court action, the district court dismissed, and the court of appeals upheld the dismissal, *inter alia,* on Younger grounds.

The Supreme Court reversed. Justice Scalia's majority opinion reasoned that: "NOPSI's challenge must stand or fall upon the answer to the question whether the Louisiana court action is the type of proceeding to which Younger applies. Viewed in isolation, it plainly is not. * * * [I]t has never been suggested that Younger requires abstention in deference to a state judicial proceeding reviewing legislative or executive action. Such a broad abstention requirement would make a mockery of the rule that only exceptional circumstances justify a federal court's refusal to decide a case in deference to the States" (pp. 367–68).

Viewing the suit as a challenge to "completed legislative action", the Court found that, "insofar as our policies of federal comity are concerned, [it was] no different in substance from a facial challenge to an allegedly unconstitutional statute or zoning ordinance—which we would assuredly not require to be brought in state courts" (p. 372).[2]

NOPSI thus appears to establish that the rationale of cases such as Huffman, Trainor, and Moore—which calls for abstention when the state brings a civil enforcement actions in its sovereign capacity—does not extend to challenges to completed legislative or executive action that do not require, or have not yet led to, enforcement suits. How helpful is this discussion in clarifying the scope of Younger? Suppose that Louisiana amended its laws so that the Council's rate orders were not self-executing, but instead had to be enforced by a judicial decree in the state courts, which were obliged to issue the decree unless they found that the rate order was contrary to law or arbitrary or capricious. If a utility such as NOPSI brought a federal action challenging a rate order while there was a pending enforcement proceeding in state court, should the federal court abstain?

(2) *Civil Actions Involving Important State Interests.* Even in cases in which the state is not enforcing its criminal or civil law, and indeed even if the state is not a party, the Supreme Court has held that Younger abstention may sometimes be justified by important state interests. Which state interests are sufficiently important to trigger Younger abstention?

(a) Juidice v. Vail, 430 U.S. 327 (1977), arose when, following a default judgment against him in a debt collection case, Vail was found in civil contempt of a New York court's order to attend a deposition to provide information relevant to satisfying the judgment. Vail then filed a federal class action to enjoin New York's judges from using the state's statutory contempt procedures, which, he alleged, denied due process. The Court held that Younger and Huffman barred the injunction. Although the underlying lawsuit was between private parties, the state's interest in its contempt processes, "through which it vindicates the regular operation of its judicial system", was deemed important enough to warrant the application of Younger, "so long as that system itself affords the opportunity to pursue federal claims within it", even though no

2. All members of the Court joined the section of the opinion dealing with Younger   abstention except Justice Blackmun, who concurred in the result.

criminal or "quasi-criminal" law was being enforced (p. 335).[3]

(b) In Pennzoil Co. v. Texaco, Inc., 481 U.S. 1 (1987), Pennzoil obtained an $11 billion jury verdict against Texaco in a Texas court and, under Texas law, acquired two important rights after the entry of judgment and pending appeal: (i) to obtain a writ of execution permitting it to levy execution on Texaco's assets unless Texaco posted a sufficient bond (Texas law appeared to call for a bond equal to the judgment and interest, though it was not certain that such an extraordinary amount would be required); and (ii) to secure liens on Texaco's real property in Texas, without regard to the posting of a bond.

Before judgment on the verdict was entered in state court, Texaco brought suit in federal court in New York (where it was headquartered) to enjoin Pennzoil from taking action to enforce its post-judgment rights. Such an injunction, Texaco argued, would not interfere with state proceedings, but, on the contrary, was necessary to permit Texaco, which could not afford to post the requisite bond, to prosecute an appeal. The district court issued a preliminary injunction along the lines requested, finding that application of the lien and bond provisions would probably force Texaco into bankruptcy and hence denied due process, and the court of appeals substantially affirmed.

The Supreme Court reversed. Without considering whether the lower courts were correct in holding that the suit was properly brought under § 1983 (and hence not barred by § 2283),[4] Justice Powell's opinion for five Justices stated that Younger applied when, as here, "the State's interests in the proceeding are so important that exercise of the federal judicial power would disregard the comity between the States and the National Government" (p. 11). As in Juidice, the pending proceeding implicated the state's interest in enforcing the orders and judgments of its courts. Justice Powell added that the Texas courts might interpret state law to provide some relief from the lien and bond provisions; federal noninterference was thus also supported by the policy of constitutional avoidance. In a footnote, he asserted that the Court was not holding Younger applicable whenever a civil case is pending in state court (p. 14 n. 12).

Four Justices concurred in the judgment but rejected the Court's Younger analysis.[5] Justice Brennan's opinion (with which Justices Marshall, Blackmun, and Stevens agreed on this point) repeated his view that Younger should be generally inapplicable to civil proceedings, and argued that since Texas law directs state officials merely to follow Pennzoil's directions in enforcing the judgment, only Pennzoil, not Texas, had an interest in the pending proceedings (pp. 19–21). (For further discussion of the Pennzoil case, see Chap. XII, pp. 1503-04, *infra*.)

(c) *Limiting Principles?* In the NOPSI case, Paragraph (1)(c), *supra*, the Supreme Court cited Juidice, *supra*, and Pennzoil, *supra*, as establishing that

---

3. Justice Stevens concurred in the result on the ground that the New York procedure was valid, but did not agree that it was appropriate to invoke Younger. Justice Brennan (joined by Justice Marshall) and Justice Stewart each dissented; the latter thought that Pullman abstention was called for.

4. The four concurring Justices addressed this issue, agreeing with the lower courts. See Justices Brennan's and Stevens' separate opinions.

5. Justices Brennan, Marshall, and Stevens concluded that Texaco's due process argument lacked merit. Justice Marshall further argued that the district court lacked jurisdiction under the "Rooker–Feldman" doctrine, pp. 1500-04, *infra*. Justice Blackmun favored Pullman abstention.

Younger abstention doctrine extends to "civil proceedings involving certain orders that are uniquely in furtherance of the state courts' ability to perform their judicial functions" (491 U.S. at 367).   Do Juidice and Pennzoil nonetheless invite further extensions whenever state interests are deemed sufficiently important?[6]

Given the difficulty of drawing principled lines once Younger is extended to civil actions, would it have been better to limit the doctrine sharply and expressly to cases involving pending criminal proceedings?[7]   Or, in light of the underlying state interests, would such a line itself be arbitrary?   When, generally, should sharp jurisdictional lines be preferred to the uncertainties generated by more case-specific inquiries?

(3) *Damages Actions Involving State Officials.*   In Juidice v. Vail, 430 U.S. at 339 n. 16, the Supreme Court noted but reserved the question "as to the applicability of Younger–Huffman principles to a § 1983 suit seeking only [damages] relief."   Unlike a federal injunction, a federal judgment in a damages action would not directly bar state court proceedings.   In some cases, however, a federal judgment might have preclusive effect.

In Deakins v. Monaghan, 484 U.S. 193 (1988), the court of appeals, reversing the district court's dismissal under Younger of a damages claim, ruled that the action should instead have been stayed.   Before the Supreme Court, the plaintiffs represented that on remand they would seek to stay the damages claims pending resolution of state prosecutions.   In this posture, the Supreme Court affirmed the court of appeals' disposition, without deciding whether Younger applied to damages actions.   Justice White (joined by Justice O'Connor) would have reached that question.   He argued that Younger's policy of avoiding the preemption of state proceedings was fully implicated by federal damages claims, whose decision would presumably be res judicata in any state prosecution.

Does Fair Assessment in Real Estate Ass'n, Inc. v. McNary, 454 U.S. 100 (1981), p. 1219, *supra,* argue for holding Younger applicable to federal damages actions?   In McNary, the Court ruled that "the principle of comity bars federal courts from granting damages relief" in a § 1983 action against state tax

---

6.   Writing for the Court in NOPSI, Justice Scalia observed that "when we inquire into the substantiality of the State's interest in its proceedings, we do not look narrowly to its interest in the *outcome* of the particular case—which could arguably be offset by a substantial federal interest in the opposite outcome.   Rather, what we look to is the importance of the generic proceedings to the state" (p. 365).   How helpful is this formulation?

For criticism of the focus on state interests, see Althouse, *The Misguided Search for State Interest in Abstention Cases: Observations on the Occasion of Pennzoil v. Texaco,* 63 N.Y.U.L.Rev. 1051 (1988), arguing that while traditional analysis would militate against abstention in Pennzoil because state interests were weak, federal interests (in avoiding delay and inefficiency and in in-

creasing the capacity of state courts to enforce federal law) strongly supported the result.

7.   For commentary on the application of Younger to civil cases, see, *e.g.,* Stravitz, *Younger Abstention Reaches a Civil Maturity: Pennzoil Co. v. Texaco, Inc.,* 57 Fordham L.Rev. 997 (1989); Vairo, *Making Younger Civil: The Consequences of Federal Court Deference to State Court Proceedings: A Reply to Professor Stravitz,* 58 Fordham L.Rev. 173 (1989); Edwards, *The Changing Notion of "Our Federalism",* 33 Wayne L.Rev. 1015 (1987); Aldisert, *On Being Civil to Younger,* 11 Conn.L.Rev. 181 (1979); Bartels, *Avoiding a Comity of Errors: A Model for Adjudicating Federal Civil Rights Suits That "Interfere" With State Civil Proceedings,* 29 Stan.L.Rev. 27 (1976).

officials.   Though the Tax Anti–Injunction Act did not itself apply, the Court found that the "principle of comity"—which was given its "fullest articulation" in Younger—was applicable and barred relief, even in the absence of a pending state proceeding (pp. 111–13); a key argument was that before damages could be awarded, the district court would "[i]n effect [have to] enter a declaratory judgment" (p. 113).   Should McNary be limited to the special problem of federal interference with state tax administration?

In Martin v. Merola, 532 F.2d 191 (2d Cir.1976), the defendants in a pending state criminal case, alleging a denial of their fair trial rights, brought a damages action against a state prosecutor.   The court of appeals held that the complaint had to be dismissed as premature.   The court went on to opine that, in any event, it would "offend the principle of comity for a federal district court to inquire into plaintiffs' ability to secure a fair trial in a pending state prosecution.   See Younger v. Harris * * *" (pp. 194–95).[8]

Isn't the court's principal holding—that a damages remedy should not be available until the damage is done—correct?   Is the citation to Younger apposite?[9]

(4) *Administrative Proceedings of a Judicial Nature*.   Although Younger has sometimes been characterized as a doctrine uniquely concerned with appropriate deference to state courts, see, *e.g.,* Steffel v. Thompson, *supra,* the Supreme Court has extended the abstention doctrine to state administrative proceedings of a judicial nature.

(a) Middlesex County Ethics Comm. v. Garden State Bar Ass'n, 457 U.S. 423 (1982), involved New Jersey's system for the discipline of attorneys, for which the state supreme court had ultimate responsibility.   By rule, the court had established local district ethics committees to investigate complaints and hold hearings on any charges issued, subject to review by a statewide board and in some cases by the state supreme court.   A lawyer who had referred to a pending murder trial as "a travesty," a "legalized lynching," and a "kangaroo court" was charged with violating a bar rule prohibiting conduct "prejudicial to the administration of justice."   Rather than defend himself before the local

---

8.   In Giulini v. Blessing, 654 F.2d 189 (2d Cir.1981), the Second Circuit indicated that its broad dictum in Martin v. Merola, *supra,* about the applicability of Younger to damage actions should not be taken seriously.   Giulini found that a § 1983 damage action challenging a local zoning ordinance was not barred by Younger, even though there was pending in state court an action against the federal plaintiff for a previous violation. The court of appeals strongly suggested, however, that on remand the district court should exercise its discretion to stay the action in view of the parallel state proceeding. See generally Sec. 2(D), *infra.*

9.   The Supreme Court seems to have disposed of most if not all of the general problems presented by § 1983 damages actions that necessarily require testing the validity of a state criminal conviction.   Heck v.

Humphrey, 114 S.Ct. 2364 (1994), p. 1504, *infra,* holds that where a plaintiff's § 1983 action seeks recovery for "allegedly unconstitutional conviction or imprisonment, or for other harm caused by actions whose unlawfulness would render a conviction or sentence invalid", a plaintiff, as a substantive element of the § 1983 cause of action, must show that the underlying "conviction or sentence has been reversed on direct appeal, expunged by executive order, declared invalid by a state tribunal * * *, or called into question by a federal court's issuance of a writ of habeas corpus" (p. 2372).   Justice Souter, concurring in an opinion joined by three other Justices, would have decided the case by imposing an exhaustion requirement in such cases (pp. 2380–81).   For further discussion, see Chapter XII, *infra.*

ethics committee, the lawyer filed a federal action challenging the rule under the First Amendment, but the Supreme Court held the suit barred by Younger.

The Court first noted that under state law, a local committee was "an arm of the [New Jersey Supreme Court]" and its disciplinary proceedings were "judicial in nature" (pp. 433–34). Because those proceedings implicate the state's extremely important interests in assuring the professional conduct of attorneys, federal interference was inappropriate, as long as the lawyer had an adequate opportunity to raise his First Amendment claim. The Court rejected his argument that the local ethics committee lacked authority to consider that claim. In addition, citing Hicks v. Miranda, p. 1291, *supra*, the Court held that it could take account of the fact that the New Jersey Supreme Court had recently undertaken review of the disciplinary case, leaving no doubt that the First Amendment issue could be raised in the pending state proceeding.

Justice Marshall, joined by Justices Brennan, Blackmun, and Stevens, concurred in the judgment, finding Younger applicable only because of the state supreme court's recent intervention. In a separate concurrence, Justice Brennan said that "[t]he traditional * * * responsibility of state courts for [bar discipline] and the quasi-criminal nature of bar disciplinary procedures call for exceptional deference by the federal courts" (p. 438).

(b) The significance of Middlesex in extending Younger doctrine to state administrative proceedings of a judicial nature became clear in Ohio Civil Rights Com'n v. Dayton Christian Schools, Inc., 477 U.S. 619 (1986). There, the Ohio Civil Rights Commission had filed a formal administrative complaint against a religious school for terminating the employment of a pregnant teacher. The school then filed a federal court § 1983 action to enjoin the administrative proceedings as a violation of the Religion Clauses of the First Amendment. Relying in part upon Middlesex County, the Court ruled that Younger bars interference with a pending state administrative proceeding involving sufficiently important state interests, of which combatting discrimination was one (pp. 627–28). The Court rejected on the merits the school's argument that the investigation itself was prohibited by the First Amendment (p. 628). It then found that the school had an adequate opportunity to raise its First Amendment objections: even if they could not be raised in the administrative hearing, it sufficed that they could be heard in state court judicial review of any administrative decision (p. 629).[10]

The Court had to distinguish Hawaii Housing Auth. v. Midkiff, 467 U.S. 229 (1984), which involved a federal challenge to a Hawaii land redistribution program. Before the federal preliminary injunction issued, a state agency had started the process for acquiring land owned by the federal plaintiffs, ordering them to submit to compulsory arbitration as provided by state law. The Supreme Court found Younger inapplicable: under Hawaii law the administrative proceedings were not "judicial", and "Younger is not a bar to federal court action when state judicial proceedings have not themselves commenced" (pp. 238–39). In the Ohio case, the Court, citing Midkiff, said "if state law expressly indicates that the administrative proceedings are not even 'judicial in nature,' abstention may not be appropriate" (477 U.S. at 627 n. 2).

---

10. The case was consistent, in the Court's view, with the rule that § 1983 plaintiffs need not exhaust state administrative remedies, *see* Patsy v. Florida Board of Regents, 457 U.S. 496 (1982), p. 1225, *supra*: "Unlike Patsy, the administrative proceedings here are coercive rather than remedial, began before any substantial advancement in the federal action took place, and involve an important state interest" (p. 627 n. 2).

Finding the school's challenge not ripe, Justice Stevens, joined by Justices Brennan, Marshall, and Blackmun, concurred in the judgment, but criticized the Court's reliance on Younger: "That disposition would presumably deny the School a federal forum to adjudicate the constitutionality of a provisional administrative remedy, such as reinstatement pending resolution of the complainant's charges, even though * * * the Commission refuses to address the merits of the constitutional claims" (p. 633–34 n. 5).

In the Midkiff case, if Hawaii had deemed the arbitration proceeding "judicial", should the Younger issue have come out the other way? Wasn't Justice Stevens correct in the Ohio case that the critical question is not the state's label, but whether the pending proceedings are before a tribunal competent to adjudicate the federal constitutional issue? Isn't federal interference justified in an otherwise ripe case if the administrative agency lacks that competence? *Cf.* Gibson v. Berryhill, p. 1274, *supra.*

(c) If a state administrative proceeding is *judicial* in character, and the administrative decision has become final, may a litigant seek to review or challenge it in federal court? This issue has arisen when a state insurance commission has denied an application for permission to acquire an interest in a regulated insurer, and the applicant (who could have sought judicial review in state court) challenged the denial as unconstitutional in a federal court action. The circuits have divided. Compare Alleghany Corp. v. Haase, 896 F.2d 1046 (7th Cir.1990), *vacated on other grounds*, 499 U.S. 933 (1991), *with* Alleghany Corp. v. Pomeroy, 898 F.2d 1314 (8th Cir.1990). Consider carefully the implications for such a case of (i) the Middlesex Ethics Committee and Dayton Christian cases, (ii) Huffman v. Pursue, p. 1300, *supra,* (iii) Patsy v. Board of Regents, p. 1225, *supra,* and (iv) Monroe v. Pape, p. 1111, *supra.* See also the discussion in NOPSI, summarized at p. 1301, *supra,* 491 U.S. at 211 n. 4, and in the separate opinions of the Chief Justice and Justice Blackmun. For further discussion, see Note, 1991 B.Y.U.L.Rev. 1445.

In thinking generally about this problem, consider if it matters (i) whether the party seeking review was effectively the "plaintiff" or the "defendant" before the agency—that is, whether the administrative proceeding was an enforcement action; (ii) whether the challenge is to the agency's specific findings, or to its power to proceed at all; (iii) whether the agency was competent to adjudicate the issues underlying the federal challenge; and (iv) whether the party seeking review could have bypassed the agency and filed suit in federal court in the first instance.

(5) *Equitable Restraint and State Executive Functions.* Rizzo v. Goode, 423 U.S. 362 (1976), was a lawsuit under § 1983 charging the mayor and other high officials of the City of Philadelphia with responsibility for a wide variety of discriminatory and arbitrary police practices. The Supreme Court held that there was no justification for equitable relief against the named defendants, since there was no showing that they had themselves invaded or authorized any invasions of the plaintiffs' constitutional rights. The opinion then went on, quite unnecessarily, to suggest that "principles of federalism" would independently bar relief. After citing Doran v. Salem Inn, p. 1296, *supra,* and Huffman, Paragraph (1), *supra,* the Court said (p. 380): "Thus the principles of federalism which play such an important part in governing the relationship between federal courts and state governments, though initially expounded and perhaps entitled to their greatest weight in cases where it was sought to enjoin a criminal prosecution in progress, have not been limited either to that situation or indeed to a criminal proceeding itself. We think these principles

likewise have applicability where injunctive relief is sought, not against the judicial branch of the state government, but against those in charge of an executive branch of an agency of state or local governments such as petitioners here."[11] Accord, City of Los Angeles v. Lyons, 461 U.S. 95, 112–13 (1983), p. 266 *supra*. *Cf.* Missouri v. Jenkins, 115 S.Ct. 2038, 2054 (1995)(suggesting that, due to "federalism concerns", federal courts should be more hesitant to award equitable relief against a state than against a federal agency).

Do you understand the *content* of a rule that would take the Younger doctrine of non-interference with state judicial proceedings and convert it by analogy into a principle of non-interference with state executive officials? Isn't Rizzo in conflict with a vast line of federal cases running back to Ex parte Young, 209 U.S. 123 (1908), p. 1058, *supra?*

The Younger-based aspect of Rizzo appears to have been applied very cautiously by the lower federal courts. See Chemerinsky, Federal Jurisdiction 750 (2d ed.1994). Commentary on the extension of Younger's equitable restraint doctrine to executive functions has been almost uniformly unfavorable. See, *e.g.,* Weinberg, *The New Judicial Federalism,* 29 Stan.L.Rev. 1191, 1219–27 (1977); Eisenberg & Yeazell, *The Ordinary and the Extraordinary in Institutional Litigation,* 93 Harv.L.Rev. 465, 503–06 (1980); Fiss, *Dombrowski,* 86 Yale L.J. 1103, 1159 (1977).

SUBSECTION D: PARALLEL PROCEEDINGS

Colorado River Water Conservation District v. United States

424 U.S. 800, 96 S.Ct. 1236, 47 L.Ed.2d 483 (1976).
Certiorari to the United States Court of Appeals for the Tenth Circuit.

■ MR. JUSTICE BRENNAN delivered the opinion of the Court.

The McCarran Amendment, 43 U.S.C. § 666, provides that "consent is hereby given to join the United States as a defendant in any suit (1) for the adjudication of rights to the use of water of a river system or other source, or (2) for the administration of such rights, where it appears that the United States is the owner of or is in the process of acquiring water rights by appropriation under State law, by purchase, by exchange, or otherwise, and the United States is a necessary party to such suit." The questions presented by this case concern the effect of the McCarran Amendment upon the jurisdiction of the federal district courts under 28 U.S.C. § 1345 over suits for determination of water rights brought by the United States as trustee for certain Indian tribes and as owner of various non-Indian Government claims.

---

11. Just two years before Rizzo, in Allee v. Medrano, 416 U.S. 802 (1974), the Court had approved a district court decree barring certain law enforcement practices, observing (p. 814) that it "creates no interference with prosecutions pending in the state courts, so that the special considerations relevant to cases like Younger v. Harris, 401 U.S. 37, do not apply here."

I

It is probable that no problem of the Southwest section of the Nation is more critical than that of scarcity of water. * * * [S]everal Southwestern States have established elaborate procedures for allocation of water and adjudication of conflicting claims to that resource. In 1969, Colorado enacted its Water Rights Determination and Administration Act in an effort to revamp its legal procedures for determining claims to water within the State.

Under the Colorado Act, the State is divided into seven Water Divisions, each Division encompassing one or more entire drainage basins for the larger rivers in Colorado. * * * Each month, Water Referees in each Division rule on applications for water rights filed within the preceding five months or refer those applications to the Water Judge of their Division. Every six months, the Water Judge passes on referred applications and contested decisions by Referees. A State Engineer and engineers for each Division are responsible for the administration and distribution of the waters of the State according to the determinations in each Division.

Colorado applies the doctrine of prior appropriation in establishing rights to the use of water. Under that doctrine, one acquires a right to water by diverting it from its natural source and applying it to some beneficial use. Continued beneficial use of the water is required in order to maintain the right. In periods of shortage, priority among confirmed rights is determined according to the date of initial diversion.

The reserved rights of the United States extend to Indian reservations and other federal lands, such as national parks and forests. The reserved rights claimed by the United States in this case affect waters within Colorado Water Division No. 7. On November 14, 1972, the Government instituted this suit in the United States District Court for the District of Colorado, invoking the court's jurisdiction under 28 U.S.C. § 1345. The District Court is located in Denver, some 300 miles from Division 7. The suit, against some 1,000 water users, sought declaration of the Government's rights to waters in certain rivers and their tributaries located in Division 7. In the suit, the Government asserted reserved rights on its own behalf and on behalf of certain Indian tribes, as well as rights based on state law. It sought appointment of a water master to administer any waters decreed to the United States. Prior to institution of this suit, the Government had pursued adjudication of non-Indian reserved rights and other water claims based on state law in Water Divisions 4, 5, and 6, and the Government continues to participate fully in those Divisions.

Shortly after the federal suit was commenced, one of the defendants in that suit filed an application in the state court for Division 7, seeking an order directing service of process on the United States in order to make it a party to proceedings in Division 7 for the purpose of adjudicating all of the Government's claims, both state and federal. On January 3, 1973, the United States was served pursuant to authority of the McCarran Amendment. Several defendants and intervenors in the federal proceeding then filed a motion in the District Court to dismiss on the ground that under the Amendment, the court was without jurisdiction to determine federal water rights. Without deciding the jurisdictional question, the District Court, on June 21, 1973, granted the motion * * *, stating that the doctrine of abstention required deference to the proceedings in Division 7. On appeal, the Court of Appeals for the Tenth Circuit reversed, holding that the suit of the United States was within district-court jurisdiction under 28 U.S.C. § 1345, and that abstention was inappropriate. * * * We reverse.

II

[Under 28 U.S.C. § 1345, the district courts have jurisdiction over all civil actions brought by the Federal Government "[e]xcept as otherwise provided by Act of Congress." The Court determined that the McCarran Amendment is not an Act of Congress excepting jurisdiction under § 1345 (or under § 1331, on which jurisdiction might also have been based), but that the Amendment merely provides for concurrent state and federal court jurisdiction over the actions that it encompasses.]

III

We turn next to the question whether this suit nevertheless was properly dismissed in view of the concurrent state proceedings in Division 7.

A

[The Court here concluded that the McCarran Amendment provided consent for the state courts to determine federal reserved rights held on behalf of Indians.]

B

Next, we consider whether the District Court's dismissal was appropriate under the doctrine of abstention. We hold that the dismissal cannot be supported under that doctrine in any of its forms.

Abstention from the exercise of federal jurisdiction is the exception, not the rule. "The doctrine of abstention, under which a District Court may decline to exercise or postpone the exercise of its jurisdiction, is an extraordinary and narrow exception to the duty of a District Court to adjudicate a controversy properly before it. Abdication of the obligation to decide cases can be justified under this doctrine only in the exceptional circumstances where the order to the parties to repair to the State court would clearly serve an important countervailing interest." County of Allegheny v. Frank Mashuda Co., 360 U.S. 185, 188–189 (1959). "[I]t was never a doctrine of equity that a federal court should exercise its judicial discretion to dismiss a suit merely because a State court could entertain it." Alabama Pub. Serv. Comm'n v. Southern R. Co., 341 U.S. 341, 361 (1951)(Frankfurter, J., concurring in result). Our decisions have confined the circumstances appropriate for abstention to three general categories.

(a) Abstention is appropriate "in cases presenting a federal constitutional issue which might be mooted or presented in a different posture by a state court determination of pertinent state law." County of Allegheny v. Frank Mashuda Co., *supra*, at 189. See, *e.g.*, Railroad Comm'n of Texas v. Pullman Co., 312 U.S. 496 (1941). This case, however, presents no federal constitutional issue for decision.

(b) Abstention is also appropriate where there have been presented difficult questions of state law bearing on policy problems of substantial public import whose importance transcends the result in the case then at bar. Louisiana Power & Light Co. v. City of Thibodaux, 360 U.S. 25 (1959), for example, involved such a question. In particular, the concern there was with the scope of the eminent domain power of municipalities under state law. See also Kaiser Steel Corp. v. W.S. Ranch Co., 391 U.S. 593 (1968). In some cases, however, the state question itself need not be determinative of state policy. It is enough that exercise of federal review of the question in a case and in similar cases would be disruptive of state efforts to establish a coherent policy with respect to a matter of substantial public concern. In Burford v. Sun Oil Co., 319 U.S. 315 (1943), for example, the Court held that a suit seeking review of the reasonableness under Texas state law of a state commission's permit to drill oil wells should have been dismissed by the District Court. The reasonableness of the permit in that case was not of transcendent importance, but review of reasonableness by the federal courts in that and future cases, where the State had established its own elaborate review system for dealing with the geological complexities of oil and gas fields, would have had an impermissibly disruptive effect on state policy for the management of those fields. See also Alabama Pub. Serv. Comm'n v. Southern R. Co., *supra*.[21]

The present case clearly does not fall within this second category of abstention. While state claims are involved in the case, the state law to be applied appears to be settled. No questions bearing on state policy are presented for decision. Nor will decision of the state claims impair efforts to implement state policy as in Burford. To be sure, the federal claims that are involved in the case go to the establishment of water rights which may conflict with similar rights based on state law. But the mere potential for conflict in the results of adjudications, does not, without more, warrant staying exercise of federal jurisdiction. See Meredith v. Winter Haven, 320 U.S. 228 (1943); Kline v. Burke Constr. Co., 260 U.S. 226 (1922); McClellan v. Carland, 217 U.S. 268 (1910). The potential conflict here, involving state claims and federal claims, would not be such as to impair impermissibly the State's effort to effect its policy respecting the allocation of state waters. Nor would exercise of federal jurisdiction here interrupt any such efforts by restraining the exercise of authority vested in state officers.

(c) Finally, abstention is appropriate where, absent bad faith, harassment, or a patently invalid state statute, federal jurisdiction has been invoked for the purpose of restraining state criminal proceedings, Younger v. Harris, 401 U.S. 37 (1971); state nuisance proceedings antecedent to a criminal prosecution, which are directed at obtaining the closure of places exhibiting obscene films, Huffman v. Pursue, Ltd., 420 U.S. 592 (1975); or collection of state taxes, Great Lakes Dredge & Dock Co. v. Huffman, 319 U.S. 293 (1943). Like the

---

21. We note that Burford v. Sun Oil Co., and Alabama Pub. Serv. Comm'n v. Southern R. Co., differ from Louisiana Power & Light Co. v. City of Thibodaux, and County of Allegheny v. Frank Mashuda Co., in that the former two cases, unlike the latter two, raised colorable constitutional claims and were therefore brought under federal-question, as well as diversity, jurisdiction. While abstention in Burford and Alabama Pub. Serv. had the effect of avoiding a federal constitutional issue, the opinions indicate that this was not an additional ground for abstention in those cases. See Alabama Pub. Serv. Comm'n v. Southern R. Co., 341 U.S., at 344; Burford v. Sun Oil Co., 319 U.S., at 334; H. Hart & H. Wechsler, The Federal Courts and the Federal System 1005 (2d ed. 1973)("The two groups of cases share at least one common characteristic: the Pullman purpose of avoiding the necessity for federal constitutional adjudication is not relevant"). We have held, of course, that the opportunity to avoid decision of a constitutional question does not alone justify abstention by a federal court. See Harman v. Forssenius, 380 U.S. 528 (1965); Baggett v. Bullitt, 377 U.S. 360 (1964). Indeed, the presence of a federal basis for jurisdiction may raise the level of justification needed for abstention. See Burford v. Sun Oil Co., *supra*, at 318 n. 5; Hawks v. Hamill, 288 U.S. [52, 61 (1933)].

previous two categories, this category also does not include this case.   * * *[23]
* * *

C

Although this case falls within none of the abstention categories, there are principles unrelated to considerations of proper constitutional adjudication and regard for federal-state relations which govern in situations involving the contemporaneous exercise of concurrent jurisdictions, either by federal courts or by state and federal courts.   These principles rest on considerations of "[w]ise judicial administration, giving regard to conservation of judicial resources and comprehensive disposition of litigation." Kerotest Mfg. Co. v. C–O–Two Fire Equipment Co., 342 U.S. 180, 183 (1952). Generally, as between state and federal courts, the rule is that "the pendency of an action in the state court is no bar to proceedings concerning the same matter in the Federal court having jurisdiction.   * * *" McClellan v. Carland, *supra*, at 282. As between federal district courts, however, though no precise rule has evolved, the general principle is to avoid duplicative litigation. See Kerotest Mfg. Co. v. C–O–Two Fire Equipment Co., *supra*. This difference in general approach between state-federal concurrent jurisdiction and wholly federal concurrent jurisdiction stems from the virtually unflagging obligation of the federal courts to exercise the jurisdiction given them. England v. Medical Examiners, 375 U.S. 411, 415 (1964); Cohens v. Virginia, 6 Wheat. 264, 404 (1821)(dictum). Given this obligation, and the absence of weightier considerations of constitutional adjudication and state-federal relations, the circumstances permitting the dismissal of a federal suit due to the presence of a concurrent state proceeding for reasons of wise judicial administration are considerably more limited than the circumstances appropriate for abstention. The former circumstances, though exceptional, do nevertheless exist.

It has been held, for example, that the court first assuming jurisdiction over property may exercise that jurisdiction to the exclusion of other courts. Donovan v. City of Dallas, [377 U.S. 408, 412 (1964)]; Princess Lida v. Thompson, 305 U.S. 456, 466 (1939). But *cf.* Markham v. Allen, 326 U.S. 490 (1946). This has been true even where the Government was a claimant in existing state proceedings and then sought to invoke district-court jurisdiction under the jurisdictional provision antecedent to 28 U.S.C. § 1345. In assessing the appropriateness of dismissal in the event of an exercise of concurrent jurisdiction, a federal court may also consider such factors as the inconvenience of the federal forum, *cf.* Gulf Oil Corp. v. Gilbert, 330 U.S. 501 (1947); the desirability of avoiding piecemeal litigation, *cf.* Brillhart v. Excess Ins. Co., 316 U.S. 491, 495 (1942); and the order in which jurisdiction was obtained by the concurrent forums, Pacific Live Stock Co. v. Lewis, 241 U.S. 440, 447 (1916). No one factor is necessarily determinative; a carefully considered judgment taking into account both the obligation to exercise jurisdiction and the combination of factors counselling against that exercise is required. Only the clearest of justifications will warrant dismissal.

Turning to the present case, a number of factors clearly counsel against concurrent federal proceedings. The most important of these is the McCarran

23. Our reasons for finding abstention inappropriate in this case make it unnecessary to consider when, if at all, abstention would be appropriate where the Federal Government seeks to invoke federal jurisdiction. *Cf.* Leiter Minerals, Inc. v. United States, 352 U.S. 220 (1957).

Amendment itself. The clear federal policy evinced by that legislation is the avoidance of piecemeal adjudication of water rights in a river system. This policy is akin to that underlying the rule requiring that jurisdiction be yielded to the court first acquiring control of property, for the concern in such instances is with avoiding the generation of additional litigation through permitting inconsistent dispositions of property. This concern is heightened with respect to water rights, the relationships among which are highly interdependent. Indeed, we have recognized that actions seeking the allocation of water essentially involve the disposition of property and are best conducted in unified proceedings. The consent to jurisdiction given by the McCarran Amendment bespeaks a policy that recognizes the availability of comprehensive state systems for adjudication of water rights as the means for achieving these goals.

As has already been observed, the Colorado Water Rights Determination and Administration Act established such a system for the adjudication and management of rights to the use of the State's waters. * * *

Beyond the congressional policy expressed by the McCarran Amendment and consistent with furtherance of that policy, we also find significant (a) the apparent absence of any proceedings in the District Court, other than the filing of the complaint, prior to the motion to dismiss, (b) the extensive involvement of state water rights occasioned by this suit naming 1,000 defendants, (c) the 300–mile distance between the District Court in Denver and the court in Division 7, and (d) the existing participation by the Government in Division 4, 5, and 6 proceedings. We emphasize, however, that we do not overlook the heavy obligation to exercise jurisdiction. We need not decide, for example, whether, despite the McCarran Amendment, dismissal would be warranted if more extensive proceedings had occurred in the District Court prior to dismissal, if the involvement of state water rights were less extensive than it is here, or if the state proceeding were in some respect inadequate to resolve the federal claims. But the opposing factors here, particularly the policy underlying the McCarran Amendment, justify the District Court's dismissal in this particular case.[26]

The judgment of the Court of Appeals is reversed and the judgment of the District Court dismissing the complaint is affirmed for the reasons here stated.

■ MR. JUSTICE STEWART, with whom MR. JUSTICE BLACKMUN and MR. JUSTICE STEVENS concur, dissenting.

The Court says that the United States District Court for the District of Colorado clearly had jurisdiction over this lawsuit. I agree. The Court further says that the McCarran Amendment "in no way diminished" the District Court's jurisdiction. I agree. The Court also says that federal courts have a "virtually unflagging obligation * * * to exercise the jurisdiction given them." I agree. And finally, the Court says that nothing in the abstention doctrine "in any of its forms" justified the District Court's dismissal of the Government's complaint. I agree. These views would seem to lead ineluctably to the conclusion that the District Court was wrong in dismissing the complaint. Yet the Court holds that the order of dismissal was "appropriate." With that conclusion I must respectfully disagree.

26. Whether similar considerations would permit dismissal of a water suit brought by a private party in federal district court is a question we need not now decide.

* * * [T]he Court relies principally on cases reflecting the rule that where "control of the property which is the subject of the suit [is necessary] in order to proceed with the cause and to grant the relief sought, the jurisdiction of one court must of necessity yield to that of the other." Penn General Casualty Co. v. Pennsylvania ex rel. Schnader, 294 U.S. 189, 195. See also Donovan v. City of Dallas, 377 U.S. 408; Princess Lida v. Thompson, 305 U.S. 456. But, as those cases make clear, this rule applies only when exclusive control over the subject matter is necessary to effectuate a court's judgment. Here the federal court did not need to obtain *in rem* or *quasi in rem* jurisdiction in order to decide the issues before it. The court was asked simply to determine as a matter of federal law whether federal reservations of water rights had occurred, and, if so, the date and scope of the reservations. The District Court could make such a determination without having control of the river.

The rule invoked by the Court thus does not support the conclusion that it reaches. In the Princess Lida case, for example, the reason for the surrender of federal jurisdiction over the administration of a trust was the fact that a state court had already assumed jurisdiction over the trust estate. But the Court in that case recognized that this rationale "ha[d] no application to a case in a federal court * * * wherein the plaintiff seeks merely an adjudication of his right or his interest as a basis of a claim against a fund in the possession of a state court. * * *" * * * Similarly, in [United States v. Bank of New York & Trust Co., 296 U.S. 463 (1936)], the Court stressed that the "object of the suits is to take the property from the depositaries and from the control of the state court, and to vest the property in the United States. * * *" "The suits are not merely to establish a debt or a right to share in property, and thus to obtain an adjudication which might be had without disturbing the control of the state court." * * *

The precedents cited by the Court thus not only fail to support the Court's decision in this case, but expressly point in the opposite direction. The present suit, in short, is not analogous to the administration of a trust, but rather to a claim of a "right to participate," since the United States in this litigation does not ask the court to control the administration of the river, but only to determine its specific rights in the flow of water in the river. This is an almost exact analogue to a suit seeking a determination of rights in the flow of income from a trust.

The Court's principal reason for deciding to close the doors of the federal courthouse to the United States in this case seems to stem from the view that its decision will avoid piecemeal adjudication of water rights.[6] * * * To the

6. The Court lists four other policy reasons for the "appropriateness" of the District Court's dismissal of this lawsuit. All of those reasons are insubstantial. First, the fact that no significant proceedings had yet taken place in the federal court at the time of the dismissal means no more than that the federal court was prompt in granting the defendants' motion to dismiss. At that time, of course, no proceedings involving the Government's claims had taken place in the state court either. Second, the geographic distance of the federal court from the rivers in question is hardly a significant factor in this age of rapid and easy transportation. Since the basic issues here involve the determination of the amount of water the Government intended to reserve rather than the amount it actually appropriated on a given date, there is little likelihood that live testimony by water district residents would be necessary. In any event, the Federal District Court in Colorado is authorized to sit at Durango, the headquarters of Water Division 7. Third, the Government's willingness to participate in some of the state proceedings certainly does not mean that it had no right to bring this action, unless the Court has today unearthed

extent that the Court's view is based on the realistic practicalities of this case, it is simply wrong, because the relegation of the Government to the state courts will not avoid piecemeal litigation.

The Colorado courts are currently engaged in two types of proceedings under the State's water-rights law. First, they are processing new claims to water based on recent appropriations. Second, they are integrating these new awards of water rights with all past decisions awarding such rights into one all-inclusive tabulation for each water source. The claims of the United States that are involved in this case have not been adjudicated in the past. Yet they do not involve recent appropriations of water. In fact, these claims are wholly dissimilar to normal state water claims, because they are not based on actual beneficial use of water but rather on an intention formed at the time the federal land use was established to reserve a certain amount of water to support the federal reservations. The state court will, therefore, have to conduct separate proceedings to determine these claims. And only after the state court adjudicates the claims will they be incorporated into the water source tabulations. If this suit were allowed to proceed in federal court the same procedures would be followed, and the federal court decree would be incorporated into the state tabulation, as other federal court decrees have been incorporated in the past. * * * Whether the virtually identical separate proceedings take place in a federal court or a state court, the adjudication of the claims will be neither more nor less "piecemeal." * * *

As the Court says, it is the virtual "unflagging obligation" of a federal court to exercise the jurisdiction that has been conferred upon it. Obedience to that obligation is particularly "appropriate" in this case, for at least two reasons.

First, the issues involved are issues of federal law. A federal court is more likely than a state court to be familiar with federal water law and to have had experience in interpreting the relevant federal statutes, regulations, and Indian treaties. * * *

Second, some of the federal claims in this lawsuit relate to water reserved for Indian reservations. It is not necessary to determine that there is no state-court jurisdiction of these claims to support the proposition that a federal court is a more appropriate forum than a state court for determination of questions of life-and-death importance to Indians. * * *

    * * *

I would affirm the judgment of the Court of Appeals.

■ MR. JUSTICE STEVENS, dissenting.

[While agreeing with Justice Stewart, Justice Stevens added three points: (1) "the holding that United States may not litigate a federal claim in a federal court having jurisdiction thereof [is] particularly anomalous"; (2) the Court's holding would restrict private water users' access to federal courts—a "surprising byproduct of the McCarran Amendment"—since private persons could hardly have greater access than the United States to a federal court;* and (3)

a new kind of waiver. Finally, the fact that there were many defendants in the federal suit is hardly relevant. It only indicates that the federal court had all the necessary parties before it in order to issue a decree finally settling the Government's claims. * * *

  * [Ed.] Justice Stevens' prophecy was fulfilled in Arizona v. San Carlos Apache Tribe

the Court should defer to the judgment of the Court of Appeals, rather than evaluate itself the balance of factors for and against the exercise of jurisdiction.]

NOTE ON FEDERAL COURT DEFERENCE TO PARALLEL STATE COURT PROCEEDINGS

(1) *Earlier Examples of Deference to Pending State Court Proceedings.* Both the majority and the dissent in Colorado River accepted (a) the principle set forth in the Kline case, p. 1185, *supra*, that the pendency of a state court action does not require a federal court to stay proceedings concerning the same matter, and (b) the exception to that principle when the state court has already exercised jurisdiction over a *res*—although the Justices differed over that exception's applicability to the circumstances at bar.

Apart from the *res* exception and the Younger line of cases (involving pending state enforcement actions), the Court had approved federal deference to pending state proceedings in only a few instances before Colorado River.

(a) In Langnes v. Green, 282 U.S. 531 (1931), the Court held that a federal district court should have stayed a shipowner's petition to limit his liability (pursuant to a federal statute) to the value of his interest in the vessel, where there was a pending state court personal injury claim and it was doubtful that other valid claims against him existed. The Court emphasized the importance of preserving, if possible, the state claimant's common-law remedy.

Can this decision be viewed as resting on ripeness grounds?

(b) Brillhart v. Excess Ins. Co., 316 U.S. 491 (1942), has broader implications. There Brillhart, after recovering a default judgment against a tortfeasor, instituted state court garnishment proceedings against the insurer. A reinsurer then brought a federal diversity action, *inter alia*, for a declaratory judgment to determine its obligations under the reinsurance agreement. After the insurer became insolvent, the reinsurer was joined as a defendant in the state garnishment proceedings, where it challenged the court's jurisdiction. That is how matters stood when the federal district court dismissed the declaratory judgment complaint, without considering whether the claims could be raised in the state garnishment proceeding. The court of appeals reversed and directed a trial on the merits.

The Supreme Court (per Frankfurter, J.,) in turn reversed, holding that the district court should consider "whether the claims of all parties in interest can satisfactorily be adjudicated in" the state proceeding (p. 495). "Although the District Court had jurisdiction of the suit under the Federal Declaratory Judgments Act, it was under no compulsion to exercise that jurisdiction. * * * Ordinarily it would be uneconomical as well as vexatious for a federal court to proceed in a declaratory judgment suit where another suit is pending in a state court presenting the same issues, not governed by federal law, between the same parties. Gratuitous interference with the orderly and comprehensive disposition of a state court litigation should be avoided" (pp. 494–45).

of Arizona, 463 U.S. 545 (1983), upholding a district court's dismissal, in deference to pending state court proceedings, of federal water rights claims brought by Indian Tribes. The Court stressed that both water rights adjudication and the McCarran Amendment were "unique" (p. 571). Justices Stevens, Marshall, and Blackmun dissented.

(c) In Scott v. Germano, 381 U.S. 407 (1965)(per curiam), the Court directed the district court to stay its hand in an action challenging a state legislative apportionment. The stay was warranted, the Court held, by a similar proceeding then pending in which the state supreme court had held the apportionment statute invalid and was awaiting legislative action.

Since a state can have only one set of legislative districts, can control over districting be analogized to jurisdiction over a res? Even if so, note that in Germano the state proceeding was filed some time *after* the federal one.[1]

(d) Kaiser Steel Corp. v. W.S. Ranch Co., 391 U.S. 593 (1968), p. 1255, *supra*, involved a private diversity action for trespass that raised questions about the construction and validity of a state statute governing water rights. After the federal court of appeals had decided the case on the merits, the defendant in the federal suit commenced a state court declaratory judgment action raising the same issues. The Supreme Court unanimously ruled that the federal court should abstain, as the dispute concerned a truly novel issue of vital concern in an arid state.

(e) Does any general principle emerge from these precedents? From Colorado River? Should Colorado River be viewed as focusing on the avoidance not merely of duplication but of piecemeal litigation? Did the decision rest not only on the unique character of disputes over water rights, but also on the specific purpose of the McCarran Amendment?[2]

(2) *The Moses H. Cone Decision.* The Court elaborated on the Colorado River holding seven years later in Moses H. Cone Memorial Hosp. v. Mercury Constr. Corp., 460 U.S. 1 (1983).[3] The case revolved around a construction contract

---

1. The holding in Germano was reaffirmed, and perhaps extended, in Growe v. Emison, 507 U.S. 25 (1993). There, different sets of plaintiffs filed parallel state and federal court suits challenging the apportionment of Minnesota's state legislative and federal congressional districts. (The state suit had been filed two months before the federal suit.) The state courts found violations of both state and federal constitutions, ordered adoption of a state legislative redistricting plan, and was considering plans for congressional redistricting. Two days later, the three-judge federal district court ordered adoption of its own districting plans and enjoined interference with their implementation. Relying on Germano, a unanimous Supreme Court reversed the three-judge court, holding that it should have stayed its hand, as "reapportionment is primarily the duty and responsibility of the state" (507 U.S. at ___, quoting Chapman v. Meier, 420 U.S. 1, 27 (1975)). Though the state plan was being formulated by a court rather than by the legislature, as in Germano, the Court declared that "the doctrine of Germano prefers *both* state branches to federal courts as agents of apportionment" (507 U.S. at ___). And although the federal suit included Voting Rights Act claims not pressed in state court,

the Court stated that Germano focuses on the nature of relief, stressing that there could be only one set of legislative districts in Minnesota.

2. For discussion of lower court decisions before Colorado River, see Comment, 44 U.Chi.L.Rev. 641, 653–66 (1977), which views Colorado River as having narrowed discretion to decline jurisdiction. For discussions of the Colorado River case itself, see Mullenix, *A Branch Too Far: Pruning the Abstention Doctrine*, 75 Geo.L.J. 99 & authorities cited at 107 n. 33 (1986).

3. An earlier decision in Will v. Calvert Fire Ins. Co., 437 U.S. 655 (1978), did little to clarify the meaning of Colorado River. In reviewing a district court's decision to stay a federal action in light of a pending state court proceeding, the Court could not muster a majority opinion, with the Justices disagreeing, *inter alia*, over (i) whether the district court's decision could appropriately be reviewed on mandamus, and (ii) whether the broad discretion recognized in Brillhart, Paragraph (1)(b), *supra*, was limited to suits based on state law or to those seeking declaratory relief. For discussion of Calvert, see the authorities in Mullenix, note 2, *supra*, at 109–10 n. 51.

between the hospital and a contractor, which provided that disputed claims, after initial referral to the architect, were subject to arbitration. After the contractor filed with the architect a claim against the hospital, the hospital sued the contractor and architect in state court, seeking declarations (i) that the hospital was not liable to the contractor, (ii) that if the hospital were liable, it would be entitled to indemnity from the architect, and (iii) that the contractor had no present right to arbitration. A stay of arbitration was also sought. Soon thereafter, the contractor filed a federal diversity action to compel arbitration under the Federal Arbitration Act (FAA), 9 U.S.C. § 4. The district court stayed the suit in view of the pending state court action, but the court of appeals reversed and instructed the district court to issue an order compelling arbitration.

The Supreme Court, with Justice Brennan writing, affirmed. Although "the decision whether to defer to the state courts is necessarily left to the discretion of the district court in the first instance", that discretion is not unreviewable, but rather must be exercised in accordance with "Colorado River's exceptional circumstances test, as elucidated by the factors discussed in that case" (p. 19). Applying that test, the Court found the district court had abused its discretion. Of the four factors supporting dismissal in Colorado River, the first two—the state court's assumption of jurisdiction over a res, and that court's greater convenience—were inapplicable.[4] Nor did the suit implicate the third, and "paramount" consideration, in Colorado River, avoidance of piecemeal litigation: because the contractor's claim against the hospital was arbitrable but the hospital's indemnity claim was not, piecemeal litigation was inevitable whether or not a stay issued. And fourth, here the order of suit did not support the stay: though the state action had been filed first, the hospital's claim of priority was "too mechanical"; "[t]his factor, as with the other Colorado River factors, is to be applied in a pragmatic, flexible manner," and here "the federal suit was running well ahead of the state suit * * *" (pp. 21–22).

Two other factors, Justice Brennan continued, were pertinent. The federal action in Moses Cone was governed by federal law (the FAA's provisions governing arbitrability of the dispute), which "must always be a major consideration weighing against surrender" (p. 26).[5] Moreover, because of uncertainty whether the FAA obliges state as well as federal courts to issue orders compelling arbitration,[6] the state court proceeding was "probabl[y] inadequa[te]" to protect the contractor's rights (p. 26).

---

4. In Moses Cone, as in Colorado River, the federal district court was located in the state in which the related proceedings were pending. When that is not so, convenience may be a more important factor. See, *e.g.*, Centronics Data Computer Corp. v. Merkle–Korff Indus., 503 F.Supp. 168 (D.N.H.1980), deferring to a suit in Illinois state court.

5. Justice Brennan noted the "anomaly" that the FAA creates a federal right to arbitration that cannot be enforced under the federal question jurisdiction (p. 25 n. 32). "But * * * our task * * * is not to find some substantial reason for the *exercise* of federal jurisdiction, [but rather] * * * to ascertain

whether there exist 'exceptional' circumstances, 'the clearest of justifications,' that can suffice under Colorado River to justify the *surrender* of that jurisdiction" (pp. 25–26).

In Medema v. Medema Builders Inc., 854 F.2d 210 (7th Cir.1988), the court (agreeing with other circuits that had faced the question) held that a district court may not stay proceedings within exclusive federal jurisdiction, notwithstanding Colorado River's insistence that no single factor is decisive.

6. The Court subsequently ruled in Southland Corp. v. Keating, 465 U.S. 1 (1984), that the FAA preempts a state law

Finally, the Court rejected the hospital's argument that a *stay* of a federal action could be justified more easily than a *dismissal* (as in Colorado River), finding that in either event, the district court must conclude "that the parallel state-court litigation will be an adequate vehicle for the complete and prompt resolution of the issues between the parties", and must contemplate "that the federal court will have nothing further to do in resolving any substantive part of the case" (p. 28).[7]

Justice Rehnquist, joined by Chief Justice Burger and Justice O'Connor, expressed no view on whether a stay should have issued, as he thought there was no appellate jurisdiction under 28 U.S.C. § 1291. See Paragraph (7), *infra*.[8]

(3) *Declaratory Judgment Actions.* In Wilton v. Seven Falls Co., 115 S.Ct. 2137 (1995), the Court faced a case very similar to Brillhart, Paragraph (1)(b), *supra*. There, as in Brillhart, there were pending (i) an insurer's federal diversity action seeking a declaratory judgment of non-coverage, and (ii) a state court action seeking to recover from the insurer. (In Wilton, unlike Brillhart, the federal suit had been filed first.)

Without dissent, the Court upheld the district court's dismissal of the federal action, finding that the "exceptional circumstances" test of Colorado River and Moses Cone did not govern a federal declaratory judgment action, in which a district court's discretion whether to proceed is far broader. Justice O'Connor noted that the Declaratory Judgment Act, 28 U.S.C. § 2201, says that a district court "*may* declare the rights and other legal relations of any interested party * * *", 28 U.S.C. § 2201, and concluded (p. 2142) that the Act's "textual commitment to discretion, and the breadth of leeway we have always understood it to suggest, distinguish the declaratory judgment context from other areas of the law in which concepts of discretion surface. See generally D. Shapiro, Jurisdiction and Discretion, 60 N.Y.U.L.Rev. 543 (1985)." Here, "the normal principle that federal courts should adjudicate claims within their jurisdiction yields to considerations of practicality and wise judicial administration" (p. 2143). Without trying "to delineate the outer boundaries of [the district court's] discretion in other cases, for example, cases raising issues of federal law or cases in which there are no parallel state proceedings" (p. 2144), the Court found no abuse of discretion.

When a claim is based on federal law, should a district court have less leeway to decline to exercise declaratory judgment jurisdiction (much as it has less leeway to abstain under Colorado River and Moses Cone when the claim is federal)?

(4) *When is Deference Appropriate?* How clear are the factors identified in Colorado River and Moses Cone? What should a court do when different factors pull in opposite directions?

---

purporting to limit state court power to enforce arbitration agreements.

7. Compare Wilton v. Seven Falls Co., Paragraph (3), *infra*, 115 S.Ct. 2137, 2143 n. 2 (1995)("where the basis for declining to proceed is the pendency of a state proceeding, a stay will often be the preferable course, insofar as it assures that the federal action can proceed without risk of a time bar if the state case, for any reason, fails to resolve the matter in controversy. See, *e.g.*, P. Bator, D. Meltzer, P. Mishkin & D. Shapiro, Hart and Wechsler's The Federal Courts and the Federal System 1451 n. 9 (3d ed.1988).").

8. For discussion of Moses Cone, see the authorities cited by Mullenix, note 2, *supra*, at 112 n. 65.

The Wilton decision, Paragraph (3), *supra*, clearly gives a district court broad discretion to decline to exercise jurisdiction in a declaratory judgment action. But in other kinds of actions, is it consistent with the Supreme Court's decisions, and otherwise appropriate, for a district court also to consider: (a) whether the federal suit is meritless or vexatious;[9] (b) whether the federal plaintiff could have filed the state proceeding in, or removed it to, federal court;[10] (c) whether the federal plaintiff is also the plaintiff in state court, having filed parallel claims in two fora, or is the state court defendant, having filed a federal claim incorporating issues that could be raised as defenses or counterclaims in state court;[11] (d) whether the subject matter implicates important state interests;[12] (e) whether either the federal or state court offers particular procedural advantages; (f) whether the state court has stayed its own proceedings;[13] or (g) whether the federal action is filed under § 1983?[14]

Even when refusing formally to defer to state proceedings, might not federal district courts in effect do so anyway in the guise of arranging priorities on their dockets?

(5) *Criticisms of Colorado River.* The practice of deferring to pending state proceedings has been criticized on various grounds.

(a) The most fundamental challenge asserts that federal courts may not legitimately decline to exercise jurisdiction conferred by Congress. Recall the discussion of that position, and of responses to it, in connection with other judge-made doctrines in this Chapter—particularly Pullman and Younger abstention.[15]

---

9. In Moses Cone, the Court said there was "considerable merit" in giving weight to vexatiousness, but did not rely on that consideration (p. 18 n. 20).

10. See, *e.g.*, Microsoftware Computer Systems, Inc. v. Ontel Corp., 686 F.2d 531, 537 (7th Cir.1982).

11. See generally Vestal, *Repetitive Litigation*, 45 Iowa L.Rev. 525 (1960).

12. Recall the discussion of this factor in Colorado River. *Cf.* Louisiana Power & Light Co. v. City of Thibodaux, p. 1252, *supra*. Compare Iowa Mutual Ins. Co. v. La-Plante, 480 U.S. 9 (1987), approving the stay of a federal diversity action arising from the same facts as a previously filed suit in an Indian tribal court, in view of the strong federal policy favoring tribal self-government. Justice Stevens' dissent complained that federal courts should not exhibit greater deference to tribal courts than to state courts.

13. *Cf.* United States v. Adair, 723 F.2d 1394, 1404–05 (9th Cir.1983), finding no abuse of discretion in a refusal to stay a federal water rights claim brought by an Indian tribe—notwithstanding San Carlos Apache Tribe, p. 1315, note *, *supra*—in part because the state court proceedings had been effectively stayed.

14. The obligation to exercise federal jurisdiction has been deemed especially weighty in such cases, see, *e.g.*, Signad, Inc. v. City of Sugar Land, 753 F.2d 1338, 1340 (5th Cir.1985), though in Lumen Constr., Inc. v. Brant Constr. Co., 780 F.2d 691, 696–98 (7th Cir.1985), the court nonetheless deferred.

See also Heck v. Humphrey, 114 S.Ct. 2364, 2373 n. 8 (1994), Chap. XII, Sec. 2, p. 1504, *infra* (citing Colorado River when stating that "if a state criminal defendant brings a federal civil-rights lawsuit during the pendency of his criminal trial, appeal, or state habeas action, abstention may be an appropriate response").

15. See also McClellan v. Carland, 217 U.S. 268 (1910), where a federal circuit court had stayed an action seeking a declaration that plaintiffs were the sole heirs at law of a decedent, to permit the state to bring a proceeding in its courts to determine an escheat that would have bound the complainants. The Supreme Court held the stay improper, criticizing the circuit court for having "practically abandoned its jurisdiction over a case of which it had cognizance, and turned the matter over for adjudication to the state court" (p. 281). But see Thompson v. Magnolia Petroleum Co., 309 U.S. 478 (1940), where the Court did approve the suggestion that a federal court should stay its hand in favor of state proceedings not yet instituted.

(b) Professor Mullenix has more specific criticisms: (i) that Colorado River extended abstention beyond its justified purpose of promoting comity and federalism into the realm of "an unprincipled judicial self-help remedy", assertedly in response to Congress' failure to restrict diversity jurisdiction; and (ii) that the ill-defined "exceptional circumstances test" permits *ad hoc* and unpredictable decisionmaking. Mullenix, note 2, *supra*, at 101, 103–04, 156. Consider these criticisms separately:

(i) Is abstention less justified in the service of judicial administration than in the service of comity and federalism? Why? Compare Shreve, *Pragmatism Without Politics—A Half Measure of Authority for Jurisdictional Common Law*, 1991 B.Y.U.L.Rev. 601 (arguing that Colorado River, because it rests on administrative concerns rather than on political choices that should be left to Congress, is more rather than less legitimate than, for example, Younger abstention). Are the decisions staying (for reasons of judicial administration) one federal action to permit a second, overlapping federal action to proceed, see Chap. XIV, Sec. 4, *infra*, inapplicable to a case like Colorado River because they still permit some federal court to adjudicate?

(ii) Do the flexibility and multiplicity of Moses Cone's criteria—not to mention additional possible criteria, see Paragraph (4), *supra*—make the jurisdictional determination too difficult and unpredictable? See, *e.g.*, In re Chicago Flood Litigation, 819 F.Supp. 762, 764 (N.D.Ill.1993) (stating that there are "at least ten factors" that must be considered, and proceeding to analyze each one). Are overburdened federal judges too likely to succumb to the temptation to find deference appropriate, so as to reduce their caseloads?

(6) *Colorado River and Kline.* Despite their disagreements in particular cases, none of the Justices appears to have questioned the premise of Kline v. Burke Construction Co., p. 1185, *supra*, that a federal court should exercise jurisdiction even when there is already pending a related state court *in personam* action. Is that premise sound in view of the duplication that it invites? Consider, *e.g.*, Burns v. Watler, 931 F.2d 140 (1st Cir.1991), where the court of appeals reversed, as an abuse of discretion, a federal district court's stay of a diversity action for personal injuries—even though a virtually identical state court action, filed by plaintiff one day after filing the federal action, was much further along. Is the premise of Kline less convincing in view of the subsequent merger of law and equity and the general trend in favor of consolidated litigation?

(a) Consider the suggestion that the judicial code should be amended to require a state or federal court to stay any action whose subject matter is already at issue in another court, so long as the other court can resolve the rights of all of the parties. See Kurland, *Toward a Co-operative Judicial Federalism: The Federal Court Abstention Doctrine*, 24 F.R.D. 481, 491–92 (1959); accord Currie, *The Federal Courts and the American Law Institute (II)*, 36 U.Chi.L.Rev. 268, 335 (1969). See also James Rehnquist, *Taking Comity Seriously: How to Neutralize the Abstention Doctrine*, 46 Stan.L.Rev. 1049, 1068 (1994)(arguing that all of the judge-made doctrines of abstention (Pullman, Burford, Thibodaux), equitable restraint (as in Younger), and deference (Colorado River) should be replaced by a single rule—that "a federal court should abstain if, and only if, the federal plaintiff has an adequate opportunity to litigate his federal claim in a duplicative suit already pending in state court").

Without doubt, a first-filed approach would sometimes generate a race to the courthouse. But isn't that race less wasteful than the race to judgment that current doctrine invites?

Still, should the dice be loaded so heavily in favor of the first filed action? Mr. Rehnquist's affirmative answer is based on the contention that the Constitution is neutral as between state and federal forums. Even if this is so, can the same be said of the federal jurisdictional statutes? Though §§ 1331–32 confer concurrent jurisdiction in federal question and diversity cases, they operate, in conjunction with the removal statute (§ 1441) to favor federal court adjudication—for when the parties disagree about forum, the preference of either party for a federal court prevails.

(b) Consider the special problems posed by class actions, and by multi-party, multi-forum litigation, involving, for example, hazardous products (like asbestos or the Dalkon Shield) or mass disasters. Permitting multiple in personam actions to go forward creates severe problems of duplication, inconsistent judgments, and delay.

For these reasons, the ALI's Study of Complex Litigation (1993) recommended new statutory authority to permit consolidation of related state and federal cases in a single forum. Proposed § 5.01 would broaden federal removal jurisdiction by authorizing a Complex Litigation Panel of federal judges to order the removal of state court actions that arise from the same transaction or occurrence (or series of transactions or occurrences) as a pending federal action with which there is a common question of fact—unless all of the parties and the state court judge object. The Panel would consider a long list of administrative concerns, as well as the presence of special state or local interests, in deciding whether to order removal.

More controversially, the Study proposed (§ 4.01) that the Panel could designate a state court as the forum to which pending federal as well as state court cases would be transferred for consolidation. Excluded from the operation of § 4.01 are actions (i) within exclusive federal jurisdiction, (ii) brought under 42 U.S.C. § 1983, or (iii) removed under 28 U.S.C. §§ 1441(d) (suits against foreign states), 1442 (federal officers), and 1443 (civil rights removal). In addition, the United States could block transfer in actions brought under § 1345 or removed under § 1444.

Proposed §§ 4.01(a) and 5.04 appear to authorize not only a federal court but also a state court that is hearing a consolidated proceeding to enjoin other lawsuits (in both state and federal courts) whose continuation would impair the consolidated action. See also Appendix A, proposed §§ 1407(e)(4), 1407A(f). The Reporter's Notes suggest that the rationale for such power is closely analogous to the "res" exception to the Anti–Injunction Act.

Are the concerns underlying these proposals persuasive reasons for Congress to depart from the "hands-off" approach of Kline and of the Anti–Injunction Act? For the courts to do so absent legislation? Cf. Allison v. Security Ben. Life Ins. Co., 980 F.2d 1213 (8th Cir.1992) (alternative holding)(district court did not abuse discretion in dismissing class action of thirty policyholders against insurer when plaintiffs were already members of a certified class in a state court action in which the claims could be litigated). To what extent are these concerns applicable not only in so-called complex cases but also in run-of-the-mill examples of duplicative litigation?

(7) *Appealability*.   A refusal to stay or dismiss an action is not appealable. Gulfstream Aerospace Corp. v. Mayacamas Corp., 485 U.S. 271 (1988), p. 1651, note 11, *infra*.   An order staying or dismissing a federal action in favor of state court proceedings is appealable—at least where the judgment in that proceeding will be res judicata.   See Moses Cone, Paragraph (2), *supra*; Wilton v. Seven Falls Co., Paragraph (3), *supra*.   See generally Chap. XV, Sec. 2, *infra*.

The Wilton case stated that a district court's decision whether to hear a declaratory judgment action is reviewable only for abuse of discretion.   But what is the scope of review of a decision to abstain under Colorado River and Moses Cone?   Compare the scope of review in related settings.   As to decisions to abstain under Pullman, the appellate court undertakes de novo review of the "essentially legal" questions whether state law is unsettled and whether a narrowing construction is possible.   See D'Iorio v. County of Delaware, 592 F.2d 681, 686 (3d Cir.1978).   A district court has some discretion to forgo abstention even where it might be proper, Shamrock Development Co. v. City of Concord, 656 F.2d 1380, 1385 (9th Cir.1981), but little or no discretion to abstain when the stated requirements are not met, United Services Auto. Ass'n v. Muir, 792 F.2d 356, 361 (3d Cir.1986).   (If review in the former situation comes only after the case has been litigated to final judgment, won't reversal be especially costly?)   By contrast, the decision whether to certify an issue to a state court rests in the "sound discretion" of the federal court, see Lehman Bros. v. Schein, p. 1245, *supra*; note that the case was remanded to permit the *court of appeals*, rather than the district court, to exercise its discretion.   In Younger cases, however, the Supreme Court appears to have recognized virtually no discretion in the lower courts.   *Cf.* also Loyd v. Loyd, 731 F.2d 393, 397 (7th Cir.1984), p. 1336, note 4, *infra*.

(8) *Bibliography*.   For commentary in addition to that previously cited, see Sonenshein, *Abstention: The Crooked Course of Colorado River*, 59 Tul.L.Rev. 651, 693–94 (1985); Note, 30 Stan.L.Rev. 1111 (1978); Friedman, *A Revisionist Theory of Abstention*, 88 Mich.L.Rev. 530, 588–94 (1989); Gibson, *Private Concurrent Litigation in Light of Younger, Pennzoil, and Colorado River*, 14 Okla.City.L.Rev. 185 (1989).

SUBSECTION E: MATTERS OF DOMESTIC RELATIONS AND PROBATE

Ankenbrandt v. Richards

504 U.S. 689, 112 S.Ct. 2206, 119 L.Ed.2d 468 (1992).
Certiorari to the Circuit Court of Appeals for the Fifth Circuit.

■ JUSTICE WHITE delivered the opinion of the Court.

* * *

I

Petitioner Carol Ankenbrandt, a citizen of Missouri, brought this lawsuit * * * on behalf of her daughters L. R. and S. R. against respondents Jon A. Richards and Debra Kesler * * *.   Alleging federal jurisdiction based on the diversity of citizenship provision of § 1332, Ankenbrandt's complaint sought monetary damages for alleged sexual and physical abuse of the children committed by Richards and Kesler.   Richards is the divorced father of the children and Kesler his female companion.   * * * [T]he District Court granted respondents' motion to dismiss this lawsuit.   Citing In re Burrus, 136 U.S. 586, 593–594 (1890), for the proposition that "[t]he whole subject of the domestic relations of husband and wife, parent and child, belongs to the laws of the States and not to the laws of the United States," the court concluded that this case fell within what has become known as the "domestic relations" exception to diversity jurisdiction, and that it lacked jurisdiction over the case.   The court also invoked the abstention principles announced in Younger v. Harris, 401 U.S. 37 (1971), to justify its decision to dismiss the complaint without prejudice.   The Court of Appeals affirmed * * *.

We granted certiorari limited to the following questions: "(1) Is there a domestic relations exception to federal jurisdiction?   (2) If so, does it permit a district court to abstain from exercising diversity jurisdiction over a tort action for damages?   (3) Did the District Court in this case err in abstaining from exercising jurisdiction under the doctrine of Younger v. Harris, [*supra*]?".   We address each of these issues in turn.

II

The domestic relations exception * * * has been invoked often by the lower federal courts.   The seeming authority for doing so originally stemmed from the announcement in Barber v. Barber, 21 How. 582 (1859), that the federal courts have no jurisdiction over suits for divorce or the allowance of alimony.   [There, a woman who had obtained a New York state award of divorce and alimony sued in equity in a federal district court in Wisconsin (to which her former husband had moved) and won an order enforcing the New York judgment.]   * * *

On appeal, it was argued that the District Court lacked jurisdiction on two grounds: first, that there was no diversity of citizenship because although divorced, the wife's citizenship necessarily remained that of her former husband;   and second, that the whole subject of divorce and alimony * * * was exclusively ecclesiastical at the time of the adoption of the Constitution and that the Constitution therefore placed the whole subject * * * beyond the jurisdiction of the United States courts.   Over the dissent of three Justices, the Court rejected both arguments.   After an exhaustive survey of the authorities, the Court concluded that * * * a suit to enforce an alimony decree rested within the federal courts' equity jurisdiction.   * * * In so stating, however, the Court also announced the following limitation on federal jurisdiction:

"Our first remark is—and we wish it to be remembered—that this is not a suit asking the court for the allowance of alimony.   That has been done by a court of competent jurisdiction.   The court in Wisconsin was asked to interfere to prevent that decree from being defeated by fraud.

"We disclaim altogether any jurisdiction in the courts of the United States upon the subject of divorce, or for the allowance of alimony, either as an original proceeding in chancery or as an incident to divorce *a vinculo*, or to one from bed and board." Barber, *supra*, at 584.

As a general matter, the [three] dissenters agreed with these statements, but took issue with the Court's holding that the instant action to enforce an alimony decree was within the equity jurisdiction of the federal courts.

The statements disclaiming jurisdiction over divorce and alimony decree suits, though technically dicta, formed the basis for excluding "domestic relations" cases from the jurisdiction of the lower federal courts, a jurisdictional limitation those courts have recognized ever since. The Barber Court, however, cited no authority and did not discuss the foundation for its announcement. Since that time, the Court has dealt only occasionally with the domestic relations limitation on federal-court jurisdiction, and it has never addressed the basis for such a limitation. Because we are unwilling to cast aside an understood rule that has been recognized for nearly a century and a half, we feel compelled to explain why we will continue to recognize this limitation on federal jurisdiction.

A

[In this section of its opinion, the Court held that "the Constitution does not exclude domestic relations cases from the jurisdiction otherwise granted by statute to the federal courts." The Court noted, *inter alia*, that it had heard appeals from territorial courts involving divorce, see *e.g.*, De La Rama v. De La Rama, 201 U.S. 303 (1906); Simms v. Simms, 175 U.S. 162 (1899), and had upheld the jurisdiction of the federal courts in the District of Columbia to decide divorce actions, see, *e.g.*, Glidden Co. v. Zdanok, 370 U.S. 530, 581 n. 54 (1962).][3]

B

* * *

* * * We thus turn our attention to the relevant jurisdictional statutes.

The Judiciary Act of 1789 [gave the circuit courts concurrent jurisdiction] *"of all suits of a civil nature at common law or in equity* [where the amount in controversy exceeds five hundred dollars], and ... an alien is a party, or the suit is *between a citizen of the State where the suit is brought, and a citizen of another State."* Act of Sept. 24, 1789, § 11, 1 Stat. 73, 78. (Emphasis added.) The defining phrase, "all suits of a civil nature at common law or in equity," remained a key element of statutory provisions demarcating the terms of diversity jurisdiction until 1948, when Congress amended the diversity jurisdiction provision to eliminate this phrase and replace in its stead the term "all civil actions." 28 U.S.C. § 1332.

The Barber majority itself did not expressly refer to the diversity statute's use of the limitation on "suits of a civil nature at common law or in equity." The dissenters in Barber, however, implicitly made such a reference, for they suggested that the federal courts had no power over certain domestic relations actions because * * * "* * * the jurisdiction of the chancery in England does not extend to or embrace the subjects of divorce and alimony, and * * * the jurisdiction of the courts of the United States in chancery is bounded by that of the chancery in England * * *." Barber, *supra*, at 605 (Daniel, J., dissenting). * * * Because the Barber Court did not disagree with this reason for accepting

---

3. [Original footnote of the Court.] We read Ohio ex rel. Popovici v. Agler, 280 U.S. 379 (1930), as in accord with this conclusion. In that case, the Court referenced the language in In re Burrus, 136 U.S. 586 (1890), regarding the domestic relations exception and then held that a state court was not precluded by the Constitution and relevant federal statutes from exercising jurisdiction over a divorce suit brought against the Roumanian vice-consul.

the jurisdictional limitation over the issuance of divorce and alimony decrees, it may be inferred fairly that the jurisdictional limitation recognized by the Court rested on this statutory basis and that the disagreement between the Court and the dissenters thus centered only on the extent of the limitation.

We have no occasion here to join the historical debate over whether the English court of chancery had jurisdiction to handle certain domestic relations matters, though we note that commentators have found some support for the Barber majority's interpretation. * * * We * * * are content to rest our conclusion that a domestic relations exception exists * * * on Congress' apparent acceptance of this construction of the diversity jurisdiction provisions in the years prior to 1948, when the statute limited jurisdiction to "suits of a civil nature at common law or in equity." * * *

When Congress amended the diversity statute in 1948 to replace the law/equity distinction with the phrase "all civil actions," we presume Congress did so with full cognizance of the Court's nearly century-long interpretation of the prior statutes * * *. * * * [W]here Congress made substantive changes to the statute in other respects, see 28 U.S.C. § 1332 note, we presume, absent any indication that Congress intended to alter this exception, that Congress "adopt[ed] that interpretation" when it reenacted the diversity statute. Lorillard v. Pons, 434 U.S. 575, 580 (1978).

III

In the more than 100 years since this Court laid the seeds for the development of the domestic relations exception, the lower federal courts have applied it in a variety of circumstances. Many of these applications go well beyond the circumscribed situations posed by Barber and its progeny. * * *

The Barber Court * * * did not intend to strip the federal courts of authority to hear cases arising from the domestic relations of persons unless they seek the granting or modification of a divorce or alimony decree. * * *

Subsequently, this Court expanded the domestic relations exception to include decrees in child custody cases. In a child custody case brought pursuant to a writ of habeas corpus, for instance, the Court held void a writ issued by a Federal District Court to restore a child to the custody of the father. "As to the right to the control and possession of this child, as it is contested by its father and its grandfather, it is one in regard to which neither the Congress of the United States nor any authority of the United States has any special jurisdiction." In re Burrus, 136 U.S. 586, 594 (1890).

Although In re Burrus technically did not involve a construction of the diversity statute, as we understand Barber to have done, its statement that "[t]he whole subject of the domestic relations of husband and wife, parent and child, belongs to the laws of the States and not to the laws of the United States," id., at 593–594, has been interpreted by the federal courts to apply with equal vigor in suits brought pursuant to diversity jurisdiction. [Citing numerous authorities.] * * * We conclude, therefore, that the domestic relations exception, as articulated by this Court since Barber, divests the federal courts of power to issue divorce, alimony, and child custody decrees. * * *

* * * [O]ur conclusion * * * is also supported by sound policy considerations. Issuance of decrees of this type not infrequently involves retention of jurisdiction by the court and deployment of social workers to monitor compliance. As a matter of judicial economy, state courts are more eminently suited

to work of this type than are federal courts, which lack the close association with state and local government organizations dedicated to handling issues that arise out of conflicts over divorce, alimony, and child custody decrees. Moreover, * * * [the state courts have developed special proficiency] * * * over the past century and a half in handling issues that arise in the granting of such decrees.

By concluding, as we do, that the domestic relations exception encompasses only cases involving the issuance of a divorce, alimony, or child custody decree, we necessarily find that the Court of Appeals erred by affirming the District Court's invocation of this exception. This lawsuit in no way seeks such a decree; rather, it alleges that respondents Richards and Kesler committed torts against L. R. and S. R., Ankenbrandt's children by Richards. * * * We now address whether, even though subject-matter jurisdiction might be proper, sufficient grounds exist to warrant abstention from the exercise of that jurisdiction.

IV

The Court of Appeals, as did the District Court, stated abstention as an alternative ground for its holding. * * * Abstention rarely should be invoked, because the federal courts have a "virtually unflagging obligation ... to exercise the jurisdiction given them." [Colorado River Water Conservation Dist. v. United States, 424 U.S. 800,] 817 [(1976)].

The courts below cited Younger v. Harris, 401 U.S. 37 (1971), to support their holdings to abstain in this case. * * * Though we have extended Younger abstention to the civil context, we have never applied the notions of comity so critical to Younger's "Our Federalism" when no state proceeding was pending nor any assertion of important state interests made. [Because no state proceedings were pending when Ankenbrandt filed suit,] * * * application by the lower courts of Younger abstention was clearly erroneous.

It is not inconceivable, however, that in certain circumstances, the abstention principles developed in Burford v. Sun Oil Co., 319 U.S. 315 (1943), might be relevant in a case involving elements of the domestic relationship even when the parties do not seek divorce, alimony, or child custody. This would be so when a case presents "difficult questions of state law bearing on policy problems of substantial public import whose importance transcends the result in the case then at bar." Colorado River Water Conservation Dist., *supra*, at 814. Such might well be the case if a federal suit were filed prior to effectuation of a divorce, alimony, or child custody decree, and the suit depended on a determination of the status of the parties. Where, as here, the status of the domestic relationship has been determined as a matter of state law, and in any event has no bearing on the underlying torts alleged, we have no difficulty concluding that Burford abstention is inappropriate in this case.

V

* * * Accordingly, we reverse the decision of the Court of Appeals and remand the case for further proceedings consistent with this opinion.

It is so ordered.

■ JUSTICE BLACKMUN, concurring in the judgment.

I agree with the Court that the District Court had jurisdiction over petitioner's claims in tort. Moreover, I agree that the federal courts should not entertain claims for divorce, alimony, and child custody. I am unable to agree, however, that the diversity statute contains any "exception" for domestic relations matters. * * * In my view, the longstanding, unbroken practice of the federal courts in refusing to hear domestic relations cases is precedent at most for continued discretionary abstention rather than mandatory limits on federal jurisdiction. * * *

I

* * *

* * * I do not see how [the 1948 change in the wording of the diversity statute] that, if anything, expands the jurisdictional scope of the statute can be said to constitute evidence of approval of a prior narrow construction.[1] Any inaction on the part of Congress in 1948 in failing expressly to mention domestic relations matters in the diversity statute reflects the fact * * * that Congress likely had no idea until the Court's decision today that the diversity statute contained an exception for domestic relations matters.

This leads to my primary concern: the Court's conclusion that Congress understood Barber as an interpretation of the diversity statute. Barber did not express any intent to construe the diversity statute * * *. As the Court puts it, it may only be "inferred" that the basis for declining jurisdiction was the diversity statute. It is inferred not from anything in the Barber majority opinion. Rather, it is inferred from the comments of a dissenting justice and the absence of rebuttal by the Barber majority. The Court today has a difficult enough time arriving at this unlikely interpretation of the Barber decision. I cannot imagine that Congress ever assembled this construction on its own.

[Justice Blackmun then discussed three decisions that, in his view, "seriously undermine any inference that Barber's recognition of a domestic relations 'exception' traces to a 'common law or equity' limitation of the diversity statute." In Simms v. Simms, 175 U.S. 162 (1899), the Court did not find that limitation to bar its authority to hear an appeal from the Supreme Court of the Territory of Arizona affirming the territorial District Court's dismissal of a husband's bill for divorce and its award to his wife of alimony and counsel fees *pendente lite*.[4]

[In De La Rama v. De La Rama, 201 U.S. 303 (1906), "the Court took jurisdiction over an appeal from the Supreme Court of the Philippine Islands in a wife's action for divorce and alimony." The Court's explanation of the reasons that federal courts have not exercised jurisdiction over actions for divorce and alimony did not include the "common law or equity" limitation. Indeed, the appellate jurisdictional statute in De La Rama extended to "all

---

1. To be sure, this modification in language was part of a wholesale revision of the Judicial Code in 1948, and this Court has recognized that "no changes in law or policy are to be presumed from changes of language in the revision unless an intent to make such changes is clearly expressed." Fourco Glass Co. v. Transmirra Products Corp., 353 U.S. 222, 227 (1957). This principle may negate an inference that the change in language expanded the scope of the statute, but it does not affirmatively authorize an inference that

Congress' recodification was designed to approve of prior constructions of the statute.

4. [Original footnote of Justice Blackmun] The Court concluded it could not review the question of divorce, because it involved "no matter of law, but mere questions of fact" and because, contrary to the statutory amount-in-controversy requirement, it involved "a matter the value of which could not be estimated in money." 175 U.S., at 168–169. It modified and affirmed the alimony award.

actions, cases, causes, and proceedings," so that Barber could easily have been distinguished on the grounds of the "common law or equity" limitation in the diversity statute. Instead, following Simms, the Court pointed to the absence of any need to defer to the states' regulation of domestic relations in an appeal from a territorial court.

[The third decision is Ohio ex rel. Popovici v. Agler, 280 U.S. 379 (1930), where a Roumanian vice-consul defended against his wife's state court action for a divorce and alimony by claiming that the state court lacked jurisdiction in view of the federal courts' *exclusive* jurisdiction over all suits and proceedings against consuls or vice-consuls. Rejecting this claim, Justice Holmes noted the absence of federal court jurisdiction over divorce, which he traced not to the diversity statute but apparently to the Constitution itself]:

"If when the Constitution was adopted the common understanding was that the domestic relations of husband and wife and parent and child were matters reserved to the States, there is no difficulty in construing the instrument accordingly and not much in dealing with the statutes. Suits against consuls and vice-consuls' must be taken to refer to ordinary civil proceedings and not to include what formerly would have belonged to the ecclesiastical Courts." *Id.*, at 383–384.

* * *

Even assuming the Court today correctly interprets Barber, its extension of any domestic relations "exception" to the diversity statute for child custody matters is not warranted by any known principles of statutory construction. The Court relies on In re Burrus, 136 U.S. 586 (1890), in which the Court denied the "jurisdiction" of a federal district court to issue a writ of habeas corpus in favor of a father to recover the care and custody of his child from the child's grandfather. That case * * * involve[d] * * * the habeas corpus statute, and the Court expressly declined to address the diversity statute. * * *

II

A

To reject the Court's construction of the diversity statute is not, however, necessarily to reject the federal courts' longstanding practice of declining to hear certain domestic relations cases. * * * [T]he common concern reflected in these earlier cases is, in modern terms, abstentional—and not jurisdictional—in nature. These cases are premised not upon a concern for the historical limitation of equity jurisdiction of the English courts, but upon the virtually exclusive primacy at that time of the States in the regulation of domestic relations. * * *

Whether the interest of States remains a sufficient justification today for abstention is uncertain in view of the expansion in recent years of federal law in the domestic relations area.[8] I am confident, nonetheless, that the unbroken and unchallenged practice of the federal courts since before the War Between

---

8. See, *e.g.*, Victims of Child Abuse Act of 1990, 104 Stat. 4792, 42 U.S.C. § 13001 *et seq.*; Family Violence Prevention and Services Act, 98 Stat. 1757, 42 U.S.C. § 10401 *et seq.*; Parental Kidnaping Prevention Act of 1980, 94 Stat. 3568, 28 U.S.C. § 1738A; Adoption Assistance and Child Welfare Act of 1980, 94 Stat. 500, 42 U.S.C. §§ 620–628, 670–679a; Child Abuse Prevention and Treatment and Adoption Reform Act of 1978, 92 Stat. 205, 42 U.S.C. § 5111 *et seq.*; Child Abuse Prevention and Treatment Act, 88 Stat. 4, 42 U.S.C. § 5101 *et seq.*

the States of declining to hear certain domestic relations cases provides the very rare justification for continuing to do so. It is not without significance, moreover, that, because of this historical practice of the federal courts, the States have developed specialized courts and institutions in family matters, while Congress and the federal courts generally have not done so. Absent a contrary command of Congress, the federal courts properly should abstain, at least from diversity actions traditionally excluded from the federal courts, such as those seeking divorce, alimony, and child custody.

* * * Although there is no occasion to resolve the issue in definitive fashion in this case, I would suggest that principles of abstention provide a more principled basis for the Court's continued disinclination to entertain domestic relations matters.[9]

B

Whether or not the domestic relations "exception" is properly grounded in principles of abstention or principles of jurisdiction, I do not believe this case falls within the exception. * * * None of this Court's prior cases that consider the domestic relations "exception" involves the type of periphery domestic relations claim at issue here.

* * * Moreover, any federal court determination of petitioner's claims will neither upset a prior state court determination of status or obligations appurtenant to status, nor pre-empt a pending state court determination of this nature. * * * While petitioner's claims do not involve a federal question or statute—the presence of which would strongly counsel against abstention, see Colorado River Water Cons. Dist. v. United States, 424 U.S. 800, 815, n. 21 (1976)— petitioner's state law tort claims for money damages are easily cognizable in a federal court. All these considerations favor the exercise of federal jurisdiction over petitioner's claims.

■ [Justice Stevens, joined by Justice Thomas, concurred in the judgment, finding that the case fell outside the scope of any plausible "domestic relations exception", and leaving for another day consideration of whether such an exception in fact exists.]

NOTE ON FEDERAL JURISDICTION IN MATTERS OF DOMESTIC RELATIONS

(1) *History.* The view, repudiated in Ankenbrandt, that Article III excludes jurisdiction in domestic relations cases was bound up with the assertion that

---

Like the diversity statute, the federal-question grant of jurisdiction in Article III * * * limits the judicial power in federal-question cases to "Cases, in Law and Equity." Assuming this limitation applies with equal force in the constitutional context as the Court finds today that it does in the statutory context, the Court's decision today casts grave doubts upon Congress' ability to confer federal-question jurisdiction (as under 28 U.S.C. § 1331) on the federal courts in any matters involving divorces, alimony, and child custody.

9. As this Court has previously observed that the various types of abstention are not "rigid pigeonholes," Pennzoil Co. v. Texaco Inc., 481 U.S. 1, 11, n. 9 (1987), there is no need to affix a label to the abstention principles I suggest. Nevertheless, I fully agree with the Court that Younger abstention is inappropriate on the facts before us, because of the absence of any pending state proceeding.

certain matters were beyond the historical scope of law and equity. See, *e.g.*, Fontain v. Ravenel, 58 U.S. (17 How.) 369 (1854)(Taney, C.J., dissenting)(arguing that the federal courts lacked power to enforce a charitable bequest, as the "chancery jurisdiction" of the federal courts conferred by Article III extended only to matters of which chancery had jurisdiction "in its judicial character as a court of equity," and not to the "prerogative powers, which the king, as *parens patriae*, in England, exercised through the courts," and which remained with the States as sovereigns).

(2) *The Spindel Decision*. In Spindel v. Spindel, 283 F.Supp. 797 (E.D.N.Y. 1968), Judge Weinstein offered a searching analysis and criticism of the whole development of the federal domestic relations exception. On the historical point, he challenged the premise that matrimonial matters were handled exclusively in the ecclesiastical courts and not in chancery acting in its judicial capacity. He also noted that Article III requires only a "controversy" (not a "case in law or equity") between citizens of different states for federal jurisdiction to exist, and that Congress could therefore confer on the federal courts authority to grant divorces in such cases. The force of his critique was broadly recognized.[1]

(3) *The Justification for Ankenbrandt*. Note that the Ankenbrandt opinion eschews historical arguments about the scope of chancery vs. ecclesiastical jurisdiction in matrimonial matters, relying instead on precedents and on Congress' failure to object to them. Were those adequate bases for upholding a limit on a statutory grant of jurisdiction? Do other circumstances support continued observance of the exception, including "the strong state interest in domestic relations matters, the competence of state courts in settling family disputes,[2] the possibility of incompatible federal and state court decrees in cases of continuing judicial supervision by the state, and the problem of congested dockets in the federal courts," Crouch v. Crouch, 566 F.2d 486, 487 (5th Cir.1978)?[3] Should federal courts be especially reluctant not to exercise jurisdiction insofar as studies suggest that gender bias is found in state family courts? Or is diversity jurisdiction meant to protect against state court prejudice against non-citizens rather than against gender bias? See Jackson, *Empiricism, Gender, and Legal Pedagogy: An Experiment in a Federal Courts Seminar at Georgetown University Law School*, 83 Geo.L.J. 494–95 & n. 113 (1994).

---

1. Some commentators suggested outright abolition. See Wand, *A Call for the Repudiation of the Domestic Relations Exception to Federal Jurisdiction*, 30 Vill.L.Rev. 307 (1985); Note, 24 B.C.L.Rev. 661 (1983); Comment, 71 Marq.L.Rev. 141 (1987). Others have urged limiting the scope of the exception, see Rush, *Domestic Relations Law: Federal Jurisdiction and State Sovereignty in Perspective*, 60 Notre Dame L. Rev. 1 (1984), Note, 83 Colum.L.Rev. 1824 (1983), or serving its purposes by use of more general abstention doctrines, see, *e.g.*, Atwood, *Domestic Relations Cases in Federal Court: Toward a Principled Exercise of Jurisdiction*, 35 Hastings L.J. 571 (1984); Note, 1983 Duke L.J. 1095.

2. [Ed.] *Cf.* Currie, *Suitcase Divorce in the Conflict of Laws: Simons, Rosenstiel, and Borax*, 34 U.Chi.L.Rev. 26, 49–53 (1966), arguing that a state whose divorce law is to be applied may properly confine divorce litigation to its own (often specialized) courts to avoid the serious risk of error in adjudication in other fora.

3. See Phillips, Nizer, Benjamin, Krim & Ballon v. Rosenstiel, 490 F.2d 509, 514 (2d Cir.1973)(Friendly, J.)("It is beyond the realm of reasonable belief that, in these days of congested dockets, Congress would wish the federal courts to seek to regain territory, even if the cession of 1859 was unjustified.")

Professor Resnik argues that the exception is part of a larger pattern of exclusion of women from the federal courts: "[W]omen and the families they sometimes inhabit are not only assumed to be outside the federal courts, they also are assumed not to be related to the 'national issues' to which the federal judiciary is to devote its interests. Jurisdictional lines have not been drawn according to the laws of nature but by men, who today are seeking to confirm their prestige as members of the most important judiciary in the country * * *. Dealing with women * * * is not how they want to frame their job." Resnik, *"Naturally" Without Gender: Women, Jurisdiction, and the Federal Courts*, 66 N.Y.U.L.Rev. 1682, 1749 (1991). See also *Cahn, Family Law, Federalism, and the Federal Courts*, 79 Iowa L.Rev. 1073 (1994); Stein, *The Domestic Relations Exception to Federal Jurisdiction: Rethinking an Unsettled Federal Courts Doctrine*, 36 B.C.L.Rev. 669 (1995).

To what extent do you believe that the exclusion of domestic relations cases from federal courts is premised on gender bias, rather than on the kinds of considerations discussed by the Court? Do any of these considerations themselves reflect gender bias? (Reconsider these questions after you have read the following Note, which discusses a similar judge-made exclusion for probate matters.) If you are persuaded by the gender-bias thesis, does it lead you to conclude that Congress should amend the jurisdictional statutes to permit federal courts to enter divorce, alimony, and custody decrees? See Cahn, *supra* (urging that domestic relations matters be treated no differently from other matters in which diversity of citizenship is present).

(4) *The Scope of the Exception.* Ankenbrandt defines the domestic relations exception rather narrowly. Before the decision, it was less certain whether the domestic relations exception extended to suits arising in a domestic relations context, but involving claims traditionally adjudicated in federal courts—for example, tort or contract claims—though the majority of cases had held no. See generally Rush, note 1, *supra*, at 8 n. 33; Note, 83 Colum.L.Rev. 1824, 1828 & nn. 29–31 (1983).

Does (should) Ankenbrandt exclude disputes about child support? About pre-nuptial agreements? About domestic partnership agreements? See Cahn, Paragraph (3), *supra*, at 1084–85.

(5) *Lack of Jurisdiction vs. Abstention.* Would acceptance of Justice Blackmun's view that the "exception" should be reconceptualized as an exercise in discretionary abstention affect the appropriateness, or scope, of the exception? Whether an objection to federal adjudication is waivable? The scope of appellate review of trial court decisions? See generally Wand, note 1, *supra*, at 323–24.

Note that while Ankenbrandt adopts the "jurisdictional" view, Part IV of the opinion leaves open the possibility of "abstention" in cases that fall outside of the jurisdictional exception. See, *e.g.*, Minot v. Eckardt–Minot, 13 F.3d 590 (2d Cir.1994)(upholding abstention in tort action based on defendant's violation of a state court custody order, and emphasizing the difficulty of the state tort law issues, the state courts' comparative expertise, and the pendency of a motion in state court to re-open the custody decision); Kahn v. Kahn, 21 F.3d 859 (8th Cir.1994)(refusing to exercise jurisdiction in tort action based on defendant's misappropriation of property during course of marriage, when property settlement in divorce action had taken account of the alleged misconduct). See generally Stein, Paragraph (3), *supra*, at 697–722 (advocating a limited abstention doctrine in cases that arise in well-marked areas of state expertise and interest—such as guardianship, adoption, and delinquency matters—or that raise difficult state law questions).

(6) *Jurisdictional Grants Other than Diversity.* What implications does Ankenbrandt have for cases in which federal jurisdiction does not rest on the diversity statute (§ 1332)?

(a) The Ankenbrandt Court's interpretation of § 1332 relied in part (over Justice Blackmun's protest) on In re Burrus, a case that arose under the habeas corpus jurisdiction. Does a similar exception attach to the habeas jurisdiction?

In Lehman v. Lycoming County Children's Services Agency, 458 U.S. 502 (1982), a mother filed a federal habeas corpus action on behalf of her children challenging, as a denial of due process, a state court's termination of her parental rights. Custody had been awarded to a county agency, which placed the children in a private foster home. In ruling (6–3) that there was no federal habeas jurisdiction, the Supreme Court distinguished the children's situation from that of a petitioner whose custody arises from a criminal conviction.[4] Though it did not advert to the domestic relations exception per se, the Court did stress the special solicitude that federal courts have traditionally shown in "family and family-property arrangements" (p. 512), and the importance to the state of certainty and finality in child custody disputes.

(b) Before Ankenbrandt, the decisions were divided on whether a federal court should exercise federal question jurisdiction in domestic relations matters.[5] What does Ankenbrandt suggest? See Thomas v. New York City, 814 F.Supp. 1139 (E.D.N.Y.1993)(upholding jurisdiction).

NOTE ON FEDERAL JURISDICTION IN MATTERS OF PROBATE AND ADMINISTRATION

(1) *Development of the Exception.* The probate of wills and the grant of letters of administration were the distinctive functions of the ecclesiastical courts in England. No federal court seems ever to have undertaken either of these tasks.

---

4. The Court reserved the question of jurisdiction when the child is confined in a state institution (p. 511 n. 12).

5. Compare, *e.g.*, Bergstrom v. Bergstrom, 623 F.2d 517 (8th Cir.1980)(abstaining in custody fight involving child's claim of a constitutional right to remain in the United States), with Hooks v. Hooks, 771 F.2d 935 (6th Cir.1985)(upholding jurisdiction over § 1983 claim that plaintiff was deprived of custody without due process). See generally Comment, 31 U.C.L.A.L.Rev. 843 (1984).

The Parental Kidnaping Prevention Act of 1980, 94 Stat. 3568–73 (1980), codified in pertinent part as 28 U.S.C. § 1738A, generally requires that a state enforce child custody decrees rendered by other states in accordance with the Act's provisions. Resolving a circuit conflict, the Supreme Court ruled in Thompson v. Thompson, 484 U.S. 174 (1988) that the Act does not create an implied federal right of action permitting federal court suit to enjoin state court proceedings in violation of the Act. The Court noted that Congress, when enacting this statute, had rejected a proposal to extend the diversity jurisdiction to actions seeking enforcement of state custody orders. Federal court determination of which of two conflicting decrees should be given effect, the Court added, would offend the "longstanding tradition of reserving domestic-relations matters to the States" (pp. 186–87 n. 4).

Before 1789 the English chancery courts took jurisdiction over the administration of estates of personalty. See Ballow, A Treatise of Equity 193 (1756); Note, 43 Harv.L.Rev. 462, 465 (1930). But the Supreme Court has regularly rebuked the few efforts of lower federal courts to take over, generally, the administration of a decedent's estate. E.g., Hook v. Payne, 81 U.S. (14 Wall.) 252 (1872); Byers v. McAuley, 149 U.S. 608 (1893). Cf. Waterman v. Canal–Louisiana Bank & Trust Co., 215 U.S. 33 (1909)(denying jurisdiction, in an otherwise proper case, of a prayer for an accounting of an estate).

(2) *The Markham Decision.* A leading decision on the "probate exception" is Markham v. Allen, 326 U.S. 490 (1946). There, the will of the decedent was admitted to probate and his estate was being administered in California state court. In 1942, six of his heirs filed a petition in the probate proceeding challenging the right under state law of German legatees to take as beneficiaries. Three months later, the federal Alien Property Custodian, who purported to vest in himself all title and interest of the German legatees, sued the executor and heirs in a federal court in California under § 24(1) of the Judicial Code (now 28 U.S.C. § 1345), which grants jurisdiction over suits brought by an officer of the United States. A judgment in favor of the Custodian was reversed by the court of appeals, which held that the district court should have dismissed for want of jurisdiction because probate matters are not "cases or controversies" within the meaning of Article III.

The Supreme Court reversed in turn. Chief Justice Stone, for the Court, acknowledged that "a federal court has no jurisdiction to probate a will or administer an estate, the reason being that the equity jurisdiction conferred by the Judiciary Act of 1789, and § 24(1) of the Judicial Code, which is that of the English Court of Chancery in 1789, did not extend to probate matters. But it has been established by a long series of decisions of this Court that federal courts of equity have jurisdiction to entertain suits 'in favor of creditors, legatees and heirs' and other claimants against a decedent's estate 'to establish their claims' so long as the federal court does not interfere with the probate proceedings or assume general jurisdiction of the probate or control of the property in the custody of the state court. Waterman v. Canal–Louisiana Bank & Trust Co., 215 U.S. 33, 43, and cases cited" (p. 444).

The district court's judgment declared only that the Alien Property Custodian was "entitled to receive [the decedent's] net estate", and left "undisturbed the orderly administration of decedent's estate in the state probate court * * *. This, as our authorities demonstrate, is not an exercise of probate jurisdiction or an interference with property in the possession or custody of a state court" (p. 495). Nor should the district court have declined to exercise jurisdiction so that the state court could decide the state law issues—particularly since the Trading With the Enemy Act, which confers district court jurisdiction (in addition to that under § 24(1)) to enter all orders necessary and proper to enforce the Act, reflects the policy of permitting the Custodian to sue in federal court.[1]

(3) *The Rationale for the Exception.* Was the jurisdiction of the English Court of Chancery an appropriate criterion of federal jurisdiction in probate matters in 1789? Is it appropriate today? Cf. the critique of the use of that criterion to define the domestic relations exception in Paragraph (2) of the preceding Note.

---

1. Justice Jackson did not participate; Justice Rutledge would have remanded the case for the district court to retain jurisdiction pending the state court's decision.

Could the probate exception instead be predicated on non-interference with the state court's possession of a *res* (see p. 1201 & note 2, *supra*)?

In Dragan v. Miller, 679 F.2d 712 (7th Cir.1982)(Posner, J.), the court concluded that "however shoddy the historical underpinnings of the probate exception, it is too well established a feature of our federal system to be lightly discarded, and by an inferior court at that" (p. 713). Uncertain whether Markham controlled the case of an action to set aside a will on the ground of undue influence, the court followed the "practical" approach of examining "the purposes that the probate exception * * * might be thought to serve," (p. 714) and proceeded to explore considerations—such as legal certainty, judicial economy, and relative judicial expertise—that might favor state court exclusivity.

If the lower courts lack the authority to abandon the probate exception, do they have the authority to redefine its boundaries in light of "practical" considerations? Is Dragan's approach likely to increase litigation about where to litigate?

(4) *The Scope of the Exception.*

(a) *Misconduct by Representatives.* Numerous cases support the holding of the Markham decision that federal courts may entertain actions *inter partes* against administrators or executors, or other claimants, for such purposes as the establishment of (a) a right to a distributive share under a will or in intestacy, Payne v. Hook, 74 U.S. (7 Wall.) 425 (1869); McClellan v. Carland, 217 U.S. 268 (1910), p. 1320, note 15, *supra*, (b) a lien on a distributive share, Ingersoll v. Coram, 211 U.S. 335 (1908), or (c) a debt due from the decedent, Hess v. Reynolds, 113 U.S. 73 (1885)—so long as any judgment does not interfere with the state court's orderly handling of an estate under administration.[2]

(b) *Challenges to Wills.* Actions to annul a will or set aside an order of probate have been treated as raising special problems. In Sutton v. English, 246 U.S. 199 (1918), a bill in equity sought a determination, *inter alia*, that that the joint will of the decedent and her husband, who had predeceased her, was inefficacious to dispose of the community property. For the Court, Justice Pitney observed (p. 205) that "matters of strict probate are not within the jurisdiction of courts of the United States". However, where a state permits independent actions "*inter partes*, either at law or in equity, to annul a will or to set aside the probate, the courts of the United States, where diversity of citizenship and a sufficient amount in controversy appear, can enforce the same remedy". Examining state law, he determined that the state courts lacked jurisdiction to annul by an original proceeding the action of a county court in probating a will; such a suit must be instituted in the county court in which the will was admitted to probate, and calls for an exercise of original probate jurisdiction. Thus, the present action was "merely supplemental" to the

---

2. It is less clear whether there is jurisdiction over an action against an executor or administrator personally for fraud or mismanagement. Compare, *e.g.*, Hamilton v. Nielsen, 678 F.2d 709 (7th Cir.1982)(allowing an action for breach of fiduciary duty), and Bassler v. Arrowood, 500 F.2d 138 (8th Cir.1974)(allowing a fraud action), with, *e.g.*, Bedo v. McGuire, 767 F.2d 305 (6th Cir.1985)(dismissing an action for breach of fiduciary duty). The courts in these cases consider whether the state probate court's jurisdiction over such actions is exclusive within the state's court system, and whether a final accounting has yet been rendered in a state probate proceeding.

probate proceedings and "cognizable only by the probate court," and hence fell outside the federal courts' jurisdiction (p. 208).[3]

Should federal jurisdiction depend upon the particular state court's jurisdictional arrangements? *Cf.* the Burford decision, p. 1247, *supra.*

(5) *The Basis for Federal Jurisdiction.* Markham is unusual in that federal jurisdiction was not premised on diversity of citizenship. Is the scope of the probate exception uniform regardless of the basis for federal jurisdiction? If the Alien Property Custodian had been advancing the claim in Sutton v. English, Paragraph (4)(b), *supra,* should the result have differed?

(6) *Abstention.* In Rice v. Rice Foundation, 610 F.2d 471 (7th Cir.1979), the court of appeals remanded for consideration of whether the proceeding was within the probate exception, and added that even if it were not, "the district court may, in its discretion, decline to exercise its jurisdiction. * * * Discretionary abstention in probate-related matters is suggested not only by the strong state interest in such matters generally but also by special circumstances in particular cases" (pp. 477–78).[4] Can workable criteria be developed for the exercise of such discretion?

A similar notion had emerged in cases involving domestic relations matters before Ankenbrandt, and perhaps was kept alive in limited form in Part IV of the opinion. (See Paragraph (5) of the preceding Note.) Is discretionary abstention more appropriate here than in other diversity cases involving state law? See Subsections 2(B) and 2(D) of this Chapter, *supra.* Consider Giardina v. Fontana, 733 F.2d 1047 (2d Cir.1984), finding that the district court erred in declining to exercise diversity jurisdiction over a plaintiff's claim that her assignment of her interest in an estate was obtained by undue influence and fraud. The court ruled that the case did not fall within any of the exceptions recognized by Colorado River and Moses Cone, pp. 1308-20, *supra,* and emphasized the district courts' "virtually unflagging obligation * * * to exercise the jurisdiction given them" (p. 1052, quoting Colorado River, 424 U.S. at 817).

---

3. See generally 13B Wright, Miller & Cooper, Federal Practice and Procedure § 3610 (1984 & 1995 Supp.); Vestal & Foster, *Implied Limitations on the Diversity Jurisdiction of Federal Courts,* 41 Minn.L.Rev. 1, 13–23 (1956); Note, 45 Ind.L.J. 387 (1970).

4. See also Loyd v. Loyd, 731 F.2d 393, 397 (7th Cir.1984). There the district court, applying Dragan's practical approach, entertained jurisdiction. In affirming that decision, the court of appeals treated it as "an exercise of discretion" and found no abuse: "[i]n candor, if the district court had found originally that the probate exception was applicable, we doubt we would have faulted him" (p. 397).

CHAPTER XI

FEDERAL HABEAS CORPUS

SECTION 1. INTRODUCTION

INTRODUCTORY NOTE ON THE FUNCTIONS OF THE WRIT

This Chapter deals with the writ of *habeas corpus ad subjiciendum*—the so-called Great Writ.[1] In McNally v. Hill, 293 U.S. 131, 136–37 (1934), the Court described the development and function of the writ:

"Originating [in England] as a writ by which the superior courts of the common law and the chancellor sought to extend their jurisdiction at the expense of inferior or rival courts, it ultimately took form and survived as the writ of *habeas corpus ad subjiciendum*, by which the legality of the detention of one in the custody of another could be tested judicially. Its use was defined and regulated by the Habeas Corpus Act of 1679, 31 Car. II, c. 2. * * *

"The purpose of the proceeding defined by the statute was to inquire into the legality of the detention, and the only judicial relief authorized was the discharge of the prisoner or his admission to bail, and that only if his detention were found to be unlawful."

The underlying premise of the Great Writ is that only legal authority can justify detention.[2] A custodian, whether an official or a private citizen,[3] must point to law to defend the restraint of liberty.

---

1. This was only one of many forms of the writ of habeas corpus at common law. The other forms enumerated by Blackstone were: (1) *ad respondendum* (to remove a prisoner confined by process of an inferior court to answer to an action in a higher court); (2) *ad satisfaciendum* (to remove a prisoner to a higher court to be charged with process of execution); (3) *ad prosequendum, testificandum, deliberandum* (to remove a prisoner to enable the prisoner to prosecute, to testify, or to be tried in the proper jurisdiction); and (4) *ad faciendum et recipiendum* (to remove a cause at the prisoner's behest from an inferior court to Westminster). 3

Commentaries 129–32. See also Ex parte Bollman, 8 U.S. (4 Cranch) 75, 97–98 (1807); Price v. Johnston, 334 U.S. 266, 281 (1948).

The Price decision held that a court of appeals has the additional power, under the All Writs Act (now 28 U.S.C. § 1651), to issue a writ "in the nature of *habeas corpus*" to compel the production of a prisoner to argue an appeal *pro se*. Use of the writ when "necessary" to bring the prisoner "into court to testify or for trial" is now specifically authorized by 28 U.S.C. § 2241(c)(5).

2, 3. See notes 2 and 3 on page 1338.

But law is not a simple concept for this purpose, consisting as it does not only of rules that govern substantive decisions, but also of rules that distribute authority to make those decisions and that determine when an institutional process for deciding should be regarded as definitive. There is a sense, therefore, in which a prisoner can be deemed to be legally detained pursuant to the judgment of a competent tribunal, even though the decision to detain rested on an error of law or fact. For absent such a limiting conception, no decision denying relief could be immune from a further claim that the decision was in error and the detention therefore illegal. See generally Bator, *Finality in Criminal Law and Federal Habeas Corpus for State Prisoners*, 76 Harv.L.Rev. 441, 447 (1963).

This Chapter focuses primarily on the use of the writ as a post-conviction remedy for prisoners claiming that an error of federal law—almost always of federal constitutional law—infected the judicial proceedings that resulted in their detention. Post-conviction relief, although not the original office of habeas corpus, has become its primary contemporary use.

Yet other uses of the writ should not be ignored. The writ provides a ready mechanism for a constitutional attack upon official claims of power to detain (other than to answer charges in a civil court).[4] Thus, it provides

2. The writ played an historic part in the English struggle with royal prerogative. See Duker, *The English Origins of the Writ of Habeas Corpus: A Peculiar Path to Fame*, 53 N.Y.U.L.Rev. 983 (1978); *Developments in the Law—Federal Habeas Corpus*, 83 Harv. L.Rev. 1038, 1042–45 & sources cited (1970). See also Walker, The Constitutional and Legal Development of Habeas Corpus as the Writ of Liberty (1960).

3. Today, restraints by private citizens are rarely reached by the federal writ. Compare Wales v. Whitney, 114 U.S. 564, 571 (1885)(describing forms of custody subject to the writ, including "arbitrary custody by private individuals").

The court in Neale v. Pfeiffer, 523 F.Supp. 164, 165–66 (S.D.Ohio), *aff'd without opinion*, 665 F.2d 1046 (6th Cir.1981), reviewed a variety of situations in which the writ had been used in suits against private individuals—against parents in child custody cases; on behalf of persons committed to mental institutions; against ship officials who are custodians of persons forbidden to enter the country—and concluded that to obtain relief against a private custodian, the custodian must have acted pursuant to a court decree or other government intervention.

That such state involvement, even if necessary, is not sufficient was made clear in Lehman v. Lycoming County Children's Ser-

vices Agency, 458 U.S. 502 (1982), Ch. X, Sec. 2(E), p. 1333, *supra*, which held that the habeas statute does not confer jurisdiction over a petition brought by a mother to challenge as unconstitutional a state adjudication terminating her parental rights and awarding custody of her children to a county agency, which placed the children in a private foster home. The Court reserved the question of federal habeas jurisdiction when a child is confined in a state institution.

The precise holding and implications of the Lehman decision are uncertain. See generally Robbins & Newell, *The Continuing Diminished Availability of Federal Habeas Corpus Review to Challenge State Court Judgments: Lehman v. Lycoming County Children's Service Agency*, 33 Am.U.L.Rev. 271 (1984). Earlier decisions had reserved the question whether the writ might issue (in a case involving a private detention) under the "all writs" section in aid of diversity jurisdiction. See Ex parte Burrus, 136 U.S. 586, 597 (1890); Matters v. Ryan, 249 U.S. 375 (1919).

4. See, *e.g.*, Ex parte Milligan, 71 U.S. (4 Wall.) 2 (1866)(power of military to try civilian); Jurney v. MacCracken, 294 U.S. 125 (1935)(power of Senate to order arrest for contempt of a Committee); Ex parte Quirin, 317 U.S. 1 (1942)(military commission); Ex parte Endo, 323 U.S. 283 (1944)(power to

judicial review—at least to the extent required by the Constitution—of decisions of other agencies resulting in detention.[5] It also performs traditional, though marginal, preliminary functions in connection with criminal charges: testing the sufficiency of cause for a commitment on complaint[6] or for removal,[7] the denial of bail,[8] the legality of interstate rendition,[9] or extradition to a foreign country.[10] Finally, the writ has been much used to test the legality of conditions of confinement.[11]

For a comprehensive survey of federal habeas corpus for state prisoners, see Liebman & Hertz, Federal Habeas Corpus Practice & Procedure (2d ed.1994); see also 17A Wright, Miller & Cooper, Federal Practice & Procedure §§ 4261–4268.5 (1988 & Supp.1995); Developments in the Law, note 2, *supra*.

NOTE ON THE JURISDICTIONAL STATUTES

(1) *The First Judiciary Act.* Section 14 of the First Judiciary Act provided (1 Stat. 81–82):

"That all the before-mentioned courts of the United States, shall have power to issue writs of *scire facias*, *habeas corpus*, and all other writs not specially provided for by statute, which may be necessary for the exercise of

hold loyal citizen of Japanese descent in Relocation Center); Ludecke v. Watkins, 335 U.S. 160 (1948)(power to repatriate enemy without due process hearing); Kwong Hai Chew v. Colding, 344 U.S. 590 (1953)(power to exclude resident alien without hearing). See also note 3, *supra*.

5. For a survey of the use of federal habeas corpus to review administrative restraints in three areas (military administrative decisions, conscription, and deportation and exclusion of aliens), see *Developments in the Law—Federal Habeas Corpus*, note 2, *supra*, at 1238–63.

6. See, *e.g.*, Ex parte Bollman, 8 U.S. (4 Cranch) 75 (1807).

7. See, *e.g.*, Tinsley v. Treat, 205 U.S. 20 (1907); United States ex rel. Kassin v. Mulligan, 295 U.S. 396 (1935). The narrow review sanctioned by these decisions has been further limited by Fed.R.Crim.Proc. 40(a), under which an indictment suffices for removal upon proof of the defendant's identity. Moreover, the Act of June 29, 1938, 52 Stat. 1232, eliminated an appeal from final orders on the writ when used to test detention for removal. See 28 U.S.C. § 2253.

8. Though one of the main purposes of the Habeas Corpus Act of 1679 was to vindicate the right to bail of persons charged with bailable offenses, the writ is rarely needed for this purpose in federal courts. Bail is normally allowed at the preliminary hearing and

an application to the court or to a judge or justice may be made if it is not. See 18 U.S.C. §§ 3142, 3144; Fed.R.Crim.Proc. 46. In Stack v. Boyle, 342 U.S. 1 (1951), the proper remedy for a reduction of excessive bail was held to be a motion in the district court and an appeal from its denial.

As to the power of a single Justice to admit to bail pending review of a denial of habeas corpus, see the opinion of Jackson, J., in Stack v. Boyle, *supra*; and compare In the Matter of Pirinsky, 70 S.Ct. 232 (1949)(opinion of Jackson, J.) with Petition of Johnson, 72 S.Ct. 1028 (1952)(opinion of Douglas, J.).

9. See, *e.g.*, Roberts v. Reilly, 116 U.S. 80 (1885); Biddinger v. Commissioner of Police, 245 U.S. 128 (1917). But *cf.* Sweeney v. Woodall, 344 U.S. 86 (1952)(escaped prisoner). For a case discussing the limits that the Extradition Act, 18 U.S.C. § 3182, imposes upon state habeas corpus challenges to extradition warrants, see California v. Superior Court, 482 U.S. 400 (1987). See generally Note, 83 Colum.L.Rev. 975 (1983); Note, 74 Yale L.J. 78 (1964).

10. See, *e.g.*, Fernandez v. Phillips, 268 U.S. 311 (1925); Factor v. Laubenheimer, 290 U.S. 276 (1933); *cf.* 18 U.S.C. § 3184 (procedure prior to issuance of warrant).

11. See, *e.g.*, Wilwording v. Swenson, 404 U.S. 249 (1971); Johnson v. Avery, 393 U.S. 483 (1969).

their respective jurisdictions, and agreeable to the principles and usages of law. And that either of the justices of the supreme court, as well as judges of the district courts, shall have power to grant writs of *habeas corpus* for the purpose of an inquiry into the cause of commitment.—*Provided*, That writs of *habeas corpus* shall in no case extend to prisoners in gaol, unless where they are in custody, under or by colour of the authority of the United States, or are committed for trial before some court of the same, or are necessary to be brought into court to testify."

(2) *Ex parte Bollman*. The decision in Ex parte Bollman, 8 U.S. (4 Cranch) 75 (1807), provided several important interpretations of the habeas jurisdiction.

First, Chief Justice Marshall's opinion rejected the view that § 14 authorized the courts to issue the writ only as an auxiliary to jurisdiction otherwise conferred upon them.[1] Rather, he read that provision as authorizing an independent action in habeas corpus. (The power that § 14 expressly conferred on the *Justices* and *judges* was held to be vested by implication in the courts.)

Second, Chief Justice Marshall declared that when (as in Bollman) a petitioner applied directly to the Supreme Court, the Court could use the writ as a means of reviewing the legality of a commitment by order of a lower federal court. Issuance of the writ by the Supreme Court was held to be an exercise of *appellate* jurisdiction, thus avoiding any difficulty under Marbury v. Madison's holding that Congress may not expand the scope of the Supreme Court's *original* jurisdiction. And § 14 permitted such review even though the First Judiciary Act provided for no appeal to the Court from a lower federal court's judgment of conviction in a criminal case. See p. 343, *supra*.

Finally, the Bollman opinion stated that the jurisdiction of the federal courts to issue the writ must be conferred by statute, and is not an "inherent" power.[2] Thus, Ex parte Dorr, 44 U.S. (3 How.) 103 (1845), affirmed that the federal courts lacked power under § 14, in view of its proviso, to issue the writ to one held under authority of *state* law.

(3) *Ante-Bellum Legislation*. Subsequent enactments progressively reduced the class of prisoners excluded from the writ by the proviso—articulating, at the same time, specific grounds on which the writ might issue.

(a) The Force Act of 1833, countering South Carolina's resistance to the "Tariff of Abominations", provided in section 7 (4 Stat. 634–35) that "either of the justices of the Supreme Court, or a judge of any district court of the United States, in addition to the authority already conferred by law, shall have power to grant writs of habeas corpus in all cases of a prisoner or prisoners, in jail or confinement, where he or they shall be committed or confined on, or by any authority or law, for any act done, or omitted to be done, in pursuance of a law of the United States, or any order, process, or decree, of any judge or court thereof, anything in any act of Congress to the contrary notwithstanding."

(b) Following British protests that the New York murder trial of a Canadian soldier violated the law of nations (the homicide was claimed to be an act of

---

1. For the contrary view—that § 14 merely ratified a court's power to employ habeas corpus in aid of jurisdiction otherwise conferred—see Paschal, *The Constitution and Habeas Corpus*, 1970 Duke L.J. 605, also discussed at p. 1369, note 2, *infra*.

2. For discussion of other aspects of Bollman, see pp. 1369–70, *infra*.

state),[3] the Act of Aug. 29, 1842, 5 Stat. 539–40, authorized Justices and district judges to "grant writs of habeas corpus" in certain cases involving prisoners who are "subjects or citizens of a foreign State, and domiciled therein" and are held under federal or state law. Decisions of Justices and judges were made appealable to the circuit court and then to the Supreme Court.

(4) *The Act of 1867.* The most significant expansion of the writ—to encompass generally persons held under *state* law—came with the Act of February 5, 1867, 14 Stat. 385. It provided broadly that "the several courts of the United States, and the several justices and judges of such courts, within their respective jurisdictions, in addition to the authority already conferred by law, shall have power to grant writs of habeas corpus in all cases where any person may be restrained of his or her liberty in violation of the constitution, or of any treaty or law of the United States * * *." The Act also prescribed the procedure on the writ; authorized appeals to the circuit court from decisions of Justices, judges or inferior courts and from the circuit court to the Supreme Court;[4] and declared void all state proceedings against the prisoner, pending a determination on the writ.[5]

(5) *Subsequent Congressional Action.* The foregoing provisions were codified in Title 13 of the Revised Statutes of 1874, §§ 751–66, and survived without important change until 1948. See 28 U.S.C. § 451 *et seq.* (1940).

   (a) The 1948 revision codified in 28 U.S.C. §§ 2241–55 the provisions relating to habeas corpus. The revision did not significantly change the grounds on which detention could be challenged or the prisoners to whom the writ extends. But it effected some important alterations of procedure; established a section (2254) dealing specifically with challenges to custody resulting from conviction in state custody;[6] and for the first time gave statutory recognition to the judge-made rule requiring exhaustion of state remedies prior to seeking the writ in federal court, see § 2254(b) and (c), discussed at pp. 1443-44, *infra.*

   In addition, the revision created a new statutory motion in § 2255 for federal prisoners collaterally attacking their convictions. The § 2255 motion is the exclusive post-conviction remedy for federal prisoners, unless it is found (as it has not been) to be "inadequate or ineffective to test the legality" of detention. See generally Sec. 3, *infra.*

---

3. See People v. McCleod, 25 Wend. 483 (1841); 2 Warren, The Supreme Court in United States History 98 (rev.ed.1947).

4. This was the provision repealed by the Act of March 27, 1868, 15 Stat. 44, involved in Ex parte McCardle, p. 356, *supra.* The right to appeal was restored by the Act of March 3, 1885, 23 Stat. 437.

5. Decisions under each of the foregoing statutory formulations are collected in 18 Fed. 68 (1884).

For further discussion of the 1867 Act, see pp. 1364-68, *infra.*

6. Prior to the 1948 revision, the statute provided that on an application for habeas, the court, Justice or judge shall "forth-with award a writ of habeas corpus, unless it appears from the petition itself that the party is not entitled thereto," and that the "person making the return shall at the same time bring the body of the party before the judge who granted the writ." Rev.Stat. § 755, 28 U.S.C. §§ 455, 458 (1940). But Walker v. Johnston, 312 U.S. 275 (1941), sustained the practice (later ratified in 1948 by § 2243) of issuing a rule to show cause rather than the writ itself, thereby avoiding a useless grant of the writ, and consequent production of the prisoner and witnesses, when the record makes clear that there is no basis for relief.

For discussion of other procedural changes, see Parker, *Limiting the Abuse of Habeas Corpus,* 8 F.R.D. 171, 174–75 (1949).

(b) In 1966 Congress added subsections 2244(b) and (c), which further specify the effect of previous federal adjudications on a federal habeas petition. It also enacted § 2254(d), which provides that if state court factfindings were made in a procedurally fair manner, a federal habeas court must treat them as presumptively correct and may not depart from them absent "convincing" evidence that they were erroneous. See p. 1372, *infra*.[7]

NOTE ON COURTS, JUSTICES, AND JUDGES AUTHORIZED TO GRANT THE WRIT

(1) *Territorial Jurisdiction: Location of The Petitioner.* Section 2241(a) vests authority to grant the writ in the Supreme Court and the district courts, any Justice of the Supreme Court and any circuit judge, but only "within their respective jurisdictions".[1] That limitation, as initially interpreted in Ahrens v. Clark, 335 U.S. 188 (1948), permitted a district court to entertain a petition only with respect to a person detained within its territorial jurisdiction. The Court thus held that the District Court for the District of Columbia could not issue the writ for persons detained at Ellis Island, New York—even though they were held by order of the U.S. Attorney General.

The provisions construed in Ahrens were legislatively modified (1) as to federal prisoners, by the 1948 revision, see 28 U.S.C. § 2255 (federal prisoners must attack their convictions in the sentencing court, not the district of incarceration); and (2) as to state prisoners, by the Act of September 19, 1966, 80 Stat. 811, see 28 U.S.C. § 2241(d)(prisoners attacking convictions in states comprising two or more federal districts may seek habeas in district where incarcerated *or* where convicting court sat). See Nelson v. George, 399 U.S. 224, 228 n. 5 (1970).

Ahrens' interpretation of § 2241(a) was overruled in Braden v. 30th Judicial Circuit Court, 410 U.S. 484 (1973)(6–3). There, a detainer had been filed against an Alabama prisoner to assure that he would be turned over to Kentucky for trial when his Alabama sentence (on an unrelated charge) expired. He filed a petition in the federal district court in Kentucky, alleging denial of his constitutional right to a speedy trial in Kentucky and seeking an order compelling his immediate trial there. The Supreme Court upheld the district court's jurisdiction, concluding that § 2241(a) requires only that the court "have jurisdiction over the custodian" (pp. 495).

The Court stated that "developments since Ahrens have had a profound impact on the continuing vitality of that decision" (p. 497). It pointed to §§ 2255 and 2241(d) as exemplifying Congress' recognition of the desirability of

---

7. Note also the provision of the Anti–Drug Abuse Act of 1988, 102 Stat. 4393, codified at 21 U.S.C. § 848(q)(4)(B), giving indigent petitioners under sentence of death the right to appointed counsel in § 2254 and § 2255 proceedings.

1. This represents a change from prior law in the unexplained exclusion of the district judges, see 28 U.S.C. § 452 (1940). The courts of appeals (as distinguished from their judges) have never been authorized to grant the writ, see Whitney v. Dick, 202 U.S. 132 (1906), except under the "all writs" provision, 28 U.S.C. § 1651, in aid of appellate jurisdiction in a pending case, see Adams v. United States, 317 U.S. 269 (1942); Price v. Johnston, 334 U.S. 266 (1948). (From 1911 until corrected by the Judiciary Act of 1925, 43 Stat. 940, circuit judges lacked authority to grant the writ unless specially assigned to hold a district court. See Craig v. Hecht, 263 U.S. 255, 271 (1923).)

resolving habeas cases in a court having close contact with the underlying controversy. Another development—"the emergence of new classes of prisoners who are able to petition for habeas corpus because of the adoption of a more expansive definition of the 'custody' requirement", see pp. 1450-54, *infra*—now permitted a "petitioner held in one State to attack a detainer lodged against him by another" (p. 498).

The Court concluded that Ahrens, rather than creating a rigid rule about jurisdiction over the petitioner, should be confined to its facts—on which it was correctly decided, since not only the prisoners but those holding them were located in New York, and no showing had been made that the District of Columbia was a more convenient forum. In Braden, by contrast, "[w]e cannot assume that Congress intended" to require "Kentucky to defend its action in a distant State" (p. 499).[2]

See also 28 U.S.C. § 1631, enacted in 1982, which provides that a court lacking jurisdiction shall, "if it is in the interest of justice", transfer the action to a court in which it could have been brought.

(2) *Territorial Jurisdiction: Location of The Custodian.* What if there is no *custodian* within the territorial reach of the district court? In Schlanger v. Seamans, 401 U.S. 487 (1971), the Court held that a federal district court in Arizona could not entertain a petition from an Air Force enlisted man on temporary duty in Arizona, since nobody who could be deemed his "custodian" (*i.e.*, his commanding officer or the Secretary of the Air Force) was in the state. But the teeth of this decision were drawn the next Term in Strait v. Laird, 406 U.S. 341 (1972), holding that an inactive Army reservist could petition for habeas (to review a failure to grant discharge as a conscientious objector) in California, where he was domiciled. Even though all of his superior officers were in Indiana, they were "present" in California because they processed his discharge application through Army personnel in that state.

Compare the decision in Ex parte Endo, 323 U.S. 283 (1944). Petitioner applied for the writ in the Northern District of California—where she was being held in a Relocation Center—and appealed from its denial. The Supreme Court held that her subsequent removal to Utah did not cause the District Court to lose jurisdiction because there remained within the district a custodian—the assistant director of the War Relocation Authority. The decision was explained in Ahrens v. Clark, Paragraph (1), *supra*, 335 U.S. at 193, as "in conformity with the policy underlying [then] Rule 45(1) of the Court", which provided that pending "review of a decision refusing a writ of habeas corpus, the custody of the prisoner shall not be disturbed." For the current, somewhat different, provision, see Sup.Ct.R. 36.[3]

---

2. A footnote suggested that the district of confinement had concurrent habeas jurisdiction—subject to possible transfer under § 1404(a) to a more convenient venue (p. 499 n. 15).

The three dissenters argued that it was for Congress, not the courts, to bring § 2241(a) into line with new developments.

3. What happens if no custodian remains within the district after the petition is filed and the custodian is served? In cases in which a member of the armed services, after filing a petition naming as respondent the commanding officer, was transferred out of the district, the Supreme Court has dismissed the petition as moot. See United States ex rel. Innes v. Crystal, 319 U.S. 755 (1943); United States ex rel. Lynn v. Downer, 322 U.S. 756 (1944).

(3) *Original Application in the Supreme Court.* Since 1789, the Supreme Court, and its Justices, have had authority to issue the writ directly. See Ex parte Bollman, p. 1340, *supra.* The Court's early practice was to exercise jurisdiction if the petition made the necessary showing of defect of "jurisdiction" in the lower court authorizing the detention. See, *e.g.,* Ex parte Siebold, 100 U.S. 371 (1879).[4] In such a case, the Court declared in Ex parte Yarbrough, 110 U.S. 651, 653 (1884), "it is not only within the authority of the Supreme Court, but it is its duty to inquire into the cause of commitment * * *, and if found to be as charged, a matter of which such a court had no jurisdiction, to discharge a prisoner from confinement."

The Court's concept of judicial duty went through drastic change.[5] As stated in Ex parte Abernathy, 320 U.S. 219, 219 (1943): "the jurisdiction conferred on this Court * * * to issue writs of habeas corpus in aid of its appellate jurisdiction * * * is discretionary * * * and this Court does not, save in exceptional circumstances, exercise it in cases where an adequate remedy may be had in a lower federal court, or, if the relief sought is from the judgment of a state court, where the petitioner has not exhausted his remedies in the state courts." *Cf.* Ex parte Peru, 318 U.S. 578 (1943), p. 336, *supra.* See generally Chap. III, Sec. 3, *supra.*

In this century, the Court appears to have granted relief in cases involving direct recourse to its habeas jurisdiction in only three instances. In Ex parte Hudgings, 249 U.S. 378, 384–85 (1919), a district court had summarily adjudged the petitioner in contempt for committing perjury. Ruling that perjury as such is not contempt, and noting the danger to liberty posed by the district court's approach, the Court held the case "an exception to the general rules of procedure to which we have at the outset referred" and proceeded to reach the merits. See also Matter of Heff, 197 U.S. 488 (1905)(petitioner's attack on constitutionality of statute under which he was convicted had already been rejected by court of appeals in another case; statute held unconstitutional and prisoner discharged); Ex parte Grossman, 267 U.S. 87 (1925)(commitment for criminal contempt despite Presidential pardon; Attorney General, urging Presidential power, supported petitioner; prisoner discharged).

The present Sup.Ct.R. 20.4(a) states: "To justify the granting of a writ of habeas corpus, the petitioner must show that exceptional circumstances warrant the exercise of the Court's discretionary powers, and that adequate relief cannot be obtained in any other form or from any other court. This writ is rarely granted."[6]

---

4. *Cf.* Ex parte Virginia, 100 U.S. 339 (1879), where the petition was entertained before trial on a challenge to the statute underlying the indictment.

5. Three major factors seem to have produced the change: (1) the Act of March 3, 1885, 23 Stat. 437, restoring an appeal to the Supreme Court from circuit court judgments in habeas cases, as provided by the Act of 1867 and withdrawn in 1868 (see p. 356, *supra*); (2) the decision in Ex parte Royall, 117 U.S. 241, 254 (1886), affirming broad discretion to deny the writ to a state prisoner seeking to challenge in advance of trial the validity of the state statute under which the

indictment was brought; and (3) the establishment in 1889 and 1891 of an appeal from convictions in federal criminal cases, see p. 1636 & note 3, *infra.*

6. The principles guiding the Supreme Court on original applications for the writ are presumably followed by its members in the exercise of their authority as Justices. For an express statement to this effect, see Justice Douglas' opinion in United States ex rel. Norris v. Swope, 72 S.Ct. 1020 (1952); *cf.* Rosoto v. Warden, 83 S.Ct. 1788 (1963)(Harlan, J.). Such applications have, however, occasionally been denied on the merits. See, *e.g.,* the unreported opinions of Justice Reed

For an admirable review, see Oaks, *The "Original" Writ of Habeas Corpus in the Supreme Court*, 1962 Sup.Ct.Rev. 153.

(4) *Transfer of Petitions from Appellate Courts.* Since 1948, the Supreme Court, Supreme Court Justices, and circuit judges have been expressly authorized to "decline to entertain an application for the writ" and to transfer it to the district court "having jurisdiction to entertain it." 28 U.S.C. § 2241(b). See, *e.g.*, Chaapel v. Cochran, 369 U.S. 869 (1962); Byrnes v. Walker, 371 U.S. 937 (1962). See generally Oaks, Paragraph (3), *supra*, at 194.

SECTION 2. COLLATERAL ATTACK ON STATE JUDGMENTS OF CONVICTION

INTRODUCTORY NOTE ON THE OPERATION OF FEDERAL HABEAS CORPUS JURISDICTION FOR STATE PRISONERS

Federal habeas corpus jurisdiction provides a method for prisoners convicted in state court to obtain federal court review of federal constitutional questions that were decided adversely to them by the state courts. Section 2254 specifically governs such cases. (Post-conviction relief for *federal prisoners* is governed by 28 U.S.C. § 2255, discussed in Sec. 3, *infra*.) Habeas corpus is not an appeal from, but rather a collateral attack upon, the state criminal conviction. And unlike most collateral attacks, habeas proceedings are not governed by the ordinary rules of res judicata, thus permitting the federal court to relitigate federal issues that were fully and fairly litigated in state court.

Decisional law has woven an intricate web of doctrinal rules shaping the habeas jurisdiction. The following general (and necessarily simplified) overview of how this jurisdiction operates today in actions commenced by state prisoners may therefore be useful.

A. Cognizable Issues

(1) *The Statutory Grant.* For all practical purposes, federal habeas corpus relief is limited to claims that the state court proceedings leading to the defendant's detention were infected with federal constitutional error. See pp. 1360-61, *infra*. Studies have found that although most state prisoners are convicted by guilty plea, roughly 70–80% of habeas petitioners were convicted after a trial.[1]

However, not all constitutional issues that the Supreme Court could consider on direct review of a state criminal conviction are open to the federal habeas court. Two limitations are of particular importance:

in Ex parte Taylor Seals, September 4 and November 23, 1943.

The power of a justice to grant a writ returnable before the full Court was affirmed in Ex parte Clarke, 100 U.S. 399, 403 (1879).

1. Flango, Habeas Corpus in State and Federal Courts 36 (1994); Robinson, An Empirical Study of Federal Habeas Corpus Review of State Court Judgments 7 (1979); Faust, Rubenstein & Yackle, *The Great Writ in Action: Empirical Light on the Federal Habeas Corpus Debate*, 18 N.Y.U.Rev.L. & Soc. Change 637, 678 (1991).

First, a habeas court lacks the power to award relief when the prisoner alleges only that the state court erred in denying a motion to suppress evidence under the Fourth Amendment. See pp. 1376-85, *infra*.

Second, subject to the narrowest possible exceptions, a habeas court lacks power to award relief when the prisoner's constitutional claim is based on "new law"—*i.e.*, a constitutional rule that was not dictated by precedent at the time that the prisoner's conviction became final on direct review. See pp. 1392-1413, *infra*.

B. Prerequisites to Review

A state prisoner seeking to obtain federal habeas relief must satisfy two preconditions.

(1) *Custody*. By its nature, habeas corpus extends only to persons in custody at the time that they file their federal petition. See 28 U.S.C. § 2241(c)(3); pp. 1450-54, *infra*. Custody is a technical term, which has been extended from one who is in physical custody to include one who is subject to parole or probation conditions. But a convict who has served the entire sentence (including parole or probation terms) before filing a habeas petition, or whose only penalty was a monetary fine, is not in custody and may not obtain relief.

(2) *Exhaustion of State Remedies*. A prisoner may not seek habeas relief without having first exhausted state remedies. See 28 U.S.C. § 2254(b-c); pp. 1443-50, *infra*. Exhaustion refers only to remedies still available at the time the habeas corpus petition is filed—not to remedies no longer available.

Typically, the exhaustion requirement obliges a prisoner to pursue direct appellate review in the state courts. There is no need, however, to seek Supreme Court review of the state court conviction. Nor, ordinarily, is there any need to pursue state post-conviction remedies as to issues decided on direct review; but those remedies do have to be exhausted as to an issue not previously presented to the state courts (as might be true, for example, of claims of ineffective assistance of counsel or of non-disclosure of exculpatory evidence). Studies suggest that 30–50% of petitions are dismissed for failure to exhaust.[2]

Note the important interaction of the custody and exhaustion requirements: in cases involving short sentences, a prisoner may no longer be in custody by the time state remedies have been exhausted.

C. Initiation and Nature of the Proceedings

(1) *Filing a Petition*. A state prisoner in custody, having exhausted state remedies, may file a petition for a writ of habeas corpus in federal district court, seeking relief on the ground that one or more federal constitutional errors infected the state court proceedings that resulted in the petitioner's detention. The state officer having custody of the petitioner (ordinarily the prison warden or the director of the state correctional system) is named as respondent. (The convention is to refer to habeas decisions by the prisoner's name. For example, the Supreme Court's decision in Wainwright v. Sykes, p. 1415, *infra*, is usually called "Sykes" rather than "Wainwright" because Wainwright was the name of the warden.)

---

2. See p. 1449, *infra*.

(2) *Civil Nature of Proceedings and Applicable Rules.* Habeas corpus actions are *civil* proceedings. Since 1977, they have been subject to the special "Rules Governing Section 2254 Cases in the United States District Courts" (the "§ 2254 Rules"), Rule 11 of which states: "The Federal Rules of Civil Procedure, to the extent that they are not inconsistent with these rules, may be applied, when appropriate, to petitions filed under these rules."

(3) *Availability of Counsel.* The great majority of petitioners are indigent, and studies have found that approximately 80–90% of petitioners lack counsel.[3] The Supreme Court has held that petitioners generally have no *constitutional* right to counsel in state or federal collateral attacks on their convictions.[4] Thus, any federal right to counsel derives from statutes or court rules.

(a) *Capital Cases.* A 1988 enactment gives indigents in habeas actions who are attacking a capital sentence or conviction a statutory right to appointed counsel. 102 Stat. 4393, codified at 21 U.S.C. § 848(q)(4)(B). In McFarland v. Scott, 114 S.Ct. 2568 (1994), the Supreme Court ruled, 6–3, that § 848(q)(4)(B) permits the appointment of counsel even before a habeas petition has been filed, in order to provide assistance in preparing the petition. The Court also ruled, 5–4, that despite the language of 28 U.S.C. § 2251 authorizing the issuance of stays of execution when "a habeas corpus proceeding is pending", the provision should be read *"in pari materia"* with § 848(q)(4)(B), and thus a stay may be issued as soon as a death row inmate requests appointment of counsel to help prepare a habeas petition.

---

3. See Flango, note 1, *supra*, at 37; Robinson, note 1, *supra*, at 9.

4. *E.g.*, Pennsylvania v. Finley, 481 U.S. 551, 554–55 (1987); Johnson v. Avery, 393 U.S. 483, 488 (1969).

However, in Bounds v. Smith, 430 U.S. 817, 828 (1977), the Court ruled that "the fundamental constitutional right of access to the courts" requires prison authorities to provide prisoners with adequate law libraries or adequate assistance from law-trained persons to permit preparation of meaningful legal papers. (In Casey v. Lewis, 43 F.3d 1261 (9th Cir.1994), the lower courts found Arizona's system of prison libraries and legal assistance to violate Bounds. The Supreme Court granted certiorari, 115 S.Ct. 1997 (1995), apparently to review the detailed remedial order, which required, *inter alia,* opening the libraries for 50 hours a week, purchasing designated collections of judicial decisions, hiring professionally trained librarians, providing legal assistance to prisoners who (because they were in segregation or did not speak English) could not use the library, and allowing prisoners at least three 20-minute calls per week to their attorneys.)

The relationship between these two lines of decision was at issue in Murray v. Giarratano, 492 U.S. 1 (1989), a class action seeking injunctive relief against Virginia officials. The lower courts ordered the defendants to develop a plan to provide counsel upon request to death row inmates seeking post-conviction relief. They found Virginia's existing efforts (providing legal advisers in penal institutions and appointing counsel after a petition was filed) to be inadequate under Bounds in view of the inmates' limited time to prepare petitions, the special complexity of their cases, and the emotional burdens upon them. The Supreme Court reversed, 5–4. Four Justices ruled that Pennsylvania v. Finley applied no differently in capital cases and therefore controlled. Justice Kennedy provided the fifth vote. He acknowledged that capital cases are unusually complex and that many death sentences are vacated in post-conviction proceedings. But stressing that Bounds can be satisfied in many ways and that judicial capacity to design a comprehensive system of representation is limited, he was not prepared to hold Virginia's approach unconstitutional.

In Coleman v. Thompson, 501 U.S. 722, 755 (1991), the Court raised but did not answer the question whether there might be "an exception to the rule of Finley and Giarratano in those cases where state collateral review is the first place a prisoner can present a challenge to his conviction."

(b) *Non-Capital Cases*. Appointment of counsel in non-capital cases is governed by Rules 6(b) and 8(c) of the § 2254 Rules. The court *must* appoint counsel for an indigent petitioner if an evidentiary hearing is required (Rule 8(c)) or when necessary for effective utilization of discovery authorized by the court (Rule 6(b))—both of which are extremely rare. Otherwise, counsel may be appointed at any stage "if the interest of justice so requires" (Rule 8(c)).

(4) *Time Limits*. There is no statute of limitations for habeas proceedings.[5] Rule 9(a) does provide that a petition may be dismissed if the state "has been prejudiced in its ability to respond to the petition by delay in filing unless the petitioner shows that it is based on grounds of which he could not have had knowledge by the exercise of reasonable diligence before the circumstances prejudicial to the state occurred."[6] In Vasquez v. Hillery, 474 U.S. 254, 265 (1986), the Court ruled that difficulties in retrying the defendant (as distinguished from difficulties in responding to the petition) are not "prejudice" within the meaning of Rule 9(a).

D. Processing of Cases

(1) *Petition and Response*. Many habeas petitions are summarily dismissed. When the judge orders the warden to respond, often the response (sometimes accompanied by excerpts from the record or by affidavits) establishes a basis for dismissal without further proceedings. Discovery in habeas proceedings proceeds only as authorized in the court's discretion, see § 2254 Rules, Rule 6(a), and in practice is extremely limited. Evidentiary hearings to develop the facts are authorized by statute but rarely conducted.[7]

In the twelve month period ending September 30, 1994, of 10,659 petitions on which court action was taken, 10,550 were terminated "Before Pretrial", 50 "During or After Pretrial", and only 59, or 0.5%, "During or After Trial". Annual Report of the Director of the Administrative Office of the United States Courts A–37 (1994)(Table C–4).

(2) *Relitigation of Facts*. Because ordinary rules of res judicata do not apply in habeas proceedings, a habeas court is not bound to follow or defer to a state court's decision on a question of law or on the application of law to the facts. But 28 U.S.C. § 2254(d) sets forth rules that essentially require the federal court to presume that state court findings of historical fact are correct unless there was some defect in the state court factfinding process. See pp. 1371-76, *infra*.

(3) *The Role of Magistrate Judges*. In many federal districts federal magistrate judges have the primary responsibility for processing habeas petitions. The Federal Magistrates Act permits a district judge to designate a magistrate judge to handle all aspects of a habeas proceeding. 28 U.S.C. § 636(b)(1)(B).

---

5. Over the years there have been legislative proposals to add a limitations period. Separate bills passed by the House and Senate in 1995 both include (i) a one-year limitations period (subject to tolling) and (ii) in states that meet specified conditions, a 180–day limitations period for petitioners under sentence of death. See pp. 1458-59, *infra*.

6. See generally Clinton, *Rule 9 of the Federal Habeas Corpus Rules: A Case Study on the Need for Reform of the Rules Enabling Acts*, 63 Iowa L.Rev. 15 (1977).

7. See Weisselberg, *Evidentiary Hearings in Federal Habeas Corpus Cases*, 1990 B.Y.U.L.Rev. 131, 165–68.

If a party objects to the magistrate judge's proposed findings and recommendations, the district judge must make a "de novo determination" with respect to any such contested matter.[8]

E. Procedural Default

(1) *Forfeiture of Federal Claims.* Sometimes a habeas petitioner failed to present the state courts with the federal claim raised in the habeas petition—or failed to present it in accordance with state procedural rules (*e.g.*, by failing to raise it on a timely basis). And as a result of that procedural default, the state courts may have refused to reach the issue. Where that is so, subject to only the narrowest exceptions, the federal habeas court will not consider the defaulted claim. See pp. 1418–40, *infra.*

Note that procedural defaults typically involve a failure to pursue opportunities to litigate in state court that once were but no longer are available. A failure to exhaust state remedies, by contrast, involves opportunities to litigate in state court that remain available as of the time that the habeas petition is filed.

F. Remedy, Appeals and Successive Petitions

(1) *Relief.* The only remedy awarded is release from custody, but as is true of reversals of conviction on appeal, the remedy is tailored to the nature of the constitutional violation. For example, if a petitioner had been convicted for conduct that was constitutionally protected (for example, burning the American flag), the remedy would be unconditional release from custody. If instead a constitutional error occurred in the state proceedings (for example, admission of a confession in violation of the Miranda rules), the remedy would be conditional, requiring release from custody only if a retrial and re-conviction do not occur within a specified period.

(2) *Appeals.* The warden may appeal a district court's grant of relief. A prisoner may appeal a denial of relief only after first obtaining a "certificate of probable cause" from the district judge, or, if the district judge refuses, from a judge of the court of appeals. 28 U.S.C. § 2253; Fed.R.App.Proc. 22(b). A certificate should issue if the appeal presents a question of substance that is "debatable among jurists of reason" or is not "squarely foreclosed by statute, rule or authoritative court decision". Barefoot v. Estelle, 463 U.S. 880, 893 n. 4, 894 (1983).

(3) *Successive Petitions.* Since 1991, a prisoner's ability to file more than one federal habeas corpus petition has been subject to very tight restrictions, which parallel the restrictions on raising in a habeas corpus petition issues not properly raised in state courts. See pp. 1440–43, *infra.*

---

8. That obligation was narrowly construed, however, in United States v. Raddatz, 447 U.S. 667 (1980), p. 439, *supra.* There, the Supreme Court ruled that after a magistrate (as they were then called) had heard a motion to suppress evidence in a federal criminal prosecution, the district judge was not obliged to rehear the evidence even with respect to critical issues of credibility.

Brown v. Allen

344 U.S. 443, 73 S.Ct. 397, 97 L.Ed. 469 (1953).
Certiorari to the United States Court of Appeals for the Fourth Circuit.

[Brown involved three consolidated habeas cases (Brown, Daniels, and Speller), each filed by a black man convicted in North Carolina of interracial rape or murder and sentenced to death. All three prisoners claimed that there had been racial discrimination in the selection of his petit jury in violation of the Equal Protection Clause; in Brown and Daniels, the prisoners also complained of discrimination in the selection of the grand jury and of the admission at trial of an allegedly coerced confession.

[In the Daniels case, the Supreme Court of North Carolina, on direct appeal from the judgment of conviction, had refused to consider the merits of these federal constitutional claims because the appeal had been filed one day late. The U.S. Supreme Court held that this state court procedural default precluded the exercise of habeas review.[1]

[The Brown and Speller petitions presented federal constitutional issues that had been fully litigated, with the aid of counsel, in the state trial courts; rejected on the merits by the Supreme Court of North Carolina (which had affirmed the convictions); and made the basis of unsuccessful efforts to obtain Supreme Court review of the judgment of the Supreme Court of North Carolina. In considering those habeas petitions, the federal district court examined the state trial court record, and, in Speller's case, took additional evidence. It then adopted the state court's findings on the federal constitutional issues and denied relief, essentially on the basis that those findings were supported by the evidence and should not be relitigated in federal court. In Speller's case, the district judge stated that a "habeas corpus proceeding is not available * * * for the purpose of raising the identical question passed upon in [the state] Courts", 99 F.Supp. 92, 95; but he added, as an alternative ground, that the petitioner had failed to substantiate his constitutional claims. The Court of Appeals for the Fourth Circuit affirmed in both cases.

[In the Supreme Court, eight opinions were filed, totalling more than 100 pages. The Justices divided both on the central question presented by the Brown and Speller petitions—whether a federal court exercising habeas jurisdiction may re-examine the merits of federal constitutional claims that were denied by the state courts—and on the merits of those constitutional claims.

[The Court's handling of the case was unusual. The "opinion of the Court" was written by Justice Reed—even though on one issue, he spoke for only a minority.[2] His opinion, joined by Chief Justice Vinson and Justices Burton, Clark, and Minton, is not a model of clarity;[3] some language suggests that federal courts should defer to the state court's substantive determination,

1. Daniels, and the general question of the impact of state court procedural defaults on the exercise of habeas corpus jurisdiction, are discussed at pp. 1413-40, *infra*.

2. That issue was whether the Supreme Court's denial of certiorari from the state supreme court's decision affirming the convictions should be taken by the habeas court as reflecting the judgment that there was no

denial of constitutional rights. The majority said no.

3. But see Liebman, *Apocalypse Next Time?: The Anachronistic Attack on Habeas Corpus/Direct Review Parity*, 92 Colum.L.Rev. 1997, 2020 (1992)(dismissing criticisms of the "terseness" of Reed's opinion because he had laid out his views in prior decisions).

while other language suggests they should not.[4] In the end, Justice Reed did reach the merits of Brown's and Speller's constitutional claims, and found them wanting.

[Justice Frankfurter filed an elaborate opinion that no other Justice formally joined, but with which four other Justices (Black, Douglas, Burton, and Clark) indicated their agreement in separate opinions. Justice Frankfurter described his opinion as "designed to make explicit and detailed matters that are also the concern of Mr. Justice Reed's opinion", and he stated that "[t]he views of the Court * * * may thus be drawn from the two opinions jointly" (p. 497).[5]

[Because Justice Frankfurter's opinion reflects the way that the case has been understood by subsequent Supreme Court decisions, substantial portions of it are presented here as best reflecting the position of the majority.]

■ Opinion of FRANKFURTER, J.

* * *

I

* * *

II

* * *

I deem it appropriate to begin by making explicit some basic considerations underlying the federal habeas corpus jurisdiction. Experience may be summoned to support the belief that most claims in these attempts to obtain review of State convictions are without merit. Presumably they are adequately dealt with in the State courts. Again, no one can feel more strongly than I do that a casual, unrestricted opening of the doors of the federal courts to these claims not only would cast an undue burden upon those courts, but would also disregard our duty to support and not weaken the sturdy enforcement of their criminal laws by the States. That wholesale opening of State prison doors by federal courts is, however, not at all the real issue before us is best indicated by

4. Part II of Justice Reed's opinion is entitled, "Effect of Former Proceedings." Here, he observed that "where there is material conflict of fact in the transcripts of evidence as to deprivation of constitutional rights, the District Court may properly depend upon the state's resolution of the issue. In other circumstances the state adjudication carries the weight that federal practice gives to the conclusion of a court of last resort of another jurisdiction on federal constitutional issues. It is not *res judicata*" (p. 458). But he stated (p. 459) that the district court had power "to reexamine federal constitutional issues even after trial and review by a state".

Justice Reed then proceeded in Part III, entitled "Right to a Plenary Hearing", to appear to conflate two issues that today would be viewed separately. The first was whether the district court was required to

hold an evidentiary hearing to develop further facts. On this point, Justice Reed said that the decision rested in the district court's discretion. The second issue was whether, in deciding the merits of the petition, the federal court was always to decide questions of federal constitutional law de novo, or could defer to the state court's prior determination. On this point, the opinion appears at some points to suggest that a district court may defer (pp. 462–65), but in the end proceeds to analyze the merits de novo.

5. On the merits, Justice Frankfurter voted to reverse on the ground that the courts below had incorrectly viewed themselves as foreclosed from considering the constitutional merits.

In a separate opinion, Justices Douglas and Black voted to reverse on the ground that the record revealed constitutional error.

a survey recently prepared in the Administrative Office of the United States Courts for the Conference of Chief Justices: of all federal question applications for habeas corpus, some not even relating to State convictions, only 67 out of 3,702 applications were granted in the last seven years. And "only a small number" of these 67 applications resulted in release from prison: "a more detailed study over the last four years * * * shows that out of 29 petitions granted, there were only 5 petitioners who were released from state penitentiaries."[11] The meritorious claims are few, but our procedures must ensure that those few claims are not stifled by undiscriminating generalities. * * *

For surely it is an abuse to deal too casually and too lightly with rights guaranteed by the Federal Constitution, even though they involve limitations upon State power and may be invoked by those morally unworthy. Under the guise of fashioning a procedural rule, we are not justified in wiping out the practical efficacy of a jurisdiction conferred by Congress on the District Courts. Rules which in effect treat all these cases indiscriminately as frivolous do not fall far short of abolishing this head of jurisdiction.

Congress could have left the enforcement of federal constitutional rights governing the administration of criminal justice in the States exclusively to the State courts. These tribunals are under the same duty as the federal courts to respect rights under the United States Constitution. See The Federalist, No. 82; Claflin v. Houseman, 93 U.S. 130; Testa v. Katt, 330 U.S. 386. Indeed, the jurisdiction given to the federal courts to issue writs of habeas corpus by the First Judiciary Act, § 14, extended only to prisoners in custody under authority of the United States. It was not until the Act of 1867 that the power to issue the writ was extended to an applicant under sentence of a State court. It is not for us to determine whether this power should have been vested in the federal courts. As Mr. Justice Bradley, with his usual acuteness, commented not long after the passage of that Act, "although it may appear unseemly that a prisoner, after conviction in a state court, should be set at liberty by a single judge on *habeas corpus*, there seems to be no escape from the law." Ex parte Bridges, 2 Woods (5th Cir.) 428, 432. * * * It is for this Court to give fair effect to the habeas corpus jurisdiction as enacted by Congress. By giving the federal courts that jurisdiction, Congress has embedded into federal legislation the historic function of habeas corpus adapted to reaching an enlarged area of claims.

In exercising the power thus bestowed, the District Judge must take due account of the proceedings that are challenged by the application for a writ. All that has gone before is not to be ignored as irrelevant. But the prior State determination of a claim under the United States Constitution cannot foreclose consideration of such a claim, else the State court would have the final say which the Congress, by the Act of 1867, provided it should not have. A State determination may help to define the claim urged in the application for the writ and may bear on the seriousness of the claim. That most claims are frivolous has an important bearing upon the procedure to be followed by a district judge. The prior State determination may guide his discretion in deciding upon the appropriate course to be followed in disposing of the application before him. The State record may serve to indicate the necessity of further pleadings or of a quick hearing to clear up an ambiguity, or the State record may show the claim

---

11. Habeas Corpus Cases in the Federal Courts Brought by State Prisoners, Administrative Office of the United States Courts 4 (Dec. 16, 1952).

to be frivolous or not within the competence of a federal court because solely dependent on State law.

It may be a matter of phrasing whether we say that the District Judge summarily denies an application for a writ by accepting the ruling of the State court or by making an independent judgment, though he does so on the basis of what the State record reveals. But since phrasing mirrors thought, it is important that the phrasing not obscure the true issue before a federal court. Our problem arises because Congress has told the District Judge to act on those occasions, however rare, when there are meritorious causes in which habeas corpus is the ultimate and only relief and designed to be such. Vague, undefined directions permitting the District Court to give "consideration" to a prior State determination fall short of appropriate guidance for bringing to the surface the meritorious case. They may serve indiscriminately to preclude a hearing where one should have been granted, and yet this basis for denial may be so woven into the texture of the result that an improper deference to a State court treatment of a constitutional issue cannot even be corrected on review. If we are to give effect to the statute and at the same time avoid improper intrusion into the State criminal process by federal judges * * *[,] we must direct them to probe the federal question while drawing on available records of prior proceedings to guide them in doing so.

Of course, experience cautions that the very nature and function of the writ of habeas corpus precludes the formulation of fool-proof standards which the 225 District Judges can automatically apply. * * * But it is important, in order to preclude individualized enforcement of the Constitution in different parts of the Nation, to lay down as specifically as the nature of the problem permits the standards or directions that should govern the District Judges in the disposition of applications for habeas corpus by prisoners under sentence of State courts.

First. Just as in all other litigation, a prima facie case must be made out by the petitioner. The application should be dismissed when it fails to state a federal question, or fails to set forth facts which, if accepted at face value, would entitle the applicant to relief. * * *

Second. Failure to exhaust an available State remedy is an obvious ground for denying the application. An attempt must have been made in the State court to present the claim now asserted in the District Court * * *. * * *

Third. If the record of the State proceedings is not filed, the judge is required to decide * * * whether it is more desirable to call for the record or to hold a hearing. * * *

Fourth. When the record of the State court proceedings is before the court, it may appear that the issue turns on basic facts and that the facts (in the sense of a recital of external events and the credibility of their narrators) have been tried and adjudicated against the applicant. Unless a vital flaw be found in the process of ascertaining such facts in the State court, the District Judge may accept their determination in the State proceeding and deny the application. On the other hand, State adjudication of questions of law cannot, under the habeas corpus statute, be accepted as binding. It is precisely these questions that the federal judge is commanded to decide. * * *

Fifth. Where the ascertainment of the historical facts does not dispose of the claim but calls for interpretation of the legal significance of such facts, the District Judge must exercise his own judgment on this blend of facts and their legal values. Thus, so-called mixed questions or the application of constitutional principles to the facts as found leave the duty of adjudication with the federal judge.

For instance, the question whether established primary facts underlying a confession prove that the confession was coerced or voluntary cannot rest on the State decision. * * * Although there is no need for the federal judge, if he could, to shut his eyes to the State consideration of such issues, no binding weight is to be attached to the State determination. The congressional requirement is greater. The State court cannot have the last say when it, though on fair consideration and what procedurally may be deemed fairness, may have misconceived a federal constitutional right.

* * *

These standards, addressed as they are to the practical situation facing the District Judge, recognize the discretion of judges to give weight to whatever may be relevant in the State proceedings, and yet preserve the full implication of the requirement of Congress that the District Judge decide constitutional questions presented by a State prisoner even after his claims have been carefully considered by the State courts. Congress has the power to distribute among the courts of the States and of the United States jurisdiction to determine federal claims. It has seen fit to give this Court power to review errors of federal law in State determinations, and in addition to give to the lower federal courts power to inquire into federal claims, by way of habeas corpus. Such power is in the spirit of our inherited law. It accords with, and is thoroughly regardful of, "the liberty of the subject" * * *.

The reliable figures of the Administrative Office of the United States Courts, showing that during the last four years five State prisoners, all told, were discharged by federal district courts, prove beyond peradventure that it is a baseless fear, a bogeyman, to worry lest State convictions be upset by allowing district courts to entertain applications for habeas corpus on behalf of prisoners under State sentence. Insofar as this jurisdiction enables federal district courts to entertain claims that State Supreme Courts have denied rights guaranteed by the United States Constitution, it is not a case of a lower court sitting in judgment on a higher court. It is merely one aspect of respecting the Supremacy Clause of the Constitution whereby federal law is higher than State law. It is for the Congress to designate the member in the hierarchy of the federal judiciary to express the higher law. The fact that Congress has authorized district courts to be the organ of the higher law rather than a Court of Appeals, or exclusively this Court, does not mean that it allows a lower court to overrule a higher court. It merely expresses the choice of Congress how the superior authority of federal law should be asserted.

* * *

The uniqueness of habeas corpus in the procedural armory of our law cannot be too often emphasized. It differs from all other remedies in that it is available to bring into question the legality of a person's restraint and to require justification for such detention. Of course this does not mean that prison doors may readily be opened. It does mean that explanation may be exacted why they should remain closed. * * *

The significance of the writ for the moral health of our kind of society has been amply attested by all the great commentators, historians and jurists, on our institutions. It has appropriately been characterized by Hallam as "the principal bulwark of English liberty." But the writ has potentialities for evil as well as for good. Abuse of the writ may undermine the orderly administration of justice and therefore weaken the forces of authority that are essential for civilization.

* * *

■ Mr. Justice Jackson, concurring in the result.

Controversy as to the undiscriminating use of the writ of habeas corpus by federal judges to set aside state court convictions is traceable to three principal causes: (1) this Court's use of the generality of the Fourteenth Amendment to subject state courts to increasing federal control, especially in the criminal law field; (2) *ad hoc* determination of due process of law issues by personal notions of justice instead of by known rules of law; and (3) the breakdown of procedural safeguards against abuse of the writ.

* * *

The fact that the substantive law of due process is and probably must remain so vague and unsettled as to invite farfetched or borderline petitions makes it important to adhere to procedures which enable courts readily to distinguish a probable constitutional grievance from a convict's mere gamble on persuading some indulgent judge to let him out of jail. Instead, this Court has sanctioned progressive trivialization of the writ until floods of stale, frivolous and repetitious petitions inundate the docket of the lower courts and swell our own. Judged by our own disposition of habeas corpus matters, they have, as a class, become peculiarly undeserving. It must prejudice the occasional meritorious application to be buried in a flood of worthless ones. He who must search a haystack for a needle is likely to end up with the attitude that the needle is not worth the search. Nor is it any answer to say that few of these petitions in any court really result in the discharge of the petitioner. That is the condemnation of the procedure which has encouraged frivolous cases. In this multiplicity of worthless cases, states are compelled to default or to defend the integrity of their judges and their official records, sometimes concerning trials or pleas that were closed many years ago. State Attorneys General recently have come habitually to ignore these proceedings, responding only when specially requested and sometimes not then. Some state courts have wearied of our repeated demands upon them and have declined to further elucidate grounds for their decisions. The assembled Chief Justices of the highest courts of the states have taken the unusual step of condemning the present practice by resolution.[13]

It cannot be denied that the trend of our decisions is to abandon rules of pleading or procedure which would protect the writ against abuse. Once upon a time the writ could not be substituted for appeal or other reviewing process but challenged only the legal competence or jurisdiction of the committing court. We have so departed from this principle that the profession now believes that the issues we *actually consider* on a federal prisoner's habeas corpus are substantially the same as would be considered on appeal.

Conflict with state courts is the inevitable result of giving the convict a virtual new trial before a federal court sitting without a jury. Whenever

13. Conference of Chief Justices—1952, 1952).
25 State Government, No. 11, p. 249 (Nov.

decisions of one court are reviewed by another, a percentage of them are reversed. That reflects a difference in outlook normally found between personnel comprising different courts. However, reversal by a higher court is not proof that justice is thereby better done. There is no doubt that if there were a super-Supreme Court, a substantial proportion of our reversals of state courts would also be reversed. We are not final because we are infallible, but we are infallible only because we are final.

* * *

It is sometimes said that *res judicata* has no application whatever in habeas corpus cases and surely it does not apply with all of its conventional severity. Habeas corpus differs from the ordinary judgment in that, although an adjudication has become final, the application is renewable, at least if new evidence and material is discovered or if, perhaps as the result of a new decision, a new law becomes applicable to the case. This is quite proper so long as its issues relate to jurisdiction. But call it *res judicata* or what one will, courts ought not to be obliged to allow a convict to litigate again and again exactly the same question on the same evidence. Nor is there any good reason why an identical contention rejected by a higher court should be reviewed on the same facts in a lower one. * * *

My conclusion is that * * * no lower federal court should entertain a petition except on the following conditions: (1) that the petition raises a jurisdictional question involving federal law on which the state law allowed no access to its courts, either by habeas corpus or appeal from the conviction, and that he therefore has no state remedy; or (2) that the petition shows that although the law allows a remedy, he was actually improperly obstructed from making a record upon which the question could be presented, so that his remedy by way of ultimate application to this Court for certiorari has been frustrated. There may be circumstances so extraordinary that I do not now think of them which would justify a departure from this rule, but the run-of-the-mill case certainly does not.

NOTE ON THE RULE OF BROWN v. ALLEN

A.   The Rationale of Brown v. Allen

(1) *The Scope of Federal Relitigation.* The basic principle of Brown v. Allen— that federal habeas courts may relitigate questions of federal constitutional law that were fully and fairly litigated in state court—has been controversial since its inception.[1] But as Justice Frankfurter noted, the scope of relitigation has never routinely extended to the basic, or historical, facts. Thus, for example, if in Brown the admissibility of the confession turned on the length of the interrogation, or on whether certain threats had been made, a federal court was permitted (though not obliged) to accept the state court's factfindings about what happened. (Statutory amendments in 1966 narrowed the federal district

---

1. Since Brown was decided, bills have repeatedly been introduced that would effectively permit federal habeas review only when the state courts did not afford the petitioner a "fair and adequate opportunity" to adjudicate his constitutional claim. A number have passed one House of Congress, but none has gone further. For discussion of these and other efforts to restrict the jurisdiction, see Note on Habeas Corpus Reform, pp. 1451–66, *infra.*

court's discretion by making state court factfindings presumptively binding. See p. 1372, *infra*.)   The federal *obligation* was limited to determining the appropriate standard for deciding whether a confession was admissible (a question of legal principle), and applying that standard to the facts as found (an application of law to fact, or "mixed" question).[2]   As a result, the vast majority of cases have been resolved on the state court record, without any evidentiary proceedings in federal court.

(2) *The Theory of Federal Relitigation.*   Justice Frankfurter viewed Congress as having clearly mandated federal relitigation of federal constitutional issues previously resolved in the state trial.   How persuasive do you find the following justifications for a congressional decision—or, insofar as the statute's meaning was less certain than Justice Frankfurter asserted, for a judicial interpretation of the habeas statute—calling for federal relitigation?

(a) *Appellate Review.*   One view of habeas begins with the premise that in view of the Supreme Court's limited docket, constitutional rights cannot be adequately protected by direct Supreme Court review of state court judgments resulting in detention.   Habeas jurisdiction, though not technically appellate review by district courts, serves as a substitute for Supreme Court appellate review to ensure that federal constitutional claims can be heard by a federal court.   See, *e.g.,* Justice Brennan's dissent in Stone v. Powell, p. 1376, *infra,* especially footnote 1; Hart, *The Supreme Court, 1958 Term, Foreword: The Time Chart of the Justices,* 73 Harv.L.Rev. 84, 105–07 (1959); Friedman, *A Tale of Two Habeas,* 73 Minn.L.Rev. 247 (1988); Liebman, *Apocalypse Next Time?: The Anachronistic Attack on Habeas Corpus/Direct Review Parity,* 92 Colum.L.Rev. 1997 (1992).

Consider these questions:

(i) Would acceptance of this view suggest that a habeas court must observe the same limitations—for example, on review of state court factual determinations, or on consideration of issues not properly raised in state court—that the Supreme Court would?   See generally Liebman, *supra* (so urging).

(ii) If state courts can be trusted to find the facts, why can't they be trusted to apply the law properly?   See Townsend v. Sain, 372 U.S. 293, 312 (1963)("It is the typical, not the rare, case in which constitutional claims turn upon the resolution of contested factual issues").

(iii) Why should federal review via habeas be only one-way—where the state courts denied claims of federal constitutional right—when on direct review the Supreme Court has jurisdiction to review state court decisions upholding federal rights?   See the *Note on Review of State Decisions Upholding Claims of Federal Right,* p. 536, *supra.*

---

2. In addition to requiring a habeas court ordinarily to defer to a state court determination of historical *facts,* § 2254(d), the 1966 amendments provide that the court shall treat as conclusive a previous *federal* adjudication (whether of law or fact) by the Supreme Court, § 2244(c), and may effectively treat as conclusive a previous *federal* adjudication by a habeas court, § 2244(b).

Should those amendments be viewed as having codified, by negative implication, Brown v. Allen's ruling that federal courts should not defer to a previous *state* adjudication on issues of *law* or on *application of law to fact?*

(iv) Why should federal court relitigation be limited to criminal cases, and then only to those eventuating in custody—thereby excluding federal adjudication of constitutional issues arising in state court civil cases, or the vast number of minor state criminal cases (those in which only a fine or short sentence has been imposed) in which the defendant is not in custody by the time state remedies have been exhausted? (For a response, see Friedman, *Pas de Deux: The Supreme Court and the Habeas Courts*, 66 S.Cal.L.Rev. 2467, 2485–90 (1993).)

(b) *Independent Inquiry Into Detention*. A quite different justification for the habeas jurisdiction was elaborated by Justice Brennan for the Court in Fay v. Noia, 372 U.S. 391, 430–31 (1963), p. 1415, *infra*: "The jurisdictional prerequisite [in habeas] is not the judgment of a state court but detention *simpliciter*. * * * And the broad power of the federal courts under 28 U.S.C. § 2243 * * * to 'determine the facts, and dispose of the matter as law and justice require,' is hardly characteristic of an appellate jurisdiction. Habeas lies to enforce the right of personal liberty * * *. * * * [I]t cannot revise the state court judgment; it can act only on the body of the petitioner".[3] See also Townsend v. Sain, p. 1371, *infra*; Reitz, *Federal Habeas Corpus: Postconviction Remedy for State Prisoners*, 108 U.Pa.L.Rev. 461 (1960); Amsterdam, *Search, Seizure and Section 2255: A Comment*, 112 U.Pa.L.Rev. 378 (1964); Wright & Sofaer, *Federal Habeas Corpus for State Prisoners: The Allocation of Fact–Finding Responsibility*, 75 Yale L.J. 895 (1966). On this view, the habeas court need not observe limits on the scope of review that would apply on direct review by the Supreme Court.

Professor Yackle offers the following argument in support of such a view: (a) in principle, federal courts ordinarily should have original or removal jurisdiction over all cases in which federal issues are raised (whether as part of the cause of action or by defense); (b) that principle is not observed as to state criminal cases in which federal constitutional issues arise, for there is no general provision for removal; (c) the absence of removal jurisdiction is justifiable, because the federal issues often arise only late in the game, and also because permitting removal would concentrate excessive coercive power in the federal courts; but (d) federal review (via habeas) must be available after conviction to provide the needed federal forum for the federal constitutional issues. See Yackle, *Explaining Habeas Corpus*, 60 N.Y.U.L.Rev. 991 (1985); Yackle, *The Habeas Hagioscope*, 66 S.Cal.L.Rev. 2331 (1993).

Is Professor Yackle's starting premise—that a party should be entitled to litigate a case raising a federal question in federal court—a convincing one? If accepted, wouldn't it imply, also, that the custody requirement—which prevents many state convicts from obtaining federal court adjudication of federal constitutional questions—should be abolished?[4] Compare Meltzer, *Habeas*

---

3. Whatever the merits of this view, wasn't Justice Harlan correct when he objected in dissent that the majority's effort to distinguish review of a judgment—though literally accurate—was formalistic, as "termination of the detention [by granting a writ of habeas corpus] necessarily nullifies the judgment" (p. 469)?

4. Yackle makes clear that his views call for broadening federal removal in civil matters to embrace cases in which the federal issue arises only by way of defense (60 N.Y.U.L.Rev. at 1032).

Corpus Jurisdiction: The Limits of Models, 66 S.Cal.L.Rev. 2507, 2507–13 (1993) with Yackle, Reclaiming the Federal Courts 287–88 n. 157 (1994).[5]

If state courts are inferior to federal courts in adjudicating constitutional rights implicated in the criminal process, is habeas relief—which comes only after the prisoner has been convicted, and, frequently, sent to prison—adequate to undo the damage?   Consider Amsterdam, *Criminal Prosecutions Affecting Federally Guaranteed Civil Rights: Federal Removal and Habeas Corpus Jurisdiction to Abort State Court Trial*, 113 U.Pa.L.Rev. 793, 801 (1965)("True, state courts are competent to administer federal law, and they may by self-denial act to vindicate federal liberties.   Theory casts them in this protective role, but the battle is not over theory.   The battle is for the streets, and on the streets conviction now is worth a hundred times reversal later.").

(3) *Finality in the Criminal Process.*   The rule of Brown v. Allen touches not only the proper relation between state and federal courts in the effectuation of constitutional rights, but also the problem of creating effective, humane, and sensible procedures for enforcing the criminal law.   What role should interests in finality play in those procedures?

In Sanders v. United States, 373 U.S. 1, 8 (1963), Justice Brennan broadly declared: "Conventional notions of finality of litigation have no place where life or liberty is at stake and infringement of constitutional rights is alleged".   Judge Friendly responded: "Why do they have *no* place?   One will readily agree that 'where life or liberty is at stake,' different rules should govern the determination of guilt than when only property is at issue * * *.   * * * But this shows only that 'conventional notions of finality' should not have *as much* place in criminal as in civil litigation, not that they should have *none*."   Friendly, *Is Innocence Irrelevant?   Collateral Attack on Criminal Judgments*, 38 U.Chi.L.Rev. 142, 149–50 (1970).

(4) *The Process View.*   A celebrated article by Professor Bator, *Finality in Criminal Law and Federal Habeas Corpus for State Prisoners*, 76 Harv.L.Rev. 441, 448 (1963), which built on Justice Jackson's opinion in Brown v. Allen, objected to routine federal relitigation.   Bator articulated a far narrower

---

5.   Consider, also, the intriguing defense of federal relitigation presented by Cover & Aleinikoff, *Dialectical Federalism: Habeas Corpus and the Court*, 86 Yale L.J. 1035 (1977).   In their view, habeas jurisdiction generates a healthy dialogue between state and federal judicial systems about the scope of federal constitutional rights.   State courts tend to possess the pragmatic perspective (and narrow view of rights) of everyday law enforcement, while federal habeas courts, because they consider the constitutional issue in relative isolation from evidence of the prisoner's guilt, are more likely to have a "utopian", rights-protective perspective.   Neither system has the power to enforce its view upon the other: although the federal district and appellate courts may effectively nullify a conviction by granting habeas relief, their decisions are not binding precedents for the state courts, which thus remain free to follow their narrower view of constitutional rights.

Do state and federal courts' perspectives differ in this way?   *Cf.* pp. 351-54, *supra.*   Doesn't the adversary process inject both pragmatic and utopian perspectives into state prosecutions and habeas proceedings alike?   And are habeas courts truly unaware of the likely guilt of the prisoner, or inattentive to concerns about the impact on law enforcement of recognizing a constitutional right?   Insofar as the perspectives do differ, will the result in fact be dialogue, or simply an accommodation of opposing power—perhaps accompanied by considerable friction?   See Meltzer, *State Court Forfeitures of Federal Rights*, 99 Harv.L.Rev. 1128, 1233–34 n. 505 (1986).

conception of the appropriate scope of habeas review that is generally called the "process" view.

Among Bator's objections to federal relitigation were these: (a) "[I]f a job can be well done once, it should not be done twice" (p. 451); (b) "I could imagine nothing more subversive of a [state] judge's sense of responsibility, of the inner subjective conscientiousness which is so essential a part of the difficult and subtle art of judging well, than an indiscriminate acceptance of the notion that all the shots will always be called by someone else" (*id.*); (c) The swiftness and the certainty of punishment—both of which are important to the educative and deterrent functions of the criminal law—and the goal of rehabilitation are undermined by broad federal habeas review; and (d) "There comes a point where a procedural system which leaves matters perpetually open no longer reflects humane concern but merely anxiety and a desire for immobility" (pp. 452–53).

Noting that no legal process can assure the ultimate correctness of the results reached, Bator doubted that when state and federal court decisions differed, the latter were necessarily more correct. He also resisted "the notion that sound remedial institutions can be built on the premise that state judges are not in sympathy with federal law" (p. 524).

He thus concluded that when a state court of competent jurisdiction has rendered a criminal judgment, a federal court should not exercise habeas jurisdiction for the purpose of deciding whether it agrees with the state court's resolution of the federal constitutional claims. Instead, the habeas jurisdiction should be exercised only to determine "whether the conditions and tools of inquiry were such as to assure a reasonable probability that the facts were correctly found and the law correctly applied" (p. 455; emphasis omitted). Thus, for example, if a prisoner alleges a deprivation of the effective assistance of counsel, or claims that evidence discovered only after the conviction was affirmed shows that the trial judge had been bribed, habeas review would be appropriate to correct such a defect in the state's process.[6]

Do you agree with Bator's dismissal of the premise that state judges are not adequately sympathetic to claims of federal constitutional right? Didn't that premise have particular force with respect to many criminal procedure decisions of the Warren Court, especially when implicated in the prosecution of black defendants or of civil rights protesters in the South during the 1950s and 1960s? Does it retain force today? See generally pp. 351-54, *supra.*

(5) *Cognizable Issues.* In practice, the rule of Brown v. Allen applies almost exclusively to questions of *constitutional* law—even though § 2254(a) speaks also of custody in violation of "law or treaties of the United States."[7]   Judge

---

6. However, for Bator, if an allegation of bribery at the trial level had been raised in a state appellate court and rejected after a fair hearing, no habeas relief should follow.

7. When might a state prisoner present a federal nonconstitutional ground in seeking habeas relief? When the state conviction was under a state criminal statute that is alleged to be preempted by federal regulation?

See also Reed v. Farley, 114 S.Ct. 2291 (1994), which involved a claim that the state had violated Article IV(c) of the Interstate Agreement on Detainers—an interstate compact, approved by Congress—which requires the trial of a prisoner transferred from one state to another to commence within 120 days of the transfer. Although the petitioner had filed numerous pretrial motions, he had not objected to the scheduling of the trial date until four days after the 120–day limit had expired, and had suffered no prejudice as a result.

Friendly, Paragraph (3), *supra*, at 156–57, noted that when Brown v. Allen was decided, "the Bill of Rights was read to protect a state criminal defendant only if the state had acted in a manner 'repugnant to the conscience of mankind.' " But after the Warren Court's vast expansion of constitutional protections of criminal procedure, "the 'constitutional' label no longer assists in appraising how far society should go in permitting relitigation of criminal convictions. It carries a connotation of outrage—the mob-dominated jury, the confession extorted by the rack, the defendant deprived of counsel—which is wholly misplaced when, for example, the claim is a pardonable but allegedly mistaken belief that probable cause existed for an arrest or that a statement by a person not available for cross-examination came within an exception to the hearsay rule."

Judge Friendly also observed that "[a] judge's overly broad construction of a [state] penal statute can be much more harmful to a defendant than unwarranted refusal to compel a prosecution witness on some peripheral element of the case to reveal his address. If a second round on the former is not permitted, and no one suggests it should be, I see no justification for one on the latter in the absence of a colorable showing of innocence." For emphatic reaffirmation that habeas corpus does not lie to correct errors of *state* law, see Estelle v. McGuire, 502 U.S. 62 (1991).

(6) *Restriction of Brown.* The broad scope of habeas relitigation authorized in Brown and reaffirmed in Fay v. Noia, 372 U.S. 391 (1963), is often seen as an important or even necessary aspect of the Warren Court's effort to ensure that its criminal procedure decisions were followed by state courts. In turn, the reach of the writ has been narrowed in a variety of ways by the Burger and Rehnquist Courts, which are seen as having a different substantive agenda—one that embraces greater reluctance to interfere with the state courts, and greater faith in their quality. Contemporary views about the Great Writ have also been influenced by the sharp increase in the use of capital punishment in the past 15 years;[8] by the central role that habeas litigation has played in challenging (and often overturning) capital convictions or sentences; and by the impatience of many (including some Justices) who view habeas litigation as a means to delay endlessly the carrying out of the death penalty. See generally Yackle, Reclaiming the Federal Courts 164–66, 177 (1994).

Despite the expression of reservations about Brown by some Justices, see, *e.g.*, Schneckloth v. Bustamonte, 412 U.S. 218, 250 (1973)(Powell, J., concurring, joined by Burger, C.J., and Rehnquist, J.); Withrow v. Williams, 507 U.S. 680, ___ (1993)(Scalia, J., joined by Thomas J.) the Court has not moved

---

The Court held, 5–4, that § 2254 (like § 2255 for federal prisoners) permits relief for statutory violations only when they give rise to a "fundamental defect". See generally pp. 1465-66, *infra.* Three Justices found no such defect in this case—leaving open the situation in which the prisoner had made a timely request under Article IV(c). Justice Scalia, joined by Justice Thomas, concluded more broadly that few if any nonconstitutional violations constitute "fundamental defects", and even an intentional violation of the 120–day requirement would not qualify. The four dissenters found the "fundamental

defect" standard inappropriate in § 2254 proceedings, and argued that Congress, by providing in Article IV(c) for dismissal of cases not brought to trial within the 120–day limit, demonstrated the fundamental nature of the violation.

8. In 1995, the House and the Senate each passed bills that not only limit the habeas jurisdiction generally, but also impose a further set of restrictions on habeas relief in capital cases—restrictions designed to expedite the carrying out of executions. See p. 1459, *infra.*

frontally to overrule it.[9]   (On the repeated, but to date unsuccessful, efforts in Congress effectively to overrule Brown, see pp. 1455–61, *infra*.)   As the remainder of this Section illustrates, however, in the past 20 years the Court has narrowed the scope of the writ in important ways.

(7) *Harmless Error*. It was long assumed that a federal habeas court, after finding a constitutional violation, should grant relief unless the state could prove that the error was harmless beyond a reasonable doubt—the standard applied by state and federal courts on direct review of criminal convictions. See Chapman v. California, 386 U.S. 18 (1967). But in Brecht v. Abrahamson, 507 U.S. 619 (1993), the Court for the first time addressed the issue expressly, and held that a less exacting standard was appropriate on habeas review.

The state courts in Brecht had found a violation of Doyle v. Ohio, 426 U.S. 610 (1976), which held it unconstitutional to impeach a defendant's trial testimony by pointing to the defendant's silence after having been given Miranda warnings. But the state courts upheld the conviction in Brecht, finding the violation harmless beyond a reasonable doubt. On federal habeas review, the district court found that the error was not harmless beyond a reasonable doubt, and hence granted relief. But the Supreme Court held that the harmlessness of the constitutional error should be judged in a habeas proceeding by the less stringent standard applied by federal courts to nonconstitutional errors—under which an error is harmless unless it "had substantial and injurious effect or influence in determining the jury's verdict," Kotteakos v. United States, 328 U.S. 750, 776 (1946).[10] The Court, in finding that application of the Chapman standard on habeas was not necessary to give incentives for state courts faithfully to apply that standard on direct review, refused to presume that state-court judges are ignoring their oath to uphold the Constitution. The Court concluded that in any event, "the costs of applying the Chapman standard on federal habeas outweigh the additional deterrent effect, if any, which would be derived from its application on collateral review" (507 U.S. at ___).

Justice Stevens' concurrence stressed that "the way we phrase the governing standard is far less important than the quality of the judgment with which it is applied" (507 U.S. at ___). Justice White's dissent, joined by Justice Blackmun and in relevant part by Justice Souter, argued that petitioner was being held " 'in custody in violation of the Constitution or laws ... of the United States,' 28 U.S.C. § 2254(a)," and hence was entitled to relief.[11] Justice O'Connor's separate dissent stated that "[a]t least where errors bearing on accuracy are at issue, I am not persuaded that the Kotteakos standard offers

---

9. In Wright v. West, 505 U.S. 277 (1992), the Supreme Court had asked the parties to address the question: "* * * should a federal [habeas] court give deference to the state court's application of law to the specific facts of the petitioner's case or should it review the state court's determination *de novo*?", 502 U.S. 1021 (1991), but decided the case without reaching that question, see p. 1408, *infra*.

10. The Court left open the possibility that a more stringent harmless error standard would govern an "unusual case, a deliberate and especially egregious error of the

trial type, or one that is combined with a pattern of prosecutorial misconduct" (507 U.S. at ___ n.9). And it noted that certain "structural defects" can never be deemed harmless.

11. Would Justice White's objection be blunted (whatever the ultimate wisdom of Brecht) if, as is argued in Meltzer, *Harmless Error and Constitutional Remedies*, 61 U.Chi. L.Rev. 1 (1993), the Chapman rule is not truly required by the Constitution but is instead a rule of constitutional common law? See generally pp. 490–91, *supra*.

an adequate assurance of reliability" (507 U.S. at ___). Doubting the wisdom of requiring a determination whether a particular error relates to accuracy in order to ascertain which harmless error standard applies, she favored retaining the Chapman rule across the board.[12]

B. Filing and Success Rates: Brown v. Allen in Practice

In evaluating the regime of Brown v. Allen, consider the following statistics:

(1) *Number of Petitions Filed.* The trend in filings is as follows:

	Number of State Prisoner Habeas Corpus Petitions[13]	Number of State Prisoners[14]	State Prisoner Habeas Petitions as % of State Prisoners	Number of Private Civil Cases Filed in the Federal Courts[15]	State Prisoner Habeas Petitions as % of Private Civil Cases
1950	560	149,031	0.37%	32,193	1.73%
1955	660	165,692	0.39%	39,225	1.68%
1960	871	189,735	0.45%	38,444	2.26%
1965	4,845	189,855	2.55%	46,027	10.52%
1970	9,063	176,403	5.13%	62,356	14.53%
1975	7,843	216,462	3.62%	85,541	9.16%
1980	7,029	305,458	2.30%	105,161	6.68%
1985	8,520	462,284	1.84%	156,182	5.45%
1990	10,817	708,393	1.52%	161,579	6.69%
1994	11,908	919,143	1.30%	189,478	6.28%

12. In O'Neal v. McAninch, 115 S.Ct. 992 (1995), the Court held, 6–3, that when a judge is in equipoise about whether an error substantially influenced the jury's decision, the petitioner is entitled to relief.

For analysis and criticism of Brecht, see Liebman & Hertz, *Brecht v. Abrahamson: Harmful Error in Habeas Corpus Law*, 84 J.Crim.L. & Criminology 1109, 1155 (1994); Gershman, *The Gate is Open But the Door is Locked—Habeas Corpus and Harmless Error*, 51 Wash. & Lee L.Rev. 115 (1994).

13. See Annual Report of the Director of the Administrative Office of the United States Courts, Table C–3, for the years indicated. Where numbers have been revised, the most recent figure is used. Statistics are for a fiscal year ending June 30, except for the 1994 figure, which is for a fiscal year ending September 30. Excluded are the very small number of petitions listed under "local jurisdiction".

One study found that 10% of the filings categorized as habeas corpus petitions by the Administrative Office during fiscal years 1975–76 in fact were not § 2254 petitions but other kinds of actions (*e.g.*, § 2255 motions or § 1983 suits). Allen, Schachtman & Wilson, *Federal Habeas Corpus and its Reform: An Empirical Analysis*, 13 Rutgers L.J. 675, 680 n. 8 (1982). Of the habeas petitions filed, roughly 70% attacked convictions or sentences; the rest related to pretrial matters, conditions of confinement, or revocation

of probation or parole. See *id.* at 755 n. 367; Meltzer, note 5, *supra*, at 1192 n. 323.

14. The 1950–1975 statistics are based on the Bureau of Justice Statistics (BJS), *Historical Statistics on Prisoners in State and Federal Institutions, Yearend 1925–86*. The 1980 statistics are based on BJS, *Prisoners in State and Federal Institutions on December 31, 1981*, Table 1. The 1985 and 1990 statistics are based on BJS, *Correctional Populations in the United States*, 1986 and 1991, respectively, Table 5.1. The 1994 statistics are based on the BJS Press Release, *State and Federal Prison Population Tops One Million* (Oct. 27, 1994). Statistics are as of December 31 for the indicated years, except for the 1994 figure, which is as of June 30.

After 1978, a distinction was made between prisoners "in custody" and prisoners "under jurisdiction". "In custody" refers to the direct physical control of a confined person. "Under jurisdiction" refers to the legal power to incarcerate the person, and includes persons not held in the state's own prisons— for example, prisoners housed in local jails, in other states, or in hospitals outside the correctional system; inmates on work release, furlough, or bail; and state prisoners held in federal prisons. Beginning with 1980, the table in text uses the "under jurisdiction" statistic.

15. See Annual Report, note 13, *supra*, Table C–2. Statistics are based on a fiscal

(2) *Success Rates Generally*. Studies conducted during the 1970s generally found that only 3–4% of petitions filed by state prisoners resulted in the district court's granting of any kind of relief[16]—and relief may result only in a further hearing or retrial that sustains the conviction. A more recent study, of petitions filed in 1990 and 1992, found a success rate of only 1%.[17]

(3) *Capital Cases*. A study of the federal courts' disposition of habeas petitions filed by death row inmates (included in the Brief Amici Curiae of Benjamin R. Civiletti et al., Wright v. West, 505 U.S. 277 (1992), at 44–45) found that from 1976–91, federal courts found reversible constitutional error in 42% of all such proceedings. The vastly greater success rate in capital cases is no doubt attributable to the greater complexity of the constitutional doctrines implicated (particularly in sentencing proceedings), the availability of counsel, ambivalent attitudes toward capital punishment, and the greater care taken by the federal courts when life is at stake.

(4) *The Scope of the System*. It has been estimated that of state prisoners committed to custody each year, no more than 0.4% even file habeas petitions—and no more than 0.003% obtain relief. See Meltzer, *Habeas Corpus Jurisdiction: The Limits of Models*, 66 S.Cal.L.Rev. 2507, 2523–24 (1993).[18] Do these statistics give reason to doubt whether any purpose that one might posit for habeas review is substantially fulfilled in practice?

C. The Historical Debate

(1) *Introduction*. In a number of cases, Supreme Court Justices have delved into the history of habeas corpus in support of particular views about the proper scope of the jurisdiction. The following brief survey of these debates identifies the key questions that the historical materials present.

(2) *The Bator View*. A 1963 article by Professor Bator, *Finality in Criminal Law and Federal Habeas Corpus for State Prisoners*, 76 Harv.L.Rev. 441 (1963)—which for many years was the most influential account of the writ's history among scholars[19]—set forth a narrow view of federal habeas corpus

---

year ending June 30, except for the 1994 figure, which is for a fiscal year ending September 30.

16. See Faust, Rubenstein & Yackle, p. 1345, note 1, *supra*, at 681; Robinson, p. 1345, note 1, *supra*, at 23; Shapiro, *Federal Habeas Corpus: A Study in Massachusetts*, 87 Harv.L.Rev. 321, 333 (1973). Capital cases aside (see Paragraph (3), *infra*), very few petitioners who lose in the district court obtain relief on appeal. See, *e.g.*, Robinson, *supra*, at 23, 35 (19 such cases of 1,899 total petitions filed in the district court).

17. Flango, p. 1345, note 1, *supra*, at 62–63.

18. Those estimates were based on a 3.2% success rate, which, as the preceding Paragraph suggests, may be higher than the rate today.

19. See, *e.g.*, Duker, A Constitutional History of Habeas Corpus (1980); *Developments in the Law: Federal Habeas Corpus*, 83 Harv.L.Rev. 1038, 1047–49 (1970); Friendly, Paragraph A(3), *supra*, at 146 n. 15, 151; Hart, Paragraph A(2)(a), *supra*, at 103–04; Mayers, *The Habeas Corpus Act of 1867: The Supreme Court as Legal Historian*, 33 U.Chi. L.Rev. 31, 56 (1965).

before Brown v. Allen. Although Justice Brennan's majority opinion in Fay v. Noia, 372 U.S. 391 (1963), rejected Bator's account a few months after its publication, Justice Harlan's dissent in that case for the most part embraced the Bator view; and more recently, many members of the Burger and Rehnquist Courts have found that view persuasive. See, *e.g.*, Wright v. West, 505 U.S. 277, ___ (1992)(opinion of Thomas J., joined by Rehnquist, C.J., and Scalia, J.); McCleskey v. Zant, 499 U.S. 467, 477–79 (1991)(Kennedy, J.); Swain v. Pressley, 430 U.S. 372, 384–86 (1977)(Burger, C.J., joined by Rehnquist & Blackmun, JJ., concurring in part and concurring in the judgment); Stone v. Powell, 428 U.S. 465, 475–76 (1976), p. 1376, *infra* (Powell, J.).

According to Bator, the historic office of habeas, both in England and in the United States, was to deal with detention by the executive, effected wholly outside the judicial process. By contrast, in the post-conviction setting, habeas petitioners were permitted to challenge only the jurisdiction of the court that had rendered the judgment under which they were in custody; they could not contest the legality of the conviction itself. See, *e.g.*, Ex parte Watkins, 28 U.S. (3 Pet.) 193 (1830).[20] The Habeas Corpus Act of 1867 for the first time made the federal writ generally available to *state* prisoners, but, Bator argued, there is no convincing evidence that the Act was designed to expand the scope of the writ beyond its well-understood meaning.

Bator conceded that some post–1867 cases reflected a "softening" of the concept of jurisdiction, embracing claims that the statute under which the defendant had been convicted was unconstitutional, *e.g.*, Ex parte Siebold, 100 U.S. 371, 376–77 (1879), or that detention was based on an illegally-imposed sentence, *e.g.*, Ex parte Lange, 85 U.S. (18 Wall.) 163, 176 (1873)(involving imposition of a second sentence after the first sentence had been carried out, under a statute that permitted only one sentence). But this softening—which was driven by the absence before 1891 of other means for obtaining Supreme Court review of federal criminal convictions—did not change the basic rule that habeas was unavailable to review claims of constitutional error not going to the sentencing court's jurisdiction.

In the early twentieth century, the Court further expanded the writ—correctly, in Bator's view—to encompass cases in which the state courts had not afforded a full and fair opportunity to litigate the prisoner's federal constitutional claims. Two key cases, discussed at length by Bator, are Frank v. Mangum, 237 U.S. 309 (1915), and Moore v. Dempsey, 261 U.S. 86 (1923), both of which involved due process claims arising from alleged mob domination of state trial proceedings. In Frank, the Court refused to grant the writ, over a dissent by Justice Holmes; eight years later, in Moore, the writ was granted, with Justice Holmes writing. Bator views the decision in Frank as premised on the fact that the state appellate court, in reviewing the trial proceedings, had already provided fair corrective process. Acknowledging that the Moore opinion was far from clear, Bator contends that the Court, rather than generally authorizing federal relitigation of constitutional claims, may have held only that there, unlike in Frank, the state appellate courts' review of the alleged mob domination had been so perfunctory as not to constitute an adequate

---

20. For agreement on this point, see Oaks, *Habeas Corpus in the States—1776–1865*, 32 U.Chi.L.Rev. 243, 258–61 (1965).

For discussion of the British development, see the authorities cited in p. 1338, note 2, *supra*.

process—therefore permitting federal habeas review. See 76 Harv.L.Rev. at 483–93.[21]

Thus, Bator concludes that, despite some murkiness in the case law, before Brown v. Allen there was no clear authority for the proposition that a habeas court should routinely relitigate a federal constitutional claim that the prisoner had been able to litigate fully and fairly in state court.

(3) *Contrasting Views of the History.* In Fay v. Noia, *supra*, Justice Brennan rejected Bator's historical reading and took the position that habeas corpus—in English common law and in this country—was not limited to challenges to executive detentions or to the jurisdiction of the committing court, but rather had always provided a means of testing whether detention comported with fundamental law. Justice Brennan's history was sharply criticized,[22] but more recently several commentators have argued, in differing and sometimes conflicting ways, that the rule of Brown v. Allen is consistent with historic practice.

(a) Professor Peller, note 21, *supra*, offered an elaboration of Justice Brennan's position in Noia. In Peller's view, the language in ante-bellum cases describing the writ as limited to jurisdictional defects was attributable to the Supreme Court's lack of jurisdiction to review federal criminal convictions directly. It would have been anomalous, he argues, for the Court effectively to have overturned, on habeas review, a federal conviction it could not review directly. Peller contends that lower federal courts, which were not circumscribed by the limit on the Supreme Court's appellate jurisdiction, exercised

21. Others have viewed Frank and Moore differently. See, *e.g.*, Wright v. West, 505 U.S. 277, 298 (1992)(O'Connor, J., concurring in the result, joined by Blackmun & Stevens, JJ.)("the absence of a full and fair hearing was *itself* the relevant violation of the Constitution; it was not a prerequisite to" habeas relief; both cases reviewed the claim of mob domination de novo, and found it meritorious in Moore (because the state appellate courts offered no corrective process) but not in Frank); Peller, *In Defense of Federal Habeas Corpus Relitigation*, 16 Harv. Civ.R–Civ.L.L.Rev. 579, 646 (1982)(also reading Frank and Moore as decisions on the merits, but unlike Justice O'Connor, finding that Moore overruled Frank and held that mob domination states a due process violation regardless of the nature of the state appellate process); Wechsler, *Habeas Corpus and the Supreme Court: Reconsidering the Reach of the Great Writ*, 59 U. Colo.L.Rev. 167, 173 (1988)(the Moore decision, though it could have been decided more narrowly, held that the habeas court had the duty to adjudicate the merits of the federal constitutional claim).

For other twentieth century decisions before Brown that might be accommodated to the view that habeas extended not to all federal constitutional claims, but only to those raising issues that could not have been fairly litigated at trial or on direct review, see Johnson v. Zerbst, 304 U.S. 458, 468 (1938)(federal prisoner who was denied effective assistance of counsel at trial); Waley v. Johnston, 316 U.S. 101 (1942)(federal prisoner who alleged that plea of guilty had been coerced); Mooney v. Holohan, 294 U.S. 103 (1935)(where prisoner claimed that perjured testimony was knowingly used by prosecution, state is required to provide adequate corrective process, and in its absence, federal habeas will lie; case remanded for exhaustion of state post-conviction remedies).

Bator acknowledged that in Waley v. Johnston, *supra*, the Court "finally dispensed with the fiction of 'jurisdiction' as applicable to this kind of case" (p. 495).

22. In addition to Justice Harlan's strong dissent in Noia, see, *e.g.*, Oaks, *Legal History in the High Court—Habeas Corpus*, 64 Mich.L.Rev. 451 (1966); Mayers, note 19, *supra*. For criticism of Mayers, see Yackle, *Form and Function in the Administration of Justice: The Bill of Rights and Federal Habeas Corpus*, 23 U.Mich.J.L.Ref. 685, 695–702 (1990).

plenary power to relitigate constitutional claims at the behest of petitioners.[23] The 1867 Act, reflecting the Reconstruction Congress' mistrust of state courts, gave state prisoners the right to relitigate federal constitutional claims in habeas corpus proceedings.[24] Thereafter, the reach of habeas jurisdiction did not change, but was always dependent on the scope of federal constitutional rights. The nineteenth century's narrow conception of due process—under which a determination that the convicting court had jurisdiction virtually established the lack of any constitutional violation—gradually gave way to far broader conceptions of due process, as in Moore v. Dempsey, Paragraph (2), *supra*. That evolution opened up correspondingly broader opportunities to relitigate federal issues in habeas proceedings.

(b) Professor Liebman, note 23, *supra*, also views Brown v. Allen as consistent with a long history—but his history differs from Peller's: "Since 1789, Congress has entitled federal and state prisoners incarcerated in violation of any fundamental legal (typically, any constitutional) principle to one meaningful federal court review as of right" (p. 2096). The preferred method of review was direct review in the Supreme Court, but when such review was unavailable, habeas "filled the breach" (*id.*) Thus, for state prisoners (who since 1789 could seek Supreme Court review of their convictions) and for federal prisoners (after they gained the right to Supreme Court review in 1891) habeas would ordinarily not lie.[25]

The scope of habeas review was also influenced by the scope of direct review. From 1789–1867, habeas review for federal prisoners was no broader than the direct review that a state criminal defendant could obtain via writ of error—which was limited to legal (rather than factual) determinations apparent on the face of the record. The 1867 Act, in Liebman's view, not only extended the writ to state prisoners generally, but also broadened the scope of both the writ of error and the writ of habeas corpus—thus making clear that state prisoners would have one full opportunity to enforce their newly-established federal rights in a federal court.

In this century, the shift from mandatory to discretionary Supreme Court review of state judgments, see pp. 493–94, *supra*, narrowed the preferred method of federal review. Habeas jurisdiction expanded (in cases like Frank and Moore) to fill the breach and to provide the same review that the Supreme Court had formerly provided.

(c) Professor Woolhandler, note 23, *supra*, agrees with Bator that numerous habeas corpus decisions (both before and after 1867) stated that the writ was limited to jurisdictional defects. But she believes that post–1867 decisions encompassing claims of conviction under unconstitutional statutes and claims of illegal sentences cannot be treated (as Bator does) merely as a "softening" of

---

23. For doubts about this aspect of Peller's argument from commentators sympathetic to broad habeas relitigation, see Woolhandler, *Demodeling Habeas*, 45 Stan.L.Rev. 575, 585–96 & n. 67 (1993); Liebman, *Apocalypse Next Time?: The Anachronistic Attack on Habeas Corpus/Direct Review Parity*, 92 Colum.L.Rev. 1997, 2046 (1992).

24. For a more limited view of the 1867 Act, see Forsythe, *The Historical Origins of Broad Federal Habeas Review Reconsidered*, 70 Notre Dame L.Rev. 1079, 1101–24

(1995)(citing many of the scholars who have debated the meaning of the 1867 Act); Mayers, note 19, *supra*.

25. Note that for Liebman, the 1891 provision of Supreme Court jurisdiction to review federal criminal cases called for a contraction of habeas review, whereas for Professor Peller it called for an expansion of the jurisdiction (at least as exercised by the Supreme Court).

the jurisdictional concept. Rather, this expansion meant that habeas jurisdiction extended to most meritorious constitutional claims—which, in the nineteenth century, were generally limited to challenges to statutes and did not encompass ad hoc or random official acts unauthorized by state law. Thus, federal relitigation of constitutional claims was common long before Brown v. Allen. The emergence of a broader understanding of constitutional wrongs—as encompassing ad hoc or random illegality—was reflected in habeas actions, and resulted in a broadening of the effective reach of federal relitigation.

(d) All three of these accounts are in turn found to be flawed in Forsythe, note 24, *supra,* at 1146–63. His review of the history leads him to conclude that Bator's view was correct and remains unimpeached.

(4) *The Significance of the History.* Part of the difficulty in seeking to draw inferences from the history is that the cases involve a broad range of variables—federal vs. state prisoners; pre-trial vs. post-trial detention; ordinary criminal cases vs. contempt proceedings; unfamiliar, and shifting, conceptions of jurisdiction; evolving conceptions of due process; changes in the Supreme Court's jurisdiction to review state and federal criminal cases—whose significance is not always clearly indicated in the judicial opinions. More generally, many of the decisions do not clearly articulate an understanding of habeas corpus—particularly one that corresponds neatly to modern categories and perceptions.[26]

How much weight should the historical debate be given today when the Court is faced with a particular doctrinal question? Even if one were persuaded by the Bator view of the history, would that justify a Supreme Court decision, some 40 years after Brown v. Allen, to overrule or sharply curtail the rule of federal relitigation? *Per contra,* even if one views Brown as firmly rooted in historical practice, would that justify an insistence on unlimited federal relitigation even in the face of contrary arguments of contemporary policy? What are—and should be—the respective roles of historical practice, congressional direction, and judicial policymaking in fleshing out the scope of the writ?

NOTE ON THE SUSPENSION CLAUSE OF THE CONSTITUTION

(1) *The Constitutional Provision.* Is the federal courts' exercise of post-conviction review for state prisoners constrained in any way by the language of the Suspension Clause (Art. I, § 9, cl. 2): "The Privilege of the Writ of Habeas Corpus shall not be suspended, unless when in cases of Rebellion or Invasion the public Safety may require it"? The proceedings of the Convention do not cast much light on just what the Framers assumed the "Privilege of the Writ" to be.

---

26. The last point is stressed in Arkin, *The Ghost at the Banquet: Slavery, Federalism, and Habeas Corpus for State Prisoners,* 70 Tulane L.Rev. 1 (1995), a discussion of the ante-Bellum period, which observes, *inter alia,* that (i) post-conviction habeas petitions were very rare because imprisonment was not then a common sanction, and thus convicts were rarely in "custody"; and (ii) the most prominent use of federal habeas jurisdiction to promote federal supremacy was in enforcing the Fugitive Slave Act—hardly a comfortable foundation for modern proponents of broad habeas review.

(2) *Original Understanding*. Any effort to draw from the Suspension Clause a constitutional right to federal post-conviction review for state prisoners must confront the fact that the text does not confer a right to habeas relief, but merely sets forth when the "Privilege of the Writ" may be suspended.[1] Thus, Collings, *Habeas Corpus for Convicts—Constitutional Right or Legislative Grace?*, 40 Calif.L.Rev. 335, 340–41 (1952), after surveying suspension of the writ in England and the Colonies, concludes that "to suspend the privilege of habeas corpus in the constitutional sense is to deprive persons accused of crime of their right either to be speedily accused and tried or to be set free. * * * Suspension statutes were aimed at suspects, never at convicts." He also notes that four of the state ratifying conventions objected to the Constitution's lack of a provision *affirmatively* guaranteeing a right to habeas corpus.[2] Compare *Developments*, note 1, *supra*, at 1267 (arguing that "[a] purposive analysis * * * supports a constitutional requirement that there be *some* court with habeas jurisdiction over federal prisoners").

Note, in addition, the following three difficulties encountered by any effort to read the Suspension Clause as providing a right to federal relitigation:

(a) *The Scope of the Writ*. Interpretation of the Clause has been tied up with debates about the historical scope of the writ. Thus, if the original understanding was that the writ's function was merely to test the legality of executive detention—and that a conviction by a criminal court of competent jurisdiction could not be reexamined on habeas corpus at all—that would argue (albeit not conclusively) against reading the Suspension Clause as protecting a constitutional writ to post-conviction review.[3] Compare Developments, *supra*, at 1269 (suggesting that the Clause "could be read to protect the product of an evolving judicial process").

(b) *The Right of State Prisoners*. The Suspension Clause was directed only to detention under *federal* authority—as was the grant of habeas jurisdiction in the Judiciary Act of 1789. Prisoners held under *state* authority did not generally have access to the writ in the federal courts until 1867. See pp. 1339-41, *supra*.

(c) *The Right to a Federal Court*. Recall the constitutional understanding (already accepted by the Convention when the Suspension Clause was adopted) that it was up to Congress to decide whether to create lower federal courts at all.[4] And Ex parte Bollman, 8 U.S. (4 Cranch) 75, 94–95 (1807), p. 1340 *supra*, held that the jurisdiction of the federal courts to issue the writ is not inherent,

---

1. On the significance of the reference to the "Privilege of the Writ" rather than simply the Writ itself, see Ex parte Milligan, 71 U.S. (4 Wall.) 2, 130–31 (1866)(dictum); *Developments in the Law—Federal Habeas Corpus*, 83 Harv.L.Rev. 1038, 1265–66 (1970).

2. See also Paschal, *The Constitution and Habeas Corpus*, 1970 Duke L.J. 605, who reads the negative phraseology as "only a circumlocution to propose a suspending power in the least offensive way" (p. 611), and asserts that the Clause "is a direction to all superior courts of record, state as well as federal, to make the habeas privilege routinely available" (p. 607).

3. For a survey of the historical materials on the Suspension Clause, see Paschal, note 2, *supra*; *Developments in the Law*, note 1, *supra*, at 1263–66. With respect to the contemporaneous understanding about habeas corpus, *see* Oaks, p. 1366, note 22, *supra*.

4. Recall, too, that even readings of Article III as mandating the vesting of the federal judicial power tend to agree that Congress need not create lower federal courts so long as the Supreme Court's jurisdiction to review state court judgments is unimpaired. See generally pp. 359-72, *supra*.

but must be conferred by statute.[5] Doesn't that make it hard to argue that there is a constitutional right to seek habeas corpus in a *federal* court? But see Developments, note 1, *supra*, at 1271–72 ("An argument can be derived from some cases * * * that once Congress has established federal courts with the power to enforce federal law, it may not—as a matter of due process—withhold habeas jurisdiction over federal prisoners"); Paschal, note 2, *supra*.

(3) *The Pertinence of the Fourteenth Amendment.* Professor Jordan Steiker, note 5, *supra*, while acknowledging the foregoing difficulties, argues for a constitutional right to federal habeas relief that is premised on the interaction of the Suspension Clause and the Fourteenth Amendment. He finds that by the time the Fourteenth Amendment was ratified, the writ had evolved far beyond its common law origins (compare Paragraph (2)(a), *supra*), and that the Fourteenth Amendment incorporated the "privilege" of that broadened writ against *state authority* (compare Paragraph (2)(b), *supra*).[6] But even if one accepts those claims, the hardest part of his argument, as he recognizes, is the further claim of a right to *federal court* review (compare Paragraph (2)(c), *supra*). Can one plausibly argue that the Fourteenth Amendment, a provision directed to the *states*, implicitly imposed an obligation on the *federal* legislature to confer, or on the *federal* courts to exercise, habeas corpus jurisdiction?

(4) *Supreme Court Interpretation.* Supreme Court decisions contain little discussion of the Suspension Clause. Two 1963 decisions that provided liberal interpretations of the scope of the jurisdiction contained passing suggestions, in dictum, that narrower interpretations might raise constitutional questions. Sanders v. United States, 373 U.S. 1, 11–12; Fay v. Noia, 372 U.S. 391, 406. (Both decisions have been overruled. See pp. 1436, 1442 *infra*.)

In Swain v. Pressley, 430 U.S. 372 (1977), the Court upheld a provision of the District of Columbia Code applying to persons convicted of local crimes in the District. The statute substituted, for the habeas corpus remedy, a statutory motion in the local D.C. courts. The majority ruled simply that the motion was "commensurate" with habeas corpus; that it was not inadequate merely because the local judges who administer it are not Article III judges; and that there accordingly was no suspension of the writ. Chief Justice Burger, joined by Justices Blackmun and Rehnquist, concurred on broader grounds, arguing

---

5. Note, however, that Chief Justice Marshall stated in Bollman that the First Congress, acting under the "immediate influence of [the] injunction" in the Suspension Clause, "must have felt * * * the obligation of providing efficient means by which this great constitutional privilege should receive life and activity; for if the means be not in existence, the privilege itself would be lost, although no law for its suspension should be enacted" (p. 95). Should this paean to the writ be read as recognizing a genuine constitutional duty in Congress to give the federal courts habeas jurisdiction—notwithstanding the Madisonian Compromise? See Steiker, *Incorporating the Suspension Clause: Is There A Constitutional Right to Federal Habeas Corpus For State Prisoners?*, 92 Mich. L.Rev. 862, 874–78 (1994), & sources cited.

6. He notes that The Slaughter–House Cases, 83 U.S. (16 Wall.) 36, 82 (1873), included the writ of habeas corpus as one of the rights of national citizenship that the Privileges and Immunities Clause protected against the states. But *if* the federal government has an obligation under the Suspension Clause to provide post-conviction review for federal prisoners, and *if* the Fourteenth Amendment incorporates the Suspension Clause, isn't the idea of incorporating the privilege of the writ against the states much less clear-cut than, for example, the idea of incorporating the First Amendment? Incorporation of the First Amendment imposes obligations upon state governmental bodies to comply with federal requirements; does that suggest that incorporation of the Suspension Clause would oblige *state courts* to provide post-conviction review?

that the Suspension Clause protects only the writ as known at the time of the Framers and therefore imposes no requirement on Congress to provide any collateral review of convictions entered by a court of competent jurisdiction.[7]

Under Chief Justice Burger's view, just what did the Suspension Clause guarantee? The availability of the writ (in state courts, since there might be no lower federal courts) to challenge detentions (other than those pursuant to a judgment of a court) by federal officials? See Duker, A Constitutional History of Habeas Corpus 155 (1980). But *cf.* Tarble's Case, p. 459, *supra.* Does the Clause mean only that Congress may not preclude the state courts from exercising whatever habeas jurisdiction they might wish? Or that the state courts have an obligation to hear claims that detainees are being held in violation of law?

NOTE ON RELITIGATING THE FACTS ON HABEAS CORPUS

(1) *Introduction.* Both Justices Reed and Frankfurter, in their opinions in Brown v. Allen, stated that a habeas court generally has discretion whether to hold an evidentiary hearing; it is obliged to do so only if there are "unusual circumstances" (Reed) or a "vital flaw" (Frankfurter) in the state proceedings (pp. 463–64, 507).

(2) *Townsend v. Sain.* In Townsend v. Sain, 372 U.S. 293 (1963), the Court transformed Brown's generalities into a detailed code specifying when a hearing must be held. Townsend's habeas petition alleged that his confession was involuntary because caused by his injection with a supposed "truth serum". Although the state trial judge had made no findings on the admissibility of the confession, leaving the issue of its voluntariness to the jury, the federal habeas court refused to hold a hearing on that issue. The Supreme Court, per Warren, C.J., held that to be error (pp. 311–12):

"* * * [T]his Court has consistently upheld the power of the federal courts on habeas corpus to take evidence relevant to claims of [unconstitutional] detention. * * *

"The rule could not be otherwise. The whole history of the writ—its unique development—refutes a construction of the federal courts' habeas corpus powers that would assimilate their task to that of courts of appellate review. The function on habeas is different. It is to test by way of an original civil proceeding, independent of the normal channels of review of criminal judgments, the very gravest allegations. * * * It is the typical, not the rare, case in which constitutional claims turn upon the resolution of contested factual issues. * * * Therefore, where an applicant for a writ of habeas corpus alleges facts which, if proved, would entitle him to relief, the federal court to which the application is made has the power to receive evidence and try the facts anew."

The Court went on (pp. 312–13) to set out "the considerations which in certain cases may make exercise of that power mandatory":

---

7. Other scattered judicial statements about the Suspension Clause are collected in Yackle, *Form and Function in The Adminis-* *tration of Justice: The Bill of Rights and Federal Habeas Corpus*, 23 U.Mich.J.L.Ref. 685, 694 nn. 39–40 (1990).

"Where the facts are in dispute, the federal court in habeas corpus must hold an evidentiary hearing if the habeas applicant did not receive a full and fair evidentiary hearing in a state court, either at the time of the trial or in a collateral proceeding. In other words a federal evidentiary hearing is required unless the state-court trier of fact has after a full hearing reliably found the relevant facts.

"It would be unwise to overly particularize this test. The federal district judges are more intimately familiar with state criminal justice, and with the trial of fact, than are we, and to their sound discretion must be left in very large part the administration of federal habeas corpus. But experience proves that a too general standard—the 'exceptional circumstances' and 'vital flaw' tests of the opinions in Brown v. Allen—does not serve adequately to explain the controlling criteria for the guidance of the federal habeas corpus courts. Some particularization may therefore be useful. We hold that a federal court must grant an evidentiary hearing to a habeas applicant under the following circumstances: If (1) the merits of the factual dispute were not resolved in the state hearing; (2) the state factual determination is not fairly supported by the record as a whole; (3) the fact-finding procedure employed by the state court was not adequate to afford a full and fair hearing; (4) there is a substantial allegation of newly discovered evidence; (5) the material facts were not adequately developed at the state-court hearing; or (6) for any reason it appears that the state trier of fact did not afford the habeas applicant a full and fair fact hearing."

The Court held that a hearing was required in Townsend's case. The state court judge had neither made factfindings nor instructed the jury on the proper constitutional standards for determining the confession's voluntariness. As a result, there was no basis for determining whether the judge had (i) applied the proper legal standard (and merely disbelieved the evidence that Townsend adduced in support of his motion to suppress), or (ii) credited that evidence but applied the wrong legal standard.

Justice Stewart, for the four dissenters, agreed that a habeas court must hold a hearing where the petitioner did not receive a full and fair evidentiary hearing in the state court, but strongly doubted the wisdom of "cataloguing in advance a set of standards which are inflexibly to compel district judges to grant evidentiary hearings in habeas corpus proceedings" (p. 326). In his view, no hearing was required in this case, for the trial judge's instructions to the jury clearly established that he was aware of the proper constitutional standard. Absent any indication to the contrary, a habeas court should presume that the judge knew the law and correctly applied it, rather than presuming, as the majority had, that he "did *not* know the law which the Constitution commands him to follow" (p. 331).

(3) *Section 2254(d)*. Three years after Townsend, Congress added a new provision, 28 U.S.C. § 2254(d), to the habeas statutes. Section 2254(d) deals not with the question when an evidentiary hearing must be held, but with the distinct (although closely related) question of what deference a habeas court that does hold a hearing should give to state court factfindings.

Section 2254(d) is a complicated burden of proof rule. It lists eight possible deficiencies in state court fact-findings, whose substance is very similar to the Townsend six. If none of the eight deficiencies is established, state factfindings are presumed to be correct, and "the burden shall rest upon the [petitioner] to establish by convincing evidence that the factual determination by the State court was erroneous."[1]   Although 2254(d) does not so state in terms, if one of the deficiencies is shown, then there is no deference to the state court findings, and the petitioner faces merely the ordinary burden of proving the constitutional claims asserted by a preponderance of the evidence.

Three of the eight statutory factors (lack of state court jurisdiction; failure to appoint counsel when constitutionally required; denial of due process in state court) are not found in Townsend, but would not appear to have changed the law.   The remaining five appear to subsume the Townsend six.   Thus, in general, when one of the eight deficiencies is present, (1) Townsend requires an evidentiary hearing, and (2) under § 2254(d) no special deference to state court factfindings is required.   *Per contra*, absent a defect in the state court proceedings, (1) Townsend does not require a hearing, and (2) state factfindings must be accepted unless the petitioner proves by convincing evidence that they were erroneous.

(4) *Keeney v. Tamayo–Reyes*.   The mandatory hearing requirements of Townsend v. Sain were sharply limited in Keeney v. Tamayo–Reyes, 504 U.S. 1 (1992).   There, the state court had rejected a prisoner's collateral attack alleging that his *nolo contendere* plea was not knowing and intelligent because the elements of the crime had not been adequately translated to him.   In his federal habeas action, the prisoner sought an evidentiary hearing, invoking Townsend's fifth circumstance ("the material facts were not adequately developed at the state court hearing") and asserting the inadequacy of his lawyer in the state post-conviction proceeding.

The district court refused to provide a hearing.   The court of appeals reversed, relying on a portion of the Townsend opinion requiring a federal hearing unless the prisoner had "deliberate[ly] bypassed" the chance to present evidence in state court.   But the Supreme Court reversed in turn, holding that a prisoner's right to a hearing, following a failure to develop a material fact in a state proceeding, was no longer governed by the "deliberate bypass" standard. That standard had been borrowed, in Townsend, from the companion case of Fay v. Noia, 372 U.S. 391 (1963), where it was held to govern when a prisoner could obtain habeas relief on a "defaulted" claim—one that had not been properly raised in state court.   But Noia had been overruled, see p. 1436, *infra*, and replaced with a rule permitting a petitioner to seek habeas relief on a defaulted claim only upon a showing that (i) there was "cause and prejudice" for the default, or (ii) a "fundamental miscarriage of justice" would occur were relitigation of the claim foreclosed.   (Those standards are discussed at pp. 1430–35, *infra*; both have been given extremely narrow scope.)   That same rule, the Court ruled in Tamayo–Reyes, should govern whether a petitioner who failed to develop the facts in state court should be afforded a federal evidentiary hearing.

Justice O'Connor, joined by Justices Blackmun, Stevens, and Kennedy, dissented.   She charged the majority with failing to respect the congressional purpose underlying § 2254(d).   Acknowledging that Townsend and § 2254(d) formally addressed different issues, Justice O'Connor saw them as intertwined. In general, § 2254(d)'s presumption of correctness can be avoided if and only if Townsend calls for a hearing.   By enacting a statute so closely tied to

---

1.   Although this language contemplates—as is usually the case—that it will be the petitioner who seeks to overcome the state court finding, § 2254(d) also applies to a warden's efforts to overcome state court findings.   See, *e.g.*, Burden v. Zant, 498 U.S. 433 (1991)(per curiam).

Townsend's mandatory hearing rules, Justice O'Connor argued, "Congress established a procedural framework that relies upon Townsend's continuing validity" (p. 21). Therefore, the petitioner was entitled to a federal evidentiary hearing in those circumstances in which, under § 2254(d), the normal presumption of correctness for state court factfindings does not apply.[2]

(5) *The Operation of § 2254(d)*. Of the many questions that have arisen under § 2254(d), two deserve special note.

(a) How should a federal habeas court treat a state court decision that does not rest on express factual findings? In LaVallee v. Delle Rose, 410 U.S. 690 (1973), the petitioner argued that a state court's decision that his confession was voluntary was not entitled to a presumption of correctness because the court had failed to articulate any finding as to the credibility of the petitioner's testimony that the confessions had been coerced—and thus had failed to resolve the merits of the factual dispute as required under § 2254(d)(1). The Supreme Court rejected this argument, ruling that it was obvious from the state court's finding of voluntariness that it had not credited the petitioner's testimony, and that that implicit finding fell within § 2254(d).

A habeas court's freedom to reconstruct state court factfindings that are not express is, however, subject to important limitations. See generally 1 Liebman & Hertz, note 2, *supra*, § 20.3.

(b) Must a *habeas* court make any special findings before refusing to treat state factfindings as presumptively correct? In Sumner v. Mata [I], 449 U.S. 539 (1981), the California Court of Appeal had rejected the prisoner's argument that a pretrial identification admitted as evidence against him at trial had been based on impermissibly suggestive procedures. On habeas, the Ninth Circuit reached the opposite conclusion and granted relief—without having required proof "by convincing evidence" that the state court's finding was erroneous. The Supreme Court reversed, holding that in order to enforce the "mandate of Congress" in enacting § 2254(d), "a habeas court should include in its opinion granting the writ the reasoning which led it to conclude that any of the first seven [§ 2254(d)] factors were present, or the reasoning which led it to

---

2. Though critical of the Court's opinion, Justice O'Connor contended that it merely restricted the circumstances in which evidentiary hearings are mandatory, and did not restrict the district courts' discretion under Townsend to provide a hearing whenever it sees fit. The Court's opinion did not directly address the point. Some lower courts have followed Justice O'Connor's view, see 1 Liebman & Hertz, Federal Habeas Corpus Practice & Procedure, § 20.4 (2d ed. 1994), although that view may be hard to square with the fact that district courts possess no similar discretion to entertain defaulted claims when the requisite showing has not been made.

On evidentiary hearings generally, see Weisselberg, *Evidentiary Hearings in Federal Habeas Corpus Cases*, 1990 B.Y.U.L.Rev. 131, 165–68. Compare Yackle, *The Habeas Hagioscope*, 66 S.Cal.L.Rev. 2331, 2428 (1993)(contending that hearings should al-ways be permitted, with district judges giving a state court factfinding "whatever persuasive power it may have") with Meltzer, *Habeas Corpus Jurisdiction: The Limits of Models*, 66 S.Cal.L.Rev. 2507, 2512–13 (1993)(limits on federal factfinding are desirable and should be governed by "some basic set of ground rules").

A bill that passed the Senate on June 7, 1995, would (a) presume state court factfindings to be correct, and make them rebuttable only by clear and convincing evidence, regardless of the quality of state factfinding processes; and (b) prohibit a habeas court from holding an evidentiary hearing unless (i) the claim relies on new law or new facts not discoverable through due diligence, and (ii) the facts underlying the claim establish that but for the constitutional error, no reasonable factfinder would have found the applicant guilty of the underlying offense. S. 735, § 604, p. 1459, *infra*.

conclude that the state finding was 'not fairly supported by the record' "(p. 551).[3]

(6) *Questions of Fact vs. Mixed Questions.* Recent cases have re-affirmed the rule—whose roots can be found in Justice Frankfurter's opinion in Brown v. Allen—that § 2254(d) requires deference to state court determinations of "historical" fact, but not to determinations requiring the application of law to fact ("mixed" questions). For elaboration of this distinction, see *Note On Control of Factfinding and of Application of Law to Fact,* Paragraph (1), p. 596, *supra.* The Court has, however, had considerable trouble distinguishing the two categories. See generally 1 Liebman & Hertz, note 2, *supra,* § 20.3.

(a) Decisions treating an issue as a mixed question, and thus subject to de novo federal relitigation, include Sumner v. Mata [II], 455 U.S. 591, 597–98 (1982)(per curiam)(question whether a state's identification procedure was impermissibly suggestive); Miller v. Fenton, 474 U.S. 104, 115 (1985)("ultimate question of the admissibility of a confession" alleged to have been coerced); and Brewer v. Williams, 430 U.S. 387, 398 (1977)(question whether suspect's conduct constituted a waiver of his right to counsel in post-indictment interrogation).

(b) Decisions treating an issue as an historical fact, and thus governed by § 2254(d), include Maggio v. Fulford, 462 U.S. 111 (1983)(determination that defendant was competent to stand trial, based upon state trial judge's observation of the defendant and disbelief of a psychiatrist's testimony); Rushen v. Spain, 464 U.S. 114 (1983)(determination that ex parte communication between trial judge and juror had no effect on juror impartiality); Wainwright v. Witt, 469 U.S. 412 (1985)(determination that a person was excludable for cause from a jury in a capital case because of opposition to the death penalty); Marshall v. Lonberger, 459 U.S. 422 (1983)(although determination whether a guilty plea is voluntary for constitutional purposes is a mixed question, determination that the defendant understood the crime to which he was pleading was an issue of fact).

(c) The decisions in Sub–Paragraph (b) prompted Justice Brennan to complain, in dissent in Witt, *supra,* about "the Court's increasingly expansive definition of 'questions of fact' calling for application of the presumption of correctness of 28 U.S.C. § 2254(d) to thwart vindication of fundamental rights in the federal courts" (469 U.S. at 463).

A number of decisions do leave the sense that the line-drawing may be influenced by the majority's lack of enthusiasm for habeas relitigation. But the categories "historical fact" and "application of law to fact", rather than being separated by a sharp line, are more points on a continuum. And in the inevitable close cases, isn't it unsurprising—and perhaps desirable—that decisions are based not so much on a priori analysis and classification of the nature of the issue as on a determination of where in the judicial system decisional

---

3. Sumner I also determined that § 2254(d) applies to factual findings by state appellate as well as trial courts. Furthermore, the majority held it proper to consider the applicability of § 2254(d) though the issue had not been raised below, because the question was one of subject matter jurisdiction: the habeas statute was the "successor to 'the first congressional grant of jurisdiction to the federal courts' * * * and the 1966 amendments embodied in § 2254(d) were intended by Congress as limitations on the exercise of that jurisdiction" (p. 547 n. 2).

Should a burden of proof statute be classified as "jurisdictional"?

authority should be allocated, and on the burden of relitigation (which may be greater for factual than for legal issues)? See pp. 596–97, *supra.*

The Court explicitly followed this institutional approach in its most recent decision on this question, Thompson v. Keohane, 116 S.Ct. 457 (1995), holding (7–2) that the issue whether a suspect is in custody for purposes of *Miranda* is a mixed question that falls outside of § 2254(d) and thus warrants independent review. Justice Ginsburg's majority opinion explained the line of cases in Sub-Paragraph (b) as presenting questions that, although "extending beyond the determination of 'what happened' ", should not be reviewed de novo because they depend heavily on the state court's appraisal of demeanor and credibility, and because the state court's decision "is unlikely to have precedential value" (pp. 464–66).[4] By contrast, a state judge has no "first person vantage" on the "in custody" question, and its resolution may in fact guide future decisions, making de novo federal review appropriate.

———————

Stone v. Powell

428 U.S. 465, 96 S.Ct. 3037, 49 L.Ed.2d 1067 (1976).
Certiorari to the United States Court of Appeals for the Ninth Circuit.

■ MR. JUSTICE POWELL delivered the opinion of the Court.

Respondents in these cases were convicted of criminal offenses in state courts, and their convictions were affirmed on appeal. The prosecution in each case relied upon evidence obtained by searches and seizures alleged by respondents to have been unlawful. Each respondent subsequently sought relief in a federal district court by filing a petition for a writ of federal habeas corpus under 28 U.S.C. § 2254. The question presented is whether a federal court should consider, in ruling on a petition for habeas corpus relief filed by a state prisoner, a claim that evidence obtained by an unconstitutional search or seizure was introduced at his trial, when he has previously been afforded an opportunity for full and fair litigation of his claim in the state courts.   * * *

I

We summarize first the relevant facts and procedural history of these cases.

A

Respondent Lloyd Powell * * * and three companions entered the Bonanza Liquor Store in San Bernardino, Cal., where Powell became involved in an altercation with Gerald Parsons, the store manager, over the theft of a bottle of wine. In the scuffling that followed Powell shot and killed Parsons' wife. Ten hours later an officer of the Henderson, Nev., Police Department arrested Powell for violation of the Henderson vagrancy ordinance, and in the search incident to the arrest discovered a .38 caliber revolver with six expended cartridges in the cylinder.

4. If the last point is correct, what justified the grant of certiorari in these cases? Or is the point that determinations of those issues *generally* have little precedential value (making independent habeas review less important), but an occasional case may be significant enough for Supreme Court review?

Powell was extradited to California and convicted of second-degree murder in the Superior Court of San Bernardino County. * * * A criminologist testified that the revolver found on Powell was the gun that killed Parsons' wife. The trial court rejected Powell's contention that testimony by the Henderson police officer as to the search and the discovery of the revolver should have been excluded because the vagrancy ordinance was unconstitutional. In October 1969, the conviction was affirmed by a California District Court of Appeal. * * * The Supreme Court of California denied Powell's petition for habeas corpus relief.

In August 1971 Powell filed an amended petition for a writ of federal habeas corpus * * * in the United States District Court for the Northern District of California, contending that the testimony concerning the .38 caliber revolver should have been excluded as the fruit of an illegal search. * * * The District Court concluded that the arresting officer had probable cause and held that even if the vagrancy ordinance was unconstitutional, the deterrent purpose of the exclusionary rule does not require that it be applied to bar admission of the fruits of a search incident to an otherwise valid arrest. In the alternative, that court agreed with the California District Court of Appeal that the admission of the evidence concerning Powell's arrest, if error, was harmless beyond a reasonable doubt.

In December 1974, the Court of Appeals for the Ninth Circuit reversed. The Court concluded that the vagrancy ordinance was unconstitutionally vague, that Powell's arrest was therefore illegal, and that although exclusion of the evidence would serve no deterrent purpose with regard to police officers who were enforcing statutes in good faith, exclusion would serve the public interest by deterring legislators from enacting unconstitutional statutes. After an independent review of the evidence the court concluded that the admission of the evidence was not harmless error * * *.

B

[The Court's description of the co-defendant Rice's case is omitted.]

II

* * *

* * * Prior to the Court's decision in Kaufman v. United States, 394 U.S. 217 (1969), * * * a substantial majority of the federal courts of appeals had concluded that collateral review of search-and-seizure claims was inappropriate on motions filed by federal prisoners under 28 U.S.C. § 2255, the modern post-conviction procedure available to federal prisoners in lieu of habeas corpus. The primary rationale advanced in support of those decisions was that Fourth Amendment violations are different in kind from denials of Fifth or Sixth Amendment rights in that claims of illegal search and seizure do not "impugn the integrity of the fact-finding process or challenge evidence as inherently unreliable; rather, the exclusion of illegally seized evidence is simply a prophylactic device intended generally to deter Fourth Amendment violations by law enforcement officers." *Id.*, at 224.

Kaufman rejected this rationale and held that search-and-seizure claims are cognizable in § 2255 proceedings. The Court noted that "the federal habeas remedy extends to state prisoners alleging that unconstitutionally obtained evidence was admitted against them at trial," 394 U.S., at 225, and concluded, as a matter of statutory construction, that there was no basis for restricting "access by federal prisoners with illegal search-and-seizure claims to federal collateral remedies, while placing no similar restriction on access by state prisoners," 394 U.S., at 226. * * * [T]he Court, without discussion or consideration of the issue, has continued to accept jurisdiction in cases raising such claims. See Lefkowitz v. Newsome, 420 U.S. 283 (1975); Cady v. Dombrowski, 413 U.S. 433 (1973).

The discussion in Kaufman * * * rests on the view that the effectuation of the Fourth Amendment, as applied to the States through the Fourteenth Amendment, requires the granting of habeas corpus relief when a prisoner has been convicted in state court on the basis of evidence obtained in an illegal search or seizure since those Amendments were held in Mapp v. Ohio, 367 U.S. 643 (1961), to require exclusion of such evidence at trial and reversal of conviction upon direct review. Until this case we have not had occasion fully to consider the validity of this view. Upon examination, we conclude, in light of the nature and purpose of the Fourth Amendment exclusionary rule, that this view is unjustified.[16] We hold, therefore, that where the State has provided an opportunity for full and fair litigation of a Fourth Amendment claim, the Constitution does not require that a state prisoner be granted federal habeas corpus relief on the ground that evidence obtained in an unconstitutional search or seizure was introduced at his trial.

III

* * *

The exclusionary rule was a judicially created means of effectuating the rights secured by the Fourth Amendment. * * *

Decisions prior to Mapp advanced two principal reasons for application of the rule in federal trials. The Court in Elkins * * * referred to the "imperative of judicial integrity," suggesting that exclusion of illegally seized evidence prevents contamination of the judicial process. 364 U.S., at 222. But even in that context a more pragmatic ground was emphasized:

"The rule is calculated to prevent, not to repair. Its purpose is to deter— to compel respect for the constitutional guaranty in the only effectively available way—by removing the incentive to disregard it." Id., at 217.

The Mapp majority justified the application of the rule to the States on several grounds, but relied principally upon the belief that exclusion would deter future unlawful police conduct. 367 U.S., at 658.

* * *

The primary justification for the exclusionary rule then is the deterrence of police conduct that violates Fourth Amendment rights. Post–Mapp decisions have established that the rule is not a personal constitutional right. It is not calculated to redress the injury to the privacy of the victim of the search or seizure, for any "[r]eparation comes too late." Linkletter v. Walker, 381 U.S.

---

16. The issue in Kaufman was the scope of § 2255. Our decision today rejects the dictum in Kaufman concerning the applicability of the exclusionary rule in federal habeas corpus review of state court decisions pursuant to § 2254. To the extent the appli-cation of the exclusionary rule in Kaufman did not rely upon the supervisory role of this Court over the lower federal courts, cf. Elkins v. United States, 364 U.S. 206 (1960), the rationale for its application in that context is also rejected.

618, 637 (1965). Instead, "the rule is a judicially created remedy designed to safeguard Fourth Amendment rights generally through its deterrent effect. * * *" United States v. Calandra, 414 U.S. at 348. * * *

* * * As in the case of any remedial device, "the application of the rule has been restricted to those areas where its remedial objectives are thought most efficaciously served." United States v. Calandra, 414 U.S. at 348.[24] * * *

IV

We turn now to the specific question presented by these cases * * *[:] whether state prisoners—who have been afforded the opportunity for full and fair consideration of their reliance upon the exclusionary rule with respect to seized evidence by the state courts at trial and on direct review—may invoke their claim again on federal habeas corpus review. The answer is to be found by weighing the utility of the exclusionary rule against the costs of extending it to collateral review of Fourth Amendment claims.

The costs of applying the exclusionary rule even at trial and on direct review are well known: the focus of the trial, and the attention of the participants therein, is diverted from the ultimate question of guilt or innocence that should be the central concern in a criminal proceeding. Moreover, the physical evidence sought to be excluded is typically reliable and often the most probative information bearing on the guilt or innocence of the defendant. * * * Application of the rule thus deflects the truthfinding process and often frees the guilty. The disparity in particular cases between the error committed by the police officer and the windfall afforded a guilty defendant by application of the rule is contrary to the idea of proportionality that is essential to the concept of justice. Thus, although the rule is thought to deter unlawful police activity in part through the nurturing of respect for Fourth Amendment values, if applied indiscriminately it may well have the opposite effect of generating disrespect for the law and administration of justice. These long-recognized costs of the rule persist when a criminal conviction is sought to be overturned on collateral review on the ground that a search-and-seizure claim was erroneously rejected by two or more tiers of state courts.[31]

---

24. As Professor Amsterdam has observed:

"The rule is unsupportable as reparation or compensatory dispensation to the injured criminal; its sole rational justification is the experience of its indispensability in 'exert[ing] general legal pressures to secure obedience to the Fourth Amendment on the part of * * * law-enforcing officers.' As it serves this function, the rule is a needed, but grud[g]ingly taken, medicament; no more should be swallowed than is needed to combat the disease. Granted that so many criminals must go free as will deter the constables from blundering, pursuance of this policy of liberation beyond the confines of necessity inflicts gratuitous harm on the public interest. * * *" Amsterdam, Search, Seizure, and Section 2255: A Comment, 112 U.Pa. L.Rev. 378, 388–389 (1964)(footnotes omitted).

31. Resort to habeas corpus, especially for purposes other than to assure that no innocent person suffers an unconstitutional loss of liberty, results in serious intrusions on values important to our system of government. They include "(i) the most effective utilization of limited judicial resources, (ii) the necessity of finality in criminal trials, (iii) the minimization of friction between our federal and state systems of justice, and (iv) the maintenance of the constitutional balance upon which the doctrine of federalism is founded." Schneckloth v. Bustamonte, 412 U.S., at 259 (Powell, J., concurring).

We nevertheless afford broad habeas corpus relief, recognizing the need in a free society for an additional safeguard against compelling an innocent man to suffer an unconstitutional loss of liberty. * * * But in the case of a typical Fourth Amendment claim, asserted on collateral attack, a convict-

* * * Despite the absence of supportive empirical evidence, we have assumed that the immediate effect of exclusion will be to discourage law enforcement officials from violating the Fourth Amendment by removing the incentive to disregard it. More importantly, over the long term, this demonstration that our society attaches serious consequences to violation of constitutional rights is thought to encourage those who formulate law enforcement policies, and the officers who implement them, to incorporate Fourth Amendment ideals into their value system.

We adhere to the view that these considerations support the implementation of the exclusionary rule at trial and its enforcement on direct appeal of state court convictions. But the additional contribution, if any, of the consideration of search-and-seizure claims of state prisoners on collateral review is small in relation to the costs. To be sure, each case in which such claim is considered may add marginally to an awareness of the values protected by the Fourth Amendment. There is no reason to believe, however, that the overall educative effect of the exclusionary rule would be appreciably diminished if search-and-seizure claims could not be raised in federal habeas corpus review of state convictions. Nor is there reason to assume that any specific disincentive already created by the risk of exclusion of evidence at trial or the reversal of convictions on direct review would be enhanced if there were the further risk that a conviction obtained in state court and affirmed on direct review might be overturned in collateral proceedings often occurring years after the incarceration of the defendant. The view that the deterrence of Fourth Amendment violations would be furthered rests on the dubious assumption that law enforcement authorities would fear that federal habeas review might reveal flaws in a search or seizure that went undetected at trial and on appeal.[35] Even if one rationally could assume that some additional incremental deterrent effect would be present in isolated cases, the resulting advance of the legitimate goal of furthering Fourth Amendment rights would be outweighed by the acknowledged costs to other values vital to a rational system of criminal justice.

In sum, we conclude that where the State has provided an opportunity for full and fair litigation of a Fourth Amendment claim,[36] a state prisoner may not

---

ed defendant is usually asking society to re-determine an issue that has no bearing on the basic justice of his incarceration.

35. The policy arguments that respondents marshal in support of the view that federal habeas corpus review is necessary to effectuate the Fourth Amendment stem from a basic mistrust of the state courts as fair and competent forums for the adjudication of federal constitutional rights. The argument is that state courts cannot be trusted to effectuate Fourth Amendment values through fair application of the rule, and the oversight jurisdiction of this Court on certiorari is an inadequate safeguard. * * * Despite differences in institutional environment and the unsympathetic attitude to federal constitutional claims of some state judges in years past, we are unwilling to assume that there now exists a general lack of appropriate sensitivity to constitutional rights in the trial and appellate courts of the several States. State courts, like federal courts, have a constitutional obligation to safeguard personal liberties and to uphold federal law. Moreover, the argument that federal judges are more expert in applying federal constitutional law is especially unpersuasive in the context of search-and-seizure claims, since they are dealt with on a daily basis by trial level judges in both systems. In sum, there is "no intrinsic reason why the fact that a man is a federal judge should make him more competent, or conscientious, or learned with respect to the [consideration of Fourth Amendment claims] than his neighbor in the state courthouse." Bator, [*Finality in Criminal Law and Federal Habeas Corpus for State Prisoners*, 76 Harv.L.Rev. 441,] 509 [(1963)].

36. *Cf.* Townsend v. Sain, 372 U.S. 293 (1963).

be granted federal habeas corpus relief on the ground that evidence obtained in an unconstitutional search or seizure was introduced at his trial.[37]   * * *

Accordingly, the judgments of the Courts of Appeals are

Reversed.

■ MR. CHIEF JUSTICE BURGER, concurring.

I concur in the Court's opinion. By way of dictum, and somewhat hesitantly, the Court notes that the holding in this case leaves undisturbed the exclusionary rule as applied to criminal trials. For reasons stated in my dissent in Bivens v. Six Unknown Named Federal Agents, 403 U.S. 388, 414 (1971), it seems clear to me that the exclusionary rule has been operative long enough to demonstrate its flaws. The time has come to modify its reach, even if it is retained for a small and limited category of cases. * * *

MR. JUSTICE BRENNAN, with whom MR. JUSTICE MARSHALL concurs, dissenting.

* * * [T]hese cases, despite the veil of Fourth Amendment terminology employed by the Court, plainly do not involve any question of the right of a defendant to have evidence excluded from use against him in his criminal trial when that evidence was seized in contravention of rights ostensibly secured by the Fourth and Fourteenth Amendments. Rather, they involve the question of the availability of a *federal forum* for vindicating those federally guaranteed rights. Today's holding portends substantial evisceration of federal habeas corpus jurisdiction, and I dissent.

* * * The Court insists that its holding is based on the Constitution, but in light of the explicit language of 28 U.S.C. § 2254 (significantly not even mentioned by the Court), I can only presume that the Court intends to be understood to hold either that respondents are not, as a matter of statutory construction, "in custody in violation of the Constitution or laws of the United States," or that "considerations of comity and concerns for the orderly administration of criminal justice," are sufficient to allow this Court to rewrite jurisdictional statutes enacted by Congress. Neither ground of decision is tenable; the former is simply illogical, and the latter is an arrogation of power committed solely to the Congress.

I

Much of the Court's analysis implies that respondents are not entitled to habeas relief because they are not being unconstitutionally detained. Although purportedly adhering to the principle that the Fourth and Fourteenth Amendments "require exclusion" of evidence seized in violation of their commands, the Court informs us that there has merely been a "view" in our cases that "the effectuation of the Fourth Amendment * * * requires the granting of habeas corpus relief when a prisoner has been convicted in state court on the basis of evidence obtained in an illegal search or seizure * * *." * * * [T]he

---

37. Mr. Justice Brennan's dissent characterizes the Court's opinion as laying the groundwork for a "drastic withdrawal of federal habeas jurisdiction, if not for all grounds * * *, then at least [for many] * * *." * * *

With all respect, the hyperbole of the dissenting opinion is misdirected. Our decision today is *not* concerned with the scope of the habeas corpus statute as authority for litigating constitutional claims generally. We do reaffirm that the exclusionary rule is a judicially created remedy rather than a personal constitutional right, and we emphasize the minimal utility of the rule when sought to be applied to Fourth Amendment claims in a habeas corpus proceeding. * * *

Court then concludes that this "view" is unjustified and that the policies of the Fourth Amendment would not be implemented if claims to the benefits of the exclusionary rule were cognizable in collateral attacks on state court convictions.

Understandably the Court must purport to cast its holding in constitutional terms, because that avoids a direct confrontation with the incontrovertible facts that the habeas statutes have heretofore always been construed to grant jurisdiction to entertain Fourth Amendment claims of both state and federal prisoners, that Fourth Amendment principles have been applied in decisions on the merits in numerous cases on collateral review of final convictions, and that Congress has legislatively accepted our interpretation of congressional intent as to the necessary scope and function of habeas relief. * * * [T]he Court asserts, in essence, that the Justices joining those prior decisions or reaching the merits of Fourth Amendment claims simply overlooked the obvious constitutional dimension to the problem in adhering to the "view" that granting collateral relief when state courts erroneously decide Fourth Amendment issues would effectuate the principles underlying that Amendment. But shorn of the rhetoric of "interest balancing" used to obscure what is at stake in this case, it is evident that today's attempt to rest the decision on the Constitution must fail so long as Mapp v. Ohio, 367 U.S. 643 (1961), remains undisturbed.

Under Mapp, as a matter of federal constitutional law, a state court *must* exclude evidence from the trial of an individual whose Fourth and Fourteenth Amendment rights were violated by a search or seizure that directly or indirectly resulted in the acquisition of that evidence. * * * When a state court admits such evidence, it has committed a *constitutional* error, and unless that error is harmless under federal standards, see, *e.g.*, Chapman v. California, 386 U.S. 18 (1967), it follows ineluctably that the defendant has been placed "in custody in violation of the Constitution" within the comprehension of 28 U.S.C. § 2254. * * *

The Court, assuming without deciding that respondents were convicted on the basis of unconstitutionally obtained evidence erroneously admitted against them by the state trial courts, acknowledges that respondents had the right to obtain a reversal of their convictions on appeal in the state courts or on certiorari to this Court. * * * It is simply inconceivable that that constitutional deprivation suddenly vanishes after the appellate process has been exhausted. And as between this Court on certiorari, and federal district courts on habeas, it is for *Congress* to decide what the most efficacious method is for enforcing *federal* constitutional rights and asserting the primacy of federal law. The Court, however, simply ignores the settled principle that for purposes of adjudicating constitutional claims Congress, which has the power to do so under Art. III of the Constitution, has effectively cast the district courts sitting in habeas in the role of surrogate Supreme Courts.[10]

* * *

---

10. The failure to confront this fact forthrightly is obviously a core defect in the Court's analysis. For to the extent Congress has accorded the Federal District Courts a role in our constitutional scheme functionally equivalent to that of the Supreme Court with respect to review of state court resolutions of federal constitutional claims, it is evident that the Court's direct/collateral review distinction for constitutional purposes simply collapses. Indeed, logically extended, the Court's analysis, which basically turns on the fact that law enforcement officials cannot anticipate a second court finding constitutional errors after one court has fully and fairly adjudicated the claim and found it to be

II

Therefore, the real ground of today's decision—a ground that is particularly troubling in light of its portent for habeas jurisdiction generally—is the Court's novel reinterpretation of the habeas statutes; this would read the statutes as requiring the District Courts routinely to deny habeas relief to prisoners "in custody in violation of the Constitution or laws of the United States" as a matter of judicial "discretion"—a "discretion" judicially manufactured today contrary to the express statutory language—because such claims are "different in kind" from other constitutional violations in that they "do not 'impugn the integrity of the fact-finding process,' " and because application of such constitutional strictures "often frees the guilty." Much in the Court's opinion suggests that a construction of the habeas statutes to deny relief for non-"guilt-related" constitutional violations, based on this Court's vague notions of comity and federalism, is the actual premise for today's decision, and although the Court attempts to bury its underlying premises in footnotes, those premises mark this case as a harbinger of future eviscerations of the habeas statutes that plainly does violence to congressional power to frame the statutory contours of habeas jurisdiction. * * * I am therefore justified in apprehending that the groundwork is being laid today for a drastic withdrawal of federal habeas jurisdiction, if not for all grounds of alleged unconstitutional detention, then at least for claims—for example, of double jeopardy, entrapment, self-incrimination, Miranda violations, and use of invalid identification procedures—that this Court later decides are not "guilt-related."

To the extent the Court is actually premising its holding on an interpretation of 28 U.S.C. § 2241 or § 2254, it is overruling the heretofore settled principle that federal habeas relief is available to redress *any* denial of asserted constitutional rights, whether or not denial of the right affected the truth or fairness of the fact-finding process. * * *

* * * In effect, habeas jurisdiction is a deterrent to unconstitutional actions by trial and appellate judges, and a safeguard to ensure that rights secured under the Constitution and federal laws are not merely honored in the breach. * * *

At least since Brown v. Allen, detention emanating from judicial proceedings in which constitutional rights were denied has been deemed "contrary to fundamental law," and all constitutional claims have thus been cognizable on federal habeas corpus. There is no foundation in the language or history of the habeas statutes for discriminating between types of constitutional transgressions, and efforts to relegate certain categories of claims to the status of "second-class rights" by excluding them from that jurisdiction have been repulsed. Today's opinion, however, marks the triumph of those who have sought to establish a hierarchy of constitutional rights, and to deny for all practical purposes a federal forum for review of those rights that this Court deems less worthy or important. * * *

* * * State judges popularly elected may have difficulty resisting popular pressures not experienced by federal judges given lifetime tenure designed to immunize them from such influences, and the federal habeas statutes reflect the Congressional judgment that such detached federal review is a salutary

meritless, would preclude any Supreme Court review on direct appeal or even state appellate review if the trial court fairly addressed the Fourth Amendment claim on the merits. * * *

* * *

safeguard against *any* detention of an individual "in violation of the Constitution or laws of the United States."

Federal courts have the duty to carry out the congressionally assigned responsibility to shoulder the ultimate burden of adjudging whether detentions violate federal law, and today's decision substantially abnegates that duty. The Court does not, because it cannot, dispute that institutional constraints totally preclude any possibility that this Court can adequately oversee whether state courts have properly applied federal law, and does not controvert the fact that federal habeas jurisdiction is partially designed to ameliorate that inadequacy. Thus, although I fully agree that state courts "have a constitutional obligation to safeguard personal liberties and to uphold federal law," and that there is no "general lack of appropriate sensitivity to constitutional rights in the trial and appellate courts of the several States," I cannot agree that it follows that, as the Court today holds, federal court determination of almost all Fourth Amendment claims of state prisoners should be barred and that state court resolution of those issues should be insulated from the federal review Congress intended.
* * *

■ Mr. Justice White, dissenting.

For many of the reasons stated by Mr. Justice Brennan, I cannot agree that the writ of habeas corpus should be any less available to those convicted of state crimes where they allege Fourth Amendment violations than where other constitutional issues are presented to the federal court. Under the amendments to the habeas corpus statute, which were adopted after Fay v. Noia, 372 U.S. 391 (1963), and represented an effort by Congress to lend a modicum of finality to state criminal judgments, I cannot distinguish between Fourth Amendment and other constitutional issues.

Suppose, for example, that two confederates in crime, Smith and Jones, are tried separately for a state crime and convicted on the very same evidence, including evidence seized incident to their arrest allegedly made without probable cause. Their constitutional claims are fully aired, rejected and preserved on appeal. Their convictions are affirmed by the State's highest court. Smith, the first to be tried, does not petition for certiorari, or does so but his petition is denied. Jones, whose conviction was considerably later, is more successful. His petition for certiorari is granted and his conviction reversed because this Court, without making any new rule of law, simply concludes that on the undisputed facts the arrests were made without probable cause and the challenged evidence was therefore seized in violation of the Fourth Amendment. The State must either retry Jones or release him, necessarily because he is deemed in custody in violation of the Constitution. It turns out that without the evidence illegally seized, the State has no case; and Jones goes free. Smith then files his petition for habeas corpus. He makes no claim that he did not have a full and fair hearing in the state courts, but asserts that his Fourth Amendment claim had been erroneously decided and that he is being held in violation of the Federal Constitution. * * * Unless the Court's reservation, in its present opinion, of those situations where the defendant has not had a full and fair hearing in the state courts is intended to encompass all those circumstances under which a state criminal judgment may be reexamined under § 2254—in which event the opinion is essentially meaningless and the judgment erroneous—Smith's petition would be dismissed, and he would spend his life in prison while his colleague is a free man. I cannot believe that Congress intended this result. * * *

I feel constrained to say, however, that I would join four or more other Justices in substantially limiting the reach of the exclusionary rule as presently administered under the Fourth Amendment in federal and state criminal trials.
* * *

FURTHER NOTE ON THE ISSUES COGNIZABLE ON HABEAS CORPUS: THE PERTINENCE OF GUILT OR INNOCENCE

(1) *The "Full and Fair Opportunity" Standard.* If one accepts the majority's theory, why should habeas relief remain available when the state court failed to provide a full and fair opportunity to litigate the claim that the Fourth Amendment requires exclusion of evidence? In such cases, isn't any incremental deterrent effect on the police from the knowledge that habeas review might be available no greater than was true in Stone v. Powell itself? If federal oversight is unnecessary to ensure that state courts will fairly apply federal substantive standards, see footnote 35 of the Court's opinion, why is it necessary to ensure that state courts will provide a fair process?

What constitutes a "full and fair opportunity"? A recurrent question has been whether that phrase should be interpreted as incorporating the standards under Townsend v. Sain, p. 1371, *supra*, for determining when a habeas court must rehear the facts. (Note the majority's cryptic "cf." reference, in footnote 36, to Townsend.) *See generally* 2 Liebman & Hertz, Federal Habeas Corpus Practice & Procedure, ch. 27 (2d ed.1994); Halpern, *Federal Habeas Corpus and the Mapp Exclusionary Rule After Stone v. Powell*, 82 Colum.L.Rev. 1, 14–16 (1982).

(2) *The Relevance of Petitioner's Guilt or Innocence.*

(a) Justice Brennan's dissent in Stone expressed concern that the majority was laying the groundwork for "a drastic withdrawal of federal habeas jurisdiction * * * for claims * * * that this Court later decides are not 'guilt-related.'" There was some basis for that concern not only in Justice Powell's opinion in Stone, but also in his concurring opinion in Schneckloth v. Bustamonte, 412 U.S. 218, 250 (1973), on which he drew in Stone. Bustamonte was also a habeas case attacking a state conviction on the ground that illegal evidence was admitted at trial. A majority of the Court reached (and rejected on the merits) the Fourth Amendment claim. Justice Powell, joined by Chief Justice Burger and Justice Rehnquist,[1] would have held that such a claim was cognizable on habeas only where the petitioner did not have a fair opportunity to litigate in state court.

Justice Powell's opinion in Bustamonte, in addition to pre-figuring arguments that appeared in Stone v. Powell, offered a more general attack on Brown v. Allen. He stated (pp. 256–58):

"Recent decisions * * * have tended to depreciate the importance of the finality of prior judgments in criminal cases. * * * This trend may be a justifiable evolution of the use of habeas corpus where the one in state custody raises a constitutional claim bearing on his innocence. But the justification for

---

1. Justice Blackmun stated that he agreed with "nearly all" of Justice Powell's opinion, but did not formally join it.

disregarding the historic scope and function of the writ is measurably less apparent in the typical Fourth Amendment claim asserted on collateral attack. * * *

* * *

"I am aware that history reveals no exact tie of the writ of habeas corpus to a constitutional claim relating to innocence or guilt. * * * We are now faced, however, with the task of accommodating the historic respect for the finality of the judgment of a committing court with recent Court expansions of the role of the writ. This accommodation can best be achieved, with due regard to all of the values implicated, by recourse to the central reason for habeas corpus: the affording of means, through an extraordinary writ, of redressing an *unjust* incarceration."

(b) Justice Powell's Bustamonte opinion was plainly influenced by Friendly, *Is Innocence Irrelevant?   Collateral Attack on Criminal Judgments*, 38 U.Chi.L.Rev. 142 (1970). Judge Friendly contended that, subject only to limited exceptions, a petitioner who received a fair hearing in state court should not be able collaterally to attack a criminal conviction without making "a colorable showing that an error, whether 'constitutional' or not, may be producing the continued punishment of an innocent" person (p. 160).[2]   A showing that, for example, the petitioner would not have escaped conviction had illegally obtained (but entirely reliable) evidence not been improperly admitted would fall short; rather, the petitioner "must show a fair probability that, in light of all the evidence, including that alleged to have been illegally admitted (but with due regard to any unreliability of it) and evidence tenably claimed to have been wrongly excluded or to have become available only after the trial, the trier of the facts would have entertained a reasonable doubt of his guilt" (p. 160).

Note, however, how Justice Powell's position in Bustamonte differs from Judge Friendly's approach. Justice Powell would limit habeas based on the general nature of the claim; coerced confession claims are permitted, fourth amendment claims are not. Judge Friendly would look more specifically to the facts of the particular prisoner's case (and to any error): if the proper showing can be made, the prisoner could raise any constitutional claim (even a fourth amendment claim); absent the requisite showing, habeas is unavailable (even on a coerced confession claim).

(c) Would acceptance of Judge Friendly's position burden habeas courts further, by requiring litigation at the threshold about the state of the evidence of the prisoner's guilt?

Would acceptance of Justice Powell's position create a set of "second-class" constitutional rights?   Under his view, should double jeopardy or selective prosecution claims be cognizable?   Claims of discrimination in selection of the petit jury, or of improper exclusion of potential jurors for cause?

2. Judge Friendly advocated exceptions where (i) the original tribunal lacked jurisdiction or the criminal process had so broken down that the defendant did not receive the kind of trial the Constitution guarantees (*e.g.*, mob domination); (ii) the constitutional claim was based on facts outside the record and only collateral attack could vindicate the claim; (iii) the state failed to provide a proper procedure for making a defense at trial and on appeal; or (iv) there had been a change in the governing constitutional law.

Under either view, would petitioners simply try to plead around any limitation, by asserting their innocence and/or by including additional guilt-related claims in their petitions?

Whatever the intuitive appeal of restricting habeas review to claims somehow related to innocence, might the pressures to under-enforce federal constitutional norms be greatest when conviction of the innocent is not at issue—making federal oversight most important in exactly the cases that Judge Friendly and Justice Powell suggested should be excluded from habeas review? On the other hand, if certain constitutional norms can be reliably enforced only by providing an additional layer of collateral litigation, does that cast doubt upon the soundness of the norms themselves?

(3) *The Limitation of Stone.* Decisions since Stone v. Powell have not expanded upon its suggestion that habeas corpus be limited to matters relating to guilt or innocence.

(a) Rose v. Mitchell, 443 U.S. 545 (1979), involved an allegation by prisoners convicted of murder that there had been racial discrimination in selecting the grand jury that had indicted them. (When a prisoner has been convicted by an untainted trial jury, which had to find guilt beyond a reasonable doubt, there is little reason to believe that discrimination in selection of the grand jury—which typically has to find only a prima facie case of guilt—led to conviction of an innocent person.) The Supreme Court decided (5–2 on this issue) not to extend the rationale of Stone v. Powell to such a claim.

Justice Blackmun wrote (p. 560) that in Stone the Court confined its ruling to "cases involving the judicially created exclusionary rule, which had minimal utility when applied in a habeas corpus proceeding. * * * [A] claim of discrimination in the selection of the grand jury differs * * * fundamentally"—a contention Justice Blackmun supported by stressing four points. First, a claim of grand jury discrimination involves an allegation that the trial court itself—rather than the police—violated the Constitution; as a result, there is doubt whether the claim can receive a full and fair hearing in the state courts. Second, the grand jury claim involves a violation of the direct commands of the Equal Protection Clause and statutes passed under it, rather than the judicially created exclusionary rule. Third, habeas corpus will serve as an effective remedy for violations of the rule prohibiting discrimination in the selection of the grand jury. Finally, the grand jury discrimination issues involve a "concern with judicial integrity" and touch on "substantially more compelling" constitutional interests than those at issue in Stone v. Powell (pp. 563–64).[3]

Justice Powell, joined by Justice Rehnquist, dissented on this issue, reiterating the arguments he advanced in Schneckloth v. Bustamonte, and complaining that the Court's ruling was an "extreme example" of the "loss of historical perspective" that has converted habeas corpus into a duplication of the appellate process (p. 581).[4]

3. The Court also rejected the argument presented in Justice Stewart's separate opinion (which Justice Rehnquist joined) that a claim of grand jury discrimination, when raised by a defendant convicted beyond a reasonable doubt by an untainted petit jury, is "harmless error" that does not warrant setting aside a conviction on either direct or collateral review.

4. Chief Justice Burger and Justice Stewart (whose opinion is described in note 3, *supra*) expressed no view on this issue.

In accord with Rose is Vasquez v. Hillery, 474 U.S. 254 (1986)(affirming the grant of a habeas petition because there had been

(b) In Kimmelman v. Morrison, 477 U.S. 365 (1986), the Court (per Justice Brennan) held that a habeas petitioner may obtain relief on a Sixth Amendment claim of ineffective assistance of counsel—even though the claim was premised on counsel's failure to file a timely motion, under the Fourth Amendment, to suppress evidence. Justice Brennan reasoned that the Sixth Amendment claim was distinct from a Fourth Amendment claim (which would be foreclosed under Stone), because in order to prevail, the defendant had to show not only that the Fourth Amendment claim would have been meritorious, but also that the lawyer's performance was deficient and that there was a reasonable probability that the verdict would have been different had the evidence been excluded.

Justice Brennan also rejected the state's argument that Stone's rationale should bar relief. He noted that the Court in Stone had distinguished personal constitutional rights—such as that to effective assistance of counsel—from the judicially created remedy excluding illegally obtained evidence. And he concluded that while the Stone Court had stressed the minimal deterrent utility of applying the exclusionary rule in habeas cases, "collateral review will frequently be the only means through which an accused can effectuate the right to counsel * * *. * * * Indeed, an accused will often not realize that he has a meritorious ineffectiveness claim until he begins collateral review proceedings, particularly if he retained trial counsel on direct appeal. * * * Thus, we cannot say, as the Court was able to say in Stone, that restriction of federal habeas review would not severely interfere with the protection of the constitutional right asserted by the habeas petitioner" (pp. 378–79). Justice Brennan added that Stone was predicated on the existence of "an opportunity for full and fair litigation" in state court of the petitioner's constitutional claim—an opportunity that generally is lacking for ineffective assistance claims.

(c) Perhaps the most notable decision refusing to extend Stone was Withrow v. Williams, 507 U.S. 680 (1993), where the petitioner claimed a violation of the Miranda rules. Justice Souter's majority opinion argued that unlike the Fourth Amendment's exclusionary rule, the Miranda decision "safeguards 'a fundamental trial right'" (507 U.S. at ___, quoting United States v. Verdugo–Urquidez, 494 U.S. 259, 264 (1990)). Moreover, that right, unlike the rights conferred by the Fourth Amendment, is not necessarily "divorced from the correct ascertainment of guilt" (507 U.S. at ___). Most importantly, eliminating habeas review of Miranda claims would not significantly unburden the federal courts or the states: petitioners would simply allege instead that their confessions were involuntary and thus in violation of the Due Process Clause, which would require difficult determinations under a totality of the circumstances test rather than under Miranda's "brighter-line" rules.[5]

Dissenting from this portion of the Court's decision, Justice O'Connor (joined by Chief Justice Rehnquist) argued that (1) Miranda announced a set of prophylactic rules, not a core constitutional right; (2) confessions that were obtained in violation of Miranda, but were not involuntary in the constitutional

---

racial discrimination in selecting the grand jury, over Justice Powell's objection in dissent that because the prisoner was convicted in 1962, the state might no longer be able to retry him).

5. Note also that if Stone were extended to Miranda claims, the state courts, too,

would have to litigate involuntary confession claims more frequently, for the procedural default and exhaustion doctrines would require defendants to raise, in state court, not only Miranda claims, but also involuntary confession claims in order to preserve the latter for federal review.

sense, are reliable; and (3) any impact of habeas review in improving police compliance with Miranda is so slight as to be outweighed by considerations of finality, equity, and federalism. She added that the Court greatly underestimated the relief to habeas courts from eliminating Miranda claims, most of which cannot easily be transformed into litigable claims that a confession was involuntary.[6]

(d) Do Rose, Kimmelman, and Withrow, taken together, make clear that, for the present at least, Stone is limited to the Fourth Amendment's exclusionary rule? Is that case truly *sui generis*?[7]

(4) *Claims Relating to Innocence.* Do habeas courts have a special responsibility for claims that go directly to the prisoner's innocence?

(a) *Jackson v. Virginia.* In Jackson v. Virginia, 443 U.S. 307 (1979), p. 612, *supra*, the Court, per Stewart, J., first ruled that the federal constitutional right not to be convicted of a crime unless the jury finds the defendant guilty beyond a reasonable doubt means that the question whether the evidence in the case supports the finding of guilt beyond reasonable doubt is itself a federal constitutional question. The Court then went on to hold that question to be fully cognizable in habeas proceedings.

On the latter point, the Court rejected the state's invitation to treat such a claim as falling within Stone v. Powell's limit on federal habeas corpus jurisdiction, in order to avoid creating friction with the state courts, eroding finality, and burdening the habeas courts with meritless petitions. Justice Stewart's opinion for the most part treated the exercise of habeas jurisdiction in this case as a routine application of Brown v. Allen, but he did note that unlike the Fourth Amendment issue in Stone, "[t]he question whether a defendant has been convicted upon inadequate evidence is central to the basic question of guilt or innocence" (p. 323).

(b) *Herrera v. Collins.* In Herrera v. Collins, 506 U.S. 390 (1993), however, the Court made clear that habeas corpus is not to be used as a general

---

6. Justice Scalia (joined by Justice Thomas) would have denied relief on the ground that the equitable discretion possessed by habeas courts is abused by granting relief to a petitioner who had a full and fair opportunity to litigate in state court, unless the claim "goes to the fairness of the trial process or to the accuracy of the ultimate result" (507 U.S. at ___). He distinguished Kimmelman on the ground that the right to counsel goes to the fairness of the trial process, and Rose on the ground that in that case there had been no full and fair opportunity to litigate the claim that the state judiciary itself had denied equal protection.

He also noted more broadly that federal prisoners who had a prior opportunity to litigate constitutional issues ordinarily may not relitigate those claims in collateral attacks under § 2255. He argued that to treat state prisoners differently—in order to give them a federal forum for their federal constitutional claims—was inconsistent with (i) the history of federal habeas corpus in the nine-

teenth century, and (ii) the presumption—drawn from Article III's failure to mandate creation of lower federal courts—that state courts will faithfully apply federal law.

7. Articles critical of Stone v. Powell include Patchel, *The New Habeas*, 42 Hastings L.J. 939, 959–65 (1991); Rosenberg, *Constricting Federal Habeas Corpus: From Great Writ to Exceptional Remedy*, 12 Hastings Const.L.Q. 597, 598–610 (1985); Seidman, *Factual Guilt and the Burger Court: An Examination of Continuity and Change in Criminal Procedure*, 80 Colum.L.Rev. 436, 449–59 (1980); Soloff, *Litigation and Relitigation: The Uncertain Status of Federal Habeas Corpus for State Prisoners*, 6 Hofstra L.Rev. 297, 304–09 (1978); Tushnet, *Constitutional and Statutory Analyses in the Law of Federal Jurisdiction*, 25 U.C.L.A.L.Rev. 1301, 1316–18 (1978). More supportive of Stone is Halpern, Paragraph (1), *supra*. See also Cover & Aleinikoff, *Dialectical Federalism: Habeas Corpus and the Court*, 86 Yale L.J. 1035, 1086–1100 (1977).

inquiry into a prisoner's guilt or innocence. The evidence at Herrera's murder trial included two eyewitness identifications and a handwritten letter in which he appeared to admit his guilt. Ten years after his conviction and death sentence, he contended that newly discovered evidence (affidavits from persons asserting that Herrera's now-dead brother had confessed to the murder) showed that Herrera was actually innocent, and argued that his execution would violate the Eighth and Fourteenth Amendments.

Holding that his petition should be denied, the Court ruled that "[c]laims of actual innocence based on newly discovered evidence have never been held to state a ground for federal habeas relief absent an independent constitutional violation occurring in the underlying state criminal proceeding" (506 U.S. at 400). The function of habeas review, the Court submitted, was to redress federal constitutional violations, not to correct factual errors, and review of innocence claims standing alone would severely disrupt the strong state interest in finality. The Court resisted petitioner's formulation of the question— whether it is constitutional to execute the innocent—stressing that in view of Herrera's conviction after a fair trial, he was to be treated as guilty of murder.

Herrera's claim, the Court reasoned, differed from the claim presented in Jackson v. Virginia. First, Jackson establishes an independent constitutional violation. Second, Jackson does not require new factfinding, but only review of the record evidence. Finally, Jackson asks only if the verdict of guilt was rational, not whether it was correct.

The Court added: "We may assume, for the sake of argument * * *, that in a capital case a truly persuasive demonstration of 'actual innocence'" would warrant habeas relief "if there were no state avenue open to process such a claim." However, the petitioner's showing in this case fell far short of the "extraordinarily high" threshold for such an "assumed right" (506 U.S. at 417).[8]

(5) *Questions About Innocence.* Is any purpose of post-conviction review more central than protecting against conviction of the innocent? If not, was the Court too grudging in Herrera? Or are there institutional arguments that support the Court's approach: (a) the burdens of habeas review of "actual innocence" would be high, for a claim of innocence can be raised in every case, and its adjudication is labor-intensive; and (b) there is less need for federal supervision here, because the claim is one that state courts care about, and often requires an interpretation of the elements of the crime (a question of state law)? Are these arguments persuasive in general? Is the second argument persuasive in the context of a capital conviction for a heinous murder in a

---

8. Concurring in the judgment, Justice White stated: "I assume that a persuasive showing of 'actual innocence' * * * would render unconstitutional the execution of petitioner in this case," but agreed that no such showing had been made (506 U.S. at 429). In a concurrence joined by Justice Kennedy, Justice O'Connor said she would not reach the "sensitive" and "troubling" issue of whether habeas jurisdiction encompasses a death row inmate's claim of innocence, because "[t]he record overwhelmingly demonstrates" that Herrera committed the murder (506 U.S. at 421). Justice Scalia, in a con-

curring opinion joined by Justice Thomas, criticized the Court for failing firmly to declare that there is no constitutional right to consideration of evidence of innocence that is discovered after conviction.

In dissent Justice Blackmun (joined by Justices Stevens and Souter) contended that it would be unconstitutional to execute a person who could prove his innocence based on newly discovered evidence, and urged a remand to permit the district court to determine whether Herrera was "probably actually innocent" (506 U.S. at 445).

region known for both strong pro-death penalty sentiment and inadequate resources for defense counsel?

What about the objection that the writ always requires as a jurisdictional pre-requisite an allegation that the custody violates the federal Constitution, or some other fundamental federal law? One response notes the role that allegations of innocence play in other areas of habeas doctrine. Despite the Court's failure generally to restrict habeas to claims relating to guilt or innocence, it has privileged such claims in other ways. Thus, a number of distinct doctrines that generally bar the exercise of habeas corpus jurisdiction contain exceptions permitting federal review if the petitioner can make a strong showing of probable innocence. See, *e.g.*, Murray v. Carrier, p. 1432, *infra* (state court procedural default); McCleskey v. Zant, p. 1442, *infra* (default in previous habeas petition); Teague v. Lane, p. 1392, *infra* (claim based on new law). Still, in each of these instances, allegations of innocence serve as a *gateway* to the consideration of a constitutional claim rather than as the sole basis for habeas relief.

Can it be argued that the Court has always re-shaped the writ based on its evaluation of competing concerns—as illustrated by (a) the evolution of the writ, through 1953, into a regime of relitigation; (b) cutbacks in the rule of Brown v. Allen in Stone v. Powell and in Brecht v. Abrahamson, p. 1362, *supra* (on harmless error standards); and (c) a range of other judicially crafted doctrines, most notably that of the next principal case, Teague v. Lane (limiting habeas jurisdiction over claims based on "new" rules of constitutional law)? See Steiker, *Innocence and Federal Habeas*, 41 U.C.L.A.L.Rev. 303, 309 (1993). If so, should the writ be re-shaped once again, to permit relief based on a showing of innocence?

(6) *The Availability of State Court Post–Conviction Remedies.* The Herrera opinion noted that every state permits motions for a new trial based on new evidence, but such proceedings are subject to a number of limitations. One relates to timing: 17 states (including Texas, where Herrera was convicted) require that such a motion be made within 60 days after judgment, while another 18 have time limits of one to three years. A second limit is the substantive standard that must be satisfied: many jurisdictions require the evidence to have come to light after trial, not to have been obtainable earlier in the exercise of due diligence, and to be likely to lead to a different result upon retrial. See Berger, *Herrera v. Collins: The Gateway of Innocence For Death–Sentenced Prisoners Leads Nowhere*, 35 Wm. & Mary L.Rev. 943, 958 (1994). Judges often exhibit considerable skepticism about such motions (based in part on the difficulties faced in retrying the prisoner should relief be granted), and it is difficult for convicts (who often lack the assistance of counsel) to prevail.

Does the Constitution require states to provide some post-conviction process for certain classes of claims not easily raised at trial or on appeal—for example, claims of newly discovered evidence, or of prosecutorial withholding of exculpatory evidence, or of ineffective assistance of counsel? The Court granted certiorari to address that question in Case v. Nebraska, 381 U.S. 336 (1965), where the state courts had held that they lacked jurisdiction to entertain a post-conviction motion asserting ineffective assistance of counsel; but in the end the Court remanded in light of a supervening state statute that appeared to afford a hearing. Dicta in Supreme Court opinions since then have asserted broadly, although with respect to quite different questions, that due process "does not establish any right to collaterally attack a final judgment of conviction". United States v. MacCollom, 426 U.S. 317, 323 (1976)(plurality opinion)(rejecting federal defendant's equal protection challenge to failure to provide a free transcript for use in a motion to vacate sentence); accord Pennsylvania v. Finley, 481 U.S. 551, 556–57 (1987)(upholding right of lawyer who had been provided by state in post-conviction proceeding to withdraw from matter he and trial court deemed frivolous); Murray v. Giarratano, 492 U.S. 1, 10–11 (1989)(plurality opinion)(death row inmates have no constitutional right to appointed counsel in state post-conviction proceedings). For an argument there is a right to seek state post-conviction relief in some circumstances, see generally Berger, *supra*.

Could Herrera have argued not simply that under state law he was innocent of the crime, but that Texas' refusal to entertain a new trial motion more than 30 days after conviction was itself a denial of due process—and/or, in a capital case, of the Eighth Amendment? What would be the content of such a due process right to state postconviction relief? If a state refused to provide a constitutionally-required hearing, could the Supreme Court order it to do so on remand? Should a federal habeas court enter an order requiring a state court to provide any hearing that federal law might require, *cf.* Testa v. Katt, p. 469, *supra*, or proceed instead to conduct the hearing itself? See Bator, *Finality in Criminal Law and Federal Habeas Corpus for State Prisoners*, 76 Harv.L.Rev. 441, 459–60, 491–93 (1963); Note, 53 Colum.L.Rev. 1143 (1953). Should the states be constitutionally obligated to create special remedies for the litigation of federal claims if those claims are in any event going to be relitigated in a federal district court? Should any such duty remain inchoate until such time as the federal courts are unavailable to hear such claims?

Teague v. Lane

489 U.S. 288, 109 S.Ct. 1060, 103 L.Ed.2d 334 (1989).
Certiorari to the United States Court of Appeals for the Seventh Circuit.

■ JUSTICE O'CONNOR announced the judgment of the Court and delivered the opinion of the Court with respect to Parts I, II, and III, and an opinion with respect to Parts IV and V, in which THE CHIEF JUSTICE, JUSTICE SCALIA, and JUSTICE KENNEDY join.

In Taylor v. Louisiana, 419 U.S. 522 (1975), this Court held that the Sixth Amendment required that the jury venire be drawn from a fair cross section of the community. The Court stated, however, that "* * * we impose no requirement that petit juries actually chosen must mirror the community and reflect the various distinctive groups in the population. Defendants are not entitled to a jury of any particular composition." The principal question presented in this case is whether the Sixth Amendment's fair cross section requirement should now be extended to the petit jury. Because we adopt Justice Harlan's approach to retroactivity for cases on collateral review, we leave the resolution of that question for another day.

I

Petitioner, a black man, was convicted by an all-white Illinois jury of three counts of attempted murder, two counts of armed robbery, and one count of aggravated battery. During jury selection for petitioner's trial, the prosecutor used all 10 of his peremptory challenges to exclude blacks.   * * *   [After petitioner moved for a mistrial, the] prosecutor defended the challenges by stating that he was trying to achieve a balance of men and women on the jury. The trial court denied the motion, reasoning that the jury "appear[ed] to be a fair [one]."

* * *

[After unsuccessful appeals, Teague filed a federal habeas corpus petition that repeated his fair cross-section claim, and also argued that the opinions of several Justices concurring in and dissenting from the denial of certiorari in McCray v. New York, 461 U.S. 961 (1983), had invited a reexamination of Swain v. Alabama, 380 U.S. 202 (1965), which had limited the reach of the Equal Protection Clause as applied to the prosecutor's use of peremptory challenges to exclude blacks from the jury. The district court denied relief, holding that it was bound by Swain and Circuit precedent.

[The Court of Appeals reversed, and rehearing en banc] was postponed until after our decision in Batson v. Kentucky, 476 U.S. 79 (1986), which overruled a portion of Swain. After Batson was decided, the Court of Appeals held that petitioner could not benefit from the rule in that case because Allen v. Hardy, 478 U.S. 255 (1986)(per curiam), had held that Batson would not be applied retroactively to cases on collateral review. * * * The Court of Appeals rejected petitioner's fair cross section claim, holding that the fair cross section requirement was limited to the jury venire. * * *

II

Petitioner's first contention is that he should receive the benefit of our decision in Batson even though his conviction became final before Batson was decided. * * *

In Batson, the Court overruled that portion of Swain setting forth the evidentiary showing necessary to make out a prima facie case of racial discrimination under the Equal Protection Clause. The Court held that a defendant can establish a prima facie case by showing that he is a "member of a cognizable racial group," that the prosecutor exercised "peremptory challenges to remove from the venire members of the defendant's race," and that those "facts and any other relevant circumstances raise an inference that the prosecutor used that practice to exclude the veniremen from the petit jury on account of their race." 476 U.S., at 96. * * *

In Allen v. Hardy, the Court held that Batson constituted an "explicit and substantial break with prior precedent" because it overruled a portion of Swain. Employing the retroactivity standard of Linkletter v. Walker, 381 U.S. 618, 636 (1965), the Court concluded that the rule announced in Batson should not be applied retroactively on collateral review of convictions that became final before Batson was announced. The Court defined final to mean a case "where the judgment of conviction was rendered, the availability of appeal exhausted, and the time for petition for certiorari had elapsed before our decision in Batson[.]"

Petitioner's conviction became final two and a half years prior to Batson * * *.

* * * We find that Allen v. Hardy is dispositive, and that petitioner cannot benefit from the rule announced in Batson.

III

* * *

IV

Petitioner's * * * final contention is that the Sixth Amendment's fair cross section requirement applies to the petit jury. * * * Petitioner * * * contends that the *ratio decidendi* of Taylor cannot be limited to the jury venire, and he urges adoption of a new rule. Because we hold that the rule urged by petitioner should not be applied retroactively to cases on collateral review, we decline to address petitioner's contention.

A

In the past, the Court has, without discussion, often applied a new constitutional rule of criminal procedure to the defendant in the case announcing the new rule, and has confronted the question of retroactivity later when a different defendant sought the benefit of that rule. In several cases, however, the Court has addressed the retroactivity question in the very case announcing the new rule. These two lines of cases do not have a unifying theme, and we think it is time to clarify how the question of retroactivity should be resolved for cases on collateral review.

* * *

In our view, the question "of whether a decision [announcing a new rule should] be given prospective or retroactive effect should be faced at the time of [that] decision." Mishkin, *Foreword: The High Court, the Great Writ, and the Due Process of Time and Law*, 79 Harv.L.Rev. 56, 64 (1965). Retroactivity is properly treated as a threshold question, for, once a new rule is applied to the defendant in the case announcing the rule, even-handed justice requires that it be applied retroactively to all who are similarly situated. Thus, before deciding whether the fair cross section requirement should be extended to the petit jury, we should ask whether such a rule would be applied retroactively to the case at issue. This retroactivity determination would normally entail application of the Linkletter standard, but we believe that our approach to retroactivity for cases on collateral review requires modification.

It is admittedly often difficult to determine when a case announces a new rule, and we do not attempt to define the spectrum of what may or may not constitute a new rule for retroactivity purposes. In general, however, a case announces a new rule when it breaks new ground or imposes a new obligation on the States or the Federal Government. See, *e.g.*, Rock v. Arkansas, 483 U.S. 44, 62 (1987)(*per se* rule excluding all hypnotically refreshed testimony infringes impermissibly on a criminal defendant's right to testify on his behalf); Ford v. Wainwright, 477 U.S. 399, 410 (1986)(Eighth Amendment prohibits the execution of prisoners who are insane). To put it differently, a case announces a new rule if the result was not dictated by precedent existing at the time the defendant's conviction became final. Given the strong language in Taylor and our statement in Akins v. Texas, 325 U.S. 398, 403 (1945), that "[f]airness in [jury] selection has never been held to require proportional representation of races upon a jury," application of the fair cross section requirement to the petit jury would be a new rule.[1]

---

1. The dissent asserts that petitioner's fair cross section claim does not embrace the concept of proportional representation on the petit jury. Although petitioner disavows

Not all new rules have been uniformly treated for retroactivity purposes. Nearly a quarter of a century ago, in Linkletter, the Court * * * [faced the question] whether Mapp v. Ohio, which made the exclusionary rule applicable to the States, should be applied retroactively to cases on collateral review. The Court determined that the retroactivity of Mapp should be determined by examining the purpose of the exclusionary rule, the reliance of the States on prior law, and the effect on the administration of justice of a retroactive application of the exclusionary rule. Using that standard, the Court held that Mapp would only apply to trials commencing after that case was decided.

* * *

Application of the Linkletter standard led to the disparate treatment of similarly situated defendants on direct review. For example, in Miranda v. Arizona, 384 U.S. 436, 467–473 (1966), the Court * * * [applied the new rules there announced] to the defendants in Miranda and its companion cases, and held that their convictions could not stand because they had been interrogated without the proper warnings. In Johnson v. New Jersey, 384 U.S. 719, 733–735 (1966), the Court held under the Linkletter standard that Miranda would only be applied to trials commencing after that decision had been announced. Because the defendant in Johnson, like the defendants in Miranda, was on direct review of his conviction, the Court's refusal to give Miranda retroactive effect resulted in unequal treatment of those who were similarly situated. * * *

Dissatisfied with the Linkletter standard, Justice Harlan advocated a different approach to retroactivity. He argued that new rules should always be applied retroactively to cases on direct review, but that generally they should not be applied retroactively to criminal cases on collateral review. See Mackey v. United States, 401 U.S. 667, 675 (1971)(separate opinion of Harlan, J.); Desist v. United States, 394 U.S. [244], 256 [(1969)] (Harlan, J., dissenting).

In Griffith v. Kentucky, 479 U.S. 314 (1987), we * * * adopted the first part of the retroactivity approach advocated by Justice Harlan. We agreed with Justice Harlan that "failure to apply a newly declared constitutional rule to criminal cases pending on direct review violates basic norms of constitutional adjudication." We gave two reasons for our decision. First, because we can only promulgate new rules in specific cases and cannot possibly decide all cases in which review is sought, "the integrity of judicial review" requires the application of the new rule to "all similar cases pending on direct review." We quoted approvingly from Justice Harlan's separate opinion in Mackey, 401 U.S., at 679:

such representation at the beginning of his brief, he later advocates adoption of the standard set forth in Duren v. Missouri, 439 U.S. 357 (1979) * * *. In order to establish a prima facie violation of the fair cross section requirement under Duren, a defendant must show: (1) that the "group alleged to be excluded is a 'distinctive' group in the community;" (2) that the representation of the group "is not fair and reasonable in relation to the number of such persons in the commu-

nity;" and (3) that the underrepresentation of the group "is due to systematic exclusion of the group in the jury selection process." The second prong of Duren is met by demonstrating that the group is underrepresented in proportion to its position in the community as documented by census figures. If petitioner must meet this prong of Duren to prevail, it is clear that his fair cross section claim is properly characterized as requiring "fair and reasonable" proportional representation on the petit jury. * * *

"If we do not resolve all cases before us on direct review in light of our best understanding of governing constitutional principles, it is difficult to see why we should so adjudicate any case at all. * * * In truth, the Court's assertion of power to disregard current law in adjudicating cases before us that have not already run the full course of appellate review is quite simply an assertion that our constitutional function is not one of adjudication but in effect of legislation."

Second, because "selective application of new rules violates the principle of treating similarly situated defendants the same," we refused to continue to tolerate the inequity that resulted from not applying new rules retroactively to defendants whose cases had not yet become final. * * *

* * *

B

Justice Harlan believed that new rules generally should not be applied retroactively to cases on collateral review. * * * [In Mackey, he wrote:]

"Habeas corpus always has been a *collateral* remedy, providing an avenue for upsetting judgments that have become otherwise final. It is not designed as a substitute for direct review. The interest in leaving concluded litigation in a state of repose, that is, reducing the controversy to a final judgment not subject to further judicial revision, may quite legitimately be found by those responsible for defining the scope of the writ to outweigh in some, many, or most instances the competing interest in readjudicating convictions according to all legal standards in effect when a habeas petition is filed." [401 U.S.] at 682–683.

* * * As he had explained in Desist, "the threat of habeas serves as a necessary incentive for trial and appellate judges throughout the land to conduct their proceedings in a manner consistent with established constitutional principles. In order to perform this deterrence function, the habeas court need only apply the constitutional standards that prevailed at the time the original proceedings took place." 394 U.S., at 262–263. * * *

Justice Harlan identified only two exceptions to his general rule of nonretroactivity for cases on collateral review. First, a new rule should be applied retroactively if it places "certain kinds of primary, private individual conduct beyond the power of the criminal law-making authority to proscribe." Mackey, 401 U.S., at 692 (separate opinion). Second, a new rule should be applied retroactively if it requires the observance of "those procedures that * * * are 'implicit in the concept of ordered liberty.'" *Id.*, at 693 (quoting Palko v. Connecticut, 302 U.S. 319, 325 (1937)(Cardozo, J.)).

* * *

We agree with Justice Harlan's description of the function of habeas corpus. * * *

* * *

* * * Application of constitutional rules not in existence at the time a conviction became final seriously undermines the principle of finality which is essential to the operation of our criminal justice system. Without finality, the criminal law is deprived of much of its deterrent effect. The fact that life and liberty are at stake in criminal prosecutions "shows only that 'conventional notions of finality' should not have *as much* place in criminal as in civil

litigation, not that they should have *none*." Friendly, *Is Innocence Irrelevant? Collateral Attacks on Criminal Judgments*, 38 U.Chi.L.Rev. 142, 150 (1970). "[I]f a criminal judgment is ever to be final, the notion of legality must at some point include the assignment of final competence to determine legality." Bator, *Finality in Criminal Law and Federal Habeas Corpus for State Prisoners*, 76 Harv.L.Rev. 441, 450–451 (1963) (emphasis omitted). * * *

As explained by Professor Mishkin:

"[F]rom this aspect, the Linkletter problem becomes not so much one of prospectivity or retroactivity of the rule but rather of the availability of collateral attack—in [that] case federal habeas corpus—to go behind the otherwise final judgment of conviction. * * * For the potential availability of collateral attack is what created the 'retroactivity' problem of Linkletter in the first place; there seems little doubt that without that possibility the Court would have given short shrift to any arguments for 'prospective limitation' of the Mapp rule." Mishkin, *Foreword*, 79 Harv.L.Rev., at 77–78 (footnote omitted).

The "costs imposed upon the State[s] by retroactive application of new rules of constitutional law on habeas corpus * * * generally far outweigh the benefits of this application." [Solem v. Stumes, 465 U.S. 638, 654 (1984)] (Powell, J., concurring in judgment). * * * [T]he application of new rules to cases on collateral review * * * continually forces the States to marshal resources in order to keep in prison defendants whose trials and appeals conformed to then-existing constitutional standards. Furthermore, as we recognized in Engle v. Isaac, "[s]tate courts are understandably frustrated when they faithfully apply existing constitutional law only to have a federal court discover, during a [habeas] proceeding, new constitutional commands." 456 U.S., at 128, n. 33. * * *

We find these criticisms to be persuasive, and we now adopt Justice Harlan's view of retroactivity for cases on collateral review. Unless they fall within an exception to the general rule, new constitutional rules of criminal procedure will not be applicable to those cases which have become final before the new rules are announced.

V

Petitioner's conviction became final in 1983. As a result, the rule petitioner urges would not be applicable to this case, which is on collateral review, unless it would fall within an exception.

The first exception suggested by Justice Harlan—that a new rule should be applied retroactively if it places "certain kinds of primary, private individual conduct beyond the power of the criminal law-making authority to proscribe"—is not relevant here. Application of the fair cross section requirement to the petit jury would not accord constitutional protection to any primary activity whatsoever.

The second exception suggested by Justice Harlan—that a new rule should be applied retroactively if it requires the observance of "those procedures that . . . are 'implicit in the concept of ordered liberty' " (quoting Palko, 302 U.S., at 325)—we apply with a modification. * * *

In Desist, Justice Harlan had reasoned that one of the two principal functions of habeas corpus was "to assure that no man has been incarcerated under a procedure which creates an impermissibly large risk that the innocent will be convicted," and concluded "from this that all 'new' constitutional rules which significantly improve the pre-existing factfinding procedures are to be retroactively applied on habeas." In Mackey, Justice Harlan gave three reasons for shifting to the less defined Palko approach. First, he observed that recent precedent * * * led "ineluctably * * * to the conclusion that it is not a principal purpose of the writ to inquire whether a criminal convict did in fact commit the deed alleged." Second, he noted that cases such as Coleman v. Alabama, 399 U.S. 1 (1970)(invalidating lineup procedures in the absence of counsel), gave him reason to doubt the marginal effectiveness of claimed improvements in factfinding. Third, he found "inherently intractable the purported distinction between those new rules that are designed to improve the factfinding process and those designed principally to further other values."

We believe it desirable to combine the accuracy element of the Desist version of the second exception with the Mackey requirement that the procedure at issue must implicate the fundamental fairness of the trial. Were we to employ the Palko test without more, we would be doing little more than importing into a very different context the terms of the debate over incorporation. Reviving the Palko test now, in this area of law, would be unnecessarily anachronistic. Moreover, since Mackey was decided, our cases have moved in the direction of reaffirming the relevance of the likely accuracy of convictions in determining the available scope of habeas review. See, *e.g.*, Kuhlmann v. Wilson, 477 U.S., at 454 (plurality opinion)(a successive habeas petition may be entertained only if the defendant makes a "colorable claim of factual innocence"); Murray v. Carrier, 477 U.S., at 496 ("where a constitutional violation has probably resulted in the conviction of one who is actually innocent, a federal habeas court may grant the writ even in the absence of a showing of cause for the procedural default"); Stone v. Powell, 428 U.S., at 491–492, n. 31 (removing Fourth Amendment claims from the scope of federal habeas review if the State has provided a full and fair opportunity for litigation creates no danger of denying a "safeguard against compelling an innocent man to suffer an unconstitutional loss of liberty"). Finally, we believe that Justice Harlan's concerns about the difficulty in identifying both the existence and the value of accuracy-enhancing procedural rules can be addressed by limiting the scope of the second exception to those new procedures without which the likelihood of an accurate conviction is seriously diminished.

Because we operate from the premise that such procedures would be so central to an accurate determination of innocence or guilt, we believe it unlikely that many such components of basic due process have yet to emerge. We are also of the view that such rules are "best illustrated by recalling the classic grounds for the issuance of a writ of habeas corpus—that the proceeding was dominated by mob violence; that the prosecutor knowingly made use of perjured testimony; or that the conviction was based on a confession extorted from the defendant by brutal methods." Rose v. Lundy, 455 U.S. 509, 544 (1982)(Stevens, J., dissenting)(footnotes omitted).[3]

---

3. Because petitioner is not under sentence of death, we need not, and do not, express any views as to how the retroactivity approach we adopt today is to be applied in the capital sentencing context. We do, however, disagree with Justice Stevens' suggestion that the finality concerns underlying Justice Harlan's approach to retroactivity are limited to "making convictions final," and are therefore "wholly inapplicable to the capital sentencing context." * * *

An examination of our decision in Taylor applying the fair cross section requirement to the jury venire leads inexorably to the conclusion that adoption of the rule petitioner urges would be a far cry from the kind of absolute prerequisite to fundamental fairness that is "implicit in the concept of ordered liberty." * * * Because the absence of a fair cross section on the jury venire does not * * * seriously diminish the likelihood of obtaining an accurate conviction, we conclude that a rule requiring that petit juries be composed of a fair cross section of the community would not be a "bedrock procedural element" that would be retroactively applied under the second exception we have articulated.

Were we to recognize the new rule urged by petitioner in this case, we would have to give petitioner the benefit of that new rule even though it would not be applied retroactively to others similarly situated. In the words of Justice Brennan, such an inequitable result would be "an unavoidable consequence of the necessity that constitutional adjudications not stand as mere dictum." Stovall v. Denno, 388 U.S., at 301. But the harm caused by the failure to treat similarly situated defendants alike cannot be exaggerated * * *. * * *

If there were no other way to avoid rendering advisory opinions, we might well agree that the inequitable treatment described above is "an insignificant cost for adherence to sound principles of decision-making." Stovall v. Denno, 388 U.S., at 301. But there is a more principled way of dealing with the problem. We can simply refuse to announce a new rule in a given case unless the rule would be applied retroactively to the defendant in the case and to all others similarly situated. * * * We think this approach is a sound one. Not only does it eliminate any problems of rendering advisory opinions, it also avoids the inequity resulting from the uneven application of new rules to similarly situated defendants. We therefore hold that, implicit in the retroactivity approach we adopt today, is the principle that habeas corpus cannot be used as a vehicle to create new constitutional rules of criminal procedure unless those rules would be applied retroactively to *all* defendants on collateral review through one of the two exceptions we have articulated. Because a decision extending the fair cross section requirement to the petit jury would not be applied retroactively to cases on collateral review under the approach we adopt today, we do not address petitioner's claim.

For the reasons set forth above, the judgment of the Court of Appeals is affirmed.

■ JUSTICE WHITE, concurring in part and concurring in the judgment.

I join Parts I, II, and III of Justice O'Connor's opinion. Otherwise, I concur only in the judgment.

Our opinion in Stovall v. Denno, 388 U.S. 293, 297 (1967), authored by Justice Brennan, articulated a three-factor formula for determining the retroactivity of decisions changing the constitutional rules of criminal procedure. The formula, which applied whether a case was on direct review or arose in collateral proceedings, involved consideration of the purpose of the new rule, the extent of reliance on the old rule, and the effect on the administration of justice of retroactive application of the new rule. In a series of cases, however, the Court has departed from Stovall and has held that decisions changing the governing rules in criminal cases will be applied retroactively to all cases then pending on direct review, *e.g.*, United States v. Johnson, 457 U.S. 537 (1982);

Shea v. Louisiana, 470 U.S. 51 (1985); Griffith v. Kentucky, 479 U.S. 314 (1987). I dissented in those cases, believing that Stovall was the sounder approach. * * *

I regret the course the Court has taken to this point, but cases like Johnson, Shea, and Griffith have been decided, and I have insufficient reason to continue to object to them. In light of those decisions, the result reached in Parts IV and V of Justice O'Connor's opinion is an acceptable application in collateral proceedings of the theories embraced by the Court in cases dealing with direct review, and I concur in that result. If we are wrong in construing the reach of the habeas corpus statutes, Congress can of course correct us; but because the Court's recent decisions dealing with direct review appear to have constitutional underpinnings, see, *e.g.*, Griffith v. Kentucky, *supra*, at 322–323, correction of our error, if error there is, perhaps lies with us, not Congress.

■ JUSTICE BLACKMUN, concurring in part and concurring in the judgment.

* * *

■ JUSTICE STEVENS, with whom JUSTICE BLACKMUN joins as to Part I, concurring in part and concurring in the judgment.

I

For the reasons stated in Part III of Justice Brennan's dissent, I am persuaded this petitioner has alleged a violation of the Sixth Amendment. I also believe the Court should decide that question in his favor. I do not agree with Justice O'Connor's assumption that a ruling in petitioner's favor on the merits of the Sixth Amendment issue would require that his conviction be set aside.

When a criminal defendant claims that a procedural error tainted his conviction, an appellate court often decides whether error occurred before deciding whether that error requires reversal or should be classified as harmless. I would follow a parallel approach in cases raising novel questions of constitutional law on collateral review, first determining whether the trial process violated any of the petitioner's constitutional rights and then deciding whether the petitioner is entitled to relief. If error occurred, factors relating to retroactivity—most importantly, the magnitude of unfairness—should be examined before granting the petitioner relief. * * *[2]

* * * I am persuaded that the Court should adopt Justice Harlan's analysis of retroactivity for habeas corpus cases as well [as] for cases still on direct review.

I do not agree, however, with the plurality's dicta proposing a "modification" of Justice Harlan's fundamental fairness exception. * * * [In Mackey, Justice Harlan wrote:]

"[T]he writ ought always to lie for claims of nonobservance of those procedures that, as so aptly described by Mr. Justice Cardozo in Palko v. Connecticut, 302 U.S. 319, 325 (1937), are 'implicit in the concept of ordered liberty.' Typically, it should be the case that any conviction free

---

2. The plurality states that retroactivity questions ought to be decided at the same time a new rule of criminal procedure is announced. I agree that this should be the approach in most instances. By declaring retroactivity to be the "threshold question," however, the plurality inverts the proper order of adjudication. Among other things, until a rule is set forth, it would be extremely difficult to evaluate whether the rule is "new" at all. If it is not, of course, no retroactivity question arises. * * *

from federal constitutional error at the time it became final, will be found, upon reflection, to have been fundamentally fair and conducted under those procedures essential to the substance of a full hearing. However, in some situations it might be that time and growth in social capacity, as well as judicial perceptions of what we can rightly demand of the adjudicatory process, will properly alter our understanding of the bedrock procedural elements that must be found to vitiate the fairness of a particular conviction.''

* * *

The plurality wrongly resuscitates Justice Harlan's early view, indicating that the only procedural errors deserving correction on collateral review are those that undermine ''an accurate determination of innocence or guilt * * *.'' I cannot agree that it is ''unnecessarily anachronistic'' to issue a writ of habeas corpus to a petitioner convicted in a manner that violates fundamental principles of liberty. Furthermore, a touchstone of factual innocence would provide little guidance in certain important types of cases, such as those challenging the constitutionality of capital sentencing hearings.[3] Even when assessing errors at the guilt phase of a trial, factual innocence is too capricious a factor by which to determine if a procedural change is sufficiently ''bedrock'' or ''watershed'' to justify application of the fundamental fairness exception. In contrast, given our century-old proclamation that the Constitution does not allow exclusion of jurors because of race, a rule promoting selection of juries free from racial bias clearly implicates concerns of fundamental fairness.

As a matter of first impression, therefore, I would conclude that a guilty verdict delivered by a jury whose impartiality might have been eroded by racial prejudice is fundamentally unfair. Constraining that conclusion is the Court's holding in Allen v. Hardy, 478 U.S. 255 (1986)(per curiam)—an opinion I did not join—that Batson v. Kentucky, 476 U.S. 79 (1986), cannot be applied retroactively to permit collateral review of convictions that became final before it was decided. * * * [I]f there is no fundamental unfairness in denying retroactive relief to a petitioner denied his Fourteenth Amendment right to a fairly chosen jury, as the Court held in Allen, there cannot be fundamental unfairness in denying this petitioner relief for the violation of his Sixth Amendment right to an impartial jury. I therefore agree that the judgment of the Court of Appeals must be affirmed.[5]

* * *

II

* * *

■ JUSTICE BRENNAN, with whom JUSTICE MARSHALL joins, dissenting.

* * *

I

* * * For well over a century, we have read [the federal habeas corpus] statute and its forbears to authorize federal courts to grant writs of habeas corpus whenever a person's liberty is unconstitutionally restrained. * * *

---

3. A major reason that Justice Harlan espoused limited retroactivity in collateral proceedings was the interest in making convictions final, an interest that is wholly inap- plicable to the capital sentencing context. * * *

5. In addition, I join Part II of this Court's opinion.

* * * I would reach the merits of Teague's Sixth Amendment argument and hold in his favor.

II

Unfortunately, the plurality turns its back on established case law and would erect a formidable new barrier to relief. * * *

* * *

The plurality does not so much as mention *stare decisis*. Indeed, from the plurality's exposition of its new rule, one might infer that its novel fabrication will work no great change in the availability of federal collateral review of state convictions. Nothing could be further from the truth. Although the plurality declines to "define the spectrum of what may or may not constitute a new rule for retroactivity purposes," it does say that generally "a case announces a new rule when it breaks new ground or imposes a new obligation on the States or the Federal Government." Otherwise phrased, "a case announces a new rule if the result was not *dictated* by precedent existing at the time the defendant's conviction became final." This account is extremely broad. Few decisions on appeal or collateral review are "dictated" by what came before. Most such cases involve a question of law that is at least debatable, permitting a rational judge to resolve the case in more than one way. Virtually no case that prompts a dissent on the relevant legal point, for example, could be said to be "dictated" by prior decisions. By the plurality's test, therefore, a great many cases could only be heard on habeas if the rule urged by the petitioner fell within one of the two exceptions the plurality has sketched. Those exceptions, however, are narrow. Rules that place "certain kinds of primary, private individual conduct beyond the power of the criminal law-making authority to proscribe" are rare. And rules that would require "new procedures without which the likelihood of an accurate conviction is seriously diminished" are not appreciably more common. The plurality admits, in fact, that it "believe[s] it unlikely that many such components of basic due process have yet to emerge." The plurality's approach today can thus be expected to contract substantially the Great Writ's sweep.

Its impact is perhaps best illustrated by noting the abundance and variety of habeas cases we have decided in recent years that could never have been adjudicated had the plurality's new rule been in effect. * * *

[Justice Brennan then noted seventeen Supreme Court decisions in habeas cases in which the constitutional claim presented (i) would surely or likely have been found to be novel, and (ii) did not relate to guilt or innocence or otherwise fall within the plurality's two exceptions.]

These are massive changes, unsupported by precedent.[6] They also lack a reasonable foundation. * * *

---

6. The plurality's claim that "our cases have moved in the direction of reaffirming the relevance of the likely accuracy of convictions in determining the available scope of habeas review" has little force. Two of the cases it cites—Kuhlmann v. Wilson, 477 U.S. 436, 454 (1986) (plurality opinion), and Murray v. Carrier, 477 U.S. 478 (1986)—discuss the conditions under which a habeas petition- er may obtain review even though his claim would otherwise be procedurally barred. They do not hold that a petitioner's likely guilt or innocence bears on the cognizability of habeas claims in the absence of procedural default. And the Court has limited Stone v. Powell, 428 U.S. 465 (1976), * * * to Fourth Amendment exclusionary rule claims, passing up several opportunities to extend it.

* * * Sometimes a claim which, if successful, would create a new rule not appropriate for retroactive application on collateral review is better presented by a habeas case than by one on direct review. In fact, sometimes the claim is *only* presented on collateral review. In that case, while we could forgo deciding the issue in the hope that it would eventually be presented squarely on direct review, that hope might be misplaced, and even if it were in time fulfilled, the opportunity to check constitutional violations and to further the evolution of our thinking in some area of the law would in the meanwhile have been lost. In addition, by preserving our right and that of the lower federal courts to hear such claims on collateral review, we would not discourage their litigation on federal habeas corpus and thus not deprive ourselves and society of the benefit of decisions by the lower federal courts when we must resolve these issues ourselves.

The plurality appears oblivious to these advantages of our settled approach to collateral review. Instead, it would deny itself these benefits because adherence to precedent would occasionally result in one habeas petitioner's obtaining redress while another petitioner with an identical claim could not qualify for relief. In my view, the uniform treatment of habeas petitioners is not worth the price the plurality is willing to pay. * * *

III

Even if one accepts the plurality's account of the appropriate limits to habeas relief, its conclusion that Teague's claim may not be heard is dubious. * * * As the plurality would have it, Teague contends "that petit juries actually chosen must mirror the community and reflect the various distinctive groups in the population," (quoting Taylor v. Louisiana, 419 U.S. 522, 538 (1975)), and that fairness in jury selection "require[s] proportional representation of races upon a jury" (quoting Akins v. Texas, 325 U.S. 398, 403 (1945)). Teague, however, makes no such claim * * *. He submits, rather, that "the Sixth Amendment guarantees the accused a jury selected in accordance with procedures that allow a *fair possibility* for the jury to reflect a cross section of the community." Brief for Petitioner 4 (emphasis added). * * * Teague's claim is therefore closely akin to that which prevailed in Batson v. Kentucky, 476 U.S. 79 (1986), where we held that the Equal Protection Clause forbids the prosecution from using its peremptory challenges to exclude venirepersons from the jury solely because they share the defendant's race. The only potentially significant difference is that Teague's claim, if valid, would bar the prosecution from excluding venirepersons from the petit jury on account of their membership in some cognizable group even when the defendant is not himself a member of that group, whereas the Equal Protection Clause might not provide a basis for relief unless the defendant himself belonged to the group whose members were improperly excluded.

Once Teague's claim is characterized correctly, the plurality's assertions that on its new standard his claim is too novel to be recognized on habeas corpus, and that the right he invokes is "a far cry from the kind of absolute prerequisite to fundamental fairness that is 'implicit in the concept of ordered liberty,'" are dubious. * * *

The plurality's assertion that Teague's claim fails to fit within Justice Harlan's second exception is also questionable. * * * Justice Jackson rightly observed:

"It is obvious that discriminatory exclusion of Negroes from a trial jury does, or at least may, prejudice a Negro's right to a fair trial, and that a conviction so obtained should not stand. The trial jury * * * is influenced by imponderables—unconscious and conscious prejudices and preferences—and a thousand things we cannot detect or isolate in its verdict and whose influence we cannot weigh. A single juror's dissent is generally enough to prevent conviction. A trial jury on which one of the defendant's race has no chance to sit may not have the substance, and cannot have the appearance, of impartiality, especially when the accused is a Negro and the alleged victim is not." Cassell v. Texas, 339 U.S. 282, 301–302 (1950)(dissenting opinion).

* * * The plurality's assertion that an allegation, like Teague's, of discrimination in the selection of the *petit* jury * * * is too tangentially connected with truth finding to warrant retroactive application on habeas corpus under its new approach therefore strains credibility.

IV

A majority of this Court's Members now share the view that cases on direct and collateral review should be handled differently for retroactivity purposes. See Griffith v. Kentucky, 479 U.S. 314 (1987); Allen v. Hardy, 478 U.S. 255 (1986)(per curiam). In Griffith, the Court adopted Justice Harlan's proposal that a new rule be applied retroactively to all convictions not yet final when the rule was announced. If we had adhered to our precedents, reached Teague's Sixth Amendment claim, and ruled in his favor, we would ultimately have had to decide whether we should continue to apply to habeas cases the three-factor approach outlined in Stovall v. Denno, 388 U.S. [293, 297 (1967)], or whether we should embrace most of the other half of Justice Harlan's proposal and ordinarily refuse to apply new rules retroactively to cases on collateral review, except in the cases where they are announced.

In my view, that is not a question we should decide here. The better course would have been to grant certiorari in another case on collateral review raising the same issue and to resolve the question after full briefing and oral argument. Justices Blackmun and Stevens disagree. They concur in the Court's judgment on this point because they find further discussion unnecessary and because they believe that, although Teague's Sixth Amendment claim is meritorious, neither he nor other habeas petitioners may benefit from a favorable ruling. As I said in Stovall v. Denno, *supra,* at 301, according a petitioner relief when his claim prevails seems to me "an unavoidable consequence of the necessity that constitutional adjudications not stand as mere dictum." But I share the view of Justices Blackmun and Stevens that the retroactivity question is one we need not address until Teague's claim has been found meritorious. Certainly it is not one the Court need decide *before* it considers the merits of Teague's claim because, as the plurality mistakenly contends, its resolution properly determines whether the merits should be reached. By repudiating our familiar approach without regard for the doctrine of *stare decisis,* the plurality would deprive us of the manifold advantages of deciding important constitutional questions when they come to us first or most cleanly on collateral review. I dissent.

NOTE ON THE RETROACTIVE EFFECT OF "NEW" RULINGS IN FEDERAL HABEAS CORPUS PROCEEDINGS

(1) *Penry v. Lynaugh.* If Justice White's cryptic concurring opinion in Teague gave rise to any doubt that a majority of Justices subscribed to the position of Justice O'Connor's plurality opinion, that doubt was quickly put to rest later the same Term in Penry v. Lynaugh, 492 U.S. 302 (1989), where Justice White joined a portion of the majority opinion that re-affirmed Justice O'Connor's approach.

The Penry decision was significant in three other respects:

(a) First, the Court ruled that Teague applies to capital cases. (And many of the subsequent Supreme Court decisions applying Teague have involved death row inmates.)

(b) Second, the Court was unanimous in finding that one of Penry's two claims—that execution of a prisoner with the mental capacity of a seven-year old violated the Eighth Amendment—fell within Teague's first exception. That exception, Justice O'Connor said, "should be understood to cover not only rules forbidding criminal punishment of certain primary conduct but also rules prohibiting a certain category of punishment for a class of defendants because of their status or offense" (p. 330). On the merits, however, a majority rejected Penry's claim.[1]

(c) Finally, Justice O'Connor (here joined by Justices Brennan, Marshall, Blackmun, and Stevens) ruled, 5–4, that Penry's other claim—that the Texas sentencing jury should have been told that it could consider mental retardation as a mitigating factor—was not "new" in light of precedents handed down before his conviction became final. The Court noted that Jurek v. Texas, 428 U.S. 262 (1976), had upheld the Texas death penalty scheme, under which the jury is asked three "special issues"; if all three are answered in the affirmative, a death sentence must be imposed. Jurek had found generally that a Texas jury could consider mitigating evidence in addressing those "special issues." But in Penry, the Court ruled that the special issues did not permit consideration of a defendant's mental retardation in mitigation. Accordingly, the defendant's sentence violated the principle reflected in Jurek, and expressed more clearly in Lockett v. Ohio, 438 U.S. 586, 604 (1978) and Eddings v. Oklahoma, 455 U.S. 104 (1982), that a state may not preclude the sentencer from considering in mitigation "any aspect of the defendant's character and record and any of the circumstances of the offense" (p. 317). Because those precedents were handed down before Penry's conviction became final, he was entitled to habeas relief as to his sentence.[2]

---

1. Justices Stevens, Blackmun, Brennan, and Marshall agreed with this application of Teague's first exception, while maintaining their objections to the decision and dissenting on the merits of the Eighth Amendment claim.

2. Justice Scalia (joined by Chief Justice Rehnquist and Justices White and Kennedy) dissented on the "new law" issue. A habeas claim should not be sustained, he argued, when "the law is so uncertain that a judge acting in all good faith and with the greatest of care could reasonably read our precedents as permitting the result the habeas petition contends is wrong. Thus, a 'new rule' must include not only a new rule that replaces an old one, but a new rule that replaces palpable uncertainty as to what the rule might be" (p. 352).

The Penry dissenters may have had the last word in Graham v. Collins, 506 U.S. 461 (1993), a similar case from Texas, in which the prisoner claimed that the jury had not been permitted to consider, in mitigation, his youth and good general character. That

(2) *Subsequent Definitions of New Law.* The following Term, several decisions considerably expanded the notion of "new law", and correspondingly narrowed the scope of federal habeas jurisdiction. The most notable of these was Butler v. McKellar, 494 U.S. 407 (1990).

The background to Butler is found in two precedents interpreting the Miranda decision. In Edwards v. Arizona, 451 U.S. 477 (1981), the Court had ruled that after a suspect in custody has requested counsel, the police may not initiate further interrogation until counsel has been made available. Then in Arizona v. Roberson, 486 U.S. 675 (1988), the Court held that the ruling in Edwards was equally applicable where the second interrogation concerned a crime unrelated to the subject of the initial questioning.

The Butler case involved facts generally similar to those in Roberson. But by the time Roberson was decided, not only had Butler's conviction become final; Butler had already been denied habeas relief in the district court and the court of appeals had affirmed that decision. Indeed, Butler's petition for rehearing in the court of appeals was denied on the very day that Roberson was decided.

On review, the Supreme Court held, 5–4, that Roberson set forth a new rule, and thus that Butler could not obtain habeas relief premised on the Roberson decision. Chief Justice Rehnquist wrote (p. 414): "The 'new rule' principle * * * validates reasonable, good-faith interpretations of existing precedents made by state courts even though they are shown to be contrary to later decisions." Although the Court in Roberson had viewed the case as within the scope of its Edwards decision, the Court asserted that "the fact that a court says that its decision * * * is 'controlled' by a prior decision, is not conclusive * * *. Courts frequently view their decisions as being 'controlled' or 'governed' by prior opinions even when aware of reasonable conclusions reached by other courts. * * * [Differing positions taken by judges in the courts of appeals indicate that] the outcome in Roberson was susceptible to debate among reasonable minds * * *. It would not have been an illogical or even a grudging application of Edwards to decide that it did not extend to the facts of Roberson" (p. 415).

For the four dissenters, the Court's approach meant that "a state prisoner can secure habeas relief only by showing that the state court's rejection of the constitutional challenge was *so* clearly invalid under then-prevailing legal standards that the decision could not be defended by any reasonable jurist" (pp. 417–18).[3]

claim, the majority ruled, depended on a "new rule". The Court interpreted Jurek as holding that the jury could adequately consider such evidence in answering the three "special issues" posed by Texas law, for similar evidence had been admitted in Jurek.

Four dissenters argued forcefully that this case differed from Penry only in the kind of mitigating evidence involved (youth and good character vs. mental retardation). The majority responded that youth and good character "had mitigating relevance" to the second of the three special issues (which addressed the likelihood of future violence),

while Penry's mental retardation was relevant to that issue in just the opposite way. Thus here, unlike Penry, the sentencer had "reliable means of giving mitigating effect to th[e] evidence" (506 U.S. at 475). As a result, "[w]e cannot say that all reasonable jurists would have deemed themselves compelled to accept Graham's claim in 1984" (506 U.S. at 477).

All four dissenters in Penry joined the majority in Graham. The fifth vote in Graham was that of Justice Thomas, who had replaced Justice Marshall (a member of the Penry majority on this point).

(3) *Novelty, Levels of Generality, and Stringer v. Black.* When a habeas claim is based on a precedent rendered after the prisoner's conviction became final, the more general the description of the precedent, the less likely the rule whose application is sought in the present case will be found to be new. The Court's decision in Stringer v. Black, 503 U.S. 222 (1992)(6–3), can be viewed as adopting a more general description of precedent—and therefore a narrower view of "new law"—than did Butler.

(a) In Stringer, the Mississippi jury that sentenced the prisoner to death had found three aggravating factors, one of which was constitutionally invalid. In Clemons v. Mississippi, 494 U.S. 738 (1990), the Court had held that in a state like Mississippi that requires the jury to weigh aggravating and mitigating factors, a capital sentence resting on an invalid aggravating factor may stand only if the appellate court has reweighed the valid aggravating and mitigating factors and found capital punishment appropriate. The state argued that the rule of Clemons—which was announced only after the prisoner's conviction became final—was "new", because the Court had not previously held that reliance on an invalid aggravating factor (where other aggravating factors were present) required resentencing in "weighing" states. But the Court (per Kennedy, J.) disagreed. The Court acknowledged that new rules include not only those not dictated by precedent but also those involving application of an established rule "in a novel setting, thereby extending the precedent" (p. 228). Nonetheless, the Court found that Clemons merely implemented a general principle—established not by "any single case" but rather by a "long line of authority"—requiring precise and individualized capital sentencing (p. 232).

(b) The Stringer opinion also considered an element of "newness" that the Court has not often addressed—the relevance of lower court decisions upholding a practice later found unconstitutional by the Supreme Court. The state argued that because Fifth Circuit decisions (prior to Clemons) had held that resentencing was not required in the circumstances at bar, Clemons plainly was not "dictated by precedent". But the Court found the existence of those decisions relevant but not dispositive.

Compare Caspari v. Bohlen, 114 S.Ct. 948, 956 (1994), where the Court's conclusion that petitioner's claim was based on "new law" relied in part on the rejection of that claim by one of two federal courts of appeals, and by two of four state courts of last resort, to consider it. The Court stressed (p. 956) that "[c]onstitutional law is not the exclusive province of the federal courts, and in the Teague analysis the reasonable views of state courts are entitled to consideration * * *." See also Chap. IX, Sec. 3, p. 1174, *supra* (discussing similar question in connection with the immunity of officials from damages when their conduct did not violate clearly established law).

(c) If Stringer reflects a somewhat narrower view of new law, more recent decisions look the other way. See especially Caspari, *supra*; Graham v. Collins,

---

3. Two other 5–4 decisions the same Term also found petitioners to be barred from obtaining relief because they relied on a new rule. See Saffle v. Parks, 494 U.S. 484, 491 (1990)(stating that "[e]ven were we to agree with Parks' assertion that [the perti-nent Supreme Court precedents] inform, or even control or govern, the analysis of the claim, it does not follow that they compel the rule that Parks seeks"); Sawyer v. Smith, 497 U.S. 227 (1990), note 7, *infra*.

note 2, *supra*. Thus, while the decisions are not all of a piece, the dominant trend is toward defining new law very broadly.

(4) *Application of Law to Fact.* Recall the Court's statement in Stringer, Paragraph (3)(a), *supra*, that new rules include applications of an established rule "in a novel setting, thereby extending the precedent". Should that be taken to mean that whenever the application of an established constitutional principle is uncertain on the facts of the particular case, the habeas claim depends upon a new rule?

(a) That question was raised in Wright v. West, 505 U.S. 277 (1992), where petitioner sought relief under the rule of Jackson v. Virginia, 443 U.S. 307 (1979), pp. 612, 1389, *supra*, that due process is denied if no rational juror could have found an essential element of the crime proven beyond a reasonable doubt. Though established well before petitioner's conviction became final, that rule had, of course, never before been applied to the particular facts of petitioner's case. The state contended that § 2254(d) requires habeas courts to defer to "reasonable" state court factual determinations, while Teague requires similar deference to state court determinations of legal principles. It followed, the state submitted, that habeas courts must also defer to "reasonable" state court decisions of "mixed" questions of law and fact—that is, to reasonable applications of established legal rules to the facts as found.

Justice Thomas' plurality opinion (joined by the Chief Justice and Justice Scalia) read Brown v. Allen and subsequent opinions as not foreclosing the state's argument, which he described in considerable and seemingly sympathetic detail. In the end, however, he did not rely on it, instead rejecting petitioner's claim on the merits. Justice Souter, while not accepting the state's position in full, declared that Teague does require deference to state court decisions on mixed questions unless "in light of authority extant when [the] conviction became final, its unlawfulness [was] apparent" (p. 313). Because that was not true here, he voted to deny relief.

Concurring in the judgment on the ground that the petitioner's claim lacked merit, Justice O'Connor, joined by Justices Blackmun and Stevens, asserted that the Court's precedents foreclosed the state's argument.

In still another concurrence, Justice Kennedy stated that Teague did not establish a rule of deference to state courts, but a principle of retroactivity, based on objective review of the precedents at the time of the state court's determination. (Justice O'Connor's opinion echoed this point.) While reaffirming Stringer's proposition that Teague extends to applications of old rules in a novel setting, he argued that only in a rare case will application of a rule like that of Jackson v. Virginia—which by its nature calls for case-by-case examination of the evidence—be "so novel that it forges a new rule" (p. 309).[4]

(b) Aren't the categories "legal rules" and "application of legal rules to fact" points on a continuum rather than sharply differentiated concepts? Did Butler v. McKellar, Paragraph (2), *supra*, present a question of the application of the existing rule of Edwards v. Arizona (that Miranda prohibits the police from initiating further interrogation after the suspect has asked to see an attorney) to a new set of facts (in which the further interrogation, unlike that in Edwards, related to a different crime)? Or did Butler ask for creation of a

---

4. Justice White did not address the question, but simply voted to deny relief be-   cause there was ample evidence to satisfy the Jackson standard.

new rule—that police may not initiate an interrogation as to a different crime after the suspect has asked to see an attorney?

Even if a distinction between legal rules and mixed questions could be formulated, why—in view of the theory of Teague—should it matter?[5]

(5) *The Teague Exceptions.*

(a) *Primary Conduct.* Penry v. Lynaugh, Paragraph (1), *supra*, is the only case in which the first Teague exception, for rules that immunize one's behavior from punishment, has been found applicable. (The claim was that capital punishment cannot constitutionally be imposed on an offender with the mental capacity of a seven year-old.)[6]

Why should there be such an exception? Does it echo the historic notion that habeas will lie when the sentencing court lacked jurisdiction—and that jurisdiction is lacking when the statute under which the defendant was convicted was unconstitutional? Is relief less prejudicial to state interests in finality because no trial should have been held and no retrial can be commenced?

(b) *Rules That Implicate Fundamental Fairness and Bear on Guilt or Innocence.* The Supreme Court has yet to find a claim that fits within the exception for fundamental or bedrock procedures "without which the likelihood of an accurate conviction is seriously diminished".[7] (Recall Justice O'Connor's statement in Teague that it is "unlikely that many such components of basic due process have yet to emerge".) One case where that exception was at issue was Gilmore v. Taylor, 508 U.S. 333 (1993). The rule in question was one recognized by a Seventh Circuit decision that the standard Illinois homicide instructions denied due process because they permitted a jury to convict for murder without considering whether the defendant had killed in the heat of passion and therefore should be convicted only of voluntary manslaughter.

5. In 1995, the House and the Senate each passed a bill that would preclude the grant of relief with respect to a claim that was decided on the merits in state court, unless the state court decision (i) "was contrary to, or involved an unreasonable interpretation of, clearly established Federal law as determined by the Supreme Court of the United States", or (ii) "was based on an unreasonable application of the facts in light of the evidence presented in the State proceeding." S. 735, § 604 (June 7, 1995); the House language in H.R. 729, § 104(b) (Feb. 8, 1995) differs only slightly. Note that these bills, in addition to extending the approach of Teague to the application of law to fact (and to factfinding itself), would treat as "new law" any rule not established by the Supreme Court—no matter how clearly established in lower court decisions.

6. In Caspari v. Bohlen, 114 S.Ct. 948 (1994), petitioner's enhanced sentence as a persistent offender was reversed on appeal for lack of proof of the predicate prior offenses. At his re-sentencing, he again received an enhanced sentence, over his objec-

tion that allowing the state a second chance to introduce proof of prior convictions violated the Double Jeopardy Clause. In his habeas proceeding, the Supreme Court first found that his double jeopardy argument was based on new law, and then summarily found the first exception inapplicable, noting that his primary conduct was not beyond punishment, since he could be sentenced to prison (whether as a persistent offender or not) on the underlying convictions.

7. Cases finding it inapplicable include Sawyer v. Smith, 497 U.S. 227, 244 (1990)(rule of Caldwell v. Mississippi, 472 U.S. 320 (1985), that Eighth Amendment prohibits imposition of death sentence by a sentencer that has been led to the false belief that responsibility for determining the appropriateness of such a sentence lies elsewhere); Butler v. McKellar, Paragraph (2), *supra*; Saffle v. Parks, 494 U.S. 484 (1990) (claim that instruction to jury in capital sentencing hearing that it should "avoid any influence of sympathy" violates the Eighth Amendment); Graham v. Collins, note 2, *supra*; Caspari v. Bohlen, note 6, *supra*.

The Supreme Court, after concluding that the Seventh Circuit had announced a "new" rule, held rather summarily that the watershed exception was inapplicable. Justice Blackmun's dissenting opinion (in which Justice Stevens joined) argued that the inadequate instructions created an ex post facto law (by effectively redefining, retroactively, the crime of murder) and denied the right to a fair trial. He concluded that this profound violation of the prisoner's constitutional rights brought the claim within Teague's second exception.

(6) *Teague and the Purposes of Habeas Jurisdiction.* How does Teague fit with the various purposes that habeas corpus jurisdiction might be thought to serve?

(a) Can Teague be reconciled with the view of habeas corpus as a surrogate for Supreme Court review, see p. 1357, *supra*? Professor Friedman, one proponent of that view, has been highly critical of Teague. See his *Habeas and Hubris*, 45 Vand.L.Rev. 797 (1992) and *Pas de Deux: The Supreme Court and the Habeas Courts*, 66 S.Cal.L.Rev. 2467 (1993). By contrast, Professor Liebman finds Teague consistent with an "appellate review" model because a habeas court is prevented from applying new rules that the Supreme Court would not have applied on direct review. See Liebman, p. 1357, *supra*, at 2006–07.

(b) Teague appears to be based on the premise (also relied on by Justice Harlan in Desist) that the major if not the sole purpose of federal habeas is to provide an incentive for state judges to adhere to constitutional norms.[8] But that premise conflicts with the rationale of other Burger and Rehnquist Courts decisions that reject the view that state courts need extra prodding to apply federal constitutional norms faithfully. See, *e.g.*, Brecht v. Abrahamson, p. 1362, *supra*; Stone v. Powell, p. 1376, *supra*. See also Withrow v. Williams, 507 U.S. 680, ___ (1993), p. 1388, *supra* (Scalia, J., dissenting).

(c) Although decisions after Stone v. Powell appeared to close the door on efforts to limit habeas corpus to claims related to guilt or innocence, see p. ___, *supra*, Teague, after citing Stone and other cases as reflecting "the relevance of the likely accuracy of convictions in determining the available scope of habeas review", builds "accuracy" into the second exception. Is accuracy more appropriate in this context than it is generally in shaping habeas jurisdiction?

(d) Is it a mistake to seek to explain the habeas jurisdiction as promoting a single purpose? Two recent articles have so asserted.

---

8. Under that rationale, should habeas relief be available if a state court erroneously denied a right that was well-established at the time, but which has since been rejected by the Supreme Court?

In Lockhart v. Fretwell, 506 U.S. 364 (1993)(7–2), the prisoner's lawyer had failed to raise, at the capital sentencing hearing, a constitutional objection based on an established lower court precedent that the Supreme Court later rejected. The prisoner's habeas petition alleged ineffective assistance of counsel, a claim that requires proof of both deficient performance by the lawyer and prejudice resulting from the deficiency. The Court (per Rehnquist, C.J.) found no prejudice resulting from the lawyer's failure to make an objection that would no longer be viewed as meritorious: "A federal habeas petitioner has no interest in the finality of the state court judgment under which he is incarcerated: indeed, the very purpose of his habeas petition is to overturn that judgment. Nor does such a petitioner ordinarily have any claim of reliance on past judicial precedent as a basis for his actions that corresponds to the State's interest * * *. The result of these differences is that the State will benefit from our Teague decision in some federal cases, while the habeas petitioner will not. The result is not, as the dissent would have it, a 'windfall' for the State, but instead is a perfectly logical limitation of Teague to the circumstances which gave rise to it" (506 U.S. at 373).

Hoffmann & Stuntz, *Habeas After the Revolution*, 1993 Sup.Ct.Rev. 65, 69, contend that habeas relief should have two tracks. The first would extend de novo review of federal claims—free of limits currently imposed by Teague or by restrictive procedural doctrines—to petitioners who can demonstrate a reasonable probability of innocence. The second, whose purpose is to deter unconstitutional behavior by state officials, would permit limited review of federal claims (whether factual, legal, or mixed) "solely to determine if the state court acted reasonably in denying them".

Lee, *The Theories of Habeas Corpus*, 72 Wash.U.L.Q. 151 (1994) also favors granting relief either when the petitioner makes a "colorable showing of innocence" or when appropriate to promote deterrence—as well as when the state courts failed to provide a full and fair hearing. But his view of deterrence leads him to endorse Brown v. Allen, to reject Stone v. Powell, and to contend that Teague's exceptions are too narrow while its definition of new law is too broad.

(7) *Criticisms of and Alternatives to Teague.*

(a) The most common criticism of Teague is that "new law" has been too broadly defined. See, *e.g.*, Fallon & Meltzer, *New Law, Non–Retroactivity, and Constitutional Remedies*, 104 Harv.L.Rev. 1731, 1816–17 (1991)("Teague reduces the incentives for state courts, and state law enforcement officials, to take account of the evolving direction of the law. A better view would emphasize the continuities in adjudication, and the reasoning process that links issues not yet clearly resolved to past decisions and principles. In short, new law should be defined more narrowly, to exclude rules and decisions that are clearly foreshadowed, or reflect ordinary legal evolution"); Liebman, *More Than "Slightly Retro": The Rehnquist Court's Rout of Habeas Corpus Jurisdiction in Teague v. Lane*, 18 N.Y.U.Rev.L. & Soc.Change 537 (1990–91); Heald, *Retroactivity, Capital Sentencing, and the Jurisdictional Contours of Habeas Corpus*, 42 Ala.L.Rev. 1273 (1991); Hoffman, *Retroactivity and the Great Writ: How Congress Should Respond to Teague v. Lane*, 1990 B.Y.U.L.Rev. 183.

Others have questioned any effort to distinguish old from new rules. See Feldman, *Diagnosing Power: Postmodernism in Legal Scholarship and Judicial Practice (with an Emphasis on the Teague Rule Against New Rules in Habeas Corpus Cases)*, 88 Nw.U.L.Rev. 1046, 1065 (1994)(arguing that every rule is both new (because interpreters must reconstruct it each time they apply it) and old (because it emerges from existing traditions and prejudices)); Meyer, *"Nothing We Say Matters": Teague and New Rules*, 61 U.Chi.L.Rev. 423 (1994)(arguing that Teague's treatment of some rules as new is incompatible with the common law tradition in which the meaning of precedents becomes clear only as they are distinguished and reshaped in subsequent cases).

(b) Given the absence of a statute of limitations in habeas corpus actions, isn't there a need for some limit on the retroactive effect of unpredictable decisions with far-reaching consequences? Would it have been tolerable, after a decision like Mapp or Miranda, for the courts to have granted habeas relief to every prisoner whose trial had not been conducted in accordance with those decisions?[9]

---

9. A prisoner who had not anticipated the claim in state court would today be barred from pursuing it on habeas corpus, but that was not true under the Warren Court's decision in Fay v. Noia, 372 U.S. 391 (1963). See generally pp. 1413-40, *infra*.

(c) The Warren Court limited the impact of its criminal procedure rulings not by restricting habeas corpus jurisdiction, but rather by making certain constitutional rulings non-retroactive, not only on collateral but also on direct review. Whether a ruling would be held non-retroactive depended on the purpose of the new rule, the extent of reliance on the old rule, and the effect on the administration of justice of retroactive application of the new rule. See Stovall v. Denno, 388 U.S. 293, 297 (1967). For discussion, see Chap. II, Sec. 1, pp. 84–88, *supra*.

In Teague, Justice O'Connor objected that that approach unjustifiably treated similarly situated litigants differently. But does Teague eliminate inequality or merely re-direct it? Consider two prisoners who filed habeas petitions in 1987 that relied on a 1986 Supreme Court decision. Both had been convicted in state court in 1985; one case moved swiftly on appeal and the conviction became final that same year; the other progressed more slowly and the conviction became final only in 1987. Teague presents a barrier to the first but not to the second.

Won't any system in which adjudication is neither fully retroactive nor fully prospective create inequalities? If so, was the Stovall regime really so bad? Note that under Stovall a non-retroactive decision did not apply to police or judicial conduct that occurred before the date of the decision—even if the conviction became final only thereafter. Didn't that make more functional sense?

(d) Habeas corpus is a remedy for constitutional wrongdoing. In Fallon & Meltzer, *supra*, the authors offer a general argument that the novelty of a finding of constitutional violation is relevant to the appropriate scope of remediation. They contend that the Court has recognized that relevance not only in habeas but also in actions seeking damages for violations of constitutional rights (in which officials' immunity from damages liability often depends on whether their conduct violated "clearly established" law, see Chap. IX, Sec. 3, *supra*). With respect to the availability of federal habeas for state prisoners, they agree that in view of the state's interest in finality, the newness of a rule of decision should have greater significance on collateral than on direct review, but they object to the narrowness of the exceptions, to the application of the same standards in capital and non-capital cases, and to the expansiveness of the definition of "new law".[10]

(e) Does the Court's insistence that new law is a threshold issue—and that where the law is new, a habeas court must dismiss without reaching the merits—threaten to freeze the development of constitutional doctrine by barring habeas courts from participating? See Friedman, *Habeas and Hubris*, 45 Vand.L.Rev. 797, 818 (1992). Or are there usually adequate opportunities for such development in the swollen dockets of the state courts (many of which are quite rights-protective) as well as in federal criminal prosecutions (which raise many of the issues that habeas courts would consider)? See Meltzer, *Habeas*

---

10. See also Kinports, *Habeas Corpus, Qualified Immunity, and Crystal Balls: Predicting the Course of Constitutional Law*, 33 Ariz.L.Rev. 115 (1991), analyzing the treatment of "new law" in three areas, and concluding that the Court has been less willing to forgive errors in interpreting constitutional norms made by public officials (who are governed by a broad qualified immunity in constitutional tort actions) and by state judges (whose decisions often may not be reviewed in habeas because of Teague) than those made by prisoners and their attorneys (whose failure to anticipate and raise a novel constitutional claim is rarely excused).

Corpus Jurisdiction: The Limits of Models, 66 S.Cal.L.Rev. 2507, 2517–23 (1993).

Even if other alternatives exist, why should habeas courts *always* be precluded from reaching the merits of a question of new law? Don't courts often discuss the merits even if relief is denied on other grounds (as in Justice Stevens' example of the harmless error doctrine)? And mightn't such an approach help establish more promptly the contours of new constitutional protections—thereby providing guidance for state officials and state courts, and making it difficult for them in the future to contend that unconstitutional action should go without remedy because the law was not sufficiently clear? See generally Fallon & Meltzer, *supra*, at 1797–1807.

(8) *Waiver*. In Collins v. Youngblood, 497 U.S. 37, 41 (1990), the Court held that the Teague rule was not "jurisdictional" and thus could be waived by the state.

In Schiro v. Farley, 114 S.Ct. 783 (1994), the Court noted that a warden, when named as the respondent in the Supreme Court, may rely on any argument to support a favorable judgment below. (The Court nonetheless refused to consider the Teague argument in view of the warden's failure to have raised it in her opposition to the petition for certiorari—but in the end ruled for the warden on the merits.)

In Caspari v. Bohlen, Paragraph (3)(b), *supra*, the warden had relied on Teague below, but her petition for certiorari had presented only the question of the correctness of the court of appeals' decision in favor of the prisoner. The Court ruled that the Teague issue was "a necessary predicate to the resolution of the question presented in the petition" (114 S.Ct. at 953) and proceeded to rule that Teague barred the exercise of habeas jurisdiction.

If non-retroactivity is a "necessary predicate" in arguing to the Supreme Court that a petition lacks merit, is it just as much a necessary predicate when so arguing to a district court? If so, how can a state ever waive an objection under Teague?

(9) *Bibliography*. See, in addition to authorities previously cited, Arkin, *The Prisoner's Dilemma: Life in the Lower Federal Courts After Teague v. Lane*, 69 N.C.L.Rev. 371 (1991); Patchel, *The New Habeas*, 42 Hastings L.J. 939 (1991); Rosenberg, *Kaddish for Federal Habeas Corpus*, 59 Geo.Wash.L.Rev. 362 (1991). See also Althouse, *Saying What Rights Are—In and Out of Context*, 1991 Wis.L.Rev. 929.

INTRODUCTORY NOTE ON FEDERAL HABEAS CORPUS AND STATE PROCEDURAL DEFAULT

(1) *Introduction*. Not infrequently, a federal habeas petition includes a claim that was not presented to the state court at all, or that was not presented in accordance with state procedural requirements. Typically, the state court will have treated the procedural default—*i.e.*, the failure properly to have raised the claim—as forfeiting the prisoner's right to obtain an adjudication on the merits. In the ordinary case, in which state remedies no longer are available at the time the federal habeas petition is filed, there is no question of exhaustion of state remedies. The question, rather, is what effect the procedural default in state court should have on the exercise of federal habeas jurisdiction.

In dealing with this question, the Supreme Court has shifted ground more than once. Two cases decided ten years apart—Daniels v. Allen, 344 U.S. 443 (1953), and Fay v. Noia, 372 U.S. 391 (1963), provide the backdrop to the next principal case, Wainwright v. Sykes, and to the more recent Supreme Court decisions dealing with the problem of procedural default.

(2) *Daniels v. Allen.* In Daniels v. Allen, a companion case to Brown v. Allen, 344 U.S. 443 (1953), p. 1350, *supra*, that was decided by the same opinions, the two petitioners had been convicted of murder in North Carolina and sentenced to death. At their trial and on appeal they raised federal claims (complaining of jury discrimination and the introduction of coerced confessions) similar to those raised in Brown v. Allen.

The North Carolina Supreme Court refused to consider the merits of petitioners' appeals, because their lawyer had been tardy in serving the "statement of the case on appeal" on the prosecutor. According to Justice Frankfurter's dissent in the case (which was unchallenged on this point), "if petitioners' lawyer had mailed his 'statement of the case on appeal' on the 60th day and the prosecutor's office had received it on the 61st day the law of North Carolina would clearly have been complied with, but because he delivered it by hand on the 61st day" it was untimely (p. 557).

In petitioners' federal habeas corpus action, the Supreme Court ruled that their failure to have made timely service of the appeal was "decisive" (p. 483); the habeas petition would not be considered. Justice Reed's opinion was not entirely clear whether the denial of relief rested on waiver, failure to exhaust state remedies, or the presence of an adequate state ground. He stated (pp. 485–87):

"* * * The state furnished an adequate and easily-complied-with method of appeal. * * * Yet petitioners' appeal was not taken and the State of North Carolina * * * refused to consider the appeal on its merits. * * *

"* * *

"North Carolina has applied its law in refusing this out-of-time review. This Court applies its jurisdictional statute in the same manner. We cannot say that North Carolina's action in refusing review after failure to perfect the case on appeal violates the Federal Constitution. A period of limitation accords with our conception of proper procedure.

"* * * A failure to use a state's available remedy, in the absence of some interference or incapacity * * * bars federal habeas corpus. The statute requires that the applicant exhaust available state remedies. To show that the time has passed for appeal is not enough to empower the Federal District Court to issue the writ. The judgment must be affirmed."

In dissent, Justice Black (joined by Justice Douglas) objected (pp. 552–54): "The State Supreme Court refused to review [evidence of jury discrimination] on state procedural grounds. Absence of state court review on this ground is now held to cut off review in federal habeas corpus proceedings. But in the two preceding cases [those of Brown and Speller, jointly decided in Brown v. Allen] where the State Supreme Court did review the evidence, this Court has also reviewed it. I find it difficult to agree with the soundness of a philosophy which prompts this Court to grant a second review where the state has granted one but to deny any review at all where the state has granted none. * * *

"* * * [T]he object of habeas corpus is to search records to prevent illegal imprisonments.   * * * [I]t is never too late for courts in habeas corpus proceedings to look straight through procedural screens in order to prevent forfeiture of life or liberty in flagrant defiance of the Constitution.   Perhaps there is no more exalted judicial function.   I am willing to agree that it should not be exercised in cases like these except under special circumstances or in extraordinary situations.   But I cannot join in any opinion that attempts to confine the Great Writ within rigid formalistic boundaries."

In a separate dissent joined by Justices Black and Douglas, Justice Frankfurter complained (pp. 557–58) that because of the minor default, "all opportunities for appeal, both in the North Carolina courts and in the federal courts, are cut off although the North Carolina courts had discretion to hear this appeal.   For me it is important to emphasize the fact that North Carolina does not have a fixed period for taking an appeal.   The decisive question is whether a refusal to exercise a discretion which the Legislature of North Carolina has vested in its judges is an act so arbitrary and so cruel in its operation, considering that life is at stake, that in the circumstances of this case it constitutes a denial of due process in its rudimentary procedural aspect."[1]

(3) *Fay v. Noia.*   Ten years later, in Fay v. Noia, 372 U.S. 391 (1963), the Court rejected the Daniels rule and sharply expanded the reach of habeas review of defaulted claims.   Noia had been convicted of a capital crime, but after he was not sentenced to death, he chose not to appeal.   His subsequent effort to obtain postconviction relief (a writ of coram nobis) in state court, on the ground that his conviction was based on a coerced confession, was rebuffed on the basis of his failure to have appealed.   (Noia's two co-defendants, who had appealed from their convictions on that ground, did obtain postconviction relief in state court.)

When Noia's federal habeas petition raising the coerced confession claim reached the Supreme Court, it held that the failure to have appealed from his conviction, although it might have barred an effort to obtain direct review by the Supreme Court of the state conviction or of the denial of state postconviction relief, did not preclude the exercise of federal habeas jurisdiction.

(a) Justice Brennan wrote for the Court (pp. 428–34, 438–39):

"* * * [A] default such as Noia's, if deemed adequate and independent (a question on which we intimate no view), would cut off review by this Court of the state *coram nobis* proceeding in which the New York Court of Appeals refused him relief.   It is contended that it follows from this that the remedy of federal habeas corpus is likewise cut off.

"The fatal weakness of this contention is its failure to recognize that the adequate state-ground rule is a function of the limitations of *appellate* review. * * * [W]e have held that the adequate state-ground rule is a consequence of

---

1. In a separate opinion in the same case, Justice Frankfurter wrote (p. 503): "Of course, nothing we have said suggests that the federal habeas corpus jurisdiction can displace a state's procedural rule requiring that certain errors be raised on appeal.   Normally rights under the Federal Constitution may be waived at the trial, and may likewise be waived by failure to assert such errors on appeal.   When a State insists that a defen-dant be held to his choice of trial strategy and not be allowed to try a different tack on State habeas corpus, he may be deemed to have waived his claim and thus have no right to assert on federal habeas corpus.   * * * However, this does not touch one of those extraordinary cases in which a substantial claim goes to the very foundation of a proceeding, as in Moore v. Dempsey, 261 U.S. 86."

the Court's obligation to refrain from rendering advisory opinions or passing upon moot questions.[40]

"But while our appellate function is concerned only with the judgments or decrees of state courts, the habeas corpus jurisdiction of the lower federal courts is not so confined. The jurisdictional prerequisite is not the judgment of a state court but detention *simpliciter*. * * * Habeas lies to enforce the right of personal liberty; when that right is denied and a person confined, the federal court has the power to release him. Indeed, it has no other power; it cannot revise the state court judgment; it can act only on the body of the petitioner.

"To be sure, this may not be the entire answer to the contention that the adequate state-ground principle should apply to the federal courts on habeas corpus as well as to the Supreme Court on direct review of state judgments. The Murdock decision may be supported not only by the factor of mootness, but in addition by certain characteristics of the federal system. The first question the Court had to decide in Murdock was whether it had the power to review state questions in cases also raising federal questions. It held that it did not, thus affirming the independence of the States in matters within the proper sphere of their lawmaking power from federal judicial interference. For the federal courts to refuse to give effect in habeas proceedings to state procedural defaults might conceivably have some effect upon the States' regulation of their criminal procedures. But the problem is crucially different from that posed in Murdock of the federal courts' deciding questions of substantive state law. In Noia's case the only relevant substantive law is federal—the Fourteenth Amendment. State law appears only in the procedural framework for adjudicating the substantive federal question. The paramount interest is federal. That is not to say that the States have not a substantial interest in exacting compliance with their procedural rules from criminal defendants asserting federal defenses. * * * But * * * the only concrete impact the assumption of federal habeas jurisdiction in the face of a procedural default has on the state interest we have described, is that it prevents the State from closing off the convicted defendant's last opportunity to vindicate his constitutional rights, thereby punishing him for his default and deterring others who might commit similar defaults in the future.

"Surely this state interest in an airtight system of forfeitures is of a different order from that, vindicated in Murdock, in the autonomy of state law within the proper sphere of its substantive regulation. * * *

"* * * A man under conviction for crime has an obvious inducement to do his very best to keep his state remedies open, and not stake his all on the outcome of a federal habeas proceeding which, in many respects, may be less advantageous to him than a state court proceeding. And if because of inadvertence or neglect he runs afoul of a state procedural requirement, and thereby forfeits his state remedies, appellate and collateral, as well as direct review thereof in this Court, those consequences should be sufficient to vindicate the State's valid interest in orderly procedure. Whatever residuum of state inter-

---

40. "* * * We need not decide whether the adequate state-ground rule is constitutionally compelled or merely a matter of the construction of the statutes defining this Court's appellate review. Murdock itself was predicated on statutory construction, and the present statute governing our review of state court decisions, 28 U.S.C. § 1257, limited as it is to '*judgments or decrees* rendered by the highest court of a State in which a decision could be had' (italics supplied), provides ample statutory warrant for our continued adherence to the principles laid down in Murdock."

est there may be under such circumstances is manifestly insufficient in the face of the federal policy, drawn from the ancient principles of the writ of habeas corpus, * * * of affording an effective remedy for restraints contrary to the Constitution. For these several reasons we reject * * * the suggestion that the federal courts are without power to grant habeas relief to an applicant whose federal claims would not be heard on direct review in this Court because of a procedural default furnishing an adequate and independent ground of state decision. * * *"

The Court did "recognize a limited discretion in the federal judge to deny relief to an applicant" when he "has deliberately bypassed the orderly procedure of the state courts and in so doing has forfeited his state court remedies." Justice Brennan added, however, that the "classic definition of waiver enunciated in Johnson v. Zerbst, 304 U.S. 458, 464—'an intentional relinquishment or abandonment of a known right or privilege'—furnishes the controlling standard. If a habeas applicant, after consultation with competent counsel or otherwise, understandingly and knowingly forewent the privilege of seeking to vindicate his federal claims in the state courts, whether for strategic, tactical, or any other reasons that can fairly be described as the deliberate by-passing of state procedures, then it is open to the federal court on habeas to deny him all relief if the state courts refused to entertain his federal claims on the merits * * *. At all events we wish it clearly understood that the standard here put forth depends on the considered choice of the petitioner. * * * A choice made by counsel not participated in by the petitioner does not automatically bar relief. * * *"

Although Noia's was one of the rare cases in which the defendant had in fact participated in a decision not to raise an issue in state court, the Court refused to treat it as a deliberate bypass, stressing the "grisly choice" (p. 440) he faced—either forgoing an appeal from his conviction or running the risk that a successful appeal might lead to a death sentence on retrial.

(b) Justice Harlan dissented, joined by Justices Clark and Stewart (pp. 468–70):

"The adequate state ground doctrine * * * finds its source in basic constitutional principles, and the question before us is whether this is as true in a collateral attack in habeas corpus as on direct review. Assume, then, that after dismissal of the writ of certiorari in * * * [a case where a state defendant failed to make a timely challenge to the composition of the grand jury], the prisoner seeks habeas corpus in a Federal District Court, again complaining of the composition of the grand jury that indicted him. Is that federal court constitutionally more free than the Supreme Court on direct review to 'ignore' the adequate state ground, proceed to the federal question, and order the prisoner's release?

"The answer must be that it is not. Of course, as the majority states, a judgment is not a 'jurisdictional prerequisite' to a habeas corpus application, but that is wholly irrelevant. The point is that if the applicant is detained *pursuant* to a judgment, termination of the detention necessarily nullifies the judgment. The fact that a District Court on habeas has fewer choices than the Supreme Court, since it can *only* act on the body of the prisoner, does not alter the significance of the exercise of its power. In habeas as on direct review, ordering the prisoner's release invalidates the judgment of conviction and renders ineffective the state rule relied upon to sustain that judgment. Try as the majority does to turn habeas corpus into a roving commission of inquiry into every possible invasion of the applicant's civil rights that may ever have occurred, it cannot divorce the writ from a judgment of conviction if that judgment is the basis of the detention.

"Thus in the present case if this Court had granted certiorari to review the State's denial of *coram nobis,* had considered the coerced confession claim, and had ordered Noia's release, the necessary effects of that disposition would have been (1) to set aside the conviction and (2) to invalidate application of the New York rule requiring the claim to be raised on direct appeal in order to be preserved. It is, I think, beyond dispute that the Court does exactly the same thing by affirming the decision below in this case. In doing so, the Court exceeds its constitutional power if in fact the state ground relied upon to sustain the judgment of conviction is an adequate one. The effect of the approach adopted by the Court is, indeed, to do away with the adequate state ground rule entirely in every state case, involving a federal question, in which detention follows from a judgment."

Wainwright v. Sykes

433 U.S. 72, 97 S.Ct. 2497, 53 L.Ed.2d 594 (1977).
Certiorari to the United States Court of Appeals for the Fifth Circuit.

■ MR. JUSTICE REHNQUIST delivered the opinion of the Court.

We granted certiorari to consider the availability of federal habeas corpus to review a state convict's claim that testimony was admitted at his trial in violation of his rights under Miranda v. Arizona, 384 U.S. 436 (1966), a claim which the Florida courts have previously refused to consider on the merits because of noncompliance with a state contemporaneous-objection rule. Petitioner Wainwright, on behalf of the State of Florida, here challenges a decision of the Court of Appeals for the Fifth Circuit ordering a hearing in state court on the merits of respondent's contention.

Respondent Sykes was convicted of third-degree murder after a jury trial * * *. He testified at trial that on the evening of January 8, 1972, he told his wife to summon the police because he had just shot Willie Gilbert. Other evidence indicated that when the police arrived at respondent's trailer home, they found Gilbert dead of a shotgun wound, lying a few feet from the front porch. Shortly after their arrival, respondent came from across the road and volunteered that he had shot Gilbert, and a few minutes later respondent's wife approached the police and told them the same thing. Sykes was immediately arrested and taken to the police station.

Once there, it is conceded that he was read his Miranda rights, and that he declined to seek the aid of counsel and indicated a desire to talk. He then made a statement, which was admitted into evidence at trial through the testimony of the two officers who heard it, to the effect that he had shot Gilbert from the front porch of his trailer home. There were several references during the trial to respondent's consumption of alcohol during the preceding day and to his apparent state of intoxication, facts which were acknowledged by the officers who arrived at the scene. At no time during the trial, however, was the admissibility of any of respondent's statements challenged by his counsel on the ground that respondent had not understood the Miranda warnings. * * *

Respondent appealed his conviction, but apparently did not challenge the admissibility of the inculpatory statements. He later filed in the trial court a motion to vacate the conviction and, in the State District Court of Appeals and Supreme Court, petitions for habeas corpus. These filings, apparently for the first time, challenged the statements made to police on grounds of involuntariness. In all of these efforts respondent was unsuccessful.

Having failed in the Florida courts, respondent initiated the present action under 28 U.S.C. § 2254, asserting the inadmissibility of his statements by reason of his lack of understanding of the Miranda warnings. * * *

The simple legal question before the Court calls for a construction of the language of 28 U.S.C. § 2254(a), which provides that the federal courts shall entertain an application for a writ of habeas corpus "in behalf of a person in custody pursuant to the judgment of a state court only on the ground that he is in custody in violation of the Constitution or laws or treaties of the United States." But, to put it mildly, we do not write on a clean slate in construing this statutory provision. * * *

* * * For more than a century since the [Act of 1867, which extended federal habeas corpus to persons held under *state* custody], this Court has grappled with the relationship between the classical common-law writ of habeas corpus and the remedy provided in 28 U.S.C. § 2254. Sharp division within the Court has been manifested on more than one aspect of the perplexing problems which have been litigated in this connection. Where the habeas petitioner challenges a final judgment of conviction rendered by a state court, this Court has been called upon to decide no fewer than four different questions, all to a degree interrelated with one another: (1) What types of federal claims may a federal habeas court properly consider? (2) Where a federal claim is cognizable by a federal habeas court, to what extent must that court defer to a resolution of the claim in prior state proceedings? (3) To what extent must the petitioner who seeks federal habeas exhaust state remedies before resorting to the federal court? (4) In what instances will an adequate and independent state ground bar consideration of otherwise cognizable federal issues on federal habeas review?

Each of these four issues has spawned its share of litigation. * * *

There is no need to consider here in greater detail these first three areas of controversy attendant to federal habeas review of state convictions. Only the fourth area—the adequacy of state grounds to bar federal habeas review—is presented in this case. * * * [D]iscussion of the other three is pertinent here only as it illustrates this Court's historic willingness to overturn or modify its earlier views of the scope of the writ, even where the statutory language authorizing judicial action has remained unchanged.

As to the role of adequate and independent state grounds, it is a well-established principle of federalism that a state decision resting on an adequate foundation of state substantive law is immune from review in the federal courts. Fox Film Corp. v. Muller, 296 U.S. 207 (1935); Murdock v. Memphis, 20 Wall. 590 (1875). The application of this principle in the context of a federal habeas proceeding has therefore excluded from consideration any questions of state *substantive* law, and thus effectively barred federal habeas review where questions of that sort are either the only ones raised by a petitioner or are in themselves dispositive of his case. The area of controversy which has developed has concerned the reviewability of federal claims which the state court has declined to pass on because they were not presented in the manner prescribed by its *procedural* rules. The adequacy of such an independent state procedural ground to prevent federal habeas review of the underlying federal issue has been treated very differently than where the state-law ground is substantive. The pertinent decisions marking the Court's somewhat tortuous efforts to deal with this problem are: Ex parte Spencer, 228 U.S. 652 (1913); Brown v. Allen, 344 U.S. 443 (1953); Fay v. Noia, [372 U.S. 391 (1963)]; Davis v. United States, 411 U.S. 233 (1973); and Francis v. Henderson, 425 U.S. 536 (1976).

In Brown, *supra*, petitioner Daniels' lawyer had failed to mail the appeal papers to the State Supreme Court on the last day provided by law for filing, and hand delivered them one day after that date. Citing the state rule requiring timely filing, the Supreme Court of North Carolina refused to hear the appeal. This Court, relying in part on its earlier decision in Ex parte Spencer, *supra*, held that federal habeas was not available to review a constitutional claim which could not have been reviewed on direct appeal here because it rested on an independent and adequate state procedural ground.

In Fay v. Noia, *supra*, respondent Noia sought federal habeas to review a claim that his state-court conviction had resulted from the introduction of a coerced confession in violation of the Fifth Amendment to the United States Constitution. While the convictions of his two codefendants were reversed on that ground in collateral proceedings following their appeals, Noia did not appeal and the New York courts ruled that his subsequent *coram nobis* action was barred on account of that failure. This Court held that petitioner was nonetheless entitled to raise the claim in federal habeas, and thereby overruled its decision 10 years earlier in Brown v. Allen, *supra*:

> "[T]he doctrine under which state procedural defaults are held to constitute an adequate and independent state law ground barring direct Supreme Court review is not to be extended to limit the power granted the federal courts under the federal habeas statute." 372 U.S., at 399.

As a matter of comity but not of federal power, the Court acknowledged "a limited discretion in the federal judge to deny relief * * * to an applicant who had deliberately by-passed the orderly procedure of the state courts and in so doing has forfeited his state court remedies." *Id.*, at 438. In so stating, the Court made clear that the waiver must be knowing and actual—"an intentional relinquishment or abandonment of a known right or privilege." *Id.*, at 439, quoting Johnson v. Zerbst, 304 U.S., at 464. Noting petitioner's "grisly choice" between acceptance of his life sentence and pursuit of an appeal which might culminate in a sentence of death, the Court concluded that there had been no deliberate bypass of the right to have the federal issues reviewed through a state appeal.

A decade later we decided Davis v. United States, *supra*, in which a federal prisoner's application under 28 U.S.C. § 2255 sought for the first time to challenge the makeup of the grand jury which indicted him. The Government contended that he was barred by the requirement of Fed.Rule Crim.Proc. 12(b)(2) providing that such challenges must be raised "by motion before trial." The Rule further provides that failure to so object constitutes a waiver of the objection, but that "the court for cause shown may grant relief from the waiver." We noted that the Rule "promulgated by this Court and, pursuant to 18 U.S.C. § 3771, 'adopted' by Congress, governs by its terms the manner in which the claims of defects in the institution of criminal proceedings may be waived," 411 U.S., at 241, and held that this standard contained in the Rule, rather than the Fay v. Noia concept of waiver, should pertain in federal habeas as on direct review. Referring to previous constructions of Rule 12(b)(2), we concluded that review of the claim should be barred on habeas, as on direct appeal, absent a showing of cause for the noncompliance and some showing of actual prejudice resulting from the alleged constitutional violation.

Last Term, in Francis v. Henderson, *supra*, the rule of Davis was applied to the parallel case of a state procedural requirement that challenges to grand jury composition be raised before trial. The Court noted that there was power in the federal courts to entertain an application in such a case, but rested its holding on "considerations of comity and concerns for the orderly administration of criminal justice * * *." 425 U.S., at 538–539. While there was no counterpart provision of the state rule which allowed an exception upon some showing of cause, the Court concluded that the standard derived from the Federal Rule should nonetheless be applied in that context since "[t]here is no reason to * * * give greater preclusive effect to procedural defaults by federal defendants than to similar defaults by state defendants." *Id.*, at 542, quoting Kaufman v. United States, 394 U.S. 217, 228 (1969). As applied to the federal petitions of state convicts, the Davis cause-and-prejudice standard was thus incorporated directly into the body of law governing the availability of federal habeas corpus review.

To the extent that the dicta of Fay v. Noia may be thought to have laid down an all-inclusive rule rendering state contemporaneous-objection rules ineffective to bar review of underlying federal claims in federal habeas proceedings—absent a "knowing waiver" or a "deliberate bypass" of the right to so object—its effect was limited by Francis, which applied a different rule and barred a habeas challenge to the makeup of a grand jury. Petitioner Wainwright in this case urges that we further confine its effect by applying the principle enunciated in Francis to a claimed error in the admission of a defendant's confession. * * *

We * * * conclude that Florida procedure did, consistently with the United States Constitution, require that respondent's confession be challenged at trial or not at all, and thus his failure to timely object to its admission amounted to an independent and adequate state procedural ground which would have prevented direct review here. We thus come to the crux of this case. Shall the rule of Francis v. Henderson, *supra*, barring federal habeas review absent a showing of "cause" and "prejudice" attendant to a state procedural waiver, be applied to a waived objection to the admission of a confession at trial? We answer that question in the affirmative.

* * * [S]ince Brown v. Allen, 344 U.S. 443 (1953), it has been the rule that the federal habeas petitioner who claims he is detained pursuant to a final judgment of a state court in violation of the United States Constitution is entitled to have the federal habeas court make its own independent determination of his federal claim, without being bound by the determination on the merits of that claim reached in the state proceedings. This rule of Brown v. Allen is in no way changed by our holding today. Rather, we deal only with contentions of federal law which were *not* resolved on the merits in the state proceeding due to respondent's failure to raise them there as required by state procedure. We leave open for resolution in future decisions the precise definition of the "cause"-and-"prejudice" standard, and note here only that it is narrower than the standard set forth in dicta in Fay v. Noia, 372 U.S. 391 (1963), which would make federal habeas review generally available to state

convicts absent a knowing and deliberate waiver of the federal constitutional contention. It is the sweeping language of Fay v. Noia, going far beyond the facts of the case eliciting it, which we today reject.[12]

The reasons for our rejection of it are several. The contemporaneous-objection rule itself is by no means peculiar to Florida, and deserves greater respect than Fay gives it, both for the fact that it is employed by a coordinate jurisdiction within the federal system and for the many interests which it serves in its own right. A contemporaneous objection enables the record to be made with respect to the constitutional claim when the recollections of witnesses are freshest, not years later in a federal habeas proceeding. It enables the judge who observed the demeanor of those witnesses to make the factual determinations necessary for properly deciding the federal constitutional question. While the 1966 amendment to § 2254 requires deference to be given to such determinations made by state courts, the determinations themselves are less apt to be made in the first instance if there is no contemporaneous objection to the admission of the evidence on federal constitutional grounds.

A contemporaneous-objection rule may lead to the exclusion of the evidence objected to, thereby making a major contribution to finality in criminal litigation. Without the evidence claimed to be vulnerable on federal constitutional grounds, the jury may acquit the defendant, and that will be the end of the case; or it may nonetheless convict the defendant, and he will have one less federal constitutional claim to assert in his federal habeas petition. If the state trial judge admits the evidence in question after a full hearing, the federal habeas court pursuant to the 1966 amendment to § 2254 will gain significant guidance from the state ruling in this regard. Subtler considerations as well militate in favor of honoring a state contemporaneous-objection rule. An objection on the spot may force the prosecution to take a hard look at its hole card, and even if the prosecutor thinks that the state trial judge will admit the evidence he must contemplate the possibility of reversal by the state appellate courts or the ultimate issuance of a federal writ of habeas corpus based on the impropriety of the state court's rejection of the federal constitutional claim.

We think that the rule of Fay v. Noia, broadly stated, may encourage "sandbagging" on the part of defense lawyers, who may take their chances on a verdict of not guilty in a state trial court with the intent to raise their constitutional claims in a federal habeas court if their initial gamble does not pay off. The refusal of federal habeas courts to honor contemporaneous-objection rules may also make state courts themselves less stringent in their enforcement. Under the rule of Fay v. Noia, state appellate courts know that a federal constitutional issue raised for the first time in the proceeding before them may well be decided in any event by a federal habeas tribunal. Thus,

---

12. We have no occasion today to consider the Fay rule as applied to the facts there confronting the Court. Whether the Francis rule should preclude federal habeas review of claims not made in accordance with state procedure where the criminal defendant has surrendered, other than for reasons of tactical advantage, the right to have all of his claims of trial error considered by a state appellate court, we leave for another day.

The Court in Fay stated its knowing-and-deliberate-waiver rule in language which applied not only to the waiver of the right to appeal, but to failures to raise individual substantive objections in the state trial. Then, with a single sentence in a footnote, the Court swept aside all decisions of this Court "to the extent that [they] may be read to suggest a standard of discretion in federal habeas corpus proceedings different from what we lay down today * * *." 372 U.S., at 439 n. 44. We do not choose to paint with a similarly broad brush here.

their choice is between addressing the issue notwithstanding the petitioner's failure to timely object, or else face the prospect that the federal habeas court will decide the question without the benefit of their views.

The failure of the federal habeas courts generally to require compliance with a contemporaneous-objection rule tends to detract from the perception of the trial of a criminal case in state court as a decisive and portentous event. A defendant has been accused of a serious crime, and this is the time and place set for him to be tried by a jury of his peers and found either guilty or not guilty by that jury. To the greatest extent possible all issues which bear on this charge should be determined in this proceeding * * *. * * * Any procedural rule which encourages the result that those proceedings be as free of error as possible is thoroughly desirable, and the contemporaneous-objection rule surely falls within this classification.

We believe the adoption of the Francis rule in this situation will have the salutary effect of making the state trial on the merits the "main event," so to speak, rather than a "tryout on the road" for what will later be the determinative federal habeas hearing. There is nothing in the Constitution or in the language of § 2254 which requires that the state trial on the issue of guilt or innocence be devoted largely to the testimony of fact witnesses directed to the elements of the state crime, while only later will there occur in a federal habeas hearing a full airing of the federal constitutional claims which were not raised in the state proceedings. If a criminal defendant thinks that an action of the state trial court is about to deprive him of a federal constitutional right there is every reason for his following state procedure in making known his objection.

The "cause"-and-"prejudice" exception of the Francis rule will afford an adequate guarantee, we think, that the rule will not prevent a federal habeas court from adjudicating for the first time the federal constitutional claim of a defendant who in the absence of such an adjudication will be the victim of a miscarriage of justice. Whatever precise content may be given those terms by later cases, we feel confident in holding without further elaboration that they do not exist here. Respondent has advanced no explanation whatever for his failure to object at trial,[14] and, as the proceeding unfolded, the trial judge is certainly not to be faulted for failing to question the admission of the confession himself. The other evidence of guilt presented at trial, moreover, was substantial to a degree that would negate any possibility of actual prejudice resulting to the respondent from the admission of his inculpatory statement.

We accordingly conclude that the judgment of the Court of Appeals for the Fifth Circuit must be reversed, and the cause remanded to the United States District Court for the Middle District of Florida with instructions to dismiss respondent's petition for a writ of habeas corpus.

It is so ordered.

---

14. In Henry v. Mississippi, 379 U.S. [443, 451 (1965)], the Court noted that decisions of counsel relating to trial strategy, even when made without the consultation of the defendant, would bar direct federal review of claims thereby forgone, except where "the circumstances are exceptional."

Last Term in Estelle v. Williams, 425 U.S. [501 (1976)], the Court reiterated the burden on a defendant to be bound by the trial judgments of his lawyer. "Under our adversary system, once a defendant has the assistance of counsel the vast array of trial decisions, strategic and tactical, which must be made before and during trial rests with the accused and his attorney." 425 U.S., at 512.

■ MR. CHIEF JUSTICE BURGER, concurring.

* * * I write separately to emphasize one point which, to me, seems of critical importance to this case. In my view, the "deliberate bypass" standard enunciated in Fay v. Noia, 372 U.S. 391 (1963), was never designed for, and is inapplicable to, errors—even of constitutional dimension—alleged to have been committed during trial.

In Fay v. Noia, the Court applied the "deliberate bypass" standard to a case where the critical procedural decision—whether to take a criminal appeal—was entrusted to a convicted defendant. Although Noia, the habeas petitioner, was represented by counsel, he himself had to make the decision whether to appeal or not; the role of the attorney was limited to giving advice and counsel. In giving content to the new deliberate-bypass standard, Fay looked to the Court's decision in Johnson v. Zerbst, 304 U.S. 458 (1938), a case where the defendant had been called upon to make the decision whether to request representation by counsel in his federal criminal trial. Because in both Fay and Zerbst, important rights hung in the balance of the *defendant's own decision*, the Court required that a waiver impairing such rights be a knowing and intelligent decision by the defendant himself. * * *

* * * In contrast, the claim in the case before us relates to events during the trial itself. Typically, habeas petitioners claim that unlawfully secured evidence was admitted, or that improper testimony was adduced, or that an improper jury charge was given, or that a particular line of examination or argument by the prosecutor was improper or prejudicial. * * * [T]he decision to assert or not to assert constitutional rights or constitutionally based objections at trial is necessarily entrusted to the defendant's attorney, who must make on-the-spot decisions at virtually all stages of a criminal trial. As a practical matter, a criminal defendant is rarely, if ever, in a position to decide, for example, whether certain testimony is hearsay and, if so, whether it implicates interests protected by the Confrontation Clause; indeed, it is because "[e]ven the intelligent and educated layman has small and sometimes no skill in the science of law" that we held it constitutionally required that every defendant who faces the possibility of incarceration be afforded counsel. Argersinger v. Hamlin, 407 U.S. 25 (1972); Gideon v. Wainwright, 372 U.S. 335, 345 (1963).

Once counsel is appointed, the day-to-day conduct of the defense rests with the attorney. He, not the client, has the immediate—and ultimate—responsibility of deciding if and when to object, which witnesses, if any, to call, and what defenses to develop. Not only do these decisions rest with the attorney, but such decisions must, as a practical matter, be made without consulting the client.[1] The trial process simply does not permit the type of frequent and protracted interruptions which would be necessary if it were required that clients give knowing and intelligent approval to each of the myriad tactical decisions as a trial proceeds.

Since trial decisions are of necessity entrusted to the accused's attorney, the Fay–Zerbst standard of "knowing and intelligent waiver" is simply inapplicable. The dissent in this case, written by the author of Fay v. Noia, implicitly

---

1. Only such basic decisions as whether to plead guilty, waive a jury, or testify in one's own behalf are ultimately for the accused to make. See ABA Project on Standards for Criminal Justice, The Prosecution Function and Defense Function § 5.2, pp. 237–238 (App.Draft 1971).

recognizes as much. According to the dissent, Fay imposes the knowing-and-intelligent-waiver standard "where possible" during the course of the trial. In an extraordinary modification of Fay, Mr. Justice Brennan would now require "that the lawyer actually exercis[e] his expertise and judgment in his client's service, and with his client's knowing and intelligent participation *where possible*"; he does not intimate what guidelines would be used to decide when or under what circumstances this would actually be "possible." (Emphasis supplied.) What had always been thought the standard governing the *accused's* waiver of his own constitutional rights the dissent would change, in the trial setting, into a standard of conduct imposed upon the defendant's *attorney*. This vague "standard" would be unmanageable to the point of impossibility.

The effort to read this expanded concept into Fay is to no avail; that case simply did not address a situation where the defendant had to look to his lawyer for vindication of constitutionally based interests. I would leave the core holding of Fay where it began, and reject this illogical uprooting of an otherwise defensible doctrine.

■ Mr. Justice Stevens, concurring.

Although the Court's decision today may be read as a significant departure from the "deliberate bypass" standard announced in Fay v. Noia, 372 U.S. 391, I am persuaded that the holding is consistent with the way other federal courts have actually been applying Fay.[1] The notion that a client must always consent to a tactical decision not to assert a constitutional objection to a proffer of evidence has always seemed unrealistic to me. Conversely, if the constitutional issue is sufficiently grave, even an express waiver by the defendant himself may sometimes be excused. Matters such as the competence of counsel, the procedural context in which the asserted waiver occurred, the character of the constitutional right at stake, and the overall fairness of the entire proceeding, may be more significant than the language of the test the Court purports to apply. I therefore believe the Court has wisely refrained from attempting to give precise content to its "cause" and "prejudice" exception to the rule of Francis v. Henderson, 425 U.S. 536.[4]

In this case I agree with the Court's holding that collateral attack on the state-court judgment should not be allowed. The record persuades me that competent trial counsel could well have made a deliberate decision not to object to the admission of the respondent's in-custody statement. That statement was consistent, in many respects, with the respondent's trial testimony. It even had some positive value, since it portrayed the respondent as having acted in response to provocation, which might have influenced the jury to return a

---

1. The suggestion in Fay that the decision must be made personally by the defendant has not fared well, although a decision by counsel may not be binding if made over the objection of the defendant. Courts have generally found a "deliberate bypass" where counsel could reasonably have decided not to object, but they have not found a bypass when they consider the right "deeply embedded" in the Constitution, Frazier v. Roberts, 441 F.2d 1224, 1230 (C.A.8 1971), or when the procedural default was not substantial. Sometimes, even a deliberate choice by trial counsel has been held not to be a "deliberate bypass" when the result would be unjust. In short, the actual disposition of these cases seems to rest on the court's perception of the totality of the circumstances, rather than on mechanical application of the "deliberate bypass" test.

4. As Fay v. Noia, *supra*, at 438, makes clear, we are concerned here with a matter of equitable discretion rather than a question of statutory authority; and equity has always been characterized by its flexibility and regard for the necessities of each case.

verdict on a lesser charge. To the extent that it was damaging, the primary harm would have resulted from its effect in impeaching the trial testimony, but it would have been admissible for impeachment in any event, Harris v. New York, 401 U.S. 222. Counsel may well have preferred to have the statement admitted without objection when it was first offered rather than making an objection which, at best, could have been only temporarily successful.

Moreover, since the police fully complied with Miranda, the deterrent purpose of the Miranda rule is inapplicable to this case. Finally, there is clearly no basis for claiming that the trial violated any standard of fundamental fairness. Accordingly, no matter how the rule is phrased, this case is plainly not one in which a collateral attack should be allowed. I therefore join the opinion of the Court.

■ Mr. Justice White, concurring in the judgment. * * *

■ Mr. Justice Brennan, with whom Mr. Justice Marshall joins, dissenting.

Over the course of the last decade, the deliberate-bypass standard announced in Fay v. Noia, 372 U.S. 391, 438–439 (1963), has played a central role in efforts by the federal judiciary to accommodate the constitutional rights of the individual with the States' interests in the integrity of their judicial procedural regimes. The Court today decides that this standard should no longer apply with respect to procedural defaults occurring during the trial of a criminal defendant. In its place, the Court adopts the two-part "cause"-and-"prejudice" test originally developed in Davis v. United States, 411 U.S. 233 (1973), and Francis v. Henderson, 425 U.S. 536 (1976). As was true with these earlier cases,[1] however, today's decision makes no effort to provide concrete guidance as to the content of those terms. More particularly, left unanswered is the thorny question that must be recognized to be central to a realistic rationalization of this area of law: How should the federal habeas court treat a procedural default in a state court that is attributable purely and simply to the error or negligence of a defendant's trial counsel? * * *[2] * * *

1. The Court began its retreat from the deliberate-bypass standard of Fay in Davis v. United States, where a congressional intent to restrict the bypass formulation with respect to collateral review under 28 U.S.C. § 2255 was found to inhere in Fed.Rule Crim.Proc., 12(b)(2). By relying upon Congress' purported intent, Davis managed to evade any consideration of the justifications and any shortcomings of the bypass test. Subsequently, in Francis v. Henderson, a controlling congressional expression of intent no longer was available, and the Court therefore employed the shibboleth of "considerations of comity and federalism" to justify application of Davis to a § 2254 proceeding. 425 U.S., at 541. Again, any coherent analysis of the bypass standard or the waivability of constitutional rights was avoided—as it was that same day in Estelle v. Williams, 425 U.S. 501 (1976), which proceeded to find a surrender of a constitutional right in an opinion that was simply oblivious to some 40 years of existing case law. Thus, while to-

day's opinion follows from Davis, Francis, and Estelle, the entire edifice is a mere house of cards whose foundation has escaped any systematic inspection.

2. * * * This Court has never taken issue with the foundation principle established by Fay v. Noia—that in considering a petition for the writ of habeas corpus, federal courts possess the *power* to look beyond a state procedural forfeiture in order to entertain the contention that a defendant's constitutional rights have been abridged. * * * Our disagreement, therefore, centers upon the standard that should govern a federal district court in the exercise of this power to adjudicate the constitutional claims of a state prisoner—which, in turn, depends upon an evaluation of the competing policies and values served by collateral review weighted against those furthered through strict deference to a State's procedural rules.

* * *

I

I begin with the threshold question: What is the meaning and import of a procedural default? If it could be assumed that a procedural default more often than not is the product of a defendant's conscious refusal to abide by the duly constituted, legitimate processes of the state courts, then I might agree that, a regime of collateral review weighted in favor of a State's procedural rules would be warranted. Fay, however, recognized that such rarely is the case; and therein lies Fay's basic unwillingness to embrace a view of habeas jurisdiction that results in "an airtight system of [procedural] forfeitures." 372 U.S., at 432.

This, of course, is not to deny that there are times when the failure to heed a state procedural requirement stems from an intentional decision to avoid the presentation of constitutional claims to the state forum. Fay was not insensitive to this possibility. Indeed, the very purpose of its bypass test is to detect and enforce such intentional procedural forfeitures of outstanding constitutionally based claims. * * * For this reason, the Court's assertion that it "think[s]" that the Fay rule encourages intentional "sandbagging" on the part of the defense lawyers is without basis; certainly the Court points to no cases or commentary arising during the past 15 years of actual use of the Fay test to support this criticism. Rather, a consistent reading of case law demonstrates that the bypass formula has provided a workable vehicle for protecting the integrity of state rules in those instances when such protection would be both meaningful and just.

But having created the bypass exception to the availability of collateral review, Fay recognized that intentional, tactical forfeitures are not the norm upon which to build a rational system of federal habeas jurisdiction. In the ordinary case, litigants simply have no incentive to slight the state tribunal, since constitutional adjudication on the state and federal levels are not mutually exclusive. * * * [N]o rational lawyer would risk the "sandbagging" feared by the Court. If a constitutional challenge is not properly raised on the state level, the explanation generally will be found elsewhere than in an intentional tactical decision.

In brief then, any realistic system of federal habeas corpus jurisdiction must be premised on the reality that the ordinary procedural default is born of the inadvertence, negligence, inexperience, or incompetence of trial counsel. The case under consideration today is typical. * * *

II

What are the interests that Sykes can assert in preserving the availability of federal collateral relief in the face of his inadvertent state procedural default? Two are paramount.

As is true with any federal habeas applicant, Sykes seeks access to the federal court for the determination of the validity of his federal constitutional claim. * * *

With respect to federal habeas corpus jurisdiction, Congress explicitly chose to effectuate the federal court's primary responsibility for preserving federal rights and privileges by authorizing the litigation of constitutional claims and defenses in a district court after the State vindicates its own interest through trial of the substantive criminal offense in the state courts. * * * [W]hether Fay was correct in penalizing a litigant solely for his intentional forfeitures properly must be read in light of Congress' desired norm of widened post-trial access to the federal courts. If the standard adopted today is later construed to require that the simple mistakes of attorneys are to be treated as binding forfeitures, it would serve to subordinate the fundamental rights contained in our constitutional charter to inadvertent defaults of rules promulgated by state agencies, and would essentially leave it to the States, through the enactment of procedure and the certification of the competence of local attorneys, to determine whether a habeas applicant will be permitted the access to the federal forum that is guaranteed him by Congress.

Thus, I remain concerned that undue deference to local procedure can only serve to undermine the ready access to a federal court to which a state defendant otherwise is entitled. But federal review is not the full measure of Sykes' interest, for there is another of even greater immediacy: assuring that his constitutional claims can be addressed to *some* court. For the obvious consequence of barring Sykes from the federal courthouse is to insulate Florida's alleged constitutional violation from any and all judicial review because of a lawyer's mistake. From the standpoint of the habeas petitioner, it is a harsh rule indeed that denies him "any review at all where the state has granted none," Brown v. Allen, 344 U.S., at 552 (Black, J., dissenting)— particularly when he would have enjoyed both state and federal consideration had his attorney not erred. * * *

                    * * *

III

A regime of federal habeas corpus jurisdiction that permits the reopening of state procedural defaults does not invalidate any state procedural rule as such; Florida's courts remain entirely free to enforce their own rules as they choose, and to deny any and all state rights and remedies to a defendant who fails to comply with applicable state procedure. The relevant inquiry is whether more is required—specifically, whether the fulfillment of important interests of the State necessitates that federal courts be called upon to impose additional sanctions for inadvertent noncompliance with state procedural requirements such as the contemporaneous-objection rule involved here. * * *

Punishing a lawyer's unintentional errors by closing the federal courthouse door to his client is both a senseless and misdirected method of deterring the slighting of state rules. It is senseless because unplanned and unintentional action of any kind generally is not subject to deterrence; and, to the extent that it is hoped that a threatened sanction addressed to the defense will induce greater care and caution on the part of trial lawyers, thereby forestalling negligent conduct or error, the potential loss of all valuable state remedies would be sufficient to this end. And it is a misdirected sanction because even if the penalization of incompetence or carelessness will encourage more thorough legal training and trial preparation, the habeas applicant, as opposed to his lawyer, hardly is the proper recipient of such a penalty. Especially with fundamental constitutional rights at stake, no fictional relationship of principal-agent or the like can justify holding the criminal defendant accountable for the naked errors of his attorney. This is especially true when so many indigent defendants are without any realistic choice in selecting who ultimately represents them at trial. Indeed, if responsibility for error must be apportioned between the parties, it is the State, through its attorney's admissions and certification policies, that is more fairly held to blame for the fact that practicing lawyers too often are ill-prepared or ill-equipped to act carefully and knowledgeably when faced with decisions governed by state procedural requirements. * * *

IV

Perhaps the primary virtue of Fay is that the bypass test at least yields a coherent yardstick for federal district courts in rationalizing their power of collateral review. In contrast, although some four years have passed since its introduction in Davis v. United States, 411 U.S. 233 (1973), the only thing clear about the Court's "cause"-and-"prejudice" standard is that it exhibits the notable tendency of keeping prisoners in jail without addressing their constitutional complaints. Hence, as of today, all we know of the "cause" standard is its requirement that habeas applicants bear an undefined burden of explanation for the failure to obey the state rule. Left unresolved is whether a habeas petitioner like Sykes can adequately discharge this burden by offering the commonplace and truthful explanation for his default: attorney ignorance or error beyond the client's control. The "prejudice" inquiry, meanwhile, appears to bear a strong resemblance to harmless-error doctrine. * * * I disagree with the Court's appraisal of the harmlessness of the admission of respondent's confession, but if this is what is meant by prejudice, respondent's constitutional contentions could be as quickly and easily disposed of in this regard by permitting federal courts to reach the merits of his complaint. In the absence of a persuasive alternative formulation to the bypass test, I would simply affirm the judgment of the Court of Appeals and allow Sykes his day in court on the ground that the failure of timely objection in this instance was not a tactical or deliberate decision but stemmed from a lawyer's error that should not be permitted to bind his client.

One final consideration deserves mention. Although the standards recently have been relaxed in various jurisdictions, it is accurate to assert that most courts, this one included, traditionally have resisted any realistic inquiry into the competency of trial counsel. There is nothing unreasonable, however, in adhering to the proposition that it is the responsibility of a trial lawyer who takes on the defense of another to be aware of his client's basic legal rights and of the legitimate rules of the forum in which he practices his profession. If he should unreasonably permit such rules to bar the assertion of the colorable constitutional claims of his client, then his conduct may well fall below the level of competence that can fairly be expected of him. For almost 40 years it has been established that inadequacy of counsel undercuts the very competence and jurisdiction of the trial court and is always open to collateral review. Obviously, as a practical matter, a trial counsel cannot procedurally waive his own inadequacy. If the scope of habeas jurisdiction previously governed by Fay v. Noia is to be redefined so as to enforce the errors and neglect of lawyers with unnecessary and unjust rigor, the time may come when conscientious and fair-minded federal and state courts * * * will have to reconsider whether they can continue to indulge the comfortable fiction that all lawyers are skilled or even competent craftsmen in representing the fundamental rights of their clients.

NOTE ON FEDERAL HABEAS CORPUS AND STATE
COURT PROCEDURAL DEFAULT

A. The Meaning of the Sykes Standard

(1) *Introduction.* Sykes left "cause and prejudice" to be defined in later cases.[1]
An elaborate series of decisions has given "cause" a very restricted meaning,
embracing only (a) reliance on a novel constitutional claim, see Paragraph (2),
infra; (b) a lawyer's inadvertence or other deficiency that is so serious as to
constitute constitutionally ineffective assistance of counsel, see Paragraphs (3–
4), *infra*; and (c) the state's creation of an "external impediment" to presentation of the claim, see Paragraph (5), *infra*. In addition, the Court has added
one other very narrow basis on which a defaulted claim may nonetheless be
heard—when the petitioner has made an adequate showing of "actual innocence", see Paragraph (7), *infra*.

(2) *Novelty as Cause.*

(a) Engle v. Isaac, 456 U.S. 107 (1982), involved habeas petitions objecting
to jury charges stating that the defendant bore the burden of persuasion on the
issue of self-defense. The Court, with Justice O'Connor writing, stated that
the petitioners had a colorable constitutional claim (under Mullaney v. Wilbur,
421 U.S. 684 (1975), and Patterson v. New York, 432 U.S. 197 (1977)) that the
state must disprove self-defense.[2] But she found no "cause" for the failure to
have complied with Ohio's rule requiring contemporaneous objection to jury
instructions. The Court rejected the notion that the supposed futility of
raising the objection—Ohio had long required defendants to prove self-defense—constituted cause, saying that "[e]ven a state court that has previously
rejected a constitutional argument may decide, upon reflection, that the contention is valid" (p. 130).

The prisoners also argued that they could not reasonably have been
expected to know of the constitutional claim at the time of their trials, which
were conducted before Mullaney and Patterson were decided. But the Court
responded that the trials took place after the decision in In re Winship, 397
U.S. 358, 364 (1970), holding that the Due Process Clause requires "proof
beyond a reasonable doubt of every fact necessary to constitute the crime with
which [a defendant] is charged." Mullaney and Patterson themselves were
based on Winship, and at the time of the prisoners' trials, some lawyers were
relying on Winship in advancing claims similar to the ones now being raised on
habeas. Thus, it could not be said in these cases that the petitioners had
"lacked the tools to construct" a constitutional argument. Though not "every
astute counsel" would have recognized in Winship the basis for a constitutional
objection to the instructions on self-defense, "the Constitution * * * does not
insure that defense counsel will recognize and raise every conceivable constitutional claim" (456 U.S. at 133–34).

(b) The Isaac opinion explicitly left open the question whether the novelty
of a constitutional claim could ever establish cause. That question was
answered affirmatively in Reed v. Ross, 468 U.S. 1 (1984)(5–4), which involved

---

1. On the evolution from Noia to Sykes,
see Hill, *The Forfeiture of Constitutional
Rights in Criminal Cases*, 78 Colum.L.Rev.
1050, 1051–62 (1978); Tague, *Federal Habeas Corpus and Ineffective Representation of*

*Counsel: The Supreme Court Has Work to
Do*, 31 Stan.L.Rev. 1, 6–19 (1978).

2. The Court has since found that claim
wanting on the merits. See Martin v. Ohio,
480 U.S. 228 (1987).

an issue similar to that in Isaac. At trial, the jury instructions, following North Carolina law, placed on the defendant the burden of proving (i) provocation—so as to reduce an intentional killing from murder to malice, and (ii) self-defense. The defendant had not challenged those instructions in his appeal, which was decided in 1969, before Winship was decided. In 1977, after the Court's ruling in Hankerson v. North Carolina, 432 U.S. 233 (1977), that the North Carolina burden of proof rules on provocation were unconstitutional under Mullaney v. Wilbur, Ross sought federal habeas relief. The Supreme Court found that relief was not precluded by Ross' failure to have challenged the instructions in his 1969 appeal. Stating that "the cause requirement may be satisfied under certain circumstances when a procedural failure is not attributable to an intentional decision by counsel made in pursuit of his client's interests" (p. 14), Justice Brennan held that here there was cause for the procedural default because at the time of appeal counsel could not reasonably have been expected to know his client had a constitutional argument. In dissent, Justice Rehnquist first questioned whether the novelty of an argument should ever constitute cause, and added that in any event Ross' claim was not novel, because the Winship approach had been adopted in two decisions—one state, one federal— reached some months prior to Ross' appeal.[3]

(c) In the rare case in which a prisoner can demonstrate that a claim is novel, today the claim is likely to be rejected under the 1989 decision in Teague v. Lane, p. 1392, *supra*—which generally bars a habeas petition based on "new law".[4] Teague's second exception does permit a habeas court to apply new constitutional rules that establish a bedrock procedure "without which the likelihood of an accurate conviction is seriously diminished"; would the constitutional claim in Reed v. Ross qualify?

(d) Under Fed.R.Crim.Proc. 52(b), in a *federal* criminal prosecution, an appellate court may not excuse a procedural default unless the error was "plain"—which the Court has interpreted to mean "clear under current law", United States v. Olano, 507 U.S. 725, ___ (1993). Why should the novelty of a

---

3. In Dugger v. Adams, 489 U.S. 401 (1989), the Court found a constitutional claim was not novel for a somewhat novel reason. The habeas petition objected to a jury instruction stating that the trial judge would ultimately decide whether to impose capital punishment; in fact, state law provided that a judge may override a jury recommendation only when the facts are "so clear and convincing that virtually no reasonable person could differ." The petition relied on Caldwell v. Mississippi, 472 U.S. 320 (1985), which held unconstitutional a prosecutor's comments that misinformed the jury about its role in capital sentencing. But the Supreme Court in Dugger found the claim barred by the prisoner's failure to have objected to the jury instruction on direct appeal from his conviction. Although that appeal pre-dated the Caldwell decision, the Court noted that a violation under Caldwell presupposes that the jury was misled about its role under state law; thus, a challenge (albeit one based on state law) to the instruction in his direct appeal would not have been novel. The Court emphasized that the failure to preserve a state law objection does not always bar a federal challenge to the same practice; but under Caldwell, an error of state law is a necessary element of the federal claim.

4. Indeed, note that the definition of legal novelty under Engle and Reed is narrower than that under Teague. Where, for example, lower courts have divided on an issue, a criminal defendant is deemed to have the tools to raise a claim, which therefore will not be deemed novel so as to establish cause under the Isaac decision. By contrast, under Teague, the same difference of judicial opinion is likely to support a finding that the claim depends on a new rule. Is there justification for this difference, or does it simply reflect the Supreme Court's desire to narrow the habeas jurisdiction? See Kinports, *Habeas Corpus, Qualified Immunity, and Crystal Balls: Predicting the Course of Constitutional Law*, 33 Ariz.L.Rev. 115, 194–95 (1991).

claim make it harder to excuse a default in that context but easier to do so in a collateral attack on a state conviction?

(3) *Counsel's Inadvertence.* In Murray v. Carrier, 477 U.S. 478 (1986), the Court refused to accept Justice Brennan's suggestion, in his majority opinion in Ross, Paragraph (2)(b), *supra*, that cause might generally be found for procedural failures not attributable to *intentional* decisions by counsel. In Carrier, counsel had inadvertently failed to include in the appeal a claim that the trial court had erred by not permitting the defense to examine the victim's statements to the police. Under Virginia law, this procedural default barred state collateral review.

In an opinion by Justice O'Connor, the Court held that the default also barred federal habeas review, emphasizing the "considerable costs" associated with habeas review, costs that "do not disappear when the default stems from counsel's ignorance or inadvertence rather than from a deliberate decision, for whatever reason, to withhold a claim" (p. 487). These costs would increase, she argued, if the treatment of procedural defaults depended on whether they were unintentional, because "federal habeas courts would routinely be required to hold evidentiary hearings to determine what prompted counsel's failure to raise the claim in question" (*id.*). The Court thus held that "[s]o long as a defendant is represented by counsel whose performance is not constitutionally ineffective under the standard established in Strickland v. Washington, [466 U.S. 668 (1984)], we discern no inequity in requiring him to bear the risk of attorney error that results in the procedural default. Instead, we think that the existence of cause for a procedural default must ordinarily turn on whether the prisoner can show that some objective factor external to the defense impeded counsel's efforts to comply with the State's procedural rule. Without attempting an exhaustive catalog * * *, we note that a showing that the factual or legal basis for a claim was not reasonably available to counsel, see Reed v. Ross * * *, or that 'some interference by officials,' Brown v. Allen, 344 U.S. [at] 486, * * * made compliance impracticable, would constitute cause under this standard.

"Similarly, if the procedural default is the result of ineffective assistance of counsel, the Sixth Amendment itself requires that responsibility for the default be imputed to the State * * *. Ineffective assistance of counsel, then, is cause for a procedural default. However, we think that the exhaustion doctrine * * * generally requires that a claim of ineffective assistance be presented to the state courts as an independent claim before it may be used to establish cause for a procedural default. [Otherwise] the federal habeas court would find itself in the anomalous position of adjudicating an unexhausted constitutional claim for which state court review might still be available * * *" (pp. 488–89).

Justices Brennan and Marshall, in dissent, repeated the assertion that Sykes was wrong to have abandoned Noia's "deliberate bypass" standard. They went on to argue that, even under Sykes, counsel's inadvertent default should constitute cause (p. 524): "Where counsel is unaware of a claim or of the duty to raise it at a particular time, the procedural default rule cannot operate as a specific deterrent to noncompliance with the State's procedural rules. Consequently, the State's interest in ensuring that the federal court help prevent circumvention of the State's procedural rules by imposing the same forfeiture sanction is much less compelling [and] simply is not sufficient to overcome the heavy presumption against a federal court's refusing to exercise jurisdiction clearly granted by Congress."

(4) *Ineffective Assistance of Counsel as Cause.* Does the statement in Carrier that ineffective assistance of counsel constitutes cause add anything to the scope of habeas relief? Suppose a lawyer's failure to have objected under Miranda to the admission of a confession constituted a denial of the effective assistance of counsel. Wouldn't that Sixth Amendment violation provide the basis for habeas relief directly? If so, would there be any need to assert that violation as "cause", so as to permit the habeas court to reach the merits of the Miranda question?

Claims of ineffective assistance of counsel, though frequently set forth in habeas petitions, rarely succeed—primarily for two reasons. First, despite (or perhaps because of) the widespread shortcomings of systems of criminal defense representation, defendants have generally had great difficulty in persuading courts to find that the lawyer's performance fell below the constitutional minimum. See, *e.g.,* Green, *Lethal Fiction: The Meaning of Counsel in the Sixth Amendment,* 78 Iowa L.Rev. 433, 499–507 (1933); McConville & Mirsky, *Criminal Defense of the Poor in New York City,* 15 N.Y.U. Rev. L. & Soc.Ch. 581, 748 (1986); Berger, *The Supreme Court and Defense Counsel: Old Roads, New Paths—A Dead End?,* 86 Colum.L.Rev. 9, 65 (1986). Second, there can be no violation of the right to counsel when the lawyer's error occurred in a stage of the state court proceedings—such as a second, discretionary appeal from a conviction, or post-conviction proceedings—in which there is no Sixth Amendment right to counsel in the first place. For example, in Coleman v. Thompson, 501 U.S. 722 (1991)(also discussed in Paragraph B(3), *infra*), Coleman's attorney had missed a deadline for filing a notice of appeal from a denial of state post-conviction relief. (The appeal included a claim of ineffective assistance of counsel during trial, sentencing, and direct appeal—a claim that under state law could be raised only in a post-conviction proceeding.) The Court held, 6–3, that because the right to counsel does not extend to post-conviction proceedings,[5] "a petitioner cannot claim constitutionally ineffective assistance of counsel in such proceedings" (p. 752).

Note that at trial or in an initial direct appeal, where the Sixth Amendment right to counsel applies, one can understand (whether or not one agrees with) the decision to use the constitutional standard of effective assistance of counsel to determine whether a client should be taxed with a lawyer's inadvertent default. But because no mistake by a lawyer in a post-conviction proceeding will violate the Sixth Amendment, no matter how egregious the mistake, Coleman leaves prisoners entirely at the mercy of incompetent lawyers in this setting. What justifies that result?

(5) *External Impediment as Cause.* In Amadeo v. Zant, 486 U.S. 214 (1988), the Supreme Court found cause to excuse a procedural default. While the defendant's direct appeal from his conviction and death sentence was pending, an independent voting rights lawsuit uncovered a handwritten memorandum from the District Attorney's Office to the jury commissioners, listing figures for the number of blacks and women to be placed on master jury lists. The document's apparent purpose was to maintain the under-representation of these groups while preventing it from becoming so large as to give rise to a

---

5. The Court actually left open the possibility that Coleman possessed a constitutional right to counsel in a state collateral proceeding with respect to his claim of ineffective assistance during trial, sentencing, and direct appeal, but held that if such a right existed, it would not extend to an appeal from denial of relief in such a proceeding—the stage at which the default had occurred.

prima facie case of discrimination. When the prisoner asserted a jury discrimination claim for the first time on appeal, the Georgia Supreme Court brushed it aside as untimely. On federal habeas corpus, the district court found that deliberate concealment by local officials constituted cause, and that there had been no deliberate bypass by the prisoner's lawyers. The court of appeals reversed, but was in turn unanimously reversed by the Supreme Court, whose opinion emphasized the deference an appellate court owes to district court fact-findings. Cause was established, the Court ruled, because the basis for the claim was "reasonably unknown" to the prisoner's lawyers as a result of "the 'objective factor' of 'some interference by officials' "(p. 222, quoting Reed v. Ross and Murray v. Carrier, Paragraphs (2–3), *supra*).[6]

(6) *Prejudice*. In the only two cases in which the Supreme Court has found cause—Reed v. Ross, Paragraph (2)(b), *supra*, and Amadeo v. Zant, Paragraph (5), *supra*—there was no dispute that prejudice was also present, and thus no occasion for defining its meaning. The major decision discussing the meaning of "prejudice" is United States v. Frady, 456 U.S. 152 (1982), p. 1465, *infra*, a case involving a § 2255 motion by a federal prisoner. There, the Court said that to establish prejudice, the prisoner must show that errors at trial "worked to his *actual* and substantial disadvantage, infecting his entire trial with error of constitutional dimensions" (p. 170). See generally Jeffries & Stuntz, *Ineffective Assistance and Procedural Default in Federal Habeas Corpus*, 57 U.Chi. L.Rev. 679, 684–85 & n. 25 (1990).

(7) *Actual Innocence*. In Murray v. Carrier, Paragraph (3), *supra*, the Court adumbrated one other circumstance—in addition to the presence of "cause and prejudice"—in which a state court default could be excused. Justice O'Connor stated that "in an extraordinary case, where a constitutional violation has probably resulted in the conviction of one who is actually innocent, a federal habeas court may grant the writ even in the absence of a showing of cause for the procedural default" (p. 496). The Court has yet to find a case satisfying that standard,[7] but has given "actual innocence" further definition in two cases raising the question whether a federal habeas court could decide a claim not raised in a prior federal habeas petition—a question governed, the Court held in McCleskey v. Zant, 499 U.S. 467 (1991), p. 1442, *infra*, by the same standards that govern state court procedural defaults.

(a) Sawyer v. Whitley, 505 U.S. 333 (1992), involved a challenge to the constitutionality of a capital sentence. The claims at issue were that (i) the police failed to make exculpatory evidence available to the defendant, and (ii) the defendant's counsel was ineffective in failing to introduce mitigating

---

6. Amadeo v. Zant was given a narrow reading in McCleskey v. Zant, 499 U.S. 467 (1991), p. 1442, *infra*. In rejecting McCleskey's argument that the state's failure to turn over a document constituted cause for an earlier procedural default, the Court said: "This case differs from Amadeo in two crucial respects. First, there is no finding that the State concealed the evidence. And second, * * * [any concealment that might have occurred] would not establish cause here because, in light of McCleskey's knowledge of the information in the document, any initial concealment would not have prevented him from raising the claim [in the earlier proceeding]" (p. 501).

7. Steiker, *Innocence and Federal Habeas*, 41 U.C.L.A.L.Rev. 303, 341 (1993), reports that "[o]f the several hundred reported [lower federal court] decisions confronting defaulted claims since Carrier, few have permitted habeas review via the innocence exception"; accord Berger, *Herrera v. Collins: The Gateway of Innocence For Death–Sentenced Prisoners Leads Nowhere*, 35 Wm. & Mary L.Rev. 943, 986 (1994). See also Garvey, *Death-Innocence and the Law of Habeas Corpus*, 56 Alb.L.Rev. 225 (1992).

evidence at the capital sentencing hearing. Both claims, the Court held, were foreclosed by not having been raised in a timely manner, as neither would have established "by clear and convincing evidence" that "no reasonable juror would find [the prisoner] eligible for the death penalty" under state law (p. 347). Petitioners can meet this standard only by showing either that they are innocent of the capital crime itself, or that no aggravating factor or "other condition of eligibility" was present (p. 345). The existence of mitigating evidence, not introduced at sentencing as the result of an alleged constitutional error, does not satisfy this standard.[8]

(b) Schlup v. Delo, 115 S.Ct. 851 (1995), also involved a death row inmate, but one who was claiming to be actually innocent of the underlying crime rather than wrongly sentenced to death. The Supreme Court held that the showing of actual innocence required in such a case, though stronger than that needed to establish "prejudice", was less strong than the showing required in Sawyer. Justice Stevens' majority opinion noted that challenges to capital sentences (as in Sawyer) are common, while claims that an innocent person was convicted are rarely made and difficult to substantiate. The latter thus pose a less serious threat to finality, comity and scarce judicial resources, while also implicating a compelling interest of the prisoner. Thus, the less exacting standard set forth in Carrier—which the Court defined as requiring a showing that, absent the constitutional error, "it is more likely than not that no reasonable juror would have convicted"—was appropriate (p. 867). Chief Justice Rehnquist, joined in dissent by Justices Kennedy and Thomas, objected that the majority's formulation mixed "apples and oranges: 'More likely than not' is a quintessential charge to a finder of fact, while 'no reasonable juror would have convicted him' [but for the constitutional error] is an equally quintessential conclusion of law", similar to the standard used to decide motions for judgment of acquittal (p. 873). The dissenters would have applied the Sawyer standard and required proof " 'by clear and convincing evidence [that] no reasonable juror would find [the prisoner guilty of murder]' " (p. 874, quoting Sawyer).[9]

B. The Extension of the Sykes Approach to All State Court Defaults

(1) *Introduction.* In Sykes, the concurring opinions of Chief Justice Burger and of Justice Stevens both stressed that the failure to challenge the admission of Sykes' statement was a default at trial, and was related to a decision (whether to object under Miranda) that was entrusted to the lawyer. The Court's opinion left open whether the "cause and prejudice" standard would be appropriate for other kinds of defaults—for example, the failure to file an appeal at all, as in Fay v. Noia, p. 1415, *supra*—proclaiming that the Court

---

8. Justice Stevens (joined by Justices Blackmun & O'Connor) argued that a default should be excused if the petitioner shows by a preponderance of the evidence that the death sentence was "clearly erroneous"—a test that would allow consideration not only of eligibility for death but also of whether mitigating circumstances so outweighed aggravating circumstances that no reasonable sentencer could have imposed a death sentence. He concurred in the judgment, finding that petitioner failed to meet that standard.

9. In a separate dissent, Justice Scalia (joined by Justice Thomas) agreed that the Sawyer standard was appropriate, but argued more broadly (i) that the habeas statute, in § 2244(b), governs a case of multiple federal habeas petitions, providing that a district court need not entertain a second petition in these circumstances; and (ii) that the district court's refusal in this case to reach the merits was not an abuse of discretion.

(unlike the majority in Noia) did "not choose to paint with a * * * broad brush" (footnote 12). But over time, the approach in Sykes has been extended, through a series of smaller brush strokes, to cover all types of state court procedural defaults.

(2) *Murray v. Carrier.* An important step along the way was taken in Murray v. Carrier, Paragraph A(3), *supra*, where counsel did file an appeal from the judgment of conviction, but inadvertently failed to include within it a claim based on the trial court's failure to permit defense counsel to examine the victim's statements to the police. In a habeas action based on that claim, the Supreme Court held that habeas review of that claim was unavailable, rejecting the argument that the standard applied to defaults on appeal should differ from that applied at trial. Justice O'Connor wrote (477 U.S. at 490–91): "A State's procedural rules serve vital purposes at trial, on appeal, and on state collateral attack. * * * [T]he standard for cause should not vary depending on the timing of a procedural default or on the strength of an uncertain and difficult assessment of the relative magnitude of the benefits attributable to the state procedural rules that attach at each successive stage of the judicial process. * * *"

Concurring in the result in Carrier (a remand), Justice Stevens (joined by Justice Blackmun) argued that "appellate procedural default should not foreclose habeas corpus review of a meritorious constitutional claim that may establish the prisoner's innocence" (p. 515). The cause and prejudice formula, he noted, "is of recent vintage, particularly in comparison to the writ for which it is invoked. It is, at most, part of a broader inquiry into the demands of justice" (p. 501). According to Justice Stevens, this inquiry "requires a consideration, not only of the nature and strength of the constitutional claim, but also of the nature and strength of the state procedural rule that has not been observed" (p. 506). And "with an appellate default, the state interest in procedural rigor is weaker than at trial, and the transcendence of the Great Writ is correspondingly clearer" (p. 507).[10]

In Smith v. Murray, 477 U.S. 527 (1986)(5–4), decided the same day as Carrier, the Court held the Carrier approach equally applicable to capital cases. Four Justices dissented, with Justices Brennan and Stevens each writing an opinion, based on his separate opinion in Carrier, that urged greater forgiveness of defaults in capital cases.

(3) *The Overruling of Noia: Coleman v. Thompson.* Fay v. Noia was squarely overruled in Coleman v. Thompson, 501 U.S. 722 (1991), in which the procedural default consisted of a failure to perfect a timely appeal. The Court held that in the absence of a showing of cause and prejudice, the existence of an independent and adequate state ground barring direct Supreme Court review would also bar review in federal habeas corpus.[11]

10. Compare Meltzer, *State Court Forfeitures of Federal Rights*, 99 Harv.L.Rev. 1130, 1224 (1986)(urging greater forgiveness of defaults that occur on appeal rather than at trial, as "there is a fresh record of the facts [relating to the constitutional claim]; the state court was given the chance to consider the claim in the first instance; [and] the prosecution was given notice" of the constitutional claim).

For discussion of Justice Brennan's dissent in Carrier, see Paragraph A(3), *supra*.

11. In Coleman, the failure to file a timely notice of appeal occurred in state postconviction proceedings, in which there is no constitutional right to counsel. See Paragraph A(4), *supra*. In a case like Noia, involving a failure to file a direct appeal from a conviction, a petitioner is very likely to have a substantial claim that the default constitut-

(4) *Questions*. Was the Court wise to extend the cause and prejudice standard across the board? More generally, should it have made irrelevant such factors as (a) whether the lawyer's default was intentional or inadvertent; (b) whether the sentence was three year's probation or death; (c) whether the default occurred at the criminal trial, on appeal, or in post-conviction proceedings; and (d) whether the challenge, if successful, would have immunized the defendant from conviction? See generally Meltzer, note 10, *supra*, at 1208–26.

(5) *Loose Threads*. Chief Justice Burger's concurrence in Sykes said (in footnote 1) that a few "basic decisions"—such as "whether to plead guilty, waive a jury, or testify in one's own behalf are ultimately for the accused to make." His opinion, however, said the same thing of the decision whether to take an appeal, but the Court held in Coleman v. Thompson, Paragraph (3), *supra*, that a failure to appeal precludes habeas relief—without inquiring whether the decision not to appeal had been made by the prisoner himself. (At the same time, Coleman involved an appeal from denial of post-conviction relief rather than an appeal from conviction.) Do there remain some rights that, as a matter of substantive constitutional law, cannot validly be waived except by the defendant personally?

C. The Grounds of a State Court Decision and the Problem of Ambiguity

(1) *State Court Excuse of Procedural Default*. None of the Court's decisions disturbs the traditional rule that if the state courts overlook a procedural default and decide the federal claim, the federal courts on habeas have jurisdiction to reach the merits. See, *e.g.*, Warden v. Hayden, 387 U.S. 294, 297 n. 3 (1967). (A similar rule is followed by the Supreme Court on direct review of state court decisions in the face of a procedural default that, had it not been excused, would have constituted an independent and adequate state ground. See Chap. V, Sec. 2(B), p. 583, *supra*.)

(2) *Ambiguous Decisions*. It is sometimes unclear whether a state court's refusal to recognize a constitutional claim presented by a criminal defendant was a decision that the claim lacked merit or rather that the claim was procedurally foreclosed due to a default. Similar problems arise on Supreme Court review of ambiguous state court decisions, a matter addressed in Michigan v. Long, see Chap. V, Sec. 2(A), p. 528, *supra*.

In three recent federal habeas cases, the Supreme Court has considered the implications of Long for federal habeas courts dealing with ambiguous state court decisions. The cases have established a presumption that an ambiguous state court decision rests on a denial of the claim on the merits, and hence is reviewable, see Harris v. Reed, 489 U.S. 255 (1989); but the presumption can be rebutted, see Coleman v. Thompson, 501 U.S. 722 (1991), and Ylst v. Nunnemaker, 501 U.S. 797 (1991).

After reviewing the discussion of these decisions in Chap. V, Sec. 2(A), pp. 541–42, *supra*, do you agree with the balance struck by the Court? Is it relevant that in habeas, unlike Supreme Court review on certiorari, a federal court lacks the option of vacating and remanding for clarification of an ambiguity? That, again unlike certiorari review, a federal habeas court lacks discretion to refuse to entertain the case at all?

ed a denial of the effective assistance of counsel.

D. Questions and Avenues of Exploration

(1) *The Relationship of Procedural Default to the Rule of Brown v. Allen.* In recent years, many Justices have expressed the view that plenary federal relitigation on habeas seriously impairs the effective administration of criminal justice and the ideals of federalism. But so long as the rule of Brown v. Allen remains, should the failure to raise a federal question in state court bar habeas relief—when, even had the issue been properly raised, any state court determination would not have been dispositive? If habeas proceedings are seen as wholly independent of the state court judgment, see p. 1358, Paragraph (2)(b), *supra*, should noncompliance with state court rules ever block prisoners from obtaining federal review of their federal constitutional claims? If, on the other hand, the habeas jurisdiction demands limitation, does the elaboration of an exquisitely detailed and narrow set of standards governing the excuse of state court procedural defaults address the central problem?[12]

(2) *The Relationship of Procedural Default to the Adequate State Ground Doctrine.* What is (or should be) the relationship of the standards for forgiving procedural defaults applied by the state courts in the first instance to the standards applied by the federal courts on direct or collateral review of state court convictions?

(a) In Dugger v. Adams, note 3, *supra*, the Court appeared to assume that a state procedural default that would not bar direct review (because the procedural ruling would not be an "adequate" state ground) would also not bar federal habeas corpus review—although the challenged ground was found to be "adequate". See 489 U.S. at 410–11 n.6. See also Coleman v. Thompson, 501 U.S. at 729–32 (stating generally that the adequate state ground doctrine applies also in habeas corpus actions).

On the other hand, certain procedural defaults that would bar Supreme Court review do not bar habeas review—for example, where the defaulted claim is novel or would establish "actual innocence". In practice, however, these avenues of excuse are so narrow that the standards applied on direct and collateral differ very little.

Should the standards differ at all? Recall the general view (see p. 1357, Paragraph (2)(a), *supra*) that the purpose of habeas jurisdiction is to provide a substitute for Supreme Court appellate review, which the Court cannot practicably afford in every case. Does that view suggest that the standards on direct and collateral review should be the same?

(b) Note that two years after Noia, the availability of habeas relief in the face of an adequate state ground was used by Justice Brennan as an argument for widening access to direct review. See Henry v. Mississippi, Chap. V, Sec. 2(B), p. 583, *supra*. Sykes, on the other hand, narrowed the excuse of procedur-

---

12. Professor Shapiro's study (conducted during the ascendancy of Fay v. Noia) found that fewer than 2% of the applications in the District of Massachusetts in 1970–72 were denied on procedural default grounds. Shapiro, *Federal Habeas Corpus: A Study in Massachusetts*, 87 Harv.L.Rev. 321, 347–48 (1973). A study of petitions filed in the Southern District of New York found that procedural default objections were raised in only a small fraction of cases—3% for the period 1973–75, and 9% for the period 1979–81; the increase was attributed to the shift from Noia to Sykes. See Faust, Rubenstein & Yackle, *The Great Writ in Action: Empirical Light on the Federal Habeas Corpus Debate*, 18 N.Y.U.Rev.L. & Soc.Change 637, 692 (1990–91). A multidistrict study of petitions filed in 1990 and 1992 found that only 7% were denied because of a procedural default. Flango, Habeas Corpus in State and Federal Courts 67 (1994).

al default on collateral review, making it not much broader than that on direct review. Do these developments suggest the essential instability of any sharp difference in the standards applied on direct and collateral review?

(c) In Fay v. Noia, p. 1415, *supra*, the Court stated that a habeas court's refusal to give effect to a state court forfeiture did not bar the state from enforcing the underlying procedural requirement in the future. The regime thus created, the Court contended, had several advantages: (i) it minimized federal interference with the state courts; (ii) it adequately deterred violations of state procedural rules by permitting forfeiture of remedies in state court and on direct review;[13] and (iii) under the deliberate bypass standard, it ensured virtually all criminal defendants an ultimate federal adjudication of their federal claims.[14]

These contentions are challenged in Meltzer, note 10, *supra*, at 1150–58, 1190–1202. On the first point, he suggests that Noia placed considerable pressure on states to excuse defaults that would ultimately be excused on habeas, and notes that during Noia's ascendancy many states did relax their procedural rules for just this reason. On the second point, he notes the dubiety of the assumption that state court forfeitures of federal rights significantly deter violation of state procedural rules. On the third point, he argues that the habeas jurisdiction does not afford a federal forum for review of all federal claims: many convicts will not be in custody by the time state remedies are exhausted; many others fail to seek relief; and any relief will come only after months or years of confinement.

(d) Meltzer also argues that the rules that permit defendants to obtain federal direct or collateral review of federal claims, notwithstanding noncompliance with state procedural rules, should be characterized as rules of federal common law. As such, they should be binding on the states, like other forms of federal common law, with the states bound to forgive any defaults that would not block direct or collateral review in federal court. "[I]f the state's interest in imposing a forfeiture * * * is not sufficiently weighty to bar the Supreme Court or a federal habeas court from reviewing the federal issue, that interest is also not weighty enough to bar review of the federal issue in state court in the first instance" (pp. 1189–90). Meltzer then proceeds to argue for more forgiveness of defaults than is provided under the cause and prejudice test.

What authority would justify the federal habeas courts in requiring state courts to exhibit more forgiveness of procedural defaults than the Constitution requires?

(3) *Procedural Default and the Adversary Process.* The procedural default cases vividly highlight the intractable difficulties that arise when lawyers are responsible for compliance with state procedural rules but their mistakes affect the constitutional rights of their clients. How should the costs of the inevitable errors be allocated between the state and criminal defendants? Does the answer depend on whether Justice Rehnquist was correct, in his opinion in

---

13. This argument is echoed in Brilmayer, *State Forfeiture Rules and Federal Review of State Criminal Convictions,* 49 U.Chi.L.Rev. 741, 770–74 (1982).

14. Accord Note, *Federal Habeas Corpus for State Prisoners: The Isolation Principle,* 39 N.Y.U.L.Rev. 78, 94 (1964); Reitz,

Federal Habeas Corpus: Impact of an Abortive State Proceeding, 74 Harv.L.Rev. 1314, 1347–48 (1961). See also Justice Brennan's lecture, *Federal Habeas Corpus and State Prisoners: An Exercise in Federalism,* 7 Utah L.Rev. 423 (1961).

Sykes, that broad excuse of procedural defaults would create a serious risk that defense lawyers will "sandbag" the prosecution? (For an argument that the risk is small, see Meltzer, note 10, *supra*, at 1196–1200.) Does it depend on the general quality of defense representation and on the strictness of constitutional standards of effective assistance of counsel?

Wasn't Justice Brennan correct, in his dissent in Sykes, that narrowing the bases for excusing procedural default will lead to more claims of ineffective assistance?[15] Even if so, many defaults result from lawyers' errors that are not deemed serious enough to violate the Sixth Amendment. Thus, some defendants obtain state and federal review of their constitutional claims, while others obtain no review whatsoever; the difference in treatment depends only on the quality of their lawyer—a circumstance over which most defendants have little control.

(4) *Alternatives*. Many have suggested that the Court's recent decisions impose a standard that, in general, is too strict.[16] But has the Court's approach been misguided in some more fundamental way?

Professors Jeffries & Stuntz, Paragraph A(6), *supra*, at 691–92, argue that excuse of procedural default should be predicated on showing that the defaulted claim, if meritorious, would establish a reasonable probability that the prisoner was innocent of the crime charged. That standard is similar to, but broader than, the "fundamental miscarriage of justice" notion of Murray v. Carrier, Paragraph A(7), *supra*. But Jeffries & Stuntz propose that their broader standard wholly displace, rather than supplement, the "cause and prejudice" rubric. They contend that if such a showing is made, procedural barriers to review should be swept aside so that a possibly innocent person can get federal review; absent such a showing, there is no reason to excuse a default. Without rejecting a more general limitation of habeas relief to claims related to innocence, see p. 1385, Paragraph (2), *supra*, they argue that such a limitation is especially appropriate as to defaulted claims: because the state court did not reach the merits, habeas review cannot help ensure that state courts properly applied federal standards.

NOTE ON SUCCESSIVE AND ABUSIVE HABEAS PETITIONS

(1) *The Sanders Decision*. The preceding Note deals with the failure properly to have raised a federal claim in *state court*. What consequences attach when a habeas petitioner failed to raise a claim in a previous *federal habeas corpus petition*? This issue—the subject of this Note—was addressed in Sanders v. United States, 373 U.S. 1 (1963) (7–2).

15. A study of habeas petitions in one district in 1973–75 (before Sykes) and in 1979–81 found that the percentage of petitions that included ineffective assistance claims rose from 16% to 29%. Faust, Rubenstein, & Yackle, note 12, *supra*, at 690–91. A multidistrict study of petitions filed from mid–1975 to mid–1977 (before Sykes) found that 40% of *petitions attacking convictions* (which themselves were only 67% of all petitions) included ineffective assistance claims. Robinson, An Empirical Study of Federal Habeas Corpus Review of State Court Judgments 10–12 (1979). A different multidistrict study found that 45% of *all petitions* filed in 1990 and 1992 included such a claim. Flango, note 12, *supra*, at 47.

16. See, *e.g.*, Meltzer, note 10, *supra*, at 1208–26.

Sanders actually involved a second collateral attack filed not by a state prisoner but rather by a *federal* prisoner under 28 U.S.C. § 2255, after an initial § 2255 motion had been denied. The Court first held that the standards governing successive applications under § 2255 are the same as the standards (codified in 1948 in 28 U.S.C. § 2244)[1] that govern state prisoners who have previously applied for federal habeas corpus. The Court then ruled (pp. 15–17) that "[c]ontrolling weight may be given to denial of a prior application for federal habeas corpus or § 2255 relief only if (1) the same ground presented in the subsequent application was determined adversely to the applicant on the prior application, (2) the prior determination was on the merits, and (3) the ends of justice would not be served by reaching the merits of the subsequent application." If, on the other hand, the ground presented was new, or had not previously been adjudicated on the merits, the federal court was obliged to entertain it absent an abuse of the writ—which the Court appeared to equate with a "deliberate bypass" within the meaning of Fay v. Noia, p. 1415, *supra*.[2]

(2) *Post-Sanders Statutory Provisions.*

(a) In 1966, Congress added subsections (b) and (c) to § 2244, which became the exclusive statutory provisions governing successive petitions from state prisoners.[3] Section 2244(b), the key provision—unlike the 1948 version of § 2244—does not condition the denial of a second petition, *inter alia*, on the court's being "satisfied that the ends of justice will not be served" by further inquiry into the legality of detention. Instead, § 2244(b) provides that after a denial of a habeas petition on the merits, a federal court need not entertain a second petition unless it was based on a ground not adjudicated in the earlier proceeding and unless "the applicant has not * * * deliberately withheld the newly asserted ground or otherwise abused the writ."

(b) Should this provision be read as codifying the doctrine of Sanders? As intended to limit a habeas court's discretion to entertain successive petitions, without restricting its power to refuse to hear them? As confirming the power of the federal courts to fashion "equitable" standards for the treatment of successive petitions? See generally Steiker, p. 1434, note 7, *supra*, at 343–49.

(c) Rule 9(b) of the § 2254 Rules, first promulgated in 1975, and since amended by Congress, see Pub.L. 94–426, § 2(7–8)(1976), provides: "A second or successive petition may be dismissed if the judge finds that it fails to allege new or different grounds for relief and the prior determination was on the merits or, if new and different grounds are alleged, the judge finds that the failure of the petitioner to assert those grounds in a prior petition constituted an abuse of the writ."

---

1. In the 1948 codification, § 2244 had but only subsection—essentially the present § 2244(a), but drafted to apply to state as well as federal prisoners. See Paragraph (2), *infra*.

2. Although 28 U.S.C. §§ 2244 and 2255 (1948) provided only that a federal court was authorized to deny a successive application in specified circumstances, Sanders held that the court was required to entertain such an application unless those circumstances were present. Thus, for example, § 2244 did not apply to successive petitions

raising claims not previously raised; Sanders interpreted that silence as requiring federal courts to hear such claims (absent a deliberate bypass).

3. Subsection (a) was amended to eliminate its application to state prisoners. In the post-conviction context, it thus would apply today only if the § 2255 remedy were deemed "inadequate or ineffective" so as to permit the federal prisoner to seek a writ of habeas corpus.

(3) *The Demise of Sanders*. The Sanders approach came under pressure for at least two reasons. First, its deliberate bypass standard had been drawn from Fay v. Noia, which was all but overruled in Wainwright v. Sykes and successive cases. Second, a number of Justices expressed concern that death row inmates were filing successive petitions (often at the eleventh hour) in order to delay their executions. See Steiker, p. 1434, note 7, *supra*, at 351.

Two decisions in the 1980s dealt with aspects of this problem. Neither generated a majority opinion, but in both a plurality of four Justices expressed support for tightening the limits on successive petitions.[4]

The other shoe finally dropped in McCleskey v. Zant, 499 U.S. 467 (1991), a capital case. There, a state prisoner made a number of claims in his first (unsuccessful) federal habeas petition, but did not include among them a claim that the admission of certain testimony violated his right to counsel as construed in Massiah v. United States, 377 U.S. 201 (1964). (That claim had been raised and rejected in the state courts.) He then filed a second federal habeas petition, which did include the Massiah claim. The Supreme Court held that the claim was properly dismissed as an abuse of the writ. That doctrine was governed by "a complex and evolving body of equitable principles informed and controlled by historical usage, statutory developments, and judicial decisions" (p. 489). "Deliberate abandonment" was not a prerequisite to a finding of abuse under § 2244(b). Rather, the importance of finality and the burden of habeas corpus litigation on the federal courts mandated adoption of a standard derived from that announced in Wainwright v. Sykes, p. 1418, *supra*, and Murray v. Carrier, p. 1432, *supra*: the failure to raise a claim in an earlier federal habeas petition will be excused only on a showing of cause and prejudice, or on a showing "that a fundamental miscarriage of justice would result from a failure to entertain the claim" (p. 494). (The Court went on to find that neither showing had been made. See p. 1434, note 6, *supra*.)

---

4. In Kuhlmann v. Wilson, 477 U.S. 436 (1986), an initial petition, challenging as a violation of the right to counsel the introduction at the prisoner's trial of statements he had made to his cellmate (a police informant), was denied. After an intervening Supreme Court decision that the prisoner claimed supported that challenge, he filed a second petition putting forward the same ground. The government argued that because the 1966 amendments eliminated language previously in § 2244 requiring consideration of the "ends of justice", the court need no longer consider them before dismissing a successive petition. The eight members of the Court who addressed the issue rejected this argument, but divided in their reasoning. Speaking for three other Justices, Justice Powell took the view that "the 'ends of justice' require federal courts to entertain such petitions only where the prisoner supplements his constitutional claim with a colorable showing of factual innocence" (p. 454). Justice Brennan's dissent (joined by Justice Marshall) objected to that limitation, while Justice Stevens' separate dissent took the intermediate view that assertion of a colorable claim of innocence is not a prerequisite to consideration of a successive petition but is relevant to whether it should be entertained.

Rose v. Lundy, 455 U.S. 509 (1982), p. 1446, *infra*, involved a petition that included some claims as to which the prisoner had satisfied the exhaustion requirement and some as to which he had not. The Court (per Justice O'Connor) first held that the petition had to be dismissed for lack of exhaustion. She then asserted (here speaking for only a plurality of four Justices) that although the prisoner could amend his petition to include only the "exhausted" claims, by doing so he would risk dismissal, as an abuse of the writ under Rule 9(b), of any subsequent petition presenting the other claims once state remedies had been exhausted. Four other Justices expressed their disagreement with this assertion.

The three dissenters objected to substituting the procedural default rules of Sykes for the approach of Sanders, which, they argued, had been codified in § 2244(b) and in Rule 9(b). Moreover, the Sykes standard was inapt because it was premised on a failure to raise a claim in state court and on the value of recognizing independent and adequate state grounds of decision. The abuse-of-the-writ doctrine, on the other hand, "presupposes that the petitioner has effectively raised his claim in state proceedings, [and thus] a decision by the habeas court to entertain the claim notwithstanding its omission from an earlier habeas petition will neither breed disrespect for state-procedural rules nor unfairly subject state courts to federal collateral review in the absence of a state-court disposition of a federal claim" (pp. 519–20).[5]

(4) *The Number of Successive Petitions.* Studies have found the percentage of petitioners who were known to have filed one or more previous petitions to be anywhere from 13% to 54%.[6]

NOTE ON EXHAUSTION OF STATE COURT REMEDIES[1]

(1) *Origins.* The requirement that state prisoners exhaust state court remedies before seeking federal habeas corpus relief derives from Ex parte Royall, 117 U.S. 241 (1886). There, the petitioner, while detained and awaiting trial on a state charge of selling a bond coupon without a license, sought federal habeas relief, alleging that the state licensing statute violated the Contract Clause. The Supreme Court affirmed the trial court's dismissal of the writ, ruling that although that court had *power* to inquire into the allegation in advance of trial, it should instead permit the question to be resolved by the state court in the normal course of trial (p. 251): "We cannot suppose that Congress intended to compel * * * [the federal] courts * * * to draw to themselves, in the first instance, the control of all criminal prosecutions commenced in State courts * * *. The injunction to hear the case summarily, and thereupon 'to dispose of the party as law and justice require' does not deprive the court of discretion as to the time and mode in which it will exert the powers conferred upon it. That discretion should be exercised in the light of the relations existing * * * between the judicial tribunals of the Union and of the States, and in recognition of the fact that the public good requires that those relations be not disturbed by unnecessary conflict between courts equally bound to guard and protect rights secured by the Constitution."

---

5. A provision in a bill that passed the Senate in 1995 would further limit successive petitions. A petitioner could not litigate a claim presented in an earlier petition, and could litigate a claim not previously presented only after first obtaining from a three-judge panel of the court of appeals a determination that (i) the claim relies on new law or new facts not discoverable through due diligence, and (ii) the facts underlying the claim establish that but for the constitutional error, no reasonable factfinder would have found the applicant guilty of the underlying offense. S. 735, § 606(b). See p. 1460, *infra.*

6. See Faust, Rubenstein and Yackle, p. 1438, note 12, *supra,* at 687 (15–20%); Flan-go, p. 1438, note 12, *supra,* at 37 (54%); Robinson, p. 1440, note 15, *supra,* at 15 (31%); Shapiro, p. 1438, note 12, *supra,* at 353–54 (13%).

1. See generally Yackle, *The Exhaustion Doctrine in Federal Habeas Corpus: An Argument for a Return to First Principles,* 44 Ohio St.L.J. 393 (1983); Amsterdam, *Criminal Prosecutions Affecting Federally Guaranteed Civil Rights: Federal Removal and Habeas Corpus Jurisdiction to Abort State Court Trial,* 113 U.Pa.L.Rev. 793, 884–96 (1965); 2 Liebman & Hertz, Federal Habeas Corpus Practice & Procedure, ch. 23 (2d ed.1994).

The Court subsequently made it clear that the references in Royall to the trial court's "discretion" were not to be taken seriously; it routinely reversed grants of the writ prior to exhaustion of state remedies where no special circumstances were present.[2]

In 1948 Congress codified some aspects of the exhaustion rule in 28 U.S.C. § 2254(b) and (c). The reviser's note states that "[t]his new section is declaratory of existing law as affirmed by the Supreme Court." H.R.Rep. No.308, 80th Cong., 1st Sess. A180 (1947).

Although the Supreme Court has raised doubts about whether judges may fashion non-statutory exceptions to the exhaustion requirement, see Duckworth v. Serrano, 454 U.S. 1, 5 (1981)(per curiam)(refusing to recognize an exception for "clear violations" of federal law), the Court reiterated in Granberry v. Greer, 481 U.S. 129, 136 (1987), Paragraph (8), *infra*, that the requirement is neither jurisdictional nor "rigid and inflexible".

(2) *The Import of Exhaustion.* Under the regime of Brown v. Allen, the exhaustion requirement operates as a rule of timing: a failure to exhaust does not entirely preclude federal habeas review, but merely postpones it until the prisoner has returned to the state courts and given them the opportunity to consider the allegations of federal error.

In Rose v. Lundy, 455 U.S. 509 (1982), the Court stated that the exhaustion requirement is meant to "protect the state courts' role in the enforcement of federal law", to "prevent disruption of state judicial proceedings", and to " 'minimize friction between our federal and state systems of justice by allowing the State an initial opportunity to pass upon and correct alleged violations of prisoners' federal rights' "(p. 518, quoting Duckworth v. Serrano, 454 U.S. 1, 3 (1981)(per curiam)). The Court also noted that exhaustion helps to generate a complete factual record to aid federal review, and that over time, exhaustion may make state courts more familiar with and hospitable to federal claims.

With the standard view expressed in Lundy, compare the argument in Amsterdam, note 1, *supra*, that federal habeas corpus should be available prior to state trial whenever the prospective state defendant makes a "colorable showing that the conduct for which he is prosecuted was conduct protected by the federal constitutional guarantees of civil rights" (113 U.Pa.L.Rev. at 804).[3] Writing in 1965, against the background of prosecutions of civil rights protesters in the South, Amsterdam contended that state courts will often flout the federal Constitution; that even if convictions are ultimately reversed on direct or collateral review, in the interim the defendants will have suffered incarceration, been required to post bail, lost educational or employment opportunities, and been chilled in the exercise of federal rights. See p. 1359, *supra*. He recognized objections that his proposal disserves federalism and invites defendants to use federal petitions to delay or disrupt state trials, but argued that such abuses can be minimized, and that the price is one that he (and more importantly, the Congress) was willing to pay.

(3) *What Constitutes Exhaustion.* A prisoner is required to exhaust only state remedies that remain available at the time that a habeas petition is filed. If, for example, a prisoner neglects to appeal from a state court conviction, and the

---

2. See, *e.g.*, New York v. Eno, 155 U.S. 89 (1894); Fitts v. McGhee, 172 U.S. 516 (1899); Urquhart v. Brown, 205 U.S. 179 (1907).

3. Amsterdam also argued that federal removal jurisdiction should be available in like circumstances. On the rejection of that view, see p. 959, *supra*.

time for doing so has elapsed at the time the habeas petition was filed, the exhaustion requirement would pose no barrier to habeas relief. The failure to appeal would, however, be treated as a procedural default, which has more serious consequences: unlike a failure to exhaust, such a default precludes rather than merely postpones the exercise of habeas jurisdiction.

A number of more specific questions have arisen in the application of the exhaustion requirement.

(a) *Proper Presentation of the Federal Issue.* Picard v. Connor, 404 U.S. 270 (1971), reaffirmed the principle that the exhaustion requirement is satisfied only where the prisoner presented the state courts with the *same* claim being raised on habeas: "[t]he rule would serve no purpose if it could be satisfied by raising one claim in the state courts and another in the federal courts" (p. 276). See also Anderson v. Harless, 459 U.S. 4, 7 n. 3 (1982)(exhaustion requirement not satisfied by presenting federal claim to state court by citing a state court decision, predicated on state law, in which another defendant had advanced the federal claim).[4]

In Duncan v. Henry, 115 S.Ct. 887 (1995)(per curiam), a bare majority ruled that a petitioner who had objected at trial to the admission of certain evidence, and on appeal had alleged that the error was a "miscarriage of justice" under the state constitution, had not properly presented a *federal* due process claim in state court and hence had not exhausted state court remedies. The Court read Picard and Harless as requiring that prisoners alert the state courts that they are asserting a *federal* constitutional claim. Justices Souter, Ginsburg, and Breyer concurred in the judgment without adopting that reading, finding only that the claim raised in the federal habeas petition differed from that raised in state court. In dissent, Justice Stevens accused the majority of imposing a new, "hypertechnical and unwise" requirement—one not supported by Picard or Harless or by the courts of appeals—that a claim raised in state court be labelled a federal claim (p. 889).[5]

(b) *Which State Remedies Must be Exhausted?* A prisoner ordinarily must exhaust state remedies available at trial and on appeal.[6] Although the language of § 2254(c) states that an applicant must exhaust "any available procedure" under state law, Justice Reed's opinion in Brown v. Allen, p. 1350, *supra*, relied on the legislative history in ruling that if the federal question had been properly presented to the trial and appellate courts, "[i]t is not necessary * * * for the prisoner to ask the state for collateral relief, based on the same evidence and issues already decided by direct review * * *" (344 U.S. at 447–

4. But in Vasquez v. Hillery, 474 U.S. 254, 260 (1986), the Court held that a claim of grand jury discrimination had been presented to state court, even though the federal habeas court had exercised its power to require the parties to provide supplemental evidence consisting of affidavits and computer analysis; the new evidence "did not fundamentally alter the legal claim already considered by the state courts".

5. None of the opinions referred to the analogous problem of determining whether a litigant seeking direct Supreme Court review of a state court judgment had properly presented the federal issue in state court—where

the Court's approach has been similar to that of the majority in Henry. See Chap. V, Sec. 2(B), p. 569, *supra*. Are there reasons for treating the two situations differently?

6. In Pitchess v. Davis, 421 U.S. 482 (1975)(per curiam), the Court unanimously reaffirmed the holding of Ex parte Hawk, 321 U.S. 114 (1944), that application to state appellate courts for an extraordinary writ does not exhaust state remedies where the state court's denial of the writ could not be taken as a decision on the merits of the federal claim and where normal channels of state appellate review remain open.

50).[7] Nor need a prisoner resubmit the federal contention to the state courts because a change in the state court's interpretation of federal law suggests that a second attempt would be successful. Francisco v. Gathright, 419 U.S. 59 (1974)(per curiam). However, when state post-conviction processes are open to a claim not previously raised in state court—for example, a claim of ineffective assistance of counsel—exhaustion of those processes is required. See Yackle, *The Misadventures of State Postconviction Remedies*, 16 N.Y.U.Rev.L. & Soc. Change 359 (1987–88)(noting but criticizing this rule, on the grounds that state post-conviction remedies rarely further and often foil the adjudication of federal claims, and that if a collateral proceeding must be commenced, the presumption that federal rightholders are entitled to a federal forum should permit petitioners to proceed immediately in federal court).

(c) *State Remedies Unavailable.* As § 2254(b) makes clear, exhaustion is not required where a state remedy is not available at all (either generally or for the particular prisoner), when the remedy is unduly burdensome or ineffective, or where resort to the state courts would clearly be futile. See, *e.g.*, Wilwording v. Swenson, 404 U.S. 249 (1971); see generally 2 Liebman & Hertz, note 1, *supra*, § 23.4a.

(d) *State Court Failure to Decide.* If a claim has been properly presented to the state court, state remedies are exhausted even if the claim is ignored in the state court's opinion. Smith v. Digmon, 434 U.S. 332 (1978).

(e) *Supreme Court Review.* Despite the omission from §§ 2254(b) and (c) of any express requirement that habeas be preceded by an application to the Supreme Court for direct review of the state court determination, Darr v. Burford, 339 U.S. 200 (1950), reaffirmed the existence of such a requirement, relying in part on the reviser's note that the "new section is declaratory of existing law as affirmed by the Supreme Court. See Ex parte Hawk, 1944, 321 U.S. 114." Darr v. Burford was overruled in Fay v. Noia, 372 U.S. 391, 435–38 (1963), on the ground that the statute specifically required only that a petitioner exhaust "remedies available in the courts of the State". See also Ulster County Court v. Allen, 442 U.S. 140, 149 n. 7 (1979)(rejecting, for the same reason, the argument that habeas review was unavailable where the prisoner had not first sought Supreme Court review under the provision (repealed in 1988) that in specified circumstances had authorized appeals as of right from state court judgments).

(4) *"Mixed" Petitions.* Most circuits had ruled that a federal court could reach the merits of a federal claim that had been properly exhausted, even if the habeas petition in which it was asserted also included unexhausted claims. The Supreme Court rejected this position, however, in Rose v. Lundy, 455 U.S. 509 (1982), with six Justices voting for a "total exhaustion" rule that requires a district court to dismiss such "mixed" habeas petitions. The total exhaustion rule, Justice O'Connor argued for the Court, not only promotes the general purposes of exhaustion, but eliminates any temptation for district courts to consider unexhausted claims and discourages piecemeal litigation in federal court.[8]

---

7. Although a prisoner must exhaust available appeals as of right, the lower courts disagree about whether discretionary appellate remedies—for example, a petition seeking certiorari from a state supreme court—

must be exhausted. See Note, 79 Minn. L.Rev. 1197 (1995).

8. Concurring only in the judgment, Justice Blackmun asserted that a district court should not dismiss the entire mixed

This decision leaves a prisoner who has filed a mixed petition with the choice of (a) returning to state court to exhaust the unexhausted claims, or (b) amending the petition to proceed with only the exhausted claims. Four Justices asserted in Lundy that if the second course were followed, any subsequent habeas petition containing the previously unexhausted claims might be dismissed as an abuse of the writ—a position that in 1991 gained majority support in McCleskey v. Zant, p. 1442, *supra*.

(5) *"Special Circumstances" Justifying Prompt Federal Intervention*. In the Royall case, Paragraph (1), *supra*, the first Justice Harlan stated that the discretion to withhold jurisdiction on habeas is "to be subordinated to any special circumstances requiring immediate action" (117 U.S. at 253), and suggested that federal interference prior to exhaustion might be justified in "cases of urgency, involving the authority and operations of the General Government, or the obligations of this country to, or its relations with, foreign nations" (p. 251). A number of cases have developed this suggestion.

(a) *Intervention Before Trial*. Determination of the federal claim on habeas before trial was deemed appropriate in Wildenhus Case, 120 U.S. 1 (1887)(state indictment of foreign seaman, for crime on vessel in port, urged to contravene treaty); In re Neagle, 135 U.S. 1 (1890)(state indictment of federal marshal for murder; claim that homicide was in justifiable performance of his duty to defend Justice Field); Thomas v. Loney, 134 U.S. 372 (1890)(state indictment for perjury in making deposition before notary for transmittal to House of Representatives in connection with election contest; claimed to infringe exclusive federal jurisdiction). But *cf.* Drury v. Lewis, 200 U.S. 1 (1906)(state indictment of military officer for murder; claim that homicide was committed in course of duty; evidence conflicting; circuit court "properly exercised" discretion not to intervene).

Note that these examples of pre-conviction relief appear to fall outside of 28 U.S.C. § 2254(b), which was amended in the course of its enactment to limit its exhaustion requirement to cases of custody pursuant to a "judgment of a state court"—excluding language that would have applied it also to custody pursuant to "authority of a State officer". See H.R.7124, 79th Cong., 2d Sess. 138 (1948).[9]

(b) *Intervention After Trial and Judgment*. In a number of decisions before the 1948 codification, the federal claim was entertained and determined after trial and judgment in state court, without exhaustion of further state remedies. See Ohio v. Thomas, 173 U.S. 276 (1899)(prosecution of governor of soldiers' home for serving oleomargarine without notice required by state statute; application of statute held interference with performance of federal

---

petition but only the unexhausted claims. He warned that the total exhaustion rule would "operate[] as a trap for the uneducated and indigent pro se prisoner-applicant" (p. 522), who "will consolidate all conceivable grounds for relief in an attempt to accelerate review and minimize costs. But, under the Court's approach, if he unwittingly includes in a § 2254 motion a claim not yet presented to the state courts, he risks dismissal of the entire petition and substantial delay before a ruling on the merits of his exhausted claims" (p. 530).

Justice Brennan (joined by Justice Marshall), Justice White, and Justice Stevens all filed separate opinions.

For criticism of Lundy, see Yackle, note 1, *supra*, at 424–40.

9. However, the broad provision in 28 U.S.C. §§ 1442(a) for removal of state prosecutions of federal officials may provide ground in some cases for declining to grant the writ.

function); Boske v. Comingore, 177 U.S. 459 (1900)(Collector of Internal Revenue committed for contempt of state court for refusing to produce copies of reports filed with Treasury pursuant to regulation of Secretary forbidding disclosure); Hunter v. Wood, 209 U.S. 205 (1908)(railroad ticket agent convicted of violating rate statute after federal interlocutory injunction restraining its enforcement). See generally Amsterdam, note 1, *supra*, at 892–99.

Is relief in such circumstances now precluded by the language of § 2254(b), quoted in Paragraph (5)(a), *supra*? Or do some or all of these decisions present circumstances in which state corrective processes were "ineffective to protect the rights of the prisoner" within the meaning of the statute? Should § 2254 have been made inapplicable to cases where habeas is sought under 28 U.S.C. § 2241(c)(2) (persons in custody for acts done under federal statutory or judicial authority) or (c)(4) (aliens in custody for acts, taken under authority of a foreign state, whose validity depends upon the law of nations)?

(6) *Time-Sensitive Federal Rights.* Is immediate federal intervention permissible when the prisoner claims a constitutional right that by its nature would evaporate if further pursuit of state court remedies were required?

(a) In Braden v. 30th Judicial Circuit Court, 410 U.S. 484 (1973), the petitioner, who was serving a sentence in Alabama while under detainer on a separate Kentucky charge, was permitted to seek relief premised on Kentucky's alleged denial of his right to a speedy trial. Acknowledging that Braden "can assert a speedy trial defense when, and if, he is finally brought to trial," the Court found that he nonetheless had "exhausted all available state court remedies for consideration of that constitutional claim. * * * He has already presented his federal constitutional claim of a *present* denial of a speedy trial to the courts of Kentucky. The state courts rejected the claim, apparently on the ground that since he had once escaped from custody the Commonwealth should not be obligated to incur the risk of another escape by returning him for trial. * * * Moreover, petitioner made no effort to abort a state proceeding or to disrupt the orderly functioning of state judicial processes. He comes to federal court, not in an effort to forestall a state prosecution, but to enforce the Commonwealth's obligation to provide him with a state court forum" (pp. 489–91).

Does Braden make pre-trial habeas automatically available to test the right to a speedy trial?[10]

(b) What about a pre-trial claim of double jeopardy? In Justices of Boston Municipal Court v. Lydon, 466 U.S. 294 (1984), a defendant had elected a bench trial in municipal court, from which there was no appeal, but after which he had the right to a trial de novo before a jury. Following his conviction in the bench trial, the defendant first requested a trial de novo, and then sought dismissal of the charge, arguing that a new jury trial would violate the Double Jeopardy Clause absent a prior determination that the evidence at the bench trial had been sufficient to sustain a conviction. After that claim was rejected by the trial court and by the state supreme court, the defendant sought habeas review. Although ruling against petitioner on the merits, the Court held that the petitioner had met the exhaustion requirement. The Court noted that the highest state court had rejected the double jeopardy claim on the merits, but

---

10. The courts of appeals have not so held. See, *e.g.*, Dickerson v. Louisiana, 816 F.2d 220, 227 (5th Cir.1987); Aktins v. Michigan, 644 F.2d 543 (6th Cir.1981). See also Note, 1977 Duke L.J. 707.

went on to note "the unique nature of the double jeopardy right", which "cannot be fully vindicated on appeal following final judgment, since in part the Double Jeopardy Clause protects 'against being twice put to *trial* for the same offense' "(pp. 302–03).

In Lydon, the petitioner had been able to obtain an authoritative decision of the state's highest court before trial. Suppose, however, that the state had permitted appellate review of the trial court's denial of the double jeopardy claim only after conviction. In such a case, should the exhaustion requirement stand in the way of a pre-trial application for federal relief?[11]

(c) As support for the "unique nature" of the double jeopardy right, the Lydon opinion relied on Abney v. United States, 431 U.S. 651 (1977), where the Court held that in a federal criminal prosecution, a district court's denial of a motion to dismiss an indictment on double jeopardy grounds is immediately appealable. With respect to time-sensitive rights such as the protection against double jeopardy, to what extent does the question whether a federal trial court judgment can be deemed "final", within the meaning of 28 U.S.C. § 1291—so as to permit immediate appellate review—implicate the same considerations as the question whether a habeas petitioner seeking immediate review of a state trial court's decision can be deemed to have exhausted state remedies?

(7) *The Exhaustion Requirement in Action.* Two empirical studies have shown that failure to exhaust state remedies is a major obstacle to adjudication of habeas petitions on the merits. In a pioneering study of Massachusetts habeas cases, Professor Shapiro found that more than half of the petitions filed from 1970–72 (135 out of 257) were dismissed wholly or in part on exhaustion grounds. Concluding that the system was not functioning well, he proposed, *inter alia*, that states limit the time available for their post-conviction processes, and that plainly unmeritorious petitions not be dismissed for lack of exhaustion. Shapiro, *Federal Habeas Corpus: A Study in Massachusetts*, 87 Harv.L.Rev. 321, 356–61 (1973). A later study found that of 1899 petitions filed in six district courts and one court of appeals between 1975 and 1977, 37% were denied for failure to exhaust state remedies, and that the average time lapse between state court conviction and the filing of a habeas corpus petition was 2.8 years. Allen, Schachtman & Wilson, *Federal Habeas Corpus and its Reform: An Empirical Analysis*, 13 Rutgers L.J. 675, 695, 703 (1982).

(8) *Waiver By the State.* One of Shapiro's proposals was subsequently adopted in part. In Granberry v. Greer, 481 U.S. 129 (1987), a unanimous Court held that when the state had failed to raise a meritorious exhaustion defense in the district court, the court of appeals was not obliged to dismiss the petition for failure to exhaust. Nor was the appellate court required to treat the default as definitively precluding the state from raising the issue on appeal. Re-affirming that the exhaustion doctrine is not jurisdictional, the Court stated: "[I]t seems unwise to adopt a rule that would permit, and might even encourage, the State to seek a favorable ruling on the merits in the district court while holding the exhaustion defense in reserve for use on appeal if necessary" (p. 131). Instead, the Court said that the court of appeals "should determine whether the interests of comity and federalism will be better served by addressing the

---

11. *Cf.* In re Shuttlesworth, 369 U.S. 35 (1962)(per curiam), discussed by Amsterdam, note 1, *supra*, at 895–96, where the Court appears to have held that habeas corpus should be available in advance of state appeal where the shortness of the sentence might moot the case.

merits forthwith or by requiring a series of additional state and district court proceedings before reviewing the merits of the petitioner's claim. * * * [I]f it is perfectly clear that the applicant does not raise even a colorable federal claim, the interests of the petitioner, the warden, the state attorney general, the state courts, and the federal courts will all be well served even if the State fails to raise the exhaustion defense, the district court denies the habeas petition, and the court of appeals affirms the judgment of the district court forthwith.'' Similarly, the nonexhaustion defense may be held waived "if a full trial has been held in the district court and it is evident that a miscarriage of justice has occurred" (pp. 134–35).

In Granberry, the exhaustion defense was raised for the first time in the court of appeals. The weight of authority suggests that district courts possess a similar discretion when the state fails to raise the issue in its pleadings but the district judge realizes that state remedies have not been exhausted. See 2 Liebman & Hertz, note 1, *supra*, § 23.2a, at 660 n. 10.[12]

(9) *Rules and Standards.* Has the Court (or Congress) made the exhaustion requirement unduly rigid? Would it be preferable to adopt the approach advocated by Yackle, note 1, *supra*, at 400: "As a general rule, petitioners should be required to pursue identifiable state remedies that promise a reasonable opportunity for litigation of their federal claims. If the federal courts reach the merits immediately notwithstanding the availability of state procedures, they should have sound reasons for concluding that prompt federal review is desirable. * * * The lower federal courts can be trusted to exercise their discretion responsibly."

(10) *Exhaustion in Civil Rights Suits.* Unlike habeas corpus actions, prisoner civil rights suits under 42 U.S.C. § 1983 may be filed in federal court without regard to exhaustion of state remedies. For consideration of the potential overlap of these two remedies, and the difficulties presented by their disparate approaches to exhaustion, see Chap. XII, pp. 1504–15, *infra*.

NOTE ON PROBLEMS OF CUSTODY AND REMEDY

(1) *The Statutory Requirement of Custody.* Like the common law, the habeas corpus statute (in § 2241(c)) confers jurisdiction only when the petitioner is "in custody". Until the 1960s, the custody requirement was strictly interpreted. See, *e.g.*, Wales v. Whitney, 114 U.S. 564 (1885)(naval officer's challenge to order confining him to city limits; no jurisdiction); Stallings v. Splain, 253 U.S. 339 (1920)(habeas will not lie if petitioner has been released on bail); Weber v. Squier, 315 U.S. 810 (1942)(habeas does not lie for convict released on parole).

(2) *Jones v. Cunningham.* The understanding of "custody" was revolutionized in Jones v. Cunningham, 371 U.S. 236 (1963), which held that a petitioner who was free on parole could obtain habeas review of the original criminal conviction.[1] The Court said that "[w]hile petitioner's parole releases him from

---

12. Provisions in two bills that each passed one House of Congress in 1995 would modify Granberry by providing that the state's failure to object to non-exhaustion may be treated as a waiver only where coun-

sel for the state *expressly* waives the defense. See H.R.729, § 104(b), and S.735, § 604, p. 1459, *infra*.

1. For criticism of the Court's use of history and precedent, see Oaks, *Legal Histo-*

immediate physical imprisonment, it imposes conditions which significantly confine and restrain his freedom" (p. 243). In concluding that petitioner was "in the 'custody' of the members of the Virginia Parole Board" (*id.*), the Court noted several different types of constraints—restrictions on lawful physical movements (*e.g.*, official permission required to leave the city or to change residence); other requirements which constrained freedom (*e.g.*, official permission required to drive an automobile; obligation to report monthly to a parole officer); the threat of re-imprisonment for violation of parole conditions; and the fact that re-imprisonment could occur (as of that time) without further judicial proceedings or other procedural safeguards. The opinion did not specify which of those constraints was essential to the conclusion that the petitioner was in custody.

Where all or most of these constraints accompany other forms of restraint, the lower courts have not hesitated since Jones to entertain applications for habeas corpus; the obvious examples are probation[2] and release on a conditionally suspended sentence.[3]

Some broad language in Jones—"besides physical imprisonment, there are other restraints on a man's liberty, restraints not shared by the public generally, which have been thought sufficient in the English-speaking world to support the issuance of habeas corpus" (p. 240)—appeared to have the potential of pushing the law even further. Is *any* special disability or constraint, not shared by the public generally, sufficient to constitute custody? Can a fully served sentence be challenged on habeas if civil disabilities still adhere? Can the imposition of a fine be tested by habeas?

The Supreme Court's answer to the last two question is no. See Maleng v. Cook, 490 U.S. 488, 492 (1989)(per curiam), Paragraph (5)(c), *infra*. But is there a principled limit once the notion of physical custody is abandoned? What of the suggestion that, absent physical custody, the petitioner must show the possibility of reincarceration by administrative action without judicial hearing? See *Developments in the Law—Federal Habeas Corpus*, 83 Harv. L.Rev. 1038, 1078–79, (1970).

Recall that in the view of some, habeas corpus jurisdiction is premised on the need to provide a sure means of federal review of state criminal convictions. See p. 1357, *supra*. Is that need limited to cases in which the prisoner remains in physical custody, or faces the threat of reincarceration? Does that understanding of the habeas jurisdiction create pressure for eliminating the custody requirement, or at least for broadening it as much as the statutory language will allow?

(3) *Hensley v. Municipal Court.* The trend towards a wider definition of "custody" continued with Hensley v. Municipal Court, 411 U.S. 345 (1973), involving a petitioner who had been sentenced to jail by a state court, and who had exhausted all available state appellate and collateral remedies. When he filed his habeas petition he was, however, still free on his own recognizance, awaiting execution of the sentence. The Court ruled that he was in "custody", because he was "subject to restraints 'not shared by the public generally' ": he

---

ry in the High Court—Habeas Corpus, 64 Mich.L.Rev. 451 (1966). For an inquiry into the reasons for expansion of the custody concept, see Yackle, *Explaining Habeas Corpus*, 60 N.Y.U.L.Rev. 991, 998–1010 (1985).

2. *E.g.*, Krantz v. Briggs, 983 F.2d 961, 962 n. 1 (9th Cir.1993); Bruno v. Greenlee, 569 F.2d 775 (3d Cir.1978).

3. *E.g.*, Sammons v. Rodgers, 785 F.2d 1343, 1345 (5th Cir.1986) & authorities cited.

could not "come and go as he pleases", and his freedom rested in the hands of state judicial officials "who may demand his presence at any time" (p. 351, quoting Jones, 371 U.S. at 240). In any event, said the Court, the petitioner remained at large only by grace of a stay granted by the federal courts; custody was imminent and certain, not speculative. Nor would any important state interest be jeopardized by acting now rather than postponing adjudication until actual imprisonment.[4]

Note that a person on bail or recognizance, even though deemed to be in custody, will often have difficulty satisfying the exhaustion requirement.

(4) *Release From Custody After Filing: The Question of Mootness.*

(a) In Carafas v. LaVallee, 391 U.S. 234 (1968), the prisoner filed a habeas petition while in prison, but during the course of the litigation his sentence expired and he was unconditionally released. Overruling its decision in Parker v. Ellis, 362 U.S. 574 (1960), the Court held that release did not moot the proceeding, stressing that civil disabilities and burdens accompanied the prisoner after his release. On the other hand the Court did not go so far as to hold that those civil disabilities by themselves constituted "custody" that would independently support an application for the writ by a petitioner not otherwise deprived of liberty. And in Maleng v. Cook, 490 U.S. 488, 492 (1989)(per curiam), the Court made clear that they do not.

(b) Carafas was limited by Lane v. Williams, 455 U.S. 624 (1982). The habeas petitioners, who had pleaded guilty, were subject upon their release from prison to a special parole term that was mandatory under state law but of which they averred that they had not been informed when entering their plea. After violating parole they were re-imprisoned. They then filed for habeas corpus, alleging a due process violation based on the state court's failure to have informed them of the parole term. They did not ask the federal court to set aside their conviction and allow them to plead anew, but rather to free them from imprisonment and from "all future liability" under the original sentence (p. 627). The district court granted their petitions. After the state had appealed from that decision, the parole terms expired and both men were released.

The Court (per Stevens, J.) held the petition moot because the sentence—which was all the petition attacked—had expired. "No civil disabilities such as those present in Carafas result from a finding that an individual has violated parole. At most, certain nonstatutory consequences may occur; employment prospects, or the sentence imposed in a future criminal proceeding, could be affected. * * * The discretionary decisions that are made by an employer or a sentencing judge, however, are not governed by the mere presence or absence of a recorded violation of parole; these decisions may take into consideration, and are more directly influenced by, the underlying conduct that formed the basis for the parole violation. Any disabilities that flow from whatever respondents did to evoke revocation of parole are not removed—or even affected—by a District Court order that simply recites that their parole terms are 'void' "(pp. 632–33).

---

4. *Cf.* Justices of Boston Municipal Court v. Lydon, p. 1448, *supra*, at 300–02 (petitioner in custody, though his conviction was vacated when he applied for trial de novo and he was released on his own recognizance, because he was required to appear for trial and not leave the jurisdiction without permission).

(5) *The Nature of Relief: Release From Custody and the Rise and Fall of the Prematurity Rule.*

(a) The correlative of the custody requirement was the notion that the only appropriate habeas corpus remedy is release from confinement. McNally v. Hill, 293 U.S. 131, 138 (1934), relied on this notion in holding that a prisoner, while serving the first of two consecutive sentences, may not attack the second sentence; a "sentence which the prisoner has not begun to serve cannot be the cause of restraint which the statute makes the subject of inquiry".

Lower courts, relying on some sweeping language in the McNally decision stating that the writ can be sought only if a ruling for the petitioner would result in "immediate release" (pp. 137–38), read it as also barring challenges to one of two concurrent sentences,[5] to the first of several consecutive sentences,[6] and to an excessively long sentence before completion of the valid portion.[7]

In 1968 the Supreme Court started the process of eroding McNally by disapproving these holdings and restricting McNally to cases where the petitioner had not yet begun to serve the sentence under attack. See Walker v. Wainwright, 390 U.S. 335 (1968), permitting attack on the validity of a sentence presently being served, even though another sentence awaited the prisoner.[8]

(b) Two months after its Walker decision, the Court overruled McNally in Peyton v. Rowe, 391 U.S. 54 (1968), holding that a prisoner may challenge the validity of the second of two consecutive sentences while still serving the first. The principal reason given was a practical one: if the first sentence is lengthy, McNally causes the validity of the second to be tested long after the event, when witnesses have disappeared and memories have dimmed. The Court added that the prematurity rule prejudices petitioners who are ultimately successful, by forcing them to enter upon confinement before litigating its validity.[9]

(c) Garlotte v. Fordice, 115 S.Ct. 1948 (1995)(7–2) was a case of Peyton in reverse: the petitioner had already fully served a sentence for a drug offense,

---

5. See, *e.g.*, Wilson v. Gray, 345 F.2d 282, 286 (9th Cir.1965); Lowther v. Maxwell, 347 F.2d 941 (6th Cir.1965).

6. See, *e.g.*, Wells v. California, 352 F.2d 439 (9th Cir.1965).

7. See, *e.g.*, Carpenter v. Crouse, 358 F.2d 701 (10th Cir.1966).

8. See also the cases holding that the writ is available to test the validity of conditions of confinement in prison, *e.g.*, Wilwording v. Swenson, 404 U.S. 249 (1971); Johnson v. Avery, 393 U.S. 483 (1969). For further light on this use of the writ, see Preiser v. Rodriguez, Chap. XII, p. 1513, *infra*.

9. Under Rowe, prisoners have generally been permitted to mount habeas attacks where the result would be to shorten the total period of confinement, though not to obtain immediate release. See, *e.g.*, Bostic v.

Carlson, 884 F.2d 1267, 1269 (9th Cir.1989); Jensen v. Satran, 688 F.2d 76 (8th Cir.1982).

May habeas be used to challenge a conviction where the prisoner is also serving a concurrent sentence, of at least equal length, on a second conviction not assailed as invalid? Compare, *e.g.*, Brewer v. Iowa, 19 F.3d 1248, 1250–51 (8th Cir.1994)(exercising jurisdiction on the ground that the allegedly invalid conviction might prejudice the prisoner's ability to obtain commutation of the sentence for the second conviction) with, *e.g.*, Scott v. Louisiana, 934 F.2d 631, 635 (5th Cir.1991) (dismissing the petition and stating that jurisdiction would be exercised in the future if, but only if, the prisoner can actually demonstrate prejudice in obtaining commutation, or some other collateral consequence, arising from the allegedly invalid conviction).

and was serving a consecutive sentence for murder when he filed a habeas petition challenging the drug conviction. The Court held, 7–2, that the prisoner remained " 'in custody' under all of his sentences until all are served" (p. 1949).

The state had argued that the decision in Maleng v. Cook, 490 U.S. 488 (1989)(per curiam), precluded a holding that Garlotte remained in custody on the earlier drug conviction. In Maleng, the Court ruled unanimously that a prisoner was not "in custody" under a 1958 conviction, for which he had served the full sentence, simply because under state law that conviction increased the mandatory minimum term imposed on him in 1978 for a different offense.[10]

In Garlotte, the Court distinguished Maleng v. Cook on the ground that the prisoner in Maleng had been suffering no present restraint from the prior conviction. The Court also noted that, given the prevalence of sentence enhancement provisions, to have accepted the prisoner's claim in Maleng that he remained "in custody" under the earlier conviction "would have left nearly all convictions perpetually open to collateral attack" (115 S.Ct. at 1942). By contrast, Garlotte was serving consecutive sentences; "[h]aving construed the statutory term 'in custody' [in Peyton v. Rowe] to require that consecutive sentences be viewed in the aggregate, we will not now adopt a different construction simply because the sentence imposed under the challenged conviction lies in the past rather than in the future" (115 S.Ct. at 1952).

(d) How does the "aggregation" principle of Rowe and Garlotte apply when a petitioner has been sentenced in two different states? In Nelson v. George, 399 U.S. 224 (1970), the Court, although ultimately finding that the prisoner had not yet exhausted state remedies, stated that a North Carolina sentence could be challenged in a federal district court in California by a prisoner presently serving a California sentence—at least where North Carolina had issued a detainer to the California warden that allegedly affected the petitioner's conditions of confinement and chances of parole in California. *Cf.* Braden v. 30th Judicial Circuit Court, p. 1448, *supra* (prisoner serving an Alabama sentence while under detainer from Kentucky may file for the writ in federal court in Kentucky to litigate the question whether Kentucky is under a constitutional obligation to grant him immediate trial).

(6) *Redetermination of Federal Claims: Federal or State Court Adjudication.* Where a federal habeas court determines that a state court resolved a federal claim under an erroneous standard or through impermissible procedures, what is the proper remedy? A few cases hold that the federal court should not itself re-determine the federal claim, but instead should grant the writ, subject to a new adjudication of the federal question by the *state* court. See, *e.g.*, Rogers v.

---

10. In Maleng, however, the Court— following Peyton v. Rowe and Braden v. 30th Judicial Circuit Court, p. 1448, *supra*—ruled that the prisoner was in custody under the 1978 sentence, even though he would not begin serving it until he had completed an intervening federal sentence. The Court expressed no view on the extent to which the 1958 conviction could be challenged in the collateral attack on the 1978 sentence.

Compare Custis v. United States, 114 S.Ct. 1732, 1746 n. 7 (1994)(Souter, J., dis-

senting)(stating that post-Maleng decisions of the courts of appeals have uniformly held that "federal habeas courts may review prior convictions relied upon for sentence enhancement and grant appropriate relief"). Justice Souter also noted that in some circumstances the writ of coram nobis may be used to challenge the validity of a prior conviction, whose sentence has been fully served, that is relied upon to enhance sentencing for another offense. See *id.*; compare United States v. Morgan, p. 1466, note 13, *infra*.

Richmond, 365 U.S. 534 (1961)(state trial judge's use of improper legal standard in testing voluntariness of confession may have "tainted" his findings of fact on that issue; federal court grants writ and orders prisoner released subject to state's right to retry him); Jackson v. Denno, 378 U.S. 368 (1964)(state may not leave the issue of the voluntariness of a confession to the jury trying guilt; petitioner must be released subject to state's right to retry him or to hold a hearing (before a judge) limited to issue of voluntariness, with release to be ordered if judge finds the confession coerced); Pate v. Robinson, 383 U.S. 375 (1966)(hearing in state court on issue of petitioner's competency to stand trial inadequate; writ will issue subject to state's right to retry him).

By what criteria should a habeas court decide whether to adjudicate the underlying federal question, or instead to issue an order whose effect is to require the state court to re-determine the question? If the latter alternative is chosen, and a state retrial or rehearing results in continued custody, the state court's second determination will presumably be cognizable anew in federal habeas corpus. Does that bear on whether the habeas court should itself undertake any re-determination that is required?

NOTE ON HABEAS CORPUS REFORM[1]

(1) *Court vs. Congress.* Proposals for "reform" of the habeas corpus jurisdiction—which has nearly always meant restriction of the jurisdiction in some respect—have abounded ever since Brown v. Allen was decided in 1953. But in the succeeding decades Congress has not significantly modified the underlying statutes, having enacted only rather limited amendments in 1966, see p. 1342, *supra.*

At the same time, as already illustrated throughout this Section, Supreme Court decisions have dramatically re-shaped the writ. In general, the Warren Court expanded it, and the Burger and Rehnquist Courts in turn cut it back. Consider these questions:

(a) Have the significant cutbacks made in recent years succeeded in accomplishing the Burger and Rehnquist Courts' stated goals of conserving judicial resources, promoting finality, and exhibiting greater respect for the states? Professor Friedman surveys the important restrictions in habeas jurisdiction fashioned since 1976, and argues that even if one accepts the Court's goals (as he does not), its decisions have backfired. He contends that the doctrines created by the Court are unclear and complex, and that the limitations they impose are riddled with exceptions that, however narrow, will be pursued by petitioners. The net result is to embroil the federal courts, and lawyers defending the states, in a morass of litigation over procedural questions antecedent to the merits, thereby disserving the Court's underlying aims. (He grants that the Court may be able to claim a measure of success in its effort to expedite the carrying out of death sentences.) See Friedman, *Failed Enterprise: The Supreme Court's Habeas Reform*, 83 Cal.L.Rev. 485 (1995).

Friedman is surely correct about the complexity of current doctrine. But are you as clear as he is that in run-of-the-mill cases, the task of determining

---

1. For comparative perspectives, see Robbins, Comparative Postconviction Remedies (1980).

the merits of constitutional claims is "familiar and often easy", whereas application of the new restrictions is "particularly difficult and time consuming" (pp. 541–42)? Moreover, *if* the Court's "reforms" can claim credit for the apparent declines in recent years in the percentage of prisoners who file habeas petitions, and in the percentage of petitioners who obtain relief,[2] does that bear on the Court's "success"?

(b) What are the appropriate roles of Congress and the courts in shaping the writ? Does Congress' failure to have significantly modified the jurisdiction, despite broad controversy about it, signal a willingness to give the courts the primary role? Should the congressional silence, when coupled with the minor provisions enacted in 1966, have been understood as ratification of the basic structure established by the Supreme Court before 1966?

Are the Supreme Court's frequent departures from *stare decisis* in habeas matters justifiable? On the ground that the habeas statute is a broad, organic provision, almost more in the nature of a constitutional provision (where *stare decisis* figures less prominently) than a typical federal statute? That habeas is a court-centered matter in which the judiciary may appropriately play a broader interpretive role?

(2) *The Number and Quality of Petitions.* Is it possible to give conscientious attention to every petition when so very few are meritorious and most are frivolous?[3] Many assert that the very low success rate demonstrates that the jurisdiction exacts few costs.[4] Judge Friendly responds (see *Is Innocence Irrelevant? Collateral Attack on Criminal Judgments*, 38 U.Chi.L.Rev. 142, 148–49 (1970)) that a "remedy that produces no result in the overwhelming majority of cases" may be a "gigantic waste of effort", and continues: "[T]he most serious evil with today's proliferation of collateral attack is its drain upon the resources of the community—judges, prosecutors, and attorneys * * *. Today of all times we should be conscious of the falsity of the bland assumption that these are in endless supply. Everyone concerned with the criminal process * * * agrees that our greatest single problem is the long delay in bringing accused persons to trial. The time of judges, prosecutors, and lawyers now devoted to collateral attacks, most of them frivolous, would be much better spent in trying cases."

See also Meltzer, *Habeas Corpus Jurisdiction: The Limits of Models*, 66 S.Cal.L.Rev. 2507, 2526 (1993)(asking—"not as a legislative reform proposal but as a stimulus for thought"—whether in non-capital cases one would "prefer to abolish habeas and invest [all of the society's resources now committed to habeas] in upgrading state criminal justice systems, focusing particularly on improving the quality of defense representation in the state courts").

(3) *Efforts to Overturn Brown v. Allen.* In 1955, two years after Brown v. Allen, the Judicial Conference of the United States recommended an amendment to § 2254, whose key provision would have limited habeas relief to claims that "present[] a substantial Federal constitutional question (1) which was not theretofore raised and determined (2) which there was no fair and adequate opportunity theretofore to raise and have determined and (3) which cannot

---

2. See pp. 1363–64 *supra.*

3. Recall Justice Jackson's complaint about the frivolous character of most petitions, in his opinion in Brown v. Allen, p. 1350, *supra.*

4. See, *e.g.*, Frankfurter, J., in Brown v. Allen, 344 U.S. at 510; Brennan, *Federal Habeas Corpus and State Prisoners: An Exercise in Federalism*, 7 Utah L.Rev. 423, 440–41 (1961).

thereafter be raised and determined in a proceeding in the State court, by an order or judgment subject to review by the Supreme Court of the United States on writ of certiorari."[5]   This bill twice passed the House but never the Senate.[6]

Similar bills have been repeatedly introduced in succeeding decades.[7]   Two such bills did pass the Senate, once in 1984 and once in 1991, but went no further.   See S. 1763, 98th Cong., 1st Sess. (1984); S. 1241, 102d Cong., 1st Sess. (1991).

(4) *The Question of Innocence.*   Recall the suggestion of Judge Friendly, Paragraph (2), *supra*—discussed more fully at p. 1386, *supra*—that "with a few important exceptions, convictions should be subject to collateral attack only when the prisoner supplements his constitutional plea with a colorable claim of innocence" (p. 142).   Compare the suggestion of then Assistant Attorney General Rehnquist, as head of the Office of Legal Counsel, that habeas be limited to cases where the "claimed constitutional right is one which has as its primary purpose the protection of the reliability of either the fact finding process at the trial or the appellate process on appeal from the judgment of conviction * * *."   Hearings on S.895 Before the Subcomm. on Constitutional Rights, Sen.Comm. on the Judiciary, 92d Cong., 1st Sess. 264–72 (1971).

(5) *Capital Cases.*   Several proposals have focused on reform of habeas corpus in capital cases.   Serious administrative difficulties—in particular, repeated and often eleventh hour petitions, coupled with last-minute requests for stays of execution—have arisen from the interaction of a multitude of factors, including: the difficulties in locating adequate counsel early on to represent death row inmates in federal habeas proceedings; the tenacity of many of the lawyers who take such cases in attempting to forestall execution; the obvious incentive for prisoners and their lawyers to delay; the complexity of the cases and the poor quality of the representation often afforded at trial and on direct review (frequently resulting in inadequate records); the seriousness of the stakes; and the far greater rate of success of those petitioners who are under sentence of death, see p. 1364, *supra.*

The Judicial Branch established an Ad Hoc Committee on Federal Habeas Corpus in Capital Cases, chaired by retired Associate Justice Powell (the "Powell Committee"), whose Report (published at 45 Crim.L.Rep. 3239 (1989)) proposed that those states providing prisoners with competent counsel on state collateral review could limit them to a single federal collateral challenge to a capital conviction or sentence, which would have to be filed within six months of the appointment of counsel.   The ABA Task Force on Death Penalty Habeas Corpus issued a report, Toward a More Just and Effective System of Review in

---

5. See Hearings on H.R.5649 Before Subcomm. No.3 of the House Comm. on the Judiciary, 84th Cong., 1st Sess., § 6, at 89–90 (1955).

6. See 102 Cong.Rec. 940 (84th Cong. 1956); 104 *id.* 4675 (85th Cong.1958).   The bill received the support of the Conference of State Chief Justices, the Association of Attorneys General, the ABA, and the Department of Justice.   See Hearings, note 5, *supra*, at 7. It was criticized in Schaefer, *Federalism and State Criminal Procedure*, 70 Harv.L.Rev. 1 (1956); Pollak, *Proposals to Curtail Federal*

Habeas Corpus for State Prisoners: Collateral Attack on the Great Writ, 66 Yale L.J. 50 (1956).

7. For the Reagan Administration proposals, see Habeas Corpus Reform Act of 1982, S.2216, 97th Cong., 2d Sess., 128 Cong. Rec. S2172 (daily ed. Apr. 1, 1982); H.R. 6050, 97th Cong., 2d Sess., Cong.Rec. H1405 (daily ed. Mar. 16, 1982).

See generally Yackle, *The Reagan Administration's Habeas Corpus Proposals*, 68 Iowa L.Rev. 609 (1983).

State Death Penalty Cases (1990), which proposed a number of changes in existing law, including a one-year limitations period "with adequate and sufficient tolling provisions," and mechanisms "to assure that the state provides competent representation and to avoid procedural delays".[8]

(6) *Changes in Institutional Structure.* Beginning in 1959 the Judicial Conference repeatedly urged that habeas corpus cases be heard by three-judge federal courts—a proposal withdrawn in 1965 after the number of petitions skyrocketed in the 1960s.[9]

In a related vein, Judge Friendly, Paragraph (2), *supra,* at 166–67, raised the possibility of routing appeals from state criminal cases to an intermediate court of appeals. See also Meador, *Straightening Out Federal Review of State Criminal Cases,* 44 Ohio St.L.J. 273 (1983).[10]

(7) *Statute of Limitations.* Responding to the difficulties of determining a claim after much time has passed and of retrying the prisoner should the writ issue—as well as, in some instances, to the distinctive incentive for delay in capital cases—proposals have been advanced for a federal statute of limitations for habeas corpus petitions. See, *e.g.,* Attorney General's Task Force on Violent Crime, Final Report, Rec. 42 (1981)(three years); Habeas Corpus Reform Act of 1982, S.2216, 97th Cong., 2d Sess., 128 Cong.Rec. S2172 (daily ed. Apr. 1, 1982)(one year in § 2254 cases, two years in § 2255 cases); Paragraph (9)(b), *infra.* For criticism, see Yackle, note 7, *supra,* at 612 n. 22.

(8) *Responses to Teague v. Lane.* Less common has been serious legislative consideration of expanding the habeas corpus jurisdiction. In 1991, however—after Supreme Court decisions had sharply restricted the availability of the

---

8. For comments on these two proposals, see Berger, *Justice Delayed or Justice Denied?—A Comment on Recent Proposals to Reform Death Penalty Habeas Corpus,* 90 Colum.L.Rev. 1665 (1990); Mello & Duffy, *Suspending Justice: The Unconstitutionality of the Proposed Six–Month Time Limit on the Filing of Habeas Corpus Petitions By State Death Row Inmates,* 18 N.Y.U.Rev.L. & Soc. Change 451 (1990–91); Tabak & Lane, *Judicial Activism and Legislative "Reform" of Federal Habeas Corpus: A Critical Analysis of Recent Developments and Current Proposals,* 55 Alb.L.Rev. 1 (1991); Lay, *The Writ of Habeas Corpus: A Complex Procedure for a Simple Process,* 77 Minn.L.Rev. 1015 (1993)(criticizing the Powell Committee). See also Hoffman, *Starting from Scratch: Rethinking Federal Habeas Review of Death Penalty Cases,* 20 Fla.St.U.L.Rev. 133 (1992), and Bonnie, *Preserving Justice in Capital Cases While Streamlining the Process of Collateral Review,* 23 U.Tol.L.Rev. 99 (1991), both suggesting some relaxation, in capital cases, of existing restrictions on habeas review generally.

Since these proposals were formulated, Supreme Court decisions have responded to some of the perceived problems. In McCleskey v. Zant, p. 1442, *supra,* the Court sharply limited a prisoner's ability to file more than one federal habeas petition. But McCleskey gave rise to another difficulty: if a prisoner had to file a petition pro se (and had to do so quickly when an execution date had been set), that petition might omit important constitutional claims, which, after McCleskey, could not be raised in a subsequent petition.

The Court's decision in McFarland v. Scott, 114 S.Ct. 2568 (1994), p. 1347, *supra,* responded to that difficulty by permitting a federal court, even before a habeas petition was actually filed, both to appoint counsel for capital petitioners and to issue a stay of execution. That decision thus gives capital prisoners the opportunity to present one federal petition with the assistance of counsel, and to have any scheduled execution stayed pending decision on that petition.

9. See H.R.Rep. No.1892, 89th Cong., 2d Sess. (1966).

10. With these proposals for direct review by federal courts of greater "dignity", compare the actual movement toward greater use of federal *magistrates* (now called magistrate judges) to screen habeas petitions, subject to district court review. See p. 1348, *supra.*

writ—a bill passed by the House dealt with the retroactivity problem addressed in Teague v. Lane, p. 1392, *supra*. Like Teague, the bill would have restricted a habeas court's ability to entertain petitions based on "new law", but it would have expanded the habeas jurisdiction by defining "new law" far more narrowly than the Court had in Teague—to mean "a clear break from precedent, announced by the Supreme Court of the United States, that could not reasonably have been anticipated at the time the claimant's sentence became final in State court." H.R.3371, 102d Cong., 1st Sess. § 1104 (1991). At the same time, the bill would have altogether precluded a habeas court from applying new law, thereby eliminating Teague's two exceptions—a provision apparently seen as politically necessary to permit enactment of the bill.[11]

(9) *Pending Proposals.* The 1994 Republican legislative victory appeared to improve the prospects for major legislative restriction of the habeas corpus jurisdiction. As this book went to press, separate bills had passed the House (H.R.729, 104th Cong., 1st Sess., Feb. 8, 1995), and Senate (S.735, 104th Cong., 1st Sess. June 7, 1995) with very similar thrusts, although they differ in their particulars. Their major proposals—many of which draw on earlier efforts—are as follows:

(a) *Deference to State Court Determinations.* The key provision of both bills would preclude the grant of relief with respect to a claim that was decided on the merits in state court, unless the state court decision (i) "was contrary to, or involved an unreasonable application of, clearly established Federal law, as determined by the Supreme Court of the United States", or (ii) "was based on an unreasonable determination of the facts in light of the evidence presented in the State court proceeding." S.735, § 604, proposed 28 U.S.C. § 2254(d); the House language in § 104(b), proposed 28 U.S.C. § 2254(g), differs only slightly.

(b) *Statute of Limitations.* Both bills contain a one-year limitation period for the filing of a federal habeas petition; although worded differently, in both bills the period in effect commences on the date that the state court judgment became final on direct review, but is subject to certain tolling provisions. H.R.729, § 101, proposed 28 U.S.C. § 2244(d); S.735, § 601, proposed 28 U.S.C. § 2244(d).

(c) *Exhaustion and Waiver.* Both bills would follow current law in permitting a habeas court to deny the writ even where state remedies have not been exhausted, but would change current law by providing that only an *express* relinquishment of the exhaustion defense by counsel for the state—and not a simple failure to plead non-exhaustion—may be treated as a waiver. H.R.729, § 104(b), proposed 28 U.S.C. § 2254(b); S.735, § 604, proposed 28 U.S.C. § 2254(b)(1–3).

(d) *State Factfindings and Federal Evidentiary Hearings.* The Senate bill would presume state court factfindings to be correct, and make them rebuttable only by clear and convincing evidence; unlike existing law, the presumption would operate regardless of the quality of state factfinding processes. S.735, § 604, proposed 28 U.S.C. § 2254(e). In addition, the bill would prohibit the holding of an evidentiary hearing unless the petitioner demonstrates that (i) the claim relies on new law or new facts not discoverable through due diligence, and (ii) the facts underlying the claim establish that but for the constitutional

---

11. For an exhaustive analysis of this and other proposals for legislative revision, see Yackle, *The Habeas Hagioscope*, 66 S.Cal. L.Rev. 2331 (1993), especially p. 2418.

error, no reasonable factfinder would have found the applicant guilty of the underlying offense. *Id.*

(e) *Successive Petitions.* The Senate bill provides that a petitioner may not litigate a claim presented in an earlier petition, and may litigate a claim not previously presented only after first obtaining from a three-judge panel of the court of appeals a determination that the two criteria described in Paragraph (9)(d), *supra*, have been satisfied. S.735, § 606(b), proposed 28 U.S.C. § 2244(b).[12]

(f) *Appellate Review.* Both bills would preserve the current requirement of a certificate of probable cause to permit appeal from a denial of relief, but provide that only a circuit judge may issue the certificate, and that it must be limited to specific issues as to which there has been "a substantial showing of the denial of" a federal right. H.R.729, § 102, proposed 28 U.S.C. § 2253; S.735, § 602, proposed 28 U.S.C. § 2253.

(g) *Capital Cases.* Both bills contain provisions, applicable only to death penalty cases, that would take effect only in those states that establish by statute or rule a system for supplying "competent" counsel in state post-conviction proceedings for indigent death row prisoners. H.R.729, § 111; S.735, § 607. Petitioners under sentence of death in qualifying states would be subject not only to the rules already summarized, but also to the following provisions:

(i) *Statute of Limitations.* Both bills would impose (subject to tolling provisions) a 180–day statute of limitations—commencing in the House bill with appointment of counsel in state post-conviction proceedings, and in the Senate bill with the conclusion of direct review in state court. H.R.729, § 111, proposed 28 U.S.C. § 2258; S.735, § 607, proposed 28 U.S.C. § 2263.

(ii) *Time Limits for Federal Court Consideration.* Both bills prescribe certain time limits within which federal district and appellate courts must dispose of habeas cases, and provide that the state can seek mandamus to enforce those limits. H.R.729, § 111, proposed § 2262; S.735, § 607, proposed 28 U.S.C. § 2266.

(iii) *Stays of Execution.* Both bills provide that when a prisoner has filed for state post-conviction relief, the federal court shall, upon application, stay any scheduled execution. The stay would expire unless the prisoner files a timely federal habeas petition and makes "a substantial showing of the denial of a federal right"; if the stay continues, it then expires if relief is denied in the district court or in any further stage of review. H.R.729, § 111, proposed 28 U.S.C. § 2257(a-b); S.735, § 607, proposed 28 U.S.C. § 2262.

(iv) *Successive Petitions.* The House Bill would bar relief or a stay of execution premised on a successive petition unless two different hurdles are surmounted. First, the petitioner must show that (A) the claim was not previously presented to a state or federal court, (B) the failure to have raised it earlier was attributable to reliance on new law or new facts or to unconstitutional action of the state, and (C) the facts underlying the claim establish by "clear and convincing evidence" that but for the constitutional error, "no reasonable factfinder would have found the petitioner guilty of the underlying

---

12. H.R.729 contains strict limits on successive petitions that apply only in capital cases in states that have opted into the bill's special death penalty provisions. See Paragraph (9)(g), *infra.*

offense". Second, the court must determine that the petition does not constitute an abuse of the writ. H.R.729, § 111, proposed 28 U.S.C. § 2257(c-d).[13]

(v) *Procedural Default.* Both bills preclude consideration of a claim not decided on the merits by the state courts, unless the prisoner's failure to have properly raised the claim is attributable to new law, new facts, or state action in violation of federal law. H.R.729, § 111, proposed 28 U.S.C. § 2259; S.735, § 607, proposed 28 U.S.C. § 2264(a).

SECTION 3.   COLLATERAL ATTACK ON FEDERAL JUDGMENTS OF CONVICTION

NOTE ON 28 U.S.C. § 2255 AND ITS RELATIONSHIP TO FEDERAL HABEAS CORPUS

(1) *The Enactment of § 2255.* Before the enactment of 28 U.S.C. § 2255 in 1948, the federal courts' habeas corpus jurisdiction extended to prisoners detained after federal criminal convictions. Such prisoners were required to file petitions in the district in which they were confined, a rule that gave rise to serious administrative problems. Facially meritorious applications were often found wholly lacking in merit when the records of the sentencing court were consulted, but those records were not readily available to the habeas court. Venue also proved inconvenient when hearings had to be conducted far from the locale of the underlying events. And a few federal districts within whose territorial jurisdiction were located the major federal correctional facilities were inundated with petitions. See generally United States v. Hayman, 342 U.S. 205, 210–14 (1952).

In 1948, § 2255 "was passed at the instance of the Judicial Conference to meet practical difficulties that had arisen in administering the habeas corpus jurisdiction of the federal courts.[1] Nowhere in the history of Section 2255 do we find any purpose to impinge upon prisoners' rights of collateral attack upon their convictions. On the contrary, the sole purpose was to minimize the difficulties encountered in habeas corpus hearings by affording the same rights in another and more convenient forum" (*id.* at 219). Accord *e.g.*, Sanders v. United States, 373 U.S. 1 (1963); United States v. Frady, 456 U.S. 152, 165 (1982).

Although entitled "Federal custody; remedies on motion attacking sentence", § 2255, like habeas corpus for state prisoners, is available to attack convictions (or sentences) resulting in custody in violation of the federal Constitution or, in some cases, federal law. This Note sketches the basic outlines of the § 2255 remedy, highlighting ways in which it resembles, and differs from, collateral relief under § 2254 for state prisoners.

---

13. The Senate bill provides in § 607, proposed § 2262(c), that once an initial stay of execution has expired, no further stay shall be issued unless the court of appeals has approved the filing of a successive application in accordance with the standards described in Paragraph (9)(e), *supra.*

1. [Ed.] The provision was drafted by a committee of the Judiciary Conference headed by Chief Judge Parker. See Parker, *Limiting the Abuse of Habeas Corpus*, 8 F.R.D. 171 (1948).

(2) *The Exclusivity of § 2255.* Although Congress, in enacting § 2255, did not repeal the pre-existing grant of habeas corpus jurisdiction over petitions by federal prisoners, § 2255 provides that a federal convict's habeas petition shall not be entertained unless the petitioner had first sought relief under § 2255, and "unless it also appears that the remedy by motion [under § 2255] is inadequate or ineffective to test the legality of his detention."

In United States v. Hayman, 342 U.S. 205 (1952), the court of appeals had held § 2255 to be an unconstitutional suspension of the writ of habeas corpus. The Supreme Court reversed. It found no need to reach the suspension question, ruling that there had been no showing that the § 2255 remedy was inadequate, and that if it were, the statute would permit resort to the writ. Accord Swain v. Pressley, 430 U.S. 372, 381 (1977), p. 1370, *supra.*

Federal habeas corpus also remains available to challenge detention by federal officials that cannot be reached in a § 2255 motion—for example, challenges to court martial proceedings, civil commitment of the mentally ill, administration of parole, prison conditions or discipline, extradition, and deportation or exclusion under the immigration laws. See generally 2 Liebman & Hertz, Federal Habeas Corpus Practice & Procedure 1185–88 (2d ed.1994).

(3) *Proceedings Under § 2255.* Unlike a state prisoner's habeas petition, a § 2255 motion is not a separate civil action, but rather a continuation of the criminal proceeding. The motion will be opposed not by a prison warden, but rather by the United States, which initiated the criminal proceeding. Nonetheless, § 2255 motions are processed in much the same way as are § 2254 petitions, and the Rules Governing § 2255 Proceedings in the United States District Courts are virtually identical to the parallel Rules Governing § 2254 Proceedings.[2] Rule 4 of the § 2255 Rules specifies that the motion shall be heard by the judge who presided at the trial and sentenced the prisoner—although, as with state prisoner petitions, § 2255 motions are often referred initially to magistrate judges.

(4) *The Analogy to Brown v. Allen.* Kaufman v. United States, 394 U.S. 217 (1969)(6–3), determined that the broad collateral relief for state prisoners recognized in Brown v. Allen in 1953, and ratified in Fay v. Noia in 1963, should extend to federal prisoners who seek relief under § 2255. The particular issue in Kaufman was whether a federal prisoner could present a Fourth Amendment challenge to the introduction at trial of evidence that he alleged had been illegally seized. (Kaufman was decided prior to the ruling in Stone v. Powell, 428 U.S. 465 (1976), that claims under the Fourth Amendment's exclusionary rule are ordinarily not cognizable in habeas corpus. After Stone, such claims are no longer cognizable under § 2255.[3])

The Court in Kaufman held that the issue was cognizable under the rule of Brown v. Allen; that Fay v. Noia's "deliberate bypass" standard, see p. 1415, *supra,* should govern the question whether the constitutional objection had

---

2. For a catalogue of minor differences, see the Advisory Committee Note to Rules 1, 8 of the § 2255 Rules. Note also that Rule 12 of the § 2255 Rules (which has no counterpart in the § 2254 Rules) authorizes a district court to apply the criminal as well as the civil rules, as the court deems appropriate.

3. See Stone, 428 U.S. at 494–95; 2 Liebman & Hertz, Paragraph (2), *supra,* at 1220–21 n. 26.

been waived; and that Townsend v. Sain, p. 1371, *supra*, should govern the question of the § 2255 court's discretion to try the facts anew.[4]

The Court rejected the government's argument that Brown v. Allen was inapposite because Kaufman had already had one fair chance to litigate his Fourth Amendment claim in a *federal* court. "The opportunity to assert federal rights in a federal forum is clearly not the sole justification for federal post-conviction relief; otherwise there would be no need to make such relief available to federal prisoners at all. The provision of federal collateral remedies rests more fundamentally upon a recognition that adequate protection of constitutional rights relating to the criminal trial process requires the continuing availability of a mechanism for relief. This is no less true for federal prisoners than it is for state prisoners. * * *

"* * * Plainly the interest in finality is the same with regard to both federal and state prisoners. With regard to both, Congress has determined that the full protection of their constitutional rights requires the availability of a mechanism for collateral attack. * * * There is no reason to treat federal trial errors as less destructive of constitutional guarantees than state trial errors, nor to give greater preclusive effect to procedural defaults by federal defendants than to similar defaults by state defendants. To hold otherwise would reflect an anomalous and erroneous view of federal-state relations" (pp. 226–28).[5]

(5) *Section 2255 in Practice.* Despite the formal equivalence between state and federal prisoner cases posited by Kaufman, § 2255 is far more restricted in practice. Suppose that a prisoner's constitutional challenge to some aspect of the criminal prosecution is rejected by the trial court and the court of appeals. A *state* prisoner can then obtain a new determination from a federal habeas court on the constitutional claim, and the federal court is not bound by the state court's determination. But a federal prisoner's § 2255 motion will be presented to the same judge who initially denied the claim, and who is likely to ask, "What's new?". So, too, with the circuit judges considering an appeal from a denial of the § 2255 motion. And even if different judges heard the § 2255 motion, they would almost certainly be bound by the precedent rejecting the claim on direct appeal. (Most circuits today require an appellate panel to follow circuit precedent; only the en banc court has the authority to depart from it.) Thus, in the ordinary case the § 2255 motion will be dismissed out of hand (even if formally the court has jurisdiction and res judicata is inapplicable). See Potuto, *The Federal Prisoner Collateral Attack: Requiescat in Pace*, 1988 B.Y.U.L.Rev. 37, 41–47.[6]

When, then, might a federal prisoner ever get relief under § 2255? At the time of the Kaufman decision, there were several such situations, though more

4. The Court held that only the third Townsend criterion, requiring that the habeas court scrutinize the trial court's fact-finding procedure, did not apply in a § 2255 case: "[F]ederal fact-finding procedures are by hypothesis adequate to assure the integrity of the underlying constitutional rights" (p. 227).

5. In footnote 8, the Court added that the effect of previous consideration of the constitutional question by the sentencing court should be assimilated to the standards announced in Sanders v. United States, 373 U.S. 1 (1963)(p. 1440, *supra*), governing *successive* motions under § 2255.

6. Of course, the en banc court of appeals, or the Supreme Court, might decide in its discretion to review the denial of relief under § 2255—and if so, the prior circuit decision would not be binding. But such review very rarely is provided.

recent Supreme Court decisions have further narrowed the reach of § 2255 proceedings:

(a) *New Law.* When legal standards have changed since the prisoner's direct appeal—for example, by virtue of a recent Supreme Court decision— there would be something "new" to decide in a § 2255 motion, and relief has sometimes been predicated on this basis.[7]   But the lower courts have held that the Supreme Court's 1989 decision in Teague v. Lane, p. 1392, *supra*—which precludes habeas courts from considering state prisoners' claims based on new law in all but the most exceptional cases—also governs § 2255 proceedings. See 2 Liebman & Hertz, Paragraph (2), *supra*, § 25.6, at 789 n. 18.   Thus, Teague nearly always precludes relief based on new legal standards.   The major exception is when an intervening decision holds that the criminal statute under which the prisoner was convicted did not, when properly interpreted, reach the prisoner's conduct.   See, *e.g.*, Davis v. United States, note 7, *supra*; Ianniello v. United States, 10 F.3d 59 (2d Cir.1993); United States v. Sood, 969 F.2d 774 (9th Cir.1992).

(b) *New Evidence.*   There are similar suggestions that a § 2255 motion may properly be based upon new evidence that could not, with due diligence, have been discovered at trial, see, *e.g.*, United States v. Johnpoll, 748 F.Supp. 86, 91 n. 3 (S.D.N.Y.1990), *aff'd without opinion*, 932 F.2d 956 (2d Cir.1991)— although it is difficult to find cases actually granting relief on this basis.[8]

(c) *No Previous Decision on the Merits.*   A third situation in which a § 2255 motion would not simply revisit ground already covered arises when the claim was not raised in the original trial or on direct review—precisely the situation in Kaufman.   Under the expansive regime of Fay v. Noia, p. 1415, *supra*, which was in effect when Kaufman was decided, a procedural default at trial or on appeal would preclude collateral review only in the highly unusual case where a "deliberate bypass" could be found.[9]

---

7.   Thus, in Davis v. United States, 417 U.S. 333 (1974), the court of appeals had affirmed Davis' conviction for refusing to obey an order of induction, rejecting his claim that the regulation authorizing his induction for "delinquency" (failing to report for a physical examination) was invalid because not authorized by the statute.   Thereafter, a different panel of the same court of appeals, in an unrelated case, upheld the same legal claim that Davis had presented, prompting Davis to seek relief under § 2255.   The Supreme Court without discussion held that the second panel's decision constituted "an intervening change in the law" within the meaning of Sanders v. United States, 373 U.S. 1 (1963), p. 1440, *supra*, and that Davis could therefore raise the question in his § 2255 motion.

Should collateral relitigation be permitted in the absence of an intervening change in law that would be *authoritative* (*e.g.*, a ruling by the Supreme Court or by the court of appeals *en banc*)?   Under Davis, may a federal prisoner collaterally relitigate a claim rejected on direct appeal if thereafter *another* court of appeals takes a different view of the law?

8.   These suggestions also predate the Court's decision in Keeney v. Tamayo–Reyes, 504 U.S. 1 (1992), p. 1373, *supra*, holding that a *state* prisoner may obtain a hearing in a habeas proceeding to develop facts not previously developed in state court only upon a showing that (i) there was "cause and prejudice" for the failure to have developed the facts in state court, or (ii) a "fundamental miscarriage of justice" would occur were the prisoner not permitted to develop those facts.

9.   Whatever the force of the Government's argument in Kaufman that state and federal prisoners are differently situated with respect to claims previously litigated, aren't the two classes of prisoner similarly situated with respect to defaulted claims?   In both cases, a refusal to excuse the default forfeits the claim altogether, while excuse of the default permits a federal decision on collateral review.   Whether one favors broad or narrow excuse of defaults, isn't the balance of inter-

But in habeas cases for state prisoners, the regime of Fay v. Noia has been displaced by the far more restrictive standards of Wainwright v. Sykes and its progeny. See pp. 1413-40, *supra*. And the Supreme Court confirmed, in United States v. Frady, 456 U.S. 152 (1982), that those standards apply equally to preclude § 2255 relief where there was a procedural default in the *federal* criminal proceedings.[10] Accord Reed v. Farley, 114 S.Ct. 2291, 2300 (1994)(dictum). Thus, when the government objects to a § 2255 motion on the ground that the prisoner failed to raise a claim at trial or on appeal, relief will be foreclosed except in the exceedingly rare case in which the prisoner establishes "cause and prejudice" or "actual innocence".

(6) *Federal Statutory Claims.* Like § 2254, § 2255 refers to sentences "imposed in violation of the Constitution *or laws* of the United States" (emphasis added). But given that federal criminal prosecutions involve far more federal non-constitutional law than do state prosecutions, in practice the inclusion of federal "laws" is far more significant in the § 2255 setting.

At the same time, under § 2255 as under § 2254, not all non-constitutional errors provide the basis for collateral relief. In Hill v. United States, 368 U.S. 424 (1962), the Court held that § 2255 did not encompass a claim that Rule 32(a) of the Criminal Rules had been violated by the sentencing judge's failure to ask whether the defendant (who was represented by counsel) had anything to say before sentence was imposed. The alleged error was "neither jurisdictional nor constitutional. It is not a fundamental defect which inherently results in a complete miscarriage of justice, nor an omission inconsistent with the rudimentary demands of fair procedure. It does not present 'exceptional circumstances where the need for the remedy afforded by the writ of habeas corpus is apparent'" (p. 428, quoting Bowen v. Johnston, 306 U.S. 19, 27 (1939)).

That language from Hill, though hardly self-applying, was recited by the Court in holding that § 2255 does not reach a claim of a purely "formal" violation of Rule 11 (governing the taking of guilty pleas), see United States v. Timmreck, 441 U.S. 780 (1979), or a claim that in imposing sentence, the judge had failed to foresee a change in parole regulations whose effect was to delay the prisoner's release, see United States v. Addonizio, 442 U.S. 178, 186 (1979).

---

ests the same for state and federal prisoners? See generally Meltzer, *State Court Forfeitures of Federal Rights*, 99 Harv.L.Rev. 1128, 1204–1205 (1986).

10. Frady's § 2255 motion alleged that 19 years previously, the jury at his federal murder trial had been wrongly instructed as to proof of malice—a contention not raised at trial, on appeal, or in his numerous prior collateral attacks. Applying the "cause and prejudice" standard of Wainwright v. Sykes, the Court refused to permit § 2255 review, holding that Frady, who admitted the killing for which he had been convicted, had suffered no prejudice as a result of the procedural default. Prejudice does not follow simply from the fact that a jury instruction is erroneous, the Court held. Rather, prejudice must be judged in the context of the whole trial, and is established only when the error

"worked to his *actual* and substantial disadvantage, infecting his entire trial with error of constitutional dimensions" (p. 170). Since Frady had never presented colorable evidence to contradict strong evidence in the record that he had acted with malice, he had failed to show prejudice.

Justice Brennan's dissent argued that Fed.R.Crim.Proc. 52(b)(the plain error rule), not the Sykes standard, governs § 2255 motions. Rule 52(b) should apply in the § 2255 context even if it does not govern § 2254 review because the latter authorizes a *civil* collateral review for state prisoners, whereas § 2255 provides a *criminal* review procedure for federal prisoners. This result, Justice Brennan said, "merely allows federal courts the discretion common to most [state] courts to waive procedural defaults where justice requires" (p. 184).

Cf. Reed v. Farley, p. 1360, n. 7, *supra* (applying the Hill standard to a federal statutory claim asserted by a state prisoner in a § 2254 proceeding, and finding not cognizable a claim that the state had violated Article IV(c) of the Interstate Agreement on Detainers—an interstate compact, approved by Congress—which requires the trial of a prisoner transferred from one state to another to commence within 120 days of the transfer).

The Hill standard was found to have been satisfied in Davis v. United States, 417 U.S. 333 (1974), note 7, *supra*. With only Justice Rehnquist dissenting on this point, the Court held that Davis could raise in a § 2255 proceeding the claim that the statute he had been convicted of violating did not in fact prohibit his conduct.[11] See also Paragraph (5)(a), *supra*.

(7) *Custody, Exhaustion, and Delayed or Successive Petitions.* Although § 2255 provides that a motion "may be made at any time", the Court, and the rulemakers, have not taken that language to displace traditional limits on collateral attacks. In addition to the procedural default doctrine discussed in Paragraph (5)(c), *supra*, note in particular:

(a) The statute extends to "a prisoner in custody under sentence of a [federal] court," and Heflin v. United States, 358 U.S. 415 (1959), held that "custody" was a jurisdictional prerequisite for § 2255 motions. The § 2255 Rules clearly reiterate that view. See the Advisory Committee Note to Rules 1–2.[12] On the meaning of custody, see pp. 1450–54, *supra*.[13]

---

11. The Court in Davis had to distinguish Sunal v. Large, 332 U.S. 174 (1947). (Sunal was decided one year before § 2255 was enacted, and thus fell under the habeas corpus statute (§ 2241(c)(3)), which likewise refers to custody in violation of the "laws" as well as of the Constitution of the United States.) There, the petitioners had been convicted of violating the Selective Training and Service Act of 1940 by refusing to submit to induction. At trial, they were not permitted to introduce evidence to show that they had been illegally denied exempt classification as ministers of religion, on the ground that their classifications were incontestable in a criminal prosecution. The petitioners had not appealed from their convictions, but later sought habeas relief following the decision in Estep v. United States, 327 U.S. 114 (1946), Chap. IV, Sec. 2, p. 384, *supra*, which established that the trial courts had erred in precluding an attack on the classification. The Supreme Court (per Douglas, J.) held that habeas corpus was not available to test whether there was a basis in fact for the classifications, stressing the rule that "the writ of habeas corpus will not be allowed to do service for an appeal" (p. 178).

Even though the Sunal opinion had acknowledged an exception to that rule for issues of jurisdictional or constitutional dimension, the Court in Davis distinguished Sunal as having been premised essentially on the fact that no appeal had been taken, rather than on the view that the issue raised was not encompassed by collateral review.

12. Those Rules also state that a prisoner presently in state custody may seek relief under § 2255 from a federal judgment that will give rise to future custody.

13. Compare United States v. Morgan, 346 U.S. 502 (1954), where a state prisoner sought to challenge the constitutionality of a previous *federal* conviction—on the ground that, although he had fully served the federal sentence, the federal conviction had resulted in enhancement of his state sentence. The Supreme Court held that the district court had power to grant relief "in the nature of a writ of error coram nobis" under the All Writs Act, 28 U.S.C. § 1651. Rule 60(b) of the Civil Rules, which had abolished coram nobis, was deemed inapplicable on the ground that the application was a step in a *criminal* case. Relief under § 2255 was deemed to be unavailable but not to preclude this alternative avenue of relief.

On the authority of Morgan, the Ninth Circuit held that coram nobis should be granted to vacate a petitioner's federal convictions—upheld more than 40 years earlier in Hirabayashi v. United States, 320 U.S. 81 (1943)—for violating wartime military orders that excluded Japanese–Americans from certain areas and imposed a curfew on them. See Hirabayashi v. United States, 828 F.2d

(b) Although § 2255 makes no mention of exhaustion of remedies, the Advisory Committee Note to Rule 5 notes that "courts have held that such a motion is inappropriate if the movant is simultaneously appealing the [conviction]."[14]

(c) Rule 9(a) and Rule 9(b) of the § 2255 Rules contain limits on consideration of delayed petitions, and successive petitions, respectively, that are in substance identical to those found in Rule 9(a) and (b) of the § 2254 Rules, see pp. 1348, 1441 *supra*. With respect to successive petitions, the lower courts have found that the interpretation of the "abuse of the writ" doctrine in McCleskey v. Zant, 499 U.S. 467 (1991), p. 1442, *supra*—which permits consideration of successive § 2254 petitions only when "cause and prejudice" or "actual innocence" can be demonstrated—applies equally to § 2255 motions. *E.g.*, Andiarena v. United States, 967 F.2d 715, 717 & cases cited (1st Cir. 1992)(per curiam); 2 Liebman & Hertz, Paragraph (2), *supra*, at 220–21.

(8) *Relief.* Because the § 2255 motion is a continuation of the criminal proceeding, the judge has some remedial options—for example, treating the motion as in effect a motion for a new trial—that are not available in § 2254 proceedings. See Advisory Committee Note to Rule 1 of the § 2255 Rules.

591 (9th Cir.1987). The court cited the War Department's concealment of a report explaining the basis for the orders and evidencing racial prejudice. See also Korematsu v. United States, 584 F.Supp. 1406 (N.D.Cal. 1984), again relying on Morgan in granting coram nobis to vacate a conviction (for violating the exclusion order) that had been upheld at 323 U.S. 214 (1944).

14. See, *e.g.*, United States v. Gordon, 634 F.2d 638 (1st Cir.1980); United States ex

rel. Calabro v. United States Marshal, 466 F.2d 1350 (2d Cir.1972)(per curiam).

However, in rare cases the courts have permitted § 2255 proceedings to continue, even when an appeal is pending, upon a showing of "extraordinary circumstances". See, *e.g.*, United States v. Cyrus, 890 F.2d 1245 (D.C.Cir.1989); United States v. Taylor, 648 F.2d 565, 572 (9th Cir.1981).

CHAPTER XII

ADVANCED PROBLEMS IN JUDICIAL FEDERALISM

SECTION 1. PROBLEMS OF RES JUDICATA

NOTE ON THE RES JUDICATA EFFECT OF FEDERAL JUDGMENTS

(1) *Introduction.* An understanding of the res judicata effects of federal judgments in federal and state courts requires an underlying grasp of the basic rules of res judicata. For the reader unfamiliar with those rules, a very brief summary is provided here; a more exhaustive treatment is available in a number of sources, especially the Restatement (Second) of Judgments (1982)(hereafter cited as Restatement 2d).

While the term "res judicata" is occasionally used in a narrower sense by the Supreme Court and others, it is used in the discussion here to embrace the entire subject of the preclusive effects of an adjudicatory proceeding in a subsequent adjudicatory proceeding. Those effects are in turn divided into "claim" and "issue" preclusion. Under the doctrine of claim preclusion, once a valid final judgment has been entered, a subsequent action on the same claim by any party to that judgment, or by one in privity with a party, is normally precluded. A range of exceptions has been recognized, covering such matters as the existence of "consent" to the splitting of a claim and a case in which the initial judgment rested on such preliminary grounds as jurisdiction or venue. Moreover, most modern courts embrace the Restatement 2d view that a claim should be defined in terms of the transaction or transactions that were the subject of the dispute, not in terms of the particular theory of recovery that was advanced.

When a second action is not entirely barred by the doctrine of claim preclusion, a party to the first action will normally be barred by the doctrine of issue preclusion (also frequently referred to as collateral estoppel, or in certain instances, direct estoppel) from relitigating an issue decided in the first action that was necessary to the judgment in that action. Again, numerous exceptions are recognized in the Restatement 2d and in virtually all jurisdictions, but in recent years, this doctrine has been extended by many courts beyond the parties to the initial action, so that a party to that action who suffered an adverse determination on an issue may be barred from relitigating that issue with any other person in a subsequent proceeding.[1]

---

1. This Note does not deal with the more limited, and more controversial, question of the instances in which one who was *not* a party to a prior action, or in privity with a party, may nevertheless be barred from litigating a claim or an issue in a subsequent proceeding.

(2) *Leading Federal Cases.*   When a federal court renders a judgment on a federal question it has generally been assumed—usually without discussion—that federal law governs the preclusive effects of that judgment in a subsequent action in a federal court.   See 18 Wright, Miller & Cooper, Federal Practice and Procedure § 4466 (1981 & 1995 Supp.)(hereafter cited "18 Federal Practice"); Degnan, *Federalized Res Judicata,* 85 Yale L.J. 741, 755–73 (1976); see also Restatement 2d § 87 ("Federal law determines the effects under the rules of res judicata of a judgment of a federal court").

Res judicata law is almost entirely judge-made.   Several significant federal decisions that have contributed to this body of law and that are of particular value in understanding the following materials in this section are summarized below.

(a) *Questions of Law Adjudicated in Government Litigation.*[2]   United States v. Moser, 266 U.S. 236 (1924), involved the question whether a retired naval captain's service at the Naval Academy had amounted to "service during the civil war" within the meaning of a federal statute; if so, he was entitled to a higher pension.   The Court of Claims said yes, and in two later actions to recover pension installments it held the issue of Moser's entitlement to be res judicata, despite an intervening decision involving another person in which the same court had declined to follow the interpretation of the applicable statute adopted in the first Moser case.   In Moser's fourth action to recover an installment of the pension, the Supreme Court held that his right to his pension was res judicata, stating that "a fact, question or right distinctly adjudged in the original action cannot be disputed in a subsequent action, even though the determination was reached upon an erroneous view or by an erroneous application of the law. * * * A determination in respect of the status of an individual upon which his right to recover depends is as conclusive as a decision upon any other matter" (p. 242).

In Commissioner v. Sunnen, 333 U.S. 591 (1948), a taxpayer had won a decision in the Board of Tax Appeals that he was not liable for taxes for the years 1929 through 1931 on royalties paid under a contract he had assigned to his wife in 1928.   The contract was renewed in 1938 and the Commissioner again sought a decision that Sunnen was liable for taxes, this time for 1937 (for royalties paid under the 1928 contract) and 1938 through 1941 (under the new contract).   As to liability for 1937, the Court held that issue preclusion did not apply, despite "complete identity of facts, issues and parties as between the earlier Board proceeding and the instant one" (p. 602), because a series of intervening Supreme Court decisions had "vitally altered" the legal situation and made it clear that the Board had reached an erroneous result (p. 600).[3]

Regarding liability under the 1938 contract, the Sunnen Court denied the Board decision preclusive effect on the distinct ground that different facts were involved.   The Court held that "if the relevant facts in the two cases are separable, even though they be similar or identical, collateral estoppel does not

---

2.   It is often said that the doctrine of res judicata does not apply to "pure" questions of law, at least where the two actions involve substantially unrelated claims.   Montana v. United States, 440 U.S. 147, 162–63 (1979); Restatement 2d § 28(2)(a).   This statement can be misleading, however, and in any event, the difference between questions

of "pure" law and questions of law application is often slighted or difficult to draw.   See, *e.g.,* p. 1480, note 1, *infra.*

3.   On the sorts of changes in legal climate that have been held sufficient to bar issue preclusion, see 18 Federal Practice § 4425, at 261–64; 1995 Supp. at 224–28.

govern the legal issues which recur in the second case. Thus the second proceeding may involve an instrument or transaction identical with, but in form separable from, the one dealt with in the first proceeding. In that situation, a court is free in the second proceeding to make an independent examination of the legal matters at issue" (p 601). (With respect to this second aspect of the decision, compare the discussion in the Stauffer case, p. 1479–80 and note 1, *infra*).

Montana v. United States, 440 U.S. 147 (1979), involved attacks by the United States on the validity of Montana's gross receipts tax on contractors for public construction projects; the government claimed the tax discriminated against the United States. The Montana Supreme Court upheld the tax in a state-court litigation brought by contractors but controlled and financed by the United States. No appeal was taken. The United States in the meantime had brought its own action to invalidate the tax in a federal district court. The Supreme Court held that the United States was bound by the state-court judgment, since it was in privity with the plaintiffs there and since there had not been the "major changes in the law governing intergovernmental tax immunity" required under Sunnen to create an exception to res judicata.[4]

(b) *The Decline of Mutuality*. The Supreme Court has also made significant contributions to the erosion of the doctrine of mutuality (noted in Paragraph (1)), under which a new plaintiff or defendant was not allowed to make offensive or defensive use of the rule of issue preclusion against a party to a prior proceeding.

In Blonder–Tongue Lab., Inc. v. University of Illinois Found., 402 U.S. 313 (1971), a patentee brought an infringement suit. In a prior infringement action by the same patentee against a different defendant, the patent had been held invalid. Emphasizing the burden on courts and defendants of permitting relitigation of the issue of validity, the Supreme Court held that the prior holding of invalidity was preclusive, provided the plaintiff had been afforded a "full and fair opportunity to litigate" the question at the first trial.

In Parklane Hosiery Co. v. Shore, 439 U.S. 322 (1979), the SEC had obtained an injunction against false and misleading proxy statements in violation of the securities laws. A private stockholders' action seeking damages on the basis of the same statements was then brought against the same defendant. The Court held that the defendant was precluded by the first judgment from relitigating the issues adjudicated in the first case. The Court noted that *offensive* nonmutual preclusion does present some special problems;[5] but it said that these problems can be solved by giving the district courts "broad discretion to determine" whether to allow a nonparty to the former litigation to make offensive use of findings made in that litigation. Such use should be

---

4. Montana involved a state court, not a federal court judgment, but the Supreme Court apparently assumed that federal law governs the preclusion question. *Cf. Note on 28 U.S.C. § 1738 and the Res Judicata Effect of State Judgments*, p. 1492, *infra*.

5. The Court observed that offensive preclusion (a) may encourage potential plaintiffs not to join the first action, because they have everything to win (by a favorable judg-

ment) and nothing to lose (by an unfavorable one); and (b) may be unfair if the defendant had little incentive to litigate in the first action (because, for instance, the amount involved was small), or if the judgment relied on was itself inconsistent with earlier judgments involving the same defendant, or if in the first action the defendant was inconvenienced by difficulties in obtaining proof or calling witnesses.

denied when the plaintiff "could easily have joined in the earlier action" or where preclusion "would be unfair to the defendants."[6]

(c) *Additional Decisions.* For other important cases developing the federal common law of res judicata, see, *e.g.,* Federated Dep't Stores, Inc. v. Moitie, 452 U.S. 394 (1981)(considering—and rejecting in the particular context—a plea for recognition of a "fairness" exception to the rules of claim preclusion); Lawlor v. National Screen Service Corp., 349 U.S. 322 (1955)(scope of claim preclusion).

(3) *Attacks on Subject Matter Jurisdiction.* Difficult res judicata problems arise when a federal judgment is collaterally attacked in a subsequent action on the ground that the first court lacked subject matter jurisdiction. Rules limiting the subject matter jurisdiction of the federal courts have always had special force. Thus, under the Mansfield rule, discussed further in Chap. XIV, Sec. 1, *infra,* a challenge to a federal court's subject matter jurisdiction may be made at any time during the course of proceedings, and the court may raise the question *sua sponte.* Does this policy go so far, however, as to permit a federal court's judgment to be collaterally attacked on this ground?

In McCormick v. Sullivant, 23 U.S. (10 Wheat.) 192 (1825), the Court was called upon to decide whether a prior "general decree of dismissal" by a federal district court acted as a bar to a second action on the same claim. The record in the first suit did not show that the parties were of diverse citizenship; on this basis, plaintiffs claimed that the previous action was *coram non judice* and the prior decree void. The Supreme Court responded that if subject matter jurisdiction "be not alleged in the proceedings, [a federal district court's] judgments and decrees are erroneous, and may, upon a writ of error or appeal, be reversed for that cause. But they are not absolute nullities." The decree in the prior suit "whilst it remains unreversed, is a valid bar of the present suit" (p. 199).

In McCormick the record in the first case merely failed to disclose the citizenship of the parties. But in Des Moines Navig. & R. Co. v. Iowa Homestead Co., 123 U.S. 552 (1887), the record showed affirmatively that there was neither diversity nor any other basis of jurisdiction. The Court held that this made no difference.

In Chicot County Drainage Dist. v. Baxter State Bank, 308 U.S. 371 (1940), a federal district court had approved a plan of municipal reorganization under a jurisdictional statute that the Supreme Court in other litigation later held unconstitutional. Relying in part on McCormick, the Court decided that the judgment was res judicata against participating bondholders in a second action in the same district court, even though the issue of constitutionality had not been litigated in the first case. *Cf.* Stoll v. Gottlieb, 305 U.S. 165 (1938), holding that an order of a district court in bankruptcy proceedings releasing a guarantor of the debtor's bonds, although assumed to have been entered without jurisdiction, was res judicata in a later action in a state court against the guarantor brought by a bondholder who had received notice of the district court's hearing and had later failed in a petition to the court to set aside its order for want of jurisdiction.[7] See also Jackson v. Irving Trust Co., 311 U.S.

---

6. The Court rejected the defendants' claim that it violated their Seventh Amendment rights to give preclusive effect in a damages action (in which they had a right to jury trial) to a decision against them in an equitable action (in which they did not).

7. The principle of McCormick and subsequent cases was applied in Willy v. Coastal

494 (1941). *Cf.* Durfee v. Duke, 375 U.S. 106 (1963), holding that a Nebraska state court decision determining after litigation that the land in issue was in Nebraska was binding in a subsequent action in federal court in Missouri, even though the Nebraska court had jurisdiction only if the land was in that state.[8]

However, in United States v. United States Fidelity & Guar. Co., 309 U.S. 506 (1940), the Court held that the United States and the Indian Nations under its tutelage were immune from suit; that the immunity could not be waived by failure to assert it; and that a judgment against them was open to collateral attack in a later proceeding. See also Kalb v. Feuerstein, 308 U.S. 433 (1940), in which a judgment of foreclosure and a foreclosure sale by a state court while a petition was pending under Section 75 of the Bankruptcy Act (the Frazier–Lemke Act) were held void in a later action by the mortgagors to recover possession.

Can these two cases be reconciled with the others? See generally Boskey & Braucher, *Jurisdiction and Collateral Attack,* 40 Colum.L.Rev. 1006 (1940); Note, 87 Yale L.J. 164 (1977). And see the formulation in Restatement 2d § 12:

"When a court has rendered a judgment in a contested action, the judgment precludes the parties from litigating the question of the court's subject matter jurisdiction in subsequent litigation except if:

"(1) The subject matter of the action was so plainly beyond the court's jurisdiction that its entertaining the action was a manifest abuse of authority; or

"(2) Allowing the judgment to stand would substantially infringe the authority of another tribunal or agency of government; or

"(3) The judgment was rendered by a court lacking capability to make an adequately informed determination of a question concerning its own jurisdiction and as a matter of procedural fairness the party seeking to avoid the judgment should have the opportunity belatedly to attack the court's subject matter jurisdiction."

Corp., 503 U.S. 131 (1992). There a federal district judge granted defendant's motions to dismiss under Rule 12(b)(6) and for sanctions under Rule 11. The court of appeals found that subject matter jurisdiction was lacking: it ordered the case remanded to the state court from which it had been removed, but affirmed the award of sanctions. The Supreme Court affirmed, rejecting the plaintiff's claim that the district court lacked power to award sanctions. A determination that there is no subject matter jurisdiction "does not automatically wipe out all proceedings had in the district court at a time when the district court operated under the misapprehension that it had jurisdiction" (p. 137, citing Chicot County and Stoll v. Gottlieb).

8. The Restatement 2d (§ 10 comment *d,* and Reporter's Note, p. 107; *cf. id.* § 11 comment *b*) suggests that Durfee involved territorial rather than subject-matter juris-

diction. Nevertheless, Durfee was relied on in Underwriters Nat'l Assurance Co. v. North Carolina Life & Acc. Health Ins. Guar. Ass'n, 455 U.S. 691 (1982), holding that North Carolina violated the Full Faith and Credit Clause by failing to give res judicata effect to an Indiana adjudication upholding jurisdiction. (The Indiana court had concluded that it had subject matter jurisdiction over an action involving rights to a $100,000 deposit that an Indiana insurance company had made in North Carolina to qualify in order to do insurance business in that state.) The issue of the Indiana court's jurisdiction had been litigated in Indiana in a proceeding in which the North Carolina objector had intervened. The Court said that since the Indiana court had "fully and fairly" considered the question of jurisdiction, its conclusion was preclusive.

(4) *The Effect of a Federal Judgment in a Subsequent State Proceeding.* No explicit constitutional or legislative provision states that the preclusive effect of federal judgments in state courts should be measured by federal law. But such a rule "is indispensable to federalism"; "[w]ere there no such rule, it would be necessary to invent one—so invent it the Supreme Court did." Degnan, Paragraph (2), *supra,* at 749. Beginning with Dupasseur v. Rochereau, 88 U.S. (21 Wall.) 130, 134 (1874), the Court has consistently held that a claim under a federal court judgment is "a title or right * * * claimed under an authority exercised under the United States," and that the court therefore has jurisdiction on review of state court decisions to determine whether proper effect has been given to such a judgment. See Metcalf v. Watertown, 153 U.S. 671 (1894); Stoll v. Gottlieb, *supra,* 305 U.S. at 167. There is, nevertheless, a good deal of confusion as to what makes the preclusive effects of federal judgments in state cases a federal matter. Compare, *e.g.,* Embry v. Palmer, 107 U.S. 3 (1883)(application of the full faith and credit statute, now 28 U.S.C. § 1738, to federal judgments was authorized), with Dupasseur v. Rochereau, *supra,* 88 U.S. at 134 (res judicata effect of circuit court judgment is a question arising under the laws "establishing the circuit court and vesting it with jurisdiction; * * * and it is clearly within the chart of appellate power given to this court, over cases arising in and decided by the State Courts").

(5) *Federal Question and Diversity Cases Contrasted.* It is clear that where the federal court decided a federal question, federal res judicata rules govern. See Deposit Bank v. Frankfort, 191 U.S. 499 (1903); Stoll v. Gottlieb, *supra.* But where the first judgment was in a diversity action (or decided questions of state law pursuant to the court's supplemental jurisdiction), the Supreme Court, in reviewing the subsequent state court action, has often applied state preclusion rules. In the Dupasseur case, for example, concerning the preclusive effect of a judgment in a diversity action, Justice Bradley said that "[t]he only effect that can be justly claimed for the judgment in the Circuit Court of the United States, is such as would belong to judgments of the State courts [in the state in which the circuit court was sitting] rendered under similar circumstances" (p. 135). Accord, *e.g.,* Crescent City Live Stock Co. v. Butchers' Union Slaughter–House Co., 120 U.S. 141, 146–47 (1887); Metcalf v. Watertown, *supra,* 153 U.S. at 676. See generally 18 Federal Practice § 4472 (1995 Supp.); Restatement 2d § 87 comment *b.*[9]

On the other hand, where the federal court finds some affirmative federal policy with respect to preclusion—at least one that is embodied in a Federal Rule of Civil Procedure—that policy governs even if the case is a diversity case. Thus, Federal Rule of Civil Procedure 41(b) provides that dismissal of an action "operates as an adjudication upon the merits." In Kern v. Hettinger, 303 F.2d 333 (2d Cir.1962), the preclusive effect of a diversity judgment rendered by a district court in California was measured by Rule 41(b) rather than by California law (under which the dismissal would have been without prejudice). Judge Medina stated, in a well-known passage, that "[o]ne of the strongest policies a court can have is that of determining the scope of its own judgments. * * * It would be destructive of the basic principles of the Federal Rules of Civil Procedure to say that the effect of a judgment of a federal court was governed

---

9. Similarly, where the question is the preclusive effect of a federal judgment on a state law issue in a second federal diversity action, state preclusion rules are frequently applied without significant discussion. See, *e.g.,* Iowa Elec. Light & Power Co. v. Mobile Aerial Towers, Inc., 723 F.2d 50 (8th Cir. 1983).

by the law of the state where the court sits simply because the source of federal jurisdiction is diversity. The rights and obligations of the parties are fixed by state law. * * * But we think it would be strange doctrine to allow a state to nullify the judgments of federal courts. * * * The Erie doctrine is not applicable here * * *'' (p. 340).

Should a federal court apply state law as the measure of the effect of a judgment in a case involving only state-created rights? In what circumstances? Even if state law is applied, would it follow that the state has legislative jurisdiction to enact provisions with regard to the effect of the judgments of federal courts sitting in the state?

In connection with all of these questions, consider Degnan, Paragraph (2), *supra,* at 773, contending that "[a] valid judgment rendered in any judicial system within the United States must be recognized by all other judicial systems within the United States, and the claims and issues precluded by that judgment, and the parties bound thereby, are determined by the law of the system which rendered the judgment." Compare Burbank, *Interjurisdictional Preclusion, Full Faith and Credit and Federal Common Law: A General Approach,* 71 Cornell L.Rev. 733, 747–97 (and especially 791–97)(1986). Professor Burbank, disagreeing with Professor Degnan, argues that neither the Full Faith and Credit Clause nor the Federal Rules of Civil Procedure provide preclusion rules for federal judgments; that the only putative federal rules on this question are rules of federal common law, and that the usual methodology regarding the use of federal common law should apply; moreover, when a federal diversity court adjudicates issues of state law, the Court's Erie precedents are also relevant and should be "integrated" with the Court's federal common law precedents.[10]

(6) *Federal Declaratory Judgments.* Do the normal rules with respect to the preclusive effects of federal judgments apply if the judgment entered by the federal court was declaratory in form? See the comprehensive discussion in Shapiro, *State Courts and Federal Declaratory Judgments,* 74 Nw.U.L.Rev. 759 (1979). Suppose that a federal district court has declared a state statute unconstitutional on the ground that it made criminal some constitutionally protected activity. Is the state precluded from prosecuting under that statute the person who prevailed in the federal suit? From prosecuting someone else under it? What if the federal court's decision was that the statute was overbroad?

As to these problems, see also the discussion in Chap. X, Sec. 2(C), pp. 1287–88, *supra.*

United States v. Mendoza

464 U.S. 154, 104 S.Ct. 568, 78 L.Ed.2d 379 (1984).
Certiorari to the United States Court of Appeals for the Ninth Circuit.

■ JUSTICE REHNQUIST delivered the opinion of the Court.

In 1978 respondent Sergio Mendoza, a Filipino national, filed a petition for naturalization under a statute which by its terms had expired 32 years earlier.

---

10. A recent comment reports that the federal courts are divided on the appropriate role of state law in such cases. Shreve, *Judgments from a Choice-of-Law Perspective,* 40 Am.J.Comp.L. 985 (1992).

Respondent's claim for naturalization was based on the assertion that the Government's administration of the Nationality Act denied him due process of law. Neither the District Court nor the Court of Appeals for the Ninth Circuit ever reached the merits of his claim, because they held that the Government was collaterally estopped from litigating that constitutional issue in view of an earlier decision against the Government in a case brought by other Filipino nationals in the United States District Court for the Northern District of California. We hold that the United States may not be collaterally estopped on an issue such as this, adjudicated against it in an earlier lawsuit brought by a different party. We therefore reverse the judgment of the Court of Appeals.

The facts bearing on respondent's claim to naturalization are not in dispute. In 1942 Congress amended the Nationality Act, § 701 of which provided that noncitizens who served honorably in the Armed Forces of the United States during World War II were exempt from some of the usual requirements for nationality. * * * Congress later provided by amendment that all naturalization petitions seeking to come under § 701 must be filed by December 31, 1946. Section 702 of the Act provided for the overseas naturalization of aliens in active service who were eligible for naturalization under § 701 but who were not within the jurisdiction of any court authorized to naturalize aliens. In order to implement that provision, the Immigration and Naturalization Service from 1943 to 1946 sent representatives abroad to naturalize eligible alien servicemen.

Respondent Mendoza served as a doctor in the Philippine Commonwealth Army from 1941 until his discharge in 1946. Because Japanese occupation of the Philippines had made naturalization of alien servicemen there impossible before the liberation of the Islands, the INS did not designate a representative to naturalize eligible servicemen there until 1945. Because of concerns expressed by the Philippine Government to the United States, however, to the effect that large numbers of Filipinos would be naturalized and would immigrate to the United States just as the Philippines gained their independence, the Attorney General subsequently revoked the naturalization authority of the INS representative. Thus all naturalizations in the Philippines were halted for a 9–month period from late October 1945 until a new INS representative was appointed in August 1946.

Respondent's claim for naturalization is based on the contention that that conduct of the Government deprived him of due process of law in violation of the Fifth Amendment to the United States Constitution, because he was present in the Philippines during part, but not all, of the 9–month period during which there was no authorized INS representative there. The naturalization examiner recommended denial of Mendoza's petition, but the District Court granted the petition * * * [concluding] that the Government could not relitigate the due process issue because that issue had already been decided against the Government in In re Naturalization of 68 Filipino War Veterans, 406 F.Supp. 931 (N.D.Cal.1975)(hereinafter 68 Filipinos), a decision which the Government had not appealed.[2]

2. * * * Although the Government initially docketed an appeal from that decision, the Court of Appeals granted the Government's motion to withdraw the appeal on November 30, 1977. The Government made that motion after a new administration and a

Noting that the doctrine of nonmutual offensive collateral estoppel has been conditionally approved by this Court in Parklane Hosiery Co. v. Shore, 439 U.S. 322 (1979), the Court of Appeals concluded that the District Court had not abused its discretion in applying that doctrine against the United States in this case. * * * For the reasons which follow, we agree with the Government that Parklane Hosiery's approval of nonmutual offensive collateral estoppel is not to be extended to the United States.

Under the judicially developed doctrine of collateral estoppel, once a court has decided an issue of fact or law necessary to its judgment, that decision is conclusive in a subsequent suit based on a different cause of action involving a party to the prior litigation. Montana v. United States, 440 U.S. 147, 153 (1979). Collateral estoppel, like the related doctrine of res judicata,[3] serves to "relieve parties of the cost and vexation of multiple lawsuits, conserve judicial resources, and, by preventing inconsistent decisions, encourage reliance on adjudication." Allen v. McCurry, 449 U.S. 90, 94 (1980). In furtherance of those policies, this Court in recent years has broadened the scope of the doctrine of collateral estoppel beyond its common-law limits. It has done so by abandoning the requirement of mutuality of parties, Blonder–Tongue Laboratories, Inc. v. University of Illinois Foundation, 402 U.S. 313 (1971), and by conditionally approving the "offensive" use of collateral estoppel by a nonparty to a prior lawsuit. Parklane Hosiery, *supra*.

In Standefer v. United States, 447 U.S. 10, 24 (1980), however, we emphasized the fact that Blonder–Tongue and Parklane Hosiery involved disputes over private rights between private litigants. We noted that "[i]n such cases, no significant harm flows from enforcing a rule that affords a litigant only one full and fair opportunity to litigate an issue, and [that] there is no sound reason for burdening the courts with repetitive litigation." Here, as in Montana v. United States [p. 1470, *supra*], the party against whom the estoppel is sought is the United States; but here, unlike in Montana, the party who seeks to preclude the Government from relitigating the issue was not a party to the earlier litigation.

We have long recognized that "the Government is not in a position identical to that of a private litigant," INS v. Hibi, 414 U.S. 5, 8 (1973)(*per curiam*), both because of the geographic breadth of Government litigation and also, most importantly, because of the nature of the issues the Government litigates. It is not open to serious dispute that the Government is a party to a far greater number of cases on a nationwide basis than even the most litigious private entity; in 1982, the United States was a party to more than 75,000 of the 206,193 filings in the United States District Courts. Administrative Office of the United States Courts, Annual Report of the Director 98 (1982). In the same year the United States was a party to just under 30% of the civil cases

new INS Commissioner had taken office. Eventually the Government reevaluated its position and decided to take appeals from all orders granting naturalization to so-called Category II petitioners, with the exception of orders granting naturalization to petitioners who filed petitions prior to the withdrawal of the appeal in 68 Filipinos. Mendoza's petition for naturalization was filed after the Government withdrew its appeal in 68 Filipinos.

3. Under res judicata, a final judgment on the merits bars further claims by parties or their privies on the same cause of action. Montana v. United States, 440 U.S., at 153; Parklane Hosiery Co. v. Shore, 439 U.S. 322, 326, n. 5 (1979). The Restatement of Judgments speaks of res judicata as "claim preclusion" and of collateral estoppel as "issue preclusion." Restatement (Second) of Judgments § 27 (1982).

appealed from the District Courts to the Court of Appeals. *Id.*, at 79, 82. Government litigation frequently involves legal questions of substantial public importance; indeed, because the proscriptions of the United States Constitution are so generally directed at governmental action, many constitutional questions can arise only in the context of litigation to which the Government is a party. Because of those facts the Government is more likely than any private party to be involved in lawsuits against different parties which nonetheless involve the same legal issues.

A rule allowing nonmutual collateral estoppel against the Government in such cases would substantially thwart the development of important questions of law by freezing the first final decision rendered on a particular legal issue. Allowing only one final adjudication would deprive this Court of the benefit it receives from permitting several courts of appeals to explore a difficult question before this Court grants certiorari. Indeed, if nonmutual estoppel were routinely applied against the Government, this Court would have to revise its practice of waiting for a conflict to develop before granting the Government's petitions for certiorari.

The Solicitor General's policy for determining when to appeal an adverse decision would also require substantial revision. The Court of Appeals faulted the Government in this case for failing to appeal a decision that it now contends is erroneous. But the Government's litigation conduct in a case is apt to differ from that of a private litigant. Unlike a private litigant who generally does not forgo an appeal if he believes that he can prevail, the Solicitor General considers a variety of factors, such as the limited resources of the Government and the crowded dockets of the courts, before authorizing an appeal. Brief for United States 30–31. The application of nonmutual estoppel against the Government would force the Solicitor General to abandon those prudential concerns and to appeal every adverse decision in order to avoid foreclosing further review.

In addition to those institutional concerns traditionally considered by the Solicitor General, the panoply of important public issues raised in governmental litigation may quite properly lead successive administrations of the Executive Branch to take differing positions with respect to the resolution of a particular issue. While the Executive Branch must of course defer to the Judicial Branch for final resolution of questions of constitutional law, the former nonetheless controls the progress of Government litigation through the federal courts. It would be idle to pretend that the conduct of Government litigation in all its myriad features, from the decision to file a complaint in the United States district court to the decision to petition for certiorari to review a judgment of the court of appeals, is a wholly mechanical procedure which involves no policy choices whatever.

For example, in recommending to the Solicitor General in 1977 that the Government's appeal in 68 Filipinos be withdrawn, newly appointed INS Commissioner Castillo commented that such a course "would be in keeping with the policy of the [new] Administration," described as "a course of compassion and amnesty." Brief for United States 11. But for the very reason that such policy choices are made by one administration, and often reevaluated by another administration, courts should be careful when they seek to apply expanding rules of collateral estoppel to Government litigation. The Government of course may not now undo the consequences of its decision not to appeal the District Court judgment in the 68 Filipinos case; it is bound by that judgment under the principles of res judicata. But we now hold that it is not further bound in a case involving a litigant who was not a party to the earlier litigation.

The Court of Appeals did not endorse a routine application of nonmutual collateral estoppel against the Government, because it recognized that the Government does litigate issues of far-reaching national significance which in some cases, it concluded, might warrant relitigation. But in this case it found no "record evidence" indicating that there was a "crucial need" in the administration of the immigration laws for a redetermination of the due process question decided in 68 Filipinos and presented again in this case. The Court of Appeals did not make clear what sort of "record evidence" would have satisfied it that there *was* a "crucial need" for redetermination of the question in this case, but we pretermit further discussion of that approach; we believe that the standard announced by the Court of Appeals for determining when relitigation of a legal issue is to be permitted is so wholly subjective that it affords no guidance to the courts or to the Government. Such a standard leaves the Government at sea because it cannot possibly anticipate, in determining whether or not to appeal an adverse decision, whether a court will bar relitigation of the issue in a later case. By the time a court makes its subjective determination that an issue cannot be relitigated, the Government's appeal of the prior ruling of course would be untimely.

We hold, therefore, that nonmutual offensive collateral estoppel simply does not apply against the Government in such a way as to preclude relitigation of issues such as those involved in this case.[7] The conduct of Government litigation in the courts of the United States is sufficiently different from the conduct of private civil litigation in those courts so that what might otherwise be economy interests underlying a broad application of collateral estoppel are outweighed by the constraints which peculiarly affect the Government. We think that our conclusion will better allow thorough development of legal doctrine by allowing litigation in multiple forums. Indeed, a contrary result might disserve the economy interests in whose name estoppel is advanced by requiring the Government to abandon virtually any exercise of discretion in seeking to review judgments unfavorable to it. The doctrine of res judicata, of course, prevents the Government from relitigating the same cause of action against the parties to a prior decision, but beyond that point principles of nonmutual collateral estoppel give way to the policies just stated.

Our holding in this case is consistent with each of our prior holdings to which the parties have called our attention, and which we reaffirm. Today in a companion case we hold that the Government may be estopped under certain circumstances from relitigating a question when the parties to the two lawsuits are the same. United States v. Stauffer Chemical Co., [464 U.S.] 165; see also Montana v. United States, 440 U.S. 147 (1979); United States v. Moser, 266 U.S. 236 (1924). None of those cases, however, involve the effort of a party to estop the Government in the absence of mutuality.

The concerns underlying our disapproval of collateral estoppel against the Government are for the most part inapplicable where mutuality is present, as

---

7. The Government does not base its argument on the exception to the doctrine of collateral estoppel for "unmixed questions of law" arising in "successive actions involving unrelated subject matter." Montana v. United States, 440 U.S., at 162. Our holding in no way depends on that exception.

in Stauffer Chemical, Montana, and Moser. The application of an estoppel when the Government is litigating the same issue with the same party avoids the problem of freezing the development of the law because the Government is still free to litigate that issue in the future with some other party. And, where the parties are the same, estopping the Government spares a party that has already prevailed once from having to relitigate—a function it would not serve in the present circumstances. We accordingly hold that the Court of Appeals was wrong in applying nonmutual collateral estoppel against the Government in this case. Its judgment is therefore reversed.

NOTE ON RES JUDICATA IN FEDERAL GOVERNMENT LITIGATION AND ON THE PROBLEM OF ACQUIESCENCE

(1) *Mutual Preclusion in Government Litigation.* As indicated at the end of the Mendoza opinion, the Supreme Court considered the applicability of *mutual* preclusion in government litigation in United States v. Stauffer Chemical Co., 464 U.S. 165 (1984), decided on the same day. Stauffer had refused to allow private contractors hired by EPA to inspect one of its chemical plants in Wyoming. In the suit that followed, the Tenth Circuit held (in Stauffer I) that private contractors were not "authorized representatives" of the Administrator of EPA with authority (under § 114(a)(2) of the Clean Air Act, 42 U.S.C. § 7414(a)(2)) to inspect the plant. Two weeks after the attempted inspection in Wyoming, the EPA tried to inspect a Stauffer plant in Tennessee, again using private contractors. When Stauffer refused to allow the contractors to enter the plant, the EPA obtained an administrative warrant authorizing the inspection. Stauffer failed to honor the warrant and the EPA then began civil contempt proceedings. The Sixth Circuit held (in Stauffer II) that the government was precluded from relitigating against Stauffer the question of statutory interpretation settled in Stauffer I. The Supreme Court affirmed. Writing for the Court, Justice Rehnquist said (p. 173):

"[W]e concluded in United States v. Mendoza that [the argument that preclusion against the government will freeze development of the law] is persuasive only to prevent the application of collateral estoppel against the Government in the absence of mutuality. When estoppel is applied in a case where the Government is litigating the same issue arising under virtually identical facts against the same party, as here, the Government's argument loses its force. * * *[6]"

6. "* * *

"The Government argues * * * that in deciding whether to appeal an adverse decision, the Solicitor General has no way of knowing whether future litigation will arise with the same or a different party. The Government thus argues that the mere possibility of being bound in the future will influence the Solicitor General to appeal or seek certiorari from adverse decisions when such action would otherwise be unwarranted. The Government lists as an example Stauffer I, from which the Government did not seek certiorari because there was no circuit conflict at the time of the Tenth Circuit's decision. Yet, taking the issue here as an example, the Government itself asserts that 'thousands of businesses are affected each year by the question of contractor participation in Section 114 inspections.' Brief for United States 28. It is thus unrealistic to assume that the Government would be driven to pursue an unwarranted appeal here because of fear of being unable to relitigate the § 114 issue in the future with a

Unlike the Tenth Circuit, the Ninth Circuit (in an unrelated case) had interpreted § 114(a)(2) to authorize inspection by private contractors. Bunker Hill Company Lead & Zinc Smelter v. EPA, 658 F.2d 1280 (9th Cir.1981). The EPA argued in Stauffer II that "if it is foreclosed from relitigating the statutory issue with Stauffer, then Stauffer plants within the Ninth Circuit will benefit from a rule precluding inspections by private contractors while plants of Stauffer's competitors will be subject to the Ninth Circuit's contrary rule," and "an inequitable administration of the law" would result (p. 174). Compare Restatement 2d § 28(2)(b) comment *c* (problems of inequality are particularly significant if "one of the parties is a government agency responsible for continuing administration of a body of law that affects members of the public generally, as in the case of tax law"). The Court, however, refused to address the question whether preclusion would operate against the EPA in an action against Stauffer in the Ninth Circuit.[1]

Justice White, concurring, agreed that further litigation on the statutory interpretation issue was foreclosed between the EPA and Stauffer in the Tenth Circuit, and (though the question was more difficult) in the Sixth Circuit as well.

But Justice White stated that he would not give Stauffer the benefit of estoppel in a circuit that had adopted a contrary rule on the merits, as had the Ninth Circuit: "Judicial economy is not served for the simple reason that no litigation is prevented; the prior litigant is subject to one black-letter rule rather than another. For the same reason, there is no concern about protecting the prior litigant from repetitious, vexatious, or harassing litigation" (p. 178). Moreover, preclusion in such circumstances would create inconsistency "more dramatic and more troublesome than a normal circuit split; by definition, it compounds that problem. It would be dubious enough were the EPA unable to employ private contractors to inspect Stauffer's plants within the Ninth Circuit even though it can use such contractors in inspecting other plants. But the disarray is more extensive. By the same application of mutual collateral estoppel, the EPA could presumably use private contractors to inspect Bunker Hill's plants in circuits like the Tenth, despite the fact that other companies are not subject to such inspections. Furthermore * * * the EPA can relitigate this matter as to other companies. As a result, in, say, the First Circuit, the EPA must follow one rule as to Bunker Hill, the opposite as to Stauffer, and, depending on any ruling by that Circuit, one or the other or a third as to other companies" (p. 178–79).

Would Justice White's solution cause complexities of its own? Suppose the Sixth Circuit were later to decide in the EPA's favor in a suit brought against a different defendant. Would Stauffer be able to rely on issue preclusion in the Sixth Circuit thereafter?

(2) *The Question of Party Identity.* Under Mendoza and Stauffer, there can be no issue preclusion against the government without mutuality. Questions can

different one of those thousands of affected parties."

1. The Government also argued in Stauffer II that the issue of statutory interpretation was "an unmixed question of law," and that under Commissioner v. Sunnen, *supra,* there is no issue preclusion unless the two cases arise from the very same transac-

tion. The Court rejected this argument, holding that under Montana v. United States, *supra,* legal issues will be res judicata in a subsequent action where there is mutuality and there has been no change in the law, unless the claims in the two actions are substantially unrelated. *Cf.* Restatement 2d § 29 comment *i.*

therefore arise whether the government party in the second suit is the same government party that was involved in the first suit. Sunshine Anthracite Coal Co. v. Adkins, 310 U.S. 381, 402–03 (1940), a case involving an IRS claim of issue preclusion resulting from a prior judgment in favor of the National Bituminous Coal Commission, held that "a judgment in a suit between a party and a representative of the United States is *res judicata* in relitigation of the same issue between that party and another officer of the government." *Cf.* Montana v. United States, 440 U.S. 147 (1979), p. 1470, *supra.* Compare the materials discussing the question of when the United States is bound by judgments rendered in actions against its individual officials, in Chap. IX, pp. 1024, *supra.*[2] Compare also the rule that double jeopardy does not bar a federal government prosecution for conduct that a state government has already prosecuted, and vice versa. See United States v. Wheeler, 435 U.S. 313 (1978); Bartkus v. Illinois, 359 U.S. 121 (1959).

(3) *Executive or Administrative Nonacquiescence.* Difficult questions about the fair administration of justice can arise when the government is faced with lower court rulings it believes to be wrong. Mendoza established that res judicata does not bar the government from relitigating the issue against a new party. And the policy arguments that the Supreme Court relied on in Mendoza make it plain that the government may relitigate issues in order to persuade other courts that the first decision was erroneous.

(a) Should there nevertheless be some limits on the government's privilege to relitigate? Suppose that the government loses on an issue in Circuit A. May it—and should it—take the position that, even in Circuit A, it will not "acquiesce" in the decision—that it will require citizens to litigate the question in district courts even though those courts are bound to reject the government's position? Why should private parties be burdened by the obligation to litigate cases that the government knows it will lose? Isn't this simply bullying, by putting pressure on those citizens who cannot afford litigation to forgo their rights? Can nonacquiescence be justified if the government's purpose is to generate either an intracircuit conflict or an *en banc* reconsideration by Circuit A? If in the meantime well considered opinions elsewhere have rejected the views of Circuit A? If the question at issue is one that demands uniform nationwide administration as a matter of effective and fair policy?

Or suppose that the government's position on an issue is rejected in three or four—or seven or eight—circuits. Is the government free to—and should it—relitigate the issue in the remaining circuits?

2. As noted in Chapter IX, the Court of Claims held in Duncan v. United States, 667 F.2d 36, 38 (Ct.Cl.1981), that plaintiffs, having previously obtained a federal court injunction forbidding certain action by the Secretary of the Interior on the ground that it would be unlawful, could estop the United States, in a separate suit for damages, from denying the illegality of the action.

Parallel issues of privity can arise in litigation involving state officials. If in a federal court action brought against a state officer (on account of the Eleventh Amendment) rather than against the state itself, it is held that a state statute is unconstitutional, is the state barred from prosecuting the federal plaintiff for violating the statute? Shapiro, *State Courts and Federal Declaratory Judgments,* 74 Nw.U.L.Rev. 759, 764 & n. 31 (1979), argues that the answer is yes. See also Jackson, *The Supreme Court, the Eleventh Amendment, and State Sovereign Immunity,* 98 Yale L.J. 1, 67 n. 276 (1988)(supporting Shapiro's view and comparing Steffel v. Thompson, 415 U.S. 452, 477 (White, J., concurring)(judgment would be conclusive in subsequent prosecution against federal plaintiff), with *id.* at 482 n. 3 (Rehnquist, J., concurring)(reserving question)).

Should these problems be solved by legal rules enforced by courts and binding on the government? Or is the matter one that should be worked out by the executive branch?

All of these issues have generated intense controversy. A number of federal agencies have regularly refused to acquiesce in circuit court decisions. Between 1981 and 1984, for example, the Social Security Administration—acting at the instance of Congress in re-evaluating all cases where disability payments were being made—terminated an unusually high number of disability payments. By 1984, all but one circuit had struck down the SSA's termination criteria. The SSA nevertheless refused to acquiesce in these decisions, prompting at least one judge to threaten the Secretary with contempt proceedings, see Hillhouse v. Harris, 715 F.2d 428, 430 (8th Cir.1983)(McMillian, J., concurring), and at one point causing the Ninth Circuit to uphold a preliminary injunction ordering the Secretary to reinstate beneficiaries terminated pursuant to the nonacquiescence policy. Lopez v. Heckler, 725 F.2d 1489 (9th Cir.), *vacated and remanded,* 469 U.S. 1082 (1984). And in the Second Circuit, a class action eventuated in a settlement agreement in which the SSA agreed, *inter alia,* to instruct all its adjudicators acting in cases falling within the circuit's jurisdiction to comply with holdings in Second Circuit disability decisions. Stieberger v. Sullivan, 792 F.Supp. 1376 (S.D.N.Y.), *modified by* 801 F.Supp. 1079 (S.D.N.Y.1992). These and related decisions are discussed in Note, 60 Brook.L.Rev. 765 (1994).[3]

(b) Judge Weis has complained that "[t]he non-acquiescence policy of an agency results in intolerable and inexcusable expense to litigants, as well as in the unnecessary and wasteful expenditure of scarce judicial resources. But perhaps most objectionable is the disrespect for the administration of justice generated by the spectacle of a federal agency which refuses to acknowledge that a court's ruling applies to it as well as to other litigants." Weis, *Agency Nonacquiescence—Respectful Lawlessness or Legitimate Disagreement?,* 48 U.Pitt.L.Rev. 845, 851–52 (1987).

In view of the policy considerations outlined in Mendoza, isn't the criticism too general? Too harsh? But are there not cases where it could be apt?[4]

For an exhaustive study of nonacquiescence, see Estreicher & Revesz, *Nonacquiescence by Federal Administrative Agencies,* 98 Yale L.J. 679 (1989). The authors contend that nonacquiescence (at least as to nonconstitutional questions) does not necessarily violate due process, equal protection, or the separation of powers. And nonacquiescence, they submit, may be desirable (a) to facilitate the development of uniform national law by the courts of appeals or the Supreme Court, through the formulation and testing of different views about the agency's mission, (b) to permit uniform administration by the agency during that process, and (c) to avoid binding the agency by a single unfavorable ruling. They suggest, however, that while *intra*circuit nonacquiescence should

---

3. During this period, SSA also adopted regulations providing that when the agency's position on an issue of law is rejected by a court of appeals, the agency will promptly publish an intracircuit acquiescence ruling unless further review is sought or other conditions are met. See 20 C.F.R. § 404.985.

4. For a proposal to deal with the problems raised by Mendoza through structural change in the federal judicial system—specifically the creation of an intercircuit tribunal "with the authority to resolve issues of national law on a national basis"—see Levin & Leeson, *Issue Preclusion Against the United States Government,* 70 Iowa L.Rev. 113, 136–39 (1984).

not be *per se* improper, it is justified only where "(1) the agency has responsibility for securing a nationally uniform policy * * *, (2) there is a justifiable basis for belief that the agency's position falls within the scope of its delegated discretion, and (3) the agency is reasonably seeking the vindication of its position both in the courts of appeals and before the Supreme Court" (p. 753). Nonacquiescence not justified under that standard, they argue, should be set aside as "arbitrary and capricious" under the Administrative Procedure Act.[5]

Whatever the case against intracircuit nonacquiescence when the venue for judicial review is confined to a particular circuit, the argument for acquiescence at the administrative stage appears to collapse when there is a choice of venue for judicial review and at least one of the circuits in which review may be sought has not declared itself on the issue. (A vivid example is presented by the National Labor Relations Act. An aggrieved party may seek review in the circuit where the case arose, in any circuit in which it transacts business, or in the District of Columbia Circuit. The NLRB may seek enforcement in the circuit where the case arose or where the respondent resides or transacts business. 29 U.S.C. § 160(e), (f).) But if review in such a case is sought in a circuit that has declared itself adversely to the agency, may the agency properly argue for a change in the circuit's law? Should the panel hearing the case be free—despite prevailing practice in the circuit in other kinds of cases—to disagree with another panel in the same circuit without an en banc hearing by the full bench? For an affirmative answer to both questions, see White, *Time for a New Approach: Why the Judiciary Should Disregard the "Law of the Circuit" When Confronting Nonacquiescence by the National Labor Relations Board,* 69 N.C.L.Rev. 639 (1991).

Suppose a court of appeals finds that in the circumstances presented, an agency's nonacquiescence is arbitrary and capricious. Would that judgment bind the agency in a subsequent action involving the same issue but a different individual, notwithstanding the rule against precluding the United States? If so, on what basis? If not, what difference does it make if in the first action, the court finds nonacquiescence to be arbitrary and capricious rather than simply ruling for the individual on the merits? Would the finding affect the award of attorney's fees or costs in the second action against the agency for having adopted a meritless position?

Suppose the court of appeals not only finds the agency's nonacquiescence to be arbitrary and capricious but also enjoins the agency from continuing its refusal to acquiesce. If the finding is correct, is an injunction (along the lines

---

5. But see Coenen, *The Constitutional Case Against Intracircuit Nonacquiescence,* 75 Minn.L.Rev. 1339 (1991)(arguing that intracircuit nonacquiescence cannot withstand the "heightened scrutiny" analysis required when important constitutional values—here the threatened affront to the judicial power by the executive branch—are implicated).

What is the relevance, if any, of the Chevron doctrine of deference to administrative interpretations (Chevron U.S.A., Inc. v. NRDC, 467 U.S. 837 (1984)) to the question of intracircuit nonacquiescence? Strauss, *One Hundred Fifty Cases Per Year: Some*

Implications of the Supreme Court's Limited Resources for Judicial Review of Agency Action, 87 Colum.L.Rev. 1093, 1122 (1987), suggests that it makes nonacquiescence less appropriate because the court, in order to invalidate an administrative interpretation, must find that interpretation to be unreasonable. But can't it also be argued that the Chevron doctrine is a recognition of the special status of administrative agencies—one that differentiates that status from the subordinate position of a federal district court in the judicial hierarchy?

of the settlement order in Stieberger, *supra*) appropriate? How does it affect the analysis of the significance of the decision in future cases?

In thinking about the practice of nonacquiescence, consider the impact of class actions (either circuit-wide or nationwide). A judgment against the agency is res judicata as to the entire class; thus, as to class members, doesn't the question whether to "acquiesce" disappear? Should this consequence lead a federal court to be reluctant to certify a nationwide class in an action against the government?[6]

(4) *Nonacquiescence by State Officers.* Problems of acquiescence can also arise, of course, in the context of litigation involving state and local governments. Should a state refrain from further prosecution after a ruling by a federal district court—for instance in a habeas case—that a state criminal statute is unconstitutional? *Cf.* p. 1474, *supra* (discussion of the effect of federal court declaratory judgments in subsequent state proceedings).

Allen v. McCurry

449 U.S. 90, 101 S.Ct. 411, 66 L.Ed.2d 308 (1980).
Certiorari to the United States Court of Appeals for the Eighth Circuit.

■ JUSTICE STEWART delivered the opinion of the Court.

At a hearing before his criminal trial in a Missouri court, the respondent, Willie McCurry, invoked the Fourth and Fourteenth Amendments to suppress evidence that had been seized by the police. The trial court denied the suppression motion in part, and McCurry was subsequently convicted after a jury trial. The conviction was later affirmed on appeal. Because he did not assert that the state courts had denied him a "full and fair opportunity" to litigate his search and seizure claim, McCurry was barred by this Court's decision in Stone v. Powell, 428 U.S. 465, from seeking a writ of habeas corpus in a federal district court. Nevertheless, he sought federal-court redress for the alleged constitutional violation by bringing a damages suit under 42 U.S.C. § 1983 against the officers who had entered his home and seized the evidence in question. We granted certiorari to consider whether the unavailability of federal habeas corpus prevented the police officers from raising the state courts' partial rejection of McCurry's constitutional claim as a collateral estoppel defense to the § 1983 suit against them for damages.

I

In April 1977, several undercover police officers, following an informant's tip that McCurry was dealing in heroin, went to his house in St. Louis, Mo., to attempt a purchase. Two officers, petitioners Allen and Jacobsmeyer, knocked on the front door, while the other officers hid nearby. When McCurry opened the door, the two officers asked to buy some heroin "caps." McCurry went back into the house and returned soon thereafter, firing a pistol at and seriously wounding Allen and Jacobsmeyer. After a gun battle with the other

---

6. For further discussion of these problems, see Diller & Morawetz, *Intracircuit Non-acquiescence and the Breakdown of the Rule of Law: A Response to Estreicher & Revesz*, 99 Yale L.J. 801 (1990); Estreicher & Revesz, *The Uneasy Case Against Intracircuit Nonacquiescence: A Reply*, 99 Yale L.J. 831 (1990); Schwartz, *Nonacquiescence, Crowell v. Benson, and Administrative Adjudication*, 77 Geo.L.J. 1815 (1989).

officers and their reinforcements, McCurry retreated into the house; he emerged again when the police demanded that he surrender. Several officers then entered the house without a warrant, purportedly to search for other persons inside. One of the officers seized drugs and other contraband that lay in plain view, as well as additional contraband he found in dresser drawers and in auto tires on the porch.

McCurry was charged with possession of heroin and assault with intent to kill. At the pretrial suppression hearing, the trial judge excluded the evidence seized from the dresser drawers and tires, but denied suppression of the evidence found in plain view. McCurry was convicted of both the heroin and assault offenses.

McCurry subsequently filed the present § 1983 action for $1 million in damages against petitioners Allen and Jacobsmeyer, other unnamed individual police officers, and the city of St. Louis and its police department. The complaint alleged a conspiracy to violate McCurry's Fourth Amendment rights, an unconstitutional search and seizure of his house, and an assault on him by unknown police officers after he had been arrested and handcuffed. The petitioners moved for summary judgment. The District Court apparently understood the gist of the complaint to be the allegedly unconstitutional search and seizure and granted summary judgment, holding that collateral estoppel prevented McCurry from relitigating the search-and-seizure question already decided against him in the state courts.

The Court of Appeals reversed the judgment and remanded the case for trial. The appellate court said it was not holding that collateral estoppel was generally inapplicable in a § 1983 suit raising issues determined against the federal plaintiff in a state criminal trial. But noting that Stone v. Powell, *supra,* barred McCurry from federal habeas corpus relief, and invoking "the special role of the federal courts in protecting civil rights," the court concluded that the § 1983 suit was McCurry's only route to a federal forum for his constitutional claim and directed the trial court to allow him to proceed to trial unencumbered by collateral estoppel.

II

The federal courts have traditionally adhered to the related doctrines of res judicata and collateral estoppel. * * *[5] As this Court and other courts have often recognized, res judicata and collateral estoppel relieve parties of the cost and vexation of multiple lawsuits, conserve judicial resources, and, by preventing inconsistent decisions, encourage reliance on adjudication.

In recent years, this Court has reaffirmed the benefits of collateral estoppel in particular, finding the policies underlying it to apply in contexts not formerly recognized at common law. Thus, the Court has eliminated the requirement of mutuality in applying collateral estoppel to bar relitigation of issues decided earlier in federal-court suits, and has allowed a litigant who was not a party to a federal case to use collateral estoppel "offensively" in a new federal suit against the party who lost on the decided issue in the first case. But one general limitation the Court has repeatedly recognized is that the concept of collateral estoppel cannot apply when the party against whom the earlier

5. Contrary to a suggestion in the dissenting opinion, n. 12, this case does not involve the question whether a § 1983 claim-

ant can litigate in federal court an issue he might have raised but did not raise in previous litigation.

decision is asserted did not have a "full and fair opportunity" to litigate that issue in the earlier case. Montana v. United States, *supra,* at 153.[7]

The federal courts generally have also consistently accorded preclusive effect to issues decided by state courts. *E.g.,* Montana v. United States, *supra;* Angel v. Bullington, 330 U.S. 183. Thus, res judicata and collateral estoppel not only reduce unnecessary litigation and foster reliance on adjudication, but also promote the comity between state and federal courts that has been recognized as a bulwark of the federal system.

Indeed, though the federal courts may look to the common law or to the policies supporting res judicata and collateral estoppel in assessing the preclusive effect of decisions of other federal courts, Congress has specifically required all federal courts to give preclusive effect to state-court judgments whenever the courts of the State from which the judgments emerged would do so:

> "[J]udicial proceedings [of any court of any State] shall have the same full faith and credit in every court within the United States and its Territories and Possessions as they have by law or usage in the courts of such State. * * *" 28 U.S.C. § 1738.[8]

It is against this background that we examine the relationship of § 1983 and collateral estoppel, and the decision of the Court of Appeals in this case.

III

This Court has never directly decided whether the rules of res judicata and collateral estoppel are generally applicable to § 1983 actions. But in Preiser v. Rodriguez, 411 U.S. 475, 497, the Court noted with implicit approval the view of other federal courts that res judicata principles fully apply to civil rights suits brought under that statute. And the virtually unanimous view of the Courts of Appeals since Preiser has been that § 1983 presents no categorical bar to the application of res judicata and collateral estoppel concepts.[10] These federal appellate court decisions have spoken with little explanation or citation in assuming the compatibility of § 1983 and rules of preclusion, but the statute and its legislative history clearly support the courts' decisions.

---

7. Other factors, of course, may require an exception to the normal rules of collateral estoppel in particular cases. *E.g.,* Montana v. United States, 440 U.S., at 162 (unmixed questions of law in successive actions between the same parties on unrelated claims).

Contrary to the suggestion of the dissent, our decision today does not "fashion" any new, more stringent doctrine of collateral estoppel, nor does it hold that the collateral-estoppel effect of a state-court decision turns on the single factor of whether the State gave the federal claimant a full and fair opportunity to litigate a federal question. Our decision does not "fashion" any doctrine of collateral estoppel at all. Rather, it construes § 1983 to determine whether the conventional doctrine of collateral estoppel applies to the case at hand. It must be emphasized that the question whether any exceptions or qualifications within the bounds of that doctrine

might ultimately defeat a collateral-estoppel defense in this case is not before us.

8. This statute has existed in essentially unchanged form since its enactment just after the ratification of the Constitution, Act of May 26, 1790, ch. 11, 1 Stat. 122, and its re-enactment soon thereafter, Act of Mar. 27, 1804, ch. 56, 2 Stat. 298–299. * * *

10. *E.g.,* Robbins v. District Court, 592 F.2d 1015 (C.A.8 1979) * * *.

A very few courts have suggested that the normal rules of claim preclusion should not apply in § 1983 suits in one peculiar circumstance: Where a § 1983 plaintiff seeks to litigate in federal court a federal issue which he could have raised but did not raise in an earlier state-court suit against the same adverse party. These cases present a narrow question not now before us, and we intimate no view as to whether they were correctly decided.

Because the requirement of mutuality of estoppel was still alive in the federal courts until well into this century * * *, the drafters of the 1871 Civil Rights Act, of which § 1983 is a part, may had less reason to concern themselves with rules of preclusion than a modern Congress would. Nevertheless, in 1871 res judicata and collateral estoppel could certainly have applied in federal suits following state-court litigation between the same parties or their privies, and nothing in the language of § 1983 remotely expresses any congressional intent to contravene the common-law rules of preclusion or to repeal the express statutory requirements of the predecessor of 28 U.S.C. § 1738. Section 1983 creates a new federal cause of action. It says nothing about the preclusive effect of state-court judgments.[12]

Moreover, the legislative history of § 1983 does not in any clear way suggest that Congress intended to repeal or restrict the traditional doctrines of preclusion. The main goal of the Act was to override the corrupting influence of the Ku Klux Klan and its sympathizers on the governments and law enforcement agencies of the Southern States, see Monroe v. Pape, 365 U.S. 167, 174, and of course the debates show that one strong motive behind its enactment was grave congressional concern that the state courts had been deficient in protecting federal rights, Mitchum v. Foster, 407 U.S. 225, 241–242; Monroe v. Pape, *supra,* at 180. But in the context of the legislative history as a whole, this congressional concern lends only the most equivocal support to any argument that, in cases where the state courts have recognized the constitutional claims asserted and provided fair procedures for determining them, Congress intended to override § 1738 or the common-law rules of collateral estoppel and res judicata. Since repeals by implication are disfavored, * * * much clearer support than this would be required to hold that § 1738 and the traditional rules of preclusion are not applicable to § 1983 suits.

As the Court has understood the history of the legislation, Congress realized that in enacting § 1983 it was altering the balance of judicial power between the state and federal courts. See Mitchum v. Foster, *supra,* at 241. But in doing so, Congress was adding to the jurisdiction of the federal courts, not subtracting from that of the state courts.[14] * * *

To the extent that it did intend to change the balance of power over federal questions between the state and federal courts, the 42d Congress was acting in a way thoroughly consistent with the doctrines of preclusion. In reviewing the

12. By contrast, the roughly contemporaneous statute extending the federal writ of habeas corpus to state prisoners expressly rendered "null and void" any state-court proceeding inconsistent with the decision of a federal habeas court, Act of Feb. 5, 1867, ch. 28, § 1, 14 Stat. 385, 386 (current version at 28 U.S.C. § 2254), and the modern habeas statute also expressly adverts to the effect of state-court criminal judgments by requiring the applicant for the writ to exhaust his state-court remedies, 28 U.S.C. § 2254(b), and by presuming a state-court resolution of a factual issue to be correct except in eight specific circumstances, § 2254(d). In any event, the traditional exception to res judicata for habeas corpus review, see Preiser v.

Rodriguez, 411 U.S. 475, 497, provides no analogy to § 1983 cases, since that exception finds its source in the unique purpose of habeas corpus—to release the applicant for the writ from unlawful confinement.

14. To the extent that Congress in the post-Civil War period did intend to deny full faith and credit to state-court decisions on constitutional issues, it expressly chose the very different means of postjudgment removal for state-court defendants whose civil rights were threatened by biased state courts and who therefore "are denied or cannot enforce [their civil rights] in the courts or judicial tribunals of the State." Act of Apr. 9, 1866, ch. 31, § 3, 14 Stat. 27.

legislative history of § 1983 in Monroe v. Pape, the Court inferred that Congress had intended a federal remedy in three circumstances: where state substantive law was facially unconstitutional, where state procedural law was inadequate to allow full litigation of a constitutional claim, and where state procedural law, though adequate in theory, was inadequate in practice. In short, the federal courts could step in where the state courts were unable or unwilling to protect federal rights. This understanding of § 1983 might well support an exception to res judicata and collateral estoppel where state law did not provide fair procedures for the litigation of constitutional claims, or where a state court failed to even acknowledge the existence of the constitutional principle on which a litigant based his claim. Such an exception, however, would be essentially the same as the important general limit on rules of preclusion that already exists: Collateral estoppel does not apply where the party against whom an earlier court decision is asserted did not have a full and fair opportunity to litigate the claim or issue decided by the first court. But the Court's view of § 1983 in Monroe lends no strength to any argument that Congress intended to allow relitigation of federal issues decided after a full and fair hearing in a state court simply because the state court's decision may have been erroneous.[17]

The Court of Appeals in this case acknowledged that every Court of Appeals that has squarely decided the question has held that collateral estoppel applies when § 1983 plaintiffs attempt to relitigate in federal court issues decided against them in state criminal proceedings. But the court * * * concluded that since Stone v. Powell had removed McCurry's right to a hearing of his Fourth Amendment claim in federal habeas corpus, collateral estoppel should not deprive him of a federal judicial hearing of that claim in a § 1983 suit.

Stone v. Powell does not provide a logical doctrinal source for the court's ruling. This Court in Stone assessed the costs and benefits of the judge-made exclusionary rule within the boundaries of the federal courts' statutory power to issue writs of habeas corpus, and decided that the incremental deterrent effect that the issuance of the writ in Fourth Amendment cases might have on police conduct did not justify the cost the writ imposed upon the fair administration of criminal justice. The Stone decision concerns only the prudent exercise of federal-court jurisdiction under 28 U.S.C. § 2254. It has no bearing on § 1983 suits or on the question of the preclusive effect of state-court judgments.

---

17. The dissent suggests that the Court's decision in England v. Medical Examiners, 375 U.S. 411, demonstrates the impropriety of affording preclusive effect to the state-court decision in this case. The England decision is inapposite to the question before us. In the England case, a party first submitted to a federal court his claim that a state statute violated his constitutional rights. The federal court abstained and remitted the plaintiff to the state courts * * *. This Court held that in such a circumstance, a plaintiff who properly reserved the federal issue by informing the state courts of his intention to return to federal court, if necessary, was not precluded from litigating the federal question in federal court. The holding in England depended entirely on this Court's view of the purpose of abstention in such a case: Where a plaintiff properly invokes federal court jurisdiction in the first instance on a federal claim, the federal court has a duty to accept that jurisdiction. Abstention may serve only to postpone, rather than to abdicate, jurisdiction, since its purpose is to determine whether resolution of the federal question is even necessary, or to obviate the risk of a federal court's erroneous construction of state law. These concerns have no bearing whatsoever on the present case.

The actual basis of the Court of Appeals' holding appears to be a generally framed principle that every person asserting a federal right is entitled to one unencumbered opportunity to litigate that right in a federal district court, regardless of the legal posture in which the federal claim arises. But the authority for this principle is difficult to discern. It cannot lie in the Constitution, which makes no such guarantee, but leaves the scope of the jurisdiction of the federal district courts to the wisdom of Congress. And no such authority is to be found in § 1983 itself. For reasons already discussed at length, nothing in the language or legislative history of § 1983 proves any congressional intent to deny binding effect to a state-court judgment or decision when the state court, acting within its proper jurisdiction, has given the parties a full and fair opportunity to litigate federal claims, and thereby has shown itself willing and able to protect federal rights. And nothing in the legislative history of § 1983 reveals any purpose to afford less deference to judgments in state criminal proceedings than to those in state civil proceedings. There is, in short, no reason to believe that Congress intended to provide a person claiming a federal right an unrestricted opportunity to relitigate an issue already decided in state court simply because the issue arose in a state proceeding in which he would rather not have been engaged at all.

Through § 1983, the 42d Congress intended to afford an opportunity for legal and equitable relief in a federal court for certain types of injuries. It is difficult to believe that the drafters of that Act considered it a substitute for a federal writ of habeas corpus, the purpose of which is not to redress civil injury, but to release the applicant from unlawful physical confinement,[24] particularly in light of the extremely narrow scope of federal habeas relief for state prisoners in 1871.

The only other conceivable basis for finding a universal right to litigate a federal claim in a federal district court is hardly a legal basis at all, but rather a general distrust of the capacity of the state courts to render correct decisions on constitutional issues. It is ironic that Stone v. Powell provided the occasion for the expression of such an attitude in the present litigation, in view of this Court's emphatic reaffirmation in that case of the constitutional obligation of the state courts to uphold federal law, and its expression of confidence in their ability to do so.

The Court of Appeals erred in holding that McCurry's inability to obtain federal habeas corpus relief upon his Fourth Amendment claim renders the doctrine of collateral estoppel inapplicable to his § 1983 suit.[25] Accordingly, the judgment is reversed, and the case is remanded to the Court of Appeals for proceedings consistent with this opinion.

It is so ordered.

■ JUSTICE BLACKMUN, with whom JUSTICE BRENNAN and JUSTICE MARSHALL join, dissenting.

---

24. Under the modern statute, federal habeas corpus is bounded by a requirement of exhaustion of state remedies and by special procedural rules, 28 U.S.C. § 2254, which have no counterparts in § 1983, and which therefore demonstrate the continuing illogic of treating federal habeas and § 1983 suits as fungible remedies for constitutional violations.

25. We do not decide *how* the body of collateral-estoppel doctrine or 28 U.S.C. § 1738 should apply in this case.

The legal principles with which the Court is concerned in this civil case obviously far transcend the ugly facts of respondent's criminal convictions in the courts of Missouri for heroin possession and assault.

The Court today holds that notions of collateral estoppel apply with full force to this suit brought under 42 U.S.C. § 1983. In my view, the Court, in so ruling, ignores the clear import of the legislative history of that statute and disregards the important federal policies that underlie its enforcement. It also shows itself insensitive both to the significant differences between the § 1983 remedy and the exclusionary rule, and to the pressures upon a criminal defendant that make a free choice of forum illusory. I do not doubt that principles of preclusion are to be given such effect as is appropriate in a § 1983 action. In many cases, the denial of res judicata or collateral estoppel effect would serve no purpose and would harm relations between federal and state tribunals. Nonetheless, the Court's analysis in this particular case is unacceptable to me. It works injustice on this § 1983 plaintiff, and it makes more difficult the consistent protection of constitutional rights, a consideration that was at the core of the enacters' intent. Accordingly, I dissent.

* * *

* * * Although the legislators of the 42d Congress did not expressly state whether the then existing common-law doctrine of preclusion would survive enactment of § 1983, they plainly anticipated more than the creation of a federal statutory remedy to be administered indifferently by either a state or a federal court. The legislative intent, as expressed by supporters and understood by opponents, was to restructure relations between the state and federal courts. Congress deliberately opened the federal courts to individual citizens in response to the States' failure to provide justice in their own courts. Contrary to the view presently expressed by the Court, the 42d Congress was not concerned solely with procedural regularity. Even where there was procedural regularity, which the Court today so stresses, Congress believed that substantive justice was unobtainable. The availability of the federal forum was not meant to turn on whether, in an individual case, the state procedures were adequate. Assessing the state of affairs as a whole, Congress specifically made a determination that federal oversight of constitutional determinations through the federal courts was necessary to ensure the effective enforcement of constitutional rights.

That the new federal jurisdiction was conceived of as concurrent with state jurisdiction does not alter the significance of Congress' opening the federal courts to these claims. * * *

[Justice Blackmun's analysis of the legislative history is omitted.]

I appreciate that the legislative history is capable of alternative interpretations. I would have thought, however, that our prior decisions made very clear which reading is required. The Court repeatedly has recognized that § 1983 embodies a strong congressional policy in favor of the federal courts' acting as the primary and final arbiters of constitutional rights. In Monroe v. Pape, 365 U.S. 167 (1961), the Court held that Congress passed the legislation in order to substitute a federal forum for the ineffective, though plainly available, state remedies. * * * The Court's conclusion was that this [federal] remedy was to be available no matter what the circumstances of state law * * *. In Mitchum v. Foster, 407 U.S. 225 (1972), the Court reiterated its understanding of the effect of § 1983 upon state and federal relations:

"Section 1983 was thus a product of a vast transformation from the concepts of federalism that had prevailed in the late 18th century.... The very purpose of § 1983 was to interpose the federal courts between the States and the people, as guardians of the people's federal rights * * *." *Id.*, at 242.

At the very least, it is inconsistent now to narrow, if not repudiate, the meaning of Monroe and Mitchum and to alter our prior understanding of the distribution of power between the state and federal courts.

One should also note that in England v. Medical Examiners, 375 U.S. 311 (1964), the Court had affirmed the federal courts' special role in protecting constitutional rights under § 1983.   * * * I do not understand why the Court today should abandon this approach.

The Court now fashions a new doctrine of preclusion, applicable only to actions brought under § 1983, that is more strict and more confining than the federal rules of preclusion applied in other cases.   In Montana v. United States, 440 U.S. 147 (1979), the Court pronounced three major factors to be considered in determining whether collateral estoppel serves as a barrier in the federal court:

"[W]hether the issues presented * * * are in substance the same * * *; whether controlling facts or legal principles have changed significantly since the state-court judgment; and finally whether other special circumstances warrant an exception to the normal rules of preclusion."

But now the Court states that the collateral-estoppel effect of prior state adjudication should turn on only one factor, namely, what it considers the "one general limitation" inherent in the doctrine of preclusion: "that the concept of collateral estoppel cannot apply when the party against whom the earlier decision is asserted did not have a 'full and fair opportunity' to litigate that issue in the earlier case."   If that one factor is present, the Court asserts, the litigant properly should be barred from relitigating the issue in federal court.[12] One cannot deny that this factor is an important one.   I do not believe, however, that the doctrine of preclusion requires the inquiry to be so narrow, and my understanding of the policies underlying § 1983 would lead me to consider all relevant factors in each case before concluding that preclusion was warranted.

In this case, the police officers seek to prevent a criminal defendant from relitigating the constitutionality of their conduct in searching his house, after the state trial court had found that conduct in part violative of the defendant's Fourth Amendment rights and in part justified by the circumstances.   I doubt that the police officers, now defendants in this § 1983 action, can be considered to have been in privity with the State in its role as prosecutor.   Therefore, only "issue preclusion" is at stake.

The following factors persuade me to conclude that this respondent should not be precluded from asserting his claim in federal court.   First, at the time § 1983 was passed, a non-party's ability, as a practical matter, to invoke collateral estoppel was nonexistent.   One could not preclude an opponent from relitigating an issue in a new cause of action, though that issue had been determined conclusively in a prior proceeding, unless there was "mutuality."

---

12. This articulation of the preclusion doctrine of course would bar a § 1983 litigant from relitigating any issue he *might* have raised, as well as any issue he actually litigated in his criminal trial.

Additionally, the definitions of "cause of action" and "issue" were narrow. As a result, and obviously, no preclusive effect could arise out of a criminal proceeding that would affect subsequent *civil* litigation. Thus, the 42d Congress could not have anticipated or approved that a criminal defendant, tried and convicted in state court, would be precluded from raising against police officers a constitutional claim arising out of his arrest.

Also, the process of deciding in a state criminal trial whether to exclude or admit evidence is not at all the equivalent of a § 1983 proceeding. The remedy sought in the latter is utterly different. In bringing the civil suit the criminal defendant does not seek to challenge his conviction collaterally. At most, he wins damages. In contrast, the exclusion of evidence may prevent a criminal conviction. A trial court, faced with the decision whether to exclude relevant evidence, confronts institutional pressures that may cause it to give a different shape to the Fourth Amendment right from what would result in civil litigation of a damages claim. Also, the issue whether to exclude evidence is subsidiary to the purpose of a criminal trial, which is to determine the guilt or innocence of the defendant, and a trial court, at least subconsciously, must weigh the potential damage to the truth-seeking process caused by excluding relevant evidence. * * *

A state criminal defendant cannot be held to have chosen "voluntarily" to litigate his Fourth Amendment claim in the state court. The risk of conviction puts pressure upon him to raise all possible defenses. He also faces uncertainty about the wisdom of forgoing litigation on *any* issue, for there is the possibility that he will be held to have waived his right to appeal on that issue. The "deliberate bypass" of state procedures, which the imposition of collateral estoppel under these circumstances encourages, surely is not a preferred goal. To hold that a criminal defendant who raises a Fourth Amendment claim at his criminal trial "freely and without reservation submits his federal claims for decision by the state courts," see England v. Medical Examiners, 375 U.S., at 419, is to deny reality. The criminal defendant is an involuntary litigant in the state tribunal, and against him all the forces of the State are arrayed. To force him to a choice between forgoing either a potential defense or a federal forum for hearing his constitutional civil claim is fundamentally unfair.

I would affirm the judgment of the Court of Appeals.

NOTE ON 28 U.S.C. § 1738 AND THE RES JUDICATA EFFECT OF STATE JUDGMENTS

(1) *The Rationale of the Allen Decision.*

(a) Although the result in Allen can be readily explained in terms of the requirements of § 1738 and the general rules of full faith and credit reflected in that provision, is the result so easily squared with the jurisprudence that has evolved under § 1983? As developed in earlier chapters, and as emphasized in Justice Blackmun's opinion, that jurisprudence recognizes the right of a litigant asserting a cause of action under § 1983 ordinarily to resort to a federal court, state law and available state remedies notwithstanding. And as both opinions in Allen recognize, when Pullman abstention is appropriate, the federal plaintiff is permitted to retain the ability to return to federal court for a determination of the federal claim. When abstention is required by the doctrine of

Younger v. Harris, should it follow that the principles of res judicata limit the person seeking federal relief to direct Supreme Court review (or collateral habeas corpus review in the case of a criminal conviction)? If one agrees with the view, shared by all the Justices in Allen, that notions of res judicata have a proper place in § 1983 jurisprudence, should the federal courts be permitted, consistently with the spirit of that statute and the context of its enactment, to give special consideration to the interest of a litigant in obtaining a federal court determination of a federal claim?

(b) The Allen Court left open a number of difficult questions. (i) The Court noted the relevance of § 1738 as "background", but at the same time insisted that it was not deciding exactly "how" res judicata applies in § 1983 actions. (ii) The Court reserved the question whether preclusion could or should apply to matters that could have been but were not raised in the state courts, and did not indicate whether this issue turned on federal or state law. (iii) Nor did the Court specify the source or content of the rule that res judicata does not apply when there was no "full and fair opportunity" to litigate. (Is the rule a constitutional principle that generally limits res judicata? Is it simply a short-hand for exceptions found inside the law of res judicata in most states? Or is it a federal rule derived from § 1983?)

Many of these questions have been resolved in the Court's later opinions— opinions that have in turn generated further controversy. See generally Shreve, *Preclusion and Federal Choice of Law,* 64 Tex.L.Rev. 1209 (1986); Burbank, p. 1474, *supra,* at 805–29.[1]

(2) *The Kremer Decision and the Role of State Law.* Kremer v. Chemical Constr. Corp., 456 U.S. 461 (1982), squarely held that § 1738 directs the federal courts to give the same preclusive effect to state court resolutions of federal questions as would be given in the courts of the rendering state, absent a countervailing command in another federal statute. Kremer involved not § 1983, but Title VII of the Civil Rights Act of 1964, which provides that employment discrimination charges must initially be filed with the state agency that administers state antidiscrimination laws. Thereafter, a complainant may file a claim with the federal EEOC, which is required to "accord substantial weight" to the state agency decision. Title VII also gives a complainant the right, after state and federal agency determinations of his claim, to a trial de novo in federal (or state) court. In Kremer the complainant had unsuccessfully appealed an unfavorable state agency determination to the New York courts before filing with the EEOC and, after failing there, bringing suit in a federal district court. By a bare majority, the Supreme Court held that neither the grant in Title VII of a right to a trial de novo, nor the provision that state findings be accorded "substantial weight" by the EEOC, worked an implied partial repeal of § 1738; the state courts' rejection of the claim was therefore

---

1. Consider also the observations of Althouse, *Tapping the State Court Resource,* 44 Vand.L.Rev. 953, 995 (1991): "Regardless of whether the Stone and McCurry doctrines grew out of an antagonism to Fourth Amendment rights, they can now produce favorable results if they are applied with a keen awareness of the need to move the state courts toward the active enforcement of federal rights. This is obviously a big 'if,' and the federal courts' chronic hesitation to scrutinize the behavior of state courts gives little reason for optimism. Yet unless the federal courts abandon their traditional hesitation and engage in vigorous scrutiny, Stone and McCurry represent mere deference to state autonomy and deserve only condemnation."

preclusive to the same extent that it would be in a second action in the New York state courts.

The state court in Kremer had determined only that the state agency's decision had not been "arbitrary or capricious". In dissent, Justice Blackmun argued that because "the Appellate Division made no finding one way or the other concerning the *merits*" of the discrimination claim, "although it claims to grant a state *court* decision preclusive effect, in fact the Court bars petitioner's suit based on the state *agency's* decision of no probable cause. The Court thereby disregards the express provisions of Title VII, for * * * Congress has decided that an adverse state agency decision will not prevent a complainant's subsequent Title VII suit" (pp. 492–93).

Is there a convincing answer to Justice Blackmun's argument?

The Court in Kremer also considered the "full and fair opportunity to litigate" exception to preclusion. Noting that neither the source nor content of the exception had been specified in previous cases, the Court stated that "for present purposes, where we are bound by the statutory directive of § 1738, state proceedings need do no more than satisfy the minimum procedural requirements of the Fourteenth Amendment's Due Process Clause in order to qualify for the full faith and credit guaranteed by federal law" (p. 481). Since a state "may not grant preclusive effect in its own courts to a constitutionally infirm judgment," this requirement is consistent with § 1738; "other state and federal courts would still be providing a state court judgment with the 'same' preclusive effect as the courts of the State from which the judgment emerged. In such a case, there could be no constitutionally recognizable preclusion at all" (pp. 482–83).[2]

(3) *The Migra Decision.* Further ambiguities in the Court's opinion in Allen v. McCurry were resolved in Migra v. Warren City School Dist., 465 U.S. 75 (1984), in an opinion—this time for a surprisingly unanimous Court—written by Justice Blackmun.[3]

Migra involved an elementary school supervisor who had been fired from her job. She brought a successful suit in the Ohio courts for damages and reinstatement, alleging only breach of contract and tortious interference with an employment contract. Thereafter she brought a second action under § 1983 in federal court, this time alleging that her dismissal violated the First, Fifth, and Fourteenth Amendments, and seeking, *inter alia,* punitive damages. The

---

2. For further extension of the reach of § 1738, see Parsons Steel, Inc. v. First Alabama Bank, 474 U.S. 518 (1986)(whether state-court rejection of res judicata claim with respect to earlier federal judgment is itself res judicata in a later federal action to enjoin the enforcement of the state court judgment depends, under § 1738, on the state's res judicata law; 28 U.S.C. § 2283 does not create an implied exception to § 1738).

3. Between Kremer and Migra the Court decided Haring v. Prosise, 462 U.S. 306 (1983), holding that a state court guilty plea to a charge of manufacturing illegal drugs did not preclude a § 1983 action against state police who had obtained the evidence leading

to the charge. The Court said that § 1738 did not require preclusion, because the relevant state law did not require it. The Court also went on, however, to suggest that preclusion may be negated as a matter of federal policy or by special circumstances. For a summary of arguments lending support to this suggestion, see Paragraph (4), *infra.* And see generally the discussion in 18 Federal Practice §§ 4471, 4474, at 521–25, 602–06 (1995 Supp.).

On the question of preclusion considered in Haring, see Shapiro, *Should a Guilty Plea Have Preclusive Effect?,* 70 Iowa L.Rev. 27 (1984).

Supreme Court held that § 1738 governs and requires claim preclusion to the same extent that preclusive effect would be given by the Ohio courts. It rejected plaintiff's argument that the Court should "interpret the interplay between § 1738 and § 1983 in such a way as to accord state-court judgments preclusive effect in § 1983 suits only as to issues actually litigated in state courts" (p. 83). The Court went on to say (pp. 83–85):

"It is difficult to see how the policy concerns underlying § 1983 would justify a distinction between the issue preclusive and claim preclusive effects of state-court judgments. The argument that state-court judgments should have less preclusive effect in § 1983 suits than in other federal suits is based on Congress' expressed concern over the adequacy of state courts as protectors of federal rights. * * * Allen recognized that the enactment of § 1983 was motivated partially out of such concern, but Allen nevertheless held that § 1983 did not open the way to relitigation of an issue that had been determined in a state criminal proceeding. Any distrust of state courts that would justify a limitation on the preclusive effect of state judgments in § 1983 suits would presumably apply equally to issues that actually were decided in a state court as well as to those that could have been. If § 1983 created an exception to the general preclusive effect accorded to state-court judgments, such an exception would seem to require similar treatment of both issue preclusion and claim preclusion. Having rejected in Allen the view that state-court judgments have no issue preclusive effect in § 1983 suits, we must reject the view that § 1983 prevents the judgment in petitioner's state-court proceeding from creating a claim preclusion bar in this case.

"* * *

"In the present litigation, petitioner does not claim that the state court would not have adjudicated her federal claims had she presented them in her original suit in state court. Alternatively, petitioner could have obtained a federal forum for her federal claim by litigating it first in a federal court.[4] Section 1983, however, does not override state preclusion law and guarantee petitioner a right to proceed to judgment in state court on her state claims and then turn to federal court for adjudication of her federal claims. We hold, therefore, that petitioner's state-court judgment in this litigation has the same claim preclusive effect in federal court that the judgment would have in the Ohio state courts."

The Court remanded the case to the district court with the order to "interpret Ohio preclusion law and apply it" (p. 87).

Justice White's concurrence, joined by Chief Justice Burger and Justice Powell, stated that it would be desirable to allow federal courts to use federal res judicata law to give state court judgments preclusive effect even if state res judicata doctrine would not bar relitigation in the state courts. However, in view of the "long standing" construction of § 1738 as allowing a federal court

---

4. "The author of this opinion was in dissent in Allen. The rationale of that dissent, however, was based largely on the fact that the § 1983 plaintiff in that case first litigated his constitutional claim in state court in the posture of his being a *defendant* in a criminal proceeding. In this case, petitioner was in an offensive posture in her state-court proceeding, and could have proceeded first in federal court had she wanted to litigate her federal claim in a federal forum. * * *"

to give a state judgment "no greater efficacy" than would the judgment-rendering state, Justice White agreed with the Court's disposition (p. 88).[5]

(4) *Arguments for Alternative Approaches.* Several commentators have taken issue with the Court's assumption that under § 1738, the preclusive effect of a state court judgment on an issue of federal law is measured entirely by state preclusion law (subject only to due process limits or to congressional repeal of § 1738 with respect to particular matters). Professor Burbank, in *Interjurisdictional Preclusion, Full Faith and Credit and Federal Common Law: A General Approach,* 71 Cornell L.Rev. 733 (1986), and in *Federal Judgments Law: Sources of Authority and Sources of Rules,* 70 Tex.L.Rev. 1551 (1992), argues that § 1738 does not invariably require a federal court to apply the preclusion law of the rendering state. Although a state court determining the preclusive effect of a prior state judgment involving federal law would usually apply the forum state's res judicata law, in some cases federal common law rules governing preclusion should supervene.

Thus, Burbank suggests that even if, in a case like Allen v. McCurry, the subsequent § 1983 action had been filed in state court, a state court might be required to apply federal common law limiting the preclusive effect of a ruling on a search and seizure question in a suppression hearing in which no discovery is available and the rules of evidence do not apply. In short, because § 1738 mandates only that the federal court apply the same law that the state court would, a federal court should apply federal common law rules in those instances when a state court would be obligated to do so.

Consider in this regard the reiteration, in ASARCO Inc. v. Kadish, 490 U.S. 605 (1989), p. 155, *supra,* of suggestions in earlier decisions that if a state court decision on a question of federal law cannot be reviewed by the Supreme Court (because the state proceedings did not satisfy Article III's justiciability requirements), the state court decision might not have res judicata effect. In ASARCO, no reference was made to the line of decisions, beginning with Allen v. McCurry, that read § 1738 as obliging the federal courts to adhere to state res judicata doctrine. Don't ASARCO and the precedents on which it relies in effect recognize federal power, when federal policy so requires, to deny res judicata effect to state court decisions on questions of federal law—even when state res judicata doctrine would dictate otherwise?

For an argument similar to Burbank's, see Luneberg, *The Opportunity to be Heard and the Doctrines of Preclusion: Federal Limits on State Law,* 31 Vill.L.Rev. 81 (1986). See also Braveman & Goldsmith, *Rules of Preclusion and Challenges to Official Action: An Essay on Finality, Fairness and Federalism, All Gone Awry,* 39 Syracuse L.Rev. 599 (1988)(advocating construction of § 1738 to permit case-by-case exceptions to preclusion as a matter of federal law to prevent unfair results).

(5) *Cases Involving Exclusive Federal Jurisdiction.*

(a) Marrese v. American Academy of Orthopaedic Surgeons, 470 U.S. 373 (1985), touches on the thorny question of the preclusive effect of a state court judgment on a later federal action within the exclusive jurisdiction of the federal courts. This case involved an action brought in state court asserting

---

5. For discussion and criticism of the implication of statements in Supreme Court opinions suggesting that federal courts may not give a state court judgment more preclu-sive effect than the state court would give it, see 18 Federal Practice § 4471, at 525 (1995 Supp.).

that the Academy's denial of membership to plaintiff violated Illinois law. After a defeat in the state courts, plaintiff brought a new action in federal court, alleging a violation of the federal antitrust laws—a claim over which the federal courts have exclusive jurisdiction and which could not, therefore, have been joined in the state action. The Seventh Circuit, in an interesting array of opinions, applied federal res judicata doctrine in holding that the federal action was barred. 726 F.2d 1150 (7th Cir.1984). In the Supreme Court, Justice O'Connor said that the lower courts had erred in not taking account of Illinois preclusion law under § 1738, which "requires a federal court to look first to state preclusion law in determining the preclusive effect of a state court judgment" (p. 381). Acknowledging that Illinois law would have no "occasion to address the specific question whether a state judgment has issue or claim preclusive effect in a later action that can be brought only in federal court," the Court pointed out that Illinois res judicata law might nevertheless address the more general question whether claim preclusion forecloses related claims that were not within the jurisdiction of the rendering court. Ordinarily, the Court said, claim preclusion does not apply in such situations. If Illinois adheres to that rule, the federal courts under § 1738 must also do so and may not give preclusive effect to the Illinois judgment. "States * * * determine the preclusive scope of their own courts' judgments. * * * These concerns certainly are not made less compelling because state courts lack jurisdiction over federal antitrust claims. We therefore reject a judicially created exception to § 1738 that effectively holds as a matter of federal law that a plaintiff can bring state law claims initially in state court only at the cost of forgoing subsequent federal antitrust claims" (pp. 385–86).

The Court went on to state that it would not determine whether preclusion would be required if the preclusion law of Illinois did apply to closely related claims even when one was not within the jurisdiction of the rendering court. The Court stated that in determining whether an exception is to be made to § 1738 for a particular class of federal claims, such as an antitrust claim, the question is "whether the concerns underlying a particular grant of exclusive jurisdiction justify a finding of an implied partial repeal of § 1738" (p. 386). The case was remanded for an inquiry into Illinois law.

Does this last point (as well as the Court's suggestion in Haring v. Prosise, note 3, *supra*) lend support to the arguments of Professor Burbank and others, discussed in Paragraph (4)?

(b) The Marrese case leaves unexplored the difficult question whether and when state preclusion rules can be defeated by the policies that led Congress to provide for exclusive federal jurisdiction over a certain class of claims. The extraordinary array of approaches to this question is explored in depth in 18 Federal Practice § 4470 (1995 Supp.). A celebrated treatment of the question in the context of issue preclusion is Judge Learned Hand's opinion in Lyons v. Westinghouse Elec. Corp., 222 F.2d 184 (2d Cir.1955), holding that a state court determination of an antitrust defense in a contract action did not bind the federal court in a later federal antitrust action. On the other hand, the Third Circuit held that where a patentee, suing to recover royalties under a license agreement, lost in state court on the ground that the patent did not cover the defendant's goods, the patentee was barred thereafter from maintaining a federal patent infringement suit with respect to the identical goods. Vanderveer v. Erie Malleable Iron Co., 238 F.2d 510 (3d Cir.1956). The question has also arisen in such areas as securities litigation and bankruptcy.

The Restatement 2d § 26 provides that rules against splitting causes of action do not apply where the plaintiff was barred from submitting a "certain theory of the case" because of limitations on the subject matter jurisdiction of the rendering court; and a specific illustration (p. 237) states that if A sues B in a state court on a state antitrust claim and loses on the merits, A is not thereafter barred from bringing a federal antitrust action against B in federal court. Compare § 28, Subsection (2) and comment *d* (flexible rule with respect to issue preclusion).

Should there be a single answer to this problem? Note the following factors: (i) the nature and strength of the policies that led Congress to the decision to make federal jurisdiction exclusive, and (ii) the particular sort of preclusion in question (*e.g.,* claim preclusion or issue preclusion? issue preclusion with respect to an issue of fact or of law? mutual or nonmutual issue preclusion?).[6]

(6) *The Res Judicata Effect of State Administrative Decisions.* In University of Tennessee v. Elliott, 478 U.S. 788 (1986), the Court extended the notion that the preclusive effect of state proceedings on the federal courts is to be measured by state law. A state administrative law judge determined that Elliott's discharge from his university job had not been motivated by racial prejudice, and this finding was upheld on administrative appeal. Rather than seeking review of these agency determinations in the Tennessee courts, Elliott filed Title VII and § 1983 claims in a federal district court. The Supreme Court ruled that § 1738 was inapplicable, because it governs only the preclusive effect of "judicial" proceedings. Nevertheless, the Court noted that it had "frequently fashioned federal common-law rules of preclusion in the absence of a governing statute", and that "because § 1738 antedates the development of administrative agencies it clearly does not represent a congressional determination that the decisions of state administrative agencies should not be given preclusive effect" (p. 794–95). The Court held that a rule giving unreviewed state administrative proceedings preclusive effect would be inconsistent with Title VII's provision for a trial de novo following agency action. As to § 1983 actions, however, the Court held that factfinding by a state agency acting in a judicial capacity was to be given the preclusive effect to which it would be entitled in the state's courts. Citing Allen v. McCurry for the proposition that Congress had not intended § 1983 "to repeal or restrict the traditional doctrines of preclusion", and United States v. Utah Constr. & Mining Co., 384 U.S. 394 (1966), for the proposition that federal agency factfinding has preclusive effect (p. 797), the Court held that the traditional purposes of preclusion are "equally implicated whether factfinding is done by a federal or state agency" (p. 798).[7]

6. Consider, for instance, a holding by a state court, in adjudicating a defense in a contract action, that the plaintiff's patent is invalid. Even if that holding is binding in a subsequent federal infringement action by the same plaintiff against the same defendant, should it be binding, under the Blonder Tongue case, in an infringement action against a different defendant?

7. Dissenting as to the § 1983 issue, Justice Stevens said preclusion would not serve finality or federalism objectives, be-cause the complainant could still take his companion Title VII claim to federal court, and because "litigants apprised of this decision will presumably forgo state administrative determinations for the same reason they currently forgo state judicial review of those determinations—to protect their entitlement to a federal forum" (p. 801).

In Astoria Federal Savings and Loan Ass'n v. Solimino, 501 U.S. 104 (1991), the Court held that a judicially unreviewed state

Recall that in Patsy v. Florida Bd. of Regents, p. 1225, *supra,* the Court held that a § 1983 plaintiff does not have to exhaust state administrative remedies. In light of that holding, was it wise for the Court to discourage voluntary resort to state administrative procedures by creating a risk that administrative findings may bar the § 1983 action entirely? On the other hand, recall also the holding in Ohio Civil Rights Comm'n v. Dayton Christian Schools, p. 1225, *supra,* that Younger bars interference with a pending state administrative enforcement proceeding. Aren't the consequences of that holding intensified by the Elliott case?

Do Patsy, Dayton Christian Schools, and Elliott, together, create a sensible system of deference to state administrative processes?[8]

(7) *The Res Judicata Effects of Determinations in State Court Class Actions.* Many of the problems discussed in this Note, as well as difficult additional questions, are raised by state court class actions that are settled or adjudicated and then are followed by federal actions presenting related issues.[9] Take, for example, a state court case in which a class is certified and the action is ultimately settled, with the court's approval, on terms that include a release by the plaintiff class of "all claims relating to the transactions complained of". Assume that a subsequent class action brought in a federal court involves the same class members (but different representative plaintiffs) and is based on a claim relating to the same transactions as the state action, but the legal theory is grounded on an alleged violation of the federal securities laws—a violation that falls within the exclusive original jurisdiction of the federal courts. If a state court would apply claim and issue preclusion to an analogous action in a state court, does § 1738, as interpreted in Marrese and other cases, require the federal court to follow state law? Clearly not, to the extent that a holding of preclusion would violate federal constitutional requirements with respect to such questions as notice, adequacy of representation, and possible opt-out rights afforded in the initial action (see, *e.g.,* Phillips Petroleum Co. v. Shutts, 472 U.S. 797 (1985)). Are there additional reasons rooted in federal substantive and procedural law for disregarding the state's preclusion rules, in whole or in part?

For an example of such a case, in which the federal action was held to be precluded under § 1738, see Grimes v. Vitalink Communications Corp., 17 F.3d 1553 (3d Cir.1994). For a case in which the subsequent federal action was held

---

administrative agency determination had no preclusive effect in a subsequent federal action under the Age Discrimination in Employment Act (ADEA). Relying on its similar holding under Title VII in Elliott, the Court in Astoria stated that the "lenient presumption" in favor of preclusion was overcome by evidence of congressional intent in enacting the ADEA (p. 112).

8. Suppose that state law does not give unreviewed administrative findings res judicata effect, but provides for a narrow scope of review of such findings by the state courts. If the Younger doctrine does not preclude a § 1983 action under these circumstances, should a federal court in such an action,

brought before any judicial review is sought in the state courts, consider such state law to be analogous to state preclusion rules and thus applicable under Elliott?

9. Indeed, many issues raised in other chapters are often acutely presented in the context of related or parallel class actions in state and federal courts—issues that have been brought into sharp focus by the advent of litigation involving mass or toxic torts. See., *e.g.,* Chap. VII, p. 805, *supra* (federal common law); Chap. X., p. 1205, *supra* (anti-suit injunction). Moreover, class actions in federal courts often raise unique issues of justiciability. See, *e.g.,* Chap. II, p. 146, 236, *supra* (standing; mootness).

not precluded, see Epstein v. MCA, Inc., 50 F.3d 644, 657–67 (9th Cir.), cert. granted *sub nom*. Matsushita Elec. Indus. Co. v. Epstein, 115 S.Ct. 2576 (1995).

SECTION 2. OTHER ASPECTS OF CONCURRENT OR SUCCESSIVE JURISDICTION

Rooker v. Fidelity Trust Company

263 U.S. 413, 44 S.Ct. 149, 68 L.Ed. 362 (1923).
Appeal From the District Court of the United States for the District of Indiana.

■ MR. JUSTICE VAN DEVANTER delivered the opinion of the Court.

This is a bill in equity to have a judgment of a circuit court in Indiana, which was affirmed by the Supreme Court of the State, declared null and void, and to obtain other relief dependent on that outcome. An effort to have the judgment reviewed by this Court on writ of error had failed because the record did not disclose the presence of any question constituting a basis for such a review. The parties to the bill are the same as in the litigation in the state court, but with an addition of two defendants whose presence does not need special notice. All are citizens of the same State. The grounds advanced for resorting to the District Court are that the judgment was rendered and affirmed in contravention of the contract clause of the Constitution of the United States and the due process of law and equal protection clauses of the Fourteenth Amendment, in that it gave effect to a state statute alleged to be in conflict with those clauses and did not give effect to a prior decision in the same cause by the Supreme Court of the State which is alleged to have become the "law of the case." The District Court was of opinion that the suit was not within its jurisdiction as defined by Congress, and on that ground dismissed the bill. The plaintiffs have appealed directly to this court * * *.

The appellees move that the appeal be dismissed, or in the alternative that the decree be affirmed.

The appeal is within the first clause of § 238; so the motion to dismiss must be overruled. But the suit is so plainly not within the District Court's jurisdiction as defined by Congress that the motion to affirm must be sustained.

It affirmatively appears from the bill that the judgment was rendered in a cause wherein the circuit court had jurisdiction of both the subject matter and the parties; that a full hearing was had therein; that the judgment was responsive to the issues, and that it was affirmed by the Supreme Court of the State on an appeal by the plaintiffs. If the constitutional questions stated in the bill actually arose in the cause, it was the province and duty of the state courts to decide them; and their decision, whether right or wrong, was an exercise of jurisdiction. If the decision was wrong, that did not make the judgment void, but merely left it open to reversal or modification in an appropriate and timely appellate proceeding. Unless and until so reversed or modified, it would be an effective and conclusive adjudication. * * * Under the legislation of Congress, no court of the United States other than this Court could entertain a proceeding to reverse or modify the judgment for errors of that character. Judicial Code, § 237. To do so would be an exercise of appellate jurisdiction. The jurisdiction possessed by the District Courts is strictly original. Judicial Code, § 24. Besides, the period within which a proceeding might be begun for the correction of errors such as are charged in the bill had expired before it was filed, Act September 6, 1916, c. 448, § 6, and * * * after that period elapses an aggrieved litigant cannot be permitted to do indirectly what he no longer can do directly.

Some parts of the bill speak of the judgment as given without jurisdiction and absolutely void; but this is merely mistaken characterization. A reading of the entire bill shows indubitably that there was full jurisdiction in the state courts and that the bill at best is merely an attempt to get rid of the judgment for alleged errors of law committed in the exercise of that jurisdiction.

In what has been said we have proceeded on the assumption that the constitutional questions alleged to have arisen in the state courts respecting the validity of a state statute, Acts 1915, c. 62, and the effect to be given to a prior decision in the same cause by the Supreme Court of the State, 185 Ind. 172, were questions of substance * * *.

Decree affirmed.

_____

NOTE ON THE ROOKER DOCTRINE AND ON THE INTERPLAY AMONG RES JUDICATA, EXCLUSIVE JURISDICTION, AND COMITY

(1) *The Feldman Decision.* The Rooker case, apparently holding that the grant of statutory jurisdiction to the Supreme Court to review state court judgments furnished an independent basis for prohibiting collateral attack on those judgments, was largely forgotten until revived in Chang, *Rediscovering the Rooker Doctrine: Section 1983, Res Judicata and the Federal Courts,* 31 Hastings L.J. 1337 (1980).

Rooker's analysis was thereafter used as the basis for the Court's decision in District of Columbia Court of Appeals v. Feldman, 460 U.S. 462 (1983). In that case two applicants for membership in the District of Columbia bar asked the District of Columbia Court of Appeals—the "local" court authorized by statute to supervise D.C. bar admission matters—to waive the normal rule that requires applicants to have graduated from an ABA-accredited law school. After various proceedings, that court by per curiam order denied the applications for waivers, notwithstanding the applicants' arguments that denial would deprive them of constitutional rights. Applicants thereafter filed complaints in the United States District Court for the District of Columbia, challenging the denial of the waiver applications and the constitutional validity of the relevant bar admission rules. The district court dismissed for lack of subject matter jurisdiction, but was reversed by the court of appeals.

The Supreme Court held that the district court did not have jurisdiction over the actions to challenge the validity of the waivers. Noting that final judgments of the D.C. Court of Appeals are reviewable by the Supreme Court under § 1257, the Supreme Court held that the district court "is without authority to review final determinations of the District of Columbia Court of Appeals in judicial proceedings [citing Rooker]" (p. 476). It then considered whether the rulings of the D.C. Court of Appeals, denying the petitions for waiver, constituted "judicial" proceedings, and concluded that they did. The proceedings were not legislative, ministerial, or administrative. * * * Instead, the proceedings * * * involved a "judicial inquiry" in which the court was called upon to investigate, declare, and enforce "liabilities as they [stood] on present or past facts and under laws supposed already to exist" [citing Prentis v. Atlantic Coast Line Co., 211 U.S. at 226, p. 1223, *supra*] (p. 479). Consequently, said the Court, the district court lacked subject matter jurisdiction over these complaints; applicants "should have sought review of the District of Columbia Court of Appeals' judgments in this Court."[1]

The Court held, on the other hand, that the applicants' "general challenge" to the constitutionality of the rule requiring graduation from a law school for bar admission was within the district court's jurisdiction. The Court stated that there is a distinction between "seeking review in a federal district court of a state court's final judgment in a bar admission matter and challenging the validity of a state bar admission rule" (pp. 483–84).

The Court "expressly" did not reach the question "whether the doctrine of res judicata forecloses litigation of the latter claims" (p. 487).[2]

Justice Stevens, dissenting, said (pp. 489–90):

"[E]ven if the refusal to grant a waiver were an adjudication, the federal statute that confers jurisdiction upon the United States District Court to entertain a constitutional challenge to the rules themselves also authorizes that court to entertain a collateral attack upon the unconstitutional application of those rules. The Court's opinion fails to distinguish between two concepts: appellate review and collateral attack. If a challenge to a state court's decision is brought in United States district court and alleges violations of the United States Constitution, then by definition it does not seek appellate review. It is plainly within the federal-question jurisdiction of the federal court. There may be other reasons for denying relief to the plaintiff—such as failure to state a cause of action, claim or issue preclusion, or failure to prove a violation of constitutional rights. But it does violence to jurisdictional concepts for this Court to hold, as it does, that the federal district court has no *jurisdiction* to conduct independent review of a specific claim that a licensing body's action did not comply with federal constitutional standards. The fact that the licensing function in the legal profession is controlled by the judiciary is not a sufficient reason to immunize allegedly unconstitutional conduct from review in the federal courts."

---

1. In an elaborate footnote (p. 482 n. 16) the Court noted that Supreme Court review of the denial of applicants' requests for admission might be barred if they failed to raise their constitutional claims in the "state" court. It then went on expressly to disapprove the holding of the Fifth Circuit in Dasher v. Supreme Court of Texas, 658 F.2d 1045 (5th Cir.1981), that in such a case a district court may review a bar admission denial precisely because the Supreme Court could not. "[T]he fact that we may not have jurisdiction to review a final state court judgment because of a petitioner's failure to raise his constitutional claims in state court does not mean that a United States district court should have jurisdiction over the claims."

2. The doctrine of the Rooker and Feldman cases has also been applied by the lower federal courts. One significant recent decision is Guarino v. Larsen, 11 F.3d 1151 (3d Cir.1993), in which, without reaching the issues of possible preclusion, the court held that there was no federal jurisdiction to entertain a § 1983 action by a retired state judge who claimed that his assignment had been unconstitutionally revoked by the state court. The Third Circuit held that while the original order revoking the assignment was not "adjudicative", the subsequent state supreme court determination upholding the revocation was, and therefore could be challenged only on review by the U.S. Supreme Court.

(2) *Critique of the Rooker–Feldman Doctrine.* What do Rooker and Feldman add to the doctrine of res judicata and to § 1738?

(a) Suppose, first, that under state res judicata doctrine, a collateral challenge to a state court judgment would be barred in the state's own courts. Wouldn't a collateral challenge in a federal court normally be barred by § 1738? Does § 1257 now furnish an independent statutory basis for that result? What turns on labeling the result a lack of jurisdiction in the district court to review the state court judgment, rather than an application of res judicata? (Does the reformulation suggest that the case might be dismissed even if the defendant does not object to the action?)

Note that the Court in Feldman held that the district court had "jurisdiction" to consider the plaintiffs' attack on the validity of the bar admission rules, but left open the question whether this latter attack was barred as a matter of claim or issue preclusion. Do the resulting distinctions make sense? Is the Court saying that the preclusive effect of a state court's ruling on the validity *as applied* of a state bar admission rule is governed by § 1257's grant of exclusive appellate jurisdiction to the Supreme Court, whereas the preclusive effect of its judgment on the question whether that same rule is valid on its face is tested by the law of res judicata? If so, why should this be so?

(b) Now assume that an original action of the sort at issue in Feldman, challenging on constitutional grounds the state supreme court's denial of waiver, *could* be maintained in the state courts. Does the Rooker–Feldman doctrine hold that a federal action is impermissible nevertheless? What would this do to the Court's insistence, in its § 1738 cases, that the preclusive effect in a federal court of a state court judgment must be measured by state law? See *Note on § 1738 and the Res Judicata Effect of State Judgments,* p. 1492, *supra.*

When a federal district court is asked to reopen issues already adjudicated by another federal district court, the law of res judicata ordinarily determines whether reopening is permissible. Would it help the analysis to ask, independently, whether the second inquiry is precluded by 28 U.S.C. § 1291—the statute governing the federal courts of appeals' "exclusive" jurisdiction to review final district court judgments?

(c) Rooker and Feldman both involved state court proceedings that were complete when district court challenges were initiated; there was no occasion to inquire whether state remedies should be exhausted before the federal action is entertained, or whether comity principles barred the action. But note that the "exclusive jurisdiction" notion underlying Rooker–Feldman could, theoretically, also be relevant in cases where state proceedings are still underway, and where the applicable doctrines in play have been thought to be those of comity, abstention, and exhaustion, rather than res judicata. (See, in this connection, the discussion of Huffman v. Pursue and related cases in Chap. X, Sec. 2(C), p. 1289, *supra.*)

(3) *The Pennzoil–Texaco Litigation: A Case Study.* The relationship among Rooker–Feldman and other doctrines canvassed in earlier chapters was dramatically presented by the celebrated case of Pennzoil Co. v. Texaco, Inc., 481 U.S. 1 (1987), a case whose facts and outcome are fully discussed in Chapter X, p. 1303, *supra.*[3] Among the themes raised by that litigation (in which the

---

3. Briefly stated, the case was one in which Texaco brought a § 1983 action in a   federal court seeking a stay of the enforcement of a multibillion dollar state court judg-

Supreme Court ultimately decided to require federal court abstention) were the following:

(a) *The Anti–Injunction Act.* Texaco's federal court action to enjoin Pennzoil from enforcing its state court judgment pending an appeal would not have been barred by § 2283 if the action was one properly brought under § 1983. (See Mitchum v. Foster, p. 1195, *supra.*) That question turned in part on whether Pennzoil's effort to enforce the judgment sufficiently involved action by or on behalf of the state (*i.e.,* "under color" of state law)—a question not reached by a majority of the Court. How do you think it should be decided?

(b) *Younger v. Harris.* The court of appeals held that the Younger rationale (pp. 1256–75, *supra*) did not apply to "private" proceedings in the state courts, and that to apply Younger would undermine Mitchum. Pennzoil argued that if there was state action for § 1983 purposes, there was also a sufficient state interest for purposes of the Younger doctrine. The Supreme Court, without explicitly addressing these issues, did hold the Younger abstention doctrine applicable. Do you agree?

(c) *Rooker–Feldman.* Pennzoil argued, in addition, that the rationale of the Rooker–Feldman doctrine, properly understood, denied the lower federal courts any authority to displace state courts (and ultimately the Supreme Court) in the appellate process. A majority of the Justices explicitly rejected this argument. Were they correct in doing so?

Where a litigant seeks to enjoin a pending state proceeding, what independent significance should the Rooker–Feldman doctrine have? If an injunction is permissible under Younger, should the doctrine cut in to prevent it? *Per contra,* if interference is prohibited by Younger (as supplemented by Huffman v. Pursue), what need is there for Rooker–Feldman?

(4) *A Proposed Reformulation.* Should Rooker–Feldman be reformulated so that, instead of operating as an independent doctrine, it would simply serve to remind courts that where a collateral attack is mounted on a pending or completed state proceeding, one of the consequences of allowing the attack is to interfere with Congress' contemplated plan for review of state court judgments by the Supreme Court under § 1257? See Note, 42 Rutgers L.Rev. 859 (1990)(supporting such a reformulation).[4]

Heck v. Humphrey

___ U.S. ___, 114 S.Ct. 2364, 129 L.Ed.2d 383 (1994).
Certiorari to the United States Court of Appeals for the Seventh Circuit.

■ JUSTICE SCALIA delivered the opinion of the Court.

This case presents the question whether a state prisoner may challenge the constitutionality of his conviction in a suit for damages under 42 U.S.C. § 1983.

ment against it that had been obtained by Pennzoil. Texaco alleged that the bond and lien provisions of state law placed such draconian requirements on Texaco in order to obtain a stay of enforcement that they imposed an unconstitutional burden on Texaco's ability to appeal the adverse judgment to a higher state court.

4. For a recent decision declining to apply the Rooker–Feldman doctrine to bar a federal court action by the United States when the US was not a party to the state litigation, see Johnson v. DeGrandy, 114 S.Ct. 2647, 2654 (1994).

I

Petitioner Roy Heck was convicted in Indiana state court of voluntary manslaughter for the killing of Rickie Heck, his wife, and is serving a 15–year sentence in an Indiana prison. While the appeal from his conviction was pending, petitioner, proceeding pro se, filed this suit in Federal District Court under 42 U.S.C. § 1983, naming as defendants respondents James Humphrey and Robert Ewbank, Dearborn County prosecutors, and Michael Krinoph, an investigator with the Indiana State Police. The complaint alleged that respondents, acting under color of state law, had engaged in an "unlawful, unreasonable, and arbitrary investigation" leading to petitioner's arrest; "knowingly destroyed" evidence "which was exculpatory in nature and could have proved [petitioner's] innocence"; and caused "an illegal and unlawful voice identification procedure" to be used at petitioner's trial. The complaint sought, among other things, compensatory and punitive monetary damages. It did not ask for injunctive relief, and petitioner has not sought release from custody in this action.

The District Court dismissed the action without prejudice, because the issues it raised "directly implicate the legality of [petitioner's] confinement." While petitioner's appeal to the Seventh Circuit was pending, the Indiana Supreme Court upheld his conviction and sentence on direct appeal; his first petition for a writ of habeas corpus in Federal District Court was dismissed because it contained unexhausted claims; and his second federal habeas petition was denied, and the denial affirmed by the Seventh Circuit.

When the Seventh Circuit reached petitioner's appeal from dismissal of his § 1983 complaint, it affirmed the judgment and approved the reasoning of the District Court: "If, regardless of the relief sought, the plaintiff [in a federal civil rights action] is challenging the legality of his conviction, so that if he won his case the state would be obliged to release him even if he hadn't sought that relief, the suit is classified as an application for habeas corpus and the plaintiff must exhaust his state remedies, on pain of dismissal if he fails to do so." Heck filed a petition for certiorari, which we granted.[2]

II

This case lies at the intersection of the two most fertile sources of federal-court prisoner litigation—the Civil Rights Act of 1871, 42 U.S.C. § 1983, and the federal habeas corpus statute, 28 U.S.C. § 2254. Both of these provide access

---

2. Neither in his petition for certiorari nor in his principal brief on the merits did petitioner contest the description of his monetary claims (by both the District Court and the Court of Appeals) as challenging the legality of his conviction. Thus, the question we understood to be before us was whether money damages premised on an unlawful conviction could be pursued under § 1983. Petitioner sought to challenge this premise in his reply brief, contending that findings validating his damages claims would not invalidate his conviction. That argument comes too late. We did not take this case to review such a fact-bound issue, and we accept the characterization of the lower courts.

We also decline to pursue, without implying the nonexistence of, another issue, suggested by the Court of Appeals' statement that, if petitioner's "conviction were proper, this suit would in all likelihood be barred by res judicata." The res judicata effect of state-court decisions in § 1983 actions is a matter of state law. See Migra v. Warren City School Dist. Bd. of Ed., 465 U.S. 75 (1984).

to a federal forum for claims of unconstitutional treatment at the hands of state officials, but they differ in their scope and operation. In general, exhaustion of state remedies "is *not* a prerequisite to an action under § 1983," Patsy v. Board of Regents of Fla., 457 U.S. 496, 501 (1982)(emphasis added), even an action by a state prisoner, *id.*, at 509. The federal habeas corpus statute, by contrast, requires that state prisoners first seek redress in a state forum.

Preiser v. Rodriguez, 411 U.S. 475 (1973), considered the potential overlap between these two provisions, and held that habeas corpus is the exclusive remedy for a state prisoner who challenges the fact or duration of his confinement and seeks immediate or speedier release, even though such a claim may come within the literal terms of § 1983. We emphasize that Preiser did not create an exception to the "no exhaustion" rule of § 1983; it merely held that certain claims by state prisoners are not cognizable under that provision, and must be brought in habeas corpus proceedings, which do contain an exhaustion requirement.

This case is clearly not covered by the holding of Preiser, for petitioner seeks not immediate or speedier release, but monetary damages, as to which he could not "have sought and obtained fully effective relief through federal habeas corpus proceedings." *Id.*, at 488. In dictum, however, Preiser asserted that since a state prisoner seeking only damages "is attacking something other than the fact or length of . . . confinement, and . . . is seeking something other than immediate or more speedy release[,] . . . a damages action by a state prisoner could be brought under [§ 1983] in federal court without any requirement of prior exhaustion of state remedies." 411 U.S., at 494. That statement may not be true, however, when establishing the basis for the damages claim necessarily demonstrates the invalidity of the conviction. In that situation, the claimant *can* be said to be "attacking the fact or length of confinement," bringing the suit within the other dictum of Preiser: "Congress has determined that habeas corpus is the appropriate remedy for state prisoners attacking the validity of the fact or length of their confinement, and that specific determination must override the general terms of § 1983." *Id.*, at 490. In the last analysis, we think the dicta of Preiser to be an unreliable, if not an unintelligible, guide: that opinion had no cause to address, and did not carefully consider, the damages question before us today.

* * * [The Court also found that the question before it had not been resolved by Wolff v. McDonnell, 418 U.S. 539 (1974), which is discussed in Paragraph (1) of the Note following the opinions in this case.]

Thus, the question posed by § 1983 damage claims that do call into question the lawfulness of conviction or confinement remains open. To answer that question correctly, we see no need to abandon, as the Seventh Circuit and those courts in agreement with it have done, our teaching that § 1983 contains no exhaustion requirement beyond what Congress has provided. The issue with respect to monetary damages challenging conviction is not, it seems to us, exhaustion; but rather, the same as the issue was with respect to injunctive relief challenging conviction in Preiser: whether the claim is cognizable under § 1983 at all. We conclude that it is not.

* * *

The common-law cause of action for malicious prosecution provides the closest analogy to claims of the type considered here because, unlike the related cause of action for false arrest or imprisonment, it permits damages for confinement imposed pursuant to legal process.   * * * [A] successful malicious prosecution plaintiff may recover, in addition to general damages, "compensation for any arrest or imprisonment, including damages for discomfort or injury to his health, or loss of time and deprivation of the society" [citing Prosser & Keeton on Torts 887–88 (5th ed. 1984)].

One element that must be alleged and proved in a malicious prosecution action is termination of the prior criminal proceeding in favor of the accused. Prosser and Keeton, supra, at 874.   * * * "[T]o permit a convicted criminal defendant to proceed with a malicious prosecution claim would permit a collateral attack on the conviction through the vehicle of a civil suit" [citing Speiser, Krause & Gans, American Law of Torts § 28:5, at 24 (1991)].[4]   This Court has long expressed similar concerns for finality and consistency and has generally declined to expand opportunities for collateral attack.   We think the hoary principle that civil tort actions are not appropriate vehicles for challenging the validity of outstanding criminal judgments applies to § 1983 damages actions that necessarily require the plaintiff to prove the unlawfulness of his conviction or confinement, just as it has always applied to actions for malicious prosecution.[5]

We hold that, in order to recover damages for allegedly unconstitutional conviction or imprisonment, or for other harm caused by actions whose unlawfulness would render a conviction or sentence invalid,[6] a § 1983 plaintiff must prove that the conviction or sentence has been reversed on direct appeal, expunged by executive order, declared invalid by a state tribunal authorized to make such determination, or called into question by a federal court's issuance of a writ of habeas corpus, 28 U.S.C. § 2254.   A claim for damages bearing that relationship to a conviction or sentence that has *not* been so invalidated is not cognizable under § 1983.   Thus, when a state prisoner seeks damages in a § 1983 suit, the district court must consider whether a judgment in favor of the

---

4.   * * * [E]ven if Justice Souter were correct [in his opinion concurring in the judgment] in asserting that a prior conviction, although reversed, "dissolved [a] claim for malicious prosecution," [and we do not believe he is,] our analysis would be unaffected. It would simply demonstrate that *no* common-law action, *not even* malicious prosecution, would permit a criminal proceeding to be impugned in a tort action, *even after* the conviction had been reversed.   That would, if anything, strengthen our belief that § 1983, which borrowed general tort principles, was not meant to permit such collateral attack.

5.   Justice Souter's discussion of abuse of process does not undermine this principle. It is true that favorable termination of prior proceedings is not an element of that cause of action—but neither is an impugning of those proceedings one of its consequences.   The gravamen of that tort is not the wrongfulness of the prosecution, but some extortionate perversion of lawfully initiated process to illegitimate ends.   Cognizable injury for abuse of process is limited to the harm caused by the misuse of process, and does not include harm (such as conviction and confinement) resulting from that process's being carried through to its lawful conclusion.   * * *

6.   An example of this latter category—a § 1983 action that does not seek damages directly attributable to conviction or confinement but whose successful prosecution would necessarily imply that the plaintiff's criminal conviction was wrongful—would be the following: A state defendant is convicted of and sentenced for the crime of resisting arrest, defined as intentionally preventing a peace officer from effecting a *lawful* arrest.   (This is a common definition of that offense.)   He then brings a § 1983 action against the arresting officer, seeking damages for violation of his Fourth Amendment right to be free from unreasonable seizures.   In order to prevail in this § 1983 action, he would have to negate an element of the offense of which he has been convicted.   Regardless of the state law concerning res judicata, the § 1983 action will not lie.

plaintiff would necessarily imply the invalidity of his conviction or sentence; if it would, the complaint must be dismissed unless the plaintiff can demonstrate that the conviction or sentence has already been invalidated. But if the district court determines that the plaintiff's action, even if successful, will *not* demonstrate the invalidity of any outstanding criminal judgment against the plaintiff, the action should be allowed to proceed,[7] in the absence of some other bar to the suit.[8]

Respondents had urged us to adopt a rule that was in one respect broader than this: exhaustion of state remedies should be required, they contended, not just when success in the § 1983 damages suit would necessarily show a conviction or sentence to be unlawful, but whenever "judgment in a § 1983 action would resolve a necessary element to a likely challenge to a conviction, even if the § 1983 court [need] not determine that the conviction is invalid." Such a broad sweep was needed, respondents contended, lest a judgment in a prisoner's favor in a federal-court § 1983 damage action claiming, for example, a Fourth Amendment violation, be given preclusive effect as to that sub-issue in a subsequent state-court post-conviction proceeding. Preclusion might result, they asserted, if the State exercised sufficient control over the officials' defense in the § 1983 action. See Montana v. United States, 440 U.S. 147, 154 (1979). While we have no occasion to rule on the matter at this time, it is at least plain that preclusion will not necessarily be an automatic, or even a permissible, effect.[9]

In another respect, however, our holding sweeps more broadly than the approach respondents had urged. We do not engraft an exhaustion requirement upon § 1983, but rather deny the existence of a cause of action. Even a prisoner who has fully exhausted available state remedies has no cause of action under § 1983 unless and until the conviction or sentence is reversed, expunged, invalidated, or impugned by the grant of a writ of habeas corpus. That makes it unnecessary for us to address the statute-of-limitations issue wrestled with by the Court of Appeals, which concluded that a federal doctrine of equitable tolling would apply to the § 1983 cause of action while state

---

7. For example, a suit for damages attributable to an allegedly unreasonable search may lie even if the challenged search produced evidence that was introduced in a state criminal trial resulting in the § 1983 plaintiff's still-outstanding conviction. Because of doctrines like independent source and inevitable discovery, and especially harmless error, such a § 1983 action, even if successful, would not *necessarily* imply that the plaintiff's conviction was unlawful. In order to recover compensatory damages, however, the § 1983 plaintiff must prove not only that the search was unlawful, but that it caused him actual, compensable injury, which, we hold today, does *not* encompass the "injury" of being convicted and imprisoned (unless his conviction has been overturned).

8. For example, if a state criminal defendant brings a federal civil-rights lawsuit during the pendency of his criminal trial, appeal, or state habeas action, abstention may be an appropriate response to the parallel state-court proceedings. See Colorado River Water Conservation Dist. v. United States, 424 U.S. 800 (1976). * * *

9. State courts are bound to apply federal rules in determining the preclusive effect of federal-court decisions on issues of federal law. See P. Bator, D. Meltzer, P. Mishkin, & D. Shapiro, Hart and Wechsler's The Federal Courts and the Federal System 1604 (3d ed. 1988)("It is clear that where the federal court decided a federal question, federal res judicata rules govern"). The federal rules on the subject of issue and claim preclusion, unlike those relating to exhaustion of state remedies, are "almost entirely judge-made." Hart & Wechsler, *supra,* at 1598. And in developing them the courts can, and indeed should, be guided by the federal policies reflected in congressional enactments. * * * [These enactments include the exhaustion requirements of § 2254.]

challenges to the conviction or sentence were being exhausted. * * * Under our analysis the statute of limitations poses no difficulty while the state challenges are being pursued, since the § 1983 claim has not yet arisen. * * *[10]

Applying these principles to the present action, in which both courts below found that the damage claims challenged the legality of the conviction, we find that the dismissal of the action was correct. The judgment of the Court of Appeals for the Seventh Circuit is

Affirmed.

■ JUSTICE THOMAS, concurring.

* * *

I write separately to note that it is we who have put § 1983 and the habeas statute on what Justice Souter appropriately terms a "collision course." It has long been recognized that we have expanded the prerogative writ of habeas corpus and § 1983 far beyond the limited scope either was originally intended to have. Expanding the two historic statutes brought them squarely into conflict in the context of suits by state prisoners, as we made clear in Preiser.

Given that the Court created the tension between the two statutes, it is proper for the Court to devise limitations aimed at ameliorating the conflict, provided that it does so in a principled fashion. Because the Court today limits the scope of § 1983 in a manner consistent both with the federalism concerns undergirding the explicit exhaustion requirement of the habeas statute, and with the state of the common law at the time § 1983 was enacted, I join the Court's opinion.

■ JUSTICE SOUTER, with whom JUSTICE BLACKMUN, JUSTICE STEVENS, and JUSTICE O'CONNOR join, concurring in the judgment.

* * *

While I do not object to referring to the common law when resolving the question this case presents, I do not think that the existence of the tort of malicious prosecution alone provides the answer. Common-law tort rules can provide a "starting point for the inquiry under § 1983," Carey v. Piphus, 435 U.S. 247, 258 (1978), but we have relied on the common law in § 1983 cases

---

10. Justice Souter also adopts the common-law principle that one cannot use the device of a civil tort action to challenge the validity of an outstanding criminal conviction, but thinks it necessary to abandon that principle in those cases (of which no real-life example comes to mind) involving former state prisoners who, because they are no longer in custody, cannot bring post-conviction challenges. We think the principle barring collateral attacks—a longstanding and deeply rooted feature of both the common law and our own jurisprudence—is not rendered inapplicable by the fortuity that a convicted criminal is no longer incarcerated. Justice Souter opines that disallowing a damages suit for a former state prisoner framed by Ku Klux Klan-dominated state officials is

"hard indeed to reconcile ... with the purpose of § 1983." Id., at 12. But if, as Justice Souter appears to suggest, the goal of our interpretive enterprise under § 1983 were to provide a remedy for all conceivable invasions of federal rights that freedmen may have suffered at the hands of officials of the former States of the Confederacy, the entire landscape of our § 1983 jurisprudence would look very different. We would not, for example, have adopted the rule that judicial officers have absolute immunity from liability for damages under § 1983, Pierson v. Ray, 386 U.S. 547 (1967), a rule that would prevent recovery by a former slave who had been tried and convicted before a corrupt state judge in league with the Ku Klux Klan.

only when doing so was thought to be consistent with ordinary rules of statutory construction * * *. At the same time, we have consistently refused to allow common-law analogies to displace statutory analysis, declining to import even well-settled common-law rules into § 1983 "if [the statute's] history or purpose counsel against applying [such rules] in § 1983 actions." Wyatt v. Cole, 504 U.S. 158, 164 (1992).[1]

An examination of common-law sources arguably relevant in this case confirms the soundness of our hierarchy of principles for resolving questions concerning § 1983. * * * Absent an independent statutory basis for doing so, importing into § 1983 the malicious-prosecution tort's favorable-termination requirement but not its probable-cause requirement would be particularly odd since it is from the latter that the former derives. See Prosser and Keeton [The Law of Torts] at 874 ("The requirement that the criminal prosecution terminate in favor of the malicious prosecution plaintiff ... is primarily important not as an independent element of the malicious prosecution action but only for what it shows about probable cause or guilt-in-fact").

If, in addition, the common law were the master of statutory analysis, not the servant (to switch metaphors), we would find ourselves with two masters to contend with here, for we would be subject not only to the tort of malicious prosecution but to the tort of abuse of process as well * * *.

Furthermore, even if the tort of malicious prosecution were today marginally more analogous than other torts to the type of § 1983 claim in the class of cases before us (because it alone may permit damages for unlawful conviction or postconviction confinement, see n. 3, *infra*), the Court overlooks a significant historical incongruity that calls into question the utility of the analogy to the tort of malicious prosecution insofar as it is used exclusively to determine the scope of § 1983: the damages sought in the type of § 1983 claim involved here, damages for unlawful conviction or postconviction confinement, were not available at all in an action for malicious prosecution at the time of § 1983's enactment. A defendant's conviction, under Reconstruction-era common law, dissolved his claim for malicious prosecution because the conviction was regarded as irrebuttable evidence that the prosecution never lacked probable cause. Thus the definition of "favorable termination" with which the framers of § 1983 were aware (if they were aware of any definition) included none of the events relevant to the type of § 1983 claim involved in this case ("revers[al] on direct appeal, expunge[ment] by executive order, [a] declaration [of] invalid[ity] by a state tribunal authorized to make such determination, or [the] call[ing] into question by a federal court's issuance of a writ of habeas corpus"), and it is easy to see why the analogy to the tort of malicious prosecution in this context has escaped the collective wisdom of the many courts and commentators to

---

1. Our recent opinion in Wyatt [504 U.S. at 163–64] summarized the manner in which the Court has analyzed the relationship between the common law and § 1983 in the context of immunity:

"Section 1983 'creates a species of tort liability that on its face admits of no immunities.' Imbler v. Pachtman, 424 U.S. 409, 417, (1976). Nonetheless, we have accorded certain government officials either absolute or qualified immunity from suit if the 'tradition of immunity was so firmly rooted in the

common law and was supported by such strong policy reasons that "Congress would have specifically so provided had it wished to abolish the doctrine." ' Owen v. City of Independence, 445 U.S. 622, 637 (1980)(quoting Pierson v. Ray, 386 U.S. 547, 555 (1967)). * * * [But] irrespective of the common law support, we will not recognize an immunity available at common law if § 1983's history or purpose counsel against applying it in § 1983 actions." * * *

have previously addressed the issue, as well as the parties to this case. Indeed, relying on the tort of malicious prosecution to dictate the outcome of this case would logically drive one to the position, untenable as a matter of statutory interpretation (and, to be clear, disclaimed by the Court), that conviction of a crime wipes out a person's § 1983 claim for damages for unconstitutional conviction or postconviction confinement.[3]

We are not, however, in any such strait, for our enquiry in this case may follow the interpretive methodology employed in Preiser v. Rodriguez. In Preiser, we read the "general" § 1983 statute in light of the "specific federal habeas corpus statute," which applies only to "person[s] in custody," 28 U.S.C. § 2254(a), and the habeas statute's policy, embodied in its exhaustion requirement, § 2254(b), that state courts be given the first opportunity to review constitutional claims bearing upon a state prisoner's release from custody. 411 U.S., at 489. Though in contrast to Preiser the state prisoner here seeks damages, not release from custody, the distinction makes no difference when the damages sought are for unconstitutional conviction or confinement. * * * Because allowing a state prisoner to proceed directly with a federal-court § 1983 attack on his conviction or sentence "would wholly frustrate explicit congressional intent" as declared in the habeas exhaustion requirement, Preiser, 411 U.S., at 489, the statutory scheme must be read as precluding such attacks. This conclusion flows not from a preference about how the habeas and § 1983 statutes ought to have been written, but from a recognition that "Congress has determined that habeas corpus is the appropriate remedy for state prisoners attacking the validity of the fact or length of their confinement, [a] specific determination [that] must override the general terms of § 1983." Id., at 490.

That leaves the question of how to implement what statutory analysis requires. It is at this point that the malicious-prosecution tort's favorable-termination requirement becomes helpful, not in dictating the elements of a § 1983 cause of action, but in suggesting a relatively simple way to avoid collisions at the intersection of habeas and § 1983. A state prisoner may seek federal-court § 1983 damages for unconstitutional conviction or confinement, but only if he has previously established the unlawfulness of his conviction or confinement, as on appeal or on habeas. This has the effect of requiring a state prisoner challenging the lawfulness of his confinement to follow habeas's rules before seeking § 1983 damages for unlawful confinement in federal court, and it is ultimately the Court's holding today. It neatly resolves a problem that has bedeviled lower courts * * * and law students (some of whom doubtless have run up against a case like this in law-school exams). The favorable-termination requirement avoids the knotty statute-of-limitations problem that arises if federal courts dismiss § 1983 suits filed before an inmate pursues federal habeas, and (because the statute-of-limitations clock does not start ticking until an inmate's conviction is set aside) it does so without

---

3. Some of the traditional common-law requirements appear to have liberalized over the years, see Prosser and Keeton, *supra*, at 882 ("[t]here is a considerable minority view which regards the conviction as creating only a presumption, which may be rebutted by any competent evidence showing that proba-ble cause for the prosecution did not in fact exist"), strengthening the analogy the Court draws. But surely the Court is not of the view that a single tort in its late 20th-century form can conclusively (and retroactively) dictate the requirements of a 19th-century stat-ute for a discrete category of cases. * * *

requiring federal courts to stay, and therefore to retain on their dockets, prematurely filed § 1983 suits.[4]

It may be that the Court's analysis takes it no further than I would thus go, and that any objection I may have to the Court's opinion is to style, not substance. * * * The Court's opinion can be read as saying nothing more than that now, after enactment of the habeas statute and because of it, prison inmates seeking § 1983 damages in federal court for unconstitutional conviction or confinement must satisfy a requirement analogous to the malicious-prosecution tort's favorable-termination requirement.

That would be a sensible way to read the opinion, in part because the alternative would needlessly place at risk the rights of those outside the intersection of § 1983 and the habeas statute, individuals not "in custody" for habeas purposes. If these individuals (people who were merely fined, for example, or who have completed short terms of imprisonment, probation or parole, or who discover (through no fault of their own) a constitutional violation after full expiration of their sentences), like state prisoners, were required to show the prior invalidation of their convictions or sentences in order to obtain § 1983 damages for unconstitutional conviction or imprisonment, the result would be to deny any federal forum for claiming a deprivation of federal rights to those who cannot first obtain a favorable state ruling. The reason, of course, is that individuals not "in custody" cannot invoke federal habeas jurisdiction, the only statutory mechanism besides § 1983 by which individuals may sue state officials in federal court for violating federal rights. That would be an untoward result.

* * *

* * * Consider the case of a former slave framed by Ku Klux Klan-controlled law-enforcement officers and convicted by a Klan-controlled state court of, for example, raping a white woman; and suppose that the unjustly convicted defendant did not (and could not) discover the proof of unconstitutionally until after his release from state custody. If it were correct to say that § 1983 independently requires a person not in custody to establish the prior invalidation of his conviction, it would have been equally right to tell the former slave that he could not seek federal relief even against the law-enforcement officers who framed him unless he first managed to convince the state courts that his conviction was unlawful.

That would be a result hard indeed to reconcile either with the purpose of § 1983 or with the origins of what was "popularly known as the Ku Klux Act," Collins v. Hardyman, 341 U.S. 651, 657 (1951), the statute having been enacted in part out of concern that many state courts were "in league with those who were bent upon abrogation of federally protected rights," Mitchum v. Foster, 407 U.S., at 240. * * *

Nor do I see any policy reflected in a congressional enactment that would justify denying to an individual today federal damages (a significantly less disruptive remedy than an order compelling release from custody) merely because he was unconstitutionally fined by a state, or to a person who discovers after his release from prison that, for example, state officials deliberately

---

4. * * * [A] state prisoner whose constitutional attacks on his confinement have been rejected by state courts cannot be said to be unlawfully confined unless a federal habeas court declares his "custody [to be] in violation of the Constitution or laws or treaties of the United States," 28 U.S.C. § 2254(a). * * *

withheld exculpatory material. And absent such a statutory policy, surely the common law can give us no authority to narrow the "broad language" of § 1983 * * *.

In sum, while the malicious-prosecution analogy provides a useful mechanism for implementing what statutory analysis requires, congressional policy as reflected in enacted statutes must ultimately be the guide. I would thus be clear that the proper resolution of this case (involving, of course, a state prisoner) is to construe § 1983 in light of the habeas statute and its explicit policy of exhaustion. I would not cast doubt on the ability of an individual unaffected by the habeas statute to take advantage of the broad reach of § 1983.

NOTE ON THE RELATIONSHIP OF HABEAS CORPUS AND SECTION 1983

(1) *The Background of the Heck Decision.* As indicated by the Court in Heck, there were two important decisions that preceded it. In the first, Preiser v. Rodriguez, 411 U.S. 475 (1973), the majority held that a federal court could not entertain a § 1983 action in which state prisoners challenged the constitutionality of the deprivation of good time credits and sought restoration of the credits—relief that, if granted, would result in their immediate release. The court held that habeas corpus, with its requirement of exhaustion of state remedies, was the only available federal remedy. Justice Brennan, dissenting for himself and Justices Douglas and Marshall, argued that since the prisoners' actions did not focus on the relations between state and federal judiciaries, but rather on the constitutionality of the state's administrative treatment of the prisoners, exhaustion should not be required and habeas should not be regarded as the exclusive remedy.

The limits of Preiser were tested in Wolff v. McDonnell, 418 U.S. 539 (1974), in which state prisoners brought § 1983 actions challenging the constitutionality of certain state disciplinary proceedings, of the state legal aid program, and of the prison mail censorship system. Plaintiffs sought both damages and the restoration of good time credits. The Court allowed the § 1983 action to go forward but ruled that the restoration of good time credits in such an action was foreclosed under Preiser.

The lower courts had struggled with the relationship between these two decisions for a number of years before Heck was decided. See generally Schwartz, *The Preiser Puzzle: Continued Frustrating Conflict Between the Civil Rights and Habeas Corpus Remedies for State Prisoners,* 37 DePaul L.Rev. 85 (1988). Does Heck resolve the questions raised by the Court's earlier rulings? If so, does it resolve them properly?

(2) *Some Questions Remaining After the Heck Decision.* The Court's unanimous agreement on the result in the Heck case masks some difficult questions, several of which are brought to the surface in the opinions.

(a) Under what circumstances is it sufficiently clear that upholding a damage claim under § 1983 would effectively invalidate the prisoner's conviction, thus requiring the prisoner to resort to habeas corpus as the exclusive federal remedy? The Court stated in footnote 2 that it was no longer open to Heck to argue that his claim would not have such an effect, but had he been allowed to argue this point, should he have prevailed? Won't the availability of

§ 1983 in a number of instances now turn on a rather delicate analysis of the harmless error rule or some variant of it? If so, what version of the rule, and what burden of proof, is applicable? Won't the state prisoner be caught between the Scylla of the Heck rule and the Charybdis of negating some substantial part of his claim for damages? Or should the test be whether upholding the prisoner's claim would *necessarily* have the effect of invalidating his conviction?[1]

(b) In a case in which a state prisoner is allowed to pursue a § 1983 claim that relates to his conviction, what will be the res judicata effects of the determinations made in the original trial leading to the conviction? Has that question, in all its aspects, been fully resolved by the decision in Allen v. McCurry, p. 1484, *supra,* and subsequent related cases?

(c) If a state prisoner who is allowed to pursue a § 1983 claim relating to his conviction prevails on the merits of his § 1983 claim, what is the res judicata effect of that determination in a later habeas corpus action? The question is not purely academic, since there are sure to be instances in which the issue determined has a bearing on the validity of the conviction, even though the determination does not "invalidate" the conviction.

(d) Heck clearly bars a § 1983 suit based on a conviction obtained by torture (if the conviction has not been invalidated in a collateral attack). But if instead of torturing the defendant to get a confession, the police have obtained evidence unlawfully, is a § 1983 damage action permitted as a result of Stone v. Powell, p. 1376, *supra*? Would the court first have to determine whether state post-conviction process was available? (Indeed, is that a general problem in applying the Heck rationale?) Is there an irony in allowing a damages action under § 1983 for what is plainly a *less serious* constitutional violation?[2]

(e) Does Justice Scalia adequately answer Justice Souter's point that the majority's reasoning has no application to a state defendant who has fully served his sentence, or who has been fined but not imprisoned, because habeas corpus does not lie for such a defendant and thus § 1983 becomes the *only* form of available federal relief? Justice Scalia, in footnote 10, notes that in view of doctrines such as that of qualified or absolute official immunity, § 1983 is not a comprehensive remedy for all violations of federal law committed by state officers. But those doctrines are presumably based on a careful balancing of the interest in vindicating individual rights against the interest in not unduly

1.   May a prisoner who is willing to stipulate that any relief would not impugn his conviction (or to waive any right to try to do so) obtain relief under § 1983?

2.   The analysis of the issues raised in subparagraphs (a)-(d) may change dramatically if legislation affecting the availability of federal habeas corpus—legislation that was pending as this edition went to press—is enacted. (For discussion of the pending proposals, see p. 1459–61, *supra*.) To the extent that the availability of federal habeas corpus is restricted by such legislation, Heck would not appear to bar a remedy under § 1983

(unless a state post-conviction remedy attacking the conviction remains available). Yet even so, the prisoner-plaintiff might end up in a Catch–22 situation: under those proposals, habeas relief would be unavailable (and thus Heck would not foreclose a § 1983 suit) where the state action was not clearly unconstitutional; but in such a case, a state official is very likely to be shielded from damages liability under § 1983 by official immunity. (This problem of official immunity would not exist in situations where a § 1983 damage remedy was available against a local government entity under the Monell doctrine, p. 1126, *supra*.)

undermining effective law enforcement. What elements should be considered in striking such a balance in Justice Souter's hypothetical cases?[3]

(3) *Actions Under § 1983 Challenging the Method of Punishment.* In Gomez v. United States District Court, 503 U.S. 653 (1992)(per curiam), several prisoners filed a § 1983 class action four days before one of them (Harris) was scheduled to be executed. The complaint alleged that the manner of execution (lethal gas) constituted cruel and unusual punishment. The district court ruled that because the suit did not challenge the legality of either a conviction or a death sentence, § 1983 was an appropriate vehicle through which to raise the claim; the court issued a temporary restraining order barring all executions by lethal gas pending a hearing on the claim. The state immediately sought a writ of mandamus or prohibition from the Ninth Circuit, a panel of which overturned the TRO, but the following day (which was the day before the execution was scheduled), ten members of the Ninth Circuit granted a stay of the execution.

Over the course of that night, the Supreme Court dissolved the stay.[4] The Court's three-paragraph per curiam opinion stated that, as Harris had filed four previous federal habeas petitions, this § 1983 action was "an obvious attempt to avoid application of McCleskey v. Zant," p. 1442, *supra,* which sharply restricts a prisoner's ability to have successive petitions entertained. The Court continued: "Even if we were to assume, however, that Harris could avoid the application of McCleskey to bar his claim, we would not consider it on the merits. Whether his claim is framed as a habeas petition or § 1983 action, Harris seeks an equitable remedy," which should be denied in view of his "abusive delay" (p. 654). Justice Stevens, joined by Justice Blackmun, dissented, arguing that any delay, even if unjustified, did not warrant the refusal to hear what Justice Stevens viewed as a meritorious challenge under the Eighth Amendment.

Suppose that the state had only recently changed its method of execution, so that Harris could not be charged with delay in challenging it. After Heck, would you agree with the district court that a challenge to the manner of execution is cognizable in a § 1983 action? If so, what principles should govern the question of how promptly such a challenge must be filed after a death sentence is imposed?

(4) *The Relation Between the Heck Decision and Other Doctrines.* Note the tension between the rationale of Heck, in which the habeas remedy (together with its state counterparts) is seen as occupying the field (even when it is unavailable), and the rationale of such cases as Monroe v. Pape, p. 1111, *supra,* in which the Court refused to permit the availability of a § 1983 remedy to hinge on the existence *vel non* of a parallel state court remedy.

---

3. Suppose a prosecutor deliberately manufactures false evidence. If the judge discovers the misconduct in time to avoid conviction, the defendant is presumably free to bring a § 1983 action. But if the defendant is convicted (perhaps because the judge is part of the conspiracy), then Heck would appear to erect an insurmountable barrier to such an action if the defendant is not imprisoned, or has been released, unless the state has available post-conviction process (like co-ram nobis) in such cases. (Compare the questions raised in subparagraph (d) of the text.)

4. The Supreme Court also dissolved other stays entered by the Ninth Circuit in other actions filed by Harris, ultimately entering an order at 7:05 a.m. (Eastern time) stating that "No further stays of * * * Harris' execution shall be entered by the federal courts except upon the order of this Court."

CONCLUDING NOTE ON THE JURISDICTION OF FEDERAL
AND STATE COURTS IN CASES INVOLVING FEDERAL
LAW CHALLENGES TO STATE OFFICIAL ACTION

(1) *A Proposed Restatement.* When an individual claims in a federal court suit that state or local government action—past, present, or threatened—violates a federal right or immunity, a myriad of jurisdictional doctrines come into play. Any effort to summarize those doctrines will inevitably be oversimplified. As you read the following attempt at a brief Restatement, consider the respects, if any, in which qualifications should be added, and the extent to which such qualifications might end by swallowing the asserted rule. Consider also whether the overall pattern makes practical sense.

I. Where No State Court Enforcement Proceeding Is Underway

A. The plaintiff, subject to justiciability requirements, may bring an action against an appropriate state official for an injunction and/or damages, alleging past, present, or future violation of a federal constitutional right (Ex parte Young; Monroe v. Pape).

B. It is irrelevant whether an adequate remedy exists in the state courts (Home Telephone; Monroe), *unless*

    1. The action falls under the Johnson Act of 1934 or the Tax Injunction Act of 1937, in which case the existence of an adequate remedy in state court ousts federal jurisdiction; *or*

    2. The existence of fair state post-deprivation procedures, constituting the "process" that is "due", negates the claimed constitutional liability under the Due Process Clause (Parratt; Zinermon).[1]

C. It is irrelevant whether the official's action was authorized by state law or state policy (Monroe), *unless* the action is against a local governmental body (Monell), or the complaint is one involving the violation of procedural due process rights (see B(2), above).

D. In a federal court action seeking specific relief, the plaintiff may not—absent consent (Smith v. Reeves)—append a state law claim to a federal claim against officials of the state (Pennhurst), but must either split that action or pursue both claims in state court.

E. If antecedent or parallel state law issues are present in the case (and their resolution may obviate the decision of federal constitutional questions, or may significantly affect the nature of those questions), the federal court may abstain and remit the plaintiff to state court for resolution of those issues (Pullman). But the plaintiff may return to the federal court for disposition of the unmooted federal claims notwithstanding normal res judicata rules, and may guarantee that the right to return is not lost by making an appropriate reservation in the state court proceeding (England).

F. Plaintiff may choose to take the federal claim first to state court, but will then be subject to normal res judicata rules (see "III", *infra*).

G. Suits for damages against persons in their "individual" capacities are subject to the limitations imposed by official immunity doctrines.

---

1. Additional qualifications on proposition I(B) arise when the claim is a "takings" claim that is not yet ripe; when the claim is one by a prisoner subject to the exhaustion requirements of 42 U.S.C. § 1997e; or when the case is one that warrants "Burford" abstention.

II. Where A State Court Proceeding Is Underway (Or Imminent) When The Federal Action Is Commenced

A. If the federal action is not a § 1983 action, injunctive relief may be barred by the Anti–Injunction Act (§ 2283).

B. If the plaintiff is in custody, and the effect of the relief sought would be to end or shorten custody, the action will be deemed a habeas corpus action, and the exhaustion requirements will apply (Preiser).

C. A convicted state defendant may not pursue a federal claim under § 1983 if the prisoner's conviction has not been previously invalidated and if the findings sustaining the claim would invalidate the conviction (Heck).

D. In a § 1983 action, § 2283 is not a bar (Mitchum). But the Younger doctrine will normally prevent a federal court from aborting, by injunction or declaratory judgment, a pending state court enforcement proceeding (Younger), or sometimes an impending one (Hicks), throughout its course (Huffman). It is uncertain whether a concurrent damage action based on the same constitutional claims is allowable.

E. In addition, the federal court may decline to adjudicate where "exceptional circumstances" call for deference to pending state proceedings (Colorado River).

F. A state court enforcement proceeding based on an asserted violation of state law may not be removed to federal court, *unless*

    1. The defendant is a federal official asserting a federal defense (§ 1441; Mesa); *or*

    2. The stringent rules for civil rights removal under § 1443 are met.

III. Where State Court Proceedings Are Complete[2]

A. If the petitioner is in custody as the result of the state court proceeding, habeas relitigation of the federal question—subject to the limitations of 28 U.S.C. § 2254(d)—is permissible (Brown), *unless*

    1. The federal issue involves a Fourth Amendment claim that a motion to suppress evidence was improperly denied, and there was a full and fair opportunity to litigate that issue in the state courts (Stone); *or*

    2. An available state remedy has not been exhausted; *or*

    3. The habeas petitioner is seeking relief on the basis of a "new rule" and cannot show a sufficient ground for permitting reliance on such a rule (Teague); *or*

    4. The federal question was not raised or decided in the state courts, and the resulting forfeiture is not excused by either an adequate showing of cause and prejudice (Sykes) or by a showing of probable innocence (Murray); *or*

    5. The petitioner filed an earlier petition for federal habeas and the failure to raise the present claim in that earlier petition is not excused by an adequate showing of cause and prejudice, nor is

---

2. The propositions stated in this section, and especially in Part A, may be significantly affected by enactment of various proposals pending in Congress as this edition went to press. See p. 1514, note 2, *supra*.

consideration of the claim warranted by the threat of a fundamental miscarriage of justice (McCleskey).

B. If the result of the state proceeding is not custody, the issue and claim preclusion rules that would be applied in the courts of the rendering state as a matter of that state's law apply in a subsequent federal action, whether the litigant was plaintiff or defendant in the state proceeding (Allen; Migra; Kremer), *unless*

1. State preclusion law is overcome by significant federal interests in allowing relitigation—for example, an interest that may be inferred from a grant of exclusive federal jurisdiction (*cf.* Marrese); *or*

2. The plaintiff began the action in a federal court, and following the court's decision to abstain on a question of state law (Pullman), the plaintiff did not forfeit the ability—after going to state court—to return to federal court to litigate the federal claim (England); *or*

3. The state's preclusion law violates due process (Allen; Kremer).

C. Resort to federal court (except by direct review) may also be independently barred by the Rooker–Feldman doctrine.

IV. Effect Of State Administrative Proceedings

A. If the federal plaintiff is seeking relief that entails the ending or shortening of confinement or that entails findings that would invalidate an outstanding conviction, exhaustion of state remedies, including administrative remedies, is required (Preiser; Heck).

B. In other cases, if the plaintiff reaches federal court before state administrative proceedings have begun (and otherwise has a proper § 1983 action), exhaustion of state administrative procedures is not required (Patsy), *unless* required by another superseding federal statute (*e.g.,* 42 U.S.C. § 1997e).

C. If state administrative enforcement proceedings of a judicial nature have begun when the plaintiff reaches federal court, an injunctive or declaratory action is prohibited by Younger (Dayton Christian Schools; NOPSI).

D. If a state administrative proceeding of a judicial nature has been completed, and there is no proceeding for judicial review underway in the state courts, it is unclear whether and under what circumstances abstention in favor of state review proceedings is required (see NOPSI; Burford). If a § 1983 action may be brought, it is subject to any relevant state law giving preclusive effect to state administrative findings (in the absence of any overriding federal interest in denying preclusive effect)(Elliott).

E. If the state administrative proceeding has gone to the state courts, the rules of "II" and "III" apply.

* * *

(2) *Some Questions About Existing Rules.*

(a) Note the enormous weight the law places on the question whether a state *court* has undertaken to inquire into the dispute between the citizen and the state. If it has not, the citizen can normally proceed immediately to federal court and ask for adjudication of the relevant federal issues without regard to state administrative or judicial remedies; even if abstention is required, an eventual federal adjudication is guaranteed. On the other hand, once a state court proceeding is underway, there is ordinarily no removal and federal suits for injunctive relief are barred by the abstention doctrine. In addition, a state judgment, once rendered, receives full res judicata effect. Even in cases where habeas is available, it must await exhaustion and is subject to harsh forfeiture rules.

Why is access to a federal court so freely available for plaintiffs not yet subject to state court enforcement actions, but so difficult for state-court defendants?

(b) Note also the extraordinary array of formulations that govern the question whether the usual rules of comity are overcome because the state courts do not provide an adequate forum for the litigation of the federal right:

(i) The Johnson Act and the Tax Injunction Act allow attacks on the constitutional validity of state rate orders and state taxes where a "plain, speedy, and efficient remedy" cannot be had in the state courts (§§ 1341, 1342).

(ii) The Younger abstention doctrine will not prevent a federal action to abort pending state enforcement proceedings if those proceedings are in "bad faith" or there are other "extraordinary circumstances".

(iii) The Anti–Injunction Act, when it applies, has its own statutory exceptions; none is couched in terms of a "fair opportunity" to litigate a question in the state courts (§ 2283).

(iv) A private state court defendant may remove an enforcement proceeding to federal court if the defendant is "denied or cannot enforce" in state courts a right under the statutes protecting equal civil rights (§ 1443).

(v) A state prisoner may raise Fourth Amendment claims on habeas corpus if the state did not provide an opportunity for a "full and fair litigation" of that claim (Stone).

(vi) Habeas exhaustion is excused if there is "an absence of available state corrective process" or if the circumstances render "such process ineffective" (§ 2254(b)).

(vii) A failure to raise a federal question in a state criminal case will not lead to forfeiture of a habeas remedy if there was "cause" for the failure and if the prisoner was "prejudiced" as a result.

(viii) Res judicata will not bar federal consideration of a federal question if there was no "full and fair opportunity" to litigate in the state courts (Allen).

Do these formulations respond to a common set of concerns? See Bator, *The State Courts and Federal Constitutional Litigation*, 22 Wm. & Mary L.Rev. 605 (1981); Collins, *The Right to Avoid Trial: Justifying Federal Court Intervention Into Ongoing State Proceedings*, 66 N.C.L.Rev. 49 (1987). If so, should we attempt to develop a unifying framework—a field theory—that could encompass them all? Consider, for instance, the realms of habeas, Younger, and res judicata. In all these contexts, the courts are grappling with the question of when failure to resort to the state courts should be excused and the doors of the federal courthouse opened because of some failing in the state court system for adjudicating federal rights.

If a common formulation were to be attempted, when would state processes or remedies be regarded as "inadequate"? Where and by whom would this question be decided? See generally Chap. IV, Sec. 1, pp. 351–54, *infra* (discussing the concept of "parity" of state and federal courts).

(c) In cases where federal court trial jurisdiction is justified, what is the best technique for affording it? Removal before or after judgment? Independent injunctive or declaratory actions in the federal courts to test the federal right? Post-judgment audit of the state court adjudication by collateral attack? Or some mix of all of the above?

CHAPTER XIII

THE DIVERSITY JURISDICTION OF THE FEDERAL DISTRICT COURTS

SECTION 1. INTRODUCTION

STATUTORY DEVELOPMENT

Federal diversity jurisdiction has existed ever since the Judiciary Act of 1789. Section 11 of that Act, 1 Stat. 79, authorized the exercise of jurisdiction when the "matter in dispute" exceeded the sum or value of five hundred dollars and (1) an alien was a party, or (2) the suit was between a citizen of the state where the action was brought and a citizen of another state. The limitation of the second category to cases in which one of the parties was a citizen of the forum state was eliminated in the Act of Mar. 3, 1875, Sec. 1, 18 Stat. 470, and, in lieu of the reference in the first category to an alien as a party, the 1875 Act authorized jurisdiction in controversies between "citizens of a State and foreign states, citizens, or subjects."

In 1887, the requisite amount in controversy was raised to two thousand dollars (Act of Mar. 3, 1887, Sec. 1, 24 Stat. 552), and in 1911 to three thousand dollars (Act of Mar. 3, 1911, Sec. 24, 36 Stat. 1087, 1091).

In 1940, an amendment extended the jurisdiction to suits "between * * * citizens of the District of Columbia, the Territory of Hawaii, or Alaska, and any State or Territory." Act of Apr. 20, 1940, 54 Stat. 143. And as part of the general revision of the Judicial Code in 1948, the operative provisions were rewritten and subdivided to cover (in subsection (a)) suits between "(1) Citizens of different states; (2) Citizens of a State and foreign states or citizens or subjects thereof; [or] (3) Citizens of different States and in which foreign states or citizens or subjects thereof are additional parties." Act of June 25, 1948, c. 85, 62 Stat. 930. Subsection (b) then went on to define "States" to include the Territories and the District of Columbia (*id.*), and that definition was extended in 1956 to the Commonwealth of Puerto Rico (Act of July 26, 1956, c. 740, 70 Stat. 658).

In 1958, the jurisdictional threshold was raised to $10,000, the definition of "States" was moved to subsection (d), and Congress added a new subsection (b) and (c). Act of July 25, 1958, Sec. 2, 72 Stat. 415. Subsection (b), dealing with cases in which the plaintiff recovers less than the jurisdictional amount, has remained unchanged to the present day (except for the subsequent increase in the dollar amount), and subsection (c) read as follows:

"(c) For the purposes of this section and section 1441 of this title, a corporation shall be deemed a citizen of any State by which it has been incorporated and of the State where it has its principal place of business."

In 1964, Congress added a proviso to subsection (c) designed to deal with "direct actions" against insurance companies. Act of Aug. 14, 1964, Sec. 1, 78 Stat. 445. It stated that "in any direct action against the insurer of a policy or contract of liability insurance, whether incorporated or unincorporated, to which action the insured is not joined as a party-defendant, such insurer shall be deemed a citizen of the State of which the insured is a citizen, as well as of any State by which the insurer has been incorporated and of the State where it has its principal place of business."

In 1976, § 1332 was amended in connection with the Foreign Sovereign Immunities Act of that year, 28 U.S.C. §§ 1602–11. The references to foreign states as parties were stricken from subsections (a)(2) and (a)(3), and a new subsection (a)(4) was added conferring jurisdiction over suits brought by foreign states as defined by the new act. Suits against foreign states, as defined by that act, were dealt with in new § 1330 of Title 28, which conferred on the district courts "original jurisdiction without regard to amount in controversy of any nonjury civil action against a foreign state as defined in section 1603(a) of this title as to any claim for relief in personam with respect to which the foreign state is not entitled to immunity either under sections 1605–1607 of this title or under any applicable international agreement." The corresponding provision for removal of actions brought in state courts was new § 1441(d) of Title 28.

Finally, in 1988, § 1332 was amended once again, this time in three significant respects. Act of Nov. 19, 1988, Sec. 201–03, 102 Stat. 4646. First, the jurisdictional threshold was raised to $50,000. Second, Congress provided that for purposes of § 1332 (as well as §§ 1335 and 1441), "an alien admitted to the United States for permanent residence shall be deemed a citizen of the State in which such an alien is domiciled." Third, the direct action proviso of subsection (c) was slightly changed and a second paragraph added to the subsection stating: "The legal representative of the estate of a decedent shall be deemed to be a citizen only of the same State as the decedent, and the legal representative of an infant or incompetent shall be deemed to be a citizen only of the same State as the infant or incompetent."

NOTE ON THE HISTORICAL BACKGROUND OF THE DIVERSITY JURISDICTION

(1) The conventional account of the diversity jurisdiction has confined it to the last of the six "descriptions of cases" that Hamilton listed as proper for federal jurisdiction at the beginning of The Federalist, No. 80. The most quoted statement is Marshall's in Bank of the United States v. Deveaux, 9 U.S. (5 Cranch) 61, 87 (1809):

"* * * However true the fact may be, that the tribunals of the states will administer justice as impartially as those of the nation, to parties of every description, it is not less true, that the constitution itself either entertains apprehensions on this subject, or views with such indulgence the possible fears and apprehensions of suitors, that it has established national tribunals for the decision of controversies between aliens and a citizen, or between citizens of different states."

In Martin v. Hunter's Lessee, 14 U.S. (1 Wheat.) 304, 347 (1816), Justice Story said of diversity cases:

"* * * The constitution has presumed (whether rightly or wrongly we do not inquire) that state attachments, state prejudices, state jealousies, and state interests, might sometimes obstruct, or control, or be supposed to obstruct or control, the regular administration of justice * * *. No other reason than that which has been stated can be assigned, why some, at least, of those cases should not have been left to the cognizance of the state courts."

(2) The evidence concerning the origins of the diversity jurisdiction is examined in Friendly, *The Historic Basis of the Diversity Jurisdiction,* 41 Harv. L.Rev. 483 (1928). The principal discussion took place in the debates on ratification, in which the proposed jurisdiction was bitterly denounced. What Friendly finds "astounding", however, "is not the vigor of the attack but the apathy of the defense" (p. 487). Hamilton's argument from the privileges and immunities clause he dismisses as "specious" (p. 492 n. 44). And he questions the "sincerity" of the argument from apprehension of local prejudice because of the failure of Madison and others who made it to adduce specific examples. Reviewing the scanty reports of contemporary decisions, he finds that the evidence "entirely fails to show the existence of prejudice on the part of the state judges".

What Friendly does find is that "the real fear was not of state courts so much as of state legislatures. * * * In summary, we may say that the desire to protect creditors against legislation favorable to debtors was a principal reason for the grant of diversity jurisdiction, and that as a reason it was "by no means without validity" (pp. 495–97). To this he adds lack of confidence in elected judges and fear of the practice of legislative review prevailing in some states. "Not unnaturally the commercial interests of the country were reluctant to expose themselves to the hazards of litigation before such courts as these. They might be good enough for the inhabitants of their respective states, but merchants from abroad felt themselves entitled to something better. There was a vague feeling that the new courts would be strong courts, creditors' courts, business men's courts" (p. 498).

Friendly's conclusions are challenged in Yntema & Jaffin, *Preliminary Analysis of Concurrent Jurisdiction,* 79 U.Pa.L.Rev. 869, 873–76 (1931), on the ground that the available evidence "precludes extensive inference", and that "the theory of no local prejudice is presumptively improbable."

Frank, *Historical Bases of the Federal Judicial System,* 13 Law & Contemp.Prob. 3, 22–28 (1948), reviews the question and concludes:

"To summarize, the diversity jurisdiction in the federal Constitution may fairly be said to be the product of three factors, the relative weights of which cannot now be assessed:

"1. The desire to avoid regional prejudice against commercial litigants, based in small part on experience and in large part on common-sense anticipation.

"2. The desire to permit commercial, manufacturing, and speculative interests to litigate their controversies, and particularly their controversies with other classes, before judges who would be firmly tied to their own interests.

"3. The desire to achieve more efficient administration of justice for the classes thus benefitted".

(3) For a description of the use made of the diversity authority in the first Judiciary Act, and the related effort in the same Congress to eliminate the diversity clause by constitutional amendment, see Warren, *New Light on the History of the Federal Judiciary Act of 1789*, 37 Harv.L.Rev. 49 (1923). For a view of the first Judiciary Act, in which the author concludes that alienage jurisdiction was "historically the single most important grant of national court jurisdiction embodied in the Act," and that the "poor record" of the state courts in enforcing the treaty obligations of the union was the main impetus behind the creation of national courts, see Holt, *The Origins of Alienage Jurisdiction*, 14 Okla. City U.L.Rev. 547, 548–49 (1989).

For discussions of the origins of the diversity jurisdiction that emphasize the nationalizing functions it served, see Marbury, *Why Should We Limit Federal Diversity Jurisdiction?*, 46 A.B.A.J. 379 (1960); Moore & Weckstein, *Diversity Jurisdiction: Past, Present, and Future*, 43 Tex. L.Rev. 1 (1964).

SECTION 2.   ELEMENTS OF DIVERSITY JURISDICTION

NOTE ON THE KINDS OF DIVERSE CITIZENSHIP THAT CONFER JURISDICTION

A.   The Meaning of State Citizenship

From the beginning, state citizenship, for the purposes of the diversity jurisdiction, was viewed as dependent upon two elements: first, United States citizenship; and second, domicile in the state, in the traditional conflict-of-laws sense of the term "domicile". See, *e.g.*, Brown v. Keene, 33 U.S. (8 Pet.) 112 (1834).[1]

The requirement of domicile has been reflected in innumerable holdings that a mere allegation of residence in a state is insufficient to found diversity jurisdiction, since such an allegation may not connote citizenship. *E.g.*, Wolfe v. Hartford Life & Annuity Ins. Co., 148 U.S. 389 (1893). This doctrine survived the Fourteenth Amendment, despite the use in the amendment of the term "resides". See the discussion in Robertson v. Cease, 97 U.S. 646, 648–50 (1879).

The doctrine, of course, is initially one of pleading, but there is an underlying point of substance. It is possible to be a citizen of the United States without being a citizen of any state or federal territory. See Paragraph B(7) of this Note. And a natural person cannot be a citizen of more than one state.

B.   The Kinds of Diverse Citizenship

1.   *Actions Between a Citizen of the Forum State and a Citizen of Another State.*

---

1. Do any of the potential applications of the 1988 amendment to § 1332 (p. 1522, *supra*), raise questions about the constitutional correctness of the first of these requirements? See Paragraph B(6) of this Note.

From 1789 to 1875 the diversity jurisdiction (apart from aliens) extended only to cases of this first type. (Here, and throughout this Note, the existence of the requisite amount in controversy is assumed.)

It made no difference, and never has, whether the out-of-state citizen was plaintiff or defendant. But if the plaintiff elected to sue in the state court, only an out-of-state defendant could, or now can, remove to the federal court. Is there a sound reason for this difference?

2. *Actions Between Citizens of Two Different Non-forum States.*

Jurisdiction in this class of cases was first conferred in 1875 and still exists. If the case is brought in a state court, the defendant can remove.

Did the Klaxon case, p. 695, *supra*, remove whatever justification there was for this jurisdiction? Or is there warrant for it in the fact that, on many occasions, one noncitizen may have much closer ties to the forum state than another?

3. *Actions Between an Alien (or a Foreign State) and a Citizen of the Forum State.*

This jurisdiction has existed since 1789. The present statute appears to exclude from the jurisdiction an alien who is "stateless" (at least if not domiciled in the U.S. and admitted here as a permanent resident), and it has been so held. *E.g.*, Shoemaker v. Malaxa, 241 F.2d 129 (2d Cir.1957). Is this result compelled by Article III?[2]

4. *Actions Between an Alien (or a Foreign State) and a Citizen of a Non-forum State.*

Unlike the comparable jurisdiction in class 2, this jurisdiction has existed since 1789. Are there special dangers of prejudice here that do not exist in class 2? Do they bear on the applicability of Klaxon in such a case?

5. *Actions Between a Citizen of the District of Columbia and* (a) *a Citizen of the Forum State; or* (b) *a Citizen of a Non-forum State; or* (c) *an Alien; or* (d) *a Citizen of Puerto Rico; or* (e) *a Citizen of a Territory.*

Actions Between a Citizen of a Territory and (a) *a Citizen of the Forum State; or* (b) *a Citizen of a Non-forum State; or* (c) *an Alien; or* (d) *a Citizen of Puerto Rico; or* (e) *a Citizen of Another Territory.*

Actions Between a Citizen of Puerto Rico and (a) *a Citizen of the Forum State; or* (b) *a Citizen of a Non-forum State; or* (c) *an Alien.*

Section 1332 now confers jurisdiction over all the subclasses in this class (with parallel removal jurisdiction under § 1441, except when a citizen of the forum state is a defendant).

Does the decision in the Tidewater case, p. 44, *supra,* settle the constitutionality of every aspect of this grant? See, *e.g.*, Americana of Puerto Rico, Inc. v. Kaplus, 368 F.2d 431 (3d Cir.1966)(upholding jurisdiction in an action by a Puerto Rican corporation against New Jersey defendants brought in a New

---

2. On the applicability of § 1332 to dual nationals, compare Aguirre v. Nagel, 270 F.Supp. 535 (E.D.Mich.1967)(upholding jurisdiction in action by a citizen of both the United States and Mexico against a citizen of the United States; both parties were domiciled in Michigan), with Sadat v. Mertes, 615 F.2d 1176 (7th Cir.1980)(denying jurisdiction in action by a citizen of both the United States and Egypt against citizens of the United States; plaintiff was domiciled abroad and defendants were domiciled in Connecticut and Wisconsin).

Jersey federal court). In which of the sub-classes is there substantial justification for the jurisdiction?

6. *Actions* (a) *Between Aliens, or* (b) *Between a Foreign State and an Alien Who Is a Subject of That or of a Different State, or* (c) *Between Different Foreign States.*

At least until 1988, there was no statutory basis for jurisdiction in any of these cases. Does the 1988 amendment authorize federal jurisdiction (on the basis of diversity) in an action between two aliens, at least one of whom is domiciled in a state and admitted to the U.S. as a permanent resident? Would such jurisdiction (or jurisdiction in any of the other categories in this part) be consistent with Article III?[3]

7. *Actions in Which One of the Parties Is a Citizen of the United States But Not of Any State or Territory or of the District of Columbia or Puerto Rico.*

This class of American citizens includes Americans domiciled abroad. See, *e.g.,* Smith v. Carter, 545 F.2d 909 (5th Cir.1977); Van Der Schelling v. U.S. News & World Report, Inc., 213 F.Supp. 756 (E.D.Pa.), *aff'd per curiam,* 324 F.2d 956 (3d Cir.1963). In both cases, motions to dismiss were sustained on the ground that such persons are not within the grant of diversity jurisdiction. Is this result compelled by Article III?

8. *Actions in Which One of the Parties Is a Citizen of a Territory But Not of the United States.*

The first question in dealing with this class—a question on which there is a notable lack of authority—is to determine the meaning of "Territory" under § 1332(d). Does it include all territories and possessions of the United States regardless of their formal designation? American Samoa and Swains Island, for example, are defined as "outlying possessions" in 8 U.S.C. § 1101(a)(29).[4]

Persons born in the outlying possessions are "nationals, but not citizens, of the United States". 8 U.S.C. § 1408(a). They are clearly not aliens. Are they within the diversity jurisdiction if domiciled in an outlying possession? In a state?

---

3. In Hodgson v. Bowerbank, 9 U.S. (5 Cranch) 303 (1809), the Court construed an ambiguous provision of the First Judiciary Act as not authorizing the exercise of jurisdiction solely on the basis of the alienage of one of the parties. See p. 444, *supra.*

In Singh v. Daimler–Benz AG, 9 F.3d 303 (3d Cir.1993), the court held that the 1988 amendment gave the district court jurisdiction over a suit brought by an alien who had been admitted to permanent residence and who was domiciled in Virginia against two defendants: a German corporation and its American subsidiary (incorporated in Delaware with its principal place of business in New Jersey). The court noted that the statute applied even though the legislative histo-

ry suggested that the major purpose of the change was to preclude diversity jurisdiction when a citizen of a state sued, or was sued by, a permanent resident alien domiciled in that state.

The constitutional question presented in Singh was not a difficult one. But what if the German corporation had been the *sole* defendant?

4. In United States v. Standard Oil Co., 404 U.S. 558 (1972)(per curiam), the Supreme Court held that American Samoa is a "Territory of the United States" within the meaning of § 3 of the Sherman Antitrust Act. The term, the Court said in quoting from an earlier opinion, was "used in its most comprehensive sense"(p. 559).

NOTE ON THE TIME WHEN JURISDICTION ATTACHES
AND ITS OUSTER BY SUBSEQUENT EVENTS

It is commonly said that the original jurisdiction of a federal trial court depends upon the facts existing when the action was begun. As a corollary, it is said that jurisdiction, once having attached, whether in an original or a removed action, will not be ousted by later events. Mollan v. Torrance, 22 U.S. (9 Wheat.) 537 (1824).

The problem of ouster of jurisdiction may arise as a result simply of extra-litigation events. These events may or may not have been within the control of a party, who in turn may or may not have been trying to defeat federal jurisdiction. The Court early said that jurisdiction, once attached, would not be defeated by a party's later change of domicile, Mollan v. Torrance, *supra,* or by the death of a party and the substitution of a non-diverse representative. Dunn v. Clarke, 33 U.S. (8 Pet.) 1, 2 (1834).

Changes in the record that are not simply unavoidable responses to external events may be thought to raise different problems. However, in Hardenbergh v. Ray, 151 U.S. 112, 118 (1894), the Court relied on the Mollan and Dunn cases in holding that the substitution, on his own motion, of a non-diverse landlord as the defendant in an action of ejectment brought originally against the tenant left the jurisdiction unimpaired. The Court relied also on Phelps v. Oaks, 117 U.S. 236, 240 (1886), which had reached the same result in a case of intervention by the landlord. See generally 13B Wright, Miller & Cooper, Federal Practice and Procedure § 3608 (1984 and 1995 Supp.).[5]

More difficult problems arise when one of the parties tries by amendment or responsive pleading to present a case or question that would not, in the first instance, have been within the court's jurisdiction. The Court has squarely held that the plaintiff may not, after removal by the defendant, defeat the jurisdiction by reducing the *ad damnum* below the jurisdictional amount. Saint Paul Mercury Indemnity Co. v. Red Cab Co., 303 U.S. 283 (1938). On the other hand, prior to the recent amendment of 28 U.S.C. § 1441(c), when a separable controversy with a diverse party could serve as the basis of removal, an amendment eliminating such a controversy was held to require the remand of the remnant of the case to the state court. Texas Transp. Co. v. Seeligson, 122 U.S. 519 (1887).

Other aspects of the question of ouster of jurisdiction are developed later in this chapter. Consider, after reflecting on these aspects, whether the cases can be reconciled on the basis that jurisdiction will be ousted by a later amendment only when the jurisdiction was ancillary and the amendment eliminated entirely the primary claim upon which it depended. Consider also the effect, if any, of the recent supplemental jurisdiction statute, 28 U.S.C. § 1367, p. 1564, *infra.*

---

5. See also Freeport–McMoRan Inc. v. K N Energy, Inc., 498 U.S. 426 (1991). In this case, plaintiffs brought a diversity action for breach of contract, and after suit was filed, the contract interest was transferred (for reasons unrelated to the litigation) to a limited partnership, some of whose members were co-citizens of the defendant. The partnership was added as a party, and after plain- tiffs prevailed at trial, the court of appeals reversed and ordered dismissal for lack of diversity. The Supreme Court reversed per curiam on the certiorari papers, citing (*inter alia*) the Mollan decision. "Diversity juris- diction, once established, is not defeated by the addition of a nondiverse party to the action" (p. 428).

Strawbridge v. Curtiss

7 U.S. (3 Cranch) 267, 2 L.Ed. 435 (1806).
Appeal from the Circuit Court for the District of Massachusetts.

■ MARSHALL, CH.J., delivered the opinion of the court.

The court has considered this case, and is of opinion that the jurisdiction cannot be supported.

The words of the act of congress are, "where an alien is a party; or the suit is between a citizen of a state where the suit is brought, and a citizen of another state."

The court understands these expressions to mean, that each distinct interest should be represented by persons, all of whom are entitled to sue, or may be sued, in the federal courts. That is, that where the interest is joint, each of the persons concerned in that interest must be competent to sue, or liable to be sued, in those courts.

But the court does not mean to give an opinion in the case where several parties represent several distinct interests, and some of those parties are, and others are not, competent to sue, or liable to be sued, in the courts of the United States.

Decree affirmed.

———

NOTE ON MULTIPLE ORIGINAL PARTIES: HEREIN OF ALIGNMENT AND INTERPLEADER

(1) *The Strawbridge Holding.* The Strawbridge opinion is certainly one of Marshall's more cryptic efforts. But under all the varying formulations of the general grant of diversity jurisdiction in successive judiciary acts, the decision has been consistently interpreted as requiring diversity of citizenship as between each plaintiff and each defendant.[1] Should application of the decision have been limited to cases in which the interests of the several plaintiffs and/or defendants were "joint"?[2] Does the co-citizenship of two adverse parties always assure impartiality in the disposition of every aspect of the litigation?

(2) *Realignment.* In applying the doctrine of Strawbridge v. Curtiss, the court is not controlled by the plaintiff's alignment of the parties. It "will look beyond the pleadings and arrange the parties according to their sides in the dispute", whether the result is to establish or to defeat jurisdiction. See Dawson v. Columbia Ave. Saving Fund, Safe Dep., Title & Trust Co., 197 U.S. 178, 180 (1905)(realigning to defeat jurisdiction); Indianapolis v. Chase Nat. Bank, 314 U.S. 63 (1941)(same).

1. Does the Strawbridge rule apply when there is an independent basis of federal jurisdiction over the controversy between the nondiverse parties? See Comment, 82 Colum.L.Rev. 784, 797 (1982)(arguing persuasively, on the basis of the Romero case, p. 975, *supra*, that the Strawbridge rule does not apply).

2. Strawbridge itself was a suit brought by co-executors, one of whom was a co-citizen of several of the defendants. Under the prevailing law, neither executor could bring suit without the other joining as plaintiff. A fuller description of the case, based on a study of the archives, is set forth in a letter from Prof. L.H. LaRue to David Shapiro (10/9/92).

Realignment is particularly important in stockholders' derivative suits, since the defendants are often directors or officers of the corporation and thus co-citizens of the corporation.[3] Such early decisions as Dodge v. Woolsey, 59 U.S. (18 How.) 331 (1856), and Hawes v. Oakland, 104 U.S. 450 (1882), established criteria for determining when a shareholder could maintain a derivative action—criteria now reflected in significant part in Fed.Rule 23.1. In Doctor v. Harrington, 196 U.S. 579 (1905), the Court, while reversing a decision realigning a corporate defendant as a plaintiff in a derivative action, apparently recognized the possibility that realignment might be appropriate. Even though a corporation stands to benefit from the suit, the Court said (p. 587) that the corporation should not be realigned as a plaintiff if it is "under a control antagonistic to him [the shareholder plaintiff], and made to act in a way detrimental to his rights".

The circumstances in which realignment was required in these cases remained cloudy at least until Smith v. Sperling, 354 U.S. 91 (1957), and its companion case, Swanson v. Traer, 354 U.S. 114 (1957). The plaintiff in Smith had brought a derivative action in a federal court on behalf of Warner Brothers (a Delaware corporation), against United States Pictures, Inc. (another Delaware corporation), certain directors of Warner, and others, challenging the fairness of various agreements between Warner and United. The district court, after a 15–day hearing, ordered Warner realigned as a plaintiff and dismissed the action for lack of diversity, finding that the stockholders, officers, and directors of Warner were not "antagonistic to the financial interests" of the company and that none of the officers and directors "wrongfully participated" in the acts complained of.

After affirmance by the court of appeals, the Supreme Court reversed, 5–4, with both sides relying on existing precedent. Justice Douglas, for the majority, said (pp. 96–97):

"It seems to us that the proper course [for deciding the alignment question] is not to try out the issues presented by the charges of wrongdoing but to determine the issue of antagonism on the face of the pleadings and by the nature of the controversy. The bill and answer normally determine whether the management is antagonistic to the stockholder * * *. Whenever the management refuses to take action to undo a business transaction or whenever, as in this case, it so solidly approves it that any demand to rescind would be futile, antagonism is evident. The cause of action, to be sure, is that of the corporation. But the corporation has become through its managers hostile and antagonistic to the enforcement of the claim.

"Collusion to satisfy the jurisdictional requirements of the District Courts may, of course, always be shown; and it will always defeat jurisdiction. Absent collusion, there is diversity jurisdiction when the real collision of issues * * * is between citizens of different States."

For Justice Frankfurter, in dissent, the Court, "purporting to interpret [a] half-century of precedents, sweeps them away" and "[i]n so doing, it greatly expands the diversity jurisdiction," perhaps beyond constitutional bounds (p. 105). In his view, a corporation on whose behalf a derivative action is brought

---

3. In determining diversity in derivative actions, the only shareholder whose citizenship is taken into account is the one in whose name the action is filed. 7C Wright, Miller & Kane, Federal Practice and Procedure § 1822 (1986).

may properly be regarded as a defendant only when it is "in fact the tool of the very people against whom a judgment is sought".

Does the Smith case hold that an allegation of antagonism and satisfaction of the other pleading requirements of Rule 23.1 is sufficient to insure that the corporation will be aligned as a defendant? Some commentators think so, *e.g.,* Wright, Federal Courts § 73 (5th ed. 1994), and it is hard to see what else the majority is asking the plaintiff to do. Is there an acceptable alternative that does not involve a lengthy hearing that is bound to duplicate in part the hearing on the merits? Do the constitutional doubts expressed by the dissent have any substance if complete diversity is not constitutionally required? See Paragraph (3), *infra.*

The majority in Smith states that collusion "may always be shown". How? Suppose that a corporation has 1000 stockholders, most of whom are co-citizens of the corporation and of its directors. If a derivative action is brought against the directors by a shareholder who is not a co-citizen, is collusion shown by the fact that he is morally and financially supported by shareholders who are? Compare Amar v. Garnier Enterprises, Inc., 41 F.R.D. 211 (C.D.Cal. 1966), where an outsider from another state was brought into a family dispute over a close corporation so that the suit might be brought in a federal court, and collusion was found. See generally 7C Wright, Miller & Kane, Federal Practice and Procedure § 1830 (1986).

Smith v. Sperling has had an impact in cases other than derivative suits. In Reed v. Robilio, 376 F.2d 392 (6th Cir.1967), the plaintiff sued on behalf of the executors of her parents' estate to set aside certain contracts, and the court relied heavily on Smith in holding that the executors, who had refused to sue and had shown considerable hostility to the plaintiff's claim, should not have been realigned as plaintiffs.

The possibility of realignment, however, is still a very real one, at least in other contexts. See, *e.g.,* Standard Oil Co. of California v. Perkins, 347 F.2d 379 (9th Cir.1965), holding that parties who had refused to join as plaintiffs and who had been added as defendants because they were indispensable (see Fed.Rule 19(a)) should be realigned as plaintiffs, thus preserving diversity jurisdiction.[4]

(3) *Statutory Jurisdiction in Cases of Less Than Complete Diversity.* Did the Strawbridge decision preclude Congress from granting jurisdiction when complete diversity was lacking? The question remained open until 1967, and generated considerable discussion. Compare McGovney, *A Supreme Court Fiction: Corporations in the Diverse Citizenship Jurisdiction of the Federal Courts,* 56 Harv.L.Rev. 853, 1090, 1103–11 (1943)(arguing that complete diversity was probably required by Article III, and that the likelihood of prejudice was obviated if either result in the case would cut against a citizen of the forum state), with ALI Study of the Division of Jurisdiction Between State and

---

4. For an in-depth analysis and critique of Indianapolis v. Chase Nat. Bank (referred to in text at the beginning of Paragraph (2)), and discussion of the varying interpretations of that opinion by the lower courts, see Note, 68 N.Y.U.L.Rev. 1072 (1993). The author recommends the adoption of a test that would "require a court to (1) align the parties with respect to the primary purpose of the suit, and (2) investigate any other conflicts that might justify aligning the parties differently" (p. 1119).

Federal Courts, Supporting Memorandum A, at 426–36 (1969)(arguing the opposite on the basis of both precedent[5] and policy).

The matter came to a head in 1967 in a federal interpleader case. There are today two kinds of federal interpleader: statutory interpleader, under the successively broadened federal interpleader acts now codified in 28 U.S.C. §§ 1335, 1397, and 2361; and what may be called equity interpleader, developed under the old equity practice now liberalized and codified in Rule 22 of the Federal Rules of Civil Procedure. In the absence of a ground for federal question jurisdiction under § 1331, jurisdiction in equity interpleader must be based on the general grant of diversity jurisdiction, and its exercise is subject to the rules of process and venue ordinarily applicable in diversity cases. Such interpleader has been treated as involving a controversy between the stakeholder on one side and all the claimants on the other, whether or not the stakeholder disputes the existence or extent of its liability. See Wright, Federal Courts § 74, at 535 (5th ed. 1994).

In statutory interpleader, the jurisdictional amount is only $500. The requirement of citizenship under § 1335 is expressed in the words: "Two or more adverse claimants, of diverse citizenship as defined in section 1332 of this title". Under the prior act, 49 Stat. 1096 (1936), the parenthetical phrase after "claimants" was "citizens of different States". Under both acts, lower courts had generally held that diversity between any two adverse claimants was sufficient. The constitutional question posed by these holdings was dealt with by the Supreme Court in State Farm Fire & Cas. Co. v. Tashire, 386 U.S. 523 (1967), an interpleader case in which there was not complete diversity among all the adverse claimants. Raising the issue of diversity jurisdiction on its own motion, the Court held with almost no discussion that "minimal diversity"— diversity between any two adverse parties—was enough. Citing its own precedents as implicitly recognizing this rule "in a variety of contexts," the Court stated that "[f]ull-dress arguments for the constitutionality of 'minimal diversity' in situations like interpleader * * * need not be rehearsed here". The ALI Study and other secondary sources were also cited (p. 531 and n. 7).

Does the Tashire case stand for the proposition that minimal diversity is always enough to satisfy Article III? Can the proposition be defended on the ground that Article III should be read as authorizing Congress in the broadest terms to decide when, if ever, it is appropriate to take jurisdiction over controversies in which there are persons of diverse citizenship on different sides?

NOTE ON THE EFFECTS OF MISJOINDER OF PARTIES

(1) *Correction of Misjoinder in the District Court.* What if the presence in the case of a person who has joined as a plaintiff, or who has been joined as a defendant, destroys the complete diversity required by § 1332? If jurisdiction is not available under the new supplemental jurisdiction statute (§ 1367, discussed in Section 4, *infra*), and the person in question is not indispensable within the meaning of Fed.Rule 19, may that person be dropped as a party

---

5. *E.g.,* Barney v. Latham, 103 U.S. 205 (1881)(removal of "separable controversy");   Supreme Tribe of Ben Hur v. Cauble, 255 U.S. 356 (1921)(class action).

without dismissal of the case? Fed.Rule 21 states that he may, "at any stage of the action and on such terms as are just".

(2) *Correction on Appeal.* Suppose that an action against two defendants, one of whom is a co-citizen of the plaintiff, goes to trial and to judgment for the plaintiff, and the jurisdictional defect is noticed for the first time on appeal. If the co-citizen defendant is dropped as a party, may the judgment stand against the other defendant? What of the rule that subsequent events cannot ordinarily create or defeat jurisdiction? See *Note on the Time When Jurisdiction Attaches and its Ouster by Subsequent Events,* p. 1527, *supra.*

In Newman–Green, Inc. v. Alfonzo–Larrain, 490 U.S. 826 (1989)(7–2), the Court ruled that a court of appeals may dismiss a party (if not indispensable) in order to correct a lack of diversity, and may then uphold relief against the remaining defendants. The Court read § 1653, which speaks of amending "*allegations* of jurisdiction" (emphasis added by the Court), as addressing "only incorrect statements about jurisdiction that actually exists, and not defects in the jurisdictional facts themselves" (p. 831). Fed.Rule 21, however, was more helpful: though the Federal Rules of Civil Procedure purport to apply only in the district courts, the Court was unwilling to disturb the courts of appeals' almost unanimous view that, by virtue of Rule 21, they have authority to dismiss a dispensable non-diverse party. That authority should be exercised sparingly, the Court cautioned, and only after considering whether dismissal would prejudice any of the parties.

Kelly v. United States Steel Corp.

284 F.2d 850 (1960).
United States Court of Appeals for the Third Circuit.

■ Before GOODRICH, KALODNER and STALEY, CIRCUIT JUDGES.

■ GOODRICH, CIRCUIT JUDGE.

These are appeals from a series of decisions in the United States District Court for the Western District of Pennsylvania in which judgment has been entered for the defendant. The appeals all raise the same question. That question is whether the United States Steel Corporation has its principal place of business in Pennsylvania. If it has, the decision of the court below is correct since all these appellants are Pennsylvania citizens and there is, consequently, no diversity of citizenship on which to base the jurisdiction of a federal court.

The question arises under the 1958 statute, § 1332(c) of Title 28 [now § 1332(c)(1)]. * * * The new provision is, as appears in its legislative history, an effort to reduce the number of cases coming to federal courts on the ground of diversity of citizenship only.

* * * The simplest case [under this statute] is probably that of a corporation which gets a charter in one state but carries on all its business operations in another state. Obviously, in such a case the connection with the state of charter is nominal and the principal place of business is where the corporate activity is carried on. But from there the question becomes more difficult. A corporation may carry on much of its activity in the state of charter but have another state or perhaps more than one state where a great deal of its business

activities take place. In such circumstances one is tempted to try to find some one criterion by which the question can be decided.

The place of the meeting of shareholders will not do. Corporations under modern statutes may have shareholders' meetings in a state other than the state of charter and that place of meeting may be the only corporate act which takes place in that state. The place of meeting of the Board of Directors offers a tempting criterion. * * * That spot, of course, may change from time to time as the seasons and the board personnel change.

One may also look to the place where physical activity is carried on. We can suppose a mining corporation where the actual digging of iron ore is on the Mesabi Range in Minnesota, the corporation has a New Jersey charter but all the directive activity of the corporation is conducted at its office in Superior, Wisconsin. Should the state of digging be called the principal place of business when all the contracts, sales and plans for expansion or contraction, the bank accounts and all the rest that make up this corporation's business activity take place in Wisconsin? In the absence of a simple single test we are forced to analyze our question further and endeavor to pick out as best we can the factor or combination of factors that seem to point to one place as the "principal" place of business. The concept may get artificial in some cases as indeed it is in the case before us. This great corporation has fourteen divisions of the parent corporation and eleven principal subordinate companies. Its various manufacturing activities are spread over practically all the United States and extend to foreign countries. It has literally dozens of important places of business one of which we must pick out as the principal one because the statute says so.

The appellants urge upon us that the test should be where the "nerve center" of the corporation's business is and they urge that the nerve center is New York. We do not find the figure of speech helpful. Dorland's Medical Dictionary tells us that a nerve center is "any group of cells of gray nerve substance having a common function." We think there will be, in the case of United States Steel Corporation, a good many collections of nerve cells serving the common function of making the corporate enterprise go.

We turn, therefore, from a pleasant and alluring figure of speech to a consideration of the facts of the Steel Corporation's life. The appellants in a very well constructed brief list for us the activities of the United States Steel Corporation which to their minds make New York its principal place of business. We make little out of the fact that the federal income tax return is filed in New York. As will be seen from enumeration of other things which take place in that state, New York would be the natural filing place for its tax return. We move then to things more important on the New York side of the question. The Board of Directors regularly meets in New York. It has, however, met in Pittsburgh and as already pointed out the Board can choose its own place of meeting. The Chairman of the Board is in New York, spending one day a week in Pittsburgh. The President divides his time evenly between New York and Pittsburgh. The Executive Committee of the Board meets regularly in New York. So does the Finance Committee. The Secretary of the corporation lives and has his office in New York and the Treasurer, Comptroller and General Counsel have their offices there. The company owns the building at 71 Broadway. From New York is mailed the annual report. Dividends are declared in New York. The Public Relations Department of the corporate enterprise is centered in New York. The Steel Corporation's major banking activities are there. The cash on hand and its government securities are managed and controlled in New York and the corporation's pension funds are invested in New York. To us this adds up to the conclusion that as at present conducted the final decisions through the Board of Directors, the President and top executive officers are made in New York state. If the test of "principal place of business" is where such final decisions are made on corporate policy, including its financing, then the appellants are right in pointing to New York as the principal place of business.

After balancing these important and significant facts with those pointing to Pennsylvania, we reach the conclusion that Pennsylvania and not New York is the principal place of business. It is in Pennsylvania that the Operation Policy Committee sits and conducts its affairs. The Board of Directors has delegated to this committee the duty of conducting the business of the corporation relating to manufacturing, mining, transportation and general operation. It is composed of the Chairman of the Board, the President, the Chairman of the Finance Committee, the General Counsel and the seven Executive Vice Presidents. It makes policy decisions, of course subject to the Board of Directors. It appoints division presidents and corporate officers through the rank of Administrative Vice President. The seven Executive Vice Presidents, one at the head of each of the seven great branches of the corporation, have headquarters and staffs in Pittsburgh. All but one of the seventeen Administrative Vice Presidents and twenty-two out of the twenty-five Vice Presidents are located in Pittsburgh with their staffs. So, too, is the General Solicitor and his staff. In Pennsylvania almost thirty-four per cent of the employees classified as exempt under the Fair Labor Standards Act (29 U.S.C.A. § 201 *et seq.*) are located. This is fourteen times as many as there are in New York.

All this points to us the conclusion that business by way of activities is centered in Pennsylvania and we think it is the activities rather than the occasional meeting of policy-making Directors which indicate the principal place of business.

To this center of corporate activity we may add some other facts having to do with physical location of employer's plants and the like. We think these elements are of lesser importance, but added to the items already enumerated pointing to the center of corporate activity, we think they have some significance. For instance, Pennsylvania has 32.13 per cent of employee personnel, twenty-five times as many as New York and more than twice as many as any other state. More than one-third of the $2,547,594,414 worth of tangible property is in Pennsylvania. In New York there is less than one per cent. Pennsylvania leads in steel productive capacity. This is about thirty-five per cent of the total capacity of the corporation. New York has none. Other items could be added to this list but we have picked those which we think most significant. It is true that Pennsylvania does not have the majority of the productive capacity of this corporation nor the majority of the employees of this corporation. It does have, however, more than any other state. These facts, added to what we have found to be the headquarters of day-to-day corporate activity and management, add up to the irresistible conclusion that the principal place of business of this giant corporation is in Pennsylvania.   * * *

The judgments of the district court will be affirmed.

NOTE ON CORPORATE CITIZENSHIP

(1) *Historical Development and Constitutional Issues.* Does the conferring of citizenship on corporations for diversity purposes raise any constitutional issues? Prior to the addition of § 1332(c) to the Code in 1958, what was the basis on which corporations were treated as citizens for diversity purposes?

In the Supreme Court's first major pronouncement on the subject, Chief Justice Marshall said: "That invisible, intangible, and artificial being, that mere legal entity, a corporation aggregate, is certainly not a citizen; * * *." Bank of the United States v. Deveaux, 9 U.S. (5 Cranch) 61, 86 (1809).

From this premise the Court might have moved to any one of three possible conclusions: first, that despite its admitted capacity to sue and be sued, a corporation was barred altogether from the diversity jurisdiction; second, that actions by and against corporations should be regarded as conducted, in behalf of the stockholders, by the president and directors, and that the citizenship of these managers controlled for diversity purposes; and third, that such actions should be treated as, in substance, actions by or against all the stockholders, and thus the citizenship of all the stockholders was controlling. In the Deveaux case, the Court reached the third of these conclusions. Taken together with the rule of Strawbridge v. Curtiss, this approach effectively barred the use of diversity jurisdiction in much corporate litigation.

Thirty-five years later, the Court yielded to the pressure of the bar for a different result. Louisville, C. & C.R.R. v. Letson, 43 U.S. (2 How.) 497 (1844). The Court said (p. 555):

"* * * A corporation created by a state to perform its functions under the authority of that state and only suable there, though it may have members out of the state, seems to us to be a person, though an artificial one, inhabiting and belonging to that state, and therefore entitled, for the purpose of suing and being sued, to be deemed a citizen of that state".

While the Letson opinion said that a corporation was "entitled to be deemed" a citizen, and elsewhere that it was "substantially" a citizen, it carefully avoided saying that it *was* a citizen. Under the hammering of a minority of the Justices, the Court ten years later rephrased its position so as to bring it into closer accord with the Deveaux decision. Marshall v. Baltimore & O.R.R., 57 U.S. (16 How.) 314, 329 (1854). As Chief Justice Taney later explained it, the Court decided "that where a corporation is created by the laws of a State, the legal presumption is, that its members are citizens of the State * * * and that a suit by or against a corporation, in its corporate name, must be presumed to be a suit by or against citizens of the State which created the corporate body; and that no averment or evidence to the contrary is admissible * * *." Ohio & M.R.R. v. Wheeler, 66 U.S. (1 Black) 286, 296 (1861). See also National Steamship Co. v. Tugman, 106 U.S. 118 (1882), applying a similar presumption to corporations created by foreign states.

The story here summarized is told in detail, but from sharply conflicting points of view, in McGovney, *A Supreme Court Fiction*, 56 Harv.L.Rev. 853, 1090, 1225 (1943), and Green, *Corporations as Persons, Citizens, and Possessors of Liberty*, 94 U.Pa.L.Rev. 202 (1946). See also Henderson, The Position of Foreign Corporations in American Constitutional Law (1918), particularly Chap. IV; Moore & Weckstein, *Corporations and Diversity of Citizenship Jurisdiction: A Supreme Court Fiction Revisited*, 77 Harv.L.Rev. 1426 (1964).

Professor McGovney saw this judicial development as part of a larger effort by the federal courts to free business interests from state control. Speaking of the presumption of the Marshall case, he concluded (56 Harv.L.Rev. at 1258):

"In this era of candor and intellectual integrity in judicial decision it is inconceivable that the present Court would now create the fiction. Nothing but *stare decisis* stands in the way of its recall, and *stare decisis* was ignored by the justices who adopted it. Is it not time for the Supreme Court to say of it, as Mr. Justice Holmes said of the doctrine of Swift v. Tyson, that it is 'an unconstitutional assumption of powers by the Courts of the United States which no lapse of time or respectable array of opinion should make us hesitate to correct'?"

The following excerpts indicate Professor Green's position (94 U.Pa.L.Rev. at 217, 218, 227–28):

"A state which calls a corporation into being endows its members with corporate existence and capacities. * * * The fulfillment of the legitimate purposes of incorporation requires that if the corporation is looked upon as a body of members it be also recognized that the members in their organized capacity are the adopted citizens of the state that has made them into a body. To that state the incorporated group stands in a relation which for the purposes of the jurisdictional clauses of the Constitution seems identical with that of an individual citizen to his state. * * *

"* * * The so-called presumption of citizenship is not a fictitious presumption as to what the facts are, but a characterization of the actual facts. It is not a presumption about persons, who happen to be members of a corporation, to the effect that they are individually citizens of the state of incorporation; it is a doctrine about corporations, to the effect that their members, as members, are citizens of the corporation's state. * * *

"It was the Deveaux case and not the later cases that was founded on fiction, for a suit by or against a corporation is not a suit by or against its members."

(2) *The 1958 Amendment.* Prior to the 1958 amendment, the Supreme Court's treatment of the problem of the corporation incorporated in more than one state was not a model of clarity. After a per curiam opinion in Jacobson v. New York, N.H. & H.R.R., 347 U.S. 909 (1954), the chances were excellent that a corporation would be considered a citizen of the forum state, and *only* of the forum state, if it was incorporated there, at least if it had not been compelled to incorporate in that state as a condition of doing business. Thus the fact of dual incorporation might sometimes be used to create and sometimes to defeat diversity jurisdiction. Did such a rule make sense?

Was all this confusion swept away by the 1958 amendment, making a corporation a citizen of "any" state in which it was incorporated? Friedenthal, *New Limitations on Federal Jurisdiction,* 11 Stan.L.Rev. 213, 236–41 (1959), expressed some doubts and noted the absence of any useful legislative history. The matter, unfortunately, is yet to be laid to rest, and some courts still hold that there is diversity if a citizen of *A* brings an action in *B* against a corporation incorporated in both *A* and *B,* at least if the corporation's principal place of business is not in *A.* See Wright, Federal Courts § 27, at 166 and authorities cited nn. 22, 24 (5th ed. 1994).

What more could Congress do to resolve the problem? Would it help to change "any" to "every"?

No matter how the statute is drafted, isn't there a problem if an *A* corporation is required to incorporate in *B* as a condition of doing business there and then is considered a citizen of *B* for diversity purposes? Can or should such a condition imposed by a state lead to the closing of the doors of the federal court for disputes between the corporation and the citizens of *B*? *Cf.* Terral v. Burke Constr. Co., 257 U.S. 529 (1922), p. 733, *supra.*

(3) *Locating the Principal Place of Business.* The most frequently litigated issue under § 1332(c)(1) is the location of a corporation's principal place of business. Is there one and only one such place for each corporation?[1] The language suggests so, and the legislative history so indicates. See S.Rep. No. 1830, 85th Cong., 2d Sess. 5 (1958); H.R.Rep. No. 1706, 85th Cong., 2d Sess. 4 (1958).

According to Professor Wright, the early cases "seemed to take two different views on how to determine the principal place of business of a corporation with significant activities in several states." On one view, the principal place was the one in which the "home office" was located, since this was "the nerve center" of the corporation. The other view looked to "the place where the corporation carried on the bulk of its activity." Later cases, however, tended to reconcile these decisions and to apply "a single rule," which "looks to the place where the bulk of the corporate activity takes place, if there is any one state in which this is true, while resorting to the location of the home office only if the corporation's activities are dispersed among several states and no one state clearly predominates." Wright, Federal Courts § 27, at 167–68 (5th ed. 1994).

How do the result and rationale of the Kelly case fit into this analysis? Should a court in deciding this issue ever consider the effect on its jurisdiction in the case as a factor in the decision?

Should U.S. Steel, if sued after Kelly in a New York federal court by a New York citizen, be allowed to argue that its principal place of business is New York? What if its New York adversary had sued in a state court and was seeking to block removal to a federal court on this ground?

(4) *Corporations Incorporated in Other Countries.* Does § 1332(c) have any impact on a corporation incorporated abroad with its principal place of business in the United States? What if, for example, a Panamanian corporation with its headquarters in Florida sues (or is sued by) a Florida citizen? One leading decision sustained diversity jurisdiction in such a case. Eisenberg v. Commercial Union Assurance Co., 189 F.Supp. 500 (S.D.N.Y.1960)(alternative holding), but several later decisions have held to the contrary. *E.g.,* Jerguson v. Blue Dot Investment, Inc., 659 F.2d 31 (5th Cir.1981); Danjaq, S.A. v. Pathe Communications Corp. 979 F.2d 772 (9th Cir.1992). If these later cases are followed, could the Panamanian corporation in the hypothetical sue a Mexican national in a federal court? (Compare the question raised by the 1988 amendment to § 1332, discussed at p. 1526, *supra.*)

(5) *Federally Chartered Corporations.* What is the status for diversity purposes of a corporation incorporated under the laws of the United States but not of any state? Section 1348 of Title 28 provides that national banking associations shall "be deemed citizens of the States in which they are respectively

1. What if a corporation has become inactive? See Midlantic Nat'l Bank v. Hansen, 48 F.3d 693 (3d Cir.1995)(discussing conflicting decisions and holding that such a corporation has no principal place of business).

located". This provision codified a result that had previously been reached without the aid of statute, and has also been reached with respect to federal corporations other than national banks. Should a similar result be reached with respect to other nationally chartered corporations, at least if "localized" within one state? See generally 13B Wright, Miller & Cooper, Federal Practice and Procedure § 3627 (1984). Would a decision sustaining jurisdiction in such a case be consistent with the provisions of 28 U.S.C. § 1349? With the rationale of the Bouligny case, which follows this Note? Observe that the only effect of such a decision would be to expand the reach of the diversity jurisdiction.

(6) *State and Local Governments.* A state itself is not a "citizen of a state". Postal Tel. Cable Co. v. Alabama, 155 U.S. 482, 487 (1894). But a political subdivision is, "unless it is merely an alter ego" of the state itself. See 13B Wright, Miller & Cooper, Federal Practice and Procedure § 3602 (1984). Note that the presumption of Marshall v. Baltimore & O.R.R., Paragraph (1), *supra,* has a real foundation of probability in such cases.

United Steelworkers v. R.H. Bouligny, Inc.

382 U.S. 145, 86 S.Ct. 272, 15 L.Ed.2d 317 (1965).
Certiorari to the United States Court of Appeals for the Fourth Circuit.

■ Mr. Justice Fortas delivered the opinion of the Court.

Respondent, a North Carolina corporation, brought this action in a North Carolina state court. It sought $200,000 in damages for defamation alleged to have occurred during the course of the United Steelworkers' campaign to unionize respondent's employees. The Steelworkers, an unincorporated labor union whose principal place of business purportedly is Pennsylvania, removed the case to a Federal District Court. The union asserted not only federal-question jurisdiction, but that for purposes of the diversity jurisdiction it was a citizen of Pennsylvania, although some of its members were North Carolinians.

The corporation sought to have the case remanded to the state courts, contending that its complaint raised no federal questions and relying upon the generally prevailing principle that an unincorporated association's citizenship is that of each of its members. But the District Court retained jurisdiction. The District Judge noted "a trend to treat unincorporated associations in the same manner as corporations and to treat them as citizens of the state wherein the principal office is located." Divining "no common sense reason for treating an unincorporated national labor union differently from a corporation," he declined to follow what he styled "the poorer reasoned but more firmly established rule" of Chapman v. Barney, 129 U.S. 677.

On interlocutory appeal the Court of Appeals for the Fourth Circuit reversed and directed that the case be remanded to the state courts. * * * Because we believe this properly a matter for legislative consideration which cannot adequately or appropriately be dealt with by this Court, we affirm the decision of the Court of Appeals.

[In 1875] Congress * * * significantly expand[ed] diversity jurisdiction by deleting the requirement imposed in 1789 that one of the parties must be a citizen of the forum State. The resulting increase in the quantity of diversity litigation, however, cooled enthusiasts of the jurisdiction, and in 1887 and 1888 Congress enacted sharp curbs. It quadrupled the jurisdictional amount, confined the right of removal to nonresident defendants, reinstituted protections against jurisdiction by collusive assignment, and narrowed venue.

It was in this climate that the Court in 1889 decided Chapman v. Barney, *supra*. On its own motion the Court observed that plaintiff was a joint stock company and not a corporation or natural person. It held that although plaintiff was endowed by New York with capacity to sue, it could not be considered a "citizen" for diversity purposes.

In recent years courts and commentators have reflected dissatisfaction with the rule of Chapman v. Barney. The distinction between the "personality" and "citizenship" of corporations and that of labor unions and other unincorporated associations, it is increasingly argued, has become artificial and unreal. * * * They assert, with considerable merit, that it is not good judicial administration, nor is it fair, to remit a labor union or other unincorporated association to vagaries of jurisdiction determined by the citizenship of its members and to disregard the fact that unions and associations may exist and have an identity and a local habitation of their own.

The force of these arguments in relation to the diversity jurisdiction is particularized by petitioner's showing in this case. Petitioner argues that one of the purposes underlying the jurisdiction—protection of the nonresident litigant from local prejudice—is especially applicable to the modern labor union. According to the argument, when the nonresident defendant is a major union, local juries may be tempted to favor local interests at its expense. Juries may also be influenced by the fear that unionization would adversely affect the economy of the community and its customs and practices in the field of race relations. * * * Extending diversity jurisdiction to unions, says petitioner, would make available the advantages of federal procedure, Article III judges less exposed to local pressures than their state court counterparts, juries selected from wider geographical areas, review in appellate courts reflecting a multistate perspective, and more effective review by this Court.

We are of the view that these arguments, however appealing, are addressed to an inappropriate forum, and that pleas for extension of the diversity jurisdiction to hitherto uncovered broad categories of litigants ought to be made to the Congress and not to the courts.

     * * *

If we were to accept petitioner's urgent invitation to amend diversity jurisdiction so as to accommodate its case, we would be faced with difficulties which we could not adequately resolve. Even if the record here were adequate, we might well hesitate to assume that petitioner's situation is sufficiently representative or typical to form the predicate of a general principle. We should, for example, be obliged to fashion a test for ascertaining of which State the labor union is a citizen. Extending the jurisdiction to corporations raised no such problem, for the State of incorporation was a natural candidate, its arguable irrelevance in terms of the policies underlying the jurisdiction being outweighed by its certainty of application. But even that easy and apparent solution did not dispose of the problem; in 1958 Congress thought it necessary to enact legislation providing that corporations are citizens both of the State of incorporation and of the State in which their principal place of business is located. Further, in contemplating a rule which would accommodate petitioner's claim, we are acutely aware of the complications arising from the circumstance that petitioner, like other labor unions, has local as well as national organizations and that these perhaps, should be reckoned with in connection with "citizenship" and its jurisdictional incidents.

Whether unincorporated labor unions ought to be assimilated to the status of corporations for diversity purposes, how such citizenship is to be determined, and what if any related rules ought to apply, are decisions which we believe suited to the legislative and not the judicial branch, regardless of our views as to the intrinsic merits of petitioner's argument—merits stoutly attested by widespread support for the recognition of labor unions as juridical personalities.

We affirm the decision below.

———

NOTE ON UNINCORPORATED ORGANIZATIONS

(1) *The Bouligny Rationale.* Did the Court in Bouligny make too much, or too little, of the addition of § 1332(c) in 1958? The legislative history shows no consideration of the Bouligny problem, or of the rule of Chapman v. Barney. Would it "amend diversity jurisdiction" for the Court to overrule its own prior decision in Chapman? Did the Court exaggerate the difficulties that overruling would bring in its wake? How would the overruling have affected an unincorporated association organized under the laws of state *A* and having its principal place of business in state *B*? Is the problem likely to arise? Aside from any practical difficulties, is there a rational basis for distinguishing between a corporation and a labor union?

(2) *Partnerships and Business Trusts.* When a partnership sues or is sued, the citizenship of each of its members must be considered in determining diversity jurisdiction. See 13B Wright, Miller & Cooper, Federal Practice and Procedure § 3630 (1984). But in Navarro Sav. Ass'n v. Lee, 446 U.S. 458 (1980), the Court decided that individual trustees of a Massachusetts business trust could invoke diversity jurisdiction on the basis of their own citizenship without regard to the citizenship of the trust's beneficial shareholders. The Court began with the proposition that diversity jurisdiction should rest on the citizenship of the "real parties to the controversy" (p. 461) and took note of a line of decisions establishing that a trustee is such a party "when he possesses certain customary powers to hold, manage, and dispose of assets for the benefit of others" (p. 464). The business trust in Navarro, though different from a conventional trust in some respects, was one in which there were "active trustees whose control over the assets held in their names is real and substantial" (p. 465). The Court stressed the value of simplicity in determining jurisdictional issues, and observed that there was a rough correspondence between the test of citizenship it had applied and that for determining capacity to sue under Fed.R.Civ.P. 17(a).

Did the Court in Navarro pay sufficient heed to the rationale of Bouligny? Or can it be said that Bouligny simply reaffirmed the unavailability of entity status to organizations other than corporations, leaving open the question of determining those individuals in an organization whose citizenship should be looked to when diversity jurisdiction is invoked?

(3) *Limited Partnerships.* Navarro resolved one conflict among the lower courts; another still remained with respect to limited partnerships in which

there are both "general" and "limited" partners.[1] In Carden v. Arkoma Associates, 494 U.S. 185 (1990), the Supreme Court held, 5–4, that a limited partnership is not itself a citizen and that in determining whether there is complete diversity, a federal court must look to the citizenship of the limited as well as the general partners. Justice Scalia, for the majority, said that the Navarro decision was "irrelevant, since it involved not a juridical person but the distinctive common-law institution of trustees" (p. 194). Citing Bouligny and Chapman v. Barney, he concluded that diversity jurisdiction in a suit by or against an artificial entity other than a corporation "depends on the citizenship of 'all the members' "(p. 195)(quoting Chapman).[2]

For the four dissenters, Navarro was squarely in point. In their view, that decision did not rest on the distinctive common-law institution of a trust but rather on a determination of the "real parties to the controversy" (p. 204). Applying that test, the dissenters concluded that the citizenship of the limited partners should not be considered, since those partners lacked power to control partnership assets or to initiate or control litigation.

Note that even after Navarro, it may still be possible—through use of the class action device—for limited partnerships, or other unincorporated entities, to sue or be sued in a federal court on the basis of diversity even though some of their members are co-citizens of the adverse party. See Paragraph (4) of this Note.

(4) *Class Actions.* Supreme Tribe of Ben Hur v. Cauble, 255 U.S. 356 (1921), established that in a class action the citizenship of the named representatives is controlling. The courts are not of one view on whether the class action device may be successfully invoked to circumvent the limitations of the Chapman rule in all its manifestations. See authorities cited in 13B Wright, Miller & Cooper, Federal Practice and Procedure § 3630 (1984) and nn. 58.1, 58.2 (1995 Supp.). Note also that Fed.Rule 23.2, added in 1966, relates specifically to actions "by or against the members of an unincorporated association as a class".

Is it sound to allow the use of the class action device in this context? It does not render the Chapman–Bouligny problem academic, since even if the other prerequisites for a class action are met, the court may conclude that the only members of the unincorporated association who would adequately represent the class are those whose citizenship would destroy diversity. And there is a danger that the named representative may be held to have been "improperly or collusively made or joined to invoke the jurisdiction" of the federal court. 28 U.S.C. § 1359. See also Underwood v. Maloney, 256 F.2d 334 (3d Cir.1958),

---

1. Under the law prevailing in every state, limited partners have narrow rights with respect to management, do not have an interest in the property of the partnership but only a right to a distributive share of the profits, are not personally liable for the debts or torts of the partnership, and cannot sue or be sued on behalf of the partnership. See Comment, 45 U.Chi.L.Rev. 384, 403–04 (1978).

2. In Puerto Rico v. Russell & Co., 288 U.S. 476 (1933), the Court held that a "sociedad", organized under the law of Puerto Rico, was itself a party for diversity purposes even though it was not a "corporation" within the meaning of American law. The Russell case was distinguished in Bouligny on the grounds that, unlike a labor union, a sociedad was an exotic entity unknown to the common law and that the court in Russell had relied on the civil law tradition of regarding such an entity as a juridical person. In Carden, the Court recognized that Russell was "[t]he one exception to the admirable consistency of our jurisprudence on this matter" but said that "the approach it espouses was proposed and specifically rejected in Bouligny" (494 U.S. at 189–90).

holding that the class action device may not be used to circumvent diversity requirements if under the forum state's law the unincorporated association in question may sue or be sued *only* as an entity. (The court relied on Rule 17(b) of the Federal Rules of Civil Procedure in reaching this result. Was the reliance warranted?)

(5) *Possible Statutory Changes.* Would enactment of a provision giving a partnership or other unincorporated association state citizenship for diversity purposes, and in particular providing that any such entity shall be deemed a citizen of the state where it has its principal place of business, be likely to reduce or to expand the number of cases falling within diversity jurisdiction? If adopted, should its applicability in a particular case depend on the capacity of the association to sue or be sued under state law? *Cf.* Fed.Rule Civ.P. 17(b).

SECTION 3.   JURISDICTIONAL AMOUNT

INTRODUCTORY NOTE

(1) The Judiciary Act of 1789, 1 Stat. 73, 78, fixed the jurisdictional amount, in those cases in which some amount was requisite, at $500.[1] Ninety-eight years later, 24 Stat. 552 (1887), this was raised to $2,000. In 1911, 36 Stat. 1087, 1091, it was set at $3,000, in 1958, 72 Stat. 415, at $10,000, and in 1988, 102 Stat. 4646, at $50,000, where it remains today in diversity cases brought under 28 U.S.C. § 1332.[2] In interpleader, the figure is far lower—$500. 28 U.S.C. § 1335. (Why the difference?)

(2) From 1875, when general federal question jurisdiction was first enacted, to 1976, there was a jurisdictional amount requirement in such cases identical to that in diversity cases. But many statutes, *e.g.*, 28 U.S.C. § 1333 (admiralty), 28 U.S.C. § 1337 (cases arising under any act of Congress regulating commerce), 28 U.S.C. § 1343 (certain civil rights cases), authorized suits to be brought without regard to that requirement. And in cases involving constitutional claims that could be brought in federal court, if at all, only under § 1331 (the general federal question statute), some decisions ignored the requirement,[3] or stretched it to accommodate the case,[4] or even raised a question about its constitutionality,[5] while others rigorously insisted that it be satisfied.[6] The

---

1. For a fuller review of the jurisdictional amount requirement, see Baker, *The History and Tradition of the Amount in Controversy Requirement: A Proposal to "Up the Ante" in Diversity Jurisdiction,* 102 F.R.D. 299 (1985). For the history of specified amounts in controversy as prerequisites for taking an appeal, see pp. 31, 36–37, *supra,* p. 1636, *infra.*

2. Note that the amount in controversy must *exceed* $50,000 to confer federal jurisdiction under § 1332. Compare 28 U.S.C. § 1346 (district court jurisdiction over certain civil actions against the United States is concurrent with that of the Claims Court

only as to claims "not exceeding $10,000 in amount").

3. See, *e.g.,* Flast v. Cohen, 392 U.S. 83 (1968); Kleindienst v. Mandel, 408 U.S. 753 (1972).

4. See, *e.g.,* Spock v. David, 469 F.2d 1047 (3d Cir.1972).

5. See, *e.g.,* Cortright v. Resor, 325 F.Supp. 797 (E.D.N.Y.1971), *reversed on other grounds,* 447 F.2d 245 (2d Cir.1971); Murray v. Vaughn, 300 F.Supp. 688 (D.R.I.1969). See also Note, 71 Colum.L.Rev. 1474 (1971).

6. See, *e.g.,* Goldsmith v. Sutherland, 426 F.2d 1395 (6th Cir.1970); McGaw v. Far-

difficulty was significantly alleviated in 1976, when Congress excepted actions against federal officers and agencies from the jurisdictional amount requirement of § 1331,[7] and was virtually eliminated in 1980 when the requirement was deleted from the section altogether.[8] Only a few federal statutes remain in which access to a federal court is conditioned on a specified amount in controversy.[9]

Thus, the principal impact of this requirement today is in diversity cases, and the materials on the requirement are therefore included in this chapter. Some of the relevant cases, however, are federal question cases decided under earlier versions of the grant of federal question jurisdiction.

(3) If it was appropriate to abolish the jurisdictional amount requirement in federal question cases, should it be retained in diversity cases? Professor Currie at one time proposed eliminating the requirement across the board. Currie, *The Federal Courts and the American Law Institute (II)*, 36 U.Chi. L.Rev. 268, 292–98 (1969). Isn't there a greater justification for imposing on a federal court the burden of litigating a "small" case when that case arises under federal law than when it arises under state law? Note too that state courts may be better equipped, through the use of special tribunals and procedures, to adjudicate small cases, especially those arising under state law. And consider the burden on a defendant who is forced to litigate a small case in a distant, unfamiliar federal court rather than in a nearby state court; isn't that burden easier to explain if the rights and liabilities at stake are themselves federal? Do the practical difficulties in administration of the amount requirement, the ease of circumventing it in many cases, and the possible unfairness of judging a case's importance in terms of a dollar figure, outweigh these considerations? You should keep these questions in mind in reading the materials that follow.

Burns v. Anderson

502 F.2d 970 (1974).
United States Court of Appeals for the Fifth Circuit.

■ Before BROWN, CHIEF JUDGE, and THORNBERRY and AINSWORTH, CIRCUIT JUDGES.

■ JOHN R. BROWN, CHIEF JUDGE:

The question on this appeal is whether a district court may dismiss a personal injury diversity suit where it appears "to a legal certainty" that the

---

row, 472 F.2d 952 (4th Cir.1973); Senate Select Comm. on Presidential Campaign Activities v. Nixon, 366 F.Supp. 51 (D.D.C. 1973).

7. Act of Oct. 21, 1976, 90 Stat. 2721.

8. Act of Dec. 1, 1980, 94 Stat. 2369.

9. *E.g.,* 15 U.S.C. § 2072 (actions under Consumer Product Safety Act); 15 U.S.C. § 2310(d)(actions under Consumer Product Warranties Act); 28 U.S.C. §§ 1337,

1445(b)(suits under 49 U.S.C. § 11707 for freight damage or loss); 42 U.S.C. § 1395 ff(b)(judicial review of the denial of benefits under the Medicare Act). With respect to the last of these provisions, see Bartlett v. Bowen, 816 F.2d 695, 697 (D.C.Cir.1987)(holding that Congress "did not intend to bar judicial review [in cases falling below the jurisdictional amount] of constitutional challenges to the underlying Act").

claim was "really for less than the jurisdictional amount."[1]

The suit grew out of an auto accident in which plaintiff Burns' automobile was struck amidships by that of defendant Anderson. Burns' principal injury was a broken thumb. He brought the action in the Eastern District of Louisiana, claiming $1,026.00 in lost wages and medical expenses and another $60,000.00 for pain and suffering. After a pre-trial conference and considerable discovery, the District Court dismissed for want of jurisdiction. Plaintiff appeals.

The test for jurisdictional amount was established by the Supreme Court in St. Paul Mercury Indemnity Co. v. Red Cab Co.[2] There, the Court held that the determinant is plaintiff's good faith claim and that to justify dismissal it must appear to a legal certainty that the claim is really for less than the jurisdictional amount. There is no question but that this is a test of liberality, and it has been treated as such by this Court. This does not mean, however, that Federal Courts must function as small claims courts. The test is an objective one and, once it is clear that as a matter of law the claim is for less than $10,000.00 [the statutory figure at that time], the Trial Judge is required to dismiss.

In the instant case, the District Judge dismissed only after examination of an extensive record. * * * The accident occurred on May 26. The evidence is without contradiction that by the middle of August only very minimal disability remained. By December, even this minor condition had disappeared. Burns' actions speak even more strongly than the medical testimony. In his deposition he testified that he took a job as a carpenter's assistant on June 21 or 22— less than a month after the accident. He did heavy manual labor for the remainder of the summer with absolutely no indication of any difficulty with his thumb. It is equally clear that any pain he suffered was not of very great magnitude or lasting duration. Burns admitted that by the end of July there was no pain whatsoever. As a matter of fact, the evidence reveals that the only medication he ever received was a single prescription on the day of the accident for Empirin, a mild aspirin compound. Nor did his special damages take him a significant way down the road to the $10,000.00 minimum. His total medical bills were less than $250.00. Although he claims $800.00 in lost wages, it is difficult to see how this could have amounted to even $300.00 at Burns' rate of pay that summer.

The point of this fact recitation is that it really does appear to a legal certainty that the amount in controversy is less than $10,000. This is no Plimsoll case,[5] where dismissal was based on "bare bones pleadings" alone. The present situation differs from that case also in that this dismissal was for lack of subject matter jurisdiction not for failure to state a claim. Here the Trial Court examined an extensive record and determined as a matter of law that the requisite amount in controversy was not present. Indeed, had the case gone to trial and had the jury returned an award of $10,000, a Gorsalitz-girded Judge would have been compelled as a matter of law to order a remittitur. He would have inescapably found that the verdict was "so inordinately large as

---

1. St. Paul Mercury Indemnity Co. v. Red Cab Co., 1938, 303 U.S. 283, 289.

2. *Id.*

5. Cook & Nichol, Inc. v. Plimsoll Club, 5 Cir., 1971, 451 F.2d 505.

obviously to exceed the maximum of the reasonable range within which the jury may properly operate.[6]" * * *

Neither are we affected by plaintiff's plaintive plea that he is being deprived of a jury trial. The question in this case is not whether Burns is entitled to a trial by jury but rather where that trial is to be. We hold only that the case cannot be tried in the Federal Court because competence over it has not been granted to that Court by Congress.

Affirmed.

NOTE ON THE EFFECT OF PLAINTIFF'S AD DAMNUM IN UNLIQUIDATED DAMAGES CASES

(1) In St. Paul Mercury Indem. Co. v. Red Cab Co., 303 U.S. 283 (1938), cited in the Burns opinion, the Court held in a removed case that jurisdiction, once having attached by virtue of the plaintiff's good faith claim in excess of $3,000, was not defeated by the plaintiff's later amendment reducing the ad damnum below $3,000. Would it ever be possible to find bad faith in a claim for unliquidated damages where the defendant rather than the plaintiff had invoked federal jurisdiction?

(2) For unliquidated damage cases in which the Supreme Court has upheld the plaintiff's invocation of federal jurisdiction against a challenge to the amount in controversy, see, *e.g.,* Bell v. Preferred Life Assurance Society, 320 U.S. 238, 243 (1943)(although actual damages could not exceed $1,000, evidence might justify a jury verdict for actual and punitive damages exceeding $3,000); Barry v. Edmunds, 116 U.S. 550 (1886).

Following these decisions, the lower federal courts had at one time held that the plaintiff's claim in an action for unliquidated damages was virtually conclusive on the issue of amount in controversy. *E.g.,* Deutsch v. Hewes St. Realty Corp., 359 F.2d 96 (2d Cir.1966); Wade v. Rogala, 270 F.2d 280 (3d Cir.1959). But a number of later decisions, of which Burns is representative, have taken a much closer look. See 14A Wright, Miller & Cooper, Federal Practice and Procedure § 3707 (1985 & 1995 Supp.)

Granted a genuine concern over crowded federal dockets, is the game worth the candle? Might motions to dismiss on this ground, coupled with extensive discovery designed to show lack of a colorable claim, lead to a net increase in the expenditure of judicial time?

Was plaintiff's jury trial argument in Burns properly disposed of? See Note, 48 Iowa L.Rev. 471 (1963); 14A Wright, Miller & Cooper, Federal Practice and Procedure § 3702, at 27–28 (1985)(arguing that there is no jury trial right on jurisdictional fact issues even if they are related to the merits).[1]

(3) Suppose it is established at trial that any recovery to which plaintiff is entitled falls short of the jurisdictional amount, or that plaintiff is not entitled to recover at all. Should the action be dismissed for lack of jurisdiction? See Rosado v. Wyman, 397 U.S. 397, 405 n. 6 (1970); Mt. Healthy City School Dist.

---

6. Gorsalitz v. Olin Mathieson Chemical Corp., 5 Cir., 1970, 429 F.2d 1033, 1046.

1. After the Burns decision, was a state court jury still free to award plaintiff more than $10,000?

Bd. of Educ. v. Doyle, 429 U.S. 274 (1977). In Mt. Healthy, the plaintiff had sought $50,000 damages and reinstatement but was awarded only $5,158 damages and reinstatement. The Court said (p. 277): "Even if the District Court had chosen to award only compensatory damages [of $5,158] and not reinstatement, it was far from a 'legal certainty' at the time of suit that Doyle would not have been entitled to more than $10,000."

Section 1332(b), enacted in 1958, provides that a plaintiff who recovers less than the jurisdictional amount may be saddled with the opponent's court costs. The provision does not seem to have had much impact. See Wright, Federal Courts § 33, at 199 (5th ed. 1994). Note the difficulty of imposing such a sanction on the plaintiff when in all probability it was plaintiff's lawyer who chose the forum. Do the provisions of Fed.R.Civ.P. 11 (subjecting a lawyer to possible sanctions for filing a pleading or other paper that is without "evidentiary support") afford a more appropriate basis for relief? See generally Note, 27 B.C.L.Rev. 385 (1986).

NOTE ON THE ADMISSIBLE ELEMENTS IN VALUATION

(1) *Introduction: The Rule of Healy v. Ratta.* The Supreme Court addressed some important questions of valuation in Healy v. Ratta, 292 U.S. 263 (1934). In this case, the plaintiff sought to enjoin as unconstitutional the application of a state's license fee imposed on peddlers and hawkers. The plaintiff alleged that the jurisdictional amount (then $3,000) was met because the inability or unwillingness of his salesmen to pay the tax meant a loss to his business in excess of that amount. He alleged in the alternative that the jurisdictional amount requirement was met because the capitalized value of the tax that would have to be paid to stay in business (at least $350 per year) also exceeded $3,000.

The Court rejected both arguments. It said (pp. 269–70) that "[t]he disputed tax is the matter in controversy, and its value, not that of the penalty or loss which payment of the tax would avoid, determines the jurisdiction. * * * [Moreover, it does not follow from the requirement of annual payment] that capitalization of the tax is the method of determining the value of the matter in controversy." The Court declined to assume that the defendant (a city official) would seek to exact compliance in future years, that the plaintiff would wish to continue his business in that city, or indeed that the statute itself (or its allegedly objectionable features) would remain on the books. Further, since the defendant who had threatened to enforce the statute was an official of a particular city, the Court declined to consider the monetary effect of the tax in other parts of the state.

Finally, the Court distinguished such cases as Berryman v. Board of Trustees of Whitman College, 222 U.S. 334 (1912), where the question involved the validity of a *permanent* exemption by contract from an annual property tax. In such a case, the Court said, the value of the permanent immunity was "more than a limited number of annual payments demanded. * * * [Thus] the burden which rests on a defendant who challenges the plaintiff's allegation of the jurisdictional amount may well not be sustained by the mere showing that the annual payment is less than the jurisdictional amount" (p. 271).

The Healy case applied doctrine that is standard in tax litigation: the amount in controversy is measured by the amount of the tax rather than the penalty. See, *e.g.,* Henneford v. Northern Pac. Ry., 303 U.S. 17 (1938). Can these cases be explained in part on the basis of a policy of avoiding undue friction with the administration of state tax laws—a policy now reflected in 28 U.S.C. § 1341? With these decisions, compare Hunt v. New York Cotton Exch., 205 U.S. 322 (1907)(in suit to enjoin unauthorized use of stock quotations, amount in controversy is value to exchange of right to control their distribution, not the cost of a subscription by the defendant).

Consider also the much-cited decision and statement in Mississippi & M.R.R. v. Ward, 67 U.S. (2 Black) 485 (1862). That was a suit, on the theory of abatement of nuisance, to enjoin the continued maintenance of a bridge over the Mississippi. The Court upheld the jurisdiction, and seemed to say that the damage to the plaintiff's navigation business was not controlling (p. 492):

"But the want of a sufficient amount of damage having been sustained to give the Federal Courts jurisdiction, will not defeat the remedy, as the removal of the obstruction is the matter of controversy, and the value of the object must govern."

(2) *The Relevance of the "Res Judicata" Value of the Judgment.* Granting that the stare decisis value of a judgment ought not to be taken into account, as the Healy case indicates, why not the res judicata value? Is the Healy Court's refusal to take future taxes into account based simply on the uncertainty of the taxes or on a general principle that only the value of the relief *currently* sought can be counted and not the value of the issue preclusive effect of the decision in future litigation?

In Clark v. Paul Gray, Inc., 306 U.S. 583, 589 (1939), a suit to enjoin enforcement of a California statute imposing license fees aggregating $15 for each automobile caravaned into the state for sale, the Court said:

"Examination of the record shows that only in the case of a single appellee, Paul Gray, Inc., is there any allegation or proof tending to show the amount in controversy [which then stood at $3,000]. As to it the bill of complaint alleged that 'it causes to be caravaned into the said state * * * approximately one hundred fifty (150) automobiles each year.' This allegation is supported by evidence that this appellee is regularly engaged in the business and tending to show that its volume exceeded that amount when the act went into effect July 2, 1937. Since the amount in controversy in a suit to restrain illegal imposition of fees or taxes is the amount of the fees or taxes which would normally be collected during the period of the litigation, Healy v. Ratta, 292 U.S. 263, we cannot say, upon this state of the record, that jurisdiction was not established as to appellee Paul Gray, Inc."

Elgin v. Marshall, 106 U.S. 578 (1882), was an action to recover the amount due on certain coupons detached from bonds, the defense being that both bonds and coupons were void. The Court held that the amount in controversy was the value of the coupons in suit only, although it recognized that a decision would be res judicata as to other coupons and as to the bonds themselves. And in cases involving the right to recover on a policy of disability insurance, the courts have generally refused to consider future installments in computing the amount in controversy unless the suit relates to the validity of the policy. *E.g.,* Mutual Life Ins. Co. v. Wright, 276 U.S. 602 (1928), *affirming* 19 F.2d 117 (5th Cir.1927); Lenox v. S.A. Healy Co., 463 F.Supp. 51 (D.Md.

1978); *cf.* New York Life Ins. Co. v. Viglas, 297 U.S. 672 (1936). Nor does it appear to avail the plaintiff to seek a declaratory judgment that he is permanently disabled and entitled to future installments. *E.g.,* Beaman v. Pacific Mut. Life Ins. Co., 369 F.2d 653 (4th Cir.1966).[1]

(3) *Capitalization of the Amount Due.* When is it proper to capitalize the amount currently due or to be expended? Does the Healy decision satisfactorily distinguish Berryman v. Whitman College?

In Aetna Cas. & Sur. Co. v. Flowers, 330 U.S. 464 (1947), a widow brought an action for death benefits under a state workers' compensation statute, and the case was removed to a federal court. The statute sued on provided for maximum payments of $18 per week, for a maximum of 400 weeks (but not to exceed $5,000), with payments to end on the death or remarriage of the widow, or on the death or attainment of the age of eighteen by the children. The Court held that a remand for lack of the jurisdictional amount was improper, distinguishing the disability cases cited in the preceding Paragraph on the ground that the state law creating liability for the award in Flowers "contemplates a single action for the determination of claimant's right to benefits and a single judgment for the award granted" (pp. 467–68). Are you satisfied with the distinction? Is it like the difference between a contingent remainder and a vested remainder subject to divestment? *Cf.* Western & A.R.R. v. Railroad Comm'n, 261 U.S. 264, 267 (1923)(in a suit to enjoin an order to build a side track, the "permanent annual burden" of interest on the cost of construction, of depreciation, and of maintenance and operation of the side track, capitalized at a reasonable rate, should be taken into account in computing the amount in controversy).

Though not cited, the Flowers case was followed (and perhaps extended) in Weinberger v. Wiesenfeld, 420 U.S. 636, 642 n. 10 (1975). In upholding jurisdiction in an action for survivors' benefits under the Social Security Act, the Court said: "[W]here an injunction commanding future payments is sought, there is no need to await accrual of $10,000 in back benefits to bring suit." The disability cases, though not cited, were implicitly distinguished: "[U]nlike disability benefits, * * * these survivors' benefits do not depend upon ability to earn, but only upon actual earnings. Thus, they give a potential recipient a choice between staying home * * * and working. This opportunity for choice * * * certainly has a present value of $10,000 * * *."

The relevance of future harm to the determination of the amount in controversy was further underscored in Hunt v. Washington State Apple Advertising Comm'n, 432 U.S. 333 (1977). In this case, an agency of the state of Washington sought a declaration of the unconstitutionality, and an injunction against enforcement, of a North Carolina law effectively prohibiting the use by Washington apple growers and dealers of their own state's system for grading apples destined for North Carolina. The requested relief was granted below and the Supreme Court unanimously affirmed. After holding that the state agency had standing to sue as representative of its constituent growers and dealers, see p. 186, *supra,* the Court held the jurisdictional amount requirement satisfied on the basis of "the losses [to growers and dealers] that will follow from the statute's enforcement" (p. 347). Such losses included lost sales in North Carolina, the costs of altering containers, and the loss of

---

1. But *cf.* Goldberg, *The Influence of Procedural Rules on Federal Jurisdiction,* 28 Stan.L.Rev. 395, 424–27 (1976), discussing some of the older decisions.

competitive advantage associated with the widely known Washington grades. Given the substantial volume of sales of Washington apples in North Carolina, and "the continuing nature of the statute's interference, * * * [we cannot say] 'to a legal certainty,' on this record, that such losses and expenses will not, *over time, if they have not done so already,* amount to the requisite $10,000 *for at least some of the individual growers and dealers.*" (p. 348)(emphasis added).

The analysis seems eminently sound, and the first italicized phrase seems consistent with Weinberger v. Wiesenfeld. Is the second phrase consistent with the Zahn case, p. 1556, *infra?* Does it at least suggest a way around the Zahn result if the right plaintiff can be found and the "class action" label avoided?

Note that Weinberger and Hunt were both federal question cases—arising before the 1980 amendment to § 1331 eliminated the amount requirement. Do you think that fact made the Court more receptive to the arguments favoring jurisdiction than it would have been in a diversity case?

(4) *The Relevance of the "Good Faith" Test in Actions for Non-monetary Relief.* In an action for other than monetary relief, is the "good faith" test applicable to the amount alleged by the plaintiff to be in controversy? Many of the cases discussed in this Note indicate that it is not—that the plaintiff must satisfy the court as to the objective facts. See Justice Roberts' opinion in Hague v. CIO, 307 U.S. 496, 507–08 (1939). See also City of Milwaukee v. Saxbe, 546 F.2d 693, 702 (7th Cir.1976). (But see, *e.g.,* Opelika Nursing Home, Inc. v. Richardson, 448 F.2d 658 (5th Cir.1971).) What if the plaintiff attempts to satisfy the burden by showing that although the value of the requested relief to the plaintiff does not meet the jurisdictional amount requirement, the cost to defendant does?[2] What if the defendant argues in the converse case that the crucial figure is the cost of the relief to him?

Glenwood Light & Water Co. v. Mutual Light, Heat & Power Co., 239 U.S. 121 (1915), was a suit to enjoin the defendant from maintaining its poles and wires so as to interfere with the complainant's poles and wires. The Court, finding that the damage to the plaintiff from the interference exceeded $3,000, held it to be irrelevant that the defendant could remove the offending equipment for $500. See also Hunt v. New York Cotton Exch., Paragraph (1), *supra.* But compare Mississippi & M.R.R. v. Ward, Paragraph (1), *supra.*

In Ronzio v. Denver & Rio Grande Co., 116 F.2d 604 (10th Cir.1940), a suit to quiet title to water rights, it appeared that while the value of the water to the plaintiff for farming purposes was less than $3,000, its value to the defendant railroad materially exceeded that amount. The court upheld the jurisdiction.[3]

---

2. Professor Currie suggests that the question—whether to look to either the value to the plaintiff or the cost to the defendant—may be meaningless because "If the * * * [right sought to be protected] is worth only $1000 to the plaintiff, cannot the defendant buy it from him for $1000.01?" Currie, Federal Courts 303–04 (4th ed. 1990). Professor Wright replies that the answer "will not always be 'Yes,' either because of stubbornness or because a right may have intangible value to a party, not included among the elements used in measuring the value of the right for

purposes of amount in controversy." Wright, Federal Courts § 34, at 206 n. 12 (5th ed. 1994).

3. Ronzio and other authorities supporting an "either party" viewpoint were cited with approval in Illinois v. City of Milwaukee, 406 U.S. 91, 98 (1972). The citation followed the cryptic comment that the "considerable interests involved in the purity of interstate waters would seem to put beyond question the jurisdictional amount provided in § 1331(a)."

If the major purpose of the jurisdictional amount limitation is to keep relatively small cases out of the federal courts, why shouldn't the value to either party suffice? Indeed, to the extent the limitation is designed to protect defendants against harassment by suit in distant courts, shouldn't the value to the defendant be critical? (Note that in some cases the presence of a readily ascertainable value to the defendant may eliminate the necessity of a highly speculative judgment as to the value to the plaintiff.) See Wright, Federal Courts § 34, at 206–07 (5th ed. 1994); *cf. Note on Joinder and Aggregation of Claims,* p. 1555, *infra.*

(5) *Declaratory Judgments.* How is the amount in controversy determined in a declaratory judgment action? "Usually the right or nonliability sought to be established in a declaratory suit might be adjudicated in a present or potential coercive action by one of the parties. The potential monetary value of the right, or amount of the liability, in such a coercive action, is normally considered to be the amount in controversy in the declaratory suit. * * * If a breach of a contractual condition is in issue, the amount of the probable liability is the amount in controversy." *Developments in the Law—Declaratory Judgments,* 62 Harv.L.Rev. 787, 801 (1949).

(6) *The Relevance of Counterclaims.* Suppose the plaintiff's claim does not exceed the jurisdictional amount: what then is the relevance of a counterclaim by the defendant? Does it matter whether the question arises in an original action, or in a removed action where the counterclaim was asserted before removal? Whether the counterclaim is permissive or compulsory? Whether the counterclaim itself exceeds the jurisdictional amount or must be added to the claim before the minimum is reached? For a survey of judicial responses to these questions, see 14A Wright, Miller & Cooper, Federal Practice and Procedure § 3706 (1985 and 1995 Supp.). Does Louisville & Nashville R.R. v. Mottley, 211 U.S. 149 (1908), p. 907, *supra,* have any bearing?

In Horton v. Liberty Mut. Ins. Co., 367 U.S. 348 (1961), Horton had filed a claim for $14,035 with the Texas Industrial Accident Board and had received an award for $1,050. Asserting diversity of citizenship, the insurance company brought an action in a Texas federal court to set aside the award, alleging that Horton had claimed and would claim $14,035. (Under Texas law, the filing of a suit by either party had the effect of nullifying the award and placing the burden of proof on the claimant of establishing the amount to which he was entitled.) Subsequently, Horton filed a suit in a Texas state court for $14,035,[4] moved to dismiss the federal action for lack of the jurisdictional amount, and filed a "conditional" compulsory counterclaim in the federal suit for $14,035. The Supreme Court held, 5–4, that the requisite jurisdictional amount existed. Relying on the facts described above, the Court said (pp. 353–54):

"* * * No denial of these allegations in the complaint has been made, no attempted disclaimer or surrender of any part of the original claim has been made by petitioner [Horton], and there has been no other showing * * * of any lack of good faith on the part of the respondent * * *. No matter which party brings it into court, the controversy remains the same; it involves the same

---

4. Under a 1958 provision, 28 U.S.C. § 1445(c), a state court action arising under the workers' compensation laws of that state is not removable. The Horton case, and cases like it, thus involve a race to the court-house by the two parties—a race often won by the insurance company. In Horton the dissenters noted that the federal action was filed within hours of the state board's award.

amount of money and is to be adjudicated under the same rules. Unquestionably, therefore, the amount in controversy is in excess of $10,000."

Does the Horton case mean that a plaintiff may always survive a challenge to the amount in controversy by making a good faith allegation that the defendant will counterclaim for more than $10,000? What if the defendant simply refuses to file the counterclaim until disposition of a motion to dismiss, as Horton could certainly have done? Can the Horton case be explained as simply an example of the principle referred to in Paragraph (5) governing actions for a declaratory judgment? Is the company's action any different from a request for a determination of non-liability? In the view of the dissenters, the analogy to a declaratory judgment proceeding was unacceptable because "[t]he complaint filed in the District Court was not styled a declaratory judgment action, and it did not seek such relief. More importantly, respondent has succeeded in avoiding the element of discretion permitted by the [declaratory judgment] statute. * * * Moreover, it is even questionable whether respondent has satisfied the jurisdictional amount requirement for such actions" (pp. 359–60).

(7) *Interest and Costs.* On the statutory exclusion of interest and costs, *see* Note, 45 Iowa L.Rev. 832 (1960). The interest exclusion has caused difficulty. There are plainly times when interest must be included in determining the amount in controversy—in an action on a bond coupon for example—but shouldn't any interest accruing *after* the cause of action arose be excluded? It would seem so if the purpose of the interest exclusion is to prevent the plaintiff from profiting from a delay in bringing suit, yet artful pleading sometimes enables the plaintiff to defeat this purpose. See cases cited in Wright, Federal Courts § 35, at 209 n. 21 (5th ed. 1994). See also Baron, *The "Amount in Controversy" Controversy: Using Interest, Costs, and Attorneys' Fees in Computing Its Value,* 41 Okla.L.Rev. 257 (1988).

Snyder v. Harris

394 U.S. 332, 89 S.Ct. 1053, 22 L.Ed.2d 319 (1969).
Certiorari to the United States Court of Appeals for the Eighth Circuit.

■ MR. JUSTICE BLACK delivered the opinion of the Court.

* * *

Each of these cases involves a single plaintiff suing on behalf of himself and "all others similarly situated." In No. 109, Mrs. Margaret E. Snyder, a shareholder of Missouri Fidelity Union Trust Life Insurance Company, brought suit against members of the company's board of directors alleging that they had sold their shares of the company's stock for an amount far in excess of its fair market value, that this excess represented payment to these particular directors to obtain complete control of the company, and that under Missouri law the excess should properly be distributed among all the shareholders of the company and not merely to a few of them. The suit was brought in the United States District Court for the Eastern District of Missouri, diversity of citizenship being alleged as the basis for federal jurisdiction. Since petitioner's allegations showed that she sought for herself only $8,740 in damages, respondent moved to dismiss on the grounds that the matter in controversy did not exceed $10,000. Petitioner contended, however, that her claim should be aggregated with those of the other members of her class, approximately 4,000 shareholders of the company stock. If all 4,000 potential claims were aggregated, the amount in controversy would be approximately $1,200,000. The District Court held that the claims could not thus be aggregated to meet the statutory test of jurisdiction and the Court of Appeals for the Eighth Circuit * * * affirmed.

In No. 117, Otto R. Coburn, a resident of Kansas, brought suit in the United States District Court for the District of Kansas against the Gas Service Company, a corporation marketing natural gas in Kansas. Jurisdiction was predicated upon diversity of citizenship. The complaint alleged that the Gas Service Company had billed and illegally collected a city franchise tax from Coburn and others living outside city limits. Coburn alleged damages to himself of only $7.81. Styling his complaint as a class action, however, Coburn sought relief on behalf of approximately 18,000 other Gas Service Company customers living outside of cities. The amount by which other members of the class had been overcharged was, and is, unknown, but the complaint alleged that the aggregation of all these claims would in any event exceed $10,000. The District Court overruled the Gas Company's motion to dismiss for failure to satisfy the jurisdictional amount and, on interlocutory appeal, the Court of Appeals for the Tenth Circuit affirmed * * *. We granted certiorari to resolve the conflict * * *.

The traditional judicial interpretation under all of [the statutes dealing with jurisdictional amount] * * * has been from the beginning that the separate and distinct claims of two or more plaintiffs cannot be aggregated in order to satisfy the jurisdictional amount requirement. Aggregation has been permitted only (1) in cases in which a single plaintiff seeks to aggregate two or more of his own claims against a single defendant and (2) in cases in which two or more plaintiffs unite to enforce a single title or right in which they have a common and undivided interest. It is contended, however, that the adoption of a 1966 amendment to Rule 23 effectuated a change in this jurisdictional doctrine. Under old Rule 23, class actions were divided into three categories which came to be known as "true", "hybrid," and "spurious." * * * The 1966 amendment to Rule 23 replaced the old categories with a functional approach to class actions. The new Rule establishes guidelines for the appropriateness of class actions, makes provision for giving notice to absent members, allows members of the class to remove themselves from the litigation and provides that the judgment will include all members of the class who have not requested exclusion. In No. 117, Gas Service Company, the Court of Appeals for the Tenth Circuit held that these changes in Rule 23 changed the jurisdictional amount doctrine as well. * * * We disagree and conclude, as did the Courts of Appeal for the Fifth and Eighth Circuits, that the adoption of amended Rule 23 did not and could not have brought about this change in the scope of the congressionally enacted grant of jurisdiction to the district courts.

The doctrine that separate and distinct claims could not be aggregated was never, and is not now, based upon the categories of old Rule 23 or of any rule of procedure. That doctrine is based rather upon this Court's interpretation of the statutory phrase "matter in controversy." The interpretation of this phrase as precluding aggregation substantially predates the 1938 Federal Rules of Civil Procedure. In 1911 this Court said in Troy Bank v. G.A. Whitehead & Co.:

"When two or more plaintiffs, having separate and distinct demands, unite for convenience and economy in a single suit, it is essential that the demand of each be of the requisite jurisdictional amount * * *." 222 U.S. 39.

By 1916 this Court was able to say in Pinel v. Pinel, 240 U.S. 594, that it was "settled doctrine" that separate and distinct claims could not be aggregated to meet the required jurisdictional amount. In Clark v. Paul Gray, Inc., 306 U.S. 583 (1939), this doctrine, which had first been declared in cases involving joinder of parties, was applied to class actions under the then recently passed Federal Rules. In that case numerous individuals, partnerships, and corporations joined in bringing a suit challenging the validity of a California statute which exacted fees of $15 on each automobile driven into the State. Raising the jurisdictional amount question *sua sponte,* this Court held that the claims of the various fee payers could not be aggregated "where there are numerous plaintiffs having no joint or common interest or title in the subject matter of the suit." 306 U.S., at 588. Nothing in the amended Rule 23 changes this doctrine. The class action plaintiffs in the two cases before us argue that since the new Rule will include in the judgment all members of the class who do not ask to be out by a certain date, the "matter in controversy" now encompasses all the claims of the entire class. But it is equally true that where two or more plaintiffs join their claims under the joinder provisions of Rule 20, each and every joined plaintiff is bound by the judgment. And it was in joinder cases of this very kind that the doctrine that distinct claims could not be aggregated was originally enunciated. The fact that judgments under class actions formerly classified as spurious may now have the same effect as claims brought under the joinder provisions is certainly no reason to treat them *differently* from joined actions for purposes of aggregation.

Any change in the Rules that did purport to effect a change in the definition of "matter in controversy" would clearly conflict with the command of Rule 82 that "[t]hese rules shall not be construed to extend or limit the jurisdiction of the United States district courts * * *." In Sibbach v. Wilson & Co., this Court held that the rule-making authority was limited by "the inability of a court, by rule, to extend or restrict the jurisdiction conferred by a statute." 312 U.S. 1, 10 (1941). We have consistently interpreted the jurisdictional statute passed by Congress as not conferring jurisdiction where the required amount in controversy can be reached only by aggregating separate and distinct claims. The interpretation of that statute cannot be changed by a change in the Rules.

For the reasons set out above, we think that it is unmistakably clear that the 1966 changes in Rule 23 did not and could not have changed the interpretation of the statutory phrase "matter in controversy." * * *

To overrule the aggregation doctrine at this late date would run counter to the congressional purpose in steadily increasing through the years the jurisdictional amount requirement. That purpose was to check, to some degree, the rising caseload of the federal courts, especially with regard to the federal courts' diversity of citizenship jurisdiction. * * *

Finally, it has been argued that unless the established aggregation principles are overturned, the functional advantages alleged to inhere in the new class action Rule will be undercut by resort to the old forms. But the disadvantageous results are overemphasized, we think, since lower courts have developed largely workable standards for determining when claims are joint and common, and therefore entitled to be aggregated, and when they are separate and distinct and therefore not aggregable. Moreover, while the class action device serves a useful function across the entire range of legal questions, the jurisdictional amount requirement applies almost exclusively to controversies based upon diversity of citizenship. * * * If there is a present need to expand the jurisdiction of those courts we cannot overlook the fact that the Constitution specifically vests that power in the Congress, not in the courts.

The judgment in No. 109 is Affirmed.

The judgment in No. 117 is Reversed.

■ MR. JUSTICE FORTAS, with whom MR. JUSTICE DOUGLAS joins, dissenting.

The Court today refuses to conform the judge-made formula for computing the amount in controversy in class actions with the 1966 amendment to Rule 23 of the Federal Rules of Civil Procedure. The effect of this refusal is substantially to undermine a generally welcomed and long-needed reform in federal procedure.

    * * *

The artificial, awkward, and unworkable distinctions between "joint," "common," and "several" claims and between "true," "hybrid," and "spurious" class actions which the amendment of Rule 23 sought to terminate is now reestablished in federal procedural law. Litigants, lawyers, and federal courts must now continue to be ensnared in their complexities in all cases where one or more of the coplaintiffs have a claim of less than the jurisdictional amount, usually $10,000.

It was precisely this morass that the 1966 amendment to Rule 23 sought to avoid. * * *

II

    * * *

The jurisdictional amount statutes require placing a value on the "matter in controversy" in a civil action. Once it is decided under the new Rule that an action may be maintained as a class action, it is the claim of the whole class and not the individual economic stakes of the separate members of the class which is the "matter in controversy." That this is so is perhaps most clearly indicated by the fact that the judgment in a class action properly maintained as such includes all members of the class. Rule 23(c)(3). This effect of the new Rule in broadening the scope of the "controversy" in a class action to include the combined interests of all the members of the class is illustrated by the facts of No. 117. That class action, if allowed to proceed, would, under the Rule, determine not merely whether the gas company wrongfully collected $7.81 in taxes from Mr. Coburn. It would also result in a judgment which, subject to the limits of due process, would determine—authoritatively and not merely as a matter of precedent—the status of the taxes collected from the 18,000 other people allegedly in the class Coburn seeks to represent. That being the case, it is hard to understand why the fact that the alleged claims are, in terms of the old Rule categories, "several" rather than "joint," means that the "matter in controversy" for jurisdictional amount purposes must be regarded as the $7.81 Mr. Coburn claims instead of the thousands of dollars of alleged overcharges of the whole class, the status of all of which would be determined by the judgment.

* * * [T]he majority result will continue to make determinative of the maintainability of a class action just that obsolete conceptualism the amended Rule sought to make irrelevant. In this sense, continued adherence to the old aggregation doctrines conflicts with the new Rule and is improper under 28 U.S.C. § 2072.

III

Permitting aggregation in class action cases does not involve any violation of the principle, expressed in Rule 82 and inherent in the whole procedure for the promulgation and amendment of the Federal Rules, that the courts cannot by rule expand their own jurisdictions. While the Rules cannot change subject-matter jurisdiction, changes in the forms and practices of the federal courts through changes in the Rules frequently and necessarily will affect the occasions on which subject-matter jurisdiction is exercised because they will in some cases make a difference in what cases the federal courts will hear and who will be authoritatively bound by the judgment. * * *

For these reasons, I would measure the value of the "matter in controversy" in a class action found otherwise proper under the amended Rule 23 by the monetary value of the claim of the whole class.

NOTE ON JOINDER AND AGGREGATION OF CLAIMS

(1) *Aggregation by an Individual Plaintiff.* The Court in Snyder implies that a single plaintiff may aggregate two or more claims against a single defendant even if there is no relationship among the claims. Why should this be so? Is it consistent with the purpose of the jurisdictional amount requirement?

For a case in which the rules on aggregation were surmounted by a transfer of claims to a small group of plaintiffs, see Bullard v. City of Cisco, 290 U.S. 179 (1933). Compare Woodside v. Beckham, 216 U.S. 117 (1910)(when transferee was not in fact the owner of the claims sued upon, jurisdiction depended on the ability of the transferors to sue). See *Note on Devices for Creating or Avoiding Federal Jurisdiction,* p. 1570, *infra.*

(2) *The Significance of the Pinel Decision.* Recall the majority's argument in Snyder that a contrary result would necessitate the overruling of cases dealing with permissive joinder (like Pinel v. Pinel, 240 U.S. 594 (1916)) because in those cases, as in class actions, each person whose claim is involved would be bound by the judgment. Is this argument adequately answered by the dissent?

(3) *Cost to the Defendant as a Basis of Determining the Amount in Controversy in a Class Action.* Why doesn't an answer to the majority in Snyder lie in the suggestion at p. 1549–50, *supra,* that the controlling amount is either the value to the plaintiff or the cost to the defendant, whichever is higher? If the suggestion is sound, why isn't the total potential liability of each defendant in a case like Snyder sufficient to meet the requirement? See Lonnquist v. J.C. Penney Co., 421 F.2d 597, 599 (10th Cir.1970), a class action in which the court refused to permit aggregation and attempted to distinguish Ronzio v. Denver & Rio Grande Co., 116 F.2d 604 (10th Cir.1940), p. 1549, *supra,* by stating: "Although the court [in Ronzio] said that the test was the pecuniary value to either party, the decision is not pertinent because a single right was asserted by a single plaintiff and the question was the value of that right. No problem of

aggregation was presented." See also, *e.g.*, Snow v. Ford Motor Co., 561 F.2d 787 (9th Cir.1977)(consumer class action seeking damages and injunctive relief). But see Committee for GI Rights v. Callaway, 518 F.2d 466, 473 (D.C.Cir.1975)(alternative holding).

Unless a theory analogous to that adopted in Ronzio is used, how could federal jurisdiction have existed in a case like Flast v. Cohen, 392 U.S. 83 (1968), p. 137, *supra?* See Note, 79 Yale L.J. 1577 (1970). The problem was not alluded to in Flast itself, or in later decisions dealing on the merits with the constitutionality of government aid to schools with religious affiliations. *E.g.,* Lemon v. Kurtzman, 403 U.S. 602 (1971).[1]

(4) *"Joint and Common" Claims.* In commenting on the Snyder majority's reference to "largely workable standards for determining when claims are joint and common", Professor Wright says: "It would have been helpful if the Court had indicated what these standards are or where they are to be found." Wright, Federal Courts § 36, at 212 (5th ed. 1994). A review of the decisions dealing with aggregation of multiple claims offers convincing evidence of Wright's skepticism. See 14A Wright, Miller & Cooper, Federal Practice and Procedure § 3704 (1985 and 1995 Supp.).[2]

(5) *The Zahn Decision.* After Snyder, the question arose whether federal jurisdiction existed in a class action in which (a) the interests were not joint and common, and (b) some but not all members of the class had the requisite amount in controversy. In Zahn v. International Paper Co., 414 U.S. 291 (1973), the Supreme Court upheld the decision of the district court that in a Rule 23(b)(3) class action "each plaintiff * * * must satisfy the jurisdictional amount, and any plaintiff who does not must be dismissed from the case * * *" (p. 301). The Court began by noting that, though the named plaintiffs did satisfy the jurisdictional amount requirement, some unnamed class members did not. Describing a Rule 23(b)(3) class action as, "in effect, but a congeries of separate suits," the Court evoked the requirement of Clark v. Paul Gray, Inc., cited and discussed in Snyder v. Harris, that named plaintiffs in such a suit who did not meet the jurisdictional requirements had to be dismissed (pp. 296–300). Reasoning that unnamed members of a class should not "enjoy advantages not shared by named plaintiffs," the Court applied "the rule governing named plaintiffs joining in an action to the unnamed members of a class" (pp. 300–01 n. 9). The Court concluded by refusing to reconsider Snyder and "the Court's longstanding construction of the 'matter in controversy' requirement of § 1332" (p. 301).

Justices Brennan, Douglas, and Marshall, dissenting, drew a distinction between "civil actions" and "individual claimants and individual claims," asserting that the "matter in controversy" requirement applied only to the former (p. 303). Arguing that the claims of the unnamed class members should be entertained as within the district court's ancillary jurisdiction, the dissent

---

1. The jurisdictional amount question in such cases was, of course, mooted by the 1980 amendment to § 1331.

2. But see Rensberger, *The Amount in Controversy: Understanding the Rules of Aggregation,* 26 Ariz.St.L.J.925 (1994), who defends the soundness and rationality of the current rules on aggregation. Rensberger pro- poses only a clarifying legislative change, that would allow aggregation against multiple de- fendants (or by multiple plaintiffs) when the liability claimed (or the right asserted) is joint or when the impossibility of joining all defendants (or all plaintiffs) would lead to a dismissal under the rules governing compul- sory joinder.

described the governing policies as "accommodations that take into account the impact of the adjudication on parties and third persons, the susceptibility of the dispute or disputes in the case to resolution in a single adjudication, and the structure of the litigation as governed by the Federal Rules of Civil Procedure" (p. 305). "Class actions were born of necessity," the dissent continued; "the alternatives were joinder of the entire class, or redundant litigation of the common issues" (p. 307). Concluding that Clark v. Paul Gray, Inc., should be limited so as to allow unnamed class members' claims to be adjudicated within a single suit, the dissent urged that both precedent (*e.g.,* Strawbridge v. Curtiss, 7 U.S. (3 Cranch) 267 (1806); Supreme Tribe of Ben Hur v. Cauble, 255 U.S. 356 (1921)), and the impact of a decision on nonappearing class members justified such a use of ancillary jurisdiction (pp. 309–10).

Prior to the enactment of the supplemental jurisdiction provision (28 U.S.C. § 1367) in 1990, the courts were divided on the impact of Zahn outside the class action context, for example in a case in which A and B join in suing C on closely related claims but only a has the requisite amount in controversy. See 14A Wright, Miller & Cooper, Federal Practice and Procedure § 3704, at 88–95 (1985). Since the enactment of that provision, the focus has shifted to the question of the effect of the provision on the rulings in Snyder and in Zahn as well as in the non-class action example just referred to. That problem is discussed in the following section.

(6) *Shareholder's Derivative Actions.* One type of class action in which aggregation is not a problem is a stockholder's derivative action. The Court has held that the measure of the amount in controversy in such cases is not the possible benefit to the plaintiff shareholder but the damage asserted to have been sustained by the corporation. Koster v. (American) Lumbermens Mut. Cas. Co., 330 U.S. 518 (1947). Was the Koster holding inconsistent with the Court's observation in the same case that the corporation was properly aligned as a defendant for diversity purposes because it was in "antagonistic hands"?

(7) *The Relevance of Federal Rule 82.* Rule 82 of the Federal Rules of Civil Procedure states that the rules "shall not be construed to extend or limit the jurisdiction of the United States district courts or the venue of actions therein." In the Snyder case, and to a lesser extent in Zahn, the Court relied on Rule 82 as a barrier to sustaining jurisdiction. Professor Goldberg, in *The Influence of Procedural Rules on Federal Jurisdiction,* 28 Stan.L.Rev. 395 (1976), has challenged this reliance. Pointing to a number of areas in which the courts, resting in part on the federal rules, sustained federal jurisdiction on a theory of pendent or ancillary jurisdiction without even alluding to the prohibition of Rule 82, she argues that Rule 82 is not required by either the Enabling Act or the Constitution but rather is a rule of judicial self-restraint. She urges that it should therefore be construed in harmony with Rule 1 with respect to procedural changes that serve "some procedural purpose in one or more situations in which jurisdiction is not a barrier to the rule's implementation" (p. 442).

Do you agree with Professor Goldberg that Rule 82 is not required by the Enabling Act or the Constitution? In the absence of Rule 82, could the rulemakers, consistently with the Enabling Act and the Constitution, abolish the diversity jurisdiction? Eliminate the jurisdictional amount limitation under § 1332?[3]

---

3. With respect to the limitations imposed by the Enabling Act, see Burbank, *The Rules Enabling Act of 1934,* 130 U.Pa.L.Rev. 1015 (1982). On the general question wheth-

SECTION 4.   SUPPLEMENTAL (ANCILLARY) JURISDICTION

Owen Equipment and Erection Company v. Kroger

437 U.S. 365, 98 S.Ct. 2396, 57 L.Ed.2d 274 (1978).
Certiorari to the United States Court of Appeals for the Eighth Circuit.

■ MR. JUSTICE STEWART delivered the opinion of the Court.

In an action in which federal jurisdiction is based on diversity of citizenship, may the plaintiff assert a claim against a third-party defendant when there is no independent basis for federal jurisdiction over that claim? The Court of Appeals for the Eighth Circuit held in this case that such a claim is within the ancillary jurisdiction of the federal courts. We granted certiorari because this decision conflicts with several recent decisions of other Courts of Appeals.

I

On January 18, 1972, James Kroger was electrocuted when the boom of a steel crane next to which he was walking came too close to a high-tension electric power line. The respondent (his widow, who is the administratrix of his estate) filed a wrongful-death action in the United States District Court for the District of Nebraska against the Omaha Public Power District (OPPD). Her complaint alleged that OPPD's negligent construction, maintenance, and operation of the power line had caused Kroger's death. Federal jurisdiction was based on diversity of citizenship, since the respondent was a citizen of Iowa and OPPD was a Nebraska corporation.

OPPD then filed a third-party complaint pursuant to Fed.Rule Civ.Proc. 14(a) against the petitioner, Owen Equipment and Erection Co. (Owen), alleging that the crane was owned and operated by Owen, and that Owen's negligence had been the proximate cause of Kroger's death.[3] OPPD later moved for summary judgment on the respondent's complaint against it. While this motion was pending, the respondent was granted leave to file an amended complaint naming Owen as an additional defendant. Thereafter, the District Court granted OPPD's motion for summary judgment * * *. The case thus went to trial between the respondent and the petitioner alone.

The respondent's amended complaint alleged that Owen was "a Nebraska corporation with its principal place of business in Nebraska." Owen's answer admitted that it was "a corporation organized and existing under the laws of the State of Nebraska," and denied every other allegation of the complaint.

er and to what extent Congress may delegate to the federal courts authority to regulate subject-matter jurisdiction, see Shapiro, *Federal Diversity Jurisdiction: A Survey and a Proposal,* 91 Harv.L.Rev. 317, 343–48 (1977).

3. Under Rule 14(a), a third-party defendant may not be impleaded merely because he may be liable to the *plaintiff.* While the third-party complaint in this case alleged merely that Owen's negligence caused Kroger's death, and the basis of Owen's alleged liability *to OPPD* is nowhere spelled out, OPPD evidently relied upon the state common-law right of contribution among joint tortfeasors. * * *

On the third day of trial, however, it was disclosed that the petitioner's principal place of business was in Iowa, not Nebraska,[5] and that the petitioner and the respondent were thus both citizens of Iowa.   The petitioner then moved to dismiss the complaint for lack of jurisdiction.   The District Court reserved decision on the motion, and the jury thereafter returned a verdict in favor of the respondent.   In an unreported opinion issued after the trial, the District Court denied the petitioner's motion to dismiss the complaint.

The judgment was affirmed on appeal.   * * *

II

It is undisputed that there was no independent basis of federal jurisdiction over the respondent's state-law tort action against the petitioner, since both are citizens of Iowa.   And although Fed.Rule Civ.Proc. 14(a) permits a plaintiff to assert a claim against a third-party defendant, it does not purport to say whether or not such a claim requires an independent basis of federal jurisdiction.   Indeed, it could not determine that question, since it is axiomatic that the Federal Rules of Civil Procedure do not create or withdraw federal jurisdiction.

In affirming the District Court's judgment, the Court of Appeals relied upon the doctrine of ancillary jurisdiction, whose contours it believed were defined by this Court's holding in Mine Workers v. Gibbs, 383 U.S. 715 [p. 962, *supra*].   * * * [8]* * * [W]e believe that the Court of Appeals failed to understand the scope of the doctrine of the Gibbs case.

* * *

Gibbs delineated the constitutional limits of federal judicial power.   But even if it be assumed that the District Court in the present case had constitutional power to decide the respondent's lawsuit against the petitioner, it does not follow that the decision of the Court of Appeals was correct.   Constitutional power is merely the first hurdle that must be overcome in determining that a federal court has jurisdiction over a particular controversy.   For the jurisdiction of the federal courts is limited not only by the provisions of Art. III of the Constitution, but also by Acts of Congress.

* * *

III

The relevant statute in this case, 28 U.S.C. § 1332(a)(1), * * * and its predecessors have consistently been held to require complete diversity of citizenship. * * * Over the years Congress has repeatedly re-enacted or amended the statute conferring diversity jurisdiction, leaving intact this rule of complete diversity.   * * *

---

5.   The problem apparently was one of geography.   Although the Missouri River generally marks the boundary between Iowa and Nebraska, Carter Lake, Iowa, where the accident occurred and where Owen had its main office, lies west of the river, adjacent to Omaha, Neb.   Apparently the river once avulsed at one of its bends, cutting Carter Lake off from the rest of Iowa.

8.   No more than in Aldinger v. Howard, 427 U.S. 1, is it necessary to determine here "whether there are any 'principled' differences between pendent and ancillary jurisdiction; or, if there are, what effect Gibbs had on such differences."   *Id.*

Thus it is clear that the respondent could not originally have brought suit in federal court naming Owen and OPPD as codefendants, since citizens of Iowa would have been on both sides of the litigation. Yet the identical lawsuit resulted when she amended her complaint. Complete diversity was destroyed just as surely as if she had sued Owen initially. In either situation, in the plain language of the statute, the "matter in controversy" could not be "between * * * citizens of different States."

It is a fundamental precept that federal courts are courts of limited jurisdiction. * * * Yet under the reasoning of the Court of Appeals in this case, a plaintiff could defeat the statutory requirement of complete diversity by the simple expedient of suing only those defendants who were of diverse citizenship and waiting for them to implead nondiverse defendants.[17] If, as the Court of Appeals thought, a "common nucleus of operative fact" were the only requirement for ancillary jurisdiction in a diversity case, there would be no principled reason why the respondent in this case could not have joined her cause of action against Owen in her original complaint as ancillary to her claim against OPPD. Congress' requirement of complete diversity would thus have been evaded completely.

It is true, as the Court of Appeals noted, that the exercise of ancillary jurisdiction over nonfederal claims has often been upheld in situations involving impleader, cross-claims or counterclaims.[18] But in determining whether jurisdiction over a nonfederal claim exists, the context in which the nonfederal claim is asserted is crucial. And the claim here arises in a setting quite different from the kinds of nonfederal claims that have been viewed in other cases as falling within the ancillary jurisdiction of the federal courts.

First, the nonfederal claim in this case was simply not ancillary to the federal one in the same sense that, for example, the impleader by a defendant of a third-party defendant always is. A third-party complaint depends at least in part upon the resolution of the primary lawsuit. Its relation to the original complaint is thus not mere factual similarity but logical dependence. The respondent's claim against the petitioner, however, was entirely separate from her original claim against OPPD, since the petitioner's liability to her depended not at all upon whether or not OPPD was also liable. Far from being an ancillary and dependent claim, it was a new and independent one.

Second, the nonfederal claim here was asserted by the plaintiff, who voluntarily chose to bring suit upon a state-law claim in a federal court. By contrast, ancillary jurisdiction typically involves claims by a defending party haled into court against his will, or by another person whose rights might be

---

17. This is not an unlikely hypothesis, since a defendant in a tort suit such as this one would surely try to limit his liability by impleading any joint tortfeasors for indemnity or contribution. * * *

18. The ancillary jurisdiction of the federal courts derives originally from cases such as Freeman v. Howe, 24 How. 450, which held that when federal jurisdiction "effectively controls the property or fund under dispute, other claimants thereto should be allowed to intervene in order to protect their interests, without regard to jurisdiction." Aldinger v. Howard, 427 U.S., at 11. More recently, it has been said to include cases that involve multiparty practice, such as compulsory counterclaims, e.g., Moore v. New York Cotton Exchange, 270 U.S. 593; impleader, e.g., H.L. Peterson Co. v. Applewhite, 383 F.2d 430, 433 (CA5); Dery v. Wyer, 265 F.2d 804 (CA2); cross-claims, e.g., LASA Per L'Industria Del Marmo Soc. Per Azioni v. Alexander, 414 F.2d 143 (CA6); or intervention as of right, e.g., Phelps v. Oaks, 117 U.S. 236, 241; Smith Petroleum Service, Inc. v. Monsanto Chemical Co., 420 F.2d 1103, 1113–1115 (CA5).

irretrievably lost unless he could assert them in an ongoing action in a federal court. A plaintiff cannot complain if ancillary jurisdiction does not encompass all of his possible claims in a case such as this one, since it is he who has chosen the federal rather than the state forum and must thus accept its limitations. * * *

* * * [N]either the convenience of litigants nor considerations of judicial economy can suffice to justify extension of the doctrine of ancillary jurisdiction to a plaintiff's cause of action against a citizen of the same State in a diversity case. Congress has established the basic rule that diversity jurisdiction exists under 28 U.S.C. § 1332 only when there is complete diversity of citizenship. "The policy of the statute calls for its strict construction." Healy v. Ratta, 292 U.S. 263, 270. To allow the requirement of complete diversity to be circumvented as it was in this case would simply flout the congressional command.[21]

Accordingly, the judgment of the Court of Appeals is reversed.

■ MR. JUSTICE WHITE, with whom MR. JUSTICE BRENNAN joins, dissenting.

* * *

* * * [A]s far as Art. III of the Constitution is concerned, the District Court had power to entertain Mrs. Kroger's claim against Owen.

The majority correctly points out, however, that the analysis cannot stop here. As Aldinger v. Howard teaches, the jurisdictional power of the federal courts may be limited by Congress, as well as by the Constitution. * * *

In the present case, the only indication of congressional intent that the Court can find is that contained in the diversity jurisdictional statute, 28 U.S.C. § 1332(a) * * *. Because this statute has been interpreted as requiring complete diversity of citizenship between each plaintiff and each defendant, the Court holds that the District Court did not have ancillary jurisdiction over Mrs. Kroger's claim against Owen. In so holding, the Court unnecessarily expands the scope of the complete-diversity requirement while substantially limiting the doctrine of ancillary jurisdiction.

The complete-diversity requirement, of course, could be viewed as meaning that in a diversity case, a federal district court may adjudicate only those claims that are between parties of different States. Thus, in order for a defendant to implead a third-party defendant, there would have to be diversity of citizenship; the same would also be true for cross-claims between defendants and for a third-party defendant's claim against a plaintiff. Even the majority, however, refuses to read the complete-diversity requirement so broadly; it recognizes with seeming approval the exercise of ancillary jurisdiction over nonfederal claims in situations involving impleader, cross-claims, and counterclaims. Given the Court's willingness to recognize ancillary jurisdiction in these contexts, despite the requirements of § 1332(a), I see no justification for the Court's refusal to approve the District Court's exercise of ancillary jurisdiction in the present case.

It is significant that a plaintiff who asserts a claim against a third-party defendant is not seeking to add a new party to the lawsuit. In the present

---

21. Our holding is that the District Court lacked power to entertain the respondent's lawsuit against the petitioner. Thus, the asserted inequity in the respondent's alleged concealment of its citizenship is irrele-

vant. Federal judicial power does not depend upon "prior action or consent of the parties." American Fire & Cas. Co. v. Finn, 341 U.S., at 17–18.

case, for example, Owen had already been brought into the suit by OPPD
* * *.

Because in the instant case Mrs. Kroger merely sought to assert a claim against someone already a party to the suit, considerations of judicial economy, convenience, and fairness to the litigants—the factors relied upon in Gibbs—support the recognition of ancillary jurisdiction here. Already before the court was the whole question of the cause of Mr. Kroger's death. Mrs. Kroger initially contended that OPPD was responsible; OPPD in turn contended that Owen's negligence had been the proximate cause of Mr. Kroger's death. In spite of the fact that the question of Owen's negligence was already before the District Court, the majority requires Mrs. Kroger to bring a separate action in state court in order to assert that very claim. Even if the Iowa statute of limitations will still permit such a suit, considerations of judicial economy are certainly not served by requiring such duplicative litigation.

The majority, however, brushes aside such considerations of convenience, judicial economy, and fairness because it concludes that recognizing ancillary jurisdiction over a plaintiff's claim against a third-party defendant would permit the plaintiff to circumvent the complete-diversity requirement and thereby "flout the congressional command." Since the plaintiff in such a case does not bring the third-party defendant into the suit, however, there is no occasion for deliberate circumvention of the diversity requirement, absent collusion with the defendant. In the case of such collusion, of which there is absolutely no indication here, the court can dismiss the action under the authority of 28 U.S.C. § 1359. In the absence of such collusion, there is no reason to adopt an absolute rule prohibiting the plaintiff from asserting those claims that he may properly assert against the third-party defendant pursuant to Fed.Rule Civ.Proc. 14(a). The plaintiff in such a situation brings suit against the defendant only with absolutely no assurance that the defendant will decide or be able to implead a particular third-party defendant. Since the plaintiff has no control over the defendant's decision to implead a third party, the fact that he could not have originally sued that party in federal court should be irrelevant. Moreover, the fact that a plaintiff in some cases may be able to foresee the subsequent chain of events leading to the impleader does not seem to me to be a sufficient reason to declare that a district court does not have the *power* to exercise ancillary jurisdiction over the plaintiff's claims against the third-party defendant.[7]

* * *

NOTE ON SUPPLEMENTAL (ANCILLARY) JURISDICTION IN DIVERSITY CASES

(1) *Historical Development to 1990.*

(a) Prior to 1990, when the supplemental jurisdiction provision (28 U.S.C. § 1367) was enacted, the scope of what was usually called "ancillary" jurisdic-

---

7. Under the Gibbs analysis, recognition of the district court's power to hear a plaintiff's nonfederal claim against a third-party defendant in a diversity suit would not mean that the court would be required to entertain such claims in all cases. The district court would have the discretion to dismiss the nonfederal claim if it concluded that the interests of judicial economy, convenience, and fairness would not be served by the retention of the claim in the federal lawsuit. * * *

tion in diversity cases was essentially judge-made. This Paragraph is a brief history of developments during that period.

(b) One of the earliest cases on this subject is Freeman v. Howe, 65 U.S. (24 How.) 450 (1860), cited in Kroger at footnote 18. In that case the Court held that a state court was without jurisdiction of a replevin action brought by claimants to obtain property that had previously been attached in a federal diversity action. Answering the objection that the claimants would then be "utterly remediless in the Federal courts, inasmuch as both parties were citizens of Massachusetts" the Court said (p. 460):

"The principle is, that a bill filed on the equity side of the [federal] court to restrain or regulate judgments or suits at law in the same court, and thereby prevent injustice, or an inequitable advantage under mesne or final process, is not an original suit, but ancillary and dependent, supplementary merely to the original suit, out of which it had arisen, and is maintained without reference to the citizenship or residence of the parties."

(c) From Freeman and related holdings, the Court moved almost imperceptibly to the recognition of an ancillary jurisdiction to effectuate or to reexamine judgments after they had become final. See, e.g., Dietzsch v. Huidekoper, 103 U.S. 494 (1880)(upholding district court jurisdiction, after judgment for the plaintiff in a removed action of replevin, to enjoin the prosecution of an action against the plaintiff in a state court on the plaintiff's replevin bond).

A key case in this development is Supreme Tribe of Ben Hur v. Cauble, 255 U.S. 356 (1921). A class action had been brought in a federal court against a fraternal benefit association organized under the laws of Indiana. The action was brought by certificate holders from states other than Indiana, and a judgment was rendered favorable to the association. Indiana certificate holders then commenced a state court action against the association, designed to litigate the same questions, and the association filed a bill in federal court against the Indiana plaintiffs seeking to enjoin them from prosecuting the state court action on the ground that they were bound by the federal decree. The Supreme Court reversed a dismissal for lack of jurisdiction and held that the requested injunction should issue. The Court stated that even though their joinder as plaintiffs at the outset of the initial federal action would have defeated jurisdiction, the Indiana certificate holders were bound by the judgment rendered in that action as members of the class represented. "The intervention of the Indiana citizens in the suit [after it had begun]", the Court noted (p. 366), "would not have defeated the jurisdiction already acquired. Stewart v. Dunham [115 U.S. 61]." The Court then disposed of the remaining jurisdictional issue—that the adversaries in the second federal proceeding were not of diverse citizenship—in a single sentence (p. 367): "As to the other question herein involved, holding, as we do, that the [Indiana certificate holders] * * * were concluded by the decree of the District Court, an ancillary bill may be prosecuted from the same court to protect the rights secured to all in the class by the decree rendered."

Was the determination that the Indiana certificate holders could have intervened in the initial action essential to the result? Consistent with Strawbridge? See Note on the Time When Jurisdiction Attaches and Its Ouster by Subsequent Events, p. 1527, supra. Was the need to uphold ancillary jurisdiction as great in Ben–Hur as in Freeman v. Howe? Could the Supreme

Court have reviewed an Indiana state court decision adverse to the contentions of the association?

(d) Several Supreme Court decisions prior to Kroger dealt directly with the question of the effect of intervention on diversity jurisdiction. *E.g.*, Phelps v. Oaks, 117 U.S. 236 (1886)(cited with apparent approval in Kroger at footnote 18); Wichita R.R. & Light Co. v. Public Util. Comm'n, 260 U.S. 48 (1922). In Wichita the Court said (p. 54):

"* * * Jurisdiction once acquired on [the ground of diversity of citizenship] * * * is not divested by a subsequent change in the citizenship of the parties. * * * Much less is such jurisdiction defeated by the intervention, by leave of the court, of a party whose presence is not essential to a decision of the controversy between the original parties."

During this period, the lower courts held, however, that if intervention was needed to cure an otherwise fatal defect of parties (*i.e.*, the absence of an "indispensable" party under Rule 19), there was no preexisting jurisdiction to which the intervention could be regarded as ancillary. See, *e.g.*, Kentucky Natural Gas Corp. v. Duggins, 165 F.2d 1011 (6th Cir.1948); Chance v. County Board, 332 F.2d 971 (7th Cir.1964). Also during this period, the lower courts generally held that permissive intervention under Rule 24(b) had to be supported by independent grounds of jurisdiction. Was this sound? Even in a case in which the applicant for intervention was trying only to prevent a judgment that would worsen his position?

See generally 7C Wright, Miller & Kane, Federal Practice and Procedure § 1917 (1986); Shapiro, *Some Thoughts on Intervention Before Courts, Agencies, and Arbitrators*, 81 Harv.L.Rev. 721, 760–64 (1968).

(e) The Ben–Hur decision itself indicated that ancillary jurisdiction would support intervention in a class action (at least one that, under the rule prevailing at that time was not "spurious") by a member of the class without regard to that member's citizenship. See 7C Wright, Miller & Kane, *supra*, at 470–72. But *Cf.* Snyder v. Harris, 394 U.S. 332 (1969), p. 1551, *supra* (relying in part on Rule 82 in disallowing aggregation of claims for purposes of satisfying the jurisdictional amount requirement in a class action).

(f) The Supreme Court did not foreclose the possibility that in a case like Kroger, the third-party defendant might be allowed to assert a claim against the original plaintiff arising out of the subject matter of the original action. Were such a claim allowed, would the door have been open for the assertion of a "compulsory" counterclaim by the plaintiff against the third-party defendant? If your answer is yes, does your response cast doubt on the central distinction between parties drawn in Kroger itself?

(2) *Supplemental Jurisdiction in Diversity Cases Under the New Statutory Provision (§ 1367).*

(a) The genesis of the supplemental jurisdiction provision enacted by Congress in 1990 is described in Chap. VIII, Sec. 5, pp. 966–73, *supra,* and the reader should refer to that discussion for consideration of a number of problems that arise in both the federal question and diversity contexts. The legislative history indicates, however, that the provision was designed primarily to deal with the "pendent party" question in the context of federal question litigation and, by and large, not to change the law dramatically in the diversity context. As it turned out, a number of questions have been raised by the provision's application in diversity cases—especially with respect to subsection (b), and there has been vigorous debate in the law reviews about the meaning and wisdom of the provision in diversity litigation. That commentary has been extensive,[1] and much of the discussion that follows is suggested by the questions raised by commentators, not all of which can be covered in this brief compass.

(b) Both the wording of subsection (b) and the legislative history indicate that the drafters did not intend to change the result in Kroger. But was that decision a sound one, in view of the powerful arguments Justice White makes in dissent? Can it be justified by a general predisposition against any expansion of the diversity jurisdiction?

Does the intent to preserve the Kroger result mean that a plaintiff cannot assert a direct claim against a third-party nondiverse defendant even if the action was originally brought in a state court or if the plaintiff's claim is asserted as a counterclaim to a claim asserted by the third-party defendant? As a *compulsory* counterclaim to such a claim?

(c) Subsection (b) excludes claims *by plaintiffs* against persons made parties under Rules 14, 19, 20, or 24, as well as claims by persons proposed to be joined as plaintiffs under Rule 19 or seeking to intervene as plaintiffs under Rule 24 "when exercising supplemental jurisdiction over such claims would be inconsistent with the jurisdictional requirements of section 1332." But, for example, what of a claim against an original defendant by a person joined as a plaintiff (at or after initiation of the action) under Rule 20? Isn't such a claim an especially clear case of an effort (in the absence of complete diversity) to take action "inconsistent with the jurisdictional requirements of section 1332"? If so, is the failure to include Rule 20 in this part of the subsection just an inadvertent omission? How should the problem be dealt with by the courts?

(d) Assume that (despite some confusing legislative history on the point) § 1367 applies to removed cases.[2] If so, do the limitations in § 1367(b) apply to claims asserted before removal?[3] What is the relevance, if any, of the provisions of 28 U.S.C. § 1447(e)?

(e) Difficult questions are raised by the new statute with respect to the addition of parties under Rule 19 and intervention under Rule 24. For example, are *all* claims excluded if they are asserted by plaintiffs against persons made parties under these rules, or only those that "would be inconsistent" with the requirements of § 1332? (And what are those?) An aspect of

---

1. Among the leading articles in the field, some of which deal with the new provision in all its aspects and some of which focus on diversity litigation, are the following: Freer, *Compounding Confusion and Hampering Diversity: Life After Finley and the Supplemental Jurisdiction Statute,* 40 Emory L.J. 445, 474–86 (1991); Oakley, *Recent Statutory Changes in the Law of Federal Jurisdiction and Venue: The Judicial Improvements Acts of 1988 and 1990,* 24 U.C. Davis L.Rev. 735 (1991); Rowe, Burbank & Mengler, *Compounding or Creating Confusion About Supplemental Jurisdiction? A Reply to Professor Freer,* 40 Emory L.J. 944 (1992)(and subsequent rebuttals and surrebuttals in the same

issue); McLaughlin, *The Federal Supplemental Jurisdiction Statute—A Constitutional and Statutory Analysis,* 24 Ariz.St.L.J. 849 (1992); Wolf, *Codification of Supplemental Jurisdiction: Anatomy of a Legislative Proposal,* 14 W.New Eng.L.Rev. 1 (1992)(discussing the legislative history); Steinman, *Supplemental Jurisdiction in § 1441 Removed Cases: An Unsurveyed Frontier of Congress' Handiwork,* 35 Ariz.L.Rev. 305 (1993); Comment, 72 Ore.L.Rev. 695 (1993); Note, 93 Mich.L.Rev. 2135 (1995).

2. See generally the discussion in Steinman, note 1, *supra.*

3. Steinman, note 1, *supra,* argues forcefully that they do not.

this question is grammatical: does the final clause of subsection (b) relate to the entire subsection, or only to claims by persons joined as, or seeking to intervene as, plaintiffs? As another example, since subsection (b) does not purport to affect claims made by persons seeking to intervene as *defendants*, the problem of alignment, and possible realignment, becomes critical.

(f) Subsection (b) does not refer to Rules 23, 23.1, or 23.2. Is the treatment of persons under those rules then unaffected by the limitations in that subsection? What if a member of a plaintiff class who is a co-citizen of the defendant seeks not merely to "appear" under Rule 23 but to intervene as an additional named party?

(g) Finally, a difficult set of questions is presented with respect to claims (in ordinary and in class actions) that satisfy all jurisdictional requirements except the requisite jurisdictional amount. What effect, if any, does § 1367 have on the availability of a federal forum in a case like Snyder v. Harris, p. 1551, *supra*, Zahn v. International Paper Co., p. 1556, *supra*, or a case in which *A* (who has a claim in excess of the jurisdictional amount) joins with *B* (who has a closely related claim for less than the requisite amount) in suing diverse defendant *C*? And what if a plaintiff wants to assert against a diverse third-party defendant a claim that is within the scope of Rule 14 but is for less than the jurisdictional amount?

Subsection (b) of § 1367, in its reference to Rule 14, appears to exclude jurisdiction in the last of the examples just given. Is such exclusion sound? And does the failure of subsection (b) to refer to Rule 23 (noted above) mean that supplemental jurisdiction is available in cases like Snyder and Zahn? Is there a difference between the two cases in that *no* class member's claim in Snyder qualified for original jurisdiction and thus the authority granted in § 1367(a) does not apply?

With respect to Zahn, it is hard to see how § 1367 could be read not to authorize supplemental jurisdiction in such a case. But the legislative history of the provision suggests that no change in jurisdiction over class actions was intended. Assuming that legislative history may be helpful in resolving uncertainties created by the statutory language, what relevance should such history have on a question of interpretation like this one?

(h) The Supreme Court has yet to rule on any of these issues.[4] In the meantime, or even after some of the answers have been given by the Court, should Congress go back to the drawing board?[5]

---

4. As this Edition went to press, many of the questions raised in text (as well as several others) had been considered primarily at the district court level, where there appeared to be a lack of consensus on the more puzzling issues. In the first appellate court decision to address the question squarely, the Fifth Circuit has held that the clear language of § 1367 (which was regarded as prevailing over any contrary legislative history) overrules the Supreme Court's decision in Zahn. In re Abbott Laboratories, 51 F.3d 524 (5th Cir.1995).

In one especially interesting district court decision, the court held that under § 1367, the plaintiff, in response to a counterclaim, could not implead a non-diverse person on the counterclaim. Guaranteed

Systems Inc. v. American Nat'l Can Co., 842 F.Supp. 855 (M.D.N.C.1994). The court reasoned that even though the Kroger rationale did not apply in such a case, the statutory prohibition in § 1367(b) precluded the exercise of supplemental jurisdiction.

In one recent discussion (Note, 93 Mich. L.Rev. 2139 (1995)), the author argues that lower courts have interpreted the bar of § 1367(b) too broadly (as in Guaranteed Systems), and proposes that the subsection be read to proscribe claims by plaintiffs if, but only if, "but for the absence of complete diversity, the plaintiff could have included the claim against the nondiverse party in the original complaint." *Id.* at 2157.

5. The doctrine of "ancillary jurisdiction" is not exhausted by the provisions of

SECTION 5. DEVICES FOR CREATING OR AVOIDING DIVERSITY JURISDICTION

Kramer v. Caribbean Mills, Inc.

394 U.S. 823, 89 S.Ct. 1487, 23 L.Ed.2d 9 (1969).
Certiorari to the United States Court of Appeals for the Fifth Circuit.

■ MR. JUSTICE HARLAN delivered the opinion of the Court.

The sole question presented by this case is whether the Federal District Court in which it was brought had jurisdiction over the cause, or whether that court was deprived of jurisdiction by 28 U.S.C. § 1359. * * *

The facts were these. Respondent Caribbean Mills, Inc. (Caribbean) is a Haitian corporation. In May 1959 it entered into a contract with an individual named Kelly and the Panama and Venezuela Finance Company (Panama), a Panamanian Corporation. The agreement provided that Caribbean would purchase from Panama 125 shares of corporate stock, in return for payment of $85,000 down and an additional $165,000 in 12 annual installments.

No installment payments ever were made, despite requests for payment by Panama. In 1964, Panama assigned its entire interest in the 1959 contract to petitioner Kramer, an attorney in Wichita Falls, Texas. The stated consideration was $1. By a separate agreement dated the same day, Kramer promised to pay back to Panama 95% of any net recovery on the assigned cause of action, "solely as a Bonus."

Kramer soon thereafter brought suit against Caribbean for $165,000 in the United States District Court for the Northern District of Texas, alleging diversity of citizenship between himself and Caribbean. The District Court denied Caribbean's motion to dismiss for want of jurisdiction. The case proceeded to trial, and a jury returned a $165,000 verdict in favor of Kramer.

On appeal, the Court of Appeals for the Fifth Circuit reversed, holding that the assignment was "improperly or collusively made" within the meaning of 28 U.S.C. § 1359, and that in consequence the District Court lacked jurisdiction. * * * For reasons which follow, we affirm the judgment of the Court of Appeals.

§ 1367. Thus in Kokkonen v. Guardian Life Ins. Co., 114 S.Ct. 1673 (1994), the Court first held that the doctrine did *not* confer authority on a federal court to enforce the terms of a settlement agreement in a diversity case, but then suggested (without reference to § 1367) that such authority would exist had the district court "embod[ied] the contract in its dismissal order (or what has the same effect, retain[ed] jurisdiction over the settlement contract) if the parties agree" (p. 1677). (Is there a reasonable distinction between the case in which jurisdiction is lacking and that in which the Court in Kokkonen indicates that jurisdiction would exist, or is the distinction one of form without substance?) *Cf.* Thomas v. Peacock, 39 F.3d 493 (4th Cir.1994)(upholding ancillary jurisdiction in separate action seeking to pierce corporate veil and to enforce judgment obtained in prior federal question suit), cert. granted, 115 S.Ct. 1997 (1995).

I

The issue before us is whether Kramer was "improperly or collusively made" a party "to invoke the jurisdiction" of the District Court, within the meaning of 28 U.S.C. § 1359. We look first to the legislative background.

Section 1359 has existed in its present form only since the 1948 revision of the Judicial Code. Prior to that time, the use of devices to create diversity was regulated by two federal statutes. The first, known as the "assignee clause," provided that, with certain exceptions not here relevant:

"No district court shall have cognizance of any suit * * * to recover upon any promissory note or other chose in action in favor of any assignee * * * unless such suit might have been prosecuted in such court * * * if no assignment had been made."[3]

The second pre–1948 statute, 28 U.S.C. § 80 (1940 ed.), stated that a district court should dismiss an action whenever: "it shall appear to the satisfaction of the * * * court * * * that such suit does not really and substantially involve a dispute or controversy properly within the jurisdiction of [the] court, or that the parties to said suit have been improperly or collusively made or joined * * * for the purpose of creating [federal jurisdiction]."

As part of the 1948 revision, § 80 was amended to produce the present § 1359. The assignee clause was simultaneously repealed. The Reviser's Note describes the amended assignee clause as a "jumble of legislative jargon,'" and states that "[t]he revised section changes this clause by confining its application to cases wherein the assignment is improperly or collusively made * * *. Furthermore, * * * the original purpose of [the assignee] clause is better served by substantially following section 80." That purpose was said to be "to prevent the manufacture of Federal jurisdiction by the device of assignment." *Ibid.*

II

* * * Because the approach of the former assignee clause was to forbid the grounding of jurisdiction upon *any* assignment, regardless of its circumstances or purpose, decisions under that clause are of little assistance. However, decisions of this Court under the other predecessor statute, 28 U.S.C. § 80 (1940 ed.), seem squarely in point. These decisions, together with the evident purpose of § 1359, lead us to conclude that the Court of Appeals was correct in finding that the assignment in question was "improperly or collusively made."

The most compelling precedent is Farmington Village Corp. v. Pillsbury, 114 U.S. 138 (1885). There Maine holders of bonds issued by a Maine village desired to test the bonds' validity in the federal courts. In an effort to accomplish this, they cut the coupons from their bonds and transferred them to a citizen of Massachusetts, who gave in return a non-negotiable two-year note for $500 and a promise to pay back 50% of the net amount recovered above $500. The jurisdictional question was certified to this Court, which held that there was no federal jurisdiction because the plaintiff had been "improperly or collusively" made a party within the meaning of the predecessor statute to 28 U.S.C. § 80 (1940 ed.). The Court pointed out that the plaintiff could easily

---

3. 28 U.S.C. § 41(1)(1940 ed.). The clause first appeared as § 11 of the Judiciary   Act of 1789, 1 Stat. 79.

have been released from his non-negotiable note, and found that apart from the hoped-for creation of federal jurisdiction the only real consequence of the transfer was to enable the Massachusetts plaintiff to "retain one-half of what he collects for the use of his name and his trouble in collecting." 114 U.S., at 146. The Court concluded that "the transfer of the coupons was 'a mere contrivance, a pretense, the result of a collusive arrangement to create'" federal jurisdiction. *Ibid.*

We find the case before us indistinguishable from Farmington and other decisions of like tenor. When the assignment to Kramer is considered together with his total lack of previous connection with the matter and his simultaneous reassignment of a 95% interest back to Panama, there can be little doubt that the assignment was for purposes of collection, with Kramer to retain 5% of the net proceeds "for the use of his name and his trouble in collecting."[9] If the suit had been unsuccessful, Kramer would have been out only $1, plus costs. Moreover, Kramer candidly admits that the "assignment was in substantial part motivated by a desire by [Panama's] counsel to make diversity jurisdiction available * * *."

The conclusion that this assignment was "improperly or collusively made" within the meaning of § 1359 is supported not only by precedent but also by consideration of the statute's purpose. If federal jurisdiction could be created by assignments of this kind, which are easy to arrange and involve few disadvantages for the assignor, then a vast quantity of ordinary contract and tort litigation could be channeled into the federal courts at the will of one of the parties. Such "manufacture of Federal jurisdiction" was the very thing which Congress intended to prevent when it enacted § 1359 and its predecessors.

III

Kramer nevertheless argues that the assignment to him was not "improperly or collusively made" within the meaning of § 1359, for two main reasons. First, he suggests that the undisputed legality of the assignment under Texas law necessarily rendered it valid for purposes of federal jurisdiction. We cannot accept this contention. * * * [To do so] would render § 1359 largely incapable of accomplishing its purpose; this very case demonstrates the ease with which a party may "manufacture" federal jurisdiction by an assignment which meets the requirements of state law.

Second, Kramer urges that this case is significantly distinguishable from earlier decisions because it involves diversity jurisdiction under 28 U.S.C. § 1332(a)(2), arising from the alienage of one of the parties, rather than the

---

9. Hence, we have no occasion to re-examine the cases in which this Court has held that where the transfer of a claim is absolute, with the transferor retaining no interest in the subject matter, then the transfer is not "improperly or collusively made," regardless of the transferor's motive.

Nor is it necessary to consider whether, in cases in which suit is required to be brought by an administrator or guardian, a motive to create diversity jurisdiction renders the appointment of an out-of-state representative "improper" or "collusive." *See, e.g.,* McSparran v. Weist, 402 F.2d 867 (3d Cir.

1968); *cf.* Mecom v. Fitzsimmons Drilling Co., 284 U.S. 183 (1931). Cases involving representatives vary in several respects from those in which jurisdiction is based on assignments: (1) in the former situation, some representative must be appointed before suit can be brought, while in the latter the assignor normally is himself capable of suing in state court; (2) under state law, different kinds of guardians and administrators may possess discrete sorts of powers; and (3) all such representatives owe their appointment to the decree of a state court, rather than solely to an action of the parties. * * *

more common diversity jurisdiction based upon the parties' residence in different States. We can perceive no substance in this argument: by its terms, § 1359 applies equally to both types of diversity jurisdiction, and there is no indication that Congress intended them to be treated differently.

IV

In short, we find that this assignment falls not only within the scope of § 1359 but within its very core. It follows that the District Court lacked jurisdiction to hear this action, and that petitioner must seek his remedy in the state courts. The judgment of the Court of Appeals is affirmed.

NOTE ON DEVICES FOR CREATING OR AVOIDING FEDERAL JURISDICTION

(1) *Appointments of Legal Representatives.*

(a) Footnote 9 of the Kramer opinion refers to the appointment of an administrator or guardian for the purpose of creating diversity jurisdiction. The problem presented by this practice had become particularly acute in the Eastern District of Pennsylvania, where it was common for lawyers in Philadelphia to arrange for the appointment—as guardians, administrators, or executors—of secretaries or other office staff who commuted to work from New Jersey, thus laying the basis for a diversity action against a Pennsylvania defendant. In McSparran v. Weist, 402 F.2d 867 (3d Cir.1968), decided a few months before Kramer, the plaintiff conceded that the fiduciary (a guardian for a minor) was "a straw party, chosen solely to create diversity jurisdiction" (p. 869). The Third Circuit, overruling its own precedent, sustained a challenge to the jurisdiction, saying (p. 873):

"* * * [A] nominal party designated simply for the purpose of creating diversity of citizenship, who has no real or substantial interest in the dispute or controversy, is improperly or collusively named."

(b) Following Kramer, and despite the effort by the Court in that case to suggest some distinctions between the facts presented and those involved in McSparran, most lower courts followed McSparran's lead and held that § 1359 barred jurisdiction on the basis of the representative's citizenship if the purpose of his appointment was to create diversity. *E.g.,* Bianca v. Parke–Davis Pharmaceutical Division, 723 F.2d 392 (5th Cir.1984).

(c) In 1988, Congress addressed the McSparran problem by adopting a "bright line" test for determining jurisdiction. A new provision, 28 U.S.C. § 1332(c)(2), specifies that the representative of an estate shall be deemed to be a citizen only of the state of citizenship of the decedent, and the representative of an infant or incompetent shall be deemed to be a citizen only of the state of citizenship of the person represented.

(2) *Variations on the Theme: Matters Not Covered by Kramer or by § 1332 (c)(2).* The Kramer Court deliberately left open the status under § 1359 of a variety of events, thus casting doubt on a number of its own precedents. As stated in the Court's footnote 9, an absolute transfer not subject to the former assignee clause had been held not improper or collusive, regardless of the transferor's motive. *E.g.,* Cross v. Allen, 141 U.S. 528 (1891). And if the plaintiff effectively changed his domicile prior to the bringing of suit, it did not

matter that his sole motive was to create jurisdiction. Williamson v. Osenton, 232 U.S. 619 (1914). Finally, although reincorporation would fail to create diversity jurisdiction if the old corporation continued in existence with power to control the new, *e.g.*, Lehigh Mining & Mfg. Co. v. Kelly, 160 U.S. 327 (1895), the device would succeed if the new corporation was a genuine one not subject to control by any predecessor, Black and White Taxicab & Transfer Co. v. Brown and Yellow Taxicab & Transfer Co., 276 U.S. 518 (1928).

Should any or all of these holdings be overruled? What is the effect, if any, of Congress' decision to deal specifically with the case of the legal representative (see Paragraph (1)(c), *supra*)?

(3) *Direct Actions Against Insurers: § 1332(c)(1)*. In its 1964 amendment to 28 U.S.C. § 1332(c), Congress dealt with another device for obtaining federal diversity jurisdiction. Statutes of a few states (notably, Louisiana) permitted an injured person to bring suit directly against a liability insurer without joining the insured, and this made it possible, for example, for a case in which one Louisiana citizen had injured another to be litigated in a federal court if the alleged tortfeasor had an out-of-state insurer. Lumbermen's Mut. Cas. Co. v. Elbert, 348 U.S. 48 (1954). Such cases were pouring into the Louisiana federal courts until Congress provided that the insurer defendant in a direct action must be deemed a citizen of the insured's state as well as of its own.[10]

Was Congress correct in concluding that such cases are less fitting for original diversity jurisdiction than other cases in which an in-state citizen sues an out-of-state citizen? See the criticism of the statute in Weckstein, *The 1964 Diversity Amendment: Congressional Indirect Action Against State "Direct Action" Laws*, 1965 Wis.L.Rev. 268.

(4) *Avoidance Devices*. No statutory provision aids a district court in disregarding devices to avoid federal jurisdiction, and such devices have often been successful. In Provident Savings Life Assurance Society v. Ford, 114 U.S. 635 (1885), the Court held that if an assignment to the plaintiff was "merely colorable" and made to prevent removal, the matter was at most one of defense to the action in the state court, and thus the case could not be removed. See also Oakley v. Goodnow, 118 U.S. 43 (1886)(assignment to defeat jurisdiction precludes removal); Mecom v. Fitzsimmons Drilling Co., 284 U.S. 183 (1931)(appointment of co-citizen administrator to defeat jurisdiction precludes removal).

But the tide appears to have turned. In Gentle v. Lamb–Weston, Inc., 302 F.Supp. 161 (D.Me.1969), each of the plaintiffs, who were citizens of Maine, transferred 1% of his claim to an Oregon citizen (a law school classmate of their Maine attorney), and the Oregon citizen then joined as a plaintiff in an action against an Oregon defendant in a Maine state court. The admitted purpose of the transfer was to prevent removal, yet Judge Gignoux denied a motion to remand the case to the state court. He managed to distinguish each of the Supreme Court cases cited above (as involving either total assignments or state-court approved appointments), and relied on the Kramer rationale as well as on cases in which "fraudulent joinder" of an in-state defendant failed to preclude

---

10. In Northbrook Nat. Ins. Co. v. Brewer, 493 U.S. 6 (1989), the Court held, 8–1, that the provision does not apply to an action brought *by* an insurer, even when the action is one for de novo review of a state workers' compensation ruling and is one in which the employee must assert and prove the merit of the claim no matter who requests review.

removal. As to the partial transfer in the case before him, "the essential diversity of citizenship of the parties at bar has not been vitiated by plaintiffs' sham transaction" (p. 166). The case was noted at 83 Harv.L.Rev. 465 (1969), and has been followed in several other courts. See, *e.g.*, Grassi v. Ciba–Geigy, Ltd., 894 F.2d 181 (5th Cir.1990); Carter v. Seaboard Coast Line R.R., 318 F.Supp. 368 (D.S.C.1970); *cf.* Miller v. Perry, 456 F.2d 63 (4th Cir.1972)(criticizing and distinguishing Mecom and holding that plaintiff's appointment of a North Carolina administrator did not preclude removal to a federal court by North Carolina defendants). See generally Wright, Federal Courts § 31, at 185–89 (5th ed. 1994).

SECTION 6.   THE FUTURE OF DIVERSITY JURISDICTION

NOTE ON THE PRESENT–DAY UTILITY OF THE JURISDICTION

(1) *The Effect of the Erie Decision.* Does Erie R.R. v. Tompkins weaken or strengthen the case for the diversity jurisdiction?[1] For a review of the problem, written after Erie and before the 1948 revision of the Judicial Code, see Wechsler, *Federal Jurisdiction and the Revision of the Judicial Code,* 13 Law & Contemp.Prob. 216, 234–40 (1948):

"Those who defend the jurisdiction point, of course, to the original fear of prejudice against the litigant from out of state and argue that the danger is not gone today. I share the view that this provides an insufficient answer, that when this sentiment exists and works unfairness, the protection must be found, as in the case of other prejudices threatening administration of state justice, in state appellate processes—including, when due process is denied, review by the Supreme Court. It is, indeed, a rather startling thought that this least troublesome of all the prejudices should be the basis of a special federal forum which none of the hostilities that flow from faction, interest, race, or creed is deemed sufficient to provide. But even if the prejudice hypothesis is thought to warrant federal intervention, it is quite plain that the diversity jurisdiction is not defined in terms that are responsive to the theory.

* * *

"There is, I think, a solid case for preservation of the jurisdiction in any instance where a concrete showing of state prejudice can be established. There may be cases, too, where there is need for process that outruns state borders, as in the interpleader under present law. I do not argue that diversity should not be utilized to grant a federal forum on such principles. To do so is to premise federal intervention on a current finding of a state inadequacy. The problem is

---

1. The controversy over the diversity jurisdiction did not begin with the Erie decision. For conflicting views in the decade prior to Erie, see Frankfurter, *Distribution of Judicial Power between United States and State Courts,* 13 Corn.L.Q. 499, 520–30 (1928); Yntema & Jaffin, *Preliminary Analysis of Concurrent Jurisdiction,* 79 U.Pa. L.Rev. 869 (1931); *Limiting Jurisdiction of* *Federal Courts—Pending Bills—Comments by Members of Chicago University Law Faculty,* 31 Mich.L.Rev. 59 (1932); Charles E. Clark, *Diversity of Citizenship Jurisdiction of the Federal Courts,* 19 A.B.A.J. 499 (1933).

For a summary of earlier views, see Frankfurter & Landis, The Business of the Supreme Court 86–102, 136–41 (1928).

to limit intervention to the situations where it is in fact responsive to such need."

(2) *The Possible Uses of the Diversity Jurisdiction.*

(a) *As a vehicle for building up and administering a uniform body of judge-made law in areas in which Congress either has not legislated or could not.*

This was the great experiment of Swift v. Tyson on which, presumably, the books are now closed.

(b) *As a means of encouraging out-of-state individuals and enterprises to engage in local investment and other activities, by providing an assurance of impartial decision of disputes growing out of those activities.*

Notice the varying kinds of injustice against which safeguard may be desired: *e.g.*, invocation of unjust or discriminatory rules of law; unjust application of law to the facts; delays and inefficiencies in judicial administration.

Consider the other instruments of federal protection against these evils: *e.g.*, the Privileges and Immunities Clause of Article IV, § 2; the Privileges or Immunities Clause of the Fourteenth Amendment; the Commerce Clause; the Due Process Clause of the Fourteenth Amendment; the Equal Protection Clause.

In view of these safeguards, as well as the lessening of provincialism and the improvement of state judicial systems, is there substantial present need on this score for maintaining the diversity jurisdiction?[2]

(c) *As a means of providing for the just resolution of conflicts of laws in controversies between citizens of different states.*

Was Klaxon Co. v. Stentor Elec. Mfg. Co., 313 U.S. 487 (1941), p. 695, *supra*, a mistake? Should legislative or judicial action be taken under the Full Faith and Credit Clause to achieve the suggested objective?[3]

(d) *As a means of facilitating the settlement of controversies that because of the multiplicity of parties and their diversity of citizenship, cannot be effectually settled in the courts of any one state.*

Consider the distinctive function served by the Federal Interpleader Act and various provisions of the federal rules with respect to multi-party litigation.

Are there amendments of the Judicial Code that would enable this function to be better performed?[4]

---

2. For an argument that the diversity jurisdiction may be justified in at least those situations in which a state's residents (including the judges they have chosen) may have an *economic* incentive to discriminate against nonresidents, see Posner, The Federal Courts: Crisis and Reform 175–77 (1985).

3. In cases involving complex litigation, especially litigation likely to take the form of lawsuits brought in a number of courts (state and/or federal), are the arguments for such action especially strong? For proposed federal legislation governing choice of law in such cases, see American Law Institute, Complex Litigation: Statutory Recommendations and Analysis (1994). See also the extensive discussion of this and other aspects of the proposals made by the ALI Project in the Symposium appearing in 54 La.L.Rev., No. 4 (1994).

4. Various proposals have been made to expand original or removal diversity jurisdiction in order to allow complex multi-party suits to be litigated in federal courts; other proposals have been designed to facilitate transfer and consolidation of such suits. For a comprehensive study of the area, see the ALI Project discussed in note 3, *supra*.

For a critique of such proposals, and a questioning of their constitutionality, see

(e) *As a means of assuring out-of-state litigants and their attorneys that a familiar procedural system will be available for the adjudication of their disputes.*

The adoption of the Federal Rules of Civil Procedure in 1938 made it possible to think about this objective as a justification for the jurisdiction. Has its value been undercut by the extent to which those very rules have influenced the development of procedural systems in virtually every state? By recent legislation and other developments that tend to encourage Balkanization of procedures within the federal system itself? (See Chap. 6, Sec. 1, pp. 668–69, *supra.*)

(f) *As a means of facilitating interchange between state and federal systems on matters of substance and procedure.*

For discussion of the possible values of diversity jurisdiction in supporting the "migration of ideas" between state and federal courts, see Shapiro, *Federal Diversity Jurisdiction: A Survey and a Proposal,* 91 Harv.L.Rev. 317, 324–27 (1977). See also Posner, note 2, *supra,* at 144, concluding that "[e]ven in the years since the Erie decision eliminated or, more realistically, confined their creative lawmaking role in diversity cases, the federal courts have made a disproportionate contribution to the shaping of the common law * * *."

Are there other uses of the diversity jurisdiction to which consideration should be given? Should it matter if the federal courts of first instance are in fact, or are perceived to be, of higher quality than their state counterparts? For an argument that it should not, see Friendly, Federal Jurisdiction: A General View 145–47 (1973).

(3) *The ALI Study of the Division of Jurisdiction, and Subsequent Developments.*

(a) Concern with the questions of policy raised by the scope of the diversity jurisdiction was brought to a head, once again, in the 1960s by the recommendations of the American Law Institute Study of the Division of Jurisdiction Between State and Federal Courts. The Study recognized that the pledge of federal justice to travelers from other states was "woven into the fabric of our society" and "should not lightly be withdrawn". Further, it saw the jurisdiction as guarding against the still-existing dangers of prejudice towards those from far-removed sections of the country and against other possible shortcomings of state justice for which the out-of-stater could not be held responsible and which were beyond his power to remedy. Finally, the Study noted that whatever the actual defects of state justice, the out-of-stater (and especially the alien[5]) who loses is far less likely to blame the defeat on the bias or incompetence of the tribunal if the case is tried in a federal court. See ALI Study 105–08 (1969).

Mullenix, *Complex Litigation Reform and Article III Jurisdiction,* 59 Fordham L.Rev. 169 (1990).

5. An (as yet) unpublished empirical study by Clermont & Eisenberg, *Xenophilia in American Courts* (Draft of 9/11/95) comes up with a counter-intuitive conclusion: "The available data indicate that foreigners do very well in federal courts. They win substantial-

ly more, whether as plaintiffs or defendants, than their United States counterparts." The authors go on to suggest that one explanation may lie in foreigners' aversion to American courts—an aversion meaning that "[f]oreigners' cases reaching judgment are consequently a strong set of cases, which might not meet the expected bias."

After rejecting other arguments in favor of diversity, the Study proposed a series of changes designed to bring the jurisdiction into harmony with its rationale. In some respects, the Study recommended expansion of the jurisdiction.[6] At the same time, it concluded that invocation of diversity jurisdiction by persons who had close ties with the forum state was inconsistent with the underlying rationale of diversity jurisdiction and should not be allowed. Thus the Study proposed to bar one who was a "citizen" of the forum state from invoking the jurisdiction. Invocation would also be barred by out-of-state corporations and other businesses having "local establishments" (as defined) in the state, if the suit arose out of the activities of that establishment, and by persons who regularly commuted to work in the state (proposed § 1302). In such instances, the Study argued, there was no basis for overcoming the normal presumption that the proper allocation of functions in a federal system requires state law cases to be tried in the state courts.

(b) In 1978, a bill abolishing the diversity jurisdiction, except in alienage and interpleader cases, was approved by the House of Representatives, H.R. 9622, 95th Cong., 2d Sess. (1978), but died in a subcommittee of the Senate Judiciary Committee. Similar bills have been introduced in later Congresses, but none has been approved in either House. Staunch opposition by the trial bar has undoubtedly been a factor in blocking so sweeping a change. Proposals for cutting back or largely eliminating the jurisdiction continue to flourish, however, with the latest including Recommendation 7 of the Judicial Conference Committee on Long Range Planning, note 10, *infra*, at 29–32. In addition, a bill under consideration in the 104th Congress would provide for limited fee shifting in certain diversity cases, thus (in the view of some) reducing the incentive for plaintiffs to file diversity cases in federal courts.[7] See 63 U.S.L.W. 2507 (1995).

6. Most notable was a proposed new head of federal jurisdiction designed to cover multi-party, multi-state cases that were thought to fall beyond the reach of the state courts. (See proposed §§ 2371–76.) For a simpler, and broader, proposal, see Rowe & Sibley, *Beyond Diversity: Federal Multistate, Multiparty Jurisdiction,* 135 U.Pa.L.Rev. 7 (1987).

7. Since the publication of the ALI Study, discussion of the desirability and appropriate scope of the diversity jurisdiction has been extensive. Among those favoring abolition of diversity jurisdiction under § 1332(a)(1) have been Judge Friendly, in Federal Jurisdiction: A General View 3–4, 139–52 (1973), and then-Chief Justice Burger in *Annual Report on the State of the Judiciary,* 62 A.B.A.J. 443, 444 (1976). See also Rowe, *Abolishing Diversity Jurisdiction: Positive Side Effects and Potential for Further Reforms,* 92 Harv.L.Rev. 963, 966 (1979) (concluding that abolition is supported not only by arguments traditionally made—"the lack of positive reasons for it, the need for a reduction in federal caseloads and jury trials, and the appropriateness of merging more ful-

ly the power to interpret state law with the responsibility of applying it"—but also by the "additional effects of abolition—elimination or reduction of some of the most vexing problems in federal practice, demystified interpretations, and facilitation of reforms"); Kramer, *Diversity Jurisdiction,* 1990 B.Y.U.L.Rev. 97 (concluding that, with limited exceptions, the jurisdiction should be abolished, a conclusion that parallelled that of the Federal Courts Study Committee (at 38–42), which he served as a reporter).

With the foregoing, compare, *e.g.,* Arnold, *The Future of the Federal Courts,* 60 Mo.L.Rev. 533, 538–39 (1995) (noting that Congress "created the lower federal courts primarily to hear diversity cases"); Frank, *The Case for Diversity Jurisdiction,* 16 Harv.J.Legis. 403 (1979); Posner, The Federal Courts: Crisis and Reform 139–47 (1985)(advocating adoption of a higher jurisdictional amount, together with the ALI's proposed limitations on invocation of diversity jurisdiction); Shapiro, Paragraph (2)(f), *supra,* at 319 (suggesting a " 'local option plan,' under which each federal district would have limited freedom to retain, curtail, or

(c) Prior to the 1988 amendment, the number of diversity cases filed in the district courts continued to increase, but the ratio of such cases to all civil actions filed in those courts declined—from approximately one-third in 1960 to one-quarter in 1988.   In the years from 1989 to 1993, overall civil filings have remained relatively stable (starting at 225,811 in 1989, dropping to 210,890 in 1991, and rising to 229,850 in 1993), while diversity filings dropped dramatically through 1992 (from 62,422 in 1989[8] to 49,432 in 1992) and then rose slightly to 51,445 in 1993.[9]   In 1994, total civil filings had reached 235,996, and diversity filings rose again to 54,917.[10]   As a result of the increase in jurisdictional amount, those diversity cases that are being filed are likely on average to be more complex and time-consuming than before the 1988 change.[11]

(4) *Empirical Studies and Surveys.*   Only in recent decades has there been any empirical investigation of the views of judges and lawyers and of the reasons why litigants and their lawyers choose one system of courts or another in diversity cases.   Two of the earliest studies, in the 1960s, seemed to point toward quite different conclusions.   Compare Summers, *Analysis of Factors That Influence Choice of Forum in Diversity Cases,* 47 Iowa L.Rev. 933 (1962)(local bias against a nonresident client was rarely indicated as a factor in choice of forum [only 7 of 164 reasons given in 82 cases], and was never the sole factor;   geographical convenience, on the other hand, was listed 30 times;   better discovery 26 times;   and higher awards 23 times), with Note, 51 Va. L.Rev. 178 (1965)(local prejudice against an out-of-state client was listed as a reason for choosing a federal court by 60.3% of the surveyed attorneys;   local prejudice against an out-of-state adversary was indicated as a reason for preferring a state court by 52.1% of the same group).[12]

In a later survey, taken in Cook County, Illinois, it was reported, *inter alia,* that 40% of the surveyed attorneys who had filed diversity cases (originally or on removal) in federal court cited "local bias against an out-of-state resident" as a relevant factor in making the choice of courts.   Goldman & Marks, *Diversity Jurisdiction and Local Bias: A Preliminary Empirical Inquiry,* 9 J.Leg.Stud. 93, 97–99 (1980).   And in Bumiller, *Choice of Forum in Diversity Cases: Analysis of a Survey and Implications for Reform,* 15 Law & Soc'y Rev. 749 (1980–81), the author found "local bias" to be a significant factor in the choice of a federal court only in rural districts.   This and other variables indicating the greater utility of diversity jurisdiction within particular geographical areas led her to support the local option plan proposed in Shapiro, Paragraph (2)(f), *supra.*

Finally, a study in 1991 examined the forum-selection choices of attorneys in tort and contract cases.   The study found that when the client is a non-

virtually eliminate diversity jurisdiction within its borders").

8.   This figure is similar to those for prior years.

9.   Annual Report of the Director of the Administrative Office of the United States Courts, Judicial Business of the United States Courts 8 (1993).

10.   See Table 3 in Committee on Long Range Planning, Judicial Conference of the United states, Proposed Long Range Plan for the Federal Courts 14 (1995).

11.   For further discussion of the dockets of the district courts, and the nature of their business, see Chap. I, pp. 47–52, *supra.*

12.   The studies differed in methodology in several respects, one of which was that the Virginia study asked attorneys about the factors that *would* lead them to prefer a federal or state court, rather than—as with the Wisconsin study—the factors that *did* influence them in actual cases.

resident of the state, the overwhelming percentage of lawyers (85% of the lawyers litigating in state court, and 96% of those litigating in federal court) prefer a federal forum.   (Among *all* lawyers surveyed, reasons for preferring a particular forum covered a broad range, from familiarity with the court system to judgments about quality, possible prejudice, and docket conditions.   See Flango, *Attorneys' Perspectives on Choice of Forum in Diversity Cases,* 25 Akron L.Rev. 41 (1991)).   See also Miller, *An Empirical Study of Forum Choices in Removal Cases Under Diversity and Federal Question Jurisdiction,* 41 Am. U.L.Rev. 369 (1992)(attorneys' decisions to remove based primarily on opinions about judicial quality, local bias, convenience, and court rules).

For a survey of federal judges showing a wide variety of opinions on the question whether diversity jurisdiction should be retained, in whole or in part, or abolished, see Shapiro, Paragraph 2(f), *supra,* at 332–39.   For the results of a survey of lawyers, see *Lawpoll,* 66 A.B.A.J. 148, 149 (1980).

The most recent survey of federal judges was conducted under the auspices of the Federal Judicial Center.   Among the many questions asked on a wide variety of issues was one on abolishing diversity jurisdiction.   On a scale of 1 to 5 (excluding such categories as no opinion or no answer), with 1 constituting strong support of abolition and 5 strong opposition, active circuit judges divided as follows: Category 1, *31.0%*; Category 2, *17.8%*; Category 3, *12.4%*; Category 4, *17.1%*; and Category 5, *20.9%*.   Active district judges leaned more toward opposition: Category 1, *23.4%*; Category 2, *13.3%*; Category 3, *14.2%*; Category 4, *13.3%*; and Category 5, *33.7%*.   Federal Judicial Center, Planning for the Future: Results of a 1992 Survey Federal Judicial Center Survey of United States Judges 7, 29 (1994).

CHAPTER XIV

ADDITIONAL PROBLEMS OF DISTRICT COURT JURISDICTION

SECTION 1. CHALLENGES TO JURISDICTION

Mansfield, Coldwater & Lake Michigan Ry. v. Swan

111 U.S. 379, 4 S.Ct. 510, 28 L.Ed. 462 (1884).
In Error to the Circuit Court of the United States for the Northern District of Ohio.

■ MR. JUSTICE MATTHEWS delivered the opinion of the Court.

This was an action at law originally brought in the court of common pleas of Fulton county, Ohio, by John Swan, S.C. Rose, F.M. Hutchinson, and Robert McMann, as partners under the name of Swan, Rose & Co., against the plaintiffs in error. * * * It was commenced June 10, 1874. Afterwards, on October 28, 1879, the cause being at issue, the defendants below filed a petition for its removal to the circuit court of the United States. They aver therein that one of the petitioners is a corporation created by the laws of Ohio alone, and the other, a corporation consolidated under the laws of Michigan and Ohio * * *. It is also alleged, in the petition for removal, "that the plaintiffs, John Swan and Frank M. Hutchinson, at the time of the commencement of this suit, were, and still are, citizens of the state of Pennsylvania; that the said Robert H. McMann was then (according to your petitioners' recollection) a citizen of the state of Ohio, but that he is not now a citizen of that state, but where he now resides or whereof he is now a citizen (except that he is a citizen of one of the states or territories comprising the United States) your petitioners are unable to state; * * *." The petition, being accompanied with a satisfactory bond, was allowed, and an order made for the removal of the cause. The plaintiffs below afterwards, on December 13, 1879, moved to remand the cause on the ground, among others, that the circuit court had no jurisdiction, because the "real and substantial controversy in the cause is between real and substantial parties who are citizens of the same state and not of different states." But the motion was denied. Subsequently a trial took place upon the merits, which resulted in a verdict and judgment in favor of the plaintiffs * * *. [T]he writ of error is prosecuted by the defendants below to reverse this judgment.

An examination of the record, however, discloses that the circuit court had no jurisdiction to try the action * * *. It appears from the petition for removal, and not otherwise by the record elsewhere, that, at the time the action was first brought in the state court, one of the plaintiffs, and a necessary party, McMann, was a citizen of Ohio, the same state of which the defendants were citizens. It does not affirmatively appear that at the time of the removal he was a citizen of any other state. The averment is that he was not then a citizen of Ohio, and that his actual citizenship was unknown, except that he was a citizen of one of the states or territories. It is consistent with this statement that he was not a citizen of any state. He may have been a citizen of a territory; and, if so, the requisite citizenship would not exist. According to the decision in Gibson v. Bruce, 108 U.S. 561, the difference of citizenship on which the right of removal depends must have existed at the time when the suit was begun, as well as at the time of the removal * * *. It was error, therefore, in the circuit court to assume jurisdiction in the case, and not to remand it, on the motion of the plaintiffs below.

It is true that the plaintiffs below, against whose objection the error was committed, do not complain of being prejudiced by it, and it seems to be an anomaly and a hardship that the party at whose instance it was committed should be permitted to derive an advantage from it; but the rule, springing from the nature and limits of the judicial power of the United States, is inflexible and without exception which requires this court, of its own motion, to deny its own jurisdiction, and, in the exercise of its appellate power, that of all other courts of the United States, in all cases where such jurisdiction does not affirmatively appear in the record on which, in the exercise of that power, it is called to act. On every writ of error or appeal the first and fundamental question is that of jurisdiction, first, of this court, and then of the court from which the record comes. * * *

In the Dred Scott Case, 19 How. 393–400, it was decided that a judgment of the circuit court, upon the sufficiency of a plea in abatement, denying its jurisdiction, was open for review upon a writ of error sued out by the party in whose favor the plea had been overruled. And in this view Mr. Justice Curtis, in his dissenting opinion, concurred; and we adopt from that opinion the following statement of the law on the point: "* * * The true question is not what either of the parties may be allowed to do, but whether this court will affirm or reverse a judgment of the circuit court on the merits, when it appears on the record, by a plea to the jurisdiction, that it is a case to which the judicial power of the United States does not extend. The course of the court is, when no motion is made by either party, on its own motion, to reverse such a judgment for want of jurisdiction, not only in cases where it is shown, negatively, by a plea to the jurisdiction, that jurisdiction does not exist, but even when it does not appear, affirmatively, that it does exist. It acts upon the principle that the judicial power of the United States must not be exerted in a case to which it does not extend, even if both parties desire to have it exerted. I consider, therefore, that when there was a plea to the jurisdiction of the circuit court in a case brought here by a writ of error, the first duty of this court is, *sua sponte,* if not moved to it by either party, to examine the sufficiency of that plea, and thus to take care that neither the circuit court nor this court shall use the judicial power of the United States in a case to which the constitution and laws of the United States have not extended that power" [19 How. 566].

This is precisely applicable to the present case, for the motion of the plaintiffs below to remand the cause was equivalent to a special plea to the jurisdiction of the court; but the doctrine applies equally in every case where the jurisdiction does not appear from the record. * * *

The judgment of the circuit court is accordingly reversed, with costs against the plaintiffs in error, and the cause is remanded to the circuit court, with directions to render a judgment against them for costs in that court, and to remand the cause to the court of common pleas of Fulton county, Ohio; and it is so ordered.

NOTE ON CHALLENGING THE EXISTENCE OF FEDERAL JURISDICTION IN THE REGULAR COURSE OF TRIAL AND APPELLATE REVIEW

(1) *Relevant Provisions of the Rules of Civil Procedure*. Requirements for alleging jurisdiction and the proper manner for raising the defense of lack of jurisdiction are specified in Rules 8(a) and 12(b)(1) of the Federal Rules of Civil Procedure. Rule 12(h)(3) requires dismissal whenever it appears that jurisdiction over the subject matter is lacking.

(2) *The Mansfield Doctrine*. The principle declared in the Mansfield case and codified in the Federal Rules is reflected not only in the requirements of proper pleadings and requests for review but in the accepted form of briefing and oral argument. See Fed.R.App.P. 28(a)(2)(requiring appellant's brief to contain a statement of appellate and subject matter jurisdiction); S.Ct.R. 24.1(e)(requiring the brief of appellant or petitioner to contain a concise statement of the grounds on which jurisdiction depends). The first duty of counsel is to make clear to a federal court the basis of its jurisdiction. The first duty of the court is to make sure that jurisdiction exists. If the record fails to disclose a basis for federal jurisdiction, the court not only will but must refuse to proceed further with the determination of the merits of the controversy unless the failure can be cured. This is true whether the case is at the trial stage or the appellate stage, and whether the defect is called to the court's attention "by suggestion of the parties or otherwise". The rest of this book might be filled with citations and thumbnail abstracts of cases illustrating the application of this principle.[1]

This is established practice. Is it fetishism? Or is it grounded on solid considerations of policy and of legislative and judicial statesmanship? Why should not a party who has invoked federal jurisdiction, or failed seasonably to object to it, be held to have waived any defect, or be estopped from asserting it?

(3) *Curing Defective Allegations*.

(a) A federal court always has jurisdiction to decide whether it has jurisdiction and, if it decides that it does not, to take appropriate action. And a federal

---

1. For a noteworthy but evidently unsuccessful effort by one lower court to depart from the principle, see Paragraph (5), *infra*.

The Supreme Court itself has shown no tendency to retreat explicitly from the principle. See, *e.g.*, Firestone Tire & Rubber Co. v. Risjord, 449 U.S. 368, 379–80 & n. 15 (1981), holding that a "jurisdictional ruling [that an appeal could not be heard for lack of a final judgment] may never be made prospective only." But the Court has not infrequently overlooked some jurisdictional issues. Thus before the 1976 repeal of the jurisdictional amount requirement under § 1331, the Court

often dealt with a case without reference to that requirement, even though a substantial question appeared to exist. See, *e.g.*, Flast v. Cohen, 392 U.S. 83 (1968); Kleindienst v. Mandel, 408 U.S. 753 (1972); United States v. Richardson, 418 U.S. 166 (1974). And the Court has occasionally refused to resolve an unusually difficult issue of jurisdiction in a case where decision in another, related case effectively disposed of the action on the merits. See Philbrook v. Glodgett, 421 U.S. 707 (1975); Secretary of the Navy v. Avrech, 418 U.S. 676 (1974).

appellate court has jurisdiction to decide whether the court or courts below had jurisdiction and, if not, to take appropriate action. Commonly the appropriate disposition will be to reverse the judgment under review with directions to the court of first instance to dismiss the action, or if it was a removed action, to remand it to the state court for want of jurisdiction. But what if jurisdiction exists in fact but merely has not been properly alleged?

At the time of the Mansfield case, the appellate court in this situation had no choice but reversal. In an original action the trial court might thereafter permit an appropriate amendment of the pleadings, if it were satisfied of the existence of jurisdiction in fact. Robertson v. Cease, 97 U.S. 646, 650–51 (1878). But no such amendment was permitted in a removed action. Cameron v. Hodges, 127 U.S. 322, 326 (1888). Why the difference?

In 1915, Congress provided (38 Stat. 956) that in a case in which "diverse citizenship in fact existed at the time the suit was brought or removed, though defectively alleged, either party may amend at any stage of the proceedings and in the appellate court upon such terms as the court may impose, so as to show on the record" the existence of jurisdiction. Why the discrimination in favor of diversity litigation?

The present statute, 28 U.S.C. § 1653, provides generally that "[d]efective allegations of jurisdiction may be amended, upon terms, in the trial or appellate courts."

(b) A lack of jurisdiction at the time the complaint is filed may be cured by a subsequent statutory change. In Andrus v. Charlestone Stone Prods. Co., Inc., 436 U.S. 604, 607–08 n. 6 (1978), and in Duke Power Co. v. Carolina Env. Study Group, Inc., 438 U.S. 59, 70 n. 14 (1978), the Supreme Court raised the issue of federal jurisdiction *sua sponte*. It then held that failure to assert any "amount in controversy" in actions against federal officers instituted in 1973 was immaterial on the basis of the 1976 amendment to § 1331 eliminating the jurisdictional amount requirement in such actions—an amendment adopted several years after each suit had been commenced. The absence from each complaint of any explicit reference to § 1331 was deemed insignificant because the facts alleged were sufficient to establish jurisdiction under the amended section.

(4) *Statutory History*. At the time of the Mansfield decision, section 5 of the Act of March 3, 1875, c. 137, 18 Stat. 470, 472, provided:

"That if, in any suit commenced in a circuit court or removed from a State court to a circuit court of the United States, it shall appear to the satisfaction of said circuit court, at any time after such suit has been brought or removed thereto, that such suit does not really and substantially involve a dispute or controversy properly within the jurisdiction of said circuit court, or that the parties to said suit have been improperly or collusively made or joined, either as plaintiffs or defendants, for the purpose of creating a case cognizable or removable under this act, the said circuit court shall proceed no further therein, but shall dismiss the suit or remand it to the court from which it was removed as justice may require, and shall make such order as to costs as shall be just * * *."

This provision was relied upon in innumerable cases decided between 1875 and 1948 in which the court at either the trial or the appellate stage, on its own motion or on the belated suggestion of a party, took notice of a defect of jurisdiction and dismissed or directed dismissal of the action. It was also the primary ground for holding that the burden of proof of all the elements requisite for federal jurisdiction rested on the party invoking the jurisdiction. See McNutt v. General Motors Acc. Corp., 298 U.S. 178 (1936). Does this mean that these results would have been different in the absence of the provision?

The question is not academic. In the 1948 revision, the provision was combined with the famous assignee clause (see pp. 354, 1568, *supra*) and the two reduced (in the present § 1359) to the following sentence:

"A district court shall not have jurisdiction of a civil action in which any party, by assignment or otherwise, has been improperly or collusively made or joined to invoke the jurisdiction of such court."

The revisers stated:

"Provisions * * * for dismissal of an action not really and substantially involving a dispute or controversy within the jurisdiction of a district court, were omitted as unnecessary. Any court will dismiss a case not within its jurisdiction when its attention is drawn to the fact, or even on its own motion."

Were the revisers well-advised in what they did?

(5) *Present Practice*. The revisers' prophecy—self-fulfilling or otherwise—has generally prevailed. The federal courts have continued to accept jurisdictional attacks at any time, *e.g.*, even when the party that had invoked federal jurisdiction challenged it after losing the case on the merits, American Fire & Cas. Co. v. Finn, 341 U.S. 6 (1951),[2] or when the objection was withheld until after the statute of limitations had run on a possible state court action, Knee v. Chemical Leaman Tank Lines, 293 F.Supp. 1094 (E.D.Pa.1968).[3]

One effort to carve out an exception occurred in Di Frischia v. New York Central R.R., 279 F.2d 141 (3d Cir.1960). Defendant in this case, after objecting to the jurisdiction of the court on the basis of lack of diversity, filed a stipulation withdrawing the objection, and the case proceeded through pretrial stages. Twenty-three months later, after the statute of limitations had run, defendant renewed its original objection. The trial court dismissed the action, but the Third Circuit reversed, tartly commenting that "[a] defendant may not play fast and loose with the judicial machinery and deceive the courts" (p. 144). Is this response to a "fast and loose" play consistent with the Mansfield rule? For an interesting argument that it is, as well as for a narrow reading of Mansfield generally,[4] see Dobbs, *Beyond Bootstrap: Foreclosing the Issue of Subject–Matter Jurisdiction Before Final Judgment*, 51 Minn.L.Rev. 491 (1967).

But the Di Frischia assault on the principle has not proved generative. See, *e.g.*, Sadat v. Mertes, 615 F.2d 1176, 1189 (7th Cir.1980); Eisler v.

---

2. The Court of Appeals did subsequently enter a new judgment on the original verdict in this case after plaintiff had dismissed as to the party whose presence had barred jurisdiction. Finn v. American Fire & Cas. Co., 207 F.2d 113 (5th Cir.1953).

3. But compare with this general rule the discussion of the "Baggs–Mackay" estop-

pel doctrine in Section 3 of this Chapter, p. 1629, *infra*.

4. Recall that in Mansfield, the jurisdictional defect was apparent on the face of the record. (Also, as the Supreme Court noted, the question of jurisdiction had been raised below by the plaintiffs. Plaintiffs, of course,

Stritzler, 535 F.2d 148, 151–52 (1st Cir.1976).[5] And it was at least implicitly disapproved by the Supreme Court in Owen Equipment & Erection Co. v. Kroger, 437 U.S. 365 (1978), p. 1558, *supra*. Defendant Owen's answer had admitted diversity jurisdiction, but on the third day of trial it appeared that the requisite diversity did not exist, and Owen then moved to dismiss for want of jurisdiction. The Third Circuit, relying in part on the view that Owen's conduct created an estoppel, affirmed denial of the motion. The Supreme Court reversed, concluding (p. 377 n. 21): "Our holding is that the District Court lacked power to entertain the respondent's lawsuit against the petitioner. Thus, the asserted inequity in the respondent's alleged concealment of its citizenship is irrelevant."

(6) *The ALI Proposal.* The American Law Institute proposed to overturn the Mansfield rule and to preclude raising of jurisdictional issues by the parties or the courts after the beginning of trial except in specified circumstances— principally involving either previously unknown and unavailable facts or collusion between the parties. ALI, Study of the Division of Jurisdiction Between State and Federal Courts § 1386 (1969). The Commentary gave as the "principal purpose of the revisions * * * to provide every incentive to both sides to seek resolution of the issue of subject-matter jurisdiction prior to the commencement of trial. At the same time, an effort has been made not to preclude the raising of issues even after the beginning of trial if those issues could not reasonably be expected to have been raised and resolved earlier."

Would the proposed jurisdictional foreclosure be constitutional? In a case that was shown, while still pending, to fall outside the competence of the federal courts under Article III?[6]

NOTE ON RAISING OTHER QUESTIONS OF "JURISDICTION" IN THE REGULAR COURSE OF THE PROCEEDING

The prior Note dealt only with questions of the jurisdiction of the court as a federal court. Usually, these are questions whether the case is founded on federal law, whether the requisite diversity of citizenship exists, or whether any applicable jurisdictional amount requirement has been satisfied.

Other types of questions, however, are in some sense jurisdictional, for example, questions of the power of the federal tribunal to decide a particular

did not press the issue on the defendant's appeal.)

5. But see Ferguson v. Neighborhood Housing Services, Inc., 780 F.2d 549, 551 (6th Cir.1986). In this case, the defendant sought on the eve of trial to amend its answer to withdraw its admission that it was an employer subject to the Fair Labor Standards Act. A divided court of appeals upheld the district court's refusal to permit the amendment, holding that although parties could not confer jurisdiction by consent, a party could be held bound to an admission of a "jurisdictional fact."

Is the suggested distinction valid? Is the fact at issue in the Ferguson case "jurisdictional" in the same sense as the question of citizenship in a diversity case?

6. The materials in this section do not deal with the problem of challenging a district court's assumption of jurisdiction, or its refusal to assume jurisdiction, either by interlocutory appeal or by seeking prohibition or mandamus from a higher court. As to the problem of appellate review, see in addition to ex parte Peru, p. 336, *supra,* the materials in Chap. XV, Sec. 1, *infra.* On challenges to subject-matter jurisdiction after final judgment, see Chap. XII, p. 1471, *supra.*

kind of case.[1] Are these questions the court should raise on its own motion, treating the objection as beyond the power of the parties to waive? The trial court only? Or the appellate court also? To which of them, if any, is Rule 12(h) applicable? Which of them, if any, is within the principle relied on by the revisers that "any court will dismiss a case not within its jurisdiction when its attention is called to the fact"?

Consider the following objections:

(1) *Lack of personal jurisdiction.* Look again at Rules 12(b) and 12(h). See also Insurance Corp. of Ireland Ltd. v. Compagnie des Bauxites de Guinee, 456 U.S. 694 (1982).

(2) *Improper venue.* In Neirbo Co. v. Bethlehem Shipbuilding Corp., 308 U.S. 165, 167–68 (1939), Justice Frankfurter said:

"The jurisdiction of the federal courts—their power to adjudicate—is a grant of authority to them by Congress and thus beyond the scope of litigants to confer. But the locality of a law suit—the place where judicial authority may be exercised—though defined by legislation relates to the convenience of litigants and as such is subject to their disposition. * * * Section 51 [the then venue statute] 'merely accords to the defendant a personal privilege respecting the venue, or place of suit, which he may assert, or may waive, at his election.' "

(3) *Lack of equity jurisdiction.* Many cases say in substance what Justice Stone said in Di Giovanni v. Camden Fire Ins. Ass'n, 296 U.S. 64, 69 (1935):

"Whether a suitor is entitled to equitable relief in the federal courts, other jurisdictional requirements being satisfied, is strictly not a question of jurisdiction in the sense of the power of a federal court to act. It is a question only of the merits; whether the case is one for the peculiar type of relief which only a federal court of equity is competent to give."

(4) *Abstention.* See Chap. X, p. 1275, *supra.*

(5) *Sovereign Immunity.* See Chap. IX, p. 1098, *supra.*

(6) *Failure to Satisfy Statutory Conditions on Availability of Habeas Corpus.* In Sumner v. Mata, 449 U.S. 539, 547–48 n. 2 (1981), the Court said: "Whether or not the petitioner specifically directed the Court of Appeals' attention to [28 U.S.C.] § 2254(d)[2] makes no difference as to the outcome of this case. * * * [The provisions of the habeas corpus statute are jurisdictional and as stated in Louisville & N. Ry. v. Mottley, 211 U.S. 149, 152 (1908)] 'it is the duty of this Court to see to it that the jurisdiction of the [District Court], which is defined and limited by the statute, is not exceeded.' "

But in Granberry v. Greer, 481 U.S. 129 (1987), the Court held that the statutory requirement of exhaustion of state remedies did not go to the jurisdiction of a federal court to entertain a habeas petition. At the same time,

---

1. A related question is the extent to which state law may permit waiver of a challenge to state court authority based on federal grounds. See, *e.g.,* International Longshoremen's Ass'n v. Davis, 476 U.S. 380, 389 (1986), holding that the defense that federal labor law preempts a state law claim for unlawful discharge involves a "nonwaivable foreclosure of the state court's very jurisdiction to adjudicate." Thus, the appellant's failure to comply with state court rules for the raising of affirmative defenses did not constitute an adequate state ground barring Supreme Court review.

2. This provision specifies what an applicant for habeas corpus must show in order to overcome the presumed correctness of a state court determination of a factual issue.

it held that when the state failed to raise an exhaustion claim, the federal court was not obligated to entertain the petition but rather had discretion to determine whether exhaustion should be required. See also Collins v. Youngblood, 497 U.S. 37, 41 (1990)(holding that the rule of Teague v. Lane, p. 1392, *supra* (restricting the scope of habeas corpus review), "is not 'jurisdictional' in the sense that this Court * * * *must* raise and decide the issue *sua sponte*").

(7) *Justiciability.*   Claims that a case is moot, or unripe, or that a plaintiff lacks standing, are considered nonwaivable.   See generally the materials in Chap. II, *supra.*

(8) *Independent and Adequate State Ground.*   In Sochor v. Florida, 504 U.S. 527, 534 n. ** (1992), the Court stated that the existence of an adequate and independent state procedural ground (here a litigant's failure properly to raise a federal issue in state court) goes to the Supreme Court's jurisdiction and bars review whether or not the defect was raised by the opposing party.

Are there any threads running through these diverse areas and holdings that make possible the formulation of general criteria with respect to waiver?

SECTION 2.   PROCESS AND VENUE IN ORIGINAL ACTIONS

Robertson v. Railroad Labor Board

268 U.S. 619, 45 S.Ct. 621, 69 L.Ed. 1119 (1925).
Appeal from the District Court of the United States for the Northern District of Illinois.

■ Mr. Justice Brandeis delivered the opinion of the Court.

[Robertson appealed from a decree of the district court overruling his motion to quash service of original process upon him in a suit brought by the Board to compel him to appear before it as a witness.   The ground of the motion was that the district court for the Northern District of Illinois lacked personal jurisdiction over him, since process had been served upon him in the Northern District of Ohio where he resided.

[Robertson had previously failed to respond to a subpoena, served upon him in Ohio, commanding him to appear and testify on a day named at the Board's offices in Chicago.   The present action was brought pursuant to § 310(b) of the Transportation Act of February 28, 1920, 41 Stat. 456, 472, which provided: "In case of failure to comply with any subpoena [to testify] * * *, the Board may invoke the aid of any United States district court.   Such court may thereupon order the witness to comply with the requirements of such subpoena * * *."]

* * * Whether the court acquired jurisdiction over Robertson is the only question requiring decision.

Robertson contends that by the term "any United States District Court" Congress meant any such court "of competent jurisdiction"; and that, under the applicable law, no District Court is of competent jurisdiction to compel a defendant to obey its decree except that of the district of which he is an inhabitant or of one in which he is found.   The Board contends that Congress intended by the phrase to confer not only liberty to invoke the aid of the court for any district, but power to compel the person named as defendant to litigate in the district selected by the Board, although he is not a citizen or inhabitant of it and is not found therein. The question presented is one of statutory construction. Congress clearly has the power to authorize a suit under a federal law to be brought in any inferior federal court. Congress has power, likewise, to provide that the process of every District Court shall run into every part of the United States. Toland v. Sprague, 12 Pet. 300; United States v. Union Pacific R.R. Co., 98 U.S. 569, 604. But it has not done so either by any general law or in terms by § 310 of Transportation Act 1920. The precise question is whether it has impliedly done so by that provision.

In a civil suit in personam, jurisdiction over the defendant, as distinguished from venue, implies, among other things, either voluntary appearance by him or service of process upon him at a place where the officer serving it has authority to execute a writ of summons. Under the general provisions of law, a United States District Court cannot issue process beyond the limits of the district. Harkness v. Hyde, 98 U.S. 476. And a defendant in a civil suit can be subjected to its jurisdiction in personam only by service within the district. Toland v. Sprague, 12 Pet. 300, 330. Such was the general rule established by Judiciary Act Sept. 24, 1789, c. 20, § 11, in accordance with the practice at the common law. And such has been the general rule ever since. No distinction has been drawn between the case where the plaintiff is the Government and where he is a private citizen.

[Former] Section 51 of the Judicial Code is a general provision regulating venue. The part pertinent here is that, with certain inapplicable exceptions, "no civil suit shall be brought in any District Court against any person by any original process or proceeding in any other district than that whereof he is an inhabitant."[2] It is obvious that jurisdiction, in the sense of personal service within a district where suit has been brought, does not dispense with the necessity of proper venue. It is equally obvious that proper venue does not eliminate the requisite of personal jurisdiction over the defendant. The general provision as to venue contained in Judicial Code, § 51, has been departed from in various specific provisions which allow the plaintiff, in actions not local in their nature, some liberty in the selection of venue. Unrestricted choice was conferred upon the Labor Board by the section of Transportation Act 1920, here involved (§ 310). So far as venue is concerned, there is no ambiguity in the words "any United States District Court."

Congress has also made a few clearly expressed and carefully guarded exceptions to the general rule of jurisdiction in personam stated above. * * * [For example,] [t]he Sherman Act provides that when "it shall appear to the court" in which a proceeding to restrain violations of the act is pending "that the ends of justice require that other parties should be brought before the court," it may cause them to be summoned although they reside in some other district. * * * But no act has come to our attention in which such power has been conferred in a proceeding in a Circuit or District Court where a private citizen is the sole defendant and where the plaintiff is at liberty to commence the suit in the district of which the defendant is an inhabitant or in which he can be found.

---

2. * * * The rule applies even where it may result in barring the jurisdiction of every federal court because all the defendants are   indispensable parties. Shields v. Barrow, 17 How. 130, 140, 142 * * *.

* * * Congress * * * granted to the [Railroad] Labor Board in explicit language the broad power of compelling a person to come from any place in the United States to any designated place of hearing to furnish evidence. The refusal of such person, who might be in any district in the United States, to comply with such a subpoena was obviously a second contingency to be provided for. Unrestricted liberty of venue in invoking the aid of a District Court, referred to before, was clearly essential to the complete exercise of the Board's powers and the effective performance of its functions. Moreover, this unrestricted choice cannot subject to undue hardship any defendant actually found within the district in which the suit is brought. But no reason is suggested why Congress should have wished to compel every person summoned either to obey the Board's administrative order without question, or to litigate his right to refuse to do so in such district, however remote from his home or temporary residence, as the Board might select. The Interstate Commerce Commission which, throughout 38 years, has dealt in many different ways with most of the railroads of the United States, has never exercised, nor asserted, or sought to secure for itself, such broad powers.

We are of opinion that by the phrase "any District Court of the United States" Congress meant any such court "of competent jurisdiction." The phrase "any court" is frequently used in the federal statutes and has been interpreted under similar circumstances as meaning "any court of competent jurisdiction." By the general rule the jurisdiction of a District Court in personam has been limited to the district of which the defendant is an inhabitant or in which he can be found. It would be an extraordinary thing if, while guarding so carefully all departure from the general rule, Congress had conferred the exceptional power here invoked upon a board whose functions are purely advisory, and which enters the District Court, not to enforce a substantive right, but in an auxiliary proceeding to secure evidence from one who may be a stranger to the matter with which the Board is dealing. We think it has made no such extension by section 310 of Transportation Act 1920. It is not lightly to be assumed that Congress intended to depart from a long-established policy.

Reversed.

NOTE ON THE DEVELOPMENT OF THE RULES GOVERNING PROCESS AND VENUE IN THE DISTRICT COURTS

(1) *Federal Process and the Fifth Amendment.* Are there any constitutional limitations on the reach of process issuing from the district courts? Language in a number of Supreme Court opinions, including Robertson, indicates that there are not, at least within national boundaries. Could Congress then authorize any action within federal jurisdiction to be brought in any federal court, with nationwide process issuing from that court, regardless of the presence or absence of connections between the district or state in which the court sits and the claim asserted? Recall that territorial limitations on process rooted in notions of sovereignty, see Pennoyer v. Neff, 95 U.S. 714 (1877), have been supplemented, and to some extent superseded, by limitations based on principles of fairness and convenience, see International Shoe Co. v. Washing-

ton, 326 U.S. 310 (1945).[1] Are not such principles to be found in the Due Process Clause of the Fifth Amendment as well as the Due Process Clause of the Fourteenth? Do they extend beyond questions of the adequacy of notice to the appropriateness of the particular forum? If so, can such questions in any event be resolved by transfer of the case to an appropriate forum (pp. 1602–15, *infra*) rather than dismissal?[2]

Isn't it clear that whatever the constitutional limitations on the reach of federal process, there is little if any significance to a state or district line, at least in a civil case, since district boundaries are matters of congressional choice? (But note that with the sole exception of the short-lived Midnight Judges Act of 1801, p. 879, *supra,* Congress has never chosen to create districts crossing state lines.) Justice Black argued that in diversity cases state lines may well be constitutionally controlling: "Whatever power Congress might have in these other areas to extend a District Court's power to serve process across state lines, such power does not, I think, provide sound argument to justify reliance upon diversity jurisdiction to destroy a man's constitutional right to have his civil lawsuit tried in his own State." National Equip. Rental, Ltd. v. Szukhent, 375 U.S. 311, 318, 331 (1964) (dissenting opinion). What effect would such a conclusion have on the provision for nationwide service in interpleader cases, 28 U.S.C. § 2361? How does the constitutional right asserted by Justice Black square with his own support of state long-arm process in such cases as International Shoe, and McGee v. International Life Ins. Co., 355 U.S. 220 (1957)?

Constitutional questions aside, what considerations should guide Congress in framing policy? What is the appropriate function of a restriction on service of process as distinguished from a venue requirement? Is there any reason why the two concepts should be kept separate?

(2) *Developments Under Rule 4 of the Federal Civil Rules.* Fed.R.Civ.P. 4, as originally promulgated in 1938, relaxed the rule for service of process in actions in the district courts by providing that process "may be served anywhere within the territorial limits of the state in which the district court is held."

In Mississippi Publishing Corp. v. Murphree, 326 U.S. 438 (1946), this rule was attacked as in violation of the provision of the Enabling Act that the rules "shall neither abridge, enlarge, nor modify the substantive rights of any

---

1. In Omni Capital Int'l v. Rudolf Wolff & Co., Ltd., 484 U.S. 97, 108 (1987), the Court relied upon the Robertson case for the rule that "[a]t common law a court lacked authority to issue process outside its district". It then noted that the principles of territoriality underlying that rule had been undercut by International Shoe, but "express[ed] no view as to the continuing validity of Robertson's rationales" (484 U.S. at 109 n. 10).

2. See the dissenting opinion in Stafford v. Briggs, 444 U.S. 527, 554 (1980), a case discussed more fully in Paragraph (7), *infra.* The dissent rejected the argument that nationwide service in a federal court suit against a federal official might violate the Fifth Amendment, since "due process re-

quires only certain minimum contacts between the defendant and the sovereign that has created the court." In the Omni case, note 1, *supra,* the Court expressly declined to consider the constitutional issues raised by this theory.

Commentators have expressed a variety of views on these questions. See, *e.g.,* Abrams, *Power, Convenience, and the Elimination of Personal Jurisdiction in the Federal Courts,* 58 Ind.L.J. 1 (1982); Fullerton, *Constitutional Limits on Nationwide Personal Jurisdiction in the Federal Courts,* 79 Nw. U.L.Rev. 1 (1984); Seidelson, *The Jurisdictional Reach of a Federal Court Hearing a Federal Cause of Action: A Path Through the Maze,* 23 Duquesne L.Rev. 323 (1984).

litigant", and as inconsistent with the provision of Rule 82 that the rules "shall not be construed to extend or limit the jurisdiction of the district courts of the United States or the venue of actions therein". Rejecting the attack, the Court explained that Rule 82 must be treated as "referring to venue and jurisdiction of the subject matter * * *, rather than the means of bringing the defendant before the court already having venue and jurisdiction of the subject matter". Concerning the charge of violation of the Enabling Act, it said that the expansion of the reach of process "relates merely to 'the manner and the means by which a right to recover * * * is enforced.' Guaranty Trust Co. v. York, 326 U.S. 99, 109. In this sense the rule is a rule of procedure and not of substantive right, and is not subject to the prohibition of the Enabling Act" (p. 446).[3]

Substantial amendments of Rule 4 became effective in 1963, 1983, and (after considerable travail) in 1993. The 1963 amendments included addition of a special subsection relating to service in a foreign country; explicit permission for federal courts to make use of state provisions for extraterritorial service and for attachment and garnishment actions against nonresidents; and creation of a "100–mile bulge" around the federal courthouse for service of persons brought in as parties under Rule 14, or as additional parties under Rule 19. The 1983 amendments contained, *inter alia,* authorization for service in most cases by mail or by any authorized person (not less than 18 years of age) who was not a party. The 1993 amendments (by far the most elaborate) included a new Rule 4(k), which, in some particulars, appears to differ little in substance from the provisions it replaces. Rule 4(k)(1) provides that service of process is effective to establish personal jurisdiction over a defendant (a) "who could be subjected to the jurisdiction of a court of general jurisdiction in the state in which the district court is located," (b) who is joined under Rule 14 or 19 and served within the "100–mile bulge" established by the 1963 amendments, (c) who is subject to federal interpleader jurisdiction, or (d) when jurisdiction over the defendant is otherwise authorized by a federal statute. The last provision is new, but merely recognizes the effect that other federal statutes would have in any event.

Rule 4(k)(2) fills a gap under the prior rule. In cases arising under federal law, the provision authorizes service of process on any defendant not subject to the long-arm jurisdiction of any state, so long as the exercise of jurisdiction would not violate the Fifth Amendment's Due Process Clause.[4]

For further discussion of the significance of Rule 4 in determining questions of personal jurisdiction, see pp. 1598–99, *infra.*

(3) *"Supplemental" Personal Jurisdiction.* May a defendant summoned under a special provision for nationwide service of process be required to answer additional claims filed by the same party, or by other parties, if they would otherwise be proper under the rules? Only if they are "supplemental" within the meaning of the new statutory provision (28 U.S.C. § 1367) providing for supplemental jurisdiction over the subject matter of certain claims (see p. 972,

---

3. For criticism of the Murphree rationale, and an argument that Rule 4 raises serious questions under the Enabling Act, see Whitten, *Separation of Powers Restrictions on Rulemaking: A Case Study of Federal Rule 4,* 40 Me.L.Rev. 41 (1988).

4. Several special provisions for service beyond the borders of a state have been mentioned in this Note; others (some of which are cited in the Robertson case) are still in existence. But the norm, even in federal question cases, remains that imposed by the provisions of Rule 4.

supra)?[5] For discussion and a survey of the cases prior to adoption of the new statutory provision, see Ferguson, *Pendent Personal Jurisdiction in the Federal Courts*, 11 Vill.L.Rev. 56 (1965); 4 Wright & Miller, Federal Practice and Procedure § 1075, at 481–82 (1987); Wright, Federal Courts §§ 9, 19 (and especially p. 121)(5th ed. 1994).

Should the Klaxon rule (Klaxon Co. v. Stentor Elec. Mfg. Co., p. 695, *supra*) apply whenever the supplemental claim in such a case is governed by state law? If your answer is yes, would you consider a modification of the rule looking to the state where the party is *served* rather than the state in which the district court sits?

(4) *Venue: Statutory Development.* Venue and personal jurisdiction were scarcely distinguishable concepts in federal practice prior to the Judiciary Act of March 3, 1887, 24 Stat. 552, as corrected by the Act of August 13, 1888, 25 Stat. 433. The earlier venue provision was as follows: "And no civil suit shall be brought before either of said courts [circuit or district] against any person by any original process or proceeding in any other district than that whereof he is an inhabitant, or in which he shall be found * * *." Act of March 3, 1875, 18 Stat. 470, based on § 11 of the Judiciary Act of 1789. By virtue of the latter clause the acquisition of personal jurisdiction automatically satisfied the requirement of venue.

Until 1963, the general venue statute (28 U.S.C. § 1391), as it applied to natural persons, did not substantially depart from the provision introduced in 1887. In 1963, the restrictions (which had been tied to party residence) were eased by a provision allowing venue, in certain motor vehicle tort cases, in the district where "the act or omission complained of occurred". 77 Stat. 473. In 1966, this provision was repealed, and venue was made proper generally in the district "in which the claim arose".

The venue provisions were further revised in 1988, 1990, and 1992. In 1988, Congress repealed § 1393 (which dealt with problems in districts containing several divisions). In 1990, in response to recommendations of the Federal Courts Study Committee, Congress significantly modified § 1391. The 1992 amendment corrected what was apparently a drafting error made in 1990. See Oakley, p. 1565, note 1, *supra*, at 717.

The revised section (i) eliminates the plaintiff's residence as, *ipso facto*, an acceptable venue in diversity cases; (ii) authorizes venue in any district where any defendant resides, if all defendants reside in the same state; (iii) authorizes venue in any district in which "a substantial part of the events or omissions giving rise to the claim occurred, or a substantial part of the property that is the subject of the action is situated"; and (iv) authorizes venue (A) in cases where jurisdiction is based only on diversity, in any district "in which the defendants are subject to personal jurisdiction at the time the action is commenced, if there is no district in which the action may otherwise be brought", and (B) in cases where jurisdiction is not based solely on diversity, in any district "in which any defendant may be found, if there is no district in which the action may otherwise be brought."

Is there a significant difference between the two formulations in item (iv)? Does the formulation applicable in diversity cases apply only when there is more than one defendant? In any event, both versions of item (iv) adopt, as

---

5. Similar questions may be raised with respect to the possibility of "supplemental" venue over certain claims. See Paragraph (10), *infra*.

fallback provisions when venue does not otherwise lie, the position that there is venue wherever there is personal jurisdiction. Should that approach be followed more generally, eliminating venue as a separate defense? Might such an approach be warranted by the availability of transfer under § 1404, as well as the ability of a plaintiff to bring an action in a *state* court having personal jurisdiction over the defendant—leaving the defendant the option in most cases within federal jurisdiction to remove and seek transfer?

(5) *The Meaning of "Reside" in the Venue Statute.* The concept of state citizenship, for purposes of diversity jurisdiction, is considered to be substantially the same as the concept of domicile in the conflict of laws; thus a natural person can be a citizen, for diversity purposes, of only one state. Should the reference to residence in the venue statute be similarly restricted? One treatise, relying in part on Ex parte Shaw, 145 U.S. 444 (1892), argues that it should, and most courts agree. See 15 Wright, Miller & Cooper, Federal Practice and Procedure § 3805, at 33–36 (1986). But see, *e.g.,* Townsend v. Bucyrus–Erie Co., 144 F.2d 106 (10th Cir.1944)(place of abode where defendant intended to remain for an indefinite period was sufficient basis for venue, though defendant was domiciled in another state); Kahane v. Carlson, 527 F.2d 492, 494 (2d Cir.1975)(though domicile is usually the best measure of residence, special considerations of fairness and convenience warrant the conclusion that a party who may be domiciled abroad is a resident of the Eastern District of New York). *Cf.* 28 U.S.C. § 1391(c)(venue in actions involving corporations), discussed at pp. 1600–01, *infra.*

(6) *Venue in Suits Against Aliens.* Section 1391(d), providing that an alien may be sued in any district, appeared for the first time in the Judicial Code of 1948.[6] As early as 1893, however, the Court held the general venue statute inapplicable in a suit against an alien defendant; thus such a defendant could be sued in any district in which valid service could be made. See generally Brunette Machine Works, Ltd. v. Kockum Industries, Inc., 406 U.S. 706, 714 (1972).[7]

(7) *Venue in Suits Against Federal Officers and Agencies.* The basic statutory provision governing venue and service of process for suits against federal officials and agencies is § 1391(e).[8] This provision gives the plaintiff a number

---

6. As part of the Foreign Sovereign Immunities Act of 1976, see p. 903, *supra,* Congress enacted a new statutory provision, 28 U.S.C. § 1391(f), governing venue in civil actions against a foreign state.

7. Does the 1988 amendment to § 1332, providing that a permanent resident alien domiciled in a state is a citizen of that state (see p. 1526, *supra*), have any impact on available venue in a suit involving such an alien? Apparently not. See 15 Wright, Miller & Cooper, Federal Practice and Procedure § 3810 (1995 Supp. at 27).

8. In federal criminal prosecutions, the Sixth Amendment gives the accused a right to trial by a jury "of the State and District wherein the crime shall have been committed," and Fed.R.Cr.P. 18 states that, except as otherwise provided by law, the prosecution

shall be had in "a district in which the offense was committed." (Rule 18 thus appears to recognize the fact that many federal crimes have no single locus of commission but rather are continuous in time and space.) In addition, 18 U.S.C. § 3238 deals with the trial of offenses "begun or committed on the high seas, or elsewhere out of the jurisdiction of any particular State or district," and 49 U.S.C. § 1473 contains similar provisions for aircraft cases.

In the absence of a special venue statute (*e.g.,* 28 U.S.C. § 1395, covering actions for fines, penalties, seizures, and forfeitures), civil actions brought by the United States are subject to the general venue provisions of § 1391(b). Civil actions brought against the United States in its own name are, for the most part, governed by 28 U.S.C. § 1402.

of choices, including the district of plaintiff's residence. Expressly preserved are the specific venue provisions of various statutes authorizing actions against federal officers or agencies to review particular administrative acts.

Prior to the enactment of § 1391(e), a litigant suing a subordinate government official frequently found the action dismissed on the ground that the superior officer was an indispensable party. Thus litigants often found it difficult or impossible to bring suit outside the District of Columbia. The Committee Report recommending the enactment of § 1391(e) concluded that this state of affairs was "contrary to the sound and equitable administration of justice", and that requiring the government to defend certain suits outside Washington would aid private citizens without imposing an undue burden on the government itself. See H.R.Rep. No. 536, 87th Cong., 1st Sess. 3–4 (1961).[9]

In Stafford v. Briggs, 444 U.S. 527 (1980), the Supreme Court came to the surprising conclusion that § 1391(e) does not apply to actions for money damages brought against federal officials in their individual capacities, even though the activity complained of was "under color of legal authority" within the meaning of the statute.[10] The Court read the legislative history of the Act to indicate that "Congress intended nothing more than to provide nationwide venue for the convenience of individual plaintiffs in actions which are nominally against an individual officer but are in reality against the Government" (p. 542). Justice Stewart, joined by Justice Brennan, dissented, emphasizing the "plain meaning" of the statutory language and the fact that the Department of Justice "has long assumed a special responsibility for representing federal officers sued for money damages for actions taken under color of legal authority" (p. 552).

Although § 1391(e) is not entirely clear on the point, courts and commentators have interpreted the section to authorize nationwide service by certified mail to the officer or agency whenever the provision's venue requirements are satisfied. This interpretation appears to have been endorsed in Stafford v. Briggs, when the Court said that § 1391(e) rendered defendants amenable to suit "in any one of the 95 federal district courts covering the 50 states and other areas within federal jurisdiction" (444 U.S. at 544).

(8) *Problems Raised by the Phrase "In Which the Claim Arose"; Statutory Revision in 1990.* The phrase "in which the claim arose" in the 1966 amendment to § 1391 was considered by the Supreme Court in Leroy v. Great Western United Corp., 443 U.S. 173 (1979)(holding that a Texas federal court lacked venue in a federal question suit involving an effort by the plaintiff, a corporation headquartered in Texas, to take over an out-of-state corporation). In the course of its decision, the Court said that venue provisions were generally designed to protect defendants and, whatever gaps the "claim arose" language was designed to fill, it was not intended to give plaintiffs an "unfettered choice among a host of different districts" (p. 185). The Court declined to decide whether a claim could ever arise in more than one district within the meaning of the law: "In our view * * * the broadest interpretation of the language of § 1391(b) that is even arguably acceptable is that in the unusual

---

See 15 Wright, Miller & Cooper, Federal Practice and Procedure § 3814 (1986).

9. A district court must still determine whether a superior officer not named as a defendant must be joined as a party. A finding of "indispensability" can usually be sur-

mounted, however, by refiling or amending to add the essential party.

10. In an earlier decision, Schlanger v. Seamans, 401 U.S. 487 (1971), the Court had held § 1391(e) inapplicable to habeas corpus proceedings.

case in which it is not clear that the claim arose in only one specific district, a plaintiff may choose between those two (or conceivably even more) districts that with approximately equal plausibility—in terms of the availability of witnesses, the accessibility of relevant evidence, and the convenience of the defendant (but *not* of the plaintiff)—may be assigned as the locus of the claim" (*id.*).

In response to the restrictive interpretation of the statute in this and other decisions, as well as a recommendation of the American Law Institute as part of its study of federal jurisdiction, Congress in 1990 abandoned the language "in which the claim arose" and substituted the less confining term "in which a substantial part of the events or omissions giving rise to the claim occurred, or a substantial part of property that is the subject of the action is situated".[11]

Under the new language, would venue lie in a diversity class action against multiple defendants for harm caused by a product if some but not all of the defendants were engaged in distribution of (or other conduct relating to) the product in the district of suit?

(9) *Waivability of the Venue Defense.* The established doctrine that venue is merely a personal privilege that may be waived is codified in Fed.R.Civ.P. 12(b), (g), and (h) and in 28 U.S.C. § 1406(b).

Waiver may take place in other ways than by failure to "interpose timely and sufficient objection" in the particular action. See, *e.g.,* General Elec. Co. v. Marvel Rare Metals Co., 287 U.S. 430 (1932), holding that the plaintiff in a federal court waived any objection on the score of venue to any counterclaim permitted under the federal rules. See also Neirbo Co. v. Bethlehem Shipbuilding Corp., 308 U.S. 165 (1939), and related problems discussed in the *Note on Bringing Corporations and Unincorporated Organizations Into Court,* p. 1598, *infra.*

Prior to 1948, a federal district court had no choice but to dismiss an action as to any defendant who duly asserted a proper objection to the venue. If there was only one defendant, or if the objecting defendant was an indispensable party, the entire action had to be dismissed.

Section 1406(a) of Title 28 introduced a striking innovation, transforming the whole theory of federal venue. In its original form this section made it mandatory for a district judge who found the venue improper, to "transfer such case to any district or division in which it could have been brought". The 1949 amendments, however, modified the direction to provide that the judge "shall dismiss, or if it be in the interest of justice, transfer such case * * *." See *Note on Forum Non Conveniens and Change of Venue,* p. 1607, *infra.*

(10) *"Supplemental Venue".* Recall the materials on supplemental jurisdiction, pp. 962–73, 1558–67, *supra.* Should any claim maintainable on a supplemental jurisdiction theory—for example, a cross-claim, counterclaim against an additional party, or third-party claim—be freed from the venue requirements on a "supplemental venue" theory? Generally, the courts answered in the affirmative during the period when notions of "pendent" and "ancillary" jurisdiction were essentially judicially developed. See Wright, Federal Courts § 9, at 39 (5th ed. 1994)(also noting that "[t]he new statute does nothing to change this, and the result seems right"). Should it matter whether the party objecting to

---

11. For an illustration of the more flexible approach that this language has encouraged, see Bates v. C & S Adjusters, Inc., 980 F.2d 865 (2d Cir.1992).

the venue on one claim is already a party to the proceeding with respect to another claim?

(11) *Special Venue Provisions.* There are a large number of special venue provisions in the United States Code. Some, like 28 U.S.C. §§ 1397 (interpleader), 1400 (patents and copyrights), 1401 (stockholders derivative actions), and 1402 (United States as defendant), are in the Judicial Code, but an extraordinary number are not. (The ALI Study, pp. 498–501, listed over 300 special venue provisions not in Title 28.) Such provisions are often combined with special provisions for service of process, as in the case of interpleader. But the reasons for many of these special venue provisions are hard to come by, and although a number may have been justified by the rigidity of the general venue law before 1966, their usefulness may now be questioned.[12]

(12) *Local Actions.* 28 U.S.C. § 1392(b) provides that any civil action "of a local nature" involving property located in different districts in the same state may be brought in any of such districts. But the phrase "of a local nature" is nowhere defined, nor does the Code specify what happens when such an action involves property in only one district.

Under the common-law doctrine of local actions, certain proceedings involving real property may be tried only in the jurisdiction where the land is located.[13] As developed in the federal courts and in many states, the doctrine extends beyond actions in rem to such in personam actions as trespass to land and nuisance. See, *e.g.,* Livingston v. Jefferson, 15 Fed.Cas. 660 (No. 8411)(C.C.D.Va.1811). The unanswered questions raised by the doctrine in the federal courts include: Is the doctrine one of subject matter jurisdiction (and thus not waivable), as Ellenwood v. Marietta Chair Co., 158 U.S. 105 (1895), would indicate, or is it one of venue, as suggested by the reference in § 1392 and by cases allowing transfer under 28 U.S.C. § 1406(a), *e.g.,* Wheatley v. Phillips, 228 F.Supp. 439, 442 (W.D.N.C.1964)? Must an action that is local also satisfy the general statutory venue requirements, as indicated by Ladew v. Tennessee Copper Co., 218 U.S. 357 (1910), or does it suffice that the action is brought where the land is located, as indicated by Casey v. Adams, 102 U.S. 66 (1880)? What is the effect in a federal diversity case of a rule in the forum state that differs from the rule developed in the federal courts? See Still v. Rossville Crushed Stone Co., 370 F.2d 324 (6th Cir.1966)(state rule is determinative); Central Transport, Inc. v. Theurer, Inc., 430 F.Supp. 1076 (E.D.Mich.1977)(venue is determined by federal law, but state substantive law must be analyzed to determine whether the action is local or transitory).[14] The question is important because some states have drastically curtailed or elimi-

---

12. There is a judge-made exception to the general venue provisions in the area of admiralty and maritime claims, where venue lies in an in personam action wherever the defendant can be served or its goods or credits can be attached. See Atkins v. Fibre Disintegrating Co., 85 U.S. (18 Wall.) 272 (1873); In re Louisville Underwriters, 134 U.S. 488 (1890). This exception is now reflected in Fed.R.Civ.P. 82, providing that admiralty and maritime claims shall not be regarded as civil actions for purposes of 28 U.S.C. §§ 1391 and other provisions.

13. One decision indicated that if an action is local, the district where the property is located becomes simply another available venue. Coffey v. Managed Properties, Inc., 85 F.2d 88 (2d Cir.1936). But other cases support the proposition in text.

14. One commentary criticizes the tendency of lower federal courts to regard state law as controlling, and attributes it to an "erroneous dictum" in Huntington v. Attrill, 146 U.S. 657, 669–70 (1892), "misreading [Chief Justice] Marshall [in Livingston v. Jefferson]." 15 Wright, Miller & Cooper, Federal Practice and Procedure § 3822, at 208 (1986).

nated the operation of the doctrine, while others may define a local action more expansively than would a federal court.

When a case falls within 28 U.S.C. § 1655, several of these questions are resolved. That section, which was derived from a provision limited to equity cases, 17 Stat. 196, 198 (1872), authorizes extraterritorial service in actions "to enforce any lien upon or claim to, or to remove any incumbrance or lien or cloud upon the title to, real or personal property within the district"; if the defendant does not appear or plead, the court is empowered to render an adjudication affecting only the property that is the subject of the action. The section has been held to authorize venue in the district where the land is located. See Shuford v. Anderson, 352 F.2d 755 (10th Cir.1965). But it does not apply to all local actions, see Ladew v. Tennessee Copper Co., *supra* (action to enjoin a nuisance), and has been limited to "a lien or title existing anterior to the suit, and not one caused by the institution of the suit itself." Dormitzer v. Illinois & St. Louis Bridge Co., 6 Fed. 217, 218 (C.C.Mass.1881); see Nowell v. Nowell, 417 F.2d 902, 905 (1st Cir.1969).

The recent amendments to § 1391 have afforded considerable relief from some of these problems (at least if the local action doctrine is one of venue and not of jurisdiction), since the district where the land is located in a local action case will almost invariably (perhaps always) be one that satisfies the provisions of the amended general venue statute. The present statute, coupled with the large number of state long-arm statutes applying to one who commits a tort in the state, makes it unlikely that, as in Livingston v. Jefferson, *supra,* the plaintiff will be remediless for lack of a forum.

Does the doctrine of local actions have any proper place in the federal courts? See Note, 70 Harv.L.Rev. 708 (1957).

(13) *State Court Proceedings Begun by Attachment or Garnishment.* Although they have long been held removable if state statutory requirements are satisfied, proceedings commenced by attachment or garnishment could not originate in the federal courts prior to the 1963 amendment of Fed.Rule 4. But the significance of this amendment was in turn reduced by later Supreme Court decisions invalidating state court assertions of "quasi in rem" jurisdiction. Shaffer v. Heitner, 433 U.S. 186 (1977); Rush v. Savchuk, 444 U.S. 320 (1980). In these cases, the Court held that the relevant standards for determining the validity of such jurisdiction under the Due Process Clause of the Fourteenth Amendment were those set forth in International Shoe Co. v. Washington, 326 U.S. 310 (1945).

The applicability of these decisions to federal court actions is not entirely clear, but they would presumably be controlling in diversity cases where the reach of federal court jurisdiction is determined by state law. For consideration of their applicability in a maritime attachment proceeding under the Supplemental Rules for Admiralty and Maritime Claims, see Culp, *Charting a New Course: Proposed Amendments to the Supplemental Rules for Admiralty Arrest and Attachment,* 103 F.R.D. 319, 334–38 (1985), and cases cited therein.

Kingsepp v. Wesleyan University

United States District Court for the Southern District of New York.
763 F.Supp. 22 (1991).

■ DAVID N. EDELSTEIN, DISTRICT JUDGE:

Defendants Wesleyan University ("Wesleyan"), The President and Trustees of Williams College ("Williams"), and the Trustees of Dartmouth College ("Dartmouth") have moved * * * to dismiss this putative class action antitrust case against them on the grounds that this Court lacks personal jurisdiction and that venue is improper, and, in the alternative, pursuant to 28 U.S.C. § 1406 to transfer this action to a district in which it could have been brought. For the following reasons, defendants' motions are denied.

I. BACKGROUND

Plaintiff Roger Kingsepp, a student at Wesleyan, * * * alleges that defendants "have engaged in a conspiracy to fix or artificially inflate the price of tuition and financial aid." As a result of the alleged conspiracy, plaintiff claims that "tuition and financial aid have been fixed, stabilized and inflated in violation of Section One of the Sherman Act" and that the class has therefore been damaged by "having to pay higher tuition than in a free competitive market."

II. DISCUSSION

Wesleyan, Williams, and Dartmouth (the "moving defendants") have moved to dismiss the complaint against them for lack of personal jurisdiction and improper venue, and, in the alternative, to transfer this action to a district in which it could have been brought. The moving defendants contend that they are not subject to jurisdiction under the nationwide service of process provisions of the antitrust laws or under the New York long-arm statute, and that venue is improper under any of the applicable venue statutes. The remaining defendants do not contest jurisdiction and venue. Plaintiff has asserted personal jurisdiction over the moving defendants under section 12 of the Clayton Act, 15 U.S.C. § 22, and New York Civil Practice Law §§ 301, 302(a)(1), and 302(a)(3). Plaintiff also claims that venue is appropriate under section 12 of the Clayton Act and under the general federal venue provision, 28 U.S.C. § 1391(b).

A. Personal Jurisdiction.

* * *

Rule 4(e) of the Federal Rules of Civil Procedure [now Rule 4(k)(1)(D)] authorizes service of process on an out of state party when authorized by a federal statute. Personal jurisdiction in an antitrust action is governed by section 12 of the Clayton Act, 15 U.S.C. § 22, which provides:

"Any suit, action, or proceeding under the antitrust laws against a corporation may be brought not only in the judicial district whereof it is an inhabitant, but also in any district wherein it may be found or transacts business; and all process in such cases may be served in the district of which it is an inhabitant, or wherever it may be found."

Section 12 authorizes out of state service on a corporate defendant in an antitrust action, but does not specifically mention the exercise of personal jurisdiction. However, the statute's authorization of service outside the state has been interpreted as authorizing federal courts to exercise nationwide personal jurisdiction over corporate antitrust defendants.

In cases where Congress authorizes nationwide federal jurisdiction, as in section 12 of the Clayton Act, the district court's jurisdiction is co-extensive with the boundaries of the United States. Thus, a defendant who resides within the territorial boundaries of the United States is subject to personal jurisdiction under nationwide service of process without regard to state jurisdictional statutes. Further, it is not necessary that the resident defendant have the requisite minimum contacts with the state that would exercise jurisdiction. * * *

* * * [Wesleyan and Williams are non-profit corporations that "reside" in the United States. As such, they] are subject to nationwide service of process under Section 12 of the Clayton Act and subject to personal jurisdiction in this action. Dartmouth, however, contends that as a trust organized under a charter issued in the name of King George III of Britain,[1] it should not be deemed a "corporation" for purposes of section 12.

Section 12's nationwide service of process provision applies to corporations, and has been narrowly construed. In McManus v. Tato, 184 F.Supp. 958 (S.D.N.Y.1959), Judge Weinfeld refused to apply section 12's nationwide service of process provision to a voluntary association * * *. * * * A number of other cases have narrowly construed section 12's nationwide service of process provision so as to exclude non-corporate defendants. Given the narrow construction of the term "corporation" in section 12 and the reluctance of courts to extend nationwide service of process under section 12 to non-corporate defendants, it would be inappropriate to extend section 12 to encompass a trust such as Dartmouth. * * *

Accordingly, Dartmouth can not be deemed a "corporation" for purposes of section 12.

Since nationwide service of process under section 12 does not extend to Dartmouth, plaintiff must turn to New York's long arm statute to provide a basis for personal jurisdiction. * * *

A defendant is subject to jurisdiction under CPLR § 301 [the relevant New York statute] if it is "engaged in such a continuous and systematic course of 'doing business' here as to warrant a finding of its 'presence' in this jurisdiction." * * *

Dartmouth is not licensed to do business in New York, it maintains no offices in New York, and it does not list a phone number in New York. Nonetheless, Dartmouth engages in a continuous and systematic course of conduct sufficient to warrant a finding that it is doing business in New York. Dartmouth College actively solicits students in New York by sending representatives to approximately 44 secondary schools in the state a year. In addition to this solicitation, Dartmouth has engaged in substantial commercial activity in the state. Dartmouth has a banking relationship with Chase Manhattan Bank that dates back to at least 1982. Since that time, Dartmouth has maintained at least two accounts in Chase, with a balance in one account as high as $14,487,051.88 in 1987. Further, from 1982 to 1987, Dartmouth has issued bonds in New York through Goldman Sachs on at least four separate

---

1. Under the terms of its charter, the founder of Dartmouth College, Eleazor Wheelock, created a charitable trust of funds owned and procured by himself and devised in trust to named trustees to continue the existence and uses of Dartmouth College. No funds were given to Dartmouth College by the charter; rather, such funds were given to the trustees as the sole legal owners of all the property acquired under the charter. Trustees of Dartmouth College v. Woodward, 17 U.S. (4 Wheat.) 518, 553–54 (1819). Thus, Dartmouth maintains some of the attributes of a corporation, such as continuity of existence and the ability to sue and be sued, but is not incorporated in any state, does not issue stock, does not have a board of directors, and does not have shareholders.

occasions. Dartmouth also owns real property in New York—a future remainder interest in a piece of residential real estate on Long Island worth approximately $65,000. Accordingly, Dartmouth has sufficient contacts with New York to establish that it engaged in a continuous and systematic course of "doing business" sufficient to warrant a finding of its presence in New York for purposes of jurisdiction.

B. Venue

The moving defendants argue that venue is not appropriate under either the special venue provisions of the Clayton Act found in section 12, or the general federal venue provision found in 28 U.S.C. § 1391(b). It is now well settled that the provisions of 28 U.S.C. § 1391(b) "are supplemental to—not superseded by—the special antitrust venue statute." General Electric v. Bucyrus–Erie Co., 550 F.Supp. 1037, 1040 & n. 3, 1042 (S.D.N.Y.1982). Thus, venue in this district may be authorized under either section 12 or under the general federal venue provisions of 28 U.S.C. § 1391(b).

Section 1391(b) provides that a federal question case may be maintained in the forum where all defendants reside. Pursuant to section 1391(c), a corporation is deemed to "reside" in any district "in which it is subject to personal jurisdiction at the time the action was commenced." Wesleyan and Williams are * * * therefore deemed to "reside" in this district pursuant to section 1391(c).

To be sure, although a trust like Dartmouth is not a "corporation" for purposes of section 12 of the Clayton Act, it is a "corporation" for purposes of section 1391(c). That section's reference to "corporations" has been liberally construed to include trust funds and other entities such as voluntary associations and partnerships. See, *e.g.,* Denver & Rio Grande Western R.R. Co. v. Brotherhood of R.R. Trainmen, 387 U.S. 556, 559–62; Penrod Drilling Co. v. Johnson, 414 F.2d 1217, 1220 (5th Cir.1969). Because Dartmouth is a "corporation" for purposes of section 1391(c) and was subject to personal jurisdiction at the time this action was commenced, Dartmouth is deemed to "reside" in this district pursuant to section 1391(c). Accordingly, all of the moving defendants are deemed to reside in this district and venue is therefore appropriate under section 1391(b).

III. CONCLUSION

Defendants' motions * * * to dismiss this action against them for lack of personal jurisdiction and improper venue, and, in the alternative, pursuant to 28 U.S.C. § 1406 to transfer this action to a district in which it might have been brought are denied.

So Ordered.

NOTE ON BRINGING CORPORATIONS AND UNINCORPORATED ORGANIZATIONS INTO COURT

(1) *Rule 4 and Amenability to Territorial Jurisdiction.*

   (a) Fed. Rule 4(h) tells *how* service of process is to be made on a corporation or on a partnership or other unincorporated association subject to suit under a common name, but does not appear to govern the *amenability* of these organizations to process. By contrast (and as more fully discussed at p.

1589, *supra*), Rule 4(k), adopted in 1993, does explicitly address the question of amenability. Notably, Rule 4(k)(2)(adopted after the Kingsepp decision) fills a gap under the former rule. In cases arising under federal law, the provision authorizes service of process on any defendant not subject to the long-arm jurisdiction of any state, so long as the exercise of jurisdiction would not violate the defendant's constitutional rights (presumably those under the Fifth Amendment's Due Process Clause).

(b) Recall the decision in Szantay v. Beech Aircraft Corp., 349 F.2d 60 (4th Cir.1965)(p. 740, *supra*)(holding that, despite the provisions of a South Carolina "door-closing" statute, a non-resident plaintiff could join a non-resident defendant in a federal court diversity action in that state). What if the state's limitation on suit by one out-of-stater against another had been built into its statutory provisions for service of process? Should the result be different? Note that in Szantay, one of the reasons for not dismissing the out-of-state defendant was the desirability of resolving a multi-party controversy in a single lawsuit. Not all such cases are covered by the nationwide service provision of the interpleader statute, 28 U.S.C. § 2361, or by the 100–mile bulge provision of Rule 4.

At least in the absence of a clear directive to the contrary in rule or statute, shouldn't state law, if constitutional, at least establish the floor for service on a defendant? Isn't it often arguable (though perhaps not in Szantay) that in litigation governed by state substantive law, that state's law should also establish a ceiling because the state may desire not to discourage foreign businesses from coming in by subjecting them to the threat of inconvenient litigation?[1]

(c) What standard should be applied in measuring amenability within the 100–mile bulge of Rule 4(k)(1)(B)(discussed at p. 1589, *supra*)? Assuming the question is presented in a case that does not arise under federal law, should the court look either to the law of the state in which suit has been brought or to the law of the bulge state? Doesn't the bulge provision (especially in light of its limited applicability to additional parties joined under Rules 14 or 19) reflect a federal policy in favor of resolving an entire controversy in a multi-party dispute, and if so, shouldn't amenability be pressed to the full extent permitted by the Constitution? See Note, 41 U.Pitt.L.Rev. 801 (1980). But if this approach is taken in a diversity case, should the forum state's choice of law rules be held to govern? *Cf.* Griffin v. McCoach, 313 U.S. 498 (1941), p. 702, *supra*.

(d) Whenever state law is controlling for purposes of amenability, is it appropriate to consider whether it would be constitutional for the state courts to apply that law in the case at hand? Assuming that the constitutional standards applicable to state and federal courts are not the same, is it possible to attach federal consequences to an unconstitutional state law? And if it is—perhaps on a theory of "incorporation" of state rules into federal law—what purpose would be served by doing so?

1. Many federal decisions in this area are collected and discussed in 4 Wright & Miller, Federal Practice and Procedure § 1075 (1987 and 1995 Supp.). Of special interest is Arrowsmith v. United Press Int'l, 320 F.2d 219 (2d Cir.1963), a case decided before the recent amendments to Rule 4 discussed in text. In Arrowsmith, an en banc court, per Judge Friendly, held state law to be controlling in the absence of a specific federal provision to the contrary. Judge Clark filed a vigorous dissent.

(2) *Venue in Actions Against Corporations.*

(a) Solutions to problems both of venue and of personal jurisdiction in actions against corporations were long thwarted by the dogma that a corporation "must dwell in the place of its creation, and cannot migrate to another sovereignty". Bank of Augusta v. Earle, 38 U.S. (13 Pet.) 519, 588 (1839).

As the Bank of Augusta case itself showed, a corporation could migrate as a plaintiff, in the absence of valid state action to exclude it. But not until 1877 did the Court work out a basis for overcoming difficulties of venue and process when a foreign corporation was a defendant. It did this through a theory of consent. At a time when venue depended, alternatively, on the defendant's being an "inhabitant" of or "found" within the district of suit, Ex parte Schollenberger, 96 U.S. 369 (1877), held that the defendant had consented to be so "found" by designating an agent for service of process in actions in courts of the state in which the federal district court was located.

However, after venue in 1887 had been made to depend solely on residence, the Court, harking back to early notions, held that a corporation could be a "resident" only of the state in which it was incorporated and of the district in that state in which its principal offices were located. Shaw v. Quincy Mining Co., 145 U.S. 444 (1892). Most lower federal courts interpreted this holding as an abandonment of the theory of venue by prior consent or waiver.

Nearly fifty years later, in Neirbo Co. v. Bethlehem Shipbuilding Corp., 308 U.S. 165 (1939), the Supreme Court reaffirmed the Schollenberger principle. There New Jersey plaintiffs brought a diversity action in a federal district court in New York against a New York corporation and a Delaware corporation. The Supreme Court held that the Delaware company had waived its venue privilege by a prior general designation of an agent "as the person upon whom a summons may be served within the State of New York".

The Neirbo decision greatly eased the problems of suing foreign corporations in federal courts. But it made federal venue in such actions dependent *pro tanto* upon state law. The state must have power to exact a valid consent. And application of the doctrine, for example, to causes of action arising outside the state, depended presumably upon the state court's construction of the consent.

(b) Section 1391(c) of Title 28, as enacted in 1948, provided, *inter alia,* for venue with respect to a corporation in any district in which the corporation was licensed to do business or was doing business, and appears to have been primarily designed to eliminate the possibility that a corporation failing to comply with state law requirements would be better off than one that had complied.[2]

(c) Important amendments of § 1391(c) in 1988 clarified a number of questions. The revised version (i) eliminates the confusion on the issue in the lower courts by expressly confining the provision's applicability to corporate

---

2. In Olberding v. Illinois Cent. R.R., 346 U.S. 338 (1953), a divided Court upheld a venue challenge by an out-of-state individual defendant who had been involved in an accident in the state but who had no other connections with it and had not designated an agent for service. Section 1391(c) was not applicable, and the fact that the state's long-arm statute reached this defendant was held to be of no help, since "implied consent" was a pure fiction not equivalent to actual consent within the meaning of Neirbo.

Note that the problem in the Olberding case would now be obviated by the provision for venue in the district in which a substantial part of the events in suit occurred.

defendants, (ii) applies to all questions of venue under "this chapter" (28 U.S.C. §§ 1391–1412)(but not to venue provisions in other federal laws), (iii) provides that "a corporation shall be deemed to reside in any judicial district in which it is subject to personal jurisdiction at the time the action is commenced," and (iv) deals with cases in which there is more than one judicial district within a state.

Was the prior version of § 1391(c) more, or less, restrictive than the present one with respect to the available venues in a suit against a corporate defendant? Is the significance of the revision reduced by the subsequent changes in the general provisions of § 1391(a) and (b) (discussed in Paragraphs (4)-(8) of the preceding *Note on the Development of the Rules Governing Process and Venue in the District Courts*)?

(3) *Venue in Actions Against Partnerships and Unincorporated Associations, and the Question of Capacity to Litigate.* As the "common name" provision of Rule 4(h) suggests, the question of litigating capacity becomes important when considering the amenability to suit of a partnership or unincorporated association. Note the provisions of Rule 17(b) on this point, particularly the distinction drawn between cases involving federal claims and all other cases. Is the distinction sound? Does it imply that for purposes of federal law, an unincorporated association may have rights and liabilities distinct from those of its members?[3] If so, is it consistent with the Enabling Act? *Cf.* § 301(b) of the Labor–Management Relations Act of 1947, 29 U.S.C. § 185(b), providing that for certain purposes a labor organization may sue or be sued "as an entity" in the federal courts and that "[a]ny money judgment against a labor organization in a district court of the United States shall be enforceable only against the organization as an entity and against its assets, and shall not be enforceable against any individual member or his assets".

(4) *The Venue Holding in Kingsepp.* In holding that venue was proper not only with respect to the corporate defendants but also with respect to Dartmouth, the court in Kingsepp relied on Denver & R.G.W.R.R. v. Brotherhood of Railroad Trainmen, 387 U.S. 556 (1967), and on the Fifth Circuit's decision in Penrod Drilling Co. v. Johnson, 414 F.2d 1217 (5th Cir.1969). In the Denver decision, rendered at a time when corporate venue was defined in terms of the corporation's doing business (or being licensed to do business) in the district, the Supreme Court noted that Congress in enacting § 1391(c) was addressing a question involving corporations "while maintaining its silence with regard to the unincorporated association" (p. 561). The Court thus decided that it was appropriate to equate a labor union with a corporation for venue purposes; it distinguished its decision in United Steelworkers v. Bouligny, p. 1538, *supra,* on the ground that unlike the rules relating to diversity jurisdiction, "[t]here was no settled construction of the [venue] law" as it applied to such associations in 1948 "and there is none yet". *Id.* Finally, the Court suggested that there could be more judicial innovation in matters of venue than in matters affecting the scope of jurisdiction. In Penrod, the Fifth Circuit followed suit with respect to partnerships.

Was the Kingsepp court on sound ground in relying on these cases? They were, after all, on the books when the venue provision was revised to allow venue against *corporate* defendants wherever personal jurisdiction could be

---

3. The provision of Rule 17(b) relating to federal claims is drawn from United Mine Workers v. Coronado Coal Co., 259 U.S. 344 (1922).

obtained, but Congress did not extend this change to any unincorporated entities. Was the silence of Congress at this point as lacking in significance as the Supreme Court thought it was when the Denver decision was rendered?

Note how a plaintiff who wishes to sue an unincorporated entity in a federal court can be squeezed between the rules governing diversity jurisdiction and those governing venue. The plaintiff may be forced to bring a class action against representative members of an association, in order to satisfy the diversity requirements, but may end up with a more limited choice of venue than if suit could be brought against the association directly.

Van Dusen v. Barrack

376 U.S. 612, 84 S.Ct. 805, 11 L.Ed.2d 945 (1964).
Certiorari to the United States Court of Appeals for the Third Circuit.

MR. JUSTICE GOLDBERG delivered the opinion of the Court.

* * * On October 4, 1960, shortly after departing from a Boston airport, a commercial airliner, scheduled to fly from Boston to Philadelphia, plunged into Boston Harbor. As a result of the crash, over 150 actions for personal injury and wrongful death have been instituted against the airline, various manufacturers, the United States, and, in some cases, the Massachusetts Port Authority. In most of these actions the plaintiffs have alleged that the crash resulted from the defendants' negligence in permitting the aircraft's engines to ingest some birds. More than 100 actions were brought in the United States District Court for the District of Massachusetts, and more than 45 actions in the United States District Court for the Eastern District of Pennsylvania.

The present case concerns 40 of the wrongful death actions brought in the Eastern District of Pennsylvania by personal representatives of victims of the crash. The defendants, petitioners in this Court, moved under [28 U.S.C.] § 1404(a) to transfer these actions to the District of Massachusetts, where it was alleged that most of the witnesses resided and where over 100 other actions are pending. The District Court granted the motion, holding that the transfer was justified regardless of whether the transferred actions would be governed by the laws and choice-of-law rules of Pennsylvania or of Massachusetts. The District Court also specifically held that transfer was not precluded by the fact that the plaintiffs had not qualified under Massachusetts law to sue as representatives of the decedents. The plaintiffs, respondents in this Court, sought a writ of mandamus from the Court of Appeals and successfully contended that the District Court erred and should vacate its order of transfer. The Court of Appeals held that a § 1404(a) transfer could be granted only if at the time the suits were brought, the plaintiffs had qualified to sue in Massachusetts, the State of the transferee District Court. The Court of Appeals relied in part upon its interpretation of Rule 17(b) of the Federal Rules of Civil Procedure.

We granted certiorari to review important questions concerning the construction and operation of § 1404(a). For reasons to be stated below, we hold that the judgment of the Court of Appeals must be reversed, that both the Court of Appeals and the District Court erred in their fundamental assumptions regarding the state law to be applied to an action transferred under

§ 1404(a), and that accordingly the case must be remanded to the District Court.[3]

I. WHERE THE ACTION "MIGHT HAVE BEEN BROUGHT."

Section 1404(a) reflects an increased desire to have federal civil suits tried in the federal system at the place called for in the particular case by considerations of convenience and justice. * * * This transfer power is, however, expressly limited by the final clause of § 1404(a) restricting transfer to those federal districts in which the action "might have been brought." Although in the present case the plaintiffs were qualified to bring suit as personal representatives under Pennsylvania law (the law of the State of the transferor federal court), the Court of Appeals ruled that the defendants' transfer motion must be denied because at the time the suits were brought in Pennsylvania (the transferor forum) the complainants had not obtained the appointments requisite to initiate such actions in Massachusetts (the transferee forum). At the outset, therefore, we must consider whether the incapacity of the plaintiffs at the time they commenced their actions in the transferor forum to sue under the state law of the transferee forum renders the latter forum impermissible under the "might-have-been-brought" limitation.

* * *

A. In Hoffman v. Blaski [363 U.S. 335 (1960),] this Court first considered the nature of the limitation imposed by the words "where it might have been brought." The plaintiff opposed the defendant's motion to transfer on the ground that the proposed transferee forum lacked both "venue over the action and ability to command jurisdiction over the * * *" defendant. 363 U.S., at 337. The question, as stated by the Court, was "whether a District Court, in which a civil action has been properly brought, is empowered by § 1404(a) to transfer the action, on the motion of the defendant, to a district in which the plaintiff did not have a *right* to bring it." *Id.*, 363 U.S. at 336. (Emphasis in original.) The defendant emphasized that "venue, like jurisdiction over the person, may be waived." *Id.*, 363 U.S. at 343. This Court held that, despite the defendant's waivers or consent, a forum which had been improper for both venue and service of process was not a forum where the action "might have been brought."

In the present case the Court of Appeals concluded that transfer could not be granted because here, as in Hoffman v. Blaski, the plaintiffs did not have an "independent" or "unqualified" right to bring the actions in the transferee forum. The propriety of this analogy to Hoffman turns, however, on the validity of the assumption that the "where-it-might-have-been-brought" clause refers not only to federal venue statutes but also to the laws applied in the State of the transferee forum. It must be noted that the instant case, unlike Hoffman, involves a motion to transfer to a district in which both venue and jurisdiction are proper. * * *

---

3. Although it is clear that this Court has jurisdiction to review the judgment of the Court of Appeals, the Government, a defendant in this case, urges that the judgment below be reversed because mandamus was an improper remedy. * * * Since in our opinion the courts below erred in interpreting the legal limitations upon and criteria for a § 1404(a) transfer, we find it unnecessary to consider the mandamus contentions advanced by the Government.

* * * [W]e hold that the words "where it might have been brought" must be construed with reference to the federal laws delimiting the districts in which such an action "may be brought" and not with reference to laws of the transferee State concerning the capacity of fiduciaries to bring suit.

B. The Court of Appeals, in reversing the District Court, relied in part upon Rule 17(b) of the Federal Rules of Civil Procedure. * * * The reliance placed on Rule 17(b) necessarily assumes that its language—which is not free from ambiguity—requires the application of the law of the State of the transferee district court rather than that of the transferor district court. * * *

* * * [I]n our opinion the underlying and fundamental question is whether, in a case such as the present, a change of venue within the federal system is to be accompanied by a change in the applicable state law. * * * In view of the facts of this case and their bearing on this basic question, we must consider first, insofar as is relevant, the relationship between a change of venue under § 1404(a) and the applicable state law.

II. "THE INTEREST OF JUSTICE": EFFECT OF A CHANGE OF VENUE UPON APPLICABLE STATE LAW.

A. The plaintiffs contend that the change of venue ordered by the District Court was necessarily precluded by the likelihood that it would be accompanied by a highly prejudicial change in the applicable state law. The prejudice alleged is not limited to that which might flow from the Massachusetts laws governing capacity to sue. Indeed, the plaintiffs emphasize the likelihood that the defendants' "ultimate reason for seeking transfer is to move to a forum where recoveries for wrongful death are restricted to sharply limited punitive damages rather than compensation for the loss suffered." It is argued that Pennsylvania choice-of-law rules would result in the application of laws substantially different from those that would be applied by courts sitting in Massachusetts. * * *

The possibilities suggested by the plaintiffs' argument illustrate the difficulties that would arise if a change of venue, granted at the motion of a defendant, were to result in a change of law. Although in the present case the contentions concern rules relating to capacity to sue and damages, in other cases the transferee forum might have a shorter statute of limitations or might refuse to adjudicate a claim which would have been actionable in the transferor State. In such cases a defendant's motion to transfer could be tantamount to a motion to dismiss. In light, therefore, of this background and the facts of the present case, we need not and do not consider the merits of the contentions concerning the meaning and proper application of Pennsylvania's laws and choice of law rules. For present purposes it is enough that the potential prejudice to the plaintiffs is so substantial as to require review of the assumption that a change of state law would be a permissible result of transfer under § 1404(a).

* * *

* * * There is nothing * * * in the language or policy of § 1404(a) to justify its use by defendants to defeat the advantages accruing to plaintiffs who have chosen a forum which, although it was inconvenient, was a proper venue. In this regard the transfer provisions of § 1404(a) may be compared with those of § 1406(a). Although both sections were broadly designed to allow transfer instead of dismissal, § 1406(a) provides for transfer from forums in which

venue is wrongly or improperly laid, whereas, in contrast, § 1404(a) operates on the premise that the plaintiff has properly exercised his venue privilege. This distinction underlines the fact that Congress, in passing § 1404(a), was primarily concerned with the problems arising where, despite the propriety of the plaintiff's venue selection, the chosen forum was an inconvenient one.

* * * The legislative history of § 1404(a) certainly does not justify the rather startling conclusion that one might "get a change of law as a bonus for a change of venue." Indeed, an interpretation accepting such a rule would go far to frustrate the remedial purposes of § 1404(a). If a change of law were in the offing, the parties might well regard the section primarily as a forum-shopping instrument. And, more importantly, courts would at least be reluctant to grant transfers, despite considerations of convenience, if to do so might conceivably prejudice the claim of a plaintiff who had initially selected a permissible forum. We believe, therefore, that both the history and purposes of § 1404(a) indicate that it should be regarded as a federal judicial housekeeping measure, dealing with the placement of litigation in the federal courts and generally intended, on the basis of convenience and fairness, simply to authorize a change of courtrooms.

Although we deal here with a congressional statute apportioning the business of the federal courts, our interpretation of that statute fully accords with and is supported by the policy underlying Erie R. Co. v. Tompkins, 304 U.S. 64. * * * [W]e should ensure that the "accident" of federal diversity jurisdiction does not enable a party to utilize a transfer to achieve a result in federal court which could not have been achieved in the courts of the State where the action was filed. This purpose would be defeated in cases such as the present if nonresident defendants, properly subjected to suit in the transferor State (Pennsylvania), could invoke § 1404(a) to gain the benefits of the laws of another jurisdiction (Massachusetts). What Erie and the cases following it have sought was an identity or uniformity between federal and state courts; and the fact that in most instances this could be achieved by directing federal courts to apply the laws of the States "in which they sit" should not obscure that, in applying the same reasoning to § 1404(a), the critical identity to be maintained is between the federal district court which decides the case and the courts of the State in which the action was filed.

We conclude, therefore, that in cases such as the present, where the defendants seek transfer, the transferee district court must be obligated to apply the state law that would have been applied if there had been no change of venue. A change of venue under § 1404(a) generally should be, with respect to state law, but a change of courtrooms.[40]

We, therefore, reject the plaintiffs' contention that the transfer was necessarily precluded by the likelihood that a prejudicial change of law would result. In so ruling, however, we do not and need not consider whether in all cases § 1404(a) would require the application of the law of the transferor, as opposed to the transferee, State.[41] We do not attempt to determine whether, for example, the same considerations would govern if a plaintiff sought transfer

---

40. Of course the transferee District Court may apply its own rules governing the conduct and dispatch of cases in its court. We are only concerned here with those state laws of the transferor State which would significantly affect the outcome of the case.

41. We do not suggest that the application of transferor state law is free from constitutional limitations. See, *e.g.,* Watson v. Employers Liability Assurance Corp., Ltd., 348 U.S. 66; Hughes v. Fetter, 341 U.S. 609. * * *

under § 1404(a) or if it was contended that the transferor State would simply have dismissed the action on the ground of *forum non conveniens.*

B.   * * *

Since in this case the transferee district court must under § 1404(a) apply the laws of the State of the transferor district court, it follows in our view that Rule 17(b) must be interpreted similarly so that the capacity to sue will also be governed by the laws of the transferor State. Where a § 1404(a) transfer is thus held not to effect a change of law but essentially only to authorize a change of courtrooms, the reference in Rule 17(b) to the law of the State "in which the district court is held" should be applied in a corresponding manner so that it will refer to the district court which sits in the State that will generally be the source of applicable laws. We conclude, therefore, that the Court of Appeals misconceived the meaning and application of Rule 17(b) and erred in holding that it required the denial of the § 1404(a) transfer.

III.   APPLICABLE LAW: EFFECT ON THE CONVENIENCE OF PARTIES AND WITNESSES.

The holding that a § 1404(a) transfer would not alter the state law to be applied does not dispose of the question of whether the proposed transfer can be justified when measured against the relevant criteria of convenience and fairness.   * * *

* * * [T]o the extent that Pennsylvania laws are difficult or unclear and might not defer to Massachusetts laws, it may be advantageous to retain the actions in Pennsylvania where the judges possess a more ready familiarity with the local laws.

If, on the other hand, Pennsylvania courts would apply the Massachusetts Death Act in its entirety, these same factors might well weigh quite differently. Consolidation of the transferred cases with those now pending in Massachusetts might be freed from any potential difficulties and rendered more desirable. The plaintiffs' need for witnesses residing in Pennsylvania might be significantly reduced. And, of course, the trial would be held in the State in which the causes of action arose and in which the federal judges are more familiar with the governing laws.

In pointing to these considerations, we are fully aware that the District Court concluded that the relevant Pennsylvania law was unsettled, that its determination involved difficult questions, and that in the near future Pennsylvania courts might provide guidance. We think that this uncertainty, however, should itself have been considered as a factor bearing on the desirability of transfer. Section 1404(a) provides for transfer to a more convenient forum, not to a forum likely to prove equally convenient or inconvenient. We do not suggest that elements of uncertainty in transferor state law would alone justify a denial of transfer; but we do think that the uncertainty is one factor, among others, to be considered in assessing the desirability of transfer.   * * *

Accordingly, the judgment of the Court of Appeals for the Third Circuit is reversed and the cause remanded to the District Court for further proceedings in conformity with this opinion.

Reversed and remanded.

■ MR. JUSTICE BLACK concurs in the reversal substantially for the reasons set forth in the opinion of the Court, but he believes that, under the circumstances shown in the opinion, this Court should now hold it was error to order these actions transferred to the District of Massachusetts.

NOTE ON FORUM NON CONVENIENS AND CHANGE OF VENUE

(1) *Decisions Prior to the Enactment of § 1404: The Gulf Oil Case.* Section 1404 of Title 28 originated in the revision of the Judicial Code in 1948.[1] Prior to that time, the Court had held the principle of forum non conveniens applicable in an action at law in the federal courts: "[A] court [by dismissing the action] may resist imposition upon its jurisdiction even when jurisdiction is authorized by the letter of a general venue statute." Gulf Oil Corp. v. Gilbert, 330 U.S. 501, 507 (1947).[2] After noting that the doctrine "presupposes at least two forums in which the defendant is amenable to process," the Court in Gulf Oil described the factors that were to be considered (pp. 508–09):

"If the combination and weight of factors requisite to given results are difficult to forecast or state, those to be considered are not difficult to name. An interest to be considered, and the one likely to be most pressed, is the private interest of the litigant. Important considerations are the relative ease of access to sources of proof; availability of compulsory process for attendance of unwilling, and the cost of obtaining attendance of willing, witnesses; possibility of view of premises, if view would be appropriate to the action; and all other practical problems that make trial of a case easy, expeditious and inexpensive. There may also be questions as to the enforceability of a judgment if one is obtained. The court will weigh relative advantages and obstacles to fair trial. It is often said that the plaintiff may not, by choice of an inconvenient forum, 'vex,' 'harass,' or 'oppress' the defendant by inflicting upon him expense or trouble not necessary to his own right to pursue his remedy. But unless the balance is strongly in favor of the defendant, the plaintiff's choice of forum should rarely be disturbed.

"Factors of public interest also have place in applying the doctrine. Administrative difficulties follow for courts when litigation is piled up in congested centers instead of being handled at its origin. * * * There is a local interest in having localized controversies decided at home. There is an appropriateness, too, in having the trial of a diversity case in a forum that is at home with the state law that must govern the case, rather than having a court in some other forum untangle problems in conflict of laws, and in law foreign to itself."

(2) *The Effect of § 1404.* The Reviser's Notes to § 1404(a) explained the provision as follows: "Subsection (a) was drafted in accordance with the

---

1. Other transfer provisions in Title 28 include § 1406 (see Paragraph (6), *infra*); § 1407 (see Paragraph (10), *infra*); 28 U.S.C. § 1631 (transfer "to cure want of jurisdiction"); and § 2112(a) (proceedings instituted in two or more courts of appeals with respect to the same administrative order). See also 46 U.S.C. § 742 (admiralty suits against the United States); Fed.R.Civ.P., Supplementary Rule F(9) (limitation proceedings); Fed. R.Cr.P. 21 (criminal proceedings).

2. Gulf Oil was a diversity action for damages resulting from alleged negligence. Earlier decisions had permitted dismissal on similar grounds in admiralty and equity proceedings. See, *e.g.*, Canada Malting Co. v. Paterson S.S., Ltd., 285 U.S. 413 (1932); Rogers v. Guaranty Trust Co., 288 U.S. 123 (1933).

doctrine of *forum non conveniens,* permitting transfer to a more convenient forum, even though the venue is proper. As an example of the need of such a provision, see Baltimore & Ohio R. Co. v. Kepner, 314 U.S. 44 (1941), which was prosecuted under the Federal Employer's Liability Act in New York, although the accident occurred and the employee resided in Ohio. The new subsection requires the court to determine that the transfer is necessary for convenience of the parties and witnesses, and further, that it is in the interest of justice to do so."[3]

The provision does not deprive the court of discretion to dismiss on grounds of forum non conveniens when it concludes that the case ought to be litigated in a forum to which it cannot be transferred. Thus in Piper Aircraft Co. v. Reyno, 454 U.S. 235 (1981), the Supreme Court upheld as within the district court's discretion a decision to dismiss a wrongful death action brought on behalf of the Scottish victims of an air crash that had occurred in Scotland—even though the defendants were American companies and Scottish law was less favorable to the plaintiffs than American law on a number of issues. Among the factors supporting the dismissal were the Scottish citizenship and residence of the victims and their survivors, the location of evidence in Scotland, the ability to implead third parties there, the interest of United States courts in avoiding complex problems of choice of law, and the danger that refusal to dismiss would "increase and further congest already crowded courts" in this country (p. 252). The Court did state, however, that dismissal might not be in the interest of justice "if the remedy provided by the alternative forum is so clearly inadequate or unsatisfactory that it is no remedy at all * * *" (p. 254).[4]

(3) *The Effect of State Law in Diversity Cases.* The doctrine of forum non conveniens is recognized in many but not all of the states. (Most state court dismissals involve suits between nonresidents on foreign causes of action. Some involve questions of the "internal affairs" of a foreign corporation.) Should a federal court transfer a diversity case (or if transfer is unavailable,

---

3. The Court in Kepner had refused to permit dismissal of the suit, reasoning, that the FELA's broad venue provision conferred an unqualified privilege on the plaintiff employee to choose the forum. Partly on the basis of the Reviser's citation of the Kepner case, the Court concluded in Ex parte Collett, 337 U.S. 55 (1949), that § 1404(a) applies in an FELA case. See also Continental Grain Co. v. Barge FBL–585, 364 U.S. 19 (1960)(upholding transfer under § 1404(a) of admiralty action in which in rem and in personam proceedings were joined).

4. The Court in Piper emphasized the fact that the action had been brought on behalf of persons who were not U.S. citizens or residents. How much weight should be accorded this factor in deciding whether to defer to the plaintiff's choice of forum? See Alcoa S.S. Co., Inc. v. M/V Nordic Regent, 654 F.2d 147 (2d Cir.1980)(upholding forum non conveniens dismissal although the plaintiff was a U.S. corporation and the law of Trinidad—the place found to be the more

appropriate forum—imposed a much lower limit on recovery than did the law of the United States); Yellen, *Forum Non Conveniens: Standards for the Dismissal of Actions From United States Federal Courts to Foreign Tribunals,* 5 Fordham Int'l L.J. 533 (1982).

The Piper decision was relied on by the Second Circuit in affirming a dismissal on forum non conveniens grounds in In re Union Carbide Corp. Gas Plant Disaster at Bhopal, India, in December 1984, 809 F.2d 195 (2d Cir.1987).

For broad-ranging criticisms of current forum non conveniens doctrine, see Stein, *Forum Non Conveniens and the Redundancy of Court Access Doctrine,* 133 U.Pa.L.Rev. 781 (1985); Stewart, *Forum Non Conveniens: A Doctrine in Search of a Role,* 74 Calif.L.Rev. 1259 (1986); Robertson, *The Federal Doctrine of Forum Non Conveniens: "An Object Lesson in Uncontrolled Discretion",* 29 Tex. Int'l L.J. 353 (1994).

dismiss) if the case is one that the forum state would dismiss on forum non conveniens grounds?[5] *Cf.* Szantay v. Beech Aircraft Corp., 349 F.2d 60 (4th Cir.1965), p. 740, *supra.* In Parsons v. Chesapeake & O. Ry. Co., 375 U.S. 71, 74 (1963), the Supreme Court held in an FELA case that a prior state court dismissal on the basis of forum non conveniens can "never serve to divest a federal district judge of the discretionary power vested in him" under § 1404(a). Noting that there were differences between the state's criteria for dismissal and the federal court's criteria for transfer, the Supreme Court sustained the trial court's refusal to transfer the action. The precise question in Parsons was the applicability of res judicata to a motion for transfer in a federal question case, but the Parsons rationale was relied on, along with a number of other factors, in a well-reasoned opinion in a diversity case refusing to follow state law on a motion to dismiss. Lapides v. Doner, 248 F.Supp. 883 (E.D.Mich.1965).

What if a state would *refuse* to dismiss an action on forum non conveniens grounds or on the closely analogous ground that the parties had agreed by contract to litigate in another forum? In Stewart Org., Inc. v. Ricoh Corp., 487 U.S. 22 (1988), p. 735, *supra,* the relevant state law would have made such an agreement unenforceable. The Court nevertheless held, over a vigorous dissent, that § 1404(a) gives district courts discretion to decide transfer motions on a case-by-case basis, taking into account a range of factors, of which a forum selection clause is only one.

(4) *The Interpretation of "Where It Might Have Been Brought" in the Hoffman Case.* The Court's decision in Hoffman v. Blaski, construing "where it might have been brought" in § 1404(a), is discussed and distinguished in Van Dusen. Although neither decision makes it completely clear whether a case can be transferred to a district in which venue is proper but personal jurisdiction over the defendant cannot be obtained, it is generally believed that such transfer is unavailable. See Wright, Federal Courts § 44, at 281–82 & n. 48 (5th ed. 1994).

A vigorous dissent in Hoffman was filed by Justice Frankfurter, who argued that the language of § 1404(a) did not compel the result reached and that the policies of the section would best be served by holding that the defendant's motion for transfer obviates any objections to process or venue in the transferee forum. But what of the argument that the venue provisions are designed for the convenience of *both* parties and that while a plaintiff who has selected the forum cannot be heard to object, the plaintiff should be able to object if the defendant is trying to choose the place of trial? Justice Frankfurter answered (363 U.S. at 361–62):

"* * * This would be a powerful argument if, under § 1404(a), a transfer were to be made whenever requested by the defendant. Such is not the case, and this bears emphasis. A transfer can be made under § 1404(a) to a place where the action might have been brought only when 'convenience' and 'justice' so dictate * * *. If the plaintiff's objection to proceedings in the

---

5. In the Gulf Oil case, the Court observed that "[t]he law of New York as to the discretion of a court to apply the doctrine of forum non conveniens, and as to the standards that guide discretion is, so far as here involved, the same as the federal rule. * * * It would not be profitable, therefore, to pursue inquiry as to the source from which our rule must flow." 330 U.S. at 509. See also Piper Aircraft Co. v. Reyno, Paragraph (2), *supra,* at 248 n. 13.

transferee court is not consonant with the interests of justice, a good reason is wanting why the transfer should not be made."

Are you satisfied with the answer? If Justice Frankfurter's position is sound, shouldn't it be applicable to a plaintiff's motion for transfer as well? Would Justice Frankfurter agree? Was he perhaps thinking of § 1404(a) as only a defendant's remedy?[6] If the answer to either of the last two questions is yes, what meaning did Justice Frankfurter attribute to "where it might have been brought"?

Given the result in Hoffman v. Blaski, should § 1404(a) be changed to delete the phrase "where it might have been brought"? What of the similar language in § 1406(a)(discussed in Paragraph (6), *infra*)?

(5) *The Criteria for Transfer.* What considerations should guide a judge in deciding whether to order a transfer? In Norwood v. Kirkpatrick, 349 U.S. 29 (1955), the Court held that the relevant factors remained those described in Gulf Oil Corp. v. Gilbert, *supra,* but that a "lesser showing of inconvenience" (p. 32) was needed to support transfer than was required for dismissal. Dismissal, the Court noted, was a far harsher remedy than transfer. Is this result sound in view of the fact that dismissal under forum non conveniens presupposes another available forum? Should a heavier burden be imposed on a plaintiff seeking transfer than is imposed on a defendant?

For informative and provocative discussions, see Kitch, *Section 1404(a) of the Judicial Code: In the Interest of Justice or Injustice?,* 40 Ind.L.J. 99, 131–37 (1965); Steinberg, *The Motion To Transfer and the Interests of Justice,* 66 Notre Dame L.Rev. 443 (1990).

(6) *Transfer Under § 1406.* 28 U.S.C. § 1406(a) authorizes transfer in lieu of dismissal in a case "laying venue in the wrong division or district". Section 1406(a) is plainly designed to aid plaintiffs who have chosen the wrong court. Somewhat surprisingly, this section has been held applicable to a case in which venue is improper *and* the defendant has not been subjected to the jurisdiction of the court. Goldlawr, Inc. v. Heiman, 369 U.S. 463 (1962). What is the advantage of transfer over dismissal in such a case?

Is transfer available if the plaintiff has selected the right venue but has not obtained personal jurisdiction over the defendant? See, *e.g.,* Dubin v. United States, 380 F.2d 813 (5th Cir.1967)(transfer allowed under § 1406(a)); Ellis v. Great Southwestern Corp., 646 F.2d 1099, 1106 (5th Cir.1981)(transfer allowed under § 1404(a)).[7]

(7) *Appellate Review of Transfer Orders.*

(a) An order granting or denying transfer is not an appealable final judgment, and is not ordinarily thought to be within the scope of the interlocutory appeal provisions of 28 U.S.C. § 1292(b). See Wright, Federal Courts

---

6. Although the question has not been squarely ruled upon by the Supreme Court, it is now generally held that transfer may be granted on plaintiff's motion under § 1404(a). See 15 Wright, Miller & Cooper, Federal Practice and Procedure § 3844, at 330 (1986 & 1995 Supp.). Why might a plaintiff want transfer if the transfer cannot be used to avoid venue and process requirements?

7. See Piper Aircraft Co. v. Reyno, Paragraph (2), *supra,* at 240–41 (district court transferred action in which venue was proper but personal jurisdiction was lacking with respect to one of the two defendants; transferee court then dismissed on forum non conveniens grounds.)

Would 28 U.S.C. § 1631 be of any assistance in such a case? See note 1, *supra.*

§ 44, at 285–86 (5th ed. 1994).[8] Thus immediate review of such an order is generally limited to an application for mandamus or prohibition, see p. 1669, *infra,* and each circuit seems to have its own standard governing the availability of the writ. While the Supreme Court has avoided any direct pronouncements, such decisions as Hoffman and Van Dusen indicate that it regards issuance of the writ to be proper when the district court has ordered a transfer to a district that is not one where the action "might have been brought". What if it is argued that the district court has relied on an inappropriate factor or refused to take a relevant factor into account? That it has evaluated relevant factors incorrectly?

Although the decisions of the circuits differ in both language and result, it seems almost impossible to obtain reversal in most courts of appeals on an application for mandamus if the argument is simply that the trial court abused its discretion in ordering or denying a transfer. For a forceful statement that such abuse should not be a basis for issuance of the writ, see Judge Friendly's concurring opinion in A. Olinick & Sons v. Dempster Bros., 365 F.2d 439, 445–48 (2d Cir.1966).

Would a party aggrieved by a grant or denial of transfer be able to obtain an effective remedy on appeal after final judgment? Would any error relating to transfer be likely to be considered harmless at that stage? See Ford Motor Co. v. Ryan, 182 F.2d 329, 330 (2d Cir.1950). If so, how can the issuance of mandamus at an earlier stage be said to be "in aid of" the court's appellate jurisdiction under 28 U.S.C. § 1651? On the basis that the phrase contemplates use of the writ when its denial would immunize a lower court decision from appellate review?

(b) One conceptual problem in these cases is to decide where a case "is" when a district court has ordered it transferred to a district in another circuit. Once a case has been transferred, can the court of appeals in the transferor circuit cause the case to be brought back by instructing the district judge to vacate the order of transfer? See In re Nine Mile Limited, 673 F.2d 242 (8th Cir.1982)(after district court in 8th circuit transferred file to district court in 4th circuit, 8th circuit had no jurisdiction to review on writ of mandamus; transferor court should request transferee court to return the record).

Conceptual questions aside, should review of a transfer order occur in the transferor or in the transferee circuit? To avoid a judicial ping-pong game, shouldn't a decision by the transferor circuit refusing to require vacation of the transfer order be considered the "law of the case" in the transferee circuit? In Hoffman v. Blaski, the transferee circuit had ordered the case transferred back after the transferor circuit had denied mandamus, and the Supreme Court affirmed over Justice Frankfurter's dissenting argument that "res judicata" should be applied.[9]

---

8. But see Continental Grain Co. v. Barge FBL–585, note 3, *supra,* in which an appeal to the court of appeals was allowed under § 1292(b). The question of appealability was not discussed by the Supreme Court.

9. It is generally held that if a case is transferred from a district court in one circuit to a district court in another, the initial decision may not be reviewed by a court of appeals in the transferee circuit. See, *e.g.,* Roofing & Sheet Metal Services, Inc. v. La Quinta Motor Inns, Inc., 689 F.2d 982 (11th Cir.1982). But this limitation may be finessed by a motion in the transferee district court to send the case back. Denial of that motion would presumably be subject to review by the court of appeals in the transferee circuit.

(8) *Choice of Law in § 1404 Cases Transferred on Motion of Defendant.* Can the result in Van Dusen be squared with the fact that, prior to the enactment of § 1404, a dismissal would have required the commencement of a new action with the applicable law being determined in and by the second forum? Does the answer lie in part in the greater availability of transfer under § 1404 (see Norwood v. Kirkpatrick, Paragraph (5), *supra*)? For an argument that, in spite of Klaxon, there should be independent federal choice of law rules in transfer cases, see Note, 75 Yale L.J. 90 (1965). For the view that the approach represented by Van Dusen is probably the best of several unsatisfactory alternatives, see B. Currie, *Change of Venue and the Conflict of Laws: A Retraction,* 27 U.Chi.L.Rev. 341 (1960). Wasn't Justice Goldberg right when he said that any other approach would lead litigants to use § 1404 to shop for the most favorable substantive rules and would make courts reluctant, for that very reason, to grant the transfer remedy?

What does the Van Dusen Court mean by the statement in footnote 40 that the transferee court may apply its own rules governing the "conduct and dispatch of cases"?

What law should govern the liability of a party who is added to the case after transfer?

Are the questions of applicable law on transfer different if state law applies interstitially in a federal question case? See note 10, *infra.*

(9) *Questions Unresolved in the Van Dusen Decision.* Several questions explicitly or implicitly reserved by the Court in Van Dusen are discussed in this Paragraph.

(a) Two of the unresolved questions involved the governing law in a diversity case when transfer is granted under § 1406(a), or at the behest of the plaintiff under § 1404(a). Should it matter in either case whether the law of the transferor state is more favorable to the plaintiff than the law of the transferee state? In Ferens v. John Deere Co., 494 U.S. 516 (1990), the Supreme Court held, 5–4, that the transferor state's law governs in all cases transferred under § 1404, whether the transfer is initiated by the defendant, the plaintiff, or the court. The plaintiffs in this case, alleging injuries caused by equipment manufactured by the defendant, filed a diversity action in a Pennsylvania federal court for breach of warranty. Since the Pennsylvania statute of limitations for tort actions had run, plaintiffs filed a tort action against the same defendant in a federal court in Mississippi, which had a longer statute of limitations for such actions and a choice-of-law rule that would apply that statute. The plaintiffs then moved under § 1404(a) to transfer the Mississippi action to Pennsylvania, and the motion was granted. The transferee court dismissed the tort action, holding that after a transfer on plaintiff's motion, the transferee state's law applied. The Third Circuit affirmed, but the Supreme Court reversed.

Justice Kennedy, for the majority, concluded that to apply the transferor's law in these circumstances would be fully consistent with the policies of Erie and Van Dusen. And he noted that not to do so would mean that the decision whether to seek or grant a transfer under § 1404, which is supposed to be based solely on considerations of convenience, would become enmeshed in questions of choice of law. Moreover, a rule requiring application of the transferee's law would simply deter plaintiffs like the Ferenses from moving for transfer; thus, "the Ferenses are seeking [in their transfer motion] to deprive

Deere only of the advantage of using against them the inconvenience of litigating in Mississippi" (p. 525).

Justice Scalia, in dissent, agreed that application of the transferee's law in these circumstances "would deter a plaintiff * * * from seeking a transfer, since that would deprive him of the favorable substantive law. But that proves only that this disposition achieves what Erie and Klaxon are designed to achieve: preventing the plaintiff from using 'the accident of diversity of citizenship' [quoting Klaxon] to obtain the application of a different law within the State where he wishes to litigate" (p. 536).

The 5–4 decision in this case, as well as the division among courts and scholars that preceded the decision, reflects the difficulty of the issue presented. But is there an effective answer to Justice Scalia's point? As long as Klaxon is on the books, should a plaintiff be able to separate his choice of forum from the question of choice of law?[10]

Whether or not the Ferens result is sound, shouldn't a different result prevail when a case is transferred under § 1406—when, in other words, the plaintiff has selected a federal forum *not open* to him (without the defendant's consent) as a matter of federal law?

(b) Isn't the weakest case for application of the transferor state's law one also reserved by the Court in Van Dusen—that in which a state court in the transferor district would have dismissed for forum non conveniens? Aside from the difficulty of determining whether the state court would have dismissed—a difficulty that may well be dispositive—wouldn't it be consistent with Klaxon, and eminently sensible, to have a federal choice of law rule in such a case? Even if the case is not transferred?[11] Might application of the transferor state's substantive law in such a case raise constitutional issues under the Due Process or Full–Faith-and-Credit Clauses.[12]

10. For criticism of Ferens—and especially of its interpretation by some lower courts with respect to transfers in federal question cases—coupled with a proposal for legislative change, see Norwood, *Double Forum Shopping and the Extension of Ferens to Federal Claims That Borrow State Limitations Periods*, 44 Emory L.J. 501 (1995).

11. But see In re Air Crash Disaster at Boston, Mass., 399 F.Supp. 1106, 1119–22 (D.Mass.1975), discussed in Caffrey, *The Role of the Transferee Judge in Multidistrict Litigation*, 69 F.R.D. 289, 294–98 (1976). In this case, Judge Caffrey held that the law of the transferor state would apply, even though the courts of that state would have dismissed for forum non conveniens. He argued that the transferor district court was not obliged to dismiss or to transfer because of state law (compare the discussion in Paragraph (3), *supra*), and had it retained the case, would have applied the transferor state's law.

12. In a federal question case, which circuit's rule should govern if the controlling precedents differ in the transferor and transferee circuits? Marcus, *Conflicts Among Circuits and Transfers Within the Federal Judicial System*, 93 Yale L.J. 677 (1984), argued that the transferee's rule should govern, and most courts considering the issue adopted that view. In a later survey and critique, Professor Ragazzo notes that Professor Marcus' view has been accepted not only in cases involving permanent transfer but also in cases involving transfer and consolidation of multi-district litigation for pretrial purposes under 28 U.S.C. § 1407 (Paragraph (10), *infra*). Ragazzo, *Transfer and Choice of Federal Law: The Appellate Model*, 93 Mich.L.Rev. 704 (1995). Ragazzo argues that in the latter cases, the law of the transferor circuit should apply because "the transferor circuit [after the case is returned to the district court in that circuit for trial] will have ultimate jurisdiction over any appeal of the case" (p. 747).

(10) *Transfer of Complex and Multidistrict Litigation.*

(a) Following the experience in handling pretrial discovery in the almost 2,000 separate antitrust suits filed in 36 districts against electrical equipment manufacturers in the early 1960s,[13] Congress enacted 28 U.S.C. § 1407 in 1968. The statute, based on the recommendations of a committee of the Judicial Conference, provides for transfers of actions involving one or more questions of fact "to any district for coordinated or consolidated pretrial proceedings." Transfers are made by a "judicial panel on multidistrict litigation," consisting of seven circuit and district judges named by the Chief Justice, no two of whom may be from the same circuit.

Although annual data are difficult to obtain, the available statistics indicate that of the cases consolidated for pretrial proceedings under § 1407, the large majority (over 75%) are terminated (by settlement or otherwise) in the transferee district. See, *e.g.,* Administrative Office of the United States Courts, Annual Report 128 (1986).

A transferee court acting under § 1407 may order some or all of the cases transferred to itself for trial under § 1404(a) or § 1406.[14]

(b) Building on the principles underlying § 1407, the American Law Institute has recently proposed an elaborate plan for transfer and consolidation of complex litigation, including consolidation of cases pending not only within the federal system but also in the courts of different states—and, in perhaps its major innovation, designation of state as well as federal courts as available forums for consolidation. See ALI, Complex Litigation: Statutory Recommendations and Analysis (1994). As a part of the plan, the project proposes the adoption of uniform choice-of-law rules to govern such cases, whether the controlling substantive law is federal or state.

(11) *Criticism and Defense of Existing Transfer Provisions.* Both Professors Kitch and Steinberg, in the articles cited in Paragraph (5), *supra,* have argued in favor of severely curtailing or eliminating the availability of transfer under § 1404. Thus, Professor Kitch proposed that Congress improve the basic venue statutes and then repeal the transfer provisions for cases in which initial venue is proper. Once defects in the general venue provisions were remedied, he contended, the marginal benefits from finding a better forum in the occasional case would be outweighed by the costs to litigants and courts of protracted disputes about the place of trial. Such costs, in his view, were amply demonstrated by the experience under present law.

But Kitch says nothing about the relationship between the number of cases transferred without substantial delay under present law and the cases in which appeals or other time consuming tactics are employed. Nor does he seek to explore the experience of judges, lawyers, and litigants since § 1404 was enacted in 1948. Aren't such empirical data essential to well-informed judgments about the utility of transfer?

---

13. See Neal & Goldberg, *The Electrical Equipment Antitrust Cases: Novel Judicial Administration,* 50 A.B.A.J. 621 (1964).

14. See Jud.Pan.Mult.Lit.Rule 14(b); Pfizer v. Lord, 447 F.2d 122 (2d Cir.1971); In re Yarn Processing Patent Validity Litigation, 472 F.Supp. 174 (S.D.Fla.1979)(also raising questions of the use of issue preclusion in actions not eligible for transfer under § 1404(a) or § 1406).

For further discussion of § 1407 and its administration, see Herndon & Higginbotham, *Complex Multidistrict Litigation—An Overview,* 31 Baylor L.Rev. 33 (1979); 15 Wright, Miller & Cooper, Federal Practice and Procedure §§ 3861–3867 (1986 and 1995 Supp.).

A recent study by Clermont & Eisenberg, *Exorcising the Evil of Forum Shopping* (forthcoming in the Cornell Law Review), seeks to develop and assess such data, and then urges that sound policy favors the preservation of the existing transfer scheme. On the benefit side, the authors note that plaintiffs' "rate of winning drops from 58% in cases where there is no transfer to 29% in transferred cases", thus suggesting that a significant effect of transfer is to strip the plaintiff of "an unjust forum advantage". (Are there other possible explanations for the drop?) On the cost side, the authors state that the percentage of cases transferred has climbed slightly in recent years but remains below 2% of all cases, that many transferred cases fall into such special categories as prisoner cases or cases transferred under § 1406, and that relatively few transfer motions are sufficiently contested to involve the expenditure of significant resources. Finally, the percentage of transfer decisions that are reviewed by appellate courts is extremely low, and of those, the overwhelming majority are affirmed.

SECTION 3. REMOVAL JURISDICTION AND PROCEDURE*

INTRODUCTORY NOTE

(1) Since 1789, the judiciary acts have continuously provided two ways of removing a case from a state to a federal court: first, by review in the Supreme Court after the state courts have had their final say; and second, by transfer to a lower federal court for trial in the first instance.

What purposes should the removal jurisdiction serve? Primarily to equalize, in cases of concurrent jurisdiction, the opportunity of both parties to gain access to a federal court? Is there justification in some cases for denying the defendant this choice even though the plaintiff had it? May there be a justification in others for allowing removal (by the defendant or by either party) even though the plaintiff's only initial choice was to sue in the state court—as, for example, if a federal defense is raised? See pp. 911–12, *supra*.

(2) From 1789 to 1887, the requirements of jurisdiction on removal were stated in terms independent of the requirements for original jurisdiction.

In the Judiciary Act of 1789, 1 Stat. 73, 79–80, the removal privilege was given only in cases in which more than five hundred dollars was in dispute, and then only to three classes of parties: (a) to a defendant who was an alien; (b) to a defendant who was a citizen of another state, sued by a citizen of the state of the forum; and (c) to either party, where title to land was in dispute under conflicting grants of different states and the non-removing party claimed under a grant of the forum state.

Between 1789 and 1872, Congress enacted a series of relatively specific removal statutes, most of them prompted by occasions of sharp conflict with state authority and designed to give added protection to federal officers or

---

* Issues relating to removal are also dealt with in several other chapters. See Chap. IV, pp. 455–59, *supra* (power of Congress to provide for removal); Chap. VIII, Sec. 4, *supra* (removal on the basis of a federal question); Chap. XV, pp. 1667–68, *infra* (appealability of remand orders).

federal law. See pp. 948, 951, *supra*. In addition the Separable Controversy Act of July 27, 1866, 14 Stat. 306, introduced a new principle of general importance, allowing removal by one or fewer than all of the defendants on the basis of the nature of the controversy with the removing defendants rather than of the case as a whole. The problems involved in the current version of this legislation are dealt with below in this section.

The Act of March 3, 1875, 18 Stat. 470, enormously broadened the removal as well as the original jurisdiction. Removal was made a privilege equally of a plaintiff and a defendant. The general removal provision did retain the jurisdictional amount requirement of five hundred dollars. But otherwise the classes of removable cases covered substantially the entire gamut authorized by Article III.

The present pattern of the removal jurisdiction was fixed by the Judiciary Act of 1887. Act of March 3, 1887, 24 Stat. 552, corrected by Act of August 13, 1888, 25 Stat. 433. For the first time the requirements of removal jurisdiction, under the general removal provision, were expressly tied to those for original jurisdiction. The general provision applied only if the case was one "of which the circuit courts of the United States are given original jurisdiction by the preceding section". The present general removal provision, 28 U.S.C. § 1441(a), states the basic condition for removal in substantially the same way: the action must be one "of which the district courts of the United States have original jurisdiction". There are, in addition, special removal provisions in the Judicial Code that contain independent requirements, *e.g.,* § 1441(d) (civil actions against foreign states); § 1442 (federal officers sued or prosecuted); § 1443 (civil rights cases); and § 1444 (foreclosure action against the United States), and in other titles of the U.S. Code, *e.g.,* 12 U.S.C. § 1441a(*l*)(3)(removal by the Resolution Trust Company).[1]

The present statute follows the 1887 act also in restricting the privilege of removal to defendants. All the defendants (or if removal is based on a separate or independent claim against some of the defendants, all defendants interested in the separate claim) must join in the petition for removal. The defendant's residence is immaterial if jurisdiction is "founded on a claim or right arising under the Constitution, treaties or laws of the United States". But any other action "shall be removable only if none of the parties in interest properly joined and served as defendants is a citizen of the State in which such action is brought".

(3) Sometimes Congress has deliberately denied to defendants the choice of forum given to plaintiffs. Notice that this is true in diversity cases in which the defendant is a resident of the state in which the action is brought. Removal is expressly forbidden also in a number of statutes creating federal rights of action. See, *e.g.,* 28 U.S.C. § 1445(a) (FELA). In these instances, plaintiff alone has the choice of forum.

1. For a recent decision in which the court held that *only* the Resolution Trust Company (and not any other defendant) could take advantage of the special removal privilege afforded by 12 U.S.C. § 1441a(*l*)(3), see California v. Keating, 986 F.2d 346 (9th Cir.1993). (This special removal provision has been held to enable the RTC to remove not only as a defendant or third-party defen- dant but also as a plaintiff in a state court action. See RTC v. Nernberg, 3 F.3d 62 (3d Cir.1993) (noting that when the RTC removes as plaintiff, it may remove only to the federal court for the district in which the action was brought or to the district court for the District of Columbia—a narrower choice of venues than is provided in those cases in which the RTC is a defendant).)

(4) Should a plaintiff against whom a counterclaim has been filed setting forth an independent cause of action be permitted to remove as a "defendant" to the counterclaim?

In Shamrock Oil & Gas Corp. v. Sheets, 313 U.S. 100 (1941), the Supreme Court, resolving conflicting decisions in the lower courts, held that the plaintiff could not remove in such a case. This was a diversity case in which both the original claim and the counterclaim exceeded $3,000. But the Court went out of its way to say that it would have made no difference if the plaintiff had never had a choice of suing in the federal court (p.108):

"[T]he question here is not of waiver but of the acquisition of a right which can only be conferred by Act of Congress. We can find no basis for saying that Congress, by omitting from the present statute all reference to 'plaintiffs,' intended to save a right of removal to some plaintiffs and not to others. * * *

"Not only does the language of the Act of 1887 evidence the Congressional purpose to restrict the jurisdiction of the federal courts on removal, but the policy of the successive acts of Congress regulating the jurisdiction of federal courts is one calling for the strict construction of such legislation."

Shamrock did not discuss the question whether the original defendant could rely on a counterclaim as a basis for removal. Should it matter whether such a counterclaim is permissive or compulsory? What is the relevance of Louisville & N.R.R. v. Mottley, 211 U.S. 149 (1908), p. 907, *supra?* For a discussion of the issues and citation of the divided cases, see Wright, Federal Courts § 37, at 216–22 (5th ed. 1994).[2]

(5) Section 1441 and succeeding sections contain their own venue provisions. Removal is "to the district court of the United States for the district and division embracing the place where such action is pending." For the tangled history of venue on removal under earlier statutes, see Lee v. Chesapeake & O. Ry., 260 U.S. 653 (1923).

(6) The privilege of removal may be lost if it is not asserted in time and in due conformity with the provisions of the statute. Moreover, even before the time for removal has expired the defendant may take steps in the state court that will be construed as a waiver. See p. 1675, *infra.* As to waiver by voluntary agreement in advance of any litigation, see p. 733, *supra.*

(7) Does a federal judge ever have power to remove a case from a state court *sua sponte,* and if so, what is the source of such authority? In an extraordinary move following settlement of the federal court Agent Orange class action suit, Judge Weinstein asserted such power under the All Writs Act (28 U.S.C. § 1651) with respect to a state court action filed against the defendants by several disgruntled members of the class. Ryan v. Dow Chemical Co., 781 F.Supp. 902, 918 (E.D.N.Y.1991), aff'd, 996 F.2d 1425 (2d Cir.1993).

---

2. Though the Supreme Court has never decided whether counterclaims (or third-party or cross claims) are removable by any party under § 1441(c) (considered in more detail at pp. 1625–28, *infra*), most commentators and lower courts have concluded that they are not. See 14A Wright, Miller & Cooper, Federal Practice and Procedure § 3724, at 388–94 (1985 and 1995 Supp.).

Granny Goose Foods, Inc. v. Brotherhood of Teamsters

415 U.S. 423, 94 S.Ct. 1113, 39 L.Ed.2d 435 (1974).
Certiorari to the United States Court of Appeals for the Ninth Circuit.

■ MR. JUSTICE MARSHALL delivered the opinion of the Court.

This case concerns the interpretation of 28 U.S.C. § 1450, which provides in pertinent part: "Whenever any action is removed from a State court to a district court of the United States * * * [a]ll injunctions, orders, and other proceedings had in such action prior to its removal shall remain in full force and effect until dissolved or modified by the district court." The District Court held respondent Union in criminal contempt for violating a temporary restraining order issued by the California Superior Court on May 18, 1970, prior to the removal of the case from the Superior Court to the District Court. The Court of Appeals reversed, one judge dissenting, on the ground that the temporary restraining order had expired long before November 30, 1970, the date of the alleged contempt. The court reasoned that under both § 527 of the California Code of Civil Procedure and Fed.Rule Civ.Proc. 65(b), the temporary restraining order must have expired no later than June 7, 1970, 20 days after its issuance. The court rejected petitioners' contention that the life of the order was indefinitely prolonged by § 1450 "until dissolved or modified by the district court" * * *.

I

On May 15, 1970, petitioners Granny Goose Foods, Inc., and Sunshine Biscuits, Inc., filed a complaint in the Superior Court of California for the county of Alameda alleging that respondent, a local Teamsters Union, and its officers and agents, were engaging in strike activity in breach of national and local collective-bargaining agreements recently negotiated by multiunion-multiemployer bargaining teams. * * *

The same day the complaint was filed, the Superior Court issued a temporary restraining order enjoining all existing strike activity and ordering the defendants to show cause on May 26, 1970, why a preliminary injunction should not issue during the pendency of the suit. * * *

On May 19, 1970, after having been served with the May 15 restraining order but before the scheduled hearing on the order to show cause, the Union and the individual defendants removed the proceeding to the District Court on the ground that the action arose under § 301 of the Labor Management Relations Act, 1974. * * *

Simultaneously with the filing of the removal petition, the defendants filed a motion in the District Court to dissolve the temporary restraining order. * * * [O]n June 4, 1970, the District Court entered a brief order denying the motion to dissolve the state court temporary restraining order * * *.

Evidently picketing and strike activity stopped and the labor dispute remained dormant after June 4. The flame was rekindled, however, when on November 9, 1970, the Union sent the employers telegrams requesting bargaining to arrive at a collective-bargaining agreement and expressing the Union's continued belief that it was not bound by the national and local agreements negotiated by the multiunion-multiemployer groups. The employers answered that there was no need to bargain because, in their view, the Union was bound by the national and local agreements. The conflict remained unresolved, and on November 30, 1970, the Union commenced its strike activity once again.

The next day the employers moved the District Court to hold the Union, its agents, and officers in contempt of the modified temporary restraining order issued by the Superior Court * * *. A hearing was held on the motion the following day. The Union's argument that the temporary restraining order had long since expired was rejected by the District Court on two grounds. First, the court concluded that its earlier action denying the motion to dissolve the temporary restraining order gave the order continuing force and effect. Second, the court found that § 1450 itself served to continue the restraining order in effect until affirmatively dissolved or modified by the court. Concluding after the hearing that the Union had willfully violated the restraining order, the District Court held it in criminal contempt and imposed a fine of $200,000.

II

* * * [I]t is clear that whether California law or Rule 65(b) is controlling, the temporary restraining order issued by the Superior Court expired long before the date of the alleged contempt. Section 527 of the California Code of Civil Procedure, under which the order was issued, provides that temporary restraining orders must be returnable no later than 15 days from the date of the order, 20 days if good cause is shown, and unless the party obtaining the order then proceeds to submit its case for a preliminary injunction, the temporary restraining order must be dissolved. Similarly, under Rule 65(b), temporary restraining orders must expire by their own terms within 10 days after entry, 20 days if good cause is shown.

Petitioners argue, however, that notwithstanding the time limitations of state law, § 1450 keeps all state court injunctions, including *ex parte* temporary restraining orders, in full force and effect after removal until affirmatively dissolved or modified by the district court. To the extent this reading of § 1450 is inconsistent with the time limitations of Rule 65(b), petitioners contend the statute must control.

In our view, however, § 1450 can and should be interpreted in a manner which fully serves its underlying purposes, yet at the same time places it in harmony with the important congressional policies reflected in the time limitations in Rule 65(b).

   * * *

* * * [W]hile Congress clearly intended to preserve the effectiveness of state court orders after removal, there is no basis for believing that § 1450 was designed to give injunctions or other orders *greater* effect after removal to federal court than they would have had if the case had remained in state court. * * *

More importantly, once a case has been removed to federal court, it is settled that federal rather than state law governs the future course of proceedings, notwithstanding state court orders issued prior to removal. Section 1450 implies as much by recognizing the district court's authority to dissolve or modify injunctions, orders, and all other proceedings had in state court prior to removal. * * *

* * * [R]espondent Union had a right to the protections of the time limitation in Rule 65(b) once the case was removed to the District Court. The Federal Rules of Civil Procedure, like other provisions of federal law, govern the mode of proceedings in federal court after removal. See Fed.Rule Civ.Proc. 81(c). * * * The stringent restrictions * * * on the availability of *ex parte* temporary restraining orders reflect the fact that our entire jurisprudence runs counter to the notion of court action taken before reasonable notice and an opportunity to be heard has been granted both sides of a dispute. *Ex parte* temporary restraining orders are no doubt necessary in certain circumstances, but under federal law they should be restricted to serving their underlying purpose of preserving the status quo and preventing irreparable harm just so long as is necessary to hold a hearing, and no longer.

We can find no indication that Congress intended § 1450 as an exception to its broader, longstanding policy of restricting the duration of *ex parte* restraining orders. The underlying purpose of § 1450—ensuring that no lapse in a state court temporary restraining order will occur simply by removing the case to federal court—and the policies reflected in Rule 65(b) can easily be accommodated by applying the following rule: An *ex parte* temporary restraining order issued by a state court prior to removal remains in force after removal no longer than it would have remained in effect under state law, but in no event does the order remain in force longer than the time limitations imposed by Rule 65(b), measured from the date of removal.

* * * Accordingly, no order was in effect on November 30, 1970, and the Union violated no order when it resumed its strike at that time.

III

We now turn to petitioners' argument that, apart from the operation of § 1450, the District Court's denial of the Union's motion to dissolve the temporary restraining order effectively converted the order into a preliminary injunction of unlimited duration. The Court of Appeals rejected this argument out of hand * * *. We reach essentially the same conclusion.

* * *

Judgment affirmed.

■ MR. JUSTICE REHNQUIST, with whom THE CHIEF JUSTICE, MR. JUSTICE STEWART, and MR. JUSTICE POWELL join, concurring in the judgment.

I agree with the Court that the judgment of the Court of Appeals for the Ninth Circuit in this case should be affirmed, since there was no injunctive order in effect at the time that respondent's allegedly contemptuous conduct occurred. But I do not join that portion of the Court's opinion which lays down a "rule" for all cases involving 28 U.S.C. § 1450, the statute which all parties agree is controlling in the case before us. In my view, the announcement of this "rule" is neither necessary to the decision of this case nor consistent with the provisions of the statute itself.

* * * Since the temporary restraining order, had the case remained in state court, concededly would have expired in early June, respondent's actions in November and December could not have constituted a contempt of that order.

The Court also persuasively demonstrates that none of the proceedings occurring after removal of the case to the United States District Court had the effect of converting the subsisting state court temporary restraining order into a preliminary injunction of indefinite duration. * * *

Having said this much, the Court has disposed of the case before it. The opinion then goes on, however, to devise a "rule" that

> "[a]n *ex parte* temporary restraining order issued by a state court prior to removal remains in force after removal no longer than it would have remained in effect under state law, but in no event does the order remain in force longer than the time limitations imposed by Rule 65(b), measured from the date of removal."

But the determination that mere removal of a case to a federal district court does not extend the duration of a previously issued state court order past its original termination date makes quite unnecessary to this case any further discussion about time limitations contained in Fed.Rules Civ.Proc. 65(b). More importantly, the second clause of the "rule" devised by the Court seems quite contrary to the specific language of 28 U.S.C. § 1450.

The Court apparently bases this latter clause of the "rule" upon the observation that "respondent Union had a right to the protections of the time limitation in Rule 65(b) once the case was removed to the District Court." While this premise probably has a good deal to recommend it as a matter of practicality or of common sense, the language of the statute gives no hint that rules of practice governing issuance of federal injunctions in the first instance were automatically to be incorporated in applying its terms. The statute says that the state court's temporary restraining order "shall remain in full force and effect until dissolved or modified by the district court." This Court's "rule," however, says that it shall *not* remain in full force and effect, even though not dissolved or modified by the District Court, if it would have a life beyond the time limitations imposed by Rule 65(b).

I think it likely that the interest in limiting the duration of temporary restraining orders which is exemplified in Rule 65(b) can be fully protected in cases removed to the district court by an application to modify or dissolve a state court restraining order which is incompatible with those terms. Such a procedure would be quite consistent with § 1450, which specifically contemplates dissolution or modification by the district court upon an appropriate showing, in a way that the "rule" devised by the Court in this case is not. It is unlikely that many orders issued under rules of state procedure, primarily designed, after all, to provide suitable procedures for state courts rather than to frustrate federal procedural rules in removed actions, would by their terms remain in effect for a period of time far longer than that contemplated by the comparable Federal Rule of Civil Procedure. But in the rare case where such a condition obtains, it is surely not asking too much of a litigant in a removed case to comply with § 1450 and affirmatively move for appropriate modification of the state order.

    * * *

NOTE ON SOME SPECIAL PROBLEMS OF THE RELATION BETWEEN STATE AND FEDERAL LAW IN REMOVED CASES

(1) *The Court's Rationale in the Granny Goose Decision.* In its interpretation of § 1450, the majority in Granny Goose (in a passage not reproduced here)

cited and relied on the decision in Ex parte Fisk, 113 U.S. 713 (1885), which held that a state court order to take a deposition was subject to reconsideration after removal. Doesn't the holding of that case actually lend support to the argument of the concurrence—that a state court order remains in effect until and unless modified or dissolved in accordance with federal law?

Federal Rule of Civil Procedure 81(c), also referred to by the majority, provides that the rules apply to removed actions and "govern procedure after removal." But the pre–1948 provision of the Judicial Code—which provided that the district court, after removal, shall "proceed therein as if the suit had been originally commenced in said district court"—was not carried forward in the new § 1447. Doesn't this omission lend further support to the position of the concurrence?

(2) *Statutory Repeal of the Doctrine That Removal Jurisdiction is "Derivative"*. Until 1986, subject matter jurisdiction in cases removed under § 1441 turned not only on the existence of original federal court jurisdiction in the removed case but also on the existence of state subject matter jurisdiction. Thus if a removed case was one within exclusive federal jurisdiction, the federal court was required to dismiss. See, *e.g.*, Lambert Run Coal Co. v. Baltimore & Ohio R.R., 258 U.S. 377 (1922).

Academic reaction to this rule was generally critical, and it was finally overturned by the 99th Congress, which added a new subsection (e) to § 1441 (100 Stat. 637 (1986)): "The court to which such civil action is removed is not precluded from hearing and determining any claim in such civil action because the State court from which such civil action is removed did not have jurisdiction over that claim."

(3) *Failure of the State Court to Obtain Territorial Jurisdiction over the Defendant*. An objection that the state court had not obtained personal jurisdiction over the defendant is not waived by removal to a federal court, Cain v. Commercial Publishing Co., 232 U.S. 124 (1914); and the state court's decision upholding jurisdiction may be reexamined by the district court, at least if the decision was interlocutory under state law, General Inv. Co. v. Lake Shore & M.S. Ry., 260 U.S. 261, 267 (1922), or is open to constitutional challenge, Goldey v. Morning News, 156 U.S. 518 (1895).

If the objection is sustained, and valid service cannot be made, the action should presumably be dismissed and not remanded. But 28 U.S.C. §§ 1447(a) and 1448 preserve the plaintiff's right to make or perfect service after removal. See 14A Wright, Miller & Cooper, Federal Practice and Procedure § 3722, at 290 (1985).[1]

(4) *Appealability of a Removed Criminal Case*. An interesting question of the relation between state and federal law in a removed criminal case arose in Arizona v. Manypenny, 451 U.S. 232 (1981). A state criminal prosecution of a federal official was removed to a federal district court under 28 U.S.C. § 1442(a)(1). After the jury rendered a guilty verdict, the trial judge upheld the defendant's immunity defense and entered a judgment of acquittal. When the state sought to appeal under the general appeal provisions of § 1291, the defendant invoked the rule of federal law that bars an appeal by the prosecu-

---

1. Thus, after removal, a plaintiff may be able to effect service under federal law (the 100–mile bulge provision of Rule 4, for example) on a party who was not amenable to service under state law.

tion in a criminal case in the absence of express authorization by Congress. The Supreme Court held, over two dissents, that since the prosecution was authorized to appeal under state law, the appeal should be allowed. "[T]he Court's prior decisions restricting the availability of § 1291 in a criminal context flow from a tradition of requiring that a prosecutorial appeal be affirmatively authorized by the same sovereign that sponsors the prosecution. * * * [Thus] Arizona can rely on § 1291 combined with appellate authorization from the Arizona Legislature" (p. 249).

NOTE ON THE PROCEDURE FOR DETERMINING REMOVABILITY AND ON THE TIME FOR REMOVAL

(1) *Procedure for Removal; Authority of a State Court with Respect to a Removed Case.*

(a) Before 1948, removal procedure varied according to the ground of removal. The 1948 revision eliminated these discrepancies, save for a few provisions peculiar to criminal prosecutions. Questions of the sufficiency of the petition and of removability are passed on by the federal court.[1]

(b) Does the 1948 revision eliminate the possibilities of inconvenience and conflict? Under the revision, state courts have generally held that once the required procedural steps are taken in a civil case,[2] all subsequent state action is void, even if the case is nonremovable, unless and until the case is remanded. See, *e.g.*, Hopson v. North Am. Ins. Co., 71 Idaho 461, 233 P.2d 799 (1951); Artists' Representatives Ass'n v. Haley, 26 A.D.2d 918, 274 N.Y.S.2d 442 (1966). But what if the removal petition reveals on its face that it has been filed out of time? What if the state court action is taken between the filing of the petition and the receipt of notice by the parties and the state court? See 14A Wright, Miller & Cooper, Federal Practice and Procedure § 3737, at 550 (1985)(suggesting that "the sounder rule" is that removal is not effective until all required steps have been taken). See also Burroughs v. Palumbo, 871 F.Supp. 870 (E.D.Va.1994)(holding that federal and state courts have concurrent jurisdiction in the period between the filing of notice in federal court and the filing of notice in state court).

(c) Do the authorities discussed in subparagraph (b) mean that if a petition for removal is filed in the middle of a state court jury trial, the trial must stop

---

1. Under the former procedure the state court had first to decide whether, on the face of the record including the petition, a case for removal had been made out. If the state court denied the petition, the defendant could (a) remain in the state courts and, if it lost on the merits, urge the denial as ground for reversal, Railroad Co. v. Koontz, 104 U.S. 5 (1881); (b) file a transcript of the record in the federal court, disregard the state proceedings and thus run the risk of a binding state judgment if the case was ultimately held nonremovable, Metropolitan Cas. Ins. Co. v. Ste-

vens, 312 U.S. 563 (1941); or (c) litigate in both courts at once in order to safeguard every flank. A federal court did have authority under the old procedure to protect the defendant from the danger of (b) or the burden of (c) by enjoining the plaintiff from further proceedings in the state court. See, *e.g.*, Madisonville Traction Co. v. Saint Bernard Mining Co., 196 U.S. 239 (1905).

2. As amended in 1977, § 1446 distinguishes between civil and criminal cases with respect to the authority of a state court over a removed action.

no matter how frivolous the claim for removal? Apparently so, at least if the petition does not reveal on its face that it has been filed out of time.[3] See ALI Study of the Division of Jurisdiction Between State and Federal Courts 358–60 and authorities there cited (1968). But see Burlington N.R.R. v. Bell, 482 U.S. 919 (1987)(White, J., dissenting from denial of certiorari).

(2) *Time Limits on Removal.*

(a) Before 1948, a petition for removal under the general removal statute had to be filed "at the time, or any time before the defendant is required by the laws of the State * * * to answer or plead to the declaration or complaint of the plaintiff". 24 Stat. 554 (1887), as amended, 25 Stat. 435 (1888). The provision yielded a mass of litigation over what happened when a case became removable only after this time had expired.

The 1948 revisers decided to replace the prior law's indefinite period for removal of a civil case with a definite period of twenty days (changed in 1965 to thirty days) from the date of filing the initial pleading. This change, they said, would "give adequate time and operate uniformly throughout the federal jurisdiction."[4] But the revisers overlooked the problem of post-filing events (such as voluntary dismissal of a party) that might make a non-removable case removable, and the provision had to be amended in 1949. Under the amended provision, the period begins to run, if the case was not at first removable, upon "receipt by the defendant, through service or otherwise, of a copy of an amended pleading, motion, order or other paper from which it may first be ascertained that the case is one which is or has become removable."[5] Even after the 1949 amendment, however, some courts have held that removal is available only if the post-commencement event that rendered the case removable was the result of a "voluntary" act of the plaintiff. See, *e.g.,* California v. Keating, 986 F.2d 346 (9th Cir.1993).[6]

(b) Some difficult questions have arisen as to when, if ever, the existence of the requisite amount in controversy is sufficiently established to start the clock running on the right to removal. In states that do not require (or do not permit) a specific sum to be demanded in the pleading, may the defendant remove if he can show that a recovery of more than $50,000 is possible, or likely? If so, when does the time start to run? In states following the pattern of Fed.R.Civ.P. 54(c)(allowing a grant of the relief to which the winner is entitled, even if not demanded in the pleadings), what is the effect of a specific demand for less than the jurisdictional amount if the complaint shows damages of more? Of a statement by counsel at the trial of such a case that more than $50,000 is sought? Of a jury verdict for $70,000 if no prior demand for

---

3. A 1988 amendment to § 1446(a) does address the problem of a frivolous effort to remove, requiring that a notice of removal be "signed pursuant to Rule 11 of the Federal Rules of Civil Procedure."

4. In the 1977 amendments to § 1446 (note 2, *supra*), Congress also changed the time limits for removal of a criminal case. Prior to that amendment, removal was allowed "at any time before trial."

5. But a 1988 amendment to § 1446(b) bars removal on the basis of diversity of citizenship more than one year after commencement of the action.

6. The private defendant in the Keating case had added the Resolution Trust Company (RTC) as a defendant in the state court, but the RTC (which had a statutory right to remove without the concurrence of any other party) had not chosen to remove, and the Ninth Circuit held that the addition of the RTC was not a "voluntary" act by a plaintiff that allowed the private defendant to remove.

judgment in excess of $50,000 has been made?[7]

(3) *Waiver*. The defendant may waive the right of removal, before the statutory period has expired, by action in the state court deemed inconsistent with that right. See Rosenthal v. Coates, 148 U.S. 142, 147 (1893), in which the Supreme Court referred to "the spirit of the removal acts, which do not contemplate that a party may experiment on his case in the state court, and, upon an adverse decision, then transfer it to the Federal court". See also 14A Wright, Miller & Cooper, Federal Practice and Procedure § 3721, at 223–24 (1985); *id.* 1995 Supp.

Given the short time limit on removal, does the waiver doctrine have any rational basis?

NOTE ON 28 U.S.C. § 1441(c): SEPARATE AND INDEPENDENT CLAIMS OR CAUSES OF ACTION

(1) *Historical Background*.

(a) The original Separable Controversy Act of July 27, 1866, 14 Stat. 306, authorized removal to the federal court of a separable controversy between citizens of different states when the entire suit was not removable under any other provision of law. But the 1875 act, as construed in Barney v. Latham, 103 U.S. 205 (1881), provided that the *whole* suit should be removed. The court, in other words, had first to inquire whether the suit included a controversy "which is wholly between citizens of different States, and which can be fully determined as between them", and then, if it found a controversy that was thus separable from the main suit, it was directed *not* to separate it. In this way the federal courts were called upon to determine many claims between co-citizens founded solely upon state law.

What was the constitutional justification, if any, for this jurisdiction? That it was ancillary to the exercise of jurisdiction over a controversy independently within Article III, and hence within the power of Congress to authorize under the Necessary and Proper Clause? That Strawbridge v. Curtiss did not state a constitutional principle, and that the whole suit was within Article III?

(b) The 1948 revision made three major changes in the former provisions relating to "separable controversies":

First, substitution for a "separable controversy" of a new standard of "a separate and independent claim or cause of action";

Second, provision for remand, at the district court's discretion, of matters not within the court's original jurisdiction; and

---

7. See Justices v. Murray, 76 U.S. (9 Wall.) 274 (1870), p. 458, *supra*. And compare Burns v. Windsor Ins. Co., 31 F.3d 1092 (11th Cir.1994)(plaintiff's refusal to stipulate that she will not amend her state court claim to seek more than $50,000 does not entitle the defendant to remove), with De Aguilar v. Boeing Co., 47 F.3d 1404 (5th Cir.1995)(if defendant shows that the amount in controversy actually exceeds $50,000, plaintiff can prevent removal only by showing that, as a matter of law, he cannot recover more than the lesser amount prayed for in the state court complaint).

See generally 14A Wright, Miller & Cooper, Federal Practice and Procedure § 3725 (1985 & 1995 Supp.).

Third, elimination of the former restriction to controversies "wholly between citizens of different States", and the extension of the authority to remove to cases in which federal jurisdiction over the separate claim was based on the presence of a federal question, alienage, or any other ground.

The Reviser's notes included the following explanation:

"Subsection (c) permits the removal of a separate cause of action but not of a separable controversy unless it constitutes a separate and independent claim or cause of action within the original jurisdiction of United States District Courts. In this respect it will somewhat decrease the volume of Federal litigation.

"Rules 18, 20, and 23 of the Federal Rules of Civil Procedure permit the most liberal joinder of parties, claims, and remedies in civil actions. Therefore there will be no procedural difficulty occasioned by the removal of the entire action. Conversely, if the court so desires, it may remand to the State court all nonremovable matters."

Was this an accurate explanation or an adequate disclosure of what was actually done?

Consider whether the following is an unfair paraphrase of § 1441(c) as revised in 1948: "When a matter that would be independently within federal jurisdiction is associated in a state court proceeding with matters that would not be independently within federal jurisdiction, the whole proceeding can be removed to the federal court if the state and federal matters are sufficiently *disconnected.*" If this paraphrase is accurate, what was the rationale of the revision?

(c) The major Supreme Court decision interpreting the provisions of § 1441(c) as enacted in 1948 is American Fire & Casualty Co. v. Finn, 341 U.S. 6 (1951). In this case, a state court action to recover for a fire loss was brought by a Texas citizen against American Fire & Casualty (a Florida corporation), Lumbermen's Insurance (an Indiana corporation), and one Reiss (a local agent of both corporations and a citizen of Texas). The two corporations removed the entire case to a federal court under § 1441(c); after trial, judgment was entered against American and for the other two defendants. On appeal, American challenged the removability of the action that it had joined in removing, and the Supreme Court agreed with the challenge.

The Court started its analysis by stating that a case was not removable under the new provision if there was "a single wrong to plaintiff, for which relief is sought, arising from an interlocked series of transactions" (p. 14). Under this test, no "separate and independent claim or cause of action" existed in the case at bar because every portion of the complaint involving either insurance company also involved Reiss as agent and because the damage claimed arose from a single incident. Since § 1441(c) was unavailable, the action was not removable.

The Court also rejected the argument that American, as the defendant who removed, was estopped from attacking removability. The Court stated that the decisions supporting an estoppel (discussed at pp. 1629–31, *infra*) all involved situations in which the federal court would have had original jurisdiction even though the case was not removable.[1] Justice Douglas, joined by Justices Black and Minton, dissented on this issue.

---

1. The Court did not consider whether vacation of the original judgment, followed by dismissal of the non-diverse defendant Reiss, would permit a new judgment against Ameri-

(d) The Report of the Federal Courts Study Committee in 1990 recommended repeal of § 1441(c). See Report 94–95; see also Rothfeld, *Rationalizing Removal,* 1990 B.Y.U.L.Rev. 221, 234–41. Congress responded, in the same year, by amending the section to apply only to separate and independent federal question claims (*i.e.,* those arising under § 1331) and by changing the district court's authority to "remand all matters not within its original jurisdiction" to an authority to "remand all matters in which State law predominates." The legislative history states that the amended provision allows removal of cases that join a federal claim with a completely unrelated state claim, as permitted by some state joinder rules, and thus avoids the need to determine whether the state claim is one over which there is pendent jurisdiction. See H.R. 101–734, 101st Cong., 2d Sess. 23 (1990).

(2) *The Constitutionality and Scope of Amended § 1441(c).* The concept of supplemental jurisdiction, as articulated in new § 1367 (a provision enacted at the same time as amended § 1441(c) and that is discussed at pp. 971–73, 1564–67, *supra*), is defined in subsection (a) as reaching to the full extent of Article III. Since § 1367 evidently applies to removed cases as well as to original federal actions, does what is left of § 1441(c) have any constitutional application,[2] or any utility, in cases not removable under the general removal provisions of § 1441(a)?

(a) Many commentators have argued that the amended section serves no valid purpose, but this position is forcefully countered by an exhaustive study by Professor Hartnett, *A New Trick from an Old and Abused Dog: Section 1441(c) Lives and Now Permits the Remand of Federal Question Cases,* 73 Fordham L.Rev. 1099 (1995).

After exploring in detail the history of § 1441(c) and its interpretation in the Finn case, Hartnett notes that in some situations, a state court plaintiff may be able to preclude removal of the entire case under the general removal provision (§ 1441(a)) by combining a removable claim with a claim made nonremovable by statute. Two instances in which both claims would fall within the scope of Article III are (i) a case in which both claims are federal question claims but in one, removal is precluded by statute (*e.g.,* an FELA claim brought in a state court, see 28 U.S.C. § 1445),[3] and (ii) a case in which the nonremovable claim is one in which there is neither a federal question nor complete diversity but in which there is minimal diversity sufficient to satisfy Article III. In both instances, removal would be allowed only under § 1441(c) and would be constitutional.[4]

---

can to be entered on remand without a new trial. For the treatment of this issue on remand, see p. 1630, *infra*.

2. Prior to the enactment of § 1367 and the revision limiting the applicability of § 1441(c) to federal question cases, similar questions were raised about the relationship between the Gibbs test for ancillary or pendent jurisdiction and the reach and validity of § 1441(c) in both the diversity and federal question contexts. See, *e.g.,* Cohen, *Problems in the Removal of a "Separate and Independent Claim or Cause of Action,"* 46 Minn. L.Rev. 1 (1961).

3. But *should* the FELA claim be adjudicated in a federal court in such a case? Does § 1441(c), in other words, trump the policy underlying § 1445?

4. Analogous to the first example is an action in which a state court plaintiff asserts two federal question claims, but in one, the claim is against a state official or entity that has an Eleventh Amendment immunity defense. If this defense deprives a federal district court of "jurisdiction", removal of the entire case would presumably be available, if

Further, Hartnett notes that in many states, liberal joinder rules allow the joinder of claims that probably extend beyond the scope of a constitutional "case" under Article III. In such instances, Hartnett argues that (i) § 1441(c) is applicable to permit removal even when the unrelated claim falls outside Article III jurisdiction (and thus the general removal provision in § 1441(a) is unavailable), and (ii) the Constitution does not bar a federal court in such a case from determining the extent of its jurisdiction, although the required disposition may be to remand to state court the claim that falls beyond the scope of Article III. (Thus a state court plaintiff is effectively deterred from barring removal of a federal question claim by combining it with a "separate and independent" nonremovable state law claim.) Finally, Hartnett suggests that the new language of § 1441(c), referring to the court's discretion to remand "all matters in which State law predominates", authorizes federal courts in some instances to remand the *entire* case, including the removable claim, to a state court.

If, as Hartnett argues, the Constitution in many instances *requires* remand of the nonremovable claim to state court, why does the text of § 1441(c) speak only of "discretion" to remand?

(b) *The Scope of § 1441(c).* Constitutional limitations aside, what kinds of cases can be removed under § 1441(c) as now interpreted? Suppose that the petitioner (American) in Finn had insured only part of the risk and that the claim against Reiss touched only the question of the remainder of the risk with the other company. Would the claim against the petitioner then have been "separate and independent"?

For the view that "separate and independent claims are presented * * * if recovery upon one of the claims would not preclude enforcement of the other", see Note, *The Supreme Court, 1950 Term*, 65 Harv.L.Rev. 107, 166–68 (1951). But language in the Finn decision is difficult to square with this approach. Would it be accurate at least to say that separate and independent claims are *not* presented if recovery on one *would* preclude enforcement of the other?

(3) *"Fraudulent Joinder" of a Defendant Who is Not Entitled to Remove.* Suppose that in the Finn case there had been no basis for the plaintiff's claim against Reiss. The doctrine has long been recognized that the "fraudulent" joinder of a defendant who is not entitled to remove (perhaps because no federal claim is asserted against her and she is a citizen of the state in which the action was brought) is no bar to removal. If a petition for removal contained allegations sufficient, if proved, to show "fraud", the state court was bound to grant the petition, leaving the proof to be made in the federal court. But a mere purpose to defeat removal did not constitute fraud, even though the resident defendant was known to be judgment-proof. Illinois Cent. R.R. v. Sheegog, 215 U.S. 308 (1909). The plaintiff must be shown to have known that his claim was groundless in fact or in law, or else to have closed his eyes to evidence that would have shown it to be so. Wecker v. National Enameling & Stamping Co., 204 U.S. 176 (1907); Parks v. New York Times Co., 308 F.2d 474 (5th Cir.1962).

---

at all, only if the removable claim constituted a "separate and independent" claim or cause of action under § 1441(c). See, *e.g.,* Frances v. Wright, 19 F.3d 337, 341 (7th Cir.1994)(holding such an action unremovable under § 1441(a)).

NOTE ON THE DOCTRINE OF ESTOPPEL AND ON THE EFFECT UPON
REMOVAL JURISDICTION OF POST–REMOVAL EVENTS

(1) *The Baggs–Mackay Doctrine.*

(a) In Baggs v. Martin, 179 U.S. 206 (1900)(cited and distinguished on the estoppel issue by the Court's opinion in Finn), a state court action against a railroad receiver had been removed by the receiver to the federal circuit court that had appointed him. After judgment had gone against the receiver on the merits, he raised the question of jurisdiction for the first time in the circuit court of appeals. Answering certified questions, the Supreme Court assumed that the case was not within the removal statute, but held "that, in the present case, the receiver, having voluntarily brought the cause into the Circuit Court by whose appointment he held his office, cannot, after that court has passed upon the matter in controversy, be heard to object to the power of that court to render judgment therein". Explaining this holding, the Court said (179 U.S. at 209):

"We do not mean to be understood to say that mere consent, or even voluntary action by the parties, can confer jurisdiction upon a court which would not have possessed it without such consent or action. But here the Circuit Court had, independently of the citizenship of the parties in the damage suit, jurisdiction over the railroad and its property in the hands of its receiver. It may be that its jurisdiction was not, by reason of the act of March 3, 1887, exclusive of that of other courts in controversies like the present one. But when the receiver, waiving any right he might have had to have the cause tried in a state court, brought it before the court whose officer he was, he cannot successfully dispute its jurisdiction."

The reasoning in Baggs v. Martin was more fully developed in Mackay v. Uinta Dev. Co., 229 U.S. 173 (1913). A Wyoming corporation had sued Mackay, a citizen of Utah, in a Wyoming state court upon a non-federal claim for less than the jurisdictional amount. Mackay then counterclaimed upon a federal claim for more than the jurisdictional amount, and thereafter removed the entire case to the federal circuit court, where the company had judgment on the merits. The circuit court of appeals raised the jurisdictional question on its own motion and certified it to the Supreme Court.

The Supreme Court assumed without deciding that the removal was improper, but upheld the jurisdiction. It said (pp. 176–77):

"* * * The case was removed in fact, and, while the parties could not give jurisdiction by consent, there was the requisite amount and the diversity of citizenship necessary to give the United States Circuit Court jurisdiction of the cause. The case, therefore, resolves itself into an inquiry as to whether, if irregularly removed, it could be lawfully tried and determined.

"* * *

"What took place in the state court may * * * be disregarded by the court because it was waived by the parties, and regardless of the manner in which the case was brought or how the attendance of the parties in the United States court was secured, there was presented to the Circuit Court a controversy between citizens of different States in which the amount claimed by one non-resident was more than $2,000, exclusive of interest and costs. As the court had jurisdiction of the subject-matter the parties could have been realigned by making Mackay plaintiff and the Development Company defendant, if that had been found proper. But if there was any irregularity in docketing the case or in the order of the pleadings such an irregularity was waivable and neither it nor the method of getting the parties before the court operated to deprive it of the power to determine the cause."

(c) Look again at the text of 28 U.S.C. § 1447(c). Does this shake the Baggs–Mackay principle? No court has so held, and the most recent Supreme Court decision applying the principle, Grubbs v. General Elec. Credit Corp., 405 U.S. 699 (1972), makes no mention of the provision.

(d) Is the Baggs–Mackay doctrine in tension with the principle, developed in Section 1 of this Chapter and exemplified by the Mansfield case, p. 1578, *supra*, that an objection to subject matter jurisdiction can not be waived, at least prior to final judgment and the completion of direct review? May the doctrine be invoked only when the case could have been filed originally in federal court under existing statutes? What if there is no existing statute but the case is within the scope of jurisdiction authorized by Article III?

(e) Should the Baggs–Mackay doctrine be extended to bar the removing defendant from objecting to any curative amendment offered by the plaintiff for the purpose of establishing jurisdiction retroactively? On remand of the Finn case, the district court allowed dismissal as to all defendants except American Fire & Casualty Co., and then ordered a second trial. On appeal by Finn from a judgment for defendant following the second trial, the court of appeals held that after dismissal of the other defendants, judgment for the plaintiff should have been entered on the original record. Finn v. American Fire & Cas. Co., 207 F.2d 113 (5th Cir.1953). See *Note on the Effects of Misjoinder of Parties*, p. 1531, *supra*.

(2) *The Effect of Amendment After Removal.* If jurisdiction exists at the time of removal, what is the effect of a later effort by the plaintiff to oust that jurisdiction?

A plaintiff unquestionably can defeat removal jurisdiction by dismissing his complaint in the federal court. Thereafter he can try to state a non-removable case in a fresh action in the state court.

What of steps short of outright dismissal, such as amendment of the complaint (a) to reduce the ad damnum below the jurisdictional amount, or (b) to eliminate the federal claim on which removal jurisdiction was based, leaving only a state claim for adjudication?[5] Although (a) has long been held not to oust jurisdiction, or to permit remand, St. Paul Mercury Indemnity Co. v. Red Cab Co., 303 U.S. 283 (1938), there was for some years a conflict on (b) in the lower courts. That conflict was resolved in 1988 when the Supreme Court held that while a district court has discretion to retain jurisdiction in such a case, it also has discretion to remand, as well as to dismiss. Carnegie–Mellon Univ. v. Cohill, 484 U.S. 343 (1988). The decision seems consistent with the discretionary scope of supplemental jurisdiction first articulated in UMW v. Gibbs, p. 962, *supra*, and later in § 1367. The Court in Carnegie–Mellon distinguished St. Paul Mercury on that ground, adding that "forum manipulation concerns" (p. 356 n. 12) could be dealt with by the court in the exercise of its discretion. Broad language in Thermtron Products, Inc. v. Hermansdorfer, p. 1667, *infra*— to the effect that a court may never remand a case to a state court on a ground

---

5. In 1988, Congress added a new § 1447(e), providing that "[i]f after removal the plaintiff seeks to join additional defendants whose joinder would destroy subject matter jurisdiction, the court may deny joinder, or permit joinder and remand the action to the State court."

not specified in the removal statute—was also distinguished on the basis of the discretionary nature of pendent jurisdiction. See generally Swing, *Federal Common Law Power to Remand a Removed Case,* 136 U.Pa.L.Rev. 583 (1987).[6]

SECTION 4. CONFLICTS OF JURISDICTION AMONG FEDERAL COURTS

Kerotest Manufacturing Co. v. C–O–Two Fire Equipment Co.

342 U.S. 180, 72 S.Ct. 219, 96 L.Ed. 200 (1952).
Certiorari to the United States Court of Appeals for the Third Circuit.

■ MR. JUSTICE FRANKFURTER delivered the opinion of the Court.

The C–O–Two Fire Equipment Company, the respondent here, owns two patents * * * for squeeze-grip valves and discharge heads for portable fire extinguishers. C–O–Two, incorporated in Delaware, has offices in Newark, New Jersey. On January 17, 1950, it commenced in the District Court for the Northern District of Illinois an action against the Acme Equipment Company for "making and causing to be made and selling and using" devices which were charged with infringing C–O–Two's patents.

On March 9, 1950, the petitioner Kerotest began in the District Court of Delaware this proceeding against C–O–Two for a declaration that the two patents sued on in the Illinois action are invalid and that the devices which Kerotest manufactures and supplies to Acme, the Illinois defendant, do not infringe the C–O–Two patents. Kerotest, a Pennsylvania corporation, has its offices in Pittsburgh, but was subject to service of process in Illinois. C–O–Two on March 22, 1950, filed an amendment to its complaint joining Kerotest as a defendant in the Illinois action.

In Delaware, C–O–Two moved for a stay of the declaratory judgment action and Kerotest sought to enjoin C–O–Two from prosecuting the Illinois suit "whether as against Kerotest alone, or generally, as [the Delaware District Court might] deem just and proper." The District Court stayed the Delaware proceeding and refused to enjoin that in Illinois, subject to reexamination of the questions after 90 days. On appeal by Kerotest, the Court of Appeals for the Third Circuit affirmed, holding that the District Court had not abused its discretion in staying the Delaware action for 90 days to permit it to get "more information concerning the controverted status of Kerotest in the Illinois suit".

6. Professor Wright objects to those lower court decisions that have interpreted Carnegie–Mellon to endorse discretionary authority to remand the entire case, including the undismissed federal claims that were the basis for removal. See Wright, Federal Courts § 41, at 252 (5th ed. 1994).

For the view that at least in some instances, a court does have discretion to remand an entire case properly removed under § 1441(a), see Hartnett, p. 1627, *supra,* at 1175–81.

For further discussion of the power to remand, see Steinman, *Removal, Remand, and Review in Pendent Claim and Pendent Party Cases,* 41 Vand.L.Rev. 923 (1988); Steinman, *Postremoval Changes in the Party Structure of Diversity Cases: The Old Law, the New Law, and Rule 19,* 38 U.Kan.L.Rev. 863 (1990).

During the 90–day period the Illinois District Court allowed the joinder of Kerotest as a defendant, denying a motion by Acme to stay the Illinois proceeding pending disposition of the Delaware suit, and Kerotest made a general appearance. After 90 days both parties renewed their motions in Delaware, with Kerotest this time asking that C–O–Two be enjoined from prosecuting the Illinois suit only as to Kerotest. The District Court, a different judge sitting, enjoined C–O–Two from proceeding in the Illinois suit against Kerotest, and denied the stay of the Delaware action, largely acting on the assumption that rulings by its own and other Courts of Appeals required such a result except in "exceptional cases," since the Delaware action between C–O–Two and Kerotest was commenced before Kerotest was made a defendant in the Illinois suit. On appeal, the Court of Appeals for the Third Circuit reversed, saying in part: "* * * the whole of the war and all the parties to it are in the Chicago theatre and there only can it be fought to a finish as the litigations are now cast. On the other hand if the battle is waged in the Delaware arena there is a strong probability that the Chicago suit nonetheless would have to be proceeded with for Acme is not and cannot be made a party to the Delaware litigation. The Chicago suit when adjudicated will bind all the parties in both cases. Why, under the circumstances, should there be two litigations where one will suffice? We can find no adequate reason. We assume, of course, that there will be prompt action in the Chicago theatre."

* * * [On rehearing en banc, the court of appeals adhered, 5–2, to the panel decision.]

* * * The conclusion which we are asked to upset derives from an extended and careful study of the circumstances of this litigation. Such an estimate has led the Court of Appeals twice to conclude that all interests will be best served by prosecution of the single suit in Illinois. Even if we had more doubts than we do about the analysis made by the Court of Appeals, we would not feel justified in displacing its judgment with ours.

It was strongly pressed upon us that the result below may encourage owners of weak patents to avoid a real test of their patents' validity by successive suits against customers in forums inconvenient for the manufacturer, or selected because of greater hospitality to patents. Such apprehension implies a lack of discipline and of disinterestedness on the part of the lower courts, hardly a worthy or wise basis for fashioning rules of procedure. It reflects an attitude against which we were warned by Mr. Justice Holmes, speaking for the whole Court, likewise in regard to a question of procedure: "Universal distrust creates universal incompetence." Graham v. United States, 231 U.S. 474, 480. If in a rare instance a district judge abuses the discretionary authority the want of which precludes an effective, independent judiciary, there is always the opportunity for corrective review by a Court of Appeals and ultimately by this Court.

The manufacturer who is charged with infringing a patent cannot stretch the Federal Declaratory Judgments Act to give him a paramount right to choose the forum for trying out questions of infringement and validity. He is given an equal start in the race to the courthouse, not a headstart. If he is forehanded, subsequent suits against him by the patentee can within the trial court's discretion be enjoined pending determination of the declaratory judgment suit, and a judgment in his favor bars suits against his customers. If he is anticipated, the court's discretion is broad enough to protect him from harassment of his customers. If the patentee's suit against a customer is brought in a district where the manufacturer cannot be joined as a defendant, the manufacturer may be permitted simultaneously to prosecute a declaratory action against the patentee elsewhere. And if the manufacturer is joined as an unwilling defendant in a *forum non conveniens,* he has available upon an appropriate showing the relief provided by § 1404(a) of the Judiciary Code. Affirmed.

■ THE CHIEF JUSTICE and MR. JUSTICE BLACK dissent.

NOTE ON THE TREATMENT OF DUPLICATIVE ACTIONS IN THE FEDERAL COURTS*

(1) *Multiple Federal Actions Between the Same Parties.*

(a) Should it be a postulate of federal judicial administration that there ought to be no more than one trial of a controversy between the same parties at the same time in the federal courts, and that accordingly, when duplicative actions of this kind are instituted, the only problem is to decide which action should be allowed to proceed?

Are the three-fold devices of stay (or abatement), injunction against the other proceeding, and transfer to the other district under 28 U.S.C. § 1404(a), adequate to accomplish such an objective? When one proceeding includes additional parties not joined in the other? When decisions in each district are subject to revision by different courts of appeals?

(b) The common law plea of a prior action pending called for the abatement of the second action, when both courts were in the same jurisdiction and the parties and cause of action were identical. See Clark, Code Pleading 505, 603 (2d ed. 1947).

A more flexible instrument than abatement is the discretionary power of a court to stay its proceedings, which may be exercised where abatement would not be permissible or appropriate. The considerable latitude of the federal courts in granting stays is illustrated by the landmark decision in Landis v. North American Co., 299 U.S. 248 (1936), recognizing a limited power to stay an action pending the outcome of other proceedings having only a stare decisis bearing on the case at bar. Justice Cardozo said (p. 254):

"* * * [T]he power to stay proceedings is incidental to the power inherent in every court to control the disposition of the causes on its docket with economy of time and effort for itself, for counsel, and for litigants".

(c) It has long been held that, where a controversy between the same parties is simultaneously before two state courts of coordinate jurisdiction, whether in the same or different states, the first court to obtain jurisdiction may in its discretion enjoin the parties (not the court) from carrying on the second proceeding. See 2 Story, Equity Jurisprudence 560 (14th ed. 1918). Assertion of the power of a federal court to enjoin proceedings in another federal court was a later development. In Steelman v. All Continent Corp., 301 U.S. 278 (1937), the Court upheld the power of a bankruptcy court to enjoin an allegedly fraudulent action against the trustee in bankruptcy in another district

---

* For extensive treatment of the problems presented by parallel proceedings in federal and state courts, see Chap. X, and especially Sec. 2(D), *supra.*

court. The power came, Justice Cardozo said, from the all-writs section, now 28 U.S.C. § 1651, and the provision of the Bankruptcy Act investing the bankruptcy court with equity jurisdiction.

(2) *Analysis and Critique of the Kerotest Rationale.*

(a) What is the precise holding in Kerotest? Whose discretion is to be left largely undisturbed? That of the courts in the first district or in the second? That of the district court or of the court of appeals? *Cf.* Semmes Motors, Inc. v. Ford Motor Co., 429 F.2d 1197, 1203 (2d Cir.1970)(there are "insufficient grounds for * * * [the district court's departure] from the general rule that in the absence of sound reasons the second action should give way to the first").

In Note, *The Supreme Court, 1951 Term,* 66 Harv.L.Rev. 89, 169–70 (1952), it is suggested that the danger of conflicting decisions in different districts and circuits might have been avoided in Kerotest "by the adoption of a strict rule to determine the proper court to decide which action should be given priority". What should be the content of such a rule?

(b) In evaluating Kerotest, what weight should be given to the fact that a declaratory judgment action was involved? *Cf.* Brillhart v. Excess Ins. Co. of America, 316 U.S. 491 (1942), discussed at p. 1316, *supra.*

(3) *The Consumers Union Litigation.* A difficult problem of conflicting federal court orders under the Freedom of Information Act, 5 U.S.C. § 552, was resolved as a matter of statutory construction in GTE Sylvania, Inc. v. Consumers Union, 445 U.S. 375 (1980). When the Consumer Product Safety Commission (CPSC) was contemplating releasing to Consumers Union (CU) certain documents CU had requested under the Freedom of Information Act, GTE and others brought suit against the CPSC in the District of Delaware and elsewhere to enjoin release, claiming that such disclosure was prohibited by the Consumer Product Safety Act, 15 U.S.C. § 2055, and other laws. The Delaware federal court issued a preliminary injunction and, ultimately, a permanent injunction against release that was affirmed by the Third Circuit. CU did not seek to intervene in that action but instead (after the filing of the Delaware action and the issuance of certain temporary restraining orders but before the Delaware court's issuance of the preliminary injunction) filed suit against the CPSC in the District of Columbia to compel release under the Freedom of Information Act. The district court dismissed the action for want of a case or controversy.

The D.C. Circuit reversed, holding that there was a sufficient controversy and that the suit was not foreclosed by the Delaware action; it adhered to this position even after the Supreme Court had remanded (434 U.S. 1030 (1978)) for reconsideration in light of the intervening issuance of a permanent injunction by the Delaware district court. The Supreme Court granted certiorari to review the decisions of both circuits.

Reversing the decision of the D.C. Circuit before deciding the Third Circuit case on the merits, the Supreme Court unanimously held that (a) there was a case or controversy within the scope of Article III and (b) the CPSC could not be ordered to release the documents because those documents had not been "improperly" withheld within the meaning of the Freedom of Information Act, 5 U.S.C. § 552(a)(4)(B). The Delaware district court plainly had jurisdiction to issue its decrees; they had more than a "frivolous pretense to validity" (p. 386, quoting Walker v. Birmingham, 388 U.S. 307, 315 (1967)); and the CPSC's lawful obedience of a federal court injunction thus could not be considered improper.

Does this decision have any implications for the doctrines of res judicata (since CU was not a party to the Delaware action) or of comity between federal courts? Or is its significance confined to the precise question of statutory construction decided by the Supreme Court? (See p. 387 n. 11, where the Court says that it "need not address" the issue of comity.)

(4) *Lower Court Practice.* When the same parties litigate the same issues in two or more federal district courts, the litigation filed first will generally take precedence. See, *e.g.,* Cianbro Corp. v. Curran–Lavoie, Inc., 814 F.2d 7, 11 (1st Cir.1987); West Gulf Maritime Ass'n v. ILA Deep Sea Local 24, 751 F.2d 721, 730 (5th Cir.1985). The "first filed" preference may be overridden, however, if the factual circumstances render the second forum significantly more suitable. See, *e.g.,* Private Medical Care Foundation, Inc. v. Califano, 451 F.Supp. 450, 452–53 (W.D.Ok.1977)(second litigation was at a more advanced stage); Columbia Pictures Indus., Inc. v. Schneider, 435 F.Supp. 742, 748 (S.D.N.Y. 1977)(doubts about personal jurisdiction in first forum).

See generally 28 Wright, Miller & Cooper, Federal Practice and Procedure § 4247 (1981 and 1995 Supp.).

CHAPTER XV

APPELLATE REVIEW OF FEDERAL DECISIONS AND THE CERTIORARI POLICY

SECTION 1.   STATUTORY DEVELOPMENT

(1) *1789–1891*.   The court structure established by the First Judiciary Act and the system of appellate review thus created are described in broad outline in Chapter I. They were maintained more than a century, with changes only of detail, before the Evarts Act[1] laid the foundation of the present plan.   Long before 1891, however, it was acknowledged that the circuit courts were ill-equipped for the performance of appellate duties and that reviewing both the circuit and the district courts placed an intolerable burden on the Supreme Court.[2]   Only the slow development of criminal appeals[3] and jurisdictional amount requirements in some cases[4] stood between most unsuccessful litigants and a determination of their cases by the highest court.

(2) *The Evarts Act of 1891*.   The Evarts Act interposed the circuit courts of appeals between the Supreme Court and the circuit and district courts, stripping the circuit courts of their appellate jurisdiction.

Section 5 provided direct Supreme Court review of circuit or district court decisions in six categories of cases (including a range of cases raising constitutional issues).   Section 6 conferred jurisdiction on the circuit courts of appeals to review a "final decision" in all other cases, "unless otherwise provided by law."   It declared that the circuit court of appeals decision "shall be final in all cases in which the jurisdiction is dependent entirely upon the opposite parties to the suit or controversy, being aliens and citizens of the United States or citizens of different States; also in all cases arising under the patent laws, under the revenue laws, and under the criminal laws and in admiralty cases," subject to the power of the court of appeals to certify to the Supreme Court "any questions or propositions of law concerning which it desires the instruction of that court for its proper decision" and the power of the Supreme Court "to require, by certiorari or otherwise, any such case to be certified * * * for its

---

1.   Act of Mar. 3, 1891, 26 Stat. 826.

2.   See Frankfurter & Landis, The Business of the Supreme Court 56–102 (1928).

3.   Until 1889, criminal cases were reviewable by the Supreme Court only in the event of a division of opinion in the circuit court on a question of law (Act of Apr. 29, 1802, § 6, 2 Stat. 156, 159–61 (certification); Act of June 1, 1872, § 1, 17 Stat. 196) or

within the limited range of issues that could be raised by habeas corpus. The Act of Feb. 6, 1889, § 6, 25 Stat. 655, 656, granted a writ of error in capital cases only, extended by the Evarts Act to "infamous crimes."

4.   The jurisdictional amount, fixed in 1789 at $2000, was raised to $5000 in 1875. Many cases were reviewable, however, without regard to amount.

review and determination * * * as if it had been carried by appeal or writ of error to the Supreme Court."

Except in cases where the decision of the circuit court of appeals was thus declared to be final, courts of appeals decisions were reviewable by the Supreme Court as of right "where the matter in controversy shall exceed one thousand dollars besides costs."

Section 7 of the Act, initiating a departure from the general finality requirement, authorized appeal to a circuit court of appeals from "an interlocutory order or decree granting or continuing" an injunction in cases in which a final decree would be appealable to the circuit court of appeals.

(3) *1891–1925.* The distribution of appellate jurisdiction effected by the Evarts Act was not drastically altered until the enactment of the Judges' Bill in 1925.[5] Among the changes in the intervening years, however, were three of note:

(a) The Criminal Appeals Act of 1907 authorized direct Supreme Court review of a judgment quashing a criminal indictment on the ground that it was based on an invalid statute.[6]

(b) The Expediting Act of 1903 and later legislation providing for a special three-judge court in certain cases also provided for direct review of the three-judge court's determinations by the Supreme Court.[7]

(c) Under the Evarts Act, decisions of the circuit courts of appeals were reviewable as of right in the Supreme Court in many types of cases, and the number grew as Congress enacted new substantive legislation.[8] The principle of discretionary review was applied, however, to cases under the Trademark Act of 1905,[9] other trademark cases, all bankruptcy cases[10] and, most important, cases under the Federal Employers' Liability Act.[11]

(4) *The Act of 1925 and the Growth of Discretionary Supreme Court Jurisdiction.* The Judges' Bill of 1925 dealt a blow to obligatory Supreme Court review of circuit court of appeals decisions. Under its terms such review was preserved only "where is drawn in question the validity of a statute of any state, on the grounds of its being repugnant to the Constitution, treaties or laws of the United States, and the decision is against its validity"; and even then obligatory review was "restricted to an examination and decision of the Federal questions presented" and could be sought only by the party relying on state law.[12] In all other situations the jurisdiction of the Supreme Court could be invoked to pass on court of appeals decisions only by certificate[13] or (before as well as after final judgment of the court of appeals) by certiorari.[14] It could, however, be invoked without regard to jurisdictional amount.

The Act also contracted greatly the area of direct Supreme Court review of the district courts. The categories of cases in which the Evarts Act preserved

---

5. Act of Feb. 13, 1925, 43 Stat. 936.

6. Act of Mar. 2, 1907, 34 Stat. 1246.

7. See pp. 1212–15, *supra.*

8. See the enumeration by Chief Justice Taft quoted in Frankfurter & Landis, note 2, *supra,* at 261–62.

9. Act of Feb. 20, 1905, § 18, 33 Stat. 724, 729.

10. Act of Jan. 28, 1915, §§ 2, 4, 38 Stat. 803, 804.

11. Act of Sept. 6, 1916, § 3, 39 Stat. 726, 727.

12. Judicial Code § 240(b), 28 U.S.C. § 347(b)(1940).

13. Judicial Code § 239, 28 U.S.C. § 346 (1940).

14. Judicial Code § 240(a), 28 U.S.C. § 347(a)(1940).

direct review were all eliminated, shifting appellate jurisdiction to the circuit courts of appeals. Direct review was maintained, however, in a group of important cases where it had been authorized by later legislation: suits in equity brought by the United States to restrain violations of the Anti–Trust or Interstate Commerce Acts; suits to enjoin enforcement of certain orders of the Interstate Commerce Commission or of the Secretary of Agriculture under the Packers and Stockyards Act; suits to enjoin enforcement of state statutes or administrative orders governed by Section 266 of the Judicial Code; and government appeals under the Criminal Appeals Act.[15] All but the criminal cases were required to be heard in the first instance by a three-judge court (some only on certificate of the Attorney General), a tribunal of comparable dignity to a circuit court of appeals. Where preserved, direct review remained as a matter of right.

(5) *Developments Since 1925: Continuing Reduction of Obligatory Review.* The provisions for direct review by the Supreme Court were extended in a number of instances after 1925,[16] but the movement towards reduction of a right of appeal to the Supreme Court from the lower federal courts began again in 1950. In that year, Congress substituted court of appeals review for the existing procedures as the mode of challenging orders issued under the Federal Communications Act, Packers and Stockyards Act, Perishable Agricultural Commodities Act, and the Shipping Acts.[17] In 1974, partly as a result of dissatisfaction expressed by Supreme Court Justices themselves, see United States v. Singer Mfg. Co., 374 U.S. 174, 175 n. 1 (1963), Congress eliminated the provision of the Expediting Act requiring direct appeals to the Supreme Court in all antitrust and Interstate Commerce Act cases in which the United States was a party.[18] And the following year, Congress repealed the require-

---

15. Judicial Code § 238, 28 U.S.C. § 345 (1940). See also California v. United States, 320 U.S. 577, 579 (1944).

16. These instances included: (a) extending the Expediting Act to civil suits to enforce Title II of the Communications Act (see Act of June 19, 1934, § 401(d), 48 Stat. 1093); (b) requiring a three-judge court in suits to restrain other administrative orders (see, *e.g.,* Act of June 10, 1930, § 11, 46 Stat. 535); (c) requiring a three-judge court in suits to enjoin the enforcement of an Act of Congress on constitutional grounds, with direct Supreme Court review of a judgment granting or denying injunctive relief (see Act of Aug. 24, 1937, § 3, 50 Stat. 752); (d) providing for an appeal to the Supreme Court from any judgment invalidating a federal statute when the United States or a federal officer or agency was a party (see *id.,* § 2); and (e) providing for a three-judge court, and a direct appeal to the Supreme Court, in certain cases arising under the Voting Rights Acts of 1965 and 1970 (see 42 U.S.C. §§ 1973b, 1973c (1965 Act); 42 U.S.C. §§ 1973aa–2, 1973bb(a)(2)(1970 Act)) and the Civil Rights Act of 1964 (see 42 U.S.C. §§ 1971(g), 2000a–5(b), 2000e–6(b)).

17. 64 Stat. 1129 (1950)(the relevant provisions are now contained in 28 U.S.C. § 2342).

18. Sections 4–6, 88 Stat. 1708–09 (1974), 15 U.S.C. §§ 28, 29, 49 U.S.C. §§ 44, 45. Section 1 now provides that if a certificate of general importance is filed by the Attorney General in an action covered by the Act, the action must be expedited but is no longer to be heard by a three-judge court. Section 2 now provides that appeals are to be taken to the court of appeals unless upon application of a party after final judgment the district judge enters an order "stating that immediate consideration of the appeal by the Supreme Court is of general public importance in the administration of justice"; in that event the Supreme Court may either dispose of the appeal and any cross appeal or, in its discretion, deny direct appeal and remand the case to the court of appeals. The end result of the statute is only marginally different from certiorari practice—under which certiorari may be granted before as well as after judgment in the courts of appeals. 28 U.S.C. § 1254(1).

ment that suits for injunctive relief from Interstate Commerce Commission orders be heard by three-judge courts, subject to direct Supreme Court review.[19]

Perhaps most important, Congress in 1976 repealed the three-judge court provisions of 28 U.S.C. §§ 2281 (relating to actions to enjoin the enforcement of state statutes) and 2282 (relating to certain actions to enjoin the operation of federal statutes), substituting a far more limited requirement of a three-judge court in certain legislative apportionment cases.[20] The effect of these repeals was to render inapplicable to cases no longer calling for the convening of a three-judge district court the provision for direct Supreme Court review of the decisions of such courts (28 U.S.C. § 1253).

(6) *The Elimination of Direct Appeals in Criminal Cases.* A further significant change in the Supreme Court's appellate jurisdiction was the elimination of direct appeals from the district courts in certain criminal cases—a change incorporated in the Omnibus Crime Control Act of 1970.[21] The Criminal Appeals Act of 1907, Paragraph (3)(a), *supra,* was not affected by the Judges' Bill of 1925, and had been carried forward, as amended, in 18 U.S.C. § 3731. The provision had caused continual difficulties for the Supreme Court—because of the statute's own ambiguities, the Court's reluctance to review directly the decisions of the district courts, and the problems of double jeopardy often posed by Government appeals in criminal cases. See, *e.g.,* United States v. Sisson, 399 U.S. 267 (1970). See also Kurland, *The Mersky Case and the Criminal Appeals Act: A Suggestion for Amendment of the Statute,* 28 U.Chi.L.Rev. 419 (1961).

The Amendment in the Act of 1970 provided that any appeal by the United States from a dismissal of one or more counts of an indictment or information shall lie to a court of appeals "except that no appeal shall lie where the double jeopardy clause of the United States Constitution prohibits further prosecution."[22]

While the 1970 Act freed the Supreme Court from the burden of direct criminal appeals, it assigned the Court the difficult task of marking the boundaries of the government's right to appeal to the court of appeals by defining the constitutional limits established by the Double Jeopardy Clause.

Two additional provisions for appeals by the United States in criminal cases were enacted in 1984. One of these provisions amended 18 U.S.C. § 3731 to authorize government appeals to the courts of appeals from certain orders granting release of a prisoner, as well as from orders "granting a new trial after verdict or judgment". In the other provision (codified, as amended, in 18 U.S.C. § 3742)—enacted in connection with the new sentencing guidelines— Congress authorized government appeals to the courts of appeals from certain sentencing decisions of the district courts.

(7) *Supreme Court Review of Decisions of the Court of Military Appeals.* As part of the Military Justice Act of 1983, Congress added to the certiorari

---

19. Section 9, 88 Stat. 1918 (1975).

20. 90 Stat. 1119 (1976). The story of these provisions and of their repeal is more fully told at pp. 1212–15, *supra.*

21. 18 U.S.C. § 3731, as amended by Act of Jan. 2, 1971, § 14(a), 84 Stat. 1890.

22. The amendment also continued, with some modification, the prior provision for appeals by the United States from certain orders suppressing or excluding evidence, or requiring the return of seized property, but provided that such appeals lie only to a court of appeals.

jurisdiction of the Supreme Court certain categories of decisions of the United States Court of Military Appeals. See 28 U.S.C. § 1259. This provision—the first authorizing direct review by an Article III court of the judgments of a military tribunal—is discussed in Boskey & Gressman, *The Supreme Court's New Certiorari Jurisdiction Over Military Appeals,* 102 F.R.D. 329 (1985).

(8) *1988: Virtual Elimination of the Supreme Court's Mandatory Appellate Jurisdiction.* In a major structural change in the Supreme Court's jurisdiction, Congress in 1988 eliminated virtually all of the Supreme Court's mandatory jurisdiction over appeals from the lower federal courts. See Pub.L. 100–352, 102 Stat. 662. Section 1254 of Title 28, which had permitted appeals as of right from decisions holding state statutes invalid, was amended to provide for review only by writ of certiorari. And 28 U.S.C. § 1252, which had authorized appeals from decisions (even of district courts) invalidating acts of Congress in civil cases to which the United States was a party, was repealed altogether. Appeals as of right to the Supreme Court remain, under 28 U.S.C. § 1253, from the judgments of three-judge district courts, but those courts have a very narrow jurisdiction. See p. 1213, *supra.*

(9) *Time Limits for Seeking Supreme Court Review.* The time limits for requesting review on appeal or certiorari in the Supreme Court appear in 28 U.S.C. § 2101 and Sup.Ct. Rules 13 and 18. For valuable discussions of these provisions and of Supreme Court procedure generally, see Stern, Gressman, Shapiro & Geller, Supreme Court Practice (7th ed. 1993).

(10) *Statutory Provision for Interlocutory Appeals to the Courts of Appeals.* One important change in the statutory jurisdiction of the courts of appeals was the enactment in 1958 of the Interlocutory Appeals Act, 28 U.S.C. § 1292(b). This act provides for an appeal of any interlocutory order of a district court when the trial judge authorizes such an appeal after finding that certain conditions exist and the court of appeals, in its discretion, decides to allow the appeal. See p. 1661, *infra,* for further discussion.

(11) *Special Provisions Governing Appeals.* There are, in addition, many special provisions relating to appeals in particular kinds of cases or from particular tribunals. (A number of these provisions appear outside the Judicial Code). Examples include provisions for appeals of federal administrative orders, of final orders in habeas corpus proceedings, 28 U.S.C. § 2253, of decisions by magistrates in cases tried by consent, 28 U.S.C. § 636(c), of decisions in bankruptcy cases, 28 U.S.C. § 158, and of cases within the jurisdiction of the Court of Appeals for the Federal Circuit, 28 U.S.C. § 1295. These provisions often raise difficult questions of interpretation. See, *e.g.,* United States v. Hohri, 482 U.S. 64 (1987)(jurisdiction of the Federal Circuit).

(12) *Time Limits for Appeals to the Courts of Appeals.* The time limits for appeals from the district courts (and from the Court of Federal Claims) to the courts of appeals appear in 28 U.S.C. §§ 1292(b), 2107, and 2522, and in the Federal Rules of Appellate Procedure (primarily Rule 4). Until 1968, the procedures governing such appeals were set out in Rules 73–76 of the Civil Rules, Rules 37–39 of the Criminal Rules, and the separately adopted and varying provisions of the rules of each of the eleven courts of appeals. In that year, the Federal Rules of Appellate Procedure, a uniform set of rules applicable to all cases in the courts of appeals, went into effect following their submission to Congress by the Supreme Court. *See* 389 U.S. 1063 (1968). For detailed discussion of these rules and their innovations, see 16 Wright, Miller,

Cooper & Gressman, Federal Practice and Procedure §§ 3945–3994 (1977 and 1995 Supp.)

(13) *Other References.* For discussion of further proposed changes in the jurisdiction of the courts of appeals and of the Supreme Court to review decisions of lower federal tribunals, see Chap. I, pp. 60–66, *supra.* For discussion of the explosive growth in the caseloads of the courts of appeals, and of responses to that growth, see Chap. I, pp. 53–55, *supra.*

SECTION 2.   JURISDICTION OF THE COURTS OF APPEALS

Firestone Tire & Rubber Co. v. Risjord

449 U.S. 368, 101 S.Ct. 669, 66 L.Ed.2d 571 (1981).
Certiorari to the United States Court of Appeals for the Eighth Circuit.

■ JUSTICE MARSHALL delivered the opinion of the Court.

This case presents the question whether a party may take an appeal, pursuant to 28 U.S.C. § 1291, from a district court order denying a motion to disqualify counsel for the opposing party in a civil case. The United States Court of Appeals for the Eighth Circuit held that such orders are not appealable, but made its decision prospective only and therefore reached the merits of the challenged order. We hold that orders denying motions to disqualify counsel are not appealable final decisions under § 1291, and we therefore vacate the judgment of the Court of Appeals and remand with instructions that the appeal be dismissed for lack of jurisdiction.

I

Respondent is lead counsel for the plaintiffs in four product liability suits seeking damages from petitioner and other manufacturers of multipiece truck tire rims for injuries caused by alleged defects in their products. * * * Plaintiffs seek both compensatory and exemplary damages.

Petitioner was at all relevant times insured by Home Insurance Company (Home) under a contract providing that Home would be responsible only for some types of liability beyond a minimum "deductible" amount. Home was also an occasional client of respondent's law firm. Based on these facts, petitioner in May 1979 filed a motion to disqualify respondent from further representation of the plaintiffs. Petitioner argued that respondent had a clear conflict of interest because his representation of Home would give him an incentive to structure plaintiff's claims for relief in such a way as to enable the insurer to avoid any liability. This in turn, petitioner argued, could increase its own potential liability. Home had in fact advised petitioner in the course of the litigation that its policy would cover neither an award of compensatory damages for willful or intentional acts nor any award of exemplary or punitive damages. The District Court entered a pretrial order requiring that respondent terminate his representation of the plaintiffs unless both the plaintiffs and Home consented to his continuing representation.

In accordance with the District Court's order, respondent filed an affidavit in which he stated that he had informed both the plaintiffs and Home of the potential conflict and that neither had any objection to his continuing representation of them both. He filed supporting affidavits executed by the plaintiffs and by a representative of Home. Because he had satisfied the requirements of the pretrial order, respondent was able to continue his representation of the plaintiffs. Petitioner objected to the District Court's decision to permit respondent to continue his representation if he met the stated conditions, and therefore filed a notice of appeal pursuant to 28 U.S.C. § 1291.[7]

Although it did not hear oral argument on the appeal, the Eighth Circuit decided the case en banc and affirmed the trial court's order permitting petitioner to continue representing the plaintiffs.[8] Before considering the merits of the appeal, the court reconsidered and overruled its prior decisions holding that orders denying disqualification motions were immediately appealable under § 1291. The Court of Appeals reasoned that such orders did not fall within the collateral order doctrine of Cohen v. Beneficial Industrial Loan Corp., 337 U.S. 541 (1949), which allows some appeals prior to final judgment. Because it was overruling prior cases, the court stated that it would reach the merits of the challenged order "[i]n fairness to the appellant in the instant case," but held that in the future, appellate review of such orders would have to await final judgment on the merits of the main proceeding. We granted certiorari, to resolve a conflict among the circuits on the appealability question.

II

Under § 1291, the Courts of Appeals are vested with "jurisdiction of appeals from all final decisions of the district courts * * * except when a direct review may be had in the Supreme Court." We have consistently interpreted this language as indicating that a party may not take an appeal under this section until there has been "a decision by the District Court that 'ends the litigation on the merits and leaves nothing for the court to do but execute the judgment.'" Coopers & Lybrand v. Livesay, 437 U.S. 463, 467 (1978), quoting Catlin v. United States, 324 U.S. 229 (1945). This rule, that a party must ordinarily raise all claims of error in a single appeal following final judgment on the merits, serves a number of important purposes. It emphasizes the deference that appellate courts owe to the trial judge as the individual initially called upon to decide the many questions of law and fact that occur in the course of a trial. Permitting piecemeal appeals would undermine the independence of the District Judge, as well as the special role that individual plays in our judicial system. In addition, the rule is in accordance with the sensible policy of "avoid[ing] the obstruction to just claims that would come from permitting the harassment and cost of a succession of separate appeals from the various rulings to which a litigation may give rise, from its initiation to entry of judgment." Cobbledick v. United States, 309 U.S. 323, 325 (1940). * * * The

---

7. The District Court certified its pretrial order on disqualification for interlocutory appeal pursuant to 28 U.S.C. § 1292(b) * * *.

Neither party elected to proceed under § 1292(b). Respondent chose to comply with the order rather than appeal. Petitioner chose to appeal the denial of its motion under § 1291 rather than under § 1292(b). * * *

8. The Court of Appeals also stated that orders *granting* motions to disqualify counsel would be appealable under § 1291. That question is not presented by the instant petition, and we express no opinion on it. Neither do we express any view on whether an order denying a disqualification motion in a criminal case would be appealable under § 1291.

rule also serves the important purpose of promoting efficient judicial administration.

Our decisions have recognized, however, a narrow exception to the requirement that all appeals under § 1291 await final judgment on the merits. In Cohen v. Beneficial Industrial Loan Corp., *supra,* we held that a "small class" of orders that did not end the main litigation were nevertheless final and appealable pursuant to § 1291. Cohen was a shareholder's derivative action in which the Federal District Court refused to apply a state statute requiring a plaintiff in such a suit to post security for costs. The defendant appealed the ruling without awaiting final judgment on the merits, and the Court of Appeals ordered the trial court to require that costs be posted. We held that the Court of Appeals properly assumed jurisdiction of the appeal pursuant to § 1291 because the District Court's order constituted a final determination of a claim "separable from, and collateral to," the merits of the main proceeding, because it was "too important to be denied review," and because it was "too independent of the cause itself to require that appellate consideration be deferred until the whole case is adjudicated." *Id.,* at 546. Cohen did not establish new law; rather, it continued a tradition of giving § 1291 a "practical rather than a technical construction." *Ibid.* See, *e.g.,* United States v. River Rouge Improvement Co., 269 U.S. 411, 413–414 (1926); Forgay v. Conrad, 47 U.S. 201, 203 (1848). We have recently defined this limited class of final "collateral orders" in these terms: "[T]he order must conclusively determine the disputed question, resolve an important issue completely separate from the merits of the action, and be effectively unreviewable on appeal from a final judgment." Coopers & Lybrand v. Livesay, *supra,* 437 U.S. at 468 * * *.

Because the litigation from which the instant petition arises had not reached final judgment at the time the notice of appeal was filed, the order denying petitioner's motion to disqualify respondent is appealable under § 1291 only if it falls within the Cohen doctrine. The Court of Appeals held that it does not, and * * * [w]e agree * * * that under Cohen such an order is not subject to appeal prior to resolution of the merits.

An order denying a disqualification motion meets the first part of the "collateral order" test. It "conclusively determine[s] the disputed question," because the only issue is whether challenged counsel will be permitted to continue his representation. In addition, we will assume, although we do not decide, that the disqualification question "resolve[s] an important issue completely separate from the merits of the action," the second part of the test. Nevertheless, petitioner is unable to demonstrate that an order denying disqualification is "effectively unreviewable on appeal from a final judgment" within the meaning of our cases.

In attempting to show why the challenged order will be effectively unreviewable on final appeal, petitioner alleges that denying immediate review will cause it irreparable harm. It is true that the finality requirement should "be construed so as not to cause crucial collateral claims to be lost and potentially irreparable injuries to be suffered," Mathews v. Eldridge, 424 U.S. 319, 331, n. 11 (1976). In support of its assertion that it will be irreparably harmed, petitioner hints at "the possibility that the course of the proceedings may be indelibly stamped or shaped with the fruits of a breach of confidence or by acts or omissions prompted by a divided loyalty," and at "the effect of such a tainted proceeding in frustrating public policy." But petitioner fails to supply a single concrete example of the indelible stamp or taint of which it warns.

The only ground that petitioner urged in the District Court was that respondent might shape the products-liability plaintiffs' claims for relief in such a way as to increase the burden on petitioner. Our cases, however, require much more before a ruling may be considered "effectively unreviewable" absent immediate appeal.

To be appealable as a final collateral order, the challenged order must constitute "a complete, formal and, in the trial court, a final rejection," Abney v. United States, *supra*, 431 U.S. at 659, of a claimed right "where denial of immediate review would render impossible any review whatsoever," United States v. Ryan, 402 U.S. 530, 533 (1971). Thus we have permitted appeals prior to criminal trials when a defendant has claimed that he is about to be subjected to forbidden double jeopardy, Abney v. United States, *supra*, or a violation of his constitutional right to bail, Stack v. Boyle, 342 U.S. 1 (1951), because those situations, like the posting of security for costs involved in Cohen, "each involved an asserted right the legal and practical value of which would be destroyed if it were not vindicated before trial." United States v. MacDonald, 435 U.S. 850, 860 (1978). By way of contrast, we have generally denied review of pretrial discovery orders, see, *e.g.*, United States v. Ryan, *supra;* Cobbledick v. United States, *supra*. Our rationale has been that in the rare case when appeal after final judgment will not cure an erroneous discovery order, a party may defy the order, permit a contempt citation to be entered against him, and challenge the order on direct appeal of the contempt ruling. See Cobbledick v. United States, *supra*, at 327. We have also rejected immediate appealability under § 1291 of claims that "may fairly be assessed" only after trial, United States v. MacDonald, *supra*, at 860, and those involving "considerations that are 'enmeshed in the factual and legal issues comprising the plaintiff's cause of action,'" Coopers & Lybrand v. Livesay, *supra*, 437 U.S. at 469, quoting Mercantile Nat'l Bank v. Langdeau, 371 U.S. 555, 558 (1963).

An order refusing to disqualify counsel plainly falls within the large class of orders that are indeed reviewable on appeal after final judgment, and not within the much smaller class of those that are not. The propriety of the District Court's denial of a disqualification motion will often be difficult to assess until its impact on the underlying litigation may be evaluated, which is normally only after final judgment. The decision whether to disqualify an attorney ordinarily turns on the peculiar factual situation of the case then at hand, and the order embodying such a decision will rarely, if ever, represent a final rejection of a claim of fundamental right that cannot effectively be reviewed following judgment on the merits. In the case before us, petitioner has made no showing that its opportunity for meaningful review will perish unless immediate appeal is permitted. On the contrary, should the Court of Appeals conclude after the trial has ended that permitting continuing representation was prejudicial error, it would retain its usual authority to vacate the judgment appealed from and order a new trial. That remedy seems plainly adequate should petitioner's concerns of possible injury ultimately prove well-founded. As the Second Circuit has recently observed, the potential harm that might be caused by requiring that a party await final judgment before it may appeal even when the denial of its disqualification motion was erroneous does not "diffe[r] in any significant way from the harm resulting from other interlocutory orders that may be erroneous, such as orders requiring discovery over a work-product objection or orders denying motions for recusal of the trial judge." Armstrong v. McAlpin, 625 F.2d 433, 438 (1980). But interlocutory orders are not appealable "on the mere ground that they may be erroneous."

Will v. United States, 389 U.S. 90, 98, n. 6 (1967). Permitting wholesale appeals on that ground not only would constitute an unjustified waste of scarce judicial resources, but would transform the limited exception carved out in Cohen into a license for broad disregard of the finality rule imposed by Congress in § 1291. This we decline to do.[13]

III

We hold that a district court's order denying a motion to disqualify counsel is not appealable under § 1291 prior to final judgment in the underlying litigation. Insofar as the Eighth Circuit reached this conclusion, its decision is correct. But because its decision was contrary to precedent in the circuit, the court went further and reached the merits of the order appealed from. This approach, however, overlooks the fact that the finality requirement embodied in § 1291 is jurisdictional in nature. If the appellate court finds that the order from which a party seeks to appeal does not fall within the statute, its inquiry is over. A court lacks discretion to consider the merits of a case over which it is without jurisdiction, and thus, by definition, a jurisdictional ruling may never be made prospective only. * * * Consequently, the judgment of the Eighth Circuit is vacated and the case remanded with instructions to dismiss the appeal for want of jurisdiction. * * *

So ordered.

JUSTICE REHNQUIST, with whom THE CHIEF JUSTICE joins, concurring.

I agree with the result in this case and the analysis of the Court so far as it concerns the question whether an order denying disqualification of counsel is "effectively unreviewable on appeal from the final judgment." The Court's answer to this question is dispositive on the appealability issue. Since it is completely unnecessary to do so, however, I would not state, as the Court does:

> "An order denying a disqualification motion meets the first part of the 'collateral order' test. It 'conclusively determines the disputed question,' because the only issue is whether challenged counsel will be permitted to continue his representation."

In Cohen v. Beneficial Industrial Loan Corp., 337 U.S. 541 (1949), Mr. Justice Jackson stressed that the order before the Court was "a final disposition of a claimed right" and specifically distinguished a case in which the matter was "subject to reconsideration from time to time." *Id.,* at 546–547. Just recently in Coopers & Lybrand v. Livesay, 437 U.S. 463 (1978), we held that an order denying class certification was not appealable under the collateral order doctrine, in part because such an order is "subject to revision in the

---

13. Although there may be situations in which a party will be irreparably damaged if forced to wait until final resolution of the underlying litigation before securing review of an order denying its motion to disqualify opposing counsel, it is not necessary, in order to resolve those situations, to create a general rule permitting the appeal of all such orders. In the proper circumstances, the moving party may seek sanctions short of disqualification, such as a protective order limiting counsel's ability to disclose or to act on purportedly confidential information. If additional facts in support of the motion develop in the course of the litigation, the moving party might ask the trial court to reconsider its decision. Ultimately, if dissatisfied with the result in the District Court and absolutely determined that it will be harmed irreparably, a party may seek to have the question certified for interlocutory appellate review pursuant to 28 U.S.C. § 1292(b), and, in the exceptional circumstances for which it was designed, a writ of mandamus from the court of appeals might be available. * * *

District Court." *Id.,* at 469. The possibility that a district judge would reconsider his determination was highly significant in United States v. Mac-Donald, 435 U.S. 850, 858–859 (1978), where the Court held that the denial of a pretrial motion to dismiss an indictment on speedy trial grounds was not appealable under the collateral order doctrine. The Court noted that speedy trial claims necessitated a careful assessment of the particular facts of the case, and that "The denial of a pretrial motion to dismiss an indictment on speedy trial grounds does not indicate that a like motion made after trial—when prejudice can be better gauged—would also be denied."

It is not at all clear to me, nor has it been to courts considering the question, that an order denying a motion for disqualification of counsel conclusively determines the disputed question. The District Court remains free to reconsider its decision at any time. * * * Petitioner's claim is that respondent will advance only those theories of liability which absolve the insurer, or will advance those theories more strenuously than others. Although it is impossible to discern if this is true before trial, the issue may become clearer as trial progresses and respondent actually does present his theories. As in Mac-Donald, it cannot be assumed that a motion made at a later point in the proceedings—"when prejudice can be better gauged"—will be denied.

Because of what seem to me to be totally unnecessary and very probably incorrect statements as to this minor point in the opinion, I concur in the result only.

———

NOTE ON "FINAL DECISIONS"

(1) *Policy Questions Raised by the Finality Rule.* The policies favoring limitation of appeals to final judgments are articulated in the Firestone opinion. There is little indication, however, that those policies underlay the development of the common law rule from which the present statutory provisions are derived. The original motives appear to have been largely formalistic. See Crick, *The Final Judgment as a Basis for Appeal,* 41 Yale L.J. 539, 540–44 (1932).

Countering the policies supporting the final judgment rule are a number of factors that may favor earlier appeals in particular cases: the avoidance of hardship that would be difficult or impossible to remedy if appeal were postponed, the need to oversee the work of the lower courts on matters that seldom if ever arise on appeal from a final judgment, and the interest in conserving the time and energy of courts and litigants by the correction of error at an early stage. The story of judicial and legislative attempts to work out a sensible system of appeals is in large part the story of the continuing effort to reconcile these conflicting interests.[1]

---

1. For a comprehensive effort to rationalize and restate the law governing appeals in the federal courts, see the collective undertaking, *Federal Civil Appellate Jurisdiction: An Interlocutory Restatement,* 47 Law & Contemp.Probs., Spring 1984, at 13. Building on this effort, Professor Carrington has proposed a revision of the governing statutes that would authorize appeals both from "final" decisions and from certain "interlocutory orders"; included under the latter heading would be appeals "essential to protect substantial rights which cannot be effectively enforced on review after final decision." Carrington, *Toward a Federal Civil Interloc-*

(2) *The Court's Practical Approach to Finality.* As the Court notes in Firestone, the final judgment rule has never been construed to mean that the litigation must be concluded in every respect before the time for appeal begins to run. In the case of actions in which declaratory or injunctive relief is granted, the possibilities of modification or of supplemental relief might prevent that point from ever being reached, and even a judgment in a routine action for damages is subject to being reopened. See Fed.R.Civ.P. 60(b). And the Court has not insisted that all incidental questions, like those of costs, for example, must be resolved before the point of finality is reached. See St. Louis, I.M. & S.R.R. v. Southern Express Co., 108 U.S. 24, 28–29 (1883). Even the denial of a temporary restraining order may be final if the likely effect of the denial is to moot the case and thus to deny the ultimate relief sought. See United States v. Wood, 295 F.2d 772 (5th Cir.1961).

But a "practical" approach of this kind, appropriate as it may be, brings difficult issues to the fore. If incidental questions of costs need not be resolved, for example, what of a question of an award of attorney's fees? That question at one time sharply divided the courts of appeals but has been resolved in favor of the finality of the judgment before the fee is determined—at least when the fee is claimed under authority of a separate statute such as 42 U.S.C. § 1988. White v. New Hampshire Dep't of Employment Security, 455 U.S. 445 (1982).[2]

(3) *The Collateral Order Rule.* The rule of Cohen v. Beneficial Industrial Loan Corp., explained and applied in Firestone, has its roots in similar practical considerations: although the litigation may not be at an end, a particular matter of importance has been finally determined, and effective review at a later stage may be difficult or impossible. Areas in which the Court has had to grapple with this rule in recent years include pretrial appeals by defendants in criminal cases, appeals from denials of immunity claims in actions against government officials, appeals from denials of certification in class action suits, and appeals from decisions to abstain in favor of state proceedings.[3]

---

utory Appeals Act, 47 Law & Contemp.Probs., Summer 1984, at 165, 167.

2. The lower courts remain divided on the question whether the White decision governs *all* disputes over attorneys' fees. See Beckwith Machinery Co. v. Travelers Indemnity Co., 815 F.2d 286 (3d Cir.1987), and authorities cited at 288–90.

In Budinich v. Becton Dickinson & Co., 486 U.S. 196 (1988), the Court ruled that the finality of a judgment in a diversity action is governed by federal rather than state law, and held final an order determining liability and damages despite the pendency of proceedings to assess costs and attorneys' fees. Compare Napier v. Thirty or More Unidentified Fed. Agents, 855 F.2d 1080 (3d Cir.1988)(holding non-final an order that dismissed the suit and found plaintiff's attorney liable for sanctions without determining their amount).

3. Another area of difficulty is presented by cases in which district courts review administrative action. In Sullivan v. Finkel-stein, 496 U.S. 617 (1990), the Court held that a district court order reversing and remanding an agency's denial of a claim for social security disability benefits was final and could be appealed by the agency. The Court relied heavily on the particular context, and on the judicial review provisions of 42 U.S.C. § 405(g). But the Court also stated, more broadly, that the district court's remand order "was unquestionably a 'judgment,' as it terminated the civil action challenging the [agency's] final determination that [the claimant] was not entitled to benefits, set aside that determination, and finally decided that the [agency] could not follow [its] own regulations in considering the disability issue" (p. 625). In view of this analysis, the case may well be interpreted to allow immediate appeals of a wide range of district court decisions remanding a proceeding to an agency for further action.

(a) *Criminal Cases*. In Abney v. United States, 431 U.S. 651 (1977), discussed in Firestone, the Court permitted appeal before trial of a denial of a motion to dismiss an indictment on grounds of double jeopardy. The Court emphasized that the rights conferred on a criminal defendant by the Double Jeopardy Clause are significantly undermined by the very occurrence of a second trial, regardless of the outcome.[4]

Was the Court in Firestone correct when it characterized Abney as involving a right whose "legal and practical value" would be "destroyed" if not vindicated before trial? Surely the Court did not mean that the defendant's right is *solely* a right not to be tried, so that a conviction in these circumstances would not be set aside. Does this verbal overkill in the description of Abney make the Firestone case seem more distinguishable than it really was?[5]

(b) *Claims of Immunity*. Relying on the Abney rationale, the Court in Nixon v. Fitzgerald, 457 U.S. 731 (1982), unanimously held immediately appealable a district court denial of a claim of absolute presidential immunity from civil prosecution for damages. But the unanimity dissolved in Mitchell v. Forsyth, 472 U.S. 511 (1985), where the question was the appealability of denial of a claim of qualified immunity in a damages action against a former Attorney General. For the majority, the denial was immediately appealable, to the extent it turned on an issue of law, because "qualified immunity is in fact an entitlement not to stand trial under certain circumstances" (p. 525).[6] For Justice Brennan (joined by Justice Marshall) in dissent, the immunity claim

---

4. After stating that a ruling falling within the Cohen rationale was a "final decision" under § 1291 even though not a "final judgment" (p. 658), the Court noted that its holding did not permit the appeal of rulings on other claims contained in the motion to dismiss.

Even after this holding, some lower courts, acting in civil cases, upheld a claim of "pendent appellate jurisdiction" over issues unappealable in themselves, at least when the issues presented questions closely related to those involved in matters appealable under the Cohen rationale. In the area of qualified immunity (Paragraph (3)(b) of this Note), for example, see Dube v. SUNY, 900 F.2d 587, 598 (2d Cir.1990). But in Swint v. Chambers County Commission, 115 S.Ct. 1203 (1995), the Supreme Court unanimously rejected a claim of pendent *party* appellate jurisdiction over an appeal by the Commission in a case in which an individual co-defendant was able to appeal a denial of a qualified immunity claim. The Court relied both on its reasoning in Abney and on the recently enacted grants of rulemaking power in this area (see pp. 1655, 1661, *infra*) as grounds for rejecting an expansive application of the collateral order rule. The Court reserved judgment, however, on the possible adoption of a pendent jurisdiction approach in the case of an unappealable ruling that was closely "inter-

twined" with an appealable ruling. *Id*. at 1212.

5. Since Abney, the Court has on several occasions refused to allow an appeal from a pretrial order in a criminal case, concluding in each instance that the right involved could be adequately protected by an appeal after conviction. United States v. MacDonald, 435 U.S. 850 (1978)(claim of right to speedy trial); United States v. Hollywood Motor Car Co., Inc., 458 U.S. 263 (1982)(claim of prosecutorial vindictiveness); *cf*. Midland Asphalt Corp. v. United States, 489 U.S. 794 (1989)(denying appeal from refusal to dismiss an indictment on the basis of an alleged error that might be considered "harmless" after conviction).

Compare Helstoski v. Meanor, 442 U.S. 500 (1979)(applying the Abney rationale to allow interlocutory appeal from denial of a claim of immunity from criminal prosecution on the basis of the Speech or Debate Clause).

6. But in Johnson v. Jones, 115 S.Ct. 2151 (1995), the Court held unanimously that the denial of a summary judgment motion asserting a qualified immunity defense is not appealable as a collateral order when the denial is based not on the district court's determination of an issue of law but on its finding of the existence of a triable issue of fact.

was not sufficiently separable from the merits and was not appropriately characterized as a right not to stand trial—any more than a claim based on the statute of limitations, a right to jury trial, or a venue limitation (p. 547 n. 4).[7]

Can a satisfactory line be drawn between those rights that would be seriously impaired by the holding of further proceedings and those rights that can be adequately vindicated when the proceedings have been concluded? Do you agree that a defendant's claim—that, as a present or former government official, he cannot be held accountable in damages for his unlawful actions—fits into the former category?[8]

(c) *Class Action Certification.* The Supreme Court first spoke on this problem in Eisen v. Carlisle & Jacquelin, 417 U.S. 156 (1974), holding final a trial court order (allowing the suit to proceed as a class action) that required the defendants to pay 90% of the costs of notifying class members. The Court analogized the order imposing costs to the order held final in Cohen and went on to uphold appellate authority to review all aspects of the class action notice problems in the case.

---

7. The question of the proper timing of appeals of claims of qualified immunity continues to trouble the courts. In the 1994 Term, the Supreme Court granted certiorari in Behrens v. Pelletier, 115 S.Ct. 1398 (1995), to review a Ninth Circuit decision dismissing a defendant's appeal from a denial of a motion for summary judgment on a claim of qualified immunity; the case was one in which the court of appeals had previously decided on the merits an appeal by the same defendant from a denial of a motion to dismiss on qualified immunity grounds.

The Mitchell decision was followed and perhaps extended in a related context in Puerto Rico Aqueduct & Sewer Auth. v. Metcalf & Eddy, Inc., 506 U.S. 139 (1993), where the Court held appealable an order denying the claim of a state governmental entity that as an "arm of the state," it is immune under the Eleventh Amendment from federal court suit. Eleventh Amendment immunity, the Court said, was not merely a protection from certain forms of relief, but also was meant to spare states the indignity of suit at the instance of private parties. Justice Stevens dissented, arguing, *inter alia,* that the Eleventh Amendment (unlike the doctrine of official immunity) was not designed to confer total immunity from suit in any court and that the indignity rationale was "embarrassingly insufficient" to overcome the final judgment rule (506 U.S. at ___, 113 S.Ct. at 691).

8. In Van Cauwenberghe v. Biard, 486 U.S. 517 (1988), the Supreme Court held unappealable a district court order denying an extradited person's claim of absolute immunity from civil process. The Court reasoned that the right not to be burdened with a civil trial is not an essential aspect of any immunity from civil process that might arise from federal treaties and statutes regulating extradition to face criminal charges. The Court also ruled that an order denying a motion to dismiss on forum non conveniens grounds is not appealable, because the applicable legal standards are entangled with the merits.

In Lauro Lines S.R.L. v. Chasser, 490 U.S. 495 (1989), the defendant moved to dismiss a damage action, citing a contractual clause requiring suit to be brought in Italy. The Supreme Court unanimously held the denial of that motion to fall outside the collateral order doctrine; the third prong of the Cohen test was not satisfied because the right to be sued only in Italy, unlike a right not to be sued at all, was "adequately vindicable" after final judgment (p. 501). Justice Scalia's concurrence conceded that the right to be sued only in Italy was "positively destroyed" by denying review, but understood the collateral order doctrine as having always taken account of whether the right in question was sufficiently important to overcome the policy against interlocutory appeals (p.502).

Finally, in Digital Equip. Corp. v. Desktop Direct, Inc., 114 S.Ct. 1992 (1994), the Court ruled that any "right not to stand trial" allegedly conferred by a settlement agreement is not sufficiently "important" for a district court ruling rescinding the settlement to come within the collateral order doctrine.

Four years later, the Court settled over a decade of controversy in the lower courts by unanimously holding that, despite the implications of Eisen, a district court order denying class certification (and, a fortiori, an order granting certification) is not final and appealable under § 1291. Coopers & Lybrand v. Livesay, 437 U.S. 463 (1978). The Cohen rule did not apply because the order denying certification was subject to later revision in the district court, because the issues were closely related to the factual and legal issues on the merits, and because such an order was "subject to effective review after final judgment at the behest of the named plaintiff or intervening class members" (p. 469).[9] The Court explicitly administered the coup de grace to the "death knell" doctrine that had been developed in some circuits—a doctrine allowing an appeal when a denial of class certification to the plaintiff made it extremely unlikely that the plaintiff could or would pursue the action on his own behalf. The Court reasoned that (a) if based solely on the lack of a sufficient amount in controversy, the death-knell approach involved an invasion of the legislative province, (b) if based on a multi-factor analysis, the approach would impose too heavy a burden on the courts, and (c) the approach would in any event authorize indiscriminate interlocutory review inconsistent with the procedures and criteria provided in the Interlocutory Appeals Act, § 1292(b).

Did the Court in Coopers & Lybrand effectively preclude any appeal as of right of a trial court's denial of class action certification whenever the plaintiff cannot afford to pursue the action on an individual basis? What if a plaintiff whose motion is denied submits to a judgment of involuntary dismissal of his individual action under Rule 41(b)—perhaps for failure to prosecute—and then raises the certification issue on appeal? See Huey v. Teledyne, Inc., 608 F.2d 1234 (9th Cir.1979)(denial of class certification not reviewable on appeal of dismissal for failure to prosecute); Comment, 48 U.Chi.L.Rev. 912, 927–35 (1981)(forcefully criticizing the Huey decision).[10]

(d) *Abstention in Favor of State Proceedings.* In Moses H. Cone Memorial Hosp. v. Mercury Construction Corp., 460 U.S. 1 (1983), the district court stayed a diversity action to compel arbitration pending resolution of a state court action between the same parties involving similar issues. The Supreme Court held that order final and appealable. It reasoned that (a) the only substantial issue in the case (that of arbitrability) would not be further litigated in federal court, since the state court's determination of that issue would be res judicata and (b) "[i]n any event," the case met the criteria for the "exception to the finality rule" under Cohen and its progeny (p. 11). (The Court went on to hold that the decision to abstain was an abuse of discretion. See p. 1317, *supra.*)

Justice Rehnquist (joined by the Chief Justice and Justice O'Connor) dissented on the question of appealability. He argued that the stay order was

---

9. Two years after Coopers & Lybrand, a sharply divided Supreme Court confronted some aspects of the appealability of a denial of class certification in the face of a claim of mootness. See United States Parole Comm'n v. Geraghty, 445 U.S. 388 (1980), p. 227, *supra,* and the following Note. In the course of his dissent from the decision allowing an appeal in Geraghty, Justice Powell referred to the statement quoted in text from Coopers & Lybrand—that an order denying certification is reviewable after final judgment "at

the behest of the named plaintiff"—as a "gratuitous sentence" that "apparently is elevated by the Court's opinion in this case to the status of new doctrine." 445 U.S. at 416–17.

10. *Cf.* Stringfellow v. Concerned Neighbors in Action, 480 U.S. 370 (1987)(order granting permissive intervention under certain restrictions but denying intervention as of right is not an appealable collateral order).

"tentative" and "subject to change at any time" and that the decision constituted "an unwarranted limitation upon the power of district courts to control their own cases" (pp. 30–31). And he urged that the decision lacked both the conclusiveness and the importance to warrant an appeal under the Cohen rationale.

Does this decision mean that any stay of proceedings is an appealable decision? How can the result be squared with the rejection of the "death knell" doctrine in Coopers & Lybrand, Paragraph (3)(c), *supra*? The Court attempted to answer both questions in its opinion (pp. 10–11, n. 11), stating that (a) "most stays do not put the plaintiff 'effectively out of court,'" and (b) unlike the death-knell cases, the order appealed from in Cone had the *legal* effect of preventing further litigation in federal court.[11]

(4) *Further Aspects of the Collateral Order Rule.*

(a) *Appealability of Orders Denying Disqualification of Counsel.* Accepting the Firestone opinion's analysis of the application of the Cohen rule to an order denying disqualification, would you distinguish the case in which a motion to disqualify is granted? If the party deprived of the counsel of choice by such an order later lost on the merits, would an appellate court simply presume that the change of counsel had been prejudicial, or would some showing of prejudice be required? If motions to disqualify are used by litigants as a dilatory tactic, would allowing an appeal of a grant of disqualification be as supportive of that tactic as allowing an appeal of a denial?

Without answering the question whether a showing of prejudice is required, the Court after Firestone held orders granting disqualification to be nonappealable in both criminal and civil contexts. See Flanagan v. United States, 465 U.S. 259 (1984)(criminal); Richardson–Merrell, Inc. v. Koller, 472 U.S. 424 (1985)(civil). The reasoning was explained in Richardson–Merrell:

"[I]f establishing a violation of one's right to counsel of choice in civil cases requires no showing of prejudice, then, 'a pretrial order violating the right does not meet the third condition for coverage by the collateral order exception: it is not "effectively unreviewable on appeal from a final judgment."'" * * * [If a showing of prejudice is required,] then a disqualification order, though 'final,' is not independent of the issues to be tried" (pp. 438–39).

(b) *Antecedents of the Rule.* Forgay v. Conrad, 47 U.S. (6 How.) 201 (1848), was a case in which a federal circuit court had ordered the defendants to turn over certain property to an assignee in bankruptcy. Although the case was to continue in the circuit court for an accounting, the Supreme Court held this order final and appealable, since immediate execution, sale of the property, and distribution of the proceeds to creditors was contemplated.

In recent years, the Forgay case has apparently not been viewed by the Supreme Court as establishing an independent rationale for determining the finality of a district court order. Rather, as in Firestone, it seems to have been assimilated to the Cohen "collateral order" rule.[12] But the order in Forgay

---

11. In Gulfstream Aerospace Corp. v. Mayacamas Corp., 485 U.S. 271 (1988), the Supreme Court held that an order *denying* a request for abstention is not immediately appealable under § 1291 or § 1292(a)(1).

12. The case has occasionally been relied on, however, as a basis for allowing re-

view of state court judgments under 28 U.S.C. § 1257. See, *e.g.*, Radio Station WOW, Inc. v. Johnson, 326 U.S. 120, 125–26 (1945), p. 636, *supra*; North Dakota State

was in no sense "collateral" to the merits of the controversy over distribution of the bankrupt's estate among his creditors. It was the element of hardship from the impending execution and sale of the property that, standing alone, supported the determination of finality. Indeed, the opinion suggested that an order simply directing transfer of the property to the control of the court would not be final. See generally 15A Wright, Miller & Cooper, Federal Practice & Procedure § 3910 (1992 & 1995 Supp.).

(5) *The Rise and Fall of the Gillespie Approach.* In the 1960s and '70s, the Court flirted with a considerably more relaxed approach to finality than that evidenced by its recent decisions under § 1291. The high water mark of this period was Gillespie v. United States Steel Corp., 379 U.S. 148 (1964), a case not even cited in Firestone. In Gillespie, the plaintiff, administrator of her son's estate, sued for damages under the Jones Act and (under Ohio's wrongful death law) for unseaworthiness. She sought recovery both for herself and for her son's surviving brother and sisters. The district court struck all references in the complaint to Ohio law, to unseaworthiness, and to recovery for the benefit of the brother and sisters. On appeal from this order, the court of appeals decided the controversy on the merits, as did the Supreme Court after holding, 7–2, that the order was appealable under § 1291. The basis of the decision on appealability appeared to be that the cost of holding the order unappealable would exceed the benefits:

"It is true that the review of this case by the Court of Appeals could be called 'piecemeal'; but it does not appear that the inconvenience and cost of trying this case will be greater because the Court of Appeals decided the issues raised instead of compelling the parties to go to trial with them unanswered. We cannot say that the Court of Appeals chose wrongly under the circumstances. And it seems clear now that the case is before us that the eventual costs, as all the parties recognize, will certainly be less if we now pass on the questions presented here rather than send the case back with those issues undecided. Moreover, delay of perhaps a number of years in having the brother's and sisters' rights determined might work a great injustice on them, since the claims for recovery for their benefit have been effectively cut off so long as the District Judge's ruling stands. * * * It is true that if the District Judge had certified the case to the Court of Appeals under 28 U.S.C. § 1292(b) * * *, the appeal unquestionably would have been proper; in light of the circumstances we believe that the Court of Appeals properly implemented the same policy Congress sought to promote in § 1292(b) by treating this obviously marginal case as final and appealable under 28 U.S.C. § 1291 * * *"(pp. 153–54).

Gillespie did have some impact in the lower courts, moving them toward a greater willingness to entertain appeals on the basis of a balance of costs and benefits. See, *e.g.,* Norman v. McKee, 431 F.2d 769 (9th Cir.1970). But its generative force in cases arising under § 1291 was not great, especially at the Supreme Court level.[13] See Redish, *The Pragmatic Approach to Appealability in the Federal Courts,* 75 Colum.L.Rev. 89, 120–24 (1975). And in 1978, in

Bd. of Pharmacy v. Snyder's Drug Stores, Inc., 414 U.S. 156, 162 (1973), p. 630, *supra.* *Cf.* Paragraph (7), *infra.*

13. Gillespie was relied on, however, in Cox Broadcasting Corp. v. Cohn, 420 U.S. 469, 478 n. 7 (1975), p. 627, *supra.*

Coopers & Lybrand, Paragraph (3)(c), *supra,* the Court confined it to the limbo of its particular facts.[14]

Assuming that the statutory language of § 1291 permits the kind of balancing employed in Gillespie, do you think the Court weighed all relevant elements in the scale? What of the impact on the costs of administration and of litigation that such an open-ended, case-by-case approach might entail? In Gillespie itself, was there any harm that could be shown aside from the delay that would result from having to wait for a final decision and the possible extra expense of a second trial?

(6) *Orders Compelling Testimony or Other Disclosure.* In general, orders to testify or to produce documents in a pending judicial proceeding are not regarded as final. See, *e.g.,* Cobbledick v. United States, 309 U.S. 323 (1940); United States v. Ryan, 402 U.S. 530 (1971). And indeed, although a criminal or civil contempt order against a nonparty is considered final, a civil contempt order against a party is not, see Doyle v. London Guar. & Accident Co., 204 U.S. 599 (1907)—a rule that is sometimes honored in the breach, as in Sibbach v. Wilson & Co., 312 U.S. 1 (1941). The distinction has been forcefully criticized on the ground that both civil and criminal contempt adjudications cause the kind of hardship that decisions like Forgay v. Conrad, Paragraph (4)(b), *supra,* have sought to prevent. Andre, *The Final Judgment Rule and Party Appeals of Civil Contempt Orders: Time for a Change,* 55 N.Y.U.L.Rev. 1041 (1980).

In two instances, appeals even prior to a contempt adjudication have been allowed. The first was a case in which the owner of documents in possession of the court petitioned to bar their use before a grand jury, and his petition was denied; the Court noted that to deny an appeal at that stage would be to deny any appeal, since the petitioner was unable to resist production by placing himself in contempt. Perlman v. United States, 247 U.S. 7 (1918). In the second, President Nixon was allowed to appeal from the denial of his motion to quash a subpoena to produce the "Watergate" tapes before a grand jury. United States v. Nixon, 418 U.S. 683 (1974). The extraordinary rationale of this case—that it would be "unseemly" to require a President to place himself in contempt just to "trigger" appellate review (pp. 691–92)—evidently does not extend to members of the President's cabinet. See In re Attorney General, 596 F.2d 58 (2d Cir.1979), and Justice White's dissent from the denial of certiorari in Socialist Workers Party v. Attorney General, 444 U.S. 903 (1979).

(7) *Finality Under §§ 1291 and 1257.* Should the criteria for determining what is a "final decision" under § 1291 be any different from those used in applying 28 U.S.C. § 1257, which provides for Supreme Court review of "final judgments or decrees" of "the highest court of a State"? See Chap. V, Sec. 3, *supra.* The Supreme Court has often cited cases under one statute when applying the other. See, *e.g.,* Cox Broadcasting Corp. v. Cohn, 420 U.S. 469, 478 (1975); National Socialist Party v. Village of Skokie, 432 U.S. 43, 44 (1977). But consider the following possible bases for drawing some distinctions:

---

14. In a parting footnote in Coopers & Lybrand, the Court emphasized the importance of the substantive issue in Gillespie and the late stage at which the finality issue had been presented to the Supreme Court. "If Gillespie were extended beyond the unique facts of that case," it concluded, "§ 1291 would be stripped of all significance" (p. 477 n. 30).

(a) The language of the two statutes;

(b) Problems of federalism and comity involved in federal review of state court judgments (see Justice Rehnquist's dissent in the Cox Broadcasting case, 420 U.S. at 502–05), p. 632, *supra*;

(c) The availability in the lower federal courts, but not on Supreme Court review of state courts, of alternative avenues to appellate review (*e.g.*, 28 U.S.C. §§ 1292(a)(1), 1292(b));

(d) The possibility that the federal issues in a case in the state courts might be finally disposed of by the highest state court long before the case is concluded, and that the federal interest might be defeated absent immediate review;[15]

(e) The relative difficulties for a court in administering a flexible standard governing its own appellate jurisdiction (§ 1257), and in supervising the administration of a standard governing the appellate jurisdiction of thirteen lower courts (§ 1291); and

(f) The fact that, at least on petitions for certiorari governed by 28 U.S.C. § 1254(1), there is no final judgment required for Supreme Court review of the decisions of the federal courts of appeals.

(8) *Problems of Waiver.* When a close question of finality is presented in the course of litigation, must the party aggrieved file an appeal in order to preserve his rights? Congress has provided thirty days for the filing of an appeal, 28 U.S.C. § 2107, and the failure to appeal from a "final" order during that time has been held fatal, even though the action did not go to judgment until more than a year later. Dickinson v. Petroleum Conversion Corp., 338 U.S. 507 (1950).[16] But in Corey v. United States, 375 U.S. 169 (1963), the Court, over Justice Harlan's dissent, held that the petitioner, a defendant in a criminal case, had an option to appeal either (1) when he was committed under 18 U.S.C. § 4208(b), pending receipt of a report from the Bureau of Prisons, or (2) when he was resentenced following receipt of the report over three months later.[17] And in several cases since Abney, Paragraph 3(a), *supra,* lower courts have held that although denial of a pretrial motion to dismiss on double jeopardy grounds is immediately appealable, appeal at that stage is not "mandatory"; the claim may be raised on appeal after conviction. *E.g.,* United States v. Gamble, 607 F.2d 820 (9th Cir.1979). Perhaps with tongue in cheek, the court in Gamble said that its holding would "avoid piecemeal appeals" (p. 823).

Are there, then, two kinds of final orders—those that may be treated as final at the option of the litigants and those that must be appealed now if at all? How are they to be distinguished? Does a case fall into the latter category if the party contemplating an appeal cannot be affected by anything remaining for determination in the trial court? Only in such circumstances? *Cf.* Chap. V, Sec. 3, p. 642, *supra* (discussing an analogous question with respect to Supreme Court review of state court decisions).

---

15. See, *e.g.,* Mercantile Nat'l Bank v. Langdeau, 371 U.S. 555 (1963), p. 631, *supra.* (Would an extraordinary writ like mandamus or prohibition be available in a case like Langdeau if an appeal did not lie? See 28 U.S.C. § 1651.)

16. See also White v. New Hampshire Dep't of Employment Security, 455 U.S. 445 (1982); Boeing Co. v. Van Gemert, 444 U.S. 472, 489 (1980)(Rehnquist, J., dissenting).

17. *Cf.* Rosenblatt v. American Cyanamid Co., 86 S.Ct. 1, 3 n. 6 (1965)(Goldberg, J., on application for a stay).

(9) *Appealability as a Question of Jurisdiction.* The notion that the statutory limits on appellate review are "jurisdictional" is of ancient lineage, and its announcement and application in Firestone was not too surprising. But this application may be seen as driving one more nail into the coffin of the Gillespie case, Paragraph (5), *supra.*[18]

(10) *Statutory Grant of Rulemaking Power.* As part of its response to the Report of the Federal Courts Study Committee, Congress in 1990 added to the Rules Enabling Act (28 U.S.C. § 2072) a new subsection (c), which (as amended) provides: "Such rules may define when a ruling of a district court is final for purposes of appeal under section 1291 of this title."

To date, no proposed rules have been issued under this authority.[19] Are there areas that call for such definitional rules? Would it be desirable, or appropriate, for such rules to depart from existing Supreme Court precedent, or should they attempt to deal, at most, with questions as yet unresolved by the Court? How much flexibility do the rulemakers have in defining finality? *Cf.* Sears, Roebuck & Co. v. Mackey, p. 1656, *infra.*

Note that the scope of the finality doctrine goes to the heart of federal appellate jurisdiction. Is such a matter appropriate for judicial rulemaking? For discussion of new subsection (c), see Martineau, *Defining Finality and Appealability By Court Rule: Right Problem, Wrong Solution,* 54 U.Pitt.L.Rev. 717 (1993); Rowe, *Defining Finality and Appealability By Court Rule: A Comment on Martineau's "Right Problem, Wrong Solution," id.* at 795. See generally Goldberg, *The Influence of Procedural Rules on Federal Jurisdiction,* 28 Stan.L.Rev. 395 (1976); Shapiro, *Federal Diversity Jurisdiction: A Survey and a Proposal,* 91 Harv.L.Rev. 317, 340–48 (1977).

NOTE ON RULE 54(b): APPEALS IN MULTI-PARTY AND MULTI-CLAIM CASES

(1) *Rule 54(b) and Its Validity Under the Enabling Act.* Before the adoption of the federal rules in 1938, the Supreme Court had held that an appeal from the disposition of one claim in a single or multi-party case could not be taken if other claims remained undecided. *E.g.,* Collins v. Miller, 252 U.S. 364 (1920). The rulemakers originally addressed the problem by providing, in Rule 54(b), that an order disposing of a single claim in a multi-claim case "shall terminate the action with respect to the claim so disposed of." But in 1946, the rule was amended to permit the resolution of doubts, and the limitation of appeals, at the district court level; the amended rule stated that "[t]he [district] court may direct the entry of a final judgment upon one or more but less than all of the claims only upon an express determination that there is no just reason for

18. Note, however, the decisions after Firestone (discussed at pp. 84–88, *supra*) that reject the notion of prospective overruling, even outside the context of "jurisdiction".

19. One proposal under discussion, however, would (as part of a general revision of Rule 23, governing class actions) authorize interlocutory appeals of rulings granting or denying certification of actions as class actions. See *Significant Developments in Federal Civil Practice and Procedure: 1990–91 Legislative and Rule–Making Changes, Proposed Amendments to the Federal Rules of Civil Procedure and Federal Rules of Evidence,* Q207 ALI–ABA 411, Rule 23(f)(1991).

delay"; in the absence of such a determination and direction, "any order * * * shall not terminate the action as to any of the claims."

In Sears, Roebuck & Co. v. Mackey, 351 U.S. 427 (1956), the Court rejected an attack on the validity of this rule, holding that it was not "an unauthorized extension of § 1291. * * * The District Court *cannot* in the exercise of its discretion, treat as 'final' that which is not 'final' within the meaning of § 1291. But the District Court *may,* by the exercise of its discretion in the interest of sound judicial administration, release for appeal final decisions upon one or more, but less than all, claims in multiple claim actions. * * * [A]ny abuse of that discretion remains reviewable by the Court of Appeals" (pp. 436–37). Such cases as Collins v. Miller were shunted aside as resting on a construction of the judicial unit "developed from the common law which had dealt with litigation generally less complicated than much of that of today" (p. 432).

(2) *The Effect of Subsequent Legislation.* Would the problem of rulemaking authority raised in Mackey be more easily resolved today, in light of the recent addition to Title 28 of § 2072(c), discussed at p. 1655, *supra,* and of § 1292(e), discussed at pp. 1661–62, *infra?*

(3) *Dimensions of a Claim for Relief Under Rule 54(b).* A 1961 amendment to Rule 54(b) explicitly made the rule applicable to a judgment in a multi-party case determining the rights of "fewer than all the parties". But the question of the dimensions of a "claim for relief" remains important. In Sears itself, the district court order, certified under Rule 54(b), had dismissed only Counts I and II of a multi-count complaint, and the Supreme Court, in upholding the appealability of the order, noted that "the claim dismissed by striking out Count I is based on the Sherman Act, while Counts III and IV do not rely on, or even refer to, that Act. They are largely predicated on common-law rights. The basis of liability in Count I is independent of that on which the claims in Counts III and IV depend. But the claim in Count I does rest in part on some of the facts that are involved in Counts III and IV. The claim stated in Count II is clearly independent of those in Counts III and IV" (p. 437 n. 9).[1]

In Seatrain Shipbldg. Co. v. Shell Oil Co., 444 U.S. 572, 579–84 (1980), the Court held that plaintiff's complaint asserted two claims: (1) that the Secretary of Commerce had no authority to grant a release from certain restrictions on the operation of a vessel, and (2) that in any event the granting of a release in the particular case was an abuse of discretion. Thus an appeal would lie under Rule 54(b) from a "final disposition" of the first claim, on proper certification by the district court, even though the second claim had not been finally disposed of. Was the Supreme Court here and in Sears using a narrower definition of a claim than the "transactional" approach adopted in the Restatement (Second) of Judgments § 24 (1982)? Is this appropriate? For example, would dividing a case into claims on the basis of legal theories, or sources of governing law, encourage too many piecemeal appeals?

(4) *The Scope of District Court Discretion.* Although the opinion in Sears indicated that the district court's exercise of discretion under Rule 54(b) was

---

1. *Cf.* Liberty Mut. Ins. Co. v. Wetzel, 424 U.S. 737, 743 n. 4 (1976)(order granting partial summary judgment on liability, but leaving unresolved requests for injunctive relief, damages, and fees, was not appealable under Rule 54(b) or on any other ground; "a complaint asserting only one legal right, even if seeking multiple remedies * * * states a single claim for relief").

subject to review, the Court later made it clear that this exercise should not be lightly set aside for abuse. In Curtiss–Wright Corp. v. General Elec. Co., 446 U.S. 1 (1980), Curtiss–Wright had sued General Electric on several claims, including a claim for a balance of $19 million due on contracts performed, and General Electric had filed a substantial counterclaim. The district court entered summary judgment for Curtiss–Wright on the $19 million claim and ruled it entitled to prejudgment interest on that claim. After full consideration of the relevant factors, the district court then determined that there was "no just reason for delay" and granted Curtiss–Wright's motion to certify the court's orders as final judgments under Rule 54(b). A divided court of appeals ruled that the district court's certification was an abuse of discretion because in the appellate court's view, the presence of a non-frivolous counterclaim that could result in a set-off weighed heavily against the decision to certify. The Supreme Court reversed the judgment of the court of appeals, noting that the presence of the counterclaim had been considered by the district court, along with other factors, and that its assessment of the equities was reasonable. "The question in cases such as this is likely to be close, but the task of weighing and balancing the contending factors is peculiarly one for the trial judge, who can explore all the facets of a case. As we have noted, that assessment merits substantial deference on review" (p. 12).[2]

(5) *Denial of Class Certification.* May Rule 54(b) be used to appeal the denial of a motion to certify an action as a class action, on the theory that the denial is a final disposition of the claim on behalf of the class (as distinct from the claim of the named plaintiff)? Compare Windham v. American Brands, Inc., 539 F.2d 1016, 1020 (4th Cir.1976)(allowing Rule 54(b) review), *rev'd on other grounds on rehearing en banc,* 565 F.2d 59 (4th Cir.1977), with West v. Capital Fed. Sav. & Loan Ass'n, 558 F.2d 977 (10th Cir.1977). Can the Windham approach survive the decisions in Coopers & Lybrand, p. 1650, *supra,* and Gardner v. Westinghouse Broadcasting Co., p. 1659, *infra?*

(6) *Relation Between Rule 54(b) and Other Statutes and Rules Governing Appealability.* To what degree is there an overlap between Rule 54(b) and other statutory and judicially developed rules allowing appeals? In theory at least, Rule 54(b) and 28 U.S.C. § 1292(b), p. 1661, *infra,* are mutually exclusive—though the line between a "final" order subject to Rule 54(b) certification and an "interlocutory" order eligible for § 1292(b) certification may often be indistinct. What of a collateral order within the rationale of the Cohen case? Clearly, not all collateral orders raise a question of the applicability of Rule 54(b). But might there be a collateral order that, for example, involved the final disposition of a single claim in a multi-claim case?[3] If so, would the absence of the requisite district court certification under Rule 54(b) bar an appeal? The commentators don't think so, but the discussion sometimes bogs down in the metaphysics of defining a "claim for relief". See, *e.g.,* 10 Wright, Miller & Kane, Federal Practice and Procedure § 2658.4 (1983 & 1995 Supp.). And though the question has not been squarely addressed by the Supreme Court, it has generally been given fairly short shrift in the lower courts. See,

2. See also Reiter v. Cooper, 507 U.S. 258, ___, 113 S.Ct. 1213, 1218 (1993)(stressing district court discretion to grant or to deny Rule 54(b) certifications).

3. In Cohen itself, for example, could the demand of security for costs be considered a separate "claim for relief"? The majority spoke of the state security-for-costs statute as creating "a new liability where none existed before" (337 U.S. at 555).

e.g., In re General Motors Corp. Engine Interchange Litigation, 594 F.2d 1106, 1118 n. 12 (7th Cir.1979)(a "collateral order" final within the Cohen doctrine is appealable without certification under Rule 54(b)).[4]

NOTE ON INTERLOCUTORY APPEALS

(1) *Section 1292(a)(1).* Section 1292 of Title 28 authorizes interlocutory appeals in a number of situations, the most important of which is that specified in subsection (a)(1): orders "granting, continuing, modifying, refusing or dissolving injunctions, or refusing to modify or dissolve injunctions, except where a direct review may be had in the Supreme Court".

(a) *The Carson Case.* Some insight into the meaning and purpose of this provision is given by the decision in Carson v. American Brands, Inc., 450 U.S. 79 (1981). There, in a case brought under Title VII of the Civil Rights Act of 1964, the district court had refused to enter a proposed consent decree that would have imposed significant obligations on the employer. The Supreme Court held that this action was appealable under § 1292(a)(1). It was not sufficient, however, that the district court's action had the practical effect of denying injunctive relief: "Unless a litigant can show that an interlocutory order of the District Court might have 'serious, perhaps irreparable consequence,' and that the order can be 'effectually challenged' only by immediate appeal, the general congressional policy against piecemeal appeal will preclude interlocutory appeal" (p. 84). In the present case, those stringent criteria were met because the district court's order might deny the parties "their right to compromise their dispute on mutually agreeable terms" (p. 88), and because the plaintiffs might be irrevocably harmed by the delay resulting from a trial.

Was the order in Carson also appealable under § 1291? (The Court noted the question in its opinion but did not resolve it.)

What basis did the Court in Carson have for saying that for an interlocutory order to be immediately appealable under § 1292(a)(1), a litigant must show *more* than that the order has the practical effect of refusing an injunction? Granted that one purpose of the statute is to facilitate prompt review in cases most likely to involve immediate hardship to the litigants, does the statute make a showing of hardship the test of appealability?

Does the Carson decision mean that, to resolve the issue of appealability under § 1292(a)(1), each case must be judged on its particular facts to determine the seriousness of the consequences? If so, does this requirement apply only to orders effectively denying injunctive relief and not to orders *granting*

---

4. A related question is whether a trial court's disposition of the claims in a case that has been consolidated with another case is appealable as a final judgment under § 1291, or only pursuant to certification under Rule 54(b). The courts of appeals are divided, and one recent comprehensive discussion of the various problems associated with consolidation favors treating the cases as a single action for purposes of determining appealability; under such an approach, appeals of judgments on claims not encompassing the entire action would ordinarily be governed by the provisions of Rule 54(b). Steinman, *The Effects of Case Consolidation on the Procedural Rights of Litigants: What They Are, What They Might Be Part I: Justiciability*

such relief?[1]   (Consider, for example, a case in which a court, in a preliminary injunction, orders the parties to maintain the status quo, and in which neither party can show any serious or irreparable harm as a result of the order.)

In Switzerland Cheese Ass'n, Inc. v. E. Horne's Mkt., Inc., 385 U.S. 23 (1966), relied on in Carson, the denial of plaintiffs' motion for summary judgment was held not immediately appealable even though its practical effect was to deny them the permanent injunction they had sought in the motion. But the denial did not preclude the plaintiffs from immediately seeking preliminary relief and only postponed the question of permanent relief until trial. Did it require a close analysis of the actual consequences to conclude that the order was not appealable under § 1292(a)(1)?

(b) *The Gardner Decision and Denial of Class Certification.*   In Gardner v. Westinghouse Broadcasting Co., 437 U.S. 478 (1978), also relied on in Carson, the Court held that an order denying class certification was not appealable under § 1292(a)(1) even though the order might significantly affect the scope of any ultimate injunctive relief. No motion for preliminary relief had been filed, the Court noted, and the district court had not "entirely disposed of" the prayer for permanent relief. Moreover, the denial of class action status was itself conditional and "did not pass on the legal sufficiency of any claims for injunctive relief"; thus, as in Switzerland Cheese, the order had "no direct or irreparable impact on the merits of the controversy" (pp. 480–82).

In Gardner, the plaintiff was also seeking injunctive relief on her own behalf. What if the equities were such that the individual plaintiff would clearly not be entitled to an injunction—that such relief could be granted only on behalf of the class? Should the conditional nature of the denial of class action status serve in itself to preclude review under § 1292(a)(1)?

(c) *Rulings Staying Proceedings or Advancing the Order of Trial: The Rise and Fall of the Enelow Doctrine.*   Among the most troublesome cases under § 1292(a)(1) are those concerned with the order of trial or with a stay of proceedings in one tribunal pending adjudication in another.

In Enelow v. New York Life Ins. Co., 293 U.S. 379 (1935), the plaintiff brought an action on a life insurance policy. Relying on then § 274b of the Judicial Code, permitting equitable defenses in actions at law, the defendant alleged that the policy had been obtained by fraud, offered to refund the premiums, prayed for cancellation of the policy and petitioned that the "equitable" issue be heard by the court without a jury prior to determination of the "legal" issues. The district court granted the petition and on appeal from the decree the court of appeals affirmed. The Supreme Court, reversing on the merits, held the decree appealable. Chief Justice Hughes said (p. 383):

---

and Jurisdiction (Original and Appellate), 42 UCLA L.Rev. 717, 807 (1995).

1. Section 1292(a)(1) had its origin in the Evarts Act of 1891, see p. 1636, *supra,* and originally provided for interlocutory appeals only from orders granting or continuing injunctions. For analysis of subsequent revisions, and the suggestion that in extending the statute to denials of relief, Congress "was thinking primarily of the case where erroneous denial of a *temporary* injunction may cause injury quite as irreparable as an erro-

neous grant of one," see Stewart–Warner Corp. v. Westinghouse Elec. Corp., 325 F.2d 822, 830 (2d Cir.1963)(Friendly, J., dissenting).

Though the final judgment rule existed at common law, it never developed in courts of equity. See Crick, *The Final Judgment Rule as a Basis for Appeal,* 41 Yale L.J. 539, 545–48 (1932). There is no clear indication of why the First Judiciary Act limited appeals to final judgments and decrees at law *and* in equity.

"[W]hen an order or decree is made under § 274b, requiring, or refusing to require, that an equitable defense shall first be tried, the court, exercising what is essentially an equitable jurisdiction, in effect grants or refuses an injunction restraining proceedings at law precisely as if the court had acted upon a bill of complaint in a separate suit for the same purpose."

Enelow and later Supreme Court decisions applying it became a source of disagreement and confusion in the lower courts, especially in cases involving requests for abstention or for a stay relating to arbitration. In the context of arbitration, the question could arise in connection with orders granting or denying a stay of an arbitration proceeding or with orders granting or denying a stay of the court's own proceedings pending arbitration. And the judicial proceeding itself could be characterized as one in equity or law, depending on the nature of the complaint.

Criticism of the Enelow line, from the standpoint both of its historical accuracy and its current value, was widespread. After a full review, the Supreme Court, in Gulfstream Aerospace Corp. v. Mayacamas Corp., 485 U.S. 271 (1988), unanimously voted to "overturn the cases establishing the Enelow * * * rule and hold that orders granting or denying stays of 'legal' proceedings on 'equitable' grounds are not automatically appealable under § 1292(a)(1)" (p. 287). "The case against perpetuation of this sterile and antiquated doctrine seems to us conclusive. * * * This holding will not prevent interlocutory review of district court orders when such review is truly needed * * * [as in the case of] orders that have the practical effect of granting or denying injunctions and have 'serious, perhaps irreparable, consequence' [citing discussion in Carson, Paragraph (1)(a), *supra*]" (pp. 287–88).[2]

(d) *Orders Granting, Denying, or Dissolving Temporary Restraining Orders.* An order granting, denying, or dissolving a temporary restraining order is not ordinarily appealable under § 1292(a)(1). See 16 Wright, Miller, Cooper & Gressman, Federal Practice and Procedure § 3922 (1977 & 1995 Supp.). But in Sampson v. Murray, 415 U.S. 61, 86–87 n. 58 (1974), the Court quoted with approval, and applied, the reasoning of the Second Circuit (in Pan American World Airways, Inc. v. Flight Engineers' Intern. Ass'n, 306 F.2d 840, 843 (2d Cir.1962)) that "continuation of the temporary restraining order beyond the period of statutory authorization [*i.e.,* the time permissible under Federal Rule 65(b)] having, as it does, the same practical effect as the issuance of a preliminary injunction, is appealable within the meaning and intent of 28 U.S.C. § 1292(a)(1)". See also International Primate Prot. League v. Adminis-

---

2. A 1988 amendment to the Federal Arbitration Act, 9 U.S.C. § 1 *et seq.*, addresses the appealability of orders compelling or refusing to compel arbitration. A new provision, 9 U.S.C. § 16, permits appeals from orders refusing to stay a lawsuit or denying a motion to compel arbitration, and from any "final decision with respect to an arbitration". It prohibits appeals (except under 28 U.S.C. § 1292(b)) from interlocutory orders compelling arbitration or granting a stay of an action pending arbitration.

The effect of this provision on the appealability of orders concerning arbitration of labor disputes is uncertain. See United Pa-

perworkers Int'l Union v. Misco, Inc., 484 U.S. 29, 40 n. 9 (1987)(the Federal Arbitration Act does not apply to collective bargaining agreements, "but the federal courts have often looked to the Act for guidance in labor arbitration cases"). The courts of appeals are divided on the general question of the appealability under § 1292(a)(1) of a refusal to grant a stay pending arbitration in cases *not* within the coverage of the Arbitration Act. Compare, *e.g.,* Nordin v. Nutri/System, Inc., 897 F.2d 339 (8th Cir.1990)(allowing appeal) with, *e.g.,* Zosky v. Boyer, 856 F.2d 554 (3d Cir.1988)(denying appeal).

trators of Tulane Educ. Fund, 500 U.S. 72, 76 (1991). Also, the grant or denial of a temporary restraining order may under special circumstances be so clear a disposition of the merits (because of the threat of mootness) as to be an appealable final order under § 1291. See, *e.g.*, Virginia v. Tenneco, Inc., 538 F.2d 1026 (4th Cir.1976).

(2) *Section 1292(b).* The enactment in 1958 of § 1292(b) added one more string to the bow of a losing party in a civil action who wants prompt review of an interlocutory order. But the statute requires approval of an appeal by both the district and appellate courts, and the courts have never allowed free and easy use of its provisions. Thus one author reported that the acceptance rate of 1292(b) applications by the appellate courts dropped from approximately 50% in the 1960s to about 35% in the 1980s, and that in the 1980s, the cases accepted represented about 0.3% of appeals terminated on the merits.[3]

(a) Among the possible reasons for permitting appeals before final judgment are the avoidance of hardship, the need to supervise the administration of the law in the lower courts on matters not often presented on appeal from final judgments, and the desire to increase efficiency and reduce costs. Does § 1292(b) contemplate the allowance of interlocutory appeals on any or all of these grounds?

(b) What is a "controlling question of law" within the meaning of the statute? Must the question be one that will be dispositive of the action? Or is it enough that reversal would have a substantial effect on the course of litigation? May a question involving the exercise of discretion ever be reviewed under this section?[4]

(c) Does the condition that an immediate appeal "may materially advance the ultimate termination of the litigation" limit the applicability of § 1292(b) to protracted cases? Must the time and expense of the appeal be countered by a greater potential saving of time and expense at the trial level?

(d) Given the specific requirements of § 1292(b), may an order to transfer a case under § 28 U.S.C. § 1404, or refusing to transfer, ever be reviewable under this section?[5]

(3) *Legislative Authorization of Supreme Court Rulemaking.* In 1992, Congress added to § 1292 a new subsection (e), which authorizes the Supreme

---

3. Solimine, *Revitalizing Interlocutory Appeals in the Federal Courts,* 58 Geo.Wash. L.Rev. 1165, 1174 (1990). Solimine suggests that part of the reluctance to accept applications is the view of many courts that § 1292(b) should be reserved for "big" cases, see *id.* at 1173, and concludes by advocating a "more positive" attitude toward the certification of appeals, *id.* at 1213.

4. In Coopers & Lybrand v. Livesay, 437 U.S. 463 (1978), p. 1650, *supra,* the Supreme Court cited with apparent approval several lower court decisions reviewing "discretionary class determinations" under § 1292(b)(pp. 475–76 n. 27).

5. In Continental Grain Co. v. Barge FBL–585, 364 U.S. 19 (1960), p. 1611, *supra,*

the court of appeals had allowed a § 1292(b) appeal of a transfer order; the question of appealability was not discussed by the Supreme Court. See also Katz v. Carte Blanche Corp., 496 F.2d 747 (3d Cir.1974)(transferor court's decision may be reviewed on appeal under § 1292(b) in appropriate circumstances).

See generally 16 Wright, Miller, Cooper & Gressman, Federal Practice and Procedure § 3930, at 159–60 (1977)(noting that a question of law may be viewed as "controlling" if interlocutory reversal "might save time for the district court, and time and expense for the litigants").

Court to prescribe rules that provide for interlocutory appeals not otherwise authorized by § 1292. No such rules have yet been promulgated.

Is this an appropriate subject for judicial rulemaking? See p. 1655, *supra*. See also Martineau, *Defining Finality and Appealability by Court Rule: Right Problem, Wrong Solution,* 54 U.Pitt.L.Rev. 718 (1993), and a comment on Martineau's article by Rowe, 54 *id.* 795. Would you approve a decision by the Court, acting pursuant to its new authority under this provision and under new § 2072(c), to promulgate rules that (a) redefined "finality" to exist only when the case was truly over in the district court and then (b) gave appellate courts broad discretion (perhaps pursuant to general criteria relating to hardship and importance) to allow interlocutory appeals from *any* district court ruling? See Note, 44 Duke L.J. 200 (1994)(advocating a similar approach). Would such a course leave too wide an opening for using up court and litigant time with requests for discretionary appeals?

Will v. United States

389 U.S. 90, 88 S.Ct. 269, 19 L.Ed.2d 305 (1967).
Certiorari to the United States Court of Appeals for the Seventh Circuit.

■ MR. CHIEF JUSTICE WARREN delivered the opinion of the Court.

The question in this case is the propriety of a writ of mandamus issued by the Court of Appeals for the Seventh Circuit to compel the petitioner, a United States District Judge, to vacate a portion of a pretrial order in a criminal case.

Simmie Horwitz, the defendant in a criminal tax evasion case pending before petitioner in the Northern District of Illinois, filed a motion for a bill of particulars, which contained thirty requests for information. * * * Ultimately the dispute centered solely on defendant's request number 25. This request sought certain information concerning any oral statements of the defendant relied upon by the Government to support the charge in the indictment. It asked the names and addresses of the persons to whom such statements were made, the times and places at which they were made, whether the witnesses to the statements were government agents and whether any transcripts or memoranda of the statements had been prepared by the witnesses and given to the Government. After considerable discussion with counsel for both sides, petitioner ordered the Government to furnish the information. The United States Attorney declined to comply with the order on the grounds that request number 25 constituted a demand for a list of prosecution witnesses and that petitioner had no power under Rule 7(f) of the Federal Rules of Criminal Procedure to require the Government to produce such a list.

Petitioner indicated his intention to dismiss the indictments against Horwitz because of the Government's refusal to comply with his order for a bill of particulars. Before the order of dismissal was entered, however, the Government sought and obtained *ex parte* from the Seventh Circuit a stay of all proceedings in the case. The Court of Appeals also granted the Government leave to file a petition for a writ of mandamus and issued a rule to show cause why such a writ should not issue to compel petitioner to strike request number 25 from his bill of particulars order. This case was submitted on the briefs, and the Court of Appeals at first denied the writ. The Government petitioned for reconsideration, however, and the Court of Appeals, without taking new briefs or hearing oral argument, reversed itself and without opinion issued a writ of mandamus directing petitioner "to vacate his order directing the Government to answer question 25 in defendant's motion for bill of particulars." We granted certiorari because of the wide implications of the decision below for the orderly administration of criminal justice in the federal courts. We vacate the writ and remand the case to the Court of Appeals for further proceedings.

Both parties have devoted substantial argument in this Court to the propriety of petitioner's order. In our view of the case, however, it is unnecessary to reach this question.[4] The peremptory writ of mandamus has traditionally been used in the federal courts only "to confine an inferior court to a lawful exercise of its prescribed jurisdiction or to compel it to exercise its authority when it is its duty to do so." Roche v. Evaporated Milk Assn., 319 U.S. 21, 26 (1943). While the courts have never confined themselves to an arbitrary and technical definition of "jurisdiction," it is clear that only exceptional circumstances amounting to a judicial "usurpation of power" will justify the invocation of this extraordinary remedy. De Beers Consol. Mines, Ltd. v. United States, 325 U.S. 212, 217 (1945). Thus the writ has been invoked where unwarranted judicial action threatened "to embarrass the executive arm of the government in conducting foreign relations," Ex parte Republic of Peru, 318 U.S. 578, 588 (1943), where it was the only means of forestalling intrusion by the federal judiciary on a delicate area of federal-state relations, State of Maryland v. Soper, 270 U.S. 9 (1926), where it was necessary to confine a lower court to the terms of an appellate tribunal's mandate, United States v. United States Dist. Court, 334 U.S. 258 (1948), and where a district judge displayed a persistent disregard of the Rules of Civil Procedure promulgated by this Court, La Buy v. Howes Leather Co., 352 U.S. 249 (1957) * * *.   And the party seeking mandamus has "the burden of showing that its right to issuance of the writ is 'clear and indisputable.' " Bankers Life & Cas. Co. v. Holland, 346 U.S. 379, 384 (1953). * * *

We also approach this case with an awareness of additional considerations which flow from the fact that the underlying proceeding is a criminal prosecution.   All our jurisprudence is strongly colored by the notion that appellate review should be postponed, except in certain narrowly defined circumstances, until after final judgment has been rendered by the trial court.   * * * This general policy against piecemeal appeals takes on added weight in criminal cases, where the defendant is entitled to a speedy resolution of the charges against him.   * * * Nor is the case against permitting the writ to be used as a substitute for interlocutory appeal "made less compelling * * * by the fact that the Government has no later right to appeal." DiBella v. United States, 369 U.S. 121, 130 (1962).[5] This is not to say that mandamus may never be used to

---

4. It is likewise unnecessary for us to reach the question whether the writ in the circumstances of this case may be said to issue in aid of an exercise of the Court of Appeals' appellate jurisdiction.   See 28 U.S.C. § 1651; Roche v. Evaporated Milk Assn., 319 U.S. 21, 25 (1943). * * * In our view, even assuming that the possible future appeal in this case would support the Court of Appeals' mandamus jurisdiction, it was an

abuse of discretion for the court to act as it did in the circumstances of this case.

5. Thus it is irrelevant, and we do not decide, whether the Government could appeal in the event petitioner dismissed the Horwitz indictments because of its refusal to comply with his bill of particulars order. * * *

[Ed.] Would a dismissal of the indictments be appealable today? See p. 1639, *supra.*

review procedural orders in criminal cases. It has been invoked successfully where the action of the trial court totally deprived the Government of its right to initiate a prosecution, Ex parte United States, 287 U.S. 241 (1932), and where the court overreached its judicial power to deny the Government the rightful fruits of a valid conviction, Ex parte United States, 242 U.S. 27 (1916). But this Court has never approved the use of the writ to review an interlocutory procedural order in a criminal case which did not have the effect of a dismissal. We need not decide under what circumstances, if any, such a use of mandamus would be appropriate. It is enough to note that we approach the decision in this case with an awareness of the constitutional precepts that a man is entitled to a speedy trial and that he may not be placed twice in jeopardy for the same offense.

In light of these considerations and criteria, neither the record before us nor the cryptic order of the Court of Appeals justifies the invocation of the extraordinary writ in this case.

We do not understand the Government to argue that petitioner was in any sense without "jurisdiction" to order it to file a bill of particulars.[6] * * *.

The Government seeks instead to justify the employment of the writ in this instance on the ground that petitioner's conduct displays a "pattern of manifest noncompliance with the rules governing federal criminal trials." It argues that the federal rules place settled limitations upon pretrial discovery in criminal cases, and that a trial court may not, in the absence of compelling justification, order the Government to produce a list of its witnesses in advance of trial. It argues further that in only one category of cases, i.e., prosecutions for treason and other capital offenses, is the Government required to turn over to the defense such a list of its witnesses. A general policy of requiring such disclosure without a particularized showing of need would, it is contended, offend the informant's privilege. Petitioner, according to the Government, adopted "a uniform rule in his courtroom requiring the government in a criminal case to furnish the defense, on motion for a bill of particulars, a list of potential witnesses." The Government concludes that since petitioner obviously had no power to adopt such a rule, mandamus will lie under this Court's decision in La Buy v. Howes Leather Co., 352 U.S. 249 (1957), to correct this studied disregard of the limitations placed upon the district courts by the federal rules.[10]

The action of the Court of Appeals cannot, on the record before us, bear the weight of this justification. There is absolutely no foundation in this record for the Government's assertions concerning petitioner's practice. The legal proposition that mandamus will lie in appropriate cases to correct willful disobedience of the rules laid down by this Court is not controverted. But the position of the Government rests on two central factual premises: (1) that

---

6. Nor do we understand the Government to argue that a judge has no "power" to enter an erroneous order. Acceptance of this semantic fallacy would undermine the settled limitations upon the power of an appellate court to review interlocutory orders. * * * Courts faced with petitions for the peremptory writs must be careful lest they suffer themselves to be misled by labels such as "abuse of discretion" and "want of power" into interlocutory review of nonappealable orders on the mere ground that they may be erroneous. * * *

10. We note in passing that La Buy and the other decisions of this Court approving the use of mandamus as a means of policing compliance with the procedural rules were civil cases. * * * We have pointed out that the fact this case involves a criminal prosecution has contextual relevance. * * *

petitioner in effect ordered it to produce a list of witnesses in advance of trial; and (2) that petitioner took this action pursuant to a deliberately adopted policy in disregard of the rules of criminal procedure. Neither of these premises finds support in the record.

     * * *

Even more important in our view, however, than these deficiencies in the record is the failure of the Court of Appeals to attempt to supply any reasoned justification of its action. * * * There is no evidence in this record concerning petitioner's practice in other cases, aside from his own remark that the Government was generally dissatisfied with it, and his statements do not reveal any intent to evade or disregard the rules. We do not know what he ordered the Government to reveal under what circumstances in other cases. This state of the record renders the silence of the Court of Appeals all the more critical. We recognized in La Buy that the familiarity of a court of appeals with the practice of the individual district courts within its circuit was relevant to an assessment of the need for mandamus as a corrective measure. But without an opinion from the Court of Appeals we do not know what role, if any, this factor played in the decision below. In fact, we are in the dark with respect to the position of the Court of Appeals on all the issues crucial to an informed exercise of our power of review. * * * We cannot properly identify the questions for decision in the case before us without illumination of this unclear record by the measured and exposed reflection of the Court of Appeals. * * *

Mandamus is not a punitive remedy. The entire thrust of the Government's justification for mandamus in this case, moreover, is that the writ serves a vital corrective and didactic function. While these aims lay at the core of this Court's decisions in La Buy and Schlagenhauf v. Holder, 379 U.S. 104 (1964), we fail to see how they can be served here without findings of fact by the issuing court and some statement of the court's legal reasoning. A mandamus from the blue without rationale is tantamount to an abdication of the very expository and supervisory functions of an appellate court upon which the Government rests its attempt to justify the action below.

* * * What might be the proper decision upon a more complete record, supplemented by the findings and conclusions of the Court of Appeals, we cannot and do not say. Hence the writ is vacated and the cause is remanded to the Court of Appeals for the Seventh Circuit for further proceedings not inconsistent with this opinion. It is so ordered.

Writ vacated and cause remanded.

■ MR. JUSTICE BLACK, concurring.

I concur in the Court's judgment to vacate and agree substantially with its opinion, but would like to add a few words, which I do not understand to be in conflict with what the Court says, concerning the writ of mandamus. I agree that mandamus is an extraordinary remedy which should not be issued except in extraordinary circumstances. And I also realize that sometimes the granting of mandamus may bring about the review of a case as would an appeal. Yet this does not deprive a court of its power to issue the writ. Where there are extraordinary circumstances, mandamus may be used to review an interlocutory order which is by no means "final" and thus appealable under federal statutes. Finality, then, while relevant to the right of appeal, is not determinative of the question when to issue mandamus. Rather than hinging on this abstruse and infinitely uncertain term, the issuance of the writ of mandamus is proper where a court finds exceptional circumstances to support such an order. In the present case it is conceivable that there are valid reasons why the Government should not be forced to turn over the requested names and that compliance with the order would inflict irreparable damage on its conduct of the case.   The trouble here, as I see it, is that neither of the courts below gave proper consideration to the possible existence of exceptional facts which might justify the Government's refusal to disclose the names.   Having no doubt as to the appropriateness of mandamus, if the circumstances exist to justify it, I would vacate the judgment below and remand the case to the Court of Appeals for further deliberation on whether there are special circumstances calling for the issuance of mandamus.

NOTE ON THE EXTRAORDINARY WRITS IN THE COURTS OF APPEALS

(1) *The Background and Aftermath of the Will decision.*   The Court in Will relied on its 1943 decision in Roche v. Evaporated Milk Ass'n, 319 U.S. 21 (1943), in which it reversed a lower court's use of mandamus to review a decision of a pretrial motion in a criminal case.   Since Roche, there has been a good deal of oscillation in the Supreme Court's approach to the availability of mandamus under the All Writs Act, now embodied in 28 U.S.C. § 1651.   But since Will, the trend has been in the direction of greater restraint,[1] although the standard is still far from precise, and the Court may take a close look at the merits in the course of holding mandamus unavailable.[2]

A particularly interesting case (also involving Judge Will) is Will v. Calvert Fire Ins. Co., 437 U.S. 655 (1978), p. 1317, *supra,* in which the Court reversed an appellate court's grant of mandamus to compel the district court to adjudicate a claim pending between the same parties in a state court.   A plurality opinion for four Justices said that mandamus did not lie because the district court had neither exceeded the bounds of its jurisdiction nor refused to exercise its authority when it had a duty to do so.   The district court's decision to defer to the state court was essentially discretionary, and the opinion strongly suggested that even an abuse of discretion was not subject to review on mandamus: "Although in at least one instance we approved the issuance of the writ upon a *mere* showing of abuse of discretion, LaBuy v. Howes Leather Co., 352 U.S. 249, 257 (1957), we warned soon thereafter against the dangers of such a practice" (p. 665 n. 7)(emphasis added).

Justice Blackmun, in a brief opinion concurring only in the judgment, said that the court below should have remanded for reconsideration in the light of Colorado River, p. 1308, *supra,* decided after the district court's action.   With respect to the appropriateness of mandamus, he said only that its issuance had

---

1.   See, *e.g.,* Kerr v. United States Dist. Court, 426 U.S. 394 (1976)(mandamus unavailable to review district court order compelling the government to disclose documents); Helstoski v. Meanor, 442 U.S. 500, 506 (1979)(mandamus unavailable to obtain pretrial review of denial of claim of immunity from criminal prosecution; though no timely appeal had been taken, denial was appealable under § 1291); Allied Chem. Corp. v. Dai-flon, Inc., 449 U.S. 33, 35 (1980)(per curiam reversal of grant of mandamus to review new trial order).   But see Mallard v. United States Dist. Court, discussed at the end of Paragraph (1) of this Note.

2.   See, *e.g.,* Kerr v. United States Dist. Court, note 1, *supra.*   For an example at the court of appeals level, see Kaufman v. Edelstein, 539 F.2d 811, 816–22 (2d Cir.1976).

been "premature" (p. 668). (How could the court of appeals have required the district court to do anything without granting the petition in some form?) Four dissenters argued that the issuance of mandamus was appropriate "[w]hether evaluated under the 'clear abuse of discretion' standard set forth [in LaBuy] or under the prong of [Will v. United States] that permits the use of mandamus 'to compel [an inferior court] to exercise its authority when it is its duty to do so' "(p. 676).

The nature of Justice Blackmun's swing vote in this case has complicated the problem of determining the applicable standard for the availability of mandamus, but some further light may have been shed by the Court's subsequent decision in Mallard v. United States Dist. Court, 490 U.S. 296 (1989). In that case, the Court upheld the availability of mandamus to an attorney who claimed that the district court lacked statutory authority to order him to represent indigent inmates in a § 1983 action against prison officials. While stressing that mandamus remains "an extraordinary remedy", the Court held that the attorney had made an adequate showing that the district lacked statutory "jurisdiction" (as that term had been broadly defined in the mandamus context) to order him to act as counsel, that the attorney had no alternative remedy, that the district judge had not been made a formal party to the action, and that the mandamus petition did not "sever one element of the merits litigation from the rest" (p.309).

(2) *Mandamus and § 1447(d)*. After the first Will decision, the Supreme Court did hold, in Thermtron Prods., Inc. v. Hermansdorfer, 423 U.S. 336 (1976), that mandamus was available to review a district court remand order, despite the prohibitory language of 28 U.S.C. § 1447(d), because the order was not issued under § 1447(c), *i.e.,* the district court had not relied on the ground that the case had been removed "improvidently and without jurisdiction". Only cases remanded under § 1447(c), the Court held, were unreviewable under § 1447(d), and this was not such a case since the district court had in effect conceded that the case had been properly removed.

Justice Rehnquist, speaking for himself and two other Justices, dissented. He disagreed with the majority's view of the legislative history of the relevant statutory provisions, urged that the plain language of § 1447(d) precluded the result, and asked what would now happen if a remanding court used "the rubric of § 1447(c), but the papers plainly demonstrate such a conclusion to be absurd? * * * If the Court's grant of certiorari and order of reversal in this case are to have any meaning, it would seem that such avenues of attack should clearly be open. * * * Yet it is equally clear that such devices would soon render meaningless Congress' express, and heretofore fully effective, directive prohibiting such tactics because of their potential for abuse by those seeking only to delay" (p. 357).

If you were a legislator determined to avoid the delays inherent in review of remand orders, and thus to prohibit *all* such review, could you have drafted clearer language than that contained in § 1447(d)? Did the majority in Thermtron imply that some errors of law are so egregious that prohibitions on review will simply be ignored? Does the recognition of judicial discretion in other areas of original and appellate jurisdiction (see, *e.g.,* p. 1265, *supra*) afford justification for such action?

Whether Thermtron was correct or not, its scope was confined by the brief per curiam decision in Gravitt v. Southwestern Bell Tel. Co., 430 U.S. 723

(1977)(holding that a remand order purporting to rest on a ground within the scope of § 1447(c) was not reviewable on mandamus).[3]

(3) *Lower Court Decisions.* Whatever the precise standard for the availability of mandamus—whether phrased in terms of "jurisdiction," "excess of power," or "clear abuse of discretion"—some courts of appeals appear willing to issue mandamus or its equivalent when the court is satisfied that judicial administration so requires.[4] There are variations in approach among and even within circuits, and there is recognition of the congressional policy favoring review only after final decision. But that policy has been subject to exception by judicial decision, by rule, and by statute. Indeed, it is not too difficult to imagine a party in a civil case who wants to bring an issue up for review seeking a certification from the trial judge under Rule 54(b) or § 1292(b) in the alternative, and failing in that, arguing to the court of appeals that (a) the decision below is final under § 1291; (b) if not, it is appealable under § 1292(a)(1); and (c) if not, mandamus should issue.

(4) *Issues in the Application of § 1651.* What is the meaning of the limitation in the All Writs Act to writs necessary or appropriate "in aid of [the courts'] respective jurisdictions"? (See footnote 4 of the Court's opinion in the *Will* case.) The phrase has not been construed to mean that the case must then be pending in the court issuing the writ. Is it enough that the case is one that may at some future time come within the court's appellate jurisdiction? If the issue would not come before the appellate court in the ordinary course of review of a final judgment, either because it would then be moot or because any

3. Solimine, *Removal, Remands, and Reforming Federal Appellate Review,* 58 Mo. L.Rev. 287 (1993), points out that Thermtron has served as the basis for a number of appellate decisions permitting review of remand orders in situations that, at the least, raise difficult questions of interpretation under § 1447(d). See, *e.g.,* TMI Litigation Cases Consol. II, 940 F.2d 832 (3d Cir.1991)(allowing appeal from a remand order based on a ruling that the provision allowing removal was unconstitutional). *But cf.* Linton v. Airbus Industrie, 30 F.3d 592 (5th Cir.1994)(refusing to allow review of remand order based on district court's rejection of allegedly "separable" claim of immunity under Foreign Sovereign Immunities Act); Liberty Mut. Ins. Co. v. Ward Trucking Corp., 48 F.3d 742 (3d Cir.1995)(review of remand order denied although district court had not given removing party opportunity to respond to motion to remand). Moreover, the Supreme Court itself has recently re-emphasized the narrow application of the Thermtron rule in its decision in Things Remembered, Inc. v. Petrarca, 116 S.Ct. 494 (1995) (holding unreviewable a remand order in removed bankruptcy proceeding). See also *id.* at 498 (Kennedy, J., concurring, suggesting that other questions as to the proper

scope of the Thermtron rule remain unresolved).

Solimine urges that because § 1447(d) runs counter to the general availability of appellate review and does so without sufficient basis, some form of review—perhaps under a modified version of § 1292(b)—be authorized by Congress. (Congress has authorized appellate review of remand orders in some specific instances—*e.g.,* in § 1447(d) itself for cases removed under § 1443, and in cases involving removal pursuant to the Financial Institutions Reform, Recovery and Enforcement Act, 12 U.S.C. § 1819(b)(2)(C).)

For further discussion of the reviewability of remand orders, see Herrmann, *Thermtron Revisited: When and How Federal Trial Court Remand Orders Are Reviewable,* 19 Ariz.St.L.J. 395 (1987); Steinman, *Removal, Remand, and Review in Pendent Claim and Pendent Party Cases,* 41 Vand.L.Rev. 923, 991–1010 (1988).

4. See, *e.g.,* Central Microfilm Serv. Corp. v. Basic/Four Corp., 688 F.2d 1206 (8th Cir.1982)(mandamus lies to review second new trial order that was erroneous as a matter of law); In re American Cable Publications, Inc., 768 F.2d 1194 (10th Cir.1985)(mandamus lies to review order disqualifying plaintiff's law partner from representing him).

error would likely be held harmless at that stage, how can the granting of mandamus aid the court in the exercise of appellate jurisdiction? If the issue would come up in ordinary course after final judgment, how can the use of mandamus simply to advance appellate consideration be defended? Is the strongest case for the exercise of mandamus one in which the trial judge has acted or failed to act in a way that would prevent the controversy from being adjudicated and thus would defeat appellate review, *e.g.,* a refusal to render a ruling or to allow the case to proceed?[5].

For discussion of similar issues as they affect the power of the Supreme Court, see Ex parte Peru, 318 U.S. 578 (1943), and the following Note, p. 336, *supra.*

(5) *Specific Rulings Subject to Review on Mandamus.* Two of the trial court actions as to which mandamus is frequently sought are denials of jury trial claims and grants or denials of requested transfers of venue. With respect to transfer, Supreme Court decisions indicate that the writ is available to review certain errors of law by the district court,[6] but there is less guidance on the availability of the writ to review the exercise of discretion.[7] With respect to a claim of the right to a jury trial, the Court has said: "Whatever differences of opinion there may be in other types of cases, we think the right to grant mandamus to require jury trial where it has been improperly denied is settled." Beacon Theatres, Inc. v. Westover, 359 U.S. 500, 511 (1959). Do you believe it has been settled correctly?

(6) *The Trial Judge as Litigant in the Reviewing Court.* When mandamus is used not as a remedy against a judge for wrongful conduct but simply as a means of reviewing the merits of his decision on an issue of law, it seems inappropriate for the judge to appear in the reviewing court as a litigant. And the problem is aggravated if after working with a party to have his ruling upheld on review, the judge returns to his role as adjudicator when the case goes forward in the district court. Fed.R.App.P. 21 provides that in an application for prohibition or mandamus, all parties other than the petitioner shall be considered respondents, along with the named judge or judges. It further provides that the judge may, if he wishes, choose not to appear in the proceeding, and such a choice shall not be taken as an admission of the allegations of the petition.[8]

(7) *Other Extraordinary Writs.* Mandamus and its fraternal twin, prohibition, are not the only writs falling within the scope of the All Writs Act. See, *e.g.,* Kanatser v. Chrysler Corp., 199 F.2d 610 (10th Cir.1952)(granting a common law writ of certiorari to review the district court's award of a new trial, more than six months after the entry of judgment, on a ground not asserted in a

---

5. See generally FTC v. Dean Foods Co., 384 U.S. 597, 603–04 (1966).

6. See Hoffman v. Blaski, 363 U.S. 335, 340 n. 9 (1960); Van Dusen v. Barrack, 376 U.S. 612, 615 n. 3 (1964). The discussion in these opinions is less than fully enlightening, but they appear to support use of the writ at least when transfer has been ordered to a district that is not one where the action "might have been brought."

7. The variation among the lower courts is set forth in 15 Wright, Miller &

Cooper, Federal Practice and Procedure, § 3855 (1986 & 1995 Supp.).

8. The local rules of several courts of appeals now provide that a petition for mandamus or prohibition shall not bear the name of the district judge and that, unless otherwise ordered, the judge shall be represented pro forma by counsel opposing the requested relief. See, *e.g.,* U.S.Ct.App. 1st Cir. Rule 21; U.S. Ct. App. 4th Cir. Rule 21.

timely new trial motion); FTC v. Dean Foods Co., 384 U.S. 597 (1966)(holding, 5–4, that a court of appeals may exercise its authority under the All Writs Act to enjoin a corporate merger pending adjudication of the lawfulness of the proposed merger before the FTC).

(8) *Infrequency of the Use of § 1651.* The quantity of applications to the courts of appeals for extraordinary writs has not been great. In fiscal 1970, of 11,662 cases filed in the courts of appeals, only 241 were original proceedings. Annual Report of the Director of the Administrative Office of the U.S. Courts 1970, Table B–1. Sixteen years later, the figure had grown to 703 of 34,292 cases docketed in the courts of appeals (Annual Report 1986, Table B–1), but by 1994 had declined to 588 of 48,322 cases docketed (Annual Report 1994, Table B–1). (The overwhelming majority of these original proceedings are applications for writs of mandamus, and most of the remainder are applications for writs of prohibition. See letter from J.A. McCafferty, Administrative Office, to David Shapiro (Aug. 26, 1982).)[9]

SECTION 3.   REVIEW OF FEDERAL DECISIONS BY THE SUPREME COURT

SUBSECTION A: OBLIGATORY REVIEW

NOTE ON APPEALS TO THE SUPREME COURT FROM THE LOWER FEDERAL COURTS

(1) *Reduction in the Supreme Court's Mandatory Appellate Jurisdiction Over Decisions of the Lower Federal Courts.* As a result of the statutory changes described in Section 1 of this chapter, and more fully detailed in Stern, Gressman, Shapiro & Geller, Supreme Court Practice §§ 2.6–2.9 (7th ed. 1993), the Supreme Court's mandatory appellate jurisdiction over decisions of the lower federal courts is now limited to only a few situations. Thus, certain acts of Congress require that some or all actions under them be heard by a three-judge district court and further provide (either in their own terms or pursuant to the provisions of 28 U.S.C. § 1253) for direct appeal to the Supreme Court. These statutes include 28 U.S.C. § 2284 (actions challenging the apportionment of congressional districts or of any statewide legislative body); two rarely used provisions of the Civil Rights Act of 1964 (actions in which the Attorney General seeks preventive relief against certain forms of discrimination in places of public accommodation or with respect to employment opportunities[1]); the

---

9. For valuable discussion of the availability of mandamus and other writs in the courts of appeals, see generally 16 Wright, Miller, Cooper & Gressman, Federal Practice and Procedure §§ 3932–3936 (1977 & 1995 Supp.).

1. 42 U.S.C. §§ 2000a–5, 2000e–6. In both instances, the statute permits the Attor-

Voting Rights Act of 1965 and related statutes;[2] and the Presidential Election Campaign Fund Act of 1971, 26 U.S.C. §§ 9001–9013.[3]

As a result of these and related changes discussed in Chap. V, pp. 492–94, *supra*, the Supreme Court's appellate docket has shrunk to a tiny fraction of its previous size. Of the cases remaining on that docket, the bulk are either apportionment cases or other controversies arising under the Voting Rights Act.

(2) *Problems of Interpretation*. Within the small category of cases still falling within the Court's mandatory appellate jurisdiction over the lower federal courts, questions of interpretation of the proper scope and exercise of that jurisdiction do remain. Because they arise so infrequently, however, they will not be discussed here (apart from the issues presented by the Notes and cases that follow). They are all explored in the sections of Stern, Gressman *et al.* cited in Paragraph (1), of this Note, and several are discussed in Chap. X, Sec. (1)(B), *supra*.

NOTE ON SUMMARY AFFIRMANCE AND ON DISMISSAL OF APPEALS FROM LOWER FEDERAL COURTS

(1) *Motions to Dismiss or Affirm*. Supreme Court Rule 18.6 authorizes motions to dismiss or affirm appeals from federal district courts, but does not specify when either motion is appropriate. The leading treatise on Supreme Court Practice concludes that a motion to dismiss or affirm should (like a brief in opposition to a certiorari petition) "present *all* reasons why full briefing and argument are not justified and why the judgment below should not be altered."[1] Stern, Gressman, Shapiro & Geller, Supreme Court Practice § 7.11, at 401 (7th ed. 1993). These reasons include the obvious correctness of the decision below, its unimportance, or the lack of a conflict.

(2) *Refusal to Exercise Jurisdiction That Is "Technically Present"*. In Socialist Labor Party v. Gilligan, 406 U.S. 583 (1972), the Party, its officers and members, brought a federal court action against the Governor of Ohio and others seeking to invalidate certain election laws of the state of Ohio. A three-judge panel, convened under 28 U.S.C. § 2281 (since repealed, see p. 1213, *supra*), ruled in favor of the plaintiffs except with respect to a provision requiring the filing of an oath in order to obtain a position on the ballot. Both sides appealed to the Supreme Court under 28 U.S.C. § 1253, but while the appeal was pending, changes in governing state law rendered moot all the issues except the validity of the oath requirement. As to that issue, the Court held that the appeal should be dismissed because of the inadequacy of the record and the abstractness of the questions presented. Relying heavily on Rescue Army v. Municipal Court, 331 U.S. 549 (1947), which involved an appeal from a state court decision under a provision that has since been repealed (see

---

ney General to request the convening of a three-judge court.

2. 42 U.S.C. §§ 1971(g), 1973b, 1973c, 1973h(c), 1973aa–2, and 1973bb(a)(2).

3. Section 9010(c) of this Act authorizes the Federal Election Commission to apply for declaratory or injunctive relief concerning any civil matter covered by the statute and to request that the matter be heard and determined by a three-judge district court.

1. On the differences and similarities between a summary disposition of an appeal and a denial of certiorari, see p. 1688, *infra*, and pp. 650–55, *supra*.

p. 650, *supra*), the Court stated (p. 588): "Problems of prematurity and abstractness may well present 'insuperable obstacles' to the exercise of the Court's jurisdiction, even though that jurisdiction is technically present."

Justice Douglas was the sole dissenter. He urged (pp. 592–93, n. 3) that it was "an undue extension of Rescue Army to apply it to an appeal from a federal court which properly heard and considered a federal constitutional question."

The Rescue Army doctrine raises troublesome questions with respect to the discretionary element of the Court's mandatory jurisdiction (see pp. 650–55, *supra*). But is it more, or less, defensible to apply that doctrine to an appeal from a lower federal court than to an appeal from a state court? Should the Court in the Socialist Labor Party case, instead of dismissing the appeal, have remanded to the district court with directions to dismiss the complaint? Does its failure to do so mean that the district court's decision on the merits was allowed to stand?

National Labor Relations Board v. White Swan Co.

313 U.S. 23, 61 S.Ct. 751, 85 L.Ed. 1165 (1941).
Certificate from the Circuit Court of Appeals for the Fourth Circuit.

■ MR. JUSTICE DOUGLAS delivered the opinion of the Court.

A certificate from the Circuit Court of Appeals for the Fourth Circuit submitted pursuant to § 239 of the Judicial Code [now 28 U.S.C. § 1254(2)] is as follows:

["]This is a petition for enforcement of an order of the National Labor Relations Board, which directed the White Swan Company * * * to cease and desist from certain unfair labor practices and to offer employment with back pay to certain employees held to have been discharged because of union affiliation and activities. The findings of the Board with respect to the unfair labor practices and discriminatory discharge of employees are sustained by substantial evidence; but a question has arisen, as to which the members of the Court are divided and in doubt, with respect to the jurisdiction of the Board in the premises.

["]The respondent, White Swan Company, operates a combined laundry and dry cleaning establishment in the city of Wheeling, West Virginia. * * * [There follows a detailed description of the nature and financial extent of respondent's operations.]

["]We recognize that the collection and delivery of garments across state lines, as above described, constitutes interstate commerce. We are advertent, however, to the admonition of the court that in applying the act we are to bear in mind 'the distinction between what is national and what is local in the activities of commerce.' National Labor Relations Board v. Jones & Laughlin Steel Corp. (301 U.S. 1, 30). And although the letter of the National Labor Relations Act may cover such collections and deliveries in interstate commerce as are here involved, the question arises whether a proper interpretation of the Act, in view of the intent of Congress, would include them. We are divided and in doubt as to whether such collection and delivery, which results from the fact that business of a local character, such as a laundry, is located on a state line, is sufficient to bring such business within the jurisdiction of the Board under the

National Labor Relations Act. To so hold would be to bring under the jurisdiction of the Board a great variety of businesses of purely local character simply because they maintain a delivery service in cities located on state lines. As there are many such cities in the United States, the question seems to us one of sufficient importance to justify us in certifying it to the Supreme Court so that it may be definitely settled.

["]Being divided and in doubt, therefore, this Court respectfully certifies to the Supreme Court of the United States, for its instruction and advice, the following questions of law, the determination of which is indispensable to a proper decision of the case.

["]1. Should the National Labor Relations Act be interpreted as having application to a business of purely local character, such as a laundry, merely because such business is located in a city on a state line and derives a substantial portion of its income from business which involves collections or deliveries of articles in a state other than that in which the business is located?

["]2. Where a local business, such as a laundry, is located in a city on a state line, and is not engaged in interstate commerce, except in so far as it may collect articles to be serviced and may make deliveries to customers living across the state line, is such business, by reason of such collections and deliveries, deemed engaged in 'commerce' within the meaning of Subsection 6 of Section 2 of the Act of July 5, 1935, ch. 372, 29 U.S.C.A. § 152(6), so that an unfair labor practice on its part would be an unfair labor practice 'affecting commerce' within the meaning of Subsection 7 of said section, 29 U.S.C.A. § 152(7), and Subsection (a) of Section 10, 29 U.S.C.A. § 160(a)? ["]

The certificate must be dismissed.

* * *

The questions do not focus "the controversy in its setting." Lowden v. Northwestern National Bank & Trust Co., 298 U.S. 160, 163. From the certificate we do not know on what grounds the Board based its jurisdiction—that the business was "in commerce" or that it was embraced within the other categories described in § 2(7) of the Act. The terms "business of purely local character" and "local business" are meaningful for purposes of § 10(a) of the Act only in light of specific findings of the Board. To answer the questions we would have to make a supposition as to the sense in which the Board made its finding under § 10(a) that the unfair labor practices were "affecting commerce". The necessity of making that supposition reveals the hypothetical and abstract quality of the questions. And the fact that on the whole record the answer might be clear whichever the theory of the Board's findings does not make the questions any the less defective. The reviewing court is passing on the validity of a specific order of the Board. Since the questions certified do not reflect the precise conclusions of the Board and the precise findings on which those conclusions were based, they necessarily have an "objectionable generality". See United States v. Mayer, 235 U.S. 55, 66 * * *. And if, in this case, they did reflect those conclusions and findings, they would be defective as calling for a "decision of the whole case". News Syndicate Co. v. New York Central Railroad Co., 275 U.S. 179, 188.

Dismissed.

———

Wisniewski v. United States

353 U.S. 901, 77 S.Ct. 633, 1 L.Ed.2d 658 (1957).
On Certificate from the United States Court of Appeals for the Eighth Circuit.

PER CURIAM.

Defendant was convicted of violation of 26 C.F.R. § 175.121, a Regulation promulgated by the Secretary of the Treasury * * * providing that:

"No liquor bottle shall be reused for the packaging of distilled spirits for sale, except as provided in § 175.63 [exceptions not here relevant], nor shall the original contents, or any portion of such original contents, remaining in a liquor bottle be increased by the addition of any substance."

The Court of Appeals for the Eighth Circuit has certified to this Court the following question: "Does the phrase 'any substance' as employed in 26 C.F.R., Section 175.121 * * *, include tax paid distilled spirits?"

It appears that the question certified by the Court of Appeals was decided by another panel of that court less than a year and a half before the present certification, on reviewing the dismissal of the indictment in this very case. Because of the volume of business, all but two Circuits have more than three Circuit Judges. This undoubtedly raises problems when one panel has doubts about a previous decision by another panel of the same court. Whatever procedure a Court of Appeals follows to resolve these problems—and desirable judicial administration commends consistency at least in the more or less contemporaneous decisions of different panels of a Court of Appeals—doubt about the respect to be accorded to a previous decision of a different panel should not be the occasion for invoking so exceptional a jurisdiction of this Court as that on certification. It is primarily the task of a Court of Appeals to reconcile its internal difficulties. It is also the task of a Court of Appeals to decide all properly presented cases coming before it, except in the rare instances, as for example the pendency of another case before this Court raising the same issue, when certification may be advisable in the proper administration and expedition of judicial business.

The certificate must be dismissed.

NOTE ON CERTIFICATION

(1) *Scope of the Supreme Court's Certification Authority*. Supreme Court Rule 19.1 provides: "A United States court of appeals may certify to this Court a question or proposition of law * * *. The certificate shall contain a statement of the nature of the case and the facts on which the question or proposition of law arises. Only questions or propositions of law may be certified, and they shall be stated separately and with precision."

Rule 19.2 provides that "When a question is certified by a United States court of appeals, this Court, on its own motion or that of a party, may consider and decide the entire matter in controversy. See 28 U.S.C. § 1254(2)."

In a case like White Swan, in which the certifying court was the first judicial tribunal to review the action of an administrative agency, would any constitutional problem be presented if the Supreme Court chose to decide the "entire matter in controversy" at the certification stage? *Cf.* Wheeler Lumber

Bridge & Supply Co. v. United States, 281 U.S. 572, 576 (1930)(stating, in dictum, that determination of the entire case on certification from the Court of Claims "would be an [unconstitutional] exercise of original jurisdiction by this Court"). But *cf.* United States v. Jones, 119 U.S. 477 (1886)(holding, without discussing any question of original vs. appellate jurisdiction, that an appeal lay from the Court of Claims to the Supreme Court at a time when the Court of Claims was not an Article III court). Would a similar problem be presented by the disposition of a single issue in White Swan? See Old Colony Trust Co. v. Commissioner, 279 U.S. 716, 728–29 (1929).

In News Syndicate Co. v. New York Cent. R.R., 275 U.S. 179, 188 (1927), the Court answered three certified questions, but declined to answer the fourth—"Did the District Court err in sustaining the demurrer to the said petition?" on the ground that "The inquiry calls for decision of the whole case. It is not specific or confined to any distinct question or proposition of law * * *." Yet it is not a difficulty that the answer to a "distinct and definite" question of law may be dispositive. United States v. Mayer, 235 U.S. 55, 66 (1914); Wheeler Lumber, Bridge & Supply Co. v. United States, *supra* at 1585.

Is the limitation endorsed in News Syndicate required by the statute? Does it rest on solid policy? Why should such an inquiry be unacceptable, if the facts on which the answer turns are adequately set forth in the certificate? Compare the questions in Chicago, B. & Q. Ry. v. Williams, 205 U.S. 444 (1907), and their restatement in 214 U.S. 492, 493–95 (1909); see also the dissent of Justice Holmes, 214 U.S. at 495.

(2) *Is the Court Obligated to Respond on the Merits to a Properly Submitted Certificate?* Assuming the wisdom of the Supreme Court's reluctance in Wisniewski to resolve an intra-circuit conflict on an insubstantial question, what is the source of its authority for refusing a certificate that poses such a question? Moore & Vestal, *Present and Potential Role of Certification in Federal Appellate Procedure,* 35 Va.L.Rev. 1, 42 (1949), state that: "One present difficulty arises from the fact that certification invokes the Supreme Court's obligatory jurisdiction", and then urge that response to certified questions should be made discretionary.[1]

(3) *Declining Frequency of Filings and Responses.* From 1927–36, 85 certificates were filed in the Supreme Court, including 13 from the Court of Claims, and from 1937–46, there were only 20, all from the courts of appeals. Moore & Vestal, *supra,* at 26. Since United States v. Rice, 327 U.S. 742 (1946), only three certificates have been accepted by the Court:[1] in United States v.

---

1. In 1988, as part of the repeal of what was then § 1254(2), authorizing appeals to the Supreme Court (as opposed to certiorari petitions) of certain court of appeals decisions, Congress renumbered the statute so that subsection (3) on certification became subsection (2). Does this "reenactment" constitute congressional recognition of the discretionary character of certification as articulated by the Court in such cases as Wisniewski?

1. In two cases in the past several years, the Court has dismissed a certificate. United States v. Fafowora, 489 U.S. 1002 (1989)(raising an issue related to cases in

which certiorari had already been granted); In re Slagle, 504 U.S. 952 (1992)(raising question whether a member of a three-judge district court was disqualified from hearing a case; Court cited only its own Rule 19 and the Wisniewski case in dismissing the certificate).

See also Atkins v. United States, 426 U.S. 944 (1976)(dismissing certificate, 6–3, without opinion), in which federal judges had brought suit in the Court of Claims alleging entitlement to a cost-of-living salary increase and the judges of the Court of Claims had certified the question whether they were disqualified for financial interest.

Barnett, 376 U.S. 681 (1964)(court of appeals, which was sitting in banc and was equally divided, certified the question whether Governor Barnett of Mississippi was entitled to a jury in an original contempt proceeding in that court); in Moody v. Albemarle Paper Co., 417 U.S. 622 (1974)(court of appeals certified the question whether a senior judge of the court, who had been a member of the original panel hearing a case, could vote to determine whether the case should be reheard in banc); and in Iran Nat'l Airlines Corp. v. Marschalk Co., Inc., 453 U.S. 919 (1981)(court of appeals certified three questions relating to the scope, validity, and effect of the Executive Orders carrying out the agreement with Iran under which American hostages were released).[2]

(4) *Should the Certification Procedure Be Abolished?* Since the certification procedure is "virtually, but not quite, a dead letter,"[3] and since the Court plainly is not happy about giving a measure of control over its docket to the courts of appeals, why shouldn't § 1254(2) be repealed? Can you think of a case in which the question raised in a certificate could not also be presented to the Court, at some point, in a petition for certiorari or for an extraordinary writ? See Bernard, *Certified Questions in the Supreme Court*, 83 Dick.L.Rev. 31 (1978), arguing that the law should be retained because it serves a useful purpose in those infrequent cases when the courts of appeals require authoritative guidance before proceeding. But see 17 Wright, Miller & Cooper, Federal Practice and Procedure § 4038, at 119–20 (1988): "The apparent unseemliness of * * * frank abdication of statutory jurisdiction doubtless accounts for the veiled nature of the statement in the Wisniewski decision. The Court may very well be right that discretionary control of its own docket requires abolition of certification. That result has been virtually accomplished in fact. The sooner it is accomplished by explicit statutory amendment, the better."

SUBSECTION B: DISCRETIONARY REVIEW*

---

2. In Marschalk, the Court on the same day had decided a similar controversy, in a full opinion, in a case in which certiorari had been granted before judgment in the court of appeals. Dames & Moore v. Regan, 453 U.S. 654 (1981). The Court answered the three questions in Marschalk—the third only in part—and appended a citation to Dames & Moore to each answer. In dissent, Justice Powell, joined by Justices Marshall and Stevens, said that he would dismiss the certificate with a citation to Dames & Moore. "Having rendered an opinion on the subject of those questions, we should not answer them in monosyllables nor attempt a syllabus of a portion of the Court's opinion" (pp. 919–20).

3. Stern, Gressman, Shapiro & Geller, Supreme Court Practice § 9.1, at 450 (7th ed. 1993).

* With respect to the use of extraordinary writs discussed in this section, *cf.* Jackson, J., in Ex parte Fahey, 332 U.S. 258, 259–60 (1947):

"Mandamus, prohibition and injunction against judges are drastic and extraordinary remedies. We do not doubt power in a proper case to issue such writs. But they have the unfortunate consequence of making the judge a litigant, obliged to obtain personal counsel or to leave his defense to one of the litigants before him. These remedies should be resorted to only when appeal is a clearly inadequate remedy. We are unwilling to utilize them as substitutes for appeals. As extraordinary remedies, they are reserved for really extraordinary causes."

Ex Parte Republic of Peru

The report of this decision appears at p. 336, *supra*.

Davis v. Jacobs

454 U.S. 911, 102 S.Ct. 417, 70 L.Ed.2d 226 (1981).
Petition for Certiorari to the United States Court of Appeals for the Second Circuit.

The petitions for writs of certiorari [in Davis and in 16 other, similar cases] are denied.

■ Opinion of JUSTICE STEVENS respecting the denial of the petitions for writs of certiorari.

The question raised by the dissenting opinion is whether the order to be entered in these seventeen cases should be a dismissal or a denial. Although this question might be characterized as a procedural technicality—because its resolution is a matter of complete indifference to the litigants—the argument made in the dissent merits a response because it creates the impression that the Court's answer to this arcane inquiry demonstrates that the Court is discharging its responsibilities in a lawless manner. The impression is quite incorrect.

The petitioners in these cases are state prisoners. None of them has a meritorious claim. Their habeas corpus petitions were all dismissed by federal district judges and they all unsuccessfully sought review in the United States Court of Appeals. Because none of the petitioners obtained a certificate of probable cause, none of these cases was properly "in" the Court of Appeals and therefore 28 U.S.C. § 1254 does not give this Court jurisdiction over the petitions for certiorari. It is perfectly clear, however, that if there were merit to the petitions, the Court would have ample authority to review them in either of two ways.

First, as the Court expressly decided in 1945 in a case that is procedurally identical to these, this Court has jurisdiction under 28 U.S.C. § 1651. In House v. Mayo, 324 U.S. 42 (1945), the Court conceded that it lacked certiorari jurisdiction under the predecessor to § 1254, but squarely held that the All Writs Act, now 28 U.S.C. § 1651, authorized the Court to "grant a writ of certiorari to review the action of the court of appeals in declining to allow an appeal to it" and to review the "questions on the merits sought to be raised by the appeal." 324 U.S., at 44–45.[1] The Court has consistently followed House v. Mayo for over 35 years.

---

1. The dissenting opinion makes the entirely unwarranted assumption that United States Alkali Export Assn. v. United States, 325 U.S. 196 (1945), and its companion case, De Beers Consolidated Mines, Ltd. v. United States, 325 U.S. 212 (1945), decided only a few weeks after House, implicitly overruled that case. In those cases, the petitioners had sought by writs of certiorari interlocutory review of orders issued by federal district courts, and the statutes that express-

ly conferred upon this Court appellate jurisdiction did not provide for interlocutory review. Despite its language that "[t]he writs may not be used as a substitute for an authorized appeal," 325 U.S., at 203, the Court reasoned that in both cases there were countervailing interests that so outweighed the interest in avoidance of piecemeal review that review by certiorari was appropriate. The holdings in Alkali and De Beers actually reinforce the holding in House because the

Second, as the dissent notes, "a Circuit Justice, or this Court itself, may issue a certificate of probable cause. * * *" Because we have that authority, it is part of our responsibility in processing these petitions to determine whether they have arguable merit notwithstanding the failure of a district or circuit judge to authorize an appeal to the Court of Appeals.

A complete explanation of the Court's conclusion that these cases have insufficient merit to warrant the exercise of its jurisdiction should therefore include three elements: (1) the petitioner has incorrectly invoked our jurisdiction under 28 U.S.C. § 1254 because no certificate of probable cause was issued; (2) the Court has decided not to exercise its jurisdiction under 28 U.S.C. § 1651; and (3) neither the Circuit Justice nor the Court has decided to issue a certificate of probable cause. Instead of entering detailed orders of this kind in all of these cases, the Court wisely has adopted the practice of entering simple denials. Ironically, the dissenters argue that this settled practice creates "more paper work."

As a practical matter, given the volume of frivolous, illegible, and sometimes unintelligible petitions that are filed in this Court, our work is facilitated by the practice of simply denying certiorari once a determination is made that there is no merit to the petitioner's claim. * * *

■ JUSTICE REHNQUIST, with whom THE CHIEF JUSTICE and JUSTICE POWELL join, dissenting.

In Jeffries v. Barksdale, 453 U.S. 914 (1981), The Chief Justice, Justice Powell, and I dissented from a simple denial of the writ of certiorari, contending that the writ should instead be *dismissed* because we had no jurisdiction to consider it. Further reflection and research has only strengthened my belief that where a specific statutory enactment dealing with our jurisdiction to consider decisions of the Courts of Appeals limits that jurisdiction to "[c]ases in the courts of appeals", 28 U.S.C. § 1254, we are bound by that statutory provision just as we would be bound by any other statutory provision, unless we were to hold it violative of some provision of the Constitution.

In each of these cases, the petitioner was convicted in a state court. He then sought habeas corpus relief in a United States District Court, and the District Court dismissed the action or denied the writ and refused to issue a certificate of probable cause to appeal. * * *

The effect of [28 U.S.C. § 2253], which could not have been drafted in plainer terms, is clear: a certificate of probable cause is an indispensable prerequisite to an appeal from the District Court to the appropriate Court of Appeals. * * * Our cases are not entirely in harmony as to their reasoning on this issue, though all concede that there is no jurisdiction to grant a writ of certiorari where both the District Court and the Court of Appeals have denied a habeas corpus petitioner a certificate of probable cause to appeal. See Bilik v. Strassheim, 212 U.S. 551, (1908); Ex parte Patrick, 212 U.S. 555, (1908); House v. Mayo, 324 U.S. 42, 44 (1945). In House, however, this Court held that although it could not entertain a petition for certiorari, it had jurisdiction under the All Writs Act to determine the merits of the habeas petition, as well as whether the Court of Appeals had abused its discretion in denying the petitioner a certificate of probable cause to appeal. In reaching this conclusion, it relied on a series of cases interpreting the scope of the common law writ of

interest in granting habeas relief in a deserving case clearly outweighs the interest in terminating frivolous appeals, especially when certiorari petitions are filed with this Court despite the refusals of the lower courts to grant certificates of probable cause.

certiorari under the All Writs Act. See, *e.g.*, * * * In re 620 Church St. Corp., 299 U.S. 24 (1936).

This reasoning, however, would seem to conflict with the principles established in United States Alkali Export Assn. v. United States, 325 U.S. 196, 203 (1945), and its companion case De Beers Consolidated Mines, Ltd. v. United States, 325 U.S. 212 (1945). These two cases hold that where Congress has withheld appellate review, the All Writs Act cannot be used as a substitute for an authorized appeal. Review by common law certiorari or any other extraordinary writ is not permissible in the face of a legislative purpose to foreclose review in a particular set of circumstances.

Congress, in enacting 28 U.S.C. § 2253, has determined that an indispensable prerequisite to an appeal in a habeas corpus proceeding is a certificate of probable cause. * * * [Thus] review by extraordinary writ in the absence of a certificate collides with Congress' express purpose to foreclose review.*

We should not fear that a more exacting application of § 2253 will result in meritorious petitions for habeas corpus slipping by unobservant or callous Courts of Appeals, thereby evading any review by this Court. Pursuant to § 2253, a Circuit Justice, or this Court itself, may issue a certificate of probable cause. * * *

But the practice from which I dissented in Jeffries, in addition to creating more paper work with no observable change in the results of a case, has at least two singularly undesirable side-effects. Presumably a case where a Court of Appeals has refused to grant leave to appeal, and thus has neither examined the accuracy of petitioner's factual assertions nor articulated the reasons for its conclusion that petitioner's legal contentions lack merit, is not an ideal candidate for certiorari here entirely apart from the importance of the issues presented by such a petition. * * *

But an even more important consequence of the disregard of congressional provisions as to our jurisdiction is a tendency to weaken the authority of this Court when it can demonstrate in a principled manner that it has either the constitutional or statutory authority to decide a particular issue. The necessary concomitant of our tri-partite system of government that the other two branches of government obey judgments rendered within our jurisdiction is sapped whenever we decline for any reason other than the exercise of our own constitutional duties to similarly follow the mandates of Congress and the Executive within their spheres of authority.

––––––––––

* Although the concurring opinion correctly notes that this Court utilized the common law writ in Alkali Export, *supra,* to review an interlocutory order by the District Court, this hardly "reinforce[s] the holding in House v. Mayo." The questions in Alkali Export involved the propriety of an exercise of the District Court's equitable jurisdiction, where there was an apparent conflict between its jurisdiction and that of the agency specifically charged by Congress with the duty of enforcing the antitrust laws under the circumstances present in that case. Thus, the common law writ was utilized by this Court in Alkali Export only to determine whether the District Court's assumption of jurisdiction *conflicted* with Congress' intent to foreclose such jurisdiction pending a determination of a particularly sensitive issue by the Federal Trade Commission. In contrast, use of the common law writ to review uncertificated petitions does not operate to ensure that a lower court is exercising its jurisdiction in accord with congressional intent. It has precisely the opposite effect of providing uncertificated petitioners with certiorari review in the teeth of a congressional mandate that such review should not be available.

NOTE ON COMMON LAW AND STATUTORY CERTIORARI

(1) *The Assumption in Davis That the Case Was Not "in" the Court of Appeals.* Both opinions in Davis start from the proposition that the case was not "in" the court of appeals for purposes of determining the availability of statutory certiorari under 28 U.S.C. § 1254(1). This proposition is squarely supported by House v. Mayo, 324 U.S. 42 (1945).

Is the proposition sound? What if an appeal to a court of appeals is dismissed by that court for lack of jurisdiction because the decision below was not "final"? The Supreme Court has statutory jurisdiction to review that dismissal, doesn't it? See, *e.g.,* Gardner v. Westinghouse Broadcasting Co., 437 U.S. 478 (1978). Indeed, in Nixon v. Fitzgerald, 457 U.S. 731 (1982), the Court first determined that the court of appeals erred in dismissing for lack of a final decision and then went on to decide the appeal on the merits. How different is the Davis situation?

Note that in Holiday v. Johnston, 313 U.S. 342, 348 (1941), the Supreme Court used the common law writ of certiorari to review and reverse a court of appeals decision refusing to allow an appeal *in forma pauperis.* But after a change in the statutory provisions governing these appeals, see 28 U.S.C. § 1915, the Court, without discussion, reviewed similar denials of leave apparently on statutory writ under § 1254(1). See, *e.g.,* Coppedge v. United States, 369 U.S. 438 (1962).[1] Similarly, although there has been no analogous statutory change in § 2253, the Court appears to have granted statutory certiorari in a few cases in which a court of appeals has denied a habeas petitioner's application for a certificate of probable cause. *E.g.,* Smith v. Digmon, 434 U.S. 332 (1978); cases cited in Justice Stevens opinion in Davis, at n. 2. See Oaks, *The "Original" Writ of Habeas Corpus in the Supreme Court,* 1962 Sup.Ct.Rev. 153, 186 nn. 151, 152.

(2) *The Question of the Availability of Common Law Certiorari in the Davis Case.* If statutory certiorari is not available in a case like Davis, is Justice Rehnquist correct that common law certiorari should not be available either? To the extent that Justice Rehnquist is relying on § 2253, how does he answer Justice Stevens' point that this provision goes only to the jurisdiction of the court of appeals? To the extent he is relying on § 1254, is he arguing that common law certiorari under the All Writs Act, 28 U.S.C. § 1651, should be available only to correct actions by lower courts in excess of their jurisdiction?[2] Professor Oaks, Paragraph (1), *supra,* at 182–89, concluded from his research that at common law, the writ was available to correct nonjurisdictional errors.

(3) *Statutory Certiorari Before Judgment in the Court of Appeals.* The statutory writ runs to the courts of appeals in any case "before or after rendition of judgment or decree". A final judgment in the court of appeals is not required. But grant of certiorari before *any* court of appeals judgment is quite rare, being generally reserved for cases of "imperative public importance" in which there is

---

1. In Coppedge and similar cases, review was granted simply on petition for certiorari, without insisting on prior resort to a motion for leave to file. (The latter procedure was then required by the Supreme Court Rules on any application for common law certiorari or other extraordinary writ. Present Sup.Ct. Rule 20 no longer requires such a preliminary motion.)

2. See n. 1 of Justice Rehnquist's opinion, discussing United States Alkali Export Ass'n v. United States, 325 U.S. 196 (1945).

a need for prompt settlement of the issues.[3] And in a few such instances, certiorari has been granted on petition by the United States even though it was the prevailing party in the district court.[4]

The policy of the Court in the exercise of its discretion to review by certiorari is examined in Section 4, *infra.*

SUBSECTION C: LIMITATIONS ON REVIEW

Schacht v. United States

398 U.S. 58, 90 S.Ct. 1555, 26 L.Ed.2d 44 (1970).
Certiorari to the United States Court of Appeals for the Fifth Circuit.

■ MR. JUSTICE BLACK delivered the opinion of the Court.

The petitioner, Daniel Jay Schacht, was indicted in a United States District Court for violating 18 U.S.C. § 702, which makes it a crime for any person "without authority [to wear] the uniform or a distinctive part thereof * * * of any of the armed forces of the United States, * * *." He was tried and convicted by a jury * * *. There is no doubt that Schacht did wear distinctive parts of the uniform of the United States Army and that he was not a member of the Armed Forces. He has defended his conduct since the beginning, however, on the ground that he was authorized to wear the uniform by an Act of Congress, 10 U.S.C. § 772(f), which provides as follows:

"When wearing by persons not on active duty authorized.

* * *

"(f) While portraying a member of the Army, Navy, Air Force, or Marine Corps, an actor in a theatrical or motion picture production may wear the uniform of that armed force *if the portrayal does not tend to discredit that armed force.*" (Emphasis added.)

Schacht argued in the trial court and in this Court that he wore the army uniform as an "actor" in a "theatrical production" performed several times between 6:30 and 8:30 A.M. on December 4, 1967, in front of the Armed Forces Induction Center at Houston, Texas. The street skit in which Schacht wore the army uniform as a costume was designed, in his view, to expose the evil of

---

3. See Sup.Ct. Rule 11; see also, *e.g.,* United States v. United Mine Workers, 330 U.S. 258 (1947); Youngstown Sheet & Tube Co. v. Sawyer, 343 U.S. 579 (1952); United States v. Nixon, 418 U.S. 683 (1974); Dames & Moore v. Regan, 453 U.S. 654 (1981).

Lindgren & Marshall, *The Supreme Court's Extraordinary Power to Grant Certiorari Before Judgment in the Court of Appeals,* 1986 Sup.Ct.Rev. 259, 265, 318, suggest that the Court's Rule (then Rule 18, now Rule 11)

should be revised to describe three other categories of cases in which certiorari may be granted before judgment: "(1) cases raising issues similar or identical to those in a case already pending before the [C]ourt, (2) cases coming back to the Court a second time, and (3) cases where the litigants have erroneously taken a direct appeal."

4. *E.g.,* United States v. United Mine Workers, note 3, *supra.*

the American presence in Vietnam and was part of a larger, peaceful anti-war demonstration at the induction center that morning.   * * *

[In Part I of the opinion, the Court held that Schacht had participated in a "theatrical production" within the meaning of § 772. It further held that, in order to preserve the constitutionality of that provision, the final clause must be stricken.]

II

The Government's brief and argument seriously contend that this Court is without jurisdiction to consider and decide the merits of this case on the ground that the petition for certiorari was not timely filed under Rule 22(2) of the Rules of this Court. This Rule provides that a petition for certiorari to review a court of appeals' judgment in a criminal case "shall be deemed in time when * * * filed with the Clerk within thirty days after the entry of such judgment."* We cannot accept the view that this time requirement is jurisdictional and cannot be waived by the Court. Rule 22(2) contains no language that calls for so harsh an interpretation, and it must be remembered that this Rule was not enacted by Congress but was promulgated by this Court under authority of Congress to prescribe rules concerning the time limitations for taking appeals and applying for certiorari in criminal cases. See 18 U.S.C. § 3772.** The procedural rules adopted by the Court for the orderly transaction of its business are not jurisdictional and can be relaxed by the Court in the exercise of its discretion when the ends of justice so require. This discretion has been expressly declared in several opinions of the Court. See Taglianetti v. United States, 394 U.S. 316 n. 1; Heflin v. United States, 358 U.S. 415, 418 n. 7. It is true that the Taglianetti and Heflin cases dealt with this time question only in footnotes. But this is no reason to disregard their holdings and in fact indicates the Court deemed a footnote adequate treatment to give the issue.

When the petition for certiorari was filed in this case it was accompanied by a motion, supported by affidavits, asking that we grant certiorari despite the fact that the petition was filed 101 days after the appropriate period for filing the petition had expired. Affidavits filed with the motion, not denied or challenged by the Government, present facts showing that petitioner had acted in good faith and that the delay in filing the petition for certiorari was brought about by circumstances largely beyond his control. Without detailing these circumstances, it is sufficient to note here that after consideration of the motion and affidavits this Court on December 15, 1969, granted the motion, three Justices dissenting. The decision of this Court waiving the time defect and permitting the untimely filing of the petition was thus made several months ago, and no new facts warranting a reconsideration of that decision have been presented to us.

For the reasons stated in Parts I and II of this opinion, the judgment of the Court of Appeals is reversed.

Reversed.

■ MR. JUSTICE HARLAN, concurring.

---

* [Ed.] Supreme Court Rule 13.1 now imposes ("[u]nless otherwise provided by law") a *90* day time limit for the review of any state or federal civil or criminal judgment.

** [Ed.] This provision was repealed in 1988, and replaced by 28 U.S.C. § 2071(a).

I join Part I of the Court's opinion. With respect to Part II, I agree with the Court's rejection of the Government's "jurisdictional" contention premised on the untimely filing of the petition for certiorari. In my view, however, that contention deserves fuller consideration than has been accorded it in the Court's opinion.

I

The Court's opinion does not fully come to grips with the Solicitor General's position. The Court rejects the argument that untimeliness under Rule 22(2) should be given jurisdictional effect by stating, in part, that the Rule "contains no language that calls for so harsh an interpretation." In this regard, however, the time limitation found in Rule 22(2) is no different from those established by statute;[1] neither makes explicit reference to waivers of the limitation. In the absence of language providing for waiver, we have without exception treated the statutory limitations as jurisdictional. The Solicitor General asks why we should not do the same under our Rule. This issue, *i.e.*, why we treat time requirements under our Rule differently from the requirements imposed by statute, is hardly acknowledged in the Court's opinion. Moreover, although it is true that Taglianetti v. United States, 394 U.S. 316 n. 1, and Heflin v. United States, 358 U.S. 415, 418 n. 7, held that the Court could waive untimeliness under our Rule, neither opinion explained why this is so. The Solicitor General does not belittle those two cases merely because each dealt with the problem in a footnote, but rather urges that they are inconclusive because neither gave reasons for the conclusion.

II

My own analysis of the issue presented here begins with an examination of the statutory authority for Rule 22(2). This is found in what is now 18 U.S.C. § 3772, a provision authorizing this Court to prescribe post-verdict rules of practice and procedure in criminal cases. Section 3772 specifically delegates to this Court the power to promulgate rules prescribing "the times for and manner of taking appeals [to the Courts of Appeals] and applying for writs of certiorari * * *." While the legislative history of this provision evinces a congressional concern over undue delays in the disposition of criminal cases, the broad terms of the statutory language, as well as what was written in the Committee reports, convince me that Congress' purpose was to give this Court the freedom to decide what time limits should apply.

Under the unqualified delegation found in § 3772, I have no doubts concerning this Court's authority to promulgate a rule that required certiorari petitions to be filed within 30 days of the judgment below but that expressly provided that this requirement could be waived for good cause shown, in order to avoid unfairness in extraordinary cases. I also think the Court might promulgate a rule that expressly provided that untimeliness could not be waived even for "excusable neglect,"—in other words a "jurisdictional rule."

Rule 22(2), as promulgated, contains no express provision allowing for waiver. It is clear from prior decisions that the Court has interpreted the rule to allow for such a waiver, however. So interpreted, I find Rule 22(2) no less

---

1. Compare Rule 22(2) with, *e.g.*, 28 U.S.C. § 2101(b), (c). Both the Rule and this statute provide for limited extensions of time. There was, however, no extension in the case before us.

authorized under 18 U.S.C. § 3772 than would be a rule that by its terms provided expressly for the possibility of a waiver.

Nor do I find it at all anomalous that this Court on occasion waives the time limitations imposed by its own Rules and yet treats time requirements imposed by statute as jurisdictional. As a matter of statutory interpretation, the Court has not presumed the right to extend time limits specified in statutes where there is no indication of a congressional purpose to authorize the Court to do so. Because we cannot "waive" congressional enactments, the statutory time limits are treated as jurisdictional. On the other hand, for the time requirement of Rule 22(2), established under a broad statutory delegation, it is appropriate to apply the "general principle" that "[i]t is always within the discretion of a court or an administrative agency to relax or modify its procedural rules adopted for the orderly transaction of business before it when in a given case the ends of justice require it," American Farm Lines v. Black Ball, 397 U.S. 532, 539 (1970), quoting from N.L.R.B. v. Monsanto Chemical Co., 205 F.2d 763, 764 (8th Cir.1953).

III

Although I therefore conclude that this Court possesses the discretion to waive the time requirements of Rule 22(2), it must be recognized that such requirements are essential to an orderly appellate process. Consequently, I believe our discretion must be exercised sparingly, and only when an adequate reason exists to excuse noncompliance with our Rules. In the present case, I agree with the Court that petitioner has adequately explained why he failed to meet our time requirements. On this basis I concur in Part II of the Court's opinion.

NOTE ON TIME LIMITATIONS FOR CERTIORARI AND APPEAL

(1) *Statutory Time Limits.* As indicated in the Schacht opinions, the statutory time limitations for certiorari and appeal, which are set forth in 28 U.S.C. § 2102, are regarded as jurisdictional. The time is calculated from the day of entry of the judgment below, without counting that day, but the period is tolled by the filing of a timely petition for rehearing in the court below and begins to run anew from the date of the order denying the petition. See Department of Banking v. Pink, 317 U.S. 264, 266 (1942). The filing of an untimely petition tolls the period for seeking review only if the court below "allows the filing and, after considering the merits, denies [or otherwise acts upon] the petition." Bowman v. Loperena, 311 U.S. 262, 266 (1940). But in FTC v. Minneapolis–Honeywell Regulator Co., 344 U.S. 206 (1952), the Court held that when no petition for rehearing is filed, a modification in a judgment that does not affect the portion on which review is sought does not extend the time for seeking review. Subsequent decisions, however, have held petitions for certiorari to be timely despite at least an arguable resemblance to the facts of Minneapolis–Honeywell. See United States v. Adams, 383 U.S. 39 (1966)(petition held timely although it was filed more than 90 days after the initial judgment and raised issues apparently unaffected by a second judgment entered in response to a timely motion to amend); FTC v. Colgate–Palmolive Co., 380 U.S. 374, 378–84 (1965)(period for filing petition commenced on the date of the second judgment below because, after the first judgment, the Commission issued a

revised order in a good-faith attempt to comply with the appellate court's first mandate). See generally Stern, Gressman, Shapiro & Geller, Supreme Court Practice §§ 6.2, 6.3, 6.4 (7th ed. 1993).

The governing statute and rule permit extensions of time for petitioning for certiorari to be granted for good cause shown. 28 U.S.C. § 2101(d); Sup.Ct. Rule 13.5. And although no extensions may be granted for filing notices of appeal to the Supreme Court, extensions of the time for docketing an appeal (payment of docket fee and filing of jurisdictional statement) are authorized. Sup.Ct. Rule 18.1, 18.3. The present rule (18.3) requires a showing of "specific reasons" why an extension is justified and states that an application for an extension "is not favored."

(2) *Time Limits in Criminal Cases.* There is no statutory time limit on the filing of petitions for certiorari in criminal cases, and 28 U.S.C. § 2101(c) explicitly states that the time for seeking review of a state court judgment in a criminal case "shall be as prescribed by rules of the Supreme Court." Under the new Supreme Court rules (as indicated in note * in the Schacht case), a uniform 90 day time limit has been adopted for all cases, bringing criminal cases into conformity with other cases. But the time limits are still regarded as waivable in criminal cases for good cause shown. In Schacht itself—in which the petition was filed 101 days after the prescribed period—it appeared from the affidavits that the petitioner "had acted in good faith in reliance on his lawyer's agreement to file the petition; but the lawyer, having advised petitioner that he must 'either come up with some money or sign a Pauper's Oath,' neglected to tell petitioner of the critical date when the petition was due to be filed and when such arrangements would have to be completed." Stern, Gressman, Shapiro & Geller, Supreme Court Practice § 6.1, at 280 (7th ed. 1993).

Redrup v. New York

386 U.S. 767, 87 S.Ct. 1414, 18 L.Ed.2d 515 (1967).
Certiorari to the Appellate Term of the Supreme Court
of New York, First Judicial Department.*

■ Per Curiam.

These three cases arise from a recurring conflict—the conflict between asserted state power to suppress the distribution of books and magazines through criminal or civil proceedings, and the guarantees of the First and Fourteenth Amendments of the United States Constitution.

I.

In No. 3, Redrup v. New York, the petitioner was a clerk at a New York City newsstand. A plainclothes patrolman approached the newsstand, saw two paperback books on a rack—Lust Pool, and Shame Agent—and asked for them by name. The petitioner handed him the books and collected the price of

---

* Together with No. 16, Austin v. Kentucky, on certiorari to the Circuit Court of McCracken County, Kentucky, argued on October 10–11, 1966, and No. 50, Gent et al. v. Arkansas, on appeal from the Supreme Court of Arkansas, argued October 11, 1966.

$1.65. As a result of this transaction, the petitioner was * * * [convicted of] violating a state criminal law. * * *

In No. 16, Austin v. Kentucky, the petitioner owned and operated a retail bookstore and newsstand in Paducah, Kentucky. A woman resident of Paducah purchased two magazines from a salesgirl in the petitioner's store, after asking for them by name—High Heels, and Spree. As a result of this transaction the petitioner stands convicted in the Kentucky courts for violating a criminal law of that State.

In No. 50, Gent v. Arkansas, the prosecuting attorney of the Eleventh Judicial District of Arkansas brought a civil proceeding under a state statute to have certain issues of various magazines declared obscene, to enjoin their distribution and to obtain a judgment ordering their surrender and destruction. The magazines proceeded against were: Gent, Swank, Bachelor, Modern Man, Cavalcade, Gentleman, Ace, and Sir. The County Chancery Court entered the requested judgment * * *, and the Supreme Court of Arkansas affirmed, with minor modifications.

In none of the cases was there a claim that the statute in question reflected a specific and limited state concern for juveniles. * * * In none was there any suggestion of an assault upon individual privacy by publication in a manner so obtrusive as to make it impossible for an unwilling individual to avoid exposure to it. * * * And in none was there evidence of the sort of "pandering" which the Court found significant in Ginzburg v. United States, 383 U.S. 463.

II.

The Court originally limited review in these cases to certain particularized questions, upon the hypothesis that the material involved in each case was of a character described as "obscene in the constitutional sense" in A Book Named "John Cleland's Memoirs of a Woman of Pleasure" v. Attorney General of Com. of Massachusetts, 383 U.S. 413, 418. But we have concluded that the hypothesis upon which the Court originally proceeded was invalid, and accordingly that the cases can and should be decided upon a common and controlling fundamental constitutional basis, without prejudice to the questions upon which review was originally granted. We have concluded, in short, that the distribution of the publications in each of these cases is protected by the First and Fourteenth Amendments from governmental suppression, whether criminal or civil, *in personam* or *in rem*.[6]

Two members of the Court have consistently adhered to the view that a State is utterly without power to suppress, control or punish the distribution of any writings or pictures upon the ground of their "obscenity." A third has held to the opinion that a State's power in this area is narrowly limited to a distinct and clearly identifiable class of material. Others have subscribed to a not dissimilar standard, holding that a State may not constitutionally inhibit the distribution of literary material as obscene unless "(a) the dominant theme of the material taken as a whole appeals to a prurient interest in sex; (b) the material is patently offensive because it affronts contemporary community standards relating to the description or representation of sexual matters; and

---

6. In each of the cases before us, the contention that the publications involved were basically protected by the First and Fourteenth Amendments was timely but unsuccessfully asserted in the state proceedings. In each of these cases, this contention was properly and explicitly presented for review here.

(c) the material is utterly without redeeming social value," emphasizing that the "three elements must coalesce," and that no such material can "be proscribed unless it is found to be *utterly* without redeeming social value." A Book Named "John Cleland's Memoirs of a Woman of Pleasure" v. Attorney General of Com. of Massachusetts, 383 U.S. 413, 418–419. Another Justice has not viewed the "social value" element as an independent factor in the judgment of obscenity. *Id.,* at 460–462 (dissenting opinion).

Whichever of these constitutional views is brought to bear upon the cases before us, it is clear that the judgments cannot stand. Accordingly, the judgment in each case is reversed. It is so ordered.

Judgments reversed.

■ Mr. Justice Harlan, whom Mr. Justice Clark joins, dissenting.

Two of these cases, Redrup v. New York and Austin v. Kentucky, were taken to consider the standards governing the application of the *scienter* requirement announced in Smith v. People of State of California, 361 U.S. 147, for obscenity prosecutions. There it was held that a defendant criminally charged with purveying obscene material must be shown to have had some kind of knowledge of the character of such material; the quality of that knowledge, however, was not defined. The third case, Gent v. Arkansas, was taken to consider the validity of a comprehensive Arkansas anti-obscenity statute, in light of the doctrines of "vagueness" and "prior restraint." The writs of certiorari in Redrup and Austin, and the notation of probable jurisdiction in Gent, were respectively limited to these issues, thus laying aside, for the purposes of these cases, the permissibility of the state determinations as to the obscenity of the challenged publications. Accordingly the obscenity *vel non* of these publications was not discussed in the briefs or oral arguments of any of the parties.

The three cases were argued together at the beginning of this Term. Today, the Court rules that the materials could not constitutionally be adjudged obscene by the States, thus rendering adjudication of the other issues unnecessary. In short, the Court disposes of the cases on the issue that was deliberately excluded from review, and refuses to pass on the questions that brought the cases here.

In my opinion these dispositions do not reflect well on the processes of the Court, and I think the issues for which the cases were taken should be decided. Failing that, I prefer to cast my vote to dismiss the writs in Redrup and Austin as improvidently granted and, in the circumstances, to dismiss the appeal in Gent for lack of a substantial federal question. I deem it more appropriate to defer an expression of my own views on the questions brought here until an occasion when the Court is prepared to come to grips with such issues.

NOTE ON LIMITED REVIEW

(1) *The Use of Limited Grants of Review.* Redrup and the companion cases all arose from state courts, but such limited grants also occur in cases coming from the federal appellate courts.[1] See, *e.g.,* Gregg v. United States, 393 U.S. 932

---

1. A study published in 1975 reported that over a period of eleven terms, the Court limited the grant of review in an average of 4.3% per term of the cases in which certiorari

(1968); Whiteley v. Warden, 401 U.S. 560, 562 n. 3 (1971). And, as in Redrup, the Court has on occasion gone beyond the scope of its grant in deciding the case. *E.g.*, Olmstead v. United States, 277 U.S. 438, 466, 468 (1928); Piper Aircraft Co. v. Reyno, 454 U.S. 235, 246–47 n. 12 (1981).[2]

(2) *The Validity of Limited Grants.*

(a) Suppose that in Redrup and Austin the Court had confined itself to the questions on which certiorari had been granted and had affirmed the convictions. Would you be troubled by the fact that the Court's decision would have sustained, on the merits, convictions for engaging in constitutionally protected activity? That the Court's failure to reverse was in no way attributable to any procedural default by the petitioners? (Similar questions could be asked about an affirmance of the civil judgment in Gent.) Can or should the Court, operating within the limits imposed by Article III, decide a case without passing on a question that is within its jurisdiction, that is properly presented, and that is not mooted by the Court's disposition of any other question in the case? Is it enough of an answer that the Court must be able to exercise control over its own docket?[3]

(b) Some of the questions raised in subparagraph (a) are illustrated by the opinions in Missouri v. Jenkins, 495 U.S. 33 (1990). In that case, the court of appeals had upheld in part a district court decree in a school desegregation case. In granting the petition for certiorari, 488 U.S. 888 (1988), the Court limited consideration of the merits to questions of the scope of federal court authority to order the raising of funds to implement the remedy, and did not grant review of other questions presented in the petition—including the question whether the remedy itself was excessive. In its decision on the merits, the majority again declined to consider whether the remedy itself was proper, and on the funding question, affirmed in part and reversed in part.

Justice Kennedy, for four dissenters, said: "I am required in light of our limited grant of certiorari to assume that the remedy chosen by the District Court was a permissible exercise of its remedial discretion" (p. 78). But he then went on to consider the remedy issue, at least to the extent of concluding that the far-reaching and expensive remedy chosen was not the only one possible under the Court's decisions. Realizing that this conclusion might strain the limited grant of certiorari, he stated: "The suggestion that our limited grant of certiorari requires us to decide this case blinkered as to the actual remedy underlying it * * * is ill-founded. A limited grant of certiorari is not a means by which the Court can pose for itself an abstract question. Our jurisdiction is limited to particular Cases and Controversies. * * * Far from being an improper invitation to go outside the question presented, attention to the extraordinary remedy here is the Court's duty. This would be a far more prudent course than recharacterizing the case in an attempt to reach prema-

---

was granted. See Bice, *The Limited Grant of Certiorari and the Justification of Judicial Review*, 1975 Wis.L.Rev. 343, 356–57 n. 61.

2. And the Court has, over strong dissent, asked the parties to brief and argue a question not presented in the certiorari petition. See Colorado v. Connelly, 474 U.S. 1050 (1986).

3. Whatever your answers to the questions in this paragraph, aren't you troubled

by Justice Harlan's vote to dismiss the appeal in the Gent case for lack of a substantial federal question? Did Justice Harlan mean that the appealable issues, which the majority did not reach, were insubstantial? (The issues are stated in the notation of probable jurisdiction, 384 U.S. 937 (1966).) If not, what did he mean?

ture decision on an important question [i.e., the extent to which a federal court can require a state or local authority to raise the funds necessary to implement a court-ordered remedy]" (pp. 79–80).

Although much of his discussion looks in that direction, Justice Kennedy stops short (by a hair's breadth) of holding that the remedy itself was beyond the authority of the district court. If the district court did abuse its discretion in ordering the remedy, is it an appropriate (or constitutional) exercise of the judicial power to ignore that defect (as the Supreme Court majority did), even though the question has been properly presented to the Court for review, and to go on to hold that the courts below were correct, at least in part, in their decision as to how to raise the funds necessary to implement that unlawful remedy?

(c) In an exhaustive analysis of the issues presented in this Paragraph, Bice, note 1, *supra,* concludes that the practice of limited grants is both desirable and legitimate. He argues that at least at the highest appellate level, the Court in its discretion may limit the issues for decision, even though a similar limitation at the trial court level might raise serious constitutional problems. He does suggest, however, that in certain areas, notably that of jurisdiction, Supreme Court consideration of an issue should not be excluded by a limited grant of certiorari. He also urges that when, as in Redrup, the Court goes outside such a limited grant, the parties should be given an opportunity to brief and argue the additional issues.

For a similar view, suggesting a distinction between the obligation of a trial court to decide all the issues fairly presented and the ability of an appellate court to limit its review to issues of particular importance, see Meltzer, *Harmless Error and Constitutional Remedies,* 61 U.Chi.L.Rev. 1, 15–17 (1994). May an analogous distinction be drawn between the ability of the legislature to limit the authority of enforcement courts to consider relevant questions of law (see Chap. IV, Sec. 1, *supra*) and the ability of a reviewing court itself to select among issues in determining the scope of review?

NOTE ON CROSS–PETITIONS, CROSS–APPEALS, AND REVIEW OF ERRORS NOT ASSIGNED

(1) *Arguments Available to a Respondent or Appellee in the Absence of a Cross–Petition or Cross–Appeal.* Without a cross-petition or cross-appeal, the respondent or appellee is precluded from attacking the judgment or decree "with a view either to enlarging his own rights thereunder or of lessening the rights of his adversary, whether what he seeks is to correct an error or to supplement the decree with respect to a matter not dealt with below."[1] Respondent or appellee is not barred, however, from urging in support of the judgment "any matter appearing in the record, although his argument may involve an attack upon the reasoning of the lower court or an insistence upon matter overlooked or ignored by it."[2]

1. United States v. American Ry. Exp. Co., 265 U.S. 425, 435 (1924). Even under these circumstances, an issue may be raised if it goes to subject matter jurisdiction. See

Lake Country Estates, Inc. v. Tahoe Regional Planning Agency, 440 U.S. 391, 398 (1979).

2. United States v. American Ry. Exp. Co., 265 U.S. 425, 435 (1924). See also, *e.g.,*

Nor is it necessary to support the judgment that the point be one urged below, if it is grounded in the record. Bondholders Comm. v. Commissioner, 315 U.S. 189, 192 n. 2 (1942). The Supreme Court may prefer, however, to reverse and permit the initial consideration of such new contentions on remand. See, *e.g.,* United States v. Ballard, 322 U.S. 78, 88 (1944).[3]

The same principles apply in the courts of appeals upon review of district court decisions. Morley Constr. Co. v. Maryland Cas. Co., 300 U.S. 185 (1937).

(2) *Arguments That Would Support a More Favorable Judgment for Respondent or Appellee.* Some question has arisen in recent years about the application of these principles in a case in which (a) the rationale urged by respondent could support a result more favorable to him than the judgment below but (b) the respondent is willing to accept that judgment. In Strunk v. United States, 412 U.S. 434 (1973), the petitioner had prevailed in the court of appeals on his claim of violation of his right to a speedy trial, and certiorari was granted on his claim that he was entitled to dismissal of the charge, not merely to a reduction of his sentence. The government, as respondent, sought to argue that petitioner's speedy trial right had not been violated, although it indicated its willingness to accept the reduced sentence ordered by the court of appeals. The Supreme Court refused to consider the argument, holding that "in the absence of a cross-petition for certiorari * * * the only question properly before us for review is the propriety of the remedy fashioned by the Court of Appeals" (p. 437).[4]

Perhaps in response to scholarly criticism,[5] the Court appears to have retreated from the implication that it lacks power to consider a question raised by a respondent in these circumstances, noting instead its discretion to do so. See, *e.g.,* United States v. ITT Continental Baking Co., 420 U.S. 223, 226–27 n. 2 (1975);[6] United States v. New York Tel. Co., 434 U.S. 159, 166 n. 8 (1977).

Thigpen v. Roberts, 468 U.S. 27 (1984); Langnes v. Green, 282 U.S. 531 (1931).

One apparent exception is a claim of improper venue, which has been held to be waived if not raised by cross-appeal. Peoria & Pekin Union Ry. v. United States, 263 U.S. 528, 536 (1924). Another possible exception involves claims of untimeliness. See Stern, Gressman, Shapiro & Geller, Supreme Court Practice § 6.35, at 365 (7th ed. 1993).

3. But *cf.* United States v. Erika, Inc., 456 U.S. 201, 211 n. 14 (1982)(refusing to consider a constitutional question raised by respondent at oral argument, when respondent had not presented the question below, or included it among the questions presented in the briefs in opposition or on the merits, or argued it to any substantial extent in the body of the brief on the merits); Zobrest v. Catalina Foothills School Dist., 113 S.Ct. 2462 (1993)(refusing, over four dissents, to consider (or to remand for consideration below) several nonconstitutional arguments for affirmance that were presented in the respondent's brief in opposition to certiorari

and its brief on the merits but that had not been urged in lower courts).

Of course, the point must not have been lost through failure to make a timely objection in the lower courts. See, *e.g.,* Fed. R.Civ.P. 12(h)(1)(waiver of certain defenses).

4. The opinion went on to say: "Whether in some circumstances, and as to some questions, the Court might deal with an issue involving constitutional claims, absent its being raised by cross-petition, we need not resolve" (p. 437).

5. Especially Stern, *When to Cross-Appeal or Cross-Petition—Certainty or Confusion?,* 87 Harv.L.Rev. 763 (1974).

6. The Court, citing Strunk and other cases, said: "Ordinarily * * * as a matter of practice and control of our docket, if not of our power, we do not entertain a challenge to a decision on the merits where the only petition for certiorari presents solely a question as to the remedy granted for a liability found to exist, even if the respondent is willing to accept whatever judgment has already been

In New York Telephone, the Court did in fact consider the questions raised, although the grounds urged by respondent might have justified greater relief than that accorded below.   The Court said that "[t]he only relief sought by the [respondent] Company is that granted by the Court of Appeals."

The result in New York Telephone, as well as the Court's emphasis on its discretion to accept or decline consideration, is applauded in Stern, Gressman, Shapiro & Geller, Supreme Court Practice § 6.35, at 368 (7th ed. 1993).

(3) *Review of Questions Not Presented in The Petition.*   Compare the limitations on review of errors not assigned or presented in the petition for certiorari. Sup.Ct. Rule 14.1(a); see Pollard v. United States, 352 U.S. 354, 358–59 (1957); Stern, Gressman, Shapiro & Geller, Supreme Court Practice § 6.26 (7th ed. 1993); *cf.* Neely v. Martin K. Eby Constr. Co., 386 U.S. 317, 320–21 (1967)(in granting certiorari, the Court requested the parties to argue certain questions not presented in the petition); Blonder–Tongue Labs., Inc. v. University of Illinois Found., 402 U.S. 313, 320 n. 6 (1971)("Rule 23(1)(c) [a predecessor of Rule 14.1(a)] * * * does not limit our power to decide important questions not raised by the parties"); Vance v. Terrazas, 444 U.S. 252, 258–59 n. 5 (1980)(same).   In Vance, the issue did not appear in the jurisdictional statement and had not been presented in the court of appeals.   Blonder–Tongue was cited in support of the holding; Vachon v. New Hampshire, p. 569, *supra,* a more debatable decision—involving as it did review of a state court judgment— was also cited as "*Cf.*"[7]

SECTION 4.   THE CERTIORARI POLICY

INTRODUCTORY NOTE: THE CONSIDERATION
AND DISPOSITION OF PETITIONS

(1) At the present time, approximately 7000 cases are docketed in the Supreme Court each Term.   Only a handful of these cases fall within the Court's original jurisdiction or within the Court's much reduced obligatory appellate jurisdiction.   Virtually all of the remainder are petitions for statutory certiorari under 28 U.S.C. § 1254(1) or § 1257.

The Court has traditionally denied the large majority of these petitions. Until the early 1980s, the number of petitions filed and granted had been growing, but in recent Terms, while the number of *in forma pauperis* petitions has grown dramatically, the number of "paid" petitions has leveled off and the

---

entered against him.   * * * We follow that rule of practice in this case, particularly because the issue of whether there were any violations * * * would not merit this Court's grant of a petition for certiorari."

7. In Evans v. United States, 504 U.S. 255 (1992), the Court, in affirming a criminal conviction, rejected an argument for reversal advanced by the dissenting Justices but not raised by the defendant-petitioner.   Writing separately, Justice O'Connor criticized major-

ity and dissent alike for resolving an issue that was not fairly included in the question on which certiorari had been granted and that had been neither briefed nor argued.

For a later case in which the majority, over two dissents, decided to dismiss a petition as improvidently granted because of the presence of a preliminary issue not fairly included in the questions presented, see Kaisha v. U.S. Philips Corp., 114 S.Ct. 425 (1993).

number and percentage of cases accepted for review has significantly declined. These changes are illustrated by the following table: [1]

Terms

	1960	1970	1981	1986	1992	1993	1994
Paid Cases[2]							
Cases docketed during term[3]	718	1540	2413	2071	2062	2100	2062
Review granted	87	101	299	242	83	78	83
	(12.1%)	(7.8%)	(12.4%)	(11.7%)	(4.0%)	(3.7%)	(4.0%)
In Forma Pauperis[4]							
Cases docketed during term	950	1771	2004	2165	4240	4796	4858
Review granted	16	83[5]	13	26	14	21	10
	(1.7%)	(4.8%)	(.6%)	(1.2%)	(.3%)	(.4%)	(.2%)

(2) The burden of considering certiorari petitions is lightened by the work of the Justices' law clerks, who prepare memoranda summarizing the petitions and recommending dispositions.[6] Moreover, the majority of petitions are not discussed by the Justices in conference. The concept of a "special" or "dead" list was introduced by Chief Justice Hughes; he and his clerks compiled and circulated, in advance, a list of cases that would not be discussed. Any Justice could remove a case from the list at or before conference, and those remaining on the list at the end of the conference would automatically be denied review. The increase in filings has changed the practice, first with the Miscellaneous Docket (unpaid cases, in which petitions are filed *in forma pauperis*, primarily by state prisoners) and then with the (paid) Appellate Docket, so that the list now consists of those cases scheduled *for* discussion, and any Justice may add a case to the list or delay its disposition.[7]

(3) Despite these time-saving devices, the burden involved in the exercise of discretion is clearly great, though the extent of that burden and the desirability of change have been the subject of vigorous debate.[8] For further discussion of

1. The figures in this table are taken from the statistics published each summer in the Supreme Court edition of United States Law Week.

2. These figures include all paid cases except those on the original docket.

3. This category (and the corresponding category under "In Forma Pauperis" filings) includes cases in which review was granted that were carried over to a subsequent Term, but not cases summarily decided without opinion. The percentage is computed by using as the divisor all cases docketed during the Term. (The divisor thus does not include cases remaining on the dockets from prior Terms.)

4. These figures include all cases filed in forma pauperis, whether filed as appeals or as petitions for certiorari.

5. This figure was disproportionately high because of a large number of capital cases that were vacated and remanded. See 403 U.S. 946–48 (1971).

6. A number of Justices (presently said to be eight) reportedly use "pool memos" prepared by a clerk of one of the Justices and distributed to the others in the group. See Stevens, *The Life Span of a Judge–Made Rule*, 58 N.Y.U.L.Rev. 1, 13–14 (1983); Perry, Deciding to Decide: Agenda Setting in the United States Supreme Court 51–64 (1991)(noting, *inter alia*, that clerks frequently annotate pool memoranda prepared in other chambers).

7. For a fuller description, see Provine, Case Selection in the United States Supreme Court 28–29 (1980).

8. See, *e.g.*, Symposium, *The Supreme Court Workload*, 11 Hastings Const. L.Q. 353–504 (1984); authorities cited pp. 61–63, *supra*. For earlier discussion, see, *e.g.*, Gressman, *Much Ado About Certiorari*, 52 Geo.L.J. 742 (1964); Hart, *Foreword—The Time Chart of the Justices*, 73 Harv.L.Rev. 84 (1959); Harlan, *Manning the Dikes*, 13 Record Ass'n B. City N.Y. 541 (1958).

this and related problems of Supreme Court caseload, and of proposals for change, see p. 1711, *infra*; Chap. I, pp. 61–63, *supra*.

———

Singleton v. Commissioner of Internal Revenue

439 U.S. 940, 99 S.Ct. 335, 58 L.Ed.2d 335 (1978).
Petition for Certiorari to the United States Court of Appeals for the Fifth Circuit.

The petition for a writ of certiorari is denied.

■ MR. JUSTICE BLACKMUN, with whom MR. JUSTICE MARSHALL and MR. JUSTICE POWELL join, dissenting.

The issue in this federal income tax case is whether a cash distribution that petitioner husband (hereafter petitioner) received in 1965 with respect to his shares in Capital Southwest Corporation (CSW) was taxable to him as a dividend, as the United States Court of Appeals for the Fifth Circuit held, or whether that distribution was a return of capital and therefore not taxable, as the Tax Court held. I regard the issue as of sufficient importance in the administration of the income tax laws to justify review here, and I dissent from the Court's failure to grant certiorari.

* * *

I hope that the Court's decision to pass this case by is not due to a natural reluctance to take on another complicated tax case that is devoid of glamour and emotion and that would be remindful of the recent struggles, upon argument and reargument, in United States v. Foster Lumber Co., 429 U.S. 32 (1976), and Laing v. United States, 423 U.S. 161 (1976).*

■ Opinion of MR. JUSTICE STEVENS respecting the denial of the petition for writ of certiorari.

What is the significance of this Court's denial of certiorari? That question is asked again and again; it is a question that is likely to arise whenever a dissenting opinion argues that certiorari should have been granted. Almost 30 years ago Mr. Justice Frankfurter provided us with an answer to that question that should be read again and again.

> "This Court now declines to review the decision of the Maryland Court of Appeals. The sole significance of such denial of a petition for writ of certiorari need not be elucidated to those versed in the Court's procedures. It simply means that fewer than four members of the Court deemed it desirable to review a decision of the lower court as a matter 'of sound judicial discretion.' Rule 38, paragraph 5. A variety of considerations underlie denials of the writ, and as to the same petition different reasons may lead different Justices to the same result. This is especially true of petitions for review on writ of certiorari to a State court. Narrowly technical reasons may lead to denials. Review may be sought too late; the judgment of the lower court may not be final; it may not be the judgment of a State court of last resort; the decision may be supportable as a matter of State law, not subject to review by this Court, even though the State

---

* The point Mr. Justice Stevens would make by his separate opinion was answered effectively 25 years ago by Mr. Justice Jack- son, concurring in the result, in Brown v. Allen, 344 U.S. 443, 542–544 (1953).

court also passed on issues of federal law. A decision may satisfy all these technical requirements and yet may commend itself for review to fewer than four members of the Court. Pertinent considerations of judicial policy here come into play. A case may raise an important question but the record may be cloudy. It may be desirable to have different aspects of an issue further illumined by the lower courts. Wise adjudication has its own time for ripening.

"Since there are these conflicting and, to the uninformed, even confusing reasons for denying petitions for certiorari, it has been suggested from time to time that the Court indicate its reasons for denial. Practical considerations preclude. In order that the Court may be enabled to discharge its indispensable duties, Congress has placed the control of the Court's business, in effect, within the Court's discretion. During the last three terms the Court disposed of 260, 217, 224 cases, respectively, on their merits. For the same three terms the Court denied, respectively, 1,260, 1,105, 1,189 petitions calling for discretionary review. If the Court is to do its work it would not be feasible to give reasons, however brief, for refusing to take these cases. The time that would be required is prohibitive, apart from the fact as already indicated that different reasons not infrequently move different members of the Court in concluding that a particular case at a particular time makes review undesirable. It becomes relevant here to note that failure to record a dissent from a denial of a petition for writ of certiorari in nowise implies that only the member of the Court who notes his dissent thought the petition should be granted.

"Inasmuch, therefore, as all that a denial of a petition for a writ of certiorari means is that fewer than four members of the Court thought it should be granted, this Court has rigorously insisted that such a denial carries with it no implication whatever regarding the Court's views on the merits of a case which it has declined to review. The Court has said this again and again; again and again the admonition has to be repeated." Opinion respecting the denial of the petition for writ of certiorari in Maryland v. Baltimore Radio Show, 338 U.S. 912, 917–919.

When those words were written, Mr. Justice Frankfurter and his colleagues were too busy to spend their scarce time writing dissents from denials of certiorari. Such opinions were almost nonexistent.[1] It was then obvious that if there was no need to explain the Court's action in denying the writ, there was even less reason for individual expressions of opinion about why certiorari should have been granted in particular cases.

Times have changed. Although the workload of the Court has dramatically increased since Mr. Justice Frankfurter's day,[2] most present Members of the Court frequently file written dissents from certiorari denials. It is appropriate to ask whether the new practice serves any important goals or contributes to the strength of the institution.

One characteristic of all opinions dissenting from the denial of certiorari is manifest. They are totally unnecessary. They are examples of the purest form

1. There were none in 1945 or 1946, and I have been able to find only one in the 1947 Term. See dissent in Chase National Bank v. Cheston, and companion cases, 332 U.S. 793, 800.

2. By way of comparison to the figures cited by Mr. Justice Frankfurter, the Court during the three most recent Terms reviewed and decided 362, 483, and 323 cases respectively. And during each of these Terms, the Court denied certiorari in well over 3,000 cases.

of dicta, since they have even less legal significance than the orders of the entire Court which, as Mr. Justice Frankfurter reiterated again and again, have no precedential significance at all.

Another attribute of these opinions is that they are potentially misleading. Since the Court provides no explanation of the reasons for denying certiorari, the dissenter's arguments in favor of a grant are not answered and therefore typically appear to be more persuasive than most other opinions. Moreover, since they often omit any reference to valid reasons for denying certiorari, they tend to imply that the Court has been unfaithful to its responsibilities or has implicitly reached a decision on the merits when, in fact, there is no basis for such an inference.

In this case, for example, the dissenting opinion suggests that the Court may have refused to grant certiorari because the case is "devoid of glamour and emotion." I am puzzled by this suggestion because I have never witnessed any indication that any of my colleagues has ever considered "glamour and emotion" as a relevant consideration in the exercise of his discretion or in his analysis of the law. With respect to the Court's action in this case, the absence of any conflict among the Circuits is plainly a sufficient reason for denying certiorari. Moreover, in allocating the Court's scarce resources, I consider it entirely appropriate to disfavor complicated cases which turn largely on unique facts. A series of decisions by the courts of appeals may well provide more meaningful guidance to the bar than an isolated or premature opinion of this Court. As Mr. Justice Frankfurter reminded us, "wise adjudication has its own time for ripening."

Admittedly these dissenting opinions may have some beneficial effects. Occasionally a written statement of reasons for granting certiorari is more persuasive than the Justice's oral contribution to the Conference. For that reason the written document sometimes persuades other Justices to change their votes and a case is granted that would otherwise have been denied. That effect, however, merely justifies the writing and circulating of these memoranda within the Court; it does not explain why a dissent which has not accomplished its primary mission should be published.

It can be argued that publishing these dissents enhances the public's understanding of the work of the Court. But because they are so seldom answered, these opinions may also give rise to misunderstanding or incorrect impressions about how the Court actually works. Moreover, the selected bits of information which they reveal tend to compromise the otherwise secret deliberations in our Conferences. There are those who believe that these Conferences should be conducted entirely in public or, at the very least, that the votes on all Conference matters should be publicly recorded. The traditional view, which I happen to share, is that confidentiality makes a valuable contribution to the full and frank exchange of views during the decisional process; such confidentiality is especially valuable in the exercise of the kind of discretion that must be employed in processing the thousands of certiorari petitions that are reviewed each year. In my judgment, the importance of preserving the tradition of confidentiality outweighs the minimal educational value of these opinions.

In all events, these are the reasons why I have thus far resisted the temptation to publish opinions dissenting from denials of certiorari.

———

NOTE ON DENIALS OF CERTIORARI

(1) *Reasons for Denying Certiorari.* Do you agree with Justice Frankfurter's statement in the Baltimore Radio Show Case, quoted by Justice Stevens in Singleton, that the Court should not state its reasons for denying certiorari? Might there not be times when the Court would want the denial to carry some specific meaning? See, *e.g.,* Bryant v. Ohio, 362 U.S. 906 (1960)(certiorari denied "in the light of the representation made by respondent in its brief in opposition that 'Petitioner may at this time perfect an appeal to the Supreme Court of Ohio *in forma pauperis,* which appeal will be heard by that Court.' ") See also Stern, Gressman, Shapiro & Geller, Supreme Court Practice § 5.5 and cases cited (7th ed. 1993).[1] Justice Frankfurter himself, in Rosenberg v. United States, 344 U.S. 889, 890 (1952), thought it appropriate to point out—in a statement attached to the Court's denial of rehearing on a certiorari petition—that "A sentence imposed by a United States district court, even though it be a death sentence, is not within the power of this Court to revise."

Is it ever proper for the Court, in denying certiorari, to purport to construe the opinion below? In United States ex rel. Rogers v. Richmond, 252 F.2d 807 (2d Cir.1958)—a habeas corpus proceeding attacking a state conviction—the court of appeals appeared to say that in the absence of some "vital flaw" or "unusual circumstance" in the state proceedings, the federal judge would not be warranted in holding a de novo hearing on the admissibility of certain confessions. The Supreme Court denied certiorari, 357 U.S. 220 (1958), saying: "We read the opinion of the Court of Appeals as holding that while the District Judge may, unless he finds a vital flaw in the State Court proceedings, accept the determination in such proceedings, he need not deem such determination binding, and may take testimony." One commentator pointedly inquired about the meaning and legal effect of the Supreme Court's "reading", observing: "If the Court had granted certiorari and remanded with a similar statement on its own authority, at least one reader would have understood its action as a modification of the decision of the court of appeals." Brown, *Foreword: Process of Law,* 72 Harv.L.Rev. 77, 93 (1958).[2]

(2) *Publicly Announced Dissents from Denials of Certiorari.* As Justice Stevens indicated, the practice of noting dissents from certiorari denials, and of writing opinions in support of such dissents, became increasingly common in

---

1. In the 1950s and '60s the Court not infrequently stated that the denial of certiorari to a state prisoner was "without prejudice to an application for writ of habeas corpus in an appropriate United States District Court." *E.g.,* Grace v. California, 360 U.S. 940 (1959). These notations might have been nothing more than gratuitous legal advice to often unrepresented prisoners. But they did carry the unfortunate connotation that a denial in which the words were omitted was *with prejudice* to such an application. *See* Reitz, *Federal Habeas Corpus: Postconviction Remedy for State Prisoners,* 108 U.Pa. L.Rev. 461, 503–13 (1960).

As a result of changes in the requirement of exhaustion of state remedies, this practice

appears to have abated. See 16 Wright, Miller, Cooper & Gressman, Federal Practice and Procedure § 4004 (1977 & 1995 Supp.). But *cf., e.g.,* O'Dell v. Thompson, 502 U.S. 995 (1991)(statement by three Justices, in connection with denial of certiorari, explaining why, in their view, petitioner could properly resort to a petition for federal habeas corpus).

2. For a later chapter in these proceedings, see Rogers v. Richmond, 365 U.S. 534 (1961)(reversing the court of appeals and instructing it to hold the case in order to give the state an opportunity to retry the petitioner under proper standards for determining the admissibility of his confession).

the 1970s (Justice Douglas alone announced a dissent from the denial of certiorari 477 times in the 1973 Term[3]), and has continued to the present.[4]

In accordance with the views expressed in Singleton, Justice Stevens has generally declined to note his dissents to denials of certiorari, but in three instances in the 1978 Term and on a number of other occasions, as in Singleton, he has defended the Court's denial against a dissent. See, *e.g.,* Castorr v. Brundage, 459 U.S. 928 (1982); Coleman v. Balkcom, 451 U.S. 949 (1981).[5]

Are published dissents from denials of certiorari always as inappropriate as Justice Stevens thinks they are? Justice Frankfurter's separate statement in Baltimore Radio Show, while not labeled a dissent, left little doubt that he had voted to grant the petition. And Justice Harlan, while saving his notations of dissent for "rare instances," was occasionally willing to go public in cases he thought to be particularly important. *E.g.,* Lance v. Plummer, 384 U.S. 929, 932–33 (1966).

Are such dissents of value in informing the bar and the public of possible directions the law may take, and of areas of interest to particular Justices? If the decision to accept or reject a petition is a judicial act, is the expression of dissent any more "unnecessary" than a dissent from any other judicial act? Is the problem with such dissents that in the absence of a defender like Justice Stevens, the majority's unexplained denial is too easy a target? Note, however, that the threat of dissent may serve to keep the Court from rejecting cases that ought to be accepted under the standards set forth by the Court in its own rules.

Linzer, note 3, *supra,* at 1267 concludes that dissents on the merits from denials of certiorari "can be put in three broad categories: those finding something offensive about the application of law in the particular case; 'irre-dentist' dissents, in which a minority reiterates its opposition to a clear precedent; and those urging the majority to consider an apparently uncontroversial point."[6]

---

3. See Linzer, *The Meaning of Certiorari Denials,* 79 Colum.L. Rev. 1227, 1257 (1979). Had certiorari been granted in all these cases, the Court's plenary docket at that time would have more than doubled.

4. But the departure from the Court of Justice White, who often dissented on the ground of an asserted conflict, and of several Justices who always at least noted a dissent from the denial of certiorari in capital cases, will doubtless affect the rate of such action.

5. In addition, Justice Stevens has on several occasions written a memorandum "respecting the denial" of certiorari, in which he underscored his belief in the importance of the case without dissenting from the denial. See, *e.g.,* Lackey v. Texas, 115 S.Ct. 1421 (1995); Frank v. United States, 113 S.Ct. 363 (1992). Both cases involved petitioners who had been convicted of crimes, and in Lackey, petitioner was under sentence of death. In both cases, Justice Stevens emphasized that

the novelty of the question presented, and the lack of a conflict in the lower courts, justified a decision by the Court to postpone consideration until the issue had been more fully considered. In both instances, Justice Stevens cited his opinion in Singleton for the proposition that the denial of certiorari was not a ruling on the merits.

What purpose was served by these opinions? Was their issuance consistent with Justice Stevens' arguments in his Singleton opinion? Was the opinion in Lackey more understandable because it involved a capital case? *Cf.* Stephens v. Kemp, 469 U.S. 1098 (1984)(Stevens, J., dissenting from a denial of certiorari in a capital case).

6. A few Justices have also used the dissent to express their views on the Supreme Court's workload and on the desirability of proposed legislation. See, *e.g.,* Brown Transport Co. v. Atcon, Inc., 439 U.S. 1014 (1978), in which Chief Justice Burger, Justice

(3) *The Significance of a Denial of Certiorari.*

(a) Justice Jackson, concurring in Brown v. Allen, 344 U.S. 443 (1953), p. 1355, *supra,* had this to say about denials of certiorari (p. 543):

"I agree that, as *stare decisis,* denial of certiorari should be given no significance whatever. It creates no precedent and approves no statement of principle entitled to weight in any other case. But, for the case in which certiorari is denied, its minimum meaning is that this Court allows the judgment below to stand with whatever consequences it may have upon the litigants involved under the doctrine of *res judicata* as applied either by state or federal courts. A civil or criminal judgment usually becomes *res judicata* in the sense that it is binding and conclusive even if new facts are discovered and even if a new theory of law were thought up, except for some provision for granting a new trial, which usually is discretionary with the trial court and limited in time."

Justice Jackson's opinion focused on the question of the significance of a denial of certiorari in a subsequent habeas corpus action brought by the same petitioner. (See generally Chap. XI, Sec. 2, *supra.*) Didn't Justice Blackmun miscite that opinion when he invoked it as a justification for his dissent in Singleton?

(b) In United States v. Kras, 409 U.S. 434 (1973), Justice Blackmun, speaking for the Court, placed heavy emphasis on the denial of certiorari in an identical case some time earlier, a denial made in the face of a claim that the decision below was wrong in light of a still earlier Supreme Court precedent. The denial, he said, was surely "not without some significance as to * * * the Court's attitude * * *" (p. 443). Justice Marshall, in dissent, was sharply critical of the Court's willingness to draw any inference whatever from the denial of certiorari.[7] Other categories of cases in which Linzer, note 3, *supra,* observes a tendency on the part of lower courts to rely on denials of certiorari as indicating the Supreme Court's view on the merits are (1) cases in which certiorari was denied despite the "great importance and controversial nature" of the holding below, (2) "cases in which the Supreme Court had remanded a case to a lower court and then had denied certiorari" after the lower court had acted on remand, and (3) "cases involving limited grants of certiorari" (p. 1278).

Do you think it is proper to place weight on the denial in any or all of these situations? Linzer concludes that a "certiorari denial is often not based on the merits and never should bind anyone * * *. Yet it seems time to stop pretending that denial of certiorari means nothing. Many times it gives us a glimpse, imperfect to be sure, into the Justices' preliminary attitudes on a

White, and Justice Brennan each wrote separate opinions dealing with the need for and possible shape of changes in the structure of the federal judicial system.

Are such questions of judicial administration appropriate subjects of debate in the pages of the U.S. Reports on the occasion of a denial of certiorari?

7. Note that Justice Marshall was one of those who joined Justice Blackmun's dissent in Singleton.

In Hughes Tool Co. v. TWA, Inc., 409 U.S. 363, 366 n. 1 (1973), decided the same day as Kras, the Court referred with approval to "the well-settled view that denial of certiorari imparts no implication or inference concerning the Court's view of the merits" [citing Justice Frankfurter's dissent in Baltimore Radio Show].

given issue." And dissents and other separate opinions "can provide starting points for reexamination of an issue" (pp. 1304–05). But whatever their value as signposts, he urges that "[w]ise litigants should continue to refrain from citing certiorari denials to bolster their arguments on the merits" and "neither the Supreme Court nor the courts below need be embarrassed about ignoring them" (*id.*).

(4) *The Likelihood of Reversal when Certiorari is Granted.* Studies indicate that the Supreme Court reverses the judgment below in 60 to 70 percent of the cases in which certiorari is granted. See Stern, Gressman, Shapiro & Geller, Supreme Court Practice § 4.17, at 195 n. 59 (7th ed. 1993). See also Hellman, *Error Correction, Lawmaking, and the Supreme Court's Exercise of Discretionary Review,* 44 U.Pitt.L.Rev. 795, 875 (1983)("[C]onsideration of the correctness of the lower court's decision also plays a role in the selection of cases for the plenary docket. This proposition is hardly novel, but the data provide some striking illustrations of its continuing validity.").

Does the Court's tendency to reverse in the cases in which it grants certiorari cast any light on its views in the cases in which certiorari is denied? Even if it tells us something about those cases as a group, does it provide any useful information about the Court's attitude in a *particular* case?[8]

Rogers v. Missouri Pacific Railroad Co.

352 U.S. 500, 77 S.Ct. 443, 1 L.Ed.2d 493 (1957).
Certiorari to the Supreme Court of Missouri.

Webb v. Illinois Central Railroad Co.

352 U.S. 512, 77 S.Ct. 451, 1 L.Ed.2d 503 (1957).
Certiorari to the United States Court of Appeals for the Seventh Circuit.

Herdman v. Pennsylvania Railroad Co.

352 U.S. 518, 77 S.Ct. 455, 1 L.Ed.2d 508 (1957).
Certiorari to the United States Court of Appeals for the Sixth Circuit.

Ferguson v. Moore–McCormack Lines, Inc.

352 U.S. 521, 77 S.Ct. 457, 1 L.Ed.2d 511 (1957).
Certiorari to the United States Court of Appeals for the Second Circuit.

[All four of these cases were decided on the same day. Three of them—Rogers, Webb, and Herdman—arose under the FELA, and the fourth—Ferguson—arose under the Jones Act. In each of the four cases, the court below had held that the evidence was not sufficient to take the case to the jury. In all but Herdman, the Supreme Court disagreed and reversed the judgment. Justice Brennan, writing for the Court in Rogers, defended the decision to grant certiorari in such cases:

8. For discussion of the issues of certiorari policy raised by Justice Blackmun's dissent in Singleton, see *Concluding Note on the Certiorari Policy,* p. 1708, *infra.*

["Cognizant of the duty to effectuate the intention of the Congress to secure the right to a jury determination, this Court is vigilant to exercise its power of review in any case where it appears that the litigants have been improperly deprived of that determination. * * * The kind of misconception evidenced in the opinion below, which fails to take into account the special features of this statutory negligence action that make it significantly different from the ordinary common-law negligence action, has required this Court to review a number of cases. In a relatively large percentage of the cases reviewed, the Court has found that lower courts have not given proper scope to this integral part of the congressional scheme. * * * Special and important reasons for the grant of certiorari in these cases are certainly present when lower federal and state courts persistently deprive litigants of their right to a jury determination."

[The opinions that follow are that of Justice Frankfurter, dissenting in all four cases, and that of Justice Harlan, concurring in Herdman and dissenting in the other three cases.]

■ MR. JUSTICE FRANKFURTER, dissenting.

"The Federal Employers' Liability Act gives to railroad employees a somewhat liberalized right of recovery for injuries on the job. A great number of cases under the Act have been brought to the Supreme Court, many of them cases in which the court of appeals had set aside, on the evidence, verdicts for the employees. Despite the human appeal of these cases, Brandeis never allowed himself to regard them as the proper business of the appellate jurisdiction of the Supreme Court." Paul A. Freund, The Liberalism of Justice Brandeis, address at a meeting of the American Historical Association in St. Louis, December 28, 1956.

In so discharging his judicial responsibility, Mr. Justice Brandeis did not disclose an idiosyncrasy in a great judge. His attitude expressed respect for the standards formulated by the Court in carrying out the mandate of Congress regarding this Court's appellate jurisdiction in cases arising under the Federal Employers' Liability Act, 45 U.S.C.A. § 51 *et seq.* For he began his work on the Court just after Congress had passed the Act of September 6, 1916, 39 Stat. 726, relieving the Court of its obligatory jurisdiction over Federal Employers' Liability Act decisions by the highest state courts and the Circuit Courts of Appeals. Mr. Justice Brandeis' general outlook on the formulation by the Supreme Court of the public law appropriate for an evolving society has more and more prevailed; his concept of the role of the Supreme Court in our judicial system, and his consequent regard for the bearing on the judicial product of what business comes to the Court and how the Court deals with it, have often been neglected in the name of "doing justice" in individual cases. To him these were not technicalities, in the derogatory sense, for the conduct of judicial business. He deemed wise decisions on substantive law within the indispensable area of the Court's jurisdiction dependent on a limited volume of business and on a truly deliberative process.

One field of conspicuous disregard of these vital considerations is that large mass of cases under the Federal Employers' Liability Act in which the sole issue is the sufficiency of the evidence for submission to the jury.[2] For many

---

2. Throughout this opinion I have dealt with the issue of granting certiorari in this type of case almost entirely in terms of the Federal Employers' Liability Act because the greatest abuse of the certiorari policy has occurred in that field. The problem is not

years, I reluctantly voted on the merits of these negligence cases that had been granted review. In the last ten years, and more particularly within the past few years, as the Court has been granting more and more of these petitions, I have found it increasingly difficult to acquiesce in a practice that I regard as wholly incompatible with the certiorari policy embodied in the 1916 Act, the Judiciary Act of 1925, 43 Stat. 936, and the Rules formulated by the Court to govern certiorari jurisdiction for its own regulation and for the guidance of the bar. I have therefore felt compelled to vote to dismiss petitions for certiorari in such cases as improvidently granted without passing on the merits. In these cases I indicated briefly the reasons why I believed that this Court should not be reviewing decisions in which the sole issue is the sufficiency of the evidence for submission to the jury. In view of the increasing number of these cases that have been brought here for review—this dissent is to four decisions of the Court—and in view of the encouragement thereby given to continuing resort to this Court, I deem it necessary to enlarge upon the considerations that have guided me in the conviction that writs in this class of cases are "improvidently granted."

At the outset, however, I should deal briefly with a preliminary problem. It is sometimes said that the "integrity of the certiorari process" as expressed in the "rule of four" (that is, this Court's practice of granting certiorari on the vote of four Justices) requires all the Justices to vote on the merits of a case when four Justices have voted to grant certiorari and no new factor emerges after argument and deliberation. There are two reasons why there can be no such requirement. Last Term, for example, the Court disposed of 1,361 petitions for certiorari. With such a volume of certiorari business, not to mention the remainder of the Court's business, the initial decision to grant a petition for certiorari must necessarily be based on a limited appreciation of the issues in a case, resting as it so largely does on the partisan claims in briefs of counsel. * * * The Court does not, indeed it cannot and should not try to, give to the initial question of granting or denying a petition the kind of attention that is demanded by a decision on the merits. The assumption that we know no more after hearing and deliberating on a case than after reading the petition for certiorari and the response is inadmissible in theory and not true in fact. Even an FELA case sometimes appears in quite a different light after argument than it appeared on the original papers. Surely this must be acknowledged regarding one of today's cases, No. 46. The course of argument and the briefs on the merits may disclose that a case appearing on the surface to warrant a writ of certiorari does not warrant it, see Layne & Bowler Corp. v. Western Well Works, Inc., 261 U.S. 387, or may reveal more clearly that the only thing in controversy is an appraisal of facts on which this Court is being asked to make a second guess, to substitute its assessment of the testimony for that of the court below.

But there is a more basic reason why the "integrity of the certiorari process" does not require me to vote on the merits of these cases. The right of a Justice to dissent from an action of the Court is historic. Of course self-restraint should guide the expression of dissent. But dissent is essential to an effective judiciary in a democratic society, and especially for a tribunal exercising the powers of this Court. Not four, not eight, Justices can require another

confined to that Act, however, since the same or similar issues arise under other Acts, such as the Jones Act, 41 Stat. 1007, 46 U.S.C. § 688 * * *. Indeed, one of the decisions to which this dissent is written, No. 59, arises under the Jones Act.

to decide a case that he regards as not properly before the Court. The failure of a Justice to persuade his colleagues does not require him to yield to their views, if he has a deep conviction that the issue is sufficiently important. Moreover, the Court operates ultimately by majority. Even though a minority may bring a case here for oral argument, that does not mean that the majority has given up its right to vote on the ultimate disposition of the case as conscience directs. This is not a novel doctrine. As a matter of practice, members of the Court have at various times exercised this right of refusing to pass on the merits of cases that in their view should not have been granted review.

This does not make the "rule of four" a hollow rule. I would not change the practice. No Justice is likely to vote to dismiss a writ of certiorari as improvidently granted after argument has been heard, even though he has not been convinced that the case is within the rules of the Court governing the granting of certiorari. In the usual instance, a doubting Justice respects the judgment of his brethren that the case does concern issues important enough for the Court's consideration and adjudication. But a different situation is presented when a class of cases is systematically taken for review. Then a Justice who believes that such cases raise insignificant and unimportant questions—insignificant and unimportant from the point of view of the Court's duties—and that an increasing amount of the Court's time is unduly drained by adjudication of these cases cannot forego his duty to voice his dissent to the Court's action.

The "rule of four" is not a command of Congress. It is a working rule devised by the Court as a practical mode of determining that a case is deserving of review, the theory being that if four Justices find that a legal question of general importance is raised, that is ample proof that the question has such importance. This is a fair enough rule of thumb on the assumption that four Justices find such importance on an individualized screening of the cases sought to be reviewed. The reason for deference to a minority view no longer holds when a class of litigation is given a special and privileged position.

The history of the Federal Employers' Liability Act reveals the continuing nature of the problem of review by this Court of the vast litigation under that Act in both the federal and state courts.   * * *

　　　　* * *

This unvarnished account of Federal Employers' Liability Act litigation in this Court relating to sufficiency of the evidence for submission of cases to the jury is surely not an exhilarating story. For the Supreme Court of the United States to spend two hours of solemn argument, plus countless other hours reading the briefs and record and writing opinions, to determine whether there was evidence to support an allegation that it could reasonably be foreseen that an ice-cream server on a ship would use a butcher's knife to scoop out ice cream that was too hard to be scooped with a regular scoop, is surely to misconceive the discretion that was entrusted to the wisdom of the Court for the control of its calendar. The Court may or may not be "doing justice" in the four insignificant cases it decides today; it certainly is doing injustice to the significant and important cases on the calendar and to its own role as the supreme judicial body of the country.   * * *

I would dismiss all four writs of certiorari as improvidently granted.

　　　　* * *

■ MR. JUSTICE HARLAN, concurring in No. 46 and dissenting in Nos. 28, 42 and 59.

I.

I am in full agreement with what my Brother Frankfurter has written in criticism of the Court's recurring willingness to grant certiorari in cases of this type. For the reasons he has given, I think the Court should not have heard any of these four cases. Nevertheless, the cases having been taken, I have conceived it to be my duty to consider them on their merits, because I cannot reconcile voting to dismiss the writs as "improvidently granted" with the Court's "rule of four." In my opinion due adherence to that rule requires that once certiorari has been granted a case should be disposed of on the premise that it is properly here, in the absence of considerations appearing which were not manifest or fully apprehended at the time certiorari was granted. In these instances I am unable to say that such considerations exist, even though I do think that the arguments on the merits underscored the views of those of us who originally felt that the cases should not be taken because they involved only issues of fact, and presented nothing of sufficient general importance to warrant this substantial expenditure of the Court's time.

I do not think that, in the absence of the considerations mentioned, voting to dismiss a writ after it has been granted can be justified on the basis of an inherent right of dissent. In the case of a petition for certiorari that right, it seems to me—again without the presence of intervening factors—is exhausted once the petition has been granted and the cause set for argument.[1] Otherwise the "rule of four" surely becomes a meaningless thing in more than one respect. *First,* notwithstanding the "rule of four," five objecting Justices could undo the grant by voting, after the case has been heard, to dismiss the writ as improvidently granted—a course which would hardly be fair to litigants who have expended time, effort, and money on the assumption that their cases would be heard and decided on the merits. While in the nature of things litigants must assume the risk of "improvidently granted" dismissals because of factors not fully apprehended when the petition for certiorari was under consideration, short of that it seems to me that the Court would stultify its own rule if it were permissible for a writ of certiorari to be annulled by the later vote of five objecting Justices. Indeed, if that were proper, it would be preferable to have the vote of annulment come into play the moment after the petition for certiorari has been granted, since then at least the litigants would be spared useless effort in briefing and preparing for the argument of their cases. *Second,* permitting the grant of a writ to be thus undone would undermine the whole philosophy of the "rule of four," which is that any case warranting consideration in the opinion of such a substantial minority of the Court will be taken and disposed of. It appears to me that such a practice would accomplish just the contrary of what representatives of this Court stated to Congress as to the "rule of four" at the time the Court's certiorari

---

1. In some instances where the Court has granted certiorari and simultaneously summarily disposed of the case on the merits, individual Justices (including the writer) have merely noted their dissent to the grant without reaching the merits. See, *e.g.,* Anderson v. Atlantic Coast Line R. Co., 350 U.S. 807; Cahill v. New York, N.H. & H.R. Co., 350 U.S. 898. Even here, I am bound to say, it would probably be better practice for a Justice, who has unsuccessfully opposed certiorari, to face the merits, and to dissent from the summary disposition rather than from the grant of certiorari if he is not prepared to reach the merits without full-dress argument.

jurisdiction was enlarged by the Judiciary Act of 1925. In effect the "rule of four" would, by indirection, become a "rule of five." *Third*, such a practice would, in my opinion, be inconsistent with the long-standing and desirable custom of not announcing the Conference vote on petitions for certiorari. For in the absence of the intervening circumstances which may cause a Justice to vote to dismiss a writ as improvidently granted, such a disposition of the case on his part is almost bound to be taken as reflecting his original Conference vote on the petition. And if such a practice is permissible, then by the same token I do not see how those who voted in favor of the petition can reasonably be expected to refrain from announcing their Conference votes at the time the petition is acted on.

My Brother Frankfurter states that the course he advocates will not result in making of the "rule of four" an empty thing, suggesting that in individual cases "a doubting Justice" will normally respect "the judgment of his brethren that the case does concern issues important enough for the Court's consideration and adjudication," and that it is only "when a class of cases is systematically taken for review" that such a Justice "cannot forego his duty to voice his dissent to the Court's action." However, it seems to me that it is precisely in that type of situation where the exercise of the right of dissent may well result in nullification of the "rule of four" by the action of five Justices. For differences of view as to the desirability of the Court's taking particular "classes" of cases—the situation we have here—are prone to lead to more or less definite lines of cleavage among the Justices, which past experience has shown may well involve an alignment of four Justices who favor granting certiorari in such cases and five who do not. If in such situations it becomes the duty of one Justice among the disagreeing five not to "forego" his right to dissent, then I do not see why it is not equally the duty of the remaining four, resulting in the "rule of four" being set at naught. I thus see no basis in the circumstance that a case is an "individual" one rather than one of a "class" for distinctions in what may be done by an individual Justice who disapproves of the Court's action in granting certiorari.

Although I feel strongly that cases of this kind do not belong in this Court, I can see no other course, consistent with the "rule of four," but to continue our Conference debates, with the hope that persuasion or the mounting calendars of the Court will eventually bring our differing brethren to another point of view.

II.

Since I can find no intervening circumstances which would justify my voting now to dismiss the writs in these cases as improvidently granted, I turn to the merits of the four cases before us. * * *

NOTE ON THE RULE OF FOUR

(1) *The Significance of the Rule for the Work of the Court.* When, if ever, is it appropriate to dismiss a writ as improvidently granted over four dissents?

"There is ample indication that Congress had the rule of four in mind when it approved the Judges Bill [in 1925]." Leiman, *The Rule of Four*, 57 Colum.L.Rev. 975, 985 (1957). The rule was frequently mentioned by the

Justices in their testimony and cited both in Committee reports and on the floor in defense of the fairness of the certiorari process. *Id.* at 985–86 (citing H.R.Rep. No. 1075, 68th Cong., 2d Sess. 3 (1925)). But how was the rule understood? In Leiman's view, it meant only that the vote of four would commit all nine to a more extended look at the case; it would not commit anyone to a vote on the merits if a majority were convinced, after briefing and oral argument, that the writ should be dismissed as improvidently granted. In the absence of such a majority, however, an individual Justice should not vote to dismiss except for a jurisdictional defect.[1]

A view similar to Leiman's was adopted by Justice Stevens (and perhaps by the majority) in New York v. Uplinger, 467 U.S. 246 (1984). In that case, the majority dismissed a writ of certiorari as improvidently granted because of the ambiguity of the state court opinion below and the possibility that it rested on state law. Four dissenters said that the merits of the decision below were "properly before us and should be addressed" (p. 252). The majority did not discuss the significance of the rule of four, but Justice Stevens, concurring, did (pp. 250–51):

"It might be suggested that [under the rule of four] the case must be decided unless there has been an intervening development that justifies a dismissal. * * * I am now persuaded, however, that there is *always* an important intervening development that may be decisive. The Members of the Court have always considered a case more carefully after full briefing and argument on the merits than they could at the time of the certiorari conference, when almost 100 petitions must be considered each week. * * * [T]he Rule of Four is a valuable, though not immutable, device for deciding when a case must be argued, but its force is largely spent once the case has been heard."

For further discussion of this question, see Triangle Improvement Council v. Ritchie, 402 U.S. 497, 502 (Harlan, J., concurring), 508 (Douglas, J., dissenting)(1971);[2] Donnelly v. DeChristoforo, 416 U.S. 637, 648 (1974);[3] Burrell v. McCray, 426 U.S. 471 (1976);[4] Blumstein, *The Supreme Court's*

---

1. Leiman notes one case, Parker v. Illinois, 334 U.S. 816 (1948), in which Justice Jackson's vote to dismiss the writ left the Court equally divided on the merits. Thus his vote was effectively a vote to affirm.

2. Justice Harlan, concurring in a 5–4 dismissal, concluded that the writ was properly dismissed because the case had "changed posture" after certiorari had been granted (p. 502). Justice Douglas, dissenting, argued that such action should not be taken by those who had originally opposed granting the writ.

3. Five Justices expressed the view that certiorari should not have been granted, but all nine voted on the merits (dividing 6–3). Justice Stewart, joined by Justice White, said he felt obligated to address the merits because as many as four colleagues "remain so minded after oral argument" (p. 648).

4. The Court, after oral argument, dismissed a writ of certiorari as improvidently granted over the dissent of three Justices who would have affirmed the judgment below. Justice Stevens, concurring, noted that he would have voted to deny certiorari had he been on the Court when the writ was granted, that the concurrence in the dismissal by one Justice who had voted to grant the petition meant the rule of four was not violated, and that there was ground for the dismissal because further study indicated the law to be sufficiently clear that there was no need for an opinion of the Court. (Was Justice Stevens expressing an opinion on the merits?) Justice Brennan, in dissent, argued that there was nothing to indicate that the conditions originally thought to warrant issuance of the writ were not in fact present and that under those circumstances, a Justice who originally voted to deny certiorari should not vote to dismiss.

Jurisdiction—Reform Proposals, Discretionary Review, and Writ Dismissals, 26 Vand.L.Rev. 895 (1973).[5]

(2) *The Special Problem of Stays of Execution in Capital Cases.* The question of the obligation imposed on the majority by a grant of certiorari has also been raised in the context of a request for a stay of execution in a capital case. In Darden v. Wainwright, 473 U.S. 927 (1985), the Court (within a few hours) first denied an application for a stay by a vote of 5–4, then granted a petition for certiorari, and then granted the application for a stay, again by a vote of 5–4. Explaining his ultimate vote to grant the stay, Justice Powell indicated that only four Justices had voted to grant certiorari and that he had not been one of them. Of the four Justices who dissented from grant of the stay, Chief Justice Burger said he thought that the case was wholly without merit and that the grant of certiorari was an abuse of discretion.

In another capital case during the same Term, the Court (after oral argument in Darden, *supra*) voted to hold the petition for certiorari pending disposition of Darden, but then, by a vote of 5–4, vacated its earlier stay of execution. Straight v. Wainwright, 476 U.S. 1132 (1986). (In his concurring opinion, Justice Powell indicated that there had been four votes to hold the case, though Justice Brennan disclosed in a later opinion that "[t]hree votes suffice to hold a case." Watson v. Butler, 483 U.S. 1037, 1038 (1987)(Brennan, J., joined by Marshall and Blackmun, JJ., dissenting from denial of a stay of execution).)[6]

What is the nature of the Court's obligation to attempt to preserve its jurisdiction once certiorari has been granted? Is that obligation greater in a capital case? Greater than in a case in which a minority of four (or three) has voted only to hold a petition for the disposition of another case? These and a number of other issues relating to the rule of four and to the "hold" rule are perceptively discussed in Revesz & Karlan, *Non–Majority Rules and the Supreme Court,* 136 U.Pa.L.Rev. 1067 (1988).

(3) *Application of the Rule of Four to the Issues To Be Decided.* In Board of Educ., Island Trees Union Free School Dist. No. 26 v. Pico, 457 U.S. 853 (1982), the majority, relying on the First Amendment, agreed with the court of appeals that summary judgment should not have been granted to the defendant school board. Justice White, concurring, said that he saw no need for a discussion of the First Amendment issue, since it was enough at this stage to conclude that there was a material issue of fact precluding summary judgment. Justice Rehnquist, dissenting for himself and two other Justices, said in a footnote that Justice White's refusal to reach the First Amendment issue was "inconsistent with the 'rule of four' "(p. 904 n. 1). Citing the Harlan opinion in Rogers *et al.,* he said that Justice White's concurrence, "although not couched in such language, is in effect a single vote to dismiss the writ of certiorari as improvidently granted" (*id.*).

---

5. *Cf.* Ticor Title Ins. Co. v. Brown, 114 S.Ct. 1359 (1994)(dismissing writ as improvidently granted over 3 dissents; dissenters argued that the important constitutional issue on which certiorari was granted was squarely and unavoidably presented).

6. In Herrera v. Thompson, a habeas corpus case ultimately decided on the merits (see p. 1389, *supra*), the Court granted certiorari but affirmed its previous denial of a stay of execution. 502 U.S. 1085 (1992). But the Texas Court of Criminal Appeals decided to stay the scheduled execution so that the case could be heard. (The story is told in Berger, *Herrera v. Collins: The Gateway of Innocence for Death–Sentenced Prisoners Leads Nowhere,* 35 Wm. & Mary L.Rev. 943, 944–45 (1994).)

Justice Rehnquist is plainly wrong, isn't he? If the rule of four does require a Justice to reach the merits of a particular case—at least when there is no objection to jurisdiction—does it also require him to submit to someone else's view of the *issues* that must be decided in order to dispose of the case?

(4) *Denial of Certiorari over Four Dissents.* In a few instances, a petition for certiorari has been denied over four dissents. In Gay v. United States, 411 U.S. 974 (1973), the four dissenters did not object to the denial; rather they would have summarily reversed. Should this be regarded as a waiver of the dissenters' power to have the petition granted?[7]

In a series of obscenity cases in 1974 and 1975, the Supreme Court denied certiorari over four dissents, but in each case three of the dissenters stated: "Although four of us would grant certiorari and reverse the judgment, the Justices who join this opinion do not insist that the case be decided on the merits." *E.g.,* Trinkler v. Alabama, 418 U.S. 917, 918 n. * (1974). In many of these cases, unlike Gay, it was clear that the dissenters were expressing a view that had already been rejected by the majority in prior decisions. But in some of the cases, the dissenters urged that denial of certiorari was improper on the basis of the Court's own prior decisions. *E.g.,* J–R Distributors, Inc. v. Washington, 418 U.S. 949 (1974).

When Justice Stevens replaced Justice Douglas in the 1975 Term, the number of votes regularly dissenting from the denial of certiorari in obscenity cases went down from four to three. Without rejecting the views of the dissenters on the merits, Justice Stevens concurred in the denial of certiorari in one such case, saying:

"* * * [T]here is no reason to believe that the majority of the Court * * * is any less adamant than the minority. Accordingly, regardless of how I might vote on the merits after full argument, it would be pointless to grant certiorari in case after case of this character only to have [our prior decisions] reaffirmed time after time.

"Since my dissenting Brethren have recognized the force of this reasoning in the past, I believe they also could properly vote to deny certiorari in this case without acting inconsistently with their principled views on the merits. In all events, until a valid reason for voting to grant one of these petitions is put forward, I shall continue to vote to deny. In the interest of conserving scarce law library space, I shall not repeat this explanation every time I cast such a vote." Liles v. Oregon, 425 U.S. 963–64 (1976).

(5) *The Rule When Not All Justices Are Sitting.* Are four votes required to grant a petition for certiorari when only eight Justices are sitting on a case? When only seven Justices are sitting? Although Justice Douglas said in 1970 that the vote of three Justices would suffice when seven were sitting,[8] the Court on several occasions has denied certiorari in these circumstances over

---

7. See also Drake v. Zant, 449 U.S. 999 (1980)(denying certiorari over four dissents). *Cf.* Hirsh v. City of Atlanta, 495 U.S. 927 (1990), in which the Court, by a 5–4 vote, denied an application for a stay. The four dissenters stated that, in their view, the Court was required "to treat the stay applica-tion as a petition for certiorari, to grant certiorari, and to reverse the denial of a stay by the [state] Supreme Court" (*id.*).

8. Douglas, *Managing the Docket of the Supreme Court of the United States,* 25 Record Ass'n B. City N.Y. 279, 298 (1970).

three dissents.[9] No objection to this practice was noted by the dissenters.

CONCLUDING NOTE ON THE CERTIORARI POLICY

(1) *Certiorari Policy in FELA Cases.* Professor Hart, agreeing with Justice Frankfurter in Rogers, described the Court's determination to engage in case-by-case policing in FELA and related cases as "a grievous frittering away of the judicial resources of the nation". Hart, *Foreword: The Time Chart of the Justices,* 73 Harv.L.Rev. 84, 98 (1959). Thurman Arnold replied that the enforcement of proper standards for jury verdicts in FELA cases is "vital to the security of lowly litigants" and "directly or indirectly affects the lives of millions". Arnold, *Professor Hart's Theology,* 73 Harv.L.Rev. 1298, 1302, 1304 (1960).

Did review of these decisions consume a substantial segment of the Court's time? Justice Douglas thought not. In a concurring opinion in a 1959 FELA case, he noted that in the more than ten years from January 31, 1949, to October 19, 1959, there had been 110 petitions for certiorari in FELA cases. Of these, 77 were denied, and of the 33 granted, 16 were reversed without oral argument. Of the 17 argued, 5 were disposed of with brief per curiam opinions, leaving an average of slightly more than one full opinion per year in FELA cases for the period in question. Harris v. Pennsylvania R.R., 361 U.S. 15, 16–25 (1959).

Justice Douglas' figures do not tell the whole story. A policy that encourages the filing of certiorari petitions on a given question increases the total workload even if many or most of the petitions are denied. And a case that requires review of the record to determine the sufficiency of the evidence may well take more time to dispose of than a case presenting a purely legal issue.

(2) *The Appropriate Criteria for Determining Whether to Grant the Writ.* The controversy over FELA cases is no longer a live one. But disagreements persist within the Court over the willingness to grant certiorari in certain categories of cases. Justice Stevens, for example, was at one time especially critical of the increase in petitions granted at the behest of the prosecution in state criminal cases. "The result," he complained, was "a docket swollen with requests by the state to reverse judgments that their courts have rendered in favor of their citizens." Michigan v. Long, 463 U.S. 1032, 1070 (1983)(dissenting opinion). (For further discussion of this issue, see Chap. V, Sec. 2, p. 536, *supra.*)

Note the provisions of Sup.Ct.Rule 10: "Considerations Governing Review on Certiorari." How satisfactory are the criteria there articulated? How consistent are they with the view that the Court sits to adjudicate only those cases, within its jurisdiction, of most far-reaching, general importance?

Rule 10 is closely patterned on a rule that became effective in 1980. That rule (like its present version) embodied a number of organizational and stylistic changes from its predecessor, and two substantive changes. First, the revised rule omits the reference in the earlier version to a federal court of appeals decision of "an important state or territorial question * * * in conflict with applicable state or territorial law"; the omission "reflects the Court's current

---

9. See, *e.g.,* Donaldson v. California, 404 U.S. 968 (1971); Stanley v. United States, 404 U.S. 996 (1971); Delaware State Bd. of Educ. v. Evans, 434 U.S. 880 (1977).

lack of interest in reviewing diversity cases where the only issue is the consistency of the court of appeals decision with applicable state substantive law." Stern, Gressman, Shapiro & Geller, Supreme Court Practice § 4.10, at 183 (7th ed. 1993). Second, the revised rule adds a reference to a decision of a federal question by a state court of last resort "that conflicts with the decision of another state court of last resort or of a United States court of appeals". This addition brought within the text of the rule a situation that "has long been recognized in practice" as a basis for certiorari. Boskey & Gressman, *The Supreme Court's New Rules for the Eighties,* 85 F.R.D. 487, 505 (1980).

Each of the subparagraphs of Rule 10 includes a reference to a conflict (for example, a conflict between decisions of the federal courts of appeals or with applicable decisions of the Supreme Court) as a basis for certiorari. Should the petitioner in such a case have to show in addition that present resolution of the conflict is required by such factors as the national importance of the issue or the nature of the interests affected? (The Court's 1995 revision of Rule 10 does state, for the first time, that an asserted conflict must be on an "important" federal matter.)

While the existence of a conflict is clearly a significant factor in the consideration of a certiorari petition, it was reported as early as 1953 that the Court would not automatically grant certiorari when there was a conflict among the federal courts of appeals. Stern, *Denial of Certiorari Despite a Conflict,* 66 Harv.L.Rev. 465, 472 (1953). And a 1975 study concluded that the Court was denying certiorari in approximately 60–65 cases each Term despite the existence of a "direct conflict".[1] (A recent reexamination of 40 of the cases in the 1975 study, however, applied different standards of evaluation and concluded that the number of "square conflicts" was considerably lower, and that the number of "intolerable conflicts" was lower still.[2])

Commentators on the work of the Court are not of one mind about the Supreme Court's responsibility for the resolution of conflicts. In the view of some, the Court should allow issues to "percolate" in the lower courts unless there is some pressing reason to resolve a conflict at an early stage; this process, they contend, will assure a wiser and more informed resolution in the long run. See, *e.g.,* Posner, The Federal Courts: Crisis and Reform 163 (1985).[3] In the view of others, this argument transforms the sensible caution against a rush to judgment into an inflated excuse for failing to take steps sorely needed to restore the health of our system of national law. See, *e.g.,* Baker & McFarland, *The Need for a New National Court,* 100 Harv.L.Rev. 1400, 1408–09 (1987); Bator, *What is Wrong with the Supreme Court?,* 50

---

1. Feeney, *Conflicts Involving Federal Law: A Review of Cases Presented to the Supreme Court,* 67 F.R.D. 301, 320 (1975). Professor Feeney's study was prepared under the aegis of the Hruska Commission (see Chap. I, p. 61, *supra*), and was relied on by that Commission in its decision to recommend the creation of a National Court of Appeals. See 67 F.R.D. 195, 298 (1975).

2. See Note, 59 N.Y.U.L.Rev. 1007 (1984). This reexamination was part of the New York University Supreme Court Project

published in three issues of the New York University Law Review.

3. Note also Justice Stevens' memorandum respecting the denial of certiorari in Hiersche v. United States, 503 U.S. 923 (1992), where he defended the Court's refusal to grant certiorari in order to resolve a circuit conflict about the scope of governmental immunity provided by a 1928 statute that he described as "an anachronism." "Some conflicts," he stated, "are tolerable. Others can be resolved more effectively by Congress. This is such a case" (p. 1305).

U.Pitt.L.Rev. 673 (1990); Bator, *The Judicial Universe of Judge Posner*, 52 U.Chi.L.Rev. 1146, 1154–55 (1985)(book review).[4]

(a) *The NYU Study.* In a book growing out of the NYU Supreme Court Project, note 2, *supra,* Professors Estreicher and Sexton propose a number of "modest reforms" of Supreme Court practice, one of which is to revise what is now Rule 10 to establish a "principled set of case selection criteria [that] would send clearer signals to the Bar." Estreicher & Sexton, Redefining the Supreme Court's Role 116, 118 (1986). Although they do not submit a suggested draft, they do refer to their own criteria, which embrace both a "priority" and "discretionary" docket. Among the cases in the first category are those involving "intolerable intercourt conflicts" (defined as conflicts involving three or more circuits, as well as those conflicts creating a substantial opportunity for forum shopping or making it difficult for multi-state actors to conduct their affairs), conflict with Supreme Court precedent, resolution of "profound vertical federalism disputes," resolution of interbranch disputes, and resolution of interstate disputes (pp. 52–62). Included in the second category are such cases as those involving "a significant interference with federal executive responsibility" and "vehicles for advances in the development of federal law" (pp. 62–69).

Do you think that such an effort to sharpen the applicable criteria would affect the rate of irresponsible certiorari petitions? Of improvident grants? Would it help on the first of these questions to fine attorneys who file frivolous petitions? See Sup.Ct. Rule 8.2.

(b) *The Federal Judicial Center Study.* A report has recently been released by the Federal Judicial Center in response to a request by Congress (Judicial Improvements Act of 1990, § 302, 104 Stat. 5089, 5104) for a study of the number and frequency of intercircuit conflicts and for a consideration of the costs of those conflicts and the range of structural alternatives. In that report, *Unresolved Intercircuit Conflicts: The Nature and Scope of the Problem* (Draft Final report to the Federal Judicial Center, Oct. 1994), the author, Professor Arthur Hellman, concluded that the number of such conflicts in petitions denied per term was substantial (in the neighborhood of 200 per term for the period studied), but that a substantial majority of these conflicts should not be regarded as "intolerable" in terms either of their persistence or their

---

4. In a recent opinion, Chief Justice Rehnquist dissented from the Court's decision to overrule one if its earlier holdings partly on the basis that lower courts had consistently recognized an exception to the scope and application of that holding. The Chief Justice, in objecting to the suggestion that a body of lower court case law can serve as a basis for overruling Supreme Court precedent, had this to say about the Supreme Court's certiorari policy as set forth in Rule 10: "One of the reasons contained in * * * [the Rule] is the existence of a conflict between one court of appeals and another. The negative implication of this ground, borne out time and again in our decisions to grant and deny certiorari, is that ordinarily a court of appeals decision interpreting one of our precedents—even one deemed to be arguably inconsistent with it—will not be reviewed unless it conflicts with a decision of another court of appeals. This fact is a necessary concomitant of the limited capacity in this Court." Hubbard v. United States, 115 S.Ct. 1754, 1767 (1995)(Rehnquist, C.J., dissenting).

Since Rule 10 states as a *separate* ground warranting certiorari the decision by a state or federal court of a federal question "in a way that conflicts with relevant decisions of this Court", is the Chief Justice's interpretation of the Rule consistent with its text? If there is empirical support for his observation (that the Court will ordinarily not review a lower court decision that appears to conflict with its own decisions unless there is a conflict among the lower courts), is this a sound exercise of the certiorari power?

harm to multi-circuit actors. In sum, "unresolved intercircuit conflicts do not constitute a problem of serious magnitude in the federal judicial system". See also Professor Hellman's article based on this study, *By Precedent Unbound: The Nature and Extent of Unresolved Circuit Conflicts,* 56 U.Pitt.L.Rev. 693 (1995).[5]

(3) *The Debate over Structural Changes in the Federal Judicial System.* The complaint typified by Justice Blackmun's dissent in the Singleton case (p. 1693, *supra*)—that there are significant areas of federal law where the Court is failing to give sufficient guidance—is one that, in the view of many observers, transcends issues of certiorari policy.[6] These critics argue that the Supreme Court simply lacks the capacity to insure the stability, clarity, and uniformity of the huge body of national law being interpreted and applied in many thousands of state and federal court cases each year. Thus they have urged that consideration be given to fundamental changes in the structure of the federal judiciary—changes that would enable the Supreme Court to share some of its responsibility for the elaboration and clarification of national law.

For a discussion of the evolution and content of these proposed changes, and of the debate over their desirability, see Chap. I, pp. 61–63, *supra.*

(4) *The Use of Discretionary Jurisdiction as an "Avoidance" Device.* Perhaps the most important of the avoidance devices discussed by Professor Bickel in The Least Dangerous Branch—The Supreme Court at the Bar of Politics (1962), is the Court's discretionary certiorari jurisdiction. Taking as an illustration the case of Times Film Corp. v. Chicago, 365 U.S. 43 (1961), Bickel suggested (pp. 141–43) that instead of rejecting the petitioner's challenge to Chicago's film censorship ordinance on its merits, the Court should have denied review. Since the issue as posed by the parties was the constitutionality of censorship per se (the film was not even in the record), since the Constitution did not in Bickel's view furnish a basis for invalidation, and since Bickel feared the impetus that would be given to the undesirable practice of censorship by a decision favoring the city, he would have opted for the "comparatively inoffensive expedient" of denying certiorari.

Professor Gunther was sharply critical of this line of argument. Gunther, *The Subtle Vices of the "Passive Virtues"—A Comment on Principle and Expediency in Judicial Review,* 64 Colum.L.Rev. 1 (1964). He suggested (p. 14) that it was "manipulative dissimilation" and "intervention in the political process" (using phrases of Bickel's) "when the Court concludes that the Constitution imposes no absolute ban on prior restraints but decides not to say so * * * because of the likely effect in current social and political circumstances, of the judgment of 'legitimation.' " Further, Gunther argued, "Bick-

---

5. Relying in part on Hellman's conclusions, the Proposed Long Range Plan for the Federal Courts (as submitted to the Judicial Conference in 1995 by the Conference Committee on Long Range Planning) determined that "at the present time, the Supreme Court appears to be capable of resolving significant differences of decisional law among the circuits with reasonable promptness." *Id.* at 44.

6. Professor Bator argued that the problem is especially severe in the private sector and in areas of business and tax law. In the latter areas, it appears that only the government can persuade the Court to take a case; in the four Terms of Court from 1980 to 1983, for example, all 15 tax cases heard on the merits in the Supreme Court were cases in which the government had either filed the certiorari petition or agreed that it should be granted because of a conflict. Bator, *What Is Wrong with the Supreme Court?*, Paragraph (2), *supra.*

el's approach to certiorari * * * undercuts his goal of a principled, candid evolution of constitutional interpretation" (p. 14). While Gunther agreed that valid reasons existed for denying certiorari in Times Film—especially the fact that the parties had framed a test case in a manner that "narrowed" the Court's "line of vision" (p. 13)—he rejected the asserted evils of "legitimation" as one of them.[7]

A similar controversy surfaced in 1978, in a dissent by Justice Rehnquist from a denial of certiorari. Ratchford v. Gay Lib, 434 U.S. 1080 (1978). Writing for himself and Justice Blackmun, he argued that the case—involving the validity of a state university's denial of recognition to a student organization—was one in which the Court's criteria in what is now Rule 10 had plainly been satisfied. The existence of discretion to decline to hear a case, he concluded, "does not imply that it should be used as a sort of judicial storm cellar to which we may flee to escape from controversial or sensitive cases" (p. 1081).

(5) *Summary Reversals.* During the Warren Court era, the Court frequently engaged in the practice of summarily reversing the judgment below on the certiorari papers and with no more than a citation or two of explanation. The practice was forcefully criticized by several observers, see, *e.g.,* Brown, *Foreword: Process of Law,* 72 Harv.L.Rev. 77 (1958), and its frequency was substantially reduced by the Burger Court. See Hellman, *Error Correction, Lawmaking, and the Supreme Court's Exercise of Discretionary Review,* 44 U.Pitt.L.Rev. 795, 824–25 (1983). But the Court continued in a number of instances to reverse the decision below on the certiorari papers and without plenary consideration, usually accompanying the disposition with a brief per curiam opinion explaining the Court's reasoning. See id. at 825–36.[8]

The Court in recent years has had its internal critics of summary reversal. The most forceful has been Justice Stevens, often joined by Justices Brennan and Marshall.[9] In some instances, they urged that the case was too unimportant to be considered at all;[10] in others that it was too important to be treated summarily.[11] On one occasion they called the majority's action "unprecedented and drastic" because the Court appeared to grant a petition for certiorari, and then to reject the petitioner's arguments in a footnote, solely to enable the Court to grant the government's cross-petition and to reverse summarily on the

---

7. Gunther is even more critical of Bickel's further suggestion that once certiorari had been granted, the appropriate disposition was a "jurisdictional dismissal for lack of ripeness". Bickel, *supra,* at 143. In Gunther's view, this prescription "is not merely bad but lawless judgment" (64 Colum.L.Rev. at 13) since the "jurisdictional" principle relied on has no basis in any statute or in the Constitution. *Cf.* the discussion of Naim v. Naim, 350 U.S. 891 (1955), and of other aspects of the Gunther–Bickel dispute, in Chap. V, Sec. 4, pp. 652–55, *supra.*

8. For statistics on the ratio of *per curiam* and memorandum decisions to the total number of cases disposed of on the merits—from 1980 through 1994—see Chap. V, Sec. 4, p. 649, *supra.*

9. *E.g.,* County of Los Angeles v. Kling, 474 U.S. 936 (1985); Florida v. Meyers, 466 U.S. 380, 383 (1984); Illinois v. Batchelder, 463 U.S. 1112, 1119 (1983); Idaho Dep't of Employment v. Smith, 434 U.S. 100, 103 (1977); Pennsylvania v. Mimms, 434 U.S. 106, 115 (1977). In the Kling case, Justice Stevens was especially critical of the Court's lack of "discipline and accountability" (p. 303) in issuing a one sentence per curiam reversal of a case in which the court of appeals had issued an unpublished opinion.

10. *E.g.,* Board of Educ. v. McCluskey, 458 U.S. 966, 971 (1982).

11. *E.g.,* Hutto v. Davis, 454 U.S. 370, 381 (1982).

basis of arguments in that cross-petition. Snepp v. United States, 444 U.S. 507, 517 (1980). On another, they complained that in these summary dispositions, which were frequently granted in favor of a government petition, the Court was "primarily concerned with vindicating the will of the majority and less interested in its role as protector of the individual's constitutional rights." Florida v. Meyers, 466 U.S. 380, 386 (1984).[12]

Perhaps in response to such criticism, the Court has adopted a "rule of six", requiring six votes to decide at the certiorari stage to dispose of a case summarily and issue a per curiam opinion. See Perry, Deciding to Decide: Agenda Setting in the United States Supreme Court 99–101 (1991).

Is there ever a case appropriate for summary reversal? What if the lower court has committed a manifest and grievous error in a case plainly not worth the time required for full briefing and argument? Should the Court in any event act summarily only when it is unanimous? Would even such action smack of unfairness to the losing party unless an opportunity were afforded for the filing of briefs on the merits?[13]

(6) *Studies of Supreme Court Practice.* In the last several decades, there has been a considerable body of literature, much of it emanating from political and social scientists, reporting and analyzing the Court's practices in the exercise of its discretionary jurisdiction. One of the earliest studies, by Professor Harper and others, reviewed the Court's dockets over four Terms and concluded that the Court was taking cases it shouldn't, not taking cases it should, and fostering unnecessary petitions by failing to articulate what it was doing.[14]

Subsequent studies have included:

• An analysis of FELA cases by Professor Schubert, suggesting that a bloc of Justices used the certiorari power in those cases to force the majority to reach certain policy results on the merits;[15]

• A study by Professor Tanenhaus and associates concluding that the existence of certain factors operated as "cues" to stimulate closer consideration and favorable response by the Court—notably the presence of the United States as petitioner; a disagreement between the trial and appellate courts; and the presence of certain civil liberties issues;[16] and

---

12. In a memorandum filed in Colorado v. Connelly, 474 U.S. 1050 (1986), Justice Brennan (joined by Justice Stevens) complained that of 30 criminal cases in which the Court had summarily reversed without briefing or oral argument in three and one half years, 26 were decided in favor of the prosecutor or warden.

13. See Montana v. Hall, 481 U.S. 400, 405–10 (1987)(Marshall, J., dissenting). For other recent objections to summary action, see, *e.g.,* Wood v. Bartholomew, 116 S.Ct. 7, 11 (1995)(Justices Stevens, Souter, Ginsburg, and Breyer); Duncan v. Henry, 115 S.Ct. 887, 891 (1995) (Justice Stevens); Dobbs v. Zant, 506 U.S. 357, ___, 113 S.Ct. 835, 836 (1993)(Chief Justice Rehnquist and Justice White); Hunter v. Bryant, 502 U.S. 224, 234 (1991)(Justice Kennedy, noting the disagree-

ment among his colleagues on the proper disposition of the case on the merits).

14. The four articles were entitled *What the Supreme Court Did Not Do During the [1949, 1950, 1951, 1952] Term* and appeared in the University of Pennsylvania Law Review: Harper & Rosenthal, 99 U.Pa.L.Rev. 293 (1950); Harper & Etherington, 100 U.Pa.L.Rev. 354 (1951); Harper & Pratt, 101 U.Pa.L.Rev. 439 (1953); Harper & Leibowitz, 102 U.Pa.L.Rev. 427 (1954).

15. Schubert, *The Certiorari Game,* in Quantitative Analysis of Judicial Behavior 210 (Schubert ed. 1959); Schubert, *Policy Without Law: An Extension of the Certiorari Game,* 14 Stan.L.Rev. 284 (1962).

16. Tanenhaus, Schick, Muraskin & Rosen, *The Supreme Court's Certiorari Juris-*

● Several studies by Professor Ulmer suggesting a close relationship between the Justices' votes to grant certiorari and their views on the merits.[17]

More recently, a thoughtful and informative analysis appeared in Provine, Case Selection in the United States Supreme Court (1980). This book is based in significant part on an intensive study of the records and papers of Justice Burton—papers that cover the 1945–1957 Terms and that include the recorded vote of every Justice on certiorari petitions during this period. Her basic conclusion—a most important one in light of other criticisms of the Court's work—is that the Justices' perceptions of their role and of the role of the Court serve as a significant intervening variable between their votes on certiorari and their policy preferences. Thus she concludes, for example, that as a result of these perceptions, the use of the certiorari power for dispute avoidance is rare (Chap. II); that "cue theory" serves as an inadequate explanation of certiorari decisions (Chap. III); that a Justice's political and policy orientation is not the sole or determining variable in the exercise of discretion, nor is there strong evidence that Justices will characteristically vote to deny certiorari if they fear that their views will not prevail on the merits (Chap. IV); and that the record in FELA cases does not substantiate the bloc voting hypothesis (Chap. V). She urges that the Court's discretionary power be retained but that, in the interest of public awareness and scholarly study, the votes on certiorari petitions should be disclosed.[18]

A particularly interesting table in this book reveals the high degree of unanimity on certiorari petitions. From the 1947 Term through the 1957 Term, a less than unanimous vote was recorded on only 18% of the petitions: 11% in which certiorari was denied and 7% in which it was granted (Table 1.4, p. 32).

Finally, a study by Perry, Deciding to Decide: Agenda Setting in the Supreme Court of the United States (1991), notes, *inter alia,* that there is virtually no discussion among the Justices about certiorari matters before the Justices' Conference, that discussion at the Conference itself is very limited, and that there is virtually no "horse-trading" in the process. Like Provine, Perry concludes (on the basis of detailed interviews of five Justices and 64 former clerks) that decisions tend not to turn on a Justice's predictions about how the case is likely to come out, but he did find more evidence than she had for occasional "strategic" behavior, including "defensive denials" based on a fear of an unacceptable outcome on the merits. Yet such strategic behavior, he states, is the exception even among Justices generally regarded as more "political" than others in their approach to their task. Finally, Perry observes that a decision to write a dissent from a denial is frequently made in an effort to garner additional votes to grant review.

diction: *Cue Theory,* in Judicial Decision–Making 111 (Schubert ed. 1963).

17. Ulmer, *The Decision to Grant Certiorari as an Indicator to Decision "On the Merits,"* 4 Polity 429 (1972); Ulmer, *Supreme Court Justices as Strict and Not–so–Strict Constructionists: Some Implications,* 8 Law & Soc.Rev. 13 (1973); *cf.* Ulmer, *Revis-*

ing the Jurisdiction of the Supreme Court: Mere Administrative Reform or Substantive Policy Change?, 58 Minn.L.Rev. 121 (1973).

18. If this policy were adopted, should disclosure of the votes on a grant of certiorari be deferred until the case has been disposed of?

INDEX

References are to Pages

FEDERAL RULES OF CRIMINAL PROCEDURE
See Criminal Law, Federal

FEDERAL TORT CLAIMS ACT
See also Torts
Enactment of, 1030
Exceptions to liability under,
    Generally, 1031–36
    Discretionary function exception, 1031–34
    Injury related to military service, 1034–35
Federal officers and agencies, actions against,
    766, 869–70, 1030, 1035–36, 1154–55
Prerequisites to suit under, 1030–31
Procedure under, 1030–31
Relationship to constitutional tort actions,
    1035–36, 1154–55
Role of state law under, 1030

FEDERALIST PAPERS
Excerpts, 20–27

FEDERALISTS, 3–4, 74–75

FEIGNED CASES
See Cases or Controversies

FINALITY
Administrative agency rulings, 387–88
As a condition of review, 1641–55
Federal criminal judgments, 1462–63
"Final decisions" rule in appeals to Court of
    Appeals, 1641–55
Requirement for case or controversy, 99–102
    See also Cases or Controversies
Role of, in habeas corpus actions, 1359,
    1384–85, 1405–07, 1430–32
State court judgments and Supreme Court
    review, 627–44

FIRST AMENDMENT CASES
See also Civil Rights Cases
Anticipatory actions, 259–60
Defamation actions in the Supreme Court,
    600–01
Federal judicial abstention, 1237, 1256–64,
    1267–68
Federal taxpayer suits, 137–41
Finality in, 639–41
Implied remedies in, 870–71
Obscenity cases in the Supreme Court,
    206–07, 210–11, 609–12
Overbreadth cases, 202–13, 252–54
Standing to sue,
    Federal taxpayers' suits, 137–41
    In religion cases, 137–38
    Vagueness problems, 200–02, 212–13,
      623–24, 1267–68

FIRST JUDICIARY ACT
See Judiciary Act of 1789

FOREIGN CORPORATIONS
Agreements not to resort to federal courts,
    733–37, 740–43

FOREIGN RELATIONS
Act of State doctrine, 806–10
Cases affecting foreign officials, 334–36

FOREIGN RELATIONS—Cont'd
Diplomatic Relations Act of 1978, 906–07
Federal common law relating to, 806–10
Federal jurisdiction over, debate in Constitu-
    tional Convention about, 15
Foreign Sovereign Immunities Act of 1976,
    903–04
Justiciability of foreign relations questions,
    289–91
Supreme Court original jurisdiction, 334–36
War crimes trials, 344–47

FORUM NON CONVENIENS
See also District Courts, Venue
District court's power to invoke, 1607–15
Effect of state rules in federal diversity ac-
    tions, 741n, 1608–09
State court's power to invoke in federal
    causes of action, 474
Transfer of actions under 28 U.S.C.
    § 1404(a), 1607–15

FORUM SHOPPING
See Diversity Jurisdiction, Law applied

FULL FAITH AND CREDIT
See also Due Process of Law; Judgments
Supreme Court review of state decisions, 564

HABEAS CORPUS
Adequacy of state grounds doctrine, 541–42,
    583–90, 1349, 1413–40
Appeals, 1349, 1460
Capital cases, 1347, 1364, 1405–06, 1434–36,
    1457–58, 1460
Cause and prejudice standard, 1413–35,
    1438–39, 1462–63
Claims of innocence, 1378, 1385–92, 1434–36,
    1457
Collateral attack on federal judgments of con-
    viction, 1461–67
    Adequacy and constitutionality of 28
      U.S.C. § 2255, 1461–62
    Bypassing appeal as bar to, 1462–63
    Non-constitutional issues as basis for,
      1465–66
    Post-conviction proceeding under 28
      U.S.C. § 2255, 1461–67
    Subsequent attacks, 1467
Collateral attack on state judgments of con-
    viction,
    Exhaustion of state remedies rule, 1346,
      1350–56, 1443–50, 1459
    Federal intervention before trial, 1447–49
    Innocence or guilt as factor for consider-
      ation, 1376–81, 1385–92, 1434–36,
      1457
    Issues cognizable on habeas corpus,
      1345–48, 1360–63, 1385–92
    Laches in, 1348
    Relationship to suits under 42 U.S.C.
      § 1983, 1450, 1504–15
    Relitigation of facts, 1342, 1349, 1356–59,
      1371–76
    Seeking direct review as prerequisite,
      1347, 1443–50
    State court procedural default as bar to,
      1413–37

†